TITLE 29—LABOR

CHAPTER 1—LABOR STATISTICS

SUBCHAPTER I—BUREAU OF LABOR STATISTICS

§ 1. Design and duties of bureau generally

The general design and duties of the Bureau of Labor Statistics shall be to acquire and diffuse among the people of the United States useful information on subjects connected with labor, in the most general and comprehensive sense of that word, and especially upon its relation to capital, the hours of labor, the earnings of laboring men and women, and the means of promoting their material, social, intellectual, and moral prosperity.

(June 13, 1888, ch. 389, §1, 25 Stat. 182; Feb. 14, 1903, ch. 552, §4, 32 Stat. 826; Mar. 18, 1904, ch. 716, 33 Stat. 136; Mar. 4, 1913, ch. 141, §3, 37 Stat. 737.)

CODIFICATION

Act June 27, 1884, created Bureau of Labor in Department of the Interior.

Section 1 of act June 13, 1888, created Department of Labor and outlined its general design and duties, and section 9 of that act transferred Bureau of Labor to Department of Labor.

Act Feb. 14, 1903, placed Department of Labor under jurisdiction and made it a part of Department of Commerce and Labor.

Act Mar. 18, 1904, changed name of Department of Labor to Bureau of Labor in Department of Commerce and Labor.

Act Mar. 4, 1913, created Department of Labor and transferred Bureau of Labor from Department of Commerce and Labor to newly created Department of Labor, redesignating such transferred Bureau as Bureau of Labor Statistics.

TRANSFER OF FUNCTIONS

For transfer of functions of other officers, employees, and agencies of Department of Labor, with certain exceptions, to Secretary of Labor, with power to delegate, see Reorg. Plan No. 6 of 1950, §§1, 2, 15 F.R. 3174, 64 Stat. 1263, set out in the Appendix to Title 5, Government Organization and Employees.

§2. Collection, collation, and reports of labor statistics

The Bureau of Labor Statistics, under the direction of the Secretary of Labor, shall collect, collate, and report at least once each year, or oftener if necessary, full and complete statistics of the conditions of labor and the products and distribution of the products of the same, and to this end said Secretary shall have power to employ any or either of the bureaus provided for his department and to rearrange such statistical work, and to distribute or consolidate the same as may be deemed desirable in the public interests; and said Secretary shall also have authority to call upon other departments of the Government for statistical data and results obtained by them; and said Secretary of Labor may collate, arrange, and publish such statistical information so obtained in such manner as to him may seem wise.

The Bureau of Labor Statistics shall also collect, collate, report, and publish at least once each month full and complete statistics of the volume of and changes in employment, as indicated by the number of persons employed, the total wages paid, and the total hours of employment, in the service of the Federal Government, the States and political subdivisions thereof, and in the following industries and their principal branches: (1) Manufacturing; (2) mining, quarrying, and crude petroleum production; (3) building construction; (4) agriculture and lumbering; (5) transportation, communication, and other public utilities; (6) the retail and wholesale trades; and such other industries as the Secretary of Labor may deem it in the public interest to include. Such statistics shall be reported for all such industries and their principal branches throughout the United States and also by States and/or Federal reserve districts and by such smaller geographical subdivisions as the said Secretary may from time to time prescribe. The said Secretary is authorized to arrange with any Federal, State, or municipal bureau or other governmental agency for the collection of such statistics in such manner as he may deem satisfactory, and may assign special agents of the Department of Labor to any such bureau or agency to assist in such collection.

(Mar. 4, 1913, ch. 141, §4, 37 Stat. 737; July 7, 1930, ch. 873, 46 Stat. 1019.)

AMENDMENTS

1930—Act July 7, 1930, inserted second par.

TRANSFER OF FUNCTIONS

For transfer of functions of other officers, employees, and agencies of Department of Labor, with certain exceptions, to Secretary of Labor, with power to delegate, see Reorg. Plan No. 6 of 1950, §§1, 2, 15 F.R. 3174, 64 Stat. 1263, set out in the Appendix to Title 5, Government Organization and Employees.

CENSUS DATA ON WOMEN-OWNED BUSINESSES; STUDY AND REPORT

For provisions requiring Bureaus of Labor Statistics and the Census to include certain data on women-owned businesses in census reports, and requiring a study and report on the most cost effective and accurate means to gather and present such data, see section 501 of Pub. L. 100–533, set out as a note under section 131 of Title 13, Census.

CONSUMER PRICE INDEX FOR OLDER AMERICANS

Pub. L. 100–175, title I, §191, Nov. 29, 1987, 101 Stat. 967, provided that: "The Secretary of Labor shall, through the Bureau of Labor Statistics, develop, from existing data sources, a reweighted index of consumer prices which reflects the expenditures for consumption by Americans 62 years of age and older. The Secretary shall furnish to the Congress the index within 180 days after the date of enactment of this Act [Nov. 29, 1987]. The Secretary shall include with the index furnished a report which explains the characteristics of the reweighted index, the research necessary to develop and measure accurately the rate of inflation affecting such Americans, and provides estimates of time and cost required for additional activities necessary to carry out the objectives of this section."

PRISON STATISTICS REPORT

Joint Res. June 17, 1940, ch. 389, 54 Stat. 401, authorized Bureau of Labor Statistics to furnish a report to Congress before May 1, 1941, on kind, amount, and value of all goods produced in State and Federal prisons.

§2a. Omitted

CODIFICATION

Section, act Feb. 24, 1927, ch. 189, title IV, 44 Stat. 1222, which related to collection of statistical reports through local special agents, was from an appropriations act for the Departments of State, Justice, the Judiciary, and Departments of Commerce and Labor for the fiscal year ending June 30, 1928, and was not repeated in subsequent appropriation acts.

§2b. Studies of productivity and labor costs in industries

The Bureau of Labor Statistics of the United States Department of Labor is authorized and directed to make continuing studies of productivity and labor costs in the manufacturing, mining, transportation, distribution, and other industries.

(June 7, 1940, ch. 267, 54 Stat. 249; Aug. 30, 1954, ch. 1076, §1(27), 68 Stat. 968.)

CODIFICATION

Provision of this section authorizing appropriations of up to $100,000 for studies by the bureau in the first fiscal year was omitted.

AMENDMENTS

1954—Act Aug. 30, 1954, repealed second par. which required Secretary of Labor to submit annually to Congress reports of findings under this section.

TRANSFER OF FUNCTIONS

For transfer of functions of other officers, employees, and agencies of Department of Labor, with certain exceptions, to Secretary of Labor, with power to delegate, see Reorg. Plan No. 6 of 1950, §§1, 2, 15 F.R. 3174, 64 Stat. 1263, set out in the Appendix to Title 5, Government Organization and Employees.

§3. Commissioner; appointment and tenure of office; compensation

The Bureau of Labor Statistics shall be under the charge of a Commissioner of Labor Statistics, who shall be appointed by the President, by and with the advice and consent of the Senate; he shall hold his office for four years, unless sooner removed, and shall receive a salary.

(June 27, 1884, ch. 127, 23 Stat. 60; June 13, 1888, ch. 389, §2, 25 Stat. 182; Mar. 18, 1904, ch. 716, 33 Stat. 136; Mar. 4, 1913, ch. 141, §3, 37 Stat. 737.)

CODIFICATION

Act June 13, 1888, raised salary from $3,000 to $5,000 per annum.

Act Mar. 18, 1904, changed name of Department of Labor to Bureau of Labor.

Act Mar. 4, 1913, authorized the substitution of "Commissioner of Labor Statistics" and "Bureau of Labor Statistics" for "Commissioner of Labor" and "Bureau of Labor", respectively.

Words "of five thousand dollars per annum" at end of section were omitted as superseded by the Classification Acts. See sections 5101 et seq. and 5331 et seq. of Title 5, Government Organization and Employees.

TRANSFER OF FUNCTIONS

For transfer of functions of other officers, employees, and agencies of Department of Labor, with certain exceptions, to Secretary of Labor, with power to delegate, see Reorg. Plan No. 6 of 1950, §§1, 2, 15 F.R. 3174, 64 Stat. 1263, set out in the Appendix to Title 5, Government Organization and Employees.

§4. Duties of Commissioner in general

It shall be the duty of the Commissioner of Labor Statistics to ascertain the effect of the customs laws, and the effect thereon of the state of the currency, in the United States, on the agricultural industry, especially as to its effect on mortgage indebtedness of farmers. He shall also establish a system of reports by which, at intervals of not less than two years, he can report the general condition, so far as production is concerned, of the leading industries of the country. He is also specially charged to investigate the causes of, and facts relating to, all controversies and disputes between employers and employees as they may occur, and which may tend to interfere with the welfare of the people of the different States. He shall also obtain such information upon the various subjects committed to him as he may deem desirable from different foreign nations, and what, if any, convict-made goods are imported into this country, and if so from whence.

(June 13, 1888, ch. 389, §7, 25 Stat. 183; Aug. 23, 1912, ch. 350, §1, 37 Stat. 407; Mar. 4, 1913, ch. 141, §3, 37 Stat. 737; May 29, 1928, ch. 901, §1(110), (111), 45 Stat. 994.)

REFERENCES IN TEXT

The customs laws, referred to in text, are classified generally to Title 19, Customs Duties.

CODIFICATION

Section is from act June 13, 1888. Act June 13, 1888, also contained other provisions relating to duties of former Commissioner of Labor to ascertain cost of producing, in leading countries, articles dutiable in United States, comparative cost of living, etc., which have been omitted from this section because of act Aug. 23, 1912, transferring those duties to Bureau of Foreign and Domestic Commerce.

Act Aug. 23, 1912, transferred the duty of former Commissioner of Labor to ascertain the cost of producing, in leading countries, articles dutiable in the United States, the profits of the manufacturers and producers of such articles, the comparative cost of such articles, comparative cost of living in such countries, what articles are controlled by trusts and the effect they have on prices and production, to the Bureau of Foreign and Domestic Commerce. Text of said act is set out as section 172 of Title 15, Commerce and Trade.

Act Mar. 4, 1913, authorized the substitution of "Commissioner of Labor Statistics" for "Commissioner of Labor".

AMENDMENTS

1928—Act May 29, 1928, repealed provisions requiring reports to Congress on investigations required by this section, and is authority for omission of "and report as to" after "ascertain" in first sentence and "and report thereon to Congress" at end of third sentence relating to information from foreign nations, and convict made goods.

TRANSFER OF FUNCTIONS

For transfer of functions of other officers, employees, and agencies of Department of Labor, with certain exceptions, to Secretary of Labor, with power to delegate, see Reorg. Plan No. 6 of 1950, §§1, 2, 15 F.R. 3174, 64 Stat. 1263, set out in the Appendix to Title 5, Government Organization and Employees.

§5. Bulletin as to labor conditions

The Commissioner of Labor Statistics is authorized to prepare and publish a bulletin of the Bureau of Labor Statistics, as to the condition of labor in this and other countries, condensations of State and foreign labor reports, facts as to conditions of employment, and such other facts as may be deemed of value to the industrial interests of the country.

(Mar. 2, 1895, ch. 177, §1, 28 Stat. 805; Mar. 18, 1904, ch. 716, 33 Stat. 136; Mar. 4, 1913, ch. 141, §3, 37 Stat. 737.)

CODIFICATION

Provision of act Mar. 2, 1895, as to printing of the bulletin for distribution is covered by section 1324 of Title 44, Public Printing and Documents.

Act Mar. 18, 1904, changed name of Department of Labor to Bureau of Labor.

Act Mar. 4, 1913, authorized substitution of "Commissioner of Labor Statistics" and "Bureau of Labor Statistics" for "Commissioner of Labor" and "Bureau of Labor", respectively.

TRANSFER OF FUNCTIONS

For transfer of functions of other officers, employees, and agencies of Department of Labor, with certain exceptions, to Secretary of Labor, with power to delegate, see Reorg. Plan No. 6 of 1950, §§1, 2, 15 F.R. 3174, 64 Stat. 1263, set out in the Appendix to Title 5, Government Organization and Employees.

STATISTICS OF CITIES

Commissioner authorized to compile, as part of bulletin of Department, an abstract of main features of official statistics of cities having over 30,000 population, by a provision of act July 1, 1898, ch. 546, §1, 30 Stat. 648.

§6. Annual and special reports to President and Congress

The Commissioner of Labor Statistics shall annually make a report in writing to the President and Congress, of the information collected and collated by him, and containing such recommendations as he may deem calculated to promote the efficiency of the department. He is also authorized to make special reports on particular subjects whenever required to do so by the President or either House of Congress, or when he shall think the subjects in his charge require it. He shall, on or before the 15th day of March in each year, make a report in detail to Congress of all moneys expended under his direction during the preceding fiscal year.

(June 13, 1888, ch. 389, § 8, 25 Stat. 183; Mar. 4, 1913, ch. 141, § 3, 37 Stat. 737; Pub. L. 94–273, § 5(3), Apr. 21, 1976, 90 Stat. 377.)

CODIFICATION

Act Mar. 4, 1913, authorized substitution of "Commissioner of Labor Statistics" for "Commissioner of Labor".

AMENDMENTS

1976—Pub. L. 94–273 substituted "March" for "December".

TERMINATION OF REPORTING REQUIREMENTS

For termination, effective May 15, 2000, of provisions in this section requiring the Commissioner of Labor Statistics, on or before March 15 each year, to report to Congress on all moneys expended under the Commissioner's direction, see section 3003 of Pub. L. 104–66, as amended, set out as a note under section 1113 of Title 31, Money and Finance, and page 124 of House Document No. 103–7.

TRANSFER OF FUNCTIONS

For transfer of functions of other officers, employees, and agencies of Department of Labor, with certain exceptions, to Secretary of Labor, with power to delegate, see Reorg. Plan No. 6 of 1950, §§ 1, 2, 15 F.R. 174, 64 Stat. 1263, set out in the Appendix to Title 5, Government Organization and Employees.

§ 7. Repealed. Pub. L. 86–3, §§ 15, 23, Mar. 18, 1959, 73 Stat. 11, 13; Pub. L. 96–470, title I, § 110, Oct. 19, 1980, 94 Stat. 2239

Section, acts Apr. 30, 1900, ch. 339, § 76, 31 Stat. 155; Apr. 8, 1904, ch. 948, 33 Stat. 164; Mar. 4, 1913, ch. 141, § 3, 37 Stat. 737, directed United States Commissioner of Labor Statistics to assemble and report on statistical details relating to all departments of labor in Territory of Hawaii.

§ 8. Unemployment data relating to Americans of Spanish origin or descent

The Department of Labor, in cooperation with the Department of Commerce, shall develop methods for improving and expanding the collection, analysis, and publication of unemployment data relating to Americans of Spanish origin or descent.

(Pub. L. 94–311, § 1, June 16, 1976, 90 Stat. 688.)

SUBCHAPTER II—SPECIAL STATISTICS

§ 9. Authorization of special studies, compilations, and transcripts on request; cost

The Department of Labor is authorized, within the discretion of the Secretary of Labor, upon the written request of any person, to make special statistical studies relating to employment, hours of work, wages, and other conditions of employment; to prepare from its records special statistical compilations; and to furnish transcripts of its studies, tables, and other records, upon the payment of the actual cost of such work by the person requesting it.

(Apr. 13, 1934, ch. 118, § 1, 48 Stat. 582; Apr. 11, 1935, ch. 59, 49 Stat. 154; June 15, 1937, ch. 349, 50 Stat. 259; Apr. 15, 1939, ch. 71, 53 Stat. 581.)

CODIFICATION

This section and sections 9a and 9b of this title comprised sections 1 to 3 of act Apr. 13, 1934. Section 4 of that act provided as follows: "This Act shall cease to be effective one year after the date of its enactment." The act was temporarily extended by acts Apr. 11, 1935, and June 15, 1937, and was made permanent by act Apr. 15, 1939.

§ 9a. Credit of receipts

All moneys hereinafter[1] received by the Department of Labor in payment of the cost of such work shall be deposited to the credit of the appropriation of that bureau, service, office, division, or other agency of the Department of Labor which supervised such work, and may be used, in the discretion of the Secretary of Labor, and notwithstanding any other provision of law, for the ordinary expenses of such agency and/or to secure the special services of persons who are neither officers nor employees of the United States.

(Apr. 13, 1934, ch. 118, § 2, 48 Stat. 582; Apr. 11, 1935, ch. 59, 49 Stat. 154; June 15, 1937, ch. 349, 50 Stat. 259; Apr. 15, 1939, ch. 71, 53 Stat. 581.)

CODIFICATION

This section and sections 9 and 9b of this title comprised sections 1 to 3 of act Apr. 13, 1934, which were to terminate one year after Apr. 13, 1934, pursuant to section 4 of act Apr. 13, 1934, set out as a Codification note under section 9 of this title. Such sections were temporarily extended by acts Apr. 11, 1935, and June 15, 1937, and were made permanent by act Apr. 15, 1939.

§ 9b. Rules and regulations

The Secretary of Labor shall prescribe rules and regulations for the enforcement of sections 9 and 9a of this title.

(Apr. 13, 1934, ch. 118, § 3, 48 Stat. 583; Apr. 11, 1935, ch. 59, 49 Stat. 154; June 15, 1937, ch. 349, 50 Stat. 259; Apr. 15, 1939, ch. 71, 53 Stat. 581; Aug. 7, 1946, ch. 770, § 1(16), 60 Stat. 867.)

CODIFICATION

This section and sections 9 and 9a of this title comprised sections 1 to 3 of act Apr. 13, 1934, which were to terminate one year after Apr. 13, 1934, pursuant to section 4 of act Apr. 13, 1934, set out as a Codification note under section 9 of this title. Such sections were temporarily extended by acts Apr. 11, 1935, and June 15, 1937, and were made permanent by act Apr. 15, 1939.

AMENDMENTS

1946—Act Aug. 7, 1946, repealed provisions requiring Secretary of the Interior to make annual reports to Congress.

CHAPTER 2—WOMEN'S BUREAU

[1] So in original. Probably should be "hereafter".

§ 11. Bureau established

There shall be established in the Department of Labor a bureau to be known as the Women's Bureau.

(June 5, 1920, ch. 248, §1, 41 Stat. 987.)

TRANSFER OF FUNCTIONS

For transfer of functions of other officers, employees, and agencies of Department of Labor, with certain exceptions, to Secretary of Labor, with power to delegate, see Reorg. Plan No. 6 of 1950, §§1, 2, 15 F.R. 3174, 64 Stat. 1263, set out in the Appendix to Title 5, Government Organization and Employees.

§ 12. Director of bureau; appointment

The Women's Bureau shall be in charge of a director, a woman, to be appointed by the President, by and with the advice and consent of the Senate.

(June 5, 1920, ch. 248, §2, 41 Stat. 987.)

CODIFICATION

Part of section 2 of act June 5, 1920, constitutes section 13 of this title.

Words "who shall receive an annual compensation of $5,000" were omitted in view of the Classification Acts. See sections 5101 et seq. and 5331 et seq. of Title 5, Government Organization and Employees.

TRANSFER OF FUNCTIONS

For transfer of functions of other officers, employees, and agencies of Department of Labor, with certain exceptions, to Secretary of Labor, with power to delegate, see Reorg. Plan No. 6 of 1950, §§1, 2, 15 F.R. 3174, 64 Stat. 1263, set out in the Appendix to Title 5, Government Organization and Employees.

§ 13. Powers and duties of bureau

It shall be the duty of the Women's Bureau to formulate standards and policies which shall promote the welfare of wage-earning women, improve their working conditions, increase their efficiency, and advance their opportunities for profitable employment. The said bureau shall have authority to investigate and report to the Department of Labor upon all matters pertaining to the welfare of women in industry. The director of said bureau may from time to time publish the results of these investigations in such a manner and to such extent as the Secretary of Labor may prescribe.

(June 5, 1920, ch. 248, §2, 41 Stat. 987.)

CODIFICATION

Part of section 2 of act June 5, 1920, constitutes section 12 of this title.

TRANSFER OF FUNCTIONS

For transfer of functions of other officers, employees, and agencies of Department of Labor, with certain exceptions, to Secretary of Labor, with power to delegate, see Reorg. Plan No. 6 of 1950, §§1, 2, 15 F.R. 3174, 64 Stat. 1263, set out in the Appendix to Title 5, Government Organization and Employees.

§ 14. Assistant director of bureau; appointment; duties

There shall be in the Women's Bureau an assistant director, to be appointed by the Secretary of Labor, who shall perform such duties as shall be prescribed by the director and approved by the Secretary of Labor.

(June 5, 1920, ch. 248, §3, 41 Stat. 987.)

CODIFICATION

Words "who shall receive an annual compensation of $5,000 and" were omitted in view of the Classification Acts. See sections 5101 et seq. and 5331 et seq. of Title 5, Government Organization and Employees.

TRANSFER OF FUNCTIONS

For transfer of functions of other officers, employees, and agencies of Department of Labor, with certain exceptions, to Secretary of Labor, with power to delegate, see Reorg. Plan No. 6 of 1950, §§1, 2, 15 F.R. 3174, 64 Stat. 1263, set out in the Appendix to Title 5, Government Organization and Employees.

§ 15. Repealed. Pub. L. 89–554, § 8(a), Sept. 6, 1966, 80 Stat. 644

Section, act June 5, 1920, ch. 248, §4, 41 Stat. 987, authorized employment by Woman's Bureau of Department of Labor of such employees at such rates of compensation as Congress may provide by appropriation.

§ 16. Repealed. Oct. 31, 1951, ch. 654, § 1(54), 65 Stat. 703

Section, act June 5, 1920, ch. 248, §5, 41 Stat. 987, related to quarters for bureau.

CHAPTER 2A—CHILDREN'S BUREAU

§§ 18 to 18c. Transferred

CODIFICATION

Section 18, acts Apr. 9, 1912, ch. 73, §1, 37 Stat. 79; Mar. 4, 1913, ch. 141, §3, 37 Stat. 737, which established a Children's Bureau in Department of Labor, was transferred to section 191 of Title 42, The Public Health and Welfare.

Section 18a, acts Apr. 9, 1912, ch. 73, §2, 37 Stat. 79; Mar. 4, 1913, ch. 141, §§3, 6, 37 Stat. 737, 738; Feb. 27, 1925, ch. 364, title IV, 43 Stat. 1050, which created office of chief of Children's Bureau, and enumerated powers and duties of said Bureau, was transferred to section 192 of Title 42.

Section 18b, acts Apr. 9, 1912, ch. 73, §3, 37 Stat. 80; Mar. 4, 1913, ch. 141, §§3, 6, 37 Stat. 737, 738, which created office of Assistant Chief of Children's Bureau, was transferred to section 193 of Title 42.

Section 18c, acts Apr. 9, 1912, ch. 73, §4, 37 Stat. 80; Mar. 4, 1913, ch. 141, §3, 37 Stat. 737, which related to quarters for Children's Bureau, was transferred to section 194 of Title 42.

CHAPTER 3—NATIONAL TRADE UNIONS

§§ 21 to 25. Repealed. July 22, 1932, ch. 524, 47 Stat. 741

Section 21, act June 29, 1886, ch. 567, §1, 24 Stat. 86, defined a National Trade Union for purposes of this chapter.

Section 22, act June 29, 1886, ch. 567, §2, 24 Stat. 86, related to rights of a National Trade Union upon incorporation in the office of the recorder of the District of Columbia.

Section 23, act June 29, 1886, ch. 567, §3, 24 Stat. 86, related to power of an incorporated National Trade Union to establish and amend its own constitution, rules, and by-laws.

Section 24, act June 29, 1886, ch. 567, § 4, 24 Stat. 86, related to power of an incorporated National Trade Union to establish and grant powers to its own officers.

Section 25, act June 29, 1886, ch. 567, § 5, 24 Stat. 86, related to establishment of a headquarters of a National Trade Union in District of Columbia.

CHAPTER 4—VOCATIONAL REHABILITATION OF PERSONS INJURED IN INDUSTRY

§§ 31 to 41c. Repealed. Pub. L. 93–112, title V, § 500(a), Sept. 26, 1973, 87 Stat. 390

Section 31, acts June 2, 1920, ch. 219, § 1, 41 Stat. 735; June 5, 1924, ch. 265, 43 Stat. 431; June 9, 1930, ch. 414, § 1, 46 Stat. 524; June 30, 1932, ch. 324, § 1, 47 Stat. 448; July 6, 1943, ch. 190, § 1, 57 Stat. 374; Aug. 3, 1954, ch. 655, § 2, 68 Stat. 652; Nov. 8, 1965, Pub. L. 89–333, § 2(a), 79 Stat. 1282; Oct. 3, 1967, Pub. L. 90–99, § 2, 81 Stat. 250; July 7, 1968, Pub. L. 90–391, §§ 2, 7(c), 82 Stat. 298, 300; Dec. 31, 1970, Pub. L. 91–610, § 1, 84 Stat. 1817, related to grants to assist in rehabilitating handicapped individuals, providing in subsec. (a) authorization to make grants and a statement of purpose and in subsec. (b) authorization of appropriations.

Section 32, acts June 2, 1920, ch. 219, § 2, 41 Stat. 735; July 6, 1943, ch. 190, § 1, 57 Stat. 374; Aug. 3, 1954, ch. 655, § 2, 68 Stat. 652; Nov. 8, 1965, Pub. L. 89–333, § 2(a), 79 Stat. 1282; July 7, 1968, Pub. L. 90–391, §§ 3, 4, 5, 82 Stat. 298, related to grants to States for vocational rehabilitation services, providing in: subsec. (a) for computation of allotments; subsec. (b) for amount of payments and adjusted Federal shares; and subsec. (c) for private contributions for construction or establishment of facilities.

Section 33, acts June 2, 1920, ch. 219, § 3, 41 Stat. 736; June 5, 1924, ch. 265, 43 Stat. 431; June 9, 1930, ch. 414, § 2, 46 Stat. 524; June 30, 1932, ch. 324, § 2, 47 Stat. 449; July 6, 1943, ch. 190, § 1, 57 Stat. 376; Aug. 3, 1954, ch. 655, § 2, 68 Stat. 654; Nov. 8, 1965, Pub. L. 89–333, § 2(a), 79 Stat. 1283; July 7, 1968, Pub. L. 90–391, § 6, 82 Stat. 299, related to grants for innovation of vocational rehabilitation services, providing in: subsec. (a) for the basis of allotments; subsec. (b) for duration of payments; subsec. (c) for restriction on payments; and subsec. (d) for additional amounts.

Section 34, acts June 2, 1920, ch. 219, § 4, 41 Stat. 736; June 9, 1930, ch. 414, § 3, 46 Stat. 525; July 6, 1943, ch. 190, § 1, 57 Stat. 377; Aug. 3, 1954, ch. 655, § 2, 68 Stat. 655; Aug. 3, 1956, ch. 903, 70 Stat. 956; Aug. 28, 1957, Pub. L. 85–198, § 1, 71 Stat. 473; Aug. 28, 1957, Pub. L. 85–213, 71 Stat. 488; Nov. 8, 1965, Pub. L. 89–333, §§ 4(a), 5(a), 12(a), (b)(1), (2), 79 Stat. 1289, 1290, 1293; Oct. 3, 1967, Pub. L. 90–99, § 3, 81 Stat. 251; July 7, 1968, Pub. L. 90–391, § 7(a), (b), (d), 82 Stat. 299, 300; Dec. 31, 1970, Pub. L. 91–610, § 2, 84 Stat. 1817, related to grants for special projects, providing in: subsec. (a) general provisions; subsec. (b) for payments; and subsec. (c) for National Advisory Council on Vocational Rehabilitation.

Section 35, acts June 2, 1920, ch. 219, § 5, 41 Stat. 736; June 30, 1932, ch. 324, § 3, 47 Stat. 450; July 6, 1943, ch. 190, § 1, 57 Stat. 377; Aug. 3, 1954, ch. 655, § 2, 68 Stat. 656; Nov. 8, 1965, Pub. L. 89–333, §§ 8(a), 12(b)(1), 79 Stat. 1291, 1293; Oct. 3, 1967, Pub. L. 90–99, § 6, 81 Stat. 253; July 7, 1968, Pub. L. 90–391, § 8, 82 Stat. 300, related to State plans, providing in: subsec. (a) for requirements for approval; subsec. (b) for approval; subsec. (c) for withholding or limitation of payments; and subsec. (d) for judicial review.

Section 36, acts June 2, 1920, ch. 219, § 6, 41 Stat. 737; June 5, 1924, ch. 265, 43 Stat. 432; June 9, 1930, ch. 414, § 4, 46 Stat. 526; June 30, 1932, ch. 324, § 4, 47 Stat. 450; July 6, 1943, ch. 190, § 1, 57 Stat. 378; Aug. 3, 1954, ch. 655, § 2, 68 Stat. 658, related to method of computing and making payments.

Pub. L. 89–554, § 8(a), Sept. 6, 1966, 80 Stat. 644, repealed section 36 of this title, insofar as section 36 authorized an appropriation to finance the operation of the Federal Board for Vocational Education, and insofar as it provided for certain salary restrictions.

Section 37, acts June 2, 1920, ch. 219, § 7, 41 Stat. 737; July 6, 1943, ch. 190, § 1, 57 Stat. 378; Aug. 3, 1954, ch. 655, § 2, 68 Stat. 658; Aug. 28, 1957, Pub. L. 85–198, § 2, 71 Stat. 474; Nov. 8, 1965, Pub. L. 89–333, §§ 5(b), 7, 12(b)(1), 79 Stat. 1290, 1291, 1293; July 7, 1968, Pub. L. 90–391, § 9, 82 Stat. 301, related to administration, providing in: subsec. (a) general provisions; subsec. (b) for rules and regulations; subsec. (c) for research and dissemination of information; subsec. (d) for authorization of appropriations; and subsec. (e) for evaluation of vocational rehabilitation program.

Section 38, act June 2, 1920, ch. 219, § 8, as added July 6, 1943, ch. 190, § 1, 57 Stat. 379; amended Aug. 3, 1954, ch. 655, § 2, 68 Stat. 659; Nov. 8, 1965, Pub. L. 89–333, § 12(b)(3), 79 Stat. 1293, related to promotion of employment opportunities.

Section 39, act June 2, 1920, ch. 219, § 9, as added July 6, 1943, ch. 190, § 1, 57 Stat. 379; amended Aug. 3, 1954, ch. 655, § 2, 68 Stat. 659, related to annual reports to Congress.

Section 40, act June 2, 1920, ch. 219, § 10, as added July 6, 1943, ch. 190, § 1, 57 Stat. 379; amended Aug. 3, 1954, ch. 655, § 2, 68 Stat. 659, related to appropriations for administration.

Section 41, act June 2, 1920, ch. 219, § 11, as added July 6, 1943, ch. 190, § 1, 57 Stat. 379; amended Aug. 3, 1954, ch. 655, § 2, 68 Stat. 659; Aug. 1, 1956, ch. 852, § 16, 70 Stat. 910; June 25, 1959, Pub. L. 86–70, § 24, 73 Stat. 147; July 12, 1960, Pub. L. 86–624, § 20, 74 Stat. 416; Nov. 8, 1965, Pub. L. 89–333, §§ 6(a), 9, 10(a), 11, 12(b)(1), (c), (d), 13, 79 Stat. 1291–1294, Oct. 3, 1967, Pub. L. 90–99, § 7, 81 Stat. 253; July 7, 1968, Pub. L. 90–391, § 10, 82 Stat. 301, related to definitions.

Section 41a, act June 2, 1920, ch. 219, § 12, as added Nov. 8, 1965, Pub. L. 89–333, § 3, 79 Stat. 1284; amended July 7, 1968, Pub. L. 90–391, § 11, 82 Stat. 303; Dec. 31, 1970, Pub. L. 91–610, § 3, 84 Stat. 1817, related to grants for construction and staffing of rehabilitation facilities, providing in: subsec. (a) for authorization to make grants; subsec. (b) for project requirements, assurances, plans and specifications, and labor standards; subsec. (c) for percentage shares; subsec. (d) for reservation of grant funds, payment, and additional payments; subsec. (e) for recovery of Federal share upon cessation of public or non-profit character of rehabilitation facilities; subsec. (f) for grants for staffing facilities with professional or technical personnel and limitation on Federal share; subsec. (g) for planning grants; subsec. (h) for adjustments for overpayments or underpayments; subsec. (i) for authorization of appropriations; and subsec. (j) for definitions of "construction", "cost" of construction, and what a project for construction of a rehabilitation facility which is primarily a workshop, may include.

Section 41b, act June 2, 1920, ch. 219, § 13, as added Nov. 8, 1965, Pub. L. 89–333, § 3, 79 Stat. 1286; amended July 7, 1968, Pub. L. 90–391, § 12, 82 Stat. 303; Dec. 31, 1970, Pub. L. 91–610, § 4, 84 Stat. 1817, related to rehabilitation facility improvement, providing in: subsec. (a) for grants for projects for training services, authorization, definition of training services, allowances, and payments; subsec. (b) for rehabilitation facility improvement grants; authorization, improvement of service capability, and payments; subsec. (c) for technical assistance to rehabilitation facilities, and compensation of experts and consultants; subsec. (d) for National Policy and Performance Council, its establishment, membership, function, and compensation of members; subsec. (e) for labor standards; and subsec. (f) for authorization of appropriations.

Section 41c, act June 2, 1920, ch. 219, § 14, as added Nov. 8, 1965, Pub. L. 89–333, § 3, 79 Stat. 1288, related to waiver in the case of locally financed activity of requirement that plan be statewide.

Sections 31 to 41c, referred to above, and sections 42–1 to 42b of this title, were known as the Vocational Rehabilitation Act. Section 500(a) of Pub. L. 93–112, which repealed that Act, also provided that references to such Vocational Rehabilitation Act in any other provision of law would, ninety days after Sept. 26, 1973, be deemed to be references to the Rehabilitation Act of 1973, which is classified generally to chapter 15 (§ 701 et seq.) of this title.

On enactment of the Rehabilitation Act of 1973, such former provisions were covered by various new sections of this title as follows:

Former sections	*New sections*
31(a)	701(1), 720(a)
31(b)(1), (2)	720(b)(1), (2)
31(b)(3)(A)	761(a), 774(a)
31(b)(3)(B)	720(b)(2)
31(b)(3)(C), (D)	774(a)(1)
31(b)(4)	See 720(b), 761(a), 774(a)
32(a)	730(a)
32(b)	731(a)
32(c)	724
33(a)(1)	740(a)(1)
33(a)(2)	741(a)
33(b)	741(b)
33(c)	709
33(d)	740(b)
34(a)	762(a), (b), 763, 774(b), 776(h)
34(a)(1)	762(a), (b)
34(a)(2)(A)	741(a), (b)
34(a)(2)(B)	774(d)
34(a)(2)(C)	763(b), 774(b)
34(a)(2)(D)	723(a)(7)
34(b)	741(c)
34(c)	Repealed
35(a)	721(a)
35(a), (1), (2)	721(a)(1), (2)
35(a)(3)	721(a)(3), (4)
35(a)(4)	721(a)(5)(A)(i)
35(a)(5), (6)	721(a)(5), (6)
35(a)(7)	723(a)(1), (2)
35(a)(8), (9)	721(a)(10), (11)
35(a)(10)	721(a)(11), (12)
35(a)(11)	721(a)(13)(A)
35(a)(12), (13)	721(a)(14), (15)
35(a)(14)	721(a)(17)
35(b)–(d)	721(b)–(d)
36	731(b)
37(a), (b)	780(a), (b)
37(c)(1)	780(c)
37(c)(2)	785(a)(5)
37(d)	See 780(d)
37(e)	783
38	See 791, 791(f)(1)
39	784
40	780(d)
41(a)(1)	706(14), 723(a)(1)
41(a)(1)(A)–(C)	723(a)(1)–(3)
41(a)(1)(D), (E)	723(a)(6), (7)
41(a)(2)	723(b)
41(a)(2)(A)(i)–(iv)	723(a)(4)(A)–(D)
41(a)(2)(B)	723(a)(5)
41(a)(2)(C)	723(a)(9)
41(a)(2)(D), (E)	723(b)(1), (2)
41(a)(2)(F)	723(a)(10)
41(a)(2)(G)	723(a)
41(a)(2)(H)	723(a)(3)
41(b)	706(4)(G), (6)
41(c)	706(10)
41(d)	See 706(L)
41(e)	706(8)
41(f)	706(3)
41(g)	706(13)
41(h)	707(a)
41(i)	706(5)
41(j)	707(b)
41(k)	706(11)
41(*l*)	706(1)
41a(a)	771(b)(1)
41a(b)	771(b)(2), 776
41a(b)(1)(A)–(C)	776(b)(1)(A)–(C)
41a(b)(2)	776(b)(4)
41a(b)(3)	See 780(h)
41a(b)(4)	776(b)(5)
41a(c)	771(b)(3)
41a(d), (e)	776(c), (d)
41a(f), (g)	771(c), (d)
41a(h)	776(e)
41a(i)	771(a)
41a(j)(1), (2)	706(1)
41a(j)(3)	776(f)
41b(a)(1)–(3)	772(b)(1)–(3)
41b(a)(4)	776(e)
41b(1), (2)	772(c)(1), (2)
41b(b)(3)	776(e)
41b(c)	774(e)
41b(d)(1)–(4)	Repealed
41b(e)	776(b)(4)
41b(f)	772(a), 774
41c	721(a)(4)

Effective Date of Repeal

Repeal effective 90 days after Sept. 26, 1973, see section 500(a) of Pub. L. 93–112, which is classified to section 790(a) of this title.

Increase of Allotment Percentages for Alaska

Pub. L. 86–624, §47(g), July 12, 1960, 74 Stat. 424, provided that the allotment percentage determined for Alaska under section 41(h) of this title for the first to fourth years for which such percentage was based on the per capita income data for Alaska was to be increased by varying amounts each of those four years, that the Federal share for Alaska determined under section 41(i) of this title, for the first year for which such share was based on per capita income data for Alaska, was to be increased, and that where the first year for which such Federal share was based on per capital income data for Alaska was a fiscal year ending prior to July 1, 1962, the adjusted Federal share for Alaska for such year for purposes of section 32(b) of this title was to be the Federal share determined pursuant to section 41(i) of this title.

Limitation on Expenditure of Funds for Special Projects

Act Aug. 1, 1955, ch. 437, title II, 69 Stat. 403, provided in part that not more than $2 of the funds made available for special projects under section 34(a)(2) of this title was to be expended for any project for each $1 that the grantee, or the grantee and the State, expended for the same purpose.

District of Columbia Vocational Rehabilitation Program

Act Aug. 3, 1954, ch. 655, § 3, 68 Stat. 662, provided that materials which the Director of the Bureau of the Budget [now the Director of the Office of Management and Budget] determined related to the provision of vocational rehabilitation services in the District of Columbia or the performance of certain functions by State licensing agencies were to be transferred within ninety days after Aug. 3, 1954, from the Department of Health, Education, and Welfare to the municipal government of the District of Columbia, authorized the Board of Commissioners of the District of Columbia [now the Mayor of the District of Columbia] to take the necessary steps to secure the benefits of act June 2, 1920, ch. 219, 41 Stat. 735, and also authorized the Secretary of Health, Education, and Welfare to continue the performance of certain functions relating to rehabilitation services in the District of Columbia until the completion of the transfer of responsibility.

Homebound Physically Handicapped Individuals

Act Aug. 3, 1954, ch. 655, § 7, 68 Stat. 665, required the Secretary of Health, Education, and Welfare to make a thorough study of existing programs for teaching and training handicapped persons, commonly known as shut-ins, whose disabilities confine them to their homes or beds, for the purpose of ascertaining whether additional or supplementary programs or services are necessary, particularly in rural areas, in order to provide adequate general ameliorative and vocational training for such handicapped persons, and provided that the Secretary shall report to the Congress not later than six months after Aug. 3, 1954, the results of such study, together with such recommendations as may be desirable.

State Compliance With Chapter

Act July 6, 1943, ch. 190, § 3(b), 57 Stat. 380, authorized particular States which were unable to comply with the preconditions of act June 2, 1920, ch. 219, 41 Stat. 735, on July 6, 1943, to secure the benefits of such act, for a period of sixty days after their particular State legislatures meet for the first time after such date.

APPROPRIATIONS FOR VOCATIONAL REHABILITATION

Act June 26, 1940, ch. 428, 54 Stat. 583, making appropriations for the fiscal year ending June 30, 1941, made certain appropriations for cooperative vocational rehabilitation, and expenses connected therewith, with provisions for apportionment to the States to be computed in accordance with act June 2, 1920, ch. 219, 41 Stat. 735, and other acts.

§§41d, 42. Repealed. Pub. L. 90–391, §13, July 7, 1968, 82 Stat. 304

Section 41d, act June 2, 1920, ch. 219, §15, as added Nov. 8, 1965, Pub. L. 89–333, §3, 79 Stat. 1289, established a National Commission on Architectural Barriers to Rehabilitation of the Handicapped in the Department of Health, Education, and Welfare, and provided for its membership and functions, appointment of experts and consultants, technical and administrative assistance, compensation of Commission members, interim and final reports, and authorization of appropriations.

Section 42, act June 2, 1920, ch. 219, §16, formerly §12, as added Aug. 3, 1954, ch. 655, §2, 68 Stat. 662; amended Sept. 10, 1965, Pub. L. 89–178, §2, 79 Stat. 676 and renumbered Nov. 8, 1965, Pub. L. 89–333, §3, 79 Stat. 1284, authorized grants for special projects in correctional rehabilitation, prescribed conditions thereof, defined "organization", established a National Advisory Council on Correctional Manpower and Training in the Department of Health, Education, and Welfare, and provided for its composition, selection of members, functions, compensation and travel expenses, appropriations, terms of grant, and additional financial support.

CORRECTIONAL REHABILITATION RESEARCH AND STUDY; TIME EXTENSION FOR FINAL REPORT

Pub. L. 91–6, Mar. 28, 1969, 83 Stat. 6, provided that the date by which the research and study initiated and the final report required by section 42 of this title (as in effect prior to July 7, 1968) was to be completed was July 31, 1969.

§§42–1 to 42b. Repealed. Pub. L. 93–112, title V, §500(a), Sept. 26, 1973, 87 Stat. 390

Section 42–1, act June 2, 1920, ch. 219, §15, as added July 7, 1968, Pub. L. 90–391, §13, 82 Stat. 304; amended Dec. 31, 1970, Pub. L. 91–610, §5, 84 Stat. 1817, related to vocational evaluation and work adjustment program, providing in: subsec. (a) for computation of allotments, authorization of appropriations, Federal payments, restriction on payments, evaluation and work adjustment services, and disadvantaged individuals; subsec. (b) for restriction on payments; subsec. (c) for State plans and requirements for approval; subsec. (d) for withholding of payments and judicial review; and subsec. (e) for payments to States adjustments, advances or reimbursement, installments, and conditions.

Section 42a, act June 2, 1920, ch. 219, §16, formerly §17, as added Oct. 3, 1967, Pub. L. 90–99, §4, 81 Stat. 251; renumbered July 7, 1968, Pub. L. 90–391, §13, 82 Stat. 304, related to National Center for Deaf-Blind Youths and Adults, providing in: subsec. (a) for statement of purpose, agreement for establishment and operation of the National Center, and its designation; subsec. (b) for proposals and preference; subsec. (c) for terms and conditions of agreement; subsec. (d) for recovery of funds for non-user of facilities for contemplated purposes or termination of agreement, and cause for release from obligation; and subsec. (e) for definition of "construction" for determination pursuant to regulations of the Secretary of who are both deaf and blind. Subsections (c)(2) to (4) of section 42a were amended by Pub. L. 93–608, §1(8), Jan. 2, 1975, 88 Stat. 1968, without reference to the repeal of this section by Pub. L. 93–112. The purported amendment would have eliminated the annual report of the National Center for Deaf-Blind Youths and Adults, through the Secretary of the Department of Health, Education, and Welfare, to the Congress with comments and recommendations as the Secretary deemed appropriate.

Section 42b, act June 2, 1920, ch. 219, §17, formerly §18, as added Oct. 3, 1967, Pub. L. 90–99, §5, 81 Stat. 252; renumbered July 7, 1968, Pub. L. 90–391, §13, 82 Stat. 304, related to grants for services for migratory agricultural workers, authorization, payments, and other related provisions.

Sections 42–1 to 42b, referred to above, and sections 31 to 41c of this title, were known as the Vocational Rehabilitation Act. Section 500(a) of Pub. L. 93–112, which repealed that Act, also provided that references to such Vocational Rehabilitation Act in any other provision of law would, ninety days after Sept. 26, 1973, be deemed to be references to the Rehabilitation Act of 1973, which is classified generally to chapter 15 (§701 et seq.) of this title.

Such former provisions are covered by various sections as follows:

Former sections	*Present sections*
42–1(a)(1)	See 730(a), 740(a)
42–1(a)(2)	720(b)(1)
42–1(a)(3)	Repealed
42–1(a)(4)(A)–(F)	706(4)(A)–(F)
42–1(a), last sentence	Repealed
42–1(b)	709
42–1(c)	See 721(a)
42–1(c)(1)	721(a)(1)
42–1(c)(2)	721(a)(3)
42–1(c)(3)	721(a)(5)(A)
42–1(c)(4), (5)	721(a)(6), (7)
42–1(c)(6)	Repealed
42–1(c)(7)	721(a)(10)
42–1(c)(8)	See 721(a)(11)
42–1(d)	See 721(c), (d)
42–1(e)	See 776(e)
42a(a), (b)	775(b), (c)
42a(c)(1)–(3)	776(b)(2), (3), (5)
42a(c)(4)	Repealed
42a(d)	776(d)
42a(e)(1)	706(1)
42a(e)(2)	See 723(a)(6)
42b	774(c)

EFFECTIVE DATE OF REPEAL

Repeal effective 90 days after Sept. 26, 1973, see section 500(a) of Pub. L. 93–112, which is classified to section 790(a) of this title.

§§43 to 45b. Omitted

CODIFICATION

Section 43, formerly constituting part of section 7 of act June 2, 1920, ch. 219, 41 Stat. 737, as amended by Ex. Ord. No. 6166, §15, June 10, 1933; 1939 Reorg. Plan No. I, §§201, 204, eff. July 1, 1939, related to report, by Federal Security Agency, of gifts or donations. Act June 2, 1920, was amended generally by act July 6, 1943, ch. 190, 57 Stat. 374, which did not contain similar provisions.

Section 44, formerly constituting part of section 7 of act June 2, 1920, ch. 219, 41 Stat. 737, related to prohibition of discrimination for or against persons entitled to benefits of act of June 2, 1920. Act June 2, 1920, was amended generally by act July 6, 1943, ch. 190, 57 Stat. 374, which did not contain similar provisions.

Section 45, act Mar. 10, 1924, ch. 46, §5, 43 Stat. 18, related to extension of provisions of sections 31 to 44 of this title to the Territory of Hawaii and appropriation authorization for allotment.

Section 45a, acts Mar. 3, 1931, ch. 404, §2, 46 Stat. 1489; May 17, 1932, ch. 190, 47 Stat. 158, related to extension of provisions of sections 31 to 44 of this title upon the same terms and conditions as any of the several states.

Section 45b, acts Aug. 14, 1935, ch. 531, title V, §531, 49 Stat. 633; Aug. 10, 1939, ch. 666, title V, §508, 53 Stat. 1381, related to an authorization of appropriations for each fiscal year after fiscal year ending June 30, 1937, and appropriations therefor together with apportionment of appropriations to the states and to the Territory of Hawaii.

CHAPTER 4A—EMPLOYMENT STABILIZATION

PRIOR PROVISIONS

A prior chapter 4A, consisting of sections 47 to 47f, act Feb. 23, 1929, ch. 303, §§1–7, 45 Stat. 1260, related to vocational rehabilitation of disabled residents of the District of Columbia.

§§48, 48a. Omitted

CODIFICATION

Sections 48 to 48g of this title comprised the Employment Stabilization Act of 1931, act Feb. 10, 1931, ch. 117, §§1–8, 46 Stat. 1084–1086, which became obsolete upon the abolition of the National Resources Planning Board effective Aug. 31, 1943, by act June 26, 1943, ch. 145, title I, §1, 57 Stat. 170.

Section 48, act Feb. 10, 1931, ch. 117, §1, 46 Stat. 1084, related to citation of "Employment Stabilization Act of 1931".

Section 48a, act Feb. 10, 1931, ch. 117, §2, 46 Stat. 1084; Ex. Ord. No. 6623, Mar. 1, 1934; 1939 Reorg. Plan No. I, §§4, 6 eff. July 1, 1939, 4 F.R. 2727, 53 Stat. 1423; 1939 Reorg. Plan No. II, §4(e), (f), eff. July 1, 1939, 4 F.R. 2731, 53 Stat. 1433; 1940 Reorg. Plan No. III, §3, eff. June 30, 1940, 5 F.R. 2108, 54 Stat. 1232, related to definitions of terms used in this chapter.

§48b. Repealed. Pub. L. 89–554, §8(a), Sept. 6, 1966, 80 Stat. 648

Section, act Feb. 10, 1931, ch. 117, §3, 46 Stat. 1085, Ex. Ord. No. 6623, Mar. 1, 1934; 1939 Reorg. Plan No. I, §§4, 6, eff. July 1, 1939, 4 F.R. 2727, 53 Stat. 1423, related to powers and duties of the National Resources Planning Board, which was abolished by act June 26, 1943, ch. 145, title I, §1, 57 Stat. 170.

§§48c to 48g. Omitted

CODIFICATION

Section 48c, act Feb. 10, 1931, ch. 117, §4, 46 Stat. 1085; Ex. Ord. No. 6623, Mar. 1, 1934; 1939 Reorg. Plan No. I, §§4, 6, eff. July 1, 1939, 4 F.R. 2727, 53 Stat. 1423, related to basis of action of the National Resources Planning Board which was abolished. See note below.

Section 48d, act Feb. 10, 1931, ch. 117, §5, 46 Stat. 1086; Ex. Ord. No. 6623, Mar. 1, 1934; 1939 Reorg. Plan No. I, §§4, 6, eff. July 1, 1939, 4 F.R. 2727, 53 Stat. 1423, related to public works emergency appropriations during existence of depression periods.

Section 48e, act Feb. 10, 1931, ch. 117, §6, 46 Stat. 1086, related to use of emergency appropriations authorized by section 48d of this title.

Section 48f, act Feb. 10, 1931, ch. 117, §7, 46 Stat. 1086, related to acceleration of emergency construction work.

Section 48g, act Feb. 10, 1931, ch. 117, §8, 46 Stat. 1086; Ex. Ord. No. 6623, Mar. 1, 1934; 1939 Reorg. Plan No. I, §§4, 6, eff. July 1, 1939, 4 F.R. 2727, 53 Stat. 1423, related to advance planning by construction agencies of the government and submission of programs, plans, and estimates to the National Resources Planning Board which was abolished. See note below.

NATIONAL RESOURCES PLANNING BOARD

The National Resources Planning Board was abolished August 31, 1943, by act June 26, 1943, ch. 145, title I, §1, 57 Stat. 170, and it was expressly provided that its functions were not to be transferred to any other agency, that the Director should exercise until January 1, 1944, such authority as was necessary to effectuate the discontinuance of the Board, and that the records and files of the Board should be transferred to the national archives.

CHAPTER 4B—FEDERAL EMPLOYMENT SERVICE

§49. United States Employment Service established

In order to promote the establishment and maintenance of a national system of public employment offices, the United States Employment Service shall be established and maintained within the Department of Labor.

(June 6, 1933, ch. 49, §1, 48 Stat. 113; Pub. L. 97–300, title VI, §601(a), formerly title V, §501(a), Oct. 13, 1982, 96 Stat. 1392; renumbered title VI, §601(a), Pub. L. 100–628, title VII, §712(a)(1), (2), Nov. 7, 1988, 102 Stat. 3248.)

AMENDMENTS

1982—Pub. L. 97–300 substituted "the United States Employment Service shall be established and maintained within the Department of Labor" for "there is created in the Department of Labor a bureau to be known as the United States Employment Service".

EFFECTIVE DATE OF 1982 AMENDMENT

Amendment by Pub. L. 97–300 effective Oct. 1, 1983, but with Secretary authorized to use funds appropriated for fiscal 1983 to plan for orderly implementation of amendment, see section 181(i) of Pub. L. 97–300, which was formerly classified to section 1591(i) of this title.

SHORT TITLE

Act June 6, 1933, ch. 49, §16, formerly §15, as added by Pub. L. 97–300, title VI, §601(h), formerly title V, §501(h), Oct. 13, 1982, 96 Stat. 1397; renumbered title VI, §601(h), Pub. L. 100–628, title VII, §712(a)(1), (2), Nov. 7, 1988, 102 Stat. 3248; renumbered §16, Pub. L. 105–220, title III, §309(1), Aug. 7, 1998, 112 Stat. 1082, provided that: "This Act [enacting this chapter] may be cited as the 'Wagner-Peyser Act'."

TRANSFER OF FUNCTIONS

Functions, powers, and duties of Secretary of Labor under this chapter, insofar as relates to prescription of personnel standards on a merit basis, transferred to Office of Personnel Management, see section 4728(a)(2)(A) of Title 42, The Public Health and Welfare.

Functions of all other officers of Department of Labor and functions of all agencies and employees of that Department were, with exception of functions vested by Administrative Procedure Act (see sections

551 et seq. and 701 et seq. of Title 5, Government Organization and Employees) in hearing examiners employed by such Department, transferred to Secretary of Labor, with power vested in him to authorize their performance or performance of any of his functions by any of those officers, agencies, and employees, by Reorg. Plan No. 6 of 1950, §§1, 2, 15 F.R. 3174, 64 Stat. 1263, set out in the Appendix to Title 5.

United States Employment Service transferred to Department of Labor, functions of Federal Security Administrator with respect to employment services, and Bureau of Employment Security transferred to Secretary of Labor by Reorg. Plan No. 2 of 1949, §1, eff. Aug. 20, 1949, 14 F.R. 5225, 63 Stat. 1065, set out in the Appendix to Title 5.

Section 1 of Reorg. Plan No. 2 of 1949, also provided that functions transferred by this section shall be performed by Secretary of Labor or, subject to his direction and control, by such officers, agencies, and employees of Department of Labor as he shall designate.

Act June 16, 1948, ch. 472, title I, 62 Stat. 446, provided in part that: "Effective July 1, 1948, the United States Employment Service, including its functions under title IV of the Servicemen's Readjustment Act of 1944, is transferred to the Federal Security Agency, and on and after such date the functions of the Secretary of Labor with respect to the United States Employment Service are transferred to the Federal Security Administrator and shall be performed by him or, under his direction and control, by such officers and employees of the Federal Security Agency as he may designate. There are transferred to the Federal Security Agency, for use in connection with the functions transferred by the provisions of this paragraph, the personnel, property, and records of the Department of Labor related to the United States Employment Service, and the balances of such prior appropriations, allocations, and other funds available to the United States Employment Service as the Director of the Bureau of the Budget may determine. The provisions of section 9 of the Reorganization Act of 1945 (Public Law 263, Seventy-ninth Congress) shall apply to the transfer effected by this paragraph in like manner as if such transfer were a reorganization of the agencies and functions concerned under the provisions of that Act."

United States Employment Service and all functions of Social Security Board in Federal Security Agency relating to employment service transferred to War Manpower Commission by Ex. Ord. No. 9247, Sept. 17, 1942, 7 F.R. 7379. That Commission was terminated by Ex. Ord. No. 9617, Sept. 19, 1945, 10 F.R. 11929, and the United States Employment Service transferred to the Department of Labor.

Reorg. Plan No. I of 1939, §201, eff. July 1, 1939, 4 F.R. 2728, 53 Stat. 1424, set out in the Appendix to Title 5, Government Organization and Employees, consolidated United States Employment Service in Department of Labor and its functions and personnel, with other offices and agencies, under one agency to be known as Federal Security Agency with a Federal Security Administrator at head thereof.

Section 203 of Reorg. Plan No. I of 1939, provided that functions of United States Employment Service should be consolidated with unemployment compensation functions of Social Security Board and should be administered in Social Security Board in connection with unemployment compensation functions under direction and supervision of Federal Security Administrator.

Section 203 of Reorg. Plan No. I of 1939, further, abolished office of Director of United States Employment Service and transferred all functions of that office to Social Security Board, to be exercised by Board, and provided that functions of Secretary of Labor relating to administration of United States Employment Service should be transferred to, and exercised by, Federal Security Administrator.

ADMINISTRATION OF MANPOWER IN DISTRICT OF COLUMBIA

Pub. L. 93–198, title II, §204(a), Dec. 24, 1973, 87 Stat. 783, provided that: "All functions of the Secretary of Labor (hereafter in this section referred to as the Secretary) under section 3 of the Act [section 49b of this title] entitled 'An Act to provide for the establishment of a national employment system and for cooperation with the States in the promotion of such system, and for other purposes', approved June 6, 1933 (29 U.S.C. 49–49k), with respect to the maintenance of a public employment service for the District [of Columbia], are transferred [effective July 1, 1974] to the Commissioner [of the District of Columbia established under Reorg. Plan No. 3 of 1967 (now the Mayor)]. After the effective date of this transfer [July 1, 1974], the Secretary shall maintain with the District the same relationship with respect to a public employment service in the District, including the financing of such service, as he has with the States (with respect to a public employment service in the States) generally."

RECRUITMENT AND DISTRIBUTION OF FARM LABOR

Act July 3, 1948, ch. 823, §1, 62 Stat. 1238, authorized the Federal Security Administrator to recruit foreign workers within the Western Hemisphere and workers in Puerto Rico for temporary agricultural employment in the continental United States and to direct, supervise, coordinate, and provide for the transportation of those workers from such places of recruitment to and between places of employment within the continental United States and return to the places of recruitment not later than June 30, 1949.

Section 2 of act July 3, 1948, appropriated $2,500,000, for fiscal year ending June 30, 1949, to carry out the purposes of section 1 of act July 3, 1948.

FARM PLACEMENT SERVICE

Act Apr. 28, 1947, ch. 43, §2, 61 Stat. 55, provided:

"(a) The provisions of the Farm Labor Supply Appropriation Act, 1944 (Public Law 229, Seventy-eighth Congress, second session, title I [sections 1351 to 1355 of Appendix to Title 50, War and National Defense]), as amended and supplemented, and as extended by this Act, shall not be construed to limit or interfere with any of the functions of the United States Employment Service or State public employment services with respect to maintaining a farm placement service as authorized under the Act of June 6, 1933 (48 Stat. 113) [this chapter].

"(b) The Secretary of Agriculture and the Secretary of Labor shall take such action as may be necessary to assure maximum cooperation between the agricultural extension services of the land-grant colleges and the State public employment agencies in the recruitment and placement of domestic farm labor and in the keeping of such records and information with respect thereto as may be necessary for the proper and efficient administration of the State unemployment compensation laws and of title V of the Servicemen's Readjustment Act of 1944, as amended (58 Stat. 295)."

§ 49a. Definitions

For purposes of this chapter—

(1) the term "chief elected official" has the same meaning given that term under the Workforce Investment Act of 1998;

(2) the term "local workforce investment board" means a local workforce investment board established under section 117 of the Workforce Investment Act of 1998 [29 U.S.C. 2832];

(3) the term "one-stop delivery system" means a one-stop delivery system described in section 134(c) of the Workforce Investment Act of 1998 [29 U.S.C. 2864(c)];

(4) the term "Secretary" means the Secretary of Labor; and

(5) the term "State" means any of the several States, the District of Columbia, the Commonwealth of Puerto Rico, Guam, and the Virgin Islands.

(June 6, 1933, ch. 49, §2, 48 Stat. 114; Pub. L. 97–300, title VI, §601(a), formerly title V, §501(a), Oct. 13, 1982, 96 Stat. 1392; renumbered title VI, §601(a), Pub. L. 100–628, title VII, §712(a)(1), (2), Nov. 7, 1988, 102 Stat. 3248; Pub. L. 105–220, title III, §301, Aug. 7, 1998, 112 Stat. 1080.)

REFERENCES IN TEXT

This chapter, referred to in text, was in the original "this Act", meaning act June 6, 1933, ch. 49, 48 Stat. 113, as amended, which was classified to this chapter and section 338 of former Title 39, The Postal Service. Section 338 of former title 39 was repealed and reenacted as section 4152 of former Title 39, The Postal Service, by Pub. L. 86–682, Sept. 2, 1960, 74 Stat. 578. Section 4152 of former title 39 was repealed and reenacted as section 3202 of Title 39, Postal Service, by Pub. L. 91–375, Aug. 12, 1970, 84 Stat. 719.

The Workforce Investment Act of 1998, referred to in par. (1), is Pub. L. 105–220, Aug. 7, 1998, 112 Stat. 936, as amended. For complete classification of this Act to the Code, see Short Title note set out under section 9201 of Title 20, Education, and Tables.

AMENDMENTS

1998—Par. (1). Pub. L. 105–220, §301(1), struck out "or officials" after "elected official" and substituted "Workforce Investment Act of 1998" for "Job Training Partnership Act".

Par. (2). Pub. L. 105–220, §301(2), (4), added par. (2) and struck out former par. (2) which read as follows: "the term 'private industry council' has the same meaning given that term under the Job Training Partnership Act;".

Par. (3). Pub. L. 105–220, §301(4), added par. (3). Former par. (3) redesignated (4).

Par. (4). Pub. L. 105–220, §301(2), (3), (5), redesignated par. (3) as (4), substituted "Labor; and" for "Labor;", and struck out former par. (4) which read as follows: "the term 'service delivery area' has the same meaning given that term under the Job Training Partnership Act; and".

1982—Pub. L. 97–300 amended section generally, substituting provisions relating to definitions for provisions which authorized appointment of personnel and payment of office expenses.

EFFECTIVE DATE OF 1998 AMENDMENT

Pub. L. 105–220, title III, §311, Aug. 7, 1998, 112 Stat. 1086, provided that: "The amendments made by this subtitle [subtitle A (§§301–311) of title III of Pub. L. 105–220, enacting section 49*l*–2 of this title and amending this section, sections 49b, 49c, 49d, 49e to 49g, 49j, and 49k of this title, and section 655a of Title 42, The Public Health and Welfare] shall take effect on July 1, 1999."

EFFECTIVE DATE OF 1982 AMENDMENT

Amendment by Pub. L. 97–300 effective Oct. 1, 1983, but with Secretary authorized to use funds appropriated for fiscal 1983 to plan for orderly implementation of amendment, see section 181(i) of Pub. L. 97–300, which was formerly classified to section 1591(i) of this title.

§ 49b. Duties of Secretary

(a) Assistance to State public employment services

The Secretary shall assist in coordinating the State public employment services throughout the country and in increasing their usefulness by developing and prescribing minimum standards of efficiency, assisting them in meeting problems peculiar to their localities, promoting uniformity in their administrative and statistical procedure, furnishing and publishing information as to opportunities for employment and other information of value in the operation of the system, and maintaining a system for clearing labor between the States.

(b) Provision of unemployment compensation information

It shall be the duty of the Secretary to assure that unemployment insurance and employment service offices in each State, as appropriate, upon request of a public agency administering or supervising the administration of a State program funded under part A of title IV of the Social Security Act [42 U.S.C. 601 et seq.], of a public agency charged with any duty or responsibility under any program or activity authorized or required under part D of title IV of such Act [42 U.S.C. 651 et seq.], or of a State agency charged with the administration of the supplemental nutrition assistance program in a State under the Food and Nutrition Act of 2008 (7 U.S.C. 2011 et seq.), shall (and, notwithstanding any other provision of law, is authorized to) furnish to such agency making the request, from any data contained in the files of any such office, information with respect to any individual specified in the request as to (1) whether such individual is receiving, has received, or has made application for, unemployment compensation, and the amount of any such compensation being received by such individual, (2) the current (or most recent) home address of such individual, and (3) whether such individual has refused an offer of employment and, if so, a description of the employment so offered and the terms, conditions, and rate of pay therefor.

(c) Public labor exchange services

The Secretary shall—

(1) assist in the coordination and development of a nationwide system of public labor exchange services, provided as part of the one-stop customer service systems of the States;

(2) assist in the development of continuous improvement models for such nationwide system that ensure private sector satisfaction with the system and meet the demands of jobseekers relating to the system; and

(3) ensure, for individuals otherwise eligible to receive unemployment compensation, the provision of reemployment services and other activities in which the individuals are required to participate to receive the compensation.

(June 6, 1933, ch. 49, §3, 48 Stat. 114; Sept. 8, 1950, ch. 933, §1, 64 Stat. 822; Aug. 3, 1954, ch. 655, §6(a), 68 Stat. 665; Aug. 1, 1956, ch. 852, §17(a), 70 Stat. 910; Pub. L. 86–624, §21(a), July 12, 1960, 74 Stat. 417; Pub. L. 93–198, title II, §204(c), Dec. 24, 1973, 87 Stat. 783; Pub. L. 94–566, title V, §508(a), Oct. 20, 1976, 90 Stat. 2689; Pub. L. 97–300, title VI, §601(a), formerly title V, §501(a), Oct. 13, 1982, 96 Stat. 1392; renumbered title VI, §601(a), Pub. L. 100–628, title VII, §712(a)(1), (2), Nov. 7, 1988, 102 Stat. 3248; Pub. L. 99–198, title XV, §1535(b)(2), Dec. 23, 1985, 99 Stat. 1584; Pub. L. 104–193, title I, §110(m), Aug. 22, 1996, 110 Stat. 2173; Pub. L. 105–220, title III, §§302(a), 310, Aug. 7, 1998, 112 Stat. 1080, 1086; Pub. L. 110–234, title IV, §4002(b)(1)(A), (B), (2)(Q), May 22, 2008, 122 Stat. 1095–1097; Pub. L. 110–246, §4(a), title IV,

§ 4002(b)(1)(A), (B), (2)(Q), June 18, 2008, 122 Stat. 1664, 1857, 1858.)

REFERENCES IN TEXT

The Social Security Act, referred to in subsec. (b), is act Aug. 14, 1935, ch. 531, 49 Stat. 620, as amended. Part A of title IV of the Social Security Act is classified generally to part A (§ 601 et seq.) of subchapter IV of chapter 7 of Title 42, The Public Health and Welfare. Part D of title IV of such Act is classified generally to part D (§ 651 et seq.) of subchapter IV of chapter 7 of Title 42. For complete classification of this Act to the Code, see section 1305 of Title 42 and Tables.

The Food and Nutrition Act of 2008, referred to in subsec. (b), is Pub. L. 88–525, Aug. 31, 1964, 78 Stat. 703, which is classified generally to chapter 51 (§ 2011 et seq.) of Title 7, Agriculture. For complete classification of this Act to the Code, see Short Title note set out under section 2011 of Title 7 and Tables.

CODIFICATION

Pub. L. 110–234 and Pub. L. 110–246 made identical amendments to this section. The amendments by Pub. L. 110–234 were repealed by section 4(a) of Pub. L. 110–246.

AMENDMENTS

2008—Subsec. (b). Pub. L. 110–246, § 4002(b)(1)(A), (B), (2)(Q), which directed amendment of the "Wagner-Peysner Act" by substituting "supplemental nutrition assistance program" for "food stamp program" wherever appearing and "Food and Nutrition Act of 2008" for "Food Stamp Act of 1977" wherever appearing, was executed by making the substitutions in subsec. (b) of this section, which is section 3 of the Wagner-Peyser Act, to reflect the probable intent of Congress.

1998—Subsec. (a). Pub. L. 105–220, § 302(a)(1), substituted "Secretary" for "United States Employment Service".

Subsec. (b). Pub. L. 105–220, § 310, substituted "Secretary" for "Secretary of Labor".

Subsec. (c). Pub. L. 105–220, § 302(a)(2), added subsec. (c).

1996—Subsec. (b). Pub. L. 104–193 substituted "State program funded under part A of title IV" for "State plan approved under part A of title IV".

1985—Subsec. (b). Pub. L. 99–198 inserted reference to a State agency charged with the administration of the food stamp program in a State under the Food Stamp Act.

1982—Pub. L. 97–300, amended section generally, substituting provisions which set out functions of the Service and duties of the Secretary of Labor for provisions which had stated the purposes of the Service, including services to veterans and supplying of data for the administration of programs in aid of families with dependent children, and defined "State".

1976—Subsec. (a). Pub. L. 94–566 provided that the bureau has a further duty to assure that the employment offices in each State, upon request of a public agency administering or supervising the administration of a State plan approved under part A of title IV of the Social Security Act or of a public agency charged with any duty or responsibility under any program or activity authorized or required under part D of title IV of such Act, furnish to such agency making the request, from any data contained in the files of any such employment office, information with respect to any individual specified in the request as to whether such individual is receiving, has received, or has made application for, unemployment compensation, and the amount of any such compensation being received by such individual, the current (or most recent) home address of such individual, and whether such individual has refused an offer of employment and, if so, a description of the employment so offered and terms, conditions, and rate of pay therefor.

1973—Subsec. (a). Pub. L. 93–198, § 204(c)(1), struck out function of maintaining a public employment service for the District of Columbia from the functions of the bureau.

Subsec. (b). Pub. L. 93–198, § 204(c)(2), included District of Columbia in definition of "State" or "States".

1960—Subsec. (b). Pub. L. 86–624 struck out "Hawaii, Alaska," before "Puerto Rico".

1956—Subsec. (b). Act Aug. 1, 1956, inserted "Guam" after "Puerto Rico".

1954—Subsec. (a). Act Aug. 3, 1954, inserted provisions relating to employment counseling and placement services for handicapped persons.

1950—Subsec. (b). Act Sept. 8, 1950, included Puerto Rico and Virgin Islands in definition of "State" or "States".

EFFECTIVE DATE OF 2008 AMENDMENT

Amendment of this section and repeal of Pub. L. 110–234 by Pub. L. 110–246 effective May 22, 2008, the date of enactment of Pub. L. 110–234, except as otherwise provided, see section 4 of Pub. L. 110–246, set out as an Effective Date note under section 8701 of Title 7, Agriculture.

Amendment by section 4002(b)(1)(A), (B), (2)(Q) of Pub. L. 110–246 effective Oct. 1, 2008, see section 4407 of Pub. L. 110–246, set out as a note under section 1161 of Title 2, The Congress.

EFFECTIVE DATE OF 1998 AMENDMENT

Amendment by Pub. L. 105–220 effective July 1, 1999, see section 311 of Pub. L. 105–220, set out as a note under section 49a of this title.

EFFECTIVE DATE OF 1996 AMENDMENT

Amendment by Pub. L. 104–193 effective July 1, 1997, with transition rules relating to State options to accelerate such date, rules relating to claims, actions, and proceedings commenced before such date, rules relating to closing out of accounts for terminated or substantially modified programs and continuance in office of Assistant Secretary for Family Support, and provisions relating to termination of entitlement under AFDC program, see section 116 of Pub. L. 104–193, as amended, set out as an Effective Date note under section 601 of Title 42, The Public Health and Welfare.

EFFECTIVE DATE OF 1982 AMENDMENT

Amendment by Pub. L. 97–300 effective Oct. 1, 1983, but with Secretary authorized to use funds appropriated for fiscal 1983 to plan for orderly implementation of amendment, see section 181(i) of Pub. L. 97–300, which was formerly classified to section 1591(i) of this title.

EFFECTIVE DATE OF 1973 AMENDMENT

Section 771(b) of Pub. L. 93–198 provided in part that title II of Pub. L. 93–198 [amending this section and section 50 of this title and enacting provisions set out as notes under section 49 of this title and section 8101 of Title 5, Government Organization and Employees], shall take effect on July 1, 1974.

EFFECTIVE DATE OF 1954 AMENDMENT

Section 8 of act Aug. 3, 1954, provided that: "The amendments made by this Act [enacting section 107e–1 of Title 20, Education, and amending this section, sections 31 to 41, 42, and 49g of this title, sections 107, 107a, 107b, 107e, and 107f of Title 20, and section 155a of former Title 36, Patriotic Societies and Observances] shall become effective July 1, 1954."

§ 49c. Acceptance by States; creation of State agencies

In order to obtain the benefits of appropriations apportioned under section 49d of this title, a State shall, pursuant to State statute, accept the provisions of this chapter and, in accordance with such State statute, the Governor shall designate or authorize the creation of a State agency vested with all powers necessary to cooperate with the Secretary under this chapter.

(June 6, 1933, ch. 49, §4, 48 Stat. 114; Pub. L. 105–220, title III, §303, Aug. 7, 1998, 112 Stat. 1081.)

AMENDMENTS

1998—Pub. L. 105–220 substituted ", pursuant to State statute," for ", through its legislature,", inserted ", in accordance with such State statute, the Governor shall" after "the provisions of this chapter and", and substituted "Secretary" for "United States Employment Service".

EFFECTIVE DATE OF 1998 AMENDMENT

Amendment by Pub. L. 105–220 effective July 1, 1999, see section 311 of Pub. L. 105–220, set out as a note under section 49a of this title.

TRANSFER OF STATE AGENCIES TO THE STATES

Act July 26, 1946, ch. 672, title I, 60 Stat. 684, provided in part: "On November 15, 1946, the Secretary of Labor shall transfer, to the State agency in each State designated under section 4 of the Act of Congress approved June 6, 1933, as amended [this section], as the agency to administer the State-wide system of public employment offices in cooperation with the United States Employment Service under said Act [this chapter], the operation of State and local public employment office facilities and properties which were transferred by such State to the Federal Government in 1942 to promote the national war effort. The Secretary of Labor shall, on request of the State agency, also provide for the transfer and assignment to such State, without reimbursement therefor, of any other public employment office facilities and properties within such State, including records, files, and office equipment: *Provided*, That as a condition to such transfer and assignment of Federal properties, the Secretary may require the recipient State to waive any claim which may then exist or thereafter arise out of the use made by the Federal Government of, or for the loss of or damage to, property and facilities transferred to the Federal Government as hereinabove described."

§ 49c–1. Transfer to States of property used by United States Employment Service

For the purpose of assisting the State employment services established and maintained in accordance with the terms of this chapter, the Secretary of Labor is authorized without payment of compensation to transfer and assign to the States in which it is located all property, including records, files, and office equipment, used by the United States Employment Service in its administrative and local employment offices in the respective States, except the records, files, and property used in the Veterans' Service and in the Farm Placement Service maintained under this chapter, as soon as such States establish and maintain systems of public employment offices, in accordance with the terms of sections 49c, 49d, and 49g of this title and the regulations promulgated thereunder.

(Aug. 11, 1939, ch. 693, 53 Stat. 1409; Ex. Ord. No. 9247, Sept. 17, 1942, 7 F.R. 7379; Ex. Ord. No. 9617, Sept. 19, 1945, 10 F.R. 11929; June 16, 1948, ch. 472, title I, 62 Stat. 446; 1949 Reorg. Plan No. 2, §1, eff. Aug. 20, 1949, 14 F.R. 5225, 63 Stat. 1065.)

CODIFICATION

This section was not enacted as part of the Wagner-Peyser Act which comprises this chapter.

TRANSFER OF FUNCTIONS

For history of transfer of functions of United States Employment Service to Secretary of Labor, see note set out under section 49 of this title.

§ 49c–2. Omitted

CODIFICATION

Section, act July 26, 1946, ch. 672, title I, 60 Stat. 684, 685, which authorized transfer to and retention in State system of public employment offices of Federal employees, was from the Department of Labor Act, 1947, and was not repeated in subsequent appropriation acts.

§ 49c–3. Repealed. Pub. L. 89–554, § 8(a), Sept. 6, 1966, 80 Stat. 653

Section, act July 26, 1946, ch. 672, title I, 60 Stat. 685, provided for refund of retirement deductions and interest to members of Social Security Boards returning to State employment.

§ 49c–4. Transferred

CODIFICATION

Section, Pub. L. 88–136, title I, Oct. 11, 1963, 77 Stat. 226, which related to personnel standards, was transferred to section 49n of this title and subsequently omitted from the Code.

§ 49c–5. Omitted

CODIFICATION

Section, act July 8, 1947, ch. 210, title I, 61 Stat. 263, which related to a joint budget, was from the Department of Labor Appropriation Act, 1948, and was not repeated in subsequent appropriation acts. Similar provisions were contained in act July 26, 1946, ch. 672, title I, § 101, 60 Stat. 686.

§ 49d. Appropriations; certification for payment to States

(a) Authorization of appropriations

There is authorized to be appropriated, out of any money in the Treasury not otherwise appropriated, such amounts from time to time as the Congress may deem necessary to carry out the purposes of this chapter.

(b) Certification for payment to States

The Secretary shall from time to time certify to the Secretary of the Treasury for payment to each State which—

(1) except in the case of Guam, has an unemployment compensation law approved by the Secretary under the Federal Unemployment Tax Act [26 U.S.C. 3301 et seq.] and is found to be in compliance with section 503 of title 42,

(2) is found to have coordinated the public employment services with the provision of unemployment insurance claimant services, and

(3) is found to be in compliance with this chapter,

such amounts as the Secretary determines to be necessary for allotment in accordance with section 49e of this title.

(c) Availability of appropriations

(1) Beginning with fiscal year 1985 and thereafter appropriations for any fiscal year for programs and activities assisted or conducted under this chapter shall be available for obligation only on the basis of a program year. The program year shall begin on July 1 in the fiscal year for which the appropriation is made.

(2) Funds obligated for any program year may be expended by the State during that program year and the two succeeding program years and no amount shall be deobligated on account of a rate of expenditure which is consistent with the program plan.

(June 6, 1933, ch. 49, § 5, 48 Stat. 114; May 10, 1935, ch. 102, 49 Stat. 216; June 29, 1938, ch. 816, 52 Stat. 1244; Sept. 8, 1950, ch. 933, § 2, 64 Stat. 822; Aug. 1, 1956, ch. 852, § 17(b), 70 Stat. 910; Pub. L. 86–778, title V, § 543(c), Sept. 13, 1960, 74 Stat. 987; Pub. L. 94–566, title I, § 116(c), Oct. 20, 1976, 90 Stat. 2672; Pub. L. 97–35, title VII, § 702, Aug. 13, 1981, 95 Stat. 521; Pub. L. 97–300, title VI, § 601(b), formerly title V, § 501(b), Oct. 13, 1982, 96 Stat. 1392; renumbered title VI, § 601(b), Pub. L. 100–628, title VII, § 712(a)(1), (2), Nov. 7, 1988, 102 Stat. 3248; Pub. L. 105–220, title III, § 304, Aug. 7, 1998, 112 Stat. 1081.)

REFERENCES IN TEXT

The Federal Unemployment Tax Act, referred to in subsec. (b)(1), is act Aug. 16, 1954, ch. 736, §§ 3301 to 3311, 68A Stat. 454, as amended, which is classified generally to chapter 23 (§ 3301 et seq.) of Title 26, Internal Revenue Code. For complete classification of this Act to the Code, see section 3311 of Title 26 and Tables.

AMENDMENTS

1998—Subsec. (c)(3). Pub. L. 105–220 struck out par. (3) which read as follows:

"(3)(A) Appropriations for fiscal year 1984 shall be available both to fund activities for the period between October 1, 1983, and July 1, 1984, and for the program year beginning July 1, 1984.

"(B) There are authorized to be appropriated such additional sums as may be necessary to carry out the provisions of this paragraph for the transition to program year funding."

1982—Subsec. (b). Pub. L. 97–300 added subsec. (b). Former subsec. (b), which related to certification of compliance by the Secretary to the Secretary of the Treasury with regard to the Federal Unemployment Tax Act by State programs and payment of monies for the operation of the State systems, was struck out.

Subsec. (c). Pub. L. 97–300 added subsec. (c).

1981—Subsec. (b). Pub. L. 97–35 inserted provisions authorizing appropriations for fiscal year beginning Oct. 1, 1981, and definition of "proper and efficient administration of its public employment offices".

1976—Subsec. (b). Pub. L. 94–566 substituted "Guam" for "Guam and the Virgin Islands".

1960—Subsec. (b). Pub. L. 86–778 substituted "Guam and the Virgin Islands" for "Puerto Rico, Guam, and the Virgin Islands".

1956—Subsec. (b). Act Aug. 1, 1956, inserted "Guam" after "Puerto Rico".

1950—Subsec. (a). Act, Sept. 8, 1950, struck out apportionment formula and requirement that States match the funds granted them.

1938—Subsec. (a). Act June 29, 1938, substituted "The annual appropriation under this chapter shall designate the amount to" for "Seventy-five per centum of the amounts appropriated under this chapter shall", at beginning of second sentence, and "the said amount among the several States" for "said 75 per centum of amounts appropriated after January 1, 1935, under this chapter" in proviso.

1935—Subsec. (a). Act May 10, 1935, inserted proviso.

EFFECTIVE DATE OF 1998 AMENDMENT

Amendment by Pub. L. 105–220 effective July 1, 1999, see section 311 of Pub. L. 105–220, set out as a note under section 49a of this title.

EFFECTIVE DATE OF 1982 AMENDMENT

Amendment by Pub. L. 97–300 effective Oct. 1, 1983, but with Secretary authorized to use funds appropriated for fiscal 1983 to plan for orderly implementation of amendment, see section 181(i) of Pub. L. 97–300, which was formerly classified to section 1591(i) of this title.

EFFECTIVE DATE OF 1976 AMENDMENT

Amendment by Pub. L. 94–566 effective on later of Oct. 1, 1976, or day after day on which Secretary of Labor approves under section 3304(a) of Title 26, Internal Revenue Code, an unemployment compensation law submitted to him by Virgin Islands for approval, see section 116(f)(1) of Pub. L. 94–566, set out as a note under section 3304 of Title 26.

EFFECTIVE DATE OF 1960 AMENDMENT

Section 543(c) of Pub. L. 86–778 provided that the amendment made by that section is effective on and after Jan. 1, 1961.

SUSPENSION OF STATE APPROPRIATION REQUIREMENTS UNTIL JULY 1, 1952

Act Sept. 6, 1950, ch. 896, Ch. V, title I, 64 Stat. 643, provided in part that: "No State shall be required to make any appropriation as provided in section 5(a) of said Act of June 6, 1933 [subsec. (a) of this section], prior to July 1, 1952."

Similar provisions suspending the requirement until July 1, 1950 were contained in acts June 16, 1948, ch. 472, title I, 62 Stat. 445; June 29, 1949, ch. 275, title II, 63 Stat. 284.

§ 49d–1. Omitted

CODIFICATION

Section, act June 16, 1937, ch. 359, title IV, 50 Stat. 302, provided for reapportionment of unexpended appropriations.

§ 49e. Allotment of funds

(a) From the amounts appropriated pursuant to section 49d of this title for each fiscal year, the Secretary shall first allot to Guam and the Virgin Islands an amount which, in relation to the total amount available for the fiscal year, is equal to the allotment percentage which each received of amounts available under this chapter in fiscal year 1983.

(b)(1) Subject to paragraphs (2), (3), and (4) of this subsection, the Secretary shall allot the remainder of the sums appropriated and certified pursuant to section 49d of this title for each fiscal year among the States as follows:

(A) two-thirds of such sums shall be allotted on the basis of the relative number of individuals in the civilian labor force in each State as compared to the total number of such individuals in all States; and

(B) one-third of such sums shall be allotted on the basis of the relative number of unemployed individuals in each State as compared to the total number of such individuals in all States.

For purposes of this paragraph, the number of individuals in the civilian labor force and the number of unemployed individuals shall be based on data for the most recent calendar year available, as determined by the Secretary.

(2) No State's allotment under this section for any fiscal year shall be less than 90 percent of its allotment percentage for the fiscal year preceding the fiscal year for which the determination is made. For the purpose of this section, the Secretary shall determine the allotment per-

centage for each State (including Guam and the Virgin Islands) for fiscal year 1984 which is the percentage that the State received under this chapter for fiscal year 1983 of the total amounts available for payments to all States for such fiscal year. For each succeeding fiscal year, the allotment percentage for each such State shall be the percentage that the State received under this chapter for the preceding fiscal year of the total amounts available for allotments for all States for such fiscal year.

(3) For each fiscal year, no State shall receive a total allotment under paragraphs (1) and (2) which is less than 0.28 percent of the total amount available for allotments for all States.

(4) The Secretary shall reserve such amount, not to exceed 3 percent of the sums available for allotments under this section for each fiscal year, as shall be necessary to assure that each State will have a total allotment under this section sufficient to provide staff and other resources necessary to carry out employment service activities and related administrative and support functions on a statewide basis.

(5) The Secretary shall, not later than March 15 of fiscal year 1983 and each succeeding fiscal year, provide preliminary planning estimates and shall, not later than May 15 of each such fiscal year, provide final planning estimates, showing each State's projected allocation for the following year.

(June 6, 1933, ch. 49, §6, as added Pub. L. 97–300, title VI, §601(c), formerly title V, §501(c), Oct. 13, 1982, 96 Stat. 1393; renumbered title VI, §601(c), Pub. L. 100–628, title VII, §712(a)(1), (2), Nov. 7, 1988, 102 Stat. 3248; amended Pub. L. 105–220, title III, §310, Aug. 7, 1998, 112 Stat. 1086.)

PRIOR PROVISIONS

A prior section 49e, act June 6, 1933, ch. 49, §6, 48 Stat. 115, related to apportionment of appropriations, and certification to Secretary of the Treasury, prior to repeal by act Sept. 8, 1950, ch. 933, §3, 64 Stat. 823.

AMENDMENTS

1998—Subsec. (b)(1). Pub. L. 105–220 substituted "Secretary" for "Secretary of Labor" in concluding provisions.

EFFECTIVE DATE OF 1998 AMENDMENT

Amendment by Pub. L. 105–220 effective July 1, 1999, see section 311 of Pub. L. 105–220, set out as a note under section 49a of this title.

EFFECTIVE DATE

Section effective Oct. 1, 1983, but with Secretary authorized to use funds appropriated for fiscal 1983 to plan for orderly implementation of section, see section 181(i) of Pub. L. 97–300, which was formerly classified to section 1591(i) of this title.

§ 49f. Percentage disposition of allotted funds

(a) Use of 90 percent of funds allotted

Ninety percent of the sums allotted to each State pursuant to section 49e of this title may be used—

(1) for job search and placement services to job seekers including counseling, testing, occupational and labor market information, assessment, and referral to employers;

(2) for appropriate recruitment services and special technical services for employers; and

(3) for any of the following activities:

(A) evaluation of programs;

(B) developing linkages between services funded under this chapter and related Federal or State legislation, including the provision of labor exchange services at education sites;

(C) providing services for workers who have received notice of permanent layoff or impending layoff, or workers in occupations which are experiencing limited demand due to technological change, impact of imports, or plant closures;

(D) developing and providing labor market and occupational information;

(E) developing a management information system and compiling and analyzing reports therefrom; and

(F) administering the work test for the State unemployment compensation system and providing job finding and placement services for unemployment insurance claimants.

(b) Use of 10 percent of funds allotted

Ten percent of the sums allotted to each State pursuant to section 49e of this title shall be reserved for use in accordance with this subsection by the Governor of each such State to provide—

(1) performance incentives for public employment service offices and programs, consistent with performance standards established by the Secretary, taking into account direct or indirect placements (including those resulting from self-directed job search or group job search activities assisted by such offices or programs), wages on entered employment, retention, and other appropriate factors;

(2) services for groups with special needs, carried out pursuant to joint agreements between the employment service and the appropriate local workforce investment board and chief elected official or officials or other public agencies or private nonprofit organizations; and

(3) the extra costs of exemplary models for delivering services of the types described in subsection (a) of this section.

(c) Joint funding

(1) Funds made available to States under this section may be used to provide additional funds under an applicable program if—

(A) such program otherwise meets the requirements of this chapter and the requirements of the applicable program;

(B) such program serves the same individuals that are served under this chapter;

(C) such program provides services in a coordinated manner with services provided under this chapter; and

(D) such funds would be used to supplement, and not supplant, funds provided from non-Federal sources.

(2) For purposes of this subsection, the term "applicable program" means any workforce investment activity carried out under the Workforce Investment Act of 1998.

(d) Performance of services and activities under contract

In addition to the services and activities otherwise authorized by this chapter, the Secretary or any State agency designated under this chapter may perform such other services and activities as shall be specified in contracts for payment or reimbursement of the costs thereof made with the Secretary or with any Federal, State, or local public agency, or administrative entity under the Workforce Investment Act of 1998, or private nonprofit organization.

(e) Provision of services as part of one-stop delivery system

All job search, placement, recruitment, labor employment statistics, and other labor exchange services authorized under subsection (a) of this section shall be provided, consistent with the other requirements of this chapter, as part of the one-stop delivery system established by the State.

(June 6, 1933, ch. 49, § 7, as added Pub. L. 97–300, title VI, § 601(c), formerly title V, § 501(c), Oct. 13, 1982, 96 Stat. 1394; renumbered title VI, § 601(c), Pub. L. 100–628, title VII, § 712(a)(1), (2), Nov. 7, 1988, 102 Stat. 3248; amended Pub. L. 101–392, § 5(b), Sept. 25, 1990, 104 Stat. 759; Pub. L. 105–220, title III, §§ 305, 310, Aug. 7, 1998, 112 Stat. 1081, 1086.)

REFERENCES IN TEXT

The Workforce Investment Act of 1998, referred to in subsecs. (c)(2) and (d), is Pub. L. 105–220, Aug. 7, 1998, 112 Stat. 936, as amended. For complete classification of this Act to the Code, see Short Title note set out under section 9201 of Title 20, Education, and Tables.

PRIOR PROVISIONS

A prior section 49f, act June 6, 1933, ch. 49, § 7, 48 Stat. 115, related to ascertainment of amounts due to States, and certification to the Secretary of the Treasury, prior to repeal by act Sept. 8, 1950, ch. 933, § 3, 64 Stat. 823.

AMENDMENTS

1998—Subsec. (b)(2). Pub. L. 105–220, § 305(1), substituted "local workforce investment board" for "private industry council".

Subsec. (c)(2). Pub. L. 105–220, § 305(2), substituted "any workforce investment activity carried out under the Workforce Investment Act of 1998." for "any program under any of the following provisions of law:

"(A) The Carl D. Perkins Vocational and Applied Technology Education Act.

"(B) Section 123, title II, and title III of the Job Training Partnership Act."

Subsec. (d). Pub. L. 105–220, § 310, substituted "Secretary or with" for "Secretary of Labor or with".

Pub. L. 105–220, § 305(3), substituted "Secretary or any State" for "United States Employment Service or any State" and "Workforce Investment Act of 1998" for "Job Training Partnership Act".

Subsec. (e). Pub. L. 105–220, § 305(4), added subsec. (e).

1990—Subsecs. (c), (d). Pub. L. 101–392 added subsec. (c) and redesignated former subsec. (c) as (d).

EFFECTIVE DATE OF 1998 AMENDMENT

Amendment by Pub. L. 105–220 effective July 1, 1999, see section 311 of Pub. L. 105–220, set out as a note under section 49a of this title.

EFFECTIVE DATE OF 1990 AMENDMENT

Amendment by Pub. L. 101–392 effective July 1, 1991, see section 702(a) of Pub. L. 101–392, set out as an Effective Date note under section 3423a of Title 20, Education.

EFFECTIVE DATE

Section effective Oct. 1, 1983, but with Secretary authorized to use funds appropriated for fiscal 1983 to plan for orderly implementation of section, see section 181(i) of Pub. L. 97–300, which was formerly classified to section 1591(i) of this title.

§ 49g. State plans

(a) Submission to Secretary

Any State desiring to receive assistance under this chapter shall submit to the Secretary, as part of the State plan submitted under section 2822 of this title, detailed plans for carrying out the provisions of this chapter within such State.

(b) Contents of plans

Such plans shall include provision for the promotion and development of employment opportunities for handicapped persons and for job counseling and placement of such persons, and for the designation of at least one person in each State or Federal employment office, whose duties shall include the effectuation of such purposes. In those States where a State board, department, or agency exists which is charged with the administration of State laws for vocational rehabilitation of physically handicapped persons, such plans shall include provision for cooperation between such board, department, or agency and the agency designated to cooperate with the United States Employment Service under this chapter.

(c) Information on coordination of workforce investment activities and one-stop delivery system development

The part of the State plan described in subsection (a) of this section shall include the information described in paragraphs (8) and (14) of section 2822(b) of this title.

(d) Approval by Secretary

If such detailed plans are in conformity with the provisions of this chapter and reasonably appropriate and adequate to carry out its purposes, they shall be approved by the Secretary and due notice of such approval shall be given to the State agency.

(June 6, 1933, ch. 49, § 8, 48 Stat. 115; Aug. 3, 1954, ch. 655, § 6(b), 68 Stat. 665; Pub. L. 97–300, title VI, § 601(d), formerly title V, § 501(d), Oct. 13, 1982, 96 Stat. 1395; renumbered title VI, § 601(d), Pub. L. 100–628, title VII, § 712(a)(1), (2), Nov. 7, 1988, 102 Stat. 3248; Pub. L. 105–220, title III, § 306, Aug. 7, 1998, 112 Stat. 1081.)

AMENDMENTS

1998—Subsec. (a). Pub. L. 105–220, § 306(1), amended subsec. (a) generally. Prior to amendment, subsec. (a) read as follows: "Any State desiring to receive the benefits of this chapter shall, by the agency designated to cooperate with the United States Employment Service, submit to the Secretary of Labor detailed plans for carrying out the provisions of this chapter within such State."

Subsec. (b). Pub. L. 105–220, § 306(2), (3), redesignated subsec. (d) as (b) and struck out former subsec. (b) which contained certain requirements for plan preparation at State and national levels.

Subsec. (c). Pub. L. 105–220, § 306(2), (4), added subsec. (c) and struck out former subsec. (c) which read as follows: "The Governor of the State shall be afforded the opportunity to review and transmit to the Secretary proposed modifications of such plans submitted."

Subsec. (d). Pub. L. 105–220, §306(5), (6), redesignated subsec. (e) as (d) and substituted "such detailed plans" for "such plans". Former subsec. (d) redesignated (b).

Subsec. (e). Pub. L. 105–220, §306(5), redesignated subsec. (e) as (d).

1982—Pub. L. 97–300, §601(d)(1), substituted "Secretary of Labor" for "Director" wherever appearing.

Subsec. (a). Pub. L. 97–300, §601(d)(2), designated provisions relating to the submission of a plan to the Secretary by any State desiring to receive benefits under certain sections of this chapter as subsec. (a).

Subsecs. (b), (c). Pub. L. 97–300, §601(d)(5), added subsecs. (b) and (c).

Subsec. (d). Pub. L. 97–300, §601(d)(3), designated provisions relating to the inclusion in State plans of provision for handicapped persons employment opportunities and coordination with State agencies similarly concerned as subsec. (d).

Subsec. (e). Pub. L. 97–300, §601(d)(4), designated provisions relating to approval and notice by the Secretary of the State plans as subsec. (e).

1954—Act Aug. 3, 1954, inserted provisions relating to promotion and development of employment opportunities and for job counseling and placement of handicapped persons.

EFFECTIVE DATE OF 1998 AMENDMENT

Amendment by Pub. L. 105–220 effective July 1, 1999, see section 311 of Pub. L. 105–220, set out as a note under section 49a of this title.

EFFECTIVE DATE OF 1982 AMENDMENT

Amendment by Pub. L. 97–300 effective Oct. 1, 1983, but with Secretary authorized to use funds appropriated for fiscal 1983 to plan for orderly implementation of amendment, see section 181(i) of Pub. L. 97–300, which was formerly classified to section 1591(i) of this title.

EFFECTIVE DATE OF 1954 AMENDMENT

Amendment by act Aug. 3, 1954, effective July 1, 1954, see section 8 of act Aug. 3, 1954, set out as a note under section 49b of this title.

TRANSFER OF FUNCTIONS

For history of transfer of functions of United States Employment Service to Secretary of Labor, see note set out under section 49 of this title.

§49h. Fiscal controls and accounting procedures

(a) Audit

(1) Each State shall establish such fiscal control and fund accounting procedures as may be necessary to assure the proper disbursal of, and accounting for, Federal funds paid to the recipient under this chapter. The Director of the Office of Management and Budget, in consultation with the Comptroller General of the United States, shall establish guidance for the proper performance of audits. Such guidance shall include a review of fiscal controls and fund accounting procedures established by States under this section.

(2) At least once every two years, the State shall prepare or have prepared an independent financial and compliance audit of funds received under this chapter.

(3) Each audit shall be conducted in accordance with applicable auditing standards set forth in the financial and compliance element of the Standards for Audit of Governmental Organizations, Programs, Activities, and Functions issued by the Comptroller General of the United States.

(b) Evaluations by Comptroller General

(1) The Comptroller General of the United States shall evaluate the expenditures by States of funds received under this chapter in order to assure that expenditures are consistent with the provisions of this chapter and to determine the effectiveness of the State in accomplishing the purposes of this chapter. The Comptroller General shall conduct evaluations whenever determined necessary and shall periodically report to the Congress on the findings of such evaluations.

(2) Nothing in this chapter shall be deemed to relieve the Inspector General of the Department of Labor of his responsibilities under the Inspector General Act.

(3) For the purpose of evaluating and reviewing programs established or provided for by this chapter, the Comptroller General shall have access to and the right to copy any books, accounts, records, correspondence, or other documents pertinent to such programs that are in the possession, custody, or control of the State.

(c) Repayment of funds by State

Each State shall repay to the United States amounts found not to have been expended in accordance with this chapter. No such finding shall be made except after notice and opportunity for a fair hearing. The Secretary may offset such amounts against any other amount to which the recipient is or may be entitled under this chapter.

(June 6, 1933, ch. 49, §9, 48 Stat. 116; Pub. L. 97–300, title VI, §601(e), formerly title V, §501(e), Oct. 13, 1982, 96 Stat. 1396; renumbered title VI, §601(e), Pub. L. 100–628, title VII, §712(a)(1), (2), Nov. 7, 1988, 102 Stat. 3248.)

REFERENCES IN TEXT

The Inspector General Act, referred to in subsec. (b)(2), probably means the Inspector General Act of 1978, Pub. L. 95–452, Oct. 12, 1978, 92 Stat. 1101, as amended, which is set out in the Appendix to Title 5, Government Organization and Employees.

AMENDMENTS

1982—Pub. L. 97–300 amended section generally, substituting provisions requiring the States to prepare accounting procedures under Federal guidance, to submit to biennial audit with evaluation of expenditures by the Comptroller General and providing for repayment of improperly expended funds, for provisions requiring reports on expenditures to the Secretary under his regulations and giving him authority to revoke State certification.

EFFECTIVE DATE OF 1982 AMENDMENT

Amendment by Pub. L. 97–300 effective Oct. 1, 1983, but with Secretary authorized to use funds appropriated for fiscal 1983 to plan for orderly implementation of amendment, see section 181(i) of Pub. L. 97–300, which was formerly classified to section 1591(i) of this title.

TERMINATION OF REPORTING REQUIREMENTS

For termination, effective May 15, 2000, of provisions of law requiring submittal to Congress of any annual, semiannual, or other regular periodic report listed in House Document No. 103–7 (in which a report required under subsec. (b)(1) of this section is listed on page 8), see section 3003 of Pub. L. 104–66, as amended, set out as a note under section 1113 of Title 31, Money and Finance.

§ 49i. Recordkeeping and accountability

(a) Records

Each State shall keep records that are sufficient to permit the preparation of reports required by this chapter and to permit the tracing of funds to a level of expenditure adequate to insure that the funds have not been spent unlawfully.

(b) Investigations

(1) The Secretary may investigate such facts, conditions, practices, or other matters which the Secretary finds necessary to determine whether any State receiving funds under this chapter or any official of such State has violated any provision of this chapter.

(2)(A) In order to evaluate compliance with the provisions of this chapter, the Secretary shall conduct investigations of the use of funds received by States under this chapter.

(B) In order to insure compliance with the provisions of this chapter, the Comptroller General of the United States may conduct investigations of the use of funds received under this chapter by any State.

(3) In conducting any investigation under this chapter, the Secretary or the Comptroller General of the United States may not request new compilation of information not readily available to such State.

(c) Reports

Each State receiving funds under this chapter shall—

(1) make such reports concerning its operations and expenditures in such form and containing such information as shall be prescribed by the Secretary, and

(2) establish and maintain a management information system in accordance with guidelines established by the Secretary designed to facilitate the compilation and analysis of programmatic and financial data necessary for reporting, monitoring, and evaluating purposes.

(June 6, 1933, ch. 49, § 10, 48 Stat. 116; Pub. L. 97–300, title VI, § 601(f), formerly title V, § 501(f), Oct. 13, 1982, 96 Stat. 1396; renumbered title VI, § 601(f), Pub. L. 100–628, title VII, § 712(a)(1), (2), Nov. 7, 1988, 102 Stat. 3248.)

AMENDMENTS

1982—Pub. L. 97–300 amended section generally, substituting provisions relating to State maintenance of records and investigations by the Secretary and Comptroller General for provisions which limited expenditures in States prior to adoption of State systems to the current fiscal year and two fiscal years thereafter.

EFFECTIVE DATE OF 1982 AMENDMENT

Amendment by Pub. L. 97–300 effective Oct. 1, 1983, but with Secretary authorized to use funds appropriated for fiscal 1983 to plan for orderly implementation of amendment, see section 181(i) of Pub. L. 97–300, which was formerly classified to section 1591(i) of this title.

§ 49j. Notice of strikes and lockouts to applicants

In carrying out the provisions of this chapter the Secretary is authorized and directed to provide for the giving of notice of strikes or lockouts to applicants before they are referred to employment.

(June 6, 1933, ch. 49, § 11, 48 Stat. 116; Pub. L. 97–300, title VI, § 601(g), formerly title V, § 501(g), Oct. 13, 1982, 96 Stat. 1397; renumbered title VI, § 601(g), Pub. L. 100–628, title VII, § 712(a)(1), (2), Nov. 7, 1988, 102 Stat. 3248; Pub. L. 105–220, title III, § 307, Aug. 7, 1998, 112 Stat. 1082.)

AMENDMENTS

1998—Pub. L. 105–220, § 307(2), which directed the substitution of "Secretary" for "Director", was executed by making the substitution for "director" to reflect the probable intent of Congress.

Pub. L. 105–220, § 307(1), redesignated subsec. (b) as entire section and struck out subsec. (a) which provided for establishment and composition of a Federal Advisory Council, and similar State advisory councils, to work on problems relating to employment.

1982—Subsec. (a). Pub. L. 97–300 inserted provision that nothing in this section should be construed to prohibit the Governor from carrying out functions of the State advisory council through the State job training coordinating council in accordance with section 1532(c) of this title.

EFFECTIVE DATE OF 1998 AMENDMENT

Amendment by Pub. L. 105–220 effective July 1, 1999, see section 311 of Pub. L. 105–220, set out as a note under section 49a of this title.

EFFECTIVE DATE OF 1982 AMENDMENT

Amendment by Pub. L. 97–300 effective Oct. 1, 1983, but with Secretary authorized to use funds appropriated for fiscal 1983 to plan for orderly implementation of amendment, see section 181(i) of Pub. L. 97–300, which was formerly classified to section 1591(i) of this title.

§ 49k. Rules and regulations

The Secretary is authorized to make such rules and regulations as may be necessary to carry out the provisions of this chapter.

(June 6, 1933, ch. 49, § 12, 48 Stat. 117; Pub. L. 105–220, title III, § 308, Aug. 7, 1998, 112 Stat. 1082.)

AMENDMENTS

1998—Pub. L. 105–220, which directed the substitution of "The Secretary" for "The Director, with the approval of the Secretary of Labor,", was executed by making the substitution for text which read in part "director" rather than "Director", to reflect the probable intent of Congress.

EFFECTIVE DATE OF 1998 AMENDMENT

Amendment by Pub. L. 105–220 effective July 1, 1999, see section 311 of Pub. L. 105–220, set out as a note under section 49a of this title.

§ 49*l*. Miscellaneous operating authorities

(a) The Secretary is authorized to establish performance standards for activities under this chapter which shall take into account the differences in priorities reflected in State plans.

(b)(1) Nothing in this chapter shall be construed to prohibit the referral of any applicant to private agencies as long as the applicant is not charged a fee.

(2) No funds paid under this chapter may be used by any State for advertising in newspapers for high paying jobs unless such State submits an annual report to the Secretary beginning in

December 1984 concerning such advertising and the justifications therefor, and the justification may include that such jobs are part of a State industrial development effort.

(June 6, 1933, ch. 49, § 13, as added Pub. L. 97–300, title VI, § 601(h), formerly title V, § 501(h), Oct. 13, 1982, 96 Stat. 1397; renumbered title VI, § 601(h), Pub. L. 100–628, title VII, § 712(a)(1), (2), Nov. 7, 1988, 102 Stat. 3248; amended Pub. L. 97–404, § 5, Dec. 31, 1982, 96 Stat. 2027.)

PRIOR PROVISIONS

A prior section 49l, act June 6, 1933, ch. 49, § 13, 48 Stat. 117, relating to mail franking privileges to employment systems, was transferred to section 338 of former Title 39, The Postal Service. Section 338 of former Title 39 was repealed and reenacted as section 4152 of former Title 39, The Postal Service by Pub. L. 86–682, Sept. 2, 1960, 74 Stat. 578. Section 4152 of former Title 39 was repealed and reenacted as section 3202 of Title 39, Postal Service, by Pub. L. 91–375, Aug. 12, 1970, 84 Stat. 719.

AMENDMENTS

1982—Subsec. (b). Pub. L. 97–404 designated existing provisions as par. (1) and added par. (2).

EFFECTIVE DATE

Section effective Oct. 1, 1983, but with Secretary authorized to use funds appropriated for fiscal 1983 to plan for orderly implementation of section, see section 181(i) of Pub. L. 97–300, which was formerly classified to section 1591(i) of this title.

§ 49l–1. Authorization of appropriations

There are authorized to be appropriated such sums as may be necessary to enable the Secretary to provide funds through reimburseable[1] agreements with the States to operate statistical programs which are essential for development of estimates of the gross national product and other national statistical series, including those related to employment and unemployment.

(June 6, 1933, ch. 49, § 14, as added Pub. L. 97–300, title VI, § 601(h), formerly title V, § 501(h), Oct. 13, 1982, 96 Stat. 1397; renumbered title VI, § 601(h), Pub. L. 100–628, title VII, § 712(a)(1), (2), Nov. 7, 1988, 102 Stat. 3248.)

EFFECTIVE DATE

Section effective Oct. 1, 1983, but with Secretary authorized to use funds appropriated for fiscal 1983 to plan for orderly implementation of section, see section 181(i) of Pub. L. 97–300, which was formerly classified to section 1591(i) of this title.

§ 49l–2. Employment statistics

(a) System content

(1) In general

The Secretary, in accordance with the provisions of this section, shall oversee the development, maintenance, and continuous improvement of a nationwide employment statistics system of employment statistics that includes—

(A) statistical data from cooperative statistical survey and projection programs and data from administrative reporting systems that, taken together, enumerate, estimate, and project employment opportunities and conditions at national, State, and local levels in a timely manner, including statistics on—

(i) employment and unemployment status of national, State, and local populations, including self-employed, part-time, and seasonal workers;

(ii) industrial distribution of occupations, as well as current and projected employment opportunities, wages, benefits (where data is available), and skill trends by occupation and industry, with particular attention paid to State and local conditions;

(iii) the incidence of, industrial and geographical location of, and number of workers displaced by, permanent layoffs and plant closings; and

(iv) employment and earnings information maintained in a longitudinal manner to be used for research and program evaluation;

(B) information on State and local employment opportunities, and other appropriate statistical data related to labor market dynamics, which—

(i) shall be current and comprehensive;

(ii) shall meet the needs identified through the consultations described in subparagraphs (A) and (B) of subsection (e)(2) of this section; and

(iii) shall meet the needs for the information identified in section 134(d);[1]

(C) technical standards (which the Secretary shall publish annually) for data and information described in subparagraphs (A) and (B) that, at a minimum, meet the criteria of chapter 35 of title 44;

(D) procedures to ensure compatibility and additivity of the data and information described in subparagraphs (A) and (B) from national, State, and local levels;

(E) procedures to support standardization and aggregation of data from administrative reporting systems described in subparagraph (A) of employment-related programs;

(F) analysis of data and information described in subparagraphs (A) and (B) for uses such as—

(i) national, State, and local policymaking;

(ii) implementation of Federal policies (including allocation formulas);

(iii) program planning and evaluation; and

(iv) researching labor market dynamics;

(G) wide dissemination of such data, information, and analysis in a user-friendly manner and voluntary technical standards for dissemination mechanisms; and

(H) programs of—

(i) training for effective data dissemination;

(ii) research and demonstration; and

(iii) programs and technical assistance.

[1] So in original. Probably should be "reimbursable".

[1] See References in Text note below.

(2) Information to be confidential

(A) In general

No officer or employee of the Federal Government or agent of the Federal Government may—

(i) use any submission that is furnished for exclusively statistical purposes under the provisions of this section for any purpose other than the statistical purposes for which the submission is furnished;

(ii) make any publication or media transmittal of the data contained in the submission described in clause (i) that permits information concerning individual subjects to be reasonably inferred by either direct or indirect means; or

(iii) permit anyone other than a sworn officer, employee, or agent of any Federal department or agency, or a contractor (including an employee of a contractor) of such department or agency, to examine an individual submission described in clause (i);

without the consent of the individual, agency, or other person who is the subject of the submission or provides that submission.

(B) Immunity from legal process

Any submission (including any data derived from the submission) that is collected and retained by a Federal department or agency, or an officer, employee, agent, or contractor of such a department or agency, for exclusively statistical purposes under this section shall be immune from the legal process and shall not, without the consent of the individual, agency, or other person who is the subject of the submission or provides that submission, be admitted as evidence or used for any purpose in any action, suit, or other judicial or administrative proceeding.

(C) Rule of construction

Nothing in this section shall be construed to provide immunity from the legal process for such submission (including any data derived from the submission) if the submission is in the possession of any person, agency, or entity other than the Federal Government or an officer, employee, agent, or contractor of the Federal Government, or if the submission is independently collected, retained, or produced for purposes other than the purposes of this chapter.

(b) System responsibilities

(1) In general

The employment statistics system described in subsection (a) of this section shall be planned, administered, overseen, and evaluated through a cooperative governance structure involving the Federal Government and States.

(2) Duties

The Secretary, with respect to data collection, analysis, and dissemination of labor employment statistics for the system, shall carry out the following duties:

(A) Assign responsibilities within the Department of Labor for elements of the employment statistics system described in subsection (a) of this section to ensure that all statistical and administrative data collected is consistent with appropriate Bureau of Labor Statistics standards and definitions.

(B) Actively seek the cooperation of other Federal agencies to establish and maintain mechanisms for ensuring complementarity and nonduplication in the development and operation of statistical and administrative data collection activities.

(C) Eliminate gaps and duplication in statistical undertakings, with the systemization of wage surveys as an early priority.

(D) In collaboration with the Bureau of Labor Statistics and States, develop and maintain the elements of the employment statistics system described in subsection (a) of this section, including the development of consistent procedures and definitions for use by the States in collecting the data and information described in subparagraphs (A) and (B) of subsection (a)(1) of this section.

(E) Establish procedures for the system to ensure that—

(i) such data and information are timely;

(ii) paperwork and reporting for the system are reduced to a minimum; and

(iii) States and localities are fully involved in the development and continuous improvement of the system at all levels, including ensuring the provision, to such States and localities, of budget information necessary for carrying out their responsibilities under subsection (e) of this section.

(c) Annual plan

The Secretary, working through the Bureau of Labor Statistics, and in cooperation with the States, and with the assistance of other appropriate Federal agencies, shall prepare an annual plan which shall be the mechanism for achieving cooperative management of the nationwide employment statistics system described in subsection (a) of this section and the statewide employment statistics systems that comprise the nationwide system. The plan shall—

(1) describe the steps the Secretary has taken in the preceding year and will take in the following 5 years to carry out the duties described in subsection (b)(2) of this section;

(2) include a report on the results of an annual consumer satisfaction review concerning the performance of the system, including the performance of the system in addressing the needs of Congress, States, localities, employers, jobseekers, and other consumers;

(3) evaluate the performance of the system and recommend needed improvements, taking into consideration the results of the consumer satisfaction review, with particular attention to the improvements needed at the State and local levels;

(4) justify the budget request for annual appropriations by describing priorities for the fiscal year succeeding the fiscal year in which the plan is developed and priorities for the 5 subsequent fiscal years for the system;

(5) describe current (as of the date of the submission of the plan) spending and spending

needs to carry out activities under this section, including the costs to States and localities of meeting the requirements of subsection (e)(2) of this section; and

(6) describe the involvement of States in the development of the plan, through formal consultations conducted by the Secretary in cooperation with representatives of the Governors of every State, and with representatives of local workforce investment boards, pursuant to a process established by the Secretary in cooperation with the States.

(d) Coordination with the States

The Secretary, working through the Bureau of Labor Statistics, and in cooperation with the States, shall—

(1) develop the annual plan described in subsection (c) of this section and address other employment statistics issues by holding formal consultations, at least once each quarter (beginning with the calendar quarter in which the Workforce Investment Act of 1998 is enacted) on the products and administration of the nationwide employment statistics system; and

(2) hold the consultations with representatives from each of the 10 Federal regions of the Department of Labor, elected (pursuant to a process established by the Secretary) by and from the State employment statistics directors affiliated with the State agencies that perform the duties described in subsection (e)(2) of this section.

(e) State responsibilities

(1) Designation of State agency

In order to receive Federal financial assistance under this section, the Governor of a State shall—

(A) designate a single State agency to be responsible for the management of the portions of the employment statistics system described in subsection (a) of this section that comprise a statewide employment statistics system and for the State's participation in the development of the annual plan; and

(B) establish a process for the oversight of such system.

(2) Duties

In order to receive Federal financial assistance under this section, the State agency shall—

(A) consult with State and local employers, participants, and local workforce investment boards about the labor market relevance of the data to be collected and disseminated through the statewide employment statistics system;

(B) consult with State educational agencies and local educational agencies concerning the provision of employment statistics in order to meet the needs of secondary school and postsecondary school students who seek such information;

(C) collect and disseminate for the system, on behalf of the State and localities in the State, the information and data described in subparagraphs (A) and (B) of subsection (a)(1) of this section;

(D) maintain and continuously improve the statewide employment statistics system in accordance with this section;

(E) perform contract and grant responsibilities for data collection, analysis, and dissemination for such system;

(F) conduct such other data collection, analysis, and dissemination activities as will ensure an effective statewide employment statistics system;

(G) actively seek the participation of other State and local agencies in data collection, analysis, and dissemination activities in order to ensure complementarity, compatibility, and usefulness of data;

(H) participate in the development of the annual plan described in subsection (c) of this section; and

(I) utilize the quarterly records described in section 136(f)(2) of the Workforce Investment Act of 1998 [29 U.S.C. 2871(f)(2)] to assist the State and other States in measuring State progress on State performance measures.

(3) Rule of construction

Nothing in this section shall be construed as limiting the ability of a State agency to conduct additional data collection, analysis, and dissemination activities with State funds or with Federal funds from sources other than this section.

(f) Nonduplication requirement

None of the functions and activities carried out pursuant to this section shall duplicate the functions and activities carried out under the Carl D. Perkins Career and Technical Education Act of 2006 (20 U.S.C. 2301 et seq.).

(g) Authorization of appropriations

There are authorized to be appropriated to carry out this section such sums as may be necessary for each of the fiscal years 1999 through 2004.

(h) "Local area" defined

In this section, the term "local area" means the smallest geographical area for which data can be produced with statistical reliability.

(June 6, 1933, ch. 49, §15, as added Pub. L. 105–220, title III, §309(2), Aug. 7, 1998, 112 Stat. 1082; amended Pub. L. 105–277, div. A, §101(f) [title VIII, §403(a)(1)], Oct. 21, 1998, 112 Stat. 2681–337, 2681–416; Pub. L. 105–332, §5(b)(1), Oct. 31, 1998, 112 Stat. 3127; Pub. L. 109–270, §2(g), Aug. 12, 2006, 120 Stat. 747.)

REFERENCES IN TEXT

Section 134(d), referred to in subsec. (a)(1)(B)(iii), probably means section 134(d) of the Workforce Investment Act of 1998, Pub. L. 105–220, which is classified to section 2864(d) of this title. The Wagner-Peyser Act, of which this section is a part, does not contain a section 134.

The Workforce Investment Act of 1998, referred to in subsec. (d)(1), is Pub. L. 105–220, Aug. 7, 1998, 112 Stat. 936, as amended. For complete classification of this Act to the Code, see Short Title note set out under section 9201 of Title 20, Education, and Tables.

The Carl D. Perkins Career and Technical Education Act of 2006, referred to in subsec. (f), is Pub. L. 88–210, Dec. 18, 1963, 77 Stat. 403, as amended generally by Pub.

L. 109–270, § 1(b), Aug. 12, 2006, 120 Stat. 683, which is classified generally to chapter 44 (§ 2301 et seq.) of Title 20, Education. For complete classification of this Act to the Code, see Short Title note set out under section 2301 of Title 20 and Tables.

PRIOR PROVISIONS

A prior section 15 of act of June 6, 1933, was renumbered section 16, and is set out as a Short Title note under section 49 of this title.

AMENDMENTS

2006—Subsec. (f). Pub. L. 109–270 substituted "Carl D. Perkins Career and Technical Education Act of 2006" for "Carl D. Perkins Vocational and Applied Technology Education Act".

1998—Subsec. (a)(2)(A)(i). Pub. L. 105–332, § 5(b)(1)(A), substituted "under the provisions of this section for any purpose other than the statistical purposes for which" for "under the provisions of this section for any purpose other than the statistical purposes for which".

Pub. L. 105–277, § 101(f) [title VIII, § 403(a)(1)(A)], struck out "of this section" after "statistical purposes".

Subsec. (e)(2)(G). Pub. L. 105–277, § 101(f) [title VIII, § 403(a)(1)(B)], and Pub. L. 105–332, § 5(b)(1)(B), amended subpar. (G) identically, substituting "complementarity" for "complementary".

EFFECTIVE DATE OF 1998 AMENDMENTS

Pub. L. 105–332, § 5(b)(2), Oct. 31, 1998, 112 Stat. 3127, provided that: "The amendments made by paragraph (1) [amending this section] take effect July 2, 1999."

Pub. L. 105–277, div. A, § 101(f) [title VIII, § 403(a)(2)], Oct. 21, 1998, 112 Stat. 2681–337, 2681–416, provided that: "The amendments made by paragraph (1) [amending this section] take effect on July 2, 1999."

EFFECTIVE DATE

Section effective July 1, 1999, see section 311 of Pub. L. 105–220, set out as an Effective Date of 1998 Amendment note under section 49a of this title.

§§ 49m, 49n. Omitted

CODIFICATION

Section 49m, Pub. L. 88–136, title I, Oct. 11, 1963, 77 Stat. 225, relating to payments to States for administrative expenses for their unemployment compensation law and their public employment offices, was from the Department of Labor Appropriation Act, 1964, and was not repeated in the Department of Labor Appropriation Act of 1965. Similar provisions were contained in the following prior appropriation acts:

Aug. 14, 1962, Pub. L. 87–582, title I, 76 Stat. 363.
Sept. 22, 1961, Pub. L. 87–290, title I, 75 Stat. 591.
Sept. 2, 1960, Pub. L. 86–703, title I, 74 Stat. 757.
Aug. 14, 1959, Pub. L. 86–158, title I, 73 Stat. 341.
Aug. 1, 1958, Pub. L. 85–580, title I, 72 Stat. 458.
June 29, 1957, Pub. L. 85–67, title I, 71 Stat. 212.
June 29, 1956, ch. 477, title I, 70 Stat. 424.
June 29, 1956, ch. 437, title I, 69 Stat. 398.
July 2, 1954, ch. 457, title I, 68 Stat. 435.
July 31, 1953, ch. 296, title I, 67 Stat. 246.
July 5, 1952, ch. 575, title I, 66 Stat. 369.
Aug. 31, 1951, ch. 373, title I, 65 Stat. 210.
Sept. 6, 1950, ch. 896, ch. V, title I, 64 Stat. 643.
June 29, 1949, ch. 275, title II, 63 Stat. 284.
June 16, 1948, ch. 472, title I, 62 Stat. 445.

Section 49n, Pub. L. 88–136, title I, Oct. 11, 1963, 77 Stat. 226, relating to personnel standards, was from the Department of Labor Appropriation Act, 1964, and was not repeated in the Department of Labor Appropriation Act of 1965. Similar provisions were contained in the following prior appropriations acts:

Aug. 14, 1962, Pub. L. 87–582, title I, 76 Stat. 363.
Sept. 22, 1961, Pub. L. 87–290, title I, 75 Stat. 591.
Sept. 2, 1960, Pub. L. 86–703, title I, 74 Stat. 757.
Aug. 14, 1959, Pub. L. 86–158, title I, 73 Stat. 341.
Aug. 1, 1958, Pub. L. 85–580, title I, 72 Stat. 458.
June 29, 1957, Pub. L. 85–67, title I, 71 Stat. 212.
June 29, 1956, ch. 477, title I, 70 Stat. 425.
Aug. 1, 1955, ch. 437, title I, 69 Stat. 398.
July 2, 1954, ch. 457, title I, 68 Stat. 435.
July 31, 1953, ch. 296, title I, 67 Stat. 246.
July 5, 1952, ch. 575, title I, 66 Stat. 359.
Aug. 31, 1951, ch. 273, title I, 65 Stat. 210.
Sept. 6, 1950, ch. 896, ch. V, title I, 64 Stat. 644.
June 29, 1949, ch. 275, title II, 63 Stat. 284.
June 16, 1948, ch. 472, title I, 62 Stat. 445.
July 8, 1947, ch. 210, title I, 61 Stat. 263.
July 26, 1946, ch. 672, title I, 60 Stat. 685.

CHAPTER 4C—APPRENTICE LABOR

§ 50. Promotion of labor standards of apprenticeship

The Secretary of Labor is authorized and directed to formulate and promote the furtherance of labor standards necessary to safeguard the welfare of apprentices, to extend the application of such standards by encouraging the inclusion thereof in contracts of apprenticeship, to bring together employers and labor for the formulation of programs of apprenticeship, to cooperate with State agencies engaged in the formulation and promotion of standards of apprenticeship, and to cooperate with the Secretary of Education in accordance with section 17 of title 20. For the purposes of this chapter the term "State" shall include the District of Columbia.

(Aug. 16, 1937, ch. 663, § 1, 50 Stat. 664; 1939 Reorg. Plan No. I, §§ 201, 204, 206, eff. July 1, 1939, 4 F.R. 2728, 53 Stat. 1424, 1425; July 12, 1943, ch. 221, title VII, 57 Stat. 518; 1953 Reorg. Plan No. 1, §§ 5, 8, eff. Apr. 11, 1953, 18 F.R. 2053, 67 Stat. 631; Pub. L. 93–198, title II, § 204(h), Dec. 24, 1973, 87 Stat. 784; Pub. L. 96–88, title III, § 301(a)(1), Oct. 17, 1979, 93 Stat. 677.)

REFERENCES IN TEXT

Section 17 of title 20, referred to in text, was repealed by Pub. L. 89–554, § 8(a), Sept. 6, 1966, 80 Stat. 643.

CODIFICATION

Words "with the National Youth Administration" were omitted from text in view of abolition of National Youth Administration by act July 12, 1943.

AMENDMENTS

1973—Pub. L. 93–198 inserted provision that "State" includes the District of Columbia.

EFFECTIVE DATE OF 1973 AMENDMENT

Amendment by Pub. L. 93–198 effective July 1, 1974, see section 771(b) of Pub. L. 93–198, set out in part as a note under section 49b of this title.

SHORT TITLE

The act of Aug. 16, 1937, ch. 663, 50 Stat. 664, which enacted this chapter, is popularly known as the "National Apprenticeship Act".

TRANSFER OF FUNCTIONS

"Secretary of Education" substituted in text for "Office of Education under the Department of Health, Education, and Welfare", pursuant to section 301(a)(1) of Pub. L. 96-88, which is classified to section 3441(a)(1) of Title 20, Education, and which transferred all functions of Office of Education to Secretary of Education.

Functions of Federal Security Administrator transferred to Secretary of Health, Education, and Welfare and all agencies of Federal Security Agency transferred to Department of Health, Education, and Welfare by section 5 of Reorg. Plan No. 1 of 1953, set out in the Appendix to Title 5, Government Organization and Employees. Federal Security Agency and office of Administrator abolished by section 8 of Reorg. Plan No. 1 of 1953.

Reorg. Plan No. I of 1939, consolidated National Youth Administration and Office of Education, with other agencies, into Federal Security Agency under supervision and direction of Federal Security Administrator.

§50a. Publication of information; national advisory committees

The Secretary of Labor may publish information relating to existing and proposed labor standards of apprenticeship, and may appoint national advisory committees to serve without compensation. Such committees shall include representatives of employers, representatives of labor, educators, and officers of other executive departments, with the consent of the head of any such department.

(Aug. 16, 1937, ch. 663, §2, 50 Stat. 665.)

§50b. Appointment of employees

The Secretary of Labor is authorized to appoint such employees as he may from time to time find necessary for the administration of this chapter, with regard to existing laws applicable to the appointment and compensation of employees of the United States.

(Aug. 16, 1937, ch. 663, §3, 50 Stat. 665; July 12, 1943, ch. 221, title VII, 57 Stat. 518.)

CODIFICATION

Proviso authorizing employment of certain persons in the division of apprentice training of National Youth Administration, was omitted in view of abolition of that agency by act July 12, 1943.

Provision formerly in this section relieved National Youth Administration, after August 16, 1937, of responsibility for promotion of labor standards of apprenticeship, and directed transfer of records and papers to Department of Labor.

CHAPTER 5—LABOR DISPUTES; MEDIATION AND INJUNCTIVE RELIEF

§51. Repealed. Pub. L. 89–554, §8(a), Sept. 6, 1966, 80 Stat. 642

Section, act Mar. 4, 1913, ch. 141, §8, 37 Stat. 738, related to mediation in labor disputes and the appointment of commissioners of conciliation. See section 172 of this title.

§52. Statutory restriction of injunctive relief

No restraining order or injunction shall be granted by any court of the United States, or a judge or the judges thereof, in any case between an employer and employees, or between employers and employees, or between employees, or between persons employed and persons seeking employment, involving, or growing out of, a dispute concerning terms or conditions of employment, unless necessary to prevent irreparable injury to property, or to a property right, of the party making the application, for which injury there is no adequate remedy at law, and such property or property right must be described with particularity in the application, which must be in writing and sworn to by the applicant or by his agent or attorney.

And no such restraining order or injunction shall prohibit any person or persons, whether singly or in concert, from terminating any relation of employment, or from ceasing to perform any work or labor, or from recommending, advising, or persuading others by peaceful means so to do; or from attending at any place where any such person or persons may lawfully be, for the purpose of peacefully obtaining or communicating information, or from peacefully persuading any person to work or to abstain from working; or from ceasing to patronize or to employ any party to such dispute, or from recommending, advising, or persuading others by peaceful and lawful means so to do; or from paying or giving to, or withholding from, any person engaged in such dispute, any strike benefits or other moneys or things of value; or from peaceably assembling in a lawful manner, and for lawful purposes; or from doing any act or thing which might lawfully be done in the absence of such dispute by any party thereto; nor shall any of the acts specified in this paragraph be considered or held to be violations of any law of the United States.

(Oct. 15, 1914, ch. 323, §20, 38 Stat. 738.)

§53. "Person" or "persons" defined

The word "person" or "persons" wherever used in section 52 of this title shall be deemed to include corporations and associations existing under or authorized by the laws of either the United States, the laws of any of the Territories, the laws of any State, or the laws of any foreign country.

(Oct. 15, 1914, ch. 323, §1, 38 Stat. 730.)

CODIFICATION

Section is based on the 3d par. of section 1(a) of the Clayton Act (Oct. 15, 1914, ch. 323, as amended by section 305(b) of Pub. L. 94-435, Sept. 30, 1976). Section 1 of the Clayton Act is classified in its entirety to section 12 of Title 15, Commerce and Trade.

CHAPTER 6—JURISDICTION OF COURTS IN MATTERS AFFECTING EMPLOYER AND EMPLOYEE

§ 101. Issuance of restraining orders and injunctions; limitation; public policy

No court of the United States, as defined in this chapter, shall have jurisdiction to issue any restraining order or temporary or permanent injunction in a case involving or growing out of a labor dispute, except in a strict conformity with the provisions of this chapter; nor shall any such restraining order or temporary or permanent injunction be issued contrary to the public policy declared in this chapter.

(Mar. 23, 1932, ch. 90, § 1, 47 Stat. 70.)

SHORT TITLE

Act Mar. 23, 1932, ch. 90, 47 Stat. 70, which enacted this chapter, is popularly known as the "Norris-LaGuardia Act".

§ 102. Public policy in labor matters declared

In the interpretation of this chapter and in determining the jurisdiction and authority of the courts of the United States, as such jurisdiction and authority are defined and limited in this chapter, the public policy of the United States is declared as follows:

Whereas under prevailing economic conditions, developed with the aid of governmental authority for owners of property to organize in the corporate and other forms of ownership association, the individual unorganized worker is commonly helpless to exercise actual liberty of contract and to protect his freedom of labor, and thereby to obtain acceptable terms and conditions of employment, wherefore, though he should be free to decline to associate with his fellows, it is necessary that he have full freedom of association, self-organization, and designation of representatives of his own choosing, to negotiate the terms and conditions of his employment, and that he shall be free from the interference, restraint, or coercion of employers of labor, or their agents, in the designation of such representatives or in self-organization or in other concerted activities for the purpose of collective bargaining or other mutual aid or protection; therefore, the following definitions of and limitations upon the jurisdiction and authority of the courts of the United States are enacted.

(Mar. 23, 1932, ch. 90, § 2, 47 Stat. 70.)

§ 103. Nonenforceability of undertakings in conflict with public policy; "yellow dog" contracts

Any undertaking or promise, such as is described in this section, or any other undertaking or promise in conflict with the public policy declared in section 102 of this title, is declared to be contrary to the public policy of the United States, shall not be enforceable in any court of the United States and shall not afford any basis for the granting of legal or equitable relief by any such court, including specifically the following:

Every undertaking or promise hereafter made, whether written or oral, express or implied, constituting or contained in any contract or agreement of hiring or employment between any individual, firm, company, association, or corporation, and any employee or prospective employee of the same, whereby

(a) Either party to such contract or agreement undertakes or promises not to join, become, or remain a member of any labor organization or of any employer organization; or

(b) Either party to such contract or agreement undertakes or promises that he will withdraw from an employment relation in the event that he joins, becomes, or remains a member of any labor organization or of any employer organization.

(Mar. 23, 1932, ch. 90, § 3, 47 Stat. 70.)

§ 104. Enumeration of specific acts not subject to restraining orders or injunctions

No court of the United States shall have jurisdiction to issue any restraining order or temporary or permanent injunction in any case involving or growing out of any labor dispute to prohibit any person or persons participating or interested in such dispute (as these terms are herein defined) from doing, whether singly or in concert, any of the following acts:

(a) Ceasing or refusing to perform any work or to remain in any relation of employment;

(b) Becoming or remaining a member of any labor organization or of any employer organization, regardless of any such undertaking or promise as is described in section 103 of this title;

(c) Paying or giving to, or withholding from, any person participating or interested in such labor dispute, any strike or unemployment benefits or insurance, or other moneys or things of value;

(d) By all lawful means aiding any person participating or interested in any labor dispute who is being proceeded against in, or is prosecuting, any action or suit in any court of the United States or of any State;

(e) Giving publicity to the existence of, or the facts involved in, any labor dispute, whether by advertising, speaking, patrolling, or by any other method not involving fraud or violence;

(f) Assembling peaceably to act or to organize to act in promotion of their interests in a labor dispute;

(g) Advising or notifying any person of an intention to do any of the acts heretofore specified;

(h) Agreeing with other persons to do or not to do any of the acts heretofore specified; and

(i) Advising, urging, or otherwise causing or inducing without fraud or violence the acts heretofore specified, regardless of any such undertaking or promise as is described in section 103 of this title.

(Mar. 23, 1932, ch. 90, § 4, 47 Stat. 70.)

§ 105. Doing in concert of certain acts as constituting unlawful combination or conspiracy subjecting person to injunctive remedies

No court of the United States shall have jurisdiction to issue a restraining order or temporary or permanent injunction upon the ground that any of the persons participating or interested in a labor dispute constitute or are engaged in an unlawful combination or conspiracy because of the doing in concert of the acts enumerated in section 104 of this title.

(Mar. 23, 1932, ch. 90, § 5, 47 Stat. 71.)

§ 106. Responsibility of officers and members of associations or their organizations for unlawful acts of individual officers, members, and agents

No officer or member of any association or organization, and no association or organization participating or interested in a labor dispute, shall be held responsible or liable in any court of the United States for the unlawful acts of individual officers, members, or agents, except upon clear proof of actual participation in, or actual authorization of, such acts, or of ratification of such acts after actual knowledge thereof.

(Mar. 23, 1932, ch. 90, § 6, 47 Stat. 71.)

§ 107. Issuance of injunctions in labor disputes; hearing; findings of court; notice to affected persons; temporary restraining order; undertakings

No court of the United States shall have jurisdiction to issue a temporary or permanent injunction in any case involving or growing out of a labor dispute, as defined in this chapter, except after hearing the testimony of witnesses in open court (with opportunity for cross-examination) in support of the allegations of a complaint made under oath, and testimony in opposition thereto, if offered, and except after findings of fact by the court, to the effect—

(a) That unlawful acts have been threatened and will be committed unless restrained or have been committed and will be continued unless restrained, but no injunction or temporary restraining order shall be issued on account of any threat or unlawful act excepting against the person or persons, association, or organization making the threat or committing the unlawful act or actually authorizing or ratifying the same after actual knowledge thereof;

(b) That substantial and irreparable injury to complainant's property will follow;

(c) That as to each item of relief granted greater injury will be inflicted upon complainant by the denial of relief than will be inflicted upon defendants by the granting of relief;

(d) That complainant has no adequate remedy at law; and

(e) That the public officers charged with the duty to protect complainant's property are unable or unwilling to furnish adequate protection.

Such hearing shall be held after due and personal notice thereof has been given, in such manner as the court shall direct, to all known persons against whom relief is sought, and also to the chief of those public officials of the county and city within which the unlawful acts have been threatened or committed charged with the duty to protect complainant's property: *Provided, however*, That if a complainant shall also allege that, unless a temporary restraining order shall be issued without notice, a substantial and irreparable injury to complainant's property will be unavoidable, such a temporary restraining order may be issued upon testimony under oath, sufficient, if sustained, to justify the court in issuing a temporary injunction upon a hearing after notice. Such a temporary restraining order shall be effective for no longer than five days and shall become void at the expiration of said five days. No temporary restraining order or temporary injunction shall be issued except on condition that complainant shall first file an undertaking with adequate security in an amount to be fixed by the court sufficient to recompense those enjoined for any loss, expense, or damage caused by the improvident or erroneous issuance of such order or injunction, including all reasonable costs (together with a reasonable attorney's fee) and expense of defense against the order or against the granting of any injunctive relief sought in the same proceeding and subsequently denied by the court.

The undertaking mentioned in this section shall be understood to signify an agreement entered into by the complainant and the surety upon which a decree may be rendered in the same suit or proceeding against said complainant and surety, upon a hearing to assess damages of which hearing complainant and surety shall have reasonable notice, the said complainant and surety submitting themselves to the jurisdiction of the court for that purpose. But nothing in this section contained shall deprive any party having a claim or cause of action under or upon such undertaking from electing to pursue his ordinary remedy by suit at law or in equity.

(Mar. 23, 1932, ch. 90, § 7, 47 Stat. 71.)

§ 108. Noncompliance with obligations involved in labor disputes or failure to settle by negotiation or arbitration as preventing injunctive relief

No restraining order or injunctive relief shall be granted to any complainant who has failed to comply with any obligation imposed by law which is involved in the labor dispute in question, or who has failed to make every reasonable effort to settle such dispute either by negotiation or with the aid of any available governmental machinery of mediation or voluntary arbitration.

(Mar. 23, 1932, ch. 90, § 8, 47 Stat. 72.)

§109. Granting of restraining order or injunction as dependent on previous findings of fact; limitation on prohibitions included in restraining orders and injunctions

No restraining order or temporary or permanent injunction shall be granted in a case involving or growing out of a labor dispute, except on the basis of findings of fact made and filed by the court in the record of the case prior to the issuance of such restraining order or injunction; and every restraining order or injunction granted in a case involving or growing out of a labor dispute shall include only a prohibition of such specific act or acts as may be expressly complained of in the bill of complaint or petition filed in such case and as shall be expressly included in said findings of fact made and filed by the court as provided in this chapter.

(Mar. 23, 1932, ch. 90, §9, 47 Stat. 72.)

§110. Review by court of appeals of issuance or denial of temporary injunctions; record

Whenever any court of the United States shall issue or deny any temporary injunction in a case involving or growing out of a labor dispute, the court shall, upon the request of any party to the proceedings and on his filing the usual bond for costs, forthwith certify as in ordinary cases the record of the case to the court of appeals for its review. Upon the filing of such record in the court of appeals, the appeal shall be heard and the temporary injunctive order affirmed, modified, or set aside expeditiously.

(Mar. 23, 1932, ch. 90, §10, 47 Stat. 72; June 25, 1948, ch. 646, §32(a), 62 Stat. 991; May 24, 1949, ch. 139, §127, 63 Stat. 107; Pub. L. 98–620, title IV, §402(30), Nov. 8, 1984, 98 Stat. 3359.)

AMENDMENTS

1984—Pub. L. 98–620 substituted "expeditiously" for "with the greatest possible expedition, giving the proceedings precedence over all other matters except older matters of the same character".

CHANGE OF NAME

Act June 25, 1948, eff. Sept. 1, 1948, as amended by act May 24, 1949, substituted "court of appeals" for "circuit court of appeals".

EFFECTIVE DATE OF 1984 AMENDMENT

Amendment by Pub. L. 98–620 not applicable to cases pending on Nov. 8, 1984, see section 403 of Pub. L. 98–620, set out as a note under section 1657 of Title 28, Judiciary and Judicial Procedure.

§§111, 112. Repealed. June 25, 1948, ch. 645, §21, 62 Stat. 862, eff. Sept. 1, 1948

Section 111, act Mar. 23, 1932, ch. 90, §11, 47 Stat. 72, related to contempts, speedy and public trial, and jury. See section 3692 of Title 18, Crimes and Criminal Procedure.

Section 112, act Mar. 23, 1932, ch. 90, §12, 47 Stat. 73, related to contempts and demand for retirement of sitting judge. See rule 42 of the Federal Rules of Criminal Procedure, set out in the Appendix to Title 18.

§113. Definitions of terms and words used in chapter

When used in this chapter, and for the purposes of this chapter—

(a) A case shall be held to involve or to grow out of a labor dispute when the case involves persons who are engaged in the same industry, trade, craft, or occupation; or have direct or indirect interests therein; or who are employees of the same employer; or who are members of the same or an affiliated organization of employers or employees; whether such dispute is (1) between one or more employers or associations of employers and one or more employees or associations of employees; (2) between one or more employers or associations of employers and one or more employers or associations of employers; or (3) between one or more employees or associations of employees and one or more employees or associations of employees; or when the case involves any conflicting or competing interests in a "labor dispute" (as defined in this section) of "persons participating or interested" therein (as defined in this section).

(b) A person or association shall be held to be a person participating or interested in a labor dispute if relief is sought against him or it, and if he or it is engaged in the same industry, trade, craft, or occupation in which such dispute occurs, or has a direct or indirect interest therein, or is a member, officer, or agent of any association composed in whole or in part of employers or employees engaged in such industry, trade, craft, or occupation.

(c) The term "labor dispute" includes any controversy concerning terms or conditions of employment, or concerning the association or representation of persons in negotiating, fixing, maintaining, changing, or seeking to arrange terms or conditions of employment, regardless of whether or not the disputants stand in the proximate relation of employer and employee.

(d) The term "court of the United States" means any court of the United States whose jurisdiction has been or may be conferred or defined or limited by Act of Congress, including the courts of the District of Columbia.

(Mar. 23, 1932, ch. 90, §13, 47 Stat. 73.)

§114. Separability

If any provision of this chapter or the application thereof to any person or circumstance is held unconstitutional or otherwise invalid, the remaining provisions of this chapter and the application of such provisions to other persons or circumstances shall not be affected thereby.

(Mar. 23, 1932, ch. 90, §14, 47 Stat. 73.)

§115. Repeal of conflicting acts

All acts and parts of acts in conflict with the provisions of this chapter are repealed.

(Mar. 23, 1932, ch. 90, §15, 47 Stat. 73.)

CHAPTER 7—LABOR-MANAGEMENT RELATIONS

SUBCHAPTER I—GENERAL PROVISIONS

SUBCHAPTER II—NATIONAL LABOR RELATIONS

SUBCHAPTER I—GENERAL PROVISIONS

§141. Short title; Congressional declaration of purpose and policy

(a) This chapter may be cited as the "Labor Management Relations Act, 1947".

(b) Industrial strife which interferes with the normal flow of commerce and with the full production of articles and commodities for commerce, can be avoided or substantially minimized if employers, employees, and labor organizations each recognize under law one another's legitimate rights in their relations with each other, and above all recognize under law that neither party has any right in its relations with any other to engage in acts or practices which jeopardize the public health, safety, or interest.

It is the purpose and policy of this chapter, in order to promote the full flow of commerce, to prescribe the legitimate rights of both employees and employers in their relations affecting commerce, to provide orderly and peaceful procedures for preventing the interference by either with the legitimate rights of the other, to protect the rights of individual employees in their relations with labor organizations whose activities affect commerce, to define and proscribe practices on the part of labor and management which affect commerce and are inimical to the general welfare, and to protect the rights of the public in connection with labor disputes affecting commerce.

(June 23, 1947, ch. 120, §1, 61 Stat. 136.)

References in Text

This chapter, referred to in subsec. (a), was in the original "This Act" meaning act June 23, 1947, ch. 120, 61 Stat. 136, as amended, which is classified principally to this subchapter and subchapters III (§171 et seq.) and IV (§185 et seq.) of this chapter. For complete classification of this act to the Code, see Tables.

Short Title of 1978 Amendment

Pub. L. 95–524, §6(a), Oct. 27, 1978, 92 Stat. 2020, provided that: "This section [enacting section 175a of this title, amending sections 173 and 186 of this title, and enacting provisions set out as notes under section 175a of this title] may be cited as the 'Labor Management Cooperation Act of 1978'."

National Commission on Technology, Automation, and Economic Progress

Pub. L. 88–444, Aug. 19, 1964, 78 Stat. 462, established the National Commission on Technology, Automation, and Economic Progress, to make a comprehensive and impartial study and make recommendations from time to time as needed for constructive action. The Commission was directed to submit a final report of its findings and recommendations to the President and the Congress by January 1, 1966, and ceased 30 days after submitting its final report.

Executive Order No. 10918

Ex. Ord. No. 10918, Feb. 16, 1961, 26 F.R. 1427, which established the President's Advisory Committee on Labor-Management Policy, was revoked by Ex. Ord. No. 11710, Apr. 4, 1973, 38 F.R. 9071, formerly set out below.

Executive Order No. 11710

Ex. Ord. No. 11710, Apr. 4, 1973, 38 F.R. 9071, as amended by Ex. Ord. No. 11729, July 12, 1973, 38 F.R. 18863, which established the National Commission for Industrial Peace, was revoked by Ex. Ord. No. 11823, Dec. 12, 1974, 39 F.R. 43529.

Executive Order No. 11809

Ex. Ord. No. 11809, Sept. 30, 1974, 39 F.R. 35565, which established the President's Labor-Management Committee, was revoked by Ex. Ord. No. 11948, Dec. 20, 1976, 41 F.R. 55705, set out as a note under section 14 of the

Federal Advisory Committee Act in the Appendix to Title 5, Government Organization and Employees.

§ 142. Definitions

When used in this chapter—

(1) The term "industry affecting commerce" means any industry or activity in commerce or in which a labor dispute would burden or obstruct commerce or tend to burden or obstruct commerce or the free flow of commerce.

(2) The term "strike" includes any strike or other concerted stoppage of work by employees (including a stoppage by reason of the expiration of a collective-bargaining agreement) and any concerted slowdown or other concerted interruption of operations by employees.

(3) The terms "commerce", "labor disputes", "employer", "employee", "labor organization", "representative", "person", and "supervisor" shall have the same meaning as when used in subchapter II of this chapter.

(June 23, 1947, ch. 120, title V, § 501, 61 Stat. 161.)

REFERENCES IN TEXT

Subchapter II of this chapter, referred to in par. (3), was in the original "the National Labor Relations Act as amended by this Act" [29 U.S.C. § 151 et seq.].

§ 143. Saving provisions

Nothing in this chapter shall be construed to require an individual employee to render labor or service without his consent, nor shall anything in this chapter be construed to make the quitting of his labor by an individual employee an illegal act; nor shall any court issue any process to compel the performance by an individual employee of such labor or service, without his consent; nor shall the quitting of labor by an employee or employees in good faith because of abnormally dangerous conditions for work at the place of employment of such employee or employees be deemed a strike under this chapter.

(June 23, 1947, ch. 120, title V, § 502, 61 Stat. 162.)

§ 144. Separability

If any provision of this chapter, or the application of such provision to any person or circumstance, shall be held invalid, the remainder of this chapter, or the application of such provision to persons or circumstances other than those as to which it is held invalid, shall not be affected thereby.

(June 23, 1947, ch. 120, title V, § 503, 61 Stat. 162.)

SUBCHAPTER II—NATIONAL LABOR RELATIONS

CODIFICATION

This subchapter is comprised of the National Labor Relations Act, and is not part of the Labor Management Relations Act, 1947, which comprises this chapter.

§ 151. Findings and declaration of policy

The denial by some employers of the right of employees to organize and the refusal by some employers to accept the procedure of collective bargaining lead to strikes and other forms of industrial strife or unrest, which have the intent or the necessary effect of burdening or obstructing commerce by (a) impairing the efficiency, safety, or operation of the instrumentalities of commerce; (b) occurring in the current of commerce; (c) materially affecting, restraining, or controlling the flow of raw materials or manufactured or processed goods from or into the channels of commerce, or the prices of such materials or goods in commerce; or (d) causing diminution of employment and wages in such volume as substantially to impair or disrupt the market for goods flowing from or into the channels of commerce.

The inequality of bargaining power between employees who do not possess full freedom of association or actual liberty of contract, and employers who are organized in the corporate or other forms of ownership association substantially burdens and affects the flow of commerce, and tends to aggravate recurrent business depressions, by depressing wage rates and the purchasing power of wage earners in industry and by preventing the stabilization of competitive wage rates and working conditions within and between industries.

Experience has proved that protection by law of the right of employees to organize and bargain collectively safeguards commerce from injury, impairment, or interruption, and promotes the flow of commerce by removing certain recognized sources of industrial strife and unrest, by encouraging practices fundamental to the friendly adjustment of industrial disputes arising out of differences as to wages, hours, or other working conditions, and by restoring equality of bargaining power between employers and employees.

Experience has further demonstrated that certain practices by some labor organizations, their officers, and members have the intent or the necessary effect of burdening or obstructing commerce by preventing the free flow of goods in such commerce through strikes and other forms of industrial unrest or through concerted activities which impair the interest of the public in the free flow of such commerce. The elimination of such practices is a necessary condition to the assurance of the rights herein guaranteed.

It is hereby declared to be the policy of the United States to eliminate the causes of certain substantial obstructions to the free flow of commerce and to mitigate and eliminate these obstructions when they have occurred by encouraging the practice and procedure of collective bargaining and by protecting the exercise by workers of full freedom of association, self-organization, and designation of representatives of their own choosing, for the purpose of negotiating the terms and conditions of their employment or other mutual aid or protection.

(July 5, 1935, ch. 372, § 1, 49 Stat. 449; June 23, 1947, ch. 120, title I, § 101, 61 Stat. 136.)

AMENDMENTS

1947—Act June 23, 1947, amended section generally to restate the declaration of policy and to make the finding and policy of this subchapter "two-sided".

EFFECTIVE DATE OF 1947 AMENDMENT

Section 104 of title I of act June 23, 1947, provided: "The amendments made by this title [amending this subchapter] shall take effect sixty days after the date of the enactment of this Act [June 23, 1947], except that the authority of the President to appoint certain officers conferred upon him by section 3 of the National Labor Relations Act as amended by this title [section 153 of this title] may be exercised forthwith."

§ 152. Definitions

When used in this subchapter—

(1) The term "person" includes one or more individuals, labor organizations, partnerships, associations, corporations, legal representatives, trustees, trustees in cases under title 11, or receivers.

(2) The term "employer" includes any person acting as an agent of an employer, directly or indirectly, but shall not include the United States or any wholly owned Government corporation, or any Federal Reserve Bank, or any State or political subdivision thereof, or any person subject to the Railway Labor Act [45 U.S.C. 151 et seq.], as amended from time to time, or any labor organization (other than when acting as an employer), or anyone acting in the capacity of officer or agent of such labor organization.

(3) The term "employee" shall include any employee, and shall not be limited to the employees of a particular employer, unless this subchapter explicitly states otherwise, and shall include any individual whose work has ceased as a consequence of, or in connection with, any current labor dispute or because of any unfair labor practice, and who has not obtained any other regular and substantially equivalent employment, but shall not include any individual employed as an agricultural laborer, or in the domestic service of any family or person at his home, or any individual employed by his parent or spouse, or any individual having the status of an independent contractor, or any individual employed as a supervisor, or any individual employed by an employer subject to the Railway Labor Act [45 U.S.C. 151 et seq.], as amended from time to time, or by any other person who is not an employer as herein defined.

(4) The term "representatives" includes any individual or labor organization.

(5) The term "labor organization" means any organization of any kind, or any agency or employee representation committee or plan, in which employees participate and which exists for the purpose, in whole or in part, of dealing with employers concerning grievances, labor disputes, wages, rates of pay, hours of employment, or conditions of work.

(6) The term "commerce" means trade, traffic, commerce, transportation, or communication among the several States, or between the District of Columbia or any Territory of the United States and any State or other Territory, or between any foreign country and any State, Territory, or the District of Columbia, or within the District of Columbia or any Territory, or between points in the same State but through any other State or any Territory or the District of Columbia or any foreign country.

(7) The term "affecting commerce" means in commerce, or burdening or obstructing commerce or the free flow of commerce, or having led or tending to lead to a labor dispute burdening or obstructing commerce or the free flow of commerce.

(8) The term "unfair labor practice" means any unfair labor practice listed in section 158 of this title.

(9) The term "labor dispute" includes any controversy concerning terms, tenure or conditions of employment, or concerning the association or representation of persons in negotiating, fixing, maintaining, changing, or seeking to arrange terms or conditions of employment, regardless of whether the disputants stand in the proximate relation of employer and employee.

(10) The term "National Labor Relations Board" means the National Labor Relations Board provided for in section 153 of this title.

(11) The term "supervisor" means any individual having authority, in the interest of the employer, to hire, transfer, suspend, lay off, recall, promote, discharge, assign, reward, or discipline other employees, or responsibly to direct them, or to adjust their grievances, or effectively to recommend such action, if in connection with the foregoing the exercise of such authority is not of a merely routine or clerical nature, but requires the use of independent judgment.

(12) The term "professional employee" means—

(a) any employee engaged in work (i) predominantly intellectual and varied in character as opposed to routine mental, manual, mechanical, or physical work; (ii) involving the consistent exercise of discretion and judgment in its performance; (iii) of such a character that the output produced or the result accomplished cannot be standardized in relation to a given period of time; (iv) requiring knowledge of an advanced type in a field of science or learning customarily acquired by a prolonged course of specialized intellectual instruction and study in an institution of higher learning or a hospital, as distinguished from a general academic education or from an apprenticeship or from training in the performance of routine mental, manual, or physical processes; or

(b) any employee, who (i) has completed the courses of specialized intellectual instruction and study described in clause (iv) of paragraph (a), and (ii) is performing related work under the supervision of a professional person to qualify himself to become a professional employee as defined in paragraph (a).

(13) In determining whether any person is acting as an "agent" of another person so as to make such other person responsible for his acts, the question of whether the specific acts performed were actually authorized or subsequently ratified shall not be controlling.

(14) The term "health care institution" shall include any hospital, convalescent hospital, health maintenance organization, health clinic, nursing home, extended care facility, or other institution devoted to the care of sick, infirm, or aged person.[1]

[1] So in original. Probably should be "persons."

(July 5, 1935, ch. 372, §2, 49 Stat. 450; June 23, 1947, ch. 120, title I, §101, 61 Stat. 137; Pub. L. 93–360, §1(a), (b), July 26, 1974, 88 Stat. 395; Pub. L. 95–598, title III, §319, Nov. 6, 1978, 92 Stat. 2678.)

REFERENCES IN TEXT

The Railway Labor Act, referred to in pars. (2) and (3), is act May 20, 1926, ch. 347, 44 Stat. 577, as amended, which is classified principally to chapter 8 (§151 et seq.) of Title 45, Railroads. For complete classification of this Act to the Code, see section 151 of Title 45 and Tables.

AMENDMENTS

1978—Par. (1). Pub. L. 95–598 substituted "cases under title 11" for "bankruptcy".

1974—Par. (2). Pub. L. 93–360, §1(a), struck out provisions which had excepted from definition of "employer" corporations and associations operating hospitals if no part of the net earnings inured to the benefit of any private shareholder or individual.

Par. (14). Pub. L. 93–360, §1(b), added par. (14).

1947—Act June 23, 1947, amended section generally to redefine terms used in this subchapter and to define several new terms.

EFFECTIVE DATE OF 1978 AMENDMENT

Amendment by Pub. L. 95–598 effective Oct. 1, 1979, see section 402(a) of Pub. L. 95–598, set out as an Effective Date note preceding section 101 of Title 11, Bankruptcy.

EFFECTIVE DATE OF 1974 AMENDMENT

Amendment by Pub. L. 93–360 effective on thirtieth day after July 26, 1974, see section 4 of Pub. L. 93–360, set out as an Effective Date note under section 169 of this title.

EFFECTIVE DATE OF 1947 AMENDMENT

For effective date of amendment by act June 23, 1947, see section 104 of act June 23, 1947, set out as a note under section 151 of this title.

§153. National Labor Relations Board

(a) Creation, composition, appointment, and tenure; Chairman; removal of members

The National Labor Relations Board (hereinafter called the "Board") created by this subchapter prior to its amendment by the Labor Management Relations Act, 1947 [29 U.S.C. 141 et seq.], is continued as an agency of the United States, except that the Board shall consist of five instead of three members, appointed by the President by and with the advice and consent of the Senate. Of the two additional members so provided for, one shall be appointed for a term of five years and the other for a term of two years. Their successors, and the successors of the other members, shall be appointed for terms of five years each, excepting that any individual chosen to fill a vacancy shall be appointed only for the unexpired term of the member whom he shall succeed. The President shall designate one member to serve as Chairman of the Board. Any member of the Board may be removed by the President, upon notice and hearing, for neglect of duty or malfeasance in office, but for no other cause.

(b) Delegation of powers to members and regional directors; review and stay of actions of regional directors; quorum; seal

The Board is authorized to delegate to any group of three or more members any or all of the powers which it may itself exercise. The Board is also authorized to delegate to its regional directors its powers under section 159 of this title to determine the unit appropriate for the purpose of collective bargaining, to investigate and provide for hearings, and determine whether a question of representation exists, and to direct an election or take a secret ballot under subsection (c) or (e) of section 159 of this title and certify the results thereof, except that upon the filing of a request therefor with the Board by any interested person, the Board may review any action of a regional director delegated to him under this paragraph, but such a review shall not, unless specifically ordered by the Board, operate as a stay of any action taken by the regional director. A vacancy in the Board shall not impair the right of the remaining members to exercise all of the powers of the Board, and three members of the Board shall, at all times, constitute a quorum of the Board, except that two members shall constitute a quorum of any group designated pursuant to the first sentence hereof. The Board shall have an official seal which shall be judicially noticed.

(c) Annual reports to Congress and the President

The Board shall at the close of each fiscal year make a report in writing to Congress and to the President summarizing significant case activities and operations for that fiscal year.

(d) General Counsel; appointment and tenure; powers and duties; vacancy

There shall be a General Counsel of the Board who shall be appointed by the President, by and with the advice and consent of the Senate, for a term of four years. The General Counsel of the Board shall exercise general supervision over all attorneys employed by the Board (other than administrative law judges and legal assistants to Board members) and over the officers and employees in the regional offices. He shall have final authority, on behalf of the Board, in respect of the investigation of charges and issuance of complaints under section 160 of this title, and in respect of the prosecution of such complaints before the Board, and shall have such other duties as the Board may prescribe or as may be provided by law. In case of a vacancy in the office of the General Counsel the President is authorized to designate the officer or employee who shall act as General Counsel during such vacancy, but no person or persons so designated shall so act (1) for more than forty days when the Congress is in session unless a nomination to fill such vacancy shall have been submitted to the Senate, or (2) after the adjournment sine die of the session of the Senate in which such nomination was submitted.

(July 5, 1935, ch. 372, §3, 49 Stat. 451; June 23, 1947, ch. 120, title I, §101, 61 Stat. 139; Pub. L. 86–257, title VII, §§701(b), 703, Sept. 14, 1959, 73 Stat. 542; Pub. L. 93–608, §3(3), Jan. 2, 1975, 88 Stat. 1972; Pub. L. 95–251, §3, Mar. 27, 1978, 92 Stat. 184; Pub. L. 97–375, title II, §213, Dec. 21, 1982, 96 Stat. 1826.)

REFERENCES IN TEXT

The Labor Management Relations Act, 1947, referred to in subsec. (a), is act June 23, 1947, ch. 120, 61 Stat.

136, as amended, which is classified principally to this chapter. For complete classification of this act to the Code, see section 141 of this title and Tables.

CODIFICATION

In subsec. (d), "administrative law judges" substituted for "trial examiners" pursuant to section 3105 of Title 5, Government Organization and Employees, and section 3 of Pub. L. 95–251, Mar. 27, 1978, 92 Stat. 184, which is set out as a note under section 3105 of Title 5.

AMENDMENTS

1982—Subsec. (c). Pub. L. 97–375 substituted "summarizing significant case activities and operations for that fiscal year" for "stating in detail the cases it has heard, the decisions it has rendered, and an account of all moneys it has disbursed".

1975—Subsec. (c). Pub. L. 93–608 struck out requirement that report contain the names, salaries, and duties of all employees and officers employed or supervised by the Board.

1959—Subsec. (b). Pub. L. 86–257, §701(b), authorized the Board to delegate to its regional directors its powers under section 159 of this title to determine the unit appropriate for the purpose of collective bargaining, to investigate and provide for hearings, and determine whether a question of representation exists, and to direct an election or take a secret ballot under section 159(c) or 159(e) of this title and certify the results thereof.

Subsec. (d). Pub. L. 86–257, §703, authorized the President to designate the officer or employee who shall act as General Counsel in the case of a vacancy in the office of the General Counsel.

1947—Act June 23, 1947, amended section generally by increasing membership from three to five, delegating its powers and duties to a quorum of any three members, and by appointing a General Counsel and outlining his powers and duties.

EFFECTIVE DATE OF 1959 AMENDMENT

Section 707 of title VII of Pub. L. 86–257 provided that: "The amendments made by this title [amending this section and sections 158, 159, and 160 of this title] shall take effect sixty days after the date of the enactment of this Act [Sept. 14, 1959] and no provision of this title shall be deemed to make an unfair labor practice, any act which is performed prior to such effective date which did not constitute an unfair labor practice prior thereto."

TERMINATION OF REPORTING REQUIREMENTS

For termination, effective May 15, 2000, of provisions in subsec. (c) of this section relating to making a report in writing to Congress at the close of each fiscal year, see section 3003 of Pub. L. 104–66, as amended, set out as a note under section 1113 of Title 31, Money and Finance, and page 184 of House Document No. 103–7.

§154. National Labor Relations Board; eligibility for reappointment; officers and employees; payment of expenses

(a) Each member of the Board and the General Counsel of the Board shall be eligible for reappointment, and shall not engage in any other business, vocation, or employment. The Board shall appoint an executive secretary, and such attorneys, examiners, and regional directors, and such other employees as it may from time to time find necessary for the proper performance of its duties. The Board may not employ any attorneys for the purpose of reviewing transcripts of hearings or preparing drafts of opinions except that any attorney employed for assignment as a legal assistant to any Board member may for such Board member review such transcripts and prepare such drafts. No administrative law judge's report shall be reviewed, either before or after its publication, by any person other than a member of the Board or his legal assistant, and no administrative law judge shall advise or consult with the Board with respect to exceptions taken to his findings, rulings, or recommendations. The Board may establish or utilize such regional, local, or other agencies, and utilize such voluntary and uncompensated services, as may from time to time be needed. Attorneys appointed under this section may, at the direction of the Board, appear for and represent the Board in any case in court. Nothing in this subchapter shall be construed to authorize the Board to appoint individuals for the purpose of conciliation or mediation, or for economic analysis.

(b) All of the expenses of the Board, including all necessary traveling and subsistence expenses outside the District of Columbia incurred by the members or employees of the Board under its orders, shall be allowed and paid on the presentation of itemized vouchers therefor approved by the Board or by any individual it designates for that purpose.

(July 5, 1935, ch. 372, §4, 49 Stat. 451; June 23, 1947, ch. 120, title I, §101, 61 Stat. 139; Pub. L. 95–251, §3, Mar. 27, 1978, 92 Stat. 184.)

CODIFICATION

Provisions of subsec. (a) which prescribed the basic compensation of members of the Board and the General Counsel were omitted to conform to the provisions of the Executive Schedule. See sections 5314 and 5315 of Title 5, Government Organization and Employees.

In subsec. (a), "administrative law judge's" and "administrative law judge" substituted for "trial examiner's" and "trial examiner", respectively, pursuant to section 3105 of Title 5, and section 3 of Pub. L. 95–251, Mar. 27, 1978, 92 Stat. 184, which is set out as a note under section 3105 of Title 5.

AMENDMENTS

1947—Act June 23, 1947, amended section generally by increasing Board members' salaries from $10,000 to $12,000 per annum, by providing a salary of $12,000 per annum for the General Counsel, striking out former subsec. (b) relating to termination of "Old Board", and redesignating subsec. (c) relating to payment of expenses of Board as subsec. (b).

EFFECTIVE DATE OF 1947 AMENDMENT

For effective date of amendment by act June 23, 1947, see section 104 of act June 23, 1947, set out as a note under section 151 of this title.

§155. National Labor Relations Board; principal office, conducting inquiries throughout country; participation in decisions or inquiries conducted by member

The principal office of the Board shall be in the District of Columbia, but it may meet and exercise any or all of its powers at any other place. The Board may, by one or more of its members or by such agents or agencies as it may designate, prosecute any inquiry necessary to its functions in any part of the United States. A member who participates in such an inquiry shall not be disqualified from subsequently participating in a decision of the Board in the same case.

(July 5, 1935, ch. 372, §5, 49 Stat. 452; June 23, 1947, ch. 120, title I, §101, 61 Stat. 140.)

AMENDMENTS

1947—Act June 23, 1947, reenacted section without change.

EFFECTIVE DATE OF 1947 AMENDMENT

For effective date of amendment by act June 23, 1947, see section 104 of act June 23, 1947, set out as a note under section 151 of this title.

§ 156. Rules and regulations

The Board shall have authority from time to time to make, amend, and rescind, in the manner prescribed by subchapter II of chapter 5 of title 5, such rules and regulations as may be necessary to carry out the provisions of this subchapter.

(July 5, 1935, ch. 372, §6, 49 Stat. 452; June 23, 1947, ch. 120, title I, §101, 61 Stat. 140.)

CODIFICATION

"Subchapter II of chapter 5 of title 5" substituted in text for "the Administrative Procedure Act" on authority of Pub. L. 89–554, §7(b), Sept. 6, 1966, 80 Stat. 631, the first section of which enacted Title 5, Government Organization and Employees.

AMENDMENTS

1947—Act June 23, 1947, amended section generally to provide that the rules and regulations issued by the Board should be in the manner prescribed by the Administrative Procedure Act.

EFFECTIVE DATE OF 1947 AMENDMENT

For effective date of amendment by act June 23, 1947, see section 104 of act June 23, 1947, set out as a note under section 151 of this title.

§ 157. Right of employees as to organization, collective bargaining, etc.

Employees shall have the right to self-organization, to form, join, or assist labor organizations, to bargain collectively through representatives of their own choosing, and to engage in other concerted activities for the purpose of collective bargaining or other mutual aid or protection, and shall also have the right to refrain from any or all of such activities except to the extent that such right may be affected by an agreement requiring membership in a labor organization as a condition of employment as authorized in section 158(a)(3) of this title.

(July 5, 1935, ch. 372, §7, 49 Stat. 452; June 23, 1947, ch. 120, title I, §101, 61 Stat. 140.)

AMENDMENTS

1947—Act June 23, 1947, restated rights of employees to bargain collectively and inserted provision that they have right to refrain from joining in concerted activities with their fellow employees.

EFFECTIVE DATE OF 1947 AMENDMENT

For effective date of amendment by act June 23, 1947, see section 104 of act June 23, 1947, set out as a note under section 151 of this title.

§ 158. Unfair labor practices

(a) Unfair labor practices by employer

It shall be an unfair labor practice for an employer—

(1) to interfere with, restrain, or coerce employees in the exercise of the rights guaranteed in section 157 of this title;

(2) to dominate or interfere with the formation or administration of any labor organization or contribute financial or other support to it: *Provided*, That subject to rules and regulations made and published by the Board pursuant to section 156 of this title, an employer shall not be prohibited from permitting employees to confer with him during working hours without loss of time or pay;

(3) by discrimination in regard to hire or tenure of employment or any term or condition of employment to encourage or discourage membership in any labor organization: *Provided*, That nothing in this subchapter, or in any other statute of the United States, shall preclude an employer from making an agreement with a labor organization (not established, maintained, or assisted by any action defined in this subsection as an unfair labor practice) to require as a condition of employment membership therein on or after the thirtieth day following the beginning of such employment or the effective date of such agreement, whichever is the later, (i) if such labor organization is the representative of the employees as provided in section 159(a) of this title, in the appropriate collective-bargaining unit covered by such agreement when made, and (ii) unless following an election held as provided in section 159(e) of this title within one year preceding the effective date of such agreement, the Board shall have certified that at least a majority of the employees eligible to vote in such election have voted to rescind the authority of such labor organization to make such an agreement: *Provided further*, That no employer shall justify any discrimination against an employee for nonmembership in a labor organization (A) if he has reasonable grounds for believing that such membership was not available to the employee on the same terms and conditions generally applicable to other members, or (B) if he has reasonable grounds for believing that membership was denied or terminated for reasons other than the failure of the employee to tender the periodic dues and the initiation fees uniformly required as a condition of acquiring or retaining membership;

(4) to discharge or otherwise discriminate against an employee because he has filed charges or given testimony under this subchapter;

(5) to refuse to bargain collectively with the representatives of his employees, subject to the provisions of section 159(a) of this title.

(b) Unfair labor practices by labor organization

It shall be an unfair labor practice for a labor organization or its agents—

(1) to restrain or coerce (A) employees in the exercise of the rights guaranteed in section 157 of this title: *Provided*, That this paragraph shall not impair the right of a labor organization to prescribe its own rules with respect to the acquisition or retention of membership therein; or (B) an employer in the selection of his representatives for the purposes of collec-

tive bargaining or the adjustment of grievances;

(2) to cause or attempt to cause an employer to discriminate against an employee in violation of subsection (a)(3) of this section or to discriminate against an employee with respect to whom membership in such organization has been denied or terminated on some ground other than his failure to tender the periodic dues and the initiation fees uniformly required as a condition of acquiring or retaining membership;

(3) to refuse to bargain collectively with an employer, provided it is the representative of his employees subject to the provisions of section 159(a) of this title;

(4)(i) to engage in, or to induce or encourage any individual employed by any person engaged in commerce or in an industry affecting commerce to engage in, a strike or a refusal in the course of his employment to use, manufacture, process, transport, or otherwise handle or work on any goods, articles, materials, or commodities or to perform any services; or (ii) to threaten, coerce, or restrain any person engaged in commerce or in an industry affecting commerce, where in either case an object thereof is—

(A) forcing or requiring any employer or self-employed person to join any labor or employer organization or to enter into any agreement which is prohibited by subsection (e) of this section;

(B) forcing or requiring any person to cease using, selling, handling, transporting, or otherwise dealing in the products of any other producer, processor, or manufacturer, or to cease doing business with any other person, or forcing or requiring any other employer to recognize or bargain with a labor organization as the representative of his employees unless such labor organization has been certified as the representative of such employees under the provisions of section 159 of this title: *Provided*, That nothing contained in this clause (B) shall be construed to make unlawful, where not otherwise unlawful, any primary strike or primary picketing;

(C) forcing or requiring any employer to recognize or bargain with a particular labor organization as the representative of his employees if another labor organization has been certified as the representative of such employees under the provisions of section 159 of this title;

(D) forcing or requiring any employer to assign particular work to employees in a particular labor organization or in a particular trade, craft, or class rather than to employees in another labor organization or in another trade, craft, or class, unless such employer is failing to conform to an order or certification of the Board determining the bargaining representative for employees performing such work:

Provided, That nothing contained in this subsection shall be construed to make unlawful a refusal by any person to enter upon the premises of any employer (other than his own employer), if the employees of such employer are engaged in a strike ratified or approved by a representative of such employees whom such employer is required to recognize under this subchapter: *Provided further*, That for the purposes of this paragraph (4) only, nothing contained in such paragraph shall be construed to prohibit publicity, other than picketing, for the purpose of truthfully advising the public, including consumers and members of a labor organization, that a product or products are produced by an employer with whom the labor organization has a primary dispute and are distributed by another employer, as long as such publicity does not have an effect of inducing any individual employed by any person other than the primary employer in the course of his employment to refuse to pick up, deliver, or transport any goods, or not to perform any services, at the establishment of the employer engaged in such distribution;

(5) to require of employees covered by an agreement authorized under subsection (a)(3) of this section the payment, as a condition precedent to becoming a member of such organization, of a fee in an amount which the Board finds excessive or discriminatory under all the circumstances. In making such a finding, the Board shall consider, among other relevant factors, the practices and customs of labor organizations in the particular industry, and the wages currently paid to the employees affected;

(6) to cause or attempt to cause an employer to pay or deliver or agree to pay or deliver any money or other thing of value, in the nature of an exaction, for services which are not performed or not to be performed; and

(7) to picket or cause to be picketed, or threaten to picket or cause to be picketed, any employer where an object thereof is forcing or requiring an employer to recognize or bargain with a labor organization as the representative of his employees, or forcing or requiring the employees of an employer to accept or select such labor organization as their collective bargaining representative, unless such labor organization is currently certified as the representative of such employees:

(A) where the employer has lawfully recognized in accordance with this subchapter any other labor organization and a question concerning representation may not appropriately be raised under section 159(c) of this title,

(B) where within the preceding twelve months a valid election under section 159(c) of this title has been conducted, or

(C) where such picketing has been conducted without a petition under section 159(c) of this title being filed within a reasonable period of time not to exceed thirty days from the commencement of such picketing: *Provided*, That when such a petition has been filed the Board shall forthwith, without regard to the provisions of section 159(c)(1) of this title or the absence of a showing of a substantial interest on the part of the labor organization, direct an election in such unit as the Board finds to be appropriate and shall certify the results thereof: *Provided further*, That nothing in this subparagraph (C) shall be construed to prohibit any picketing or other publicity for the purpose of truthfully advising the public (including consumers) that an employer does not employ members of, or have a contract with, a labor organization, unless an effect of such picketing is to induce any individual employed by any other person in the course of his employment, not to pick up, deliver or transport any goods or not to perform any services.

Nothing in this paragraph (7) shall be construed to permit any act which would otherwise be an unfair labor practice under this subsection.

(c) Expression of views without threat of reprisal or force or promise of benefit

The expressing of any views, argument, or opinion, or the dissemination thereof, whether in written, printed, graphic, or visual form, shall not constitute or be evidence of an unfair labor practice under any of the provisions of this subchapter, if such expression contains no threat of reprisal or force or promise of benefit.

(d) Obligation to bargain collectively

For the purposes of this section, to bargain collectively is the performance of the mutual obligation of the employer and the representative of the employees to meet at reasonable times and confer in good faith with respect to wages, hours, and other terms and conditions of employment, or the negotiation of an agreement, or any question arising thereunder, and the execution of a written contract incorporating any agreement reached if requested by either party, but such obligation does not compel either party to agree to a proposal or require the making of a concession: *Provided*, That where there is in effect a collective-bargaining contract covering employees in an industry affecting commerce, the duty to bargain collectively shall also mean that no party to such contract shall terminate or modify such contract, unless the party desiring such termination or modification—

(1) serves a written notice upon the other party to the contract of the proposed termination or modification sixty days prior to the expiration date thereof, or in the event such contract contains no expiration date, sixty days prior to the time it is proposed to make such termination or modification;

(2) offers to meet and confer with the other party for the purpose of negotiating a new contract or a contract containing the proposed modifications;

(3) notifies the Federal Mediation and Conciliation Service within thirty days after such notice of the existence of a dispute, and simultaneously therewith notifies any State or Territorial agency established to mediate and conciliate disputes within the State or Territory where the dispute occurred, provided no agreement has been reached by that time; and

(4) continues in full force and effect, without resorting to strike or lock-out, all the terms and conditions of the existing contract for a period of sixty days after such notice is given or until the expiration date of such contract, whichever occurs later:

The duties imposed upon employers, employees, and labor organizations by paragraphs (2) to (4) of this subsection shall become inapplicable upon an intervening certification of the Board, under which the labor organization or individual, which is a party to the contract, has been superseded as or ceased to be the representative of the employees subject to the provisions of section 159(a) of this title, and the duties so imposed shall not be construed as requiring either party to discuss or agree to any modification of the terms and conditions contained in a contract for a fixed period, if such modification is to become effective before such terms and conditions can be reopened under the provisions of the contract. Any employee who engages in a strike within any notice period specified in this subsection, or who engages in any strike within the appropriate period specified in subsection (g) of this section, shall lose his status as an employee of the employer engaged in the particular labor dispute, for the purposes of sections 158, 159, and 160 of this title, but such loss of status for such employee shall terminate if and when he is reemployed by such employer. Whenever the collective bargaining involves employees of a health care institution, the provisions of this subsection shall be modified as follows:

(A) The notice of paragraph (1) of this subsection shall be ninety days; the notice of paragraph (3) of this subsection shall be sixty days; and the contract period of paragraph (4) of this subsection shall be ninety days.

(B) Where the bargaining is for an initial agreement following certification or recognition, at least thirty days' notice of the existence of a dispute shall be given by the labor organization to the agencies set forth in paragraph (3) of this subsection.

(C) After notice is given to the Federal Mediation and Conciliation Service under either clause (A) or (B) of this sentence, the Service shall promptly communicate with the parties and use its best efforts, by mediation and conciliation, to bring them to agreement. The parties shall participate fully and promptly in such meetings as may be undertaken by the Service for the purpose of aiding in a settlement of the dispute.

(e) Enforceability of contract or agreement to boycott any other employer; exception

It shall be an unfair labor practice for any labor organization and any employer to enter into any contract or agreement, express or implied, whereby such employer ceases or refrains or agrees to cease or refrain from handling, using, selling, transporting or otherwise dealing in any of the products of any other employer, or to cease doing business with any other person, and any contract or agreement entered into heretofore or hereafter containing such an agreement shall be to such extent unenforcible[1] and void: *Provided*, That nothing in this subsection shall apply to an agreement between a labor organization and an employer in the construction industry relating to the contracting or subcontracting of work to be done at the site of the construction, alteration, painting, or repair

[1] So in original. Probably should be "unenforceable".

of a building, structure, or other work: *Provided further*, That for the purposes of this subsection and subsection (b)(4)(B) of this section the terms "any employer", "any person engaged in commerce or an industry affecting commerce", and "any person" when used in relation to the terms "any other producer, processor, or manufacturer", "any other employer", or "any other person" shall not include persons in the relation of a jobber, manufacturer, contractor, or subcontractor working on the goods or premises of the jobber or manufacturer or performing parts of an integrated process of production in the apparel and clothing industry: *Provided further*, That nothing in this subchapter shall prohibit the enforcement of any agreement which is within the foregoing exception.

(f) Agreement covering employees in the building and construction industry

It shall not be an unfair labor practice under subsections (a) and (b) of this section for an employer engaged primarily in the building and construction industry to make an agreement covering employees engaged (or who, upon their employment, will be engaged) in the building and construction industry with a labor organization of which building and construction employees are members (not established, maintained, or assisted by any action defined in subsection (a) of this section as an unfair labor practice) because (1) the majority status of such labor organization has not been established under the provisions of section 159 of this title prior to the making of such agreement, or (2) such agreement requires as a condition of employment, membership in such labor organization after the seventh day following the beginning of such employment or the effective date of the agreement, whichever is later, or (3) such agreement requires the employer to notify such labor organization of opportunities for employment with such employer, or gives such labor organization an opportunity to refer qualified applicants for such employment, or (4) such agreement specifies minimum training or experience qualifications for employment or provides for priority in opportunities for employment based upon length of service with such employer, in the industry or in the particular geographical area: *Provided*, That nothing in this subsection shall set aside the final proviso to subsection (a)(3) of this section: *Provided further*, That any agreement which would be invalid, but for clause (1) of this subsection, shall not be a bar to a petition filed pursuant to section 159(c) or 159(e) of this title.

(g) Notification of intention to strike or picket at any health care institution

A labor organization before engaging in any strike, picketing, or other concerted refusal to work at any health care institution shall, not less than ten days prior to such action, notify the institution in writing and the Federal Mediation and Conciliation Service of that intention, except that in the case of bargaining for an initial agreement following certification or recognition the notice required by this subsection shall not be given until the expiration of the period specified in clause (B) of the last sentence of subsection (d) of this section. The notice shall state the date and time that such action will commence. The notice, once given, may be extended by the written agreement of both parties.

(July 5, 1935, ch. 372, §8, 49 Stat. 452; June 23, 1947, ch. 120, title I, §101, 61 Stat. 140; Oct. 22, 1951, ch. 534, §1(b), 65 Stat. 601; Pub. L. 86–257, title II, §201(e), title VII, §§704(a)–(c), 705(a), Sept. 14, 1959, 73 Stat. 525, 542–545; Pub. L. 93–360, §1(c)–(e), July 26, 1974, 88 Stat. 395, 396.)

AMENDMENTS

1974—Subsec. (d). Pub. L. 93–360, §1(c), (d), substituted "any notice" for "the sixty-day" and inserted ", or who engages in any strike within the appropriate period specified in subsection (g) of this section," in loss-of-employee-status provision and inserted enumeration of modifications to this subsection which are to be applied whenever the collective bargaining involves employees of a health care institution.

Subsec. (g). Pub. L. 93–360, §1(e), added subsec. (g).

1959—Subsec. (a)(3). Pub. L. 86–257, §201(e), struck out "and has at the time the agreement was made or within the preceding twelve months received from the Board a notice of compliance with sections 159(f), (g), (h) of this title" after "such agreement when made" in cl. (i).

Subsec. (b)(4). Pub. L. 86–257, §704(a), among other changes, substituted "induce or encourage any individual employed by any person engaged in commerce or in an industry affecting commerce to engage in, a strike or a refusal in the course of his employment" for "induce or encourage the employees of any employer to engage in, a strike or a concerted refusal in the course of their employment" in cl. (i), added cl. (ii), and inserted provisions relating to agreements prohibited by subsection (e) of this section in cl. (A), the proviso relating to primary strikes and primary picketing in cl. (B), and the last proviso relating to publicity.

Subsec. (b)(7). Pub. L. 86–257, §704(c), added par. (7).

Subsec. (e). Pub. L. 86–257, §704(b), added subsec. (e).

Subsec. (f). Pub. L. 86–257, §705(a), added subsec. (f).

1951—Subsec. (a)(3). Act Oct. 22, 1951, substituted "and has at the time the agreement was made or within the preceding twelve months received from the Board a notice of compliance with section 159(f), (g), (h) of this title, and (ii) unless following an election held as provided in section 159(e) of this title within one year preceding the effective date of such agreement, the Board shall have certified that at least a majority of the employees eligible to vote in such election have voted to rescind the authority of such labor organization to make such an agreement:" for "; and (ii) if, following the most recent election held as provided in section 159(e) of this title the Board shall have certified that at least a majority of the employees eligible to vote in such election have voted to authorize such labor organization to make such an agreement:".

1947—Act June 23, 1947, amended section generally by stating what were unfair labor practices by a union as well as by an employer, and by inserting provisions protecting the right of free speech for both employers and unions.

EFFECTIVE DATE OF 1974 AMENDMENT

Amendment by Pub. L. 93–360 effective on thirtieth day after July 26, 1974, see section 4 of Pub. L. 93–360, set out as an Effective Date note under section 169 of this title.

EFFECTIVE DATE OF 1959 AMENDMENT

Amendment by sections 704(a)–(c) and 705(a) of Pub. L. 86–257 effective sixty days after Sept. 14, 1959, see section 707 of Pub. L. 86–257, set out as a note under section 153 of this title.

EFFECTIVE DATE OF 1947 AMENDMENT

For effective date of amendment by act June 23, 1947, see section 104 of act June 23, 1947, set out as a note under section 151 of this title.

AGREEMENTS REQUIRING MEMBERSHIP IN A LABOR ORGANIZATION AS A CONDITION OF EMPLOYMENT

Section 705(b) of Pub. L. 86–257 provided that: "Nothing contained in the amendment made by subsection (a) [amending this section] shall be construed as authorizing the execution or application of agreements requiring membership in a labor organization as a condition of employment in any State or Territory in which such execution or application is prohibited by State or Territorial Law."

UNFAIR LABOR PRACTICES PRIOR TO JUNE 23, 1947

Section 102 of title I of act June 23, 1947, provided that: "No provision of this title [amending this subchapter] shall be deemed to make an unfair labor practice any act which was performed prior to the date of the enactment of this act [June 23, 1947] which did not constitute an unfair labor practice prior thereto, and the provisions of section 8(a)(3) and section 8(b)(2) of the National Labor Relations Act as amended by this title [subsecs. (a)(3) and (b)(2) of this section] shall not make an unfair labor practice the performance of any obligation under a collective-bargaining agreement entered into prior to the date of the enactment of this Act [June 23, 1947], or (in the case of an agreement for a period of not more than one year) entered into on or after such date of enactment, but prior to the effective date of this title, if the performance of such obligation would not have constituted an unfair labor practice under section 8(3) [see subsec. (a)(3) of this section] of the National Labor Relations Act prior to the effective date of this title [sixty days after June 23, 1947] unless such agreement was renewed or extended subsequent thereto."

§ 158a. Providing facilities for operations of Federal Credit Unions

Provision by an employer of facilities for the operations of a Federal Credit Union on the premises of such employer shall not be deemed to be intimidation, coercion, interference, restraint or discrimination within the provisions of sections 157 and 158 of this title, or acts amendatory thereof.

(Dec. 6, 1937, ch. 3, § 5, 51 Stat. 5.)

CODIFICATION

This section was not enacted either as part of the Labor Management Relations Act, 1947, which comprises this chapter, or as part of the National Labor Relations Act, which comprises this subchapter.

§ 159. Representatives and elections

(a) Exclusive representatives; employees' adjustment of grievances directly with employer

Representatives designated or selected for the purposes of collective bargaining by the majority of the employees in a unit appropriate for such purposes, shall be the exclusive representatives of all the employees in such unit for the purposes of collective bargaining in respect to rates of pay, wages, hours of employment, or other conditions of employment: *Provided*, That any individual employee or a group of employees shall have the right at any time to present grievances to their employer and to have such grievances adjusted, without the intervention of the bargaining representative, as long as the adjustment is not inconsistent with the terms of a collective-bargaining contract or agreement then in effect: *Provided further*, That the bargaining representative has been given opportunity to be present at such adjustment.

(b) Determination of bargaining unit by Board

The Board shall decide in each case whether, in order to assure to employees the fullest freedom in exercising the rights guaranteed by this subchapter, the unit appropriate for the purposes of collective bargaining shall be the employer unit, craft unit, plant unit, or subdivision thereof: *Provided*, That the Board shall not (1) decide that any unit is appropriate for such purposes if such unit includes both professional employees and employees who are not professional employees unless a majority of such professional employees vote for inclusion in such unit; or (2) decide that any craft unit is inappropriate for such purposes on the ground that a different unit has been established by a prior Board determination, unless a majority of the employees in the proposed craft unit vote against separate representation or (3) decide that any unit is appropriate for such purposes if it includes, together with other employees, any individual employed as a guard to enforce against employees and other persons rules to protect property of the employer or to protect the safety of persons on the employer's premises; but no labor organization shall be certified as the representative of employees in a bargaining unit of guards if such organization admits to membership, or is affiliated directly or indirectly with an organization which admits to membership, employees other than guards.

(c) Hearings on questions affecting commerce; rules and regulations

(1) Whenever a petition shall have been filed, in accordance with such regulations as may be prescribed by the Board—

(A) by an employee or group of employees or any individual or labor organization acting in their behalf alleging that a substantial number of employees (i) wish to be represented for collective bargaining and that their employer declines to recognize their representative as the representative defined in subsection (a) of this section, or (ii) assert that the individual or labor organization, which has been certified or is being currently recognized by their employer as the bargaining representative, is no longer a representative as defined in subsection (a) of this section; or

(B) by an employer, alleging that one or more individuals or labor organizations have presented to him a claim to be recognized as the representative defined in subsection (a) of this section;

the Board shall investigate such petition and if it has reasonable cause to believe that a question of representation affecting commerce exists shall provide for an appropriate hearing upon due notice. Such hearing may be conducted by an officer or employee of the regional office, who shall not make any recommendations with respect thereto. If the Board finds upon the record of such hearing that such a question of representation exists, it shall direct an election by secret ballot and shall certify the results thereof.

(2) In determining whether or not a question of representation affecting commerce exists, the same regulations and rules of decision shall apply irrespective of the identity of the persons

filing the petition or the kind of relief sought and in no case shall the Board deny a labor organization a place on the ballot by reason of an order with respect to such labor organization or its predecessor not issued in conformity with section 160(c) of this title.

(3) No election shall be directed in any bargaining unit or any subdivision within which in the preceding twelve-month period, a valid election shall have been held. Employees engaged in an economic strike who are not entitled to reinstatement shall be eligible to vote under such regulations as the Board shall find are consistent with the purposes and provisions of this subchapter in any election conducted within twelve months after the commencement of the strike. In any election where none of the choices on the ballot receives a majority, a run-off shall be conducted, the ballot providing for a selection between the two choices receiving the largest and second largest number of valid votes cast in the election.

(4) Nothing in this section shall be construed to prohibit the waiving of hearings by stipulation for the purpose of a consent election in conformity with regulations and rules of decision of the Board.

(5) In determining whether a unit is appropriate for the purposes specified in subsection (b) of this section the extent to which the employees have organized shall not be controlling.

(d) Petition for enforcement or review; transcript

Whenever an order of the Board made pursuant to section 160(c) of this title is based in whole or in part upon facts certified following an investigation pursuant to subsection (c) of this section and there is a petition for the enforcement or review of such order, such certification and the record of such investigation shall be included in the transcript of the entire record required to be filed under subsection (e) or (f) of section 160 of this title, and thereupon the decree of the court enforcing, modifying, or setting aside in whole or in part the order of the Board shall be made and entered upon the pleadings, testimony, and proceedings set forth in such transcript.

(e) Secret ballot; limitation of elections

(1) Upon the filing with the Board, by 30 per centum or more of the employees in a bargaining unit covered by an agreement between their employer and a labor organization made pursuant to section 158(a)(3) of this title, of a petition alleging they desire that such authority be rescinded, the Board shall take a secret ballot of the employees in such unit and certify the results thereof to such labor organization and to the employer.

(2) No election shall be conducted pursuant to this subsection in any bargaining unit or any subdivision within which, in the preceding twelve-month period, a valid election shall have been held.

(July 5, 1935, ch. 372, §9, 49 Stat. 453; June 23, 1947, ch. 120, title I, §101, 61 Stat. 143; Oct. 22, 1951, ch. 534, §1(c), (d), 65 Stat. 601; Pub. L. 86–257, title II, §201(d), title VII, §702, Sept. 14, 1959, 73 Stat. 525, 542.)

AMENDMENTS

1959—Subsec. (c)(3). Pub. L. 86–257, §702, substituted "Employees engaged in an economic strike who are not entitled to reinstatement shall be eligible to vote under such regulations as the Board shall find are consistent with the purposes and provisions of this subchapter in any election conducted within twelve months after the commencement of the strike" for "Employees on strike who are not entitled to reinstatement shall not be eligible to vote."

Subsecs. (f), (g). Pub. L. 86–257, §201(d), repealed subsecs. (f) and (g) which required unions to file their constitutions, bylaws and a report, prescribed the contents of the report and directed the filing of annual financial reports, and are now covered by section 431 of this title.

Subsec. (h). Pub. L. 86–257, §201(d), repealed subsec. (h) which related to affidavits showing union's officers free from Communist Party affiliation or belief.

1951—Subsec. (e). Act Oct. 22, 1951, §1(c), struck out par. (1) and renumbered pars. (2) and (3) as (1) and (2).

Subsecs. (f) to (h). Act Oct. 22, 1951, §1(d), struck out "No petition under section 159(e)(1) shall be entertained" wherever appearing.

1947—Act June 23, 1947, amended section generally to allow employees to carry their grievances directly to the employer, to circumscribe certain powers of the Board, to make the union file with the Secretary of Labor its constitution, bylaws, and report before being certified as a bargaining agent, to require annual reports by labor unions, and to require labor unions to file affidavits with the Board showing that none of its officers are affiliated with or believe in the Communist Party.

EFFECTIVE DATE OF 1959 AMENDMENT

Amendment by section 702 of Pub. L. 86–257 effective sixty days after Sept. 14, 1959, see section 707 of Pub. L. 86–257, set out as a note under section 153 of this title.

EFFECTIVE DATE OF 1947 AMENDMENT

For effective date of amendment by act June 23, 1947, see section 104 of act June 23, 1947, set out as a note under section 151 of this title.

CERTAIN CERTIFICATIONS OF BARGAINING UNITS UNAFFECTED

Section 103 of title I of act June 23, 1947, provided that: "No provisions of this title [amending this subchapter] shall affect any certification of representatives or any determination as to the appropriate collective-bargaining unit, which was made under section 9 of the National Labor Relations Act [this section] prior to the effective date of this title [sixty days after June 23, 1947] until one year after the date of such certification or if, in respect of any such certification, a collective-bargaining contract was entered into prior to the effective date of this title [sixty days after June 23, 1947], until the end of the contract period or until one year after such date, whichever first occurs."

§160. Prevention of unfair labor practices

(a) Powers of Board generally

The Board is empowered, as hereinafter provided, to prevent any person from engaging in any unfair labor practice (listed in section 158 of this title) affecting commerce. This power shall not be affected by any other means of adjustment or prevention that has been or may be established by agreement, law, or otherwise: *Provided*, That the Board is empowered by agreement with any agency of any State or Territory to cede to such agency jurisdiction over any cases in any industry (other than mining, manufacturing, communications, and transportation except where predominantly local in character) even though such cases may involve labor disputes affecting commerce, unless the provision of the State or Territorial statute applicable to the determination of such cases by such agency is inconsistent with the corresponding provision of this subchapter or has received a construction inconsistent therewith.

(b) Complaint and notice of hearing; answer; court rules of evidence inapplicable

Whenever it is charged that any person has engaged in or is engaging in any such unfair labor practice, the Board, or any agent or agency designated by the Board for such purposes, shall have power to issue and cause to be served upon such person a complaint stating the charges in that respect, and containing a notice of hearing before the Board or a member thereof, or before a designated agent or agency, at a place therein fixed, not less than five days after the serving of said complaint: *Provided*, That no complaint shall issue based upon any unfair labor practice occurring more than six months prior to the filing of the charge with the Board and the service of a copy thereof upon the person against whom such charge is made, unless the person aggrieved thereby was prevented from filing such charge by reason of service in the armed forces, in which event the six-month period shall be computed from the day of his discharge. Any such complaint may be amended by the member, agent, or agency conducting the hearing or the Board in its discretion at any time prior to the issuance of an order based thereon. The person so complained of shall have the right to file an answer to the original or amended complaint and to appear in person or otherwise and give testimony at the place and time fixed in the complaint. In the discretion of the member, agent, or agency conducting the hearing or the Board, any other person may be allowed to intervene in the said proceeding and to present testimony. Any such proceeding shall, so far as practicable, be conducted in accordance with the rules of evidence applicable in the district courts of the United States under the rules of civil procedure for the district courts of the United States, adopted by the Supreme Court of the United States pursuant to section 2072 of title 28.

(c) Reduction of testimony to writing; findings and orders of Board

The testimony taken by such member, agent, or agency or the Board shall be reduced to writing and filed with the Board. Thereafter, in its discretion, the Board upon notice may take further testimony or hear argument. If upon the preponderance of the testimony taken the Board shall be of the opinion that any person named in the complaint has engaged in or is engaging in any such unfair labor practice, then the Board shall state its findings of fact and shall issue and cause to be served on such person an order requiring such person to cease and desist from such unfair labor practice, and to take such affirmative action including reinstatement of employees with or without back pay, as will effectuate the policies of this subchapter: *Provided*, That where an order directs reinstatement of an employee, back pay may be required of the employer or labor organization, as the case may be, responsible for the discrimination suffered by him: *And provided further*, That in determining whether a complaint shall issue alleging a violation of subsection (a)(1) or (a)(2) of section 158 of this title, and in deciding such cases, the same regulations and rules of decision shall apply irrespective of whether or not the labor organization affected is affiliated with a labor organization national or international in scope. Such order may further require such person to make reports from time to time showing the extent to which it has complied with the order. If upon the preponderance of the testimony taken the Board shall not be of the opinion that the person named in the complaint has engaged in or is engaging in any such unfair labor practice, then the Board shall state its findings of fact and shall issue an order dismissing the said complaint. No order of the Board shall require the reinstatement of any individual as an employee who has been suspended or discharged, or the payment to him of any back pay, if such individual was suspended or discharged for cause. In case the evidence is presented before a member of the Board, or before an administrative law judge or judges thereof, such member, or such judge or judges as the case may be, shall issue and cause to be served on the parties to the proceeding a proposed report, together with a recommended order, which shall be filed with the Board, and if no exceptions are filed within twenty days after service thereof upon such parties, or within such further period as the Board may authorize, such recommended order shall become the order of the Board and become effective as therein prescribed.

(d) Modification of findings or orders prior to filing record in court

Until the record in a case shall have been filed in a court, as hereinafter provided, the Board may at any time upon reasonable notice and in such manner as it shall deem proper, modify or set aside, in whole or in part, any finding or order made or issued by it.

(e) Petition to court for enforcement of order; proceedings; review of judgment

The Board shall have power to petition any court of appeals of the United States, or if all the courts of appeals to which application may be made are in vacation, any district court of the United States, within any circuit or district, respectively, wherein the unfair labor practice in question occurred or wherein such person resides or transacts business, for the enforcement of such order and for appropriate temporary relief or restraining order, and shall file in the court the record in the proceedings, as provided in section 2112 of title 28. Upon the filing of such petition, the court shall cause notice thereof to be served upon such person, and thereupon shall have jurisdiction of the proceeding and of the question determined therein, and shall have power to grant such temporary relief or restraining order as it deems just and proper, and to make and enter a decree enforcing, modifying and enforcing as so modified, or setting aside in whole or in part the order of the Board. No objection that has not been urged before the Board, its member, agent, or agency, shall be considered by the court, unless the failure or neglect to urge such objection shall be excused because of extraordinary circumstances. The findings of the Board with respect to questions of fact if supported by substantial evidence on the record considered as a whole shall be conclusive. If either party shall apply to the court for leave to adduce additional evidence and shall show to the satisfaction of the court that such additional evidence is material and that there were reasonable grounds for the failure to adduce such evidence in the hearing before the Board, its member, agent, or agency, the court may order such additional evidence to be taken before the Board, its member, agent, or agency, and to be made a part of the record. The Board may modify its findings as to the facts, or make new findings by reason of additional evidence so taken and filed, and it shall file such modified or new findings, which findings with respect to questions of fact if supported by substantial evidence on the record considered as a whole shall be conclusive, and shall file its recommendations, if any, for the modification or setting aside of its original order. Upon the filing of the record with it the jurisdiction of the court shall be exclusive and its judgment and decree shall be final, except that the same shall be subject to review by the appropriate United States court of appeals if application was made to the district court as hereinabove provided, and by the Supreme Court of the United States upon writ of certiorari or certification as provided in section 1254 of title 28.

(f) Review of final order of Board on petition to court

Any person aggrieved by a final order of the Board granting or denying in whole or in part the relief sought may obtain a review of such order in any United States court of appeals in the circuit wherein the unfair labor practice in question was alleged to have been engaged in or wherein such person resides or transacts business, or in the United States Court of Appeals for the District of Columbia, by filing in such a court a written petition praying that the order of the Board be modified or set aside. A copy of such petition shall be forthwith transmitted by the clerk of the court to the Board, and thereupon the aggrieved party shall file in the court the record in the proceeding, certified by the Board, as provided in section 2112 of title 28. Upon the filing of such petition, the court shall proceed in the same manner as in the case of an application by the Board under subsection (e) of this section, and shall have the same jurisdiction to grant to the Board such temporary relief or restraining order as it deems just and proper, and in like manner to make and enter a decree enforcing, modifying, and enforcing as so modified, or setting aside in whole or in part the order of the Board; the findings of the Board with respect to questions of fact if supported by substantial evidence on the record considered as a whole shall in like manner be conclusive.

(g) Institution of court proceedings as stay of Board's order

The commencement of proceedings under subsection (e) or (f) of this section shall not, unless specifically ordered by the court, operate as a stay of the Board's order.

(h) Jurisdiction of courts unaffected by limitations prescribed in chapter 6 of this title

When granting appropriate temporary relief or a restraining order, or making and entering a decree enforcing, modifying, and enforcing as so modified or setting aside in whole or in part an order of the Board, as provided in this section, the jurisdiction of courts sitting in equity shall not be limited by chapter 6 of this title.

(i) Repealed. Pub. L. 98–620, title IV, § 402(31), Nov. 8, 1984, 98 Stat. 3360

(j) Injunctions

The Board shall have power, upon issuance of a complaint as provided in subsection (b) of this section charging that any person has engaged in or is engaging in an unfair labor practice, to petition any United States district court, within any district wherein the unfair labor practice in question is alleged to have occurred or wherein such person resides or transacts business, for appropriate temporary relief or restraining order. Upon the filing of any such petition the court shall cause notice thereof to be served upon such person, and thereupon shall have jurisdiction to grant to the Board such temporary relief or restraining order as it deems just and proper.

(k) Hearings on jurisdictional strikes

Whenever it is charged that any person has engaged in an unfair labor practice within the meaning of paragraph (4)(D) of section 158(b) of this title, the Board is empowered and directed to hear and determine the dispute out of which such unfair labor practice shall have arisen, unless, within ten days after notice that such charge has been filed, the parties to such dispute submit to the Board satisfactory evidence that they have adjusted, or agreed upon methods for the voluntary adjustment of, the dispute. Upon compliance by the parties to the dispute with the decision of the Board or upon such voluntary adjustment of the dispute, such charge shall be dismissed.

***(l)* Boycotts and strikes to force recognition of uncertified labor organizations; injunctions; notice; service of process**

Whenever it is charged that any person has engaged in an unfair labor practice within the meaning of paragraph (4)(A), (B), or (C) of section 158(b) of this title, or section 158(e) of this title or section 158(b)(7) of this title, the preliminary investigation of such charge shall be made forthwith and given priority over all other cases except cases of like character in the office where it is filed or to which it is referred. If, after such investigation, the officer or regional attorney to whom the matter may be referred has reasonable cause to believe such charge is true and that a complaint should issue, he shall, on behalf of the Board, petition any United States district court within any district where the unfair labor practice in question has occurred, is alleged to have occurred, or wherein such person resides or transacts business, for appropriate injunctive relief pending the final adjudication of the Board with respect to such matter. Upon the filing of any such petition the district court shall have jurisdiction to grant such injunctive relief or temporary restraining order as it deems just and proper, notwithstanding any other provision of law: *Provided further*, That no temporary restraining order shall be issued without notice unless a petition alleges that substantial and irreparable injury to the charging party will be unavoidable and such temporary restraining order shall be effective for no longer than five days and will become void at the expiration of such period: *Provided further*, That such officer or regional attorney shall not apply for any restraining order under section 158(b)(7) of this title if a charge against the employer under section 158(a)(2) of this title has been filed and after the preliminary investigation, he has reasonable cause to believe that such charge is true and that a complaint should issue. Upon filing of any such petition the courts shall cause notice thereof to be served upon any person involved in the charge and such person, including the charging party, shall be given an opportunity to appear by counsel and present any relevant testimony: *Provided further*, That for the purposes of this subsection district courts shall be deemed to have jurisdiction of a labor organization (1) in the district in which such organization maintains its principal office, or (2) in any district in which its duly authorized officers or agents are engaged in promoting or protecting the interests of employee members. The service of legal process upon such officer or agent shall constitute service upon the labor organization and make such organization a party to the suit. In situations where such relief is appropriate the procedure specified herein shall apply to charges with respect to section 158(b)(4)(D) of this title.

(m) Priority of cases

Whenever it is charged that any person has engaged in an unfair labor practice within the meaning of subsection (a)(3) or (b)(2) of section 158 of this title, such charge shall be given priority over all other cases except cases of like character in the office where it is filed or to which it is referred and cases given priority under subsection (*l*) of this section.

(July 5, 1935, ch. 372, § 10, 49 Stat. 453; June 23, 1947, ch. 120, title I, § 101, 61 Stat. 146; June 25, 1948, ch. 646, § 32(a), (b), 62 Stat. 991; May 24, 1949, ch. 139, § 127, 63 Stat. 107; Pub. L. 85–791, § 13, Aug. 28, 1958, 72 Stat. 945; Pub. L. 86–257, title VII, §§ 704(d), 706, Sept. 14, 1959, 73 Stat. 544; Pub. L. 95–251, § 3, Mar. 27, 1978, 92 Stat. 184; Pub. L. 98–620, title IV, § 402(31), Nov. 8, 1984, 98 Stat. 3360.)

References in Text

The rules of evidence applicable in the district courts of the United States, referred to in subsec. (b), are set out in the Appendix to Title 28, Judiciary and Judicial Procedure.

The rules of civil procedure for the district courts of the United States, referred to in subsec. (b), are set out in the Appendix to Title 28.

Chapter 6 (§ 101 et seq.) of this title, referred to in subsec. (h), is a reference to act Mar. 23, 1932, ch. 90, 47 Stat. 70, popularly known as the Norris-LaGuardia Act.

Codification

In subsec. (b), "section 2072 of title 28" substituted for "the Act of June 19, 1934 (U.S.C., title 28, secs. 723-B, 723-C)" on authority of act June 25, 1948, ch. 646, 62 Stat. 869, section 1 of which enacted Title 28, Judiciary and Judicial Procedure.

In subsec. (c), "administrative law judge or judges" and "such judge or judges" substituted for "examiner or examiners" and "such examiner or examiners", respectively, pursuant to section 3105 of Title 5, Government Organization and Employees, and section 3 of Pub. L. 95–251, Mar. 27, 1978, 92 Stat. 184, which is set out as a note under section 3105 of Title 5.

In subsec. (f), "United States court of appeals" substituted for "circuit court of appeals of the United States" on authority of act June 25, 1948, as amended by act May 24, 1949.

As originally enacted subsecs. (j) and (*l*) contained references to the District Court of the United States for the District of Columbia. Act June 25, 1948, as amended by act May 24, 1949, substituted "United States District Court for the District of Columbia" for "District Court of the United States for the District of Columbia". However, the words "United States District Court for the District of Columbia" have now been deleted entirely as superfluous in view of section 132(a) of Title 28, Judiciary and Judicial Procedure, which states that "There shall be in each judicial district a district court which shall be a court of record known as the United States District Court for the district", and section 88 of Title 28 which states that "the District of Columbia constitutes one judicial district".

Amendments

1984—Subsec. (i). Pub. L. 98–620 struck out subsec. (i) which provided for expeditious hearings on petitions.

1959—Subsec. (*l*). Pub. L. 86–257, § 704(d), included unfair labor practices within the meaning of sections 158(e) and 158(b)(7) of this title, and inserted proviso prohibiting the officer or regional attorney from applying for any restraining order under section 158(b)(7) of this title if a charge against the employer under section 158(a)(2) of this title has been filed and after the preliminary investigation, he has reasonable cause to believe that such charge is true and that a complaint should issue.

Subsec. (m). Pub. L. 86–257, § 706, added subsec. (m).

1958—Subsec. (d). Pub. L. 85–791, § 13(a), struck out "a transcript of" after "until".

Subsec. (e). Pub. L. 85–791, § 13(b), struck out "(including the United States Court of Appeals for the District of Columbia)" before ", or if all the courts", and substituted "file in the court the record in the proceedings, as provided in section 2112 of title 28" for "certify and file in the court a transcript of the entire record in the proceedings including the pleadings and testimony upon which such order was entered and the findings and order of the Board" in first sentence, in second sentence substituted "the filing of such petition" for "such filing of" and struck out "upon the pleadings, testimony and proceedings set forth in such transcript" after "make and enter", in fifth sentence substituted "member" for "members" after "before the Board, its", and substituted "record" for "transcript", and in seventh sentence, substituted "Upon the filing of the record with it the" for "The", and "section 1254 of title 28" for "sections 346 and 347 of title 28".

Subsec. (f). Pub. L. 85–791, § 13(c), substituted "transmitted by the clerk of the court to" for "served upon" and "the record in the proceeding, certified by the Board, as provided in section 2112 of title 28" for "a transcript of the entire record in the proceeding, certified by the Board including the pleading and testimony upon which the order complained of was entered, and the findings and order of the Board" in second sentence, and in third sentence substituted "the filing of such petition," for "such filing", and struck out "exclusive" before "jurisdiction".

1947—Act June 23, 1947, amended section generally and added subsecs. (j) to (*l*) which gives the Board general power to petition district court for temporary relief or restraining order, directs Board to hear and determine jurisdictional strikes, and to investigate boycotts and strikes to force recognition of an uncertified labor union and to petition district court for injunctive relief.

EFFECTIVE DATE OF 1984 AMENDMENT

Amendment by Pub. L. 98–620 not applicable to cases pending on Nov. 8, 1984, see section 403 of Pub. L. 98–620, set out as a note under section 1657 of Title 28, Judiciary and Judicial Procedure.

EFFECTIVE DATE OF 1959 AMENDMENT

Amendment by Pub. L. 86–257 effective sixty days after Sept. 14, 1959, see section 707 of Pub. L. 86–257, set out as a note under section 153 of this title.

EFFECTIVE DATE OF 1947 AMENDMENT

For effective date of amendment by act June 23, 1947, see section 104 of act June 23, 1947, set out as a note under section 151 of this title.

§161. Investigatory powers of Board

For the purpose of all hearings and investigations, which, in the opinion of the Board, are necessary and proper for the exercise of the powers vested in it by sections 159 and 160 of this title—

(1) Documentary evidence; summoning witnesses and taking testimony

The Board, or its duly authorized agents or agencies, shall at all reasonable times have access to, for the purpose of examination, and the right to copy any evidence of any person being investigated or proceeded against that relates to any matter under investigation or in question. The Board, or any member thereof, shall upon application of any party to such proceedings, forthwith issue to such party subpenas requiring the attendance and testimony of witnesses or the production of any evidence in such proceedings or investigation requested in such application. Within five days after the service of a subpena on any person requiring the production of any evidence in his possession or under his control, such person may petition the Board to revoke, and the Board shall revoke, such subpena if in its opinion the evidence whose production is required does not relate to any matter under investigation, or any matter in question in such proceedings, or if in its opinion such subpena does not describe with sufficient particularity the evidence whose production is required. Any member of the Board, or any agent or agency designated by the Board for such purposes, may administer oaths and affirmations, examine witnesses, and receive evidence. Such attendance of witnesses and the production of such evidence may be required from any place in the United States or any Territory or possession thereof, at any designated place of hearing.

(2) Court aid in compelling production of evidence and attendance of witnesses

In case of contumacy or refusal to obey a subpena issued to any person, any district court of the United States or the United States courts of any Territory or possession, within the jurisdiction of which the inquiry is carried on or within the jurisdiction of which said person guilty of contumacy or refusal to obey is found or resides or transacts business, upon application by the Board shall have jurisdiction to issue to such person an order requiring such person to appear before the Board, its member, agent, or agency, there to produce evidence if so ordered, or there to give testimony touching the matter under investigation or in question; and any failure to obey such order of the court may be punished by said court as a contempt thereof.

(3) Repealed. Pub. L. 91–452, title II, §234, Oct. 15, 1970, 84 Stat. 930

(4) Process, service and return; fees of witnesses

Complaints, orders, and other process and papers of the Board, its member, agent, or agency, may be served either personally or by registered or certified mail or by telegraph or by leaving a copy thereof at the principal office or place of business of the person required to be served. The verified return by the individual so serving the same setting forth the manner of such service shall be proof of the same, and the return post office receipt or telegraph receipt therefor when registered or certified and mailed or when telegraphed as aforesaid shall be proof of service of the same. Witnesses summoned before the Board, its member, agent, or agency, shall be paid the same fees and mileage that are paid witnesses in the courts of the United States, and witnesses whose depositions are taken and the persons taking the same shall severally be entitled to the same fees as are paid for like services in the courts of the United States.

(5) Process, where served

All process of any court to which application may be made under this subchapter may be served in the judicial district wherein the defendant or other person required to be served resides or may be found.

(6) Information and assistance from departments

The several departments and agencies of the Government, when directed by the President, shall furnish the Board, upon its request, all records, papers, and information in their possession relating to any matter before the Board.

(July 5, 1935, ch. 372, §11, 49 Stat. 455; June 23, 1947, ch. 120, title I, §101, 61 Stat. 150; June 25, 1948, ch. 646, §32(b), 62 Stat. 991; May 24, 1949, ch. 139, §127, 63 Stat. 107; Pub. L. 91–452, title II, §234, Oct. 15, 1970, 84 Stat. 930; Pub. L. 86–507, §1(57), June 11, 1960, as added Pub. L. 96–245, May 21, 1980, 94 Stat. 347.)

CODIFICATION

The original text of par. (2) contained a reference to the District Court of the United States for the District of Columbia. Act June 25, 1948, as amended by act May 24, 1949, substituted "United States District Court for the District of Columbia" for "District Court of the United States for the District of Columbia". However, the words "United States District Court for the District of Columbia" have now been deleted entirely as superfluous in view of section 132(a) of Title 28, Judiciary and Judicial Procedure, which states that "There shall be in each judicial district a district court which shall be a court of record known as the United States District Court for the district", and section 88 of Title 28 which states that "the District of Columbia constitutes one judicial district".

AMENDMENTS

1980—Par. (4). Pub. L. 96–245 inserted provisions authorizing service by certified mail.

1970—Par. (3). Pub. L. 91–452 struck out par. (3) which related to the immunity from prosecution of any individual compelled to testify or produce evidence after claiming his privilege against self-incrimination.

1947—Act June 23, 1947, restated section with addition of provisions requiring the issuance of subpenas as a matter of course on the request of any party.

EFFECTIVE DATE OF 1970 AMENDMENT

Amendment by Pub. L. 91–452 effective on sixtieth day following Oct. 15, 1970, and not to affect any immunity to which any individual is entitled under this section by reason of any testimony given before sixtieth day following Oct. 15, 1970, see section 260 of Pub. L. 91–452, set out as an Effective Date; Savings Provisions note under section 6001 of Title 18, Crimes and Criminal Procedure.

EFFECTIVE DATE OF 1947 AMENDMENT

For effective date of amendment by act June 23, 1947, see section 104 of act June 23, 1947, set out as a note under section 151 of this title.

§ 162. Offenses and penalties

Any person who shall willfully resist, prevent, impede, or interfere with any member of the Board or any of its agents or agencies in the performance of duties pursuant to this subchapter shall be punished by a fine of not more than $5,000 or by imprisonment for not more than one year, or both.

(July 5, 1935, ch. 372, § 12, 49 Stat. 456; June 23, 1947, ch. 120, title I, § 101, 61 Stat. 151.)

AMENDMENTS

1947—Act June 23, 1947, reenacted section without change.

EFFECTIVE DATE OF 1947 AMENDMENT

For effective date of amendment by act June 23, 1947, see section 104 of act June 23, 1947, set out as a note under section 151 of this title.

§ 163. Right to strike preserved

Nothing in this subchapter, except as specifically provided for herein, shall be construed so as either to interfere with or impede or diminish in any way the right to strike, or to affect the limitations or qualifications on that right.

(July 5, 1935, ch. 372, § 13, 49 Stat. 457; June 23, 1947, ch. 120, title I, § 101, 61 Stat. 151.)

AMENDMENTS

1947—Act June 23, 1947, amended section so as to provide that except as specifically provided for in this subchapter nothing shall interfere with or diminish the right to strike and that nothing was to be construed to affect the limitations or qualifications on the right to strike, thus recognizing that the right to strike is not an unlimited and unqualified right.

EFFECTIVE DATE OF 1947 AMENDMENT

For effective date of amendment by act June 23, 1947, see section 104 of act June 23, 1947, set out as a note under section 151 of this title.

§ 164. Construction of provisions

(a) Supervisors as union members

Nothing herein shall prohibit any individual employed as a supervisor from becoming or remaining a member of a labor organization, but no employer subject to this subchapter shall be compelled to deem individuals defined herein as supervisors as employees for the purpose of any law, either national or local, relating to collective bargaining.

(b) Agreements requiring union membership in violation of State law

Nothing in this subchapter shall be construed as authorizing the execution or application of agreements requiring membership in a labor organization as a condition of employment in any State or Territory in which such execution or application is prohibited by State or Territorial law.

(c) Power of Board to decline jurisdiction of labor disputes; assertion of jurisdiction by State and Territorial courts

(1) The Board, in its discretion, may, by rule of decision or by published rules adopted pursuant to subchapter II of chapter 5 of title 5, decline to assert jurisdiction over any labor dispute involving any class or category of employers, where, in the opinion of the Board, the effect of such labor dispute on commerce is not sufficiently substantial to warrant the exercise of its jurisdiction: *Provided*, That the Board shall not decline to assert jurisdiction over any labor dispute over which it would assert jurisdiction under the standards prevailing upon August 1, 1959.

(2) Nothing in this subchapter shall be deemed to prevent or bar any agency or the courts of any State or Territory (including the Commonwealth of Puerto Rico, Guam, and the Virgin Islands), from assuming and asserting jurisdiction over labor disputes over which the Board declines, pursuant to paragraph (1) of this subsection, to assert jurisdiction.

(July 5, 1935, ch. 372, § 14, 49 Stat. 457; June 23, 1947, ch. 120, title I, § 101, 61 Stat. 151; Pub. L. 86–257, title VII, § 701(a), Sept. 14, 1959, 73 Stat. 541.)

CODIFICATION

In subsec. (c)(1), "subchapter II of chapter 5 of title 5" substituted for "the Administrative Procedure Act" on authority of Pub. L. 89–554, § 7(b), Sept. 6, 1966, 80 Stat. 631, the first section of which enacted Title 5, Government Organization and Employees.

AMENDMENTS

1959—Subsec. (c). Pub. L. 86–257 added subsec. (c).

1947—Act June 23, 1947, amended section generally by inserting new subject matter. Section formerly referred to conflict of laws, see section 165 of this title.

EFFECTIVE DATE OF 1947 AMENDMENT

For effective date of amendment by act June 23, 1947, see section 104 of act June 23, 1947, set out as a note under section 151 of this title.

§ 165. Conflict of laws

Wherever the application of the provisions of section 272 of chapter 10 of the Act entitled "An Act to establish a uniform system of bankruptcy throughout the United States", approved July 1, 1898, and Acts amendatory thereof and supplementary thereto (U.S.C., title 11, sec. 672), conflicts with the application of the provisions of this subchapter, this subchapter shall prevail: *Provided*, That in any situation where the provisions of this subchapter cannot be validly enforced, the provisions of such other Acts shall remain in full force and effect.

(July 5, 1935, ch. 372, §15, 49 Stat. 457; June 23, 1947, ch. 120, title I, §101, 61 Stat. 151.)

REFERENCES IN TEXT

The Act approved July 1, 1898, referred to in text, popularly known as the Bankruptcy Act, was classified generally to former Title 11, Bankruptcy, and was repealed effective Oct. 1, 1979, by Pub. L. 95–598, §§401(a), 402(a), Nov. 6, 1978, 92 Stat. 2682, section 101 of which enacted revised Title 11.

AMENDMENTS

1947—Act June 23, 1947, amended section generally by inserting new subject matter which was formerly covered by section 164 of this title. Section formerly referred to separability provisions, see section 166 of this title.

EFFECTIVE DATE OF 1947 AMENDMENT

For effective date of amendment by act June 23, 1947, see section 104 of act June 23, 1947, set out as a note under section 151 of this title.

§166. Separability

If any provision of this subchapter, or the application of such provision to any person or circumstances, shall be held invalid, the remainder of this subchapter, or the application of such provision to persons or circumstances other than those as to which it is held invalid, shall not be affected thereby.

(July 5, 1935, ch. 372, §16, 49 Stat. 457; June 23, 1947, ch. 120, title I, §101, 61 Stat. 151.)

AMENDMENTS

1947—Act June 23, 1947, amended section generally by inserting new subject matter which was formerly covered by section 165 of this title. Section formerly referred to short title of chapter, see section 167 of this title.

EFFECTIVE DATE OF 1947 AMENDMENT

For effective date of amendment by act June 23, 1947, see section 104 of act June 23, 1947, set out as a note under section 151 of this title.

§167. Short title of subchapter

This subchapter may be cited as the "National Labor Relations Act".

(July 5, 1935, ch. 372, §17, as added June 23, 1947, ch. 120, title I, §101, 61 Stat. 152.)

EFFECTIVE DATE

For effective date of amendment by act June 23, 1947, see section 104 of act June 23, 1947, set out as a note under section 151 of this title.

§168. Validation of certificates and other Board actions

No petition entertained, no investigation made, no election held, and no certification issued by the National Labor Relations Board, under any of the provisions of section 159 of this title, shall be invalid by reason of the failure of the Congress of Industrial Organizations to have complied with the requirements of section 159(f), (g), or (h) of this title prior to December 22, 1949, or by reason of the failure of the American Federation of Labor to have complied with the provisions of section 159(f), (g), or (h) of this title prior to November 7, 1947: *Provided*, That no liability shall be imposed under any provision of this chapter upon any person for failure to honor any election or certificate referred to above, prior to October 22, 1951: *Provided, however*, That this proviso shall not have the effect of setting aside or in any way affecting judgments or decrees heretofore entered under section 160(e) or (f) of this title and which have become final.

(July 5, 1935, ch. 372, §18, as added Oct. 22, 1951, ch. 534, §1(a), 65 Stat. 601.)

REFERENCES IN TEXT

Section 159(f), (g), or (h) of this title, referred to in text, was repealed by Pub. L. 86–257, title II, §201(d), 73 Stat. 525. See section 431 of this title.

§169. Employees with religious convictions; payment of dues and fees

Any employee who is a member of and adheres to established and traditional tenets or teachings of a bona fide religion, body, or sect which has historically held conscientious objections to joining or financially supporting labor organizations shall not be required to join or financially support any labor organization as a condition of employment; except that such employee may be required in a contract between such employees' employer and a labor organization in lieu of periodic dues and initiation fees, to pay sums equal to such dues and initiation fees to a nonreligious, nonlabor organization charitable fund exempt from taxation under section 501(c)(3) of title 26, chosen by such employee from a list of at least three such funds, designated in such contract or if the contract fails to designate such funds, then to any such fund chosen by the employee. If such employee who holds conscientious objections pursuant to this section requests the labor organization to use the grievance-arbitration procedure on the employee's behalf, the labor organization is authorized to charge the employee for the reasonable cost of using such procedure.

(July 5, 1935, ch. 372, §19, as added Pub. L. 93–360, §3, July 26, 1974, 88 Stat. 397; amended Pub. L. 96–593, Dec. 24, 1980, 94 Stat. 3452.)

AMENDMENTS

1980—Pub. L. 96–593 inserted reference to nonlabor organization and provisions respecting charges to employee for use of grievance-arbitration procedure, and struck out applicability of provisions to employees of health care institutions only.

EFFECTIVE DATE

Section 4 of Pub. L. 93–360 provided that: "The amendments made by this Act [enacting this section and section 183 of this title and amending sections 152 and 158 of this title] shall become effective on the thirtieth day after its date of enactment [July 26, 1974]."

SUBCHAPTER III—CONCILIATION OF LABOR DISPUTES; NATIONAL EMERGENCIES

§171. Declaration of purpose and policy

It is the policy of the United States that—

(a) sound and stable industrial peace and the advancement of the general welfare, health, and safety of the Nation and of the best interests of employers and employees can most satisfactorily be secured by the settlement of issues between employers and employees through the processes of conference and collective bargaining between employers and the representatives of their employees;

(b) the settlement of issues between employers and employees through collective bargaining may be advanced by making available full and adequate governmental facilities for conciliation, mediation, and voluntary arbitration to aid and encourage employers and the representatives of their employees to reach and maintain agreements concerning rates of pay, hours, and working conditions, and to make all reasonable efforts to settle their differences by mutual agreement reached through conferences and collective bargaining or by such methods as may be provided for in any applicable agreement for the settlement of disputes; and

(c) certain controversies which arise between parties to collective-bargaining agreements may be avoided or minimized by making available full and adequate governmental facilities for furnishing assistance to employers and the representatives of their employees in formulating for inclusion within such agreements provision for adequate notice of any proposed changes in the terms of such agreements, for the final adjustment of grievances or questions regarding the application or interpretation of such agreements, and other provisions designed to prevent the subsequent arising of such controversies.

(June 23, 1947, ch. 120, title II, §201, 61 Stat. 152.)

EXECUTIVE ORDER NO. 11482

Ex. Ord. No. 11482, Sept. 22, 1969, 34 F.R. 14723, which related to the Construction Industry Collective Bargaining Commission, was revoked by Ex. Ord. No. 12110, Dec. 28, 1978, 44 F.R. 1069, set out as a note under section 14 of the Federal Advisory Committee Act in the Appendix to Title 5, Government Organization and Employees.

EXECUTIVE ORDER NO. 11849

Ex. Ord. No. 11849, Apr. 1, 1975, 40 F.R. 14887, which related to the Collective Bargaining Committee in Construction, was revoked by Ex. Ord. No. 12110, Dec. 28, 1978, 44 F.R. 1069, set out as a note under section 14 of the Federal Advisory Committee Act in the Appendix to Title 5, Government Organization and Employees.

§172. Federal Mediation and Conciliation Service

(a) Creation; appointment of Director

There is created an independent agency to be known as the Federal Mediation and Conciliation Service (herein referred to as the "Service", except that for sixty days after June 23, 1947, such term shall refer to the Conciliation Service of the Department of Labor). The Service shall be under the direction of a Federal Mediation and Conciliation Director (hereinafter referred to as the "Director"), who shall be appointed by the President by and with the advice and consent of the Senate. The Director shall not engage in any other business, vocation, or employment.

(b) Appointment of officers and employees; expenditures for supplies, facilities, and services

The Director is authorized, subject to the civil service laws, to appoint such clerical and other personnel as may be necessary for the execution of the functions of the Service, and shall fix their compensation in accordance with chapter 51 and subchapter III of chapter 53 of title 5, and may, without regard to the provisions of the civil service laws, appoint such conciliators and mediators as may be necessary to carry out the functions of the Service. The Director is authorized to make such expenditures for supplies, facilities, and services as he deems necessary. Such expenditures shall be allowed and paid upon presentation of itemized vouchers therefor approved by the Director or by any employee designated by him for that purpose.

(c) Principal and regional offices; delegation of authority by Director; annual report to Congress

The principal office of the Service shall be in the District of Columbia, but the Director may establish regional offices convenient to localities in which labor controversies are likely to arise. The Director may by order, subject to revocation at any time, delegate any authority and discretion conferred upon him by this chapter to any regional director, or other officer or employee of the Service. The Director may establish suitable procedures for cooperation with State and local mediation agencies. The Director shall make an annual report in writing to Congress at the end of the fiscal year.

(d) Transfer of all mediation and conciliation services to Service; effective date; pending proceedings unaffected

All mediation and conciliation functions of the Secretary of Labor or the United States Conciliation Service under section 51 of this title, and all functions of the United States Conciliation Service under any other law are transferred to the Federal Mediation and Conciliation Service, together with the personnel and records of the United States Conciliation Service. Such transfer shall take effect upon the sixtieth day after June 23, 1947. Such transfer shall not affect any proceedings pending before the United States Conciliation Service or any certification, order, rule, or regulation theretofore made by it or by the Secretary of Labor. The Director and the Service shall not be subject in any way to the jurisdiction or authority of the Secretary of Labor or any official or division of the Department of Labor.

(June 23, 1947, ch. 120, title II, §202, 61 Stat. 153; Oct. 28, 1949, ch. 782, title XI, §1106(a), 63 Stat. 972.)

REFERENCES IN TEXT

The civil service laws, referred to in subsec. (b), are set forth in Title 5, Government Organization and Employees. See, particularly, section 3301 et seq. of Title 5.

Section 51 of this title, referred to in subsec. (d), was repealed by Pub. L. 89–554, §8(a), Sept. 6, 1966, 80 Stat. 642.

CODIFICATION

Provisions of subsec. (a) which prescribed the basic annual compensation of the Director were omitted to conform to the provisions of the Executive Schedule. See section 5314 of Title 5, Government Organization and Employees.

In subsec. (b), "chapter 51 and subchapter III of chapter 53 of title 5" substituted for "the Classification Act of 1949, as amended" on authority of Pub. L. 89–554, § 7(b), Sept. 6, 1966, 80 Stat. 631, the first section of which enacted Title 5.

Provisions of subsec. (b) that authorized the Director to fix the compensation of conciliators and mediators without regard to the Classification Act of 1923, as amended, have been omitted as obsolete. Sections 1202 and 1204 of the Classification Act of 1949, 63 Stat. 972, 973, repealed the Classification Act of 1923 and all other laws or parts of laws inconsistent with the 1949 Act. While section 1106(a) of the 1949 Act provided that references in other laws to the 1923 Act should be held and considered to mean the 1949 Act, it did not have the effect of continuing the exceptions contained in this section because of section 1106(b) which provided that the application of the 1949 Act to any position, officer, or employee shall not be affected by section 1106(a). The Classification Act of 1949 was repealed by Pub. L. 89–554, Sept. 6, 1966, § 8(a), 80 Stat. 632 (of which section 1 revised and enacted Title 5, Government Organization and Employees, into law). Section 5102 of Title 5 contains the applicability provisions of the 1949 Act, and section 5103 of Title 5 authorizes the Office of Personnel Management to determine the applicability to specific positions and employees.

AMENDMENTS

1949—Subsec. (b). Act Oct. 28, 1949, substituted "Classification Act of 1949" for "Classification Act of 1923".

REPEALS

Act Oct. 28, 1949, ch. 782, cited as a credit to this section, was repealed (subject to a savings clause) by Pub. L. 89–554, Sept. 6, 1966, § 8, 80 Stat. 632, 655.

TERMINATION OF REPORTING REQUIREMENTS

For termination, effective May 15, 2000, of provisions in subsec. (c) of this section requiring the Director to make an annual report in writing to Congress at the end of the fiscal year, see section 3003 of Pub. L. 104–66, as amended, set out as a note under section 1113 of Title 31, Money and Finance, and page 171 of House Document No. 103–7.

§ 173. Functions of Service

(a) Settlement of disputes through conciliation and mediation

It shall be the duty of the Service, in order to prevent or minimize interruptions of the free flow of commerce growing out of labor disputes, to assist parties to labor disputes in industries affecting commerce to settle such disputes through conciliation and mediation.

(b) Intervention on motion of Service or request of parties; avoidance of mediation of minor disputes

The Service may proffer its services in any labor dispute in any industry affecting commerce, either upon its own motion or upon the request of one or more of the parties to the dispute, whenever in its judgment such dispute threatens to cause a substantial interruption of commerce. The Director and the Service are directed to avoid attempting to mediate disputes which would have only a minor effect on interstate commerce if State or other conciliation services are available to the parties. Whenever the Service does proffer its services in any dispute, it shall be the duty of the Service promptly to put itself in communication with the parties and to use its best efforts, by mediation and conciliation, to bring them to agreement.

(c) Settlement of disputes by other means upon failure of conciliation

If the Director is not able to bring the parties to agreement by conciliation within a reasonable time, he shall seek to induce the parties voluntarily to seek other means of settling the dispute without resort to strike, lock-out, or other coercion, including submission to the employees in the bargaining unit of the employer's last offer of settlement for approval or rejection in a secret ballot. The failure or refusal of either party to agree to any procedure suggested by the Director shall not be deemed a violation of any duty or obligation imposed by this chapter.

(d) Use of conciliation and mediation services as last resort

Final adjustment by a method agreed upon by the parties is declared to be the desirable method for settlement of grievance disputes arising over the application or interpretation of an existing collective-bargaining agreement. The Service is directed to make its conciliation and mediation services available in the settlement of such grievance disputes only as a last resort and in exceptional cases.

(e) Encouragement and support of establishment and operation of joint labor management activities conducted by committees

The Service is authorized and directed to encourage and support the establishment and operation of joint labor management activities conducted by plant, area, and industrywide committees designed to improve labor management relationships, job security and organizational effectiveness, in accordance with the provisions of section 175a of this title.

(f) Use of alternative means of dispute resolution procedures; assignment of neutrals and arbitrators

The Service may make its services available to Federal agencies to aid in the resolution of disputes under the provisions of subchapter IV of chapter 5 of title 5. Functions performed by the Service may include assisting parties to disputes related to administrative programs, training persons in skills and procedures employed in alternative means of dispute resolution, and furnishing officers and employees of the Service to act as neutrals. Only officers and employees who are qualified in accordance with section 573 of title 5 may be assigned to act as neutrals. The Service shall consult with the agency designated by, or the interagency committee designated or established by, the President under section 573 of title 5 in maintaining rosters of neutrals and arbitrators, and to adopt such procedures and rules as are necessary to carry out the services authorized in this subsection.

(June 23, 1947, ch. 120, title II, § 203, 61 Stat. 153; Pub. L. 95–524, § 6(c)(1), Oct. 27, 1978, 92 Stat. 2020; Pub. L. 101–552, § 7, Nov. 15, 1990, 104 Stat. 2746; Pub. L. 102–354, § 5(b)(5), Aug. 26, 1992, 106 Stat.

946; Pub. L. 104–320, §4(c), Oct. 19, 1996, 110 Stat. 3871.)

REFERENCES IN TEXT

This chapter, referred to in subsec. (c), was in the original "this Act" meaning act June 23, 1947, ch. 120, 61 Stat. 136, as amended, known as the Labor Management Relations Act, 1947, which is classified principally to this subchapter and subchapters III (§171 et seq.) and IV (§185 et seq.) of this chapter. For complete classification of this act to the Code, see Tables.

AMENDMENTS

1996—Subsec. (f). Pub. L. 104–320 substituted "the agency designated by, or the interagency committee designated or established by, the President under section 573 of title 5" for "the Administrative Conference of the United States and other agencies".

1992—Subsec. (f). Pub. L. 102–354 substituted "section 573" for "section 583".

1990—Subsec. (f). Pub. L. 101–552 added subsec. (f).

1978—Subsec. (e). Pub. L. 95–524 added subsec. (e).

APPLICABILITY TO COLLECTIVE BARGAINING AGREEMENTS

Amendment by Pub. L. 95–524 not to affect terms and conditions of any collective bargaining agreement whether in effect prior to or entered into after Oct. 27, 1978, see section 6(e) of Pub. L. 95–524, set out as a note under section 175a of this title.

§174. Co-equal obligations of employees, their representatives, and management to minimize labor disputes

(a)[1] In order to prevent or minimize interruptions of the free flow of commerce growing out of labor disputes, employers and employees and their representatives, in any industry affecting commerce, shall—

(1) exert every reasonable effort to make and maintain agreements concerning rates of pay, hours, and working conditions, including provision for adequate notice of any proposed change in the terms of such agreements;

(2) whenever a dispute arises over the terms or application of a collective-bargaining agreement and a conference is requested by a party or prospective party thereto, arrange promptly for such a conference to be held and endeavor in such conference to settle such dispute expeditiously; and

(3) in case such dispute is not settled by conference, participate fully and promptly in such meetings as may be undertaken by the Service under this chapter for the purpose of aiding in a settlement of the dispute.

(June 23, 1947, ch. 120, title II, §204, 61 Stat. 154.)

§175. National Labor-Management Panel; creation and composition; appointment, tenure, and compensation; duties

(a) There is created a National Labor-Management Panel which shall be composed of twelve members appointed by the President, six of whom shall be selected from among persons outstanding in the field of management and six of whom shall be selected from among persons outstanding in the field of labor. Each member shall hold office for a term of three years, except that any member appointed to fill a vacancy occurring prior to the expiration of the term for which his predecessor was appointed shall be appointed for the remainder of such term, and the terms of office of the members first taking office shall expire, as designated by the President at the time of appointment, four at the end of the first year, four at the end of the second year, and four at the end of the third year after the date of appointment. Members of the panel, when serving on business of the panel, shall be paid compensation at the rate of $25 per day, and shall also be entitled to receive an allowance for actual and necessary travel and subsistence expenses while so serving away from their places of residence.

(b) It shall be the duty of the panel, at the request of the Director, to advise in the avoidance of industrial controversies and the manner in which mediation and voluntary adjustment shall be administered, particularly with reference to controversies affecting the general welfare of the country.

(June 23, 1947, ch. 120, title II, §205, 61 Stat. 154.)

§175a. Assistance to plant, area, and industrywide labor management committees

(a) Establishment and operation of plant, area, and industrywide committees

(1) The Service is authorized and directed to provide assistance in the establishment and operation of plant, area and industrywide labor management committees which—

(A) have been organized jointly by employers and labor organizations representing employees in that plant, area, or industry; and

(B) are established for the purpose of improving labor management relationships, job security, organizational effectiveness, enhancing economic development or involving workers in decisions affecting their jobs including improving communication with respect to subjects of mutual interest and concern.

(2) The Service is authorized and directed to enter into contracts and to make grants, where necessary or appropriate, to fulfill its responsibilities under this section.

(b) Restrictions on grants, contracts, or other assistance

(1) No grant may be made, no contract may be entered into and no other assistance may be provided under the provisions of this section to a plant labor management committee unless the employees in that plant are represented by a labor organization and there is in effect at that plant a collective bargaining agreement.

(2) No grant may be made, no contract may be entered into and no other assistance may be provided under the provisions of this section to an area or industrywide labor management committee unless its participants include any labor organizations certified or recognized as the representative of the employees of an employer participating in such committee. Nothing in this clause shall prohibit participation in an area or industrywide committee by an employer whose employees are not represented by a labor organization.

(3) No grant may be made under the provisions of this section to any labor management com-

[1] So in original. No subsec. (b) has been enacted.

mittee which the Service finds to have as one of its purposes the discouragement of the exercise of rights contained in section 157 of this title, or the interference with collective bargaining in any plant, or industry.

(c) Establishment of office

The Service shall carry out the provisions of this section through an office established for that purpose.

(d) Authorization of appropriations

There are authorized to be appropriated to carry out the provisions of this section $10,000,000 for the fiscal year 1979, and such sums as may be necessary thereafter.

(June 23, 1947, ch. 120, title II, §205A, as added Pub. L. 95–524, §6(c)(2), Oct. 27, 1978, 92 Stat. 2020.)

SHORT TITLE

For short title of section 6 of Pub. L. 95–524 as the Labor Management Cooperation Act of 1978, see Short Title of 1978 Amendment note set out under section 141 of this title.

CONGRESSIONAL STATEMENT OF PURPOSE

Section 6(b) of Pub. L. 95–524 provided that: "It is the purpose of this section [enacting this section and amending sections 173 and 186 of this title]—

"(1) to improve communication between representatives of labor and management;

"(2) to provide workers and employers with opportunities to study and explore new and innovative joint approaches to achieving organizational effectiveness;

"(3) to assist workers and employers in solving problems of mutual concern not susceptible to resolution within the collective bargaining process;

"(4) to study and explore ways of eliminating potential problems which reduce the competitiveness and inhibit the economic development of the plant, area or industry;

"(5) to enhance the involvement of workers in making decisions that affect their working lives;

"(6) to expand and improve working relationships between workers and managers; and

"(7) to encourage free collective bargaining by establishing continuing mechanisms for communication between employers and their employees through Federal assistance to the formation and operation of labor management committees."

APPLICABILITY TO COLLECTIVE BARGAINING AGREEMENTS

Section 6(e) of Pub. L. 95–524 provided that: "Nothing in this section or the amendments made by this section [enacting this section, amending sections 173 and 186 of this title, and enacting provisions set out as notes under this section] shall affect the terms and conditions of any collective bargaining agreement whether in effect prior to or entered into after the date of enactment of this section [Oct. 27, 1978]."

§176. National emergencies; appointment of board of inquiry by President; report; contents; filing with Service

Whenever in the opinion of the President of the United States, a threatened or actual strike or lockout affecting an entire industry or a substantial part thereof engaged in trade, commerce, transportation, transmission, or communication among the several States or with foreign nations, or engaged in the production of goods for commerce, will, if permitted to occur or to continue, imperil the national health or safety, he may appoint a board of inquiry to inquire into the issues involved in the dispute and to make a written report to him within such time as he shall prescribe. Such report shall include a statement of the facts with respect to the dispute, including each party's statement of its position but shall not contain any recommendations. The President shall file a copy of such report with the Service and shall make its contents available to the public.

(June 23, 1947, ch. 120, title II, §206, 61 Stat. 155.)

EXECUTIVE ORDER NO. 11621

Ex. Ord. No. 11621, Oct. 4, 1971, 36 F.R. 19435, as amended by Ex. Ord. No. 11622, Oct. 5, 1971, 36 F.R. 19491, which created a Board of Inquiry to inquire into issues involved in certain labor disputes, was revoked by Ex. Ord. No. 12553, Feb. 25, 1986, 51 F.R. 7237.

§177. Board of inquiry

(a) Composition

A board of inquiry shall be composed of a chairman and such other members as the President shall determine, and shall have power to sit and act in any place within the United States and to conduct such hearings either in public or in private, as it may deem necessary or proper, to ascertain the facts with respect to the causes and circumstances of the dispute.

(b) Compensation

Members of a board of inquiry shall receive compensation at the rate of $50 for each day actually spent by them in the work of the board, together with necessary travel and subsistence expenses.

(c) Powers of discovery

For the purpose of any hearing or inquiry conducted by any board appointed under this title, the provisions of sections 49 and 50 of title 15 (relating to the attendance of witnesses and the production of books, papers, and documents) are made applicable to the powers and duties of such board.

(June 23, 1947, ch. 120, title II, §207, 61 Stat. 155.)

§178. Injunctions during national emergency

(a) Petition to district court by Attorney General on direction of President

Upon receiving a report from a board of inquiry the President may direct the Attorney General to petition any district court of the United States having jurisdiction of the parties to enjoin such strike or lock-out or the continuing thereof, and if the court finds that such threatened or actual strike or lock-out—

(i) affects an entire industry or a substantial part thereof engaged in trade, commerce, transportation, transmission, or communication among the several States or with foreign nations, or engaged in the production of goods for commerce; and

(ii) if permitted to occur or to continue, will imperil the national health or safety, it shall have jurisdiction to enjoin any such strike or lockout, or the continuing thereof, and to make such other orders as may be appropriate.

(b) Inapplicability of chapter 6

In any case, the provisions of chapter 6 of this title shall not be applicable.

(c) Review of orders

The order or orders of the court shall be subject to review by the appropriate United States court of appeals and by the Supreme Court upon writ of certiorari or certification as provided in section 1254 of title 28.

(June 23, 1947, ch. 120, title II, §208, 61 Stat. 155; June 25, 1948, ch. 646, §32(a), 62 Stat. 991; May 24, 1949, ch. 139, §127, 63 Stat. 107.)

REFERENCES IN TEXT

Chapter 6 (§101 et seq.) of this title, referred to in subsec. (b), is a reference to act Mar. 23, 1932, ch. 90, 47 Stat. 70, popularly known as the Norris-LaGuardia Act.

CODIFICATION

In subsec. (c), "court of appeals" substituted for "circuit court of appeals" on authority of act June 25, 1948, as amended by act May 24, 1949. The words "United States" immediately preceding "Court of appeals" were inserted on authority of section 43 of Title 28, Judiciary and Judicial Procedure.

In subsec. (c), "section 1254 of title 28" substituted for "sections 239 and 240 of the Judicial Code, as amended (U.S.C. title 28, secs. 346 and 347)" on authority of act June 25, 1948, ch. 646, 62 Stat. 869, section 1 of which enacted Title 28, Judiciary and Judicial Procedure.

§179. Injunctions during national emergency; adjustment efforts by parties during injunction period

(a) Assistance of Service; acceptance of Service's proposed settlement

Whenever a district court has issued an order under section 178 of this title enjoining acts or practices which imperil or threaten to imperil the national health or safety, it shall be the duty of the parties to the labor dispute giving rise to such order to make every effort to adjust and settle their differences, with the assistance of the Service created by this chapter. Neither party shall be under any duty to accept, in whole or in part, any proposal of settlement made by the Service.

(b) Reconvening of board of inquiry; report by board; contents; secret ballot of employees by National Labor Relations Board; certification of results to Attorney General

Upon the issuance of such order, the President shall reconvene the board of inquiry which has previously reported with respect to the dispute. At the end of a sixty-day period (unless the dispute has been settled by that time), the board of inquiry shall report to the President the current position of the parties and the efforts which have been made for settlement, and shall include a statement by each party of its position and a statement of the employer's last offer of settlement. The President shall make such report available to the public. The National Labor Relations Board, within the succeeding fifteen days, shall take a secret ballot of the employees of each employer involved in the dispute on the question of whether they wish to accept the final offer of settlement made by their employer as stated by him and shall certify the results thereof to the Attorney General within five days thereafter.

(June 23, 1947, ch. 120, title II, §209, 61 Stat. 155.)

§180. Discharge of injunction upon certification of results of election or settlement; report to Congress

Upon the certification of the results of such ballot or upon a settlement being reached, whichever happens sooner, the Attorney General shall move the court to discharge the injunction, which motion shall then be granted and the injunction discharged. When such motion is granted, the President shall submit to the Congress a full and comprehensive report of the proceedings, including the findings of the board of inquiry and the ballot taken by the National Labor Relations Board, together with such recommendations as he may see fit to make for consideration and appropriate action.

(June 23, 1947, ch. 120, title II, §210, 61 Stat. 156.)

§181. Compilation of collective bargaining agreements, etc.; use of data

(a) For the guidance and information of interested representatives of employers, employees, and the general public, the Bureau of Labor Statistics of the Department of Labor shall maintain a file of copies of all available collective bargaining agreements and other available agreements and actions thereunder settling or adjusting labor disputes. Such file shall be open to inspection under appropriate conditions prescribed by the Secretary of Labor, except that no specific information submitted in confidence shall be disclosed.

(b) The Bureau of Labor Statistics in the Department of labor is authorized to furnish upon request of the Service, or employers, employees, or their representatives, all available data and factual information which may aid in the settlement of any labor dispute, except that no specific information submitted in confidence shall be disclosed.

(June 23, 1947, ch. 120, title II, §211, 61 Stat. 156.)

§182. Exemption of Railway Labor Act from subchapter

The provisions of this subchapter shall not be applicable with respect to any matter which is subject to the provisions of the Railway Labor Act [45 U.S.C. 151 et seq.], as amended from time to time.

(June 23, 1947, ch. 120, title II, §212, 61 Stat. 156.)

REFERENCES IN TEXT

The Railway Labor Act, as amended, referred to in text, is act May 20, 1926, ch. 347, 44 Stat. 577, as amended, which is classified principally to chapter 8 (§151 et seq.) of Title 45, Railroads. For complete classification of this Act to the Code, see section 151 of Title 45 and Tables.

§183. Conciliation of labor disputes in the health care industry

(a) Establishment of Boards of Inquiry; membership

If, in the opinion of the Director of the Federal Mediation and Conciliation Service, a threatened or actual strike or lockout affecting a health care institution will, if permitted to occur or to continue, substantially interrupt the delivery of health care in the locality concerned, the Director may further assist in the resolution of the impasse by establishing within 30 days after the notice to the Federal Mediation and Conciliation Service under clause (A) of the last sentence of section 158(d) of this title (which is required by clause (3) of such section 158(d) of this title), or within 10 days after the notice under clause (B), an impartial Board of Inquiry to investigate the issues involved in the dispute and to make a written report thereon to the parties within fifteen (15) days after the establishment of such a Board. The written report shall contain the findings of fact together with the Board's recommendations for settling the dispute, with the objective of achieving a prompt, peaceful and just settlement of the dispute. Each such Board shall be composed of such number of individuals as the Director may deem desirable. No member appointed under this section shall have any interest or involvement in the health care institutions or the employee organizations involved in the dispute.

(b) Compensation of members of Boards of Inquiry

(1) Members of any board established under this section who are otherwise employed by the Federal Government shall serve without compensation but shall be reimbursed for travel, subsistence, and other necessary expenses incurred by them in carrying out its duties under this section.

(2) Members of any board established under this section who are not subject to paragraph (1) shall receive compensation at a rate prescribed by the Director but not to exceed the daily rate prescribed for GS–18 of the General Schedule under section 5332 of title 5, including travel for each day they are engaged in the performance of their duties under this section and shall be entitled to reimbursement for travel, subsistence, and other necessary expenses incurred by them in carrying out their duties under this section.

(c) Maintenance of status quo

After the establishment of a board under subsection (a) of this section and for 15 days after any such board has issued its report, no change in the status quo in effect prior to the expiration of the contract in the case of negotiations for a contract renewal, or in effect prior to the time of the impasse in the case of an initial beginning negotiation, except by agreement, shall be made by the parties to the controversy.

(d) Authorization of appropriations

There are authorized to be appropriated such sums as may be necessary to carry out the provisions of this section.

(June 23, 1947, ch. 120, title II, §213, as added Pub. L. 93–360, §2, July 26, 1974, 88 Stat. 396.)

EFFECTIVE DATE

Section effective on thirtieth day after July 26, 1974, see section 4 of Pub. L. 93–360, set out as a note under section 169 of this title.

REFERENCES IN OTHER LAWS TO GS–16, 17, OR 18 PAY RATES

References in laws to the rates of pay for GS–16, 17, or 18, or to maximum rates of pay under the General Schedule, to be considered references to rates payable under specified sections of Title 5, Government Organization and Employees, see section 529 [title I, §101(c)(1)] of Pub. L. 101–509, set out in a note under section 5376 of Title 5.

SUBCHAPTER IV—LIABILITIES OF AND RESTRICTIONS ON LABOR AND MANAGEMENT

§185. Suits by and against labor organizations

(a) Venue, amount, and citizenship

Suits for violation of contracts between an employer and a labor organization representing employees in an industry affecting commerce as defined in this chapter, or between any such labor organizations, may be brought in any district court of the United States having jurisdiction of the parties, without respect to the amount in controversy or without regard to the citizenship of the parties.

(b) Responsibility for acts of agent; entity for purposes of suit; enforcement of money judgments

Any labor organization which represents employees in an industry affecting commerce as defined in this chapter and any employer whose activities affect commerce as defined in this chapter shall be bound by the acts of its agents. Any such labor organization may sue or be sued as an entity and in behalf of the employees whom it represents in the courts of the United States. Any money judgment against a labor organization in a district court of the United States shall be enforceable only against the organization as an entity and against its assets, and shall not be enforceable against any individual member or his assets.

(c) Jurisdiction

For the purposes of actions and proceedings by or against labor organizations in the district courts of the United States, district courts shall be deemed to have jurisdiction of a labor organization (1) in the district in which such organization maintains its principal office, or (2) in any district in which its duly authorized officers or agents are engaged in representing or acting for employee members.

(d) Service of process

The service of summons, subpena, or other legal process of any court of the United States upon an officer or agent of a labor organization, in his capacity as such, shall constitute service upon the labor organization.

(e) Determination of question of agency

For the purposes of this section, in determining whether any person is acting as an "agent" of another person so as to make such other person responsible for his acts, the question of whether the specific acts performed were actually authorized or subsequently ratified shall not be controlling.

(June 23, 1947, ch. 120, title III, §301, 61 Stat. 156.)

REFERENCES IN TEXT

This chapter, referred to in subsecs. (a) and (b), was in the original "this Act" meaning act June 23, 1947, ch. 120, 61 Stat. 136, as amended, known as the Labor Management Relations Act, 1947, which is classified principally to this subchapter and subchapters III (§171 et seq.) and IV (§185 et seq.) of this chapter. For complete classification of this act to the Code, see Tables.

§186. Restrictions on financial transactions

(a) Payment or lending, etc., of money by employer or agent to employees, representatives, or labor organizations

It shall be unlawful for any employer or association of employers or any person who acts as a labor relations expert, adviser, or consultant to an employer or who acts in the interest of an employer to pay, lend, or deliver, or agree to pay, lend, or deliver, any money or other thing of value—

(1) to any representative of any of his employees who are employed in an industry affecting commerce; or

(2) to any labor organization, or any officer or employee thereof, which represents, seeks to represent, or would admit to membership, any of the employees of such employer who are employed in an industry affecting commerce; or

(3) to any employee or group or committee of employees of such employer employed in an industry affecting commerce in excess of their normal compensation for the purpose of causing such employee or group or committee directly or indirectly to influence any other employees in the exercise of the right to organize and bargain collectively through representatives of their own choosing; or

(4) to any officer or employee of a labor organization engaged in an industry affecting commerce with intent to influence him in respect to any of his actions, decisions, or duties as a representative of employees or as such officer or employee of such labor organization.

(b) Request, demand, etc., for money or other thing of value

(1) It shall be unlawful for any person to request, demand, receive, or accept, or agree to receive or accept, any payment, loan, or delivery of any money or other thing of value prohibited by subsection (a) of this section.

(2) It shall be unlawful for any labor organization, or for any person acting as an officer, agent, representative, or employee of such labor organization, to demand or accept from the operator of any motor vehicle (as defined in section 13102 of title 49) employed in the transportation of property in commerce, or the employer of any such operator, any money or other thing of value payable to such organization or to an officer, agent, representative or employee thereof as a fee or charge for the unloading, or in connection with the unloading, of the cargo of such vehicle: *Provided*, That nothing in this paragraph shall be construed to make unlawful any payment by an employer to any of his employees as compensation for their services as employees.

(c) Exceptions

The provisions of this section shall not be applicable (1) in respect to any money or other thing of value payable by an employer to any of his employees whose established duties include acting openly for such employer in matters of labor relations or personnel administration or to any representative of his employees, or to any officer or employee of a labor organization, who is also an employee or former employee of such employer, as compensation for, or by reason of, his service as an employee of such employer; (2) with respect to the payment or delivery of any money or other thing of value in satisfaction of a judgment of any court or a decision or award of an arbitrator or impartial chairman or in compromise, adjustment, settlement, or release of any claim, complaint, grievance, or dispute in the absence of fraud or duress; (3) with respect to the sale or purchase of an article or commodity at the prevailing market price in the regular course of business; (4) with respect to money deducted from the wages of employees in payment of membership dues in a labor organization: *Provided*, That the employer has received from each employee, on whose account such deductions are made, a written assignment which shall not be irrevocable for a period of more than one year, or beyond the termination date of the applicable collective agreement, whichever occurs sooner; (5) with respect to money or other thing of value paid to a trust fund established by such representative, for the sole and exclusive benefit of the employees of such employer, and their families and dependents (or of such employees, families, and dependents jointly with the employees of other employers making similar payments, and their families and dependents): *Provided*, That (A) such payments are held in trust for the purpose of paying, either from principal or income or both, for the benefit of employees, their families and dependents, for medical or hospital care, pensions on retirement or death of employees, compensation for injuries or illness resulting from occupational activity or insurance to provide any of the foregoing, or unemployment benefits or life insurance, disability and sickness insurance, or accident insurance; (B) the detailed basis on which such payments are to be made is specified in a written agreement with the employer, and employees and employers are equally represented in the administration of such fund, together with such neutral persons as the representatives of the employers and the representatives of employees may agree upon and in the event the employer and employee groups deadlock on the administration of such fund and there are no neutral persons empowered to break such deadlock, such agreement provides that the two groups shall agree on an impartial umpire to decide such dispute, or in event of their failure to agree within a reasonable length of time, an impartial umpire to decide such dispute shall, on petition of either group, be appointed by the district court of the United States for the district where the trust fund has its principal office, and shall also contain provisions for an annual audit of the trust fund, a statement of the results of which shall be available for inspection by interested persons at the principal office of the trust fund and at such other places as may be designated in such written agreement; and (C) such payments as are intended to be used for the purpose of providing pensions or annuities for employees are made to a separate trust which provides that the funds held therein cannot be used for any purpose other than paying such pensions or annuities; (6) with respect to money or other thing of value paid by any employer to a trust fund established by such representative for the purpose of pooled vacation, holiday, severance or similar benefits, or defraying costs of apprenticeship or other training programs: *Provided*, That the requirements of clause (B) of the proviso to clause (5) of this subsection shall apply to such trust funds; (7) with respect to money or other thing of value paid by any employer to a pooled or individual trust fund established by such representative for the purpose of (A) scholarships for the benefit of employees, their families, and dependents for study at educational institutions, (B) child care centers for preschool and school age dependents of employees, or (C) financial assistance for employee housing: *Provided*, That no labor organization or employer shall be required to bargain on the establishment of any such trust fund, and refusal to do so shall not constitute an unfair labor practice: *Provided further*, That the requirements of clause (B) of the proviso to clause (5) of this subsection shall apply to such trust funds; (8) with respect to money or any other thing of value paid by any employer to a trust fund established by such representative for the purpose of defraying the costs of legal services for employees, their families, and dependents for counsel or plan of their choice: *Provided*, That the requirements of clause (B) of the proviso to clause (5) of this subsection shall apply to such trust funds: *Provided further*, That no such legal services shall be furnished: (A) to initiate any proceeding directed (i) against any such employer or its officers or agents except in workman's compensation cases, or (ii) against such labor organization, or its parent or subordinate bodies, or their officers or agents, or (iii) against any other employer or labor organization, or their officers or agents, in any matter arising under subchapter II of this chapter or this chapter; and (B) in any proceeding where a labor organization would be prohibited from defraying the costs of legal services by the provisions of the Labor-Management Reporting and Disclosure Act of 1959 [29 U.S.C. 401 et seq.]; or (9) with respect to money or other things of value paid by an employer to a plant, area or industrywide labor management committee established for one or more of the purposes set forth in section 5(b) of the Labor Management Cooperation Act of 1978.

(d) Penalties for violations

(1) Any person who participates in a transaction involving a payment, loan, or delivery of money or other thing of value to a labor organization in payment of membership dues or to a joint labor-management trust fund as defined by clause (B) of the proviso to clause (5) of subsection (c) of this section or to a plant, area, or industry-wide labor-management committee that is received and used by such labor organization, trust fund, or committee, which transaction does not satisfy all the applicable requirements of subsections (c)(4) through (c)(9) of this section, and willfully and with intent to benefit himself or to benefit other persons he knows are not permitted to receive a payment, loan, money, or other thing of value under subsections (c)(4) through (c)(9) violates this subsection, shall, upon conviction thereof, be guilty of a felony and be subject to a fine of not more than $15,000, or imprisoned for not more than five years, or both; but if the value of the amount of money or thing of value involved in any violation of the provisions of this section does not exceed $1,000, such person shall be guilty of a misdemeanor and be subject to a fine of not more than $10,000, or imprisoned for not more than one year, or both.

(2) Except for violations involving transactions covered by subsection (d)(1) of this section, any person who willfully violates this section shall, upon conviction thereof, be guilty of a felony and be subject to a fine of not more than $15,000, or imprisoned for not more than five years, or both; but if the value of the amount of money or thing of value involved in any violation of the provisions of this section does not exceed $1,000, such person shall be guilty of a misdemeanor and be subject to a fine of not more than $10,000, or imprisoned for not more than one year, or both.

(e) Jurisdiction of courts

The district courts of the United States and the United States courts of the Territories and possessions shall have jurisdiction, for cause shown, and subject to the provisions of section 381 of title 28 (relating to notice to opposite party) to restrain violations of this section, without regard to the provisions of section 17 of title 15 and section 52 of this title, and the provisions of chapter 6 of this title.

(f) Effective date of provisions

This section shall not apply to any contract in force on June 23, 1947, until the expiration of such contract, or until July 1, 1948, whichever first occurs.

(g) Contributions to trust funds

Compliance with the restrictions contained in subsection (c)(5)(B) of this section upon contributions to trust funds, otherwise lawful, shall not be applicable to contributions to such trust funds established by collective agreement prior to January 1, 1946, nor shall subsection (c)(5)(A) of this section be construed as prohibiting contributions to such trust funds if prior to January 1, 1947, such funds contained provisions for pooled vacation benefits.

(June 23, 1947, ch. 120, title III, §302, 61 Stat. 157; Pub. L. 86–257, title V, §505, Sept. 14, 1959, 73 Stat. 537; Pub. L. 91–86, Oct. 14, 1969, 83 Stat. 133; Pub. L. 93–95, Aug. 15, 1973, 87 Stat. 314; Pub. L. 95–524, §6(d), Oct. 27, 1978, 92 Stat. 2021; Pub. L. 98–473, title II, §801, Oct. 12, 1984, 98 Stat. 2131; Pub. L. 101–273, §1, Apr. 18, 1990, 104 Stat. 138; Pub. L. 104–88, title III, §337, Dec. 29, 1995, 109 Stat. 954.)

REFERENCES IN TEXT

The Labor-Management Reporting and Disclosure Act of 1959, referred to in subsec. (c)(8), is Pub. L. 86–257, Sept. 14, 1959, 73 Stat. 519, as amended, which is classified principally to chapter 11 (§401 et seq.) of this title. For complete classification of this Act to the Code, see Short Title note set out under section 401 of this title and Tables.

Section 5(b) of the Labor Management Cooperation Act of 1978, referred to in subsec. (c)(9), probably means section 6(b) of Pub. L. 95–524, which is set out as a note under section 175a of this title.

Section 381 of title 28, referred to in subsec. (e), was omitted from the revision of Title 28, Judiciary and Judicial Procedure, by act June 25, 1948, ch. 646, 62 Stat. 869. See rule 65 of Federal Rules of Civil Procedure set out in the Appendix to Title 28.

Chapter 6 (§ 101 et seq.) of this title, referred to in subsec. (e), is a reference to act Mar. 23, 1932, ch. 90, 47 Stat. 70, popularly known as the Norris-LaGuardia Act.

AMENDMENTS

1995—Subsec. (b)(2). Pub. L. 104–88 substituted "(as defined in section 13102 of title 49)" for "(as defined in part II of the Interstate Commerce Act)".

1990—Subsec. (c)(7)(C). Pub. L. 101–273 added subcl. (C).

1984—Subsec. (d). Pub. L. 98–473, in amending subsec. (d) generally, added par. (1), designated existing provisions as par. (2), inserted reference to par. (1), and inserted provisions relating to commission of a felony.

1978—Subsec. (c)(9). Pub. L. 95–524 added cl. (9).

1973—Subsec. (c)(8). Pub. L. 93–95 added cl. (8).

1969—Subsec. (c)(7). Pub. L. 91–86 added cl. (7).

1959—Subsec. (a). Pub. L. 86–257 amended subsec. (a) generally. Prior to amendment subsec. (a) read as follows: "It shall be unlawful for any employer to pay or deliver, or to agree to pay or deliver, any money or other thing of value to any representative of any of his employees who are employed in an industry affecting commerce."

Subsec. (b). Pub. L. 86–257 amended subsec. (b) generally. Prior to amendment subsec. (b) read as follows: "It shall be unlawful for any representative of any employees who are employed in an industry affecting commerce to receive or accept, or to agree to receive or accept, from the employer of such employees any money or other thing of value."

Subsec. (c). Pub. L. 86–257 substituted "in respect to any money or other thing of value payable by an employer to any of his employees whose established duties include acting openly for such employer in matters of labor relations or personnel administration or to any representative of his employees, or to any officer or employee of a labor organization, who is also an employee or former employee of such employer, as compensation for, or by reason of, his service as an employee of such employer" for "with respect to any money or other thing of value payable by an employer to any representative who is an employee or former employee of such employer, as compensation for, or by reason of, his services as an employee of such employer" in cl. (1), and added cl. (6).

EFFECTIVE DATE OF 1995 AMENDMENT

Amendment by Pub. L. 104–88 effective Jan. 1, 1996, see section 2 of Pub. L. 104–88, set out as an Effective Date note under section 701 of Title 49, Transportation.

APPLICABILITY TO COLLECTIVE BARGAINING AGREEMENTS

Amendment by Pub. L. 95–524 not to affect terms and conditions of any collective bargaining agreement whether in effect prior to or entered into after Oct. 27, 1978, see section 6(e) of Pub. L. 95–524, set out as an Effective Date note under section 175a of this title.

§ 187. Unlawful activities or conduct; right to sue; jurisdiction; limitations; damages

(a) It shall be unlawful, for the purpose of this section only, in an industry or activity affecting commerce, for any labor organization to engage in any activity or conduct defined as an unfair labor practice in section 158(b)(4) of this title.

(b) Whoever shall be injured in his business or property by reason or[1] any violation of subsection (a) of this section may sue therefor in any district court of the United States subject to the limitations and provisions of section 185 of this title without respect to the amount in controversy, or in any other court having jurisdiction of the parties, and shall recover the damages by him sustained and the cost of the suit.

(June 23, 1947, ch. 120, title III, § 303, 61 Stat. 158; Pub. L. 86–257, title VII, § 704(e), Sept. 14, 1959, 73 Stat. 545.)

AMENDMENTS

1959—Subsec. (a). Pub. L. 86–257 struck out provisions which specified particular practices that were unlawful, and inserted reference to practices defined in section 158(b)(4) of this title, which section defines the unfair labor practices formerly enumerated in this subsection.

§ 188. Repealed. Aug. 9, 1955, ch. 690, § 4(3), 69 Stat. 625

Section, act June 23, 1947, ch. 120, title III, § 305, 61 Stat. 160, forbade striking by Government employees, required discharge of striking employee and forfeiture of his civil-service status, and made him ineligible for employment for three years. See sections 3333 and 7311 of Title 5, Government Organization and Employees, and section 1918 of Title 18, Crimes and Criminal Procedure.

SUBCHAPTER V—CONGRESSIONAL JOINT COMMITTEE ON LABOR-MANAGEMENT RELATIONS

§§ 191 to 197. Omitted

CODIFICATION

Section 191, act June 23, 1947, ch. 120, title IV, § 401, 61 Stat. 160, related to establishment and composition of Joint Committee on Labor-Management Relations.

Section 192, act June 23, 1947, ch. 120, title IV, § 402, 61 Stat. 160, related to a study by committee of the entire field of labor-management relations.

Section 193, acts June 23, 1947, ch. 120, title IV, § 403, 61 Stat. 160; Aug. 10, 1948, ch. 833, 62 Stat. 1286, related to a final report to Congress to be submitted no later than March 1, 1949.

Section 194, act June 23, 1947, ch. 120, title IV, § 404, 61 Stat. 161, related to employment and compensation of experts and other personnel.

Section 195, act June 23, 1947, ch. 120, title IV, § 405, 61 Stat. 161, related to hearings, calling of witnesses, production of evidence.

Section 196, act June 23, 1947, ch. 120, title IV, § 406, 61 Stat. 161, related to reimbursement of committee members for expenses.

Section 197, act June 23, 1947, ch. 120, title IV, § 407, 61 Stat. 161, related to appropriation of funds.

CHAPTER 8—FAIR LABOR STANDARDS

[1] So in original. Probably should be "of".

§201. Short title

This chapter may be cited as the "Fair Labor Standards Act of 1938".

(June 25, 1938, ch. 676, §1, 52 Stat. 1060.)

SHORT TITLE OF 2007 AMENDMENT

Pub. L. 110–28, title VIII, §8101, May 25, 2007, 121 Stat. 188, provided that: "This subtitle [subtitle A (§§8101–8104) of title VIII of Pub. L. 110–28, amending section 206 of this title, repealing sections 205 and 208 of this title, and enacting provisions set out as notes under section 206 of this title] may be cited as the 'Fair Minimum Wage Act of 2007'."

SHORT TITLE OF 2000 AMENDMENT

Pub. L. 106–202, §1, May 18, 2000, 114 Stat. 308, provided that: "This Act [amending section 207 of this title and enacting provisions set out as notes under section 207 of this title] may be cited as the 'Worker Economic Opportunity Act'."

SHORT TITLE OF 1998 AMENDMENTS

Pub. L. 105–334, §1, Oct. 31, 1998, 112 Stat. 3137, provided that: "This Act [amending section 213 of this title and enacting provisions set out as a note under section 213 of this title] may be cited as the 'Drive for Teen Employment Act'."

Pub. L. 105–221, §1, Aug. 7, 1998, 112 Stat. 1248, provided that: "This Act [amending section 203 of this title] may be cited as the 'Amy Somers Volunteers at Food Banks Act'."

SHORT TITLE OF 1996 AMENDMENT

Pub. L. 104–188, [title II], §2104(a), Aug. 20, 1996, 110 Stat. 1928, provided that: "This section [amending section 206 of this title] may be cited as the 'Minimum Wage Increase Act of 1996'."

SHORT TITLE OF 1995 AMENDMENT

Pub. L. 104–26, §1, Sept. 6, 1995, 109 Stat. 264, provided that: "This Act [amending section 207 of this title and enacting provisions set out as a note under section 207 of this title] may be cited as the 'Court Reporter Fair Labor Amendments of 1995'."

SHORT TITLE OF 1989 AMENDMENT

Pub. L. 101–157, §1(a), Nov. 17, 1989, 103 Stat. 938, provided that: "This Act [enacting section 60k of Title 2, The Congress, amending sections 203, 205 to 208, 213, 214, and 216 of this title, and enacting provisions set out as notes under sections 203 and 206 of this title] may be cited as the 'Fair Labor Standards Amendments of 1989'."

SHORT TITLE OF 1985 AMENDMENT

Pub. L. 99–150, §1(a), Nov. 13, 1985, 99 Stat. 787, provided that: "This Act [amending sections 203, 207, and 211 of this title and enacting provisions set out as notes under sections 203, 207, 215, and 216 of this title] may be cited as the 'Fair Labor Standards Amendments of 1985'."

SHORT TITLE OF 1977 AMENDMENT

Pub. L. 95–151, §1(a), Nov. 1, 1977, 91 Stat. 1245, provided that: "This Act [amending sections 203, 206, 208, 213, 214, and 216 of this title and enacting provisions set out as notes under sections 203, 204, and 213 of this title] may be cited as the 'Fair Labor Standards Amendments of 1977'."

SHORT TITLE OF 1974 AMENDMENT

Pub. L. 93–259, §1(a), Apr. 8, 1974, 88 Stat. 55, provided that: "This Act [enacting section 633a of this title, amending sections 202 to 208, 210, 212 to 214, 216, 255, 260, 630, and 634 of this title, and enacting provisions set out as notes under this section and sections 202, 206, 207, 213, and 621 of this title] may be cited as the 'Fair Labor Standards Amendments of 1974'."

SHORT TITLE OF 1966 AMENDMENT

Pub. L. 89–601, §1, Sept. 23, 1966, 80 Stat. 830, provided: "That this Act [amending sections 203, 206, 207, 213, 214, 216, 218, and 255 of this title, and enacting provisions set out as notes under sections 207 and 214 of this title, section 1082 of former Title 5, Executive Departments and Government Officers and Employees, and section 2000e–14 of Title 42, The Public Health and Welfare] may be cited as the 'Fair Labor Standards Amendments of 1966'."

SHORT TITLE OF 1963 AMENDMENT

Pub. L. 88–38, §1, June 10, 1963, 77 Stat. 56, provided: "That this Act [amending section 206 of this title and enacting provisions set out as notes under section 206 of this title] may be cited as the 'Equal Pay Act of 1963'."

SHORT TITLE OF 1961 AMENDMENT

Pub. L. 87–30, §1, May 5, 1961, 75 Stat. 65, provided: "That this Act [amending sections 203 to 208, 212 to 214, 216, and 217 of this title and enacting provisions set out as a note under section 213 of this title] may be cited as the 'Fair Labor Standards Amendments of 1961'."

SHORT TITLE OF 1956 AMENDMENT

Act Aug. 8, 1956, ch. 1035, §1, 70 Stat. 1118, provided: "That this Act [amending sections 206, 213, and 216 of this title] may be cited as the 'American Samoa Labor Standards Amendments of 1956'."

SHORT TITLE OF 1955 AMENDMENT

Act Aug. 12, 1955, ch. 867, §1, 69 Stat. 711, provided: "That this Act [amending sections 204–206, 208, and 210 of this title and enacting provisions set out as notes under sections 204, 206, and 208 of this title] may be cited as the 'Fair Labor Standards Amendments of 1955'."

SHORT TITLE OF 1949 AMENDMENT

Act Oct. 26, 1949, ch. 736, §1, 63 Stat. 910, provided: "That this Act [enacting section 216b of this title, amending sections 202 to 208, 211 to 216, and 217 of this title, and repealing section 216a of this title] may be cited as the 'Fair Labor Standards Amendments of 1949'."

§202. Congressional finding and declaration of policy

(a) The Congress finds that the existence, in industries engaged in commerce or in the production of goods for commerce, of labor conditions detrimental to the maintenance of the minimum standard of living necessary for health, efficiency, and general well-being of workers (1) causes commerce and the channels and instrumentalities of commerce to be used to spread and perpetuate such labor conditions among the workers of the several States; (2) burdens commerce and the free flow of goods in commerce; (3) constitutes an unfair method of competition in commerce; (4) leads to labor disputes burdening and obstructing commerce and the free flow of goods in commerce; and (5) interferes with the orderly and fair marketing of goods in commerce. That Congress further finds that the employment of persons in domestic service in households affects commerce.

(b) It is declared to be the policy of this chapter, through the exercise by Congress of its power to regulate commerce among the several States and with foreign nations, to correct and as rapidly as practicable to eliminate the conditions above referred to in such industries without substantially curtailing employment or earning power.

(June 25, 1938, ch. 676, §2, 52 Stat. 1060; Oct. 26, 1949, ch. 736, §2, 63 Stat. 910; Pub. L. 93–259, §7(a), Apr. 8, 1974, 88 Stat. 62.)

AMENDMENTS

1974—Subsec. (a). Pub. L. 93–259 inserted finding of Congress that employment of persons in domestic service in households affects commerce.

1949—Subsec. (b). Act Oct. 26, 1949, inserted reference to regulation of commerce with foreign nations.

EFFECTIVE DATE OF 1974 AMENDMENT

Section 29(a) of Pub. L. 93–259 provided that: "Except as otherwise specifically provided, the amendments made by this Act [see Short Title of 1974 Amendment note set out under section 201 of this title] shall take effect on May 1, 1974."

EFFECTIVE DATE OF 1949 AMENDMENT

Section 16(a) of act Oct. 26, 1949, provided that: "The amendments made by this Act [enacting section 216b of this title, amending this section and sections 203 to 208, 211 to 216, and 217 of this title, and repealing section 216a of this title] shall take effect upon the expiration of ninety days from the date of its enactment [Oct. 26, 1947]; except that the amendment made by section 4 [amending section 204 of this title] shall take effect on the date of its enactment [Oct. 26, 1949]."

RULES, REGULATIONS, AND ORDERS WITH REGARD TO FAIR LABOR STANDARDS AMENDMENTS OF 1974

Section 29(b) of Pub. L. 93–259 provided that: "Notwithstanding subsection (a) [set out as an Effective Date of 1974 Amendment note above], on and after the date of the enactment of this Act [Apr. 8, 1974] the Secretary of Labor is authorized to prescribe necessary rules, regulations, and orders with regard to the amendments made by this Act [see Short Title of 1974 Amendment note set out under section 201 of this title]."

§203. Definitions

As used in this chapter—

(a) "Person" means an individual, partnership, association, corporation, business trust, legal representative, or any organized group of persons.

(b) "Commerce" means trade, commerce, transportation, transmission, or communication among the several States or between any State and any place outside thereof.

(c) "State" means any State of the United States or the District of Columbia or any Territory or possession of the United States.

(d) "Employer" includes any person acting directly or indirectly in the interest of an employer in relation to an employee and includes a public agency, but does not include any labor organization (other than when acting as an employer) or anyone acting in the capacity of officer or agent of such labor organization.

(e)(1) Except as provided in paragraphs (2), (3), and (4), the term "employee" means any individual employed by an employer.

(2) In the case of an individual employed by a public agency, such term means—

(A) any individual employed by the Government of the United States—

(i) as a civilian in the military departments (as defined in section 102 of title 5),

(ii) in any executive agency (as defined in section 105 of such title),

(iii) in any unit of the judicial branch of the Government which has positions in the competitive service,

(iv) in a nonappropriated fund instrumentality under the jurisdiction of the Armed Forces,

(v) in the Library of Congress, or

(vi) the[1] Government Printing Office;

(B) any individual employed by the United States Postal Service or the Postal Regulatory Commission; and

(C) any individual employed by a State, political subdivision of a State, or an interstate governmental agency, other than such an individual—

(i) who is not subject to the civil service laws of the State, political subdivision, or agency which employs him; and

(ii) who—

(I) holds a public elective office of that State, political subdivision, or agency,

(II) is selected by the holder of such an office to be a member of his personal staff,

(III) is appointed by such an officeholder to serve on a policymaking level,

(IV) is an immediate adviser to such an officeholder with respect to the constitutional or legal powers of his office, or

(V) is an employee in the legislative branch or legislative body of that State, political subdivision, or agency and is not employed by the legislative library of such State, political subdivision, or agency.

(3) For purposes of subsection (u) of this section, such term does not include any individual employed by an employer engaged in agriculture if such individual is the parent, spouse, child, or other member of the employer's immediate family.

(4)(A) The term "employee" does not include any individual who volunteers to perform services for a public agency which is a State, a political subdivision of a State, or an interstate governmental agency, if—

(i) the individual receives no compensation or is paid expenses, reasonable benefits, or a nominal fee to perform the services for which the individual volunteered; and

(ii) such services are not the same type of services which the individual is employed to perform for such public agency.

(B) An employee of a public agency which is a State, political subdivision of a State, or an interstate governmental agency may volunteer to perform services for any other State, political

[1] So in original. Probably should be preceded by "in".

subdivision, or interstate governmental agency, including a State, political subdivision or agency with which the employing State, political subdivision, or agency has a mutual aid agreement.

(5) The term "employee" does not include individuals who volunteer their services solely for humanitarian purposes to private non-profit food banks and who receive from the food banks groceries.

(f) "Agriculture" includes farming in all its branches and among other things includes the cultivation and tillage of the soil, dairying, the production, cultivation, growing, and harvesting of any agricultural or horticultural commodities (including commodities defined as agricultural commodities in section 1141j(g)[2] of title 12), the raising of livestock, bees, fur-bearing animals, or poultry, and any practices (including any forestry or lumbering operations) performed by a farmer or on a farm as an incident to or in conjunction with such farming operations, including preparation for market, delivery to storage or to market or to carriers for transportation to market.

(g) "Employ" includes to suffer or permit to work.

(h) "Industry" means a trade, business, industry, or other activity, or branch or group thereof, in which individuals are gainfully employed.

(i) "Goods" means goods (including ships and marine equipment), wares, products, commodities, merchandise, or articles or subjects of commerce of any character, or any part or ingredient thereof, but does not include goods after their delivery into the actual physical possession of the ultimate consumer thereof other than a producer, manufacturer, or processor thereof.

(j) "Produced" means produced, manufactured, mined, handled, or in any other manner worked on in any State; and for the purposes of this chapter an employee shall be deemed to have been engaged in the production of goods if such employee was employed in producing, manufacturing, mining, handling, transporting, or in any other manner working on such goods, or in any closely related process or occupation directly essential to the production thereof, in any State.

(k) "Sale" or "sell" includes any sale, exchange, contract to sell, consignment for sale, shipment for sale, or other disposition.

(*l*) "Oppressive child labor" means a condition of employment under which (1) any employee under the age of sixteen years is employed by an employer (other than a parent or a person standing in place of a parent employing his own child or a child in his custody under the age of sixteen years in an occupation other than manufacturing or mining or an occupation found by the Secretary of Labor to be particularly hazardous for the employment of children between the ages of sixteen and eighteen years or detrimental to their health or well-being) in any occupation, or (2) any employee between the ages of sixteen and eighteen years is employed by an employer in any occupation which the Secretary of Labor shall find and by order declare to be particularly hazardous for the employment of children between such ages or detrimental to their health or well-being; but oppressive child labor shall not be deemed to exist by virtue of the employment in any occupation of any person with respect to whom the employer shall have on file an unexpired certificate issued and held pursuant to regulations of the Secretary of Labor certifying that such person is above the oppressive child-labor age. The Secretary of Labor shall provide by regulation or by order that the employment of employees between the ages of fourteen and sixteen years in occupations other than manufacturing and mining shall not be deemed to constitute oppressive child labor if and to the extent that the Secretary of Labor determines that such employment is confined to periods which will not interfere with their schooling and to conditions which will not interfere with their health and well-being.

(m) "Wage" paid to any employee includes the reasonable cost, as determined by the Administrator, to the employer of furnishing such employee with board, lodging, or other facilities, if such board, lodging or other facilities are customarily furnished by such employer to his employees: *Provided*, That the cost of board, lodging, or other facilities shall not be included as a part of the wage paid to any employee to the extent it is excluded therefrom under the terms of a bona fide collective-bargaining agreement applicable to the particular employee: *Provided further*, That the Secretary is authorized to determine the fair value of such board, lodging, or other facilities for defined classes of employees and in defined areas, based on average cost to the employer or to groups of employers similarly situated, or average value to groups of employees, or other appropriate measures of fair value. Such evaluations, where applicable and pertinent, shall be used in lieu of actual measure of cost in determining the wage paid to any employee. In determining the wage an employer is required to pay a tipped employee, the amount paid such employee by the employee's employer shall be an amount equal to—

(1) the cash wage paid such employee which for purposes of such determination shall be not less than the cash wage required to be paid such an employee on August 20, 1996; and

(2) an additional amount on account of the tips received by such employee which amount is equal to the difference between the wage specified in paragraph (1) and the wage in effect under section 206(a)(1) of this title.

The additional amount on account of tips may not exceed the value of the tips actually received by an employee. The preceding 2 sentences shall not apply with respect to any tipped employee unless such employee has been informed by the employer of the provisions of this subsection, and all tips received by such employee have been retained by the employee, except that this subsection shall not be construed to prohibit the pooling of tips among employees who customarily and regularly receive tips.

(n) "Resale" shall not include the sale of goods to be used in residential or farm building construction, repair, or maintenance: *Provided*, That the sale is recognized as a bona fide retail sale in the industry.

[2] See References in Text note below.

(*o*) Hours Worked.—In determining for the purposes of sections 206 and 207 of this title the hours for which an employee is employed, there shall be excluded any time spent in changing clothes or washing at the beginning or end of each workday which was excluded from measured working time during the week involved by the express terms of or by custom or practice under a bona fide collective-bargaining agreement applicable to the particular employee.

(p) "American vessel" includes any vessel which is documented or numbered under the laws of the United States.

(q) "Secretary" means the Secretary of Labor.

(r)(1) "Enterprise" means the related activities performed (either through unified operation or common control) by any person or persons for a common business purpose, and includes all such activities whether performed in one or more establishments or by one or more corporate or other organizational units including departments of an establishment operated through leasing arrangements, but shall not include the related activities performed for such enterprise by an independent contractor. Within the meaning of this subsection, a retail or service establishment which is under independent ownership shall not be deemed to be so operated or controlled as to be other than a separate and distinct enterprise by reason of any arrangement, which includes, but is not necessarily limited to, an agreement, (A) that it will sell, or sell only, certain goods specified by a particular manufacturer, distributor, or advertiser, or (B) that it will join with other such establishments in the same industry for the purpose of collective purchasing, or (C) that it will have the exclusive right to sell the goods or use the brand name of a manufacturer, distributor, or advertiser within a specified area, or by reason of the fact that it occupies premises leased to it by a person who also leases premises to other retail or service establishments.

(2) For purposes of paragraph (1), the activities performed by any person or persons—

(A) in connection with the operation of a hospital, an institution primarily engaged in the care of the sick, the aged, the mentally ill or defective who reside on the premises of such institution, a school for mentally or physically handicapped or gifted children, a preschool, elementary or secondary school, or an institution of higher education (regardless of whether or not such hospital, institution, or school is operated for profit or not for profit), or

(B) in connection with the operation of a street, suburban or interurban electric railway, or local trolley or motorbus carrier, if the rates and services of such railway or carrier are subject to regulation by a State or local agency (regardless of whether or not such railway or carrier is public or private or operated for profit or not for profit), or

(C) in connection with the activities of a public agency,

shall be deemed to be activities performed for a business purpose.

(s)(1) "Enterprise engaged in commerce or in the production of goods for commerce" means an enterprise that—

(A)(i) has employees engaged in commerce or in the production of goods for commerce, or that has employees handling, selling, or otherwise working on goods or materials that have been moved in or produced for commerce by any person; and

(ii) is an enterprise whose annual gross volume of sales made or business done is not less than $500,000 (exclusive of excise taxes at the retail level that are separately stated);

(B) is engaged in the operation of a hospital, an institution primarily engaged in the care of the sick, the aged, or the mentally ill or defective who reside on the premises of such institution, a school for mentally or physically handicapped or gifted children, a preschool, elementary or secondary school, or an institution of higher education (regardless of whether or not such hospital, institution, or school is public or private or operated for profit or not for profit); or

(C) is an activity of a public agency.

(2) Any establishment that has as its only regular employees the owner thereof or the parent, spouse, child, or other member of the immediate family of such owner shall not be considered to be an enterprise engaged in commerce or in the production of goods for commerce or a part of such an enterprise. The sales of such an establishment shall not be included for the purpose of determining the annual gross volume of sales of any enterprise for the purpose of this subsection.

(t) "Tipped employee" means any employee engaged in an occupation in which he customarily and regularly receives more than $30 a month in tips.

(u) "Man-day" means any day during which an employee performs any agricultural labor for not less than one hour.

(v) "Elementary school" means a day or residential school which provides elementary education, as determined under State law.

(w) "Secondary school" means a day or residential school which provides secondary education, as determined under State law.

(x) "Public agency" means the Government of the United States; the government of a State or political subdivision thereof; any agency of the United States (including the United States Postal Service and Postal Regulatory Commission), a State, or a political subdivision of a State; or any interstate governmental agency.

(y) "Employee in fire protection activities" means an employee, including a firefighter, paramedic, emergency medical technician, rescue worker, ambulance personnel, or hazardous materials worker, who—

(1) is trained in fire suppression, has the legal authority and responsibility to engage in fire suppression, and is employed by a fire department of a municipality, county, fire district, or State; and

(2) is engaged in the prevention, control, and extinguishment of fires or response to emergency situations where life, property, or the environment is at risk.

(June 25, 1938, ch. 676, §3, 52 Stat. 1060; 1946 Reorg. Plan No. 2, §1(b), eff. July 16, 1946, 11 F.R. 7873, 60 Stat. 1095; Oct. 26, 1949, ch. 736, §3, 63

Stat. 911; Pub. L. 87–30, §2, May 5, 1961, 75 Stat. 65; Pub. L. 89–601, title I, §§101–103, title II, §215(a), Sept. 23, 1966, 80 Stat. 830–832, 837; Pub. L. 92–318, title IX, §906(b)(2), (3), June 23, 1972, 86 Stat. 375; Pub. L. 93–259, §§6(a), 13(e), Apr. 8, 1974, 88 Stat. 58, 64; Pub. L. 95–151, §§3(a), (b), 9(a)–(c), Nov. 1, 1977, 91 Stat. 1249, 1251; Pub. L. 99–150, §§4(a), 5, Nov. 13, 1985, 99 Stat. 790; Pub. L. 101–157, §§3(a), (d), 5, Nov. 17, 1989, 103 Stat. 938, 939, 941; Pub. L. 104–1, title II, §203(d), Jan. 23, 1995, 109 Stat. 10; Pub. L. 104–188, [title II], §2105(b), Aug. 20, 1996, 110 Stat. 1929; Pub. L. 105–221, §2, Aug. 7, 1998, 112 Stat. 1248; Pub. L. 106–151, §1, Dec. 9, 1999, 113 Stat. 1731; Pub. L. 109–435, title VI, §604(f), Dec. 20, 2006, 120 Stat. 3242.)

References in Text

Section 1141j(g) of title 12, referred to in subsec. (f), was redesignated section 1141j(f) by Pub. L. 110–246, title I, §1610, June 18, 2008, 122 Stat. 1746.

Amendments

2006—Subsecs. (e)(2)(B), (x). Pub. L. 109–435 substituted "Postal Regulatory Commission" for "Postal Rate Commission".

1999—Subsec. (y). Pub. L. 106–151 added subsec. (y).

1998—Subsec. (e)(5). Pub. L. 105–221 added par. (5).

1996—Subsec. (m). Pub. L. 104–188 inserted "In determining the wage an employer is required to pay a tipped employee, the amount paid such employee by the employee's employer shall be an amount equal to—

"(1) the cash wage paid such employee which for purposes of such determination shall be not less than the cash wage required to be paid such an employee on August 20, 1996; and

"(2) an additional amount on account of the tips received by such employee which amount is equal to the difference between the wage specified in paragraph (1) and the wage in effect under section 206(a)(1) of this title.

The additional amount on account of tips may not exceed the value of the tips actually received by an employee.", and struck out former penultimate sentence which read as follows: "In determining the wage of a tipped employee, the amount paid such employee by his employer shall be deemed to be increased on account of tips by an amount determined by the employer, but not by an amount in excess of (1) 45 percent of the applicable minimum wage rate during the year beginning April 1, 1990, and (2) 50 percent of the applicable minimum wage rate after March 31, 1991, except that the amount of the increase on account of tips determined by the employer may not exceed the value of tips actually received by the employee."

Pub. L. 104–188 in last sentence substituted "preceding 2 sentences" for "previous sentence" and struck out "(1)" after "employee unless" and "(2)" after "subsection, and".

1995—Subsec. (e)(2)(A). Pub. L. 104–1 struck out "legislative or" before "judicial branch" in cl. (iii) and added cl. (vi).

1989—Subsec. (m). Pub. L. 101–157, §5, substituted "in excess of (1) 45 percent of the applicable minimum wage rate during the year beginning April 1, 1990, and (2) 50 percent of the applicable minimum wage rate after March 31, 1991," for "in excess of 40 per centum of the applicable minimum wage rate,".

Subsec. (r). Pub. L. 101–157, §3(d), designated first sentence as par. (1), made a separate sentence out of the existing proviso and redesignated cls. (1), (2), and (3) as (A), (B), and (C), respectively, designated second sentence as par. (2), in par. (2) as so designated, redesignated existing pars. (1), (2), and (3) as subpars. (A), (B), and (C), respectively, and, in subpar. (A) as so redesignated, substituted "school is operated" for "school is public or private or operated".

Subsec. (s). Pub. L. 101–157, §3(a), amended subsec. (s) generally, completely revising definition of "enterprise engaged in commerce or in the production of goods for commerce".

1985—Subsec. (e)(1). Pub. L. 99–150, §4(a)(1), substituted "paragraphs (2), (3), and (4)" for "paragraphs (2) and (3)".

Subsec. (e)(2)(C)(ii). Pub. L. 99–150, §5, struck out "or" at end of subcl. (III), struck out "who" in subcl. (IV) before "is an", substituted ", or" for period at end of subcl. (IV), and added subcl. (V).

Subsec. (e)(4). Pub. L. 99–150, §4(a)(2), added par. (4).

1977—Subsec. (m). Pub. L. 95–151, §3(b), substituted "45 per centum" for "50 per centum", effective Jan. 1, 1979, and "40 per centum" for "45 per centum", effective Jan. 1, 1980.

Subsec. (s). Pub. L. 95–151, §9(a)–(c), in par. (1) inserted exception for enterprises comprised exclusively of retail or service establishments and described in par. (2), added par. (2), redesignated former pars. (2) to (5) as (3) to (6), respectively, and in text following par. (6), as so redesignated, inserted provisions relating to coverage of retail or service establishments subject to section 206(a)(1) of this title on June 30, 1978, and provisions relating to violations of such coverage requirements.

Subsec. (t). Pub. L. 95–151, §3(a), substituted "$30" for "$20".

1974—Subsec. (d). Pub. L. 93–259, §6(a)(1), redefined "employer" to include a public agency and struck out text which excluded from such term the United States or any State or political subdivision of a State (except with respect to employees of a State, or a political subdivision thereof, employed (1) in a hospital, institution, or school referred to in last sentence of subsec. (r) of this section, or (2) in the operation of a railway or carrier referred to in such sentence).

Subsec. (e). Pub. L. 93–259, §6(a)(2), in revising definition of "employee", incorporated existing introductory text in provisions designated as par. (1), inserting exception provision; added par. (2); incorporated existing cl. (1) in provisions designated as par. (3); and struck out former cl. (2) excepting from "employee", "any individual who is employed by an employer engaged in agriculture if such individual (A) is employed as a hand harvest laborer and is paid on a piece rate basis in an operation which has been, and is customarily and generally recognized as having been, paid on a piece rate basis in the region of employment, (B) commutes daily from his permanent residence to the farm on which he is so employed, and (C) has been engaged in agriculture less than thirteen weeks during the preceding calendar year".

Subsec. (h). Pub. L. 93–259, §6(a)(3), substituted "other activity, or branch or group thereof" for "branch thereof, or group of industries".

Subsec. (m). Pub. L. 93–259, §13(e), substituted in provision respecting wage of tipped employee "the amount of the increase on account of tips determined by the employer may not exceed the value of tips actually received by the employee" for "in the case of an employee who (either himself or acting through his representative) shows to the satisfaction of the Secretary that the actual amount of tips received by him was less than the amount determined by the employer as the amount by which the wage paid him was deemed to be increased under this sentence, the amount paid such employee by his employer shall be deemed to have been increased by such lesser amount" and inserted "The previous sentence shall not apply with respect to any tipped employee unless (1) such employee has been informed by the employer of the provisions of this subsection, and (2) all tips received by such employee have been retained by the employee, except that this subsection shall not be construed to prohibit the pooling of tips among employees who customarily and regularly receive tips."

Subsec. (r)(3). Pub. L. 93–259, §6(a)(4), added par. (3).

Subsec. (s). Pub. L. 93–259, §6(a)(5), in first sentence substituted preceding par. (1) "or employees handling, selling, or otherwise working on goods or materials" for "including employees handling, selling, or otherwise working on goods" and added par. (5), and inserted third sentence deeming employees of an enterprise which is a public agency to be employees engaged in commerce, or in production of goods for commerce, or employees handling, selling, or otherwise working on goods or materials that have been moved in or produced for commerce.

Subsec. (x). Pub. L. 93–259, § 6(a)(6), added subsec. (x).

1972—Subsecs. (r)(1), (s)(4). Pub. L. 92–318, § 906(b)(2), (3), inserted reference to a preschool.

1966—Subsec. (d). Pub. L. 89–601, § 102(b), expanded definition of employer to include a State or a political subdivision thereof with respect to employees in a hospital, institution, or school referred to in last sentence of subsec. (r) of this section, or in the operation of a railway or carrier referred to in such sentence.

Subsec. (e). Pub. L. 89–601, § 103(a), excluded from definition of "employee," when that term is used in definition of "man-day," any agricultural employee who is the parent, spouse, child, or other member of his employer's immediate family and any agricultural hand harvest laborer, paid on a piece rate basis, who commutes daily from his permanent residence to the farm on which he is so employed, and who has been employed in agriculture less than 13 weeks during the preceding calendar year.

Subsec. (m). Pub. L. 89–601, § 101(a), inserted provisions for determining the wage of a tipped employee.

Subsec. (n). Pub. L. 89–601, § 215(a), struck out provision which directed that definition of "resale" was not applicable when "resale" was used in subsection (s)(1) of this section.

Subsec. (r). Pub. L. 89–601, § 102(a), extended activities performed for a business purpose to include activities in the operation of hospitals, institutions for the sick, aged, or mentally ill or defective, schools for the handicapped, elementary and secondary schools, institutions of higher learning, or street, suburban, or interurban electric railway or local trolley or motorbus carriers if subject to regulation by a State or local agency regardless of whether public or private or whether operated for profit or not for profit.

Subsec. (s). Pub. L. 89–601, § 102(c), removed gross annual business level tests of $1,000,000 for retail and service enterprises, street, suburban, or interurban electric railways or local trolley or motorbus carriers, and brought within the coverage of the gross annual business test all enterprises having employees engaged in commerce in the production of goods for commerce, including employees handling, selling, or otherwise working on goods that have been moved in or produced for commerce, lowered the minimum gross annual volume test for covered enterprises from $1,000,000 to $500,000 for the period from Feb. 1, 1967, through Jan. 31, 1969, and to $250,000 for the period after Jan. 31, 1969, retained the $250,000 annual gross volume test for coverage of gasoline service establishments, and expanded coverage to include laundering or cleaning services, construction or reconstruction activities, or operation of hospitals, certain institutions for the care of the sick, aged, or mentally ill, certain special schools, and institutions of higher learning regardless of annual gross volume.

Subsec. (t). Pub. L. 89–601, § 101(b), added subsec. (t).

Subsec. (u). Pub. L. 89–601, § 103(b), added subsec. (u).

Subsecs. (v), (w). Pub. L. 89–601, § 102(d), added subsecs. (v) and (w).

1961—Subsec. (m). Pub. L. 87–30, § 2(a), provided for exclusion from wages under a collective-bargaining agreement the cost of board, lodging, or other facilities and authorized the Secretary to determine the fair value of board, lodging, or other facilities for defined classes of employees in defined areas to be used in lieu of actual cost.

Subsec. (n). Pub. L. 87–30, § 2(b), inserted ", except as used in subsection (s)(1) of this section,".

Subsecs. (p) to (s). Pub. L. 87–30, § 2(c), added subsecs. (p) to (s).

1949—Subsec. (b). Act Oct. 26, 1949, § 3(a), substituted "between" for "from" after "States or", and "and" for "to" before "any place".

Subsec. (j). Act Oct. 26, 1949, § 3(b), inserted "closely related" before "process" and substituted "directly essential" for "necessary" after "occupation".

Subsec. (*l*)(1). Act Oct. 26, 1949, § 3(c), included parental employment of a child under 16 years of age in an occupation found by the Secretary of Labor to be hazardous for children between the ages of 16 and 18 years, in definition of oppressive child labor.

Subsecs. (n), (*o*). Act Oct. 26, 1949, § 3(d), added subsecs. (n) and (*o*).

CONSTRUCTION OF 1999 AMENDMENT

Pub. L. 106–151, § 2, Dec. 9, 1999, 113 Stat. 1731, provided that: "The amendment made by section 1 [amending this section] shall not be construed to reduce or substitute for compensation standards: (1) contained in any existing or future agreement or memorandum of understanding reached through collective bargaining by a bona fide representative of employees in accordance with the laws of a State or political subdivision of a State; and (2) which result in compensation greater than the compensation available to employees under the overtime exemption under section 7(k) of the Fair Labor Standards Act of 1938 [29 U.S.C. 207(k)]."

EFFECTIVE DATE OF 1989 AMENDMENT

Section 3(e) of Pub. L. 101–157 provided that: "The amendments made by this section [amending this section and section 213 of this title] shall become effective on April 1, 1990."

Section 5 of Pub. L. 101–157 provided that the amendment made by that section is effective Apr. 1, 1990.

EFFECTIVE DATE OF 1985 AMENDMENT; PROMULGATION OF REGULATIONS

Section 6 of Pub. L. 99–150 provided that: "The amendments made by this Act [amending this section and sections 207 and 211 of this title and enacting provisions set out as notes under this section and sections 201, 207, 215, and 216 of this title] shall take effect April 15, 1986. The Secretary of Labor shall before such date promulgate such regulations as may be required to implement such amendments."

EFFECTIVE DATE OF 1977 AMENDMENT

Section 3(a) of Pub. L. 95–151 provided that the amendment made by that section is effective Jan. 1, 1978.

Section 3(b)(1) of Pub. L. 95–151 provided that the amendment made by that section, reducing the maximum percentage of the minimum wage used in determining tips as wages from 50 to 45 per centum, is effective Jan. 1, 1979.

Section 3(b)(2) of Pub. L. 95–151 provided that the amendment made by that section, reducing the maximum percentage of the minimum wage used in determining tips as wages from 45 to 40 per centum, is effective Jan. 1, 1980.

Section 15(a), (b) of Pub. L. 95–151 provided that:

"(a) Except as provided in sections 3, 14, and subsection (b) of this section, the amendments made by this Act [amending sections 206, 208, 213, and 216 of this title and enacting provisions set out as a note under section 204 of this title] shall take effect January 1, 1978.

"(b) The amendments made by sections 8, 9, 11, 12, and 13 [amending this section and sections 213 and 214 of this title] shall take effect on the date of the enactment of this Act [Nov. 1, 1977]."

EFFECTIVE DATE OF 1974 AMENDMENT

Amendment by Pub. L. 93–259 effective May 1, 1974, see section 29(a) of Pub. L. 93–259, set out as a note under section 202 of this title.

EFFECTIVE DATE OF 1966 AMENDMENT

Section 602 of Pub. L. 89–601 provided in part that: "Except as otherwise provided in this Act, the amendments made by this Act [amending this section and sections 206, 207, 213, 214, 216, 218, and 255 of this title] shall take effect on February 1, 1967."

EFFECTIVE DATE OF 1961 AMENDMENT

Section 14 of Pub. L. 87–30 provided that: "The amendments made by this Act [amending this section and sections 204 to 208, 212 to 214, 216, and 217 of this title] shall take effect upon the expiration of one hundred and twenty days after the date of its enactment [May 5, 1961], except as otherwise provided in such amendments and except that the authority to promulgate necessary rules, regulations, or orders with regard to amendments made by this Act, under the Fair Labor Standards Act of 1938 and amendments thereto [this chapter], including amendments made by this Act, may be exercised by the Secretary on and after the date of enactment of this Act [May 5, 1961]."

EFFECTIVE DATE OF 1949 AMENDMENT

Amendment by act Oct. 26, 1949, effective ninety days after Oct. 26, 1949, see section 16(a) of act Oct. 26, 1949, set out as a note under section 202 of this title.

TRANSFER OF FUNCTIONS

In subsec. (*l*), "Secretary of Labor" substituted for "Chief of the Children's Bureau in the Department of Labor" and for "Chief of the Children's Bureau" pursuant to Reorg. Plan No. 2 of 1946, §1(b), eff. July 16, 1946, 11 F.R. 7873, 60 Stat. 1095, set out in the Appendix to Title 5, Government Organization and Employees, which transferred functions of Children's Bureau and its Chief under sections 201 to 216 and 217 to 219 of this title to Secretary of Labor to be performed under his direction and control by such officers and employees of Department of Labor as he designates.

PRESERVATION OF COVERAGE

Section 3(b) of Pub. L. 101–157 provided that:

"(1) IN GENERAL.—Any enterprise that on March 31, 1990, was subject to section 6(a)(1) of the Fair Labor Standards Act of 1938 (29 U.S.C. 206(a)(1)) and that because of the amendment made by subsection (a) [amending this section] is not subject to such section shall—

"(A) pay its employees not less than the minimum wage in effect under such section on March 31, 1990;

"(B) pay its employees in accordance with section 7 of such Act (29 U.S.C. 207); and

"(C) remain subject to section 12 of such Act (29 U.S.C. 212).

"(2) VIOLATIONS.—A violation of paragraph (1) shall be considered a violation of section 6, 7, or 12 of the Fair Labor Standards Act of 1938 [29 U.S.C. 206, 207, 212], as the case may be."

VOLUNTEERS; PROMULGATION OF REGULATIONS

Section 4(b) of Pub. L. 99–150 provided that: "Not later than March 15, 1986, the Secretary of Labor shall issue regulations to carry out paragraph (4) of section 3(e) (as amended by subsection (a) of this section) [29 U.S.C. 203(e)(4)]."

PRACTICE OF PUBLIC AGENCY IN TREATING CERTAIN INDIVIDUALS AS VOLUNTEERS PRIOR TO APRIL 15, 1986; LIABILITY

Section 4(c) of Pub. L. 99–150 provided that: "If, before April 15, 1986, the practice of a public agency was to treat certain individuals as volunteers, such individuals shall until April 15, 1986, be considered, for purposes of the Fair Labor Standards Act of 1938 [this chapter], as volunteers and not as employees. No public agency which is a State, a political subdivision of a State, or an interstate governmental agency shall be liable for a violation of section 6 [29 U.S.C. 206] occurring before April 15, 1986, with respect to services deemed by that agency to have been performed for it by an individual on a voluntary basis."

STATUS OF BAGGERS AT COMMISSARY OF MILITARY DEPARTMENT

Pub. L. 95–485, title VIII, §819, Oct. 20, 1978, 92 Stat. 1626, provided that: "Notwithstanding any other provision of law, an individual who performs bagger or carryout service for patrons of a commissary of a military department may not be considered to be an employee for purposes of the Fair Labor Standards Act of 1938 [this chapter] by virtue of such service if the sole compensation of such individual for such service is derived from tips."

ADMINISTRATIVE ACTION BY SECRETARY OF LABOR WITH REGARD TO IMPLEMENTATION OF FAIR LABOR STANDARDS AMENDMENTS OF 1977

Section 15(c) of Pub. L. 95–151 provided that: "On and after the date of the enactment of this Act [Nov. 1, 1977], the Secretary of Labor shall take such administrative action as may be necessary for the implementation of the amendments made by this Act [See Short Title of 1977 Amendment note set out under section 201 of this title]."

RULES, REGULATIONS, AND ORDERS PROMULGATED WITH REGARD TO 1966 AMENDMENTS

Section 602 of Pub. L. 89–601 provided in part that: "On and after the date of the enactment of this Act [Sept. 23, 1966] the Secretary is authorized to promulgate necessary rules, regulations, or orders with regard to the amendments made by this Act [see Short Title of 1966 Amendment note set out under section 201 of this title]."

§ 204. Administration

(a) Creation of Wage and Hour Division in Department of Labor; Administrator

There is created in the Department of Labor a Wage and Hour Division which shall be under the direction of an Administrator, to be known as the Administrator of the Wage and Hour Division (in this chapter referred to as the "Administrator"). The Administrator shall be appointed by the President, by and with the advice and consent of the Senate.

(b) Appointment, selection, classification, and promotion of employees by Administrator

The Administrator may, subject to the civil-service laws, appoint such employees as he deems necessary to carry out his functions and duties under this chapter and shall fix their compensation in accordance with chapter 51 and subchapter III of chapter 53 of title 5. The Administrator may establish and utilize such regional, local, or other agencies, and utilize such voluntary and uncompensated services, as may from time to time be needed. Attorneys appointed under this section may appear for and represent the Administrator in any litigation, but all such litigation shall be subject to the direction and control of the Attorney General. In the appointment, selection, classification, and promotion of officers and employees of the Administrator, no political test or qualification shall be permitted or given consideration, but all such appointments and promotions shall be given and made on the basis of merit and efficiency.

(c) Principal office of Administrator; jurisdiction

The principal office of the Administrator shall be in the District of Columbia, but he or his duly authorized representative may exercise any or all of his powers in any place.

(d) Biennial report to Congress; studies of exemptions to hour and wage provisions and means to prevent curtailment of employment opportunities

(1) The Secretary shall submit biennially in January a report to the Congress covering his activities for the preceding two years and including such information, data, and recommendations for further legislation in connection with the matters covered by this chapter as he may find advisable. Such report shall contain an evaluation and appraisal by the Secretary of the minimum wages and overtime coverage established by this chapter, together with his recommendations to the Congress. In making such evaluation and appraisal, the Secretary shall take into consideration any changes which may have occurred in the cost of living and in productivity and the level of wages in manufacturing, the ability of employers to absorb wage increases, and such other factors as he may deem pertinent. Such report shall also include a summary of the special certificates issued under section 214(b) of this title.

(2) The Secretary shall conduct studies on the justification or lack thereof for each of the special exemptions set forth in section 213 of this title, and the extent to which such exemptions apply to employees of establishments described in subsection (g) of such section and the economic effects of the application of such exemptions to such employees. The Secretary shall submit a report of his findings and recommendations to the Congress with respect to the studies conducted under this paragraph not later than January 1, 1976.

(3) The Secretary shall conduct a continuing study on means to prevent curtailment of employment opportunities for manpower groups which have had historically high incidences of unemployment (such as disadvantaged minorities, youth, elderly, and such other groups as the Secretary may designate). The first report of the results of such study shall be transmitted to the Congress not later than one year after the effective date of the Fair Labor Standards Amendments of 1974. Subsequent reports on such study shall be transmitted to the Congress at two-year intervals after such effective date. Each such report shall include suggestions respecting the Secretary's authority under section 214 of this title.

(e) Study of effects of foreign production on unemployment; report to President and Congress

Whenever the Secretary has reason to believe that in any industry under this chapter the competition of foreign producers in United States markets or in markets abroad, or both, has resulted, or is likely to result, in increased unemployment in the United States, he shall undertake an investigation to gain full information with respect to the matter. If he determines such increased unemployment has in fact resulted, or is in fact likely to result, from such competition, he shall make a full and complete report of his findings and determinations to the President and to the Congress: *Provided*, That he may also include in such report information on the increased employment resulting from additional exports in any industry under this chapter as he may determine to be pertinent to such report.

(f) Employees of Library of Congress; administration of provisions by Office of Personnel Management

The Secretary is authorized to enter into an agreement with the Librarian of Congress with respect to individuals employed in the Library of Congress to provide for the carrying out of the Secretary's functions under this chapter with respect to such individuals. Notwithstanding any other provision of this chapter, or any other law, the Director of the Office of Personnel Management is authorized to administer the provisions of this chapter with respect to any individual employed by the United States (other than an individual employed in the Library of Congress, United States Postal Service, Postal Regulatory Commission, or the Tennessee Valley Authority). Nothing in this subsection shall be construed to affect the right of an employee to bring an action for unpaid minimum wages, or unpaid overtime compensation, and liquidated damages under section 216(b) of this title.

(June 25, 1938, ch. 676, §4, 52 Stat. 1061; Oct. 26, 1949, ch. 736, §4, 63 Stat. 911; Oct. 28, 1949, ch. 782, title XI, §1106(a), 63 Stat. 972; Aug. 12, 1955, ch. 867, §2, 69 Stat. 711; Pub. L. 87–30, §3, May 5, 1961, 75 Stat. 66; Pub. L. 93–259, §§6(b), 24(c), 27, Apr. 8, 1974, 88 Stat. 60, 72, 73; 1978 Reorg. Plan No. 2, §102, eff. Jan. 1, 1979, 43 F.R. 36037, 92 Stat. 3783; Pub. L. 104–66, title I, §1102(a), Dec. 21, 1995, 109 Stat. 722; Pub. L. 109–435, title VI, §604(f), Dec. 20, 2006, 120 Stat. 3242.)

REFERENCES IN TEXT

The civil service laws, referred to in subsec. (b), are set forth in Title 5, Government Organization and Employees. See, particularly, section 3301 et seq. of Title 5.

The effective date of the Fair Labor Standards Amendments of 1974, referred to in subsec. (d)(3), is the effective date of Pub. L. 93–259, which is May 1, 1974, except as otherwise specifically provided, see section 29(a) of Pub. L. 93–259, set out as an Effective Date of 1974 Amendment note under section 202 of this title.

CODIFICATION

In subsec. (a), provisions that prescribed the compensation of the Administrator were omitted to conform to the provisions of the Executive Schedule. See section 5316 of Title 5, Government Organization and Employees.

In subsec. (b), "chapter 51 and subchapter III of chapter 53 of title 5" substituted for "the Classification Act of 1949, as amended" on authority of Pub. L. 89–554, §7(b), Sept. 6, 1966, 80 Stat. 631, the first section of which enacted Title 5.

AMENDMENTS

2006—Subsec. (f). Pub. L. 109–435 substituted "Postal Regulatory Commission" for "Postal Rate Commission".

1995—Subsec. (d)(1). Pub. L. 104–66 in first sentence substituted "biennially" and "preceding two years" for "annually" and "preceding year", respectively.

1974—Subsec. (d)(1). Pub. L. 93–259, §§24(c), 27(1), (2), inserted provision at end of subsec. (d) requiring the report to Congress to include a summary of the special certificates issued under section 214(b) of this title, designated subsec. (d) provisions as subsec. (d)(1), and required the report to contain an evaluation and appraisal of overtime coverage established by this chapter, respectively.

Subsec. (d)(2), (3). Pub. L. 93–259, §27(3), added pars. (2) and (3).

Subsec. (f). Pub. L. 93–259, §6(b), added subsec. (f).

1961—Subsec. (e). Pub. L. 87–30 added subsec. (e).

1955—Subsec. (d). Act Aug. 12, 1955, required an evaluation and appraisal by the Secretary of the minimum wages, together with his recommendations to Congress, to be included in the annual report.

1949—Subsec. (b). Act Oct. 28, 1949, substituted "Classification Act of 1949" for "Classification Act of 1923".

Subsec. (a). Act Oct. 26, 1949, increased compensation of Administrator to $15,000.

EFFECTIVE DATE OF 1974 AMENDMENT

Amendment by Pub. L. 93–259 effective May 1, 1974, see section 29(a) of Pub. L. 93–259, set out as a note under section 202 of this title.

EFFECTIVE DATE OF 1961 AMENDMENT

Amendment by Pub. L. 87–30 effective upon expiration of one hundred and twenty days after May 5, 1961, except as otherwise provided, see section 14 of Pub. L. 87–30, set out as a note under section 203 of this title.

EFFECTIVE DATE OF 1949 AMENDMENT

Amendment by act Oct. 26, 1949, effective Oct. 26, 1949, see section 16(a) of act Oct. 26, 1949, set out as a note under section 202 of this title.

REPEALS

Acts Oct. 26, 1949, ch. 736, §4, 63 Stat. 911, and Oct. 28, 1949, ch. 782, cited as a credit to this section, were repealed (subject to a savings clause) by Pub. L. 89–554, Sept. 6, 1966, §8, 80 Stat. 632, 655.

TERMINATION OF REPORTING REQUIREMENTS

For termination, effective May 15, 2000, of provisions of law requiring submittal to Congress of any annual, semiannual, or other regular periodic report listed in House Document No. 103–7 (in which reports required under paragraphs (1) and (3) of subsec. (d) of this section are listed on page 124), see section 3003 of Pub. L. 104–66, as amended, set out as a note under section 1113 of Title 31, Money and Finance.

TRANSFER OF FUNCTIONS

Functions relating to enforcement and administration of equal pay provisions vested by subsecs. (d)(1) and (f) of this section in Secretary of Labor and Civil Service Commission transferred to Equal Employment Opportunity Commission by Reorg. Plan No. 1 of 1978, §1, 43 F.R. 19807, 92 Stat. 3781, set out in the Appendix to Title 5, Government Organization and Employees, effective Jan. 1, 1979, as provided by section 1–101 of Ex. Ord. No. 12106, Dec. 28, 1978, 44 F.R. 1053.

"Director of the Office of Personnel Management" substituted for "Civil Service Commission" in subsec. (f), pursuant to Reorg. Plan No. 2 of 1978, §102, 43 F.R. 36037, 92 Stat. 3783, set out under section 1101 of Title 5, Government Organization and Employees, which transferred all functions vested by statute in United States Civil Service Commission to Director of the Office of Personnel Management (except as otherwise specified), effective Jan. 1, 1979, as provided by section 1 102 of Ex. Ord. No. 12107, Dec. 28, 1978, 44 F.R. 1055, set out under section 1101 of Title 5.

Functions of all other officers of Department of Labor and functions of all agencies and employees of that Department, with exception of functions vested by Administrative Procedure Act (now covered by sections 551 et seq. and 701 et seq. of Title 5, Government Organization and Employees) in hearing examiners employed by Department, transferred to Secretary of Labor, with power vested in him to authorize their performance or performance of any of his functions by any of those officers, agencies, and employees, by Reorg. Plan No. 6 of 1950, §§1, 2, 15 F.R. 3174, 64 Stat. 1263, set out in the Appendix to Title 5.

MINIMUM WAGE STUDY COMMISSION; ESTABLISHMENT, PURPOSES, COMPOSITION, ETC.

Pub. L. 95–151, §2(e), Nov. 1, 1977, 91 Stat. 1246, provided for the establishment, purposes, composition, etc., of the Minimum Wage Study Commission, the submission of reports, with the latest report being submitted to the President and Congress thirty six months after the date of the appointment of the members of the Commission and such appointments being made within 180 days after Nov. 1, 1977, and the Commission to cease to exist thirty days after submission of the report.

DEFINITION OF "SECRETARY"

Section 6 of act Aug. 12, 1955, provided that: "The term 'Secretary' as used in this Act and in amendments made by this Act [amending this section and sections 205, 206, 208, and 210 of this title] means the Secretary of Labor."

§205. Repealed. Pub. L. 110–28, title VIII, §8103(c)(1)(A), May 25, 2007, 121 Stat. 189

Section, acts June 25, 1938, ch. 676, §5, 52 Stat. 1062; June 26, 1940, ch. 432, §3(c), 54 Stat. 615; Oct. 26, 1949, ch. 736, §5, 63 Stat. 911; Aug. 12, 1955, ch. 867, §5(a), 69 Stat. 711; Pub. L. 87–30, §4, May 5, 1961, 75 Stat. 67; Pub. L. 93–259, §5(a), Apr. 8, 1974, 88 Stat. 56; Pub. L. 101–157, §4(a), Nov. 17, 1989, 103 Stat. 939, related to establishment of special industry committees for American Samoa to recommend the minimum rate or rates of wages. See section 8103 of Pub. L. 110–28, set out as a note under section 206 of this title.

EFFECTIVE DATE OF REPEAL

Repeal effective 60 days after May 25, 2007, see section 8103(c)(2) of Pub. L. 110–28, set out as an Effective Date of 2007 Amendment note under section 206 of this title.

§206. Minimum wage

(a) Employees engaged in commerce; home workers in Puerto Rico and Virgin Islands; employees in American Samoa; seamen on American vessels; agricultural employees

Every employer shall pay to each of his employees who in any workweek is engaged in commerce or in the production of goods for commerce, or is employed in an enterprise engaged in commerce or in the production of goods for commerce, wages at the following rates:

(1) except as otherwise provided in this section, not less than—

(A) $5.85 an hour, beginning on the 60th day after May 25, 2007;

(B) $6.55 an hour, beginning 12 months after that 60th day; and

(C) $7.25 an hour, beginning 24 months after that 60th day;

(2) if such employee is a home worker in Puerto Rico or the Virgin Islands, not less than the minimum piece rate prescribed by regulation or order; or, if no such minimum piece rate is in effect, any piece rate adopted by such employer which shall yield, to the proportion or class of employees prescribed by regulation or order, not less than the applicable minimum hourly wage rate. Such minimum piece rates or employer piece rates shall be commensurate with, and shall be paid in lieu of, the minimum hourly wage rate appli-

cable under the provisions of this section. The Administrator, or his authorized representative, shall have power to make such regulations or orders as are necessary or appropriate to carry out any of the provisions of this paragraph, including the power without limiting the generality of the foregoing, to define any operation or occupation which is performed by such home work employees in Puerto Rico or the Virgin Islands; to establish minimum piece rates for any operation or occupation so defined; to prescribe the method and procedure for ascertaining and promulgating minimum piece rates; to prescribe standards for employer piece rates, including the proportion or class of employees who shall receive not less than the minimum hourly wage rate; to define the term "home worker"; and to prescribe the conditions under which employers, agents, contractors, and subcontractors shall cause goods to be produced by home workers;

(3) if such employee is employed as a seaman on an American vessel, not less than the rate which will provide to the employee, for the period covered by the wage payment, wages equal to compensation at the hourly rate prescribed by paragraph (1) of this subsection for all hours during such period when he was actually on duty (including periods aboard ship when the employee was on watch or was, at the direction of a superior officer, performing work or standing by, but not including off-duty periods which are provided pursuant to the employment agreement); or

(4) if such employee is employed in agriculture, not less than the minimum wage rate in effect under paragraph (1) after December 31, 1977.

(b) Additional applicability to employees pursuant to subsequent amendatory provisions

Every employer shall pay to each of his employees (other than an employee to whom subsection (a)(5) of this section applies) who in any workweek is engaged in commerce or in the production of goods for commerce, or is employed in an enterprise engaged in commerce or in the production of goods for commerce, and who in such workweek is brought within the purview of this section by the amendments made to this chapter by the Fair Labor Standards Amendments of 1966, title IX of the Education Amendments of 1972 [20 U.S.C. 1681 et seq.], or the Fair Labor Standards Amendments of 1974, wages at the following rate: Effective after December 31, 1977, not less than the minimum wage rate in effect under subsection (a)(1) of this section.

(c) Repealed. Pub. L. 104–188, [title II], §2104(c), Aug. 20, 1996, 110 Stat. 1929

(d) Prohibition of sex discrimination

(1) No employer having employees subject to any provisions of this section shall discriminate, within any establishment in which such employees are employed, between employees on the basis of sex by paying wages to employees in such establishment at a rate less than the rate at which he pays wages to employees of the opposite sex in such establishment for equal work on jobs the performance of which requires equal skill, effort, and responsibility, and which are performed under similar working conditions, except where such payment is made pursuant to (i) a seniority system; (ii) a merit system; (iii) a system which measures earnings by quantity or quality of production; or (iv) a differential based on any other factor other than sex: *Provided*, That an employer who is paying a wage rate differential in violation of this subsection shall not, in order to comply with the provisions of this subsection, reduce the wage rate of any employee.

(2) No labor organization, or its agents, representing employees of an employer having employees subject to any provisions of this section shall cause or attempt to cause such an employer to discriminate against an employee in violation of paragraph (1) of this subsection.

(3) For purposes of administration and enforcement, any amounts owing to any employee which have been withheld in violation of this subsection shall be deemed to be unpaid minimum wages or unpaid overtime compensation under this chapter.

(4) As used in this subsection, the term "labor organization" means any organization of any kind, or any agency or employee representation committee or plan, in which employees participate and which exists for the purpose, in whole or in part, of dealing with employers concerning grievances, labor disputes, wages, rates of pay, hours of employment, or conditions of work.

(e) Employees of employers providing contract services to United States

(1) Notwithstanding the provisions of section 213 of this title (except subsections (a)(1) and (f) thereof), every employer providing any contract services (other than linen supply services) under a contract with the United States or any subcontract thereunder shall pay to each of his employees whose rate of pay is not governed by the Service Contract Act of 1965 (41 U.S.C. 351–357) or to whom subsection (a)(1) of this section is not applicable, wages at rates not less than the rates provided for in subsection (b) of this section.

(2) Notwithstanding the provisions of section 213 of this title (except subsections (a)(1) and (f) thereof) and the provisions of the Service Contract Act of 1965 [41 U.S.C. 351 et seq.] every employer in an establishment providing linen supply services to the United States under a contract with the United States or any subcontract thereunder shall pay to each of his employees in such establishment wages at rates not less than those prescribed in subsection (b) of this section, except that if more than 50 per centum of the gross annual dollar volume of sales made or business done by such establishment is derived from providing such linen supply services under any such contracts or subcontracts, such employer shall pay to each of his employees in such establishment wages at rates not less than those prescribed in subsection (a)(1) of this section.

(f) Employees in domestic service

Any employee—

(1) who in any workweek is employed in domestic service in a household shall be paid wages at a rate not less than the wage rate in effect under subsection (b) of this section unless such employee's compensation for such service would not because of section 209(a)(6)

of the Social Security Act [42 U.S.C. 409(a)(6)] constitute wages for the purposes of title II of such Act [42 U.S.C. 401 et seq.], or

(2) who in any workweek—

(A) is employed in domestic service in one or more households, and

(B) is so employed for more than 8 hours in the aggregate,

shall be paid wages for such employment in such workweek at a rate not less than the wage rate in effect under subsection (b) of this section.

(g) Newly hired employees who are less than 20 years old

(1) In lieu of the rate prescribed by subsection (a)(1) of this section, any employer may pay any employee of such employer, during the first 90 consecutive calendar days after such employee is initially employed by such employer, a wage which is not less than $4.25 an hour.

(2) No employer may take any action to displace employees (including partial displacements such as reduction in hours, wages, or employment benefits) for purposes of hiring individuals at the wage authorized in paragraph (1).

(3) Any employer who violates this subsection shall be considered to have violated section 215(a)(3) of this title.

(4) This subsection shall only apply to an employee who has not attained the age of 20 years.

(June 25, 1938, ch. 676, §6, 52 Stat. 1062; June 26, 1940, ch. 432, §3(e), (f), 54 Stat. 616; Oct. 26, 1949, ch. 736, §6, 63 Stat. 912; Aug. 12, 1955, ch. 867, §3, 69 Stat. 711; Aug. 8, 1956, ch. 1035, §2, 70 Stat. 1118; Pub. L. 87–30, §5, May 5, 1961, 75 Stat. 67; Pub. L. 88–38, §3, June 10, 1963, 77 Stat. 56; Pub. L. 89–601, title III, §§301–305, Sept. 23, 1966, 80 Stat. 838, 839, 841; Pub. L. 93–259, §§2–4, 5(b), 7(b)(1), Apr. 8, 1974, 88 Stat. 55, 56, 62; Pub. L. 95–151, §2(a)–(d)(2), Nov. 1, 1977, 91 Stat. 1245, 1246; Pub. L. 101–157, §§2, 4(b), Nov. 17, 1989, 103 Stat. 938, 940; Pub. L. 101–239, title X, §10208(d)(2)(B)(i), Dec. 19, 1989, 103 Stat. 2481; Pub. L. 104–188, [title II], §§2104(b), (c), 2105(c), Aug. 20, 1996, 110 Stat. 1928, 1929; Pub. L. 110–28, title VIII, §§8102(a), 8103(c)(1)(B), May 25, 2007, 121 Stat. 188, 189.)

REFERENCES IN TEXT

The Fair Labor Standards Amendments of 1966, referred to in subsec. (b), is Pub. L. 89–601, Sept. 23, 1966, 80 Stat. 830. For complete classification of this Act to the Code, see Short Title of 1966 Amendment note set out under section 201 of this title and Tables.

The Education Amendments of 1972, referred to in subsec. (b), is Pub. L. 92–318, June 23, 1972, 86 Stat. 235, as amended. Title IX of the Act, known as the Patsy Takemoto Mink Equal Opportunity in Education Act, is classified principally to chapter 38 (§1681 et seq.) of Title 20, Education. For complete classification of title IX to the Code, see Short Title note set out under section 1681 of Title 20 and Tables.

The Fair Labor Standards Amendments of 1974, referred to in subsec. (b), is Pub. L. 93–259, Apr. 8, 1974, 88 Stat. 55. For complete classification of this Act to the Code, see Short Title of 1974 Amendment note set out under section 201 of this title and Tables.

The Service Contract Act of 1965, referred to in subsec. (e)(1), (2), is Pub. L. 89–286, Oct. 22, 1965, 79 Stat. 1034, as amended, which is classified generally to chapter 6 (§351 et seq.) of Title 41, Public Contracts. For complete classification of this Act to the Code, see Short Title note set out under section 351 of Title 41 and Tables.

The Social Security Act, referred to in subsec. (f)(1), is act Aug. 14, 1935, ch. 531, 49 Stat. 620, as amended. Title II of such Act is classified generally to subchapter II (§401 et seq.) of chapter 7 of Title 42, The Public Health and Welfare. For complete classification of this Act to the Code, see section 1305 of Title 42 and Tables.

AMENDMENTS

2007—Subsec. (a)(1). Pub. L. 110–28, §8102(a), amended par. (1) generally. Prior to amendment, par. (1) read as follows: "except as otherwise provided in this section, not less than $4.25 an hour during the period ending on September 30, 1996, not less than $4.75 an hour during the year beginning on October 1, 1996, and not less than $5.15 an hour beginning September 1, 1997;".

Subsec. (a)(3) to (5). Pub. L. 110–28, §8103(c)(1)(B), redesignated pars. (4) and (5) as (3) and (4), respectively, and struck out former par. (3) which read as follows: "if such employee is employed in American Samoa, in lieu of the rate or rates provided by this subsection or subsection (b) of this section, not less than the applicable rate established by the Secretary of Labor in accordance with recommendations of a special industry committee or committees which he shall appoint pursuant to sections 205 and 208 of this title. The minimum wage rate thus established shall not exceed the rate prescribed in paragraph (1) of this subsection;".

1996—Subsec. (a)(1). Pub. L. 104–188, §2104(b), amended par. (1) generally. Prior to amendment, par. (1) read as follows: "except as otherwise provided in this section, not less than $3.35 an hour during the period ending March 31, 1990, not less than $3.80 an hour during the year beginning April 1, 1990, and not less than $4.25 an hour after March 31, 1991;".

Subsec. (c). Pub. L. 104–188, §2104(c), struck out subsec. (c) which related to employees in Puerto Rico.

Subsec. (g). Pub. L. 104–188, §2105(c), added subsec. (g).

1989—Subsec. (a)(1). Pub. L. 101–157, §2, amended par. (1) generally. Prior to amendment, par. (1) read as follows: "not less than $2.65 an hour during the year beginning January 1, 1978, not less than $2.90 an hour during the year beginning January 1, 1979, not less than $3.10 an hour during the year beginning January 1, 1980, and not less than $3.35 an hour after December 31, 1980, except as otherwise provided in this section;".

Subsec. (a)(3). Pub. L. 101–157, §4(b)(1), substituted "pursuant to sections 205 and 208 of this title" for "in the same manner and pursuant to the same provisions as are applicable to the special industry committees provided for Puerto Rico and the Virgin Islands by this chapter as amended from time to time. Each such committee shall have the same powers and duties and shall apply the same standards with respect to the application of the provisions of this chapter to employees employed in American Samoa as pertain to special industry committees established under section 205 of this title with respect to employees employed in Puerto Rico or the Virgin Islands".

Subsec. (c). Pub. L. 101–157, §4(b)(2), amended subsec. (c) generally, substituting provisions relating to the application of wage rates under subsec. (a)(1) to employees in Puerto Rico for provisions relating to the superseding of subsec. (a)(1) wage rates by wage orders of a special industry committee for employees in Puerto Rico and the Virgin Islands.

Subsec. (f)(1). Pub. L. 101–239 substituted "209(a)(6)" for "209(g)".

1977—Subsec. (a)(1). Pub. L. 95–151, §2(a), substituted "not less than $2.65 an hour during the year beginning January 1, 1978, not less than $2.90 an hour during the year beginning January 1, 1979, not less than $3.10 an hour during the year beginning January 1, 1980, and not less than $3.35 an hour after December 1, 1980" for "not less than $2 an hour during the period ending December 31, 1974, not less than $2.10 an hour during the year beginning January 1, 1975, and not less than $2.30 an hour after December 31, 1975".

Subsec. (a)(5). Pub. L. 95–151, §2(b), substituted provisions for a minimum wage rate of not less than the minimum wage rate in effect under par. (1) after Dec.

31, 1977, for provisions for a minimum wage rate of not less than $1.60 an hour during the period ending Dec. 31, 1974, $1.80 an hour during the year beginning Jan. 1, 1975, $2 an hour during the year beginning Jan. 1, 1976, $2.20 an hour during the year beginning Jan. 1, 1977, and $2.30 an hour after Dec. 31, 1977.

Subsec. (b). Pub. L. 95–151, §2(c), substituted provisions for a minimum wage rate, effective after Dec. 31, 1977, of not less than the minimum wage rate in effect under subsec. (a)(1) of this section, for provisions for a minimum wage rate of not less than $1.90 an hour during the period ending Dec. 31, 1974, not less than $2 an hour during the year beginning Jan. 1, 1975, not less than $2.20 an hour during the year beginning Jan. 1, 1976, and not less than $2.30 an hour after Dec. 31, 1976.

Subsec. (c)(1). Pub. L. 95–151, §2(d)(2)(A), inserted "(A)" before "heretofore" and cl. (B), and substituted "subsection (a)(1)" for "subsections (a) and (b)".

Subsec. (c)(2). Pub. L. 95–151, §2(d)(1), added par. (2). Former par. (2), relating to applicability, etc., of wage rate orders effective on the effective date of the Fair Labor Standards Amendments of 1974, and effective on the first day of the second and each subsequent year after such date, was struck out.

Subsec. (c)(3). Pub. L. 95–151, §2(d)(1), (2)(B), (C), redesignated par. (5) as (3) and substituted references to subsec. (a)(1) of this section, for references to subsec. (a) or (b) of this section. Former par. (3), relating to appointment of a special industry committee for recommendations with respect to highest minimum wage rates for employees employed in Puerto Rico or the Virgin Islands subject to the amendments to this chapter by the Fair Labor Standards Amendments of 1974, was struck out.

Subsec. (c)(4). Pub. L. 95–151, §2(d)(1), (2)(B), (D), redesignated par. (6) as (4) and struck out "or (3)" after "(2)". Former par. (4), relating to wage rates of employees in Puerto Rico or the Virgin Islands subject to the former provisions of subsec. (c)(2)(A) or (3) of this section, was struck out.

Subsec. (c)(5), (6). Pub. L. 95–151, §2(d)(2)(B), redesignated pars. (5) and (6) as (3) and (4), respectively.

1974—Subsec. (a)(1). Pub. L. 93–259, §2, substituted "not less than $2 an hour during the period ending December 31, 1974, not less than $2.10 an hour during the year beginning January 1, 1975, and not less than $2.30 an hour after December 31, 1975" for "not less than $1.40 an hour during the first year from the effective date of the Fair Labor Standards Amendments of 1966 and not less than $1.60 an hour thereafter".

Subsec. (a)(5). Pub. L. 93–259, §4, substituted provisions for a minimum wage rate not less than: $1.60 an hour during period ending Dec. 31, 1974; $1.80, $2, and $2.20 an hour during years beginning Jan. 1, 1975, 1976, and 1977, respectively; and $2.30 an hour after Dec. 31, 1977 for former provisions for a minimum wage rate not less than $1 an hour during first year from the effective date of the Fair Labor Standards Amendments of 1966, not less than $1.15 an hour during second year from such date, and not less than $1.30 an hour thereafter.

Subsec. (b). Pub. L. 93–259, §3, inserted references to "title II of the Education Amendments of 1972" and "Fair Labor Standards Amendments of 1974" and substituted provisions for a minimum wage rate not less than $1.90 an hour during period ending Dec. 31, 1974; $2 and $2.20 an hour during years beginning Jan. 1, 1975, and 1976, respectively; and $2.30 an hour after Dec. 31, 1976 for former provisions for a minimum wage rate not less than: $1 an hour during first year from effective date of Fair Labor Standards Amendments of 1966; $1.15, $1.30, and $1.45 an hour during second, third, and fourth years from such date; and $1.60 an hour thereafter.

Subsec. (c)(2) to (6). Pub. L. 93–259, §5(b), added pars. (2) to (6) and struck out former pars. (2) to (4) which had provided:

"(2) In the case of any such employee who is covered by such a wage order and to whom the rate or rates prescribed by subsection (a) of this section would otherwise apply, the following rates shall apply:

"(A) The rate or rates applicable under the most recent wage order issued by the Secretary prior to the effective date of the Fair Labor Standards Amendments of 1966, increased by 12 per centum, unless such rate or rates are superseded by the rate or rates prescribed in a wage order issued by the Secretary pursuant to the recommendations of a review committee appointed under paragraph (C). Such rate or rates shall become effective sixty days after the effective date of the Fair Labor Standards Amendments of 1966 or one year from the effective date of the most recent wage order applicable to such employee therefore issued by the Secretary pursuant to the recommendations of a special industry committee appointed under section 205 of this title, whichever is later.

"(B) Beginning one year after the applicable effective date under paragraph (A), not less than the rate or rates prescribed by paragraph (A), increased by an amount equal to 16 per centum of the rate or rates applicable under the most recent wage order issued by the Secretary prior to the effective date of the Fair Labor Standards Amendments of 1966, unless such rate or rates are superseded by the rate or rates prescribed in a wage order issued by the Secretary pursuant to the recommendations of a review committee appointed under paragraph (C).

"(C) Any employer, or group of employers, employing a majority of the employees in an industry in Puerto Rico or the Virgin Islands, may apply to the Secretary in writing for the appointment of a review committee to recommend the minimum rate or rates to be paid such employees in lieu of the rate or rates provided by paragraph (A) or (B). Any such application with respect to any rate or rates provided for under paragraph (A) shall be filed within sixty days following the enactment of the Fair Labor Standards Amendments of 1966 and any such application with respect to any rate or rates provided for under paragraph (B) shall be filed not more than one hundred and twenty days and not less than sixty days prior to the effective date of the applicable rate or rates under paragraph (B). The Secretary shall promptly consider such application and may appoint a review committee if he has reasonable cause to believe, on the basis of financial and other information contained in the application, that compliance with any applicable rate or rates prescribed by paragraph (A) or (B) will substantially curtail employment in such industry. The Secretary's decision upon any such application shall be final. Any wage order issued pursuant to the recommendations of a review committee appointed under this paragraph shall take effect on the applicable effective date provided in paragraph (A) or (B).

"(D) In the event a wage order has not been issued pursuant to the recommendation of a review committee prior to the applicable effective date under paragraph (A) or (B), the applicable percentage increase provided by any such paragraph shall take effect on the effective date prescribed therein, except with respect to the employees of an employer who filed an application under paragraph (C) and who files with the Secretary an undertaking with a surety or sureties satisfactory to the Secretary for payment to his employees of an amount sufficient to compensate such employees for the difference between the wages they actually receive and the wages to which they are entitled under this subsection. The Secretary shall be empowered to enforce such undertaking and any sums recovered by him shall be held on a special deposit account and shall be paid, on order of the Secretary, directly to the employee or employees affected. Any such sum not paid to an employee because of inability to do so within a period of three years shall be covered into the Treasury of the United States as miscellaneous receipts.

"(3) In the case of any such employee to whom subsection (a)(5) or subsection (b) of this section would otherwise apply, the Secretary shall within sixty days after the effective date of the Fair Labor Standards

Amendments of 1966 appoint a special industry committee in accordance with section 205 of this title to recommend the highest minimum wage rate or rates in accordance with the standards prescribed by section 208 of this title, but not in excess of the applicable rate provided by subsection (a)(5) or subsection (b) of this section, to be applicable to such employee in lieu of the rate or rates prescribed by subsection (a)(5) or subsection (b) of this section, as the case may be. The rate or rates recommended by the special industry committee shall be effective with respect to such employee upon the effective date of the wage order issued pursuant to such recommendation but not before sixty days after the effective date of the Fair Labor Standards Amendments of 1966.

"(4) The provisions of sections 205 and 208 of this title, relating to special industry committees, shall be applicable to review committees appointed under this subsection. The appointment of a review committee shall be in addition to and not in lieu of any special industry committee required to be appointed pursuant to the provisions of subsection (a) of section 208 of this title, except that no special industry committee shall hold any hearing within one year after a minimum wage rate or rates for such industry shall have been recommended to the Secretary by a review committee to be paid in lieu of the rate or rates provided for under paragraph (A) or (B). The minimum wage rate or rates prescribed by this subsection shall be in effect only for so long as and insofar as such minimum wage rate or rates have not been superseded by a wage order fixing a higher minimum wage rate or rates (but not in excess of the applicable rate prescribed in subsection (a) or subsection (b) of this section) hereafter issued by the Secretary pursuant to the recommendation of a special industry committee."

Subsec. (f). Pub. L. 93–259, §7(b)(1), added subsec. (f).

1966—Subsec. (a). Pub. L. 89–601, §301(a), inserted ", or is employed in an enterprise engaged in commerce or in the production of goods for commerce," in opening provisions.

Subsec. (a)(1). Pub. L. 89–601, §301(a), raised minimum wage to not less than $1.40 an hour during first year from the effective date of the Fair Labor Standards Amendments of 1966, and not less than $1.60 thereafter, except as otherwise provided in this section.

Subsec. (a)(4). Pub. L. 89–601, §301(b), added par. (4).

Subsec. (a)(5). Pub. L. 89–601, §302, added par. (5).

Subsec. (b). Pub. L. 89–601, §303, substituted provisions for a minimum wage for employees covered for first time by the Fair Labor Standards Amendments of 1966 (other than newly covered agricultural employees) at not less than $1 an hour during first year from the effective date of the 1966 amendments, not less than $1.15 an hour during second year from such date, not less than $1.30 an hour during third year from such date, not less than $1.45 an hour during fourth year from such date, and not less than $1.60 an hour thereafter, for provisions setting a timetable for increases in the minimum wage of employees first covered by the Fair Labor Standards Amendments of 1961.

Subsec. (c). Pub. L. 89–601, §304, provided for a percentage minimum wage increase for employees in Puerto Rico and the Virgin Islands who are covered by wage orders already in effect as the equivalent of the percentage increase on the mainland, provided for minimum wages for employees brought within coverage of this chapter for the first time by the Fair Labor Standards Amendments of 1966 at rates to be set by special industry committees so as to reach as rapidly as is economically feasible without substantially curtailing employment the objectives of the minimum wage prescribed for mainland employees, and eliminated the review committees that has been established by the Fair Labor Standards Amendments of 1961.

Subsec. (e). Pub. L. 89–601, §305, added subsec. (e).

1963—Subsec. (d). Pub. L. 88–38 added subsec. (d).

1961—Subsec. (a). Pub. L. 87–30, §5(a)(1), inserted "in any workweek" in opening provisions.

Subsec. (a)(1). Pub. L. 87–30, §5(a)(2), increased minimum wage from not less than $1 an hour to not less than $1.15 an hour during first two years from the effective date of the Fair Labor Standards Amendments of 1961, and not less than $1.25 an hour thereafter.

Subsec. (a)(3). Pub. L. 87–30, §5(a)(3), inserted "in lieu of the rate or rates provided by this subsection or subsection (b) of this section" and "as amended from time to time" and struck out "now" before "applicable to".

Subsec. (b). Pub. L. 87–30, §5(b), added subsec. (b). Former subsec. (b) had provided that "This section shall take effect upon the expiration of one hundred and twenty days from June 25, 1938."

Subsec. (c). Pub. L. 87–30, §5(c), added subsec. (c). Former subsec. (c) had provided for wage orders recommended by special industrial committees and covering employees in Puerto Rico and the Virgin Islands to supersede minimum wages of $1 an hour and for continuance of wage orders in effect prior to effective date of this chapter until superseded by wage orders recommended by the special industrial committees.

1956—Subsec. (a)(3). Act Aug. 8, 1956, added par. (3).

1955—Subsec. (a)(1). Act Aug. 12, 1955, increased minimum wage from not less than 75 cents an hour to not less than $1 an hour.

1949—Subsec. (a). Act Oct. 26, 1949, §6(a), (b), struck out subpars. (1), (2), (3), and (4), inserted subpar. (1) fixing the minimum wage rate at not less than 75 cents an hour, and redesignated subpar. (5) as (2).

Subsec. (c). Act Oct. 26, 1949, §6(c), continued existing minimum wage rates in Puerto Rico and the Virgin Islands until superseded by special industry committee wage orders.

1940—Subsec. (a)(5). Act June 26, 1940, added par. (5).

Effective Date of 2007 Amendment

Pub. L. 110–28, title VIII, §8102(b), May 25, 2007, 121 Stat. 188, provided that: "The amendment made by subsection (a) [amending this section] shall take effect 60 days after the date of enactment of this Act [May 25, 2007]."

Pub. L. 110–28, title VIII, §8103(c)(2), May 25, 2007, 121 Stat. 189, provided that: "The amendments made by this subsection [amending this section and repealing sections 205 and 208 of this title] shall take effect 60 days after the date of enactment of this Act [May 25, 2007]."

Effective Date of 1977 Amendment

Amendment by Pub. L. 95–151 effective Jan. 1, 1978, see section 15(a) of Pub. L. 95–151, set out as a note under section 203 of this title.

Effective Date of 1974 Amendment

Amendment by sections 2 to 4 and 7(b)(1) of Pub. L. 93–259 effective May 1, 1974, see section 29(a) of Pub. L. 93–259, set out as a note under section 202 of this title.

Section 5(b) of Pub. L. 93–259 provided that the amendment made by that section is effective Apr. 8, 1974.

Effective Date of 1966 Amendment

Amendment by Pub. L. 89–601 effective Feb. 1, 1967, except as otherwise provided, see section 602 of Pub. L. 89–601, set out as a note under section 203 of this title.

Effective Date of 1963 Amendment

Section 4 of Pub. L. 88–38 provided that: "The amendments made by this Act [amending this section and enacting provisions set out below] shall take effect upon the expiration of one year from the date of its enactment [June 10, 1963]: *Provided*, That in the case of employees covered by a bona fide collective bargaining agreement in effect at least thirty days prior to the date of enactment of this Act [June 10, 1963], entered into by a labor organization as defined in section 6(d)(4) of the Fair Labor Standards Act of 1938, as amended [subsec. (d)(4) of this section], the amendments made by this Act shall take effect upon the termination of such collective bargaining agreement or upon the expiration of two years from the date of enactment of this Act [June 10, 1963], whichever shall first occur."

EFFECTIVE DATE OF 1961 AMENDMENT

Amendment by Pub. L. 87–30 effective upon expiration of one hundred and twenty days after May 5, 1961, except as otherwise provided, see section 14 of Pub. L. 87–30, set out as a note under section 203 of this title.

EFFECTIVE DATE OF 1955 AMENDMENT

Section 3 of act Aug. 12, 1955, provided that the amendment made by that section is effective Mar. 1, 1956.

EFFECTIVE DATE OF 1949 AMENDMENT

Amendment by act Oct. 26, 1949, effective ninety days after Oct. 26, 1949, see section 16(a) of act Oct. 26, 1949, set out as a note under section 202 of this title.

TRANSFER OF FUNCTIONS

Functions relating to enforcement and administration of equal pay provisions vested by this section in Secretary of Labor and Administrator of Wage and Hour Division of Department of Labor transferred to Equal Employment Opportunity Commission by Reorg. Plan No. 1 of 1978, §1, 43 F.R. 19807, 92 Stat. 3781, set out in the Appendix to Title 5, Government Organization and Employees, effective Jan. 1, 1979, as provided by section 1–101 of Ex. Ord. No. 12106, Dec. 28, 1978, 44 F.R. 1053.

Functions of all other officers of Department of Labor and functions of all agencies and employees of that Department, with exception of functions vested by Administrative Procedure Act (now covered by sections 551 et seq. and 701 et seq. of Title 5, Government Organization and Employees) in hearing examiners employed by Department, transferred to Secretary of Labor, with power vested in him to authorize their performance or performance of any of his functions by any of those officers, agencies, and employees, by Reorg. Plan No. 6 of 1950, §§1, 2, 15 F.R. 3174, 64 Stat. 1263, set out in the Appendix to Title 5.

APPLICABILITY OF MINIMUM WAGE TO AMERICAN SAMOA AND THE COMMONWEALTH OF THE NORTHERN MARIANA ISLANDS

Pub. L. 110–28, title VIII, §8103(a), (b), May 25, 2007, 121 Stat. 188, 189, provided that:

"(a) IN GENERAL.—Section 6 of the Fair Labor Standards Act of 1938 (29 U.S.C. 206) shall apply to American Samoa and the Commonwealth of the Northern Mariana Islands.

"(b) TRANSITION.—Notwithstanding subsection (a)—

"(1) the minimum wage applicable to the Commonwealth of the Northern Mariana Islands under section 6(a)(1) of the Fair Labor Standards Act of 1938 (29 U.S.C. 206(a)(1)) shall be—

"(A) $3.55 an hour, beginning on the 60th day after the date of enactment of this Act [May 25, 2007]; and

"(B) increased by $0.50 an hour (or such lesser amount as may be necessary to equal the minimum wage under section 6(a)(1) of such Act), beginning 1 year after the date of enactment of this Act and each year thereafter until the minimum wage applicable to the Commonwealth of the Northern Mariana Islands under this paragraph is equal to the minimum wage set forth in such section; and

"(2) the minimum wage applicable to American Samoa under section 6(a)(1) of the Fair Labor Standards Act of 1938 (29 U.S.C. 206(a)(1)) shall be—

"(A) the applicable wage rate in effect for each industry and classification under section 697 of title 29, Code of Federal Regulations, on the date of enactment of this Act;

"(B) increased by $0.50 an hour, beginning on the 60th day after the date of enactment of this Act; and

"(C) increased by $0.50 an hour (or such lesser amount as may be necessary to equal the minimum wage under section 6(a)(1) of such Act), beginning 1 year after the date of enactment of this Act and each year thereafter until the minimum wage applicable to American Samoa under this paragraph is equal to the minimum wage set forth in such section."

TRAINING WAGE

Pub. L. 101–157, §6, Nov. 17, 1989, 103 Stat. 941, provided that:

"(a) IN GENERAL.—

"(1) AUTHORITY.—Any employer may, in lieu of the minimum wage prescribed by section 6 of the Fair Labor Standards Act of 1938 (29 U.S.C. 206), pay an eligible employee the wage prescribed by paragraph (2)—

"(A) while such employee is employed for the period authorized by subsection (g)(1)(B)(i), or

"(B) while such employee is engaged in on-the-job training for the period authorized by subsection (g)(1)(B)(ii).

"(2) WAGE RATE.—The wage referred to in paragraph (1) shall be a wage—

"(A) of not less than $3.35 an hour during the year beginning April 1, 1990; and

"(B) beginning April 1, 1991, of not less than $3.35 an hour or 85 percent of the wage prescribed by section 6 of such Act, whichever is greater.

"(b) WAGE PERIOD.—An employer may pay an eligible employee the wage authorized by subsection (a) for a period that—

"(1) begins on or after April 1, 1990;

"(2) does not exceed the maximum period during which an employee may be paid such wage as determined under subsection (g)(1)(B); and

"(3) ends before April 1, 1993.

"(c) WAGE CONDITIONS.—No eligible employee may be paid the wage authorized by subsection (a) by an employer if—

"(1) any other individual has been laid off by such employer from the position to be filled by such eligible employee or from any substantially equivalent position; or

"(2) such employer has terminated the employment of any regular employee or otherwise reduced the number of employees with the intention of filling the vacancy so created by hiring an employee to be paid such wage.

"(d) LIMITATIONS.—

"(1) EMPLOYEE HOURS.—During any month in which employees are to be employed in an establishment under this section, the proportion of employee hours of employment to the total hours of employment of all employees in such establishment may not exceed a proportion equal to one-fourth of the total hours of employment of all employees in such establishment.

"(2) DISPLACEMENT.—

"(A) PROHIBITION.—No employer may take any action to displace employees (including partial displacements such as reduction in hours, wages, or employment benefits) for purposes of hiring individuals at the wage authorized in subsection (a).

"(B) DISQUALIFICATION.—If the Secretary determines that an employer has taken an action in violation of subparagraph (A), the Secretary shall issue an order disqualifying such employer from employing any individual at such wage.

"(e) NOTICE.—Each employer shall provide to any eligible employee who is to be paid the wage authorized by subsection (a) a written notice before the employee begins employment stating the requirements of this section and the remedies provided by subsection (f) for violations of this section. The Secretary shall provide to employers the text of the notice to be provided under this subsection.

"(f) ENFORCEMENT.—Any employer who violates this section shall be considered to have violated section 15(a)(3) of the Fair Labor Standards Act of 1938 (29 U.S.C. 215(a)(3)). Sections 16 and 17 of such Act (29 U.S.C. 216 and 217) shall apply with respect to the violation.

"(g) DEFINITIONS.—For purposes of this section:

"(1) ELIGIBLE EMPLOYEE.—

"(A) IN GENERAL.—The term 'eligible employee' means with respect to an employer an individual who—

"(i) is not a migrant agricultural worker or a seasonal agricultural worker (as defined in paragraphs (8) and (10) of section 3 of the Migrant and Seasonal Agricultural Worker Protection Act (29 U.S.C. 1802(8) and (10)) without regard to subparagraph (B) of such paragraphs and is not a nonimmigrant described in section 101(a)(15)(H)(ii)(a) of the Immigration and Nationality Act (8 U.S.C. 1101(a)(15)(H)(ii)(a));

"(ii) has not attained the age of 20 years; and

"(iii) is eligible to be paid the wage authorized by subsection (a) as determined under subparagraph (B).

"(B) DURATION.—

"(i) An employee shall initially be eligible to be paid the wage authorized by subsection (a) until the employee has been employed a cumulative total of 90 days at such wage.

"(ii) An employee who has been employed by an employer at the wage authorized by subsection (a) for the period authorized by clause (i) may be employed by any other employer for an additional 90 days if the employer meets the requirements of subsection (h).

"(iii) The total period, as authorized by clauses (i) and (ii), that an employee may be paid the wage authorized by subsection (a) may not exceed 180 days.

"(iv) For purposes of this subparagraph, the term 'employer' means with respect to an employee an employer who is required to withhold payroll taxes for such employee.

"(C) PROOF.—

"(i) IN GENERAL.—An individual is responsible for providing the requisite proof of previous period or periods of employment with other employers. An employer's good faith reliance on the proof presented to the employer by an individual shall constitute a complete defense to a charge that the employer has violated subsection (b)(2) with respect to such individual.

"(ii) REGULATIONS.—The Secretary of Labor shall issue regulations defining the requisite proof required of an individual. Such regulations shall establish minimal requirements for requisite proof and may prescribe that an accurate list of the individual's employers and a statement of the dates and duration of employment with each employer constitute requisite proof.

"(2) ON-THE-JOB TRAINING.—The term 'on-the-job training' means training that is offered to an individual while employed in productive work that provides training, technical and other related skills, and personal skills that are essential to the full and adequate performance of such employment.

"(h) EMPLOYER REQUIREMENTS.—An employer who wants to employ employees at the wage authorized by subsection (a) for the period authorized by subsection (g)(1)(B)(ii) shall—

"(1) notify the Secretary annually of the positions at which such employees are to be employed at such wage,

"(2) provide on-the-job training to such employees which meets general criteria of the Secretary issued by regulation after consultation with the Committee on Labor and Human Resources [now Committee on Health, Education, Labor, and Pensions] of the Senate and the Committee on Education and Labor of the House of Representatives and other interested persons,

"(3) keep on file a copy of the training program which the employer will provide such employees,

"(4) provide a copy of the training program to the employees,

"(5) post in a conspicuous place in places of employment a notice of the types of jobs for which the employer is providing on-the-job training, and

"(6) send to the Secretary on an annual basis a copy of such notice.

The Secretary shall make available to the public upon request notices provided to the Secretary by employers in accordance with paragraph (6).

"(i) REPORT.—The Secretary of Labor shall report to Congress not later than March 1, 1993, on the effectiveness of the wage authorized by subsection (a). The report shall include—

"(1) an analysis of the impact of such wage on employment opportunities for inexperienced workers;

"(2) any reduction in employment opportunities for experienced workers resulting from the employment of employees under such wage;

"(3) the nature and duration of the training provided under such wage; and

"(4) the degree to which employers used the authority to pay such wage."

PRACTICE OF PUBLIC AGENCY IN TREATING CERTAIN INDIVIDUALS AS VOLUNTEERS PRIOR TO APRIL 15, 1986; LIABILITY

Certain public agencies not to be liable for violations of this section occurring before Apr. 15, 1986, with respect to services deemed by that agency to have been performed for it by an individual on a voluntary basis, see section 4(c) of Pub. L. 99–150, set out as a note under section 203 of this title.

EFFECT OF AMENDMENTS BY PUBLIC LAW 99–150 ON PUBLIC AGENCY LIABILITY RESPECTING ANY EMPLOYEE COVERED UNDER SPECIAL ENFORCEMENT POLICY

Amendment by Pub. L. 99–150 not to affect liability of certain public agencies under section 216 of this title for violation of this section occurring before Apr. 15, 1986, see section 7 of Pub. L. 99–150, set out as a note under section 216 of this title.

INAPPLICABILITY TO NORTHERN MARIANA ISLANDS

Pursuant to section 503(c) of the Covenant to Establish a Commonwealth of the Northern Mariana Islands with the United States of America, as set forth in Pub. L. 94–241, Mar. 24, 1976, 90 Stat. 263, set out as a note under section 1801 of Title 48, Territories and Insular Possessions, this section is inapplicable to the Northern Mariana Islands.

RULES, REGULATIONS, AND ORDERS PROMULGATED WITH REGARD TO 1966 AMENDMENTS

Secretary authorized to promulgate necessary rules, regulations, or orders on and after the date of the enactment of Pub. L. 89–601, Sept. 23, 1966, with regard to the amendments made by Pub. L. 89–601, see section 602 of Pub. L. 89–601, set out as a note under section 203 of this title.

CONGRESSIONAL FINDING AND DECLARATION OF POLICY

Section 2 of Pub. L. 88–38 provided that:

"(a) The Congress hereby finds that the existence in industries engaged in commerce or in the production of goods for commerce of wage differentials based on sex—

"(1) depresses wages and living standards for employees necessary for their health and efficiency;

"(2) prevents the maximum utilization of the available labor resources;

"(3) tends to cause labor disputes, thereby burdening, affecting, and obstructing commerce;

"(4) burdens commerce and the free flow of goods in commerce; and

"(5) constitutes an unfair method of competition.

"(b) It is hereby declared to be the policy of this Act [amending this section, and enacting provisions set out as notes under this section], through exercise by Congress of its power to regulate commerce among the several States and with foreign nations, to correct the conditions above referred to in such industries."

DEFINITION OF "ADMINISTRATOR"

The term "Administrator" as meaning the Administrator of the Wage and Hour Division, see section 204 of this title.

§207. Maximum hours

(a) Employees engaged in interstate commerce; additional applicability to employees pursuant to subsequent amendatory provisions

(1) Except as otherwise provided in this section, no employer shall employ any of his employees who in any workweek is engaged in commerce or in the production of goods for commerce, or is employed in an enterprise engaged in commerce or in the production of goods for commerce, for a workweek longer than forty hours unless such employee receives compensation for his employment in excess of the hours above specified at a rate not less than one and one-half times the regular rate at which he is employed.

(2) No employer shall employ any of his employees who in any workweek is engaged in commerce or in the production of goods for commerce, or is employed in an enterprise engaged in commerce or in the production of goods for commerce, and who in such workweek is brought within the purview of this subsection by the amendments made to this chapter by the Fair Labor Standards Amendments of 1966—

(A) for a workweek longer than forty-four hours during the first year from the effective date of the Fair Labor Standards Amendments of 1966,

(B) for a workweek longer than forty-two hours during the second year from such date, or

(C) for a workweek longer than forty hours after the expiration of the second year from such date,

unless such employee receives compensation for his employment in excess of the hours above specified at a rate not less than one and one-half times the regular rate at which he is employed.

(b) Employment pursuant to collective bargaining agreement; employment by independently owned and controlled local enterprise engaged in distribution of petroleum products

No employer shall be deemed to have violated subsection (a) of this section by employing any employee for a workweek in excess of that specified in such subsection without paying the compensation for overtime employment prescribed therein if such employee is so employed—

(1) in pursuance of an agreement, made as a result of collective bargaining by representatives of employees certified as bona fide by the National Labor Relations Board, which provides that no employee shall be employed more than one thousand and forty hours during any period of twenty-six consecutive weeks; or

(2) in pursuance of an agreement, made as a result of collective bargaining by representatives of employees certified as bona fide by the National Labor Relations Board, which provides that during a specified period of fifty-two consecutive weeks the employee shall be employed not more than two thousand two hundred and forty hours and shall be guaranteed not less than one thousand eight hundred and forty-hours (or not less than forty-six weeks at the normal number of hours worked per week, but not less than thirty hours per week) and not more than two thousand and eighty hours of employment for which he shall receive compensation for all hours guaranteed or worked at rates not less than those applicable under the agreement to the work performed and for all hours in excess of the guaranty which are also in excess of the maximum workweek applicable to such employee under subsection (a) of this section or two thousand and eighty in such period at rates not less than one and one-half times the regular rate at which he is employed; or

(3) by an independently owned and controlled local enterprise (including an enterprise with more than one bulk storage establishment) engaged in the wholesale or bulk distribution of petroleum products if—

(A) the annual gross volume of sales of such enterprise is less than $1,000,000 exclusive of excise taxes,

(B) more than 75 per centum of such enterprise's annual dollar volume of sales is made within the State in which such enterprise is located, and

(C) not more than 25 per centum of the annual dollar volume of sales of such enterprise is to customers who are engaged in the bulk distribution of such products for resale,

and such employee receives compensation for employment in excess of forty hours in any workweek at a rate not less than one and one-half times the minimum wage rate applicable to him under section 206 of this title,

and if such employee receives compensation for employment in excess of twelve hours in any workday, or for employment in excess of fifty-six hours in any workweek, as the case may be, at a rate not less than one and one-half times the regular rate at which he is employed.

(c), (d) Repealed. Pub. L. 93–259, §19(e), Apr. 8, 1974, 88 Stat. 66

(e) "Regular rate" defined

As used in this section the "regular rate" at which an employee is employed shall be deemed to include all remuneration for employment paid to, or on behalf of, the employee, but shall not be deemed to include—

(1) sums paid as gifts; payments in the nature of gifts made at Christmas time or on other special occasions, as a reward for service, the amounts of which are not measured by or dependent on hours worked, production, or efficiency;

(2) payments made for occasional periods when no work is performed due to vacation, holiday, illness, failure of the employer to provide sufficient work, or other similar cause; reasonable payments for traveling expenses, or other expenses, incurred by an employee in the furtherance of his employer's interests and properly reimbursable by the employer; and other similar payments to an employee which are not made as compensation for his hours of employment;

(3) Sums[1] paid in recognition of services performed during a given period if either, (a) both

[1] So in original. Probably should not be capitalized.

the fact that payment is to be made and the amount of the payment are determined at the sole discretion of the employer at or near the end of the period and not pursuant to any prior contract, agreement, or promise causing the employee to expect such payments regularly; or (b) the payments are made pursuant to a bona fide profit-sharing plan or trust or bona fide thrift or savings plan, meeting the requirements of the Administrator set forth in appropriate regulations which he shall issue, having due regard among other relevant factors, to the extent to which the amounts paid to the employee are determined without regard to hours of work, production, or efficiency; or (c) the payments are talent fees (as such talent fees are defined and delimited by regulations of the Administrator) paid to performers, including announcers, on radio and television programs;

(4) contributions irrevocably made by an employer to a trustee or third person pursuant to a bona fide plan for providing old-age, retirement, life, accident, or health insurance or similar benefits for employees;

(5) extra compensation provided by a premium rate paid for certain hours worked by the employee in any day of workweek because such hours are hours worked in excess of eight in a day or in excess of the maximum workweek applicable to such employee under subsection (a) of this section or in excess of the employee's normal working hours or regular working hours, as the case may be;

(6) extra compensation provided by a premium rate paid for work by the employee on Saturdays, Sundays, holidays, or regular days of rest, or on the sixth or seventh day of the workweek, where such premium rate is not less than one and one-half times the rate established in good faith for like work performed in nonovertime hours on other days;

(7) extra compensation provided by a premium rate paid to the employee, in pursuance of an applicable employment contract or collective-bargaining agreement, for work outside of the hours established in good faith by the contract or agreement as the basic, normal, or regular workday (not exceeding eight hours) or workweek (not exceeding the maximum workweek applicable to such employee under subsection (a) of this section,[2] where such premium rate is not less than one and one-half times the rate established in good faith by the contract or agreement for like work performed during such workday or workweek; or

(8) any value or income derived from employer-provided grants or rights provided pursuant to a stock option, stock appreciation right, or bona fide employee stock purchase program which is not otherwise excludable under any of paragraphs (1) through (7) if—

(A) grants are made pursuant to a program, the terms and conditions of which are communicated to participating employees either at the beginning of the employee's participation in the program or at the time of the grant;

(B) in the case of stock options and stock appreciation rights, the grant or right cannot be exercisable for a period of at least 6 months after the time of grant (except that grants or rights may become exercisable because of an employee's death, disability, retirement, or a change in corporate ownership, or other circumstances permitted by regulation), and the exercise price is at least 85 percent of the fair market value of the stock at the time of grant;

(C) exercise of any grant or right is voluntary; and

(D) any determinations regarding the award of, and the amount of, employer-provided grants or rights that are based on performance are—

(i) made based upon meeting previously established performance criteria (which may include hours of work, efficiency, or productivity) of any business unit consisting of at least 10 employees or of a facility, except that, any determinations may be based on length of service or minimum schedule of hours or days of work; or

(ii) made based upon the past performance (which may include any criteria) of one or more employees in a given period so long as the determination is in the sole discretion of the employer and not pursuant to any prior contract.

(f) Employment necessitating irregular hours of work

No employer shall be deemed to have violated subsection (a) of this section by employing any employee for a workweek in excess of the maximum workweek applicable to such employee under subsection (a) of this section if such employee is employed pursuant to a bona fide individual contract, or pursuant to an agreement made as a result of collective bargaining by representatives of employees, if the duties of such employee necessitate irregular hours of work, and the contract or agreement (1) specifies a regular rate of pay of not less than the minimum hourly rate provided in subsection (a) or (b) of section 206 of this title (whichever may be applicable) and compensation at not less than one and one-half times such rate for all hours worked in excess of such maximum workweek, and (2) provides a weekly guaranty of pay for not more than sixty hours based on the rates so specified.

(g) Employment at piece rates

No employer shall be deemed to have violated subsection (a) of this section by employing any employee for a workweek in excess of the maximum workweek applicable to such employee under such subsection if, pursuant to an agreement or understanding arrived at between the employer and the employee before performance of the work, the amount paid to the employee for the number of hours worked by him in such workweek in excess of the maximum workweek applicable to such employee under such subsection—

(1) in the case of an employee employed at piece rates, is computed at piece rates not less than one and one-half times the bona fide piece rates applicable to the same work when performed during nonovertime hours; or

[2] So in original. The comma probably should be preceded by a closing parenthesis.

(2) in the case of an employee performing two or more kinds of work for which different hourly or piece rates have been established, is computed at rates not less than one and one-half times such bona fide rates applicable to the same work when performed during non-overtime hours; or

(3) is computed at a rate not less than one and one-half times the rate established by such agreement or understanding as the basic rate to be used in computing overtime compensation thereunder: *Provided*, That the rate so established shall be authorized by regulation by the Administrator as being substantially equivalent to the average hourly earnings of the employee, exclusive of overtime premiums, in the particular work over a representative period of time;

and if (i) the employee's average hourly earnings for the workweek exclusive of payments described in paragraphs (1) through (7) of subsection (e) of this section are not less than the minimum hourly rate required by applicable law, and (ii) extra overtime compensation is properly computed and paid on other forms of additional pay required to be included in computing the regular rate.

(h) Credit toward minimum wage or overtime compensation of amounts excluded from regular rate

(1) Except as provided in paragraph (2), sums excluded from the regular rate pursuant to subsection (e) of this section shall not be creditable toward wages required under section 206 of this title or overtime compensation required under this section.

(2) Extra compensation paid as described in paragraphs (5), (6), and (7) of subsection (e) of this section shall be creditable toward overtime compensation payable pursuant to this section.

(i) Employment by retail or service establishment

No employer shall be deemed to have violated subsection (a) of this section by employing any employee of a retail or service establishment for a workweek in excess of the applicable workweek specified therein, if (1) the regular rate of pay of such employee is in excess of one and one-half times the minimum hourly rate applicable to him under section 206 of this title, and (2) more than half his compensation for a representative period (not less than one month) represents commissions on goods or services. In determining the proportion of compensation representing commissions, all earnings resulting from the application of a bona fide commission rate shall be deemed commissions on goods or services without regard to whether the computed commissions exceed the draw or guarantee.

(j) Employment in hospital or establishment engaged in care of sick, aged, or mentally ill

No employer engaged in the operation of a hospital or an establishment which is an institution primarily engaged in the care of the sick, the aged, or the mentally ill or defective who reside on the premises shall be deemed to have violated subsection (a) of this section if, pursuant to an agreement or understanding arrived at between the employer and the employee before performance of the work, a work period of fourteen consecutive days is accepted in lieu of the workweek of seven consecutive days for purposes of overtime computation and if, for his employment in excess of eight hours in any workday and in excess of eighty hours in such fourteen-day period, the employee receives compensation at a rate not less than one and one-half times the regular rate at which he is employed.

(k) Employment by public agency engaged in fire protection or law enforcement activities

No public agency shall be deemed to have violated subsection (a) of this section with respect to the employment of any employee in fire protection activities or any employee in law enforcement activities (including security personnel in correctional institutions) if—

(1) in a work period of 28 consecutive days the employee receives for tours of duty which in the aggregate exceed the lesser of (A) 216 hours, or (B) the average number of hours (as determined by the Secretary pursuant to section 6(c)(3) of the Fair Labor Standards Amendments of 1974) in tours of duty of employees engaged in such activities in work periods of 28 consecutive days in calendar year 1975; or

(2) in the case of such an employee to whom a work period of at least 7 but less than 28 days applies, in his work period the employee receives for tours of duty which in the aggregate exceed a number of hours which bears the same ratio to the number of consecutive days in his work period as 216 hours (or if lower, the number of hours referred to in clause (B) of paragraph (1)) bears to 28 days,

compensation at a rate not less than one and one-half times the regular rate at which he is employed.

(*l*) Employment in domestic service in one or more households

No employer shall employ any employee in domestic service in one or more households for a workweek longer than forty hours unless such employee receives compensation for such employment in accordance with subsection (a) of this section.

(m) Employment in tobacco industry

For a period or periods of not more than fourteen workweeks in the aggregate in any calendar year, any employer may employ any employee for a workweek in excess of that specified in subsection (a) of this section without paying the compensation for overtime employment prescribed in such subsection, if such employee—

(1) is employed by such employer—

(A) to provide services (including stripping and grading) necessary and incidental to the sale at auction of green leaf tobacco of type 11, 12, 13, 14, 21, 22, 23, 24, 31, 35, 36, or 37 (as such types are defined by the Secretary of Agriculture), or in auction sale, buying, handling, stemming, redrying, packing, and storing of such tobacco,

(B) in auction sale, buying, handling, sorting, grading, packing, or storing green leaf tobacco of type 32 (as such type is defined by the Secretary of Agriculture), or

(C) in auction sale, buying, handling, stripping, sorting, grading, sizing, packing, or stemming prior to packing, of perishable cigar leaf tobacco of type 41, 42, 43, 44, 45, 46, 51, 52, 53, 54, 55, 61, or 62 (as such types are defined by the Secretary of Agriculture); and

(2) receives for—

(A) such employment by such employer which is in excess of ten hours in any workday, and

(B) such employment by such employer which is in excess of forty-eight hours in any workweek,

compensation at a rate not less than one and one-half times the regular rate at which he is employed.

An employer who receives an exemption under this subsection shall not be eligible for any other exemption under this section.

(n) Employment by street, suburban, or interurban electric railway, or local trolley or motorbus carrier

In the case of an employee of an employer engaged in the business of operating a street, suburban or interurban electric railway, or local trolley or motorbus carrier (regardless of whether or not such railway or carrier is public or private or operated for profit or not for profit), in determining the hours of employment of such an employee to which the rate prescribed by subsection (a) of this section applies there shall be excluded the hours such employee was employed in charter activities by such employer if (1) the employee's employment in such activities was pursuant to an agreement or understanding with his employer arrived at before engaging in such employment, and (2) if employment in such activities is not part of such employee's regular employment.

(*o*) Compensatory time

(1) Employees of a public agency which is a State, a political subdivision of a State, or an interstate governmental agency may receive, in accordance with this subsection and in lieu of overtime compensation, compensatory time off at a rate not less than one and one-half hours for each hour of employment for which overtime compensation is required by this section.

(2) A public agency may provide compensatory time under paragraph (1) only—

(A) pursuant to—

(i) applicable provisions of a collective bargaining agreement, memorandum of understanding, or any other agreement between the public agency and representatives of such employees; or

(ii) in the case of employees not covered by subclause (i), an agreement or understanding arrived at between the employer and employee before the performance of the work; and

(B) if the employee has not accrued compensatory time in excess of the limit applicable to the employee prescribed by paragraph (3).

In the case of employees described in clause (A)(ii) hired prior to April 15, 1986, the regular practice in effect on April 15, 1986, with respect to compensatory time off for such employees in lieu of the receipt of overtime compensation, shall constitute an agreement or understanding under such clause (A)(ii). Except as provided in the previous sentence, the provision of compensatory time off to such employees for hours worked after April 14, 1986, shall be in accordance with this subsection.

(3)(A) If the work of an employee for which compensatory time may be provided included work in a public safety activity, an emergency response activity, or a seasonal activity, the employee engaged in such work may accrue not more than 480 hours of compensatory time for hours worked after April 15, 1986. If such work was any other work, the employee engaged in such work may accrue not more than 240 hours of compensatory time for hours worked after April 15, 1986. Any such employee who, after April 15, 1986, has accrued 480 or 240 hours, as the case may be, of compensatory time off shall, for additional overtime hours of work, be paid overtime compensation.

(B) If compensation is paid to an employee for accrued compensatory time off, such compensation shall be paid at the regular rate earned by the employee at the time the employee receives such payment.

(4) An employee who has accrued compensatory time off authorized to be provided under paragraph (1) shall, upon termination of employment, be paid for the unused compensatory time at a rate of compensation not less than—

(A) the average regular rate received by such employee during the last 3 years of the employee's employment, or

(B) the final regular rate received by such employee,

whichever is higher[3]

(5) An employee of a public agency which is a State, political subdivision of a State, or an interstate governmental agency—

(A) who has accrued compensatory time off authorized to be provided under paragraph (1), and

(B) who has requested the use of such compensatory time,

shall be permitted by the employee's employer to use such time within a reasonable period after making the request if the use of the compensatory time does not unduly disrupt the operations of the public agency.

(6) The hours an employee of a public agency performs court reporting transcript preparation duties shall not be considered as hours worked for the purposes of subsection (a) of this section if—

(A) such employee is paid at a per-page rate which is not less than—

(i) the maximum rate established by State law or local ordinance for the jurisdiction of such public agency,

(ii) the maximum rate otherwise established by a judicial or administrative officer and in effect on July 1, 1995, or

(iii) the rate freely negotiated between the employee and the party requesting the transcript, other than the judge who presided over the proceedings being transcribed, and

[3] So in original. Probably should be followed by a period.

(B) the hours spent performing such duties are outside of the hours such employee performs other work (including hours for which the agency requires the employee's attendance) pursuant to the employment relationship with such public agency.

For purposes of this section, the amount paid such employee in accordance with subparagraph (A) for the performance of court reporting transcript preparation duties, shall not be considered in the calculation of the regular rate at which such employee is employed.

(7) For purposes of this subsection—

(A) the term "overtime compensation" means the compensation required by subsection (a), and

(B) the terms "compensatory time" and "compensatory time off" mean hours during which an employee is not working, which are not counted as hours worked during the applicable workweek or other work period for purposes of overtime compensation, and for which the employee is compensated at the employee's regular rate.

(p) Special detail work for fire protection and law enforcement employees; occasional or sporadic employment; substitution

(1) If an individual who is employed by a State, political subdivision of a State, or an interstate governmental agency in fire protection or law enforcement activities (including activities of security personnel in correctional institutions) and who, solely at such individual's option, agrees to be employed on a special detail by a separate or independent employer in fire protection, law enforcement, or related activities, the hours such individual was employed by such separate and independent employer shall be excluded by the public agency employing such individual in the calculation of the hours for which the employee is entitled to overtime compensation under this section if the public agency—

(A) requires that its employees engaged in fire protection, law enforcement, or security activities be hired by a separate and independent employer to perform the special detail,

(B) facilitates the employment of such employees by a separate and independent employer, or

(C) otherwise affects the condition of employment of such employees by a separate and independent employer.

(2) If an employee of a public agency which is a State, political subdivision of a State, or an interstate governmental agency undertakes, on an occasional or sporadic basis and solely at the employee's option, part-time employment for the public agency which is in a different capacity from any capacity in which the employee is regularly employed with the public agency, the hours such employee was employed in performing the different employment shall be excluded by the public agency in the calculation of the hours for which the employee is entitled to overtime compensation under this section.

(3) If an individual who is employed in any capacity by a public agency which is a State, political subdivision of a State, or an interstate governmental agency, agrees, with the approval of the public agency and solely at the option of such individual, to substitute during scheduled work hours for another individual who is employed by such agency in the same capacity, the hours such employee worked as a substitute shall be excluded by the public agency in the calculation of the hours for which the employee is entitled to overtime compensation under this section.

(q) Maximum hour exemption for employees receiving remedial education

Any employer may employ any employee for a period or periods of not more than 10 hours in the aggregate in any workweek in excess of the maximum workweek specified in subsection (a) of this section without paying the compensation for overtime employment prescribed in such subsection, if during such period or periods the employee is receiving remedial education that is—

(1) provided to employees who lack a high school diploma or educational attainment at the eighth grade level;

(2) designed to provide reading and other basic skills at an eighth grade level or below; and

(3) does not include job specific training.

(June 25, 1938, ch. 676, §7, 52 Stat. 1063; Oct. 29, 1941, ch. 461, 55 Stat. 756; July 20, 1949, ch. 352, §1, 63 Stat. 446; Oct. 26, 1949, ch. 736, §7, 63 Stat. 912; Pub. L. 87–30, §6, May 5, 1961, 75 Stat. 69; Pub. L. 89–601, title II, §§204(c), (d), 212(b), title IV, §§401–403, Sept. 23, 1966, 80 Stat. 835–837, 841, 842; Pub. L. 93–259, §§6(c)(1), 7(b)(2), 9(a), 12(b), 19, 21(a), Apr. 8, 1974, 88 Stat. 60, 62, 64, 66, 68; Pub. L. 99–150, §§2(a), 3(a)–(c)(1), Nov. 13, 1985, 99 Stat. 787, 789; Pub. L. 101–157, §7, Nov. 17, 1989, 103 Stat. 944; Pub. L. 104–26, §2, Sept. 6, 1995, 109 Stat. 264; Pub. L. 106–202, §2(a), (b), May 18, 2000, 114 Stat. 308, 309.)

REFERENCES IN TEXT

The Fair Labor Standards Amendments of 1966, referred to in subsec. (a)(2), is Pub. L. 89–601, Sept. 23, 1966, 80 Stat. 830. For complete classification of this Act to the Code, see Short Title of 1966 Amendment note set out under section 201 of this title and Tables.

The effective date of the Fair Labor Standards Amendments of 1966, referred to in subsec. (a)(2)(A), means the effective date of Pub. L. 89–601, which is Feb. 1, 1967 except as otherwise provided, see section 602 of Pub. L. 89–601, set out as an Effective Date of 1966 Amendment note under section 203 of this title.

Section 6(c)(3) of the Fair Labor Standards Amendments of 1974, referred to in subsec. (k)(1), is Pub. L. 93–259, §6(c)(3), Apr. 8, 1974, 88 Stat. 61, which is set out as a note under section 213 of this title.

AMENDMENTS

2000—Subsec. (e)(8). Pub. L. 106–202, §2(a), added par. (8).

Subsec. (h). Pub. L. 106–202, §2(b), designated existing provisions as par. (2) and added par. (1).

1995—Subsec. (*o*)(6), (7). Pub. L. 104–26 added par. (6) and redesignated former par. (6) as (7).

1989—Subsec. (q). Pub. L. 101–157 added subsec. (q).

1985—Subsec. (*o*). Pub. L. 99–150, §2(a), added subsec. (*o*).

Subsec. (p). Pub. L. 99–150, §3(a)–(c)(1), added subsec. (p).

1974—Subsec. (c). Pub. L. 93–259, §19(a), (b), substituted "seven workweeks" for "ten workweeks", "ten workweeks" for "fourteen workweeks" and "forty-eight hours" for "fifty hours" effective May 1, 1974. Pub. L. 93–259, §19(c), substituted "five workweeks" for "seven workweeks" and "seven workweeks" for "ten workweeks" effective Jan. 1, 1975. Pub. L. 93–259, §19(d), substituted "three workweeks" for "five workweeks" and "five workweeks" for "seven workweeks" effective Jan. 1, 1976. Pub. L. 93–259, §19(e), repealed subsec. (c) effective Dec. 31, 1976.

Subsec. (d). Pub. L. 93–259, §19(a), (b), substituted "seven workweeks" for "ten workweeks", "ten workweeks" for "fourteen workweeks" and "forty-eight hours" for "fifty hours" effective May 1, 1974. Pub. L. 93–259, §19(c), substituted "five workweeks" for "seven workweeks" and "seven workweeks" for "ten workweeks" effective Jan. 1, 1975. Pub. L. 93–259, §19(d), substituted "three workweeks" for "five workweeks" and "five workweeks" for "seven workweeks" effective Jan. 1, 1976. Pub. L. 93–259, §19(e), repealed subsec. (d) effective Dec. 31, 1976.

Subsec. (j). Pub. L. 93–259, §12(b), extended provision excepting from being considered a subsec. (a) violation agreements or undertakings between employers and employees respecting consecutive work period and overtime compensation to agreements between employers engaged in operation of an establishment which is an institution primarily engaged in the care of the sick, the aged, or the mentally ill or defective who reside on the premises and employees respecting consecutive work period and overtime compensation.

Subsec. (k). Pub. L. 93–259, §6(c)(1)(D), effective Jan. 1, 1978, substituted in par. (1) "exceed the lesser of (A) 216 hours, or (B) the average number of hours (as determined by the Secretary pursuant to section 6(c)(3) of the Fair Labor Standards Amendments of 1974) in tours of duty of employees engaged in such activities in work periods of 28 consecutive days in calendar year 1975" for "exceed 216 hours" and inserted in par. (2) "(or if lower, the number of hours referred to in clause (B) of paragraph (1)".

Pub. L. 93–259, §6(c)(1)(C), substituted "216 hours" for "232 hours", wherever appearing, effective Jan. 1, 1977.

Pub. L. 93–259, §6(c)(1)(B), substituted "232 hours" for "240 hours", wherever appearing, effective Jan. 1, 1976.

Pub. L. 93–259, §6(c)(1)(A), added subsec. (k), effective Jan. 1, 1975.

Subsec. (*l*). Pub. L. 93–259, §7(b)(2), added subsec. (*l*).

Subsec. (m). Pub. L. 93–259, §9(a), added subsec. (m).

Subsec. (n). Pub. L. 93–259, §21(a), added subsec. (n).

1966—Subsec. (a). Pub. L. 89–601, §401, retained provision for 40-hour workweek and compensation for employment in excess of 40 hours at not less than one and one-half times the regular rate of pay and substituted provisions setting out a phased timetable for the workweek in the case of employees covered by the overtime provisions for the first time under the Fair Labor Standards Amendments of 1966 beginning at 44 hours during the first year from the effective date of the Fair Labor Standards Amendments of 1966, 42 hours during the second year from such date, and 40 hours after the expiration of the second year from such date, for provisions giving a phased timetable for workweeks in the case of employees first covered under the provisions of the Fair Labor Standards Amendments of 1961.

Subsec. (b)(3). Pub. L. 89–601, §212(b), substituted provisions granting an overtime exemption for petroleum distribution employees if they receive compensation for the hours of employment in excess of 40 hours in any workweek at a rate not less than one and one-half times the applicable minimum wage rate and if the enterprises do an annual gross sales volume of less than $1,000,000, if more than 75 per centum of such enterprise's annual dollar volume of sales is made within the state in which the enterprise is located, and not more than 25 per centum of the annual dollar volume is to customers who are engaged in the bulk distribution of such products for resale for provisions covering employees for a period of not more than 14 workweeks in the aggregate in any calendar year in an industry found to be of a seasonal nature.

Subsec. (c). Pub. L. 89–601, §204(c), substituted provisions for an overtime exemption of 10 weeks in any calendar year or 14 weeks in the case of an employer not qualifying for the exemption in subsec. (d) of this section, limited to 10 hours a day and 50 hours a week, applicable to employees employed in seasonal industries which are not engaged in agricultural processing, for provisions granting a year-round unlimited exemption applicable to employees of employers engaged in first processing of milk into dairy products, cotton compressing and ginning, cottonseed processing, and the processing of certain farm products into sugar, and granting a 14-week unlimited exemption applicable to employees of employers engaged in first processing of perishable or seasonal fresh fruits or vegetables first processing within the area of production of any agricultural commodity during a seasonal operation, or the handling or slaughtering of livestock and poultry.

Subsec. (d). Pub. L. 89–601, §204(c), added subsec. (d). Former subsec. (d) redesignated (e).

Subsecs. (e), (f). Pub. L. 89–601, §204(d)(1), redesignated former subsecs. (d) and (e) as (e) and (f) respectively. Former subsec. (f) redesignated (g).

Subsecs. (g), (h). Pub. L. 89–601, §204(d)(1), (2), redesignated former subsecs. (f) and (g) as subsecs. (g) and (h) respectively, and in subsecs. (g) and (h) as so redesignated, substituted reference to "subsection (e)" for reference to "subsection (d)." Former subsec. (h) redesignated (i).

Subsec. (i). Pub. L. 89–601, §§204(d)(1), 402, redesignated former subsec. (h) as (i) and inserted provision that, in determining the proportion of compensation representing commissions, all earnings resulting from the application of a bona fide commission rate shall be deemed commissions on goods or services without regard to whether the computed commissions exceed the draw or guarantee.

Subsec. (j). Pub. L. 89–601, §403, added subsec. (j).

1961—Subsec. (a). Pub. L. 87–30, §6(a), designated existing provisions as par. (1), inserted "in any workweek", and added par. (2).

Subsec. (b)(2). Pub. L. 87–30, §6(b), substituted "in excess of the maximum workweek applicable to such employee under subsection (a) of this section" for "in excess of forty hours in the workweek".

Subsec. (d)(5), (7). Pub. L. 87–30, §6(c), (d), substituted "in excess of the maximum workweek applicable to such employee under subsection (a) of this section" for "forty in a workweek" in par. (5) and "the maximum workweek applicable to such employee under subsection (a) of this section" for "forty hours" in par. (7).

Subsec. (e). Pub. L. 87–30, §6(e), substituted "the maximum workweek applicable to such employee under subsection (a) of this section", "subsection (a) or (b) of section 206 of this title (whichever may be applicable" and "such maximum" for "forty hours", "section 206(a) of this title" and "forty in any", respectively.

Subsec. (f). Pub. L. 87–30, §6(f), substituted "the maximum workweek applicable to such employee under subsection" for "forty hours" in two places.

Subsec. (h). Pub. L. 87–30, §6(g), added subsec. (h).

1949—Subsec. (a). Act Oct. 26, 1949, continued requirement that employment in excess of 40 hours in a workweek be compensated at rate not less than 1½ times regular rate except as to employees specifically exempted.

Subsec. (b)(1). Act Oct. 26, 1949, increased employment period limitation from one thousand hours to one thousand and forty hours in semi-annual agreements.

Subsec. (b)(2). Act Oct. 26, 1949, increased employment period limitation from two thousand and eighty hours to two thousand two hundred and forty hours in annual agreements, fixed minimum and maximum guaranteed employment periods, and provided for overtime rate for hours worked in excess of the guaranty.

Subsec. (c). Act Oct. 26, 1949, added buttermilk to commodities listed for first processing.

Subsec. (d). Act Oct. 26, 1949, struck out former subsec. (d) and inserted a new subsec. (d) defining regular rate with certain specified types of payments excepted.

Subsec. (e) added by act July 20, 1949, and amended by act Oct. 26, 1949, which determined compensation to be paid for irregular hours of work.

Subsecs. (f) and (g). Act Oct. 26, 1949, added subsecs. (f) and (g).

1941—Subsec. (b)(2) amended by act Oct. 29, 1941.

EFFECTIVE DATE OF 2000 AMENDMENT

Pub. L. 106–202, § 2(c), May 18, 2000, 114 Stat. 309, provided that: "The amendments made by this section [amending this section] shall take effect on the date that is 90 days after the date of enactment of this Act [May 18, 2000]."

EFFECTIVE DATE OF 1995 AMENDMENT

Section 3 of Pub. L. 104–26 provided that: "The amendments made by section 2 [amending this section] shall apply after the date of the enactment of this Act [Sept. 6, 1995] and with respect to actions brought in a court after the date of the enactment of this Act."

EFFECTIVE DATE OF 1985 AMENDMENT

Amendment by Pub. L. 99–150 effective Apr. 15, 1986, see section 6 of Pub. L. 99–150, set out as a note under section 203 of this title.

EFFECTIVE DATE OF 1974 AMENDMENT

Section 6(c)(1)(A)–(D) of Pub. L. 93–259 provided that the amendments made by that section are effective Jan. 1, 1975, 1976, 1977, and 1978, respectively.

Amendment by sections 7(b)(2), 9(a), 12(b), 19(a), (b), and 21(a) of Pub. L. 93–259 effective May 1, 1974, see section 29(a) of Pub. L. 93–259, set out as a note under section 202 of this title.

Section 19(c)–(e) of Pub. L. 93–259 provided that the amendments and repeals made by that section are effective Jan. 1, 1975, Jan. 1, 1976, and Dec. 31, 1976, respectively.

EFFECTIVE DATE OF 1966 AMENDMENT

Amendment by Pub. L. 89–601 effective Feb. 1, 1967, except as otherwise provided, see section 602 of Pub. L. 89–601, set out as a note under section 203 of this title.

EFFECTIVE DATE OF 1961 AMENDMENT

Amendment by Pub. L. 87–30 effective upon expiration of one hundred and twenty days after May 5, 1961, except as otherwise provided, see section 14 of Pub. L. 87–30, set out as a note under section 203 of this title.

EFFECTIVE DATE OF 1949 AMENDMENT

Amendment by act Oct. 26, 1949, effective ninety days after Oct. 26, 1949, see section 16(a) of act Oct. 26, 1949, set out as a note under section 202 of this title.

REGULATIONS

Pub. L. 106–202, § 2(e), May 18, 2000, 114 Stat. 309, provided that: "The Secretary of Labor may promulgate such regulations as may be necessary to carry out the amendments made by this Act [amending this section]."

TRANSFER OF FUNCTIONS

Functions of all other officers of Department of Labor and functions of all agencies and employees of that Department, with exception of functions vested by Administrative Procedure Act (now covered by sections 551 et seq. and 701 et seq. of Title 5, Government Organization and Employees) in hearing examiners employed by Department, transferred to Secretary of Labor, with power vested in him to authorize their performance or performance of any of his functions by any of those officers, agencies, and employees, by Reorg. Plan No. 6 of 1950, §§ 1, 2, 15 F.R. 3174, 64 Stat. 1263, set out in the Appendix to Title 5.

APPLICABILITY; LIABILITY OF EMPLOYERS

Pub. L. 110–244, title III, § 306, June 6, 2008, 122 Stat. 1620, provided that:

"(a) APPLICABILITY FOLLOWING THIS ACT.—Beginning on the date of enactment of this Act [June 6, 2008], section 7 of the Fair Labor Standards Act of 1938 (29 U.S.C. 207) shall apply to a covered employee notwithstanding section 13(b)(1) of that Act (29 U.S.C. 213(b)(1)).

"(b) LIABILITY LIMITATION FOLLOWING SAFETEA-LU.—

"(1) LIMITATION ON LIABILITY.—An employer shall not be liable for a violation of section 7 of the Fair Labor Standards Act of 1938 (29 U.S.C. 207) with respect to a covered employee if—

"(A) the violation occurred in the 1-year period beginning on August 10, 2005; and

"(B) as of the date of the violation, the employer did not have actual knowledge that the employer was subject to the requirements of such section with respect to the covered employee.

"(2) ACTIONS TO RECOVER AMOUNTS PREVIOUSLY PAID.—Nothing in paragraph (1) shall be construed to establish a cause of action for an employer to recover amounts paid before the date of enactment of this Act [June 6, 2008] in settlement of, in compromise of, or pursuant to a judgment rendered regarding a claim or potential claim based on an alleged or proven violation of section 7 of the Fair Labor Standards Act of 1938 (29 U.S.C. 207) occurring in the 1-year period referred to in paragraph (1)(A) with respect to a covered employee.

"(c) COVERED EMPLOYEE DEFINED.—In this section, the term 'covered employee' means an individual—

"(1) who is employed by a motor carrier or motor private carrier (as such terms are defined by section 13102 of title 49, United States Code, as amended by section 305);

"(2) whose work, in whole or in part, is defined—

"(A) as that of a driver, driver's helper, loader, or mechanic; and

"(B) as affecting the safety of operation of motor vehicles weighing 10,000 pounds or less in transportation on public highways in interstate or foreign commerce, except vehicles—

"(i) designed or used to transport more than 8 passengers (including the driver) for compensation;

"(ii) designed or used to transport more than 15 passengers (including the driver) and not used to transport passengers for compensation; or

"(iii) used in transporting material found by the Secretary of Transportation to be hazardous under section 5103 of title 49, United States Code, and transported in a quantity requiring placarding under regulations prescribed by the Secretary under section 5103 of title 49, United States Code; and

"(3) who performs duties on motor vehicles weighing 10,000 pounds or less."

LIABILITY OF EMPLOYERS

Pub. L. 106–202, § 2(d), May 18, 2000, 114 Stat. 309, provided that: "No employer shall be liable under the Fair Labor Standards Act of 1938 [29 U.S.C. 201 et seq.] for any failure to include in an employee's regular rate (as defined for purposes of such Act) any income or value derived from employer-provided grants or rights obtained pursuant to any stock option, stock appreciation right, or employee stock purchase program if—

"(1) the grants or rights were obtained before the effective date described in subsection (c) [set out as an Effective Date of 2000 Amendment note above];

"(2) the grants or rights were obtained within the 12-month period beginning on the effective date described in subsection (c), so long as such program was in existence on the date of enactment of this Act [May 18, 2000] and will require shareholder approval to modify such program to comply with section 7(e)(8) of the Fair Labor Standards Act of 1938 [29 U.S.C. 207(e)(8)] (as added by the amendments made by subsection (a)); or

"(3) such program is provided under a collective bargaining agreement that is in effect on the effective date described in subsection (c)."

COMPENSATORY TIME; COLLECTIVE BARGAINING AGREEMENTS IN EFFECT ON APRIL 15, 1986

Section 2(b) of Pub. L. 99–150 provided that: "A collective bargaining agreement which is in effect on April 15, 1986, and which permits compensatory time off in lieu of overtime compensation shall remain in effect until its expiration date unless otherwise modified, except that compensatory time shall be provided after April 14, 1986, in accordance with section 7(*o*) of the Fair Labor Standards Act of 1938 (as added by subsection (a)) [29 U.S.C. 207(*o*)]."

DEFERMENT OF MONETARY OVERTIME COMPENSATION

Section 2(c)(2) of Pub. L. 99–150 provided that: "A State, political subdivision of a State, or interstate governmental agency may defer until August 1, 1986, the payment of monetary overtime compensation under section 7 of the Fair Labor Standards Act of 1938 [29 U.S.C. 207] for hours worked after April 14, 1986."

EFFECT OF AMENDMENTS BY PUBLIC LAW 99–150 ON PUBLIC AGENCY LIABILITY RESPECTING ANY EMPLOYEE COVERED UNDER SPECIAL ENFORCEMENT POLICY

Amendment by Pub. L. 99–150 not to affect liability of certain public agencies under section 216 of this title for violation of this section occurring before Apr. 15, 1986, see section 7 of Pub. L. 99–150, set out as a note under section 216 of this title.

RULES, REGULATIONS, AND ORDERS PROMULGATED WITH REGARD TO 1966 AMENDMENTS

Secretary authorized to promulgate necessary rules, regulations, or orders on and after the date of the enactment of Pub. L. 89–601, Sept. 23, 1966, with regard to the amendments made by Pub. L. 89–601, see section 602 of Pub. L. 89–601, set out as a note under section 203 of this title.

STUDY BY SECRETARY OF LABOR OF EXCESSIVE OVERTIME

Pub. L. 89–601, title VI, §603, Sept. 23, 1966, 80 Stat. 844, directed Secretary of Labor to make a complete study of practices dealing with overtime payments for work in excess of forty hours per week and the extent to which such overtime work impeded the creation of new job opportunities in American industry and instructed him to report to the Congress by July 1, 1967, the findings of such survey with appropriate recommendations.

EX. ORD. NO. 9607. FORTY-EIGHT HOUR WARTIME WORKWEEK

Ex. Ord. No. 9607, Aug. 30, 1945, 10 F.R. 11191, provided:

By virtue of the authority vested in me by the Constitution and statutes as President of the United States it is ordered that Executive Order 9301 of February 9, 1943 [8 F.R. 1825] (formerly set out as note under this section), establishing a minimum wartime workweek of forty-eight hours, be, and it is hereby, revoked.

HARRY S TRUMAN.

DEFINITION OF "ADMINISTRATOR"

The term "Administrator" as meaning the Administrator of the Wage and Hour Division, see section 204 of this title.

§208. Repealed. Pub. L. 110–28, title VIII, §8103(c)(1)(A), May 25, 2007, 121 Stat. 189

Section, acts June 25, 1938, ch. 676, §8, 52 Stat. 1064; Oct. 26, 1949, ch. 736, §8, 63 Stat. 915; Aug. 12, 1955, ch. 867, §§4, 5(b)–(e), 69 Stat. 711, 712; Pub. L. 85–750, Aug. 25, 1958, 72 Stat. 844; Pub. L. 87–30, §7, May 5, 1961, 75 Stat. 70; Pub. L. 93–259, §5(c)(1), (d), Apr. 8, 1974, 88 Stat. 58; Pub. L. 95–151, §2(d)(3), Nov. 1, 1977, 91 Stat. 1246; Pub. L. 101–157, §4(c), Nov. 17, 1989, 103 Stat. 940; Pub. L. 101–583, §1, Nov. 15, 1990, 104 Stat. 2871, related to wage orders in American Samoa.

EFFECTIVE DATE OF REPEAL

Repeal effective 60 days after May 25, 2007, see section 8103(c)(2) of Pub. L. 110–28, set out as an Effective Date of 2007 Amendment note under section 206 of this title.

§209. Attendance of witnesses

For the purpose of any hearing or investigation provided for in this chapter, the provisions of sections 49 and 50 of title 15 (relating to the attendance of witnesses and the production of books, papers, and documents), are made applicable to the jurisdiction, powers, and duties of the Administrator, the Secretary of Labor, and the industry committees.

(June 25, 1938, ch. 676, §9, 52 Stat. 1065; 1946 Reorg. Plan No. 2, §1(b), eff. July 16, 1946, 11 F.R. 7873, 60 Stat. 1095.)

TRANSFER OF FUNCTIONS

Functions relating to enforcement and administration of equal pay provisions vested by this section in Secretary of Labor and Administrator of Wage and Hour Division of Department of Labor transferred to Equal Employment Opportunity Commission by Reorg. Plan No. 1 of 1978, §1, 43 F.R. 19807, 92 Stat. 3781, set out in the Appendix to Title 5, Government Organization and Employees, effective Jan. 1, 1979, as provided by section 1–101 of Ex. Ord. No. 12106, Dec. 28, 1978, 44 F.R. 1053.

Functions of all other officers of Department of Labor and functions of all agencies and employees of that Department, with exception of functions vested by Administrative Procedure Act (now covered by sections 551 et seq. and 701 et seq. of Title 5, Government Organization and Employees) in hearing examiners employed by Department, transferred to Secretary of Labor, with power vested in him to authorize their performance or performance of any of his functions by any of those officers, agencies, and employees, by Reorg. Plan No. 6 of 1950, §§1, 2, 15 F.R. 3174, 64 Stat. 1263, set out in the Appendix to Title 5.

"Secretary of Labor" substituted in text for "Chief of the Children's Bureau" by 1946 Reorg. Plan No. 2. See Transfer of Functions note set out under section 203 of this title.

DEFINITION OF "ADMINISTRATOR"

The term "Administrator" as meaning the Administrator of the Wage and Hour Division, see section 204 of this title.

§210. Court review of wage orders in Puerto Rico and the Virgin Islands

(a) Any person aggrieved by an order of the Secretary issued under section 208[1] of this title may obtain a review of such order in the United States Court of Appeals for any circuit wherein such person resides or has his principal place of business, or in the United States Court of Appeals for the District of Columbia, by filing in such court, within 60 days after the entry of such order a written petition praying that the order of the Secretary be modified or set aside in whole or in part. A copy of such petition shall forthwith be transmitted by the clerk of the court to the Secretary, and thereupon the Secretary shall file in the court the record of the industry committee upon which the order complained of was entered, as provided in section 2112 of title 28. Upon the filing of such petition such court shall have exclusive jurisdiction to

[1] See References in Text note below.

affirm, modify (including provision for the payment of an appropriate minimum wage rate), or set aside such order in whole or in part, so far as it is applicable to the petitioner. The review by the court shall be limited to questions of law, and findings of fact by such industry committee when supported by substantial evidence shall be conclusive. No objection to the order of the Secretary shall be considered by the court unless such objection shall have been urged before such industry committee or unless there were reasonable grounds for failure so to do. If application is made to the court for leave to adduce additional evidence, and it is shown to the satisfaction of the court that such additional evidence may materially affect the result of the proceeding and that there were reasonable grounds for failure to adduce such evidence in the proceedings before such industry committee, the court may order such additional evidence to be taken before an industry committee and to be adduced upon the hearing in such manner and upon such terms and conditions as to the court may seem proper. Such industry committee may modify the initial findings by reason of the additional evidence so taken, and shall file with the court such modified or new findings which if supported by substantial evidence shall be conclusive, and shall also file its recommendation, if any, for the modification or setting aside of the original order. The judgment and decree of the court shall be final, subject to review by the Supreme Court of the United States upon certiorari or certification as provided in section 1254 of title 28.

(b) The commencement of proceedings under subsection (a) of this section shall not, unless specifically ordered by the court, operate as a stay of the Administrator's order. The court shall not grant any stay of the order unless the person complaining of such order shall file in court an undertaking with a surety or sureties satisfactory to the court for the payment to the employees affected by the order, in the event such order is affirmed, of the amount by which the compensation such employees are entitled to receive under the order exceeds the compensation they actually receive while such stay is in effect.

(June 25, 1938, ch. 676, §10, 52 Stat. 1065; Aug. 12, 1955, ch. 867, §5(f), 69 Stat. 712; Pub. L. 85–791, §22, Aug. 28, 1958, 72 Stat. 948; Pub. L. 93–259, §5(c)(2), Apr. 8, 1974, 88 Stat. 58.)

REFERENCES IN TEXT

Section 208 of this title, referred to in subsec. (a), was repealed by Pub. L. 110–28, title VIII, §8103(c)(1)(A), May 25, 2007, 121 Stat. 189.

AMENDMENTS

1974—Subsec. (a). Pub. L. 93–259 inserted "(including provision for the payment of an appropriate minimum wage rate)" in third sentence after "modify".

1958—Subsec. (a). Pub. L. 85–791 substituted "transmitted by the clerk of the court to the Secretary, and thereupon the Secretary shall file in the court the record of the industry committee" for "served upon the Secretary, and thereupon the Secretary shall certify and file in the court a transcript of the record" in second sentence, and inserted "as provided in section 2112 of title 28", and substituted "petition" for "transcript" in third sentence.

1955—Subsec. (a). Act Aug. 12, 1955, amended subsec. (a) generally to make subsection conform to new procedure applicable to Puerto Rico and Virgin Islands.

EFFECTIVE DATE OF 1974 AMENDMENT

Amendment by Pub. L. 93–259 effective May 1, 1974, see section 29(a) of Pub. L. 93–259, set out as a note under section 202 of this title.

TRANSFER OF FUNCTIONS

For transfer of functions of other officers, employees, and agencies of Department of Labor, with certain exceptions, to Secretary of Labor, with power to delegate, see Reorg. Plan No. 6 of 1950, §§1, 2, 15 F.R. 3174, 64 Stat. 1263, set out in the Appendix to Title 5, Government Organization and Employees.

DEFINITION OF "ADMINISTRATOR"

The term "Administrator" as meaning the Administrator of the Wage and Hour Division, see section 204 of this title.

DEFINITION OF "SECRETARY"

The term "Secretary" as meaning the Secretary of Labor, see section 6 of act Aug. 12, 1955, set out as a note under section 204 of this title.

§211. Collection of data

(a) Investigations and inspections

The Administrator or his designated representatives may investigate and gather data regarding the wages, hours, and other conditions and practices of employment in any industry subject to this chapter, and may enter and inspect such places and such records (and make such transcriptions thereof), question such employees, and investigate such facts, conditions, practices, or matters as he may deem necessary or appropriate to determine whether any person has violated any provision of this chapter, or which may aid in the enforcement of the provisions of this chapter. Except as provided in section 212 of this title and in subsection (b) of this section, the Administrator shall utilize the bureaus and divisions of the Department of Labor for all the investigations and inspections necessary under this section. Except as provided in section 212 of this title, the Administrator shall bring all actions under section 217 of this title to restrain violations of this chapter.

(b) State and local agencies and employees

With the consent and cooperation of State agencies charged with the administration of State labor laws, the Administrator and the Secretary of Labor may, for the purpose of carrying out their respective functions and duties under this chapter, utilize the services of State and local agencies and their employees and, notwithstanding any other provision of law, may reimburse such State and local agencies and their employees for services rendered for such purposes.

(c) Records

Every employer subject to any provision of this chapter or of any order issued under this chapter shall make, keep, and preserve such records of the persons employed by him and of the wages, hours, and other conditions and practices of employment maintained by him, and shall preserve such records for such periods of time, and shall make such reports therefrom to the Administrator as he shall prescribe by regulation or order as necessary or appropriate for the enforcement of the provisions of this chapter or the regulations or orders thereunder. The employer of an employee who performs substitute work described in section 207(p)(3) of this title may not be required under this subsection to keep a record of the hours of the substitute work.

(d) Homework regulations

The Administrator is authorized to make such regulations and orders regulating, restricting, or prohibiting industrial homework as are necessary or appropriate to prevent the circumvention or evasion of and to safeguard the minimum wage rate prescribed in this chapter, and all existing regulations or orders of the Administrator relating to industrial homework are continued in full force and effect.

(June 25, 1938, ch. 676, §11, 52 Stat. 1066; 1946 Reorg. Plan No. 2, §1(b), eff. July 16, 1946, 11 F.R. 7873, 60 Stat. 1095; Oct. 26, 1949, ch. 736, §9, 63 Stat. 916; Pub. L. 99–150, §3(c)(2), Nov. 13, 1985, 99 Stat. 789.)

AMENDMENTS

1985—Subsec. (c). Pub. L. 99–150 inserted "The employer of an employee who performs substitute work described in section 207(p)(3) of this title may not be required under this subsection to keep a record of the hours of the substitute work."

1949—Subsec. (d). Act Oct. 26, 1949, added subsec. (d).

EFFECTIVE DATE OF 1985 AMENDMENT

Amendment by Pub. L. 99–150 effective Apr. 15, 1986, see section 6 of Pub. L. 99–150, set out as a note under section 203 of this title.

EFFECTIVE DATE OF 1949 AMENDMENT

Amendment by act Oct. 26, 1949, effective ninety days after Oct. 26, 1949, see section 16(a) of act Oct. 26, 1949, set out as a note under section 202 of this title.

TRANSFER OF FUNCTIONS

Functions relating to enforcement and administration of equal pay provisions vested by subsecs. (a), (b), and (c) of this section in Secretary of Labor and Administrator of Wage and Hour Division of Department of Labor transferred to Equal Employment Opportunity Commission by Reorg. Plan No. 1 of 1978, §1, 43 F.R. 19807, 92 Stat. 3781, set out in the Appendix to Title 5, Government Organization and Employees, effective Jan. 1, 1979, as provided by section 1–101 of Ex. Ord. No. 12106, Dec. 28, 1978, 44 F.R. 1053.

For transfer of functions of other officers, employees, and agencies of Department of Labor, with certain exceptions, to Secretary of Labor, with power to delegate, see Reorg. Plan No. 6 of 1950, §§1, 2, 15 F.R. 3174, 64 Stat. 1263, set out in the Appendix to Title 5, Government Organization and Employees.

"Secretary of Labor" substituted for "Chief of the Children's Bureau" in subsec. (b) by 1946 Reorg. Plan No. 2. See note set out under section 203 of this title.

EFFECT OF AMENDMENTS BY PUBLIC LAW 99–150 ON PUBLIC AGENCY LIABILITY RESPECTING ANY EMPLOYEE COVERED UNDER SPECIAL ENFORCEMENT POLICY

Amendment by Pub. L. 99–150 not to affect liability of certain public agencies under section 216 of this title for violation of this section occurring before Apr. 15, 1986, see section 7 of Pub. L. 99–150, set out as a note under section 216 of this title.

DEFINITION OF "ADMINISTRATOR"

The term "Administrator" as meaning the Administrator of the Wage and Hour Division, see section 204 of this title.

§212. Child labor provisions

(a) Restrictions on shipment of goods; prosecution; conviction

No producer, manufacturer, or dealer shall ship or deliver for shipment in commerce any goods produced in an establishment situated in the United States in or about which within thirty days prior to the removal of such goods therefrom any oppressive child labor has been employed: *Provided*, That any such shipment or delivery for shipment of such goods by a purchaser who acquired them in good faith in reliance on written assurance from the producer, manufacturer, or dealer that the goods were produced in compliance with the requirements of this section, and who acquired such goods for value without notice of any such violation, shall not be deemed prohibited by this subsection: *And provided further*, That a prosecution and conviction of a defendant for the shipment or delivery for shipment of any goods under the conditions herein prohibited shall be a bar to any further prosecution against the same defendant for shipments or deliveries for shipment of any such goods before the beginning of said prosecution.

(b) Investigations and inspections

The Secretary of Labor or any of his authorized representatives, shall make all investigations and inspections under section 211(a) of this title with respect to the employment of minors, and, subject to the direction and control of the Attorney General, shall bring all actions under section 217 of this title to enjoin any act or practice which is unlawful by reason of the existence of oppressive child labor, and shall administer all other provisions of this chapter relating to oppressive child labor.

(c) Oppressive child labor

No employer shall employ any oppressive child labor in commerce or in the production of goods for commerce or in any enterprise engaged in commerce or in the production of goods for commerce.

(d) Proof of age

In order to carry out the objectives of this section, the Secretary may by regulation require employers to obtain from any employee proof of age.

(June 25, 1938, ch. 676, §12, 52 Stat. 1067; 1946 Reorg. Plan No. 2, §1(b), eff. July 16, 1946, 11 F.R. 7873, 60 Stat. 1095; Oct. 26, 1949, ch. 736, §10, 63 Stat. 917; Pub. L. 87–30, §8, May 5, 1961, 75 Stat. 70; Pub. L. 93–259, §25(a), Apr. 8, 1974, 88 Stat. 72.)

AMENDMENTS

1974—Subsec. (d). Pub. L. 93–259 added subsec. (d).

1961—Subsec. (c). Pub. L. 87–30 inserted "or in any enterprise engaged in commerce or in the production of goods for commerce".

1949—Subsec. (a). Act Oct. 26, 1949, §10(a), struck out effective date at beginning of subsection and inserted proviso excepting good faith purchaser of goods produced by oppressive child labor.

Subsec. (c). Act Oct. 26, 1949, §10(b), added subsec. (c).

EFFECTIVE DATE OF 1974 AMENDMENT

Amendment by Pub. L. 93–259 effective May 1, 1974, see section 29(a) of Pub. L. 93–259, set out as a note under section 202 of this title.

EFFECTIVE DATE OF 1961 AMENDMENT

Amendment by Pub. L. 87–30 effective upon expiration of one hundred and twenty days after May 5, 1961, except as otherwise provided, see section 14 of Pub. L. 87–30, set out as a note under section 203 of this title.

EFFECTIVE DATE OF 1949 AMENDMENT

Amendment by act Oct. 26, 1949, effective ninety days after Oct. 26, 1949, see section 16(a) of act Oct. 26, 1949, set out as a note under section 202 of this title.

TRANSFER OF FUNCTIONS

For transfer of functions of other officers, employees, and agencies of Department of Labor, with certain exceptions, to Secretary of Labor, with power to delegate, see Reorg. Plan No. 6 of 1950, §§1, 2, 15 F.R. 3174, 64 Stat. 1263, set out in the Appendix to Title 5, Government Organization and Employees.

"Secretary of Labor" substituted for "Chief of the Children's Bureau in the Department of Labor" in subsec. (b) by 1946 Reorg. Plan No. 2. See note set out under section 203 of this title.

§213. Exemptions

(a) Minimum wage and maximum hour requirements

The provisions of sections 206 (except subsection (d) in the case of paragraph (1) of this subsection) and 207 of this title shall not apply with respect to—

(1) any employee employed in a bona fide executive, administrative, or professional capacity (including any employee employed in the capacity of academic administrative personnel or teacher in elementary or secondary schools), or in the capacity of outside salesman (as such terms are defined and delimited from time to time by regulations of the Secretary, subject to the provisions of subchapter II of chapter 5 of title 5, except that an employee of a retail or service establishment shall not be excluded from the definition of employee employed in a bona fide executive or administrative capacity because of the number of hours in his workweek which he devotes to activities not directly or closely related to the performance of executive or administrative activities, if less than 40 per centum of his hours worked in the workweek are devoted to such activities); or

(2) Repealed. Pub. L. 101–157, §3(c)(1), Nov. 17, 1989, 103 Stat. 939.

(3) any employee employed by an establishment which is an amusement or recreational establishment, organized camp, or religious or non-profit educational conference center, if (A) it does not operate for more than seven months in any calendar year, or (B) during the preceding calendar year, its average receipts for any six months of such year were not more than 33⅓ per centum of its average receipts for the other six months of such year, except that the exemption from sections 206 and 207 of this title provided by this paragraph does not apply with respect to any employee of a private entity engaged in providing services or facilities (other than, in the case of the exemption from section 206 of this title, a private entity engaged in providing services and facilities directly related to skiing) in a national park or a national forest, or on land in the National Wildlife Refuge System, under a contract with the Secretary of the Interior or the Secretary of Agriculture; or

(4) Repealed. Pub. L. 101–157, §3(c)(1), Nov. 17, 1989, 103 Stat. 939.

(5) any employee employed in the catching, taking, propagating, harvesting, cultivating, or farming of any kind of fish, shellfish, crustacea, sponges, seaweeds, or other aquatic forms of animal and vegetable life, or in the first processing, canning or packing such marine products at sea as an incident to, or in conjunction with, such fishing operations, including the going to and returning from work and loading and unloading when performed by any such employee; or

(6) any employee employed in agriculture (A) if such employee is employed by an employer who did not, during any calendar quarter during the preceding calendar year, use more than five hundred man-days of agricultural labor, (B) if such employee is the parent, spouse, child, or other member of his employer's immediate family, (C) if such employee (i) is employed as a hand harvest laborer and is paid on a piece rate basis in an operation which has been, and is customarily and generally recognized as having been, paid on a piece rate basis in the region of employment, (ii) commutes daily from his permanent residence to the farm on which he is so employed, and (iii) has been employed in agriculture less than thirteen weeks during the preceding calendar year, (D) if such employee (other than an employee described in clause (C) of this subsection) (i) is sixteen years of age or under and is employed as a hand harvest laborer, is paid on a piece rate basis in an operation which has been, and is customarily and generally recognized as having been, paid on a piece rate basis in the region of employment, (ii) is employed on the same farm as his parent or person standing in the place of his parent, and (iii) is paid at the same piece rate as employees over age sixteen are paid on the same farm, or (E) if such employee is principally engaged in the range production of livestock; or

(7) any employee to the extent that such employee is exempted by regulations, order, or certificate of the Secretary issued under section 214 of this title; or

(8) any employee employed in connection with the publication of any weekly, semiweekly, or daily newspaper with a circulation of less than four thousand the major part of which circulation is within the county where published or counties contiguous thereto; or

(9) Repealed. Pub. L. 93–259, §23(a)(1), Apr. 8, 1974, 88 Stat. 69.

(10) any switchboard operator employed by an independently owned public telephone company which has not more than seven hundred and fifty stations; or

(11) Repealed. Pub. L. 93–259, §10(a), Apr. 8, 1974, 88 Stat. 63.

(12) any employee employed as a seaman on a vessel other than an American vessel; or

(13), (14) Repealed. Pub. L. 93–259, §§9(b)(1), 23(b)(1), Apr. 8, 1974, 88 Stat. 63, 69.

(15) any employee employed on a casual basis in domestic service employment to provide babysitting services or any employee employed in domestic service employment to provide companionship services for individuals who (because of age or infirmity) are unable to care for themselves (as such terms are defined and delimited by regulations of the Secretary); or

(16) a criminal investigator who is paid availability pay under section 5545a of title 5; or

(17) any employee who is a computer systems analyst, computer programmer, software engineer, or other similarly skilled worker, whose primary duty is—

(A) the application of systems analysis techniques and procedures, including consulting with users, to determine hardware, software, or system functional specifications;

(B) the design, development, documentation, analysis, creation, testing, or modification of computer systems or programs, including prototypes, based on and related to user or system design specifications;

(C) the design, documentation, testing, creation, or modification of computer programs related to machine operating systems; or

(D) a combination of duties described in subparagraphs (A), (B), and (C) the performance of which requires the same level of skills, and

who, in the case of an employee who is compensated on an hourly basis, is compensated at a rate of not less than $27.63 an hour.

(b) Maximum hour requirements

The provisions of section 207 of this title shall not apply with respect to—

(1) any employee with respect to whom the Secretary of Transportation has power to establish qualifications and maximum hours of service pursuant to the provisions of section 31502 of title 49; or

(2) any employee of an employer engaged in the operation of a rail carrier subject to part A of subtitle IV of title 49; or

(3) any employee of a carrier by air subject to the provisions of title II of the Railway Labor Act [45 U.S.C. 181 et seq.]; or

(4) Repealed. Pub. L. 93–259, §11(c), Apr. 8, 1974, 88 Stat. 64.

(5) any individual employed as an outside buyer of poultry, eggs, cream, or milk, in their raw or natural state; or

(6) any employee employed as a seaman; or

(7) Repealed. Pub. L. 93–259, §21(b)(3), Apr. 8, 1974, 88 Stat. 68.

(8) Repealed. Pub. L. 95–151, §14(b), Nov. 1, 1977, 91 Stat. 1252.

(9) any employee employed as an announcer, news editor, or chief engineer by a radio or television station the major studio of which is located (A) in a city or town of one hundred thousand population or less, according to the latest available decennial census figures as compiled by the Bureau of the Census, except where such city or town is part of a standard metropolitan statistical area, as defined and designated by the Office of Management and Budget, which has a total population in excess of one hundred thousand, or (B) in a city or town of twenty-five thousand population or less, which is part of such an area but is at least 40 airline miles from the principal city in such area; or

(10)(A) any salesman, partsman, or mechanic primarily engaged in selling or servicing automobiles, trucks, or farm implements, if he is employed by a nonmanufacturing establishment primarily engaged in the business of selling such vehicles or implements to ultimate purchasers; or

(B) any salesman primarily engaged in selling trailers, boats, or aircraft, if he is employed by a nonmanufacturing establishment primarily engaged in the business of selling trailers, boats, or aircraft to ultimate purchasers; or

(11) any employee employed as a driver or driver's helper making local deliveries, who is compensated for such employment on the basis of trip rates, or other delivery payment plan, if the Secretary shall find that such plan has the general purpose and effect of reducing hours worked by such employees to, or below, the maximum workweek applicable to them under section 207(a) of this title; or

(12) any employee employed in agriculture or in connection with the operation or maintenance of ditches, canals, reservoirs, or waterways, not owned or operated for profit, or operated on a sharecrop basis, and which are used exclusively for supply and storing of water, at least 90 percent of which was ultimately delivered for agricultural purposes during the preceding calendar year; or

(13) any employee with respect to his employment in agriculture by a farmer, notwithstanding other employment of such employee in connection with livestock auction operations in which such farmer is engaged as an adjunct to the raising of livestock, either on his own account or in conjunction with other farmers, if such employee (A) is primarily employed during his workweek in agriculture by such farmer, and (B) is paid for his employment in connection with such livestock auction operations at a wage rate not less than that prescribed by section 206(a)(1) of this title; or

(14) any employee employed within the area of production (as defined by the Secretary) by an establishment commonly recognized as a country elevator, including such an establishment which sells products and services used in the operation of a farm, if no more than five employees are employed in the establishment in such operations; or

(15) any employee engaged in the processing of maple sap into sugar (other than refined sugar) or syrup; or

(16) any employee engaged (A) in the transportation and preparation for transportation of fruits or vegetables, whether or not performed by the farmer, from the farm to a place of first processing or first marketing within the same State, or (B) in transportation,

whether or not performed by the farmer, between the farm and any point within the same State of persons employed or to be employed in the harvesting of fruits or vegetables; or

(17) any driver employed by an employer engaged in the business of operating taxicabs; or

(18), (19) Repealed. Pub. L. 93–259, §§15(c), 16(b), Apr. 8, 1974, 88 Stat. 65.

(20) any employee of a public agency who in any workweek is employed in fire protection activities or any employee of a public agency who in any workweek is employed in law enforcement activities (including security personnel in correctional institutions), if the public agency employs during the workweek less than 5 employees in fire protection or law enforcement activities, as the case may be; or

(21) any employee who is employed in domestic service in a household and who resides in such household; or

(22) Repealed. Pub. L. 95–151, §5, Nov. 1, 1977, 91 Stat. 1249.

(23) Repealed. Pub. L. 93–259, §10(b)(3), Apr. 8, 1974, 88 Stat. 64.

(24) any employee who is employed with his spouse by a nonprofit educational institution to serve as the parents of children—

(A) who are orphans or one of whose natural parents is deceased, or

(B) who are enrolled in such institution and reside in residential facilities of the institution,

while such children are in residence at such institution, if such employee and his spouse reside in such facilities, receive, without cost, board and lodging from such institution, and are together compensated, on a cash basis, at an annual rate of not less than $10,000; or

(25), (26) Repealed. Pub. L. 95–151, §§6(a), 7(a), Nov. 1, 1977, 91 Stat. 1249, 1250.

(27) any employee employed by an establishment which is a motion picture theater; or

(28) any employee employed in planting or tending trees, cruising, surveying, or felling timber, or in preparing or transporting logs or other forestry products to the mill, processing plant, railroad, or other transportation terminal, if the number of employees employed by his employer in such forestry or lumbering operations does not exceed eight;

(29) any employee of an amusement or recreational establishment located in a national park or national forest or on land in the National Wildlife Refuge System if such employee (A) is an employee of a private entity engaged in providing services or facilities in a national park or national forest, or on land in the National Wildlife Refuge System, under a contract with the Secretary of the Interior or the Secretary of Agriculture, and (B) receives compensation for employment in excess of fifty-six hours in any workweek at a rate not less than one and one-half times the regular rate at which he is employed; or

(30) a criminal investigator who is paid availability pay under section 5545a of title 5.

(c) Child labor requirements

(1) Except as provided in paragraph (2) or (4), the provisions of section 212 of this title relating to child labor shall not apply to any employee employed in agriculture outside of school hours for the school district where such employee is living while he is so employed, if such employee—

(A) is less than twelve years of age and (i) is employed by his parent, or by a person standing in the place of his parent, on a farm owned or operated by such parent or person, or (ii) is employed, with the consent of his parent or person standing in the place of his parent, on a farm, none of the employees of which are (because of subsection (a)(6)(A) of this section) required to be paid at the wage rate prescribed by section 206(a)(5)[1] of this title,

(B) is twelve years or thirteen years of age and (i) such employment is with the consent of his parent or person standing in the place of his parent, or (ii) his parent or such person is employed on the same farm as such employee, or

(C) is fourteen years of age or older.

(2) The provisions of section 212 of this title relating to child labor shall apply to an employee below the age of sixteen employed in agriculture in an occupation that the Secretary of Labor finds and declares to be particularly hazardous for the employment of children below the age of sixteen, except where such employee is employed by his parent or by a person standing in the place of his parent on a farm owned or operated by such parent or person.

(3) The provisions of section 212 of this title relating to child labor shall not apply to any child employed as an actor or performer in motion pictures or theatrical productions, or in radio or television productions.

(4)(A) An employer or group of employers may apply to the Secretary for a waiver of the application of section 212 of this title to the employment for not more than eight weeks in any calendar year of individuals who are less than twelve years of age, but not less than ten years of age, as hand harvest laborers in an agricultural operation which has been, and is customarily and generally recognized as being, paid on a piece rate basis in the region in which such individuals would be employed. The Secretary may not grant such a waiver unless he finds, based on objective data submitted by the applicant, that—

(i) the crop to be harvested is one with a particularly short harvesting season and the application of section 212 of this title would cause severe economic disruption in the industry of the employer or group of employers applying for the waiver;

(ii) the employment of the individuals to whom the waiver would apply would not be deleterious to their health or well-being;

(iii) the level and type of pesticides and other chemicals used would not have an adverse effect on the health or well-being of the individuals to whom the waiver would apply;

(iv) individuals age twelve and above are not available for such employment; and

(v) the industry of such employer or group of employers has traditionally and substantially employed individuals under twelve years of

[1] See References in Text note below.

age without displacing substantial job opportunities for individuals over sixteen years of age.

(B) Any waiver granted by the Secretary under subparagraph (A) shall require that—

(i) the individuals employed under such waiver be employed outside of school hours for the school district where they are living while so employed;

(ii) such individuals while so employed commute daily from their permanent residence to the farm on which they are so employed; and

(iii) such individuals be employed under such waiver (I) for not more than eight weeks between June 1 and October 15 of any calendar year, and (II) in accordance with such other terms and conditions as the Secretary shall prescribe for such individuals' protection.

(5)(A) In the administration and enforcement of the child labor provisions of this chapter, employees who are 16 and 17 years of age shall be permitted to load materials into, but not operate or unload materials from, scrap paper balers and paper box compactors—

(i) that are safe for 16- and 17-year-old employees loading the scrap paper balers or paper box compactors; and

(ii) that cannot be operated while being loaded.

(B) For purposes of subparagraph (A), scrap paper balers and paper box compactors shall be considered safe for 16- or 17-year-old employees to load only if—

(i)(I) the scrap paper balers and paper box compactors meet the American National Standards Institute's Standard ANSI Z245.5–1990 for scrap paper balers and Standard ANSI Z245.2–1992 for paper box compactors; or

(II) the scrap paper balers and paper box compactors meet an applicable standard that is adopted by the American National Standards Institute after August 6, 1996, and that is certified by the Secretary to be at least as protective of the safety of minors as the standard described in subclause (I);

(ii) the scrap paper balers and paper box compactors include an on-off switch incorporating a key-lock or other system and the control of the system is maintained in the custody of employees who are 18 years of age or older;

(iii) the on-off switch of the scrap paper balers and paper box compactors is maintained in an off position when the scrap paper balers and paper box compactors are not in operation; and

(iv) the employer of 16- and 17-year-old employees provides notice, and posts a notice, on the scrap paper balers and paper box compactors stating that—

(I) the scrap paper balers and paper box compactors meet the applicable standard described in clause (i);

(II) 16- and 17-year-old employees may only load the scrap paper balers and paper box compactors; and

(III) any employee under the age of 18 may not operate or unload the scrap paper balers and paper box compactors.

The Secretary shall publish in the Federal Register a standard that is adopted by the American National Standards Institute for scrap paper balers or paper box compactors and certified by the Secretary to be protective of the safety of minors under clause (i)(II).

(C)(i) Employers shall prepare and submit to the Secretary reports—

(I) on any injury to an employee under the age of 18 that requires medical treatment (other than first aid) resulting from the employee's contact with a scrap paper baler or paper box compactor during the loading, operation, or unloading of the baler or compactor; and

(II) on any fatality of an employee under the age of 18 resulting from the employee's contact with a scrap paper baler or paper box compactor during the loading, operation, or unloading of the baler or compactor.

(ii) The reports described in clause (i) shall be used by the Secretary to determine whether or not the implementation of subparagraph (A) has had any effect on the safety of children.

(iii) The reports described in clause (i) shall provide—

(I) the name, telephone number, and address of the employer and the address of the place of employment where the incident occurred;

(II) the name, telephone number, and address of the employee who suffered an injury or death as a result of the incident;

(III) the date of the incident;

(IV) a description of the injury and a narrative describing how the incident occurred; and

(V) the name of the manufacturer and the model number of the scrap paper baler or paper box compactor involved in the incident.

(iv) The reports described in clause (i) shall be submitted to the Secretary promptly, but not later than 10 days after the date on which an incident relating to an injury or death occurred.

(v) The Secretary may not rely solely on the reports described in clause (i) as the basis for making a determination that any of the employers described in clause (i) has violated a provision of section 212 of this title relating to oppressive child labor or a regulation or order issued pursuant to section 212 of this title. The Secretary shall, prior to making such a determination, conduct an investigation and inspection in accordance with section 212(b) of this title.

(vi) The reporting requirements of this subparagraph shall expire 2 years after August 6, 1996.

(6) In the administration and enforcement of the child labor provisions of this chapter, employees who are under 17 years of age may not drive automobiles or trucks on public roadways. Employees who are 17 years of age may drive automobiles or trucks on public roadways only if—

(A) such driving is restricted to daylight hours;

(B) the employee holds a State license valid for the type of driving involved in the job performed and has no records of any moving violation at the time of hire;

(C) the employee has successfully completed a State approved driver education course;

(D) the automobile or truck is equipped with a seat belt for the driver and any passengers and the employee's employer has instructed the employee that the seat belts must be used when driving the automobile or truck;

(E) the automobile or truck does not exceed 6,000 pounds of gross vehicle weight;

(F) such driving does not involve—

(i) the towing of vehicles;

(ii) route deliveries or route sales;

(iii) the transportation for hire of property, goods, or passengers;

(iv) urgent, time-sensitive deliveries;

(v) more than two trips away from the primary place of employment in any single day for the purpose of delivering goods of the employee's employer to a customer (other than urgent, time-sensitive deliveries);

(vi) more than two trips away from the primary place of employment in any single day for the purpose of transporting passengers (other than employees of the employer);

(vii) transporting more than three passengers (including employees of the employer); or

(viii) driving beyond a 30 mile radius from the employee's place of employment; and

(G) such driving is only occasional and incidental to the employee's employment.

For purposes of subparagraph (G), the term "occasional and incidental" is no more than one-third of an employee's worktime in any workday and no more than 20 percent of an employee's worktime in any workweek.

(7)(A)(i) Subject to subparagraph (B), in the administration and enforcement of the child labor provisions of this chapter, it shall not be considered oppressive child labor for a new entrant into the workforce to be employed inside or outside places of business where machinery is used to process wood products.

(ii) In this paragraph, the term "new entrant into the workforce" means an individual who—

(I) is under the age of 18 and at least the age of 14, and

(II) by statute or judicial order is exempt from compulsory school attendance beyond the eighth grade.

(B) The employment of a new entrant into the workforce under subparagraph (A) shall be permitted—

(i) if the entrant is supervised by an adult relative of the entrant or is supervised by an adult member of the same religious sect or division as the entrant;

(ii) if the entrant does not operate or assist in the operation of power-driven woodworking machines;

(iii) if the entrant is protected from wood particles or other flying debris within the workplace by a barrier appropriate to the potential hazard of such wood particles or flying debris or by maintaining a sufficient distance from machinery in operation; and

(iv) if the entrant is required to use personal protective equipment to prevent exposure to excessive levels of noise and saw dust.

(d) Delivery of newspapers and wreathmaking

The provisions of sections 206, 207, and 212 of this title shall not apply with respect to any employee engaged in the delivery of newspapers to the consumer or to any homeworker engaged in the making of wreaths composed principally of natural holly, pine, cedar, or other evergreens (including the harvesting of the evergreens or other forest products used in making such wreaths).

(e) Maximum hour requirements and minimum wage employees

The provisions of section 207 of this title shall not apply with respect to employees for whom the Secretary of Labor is authorized to establish minimum wage rates as provided in section 206(a)(3)[1] of this title, except with respect to employees for whom such rates are in effect; and with respect to such employees the Secretary may make rules and regulations providing reasonable limitations and allowing reasonable variations, tolerances, and exemptions to and from any or all of the provisions of section 207 of this title if he shall find, after a public hearing on the matter, and taking into account the factors set forth in section 206(a)(3)[1] of this title, that economic conditions warrant such action.

(f) Employment in foreign countries and certain United States territories

The provisions of sections 206, 207, 211, and 212 of this title shall not apply with respect to any employee whose services during the workweek are performed in a workplace within a foreign country or within territory under the jurisdiction of the United States other than the following: a State of the United States; the District of Columbia; Puerto Rico; the Virgin Islands; outer Continental Shelf lands defined in the Outer Continental Shelf Lands Act (ch. 345, 67 Stat. 462) [43 U.S.C. 1331 et seq.]; American Samoa; Guam; Wake Island; Eniwetok Atoll; Kwajalein Atoll; and Johnston Island.

(g) Certain employment in retail or service establishments, agriculture

The exemption from section 206 of this title provided by paragraph (6) of subsection (a) of this section shall not apply with respect to any employee employed by an establishment (1) which controls, is controlled by, or is under common control with, another establishment the activities of which are not related for a common business purpose to, but materially support the activities of the establishment employing such employee; and (2) whose annual gross volume of sales made or business done, when combined with the annual gross volume of sales made or business done by each establishment which controls, is controlled by, or is under common control with, the establishment employing such employee, exceeds $10,000,000 (exclusive of excise taxes at the retail level which are separately stated).

(h) Maximum hour requirement: fourteen workweek limitation

The provisions of section 207 of this title shall not apply for a period or periods of not more than fourteen workweeks in the aggregate in any calendar year to any employee who—

(1) is employed by such employer—

(A) exclusively to provide services necessary and incidental to the ginning of cotton in an establishment primarily engaged in the ginning of cotton;

(B) exclusively to provide services necessary and incidental to the receiving, handling, and storing of raw cotton and the compressing of raw cotton when performed at a cotton warehouse or compress-warehouse facility, other than one operated in conjunction with a cotton mill, primarily engaged in storing and compressing;

(C) exclusively to provide services necessary and incidental to the receiving, handling, storing, and processing of cottonseed in an establishment primarily engaged in the receiving, handling, storing, and processing of cottonseed; or

(D) exclusively to provide services necessary and incidental to the processing of sugar cane or sugar beets in an establishment primarily engaged in the processing of sugar cane or sugar beets; and

(2) receives for—

(A) such employment by such employer which is in excess of ten hours in any workday, and

(B) such employment by such employer which is in excess of forty-eight hours in any workweek,

compensation at a rate not less than one and one-half times the regular rate at which he is employed.

Any employer who receives an exemption under this subsection shall not be eligible for any other exemption under this section or section 207 of this title.

(i) Cotton ginning

The provisions of section 207 of this title shall not apply for a period or periods of not more than fourteen workweeks in the aggregate in any period of fifty-two consecutive weeks to any employee who—

(1) is engaged in the ginning of cotton for market in any place of employment located in a county where cotton is grown in commercial quantities; and

(2) receives for any such employment during such workweeks—

(A) in excess of ten hours in any workday, and

(B) in excess of forty-eight hours in any workweek,

compensation at a rate not less than one and one-half times the regular rate at which he is employed. No week included in any fifty-two week period for purposes of the preceding sentence may be included for such purposes in any other fifty-two week period.

(j) Processing of sugar beets, sugar beet molasses, or sugar cane

The provisions of section 207 of this title shall not apply for a period or periods of not more than fourteen workweeks in the aggregate in any period of fifty-two consecutive weeks to any employee who—

(1) is engaged in the processing of sugar beets, sugar beet molasses, or sugar cane into sugar (other than refined sugar) or syrup; and

(2) receives for any such employment during such workweeks—

(A) in excess of ten hours in any workday, and

(B) in excess of forty-eight hours in any workweek,

compensation at a rate not less than one and one-half times the regular rate at which he is employed. No week included in any fifty-two week period for purposes of the preceding sentence may be included for such purposes in any other fifty-two week period.

(June 25, 1938, ch. 676, §13, 52 Stat. 1067; Aug. 9, 1939, ch. 605, 53 Stat. 1266; Oct. 26, 1949, ch. 736, §11, 63 Stat. 917; Aug. 8, 1956, ch. 1035, §3, 70 Stat. 1118; Pub. L. 85–231, §1(1), Aug. 30, 1957, 71 Stat. 514; Pub. L. 86–624, §21(b), July 12, 1960, 74 Stat. 417; Pub. L. 87–30, §§9, 10, May 5, 1961, 75 Stat. 71, 74; Pub. L. 89–601, title II, §§201–204(a), (b), 205–212(a), 213, 214, 215(b), (c), Sept. 23, 1966, 80 Stat. 833–838; Pub. L. 89–670, §8(e), Oct. 15, 1966, 80 Stat. 943; 1970 Reorg. Plan No. 2, §102, eff. July 1, 1970, 35 F.R. 7959, 84 Stat. 2085; Pub. L. 92–318, title IX, §906(b)(1), June 23, 1972, 86 Stat. 375; Pub. L. 93–259, §§6(c)(2), 7(b)(3), (4), 8, 9(b), 10, 11, 12(a), 13(a)–(d), 14–18, 20(a)–(c), 21(b), 22, 23, 25(b), Apr. 8, 1974, 88 Stat. 61–69, 72; Pub. L. 95–151, §§4–8, 9(d), 11, 14, Nov. 1, 1977, 91 Stat. 1249, 1250–1252; Pub. L. 96–70, title I, §1225(a), Sept. 27, 1979, 93 Stat. 468; Pub. L. 101–157, §3(c), Nov. 17, 1989, 103 Stat. 939; Pub. L. 103–329, title VI, §633(d), Sept. 30, 1994, 108 Stat. 2428; Pub. L. 104–88, title III, §340, Dec. 29, 1995, 109 Stat. 955; Pub. L. 104–174, §1, Aug. 6, 1996, 110 Stat. 1553; Pub. L. 104–188, [title II], §2105(a), Aug. 20, 1996, 110 Stat. 1929; Pub. L. 105–78, title I, §105, Nov. 13, 1997, 111 Stat. 1477; Pub. L. 105–334, §2(a), Oct. 31, 1998, 112 Stat. 3137; Pub. L. 108–199, div. E, title I, §108, Jan. 23, 2004, 118 Stat. 236.)

REFERENCES IN TEXT

The Railway Labor Act, referred to in subsec. (b)(3), is act May 20, 1926, ch. 347, 44 Stat. 577, as amended. Title II of the Railway Labor Act was added by act Apr. 10, 1936, ch. 166, 49 Stat. 1189, and is classified generally to subchapter II (§181 et seq.) of Title 45, Railroads. For complete classification of this Act to the Code see section 151 of Title 45 and Tables.

Section 206(a)(5) of this title, referred to in subsec. (c)(1)(A), was redesignated section 206(a)(4) of this title by Pub. L. 110–28, title VIII, §8103(c)(1)(B), May 25, 2007, 121 Stat. 189.

Section 206(a)(3) of this title, referred to in subsec. (e), was repealed and section 206(a)(4) of this title was redesignated section 206(a)(3) by Pub. L. 110–28, title VIII, §8103(c)(1)(B), May 25, 2007, 121 Stat. 189.

The Outer Continental Shelf Lands Act, referred to in subsec. (f), is act Aug. 7, 1953, ch. 345, 67 Stat. 462, as amended, which is classified generally to subchapter III (§1331 et seq.) of chapter 29 of Title 43, Public Lands. For complete classification of this Act to the Code, see Short Title note set out under section 1331 of Title 43 and Tables.

CODIFICATION

In subsec. (a)(1), "subchapter II of chapter 5 of title 5" substituted for "the Administrative Procedure Act" on authority of Pub. L. 89–554, §7(b), Sept. 6, 1966, 80 Stat. 631, the first section of which enacted Title 5, Government Organization and Employees.

In subsec. (b)(1), "section 31502 of title 49" substituted for "section 3102 of title 49" on authority of Pub. L. 103–272, §§1(c), (e), 6(b), July 5, 1994, 108 Stat. 745, 862, 1029, 1378. Previously, "section 3102 of title 49" substituted for "section 204 of the Motor Carrier Act, 1935 [49 U.S.C. 304]", on authority of Pub. L. 97–449, §6(b),

Jan. 12, 1983, 96 Stat. 2443, the first section of which enacted subtitle I (§101 et seq.) and chapter 31 (§3101 et seq.) of subtitle II of Title 49, Transportation.

AMENDMENTS

2004—Subsec. (c)(7). Pub. L. 108–199 added par. (7).

1998—Subsec. (c)(6). Pub. L. 105–334 added par. (6).

1997—Subsec. (b)(12). Pub. L. 105–78 substituted "water, at least 90 percent of which was ultimately delivered for agricultural purposes during the preceding calendar year" for "water for agricultural purposes".

1996—Subsec. (a)(17). Pub. L. 104–188 added par. (17).

Subsec. (c)(5). Pub. L. 104–174 added par. (5).

1995—Subsec. (b)(2). Pub. L. 104–88 substituted "rail carrier subject to part A of subtitle IV of title 49" for "common carrier by rail and subject to the provisions of part I of the Interstate Commerce Act".

1994—Subsec. (a)(16). Pub. L. 103–329, §633(d)(1), added par. (16).

Subsec. (b)(30). Pub. L. 103–329, §633(d)(2), added par. (30).

1989—Subsec. (a)(2). Pub. L. 101–157, §3(c)(1), struck out par. (2) which related to employees employed by a retail or service establishment.

Subsec. (a)(4). Pub. L. 101–157, §3(c)(1), struck out par. (4) which related to employees employed by an establishment which qualified as an exempt retail establishment under clause (2) of this subsection and was recognized as a retail establishment in the particular industry notwithstanding that such establishment made or processed at the retail establishment the goods that it sold.

Subsec. (g). Pub. L. 101–157, §3(c)(2), substituted "provided by paragraph (6) of subsection (a) of this section" for "provided by paragraphs (2) and (6) of subsection (a) of this section" and struck out before period at end ", except that the exemption from section 206 of this title provided by paragraph (2) of subsection (a) of this section shall apply with respect to any establishment described in this subsection which has an annual dollar volume of sales which would permit it to qualify for the exemption provided in paragraph (2) of subsection (a) of this section if it were in an enterprise described in section 203(s) of this title".

1979—Subsec. (f). Pub. L. 96–70 struck out "; and the Canal Zone" after "Johnston Island".

1977—Subsec. (a)(2). Pub. L. 95–151, §9(d), substituted "section 203(s)(5)" for "section 203(s)(4)".

Subsec. (a)(3). Pub. L. 95–151, §§4(a), 11, inserted "organized camp, or religious or non-profit educational conference center," after "recreational establishment,", and inserted provisions relating to applicability of exemption from sections 206 and 207 of this title authorized by this paragraph for private employees in national parks, etc.

Subsec. (b)(8). Pub. L. 95–151, §14(a), substituted "forty-four" for "forty-six".

Pub. L. 95–151, §14(b), struck out par. (8) which related to exemption of hotel, motel, and restaurant employees, effective Jan. 1, 1979.

Subsec. (b)(22). Pub. L. 95–151, §5, struck out par. (22) which related to exemption of shade-grown tobacco employees.

Subsec. (b)(25). Pub. L. 95–151, §6(a), struck out par. (25) which related to exemption of cotton ginning employees. See subsec. (i) of this section.

Subsec. (b)(26). Pub. L. 95–151, §7(a), struck out par. (26) which related to exemption of sugar employees. See subsec. (j) of this section.

Subsec. (b)(29). Pub. L. 95–151, §4(b), added par. (29).

Subsec. (c). Pub. L. 95–151, §8, in par. (1) inserted reference to par. (4), and added par. (4).

Subsec. (i). Pub. L. 95–151, §6(b), added subsec. (i).

Subsec. (j). Pub. L. 95–151, §7(b), added subsec. (j).

1974—Subsec. (a)(2). Pub. L. 93–259, §8(a), substituted "$225,000" for "$250,000" effective Jan. 1, 1975. Pub. L. 93–259, §8(b), substituted "$200,000" for "$225,000" effective Jan. 1, 1976. Pub. L. 93–259, §8(c), struck out "or such establishment has an annual dollar volume of sales which is less than $200,000 (exclusive of excise taxes at the retail level which are separately stated)" after "section 203(s) of this title" effective Jan. 1, 1977.

Subsec. (a)(9). Pub. L. 93–259, §23(a)(1), repealed exemption provision respecting any employee employed by an establishment which is a motion picture theater. See subsec. (b)(27) of this section.

Subsec. (a)(11). Pub. L. 93–259, §10(a), repealed exemption provision respecting any employee or proprietor in a retail or service establishment which qualifies as an exempt retail or service establishment under former par. (2) of subsec. (a) with respect to whom provisions of sections 206 and 207 of this title would not otherwise apply, engaged in handling telegraphic messages for public under an agency or contract arrangement with a telegraph company where telegraph message revenue of such agency does not exceed $500 a month.

Subsec. (a)(13). Pub. L. 93–259, §23(b)(1), repealed exemption provision respecting any employee employed in planting or tending trees, cruising, surveying, or felling timber, or in preparing or transporting logs or other forestry products to mill, processing plant, railroad, or other transportation terminal, if number of employees employed by his employer in such forestry or lumbering operations does not exceed eight. See subsec. (b)(28) of this section.

Subsec. (a)(14). Pub. L. 93–259, §9(b)(1), repealed exemption provision respecting any agricultural employee employed in the growing and harvesting of shade-grown tobacco who is engaged in processing (including, but not limited to, drying, curing, fermenting, bulking, rebulking, sorting, grading, aging, and baling) of such tobacco, prior to the stemming process, for use as cigar wrapper tobacco. See subsec. (b)(22) of this section.

Subsec. (a)(15). Pub. L. 93–259, §7(b)(3), added par. (15).

Subsec. (b)(2). Pub. L. 93–259, §23(c), amended par. (2) (insofar as it relates to pipeline employees), inserting "engaged in the operation of a common carrier by rail and" after "employer".

Subsec. (b)(4). Pub. L. 93–259, §11(a), effective May 1, 1974, inserted "who is" after "employee" and ", and who receives compensation for employment in excess of forty-eight hours in any workweek at a rate not less than one and one-half times the regular rate at which he is employed" before the semi-colon. Pub. L. 93–259, §11(b), substituted "forty-four hours" for "forty-eight hours" effective one year after May 1, 1974. Pub. L. 93–259, §11(c), repealed subsec. (b)(4) effective two years after May 1, 1974.

Subsec. (b)(7). Pub. L. 93–259, §21(b)(1), substituted "(regardless of whether or not such railway or carrier is public or private or operated for profit or not for profit), if such employee receives compensation for employment in excess of forty-eight hours in any workweek at a rate not less than one and one-half times the regular rate at which he is employed" for ", if the rates and services of such railway or carrier are subject to regulation by a State or local agency" effective May 1, 1974. Pub. L. 93–259, §21(b)(2), substituted "forty-four hours" for "forty-eight hours" effective one year after May 1, 1974. Pub. L. 93–259, §21(b)(3) repealed subsec. (b)(7) effective two years after May 1, 1974.

Subsec. (b)(8). Pub. L. 93–259, §§12(a), 13(a), effective May 1, 1974, insofar as relating to nursing home employees, struck out exemption provision respecting any employee who is employed by an establishment which is an institution (other than a hospital) primarily engaged in the care of the sick, the aged, or the mentally ill or defective who reside on the premises, and receives compensation for employment in excess of forty-eight hours in any workweek at a rate not less than one and one-half times the regular rate at which he is employed, and insofar as relating to a hotel, motel, and restaurant employees, substituted "(A) any employee (other than an employee of a hotel or motel who performs maid or custodial services) who is" for "any employee", inserted before the semicolon "and who receives compensation for employment in excess of forty-eight hours in any workweek at a rate not less than one and one-half times the regular rate at which he is employed", and added subpar. (B). Pub. L. 93-259, §13(b), effective one year after May 1, 1974, substituted "forty-six hours" for "forty-eight hours" in subparas. (A) and (B). Pub. L. 93-259, §13(c), effective two years after May 1, 1974, substituted "forty-four hours" for "forty-six hours" in subpar. (B). Pub. L. 93-259, §13(d), repealed subsec. (b)(8)(B) and eliminated the designation (A), effective three years after May 1, 1974.

Subsec. (b)(10). Pub. L. 93-259, §14, incorporated existing paragraph in provisions designated as subpar. (A), struck out from the list references to trailers and aircraft, inserted reference to implements, and added subpar. (B) incorporating references to trailers and aircraft.

Subsec. (b)(15). Pub. L. 93-259, §20(a), struck out exemption provision respecting any employee engaged in ginning of cotton for market, in any place of employment located in a county where cotton is grown in commercial quantities or in the processing of sugar beets, sugar-beet molasses, and sugarcane into sugar. See subsec. (b)(25) and (26) of this section.

Subsec. (b)(18). Pub. L. 93-259, §15(a), effective May 1, 1974, inserted "and who receives compensation for employment in excess of forty-eight hours in any workweek at a rate not less than one and one-half times the regular rate at which he is employed." Pub. L. 93-259, §15(b), effective one year after May 1, 1974, substituted "forty-four hours" for "forty-eight hours." Pub. L. 93-259, §15(c), repealed par. (18) effective two years after May 1, 1974.

Subsec. (b)(19). Pub. L. 93-259, §16(a), effective one year after May 1, 1974, substituted "forty-four hours" for "forty-eight hours". Pub. L. 93-259, §16(b), repealed par. (19), effective two years after May 1, 1974.

Subsec. (b)(20). Pub. L. 93-259, §6(c)(2)(A), added par. (20) effective May 1, 1974. Pub. L. 93-259, §6(c)(2)(B), effective Jan. 1, 1975, made maximum hours provisions inapplicable during any workweek to any employee of a public agency employing during the workweek less than 5 employees.

Subsec. (b)(21). Pub. L. 93-259, §7(b)(4), added par. (21).

Subsec. (b)(22). Pub. L. 93-259, §9(b)(2), added par. (22).

Subsec. (b)(23). Pub. L. 93-259, §10(b)(1), added par. (23), effective May 1, 1974. Pub. L. 93-259, §10(b)(2), substituted "forty-four hours" for "forty-eight hours" effective one year after May 1, 1974. Pub. L. 93-259, §10(b)(3), repealed par. (23) effective two years after May 1, 1974.

Subsec. (b)(24). Pub. L. 93-259, §17, added par. (24).

Subsec. (b)(25). Pub. L. 93-259, §20(b)(1), added par. (25) effective May 1, 1974. Pub. L. 93-259, §20(b)(2), effective Jan. 1, 1975, substituted "sixty-six" for "seventy-two" in subpar. (A), "sixty" for "sixty-four" in subpar. (B), and "forty-six hours in any workweek for not more than two workweeks in that year, and" for "forty-eight hours in any other workweek in that year," in subpar. (D), and added subpar. (E). Pub. L. 93-259, §20(b)(3), effective Jan. 1, 1976, substituted "sixty" for "sixty-six", "fifty-six" for "sixty", "forty-eight" for "fifty", "forty-four" for "forty-six", and "forty" for "forty-four".

Subsec. (b)(26). Pub. L. 93-259, §20(c)(1), added par. (26) effective May 1, 1974. Pub. L. 93-259, §20(c)(2), effective Jan. 1, 1975, substituted "sixty-six" for "seventy-two" in subpar. (A), "sixty" for "sixty-four" in subpar. (B), and "forty-six hours in any workweek for not more than two workweeks in that year, and" for "forty-eight hours in any other workweek in that year," in subpar. (D), and added subpar. (E). Pub. L. 93-259, §20(c)(3), effective Jan. 1, 1976, substituted "sixty" for "sixty-six", "fifty-six" for "sixty", "forty-eight" for "fifty", "forty-four" for "forty-six", and "forty" for "forty-four".

Subsec. (b)(27). Pub. L. 93-259, §23(a)(2), added par. (27).

Subsec. (b)(28). Pub. L. 93-259, §23(b)(2), added par. (28).

Subsec. (c)(1). Pub. L. 93-259, §25(b), amended par. (1) generally, striking out "with respect" after "shall not apply", inserting ", if such employee—", and adding subpars. (A) to (C).

Subsec. (g). Pub. L. 93-259, §18, added subsec. (g).

Subsec. (h). Pub. L. 93-259, §22, added subsec. (h).

1972—Subsec. (a). Pub. L. 92-318 inserted "(except subsection (d) in the case of paragraph (1) of this subsection)" after introductory text "sections 206".

1966—Subsec. (a)(1). Pub. L. 89-601, §214, inserted "(including any employee employed in the capacity of academic administrative personnel or teacher in elementary or secondary schools)" after "professional capacity".

Subsec. (a)(2). Pub. L. 89-601, §201(a), revised the retail or service establishment exemption so as to exempt employees of a retail or service establishment (other than an establishment or employee engaged in laundering or drycleaning or an establishment engaged in the operation of a hospital, school, or institution specifically included in the definition of the term "enterprise engaged in commerce or in the production of goods for commerce") if more than 50 per centum of the establishment's annual dollar volume of sales of goods or services is made within the state in which the establishment is located and the establishment is not an enterprise described in section 203(s) of this title or the establishment has an annual dollar volume of sales which is less than $250,000.

Subsec. (a)(3). Pub. L. 89-601, §§201(b)(2), 202, repealed par. (3) relating to employees of laundry, cleaning, and fabric or clothing repair establishments doing more than 50 per centum of their annual dollar volume of business within the state in which the establishment is located and enacted a new par. (3) relating to employees of amusement or recreational establishments which do not operate for more than seven months in any calendar year or which had receipts over a six-month period which were not more than 33⅓ per centum of its average receipts for the other six months of such year.

Subsec. (a)(6). Pub. L. 89-601, §203(a), limited the provisions exempting agricultural employees from application of sections 206 and 207 of this title by narrowing the class of exempted agricultural employees to include only an employee employed by an employer who did not, during any calendar quarter during the preceding calendar year, use more than 500 man-days of agricultural labor, an employee who is the spouse, parent, child, or other member of his employer's immediate family, certain hand harvest laborers, or an employee principally engaged in the range production of livestock. See subsec. (b)(12) of this section.

Subsec. (a)(7). Pub. L. 89-601, §215(c), extended coverage to include employees exempted by a certificate of the Secretary.

Subsec. (a)(8). Pub. L. 89-601, §205, substituted "where published" for "where printed and published".

Subsec. (a)(9). Pub. L. 89-601, §§206(a), 207, repealed par. (9) relating to employees of street, suburban, or interurban electric railways, or local trolleys or motor bus carriers not in a section 203(s) enterprise and enacted a new par. (9) relating to employees employed by motion picture theaters. See subsec. (b)(7) of this section.

Subsec. (a)(10). Pub. L. 89-601, §§204(a), 215(b)(1), repealed par. (10) relating to employees engaged in handling and processing of agricultural, horticultural, and dairy products and redesignated par. (11) as (10). See section 207(d) of this title.

Subsec. (a)(11). Pub. L. 89-601, §215(b)(1), redesignated par. (13) as (11). Former par. (11) redesignated (10).

Subsec. (a)(12). Pub. L. 89-601, §§206(b)(1), 215(b)(1), repealed par. (12) relating to employees of employers engaged in the business of operating taxicabs and redesignated par. (14) as (12). See subsec. (b)(17) of this section.

Subsec. (a)(13). Pub. L. 89-601, §§208, 215(b)(1), redesignated par. (15) as (13) and substituted "eight" for "twelve". Former par. (13) redesignated (11).

Subsec. (a)(14). Pub. L. 89-601, §215(b), redesignated par. (21) as (14) and substituted a period for "; or" at end. Former par. (14) redesignated (12).

Subsec. (a)(15). Pub. L. 89-601, §215(b)(1), redesignated par. (15) as (13).

Subsec. (a)(16). Pub. L. 89-601, §203(b), repealed par. (16) relating to agricultural employees employed in livestock auctions. See subsec. (b)(13) of this section.

Subsec. (a)(17). Pub. L. 89–601, §204(a), repealed par. (17) relating to country elevator operators. See subsec. (b)(14) of this section.

Subsec. (a)(18). Pub. L. 89–601, §204(a), repealed par. (18) relating to cotton ginning employees. See subsec. (b)(15) of this section.

Subsec. (a)(19). Pub. L. 89–601, §209(a), repealed par. (19) relating to employees of retail and service establishments that are primarily engaged in the business of selling automobiles, trucks, or farm implements. See subsec. (b)(10) of this section.

Subsec. (a)(20). Pub. L. 89–601, §210(a), repealed par. (20) relating to employees of food retail or service establishments. See subsec. (b)(18) of this section.

Subsec. (a)(21). Pub. L. 89–601, §215(b)(1), redesignated par. (21) as (14).

Subsec. (a)(22). Pub. L. 89–601, §204(a), repealed par. (22) relating to fruit and vegetable transportation employees. See subsec. (b)(16) of this section.

Subsec. (b)(1). Pub. L. 89–670 substituted "Secretary of Transportation" for "Interstate Commerce Commission".

Subsec. (b)(7). Pub. L. 89–601, §206(c), narrowed the scope of the exemption from any employee of the covered transportation companies to drivers, operators, and conductors only and narrowed the range of covered transportation companies from any street, suburban, or interurban electric railway, or local trolley or motorbus carrier to only those of such named enterprises as have their rates and service subject to regulation by a state or local agency.

Subsec. (b)(8). Pub. L. 89–601, §§201(b)(1), 211, repealed par. (8) which named employees of gasoline service stations as a group to which section 207 of this title shall not apply and enacted a new par. (8) providing that section 207 of this title shall not apply with respect to hotel, motel, or restaurant employees and employees who receive compensation for employment in excess 48 hours in any workweek at a rate not less than one and one-half times the regular rate at which he is employed and who is employed by an institution other than a hospital primarily engaged in the care of the sick, the aged, or the mentally ill or defective residing on the premises.

Subsec. (b)(10). Pub. L. 89–601, §§209(b), 212(a), repealed par. (10) which granted an unlimited overtime exemption relating to petroleum distribution employees and enacted a new par. (10) relating to salesmen, partsmen, or mechanics primarily engaged in selling or servicing automobiles, trailers, trucks, farm implements, or aircraft if employed by a nonmanufacturing establishment primarily engaged in the business of selling such vehicles to ultimate purchasers. See subsec. (b)(3) of this section.

Subsec. (b)(12) to (19). Pub. L. 89–601, §§203(c)(B), 204(b), 206(b)(2), 210(b), added pars. (12) to (19).

Subsec. (c). Pub. L. 89–601, §203(d), inserted provision making section 212 of this title relating to child labor applicable to an employee below the age of sixteen employed in agriculture in an occupation that the Secretary of Labor finds and declares to be particularly hazardous for the employment of children below the age of sixteen, except where such employee is employed by his parent or by a person standing in the place of his parent on a farm owned or operated by such parent or person.

Subsec. (f). Pub. L. 89–601, §213, inserted reference to Eniwetok Atoll, Kwajalein Atoll, and Johnston Island.

1961—Subsec. (a)(1). Pub. L. 87–30, §9, substituted "any employee employed in a bona fide executive, administrative, or professional capacity, or in the capacity of outside salesman (as such terms are defined and delimited from time to time by regulations of the Secretary, subject to, the provisions of the Administrative Procedure Act" and exception provision for "any employee employed in a bona fide executive, administrative, professional, or local retailing capacity, or in the capacity of outside salesman (as such terms are defined and delimited by regulations of the Administrator)".

Subsec. (a)(2). Pub. L. 87–30, §9, inserted conditional provision, including subclauses (i) to (iv).

Subsec. (a)(5). Pub. L. 87–30, §9, inserted "propagating" and "or in the first processing, canning or packing such marine products at sea as an incident to, or in conjunction with, such fishing operations" after "taking" and "life", respectively, and substituted "loading and unloading when performed by any such employee" for "including employment in the loading, unloading, or packing of such products for shipment or in propagating, processing (other than canning), marketing, freezing, curing, storing, or distributing the above products or byproducts thereof". See subsec. (b)(4) of this section.

Subsec. (a)(7). Pub. L. 87–30, §9, substituted "Secretary" for "Administrator".

Subsec. (a)(9). Pub. L. 87–30, §9, substituted "not in an enterprise described in section 203(s)(2) of this title" for "not included in other exemptions contained in this section.".

Subsec. (a)(10). Pub. L. 87–30, §9, substituted "Secretary" for "Administrator" and struck out "ginning" after "storing".

Subsec. (a)(11). Pub. L. 87–30, §9, substituted "by an independently owned public telephone company" for "in a public telephone exchange".

Subsec. (a)(13). Pub. L. 87–30, §9, substituted "which qualifies as an exempt retail or service establishment under clause (2) of this subsection" for "as defined in clause (2) of this subsection".

Subsec. (a)(14). Pub. L. 87–30, §9, inserted "on a vessel other than an American vessel".

Subsec. (a)(16) to (22). Pub. L. 87–30, §9, added pars. (16) to (22).

Subsec. (b)(4). Pub. L. 87–30, §9, extended exemption to any employee in the processing, marketing, freezing, curing, storing, packing for shipment, or distributing of aquatic forms of life, formerly contained in subsec. (a)(5) of this section.

Subsec. (b)(6) to (11). Pub. L. 87–30, §9, added pars. (6) to (11).

Subsec. (d). Pub. L. 87–30, §10, extended the nonapplicability of sections 206, 207, and 212 of this title to any homeworker engaged in the making of evergreen wreaths.

1960—Subsec. (f). Pub. L. 86–624 struck out "Alaska; Hawaii;" before "Puerto Rico".

1957—Subsec. (f). Pub. L. 85–231 added subsec. (f).

1956—Subsec. (e). Act Aug. 8, 1956, added subsec. (b).

1949—Subsec. (a)(2). Act Oct. 26, 1949, clarified exemption by defining term "retail or service establishment" and stated conditions under which exemption shall apply.

Subsec. (a)(3). Act Oct. 26, 1949, redesignated par. (3) as (14) and added par. (3) providing a limited exemption to employees of laundries and establishments engaged in laundering, cleaning, or repairing clothing of fabrics.

Subsec. (a)(4). Act Oct. 26, 1949, redesignated par. (4) as subsec. (b)(3) and added par. (4) providing limited exemption to employees of retail establishments making or processing goods.

Subsec. (a)(5). Act Oct. 26, 1949, struck out canning of fish, shellfish, etc. See subsec. (b)(4).

Subsec. (a)(6). Act Oct. 26, 1949, added irrigation workers to the exemption.

Subsec. (a)(8). Act Oct. 26, 1949, extended exemption to employees of newspapers published daily, increased circulation limitation from 3,000 to 4,000, and increased circulation area to include counties contiguous to county of publication.

Subsec. (a)(10). Act Oct. 26, 1949, struck out "to" before "any individual".

Subsec. (a)(11). Act Oct. 26, 1949, increased number of stations from, less than 500, to, not more than 750.

Subsec. (a)(12), (13). Act Oct. 26, 1949, added pars. (12) and (13).

Subsec. (a)(14). Act Oct. 26, 1949, redesignated par. (3) as (14).

Subsec. (a)(15). Act Oct. 26, 1949, added par. (15).

Subsec. (b)(3) to (5). Act Oct. 26, 1949, added pars. (3) to (5).

Subsec. (c). Act Oct. 26, 1949, substituted "outside of school hours for the school district where such employee is living while he is so employed" for prior provision relating to school attendance following "in agricultural", and added radio or television productions to the exemption.

Subsec. (d). Act Oct. 26, 1949, added par. (d).

1939—Subsec. (a)(11). Act Aug. 9, 1939, added par. (11).

EFFECTIVE DATE OF 1998 AMENDMENT

Pub. L. 105–334, §2(b), Oct. 31, 1998, 112 Stat. 3138, provided that:

"(1) IN GENERAL.—This Act [amending this section and enacting provisions set out as a note under section 201 of this title] shall become effective on the date of the enactment of this Act [Oct. 31, 1998].

"(2) EXCEPTION.—The amendment made by subsection (a) [amending this section] defining the term 'occasional and incidental' shall also apply to any case, action, citation, or appeal pending on the date of the enactment of this Act unless such case, action, citation, or appeal involves property damage or personal injury."

EFFECTIVE DATE OF 1995 AMENDMENT

Amendment by Pub. L. 104–88 effective Jan. 1, 1996, see section 2 of Pub. L. 104–88, set out as an Effective Date note under section 701 of Title 49, Transportation.

EFFECTIVE DATE OF 1994 AMENDMENT

Amendment by Pub. L. 103–329 effective on first day of first applicable pay period beginning on or after 30th day following Sept. 30, 1994, with exceptions relating to criminal investigators employed in Offices of Inspectors General, see section 633(e) of Pub. L. 103–329, set out as an Effective Date note under section 5545a of Title 5, Government Organization and Employees.

EFFECTIVE DATE OF 1989 AMENDMENT

Amendment by Pub. L. 101–157 effective Apr. 1, 1990, see section 3(e) of Pub. L. 101–157, set out as a note under section 203 of this title.

EFFECTIVE DATE OF 1979 AMENDMENT

Amendment by Pub. L. 96–70 effective Oct. 1, 1979, see section 3304 of Pub. L. 96–70, set out as an Effective Date note under section 3601 of Title 22, Foreign Relations and Intercourse.

EFFECTIVE DATE OF 1977 AMENDMENT

Section 14(a), (b) of Pub. L. 95–151 provided that the amendments by that section are effective Jan. 1, 1978, and Jan. 1, 1979, respectively.

Amendment by sections 4 to 7 of Pub. L. 95–151 effective Jan. 1, 1978, see section 15(a) of Pub. L. 95–151, set out as a note under section 203 of this title.

Amendment by sections 8, 9(d), and 11 of Pub. L. 95–151 effective on Nov. 1, 1977, see section 15(b) of Pub. L. 95–151, set out as a note under section 203 of this title.

EFFECTIVE DATE OF 1974 AMENDMENT

Section 6(c)(2)(A), (B) of Pub. L. 93–259 provided that the amendments made by that section are effective May 1, 1974, and Jan. 1, 1975, respectively.

Section 8(a)–(c) of Pub. L. 93–259 provided that the amendments made by that section are effective Jan. 1, 1975, 1976, and 1977, respectively.

Section 10(b)(2), (3) of Pub. L. 93–259 provided that the amendment and repeal made by that section are effective one year and two years after May 1, 1974, respectively.

Section 11(b), (c) of Pub. L. 93–259 provided that the amendment and repeal made by that section are effective one year and two years after May 1, 1974, respectively.

Section 13(b)–(d) of Pub. L. 93–259 provided that the amendments made by that section are effective one year, two years, and three years after May 1, 1974, respectively.

Section 15(b), (c) of Pub. L. 93–259 provided that the amendment and repeal made by that section are effective one year and two years after May 1, 1974, respectively.

Section 16(a), (b) of Pub. L. 93–259 provided that the amendment and repeal made by that section are effective one year and two years after May 1, 1974, respectively.

Section 20(b)(2), (3) of Pub. L. 93–259 provided that the amendments made by that section are effective Jan. 1, 1975, and 1976, respectively.

Section 20(c)(2), (3) of Pub. L. 93–259 provided that the amendments made by that section are effective Jan. 1, 1975, and 1976, respectively.

Section 21(b)(2), (3) of Pub. L. 93–259 provided that the amendment and repeal made by that section are effective one year and two years after May 1, 1974, respectively.

Amendment by sections 7(b)(3), (4), 9(b), 10(a), (b)(1), 11(a), 12(a), 13(a), 14, 15(a), 17, 18, 20(a), (b)(1), (c)(1), 21(b)(1), 22, 23, and 25(b) of Pub. L. 93–259 effective May 1, 1974, see section 29(a) of Pub. L. 93–259, set out as a note under section 202 of this title.

EFFECTIVE DATE OF 1966 AMENDMENTS

Amendment by Pub. L. 89–670 effective Apr. 1, 1967, as prescribed by President and published in Federal Register, see section 16(a), formerly §15(a), of Pub. L. 89–670 and Ex. Ord. No. 11340, Mar. 30, 1967, 32 F.R. 5453.

Amendment by Pub. L. 89–601 effective Feb. 1, 1967, except as otherwise provided, see section 602 of Pub. L. 89–601, set out as a note under section 203 of this title.

EFFECTIVE DATE OF 1961 AMENDMENT

Amendment by Pub. L. 87–30 effective upon expiration of one hundred and twenty days after May 5, 1961, except as otherwise provided, see section 14 of Pub. L. 87–30, set out as a note under section 203 of this title.

EFFECTIVE DATE OF 1957 AMENDMENT

Pub. L. 85–231, §2, provided that: "The amendments made by this Act [amending this section and sections 216 and 217 of this title] shall take effect upon the expiration of ninety days from the date of its enactment [Aug. 30, 1957]."

EFFECTIVE DATE OF 1949 AMENDMENT

Amendment by act Oct. 26, 1949, effective ninety days after Oct. 26, 1949, see section 16(a) of act Oct. 26, 1949, set out as a note under section 202 of this title.

TRANSFER OF FUNCTIONS

Functions vested by law (including reorganization plans) in Bureau of the Budget or Director of Bureau of the Budget transferred to President of the United States by section 101 of Reorg. Plan No. 2 of 1970, eff. July 1, 1970, 35 F.R. 7959, 84 Stat. 2085, set out in the Appendix to Title 5, Government Organization and Employees. Section 102 of Reorg. Plan No. 2 of 1970 redesignated Bureau of the Budget as Office of Management and Budget.

For transfer of functions of other officers, employees, and agencies of Department of Labor, with certain exceptions, to Secretary of Labor, with power to delegate, see Reorg. Plan No. 6 of 1950, §§1, 2, 15 F.R. 3174, 64 Stat. 1263, set out in the Appendix to Title 5.

EXEMPTIONS FOR APPRENTICES AND STUDENT LEARNERS

Section 3 of Pub. L. 104–174 provided that: "Section 1 [amending this section] shall not be construed as affecting the exemption for apprentices and student learners published in section 570.63 of title 29, Code of Federal Regulations."

REGULATIONS CONCERNING COMPUTER, SOFTWARE, AND OTHER SIMILARLY SKILLED PROFESSIONALS

Pub. L. 101–583, §2, Nov. 15, 1990, 104 Stat. 2871, provided that: "Not later than 90 days after the date of enactment of this Act [Nov. 15, 1990], the Secretary of Labor shall promulgate regulations that permit computer systems analysts, computer programmers, software engineers, and other similarly skilled professional workers as defined in such regulations to qualify as exempt executive, administrative, or professional employees under section 13(a)(1) of the Fair Labor Standards Act of 1938 (29 U.S.C. 213(a)(1)). Such regulations shall provide that if such employees are paid on an hourly basis they shall be exempt only if their hourly rate of pay is at least 6½ times greater than the applicable minimum wage rate under section 6 of such Act (29 U.S.C. 206)."

PUBLIC AGENCY EMPLOYEES IN FIRE PROTECTION AND LAW ENFORCEMENT ACTIVITIES; STUDIES IN 1976 OF 1975 TOURS OF DUTY

Section 6(c)(3) of Pub. L. 93–259 authorized Secretary of Labor to conduct a study in 1976 of average number of hours in tours of duty in work periods in 1975 of certain employees of public agencies employed in fire protection and law enforcement activities, and publish results of such studies in Federal Register.

PIPELINE EMPLOYEES UNDER SUBSEC. (b)(2)

Section 23(c) of Pub. L. 93–259 provided in part for amendment of subsec. (b)(2) of this section "insofar as it relates to pipeline employees".

RULES, REGULATIONS, AND ORDERS PROMULGATED WITH REGARD TO 1966 AMENDMENTS

Secretary authorized to promulgate necessary rules, regulations, or orders on and after the date of the enactment of Pub. L. 89–601, Sept. 23, 1966, with regard to the amendments made by Pub. L. 89–601, see section 602 of Pub. L. 89–601, set out as a note under section 203 of this title.

STUDY OF AGRICULTURAL HANDLING AND PROCESSING EXEMPTIONS AND RATES OF PAY IN EXEMPT FOOD SERVICE ENTERPRISES

Section 13 of Pub. L. 87–30 directed Secretary of Labor to study complicated system of exemptions available for handling and processing agricultural products under this chapter and complex problems involving rates of pay of certain employees exempted from provisions of this chapter, and submit results of his studies along with his recommendations for proposed legislation to second session of Eighty-seventh Congress.

TRANSPORTATION OF MIGRANT FARM WORKERS

Section 3 of act Aug. 3, 1956, provided that: "Section 13(b)(1) of the Fair Labor Standards Act, as amended [subsec. (b)(1) of this section] shall not apply in the case of any employee with respect to whom the Interstate Commerce Commission [now Secretary of Transportation] has power to establish qualifications and maximum hours of service solely by virtue of section 204(a)(3a) of the Interstate Commerce Act [now 49 U.S.C. 31502]."

§214. Employment under special certificates

(a) Learners, apprentices, messengers

The Secretary, to the extent necessary in order to prevent curtailment of opportunities for employment, shall by regulations or by orders provide for the employment of learners, of apprentices, and of messengers employed primarily in delivering letters and messages, under special certificates issued pursuant to regulations of the Secretary, at such wages lower than the minimum wage applicable under section 206 of this title and subject to such limitations as to time, number, proportion, and length of service as the Secretary shall prescribe.

(b) Students

(1)(A) The Secretary, to the extent necessary in order to prevent curtailment of opportunities for employment, shall by special certificate issued under a regulation or order provide, in accordance with subparagraph (B), for the employment, at a wage rate not less than 85 per centum of the otherwise applicable wage rate in effect under section 206 of this title or not less than $1.60 an hour, whichever is the higher, of full-time students (regardless of age but in compliance with applicable child labor laws) in retail or service establishments.

(B) Except as provided in paragraph (4)(B), during any month in which full-time students are to be employed in any retail or service establishment under certificates issued under this subsection the proportion of student hours of employment to the total hours of employment of all employees in such establishment may not exceed—

(i) in the case of a retail or service establishment whose employees (other than employees engaged in commerce or in the production of goods for commerce) were covered by this chapter before the effective date of the Fair Labor Standards Amendments of 1974—

(I) the proportion of student hours of employment to the total hours of employment of all employees in such establishment for the corresponding month of the immediately preceding twelve-month period,

(II) the maximum proportion for any corresponding month of student hours of employment to the total hours of employment of all employees in such establishment applicable to the issuance of certificates under this section at any time before the effective date of the Fair Labor Standards Amendments of 1974 for the employment of students by such employer, or

(III) a proportion equal to one-tenth of the total hours of employment of all employees in such establishment,

whichever is greater;

(ii) in the case of retail or service establishment whose employees (other than employees engaged in commerce or in the production of goods for commerce) are covered for the first time on or after the effective date of the Fair Labor Standards Amendments of 1974—

(I) the proportion of hours of employment of students in such establishment to the total hours of employment of all employees in such establishment for the corresponding month of the twelve-month period immediately prior to the effective date of such Amendments,

(II) the proportion of student hours of employment to the total hours of employment of all employees in such establishment for the corresponding month of the immediately preceding twelve-month period, or

(III) a proportion equal to one-tenth of the total hours of employment of all employees in such establishment,

whichever is greater; or

(iii) in the case of a retail or service establishment for which records of student hours worked are not available, the proportion of student hours of employment to the total hours of employment of all employees based on the practice during the immediately preceding twelve-month period in (I) similar establishments of the same employer in the same general metropolitan area in which such establishment is located, (II) similar establishments of the same or nearby communities if such establishment is not in a metropolitan area, or (III) other establishments of the same general character operating in the community or the nearest comparable community.

For purpose of clauses (i), (ii), and (iii) of this subparagraph, the term "student hours of employment" means hours during which students are employed in a retail or service establishment under certificates issued under this subsection.

(2) The Secretary, to the extent necessary in order to prevent curtailment of opportunities for employment, shall by special certificate issued under a regulation or order provide for the employment, at a wage rate not less than 85 per centum of the wage rate in effect under section 206(a)(5)[1] of this title or not less than $1.30 an hour, whichever is the higher, of full-time students (regardless of age but in compliance with applicable child labor laws) in any occupation in agriculture.

(3) The Secretary, to the extent necessary in order to prevent curtailment of opportunities for employment, shall by special certificate issued under a regulation or order provide for the employment by an institution of higher education, at a wage rate not less than 85 per centum of the otherwise applicable wage rate in effect under section 206 of this title or not less than $1.60 an hour, whichever is the higher, of full-time students (regardless of age but in compliance with applicable child labor laws) who are enrolled in such institution. The Secretary shall by regulation prescribe standards and requirements to insure that this paragraph will not create a substantial probability of reducing the full-time employment opportunities of persons other than those to whom the minimum wage rate authorized by this paragraph is applicable.

(4)(A) A special certificate issued under paragraph (1), (2), or (3) shall provide that the student or students for whom it is issued shall, except during vacation periods, be employed on a part-time basis and not in excess of twenty hours in any workweek.

(B) If the issuance of a special certificate under paragraph (1) or (2) for an employer will cause the number of students employed by such employer under special certificates issued under this subsection to exceed six, the Secretary may not issue such a special certificate for the employment of a student by such employer unless the Secretary finds employment of such student will not create a substantial probability of reducing the full-time employment opportunities of persons other than those employed under special certificates issued under this subsection. If the issuance of a special certificate under paragraph (1) or (2) for an employer will not cause the number of students employed by such employer under special certificates issued under this subsection to exceed six—

(i) the Secretary may issue a special certificate under paragraph (1) or (2) for the employment of a student by such employer if such employer certifies to the Secretary that the employment of such student will not reduce the full-time employment opportunities of persons other than those employed under special certificates issued under this subsection, and

(ii) in the case of an employer which is a retail or service establishment, subparagraph (B) of paragraph (1) shall not apply with respect to the issuance of special certificates for such employer under such paragraph.

The requirement of this subparagraph shall not apply in the case of the issuance of special certificates under paragraph (3) for the employment of full-time students by institutions of higher education; except that if the Secretary determines that an institution of higher education is employing students under certificates issued under paragraph (3) but in violation of the requirements of that paragraph or of regulations issued thereunder, the requirements of this subparagraph shall apply with respect to the issuance of special certificates under paragraph (3) for the employment of students by such institution.

(C) No special certificate may be issued under this subsection unless the employer for whom the certificate is to be issued provides evidence satisfactory to the Secretary of the student status of the employees to be employed under such special certificate.

(D) To minimize paperwork for, and to encourage, small businesses to employ students under special certificates issued under paragraphs (1) and (2), the Secretary shall, by regulation or order, prescribe a simplified application form to be used by employers in applying for such a certificate for the employment of not more than six full-time students. Such an application shall require only—

(i) a listing of the name, address, and business of the applicant employer,

(ii) a listing of the date the applicant began business, and

(iii) the certification that the employment of such full-time students will not reduce the full-time employment opportunities of persons other than persons employed under special certificates.

(c) Handicapped workers

(1) The Secretary, to the extent necessary to prevent curtailment of opportunities for employment, shall by regulation or order provide for the employment, under special certificates, of individuals (including individuals employed in agriculture) whose earning or productive capacity is impaired by age, physical or mental deficiency, or injury, at wages which are—

(A) lower than the minimum wage applicable under section 206 of this title,

(B) commensurate with those paid to nonhandicapped workers, employed in the vicinity in which the individuals under the certificates are employed, for essentially the same type, quality, and quantity of work, and

[1] See References in Text note below.

(C) related to the individual's productivity.

(2) The Secretary shall not issue a certificate under paragraph (1) unless the employer provides written assurances to the Secretary that—

(A) in the case of individuals paid on an hourly rate basis, wages paid in accordance with paragraph (1) will be reviewed by the employer at periodic intervals at least once every six months, and

(B) wages paid in accordance with paragraph (1) will be adjusted by the employer at periodic intervals, at least once each year, to reflect changes in the prevailing wage paid to experienced nonhandicapped individuals employed in the locality for essentially the same type of work.

(3) Notwithstanding paragraph (1), no employer shall be permitted to reduce the hourly wage rate prescribed by certificate under this subsection in effect on June 1, 1986, of any handicapped individual for a period of two years from such date without prior authorization of the Secretary.

(4) Nothing in this subsection shall be construed to prohibit an employer from maintaining or establishing work activities centers to provide therapeutic activities for handicapped clients.

(5)(A) Notwithstanding any other provision of this subsection, any employee receiving a special minimum wage at a rate specified pursuant to this subsection or the parent or guardian of such an employee may petition the Secretary to obtain a review of such special minimum wage rate. An employee or the employee's parent or guardian may file such a petition for and in behalf of the employee or in behalf of the employee and other employees similarly situated. No employee may be a party to any such action unless the employee or the employee's parent or guardian gives consent in writing to become such a party and such consent is filed with the Secretary.

(B) Upon receipt of a petition filed in accordance with subparagraph (A), the Secretary within ten days shall assign the petition to an administrative law judge appointed pursuant to section 3105 of title 5. The administrative law judge shall conduct a hearing on the record in accordance with section 554 of title 5 with respect to such petition within thirty days after assignment.

(C) In any such proceeding, the employer shall have the burden of demonstrating that the special minimum wage rate is justified as necessary in order to prevent curtailment of opportunities for employment.

(D) In determining whether any special minimum wage rate is justified pursuant to subparagraph (C), the administrative law judge shall consider—

(i) the productivity of the employee or employees identified in the petition and the conditions under which such productivity was measured; and

(ii) the productivity of other employees performing work of essentially the same type and quality for other employers in the same vicinity.

(E) The administrative law judge shall issue a decision within thirty days after the hearing provided for in subparagraph (B). Such action shall be deemed to be a final agency action unless within thirty days the Secretary grants a request to review the decision of the administrative law judge. Either the petitioner or the employer may request review by the Secretary within fifteen days of the date of issuance of the decision by the administrative law judge.

(F) The Secretary, within thirty days after receiving a request for review, shall review the record and either adopt the decision of the administrative law judge or issue exceptions. The decision of the administrative law judge, together with any exceptions, shall be deemed to be a final agency action.

(G) A final agency action shall be subject to judicial review pursuant to chapter 7 of title 5. An action seeking such review shall be brought within thirty days of a final agency action described in subparagraph (F).

(d) Employment by schools

The Secretary may by regulation or order provide that sections 206 and 207 of this title shall not apply with respect to the employment by any elementary or secondary school of its students if such employment constitutes, as determined under regulations prescribed by the Secretary, an integral part of the regular education program provided by such school and such employment is in accordance with applicable child labor laws.

(June 25, 1938, ch. 676, §14, 52 Stat. 1068; Oct. 26, 1949, ch. 736, §12, 63 Stat. 918; Pub. L. 87–30, §11, May 5, 1961, 75 Stat. 74; Pub. L. 89–601, title V, §501, Sept. 23, 1966, 80 Stat. 842; Pub. L. 93–259, §24(a), (b), Apr. 8, 1974, 88 Stat. 69, 72; Pub. L. 95–151, §§12, 13, Nov. 1, 1977, 91 Stat. 1252; Pub. L. 99–486, Oct. 16, 1986, 100 Stat. 1229; Pub. L. 101–157, §4(d), Nov. 17, 1989, 103 Stat. 941.)

REFERENCES IN TEXT

Effective date of the Fair Labor Standards Amendments of 1974, referred to in subsec. (b)(1)(B)(i), (ii), means May 1, 1974, except as otherwise specifically provided, under provisions of section 29(a) of Pub. L. 93–259, set out as an Effective Date of 1974 Amendment note under section 202 of this title.

Section 206(a)(5) of this title, referred to in subsec. (b)(2), was redesignated section 206(a)(4) of this title by Pub. L. 110–28, title VIII, §8103(c)(1)(B), May 25, 2007, 121 Stat. 189.

AMENDMENTS

1989—Subsec. (b)(1)(A). Pub. L. 101–157 struck out "(or in the case of employment in Puerto Rico or the Virgin Islands not described in section 205(e) of this title, at a wage rate not less than 85 per centum of the otherwise applicable wage rate in effect under section 206(c) of this title)" after "whichever is the higher".

Subsec. (b)(2), (3). Pub. L. 101–157 struck out "(or in the case of employment in Puerto Rico or the Virgin Islands not described in section 205(e) of this title, at a wage rate not less than 85 per centum of the wage rate in effect under section 206(c) of this title)" after "whichever is the higher".

1986—Subsec. (c). Pub. L. 99–486 amended subsec. (c) generally, revising and restating as pars. (1) to (5) provisions formerly contained in pars. (1) to (3).

1977—Subsec. (b)(4)(B). Pub. L. 95–151, §12(a), substituted "six" for "four" wherever appearing.

Subsec. (b)(4)(D). Pub. L. 95–151, §13, added subpar. (D).

1974—Subsec. (a). Pub. L. 93–259, §24(a), added subsec. (a) and struck out former subsec. (a) which had provided: "The Secretary of Labor, to the extent necessary in order to prevent curtailment of opportunities for employment, shall by regulations or by orders provide for the employment of learners, of apprentices, and of messengers employed primarily in delivery letters and messages, under special certificates issued pursuant to regulations of the Secretary, at such wages lower than the minimum wage applicable under section 206 of this title and subject to such limitations as to time, number, proportion, and length of service as the Secretary shall prescribe."

Subsec. (b). Pub. L. 93–259, §24(a), added subsec. (b) and struck out former subsec. (b) which had provided: "The Secretary, to the extent necessary in order to prevent curtailment of opportunities for employment, shall by regulation or order provide for the employment of full-time students, regardless of age but in compliance with applicable child labor laws, on a part-time basis in retail or service establishments (not to exceed twenty hours in any workweek) or on a part-time or full-time basis in such establishments during school vacations, under special certificates issued pursuant to regulations of the Secretary, at a wage rate not less than 85 per centum of the minimum wage applicable under section 206 of this title, except that the proportion of student hours of employment to total hours of employment of all employees in any establishment may not exceed (1) such proportion for the corresponding month of the twelve-month period preceding May 1, 1961, (2) in the case of a retail or service establishment whose employees (other than employees engaged in commerce or in the production of goods for commerce) are covered by this chapter for the first time on or after the effective date of the Fair Labor Standards Amendments of 1966, such proportion for the corresponding month of the twelve-month period immediately prior to such date, or (3) in the case of a retail or service establishment coming into existence after May 1, 1961, or a retail or service establishment for which records of student hours worked are not available, a proportion of student hours of employment to total hours of employment of all employees based on the practice during the twelve-month period preceding May 1, 1961, in (A) similar establishments of the same employer in the same general metropolitan area in which the new establishment is located, (B) similar establishments of the same employer in the same or nearby counties if the new establishment is not in a metropolitan area, or (C) other establishments of the same general character operating in the community or the nearest comparable community. Before the Secretary may issue a certificate under this subsection he must find that such employment will not create a substantial probability of reducing the full-time employment opportunities of persons other than those employed under this subsection."

Subsecs. (c), (d). Pub. L. 93–259, §24(a), (b), struck out subsec. (c) and redesignated subsec. (d) as (c). Former subsec. (c) had provided: "The Secretary, to the extent necessary in order to prevent curtailment of opportunities for employment, shall by certificate or order provide for the employment of full-time students, regardless of age but in compliance with applicable child labor laws, on a part-time basis in agriculture (not to exceed twenty hours in any workweek) or on a part-time or full-time basis in agriculture during school vacations, at a wage rate not less than 85 per centum of the minimum wage applicable under section 206 of this title. Before the Secretary may issue a certificate or order under this subsection he must find that such employment will not create a substantial probability of reducing the full-time employment opportunities of persons other than those employed under this subsection."

1966—Pub. L. 89–601 provided for employment of full-time students regardless of age but in compliance with applicable child labor laws outside of their school hours in retail or service establishments or in agriculture at not less than 85 percent of the minimum wage in full-time positions during school vacations or in part-time positions not to exceed 20 hours in any workweek under certificates issued by the Secretary, set out the formula for the allowable proportion of student hours of employment to total hours of employment, provided for the employment of handicapped workers at rates down to 50 percent of the applicable minimum wage and at even lower rates for persons suffering severe impairment, authorized the establishment of special rates for handicapped workers employed in work activities centers, and defined work activity centers.

1961—Pub. L. 87–30 provided for employment of students in cl. (1).

1949—Act Oct. 26, 1949, substituted "primarily" for "exclusively" after "messengers employed".

EFFECTIVE DATE OF 1977 AMENDMENT

Amendment by Pub. L. 95–151 effective Nov. 1, 1977, see section 15(b) of Pub. L. 95–151, set out as a note under section 203 of this title.

EFFECTIVE DATE OF 1974 AMENDMENT

Amendment by Pub. L. 93–259 effective May 1, 1974, see section 29(a) of Pub. L. 93–259, set out as a note under section 202 of this title.

EFFECTIVE DATE OF 1966 AMENDMENT

Amendment by Pub. L. 89–601 effective Feb. 1, 1967, except as otherwise provided, see section 602 of Pub. L. 89–601, set out as a note under section 203 of this title.

EFFECTIVE DATE OF 1961 AMENDMENT

Amendment by Pub. L. 87–30 effective upon expiration of one hundred and twenty days after May 5, 1961, except as otherwise provided, see section 14 of Pub. L. 87–30, set out as a note under section 203 of this title.

EFFECTIVE DATE OF 1949 AMENDMENT

Amendment by act Oct. 26, 1949, effective ninety days after Oct. 26, 1949, see section 16(a) of act Oct. 26, 1949, set out as a note under section 202 of this title.

TRANSFER OF FUNCTIONS

For transfer of functions of other officers, employees, and agencies of Department of Labor, with certain exceptions, to Secretary of Labor, with power to delegate, see Reorg. Plan No. 6 of 1950, §§1, 2, 15 F.R. 3174, 64 Stat. 1263, set out in the Appendix to Title 5, Government Organization and Employees.

RULES, REGULATIONS, AND ORDERS PROMULGATED WITH REGARD TO 1966 AMENDMENTS

Secretary authorized to promulgate necessary rules, regulations, or orders on and after the date of the enactment of Pub. L. 89–601, Sept. 23, 1966, with regard to the amendments made by Pub. L. 89–601, see section 602 of Pub. L. 89–601, set out as a note under section 203 of this title.

STUDY OF WAGES PAID HANDICAPPED CLIENTS IN SHELTERED WORKSHOPS

Section 605 of Pub. L. 89–601 instructed Secretary of Labor to commence a complete study of wage payments to handicapped clients of sheltered workshops and of feasibility of raising existing wage standards in such workshops. The Secretary was directed to report to Congress by July 1, 1967, findings of such study with appropriate recommendations.

§215. Prohibited acts; prima facie evidence

(a) After the expiration of one hundred and twenty days from June 25, 1938, it shall be unlawful for any person—

(1) to transport, offer for transportation, ship, deliver, or sell in commerce, or to ship, deliver, or sell with knowledge that shipment or delivery or sale thereof in commerce is in-

tended, any goods in the production of which any employee was employed in violation of section 206 or section 207 of this title, or in violation of any regulation or order of the Secretary issued under section 214 of this title; except that no provision of this chapter shall impose any liability upon any common carrier for the transportation in commerce in the regular course of its business of any goods not produced by such common carrier, and no provision of this chapter shall excuse any common carrier from its obligation to accept any goods for transportation; and except that any such transportation, offer, shipment, delivery, or sale of such goods by a purchaser who acquired them in good faith in reliance on written assurance from the producer that the goods were produced in compliance with the requirements of this chapter, and who acquired such goods for value without notice of any such violation, shall not be deemed unlawful;

(2) to violate any of the provisions of section 206 or section 207 of this title, or any of the provisions of any regulation or order of the Secretary issued under section 214 of this title;

(3) to discharge or in any other manner discriminate against any employee because such employee has filed any complaint or instituted or caused to be instituted any proceeding under or related to this chapter, or has testified or is about to testify in any such proceeding, or has served or is about to serve on an industry committee;

(4) to violate any of the provisions of section 212 of this title;

(5) to violate any of the provisions of section 211(c) of this title, or any regulation or order made or continued in effect under the provisions of section 211(d) of this title, or to make any statement, report, or record filed or kept pursuant to the provisions of such section or of any regulation or order thereunder, knowing such statement, report, or record to be false in a material respect.

(b) For the purposes of subsection (a)(1) of this section proof that any employee was employed in any place of employment where goods shipped or sold in commerce were produced, within ninety days prior to the removal of the goods from such place of employment, shall be prima facie evidence that such employee was engaged in the production of such goods.

(June 25, 1938, ch. 676, §15, 52 Stat. 1068; Oct. 26, 1949, ch. 736, §13, 63 Stat. 919; 1950 Reorg. Plan No. 6, §§1, 2, eff. May 24, 1950, 15 F.R. 3174, 64 Stat. 1263.)

AMENDMENTS

1949—Subsec. (a)(1). Act Oct. 26, 1949, §13(a), inserted provision protecting purchaser in good faith in sale of goods produced in violation of this chapter.

Subsec. (a)(5). Act Oct. 26, 1949, §13(b), inserted "or any regulation or order made or continued in effect under the provisions of section 211(d) of this title" after "211(c) of this title".

EFFECTIVE DATE OF 1949 AMENDMENT

Amendment by act Oct. 26, 1949, effective ninety days after Oct. 26, 1949, see section 16(a) of act Oct. 26, 1949, set out as a note under section 202 of this title.

TRANSFER OF FUNCTIONS

For transfer of functions of other officers, employees, and agencies of Department of Labor, with certain exceptions, to Secretary of Labor, with power to delegate, see Reorg. Plan No. 6 of 1950, §§1, 2, 15 F.R. 3174, 64 Stat. 1263, set out in the Appendix to Title 5, Government Organization and Employees.

LIABILITY OF PUBLIC AGENCY FOR DISCRIMINATION AGAINST EMPLOYEE FOR ASSERTION OF COVERAGE

Pub. L. 99–150, §8, Nov. 13, 1985, 99 Stat. 791, provided that: "A public agency which is a State, political subdivision of a State, or an interstate governmental agency and which discriminates or has discriminated against an employee with respect to the employee's wages or other terms or conditions of employment because on or after February 19, 1985, the employee asserted coverage under section 7 of the Fair Labor Standards Act of 1938 [29 U.S.C. 207] shall be held to have violated section 15(a)(3) of such Act [29 U.S.C. 215(a)(3)]. The protection against discrimination afforded by the preceding sentence shall be available after August 1, 1986, only for an employee who takes an action described in section 15(a)(3) of such Act."

§216. Penalties

(a) Fines and imprisonment

Any person who willfully violates any of the provisions of section 215 of this title shall upon conviction thereof be subject to a fine of not more than $10,000, or to imprisonment for not more than six months, or both. No person shall be imprisoned under this subsection except for an offense committed after the conviction of such person for a prior offense under this subsection.

(b) Damages; right of action; attorney's fees and costs; termination of right of action

Any employer who violates the provisions of section 206 or section 207 of this title shall be liable to the employee or employees affected in the amount of their unpaid minimum wages, or their unpaid overtime compensation, as the case may be, and in an additional equal amount as liquidated damages. Any employer who violates the provisions of section 215(a)(3) of this title shall be liable for such legal or equitable relief as may be appropriate to effectuate the purposes of section 215(a)(3) of this title, including without limitation employment, reinstatement, promotion, and the payment of wages lost and an additional equal amount as liquidated damages. An action to recover the liability prescribed in either of the preceding sentences may be maintained against any employer (including a public agency) in any Federal or State court of competent jurisdiction by any one or more employees for and in behalf of himself or themselves and other employees similarly situated. No employee shall be a party plaintiff to any such action unless he gives his consent in writing to become such a party and such consent is filed in the court in which such action is brought. The court in such action shall, in addition to any judgment awarded to the plaintiff or plaintiffs, allow a reasonable attorney's fee to be paid by the defendant, and costs of the action. The right provided by this subsection to bring an action by or on behalf of any employee, and the right of any employee to become a party plaintiff to any such action, shall terminate upon the filing of a complaint by the Secretary of Labor in an action under section 217 of this title in which (1) restraint is sought of any further delay in the payment of unpaid minimum wages, or the amount of unpaid overtime compensation, as the case may be, owing to such employee under section 206 or section 207 of this title by an employer liable therefor under the provisions of this subsection or (2) legal or equitable relief is sought as a result of alleged violations of section 215(a)(3) of this title.

(c) Payment of wages and compensation; waiver of claims; actions by the Secretary; limitation of actions

The Secretary is authorized to supervise the payment of the unpaid minimum wages or the unpaid overtime compensation owing to any employee or employees under section 206 or section 207 of this title, and the agreement of any employee to accept such payment shall upon payment in full constitute a waiver by such employee of any right he may have under subsection (b) of this section to such unpaid minimum wages or unpaid overtime compensation and an additional equal amount as liquidated damages. The Secretary may bring an action in any court of competent jurisdiction to recover the amount of unpaid minimum wages or overtime compensation and an equal amount as liquidated damages. The right provided by subsection (b) of this section to bring an action by or on behalf of any employee to recover the liability specified in the first sentence of such subsection and of any employee to become a party plaintiff to any such action shall terminate upon the filing of a complaint by the Secretary in an action under this subsection in which a recovery is sought of unpaid minimum wages or unpaid overtime compensation under sections 206 and 207 of this title or liquidated or other damages provided by this subsection owing to such employee by an employer liable under the provisions of subsection (b) of this section, unless such action is dismissed without prejudice on motion of the Secretary. Any sums thus recovered by the Secretary of Labor on behalf of an employee pursuant to this subsection shall be held in a special deposit account and shall be paid, on order of the Secretary of Labor, directly to the employee or employees affected. Any such sums not paid to an employee because of inability to do so within a period of three years shall be covered into the Treasury of the United States as miscellaneous receipts. In determining when an action is commenced by the Secretary of Labor under this subsection for the purposes of the statutes of limitations provided in section 255(a) of this title, it shall be considered to be commenced in the case of any individual claimant on the date when the complaint is filed if he is specifically named as a party plaintiff in the complaint, or if his name did not so appear, on the subsequent date on which his name is added as a party plaintiff in such action.

(d) Savings provisions

In any action or proceeding commenced prior to, on, or after August 8, 1956, no employer shall be subject to any liability or punishment under this chapter or the Portal-to-Portal Act of 1947 [29 U.S.C. 251 et seq.] on account of his failure to comply with any provision or provisions of this chapter or such Act (1) with respect to work heretofore or hereafter performed in a workplace to which the exemption in section 213(f) of this title is applicable, (2) with respect to work performed in Guam, the Canal Zone or Wake Island before the effective date of this amendment of subsection (d), or (3) with respect to work performed in a possession named in section 206(a)(3)[1] of this title at any time prior to the establishment by the Secretary, as provided therein, of a minimum wage rate applicable to such work.

(e) Civil penalties for child labor violations

(1)(A) Any person who violates the provisions of sections[2] 212 or 213(c) of this title, relating to child labor, or any regulation issued pursuant to such sections, shall be subject to a civil penalty not to exceed—

(i) $11,000 for each employee who was the subject of such a violation; or

(ii) $50,000 with regard to each such violation that causes the death or serious injury of any employee under the age of 18 years, which penalty may be doubled where the violation is a repeated or willful violation.

(B) For purposes of subparagraph (A), the term "serious injury" means—

(i) permanent loss or substantial impairment of one of the senses (sight, hearing, taste, smell, tactile sensation);

(ii) permanent loss or substantial impairment of the function of a bodily member, organ, or mental faculty, including the loss of all or part of an arm, leg, foot, hand or other body part; or

(iii) permanent paralysis or substantial impairment that causes loss of movement or mobility of an arm, leg, foot, hand or other body part.

(2) Any person who repeatedly or willfully violates section 206 or 207 of this title, relating to wages, shall be subject to a civil penalty not to exceed $1,100 for each such violation.

(3) In determining the amount of any penalty under this subsection, the appropriateness of such penalty to the size of the business of the person charged and the gravity of the violation shall be considered. The amount of any penalty under this subsection, when finally determined, may be—

(A) deducted from any sums owing by the United States to the person charged;

(B) recovered in a civil action brought by the Secretary in any court of competent jurisdiction, in which litigation the Secretary shall be represented by the Solicitor of Labor; or

(C) ordered by the court, in an action brought for a violation of section 215(a)(4) of this title or a repeated or willful violation of section 215(a)(2) of this title, to be paid to the Secretary.

(4) Any administrative determination by the Secretary of the amount of any penalty under this subsection shall be final, unless within 15 days after receipt of notice thereof by certified

[1] See References in Text note below.

[2] So in original. Probably should be "section".

mail the person charged with the violation takes exception to the determination that the violations for which the penalty is imposed occurred, in which event final determination of the penalty shall be made in an administrative proceeding after opportunity for hearing in accordance with section 554 of title 5 and regulations to be promulgated by the Secretary.

(5) Except for civil penalties collected for violations of section 212 of this title, sums collected as penalties pursuant to this section shall be applied toward reimbursement of the costs of determining the violations and assessing and collecting such penalties, in accordance with the provision of section 9a of this title. Civil penalties collected for violations of section 212 of this title shall be deposited in the general fund of the Treasury.

(June 25, 1938, ch. 676, §16, 52 Stat. 1069; May 14, 1947, ch. 52, §5(a), 61 Stat. 87; Oct. 26, 1949, ch. 736, §14, 63 Stat. 919; 1950 Reorg. Plan No. 6, §§1, 2, 15 F.R. 3174, 64 Stat. 1263; Aug. 8, 1956, ch. 1035, §4, 70 Stat. 1118; Pub. L. 85–231, §1(2), Aug. 30, 1957, 71 Stat. 514; Pub. L. 87–30, §12(a), May 5, 1961, 75 Stat. 74; Pub. L. 89–601, title VI, §601(a), Sept. 23, 1966, 80 Stat. 844; Pub. L. 93–259, §§6(d)(1), 25(c), 26, Apr. 8, 1974, 88 Stat. 61, 72, 73; Pub. L. 95–151, §10, Nov. 1, 1977, 91 Stat. 1252; Pub. L. 101–157, §9, Nov. 17, 1989, 103 Stat. 945; Pub. L. 101–508, title III, §3103, Nov. 5, 1990, 104 Stat. 1388–29; Pub. L. 104–174, §2, Aug. 6, 1996, 110 Stat. 1554; Pub. L. 110–233, title III, §302(a), May 21, 2008, 122 Stat. 920.)

REFERENCES IN TEXT

The Portal-to-Portal Act of 1947, referred to in subsec. (d), is act May 14, 1947, ch. 52, 61 Stat. 84, as amended, which is classified principally to chapter 9 (§251 et seq.) of this title. For complete classification of this Act to the Code, see Short Title note set out under section 251 of this title and Tables.

The effective date of this amendment of subsection (d), referred to in subsec. (d), occurred upon the expiration of 90 days after Aug. 30, 1957. See section 2 of Pub. L. 85–231, set out as an Effective Date of 1957 Amendment note under section 213 of this title.

Section 206(a)(3) of this title, referred to in subsec. (d)(3), was repealed and section 206(a)(4) of this title was redesignated section 206(a)(3) by Pub. L. 110–28, title VIII, §8103(c)(1)(B), May 25, 2007, 121 Stat. 189.

AMENDMENTS

2008—Subsec. (e). Pub. L. 110–233 amended subsec. (e) generally. Prior to amendment, subsec. (e) related to civil penalties for child labor violations.

1996—Subsec. (e). Pub. L. 104–174 in first sentence substituted "of section 212 of this title or section 213(c)(5) of this title" for "of section 212 of this title" and "under section 212 of this title or section 213(c)(5) of this title" for "under that section".

1990—Subsec. (e). Pub. L. 101–508 struck out "or any person who repeatedly or willfully violates section 206 or 207 of this title" after "issued under that section," in first sentence, substituted "not to exceed $10,000 for each employee who was the subject of such a violation" for "not to exceed $1,000 for each such violation" in first sentence, inserted after first sentence "Any person who repeatedly or willfully violates section 206 or 207 of this title shall be subject to a civil penalty of not to exceed $1,000 for each such violation.", substituted "any penalty under this subsection" for "such penalty" wherever appearing except after "appropriateness of", substituted "Except for civil penalties collected for violations of section 212 of this title, sums" for "Sums" in last sentence, and inserted at end "Civil penalties collected for violations of section 212 of this title shall be deposited in the general fund of the Treasury."

1989—Subsec. (e). Pub. L. 101–157 inserted "or any person who repeatedly or willfully violates section 206 or 207 of this title" in introductory provisions and inserted "or a repeated or willful violation of section 215(a)(2) of this title" in par. (3).

1977—Subsec. (b). Pub. L. 95–151, §10(a), (b), inserted provisions relating to violations of section 215(a)(3) of this title by employers, "(1)" after "section 217 of this title in which", and cl. (2), and substituted "An action to recover the liability prescribed in either of the preceding sentences" for "Action to recover such liability".

Subsec. (c). Pub. L. 95–151, §10(c), inserted "to recover the liability specified in the first sentence of such subsection" after "an action by or on behalf of any employee".

1974—Subsec. (b). Pub. L. 93–259, §6(d)(1), substituted in second sentence "maintained against any employer (including a public agency) in any Federal or State court" for "maintained in any court".

Subsec. (c). Pub. L. 93–259, §26, in revising first three sentences, reenacted first sentence, substituting "Secretary" for "Secretary of Labor"; included in second sentence provision for an action by the Secretary for liquidated damaged and deleted requirement of a written request by an employee claiming unpaid minimum wages or unpaid overtime compensation with the Secretary of Labor prior to an action by the Secretary and proviso prohibiting any action in any case involving an issue of law not settled finally by the courts and depriving courts of jurisdiction of any action or proceeding involving the issue of law not settled finally; and substituted third sentence "The right provided by subsection (b) of this section to bring by or on behalf of any employee and of any employees to become a party plaintiff to any such action shall terminate upon the filing of a complaint by the Secretary in an action under this subsection in which a recovery is sought of unpaid minimum wages or unpaid overtime compensation under sections 206 and 207 of this title or liquidated or other damages provided by this subsection owing to such employee by an employer liable under the provisions of subsection (b) of this section, unless such action is dismissed without prejudice on motion of the Secretary." for "The consent of any employee to the bringing of any such action by the Secretary of Labor, unless such action is dismissed without prejudice on motion of the Secretary of Labor, shall constitute a waiver by such employee of any right of action he may have under subsection (b) of this section for such unpaid wages or unpaid overtime compensation and an additional equal amount as liquidated damages."

Subsec. (e). Pub. L. 93–259, §25(c), added subsec. (e).

1966—Subsec. (c). Pub. L. 89–601 substituted "statutes of limitations" for "two-year statute of limitations".

1961—Subsec. (b). Pub. L. 87–30 provided for termination of right of action upon commencement of injunction proceedings by the Secretary of Labor.

1957—Subsec. (d). Pub. L. 85–231 added cls. (1) and (2) and designated existing provisions as cl. (3).

1956—Subsec. (d). Act Aug. 8, 1956, added subsec. (d).

1949—Subsec. (c). Act Oct. 26, 1949, added subsec. (c).

1947—Subsec. (b). Act May 14, 1947, struck out provisions relating to the designation by employee or employees of an agent or representative to maintain an action under this section for and on behalf of all employees similarly situated and inserted provisions relating to the requirement that no employee shall be a party plaintiff unless he gives his consent in writing and such consent is filed with the court.

EFFECTIVE DATE OF 2008 AMENDMENT

Pub. L. 110–233, title III, §302(b), May 21, 2008, 122 Stat. 922, provided that: "The amendments made by this section [amending this section] shall take effect on the date of the enactment of this Act [May 21, 2008]."

EFFECTIVE DATE OF 1977 AMENDMENT

Amendment by Pub. L. 95–151 effective Jan. 1, 1978, see section 15(a) of Pub. L. 95–151, set out as a note under section 203 of this title.

EFFECTIVE DATE OF 1974 AMENDMENT

Amendment by Pub. L. 93–259 effective May 1, 1974, see section 29(a) of Pub. L. 93–259, set out as a note under section 202 of this title.

EFFECTIVE DATE OF 1966 AMENDMENT

Amendment by Pub. L. 89–601 effective Feb. 1, 1967, except as otherwise provided, see section 602 of Pub. L. 89–601, set out as a note under section 203 of this title.

EFFECTIVE DATE OF 1961 AMENDMENT

Amendment by Pub. L. 87–30 effective upon expiration of one hundred and twenty days after May 5, 1961, except as otherwise provided, see section 14 of Pub. L. 87–30, set out as a note under section 203 of this title.

EFFECTIVE DATE OF 1957 AMENDMENT

Amendment by Pub. L. 85–231 effective upon expiration of ninety days from Aug. 30, 1957, see section 2 of Pub. L. 85–231, set out as a note under section 213 of this title.

EFFECTIVE DATE OF 1949 AMENDMENT

Amendment by act Oct. 26, 1949, effective ninety days after Oct. 26, 1949, see section 16(a) of act Oct. 26, 1949, set out as a note under section 202 of this title.

EFFECTIVE DATE OF 1947 AMENDMENT

Section 5(b) of act May 14, 1947, provided that: "The amendment made by subsection (a) of this section [amending this section] shall be applicable only with respect to actions commenced under the Fair Labor Standards Act of 1938, as amended [this chapter], on or after the date of the enactment of this Act [May 14, 1947]."

TRANSFER OF FUNCTIONS

Functions relating to enforcement and administration of equal pay provisions vested by subsecs. (b) and (c) of this section in Secretary of Labor transferred to Equal Employment Opportunity Commission by Reorg. Plan No. 1 of 1978, §1, 43 F.R. 19807, 92 Stat. 3781, set out in the Appendix to Title 5, Government Organization and Employees, effective Jan. 1, 1979, as provided by section 1–101 of Ex. Ord. No. 12106, Dec. 28, 1978, 44 F.R. 1053.

For transfer of functions of other officers, employees, and agencies of Department of Labor, with certain exceptions, to Secretary of Labor, with power to delegate, see Reorg. Plan No. 6 of 1950, §§1, 2, 15 F.R. 3174, 64 Stat. 1263, set out in the Appendix to Title 5.

LIABILITY OF STATE, POLITICAL SUBDIVISION, OR INTERSTATE GOVERNMENTAL AGENCY FOR VIOLATIONS BEFORE APRIL 15, 1986, RESPECTING ANY EMPLOYEE NOT COVERED UNDER SPECIAL ENFORCEMENT POLICY

Pub. L. 99–150, §2(c)(1), Nov. 13, 1985, 99 Stat. 788, provided that: "No State, political subdivision of a State, or interstate governmental agency shall be liable under section 16 of the Fair Labor Standards Act of 1938 [29 U.S.C. 216] for a violation of section 6 [29 U.S.C. 206] (in the case of a territory or possession of the United States), 7 [29 U.S.C. 207], or 11(c) [29 U.S.C. 211(c)] (as it relates to section 7) of such Act occurring before April 15, 1986, with respect to any employee of the State, political subdivision, or agency who would not have been covered by such Act [this chapter] under the Secretary of Labor's special enforcement policy on January 1, 1985, and published in sections 775.2 and 775.4 of title 29 of the Code of Federal Regulations."

EFFECT OF AMENDMENTS BY PUBLIC LAW 99–150 ON PUBLIC AGENCY LIABILITY RESPECTING ANY EMPLOYEE COVERED UNDER SPECIAL ENFORCEMENT POLICY

Pub. L. 99–150, §7, Nov. 13, 1985, 99 Stat. 791, provided that: "The amendments made by this Act [see Short Title of 1985 Amendment note set out under section 201 of this title] shall not affect whether a public agency which is a State, political subdivision of a State, or an interstate governmental agency is liable under section 16 of the Fair Labor Standards Act of 1938 [29 U.S.C. 216] for a violation of section 6, 7, or 11 of such Act [29 U.S.C. 206, 207, 211] occurring before April 15, 1986, with respect to any employee of such public agency who would have been covered by such Act [this chapter] under the Secretary of Labor's special enforcement policy on January 1, 1985, and published in section 775.3 of title 29 of the Code of Federal Regulations."

RULES, REGULATIONS, AND ORDERS PROMULGATED WITH REGARD TO 1966 AMENDMENTS

Secretary authorized to promulgate necessary rules, regulations, or orders on and after the date of the enactment of Pub. L. 89–601, Sept. 23, 1966, with regard to the amendments made by Pub. L. 89–601, see section 602 of Pub. L. 89–601, set out as a note under section 203 of this title.

CONSTRUCTION OF 1949 AMENDMENTS WITH PORTAL-TO-PORTAL ACT OF 1947

Section 16(b) of act Oct. 26, 1949, provided that: "Except as provided in section 3(*o*) [section 203(*o*) of this title] and in the last sentence of section 16(c) of the Fair Labor Standards Act of 1938, as amended [section 216(e) of this title], no amendment made by this Act [amending sections 202, 208, 211 to 217 of this title] shall be construed as amending, modifying, or repealing any provisions of the Portal-to-Portal Act of 1947."

RETROACTIVE EFFECT OF 1949 AMENDMENTS; LIMITATION OF ACTIONS

Section 16(d) of act Oct. 26, 1949, provided that actions based upon acts or omissions occurring prior to the effective date of act Oct. 26, 1949, which was to be effective ninety days after Oct. 26, 1949, were not prevented by the amendments made to sections 202 to 208, and 211 to 217 of this title by such act, so long as such actions were instituted within two years from such effective date.

§216a. Repealed. Oct. 26, 1949, ch. 736, §16(f), 63 Stat. 920

Section, act July 20, 1949, ch. 352, §2, 63 Stat. 446, related to liability for overtime work performed prior to July 20, 1949. See section 216b of this title.

§216b. Liability for overtime work performed prior to July 20, 1949

No employer shall be subject to any liability or punishment under this chapter (in any action or proceeding commenced prior to or on or after January 24, 1950), on account of the failure of said employer to pay an employee compensation for any period of overtime work performed prior to July 20, 1949, if the compensation paid prior to July 20, 1949, for such work was at least equal to the compensation which would have been payable for such work had subsections (d)(6), (7) and (g) of section 207 of this title been in effect at the time of such payment.

(Oct. 26, 1949, ch. 736, §16(e), 63 Stat. 920.)

CODIFICATION

Section was enacted as part of the Fair Labor Standards Amendments of 1949, and not as part of the Fair Labor Standards Act of 1938 which comprises this chapter.

"January 24, 1950" substituted in text for "the effective date of this Act". See Effective Date of 1949 Amendment note set out under section 202 of this title.

§217. Injunction proceedings

The district courts, together with the United States District Court for the District of the Canal Zone, the District Court of the Virgin Islands, and the District Court of Guam shall have jurisdiction, for cause shown, to restrain violations of section 215 of this title, including in the case of violations of section 215(a)(2) of this title the restraint of any withholding of payment of minimum wages or overtime compensation found by the court to be due to employees under this chapter (except sums which employees are barred from recovering, at the time of the commencement of the action to restrain the violations, by virtue of the provisions of section 255 of this title).

(June 25, 1938, ch. 676, §17, 52 Stat. 1069; Oct. 26, 1949, ch. 736, §15, 63 Stat. 919; Pub. L. 85–231, §1(3), Aug. 30, 1957, 71 Stat. 514; Pub. L. 86–624, §21(c), July 12, 1960, 74 Stat. 417; Pub. L. 87–30, §12(b), May 5, 1961, 75 Stat. 74.)

AMENDMENTS

1961—Pub. L. 87–30 substituted ", including in the case of violations of section 215(a)(2) of this title the restraint of any withholding of payment of minimum wages or overtime compensation found by the court to be due to employees under this chapter (except sums which employees are barred from recovering, at the time of the commencement of the action to restrain the violations, by virtue of the provisions of section 255 of this title" for ": *Provided*, That no court shall have jurisdiction, in any action brought by the Administrator to restrain such violations, to order the payment to employees of unpaid minimum wages or unpaid overtime compensation or an additional equal amount as liquidated damages in such action".

1960—Pub. L. 86–624 struck out reference to the District Court for Territory of Alaska.

1957—Pub. L. 85–231 included the District Court of Guam within the enumeration of courts having jurisdiction of injunction proceedings.

1949—Act Oct. 26, 1949, included a more precise description of United States courts having jurisdiction to restrain violations and inserted proviso denying jurisdiction to order payment of unpaid minimum wages, overtime, and liquidated damages in injunction proceedings.

EFFECTIVE DATE OF 1961 AMENDMENT

Amendment by Pub. L. 87–30 effective upon expiration of one hundred and twenty days after May 5, 1961, except as otherwise provided, see section 14 of Pub. L. 87–30, set out as a note under section 203 of this title.

EFFECTIVE DATE OF 1957 AMENDMENT

Amendment by Pub. L. 85–231 effective upon expiration of ninety days from Aug. 30, 1957, see section 2 of Pub. L. 85–231, set out as a note under section 213 of this title.

EFFECTIVE DATE OF 1949 AMENDMENT

Amendment by act Oct. 26, 1949, effective ninety days after Oct. 26, 1949, see section 16(a) of act Oct. 26, 1949, set out as a note under section 202 of this title.

TERMINATION OF UNITED STATES DISTRICT COURT FOR THE DISTRICT OF THE CANAL ZONE

For termination of the United States District Court for the District of the Canal Zone at end of the "transition period", being the 30-month period beginning Oct. 1, 1979, and ending midnight Mar. 31, 1982, see Paragraph 5 of Article XI of the Panama Canal Treaty of 1977 and sections 2101 and 2201 to 2203 of Pub. L. 96–70, title II, Sept. 27, 1979, 93 Stat. 493, formerly classified to sections 3831 and 3841 to 3843, respectively, of Title 22, Foreign Relations and Intercourse.

TRANSFER OF FUNCTIONS

Functions relating to enforcement and administration of equal pay provisions vested by this section in Secretary of Labor transferred to Equal Employment Opportunity Commission by Reorg. Plan No. 1 of 1978, §1, 43 F.R. 19807, 92 Stat. 3781, set out in the Appendix to Title 5, Government Organization and Employees, effective Jan. 1, 1979, as provided by section 1–101 of Ex. Ord. No. 12106, Dec. 28, 1978, 44 F.R. 1053.

§218. Relation to other laws

(a) No provision of this chapter or of any order thereunder shall excuse noncompliance with any Federal or State law or municipal ordinance establishing a minimum wage higher than the minimum wage established under this chapter or a maximum work week lower than the maximum workweek established under this chapter, and no provision of this chapter relating to the employment of child labor shall justify noncompliance with any Federal or State law or municipal ordinance establishing a higher standard than the standard established under this chapter. No provision of this chapter shall justify any employer in reducing a wage paid by him which is in excess of the applicable minimum wage under this chapter, or justify any employer in increasing hours of employment maintained by him which are shorter than the maximum hours applicable under this chapter.

(b) Notwithstanding any other provision of this chapter (other than section 213(f) of this title) or any other law—

(1) any Federal employee in the Canal Zone engaged in employment of the kind described in section 5102(c)(7) of title 5, or

(2) any employee employed in a nonappropriated fund instrumentality under the jurisdiction of the Armed Forces,

shall have his basic compensation fixed or adjusted at a wage rate that is not less than the appropriate wage rate provided for in section 206(a)(1) of this title (except that the wage rate provided for in section 206(b) of this title shall apply to any employee who performed services during the workweek in a work place within the Canal Zone), and shall have his overtime compensation set at an hourly rate not less than the overtime rate provided for in section 207(a)(1) of this title.

(June 25, 1938, ch. 676, §18, 52 Stat. 1069; Pub. L. 89–601, title III, §306, Sept. 23, 1966, 80 Stat. 841; Pub. L. 90–83, §8, Sept. 11, 1967, 81 Stat. 222.)

REFERENCES IN TEXT

For definition of Canal Zone, referred to in subsec. (b), see section 3602(b) of Title 22, Foreign Relations and Intercourse.

AMENDMENTS

1967—Subsec. (b). Pub. L. 90–83 substituted reference to section 5102(c)(7) of title 5 for reference to par. (7) of section 202 of the Classification Act of 1949 to reflect the amendment of section 5341(a) of title 5 by section 1(97) of Pub. L. 90–83 and struck out provision covering employees described in section 7474 of title 10 in view of the repeal of section 7474 of title 10 by Pub. L. 89–554.

1966—Pub. L. 89–601 designated existing provisions as subsec. (a) and added subsec. (b).

EFFECTIVE DATE OF 1966 AMENDMENT

Amendment by Pub. L. 89–601 effective Feb. 1, 1967, except as otherwise provided, see section 602 of Pub. L. 89–601, set out as a note under section 203 of this title.

RULES, REGULATIONS, AND ORDERS PROMULGATED WITH REGARD TO 1966 AMENDMENTS

Secretary authorized to promulgate necessary rules, regulations, or orders on and after the date of the enactment of Pub. L. 89–601, Sept. 23, 1966, with regard to the amendments made by Pub. L. 89–601, see section 602 of Pub. L. 89–601, set out as a note under section 203 of this title.

§219. Separability

If any provision of this chapter or the application of such provision to any person or circumstance is held invalid, the remainder of this chapter and the application of such provision to other persons or circumstances shall not be affected thereby.

(June 25, 1938, ch. 676, §19, 52 Stat. 1069.)

CHAPTER 9—PORTAL-TO-PORTAL PAY

§251. Congressional findings and declaration of policy

(a) The Congress finds that the Fair Labor Standards Act of 1938, as amended [29 U.S.C. 201 et seq.], has been interpreted judicially in disregard of long-established customs, practices, and contracts between employers and employees, thereby creating wholly unexpected liabilities, immense in amount and retroactive in operation, upon employers with the results that, if said Act as so interpreted or claims arising under such interpretations were permitted to stand, (1) the payment of such liabilities would bring about financial ruin of many employers and seriously impair the capital resources of many others, thereby resulting in the reduction of industrial operations, halting of expansion and development, curtailing employment, and the earning power of employees; (2) the credit of many employers would be seriously impaired; (3) there would be created both an extended and continuous uncertainty on the part of industry, both employer and employee, as to the financial condition of productive establishments and a gross inequality of competitive conditions between employers and between industries; (4) employees would receive windfall payments, including liquidated damages, of sums for activities performed by them without any expectation of reward beyond that included in their agreed rates of pay; (5) there would occur the promotion of increasing demands for payment to employees for engaging in activities no compensation for which had been contemplated by either the employer or employee at the time they were engaged in; (6) voluntary collective bargaining would be interfered with and industrial disputes between employees and employers and between employees and employees would be created; (7) the courts of the country would be burdened with excessive and needless litigation and champertous practices would be encouraged; (8) the Public Treasury would be deprived of large sums of revenues and public finances would be seriously deranged by claims against the Public Treasury for refunds of taxes already paid; (9) the cost to the Government of goods and services heretofore and hereafter purchased by its various departments and agencies would be unreasonably increased and the Public Treasury would be seriously affected by consequent increased cost of war contracts; and (10) serious and adverse effects upon the revenues of Federal, State, and local governments would occur.

The Congress further finds that all of the foregoing constitutes a substantial burden on commerce and a substantial obstruction to the free flow of goods in commerce.

The Congress, therefore, further finds and declares that it is in the national public interest and for the general welfare, essential to national defense, and necessary to aid, protect, and foster commerce, that this chapter be enacted.

The Congress further finds that the varying and extended periods of time for which, under the laws of the several States, potential retroactive liability may be imposed upon employers, have given and will give rise to great difficulties in the sound and orderly conduct of business and industry.

The Congress further finds and declares that all of the results which have arisen or may arise under the Fair Labor Standards Act of 1938, as amended, as aforesaid, may (except as to liability for liquidated damages) arise with respect to the Walsh-Healey [41 U.S.C. 35 et seq.] and Bacon-Davis[1] Acts and that it is, therefore, in the national public interest and for the general welfare, essential to national defense, and necessary to aid, protect, and foster commerce, that this chapter shall apply to the Walsh-Healey Act and the Bacon-Davis Act.[1]

(b) It is declared to be the policy of the Congress in order to meet the existing emergency and to correct existing evils (1) to relieve and

[1] See References in Text note below.

protect interstate commerce from practices which burden and obstruct it; (2) to protect the right of collective bargaining; and (3) to define and limit the jurisdiction of the courts.

(May 14, 1947, ch. 52, §1, 61 Stat. 84.)

REFERENCES IN TEXT

The Fair Labor Standards Act of 1938, as amended, referred to in subsec. (a), is act June 25, 1938, ch. 676, 52 Stat. 1060, as amended, which is classified generally to chapter 8 (§201 et seq.) of this title. For complete classification of this Act to the Code, see section 201 of this title and Tables.

This chapter, referred to in subsec. (a), was in the original "this Act", meaning act May 14, 1947, ch. 52, 61 Stat. 84, as amended, known as the Portal-to-Portal Act of 1947, which enacted this chapter and amended section 216 of this title. For complete classification of this Act to the Code, see Short Title note set out below and Tables.

The Walsh-Healey and Bacon-Davis Acts, referred to in subsec. (a), are defined for purposes of this chapter in section 262 of this title.

SHORT TITLE OF 1996 AMENDMENT

Pub. L. 104–188, [title II], §2101, Aug. 20, 1996, 110 Stat. 1928, provided that: "This section and sections 2102 [amending section 254 of this title] and 2103 [enacting provisions set out as a note under section 254 of this title] may be cited as the 'Employee Commuting Flexibility Act of 1996'."

SHORT TITLE

Section 15 of act May 14, 1947, provided that: "This Act [enacting this chapter and amending section 216 of this title] may be cited as the 'Portal-to-Portal Act of 1947'."

SEPARABILITY

Section 14 of act May 14, 1947, provided: "If any provision of this Act [see Short Title note above] or the application of such provision to any person or circumstance is held invalid, the remainder of this Act and the application of such provision to other persons or circumstances shall not be affected thereby."

§252. Relief from certain existing claims under the Fair Labor Standards Act of 1938, as amended, the Walsh-Healey Act, and the Bacon-Davis Act

(a) Liability of employer

No employer shall be subject to any liability or punishment under the Fair Labor Standards Act of 1938, as amended [29 U.S.C. 201 et seq.] the Walsh-Healey Act [41 U.S.C. 35 et seq.], or the Bacon-Davis Act[1] (in any action or proceeding commenced prior to or on or after May 14, 1947), on account of the failure of such employer to pay an employee minimum wages, or to pay an employee overtime compensation, for or on account of any activity of an employee engaged in prior to May 14, 1947, except an activity which was compensable by either—

(1) an express provision of a written or nonwritten contract in effect, at the time of such activity, between such employee, his agent, or collective-bargaining representative and his employer; or

(2) a custom or practice in effect, at the time of such activity, at the establishment or other place where such employee was employed, covering such activity, not inconsistent with a written or nonwritten contract, in effect at the time of such activity, between such employee, his agent, or collective-bargaining representative and his employer.

[1] See References in Text note below.

(b) Compensable activity

For the purposes of subsection (a) of this section, an activity shall be considered as compensable under such contract provision or such custom or practice only when it was engaged in during the portion of the day with respect to which it was so made compensable.

(c) Time of employment

In the application of the minimum wage and overtime compensation provisions of the Fair Labor Standards Act of 1938, as amended [29 U.S.C. 201 et seq.], of the Walsh-Healey Act [41 U.S.C. 35 et seq.], or of the Bacon-Davis Act,[1] in determining the time for which an employer employed an employee there shall be counted all that time, but only that time, during which the employee engaged in activities which were compensable within the meaning of subsections (a) and (b) of this section.

(d) Jurisdiction

No court of the United States, of any State, Territory, or possession of the United States, or of the District of Columbia, shall have jurisdiction of any action or proceeding, whether instituted prior to or on or after May 14, 1947, to enforce liability or impose punishment for or on account of the failure of the employer to pay minimum wages or overtime compensation under the Fair Labor Standards Act of 1938, as amended [29 U.S.C. 201 et seq.], under the Walsh-Healey Act [41 U.S.C. 35 et seq.], or under the Bacon-Davis Act,[1] to the extent that such action or proceeding seeks to enforce any liability or impose any punishment with respect to an activity which was not compensable under subsections (a) and (b) of this section.

(e) Assignment of actions

No cause of action based on unpaid minimum wages, unpaid overtime compensation, or liquidated damages, under the Fair Labor Standards Act of 1938, as amended [29 U.S.C. 201 et seq.], the Walsh-Healey Act [41 U.S.C. 35 et seq.], or the Bacon-Davis Act,[1] which accrued prior to May 14, 1947, or any interest in such cause of action, shall hereafter be assignable, in whole or in part, to the extent that such cause of action is based on an activity which was not compensable within the meaning of subsections (a) and (b) of this section.

(May 14, 1947, ch. 52, §2, 61 Stat. 85.)

REFERENCES IN TEXT

The Fair Labor Standards Act of 1938, as amended, referred to in subsecs. (a), (c) to (e), is act June 25, 1938, ch. 676, 52 Stat. 1060, as amended, which is classified generally to chapter 8 (§201 et seq.) of this title. For complete classification of this Act to the Code, see section 201 of this title and Tables.

The Walsh-Healey and Bacon-Davis Acts, referred to in subsecs. (a), (c) to (e), are defined for purposes of this chapter in section 262 of this title.

§253. Compromise and waiver

(a) Compromise of certain existing claims under the Fair Labor Standards Act of 1938, the Walsh-Healey Act, or the Bacon-Davis Act; limitations

Any cause of action under the Fair Labor Standards Act of 1938, as amended [29 U.S.C. 201 et seq.], the Walsh-Healey Act [41 U.S.C. 35 et seq.], or the Bacon-Davis Act,[1] which accrued prior to May 14, 1947, or any action (whether instituted prior to or on or after May 14, 1947) to enforce such a cause of action, may hereafter be compromised in whole or in part, if there exists a bona fide dispute as to the amount payable by the employer to his employee; except that no such action or cause of action may be so compromised to the extent that such compromise is based on an hourly wage rate less than the minimum required under such Act, or on a payment for overtime at a rate less than one and one-half times such minimum hourly wage rate.

(b) Waiver of liquidated damages under Fair Labor Standards Act of 1938

Any employee may hereafter waive his right under the Fair Labor Standards Act of 1938, as amended [29 U.S.C. 201 et seq.], to liquidated damages, in whole or in part, with respect to activities engaged in prior to May 14, 1947.

(c) Satisfaction

Any such compromise or waiver, in the absence of fraud or duress, shall, according to the terms thereof, be a complete satisfaction of such cause of action and a complete bar to any action based on such cause of action.

(d) Retroactive effect of section

The provisions of this section shall also be applicable to any compromise or waiver heretofore so made or given.

(e) "Compromise" defined

As used in this section, the term "compromise" includes "adjustment", "settlement", and "release".

(May 14, 1947, ch. 52, §3, 61 Stat. 86.)

REFERENCES IN TEXT

The Fair Labor Standards Act of 1938, as amended, referred to in subsecs. (a) and (b), is act June 25, 1938, ch. 676, 52 Stat. 1060, as amended, which is classified generally to chapter 8 (§201 et seq.) of this title. For complete classification of this Act to the Code, see section 201 of this title and Tables.

The Walsh-Healey and Bacon-Davis Acts, referred to in subsec. (a), are defined for purposes of this chapter in section 262 of this title.

§254. Relief from liability and punishment under the Fair Labor Standards Act of 1938, the Walsh-Healey Act, and the Bacon-Davis Act for failure to pay minimum wage or overtime compensation

(a) Activities not compensable

Except as provided in subsection (b) of this section, no employer shall be subject to any liability or punishment under the Fair Labor Standards Act of 1938, as amended [29 U.S.C. 201 et seq.], the Walsh-Healey Act [41 U.S.C. 35 et seq.], or the Bacon-Davis Act,[1] on account of the failure of such employer to pay an employee minimum wages, or to pay an employee overtime compensation, for or on account of any of the following activities of such employee engaged in on or after May 14, 1947—

(1) walking, riding, or traveling to and from the actual place of performance of the principal activity or activities which such employee is employed to perform, and

(2) activities which are preliminary to or postliminary to said principal activity or activities,

which occur either prior to the time on any particular workday at which such employee commences, or subsequent to the time on any particular workday at which he ceases, such principal activity or activities. For purposes of this subsection, the use of an employer's vehicle for travel by an employee and activities performed by an employee which are incidental to the use of such vehicle for commuting shall not be considered part of the employee's principal activities if the use of such vehicle for travel is within the normal commuting area for the employer's business or establishment and the use of the employer's vehicle is subject to an agreement on the part of the employer and the employee or representative of such employee.

(b) Compensability by contract or custom

Notwithstanding the provisions of subsection (a) of this section which relieve an employer from liability and punishment with respect to any activity, the employer shall not be so relieved if such activity is compensable by either—

(1) an express provision of a written or nonwritten contract in effect, at the time of such activity, between such employee, his agent, or collective-bargaining representative and his employer; or

(2) a custom or practice in effect, at the time of such activity, at the establishment or other place where such employee is employed, covering such activity, not inconsistent with a written or nonwritten contract, in effect at the time of such activity, between such employee, his agent, or collective-bargaining representative and his employer.

(c) Restriction on activities compensable under contract or custom

For the purposes of subsection (b) of this section, an activity shall be considered as compensable under such contract provision or such custom or practice only when it is engaged in during the portion of the day with respect to which it is so made compensable.

(d) Determination of time employed with respect to activities

In the application of the minimum wage and overtime compensation provisions of the Fair Labor Standards Act of 1938, as amended [29 U.S.C. 201 et seq.], of the Walsh-Healey Act [41 U.S.C. 35 et seq.], or of the Bacon-Davis Act,[1] in determining the time for which an employer em-

[1] See References in Text note below.

ploys an employee with respect to walking, riding, traveling, or other preliminary or postliminary activities described in subsection (a) of this section, there shall be counted all that time, but only that time, during which the employee engages in any such activity which is compensable within the meaning of subsections (b) and (c) of this section.

(May 14, 1947, ch. 52, §4, 61 Stat. 86; Pub. L. 104–188, [title II], §2102, Aug. 20, 1996, 110 Stat. 1928.)

REFERENCES IN TEXT

The Fair Labor Standards Act of 1938, as amended, referred to in subsecs. (a) and (d), is act June 25, 1938, ch. 676, 52 Stat. 1060, as amended, which is classified generally to chapter 8 (§201 et seq.) of this title. For complete classification of this Act to the Code, see section 201 of this title and Tables.

The Walsh-Healey and Bacon-Davis Acts, referred to in subsecs. (a) and (d), are defined for purposes of this chapter in section 262 of this title.

AMENDMENTS

1996—Subsec. (a). Pub. L. 104–188 in closing provisions inserted at end "For purposes of this subsection, the use of an employer's vehicle for travel by an employee and activities performed by an employee which are incidental to the use of such vehicle for commuting shall not be considered part of the employee's principal activities if the use of such vehicle for travel is within the normal commuting area for the employer's business or establishment and the use of the employer's vehicle is subject to an agreement on the part of the employer and the employee or representative of such employee."

EFFECTIVE DATE OF 1996 AMENDMENT

Section 2103 of Pub. L. 104–188 provided that: "The amendment made by section 2101 [probably means section 2102 of Pub. L. 104–188, amending this section] shall take effect on the date of the enactment of this Act [Aug. 20, 1996] and shall apply in determining the application of section 4 of the Portal-to-Portal Act of 1947 [this section] to an employee in any civil action brought before such date of enactment but pending on such date."

§ 255. Statute of limitations

Any action commenced on or after May 14, 1947, to enforce any cause of action for unpaid minimum wages, unpaid overtime compensation, or liquidated damages, under the Fair Labor Standards Act of 1938, as amended [29 U.S.C. 201 et seq.], the Walsh-Healey Act [41 U.S.C. 35 et seq.], or the Bacon-Davis Act[1]—

(a) if the cause of action accrues on or after May 14, 1947—may be commenced within two years after the cause of action accrued, and every such action shall be forever barred unless commenced within two years after the cause of action accrued, except that a cause of action arising out of a willful violation may be commenced within three years after the cause of action accrued;

(b) if the cause of action accrued prior to May 14, 1947—may be commenced within whichever of the following periods is the shorter: (1) two years after the cause of action accrued, or (2) the period prescribed by the applicable State statute of limitations; and, except as provided in paragraph (c) of this section, every such action shall be forever barred unless commenced within the shorter of such two periods;

(c) if the cause of action accrued prior to May 14, 1947, the action shall not be barred by paragraph (b) of this section if it is commenced within one hundred and twenty days after May 14, 1947 unless at the time commenced it is barred by an applicable State statute of limitations;

(d) with respect to any cause of action brought under section 216(b) of this title against a State or a political subdivision of a State in a district court of the United States on or before April 18, 1973, the running of the statutory periods of limitation shall be deemed suspended during the period beginning with the commencement of any such action and ending one hundred and eighty days after the effective date of the Fair Labor Standards Amendments of 1974, except that such suspension shall not be applicable if in such action judgment has been entered for the defendant on the grounds other than State immunity from Federal jurisdiction.

(May 14, 1947, ch. 52, §6, 61 Stat. 87; Pub. L. 89–601, title VI, §601(b), Sept. 23, 1966, 80 Stat. 844; Pub. L. 93–259, §6(d)(2)(A), Apr. 8, 1974, 88 Stat. 61.)

REFERENCES IN TEXT

The Fair Labor Standards Act of 1938, as amended, referred to in subsecs. (a) and (d), is act June 25, 1938, ch. 676, 52 Stat. 1060, as amended, which is classified generally to chapter 8 (§201 et seq.) of this title. For complete classification of this Act to the Code, see section 201 of this title and Tables.

The Walsh-Healey and Bacon-Davis Acts, referred to in subsec. (a), are defined for purposes of this chapter in section 262 of this title.

Effective date of the Fair Labor Standards Amendments of 1974, referred to in subsec. (d), means May 1, 1974, except as otherwise specifically provided, under provisions of section 29(a) of Pub. L. 93–259, set out as an Effective Date of 1974 Amendment note under section 202 of this title.

AMENDMENTS

1974—Subsec. (d). Pub. L. 93–259 added subsec. (d).

1966—Subsec. (a). Pub. L. 89–601 inserted provision allowing causes of action arising out of willful violations to be commenced within three years after the cause of action accrued.

EFFECTIVE DATE OF 1974 AMENDMENT

Amendment by Pub. L. 93–259 effective May 1, 1974, see section 29(a) of Pub. L. 93–259, set out as a note under section 202 of this title.

EFFECTIVE DATE OF 1966 AMENDMENT

Amendment by Pub. L. 89–601 effective Feb. 1, 1967, except as otherwise provided, see section 602 of Pub. L. 89–601, set out as a note under section 203 of this title.

RULES, REGULATIONS, AND ORDERS PROMULGATED WITH REGARD TO 1966 AMENDMENTS

Secretary authorized to promulgate necessary rules, regulations, or orders on and after the date of the enactment of Pub. L. 89–601, Sept. 23, 1966, with regard to the amendments made by Pub. L. 89–601, see section 602 of Pub. L. 89–601, set out as a note under section 203 of this title.

[1] See References in Text note below.

§256. Determination of commencement of future actions

In determining when an action is commenced for the purposes of section 255 of this title, an action commenced on or after May 14, 1947 under the Fair Labor Standards Act of 1938, as amended [29 U.S.C. 201 et seq.], the Walsh-Healey Act [41 U.S.C. 35 et seq.], or the Bacon-Davis Act,[1] shall be considered to be commenced on the date when the complaint is filed; except that in the case of a collective or class action instituted under the Fair Labor Standards Act of 1938, as amended, or the Bacon-Davis Act, it shall be considered to be commenced in the case of any individual claimant—

(a) on the date when the complaint is filed, if he is specifically named as a party plaintiff in the complaint and his written consent to become a party plaintiff is filed on such date in the court in which the action is brought; or

(b) if such written consent was not so filed or if his name did not so appear—on the subsequent date on which such written consent is filed in the court in which the action was commenced.

(May 14, 1947, ch. 52, §7, 61 Stat. 88.)

REFERENCES IN TEXT

The Fair Labor Standards Act of 1938, as amended, referred to in text, is act June 25, 1938, ch. 676, 52 Stat. 1060, as amended, which is classified generally to chapter 8 (§201 et seq.) of this title. For complete classification of this Act to the Code, see section 201 of this title and Tables.

The Walsh-Healey and Bacon-Davis Acts, referred to in text, are defined for purposes of this chapter in section 262 of this title.

§257. Pending collective and representative actions

The statute of limitations prescribed in section 255(b) of this title shall also be applicable (in the case of a collective or representative action commenced prior to May 14, 1947 under the Fair Labor Standards Act of 1938, as amended [29 U.S.C. 201 et seq.]) to an individual claimant who has not been specifically named as a party plaintiff to the action prior to the expiration of one hundred and twenty days after May 14, 1947. In the application of such statute of limitations such action shall be considered to have been commenced as to him when, and only when, his written consent to become a party plaintiff to the action is filed in the court in which the action was brought.

(May 14, 1947, ch. 52, §8, 61 Stat. 88.)

REFERENCES IN TEXT

The Fair Labor Standards Act of 1938, as amended, referred to in text, is act June 25, 1938, ch. 676, 52 Stat. 1060, as amended, which is classified generally to chapter 8 (§201 et seq.) of this title. For complete classification of this Act to the Code, see section 201 of this title and Tables.

§258. Reliance on past administrative rulings, etc.

In any action or proceeding commenced prior to or on or after May 14, 1947 based on any act or omission prior to May 14, 1947, no employer shall be subject to any liability or punishment for or on account of the failure of the employer to pay minimum wages or overtime compensation under the Fair Labor Standards Act of 1938, as amended [29 U.S.C. 201 et seq.], the Walsh-Healey Act [41 U.S.C. 35 et seq.], or the Bacon-Davis Act,[1] if he pleads and proves that the act or omission complained of was in good faith in conformity with and in reliance on any administrative regulation, order, ruling, approval, or interpretation, of any agency of the United States, or any administrative practice or enforcement policy of any such agency with respect to the class of employers to which he belonged. Such a defense, if established, shall be a bar to the action or proceeding, notwithstanding that after such act or omission, such administrative regulation, order, ruling, approval, interpretation, practice, or enforcement policy is modified or rescinded or is determined by judicial authority to be invalid or of no legal effect.

(May 14, 1947, ch. 52, §9, 61 Stat. 88.)

REFERENCES IN TEXT

The Fair Labor Standards Act of 1938, as amended, referred to in text, is act June 25, 1938, ch. 676, 52 Stat. 1060, as amended, which is classified generally to chapter 8 (§201 et seq.) of this title. For complete classification of this Act to the Code, see section 201 of this title and Tables.

The Walsh-Healey and Bacon-Davis Acts, referred to in text, are defined for purposes of this chapter in section 262 of this title.

§259. Reliance in future on administrative rulings, etc.

(a) In any action or proceeding based on any act or omission on or after May 14, 1947, no employer shall be subject to any liability or punishment for or on account of the failure of the employer to pay minimum wages or overtime compensation under the Fair Labor Standards Act of 1938, as amended [29 U.S.C. 201 et seq.], the Walsh-Healey Act [41 U.S.C. 35 et seq.], or the Bacon-Davis Act,[1] if he pleads and proves that the act or omission complained of was in good faith in conformity with and in reliance on any written administrative regulation, order, ruling, approval, or interpretation, of the agency of the United States specified in subsection (b) of this section, or any administrative practice or enforcement policy of such agency with respect to the class of employers to which he belonged. Such a defense, if established, shall be a bar to the action or proceeding, notwithstanding that after such act or omission, such administrative regulation, order, ruling, approval, interpretation, practice, or enforcement policy is modified or rescinded or is determined by judicial authority to be invalid or of no legal effect.

(b) The agency referred to in subsection (a) of this section shall be—

(1) in the case of the Fair Labor Standards Act of 1938, as amended [29 U.S.C. 201 et seq.]—the Administrator of the Wage and Hour Division of the Department of Labor;

(2) in the case of the Walsh-Healey Act [41 U.S.C. 35 et seq.]—the Secretary of Labor, or

[1] See References in Text note below.

[1] See References in Text note below.

[1] See References in Text note below.

any Federal officer utilized by him in the administration of such Act; and

(3) in the case of the Bacon-Davis Act[1]—the Secretary of Labor.

(May 14, 1947, ch. 52, § 10, 61 Stat. 89.)

REFERENCES IN TEXT

The Fair Labor Standards Act of 1938, as amended, referred to in text, is act June 25, 1938, ch. 676, 52 Stat. 1060, as amended, which is classified generally to chapter 8 (§ 201 et seq.) of this title. For complete classification of this Act to the Code, see section 201 of this title and Tables.

The Walsh-Healey and Bacon-Davis Acts, referred to in text, are defined for purposes of this chapter in section 262 of this title.

TRANSFER OF FUNCTIONS

Functions relating to enforcement and administration of equal pay provisions vested by subsec. (b)(1) of this section in Administrator of Wage and Hour Division of Department of Labor transferred to Equal Employment Opportunity Commission by Reorg. Plan No. 1 of 1978, § 1, 43 F.R. 19807, 92 Stat. 3781, set out in the Appendix to Title 5, Government Organization and Employees, effective Jan. 1, 1979, as provided by section 1–101 of Ex. Ord. No. 12106, Dec. 28, 1978, 44 F.R. 1053.

For transfer of functions of other officers, employees, and agencies of Department of Labor, with certain exceptions, to Secretary of Labor, with power to delegate, see Reorg. Plan No. 6, of 1950, §§ 1, 2, 15 F.R. 3174, 64 Stat. 1263, set out in the Appendix to Title 5.

§ 260. Liquidated damages

In any action commenced prior to or on or after May 14, 1947 to recover unpaid minimum wages, unpaid overtime compensation, or liquidated damages, under the Fair Labor Standards Act of 1938, as amended [29 U.S.C. 201 et seq.], if the employer shows to the satisfaction of the court that the act or omission giving rise to such action was in good faith and that he had reasonable grounds for believing that his act or omission was not a violation of the Fair Labor Standards Act of 1938, as amended, the court may, in its sound discretion, award no liquidated damages or award any amount thereof not to exceed the amount specified in section 216 of this title.

(May 14, 1947, ch. 52, § 11, 61 Stat. 89; Pub. L. 93–259, § 6(d)(2)(B), Apr. 8, 1974, 88 Stat. 62.)

REFERENCES IN TEXT

The Fair Labor Standards Act of 1938, as amended, referred to in text, is act June 25, 1938, ch. 676, 52 Stat. 1060, as amended, which is classified generally to chapter 8 (§ 201 et seq.) of this title. For complete classification of this Act to the Code, see section 201 of this title and Tables.

AMENDMENTS

1974—Pub. L. 93–259 substituted "section 216 of this title" for "section 216(b) of this title".

EFFECTIVE DATE OF 1974 AMENDMENT

Amendment by Pub. L. 93–259 effective May 1, 1974, see section 29(a) of Pub. L. 93–259, set out as a note under section 202 of this title.

§ 261. Applicability of "area of production" regulations

No employer shall be subject to any liability or punishment under the Fair Labor Standards Act of 1938, as amended [29 U.S.C. 201 et seq.], on account of the failure of such employer to pay an employee minimum wages, or to pay an employee overtime compensation, for or on account of an activity engaged in by such employee prior to December 26, 1946, if such employer—

(1) was not so subject by reason of the definition of an "area of production", by a regulation of the Administrator of the Wage and Hour Division of the Department of Labor, which regulation was applicable at the time of performance of the activity even though at that time the regulation was invalid; or

(2) would not have been so subject if the regulation signed on December 18, 1946 (Federal Register, Vol. 11, p. 14648) had been in force on and after October 24, 1938.

(May 14, 1947, ch. 52, § 12, 61 Stat. 89.)

REFERENCES IN TEXT

The Fair Labor Standards Act of 1938, as amended, referred to in text, is act June 25, 1938, ch. 676, 52 Stat. 1060, as amended, which is classified generally to chapter 8 (§ 201 et seq.) of this title. For complete classification of this Act to the Code, see section 201 of this title and Tables.

TRANSFER OF FUNCTIONS

For transfer of functions of other officers, employees, and agencies of Department of Labor, with certain exceptions, to Secretary of Labor, with power to delegate, see Reorg. Plan No. 6, of 1950, §§ 1, 2, 15 F.R. 3174, 64 Stat. 1263, set out in the Appendix to Title 5, Government Organization and Employees.

§ 262. Definitions

(a) When the terms "employer", "employee", and "wage" are used in this chapter in relation to the Fair Labor Standards Act of 1938, as amended [29 U.S.C. 201 et seq.], they shall have the same meaning as when used in such Act of 1938.

(b) When the term "employer" is used in this chapter in relation to the Walsh-Healey Act [41 U.S.C. 35 et seq.] or Bacon-Davis Act[1] it shall mean the contractor or subcontractor covered by such Act.

(c) When the term "employee" is used in this chapter in relation to the Walsh-Healey Act [41 U.S.C. 35 et seq.] or the Bacon-Davis Act[1] it shall mean any individual employed by the contractor or subcontractor covered by such Act in the performance of his contract or subcontract.

(d) The term "Wash-Healey Act"[2] means the Act entitled "An Act to provide conditions for the purchase of supplies and the making of contracts by the United States, and for other purposes", approved June 30, 1936 (49 Stat. 2036), as amended [41 U.S.C. 35 et seq.]; and the term "Bacon-Davis Act" means the Act entitled "An Act to amend the Act approved March 3, 1931, relating to the rate of wages for laborers and mechanics employed by contractors and subcontractors on public buildings", approved August 30, 1935 (49 Stat. 1011), as amended.[1]

(e) As used in section 255 of this title the term "State" means any State of the United States or the District of Columbia or any Territory or possession of the United States.

[1] See References in Text note below.

[2] So in original. Probably should be "Walsh-Healey Act".

(May 14, 1947, ch. 52, § 13, 61 Stat. 90.)

REFERENCES IN TEXT

The Fair Labor Standards Act of 1938, as amended, referred to in subsec. (a), is act June 25, 1938, ch. 676, 52 Stat. 1060, as amended, which is classified generally to chapter 8 (§ 201 et seq.) of this title. For complete classification of this Act to the Code, see see section 201 of this title and Tables.

The "Bacon-Davis Act", as defined for purposes of this chapter in subsec. (d), is act Aug. 30, 1935, ch. 825, 49 Stat. 1011, which generally amended act Mar. 3, 1931, ch. 411, 46 Stat. 1494, popularly known as the "Davis-Bacon Act", and which was classified to sections 276a to 276a–6 of former Title 40, Public Buildings, Property, and Works. Sections 276a to 276a–6 of former Title 40 were repealed and reenacted as sections 3141–3144, 3146, and 3147 of Title 40, Public Buildings, Property, and Works, by Pub. L. 107–217, §§ 1, 6(b), Aug. 21, 2002, 116 Stat. 1062, 1304.

CHAPTER 10—DISCLOSURE OF WELFARE AND PENSION PLANS

§§ 301 to 309. Repealed. Pub. L. 93–406, title I, § 111(a)(1), Sept. 2, 1974, 88 Stat. 851

Section 301, Pub. L. 85–836, § 2, Aug. 28, 1958, 72 Stat. 997, set forth Congressional findings and policy with respect to welfare and pension plan disclosure. See section 1001 of this title.

Section 302, Pub. L. 85–836, § 3, Aug. 28, 1958, 72 Stat. 997; Pub. L. 86–624, § 21(d), July 12, 1960, 74 Stat. 417; Pub. L. 87–420, §§ 2–5, Mar. 20, 1962, 76 Stat. 35, provided definitions for this chapter. See section 1002 of this title.

Section 303, Pub. L. 85–836, § 4, Aug. 28, 1958, 72 Stat. 998; Pub. L. 87–420, § 6, Mar. 20, 1962, 76 Stat. 35, related to plans covered within chapter. See section 1003 of this title.

Section 304, Pub. L. 85–836, § 5, Aug. 28, 1958, 72 Stat. 998; Pub. L. 87–420, § 7, Mar. 20, 1962, 76 Stat. 36, related to duties of administrator and definition of "administrator". See sections 1002(16)(A) and 1021 of this title.

Section 305, Pub. L. 85–836, § 6, Aug. 28, 1958, 72 Stat. 999; Pub. L. 87–420, § 8, Mar. 20, 1962, 76 Stat. 36, related to time for publication and contents of plan. See section 1022 of this title.

Section 306, Pub. L. 85–836, § 7, Aug. 28, 1958, 72 Stat. 1000; Pub. L. 87–420, §§ 9–13, Mar. 20, 1962, 76 Stat. 36, 37, related to time for publication, contents, etc., of annual reports. See section 1023 of this title.

Section 307, Pub. L. 85–836, § 8, Aug. 28, 1958, 72 Stat. 1002; Pub. L. 87–420, §§ 14, 18, Mar. 20, 1962, 76 Stat. 37, 43, related to publication of description of plan and annual report. See section 1024 of this title.

Section 308, Pub. L. 85–836, § 9, Aug. 28, 1958, 72 Stat. 1002; Pub. L. 87–420, § 15, Mar. 20, 1962, 76 Stat. 37, related to enforcement provisions. See section 1131 et seq. of this title.

Section 308a, Pub. L. 85–836, § 10, as added Pub. L. 87–420, § 16(a), Mar. 20, 1962, 76 Stat. 38, related to reports as public information. See section 1026 of this title.

Section 308b, Pub. L. 85–836, § 11, as added Pub. L. 87–420, § 16(a), Mar. 20, 1962, 76 Stat. 38, related to retention of records. See section 1027 of this title.

Section 308c, Pub. L. 85–836, § 12, as added Pub. L. 87–420, § 16(a), Mar. 20, 1962, 76 Stat. 38, related to reliance on administrative interpretations and forms. See section 1028 of this title.

Section 308d, Pub. L. 85–836, § 13, as added Pub. L. 87–420, § 16(a), Mar. 20, 1962, 76 Stat. 39, related to bonding requirements. See section 1112 of this title.

Section 308e, Pub. L. 85–836, § 14, as added Pub. L. 87–420, § 16(a), Mar. 20, 1962, 76 Stat. 40, related to establishment, membership, duties, etc., of Advisory Council on Employee Welfare and Pension Benefit Plans. See section 1142 of this title.

Section 308f, Pub. L. 85–836, § 15, as added Pub. L. 87–420, § 16(a), Mar. 20, 1962, 76 Stat. 41, related to administration of provisions of chapter. See section 1137 of this title.

Section 309, Pub. L. 85–836, § 16, formerly § 10, Aug. 28, 1958, 72 Stat. 1002, renumbered and amended Pub. L. 87–420, § 16(a), (b), Mar. 20, 1962, 76 Stat. 38, 41, related to effect of other laws on provisions of this chapter. See section 1144 of this title.

EFFECTIVE DATE OF REPEAL

Repeal effective Jan. 1, 1975, except that chapter to remain applicable to any conduct and events which occurred before Jan. 1, 1975, see section 1031 of this title.

The Secretary of Labor was empowered, in the case of a plan which has a plan year which begins before Jan. 1, 1975, and ends after Dec. 31, 1974, to postpone by regulation the effective date of the repeal of any provision of this chapter until the beginning of the first plan year of such plan which begins after Jan. 1, 1975, pursuant to section 1031(b)(2) of this title.

CHAPTER 11—LABOR-MANAGEMENT REPORTING AND DISCLOSURE PROCEDURE

SUBCHAPTER I—GENERAL PROVISIONS

SUBCHAPTER II—BILL OF RIGHTS OF MEMBERS OF LABOR ORGANIZATIONS

SUBCHAPTER III—REPORTING BY LABOR ORGANIZATIONS, OFFICERS AND EMPLOYEES OF LABOR ORGANIZATIONS, AND EMPLOYERS

SUBCHAPTER IV—TRUSTEESHIPS

SUBCHAPTER V—ELECTIONS

SUBCHAPTER I—GENERAL PROVISIONS

§401. Congressional declaration of findings, purposes, and policy

(a) Standards for labor-management relations

The Congress finds that, in the public interest, it continues to be the responsibility of the Federal Government to protect employees' rights to organize, choose their own representatives, bargain collectively, and otherwise engage in concerted activities for their mutual aid or protection; that the relations between employers and labor organizations and the millions of workers they represent have a substantial impact on the commerce of the Nation; and that in order to accomplish the objective of a free flow of commerce it is essential that labor organizations, employers, and their officials adhere to the highest standards of responsibility and ethical conduct in administering the affairs of their organizations, particularly as they affect labor-management relations.

(b) Protection of rights of employees and the public

The Congress further finds, from recent investigations in the labor and management fields, that there have been a number of instances of breach of trust, corruption, disregard of the rights of individual employees, and other failures to observe high standards of responsibility and ethical conduct which require further and supplementary legislation that will afford necessary protection of the rights and interests of employees and the public generally as they relate to the activities of labor organizations, employers, labor relations consultants, and their officers and representatives.

(c) Necessity to eliminate or prevent improper practices

The Congress, therefore, further finds and declares that the enactment of this chapter is necessary to eliminate or prevent improper practices on the part of labor organizations, employers, labor relations consultants, and their officers and representatives which distort and defeat the policies of the Labor Management Relations Act, 1947, as amended [29 U.S.C. 141 et seq.], and the Railway Labor Act, as amended [45 U.S.C. 151 et seq.], and have the tendency or necessary effect of burdening or obstructing commerce by (1) impairing the efficiency, safety, or operation of the instrumentalities of commerce; (2) occurring in the current of commerce; (3) materially affecting, restraining, or controlling the flow of raw materials or manufactured or processed goods into or from the channels of commerce, or the prices of such materials or goods in commerce; or (4) causing diminution of employment and wages in such volume as substantially to impair or disrupt the market for goods flowing into or from the channels of commerce.

(Pub. L. 86–257, §2, Sept. 14, 1959, 73 Stat. 519.)

REFERENCES IN TEXT

This chapter, referred to in subsec. (c), was in the original "this Act", meaning Pub. L. 86–257, Sept. 14, 1959, 73 Stat. 519, as amended, known as the Labor-Management Reporting and Disclosure Act of 1959, which enacted this chapter, amended sections 153, 158, 159, 160, 164, 186, and 187 of this title, and enacted provisions set out as notes under sections 153, 158, and 481 of this title. For complete classification of this Act to the Code, see Short Title note set out below and Tables.

The Labor Management Relations Act, 1947, referred to in subsec. (c), is act June 23, 1947, ch. 120, 61 Stat. 136, as amended, which is classified principally to chapter 7 (§141 et seq.) of this title. For complete classification of this Act to the Code, see section 141 of this title and Tables.

The Railway Labor Act, referred to in subsec. (c), is act May 20, 1926, ch. 347, 44 Stat. 577, as amended, which is classified principally to chapter 8 (§151 et seq.) of Title 45, Railroads. For complete classification of this Act to the Code, see section 151 of Title 45 and Tables.

SHORT TITLE

Section 1 of Pub. L. 86–257 provided that: "This Act [enacting this chapter, amending sections 153, 158, 159, 160, 164, 186, and 187 of this title, and enacting provisions set out as notes under sections 153, 158, and 481 of this title] may be cited as the 'Labor-Management Reporting and Disclosure Act of 1959'."

§402. Definitions

For the purposes of this chapter—

(a) "Commerce" means trade, traffic, commerce, transportation, transmission, or communication among the several States or between any State and any place outside thereof.

(b) "State" includes any State of the United States, the District of Columbia, Puerto Rico, the Virgin Islands, American Samoa, Guam, Wake Island, the Canal Zone, and Outer Continental Shelf lands defined in the Outer Continental Shelf Lands Act [43 U.S.C. 1331 et seq.].

(c) "Industry affecting commerce" means any activity, business, or industry in commerce or in which a labor dispute would hinder or obstruct commerce or the free flow of commerce and includes any activity or industry "affecting commerce" within the meaning of the Labor Management Relations Act, 1947, as amended [29 U.S.C. 141 et seq.], or the Railway Labor Act, as amended [45 U.S.C. 151 et seq.].

(d) "Person" includes one or more individuals, labor organizations, partnerships, associations, corporations, legal representatives, mutual companies, joint-stock companies, trusts, unincorporated organizations, trustees, trustees in cases under title 11, or receivers.

(e) "Employer" means any employer or any group or association of employers engaged in an industry affecting commerce (1) which is, with respect to employees engaged in an industry affecting commerce, an employer within the meaning of any law of the United States relating to the employment of any employees or (2) which may deal with any labor organization concerning grievances, labor disputes, wages, rates of pay, hours of employment, or conditions of work, and includes any person acting directly or indirectly as an employer or as an agent of an employer in relation to an employee but does not include the United States or any corporation wholly owned by the Government of the United States or any State or political subdivision thereof.

(f) "Employee" means any individual employed by an employer, and includes any individual whose work has ceased as a consequence of, or in connection with, any current labor dispute or because of any unfair labor practice or because of exclusion or expulsion from a labor organization in any manner or for any reason inconsistent with the requirements of this chapter.

(g) "Labor dispute" includes any controversy concerning terms, tenure, or conditions of employment, or concerning the association or representation of persons in negotiating, fixing, maintaining, changing, or seeking to arrange terms or conditions of employment, regardless of whether the disputants stand in the proximate relation of employer and employee.

(h) "Trusteeship" means any receivership, trusteeship, or other method of supervision or control whereby a labor organization suspends the autonomy otherwise available to a subordinate body under its constitution or bylaws.

(i) "Labor organization" means a labor organization engaged in an industry affecting commerce and includes any organization of any kind, any agency, or employee representation committee, group, association, or plan so engaged in which employees participate and which exists for the purpose, in whole or in part, of dealing with employers concerning grievances, labor disputes, wages, rates of pay, hours, or other terms or conditions of employment, and any conference, general committee, joint or system board, or joint council so engaged which is subordinate to a national or international labor organization, other than a State or local central body.

(j) A labor organization shall be deemed to be engaged in an industry affecting commerce if it—

(1) is the certified representative of employees under the provisions of the National Labor Relations Act, as amended [29 U.S.C. 151 et seq.], or the Railway Labor Act, as amended [45 U.S.C. 151 et seq.]; or

(2) although not certified, is a national or international labor organization or a local labor organization recognized or acting as the representative of employees of an employer or employers engaged in an industry affecting commerce; or

(3) has chartered a local labor organization or subsidiary body which is representing or actively seeking to represent employees of employers within the meaning of paragraph (1) or (2); or

(4) has been chartered by a labor organization representing or actively seeking to represent employees within the meaning of paragraph (1) or (2) as the local or subordinate body through which such employees may enjoy membership or become affiliated with such labor organization; or

(5) is a conference, general committee, joint or system board, or joint council, subordinate to a national or international labor organization, which includes a labor organization engaged in an industry affecting commerce within the meaning of any of the preceding paragraphs of this subsection, other than a State or local central body.

(k) "Secret ballot" means the expression by ballot, voting machine, or otherwise, but in no event by proxy, of a choice with respect to any election or vote taken upon any matter, which is cast in such a manner that the person expressing such choice cannot be identified with the choice expressed.

(*l*) "Trust in which a labor organization is interested" means a trust or other fund or organization (1) which was created or established by a labor organization, or one or more of the trustees or one or more members of the governing body of which is selected or appointed by a labor organization, and (2) a primary purpose of which is to provide benefits for the members of such labor organization or their beneficiaries.

(m) "Labor relations consultant" means any person who, for compensation, advises or represents an employer, employer organization, or labor organization concerning employee organizing, concerted activities, or collective bargaining activities.

(n) "Officer" means any constitutional officer, any person authorized to perform the functions of president, vice president, secretary, treasurer, or other executive functions of a labor organization, and any member of its executive board or similar governing body.

(*o*) "Member" or "member in good standing", when used in reference to a labor organization, includes any person who has fulfilled the requirements for membership in such organization, and who neither has voluntarily withdrawn from membership nor has been expelled or suspended from membership after appropriate proceedings consistent with lawful provisions of the constitution and bylaws of such organization.

(p) "Secretary" means the Secretary of Labor.

(q) "Officer, agent, shop steward, or other representative", when used with respect to a labor organization, includes elected officials and key administrative personnel, whether elected or appointed (such as business agents, heads of departments or major units, and organizers who exercise substantial independent authority), but does not include salaried nonsupervisory professional staff, stenographic, and service personnel.

(r) "District court of the United States" means a United States district court and a

United States court of any place subject to the jurisdiction of the United States.

(Pub. L. 86–257, §3, Sept. 14, 1959, 73 Stat. 520; Pub. L. 95–598, title III, §320, Nov. 6, 1978, 92 Stat. 2678.)

REFERENCES IN TEXT

This chapter, referred to in the opening phrase, was in the original "titles I, II, III, IV, V (except section 505), and VI of this Act", which reference includes those sections of the Act which are classified principally to this chapter. For complete classification of such titles to the Code, see Tables.

For definition of Canal Zone, referred to in subsec. (b), see section 3602(b) of Title 22, Foreign Relations and Intercourse.

The Outer Continental Shelf Lands Act, referred to in subsec. (b), is act Aug. 7, 1953, ch. 345, 67 Stat. 462, as amended, which is classified generally to subchapter III (§1331 et seq.) of chapter 29 of Title 43, Public Lands. For complete classification of this Act to the Code, see Short Title note set out under section 1331 of Title 43 and Tables.

The Labor Management Relations Act, 1947, referred to in subsec. (c), is act June 23, 1947, ch. 120, 61 Stat. 136, as amended, which is classified principally to chapter 7 (§141 et seq.) of this title. For complete classification of this Act to the Code, see section 141 of this title and Tables.

This chapter, referred to in subsec. (f), was in the original "this Act", meaning Pub. L. 86–257, Sept. 14, 1959, 73 Stat. 519, as amended, known as the Labor-Management Reporting and Disclosure Act of 1959, which enacted this chapter, amended sections 153, 158, 159, 160, 164, 186, and 187 of this title, and enacted provisions set out as notes under sections 153, 158, and 481 of this title. For complete classification of this Act to the Code, see Short Title note set out under section 401 of this title and Tables.

The Railway Labor Act, referred to in subsecs. (c) and (j)(1), is act May 20, 1926, ch. 347, 44 Stat. 577, as amended, which is classified principally to chapter 8 (§151 et seq.) of Title 45, Railroads. For complete classification of this Act to the Code, see section 151 of Title 45 and Tables.

The National Labor Relations Act, referred to in subsec. (j)(1), is act July 5, 1935, ch. 372, 49 Stat. 452, as amended, which is classified generally to subchapter II (§151 et seq.) of chapter 7 of this title. For complete classification of this Act to the Code, see section 167 of this title and Tables.

AMENDMENTS

1978—Subsec. (d). Pub. L. 95–598 substituted "cases under title 11" for "bankruptcy".

EFFECTIVE DATE OF 1978 AMENDMENT

Amendment by Pub. L. 95–598 effective Oct. 1, 1979, see section 402(a) of Pub. L. 95–598, set out as an Effective Date note preceding section 101 of Title 11, Bankruptcy.

SUBCHAPTER II—BILL OF RIGHTS OF MEMBERS OF LABOR ORGANIZATIONS

§411. Bill of rights; constitution and bylaws of labor organizations

(a)(1) Equal rights

Every member of a labor organization shall have equal rights and privileges within such organization to nominate candidates, to vote in elections or referendums of the labor organization, to attend membership meetings, and to participate in the deliberations and voting upon the business of such meetings, subject to reasonable rules and regulations in such organization's constitution and bylaws.

(2) Freedom of speech and assembly

Every member of any labor organization shall have the right to meet and assemble freely with other members; and to express any views, arguments, or opinions; and to express at meetings of the labor organization his views, upon candidates in an election of the labor organization or upon any business properly before the meeting, subject to the organization's established and reasonable rules pertaining to the conduct of meetings: *Provided*, That nothing herein shall be construed to impair the right of a labor organization to adopt and enforce reasonable rules as to the responsibility of every member toward the organization as an institution and to his refraining from conduct that would interfere with its performance of its legal or contractual obligations.

(3) Dues, initiation fees, and assessments

Except in the case of a federation of national or international labor organizations, the rates of dues and initiation fees payable by members of any labor organization in effect on September 14, 1959 shall not be increased, and no general or special assessment shall be levied upon such members, except—

(A) in the case of a local labor organization, (i) by majority vote by secret ballot of the members in good standing voting at a general or special membership meeting, after reasonable notice of the intention to vote upon such question, or (ii) by majority vote of the members in good standing voting in a membership referendum conducted by secret ballot; or

(B) in the case of a labor organization, other than a local labor organization or a federation of national or international labor organizations, (i) by majority vote of the delegates voting at a regular convention, or at a special convention of such labor organization held upon not less than thirty days' written notice to the principal office of each local or constituent labor organization entitled to such notice, or (ii) by majority vote of the members in good standing of such labor organization voting in a membership referendum conducted by secret ballot, or (iii) by majority vote of the members of the executive board or similar governing body of such labor organization, pursuant to express authority contained in the constitution and bylaws of such labor organization: *Provided*, That such action on the part of the executive board or similar governing body shall be effective only until the next regular convention of such labor organization.

(4) Protection of the right to sue

No labor organization shall limit the right of any member thereof to institute an action in any court, or in a proceeding before any administrative agency, irrespective of whether or not the labor organization or its officers are named as defendants or respondents in such action or proceeding, or the right of any member of a labor organization to appear as a witness in any judicial, administrative, or legislative proceeding, or to petition any legislature or to communicate with any legislator: *Provided*, That any such member may be required to exhaust reasonable hearing procedures (but not to exceed a four-month lapse of time) within such organization, before instituting legal or administrative proceedings against such organizations or any officer thereof: *And provided further*, That no interested employer or employer association shall directly or indirectly finance, encourage, or participate in, except as a party, any such action, proceeding, appearance, or petition.

(5) Safeguards against improper disciplinary action

No member of any labor organization may be fined, suspended, expelled, or otherwise disciplined except for nonpayment of dues by such organization or by any officer thereof unless such member has been (A) served with written specific charges; (B) given a reasonable time to prepare his defense; (C) afforded a full and fair hearing.

(b) Invalidity of constitution and bylaws

Any provision of the constitution and bylaws of any labor organization which is inconsistent with the provisions of this section shall be of no force or effect.

(Pub. L. 86–257, title I, §101, Sept. 14, 1959, 73 Stat. 522.)

§412. Civil action for infringement of rights; jurisdiction

Any person whose rights secured by the provisions of this subchapter have been infringed by any violation of this subchapter may bring a civil action in a district court of the United States for such relief (including injunctions) as may be appropriate. Any such action against a labor organization shall be brought in the district court of the United States for the district where the alleged violation occurred, or where the principal office of such labor organization is located.

(Pub. L. 86–257, title I, §102, Sept. 14, 1959, 73 Stat. 523.)

§413. Retention of existing rights of members

Nothing contained in this subchapter shall limit the rights and remedies of any member of a labor organization under any State or Federal law or before any court or other tribunal, or under the constitution and bylaws of any labor organization.

(Pub. L. 86–257, title I, §103, Sept. 14, 1959, 73 Stat. 523.)

§414. Right to copies of collective bargaining agreements

It shall be the duty of the secretary or corresponding principal officer of each labor organization, in the case of a local labor organization, to forward a copy of each collective bargaining agreement made by such labor organization with any employer to any employee who requests such a copy and whose rights as such employee are directly affected by such agreement, and in the case of a labor organization other than a local labor organization, to forward a copy of any such agreement to each constituent unit which has members directly affected by such agreement; and such officer shall maintain at the principal office of the labor organization of which he is an officer copies of any such agreement made or received by such labor organization, which copies shall be available for inspection by any member or by any employee whose rights are affected by such agreement. The provisions of section 440 of this title shall be applicable in the enforcement of this section.

(Pub. L. 86–257, title I, §104, Sept. 14, 1959, 73 Stat. 523.)

§415. Information to members of provisions of chapter

Every labor organization shall inform its members concerning the provisions of this chapter.

(Pub. L. 86–257, title I, §105, Sept. 14, 1959, 73 Stat. 523.)

SUBCHAPTER III—REPORTING BY LABOR ORGANIZATIONS, OFFICERS AND EMPLOYEES OF LABOR ORGANIZATIONS, AND EMPLOYERS

§431. Report of labor organizations

(a) Adoption and filing of constitution and bylaws; contents of report

Every labor organization shall adopt a constitution and bylaws and shall file a copy thereof with the Secretary, together with a report, signed by its president and secretary or corresponding principal officers, containing the following information—

(1) the name of the labor organization, its mailing address, and any other address at which it maintains its principal office or at which it keeps the records referred to in this subchapter;

(2) the name and title of each of its officers;

(3) the initiation fee or fees required from a new or transferred member and fees for work permits required by the reporting labor organization;

(4) the regular dues or fees or other periodic payments required to remain a member of the reporting labor organization; and

(5) detailed statements, or references to specific provisions of documents filed under this subsection which contain such statements, showing the provision made and procedures followed with respect to each of the following: (A) qualifications for or restrictions on membership, (B) levying of assessments, (C) participation in insurance or other benefit plans, (D) authorization for disbursement of funds of the labor organization, (E) audit of financial transactions of the labor organization, (F) the calling of regular and special meetings, (G) the selection of officers and stewards and of any representatives to other bodies composed of labor organizations' representatives, with a specific statement of the manner in which each officer was elected, appointed, or otherwise selected, (H) discipline or removal of officers or agents for breaches of their trust, (I) imposition of fines, suspensions, and expulsions of members, including the grounds for such action and any provision made for notice, hearing, judgment on the evidence, and appeal

procedures, (J) authorization for bargaining demands, (K) ratification of contract terms, (L) authorization for strikes, and (M) issuance of work permits. Any change in the information required by this subsection shall be reported to the Secretary at the time the reporting labor organization files with the Secretary the annual financial report required by subsection (b) of this section.

(b) Annual financial report; filing; contents

Every labor organization shall file annually with the Secretary a financial report signed by its president and treasurer or corresponding principal officers containing the following information in such detail as may be necessary accurately to disclose its financial condition and operations for its preceding fiscal year—

(1) assets and liabilities at the beginning and end of the fiscal year;

(2) receipts of any kind and the sources thereof;

(3) salary, allowances, and other direct or indirect disbursements (including reimbursed expenses) to each officer and also to each employee who, during such fiscal year, received more than $10,000 in the aggregate from such labor organization and any other labor organization affiliated with it or with which it is affiliated, or which is affiliated with the same national or international labor organization;

(4) direct and indirect loans made to any officer, employee, or member, which aggregated more than $250 during the fiscal year, together with a statement of the purpose, security, if any, and arrangements for repayment;

(5) direct and indirect loans to any business enterprise, together with a statement of the purpose, security, if any, and arrangements for repayment; and

(6) other disbursements made by it including the purposes thereof;

all in such categories as the Secretary may prescribe.

(c) Availability of information to members; examination of books, records, and accounts

Every labor organization required to submit a report under this subchapter shall make available the information required to be contained in such report to all of its members, and every such labor organization and its officers shall be under a duty enforceable at the suit of any member of such organization in any State court of competent jurisdiction or in the district court of the United States for the district in which such labor organization maintains its principal office, to permit such member for just cause to examine any books, records, and accounts necessary to verify such report. The court in such action may, in its discretion, in addition to any judgment awarded to the plaintiff or plaintiffs, allow a reasonable attorney's fee to be paid by the defendant, and costs of the action.

(Pub. L. 86–257, title II, §201(a)–(c), Sept. 14, 1959, 73 Stat. 524, 525.)

CODIFICATION

Section is comprised of subsecs. (a) to (c) of section 201 of Pub. L. 86–257. Subsec. (d) of section 201 repealed subsecs. (f) to (h) of section 159 of this title, and subsec. (e) of section 201 amended section 158(a)(3)(i) of this title.

§432. Report of officers and employees of labor organizations

(a) Filing; contents of report

Every officer of a labor organization and every employee of a labor organization (other than an employee performing exclusively clerical or custodial services) shall file with the Secretary a signed report listing and describing for his preceding fiscal year—

(1) any stock, bond, security, or other interest, legal or equitable, which he or his spouse or minor child directly or indirectly held in, and any income or any other benefit with monetary value (including reimbursed expenses) which he or his spouse or minor child derived directly or indirectly from, an employer whose employees such labor organization represents or is actively seeking to represent, except payments and other benefits received as a bona fide employee of such employer;

(2) any transaction in which he or his spouse or minor child engaged, directly or indirectly, involving any stock, bond, security, or loan to or from, or other legal or equitable interest in the business of an employer whose employees such labor organization represents or is actively seeking to represent;

(3) any stock, bond, security, or other interest, legal or equitable, which he or his spouse or minor child directly or indirectly held in, and any income or any other benefit with monetary value (including reimbursed expenses) which he or his spouse or minor child directly or indirectly derived from, any business a substantial part of which consists of buying from, selling or leasing to, or otherwise dealing with, the business of an employer whose employees such labor organization represents or is actively seeking to represent;

(4) any stock, bond, security, or other interest, legal or equitable, which he or his spouse or minor child directly or indirectly held in, and any income or any other benefit with monetary value (including reimbursed expenses) which he or his spouse or minor child directly or indirectly derived from, a business any part of which consists of buying from, or selling or leasing directly or indirectly to, or otherwise dealing with such labor organization;

(5) any direct or indirect business transaction or arrangement between him or his spouse or minor child and any employer whose employees his organization represents or is actively seeking to represent, except work performed and payments and benefits received as a bona fide employee of such employer and except purchases and sales of goods or services in the regular course of business at prices generally available to any employee of such employer; and

(6) any payment of money or other thing of value (including reimbursed expenses) which he or his spouse or minor child received directly or indirectly from any employer or any person who acts as a labor relations consultant to an employer, except payments of the kinds referred to in section 186(c) of this title.

(b) Report of certain bona fide investments

The provisions of paragraphs (1), (2), (3), (4), and (5) of subsection (a) of this section shall not be construed to require any such officer or employee to report his bona fide investments in securities traded on a securities exchange registered as a national securities exchange under the Securities Exchange Act of 1934 [15 U.S.C. 78a et seq.], in shares in an investment company registered under the Investment Company Act of 1940 [15 U.S.C. 80a–1 et seq.], or in securities of a public utility holding company registered under the Public Utility Holding Company Act of 1935, or to report any income derived therefrom.

(c) Exemption from filing requirement

Nothing contained in this section shall be construed to require any officer or employee of a labor organization to file a report under subsection (a) of this section unless he or his spouse or minor child holds or has held an interest, has received income or any other benefit with monetary value or a loan, or has engaged in a transaction described therein.

(Pub. L. 86–257, title II, §202, Sept. 14, 1959, 73 Stat. 525.)

REFERENCES IN TEXT

The Securities Exchange Act of 1934, referred to in subsec. (b), is act June 6, 1934, ch. 404, 48 Stat. 881, as amended, which is classified principally to chapter 2B (§78a et seq.) of Title 15, Commerce and Trade. For complete classification of this Act to the Code, see section 78a of Title 15 and Tables.

The Investment Company Act of 1940, referred to in subsec. (b), is title I of act Aug. 22, 1940, ch. 686, 54 Stat. 789, as amended, which is classified generally to subchapter I (§80a–1 et seq.) of chapter 2D of Title 15. For complete classification of this Act to the Code, see section 80a–51 of Title 15 and Tables.

The Public Utility Holding Company Act of 1935, referred to in subsec. (b), is title I of act Aug. 26, 1935, ch. 687, 49 Stat. 803, as amended, which was classified generally to chapter 2C (§79 et seq.) of Title 15, Commerce and Trade, prior to repeal by Pub. L. 109–58, title XII, §1263, Aug. 8, 2005, 119 Stat. 974. For complete classification of this Act to the Code, see Tables.

§ 433. Report of employers

(a) Filing and contents of report of payments, loans, promises, agreements, or arrangements

Every employer who in any fiscal year made—

(1) any payment or loan, direct or indirect, of money or other thing of value (including reimbursed expenses), or any promise or agreement therefor, to any labor organization or officer, agent, shop steward, or other representative of a labor organization, or employee of any labor organization, except (A) payments or loans made by any national or State bank, credit union, insurance company, savings and loan association or other credit institution and (B) payments of the kind referred to in section 186(c) of this title;

(2) any payment (including reimbursed expenses) to any of his employees, or any group or committee of such employees, for the purpose of causing such employee or group or committee of employees to persuade other employees to exercise or not to exercise, or as the manner of exercising, the right to organize and bargain collectively through representatives of their own choosing unless such payments were contemporaneously or previously disclosed to such other employees;

(3) any expenditure, during the fiscal year, where an object thereof, directly or indirectly, is to interfere with, restrain, or coerce employees in the exercise of the right to organize and bargain collectively through representatives of their own choosing, or is to obtain information concerning the activities of employees or a labor organization in connection with a labor dispute involving such employer, except for use solely in conjunction with an administrative or arbitral proceeding or a criminal or civil judicial proceeding;

(4) any agreement or arrangement with a labor relations consultant or other independent contractor or organization pursuant to which such person undertakes activities where an object thereof, directly or indirectly, is to persuade employees to exercise or not to exercise, or persuade employees as to the manner of exercising, the right to organize and bargain collectively through representatives of their own choosing, or undertakes to supply such employer with information concerning the activities of employees or a labor organization in connection with a labor dispute involving such employer, except information for use solely in conjunction with an administrative or arbitral proceeding or a criminal or civil judicial proceeding; or

(5) any payment (including reimbursed expenses) pursuant to an agreement or arrangement described in subdivision (4);

shall file with the Secretary a report, in a form prescribed by him, signed by its president and treasurer or corresponding principal officers showing in detail the date and amount of each such payment, loan, promise, agreement, or arrangement and the name, address, and position, if any, in any firm or labor organization of the person to whom it was made and a full explanation of the circumstances of all such payments, including the terms of any agreement or understanding pursuant to which they were made.

(b) Persuasive activities relating to the right to organize and bargain collectively; supplying information of activities in connection with labor disputes; filing and contents of report of agreement or arrangement

Every person who pursuant to any agreement or arrangement with an employer undertakes activities where an object thereof is, directly or indirectly—

(1) to persuade employees to exercise or not to exercise, or persuade employees as to the manner of exercising, the right to organize and bargain collectively through representatives of their own choosing; or

(2) to supply an employer with information concerning the activities of employees or a labor organization in connection with a labor dispute involving such employer, except information for use solely in conjunction with an administrative or arbitral proceeding or a criminal or civil judicial proceeding;

shall file within thirty days after entering into such agreement or arrangement a report with the Secretary, signed by its president and treasurer or corresponding principal officers, containing the name under which such person is engaged in doing business and the address of its principal office, and a detailed statement of the terms and conditions of such agreement or arrangement. Every such person shall file annually, with respect to each fiscal year during which payments were made as a result of such an agreement or arrangement, a report with the Secretary, signed by its president and treasurer or corresponding principal officers, containing a statement (A) of its receipts of any kind from employers on account of labor relations advice or services, designating the sources thereof, and (B) of its disbursements of any kind, in connection with such services and the purposes thereof. In each such case such information shall be set forth in such categories as the Secretary may prescribe.

(c) Advisory or representative services exempt from filing requirements

Nothing in this section shall be construed to require any employer or other person to file a report covering the services of such person by reason of his giving or agreeing to give advice to such employer or representing or agreeing to represent such employer before any court, administrative agency, or tribunal of arbitration or engaging or agreeing to engage in collective bargaining on behalf of such employer with respect to wages, hours, or other terms or conditions of employment or the negotiation of an agreement or any question arising thereunder.

(d) Exemption from filing requirements generally

Nothing contained in this section shall be construed to require an employer to file a report under subsection (a) of this section unless he has made an expenditure, payment, loan, agreement, or arrangement of the kind described therein. Nothing contained in this section shall be construed to require any other person to file a report under subsection (b) of this section unless he was a party to an agreement or arrangement of the kind described therein.

(e) Services by and payments to regular officers, supervisors, and employees of employer

Nothing contained in this section shall be construed to require any regular officer, supervisor, or employee of an employer to file a report in connection with services rendered to such employer nor shall any employer be required to file a report covering expenditures made to any regular officer, supervisor, or employee of an employer as compensation for service as a regular officer, supervisor, or employee of such employer.

(f) Rights protected by section 158(c) of this title

Nothing contained in this section shall be construed as an amendment to, or modification of the rights protected by, section 158(c) of this title.

(g) "Interfere with, restrain, or coerce" defined

The term "interfere with, restrain, or coerce" as used in this section means interference, restraint, and coercion which, if done with respect to the exercise of rights guaranteed in section 157 of this title, would, under section 158(a) of this title, constitute an unfair labor practice.

(Pub. L. 86–257, title II, §203, Sept. 14, 1959, 73 Stat. 526.)

§ 434. Exemption of attorney-client communications

Nothing contained in this chapter shall be construed to require an attorney who is a member in good standing of the bar of any State, to include in any report required to be filed pursuant to the provisions of this chapter any information which was lawfully communicated to such attorney by any of his clients in the course of a legitimate attorney-client relationship.

(Pub. L. 86–257, title II, §204, Sept. 14, 1959, 73 Stat. 528.)

§ 435. Reports and documents as public information

(a) Publication; statistical and research purposes

The contents of the reports and documents filed with the Secretary pursuant to sections 431, 432, 433, and 441 of this title shall be public information, and the Secretary may publish any information and data which he obtains pursuant to the provisions of this subchapter. The Secretary may use the information and data for statistical and research purposes, and compile and publish such studies, analyses, reports, and surveys based thereon as he may deem appropriate.

(b) Inspection and examination of information and data

The Secretary shall by regulation make reasonable provision for the inspection and examination, on the request of any person, of the information and data contained in any report or other document filed with him pursuant to section 431, 432, 433, or 441 of this title.

(c) Copies of reports or documents; availability to State agencies

The Secretary shall by regulation provide for the furnishing by the Department of Labor of copies of reports or other documents filed with the Secretary pursuant to this subchapter, upon payment of a charge based upon the cost of the service. The Secretary shall make available without payment of a charge, or require any person to furnish, to such State agency as is designated by law or by the Governor of the State in which such person has his principal place of business or headquarters, upon request of the Governor of such State, copies of any reports and documents filed by such person with the Secretary pursuant to section 431, 432, 433, or 441 of this title, or of information and data contained therein. No person shall be required by reason of any law of any State to furnish to any officer or agency of such State any information included in a report filed by such person with the Secretary pursuant to the provisions of this subchapter, if a copy of such report, or of the portion thereof containing such information, is furnished to such officer or agency. All moneys received in payment of such charges fixed by the Secretary pursuant to this subsection shall be deposited in the general fund of the Treasury.

(Pub. L. 86–257, title II, §205, Sept. 14, 1959, 73 Stat. 528; Pub. L. 89–216, §2(a)–(c), Sept. 29, 1965, 79 Stat. 888.)

AMENDMENTS

1965—Pub. L. 89–216 inserted references to section 441 of this title.

§436. Retention of records

Every person required to file any report under this subchapter shall maintain records on the matters required to be reported which will provide in sufficient detail the necessary basic information and data from which the documents filed with the Secretary may be verified, explained, or clarified, and checked for accuracy and completeness, and shall include vouchers, worksheets, receipts, and applicable resolutions, and shall keep such records available for examination for a period of not less than five years after the filing of the documents based on the information which they contain.

(Pub. L. 86–257, title II, §206, Sept. 14, 1959, 73 Stat. 529.)

§437. Time for making reports

(a) Each labor organization shall file the initial report required under section 431(a) of this title within ninety days after the date on which it first becomes subject to this chapter.

(b) Each person required to file a report under section 431(b), 432, 433(a), the second sentence of 433(b), or section 441 of this title shall file such report within ninety days after the end of each of its fiscal years; except that where such person is subject to section 431(b), 432, 433(a), the second sentence of 433(b), or section 441 of this title, as the case may be, for only a portion of such a fiscal year (because September 14, 1959, occurs during such person's fiscal year) such person becomes subject to this chapter during its fiscal year or such person may consider that portion as the entire fiscal year in making such report.

(Pub. L. 86–257, title II, §207, Sept. 14, 1959, 73 Stat. 529; Pub. L. 89–216, §2(d), Sept. 29, 1965, 79 Stat. 888.)

AMENDMENTS

1965—Subsec. (b). Pub. L. 89–216 inserted reference to section 441 of this title in two places.

§438. Rules and regulations; simplified reports

The Secretary shall have authority to issue, amend, and rescind rules and regulations prescribing the form and publication of reports required to be filed under this subchapter and such other reasonable rules and regulations (including rules prescribing reports concerning trusts in which a labor organization is interested) as he may find necessary to prevent the circumvention or evasion of such reporting requirements. In exercising his power under this section the Secretary shall prescribe by general rule simplified reports for labor organizations or employers for whom he finds that by virtue of their size a detailed report would be unduly burdensome, but the Secretary may revoke such provision for simplified forms of any labor organization or employer if he determines, after such investigation as he deems proper and due notice and opportunity for a hearing, that the purposes of this section would be served thereby.

(Pub. L. 86–257, title II, §208, Sept. 14, 1959, 73 Stat. 529.)

§439. Violations and penalties

(a) Willful violations of provisions of subchapter

Any person who willfully violates this subchapter shall be fined not more than $10,000 or imprisoned for not more than one year, or both.

(b) False statements or representations of fact with knowledge of falsehood

Any person who makes a false statement or representation of a material fact, knowing it to be false, or who knowingly fails to disclose a material fact, in any document, report, or other information required under the provisions of this subchapter shall be fined not more than $10,000 or imprisoned for not more than one year, or both.

(c) False entry in or willful concealment, etc., of books and records

Any person who willfully makes a false entry in or willfully conceals, withholds, or destroys any books, records, reports, or statements required to be kept by any provision of this subchapter shall be fined not more than $10,000 or imprisoned for not more than one year, or both.

(d) Personal responsibility of individuals required to sign reports

Each individual required to sign reports under sections 431 and 433 of this title shall be personally responsible for the filing of such reports and for any statement contained therein which he knows to be false.

(Pub. L. 86–257, title II, §209, Sept. 14, 1959, 73 Stat. 529.)

§440. Civil action for enforcement by Secretary; jurisdiction

Whenever it shall appear that any person has violated or is about to violate any of the provisions of this subchapter, the Secretary may bring a civil action for such relief (including injunctions) as may be appropriate. Any such action may be brought in the district court of the United States where the violation occurred or, at the option of the parties, in the United States District Court for the District of Columbia.

(Pub. L. 86–257, title II, §210, Sept. 14, 1959, 73 Stat. 530.)

§441. Surety company reports; contents; waiver or modification of requirements respecting contents of reports

Each surety company which issues any bond required by this chapter or the Employee Retirement Income Security Act of 1974 [29 U.S.C. 1001 et seq.] shall file annually with the Secretary, with respect to each fiscal year during which any such bond was in force, a report, in such form and detail as he may prescribe by regulation, filed by the president and treasurer or corresponding principal officers of the surety company, describing its bond experience under each such chapter or Act, including information as to the premiums received, total claims paid, amounts recovered by way of subrogation, administrative and legal expenses and such related data and information as the Secretary shall determine to be necessary in the public interest and to carry out the policy of the chapter. Notwithstanding the foregoing, if the Secretary finds that any such specific information cannot be practicably ascertained or would be uninformative, the Secretary may modify or waive the requirement for such information.

(Pub. L. 86–257, title II, §211, as added Pub. L. 89–216, §3, Sept. 29, 1965, 79 Stat. 888; amended Pub. L. 93–406, title I, §111(a)(2)(D), Sept. 2, 1974, 88 Stat. 852.)

REFERENCES IN TEXT

The Employee Retirement Income Security Act of 1974, referred to in text, is Pub. L. 93–406, Sept. 2, 1974, 88 Stat. 829, as amended, which is classified principally to chapter 18 (§1001 et seq.) of this title. For complete classification of this Act to the Code, see Short Title note set out under section 1001 of this title and Tables.

AMENDMENTS

1974—Pub. L. 93–406 substituted "Employee Retirement Income Security Act of 1974" for "Welfare and Pension Plans Disclosure Act".

EFFECTIVE DATE OF 1974 AMENDMENT

Amendment by Pub. L. 93–406 effective Jan. 1, 1975, except as provided in section 1031(b)(2) of this title, see section 1031(b)(1) of this title.

SUBCHAPTER IV—TRUSTEESHIPS

§ 461. Reports

(a) Filing and contents; annual financial report

Every labor organization which has or assumes trusteeship over any subordinate labor organization shall file with the Secretary within thirty days after September 14, 1959 or the imposition of any such trusteeship, and semiannually thereafter, a report, signed by its president and treasurer or corresponding principal officers, as well as by the trustees of such subordinate labor organization, containing the following information: (1) the name and address of the subordinate organization; (2) the date of establishing the trusteeship; (3) a detailed statement of the reason or reasons for establishing or continuing the trusteeship; and (4) the nature and extent of participation by the membership of the subordinate organization in the selection of delegates to represent such organization in regular or special conventions or other policy-determining bodies and in the election of officers of the labor organization which has assumed trusteeship over such subordinate organization. The initial report shall also include a full and complete account of the financial condition of such subordinate organization as of the time trusteeship was assumed over it. During the continuance of a trusteeship the labor organization which has assumed trusteeship over a subordinate labor organization shall file on behalf of the subordinate labor organization the annual financial report required by section 431(b) of this title signed by the president and treasurer or corresponding principal officers of the labor organization which has assumed such trusteeship and the trustees of the subordinate labor organization.

(b) Applicability of other laws

The provisions of sections 431(c), 435, 436, 438, and 440 of this title shall be applicable to reports filed under this subchapter.

(c) Penalty for violations

Any person who willfully violates this section shall be fined not more than $10,000 or imprisoned for not more than one year, or both.

(d) False statements and entries; failure to disclose material facts; withholding, concealing or destroying documents, books, records, reports, or statements; penalty

Any person who makes a false statement or representation of a material fact, knowing it to be false, or who knowingly fails to disclose a material fact, in any report required under the provisions of this section or willfully makes any false entry in or willfully withholds, conceals, or destroys any documents, books, records, reports, or statements upon which such report is based, shall be fined not more than $10,000 or imprisoned for not more than one year, or both.

(e) Personal liability

Each individual required to sign a report under this section shall be personally responsible for the filing of such report and for any statement contained therein which he knows to be false.

(Pub. L. 86–257, title III, §301, Sept. 14, 1959, 73 Stat. 530.)

§ 462. Purposes for establishment of trusteeship

Trusteeships shall be established and administered by a labor organization over a subordinate body only in accordance with the constitution and bylaws of the organization which has assumed trusteeship over the subordinate body and for the purpose of correcting corruption or financial malpractice, assuring the performance of collective bargaining agreements or other duties of a bargaining representative, restoring democratic procedures, or otherwise carrying out the legitimate objects of such labor organization.

(Pub. L. 86–257, title III, §302, Sept. 14, 1959, 73 Stat. 531.)

§ 463. Unlawful acts relating to labor organization under trusteeship

(a) During any period when a subordinate body of a labor organization is in trusteeship, it shall be unlawful (1) to count the vote of delegates from such body in any convention or election of officers of the labor organization unless the delegates have been chosen by secret ballot in an election in which all the members in good standing of such subordinate body were eligible to participate, or (2) to transfer to such organization any current receipts or other funds of the subordinate body except the normal per capita tax and assessments payable by subordinate bodies not in trusteeship: *Provided*, That nothing herein contained shall prevent the distribution of the assets of a labor organization in accordance with its constitution and bylaws upon the bona fide dissolution thereof.

(b) Any person who willfully violates this section shall be fined not more than $10,000 or imprisoned for not more than one year, or both.

(Pub. L. 86–257, title III, §303, Sept. 14, 1959, 73 Stat. 531.)

§464. Civil action for enforcement

(a) Complaint; investigation; commencement of action by Secretary, member or subordinate body of labor organization; jurisdiction

Upon the written complaint of any member or subordinate body of a labor organization alleging that such organization has violated the provisions of this subchapter (except section 461 of this title) the Secretary shall investigate the complaint and if the Secretary finds probable cause to believe that such violation has occurred and has not been remedied he shall, without disclosing the identity of the complainant, bring a civil action in any district court of the United States having jurisdiction of the labor organization for such relief (including injunctions) as may be appropriate. Any member or subordinate body of a labor organization affected by any violation of this subchapter (except section 461 of this title) may bring a civil action in any district court of the United States having jurisdiction of the labor organization for such relief (including injunctions) as may be appropriate.

(b) Venue

For the purpose of actions under this section, district courts of the United States shall be deemed to have jurisdiction of a labor organization (1) in the district in which the principal office of such labor organization is located, or (2) in any district in which its duly authorized officers or agents are engaged in conducting the affairs of the trusteeship.

(c) Presumptions of validity or invalidity of trusteeship

In any proceeding pursuant to this section a trusteeship established by a labor organization in conformity with the procedural requirements of its constitution and bylaws and authorized or ratified after a fair hearing either before the executive board or before such other body as may be provided in accordance with its constitution or bylaws shall be presumed valid for a period of eighteen months from the date of its establishment and shall not be subject to attack during such period except upon clear and convincing proof that the trusteeship was not established or maintained in good faith for a purpose allowable under section 462 of this title. After the expiration of eighteen months the trusteeship shall be presumed invalid in any such proceeding and its discontinuance shall be decreed unless the labor organization shall show by clear and convincing proof that the continuation of the trusteeship is necessary for a purpose allowable under section 462 of this title. In the latter event the court may dismiss the complaint or retain jurisdiction of the cause on such conditions and for such period as it deems appropriate.

(Pub. L. 86–257, title III, §304, Sept. 14, 1959, 73 Stat. 531.)

§465. Report to Congress

The Secretary shall submit to the Congress at the expiration of three years from September 14, 1959, a report upon the operation of this subchapter.

(Pub. L. 86–257, title III, §305, Sept. 14, 1959, 73 Stat. 532.)

§466. Additional rights and remedies; exclusive jurisdiction of district court; res judicata

The rights and remedies provided by this subchapter shall be in addition to any and all other rights and remedies at law or in equity: *Provided*, That upon the filing of a complaint by the Secretary the jurisdiction of the district court over such trusteeship shall be exclusive and the final judgment shall be res judicata.

(Pub. L. 86–257, title III, §306, Sept. 14, 1959, 73 Stat. 532.)

SUBCHAPTER V—ELECTIONS

§481. Terms of office and election procedures

(a) Officers of national or international labor organizations; manner of election

Every national or international labor organization, except a federation of national or international labor organizations, shall elect its officers not less often than once every five years either by secret ballot among the members in good standing or at a convention of delegates chosen by secret ballot.

(b) Officers of local labor organizations; manner of election

Every local labor organization shall elect its officers not less often than once every three years by secret ballot among the members in good standing.

(c) Requests for distribution of campaign literature; civil action for enforcement; jurisdiction; inspection of membership lists; adequate safeguards to insure fair election

Every national or international labor organization, except a federation of national or international labor organizations, and every local labor organization, and its officers, shall be under a duty, enforceable at the suit of any bona fide candidate for office in such labor organization in the district court of the United States in which such labor organization maintains its principal office, to comply with all reasonable requests of any candidate to distribute by mail or otherwise at the candidate's expense campaign literature in aid of such person's candidacy to all members in good standing of such labor organization and to refrain from discrimination in favor of or against any candidate with respect to the use of lists of members, and whenever such labor organizations or its officers authorize the distribution by mail or otherwise to members of campaign literature on behalf of any candidate or of the labor organization itself with reference to such election, similar distribution at the request of any other bona fide candidate shall be made by such labor organization and its officers, with equal treatment as to the expense of such distribution. Every bona fide candidate shall have the right, once within 30 days prior to an election of a labor organization in which he is a candidate, to inspect a list containing the names and last known addresses of all members of the labor organization who are subject to a collective bargaining agreement requiring membership therein as a condition of employment, which list shall be maintained and kept at the principal office of such labor organization by a designated official thereof. Adequate safeguards to insure a fair election shall be provided, including the right of any candidate to have an observer at the polls and at the counting of the ballots.

(d) Officers of intermediate bodies; manner of election

Officers of intermediate bodies, such as general committees, system boards, joint boards, or joint councils, shall be elected not less often than once every four years by secret ballot among the members in good standing or by labor organization officers representative of such members who have been elected by secret ballot.

(e) Nomination of candidates; eligibility; notice of election; voting rights; counting and publication of results; preservation of ballots and records

In any election required by this section which is to be held by secret ballot a reasonable opportunity shall be given for the nomination of candidates and every member in good standing shall be eligible to be a candidate and to hold office (subject to section 504 of this title and to reasonable qualifications uniformly imposed) and shall have the right to vote for or otherwise support the candidate or candidates of his choice, without being subject to penalty, discipline, or improper interference or reprisal of any kind by such organization or any member thereof. Not less than fifteen days prior to the election notice thereof shall be mailed to each member at his last known home address. Each member in good standing shall be entitled to one vote. No member whose dues have been withheld by his employer for payment to such organization pursuant to his voluntary authorization provided for in a collective bargaining agreement shall be declared ineligible to vote or be a candidate for office in such organization by reason of alleged delay or default in the payment of dues. The votes cast by members of each local labor organization shall be counted, and the results published, separately. The election officials designated in the constitution and bylaws or the secretary, if no other official is designated, shall preserve for one year the ballots and all other records pertaining to the election. The election shall be conducted in accordance with the constitution and bylaws of such organization insofar as they are not inconsistent with the provisions of this subchapter.

(f) Election of officers by convention of delegates; manner of conducting convention; preservation of records

When officers are chosen by a convention of delegates elected by secret ballot, the convention shall be conducted in accordance with the constitution and bylaws of the labor organization insofar as they are not inconsistent with the provisions of this subchapter. The officials designated in the constitution and bylaws or the secretary, if no other is designated, shall preserve for one year the credentials of the delegates and all minutes and other records of the convention pertaining to the election of officers.

(g) Use of dues, assessments or similar levies, and funds of employer for promotion of candidacy of person

No moneys received by any labor organization by way of dues, assessment, or similar levy, and no moneys of an employer shall be contributed or applied to promote the candidacy of any person in any election subject to the provisions of this subchapter. Such moneys of a labor organization may be utilized for notices, factual statements of issues not involving candidates, and other expenses necessary for the holding of an election.

(h) Removal of officers guilty of serious misconduct

If the Secretary, upon application of any member of a local labor organization, finds after hearing in accordance with subchapter II of chapter 5 of title 5 that the constitution and bylaws of such labor organization do not provide an adequate procedure for the removal of an elected officer guilty of serious misconduct, such officer may be removed, for cause shown and after notice and hearing, by the members in good standing voting in a secret ballot, conducted by the officers of such labor organization in accordance with its constitution and bylaws insofar as they are not inconsistent with the provisions of this subchapter.

(i) Rules and regulations for determining adequacy of removal procedures

The Secretary shall promulgate rules and regulations prescribing minimum standards and procedures for determining the adequacy of the removal procedures to which reference is made in subsection (h) of this section.

(Pub. L. 86–257, title IV, §401, Sept. 14, 1959, 73 Stat. 532.)

CODIFICATION

In subsec. (h), "subchapter II of chapter 5 of title 5" substituted for "the Administrative Procedure Act" on authority of Pub. L. 89–554, §7(b), Sept. 6, 1966, 80 Stat. 631, the first section of which enacted Title 5, Government Organization and Employees.

EFFECTIVE DATE

Section 404 of Pub. L. 86–257 provided that: "The provisions of this title [enacting this subchapter] shall become applicable—

"(1) ninety days after the date of enactment of this Act [Sept. 14, 1959] in the case of a labor organization whose constitution and bylaws can lawfully be modified or amended by action of its constitutional officers or governing body, or

"(2) where such modification can only be made by a constitutional convention of the labor organization, not later than the next constitutional convention of such labor organization after the date of enactment of this Act [Sept. 14, 1959], or one year after such date, whichever is sooner. If no such convention is held within such one-year period, the executive board or similar governing body empowered to act for such labor organization between conventions is empowered to make such interim constitutional changes as are necessary to carry out the provisions of this title [enacting this subchapter]."

§ 482. Enforcement

(a) Filing of complaint; presumption of validity of challenged election

A member of a labor organization—

(1) who has exhausted the remedies available under the constitution and bylaws of such organization and of any parent body, or

(2) who has invoked such available remedies without obtaining a final decision within three calendar months after their invocation,

may file a complaint with the Secretary within one calendar month thereafter alleging the violation of any provision of section 481 of this title (including violation of the constitution and bylaws of the labor organization pertaining to the election and removal of officers). The challenged election shall be presumed valid pending a final decision thereon (as hereinafter provided) and in the interim the affairs of the organization shall be conducted by the officers elected or in such other manner as its constitution and bylaws may provide.

(b) Investigation of complaint; commencement of civil action by Secretary; jurisdiction; preservation of assets

The Secretary shall investigate such complaint and, if he finds probable cause to believe that a violation of this subchapter has occurred and has not been remedied, he shall, within sixty days after the filing of such complaint, bring a civil action against the labor organization as an entity in the district court of the United States in which such labor organization maintains its principal office to set aside the invalid election, if any, and to direct the conduct of an election or hearing and vote upon the removal of officers under the supervision of the Secretary and in accordance with the provisions of this subchapter and such rules and regulations as the Secretary may prescribe. The court shall have power to take such action as it deems proper to preserve the assets of the labor organization.

(c) Declaration of void election; order for new election; certification of election to court; decree; certification of result of vote for removal of officers

If, upon a preponderance of the evidence after a trial upon the merits, the court finds—

(1) that an election has not been held within the time prescribed by section 481 of this title, or

(2) that the violation of section 481 of this title may have affected the outcome of an election,

the court shall declare the election, if any, to be void and direct the conduct of a new election under supervision of the Secretary and, so far as lawful and practicable, in conformity with the constitution and bylaws of the labor organization. The Secretary shall promptly certify to the court the names of the persons elected, and the court shall thereupon enter a decree declaring such persons to be the officers of the labor organization. If the proceeding is for the removal of officers pursuant to subsection (h) of section 481 of this title, the Secretary shall certify the results of the vote and the court shall enter a decree declaring whether such persons have been removed as officers of the labor organization.

(d) Review of orders; stay of order directing election

An order directing an election, dismissing a complaint, or designating elected officers of a labor organization shall be appealable in the same manner as the final judgment in a civil action, but an order directing an election shall not be stayed pending appeal.

(Pub. L. 86–257, title IV, § 402, Sept. 14, 1959, 73 Stat. 534.)

§ 483. Application of other laws; existing rights and remedies; exclusiveness of remedy for challenging election

No labor organization shall be required by law to conduct elections of officers with greater frequency or in a different form or manner than is required by its own constitution or bylaws, except as otherwise provided by this subchapter. Existing rights and remedies to enforce the constitution and bylaws of a labor organization with respect to elections prior to the conduct thereof shall not be affected by the provisions of this subchapter. The remedy provided by this subchapter for challenging an election already conducted shall be exclusive.

(Pub. L. 86–257, title IV, § 403, Sept. 14, 1959, 73 Stat. 534.)

SUBCHAPTER VI—SAFEGUARDS FOR LABOR ORGANIZATIONS

§ 501. Fiduciary responsibility of officers of labor organizations

(a) Duties of officers; exculpatory provisions and resolutions void

The officers, agents, shop stewards, and other representatives of a labor organization occupy positions of trust in relation to such organization and its members as a group. It is, therefore, the duty of each such person, taking into account the special problems and functions of a labor organization, to hold its money and property solely for the benefit of the organization and its members and to manage, invest, and expend the same in accordance with its constitution and bylaws and any resolutions of the governing bodies adopted thereunder, to refrain from dealing with such organization as an adverse party or in behalf of an adverse party in any matter connected with his duties and from holding or acquiring any pecuniary or personal interest which conflicts with the interests of such organization, and to account to the organization for any profit received by him in whatever capacity in connection with transactions conducted by him or under his direction on behalf of the organization. A general exculpatory provision in the constitution and bylaws of such a labor organization or a general exculpatory resolution of a governing body purporting to relieve any such person of liability for breach of the duties declared by this section shall be void as against public policy.

(b) Violation of duties; action by member after refusal or failure by labor organization to commence proceedings; jurisdiction; leave of court; counsel fees and expenses

When any officer, agent, shop steward, or representative of any labor organization is alleged to have violated the duties declared in subsection (a) of this section and the labor organization or its governing board or officers refuse or fail to sue or recover damages or secure an accounting or other appropriate relief within a reasonable time after being requested to do so by any member of the labor organization, such member may sue such officer, agent, shop steward, or representative in any district court of the United States or in any State court of competent jurisdiction to recover damages or secure an accounting or other appropriate relief for the benefit of the labor organization. No such proceeding shall be brought except upon leave of the court obtained upon verified application and for good cause shown, which application may be made ex parte. The trial judge may allot a reasonable part of the recovery in any action under this subsection to pay the fees of counsel prosecuting the suit at the instance of the member of the labor organization and to compensate such member for any expenses necessarily paid or incurred by him in connection with the litigation.

(c) Embezzlement of assets; penalty

Any person who embezzles, steals, or unlawfully and willfully abstracts or converts to his own use, or the use of another, any of the moneys, funds, securities, property, or other assets of a labor organization of which he is an officer, or by which he is employed, directly or indirectly, shall be fined not more than $10,000 or imprisoned for not more than five years, or both.

(Pub. L. 86–257, title V, §501, Sept. 14, 1959, 73 Stat. 535.)

§ 502. Bonding of officers and employees of labor organizations; amount, form, and placement of bonds; penalty for violation

(a) Every officer, agent, shop steward, or other representative or employee of any labor organization (other than a labor organization whose property and annual financial receipts do not exceed $5,000 in value), or of a trust in which a labor organization is interested, who handles funds or other property thereof shall be bonded to provide protection against loss by reason of acts of fraud or dishonesty on his part directly or through connivance with others. The bond of each such person shall be fixed at the beginning of the organization's fiscal year and shall be in an amount not less than 10 per centum of the funds handled by him and his predecessor or predecessors, if any, during the preceding fiscal year, but in no case more than $500,000. If the labor organization or the trust in which a labor organization is interested does not have a preceding fiscal year, the amount of the bond shall be, in the case of a local labor organization, not less than $1,000, and in the case of any other labor organization or of a trust in which a labor organization is interested, not less than $10,000. Such bonds shall be individual or schedule in form, and shall have a corporate surety company as surety thereon. Any person who is not covered by such bonds shall not be permitted to receive, handle, disburse, or otherwise exercise custody or control of the funds or other property of a labor organization or of a trust in which a labor organization is interested. No such bond shall be placed through an agent or broker or with a surety company in which any labor organization or any officer, agent, shop steward, or other representative of a labor organization has any direct or indirect interest. Such surety company shall be a corporate surety which holds a grant of authority from the Secretary of the Treasury under sections 9304–9308 of title 31, as an acceptable surety on Federal bonds: *Provided*, That when in the opinion of the Secretary a labor organization has made other bonding arrangements which would provide the protection required by this section at comparable cost or less, he may exempt such labor organization from placing a bond through a surety company holding such grant of authority.

(b) Any person who willfully violates this section shall be fined not more than $10,000 or imprisoned for not more than one year, or both.

(Pub. L. 86–257, title V, §502, Sept. 14, 1959, 73 Stat. 536; Pub. L. 89–216, §1, Sept. 29, 1965, 79 Stat. 888.)

CODIFICATION

In subsec. (a), "sections 9304–9308 of title 31" substituted for "the Act of July 30, 1947 (6 U.S.C. 6–13)" on authority of Pub. L. 97–258, §4(b), Sept. 13, 1982, 96 Stat. 1067, the first section of which enacted Title 31, Money and Finance.

AMENDMENTS

1965—Subsec. (a). Pub. L. 89–216 substituted "to provide protection against loss by reason of act of fraud or dishonesty on his part directly or through connivance with others" for "for the faithful discharge of his duties" in first sentence and inserted proviso allowing Secretary to permit other arrangements to provide necessary protection.

§ 503. Financial transactions between labor organization and officers and employees

(a) Direct and indirect loans

No labor organization shall make directly or indirectly any loan or loans to any officer or employee of such organization which results in a total indebtedness on the part of such officer or employee to the labor organization in excess of $2,000.

(b) Direct or indirect payment of fines

No labor organization or employer shall directly or indirectly pay the fine of any officer or employee convicted of any willful violation of this chapter.

(c) Penalty for violations

Any person who willfully violates this section shall be fined not more than $5,000 or imprisoned for not more than one year, or both.

(Pub. L. 86–257, title V, §503, Sept. 14, 1959, 73 Stat. 536.)

§ 504. Prohibition against certain persons holding office

(a) Membership in Communist Party; persons convicted of robbery, bribery, etc.

No person who is or has been a member of the Communist Party or who has been convicted of, or served any part of a prison term resulting from his conviction of, robbery, bribery, extortion, embezzlement, grand larceny, burglary, arson, violation of narcotics laws, murder, rape, assault with intent to kill, assault which inflicts grievous bodily injury, or a violation of subchapter III or IV of this chapter[1] any felony involving abuse or misuse of such person's position or employment in a labor organization or employee benefit plan to seek or obtain an illegal gain at the expense of the members of the labor organization or the beneficiaries of the employee benefit plan, or conspiracy to commit any such crimes or attempt to commit any such crimes, or a crime in which any of the foregoing crimes is an element, shall serve or be permitted to serve—

(1) as a consultant or adviser to any labor organization,

(2) as an officer, director, trustee, member of any executive board or similar governing body, business agent, manager, organizer, employee, or representative in any capacity of any labor organization,

(3) as a labor relations consultant or adviser to a person engaged in an industry or activity affecting commerce, or as an officer, director, agent, or employee of any group or association of employers dealing with any labor organization, or in a position having specific collective bargaining authority or direct responsibility in the area of labor-management relations in any corporation or association engaged in an industry or activity affecting commerce, or

(4) in a position which entitles its occupant to a share of the proceeds of, or as an officer or executive or administrative employee of, any entity whose activities are in whole or substantial part devoted to providing goods or services to any labor organization, or

(5) in any capacity, other than in his capacity as a member of such labor organization, that involves decisionmaking authority concerning, or decisionmaking authority over, or custody of, or control of the moneys, funds, assets, or property of any labor organization,

during or for the period of thirteen years after such conviction or after the end of such imprisonment, whichever is later, unless the sentencing court on the motion of the person convicted sets a lesser period of at least three years after such conviction or after the end of such imprisonment, whichever is later, or unless prior to the end of such period, in the case of a person so convicted or imprisoned, (A) his citizenship rights, having been revoked as a result of such conviction, have been fully restored, or (B) if the offense is a Federal offense, the sentencing judge or, if the offense is a State or local offense, the United States district court for the district in which the offense was committed, pursuant to sentencing guidelines and policy statements under section 994(a) of title 28, determines that such person's service in any capacity referred to in clauses (1) through (5) would not be contrary to the purposes of this chapter. Prior to making any such determination the court shall hold a hearing and shall give notice of such proceeding by certified mail to the Secretary of Labor and to State, county, and Federal prosecuting officials in the jurisdiction or jurisdictions in which such person was convicted. The court's determination in any such proceeding shall be final. No person shall knowingly hire, retain, employ, or otherwise place any other person to serve in any capacity in violation of this subsection.

(b) Penalty for violations

Any person who willfully violates this section shall be fined not more than $10,000 or imprisoned for not more than five years, or both.

(c) Definitions

For the purpose of this section—

(1) A person shall be deemed to have been "convicted" and under the disability of "conviction" from the date of the judgment of the trial court, regardless of whether that judgment remains under appeal.

(2) A period of parole shall not be considered as part of a period of imprisonment.

(d) Salary of person barred from labor organization office during appeal of conviction

Whenever any person—

(1) by operation of this section, has been barred from office or other position in a labor organization as a result of a conviction, and

(2) has filed an appeal of that conviction,

any salary which would be otherwise due such person by virtue of such office or position, shall be placed in escrow by the individual employer or organization responsible for payment of such salary. Payment of such salary into escrow shall continue for the duration of the appeal or for the period of time during which such salary would be otherwise due, whichever period is shorter. Upon the final reversal of such person's conviction on appeal, the amounts in escrow shall be paid to such person. Upon the final sustaining of such person's conviction on appeal, the amounts in escrow shall be returned to the individual employer or organization responsible for payments of those amounts. Upon final reversal of such person's conviction, such person shall no longer be barred by this statute[2] from assuming any position from which such person was previously barred.

(Pub. L. 86–257, title V, § 504, Sept. 14, 1959, 73 Stat. 536; Pub. L. 98–473, title II, §§ 229, 803, Oct. 12, 1984, 98 Stat. 2031, 2133; Pub. L. 100–182, § 15(a), Dec. 7, 1987, 101 Stat. 1269.)

AMENDMENTS

1987—Subsec. (a). Pub. L. 100–182, in concluding provisions, substituted "if the offense is a Federal offense, the sentencing judge or, if the offense is a State or local offense, the United States district court for the district in which the offense was committed, pursuant to sentencing guidelines and policy statements under section 994(a) of title 28," for "the United States Parole Commission", "court" and "court's" for "Commission"

[1] So in original. Probably should be followed by a comma.

[2] So in original. Probably should be "section".

and "Commission's", respectively, and "a hearing" for "an administrative hearing".

1984—Subsec. (a). Pub. L. 98–473, § 229, which directed substitution of "if the offense is a Federal offense, the sentencing judge or, if the offense is a State or local offense, on motion of the United States Department of Justice, the district court of the United States for the district in which the offense was committed, pursuant to sentencing guidelines and policy statements issued pursuant to section 994(a) of title 28," for "the Board of Parole of the United States Justice Department", "court" and "court's" for "Board" and "Board's", respectively, and "a" for "an administrative", was (except for the last substitution) incapable of execution in view of the previous amendment by section 803(a) of Pub. L. 98–473 which became effective prior to the effective date of the amendment by section 229. See note below.

Pub. L. 98–473, § 803(a), in amending provisions after "or a violation of subchapter III or IV of the chapter" generally, inserted provisions relating to abuse or misuse of employment in a labor organization or employee benefit plan, substituted "conspiracy to commit any such crimes or attempt to commit any such crimes, or a crime in which any of the foregoing crimes is an element" for "conspiracy to commit any such crimes", added par. (1), redesignated former par. (1) as (2) and in par. (2) as so redesignated substituted "employee, or representative in any capacity of any labor organization" for "or other employee (other than as an employee performing exclusively clerical or custodial duties) of any labor organization, or", redesignated former par. (2) as (3) and in par. (3) as so redesignated inserted "or advisor" after "consultant", struck out "(other than as an employee performing exclusively clerical or custodial duties)" after "employee", and inserted "or in a position having specific collective bargaining authority or direct responsibility in the area of labor-management relations in any corporation or association engaged in an industry or activity affecting commerce, or", added pars. (4) and (5), struck out "or for five years after the termination of his membership in the Communist Party," substituted "the period of thirteen years" for "five years", inserted "whichever is later, unless the sentencing court on the motion of the person convicted sets a lesser period of at least three years after such conviction or after the end of such imprisonment, whichever is later, or", substituted in cl. (B) "United States Parole Commission" for "Board of Parole of the United States Department of Justice", and in the provisions following cl. (B) substituted "Commission" and "Commission's" for "Board" and "Board's", respectively, inserted provision of notice to the Secretary of Labor, and substituted "No person shall knowingly hire, retain, employ, or otherwise place any other person to serve in any capacity in violation of this subsection" for "No labor organization or officer thereof shall knowingly permit any person to assume or hold any office or paid position in violation of this subsection".

Subsec. (b). Pub. L. 98–473, § 803(b), amended subsec. (b) generally, substituting "five years" for "one year".

Subsec. (c). Pub. L. 98–473, § 803(c), designated existing provisions as par. (1), substituted provisions defining conviction as from date of judgment of trial court, regardless of appeal, for former provisions defining it as from date of judgment of trial court or date of final sustaining of judgment on appeal, whichever is later, regardless of whether such conviction occurred before or after Sept. 14, 1959, and added par. (2).

Subsec. (d). Pub. L. 98–473, § 803(d), added subsec. (d).

EFFECTIVE DATE OF 1987 AMENDMENT

Amendment by Pub. L. 100–182 applicable with respect to offenses committed after Dec. 7, 1987, see section 26 of Pub. L. 100–182, set out as a note under section 3006A of Title 18, Crimes and Criminal Procedure.

EFFECTIVE DATE OF 1984 AMENDMENT

Amendment by section 229 of Pub. L. 98–473 effective Nov. 1, 1987, and applicable only to offenses committed after the taking effect of such amendment, see section 235(a)(1) of Pub. L. 98–473, set out as an Effective Date note under section 3551 of Title 18, Crimes and Criminal Procedure.

Section 804 of title II of Pub. L. 98–473 provided that:

"(a) The amendments made by section 802 [amending section 1111 of this title] and section 803 [amending this section] of this title shall take effect with respect to any judgment of conviction entered by the trial court after the date of enactment of this title [Oct. 12, 1984], except that that portion of such amendments relating to the commencement of the period of disability shall apply to any judgment of conviction entered prior to the date of enactment of this title if a right of appeal or an appeal from such judgment is pending on the date of enactment of this title.

"(b) Subject to subsection (a) the amendments made by sections 803 and 804 [probably should be sections 802 and 803] shall not affect any disability under section 411 of the Employee Retirement Income Security Act of 1974 [section 1111 of this title] or under section 504 of the Labor-Management Reporting and Disclosure Act of 1959 [this section] in effect on the date of enactment of this title [Oct. 12, 1984]."

SUBCHAPTER VII—MISCELLANEOUS PROVISIONS

§ 521. Investigations by Secretary; applicability of other laws

(a) The Secretary shall have power when he believes it necessary in order to determine whether any person has violated or is about to violate any provision of this chapter (except subchapter II of this chapter) to make an investigation and in connection therewith he may enter such places and inspect such records and accounts and question such persons as he may deem necessary to enable him to determine the facts relative thereto. The Secretary may report to interested persons or officials concerning the facts required to be shown in any report required by this chapter and concerning the reasons for failure or refusal to file such a report or any other matter which he deems to be appropriate as a result of such an investigation.

(b) For the purpose of any investigation provided for in this chapter, the provisions of sections 49 and 50 of title 15 (relating to the attendance of witnesses and the production of books, papers, and documents), are made applicable to the jurisdiction, powers, and duties of the Secretary or any officers designated by him.

(Pub. L. 86–257, title VI, § 601, Sept. 14, 1959, 73 Stat. 539.)

REFERENCES IN TEXT

The phrase "this chapter (except subchapter II of this chapter)", referred to in subsec. (a), was in the original "this Act (except title I or amendments made by this Act to other statutes)". "This chapter", referred to later in subsec. (a) and also in subsec. (b), was in the original "this Act". "This Act" is Pub. L. 86–257, Sept. 14, 1959, 73 Stat. 519, as amended, known as the Labor-Management Reporting and Disclosure Act of 1959, which enacted this chapter, amended sections 153, 158, 159, 160, 164, 186, and 187 of this title, and enacted provisions set out as notes under sections 153, 158, and 481 of this title. For complete classification of this Act to the Code, see Short Title note set out under section 401 of this title and Tables.

§ 522. Extortionate picketing; penalty for violation

(a) It shall be unlawful to carry on picketing on or about the premises of any employer for the purpose of, or as part of any conspiracy or in furtherance of any plan or purpose for, the personal profit or enrichment of any individual (except a bona fide increase in wages or other employee benefits) by taking or obtaining any money or other thing of value from such employer against his will or with his consent.

(b) Any person who willfully violates this section shall be fined not more than $10,000 or imprisoned not more than twenty years, or both.

(Pub. L. 86–257, title VI, §602, Sept. 14, 1959, 73 Stat. 539.)

§523. Retention of rights under other Federal and State laws

(a) Except as explicitly provided to the contrary, nothing in this chapter shall reduce or limit the responsibilities of any labor organization or any officer, agent, shop steward, or other representative of a labor organization, or of any trust in which a labor organization is interested, under any other Federal law or under the laws of any State, and, except as explicitly provided to the contrary, nothing in this chapter shall take away any right or bar any remedy to which members of a labor organization are entitled under such other Federal law or law of any State.

(b) Nothing contained in this chapter and section 186(a)–(c) of this title shall be construed to supersede or impair or otherwise affect the provisions of the Railway Labor Act, as amended [45 U.S.C. 151 et seq.], or any of the obligations, rights, benefits, privileges, or immunities of any carrier, employee, organization, representative, or person subject thereto; nor shall anything contained in this chapter be construed to confer any rights, privileges, immunities, or defenses upon employers, or to impair or otherwise affect the rights of any person under the National Labor Relations Act, as amended [29 U.S.C. 151 et seq.].

(Pub. L. 86–257, title VI, §603, Sept. 14, 1959, 73 Stat. 540.)

References in Text

This chapter, referred to in subsec. (a), was in the original "this Act", meaning Pub. L. 86–257, Sept. 14, 1959, 73 Stat. 519, as amended, known as the Labor-Management Reporting and Disclosure Act of 1959, which enacted this chapter, amended sections 153, 158, 159, 160, 164, 186, and 187 of this title, and enacted provisions set out as notes under sections 153, 158, and 481 of this title. For complete classification of this Act to the Code, see Short Title note set out under section 401 of this title and Tables.

The phrase "this chapter and section 186(a)–(c) of this title", referred to in subsec. (b), was in original "titles I, II, III, IV, V, or VI of this Act". The phrase "this chapter" later appearing in subsec. (b), was in original "said titles (except section 505) of this Act". Original text reference, in both instances, includes those sections of the Act which are classified principally to this chapter. For complete classification of such titles to the Code, see Tables.

The Railway Labor Act, referred to in subsec. (b), is act May 20, 1926, ch. 347, 44 Stat. 577, as amended, which is classified principally to chapter 8 (§151 et seq.) of Title 45, Railroads. For complete classification of this Act to the Code, see section 151 of Title 45 and Tables.

The National Labor Relations Act, referred to in subsec. (b), is act July 5, 1935, ch. 372, 49 Stat. 452, as amended, which is classified generally to subchapter II (§151 et seq.) of chapter 7 of this title. For complete classification of this Act to the Code, see section 167 of this title and Tables.

§524. Effect on State laws

Nothing in this chapter shall be construed to impair or diminish the authority of any State to enact and enforce general criminal laws with respect to robbery, bribery, extortion, embezzlement, grand larceny, burglary, arson, violation of narcotics laws, murder, rape, assault with intent to kill, or assault which inflicts grievous bodily injury, or conspiracy to commit any of such crimes.

(Pub. L. 86–257, title VI, §604, Sept. 14, 1959, 73 Stat. 540.)

§524a. Elimination of racketeering activities threat; State legislation governing collective bargaining representative

Notwithstanding this or any other Act regulating labor-management relations, each State shall have the authority to enact and enforce, as part of a comprehensive statutory system to eliminate the threat of pervasive racketeering activity in an industry that is, or over time has been, affected by such activity, a provision of law that applies equally to employers, employees, and collective bargaining representatives, which provision of law governs service in any position in a local labor organization which acts or seeks to act in that State as a collective bargaining representative pursuant to the National Labor Relations Act [29 U.S.C. 151 et seq.], in the industry that is subject to that program.

(Pub. L. 98–473, title II, §2201, Oct. 12, 1984, 98 Stat. 2192.)

References in Text

This Act, referred to in text, probably means title II of Pub. L. 98–473, Oct. 12, 1984, 98 Stat. 1976, known as the Comprehensive Crime Control Act of 1984. For complete classification of this Act to the Code, see Short Title of 1984 Amendment note set out under section 1 of Title 18, Crimes and Criminal Procedure, and Tables.

The National Labor Relations Act, referred to in text, is act July 5, 1935, ch. 372, 49 Stat. 449, as amended, which is classified generally to subchapter II (§151 et seq.) of chapter 7 of this title. For complete classification of this Act to the Code, see section 167 of this title and Tables.

Codification

Section was not enacted as part of the Labor-Management Reporting and Disclosure Act of 1959, which comprises this chapter.

§525. Service of process

For the purposes of this chapter, service of summons, subpena, or other legal process of a court of the United States upon an officer or agent of a labor organization in his capacity as such shall constitute service upon the labor organization.

(Pub. L. 86–257, title VI, §605, Sept. 14, 1959, 73 Stat. 540.)

§526. Applicability of administrative procedure provisions

The provisions of subchapter II of chapter 5, and chapter 7, of title 5 shall be applicable to the issuance, amendment, or rescission of any rules or regulations, or any adjudication authorized or required pursuant to the provisions of this chapter.

(Pub. L. 86–257, title VI, § 606, Sept. 14, 1959, 73 Stat. 540.)

CODIFICATION

"Subchapter II of chapter 5, and chapter 7, of title 5" substituted in text for "the Administrative Procedure Act" on authority of Pub. L. 89–554, § 7(b), Sept. 6, 1966, 80 Stat. 631, the first section of which enacted Title 5, Government Organization and Employees.

§ 527. Cooperation with other agencies and departments

In order to avoid unnecessary expense and duplication of functions among Government agencies, the Secretary may make such arrangements or agreements for cooperation or mutual assistance in the performance of his functions under this chapter and the functions of any such agency as he may find to be practicable and consistent with law. The Secretary may utilize the facilities or services of any department, agency, or establishment of the United States or of any State or political subdivision of a State, including the services of any of its employees, with the lawful consent of such department, agency, or establishment; and each department, agency, or establishment of the United States is authorized and directed to cooperate with the Secretary and, to the extent permitted by law, to provide such information and facilities as he may request for his assistance in the performance of his functions under this chapter. The Attorney General or his representative shall receive from the Secretary for appropriate action such evidence developed in the performance of his functions under this chapter as may be found to warrant consideration for criminal prosecution under the provisions of this chapter or other Federal law.

(Pub. L. 86–257, title VI, § 607, Sept. 14, 1959, 73 Stat. 540.)

§ 528. Criminal contempt

No person shall be punished for any criminal contempt allegedly committed outside the immediate presence of the court in connection with any civil action prosecuted by the Secretary or any other person in any court of the United States under the provisions of this chapter unless the facts constituting such criminal contempt are established by the verdict of the jury in a proceeding in the district court of the United States, which jury shall be chosen and empaneled in the manner prescribed by the law governing trial juries in criminal prosecutions in the district courts of the United States.

(Pub. L. 86–257, title VI, § 608, Sept. 14, 1959, 73 Stat. 541.)

§ 529. Prohibition on certain discipline by labor organization

It shall be unlawful for any labor organization, or any officer, agent, shop steward, or other representative of a labor organization, or any employee thereof to fine, suspend, expel, or otherwise discipline any of its members for exercising any right to which he is entitled under the provisions of this chapter. The provisions of section 412 of this title shall be applicable in the enforcement of this section.

(Pub. L. 86–257, title VI, § 609, Sept. 14, 1959, 73 Stat. 541.)

§ 530. Deprivation of rights by violence; penalty

It shall be unlawful for any person through the use of force or violence, or threat of the use of force or violence, to restrain, coerce, or intimidate, or attempt to restrain, coerce, or intimidate any member of a labor organization for the purpose of interfering with or preventing the exercise of any right to which he is entitled under the provisions of this chapter. Any person who willfully violates this section shall be fined not more than $1,000 or imprisoned for not more than one year, or both.

(Pub. L. 86–257, title VI, § 610, Sept. 14, 1959, 73 Stat. 541.)

§ 531. Separability

If any provision of this chapter, or the application of such provision to any person or circumstances, shall be held invalid, the remainder of this chapter or the application of such provision to persons or circumstances other than those as to which it is held invalid, shall not be affected thereby.

(Pub. L. 86–257, title VI, § 611, Sept. 14, 1959, 73 Stat. 541.)

CHAPTER 12—DEPARTMENT OF LABOR

§ 551. Establishment of Department; Secretary; seal

There shall be an executive department in the Government to be called the Department of Labor, with a Secretary of Labor, who shall be the head thereof, to be appointed by the President, by and with the advice and consent of the Senate, and whose tenure of office shall be like that of the heads of the other executive departments. The provisions of title 4 of the Revised Statutes, including all amendments thereto, shall be applicable to said department. The purpose of the Department of Labor shall be to foster, promote, and develop the welfare of the wage earners of the United States, to improve their working conditions, and to advance their opportunities for profitable employment. The said Secretary shall cause a seal of office to be made for the said department of such device as the President shall approve and judicial notice shall be taken of the said seal.

(Mar. 4, 1913, ch. 141, § 1, 37 Stat. 736; Mar. 4, 1925, ch. 549, § 4, 43 Stat. 1301.)

REFERENCES IN TEXT

Title 4 of the Revised Statutes, referred to in text, was entitled "Provisions Applicable to All Executive Departments", and consisted of R.S. §§ 158 to 198. For provisions of the Code derived from such title 4, see sections 101, 301, 303, 304, 503, 2952, 3101, 3106, 3341, 3345 to 3349, 5535, 5536 of Title 5, Government Organization and Employees; section 207 of Title 18, Crimes and Criminal Procedure; sections 514, 520 of Title 28, Judiciary and Judicial Procedure; section 3321 of Title 31, Money and Finance.

CODIFICATION

Section was formerly classified to section 611 of Title 5 prior to the general revision and enactment of Title 5, Government Organization and Employees, by Pub. L. 89–554, § 1, Sept. 1, 1966, 80 Stat. 378.

SHORT TITLE OF 1986 AMENDMENT

Pub. L. 99–619, § 1, Nov. 6, 1986, 100 Stat. 3491, provided that: "This Act [amending sections 552 and 553 of this title and sections 5313 to 5316 of Title 5, Government Organization and Employees, repealing section 3 of Reorganization Plan No. 6 of 1950, set out in the Appendix to Title 5, and enacting provisions set out as notes under sections 552 and 553 of this title and section 5316 of Title 5] may be cited as the 'Department of Labor Executive Level Conforming Amendments of 1986'."

TRANSFER OF FUNCTIONS

For transfer of functions of other officers, employees, and agencies of Department of Labor, with certain exceptions, to Secretary of Labor, with power to delegate, see Reorg. Plan No. 6, of 1950, §§ 1, 2, 15 F.R. 3174, 64 Stat. 1263, set out in the Appendix to Title 5, Government Organization and Employees.

EMERGENCY PREPAREDNESS FUNCTIONS

For assignment of certain emergency preparedness functions to Secretary of Labor, see Parts 1, 2, and 12 of Ex. Ord. No. 12656, Nov. 18, 1988, 53 F.R. 47491, set out as a note under section 5195 of Title 42, The Public Health and Welfare.

HISTORY OF DEPARTMENT

A Department of Labor under the charge of a Commissioner of Labor was first established by act June 13, 1888, ch. 389, 25 Stat. 182. That Department was placed under the jurisdiction and made a part of a new department, called the Department of Commerce and Labor, by act Feb. 14, 1903, ch. 552, § 4, 32 Stat. 827. The name Department of Labor was changed to Bureau of Labor by act Mar. 18, 1904, ch. 716, 33 Stat. 136. The present Department of Labor was created by act Mar. 4, 1913. The Bureau of Labor in the Department of Commerce and Labor was transferred to the present Department of Labor by said act.

ORDER OF SUCCESSION

For order of succession during any period when both Secretary and Deputy Secretary of Labor are unable to perform functions and duties of office of Secretary, see Ex. Ord. No. 13245, Dec. 18, 2001, 66 F.R. 66268, set out as a note under section 3345 of Title 5, Government Organization and Employees.

COMPENSATION OF SECRETARY

Compensation of Secretary, see section 5312 of Title 5, Government Organization and Employees.

§ 552. Deputy Secretary; appointment; duties

There is established in the Department of Labor the office of Deputy Secretary of Labor, which shall be filled by appointment by the President, by and with the advice and consent of the Senate. The Deputy Secretary shall perform such duties as may be prescribed by the Secretary of Labor or required by law. The Deputy Secretary shall (1) in case of the death, resignation, or removal from office of the Secretary, perform the duties of the Secretary until a successor is appointed, and (2) in case of the absence or sickness of the Secretary, perform the duties of the Secretary until such absence or sickness shall terminate.

(Apr. 17, 1946, ch. 140, § 1, 60 Stat. 91; Pub. L. 99–619, § 2(a)(1), Nov. 6, 1986, 100 Stat. 3491.)

CODIFICATION

Provisions of this section which prescribed the basic annual compensation of the Under [Deputy] Secretary were omitted to conform to the provisions of the Executive Schedule. See section 5314 of Title 5, Government Organization and Employees.

Section was formerly classified to section 611a of Title 5 prior to the general revision and enactment of Title 5, Government Organization and Employees, by Pub. L. 89–554, § 1, Sept. 1, 1966, 80 Stat. 378.

AMENDMENTS

1986—Pub. L. 99–619 substituted "Deputy Secretary" for "Under Secretary" in three places.

TRANSFER OF FUNCTIONS

For transfer of functions of other officers, employees, and agencies of Department of Labor, with certain exceptions, to Secretary of Labor, with power to delegate, see Reorg. Plan No. 6, of 1950, §§ 1, 2, 15 F.R. 3174, 64 Stat. 1263, set out in the Appendix to Title 5, Government Organization and Employees.

REFERENCES IN OTHER LAWS

Section 2(a)(4) of Pub. L. 99–619 provided that: "Any reference to the Under Secretary of Labor in any law, rule, regulation, certificate, directive, or other document in force on the date of enactment of this Act [Nov. 6, 1986] shall be deemed to refer and apply to the Deputy Secretary of Labor."

PRESENT INCUMBENT

Section 2(f)(1) of Pub. L. 99–619 provided that: "The incumbent in the position of Under Secretary of Labor on the date of enactment of this Act [Nov. 6, 1986] may serve as Deputy Secretary of Labor at the pleasure of the President after such date and the amendments made by subsection (a)(2) [amending section 5313 of Title 5, Government Organization and Employees] shall apply to such incumbent."

ORDER OF SUCCESSION

For order of succession during any period when both Secretary and Deputy Secretary of Labor are unable to perform functions and duties of office of Secretary, see Ex. Ord. No. 13245, Dec. 18, 2001, 66 F.R. 66268, set out as a note under section 3345 of Title 5, Government Organization and Employees.

§ 553. Assistant Secretaries; appointment; duties

There are established in the Department of Labor nine offices of Assistant Secretary of Labor, which shall be filled by appointment by the President, by and with the advice and consent of the Senate. Each of the Assistant Secretaries of Labor shall perform such duties as may be prescribed by the Secretary of Labor or required by law. One of such Assistant Secretaries shall be an Assistant Secretary of Labor for Occupational Safety and Health.

(Apr. 17, 1946, ch. 140, §2, 60 Stat. 91; Pub. L. 87–137, §1, Aug. 11, 1961, 75 Stat. 338; Pub. L. 91–596, §29(a), Dec. 29, 1970, 84 Stat. 1618; Pub. L. 99–619, §2(b)(1), Nov. 6, 1986, 100 Stat. 3491.)

Codification

Provisions of this section which prescribed the basic annual compensation of the Assistant Secretaries were omitted to conform to the provisions of the Executive Schedule. See section 5315 of Title 5, Government Organization and Employees.

Section was formerly classified to section 611b of Title 5 prior to the general revision and enactment of Title 5, Government Organization and Employees, by Pub. L. 89–554, §1, Sept. 1, 1966, 80 Stat. 378.

Amendments

1986—Pub. L. 99–619 substituted "nine offices" for "five offices".

1970—Pub. L. 91–596 increased the number of Assistant Secretaries of Labor from four to five and inserted provision that one of such Assistant Secretaries be an Assistant Secretary of Labor for Occupational Safety and Health.

1961—Pub. L. 87–137 increased the number of Assistant Secretaries of Labor from three to four.

Effective Date of 1970 Amendment

Amendment by Pub. L. 91–596 effective 120 days after Dec. 29, 1970 see section 34 of Pub. L. 91–596, set out as an Effective Date note under section 651 of this title.

Transfer of Functions

For transfer of functions of other officers, employees, and agencies of Department of Labor, with certain exceptions, to Secretary of Labor, with power to delegate, see Reorg. Plan No. 6, of 1950, §§1, 2, 15 F.R. 3174, 64 Stat. 1263, set out in the Appendix to Title 5, Government Organization and Employees.

References in Other Laws

Section 2(b)(3) of Pub. L. 99–619 provided that: "Any reference in any law, regulation, certificate, directive, or other document to the Assistant Secretary of Labor for Veterans' Employment in force on the date of enactment of this Act [Nov. 6, 1986] shall be deemed to be a reference to the Assistant Secretary of Labor for Veterans' Employment and Training."

Present Incumbent

Section 2(f)(2) of Pub. L. 99–619 provided that: "The incumbent in the position of Assistant Secretary of Labor for Veterans' Employment on the date of enactment of this Act [Nov. 6, 1986] may serve as Assistant Secretary of Labor for Veterans' Employment and Training at the pleasure of the President after such date and the amendments made by subsection (b)(2) [amending section 5315 of Title 5, Government Organization and Employees] shall apply to such incumbent."

§ 554. Assistants to Secretary

There shall be in the Department of Labor not more than two assistants to the Secretary, who shall be appointed by the President and shall perform such duties as may be prescribed by the Secretary of Labor or required by law.

(Mar. 4, 1927, ch. 498, 44 Stat. 1415.)

Codification

Section was formerly classified to section 613a of Title 5 prior to the general revision and enactment of Title 5, Government Organization and Employees, by Pub. L. 89–554, §1, Sept. 1, 1966, 80 Stat. 378.

Transfer of Functions

For transfer of functions of other officers, employees, and agencies of Department of Labor, with certain exceptions, to Secretary of Labor, with power to delegate, see Reorg. Plan No. 6, of 1950, §§1, 2, 15 F.R. 3174, 64 Stat. 1263, set out in the Appendix to Title 5, Government Organization and Employees.

§ 555. Solicitor

There shall be a solicitor for the Department of Labor.

(Mar. 18, 1904, ch. 716, §1, 33 Stat. 135; Mar. 4, 1913, ch. 141, §7, 37 Stat. 738; Ex. Ord. No. 6166, §7, June 10, 1933.)

Codification

The words "of the Department of Justice" were omitted from text on authority of section 7 of Ex. Ord. No. 6166, which transferred the Solicitor for the Department of Labor from the Department of Justice to the Department of Labor.

Section was formerly classified to section 613b of Title 5 prior to the general revision and enactment of Title 5, Government Organization and Employees, by Pub. L. 89–554, §1, Sept. 1, 1966, 80 Stat. 378.

Transfer of Functions

For transfer of functions of other officers, employees, and agencies of Department of Labor, with certain exceptions, to Secretary of Labor, with power to delegate, see Reorg. Plan No. 6, of 1950, §§1, 2, 15 F.R. 3174, 64 Stat. 1263, set out in the Appendix to Title 5, Government Organization and Employees.

Compensation of Solicitor

Compensation of solicitor, see section 5315 of Title 5, Government Organization and Employees.

§ 556. Chief clerk; other employees

There shall be in said department a chief clerk and such other clerical assistants, inspectors, and special agents as may from time to time be provided for by Congress.

(Mar. 4, 1913, ch. 141, §2, 37 Stat. 736; Ex. Ord. No. 6166, §4, June 10, 1933.)

Codification

The words "a disbursing clerk" were omitted from text on authority of Ex. Ord. No. 6166, which transferred all functions relating to the disbursement of moneys of the United States to the Treasury Department. See section 3321 of Title 31, Money and Finance.

Section was formerly classified to section 615 of Title 5 prior to the general revision and enactment of Title 5, Government Organization and Employees, by Pub. L. 89–554, §1, Sept. 1, 1966, 80 Stat. 378.

Transfer of Functions

For transfer of functions of other officers, employees, and agencies of Department of Labor, with certain exceptions, to Secretary of Labor, with power to delegate, see Reorg. Plan No. 6, of 1950, §§1, 2, 15 F.R. 3174, 64 Stat. 1263, set out in the Appendix to Title 5, Government Organization and Employees.

§557. Bureaus and offices in Department

The following-named offices, bureaus, divisions, and branches of the public service, and all that pertains to the same, shall be under the jurisdiction and supervision of the Department of Labor:

1. Bureau of Employees' Compensation.
2. Bureau of Labor Standards.
3. Bureau of Labor Statistics.
4. Division of Public Contracts.
5. Employees' Compensation Appeals Board.
6. United States Employment Service.
7. Wage and Hour Division.
8. Women's Bureau.

(Mar. 4, 1913, ch. 141, §3, 37 Stat. 737; June 5, 1920, ch. 248, §1, 41 Stat. 987; June 6, 1933, ch. 49, §1, 48 Stat. 113; Ex. Ord. No. 6166, §14, June 10, 1933; June 30, 1936, ch. 881, §4, 49 Stat. 2038; June 25, 1938, ch. 676, §4, 52 Stat. 1061; 1939 Reorg. Plan No. I, §201, eff. July 1, 1939, 4 F.R. 2728, 53 Stat. 1424; 1940 Reorg. Plan No. V, §1, eff. June 4, 1940, 5 F.R. 2223, 54 Stat. 1238; Ex. Ord. No. 9247, Sept. 17, 1942, 7 F.R. 7379; Ex. Ord. No. 9617, Sept. 19, 1945, 10 F.R. 11929; 1946 Reorg. Plan No. 2, §1, eff. July 16, 1946, 11 F.R. 7873, 60 Stat. 1095; June 23, 1947, ch. 120, title II, §202, 61 Stat. 153; 1949 Reorg. Plan No. 2, §1, eff. Aug. 20, 1949, 14 F.R. 5225, 63 Stat. 1065; 1950 Reorg. Plan No. 19, §§1, 2, eff. May 24, 1952, 15 F.R. 3178, 64 Stat. 1271, 1272.)

Codification

Section was formerly classified to section 616 of Title 5 prior to the general revision and enactment of Title 5, Government Organization and Employees, by Pub. L. 89–554, §1, Sept. 1, 1966, 80 Stat. 378.

Transfer of Functions

For transfer of functions of other officers, employees, and agencies of Department of Labor, with certain exceptions, to Secretary of Labor, with power to delegate, see Reorg. Plan No. 6, of 1950, §§1, 2, 15 F.R. 3174, 64 Stat. 1263, set out in the Appendix to Title 5, Government Organization and Employees.

Bureau of Employees' Compensation transferred to Department of Labor from Federal Security Agency by Reorg. Plan No. 19 of 1950, §1, which was repealed by Pub. L. 89–554, §8(a), Sept. 6, 1966, 80 Stat. 662, the subject matter of which is covered by section 8101 et seq. of Title 5. Subsequently, Bureau of Compensation absorbed by Employment Standards Administration in Department of Labor.

Bureau of Labor Standards established in Department of Labor by departmental order in 1934, and its functions absorbed by Occupational Safety and Health Administration in May 1971.

Division of Public Contracts established in Department of Labor by virtue of act June 30, 1936, and was consolidated with Wage and Hour Division by order of Secretary of Labor on Aug. 21, 1942. Subsequently, by order of Secretary of Labor in May 1971, Division of Public Contracts absorbed by Wage and Hour Division.

Employees' Compensation Appeals Board transferred to Department of Labor from Federal Security Agency by Reorg. Plan No. 19 of 1950, §2, which was repealed by Pub. L. 89–554, §8(a), Sept. 6, 1966, 80 Stat. 662, the subject matter of which is covered by section 8101 et seq. of Title 5, Government Organization and Employees.

United States Employment Service created in Department of Labor by act June 6, 1933. Service transferred to Federal Security Agency by Reorg. Plan No. I of 1939, and its functions consolidated with unemployment compensation functions of Social Security Board in Bureau of Employment Security. Ex. Ord. No. 9247, Sept. 17, 1942, transferred United States Employment Service from Social Security Board to War Manpower Commission and became a part of Bureau of Placement. Service transferred to Department of Labor by Ex. Ord. No. 9617, Sept. 19, 1945, to be administered as an organizational entity. Act June 16, 1948, ch. 472, 62 Stat. 443, transferred Service to Federal Security Agency to function as a part of Bureau of Employment Security in Social Security Administration. Reorg. Plan No. 2 of 1949, eff. Aug. 20, 1949, transferred Bureau of Employment Security, including United States Employment Service, to Department of Labor.

Wage and Hour Division established in Department of Labor by act June 25, 1938, and consolidated with Division of Public Contracts by order of Secretary of Labor on Aug. 21, 1942.

Women's Bureau established in Department of Labor by act June 5, 1920.

Bureau of Immigration and Bureau of Naturalization, placed under jurisdiction of Department of Labor upon its creation by act Mar. 4, 1913, consolidated as Immigration and Naturalization Service by Ex. Ord. No. 6166, §14. Immigration and Naturalization Service of Department of Labor, including Office of Commissioner of Immigration and Naturalization, transferred to Department of Justice by Reorg. Plan No. V of 1940, set out in the Appendix to Title 5, Government Organization and Employees.

Children's Bureau transferred from Department of Labor to Federal Security Agency by Reorg. Plan No. 2 of 1946, set out in the Appendix to Title 5. For status of Children's Bureau, see note under section 191 of Title 42, The Public Health and Welfare.

United States Conciliation Service established in Department of Labor by virtue of act Mar. 4, 1913, §8, formerly set out as section 619 of former Title 5, Executive Departments and Government Officers and Employees, and section 51 of this title, but was discontinued in view of act June 23, 1947, §202, and set out as section 172 of this title, which transferred to Federal Mediation and Conciliation Service, an independent agency, all powers and functions vested in Secretary of Labor by act Mar. 4, 1913, §8, formerly cited as a credit to this section.

§557a. Mine Safety and Health Administration

There is established in the Department of Labor a Mine Safety and Health Administration to be headed by an Assistant Secretary of Labor for Mine Safety and Health appointed by the President, by and with the advice and consent of the Senate. The Secretary, acting through the Assistant Secretary for Mine Safety and Health, shall have authority to appoint, subject to the civil service laws, such officers and employees as he may deem necessary for the administration of this Act, and to prescribe powers, duties, and responsibilities of all officers and employees engaged in the administration of this Act. The Secretary is authorized and directed, except as specifically provided otherwise to carry out his functions under the Federal Mine Safety and Health Act of 1977 [30 U.S.C. 801 et seq.] through the Mine Safety and Health Administration.

(Pub. L. 95–164, title III, §302(a), Nov. 9, 1977, 91 Stat. 1319.)

References in Text

The civil service laws, referred to in text, are set out in Title 5, Government Organization and Employees. See particularly section 3301 et seq. of Title 5.

This Act, referred to in text, means Pub. L. 95–164, Nov. 9, 1977, 91 Stat. 1290, as amended, known as the

Federal Mine Safety and Health Amendments Act of 1977, which enacted this section, sections 822 to 825 and 961 of Title 30, Mineral Lands and Mining, amended sections 5314 and 5315 of Title 5, and sections 801 to 804, 811 to 821, 842, 861, 878, 951 to 955, 958 and 959 of Title 30, repealed sections 721 to 740 of Title 30 and section 1456a of Title 43, Public Lands, and enacted provisions set out as notes under sections 801 and 954 of Title 30 and section 11 of former Title 31, Money and Finance. For complete classification of this Act to the Code, see Short Title of 1977 Amendment note set out under section 801 of Title 30 and Tables.

The Federal Mine Safety and Health Act of 1977, referred to in text, is Pub. L. 91–173, Dec. 30, 1969, 83 Stat. 742, as amended by Pub. L. 95–164, title I, §101, Nov. 9, 1977, 91 Stat. 1290, which is classified principally to chapter 22 (§801 et seq.) of Title 30. For complete classification of this Act to the Code, see Short Title note set out under section 801 of Title 30 and Tables.

EFFECTIVE DATE

Section effective 120 days after Nov. 9, 1977, see section 307 of Pub. L. 95–164, set out as an Effective Date of 1977 Amendment note under section 801 of Title 30, Mineral Lands and Mining.

§ 557b. Office of disability employment policy

Beginning in fiscal year 2001, there is established in the Department of Labor an office of disability employment policy which shall, under the overall direction of the Secretary, provide leadership, develop policy and initiatives, and award grants furthering the objective of eliminating barriers to the training and employment of people with disabilities. Such office shall be headed by an Assistant Secretary.

(Pub. L. 106–554, §1(a)(1) [title I], Dec. 21, 2000, 114 Stat. 2763, 2763A–10.)

§ 558. Library, records, etc., of Department

The Secretary of Labor shall have charge in the buildings or premises occupied by or appropriated to the Department of Labor, of the library, furniture, fixtures, records, and other property pertaining to it or acquired for use in its business. He shall be allowed to expend for periodicals and the purposes of the library and for rental of appropriate quarters for the accommodation of the Department of Labor within the District of Columbia, and for all other incidental expenses, such sums as Congress may provide from time to time.

(Mar. 4, 1913, ch. 141, §6, 37 Stat. 738.)

CODIFICATION

Section was formerly classified to section 617 of Title 5 prior to the general revision and enactment of Title 5, Government Organization and Employees, by Pub. L. 89–554, §1, Sept. 1, 1966, 80 Stat. 378.

TRANSFER OF FUNCTIONS

For transfer of functions of other officers, employees, and agencies of Department of Labor, with certain exceptions, to Secretary of Labor, with power to delegate, see Reorg. Plan No. 6, of 1950, §§1, 2, 15 F.R. 3174, 64 Stat. 1263, set out in the Appendix to Title 5, Government Organization and Employees.

§ 559. Rented quarters

Where any office, bureau, or branch of the public service transferred to the Department of Labor by this Act is occupying rented buildings or premises, it may continue to do so until other suitable quarters are provided for its use.

(Mar. 4, 1913, ch. 141, §6, 37 Stat. 738.)

REFERENCES IN TEXT

This Act, referred to in text, is act Mar. 4, 1913, ch. 141, 37 Stat. 736, as amended, which is classified principally to sections 2, 551, and 555 to 562 of this title. For complete classification of this Act to the Code, see Tables.

CODIFICATION

Section was formerly classified to section 618 of Title 5 prior to the general revision and enactment of Title 5, Government Organization and Employees, by Pub. L. 89–554, §1, Sept. 1, 1966, 80 Stat. 378.

TRANSFER OF FUNCTIONS

For transfer of functions of other officers, employees, and agencies of Department of Labor, with certain exceptions, to Secretary of Labor, with power to delegate, see Reorg. Plan No. 6, of 1950, §§1, 2, 15 F.R. 3174, 64 Stat. 1263, set out in the Appendix to Title 5, Government Organization and Employees.

§ 560. Reports and investigations

The Secretary of Labor shall annually, at the close of each fiscal year, prepare and submit to Congress the financial statements of the Department that have been audited. He shall also, from time to time, make such special investigations and reports as he may be required to do by the President, or by Congress, or which he himself may deem necessary.

(Mar. 4, 1913, ch. 141, §9, 37 Stat. 738; Pub. L. 104–66, title I, §1102(c), Dec. 21, 1995, 109 Stat. 723.)

CODIFICATION

Section was formerly classified to section 620 of Title 5 prior to the general revision and enactment of Title 5, Government Organization and Employees, by Pub. L. 89–554, §1, Sept. 1, 1966, 80 Stat. 378.

AMENDMENTS

1995—Pub. L. 104–66 in first sentence substituted "prepare and submit to Congress the financial statements of the Department that have been audited" for "make a report in writing to Congress, giving an account of all moneys received and disbursed by him and his department and describing the work done by the department".

TERMINATION OF REPORTING REQUIREMENTS

For termination, effective May 15, 2000, of provisions of law requiring submittal to Congress of any annual, semiannual, or other regular periodic report listed in House Document No. 103–7 (in which a report required under this section is listed on page 124), see section 3003 of Pub. L. 104–66, as amended, set out as a note under section 1113 of Title 31, Money and Finance.

§ 561. Records and papers and furniture transferred to Department

The official records and papers on file in and pertaining exclusively to the business of any bureau, office, department, or branch of the public service in this Act transferred to the Department of Labor, together with the furniture in use in such bureau, office, department, or branch of the public service, are transferred to the Department of Labor.

(Mar. 4, 1913, ch. 141, §5, 37 Stat. 737.)

REFERENCES IN TEXT

This Act, referred to in text, is act Mar. 4, 1913, ch. 141, 37 Stat. 736, as amended, which is classified principally to sections 2, 551, and 555 to 562 of this title. For complete classification of this Act to the Code, see Tables.

CODIFICATION

Section was formerly classified to section 621 of Title 5 prior to the general revision and enactment of Title 5, Government Organization and Employees, by Pub. L. 89–554, § 1, Sept. 1, 1966, 80 Stat. 378.

§ 562. Laws operative

All laws prescribing the work and defining the duties of the several bureaus, offices, departments, or branches of the public service by this Act transferred to and made a part of the Department of Labor shall, so far as the same are not in conflict with the provisions of this Act, remain in full force and effect, to be executed under the direction of the Secretary of Labor.

(Mar. 4, 1913, ch. 141, § 6, 37 Stat. 738.)

REFERENCES IN TEXT

This Act, referred to in text, is act Mar. 4, 1913, ch. 141, 37 Stat. 736, as amended, which is classified principally to sections 2, 551, and 555 to 562 of this title. For complete classification of this Act to the Code, see Tables.

CODIFICATION

Section was formerly classified to section 622 of Title 5 prior to the general revision and enactment of Title 5, Government Organization and Employees, by Pub. L. 89–554, § 1, Sept. 1, 1966, 80 Stat. 378.

TRANSFER OF FUNCTIONS

For transfer of functions of other officers, employees, and agencies of Department of Labor, with certain exceptions, to Secretary of Labor, with power to delegate, see Reorg. Plan No. 6, of 1950, §§ 1, 2, 15 F.R. 3174, 64 Stat. 1263, set out in the Appendix to Title 5, Government Organization and Employees.

§ 563. Working capital fund; establishment; availability; capitalization; reimbursement

There is established a working capital fund, to be available without fiscal year limitation, for expenses necessary for the maintenance and operation of (1) a central reproduction service; (2) a central visual exhibit service; (3) a central supply service for supplies and equipment for which adequate stocks may be maintained to meet in whole or in part the requirements of the Department; (4) a central tabulating service; (5) telephone, mail and messenger services; (6) a central accounting and payroll service; and (7) a central laborers' service: *Provided*, That any stocks of supplies and equipment on hand or on order shall be used to capitalize such fund: *Provided further*, That such fund shall be reimbursed in advance from funds available to bureaus, offices, and agencies for which such centralized services are performed at rates which will return in full all expenses of operation, including reserves for accrued annual leave and depreciation of equipment: *Provided further*, That within the Working Capital Fund, there is established an Investment in Reinvention Fund (IRF), which shall be available to invest in projects of the Department designed to produce measurable improvements in agency efficiency and significant taxpayer savings. Notwithstanding any other provision of law, the Secretary of Labor may retain up to $3,900,000 of the unobligated balances in the Department's annual Salaries and Expenses accounts as of September 30, 1995, and transfer those amounts to the IRF to provide the initial capital for the IRF, to remain available until expended, to make loans to agencies of the Department for projects designed to enhance productivity and generate cost savings. Such loans shall be repaid to the IRF no later than September 30 of the fiscal year following the fiscal year in which the project is completed. Such repayments shall be deposited in the IRF, to be available without further appropriation action: *Provided further*, That the Secretary of Labor may transfer annually an amount not to exceed $3,000,000 from unobligated balances in the Department's salaries and expenses accounts, to the unobligated balance of the Working Capital Fund, to be merged with such Fund and used for the acquisition of capital equipment and the improvement of financial management, information technology and other support systems, and to remain available until expended: *Provided further*, That the unobligated balance of the Fund shall not exceed $20,000,000..[1]

(Pub. L. 85–67, title I, § 101, June 29, 1957, 71 Stat. 210; Pub. L. 86–703, title I, § 101, Sept. 2, 1960, 74 Stat. 755; Pub. L. 104–134, title I, § 101(d) [title I], Apr. 26, 1996, 110 Stat. 1321–211, 1321–219; renumbered title I, Pub. L. 104–140, § 1(a), May 2, 1996, 110 Stat. 1327; Pub. L. 105–78, title I, Nov. 13, 1997, 111 Stat. 1476.)

CODIFICATION

Section was formerly classified to section 622a of Title 5 prior to the general revision and enactment of Title 5, Government Organization and Employees, by Pub. L. 89–554, § 1, Sept. 1, 1966, 80 Stat. 378.

AMENDMENTS

1997—Pub. L. 105–78 struck out period at end and inserted ": *Provided further*, That the Secretary of Labor may transfer annually an amount not to exceed $3,000,000 from unobligated balances in the Department's salaries and expenses accounts, to the unobligated balance of the Working Capital Fund, to be merged with such Fund and used for the acquisition of capital equipment and the improvement of financial management, information technology and other support systems, and to remain available until expended: *Provided further*, That the unobligated balance of the Fund shall not exceed $20,000,000." after "appropriation action".

1996—Pub. L. 104–134 inserted before period at end ": *Provided further*, That within the Working Capital Fund, there is established an Investment in Reinvention Fund (IRF), which shall be available to invest in projects of the Department designed to produce measurable improvements in agency efficiency and significant taxpayer savings. Notwithstanding any other provision of law, the Secretary of Labor may retain up to $3,900,000 of the unobligated balances in the Department's annual Salaries and Expenses accounts as of September 30, 1995, and transfer those amounts to the IRF to provide the initial capital for the IRF, to remain available until expended, to make loans to agencies of the Department for projects designed to enhance productivity and generate cost savings. Such loans shall be repaid to the IRF no later than September 30 of the fiscal year following the fiscal year in which the project is completed. Such repayments shall be depos-

[1] So in original.

ited in the IRF, to be available without further appropriation action."

1960—Pub. L. 86–703 made fund available for maintenance and operation of a central tabulating service, a central accounting and payroll service, and a central laborers' service.

§ 563a. Working capital fund; comprehensive program of centralized services

There is appropriated for expenses necessary during the fiscal year ending September 30, 1994, and each fiscal year thereafter, for the maintenance and operation of a comprehensive program of centralized services which the Secretary of Labor may prescribe and deem appropriate and advantageous to provide on a reimbursable basis under the provisions of sections 1535 and 1536 of title 31 (subject to prior notice to OMB) in the national office and field: *Provided*, That such fund shall be reimbursed in advance from funds available to agencies, bureaus, and offices for which such centralized services are performed at rates which will return in full cost of operations including services obtained through cooperative administrative services units under sections 1535 and 1536 of title 31, including reserves for accrued annual leave, worker's compensation, depreciation of capitalized equipment, and amortization of ADP software and systems (either acquired or donated): *Provided further*, That funds received for services rendered to any entity or person for use of Departmental facilities, including associated utilities and security services, shall be credited to and merged with this fund.

(Pub. L. 103–112, title I, Oct. 21, 1993, 107 Stat. 1088.)

CODIFICATION

Section is based on paragraph under headings "DEPARTMENTAL MANAGEMENT" and "WORKING CAPITAL FUND" of Department of Labor Appropriations Act, 1994.

"Sections 1535 and 1536 of title 31" was substituted in text for "the Economy Act" on authority of Pub. L. 97–258, § 4(b), Sept. 13, 1982, 96 Stat. 1067, the first section of which enacted Title 31, Money and Finance.

§ 564. Working capital fund; availability for personnel functions in regional administrative offices

The Working Capital Fund of the Department of Labor shall be available on and after March 5, 1970, for expenses necessary for personnel functions in regional administrative offices.

(Pub. L. 91–204, title I, § 100, Mar. 5, 1970, 84 Stat. 26.)

§ 565. Repealed. Pub. L. 103–382, title III, § 391(i), Oct. 20, 1994, 108 Stat. 4023

Section, Pub. L. 100–418, title VI, § 6306(b), Aug. 23, 1988, 102 Stat. 1541, related to study and report respecting failure to provide internationally recognized worker rights.

§ 566. Employee drug and alcohol abuse assistance programs

(a) Establishment

The Secretary of Labor shall establish a program through which the Secretary shall provide grants to, or enter into contracts with, employers to enable such employers to develop employee drug and alcohol abuse assistance programs.

(b) Applications

Employers desiring to receive a grant or contract under this section shall submit to the Secretary of Labor, an application, in such form and containing such information as the Secretary may require.

(c) Regulations

The Secretary of Labor shall promulgate regulations necessary to carry out this section.

(d) Authorization of appropriations

There are authorized to be appropriated to carry out this section, $4,000,000 for fiscal year 1989, and $5,000,000 for each of the fiscal years 1990 and 1991.

(Pub. L. 100–690, title II, § 2101, Nov. 18, 1988, 102 Stat. 4216.)

§ 567. Labor-management dispute settlement expenses

Appropriations in this Act or subsequent Departments of Labor, Health and Human Services, and Education, and Related Agencies Appropriations Acts available for salaries and expenses shall be available for supplies, services, and rental of conference space within the District of Columbia, as the Secretary of Labor shall deem necessary for settlement of labor-management disputes.

(Pub. L. 102–394, title I, § 101, Oct. 6, 1992, 106 Stat. 1798.)

PRIOR PROVISIONS

Provisions similar to those in this section were contained in the following prior appropriation acts:

Pub. L. 102–170, title I, § 101, Nov. 26, 1991, 105 Stat. 1114.

Pub. L. 101–517, title I, § 101, Nov. 5, 1990, 104 Stat. 2196.

Pub. L. 101–166, title I, § 101, Nov. 21, 1989, 103 Stat. 1165.

Pub. L. 100–202, § 101(h) [title I, § 101], Dec. 22, 1987, 101 Stat. 1329–256, 1329–263.

Pub. L. 99–500, § 101(i) [H.R. 5233, title I, § 101], Oct. 18, 1986, 100 Stat. 1783–287, and Pub. L. 99–591, § 101(i) [H.R. 5233, title I, § 101], Oct. 30, 1986, 100 Stat. 3341–287.

Pub. L. 99–178, title I, § 101, Dec. 12, 1985, 99 Stat. 1108.

Pub. L. 98–619, title I, § 101, Nov. 8, 1984, 98 Stat. 3311.

Pub. L. 98–139, title I, § 101, Oct. 31, 1983, 97 Stat. 877.

Pub. L. 97–377, title I, § 101(e)(1) [title I, § 101], Dec. 21, 1982, 96 Stat. 1878, 1884.

§ 568. Acceptance of donations by Secretary

The Secretary of Labor is authorized to accept, in the name of the Department of Labor, and employ or dispose of in furtherance of authorized activities of the Department of Labor, during the fiscal year ending September 30, 1995, and each fiscal year thereafter, any money or property, real, personal, or mixed, tangible or intangible, received by gift, devise, bequest, or otherwise.

(Pub. L. 103–333, title I, § 105, Sept. 30, 1994, 108 Stat. 2548.)

PRIOR PROVISIONS

Provisions similar to those in this section were contained in the following prior appropriation acts:

Pub. L. 103–112, title I, §101, Oct. 21, 1993, 107 Stat. 1089.

Pub. L. 102–394, title I, §105, Oct. 6, 1992, 106 Stat. 1799.

CHAPTER 13—EXEMPLARY REHABILITATION CERTIFICATES

§§601 to 605. Repealed. Pub. L. 97–306, title III, §311, Oct. 14, 1982, 96 Stat. 1442

Section 601, Pub. L. 90–83, §6(a), Sept. 11, 1967, 81 Stat. 221, provided that Secretary of Labor act on any application for an Exemplary Rehabilitation Certificate received under this chapter from any person discharged or dismissed under conditions other than honorable, or who received a general discharge, at least three years before date of receipt of such application.

Section 602, Pub. L. 90–83, §6(b), Sept. 11, 1967, 81 Stat. 221, provided criteria for issuance of an Exemplary Rehabilitation Certificate and required notification of issuance of such certificate to Secretary of Defense and placement of certificate in military personnel file of person to whom it is issued.

Section 603, Pub. L. 90–83, §6(c), Sept. 11, 1967, 81 Stat. 221, specified certain types of notarized statements that might be used in support of an application for an Exemplary Rehabilitation Certificate, and provided for independent investigations by Secretary of Labor and personal appearances by applicant or appearance by counsel before Secretary.

Section 604, Pub. L. 90–83, §6(d), Sept. 11, 1967, 81 Stat. 221, provided that no benefits under any laws of United States (including but not limited to those relating to pensions, compensation, hospitalization, military pay and allowances, education, loan guarantees, retired pay, or other benefits based on military service) accrue to any person to whom an Exemplary Rehabilitation Certificate was issued under section 602 of this title unless he would have been entitled to those benefits under his original discharge or dismissal.

Section 605, Pub. L. 90–83, §6(e), Sept. 11, 1967, 81 Stat. 221, provided that Secretary of Labor require national system of public employment offices established under chapter 4B of this title to accord special counseling and job development assistance to any person who had been discharged or dismissed under conditions other than honorable but who had been issued an Exemplary Rehabilitation Certificate.

§606. Repealed. Pub. L. 97–306, title III, §311, Oct. 14, 1982, 96 Stat. 1442; Pub. L. 97–375, title I, §110(a), Dec. 21, 1982, 96 Stat. 1820

Section, Pub. L. 90–83, §6(f), Sept. 11, 1967, 81 Stat. 221, directed Secretary of Labor to report to Congress not later than Jan. 15 of each year the number of cases reviewed under this chapter and the number of certificates issued.

§607. Repealed. Pub. L. 97–306, title III, §311, Oct. 14, 1982, 96 Stat. 1442

Section, Pub. L. 90–83, §6(g), Sept. 11, 1967, 81 Stat. 221, provided that in carrying out provisions of this chapter Secretary of Labor was authorized to issued regulations, delegate authority, and utilize services of the Civil Service Commission for making such investigations as might have been mutually agreeable.

CHAPTER 14—AGE DISCRIMINATION IN EMPLOYMENT

§621. Congressional statement of findings and purpose

(a) The Congress hereby finds and declares that—

(1) in the face of rising productivity and affluence, older workers find themselves disadvantaged in their efforts to retain employment, and especially to regain employment when displaced from jobs;

(2) the setting of arbitrary age limits regardless of potential for job performance has become a common practice, and certain otherwise desirable practices may work to the disadvantage of older persons;

(3) the incidence of unemployment, especially long-term unemployment with resultant deterioration of skill, morale, and employer acceptability is, relative to the younger ages, high among older workers; their numbers are great and growing; and their employment problems grave;

(4) the existence in industries affecting commerce, of arbitrary discrimination in employment because of age, burdens commerce and the free flow of goods in commerce.

(b) It is therefore the purpose of this chapter to promote employment of older persons based on their ability rather than age; to prohibit arbitrary age discrimination in employment; to help employers and workers find ways of meeting problems arising from the impact of age on employment.

(Pub. L. 90–202, §2, Dec. 15, 1967, 81 Stat. 602.)

EFFECTIVE DATE; RULES AND REGULATIONS

Section 16, formerly §15, of Pub. L. 90–202, renumbered by Pub. L. 93–259, §28(b)(1), Apr. 8, 1974, 88 Stat. 74, provided that: "This Act [enacting this chapter] shall become effective one hundred and eighty days after enactment [Dec. 15, 1967], except (a) that the Secretary of Labor may extend the delay in effective date of any provision of this Act up to and additional ninety days thereafter if he finds that such time is necessary in permitting adjustments to the provisions hereof, and (b) that on or after the date of enactment [Dec. 15, 1967] the Secretary of Labor is authorized to issue such rules and regulations as may be necessary to carry out its provisions."

SHORT TITLE OF 1996 AMENDMENT

Pub. L. 104–208, div. A, title I, §101(a) [title I, §119], Sept. 30, 1996, 110 Stat. 3000, 3009–23, provided in part that: "This section [amending section 623 of this title, enacting provisions set out as notes under section 623 of this title, and repealing provisions set out as a note under section 623 of this title] may be cited as the 'Age Discrimination in Employment Amendments of 1996'."

SHORT TITLE OF 1990 AMENDMENT

Pub. L. 101–433, §1, Oct. 16, 1990, 104 Stat. 978, provided that: "This Act [amending sections 623, 626, and 630 of this title and enacting provisions set out as notes under this section and sections 623 and 626 of this title] may be cited as the 'Older Workers Benefit Protection Act'."

SHORT TITLE OF 1986 AMENDMENT

Pub. L. 99–592, § 1, Oct. 31, 1986, 100 Stat. 3342, provided that: "This Act [amending sections 623, 630, and 631 of this title and enacting provisions set out as notes under sections 622 to 624 and 631 of this title] may be cited as the 'Age Discrimination in Employment Amendments of 1986'."

SHORT TITLE OF 1978 AMENDMENT

Pub. L. 95–256, § 1, Apr. 6, 1978, 92 Stat. 189, provided that: "This Act [amending sections 623, 624, 626, 631, 633a, and 634 of this title and sections 8335 and 8339 of Title 5, Government Organization and Employees, repealing section 3322 of Title 5, and enacting provisions set out as notes under sections 623, 626, 631, and 633a of this title] may be cited as the 'Age Discrimination in Employment Act Amendments of 1978'."

SHORT TITLE

Section 1 of Pub. L. 90–202 provided: "That this Act [enacting this chapter] may be cited as the 'Age Discrimination in Employment Act of 1967'."

TRANSFER OF FUNCTIONS

Functions vested by this section in Secretary of Labor or Civil Service Commission transferred to Equal Employment Opportunity Commission by Reorg. Plan No. 1 of 1978, § 2, 43 F.R. 19807, 92 Stat. 3781, set out in the Appendix to Title 5, Government Organization and Employees, effective Jan. 1, 1979, as provided by section 1–101 of Ex. Ord. No. 12106, Dec. 28, 1978, 44 F.R. 1053.

SEVERABILITY

Pub. L. 101–433, title III, § 301, Oct. 16, 1990, 104 Stat. 984, provided that: "If any provision of this Act [see Short Title of 1990 Amendment note above], or an amendment made by this Act, or the application of such provision to any person or circumstances is held to be invalid, the remainder of this Act and the amendments made by this Act, and the application of such provision to other persons and circumstances, shall not be affected thereby."

CONGRESSIONAL FINDING

Pub. L. 101–433, title I, § 101, Oct. 16, 1990, 104 Stat. 978, provided that: "The Congress finds that, as a result of the decision of the Supreme Court in Public Employees Retirement System of Ohio v. Betts, 109 S.Ct. 256 (1989), legislative action is necessary to restore the original congressional intent in passing and amending the Age Discrimination in Employment Act of 1967 (29 U.S.C. 621 et seq.), which was to prohibit discrimination against older workers in all employee benefits except when age-based reductions in employee benefit plans are justified by significant cost considerations."

§ 622. Education and research program; recommendation to Congress

(a) The Secretary of Labor shall undertake studies and provide information to labor unions, management, and the general public concerning the needs and abilities of older workers, and their potentials for continued employment and contribution to the economy. In order to achieve the purposes of this chapter, the Secretary of Labor shall carry on a continuing program of education and information, under which he may, among other measures—

(1) undertake research, and promote research, with a view to reducing barriers to the employment of older persons, and the promotion of measures for utilizing their skills;

(2) publish and otherwise make available to employers, professional societies, the various media of communication, and other interested persons the findings of studies and other materials for the promotion of employment;

(3) foster through the public employment service system and through cooperative effort the development of facilities of public and private agencies for expanding the opportunities and potentials of older persons;

(4) sponsor and assist State and community informational and educational programs.

(b) Not later than six months after the effective date of this chapter, the Secretary shall recommend to the Congress any measures he may deem desirable to change the lower or upper age limits set forth in section 631 of this title.

(Pub. L. 90–202, § 3, Dec. 15, 1967, 81 Stat. 602.)

REFERENCES IN TEXT

The effective date of this chapter, referred to in subsec. (b), means the effective date of Pub. L. 90–202, which is one hundred and eighty days after the enactment of this chapter, except that the Secretary of Labor may extend the delay in effective date an additional ninety days thereafter for any provision to permit adjustments to such provisions. See section 16 of Pub. L. 90–202, set out as a note under section 621 of this title.

STUDY AND PROPOSED GUIDELINES RELATING TO POLICE OFFICERS AND FIREFIGHTERS

Pub. L. 99–592, § 5, Oct. 31, 1986, 100 Stat. 3343, provided that:

"(a) STUDY.—Not later than 4 years after the date of enactment of this Act [Oct. 31, 1986], the Secretary of Labor and the Equal Employment Opportunity Commission, jointly, shall—

"(1) conduct a study—

"(A) to determine whether physical and mental fitness tests are valid measurements of the ability and competency of police officers and firefighters to perform the requirements of their jobs,

"(B) if such tests are found to be valid measurements of such ability and competency, to determine which particular types of tests most effectively measure such ability and competency, and

"(C) to develop recommendations with respect to specific standards that such tests, and the administration of such tests should satisfy, and

"(2) submit a report to the Speaker of the House of Representatives and the President pro tempore of the Senate that includes—

"(A) a description of the results of such study, and

"(B) a statement of the recommendations developed under paragraph (1)(C).

"(b) CONSULTATION REQUIREMENT.—The Secretary of Labor and the Equal Employment Opportunity Commission shall, during the conduct of the study required under subsection (a) and prior to the development of recommendations under paragraph (1)(C), consult with the United States Fire Administration, the Federal Emergency Management Agency, organizations representing law enforcement officers, firefighters, and their employers, and organizations representing older Americans.

"(c) PROPOSED GUIDELINES.—Not later than 5 years after the date of the enactment of this Act [Oct. 31, 1986], the Equal Employment Opportunity Commission shall propose, in accordance with subchapter II of chapter 5 of title 5 of the United States Code, guidelines for the administration and use of physical and mental fitness tests to measure the ability and competency of police officers and firefighters to perform the requirements of their jobs."

§ 623. Prohibition of age discrimination

(a) Employer practices

It shall be unlawful for an employer—

(1) to fail or refuse to hire or to discharge any individual or otherwise discriminate against any individual with respect to his compensation, terms, conditions, or privileges of employment, because of such individual's age;

(2) to limit, segregate, or classify his employees in any way which would deprive or tend to deprive any individual of employment opportunities or otherwise adversely affect his status as an employee, because of such individual's age; or

(3) to reduce the wage rate of any employee in order to comply with this chapter.

(b) Employment agency practices

It shall be unlawful for an employment agency to fail or refuse to refer for employment, or otherwise to discriminate against, any individual because of such individual's age, or to classify or refer for employment any individual on the basis of such individual's age.

(c) Labor organization practices

It shall be unlawful for a labor organization—

(1) to exclude or to expel from its membership, or otherwise to discriminate against, any individual because of his age;

(2) to limit, segregate, or classify its membership, or to classify or fail or refuse to refer for employment any individual, in any way which would deprive or tend to deprive any individual of employment opportunities, or would limit such employment opportunities or otherwise adversely affect his status as an employee or as an applicant for employment, because of such individual's age;

(3) to cause or attempt to cause an employer to discriminate against an individual in violation of this section.

(d) Opposition to unlawful practices; participation in investigations, proceedings, or litigation

It shall be unlawful for an employer to discriminate against any of his employees or applicants for employment, for an employment agency to discriminate against any individual, or for a labor organization to discriminate against any member thereof or applicant for membership, because such individual, member or applicant for membership has opposed any practice made unlawful by this section, or because such individual, member or applicant for membership has made a charge, testified, assisted, or participated in any manner in an investigation, proceeding, or litigation under this chapter.

(e) Printing or publication of notice or advertisement indicating preference, limitation, etc.

It shall be unlawful for an employer, labor organization, or employment agency to print or publish, or cause to be printed or published, any notice or advertisement relating to employment by such an employer or membership in or any classification or referral for employment by such a labor organization, or relating to any classification or referral for employment by such an employment agency, indicating any preference, limitation, specification, or discrimination, based on age.

(f) Lawful practices; age an occupational qualification; other reasonable factors; laws of foreign workplace; seniority system; employee benefit plans; discharge or discipline for good cause

It shall not be unlawful for an employer, employment agency, or labor organization—

(1) to take any action otherwise prohibited under subsections (a), (b), (c), or (e) of this section where age is a bona fide occupational qualification reasonably necessary to the normal operation of the particular business, or where the differentiation is based on reasonable factors other than age, or where such practices involve an employee in a workplace in a foreign country, and compliance with such subsections would cause such employer, or a corporation controlled by such employer, to violate the laws of the country in which such workplace is located;

(2) to take any action otherwise prohibited under subsection (a), (b), (c), or (e) of this section—

(A) to observe the terms of a bona fide seniority system that is not intended to evade the purposes of this chapter, except that no such seniority system shall require or permit the involuntary retirement of any individual specified by section 631(a) of this title because of the age of such individual; or

(B) to observe the terms of a bona fide employee benefit plan—

(i) where, for each benefit or benefit package, the actual amount of payment made or cost incurred on behalf of an older worker is no less than that made or incurred on behalf of a younger worker, as permissible under section 1625.10, title 29, Code of Federal Regulations (as in effect on June 22, 1989); or

(ii) that is a voluntary early retirement incentive plan consistent with the relevant purpose or purposes of this chapter.

Notwithstanding clause (i) or (ii) of subparagraph (B), no such employee benefit plan or voluntary early retirement incentive plan shall excuse the failure to hire any individual, and no such employee benefit plan shall require or permit the involuntary retirement of any individual specified by section 631(a) of this title, because of the age of such individual. An employer, employment agency, or labor organization acting under subparagraph (A), or under clause (i) or (ii) of subparagraph (B), shall have the burden of proving that such actions are lawful in any civil enforcement proceeding brought under this chapter; or

(3) to discharge or otherwise discipline an individual for good cause.

(g) Repealed. Pub. L. 101–239, title VI, § 6202(b)(3)(C)(i), Dec. 19, 1989, 103 Stat. 2233

(h) Practices of foreign corporations controlled by American employers; foreign employers not controlled by American employers; factors determining control

(1) If an employer controls a corporation whose place of incorporation is in a foreign

country, any practice by such corporation prohibited under this section shall be presumed to be such practice by such employer.

(2) The prohibitions of this section shall not apply where the employer is a foreign person not controlled by an American employer.

(3) For the purpose of this section the determination of whether an employer controls a corporation shall be based upon the—

(A) interrelation of operations,

(B) common management,

(C) centralized control of labor relations, and

(D) common ownership or financial control,

of the employer and the corporation.

(i) Employee pension benefit plans; cessation or reduction of benefit accrual or of allocation to employee account; distribution of benefits after attainment of normal retirement age; compliance; highly compensated employees

(1) Except as otherwise provided in this subsection, it shall be unlawful for an employer, an employment agency, a labor organization, or any combination thereof to establish or maintain an employee pension benefit plan which requires or permits—

(A) in the case of a defined benefit plan, the cessation of an employee's benefit accrual, or the reduction of the rate of an employee's benefit accrual, because of age, or

(B) in the case of a defined contribution plan, the cessation of allocations to an employee's account, or the reduction of the rate at which amounts are allocated to an employee's account, because of age.

(2) Nothing in this section shall be construed to prohibit an employer, employment agency, or labor organization from observing any provision of an employee pension benefit plan to the extent that such provision imposes (without regard to age) a limitation on the amount of benefits that the plan provides or a limitation on the number of years of service or years of participation which are taken into account for purposes of determining benefit accrual under the plan.

(3) In the case of any employee who, as of the end of any plan year under a defined benefit plan, has attained normal retirement age under such plan—

(A) if distribution of benefits under such plan with respect to such employee has commenced as of the end of such plan year, then any requirement of this subsection for continued accrual of benefits under such plan with respect to such employee during such plan year shall be treated as satisfied to the extent of the actuarial equivalent of in-service distribution of benefits, and

(B) if distribution of benefits under such plan with respect to such employee has not commenced as of the end of such year in accordance with section 1056(a)(3) of this title and section 401(a)(14)(C) of title 26, and the payment of benefits under such plan with respect to such employee is not suspended during such plan year pursuant to section 1053(a)(3)(B) of this title or section 411(a)(3)(B) of title 26, then any requirement of this subsection for continued accrual of benefits under such plan with respect to such employee during such plan year shall be treated as satisfied to the extent of any adjustment in the benefit payable under the plan during such plan year attributable to the delay in the distribution of benefits after the attainment of normal retirement age.

The provisions of this paragraph shall apply in accordance with regulations of the Secretary of the Treasury. Such regulations shall provide for the application of the preceding provisions of this paragraph to all employee pension benefit plans subject to this subsection and may provide for the application of such provisions, in the case of any such employee, with respect to any period of time within a plan year.

(4) Compliance with the requirements of this subsection with respect to an employee pension benefit plan shall constitute compliance with the requirements of this section relating to benefit accrual under such plan.

(5) Paragraph (1) shall not apply with respect to any employee who is a highly compensated employee (within the meaning of section 414(q) of title 26) to the extent provided in regulations prescribed by the Secretary of the Treasury for purposes of precluding discrimination in favor of highly compensated employees within the meaning of subchapter D of chapter 1 of title 26.

(6) A plan shall not be treated as failing to meet the requirements of paragraph (1) solely because the subsidized portion of any early retirement benefit is disregarded in determining benefit accruals or it is a plan permitted by subsection (m) of this section..[1]

(7) Any regulations prescribed by the Secretary of the Treasury pursuant to clause (v) of section 411(b)(1)(H) of title 26 and subparagraphs (C) and (D)[2] of section 411(b)(2) of title 26 shall apply with respect to the requirements of this subsection in the same manner and to the same extent as such regulations apply with respect to the requirements of such sections 411(b)(1)(H) and 411(b)(2).

(8) A plan shall not be treated as failing to meet the requirements of this section solely because such plan provides a normal retirement age described in section 1002(24)(B) of this title and section 411(a)(8)(B) of title 26.

(9) For purposes of this subsection—

(A) The terms "employee pension benefit plan", "defined benefit plan", "defined contribution plan", and "normal retirement age" have the meanings provided such terms in section 1002 of this title.

(B) The term "compensation" has the meaning provided by section 414(s) of title 26.

(10) SPECIAL RULES RELATING TO AGE.—

(A) COMPARISON TO SIMILARLY SITUATED YOUNGER INDIVIDUAL.—

(i) IN GENERAL.—A plan shall not be treated as failing to meet the requirements of paragraph (1) if a participant's accrued benefit, as determined as of any date under the terms of the plan, would be equal to or greater than that of any similarly situated, younger individual who is or could be a participant.

[1] So in original.

[2] See References in Text note below.

(ii) SIMILARLY SITUATED.—For purposes of this subparagraph, a participant is similarly situated to any other individual if such participant is identical to such other individual in every respect (including period of service, compensation, position, date of hire, work history, and any other respect) except for age.

(iii) DISREGARD OF SUBSIDIZED EARLY RETIREMENT BENEFITS.—In determining the accrued benefit as of any date for purposes of this clause, the subsidized portion of any early retirement benefit or retirement-type subsidy shall be disregarded.

(iv) ACCRUED BENEFIT.—For purposes of this subparagraph, the accrued benefit may, under the terms of the plan, be expressed as an annuity payable at normal retirement age, the balance of a hypothetical account, or the current value of the accumulated percentage of the employee's final average compensation.

(B) APPLICABLE DEFINED BENEFIT PLANS.—

(i) INTEREST CREDITS.—

(I) IN GENERAL.—An applicable defined benefit plan shall be treated as failing to meet the requirements of paragraph (1) unless the terms of the plan provide that any interest credit (or an equivalent amount) for any plan year shall be at a rate which is not greater than a market rate of return. A plan shall not be treated as failing to meet the requirements of this subclause merely because the plan provides for a reasonable minimum guaranteed rate of return or for a rate of return that is equal to the greater of a fixed or variable rate of return.

(II) PRESERVATION OF CAPITAL.—An interest credit (or an equivalent amount) of less than zero shall in no event result in the account balance or similar amount being less than the aggregate amount of contributions credited to the account.

(III) MARKET RATE OF RETURN.—The Secretary of the Treasury may provide by regulation for rules governing the calculation of a market rate of return for purposes of subclause (I) and for permissible methods of crediting interest to the account (including fixed or variable interest rates) resulting in effective rates of return meeting the requirements of subclause (I). In the case of a governmental plan (as defined in the first sentence of section 414(d) of title 26), a rate of return or a method of crediting interest established pursuant to any provision of Federal, State, or local law (including any administrative rule or policy adopted in accordance with any such law) shall be treated as a market rate of return for purposes of subclause (I) and a permissible method of crediting interest for purposes of meeting the requirements of subclause (I), except that this sentence shall only apply to a rate of return or method of crediting interest if such rate or method does not violate any other requirement of this chapter.

(ii) SPECIAL RULE FOR PLAN CONVERSIONS.—If, after June 29, 2005, an applicable plan amendment is adopted, the plan shall be treated as failing to meet the requirements of paragraph (1)(H) unless the requirements of clause (iii) are met with respect to each individual who was a participant in the plan immediately before the adoption of the amendment.

(iii) RATE OF BENEFIT ACCRUAL.—Subject to clause (iv), the requirements of this clause are met with respect to any participant if the accrued benefit of the participant under the terms of the plan as in effect after the amendment is not less than the sum of—

(I) the participant's accrued benefit for years of service before the effective date of the amendment, determined under the terms of the plan as in effect before the amendment, plus

(II) the participant's accrued benefit for years of service after the effective date of the amendment, determined under the terms of the plan as in effect after the amendment.

(iv) SPECIAL RULES FOR EARLY RETIREMENT SUBSIDIES.—For purposes of clause (iii)(I), the plan shall credit the accumulation account or similar amount[3] with the amount of any early retirement benefit or retirement-type subsidy for the plan year in which the participant retires if, as of such time, the participant has met the age, years of service, and other requirements under the plan for entitlement to such benefit or subsidy.

(v) APPLICABLE PLAN AMENDMENT.—For purposes of this subparagraph—

(I) IN GENERAL.—The term "applicable plan amendment" means an amendment to a defined benefit plan which has the effect of converting the plan to an applicable defined benefit plan.

(II) SPECIAL RULE FOR COORDINATED BENEFITS.—If the benefits of 2 or more defined benefit plans established or maintained by an employer are coordinated in such a manner as to have the effect of the adoption of an amendment described in subclause (I), the sponsor of the defined benefit plan or plans providing for such coordination shall be treated as having adopted such a plan amendment as of the date such coordination begins.

(III) MULTIPLE AMENDMENTS.—The Secretary of the Treasury shall issue regulations to prevent the avoidance of the purposes of this subparagraph through the use of 2 or more plan amendments rather than a single amendment.

(IV) APPLICABLE DEFINED BENEFIT PLAN.—For purposes of this subparagraph, the term "applicable defined benefit plan" has the meaning given such term by section 1053(f)(3) of this title.

(vi) TERMINATION REQUIREMENTS.—An applicable defined benefit plan shall not be treated as meeting the requirements of clause (i) unless the plan provides that, upon the termination of the plan—

[3] So in original. Probably should be "similar account".

(I) if the interest credit rate (or an equivalent amount) under the plan is a variable rate, the rate of interest used to determine accrued benefits under the plan shall be equal to the average of the rates of interest used under the plan during the 5-year period ending on the termination date, and

(II) the interest rate and mortality table used to determine the amount of any benefit under the plan payable in the form of an annuity payable at normal retirement age shall be the rate and table specified under the plan for such purpose as of the termination date, except that if such interest rate is a variable rate, the interest rate shall be determined under the rules of subclause (I).

(C) CERTAIN OFFSETS PERMITTED.—A plan shall not be treated as failing to meet the requirements of paragraph (1) solely because the plan provides offsets against benefits under the plan to the extent such offsets are allowable in applying the requirements of section 401(a) of title 26.

(D) PERMITTED DISPARITIES IN PLAN CONTRIBUTIONS OR BENEFITS.—A plan shall not be treated as failing to meet the requirements of paragraph (1) solely because the plan provides a disparity in contributions or benefits with respect to which the requirements of section 401(*l*) of title 26 are met.

(E) INDEXING PERMITTED.—

(i) IN GENERAL.—A plan shall not be treated as failing to meet the requirements of paragraph (1) solely because the plan provides for indexing of accrued benefits under the plan.

(ii) PROTECTION AGAINST LOSS.—Except in the case of any benefit provided in the form of a variable annuity, clause (i) shall not apply with respect to any indexing which results in an accrued benefit less than the accrued benefit determined without regard to such indexing.

(iii) INDEXING.—For purposes of this subparagraph, the term "indexing" means, in connection with an accrued benefit, the periodic adjustment of the accrued benefit by means of the application of a recognized investment index or methodology.

(F) EARLY RETIREMENT BENEFIT OR RETIREMENT-TYPE SUBSIDY.—For purposes of this paragraph, the terms "early retirement benefit" and "retirement-type subsidy" have the meaning given such terms in section 1054(g)(2)(A) of this title.[2]

(G) BENEFIT ACCRUED TO DATE.—For purposes of this paragraph, any reference to the accrued benefit shall be a reference to such benefit accrued to date.

(j) Employment as firefighter or law enforcement officer

It shall not be unlawful for an employer which is a State, a political subdivision of a State, an agency or instrumentality of a State or a political subdivision of a State, or an interstate agency to fail or refuse to hire or to discharge any individual because of such individual's age if such action is taken—

(1) with respect to the employment of an individual as a firefighter or as a law enforcement officer, the employer has complied with section 3(d)(2) of the Age Discrimination in Employment Amendments of 1996[2] if the individual was discharged after the date described in such section, and the individual has attained—

(A) the age of hiring or retirement, respectively, in effect under applicable State or local law on March 3, 1983; or

(B)(i) if the individual was not hired, the age of hiring in effect on the date of such failure or refusal to hire under applicable State or local law enacted after September 30, 1996; or

(ii) if applicable State or local law was enacted after September 30, 1996, and the individual was discharged, the higher of—

(I) the age of retirement in effect on the date of such discharge under such law; and

(II) age 55; and

(2) pursuant to a bona fide hiring or retirement plan that is not a subterfuge to evade the purposes of this chapter.

(k) Seniority system or employee benefit plan; compliance

A seniority system or employee benefit plan shall comply with this chapter regardless of the date of adoption of such system or plan.

(*l*) Lawful practices; minimum age as condition of eligibility for retirement benefits; deductions from severance pay; reduction of long-term disability benefits

Notwithstanding clause (i) or (ii) of subsection (f)(2)(B) of this section—

(1)(A) It shall not be a violation of subsection (a), (b), (c), or (e) of this section solely because—

(i) an employee pension benefit plan (as defined in section 1002(2) of this title) provides for the attainment of a minimum age as a condition of eligibility for normal or early retirement benefits; or

(ii) a defined benefit plan (as defined in section 1002(35) of this title) provides for—

(I) payments that constitute the subsidized portion of an early retirement benefit; or

(II) social security supplements for plan participants that commence before the age and terminate at the age (specified by the plan) when participants are eligible to receive reduced or unreduced old-age insurance benefits under title II of the Social Security Act (42 U.S.C. 401 et seq.), and that do not exceed such old-age insurance benefits.

(B) A voluntary early retirement incentive plan that—

(i) is maintained by—

(I) a local educational agency (as defined in section 7801 of title 20,[4] or

(II) an education association which principally represents employees of 1 or more agencies described in subclause (I) and

[4] So in original. A closing parenthesis probably should follow "20".

which is described in section 501(c)(5) or (6) of title 26 and exempt from taxation under section 501(a) of title 26, and

(ii) makes payments or supplements described in subclauses (I) and (II) of subparagraph (A)(ii) in coordination with a defined benefit plan (as so defined) maintained by an eligible employer described in section 457(e)(1)(A) of title 26 or by an education association described in clause (i)(II),

shall be treated solely for purposes of subparagraph (A)(ii) as if it were a part of the defined benefit plan with respect to such payments or supplements. Payments or supplements under such a voluntary early retirement incentive plan shall not constitute severance pay for purposes of paragraph (2).

(2)(A) It shall not be a violation of subsection (a), (b), (c), or (e) of this section solely because following a contingent event unrelated to age—

(i) the value of any retiree health benefits received by an individual eligible for an immediate pension;

(ii) the value of any additional pension benefits that are made available solely as a result of the contingent event unrelated to age and following which the individual is eligible for not less than an immediate and unreduced pension; or

(iii) the values described in both clauses (i) and (ii);

are deducted from severance pay made available as a result of the contingent event unrelated to age.

(B) For an individual who receives immediate pension benefits that are actuarially reduced under subparagraph (A)(i), the amount of the deduction available pursuant to subparagraph (A)(i) shall be reduced by the same percentage as the reduction in the pension benefits.

(C) For purposes of this paragraph, severance pay shall include that portion of supplemental unemployment compensation benefits (as described in section 501(c)(17) of title 26) that—

(i) constitutes additional benefits of up to 52 weeks;

(ii) has the primary purpose and effect of continuing benefits until an individual becomes eligible for an immediate and unreduced pension; and

(iii) is discontinued once the individual becomes eligible for an immediate and unreduced pension.

(D) For purposes of this paragraph and solely in order to make the deduction authorized under this paragraph, the term "retiree health benefits" means benefits provided pursuant to a group health plan covering retirees, for which (determined as of the contingent event unrelated to age)—

(i) the package of benefits provided by the employer for the retirees who are below age 65 is at least comparable to benefits provided under title XVIII of the Social Security Act (42 U.S.C. 1395 et seq.);

(ii) the package of benefits provided by the employer for the retirees who are age 65 and above is at least comparable to that offered under a plan that provides a benefit package with one-fourth the value of benefits provided under title XVIII of such Act; or

(iii) the package of benefits provided by the employer is as described in clauses (i) and (ii).

(E)(i) If the obligation of the employer to provide retiree health benefits is of limited duration, the value for each individual shall be calculated at a rate of $3,000 per year for benefit years before age 65, and $750 per year for benefit years beginning at age 65 and above.

(ii) If the obligation of the employer to provide retiree health benefits is of unlimited duration, the value for each individual shall be calculated at a rate of $48,000 for individuals below age 65, and $24,000 for individuals age 65 and above.

(iii) The values described in clauses (i) and (ii) shall be calculated based on the age of the individual as of the date of the contingent event unrelated to age. The values are effective on October 16, 1990, and shall be adjusted on an annual basis, with respect to a contingent event that occurs subsequent to the first year after October 16, 1990, based on the medical component of the Consumer Price Index for all-urban consumers published by the Department of Labor.

(iv) If an individual is required to pay a premium for retiree health benefits, the value calculated pursuant to this subparagraph shall be reduced by whatever percentage of the overall premium the individual is required to pay.

(F) If an employer that has implemented a deduction pursuant to subparagraph (A) fails to fulfill the obligation described in subparagraph (E), any aggrieved individual may bring an action for specific performance of the obligation described in subparagraph (E). The relief shall be in addition to any other remedies provided under Federal or State law.

(3) It shall not be a violation of subsection (a), (b), (c), or (e) of this section solely because an employer provides a bona fide employee benefit plan or plans under which long-term disability benefits received by an individual are reduced by any pension benefits (other than those attributable to employee contributions)—

(A) paid to the individual that the individual voluntarily elects to receive; or

(B) for which an individual who has attained the later of age 62 or normal retirement age is eligible.

(m) Voluntary retirement incentive plans

Notwithstanding subsection (f)(2)(B) of this section, it shall not be a violation of subsection (a), (b), (c), or (e) of this section solely because a plan of an institution of higher education (as defined in section 1001 of title 20) offers employees who are serving under a contract of unlimited tenure (or similar arrangement providing for unlimited tenure) supplemental benefits upon voluntary retirement that are reduced or eliminated on the basis of age, if—

(1) such institution does not implement with respect to such employees any age-based re-

duction or cessation of benefits that are not such supplemental benefits, except as permitted by other provisions of this chapter;

(2) such supplemental benefits are in addition to any retirement or severance benefits which have been offered generally to employees serving under a contract of unlimited tenure (or similar arrangement providing for unlimited tenure), independent of any early retirement or exit-incentive plan, within the preceding 365 days; and

(3) any employee who attains the minimum age and satisfies all non-age-based conditions for receiving a benefit under the plan has an opportunity lasting not less than 180 days to elect to retire and to receive the maximum benefit that could then be elected by a younger but otherwise similarly situated employee, and the plan does not require retirement to occur sooner than 180 days after such election.

(Pub. L. 90–202, §4, Dec. 15, 1967, 81 Stat. 603; Pub. L. 95–256, §2(a), Apr. 6, 1978, 92 Stat. 189; Pub. L. 97–248, title I, §116(a), Sept. 3, 1982, 96 Stat. 353; Pub. L. 98–369, div. B, title III, §2301(b), July 18, 1984, 98 Stat. 1063; Pub. L. 98–459, title VIII, §802(b), Oct. 9, 1984, 98 Stat. 1792; Pub. L. 99–272, title IX, §9201(b)(1), (3), Apr. 7, 1986, 100 Stat. 171; Pub. L. 99–509, title IX, §9201, Oct. 21, 1986, 100 Stat. 1973; Pub. L. 99–514, §2, Oct. 22, 1986, 100 Stat. 2095; Pub. L. 99–592, §§2(a), (b), 3(a), Oct. 31, 1986, 100 Stat. 3342; Pub. L. 101–239, title VI, §6202(b)(3)(C)(i), Dec. 19, 1989, 103 Stat. 2233; Pub. L. 101–433, title I, §103, Oct. 16, 1990, 104 Stat. 978; Pub. L. 101–521, Nov. 5, 1990, 104 Stat. 2287; Pub. L. 104–208, div. A, title I, §101(a) [title I, §119[1(b)]], Sept. 30, 1996, 110 Stat. 3009, 3009–23; Pub. L. 105–244, title IX, §941(a), (b), Oct. 7, 1998, 112 Stat. 1834, 1835; Pub. L. 109–280, title VII, §701(c), title XI, §1104(a)(2), Aug. 17, 2006, 120 Stat. 988, 1058; Pub. L. 110–458, title I, §123(a), Dec. 23, 2008, 122 Stat. 5114.)

References in Text

Subparagraphs (C) and (D) of section 411(b)(2) of title 26, referred to in subsec. (i)(7), were redesignated subpars. (B) and (C) of section 411(b)(2) of Title 26, Internal Revenue Code, by Pub. L. 101–239, title VII, §7871(a)(1), Dec. 19, 1989, 103 Stat. 2435.

Section 1054(g)(2)(A) of this title, referred to in subsec. (i)(10)(F), was in the original "section 203(g)(2)(A) of the Employee Retirement Income Security Act of 1974", and was translated as reading section 204(g)(2)(A) of that Act to reflect the probable intent of Congress, because section 203 does not contain a subsec. (g).

Section 3(d)(2) of the Age Discrimination in Employment Amendments of 1996, referred to in subsec. (j)(1), probably means Pub. L. 104–208, div. A, title I, §101(a) [title I, §119[2(d)(2)]], Sept. 30, 1996, 110 Stat. 3009, 3009–23, 3009–25, which is set out as a note under this section.

The Social Security Act, referred to in subsec. (*l*)(1)(A)(ii)(II), (2)(D)(i), (ii), is act Aug. 14, 1935, ch. 531, 49 Stat. 620, as amended. Titles II and XVIII of the Act are classified generally to subchapters II (§401 et seq.) and XVIII (§1395 et seq.), respectively, of chapter 7 of Title 42, The Public Health and Welfare. For complete classification of this Act to the Code, see section 1305 of Title 42 and Tables.

Amendments

2008—Subsec. (i)(10)(B)(i)(III). Pub. L. 110–458 inserted at end "In the case of a governmental plan (as defined in the first sentence of section 414(d) of title 26), a rate of return or a method of crediting interest established pursuant to any provision of Federal, State, or local law (including any administrative rule or policy adopted in accordance with any such law) shall be treated as a market rate of return for purposes of subclause (I) and a permissible method of crediting interest for purposes of meeting the requirements of subclause (I), except that this sentence shall only apply to a rate of return or method of crediting interest if such rate or method does not violate any other requirement of this chapter."

2006—Subsec. (i)(10). Pub. L. 109–280, §701(c), added par. (10).

Subsec. (*l*)(1). Pub. L. 109–280, §1104(a)(2), designated existing provisions as subpar. (A), redesignated former subpars. (A) and (B) as cls. (i) and (ii), respectively, and former cls. (i) and (ii) of former subpar. (B) as subcls. (I) and (II) of cl. (ii), respectively, and added subpar. (B).

1998—Subsec. (i)(6). Pub. L. 105–244, §941(b), inserted "or it is a plan permitted by subsection (m) of this section." after "accruals".

Subsec. (m). Pub. L. 105–244, §941(a), added subsec. (m).

1996—Subsec. (j). Pub. L. 104–208, §101(a) [title I, §119[1(b)(1)]], reenacted subsec. (j) of this section, as in effect immediately before Dec. 31, 1993.

Subsec. (j)(1). Pub. L. 104–208, §101(a) [title I, §119[1(b)(2)]], substituted ", the employer has complied with section 3(d)(2) of the Age Discrimination in Employment Amendments of 1996 if the individual was discharged after the date described in such section, and the individual has attained—

"(A) the age of hiring or retirement, respectively, in effect under applicable State or local law on March 3, 1983; or

"(B)(i) if the individual was not hired, the age of hiring in effect on the date of such failure or refusal to hire under applicable State or local law enacted after September 30, 1996; or

"(ii) if applicable State or local law was enacted after September 30, 1996, and the individual was discharged, the higher of—

"(I) the age of retirement in effect on the date of such discharge under such law; and

"(II) age 55; and" for "and the individual has attained the age of hiring or retirement in effect under applicable State or local law on March 3, 1983, and".

1990—Subsec. (f)(2). Pub. L. 101–433, §103(1), added par. (2) and struck out former par. (2) which read as follows: "to observe the terms of a bona fide seniority system or any bona fide employee benefit plan such as a retirement, pension, or insurance plan, which is not a subterfuge to evade the purposes of this chapter, except that no such employee benefit plan shall excuse the failure to hire any individual, and no such seniority system or employee benefit plan shall require or permit the involuntary retirement of any individual specified by section 631(a) of this title because of the age of such individual; or".

Subsecs. (i), (j). Pub. L. 101–433, §103(2), redesignated subsec. (i), relating to employment as firefighter or law enforcement officer, as (j).

Subsec. (k). Pub. L. 101–433, §103(3), added subsec. (k).

Subsec. (*l*). Pub. L. 101–521 added cl. (iii) in par. (2)(A), and in par. (2)(D) inserted "and solely in order to make the deduction authorized under this paragraph" after "For purposes of this paragraph" and added cl. (iii).

Pub. L. 101–433, §103(3), added subsec. (*l*).

1989—Subsec. (g). Pub. L. 101–239 struck out subsec. (g) which read as follows:

"(1) For purposes of this section, any employer must provide that any employee aged 65 or older, and any employee's spouse aged 65 or older, shall be entitled to coverage under any group health plan offered to such employees under the same conditions as any employee, and the spouse of such employee, under age 65.

"(2) For purposes of paragraph (1), the term 'group health plan' has the meaning given to such term in section 162(i)(2) of title 26."

1986—Subsec. (g)(1). Pub. L. 99–272, §9201(b)(1), and Pub. L. 99–592, §2(a), made identical amendments, substituting "or older" for "through 69" in two places.

Subsec. (g)(2). Pub. L. 99–514 substituted "Internal Revenue Code of 1986" for "Internal Revenue Code of 1954", which for purposes of codification was translated as "title 26" thus requiring no change in text.

Subsec. (h). Pub. L. 99–272, §9201(b)(3), and Pub. L. 99–592, §2(b), made identical amendments, redesignating subsec. (g), relating to practices of foreign corporations controlled by American employers, as (h).

Subsec. (i). Pub. L. 99–592, §3, temporarily added subsec. (i) which read as follows: "It shall not be unlawful for an employer which is a State, a political subdivision of a State, an agency or instrumentality of a State or a political subdivision of a State, or an interstate agency to fail or refuse to hire or to discharge any individual because of such individual's age if such action is taken—

"(1) with respect to the employment of an individual as a firefighter or as a law enforcement officer and the individual has attained the age of hiring or retirement in effect under applicable State or local law on March 3, 1983, and

"(2) pursuant to a bona fide hiring or retirement plan that is not a subterfuge to evade the purposes of this chapter."

See Effective and Termination Dates of 1986 Amendments note below.

Pub. L. 99–509 added subsec. (i) relating to employee pension benefit plans.

1984—Subsec. (f)(1). Pub. L. 98–459, §802(b)(1), inserted ", or where such practices involve an employee in a workplace in a foreign country, and compliance with such subsections would cause such employer, or a corporation controlled by such employer, to violate the laws of the country in which such workplace is located".

Subsec. (g). Pub. L. 98–459, §802(b)(2), added subsec. (g) relating to practices of foreign corporations controlled by American employers.

Subsec. (g)(1). Pub. L. 98–369 inserted ", and any employee's spouse aged 65 through 69," after "aged 65 through 69" and ", and the spouse of such employee," after "as any employee", in subsec. (g) relating to entitlement to coverage under group health plan.

1982—Subsec. (g). Pub. L. 97–248 added subsec. (g) relating to entitlement to coverage under group health plans.

1978—Subsec. (f)(2). Pub. L. 95–256 provided that no seniority system or employee benefit plan require or permit the involuntary retirement of any individual specified by section 631(a) of this title because of the age of the individual.

Effective Date of 2008 Amendment

Pub. L. 110–458, title I, §123(b), Dec. 23, 2008, 122 Stat. 5114, provided that: "The amendment made by this section [amending this section] shall take effect as if included in the provisions of the Pension Protection Act of 2006 [Pub. L. 109–280] to which such amendment relates."

Effective Date of 2006 Amendment

Amendment by section 701(c) of Pub. L. 109–280 applicable to periods beginning on or after June 29, 2005, with provisions relating to vesting and interest credit requirements for plans in existence on June 29, 2005, special rule for collectively bargained plans, and provisions relating to conversions of plan amendments adopted after, and taking effect after, June 29, 2005, see section 701(e) of Pub. L. 109–280, set out as a note under section 411 of Title 26, Internal Revenue Code.

Effective Date of 1998 Amendment

Pub. L. 105–244, title IX, §941(d), Oct. 7, 1998, 112 Stat. 1835, provided that:

"(1) In general.—This section [amending this section and enacting provisions set out as a note below] shall take effect on the date of enactment of this Act [Oct. 7, 1998].

"(2) Effect on causes of action existing before date of enactment.—The amendment made by subsection (a) [amending this section] shall not apply with respect to any cause of action arising under the Age Discrimination in Employment Act of 1967 [29 U.S.C. 621 et seq.] prior to the date of enactment of this Act."

Effective Date of 1996 Amendment

Section 101(a) [title I, §119[3]] of Pub. L. 104–208 provided that:

"(a) General Effective Date.—Except as provided in subsection (b), this title [probably means section 101(a) [title I, §119] of Pub. L. 104–208, amending this section and enacting and repealing provisions set out as notes under this section] and the amendments made by this title shall take effect on the date of enactment of this Act [Sept. 30, 1996].

"(b) Special Effective Date.—The repeal made by section 2(a) and the reenactment made by section 2(b)(1) [probably means section 101(a) [title I, §119[1(a), (b)(1)]] of Pub. L. 104–208, amending this section and repealing provisions set out as a note under this section] shall take effect on December 31, 1993."

Effective Date of 1990 Amendment

Section 105 of title I of Pub. L. 101–433, as amended by Pub. L. 102–236, §9, Dec. 12, 1991, 105 Stat. 1816, provided that:

"(a) In General.—Except as otherwise provided in this section, this title [amending this section and section 630 of this title and enacting provisions set out as notes under this section and section 621 of this title] and the amendments made by this title shall apply only to—

"(1) any employee benefit established or modified on or after the date of enactment of this Act [Oct. 16, 1990]; and

"(2) other conduct occurring more than 180 days after the date of enactment of this Act.

"(b) Collectively Bargained Agreements.—With respect to any employee benefits provided in accordance with a collective bargaining agreement—

"(1) that is in effect as of the date of enactment of this Act [Oct. 16, 1990]; or that is a result of pattern collective bargaining in an industry where the agreement setting the pattern was ratified after September 20, 1990, but prior to the date of enactment, and the final agreement in the industry adhering to the pattern was ratified after the date of enactment, but not later than November 20, 1990;

"(2) that terminates after such date of enactment;

"(3) any provision of which was entered into by a labor organization (as defined by section 6(d)(4) of the Fair Labor Standards Act of 1938 (29 U.S.C. 206(d)(4))); and

"(4) that contains any provision that would be superseded (in whole or part) by this title [amending this section and section 630 of this title and enacting provisions set out as notes under this section and section 621 of this title] and the amendments made by this title, but for the operation of this section,

this title and the amendments made by this title shall not apply until the termination of such collective bargaining agreement or June 1, 1992, whichever occurs first.

"(c) States and Political Subdivisions.—

"(1) In general.—With respect to any employee benefits provided by an employer—

"(A) that is a State or political subdivision of a State or any agency or instrumentality of a State or political subdivision of a State; and

"(B) that maintained an employee benefit plan at any time between June 23, 1989, and the date of enactment of this Act [Oct. 16, 1990] that would be superseded (in whole or part) by this title [amending this section and section 630 of this title and enacting provisions set out as notes under this section and section 621 of this title] and the amendments made by this title but for the operation of this subsection, and which plan may be modified only through a change in applicable State or local law, this title and the amendments made by this title shall not apply until the date that is 2 years after the date of enactment of this Act.

"(2) ELECTION OF DISABILITY COVERAGE FOR EMPLOYEES HIRED PRIOR TO EFFECTIVE DATE.—

"(A) IN GENERAL.—An employer that maintains a plan described in paragraph (1)(B) may, with regard to disability benefits provided pursuant to such a plan—

"(i) following reasonable notice to all employees, implement new disability benefits that satisfy the requirements of the Age Discrimination in Employment Act of 1967 [29 U.S.C. 621 et seq.] (as amended by this title); and

"(ii) then offer to each employee covered by a plan described in paragraph (1)(B) the option to elect such new disability benefits in lieu of the existing disability benefits, if—

"(I) the offer is made and reasonable notice provided no later than the date that is 2 years after the date of enactment of this Act [Oct. 16, 1990]; and

"(II) the employee is given up to 180 days after the offer in which to make the election.

"(B) PREVIOUS DISABILITY BENEFITS.—If the employee does not elect to be covered by the new disability benefits, the employer may continue to cover the employee under the previous disability benefits even though such previous benefits do not otherwise satisfy the requirements of the Age Discrimination in Employment Act of 1967 (as amended by this title).

"(C) ABROGATION OF RIGHT TO RECEIVE BENEFITS.—An election of coverage under the new disability benefits shall abrogate any right the electing employee may have had to receive existing disability benefits. The employee shall maintain any years of service accumulated for purposes of determining eligibility for the new benefits.

"(3) STATE ASSISTANCE.—The Equal Employment Opportunity Commission, the Secretary of Labor, and the Secretary of the Treasury shall, on request, provide to States assistance in identifying and securing independent technical advice to assist in complying with this subsection.

"(4) DEFINITIONS.—For purposes of this subsection:

"(A) EMPLOYER AND STATE.—The terms 'employer' and 'State' shall have the respective meanings provided such terms under subsections (b) and (i) of section 11 of the Age Discrimination in Employment Act of 1967 (29 U.S.C. 630).

"(B) DISABILITY BENEFITS.—The term 'disability benefits' means any program for employees of a State or political subdivision of a State that provides long-term disability benefits, whether on an insured basis in a separate employee benefit plan or as part of an employee pension benefit plan.

"(C) REASONABLE NOTICE.—The term 'reasonable notice' means, with respect to notice of new disability benefits described in paragraph (2)(A) that is given to each employee, notice that—

"(i) is sufficiently accurate and comprehensive to appraise the employee of the terms and conditions of the disability benefits, including whether the employee is immediately eligible for such benefits; and

"(ii) is written in a manner calculated to be understood by the average employee eligible to participate.

"(d) DISCRIMINATION IN EMPLOYEE PENSION BENEFIT PLANS.—Nothing in this title [amending this section and section 630 of this title and enacting provisions set out as notes under this section and section 621 of this title], or the amendments made by this title, shall be construed as limiting the prohibitions against discrimination that are set forth in section 4(j) of the Age Discrimination in Employment Act of 1967 [29 U.S.C. 623(j)] (as redesignated by section 103(2) of this Act).

"(e) CONTINUED BENEFIT PAYMENTS.—Notwithstanding any other provision of this section, on and after the effective date of this title and the amendments made by this title (as determined in accordance with subsections (a), (b), and (c)), this title and the amendments made by this title shall not apply to a series of benefit payments made to an individual or the individual's representative that began prior to the effective date and that continue after the effective date pursuant to an arrangement that was in effect on the effective date, except that no substantial modification to such arrangement may be made after the date of enactment of this Act [Oct. 16, 1990] if the intent of the modification is to evade the purposes of this Act."

EFFECTIVE DATE OF 1989 AMENDMENT

Amendment by Pub. L. 101–239 applicable to items and services furnished after Dec. 19, 1989, see section 6202(b)(5) of Pub. L. 101–239, set out as a note under section 162 of Title 26, Internal Revenue Code.

EFFECTIVE AND TERMINATION DATES OF 1986 AMENDMENTS

Section 7 of Pub. L. 99–592 provided that:

"(a) IN GENERAL.—Except as provided in subsection (b), this Act and the amendments made by this Act [amending this section and sections 630 and 631 of this title and enacting provisions set out as notes under this section and sections 621, 622, 624, and 631 of this title] shall take effect on January 1, 1987, except that with respect to any employee who is subject to a collective-bargaining agreement—

"(1) which is in effect on June 30, 1986,

"(2) which terminates after January 1, 1987,

"(3) any provision of which was entered into by a labor organization (as defined by section 6(d)(4) of the Fair Labor Standards Act of 1938 (29 U.S.C. 206(d)(4)), and

"(4) which contains any provision that would be superseded by such amendments, but for the operation of this section,

such amendments shall not apply until the termination of such collective bargaining agreement or January 1, 1990, whichever occurs first.

"(b) EFFECT ON EXISTING CAUSES OF ACTION.—The amendments made by sections 3 and 4 of this Act [amending this section and section 630 of this title and enacting provisions set out as a note below] shall not apply with respect to any cause of action arising under the Age Discrimination in Employment Act of 1967 [29 U.S.C. 621 et seq.] as in effect before January 1, 1987."

Section 3(b) of Pub. L. 99–592 which provided that the amendment made by section 3(a) of Pub. L. 99–592, which amended this section, was repealed Dec. 31, 1993, was itself repealed, effective Dec. 31, 1993, by Pub. L. 104–208, div. A, title I, § 101(a) [title I, § 119[1(a)]], Sept. 30, 1996, 110 Stat. 3009, 3009–23.

Section 9204 of subtitle C (§§ 9201–9204) of title IX of Pub. L. 99–509 provided that:

"(a) APPLICABILITY TO EMPLOYEES WITH SERVICE AFTER 1988.—

"(1) IN GENERAL.—The amendments made by sections 9201 and 9202 [amending this section, section 1054 of this title, and section 411 of Title 26, Internal Revenue Code] shall apply only with respect to plan years beginning on or after January 1, 1988, and only to employees who have 1 hour of service in any plan year to which such amendments apply.

"(2) SPECIAL RULE FOR COLLECTIVELY BARGAINED PLANS.—In the case of a plan maintained pursuant to 1 or more collective bargaining agreements between employee representatives and 1 or more employers ratified before March 1, 1986, paragraph (1) shall be applied to benefits pursuant to, and individuals covered by, any such agreement by substituting for 'January 1, 1988' the date of the commencement of the first plan year beginning on or after the earlier of—

"(A) the later of—

"(i) January 1, 1988, or

"(ii) the date on which the last of such collective bargaining agreements terminate (determined without regard to any extension thereof after February 28, 1986), or

"(B) January 1, 1990.

"(b) APPLICABILITY OF AMENDMENTS RELATING TO NORMAL RETIREMENT AGE.—The amendments made by section 9203 [amending sections 1002 and 1052 of this title and sections 410 and 411 of Title 26] shall apply only with respect to plan years beginning on or after January 1, 1988, and only with respect to service performed on or after such date.

"(c) PLAN AMENDMENTS.—If any amendment made by this subtitle [amending this section, sections 1002, 1052, and 1054 of this title, and sections 410 and 411 of Title 26] requires an amendment to any plan, such plan amendment shall not be required to be made before the first plan year beginning on or after January 1, 1989, if—

"(1) during the period after such amendment takes effect and before such first plan year, the plan is operated in accordance with the requirements of such amendment, and

"(2) such plan amendment applies retroactively to the period after such amendment takes effect and such first plan year.

A pension plan shall not be treated as failing to provide definitely determinable benefits or contributions, or to be operated in accordance with the provisions of the plan, merely because it operates in accordance with this subsection.

"(d) INTERAGENCY COORDINATION.—The regulations and rulings issued by the Secretary of Labor, the regulations and rulings issued by the Secretary of the Treasury, and the regulations and rulings issued by the Equal Employment Opportunity Commission pursuant to the amendments made by this subtitle shall each be consistent with the others. The Secretary of Labor, the Secretary of the Treasury, and the Equal Employment Opportunity Commission shall each consult with the others to the extent necessary to meet the requirements of the preceding sentence.

"(e) FINAL REGULATIONS.—The Secretary of Labor, the Secretary of the Treasury, and the Equal Employment Opportunity Commission shall each issue before February 1, 1988, such final regulations as may be necessary to carry out the amendments made by this subtitle."

Amendment by Pub. L. 99–272 effective May 1, 1986, see section 9201(d)(2) of Pub. L. 99–272, set out as an Effective Date of 1986 Amendment note under section 1395p of Title 42, The Public Health and Welfare.

EFFECTIVE DATE OF 1984 AMENDMENTS

Section 2301(c)(2) of Pub. L. 98–369 provided that: "The amendment made by subsection (b) [amending this section] shall become effective on January 1, 1985."

Amendment by Pub. L. 98–459 effective Oct. 9, 1984, see section 803(a) of Pub. L. 98–459, set out as a note under section 3001 of Title 42, The Public Health and Welfare.

EFFECTIVE DATE OF 1982 AMENDMENT

Section 116(c) of Pub. L. 97–248 provided that: "The amendment made by subsection (a) [amending this section] shall become effective on January 1, 1983, and the amendment made by subsection (b) [enacting section 1395y(b)(3) of Title 42, The Public Health and Welfare] shall apply with respect to items and services furnished on or after such date."

EFFECTIVE DATE OF 1978 AMENDMENT

Section 2(b) of Pub. L. 95–256 provided that: "The amendment made by subsection (a) of this section [amending this section] shall take effect on the date of enactment of this Act [Apr. 6, 1978], except that, in the case of employees covered by a collective bargaining agreement which is in effect on September 1, 1977, which was entered into by a labor organization (as defined by section 6(d)(4) of the Fair Labor Standards Act of 1938 [section 206(d)(4) of this title]), and which would otherwise be prohibited by the amendment made by section 3(a) of this Act [amending section 631 of this title], the amendment made by subsection (a) of this section [amending this section] shall take effect upon the termination of such agreement or on January 1, 1980, whichever occurs first."

REGULATIONS

Section 104 of title I of Pub. L. 101–433 provided that: "Notwithstanding section 9 of the Age Discrimination in Employment Act of 1967 (29 U.S.C. 628), the Equal Employment Opportunity Commission may issue such rules and regulations as the Commission may consider necessary or appropriate for carrying out this title [amending this section and section 630 of this title and enacting provisions set out as notes under this section and section 621 of this title], and the amendments made by this title, only after consultation with the Secretary of the Treasury and the Secretary of Labor."

CONSTRUCTION OF 1998 AMENDMENT

Pub. L. 105–244, title IX, § 941(c), Oct. 7, 1998, 112 Stat. 1835, provided that: "Nothing in the amendment made by subsection (a) [amending this section] shall affect the application of section 4 of the Age Discrimination in Employment Act of 1967 (29 U.S.C. 623) with respect to—

"(1) any plan described in subsection (m) of section 4 of such Act (as added by subsection (a)), for any period prior to enactment of such Act [Dec. 15, 1967];

"(2) any plan not described in subsection (m) of section 4 of such Act (as added by subsection (a)); or

"(3) any employer other than an institution of higher education (as defined in section 101 of the Higher Education Act of 1965 [20 U.S.C. 1001])."

CONSTRUCTION OF 1996 AMENDMENT

Section 101(a) [title I, § 119[1(c)]] of Pub. L. 104–208 provided that: "Nothing in the repeal, reenactment, and amendment made by subsections (a) and (b) [section 101(a) [title I, § 119[1(a), (b)]] of Pub. L. 104–208, amending this section and repealing provisions set out as a note under this section] shall be construed to make lawful the failure or refusal to hire, or the discharge of, an individual pursuant to a law that—

"(1) was enacted after March 3, 1983 and before the date of enactment of the Age Discrimination in Employment Amendments of 1996 [Sept. 30, 1996]; and

"(2) lowered the age of hiring or retirement, respectively, for firefighters or law enforcement officers that was in effect under applicable State or local law on March 3, 1983."

TRANSFER OF FUNCTIONS

Functions vested by this section in Secretary of Labor or Civil Service Commission transferred to Equal Employment Opportunity Commission by Reorg. Plan No. 1 of 1978, § 2, 43 F.R. 19807, 92 Stat. 3781, set out in the Appendix to Title 5, Government Organization and Employees, effective Jan. 1, 1979, as provided by section 1–101 of Ex. Ord. No. 12106, Dec. 28, 1978, 44 F.R. 1053.

STUDY AND GUIDELINES FOR PERFORMANCE TESTS

Pub. L. 104–208, div. A, title I, § 101(a) [title I, § 119[2]], Sept. 30, 1996, 110 Stat. 3009, 3009–24, required the Secretary of Health and Human Services to conduct a study on tests assessing the abilities important for the completion of public safety tasks performed by law enforcement officers and firefighters no later than 3 years after Sept. 30, 1996, and to develop and issue advisory guidelines based on the results of the study no later than 4 years after Sept. 30, 1996, and authorized appropriations.

§ 624. Study by Secretary of Labor; reports to President and Congress; scope of study; implementation of study; transmittal date of reports

(a)(1) The Secretary of Labor is directed to undertake an appropriate study of institutional and other arrangements giving rise to involuntary retirement, and report his findings and any appropriate legislative recommendations to the President and to the Congress. Such study shall include—

(A) an examination of the effect of the amendment made by section 3(a) of the Age Discrimination in Employment Act Amendments of 1978 in raising the upper age limitation established by section 631(a) of this title to 70 years of age;

(B) a determination of the feasibility of eliminating such limitation;

(C) a determination of the feasibility of raising such limitation above 70 years of age; and

(D) an examination of the effect of the exemption contained in section 631(c) of this title, relating to certain executive employees, and the exemption contained in section 631(d) of this title, relating to tenured teaching personnel.

(2) The Secretary may undertake the study required by paragraph (1) of this subsection directly or by contract or other arrangement.

(b) The report required by subsection (a) of this section shall be transmitted to the President and to the Congress as an interim report not later than January 1, 1981, and in final form not later than January 1, 1982.

(Pub. L. 90–202, § 5, Dec. 15, 1967, 81 Stat. 604; Pub. L. 95–256, § 6, Apr. 6, 1978, 92 Stat. 192.)

REFERENCES IN TEXT

Section 3(a) of the Age Discrimination in Employment Act Amendments of 1978, referred to in subsec. (a)(1)(A), is section 3(a) of Pub. L. 95–256, Apr. 6, 1978, 92 Stat. 189, which amended section 631 of this title.

AMENDMENTS

1978—Pub. L. 95–256 designated existing provisions as par. (1), added cls. (A) to (D), added par. (2), and added subsec. (b).

STUDY TO ANALYZE POTENTIAL CONSEQUENCES OF ELIMINATION OF MANDATORY RETIREMENT ON INSTITUTIONS OF HIGHER EDUCATION

Pub. L. 99–592, § 6(c), Oct. 31, 1986, 100 Stat. 3344, provided that:

"(1) The Equal Employment Opportunity Commission shall, not later than 12 months after the date of enactment of this Act [Oct. 31, 1986], enter into an agreement with the National Academy of Sciences for the conduct of a study to analyze the potential consequences of the elimination of mandatory retirement on institutions of higher education.

"(2) The study required by paragraph (1) of this subsection shall be conducted under the general supervision of the National Academy of Sciences by a study panel composed of 9 members. The study panel shall consist of—

"(A) 4 members who shall be administrators at institutions of higher education selected by the National Academy of Sciences after consultation with the American Council of Education, the Association of American Universities, and the National Association of State Universities and Land Grant Colleges;

"(B) 4 members who shall be teachers or retired teachers at institutions of higher education (who do not serve in an administrative capacity at such institutions), selected by the National Academy of Sciences after consultation with the American Federation of Teachers, the National Education Association, the American Association of University Professors, and the American Association of Retired Persons; and

"(C) one member selected by the National Academy of Sciences.

"(3) The results of the study shall be reported, with recommendations, to the President and to the Congress not later than 5 years after the date of enactment of this Act [Oct. 31, 1986].

"(4) The expenses of the study required by this subsection shall be paid from funds available to the Equal Employment Opportunity Commission."

§ 625. Administration

The Secretary shall have the power—

(a) Delegation of functions; appointment of personnel; technical assistance

to make delegations, to appoint such agents and employees, and to pay for technical assistance on a fee for service basis, as he deems necessary to assist him in the performance of his functions under this chapter;

(b) Cooperation with other agencies, employers, labor organizations, and employment agencies

to cooperate with regional, State, local, and other agencies, and to cooperate with and furnish technical assistance to employers, labor organizations, and employment agencies to aid in effectuating the purposes of this chapter.

(Pub. L. 90–202, § 6, Dec. 15, 1967, 81 Stat. 604.)

TRANSFER OF FUNCTIONS

Functions relating to age discrimination administration and enforcement vested by this section in Secretary of Labor or Civil Service Commission transferred to Equal Employment Opportunity Commission by Reorg. Plan No. 1 of 1978, § 2, 43 F.R. 19807, 92 Stat. 3781, set out in the Appendix to Title 5, Government Organization and Employees, effective Jan. 1, 1979, as provided by section 1–101 of Ex. Ord. No. 12106, Dec. 28, 1978, 44 F.R. 1053.

§ 626. Recordkeeping, investigation, and enforcement

(a) Attendance of witnesses; investigations, inspections, records, and homework regulations

The Equal Employment Opportunity Commission shall have the power to make investigations and require the keeping of records necessary or appropriate for the administration of this chapter in accordance with the powers and procedures provided in sections 209 and 211 of this title.

(b) Enforcement; prohibition of age discrimination under fair labor standards; unpaid minimum wages and unpaid overtime compensation; liquidated damages; judicial relief; conciliation, conference, and persuasion

The provisions of this chapter shall be enforced in accordance with the powers, remedies, and procedures provided in sections 211(b), 216 (except for subsection (a) thereof), and 217 of this title, and subsection (c) of this section. Any act prohibited under section 623 of this title shall be deemed to be a prohibited act under section 215 of this title. Amounts owing to a person as a result of a violation of this chapter shall be deemed to be unpaid minimum wages or unpaid overtime compensation for purposes of sections 216 and 217 of this title: *Provided*, That liquidated damages shall be payable only in cases of willful violations of this chapter. In any action brought to enforce this chapter the court shall have jurisdiction to grant such legal or equitable relief as may be appropriate to effectuate the purposes of this chapter, including without limitation judgments compelling employment, reinstatement or promotion, or enforcing the liability for amounts deemed to be unpaid minimum wages or unpaid overtime compensation under this section. Before instituting any action under this section, the Equal Employment Opportunity Commission shall attempt to eliminate the discriminatory practice or practices alleged, and to effect voluntary compliance with the requirements of this chapter through informal methods of conciliation, conference, and persuasion.

(c) Civil actions; persons aggrieved; jurisdiction; judicial relief; termination of individual action upon commencement of action by Commission; jury trial

(1) Any person aggrieved may bring a civil action in any court of competent jurisdiction for such legal or equitable relief as will effectuate the purposes of this chapter: *Provided*, That the right of any person to bring such action shall terminate upon the commencement of an action by the Equal Employment Opportunity Commission to enforce the right of such employee under this chapter.

(2) In an action brought under paragraph (1), a person shall be entitled to a trial by jury of any issue of fact in any such action for recovery of amounts owing as a result of a violation of this chapter, regardless of whether equitable relief is sought by any party in such action.

(d) Filing of charge with Commission; timeliness; conciliation, conference, and persuasion

No civil action may be commenced by an individual under this section until 60 days after a charge alleging unlawful discrimination has been filed with the Equal Employment Opportunity Commission. Such a charge shall be filed—

(1) within 180 days after the alleged unlawful practice occurred; or

(2) in a case to which section 633(b) of this title applies, within 300 days after the alleged unlawful practice occurred, or within 30 days after receipt by the individual of notice of termination of proceedings under State law, whichever is earlier.

Upon receiving such a charge, the Commission shall promptly notify all persons named in such charge as prospective defendants in the action and shall promptly seek to eliminate any alleged unlawful practice by informal methods of conciliation, conference, and persuasion.

(e) Reliance on administrative rulings; notice of dismissal or termination; civil action after receipt of notice

Section 259 of this title shall apply to actions under this chapter. If a charge filed with the Commission under this chapter is dismissed or the proceedings of the Commission are otherwise terminated by the Commission, the Commission shall notify the person aggrieved. A civil action may be brought under this section by a person defined in section 630(a) of this title against the respondent named in the charge within 90 days after the date of the receipt of such notice.

(f) Waiver

(1) An individual may not waive any right or claim under this chapter unless the waiver is knowing and voluntary. Except as provided in paragraph (2), a waiver may not be considered knowing and voluntary unless at a minimum—

(A) the waiver is part of an agreement between the individual and the employer that is written in a manner calculated to be understood by such individual, or by the average individual eligible to participate;

(B) the waiver specifically refers to rights or claims arising under this chapter;

(C) the individual does not waive rights or claims that may arise after the date the waiver is executed;

(D) the individual waives rights or claims only in exchange for consideration in addition to anything of value to which the individual already is entitled;

(E) the individual is advised in writing to consult with an attorney prior to executing the agreement;

(F)(i) the individual is given a period of at least 21 days within which to consider the agreement; or

(ii) if a waiver is requested in connection with an exit incentive or other employment termination program offered to a group or class of employees, the individual is given a period of at least 45 days within which to consider the agreement;

(G) the agreement provides that for a period of at least 7 days following the execution of such agreement, the individual may revoke the agreement, and the agreement shall not become effective or enforceable until the revocation period has expired;

(H) if a waiver is requested in connection with an exit incentive or other employment termination program offered to a group or class of employees, the employer (at the commencement of the period specified in subparagraph (F)) informs the individual in writing in a manner calculated to be understood by the average individual eligible to participate, as to—

(i) any class, unit, or group of individuals covered by such program, any eligibility factors for such program, and any time limits applicable to such program; and

(ii) the job titles and ages of all individuals eligible or selected for the program, and the ages of all individuals in the same job classification or organizational unit who are not eligible or selected for the program.

(2) A waiver in settlement of a charge filed with the Equal Employment Opportunity Commission, or an action filed in court by the individual or the individual's representative, alleging age discrimination of a kind prohibited under section 623 or 633a of this title may not be considered knowing and voluntary unless at a minimum—

(A) subparagraphs (A) through (E) of paragraph (1) have been met; and

(B) the individual is given a reasonable period of time within which to consider the settlement agreement.

(3) In any dispute that may arise over whether any of the requirements, conditions, and circumstances set forth in subparagraph (A), (B), (C), (D), (E), (F), (G), or (H) of paragraph (1), or subparagraph (A) or (B) of paragraph (2), have been met, the party asserting the validity of a waiver shall have the burden of proving in a court of competent jurisdiction that a waiver was knowing and voluntary pursuant to paragraph (1) or (2).

(4) No waiver agreement may affect the Commission's rights and responsibilities to enforce this chapter. No waiver may be used to justify interfering with the protected right of an employee to file a charge or participate in an investigation or proceeding conducted by the Commission.

(Pub. L. 90–202, §7, Dec. 15, 1967, 81 Stat. 604; Pub. L. 95–256, §4(a), (b)(1), (c)(1), Apr. 6, 1978, 92 Stat. 190, 191; 1978 Reorg. Plan No. 1, §2, eff. Jan. 1, 1979, 43 F.R. 19807, 92 Stat. 3781; Pub. L. 101–433, title II, §201, Oct. 16, 1990, 104 Stat. 983; Pub. L. 102–166, title I, §115, Nov. 21, 1991, 105 Stat. 1079.)

AMENDMENTS

1991—Subsec. (e). Pub. L. 102–166 struck out par. (1) designation, substituted "Section" for "Sections 255 and", inserted at end "If a charge filed with the Commission under this chapter is dismissed or the proceedings of the Commission are otherwise terminated by the Commission, the Commission shall notify the person aggrieved. A civil action may be brought under this section by a person defined in section 630(a) of this title against the respondent named in the charge within 90 days after the date of the receipt of such notice.", and struck out par. (2) which read as follows: "For the period during which the Equal Employment Opportunity Commission is attempting to effect voluntary compliance with requirements of this chapter through informal methods of conciliation, conference, and persuasion pursuant to subsection (b) of this section, the statute of limitations as provided in section 255 of this title shall be tolled, but in no event for a period in excess of one year."

1990—Subsec. (f). Pub. L. 101–433 added subsec. (f).

1978—Subsec. (c). Pub. L. 95–256, §4(a), designated existing provisions as par. (1) and added par. (2).

Subsec. (d). Pub. L. 95–256, §4(b)(1), substituted references to the filing of a charge with the Secretary alleging unlawful discrimination for references to the filing with the Secretary of notice of intent to sue.

Subsec. (e). Pub. L. 95–256, §4(c)(1), designated existing provisions as par. (1) and added par. (2).

EFFECTIVE DATE OF 1991 AMENDMENT

Amendment by Pub. L. 102–166 effective Nov. 21, 1991, except as otherwise provided, see section 402 of Pub. L. 102–166, set out as a note under section 1981 of Title 42, The Public Health and Welfare.

EFFECTIVE DATE OF 1990 AMENDMENT

Section 202(a) of Pub. L. 101–433 provided that: "The amendment made by section 201 [amending this section] shall not apply with respect to waivers that occur before the date of enactment of this Act [Oct. 16, 1990]."

EFFECTIVE DATE OF 1978 AMENDMENT

Section 4(b)(2) of Pub. L. 95–256 provided that: "The amendment made by paragraph (1) of this subsection [amending this section] shall take effect with respect to civil actions brought after the date of enactment of this Act [Apr. 6, 1978]."

Section 4(c)(2) of Pub. L. 95–256 provided that: "The amendment made by paragraph (1) of this subsection [amending this section] shall take effect with respect to conciliations commenced by the Secretary of Labor after the date of enactment of this Act [Apr. 6, 1978]."

TRANSFER OF FUNCTIONS

"Equal Employment Opportunity Commission" and "Commission" substituted for "Secretary", meaning Secretary of Labor, pursuant to Reorg. Plan No. 1 of 1978, §2, 43 F.R. 19807, 92 Stat. 3781, set out in the Appendix to Title 5, Government Organization and Employees, which transferred all functions vested by this section in Secretary of Labor to Equal Employment Opportunity Commission, effective Jan. 1, 1979, as provided by section 1–101 of Ex. Ord. No. 12106, Dec. 28, 1978, 44 F.R. 1053.

RULE ON WAIVERS

Section 202(b) of Pub. L. 101–433 provided that: "Effective on the date of enactment of this Act [Oct. 16, 1990], the rule on waivers issued by the Equal Employment Opportunity Commission and contained in section 1627.16(c) of title 29, Code of Federal Regulations, shall have no force and effect."

AGE DISCRIMINATION CLAIMS ASSISTANCE

Pub. L. 100–283, Apr. 7, 1988, 102 Stat. 78, as amended by Pub. L. 101–504, §2, Nov. 3, 1990, 104 Stat. 1298, provided extension period for filing civil actions under this section, such period consisting of 450 days beginning on Apr. 7, 1988, in cases where a charge was timely filed with the Equal Employment Opportunity Commission after Dec. 31, 1983, and 450 days beginning on Nov. 3, 1990, in cases where a charge was timely filed after Apr. 6, 1985, but the Commission did not, within the applicable period set forth in subsec. (e) of this section either eliminate the alleged unlawful practice or notify the complainant, in writing, of the disposition of the charge and of right of such person to bring civil action on such claim; required the Commission to provide notice regarding claims for which extension period was applicable; and required the Commission to submit reports to Congress containing, among other things, information as to number of persons eligible for extension period and number of persons who were provided notice regarding claims for which extension period was provided.

§627. Notices to be posted

Every employer, employment agency, and labor organization shall post and keep posted in conspicuous places upon its premises a notice to be prepared or approved by the Equal Employment Opportunity Commission setting forth information as the Commission deems appropriate to effectuate the purposes of this chapter.

(Pub. L. 90–202, §8, Dec. 15, 1967, 81 Stat. 605; 1978 Reorg. Plan No. 1, §2, eff. Jan. 1, 1979, 43 F.R. 19807, 92 Stat. 3781.)

TRANSFER OF FUNCTIONS

"Equal Employment Opportunity Commission" and "Commission" substituted in text for "Secretary", meaning Secretary of Labor, pursuant to Reorg. Plan No. 1 of 1978, §2, 43 F.R. 19807, 92 Stat. 3781, set out in the Appendix to Title 5, Government Organization and

Employees, which transferred all functions vested by this section in Secretary of Labor to Equal Employment Opportunity Commission, effective Jan. 1, 1979, as provided by section 1–101 of Ex. Ord. No. 12106, Dec. 28, 1978, 44 F.R. 1053.

§ 628. Rules and regulations; exemptions

In accordance with the provisions of subchapter II of chapter 5 of title 5, the Equal Employment Opportunity Commission may issue such rules and regulations as it may consider necessary or appropriate for carrying out this chapter, and may establish such reasonable exemptions to and from any or all provisions of this chapter as it may find necessary and proper in the public interest.

(Pub. L. 90–202, § 9, Dec. 15, 1967, 81 Stat. 605; 1978 Reorg. Plan No. 1, § 2, eff. Jan. 1, 1979, 43 F.R. 19807, 92 Stat. 3781.)

TRANSFER OF FUNCTIONS

"Equal Employment Opportunity Commission" and "it" substituted in text for "Secretary of Labor" and "he", respectively, pursuant to Reorg. Plan No. 1 of 1978, § 2, 43 F.R. 19807, 92 Stat. 3781, set out in the Appendix to Title 5, Government Organization and Employees, which transferred all functions vested by this section in Secretary of Labor to Equal Employment Opportunity Commission, effective Jan. 1, 1979, as provided by section 1–101 of Ex. Ord. No. 12106, Dec. 28, 1978, 44 F.R. 1053.

§ 629. Criminal penalties

Whoever shall forcibly resist, oppose, impede, intimidate or interfere with a duly authorized representative of the Equal Employment Opportunity Commission while it is engaged in the performance of duties under this chapter shall be punished by a fine of not more than $500 or by imprisonment for not more than one year, or by both: *Provided, however*, That no person shall be imprisoned under this section except when there has been a prior conviction hereunder.

(Pub. L. 90–202, § 10, Dec. 15, 1967, 81 Stat. 605; 1978 Reorg. Plan No. 1, § 2, eff. Jan. 1, 1979, 43 F.R. 19807, 92 Stat. 3781.)

TRANSFER OF FUNCTIONS

"Equal Employment Opportunity Commission" and "it" substituted in text for "Secretary", meaning Secretary of Labor, and "he", respectively, pursuant to Reorg. Plan No. 1 of 1978, § 2, 43 F.R. 19807, 92 Stat. 3781, set out in the Appendix to Title 5, Government Organization and Employees, which transferred all functions vested by this section in Secretary of Labor to Equal Employment Opportunity Commission, effective Jan. 1, 1979, as provided by section 1–101 of Ex. Ord. No. 12106, Dec. 28, 1978, 44 F.R. 1053.

§ 630. Definitions

For the purposes of this chapter—

(a) The term "person" means one or more individuals, partnerships, associations, labor organizations, corporations, business trusts, legal representatives, or any organized groups of persons.

(b) The term "employer" means a person engaged in an industry affecting commerce who has twenty or more employees for each working day in each of twenty or more calendar weeks in the current or preceding calendar year: *Provided*, That prior to June 30, 1968, employers having fewer than fifty employees shall not be considered employers. The term also means (1) any agent of such a person, and (2) a State or political subdivision of a State and any agency or instrumentality of a State or a political subdivision of a State, and any interstate agency, but such term does not include the United States, or a corporation wholly owned by the Government of the United States.

(c) The term "employment agency" means any person regularly undertaking with or without compensation to procure employees for an employer and includes an agent of such a person; but shall not include an agency of the United States.

(d) The term "labor organization" means a labor organization engaged in an industry affecting commerce, and any agent of such an organization, and includes any organization of any kind, any agency, or employee representation committee, group, association, or plan so engaged in which employees participate and which exists for the purpose, in whole or in part, of dealing with employers concerning grievances, labor disputes, wages, rates of pay, hours, or other terms or conditions of employment, and any conference, general committee, joint or system board, or joint council so engaged which is subordinate to a national or international labor organization.

(e) A labor organization shall be deemed to be engaged in an industry affecting commerce if (1) it maintains or operates a hiring hall or hiring office which procures employees for an employer or procures for employees opportunities to work for an employer, or (2) the number of its members (or, where it is a labor organization composed of other labor organizations or their representatives, if the aggregate number of the members of such other labor organization) is fifty or more prior to July 1, 1968, or twenty-five or more on or after July 1, 1968, and such labor organization—

(1) is the certified representative of employees under the provisions of the National Labor Relations Act, as amended [29 U.S.C. 151 et seq.], or the Railway Labor Act, as amended [45 U.S.C. 151 et seq.]; or

(2) although not certified, is a national or international labor organization or a local labor organization recognized or acting as the representative of employees of an employer or employers engaged in an industry affecting commerce; or

(3) has chartered a local labor organization or subsidiary body which is representing or actively seeking to represent employees of employers within the meaning of paragraph (1) or (2); or

(4) has been chartered by a labor organization representing or actively seeking to represent employees within the meaning of paragraph (1) or (2) as the local or subordinate body through which such employees may enjoy membership or become affiliated with such labor organization; or

(5) is a conference, general committee, joint or system board, or joint council subordinate to a national or international labor organization, which includes a labor organization engaged in an industry affecting commerce with-

in the meaning of any of the preceding paragraphs of this subsection.

(f) The term "employee" means an individual employed by any employer except that the term "employee" shall not include any person elected to public office in any State or political subdivision of any State by the qualified voters thereof, or any person chosen by such officer to be on such officer's personal staff, or an appointee on the policymaking level or an immediate adviser with respect to the exercise of the constitutional or legal powers of the office. The exemption set forth in the preceding sentence shall not include employees subject to the civil service laws of a State government, governmental agency, or political subdivision. The term "employee" includes any individual who is a citizen of the United States employed by an employer in a workplace in a foreign country.

(g) The term "commerce" means trade, traffic, commerce, transportation, transmission, or communication among the several States; or between a State and any place outside thereof; or within the District of Columbia, or a possession of the United States; or between points in the same State but through a point outside thereof.

(h) The term "industry affecting commerce" means any activity, business, or industry in commerce or in which a labor dispute would hinder or obstruct commerce or the free flow of commerce and includes any activity or industry "affecting commerce" within the meaning of the Labor-Management Reporting and Disclosure Act of 1959 [29 U.S.C. 401 et seq.].

(i) The term "State" includes a State of the United States, the District of Columbia, Puerto Rico, the Virgin Islands, American Samoa, Guam, Wake Island, the Canal Zone, and Outer Continental Shelf lands defined in the Outer Continental Shelf Lands Act [43 U.S.C. 1331 et seq.].

(j) The term "firefighter" means an employee, the duties of whose position are primarily to perform work directly connected with the control and extinguishment of fires or the maintenance and use of firefighting apparatus and equipment, including an employee engaged in this activity who is transferred to a supervisory or administrative position.

(k) The term "law enforcement officer" means an employee, the duties of whose position are primarily the investigation, apprehension, or detention of individuals suspected or convicted of offenses against the criminal laws of a State, including an employee engaged in this activity who is transferred to a supervisory or administrative position. For the purpose of this subsection, "detention" includes the duties of employees assigned to guard individuals incarcerated in any penal institution.

(*l*) The term "compensation, terms, conditions, or privileges of employment" encompasses all employee benefits, including such benefits provided pursuant to a bona fide employee benefit plan.

(Pub. L. 90–202, § 11, Dec. 15, 1967, 81 Stat. 605; Pub. L. 93–259, § 28(a)(1)–(4), Apr. 8, 1974, 88 Stat. 74; Pub. L. 98–459, title VIII, § 802(a), Oct. 9, 1984, 98 Stat. 1792; Pub. L. 99–592, § 4, Oct. 31, 1986, 100 Stat. 3343; Pub. L. 101–433, title I, § 102, Oct. 16, 1990, 104 Stat. 978.)

References in Text

The National Labor Relations Act, referred to in subsec. (e)(1), is act July 5, 1935, ch. 372, 49 Stat. 452, as amended, which is classified generally to subchapter II (§ 151 et seq.) of chapter 7 of this title. For complete classification of this Act to the Code, see section 167 of this title and Tables.

The Railway Labor Act, referred to in subsec. (e)(1), is act May 20, 1926, ch. 347, 44 Stat. 577, as amended, which is classified principally to chapter 8 (§ 151 et seq.) of Title 45, Railroads. For complete classification of this Act to the Code, see section 151 of Title 45 and Tables.

The Labor-Management Reporting and Disclosure Act of 1959, referred to in subsec. (h), is Pub. L. 86–257, Sept. 14, 1959, 73 Stat. 519, as amended, which is classified principally to chapter 11 (§ 401 et seq.) of this title. For complete classification of this Act to the Code, see Short Title note set out under section 401 of this title, and Tables.

For definition of Canal Zone, referred to in subsec. (i), see section 3602(b) of Title 22, Foreign Relations and Intercourse.

The Outer Continental Shelf Lands Act, referred to in subsec. (i), is act Aug. 7, 1953, ch. 345, 67 Stat. 462, as amended, which is classified generally to subchapter III (§ 1331 et seq.) of chapter 29 of Title 43, Public Lands. For complete classification of this Act to the Code, see Short Title note set out under section 1331 of Title 43 and Tables.

Amendments

1990—Subsec. (*l*). Pub. L. 101–433 added subsec. (*l*).

1986—Subsecs. (j), (k). Pub. L. 99–592 added subsecs. (j) and (k).

1984—Subsec. (f). Pub. L. 98–459 inserted provision defining "employee" as including any individual who is a citizen of the United States employed by an employer in a workplace in a foreign country.

1974—Subsec. (b). Pub. L. 93–259, § 28(a)(1), (2), substituted in first sentence "twenty" for "twenty-five" and, in second sentence, defined term "employer" to include a State or political subdivision of a State and any agency or instrumentality of a State or a political subdivision of a State, and any interstate agency, and deleted text excluding from such term a State or political subdivision thereof.

Subsec. (c). Pub. L. 93–259, § 28(a)(3), struck out text excluding from term "employment agency" an agency of a State or political subdivision of a State, but including the United States Employment Service and the system of State and local employment services receiving Federal assistance.

Subsec. (f). Pub. L. 93–259, § 28(a)(4), excepted from the term "employee" elected public officials, persons chosen by such officials for such officials' personal staff, appointees on policymaking level, and immediate advisers with respect to exercise of constitutional or legal powers of the public office but excluded from such exemption employees subject to civil laws of a State government, governmental agency, or political subdivision.

Effective Date of 1990 Amendment

Amendment by Pub. L. 101–433 applicable only to any employee benefit established or modified on or after Oct. 16, 1990, and other conduct occurring more than 180 days after Oct. 16, 1990, except as otherwise provided, see section 105 of Pub. L. 101–433, set out as a note under section 623 of this title.

Effective Date of 1986 Amendment

Amendment by Pub. L. 99–592 effective Jan. 1, 1987, with certain exceptions, but not applicable with respect to any cause of action arising under this chapter as in effect before Jan. 1, 1987, see section 7 of Pub. L. 99–592, set out as an Effective and Termination Dates of 1986 Amendment note under section 623 of this title.

EFFECTIVE DATE OF 1984 AMENDMENT

Amendment by Pub. L. 98–459 effective Oct. 9, 1984, see section 803(a) of Pub. L. 98–459, set out as a note under section 3001 of Title 42, The Public Health and Welfare.

EFFECTIVE DATE OF 1974 AMENDMENT

Amendment by Pub. L. 93–259 effective May 1, 1974, see section 29(a) of Pub. L. 93–259, set out as a note under section 202 of this title.

TRANSFER OF FUNCTIONS

Functions vested by this section in Secretary of Labor or Civil Service Commission transferred to Equal Employment Opportunity Commission by Reorg. Plan No. 1 of 1978, §2, 43 F.R. 19807, 92 Stat. 3781, set out in the Appendix to Title 5, Government Organization and Employees, effective Jan. 1, 1979, as provided by section 1–101 of Ex. Ord. No. 12106, Dec. 28, 1978, 44 F.R. 1053.

§631. Age limits

(a) Individuals at least 40 years of age

The prohibitions in this chapter shall be limited to individuals who are at least 40 years of age.

(b) Employees or applicants for employment in Federal Government

In the case of any personnel action affecting employees or applicants for employment which is subject to the provisions of section 633a of this title, the prohibitions established in section 633a of this title shall be limited to individuals who are at least 40 years of age.

(c) Bona fide executives or high policymakers

(1) Nothing in this chapter shall be construed to prohibit compulsory retirement of any employee who has attained 65 years of age and who, for the 2-year period immediately before retirement, is employed in a bona fide executive or a high policymaking position, if such employee is entitled to an immediate nonforfeitable annual retirement benefit from a pension, profit-sharing, savings, or deferred compensation plan, or any combination of such plans, of the employer of such employee, which equals, in the aggregate, at least $44,000.

(2) In applying the retirement benefit test of paragraph (1) of this subsection, if any such retirement benefit is in a form other than a straight life annuity (with no ancillary benefits), or if employees contribute to any such plan or make rollover contributions, such benefit shall be adjusted in accordance with regulations prescribed by the Equal Employment Opportunity Commission, after consultation with the Secretary of the Treasury, so that the benefit is the equivalent of a straight life annuity (with no ancillary benefits) under a plan to which employees do not contribute and under which no rollover contributions are made.

(Pub. L. 90–202, §12, Dec. 15, 1967, 81 Stat. 607; Pub. L. 95–256, §3(a), (b)(3), Apr. 6, 1978, 92 Stat. 189, 190; 1978 Reorg. Plan No. 1, §2, eff. Jan. 1, 1979, 43 F.R. 19807, 92 Stat. 3781; Pub. L. 98–459, title VIII, §802(c)(1), Oct. 9, 1984, 98 Stat. 1792; Pub. L. 99–272, title IX, §9201(b)(2), Apr. 7, 1986, 100 Stat. 171; Pub. L. 99–592, §§2(c), 6(a), Oct. 31, 1986, 100 Stat. 3342, 3344; Pub. L. 101–239, title VI, §6202(b)(3)(C)(ii), Dec. 19, 1989, 103 Stat. 2233.)

AMENDMENTS

1989—Subsec. (a). Pub. L. 101–239 struck out "(except the provisions of section 623(g) of this title)" after "in this chapter".

1986—Subsec. (a). Pub. L. 99–592, §2(c)(1), which directed that "but less than seventy years of age" be struck out was executed by striking out "but less than 70 years of age" after "40 years of age" as the probable intent of Congress.

Pub. L. 99–272 inserted "(except the provisions of section 623(g) of this title)" after "this chapter".

Subsec. (c)(1). Pub. L. 99–592, §2(c)(2), which directed that "but not seventy years of age," be struck out was executed by striking out "but not 70 years of age," after "65 years of age" as the probable intent of Congress.

Subsec. (d). Pub. L. 99–592, §6(a), (b), temporarily added subsec. (d) which read as follows: "Nothing in this chapter shall be construed to prohibit compulsory retirement of any employee who has attained 70 years of age, and who is serving under a contract of unlimited tenure (or similar arrangement providing for unlimited tenure) at an institution of higher education (as defined by section 1141(a) of title 20)." See Effective and Termination Dates of 1986 Amendments note below.

1984—Subsec. (c)(1). Pub. L. 98–459 substituted "$44,000" for "$27,000".

Pub. L. 95–256, §3(a), designated existing provisions as subsec. (a), substituted "40 years of age but less than 70 years of age" for "forty years of age but less than sixty-five years of age", added subsecs. (b) and (c), and temporarily added subsec. (d). See Effective and Termination Dates of 1978 Amendment note below.

EFFECTIVE DATE OF 1989 AMENDMENT

Amendment by Pub. L. 101–239 applicable to items and services furnished after Dec. 19, 1989, see section 6202(b)(5) of Pub. L. 101–239, set out as a note under section 162 of Title 26, Internal Revenue Code.

EFFECTIVE AND TERMINATION DATES OF 1986 AMENDMENTS

Amendment by Pub. L. 99–592 effective Jan. 1, 1987, with certain exceptions, see section 7(a) of Pub. L. 99–592 set out as a note under section 623 of this title.

Section 6(b) of Pub. L. 99–592 provided that: "The amendment made by subsection (a) of this section [amending this section] is repealed December 31, 1993."

Amendment by Pub. L. 99–272 effective May 1, 1986, see section 9201(d)(2) of Pub. L. 99–272, set out as an Effective Date of 1986 Amendment note under section 1395p of Title 42, The Public Health and Welfare.

EFFECTIVE DATE OF 1984 AMENDMENT

Section 802(c)(2) of Pub. L. 98–459 provided that: "The amendment made by paragraph (1) of this subsection [amending this section] shall not apply with respect to any individual who retires, or is compelled to retire, before the date of the enactment of this Act [Oct. 9, 1984]."

EFFECTIVE AND TERMINATION DATES OF 1978 AMENDMENT

Section 3(b) of Pub. L. 95–256 provided that:

"(1) Sections 12(a), 12(c), and 12(d) of the Age Discrimination in Employment Act of 1967, as amended by subsection (a) of this section [subsecs. (a), (c), and (d) of this section] shall take effect on January 1, 1979.

"(2) Section 12(b) of such Act, as amended by subsection (a) of this section [subsec. (b) of this section], shall take effect on September 30, 1978.

"(3) Section 12(d) of such Act, as amended by subsection (a) of this section [enacting subsec. (d) of this section], is repealed on July 1, 1982."

TRANSFER OF FUNCTIONS

"Equal Employment Opportunity Commission" substituted for "Secretary", meaning Secretary of Labor, in subsec. (c)(2) pursuant to Reorg. Plan No. 1 of 1978, §2, 43 F.R. 19807, 92 Stat. 3781, set out in the Appendix to Title 5, Government Organization and Employees, which transferred all functions vested by this section in Secretary of Labor to Equal Employment Opportunity Commission, effective Jan. 1, 1979, as provided by section 1–101 of Ex. Ord. No. 12106, Dec. 28, 1978, 44 F.R. 1053.

§ 632. Omitted

CODIFICATION

Section, Pub. L. 90–202, §13, Dec. 15, 1967, 81 Stat. 607; 1978 Reorg. Plan No. 1, §2, eff. Jan. 1, 1979, 43 F.R. 19807, 92 Stat. 3781, which required the Equal Employment Opportunity Commission to submit to Congress an annual report on the Commission's activities including an evaluation and appraisal of the effect of the minimum and maximum ages established by this chapter, terminated, effective May 15, 2000, pursuant to section 3003 of Pub. L. 104–66, as amended, set out as a note under section 1113 of Title 31, Money and Finance. See, also, page 123 of House Document No. 103–7.

§ 633. Federal-State relationship

(a) Federal action superseding State action

Nothing in this chapter shall affect the jurisdiction of any agency of any State performing like functions with regard to discriminatory employment practices on account of age except that upon commencement of action under this chapter such action shall supersede any State action.

(b) Limitation of Federal action upon commencement of State proceedings

In the case of an alleged unlawful practice occurring in a State which has a law prohibiting discrimination in employment because of age and establishing or authorizing a State authority to grant or seek relief from such discriminatory practice, no suit may be brought under section 626 of this title before the expiration of sixty days after proceedings have been commenced under the State law, unless such proceedings have been earlier terminated: *Provided*, That such sixty-day period shall be extended to one hundred and twenty days during the first year after the effective date of such State law. If any requirement for the commencement of such proceedings is imposed by a State authority other than a requirement of the filing of a written and signed statement of the facts upon which the proceeding is based, the proceeding shall be deemed to have been commenced for the purposes of this subsection at the time such statement is sent by registered mail to the appropriate State authority.

(Pub. L. 90–202, §14, Dec. 15, 1967, 81 Stat. 607.)

TRANSFER OF FUNCTIONS

Functions vested by this section in Secretary of Labor or Civil Service Commission transferred to Equal Employment Opportunity Commission by Reorg. Plan No. 1 of 1978, §2, 43 F.R. 19807, 92 Stat. 3781, set out in the Appendix to Title 5, Government Organization and Employees, effective Jan. 1, 1979, as provided by section 1–101 of Ex. Ord. No. 12106, Dec. 28, 1978, 44 F.R. 1053.

§ 633a. Nondiscrimination on account of age in Federal Government employment

(a) Federal agencies affected

All personnel actions affecting employees or applicants for employment who are at least 40 years of age (except personnel actions with regard to aliens employed outside the limits of the United States) in military departments as defined in section 102 of title 5, in executive agencies as defined in section 105 of title 5 (including employees and applicants for employment who are paid from nonappropriated funds), in the United States Postal Service and the Postal Regulatory Commission, in those units in the government of the District of Columbia having positions in the competitive service, and in those units of the judicial branch of the Federal Government having positions in the competitive service, in the Smithsonian Institution, and in the Government Printing Office, the Government Accountability Office, and the Library of Congress shall be made free from any discrimination based on age.

(b) Enforcement by Equal Employment Opportunity Commission and by Librarian of Congress in the Library of Congress; remedies; rules, regulations, orders, and instructions of Commission: compliance by Federal agencies; powers and duties of Commission; notification of final action on complaint of discrimination; exemptions: bona fide occupational qualification

Except as otherwise provided in this subsection, the Equal Employment Opportunity Commission is authorized to enforce the provisions of subsection (a) of this section through appropriate remedies, including reinstatement or hiring of employees with or without backpay, as will effectuate the policies of this section. The Equal Employment Opportunity Commission shall issue such rules, regulations, orders, and instructions as it deems necessary and appropriate to carry out its responsibilities under this section. The Equal Employment Opportunity Commission shall—

(1) be responsible for the review and evaluation of the operation of all agency programs designed to carry out the policy of this section, periodically obtaining and publishing (on at least a semiannual basis) progress reports from each department, agency, or unit referred to in subsection (a) of this section;

(2) consult with and solicit the recommendations of interested individuals, groups, and organizations relating to nondiscrimination in employment on account of age; and

(3) provide for the acceptance and processing of complaints of discrimination in Federal employment on account of age.

The head of each such department, agency, or unit shall comply with such rules, regulations, orders, and instructions of the Equal Employment Opportunity Commission which shall include a provision that an employee or applicant for employment shall be notified of any final action taken on any complaint of discrimination filed by him thereunder. Reasonable exemptions to the provisions of this section may be established by the Commission but only when the Commission has established a maximum age requirement on the basis of a determination that age is a bona fide occupational qualification necessary to the performance of the duties of the position. With respect to employment in the Library of Congress, authorities granted in this subsection to the Equal Employment Opportunity Commission shall be exercised by the Librarian of Congress.

(c) Civil actions; jurisdiction; relief

Any person aggrieved may bring a civil action in any Federal district court of competent jurisdiction for such legal or equitable relief as will effectuate the purposes of this chapter.

(d) Notice to Commission; time of notice; Commission notification of prospective defendants; Commission elimination of unlawful practices

When the individual has not filed a complaint concerning age discrimination with the Commission, no civil action may be commenced by any individual under this section until the individual has given the Commission not less than thirty days' notice of an intent to file such action. Such notice shall be filed within one hundred and eighty days after the alleged unlawful practice occurred. Upon receiving a notice of intent to sue, the Commission shall promptly notify all persons named therein as prospective defendants in the action and take any appropriate action to assure the elimination of any unlawful practice.

(e) Duty of Government agency or official

Nothing contained in this section shall relieve any Government agency or official of the responsibility to assure nondiscrimination on account of age in employment as required under any provision of Federal law.

(f) Applicability of statutory provisions to personnel action of Federal departments, etc.

Any personnel action of any department, agency, or other entity referred to in subsection (a) of this section shall not be subject to, or affected by, any provision of this chapter, other than the provisions of section 631(b) of this title and the provisions of this section.

(g) Study and report to President and Congress by Equal Employment Opportunity Commission; scope

(1) The Equal Employment Opportunity Commission shall undertake a study relating to the effects of the amendments made to this section by the Age Discrimination in Employment Act Amendments of 1978, and the effects of section 631(b) of this title.

(2) The Equal Employment Opportunity Commission shall transmit a report to the President and to the Congress containing the findings of the Commission resulting from the study of the Commission under paragraph (1) of this subsection. Such report shall be transmitted no later than January 1, 1980.

(Pub. L. 90–202, §15, as added Pub. L. 93–259, §28(b)(2), Apr. 8, 1974, 88 Stat. 74; amended Pub. L. 95–256, §5(a), (e), Apr. 6, 1978, 92 Stat. 191; 1978 Reorg. Plan No. 1, eff. Jan. 1, 1979, §2, 43 F.R. 19807, 92 Stat. 3781; Pub. L. 104–1, title II, §201(c)(2), Jan. 23, 1995, 109 Stat. 8; Pub. L. 105–220, title III, §341(b), Aug. 7, 1998, 112 Stat. 1092; Pub. L. 108–271, §8(b), July 7, 2004, 118 Stat. 814; Pub. L. 109–435, title VI, §604(f), Dec. 20, 2006, 120 Stat. 3242.)

REFERENCES IN TEXT

The amendments made to this section by the Age Discrimination in Employment Act Amendments of 1978, referred to in subsec. (g)(1), are amendments by section 5(a) and (e) of Pub. L. 95–256, which amended subsecs. (a), (f), and (g) of this section.

AMENDMENTS

2006—Subsec. (a). Pub. L. 109–435 substituted "Postal Regulatory Commission" for "Postal Rate Commission".

2004—Subsec. (a). Pub. L. 108–271 substituted "Government Accountability Office" for "General Accounting Office".

1998—Subsec. (a). Pub. L. 105–220 inserted "in the Smithsonian Institution," before "and in the Government Printing Office".

1995—Subsec. (a). Pub. L. 104–1 substituted "units of the judicial branch" for "units of the legislative and judicial branches" and inserted "Government Printing Office, the General Accounting Office, and the" before "Library of Congress".

1978—Subsec. (a). Pub. L. 95–256, §5(a), inserted age requirement of at least 40 years of age, and "personnel actions" after "except".

Subsecs. (f), (g). Pub. L. 95–256, §5(e), added subsecs. (f) and (g).

EFFECTIVE DATE OF 1998 AMENDMENT

Pub. L. 105–220, title III, §341(d), Aug. 7, 1998, 112 Stat. 1092, provided that: "The amendments made by subsections (a), (b), and (c) [amending this section, section 791 of this title, and section 2000e–16 of Title 42, The Public Health and Welfare] shall take effect on the date of enactment of this Act [Aug. 7, 1998] and shall apply to and may be raised in any administrative or judicial claim or action brought before such date of enactment but pending on such date, and any administrative or judicial claim or action brought after such date regardless of whether the claim or action arose prior to such date, if the claim or action was brought within the applicable statute of limitations."

EFFECTIVE DATE OF 1995 AMENDMENT

Amendment by Pub. L. 104–1 effective 1 year after Jan. 23, 1995, see section 1311(d) of Title 2, The Congress.

EFFECTIVE DATE OF 1978 AMENDMENT

Section 5(f) of Pub. L. 95–256 provided that: "The amendments made by this section [amending this section and sections 8335 and 8339 of Title 5, Government Organization and Employees, and repealing section 3322 of Title 5] shall take effect on September 30, 1978, except that section 15(g) of the Age Discrimination in Employment Act of 1967, as amended by subsection (e) of this section [subsec. (g) of this section], shall take effect on the date of enactment of this Act [Apr. 6, 1978]."

EFFECTIVE DATE

Section effective May 1, 1974, see section 29(a) of Pub. L. 93–259, set out as an Effective Date of 1974 Amendment note under section 202 of this title.

TRANSFER OF FUNCTIONS

"Equal Employment Opportunity Commission" substituted for "Civil Service Commission" in subsecs. (b) and (g) pursuant to Reorg. Plan No. 1 of 1978, §2, 43 F.R. 19807, 92 Stat. 3781, set out in the Appendix to Title 5, Government Organization and Employees, which transferred all functions vested by this section in Civil Service Commission to Equal Employment Opportunity Commission, effective Jan. 1, 1979, as provided by section 1–101 of Ex. Ord. No. 12106, Dec. 28, 1978, 44 F.R. 1053.

§ 634. Authorization of appropriations

There are hereby authorized to be appropriated such sums as may be necessary to carry out this chapter.

(Pub. L. 90–202, § 17, formerly § 16, Dec. 15, 1967, 81 Stat. 608; renumbered and amended Pub. L. 93–259, § 28(a)(5), (b)(1), Apr. 8, 1974, 88 Stat. 74; Pub. L. 95–256, § 7, Apr. 6, 1978, 92 Stat. 193.)

AMENDMENTS

1978—Pub. L. 95–256 struck out ", not in excess of $5,000,000 for any fiscal year," after "sums".

1974—Pub. L. 93–259, § 28(a)(5), increased appropriations authorization to $5,000,000 from $3,000,000.

EFFECTIVE DATE OF 1974 AMENDMENT

Amendment by Pub. L. 93–259 effective May 1, 1974, see section 29(a) of Pub. L. 93–259, set out as a note under section 202 of this title.

TRANSFER OF FUNCTIONS

Functions relating to age discrimination administration and enforcement vested by this section in Secretary of Labor or Civil Service Commission transferred to Equal Employment Opportunity Commission by Reorg. Plan No. 1 of 1978, § 2, 43 F.R. 19807, 92 Stat. 3781, set out in the Appendix to Title 5, Government Organization and Employees, effective Jan. 1, 1979, as provided by section 1–101 of Ex. Ord. No. 12106, Dec. 28, 1978, 44 F.R. 1053.

CHAPTER 15—OCCUPATIONAL SAFETY AND HEALTH

§ 651. Congressional statement of findings and declaration of purpose and policy

(a) The Congress finds that personal injuries and illnesses arising out of work situations impose a substantial burden upon, and are a hindrance to, interstate commerce in terms of lost production, wage loss, medical expenses, and disability compensation payments.

(b) The Congress declares it to be its purpose and policy, through the exercise of its powers to regulate commerce among the several States and with foreign nations and to provide for the general welfare, to assure so far as possible every working man and woman in the Nation safe and healthful working conditions and to preserve our human resources—

(1) by encouraging employers and employees in their efforts to reduce the number of occupational safety and health hazards at their places of employment, and to stimulate employers and employees to institute new and to perfect existing programs for providing safe and healthful working conditions;

(2) by providing that employers and employees have separate but dependent responsibilities and rights with respect to achieving safe and healthful working conditions;

(3) by authorizing the Secretary of Labor to set mandatory occupational safety and health standards applicable to businesses affecting interstate commerce, and by creating an Occupational Safety and Health Review Commission for carrying out adjudicatory functions under this chapter;

(4) by building upon advances already made through employer and employee initiative for providing safe and healthful working conditions;

(5) by providing for research in the field of occupational safety and health, including the psychological factors involved, and by developing innovative methods, techniques, and approaches for dealing with occupational safety and health problems;

(6) by exploring ways to discover latent diseases, establishing causal connections between diseases and work in environmental conditions, and conducting other research relating to health problems, in recognition of the fact that occupational health standards present problems often different from those involved in occupational safety;

(7) by providing medical criteria which will assure insofar as practicable that no employee will suffer diminished health, functional capacity, or life expectancy as a result of his work experience;

(8) by providing for training programs to increase the number and competence of personnel engaged in the field of occupational safety and health;

(9) by providing for the development and promulgation of occupational safety and health standards;

(10) by providing an effective enforcement program which shall include a prohibition against giving advance notice of any inspection and sanctions for any individual violating this prohibition;

(11) by encouraging the States to assume the fullest responsibility for the administration and enforcement of their occupational safety and health laws by providing grants to the States to assist in identifying their needs and responsibilities in the area of occupational

safety and health, to develop plans in accordance with the provisions of this chapter, to improve the administration and enforcement of State occupational safety and health laws, and to conduct experimental and demonstration projects in connection therewith;

(12) by providing for appropriate reporting procedures with respect to occupational safety and health which procedures will help achieve the objectives of this chapter and accurately describe the nature of the occupational safety and health problem;

(13) by encouraging joint labor-management efforts to reduce injuries and disease arising out of employment.

(Pub. L. 91–596, §2, Dec. 29, 1970, 84 Stat. 1590.)

REFERENCES IN TEXT

This chapter, referred to in subsec. (b)(3), (11), and (12), was in the original "this Act", meaning Pub. L. 91–596, Dec. 29, 1970, 84 Stat. 1590, as amended. For complete classification of this Act to the Code, see Short Title note set out under this section and Tables.

EFFECTIVE DATE

Section 34 of Pub. L. 91–596 provided that: "This Act [enacting this chapter and section 3142–1 of Title 42, The Public Health and Welfare, amending section 553 of this title, sections 5108, 5314, 5315, and 7902 of Title 5, Government Organization and Employees, sections 633 and 636 of Title 15, Commerce and Trade, section 1114 of Title 18, Crimes and Criminal Procedure, and section 1421 of former Title 49, Transportation, and enacting provisions set out as notes under this section and section 1114 of Title 18] shall take effect one hundred and twenty days after the date of its enactment [Dec. 29, 1970]."

SHORT TITLE OF 1998 AMENDMENT

Pub. L. 105–197, §1, July 16, 1998, 112 Stat. 638, provided that: "This Act [amending section 670 of this title] may be cited as the 'Occupational Safety and Health Administration Compliance Assistance Authorization Act of 1998'."

SHORT TITLE

Section 1 of Pub. L. 91–596 provided: "That this Act [enacting this chapter and section 3142–1 of Title 42, The Public Health and Welfare, amending section 553 of this title, sections 5108, 5314, 5315, and 7902 of Title 5, Government Organization and Employees, sections 633 and 636 of Title 15, Commerce and Trade, section 1114 of Title 18, Crimes and Criminal Procedure, and section 1421 of former Title 49, Transportation, and enacting provisions set out as notes under this section and section 1114 of Title 18] may be cited as the 'Occupational Safety and Health Act of 1970'."

§652. Definitions

For the purposes of this chapter—

(1) The term "Secretary" mean[1] the Secretary of Labor.

(2) The term "Commission" means the Occupational Safety and Health Review Commission established under this chapter.

(3) The term "commerce" means trade, traffic, commerce, transportation, or communication among the several States, or between a State and any place outside thereof, or within the District of Columbia, or a possession of the United States (other than the Trust Territory of the Pacific Islands), or between points in the same State but through a point outside thereof.

(4) The term "person" means one or more individuals, partnerships, associations, corporations, business trusts, legal representatives, or any organized group of persons.

(5) The term "employer" means a person engaged in a business affecting commerce who has employees, but does not include the United States (not including the United States Postal Service) or any State or political subdivision of a State.

(6) The term "employee" means an employee of an employer who is employed in a business of his employer which affects commerce.

(7) The term "State" includes a State of the United States, the District of Columbia, Puerto Rico, the Virgin Islands, American Samoa, Guam, and the Trust Territory of the Pacific Islands.

(8) The term "occupational safety and health standard" means a standard which requires conditions, or the adoption or use of one or more practices, means, methods, operations, or processes, reasonably necessary or appropriate to provide safe or healthful employment and places of employment.

(9) The term "national consensus standard" means any occupational safety and health standard or modification thereof which (1),[2] has been adopted and promulgated by a nationally recognized standards-producing organization under procedures whereby it can be determined by the Secretary that persons interested and affected by the scope or provisions of the standard have reached substantial agreement on its adoption, (2) was formulated in a manner which afforded an opportunity for diverse views to be considered and (3) has been designated as such a standard by the Secretary, after consultation with other appropriate Federal agencies.

(10) The term "established Federal standard" means any operative occupational safety and health standard established by any agency of the United States and presently in effect, or contained in any Act of Congress in force on December 29, 1970.

(11) The term "Committee" means the National Advisory Committee on Occupational Safety and Health established under this chapter.

(12) The term "Director" means the Director of the National Institute for Occupational Safety and Health.

(13) The term "Institute" means the National Institute for Occupational Safety and Health established under this chapter.

(14) The term "Workmen's Compensation Commission" means the National Commission on State Workmen's Compensation Laws established under this chapter.

(Pub. L. 91–596, §3, Dec. 29, 1970, 84 Stat. 1591; Pub. L. 105–241, §2(a), Sept. 28, 1998, 112 Stat. 1572.)

AMENDMENTS

1998—Par. (5). Pub. L. 105–241 inserted "(not including the United States Postal Service)" after "the United States".

[1] So in original. Probably should be "means".

[2] So in original. The comma probably should not appear.

TERMINATION OF TRUST TERRITORY OF THE PACIFIC ISLANDS

For termination of Trust Territory of the Pacific Islands, see note set out preceding section 1681 of Title 48, Territories and Insular Possessions.

TERMINATION OF ADVISORY COMMITTEES

Advisory committees in existence on January 5, 1973, to terminate not later than the expiration of the 2-year period following January 5, 1973, unless, in the case of a committee established by the President or an officer of the Federal Government, such committee is renewed by appropriate action prior to the expiration of such 2-year period, or in the case of a committee established by the Congress, its duration is otherwise provided by law. See section 14 of Pub. L. 92–463, Oct. 6, 1972, 86 Stat. 776, set out in the Appendix to Title 5, Government Organization and Employees.

§ 653. Geographic applicability; judicial enforcement; applicability to existing standards; report to Congress on duplication and coordination of Federal laws; workmen's compensation law or common law or statutory rights, duties, or liabilities of employers and employees unaffected

(a) This chapter shall apply with respect to employment performed in a workplace in a State, the District of Columbia, the Commonwealth of Puerto Rico, the Virgin Islands, American Samoa, Guam, the Trust Territory of the Pacific Islands, Lake Island, Outer Continental Shelf lands defined in the Outer Continental Shelf Lands Act [43 U.S.C. 1331 et seq.], Johnston Island, and the Canal Zone. The Secretary of the Interior shall, by regulation, provide for judicial enforcement of this chapter by the courts established for areas in which there are no United States district courts having jurisdiction.

(b)(1) Nothing in this chapter shall apply to working conditions of employees with respect to which other Federal agencies, and State agencies acting under section 2021 of title 42, exercise statutory authority to prescribe or enforce standards or regulations affecting occupational safety or health.

(2) The safety and health standards promulgated under the Act of June 30, 1936, commonly known as the Walsh-Healey Act [41 U.S.C. 35 et seq.], the Service Contract Act of 1965 [41 U.S.C. 351 et seq.], Public Law 91–54, Act of August 9, 1969, Public Law 85–742, Act of August 23, 1958, and the National Foundation on Arts and Humanities Act [20 U.S.C. 951 et seq.] are superseded on the effective date of corresponding standards, promulgated under this chapter, which are determined by the Secretary to be more effective. Standards issued under the laws listed in this paragraph and in effect on or after the effective date of this chapter shall be deemed to be occupational safety and health standards issued under this chapter, as well as under such other Acts.

(3) The Secretary shall, within three years after the effective date of this chapter, report to the Congress his recommendations for legislation to avoid unnecessary duplication and to achieve coordination between this chapter and other Federal laws.

(4) Nothing in this chapter shall be construed to supersede or in any manner affect any workmen's compensation law or to enlarge or diminish or affect in any other manner the common law or statutory rights, duties, or liabilities of employers and employees under any law with respect to injuries, diseases, or death of employees arising out of, or in the course of, employment.

(Pub. L. 91–596, § 4, Dec. 29, 1970, 84 Stat. 1592.)

REFERENCES IN TEXT

The Outer Continental Shelf Lands Act, referred to in subsec. (a), is act Aug. 7, 1953, ch. 345, 67 Stat. 462, as amended, which is classified generally to subchapter III (§ 1331 et seq.) of chapter 29 of Title 43, Public Lands. For complete classification of this Act to the Code, see Short Title note set out under section 1331 of Title 43 and Tables.

For definition of Canal Zone, referred to in subsec. (a), see section 3602(b) of Title 22, Foreign Relations and Intercourse.

Act of June 30, 1936, commonly known as the Walsh-Healey Act, referred to in subsec. (b)(2), is act June 30, 1936, ch. 881, 49 Stat. 2036, as amended, which is classified generally to section 35 et seq. of Title 41, Public Contracts. For complete classification of this Act to the Code, see Short Title note set out under section 35 of Title 41 and Tables. See section 262 of this title.

The Service Contract Act of 1965, referred to in subsec. (b)(2), is Pub. L. 89–286, Oct. 22, 1965, 79 Stat. 1034, as amended, which is classified generally to chapter 6 (§ 351 et seq.) of Title 41. For complete classification of this Act to the Code, see Short Title note set out under section 351 of Title 41 and Tables.

Public Law 91–54, Act of August 9, 1969, referred to in subsec. (b)(2), is Pub. L. 91–54, Aug. 9, 1969, 83 Stat. 96, which amended sections 1 and 2 and added section 107 of Pub. L. 87–581, Aug. 13, 1962, 76 Stat. 357. Sections 1 and 2 of Pub. L. 87–581 were set out as notes under section 327, and section 107 of Pub. L. 87–581 was classified to section 333, of former Title 40, Public Buildings, Property, and Works. Sections 1 and 2 of Pub. L. 87–581 were repealed, and section 107 of Pub. L. 87–581 was repealed and reenacted as sections 3704 and 3705 of Title 40, Public Buildings, Property, and Works, by Pub. L. 107–217, §§ 1, 6(b), Aug. 21, 2002, 116 Stat. 1062, 1304.

Public Law 85–742, Act of August 23, 1958, referred to in subsec. (b)(2), is Pub. L. 85–742, Aug. 23, 1958, 72 Stat. 835, which amended section 941 of Title 33, Navigation and Navigable Waters, and enacted provisions set out as a note under section 941 of Title 33. For complete classification of this Act to the Code, see Tables.

The National Foundation on the Arts and the Humanities Act, referred to in subsec. (b)(2), is Pub. L. 89–209, Sept. 29, 1965, 79 Stat. 845, as amended, known as the National Foundation on the Arts and the Humanities Act of 1965, which is classified principally to subchapter I (§ 951 et seq.) of chapter 26 of Title 20, Education. For complete classification of this Act to the Code, see Short Title note set out under section 951 of Title 20 and Tables.

The effective date of this chapter, referred to in subsec. (b)(2), (3), is the effective date of Pub. L. 91–596, which is 120 days after Dec. 29, 1970, see section 34 of Pub. L. 91–596, set out as an Effective Date note under section 651 of this title.

TERMINATION OF TRUST TERRITORY OF THE PACIFIC ISLANDS

For termination of Trust Territory of the Pacific Islands, see note set out preceding section 1681 of Title 48, Territories and Insular Possessions.

EPA ADMINISTRATOR NOT EXERCISING "STATUTORY AUTHORITY" UNDER THIS SECTION IN EXERCISING ANY AUTHORITY UNDER TOXIC SUBSTANCES CONTROL ACT

In exercising any authority under the Toxic Substances Control Act (15 U.S.C. 2601 et seq.) in connection with amendment made by section 15(a) of Pub. L. 101–637, the Administrator of the Environmental Protection Agency not, for purposes of subsection (b)(1) of this section, to be considered to be exercising statutory authority to prescribe or enforce standards or regulations affecting occupational safety and health, see section 15(b) of Pub. L. 101–637, set out as a note under section 2646 of Title 15, Commerce and Trade.

§654. Duties of employers and employees

(a) Each employer—

(1) shall furnish to each of his employees employment and a place of employment which are free from recognized hazards that are causing or are likely to cause death or serious physical harm to his employees;

(2) shall comply with occupational safety and health standards promulgated under this chapter.

(b) Each employee shall comply with occupational safety and health standards and all rules, regulations, and orders issued pursuant to this chapter which are applicable to his own actions and conduct.

(Pub. L. 91–596, §5, Dec. 29, 1970, 84 Stat. 1593.)

§655. Standards

(a) Promulgation by Secretary of national consensus standards and established Federal standards; time for promulgation; conflicting standards

Without regard to chapter 5 of title 5 or to the other subsections of this section, the Secretary shall, as soon as practicable during the period beginning with the effective date of this chapter and ending two years after such date, by rule promulgate as an occupational safety or health standard any national consensus standard, and any established Federal standard, unless he determines that the promulgation of such a standard would not result in improved safety or health for specifically designated employees. In the event of conflict among any such standards, the Secretary shall promulgate the standard which assures the greatest protection of the safety or health of the affected employees.

(b) Procedure for promulgation, modification, or revocation of standards

The Secretary may by rule promulgate, modify, or revoke any occupational safety or health standard in the following manner:

(1) Whenever the Secretary, upon the basis of information submitted to him in writing by an interested person, a representative of any organization of employers or employees, a nationally recognized standards-producing organization, the Secretary of Health and Human Services, the National Institute for Occupational Safety and Health, or a State or political subdivision, or on the basis of information developed by the Secretary or otherwise available to him, determines that a rule should be promulgated in order to serve the objectives of this chapter, the Secretary may request the recommendations of an advisory committee appointed under section 656 of this title. The Secretary shall provide such an advisory committee with any proposals of his own or of the Secretary of Health and Human Services, together with all pertinent factual information developed by the Secretary or the Secretary of Health and Human Services, or otherwise available, including the results of research, demonstrations, and experiments. An advisory committee shall submit to the Secretary its recommendations regarding the rule to be promulgated within ninety days from the date of its appointment or within such longer or shorter period as may be prescribed by the Secretary, but in no event for a period which is longer than two hundred and seventy days.

(2) The Secretary shall publish a proposed rule promulgating, modifying, or revoking an occupational safety or health standard in the Federal Register and shall afford interested persons a period of thirty days after publication to submit written data or comments. Where an advisory committee is appointed and the Secretary determines that a rule should be issued, he shall publish the proposed rule within sixty days after the submission of the advisory committee's recommendations or the expiration of the period prescribed by the Secretary for such submission.

(3) On or before the last day of the period provided for the submission of written data or comments under paragraph (2), any interested person may file with the Secretary written objections to the proposed rule, stating the grounds therefor and requesting a public hearing on such objections. Within thirty days after the last day for filing such objections, the Secretary shall publish in the Federal Register a notice specifying the occupational safety or health standard to which objections have been filed and a hearing requested, and specifying a time and place for such hearing.

(4) Within sixty days after the expiration of the period provided for the submission of written data or comments under paragraph (2), or within sixty days after the completion of any hearing held under paragraph (3), the Secretary shall issue a rule promulgating, modifying, or revoking an occupational safety or health standard or make a determination that a rule should not be issued. Such a rule may contain a provision delaying its effective date for such period (not in excess of ninety days) as the Secretary determines may be necessary to insure that affected employers and employees will be informed of the existence of the standard and of its terms and that employers affected are given an opportunity to familiarize themselves and their employees with the existence of the requirements of the standard.

(5) The Secretary, in promulgating standards dealing with toxic materials or harmful physical agents under this subsection, shall set the standard which most adequately assures, to the extent feasible, on the basis of the best available evidence, that no employee will suffer material impairment of health or functional capacity even if such employee has regular exposure to the hazard dealt with by such standard for the period of his working life. Development of standards under this subsection shall be based upon research, demonstrations, experiments, and such other information as may be appropriate. In addition to the attainment of the highest degree of health and safety protection for the employee, other considerations shall be the latest available scientific data in the field, the feasibility of the standards, and experience gained under this and other health and safety laws. Whenever practicable, the standard promulgated shall be

expressed in terms of objective criteria and of the performance desired.

(6)(A) Any employer may apply to the Secretary for a temporary order granting a variance from a standard or any provision thereof promulgated under this section. Such temporary order shall be granted only if the employer files an application which meets the requirements of clause (B) and establishes that (i) he is unable to comply with a standard by its effective date because of unavailability of professional or technical personnel or of materials and equipment needed to come into compliance with the standard or because necessary construction or alteration of facilities cannot be completed by the effective date, (ii) he is taking all available steps to safeguard his employees against the hazards covered by the standard, and (iii) he has an effective program for coming into compliance with the standard as quickly as practicable. Any temporary order issued under this paragraph shall prescribe the practices, means, methods, operations, and processes which the employer must adopt and use while the order is in effect and state in detail his program for coming into compliance with the standard. Such a temporary order may be granted only after notice to employees and an opportunity for a hearing: *Provided*, That the Secretary may issue one interim order to be effective until a decision is made on the basis of the hearing. No temporary order may be in effect for longer than the period needed by the employer to achieve compliance with the standard or one year, whichever is shorter, except that such an order may be renewed not more than twice (I) so long as the requirements of this paragraph are met and (II) if an application for renewal is filed at least 90 days prior to the expiration date of the order. No interim renewal of an order may remain in effect for longer than 180 days.

(B) An application for a temporary order under this paragraph (6) shall contain:

(i) a specification of the standard or portion thereof from which the employer seeks a variance,

(ii) a representation by the employer, supported by representations from qualified persons having firsthand knowledge of the facts represented, that he is unable to comply with the standard or portion thereof and a detailed statement of the reasons therefor,

(iii) a statement of the steps he has taken and will take (with specific dates) to protect employees against the hazard covered by the standard,

(iv) a statement of when he expects to be able to comply with the standard and what steps he has taken and what steps he will take (with dates specified) to come into compliance with the standard, and

(v) a certification that he has informed his employees of the application by giving a copy thereof to their authorized representative, posting a statement giving a summary of the application and specifying where a copy may be examined at the place or places where notices to employees are normally posted, and by other appropriate means.

A description of how employees have been informed shall be contained in the certification. The information to employees shall also inform them of their right to petition the Secretary for a hearing.

(C) The Secretary is authorized to grant a variance from any standard or portion thereof whenever he determines, or the Secretary of Health and Human Services certifies, that such variance is necessary to permit an employer to participate in an experiment approved by him or the Secretary of Health and Human Services designed to demonstrate or validate new and improved techniques to safeguard the health or safety of workers.

(7) Any standard promulgated under this subsection shall prescribe the use of labels or other appropriate forms of warning as are necessary to insure that employees are apprised of all hazards to which they are exposed, relevant symptoms and appropriate emergency treatment, and proper conditions and precautions of safe use or exposure. Where appropriate, such standard shall also prescribe suitable protective equipment and control or technological procedures to be used in connection with such hazards and shall provide for monitoring or measuring employee exposure at such locations and intervals, and in such manner as may be necessary for the protection of employees. In addition, where appropriate, any such standard shall prescribe the type and frequency of medical examinations or other tests which shall be made available, by the employer or at his cost, to employees exposed to such hazards in order to most effectively determine whether the health of such employees is adversely affected by such exposure. In the event such medical examinations are in the nature of research, as determined by the Secretary of Health and Human Services, such examinations may be furnished at the expense of the Secretary of Health and Human Services. The results of such examinations or tests shall be furnished only to the Secretary or the Secretary of Health and Human Services, and, at the request of the employee, to his physician. The Secretary, in consultation with the Secretary of Health and Human Services, may by rule promulgated pursuant to section 553 of title 5, make appropriate modifications in the foregoing requirements relating to the use of labels or other forms of warning, monitoring or measuring, and medical examinations, as may be warranted by experience, information, or medical or technological developments acquired subsequent to the promulgation of the relevant standard.

(8) Whenever a rule promulgated by the Secretary differs substantially from an existing national consensus standard, the Secretary shall, at the same time, publish in the Federal Register a statement of the reasons why the rule as adopted will better effectuate the purposes of this chapter than the national consensus standard.

(c) Emergency temporary standards

(1) The Secretary shall provide, without regard to the requirements of chapter 5 of title 5, for an emergency temporary standard to take immediate effect upon publication in the Federal Register if he determines (A) that employees are exposed to grave danger from exposure

to substances or agents determined to be toxic or physically harmful or from new hazards, and (B) that such emergency standard is necessary to protect employees from such danger.

(2) Such standard shall be effective until superseded by a standard promulgated in accordance with the procedures prescribed in paragraph (3) of this subsection.

(3) Upon publication of such standard in the Federal Register the Secretary shall commence a proceeding in accordance with subsection (b) of this section, and the standard as published shall also serve as a proposed rule for the proceeding. The Secretary shall promulgate a standard under this paragraph no later than six months after publication of the emergency standard as provided in paragraph (2) of this subsection.

(d) Variances from standards; procedure

Any affected employer may apply to the Secretary for a rule or order for a variance from a standard promulgated under this section. Affected employees shall be given notice of each such application and an opportunity to participate in a hearing. The Secretary shall issue such rule or order if he determines on the record, after opportunity for an inspection where appropriate and a hearing, that the proponent of the variance has demonstrated by a preponderance of the evidence that the conditions, practices, means, methods, operations, or processes used or proposed to be used by an employer will provide employment and places of employment to his employees which are as safe and healthful as those which would prevail if he complied with the standard. The rule or order so issued shall prescribe the conditions the employer must maintain, and the practices, means, methods, operations, and processes which he must adopt and utilize to the extent they differ from the standard in question. Such a rule or order may be modified or revoked upon application by an employer, employees, or by the Secretary on his own motion, in the manner prescribed for its issuance under this subsection at any time after six months from its issuance.

(e) Statement of reasons for Secretary's determinations; publication in Federal Register

Whenever the Secretary promulgates any standard, makes any rule, order, or decision, grants any exemption or extension of time, or compromises, mitigates, or settles any penalty assessed under this chapter, he shall include a statement of the reasons for such action, which shall be published in the Federal Register.

(f) Judicial review

Any person who may be adversely affected by a standard issued under this section may at any time prior to the sixtieth day after such standard is promulgated file a petition challenging the validity of such standard with the United States court of appeals for the circuit wherein such person resides or has his principal place of business, for a judicial review of such standard. A copy of the petition shall be forthwith transmitted by the clerk of the court to the Secretary. The filing of such petition shall not, unless otherwise ordered by the court, operate as a stay of the standard. The determinations of the Secretary shall be conclusive if supported by substantial evidence in the record considered as a whole.

(g) Priority for establishment of standards

In determining the priority for establishing standards under this section, the Secretary shall give due regard to the urgency of the need for mandatory safety and health standards for particular industries, trades, crafts, occupations, businesses, workplaces or work environments. The Secretary shall also give due regard to the recommendations of the Secretary of Health and Human Services regarding the need for mandatory standards in determining the priority for establishing such standards.

(Pub. L. 91–596, § 6, Dec. 29, 1970, 84 Stat. 1593; Pub. L. 96–88, title V, § 509(b), Oct. 17, 1979, 93 Stat. 695.)

REFERENCES IN TEXT

The effective date of this chapter, referred to in subsec. (a), is the effective date of Pub. L. 91–596, Dec. 29, 1970, 84 Stat. 1590, which is 120 days after Dec. 29, 1970, see section 34 of Pub. L. 91–596, set out as an Effective Date note under section 651 of this title.

CHANGE OF NAME

"Secretary of Health and Human Services" substituted for "Secretary of Health, Education, and Welfare" in subsecs. (b)(1), (6)(C), (7), and (g) pursuant to section 509(b) of Pub. L. 96–88 which is classified to section 3508(b) of Title 20, Education.

TERMINATION OF ADVISORY COMMITTEES

Advisory committees in existence on January 5, 1973, to terminate not later than the expiration of the 2-year period following January 5, 1973, unless, in the case of a committee established by the President or an officer of the Federal Government, such committee is renewed by appropriate action prior to the expiration of such 2-year period, or in the case of a committee established by the Congress, its duration is otherwise provided by law. See section 14 of Pub. L. 92–463, Oct. 6, 1972, 86 Stat. 776, set out in the Appendix to Title 5, Government Organization and Employees.

PROHIBITION ON EXPOSURE OF WORKERS TO CHEMICAL OR OTHER HAZARDS FOR PURPOSE OF CONDUCTING EXPERIMENTS

Pub. L. 102–394, title I, § 102, Oct. 6, 1992, 106 Stat. 1799, provided that: "None of the funds appropriated under this Act or subsequent Departments of Labor, Health and Human Services, and Education, and Related Agencies Appropriations Acts shall be used to grant variances, interim orders or letters of clarification to employers which will allow exposure of workers to chemicals or other workplace hazards in excess of existing Occupational Safety and Health Administration standards for the purpose of conducting experiments on workers' health or safety."

Similar provisions were contained in the following prior appropriation acts:

Pub. L. 102–170, title I, § 102, Nov. 26, 1991, 105 Stat. 1114.

Pub. L. 101–517, title I, § 102, Nov. 5, 1990, 104 Stat. 2196.

Pub. L. 101–166, title I, § 102, Nov. 21, 1989, 103 Stat. 1165.

Pub. L. 100–202, § 101(h) [title I, § 102], Dec. 22, 1987, 101 Stat. 1329–256, 1329–263.

Pub. L. 99–500, § 101(i) [H.R. 5233, title I, § 102], Oct. 18, 1986, 100 Stat. 1783–287, and Pub. L. 99–591, § 101(i) [H.R. 5233, title I, § 102], Oct. 30, 1986, 100 Stat. 3341–287.

Pub. L. 99–178, title I, § 102, Dec. 12, 1985, 99 Stat. 1109.

Pub. L. 98–619, title I, § 102, Nov. 8, 1984, 98 Stat. 3311.

OCCUPATIONAL HEALTH STANDARD CONCERNING EXPOSURE TO BLOODBORNE PATHOGENS

Pub. L. 102–170, title I, § 100, Nov. 26, 1991, 105 Stat. 1113, provided that:

"(a) Notwithstanding any other provision of law, on or before December 1, 1991, the Secretary of Labor, acting under the Occupational Safety and Health Act of 1970 [29 U.S.C. 651 et seq.], shall promulgate a final occupational health standard concerning occupational exposure to bloodborne pathogens. The final standard shall be based on the proposed standard as published in the Federal Register on May 30, 1989 (54 FR 23042), concerning occupational exposures to the hepatitis B virus, the human immunodeficiency virus and other bloodborne pathogens.

"(b) In the event that the final standard referred to in subsection (a) is not promulgated by the date required under such subsection, the proposed standard on occupational exposure to bloodborne pathogens as published in the Federal Register on May 30, 1989 (54 FR 23042) shall become effective as if such proposed standard had been promulgated as a final standard by the Secretary of Labor, and remain in effect until the date on which such Secretary promulgates the final standard referred to in subsection (a).

"(c) Nothing in this Act [enacting section 962 of Title 30, Mineral Lands and Mining, amending section 290b of Title 42, The Public Health and Welfare, enacting provisions set out as notes under section 1070a of Title 20, Education and section 1383 of Title 42, and amending provisions set out as notes under section 1255a of Title 8, Aliens and Nationality, and section 1221–1 of Title 20] shall be construed to require the Secretary of Labor (acting through the Occupational Safety and Health Administration) to revise the employment accident reporting regulations published at 29 C.F.R. 1904.8."

RETENTION OF MARKINGS AND PLACARDS

Pub. L. 101–615, § 29, Nov. 16, 1990, 104 Stat. 3277, provided that: "Not later than 18 months after the date of enactment of this Act [Nov. 16, 1990], the Secretary of Labor, in consultation with the Secretary of Transportation and the Secretary of the Treasury, shall issue under section 6(b) of the Occupational Safety and Health Act of 1970 (29 U.S.C. 655(b)) standards requiring any employer who receives a package, container, motor vehicle, rail freight car, aircraft, or vessel which contains a hazardous material and which is required to be marked, placarded, or labeled in accordance with regulations issued under the Hazardous Materials Transportation Act [former 49 U.S.C. 1801 et seq.] to retain the markings, placards, and labels, and any other information as may be required by such regulations on the package, container, motor vehicle, rail freight car, aircraft, or vessel, until the hazardous materials have been removed therefrom."

CHEMICAL PROCESS SAFETY MANAGEMENT

Pub. L. 101–549, title III, § 304, Nov. 15, 1990, 104 Stat. 2576, provided that:

"(a) CHEMICAL PROCESS SAFETY STANDARD.—The Secretary of Labor shall act under the Occupational Safety and Health Act of 1970 (29 U.S.C. 653) [29 U.S.C. 651 et seq.] to prevent accidental releases of chemicals which could pose a threat to employees. Not later than 12 months after the date of enactment of the Clean Air Act Amendments of 1990 [Nov. 15, 1990], the Secretary of Labor, in coordination with the Administrator of the Environmental Protection Agency, shall promulgate, pursuant to the Occupational Safety and Health Act, a chemical process safety standard designed to protect employees from hazards associated with accidental releases of highly hazardous chemicals in the workplace.

"(b) LIST OF HIGHLY HAZARDOUS CHEMICALS.—The Secretary shall include as part of such standard a list of highly hazardous chemicals, which include toxic, flammable, highly reactive and explosive substances. The list of such chemicals may include those chemicals listed by the Administrator under section 302 of the Emergency Planning and Community Right to Know Act of 1986 [42 U.S.C. 11002]. The Secretary may make additions to such list when a substance is found to pose a threat of serious injury or fatality in the event of an accidental release in the workplace.

"(c) ELEMENTS OF SAFETY STANDARD.—Such standard shall, at minimum, require employers to—

"(1) develop and maintain written safety information identifying workplace chemical and process hazards, equipment used in the processes, and technology used in the processes;

"(2) perform a workplace hazard assessment, including, as appropriate, identification of potential sources of accidental releases, an identification of any previous release within the facility which had a likely potential for catastrophic consequences in the workplace, estimation of workplace effects of a range of releases, estimation of the health and safety effects of such range on employees;

"(3) consult with employees and their representatives on the development and conduct of hazard assessments and the development of chemical accident prevention plans and provide access to these and other records required under the standard;

"(4) establish a system to respond to the workplace hazard assessment findings, which shall address prevention, mitigation, and emergency responses;

"(5) periodically review the workplace hazard assessment and response system;

"(6) develop and implement written operating procedures for the chemical process including procedures for each operating phase, operating limitations, and safety and health considerations;

"(7) provide written safety and operating information to employees and train employees in operating procedures, emphasizing hazards and safe practices;

"(8) ensure contractors and contract employees are provided appropriate information and training;

"(9) train and educate employees and contractors in emergency response in a manner as comprehensive and effective as that required by the regulation promulgated pursuant to section 126(d) of the Superfund Amendments and Reauthorization Act [of 1986] [Pub. L. 99–499, set out in a note below];

"(10) establish a quality assurance program to ensure that initial process related equipment, maintenance materials, and spare parts are fabricated and installed consistent with design specifications;

"(11) establish maintenance systems for critical process related equipment including written procedures, employee training, appropriate inspections, and testing of such equipment to ensure ongoing mechanical integrity;

"(12) conduct pre-start-up safety reviews of all newly installed or modified equipment;

"(13) establish and implement written procedures to manage change to process chemicals, technology, equipment and facilities; and

"(14) investigate every incident which results in or could have resulted in a major accident in the workplace, with any findings to be reviewed by operating personnel and modifications made if appropriate.

"(d) STATE AUTHORITY.—Nothing in this section may be construed to diminish the authority of the States and political subdivisions thereof as described in section 112(r)(11) of the Clean Air Act [42 U.S.C. 7412(r)(11)]."

WORKER PROTECTION STANDARDS

Pub. L. 99–499, title I, § 126(a)–(f), Oct. 17, 1986, 100 Stat. 1690–1692, as amended by Pub. L. 100–202, § 101(f) [title II, § 201], Dec. 22, 1987, 101 Stat. 1329–187, 1329–198, provided:

"(a) PROMULGATION.—Within one year after the date of the enactment of this section [Oct. 17, 1986], the Secretary of Labor shall, pursuant to section 6 of the Occupational Safety and Health Act of 1970 [29 U.S.C. 655], promulgate standards for the health and safety protection of employees engaged in hazardous waste operations.

"(b) PROPOSED STANDARDS.—The Secretary of Labor shall issue proposed regulations on such standards which shall include, but need not be limited to, the following worker protection provisions:

"(1) SITE ANALYSIS.—Requirements for a formal hazard analysis of the site and development of a site specific plan for worker protection.

"(2) TRAINING.—Requirements for contractors to provide initial and routine training of workers before such workers are permitted to engage in hazardous waste operations which would expose them to toxic substances.

"(3) MEDICAL SURVEILLANCE.—A program of regular medical examination, monitoring, and surveillance of workers engaged in hazardous waste operations which would expose them to toxic substances.

"(4) PROTECTIVE EQUIPMENT.—Requirements for appropriate personal protective equipment, clothing, and respirators for work in hazardous waste operations.

"(5) ENGINEERING CONTROLS.—Requirements for engineering controls concerning the use of equipment and exposure of workers engaged in hazardous waste operations.

"(6) MAXIMUM EXPOSURE LIMITS.—Requirements for maximum exposure limitations for workers engaged in hazardous waste operations, including necessary monitoring and assessment procedures.

"(7) INFORMATIONAL PROGRAM.—A program to inform workers engaged in hazardous waste operations of the nature and degree of toxic exposure likely as a result of such hazardous waste operations.

"(8) HANDLING.—Requirements for the handling, transporting, labeling, and disposing of hazardous wastes.

"(9) NEW TECHNOLOGY PROGRAM.—A program for the introduction of new equipment or technologies that will maintain worker protections.

"(10) DECONTAMINATION PROCEDURES.—Procedures for decontamination.

"(11) EMERGENCY RESPONSE.—Requirements for emergency response and protection of workers engaged in hazardous waste operations.

"(c) FINAL REGULATIONS.—Final regulations under subsection (a) shall take effect one year after the date they are promulgated. In promulgating final regulations on standards under subsection (a), the Secretary of Labor shall include each of the provisions listed in paragraphs (1) through (11) of subsection (b) unless the Secretary determines that the evidence in the public record considered as a whole does not support inclusion of any such provision.

"(d) SPECIFIC TRAINING STANDARDS.—

"(1) OFFSITE INSTRUCTION; FIELD EXPERIENCE.—Standards promulgated under subsection (a) shall include training standards requiring that general site workers (such as equipment operators, general laborers, and other supervised personnel) engaged in hazardous substance removal or other activities which expose or potentially expose such workers to hazardous substances receive a minimum of 40 hours of initial instruction off the site, and a minimum of three days of actual field experience under the direct supervision of a trained, experienced supervisor, at the time of assignment. The requirements of the preceding sentence shall not apply to any general site worker who has received the equivalent of such training. Workers who may be exposed to unique or special hazards shall be provided additional training.

"(2) TRAINING OF SUPERVISORS.—Standards promulgated under subsection (a) shall include training standards requiring that onsite managers and supervisors directly responsible for the hazardous waste operations (such as foremen) receive the same training as general site workers set forth in paragraph (1) of this subsection and at least eight additional hours of specialized training on managing hazardous waste operations. The requirements of the preceding sentence shall not apply to any person who has received the equivalent of such training.

"(3) CERTIFICATION; ENFORCEMENT.—Such training standards shall contain provisions for certifying that general site workers, onsite managers, and supervisors have received the specified training and shall prohibit any individual who has not received the specified training from engaging in hazardous waste operations covered by the standard. The certification procedures shall be no less comprehensive than those adopted by the Environmental Protection Agency in its Model Accreditation Plan for Asbestos Abatement Training as required under the Asbestos Hazard Emergency Response Act of 1986 [Pub. L. 99–519, see Short Title of 1986 Amendment note, set out under section 2601 of Title 15, Commerce and Trade].

"(4) TRAINING OF EMERGENCY RESPONSE PERSONNEL.—Such training standards shall set forth requirements for the training of workers who are responsible for responding to hazardous emergency situations who may be exposed to toxic substances in carrying out their responsibilities.

"(e) INTERIM REGULATIONS.—The Secretary of Labor shall issue interim final regulations under this section within 60 days after the enactment of this section [Oct. 17, 1986] which shall provide no less protection under this section for workers employed by contractors and emergency response workers than the protections contained in the Environmental Protection Agency Manual (1981) 'Health and Safety Requirements for Employees Engaged in Field Activities' and existing standards under the Occupational Safety and Health Act of 1970 [29 U.S.C. 651 et seq.] found in subpart C of part 1926 of title 29 of the Code of Federal Regulations. Such interim final regulations shall take effect upon issuance and shall apply until final regulations become effective under subsection (c).

"(f) COVERAGE OF CERTAIN STATE AND LOCAL EMPLOYEES.—Not later than 90 days after the promulgation of final regulations under subsection (a), the Administrator shall promulgate standards identical to those promulgated by the Secretary of Labor under subsection (a). Standards promulgated under this subsection shall apply to employees of State and local governments in each State which does not have in effect an approved State plan under section 18 of the Occupational Safety and Health Act of 1970 [29 U.S.C. 667] providing for standards for the health and safety protection of employees engaged in hazardous waste operations."

§ 656. Administration

(a) National Advisory Committee on Occupational Safety and Health; establishment; membership; appointment; Chairman; functions; meetings; compensation; secretarial and clerical personnel

(1) There is hereby established a National Advisory Committee on Occupational Safety and Health consisting of twelve members appointed by the Secretary, four of whom are to be designated by the Secretary of Health and Human Services, without regard to the provisions of title 5 governing appointments in the competitive service, and composed of representatives of management, labor, occupational safety and occupational health professions, and of the public. The Secretary shall designate one of the public members as Chairman. The members shall be selected upon the basis of their experience and competence in the field of occupational safety and health.

(2) The Committee shall advise, consult with, and make recommendations to the Secretary and the Secretary of Health and Human Services on matters relating to the administration of this chapter. The Committee shall hold no fewer than two meetings during each calendar year.

All meetings of the Committee shall be open to the public and a transcript shall be kept and made available for public inspection.

(3) The members of the Committee shall be compensated in accordance with the provisions of section 3109 of title 5.

(4) The Secretary shall furnish to the Committee an executive secretary and such secretarial, clerical, and other services as are deemed necessary to the conduct of its business.

(b) Advisory committees; appointment; duties; membership; compensation; reimbursement to member's employer; meetings; availability of records; conflict of interest

An advisory committee may be appointed by the Secretary to assist him in his standard-setting functions under section 655 of this title. Each such committee shall consist of not more than fifteen members and shall include as a member one or more designees of the Secretary of Health and Human Services, and shall include among its members an equal number of persons qualified by experience and affiliation to present the viewpoint of the employers involved, and of persons similarly qualified to present the viewpoint of the workers involved, as well as one or more representatives of health and safety agencies of the States. An advisory committee may also include such other persons as the Secretary may appoint who are qualified by knowledge and experience to make a useful contribution to the work of such committee, including one or more representatives of professional organizations of technicians or professionals specializing in occupational safety or health, and one or more representatives of nationally recognized standards-producing organizations, but the number of persons so appointed to any such advisory committee shall not exceed the number appointed to such committee as representatives of Federal and State agencies. Persons appointed to advisory committees from private life shall be compensated in the same manner as consultants or experts under section 3109 of title 5. The Secretary shall pay to any State which is the employer of a member of such a committee who is a representative of the health or safety agency of that State, reimbursement sufficient to cover the actual cost to the State resulting from such representative's membership on such committee. Any meeting of such committee shall be open to the public and an accurate record shall be kept and made available to the public. No member of such committee (other than representatives of employers and employees) shall have an economic interest in any proposed rule.

(c) Use of services, facilities, and personnel of Federal, State, and local agencies; reimbursement; employment of experts and consultants or organizations; renewal of contracts; compensation; travel expenses

In carrying out his responsibilities under this chapter, the Secretary is authorized to—

(1) use, with the consent of any Federal agency, the services, facilities, and personnel of such agency, with or without reimbursement, and with the consent of any State or political subdivision thereof, accept and use the services, facilities, and personnel of any agency of such State or subdivision with reimbursement; and

(2) employ experts and consultants or organizations thereof as authorized by section 3109 of title 5, except that contracts for such employment may be renewed annually; compensate individuals so employed at rates not in excess of the rate specified at the time of service for grade GS–18 under section 5332 of title 5, including traveltime, and allow them while away from their homes or regular places of business, travel expenses (including per diem in lieu of subsistence) as authorized by section 5703 of title 5 for persons in the Government service employed intermittently, while so employed.

(Pub. L. 91–596, § 7, Dec. 29, 1970, 84 Stat. 1597; Pub. L. 96–88, title V, § 509(b), Oct. 17, 1979, 93 Stat. 695.)

CHANGE OF NAME

"Secretary of Health and Human Services" substituted for "Secretary of Health, Education, and Welfare" in subsecs. (a)(1), (2) and (b) pursuant to section 509(b) of Pub. L. 96–88 which is classified to section 3508(b) of Title 20, Education.

TERMINATION OF ADVISORY COMMITTEES

Advisory committees in existence on January 5, 1973, to terminate not later than the expiration of the 2-year period following January 5, 1973, unless, in the case of a committee established by the President or an officer of the Federal Government, such committee is renewed by appropriate action prior to the expiration of such 2-year period, or in the case of a committee established by the Congress, its duration is otherwise provided by law. See section 14 of Pub. L. 92–463, Oct. 6, 1972, 86 Stat. 776, set out in the Appendix to Title 5, Government Organization and Employees.

REFERENCES IN OTHER LAWS TO GS–16, 17, OR 18 PAY RATES

References in laws to the rates of pay for GS–16, 17, or 18, or to maximum rates of pay under the General Schedule, to be considered references to rates payable under specified sections of Title 5, Government Organization and Employees, see section 529 [title I, § 101(c)(1)] of Pub. L. 101–509, set out in a note under section 5376 of Title 5.

§ 657. Inspections, investigations, and recordkeeping

(a) Authority of Secretary to enter, inspect, and investigate places of employment; time and manner

In order to carry out the purposes of this chapter, the Secretary, upon presenting appropriate credentials to the owner, operator, or agent in charge, is authorized—

(1) to enter without delay and at reasonable times any factory, plant, establishment, construction site, or other area, workplace or environment where work is performed by an employee of an employer; and

(2) to inspect and investigate during regular working hours and at other reasonable times, and within reasonable limits and in a reasonable manner, any such place of employment and all pertinent conditions, structures, machines, apparatus, devices, equipment, and materials therein, and to question privately any such employer, owner, operator, agent, or employee.

(b) Attendance and testimony of witnesses and production of evidence; enforcement of subpoena

In making his inspections and investigations under this chapter the Secretary may require the attendance and testimony of witnesses and the production of evidence under oath. Witnesses shall be paid the same fees and mileage that are paid witnesses in the courts of the United States. In case of a contumacy, failure, or refusal of any person to obey such an order, any district court of the United States or the United States courts of any territory or possession, within the jurisdiction of which such person is found, or resides or transacts business, upon the application by the Secretary, shall have jurisdiction to issue to such person an order requiring such person to appear to produce evidence if, as, and when so ordered, and to give testimony relating to the matter under investigation or in question, and any failure to obey such order of the court may be punished by said court as a contempt thereof.

(c) Maintenance, preservation, and availability of records; issuance of regulations; scope of records; periodic inspections by employer; posting of notices by employer; notification of employee of corrective action

(1) Each employer shall make, keep and preserve, and make available to the Secretary or the Secretary of Health and Human Services, such records regarding his activities relating to this chapter as the Secretary, in cooperation with the Secretary of Health and Human Services, may prescribe by regulation as necessary or appropriate for the enforcement of this chapter or for developing information regarding the causes and prevention of occupational accidents and illnesses. In order to carry out the provisions of this paragraph such regulations may include provisions requiring employers to conduct periodic inspections. The Secretary shall also issue regulations requiring that employers, through posting of notices or other appropriate means, keep their employees informed of their protections and obligations under this chapter, including the provisions of applicable standards.

(2) The Secretary, in cooperation with the Secretary of Health and Human Services, shall prescribe regulations requiring employers to maintain accurate records of, and to make periodic reports on, work-related deaths, injuries and illnesses other than minor injuries requiring only first aid treatment and which do not involve medical treatment, loss of consciousness, restriction of work or motion, or transfer to another job.

(3) The Secretary, in cooperation with the Secretary of Health and Human Services, shall issue regulations requiring employers to maintain accurate records of employee exposures to potentially toxic materials or harmful physical agents which are required to be monitored or measured under section 655 of this title. Such regulations shall provide employees or their representatives with an opportunity to observe such monitoring or measuring, and to have access to the records thereof. Such regulations shall also make appropriate provision for each employee or former employee to have access to such records as will indicate his own exposure to toxic materials or harmful physical agents. Each employer shall promptly notify any employee who has been or is being exposed to toxic materials or harmful physical agents in concentrations or at levels which exceed those prescribed by an applicable occupational safety and health standard promulgated under section 655 of this title, and shall inform any employee who is being thus exposed of the corrective action being taken.

(d) Obtaining of information

Any information obtained by the Secretary, the Secretary of Health and Human Services, or a State agency under this chapter shall be obtained with a minimum burden upon employers, especially those operating small businesses. Unnecessary duplication of efforts in obtaining information shall be reduced to the maximum extent feasible.

(e) Employer and authorized employee representatives to accompany Secretary or his authorized representative on inspection of workplace; consultation with employees where no authorized employee representative is present

Subject to regulations issued by the Secretary, a representative of the employer and a representative authorized by his employees shall be given an opportunity to accompany the Secretary or his authorized representative during the physical inspection of any workplace under subsection (a) of this section for the purpose of aiding such inspection. Where there is no authorized employee representative, the Secretary or his authorized representative shall consult with a reasonable number of employees concerning matters of health and safety in the workplace.

(f) Request for inspection by employees or representative of employees; grounds; procedure; determination of request; notification of Secretary or representative prior to or during any inspection of violations; procedure for review of refusal by representative of Secretary to issue citation for alleged violations

(1) Any employees or representative of employees who believe that a violation of a safety or health standard exists that threatens physical harm, or that an imminent danger exists, may request an inspection by giving notice to the Secretary or his authorized representative of such violation or danger. Any such notice shall be reduced to writing, shall set forth with reasonable particularity the grounds for the notice, and shall be signed by the employees or representative of employees, and a copy shall be provided the employer or his agent no later than at the time of inspection, except that, upon the request of the person giving such notice, his name and the names of individual employees referred to therein shall not appear in such copy or on any record published, released, or made available pursuant to subsection (g) of this section. If upon receipt of such notification the Secretary determines there are reasonable grounds to believe that such violation or danger exists, he shall make a special inspection in ac-

cordance with the provisions of this section as soon as practicable, to determine if such violation or danger exists. If the Secretary determines there are no reasonable grounds to believe that a violation or danger exists he shall notify the employees or representative of the employees in writing of such determination.

(2) Prior to or during any inspection of a workplace, any employees or representative of employees employed in such workplace may notify the Secretary or any representative of the Secretary responsible for conducting the inspection, in writing, of any violation of this chapter which they have reason to believe exists in such workplace. The Secretary shall, by regulation, establish procedures for informal review of any refusal by a representative of the Secretary to issue a citation with respect to any such alleged violation and shall furnish the employees or representative of employees requesting such review a written statement of the reasons for the Secretary's final disposition of the case.

(g) Compilation, analysis, and publication of reports and information; rules and regulations

(1) The Secretary and Secretary of Health and Human Services are authorized to compile, analyze, and publish, either in summary or detailed form, all reports or information obtained under this section.

(2) The Secretary and the Secretary of Health and Human Services shall each prescribe such rules and regulations as he may deem necessary to carry out their responsibilities under this chapter, including rules and regulations dealing with the inspection of an employer's establishment.

(h) Use of results of enforcement activities

The Secretary shall not use the results of enforcement activities, such as the number of citations issued or penalties assessed, to evaluate employees directly involved in enforcement activities under this chapter or to impose quotas or goals with regard to the results of such activities.

(Pub. L. 91–596, §8, Dec. 29, 1970, 84 Stat. 1598; Pub. L. 96–88, title V, §509(b), Oct. 17, 1979, 93 Stat. 695; Pub. L. 105–198, §1, July 16, 1998, 112 Stat. 640.)

AMENDMENTS

1998—Subsec. (h). Pub. L. 105–198 added subsec. (h).

CHANGE OF NAME

"Secretary of Health and Human Services" substituted for "Secretary of Health, Education, and Welfare" in subsecs. (c), (d), and (g) pursuant to section 509(b) of Pub. L. 96–88 which is classified to section 3508(b) of Title 20, Education.

§ 658. Citations

(a) Authority to issue; grounds; contents; notice in lieu of citation for de minimis violations

If, upon inspection or investigation, the Secretary or his authorized representative believes that an employer has violated a requirement of section 654 of this title, of any standard, rule or order promulgated pursuant to section 655 of this title, or of any regulations prescribed pursuant to this chapter, he shall with reasonable promptness issue a citation to the employer. Each citation shall be in writing and shall describe with particularity the nature of the violation, including a reference to the provision of the chapter, standard, rule, regulation, or order alleged to have been violated. In addition, the citation shall fix a reasonable time for the abatement of the violation. The Secretary may prescribe procedures for the issuance of a notice in lieu of a citation with respect to de minimis violations which have no direct or immediate relationship to safety or health.

(b) Posting

Each citation issued under this section, or a copy or copies thereof, shall be prominently posted, as prescribed in regulations issued by the Secretary, at or near each place a violation referred to in the citation occurred.

(c) Time for issuance

No citation may be issued under this section after the expiration of six months following the occurrence of any violation.

(Pub. L. 91–596, §9, Dec. 29, 1970, 84 Stat. 1601.)

§ 659. Enforcement procedures

(a) Notification of employer of proposed assessment of penalty subsequent to issuance of citation; time for notification of Secretary by employer of contest by employer of citation or proposed assessment; citation and proposed assessment as final order upon failure of employer to notify of contest and failure of employees to file notice

If, after an inspection or investigation, the Secretary issues a citation under section 658(a) of this title, he shall, within a reasonable time after the termination of such inspection or investigation, notify the employer by certified mail of the penalty, if any, proposed to be assessed under section 666 of this title and that the employer has fifteen working days within which to notify the Secretary that he wishes to contest the citation or proposed assessment of penalty. If, within fifteen working days from the receipt of the notice issued by the Secretary the employer fails to notify the Secretary that he intends to contest the citation or proposed assessment of penalty, and no notice is filed by any employee or representative of employees under subsection (c) of this section within such time, the citation and the assessment, as proposed, shall be deemed a final order of the Commission and not subject to review by any court or agency.

(b) Notification of employer of failure to correct in allotted time period violation for which citation was issued and proposed assessment of penalty for failure to correct; time for notification of Secretary by employer of contest by employer of notification of failure to correct or proposed assessment; notification or proposed assessment as final order upon failure of employer to notify of contest

If the Secretary has reason to believe that an employer has failed to correct a violation for which a citation has been issued within the period permitted for its correction (which period shall not begin to run until the entry of a final order by the Commission in the case of any review proceedings under this section initiated by the employer in good faith and not solely for delay or avoidance of penalties), the Secretary shall notify the employer by certified mail of such failure and of the penalty proposed to be assessed under section 666 of this title by reason of such failure, and that the employer has fifteen working days within which to notify the Secretary that he wishes to contest the Secretary's notification or the proposed assessment of penalty. If, within fifteen working days from the receipt of notification issued by the Secretary, the employer fails to notify the Secretary that he intends to contest the notification or proposed assessment of penalty, the notification or proposed assessment of penalty, the notification and assessment, as proposed, shall be deemed a final order of the Commission and not subject to review by any court or agency.

(c) Advisement of Commission by Secretary of notification of contest by employer of citation or notification or of filing of notice by any employee or representative of employees; hearing by Commission; orders of Commission and Secretary; rules of procedure

If an employer notifies the Secretary that he intends to contest a citation issued under section 658(a) of this title or notification issued under subsection (a) or (b) of this section, or if, within fifteen working days of the issuance of a citation under section 658(a) of this title, any employee or representative of employees files a notice with the Secretary alleging that the period of time fixed in the citation for the abatement of the violation is unreasonable, the Secretary shall immediately advise the Commission of such notification, and the Commission shall afford an opportunity for a hearing (in accordance with section 554 of title 5 but without regard to subsection (a)(3) of such section). The Commission shall thereafter issue an order, based on findings of fact, affirming, modifying, or vacating the Secretary's citation or proposed penalty, or directing other appropriate relief, and such order shall become final thirty days after its issuance. Upon a showing by an employer of a good faith effort to comply with the abatement requirements of a citation, and that abatement has not been completed because of factors beyond his reasonable control, the Secretary, after an opportunity for a hearing as provided in this subsection, shall issue an order affirming or modifying the abatement requirements in such citation. The rules of procedure prescribed by the Commission shall provide affected employees or representatives of affected employees an opportunity to participate as parties to hearings under this subsection.

(Pub. L. 91–596, §10, Dec. 29, 1970, 84 Stat. 1601.)

§660. Judicial review

(a) Filing of petition by persons adversely affected or aggrieved; orders subject to review; jurisdiction; venue; procedure; conclusiveness of record and findings of Commission; appropriate relief; finality of judgment

Any person adversely affected or aggrieved by an order of the Commission issued under subsection (c) of section 659 of this title may obtain a review of such order in any United States court of appeals for the circuit in which the violation is alleged to have occurred or where the employer has its principal office, or in the Court of Appeals for the District of Columbia Circuit, by filing in such court within sixty days following the issuance of such order a written petition praying that the order be modified or set aside. A copy of such petition shall be forthwith transmitted by the clerk of the court to the Commission and to the other parties, and thereupon the Commission shall file in the court the record in the proceeding as provided in section 2112 of title 28. Upon such filing, the court shall have jurisdiction of the proceeding and of the question determined therein, and shall have power to grant such temporary relief or restraining order as it deems just and proper, and to make and enter upon the pleadings, testimony, and proceedings set forth in such record a decree affirming, modifying, or setting aside in whole or in part, the order of the Commission and enforcing the same to the extent that such order is affirmed or modified. The commencement of proceedings under this subsection shall not, unless ordered by the court, operate as a stay of the order of the Commission. No objection that has not been urged before the Commission shall be considered by the court, unless the failure or neglect to urge such objection shall be excused because of extraordinary circumstances. The findings of the Commission with respect to questions of fact, if supported by substantial evidence on the record considered as a whole, shall be conclusive. If any party shall apply to the court for leave to adduce additional evidence and shall show to the satisfaction of the court that such additional evidence is material and that there were reasonable grounds for the failure to adduce such evidence in the hearing before the Commission, the court may order such additional evidence to be taken before the Commission and to be made a part of the record. The Commission may modify its findings as to the facts, or make new findings, by reason of additional evidence so taken and filed, and it shall file such modified or new findings, which findings with respect to questions of fact, if supported by substantial evidence on the record considered as a whole, shall be conclusive, and its recommendations, if any, for the modification or setting aside of its original order. Upon the filing of the record with it, the jurisdiction of the court shall be exclusive and its judgment and decree shall be final, except that the same shall be subject to review by the Supreme Court of the United States, as provided in section 1254 of title 28.

(b) Filing of petition by Secretary; orders subject to review; jurisdiction; venue; procedure; conclusiveness of record and findings of Commission; enforcement of orders; contempt proceedings

The Secretary may also obtain review or enforcement of any final order of the Commission by filing a petition for such relief in the United States court of appeals for the circuit in which the alleged violation occurred or in which the employer has its principal office, and the provisions of subsection (a) of this section shall govern such proceedings to the extent applicable. If no petition for review, as provided in subsection (a) of this section, is filed within sixty days after service of the Commission's order, the Commission's findings of fact and order shall be conclusive in connection with any petition for enforcement which is filed by the Secretary after the expiration of such sixty-day period. In any such case, as well as in the case of a noncontested citation or notification by the Secretary which has become a final order of the Commission under subsection (a) or (b) of section 659 of this title, the clerk of the court, unless otherwise ordered by the court, shall forthwith enter a decree enforcing the order and shall transmit a copy of such decree to the Secretary and the employer named in the petition. In any contempt proceeding brought to enforce a decree of a court of appeals entered pursuant to this subsection or subsection (a) of this section, the court of appeals may assess the penalties provided in section 666 of this title, in addition to invoking any other available remedies.

(c) Discharge or discrimination against employee for exercise of rights under this chapter; prohibition; procedure for relief

(1) No person shall discharge or in any manner discriminate against any employee because such employee has filed any complaint or instituted or caused to be instituted any proceeding under or related to this chapter or has testified or is about to testify in any such proceeding or because of the exercise by such employee on behalf of himself or others of any right afforded by this chapter.

(2) Any employee who believes that he has been discharged or otherwise discriminated against by any person in violation of this subsection may, within thirty days after such violation occurs, file a complaint with the Secretary alleging such discrimination. Upon receipt of such complaint, the Secretary shall cause such investigation to be made as he deems appropriate. If upon such investigation, the Secretary determines that the provisions of this subsection have been violated, he shall bring an action in any appropriate United States district court against such person. In any such action the United States district courts shall have jurisdiction, for cause shown to restrain violations of paragraph (1) of this subsection and order all appropriate relief including rehiring or reinstatement of the employee to his former position with back pay.

(3) Within 90 days of the receipt of a complaint filed under this subsection the Secretary shall notify the complainant of his determination under paragraph (2) of this subsection.

(Pub. L. 91–596, § 11, Dec. 29, 1970, 84 Stat. 1602; Pub. L. 98–620, title IV, § 402(32), Nov. 8, 1984, 98 Stat. 3360.)

AMENDMENTS

1984—Subsec. (a). Pub. L. 98–620 struck out provision requiring expeditious hearing of petitions filed under this subsection.

EFFECTIVE DATE OF 1984 AMENDMENT

Amendment by Pub. L. 98–620 not applicable to cases pending on Nov. 8, 1984, see section 403 of Pub. L. 98–620, set out as a note under section 1657 of Title 28, Judiciary and Judicial Procedure.

§ 661. Occupational Safety and Health Review Commission

(a) Establishment; membership; appointment; Chairman

The Occupational Safety and Health Review Commission is hereby established. The Commission shall be composed of three members who shall be appointed by the President, by and with the advice and consent of the Senate, from among persons who by reason of training, education, or experience are qualified to carry out the functions of the Commission under this chapter. The President shall designate one of the members of the Commission to serve as Chairman.

(b) Terms of office; removal by President

The terms of members of the Commission shall be six years except that (1) the members of the Commission first taking office shall serve, as designated by the President at the time of appointment, one for a term of two years, one for a term of four years, and one for a term of six years, and (2) a vacancy caused by the death, resignation, or removal of a member prior to the expiration of the term for which he was appointed shall be filled only for the remainder of such unexpired term. A member of the Commission may be removed by the President for inefficiency, neglect of duty, or malfeasance in office.

(c) Omitted

(d) Principal office; hearings or other proceedings at other places

The principal office of the Commission shall be in the District of Columbia. Whenever the Commission deems that the convenience of the public or of the parties may be promoted, or delay or expense may be minimized, it may hold hearings or conduct other proceedings at any other place.

(e) Functions and duties of Chairman; appointment and compensation of administrative law judges and other employees

The Chairman shall be responsible on behalf of the Commission for the administrative operations of the Commission and shall appoint such administrative law judges and other employees as he deems necessary to assist in the performance of the Commission's functions and to fix their compensation in accordance with the provisions of chapter 51 and subchapter III of chapter 53 of title 5 relating to classification and General Schedule pay rates: *Provided*, That assignment, removal and compensation of administrative law judges shall be in accordance with sections 3105, 3344, 5372, and 7521 of title 5.

(f) Quorum; official action

For the purpose of carrying out its functions under this chapter, two members of the Commission shall constitute a quorum and official action can be taken only on the affirmative vote of at least two members.

(g) Hearings and records open to public; promulgation of rules; applicability of Federal Rules of Civil Procedure

Every official act of the Commission shall be entered of record, and its hearings and records shall be open to the public. The Commission is authorized to make such rules as are necessary for the orderly transaction of its proceedings. Unless the Commission has adopted a different rule, its proceedings shall be in accordance with the Federal Rules of Civil Procedure.

(h) Depositions and production of documentary evidence; fees

The Commission may order testimony to be taken by deposition in any proceeding pending before it at any state of such proceeding. Any person may be compelled to appear and depose, and to produce books, papers, or documents, in the same manner as witnesses may be compelled to appear and testify and produce like documentary evidence before the Commission. Witnesses whose depositions are taken under this subsection, and the persons taking such depositions, shall be entitled to the same fees as are paid for like services in the courts of the United States.

(i) Investigatory powers

For the purpose of any proceeding before the Commission, the provisions of section 161 of this title are hereby made applicable to the jurisdiction and powers of the Commission.

(j) Administrative law judges; determinations; report as final order of Commission

A[1] administrative law judge appointed by the Commission shall hear, and make a determination upon, any proceeding instituted before the Commission and any motion in connection therewith, assigned to such administrative law judge by the Chairman of the Commission, and shall make a report of any such determination which constitutes his final disposition of the proceedings. The report of the administrative law judge shall become the final order of the Commission within thirty days after such report by the administrative law judge, unless within such period any Commission member has directed that such report shall be reviewed by the Commission.

(k) Appointment and compensation of administrative law judges

Except as otherwise provided in this chapter, the administrative law judges shall be subject to the laws governing employees in the classified civil service, except that appointments shall be made without regard to section 5108 of title 5. Each administrative law judge shall receive compensation at a rate not less than that prescribed for GS–16 under section 5332 of title 5.

(Pub. L. 91–596, § 12, Dec. 29, 1970, 84 Stat. 1603; Pub. L. 95–251, § 2(a)(7), Mar. 27, 1978, 92 Stat. 183.)

REFERENCES IN TEXT

The General Schedule, referred to in subsec. (e), is set out under section 5332 of Title 5, Government Organization and Employees.

The Federal Rules of Civil Procedure, referred to in subsec. (g), are set out in the Appendix to Title 28, Judiciary and Judicial Procedure.

CODIFICATION

Subsec. (c) of this section amended sections 5314 and 5315 of Title 5, Government Organization and Employees.

In subsec. (e), reference to section 5372 of title 5 was substituted for section 5362 on authority of Pub. L. 95–454, § 801(a)(3)(A)(ii), Oct. 13, 1978, 92 Stat. 1221, which redesignated sections 5361 through 5365 of title 5 as sections 5371 through 5375.

AMENDMENTS

1978—Subsecs. (e), (j), (k). Pub. L. 95–251 substituted "administrative law judge" and "administrative law judges" for "hearing examiner" and "hearing examiners", respectively, wherever appearing.

REFERENCES IN OTHER LAWS TO GS–16, 17, OR 18 PAY RATES

References in laws to the rates of pay for GS–16, 17, or 18, or to maximum rates of pay under the General Schedule, to be considered references to rates payable under specified sections of Title 5, Government Organization and Employees, see section 529 [title I, § 101(c)(1)] of Pub. L. 101–509, set out in a note under section 5376 of Title 5.

§ 662. Injunction proceedings

(a) Petition by Secretary to restrain imminent dangers; scope of order

The United States district courts shall have jurisdiction, upon petition of the Secretary, to restrain any conditions or practices in any place of employment which are such that a danger exists which could reasonably be expected to cause death or serious physical harm immediately or before the imminence of such danger can be eliminated through the enforcement procedures otherwise provided by this chapter. Any order issued under this section may require such steps to be taken as may be necessary to avoid, correct, or remove such imminent danger and prohibit the employment or presence of any individual in locations or under conditions where such imminent danger exists, except individuals whose presence is necessary to avoid, correct, or remove such imminent danger or to maintain the capacity of a continuous process operation to resume normal operations without a complete cessation of operations, or where a cessation of operations is necessary, to permit such to be accomplished in a safe and orderly manner.

(b) Appropriate injunctive relief or temporary restraining order pending outcome of enforcement proceeding; applicability of Rule 65 of Federal Rules of Civil Procedure

Upon the filing of any such petition the district court shall have jurisdiction to grant such injunctive relief or temporary restraining order pending the outcome of an enforcement proceeding pursuant to this chapter. The proceeding shall be as provided by Rule 65 of the Federal Rules, Civil Procedure, except that no temporary restraining order issued without notice shall be effective for a period longer than five days.

(c) Notification of affected employees and employers by inspector of danger and of recommendation to Secretary to seek relief

Whenever and as soon as an inspector concludes that conditions or practices described in subsection (a) of this section exist in any place of employment, he shall inform the affected employees and employers of the danger and that he is recommending to the Secretary that relief be sought.

[1] So in original. Probably should be "An".

(d) Failure of Secretary to seek relief; writ of mandamus

If the Secretary arbitrarily or capriciously fails to seek relief under this section, any employee who may be injured by reason of such failure, or the representative of such employees, might bring an action against the Secretary in the United States district court for the district in which the imminent danger is alleged to exist or the employer has its principal office, or for the District of Columbia, for a writ of mandamus to compel the Secretary to seek such an order and for such further relief as may be appropriate.

(Pub. L. 91–596, § 13, Dec. 29, 1970, 84 Stat. 1605.)

REFERENCES IN TEXT

Rule 65 of the Federal Rules of Civil Procedure, referred to in subsec. (b), is set out in the Appendix to Title 28, Judiciary and Judicial Procedure.

§ 663. Representation in civil litigation

Except as provided in section 518(a) of title 28 relating to litigation before the Supreme Court, the Solicitor of Labor may appear for and represent the Secretary in any civil litigation brought under this chapter but all such litigations shall be subject to the direction and control of the Attorney General.

(Pub. L. 91–596, § 14, Dec. 29, 1970, 84 Stat. 1606.)

§ 664. Disclosure of trade secrets; protective orders

All information reported to or otherwise obtained by the Secretary or his representative in connection with any inspection or proceeding under this chapter which contains or which might reveal a trade secret referred to in section 1905 of title 18 shall be considered confidential for the purpose of that section, except that such information may be disclosed to other officers or employees concerned with carrying out this chapter or when relevant in any proceeding under this chapter. In any such proceeding the Secretary, the Commission, or the court shall issue such orders as may be appropriate to protect the confidentiality of trade secrets.

(Pub. L. 91–596, § 15, Dec. 29, 1970, 84 Stat. 1606.)

§ 665. Variations, tolerances, and exemptions from required provisions; procedure; duration

The Secretary, on the record, after notice and opportunity for a hearing may provide such reasonable limitations and may make such rules and regulations allowing reasonable variations, tolerances, and exemptions to and from any or all provisions of this chapter as he may find necessary and proper to avoid serious impairment of the national defense. Such action shall not be in effect for more than six months without notification to affected employees and an opportunity being afforded for a hearing.

(Pub. L. 91–596, § 16, Dec. 29, 1970, 84 Stat. 1606.)

§ 666. Civil and criminal penalties

(a) Willful or repeated violation

Any employer who willfully or repeatedly violates the requirements of section 654 of this title, any standard, rule, or order promulgated pursuant to section 655 of this title, or regulations prescribed pursuant to this chapter may be assessed a civil penalty of not more than $70,000 for each violation, but not less than $5,000 for each willful violation.

(b) Citation for serious violation

Any employer who has received a citation for a serious violation of the requirements of section 654 of this title, of any standard, rule, or order promulgated pursuant to section 655 of this title, or of any regulations prescribed pursuant to this chapter, shall be assessed a civil penalty of up to $7,000 for each such violation.

(c) Citation for violation determined not serious

Any employer who has received a citation for a violation of the requirements of section 654 of this title, of any standard, rule, or order promulgated pursuant to section 655 of this title, or of regulations prescribed pursuant to this chapter, and such violation is specifically determined not to be of a serious nature, may be assessed a civil penalty of up to $7,000 for each such violation.

(d) Failure to correct violation

Any employer who fails to correct a violation for which a citation has been issued under section 658(a) of this title within the period permitted for its correction (which period shall not begin to run until the date of the final order of the Commission in the case of any review proceeding under section 659 of this title initiated by the employer in good faith and not solely for delay or avoidance of penalties), may be assessed a civil penalty of not more than $7,000 for each day during which such failure or violation continues.

(e) Willful violation causing death to employee

Any employer who willfully violates any standard, rule, or order promulgated pursuant to section 655 of this title, or of any regulations prescribed pursuant to this chapter, and that violation caused death to any employee, shall, upon conviction, be punished by a fine of not more than $10,000 or by imprisonment for not more than six months, or by both; except that if the conviction is for a violation committed after a first conviction of such person, punishment shall be by a fine of not more than $20,000 or by imprisonment for not more than one year, or by both.

(f) Giving advance notice of inspection

Any person who gives advance notice of any inspection to be conducted under this chapter, without authority from the Secretary or his designees, shall, upon conviction, be punished by a fine of not more than $1,000 or by imprisonment for not more than six months, or by both.

(g) False statements, representations or certification

Whoever knowingly makes any false statement, representation, or certification in any application, record, report, plan, or other document filed or required to be maintained pursuant to this chapter shall, upon conviction, be punished by a fine of not more than $10,000, or by imprisonment for not more than six months, or by both.

(h) Omitted

(i) Violation of posting requirements

Any employer who violates any of the posting requirements, as prescribed under the provisions of this chapter, shall be assessed a civil penalty of up to $7,000 for each violation.

(j) Authority of Commission to assess civil penalties

The Commission shall have authority to assess all civil penalties provided in this section, giving due consideration to the appropriateness of the penalty with respect to the size of the business of the employer being charged, the gravity of the violation, the good faith of the employer, and the history of previous violations.

(k) Determination of serious violation

For purposes of this section, a serious violation shall be deemed to exist in a place of employment if there is a substantial probability that death or serious physical harm could result from a condition which exists, or from one or more practices, means, methods, operations, or processes which have been adopted or are in use, in such place of employment unless the employer did not, and could not with the exercise of reasonable diligence, know of the presence of the violation.

(*l*) Procedure for payment of civil penalties

Civil penalties owed under this chapter shall be paid to the Secretary for deposit into the Treasury of the United States and shall accrue to the United States and may be recovered in a civil action in the name of the United States brought in the United States district court for the district where the violation is alleged to have occurred or where the employer has its principal office.

(Pub. L. 91–596, §17, Dec. 29, 1970, 84 Stat. 1606, 1607; Pub. L. 101–508, title III, §3101, Nov. 5, 1990, 104 Stat. 1388–29.)

CODIFICATION

Subsec. (h) of this section amended section 1114 of Title 18, Crimes and Criminal Procedure, and enacted note set out thereunder.

AMENDMENTS

1990—Subsec. (a). Pub. L. 101–508, §3101(1), substituted "$70,000 for each violation, but not less than $5,000 for each willful violation" for "$10,000 for each violation".

Subsecs. (b) to (d), (i). Pub. L. 101–508, §3101(2), substituted "$7,000" for "$1,000".

§667. State jurisdiction and plans

(a) Assertion of State standards in absence of applicable Federal standards

Nothing in this chapter shall prevent any State agency or court from asserting jurisdiction under State law over any occupational safety or health issue with respect to which no standard is in effect under section 655 of this title.

(b) Submission of State plan for development and enforcement of State standards to preempt applicable Federal standards

Any State which, at any time, desires to assume responsibility for development and enforcement therein of occupational safety and health standards relating to any occupational safety or health issue with respect to which a Federal standard has been promulgated under section 655 of this title shall submit a State plan for the development of such standards and their enforcement.

(c) Conditions for approval of plan

The Secretary shall approve the plan submitted by a State under subsection (b) of this section, or any modification thereof, if such plan in his judgment—

(1) designates a State agency or agencies as the agency or agencies responsible for administering the plan throughout the State,

(2) provides for the development and enforcement of safety and health standards relating to one or more safety or health issues, which standards (and the enforcement of which standards) are or will be at least as effective in providing safe and healthful employment and places of employment as the standards promulgated under section 655 of this title which relate to the same issues, and which standards, when applicable to products which are distributed or used in interstate commerce, are required by compelling local conditions and do not unduly burden interstate commerce,

(3) provides for a right of entry and inspection of all workplaces subject to this chapter which is at least as effective as that provided in section 657 of this title, and includes a prohibition on advance notice of inspections,

(4) contains satisfactory assurances that such agency or agencies have or will have the legal authority and qualified personnel necessary for the enforcement of such standards,

(5) gives satisfactory assurances that such State will devote adequate funds to the administration and enforcement of such standards,

(6) contains satisfactory assurances that such State will, to the extent permitted by its law, establish and maintain an effective and comprehensive occupational safety and health program applicable to all employees of public agencies of the State and its political subdivisions, which program is as effective as the standards contained in an approved plan,

(7) requires employers in the State to make reports to the Secretary in the same manner and to the same extent as if the plan were not in effect, and

(8) provides that the State agency will make such reports to the Secretary in such form and containing such information, as the Secretary shall from time to time require.

(d) Rejection of plan; notice and opportunity for hearing

If the Secretary rejects a plan submitted under subsection (b) of this section, he shall afford the State submitting the plan due notice and opportunity for a hearing before so doing.

(e) Discretion of Secretary to exercise authority over comparable standards subsequent to approval of State plan; duration; retention of jurisdiction by Secretary upon determination of enforcement of plan by State

After the Secretary approves a State plan submitted under subsection (b) of this section, he may, but shall not be required to, exercise his authority under sections 657, 658, 659, 662, and 666 of this title with respect to comparable standards promulgated under section 655 of this title, for the period specified in the next sentence. The Secretary may exercise the authority referred to above until he determines, on the basis of actual operations under the State plan, that the criteria set forth in subsection (c) of this section are being applied, but he shall not make such determination for at least three years after the plan's approval under subsection (c) of this section. Upon making the determination referred to in the preceding sentence, the provisions of sections 654(a)(2), 657 (except for the purpose of carrying out subsection (f) of this section), 658, 659, 662, and 666 of this title, and standards promulgated under section 655 of this title, shall not apply with respect to any occupational safety or health issues covered under the plan, but the Secretary may retain jurisdiction under the above provisions in any proceeding commenced under section 658 or 659 of this title before the date of determination.

(f) Continuing evaluation by Secretary of State enforcement of approved plan; withdrawal of approval of plan by Secretary; grounds; procedure; conditions for retention of jurisdiction by State

The Secretary shall, on the basis of reports submitted by the State agency and his own inspections make a continuing evaluation of the manner in which each State having a plan approved under this section is carrying out such plan. Whenever the Secretary finds, after affording due notice and opportunity for a hearing, that in the administration of the State plan there is a failure to comply substantially with any provision of the State plan (or any assurance contained therein), he shall notify the State agency of his withdrawal of approval of such plan and upon receipt of such notice such plan shall cease to be in effect, but the State may retain jurisdiction in any case commenced before the withdrawal of the plan in order to enforce standards under the plan whenever the issues involved do not relate to the reasons for the withdrawal of the plan.

(g) Judicial review of Secretary's withdrawal of approval or rejection of plan; jurisdiction; venue; procedure; appropriate relief; finality of judgment

The State may obtain a review of a decision of the Secretary withdrawing approval of or rejecting its plan by the United States court of appeals for the circuit in which the State is located by filing in such court within thirty days following receipt of notice of such decision a petition to modify or set aside in whole or in part the action of the Secretary. A copy of such petition shall forthwith be served upon the Secretary, and thereupon the Secretary shall certify and file in the court the record upon which the decision complained of was issued as provided in section 2112 of title 28. Unless the court finds that the Secretary's decision in rejecting a proposed State plan or withdrawing his approval of such a plan is not supported by substantial evidence the court shall affirm the Secretary's decision. The judgment of the court shall be subject to review by the Supreme Court of the United States upon certiorari or certification as provided in section 1254 of title 28.

(h) Temporary enforcement of State standards

The Secretary may enter into an agreement with a State under which the State will be permitted to continue to enforce one or more occupational health and safety standards in effect in such State until final action is taken by the Secretary with respect to a plan submitted by a State under subsection (b) of this section, or two years from December 29, 1970, whichever is earlier.

(Pub. L. 91–596, §18, Dec. 29, 1970, 84 Stat. 1608.)

§668. Programs of Federal agencies

(a) Establishment, development, and maintenance by head of each Federal agency

It shall be the responsibility of the head of each Federal agency (not including the United States Postal Service) to establish and maintain an effective and comprehensive occupational safety and health program which is consistent with the standards promulgated under section 655 of this title. The head of each agency shall (after consultation with representatives of the employees thereof)—

(1) provide safe and healthful places and conditions of employment, consistent with the standards set under section 655 of this title;

(2) acquire, maintain, and require the use of safety equipment, personal protective equipment, and devices reasonably necessary to protect employees;

(3) keep adequate records of all occupational accidents and illnesses for proper evaluation and necessary corrective action;

(4) consult with the Secretary with regard to the adequacy as to form and content of records kept pursuant to subsection (a)(3) of this section; and

(5) make an annual report to the Secretary with respect to occupational accidents and injuries and the agency's program under this section. Such report shall include any report submitted under section 7902(e)(2) of title 5.

(b) Report by Secretary to President

The Secretary shall report to the President a summary or digest of reports submitted to him under subsection (a)(5) of this section, together with his evaluations of and recommendations derived from such reports.

(c) Omitted

(d) Access by Secretary to records and reports required of agencies

The Secretary shall have access to records and reports kept and filed by Federal agencies pursuant to subsections (a)(3) and (5) of this section unless those records and reports are specifically required by Executive order to be kept secret in the interest of the national defense or foreign policy, in which case the Secretary shall have access to such information as will not jeopardize national defense or foreign policy.

(Pub. L. 91–596, §19, Dec. 29, 1970, 84 Stat. 1609; Pub. L. 97–375, title I, §110(c), Dec. 21, 1982, 96 Stat. 1821; Pub. L. 105–241, §2(b)(1), Sept. 28, 1998, 112 Stat. 1572.)

CODIFICATION

Subsec. (c) of this section amended section 7902 of Title 5, Government Organization and Employees.

AMENDMENTS

1998—Subsec. (a). Pub. L. 105–241 inserted "(not including the United States Postal Service)" after "each Federal agency".

1982—Subsec. (b). Pub. L. 97–375 struck out direction that the President transmit annually to the Senate and House a report of the activities of Federal agencies under this section.

OCCUPATIONAL SAFETY AND HEALTH PROGRAMS FOR FEDERAL EMPLOYEES

Occupational safety and health programs for Federal employees and continuation of Federal Advisory Council on Occupational Safety and Health, see Ex. Ord. No. 12196, Feb. 26, 1980, 45 F.R. 12769, set out as a note under section 7902 of Title 5, Government Organization and Employees.

§ 669. Research and related activities

(a) Authority of Secretary of Health and Human Services to conduct research, experiments, and demonstrations, develop plans, establish criteria, promulgate regulations, authorize programs, and publish results and industrywide studies; consultations

(1) The Secretary of Health and Human Services, after consultation with the Secretary and with other appropriate Federal departments or agencies, shall conduct (directly or by grants or contracts) research, experiments, and demonstrations relating to occupational safety and health, including studies of psychological factors involved, and relating to innovative methods, techniques, and approaches for dealing with occupational safety and health problems.

(2) The Secretary of Health and Human Services shall from time to time consult with the Secretary in order to develop specific plans for such research, demonstrations, and experiments as are necessary to produce criteria, including criteria identifying toxic substances, enabling the Secretary to meet his responsibility for the formulation of safety and health standards under this chapter; and the Secretary of Health and Human Services, on the basis of such research, demonstrations, and experiments and any other information available to him, shall develop and publish at least annually such criteria as will effectuate the purposes of this chapter.

(3) The Secretary of Health and Human Services, on the basis of such research, demonstrations, and experiments, and any other information available to him, shall develop criteria dealing with toxic materials and harmful physical agents and substances which will describe exposure levels that are safe for various periods of employment, including but not limited to the exposure levels at which no employee will suffer impaired health or functional capacities or diminished life expectancy as a result of his work experience.

(4) The Secretary of Health and Human Services shall also conduct special research, experiments, and demonstrations relating to occupational safety and health as are necessary to explore new problems, including those created by new technology in occupational safety and health, which may require ameliorative action beyond that which is otherwise provided for in the operating provisions of this chapter. The Secretary of Health and Human Services shall also conduct research into the motivational and behavioral factors relating to the field of occupational safety and health.

(5) The Secretary of Health and Human Services, in order to comply with his responsibilities under paragraph (2), and in order to develop needed information regarding potentially toxic substances or harmful physical agents, may prescribe regulations requiring employers to measure, record, and make reports on the exposure of employees to substances or physical agents which the Secretary of Health and Human Services reasonably believes may endanger the health or safety of employees. The Secretary of Health and Human Services also is authorized to establish such programs of medical examinations and tests as may be necessary for determining the incidence of occupational illnesses and the susceptibility of employees to such illnesses. Nothing in this or any other provision of this chapter shall be deemed to authorize or require medical examination, immunization, or treatment for those who object thereto on religious grounds, except where such is necessary for the protection of the health or safety of others. Upon the request of any employer who is required to measure and record exposure of employees to substances or physical agents as provided under this subsection, the Secretary of Health and Human Services shall furnish full financial or other assistance to such employer for the purpose of defraying any additional expense incurred by him in carrying out the measuring and recording as provided in this subsection.

(6) The Secretary of Health and Human Services shall publish within six months of December 29, 1970, and thereafter as needed but at least annually a list of all known toxic substances by generic family or other useful grouping, and the concentrations at which such toxicity is known to occur. He shall determine following a written request by any employer or authorized representative of employees, specifying with reasonable particularity the grounds on which the request is made, whether any substance normally found in the place of employment has potentially toxic effects in such concentrations as used or found; and shall submit such determination both to employers and affected employees as soon as possible. If the Secretary of Health and Human Services determines that any substance is potentially toxic at the concentrations in which it is used or found in a place of employment, and such substance is not covered by an occupational safety or health standard promulgated under section 655 of this title, the Secretary of Health and Human Services shall immediately submit such determination to the Secretary, together with all pertinent criteria.

(7) Within two years of December 29, 1970, and annually thereafter the Secretary of Health and Human Services shall conduct and publish industrywide studies of the effect of chronic or low-level exposure to industrial materials, processes, and stresses on the potential for illness, disease, or loss of functional capacity in aging adults.

(b) Authority of Secretary of Health and Human Services to make inspections and question employers and employees

The Secretary of Health and Human Services is authorized to make inspections and question employers and employees as provided in section 657 of this title in order to carry out his functions and responsibilities under this section.

(c) Contracting authority of Secretary of Labor; cooperation between Secretary of Labor and Secretary of Health and Human Services

The Secretary is authorized to enter into contracts, agreements, or other arrangements with appropriate public agencies or private organizations for the purpose of conducting studies relating to his responsibilities under this chapter. In carrying out his responsibilities under this subsection, the Secretary shall cooperate with the Secretary of Health and Human Services in order to avoid any duplication of efforts under this section.

(d) Dissemination of information to interested parties

Information obtained by the Secretary and the Secretary of Health and Human Services under this section shall be disseminated by the Secretary to employers and employees and organizations thereof.

(e) Delegation of functions of Secretary of Health and Human Services to Director of the National Institute for Occupational Safety and Health

The functions of the Secretary of Health and Human Services under this chapter shall, to the extent feasible, be delegated to the Director of the National Institute for Occupational Safety and Health established by section 671 of this title.

(Pub. L. 91–596, § 20, Dec. 29, 1970, 84 Stat. 1610; Pub. L. 96–88, title V, § 509(b), Oct. 17, 1979, 93 Stat. 695.)

CHANGE OF NAME

"Secretary of Health and Human Services" substituted in text for "Secretary of Health, Education, and Welfare" pursuant to section 509(b) of Pub. L. 96–88 which is classified to section 3508(b) of Title 20, Education.

§ 669a. Expanded research on worker health and safety

The Secretary of Health and Human Services (referred to in this section as the "Secretary"), acting through the Director of the National Institute of Occupational Safety and Health, shall enhance and expand research as deemed appropriate on the health and safety of workers who are at risk for bioterrorist threats or attacks in the workplace, including research on the health effects of measures taken to treat or protect such workers for diseases or disorders resulting from a bioterrorist threat or attack. Nothing in this section may be construed as establishing new regulatory authority for the Secretary or the Director to issue or modify any occupational safety and health rule or regulation.

(Pub. L. 107–188, title I, § 153, June 12, 2002, 116 Stat. 631.)

CODIFICATION

Section was enacted as part of the Public Health Security and Bioterrorism Preparedness and Response Act of 2002, and not as part of the Occupational Safety and Health Act of 1970 which comprises this chapter.

§ 670. Training and employee education

(a) Authority of Secretary of Health and Human Services to conduct education and informational programs; consultations

The Secretary of Health and Human Services, after consultation with the Secretary and with other appropriate Federal departments and agencies, shall conduct, directly or by grants or contracts (1) education programs to provide an adequate supply of qualified personnel to carry out the purposes of this chapter, and (2) informational programs on the importance of and proper use of adequate safety and health equipment.

(b) Authority of Secretary of Labor to conduct short-term training of personnel

The Secretary is also authorized to conduct, directly or by grants or contracts, short-term training of personnel engaged in work related to his responsibilities under this chapter.

(c) Authority of Secretary of Labor to establish and supervise education and training programs and consult and advise interested parties

The Secretary, in consultation with the Secretary of Health and Human Services, shall (1) provide for the establishment and supervision of programs for the education and training of employers and employees in the recognition, avoidance, and prevention of unsafe or unhealthful working conditions in employments covered by this chapter, and (2) consult with and advise employers and employees, and organizations representing employers and employees as to effective means of preventing occupational injuries and illnesses.

(d) Compliance assistance program

(1) The Secretary shall establish and support cooperative agreements with the States under which employers subject to this chapter may consult with State personnel with respect to—

(A) the application of occupational safety and health requirements under this chapter or under State plans approved under section 667 of this title; and

(B) voluntary efforts that employers may undertake to establish and maintain safe and healthful employment and places of employment.

Such agreements may provide, as a condition of receiving funds under such agreements, for contributions by States towards meeting the costs of such agreements.

(2) Pursuant to such agreements the State shall provide on-site consultation at the employer's worksite to employers who request such assistance. The State may also provide other education and training programs for employers and employees in the State. The State shall ensure that on-site consultations conducted pursuant to such agreements include provision for the participation by employees.

(3) Activities under this subsection shall be conducted independently of any enforcement activity. If an employer fails to take immediate action to eliminate employee exposure to an imminent danger identified in a consultation or fails to correct a serious hazard so identified within a reasonable time, a report shall be made to the appropriate enforcement authority for such action as is appropriate.

(4) The Secretary shall, by regulation after notice and opportunity for comment, establish rules under which an employer—

(A) which requests and undergoes an on-site consultative visit provided under this subsection;

(B) which corrects the hazards that have been identified during the visit within the time frames established by the State and agrees to request a subsequent consultative visit if major changes in working conditions or work processes occur which introduce new hazards in the workplace; and

(C) which is implementing procedures for regularly identifying and preventing hazards regulated under this chapter and maintains appropriate involvement of, and training for, management and non-management employees in achieving safe and healthful working conditions,

may be exempt from an inspection (except an inspection requested under section 657(f) of this title or an inspection to determine the cause of a workplace accident which resulted in the death of one or more employees or hospitalization for three or more employees) for a period of 1 year from the closing of the consultative visit.

(5) A State shall provide worksite consultations under paragraph (2) at the request of an employer. Priority in scheduling such consultations shall be assigned to requests from small businesses which are in higher hazard industries or have the most hazardous conditions at issue in the request.

(Pub. L. 91–596, §21, Dec. 29, 1970, 84 Stat. 1612; Pub. L. 96–88, title V, §509(b), Oct. 17, 1979, 93 Stat. 695; Pub. L. 105–197, §2, July 16, 1998, 112 Stat. 638.)

AMENDMENTS

1998—Subsec. (d). Pub. L. 105–197 added subsec. (d).

CHANGE OF NAME

"Secretary of Health and Human Services" substituted for "Secretary of Health, Education, and Welfare" in subsecs. (a) and (c) pursuant to section 509(b) of Pub. L. 96–88 which is classified to section 3508(b) of Title 20, Education.

RETENTION OF TRAINING INSTITUTE COURSE TUITION FEES BY OSHA

Provisions stating that notwithstanding 31 U.S.C. 3302, the Occupational Safety and Health Administration could retain up to $750,000 per fiscal year of training institute course tuition fees, otherwise authorized by law to be collected, and could utilize such sums for occupational safety and health training and education grants, were contained in Department of Labor Appropriations Act, 2006, Pub. L. 109–149, title I, Dec. 30, 2005, 119 Stat. 2839, and were repeated in provisions of subsequent appropriations acts which are not set out in the Code. Similar provisions were also contained in the following prior appropriations acts:

Pub. L. 108–447, div. F, title I, Dec. 8, 2004, 118 Stat. 3118.

Pub. L. 108–199, div. E, title I, Jan. 23, 2004, 118 Stat. 232.

Pub. L. 108–7, div. G, title I, Feb. 20, 2003, 117 Stat. 303.

Pub. L. 107–116, title I, Jan. 10, 2002, 115 Stat. 2182.

Pub. L. 106–554, §1(a)(1) [title I], Dec. 21, 2000, 114 Stat. 2763, 2763A–8.

Pub. L. 106–113, div. B, §1000(a)(4) [title I], Nov. 29, 1999, 113 Stat. 1535, 1501A–222.

Pub. L. 105–277, div. A, §101(f) [title I], Oct. 21, 1998, 112 Stat. 2681–337, 2681–343.

Pub. L. 105–78, title I, Nov. 13, 1997, 111 Stat. 1474.

Pub. L. 104–208, div. A, title I, §101(e) [title I], Sept. 30, 1996, 110 Stat. 3009–233, 3009–239.

Pub. L. 104–134, title I, §101(d) [title I], Apr. 26, 1996, 110 Stat. 1321–211, 1321–217; renumbered title I, Pub. L. 104–140, §1(a), May 2, 1996, 110 Stat. 1327.

Pub. L. 103–333, title I, Sept. 30, 1994, 108 Stat. 2544.

§ 671. National Institute for Occupational Safety and Health

(a) Statement of purpose

It is the purpose of this section to establish a National Institute for Occupational Safety and Health in the Department of Health and Human Services in order to carry out the policy set forth in section 651 of this title and to perform the functions of the Secretary of Health and Human Services under sections 669 and 670 of this title.

(b) Establishment; Director; appointment; term

There is hereby established in the Department of Health and Human Services a National Institute for Occupational Safety and Health. The Institute shall be headed by a Director who shall be appointed by the Secretary of Health and Human Services, and who shall serve for a term of six years unless previously removed by the Secretary of Health and Human Services.

(c) Development and establishment of standards; performance of functions of Secretary of Health and Human Services

The Institute is authorized to—

(1) develop and establish recommended occupational safety and health standards; and

(2) perform all functions of the Secretary of Health and Human Services under sections 669 and 670 of this title.

(d) Authority of Director

Upon his own initiative, or upon the request of the Secretary or the Secretary of Health and Human Services, the Director is authorized (1) to conduct such research and experimental programs as he determines are necessary for the development of criteria for new and improved occupational safety and health standards, and (2) after consideration of the results of such research and experimental programs make recommendations concerning new or improved occupational safety and health standards. Any occupational safety and health standard recommended pursuant to this section shall immediately be forwarded to the Secretary of Labor, and to the Secretary of Health and Human Services.

(e) Additional authority of Director

In addition to any authority vested in the Institute by other provisions of this section, the Director, in carrying out the functions of the Institute, is authorized to—

(1) prescribe such regulations as he deems necessary governing the manner in which its functions shall be carried out;

(2) receive money and other property donated, bequeathed, or devised, without condition or restriction other than that it be used for the purposes of the Institute and to use, sell, or otherwise dispose of such property for the purpose of carrying out its functions;

(3) receive (and use, sell, or otherwise dispose of, in accordance with paragraph (2)), money and other property donated, bequeathed or devised to the Institute with a condition or restriction, including a condition that the Institute use other funds of the Institute for the purposes of the gift;

(4) in accordance with the civil service laws, appoint and fix the compensation of such personnel as may be necessary to carry out the provisions of this section;

(5) obtain the services of experts and consultants in accordance with the provisions of section 3109 of title 5;

(6) accept and utilize the services of voluntary and noncompensated personnel and reimburse them for travel expenses, including per diem, as authorized by section 5703 of title 5;

(7) enter into contracts, grants or other arrangements, or modifications thereof to carry out the provisions of this section, and such contracts or modifications thereof may be entered into without performance or other bonds, and without regard to section 5 of title 41, or any other provision of law relating to competitive bidding;

(8) make advance, progress, and other payments which the Director deems necessary under this title without regard to the provisions of section 3324(a) and (b) of title 31; and

(9) make other necessary expenditures.

(f) Annual reports

The Director shall submit to the Secretary of Health and Human Services, to the President, and to the Congress an annual report of the operations of the Institute under this chapter, which shall include a detailed statement of all private and public funds received and expended by it, and such recommendations as he deems appropriate.

(g) Lead-based paint activities

(1) Training grant program

(A) The Institute, in conjunction with the Administrator of the Environmental Protection Agency, may make grants for the training and education of workers and supervisors who are or may be directly engaged in lead-based paint activities.

(B) Grants referred to in subparagraph (A) shall be awarded to nonprofit organizations (including colleges and universities, joint labor-management trust funds, States, and nonprofit government employee organizations)—

(i) which are engaged in the training and education of workers and supervisors who are or who may be directly engaged in lead-based paint activities (as defined in title IV of the Toxic Substances Control Act [15 U.S.C. 2681 et seq.]),

(ii) which have demonstrated experience in implementing and operating health and safety training and education programs, and

(iii) with a demonstrated ability to reach, and involve in lead-based paint training programs, target populations of individuals who are or will be engaged in lead-based paint activities.

Grants under this subsection shall be awarded only to those organizations that fund at least 30 percent of their lead-based paint activities training programs from non-Federal sources, excluding in-kind contributions. Grants may also be made to local governments to carry out such training and education for their employees.

(C) There are authorized to be appropriated, at a minimum, $10,000,000 to the Institute for each of the fiscal years 1994 through 1997 to make grants under this paragraph.

(2) Evaluation of programs

The Institute shall conduct periodic and comprehensive assessments of the efficacy of the worker and supervisor training programs developed and offered by those receiving grants under this section. The Director shall prepare reports on the results of these assessments addressed to the Administrator of the Environmental Protection Agency to include recommendations as may be appropriate for the revision of these programs. The sum of $500,000 is authorized to be appropriated to the Institute for each of the fiscal years 1994 through 1997 to carry out this paragraph.

(h) Office of Mine Safety and Health

(1) In general

There shall be permanently established within the Institute an Office of Mine Safety and Health which shall be administered by an Associate Director to be appointed by the Director.

(2) Purpose

The purpose of the Office is to enhance the development of new mine safety technology and technological applications and to expedite the commercial availability and implementation of such technology in mining environments.

(3) Functions

In addition to all purposes and authorities provided for under this section, the Office of Mine Safety and Health shall be responsible for research, development, and testing of new technologies and equipment designed to enhance mine safety and health. To carry out such functions the Director of the Institute, acting through the Office, shall have the authority to—

(A) award competitive grants to institutions and private entities to encourage the development and manufacture of mine safety equipment;

(B) award contracts to educational institutions or private laboratories for the performance of product testing or related work with respect to new mine technology and equipment; and

(C) establish an interagency working group as provided for in paragraph (5).

(4) Grant authority

To be eligible to receive a grant under the authority provided for under paragraph (3)(A), an entity or institution shall—

(A) submit to the Director of the Institute an application at such time, in such manner, and containing such information as the Director may require; and

(B) include in the application under subparagraph (A), a description of the mine safety equipment to be developed and manufactured under the grant and a description of the reasons that such equipment would otherwise not be developed or manufactured, including reasons relating to the limited potential commercial market for such equipment.

(5) Interagency working group

(A) Establishment

The Director of the Institute, in carrying out paragraph (3)(D) shall establish an interagency working group to share technology and technological research and developments that could be utilized to enhance mine safety and accident response.

(B) Membership

The working group under subparagraph (A) shall be chaired by the Associate Director of the Office who shall appoint the members of the working group, which may include representatives of other Federal agencies or departments as determined appropriate by the Associate Director.

(C) Duties

The working group under subparagraph (A) shall conduct an evaluation of research conducted by, and the technological developments of, agencies and departments who are represented on the working group that may have applicability to mine safety and accident response and make recommendations to the Director for the further development and eventual implementation of such technology.

(6) Annual report

Not later than 1 year after the establishment of the Office under this subsection, and annually thereafter, the Director of the Institute shall submit to the Committee on Health, Education, Labor, and Pensions of the Senate and the Committee on Education and the Workforce of the House of Representatives a report that, with respect to the year involved, describes the new mine safety technologies and equipment that have been studied, tested, and certified for use, and with respect to those instances of technologies and equipment that have been considered but not yet certified for use, the reasons therefore.

(7) Authorization of appropriations

There is authorized to be appropriated, such sums as may be necessary to enable the Institute and the Office of Mine Safety and Health to carry out this subsection.

(Pub. L. 91–596, §22, Dec. 29, 1970, 84 Stat. 1612; Pub. L. 96–88, title V, §509(b), Oct. 17, 1979, 93 Stat. 695; Pub. L. 102–550, title X, §1033, Oct. 28, 1992, 106 Stat. 3924; Pub. L. 109–236, §6(a), June 15, 2006, 120 Stat. 498.)

REFERENCES IN TEXT

The civil service laws, referred to in subsec. (e)(4), are set forth in Title 5, Government Organization and Employees. See, particularly, section 3301 et seq. of Title 5.

The Toxic Substances Control Act, referred to in subsec. (g)(1)(B)(i), is Pub. L. 94–469, Oct. 11, 1976, 90 Stat. 2003, as amended. Title IV of the Act is classified generally to subchapter IV (§2681 et seq.) of chapter 53 of Title 15, Commerce and Trade. For complete classification of this Act to the Code, see Short Title note set out under section 2601 of Title 15 and Tables.

CODIFICATION

In subsec. (e)(8), "section 3324(a) and (b) of title 31" substituted for "section 3648 of the Revised Statutes, as amended (31 U.S.C. 529)" on authority of Pub. L. 97–258, §4(b), Sept. 13, 1982, 96 Stat. 1067, the first section of which enacted Title 31, Money and Finance.

AMENDMENTS

2006—Subsec. (h). Pub. L. 109–236 added subsec. (h).
1992—Subsec. (g). Pub. L. 102–550 added subsec. (g).

CHANGE OF NAME

"Secretary of Health and Human Services" substituted for "Secretary of Health, Education, and Welfare" in subsecs. (a) to (d) and (f) pursuant to section 509(b) of Pub. L. 96–88 which is classified to section 3508(b) of Title 20, Education.

Committee on Education and the Workforce of House of Representatives changed to Committee on Education and Labor of House of Representatives by House Resolution No. 6, One Hundred Tenth Congress, Jan. 5, 2007.

TERMINATION OF REPORTING REQUIREMENTS

For termination, effective May 15, 2000, of provisions in subsec. (f) of this section relating to submitting annual report to Congress, see section 3003 of Pub. L. 104–66, as amended, set out as a note under section 1113 of Title 31, Money and Finance, and page 97 of House Document No. 103–7.

§671a. Workers' family protection

(a) Short title

This section may be cited as the "Workers' Family Protection Act".

(b) Findings and purpose

(1) Findings

Congress finds that—

(A) hazardous chemicals and substances that can threaten the health and safety of workers are being transported out of industries on workers' clothing and persons;

(B) these chemicals and substances have the potential to pose an additional threat to the health and welfare of workers and their families;

(C) additional information is needed concerning issues related to employee transported contaminant releases; and

(D) additional regulations may be needed to prevent future releases of this type.

(2) Purpose

It is the purpose of this section to—

(A) increase understanding and awareness concerning the extent and possible health impacts of the problems and incidents described in paragraph (1);

(B) prevent or mitigate future incidents of home contamination that could adversely affect the health and safety of workers and their families;

(C) clarify regulatory authority for preventing and responding to such incidents; and

(D) assist workers in redressing and responding to such incidents when they occur.

(c) Evaluation of employee transported contaminant releases

(1) Study

(A) In general

Not later than 18 months after October 26, 1992, the Director of the National Institute for Occupational Safety and Health (hereafter in this section referred to as the "Director"), in cooperation with the Secretary of Labor, the Administrator of the Environmental Protection Agency, the Administrator of the Agency for Toxic Substances and Disease Registry, and the heads of other Federal Government agencies as determined to be appropriate by the Director, shall conduct a study to evaluate the potential for, the prevalence of, and the issues related to the contamination of workers' homes with hazardous chemicals and substances, including infectious agents, transported from the workplaces of such workers.

(B) Matters to be evaluated

In conducting the study and evaluation under subparagraph (A), the Director shall—

(i) conduct a review of past incidents of home contamination through the utilization of literature and of records concerning past investigations and enforcement actions undertaken by—

(I) the National Institute for Occupational Safety and Health;

(II) the Secretary of Labor to enforce the Occupational Safety and Health Act of 1970 (29 U.S.C. 651 et seq.);

(III) States to enforce occupational safety and health standards in accordance with section 18 of such Act (29 U.S.C. 667); and

(IV) other government agencies (including the Department of Energy and the Environmental Protection Agency), as the Director may determine to be appropriate;

(ii) evaluate current statutory, regulatory, and voluntary industrial hygiene or other measures used by small, medium and large employers to prevent or remediate home contamination;

(iii) compile a summary of the existing research and case histories conducted on incidents of employee transported contaminant releases, including—

(I) the effectiveness of workplace housekeeping practices and personal protective equipment in preventing such incidents;

(II) the health effects, if any, of the resulting exposure on workers and their families;

(III) the effectiveness of normal house cleaning and laundry procedures for removing hazardous materials and agents from workers' homes and personal clothing;

(IV) indoor air quality, as the research concerning such pertains to the fate of chemicals transported from a workplace into the home environment; and

(V) methods for differentiating exposure health effects and relative risks associated with specific agents from other sources of exposure inside and outside the home;

(iv) identify the role of Federal and State agencies in responding to incidents of home contamination;

(v) prepare and submit to the Task Force established under paragraph (2) and to the appropriate committees of Congress, a report concerning the results of the matters studied or evaluated under clauses (i) through (iv); and

(vi) study home contamination incidents and issues and worker and family protection policies and practices related to the special circumstances of firefighters and prepare and submit to the appropriate committees of Congress a report concerning the findings with respect to such study.

(2) Development of investigative strategy

(A) Task Force

Not later than 12 months after October 26, 1992, the Director shall establish a working group, to be known as the "Workers' Family Protection Task Force". The Task Force shall—

(i) be composed of not more than 15 individuals to be appointed by the Director from among individuals who are representative of workers, industry, scientists, industrial hygienists, the National Research Council, and government agencies, except that not more than one such individual shall be from each appropriate government agency and the number of individuals appointed to represent industry and workers shall be equal in number;

(ii) review the report submitted under paragraph (1)(B)(v);

(iii) determine, with respect to such report, the additional data needs, if any, and the need for additional evaluation of the scientific issues related to and the feasibility of developing such additional data; and

(iv) if additional data are determined by the Task Force to be needed, develop a recommended investigative strategy for use in obtaining such information.

(B) Investigative strategy

(i) Content

The investigative strategy developed under subparagraph (A)(iv) shall identify data gaps that can and cannot be filled, assumptions and uncertainties associated with various components of such strategy, a timetable for the implementation of such strategy, and methodologies used to gather any required data.

(ii) Peer review

The Director shall publish the proposed investigative strategy under subparagraph (A)(iv) for public comment and utilize other methods, including technical conferences or seminars, for the purpose of obtaining comments concerning the proposed strategy.

(iii) Final strategy

After the peer review and public comment is conducted under clause (ii), the Director, in consultation with the heads of other government agencies, shall propose a final strategy for investigating issues related to home contamination that shall be implemented by the National Institute for Occupational Safety and Health and other Federal agencies for the period of time necessary to enable such agencies to obtain the information identified under subparagraph (A)(iii).

(C) Construction

Nothing in this section shall be construed as precluding any government agency from investigating issues related to home contamination using existing procedures until such time as a final strategy is developed or from taking actions in addition to those proposed in the strategy after its completion.

(3) Implementation of investigative strategy

Upon completion of the investigative strategy under subparagraph (B)(iii), each Federal agency or department shall fulfill the role assigned to it by the strategy.

(d) Regulations

(1) In general

Not later than 4 years after October 26, 1992, and periodically thereafter, the Secretary of Labor, based on the information developed under subsection (c) of this section and on other information available to the Secretary, shall—

(A) determine if additional education about, emphasis on, or enforcement of existing regulations or standards is needed and will be sufficient, or if additional regulations or standards are needed with regard to employee transported releases of hazardous materials; and

(B) prepare and submit to the appropriate committees of Congress a report concerning the result of such determination.

(2) Additional regulations or standards

If the Secretary of Labor determines that additional regulations or standards are needed under paragraph (1), the Secretary shall promulgate, pursuant to the Secretary's authority under the Occupational Safety and Health Act of 1970 (29 U.S.C. 651 et seq.), such regulations or standards as determined to be appropriate not later than 3 years after such determination.

(e) Authorization of appropriations

There are authorized to be appropriated from sums otherwise authorized to be appropriated, for each fiscal year such sums as may be necessary to carry out this section.

(Pub. L. 102–522, title II, §209, Oct. 26, 1992, 106 Stat. 3420.)

REFERENCES IN TEXT

The Occupational Safety and Health Act of 1970, referred to in subsecs. (c)(1)(B)(i)(II) and (d)(2), is Pub. L. 91–596, Dec. 29, 1970, 84 Stat. 1590, as amended, which is classified principally to this chapter. For complete classification of this Act to the Code, see Short Title note set out under section 651 of this title and Tables.

CODIFICATION

Section was enacted as part of the Fire Administration Authorization Act of 1992, and not as part of the Occupational Safety and Health Act of 1970 which comprises this chapter.

§672. Grants to States

(a) Designation of State agency to assist State in identifying State needs and responsibilities and in developing State plans

The Secretary is authorized, during the fiscal year ending June 30, 1971, and the two succeeding fiscal years, to make grants to the States which have designated a State agency under section 667 of this title to assist them—

(1) in identifying their needs and responsibilities in the area of occupational safety and health,

(2) in developing State plans under section 667 of this title, or

(3) in developing plans for—

(A) establishing systems for the collection of information concerning the nature and frequency of occupational injuries and diseases;

(B) increasing the expertise and enforcement capabilities of their personnel engaged in occupational safety and health programs; or

(C) otherwise improving the administration and enforcement of State occupational safety and health laws, including standards thereunder, consistent with the objectives of this chapter.

(b) Experimental and demonstration projects

The Secretary is authorized, during the fiscal year ending June 30, 1971, and the two succeeding fiscal years, to make grants to the States for experimental and demonstration projects consistent with the objectives set forth in subsection (a) of this section.

(c) Designation by Governor of appropriate State agency for receipt of grant

The Governor of the State shall designate the appropriate State agency for receipt of any grant made by the Secretary under this section.

(d) Submission of application

Any State agency designated by the Governor of the State desiring a grant under this section shall submit an application therefor to the Secretary.

(e) Approval or rejection of application

The Secretary shall review the application, and shall, after consultation with the Secretary of Health and Human Services, approve or reject such application.

(f) Federal share

The Federal share for each State grant under subsection (a) or (b) of this section may not exceed 90 per centum of the total cost of the application. In the event the Federal share for all States under either such subsection is not the same, the differences among the States shall be established on the basis of objective criteria.

(g) Administration and enforcement of programs contained in approved State plans; Federal share

The Secretary is authorized to make grants to the States to assist them in administering and enforcing programs for occupational safety and health contained in State plans approved by the Secretary pursuant to section 667 of this title. The Federal share for each State grant under this subsection may not exceed 50 per centum of the total cost to the State of such a program. The last sentence of subsection (f) of this section shall be applicable in determining the Federal share under this subsection.

(h) Report to President and Congress

Prior to June 30, 1973, the Secretary shall, after consultation with the Secretary of Health and Human Services, transmit a report to the President and to the Congress, describing the experience under the grant programs authorized by this section and making any recommendations he may deem appropriate.

(Pub. L. 91–596, §23, Dec. 29, 1970, 84 Stat. 1613; Pub. L. 96–88, title V, §509(b), Oct. 17, 1979, 93 Stat. 695.)

CHANGE OF NAME

"Secretary of Health and Human Services" substituted for "Secretary of Health, Education, and Welfare" in subsec. (c), pursuant to section 509(b) of Pub. L. 96–88 which is classified to section 3508(b) of Title 20, Education.

§673. Statistics

(a) Development and maintenance of program of collection, compilation, and analysis; employments subject to coverage; scope

In order to further the purposes of this chapter, the Secretary, in consultation with the Secretary of Health and Human Services, shall develop and maintain an effective program of collection, compilation, and analysis of occupational safety and health statistics. Such program may cover all employments whether or not subject to any other provisions of this chapter but shall not cover employments excluded by section 653 of this title. The Secretary shall compile accurate statistics on work injuries and illnesses which shall include all disabling, serious, or significant injuries and illnesses, whether or not involving loss of time from work, other than minor injuries requiring only first aid treatment and which do not involve medical treatment, loss of consciousness, restriction of work or motion, or transfer to another job.

(b) Authority of Secretary to promote, encourage, or engage in programs, make grants, and grant or contract for research and investigations

To carry out his duties under subsection (a) of this section, the Secretary may—

(1) promote, encourage, or directly engage in programs of studies, information and communication concerning occupational safety and health statistics;

(2) make grants to States or political subdivisions thereof in order to assist them in developing and administering programs dealing with occupational safety and health statistics; and

(3) arrange, through grants or contracts, for the conduct of such research and investigations as give promise of furthering the objectives of this section.

(c) Federal share for grants

The Federal share for each grant under subsection (b) of this section may be up to 50 per centum of the State's total cost.

(d) Utilization by Secretary of State or local services, facilities, and employees; consent; reimbursement

The Secretary may, with the consent of any State or political subdivision thereof, accept and use the services, facilities, and employees of the agencies of such State or political subdivision, with or without reimbursement, in order to assist him in carrying out his functions under this section.

(e) Reports by employers

On the basis of the records made and kept pursuant to section 657(c) of this title, employers shall file such reports with the Secretary as he shall prescribe by regulation, as necessary to carry out his functions under this chapter.

(f) Supersedure of agreements between Department of Labor and States for collection of statistics

Agreements between the Department of Labor and States pertaining to the collection of occupational safety and health statistics already in effect on the effective date of this chapter shall remain in effect until superseded by grants or contracts made under this chapter.

(Pub. L. 91–596, §24, Dec. 29, 1970, 84 Stat. 1614; Pub. L. 96–88, title V, §509(b), Oct. 17, 1979, 93 Stat. 695.)

REFERENCES IN TEXT

The effective date of this chapter, referred to in subsec. (f), means the effective date of Pub. L. 91–596, Dec. 29, 1970, 84 Stat. 1590, which is 120 days after Dec. 29, 1970, see section 34 of Pub. L. 91–596, set out as an Effective Date note under section 651 of this title.

CHANGE OF NAME

"Secretary of Health and Human Services" substituted for "Secretary of Health, Education, and Welfare" in subsec. (a) pursuant to section 509(b) of Pub. L. 96–88 which is classified to section 3508(b) of Title 20, Education.

§674. Audit of grant recipient; maintenance of records; contents of records; access to books, etc.

(a) Each recipient of a grant under this chapter shall keep such records as the Secretary or the Secretary of Health and Human Services shall prescribe, including records which fully disclose the amount and disposition by such recipient of the proceeds of such grant, the total cost of the project or undertaking in connection with which such grant is made or used, and the amount of that portion of the cost of the project or undertaking supplied by other sources, and such other records as will facilitate an effective audit.

(b) The Secretary or the Secretary of Health and Human Services, and the Comptroller General of the United States, or any of their duly authorized representatives, shall have access for the purpose of audit and examination to any books, documents, papers, and records of the recipients of any grant under this chapter that are pertinent to any such grant.

(Pub. L. 91–596, §25, Dec. 29, 1970, 84 Stat. 1615; Pub. L. 96–88, title V, §509(b), Oct. 17, 1979, 93 Stat. 695.)

CHANGE OF NAME

"Secretary of Health and Human Services" substituted in text for "Secretary of Health, Education, and Welfare" pursuant to section 509(b) of Pub. L. 96–88 which is classified to section 3508(b) of Title 20, Education.

§675. Annual reports by Secretary of Labor and Secretary of Health and Human Services; contents

Within one hundred and twenty days following the convening of each regular session of each Congress, the Secretary and the Secretary of Health and Human Services shall each prepare and submit to the President for transmittal to the Congress a report upon the subject matter of this chapter, the progress toward achievement of the purpose of this chapter, the needs and requirements in the field of occupational safety and health, and any other relevant information. Such reports shall include information regarding occupational safety and health standards, and criteria for such standards, developed during the preceding year; evaluation of standards and criteria previously developed under this chapter, defining areas of emphasis for new criteria and standards; an evaluation of the degree of observance of applicable occupational safety and health standards, and a summary of inspection and enforcement activity undertaken; analysis and evaluation of research activities for which results have been obtained under governmental and nongovernmental sponsorship; an analysis of major occupational diseases; evaluation of available control and measurement technology for hazards for which standards or criteria have been developed during the preceding year; description of cooperative efforts undertaken between Government agencies and other interested parties in the implementation of this chapter during the preceding year; a progress report on the development of an adequate supply of trained manpower in the field of occupational safety and health, including estimates of future needs and the efforts being made by Government and others to meet those needs; listing of all toxic substances in industrial usage for which labeling requirements, criteria, or standards have not yet been established; and such recommendations for additional legislation as are deemed necessary to protect the safety and health of the worker and improve the administration of this chapter.

(Pub. L. 91–596, §26, Dec. 29, 1970, 84 Stat. 1615; Pub. L. 96–88, title V, §509(b), Oct. 17, 1979, 93 Stat. 695.)

CHANGE OF NAME

"Secretary of Health and Human Services" substituted in text for "Secretary of Health, Education, and Welfare" in text pursuant to section 509(b) of Pub. L. 96–88 which is classified to section 3508(b) of Title 20, Education.

TERMINATION OF REPORTING REQUIREMENTS

For termination, effective May 15, 2000, of provisions in this section relating to the transmittal to Congress of reports prepared by the Secretary of Labor and the Secretary of Health and Human Services, see section 3003 of Pub. L. 104–66, as amended, set out as a note under section 1113 of Title 31, Money and Finance, and pages 98 and 124 of House Document No. 103–7.

STUDY OF OCCUPATIONALLY RELATED PULMONARY AND RESPIRATORY DISEASES; STUDY TO BE COMPLETED AND REPORT SUBMITTED BY SEPTEMBER 1, 1979

Pub. L. 95–239, §17, Mar. 1, 1978, 92 Stat. 105, authorized Secretary of Labor, in cooperation with Director of National Institute for Occupational Safety and Health, to conduct a study of occupationally related pulmonary and respiratory diseases and to complete such study and report findings to President and Congress not later than 18 months after Mar. 1, 1978.

§676. Omitted

CODIFICATION

Section, Pub. L. 91–596, §27, Dec. 29, 1970, 84 Stat. 1616, provided for establishment of a National Commission on State Workmen's Compensation Laws to make an effective study and evaluation of State workmen's compensation laws to determine whether such laws provide an adequate, prompt, and equitable system of compensation for injury or death, with a final report to be transmitted to President and Congress not later than July 31, 1972, ninety days after which the Commission ceased to exist.

§677. Separability

If any provision of this chapter, or the application of such provision to any person or circumstance, shall be held invalid, the remainder of this chapter, or the application of such provision to persons or circumstances other than those as to which it is held invalid, shall not be affected thereby.

(Pub. L. 91–596, §32, Dec. 29, 1970, 84 Stat. 1619.)

§678. Authorization of appropriations

There are authorized to be appropriated to carry out this chapter for each fiscal year such sums as the Congress shall deem necessary.

(Pub. L. 91–596, §33, Dec. 29, 1970, 84 Stat. 1620.)

CHAPTER 16—VOCATIONAL REHABILITATION AND OTHER REHABILITATION SERVICES

GENERAL PROVISIONS

GENERAL PROVISIONS

§ 701. Findings; purpose; policy

(a) Findings

Congress finds that—

(1) millions of Americans have one or more physical or mental disabilities and the number of Americans with such disabilities is increasing;

(2) individuals with disabilities constitute one of the most disadvantaged groups in society;

(3) disability is a natural part of the human experience and in no way diminishes the right of individuals to—

(A) live independently;

(B) enjoy self-determination;

(C) make choices;

(D) contribute to society;

(E) pursue meaningful careers; and

(F) enjoy full inclusion and integration in the economic, political, social, cultural, and educational mainstream of American society;

(4) increased employment of individuals with disabilities can be achieved through implementation of statewide workforce investment systems under title I of the Workforce Investment Act of 1998 [29 U.S.C. 2801 et seq.] that provide meaningful and effective participation for individuals with disabilities in workforce investment activities and activities carried out under the vocational rehabilitation program established under subchapter I of this chapter, and through the provision of independent living services, support services, and meaningful opportunities for employment in integrated work settings through the provision of reasonable accommodations;

(5) individuals with disabilities continually encounter various forms of discrimination in such critical areas as employment, housing, public accommodations, education, transportation, communication, recreation, institutionalization, health services, voting, and public services; and

(6) the goals of the Nation properly include the goal of providing individuals with disabilities with the tools necessary to—

(A) make informed choices and decisions; and

(B) achieve equality of opportunity, full inclusion and integration in society, employment, independent living, and economic and social self-sufficiency, for such individuals.

(b) Purpose

The purposes of this chapter are—

(1) to empower individuals with disabilities to maximize employment, economic self-sufficiency, independence, and inclusion and integration into society, through—

(A) statewide workforce investment systems implemented in accordance with title I of the Workforce Investment Act of 1998 [29 U.S.C. 2801 et seq.] that include, as integral components, comprehensive and coordinated state-of-the-art programs of vocational rehabilitation;

(B) independent living centers and services;

(C) research;

(D) training;

(E) demonstration projects; and

(F) the guarantee of equal opportunity; and

(2) to ensure that the Federal Government plays a leadership role in promoting the employment of individuals with disabilities, especially individuals with significant disabilities, and in assisting States and providers of services in fulfilling the aspirations of such individuals with disabilities for meaningful and gainful employment and independent living.

(c) Policy

It is the policy of the United States that all programs, projects, and activities receiving assistance under this chapter shall be carried out in a manner consistent with the principles of—

(1) respect for individual dignity, personal responsibility, self-determination, and pursuit of meaningful careers, based on informed choice, of individuals with disabilities;

(2) respect for the privacy, rights, and equal access (including the use of accessible formats), of the individuals;

(3) inclusion, integration, and full participation of the individuals;

(4) support for the involvement of an individual's representative if an individual with a disability requests, desires, or needs such support; and

(5) support for individual and systemic advocacy and community involvement.

(Pub. L. 93–112, §2, as added Pub. L. 105–220, title IV, §403, Aug. 7, 1998, 112 Stat. 1095; amended Pub. L. 105–277, div. A, §101(f) [title VIII, §402(b)(2)], Oct. 21, 1998, 112 Stat. 2681–337, 2681–413.)

REFERENCES IN TEXT

The Workforce Investment Act of 1998, referred to in subsecs. (a)(4) and (b)(1)(A), is Pub. L. 105–220, Aug. 7, 1998, 112 Stat. 936, as amended. Title I of the Act is classified principally to chapter 30 (§2801 et seq.) of this title. For complete classification of this Act to the Code, see Short Title note set out under section 9201 of Title 20, Education, and Tables.

PRIOR PROVISIONS

A prior section 701, Pub. L. 93–112, §2, Sept. 26, 1973, 87 Stat. 357; Pub. L. 95–602, title I, §122(a)(1), Nov. 6, 1978, 92 Stat. 2984; Pub. L. 99–506, title I, §101, Oct. 21, 1986, 100 Stat. 1808; Pub. L. 102–569, title I, §101, Oct. 29, 1992, 106 Stat. 4346, related to findings, purpose, and policy, prior to repeal by Pub. L. 105–220, title IV, §403, Aug. 7, 1998, 112 Stat. 1093.

AMENDMENTS

1998—Pub. L. 105–277 made technical amendment in original to section designation and catchline.

SHORT TITLE OF 1998 AMENDMENT

Pub. L. 105–220, title IV, §401, Aug. 7, 1998, 112 Stat. 1092, provided that: "This title [see Tables for classification] may be cited as the 'Rehabilitation Act Amendments of 1998'."

SHORT TITLE OF 1993 AMENDMENT

Pub. L. 103–73, §1, Aug. 11, 1993, 107 Stat. 718, provided that: "This Act [enacting sections 753 and 753a of this title, amending sections 706, 718 to 718b, 721 to 723, 725, 730 to 732, 744, 761a, 762, 771a, 777, 777a, 777f, 783, 791, 792, 794e, 795*l*, 796, 796c, 796d to 796e–2, 796f to 796f–4, and 796k of this title, sections 1431, 4301 to 4305, 4331, 4332, 4351, 4353 to 4357, 4359, 4359a, and 4360 of Title 20, Education, and section 46 of Title 41, Public Contracts, enacting provisions set out as notes under section 725 of this title and section 4301 of Title 20, and amending provisions set out as a note under this section] may be cited as the 'Rehabilitation Act Amendments of 1993'."

SHORT TITLE OF 1992 AMENDMENT

Section 1(a) of Pub. L. 102–569 provided that: "This Act [see Tables for classification] may be cited as the 'Rehabilitation Act Amendments of 1992'."

SHORT TITLE OF 1991 AMENDMENT

Pub. L. 102–52, §1, June 6, 1991, 105 Stat. 260, provided that: "This Act [amending sections 720, 732, 741, 761, 771, 772, 774, 775, 777, 777a, 777f, 785, 792, 795f, 795i, 795q, 796i, and 1904 of this title and section 1475 of Title 20, Education] may be cited as the 'Rehabilitation Act Amendments of 1991'."

SHORT TITLE OF 1986 AMENDMENT

Section 1(a) of Pub. L. 99–506 provided that: "This Act [enacting sections 716, 717, 752, 794d, 795j to 795q, and 796d–1 of this title and section 2000d–7 of Title 42, The Public Health and Welfare, amending this section and sections 702, 705, 706, 711 to 715, 720 to 724, 730 to 732, 740, 741, 750, 751, 760 to 761b, 762, 762a, 770 to 777b, 777f, 780, 781, 783, 785, 791 to 794, 794c, 795, 795d to 795i, 796a, 796b, 796d to 796i, and 1904 of this title, and section 155a of former Title 36, Patriotic Societies and Observances, repealing section 751 of this title, and enacting provisions set out as notes under this section and sections 706, 730, 761a, and 795m of this title and section 1414 of Title 20, Education] may be cited as the 'Rehabilitation Act Amendments of 1986'."

SHORT TITLE OF 1984 AMENDMENT

Pub. L. 98–221, §1, Feb. 22, 1984, 98 Stat. 17, provided: "That this Act [enacting sections 780a and 1901 to 1906 of this title, amending sections 706, 712 to 714, 720 to 722, 730, 732, 741, 761 to 762a, 771, 772, 774, 775, 777, 777a, 777f, 780, 781, 783, 791, 792, 794c, 795a, 795c, 795f, 795g, 795i, 796e, and 796i of this title and sections 6001, 6012, 6033, 6061, and 6081 of Title 42, The Public Health and Welfare, repealing section 777c of this title, enacting provisions set out as a note under section 1901 of this title and amending provisions set out as a note under section 713 of this title] may be cited as the 'Rehabilitation Amendments of 1984'."

SHORT TITLE OF 1978 AMENDMENT

Section 1 of Pub. L. 95–602 provided that: "This Act [enacting sections 710 to 715, 751, 761a, 761b, 762a, 775, 777 to 777f, 780 to 785, 794a to 794c, 795 to 795i, and 796 to 796i of this title and section 6000 of Title 42, The Public Health and Welfare, amending this section, sections 702, 706, 709, 720 to 724, 730 to 732, 740, 741, 750, 760 to 762, 770 to 774, 776, and 792 to 794 of this title, section 1904 [now 3904] of Title 38, Veterans' Benefits, and sections 6001, 6008 to 6012, 6031 to 6033, 6061 to 6065, 6067, 6081, and 6862 of Title 42, repealing sections 764, 786, and 787 of this title and section 6007 of Title 42, omitting sections 6041 to 6043 of Title 42, enacting provisions set out as notes under sections 713 and 795 of this title and sections 6000 and 6001 of Title 42, and repealing a provision set out as a note under section 6001 of Title 42] may be cited as the 'Rehabilitation, Comprehensive Services, and Developmental Disabilities Amendments of 1978'."

SHORT TITLE OF 1976 AMENDMENT

Pub. L. 94–230, §1, Mar. 15, 1976, 90 Stat. 211, provided that: "This Act [amending sections 720, 732, 741, 761, 771, 772, 774, 775, 783, 785, and 792 of this title and enacting provisions set out as a note under section 720 of this title] may be cited as the 'Rehabilitation Act Extension of 1976'."

SHORT TITLE OF 1974 AMENDMENT

Pub. L. 93–516, title I, §100, Dec. 7, 1974, 88 Stat. 1617, provided that: "This title [amending sections 702, 706, 720 to 722, 732, 741, 750, 761, 762, 771, 772, 774 to 776, 783, 785, and 792 of this title and enacting provisions set out as a note under section 702 of this title] shall be known as the 'Rehabilitation Act Amendments of 1974'."

An identical provision is contained in Pub. L. 93–651, title I, §100, Nov. 21, 1974, 89 Stat. 2–3.

SHORT TITLE

Pub. L. 93–112, §1(a), as added by Pub. L. 105–220, title IV, §403, Aug. 7, 1998, 112 Stat. 1093, and amended by Pub. L. 105–277, div. A, §101(f) [title VIII, §402(b)(1)], Oct. 21, 1998, 112 Stat. 2681–337, 2681–412, provided that: "This Act [enacting this chapter] may be cited as the 'Rehabilitation Act of 1973'."

Pub. L. 93–112, title VI, §601, as added by Pub. L. 105–220, title IV, §409, Aug. 7, 1998, 112 Stat. 1210, provided that: "This title [enacting subchapter VI of this chapter] may be cited as the 'Employment Opportunities for Individuals With Disabilities Act'."

Pub. L. 93–112, §1, Sept. 26, 1973, 87 Stat. 355, provided in part that Pub. L. 93–112, which enacted this chapter and repealed sections 31 to 41c and 42–1 to 42b of this title, could be cited as the "Rehabilitation Act of 1973", prior to repeal by Pub. L. 105–220, title IV, §403, Aug. 7, 1998, 112 Stat. 1093.

Pub. L. 93–112, title VI, §601, as added by Pub. L. 95–602, title II, §201, Nov. 6, 1978, 92 Stat. 2989, and amended by Pub. L. 102–569, title I, §102(p)(34), Oct. 29, 1992, 106 Stat. 4360, provided that title VI of Pub. L. 93–112, enacting former subchapter VI of this chapter, could be cited as the "Employment Opportunities for Handicapped Individuals Act", prior to the general amendment of title VI of Pub. L. 93–112 by Pub. L. 105–220, title IV, §409, Aug. 7, 1998, 112 Stat. 1210.

EX. ORD. NO. 11758. DELEGATION OF AUTHORITY OF THE PRESIDENT

Ex. Ord. No. 11758, Jan. 15, 1974, 39 F.R. 2075, as amended by Ex. Ord. No. 11784, May 30, 1974, 39 F.R. 19443; Ex. Ord. No. 11867, June 19, 1975, 40 F.R. 26253; Ex. Ord. No. 12608, Sept. 9, 1987, 52 F.R. 34617, provided:

By virtue of the authority vested in me by section 301 of title 3 of the United States Code and as President of the United States of America, it is hereby ordered as follows:

SECTION 1. The Director of the Office of Management and Budget is hereby designated and empowered to exercise, without approval, ratification, or other action of the President, the authority of the President under section 500(a) of the Rehabilitation Act of 1973 (87 Stat. 390, 29 U.S.C. 790) with respect to the transfer of unexpended appropriations.

SEC. 2. The Secretary of Labor is hereby designated and empowered to exercise, without approval, ratification, or other action of the President, the authority of the President (1) under section 503(a) of the Rehabilitation Act of 1973 [29 U.S.C. 793(a)] to prescribe regulations, after consultation with the Secretary of Defense and the Administrator of General Services, with respect to the employment of qualified handicapped individuals under Federal procurement contracts, and (2) under section 503(c) of that act [29 U.S.C. 793(c)] with respect to prescribing, by regulation, guidelines for waiving the requirements of section 503 of the act [29 U.S.C. 793]. Changes in any regulations prescribed by the Secretary pursuant to the preceding sentence shall be made only after consultation with the Secretary of Defense and the Administrator of General Services.

SEC. 3. The head of a Federal agency may, in conformity with the provisions of section 503(c) of the Rehabilitation Act of 1973 [29 U.S.C. 793(c)], and regulations issued by the Secretary of Labor pursuant to section 2 of this order, exempt any contract and, following consultation with the Secretary of Labor, any class of contracts, from the requirements of section 503 of the act [29 U.S.C. 793].

SEC. 4. The Federal Acquisition Regulations and, to the extent necessary, any supplemental or comparable regulation issued by any agency of the executive branch shall, following consultation with the Secretary of Labor, be amended to require, as a condition of entering into, renewing or extending any contract subject to the provisions of section 503 of the Rehabilitation Act of 1973 [29 U.S.C. 793], inclusion of a provision requiring compliance with that section and regulations issued by the Secretary pursuant to section 2 of this order.

EX. ORD. NO. 13078. INCREASING EMPLOYMENT OF ADULTS WITH DISABILITIES

Ex. Ord. No. 13078, Mar. 13, 1998, 63 F.R. 13111, as amended by Ex. Ord. No. 13172, Oct. 25, 2000, 65 F.R. 64577; Ex. Ord. No. 13187, § 4(b), Jan. 10, 2001, 66 F.R. 3858, provided:

By the authority vested in me as President by the Constitution and the laws of the United States of America, and in order to increase the employment of adults with disabilities to a rate that is as close as possible to the employment rate of the general adult population and to support the goals articulated in the findings and purpose section of the Americans with Disabilities Act of 1990 [42 U.S.C. 12101 et seq.], it is hereby ordered as follows:

SECTION 1. Establishment of National Task Force on Employment of Adults with Disabilities.

(a) There is established the "National Task Force on Employment of Adults with Disabilities" ("Task Force"). The Task Force shall comprise the Secretary of Labor, Secretary of Education, Secretary of Veterans Affairs, Secretary of Health and Human Services, Commissioner of Social Security, Secretary of the Treasury, Secretary of Commerce, Secretary of Transportation, Director of the Office of Personnel Management, Administrator of the Small Business Administration, the Chair of the Equal Employment Opportunity Commission, the Chairperson of the National Council on Disability, the Chairperson of the President's Disability Employment Partnership Board., [sic] and such other senior executive branch officials as may be determined by the Chair of the Task Force.

(b) The Secretary of Labor shall be the Chair of the Task Force; the Chairperson of the President's Disability Employment Partnership Board. [sic] shall be the Vice Chair of the Task Force.

(c) The purpose of the Task Force is to create a coordinated and aggressive national policy to bring adults with disabilities into gainful employment at a rate that is as close as possible to that of the general adult population. The Task Force shall develop and recommend to the President, through the Chair of the Task Force, a coordinated Federal policy to reduce employment barriers for persons with disabilities. Policy recommendations may cover such areas as discrimination, reasonable accommodations, inadequate access to health care, lack of consumer-driven, long-term supports and services, transportation, accessible and integrated housing, telecommunications, assistive technology, community services, child care, education, vocational rehabilitation, training services, job retention, on-the-job supports, and economic incentives to work. Specifically, the Task Force shall:

(1) analyze the existing programs and policies of Task Force member agencies to determine what changes, modifications, and innovations may be necessary to remove barriers to work faced by people with disabilities;

(2) develop and recommend options to address health insurance coverage as a barrier to employment for people with disabilities;

(3) subject to the availability of appropriations, analyze State and private disability systems (e.g., workers' compensation, unemployment insurance, private insurance, and State mental health and mental retardation systems) and their effect on Federal programs and employment of adults with disabilities;

(4) consider statistical and data analysis, cost data, research, and policy studies on public subsidies, employment, employment discrimination, and rates of return-to-work for individuals with disabilities;

(5) evaluate and, where appropriate, coordinate and collaborate on, research and demonstration priorities of Task Force member agencies related to employment of adults with disabilities;

(6) evaluate whether Federal studies related to employment and training can, and should, include a statistically significant sample of adults with disabilities;

(7) subject to the availability of appropriations, analyze youth programs related to employment (e.g., Employment and Training Administration programs, special education, vocational rehabilitation, school-to-work transition, vocational education, and Social Security Administration work incentives and other programs, as may be determined by the Chair and Vice Chair of the Task Force) and the outcomes of those programs for young people with disabilities;

(8) evaluate whether a single governmental entity or program should be established to provide computer and electronic accommodations for Federal employees with disabilities;

(9) consult with the President's Committee on Mental Retardation on policies to increase the employment of people with mental retardation and cognitive disabilities; and

(10) recommend to the President any additional steps that can be taken to advance the employment of adults with disabilities, including legislative proposals, regulatory changes, and program and budget initiatives.

(d)(1) The members of the Task Force shall make the activities and initiatives set forth in this order a high priority within their respective agencies within the levels provided in the President's budget.

(2) The Task Force shall issue its first report to the President by November 15, 1998. The Task Force shall issue a report to the President on November 15, 1999, November 15, 2000, and a final report on July 26, 2002, the 10th anniversary of the initial implementation of the employment provisions of the Americans with Disabilities Act of 1990 [42 U.S.C. 12101 et seq.]. The reports shall describe the actions taken by, and progress of, each member of the Task Force in carrying out this order. The Task Force shall terminate 30 days after submitting its final report.

(e) As used herein, an adult with a disability is a person with a physical or mental impairment that substantially limits at least one major life activity.

SEC. 2. Specific activities by Task Force members and other agencies.

(a) To ensure that the Federal Government is a model employer of adults with disabilities, by November 15, 1998, the Office of Personnel Management, the Department of Labor, and the Equal Employment Opportunity Commission shall submit to the Task Force a review of Federal Government personnel laws, regulations, and policies and, as appropriate, shall recommend or implement changes necessary to improve Federal employment policy for adults with disabilities. This review shall include personnel practices and actions such as: hiring, promotion, benefits, retirement, workers' compensation, retention, accessible facilities, job accommodations, layoffs, and reductions in force.

(b) The Departments of Justice, Labor, Education, and Health and Human Services shall report to the Task Force by November 15, 1998, on their work with the States and others to ensure that the Personal Responsibility and Work Opportunity Reconciliation Act [probably means the Personal Responsibility and Work Opportunity Reconciliation Act of 1996, Pub. L. 104–193, see Tables for classification] is carried out in accordance with section 504 of the Rehabilitation Act of 1973 [29 U.S.C. 794], as amended, and the Americans with Disabilities Act of 1990 [42 U.S.C. 12101 et seq.], so that individuals with disabilities and their families can realize the full promise of welfare reform by having an equal opportunity for employment.

(c) The Departments of Education, Labor, Commerce, and Health and Human Services, the Small Business Administration, and the President's Committee on Employment of People with Disabilities shall work together and report to the Task Force by November 15,

1998, on their work to develop small business and entrepreneurial opportunities for adults with disabilities and strategies for assisting low-income adults, including those with disabilities[,] to create small businesses and micro-enterprises. These same agencies, in consultation with the Committee for Purchase from People Who Are Blind or Severely Disabled, shall assess the impact of the Randolph-Sheppard Act [20 U.S.C. 107 et seq.] vending program and the Javits-Wagner-O'Day Act [41 U.S.C. 46 et seq.] on employment and small business opportunities for people with disabilities.

(d) The Departments of Transportation and Housing and Urban Development shall report to the Task Force by November 15, 1998, on their examination of their programs to see if they can be used to create new work incentives and to remove barriers to work for adults with disabilities.

(e) The Departments of Justice, Education, and Labor, the Equal Employment Opportunity Commission, and the Social Security Administration shall work together and report to the Task Force by November 15, 1998, on their work to propose remedies to the prevention of people with disabilities from successfully exercising their employment rights under the Americans with Disabilities Act of 1990 [42 U.S.C. 12101 et seq.] because of the receipt of monetary benefits based on their disability and lack of gainful employment.

(f) The Bureau of Labor Statistics of the Department of Labor and the Census Bureau of the Department of Commerce, in cooperation with the Departments of Education and Health and Human Services, the National Council on Disability, and the President's Committee on Employment of People with Disabilities shall design and implement a statistically reliable and accurate method to measure the employment rate of adults with disabilities as soon as possible, but no later than the date of termination of the Task Force. Data derived from this methodology shall be published on as frequent a basis as possible.

(g) All executive agencies that are not members of the Task Force shall: (1) coordinate and cooperate with the Task Force; and (2) review their programs and policies to ensure that they are being conducted and delivered in a manner that facilitates and promotes the employment of adults with disabilities. Each agency shall file a report with the Task Force on the results of its review on November 15, 1998.

(h) To improve employment outcomes for persons with disabilities by addressing, among other things, the education, transition, employment, health and rehabilitation, and independent living issues affecting young people with disabilities, executive departments and agencies shall coordinate and cooperate with the Task Force to: (1) strengthen interagency research, demonstration, and training activities relating to young people with disabilities; (2) create a public awareness campaign focused on access to equal opportunity for young people with disabilities; (3) promote the views of young people with disabilities through collaboration with the Youth Councils authorized under the Workforce Investment Act of 1998 [Pub. L. 105–220, see Short Title note set out under section 9201 of Title 20, Education]; (4) increase access to and utilization of health insurance and health care for young people with disabilities through the formalization of the Federal Healthy and Ready to Work Interagency Council; (5) increase participation by young people with disabilities in postsecondary education and training programs; and (6) create a nationally representative Youth Advisory Council, to be funded and chaired by the Department of Labor, to advise the Task Force in conducting these and other appropriate activities.

SEC. 3. Cooperation. All efforts taken by executive departments and agencies under sections 1 and 2 of this order shall, as appropriate, further partnerships and cooperation with public and private sector employers, organizations that represent people with disabilities, organized labor, veteran service organizations, and State and local governments whenever such partnerships and cooperation are possible and would promote the employment and gainful economic activities of individuals with disabilities.

SEC. 4. Judicial Review. This order does not create any right or benefit, substantive or procedural, enforceable at law by a party against the United States, its agencies, its officers, or any person.

WILLIAM J. CLINTON.

EX. ORD. NO. 13187. THE PRESIDENT'S DISABILITY EMPLOYMENT PARTNERSHIP BOARD

Ex. Ord. No. 13187, Jan. 10, 2001, 66 F.R. 3857, provided:

By the authority vested in me as President by the Constitution and the laws of the United States of America, including the Federal Advisory Committee Act, as amended (5 U.S.C. App.), and in order to promote the employment of people with disabilities, it is hereby ordered as follows:

SECTION 1. *Establishment and Composition of the Board.* (a) There is hereby established the President's Disability Employment Partnership Board (Board).

(b) The Board shall be composed of not more than 15 members who shall be appointed by the President for terms of 2 years. The membership shall include individuals who are representatives of business (including small business), labor organizations, State or local government, disabled veterans, people with disabilities, organizations serving people with disabilities, and researchers or academicians focusing on issues relating to the employment of people with disabilities, and may include other individuals representing entities involved in issues relating to the employment of people with disabilities as the President finds appropriate.

(c) The President shall designate a Chairperson from among the members of the Board to serve a term of two years.

(d) Members and the Chairperson may be reappointed for subsequent terms and may continue to serve until their successors have been appointed.

SEC. 2. *Functions.* (a) The Board shall provide advice and information to the President, the Vice President, the Secretary of Labor, and other appropriate Federal officials with respect to facilitating the employment of people with disabilities, and shall assist in other activities that promote the formation of public-private partnerships, the use of economic incentives, the provision of technical assistance regarding entrepreneurship, and other actions that may enhance employment opportunities for people with disabilities.

(b) In carrying out paragraph (a) of this section, the Board shall:

(i) develop and submit to the Office of Disability Employment Policy in the Department of Labor a comprehensive written plan for joint public-private efforts to promote employment opportunities for people with disabilities and improve their access to financial institutions and commercial and business enterprises;

(ii) identify strategies that may be used by employers, labor unions, national and international organizations, and Federal, State, and local officials to increase employment opportunities for people with disabilities; and

(iii) coordinate with the Office of Disability Employment Policy in the Department of Labor in promoting the collaborative use of public and private resources to assist people with disabilities in forming and expanding small business concerns and in enhancing their access to Federal procurement and other relevant business opportunities. Public resources include those of the Department of Labor, the Small Business Administration, the Department of Commerce, the Department of Education, the Department of Defense, the Department of Treasury, the Department of Veterans Affairs, the Federal Communications Commission, and of executive departments and agency offices responsible for small, disadvantaged businesses utilization.

(c) The Board shall submit annual written reports to the President, who may apprise the Congress and other interested organizations and individuals on its activities, progress, and problems relating to maximizing employment opportunities for people with disabilities.

(d) The Chairperson of the Board shall serve as a member and Vice Chair of the National Task Force on Employment of Adults with Disabilities established under Executive Order 13078 of March 13, 1998 [set out above].

SEC. 3. *Administration.* (a) The Board shall meet when called by the Chairperson, at a time and place designated by the Chairperson. The Chairperson shall call at least two meetings per calendar year. The Chairperson may form subcommittees or working groups within the Board to address particular matters.

(b) The Chairperson may from time to time prescribe such rules, procedures, and policies relating to the activities of the Board as are not inconsistent with law or with the provisions of this order.

(c) Members of the Board shall serve without compensation but shall be allowed travel expenses, including per diem in lieu of subsistence, as authorized by law for persons serving intermittently in Federal service (5 U.S.C. 5701-5707).

(d) The Department of Labor shall provide funding and appropriate support to assist the Board in carrying out the activities described in section 2 of this order, including necessary office space, equipment, supplies, services, and staff. The functions of the President under the Federal Advisory Committee Act, as amended, except that of reporting to the Congress, that are applicable to the Commission, shall be performed by the Department of Labor in accordance with guidelines that have been issued by the Administrator of General Services.

(e) The heads of executive departments and agencies shall, to the extent permitted by law, provide the Board such information as it may need for purposes of carrying out the functions described in section 2 of this order.

SEC. 4. *Prior Orders and Transition.* (a) Executive Order 12640 of May 10, 1988, as amended, relating to the establishment of the President's Committee on Employment of People with Disabilities, is hereby revoked. The employees, records, property, and funds of the Committee shall become the employees, records, property, and funds of the Department of Labor.

(b) Executive Order 13078 of March 13, 1998 [set out above], is amended in sections 1(a) and (b) by striking "Chair of the President's Committee on Employment of People with Disabilities" and inserting "Chairperson of the President's Disability Employment Partnership Board."

WILLIAM J. CLINTON.

§ 702. Rehabilitation Services Administration

(a) There is established in the Office of the Secretary a Rehabilitation Services Administration which shall be headed by a Commissioner (hereinafter in this chapter referred to as the "Commissioner") appointed by the President by and with the advice and consent of the Senate. Except for subchapters IV and V of this chapter and as otherwise specifically provided in this chapter, such Administration shall be the principal agency, and the Commissioner shall be the principal officer, of such Department for carrying out this chapter. The Commissioner shall be an individual with substantial experience in rehabilitation and in rehabilitation program management. In the performance of the functions of the office, the Commissioner shall be directly responsible to the Secretary or to the Under Secretary or an appropriate Assistant Secretary of such Department, as designated by the Secretary. The functions of the Commissioner shall not be delegated to any officer not directly responsible, both with respect to program operation and administration, to the Commissioner. Any reference in this chapter to duties to be carried out by the Commissioner shall be considered to be a reference to duties to be carried out by the Secretary acting through the Commissioner. In carrying out any of the functions of the office under this chapter, the Commissioner shall be guided by general policies of the National Council on Disability established under subchapter IV of this chapter.

(b) The Secretary shall take whatever action is necessary to ensure that funds appropriated pursuant to this chapter are expended only for the programs, personnel, and administration of programs carried out under this chapter.

(Pub. L. 93–112, § 3, as added Pub. L. 105–220, title IV, § 403, Aug. 7, 1998, 112 Stat. 1096.)

PRIOR PROVISIONS

A prior section 702, Pub. L. 93–112, § 3, Sept. 26, 1973, 87 Stat. 357; Pub. L. 93–516, title I, § 101(a), Dec. 7, 1974, 88 Stat. 1617; Pub. L. 93–651, title I, § 101(a), Nov. 21, 1974, 89 Stat. 2–3; Pub. L. 95–602, title I, § 122(a)(2), (3), Nov. 6, 1978, 92 Stat. 2984; Pub. L. 99–506, title I, § 102, title X, § 1001(a)(1), Oct. 21, 1986, 100 Stat. 1808, 1841; Pub. L. 100–630, title II, § 201(a), Nov. 7, 1988, 102 Stat. 3303, related to the Rehabilitation Services Administration, prior to repeal by Pub. L. 105–220, title IV, § 403, Aug. 7, 1998, 112 Stat. 1093.

ADDITIONAL PERSONNEL FOR OFFICE FOR THE BLIND AND VISUALLY HANDICAPPED

Pub. L. 93–516, title II, § 208(a), Dec. 7, 1974, 88 Stat. 1629, provided that: "The Secretary of Health, Education, and Welfare [now Secretary of Education] is directed to assign to the Office for the Blind and Visually Handicapped of the Rehabilitation Services Administration of the Department of Health, Education, and Welfare [now Department of Education] ten additional full-time personnel (or their equivalent), five of whom shall be supportive personnel, to carry out duties related to the administration of the Randolph-Sheppard Act [section 107 et seq. of Title 20, Education]."

An identical provision is contained in Pub. L. 93–651, title II, § 208(a), Nov. 21, 1974, 89 Stat. 2–14.

PREFERENCE TO BLIND IN SELECTING PERSONNEL

Pub. L. 93–516, title II, § 208(c), Dec. 7, 1974, 88 Stat. 1629, provided that: "In selecting personnel to fill any position under this section [authorizing assignment of 11 additional full-time personnel to the Office for the Blind and Visually Handicapped of the Rehabilitation Service Administration of the Department of Health, Education, and Welfare under subsecs. (a) and (b) of Pub. L. 93–516], the Secretary of Health, Education, and Welfare [now Secretary of Education] shall give preference to blind individuals."

An identical provision is contained in Pub. L. 93–651, title II, § 208(c), Nov. 21, 1974, 89 Stat. 2–14.

§ 703. Advance funding

(a) For the purpose of affording adequate notice of funding available under this chapter, appropriations under this chapter are authorized to be included in the appropriation Act for the fiscal year preceding the fiscal year for which they are available for obligation.

(b) In order to effect a transition to the advance funding method of timing appropriation action, the authority provided by subsection (a) of this section shall apply notwithstanding that its initial application will result in the enactment in the same year (whether in the same appropriation Act or otherwise) of two separate appropriations, one for the then current fiscal year and one for the succeeding fiscal year.

(Pub. L. 93–112, § 4, as added Pub. L. 105–220, title IV, § 403, Aug. 7, 1998, 112 Stat. 1097.)

PRIOR PROVISIONS

A prior section 703, Pub. L. 93–112, § 4, Sept. 26, 1973, 87 Stat. 358, related to advance funding, prior to repeal by Pub. L. 105–220, title IV, § 403, Aug. 7, 1998, 112 Stat. 1093.

§ 704. Joint funding

Pursuant to regulations prescribed by the President, and to the extent consistent with the other provisions of this chapter, where funds are provided for a single project by more than one Federal agency to an agency or organization assisted under this chapter, the Federal agency principally involved may be designated to act for all in administering the funds provided, and, in such cases, a single non-Federal share requirement may be established according to the proportion of funds advanced by each agency. When the principal agency involved is the Rehabilitation Services Administration, it may waive any grant or contract requirement (as defined by such regulations) under or pursuant to any law other than this chapter, which requirement is inconsistent with the similar requirements of the administering agency under or pursuant to this chapter.

(Pub. L. 93–112, § 5, as added Pub. L. 105–220, title IV, § 403, Aug. 7, 1998, 112 Stat. 1097.)

PRIOR PROVISIONS

A prior section 704, Pub. L. 93–112, § 5, Sept. 26, 1973, 87 Stat. 359, related to joint funding, prior to repeal by Pub. L. 105–220, title IV, § 403, Aug. 7, 1998, 112 Stat. 1093.

DELEGATION OF FUNCTIONS

Authority of the President under this section delegated to Director of Office of Management and Budget by section 1 of Ex. Ord. No. 11893, Dec. 31, 1975, 41 F.R. 1040, set out as a note under section 7103 of Title 31, Money and Finance.

§ 705. Definitions

For the purposes of this chapter:

(1) Administrative costs

The term "administrative costs" means expenditures incurred in the performance of administrative functions under the vocational rehabilitation program carried out under subchapter I of this chapter, including expenses related to program planning, development, monitoring, and evaluation, including expenses for—

(A) quality assurance;

(B) budgeting, accounting, financial management, information systems, and related data processing;

(C) providing information about the program to the public;

(D) technical assistance and support services to other State agencies, private nonprofit organizations, and businesses and industries, except for technical assistance and support services described in section 723(b)(5) of this title;

(E) the State Rehabilitation Council and other advisory committees;

(F) professional organization membership dues for designated State unit employees;

(G) the removal of architectural barriers in State vocational rehabilitation agency offices and State operated rehabilitation facilities;

(H) operating and maintaining designated State unit facilities, equipment, and grounds;

(I) supplies;

(J) administration of the comprehensive system of personnel development described in section 721(a)(7) of this title, including personnel administration, administration of affirmative action plans, and training and staff development;

(K) administrative salaries, including clerical and other support staff salaries, in support of these administrative functions;

(L) travel costs related to carrying out the program, other than travel costs related to the provision of services;

(M) costs incurred in conducting reviews of rehabilitation counselor or coordinator determinations under section 722(c) of this title; and

(N) legal expenses required in the administration of the program.

(2) Assessment for determining eligibility and vocational rehabilitation needs

The term "assessment for determining eligibility and vocational rehabilitation needs" means, as appropriate in each case—

(A)(i) a review of existing data—

(I) to determine whether an individual is eligible for vocational rehabilitation services; and

(II) to assign priority for an order of selection described in section 721(a)(5)(A) of this title in the States that use an order of selection pursuant to section 721(a)(5)(A) of this title; and

(ii) to the extent necessary, the provision of appropriate assessment activities to obtain necessary additional data to make such determination and assignment;

(B) to the extent additional data is necessary to make a determination of the employment outcomes, and the nature and scope of vocational rehabilitation services, to be included in the individualized plan for employment of an eligible individual, a comprehensive assessment to determine the unique strengths, resources, priorities, concerns, abilities, capabilities, interests, and informed choice, including the need for supported employment, of the eligible individual, which comprehensive assessment—

(i) is limited to information that is necessary to identify the rehabilitation needs of the individual and to develop the individualized plan for employment of the eligible individual;

(ii) uses, as a primary source of such information, to the maximum extent possible and appropriate and in accordance with confidentiality requirements—

(I) existing information obtained for the purposes of determining the eligibility of the individual and assigning priority for an order of selection described in section 721(a)(5)(A) of this title for the individual; and

(II) such information as can be provided by the individual and, where appropriate, by the family of the individual;

(iii) may include, to the degree needed to make such a determination, an assessment of the personality, interests, interpersonal skills, intelligence and related functional capacities, educational achievements, work experience, vocational aptitudes, personal and social adjustments, and employment opportunities of the individual, and the medical, psychiatric, psychological, and other pertinent vocational, educational, cultural, social, recreational, and environmental factors, that affect the employment and rehabilitation needs of the individual; and

(iv) may include, to the degree needed, an appraisal of the patterns of work behavior of the individual and services needed for the individual to acquire occupational skills, and to develop work attitudes, work habits, work tolerance, and social and behavior patterns necessary for successful job performance, including the utilization of work in real job situations to assess and develop the capacities of the individual to perform adequately in a work environment;

(C) referral, for the provision of rehabilitation technology services to the individual, to assess and develop the capacities of the individual to perform in a work environment; and

(D) an exploration of the individual's abilities, capabilities, and capacity to perform in work situations, which shall be assessed periodically during trial work experiences, including experiences in which the individual is provided appropriate supports and training.

(3) Assistive technology device

The term "assistive technology device" has the meaning given such term in section 3002 of this title, except that the reference in such section to the term "individuals with disabilities" shall be deemed to mean more than one individual with a disability as defined in paragraph (20)(A).

(4) Assistive technology service

The term "assistive technology service" has the meaning given such term in section 3002 of this title, except that the reference in such section—

(A) to the term "individual with a disability" shall be deemed to mean an individual with a disability, as defined in paragraph (20)(A); and

(B) to the term "individuals with disabilities" shall be deemed to mean more than one such individual.

(5) Community rehabilitation program

The term "community rehabilitation program" means a program that provides directly or facilitates the provision of vocational rehabilitation services to individuals with disabilities, and that provides, singly or in combination, for an individual with a disability to enable the individual to maximize opportunities for employment, including career advancement—

(A) medical, psychiatric, psychological, social, and vocational services that are provided under one management;

(B) testing, fitting, or training in the use of prosthetic and orthotic devices;

(C) recreational therapy;

(D) physical and occupational therapy;

(E) speech, language, and hearing therapy;

(F) psychiatric, psychological, and social services, including positive behavior management;

(G) assessment for determining eligibility and vocational rehabilitation needs;

(H) rehabilitation technology;

(I) job development, placement, and retention services;

(J) evaluation or control of specific disabilities;

(K) orientation and mobility services for individuals who are blind;

(L) extended employment;

(M) psychosocial rehabilitation services;

(N) supported employment services and extended services;

(O) services to family members when necessary to the vocational rehabilitation of the individual;

(P) personal assistance services; or

(Q) services similar to the services described in one of subparagraphs (A) through (P).

(6) Construction; cost of construction

(A) Construction

The term "construction" means—

(i) the construction of new buildings;

(ii) the acquisition, expansion, remodeling, alteration, and renovation of existing buildings; and

(iii) initial equipment of buildings described in clauses (i) and (ii).

(B) Cost of construction

The term "cost of construction" includes architects' fees and the cost of acquisition of land in connection with construction but does not include the cost of offsite improvements.

(7) Repealed. Pub. L. 105–277, div. A, §101(f) [title VIII, §402(c)(1)(B)], Oct. 21, 1998, 112 Stat. 2681–337, 2681–415

(8) Designated State agency; designated State unit

(A) Designated State agency

The term "designated State agency" means an agency designated under section 721(a)(2)(A) of this title.

(B) Designated State unit

The term "designated State unit" means—

(i) any State agency unit required under section 721(a)(2)(B)(ii) of this title; or

(ii) in cases in which no such unit is so required, the State agency described in section 721(a)(2)(B)(i) of this title.

(9) Disability

The term "disability" means—

(A) except as otherwise provided in subparagraph (B), a physical or mental impairment that constitutes or results in a substantial impediment to employment; or

(B) for purposes of sections 701, 711, and 712 of this title, and subchapters II, IV, V, and VII of this chapter, the meaning given it in section 12102 of title 42.

(10) Drug and illegal use of drugs

(A) Drug

The term "drug" means a controlled substance, as defined in schedules I through V of section 202 of the Controlled Substances Act (21 U.S.C. 812).

(B) Illegal use of drugs

The term "illegal use of drugs" means the use of drugs, the possession or distribution of which is unlawful under the Controlled Substances Act [21 U.S.C. 801 et seq.]. Such term does not include the use of a drug taken under supervision by a licensed health care professional, or other uses authorized by the Controlled Substances Act or other provisions of Federal law.

(11) Employment outcome

The term "employment outcome" means, with respect to an individual—

(A) entering or retaining full-time or, if appropriate, part-time competitive employment in the integrated labor market;

(B) satisfying the vocational outcome of supported employment; or

(C) satisfying any other vocational outcome the Secretary may determine to be appropriate (including satisfying the vocational outcome of self-employment, telecommuting, or business ownership),

in a manner consistent with this chapter.

(12) Establishment of a community rehabilitation program

The term "establishment of a community rehabilitation program" includes the acquisition, expansion, remodeling, or alteration of existing buildings necessary to adapt them to community rehabilitation program purposes or to increase their effectiveness for such purposes (subject, however, to such limitations as the Secretary may determine, in accordance with regulations the Secretary shall prescribe, in order to prevent impairment of the objectives of, or duplication of, other Federal laws providing Federal assistance in the construction of facilities for community rehabilitation programs), and may include such additional equipment and staffing as the Commissioner considers appropriate.

(13) Extended services

The term "extended services" means ongoing support services and other appropriate services, needed to support and maintain an individual with a most significant disability in supported employment, that—

(A) are provided singly or in combination and are organized and made available in such a way as to assist an eligible individual in maintaining supported employment;

(B) are based on a determination of the needs of an eligible individual, as specified in an individualized plan for employment; and

(C) are provided by a State agency, a nonprofit private organization, employer, or any other appropriate resource, after an individual has made the transition from support provided by the designated State unit.

(14) Federal share

(A) In general

Subject to subparagraph (B), the term "Federal share" means 78.7 percent.

(B) Exception

The term "Federal share" means the share specifically set forth in section 731(a)(3) of this title, except that with respect to payments pursuant to part B of subchapter I of this chapter to any State that are used to meet the costs of construction of those rehabilitation facilities identified in section 723(b)(2) of this title in such State, the Federal share shall be the percentages determined in accordance with the provisions of section 731(a)(3) of this title applicable with respect to the State.

(C) Relationship to expenditures by a political subdivision

For the purpose of determining the non-Federal share with respect to a State, expenditures by a political subdivision thereof or by a local agency shall be regarded as expenditures by such State, subject to such limitations and conditions as the Secretary shall by regulation prescribe.

(15) Governor

The term "Governor" means a chief executive officer of a State.

(16) Impartial hearing officer

(A) In general

The term "impartial hearing officer" means an individual—

(i) who is not an employee of a public agency (other than an administrative law judge, hearing examiner, or employee of an institution of higher education);

(ii) who is not a member of the State Rehabilitation Council described in section 725 of this title;

(iii) who has not been involved previously in the vocational rehabilitation of the applicant or eligible individual;

(iv) who has knowledge of the delivery of vocational rehabilitation services, the State plan under section 721 of this title, and the Federal and State rules governing the provision of such services and training with respect to the performance of official duties; and

(v) who has no personal or financial interest that would be in conflict with the objectivity of the individual.

(B) Construction

An individual shall not be considered to be an employee of a public agency for purposes of subparagraph (A)(i) solely because the individual is paid by the agency to serve as a hearing officer.

(17) Independent living core services

The term "independent living core services" means—

(A) information and referral services;

(B) independent living skills training;

(C) peer counseling (including cross-disability peer counseling); and

(D) individual and systems advocacy.

(18) Independent living services

The term "independent living services" includes—

(A) independent living core services; and

(B)(i) counseling services, including psychological, psychotherapeutic, and related services;

(ii) services related to securing housing or shelter, including services related to community group living, and supportive of the purposes of this chapter and of the subchapters of this chapter, and adaptive housing services (including appropriate accommodations to and modifications of any space used to serve, or occupied by, individuals with disabilities);

(iii) rehabilitation technology;

(iv) mobility training;

(v) services and training for individuals with cognitive and sensory disabilities, including life skills training, and interpreter and reader services;

(vi) personal assistance services, including attendant care and the training of personnel providing such services;

(vii) surveys, directories, and other activities to identify appropriate housing, recreation opportunities, and accessible transportation, and other support services;

(viii) consumer information programs on rehabilitation and independent living services available under this chapter, especially for minorities and other individuals with disabilities who have traditionally been unserved or underserved by programs under this chapter;

(ix) education and training necessary for living in a community and participating in community activities;

(x) supported living;

(xi) transportation, including referral and assistance for such transportation and training in the use of public transportation vehicles and systems;

(xii) physical rehabilitation;

(xiii) therapeutic treatment;

(xiv) provision of needed prostheses and other appliances and devices;

(xv) individual and group social and recreational services;

(xvi) training to develop skills specifically designed for youths who are individuals with disabilities to promote self-awareness and esteem, develop advocacy and self-empowerment skills, and explore career options;

(xvii) services for children;

(xviii) services under other Federal, State, or local programs designed to provide resources, training, counseling, or other assistance, of substantial benefit in enhancing the independence, productivity, and quality of life of individuals with disabilities;

(xix) appropriate preventive services to decrease the need of individuals assisted under this chapter for similar services in the future;

(xx) community awareness programs to enhance the understanding and integration into society of individuals with disabilities; and

(xxi) such other services as may be necessary and not inconsistent with the provisions of this chapter.

(19) Indian; American Indian; Indian American; Indian tribe

(A) In general

The terms "Indian", "American Indian", and "Indian American" mean an individual who is a member of an Indian tribe.

(B) Indian tribe

The term "Indian tribe" means any Federal or State Indian tribe, band, rancheria, pueblo, colony, or community, including any Alaskan native village or regional village corporation (as defined in or established pursuant to the Alaska Native Claims Settlement Act [43 U.S.C. 1601 et seq.]).

(20) Individual with a disability

(A) In general

Except as otherwise provided in subparagraph (B), the term "individual with a disability" means any individual who—

(i) has a physical or mental impairment which for such individual constitutes or results in a substantial impediment to employment; and

(ii) can benefit in terms of an employment outcome from vocational rehabilitation services provided pursuant to subchapter I, III, or VI of this chapter.

(B) Certain programs; limitations on major life activities

Subject to subparagraphs (C), (D), (E), and (F), the term "individual with a disability" means, for purposes of sections 701, 711, and 712 of this title, and subchapters II, IV, V, and VII of this chapter, any person who has a disability as defined in section 12102 of title 42.

(C) Rights and advocacy provisions

(i) In general; exclusion of individuals engaging in drug use

For purposes of subchapter V of this chapter, the term "individual with a disability" does not include an individual who is currently engaging in the illegal use of drugs, when a covered entity acts on the basis of such use.

(ii) Exception for individuals no longer engaging in drug use

Nothing in clause (i) shall be construed to exclude as an individual with a disability an individual who—

(I) has successfully completed a supervised drug rehabilitation program and is no longer engaging in the illegal use of drugs, or has otherwise been rehabilitated successfully and is no longer engaging in such use;

(II) is participating in a supervised rehabilitation program and is no longer engaging in such use; or

(III) is erroneously regarded as engaging in such use, but is not engaging in such use;

except that it shall not be a violation of this chapter for a covered entity to adopt or administer reasonable policies or procedures, including but not limited to drug testing, designed to ensure that an individual described in subclause (I) or (II) is no longer engaging in the illegal use of drugs.

(iii) Exclusion for certain services

Notwithstanding clause (i), for purposes of programs and activities providing health services and services provided under subchapters I, II, and III of this chapter, an individual shall not be excluded from the benefits of such programs or activities on the basis of his or her current illegal use of drugs if he or she is otherwise entitled to such services.

(iv) Disciplinary action

For purposes of programs and activities providing educational services, local educational agencies may take disciplinary action pertaining to the use or possession of illegal drugs or alcohol against any student who is an individual with a disability and who currently is engaging in the illegal use of drugs or in the use of alcohol to the same extent that such disciplinary action is taken against students who are not individuals with disabilities. Furthermore, the due process procedures at section 104.36 of title 34, Code of Federal Regulations (or any corresponding similar regulation or ruling) shall not apply to such disciplinary actions.

(v) Employment; exclusion of alcoholics

For purposes of sections 793 and 794 of this title as such sections relate to employment, the term "individual with a disability" does not include any individual who is an alcoholic whose current use of alcohol prevents such individual from performing the duties of the job in question or whose employment, by reason of such current alcohol abuse, would constitute a direct threat to property or the safety of others.

(D) Employment; exclusion of individuals with certain diseases or infections

For the purposes of sections 793 and 794 of this title, as such sections relate to employment, such term does not include an individual who has a currently contagious disease or infection and who, by reason of such disease or infection, would constitute a direct threat to the health or safety of other individuals or who, by reason of the currently contagious disease or infection, is unable to perform the duties of the job.

(E) Rights provisions; exclusion of individuals on basis of homosexuality or bisexuality

For the purposes of sections 791, 793, and 794 of this title—

(i) for purposes of the application of subparagraph (B) to such sections, the term "impairment" does not include homosexuality or bisexuality; and

(ii) therefore the term "individual with a disability" does not include an individual on the basis of homosexuality or bisexuality.

(F) Rights provisions; exclusion of individuals on basis of certain disorders

For the purposes of sections 791, 793, and 794 of this title, the term "individual with a disability" does not include an individual on the basis of—

(i) transvestism, transsexualism, pedophilia, exhibitionism, voyeurism, gender identity disorders not resulting from physical impairments, or other sexual behavior disorders;

(ii) compulsive gambling, kleptomania, or pyromania; or

(iii) psychoactive substance use disorders resulting from current illegal use of drugs.

(G) Individuals with disabilities

The term "individuals with disabilities" means more than one individual with a disability.

(21) Individual with a significant disability

(A) In general

Except as provided in subparagraph (B) or (C), the term "individual with a significant disability" means an individual with a disability—

(i) who has a severe physical or mental impairment which seriously limits one or more functional capacities (such as mobility, communication, self-care, self-direction, interpersonal skills, work tolerance, or work skills) in terms of an employment outcome;

(ii) whose vocational rehabilitation can be expected to require multiple vocational rehabilitation services over an extended period of time; and

(iii) who has one or more physical or mental disabilities resulting from amputation, arthritis, autism, blindness, burn injury, cancer, cerebral palsy, cystic fibrosis, deafness, head injury, heart disease, hemiplegia, hemophilia, respiratory or pulmonary dysfunction, mental retardation, mental illness, multiple sclerosis, muscular dystrophy, musculo-skeletal disorders, neurological disorders (including stroke and epilepsy), paraplegia, quadriplegia, and other spinal cord conditions, sickle cell anemia, specific learning disability, end-stage renal disease, or another disability or combination of disabilities determined on the basis of an assessment for determining eligibility and vocational rehabilitation needs described in subparagraphs (A) and (B) of paragraph (2) to cause comparable substantial functional limitation.

(B) Independent living services and centers for independent living

For purposes of subchapter VII of this chapter, the term "individual with a significant disability" means an individual with a severe physical or mental impairment whose ability to function independently in the family or community or whose ability to obtain, maintain, or advance in employment is substantially limited and for whom the delivery of independent living services will improve the ability to function, continue functioning, or move toward functioning independently in the family or community or to continue in employment, respectively.

(C) Research and training

For purposes of subchapter II of this chapter, the term "individual with a significant disability" includes an individual described in subparagraph (A) or (B).

(D) Individuals with significant disabilities

The term "individuals with significant disabilities" means more than one individual with a significant disability.

(E) Individual with a most significant disability

(i) In general

The term "individual with a most significant disability", used with respect to an individual in a State, means an individual with a significant disability who meets criteria established by the State under section 721(a)(5)(C) of this title.

(ii) Individuals with the most significant disabilities

The term "individuals with the most significant disabilities" means more than one individual with a most significant disability.

(22) Individual's representative; applicant's representative

The terms "individual's representative" and "applicant's representative" mean a parent, a family member, a guardian, an advocate, or an authorized representative of an individual or applicant, respectively.

(23) Institution of higher education

The term "institution of higher education" has the meaning given the term in section 1001 of title 20.

(24) Local agency

The term "local agency" means an agency of a unit of general local government or of an Indian tribe (or combination of such units or tribes) which has an agreement with the designated State agency to conduct a vocational rehabilitation program under the supervision of such State agency in accordance with the State plan approved under section 721 of this title. Nothing in the preceding sentence of this paragraph or in section 721 of this title shall be construed to prevent the local agency from arranging to utilize another local public or nonprofit agency to provide vocational rehabilitation services if such an arrangement is made part of the agreement specified in this paragraph.

(25) Local workforce investment board

The term "local workforce investment board" means a local workforce investment board established under section 117 of the Workforce Investment Act of 1998 [29 U.S.C. 2832].

(26) Nonprofit

The term "nonprofit", when used with respect to a community rehabilitation program, means a community rehabilitation program carried out by a corporation or association, no part of the net earnings of which inures, or may lawfully inure, to the benefit of any private shareholder or individual and the income of which is exempt from taxation under section 501(c)(3) of title 26.

(27) Ongoing support services

The term "ongoing support services" means services—

(A) provided to individuals with the most significant disabilities;

(B) provided, at a minimum, twice monthly—

(i) to make an assessment, regarding the employment situation, at the worksite of each such individual in supported employment, or, under special circumstances, especially at the request of the client, off site; and

(ii) based on the assessment, to provide for the coordination or provision of specific intensive services, at or away from the worksite, that are needed to maintain employment stability; and

(C) consisting of—

(i) a particularized assessment supplementary to the comprehensive assessment described in paragraph (2)(B);

(ii) the provision of skilled job trainers who accompany the individual for intensive job skill training at the worksite;

(iii) job development, job retention, and placement services;

(iv) social skills training;

(v) regular observation or supervision of the individual;

(vi) followup services such as regular contact with the employers, the individuals, the individuals' representatives, and other appropriate individuals, in order to reinforce and stabilize the job placement;

(vii) facilitation of natural supports at the worksite;

(viii) any other service identified in section 723 of this title; or

(ix) a service similar to another service described in this subparagraph.

(28) Personal assistance services

The term "personal assistance services" means a range of services, provided by one or more persons, designed to assist an individual with a disability to perform daily living activities on or off the job that the individual would typically perform if the individual did not have a disability. Such services shall be designed to increase the individual's control in life and ability to perform everyday activities on or off the job.

(29) Public or nonprofit

The term "public or nonprofit", used with respect to an agency or organization, includes an Indian tribe.

(30) Rehabilitation technology

The term "rehabilitation technology" means the systematic application of technologies, engineering methodologies, or scientific principles to meet the needs of and address the barriers confronted by individuals with disabilities in areas which include education, rehabilitation, employment, transportation, independent living, and recreation. The term includes rehabilitation engineering, assistive technology devices, and assistive technology services.

(31) Secretary

The term "Secretary", except when the context otherwise requires, means the Secretary of Education.

(32) State

The term "State" includes, in addition to each of the several States of the United States, the District of Columbia, the Commonwealth of Puerto Rico, the United States Virgin Islands, Guam, American Samoa, and the Commonwealth of the Northern Mariana Islands.

(33) State workforce investment board

The term "State workforce investment board" means a State workforce investment board established under section 111 of the Workforce Investment Act of 1998 [29 U.S.C. 2821].

(34) Statewide workforce investment system

The term "statewide workforce investment system" means a system described in section 111(d)(2) of the Workforce Investment Act of 1998 [29 U.S.C. 2821(d)(2)].

(35) Supported employment

(A) In general

The term "supported employment" means competitive work in integrated work settings, or employment in integrated work settings in which individuals are working toward competitive work, consistent with the strengths, resources, priorities, concerns, abilities, capabilities, interests, and informed choice of the individuals, for individuals with the most significant disabilities—

(i)(I) for whom competitive employment has not traditionally occurred; or

(II) for whom competitive employment has been interrupted or intermittent as a result of a significant disability; and

(ii) who, because of the nature and severity of their disability, need intensive supported employment services for the period, and any extension, described in paragraph (36)(C) and extended services after the transition described in paragraph (13)(C) in order to perform such work.

(B) Certain transitional employment

Such term includes transitional employment for persons who are individuals with the most significant disabilities due to mental illness.

(36) Supported employment services

The term "supported employment services" means ongoing support services and other appropriate services needed to support and maintain an individual with a most significant disability in supported employment, that—

(A) are provided singly or in combination and are organized and made available in such a way as to assist an eligible individual to achieve competitive employment;

(B) are based on a determination of the needs of an eligible individual, as specified in an individualized plan for employment; and

(C) are provided by the designated State unit for a period of time not to extend beyond 18 months, unless under special circumstances the eligible individual and the rehabilitation counselor or coordinator involved jointly agree to extend the time in order to achieve the employment outcome identified in the individualized plan for employment.

(37) Transition services

The term "transition services" means a coordinated set of activities for a student, designed within an outcome-oriented process, that promotes movement from school to post school activities, including postsecondary education, vocational training, integrated employment (including supported employment), continuing and adult education, adult services, independent living, or community participation. The coordinated set of activities shall be based upon the individual student's needs, taking into account the student's preferences and interests, and shall include instruction, community experiences, the development of employment and other post school adult living objectives, and, when appropriate, acquisition of daily living skills and functional vocational evaluation.

(38) Vocational rehabilitation services

The term "vocational rehabilitation services" means those services identified in section 723 of this title which are provided to individuals with disabilities under this chapter.

(39) Workforce investment activities

The term "workforce investment activities" means workforce investment activities, as defined in section 101 of the Workforce Investment Act of 1998 [29 U.S.C. 2801], that are carried out under that Act.

(Pub. L. 93–112, § 7, formerly § 6, as added Pub. L. 105–220, title IV, § 403, Aug. 7, 1998, 112 Stat. 1097; amended Pub. L. 105–244, title I, § 102(a)(9)(A), Oct. 7, 1998, 112 Stat. 1619; renumbered § 7 and amended Pub. L. 105–277, div. A, § 101(f) [title VIII, § 402(a)(1), (b)(3), (c)(1)], Oct. 21, 1998, 112 Stat. 2681–337, 2681–412, 2681–413, 2681–415; Pub. L. 105–394, title IV, § 402(a), Nov. 13, 1998, 112 Stat. 3661; Pub. L. 110–325, § 7, Sept. 25, 2008, 122 Stat. 3558.)

REFERENCES IN TEXT

The Controlled Substances Act, referred to in par. (10)(B), is title II of Pub. L. 91–513, Oct. 27, 1970, 84 Stat. 1242, as amended, which is classified principally to subchapter I (§ 801 et seq.) of chapter 13 of Title 21, Food and Drugs. For complete classification of this Act to the Code, see Short Title note set out under section 801 of Title 21 and Tables.

The Alaska Native Claims Settlement Act, referred to in par. (19)(B), is Pub. L. 92–203, Dec. 18, 1971, 85 Stat. 688, as amended, which is classified generally to chapter 33 (§ 1601 et seq.) of Title 43, Public Lands. For complete classification of this Act to the Code, see Short Title note set out under section 1601 of Title 43 and Tables.

The Workforce Investment Act of 1998, referred to in par. (39), is Pub. L. 105–220, Aug. 7, 1998, 112 Stat. 936, as amended. For complete classification of this Act to the Code, see Short Title note set out under section 9201 of Title 20, Education, and Tables.

PRIOR PROVISIONS

Provisions similar to this section were contained in section 706 of this title prior to repeal by Pub. L. 105–220.

A prior section 705, Pub. L. 93–112, § 6, Sept. 26, 1973, 87 Stat. 359; Pub. L. 99–506, title X, § 1001(a)(2), Oct. 21, 1986, 100 Stat. 1841; Pub. L. 100–630, title II, § 201(b), Nov. 7, 1988, 102 Stat. 3303; Pub. L. 102–569, title I, § 128(b)(1), Oct. 29, 1992, 106 Stat. 4388, related to consolidated rehabilitation plan, prior to repeal by Pub. L. 105–220, title IV, § 403, Aug. 7, 1998, 112 Stat. 1093.

A prior section 7 of Pub. L. 93–112 was renumbered section 8 and is classified to section 706 of this title.

Another prior section 7 of Pub. L. 93–112 was classified to section 706 of this title prior to repeal by Pub. L. 105–220.

AMENDMENTS

2008—Par. (9)(B). Pub. L. 110–325, § 7(1), substituted "the meaning given it in section 12102 of title 42" for "a physical or mental impairment that substantially limits one or more major life activities".

Par. (20)(B). Pub. L. 110–325, § 7(2), substituted "any person who has a disability as defined in section 12102 of title 42." for "any person who—

"(i) has a physical or mental impairment which substantially limits one or more of such person's major life activities;

"(ii) has a record of such an impairment; or

"(iii) is regarded as having such an impairment."

1998—Pub. L. 105–277, § 101(f) [title VIII, § 402(b)(3)], made technical amendment to section designation and catchline in the original and inserted par. (1) heading.

Par. (2)(B). Pub. L. 105–277, § 101(f) [title VIII, § 402(c)(1)(A)], substituted "nature" for "objectives, nature,".

Par. (3). Pub. L. 105–394, § 402(a)(1), which directed the amendment of section 6 of the Rehabilitation Act of 1973 by substituting "3002" for "2202(2)", was executed to this section, which is section 7 of that act, to reflect the probable intent of Congress and the renumbering of section 6 as 7 by Pub. L. 105–277, § 101(f) [title VIII, § 402(a)(1)].

Par. (4). Pub. L. 105–394, § 402(a)(2), which directed the amendment of section 6 of the Rehabilitation Act of 1973 by substituting "3002" for "2202(3)", was executed to this section, which is section 7 of that act, to reflect the probable intent of Congress and the renumbering of section 6 as 7 by Pub. L. 105–277, § 101(f) [title VIII, § 402(a)(1)].

Par. (7). Pub. L. 105–277, § 101(f) [title VIII, § 402(c)(1)(B)], struck out heading and text of par. (7). Text read as follows: "The term 'criminal act' means any crime, including an act, omission, or possession under the laws of the United States or a State or unit of general local government, which poses a substantial threat of personal injury, notwithstanding that by reason of age, insanity, or intoxication or otherwise the person engaging in the act, omission, or possession was legally incapable of committing a crime."

Par. (16)(A)(iii). Pub. L. 105–277, § 101(f) [title VIII, § 402(c)(1)(C)], substituted "eligible individual" for "client".

Par. (23). Pub. L. 105–244 substituted "section 1001 of title 20" for "section 1141(a) of title 20".

Par. (36)(C). Pub. L. 105–277, § 101(f) [title VIII, § 402(c)(1)(D)], substituted "employment outcome" for "rehabilitation objectives".

EFFECTIVE DATE OF 2008 AMENDMENT

Pub. L. 110–325, § 8, Sept. 25, 2008, 122 Stat. 3559, provided that: "This Act [enacting sections 12103 and 12205a of Title 42, The Public Health and Welfare, amending this section, former section 706 of this title, and sections 12101, 12102, 12111 to 12114, 12201, and 12206 to 12213 of Title 42, and enacting provisions set out as notes under section 12101 of Title 42] and the amendments made by this Act shall become effective on January 1, 2009."

EFFECTIVE DATE OF 1998 AMENDMENT

Amendment by Pub. L. 105–244 effective Oct. 1, 1998, except as otherwise provided in Pub. L. 105–244, see section 3 of Pub. L. 105–244, set out as a note under section 1001 of Title 20, Education.

§ 706. Allotment percentage

(a)(1) For purposes of section 730 of this title, the allotment percentage for any State shall be 100 per centum less that percentage which bears the same ratio to 50 per centum as the per capita income of such State bears to the per capita income of the United States, except that—

(A) the allotment percentage shall in no case be more than 75 per centum or less than 33⅓ per centum; and

(B) the allotment percentage for the District of Columbia, Puerto Rico, Guam, the Virgin Islands, American Samoa, and the Commonwealth of the Northern Mariana Islands shall be 75 per centum.

(2) The allotment percentages shall be promulgated by the Secretary between October 1 and December 31 of each even-numbered year, on the basis of the average of the per capita incomes of the States and of the United States for the three most recent consecutive years for which satisfactory data are available from the Department of Commerce. Such promulgation shall be conclusive for each of the 2 fiscal years in the period beginning on the October 1 next succeeding such promulgation.

(3) The term "United States" means (but only for purposes of this subsection) the 50 States and the District of Columbia.

(b) The population of the several States and of the United States shall be determined on the basis of the most recent data available, to be furnished by the Department of Commerce by October 1 of the year preceding the fiscal year for which funds are appropriated pursuant to statutory authorizations.

(Pub. L. 93–112, § 8, formerly § 7, as added Pub. L. 105–220, title IV, § 403, Aug. 7, 1998, 112 Stat. 1110; renumbered § 8, Pub. L. 105–277, div. A, § 101(f) [title VIII, § 402(a)(1)], Oct. 21, 1998, 112 Stat. 2681–337, 2681–412.)

PRIOR PROVISIONS

Provisions similar to this section were contained in section 707 of this title prior to repeal by Pub. L. 105–220.

A prior section 706, Pub. L. 93–112, § 7, Sept. 26, 1973, 87 Stat. 359; Pub. L. 93–516, title I, § 111(a), Dec. 7, 1974, 88 Stat. 1619; Pub. L. 93–651, title I, § 111(a), Nov. 21, 1974, 89 Stat. 2–5; Pub. L. 95–602, title I, § 122(a)(4)–(8), Nov. 6, 1978, 92 Stat. 2984, 2985; Pub. L. 98–221, title I, § 101, Feb. 22, 1984, 98 Stat. 17; Pub. L. 99–506, title I, § 103(a), (b), (c)(1), (d)(1), (2)(A), (C), (e)–(h)(1), (i), (j), title X, §§ 1001(a)(3), 1002(a), Oct. 21, 1986, 100 Stat. 1809–1811, 1841, 1844; Pub. L. 99–514, § 2, Oct. 22, 1986, 100 Stat. 2095; Pub. L. 100–259, § 9, Mar. 22, 1988, 102 Stat. 31; Pub. L. 100–630, title II, § 201(c), Nov. 7, 1988, 102 Stat. 3303; Pub. L. 101–336, title V, § 513, formerly § 512, July 26, 1990, 104 Stat. 376, renumbered § 513, Pub. L. 110–325, § 6(a)(2), Sept. 25, 2008, 122 Stat. 3558; Pub. L. 102–569, title I, § 102(a)–(n), (p)(3), Oct. 29, 1992, 106 Stat. 4347–4350, 4356; Pub. L. 103–73, title I, §§ 102(1), 103, Aug. 11, 1993, 107 Stat. 718; Pub. L. 103–218, title IV, § 404, Mar. 9, 1994, 108 Stat. 97, defined terms for purposes of this chapter, prior to repeal by Pub. L. 105–220, title IV, § 403, Aug. 7, 1998, 112 Stat. 1093. See section 705 of this title.

A prior section 8 of Pub. L. 93–112 was renumbered section 10 and is classified to section 707 of this title.

Another prior section 8 of Pub. L. 93–112 was classified to section 707 of this title prior to repeal by Pub. L. 105–220.

§ 707. Nonduplication

In determining the amount of any State's Federal share of expenditures for planning, administration, and services incurred by it under a State plan approved in accordance with section 721 of this title, there shall be disregarded—

(1) any portion of such expenditures which are financed by Federal funds provided under any other provision of law; and

(2) the amount of any non-Federal funds required to be expended as a condition of receipt of such Federal funds.

No payment may be made from funds provided under one provision of this chapter relating to any cost with respect to which any payment is made under any other provision of this chapter, except that this section shall not be construed to limit or reduce fees for services rendered by community rehabilitation programs.

(Pub. L. 93–112, § 10, formerly § 8, as added Pub. L. 105–220, title IV, § 403, Aug. 7, 1998, 112 Stat. 1110; renumbered § 10 and amended Pub. L. 105–277, div. A, § 101(f) [title VIII, § 402(a)(1), (c)(2)], Oct. 21, 1998, 112 Stat. 2681–337, 2681–412, 2681–415.)

Prior Provisions

Provisions similar to this section were contained in section 709 of this title prior to repeal by Pub. L. 105–220.

A prior section 707, Pub. L. 93–112, § 8, Sept. 26, 1973, 87 Stat. 362; Pub. L. 94–273, § 10, Apr. 21, 1976, 90 Stat. 378; Pub. L. 102–569, title I, § 103, Oct. 29, 1992, 106 Stat. 4361, related to allotment percentage, prior to repeal by Pub. L. 105–220, title IV, § 403, Aug. 7, 1998, 112 Stat. 1093. See section 706 of this title.

A prior section 10 of Pub. L. 93–112 was renumbered section 12 and is classified to section 709 of this title.

Another prior section 10 of Pub. L. 93–112 was classified to section 709 of this title prior to repeal by Pub. L. 105–220.

Amendments

1998—Pub. L. 105–277, § 101(f) [title VIII, § 402(c)(2)], substituted a dash for a colon after "disregarded" and amended text to set out cls. (1) and (2) as indented pars. and last sentence as flush provision.

§ 708. Application of other laws

The provisions of chapter 71 of title 31 and of title V of the Act of October 15, 1977 (Public Law 95–134) shall not apply to the administration of the provisions of this chapter or to the administration of any program or activity under this chapter.

(Pub. L. 93–112, § 11, formerly § 9, as added Pub. L. 105–220, title IV, § 403, Aug. 7, 1998, 112 Stat. 1110; renumbered § 11, Pub. L. 105–277, div. A, § 101(f) [title VIII, § 402(a)(1)], Oct. 21, 1998, 112 Stat. 2681–337, 2681–412.)

References in Text

Act of October 15, 1977, referred to in text, is Pub. L. 95–134, Oct. 15, 1977, 91 Stat. 1159, as amended, popularly known as the Omnibus Territories Act of 1977. Title V of the Act enacted section 4368b of Title 42, The Public Health and Welfare, and section 1469a of Title 48, Territories and Insular Possessions. For complete classification of this Act to the Code, see Tables.

Codification

"Chapter 71 of title 31" substituted in text for "the Act of December 5, 1974 (Public Law 93–510) on authority of Pub. L. 97–258, § 4(b), Sept. 13, 1982, 96 Stat. 1067, the first section of which enacted Title 31, Money and Finance.

Prior Provisions

Provisions similar to this section were contained in section 710 of this title prior to repeal by Pub. L. 105–220.

A prior section 708, Pub. L. 93–112, § 9, Sept. 26, 1973, 87 Stat. 362, related to audit and examination of records, scope of disclosure, and access to representatives, prior to repeal by Pub. L. 103–382, title II, § 272, Oct. 20, 1994, 108 Stat. 3931.

A prior section 11 of Pub. L. 93–112 was renumbered section 13 and is classified to section 710 of this title.

Another prior section 11 of Pub. L. 93–112 was classified to section 710 of this title prior to repeal by Pub. L. 105–220.

§ 709. Administration

(a) Technical assistance; short-term traineeships; special projects; dissemination of information; monitoring and evaluations

In carrying out the purposes of this chapter, the Commissioner may—

(1) provide consultative services and technical assistance to public or nonprofit private agencies and organizations, including assistance to enable such agencies and organizations to facilitate meaningful and effective participation by individuals with disabilities in workforce investment activities;

(2) provide short-term training and technical instruction, including training for the personnel of community rehabilitation programs, centers for independent living, and other providers of services (including job coaches);

(3) conduct special projects and demonstrations;

(4) collect, prepare, publish, and disseminate special educational or informational materials, including reports of the projects for which funds are provided under this chapter; and

(5) provide monitoring and conduct evaluations.

(b) Utilization of services and facilities; information task forces

(1) In carrying out the duties under this chapter, the Commissioner may utilize the services and facilities of any agency of the Federal Government and of any other public or nonprofit agency or organization, in accordance with agreements between the Commissioner and the head thereof, and may pay therefor, in advance or by way of reimbursement, as may be provided in the agreement.

(2) In carrying out the provisions of this chapter, the Commissioner shall appoint such task forces as may be necessary to collect and disseminate information in order to improve the ability of the Commissioner to carry out the provisions of this chapter.

(c) Rules and regulations

The Commissioner may promulgate such regulations as are considered appropriate to carry out the Commissioner's duties under this chapter.

(d) Regulations for implementation of order of selection for vocational rehabilitation services

The Secretary shall promulgate regulations regarding the requirements for the implementation of an order of selection for vocational rehabilitation services under section 721(a)(5)(A) of this title if such services cannot be provided to all eligible individuals with disabilities who apply for such services.

(e) Regulations to implement amendments

Not later than 180 days after August 7, 1998, the Secretary shall receive public comment and promulgate regulations to implement the amendments made by the Rehabilitation Act Amendments of 1998.

(f) Limitation on regulations

In promulgating regulations to carry out this chapter, the Secretary shall promulgate only regulations that are necessary to administer and ensure compliance with the specific requirements of this chapter.

(g) Authorization of appropriations

There are authorized to be appropriated to carry out this section such sums as may be necessary.

(Pub. L. 93–112, §12, formerly §10, as added Pub. L. 105–220, title IV, §403, Aug. 7, 1998, 112 Stat. 1111; renumbered §12, Pub. L. 105–277, div. A, §101(f) [title VIII, §402(a)(1)], Oct. 21, 1998, 112 Stat. 2681–337, 2681–412.)

REFERENCES IN TEXT

The Rehabilitation Act Amendments of 1998, referred to in subsec. (e), is title IV of Pub. L. 105–220, Aug. 7, 1998, 112 Stat. 1092. For complete classification of this Act to the Code, see Tables.

PRIOR PROVISIONS

Provisions similar to this section were contained in section 711 of this title prior to repeal by Pub. L. 105–220.

A prior section 709, Pub. L. 93–112, §10, Sept. 26, 1973, 87 Stat. 363; Pub. L. 95–602, title I, §122(a)(9), Nov. 6, 1978, 92 Stat. 2985; Pub. L. 100–630, title II, §201(d), Nov. 7, 1988, 102 Stat. 3304; Pub. L. 102–569, title I, §104, Oct. 29, 1992, 106 Stat. 4361, related to nonduplication prohibition, prior to repeal by Pub. L. 105–220, title IV, §403, Aug. 7, 1998, 112 Stat. 1093. See section 707 of this title.

A prior section 12 of Pub. L. 93–112 was renumbered section 14 and is classified to section 711 of this title.

Another prior section 12 of Pub. L. 93–112 was classified to section 711 of this title prior to repeal by Pub. L. 105–220.

§710. Reports

(a) Annual reports required

Not later than one hundred and eighty days after the close of each fiscal year, the Commissioner shall prepare and submit to the President and to the Congress a full and complete report on the activities carried out under this chapter, including the activities and staffing of the information clearinghouse under section 712 of this title.

(b) Collection of information

The Commissioner shall collect information to determine whether the purposes of this chapter are being met and to assess the performance of programs carried out under this chapter. The Commissioner shall take whatever action is necessary to assure that the identity of each individual for which information is supplied under this section is kept confidential, except as otherwise required by law (including regulation).

(c) Information to be included in reports

In preparing the report, the Commissioner shall annually collect and include in the report information based on the information submitted by States in accordance with section 721(a)(10) of this title, including information on administrative costs as required by section 721(a)(10)(D) of this title. The Commissioner shall, to the maximum extent appropriate, include in the report all information that is required to be submitted in the reports described in section 2871(d) of this title and that pertains to the employment of individuals with disabilities.

(Pub. L. 93–112, §13, formerly §11, as added Pub. L. 105–220, title IV, §403, Aug. 7, 1998, 112 Stat. 1111; renumbered §13, Pub. L. 105–277, div. A, §101(f) [title VIII, §402(a)(1)], Oct. 21, 1998, 112 Stat. 2681–337, 2681–412.)

PRIOR PROVISIONS

Provisions similar to this section were contained in section 712 of this title prior to repeal by Pub. L. 105–220.

A prior section 710, Pub. L. 93–112, §11, as added Pub. L. 95–602, title I, §121, Nov. 6, 1978, 92 Stat. 2984, related to application of other laws, prior to repeal by Pub. L. 105–220, title IV, §403, Aug. 7, 1998, 112 Stat. 1093. See section 708 of this title.

A prior section 13 of Pub. L. 93–112 was renumbered section 15 and is classified to section 712 of this title.

Another prior section 13 of Pub. L. 93–112 was classified to section 712 of this title prior to repeal by Pub. L. 105–220.

EXCHANGE OF DATA

Pub. L. 102–569, title I, §137, Oct. 29, 1992, 106 Stat. 4397, provided that: "The Secretary of Education and the Secretary of Health and Human Services shall enter into a memorandum of understanding for the purpose of exchanging data of mutual importance, regarding clients of State vocational rehabilitation agencies, that are contained in databases maintained by the Rehabilitation Services Administration, as required under section 13 of the Rehabilitation Act of 1973 ([former] 29 U.S.C. 712), and the Social Security Administration, from its Summary Earnings and Records and Master Beneficiary Records. For purposes of the exchange, the Social Security data shall not be considered tax information and, as appropriate, the confidentiality of all client information shall be maintained by both agencies.''

§ 711. Evaluation

(a) Statement of purpose; standards; persons eligible to conduct evaluations

For the purpose of improving program management and effectiveness, the Secretary, in consultation with the Commissioner, shall evaluate all the programs authorized by this chapter, their general effectiveness in relation to their cost, their impact on related programs, and their structure and mechanisms for delivery of services, using appropriate methodology and evaluative research designs. The Secretary shall establish and use standards for the evaluations required by this subsection. Such an evaluation shall be conducted by a person not immediately involved in the administration of the program evaluated.

(b) Opinions of program and project participants

In carrying out evaluations under this section, the Secretary shall obtain the opinions of program and project participants about the strengths and weaknesses of the programs and projects.

(c) Data as property of United States

The Secretary shall take the necessary action to assure that all studies, evaluations, proposals, and data produced or developed with Federal funds under this chapter shall become the property of the United States.

(d) Information from other departments and agencies

Such information as the Secretary may determine to be necessary for purposes of the evaluations conducted under this section shall be made available upon request of the Secretary, by the departments and agencies of the executive branch.

(e) Longitudinal study

(1) To assess the linkages between vocational rehabilitation services and economic and noneconomic outcomes, the Secretary shall continue to conduct a longitudinal study of a national sample of applicants for the services.

(2) The study shall address factors related to attrition and completion of the program through which the services are provided and factors within and outside the program affecting results. Appropriate comparisons shall be used to contrast the experiences of similar persons who do not obtain the services.

(3) The study shall be planned to cover the period beginning on the application of individuals with disabilities for the services, through the eligibility determination and provision of services for the individuals, and a further period of not less than 2 years after the termination of services.

(f) Information on exemplary practices

(1) The Commissioner shall identify and disseminate information on exemplary practices concerning vocational rehabilitation.

(2) To facilitate compliance with paragraph (1), the Commissioner shall conduct studies and analyses that identify exemplary practices concerning vocational rehabilitation, including studies in areas relating to providing informed choice in the rehabilitation process, promoting consumer satisfaction, promoting job placement and retention, providing supported employment, providing services to particular disability populations, financing personal assistance services, providing assistive technology devices and assistive technology services, entering into cooperative agreements, establishing standards and certification for community rehabilitation programs, converting from nonintegrated to integrated employment, and providing caseload management.

(g) Authorization of appropriations

There are authorized to be appropriated to carry out this section such sums as may be necessary.

(Pub. L. 93–112, § 14, formerly § 12, as added Pub. L. 105–220, title IV, § 403, Aug. 7, 1998, 112 Stat. 1110; renumbered § 14, Pub. L. 105–277, div. A, § 101(f) [title VIII, § 402(a)(1)], Oct. 21, 1998, 112 Stat. 2681–337, 2681–412.)

PRIOR PROVISIONS

Provisions similar to this section were contained in section 713 of this title prior to repeal by Pub. L. 105–220.

A prior section 711, Pub. L. 93–112, § 12, as added Pub. L. 95–602, title I, § 122(a)(10), Nov. 6, 1978, 92 Stat. 2985; amended Pub. L. 99–506, title I, § 104, title X, § 1001(a)(4), Oct. 21, 1986, 100 Stat. 1811, 1841; Pub. L. 100–630, title II, § 201(e), Nov. 7, 1988, 102 Stat. 3304; Pub. L. 102–569, title I, § 105, Oct. 29, 1992, 106 Stat. 4361, related to administration of this chapter, prior to repeal by Pub. L. 105–220, title IV, § 403, Aug. 7, 1998, 112 Stat. 1093. See section 709 of this title.

A prior section 14 of Pub. L. 93–112 was renumbered section 16 and is classified to section 713 of this title.

Another prior section 14 of Pub. L. 93–112 was classified to section 713 of this title prior to repeal by Pub. L. 105–220.

§ 712. Information clearinghouse

(a) Establishment; information and resources for individuals with disabilities

The Secretary shall establish a central clearinghouse for information and resource availability for individuals with disabilities which shall provide information and data regarding—

(1) the location, provision, and availability of services and programs for individuals with disabilities, including such information and data provided by State workforce investment boards regarding such services and programs authorized under title I of such Act;[1]

(2) research and recent medical and scientific developments bearing on disabilities (and their prevention, amelioration, causes, and cures); and

(3) the current numbers of individuals with disabilities and their needs.

[1] See References in Text note below.

The clearinghouse shall also provide any other relevant information and data which the Secretary considers appropriate.

(b) Information and data retrieval system

The Commissioner may assist the Secretary to develop within the Department of Education a coordinated system of information and data retrieval, which will have the capacity and responsibility to provide information regarding the information and data referred to in subsection (a) of this section to the Congress, public and private agencies and organizations, individuals with disabilities and their families, professionals in fields serving such individuals, and the general public.

(c) Office of Information and Resources for Individuals with Disabilities

The office established to carry out the provisions of this section shall be known as the "Office of Information and Resources for Individuals with Disabilities".

(d) Authorization of appropriations

There are authorized to be appropriated to carry out this section such sums as may be necessary.

(Pub. L. 93–112, § 15, formerly § 13, as added Pub. L. 105–220, title IV, § 403, Aug. 7, 1998, 112 Stat. 1113; renumbered § 15, Pub. L. 105–277, div. A, § 101(f) [title VIII, § 402(a)(1)], Oct. 21, 1998, 112 Stat. 2681–337, 2681–412.)

REFERENCES IN TEXT

Such Act, referred to in subsec. (a)(1), probably means the Workforce Investment Act of 1998, which is Pub. L. 105–220, Aug. 7, 1998, 112 Stat. 936, as amended. Title I of the Act is classified principally to chapter 30 (§ 2801 et seq.) of this title. For complete classification of this Act to the Code, see Short Title note set out under section 9201 of Title 20, Education, and Tables.

PRIOR PROVISIONS

Provisions similar to this section were contained in section 714 of this title prior to repeal by Pub. L. 105–220.

A prior section 712, Pub. L. 93–112, § 13, as added Pub. L. 95–602, title I, § 122(a)(10), Nov. 6, 1978, 92 Stat. 2985; amended Pub. L. 98–221, title I, § 102, Feb. 22, 1984, 98 Stat. 17; Pub. L. 99–506, title I, § 105, Oct. 21, 1986, 100 Stat. 1812; Pub. L. 102–569, title I, §§ 102(p)(4), 106, Oct. 29, 1992, 106 Stat. 4356, 4362; Pub. L. 104–66, title I, § 1042(c), Dec. 21, 1995, 109 Stat. 715, related to reports to President and Congress, prior to repeal by Pub. L. 105–220, title IV, § 403, Aug. 7, 1998, 112 Stat. 1093. See section 710 of this title.

A prior section 15 of Pub. L. 93–112 was renumbered section 17 and is classified to section 714 of this title.

Another prior section 15 of Pub. L. 93–112 was classified to section 714 of this title prior to repeal by Pub. L. 105–220.

§ 713. Transfer of funds

(a) Except as provided in subsection (b) of this section, no funds appropriated under this chapter for any program or activity may be used for any purpose other than that for which the funds were specifically authorized.

(b) No more than 1 percent of funds appropriated for discretionary grants, contracts, or cooperative agreements authorized by this chapter may be used for the purpose of providing non-Federal panels of experts to review applications for such grants, contracts, or cooperative agreements.

(Pub. L. 93–112, § 16, formerly § 14, as added Pub. L. 105–220, title IV, § 403, Aug. 7, 1998, 112 Stat. 1113; renumbered § 16, Pub. L. 105–277, div. A, § 101(f) [title VIII, § 402(a)(1)], Oct. 21, 1998, 112 Stat. 2681–337, 2681–412.)

PRIOR PROVISIONS

Provisions similar to this section were contained in section 715 of this title prior to repeal by Pub. L. 105–220.

A prior section 713, Pub. L. 93–112, § 14, as added Pub. L. 95–602, title I, § 122(a)(10), Nov. 6, 1978, 92 Stat. 2986; amended Pub. L. 98–221, title I, § 103, Feb. 22, 1984, 98 Stat. 17; Pub. L. 99–506, title I, §§ 103(d)(2)(C), 106, title X, § 1001(a)(5), Oct. 21, 1986, 100 Stat. 1810, 1812, 1841; Pub. L. 100–630, title II, § 201(f), Nov. 7, 1988, 102 Stat. 3304; Pub. L. 102–569, title I, §§ 102(p)(5), 107, Oct. 29, 1992, 106 Stat. 4356, 4362, related to program and project evaluation, prior to repeal by Pub. L. 105–220, title IV, § 403, Aug. 7, 1998, 112 Stat. 1093. See section 711 of this title.

A prior section 16 of Pub. L. 93–112 was renumbered section 18 and is classified to section 715 of this title.

Another prior section 16 of Pub. L. 93–112 was classified to section 715 of this title prior to repeal by Pub. L. 105–220.

§ 714. State administration

The application of any State rule or policy relating to the administration or operation of programs funded by this chapter (including any rule or policy based on State interpretation of any Federal law, regulation, or guideline) shall be identified as a State imposed requirement.

(Pub. L. 93–112, § 17, formerly § 15, as added Pub. L. 105–220, title IV, § 403, Aug. 7, 1998, 112 Stat. 1114; renumbered § 17, Pub. L. 105–277, div. A, § 101(f) [title VIII, § 402(a)(1)], Oct. 21, 1998, 112 Stat. 2681–337, 2681–412.)

PRIOR PROVISIONS

Provisions similar to this section were contained in section 716 of this title prior to repeal by Pub. L. 105–220.

A prior section 714, Pub. L. 93–112, § 15, as added Pub. L. 95–602, title I, § 122(a)(10), Nov. 6, 1978, 92 Stat. 2986; amended Pub. L. 96–374, title XIII, § 1322, Oct. 3, 1980, 94 Stat. 1499; Pub. L. 98–221, title I, § 104(a)(1), Feb. 22, 1984, 98 Stat. 18; Pub. L. 99–506, title I, § 103(d)(2)(C), Oct. 21, 1986, 100 Stat. 1810; Pub. L. 102–569, title I, § 102(p)(6), Oct. 29, 1992, 106 Stat. 4356, related to information clearinghouse, prior to repeal by Pub. L. 105–220, title IV, § 403, Aug. 7, 1998, 112 Stat. 1093. See section 712 of this title.

A prior section 17 of Pub. L. 93–112 was renumbered section 19 and is classified to section 716 of this title.

Another prior section 17 of Pub. L. 93–112 was classified to section 716 of this title prior to repeal by Pub. L. 105–220.

§ 715. Review of applications

Applications for grants in excess of $100,000 in the aggregate authorized to be funded under this chapter, other than grants primarily for the purpose of conducting dissemination or conferences, shall be reviewed by panels of experts which shall include a majority of non-Federal members. Non-Federal members may be provided travel, per diem, and consultant fees not to exceed the daily equivalent of the rate of pay for level 4 of the Senior Executive Service Schedule under section 5382 of title 5.

(Pub. L. 93–112, § 18, formerly § 16, as added Pub. L. 105–220, title IV, § 403, Aug. 7, 1998, 112 Stat. 1114; renumbered § 18, Pub. L. 105–277, div. A, § 101(f) [title VIII, § 402(a)(1)], Oct. 21, 1998, 112 Stat. 2681–337, 2681–412.)

PRIOR PROVISIONS

Provisions similar to this section were contained in section 717 of this title prior to repeal by Pub. L. 105–220.

A prior section 715, Pub. L. 93–112, § 16, as added Pub. L. 95–602, title I, § 122(a)(10), Nov. 6, 1978, 92 Stat. 2987; amended Pub. L. 99–506, title I, § 107, Oct. 21, 1986, 100 Stat. 1812; Pub. L. 102–569, title I, § 108(a), Oct. 29, 1992, 106 Stat. 4363, related to transfer of funds, prior to repeal by Pub. L. 105–220, title IV, § 403, Aug. 7, 1998, 112 Stat. 1093. See section 713 of this title.

A prior section 18 of Pub. L. 93–112 was renumbered section 20 and is classified to section 717 of this title.

Another prior section 18 of Pub. L. 93–112 was classified to section 717 of this title prior to repeal by Pub. L. 105–220.

§ 716. Carryover

(a) In general

Except as provided in subsection (b) of this section, and notwithstanding any other provision of law—

(1) any funds appropriated for a fiscal year to carry out any grant program under part B of subchapter I of this chapter, section 794e of this title (except as provided in section 794e(b) of this title), part B of subchapter VI of this chapter, subpart 2 or 3 of part A of subchapter VII of this chapter, or part B of subchapter VII of this chapter (except as provided in section 796k(b) of this title), including any funds reallotted under any such grant program, that are not obligated and expended by recipients prior to the beginning of the succeeding fiscal year; or

(2) any amounts of program income, including reimbursement payments under the Social Security Act (42 U.S.C. 301 et seq.), received by recipients under any grant program specified in paragraph (1) that are not obligated and expended by recipients prior to the beginning of the fiscal year succeeding the fiscal year in which such amounts were received,

shall remain available for obligation and expenditure by such recipients during such succeeding fiscal year.

(b) Non-Federal share

Such funds shall remain available for obligation and expenditure by a recipient as provided in subsection (a) of this section only to the extent that the recipient complied with any Federal share requirements applicable to the program for the fiscal year for which the funds were appropriated.

(Pub. L. 93–112, § 19, formerly § 17, as added Pub. L. 105–220, title IV, § 403, Aug. 7, 1998, 112 Stat. 1114; renumbered § 19 and amended Pub. L. 105–277, div. A, § 101(f) [title VIII, § 402(a)(1), (b)(4)], Oct. 21, 1998, 112 Stat. 2681–337, 2681–412, 2681–413.)

REFERENCES IN TEXT

The Social Security Act, referred to in subsec. (a)(2), is act Aug. 14, 1935, ch. 531, 49 Stat. 620, as amended, which is classified generally to chapter 7 (§ 301 et seq.) of Title 42, The Public Health and Welfare. For complete classification of this Act to the Code, see section 1305 of Title 42 and Tables.

PRIOR PROVISIONS

Provisions similar to this section were contained in section 718 of this title prior to repeal by Pub. L. 105–220.

A prior section 716, Pub. L. 93–112, § 17, as added Pub. L. 99–506, title I, § 108(a), Oct. 21, 1986, 100 Stat. 1812, related to State administration, prior to repeal by Pub. L. 105–220, title IV, § 403, Aug. 7, 1998, 112 Stat. 1093. See section 714 of this title.

A prior section 19 of Pub. L. 93–112 was renumbered section 21 and is classified to section 718 of this title.

Another prior section 19 of Pub. L. 93–112 was classified to section 718 of this title prior to repeal by Pub. L. 105–220.

AMENDMENTS

1998—Pub. L. 105–277, § 101(f) [title VIII, § 402(b)(4)], made technical amendment in the original to section designation and catchline.

§ 717. Client assistance information

All programs, including community rehabilitation programs, and projects, that provide services to individuals with disabilities under this chapter shall advise such individuals who are applicants for or recipients of the services, or the applicants' representatives or individuals' representatives, of the availability and purposes of the client assistance program under section 732 of this title, including information on means of seeking assistance under such program.

(Pub. L. 93–112, § 20, formerly § 18, as added Pub. L. 105–220, title IV, § 403, Aug. 7, 1998, 112 Stat. 1114; renumbered § 20 and amended Pub. L. 105–277, div. A, § 101(f) [title VIII, § 402(a)(1), (b)(5)], Oct. 21, 1998, 112 Stat. 2681–337, 2681–412, 2681–413.)

PRIOR PROVISIONS

Provisions similar to this section were contained in section 718a of this title prior to repeal by Pub. L. 105–220.

A prior section 717, Pub. L. 93–112, § 18, as added Pub. L. 99–506, title I, § 109(a), Oct. 21, 1986, 100 Stat. 1813; amended Pub. L. 100–630, title II, § 201(g), Nov. 7, 1988, 102 Stat. 3304; Pub. L. 102–569, title I, § 108(b), Oct. 29, 1992, 106 Stat. 4363, related to review of applications, prior to repeal by Pub. L. 105–220, title IV, § 403, Aug. 7, 1998, 112 Stat. 1093. See section 715 of this title.

A prior section 20 of Pub. L. 93–112 was classified to section 718a of this title prior to repeal by Pub. L. 105–220.

AMENDMENTS

1998—Pub. L. 105–277, § 101(f) [title VIII, § 402(b)(5)], made technical amendment to section designation and catchline in the original.

§ 718. Traditionally underserved populations

(a) Findings

With respect to the programs authorized in subchapters II through VII of this chapter, the Congress finds as follows:

(1) Racial profile

The racial profile of America is rapidly changing. While the rate of increase for white Americans is 3.2 percent, the rate of increase for racial and ethnic minorities is much higher: 38.6 percent for Latinos, 14.6 percent for African-Americans, and 40.1 percent for Asian-Americans and other ethnic groups. By the year 2000, the Nation will have 260,000,000 people, one of every three of whom will be either African-American, Latino, or Asian-American.

(2) Rate of disability

Ethnic and racial minorities tend to have disabling conditions at a disproportionately high rate. The rate of work-related disability for American Indians is about one and one-half times that of the general population. African-Americans are also one and one-half times more likely to be disabled than whites and twice as likely to be significantly disabled.

(3) Inequitable treatment

Patterns of inequitable treatment of minorities have been documented in all major junctures of the vocational rehabilitation process. As compared to white Americans, a larger percentage of African-American applicants to the vocational rehabilitation system is denied acceptance. Of applicants accepted for service, a larger percentage of African-American cases is closed without being rehabilitated. Minorities are provided less training than their white counterparts. Consistently, less money is spent on minorities than on their white counterparts.

(4) Recruitment

Recruitment efforts within vocational rehabilitation at the level of preservice training, continuing education, and in-service training must focus on bringing larger numbers of minorities into the profession in order to provide appropriate practitioner knowledge, role models, and sufficient manpower to address the clearly changing demography of vocational rehabilitation.

(b) Outreach to minorities

(1) In general

For each fiscal year, the Commissioner and the Director of the National Institute on Disability and Rehabilitation Research (referred to in this subsection as the "Director") shall reserve 1 percent of the funds appropriated for the fiscal year for programs authorized under subchapters II, III, VI, and VII of this chapter to carry out this subsection. The Commissioner and the Director shall use the reserved funds to carry out one or more of the activities described in paragraph (2) through a grant, contract, or cooperative agreement.

(2) Activities

The activities carried out by the Commissioner and the Director shall include one or more of the following:

(A) Making awards to minority entities and Indian tribes to carry out activities under the programs authorized under subchapters II, III, VI, and VII of this chapter.

(B) Making awards to minority entities and Indian tribes to conduct research, training, technical assistance, or a related activity, to improve services provided under this chapter, especially services provided to individuals from minority backgrounds.

(C) Making awards to entities described in paragraph (3) to provide outreach and technical assistance to minority entities and Indian tribes to promote their participation in activities funded under this chapter, including assistance to enhance their capacity to carry out such activities.

(3) Eligibility

To be eligible to receive an award under paragraph (2)(C), an entity shall be a State or a public or private nonprofit agency or organization, such as an institution of higher education or an Indian tribe.

(4) Report

In each fiscal year, the Commissioner and the Director shall prepare and submit to Congress a report that describes the activities funded under this subsection for the preceding fiscal year.

(5) Definitions

In this subsection:

(A) Historically Black college or university

The term "historically Black college or university" means a part B institution, as defined in section 1061(2) of title 20.

(B) Minority entity

The term "minority entity" means an entity that is a historically Black college or university, a Hispanic-serving institution of higher education, an American Indian tribal college or university, or another institution of higher education whose minority student enrollment is at least 50 percent.

(c) Demonstration

In awarding grants, or entering into contracts or cooperative agreements under subchapters I, II, III, VI, and VII of this chapter, and section 794e of this title, the Commissioner and the Director, in appropriate cases, shall require applicants to demonstrate how the applicants will address, in whole or in part, the needs of individuals with disabilities from minority backgrounds.

(Pub. L. 93–112, §21, formerly §19, as added Pub. L. 105–220, title IV, §403, Aug. 7, 1998, 112 Stat. 1115; renumbered §21 and amended Pub. L. 105–277, div. A, §101(f) [title VIII, §402(a)(1), (b)(6), (c)(3)], Oct. 21, 1998, 112 Stat. 2681–337, 2681–412, 2681–413, 2681–415.)

PRIOR PROVISIONS

Provisions similar to this section were contained in section 718b of this title prior to repeal by Pub. L. 105–220.

Prior sections 718 to 718b were repealed by Pub. L. 105–220, title IV, §403, Aug. 7, 1998, 112 Stat. 1093.

Section 718, Pub. L. 93–112, §19, as added Pub. L. 102–569, title I, §109(a), Oct. 29, 1992, 106 Stat. 4363; amended Pub. L. 103–73, title I, §104, Aug. 11, 1993, 107 Stat. 719, related to carryover of funds. See section 716 of this title.

Section 718a, Pub. L. 93–112, §20, as added Pub. L. 102–569, title I, §110(a), Oct. 29, 1992, 106 Stat. 4363; amended Pub. L. 103–73, title I, §105, Aug. 11, 1993, 107 Stat. 719, related to client assistance information. See section 717 of this title.

Section 718b, Pub. L. 93–112, §21, as added Pub. L. 102–569, title I, §111(a), Oct. 29, 1992, 106 Stat. 4363; amended Pub. L. 103–73, title I, §106, Aug. 11, 1993, 107 Stat. 719, related to traditionally underserved populations.

AMENDMENTS

1998—Pub. L. 105–277, § 101(f) [title VIII, § 402(b)(6)], made technical amendment in original to section designation and catchline.

Subsec. (a)(3). Pub. L. 105–277, § 101(f) [title VIII, § 402(c)(3)], substituted "is denied" for "are denied" and "is closed" for "are closed".

SUBCHAPTER I—VOCATIONAL REHABILITATION SERVICES

CODIFICATION

Title I of the Rehabilitation Act of 1973, comprising this subchapter, was originally enacted by Pub. L. 93–112, title I, Sept. 26, 1973, 87 Stat. 363, and amended by Pub. L. 93–516, Dec. 7, 1974, 88 Stat. 1617; Pub. L. 93–651, Nov. 21, 1974, 89 Stat. 2–3; Pub. L. 94–230, Mar. 15, 1976, 90 Stat. 211; Pub. L. 95–602, Nov. 6, 1978, 92 Stat. 2955; Pub. L. 97–375, Dec. 21, 1982, 96 Stat. 1819; Pub. L. 98–221, Feb. 22, 1984, 98 Stat. 17; Pub. L. 98–524, Oct. 19, 1984, 98 Stat. 2435; Pub. L. 99–506, Oct. 21, 1986, 100 Stat. 1807; Pub. L. 100–630, Nov. 7, 1988, 102 Stat. 3289; Pub. L. 102–52, June 6, 1991, 105 Stat. 260; Pub. L. 102–54, June 13, 1991, 105 Stat. 267; Pub. L. 102–119, Oct. 7, 1991, 105 Stat. 587; Pub. L. 102–569, Oct. 29, 1992, 106 Stat. 4344; Pub. L. 103–73, Aug. 11, 1993, 107 Stat. 718; Pub. L. 104–66, Dec. 21, 1995, 109 Stat. 707; Pub. L. 104–106, Feb. 10, 1996, 110 Stat. 186. Title I is shown herein, however, as having been added by Pub. L. 105–220, title IV, § 404, Aug. 7, 1998, 112 Stat. 1116, without reference to those intervening amendments because of the extensive revision of title I by Pub. L. 105–220.

PART A—GENERAL PROVISIONS

§ 720. Declaration of policy; authorization of appropriations

(a) Findings; purpose; policy

(1) Findings

Congress finds that—

(A) work—

(i) is a valued activity, both for individuals and society; and

(ii) fulfills the need of an individual to be productive, promotes independence, enhances self-esteem, and allows for participation in the mainstream of life in the United States;

(B) as a group, individuals with disabilities experience staggering levels of unemployment and poverty;

(C) individuals with disabilities, including individuals with the most significant disabilities, have demonstrated their ability to achieve gainful employment in integrated settings if appropriate services and supports are provided;

(D) reasons for significant numbers of individuals with disabilities not working, or working at levels not commensurate with their abilities and capabilities, include—

(i) discrimination;

(ii) lack of accessible and available transportation;

(iii) fear of losing health coverage under the medicare and medicaid programs carried out under titles XVIII and XIX of the Social Security Act (42 U.S.C. 1395 et seq. and 1396 et seq.) or fear of losing private health insurance; and

(iv) lack of education, training, and supports to meet job qualification standards necessary to secure, retain, regain, or advance in employment;

(E) enforcement of subchapter V of this chapter and of the Americans with Disabilities Act of 1990 (42 U.S.C. 12101 et seq.) holds the promise of ending discrimination for individuals with disabilities;

(F) the provision of workforce investment activities and vocational rehabilitation services can enable individuals with disabilities, including individuals with the most significant disabilities, to pursue meaningful careers by securing gainful employment commensurate with their abilities and capabilities; and

(G) linkages between the vocational rehabilitation programs established under this subchapter and other components of the statewide workforce investment systems are critical to ensure effective and meaningful participation by individuals with disabilities in workforce investment activities.

(2) Purpose

The purpose of this subchapter is to assist States in operating statewide comprehensive, coordinated, effective, efficient, and accountable programs of vocational rehabilitation, each of which is—

(A) an integral part of a statewide workforce investment system; and

(B) designed to assess, plan, develop, and provide vocational rehabilitation services for individuals with disabilities, consistent with their strengths, resources, priorities, concerns, abilities, capabilities, interests, and informed choice, so that such individuals may prepare for and engage in gainful employment.

(3) Policy

It is the policy of the United States that such a program shall be carried out in a manner consistent with the following principles:

(A) Individuals with disabilities, including individuals with the most significant disabilities, are generally presumed to be capable of engaging in gainful employment and the provision of individualized vocational rehabilitation services can improve their ability to become gainfully employed.

(B) Individuals with disabilities must be provided the opportunities to obtain gainful employment in integrated settings.

(C) Individuals who are applicants for such programs or eligible to participate in such programs must be active and full partners in the vocational rehabilitation process, making meaningful and informed choices—

(i) during assessments for determining eligibility and vocational rehabilitation needs; and

(ii) in the selection of employment outcomes for the individuals, services needed to achieve the outcomes, entities providing such services, and the methods used to secure such services.

(D) Families and other natural supports can play important roles in the success of a vocational rehabilitation program, if the individual with a disability involved requests, desires, or needs such supports.

(E) Vocational rehabilitation counselors that are trained and prepared in accordance with State policies and procedures as described in section 721(a)(7)(B) of this title (referred to individually in this subchapter as a "qualified vocational rehabilitation counselor"), other qualified rehabilitation personnel, and other qualified personnel facilitate the accomplishment of the employment outcomes and objectives of an individual.

(F) Individuals with disabilities and the individuals' representatives are full partners in a vocational rehabilitation program and must be involved on a regular basis and in a meaningful manner with respect to policy development and implementation.

(G) Accountability measures must facilitate the accomplishment of the goals and objectives of the program, including providing vocational rehabilitation services to, among others, individuals with the most significant disabilities.

(b) Authorization of appropriations

(1) In general

For the purpose of making grants to States under part B of this subchapter to assist States in meeting the costs of vocational rehabilitation services provided in accordance with State plans under section 721 of this title, there are authorized to be appropriated such sums as may be necessary for fiscal years 1999 through 2003, except that the amount to be appropriated for a fiscal year shall not be less than the amount of the appropriation under this paragraph for the immediately preceding fiscal year, increased by the percentage change in the Consumer Price Index determined under subsection (c) of this section for the immediately preceding fiscal year.

(2) Reference

The reference in paragraph (1) to grants to States under part B of this subchapter shall not be considered to refer to grants under section 732 of this title.

(c) Consumer Price Index

(1) Percentage change

No later than November 15 of each fiscal year (beginning with fiscal year 1979), the Secretary of Labor shall publish in the Federal Register the percentage change in the Consumer Price Index published for October of the preceding fiscal year and October of the fiscal year in which such publication is made.

(2) Application

(A) Increase

If in any fiscal year the percentage change published under paragraph (1) indicates an increase in the Consumer Price Index, then the amount to be appropriated under subsection (b)(1) of this section for the subsequent fiscal year shall be at least the amount appropriated under subsection (b)(1) of this section for the fiscal year in which the publication is made under paragraph (1) increased by such percentage change.

(B) No increase or decrease

If in any fiscal year the percentage change published under paragraph (1) does not indicate an increase in the Consumer Price Index, then the amount to be appropriated under subsection (b)(1) of this section for the subsequent fiscal year shall be at least the amount appropriated under subsection (b)(1) of this section for the fiscal year in which the publication is made under paragraph (1).

(3) Definition

For purposes of this section, the term "Consumer Price Index" means the Consumer Price Index for All Urban Consumers, published monthly by the Bureau of Labor Statistics.

(d) Extension

(1) In general

(A) Authorization or duration of program

Unless the Congress in the regular session which ends prior to the beginning of the terminal fiscal year—

(i) of the authorization of appropriations for the program authorized by the State grant program under part B of this subchapter; or

(ii) of the duration of the program authorized by the State grant program under part B of this subchapter;

has passed legislation which would have the effect of extending the authorization or duration (as the case may be) of such program, such authorization or duration is automatically extended for 1 additional year for the program authorized by this subchapter.

(B) Calculation

The amount authorized to be appropriated for the additional fiscal year described in subparagraph (A) shall be an amount equal to the amount appropriated for such program for fiscal year 2003, increased by the percentage change in the Consumer Price Index determined under subsection (c) of this section for the immediately preceding fiscal year, if the percentage change indicates an increase.

(2) Construction

(A) Passage of legislation

For the purposes of paragraph (1)(A), Congress shall not be deemed to have passed legislation unless such legislation becomes law.

(B) Acts or determinations of Commissioner

In any case where the Commissioner is required under an applicable statute to carry out certain acts or make certain determinations which are necessary for the continuation of the program authorized by this subchapter, if such acts or determinations are required during the terminal year of such program, such acts and determinations shall be required during any fiscal year in which the extension described in that part of paragraph (1) that follows clause (ii) of paragraph (1)(A) is in effect.

(Pub. L. 93–112, title I, § 100, as added Pub. L. 105–220, title IV, § 404, Aug. 7, 1998, 112 Stat. 1116.)

REFERENCES IN TEXT

The Social Security Act, referred to in subsec. (a)(1)(D)(iii), is act Aug. 14, 1935, ch. 531, 49 Stat. 620, as amended. Titles XVIII and XIX of the Act are classified generally to subchapters XVIII (§ 1395 et seq.) and XIX (§ 1396 et seq.), respectively, of chapter 7 of Title 42, The Public Health and Welfare. For complete classification of this Act to the Code, see section 1305 of Title 42 and Tables.

The Americans with Disabilities Act of 1990, referred to in subsec. (a)(1)(E), is Pub. L. 101–336, July 26, 1990, 104 Stat. 327, as amended, which is classified principally to chapter 126 (§ 12101 et seq.) of Title 42, The Public Health and Welfare. For complete classification of this Act to the Code, see Short Title note set out under section 12101 of Title 42 and Tables.

PRIOR PROVISIONS

A prior section 720, Pub. L. 93–112, title I, § 100, Sept. 26, 1973, 87 Stat. 363; Pub. L. 93–516, title I, § 102(a), Dec. 7, 1974, 88 Stat. 1618; Pub. L. 93–651, title I, § 102(a), Nov. 21, 1974, 89 Stat. 2-3; Pub. L. 94–230, §§ 2(a), 11(b)(2), (3), Mar. 15, 1976, 90 Stat. 211, 213; Pub. L. 95–602, title I, § 101(a), (b), Nov. 6, 1978, 92 Stat. 2955; Pub. L. 98–221, title I, § 111(a)–(d), Feb. 22, 1984, 98 Stat. 19; Pub. L. 99–506, title I, § 103(d)(2)(C), title II, § 201, Oct. 21, 1986, 100 Stat. 1810, 1813; Pub. L. 100–630, title II, § 202(a), Nov. 7, 1988, 102 Stat. 3304; Pub. L. 102–52, § 2(a), (b)(1), June 6, 1991, 105 Stat. 260; Pub. L. 102–569, title I, § 121(a), (b), Oct. 29, 1992, 106 Stat. 4365, 4367, related to congressional findings, purpose, policy, authorization of appropriations, change in Consumer Price Index, and extension of program, prior to the general amendment of this subchapter by Pub. L. 105–220.

§ 721. State plans

(a) Plan requirements

(1) In general

(A) Submission

To be eligible to participate in programs under this subchapter, a State shall submit to the Commissioner a State plan for vocational rehabilitation services that meets the requirements of this section, on the same date that the State submits a State plan under section 112 of the Workforce Investment Act of 1998 [29 U.S.C. 2822].

(B) Nonduplication

The State shall not be required to submit, in the State plan for vocational rehabilitation services, policies, procedures, or descriptions required under this subchapter that have been previously submitted to the Commissioner and that demonstrate that such State meets the requirements of this subchapter, including any policies, procedures, or descriptions submitted under this subchapter as in effect on the day before August 7, 1998.

(C) Duration

The State plan shall remain in effect subject to the submission of such modifications as the State determines to be necessary or as the Commissioner may require based on a change in State policy, a change in Federal law (including regulations), an interpretation of this chapter by a Federal court or the highest court of the State, or a finding by the Commissioner of State noncompliance with the requirements of this chapter, until the State submits and receives approval of a new State plan.

(2) Designated State agency; designated State unit

(A) Designated State agency

The State plan shall designate a State agency as the sole State agency to administer the plan, or to supervise the administration of the plan by a local agency, except that—

(i) where, under State law, the State agency for individuals who are blind or another agency that provides assistance or services to adults who are blind is authorized to provide vocational rehabilitation services to individuals who are blind, that agency may be designated as the sole State agency to administer the part of the plan under which vocational rehabilitation services are provided for individuals who are blind (or to supervise the administration of such part by a local agency) and a separate State agency may be designated as the sole State agency to administer or supervise the administration of the rest of the State plan;

(ii) the Commissioner, on the request of a State, may authorize the designated State agency to share funding and administrative responsibility with another agency of the State or with a local agency in order to permit the agencies to carry out a joint program to provide services to individuals with disabilities, and may waive compliance, with respect to vocational rehabilitation services furnished under the joint program, with the requirement of paragraph (4) that the plan be in effect in all political subdivisions of the State; and

(iii) in the case of American Samoa, the appropriate State agency shall be the Governor of American Samoa.

(B) Designated State unit

The State agency designated under subparagraph (A) shall be—

(i) a State agency primarily concerned with vocational rehabilitation, or vocational and other rehabilitation, of individuals with disabilities; or

(ii) if not such an agency, the State agency (or each State agency if 2 are so designated) shall include a vocational rehabilitation bureau, division, or other organizational unit that—

(I) is primarily concerned with vocational rehabilitation, or vocational and other rehabilitation, of individuals with disabilities, and is responsible for the vocational rehabilitation program of the designated State agency;

(II) has a full-time director;

(III) has a staff employed on the rehabilitation work of the organizational unit all or substantially all of whom are employed full time on such work; and

(IV) is located at an organizational level and has an organizational status within the designated State agency comparable to that of other major organizational units of the designated State agency.

(C) Responsibility for services for the blind

If the State has designated only 1 State agency pursuant to subparagraph (A), the State may assign responsibility for the part of the plan under which vocational rehabilitation services are provided for individuals who are blind to an organizational unit of the designated State agency and assign responsibility for the rest of the plan to another organizational unit of the designated State agency, with the provisions of subparagraph (B) applying separately to each of the designated State units.

(3) Non-Federal share

The State plan shall provide for financial participation by the State, or if the State so elects, by the State and local agencies, to provide the amount of the non-Federal share of the cost of carrying out part B of this subchapter.

(4) Statewideness

The State plan shall provide that the plan shall be in effect in all political subdivisions of the State, except that—

(A) in the case of any activity that, in the judgment of the Commissioner, is likely to assist in promoting the vocational rehabilitation of substantially larger numbers of individuals with disabilities or groups of individuals with disabilities, the Commissioner may waive compliance with the requirement that the plan be in effect in all political subdivisions of the State to the extent and for such period as may be provided in accordance with regulations prescribed by the Commissioner, but only if the non-Federal share of the cost of the vocational rehabilitation services involved is met from funds made available by a local agency (including funds contributed to such agency by a private agency, organization, or individual); and

(B) in a case in which earmarked funds are used toward the non-Federal share and such funds are earmarked for particular geographic areas within the State, the earmarked funds may be used in such areas if the State notifies the Commissioner that the State cannot provide the full non-Federal share without such funds.

(5) Order of selection for vocational rehabilitation services

In the event that vocational rehabilitation services cannot be provided to all eligible individuals with disabilities in the State who apply for the services, the State plan shall—

(A) show the order to be followed in selecting eligible individuals to be provided vocational rehabilitation services;

(B) provide the justification for the order of selection;

(C) include an assurance that, in accordance with criteria established by the State for the order of selection, individuals with the most significant disabilities will be selected first for the provision of vocational rehabilitation services; and

(D) provide that eligible individuals, who do not meet the order of selection criteria, shall have access to services provided through the information and referral system implemented under paragraph (20).

(6) Methods for administration

(A) In general

The State plan shall provide for such methods of administration as are found by the Commissioner to be necessary for the proper and efficient administration of the plan.

(B) Employment of individuals with disabilities

The State plan shall provide that the designated State agency, and entities carrying out community rehabilitation programs in the State, who are in receipt of assistance under this subchapter shall take affirmative action to employ and advance in employment qualified individuals with disabilities covered under, and on the same terms and conditions as set forth in, section 793 of this title.

(C) Facilities

The State plan shall provide that facilities used in connection with the delivery of services assisted under the State plan shall comply with the Act entitled "An Act to insure that certain buildings financed with Federal funds are so designed and constructed as to be accessible to the physically handicapped", approved on August 12, 1968 (commonly known as the "Architectural Barriers Act of 1968") [42 U.S.C. 4151 et seq.], with section 794 of this title, and with the Americans with Disabilities Act of 1990 [42 U.S.C. 12101 et seq.].

(7) Comprehensive system of personnel development

The State plan shall—

(A) include a description (consistent with the purposes of this chapter) of a comprehensive system of personnel development, which shall include—

(i) a description of the procedures and activities the designated State agency will undertake to ensure an adequate supply of qualified State rehabilitation professionals and paraprofessionals for the designated State unit, including the development and maintenance of a system for determining, on an annual basis—

(I) the number and type of personnel that are employed by the designated State unit in the provision of vocational rehabilitation services, including ratios of qualified vocational rehabilitation counselors to clients; and

(II) the number and type of personnel needed by the State, and a projection of tho numbers of such personnel that will be needed in 5 years, based on projections of the number of individuals to be served, the number of such personnel who are expected to retire or leave the vocational rehabilitation field, and other relevant factors;

(ii) where appropriate, a description of the manner in which activities will be undertaken under this section to coordinate the system of personnel development with personnel development activities under the Individuals with Disabilities Education Act (20 U.S.C. 1400 et seq.);

(iii) a description of the development and maintenance of a system of determining, on an annual basis, information on the programs of institutions of higher education within the State that are preparing rehabilitation professionals, including—

(I) the numbers of students enrolled in such programs; and

(II) the number of such students who graduated with certification or licensure, or with credentials to qualify for certification or licensure, as a rehabilitation professional during the past year;

(iv) a description of the development, updating, and implementation of a plan that—

(I) will address the current and projected vocational rehabilitation services personnel training needs for the designated State unit; and

(II) provides for the coordination and facilitation of efforts between the designated State unit, institutions of higher education, and professional associations to recruit, prepare, and retain qualified personnel, including personnel from minority backgrounds, and personnel who are individuals with disabilities; and

(v) a description of the procedures and activities the designated State agency will undertake to ensure that all personnel employed by the designated State unit are appropriately and adequately trained and prepared, including—

(I) a system for the continuing education of rehabilitation professionals and paraprofessionals within the designated State unit, particularly with respect to rehabilitation technology; and

(II) procedures for acquiring and disseminating to rehabilitation professionals and paraprofessionals within the designated State unit significant knowledge from research and other sources, including procedures for providing training regarding the amendments to this chapter made by the Rehabilitation Act Amendments of 1998;

(B) set forth policies and procedures relating to the establishment and maintenance of standards to ensure that personnel, including rehabilitation professionals and paraprofessionals, needed within the designated State unit to carry out this part are appropriately and adequately prepared and trained, including—

(i) the establishment and maintenance of standards that are consistent with any national or State approved or recognized certification, licensing, registration, or other comparable requirements that apply to the area in which such personnel are providing vocational rehabilitation services; and

(ii) to the extent that such standards are not based on the highest requirements in the State applicable to a specific profession or discipline, the steps the State is taking to require the retraining or hiring of personnel within the designated State unit that meet appropriate professional requirements in the State; and

(C) contain provisions relating to the establishment and maintenance of minimum standards to ensure the availability of personnel within the designated State unit, to the maximum extent feasible, trained to communicate in the native language or mode of communication of an applicant or eligible individual.

(8) Comparable services and benefits

(A) Determination of availability

(i) In general

The State plan shall include an assurance that, prior to providing any vocational rehabilitation service to an eligible individual, except those services specified in paragraph (5)(D) and in paragraphs (1) through (4) and (14) of section 723(a) of this title, the designated State unit will determine whether comparable services and benefits are available under any other program (other than a program carried out under this subchapter) unless such a determination would interrupt or delay—

(I) the progress of the individual toward achieving the employment outcome identified in the individualized plan for employment of the individual in accordance with section 722(b) of this title;

(II) an immediate job placement; or

(III) the provision of such service to any individual at extreme medical risk.

(ii) Awards and scholarships

For purposes of clause (i), comparable benefits do not include awards and scholarships based on merit.

(B) Interagency agreement

The State plan shall include an assurance that the Governor of the State, in consultation with the entity in the State responsible for the vocational rehabilitation program and other appropriate agencies, will ensure that an interagency agreement or other mechanism for interagency coordination takes effect between any appropriate public entity, including the State entity responsible for administering the State medicaid program, a public institution of higher education, and a component of the statewide workforce investment system, and the designated State unit, in order to ensure the provision of vocational rehabilitation services described in subparagraph (A) (other than those services specified in paragraph (5)(D), and in paragraphs (1) through (4) and (14) of section 723(a) of this title), that are included in the individualized plan for employment of an eligible individual, including the provision of such vocational rehabilitation services during the pendency of any dispute described in clause (iii). Such agreement or mechanism shall include the following:

(i) **Agency financial responsibility**

An identification of, or a description of a method for defining, the financial responsibility of such public entity for providing such services, and a provision stating the financial responsibility of such public entity for providing such services.

(ii) **Conditions, terms, and procedures of reimbursement**

Information specifying the conditions, terms, and procedures under which a designated State unit shall be reimbursed by other public entities for providing such services, based on the provisions of such agreement or mechanism.

(iii) **Interagency disputes**

Information specifying procedures for resolving interagency disputes under the agreement or other mechanism (including procedures under which the designated State unit may initiate proceedings to secure reimbursement from other public entities or otherwise implement the provisions of the agreement or mechanism).

(iv) **Coordination of services procedures**

Information specifying policies and procedures for public entities to determine and identify the interagency coordination responsibilities of each public entity to promote the coordination and timely delivery of vocational rehabilitation services (except those services specified in paragraph (5)(D) and in paragraphs (1) through (4) and (14) of section 723(a) of this title).

(C) Responsibilities of other public entities

(i) **Responsibilities under other law**

Notwithstanding subparagraph (B), if any public entity other than a designated State unit is obligated under Federal or State law, or assigned responsibility under State policy or under this paragraph, to provide or pay for any services that are also considered to be vocational rehabilitation services (other than those specified in paragraph (5)(D) and in paragraphs (1) through (4) and (14) of section 723(a) of this title), such public entity shall fulfill that obligation or responsibility, either directly or by contract or other arrangement.

(ii) **Reimbursement**

If a public entity other than the designated State unit fails to provide or pay for the services described in clause (i) for an eligible individual, the designated State unit shall provide or pay for such services to the individual. Such designated State unit may claim reimbursement for the services from the public entity that failed to provide or pay for such services. Such public entity shall reimburse the designated State unit pursuant to the terms of the interagency agreement or other mechanism described in this paragraph according to the procedures established in such agreement or mechanism pursuant to subparagraph (B)(ii).

(D) Methods

The Governor of a State may meet the requirements of subparagraph (B) through—

(i) a State statute or regulation;

(ii) a signed agreement between the respective officials of the public entities that clearly identifies the responsibilities of each public entity relating to the provision of services; or

(iii) another appropriate method, as determined by the designated State unit.

(9) Individualized plan for employment

(A) Development and implementation

The State plan shall include an assurance that an individualized plan for employment meeting the requirements of section 722(b) of this title will be developed and implemented in a timely manner for an individual subsequent to the determination of the eligibility of the individual for services under this subchapter, except that in a State operating under an order of selection described in paragraph (5), the plan will be developed and implemented only for individuals meeting the order of selection criteria of the State.

(B) Provision of services

The State plan shall include an assurance that such services will be provided in accordance with the provisions of the individualized plan for employment.

(10) Reporting requirements

(A) In general

The State plan shall include an assurance that the designated State agency will submit reports in the form and level of detail and at the time required by the Commissioner regarding applicants for, and eligible individuals receiving, services under this subchapter.

(B) Annual reporting

In specifying the information to be submitted in the reports, the Commissioner shall require annual reporting on the eligible individuals receiving the services, on those specific data elements described in section 136(d)(2) of the Workforce Investment Act of 1998 [29 U.S.C. 2871(d)(2)] that are determined by the Secretary to be relevant in assessing the performance of designated State units in carrying out the vocational rehabilitation program established under this subchapter.

(C) Additional data

In specifying the information required to be submitted in the reports, the Commissioner shall require additional data with regard to applicants and eligible individuals related to—

(i) the number of applicants and the number of individuals determined to be eligible or ineligible for the program carried out under this subchapter, including—

(I) the number of individuals determined to be ineligible because they did not require vocational rehabilitation services, as provided in section 722(a) of this title; and

(II) the number of individuals determined, on the basis of clear and convincing evidence, to be too severely disabled to benefit in terms of an employment outcome from vocational rehabilitation services;

(ii) the number of individuals who received vocational rehabilitation services through the program, including—

(I) the number who received services under paragraph (5)(D), but not assistance under an individualized plan for employment;

(II) of those recipients who are individuals with significant disabilities, the number who received assistance under an individualized plan for employment consistent with section 722(b) of this title; and

(III) of those recipients who are not individuals with significant disabilities, the number who received assistance under an individualized plan for employment consistent with section 722(b) of this title;

(iii) of those applicants and eligible recipients who are individuals with significant disabilities—

(I) the number who ended their participation in the program carried out under this subchapter and the number who achieved employment outcomes after receiving vocational rehabilitation services; and

(II) the number who ended their participation in the program and who were employed 6 months and 12 months after securing or regaining employment, or, in the case of individuals whose employment outcome was to retain or advance in employment, who were employed 6 months and 12 months after achieving their employment outcome, including—

(aa) the number who earned the minimum wage rate specified in section 6(a)(1) of the Fair Labor Standards Act of 1938 (29 U.S.C. 206(a)(1)) or another wage level set by the Commissioner, during such employment; and

(bb) the number who received employment benefits from an employer during such employment; and

(iv) of those applicants and eligible recipients who are not individuals with significant disabilities—

(I) the number who ended their participation in the program carried out under this subchapter and the number who achieved employment outcomes after receiving vocational rehabilitation services; and

(II) the number who ended their participation in the program and who were employed 6 months and 12 months after securing or regaining employment, or, in the case of individuals whose employment outcome was to retain or advance in employment, who were employed 6 months and 12 months after achieving their employment outcome, including—

(aa) the number who earned the minimum wage rate specified in section 6(a)(1) of the Fair Labor Standards Act of 1938 (29 U.S.C. 206(a)(1)) or another wage level set by the Commissioner, during such employment; and

(bb) the number who received employment benefits from an employer during such employment.

(D) Costs and results

The Commissioner shall also require that the designated State agency include in the reports information on—

(i) the costs under this subchapter of conducting administration, providing assessment services, counseling and guidance, and other direct services provided by designated State agency staff, providing services purchased under individualized plans for employment, supporting small business enterprises, establishing, developing, and improving community rehabilitation programs, providing other services to groups, and facilitating use of other programs under this chapter and title I of the Workforce Investment Act of 1998 [29 U.S.C. 2801 et seq.] by eligible individuals; and

(ii) the results of annual evaluation by the State of program effectiveness under paragraph (15)(E).

(E) Additional information

The Commissioner shall require that each designated State unit include in the reports additional information related to the applicants and eligible individuals, obtained either through a complete count or sampling, including—

(i) information on—

(I) age, gender, race, ethnicity, education, category of impairment, severity of disability, and whether the individuals are students with disabilities;

(II) dates of application, determination of eligibility or ineligibility, initiation of the individualized plan for employment, and termination of participation in the program;

(III) earnings at the time of application for the program and termination of participation in the program;

(IV) work status and occupation;

(V) types of services, including assistive technology services and assistive technology devices, provided under the program;

(VI) types of public or private programs or agencies that furnished services under the program; and

(VII) the reasons for individuals terminating participation in the program without achieving an employment outcome; and

(ii) information necessary to determine the success of the State in meeting—

(I) the State performance measures established under section 136(b) of the Workforce Investment Act of 1998 [29 U.S.C. 2871(b)], to the extent the measures are applicable to individuals with disabilities; and

(II) the standards and indicators established pursuant to section 726 of this title.

(F) Completeness and confidentiality

The State plan shall include an assurance that the information submitted in the reports will include a complete count, except as provided in subparagraph (E), of the applicants and eligible individuals, in a manner permitting the greatest possible cross-classification of data and that the identity of each individual for which information is supplied under this paragraph will be kept confidential.

(11) Cooperation, collaboration, and coordination

(A) Cooperative agreements with other components of statewide workforce investment systems

The State plan shall provide that the designated State unit or designated State agency shall enter into a cooperative agreement with other entities that are components of the statewide workforce investment system of the State, regarding the system, which agreement may provide for—

(i) provision of intercomponent staff training and technical assistance with regard to—

(I) the availability and benefits of, and information on eligibility standards for, vocational rehabilitation services; and

(II) the promotion of equal, effective, and meaningful participation by individuals with disabilities in workforce investment activities in the State through the promotion of program accessibility, the use of nondiscriminatory policies and procedures, and the provision of reasonable accommodations, auxiliary aids and services, and rehabilitation technology, for individuals with disabilities;

(ii) use of information and financial management systems that link all components of the statewide workforce investment system, that link the components to other electronic networks, including nonvisual electronic networks, and that relate to such subjects as employment statistics, and information on job vacancies, career planning, and workforce investment activities;

(iii) use of customer service features such as common intake and referral procedures, customer databases, resource information, and human services hotlines;

(iv) establishment of cooperative efforts with employers to—

(I) facilitate job placement; and

(II) carry out any other activities that the designated State unit and the employers determine to be appropriate;

(v) identification of staff roles, responsibilities, and available resources, and specification of the financial responsibility of each component of the statewide workforce investment system with regard to paying for necessary services (consistent with State law and Federal requirements); and

(vi) specification of procedures for resolving disputes among such components.

(B) Replication of cooperative agreements

The State plan shall provide for the replication of such cooperative agreements at the local level between individual offices of the designated State unit and local entities carrying out activities through the statewide workforce investment system.

(C) Interagency cooperation with other agencies

The State plan shall include descriptions of interagency cooperation with, and utilization of the services and facilities of, Federal, State, and local agencies and programs, including programs carried out by the Under Secretary for Rural Development of the Department of Agriculture and State use contracting programs, to the extent that such agencies and programs are not carrying out activities through the statewide workforce investment system.

(D) Coordination with education officials

The State plan shall contain plans, policies, and procedures for coordination between the designated State agency and education officials responsible for the public education of students with disabilities, that are designed to facilitate the transition of the students with disabilities from the receipt of educational services in school to the receipt of vocational rehabilitation services under this subchapter, including information on a formal interagency agreement with the State educational agency that, at a minimum, provides for—

(i) consultation and technical assistance to assist educational agencies in planning for the transition of students with disabilities from school to post-school activities, including vocational rehabilitation services;

(ii) transition planning by personnel of the designated State agency and educational agency personnel for students with disabilities that facilitates the development and completion of their individualized education programs under section 614(d) of the Individuals with Disabilities Education Act [20 U.S.C. 1414(d)];

(iii) the roles and responsibilities, including financial responsibilities, of each agency, including provisions for determining State lead agencies and qualified personnel responsible for transition services; and

(iv) procedures for outreach to and identification of students with disabilities who need the transition services.

(E) Coordination with Statewide Independent Living Councils and independent living centers

The State plan shall include an assurance that the designated State unit, the Statewide Independent Living Council established under section 796d of this title, and the independent living centers described in subpart 3[1] of part A of subchapter VII of this chapter within the State have developed working relationships and coordinate their activities.

(F) Cooperative agreement with recipients of grants for services to American Indians

In applicable cases, the State plan shall include an assurance that the State has entered into a formal cooperative agreement with each grant recipient in the State that receives funds under part C of this subchapter. The agreement shall describe strategies for collaboration and coordination in providing vocational rehabilitation services to American Indians who are individuals with disabilities, including—

(i) strategies for interagency referral and information sharing that will assist in eligibility determinations and the development of individualized plans for employment;

(ii) procedures for ensuring that American Indians who are individuals with disabilities and are living near a reservation or tribal service area are provided vocational rehabilitation services; and

(iii) provisions for sharing resources in cooperative studies and assessments, joint training activities, and other collaborative activities designed to improve the provision of services to American Indians who are individuals with disabilities.

(12) Residency

The State plan shall include an assurance that the State will not impose a residence requirement that excludes from services provided under the plan any individual who is present in the State.

(13) Services to American Indians

The State plan shall include an assurance that, except as otherwise provided in part C of this subchapter, the designated State agency will provide vocational rehabilitation services to American Indians who are individuals with disabilities residing in the State to the same extent as the designated State agency provides such services to other significant populations of individuals with disabilities residing in the State.

(14) Annual review of individuals in extended employment or other employment under special certificate provisions of the Fair Labor Standards Act of 1938

The State plan shall provide for—

(A) an annual review and reevaluation of the status of each individual with a disability served under this subchapter who has achieved an employment outcome either in an extended employment setting in a community rehabilitation program or any other employment under section 14(c) of the Fair Labor Standards Act (29 U.S.C. 214(c)) for 2 years after the achievement of the outcome (and thereafter if requested by the individual or, if appropriate, the individual's representative), to determine the interests, priorities, and needs of the individual with respect to competitive employment or training for competitive employment;

(B) input into the review and reevaluation, and a signed acknowledgment that such review and reevaluation have been conducted, by the individual with a disability, or, if appropriate, the individual's representative; and

(C) maximum efforts, including the identification and provision of vocational rehabilitation services, reasonable accommodations, and other necessary support services, to assist the individuals described in subparagraph (A) in engaging in competitive employment.

(15) Annual State goals and reports of progress

(A) Assessments and estimates

The State plan shall—

(i) include the results of a comprehensive, statewide assessment, jointly conducted by the designated State unit and the State Rehabilitation Council (if the State has such a Council) every 3 years, describing the rehabilitation needs of individuals with disabilities residing within the State, particularly the vocational rehabilitation services needs of—

(I) individuals with the most significant disabilities, including their need for supported employment services;

(II) individuals with disabilities who are minorities and individuals with disabilities who have been unserved or underserved by the vocational rehabilitation program carried out under this subchapter; and

(III) individuals with disabilities served through other components of the statewide workforce investment system (other than the vocational rehabilitation program), as identified by such individuals and personnel assisting such individuals through the components;

(ii) include an assessment of the need to establish, develop, or improve community rehabilitation programs within the State; and

(iii) provide that the State shall submit to the Commissioner a report containing information regarding updates to the assessments, for any year in which the State updates the assessments.

(B) Annual estimates

The State plan shall include, and shall provide that the State shall annually submit a report to the Commissioner that includes, State estimates of—

(i) the number of individuals in the State who are eligible for services under this subchapter;

(ii) the number of such individuals who will receive services provided with funds provided under part B of this subchapter and under part B of subchapter VI of this chapter, including, if the designated State agency uses an order of selection in ac-

[1] See References in Text note below.

cordance with paragraph (5), estimates of the number of individuals to be served under each priority category within the order; and

(iii) the costs of the services described in clause (i), including, if the designated State agency uses an order of selection in accordance with paragraph (5), the service costs for each priority category within the order.

(C) Goals and priorities

(i) In general

The State plan shall identify the goals and priorities of the State in carrying out the program. The goals and priorities shall be jointly developed, agreed to, and reviewed annually by the designated State unit and the State Rehabilitation Council, if the State has such a Council. Any revisions to the goals and priorities shall be jointly agreed to by the designated State unit and the State Rehabilitation Council, if the State has such a Council. The State plan shall provide that the State shall submit to the Commissioner a report containing information regarding revisions in the goals and priorities, for any year in which the State revises the goals and priorities.

(ii) Basis

The State goals and priorities shall be based on an analysis of—

(I) the comprehensive assessment described in subparagraph (A), including any updates to the assessment;

(II) the performance of the State on the standards and indicators established under section 726 of this title; and

(III) other available information on the operation and the effectiveness of the vocational rehabilitation program carried out in the State, including any reports received from the State Rehabilitation Council, under section 725(c) of this title and the findings and recommendations from monitoring activities conducted under section 727 of this title.

(iii) Service and outcome goals for categories in order of selection

If the designated State agency uses an order of selection in accordance with paragraph (5), the State shall also identify in the State plan service and outcome goals and the time within which these goals may be achieved for individuals in each priority category within the order.

(D) Strategies

The State plan shall contain a description of the strategies the State will use to address the needs identified in the assessment conducted under subparagraph (A) and achieve the goals and priorities identified in subparagraph (C), including—

(i) the methods to be used to expand and improve services to individuals with disabilities, including how a broad range of assistive technology services and assistive technology devices will be provided to such individuals at each stage of the rehabilitation process and how such services and devices will be provided to such individuals on a statewide basis;

(ii) outreach procedures to identify and serve individuals with disabilities who are minorities and individuals with disabilities who have been unserved or underserved by the vocational rehabilitation program;

(iii) where necessary, the plan of the State for establishing, developing, or improving community rehabilitation programs;

(iv) strategies to improve the performance of the State with respect to the evaluation standards and performance indicators established pursuant to section 726 of this title; and

(v) strategies for assisting entities carrying out other components of the statewide workforce investment system (other than the vocational rehabilitation program) in assisting individuals with disabilities.

(E) Evaluation and reports of progress

The State plan shall—

(i) include the results of an evaluation of the effectiveness of the vocational rehabilitation program, and a joint report by the designated State unit and the State Rehabilitation Council, if the State has such a Council, to the Commissioner on the progress made in improving the effectiveness from the previous year, which evaluation and report shall include—

(I) an evaluation of the extent to which the goals identified in subparagraph (C) were achieved;

(II) a description of strategies that contributed to achieving the goals;

(III) to the extent to which the goals were not achieved, a description of the factors that impeded that achievement; and

(IV) an assessment of the performance of the State on the standards and indicators established pursuant to section 726 of this title; and

(ii) provide that the designated State unit and the State Rehabilitation Council, if the State has such a Council, shall jointly submit to the Commissioner an annual report that contains the information described in clause (i).

(16) Public comment

The State plan shall—

(A) provide that the designated State agency, prior to the adoption of any policies or procedures governing the provision of vocational rehabilitation services under the State plan (including making any amendment to such policies and procedures), shall conduct public meetings throughout the State, after providing adequate notice of the meetings, to provide the public, including individuals with disabilities, an opportunity to comment on the policies or procedures, and actively consult with the Director of the client assistance program carried out under section 732 of this title, and, as appropriate,

Indian tribes, tribal organizations, and Native Hawaiian organizations on the policies or procedures; and

(B) provide that the designated State agency (or each designated State agency if two agencies are designated) and any sole agency administering the plan in a political subdivision of the State, shall take into account, in connection with matters of general policy arising in the administration of the plan, the views of—

(i) individuals and groups of individuals who are recipients of vocational rehabilitation services, or in appropriate cases, the individuals' representatives;

(ii) personnel working in programs that provide vocational rehabilitation services to individuals with disabilities;

(iii) providers of vocational rehabilitation services to individuals with disabilities;

(iv) the director of the client assistance program; and

(v) the State Rehabilitation Council, if the State has such a Council.

(17) Use of funds for construction of facilities

The State plan shall provide that if, under special circumstances, the State plan includes provisions for the construction of facilities for community rehabilitation programs—

(A) the Federal share of the cost of construction for the facilities for a fiscal year will not exceed an amount equal to 10 percent of the State's allotment under section 730 of this title for such year;

(B) the provisions of section 776 of this title (as in effect on the day before August 7, 1998) shall be applicable to such construction and such provisions shall be deemed to apply to such construction; and

(C) there shall be compliance with regulations the Commissioner shall prescribe designed to assure that no State will reduce its efforts in providing other vocational rehabilitation services (other than for the establishment of facilities for community rehabilitation programs) because the plan includes such provisions for construction.

(18) Innovation and expansion activities

The State plan shall—

(A) include an assurance that the State will reserve and use a portion of the funds allotted to the State under section 730 of this title—

(i) for the development and implementation of innovative approaches to expand and improve the provision of vocational rehabilitation services to individuals with disabilities under this subchapter, particularly individuals with the most significant disabilities, consistent with the findings of the statewide assessment and goals and priorities of the State as described in paragraph (15); and

(ii) to support the funding of—

(I) the State Rehabilitation Council, if the State has such a Council, consistent with the plan prepared under section 725(d)(1) of this title; and

(II) the Statewide Independent Living Council, consistent with the plan prepared under section 796d(e)(1) of this title;

(B) include a description of how the reserved funds will be utilized; and

(C) provide that the State shall submit to the Commissioner an annual report containing a description of how the reserved funds were utilized during the preceding year.

(19) Choice

The State plan shall include an assurance that applicants and eligible individuals or, as appropriate, the applicants' representatives or individuals' representatives, will be provided information and support services to assist the applicants and individuals in exercising informed choice throughout the rehabilitation process, consistent with the provisions of section 722(d) of this title.

(20) Information and referral services

(A) In general

The State plan shall include an assurance that the designated State agency will implement an information and referral system adequate to ensure that individuals with disabilities will be provided accurate vocational rehabilitation information and guidance, using appropriate modes of communication, to assist such individuals in preparing for, securing, retaining, or regaining employment, and will be appropriately referred to Federal and State programs (other than the vocational rehabilitation program carried out under this subchapter), including other components of the statewide workforce investment system in the State.

(B) Referrals

An appropriate referral made through the system shall—

(i) be to the Federal or State programs, including programs carried out by other components of the statewide workforce investment system in the State, best suited to address the specific employment needs of an individual with a disability; and

(ii) include, for each of these programs, provision to the individual of—

(I) a notice of the referral by the designated State agency to the agency carrying out the program;

(II) information identifying a specific point of contact within the agency carrying out the program; and

(III) information and advice regarding the most suitable services to assist the individual to prepare for, secure, retain, or regain employment.

(21) State independent consumer-controlled commission; State Rehabilitation Council

(A) Commission or Council

The State plan shall provide that either—

(i) the designated State agency is an independent commission that—

(I) is responsible under State law for operating, or overseeing the operation of, the vocational rehabilitation program in the State;

(II) is consumer-controlled by persons who—

(aa) are individuals with physical or mental impairments that substantially limit major life activities; and

(bb) represent individuals with a broad range of disabilities, unless the designated State unit under the direction of the commission is the State agency for individuals who are blind;

(III) includes family members, advocates, or other representatives, of individuals with mental impairments; and

(IV) undertakes the functions set forth in section 725(c)(4) of this title; or

(ii) the State has established a State Rehabilitation Council that meets the criteria set forth in section 725 of this title and the designated State unit—

(I) in accordance with paragraph (15), jointly develops, agrees to, and reviews annually State goals and priorities, and jointly submits annual reports of progress with the Council;

(II) regularly consults with the Council regarding the development, implementation, and revision of State policies and procedures of general applicability pertaining to the provision of vocational rehabilitation services;

(III) includes in the State plan and in any revision to the State plan, a summary of input provided by the Council, including recommendations from the annual report of the Council described in section 725(c)(5) of this title, the review and analysis of consumer satisfaction described in section 725(c)(4) of this title, and other reports prepared by the Council, and the response of the designated State unit to such input and recommendations, including explanations for rejecting any input or recommendation; and

(IV) transmits to the Council—

(aa) all plans, reports, and other information required under this subchapter to be submitted to the Secretary;

(bb) all policies, and information on all practices and procedures, of general applicability provided to or used by rehabilitation personnel in carrying out this subchapter; and

(cc) copies of due process hearing decisions issued under this subchapter, which shall be transmitted in such a manner as to ensure that the identity of the participants in the hearings is kept confidential.

(B) More than one designated State agency

In the case of a State that, under subsection (a)(2) of this section, designates a State agency to administer the part of the State plan under which vocational rehabilitation services are provided for individuals who are blind (or to supervise the administration of such part by a local agency) and designates a separate State agency to administer the rest of the State plan, the State shall either establish a State Rehabilitation Council for each of the two agencies that does not meet the requirements in subparagraph (A)(i), or establish one State Rehabilitation Council for both agencies if neither agency meets the requirements of subparagraph (A)(i).

(22) Supported employment State plan supplement

The State plan shall include an assurance that the State has an acceptable plan for carrying out part B of subchapter VI of this chapter, including the use of funds under that part to supplement funds made available under part B of this subchapter to pay for the cost of services leading to supported employment.

(23) Annual updates

The plan shall include an assurance that the State will submit to the Commissioner reports containing annual updates of the information required under paragraph (7) (relating to a comprehensive system of personnel development) and any other updates of the information required under this section that are requested by the Commissioner, and annual reports as provided in paragraphs (15) (relating to assessments, estimates, goals and priorities, and reports of progress) and (18) (relating to innovation and expansion), at such time and in such manner as the Secretary may determine to be appropriate.

(24) Certain contracts and cooperative agreements

(A) Contracts with for-profit organizations

The State plan shall provide that the designated State agency has the authority to enter into contracts with for-profit organizations for the purpose of providing, as vocational rehabilitation services, on-the-job training and related programs for individuals with disabilities under part A of subchapter VI of this chapter, upon a determination by such agency that such for-profit organizations are better qualified to provide such rehabilitation services than nonprofit agencies and organizations.

(B) Cooperative agreements with private nonprofit organizations

The State plan shall describe the manner in which cooperative agreements with private nonprofit vocational rehabilitation service providers will be established.

(b) Approval; disapproval of the State plan

(1) Approval

The Commissioner shall approve any plan that the Commissioner finds fulfills the conditions specified in this section, and shall disapprove any plan that does not fulfill such conditions.

(2) Disapproval

Prior to disapproval of the State plan, the Commissioner shall notify the State of the intention to disapprove the plan and shall afford the State reasonable notice and opportunity for a hearing.

(Pub. L. 93–112, title I, §101, as added Pub. L. 105–220, title IV, §404, Aug. 7, 1998, 112 Stat. 1119;

amended Pub. L. 105–277, div. A, § 101(f) [title VIII, § 402(c)(4)], Oct. 21, 1998, 112 Stat. 2681–337, 2681–415; Pub. L. 108–446, title III, § 305(h)(1), Dec. 3, 2004, 118 Stat. 2805.)

REFERENCES IN TEXT

The Architectural Barriers Act of 1968, referred to in subsec. (a)(6)(C), is Pub. L. 90–480, Aug. 12, 1968, 82 Stat. 718, as amended, which is classified generally to chapter 51 (§ 4151 et seq.) of Title 42, The Public Health and Welfare. For complete classification of this Act to the Code, see Short Title note set out under section 4151 of Title 42 and Tables.

The Americans with Disabilities Act of 1990, referred to in subsec. (a)(6)(C), is Pub. L. 101–336, July 26, 1990, 104 Stat. 327, as amended, which is classified principally to chapter 126 (§ 12101 et seq.) of Title 42, The Public Health and Welfare. For complete classification of this Act to the Code, see Short Title note set out under section 12101 of Title 42 and Tables.

The Individuals with Disabilities Education Act, referred to in subsec. (a)(7)(A)(ii), is title VI of Pub. L. 91–230, Apr. 13, 1970, 84 Stat. 175, as amended, which is classified generally to chapter 33 (§ 1400 et seq.) of Title 20, Education. For complete classification of this Act to the Code, see section 1400 of Title 20 and Tables.

The Rehabilitation Act Amendments of 1998, referred to in subsec. (a)(7)(A)(v)(II), is title IV of Pub. L. 105–220, Aug. 7, 1998, 112 Stat. 1092. For complete classification of this Act to the Code, see Short Title of 1998 Amendment note set out under section 701 of this title and Tables.

The Workforce Investment Act of 1998, referred to in subsec. (a)(10)(D)(i), is Pub. L. 105–220, Aug. 7, 1998, 112 Stat. 936, as amended. Title I of the Act is classified principally to chapter 30 (§ 2801 et seq.) of this title. For complete classification of this Act to the Code, see Short Title note set out under section 9201 of Title 20, Education, and Tables.

Subpart 3 of part A of subchapter VII of this chapter, referred to in subsec. (a)(11)(E), was in the original a reference to "part C of title VII", meaning part C of title VII of the Rehabilitation Act of 1973, and was translated as if it referred to part C of chapter I of title VII of the Act to reflect the probable intent of Congress.

PRIOR PROVISIONS

A prior section 721, Pub. L. 93–112, title I, § 101, Sept. 26, 1973, 87 Stat. 363; Pub. L. 93–516, title I, § 111(b)–(d), Dec. 7, 1974, 88 Stat. 1619, 1620; Pub. L. 93–651, title I, § 111(b)–(d), Nov. 21, 1974, 89 Stat. 2–5; Pub. L. 95–602, title I, §§ 102, 122(b)(1), Nov. 6, 1978, 92 Stat. 2957, 2987; Pub. L. 98–221, title I, § 104(a)(2), Feb. 22, 1984, 98 Stat. 18; Pub. L. 98–524, § 4(f), Oct. 19, 1984, 98 Stat. 2489; Pub. L. 99–506, title I, § 103(d)(2), title II, § 202, title X, § 1001(b)(1)–(4), Oct. 21, 1986, 100 Stat. 1810, 1814, 1841, 1842; Pub. L. 100–630, title II, § 202(b), Nov. 7, 1988, 102 Stat. 3304; Pub. L. 102–54, § 13(k)(1)(A), June 13, 1991, 105 Stat. 276; Pub. L. 102–119, § 26(e), Oct. 7, 1991, 105 Stat. 607; Pub. L. 102–569, title I, §§ 102(*o*), (p)(7), 122, Oct. 29, 1992, 106 Stat. 4355, 4356, 4367; Pub. L. 103–73, title I, §§ 102(2), 107(a), Aug. 11, 1993, 107 Stat. 718, 719; Pub. L. 104–106, div. D, title XLIII, § 4321(i)(7), Feb. 10, 1996, 110 Stat. 676, related to State plans, prior to the general amendment of this subchapter by Pub. L. 105–220.

AMENDMENTS

2004—Subsec. (a)(11)(D)(ii). Pub. L. 108–446 struck out "(as added by section 101 of Public Law 105–17)" before semicolon at end.

1998—Subsec. (a)(18)(C). Pub. L. 105–277, § 101(f) [title VIII, § 402(c)(4)(A)], substituted "were utilized during the preceding year" for "will be utilized".

Subsec. (a)(21)(A)(i)(II)(bb). Pub. L. 105–277, § 101(f) [title VIII, § 402(c)(4)(B)], substituted "commission" for "Commission".

§ 722. Eligibility and individualized plan for employment

(a) Eligibility

(1) Criterion for eligibility

An individual is eligible for assistance under this subchapter if the individual—

(A) is an individual with a disability under section 705(20)(A) of this title; and

(B) requires vocational rehabilitation services to prepare for, secure, retain, or regain employment.

(2) Presumption of benefit

(A) Demonstration

For purposes of this section, an individual shall be presumed to be an individual that can benefit in terms of an employment outcome from vocational rehabilitation services under section 705(20)(A) of this title, unless the designated State unit involved can demonstrate by clear and convincing evidence that such individual is incapable of benefiting in terms of an employment outcome from vocational rehabilitation services due to the severity of the disability of the individual.

(B) Methods

In making the demonstration required under subparagraph (A), the designated State unit shall explore the individual's abilities, capabilities, and capacity to perform in work situations, through the use of trial work experiences, as described in section 705(2)(D) of this title, with appropriate supports provided through the designated State unit, except under limited circumstances when an individual cannot take advantage of such experiences. Such experiences shall be of sufficient variety and over a sufficient period of time to determine the eligibility of the individual or to determine the existence of clear and convincing evidence that the individual is incapable of benefiting in terms of an employment outcome from vocational rehabilitation services due to the severity of the disability of the individual.

(3) Presumption of eligibility

(A) In general

For purposes of this section, an individual who has a disability or is blind as determined pursuant to title II or title XVI of the Social Security Act (42 U.S.C. 401 et seq. and 1381 et seq.) shall be—

(i) considered to be an individual with a significant disability under section 705(21)(A) of this title; and

(ii) presumed to be eligible for vocational rehabilitation services under this subchapter (provided that the individual intends to achieve an employment outcome consistent with the unique strengths, resources, priorities, concerns, abilities, capabilities, interests, and informed choice of the individual) unless the designated State unit involved can demonstrate by clear and convincing evidence that such individual is incapable of benefiting in terms of an employment outcome from vocational rehabilitation services due to the severity of the disability of the individual in accordance with paragraph (2).

(B) Construction

Nothing in this paragraph shall be construed to create an entitlement to any vocational rehabilitation service.

(4) Use of existing information

(A) In general

To the maximum extent appropriate and consistent with the requirements of this part, for purposes of determining the eligibility of an individual for vocational rehabilitation services under this subchapter and developing the individualized plan for employment described in subsection (b) of this section for the individual, the designated State unit shall use information that is existing and current (as of the date of the determination of eligibility or of the development of the individualized plan for employment), including information available from other programs and providers, particularly information used by education officials and the Social Security Administration, information provided by the individual and the family of the individual, and information obtained under the assessment for determining eligibility and vocational rehabilitation needs.

(B) Determinations by officials of other agencies

Determinations made by officials of other agencies, particularly education officials described in section 721(a)(11)(D) of this title, regarding whether an individual satisfies one or more factors relating to whether an individual is an individual with a disability under section 705(20)(A) of this title or an individual with a significant disability under section 705(21)(A) of this title shall be used, to the extent appropriate and consistent with the requirements of this part, in assisting the designated State unit in making such determinations.

(C) Basis

The determination of eligibility for vocational rehabilitation services shall be based on—

(i) the review of existing data described in section 705(2)(A)(i) of this title; and

(ii) to the extent that such data is unavailable or insufficient for determining eligibility, the provision of assessment activities described in section 705(2)(A)(ii) of this title.

(5) Determination of ineligibility

If an individual who applies for services under this subchapter is determined, based on the review of existing data and, to the extent necessary, the assessment activities described in section 705(2)(A)(ii) of this title, not to be eligible for the services, or if an eligible individual receiving services under an individualized plan for employment is determined to be no longer eligible for the services—

(A) the ineligibility determination involved shall be made only after providing an opportunity for full consultation with the individual or, as appropriate, the individual's representative;

(B) the individual or, as appropriate, the individual's representative, shall be informed in writing (supplemented as necessary by other appropriate modes of communication consistent with the informed choice of the individual) of the ineligibility determination, including—

(i) the reasons for the determination; and

(ii) a description of the means by which the individual may express, and seek a remedy for, any dissatisfaction with the determination, including the procedures for review by an impartial hearing officer under subsection (c) of this section;

(C) the individual shall be provided with a description of services available from the client assistance program under section 732 of this title and information on how to contact that program; and

(D) any ineligibility determination that is based on a finding that the individual is incapable of benefiting in terms of an employment outcome shall be reviewed—

(i) within 12 months; and

(ii) thereafter, if such a review is requested by the individual or, if appropriate, by the individual's representative.

(6) Timeframe for making an eligibility determination

The designated State unit shall determine whether an individual is eligible for vocational rehabilitation services under this subchapter within a reasonable period of time, not to exceed 60 days, after the individual has submitted an application for the services unless—

(A) exceptional and unforeseen circumstances beyond the control of the designated State unit preclude making an eligibility determination within 60 days and the designated State unit and the individual agree to a specific extension of time; or

(B) the designated State unit is exploring an individual's abilities, capabilities, and capacity to perform in work situations under paragraph (2)(B).

(b) Development of an individualized plan for employment

(1) Options for developing an individualized plan for employment

If an individual is determined to be eligible for vocational rehabilitation services as described in subsection (a) of this section, the designated State unit shall complete the assessment for determining eligibility and vocational rehabilitation needs, as appropriate, and shall provide the eligible individual or the individual's representative, in writing and in an appropriate mode of communication, with information on the individual's options for developing an individualized plan for employment, including—

(A) information on the availability of assistance, to the extent determined to be appropriate by the eligible individual, from a qualified vocational rehabilitation counselor in developing all or part of the individualized plan for employment for the individual, and the availability of technical assistance in developing all or part of the individualized plan for employment for the individual;

(B) a description of the full range of components that shall be included in an individualized plan for employment;

(C) as appropriate—

(i) an explanation of agency guidelines and criteria associated with financial commitments concerning an individualized plan for employment;

(ii) additional information the eligible individual requests or the designated State unit determines to be necessary; and

(iii) information on the availability of assistance in completing designated State agency forms required in developing an individualized plan for employment; and

(D)(i) a description of the rights and remedies available to such an individual including, if appropriate, recourse to the processes set forth in subsection (c) of this section; and

(ii) a description of the availability of a client assistance program established pursuant to section 732 of this title and information about how to contact the client assistance program.

(2) Mandatory procedures

(A) Written document

An individualized plan for employment shall be a written document prepared on forms provided by the designated State unit.

(B) Informed choice

An individualized plan for employment shall be developed and implemented in a manner that affords eligible individuals the opportunity to exercise informed choice in selecting an employment outcome, the specific vocational rehabilitation services to be provided under the plan, the entity that will provide the vocational rehabilitation services, and the methods used to procure the services, consistent with subsection (d) of this section.

(C) Signatories

An individualized plan for employment shall be—

(i) agreed to, and signed by, such eligible individual or, as appropriate, the individual's representative; and

(ii) approved and signed by a qualified vocational rehabilitation counselor employed by the designated State unit.

(D) Copy

A copy of the individualized plan for employment for an eligible individual shall be provided to the individual or, as appropriate, to the individual's representative, in writing and, if appropriate, in the native language or mode of communication of the individual or, as appropriate, of the individual's representative.

(E) Review and amendment

The individualized plan for employment shall be—

(i) reviewed at least annually by—

(I) a qualified vocational rehabilitation counselor; and

(II) the eligible individual or, as appropriate, the individual's representative; and

(ii) amended, as necessary, by the individual or, as appropriate, the individual's representative, in collaboration with a representative of the designated State agency or a qualified vocational rehabilitation counselor (to the extent determined to be appropriate by the individual), if there are substantive changes in the employment outcome, the vocational rehabilitation services to be provided, or the service providers of the services (which amendments shall not take effect until agreed to and signed by the eligible individual or, as appropriate, the individual's representative, and by a qualified vocational rehabilitation counselor employed by the designated State unit).

(3) Mandatory components of an individualized plan for employment

Regardless of the approach selected by an eligible individual to develop an individualized plan for employment, an individualized plan for employment shall, at a minimum, contain mandatory components consisting of—

(A) a description of the specific employment outcome that is chosen by the eligible individual, consistent with the unique strengths, resources, priorities, concerns, abilities, capabilities, interests, and informed choice of the eligible individual, and, to the maximum extent appropriate, results in employment in an integrated setting;

(B)(i) a description of the specific vocational rehabilitation services that are—

(I) needed to achieve the employment outcome, including, as appropriate, the provision of assistive technology devices and assistive technology services, and personal assistance services, including training in the management of such services; and

(II) provided in the most integrated setting that is appropriate for the service involved and is consistent with the informed choice of the eligible individual; and

(ii) timelines for the achievement of the employment outcome and for the initiation of the services;

(C) a description of the entity chosen by the eligible individual or, as appropriate, the individual's representative, that will provide the vocational rehabilitation services, and the methods used to procure such services;

(D) a description of criteria to evaluate progress toward achievement of the employment outcome;

(E) the terms and conditions of the individualized plan for employment, including, as appropriate, information describing—

(i) the responsibilities of the designated State unit;

(ii) the responsibilities of the eligible individual, including—

(I) the responsibilities the eligible individual will assume in relation to the employment outcome of the individual;

(II) if applicable, the participation of the eligible individual in paying for the costs of the plan; and

(III) the responsibility of the eligible individual with regard to applying for and securing comparable benefits as described in section 721(a)(8) of this title; and

(iii) the responsibilities of other entities as the result of arrangements made pursuant to comparable services or benefits requirements as described in section 721(a)(8) of this title;

(F) for an eligible individual with the most significant disabilities for whom an employment outcome in a supported employment setting has been determined to be appropriate, information identifying—

(i) the extended services needed by the eligible individual; and

(ii) the source of extended services or, to the extent that the source of the extended services cannot be identified at the time of the development of the individualized plan for employment, a description of the basis for concluding that there is a reasonable expectation that such source will become available; and

(G) as determined to be necessary, a statement of projected need for post-employment services.

(c) Procedures

(1) In general

Each State shall establish procedures for mediation of, and procedures for review through an impartial due process hearing of, determinations made by personnel of the designated State unit that affect the provision of vocational rehabilitation services to applicants or eligible individuals.

(2) Notification

(A) Rights and assistance

The procedures shall provide that an applicant or an eligible individual or, as appropriate, the applicant's representative or individual's representative shall be notified of—

(i) the right to obtain review of determinations described in paragraph (1) in an impartial due process hearing under paragraph (5);

(ii) the right to pursue mediation with respect to the determinations under paragraph (4); and

(iii) the availability of assistance from the client assistance program under section 732 of this title.

(B) Timing

Such notification shall be provided in writing—

(i) at the time an individual applies for vocational rehabilitation services provided under this subchapter;

(ii) at the time the individualized plan for employment for the individual is developed; and

(iii) upon reduction, suspension, or cessation of vocational rehabilitation services for the individual.

(3) Evidence and representation

The procedures required under this subsection shall, at a minimum—

(A) provide an opportunity for an applicant or an eligible individual, or, as appropriate, the applicant's representative or individual's representative, to submit at the mediation session or hearing evidence and information to support the position of the applicant or eligible individual; and

(B) include provisions to allow an applicant or an eligible individual to be represented in the mediation session or hearing by a person selected by the applicant or eligible individual.

(4) Mediation

(A) Procedures

Each State shall ensure that procedures are established and implemented under this subsection to allow parties described in paragraph (1) to disputes involving any determination described in paragraph (1) to resolve such disputes through a mediation process that, at a minimum, shall be available whenever a hearing is requested under this subsection.

(B) Requirements

Such procedures shall ensure that the mediation process—

(i) is voluntary on the part of the parties;

(ii) is not used to deny or delay the right of an individual to a hearing under this subsection, or to deny any other right afforded under this subchapter; and

(iii) is conducted by a qualified and impartial mediator who is trained in effective mediation techniques.

(C) List of mediators

The State shall maintain a list of individuals who are qualified mediators and knowledgeable in laws (including regulations) relating to the provision of vocational rehabilitation services under this subchapter, from which the mediators described in subparagraph (B) shall be selected.

(D) Cost

The State shall bear the cost of the mediation process.

(E) Scheduling

Each session in the mediation process shall be scheduled in a timely manner and shall be held in a location that is convenient to the parties to the dispute.

(F) Agreement

An agreement reached by the parties to the dispute in the mediation process shall be set forth in a written mediation agreement.

(G) Confidentiality

Discussions that occur during the mediation process shall be confidential and may not be used as evidence in any subsequent due process hearing or civil proceeding. The parties to the mediation process may be required to sign a confidentiality pledge prior to the commencement of such process.

(H) Construction

Nothing in this subsection shall be construed to preclude the parties to such a dispute from informally resolving the dispute prior to proceedings under this paragraph or paragraph (5), if the informal process used is not used to deny or delay the right of the applicant or eligible individual to a hearing under this subsection or to deny any other right afforded under this subchapter.

(5) Hearings

(A) Officer

A due process hearing described in paragraph (2) shall be conducted by an impartial hearing officer who shall issue a decision based on the provisions of the approved State plan, this chapter (including regulations implementing this chapter), and State regulations and policies that are consistent with the Federal requirements specified in this subchapter. The officer shall provide the decision in writing to the applicant or eligible individual, or, as appropriate, the applicant's representative or individual's representative, and to the designated State unit.

(B) List

The designated State unit shall maintain a list of qualified impartial hearing officers who are knowledgeable in laws (including regulations) relating to the provision of vocational rehabilitation services under this subchapter from which the officer described in subparagraph (A) shall be selected. For the purposes of maintaining such list, impartial hearing officers shall be identified jointly by—

(i) the designated State unit; and

(ii) members of the Council or commission, as appropriate, described in section 721(a)(21) of this title.

(C) Selection

Such an impartial hearing officer shall be selected to hear a particular case relating to a determination—

(i) on a random basis; or

(ii) by agreement between—

(I) the Director of the designated State unit and the individual with a disability; or

(II) in appropriate cases, the Director and the individual's representative.

(D) Procedures for seeking review

A State may establish procedures to enable a party involved in a hearing under this paragraph to seek an impartial review of the decision of the hearing officer under subparagraph (A) by—

(i) the chief official of the designated State agency if the State has established both a designated State agency and a designated State unit under section 721(a)(2) of this title; or

(ii) an official from the office of the Governor.

(E) Review request

If the State establishes impartial review procedures under subparagraph (D), either party may request the review of the decision of the hearing officer within 20 days after the decision.

(F) Reviewing official

The reviewing official described in subparagraph (D) shall—

(i) in conducting the review, provide an opportunity for the submission of additional evidence and information relevant to a final decision concerning the matter under review;

(ii) not overturn or modify the decision of the hearing officer, or part of the decision, that supports the position of the applicant or eligible individual unless the reviewing official concludes, based on clear and convincing evidence, that the decision of the impartial hearing officer is clearly erroneous on the basis of being contrary to the approved State plan, this chapter (including regulations implementing this chapter) or any State regulation or policy that is consistent with the Federal requirements specified in this subchapter;

(iii) make a final decision with respect to the matter in a timely manner and provide such decision in writing to the applicant or eligible individual, or, as appropriate, the applicant's representative or individual's representative, and to the designated State unit, including a full report of the findings and the grounds for such decision; and

(iv) not delegate the responsibility for making the final decision to any officer or employee of the designated State unit.

(G) Finality of hearing decision

A decision made after a hearing under subparagraph (A) shall be final, except that a party may request an impartial review if the State has established procedures for such review under subparagraph (D) and a party involved in a hearing may bring a civil action under subparagraph (J).

(H) Finality of review

A decision made under subparagraph (F) shall be final unless such a party brings a civil action under subparagraph (J).

(I) Implementation

If a party brings a civil action under subparagraph (J) to challenge a final decision of a hearing officer under subparagraph (A) or to challenge a final decision of a State reviewing official under subparagraph (F), the final decision involved shall be implemented pending review by the court.

(J) Civil action

(i) In general

Any party aggrieved by a final decision described in subparagraph (I), may bring a civil action for review of such decision. The action may be brought in any State court of competent jurisdiction or in a district court of the United States of competent jurisdiction without regard to the amount in controversy.

(ii) Procedure

In any action brought under this subparagraph, the court—

(I) shall receive the records relating to the hearing under subparagraph (A) and the records relating to the State review under subparagraphs (D) through (F), if applicable;

(II) shall hear additional evidence at the request of a party to the action; and

(III) basing the decision of the court on the preponderance of the evidence, shall grant such relief as the court determines to be appropriate.

(6) Hearing board

(A) In general

A fair hearing board, established by a State before January 1, 1985, and authorized under State law to review determinations or decisions under this chapter, is authorized to carry out the responsibilities of the impartial hearing officer under this subsection.

(B) Application

The provisions of paragraphs (1), (2), and (3) that relate to due process hearings do not apply, and paragraph (5) (other than subparagraph (J)) does not apply, to any State to which subparagraph (A) applies.

(7) Impact on provision of services

Unless the individual with a disability so requests, or, in an appropriate case, the individual's representative, so requests, pending a decision by a mediator, hearing officer, or reviewing officer under this subsection, the designated State unit shall not institute a suspension, reduction, or termination of services being provided for the individual, including evaluation and assessment services and plan development, unless such services have been obtained through misrepresentation, fraud, collusion, or criminal conduct on the part of the individual, or the individual's representative.

(8) Information collection and report

(A) In general

The Director of the designated State unit shall collect information described in subparagraph (B) and prepare and submit to the Commissioner a report containing such information. The Commissioner shall prepare a summary of the information furnished under this paragraph and include the summary in the annual report submitted under section 710 of this title. The Commissioner shall also collect copies of the final decisions of impartial hearing officers conducting hearings under this subsection and State officials conducting reviews under this subsection.

(B) Information

The information required to be collected under this subsection includes—

(i) a copy of the standards used by State reviewing officials for reviewing decisions made by impartial hearing officers under this subsection;

(ii) information on the number of hearings and reviews sought from the impartial hearing officers and the State reviewing officials, including the type of complaints and the issues involved;

(iii) information on the number of hearing decisions made under this subsection that were not reviewed by the State reviewing officials; and

(iv) information on the number of the hearing decisions that were reviewed by the State reviewing officials, and, based on such reviews, the number of hearing decisions that were—

(I) sustained in favor of an applicant or eligible individual;

(II) sustained in favor of the designated State unit;

(III) reversed in whole or in part in favor of the applicant or eligible individual; and

(IV) reversed in whole or in part in favor of the designated State unit.

(C) Confidentiality

The confidentiality of records of applicants and eligible individuals maintained by the designated State unit shall not preclude the access of the Commissioner to those records for the purposes described in subparagraph (A).

(d) Policies and procedures

Each designated State agency, in consultation with the State Rehabilitation Council, if the State has such a council, shall, consistent with section 720(a)(3)(C) of this title, develop and implement written policies and procedures that enable each individual who is an applicant for or eligible to receive vocational rehabilitation services under this subchapter to exercise informed choice throughout the vocational rehabilitation process carried out under this subchapter, including policies and procedures that require the designated State agency—

(1) to inform each such applicant and eligible individual (including students with disabilities who are making the transition from programs under the responsibility of an educational agency to programs under the responsibility of the designated State unit), through appropriate modes of communication, about the availability of, and opportunities to exercise, informed choice, including the availability of support services for individuals with cognitive or other disabilities who require assistance in exercising informed choice, throughout the vocational rehabilitation process;

(2) to assist applicants and eligible individuals in exercising informed choice in decisions related to the provision of assessment services under this subchapter;

(3) to develop and implement flexible procurement policies and methods that facilitate the provision of services, and that afford eligible individuals meaningful choices among the methods used to procure services, under this subchapter;

(4) to provide or assist eligible individuals in acquiring information that enables those individuals to exercise informed choice under this subchapter in the selection of—

(A) the employment outcome;

(B) the specific vocational rehabilitation services needed to achieve the employment outcome;

(C) the entity that will provide the services;

(D) the employment setting and the settings in which the services will be provided; and

(E) the methods available for procuring the services; and

(5) to ensure that the availability and scope of informed choice provided under this section is consistent with the obligations of the designated State agency under this subchapter.

(Pub. L. 93–112, title I, § 102, as added Pub. L. 105–220, title IV, § 404, Aug. 7, 1998, 112 Stat. 1138; amended Pub. L. 105–277, div. A, § 101(f) [title VIII, § 402(c)(5)], Oct. 21, 1998, 112 Stat. 2681–337, 2681–415.)

REFERENCES IN TEXT

The Social Security Act, referred to in subsec. (a)(3)(A), is act Aug. 14, 1935, ch. 531, 49 Stat. 620, as amended. Titles II and XVI of the Act are classified generally to subchapters II (§ 401 et seq.) and XVI (§ 1381 et seq.), respectively, of chapter 7 of Title 42, The Public Health and Welfare. For complete classification of this Act to the Code, see section 1305 of Title 42 and Tables.

PRIOR PROVISIONS

A prior section 722, Pub. L. 93–112, title I, § 102, Sept. 26, 1973, 87 Stat. 368; Pub. L. 93–516, title I, § 111(e), Dec. 7, 1974, 88 Stat. 1620; Pub. L. 93–651, title I, § 111(e), Nov. 21, 1974, 89 Stat. 2–5; Pub. L. 95–602, title I, §§ 103, 122(b)(1), Nov. 6, 1978, 92 Stat. 2959, 2987; Pub. L. 98–221, title I, §§ 104(a)(3), 112, Feb. 22, 1984, 98 Stat. 18, 20; Pub. L. 99–506, title I, § 103(d)(2)(A), (B), title II, § 203, title X, § 1001(b)(5), Oct. 21, 1986, 100 Stat. 1810, 1815, 1842; Pub. L. 100–630, title II, § 202(c), Nov. 7, 1988, 102 Stat. 3305; Pub. L. 102–569, title I, §§ 102(p)(8), 123, Oct. 29, 1992, 106 Stat. 4357, 4375; Pub. L. 103–73, title I, § 107(b), Aug. 11, 1993, 107 Stat. 720, related to individualized written rehabilitation program, prior to the general amendment of this subchapter by Pub. L. 105–220.

AMENDMENTS

1998—Subsec. (c)(5)(F)(iv). Pub. L. 105–277 added cl. (iv).

§ 723. Vocational rehabilitation services

(a) Vocational rehabilitation services for individuals

Vocational rehabilitation services provided under this subchapter are any services described in an individualized plan for employment necessary to assist an individual with a disability in preparing for, securing, retaining, or regaining an employment outcome that is consistent with the strengths, resources, priorities, concerns, abilities, capabilities, interests, and informed choice of the individual, including—

(1) an assessment for determining eligibility and vocational rehabilitation needs by qualified personnel, including, if appropriate, an assessment by personnel skilled in rehabilitation technology;

(2) counseling and guidance, including information and support services to assist an individual in exercising informed choice consistent with the provisions of section 722(d) of this title;

(3) referral and other services to secure needed services from other agencies through agreements developed under section 721(a)(11) of this title, if such services are not available under this subchapter;

(4) job-related services, including job search and placement assistance, job retention services, followup services, and follow-along services;

(5) vocational and other training services, including the provision of personal and vocational adjustment services, books, tools, and other training materials, except that no training services provided at an institution of higher education shall be paid for with funds under this subchapter unless maximum efforts have been made by the designated State unit and the individual to secure grant assistance, in whole or in part, from other sources to pay for such training;

(6) to the extent that financial support is not readily available from a source (such as through health insurance of the individual or through comparable services and benefits consistent with section 721(a)(8)(A) of this title), other than the designated State unit, diagnosis and treatment of physical and mental impairments, including—

(A) corrective surgery or therapeutic treatment necessary to correct or substantially modify a physical or mental condition that constitutes a substantial impediment to employment, but is of such a nature that such correction or modification may reasonably be expected to eliminate or reduce such impediment to employment within a reasonable length of time;

(B) necessary hospitalization in connection with surgery or treatment;

(C) prosthetic and orthotic devices;

(D) eyeglasses and visual services as prescribed by qualified personnel who meet State licensure laws and who are selected by the individual;

(E) special services (including transplantation and dialysis), artificial kidneys, and supplies necessary for the treatment of individuals with end-stage renal disease; and

(F) diagnosis and treatment for mental and emotional disorders by qualified personnel who meet State licensure laws;

(7) maintenance for additional costs incurred while participating in an assessment for determining eligibility and vocational rehabilitation needs or while receiving services under an individualized plan for employment;

(8) transportation, including adequate training in the use of public transportation vehicles and systems, that is provided in connection with the provision of any other service described in this section and needed by the individual to achieve an employment outcome;

(9) on-the-job or other related personal assistance services provided while an individual is receiving other services described in this section;

(10) interpreter services provided by qualified personnel for individuals who are deaf or hard of hearing, and reader services for individuals who are determined to be blind, after an examination by qualified personnel who meet State licensure laws;

(11) rehabilitation teaching services, and orientation and mobility services, for individuals who are blind;

(12) occupational licenses, tools, equipment, and initial stocks and supplies;

(13) technical assistance and other consultation services to conduct market analyses, develop business plans, and otherwise provide resources, to the extent such resources are authorized to be provided through the statewide workforce investment system, to eligible individuals who are pursuing self-employment or telecommuting or establishing a small business operation as an employment outcome;

(14) rehabilitation technology, including telecommunications, sensory, and other technological aids and devices;

(15) transition services for students with disabilities, that facilitate the achievement of the employment outcome identified in the individualized plan for employment;

(16) supported employment services;

(17) services to the family of an individual with a disability necessary to assist the individual to achieve an employment outcome; and

(18) specific post-employment services necessary to assist an individual with a disability to, retain, regain, or advance in employment.

(b) Vocational rehabilitation services for groups of individuals

Vocational rehabilitation services provided for the benefit of groups of individuals with disabilities may also include the following:

(1) In the case of any type of small business operated by individuals with significant disabilities the operation of which can be improved by management services and supervision provided by the designated State agency, the provision of such services and supervision, along or together with the acquisition by the designated State agency of vending facilities or other equipment and initial stocks and supplies.

(2)(A) The establishment, development, or improvement of community rehabilitation programs, including, under special circumstances, the construction of a facility. Such programs shall be used to provide services that promote integration and competitive employment.

(B) The provision of other services, that promise to contribute substantially to the rehabilitation of a group of individuals but that are not related directly to the individualized plan for employment of any 1 individual with a disability.

(3) The use of telecommunications systems (including telephone, television, satellite, radio, and other similar systems) that have the potential for substantially improving delivery methods of activities described in this section and developing appropriate programming to meet the particular needs of individuals with disabilities.

(4)(A) Special services to provide nonvisual access to information for individuals who are blind, including the use of telecommunications, Braille, sound recordings, or other appropriate media.

(B) Captioned television, films, or video cassettes for individuals who are deaf or hard of hearing.

(C) Tactile materials for individuals who are deaf-blind.

(D) Other special services that provide information through tactile, vibratory, auditory, and visual media.

(5) Technical assistance and support services to businesses that are not subject to title I of the Americans with Disabilities Act of 1990 (42 U.S.C. 12111 et seq.) and that are seeking to employ individuals with disabilities.

(6) Consultative and technical assistance services to assist educational agencies in planning for the transition of students with disabilities from school to post-school activities, including employment.

(Pub. L. 93–112, title I, § 103, as added Pub. L. 105–220, title IV, § 404, Aug. 7, 1998, 112 Stat. 1148.)

REFERENCES IN TEXT

The Americans with Disabilities Act of 1990, referred to in subsec. (b)(5), is Pub. L. 101–336, July 26, 1990, 104 Stat. 327, as amended. Title I of the Act is classified generally to subchapter I (§ 12111 et seq.) of chapter 126 of Title 42, The Public Health and Welfare. For complete classification of this Act to the Code, see Short Title note set out under section 12101 of Title 42 and Tables.

PRIOR PROVISIONS

A prior section 723, Pub. L. 93–112, title I, § 103, Sept. 26, 1973, 87 Stat. 368; Pub. L. 95–602, title I, § 104, Nov. 6, 1978, 92 Stat. 2960; Pub. L. 99–506, title I, § 103(d)(2), title II, § 204, Oct. 21, 1986, 100 Stat. 1810, 1817; Pub. L. 100–630, title II, § 202(d), Nov. 7, 1988, 102 Stat. 3305; Pub. L. 102–569, title I, §§ 102(p)(9), 124, Oct. 29, 1992, 106 Stat. 4357, 4379; Pub. L. 103–73, title I, § 107(c), Aug. 11, 1993, 107 Stat. 721, related to scope of vocational rehabilitation services, prior to the general amendment of this subchapter by Pub. L. 105–220.

§ 724. Non-Federal share for establishment of program or construction

For the purpose of determining the amount of payments to States for carrying out part B of this subchapter (or to an Indian tribe under part C of this subchapter), the non-Federal share, subject to such limitations and conditions as may be prescribed in regulations by the Commissioner, shall include contributions of funds made by any private agency, organization, or individual to a State or local agency to assist in meeting the costs of establishment of a community rehabilitation program or construction, under special circumstances, of a facility for such a program, which would be regarded as State or local funds except for the condition, imposed by the contributor, limiting use of such funds to establishment of such a program or construction of such a facility.

(Pub. L. 93–112, title I, § 104, as added Pub. L. 105–220, title IV, § 404, Aug. 7, 1998, 112 Stat. 1151.)

PRIOR PROVISIONS

A prior section 724, Pub. L. 93–112, title I, § 104, Sept. 26, 1973, 87 Stat. 370; Pub. L. 95–602, title I, § 122(b)(1),

Nov. 6, 1978, 92 Stat. 2987; Pub. L. 99–506, title II, § 205, Oct. 21, 1986, 100 Stat. 1817; Pub. L. 102–569, title I, § 125, Oct. 29, 1992, 106 Stat. 4381, related to non-Federal share for construction, prior to the general amendment of this subchapter by Pub. L. 105–220.

§ 725. State Rehabilitation Council

(a) Establishment

(1) In general

Except as provided in section 721(a)(21)(A)(i) of this title, to be eligible to receive financial assistance under this subchapter a State shall establish a State Rehabilitation Council (referred to in this section as the "Council") in accordance with this section.

(2) Separate agency for individuals who are blind

A State that designates a State agency to administer the part of the State plan under which vocational rehabilitation services are provided for individuals who are blind under section 721(a)(2)(A)(i) of this title may establish a separate Council in accordance with this section to perform the duties of such a Council with respect to such State agency.

(b) Composition and appointment

(1) Composition

(A) In general

Except in the case of a separate Council established under subsection (a)(2) of this section, the Council shall be composed of—

(i) at least one representative of the Statewide Independent Living Council established under section 796d of this title, which representative may be the chairperson or other designee of the Council;

(ii) at least one representative of a parent training and information center established pursuant to section 671 of the Individuals with Disabilities Education Act [20 U.S.C. 1471];

(iii) at least one representative of the client assistance program established under section 732 of this title;

(iv) at least one qualified vocational rehabilitation counselor, with knowledge of and experience with vocational rehabilitation programs, who shall serve as an ex officio, nonvoting member of the Council if the counselor is an employee of the designated State agency;

(v) at least one representative of community rehabilitation program service providers;

(vi) four representatives of business, industry, and labor;

(vii) representatives of disability advocacy groups representing a cross section of—

(I) individuals with physical, cognitive, sensory, and mental disabilities; and

(II) individuals' representatives of individuals with disabilities who have difficulty in representing themselves or are unable due to their disabilities to represent themselves;

(viii) current or former applicants for, or recipients of, vocational rehabilitation services;

(ix) in a State in which one or more projects are carried out under section 741 of this title, at least one representative of the directors of the projects;

(x) at least one representative of the State educational agency responsible for the public education of students with disabilities who are eligible to receive services under this subchapter and part B of the Individuals with Disabilities Education Act [20 U.S.C. 1411 et seq.]; and

(xi) at least one representative of the State workforce investment board.

(B) Separate Council

In the case of a separate Council established under subsection (a)(2) of this section, the Council shall be composed of—

(i) at least one representative described in subparagraph (A)(i);

(ii) at least one representative described in subparagraph (A)(ii);

(iii) at least one representative described in subparagraph (A)(iii);

(iv) at least one vocational rehabilitation counselor described in subparagraph (A)(iv), who shall serve as described in such subparagraph;

(v) at least one representative described in subparagraph (A)(v);

(vi) four representatives described in subparagraph (A)(vi);

(vii) at least one representative of a disability advocacy group representing individuals who are blind;

(viii) at least one individual's representative, of an individual who—

(I) is an individual who is blind and has multiple disabilities; and

(II) has difficulty in representing himself or herself or is unable due to disabilities to represent himself or herself;

(ix) applicants or recipients described in subparagraph (A)(viii);

(x) in a State described in subparagraph (A)(ix), at least one representative described in such subparagraph;

(xi) at least one representative described in subparagraph (A)(x); and

(xii) at least one representative described in subparagraph (A)(xi).

(C) Exception

In the case of a separate Council established under subsection (a)(2) of this section, any Council that is required by State law, as in effect on October 29, 1992, to have fewer than 15 members shall be deemed to be in compliance with subparagraph (B) if the Council—

(i) meets the requirements of subparagraph (B), other than the requirements of clauses (vi) and (ix) of such subparagraph; and

(ii) includes at least—

(I) one representative described in subparagraph (B)(vi); and

(II) one applicant or recipient described in subparagraph (B)(ix).

(2) Ex officio member

The Director of the designated State unit shall be an ex officio, nonvoting member of the Council.

(3) Appointment

Members of the Council shall be appointed by the Governor or, in the case of a State that, under State law, vests authority for the administration of the activities carried out under this chapter in an entity other than the Governor (such as one or more houses of the State legislature or an independent board), the chief officer of that entity. The appointing authority shall select members after soliciting recommendations from representatives of organizations representing a broad range of individuals with disabilities and organizations interested in individuals with disabilities. In selecting members, the appointing authority shall consider, to the greatest extent practicable, the extent to which minority populations are represented on the Council.

(4) Qualifications

(A) In general

A majority of Council members shall be persons who are—

(i) individuals with disabilities described in section 705(20)(B) of this title; and

(ii) not employed by the designated State unit.

(B) Separate Council

In the case of a separate Council established under subsection (a)(2) of this section, a majority of Council members shall be persons who are—

(i) blind; and

(ii) not employed by the designated State unit.

(5) Chairperson

(A) In general

Except as provided in subparagraph (B), the Council shall select a chairperson from among the membership of the Council.

(B) Designation by chief executive officer

In States in which the chief executive officer does not have veto power pursuant to State law, the appointing authority described in paragraph (3) shall designate a member of the Council to serve as the chairperson of the Council or shall require the Council to so designate such a member.

(6) Terms of appointment

(A) Length of term

Each member of the Council shall serve for a term of not more than 3 years, except that—

(i) a member appointed to fill a vacancy occurring prior to the expiration of the term for which a predecessor was appointed, shall be appointed for the remainder of such term; and

(ii) the terms of service of the members initially appointed shall be (as specified by the appointing authority described in paragraph (3)) for such fewer number of years as will provide for the expiration of terms on a staggered basis.

(B) Number of terms

No member of the Council, other than a representative described in clause (iii) or (ix) of paragraph (1)(A), or clause (iii) or (x) of paragraph (1)(B), may serve more than two consecutive full terms.

(7) Vacancies

(A) In general

Except as provided in subparagraph (B), any vacancy occurring in the membership of the Council shall be filled in the same manner as the original appointment. The vacancy shall not affect the power of the remaining members to execute the duties of the Council.

(B) Delegation

The appointing authority described in paragraph (3) may delegate the authority to fill such a vacancy to the remaining members of the Council after making the original appointment.

(c) Functions of Council

The Council shall, after consulting with the State workforce investment board—

(1) review, analyze, and advise the designated State unit regarding the performance of the responsibilities of the unit under this subchapter, particularly responsibilities relating to—

(A) eligibility (including order of selection);

(B) the extent, scope, and effectiveness of services provided; and

(C) functions performed by State agencies that affect or that potentially affect the ability of individuals with disabilities in achieving employment outcomes under this subchapter;

(2) in partnership with the designated State unit—

(A) develop, agree to, and review State goals and priorities in accordance with section 721(a)(15)(C) of this title; and

(B) evaluate the effectiveness of the vocational rehabilitation program and submit reports of progress to the Commissioner in accordance with section 721(a)(15)(E) of this title;

(3) advise the designated State agency and the designated State unit regarding activities authorized to be carried out under this subchapter, and assist in the preparation of the State plan and amendments to the plan, applications, reports, needs assessments, and evaluations required by this subchapter;

(4) to the extent feasible, conduct a review and analysis of the effectiveness of, and consumer satisfaction with—

(A) the functions performed by the designated State agency;

(B) vocational rehabilitation services provided by State agencies and other public and private entities responsible for providing vocational rehabilitation services to individuals with disabilities under this chapter; and

(C) employment outcomes achieved by eligible individuals receiving services under this subchapter, including the availability of health and other employment benefits in connection with such employment outcomes;

(5) prepare and submit an annual report to the Governor and the Commissioner on the status of vocational rehabilitation programs operated within the State, and make the report available to the public;

(6) to avoid duplication of efforts and enhance the number of individuals served, coordinate activities with the activities of other councils within the State, including the Statewide Independent Living Council established under section 796d of this title, the advisory panel established under section 612(a)(20) of the Individuals with Disabilities Education Act [20 U.S.C. 1412(a)(20)], the State Council on Developmental Disabilities established under section 15025 of title 42, the State mental health planning council established under section 300x–3(a) of title 42, and the State workforce investment board;

(7) provide for coordination and the establishment of working relationships between the designated State agency and the Statewide Independent Living Council and centers for independent living within the State; and

(8) perform such other functions, consistent with the purpose of this subchapter, as the State Rehabilitation Council determines to be appropriate, that are comparable to the other functions performed by the Council.

(d) Resources

(1) Plan

The Council shall prepare, in conjunction with the designated State unit, a plan for the provision of such resources, including such staff and other personnel, as may be necessary and sufficient to carry out the functions of the Council under this section. The resource plan shall, to the maximum extent possible, rely on the use of resources in existence during the period of implementation of the plan.

(2) Resolution of disagreements

To the extent that there is a disagreement between the Council and the designated State unit in regard to the resources necessary to carry out the functions of the Council as set forth in this section, the disagreement shall be resolved by the Governor consistent with paragraph (1).

(3) Supervision and evaluation

Each Council shall, consistent with State law, supervise and evaluate such staff and other personnel as may be necessary to carry out its functions under this section.

(4) Personnel conflict of interest

While assisting the Council in carrying out its duties, staff and other personnel shall not be assigned duties by the designated State unit or any other agency or office of the State, that would create a conflict of interest.

(e) Conflict of interest

No member of the Council shall cast a vote on any matter that would provide direct financial benefit to the member or otherwise give the appearance of a conflict of interest under State law.

(f) Meetings

The Council shall convene at least four meetings a year in such places as it determines to be necessary to conduct Council business and conduct such forums or hearings as the Council considers appropriate. The meetings, hearings, and forums shall be publicly announced. The meetings shall be open and accessible to the general public unless there is a valid reason for an executive session.

(g) Compensation and expenses

The Council may use funds allocated to the Council by the designated State unit under this subchapter (except for funds appropriated to carry out the client assistance program under section 732 of this title and funds reserved pursuant to section 730(c) of this title to carry out part C of this subchapter) to reimburse members of the Council for reasonable and necessary expenses of attending Council meetings and performing Council duties (including child care and personal assistance services), and to pay compensation to a member of the Council, if such member is not employed or must forfeit wages from other employment, for each day the member is engaged in performing the duties of the Council.

(h) Hearings and forums

The Council is authorized to hold such hearings and forums as the Council may determine to be necessary to carry out the duties of the Council.

(Pub. L. 93–112, title I, § 105, as added Pub. L. 105–220, title IV, § 404, Aug. 7, 1998, 112 Stat. 1151; amended Pub. L. 105–277, div. A, § 101(f) [title VIII, § 402(c)(6)], Oct. 21, 1998, 112 Stat. 2681–337, 2681–415; Pub. L. 106–402, title IV, § 401(b)(3)(A), Oct. 30, 2000, 114 Stat. 1737; Pub. L. 108–446, title III, § 305(h)(2), (3), Dec. 3, 2004, 118 Stat. 2805.)

REFERENCES IN TEXT

The Individuals with Disabilities Education Act, referred to in subsec. (b)(1)(A)(x), is title VI of Pub. L. 91–230, Apr. 13, 1970, 84 Stat. 175, as amended. Part B of the Act is classified generally to subchapter II (§ 1411 et seq.) of chapter 33 of Title 20, Education. For complete classification of this Act to the Code, see section 1400 of Title 20 and Tables.

PRIOR PROVISIONS

A prior section 725, Pub. L. 93–112, title I, § 105, as added Pub. L. 102–569, title I, § 126(a), Oct. 29, 1992, 106 Stat. 4381; amended Pub. L. 103–73, title I, § 107(d)(1), Aug. 11, 1993, 107 Stat. 721, related to State Rehabilitation Advisory Council, prior to the general amendment of this subchapter by Pub. L. 105–220.

AMENDMENTS

2004—Subsec. (b)(1)(A)(ii). Pub. L. 108–446, § 305(h)(2), substituted "671 of the Individuals with Disabilities Education Act" for "682(a) of the Individuals with Disabilities Education Act (as added by section 101 of the Individuals with Disabilities Education Act Amendments of 1997; Public Law 105–17)".

Subsec. (c)(6). Pub. L. 108–446, § 305(h)(3), substituted "section 612(a)(20)" for "section 612(a)(21)" and "Individuals with" for "Individual with" and struck out "(as amended by section 101 of the Individuals with Disabilities Education Act Amendments of 1997; Public Law 105–17)" before ", the State Council".

2000—Subsec. (c)(6). Pub. L. 106–402 substituted "the State Council on Developmental Disabilities established under section 15025 of title 42" for "the State Developmental Disabilities Council described in section 6024 of title 42".

1998—Subsec. (b)(3). Pub. L. 105–277, § 101(f) [title VIII, § 402(c)(6)(A)], substituted "Governor or, in the case of a State that, under State law, vests authority for the administration of the activities carried out under this chapter in an entity other than the Governor (such as one or more houses of the State legislature or an independent board), the chief officer of that entity" for "Governor" in first sentence and "appointing authority" for "Governor" in second and third sentences.

Subsec. (b)(4)(A)(i). Pub. L. 105–277, §101(f) [title VIII, §402(c)(6)(B)], substituted "section 705(20)(B)" for "section 705(20)(A)".

Subsec. (b)(5)(B). Pub. L. 105–277, §101(f) [title VIII, §402(c)(6)(C)], substituted "chief executive officer" for "Governor" in heading and "appointing authority described in paragraph (3) shall" for "Governor shall" in text.

Subsec. (b)(6)(A)(ii), (7)(B). Pub. L. 105–277, §101(f) [title VIII, §402(c)(6)(D)], substituted "appointing authority described in paragraph (3)" for "Governor".

§ 726. Evaluation standards and performance indicators

(a) Establishment

(1) In general

(A) Establishment of standards and indicators

The Commissioner shall, not later than July 1, 1999, establish and publish evaluation standards and performance indicators for the vocational rehabilitation program carried out under this subchapter.

(B) Review and revision

Effective July 1, 1999, the Commissioner shall review and, if necessary, revise the evaluation standards and performance indicators every 3 years. Any revisions of the standards and indicators shall be developed with input from State vocational rehabilitation agencies, related professional and consumer organizations, recipients of vocational rehabilitation services, and other interested parties. Any revisions of the standards and indicators shall be subject to the publication, review, and comment provisions of paragraph (3).

(C) Bases

Effective July 1, 1999, to the maximum extent practicable, the standards and indicators shall be consistent with the core indicators of performance established under section 2871(b) of this title.

(2) Measures

The standards and indicators shall include outcome and related measures of program performance that facilitate the accomplishment of the purpose and policy of this subchapter.

(3) Comment

The standards and indicators shall be developed with input from State vocational rehabilitation agencies, related professional and consumer organizations, recipients of vocational rehabilitation services, and other interested parties. The Commissioner shall publish in the Federal Register a notice of intent to regulate regarding the development of proposed standards and indicators. Proposed standards and indicators shall be published in the Federal Register for review and comment. Final standards and indicators shall be published in the Federal Register.

(b) Compliance

(1) State reports

In accordance with regulations established by the Secretary, each State shall report to the Commissioner after the end of each fiscal year the extent to which the State is in compliance with the standards and indicators.

(2) Program improvement

(A) Plan

If the Commissioner determines that the performance of any State is below established standards, the Commissioner shall provide technical assistance to the State, and the State and the Commissioner shall jointly develop a program improvement plan outlining the specific actions to be taken by the State to improve program performance.

(B) Review

The Commissioner shall—

(i) review the program improvement efforts of the State on a biannual basis and, if necessary, request the State to make further revisions to the plan to improve performance; and

(ii) continue to conduct such reviews and request such revisions until the State sustains satisfactory performance over a period of more than 1 year.

(c) Withholding

If the Commissioner determines that a State whose performance falls below the established standards has failed to enter into a program improvement plan, or is not complying substantially with the terms and conditions of such a program improvement plan, the Commissioner shall, consistent with subsections (c) and (d) of section 727 of this title, reduce or make no further payments to the State under this program, until the State has entered into an approved program improvement plan, or satisfies the Commissioner that the State is complying substantially with the terms and conditions of such a program improvement plan, as appropriate.

(d) Report to Congress

Beginning in fiscal year 1999, the Commissioner shall include in each annual report to the Congress under section 710 of this title an analysis of program performance, including relative State performance, based on the standards and indicators.

(Pub. L. 93–112, title I, §106, as added Pub. L. 105–220, title IV, §404, Aug. 7, 1998, 112 Stat. 1156.)

PRIOR PROVISIONS

A prior section 726, Pub. L. 93–112, title I, §106, as added Pub. L. 102–569, title I, §127(a), Oct. 29, 1992, 106 Stat. 4385, related to evaluation standards and performance indicators, prior to the general amendment of this subchapter by Pub. L. 105–220.

§ 727. Monitoring and review

(a) In general

(1) Duties

In carrying out the duties of the Commissioner under this subchapter, the Commissioner shall—

(A) provide for the annual review and periodic onsite monitoring of programs under this subchapter; and

(B) determine whether, in the administration of the State plan, a State is complying substantially with the provisions of such plan and with evaluation standards and performance indicators established under section 726 of this title.

(2) Procedures for reviews

In conducting reviews under this section the Commissioner shall consider, at a minimum—

(A) State policies and procedures;

(B) guidance materials;

(C) decisions resulting from hearings conducted in accordance with due process;

(D) State goals established under section 721(a)(15) of this title and the extent to which the State has achieved such goals;

(E) plans and reports prepared under section 726(b) of this title;

(F) consumer satisfaction reviews and analyses described in section 725(c)(4) of this title;

(G) information provided by the State Rehabilitation Council established under section 725 of this title, if the State has such a Council, or by the commission described in section 721(a)(21)(A)(i) of this title, if the State has such a commission;

(H) reports; and

(I) budget and financial management data.

(3) Procedures for monitoring

In conducting monitoring under this section the Commissioner shall conduct—

(A) onsite visits, including onsite reviews of records to verify that the State is following requirements regarding the order of selection set forth in section 721(a)(5)(A) of this title;

(B) public hearings and other strategies for collecting information from the public;

(C) meetings with the State Rehabilitation Council, if the State has such a Council or with the commission described in section 721(a)(21)(A)(i) of this title, if the State has such a commission;

(D) reviews of individual case files, including individualized plans for employment and ineligibility determinations; and

(E) meetings with qualified vocational rehabilitation counselors and other personnel.

(4) Areas of inquiry

In conducting the review and monitoring, the Commissioner shall examine—

(A) the eligibility process;

(B) the provision of services, including, if applicable, the order of selection;

(C) such other areas as may be identified by the public or through meetings with the State Rehabilitation Council, if the State has such a Council or with the commission described in section 721(a)(21)(A)(i) of this title, if the State has such a commission; and

(D) such other areas of inquiry as the Commissioner may consider appropriate.

(5) Reports

If the Commissioner issues a report detailing the findings of an annual review or onsite monitoring conducted under this section, the report shall be made available to the State Rehabilitation Council, if the State has such a Council, for use in the development and modification of the State plan described in section 721 of this title.

(b) Technical assistance

The Commissioner shall—

(1) provide technical assistance to programs under this subchapter regarding improving the quality of vocational rehabilitation services provided; and

(2) provide technical assistance and establish a corrective action plan for a program under this subchapter if the Commissioner finds that the program fails to comply substantially with the provisions of the State plan, or with evaluation standards or performance indicators established under section 726 of this title, in order to ensure that such failure is corrected as soon as practicable.

(c) Failure to comply with plan

(1) Withholding payments

Whenever the Commissioner, after providing reasonable notice and an opportunity for a hearing to the State agency administering or supervising the administration of the State plan approved under section 721 of this title, finds that—

(A) the plan has been so changed that it no longer complies with the requirements of section 721(a) of this title; or

(B) in the administration of the plan there is a failure to comply substantially with any provision of such plan or with an evaluation standard or performance indicator established under section 726 of this title,

the Commissioner shall notify such State agency that no further payments will be made to the State under this subchapter (or, in the discretion of the Commissioner, that such further payments will be reduced, in accordance with regulations the Commissioner shall prescribe, or that further payments will not be made to the State only for the projects under the parts of the State plan affected by such failure), until the Commissioner is satisfied there is no longer any such failure.

(2) Period

Until the Commissioner is so satisfied, the Commissioner shall make no further payments to such State under this subchapter (or shall reduce payments or limit payments to projects under those parts of the State plan in which there is no such failure).

(3) Disbursal of withheld funds

The Commissioner may, in accordance with regulations the Secretary shall prescribe, disburse any funds withheld from a State under paragraph (1) to any public or nonprofit private organization or agency within such State or to any political subdivision of such State submitting a plan meeting the requirements of section 721(a) of this title. The Commissioner may not make any payment under this paragraph unless the entity to which such payment is made has provided assurances to the Commissioner that such entity will contribute, for purposes of carrying out such plan, the same amount as the State would have been obligated to contribute if the State received such payment.

(d) Review

(1) Petition

Any State that is dissatisfied with a final determination of the Commissioner under section 721(b) of this title or subsection (c) of this section may file a petition for judicial review of such determination in the United States Court of Appeals for the circuit in which the State is located. Such a petition may be filed only within the 30-day period beginning on the date that notice of such final determination was received by the State. The clerk of the court shall transmit a copy of the petition to the Commissioner or to any officer designated by the Commissioner for that purpose. In accordance with section 2112 of title 28, the Commissioner shall file with the court a record of the proceeding on which the Commissioner based the determination being appealed by the State. Until a record is so filed, the Commissioner may modify or set aside any determination made under such proceedings.

(2) Submissions and determinations

If, in an action under this subsection to review a final determination of the Commissioner under section 721(b) of this title or subsection (c) of this section, the petitioner or the Commissioner applies to the court for leave to have additional oral submissions or written presentations made respecting such determination, the court may, for good cause shown, order the Commissioner to provide within 30 days an additional opportunity to make such submissions and presentations. Within such period, the Commissioner may revise any findings of fact, modify or set aside the determination being reviewed, or make a new determination by reason of the additional submissions and presentations, and shall file such modified or new determination, and any revised findings of fact, with the return of such submissions and presentations. The court shall thereafter review such new or modified determination.

(3) Standards of review

(A) In general

Upon the filing of a petition under paragraph (1) for judicial review of a determination, the court shall have jurisdiction—

(i) to grant appropriate relief as provided in chapter 7 of title 5, except for interim relief with respect to a determination under subsection (c) of this section; and

(ii) except as otherwise provided in subparagraph (B), to review such determination in accordance with chapter 7 of title 5.

(B) Substantial evidence

Section 706 of title 5 shall apply to the review of any determination under this subsection, except that the standard for review prescribed by paragraph (2)(E) of such section 706 shall not apply and the court shall hold unlawful and set aside such determination if the court finds that the determination is not supported by substantial evidence in the record of the proceeding submitted pursuant to paragraph (1), as supplemented by any additional submissions and presentations filed under paragraph (2).

(Pub. L. 93–112, title I, § 107, as added Pub. L. 105–220, title IV, § 404, Aug. 7, 1998, 112 Stat. 1157.)

PRIOR PROVISIONS

A prior section 727, Pub. L. 93–112, title I, § 107, as added Pub. L. 102–569, title I, § 128(a), Oct. 29, 1992, 106 Stat. 4386, related to monitoring and review, prior to the general amendment of this subchapter by Pub. L. 105–220.

§ 728. Expenditure of certain amounts

(a) Expenditure

Amounts described in subsection (b) of this section may not be expended by a State for any purpose other than carrying out programs for which the State receives financial assistance under this subchapter, under part B of subchapter VI of this chapter, or under subchapter VII of this chapter.

(b) Amounts

The amounts referred to in subsection (a) of this section are amounts provided to a State under the Social Security Act (42 U.S.C. 301 et seq.) as reimbursement for the expenditure of payments received by the State from allotments under section 730 of this title.

(Pub. L. 93–112, title I, § 108, as added Pub. L. 105–220, title IV, § 404, Aug. 7, 1998, 112 Stat. 1160.)

REFERENCES IN TEXT

The Social Security Act, referred to in subsec. (b), is act Aug. 14, 1935, ch. 531, 49 Stat. 620, as amended, which is classified generally to chapter 7 (§ 301 et seq.) of Title 42, The Public Health and Welfare. For complete classification of this Act to the Code, see section 1305 of Title 42 and Tables.

PRIOR PROVISIONS

A prior section 728, Pub. L. 93–112, title I, § 108, as added Pub. L. 102–569, title I, § 129(a), Oct. 29, 1992, 106 Stat. 4389, related to expenditure of certain amounts, prior to the general amendment of this subchapter by Pub. L. 105–220.

§ 728a. Training of employers with respect to Americans with Disabilities Act of 1990

A State may expend payments received under section 731 of this title—

(1) to carry out a program to train employers with respect to compliance with the requirements of title I of the Americans with Disabilities Act of 1990 (42 U.S.C. 12111 et seq.); and

(2) to inform employers of the existence of the program and the availability of the services of the program.

(Pub. L. 93–112, title I, § 109, as added Pub. L. 105–220, title IV, § 404, Aug. 7, 1998, 112 Stat. 1160.)

REFERENCES IN TEXT

The Americans with Disabilities Act of 1990, referred to in par. (1), is Pub. L. 101–336, July 26, 1990, 104 Stat. 327, as amended. Title I of the Act is classified generally to subchapter I (§ 12111 et seq.) of chapter 126 of Title 42, The Public Health and Welfare. For complete classification of this Act to the Code, see Short Title note set out under section 12101 of Title 42 and Tables.

PRIOR PROVISIONS

A prior section 728a, Pub. L. 93–112, title I, §109, as added Pub. L. 102–569, title I, §130(a), Oct. 29, 1992, 106 Stat. 4389, related to training of employers with respect to Americans with Disabilities Act of 1990, prior to the general amendment of this subchapter by Pub. L. 105–220.

PART B—BASIC VOCATIONAL REHABILITATION SERVICES

§730. State allotments

(a) Computation; additional amount; minimum amount; adjustments

(1) Subject to the provisions of subsection (c) of this section, for each fiscal year beginning before October 1, 1978, each State shall be entitled to an allotment of an amount bearing the same ratio to the amount authorized to be appropriated under section 720(b)(1) of this title for allotment under this section as the product of—

(A) the population of the State; and

(B) the square of its allotment percentage,

bears to the sum of the corresponding products for all the States.

(2)(A) For each fiscal year beginning on or after October 1, 1978, each State shall be entitled to an allotment in an amount equal to the amount such State received under paragraph (1) for the fiscal year ending September 30, 1978, and an additional amount determined pursuant to subparagraph (B) of this paragraph.

(B) For each fiscal year beginning on or after October 1, 1978, each State shall be entitled to an allotment, from any amount authorized to be appropriated for such fiscal year under section 720(b)(1) of this title for allotment under this section in excess of the amount appropriated under section 720(b)(1)(A)[1] of this title for the fiscal year ending September 30, 1978, in an amount equal to the sum of—

(i) an amount bearing the same ratio to 50 percent of such excess amount as the product of the population of the State and the square of its allotment percentage bears to the sum of the corresponding products for all the States; and

(ii) an amount bearing the same ratio to 50 percent of such excess amount as the product of the population of the State and its allotment percentage bears to the sum of the corresponding products for all the States.

(3) The sum of the payment to any State (other than Guam, American Samoa, the Virgin Islands, and the Commonwealth of the Northern Mariana Islands) under this subsection for any fiscal year which is less than ⅓ of 1 percent of the amount appropriated under section 720(b)(1) of this title, or $3,000,000, whichever is greater, shall be increased to that amount, the total of the increases thereby required being derived by proportionately reducing the allotment to each of the remaining such States under this subsection, but with such adjustments as may be necessary to prevent the sum of the allotments made under this subsection to any such remaining State from being thereby reduced to less than that amount.

(b) Unused funds; redistribution; increase in amount

(1) Not later than 45 days prior to the end of the fiscal year, the Commissioner shall determine, after reasonable opportunity for the submission to the Commissioner of comments by the State agency administering or supervising the program established under this subchapter, that any payment of an allotment to a State under section 731(a) of this title for any fiscal year will not be utilized by such State in carrying out the purposes of this subchapter.

(2) As soon as practicable but not later than the end of the fiscal year, the Commissioner shall make such amount available for carrying out the purposes of this subchapter to one or more other States to the extent the Commissioner determines such other State will be able to use such additional amount during that fiscal year or the subsequent fiscal year for carrying out such purposes. The Commissioner shall make such amount available only if such other State will be able to make sufficient payments from non-Federal sources to pay for the non-Federal share of the cost of vocational rehabilitation services under the State plan for the fiscal year for which the amount was appropriated.

(3) For the purposes of this part, any amount made available to a State for any fiscal year pursuant to this subsection shall be regarded as an increase of such State's allotment (as determined under the preceding provisions of this section) for such year.

(c) Funds for American Indian vocational rehabilitation services

(1) For fiscal year 1987 and for each subsequent fiscal year, the Commissioner shall reserve from the amount appropriated under section 720(b)(1) of this title for allotment under this section a sum, determined under paragraph (2), to carry out the purposes of part C of this subchapter.

(2) The sum referred to in paragraph (1) shall be, as determined by the Secretary—

(A) not less than three-quarters of 1 percent and not more than 1.5 percent of the amount referred to in paragraph (1), for fiscal year 1999; and

(B) not less than 1 percent and not more than 1.5 percent of the amount referred to in paragraph (1), for each of fiscal years 2000 through 2003.

(Pub. L. 93–112, title I, §110, as added Pub. L. 105–220, title IV, §404, Aug. 7, 1998, 112 Stat. 1160; amended Pub. L. 105–277, div. A, §101(f) [title VIII, §402(b)(7)], Oct. 21, 1998, 112 Stat. 2681–337, 2681–413.)

REFERENCES IN TEXT

Section 720(b)(1)(A) of this title, referred to in subsec. (a)(2)(B), means section 720(b)(1)(A) prior to the general amendment of section 720(b) by Pub. L. 102–569, title I, §121(b)(1), Oct. 29, 1992, 106 Stat. 4367, which restated subsec. (b)(1) without a subpar. (A). Section 720 was subsequently omitted, and a new section 720 added, in the general amendment of this subchapter by Pub. L. 105–220, title IV, §404, Aug. 7, 1998, 112 Stat. 1116.

[1] See References in Text note below.

PRIOR PROVISIONS

A prior section 730, Pub. L. 93–112, title I, § 110, Sept. 26, 1973, 87 Stat. 370; Pub. L. 95–602, title I, §§ 101(c), (d), 122(b)(1), Nov. 6, 1978, 92 Stat. 2956, 2957, 2987; Pub. L. 98–221, title I, § 111(e), Feb. 22, 1984, 98 Stat. 20; Pub. L. 99–506, title I, § 103(c)(2), title II, §§ 206, 207, Oct. 21, 1986, 100 Stat. 1810, 1817, 1818; Pub. L. 102–569, title I, § 131, Oct. 29, 1992, 106 Stat. 4389; Pub. L. 103–73, title I, § 107(e), Aug. 11, 1993, 107 Stat. 723, related to State allotments, prior to the general amendment of this subchapter by Pub. L. 105–220.

AMENDMENTS

1998—Pub. L. 105–277 made technical amendment to section designation and catchline in original.

§ 731. Payments to States

(a) Amount

(1) Except as provided in paragraph (2), from each State's allotment under this part for any fiscal year, the Commissioner shall pay to a State an amount equal to the Federal share of the cost of vocational rehabilitation services under the plan for that State approved under section 721 of this title, including expenditures for the administration of the State plan.

(2)(A) The total of payments under paragraph (1) to a State for a fiscal year may not exceed its allotment under subsection (a) of section 730 of this title for such year.

(B) For fiscal year 1994 and each fiscal year thereafter, the amount otherwise payable to a State for a fiscal year under this section shall be reduced by the amount by which expenditures from non-Federal sources under the State plan under this subchapter for the previous fiscal year are less than the total of such expenditures for the second fiscal year preceding the previous fiscal year.

(C) The Commissioner may waive or modify any requirement or limitation under subparagraph (B) or section 721(a)(17) of this title if the Commissioner determines that a waiver or modification is an equitable response to exceptional or uncontrollable circumstances affecting the State.

(3)(A) Except as provided in subparagraph (B), the amount of a payment under this section with respect to any construction project in any State shall be equal to the same percentage of the cost of such project as the Federal share that is applicable in the case of rehabilitation facilities (as defined in section 291*o*(g) of title 42), in such State.

(B) If the Federal share with respect to rehabilitation facilities in such State is determined pursuant to section 291*o*(b)(2) of title 42, the percentage of the cost for purposes of this section shall be determined in accordance with regulations prescribed by the Commissioner designed to achieve as nearly as practicable results comparable to the results obtained under such section.

(b) Method of computation and payment

The method of computing and paying amounts pursuant to subsection (a) of this section shall be as follows:

(1) The Commissioner shall, prior to the beginning of each calendar quarter or other period prescribed by the Commissioner, estimate the amount to be paid to each State under the provisions of such subsection for such period, such estimate to be based on such records of the State and information furnished by it, and such other investigation as the Commissioner may find necessary.

(2) The Commissioner shall pay, from the allotment available therefor, the amount so estimated by the Commissioner for such period, reduced or increased, as the case may be, by any sum (not previously adjusted under this paragraph) by which the Commissioner finds that the estimate of the amount to be paid the State for any prior period under such subsection was greater or less than the amount which should have been paid to the State for such prior period under such subsection. Such payment shall be made prior to audit or settlement by the Government Accountability Office, shall be made through the disbursing facilities of the Treasury Department, and shall be made in such installments as the Commissioner may determine.

(Pub. L. 93–112, title I, § 111, as added Pub. L. 105–220, title IV, § 404, Aug. 7, 1998, 112 Stat. 1162; amended Pub. L. 105–277, div. A, § 101(f) [title VIII, § 402(b)(8)], Oct. 21, 1998, 112 Stat. 2681–337, 2681–413; Pub. L. 108–271, § 8(b), July 7, 2004, 118 Stat. 814.)

PRIOR PROVISIONS

A prior section 731, Pub. L. 93–112, title I, § 111, Sept. 26, 1973, 87 Stat. 371; Pub. L. 95–602, title I, § 122(b)(1), Nov. 6, 1978, 92 Stat. 2987; Pub. L. 99–506, title II, § 208, title X, § 1001(b)(6), Oct. 21, 1986, 100 Stat. 1818, 1842; Pub. L. 100–630, title II, § 202(e)(1), (2)(A), (3), Nov. 7, 1988, 102 Stat. 3306; Pub. L. 102–569, title I, § 132, Oct. 29, 1992, 106 Stat. 4390; Pub. L. 103–73, title I, § 107(f), Aug. 11, 1993, 107 Stat. 723, related to payments to States, prior to the general amendment of this subchapter by Pub. L. 105–220.

AMENDMENTS

2004—Subsec. (b)(2). Pub. L. 108–271 substituted "Government Accountability Office" for "General Accounting Office".

1998—Pub. L. 105–277 made technical amendment to section designation and catchline in original.

§ 732. Client assistance program

(a) Establishment of grant program

From funds appropriated under subsection (h) of this section, the Secretary shall, in accordance with this section, make grants to States to establish and carry out client assistance programs to provide assistance in informing and advising all clients and client applicants of all available benefits under this chapter, and, upon request of such clients or client applicants, to assist and advocate for such clients or applicants in their relationships with projects, programs, and services provided under this chapter, including assistance and advocacy in pursuing legal, administrative, or other appropriate remedies to ensure the protection of the rights of such individuals under this chapter and to facilitate access to the services funded under this chapter through individual and systemic advocacy. The client assistance program shall provide information on the available services and benefits under this chapter and title I of the Americans with Disabilities Act of 1990 (42 U.S.C. 12111 et seq.) to individuals with disabilities in the State, especially with regard to individuals with disabilities who have traditionally been unserved or underserved by vocational rehabilitation programs. In providing assistance and advocacy under this subsection with respect to services under this subchapter, a client assistance program may provide the assistance and advocacy with respect to services that are directly related to facilitating the employment of the individual.

(b) Existence of State program as requisite to receiving payments

No State may receive payments from its allotment under this chapter in any fiscal year unless the State has in effect not later than October 1, 1984, a client assistance program which—

(1) has the authority to pursue legal, administrative, and other appropriate remedies to ensure the protection of rights of individuals with disabilities who are receiving treatments, services, or rehabilitation under this chapter within the State; and

(2) meets the requirements of designation under subsection (c) of this section.

(c) Designation of agency to conduct program

(1)(A) The Governor shall designate a public or private agency to conduct the client assistance program under this section. Except as provided in the last sentence of this subparagraph, the Governor shall designate an agency which is independent of any agency which provides treatment, services, or rehabilitation to individuals under this chapter. If there is an agency in the State which has, or had, prior to February 22, 1984, served as a client assistance agency under this section and which received Federal financial assistance under this chapter, the Governor may, in the initial designation, designate an agency which provides treatment, services, or rehabilitation to individuals with disabilities under this chapter.

(B)(i) The Governor may not redesignate the agency designated under subparagraph (A) without good cause and unless—

(I) the Governor has given the agency 30 days notice of the intention to make such redesignation, including specification of the good cause for such redesignation and an opportunity to respond to the assertion that good cause has been shown;

(II) individuals with disabilities or the individuals' representatives have timely notice of the redesignation and opportunity for public comment; and

(III) the agency has the opportunity to appeal to the Commissioner on the basis that the redesignation was not for good cause.

(ii) If, after August 7, 1998—

(I) a designated State agency undergoes any change in the organizational structure of the agency that results in the creation of one or more new State agencies or departments or results in the merger of the designated State agency with one or more other State agencies or departments; and

(II) an agency (including an office or other unit) within the designated State agency was conducting a client assistance program before the change under the last sentence of subparagraph (A),

the Governor shall redesignate the agency conducting the program. In conducting the redesignation, the Governor shall designate to conduct the program an agency that is independent of any agency that provides treatment, services, or rehabilitation to individuals with disabilities under this chapter.

(2) In carrying out the provisions of this section, the Governor shall consult with the director of the State vocational rehabilitation agency, the head of the developmental disability protection and advocacy agency, and with representatives of professional and consumer organizations serving individuals with disabilities in the State.

(3) The agency designated under this subsection shall be accountable for the proper use of funds made available to the agency.

(d) Class action by designated agency prohibited

The agency designated under subsection (c) of this section may not bring any class action in carrying out its responsibilities under this section.

(e) Allotment and reallotment of funds

(1)(A) The Secretary shall allot the sums appropriated for each fiscal year under this section among the States on the basis of relative population of each State, except that no State shall receive less than $50,000.

(B) The Secretary shall allot $30,000 each to American Samoa, Guam, the Virgin Islands, and the Commonwealth of the Northern Mariana Islands.

(C) For the purpose of this paragraph, the term "State" does not include American Samoa, Guam, the Virgin Islands, and the Commonwealth of the Northern Mariana Islands.

(D)(i) In any fiscal year that the funds appropriated for such fiscal year exceed $7,500,000, the minimum allotment shall be $100,000 for States and $45,000 for territories.

(ii) For any fiscal year in which the total amount appropriated under subsection (h) of this section exceeds the total amount appropriated under such subsection for the preceding fiscal year, the Secretary shall increase each of the minimum allotments under clause (i) by a percentage that shall not exceed the percentage increase in the total amount appropriated under such subsection between the preceding fiscal year and the fiscal year involved.

(2) The amount of an allotment to a State for a fiscal year which the Secretary determines will not be required by the State during the period for which it is available for the purpose for which allotted shall be available for reallotment by the Secretary at appropriate times to other States with respect to which such a determination has not been made, in proportion to the original allotments of such States for such fiscal year, but with such proportionate amount for any of such other States being reduced to the extent it exceeds the sum the Secretary estimates such State needs and will be able to use during such period, and the total of such reduction shall be similarly reallotted among the States whose proportionate amounts were not so reduced. Any such amount so reallotted to a State for a fiscal year shall be deemed to be a part of its allotment for such fiscal year.

(3) Except as specifically prohibited by or as otherwise provided in State law, the Secretary shall pay to the agency designated under subsection (c) of this section the amount specified in the application approved under subsection (f) of this section.

(f) Application by State for grant funds

No grant may be made under this section unless the State submits an application to the Secretary at such time, in such manner, and containing or accompanied by such information as the Secretary deems necessary to meet the requirements of this section.

(g) Regulations; minimum requirements

The Secretary shall prescribe regulations applicable to the client assistance program which shall include the following requirements:

(1) No employees of such programs shall, while so employed, serve as staff or consultants of any rehabilitation project, program, or facility receiving assistance under this chapter in the State.

(2) Each program shall be afforded reasonable access to policymaking and administrative personnel in the State and local rehabilitation programs, projects, or facilities.

(3)(A) Each program shall contain provisions designed to assure that to the maximum extent possible alternative means of dispute resolution are available for use at the discretion of an applicant or client of the program prior to resorting to litigation or formal adjudication to resolve a dispute arising under this section.

(B) In subparagraph (A), the term "alternative means of dispute resolution" means any procedure, including good faith negotiation, conciliation, facilitation, mediation, factfinding, and arbitration, and any combination of procedures, that is used in lieu of litigation in a court or formal adjudication in an administrative forum, to resolve a dispute arising under this section.

(4) For purposes of any periodic audit, report, or evaluation of the performance of a client assistance program under this section, the Secretary shall not require such a program to disclose the identity of, or any other personally identifiable information related to, any individual requesting assistance under such program.

(h) Authorization of appropriations

There are authorized to be appropriated such sums as may be necessary for fiscal years 1999 through 2003 to carry out the provisions of this section.

(Pub. L. 93–112, title I, § 112, as added Pub. L. 105–220, title IV, § 404, Aug. 7, 1998, 112 Stat. 1163; amended Pub. L. 105–277, div. A, § 101(f) [title VIII, § 402(b)(9)], Oct. 21, 1998, 112 Stat. 2681–337, 2681–413.)

REFERENCES IN TEXT

The Americans with Disabilities Act of 1990, referred to in subsec. (a), is Pub. L. 101–336, July 26, 1990, 104 Stat. 327, as amended. Title I of the Act is classified generally to subchapter I (§ 12111 et seq.) of chapter 126 of Title 42, The Public Health and Welfare. For complete classification of this Act to the Code, see Short Title note set out under section 12101 of Title 42 and Tables.

PRIOR PROVISIONS

Prior sections 732 and 740 were omitted in the general amendment of this subchapter by Pub. L. 105–220.

Section 732, Pub. L. 93–112, title I, § 112, Sept. 26, 1973, 87 Stat. 371; Pub. L. 93–516, title I, §§ 102(b), 111(f), Dec. 7, 1974, 88 Stat. 1618, 1620; Pub. L. 93–651, title I, §§ 102(b), 111(f), Nov. 21, 1974, 89 Stat. 2–3, 2–5; Pub. L. 94–230, §§ 2(b), 11(b)(4), Mar. 15, 1976, 90 Stat. 211, 213; Pub. L. 95–602, title I, §§ 105, 122(b)(1), Nov. 6, 1978, 92 Stat. 2960, 2987; Pub. L. 97–375, title I, § 105, Dec. 21, 1982, 96 Stat. 1820; Pub. L. 98–221, title I, § 113(a), Feb. 22, 1984, 98 Stat. 20; Pub. L. 99–506, title I, § 103(d)(2)(C), title II, § 209, title X, § 1001(b)(7), Oct. 21, 1986, 100 Stat. 1810, 1818, 1842; Pub. L. 100–630, title II, § 202(f), Nov. 7, 1988, 102 Stat. 3306; Pub. L. 102–52, § 2(c), June 6, 1991, 105 Stat. 260; Pub. L. 102–569, title I, §§ 102(p)(10), 133, Oct. 29, 1992, 106 Stat. 4357, 4391; Pub. L. 103–73, title I, § 107(g), Aug. 11, 1993, 107 Stat. 723; Pub. L. 104–66, title I, § 1041(c), Dec. 21, 1995, 109 Stat. 714, related to client assistance program.

Section 740, Pub. L. 93–112, title I, § 120, as added Pub. L. 102–569, title I, § 134(a), Oct. 29, 1992, 106 Stat. 4392, related to State eligibility for grants.

Another prior section 740, Pub. L. 93–112, title I, § 120, Sept. 26, 1973, 87 Stat. 372; Pub. L. 95–602, title I, §§ 101(e)(1), 122(b)(1), Nov. 6, 1978, 92 Stat. 2957, 2987; Pub. L. 99–506, title X, § 1001(b)(8), Oct. 21, 1986, 100 Stat. 1842; Pub. L. 100–630, title II, § 202(g), Nov. 7, 1988, 102 Stat. 3306, provided for State allotments to assist in meeting the cost of vocational rehabilitation services, prior to the general amendment of part C of former subchapter I of this chapter by Pub. L. 102–569.

AMENDMENTS

1998—Pub. L. 105–277 made technical amendment to section designation and catchline in original.

PART C—AMERICAN INDIAN VOCATIONAL REHABILITATION SERVICES

§ 741. Vocational rehabilitation services grants

(a) Governing bodies of Indian tribes; amount; non-Federal share

The Commissioner, in accordance with the provisions of this part, may make grants to the governing bodies of Indian tribes located on Federal and State reservations (and consortia of such governing bodies) to pay 90 percent of the costs of vocational rehabilitation services for American Indians who are individuals with disabilities residing on or near such reservations. The non-Federal share of such costs may be in cash or in kind, fairly valued, and the Commissioner may waive such non-Federal share requirement in order to carry out the purposes of this chapter.

(b) Application; effective period; continuation of programs and services; separate service delivery systems

(1) No grant may be made under this part for any fiscal year unless an application therefor has been submitted to and approved by the Commissioner. The Commissioner may not approve an application unless the application—

(A) is made at such time, in such manner, and contains such information as the Commissioner may require;

(B) contains assurances that the rehabilitation services provided under this part to American Indians who are individuals with disabilities residing on or near a reservation in a State shall be, to the maximum extent feasible, comparable to rehabilitation services provided under this subchapter to other individuals with disabilities residing in the State and that, where appropriate, may include services traditionally used by Indian tribes; and

(C) contains assurances that the application was developed in consultation with the designated State unit of the State.

(2) The provisions of sections 450c, 450d, 450e, and 450f(a) of title 25 shall be applicable to any application submitted under this part. For purposes of this paragraph, any reference in any such provision to the Secretary of Education or to the Secretary of the Interior shall be considered to be a reference to the Commissioner.

(3) Any application approved under this part shall be effective for not more than 60 months, except as determined otherwise by the Commissioner pursuant to prescribed regulations. The State shall continue to provide vocational rehabilitation services under its State plan to American Indians residing on or near a reservation whenever such State includes any such American Indians in its State population under section 730(a)(1) of this title.

(4) In making grants under this part, the Secretary shall give priority consideration to applications for the continuation of programs which have been funded under this part.

(5) Nothing in this section may be construed to authorize a separate service delivery system for Indian residents of a State who reside in non-reservation areas.

(c) "Reservation" defined

The term "reservation" includes Indian reservations, public domain Indian allotments, former Indian reservations in Oklahoma, and land held by incorporated Native groups, regional corporations, and village corporations under the provisions of the Alaska Native Claims Settlement Act [43 U.S.C. 1601 et seq.].

(Pub. L. 93–112, title I, §121, as added Pub. L. 105–220, title IV, §404, Aug. 7, 1998, 112 Stat. 1166; amended Pub. L. 105–277, div. A, §101(f) [title VIII, §402(b)(10)], Oct. 21, 1998, 112 Stat. 2681–337, 2681–413.)

REFERENCES IN TEXT

The Alaska Native Claims Settlement Act, referred to in subsec. (c), is Pub. L. 92–203, Dec. 18, 1971, 85 Stat. 688, as amended, which is classified generally to chapter 33 (§1601 et seq.) of Title 43, Public Lands. For complete classification of this Act to the Code, see Short Title note set out under section 1601 of Title 43 and Tables.

PRIOR PROVISIONS

Prior sections 741 to 744 and 750 were omitted in the general amendment of this subchapter by Pub. L. 105–220.

Section 741, Pub. L. 93–112, title I, §121, as added Pub. L. 102–569, title I, §134(a), Oct. 29, 1992, 106 Stat. 4392, related to contents of strategic plans.

Another prior section 741, Pub. L. 93–112, title I, §121, Sept. 26, 1973, 87 Stat. 373; Pub. L. 93–516, title I, §102(c), Dec. 7, 1974, 88 Stat. 1618; Pub. L. 93–651, title I, §102(c), Nov. 21, 1974, 89 Stat. 2–3; Pub. L. 94–230, §2(c), Mar. 15, 1976, 90 Stat. 211; Pub. L. 95–602, title I, §§101(e)(2), 122(b), Nov. 6, 1978, 92 Stat. 2957, 2987; Pub. L. 98–221, title I, §114, Feb. 22, 1984, 98 Stat. 23; Pub. L. 99–506, title I, §103(d)(2)(C), title II, §210, Oct. 21, 1986, 100 Stat. 1810, 1819; Pub. L. 100–630, title II, §202(h), Nov. 7, 1988, 102 Stat. 3306; Pub. L. 102–52, §2(b)(2), June 6, 1991, 105 Stat. 260, related to payments to States for planning, preparing, and initiating special programs under approved State plans and payments for the costs of constructing facilities to be used in providing services under such State plans, prior to the general amendment of part C of former subchapter I of this chapter by Pub. L. 102–569.

Section 742, Pub. L. 93–112, title I, §122, as added Pub. L. 102–569, title I, §134(a), Oct. 29, 1992, 106 Stat. 4393, related to process for developing strategic plans.

Section 743, Pub. L. 93–112, title I, §123, as added Pub. L. 102–569, title I, §134(a), Oct. 29, 1992, 106 Stat. 4393, related to use of funds.

Section 744, Pub. L. 93–112, title I, §124, as added Pub. L. 102–569, title I, §134(a), Oct. 29, 1992, 106 Stat. 4395; amended Pub. L. 103–73, title I, §107(h), Aug. 11, 1993, 107 Stat. 723, related to allotments among States.

Section 750, Pub. L. 93–112, title I, §130, Sept. 26, 1973, 87 Stat. 374; Pub. L. 93–516, title I, §111(g), Dec. 7, 1974, 88 Stat. 1621; Pub. L. 93–651, title I, §111(g), Nov. 21, 1974, 89 Stat. 2–6; Pub. L. 95–602, title I, §106, Nov. 6, 1978, 92 Stat. 2960; Pub. L. 99–506, title I, §103(d)(2)(C), title II, §211, title X, §1002(b)(1), Oct. 21, 1986, 100 Stat. 1810, 1819, 1844; Pub. L. 100–630, title II, §202(i), Nov. 7, 1988, 102 Stat. 3306; Pub. L. 102–569, title I, §102(p)(11), Oct. 29, 1992, 106 Stat. 4357, related to American Indian vocational rehabilitation services grants.

AMENDMENTS

1998—Pub. L. 105–277 made technical amendment to section designation and catchline in original.

PART D—VOCATIONAL REHABILITATION SERVICES CLIENT INFORMATION

§751. Data sharing

(a) In general

(1) Memorandum of understanding

The Secretary of Education and the Secretary of Health and Human Services shall enter into a memorandum of understanding for the purposes of exchanging data of mutual importance—

(A) that concern clients of designated State agencies; and

(B) that are data maintained either by—

(i) the Rehabilitation Services Administration, as required by section 710 of this title; or

(ii) the Social Security Administration, from its Summary Earnings and Records and Master Beneficiary Records.

(2) Employment statistics

The Secretary of Labor shall provide the Commissioner with employment statistics specified in section 49*l*–2 of this title, that facilitate evaluation by the Commissioner of the program carried out under part B of this subchapter, and allow the Commissioner to compare the progress of individuals with disabilities who are assisted under the program in securing, retaining, regaining, and advancing in employment with the progress made by individuals who are assisted under title I of the Workforce Investment Act of 1998 [29 U.S.C. 2801 et seq.].

(b) Treatment of information

For purposes of the exchange described in subsection (a)(1) of this section, the data described in subsection (a)(1)(B)(ii) of this section shall not be considered return information (as defined in section 6103(b)(2) of title 26) and, as appropriate, the confidentiality of all client information shall be maintained by the Rehabilitation Services Administration and the Social Security Administration.

(Pub. L. 93–112, title I, § 131, as added Pub. L. 105–220, title IV, § 404, Aug. 7, 1998, 112 Stat. 1167.)

REFERENCES IN TEXT

The Workforce Investment Act of 1998, referred to in subsec. (a)(2), is Pub. L. 105–220, Aug. 7, 1998, 112 Stat. 936, as amended. Title I of the Act is classified principally to chapter 30 (§ 2801 et seq.) of this title. For complete classification of this Act to the Code, see Short Title note set out under section 9201 of Title 20, Education, and Tables.

PRIOR PROVISIONS

A prior section 751, Pub. L. 93–112, title I, § 131, as added Pub. L. 95–602, title I, § 106, Nov. 6, 1978, 92 Stat. 2961, and amended Pub. L. 99–506, title I, § 103(d)(2)(C), Oct. 21, 1986, 100 Stat. 1810, directed Secretary to submit to Congress, not less than thirty months after Nov. 6, 1978, an evaluation of programs conducted under part D of former subchapter I of this chapter, prior to repeal by Pub. L. 99–506, title X, § 1002(b)(2)(A), Oct. 21, 1986, 100 Stat. 1844.

A prior section 752, Pub. L. 93–112, title I, § 131, formerly § 132, as added Pub. L. 99–506, title II, § 212(a), Oct. 21, 1986, 100 Stat. 1820; renumbered § 132, Pub. L. 100–630, title II, § 202(j), Nov. 7, 1988, 102 Stat. 3307, provided for study on special problems and needs of Indians with handicaps both on and off the reservation, prior to repeal by Pub. L. 102–569, title I, § 135(a), Oct. 29, 1992, 106 Stat. 4396.

Prior sections 753 and 753a were omitted in the general amendment of this subchapter by Pub. L. 105–220.

Section 753, Pub. L. 93–112, title I, § 140, as added Pub. L. 103–73, title I, § 108, Aug. 11, 1993, 107 Stat. 724, related to review of data collection and reporting system.

Section 753a, Pub. L. 93–112, title I, § 141, as added Pub. L. 103–73, title I, § 108, Aug. 11, 1993, 107 Stat. 725, related to exchange of data.

SUBCHAPTER II—RESEARCH AND TRAINING

CODIFICATION

Title II of the Rehabilitation Act of 1973, comprising this subchapter, was originally enacted by Pub. L. 93–112, title II, Sept. 26, 1973, 87 Stat. 374, and amended by Pub. L. 93–516, Dec. 7, 1974, 88 Stat. 1617; Pub. L. 93–651, Nov. 21, 1974, 89 Stat. 2–3; Pub. L. 94–230, Mar. 15, 1976, 90 Stat. 211; Pub. L. 95–602, Nov. 6, 1978, 92 Stat. 2955; Pub. L. 96–88, Oct. 17, 1979, 93 Stat. 668; Pub. L. 98–221, Feb. 22, 1984, 98 Stat. 17; Pub. L. 99–506, Oct. 21, 1986, 100 Stat. 1807; Pub. L. 100–630, Nov. 7, 1988, 102 Stat. 3289; Pub. L. 102–52, June 6, 1991, 105 Stat. 260; Pub. L. 102–54, June 13, 1991, 105 Stat. 267; Pub. L. 102–569, Oct. 29, 1992, 106 Stat. 4344; Pub. L. 103–73, Aug. 11, 1993, 107 Stat. 718; Pub. L. 103–218, Mar. 9, 1994, 108 Stat. 50; Pub. L. 103–382, Oct. 20, 1994, 108 Stat. 3518. Title II is shown herein, however, as having been added by Pub. L. 105–220, title IV, § 405, Aug. 7, 1998, 112 Stat. 1167, without reference to those intervening amendments because of the extensive revision of title II by Pub. L. 105–220.

§ 760. Declaration of purpose

The purpose of this subchapter is to—

(1) provide for research, demonstration projects, training, and related activities to maximize the full inclusion and integration into society, employment, independent living, family support, and economic and social self-sufficiency of individuals with disabilities of all ages, with particular emphasis on improving the effectiveness of services authorized under this chapter;

(2) provide for a comprehensive and coordinated approach to the support and conduct of such research, demonstration projects, training, and related activities and to ensure that the approach is in accordance with the 5-year plan developed under section 762(h) of this title;

(3) promote the transfer of rehabilitation technology to individuals with disabilities through research and demonstration projects relating to—

(A) the procurement process for the purchase of rehabilitation technology;

(B) the utilization of rehabilitation technology on a national basis;

(C) specific adaptations or customizations of products to enable individuals with disabilities to live more independently; and

(D) the development or transfer of assistive technology;

(4) ensure the widespread distribution, in usable formats, of practical scientific and technological information—

(A) generated by research, demonstration projects, training, and related activities; and

(B) regarding state-of-the-art practices, improvements in the services authorized under this chapter, rehabilitation technology, and new knowledge regarding disabilities,

to rehabilitation professionals, individuals with disabilities, and other interested parties, including the general public;

(5) identify effective strategies that enhance the opportunities of individuals with disabilities to engage in employment, including employment involving telecommuting and self-employment; and

(6) increase opportunities for researchers who are members of traditionally underserved populations, including researchers who are members of minority groups and researchers who are individuals with disabilities.

(Pub. L. 93–112, title II, § 200, as added Pub. L. 105–220, title IV, § 405, Aug. 7, 1998, 112 Stat. 1167; amended Pub. L. 105–277, div. A, § 101(f) [title VIII, § 401(16)], Oct. 21, 1998, 112 Stat. 2681–337, 2681–412.)

PRIOR PROVISIONS

A prior section 760, Pub. L. 93–112, title II, § 200, Sept. 26, 1973, 87 Stat. 374; Pub. L. 95–602, title I, § 107, Nov. 6, 1978, 92 Stat. 2962; Pub. L. 99–506, title I, § 103(d)(2)(C), Oct. 21, 1986, 100 Stat. 1810; Pub. L. 102–569, title II, § 201, Oct. 29, 1992, 106 Stat. 4398, contained congressional declaration of purpose, prior to the general amendment of this subchapter by Pub. L. 105–220.

AMENDMENTS

1998—Pub. L. 105–277 made technical amendment to directory language of Pub. L. 105–220, § 405, which enacted this section.

§ 761. Authorization of appropriations

(a) There are authorized to be appropriated—

(1) for the purpose of providing for the expenses of the National Institute on Disability

and Rehabilitation Research under section 762 of this title, which shall include the expenses of the Rehabilitation Research Advisory Council under section 765 of this title, and shall not include the expenses of such Institute to carry out section 764 of this title, such sums as may be necessary for each of fiscal years 1999 through 2003; and

(2) to carry out section 764 of this title, such sums as may be necessary for each of fiscal years 1999 through 2003.

(b) Funds appropriated under this subchapter shall remain available until expended.

(Pub. L. 93–112, title II, § 201, as added Pub. L. 105–220, title IV, § 405, Aug. 7, 1998, 112 Stat. 1168; amended Pub. L. 105–277, div. A, § 101(f) [title VIII, § 401(16)], Oct. 21, 1998, 112 Stat. 2681–337, 2681–412.)

PRIOR PROVISIONS

Prior sections 761 to 761b were omitted in the general amendment of this subchapter by Pub. L. 105–220.

Section 761, Pub. L. 93–112, title II, § 201, Sept. 26, 1973, 87 Stat. 374; Pub. L. 93–516, title I, § 103, Dec. 7, 1974, 88 Stat. 1618; Pub. L. 93–651, title I, § 103, Nov. 21, 1974, 89 Stat. 2–3; Pub. L. 94–230, §§ 3, 11(b)(5), (6), Mar. 15, 1976, 90 Stat. 211, 213; Pub. L. 95–602, title I, § 108, Nov. 6, 1978, 92 Stat. 2962; Pub. L. 98–221, title I, § 121, Feb. 22, 1984, 98 Stat. 23; Pub. L. 99–506, title III, § 301, Oct. 21, 1986, 100 Stat. 1820; Pub. L. 100–630, title II, § 203(a), Nov. 7, 1988, 102 Stat. 3307; Pub. L. 102–52, § 3, June 6, 1991, 105 Stat. 260; Pub. L. 102–569, title II, § 202, Oct. 29, 1992, 106 Stat. 4398, authorized appropriations.

Section 761a, Pub. L. 93–112, title II, § 202, as added Pub. L. 95–602, title I, § 109(4), Nov. 6, 1978, 92 Stat. 2963; amended Pub. L. 98–221, title I, §§ 104(a)(4), (b)(1), 122, Feb. 22, 1984, 98 Stat. 18, 23; Pub. L. 99–506, title I, § 103(d)(2)(C), title III, §§ 302, 303, title X, §§ 1001(c), 1002(c), Oct. 21, 1986, 100 Stat. 1810, 1820, 1821, 1842, 1844; Pub. L. 100–630, title II, § 203(b), Nov. 7, 1988, 102 Stat. 3307; Pub. L. 102–54, § 13(k)(1)(A), June 13, 1991, 105 Stat. 276; Pub. L. 102–569, title I, § 102(p)(12), title II, § 203, Oct. 29, 1992, 106 Stat. 4357, 4399; Pub. L. 103–73, title I, §§ 102(4), 109(a), Aug. 11, 1993, 107 Stat. 718, 725; Pub. L. 103–218, title IV, § 402(a), Mar. 9, 1994, 108 Stat. 96; Pub. L. 103–382, title III, § 394(i)(1), Oct. 20, 1994, 108 Stat. 4028, related to National Institute on Disability and Rehabilitation Research. See section 762 of this title.

Section 761b, Pub. L. 93–112, title II, § 203, as added Pub. L. 95–602, title I, § 109(4), Nov. 6, 1978, 92 Stat. 2965; amended Pub. L. 96–88, title V, § 508(m)(1), Oct. 17, 1979, 93 Stat. 694; Pub. L. 98–221, title I, § 104(b)(2), Feb. 22, 1984, 98 Stat. 18; Pub. L. 99–506, title I, § 103(d)(2)(C), title III, § 304, Oct. 21, 1986, 100 Stat. 1810, 1822; Pub. L. 100–630, title II, § 203(c), Nov. 7, 1988, 102 Stat. 3307; Pub. L. 102–54, § 13(k)(1)(B), June 13, 1991, 105 Stat. 276; Pub. L. 102–569, title I, § 102(p)(13), title II, § 204, Oct. 29, 1992, 106 Stat. 4358, 4403, related to Interagency Committee on Disability Research. See section 763 of this title.

AMENDMENTS

1998—Pub. L. 105–277 made technical amendment to directory language of Pub. L. 105–220, § 405, which enacted this section.

§ 762. National Institute on Disability and Rehabilitation Research

(a) Establishment; Director as principal officer

(1) There is established within the Department of Education a National Institute on Disability and Rehabilitation Research (hereinafter in this subchapter referred to as the "Institute"), which shall be headed by a Director (hereinafter in this subchapter referred to as the "Director"), in order to—

(A) promote, coordinate, and provide for—

(i) research;

(ii) demonstration projects and training; and

(iii) related activities,

with respect to individuals with disabilities;

(B) more effectively carry out activities through the programs under section 764 of this title and activities under this section;

(C) widely disseminate information from the activities described in subparagraphs (A) and (B); and

(D) provide leadership in advancing the quality of life of individuals with disabilities.

(2) In the performance of the functions of the office, the Director shall be directly responsible to the Secretary or to the same Under Secretary or Assistant Secretary of the Department of Education to whom the Commissioner is responsible under section 702(a) of this title.

(b) Duties of Director

The Director, through the Institute, shall be responsible for—

(1) administering the programs described in section 764 of this title and activities under this section;

(2) widely disseminating findings, conclusions, and recommendations, resulting from research, demonstration projects, training, and related activities (referred to in this subchapter as "covered activities") funded by the Institute, to—

(A) other Federal, State, tribal, and local public agencies;

(B) private organizations engaged in research relating to rehabilitation or providing rehabilitation services;

(C) rehabilitation practitioners; and

(D) individuals with disabilities and the individuals' representatives;

(3) coordinating, through the Interagency Committee established by section 763 of this title, all Federal programs and policies relating to research in rehabilitation;

(4) widely disseminating educational materials and research results, concerning ways to maximize the full inclusion and integration into society, employment, independent living, family support, and economic and social self-sufficiency of individuals with disabilities, to—

(A) public and private entities, including—

(i) elementary and secondary schools (as defined in section 7801 of title 20;[1] and

(ii) institutions of higher education;

(B) rehabilitation practitioners;

(C) individuals with disabilities (especially such individuals who are members of minority groups or of populations that are unserved or underserved by programs under this chapter); and

(D) the individuals' representatives for the individuals described in subparagraph (C);

(5)(A) conducting an education program to inform the public about ways of providing for

[1] So in original. A closing parenthesis probably should precede the semicolon.

the rehabilitation of individuals with disabilities, including information relating to—

(i) family care;

(ii) self-care; and

(iii) assistive technology devices and assistive technology services; and

(B) as part of the program, disseminating engineering information about assistive technology devices;

(6) conducting conferences, seminars, and workshops (including in-service training programs and programs for individuals with disabilities) concerning advances in rehabilitation research and rehabilitation technology (including advances concerning the selection and use of assistive technology devices and assistive technology services), pertinent to the full inclusion and integration into society, employment, independent living, family support, and economic and social self-sufficiency of individuals with disabilities;

(7) taking whatever action is necessary to keep the Congress fully and currently informed with respect to the implementation and conduct of programs and activities carried out under this subchapter, including dissemination activities;

(8) producing, in conjunction with the Department of Labor, the National Center for Health Statistics, the Bureau of the Census, the Centers for Medicare & Medicaid Services, the Social Security Administration, the Bureau of Indian Affairs, the Indian Health Service, and other Federal departments and agencies, as may be appropriate, statistical reports and studies on the employment, self-employment, telecommuting, health, income, and other demographic characteristics of individuals with disabilities, including information on individuals with disabilities who live in rural or inner-city settings, with particular attention given to underserved populations, and widely disseminating such reports and studies to rehabilitation professionals, individuals with disabilities, the individuals' representatives, and others to assist in the planning, assessment, and evaluation of vocational and other rehabilitation services for individuals with disabilities;

(9) conducting research on consumer satisfaction with vocational rehabilitation services for the purpose of identifying effective rehabilitation programs and policies that promote the independence of individuals with disabilities and achievement of long-term vocational goals;

(10) conducting research to examine the relationship between the provision of specific services and successful, sustained employment outcomes, including employment outcomes involving self-employment and telecommuting; and

(11) coordinating activities with the Attorney General regarding the provision of information, training, or technical assistance regarding the Americans with Disabilities Act of 1990 (42 U.S.C. 12101 et seq.) to ensure consistency with the plan for technical assistance required under section 506[2] of such Act (42 U.S.C. 12206).

[2] See References in Text note below.

(c) Development and dissemination of models

(1) The Director, acting through the Institute or one or more entities funded by the Institute, shall provide for the development and dissemination of models to address consumer-driven information needs related to assistive technology devices and assistive technology services.

(2) The development and dissemination of models may include—

(A) convening groups of individuals with disabilities, family members and advocates of such individuals, commercial producers of assistive technology, and entities funded by the Institute to develop, assess, and disseminate knowledge about information needs related to assistive technology;

(B) identifying the types of information regarding assistive technology devices and assistive technology services that individuals with disabilities find especially useful;

(C) evaluating current models, and developing new models, for transmitting the information described in subparagraph (B) to consumers and to commercial producers of assistive technology; and

(D) disseminating through one or more entities funded by the Institute, the models described in subparagraph (C) and findings regarding the information described in subparagraph (B) to consumers and commercial producers of assistive technology.

(d) Appointment of Director; employment of technical and professional personnel; consultants

(1) The Director of the Institute shall be appointed by the Secretary. The Director shall be an individual with substantial experience in rehabilitation and in research administration.

(2) The Director, subject to the approval of the President, may appoint, for terms not to exceed three years, without regard to the provisions of title 5 governing appointment in the competitive service, and may compensate, without regard to the provisions of chapter 51 and subchapter III of chapter 53 of such title relating to classification and General Schedule pay rates, such technical and professional employees of the Institute as the Director determines to be necessary to accomplish the functions of the Institute and also appoint and compensate without regard to such provisions, in a number not to exceed one-fifth of the number of full-time, regular technical and professional employees of the Institute.

(3) The Director may obtain the services of consultants, without regard to the provisions of title 5 governing appointments in the competitive service.

(e) Fellowships

The Director, pursuant to regulations which the Secretary shall prescribe, may establish and maintain fellowships with such stipends and allowances, including travel and subsistence expenses provided for under title 5, as the Director considers necessary to procure the assistance of highly qualified research fellows, including individuals with disabilities, from the United States and foreign countries.

(f) Scientific peer review of research, training, and demonstration projects

(1) The Director shall provide for scientific peer review of all applications for financial assistance for research, training, and demonstration projects over which the Director has authority. The scientific peer review shall be conducted by individuals who are not Federal employees, who are scientists or other experts in the rehabilitation field (including the independent living field), including knowledgeable individuals with disabilities, and the individuals' representatives, and who are competent to review applications for the financial assistance.

(2) In providing for such scientific peer review, the Secretary shall provide for training, as necessary and appropriate, to facilitate the effective participation of those individuals selected to participate in such review.

(g) Use of funds

Not less than 90 percent of the funds appropriated under this subchapter for any fiscal year shall be expended by the Director to carry out activities under this subchapter through grants, contracts, or cooperative agreements. Up to 10 percent of the funds appropriated under this subchapter for any fiscal year may be expended directly for the purpose of carrying out the functions of the Director under this section.

(h) 5-year plan

(1) The Director shall—

(A) by October 1, 1998, and every fifth October 1 thereafter, prepare and publish in the Federal Register for public comment a draft of a 5-year plan that outlines priorities for rehabilitation research, demonstration projects, training, and related activities and explains the basis for such priorities;

(B) by June 1, 1999, and every fifth June 1 thereafter, after considering public comments, submit the plan in final form to the appropriate committees of Congress;

(C) at appropriate intervals, prepare and submit revisions in the plan to the appropriate committees of Congress; and

(D) annually prepare and submit progress reports on the plan to the appropriate committees of Congress.

(2) Such plan shall—

(A) identify any covered activity that should be conducted under this section and section 764 of this title respecting the full inclusion and integration into society of individuals with disabilities, especially in the area of employment;

(B) determine the funding priorities for covered activities to be conducted under this section and section 764 of this title;

(C) specify appropriate goals and timetables for covered activities to be conducted under this section and section 764 of this title;

(D) be developed by the Director—

(i) after consultation with the Rehabilitation Research Advisory Council established under section 765 of this title;

(ii) in coordination with the Commissioner;

(iii) after consultation with the National Council on Disability established under subchapter IV of this chapter, the Secretary of Education, officials responsible for the administration of the Developmental Disabilities Assistance and Bill of Rights Act of 2000 [42 U.S.C. 15001 et seq.], and the Interagency Committee on Disability Research established under section 763 of this title; and

(iv) after full consideration of the input of individuals with disabilities and the individuals' representatives, organizations representing individuals with disabilities, providers of services furnished under this chapter, researchers in the rehabilitation field, and any other persons or entities the Director considers to be appropriate;

(E) specify plans for widespread dissemination of the results of covered activities, in accessible formats, to rehabilitation practitioners, individuals with disabilities, and the individuals' representatives; and

(F) specify plans for widespread dissemination of the results of covered activities that concern individuals with disabilities who are members of minority groups or of populations that are unserved or underserved by programs carried out under this chapter.

(i) Cooperation and consultation with other agencies and departments on design of research programs

In order to promote cooperation among Federal departments and agencies conducting research programs, the Director shall consult with the administrators of such programs, and with the Interagency Committee established by section 763 of this title, regarding the design of research projects conducted by such entities and the results and applications of such research.

(j) Comprehensive and coordinated research program; interagency cooperation; research and training center

(1) The Director shall take appropriate actions to provide for a comprehensive and coordinated research program under this subchapter. In providing such a program, the Director may undertake joint activities with other Federal entities engaged in research and with appropriate private entities. Any Federal entity proposing to establish any research project related to the purposes of this chapter shall consult, through the Interagency Committee established by section 763 of this title, with the Director as Chairperson of such Committee and provide the Director with sufficient prior opportunity to comment on such project.

(2) Any person responsible for administering any program of the National Institutes of Health, the Department of Veterans Affairs, the National Science Foundation, the National Aeronautics and Space Administration, the Office of Special Education and Rehabilitative Services, or of any other Federal entity, shall, through the Interagency Committee established by section 763 of this title, consult and cooperate with the Director in carrying out such program if the program is related to the purposes of this subchapter.

(3) The Director shall support, directly or by grant or contract, a center associated with an

institution of higher education, for research and training concerning the delivery of vocational rehabilitation services to rural areas.

(k) Grants for training

The Director shall make grants to institutions of higher education for the training of rehabilitation researchers, including individuals with disabilities, with particular attention to research areas that support the implementation and objectives of this chapter and that improve the effectiveness of services authorized under this chapter.

(Pub. L. 93–112, title II, § 202, as added Pub. L. 105–220, title IV, § 405, Aug. 7, 1998, 112 Stat. 1168; amended Pub. L. 105–277, div. A, § 101(f) [title VIII, § 401(16)], Oct. 21, 1998, 112 Stat. 2681–337, 2681–412; Pub. L. 106–402, title IV, § 401(b)(3)(B), Oct. 30, 2000, 114 Stat. 1737; Pub. L. 107–110, title X, § 1076(u)(1), Jan. 8, 2002, 115 Stat. 2092; Pub. L. 108–173, title IX, § 900(e)(6)(A), Dec. 8, 2003, 117 Stat. 2373.)

REFERENCES IN TEXT

The Americans with Disabilities Act of 1990, referred to in subsec. (b)(11), is Pub. L. 101–336, July 26, 1990, 104 Stat. 327, which is classified principally to chapter 126 (§ 12101 et seq.) of Title 42, The Public Health and Welfare. Section 506 of the Act was renumbered section 507 by Pub. L. 110–325, § 6(a)(2), Sept. 25, 2008, 122 Stat. 3558. For complete classification of this Act to the Code, see Short Title note set out under section 12101 of Title 42 and Tables.

The provisions of title 5 governing appointments in the competitive service, referred to in subsec. (d)(2), (3), are classified generally to section 3301 et seq. of Title 5, Government Organization and Employees.

The Developmental Disabilities Assistance and Bill of Rights Act of 2000, referred to in subsec. (h)(2)(D)(iii), is Pub. L. 106–402, Oct. 30, 2000, 114 Stat. 1677, which is classified principally to chapter 144 (§ 15001 et seq.) of Title 42, The Public Health and Welfare. For complete classification of this Act to the Code, see Short Title note set out under section 15001 of Title 42 and Tables.

PRIOR PROVISIONS

Provisions similar to this section were contained in section 761a of this title prior to the general amendment of this subchapter by Pub. L. 105–220.

A prior section 762, Pub. L. 93–112, title II, § 204, formerly § 202, Sept. 26, 1973, 87 Stat. 375, amended Pub. L. 93–516, title I, § 111(h), Dec. 7, 1974, 88 Stat. 1621; Pub. L. 93–651, title I, § 111(h), Nov. 21, 1974, 89 Stat. 2–6; renumbered and amended Pub. L. 95–602, title I, §§ 109(3), 110, 111, Nov. 6, 1978, 92 Stat. 2963, 2966; Pub. L. 98–221, title I, §§ 104(a)(5), 123, Feb. 22, 1984, 98 Stat. 18, 24; Pub. L. 99–506, title I, § 103(d)(2)(C), (h)(2), title III, §§ 302(b), 305, Oct. 21, 1986, 100 Stat. 1810, 1811, 1821, 1822; Pub. L. 100–630, title II, § 203(d), Nov. 7, 1988, 102 Stat. 3308; Pub. L. 102–569, title I, § 102(p)(14), title II, § 205, Oct. 29, 1992, 106 Stat. 4358, 4403; Pub. L. 103–73, title I, § 109(b), Aug. 11, 1993, 107 Stat. 726, related to research, prior to the general amendment of this subchapter by Pub. L. 105–220. See section 764 of this title.

AMENDMENTS

2003—Subsec. (b)(8). Pub. L. 108–173 substituted "Centers for Medicare & Medicaid Services" for "Health Care Financing Administration".

2002—Subsec. (b)(4)(A)(i). Pub. L. 107–110 substituted "7801" for "8801".

2000—Subsec. (h)(2)(D)(iii). Pub. L. 106–402 substituted "Developmental Disabilities Assistance and Bill of Rights Act of 2000" for "Developmental Disabilities Assistance and Bill of Rights Act (42 U.S.C. 6000 et seq.)".

1998—Pub. L. 105–277 made technical amendment to directory language of Pub. L. 105–220, § 405, which enacted this section.

EFFECTIVE DATE OF 2002 AMENDMENT

Amendment by Pub. L. 107–110 effective Jan. 8, 2002, except with respect to certain noncompetitive programs and competitive programs, see section 5 of Pub. L. 107–110, set out as an Effective Date note under section 6301 of Title 20, Education.

REFERENCES TO NATIONAL INSTITUTE OF HANDICAPPED RESEARCH AMENDED OR DEEMED TO BE REFERENCES TO NATIONAL INSTITUTE ON DISABILITY AND REHABILITATION RESEARCH

Pub. L. 99–506, title III, § 302(b), Oct. 21, 1986, 100 Stat. 1821, provided that: "The Act [this chapter] is amended by striking out 'National Institute of Handicapped Research' each place it appears in the Act (including the table of contents) and inserting in lieu thereof 'National Institute on Disability and Rehabilitation Research'. Any reference in any other provision of law to the 'National Institute of Handicapped Research' shall be considered to be a reference to the 'National Institute on Disability and Rehabilitation Research'."

§ 762a. Research and demonstration projects

(a) Multiple and interrelated service needs of individuals with handicaps; report to Congress

The Secretary of Education is authorized to make grants to, and to enter into contract with, public and nonprofit agencies and organizations for the purpose of research and demonstration projects specifically designed to address the multiple and interrelated service needs of individuals with handicaps, the elderly, and children, youths, adults, and families. A report evaluating each project funded under this section shall be submitted to appropriate committees of the Congress within four months after the date each such project is completed.

(b) Authorization of appropriations

There are authorized to be appropriated to carry out this section such sums as may be necessary.

No funds other than those appropriated pursuant to this subsection can be used for the conduct of research specifically authorized by this section.

(c) Study on impact of vocational rehabilitation services; transmittal to Congress

Within one year after the date appropriations are made under subsection (b) of this section for purposes of research and demonstration projects under subsection (a) of this section, the Secretary shall prepare and transmit to the Congress a study concerning the impact of vocational rehabilitation services provided under the Rehabilitation Act of 1973 [29 U.S.C. 701 et seq.] on recipients of disability payments under titles II and XVI of the Social Security Act [42 U.S.C. 401 et seq., 1381 et seq.]. The study shall examine the relationship between the vocational rehabilitation services provided under the Rehabilitation Act of 1973 and the programs under sections 222 and 1615 of the Social Security Act [42 U.S.C. 422, 1382d], and shall include—

(1) an analysis of the savings in disability benefit payments under titles II and XVI of the Social Security Act as a result of the provision of vocational rehabilitation services under the Rehabilitation Act of 1973;

(2) a specification of the rate of return to the active labor force by recipients of services under sections 222 and 1615 of the Social Security Act;

(3) a specification of the total amount of expenditures, in the five fiscal years preceding the date of submission of the report, for vocational rehabilitation services under the Rehabilitation Act of 1973 and under sections 222 and 1615 of the Social Security Act, and recommendations for the coordinated presentation of such expenditures in the Budget submitted by the President pursuant to section 1105 of title 31; and

(4) recommendations to improve the coordination of services under the Rehabilitation Act of 1973 with programs under sections 222 and 1615 of the Social Security Act, including recommendations for increasing savings in disability benefits payments and the rate of return to the active labor force by recipients of services under sections 222 and 1615 of the Social Security Act.

(Pub. L. 95–602, title IV, § 401, Nov. 6, 1978, 92 Stat. 3002; Pub. L. 98–221, title I, § 104(c)(1), Feb. 22, 1984, 98 Stat. 18; Pub. L. 99–506, title I, § 103(d)(2)(C), Oct. 21, 1986, 100 Stat. 1810.)

REFERENCES IN TEXT

The Rehabilitation Act of 1973, referred to in subsec. (c), is Pub. L. 93–112, Sept. 26, 1973, 87 Stat. 355, as amended, which is classified generally to this chapter (§ 701 et seq.). For complete classification of this Act to the Code, see Short Title note set out under section 701 of this title and Tables.

The Social Security Act, referred to in subsec. (c), is act Aug. 14, 1935, ch. 531, 49 Stat. 620, as amended. Titles II and XVI of the Social Security Act are classified generally to subchapters II (§ 401 et seq.) and XVI (§ 1381 et seq.), respectively, of chapter 7 of Title 42, The Public Health and Welfare. For complete classification of this Act to the Code, see section 1305 of Title 42 and Tables.

CODIFICATION

In subsec. (c)(3), "section 1105 of title 31" was substituted for "section 201 of the Budget and Accounting Act, 1921 [31 U.S.C. 11]" on authority of Pub. L. 97–258, § 4(b), Sept. 13, 1982, 96 Stat. 1067, the first section of which enacted Title 31, Money and Finance.

Section was enacted as part of the Rehabilitation, Comprehensive Services, and Developmental Disabilities Amendments of 1978, and not as part of Rehabilitation Act of 1973 which comprises this chapter.

AMENDMENTS

1986—Subsec. (a). Pub. L. 99–506 substituted "individuals with handicaps" for "handicapped individuals".

1984—Subsec. (a). Pub. L. 98–221 substituted "Secretary of Education" for "Secretary of Health, Education, and Welfare".

§ 763. Interagency Committee

(a) Establishment; membership; meetings

(1) In order to promote coordination and cooperation among Federal departments and agencies conducting rehabilitation research programs, including programs relating to assistive technology research and research that incorporates the principles of universal design, there is established within the Federal Government an Interagency Committee on Disability Research (hereinafter in this section referred to as the "Committee"), chaired by the Director and comprised of such members as the President may designate, including the following (or their designees): the Director, the Commissioner of the Rehabilitation Services Administration, the Assistant Secretary for Special Education and Rehabilitative Services, the Secretary of Education, the Secretary of Veterans Affairs, the Director of the National Institutes of Health, the Director of the National Institute of Mental Health, the Administrator of the National Aeronautics and Space Administration, the Secretary of Transportation, the Assistant Secretary of the Interior for Indian Affairs, the Director of the Indian Health Service, and the Director of the National Science Foundation.

(2) The Committee shall meet not less than four times each year.

(b) Duties

(1) After receiving input from targeted individuals, the Committee shall identify, assess, and seek to coordinate all Federal programs, activities, and projects, and plans for such programs, activities, and projects with respect to the conduct of research (including assistive technology research and research that incorporates the principles of universal design) related to rehabilitation of individuals with disabilities.

(2) In carrying out its duties with respect to the conduct of Federal research (including assistive technology research and research that incorporates the principles of universal design) related to rehabilitation of individuals with disabilities, the Committee shall—

(A) share information regarding the range of assistive technology research, and research that incorporates the principles of universal design, that is being carried out by members of the Committee and other Federal departments and organizations;

(B) identify, and make efforts to address, gaps in assistive technology research and research that incorporates the principles of universal design that are not being adequately addressed;

(C) identify, and establish, clear research priorities related to assistive technology research and research that incorporates the principles of universal design for the Federal Government;

(D) promote interagency collaboration and joint research activities relating to assistive technology research and research that incorporates the principles of universal design at the Federal level, and reduce unnecessary duplication of effort regarding these types of research within the Federal Government; and

(E) optimize the productivity of Committee members through resource sharing and other cost-saving activities, related to assistive technology research and research that incorporates the principles of universal design.

(c) Annual report

Not later than December 31 of each year, the Committee shall prepare and submit, to the President and to the Committee on Education and the Workforce of the House of Representatives and the Committee on Labor and Human Resources of the Senate, a report that—

(1) describes the progress of the Committee in fulfilling the duties described in subsection (b) of this section;

(2) makes such recommendations as the Committee determines to be appropriate with respect to coordination of policy and develop-

ment of objectives and priorities for all Federal programs relating to the conduct of research (including assistive technology research and research that incorporates the principles of universal design) related to rehabilitation of individuals with disabilities; and

(3) describes the activities that the Committee recommended to be funded through grants, contracts, cooperative agreements, and other mechanisms, for assistive technology research and development and research and development that incorporates the principles of universal design.

(d) Recommendations

(1) In order to promote coordination and cooperation among Federal departments and agencies conducting assistive technology research programs, to reduce duplication of effort among the programs, and to increase the availability of assistive technology for individuals with disabilities, the Committee may recommend activities to be funded through grants, contracts or cooperative agreements, or other mechanisms—

(A) in joint research projects for assistive technology research and research that incorporates the principles of universal design; and

(B) in other programs designed to promote a cohesive, strategic Federal program of research described in subparagraph (A).

(2) The projects and programs described in paragraph (1) shall be jointly administered by at least 2 agencies or departments with representatives on the Committee.

(3) In recommending activities to be funded in the projects and programs, the Committee shall obtain input from targeted individuals, and other organizations and individuals the Committee determines to be appropriate, concerning the availability and potential of technology for individuals with disabilities.

(e) Definitions

In this section—

(1) the terms "assistive technology" and "universal design" have the meanings given the terms in section 3002 of this title; and

(2) the term "targeted individuals" has the meaning given the term "targeted individuals and entities" in section 3002 of this title.

(Pub. L. 93–112, title II, § 203, as added Pub. L. 105–220, title IV, § 405, Aug. 7, 1998, 112 Stat. 1173; amended Pub. L. 105–277, div. A, § 101(f) [title VIII, § 401(16)], Oct. 21, 1998, 112 Stat. 2681–337, 2681–412; Pub. L. 105–394, title II, § 201, Nov. 13, 1998, 112 Stat. 3651; Pub. L. 108–364, § 3(b)(1), Oct. 25, 2004, 118 Stat. 1737.)

PRIOR PROVISIONS

Provisions similar to this section were contained in section 761b of this title prior to the general amendment of this subchapter by Pub. L. 105–220.

A prior section 763, Pub. L. 93–112, title II, § 203, Sept. 26, 1973, 87 Stat. 376, relating to making of grants and contracts for training of personnel involved in vocational services to handicapped individuals, was renumbered section 304 of Pub. L. 93–112 and transferred to section 774 of this title.

AMENDMENTS

2004—Subsec. (e). Pub. L. 108–364 added subsec. (e) and struck out former subsec. (e) which read as follows: "In this section, the terms 'assistive technology', 'targeted individuals', and 'universal design' have the meanings given the terms in section 3002 of this title."

1998—Pub. L. 105–277 made technical amendment to directory language of Pub. L. 105–220, § 405, which enacted this section.

Subsec. (a)(1). Pub. L. 105–394, § 201(1), inserted "including programs relating to assistive technology research and research that incorporates the principles of universal design," after "programs,".

Subsec. (b). Pub. L. 105–394, § 201(2), designated existing provisions as par. (1), substituted "targeted individuals" for "individuals with disabilities and the individuals' representatives", inserted "(including assistive technology research and research that incorporates the principles of universal design)" after "research", and added par. (2).

Subsec. (c). Pub. L. 105–394, § 201(3), added subsec. (c) and struck out former subsec. (c) which read as follows: "The Committee shall annually submit to the President and to the appropriate committees of the Congress a report making such recommendations as the Committee deems appropriate with respect to coordination of policy and development of objectives and priorities for all Federal programs relating to the conduct of research related to rehabilitation of individuals with disabilities."

Subsecs. (d), (e). Pub. L. 105–394, § 201(4), added subsecs. (d) and (e).

CHANGE OF NAME

Committee on Education and the Workforce of House of Representatives changed to Committee on Education and Labor of House of Representatives by House Resolution No. 6, One Hundred Tenth Congress, Jan. 5, 2007.

Committee on Labor and Human Resources of Senate changed to Committee on Health, Education, Labor, and Pensions of Senate by Senate Resolution No. 20, One Hundred Sixth Congress, Jan. 19, 1999.

§ 764. Research and other covered activities

(a) Federal grants and contracts for certain research projects and related activities

(1) To the extent consistent with priorities established in the 5-year plan described in section 762(h) of this title, the Director may make grants to and contracts with States and public or private agencies and organizations, including institutions of higher education, Indian tribes, and tribal organizations, to pay part of the cost of projects for the purpose of planning and conducting research, demonstration projects, training, and related activities, the purposes of which are to develop methods, procedures, and rehabilitation technology, that maximize the full inclusion and integration into society, employment, independent living, family support, and economic and social self-sufficiency of individuals with disabilities, especially individuals with the most significant disabilities, and improve the effectiveness of services authorized under this chapter.

(2)(A) In carrying out this section, the Director shall emphasize projects that support the implementation of subchapters I, III, V, VI, and VII of this chapter, including projects addressing the needs described in the State plans submitted under section 721 or 796c of this title by State agencies.

(B) Such projects, as described in the State plans submitted by State agencies, may include—

(i) medical and other scientific, technical, methodological, and other investigations into the nature of disability, methods of analyzing it, and restorative techniques, including basic research where related to rehabilitation techniques or services;

(ii) studies and analysis of industrial, vocational, social, recreational, psychiatric, psychological, economic, and other factors affecting rehabilitation of individuals with disabilities;

(iii) studies and analysis of special problems of individuals who are homebound and individuals who are institutionalized;

(iv) studies, analyses, and demonstrations of architectural and engineering design adapted to meet the special needs of individuals with disabilities;

(v) studies, analyses, and other activities related to supported employment;

(vi) related activities which hold promise of increasing knowledge and improving methods in the rehabilitation of individuals with disabilities and individuals with the most significant disabilities, particularly individuals with disabilities, and individuals with the most significant disabilities, who are members of populations that are unserved or underserved by programs under this chapter; and

(vii) studies, analyses, and other activities related to job accommodations, including the use of rehabilitation engineering and assistive technology.

(b) Research grants

(1) In addition to carrying out projects under subsection (a) of this section, the Director may make grants under this subsection (referred to in this subsection as "research grants") to pay part or all of the cost of the research or other specialized covered activities described in paragraphs (2) through (18). A research grant made under any of paragraphs (2) through (18) may only be used in a manner consistent with priorities established in the 5-year plan described in section 762(h) of this title.

(2)(A) Research grants may be used for the establishment and support of Rehabilitation Research and Training Centers, for the purpose of providing an integrated program of research, which Centers shall—

(i) be operated in collaboration with institutions of higher education or providers of rehabilitation services or other appropriate services; and

(ii) serve as centers of national excellence and national or regional resources for providers and individuals with disabilities and the individuals' representatives.

(B) The Centers shall conduct research and training activities by—

(i) conducting coordinated and advanced programs of research in rehabilitation targeted toward the production of new knowledge that will improve rehabilitation methodology and service delivery systems, alleviate or stabilize disabling conditions, and promote maximum social and economic independence of individuals with disabilities, especially promoting the ability of the individuals to prepare for, secure, retain, regain, or advance in employment;

(ii) providing training (including graduate, pre-service, and in-service training) to assist individuals to more effectively provide rehabilitation services;

(iii) providing training (including graduate, pre-service, and in-service training) for rehabilitation research personnel and other rehabilitation personnel; and

(iv) serving as an informational and technical assistance resource to providers, individuals with disabilities, and the individuals' representatives, through conferences, workshops, public education programs, in-service training programs, and similar activities.

(C) The research to be carried out at each such Center may include—

(i) basic or applied medical rehabilitation research;

(ii) research regarding the psychological and social aspects of rehabilitation, including disability policy;

(iii) research related to vocational rehabilitation;

(iv) continuation of research that promotes the emotional, social, educational, and functional growth of children who are individuals with disabilities;

(v) continuation of research to develop and evaluate interventions, policies, and services that support families of those children and adults who are individuals with disabilities; and

(vi) continuation of research that will improve services and policies that foster the productivity, independence, and social integration of individuals with disabilities, and enable individuals with disabilities, including individuals with mental retardation and other developmental disabilities, to live in their communities.

(D) Training of students preparing to be rehabilitation personnel shall be an important priority for such a Center.

(E) The Director shall make grants under this paragraph to establish and support both comprehensive centers dealing with multiple disabilities and centers primarily focused on particular disabilities.

(F) Grants made under this paragraph may be used to provide funds for services rendered by such a Center to individuals with disabilities in connection with the research and training activities.

(G) Grants made under this paragraph may be used to provide faculty support for teaching—

(i) rehabilitation-related courses of study for credit; and

(ii) other courses offered by the Centers, either directly or through another entity.

(H) The research and training activities conducted by such a Center shall be conducted in a manner that is accessible to and usable by individuals with disabilities.

(I) The Director shall encourage the Centers to develop practical applications for the findings of the research of the Centers.

(J) In awarding grants under this paragraph, the Director shall take into consideration the location of any proposed Center and the appropriate geographic and regional allocation of such Centers.

(K) To be eligible to receive a grant under this paragraph, each such institution or provider described in subparagraph (A) shall—

(i) be of sufficient size, scope, and quality to effectively carry out the activities in an efficient manner consistent with appropriate Federal and State law; and

(ii) demonstrate the ability to carry out the training activities either directly or through another entity that can provide such training.

(L) The Director shall make grants under this paragraph for periods of 5 years, except that the Director may make a grant for a period of less than 5 years if—

(i) the grant is made to a new recipient; or

(ii) the grant supports new or innovative research.

(M) Grants made under this paragraph shall be made on a competitive basis. To be eligible to receive a grant under this paragraph, a prospective grant recipient shall submit an application to the Director at such time, in such manner, and containing such information as the Director may require.

(N) In conducting scientific peer review under section 762(f) of this title of an application for the renewal of a grant made under this paragraph, the peer review panel shall take into account the past performance of the applicant in carrying out the grant and input from individuals with disabilities and the individuals' representatives.

(O) An institution or provider that receives a grant under this paragraph to establish such a Center may not collect more than 15 percent of the amount of the grant received by the Center in indirect cost charges.

(3)(A) Research grants may be used for the establishment and support of Rehabilitation Engineering Research Centers, operated by or in collaboration with institutions of higher education or nonprofit organizations, to conduct research or demonstration activities, and training activities, regarding rehabilitation technology, including rehabilitation engineering, assistive technology devices, and assistive technology services, for the purposes of enhancing opportunities for better meeting the needs of, and addressing the barriers confronted by, individuals with disabilities in all aspects of their lives.

(B) In order to carry out the purposes set forth in subparagraph (A), such a Center shall carry out the research or demonstration activities by—

(i) developing and disseminating innovative methods of applying advanced technology, scientific achievement, and psychological and social knowledge to—

(I) solve rehabilitation problems and remove environmental barriers through planning and conducting research, including cooperative research with public or private agencies and organizations, designed to produce new scientific knowledge, and new or improved methods, equipment, and devices; and

(II) study new or emerging technologies, products, or environments, and the effectiveness and benefits of such technologies, products, or environments;

(ii) demonstrating and disseminating—

(I) innovative models for the delivery, to rural and urban areas, of cost-effective rehabilitation technology services that promote utilization of assistive technology devices; and

(II) other scientific research to assist in meeting the employment and independent living needs of individuals with significant disabilities; or

(iii) conducting research or demonstration activities that facilitate service delivery systems change by demonstrating, evaluating, documenting, and disseminating—

(I) consumer responsive and individual and family-centered innovative models for the delivery to both rural and urban areas, of innovative cost-effective rehabilitation technology services that promote utilization of rehabilitation technology; and

(II) other scientific research to assist in meeting the employment and independent living needs of, and addressing the barriers confronted by, individuals with disabilities, including individuals with significant disabilities.

(C) To the extent consistent with the nature and type of research or demonstration activities described in subparagraph (B), each Center established or supported through a grant made available under this paragraph shall—

(i) cooperate with programs established under the Assistive Technology Act of 1998 [29 U.S.C. 3001 et seq.] and other regional and local programs to provide information to individuals with disabilities and the individuals' representatives to—

(I) increase awareness and understanding of how rehabilitation technology can address their needs; and

(II) increase awareness and understanding of the range of options, programs, services, and resources available, including financing options for the technology and services covered by the area of focus of the Center;

(ii) provide training opportunities to individuals, including individuals with disabilities, to become researchers of rehabilitation technology and practitioners of rehabilitation technology in conjunction with institutions of higher education and nonprofit organizations; and

(iii) respond, through research or demonstration activities, to the needs of individuals with all types of disabilities who may benefit from the application of technology within the area of focus of the Center.

(D)(i) In establishing Centers to conduct the research or demonstration activities described in subparagraph (B)(iii), the Director may establish one Center in each of the following areas of focus:

(I) Early childhood services, including early intervention and family support.

(II) Education at the elementary and secondary levels, including transition from school to postschool activities.

(III) Employment, including supported employment, and reasonable accommodations and the reduction of environmental barriers as required by the Americans with Disabilities Act of 1990 (42 U.S.C. 12101 et seq.) and subchapter V of this chapter.

(IV) Independent living, including transition from institutional to community living, maintenance of community living on leaving the workforce, self-help skills, and activities of daily living.

(ii) Each Center conducting the research or demonstration activities described in subparagraph (B)(iii) shall have an advisory committee, of which the majority of members are individuals with disabilities who are users of rehabilitation technology, and the individuals' representatives.

(E) Grants made under this paragraph shall be made on a competitive basis and shall be for a period of 5 years, except that the Director may make a grant for a period of less than 5 years if—

(i) the grant is made to a new recipient; or

(ii) the grant supports new or innovative research.

(F) To be eligible to receive a grant under this paragraph, a prospective grant recipient shall submit an application to the Director at such time, in such manner, and containing such information as the Director may require.

(G) Each Center established or supported through a grant made available under this paragraph shall—

(i) cooperate with State agencies and other local, State, regional, and national programs and organizations developing or delivering rehabilitation technology, including State programs funded under the Assistive Technology Act of 1998 [29 U.S.C. 3001 et seq.]; and

(ii) prepare and submit to the Director as part of an application for continuation of a grant, or as a final report, a report that documents the outcomes of the program of the Center in terms of both short- and long-term impact on the lives of individuals with disabilities, and such other information as may be requested by the Director.

(4)(A) Research grants may be used to conduct a program for spinal cord injury research, including conducting such a program by making grants to public or private agencies and organizations to pay part or all of the costs of special projects and demonstration projects for spinal cord injuries, that will—

(i) ensure widespread dissemination of research findings among all Spinal Cord Injury Centers, to rehabilitation practitioners, individuals with spinal cord injury, the individuals' representatives, and organizations receiving financial assistance under this paragraph;

(ii) provide encouragement and support for initiatives and new approaches by individual and institutional investigators; and

(iii) establish and maintain close working relationships with other governmental and voluntary institutions and organizations engaged in similar efforts in order to unify and coordinate scientific efforts, encourage joint planning, and promote the interchange of data and reports among spinal cord injury investigations.

(B) Any agency or organization carrying out a project or demonstration project assisted by a grant under this paragraph that provides services to individuals with spinal cord injuries shall—

(i) establish, on an appropriate regional basis, a multidisciplinary system of providing vocational and other rehabilitation services, specifically designed to meet the special needs of individuals with spinal cord injuries, including acute care as well as periodic inpatient or outpatient followup and services;

(ii) demonstrate and evaluate the benefits to individuals with spinal cord injuries served in, and the degree of cost-effectiveness of, such a regional system;

(iii) demonstrate and evaluate existing, new, and improved methods and rehabilitation technology essential to the care, management, and rehabilitation of individuals with spinal cord injuries; and

(iv) demonstrate and evaluate methods of community outreach for individuals with spinal cord injuries and community education in connection with the problems of such individuals in areas such as housing, transportation, recreation, employment, and community activities.

(C) In awarding grants under this paragraph, the Director shall take into account the location of any proposed Spinal Cord Injury Center and the appropriate geographic and regional allocation of such Centers.

(5) Research grants may be used to conduct a program for end-stage renal disease research, to include support of projects and demonstrations for providing special services (including transplantation and dialysis), artificial kidneys, and supplies necessary for the rehabilitation of individuals with such disease and which will—

(A) ensure dissemination of research findings;

(B) provide encouragement and support for initiatives and new approaches by individuals and institutional investigators; and

(C) establish and maintain close working relationships with other governmental and voluntary institutions and organizations engaged in similar efforts,

in order to unify and coordinate scientific efforts, encourage joint planning, and promote the interchange of data and reports among investigators in the field of end-stage renal disease. No person shall be selected to participate in such program who is eligible for services for such disease under any other provision of law.

(6) Research grants may be used to conduct a program for international rehabilitation research, demonstration, and training for the purpose of developing new knowledge and methods in the rehabilitation of individuals with disabilities in the United States, cooperating with and assisting in developing and sharing information found useful in other nations in the rehabilitation of individuals with disabilities, and initiating a program to exchange experts and technical assistance in the field of rehabilitation of individuals with disabilities with other nations as a means of increasing the levels of skill of rehabilitation personnel.

(7) Research grants may be used to conduct a research program concerning the use of existing

telecommunications systems (including telephone, television, satellite, radio, and other similar systems) which have the potential for substantially improving service delivery methods, and the development of appropriate programming to meet the particular needs of individuals with disabilities.

(8) Research grants may be used to conduct a program of joint projects with the National Institutes of Health, the National Institute of Mental Health, the Health Services Administration, the Administration on Aging, the National Science Foundation, the Veterans' Administration, the Department of Health and Human Services, the National Aeronautics and Space Administration, other Federal agencies, and private industry in areas of joint interest involving rehabilitation.

(9) Research grants may be used to conduct a program of research related to the rehabilitation of children, or older individuals, who are individuals with disabilities, including older American Indians who are individuals with disabilities. Such research program may include projects designed to assist the adjustment of, or maintain as residents in the community, older workers who are individuals with disabilities on leaving the workforce.

(10) Research grants may be used to conduct a research program to develop and demonstrate innovative methods to attract and retain professionals to serve in rural areas in the rehabilitation of individuals with disabilities, including individuals with significant disabilities.

(11) Research grants may be used to conduct a model research and demonstration project designed to assess the feasibility of establishing a center for producing and distributing to individuals who are deaf or hard of hearing captioned video cassettes providing a broad range of educational, cultural, scientific, and vocational programming.

(12) Research grants may be used to conduct a model research and demonstration program to develop innovative methods of providing services for preschool age children who are individuals with disabilities, including—

(A) early intervention, assessment, parent counseling, infant stimulation, early identification, diagnosis, and evaluation of children who are individuals with significant disabilities up to the age of five, with a special emphasis on children who are individuals with significant disabilities up to the age of three;

(B) such physical therapy, language development, pediatric, nursing, psychological, and psychiatric services as are necessary for such children; and

(C) appropriate services for the parents of such children, including psychological and psychiatric services, parent counseling, and training.

(13) Research grants may be used to conduct a model research and training program under which model training centers shall be established to develop and use more advanced and effective methods of evaluating and addressing the employment needs of individuals with disabilities, including programs that—

(A) provide training and continuing education for personnel involved with the employment of individuals with disabilities;

(B) develop model procedures for testing and evaluating the employment needs of individuals with disabilities;

(C) develop model training programs to teach individuals with disabilities skills which will lead to appropriate employment;

(D) develop new approaches for job placement of individuals with disabilities, including new followup procedures relating to such placement;

(E) provide information services regarding education, training, employment, and job placement for individuals with disabilities; and

(F) develop new approaches and provide information regarding job accommodations, including the use of rehabilitation engineering and assistive technology.

(14) Research grants may be used to conduct a rehabilitation research program under which financial assistance is provided in order to—

(A) test new concepts and innovative ideas;

(B) demonstrate research results of high potential benefits;

(C) purchase prototype aids and devices for evaluation;

(D) develop unique rehabilitation training curricula; and

(E) be responsive to special initiatives of the Director.

No single grant under this paragraph may exceed $50,000 in any fiscal year and all payments made under this paragraph in any fiscal year may not exceed 5 percent of the amount available for this section to the National Institute on Disability and Rehabilitation Research in any fiscal year. Regulations and administrative procedures with respect to financial assistance under this paragraph shall, to the maximum extent possible, be expedited.

(15) Research grants may be used to conduct studies of the rehabilitation needs of American Indian populations and of effective mechanisms for the delivery of rehabilitation services to Indians residing on and off reservations.

(16) Research grants may be used to conduct a demonstration program under which one or more projects national in scope shall be established to develop procedures to provide incentives for the development, manufacturing, and marketing of orphan technological devices, including technology transfer concerning such devices, designed to enable individuals with disabilities to achieve independence and access to gainful employment.

(17)(A) Research grants may be used to conduct a research program related to quality assurance in the area of rehabilitation technology.

(B) Activities carried out under the research program may include—

(i) the development of methodologies to evaluate rehabilitation technology products and services and the dissemination of the methodologies to consumers and other interested parties;

(ii) identification of models for service provider training and evaluation and certification of the effectiveness of the models;

(iii) identification and dissemination of outcome measurement models for the assessment of rehabilitation technology products and services; and

(iv) development and testing of research-based tools to enhance consumer decision-making about rehabilitation technology products and services.

(18) Research grants may be used to provide for research and demonstration projects and related activities that explore the use and effectiveness of specific alternative or complementary medical practices for individuals with disabilities. Such projects and activities may include projects and activities designed to—

(A) determine the use of specific alternative or complementary medical practices among individuals with disabilities and the perceived effectiveness of the practices;

(B) determine the specific information sources, decisionmaking methods, and methods of payment used by individuals with disabilities who access alternative or complementary medical services;

(C) develop criteria to screen and assess the validity of research studies of such practices for individuals with disabilities; and

(D) determine the effectiveness of specific alternative or complementary medical practices that show promise for promoting increased functioning, prevention of secondary disabilities, or other positive outcomes for individuals with certain types of disabilities, by conducting controlled research studies.

(c) Site visits; grant limitations

(1) In carrying out evaluations of covered activities under this section, the Director is authorized to make arrangements for site visits to obtain information on the accomplishments of the projects.

(2) The Director shall not make a grant under this section that exceeds $500,000 unless the peer review of the grant application has included a site visit.

(Pub. L. 93–112, title II, §204, as added Pub. L. 105–220, title IV, §405, Aug. 7, 1998, 112 Stat. 1173; amended Pub. L. 105–277, div. A, §101(f) [title VIII, §401(16)], Oct. 21, 1998, 112 Stat. 2681–337, 2681–412; Pub. L. 105–394, title IV, §402(b), Nov. 13, 1998, 112 Stat. 3661.)

References in Text

The Assistive Technology Act of 1998, referred to in subsec. (b)(3)(C)(i), (G)(i), is Pub. L. 105–394, Nov. 13, 1998, 112 Stat. 3627, which is classified principally to chapter 31 (§3001 et seq.) of this title. For complete classification of this Act to the Code, see Short Title note set out under section 3001 of this title and Tables.

The Americans with Disabilities Act of 1990, referred to in subsec. (b)(3)(D)(i)(III), is Pub. L. 101–336, July 26, 1990, 104 Stat. 327, as amended, which is classified principally to chapter 126 (§12101 et seq.) of Title 42, The Public Health and Welfare. For complete classification of this Act to the Code, see Short Title note set out under section 12101 of Title 42 and Tables.

Prior Provisions

Provisions similar to this section were contained in section 762 of this title prior to the general amendment of this subchapter by Pub. L. 105–220.

A prior section 764, Pub. L. 93–112, title II, §204, Sept. 26, 1973, 87 Stat. 376, provided that a full report on research and training activities be included in annual report to Congress, prior to repeal by Pub. L. 95–602, title I, §109(3), Nov. 6, 1978, 92 Stat. 2963.

Amendments

1998—Pub. L. 105–277 made technical amendment to directory language of Pub. L. 105–220, §405, which enacted this section.

Subsec. (b)(3)(C)(i), (G)(i). Pub. L. 105–394 substituted "the Assistive Technology Act of 1998" for "the Technology-Related Assistance for Individuals With Disabilities Act of 1988 (29 U.S.C. 2201 et seq.)".

§765. Rehabilitation Research Advisory Council

(a) Establishment

Subject to the availability of appropriations, the Secretary shall establish in the Department of Education a Rehabilitation Research Advisory Council (referred to in this section as the "Council") composed of 12 members appointed by the Secretary.

(b) Duties

The Council shall advise the Director with respect to research priorities and the development and revision of the 5-year plan required by section 762(h) of this title.

(c) Qualifications

Members of the Council shall be generally representative of the community of rehabilitation professionals, the community of rehabilitation researchers, the community of individuals with disabilities, and the individuals' representatives. At least one-half of the members shall be individuals with disabilities or the individuals' representatives.

(d) Terms of appointment

(1) Length of term

Each member of the Council shall serve for a term of up to 3 years, determined by the Secretary, except that—

(A) a member appointed to fill a vacancy occurring prior to the expiration of the term for which a predecessor was appointed, shall be appointed for the remainder of such term; and

(B) the terms of service of the members initially appointed shall be (as specified by the Secretary) for such fewer number of years as will provide for the expiration of terms on a staggered basis.

(2) Number of terms

No member of the Council may serve more than two consecutive full terms. Members may serve after the expiration of their terms until their successors have taken office.

(e) Vacancies

Any vacancy occurring in the membership of the Council shall be filled in the same manner as the original appointment for the position being vacated. The vacancy shall not affect the power of the remaining members to execute the duties of the Council.

(f) Payment and expenses

(1) Payment

Each member of the Council who is not an officer or full-time employee of the Federal Government shall receive a payment of $150 for each day (including travel time) during which the member is engaged in the performance of duties for the Council. All members of the Council who are officers or full-time employees of the United States shall serve without compensation in addition to compensation received for their services as officers or employees of the United States.

(2) Travel expenses

Each member of the Council may receive travel expenses, including per diem in lieu of subsistence, as authorized by section 5703 of title 5 for employees serving intermittently in the Government service, for each day the member is engaged in the performance of duties away from the home or regular place of business of the member.

(g) Detail of Federal employees

On the request of the Council, the Secretary may detail, with or without reimbursement, any of the personnel of the Department of Education to the Council to assist the Council in carrying out its duties. Any detail shall not interrupt or otherwise affect the civil service status or privileges of the Federal employee.

(h) Technical assistance

On the request of the Council, the Secretary shall provide such technical assistance to the Council as the Council determines to be necessary to carry out its duties.

(i) Termination

Section 14 of the Federal Advisory Committee Act (5 U.S.C. App.) shall not apply with respect to the Council.

(Pub. L. 93–112, title II, §205, as added Pub. L. 105–220, title IV, §405, Aug. 7, 1998, 112 Stat. 1182; amended Pub. L. 105–277, div. A, §101(f) [title VIII, §§401(16), 402(b)(11)], Oct. 21, 1998, 112 Stat. 2681–337, 2681–412, 2681–414.)

REFERENCES IN TEXT

Section 14 of the Federal Advisory Committee Act, referred to in subsec. (i), is section 14 of Pub. L. 92–463, which is set out in the Appendix to Title 5, Government Organization and Employees.

PRIOR PROVISIONS

A prior section 765, Pub. L. 93–112, title II, §205, as added Pub. L. 102–569, title II, §206(a), Oct. 29, 1992, 106 Stat. 4409, related to the Rehabilitation Research Advisory Council, prior to the general amendment of this subchapter by Pub. L. 105–220.

A prior section 770, Pub. L. 93–112, title III, §301, formerly §300, Sept. 26, 1973, 87 Stat. 377; Pub. L. 95–602, title I, §122(c)(1), Nov. 6, 1978, 92 Stat. 2987; Pub. L. 99–506, title I, §103(d)(2)(C), Oct. 21, 1986, 100 Stat. 1810; Pub. L. 100–630, title II, §204(a), Nov. 7, 1988, 102 Stat. 3308; renumbered §301 and amended Pub. L. 102–569, title I, §102(p)(15), title III, §301(a), (b)(3), Oct. 29, 1992, 106 Stat. 4358, 4410, 4411, contained congressional declaration of purpose, prior to the general amendment of subchapter III of this chapter by Pub. L. 105–220.

AMENDMENTS

1998—Pub. L. 105–277, §101(f) [title VIII, §402(b)(11)], made technical amendment to section designation and catchline in original.

Pub. L. 105–277, §101(f) [title VIII, §401(16)], made technical amendment to directory language of Pub. L. 105–220, §405, which enacted this section.

SUBCHAPTER III—PROFESSIONAL DEVELOPMENT AND SPECIAL PROJECTS AND DEMONSTRATIONS

CODIFICATION

Title III of the Rehabilitation Act of 1973, comprising this subchapter, was originally enacted by Pub. L. 93–112, title III, Sept. 26, 1973, 87 Stat. 377, and amended by Pub. L. 93–516, Dec. 7, 1974, 88 Stat. 1617; Pub. L. 93–651, Nov. 21, 1974, 89 Stat. 2–3; Pub. L. 94–230, Mar. 15, 1976, 90 Stat. 211; Pub. L. 94–273, Apr. 21, 1976, 90 Stat. 375; Pub. L. 94–288, May 21, 1976, 90 Stat. 520; Pub. L. 95–602, Nov. 6, 1978, 92 Stat. 2955; Pub. L. 98–221, Feb. 22, 1984, 98 Stat. 17; Pub. L. 99–506, Oct. 21, 1986, 100 Stat. 1807; Pub. L. 100–630, Nov. 7, 1988, 102 Stat. 3289; Pub. L. 102–52, June 6, 1991, 105 Stat. 260; Pub. L. 102–119, Oct. 7, 1991, 105 Stat. 587; Pub. L. 102–569, Oct. 29, 1992, 106 Stat. 4344; Pub. L. 103–73, Aug. 11, 1993, 107 Stat. 718; Pub. L. 103–218, Mar. 9, 1994, 108 Stat. 50; Pub. L. 104–66, Dec. 21, 1995, 109 Stat. 707. Title III is shown herein, however, as having been added by Pub. L. 105–220, title IV, §406, Aug. 7, 1998, 112 Stat. 1183, without reference to those intervening amendments because of the extensive revision of title III by Pub. L. 105–220.

§771. Declaration of purpose and competitive basis of grants and contracts

(a) Purpose

It is the purpose of this subchapter to authorize grants and contracts to—

(1)(A) provide academic training to ensure that skilled personnel are available to provide rehabilitation services to individuals with disabilities through vocational, medical, social, and psychological rehabilitation programs (including supported employment programs), through economic and business development programs, through independent living services programs, and through client assistance programs; and

(B) provide training to maintain and upgrade basic skills and knowledge of personnel (including personnel specifically trained to deliver services to individuals with disabilities whose employment outcome is self-employment or telecommuting) employed to provide state-of-the-art service delivery and rehabilitation technology services;

(2) conduct special projects and demonstrations that expand and improve the provision of rehabilitation and other services (including those services provided through community rehabilitation programs) authorized under this chapter, or that otherwise further the purposes of this chapter, including related research and evaluation;

(3) provide vocational rehabilitation services to individuals with disabilities who are migrant or seasonal farmworkers;

(4) initiate recreational programs to provide recreational activities and related experiences for individuals with disabilities to aid such individuals in employment, mobility, socialization, independence, and community integration; and

(5) provide training and information to individuals with disabilities and the individuals' representatives, and other appropriate parties to develop the skills necessary for individuals with disabilities to gain access to the rehabilitation system and statewide workforce investment systems and to become active decisionmakers in the rehabilitation process.

(b) Competitive basis of grants and contracts

The Secretary shall ensure that all grants and contracts are awarded under this subchapter on a competitive basis.

(Pub. L. 93–112, title III, §301, as added Pub. L. 105–220, title IV, §406, Aug. 7, 1998, 112 Stat. 1183.)

PRIOR PROVISIONS

A prior section 771, Pub. L. 93–112, title III, §301, Sept. 26, 1973, 87 Stat. 377; Pub. L. 93–516, title I, §104, Dec. 7, 1974, 88 Stat. 1618; Pub. L. 93–651, title I, §104, Nov. 21, 1974, 89 Stat. 2-4; Pub. L. 94–230, §§4, 11(b)(7), Mar. 15, 1976, 90 Stat. 211, 213; Pub. L. 94–273, §3(18), Apr. 21, 1976, 90 Stat. 377; Pub. L. 95–602, title I, §§112(a), 122(c)(2), Nov. 6, 1978, 92 Stat. 2967, 2987; Pub. L. 98–221, title I, §131, Feb. 22, 1984, 98 Stat. 24; Pub. L. 99–506, title IV, §401, title X, §1002(d)(1), Oct. 21, 1986, 100 Stat. 1823, 1844; Pub. L. 102–52, §4(a), June 6, 1991, 105 Stat. 261, related to grants for construction of rehabilitation facilities, staffing, and planning assistance, prior to repeal by Pub. L. 102–569, title III, §301(b)(2), Oct. 29, 1992, 106 Stat. 4411.

A prior section 301 of Pub. L. 93–112 was classified to section 770 of this title prior to the general amendment of this subchapter by Pub. L. 105–220.

A prior section 771a, Pub. L. 93–112, title III, §302, formerly title II, §203, Sept. 26, 1973, 87 Stat. 376; renumbered title III, §304, and amended Pub. L. 95–602, title I, §§109(2), 114, Nov. 6, 1978, 92 Stat. 2963, 2970; Pub. L. 98–221, title I, §133, Feb. 22, 1984, 98 Stat. 24; Pub. L. 99–506, title I, §103(d)(2)(C), title IV, §403, title X, §1002(d)(2), Oct. 21, 1986, 100 Stat. 1810, 1824, 1844; Pub. L. 100–630, title II, §204(c), Nov. 7, 1988, 102 Stat. 3308; Pub. L. 102–52, §4(c), June 6, 1991, 105 Stat. 261; Pub. L. 102–119, §26(e), Oct. 7, 1991, 105 Stat. 607; renumbered §302 and amended Pub. L. 102–569, title I, §102(p)(18), title III, §§301(b)(3), (4), 302, Oct. 29, 1992, 106 Stat. 4358, 4411; Pub. L. 103–73, title I, §110(a), Aug. 11, 1993, 107 Stat. 726; Pub. L. 103–218, title IV, §402(b), Mar. 9, 1994, 108 Stat. 96; Pub. L. 104–66, title I, §1042(d), Dec. 21, 1995, 109 Stat. 715, related to assistance for training, prior to the general amendment of this subchapter by Pub. L. 105–220. See section 772 of this title.

§772. Training

(a) Grants and contracts for personnel training

(1) Authority

The Commissioner shall make grants to, and enter into contracts with, States and public or nonprofit agencies and organizations (including institutions of higher education) to pay part of the cost of projects to provide training, traineeships, and related activities, including the provision of technical assistance, that are designed to assist in increasing the numbers of, and upgrading the skills of, qualified personnel (especially rehabilitation counselors) who are trained in providing vocational, medical, social, and psychological rehabilitation services, who are trained to assist individuals with communication and related disorders, who are trained to provide other services provided under this chapter, to individuals with disabilities, and who may include—

(A) personnel specifically trained in providing employment assistance to individuals with disabilities through job development and job placement services;

(B) personnel specifically trained to identify, assess, and meet the individual rehabilitation needs of individuals with disabilities, including needs for rehabilitation technology;

(C) personnel specifically trained to deliver services to individuals who may benefit from receiving independent living services;

(D) personnel specifically trained to deliver services in the client assistance programs;

(E) personnel specifically trained to deliver services, through supported employment programs, to individuals with a most significant disability; and

(F) personnel specifically trained to deliver services to individuals with disabilities pursuing self-employment, business ownership, and telecommuting; and

(G) personnel trained in performing other functions necessary to the provision of vocational, medical, social, and psychological rehabilitation services, and other services provided under this chapter.

(2) Authority to provide scholarships

Grants and contracts under paragraph (1) may be expended for scholarships and may include necessary stipends and allowances.

(3) Related Federal statutes

In carrying out this subsection, the Commissioner may make grants to and enter into contracts with States and public or nonprofit agencies and organizations, including institutions of higher education, to furnish training regarding provisions of Federal statutes, including section 794 of this title, title I of the Americans with Disabilities Act of 1990 (42 U.S.C. 12111 et seq.), and the provisions of titles II and XVI of the Social Security Act (42 U.S.C. 401 et seq. and 1381 et seq.), that are related to work incentives for individuals with disabilities.

(4) Training for statewide workforce systems personnel

The Commissioner may make grants to and enter into contracts under this subsection with States and public or nonprofit agencies and organizations, including institutions of higher education, to furnish training to personnel providing services to individuals with disabilities under title I of the Workforce Investment Act of 1998 [29 U.S.C. 2801 et seq.]. Under this paragraph, personnel may be trained—

(A) in evaluative skills to determine whether an individual with a disability may be served by the State vocational rehabilitation program or another component of a statewide workforce investment system; or

(B) to assist individuals with disabilities seeking assistance through one-stop delivery systems described in section 134(c) of the Workforce Investment Act of 1998 [29 U.S.C. 2864(c)].

(5) Joint funding

Training and other activities provided under paragraph (4) for personnel may be jointly funded with the Department of Labor, using funds made available under title I of the Workforce Investment Act of 1998 [29 U.S.C. 2801 et seq.].

(b) Grants and contracts for academic degrees and academic certificate granting training projects

(1) Authority

(A) In general

The Commissioner may make grants to, and enter into contracts with, States and public or nonprofit agencies and organizations (including institutions of higher education) to pay part of the costs of academic training projects to provide training that leads to an academic degree or academic certificate. In making such grants or entering into such contracts, the Commissioner shall target funds to areas determined under subsection (e) of this section to have shortages of qualified personnel.

(B) Types of projects

Academic training projects described in this subsection may include—

(i) projects to train personnel in the areas of assisting and supporting individuals with disabilities pursuing self-employment, business ownership, and telecommuting, and of vocational rehabilitation counseling, rehabilitation technology, rehabilitation medicine, rehabilitation nursing, rehabilitation social work, rehabilitation psychiatry, rehabilitation psychology, rehabilitation dentistry, physical therapy, occupational therapy, speech pathology and audiology, physical education, therapeutic recreation, community rehabilitation programs, or prosthetics and orthotics;

(ii) projects to train personnel to provide—

(I) services to individuals with specific disabilities or individuals with disabilities who have specific impediments to rehabilitation, including individuals who are members of populations that are unserved or underserved by programs under this chapter;

(II) job development and job placement services to individuals with disabilities;

(III) supported employment services, including services of employment specialists for individuals with disabilities;

(IV) specialized services for individuals with significant disabilities; or

(V) recreation for individuals with disabilities;

(iii) projects to train personnel in other fields contributing to the rehabilitation of individuals with disabilities; and

(iv) projects to train personnel in the use, applications, and benefits of rehabilitation technology.

(2) Application

No grant shall be awarded or contract entered into under this subsection unless the applicant has submitted to the Commissioner an application at such time, in such form, in accordance with such procedures, and including such information as the Secretary may require, including—

(A) a description of how the designated State unit or units will participate in the project to be funded under the grant or contract, including, as appropriate, participation on advisory committees, as practicum sites, in curriculum development, and in other ways so as to build closer relationships between the applicant and the designated State unit and to encourage students to pursue careers in public vocational rehabilitation programs;

(B) the identification of potential employers that provide employment that meets the requirements of paragraph (5)(A)(i); and

(C) an assurance that data on the employment of graduates or trainees who participate in the project is accurate.

(3) Limitation

(A) In general

Except as provided in subparagraph (B), no grant or contract under this subsection may be used to provide any one course of study to an individual for a period of more than 4 years.

(B) Exception

If a grant or contract recipient under this subsection determines that an individual has a disability which seriously affects the completion of training under this subsection, the grant or contract recipient may extend the period referred to in subparagraph (A).

(4) Authority to provide scholarships

Grants and contracts under paragraph (1) may be expanded to provide services that include the provision of scholarships and necessary stipends and allowances.

(5) Agreements

(A) Contents

A recipient of a grant or contract under this subsection shall provide assurances to the Commissioner that each individual who receives a scholarship, for any academic year beginning after June 1, 1992, utilizing funds provided under such grant or contract shall enter into an agreement with the recipient under which the individual shall—

(i) maintain employment—

(I) in a nonprofit rehabilitation agency or related agency or in a State rehabilitation agency or related agency, including a professional corporation or professional practice group through which the individual has a service arrangement with the designated State agency;

(II) on a full- or part-time basis; and

(III) for a period of not less than the full-time equivalent of 2 years for each year for which assistance under this section was received by the individual,

within a period, beginning after the recipient completes the training for which the scholarship was awarded, of not more than the sum of the number of years in the period described in subclause (III) and 2 additional years; and

(ii) repay all or part of any scholarship received, plus interest, if the individual does not fulfill the requirements of clause (i), except as the Commissioner by regulation may provide for repayment exceptions and deferrals.

(B) Enforcement

The Commissioner shall be responsible for the enforcement of each agreement entered into under subparagraph (A) upon completion of the training involved under such subparagraph.

(c) Grants to historically Black colleges and universities

The Commissioner, in carrying out this section, shall make grants to historically Black colleges and universities and other institutions of higher education whose minority student enrollment is at least 50 percent of the total enrollment of the institution.

(d) Application

A grant may not be awarded to a State or other organization under this section unless the State or organization has submitted an application to the Commissioner at such time, in such form, in accordance with such procedures, and containing such information as the Commissioner may require. Any such application shall include a detailed description of strategies that will be utilized to recruit and train individuals so as to reflect the diverse populations of the United States as part of the effort to increase the number of individuals with disabilities, and individuals who are from linguistically and culturally diverse backgrounds, who are available to provide rehabilitation services.

(e) Evaluation and collection of data

The Commissioner shall evaluate the impact of the training programs conducted under this section, and collect information on the training needs of, and data on shortages of qualified personnel necessary to provide services to individuals with disabilities. The Commissioner shall prepare and submit to Congress, by September 30 of each fiscal year, a report setting forth and justifying in detail how the funds made available for training under this section for the fiscal year prior to such submission are allocated by professional discipline and other program areas. The report shall also contain findings on such personnel shortages, how funds proposed for the succeeding fiscal year will be allocated under the President's budget proposal, and how the findings on personnel shortages justify the allocations.

(f) Grants for the training of interpreters

(1) Authority

(A) In general

For the purpose of training a sufficient number of qualified interpreters to meet the communications needs of individuals who are deaf or hard of hearing, and individuals who are deaf-blind, the Commissioner, acting through a Federal office responsible for deafness and communicative disorders, may award grants to public or private nonprofit agencies or organizations to pay part of the costs—

(i) for the establishment of interpreter training programs; or

(ii) to enable such agencies or organizations to provide financial assistance for ongoing interpreter training programs.

(B) Geographic areas

The Commissioner shall award grants under this subsection for programs in geographic areas throughout the United States that the Commissioner considers appropriate to best carry out the objectives of this section.

(C) Priority

In awarding grants under this subsection, the Commissioner shall give priority to public or private nonprofit agencies or organizations with existing programs that have a demonstrated capacity for providing interpreter training services.

(D) Funding

The Commissioner may award grants under this subsection through the use of—

(i) amounts appropriated to carry out this section; or

(ii) pursuant to an agreement with the Director of the Office of the Special Education Program (established under section 1402 of title 20), amounts appropriated under section 1486 of title 20.

(2) Application

A grant may not be awarded to an agency or organization under paragraph (1) unless the agency or organization has submitted an application to the Commissioner at such time, in such form, in accordance with such procedures, and containing such information as the Commissioner may require, including—

(A) a description of the manner in which an interpreter training program will be developed and operated during the 5-year period following the date on which a grant is received by the applicant under this subsection;

(B) a demonstration of the applicant's capacity or potential for providing training for interpreters for individuals who are deaf or hard of hearing, and individuals who are deaf-blind;

(C) assurances that any interpreter trained or retrained under a program funded under the grant will meet such minimum standards of competency as the Commissioner may establish for purposes of this subsection; and

(D) such other information as the Commissioner may require.

(g) Technical assistance and in-service training

(1) Technical assistance

The Commissioner is authorized to provide technical assistance to State designated agencies and community rehabilitation programs, directly or through contracts with State designated agencies or nonprofit organizations.

(2) Compensation

An expert or consultant appointed or serving under contract pursuant to this section shall be compensated at a rate, subject to approval of the Commissioner, that shall not exceed the daily equivalent of the rate of pay for level 4 of the Senior Executive Service Schedule under section 5382 of title 5. Such an expert or consultant may be allowed travel and transportation expenses in accordance with section 5703 of title 5.

(3) In-service training of rehabilitation personnel

(A) Projects

Subject to subparagraph (B), at least 15 percent of the sums appropriated to carry out this section shall be allocated to designated State agencies to be used, directly or indirectly, for projects for in-service training for rehabilitation personnel, consistent with the needs identified through the comprehensive system for personnel development required by section 721(a)(7) of this title, including projects designed—

(i) to address recruitment and retention of qualified rehabilitation professionals;

(ii) to provide for succession planning;

(iii) to provide for leadership development and capacity building; and

(iv) for fiscal years 1999 and 2000, to provide training regarding the Workforce Investment Act of 1998 and the amendments to this chapter made by the Rehabilitation Act Amendments of 1998.

(B) Limitation

If the allocation to designated State agencies required by subparagraph (A) would result in a lower level of funding for projects being carried out on August 7, 1998, by other recipients of funds under this section, the Commissioner may allocate less than 15 percent of the sums described in subparagraph (A) to designated State agencies for such in-service training.

(h) Provision of information

The Commissioner, subject to the provisions of section 776 of this title, may require that recipients of grants or contracts under this section provide information, including data, with regard to the impact of activities funded under this section.

(i) Authorization of appropriations

There are authorized to be appropriated to carry out this section such sums as may be necessary for each of the fiscal years 1999 through 2003.

(Pub. L. 93–112, title III, §302, as added Pub. L. 105–220, title IV, §406, Aug. 7, 1998, 112 Stat. 1184; amended Pub. L. 108–446, title III, §305(h)(4), Dec. 3, 2004, 118 Stat. 2805.)

REFERENCES IN TEXT

The Americans with Disabilities Act of 1990, referred to in subsec. (a)(3), is Pub. L. 101–336, July 26, 1990, 104 Stat. 327, as amended. Title I of the Act is classified generally to subchapter I (§12111 et seq.) of chapter 126 of Title 42, The Public Health and Welfare. For complete classification of this Act to the Code, see Short Title note set out under section 12101 of Title 42 and Tables.

The Social Security Act, referred to in subsec. (a)(3), is act Aug. 14, 1935, ch. 531, 49 Stat. 620, as amended. Titles II and XVI of the Act are classified generally to subchapters II (§401 et seq.) and XVI (§1381 et seq.), respectively, of chapter 7 of Title 42, The Public Health and Welfare. For complete classification of this Act to the Code, see section 1305 of Title 42 and Tables.

The Workforce Investment Act of 1998, referred to in subsecs. (a)(4), (5) and (g)(3)(A)(iv), is Pub. L. 105–220, Aug. 7, 1998, 112 Stat. 936, as amended. Title I of the Act is classified principally to chapter 30 (§2801 et seq.) of this title. For complete classification of this Act to the Code, see Short Title note set out under section 9201 of Title 20, Education, and Tables.

The Rehabilitation Act Amendments of 1998, referred to in subsec. (g)(3)(A)(iv), is title IV of Pub. L. 105–220, Aug. 7, 1998, 112 Stat. 1092. For complete classification of this Act to the Code, see Short Title of 1998 Amendment note set out under section 701 of this title and Tables.

PRIOR PROVISIONS

Provisions similar to this section were contained in section 771a of this title prior to the general amendment of this subchapter by Pub. L. 105–220.

A prior section 772, Pub. L. 93–112, title III, §303, formerly §302, Sept. 26, 1973, 87 Stat. 378; Pub. L. 93–516, title I, §105, Dec. 7, 1974, 88 Stat. 1619; Pub. L. 93–651, title I, §105, Nov. 21, 1974, 89 Stat. 2-4; Pub. L. 94–230, §§5, 11(b)(8), Mar. 15, 1976, 90 Stat. 212, 213; Pub. L. 95–602, title I, §§112(b), 122(c)(3), Nov. 6, 1978, 92 Stat. 2968, 2987; Pub. L. 98–221, title I, §132, Feb. 22, 1984, 98 Stat. 24; Pub. L. 99–506, title I, §103(d)(2)(C), title IV, §402, title X, §1001(d)(1), Oct. 21, 1986, 100 Stat. 1810, 1824, 1842; Pub. L. 100–630, title II, §204(b), Nov. 7, 1988, 102 Stat. 3308; Pub. L. 102–52, §4(b), June 6, 1991, 105 Stat. 261; renumbered §303 and amended Pub. L. 102–569, title I, §102(p)(16), title III, §§301(b)(3), 303, Oct. 29, 1992, 106 Stat. 4358, 4411, 4416, related to vocational rehabilitation services for individuals with disabilities, prior to the general amendment of this subchapter by Pub. L. 105–220.

A prior section 302 of Pub. L. 93–112 was classified to section 771a of this title prior to the general amendment of this subchapter by Pub. L. 105–220.

AMENDMENTS

2004—Subsec. (f)(1)(D)(ii). Pub. L. 108–446 made technical amendment to reference in original act which appears in text as reference to section 1402 of title 20.

§773. Demonstration and training programs

(a) Demonstration projects to increase client choice

(1) Grants

The Commissioner may make grants to States and public or nonprofit agencies and organizations to pay all or part of the costs of projects to demonstrate ways to increase client choice in the rehabilitation process, including the selection of providers of vocational rehabilitation services.

(2) Use of funds

An entity that receives a grant under this subsection shall use the grant only—

(A) for activities that are directly related to planning, operating, and evaluating the demonstration projects; and

(B) to supplement, and not supplant, funds made available from Federal and non-Federal sources for such projects.

(3) Application

Any eligible entity that desires to receive a grant under this subsection shall submit an application at such time, in such manner, and containing such information and assurances as the Commissioner may require, including—

(A) a description of—

(i) how the entity intends to promote increased client choice in the rehabilitation process, including a description, if appropriate, of how an applicant will determine the cost of any service or product offered to an eligible client;

(ii) how the entity intends to ensure that any vocational rehabilitation service or related service is provided by a qualified provider who is accredited or meets such other quality assurance and cost-control criteria as the State may establish; and

(iii) the outreach activities to be conducted by the applicant to obtain eligible clients; and

(B) assurances that a written plan will be established with the full participation of the client, which plan shall, at a minimum, include—

(i) a statement of the vocational rehabilitation goals to be achieved;

(ii) a statement of the specific vocational rehabilitation services to be provided, the projected dates for their initiation, and the anticipated duration of each such service; and

(iii) objective criteria, an evaluation procedure, and a schedule, for determining whether such goals are being achieved.

(4) Award of grants

In selecting entities to receive grants under paragraph (1), the Commissioner shall take into consideration—

(A) the diversity of strategies used to increase client choice, including selection among qualified service providers;

(B) the geographic distribution of projects; and

(C) the diversity of clients to be served.

(5) Records

Entities that receive grants under paragraph (1) shall maintain such records as the Commissioner may require and comply with any request from the Commissioner for such records.

(6) Direct services

At least 80 percent of the funds awarded for any project under this subsection shall be used for direct services, as specifically chosen by eligible clients.

(7) Evaluation

The Commissioner may conduct an evaluation of the demonstration projects with respect to the services provided, clients served, client outcomes obtained, implementation issues addressed, the cost-effectiveness of the project, and the effects of increased choice on clients and service providers. The Commissioner may reserve funds for the evaluation for a fiscal year from the amounts appropriated to carry out projects under this section for the fiscal year.

(8) Definitions

For the purposes of this subsection:

(A) Direct services

The term "direct services" means vocational rehabilitation services, as described in section 723(a) of this title.

(B) Eligible client

The term "eligible client" means an individual with a disability, as defined in section 705(20)(A) of this title, who is not currently receiving services under an individualized plan for employment established through a designated State unit.

(b) Special demonstration programs

(1) Grants; contracts

The Commissioner, subject to the provisions of section 776 of this title, may provide grants to, or enter into contracts with, eligible entities to pay all or part of the cost of programs that expand and improve the provision of rehabilitation and other services authorized under this chapter or that further the purposes of the chapter, including related research and evaluation activities.

(2) Eligible entities; terms and conditions

(A) Eligible entities

To be eligible to receive a grant, or enter into a contract, under paragraph (1), an entity shall be a State vocational rehabilitation agency, community rehabilitation program, Indian tribe or tribal organization, or other public or nonprofit agency or organization, or as the Commissioner determines appropriate, a for-profit organization. The Commissioner may limit competitions to one or more types of organizations described in this subparagraph.

(B) Terms and conditions

A grant or contract under paragraph (1) shall contain such terms and conditions as the Commissioner may require.

(3) Application

An eligible entity that desires to receive a grant, or enter into a contract, under paragraph (1) shall submit an application to the Secretary at such time, in such form, and containing such information and assurances as the Commissioner may require, including, if the Commissioner determines appropriate, a description of how the proposed project or demonstration program—

(A) is based on current research findings, which may include research conducted by the National Institute on Disability and Rehabilitation Research, the National Institutes of Health, and other public or private organizations; and

(B) is of national significance.

(4) Types of projects

The programs that may be funded under this subsection may include—

(A) special projects and demonstrations of service delivery;

(B) model demonstration projects;

(C) technical assistance projects;

(D) systems change projects;

(E) special studies and evaluations; and

(F) dissemination and utilization activities.

(5) Priority for competitions

(A) In general

In announcing competitions for grants and contracts under this subsection, the Commissioner shall give priority consideration to—

(i) special projects and demonstration programs of service delivery for adults who are either low-functioning and deaf or low-functioning and hard of hearing;

(ii) supported employment, including community-based supported employment programs to meet the needs of individuals with the most significant disabilities or to provide technical assistance to States and community organizations to improve and expand the provision of supported employment services; and

(iii) model transitional planning services for youths with disabilities.

(B) Additional competitions

In announcing competitions for grants and contracts under this subsection, the Commissioner may require that applicants address one or more of the following:

(i) Age ranges.

(ii) Types of disabilities.

(iii) Types of services.

(iv) Models of service delivery.

(v) Stage of the rehabilitation process.

(vi) The needs of underserved populations, unserved and underserved areas, individuals with significant disabilities, low-incidence disability population or individuals residing in federally designated empowerment zones and enterprise communities.

(vii) Expansion of employment opportunities for individuals with disabilities.

(viii) Systems change projects to promote meaningful access of individuals with disabilities to employment-related services under title I of the Workforce Investment Act of 1998 [29 U.S.C. 2801 et seq.] and under other Federal laws.

(ix) Innovative methods of promoting achievement of high-quality employment outcomes.

(x) The demonstration of the effectiveness of early intervention activities in improving employment outcomes.

(xi) Alternative methods of providing affordable transportation services to individuals with disabilities who are employed, seeking employment, or receiving vocational rehabilitation services from public or private organizations and who reside in geographic areas in which public transportation or paratransit service is not available.

(6) Use of funds for continuation awards

The Commissioner may use funds made available to carry out this section for continuation awards for projects that were funded under sections 711 and 777a of this title (as such sections were in effect on the day before August 7, 1998).

(c) Parent information and training program

(1) Grants

The Commissioner is authorized to make grants to private nonprofit organizations for the purpose of establishing programs to provide training and information to enable individuals with disabilities, and the parents, family members, guardians, advocates, or other authorized representatives of the individuals to participate more effectively with professionals in meeting the vocational, independent living, and rehabilitation needs of individuals with disabilities. Such grants shall be designed to meet the unique training and information needs of the individuals described in the preceding sentence, who live in the area to be served, particularly those who are members of populations that have been unserved or underserved by programs under this chapter.

(2) Use of grants

An organization that receives a grant to establish training and information programs under this subsection shall use the grant to assist individuals with disabilities, and the parents, family members, guardians, advocates, or authorized representatives of the individuals—

(A) to better understand vocational rehabilitation and independent living programs and services;

(B) to provide followup support for transition and employment programs;

(C) to communicate more effectively with transition and rehabilitation personnel and other relevant professionals;

(D) to provide support in the development of the individualized plan for employment;

(E) to provide support and expertise in obtaining information about rehabilitation and independent living programs, services, and resources that are appropriate; and

(F) to understand the provisions of this chapter, particularly provisions relating to employment, supported employment, and independent living.

(3) Award of grants

The Commissioner shall ensure that grants under this subsection—

(A) shall be distributed geographically to the greatest extent possible throughout all States; and

(B) shall be targeted to individuals with disabilities, and the parents, family members, guardians, advocates, or authorized representatives of the individuals, in both urban and rural areas or on a State or regional basis.

(4) Eligible organizations

In order to receive a grant under this subsection, an organization—

(A) shall submit an application to the Commissioner at such time, in such manner, and containing such information as the Commissioner may require, including information demonstrating the capacity and expertise of the organization—

(i) to coordinate training and information activities with Centers for Independent Living;

(ii) to coordinate and work closely with parent training and information centers established pursuant to section 1471 of title 20; and

(iii) to effectively conduct the training and information activities authorized under this subsection;

(B)(i) shall be governed by a board of directors—

(I) that includes professionals in the field of vocational rehabilitation; and

(II) on which a majority of the members are individuals with disabilities or the parents, family members, guardians, advocates, or authorized representatives of the individuals; or

(ii)(I) shall have a membership that represents the interests of individuals with disabilities; and

(II) shall establish a special governing committee that meets the requirements specified in subclauses (I) and (II) of clause (i) to operate a training and information program under this subsection; and

(C) shall serve individuals with a full range of disabilities, and the parents, family members, guardians, advocates, or authorized representatives of the individuals.

(5) Consultation

Each organization carrying out a program receiving assistance under this subsection shall consult with appropriate agencies that serve or assist individuals with disabilities, and the parents, family members, guardians, advocates, or authorized representatives of the individuals, located in the jurisdiction served by the program.

(6) Coordination

The Commissioner shall provide coordination and technical assistance by grant or cooperative agreement for establishing, developing, and coordinating the training and information programs. To the extent practicable, such assistance shall be provided by the parent training and information centers established pursuant to section 1471 of title 20.

(7) Review

(A) Quarterly review

The board of directors or special governing committee of an organization receiving a grant under this subsection shall meet at least once in each calendar quarter to review the training and information program, and each such committee shall directly advise the governing board regarding the views and recommendations of the committee.

(B) Review for grant renewal

If a nonprofit private organization requests the renewal of a grant under this subsection, the board of directors or the special governing committee shall prepare and submit to the Commissioner a written review of the training and information program conducted by the organization during the preceding fiscal year.

(d) Braille training programs

(1) Establishment

The Commissioner shall make grants to, and enter into contracts with, States and public or nonprofit agencies and organizations, including institutions of higher education, to pay all or part of the cost of training in the use of braille for personnel providing vocational rehabilitation services or educational services to youth and adults who are blind.

(2) Projects

Such grants shall be used for the establishment or continuation of projects that may provide—

(A) development of braille training materials;

(B) in-service or pre-service training in the use of braille, the importance of braille literacy, and methods of teaching braille to youth and adults who are blind; and

(C) activities to promote knowledge and use of braille and nonvisual access technology for blind youth and adults through a program of training, demonstration, and evaluation conducted with leadership of experienced blind individuals, including the use of comprehensive, state-of-the-art technology.

(3) Application

To be eligible to receive a grant, or enter into a contract, under paragraph (1), an agency or organization shall submit an application to the Commissioner at such time, in such manner, and containing such information as the Commissioner may require.

(e) Authorization of appropriations

There are authorized to be appropriated to carry out this section such sums as may be necessary for each of the fiscal years 1999 through 2003.

(Pub. L. 93–112, title III, §303, as added Pub. L. 105–220, title IV, §406, Aug. 7, 1998, 112 Stat. 1190; amended Pub. L. 108–446, title III, §305(h)(5), (6), Dec. 3, 2004, 118 Stat. 2805.)

REFERENCES IN TEXT

The Workforce Investment Act of 1998, referred to in subsec. (b)(5)(B)(viii), is Pub. L. 105–220, Aug. 7, 1998, 112 Stat. 936, as amended. Title I of the Act is classified principally to chapter 30 (§2801 et seq.) of this title. For complete classification of this Act to the Code, see Short Title note set out under section 9201 of Title 20, Education, and Tables.

Sections 711 and 777a of this title (as in effect on the day before August 7, 1998), referred to in subsec. (b)(6), means section 711 of this title prior to repeal by Pub. L. 105–220, title IV, §403, Aug. 7, 1998, 112 Stat. 1093, and section 777a of this title prior to the general amendment of this subchapter by Pub. L. 105–220, title IV, §406, Aug. 7, 1998, 112 Stat. 1183.

PRIOR PROVISIONS

A prior section 773, Pub. L. 93–112, title III, §304, formerly §303, Sept. 26, 1973, 87 Stat. 379; Pub. L. 95–602, title I, §113, Nov. 6, 1978, 92 Stat. 2968; Pub. L. 99–506, title I, §103(d)(2)(C), title X, §1001(d)(2), Oct. 21, 1986, 100 Stat. 1810, 1843; renumbered §304 and amended Pub. L. 102–569, title I, §102(p)(17), title III, §§301(b)(3), 304, Oct. 29, 1992, 106 Stat. 4358, 4411, 4417, related to loan guarantees for community rehabilitation programs, prior to the general amendment of this subchapter by Pub. L. 105–220.

A prior section 303 of Pub. L. 93–112 was classified to section 772 of this title prior to the general amendment of this subchapter by Pub. L. 105–220.

AMENDMENTS

2004—Subsec. (c)(4)(A)(ii). Pub. L. 108–446, §305(h)(6), substituted "section 1471" for "section 1482(a)".

Subsec. (c)(6). Pub. L. 108–446, §305(h)(5), substituted "section 1471" for "section 1482(a)".

§774. Migrant and seasonal farmworkers

(a) Grants

(1) Authority

The Commissioner, subject to the provisions of section 776 of this title, may make grants to eligible entities to pay up to 90 percent of the cost of projects or demonstration programs for the provision of vocational rehabilitation services to individuals with disabilities who are migrant or seasonal farmworkers, as determined in accordance with rules prescribed by the Secretary of Labor, and to the family members who are residing with such individuals (whether or not such family members are individuals with disabilities).

(2) Eligible entities

To be eligible to receive a grant under paragraph (1), an entity shall be—

(A) a State designated agency;

(B) a nonprofit agency working in collaboration with a State agency described in subparagraph (A); or

(C) a local agency working in collaboration with a State agency described in subparagraph (A).

(3) Maintenance and transportation

(A) In general

Amounts provided under a grant under this section may be used to provide for the maintenance of and transportation for individuals and family members described in paragraph (1) as necessary for the rehabilitation of such individuals.

(B) Requirement

Maintenance payments under this paragraph shall be provided in a manner consistent with any maintenance payments provided to other individuals with disabilities in the State under this chapter.

(4) Assurance of cooperation

To be eligible to receive a grant under this section an entity shall provide assurances (satisfactory to the Commissioner) that in the provision of services under the grant there will be appropriate cooperation between the grantee and other public or nonprofit agencies and organizations having special skills and experience in the provision of services to migrant or seasonal farmworkers or their families.

(5) Coordination with other programs

The Commissioner shall administer this section in coordination with other programs serving migrant and seasonal farmworkers, including programs under title I of the Elementary and Secondary Education Act of 1965 (20 U.S.C. 6301 et seq.), section 254b of title 42, the Migrant and Seasonal Agricultural Worker Protection Act (29 U.S.C. 1801 et seq.), and the Workforce Investment Act of 1998.

(b) Authorization of appropriations

There are authorized to be appropriated such sums as may be necessary to carry out this section, for each of the fiscal years 1999 through 2003.

(Pub. L. 93–112, title III, §304, as added Pub. L. 105–220, title IV, §406, Aug. 7, 1998, 112 Stat. 1195.)

REFERENCES IN TEXT

The Elementary and Secondary Education Act of 1965, referred to in subsec. (a)(5), is Pub. L. 89–10, Apr. 11, 1965, 79 Stat. 27, as amended. Title I of the Act is classified generally to subchapter I (§6301 et seq.) of chapter 70 of Title 20, Education. For complete classification of this Act to the Code, see Short Title note set out under section 6301 of Title 20 and Tables.

The Migrant and Seasonal Agricultural Worker Protection Act, referred to in subsec. (a)(5), is Pub. L. 97–470, Jan. 14, 1983, 96 Stat. 2584, as amended, which is classified generally to chapter 20 (§1801 et seq.) of this title. For complete classification of this Act to the Code, see Short Title note set out under section 1801 of this title and Tables.

The Workforce Investment Act of 1998, referred to in subsec. (a)(5), is Pub. L. 105–220, Aug. 7, 1998, 112 Stat. 936, as amended. For complete classification of this Act to the Code, see Short Title note set out under section 9201 of Title 20, Education, and Tables.

PRIOR PROVISIONS

Provisions similar to this section were contained in section 777b of this title prior to the general amendment of this subchapter by Pub. L. 105–220.

A prior section 774, Pub. L. 93–112, title III, §304, formerly title II, §203, Sept. 26, 1973, 87 Stat. 376, renumbered and amended, which related to Federal grants, contracts, and programs for training in rehabilitation services, was renumbered section 302 of Pub. L. 93–112, by Pub. L. 102–569, title III, §301(b)(3), Oct. 29, 1992, 106 Stat. 4411, and transferred to section 771a of this title, prior to the general amendment of this subchapter by Pub. L. 105–220.

Another prior section 774, Pub. L. 93–112, title III, §304, Sept. 26, 1973, 87 Stat. 381; Pub. L. 93–516, title I, §§106, 111(i)–(k), Dec. 7, 1974, 88 Stat. 1619, 1621; Pub. L. 93–651, title I, §§106, 111(i)–(k), Nov. 21, 1974, 89 Stat. 2–4, 2–6; Pub. L. 94–230, §§6, 11(b)(9), Mar. 15, 1976, 90 Stat. 212, 213, related to special projects and demonstrations, prior to repeal by Pub. L. 95–602, title I, §109(1), Nov. 6, 1978, 92 Stat. 2962.

§775. Recreational programs

(a) Grants

(1) Authority

(A) In general

The Commissioner, subject to the provisions of section 776 of this title, shall make grants to States, public agencies, and nonprofit private organizations to pay the Federal share of the cost of the establishment and operation of recreation programs to provide individuals with disabilities with recreational activities and related experiences to aid in the employment, mobility, socialization, independence, and community integration of such individuals.

(B) Recreation programs

The recreation programs that may be funded using assistance provided under a grant under this section may include vocational skills development, leisure education, leisure networking, leisure resource development, physical education and sports, scouting and camping, 4–H activities, construction of facilities for aquatic rehabilitation therapy, music, dancing, handicrafts, art, and homemaking. When possible and appropriate, such programs and activities should be provided in settings with peers who are not individuals with disabilities.

(C) Design of program

Programs and activities carried out under this section shall be designed to demonstrate ways in which such programs assist in maximizing the independence and integration of individuals with disabilities.

(2) Maximum term of grant

A grant under this section shall be made for a period of not more than 3 years.

(3) Availability of nongrant resources

(A) In general

A grant may not be made to an applicant under this section unless the applicant provides assurances that, with respect to costs of the recreation program to be carried out under the grant, the applicant, to the maximum extent practicable, will make available non-Federal resources (in cash or in-kind) to pay the non-Federal share of such costs.

(B) Federal share

The Federal share of the costs of the recreation programs carried out under this section shall be—

(i) with respect to the first year in which assistance is provided under a grant under this section, 100 percent;

(ii) with respect to the second year in which assistance is provided under a grant under this section, 75 percent; and

(iii) with respect to the third year in which assistance is provided under a grant under this section, 50 percent.

(4) Application

To be eligible to receive a grant under this section, a State, agency, or organization shall submit an application to the Commissioner at such time, in such manner, and containing such information as the Commissioner may require, including a description of—

(A) the manner in which the findings and results of the project to be funded under the grant, particularly information that facilitates the replication of the results of such projects, will be made generally available; and

(B) the manner in which the service program funded under the grant will be continued after Federal assistance ends.

(5) Level of services

Recreation programs funded under this section shall maintain, at a minimum, the same level of services over a 3-year project period.

(6) Reports by grantees

(A) Requirement

The Commissioner shall require that each recipient of a grant under this section annually prepare and submit to the Commissioner a report concerning the results of the activities funded under the grant.

(B) Limitation

The Commissioner may not make financial assistance available to a grant recipient for a subsequent year until the Commissioner has received and evaluated the annual report of the recipient under subparagraph (A) for the current year.

(b) Authorization of appropriations

There are authorized to be appropriated to carry out this section, such sums as may be necessary for each of the fiscal years 1999 through 2003.

(Pub. L. 93–112, title III, § 305, as added Pub. L. 105–220, title IV, § 406, Aug. 7, 1998, 112 Stat. 1196.)

PRIOR PROVISIONS

Provisions similar to this section were contained in section 777f of this title prior to the general amendment of this subchapter by Pub. L. 105–220.

A prior section 775, Pub. L. 93–112, title III, § 305, as added Pub. L. 95–602, title I, § 115(a), Nov. 6, 1978, 92 Stat. 2971; amended Pub. L. 98–221, title I, § 134, Feb. 22, 1984, 98 Stat. 25; Pub. L. 99–506, title I, § 103(d)(2)(C), title IV, § 404, title X, § 1002(d)(3), Oct. 21, 1986, 100 Stat. 1810, 1825, 1844; Pub. L. 100–630, title II, § 204(d), Nov. 7, 1988, 102 Stat. 3309; Pub. L. 102–52, § 4(d), June 6, 1991, 105 Stat. 261; Pub. L. 102–569, title I, § 102(p)(19), title III, § 305, Oct. 29, 1992, 106 Stat. 4358, 4417, related to comprehensive rehabilitation centers, prior to the general amendment of this subchapter by Pub. L. 105–220.

Another prior section 775, Pub. L. 93–112, title III, § 305, Sept. 26, 1973, 87 Stat. 383, as amended, which authorized appropriations for fiscal years ending June 30, 1974, June 30, 1975, June 30, 1976, Sept. 30, 1977, and Sept. 30, 1978, for the establishment of the Helen Keller National Center for Deaf-Blind Youths and Adults, was renumbered section 313 of Pub. L. 93–112 by Pub. L. 95–602, title I, § 109(1), Nov. 6, 1978, 92 Stat. 2962, transferred to section 777c of this title, and subsequently repealed by Pub. L. 100–630.

§ 776. Measuring of project outcomes and performance

The Commissioner may require that recipients of grants under this subchapter submit information, including data, as determined by the Commissioner to be necessary to measure project outcomes and performance, including any data needed to comply with the Government Performance and Results Act.

(Pub. L. 93–112, title III, § 306, as added Pub. L. 105–220, title IV, § 406, Aug. 7, 1998, 112 Stat. 1197.)

REFERENCES IN TEXT

The Government Performance and Results Act, referred to in text, probably means the Government Performance and Results Act of 1993, Pub. L. 103–62, Aug. 3, 1993, 107 Stat. 285, which enacted section 306 of Title 5, Government Organization and Employees, sections 1115 to 1119, 9703, and 9704 of Title 31, Money and Finance, and sections 2801 to 2805 of Title 39, Postal Service, amended section 1105 of Title 31, and enacted provisions set out as notes under sections 1101 and 1115 of Title 31. For complete classification of this Act to the Code, see Short Title of 1993 Amendment note set out under section 1101 of Title 31 and Tables.

PRIOR PROVISIONS

Prior sections 776 to 777b were omitted in the general amendment of this subchapter by Pub. L. 105–220.

Section 776, Pub. L. 93–112, title III, § 306, Sept. 26, 1973, 87 Stat. 384; Pub. L. 93–516, title I, § 111(*l*), Dec. 7, 1974, 88 Stat. 1621; Pub. L. 93–651, title I, § 111(*l*), Nov. 21, 1974, 89 Stat. 2–6; Pub. L. 95–602, title I, §§ 115(b), 122(c)(4)–(6), Nov. 6, 1978, 92 Stat. 2972, 2987; Pub. L. 99–506, title I, § 103(d)(2)(C), title X, § 1002(d)(4), Oct. 21, 1986, 100 Stat. 1810, 1844; Pub. L. 100–630, title II, § 204(e), Nov. 7, 1988, 102 Stat. 3309; Pub. L. 102–569, title I,

§ 102(p)(20), title III, § 306, Oct. 29, 1992, 106 Stat. 4359, 4417, related to general grant and contract requirements.

Section 777, Pub. L. 93–112, title III, § 310, as added Pub. L. 95–602, title I, § 116(2), Nov. 6, 1978, 92 Stat. 2973; amended Pub. L. 98–221, title I, § 135, title II, § 208(b), Feb. 22, 1984, 98 Stat. 25, 34; Pub. L. 99–506, title IV, § 405, Oct. 21, 1986, 100 Stat. 1825; Pub. L. 100–630, title II, § 204(f), Nov. 7, 1988, 102 Stat. 3309; Pub. L. 102–52, § 4(e)(1), June 6, 1991, 105 Stat. 261; Pub. L. 102–569, title III, § 307, Oct. 29, 1992, 106 Stat. 4418; Pub. L. 103–73, title I, § 110(b), Aug. 11, 1993, 107 Stat. 726, authorized appropriations.

Section 777a, Pub. L. 93–112, title III, § 311, as added Pub. L. 95–602, title I, § 116(2), Nov. 6, 1978, 92 Stat. 2973; amended Pub. L. 98–221, title I, § 136, Feb. 22, 1984, 98 Stat. 26; Pub. L. 99–506, title I, § 103(d)(2)(C), title III, § 302(b), title IV, § 406, Oct. 21, 1986, 100 Stat. 1810, 1821, 1826; Pub. L. 100–630, title II, § 204(g), Nov. 7, 1988, 102 Stat. 3309; Pub. L. 102–52, § 4(e)(2), June 6, 1991, 105 Stat. 261; Pub. L. 102–119, § 26(e), Oct. 7, 1991, 105 Stat. 607; Pub. L. 102–569, title I, § 102(p)(21), title III, § 308, Oct. 29, 1992, 106 Stat. 4359, 4418; Pub. L. 103–73, title I, § 110(c), Aug. 11, 1993, 107 Stat. 726; Pub. L. 104–66, title I, § 1041(b), Dec. 21, 1995, 109 Stat. 714, related to special demonstration programs.

Section 777b, Pub. L. 93–112, title III, § 312, as added Pub. L. 95–602, title I, § 116(2), Nov. 6, 1978, 92 Stat. 2974; amended Pub. L. 99–506, title I, § 103(d)(2)(C), Oct. 21, 1986, 100 Stat. 1810; Pub. L. 100–630, title II, § 204(h), Nov. 7, 1988, 102 Stat. 3309; Pub. L. 102–569, title I, § 102(p)(22), title III, § 309, Oct. 29, 1992, 106 Stat. 4359, 4420, related to migratory workers, maintenance payments, and coordination with other programs. See section 774 of this title.

A prior section 777c, Pub. L. 93–112, title III, § 313, as added Pub. L. 95–602, title I, § 116(2), Nov. 6, 1978, 92 Stat. 2974, related to Helen Keller National Center for Deaf-Blind Youths and Adults, prior to repeal by Pub. L. 98–221, title II, § 203(a), Feb. 22, 1984, 98 Stat. 33. See chapter 21 (§ 1901 et seq.) of this title.

Another prior section 777c, Pub. L. 93–112, title III, § 313, formerly § 305, Sept. 26, 1973, 87 Stat. 383; Pub. L. 93–516, title I, § 107, Dec. 7, 1974, 88 Stat. 1619; Pub. L. 93–651, title I, § 107, Nov. 21, 1974, 89 Stat. 2–4; Pub. L. 94–230, §§ 7, 11(b)(10), Mar. 15, 1976, 90 Stat. 212, 213; Pub. L. 94–288, §§ 1, 2, May 21, 1976, 90 Stat. 520; renumbered § 313, Pub. L. 95–602, title I, § 109(1), Nov. 6, 1978, 92 Stat. 2962, formerly classified to section 775 of this title, authorized appropriations for fiscal years ending June 30, 1974, June 30, 1975, June 30, 1976, Sept. 30, 1977, and Sept. 30, 1978, for establishment of Helen Keller National Center for Deaf-Blind Youths and Adults, prior to repeal by Pub. L. 100–630, title II, § 204(k), Nov. 7, 1988, 102 Stat. 3309.

Prior sections 777d to 777f were omitted in the general amendment of this subchapter by Pub. L. 105–220.

Section 777d, Pub. L. 93–112, title III, § 314, as added Pub. L. 95–602, title I, § 116(2), Nov. 6, 1978, 92 Stat. 2975; amended Pub. L. 100–630, title II, § 204(i), Nov. 7, 1988, 102 Stat. 3309; Pub. L. 102–569, title I, § 102(p)(23), Oct. 29, 1992, 106 Stat. 4359, related to reader services for individuals who are blind.

Section 777e, Pub. L. 93–112, title III, § 315, as added Pub. L. 95–602, title I, § 116(2), Nov. 6, 1978, 92 Stat. 2975; amended Pub. L. 102–569, title I, § 102(p)(24), Oct. 29, 1992, 106 Stat. 4359, related to interpreter services for individuals who are deaf.

Section 777f, Pub. L. 93–112, title III, § 316, as added Pub. L. 95–602, title I, § 116(2), Nov. 6, 1978, 92 Stat. 2976; amended Pub. L. 98–221, title I, § 137, Feb. 22, 1984, 98 Stat. 26; Pub. L. 99–506, title I, § 103(d)(2)(C), title IV, § 407, Oct. 21, 1986, 100 Stat. 1810, 1827; Pub. L. 100–630, title II, § 204(j), Nov. 7, 1988, 102 Stat. 3309; Pub. L. 102–52, § 4(e)(3), June 6, 1991, 105 Stat. 261; Pub. L. 102–569, title I, § 102(p)(25), title III, § 310, Oct. 29, 1992, 106 Stat. 4359, 4420; Pub. L. 103–73, title I, § 110(d), Aug. 11, 1993, 107 Stat. 726, related to special recreational programs. See section 775 of this title.

SUBCHAPTER IV—NATIONAL COUNCIL ON DISABILITY

CODIFICATION

Title IV of the Rehabilitation Act of 1973, comprising this subchapter, was originally enacted by Pub. L. 93–112, title IV, Sept. 26, 1973, 87 Stat. 385, and amended by Pub. L. 93–516, Dec. 7, 1974, 88 Stat. 1617; Pub. L. 93–651, Nov. 21, 1974, 89 Stat. 2–3; Pub. L. 94–230, Mar. 15, 1976, 90 Stat. 211; Pub. L. 95–602, Nov. 6, 1978, 92 Stat. 2955; Pub. L. 98–221, Feb. 22, 1984, 98 Stat. 17; Pub. L. 99–506, Oct. 21, 1986, 100 Stat. 1807; Pub. L. 100–630, Nov. 7, 1988, 102 Stat. 3289; Pub. L. 102–52, June 6, 1991, 105 Stat. 260; Pub. L. 102–569, Oct. 29, 1992, 106 Stat. 4344; Pub. L. 103–73, Aug. 11, 1993, 107 Stat. 718; Pub. L. 104–66, Dec. 21, 1995, 109 Stat. 707. Title IV is shown herein, however, as having been added by Pub. L. 105–220, title IV, § 407, Aug. 7, 1998, 112 Stat. 1198, without reference to those intervening amendments because of the extensive revision of title IV by Pub. L. 105–220.

§ 780. Establishment of National Council on Disability

(a) Membership; purpose

(1)(A) There is established within the Federal Government a National Council on Disability (hereinafter in this subchapter referred to as the "National Council"), which shall be composed of fifteen members appointed by the President, by and with the advice and consent of the Senate.

(B) The President shall select members of the National Council after soliciting recommendations from representatives of—

(i) organizations representing a broad range of individuals with disabilities; and

(ii) organizations interested in individuals with disabilities.

(C) The members of the National Council shall be individuals with disabilities, parents or guardians of individuals with disabilities, or other individuals who have substantial knowledge or experience relating to disability policy or programs. The members of the National Council shall be appointed so as to be representative of individuals with disabilities, national organizations concerned with individuals with disabilities, providers and administrators of services to individuals with disabilities, individuals engaged in conducting medical or scientific research relating to individuals with disabilities, business concerns, and labor organizations. A majority of the members of the National Council shall be individuals with disabilities. The members of the National Council shall be broadly representative of minority and other individuals and groups.

(2) The purpose of the National Council is to promote policies, programs, practices, and procedures that—

(A) guarantee equal opportunity for all individuals with disabilities, regardless of the nature or severity of the disability; and

(B) empower individuals with disabilities to achieve economic self-sufficiency, independent living, and inclusion and integration into all aspects of society.

(b) Term of office

(1) Each member of the National Council shall serve for a term of 3 years, except that the terms of service of the members initially appointed after November 6, 1978, shall be (as spec-

ified by the President) for such fewer number of years as will provide for the expiration of terms on a staggered basis.

(2)(A) No member of the National Council may serve more than two consecutive full terms beginning on the date of commencement of the first full term on the Council. Members may serve after the expiration of their terms until their successors have taken office.

(B) As used in this paragraph, the term "full term" means a term of 3 years.

(3) Any member appointed to fill a vacancy occurring before the expiration of the term for which such member's predecessor was appointed shall be appointed only for the remainder of such term.

(c) Chairperson; meetings

The President shall designate the Chairperson from among the members appointed to the National Council. The National Council shall meet at the call of the Chairperson, but not less often than four times each year.

(d) Quorum; vacancies

Eight members of the National Council shall constitute a quorum and any vacancy in the National Council shall not affect its power to function.

(Pub. L. 93–112, title IV, § 400, as added Pub. L. 105–220, title IV, § 407, Aug. 7, 1998, 112 Stat. 1198.)

PRIOR PROVISIONS

A prior section 780, Pub. L. 93–112, title IV, § 400, as added Pub. L. 95–602, title I, § 117, Nov. 6, 1978, 92 Stat. 2977; amended Pub. L. 98–221, title I, § 141(a), Feb. 22, 1984, 98 Stat. 26; Pub. L. 99–506, title I, § 103(d)(2)(C), title V, § 501, title X, § 1001(e), Oct. 21, 1986, 100 Stat. 1810, 1828, 1843; Pub. L. 100–630, title II, § 205(b), Nov. 7, 1988, 102 Stat. 3310; Pub. L. 102–569, title I, § 102(p)(26), title IV, § 401, Oct. 29, 1992, 106 Stat. 4360, 4421, related to establishment of the National Council on Disability, prior to the general amendment of this subchapter by Pub. L. 105–220.

Another prior section 780, Pub. L. 93–112, title IV, § 400, Sept. 26, 1973, 87 Stat. 385, related to general administrative powers of Secretary under this chapter, prior to repeal by Pub. L. 95–602, § 117.

§ 780a. Independent status of National Council on the Handicapped

(1) Council as independent agency within Federal Government

Effective on February 22, 1984, the National Council on the Handicapped shall be an independent agency within the Federal Government and shall not be an agency within the Department of Education or any other department or agency of the United States.

(2) Transfer of functions to Council Chairman

There are transferred to the Chairman of the National Council on the Handicapped all functions relating to the Council which were vested in the Secretary of Education on the day before February 22, 1984. The Chairman of the National Council on the Handicapped shall continue to exercise all the functions under the Rehabilitation Act of 1973 [29 U.S.C. 701 et seq.] or any other law or authority which the Chairman was performing before February 22, 1984.

(3) Changes in statutory and other references

References in any statute, reorganization plan, Executive order, regulation, or other official document or proceeding to the Department of Education or the Secretary of Education with respect to functions or activities relating to the National Council on the Handicapped shall be deemed to refer to the National Council on the Handicapped or the Chairman of the National Council on the Handicapped, respectively.

(Pub. L. 98–221, title I, § 141(b), Feb. 22, 1984, 98 Stat. 26.)

REFERENCES IN TEXT

The Rehabilitation Act of 1973, referred to in par. (2), is Pub. L. 93–112, Sept. 26, 1973, 87 Stat. 355, as amended, which is classified generally to this chapter (§ 701 et seq.). For complete classification of this Act to the Code, see Short Title note set out under section 701 of this title and Tables.

CODIFICATION

Section was enacted as part of the Rehabilitation Amendments of 1984, and not as part of Rehabilitation Act of 1973 which comprises this chapter.

CHANGE OF NAME

The National Council on the Handicapped was established by former section 780 of this title and was redesignated the National Council on Disability by an amendment to that section by Pub. L. 100–630, title II, § 205(b), Nov. 7, 1988, 102 Stat. 3310.

§ 781. Duties of National Council

(a) In general

The National Council shall—

(1) provide advice to the Director with respect to the policies and conduct of the National Institute on Disability and Rehabilitation Research, including ways to improve research concerning individuals with disabilities and the methods of collecting and disseminating findings of such research;

(2) provide advice to the Commissioner with respect to the policies of and conduct of the Rehabilitation Services Administration;

(3) advise the President, the Congress, the Commissioner, the appropriate Assistant Secretary of the Department of Education, and the Director of the National Institute on Disability and Rehabilitation Research on the development of the programs to be carried out under this chapter;

(4) provide advice regarding priorities for the activities of the Interagency Disability Coordinating Council and review the recommendations of such Council for legislative and administrative changes to ensure that such recommendations are consistent with the purposes of the Council to promote the full integration, independence, and productivity of individuals with disabilities;

(5) review and evaluate on a continuing basis—

(A) policies, programs, practices, and procedures concerning individuals with disabilities conducted or assisted by Federal departments and agencies, including programs established or assisted under this chapter or under the Developmental Disabilities Assistance and Bill of Rights Act of 2000 [42 U.S.C. 15001 et seq.]; and

(B) all statutes and regulations pertaining to Federal programs which assist such individuals with disabilities;

in order to assess the effectiveness of such policies, programs, practices, procedures, statutes, and regulations in meeting the needs of individuals with disabilities;

(6) assess the extent to which such policies, programs, practices, and procedures facilitate or impede the promotion of the policies set forth in subparagraphs (A) and (B) of section 780(a)(2) of this title;

(7) gather information about the implementation, effectiveness, and impact of the Americans with Disabilities Act of 1990 (42 U.S.C. 12101 et seq.);

(8) make recommendations to the President, the Congress, the Secretary, the Director of the National Institute on Disability and Rehabilitation Research, and other officials of Federal agencies or other Federal entities, respecting ways to better promote the policies set forth in section 780(a)(2) of this title;

(9) provide to the Congress on a continuing basis advice, recommendations, legislative proposals, and any additional information that the National Council or the Congress deems appropriate; and

(10) review and evaluate on a continuing basis new and emerging disability policy issues affecting individuals with disabilities at the Federal, State, and local levels, and in the private sector, including the need for and coordination of adult services, access to personal assistance services, school reform efforts and the impact of such efforts on individuals with disabilities, access to health care, and policies that operate as disincentives for the individuals to seek and retain employment.

(b) Annual reports

(1) Not later than October 31, 1998, and annually thereafter, the National Council shall prepare and submit to the President and the appropriate committees of the Congress a report entitled "National Disability Policy: A Progress Report".

(2) The report shall assess the status of the Nation in achieving the policies set forth in section 780(a)(2) of this title, with particular focus on the new and emerging issues impacting on the lives of individuals with disabilities. The report shall present, as appropriate, available data on health, housing, employment, insurance, transportation, recreation, training, prevention, early intervention, and education. The report shall include recommendations for policy change.

(3) In determining the issues to focus on and the findings, conclusions, and recommendations to include in the report, the National Council shall seek input from the public, particularly individuals with disabilities, representatives of organizations representing a broad range of individuals with disabilities, and organizations and agencies interested in individuals with disabilities.

(c) Report describing barriers

(1) Not later than December 31, 1999, the Council shall prepare a report describing the barriers in Federal assistive technology policy to increasing the availability of and access to assistive technology devices and assistive technology services for individuals with disabilities.

(2) In preparing the report, the Council shall obtain input from the National Institute on Disability and Rehabilitation Research and the Association of Tech Act Projects, and from targeted individuals and entities, as defined in section 3002 of this title.

(3) The Council shall submit the report, along with such recommendations as the Council determines to be appropriate, to the Committee on Labor and Human Resources of the Senate and the Committee on Education and the Workforce of the House of Representatives.

(Pub. L. 93–112, title IV, §401, as added Pub. L. 105–220, title IV, §407, Aug. 7, 1998, 112 Stat. 1199; amended Pub. L. 105–394, title II, §202, Nov. 13, 1998, 112 Stat. 3653; Pub. L. 106–402, title IV, §401(b)(3)(B), Oct. 30, 2000, 114 Stat. 1737; Pub. L. 108–364, §3(b)(2), Oct. 25, 2004, 118 Stat. 1737.)

REFERENCES IN TEXT

The Developmental Disabilities Assistance and Bill of Rights Act of 2000, referred to in subsec. (a)(5)(A), is Pub. L. 106–402, Oct. 30, 2000, 114 Stat. 1677, which is classified principally to chapter 144 (§15001 et seq.) of Title 42, The Public Health and Welfare. For complete classification of this Act to the Code, see Short Title note set out under section 15001 of Title 42 and Tables.

The Americans with Disabilities Act of 1990, referred to in subsec. (a)(7), is Pub. L. 101–336, July 26, 1990, 104 Stat. 327, as amended, which is classified principally to chapter 126 (§12101 et seq.) of Title 42, The Public Health and Welfare. For complete classification of this Act to the Code, see Short Title note set out under section 12101 of Title 42 and Tables.

PRIOR PROVISIONS

A prior section 781, Pub. L. 93–112, title IV, §401, as added Pub. L. 95–602, title I, §117, Nov. 6, 1978, 92 Stat. 2977; amended Pub. L. 98–221, title I, §142, Feb. 22, 1984, 98 Stat. 27; Pub. L. 99–506, title I, §103(d)(2)(C), title III, §302(b), title V, §502, Oct. 21, 1986, 100 Stat. 1810, 1821, 1828; Pub. L. 100–630, title II, §205(c), Nov. 7, 1988, 102 Stat. 3310; Pub. L. 102–569, title I, §102(p)(27), title IV, §402, Oct. 29, 1992, 106 Stat. 4360, 4422; Pub. L. 104–66, title II, §2131, Dec. 21, 1995, 109 Stat. 731, related to duties of National Council on Disability, prior to the general amendment of this subchapter by Pub. L. 105–220.

Another prior section 781, Pub. L. 93–112, title IV, §401, Sept. 26, 1973, 87 Stat. 386, related to program and project evaluation, prior to repeal by Pub. L. 95–602, §117.

AMENDMENTS

2004—Subsec. (c)(2). Pub. L. 108–364 substituted "targeted individuals and entities" for "targeted individuals".

2000—Subsec. (a)(5)(A). Pub. L. 106–402, which directed substitution of "Developmental Disabilities Assistance and Bill of Rights Act of 2000" for "Developmental Disabilities Assistance and Bill of Rights Act (42 U.S.C. 6000 et seq.)", was executed by making the substitution for "Developmental Disabilities Assistance and Bill of Rights Act" to reflect the probable intent of Congress.

1998—Subsec. (c). Pub. L. 105–394 added subsec. (c).

CHANGE OF NAME

Committee on Labor and Human Resources of Senate changed to Committee on Health, Education, Labor, and Pensions of Senate by Senate Resolution No. 20, One Hundred Sixth Congress, Jan. 19, 1999.

Committee on Education and the Workforce of House of Representatives changed to Committee on Education and Labor of House of Representatives by House Resolution No. 6, One Hundred Tenth Congress, Jan. 5, 2007.

TERMINATION OF REPORTING REQUIREMENTS

For termination, effective May 15, 2000, of provisions of law requiring submittal to Congress of any annual, semiannual, or other regular periodic report listed in House Document No. 103–7 (in which a report to Congress required under subsec. (b) of this section is listed on page 182), see section 3003 of Pub. L. 104–66, as amended, set out as a note under section 1113 of Title 31, Money and Finance.

§ 782. Compensation of National Council members

(a) Rate

Members of the National Council shall be entitled to receive compensation at a rate equal to the rate of pay for level 4 of the Senior Executive Service Schedule under section 5382 of title 5, including travel time, for each day they are engaged in the performance of their duties as members of the National Council.

(b) Full-time officers or employees of United States

Members of the National Council who are full-time officers or employees of the United States shall receive no additional pay on account of their service on the National Council except for compensation for travel expenses as provided under subsection (c) of this section.

(c) Travel expenses

While away from their homes or regular places of business in the performance of services for the National Council, members of the National Council shall be allowed travel expenses, including per diem in lieu of subsistence, in the same manner as persons employed intermittently in the Government service are allowed expenses under section 5703 of title 5.

(Pub. L. 93–112, title IV, § 402, as added Pub. L. 105–220, title IV, § 407, Aug. 7, 1998, 112 Stat. 1200.)

PRIOR PROVISIONS

A prior section 782, Pub. L. 93–112, title IV, § 402, as added Pub. L. 95–602, title I, § 117, Nov. 6, 1978, 92 Stat. 2978; amended Pub. L. 100–630, title II, § 205(d), Nov. 7, 1988, 102 Stat. 3310; Pub. L. 102–569, title IV, § 403, Oct. 29, 1992, 106 Stat. 4423, related to compensation of National Council members, prior to the general amendment of this subchapter by Pub. L. 105–220.

Another prior section 782, Pub. L. 93–112, title IV, § 402, Sept. 26, 1973, 87 Stat. 387, authorized the Secretary to obtain information from Federal agencies, prior to repeal by Pub. L. 95–602, § 117.

§ 783. Staff of National Council

(a) Executive Director; technical and professional employees

(1) The Chairperson of the National Council may appoint and remove, without regard to the provisions of title 5 governing appointments, the provisions of chapter 75 of such title (relating to adverse actions), the provisions of chapter 77 of such title (relating to appeals), or the provisions of chapter 51 and subchapter III of chapter 53 of such title (relating to classification and General Schedule pay rates), an Executive Director to assist the National Council to carry out its duties. The Executive Director shall be appointed from among individuals who are experienced in the planning or operation of programs for individuals with disabilities.

(2) The Executive Director is authorized to hire technical and professional employees to assist the National Council to carry out its duties.

(b) Temporary or intermittent services; voluntary and uncompensated services; gifts, etc.; contracts and agreements; official representation and reception

(1) The National Council may procure temporary and intermittent services to the same extent as is authorized by section 3109(b) of title 5 (but at rates for individuals not to exceed the daily equivalent of the rate of pay for level 4 of the Senior Executive Service Schedule under section 5382 of title 5).

(2) The National Council may—

(A) accept voluntary and uncompensated services, notwithstanding the provisions of section 1342 of title 31;

(B) in the name of the Council, solicit, accept, employ, and dispose of, in furtherance of this chapter, any money or property, real or personal, or mixed, tangible or nontangible, received by gift, devise, bequest, or otherwise; and

(C) enter into contracts and cooperative agreements with Federal and State agencies, private firms, institutions, and individuals for the conduct of research and surveys, preparation of reports and other activities necessary to the discharge of the Council's duties and responsibilities.

(3) Not more than 10 per centum of the total amounts available to the National Council in each fiscal year may be used for official representation and reception.

(c) Administrative support services

The Administrator of General Services shall provide to the National Council on a reimbursable basis such administrative support services as the Council may request.

(d) Investment of amounts not required for current withdrawals

(1) It shall be the duty of the Secretary of the Treasury to invest such portion of the amounts made available under subsection (a)(2)(B)[1] of this section as is not, in the Secretary's judgment, required to meet current withdrawals. Such investments may be made only in interest-bearing obligations of the United States or in obligations guaranteed as to both principal and interest by the United States.

(2) The amounts described in paragraph (1), and the interest on, and the proceeds from the sale or redemption of, the obligations described in paragraph (1) shall be available to the National Council to carry out this subchapter.

(Pub. L. 93–112, title IV, § 403, as added Pub. L. 105–220, title IV, § 407, Aug. 7, 1998, 112 Stat. 1200.)

REFERENCES IN TEXT

The provisions of title 5 governing appointments, referred to in subsec. (a)(1), are classified generally to section 3301 et seq. of Title 5, Government Organization and Employees.

PRIOR PROVISIONS

A prior section 783, Pub. L. 93–112, title IV, § 403, as added Pub. L. 95–602, title I, § 117, Nov. 6, 1978, 92 Stat. 2978; amended Pub. L. 98–221, title I, § 143, Feb. 22, 1984, 98 Stat. 28; Pub. L. 99–506, title I, § 103(d)(2)(C), title V,

[1] So in original. Probably should be subsection "(b)(2)(B)".

§503, Oct. 21, 1986, 100 Stat. 1810, 1829; Pub. L. 100–630, title II, §205(e), Nov. 7, 1988, 102 Stat. 3310; Pub. L. 102–569, title I, §102(p)(28), title IV, §404, Oct. 29, 1992, 106 Stat. 4360, 4423; Pub. L. 103–73, title I, §111, Aug. 11, 1993, 107 Stat. 727, related to National Council staff, prior to the general amendment of this subchapter by Pub. L. 105–220.

Another prior section 783, Pub. L. 93–112, title IV, §403, Sept. 26, 1973, 87 Stat. 387; Pub. L. 93–516, title I, §108, Dec. 7, 1974, 88 Stat. 1619; Pub. L. 93–651, title I, §108, Nov. 21, 1974, 89 Stat. 2–4; Pub. L. 94–230, §§8, 11(b)(11), Mar. 15, 1976, 90 Stat. 212, 213, authorized appropriations to conduct program and project evaluations, prior to repeal by Pub. L. 95–602, §117.

§784. Administrative powers of National Council

(a) Bylaws and rules

The National Council may prescribe such bylaws and rules as may be necessary to carry out its duties under this subchapter.

(b) Hearings

The National Council may hold such hearings, sit and act at such times and places, take such testimony, and receive such evidence as it deems advisable.

(c) Advisory committees

The National Council may appoint advisory committees to assist the National Council in carrying out its duties. The members thereof shall serve without compensation.

(d) Use of mails

The National Council may use the United States mails in the same manner and upon the same conditions as other departments and agencies of the United States.

(e) Use of services, personnel, information, and facilities

The National Council may use, with the consent of the agencies represented on the Interagency Disability Coordinating Council, and as authorized in subchapter V of this chapter, such services, personnel, information, and facilities as may be needed to carry out its duties under this subchapter, with or without reimbursement to such agencies.

(Pub. L. 93–112, title IV, §404, as added Pub. L. 105–220, title IV, §407, Aug. 7, 1998, 112 Stat. 1201.)

Prior Provisions

A prior section 784, Pub. L. 93–112, title IV, §404, as added Pub. L. 95–602, title I, §117, Nov. 6, 1978, 92 Stat. 2979; amended Pub. L. 102–569, title IV, §405, Oct. 29, 1992, 106 Stat. 4423, related to administrative powers of National Council, prior to the general amendment of this subchapter by Pub. L. 105–220.

Another prior section 784, Pub. L. 93–112, title IV, §404, Sept. 26, 1973, 87 Stat. 387, directed Secretary to submit annual reports to the President and to Congress on activities carried out under this chapter, prior to repeal by Pub. L. 95–602, §117.

Termination of Advisory Committees

Advisory committees established after Jan. 5, 1973, to terminate not later than the expiration of the 2-year period beginning on the date of their establishment, unless, in the case of a committee established by the President or an officer of the Federal Government, such committee is renewed by appropriate action prior to the expiration of such 2-year period, or in the case of a committee established by the Congress, its duration is otherwise provided for by law. See section 14 of Pub. L. 92–463, Oct. 6, 1972, 86 Stat. 776, set out in the Appendix to Title 5, Government Organization and Employees.

§785. Authorization of appropriations

There are authorized to be appropriated to carry out this subchapter such sums as may be necessary for each of the fiscal years 1999 through 2003.

(Pub. L. 93–112, title IV, §405, as added Pub. L. 105–220, title IV, §407, Aug. 7, 1998, 112 Stat. 1202.)

Prior Provisions

A prior section 785, Pub. L. 93–112, title IV, §405, as added Pub. L. 95–602, title I, §117, Nov. 6, 1978, 92 Stat. 2979; amended Pub. L. 99–506, title V, §504, Oct. 21, 1986, 100 Stat. 1829; Pub. L. 102–52, §5, June 6, 1991, 105 Stat. 262; Pub. L. 102–569, title IV, §406, Oct. 29, 1992, 106 Stat. 4423, authorized appropriations, prior to the general amendment of this subchapter by Pub. L. 105–220.

Another prior section 785, Pub. L. 93–112, title IV, §405, Sept. 26, 1973, 87 Stat. 388; Pub. L. 93–516, title I, §§109, 111(m), Dec. 7, 1974, 88 Stat. 1619, 1621; Pub. L. 93–651, title I, §§109, 111(m), Nov. 21, 1974, 89 Stat. 2–4, 2–6; Pub. L. 94–230, §§9, 11(b)(12), Mar. 15, 1976, 90 Stat. 212, 213, specified certain responsibilities of the Secretary, prior to repeal by Pub. L. 95–602, §117.

Prior sections 786 and 787 were repealed by Pub. L. 95–602, title I, §117, Nov. 6, 1978, 92 Stat. 2977.

Section 786, Pub. L. 93–112, title IV, §406, Sept. 26, 1973, 87 Stat. 389; S. Res. 4, Feb. 4, 1977, provided that the Secretary conduct a study on the role of sheltered workshops in the rehabilitation and employment of handicapped individuals and report the results of this study to Congress within twenty-four months after Sept. 26, 1973.

Section 787, Pub. L. 93–112, title IV, §407, Sept. 26, 1973, 87 Stat. 389, provided that the Secretary conduct a study on allotment of funds among the States for grants for basic vocational rehabilitation and report the results of this study to Congress not later than June 30, 1974.

SUBCHAPTER V—RIGHTS AND ADVOCACY

§790. Repealed. Pub. L. 102–569, title V, §502(a), Oct. 29, 1992, 106 Stat. 4424

Section, Pub. L. 93–112, title V, §500, Sept. 26, 1973, 87 Stat. 390, related to effects on existing law, references in other provisions, availability of unexpended appropriations, savings provision, and extension of appropriations.

§791. Employment of individuals with disabilities

(a) Interagency Committee on Employees who are Individuals with Disabilities; establishment; membership; co-chairmen; availability of other Committee resources; purpose and functions

There is established within the Federal Government an Interagency Committee on Employees who are Individuals with Disabilities (hereinafter in this section referred to as the "Committee"), comprised of such members as the President may select, including the following (or their designees whose positions are Executive Level IV or higher): the Chairman of the Equal Employment Opportunity Commission (hereafter in this section referred to as the "Commission"), the Director of the Office of Personnel Management, the Secretary of Veterans Affairs, the Secretary of Labor, the Secretary of Education, and the Secretary of Health and Human Services. Either the Director of the Office of Personnel Management and the Chairman of the Commission shall serve as co-chairpersons of the Committee or the Director or Chairman shall serve as the sole chairperson of the Committee, as the Director and Chairman jointly determine, from time to time, to be appropriate. The resources of the President's Committees on Employment of People With Disabilities and on Mental Retardation shall be made fully available to the Committee. It shall be the purpose and function of the Committee (1) to provide a focus for Federal and other employment of individuals with disabilities, and to review, on a periodic basis, in cooperation with the Commission, the adequacy of hiring, placement, and advancement practices with respect to individuals with disabilities, by each department, agency, and instrumentality in the executive branch of Government and the Smithsonian Institution, and to insure that the special needs of such individuals are being met; and (2) to consult with the Commission to assist the Commission to carry out its responsibilities under subsections (b), (c), and (d) of this section. On the basis of such review and consultation, the Committee shall periodically make to the Commission such recommendations for legislative and administrative changes as it deems necessary or desirable. The Commission shall timely transmit to the appropriate committees of Congress any such recommendations.

(b) Federal agencies; affirmative action program plans

Each department, agency, and instrumentality (including the United States Postal Service and the Postal Regulatory Commission) in the executive branch and the Smithsonian Institution shall, within one hundred and eighty days after September 26, 1973, submit to the Commission and to the Committee an affirmative action program plan for the hiring, placement, and advancement of individuals with disabilities in such department, agency, instrumentality, or Institution. Such plan shall include a description of the extent to which and methods whereby the special needs of employees who are individuals with disabilities are being met. Such plan shall be updated annually, and shall be reviewed annually and approved by the Commission, if the Commission determines, after consultation with the Committee, that such plan provides sufficient assurances, procedures and commitments to provide adequate hiring, placement, and advancement opportunities for individuals with disabilities.

(c) State agencies; rehabilitated individuals, employment

The Commission, after consultation with the Committee, shall develop and recommend to the Secretary for referral to the appropriate State agencies, policies and procedures which will facilitate the hiring, placement, and advancement in employment of individuals who have received rehabilitation services under State vocational rehabilitation programs, veterans' programs, or any other program for individuals with disabilities, including the promotion of job opportunities for such individuals. The Secretary shall encourage such State agencies to adopt and implement such policies and procedures.

(d) Report to Congressional committees

The Commission, after consultation with the Committee, shall, on June 30, 1974, and at the end of each subsequent fiscal year, make a complete report to the appropriate committees of the Congress with respect to the practices of and achievements in hiring, placement, and advancement of individuals with disabilities by each department, agency, and instrumentality and the Smithsonian Institution and the effectiveness of the affirmative action programs required by subsection (b) of this section, together with recommendations as to legislation which have been submitted to the Commission under subsection (a) of this section, or other appropriate action to insure the adequacy of such practices. Such report shall also include an evaluation by the Committee of the effectiveness of the activities of the Commission under subsections (b) and (c) of this section.

(e) Federal work experience without pay; non-Federal status

An individual who, as a part of an individualized plan for employment under a State plan approved under this chapter, participates in a program of unpaid work experience in a Federal agency, shall not, by reason thereof, be considered to be a Federal employee or to be subject to the provisions of law relating to Federal employment, including those relating to hours of work, rates of compensation, leave, unemployment compensation, and Federal employee benefits.

(f) Federal agency cooperation; special consideration for positions on President's Committee on Employment of People With Disabilities

(1) The Secretary of Labor and the Secretary of Education are authorized and directed to cooperate with the President's Committee on Employment of People With Disabilities in carrying out its functions.

(2) In selecting personnel to fill all positions on the President's Committee on Employment of People With Disabilities, special consideration shall be given to qualified individuals with disabilities.

(g) Standards used in determining violation of section

The standards used to determine whether this section has been violated in a complaint alleging nonaffirmative action employment discrimination under this section shall be the standards applied under title I of the Americans with Disabilities Act of 1990 (42 U.S.C. 12111 et seq.) and the provisions of sections 501 through 504, and 510,[1] of the Americans with Disabilities Act of 1990 (42 U.S.C. 12201–12204 and 12210), as such sections relate to employment.

(Pub. L. 93–112, title V, §501, Sept. 26, 1973, 87 Stat. 390; Pub. L. 98–221, title I, §104(b)(3), Feb. 22, 1984, 98 Stat. 18; Pub. L. 99–506, title I, §103(d)(2)(C), title X, §§1001(f)(1), 1002(e)(1), (2)(A), Oct. 21, 1986, 100 Stat. 1810, 1843, 1844; Pub. L. 100–630, title II, §206(a), Nov. 7, 1988, 102 Stat.

[1] See References in Text note below.

3310; Pub. L. 102–54, § 13(k)(1)(B), June 13, 1991, 105 Stat. 276; Pub. L. 102–569, title I, § 102(p)(29), title V, § 503, Oct. 29, 1992, 106 Stat. 4360, 4424; Pub. L. 103–73, title I, § 112(a), Aug. 11, 1993, 107 Stat. 727; Pub. L. 105–220, title III, § 341(c), title IV, § 408(a)(1), Aug. 7, 1998, 112 Stat. 1092, 1202; Pub. L. 109–435, title VI, § 604(d), Dec. 20, 2006, 120 Stat. 3242.)

REFERENCES IN TEXT

Level IV of the Executive Schedule, referred to in subsec. (a), is set out in section 5315 of Title 5, Government Organization and Employees.

The Americans with Disabilities Act of 1990, referred to in subsec. (g), is Pub. L. 101–336, July 26, 1990, 104 Stat. 327. Title I of the Act is classified generally to subchapter I (§ 12111 et seq.) of chapter 126 of Title 42, The Public Health and Welfare. Section 510 of the Act was renumbered section 511 by Pub. L. 110–325, § 6(a)(2), Sept. 25, 2008, 122 Stat. 3558. For complete classification of this Act to the Code, see Short Title note set out under section 12101 of Title 42 and Tables.

PRIOR PROVISIONS

Prior similar provisions were set out in section 38 of this title.

AMENDMENTS

2006—Subsec. (b). Pub. L. 109–435, § 604(d), substituted "Postal Regulatory Commission" for "Postal Rate Office".

1998—Subsec. (a). Pub. L. 105–220, § 408(a)(1)(A), substituted "President's Committees on Employment of People With Disabilities" for "President's Committees on Employment of the Handicapped" in third sentence.

Pub. L. 105–220, § 341(c)(1), inserted "and the Smithsonian Institution" after "Government" in fourth sentence.

Subsec. (b). Pub. L. 105–220, § 341(c)(2), in first sentence, inserted "and the Smithsonian Institution" after "in the executive branch" and substituted "such department, agency, instrumentality, or Institution" for "such department, agency, or instrumentality".

Subsec. (d). Pub. L. 105–220, § 341(c)(3), inserted "and the Smithsonian Institution" after "instrumentality".

Subsec. (e). Pub. L. 105–220, § 408(a)(1)(B), substituted "individualized plan for employment" for "individualized written rehabilitation program".

1993—Subsec. (a). Pub. L. 103–73 in first sentence inserted comma after "Veterans Affairs".

1992—Pub. L. 102–569, § 102(p)(29)(A), substituted "disabilities" for "handicaps" in section catchline.

Subsec. (a). Pub. L. 102–569, § 503(a), substituted "the Director of the Office of Personnel Management, the Secretary of Veterans Affairs" for "the Secretary of Veterans Affairs, and", and amended second sentence generally. Prior to amendment, second sentence read as follows: "The Secretary of Education and the Chairman of the Commission shall serve as co-chairpersons of the Committee."

Pub. L. 102–569, § 102(p)(29)(B), (C), substituted "Interagency Committee on Employees who are Individuals with Disabilities" for "Interagency Committee on Handicapped Employees" and "individuals with disabilities" for "individuals with handicaps" in two places.

Subsec. (b). Pub. L. 102–569, § 102(p)(29)(C), (D), substituted "individuals with disabilities" for "individuals with handicaps" after "advancement of" and after "opportunities for" and "employees who are individuals with disabilities" for "employees with handicaps".

Subsecs. (c), (d), (f)(2). Pub. L. 102–569, § 102(p)(29)(C), substituted "individuals with disabilities" for "individuals with handicaps".

Subsec. (g). Pub. L. 102–569, § 503(b), added subsec. (g).

1991—Subsec. (a). Pub. L. 102–54 substituted "Secretary of Veterans Affairs" for "Administrator of Veterans' Affairs".

1988—Subsec. (a). Pub. L. 100–630, § 206(a)(3)(C), which directed substitution of "Employment of People With Disabilities" for "Employment of the Handicapped" in second sentence, could not be executed because the words did not appear in second sentence.

Pub. L. 100–630, § 206(a)(1)–(3)(B), (4), inserted "(hereafter in this section referred to as the 'Commission')" after first reference to "Equal Employment Opportunity Commission" and substituted "Commission" for "Equal Opportunity Employment Commission" wherever appearing, "Secretary of Labor, the Secretary of Education, and the Secretary of Health and Human Services" for "Secretaries of Labor and Education and Health and Human Services" in first sentence, "co-chairpersons" for "co-chairmen" in second sentence, and "Commission" for "Office" in cl. (2).

Subsec. (b). Pub. L. 100–630, § 206(a)(2), (5), substituted "submit to the Commission" for "submit to the Equal Employment Opportunity Commission", "employees with handicaps" for "handicapped employees", and "Commission, if the Commission determines" for "Office, if the Office determines".

Subsecs. (c), (d). Pub. L. 100–630, § 206(a)(2), substituted "Commission" for "Equal Opportunity Employment Commission" wherever appearing.

Subsec. (e). Pub. L. 100–630, § 206(a)(6), substituted "an individualized" for "a individualized".

Subsec. (f)(1), (2). Pub. L. 100–630, § 206(a)(7), substituted "Employment of People With Disabilities" for "Employment of the Handicapped".

1986—Pub. L. 99–506, § 103(d)(2)(C), substituted "individuals with handicaps" for "handicapped individuals" in section catchline.

Subsecs. (a) to (c). Pub. L. 99–506, §§ 103(d)(2)(C), 1002(e)(1), substituted "Equal Employment Opportunity Commission" for "Office of Personnel Management" and "individuals with handicaps" for "handicapped individuals" wherever appearing.

Subsec. (d). Pub. L. 99–506, §§ 103(d)(2)(C), 1002(e)(1), (2)(A), substituted "Equal Employment Opportunity Commission" for "Office of Personnel Management" wherever appearing, "individuals with handicaps" for "handicapped individuals", and "of the activities" for "of the the activities".

Subsec. (e). Pub. L. 99–506, § 1001(f)(1), substituted "a individualized" for "his individualized".

Subsec. (f)(2). Pub. L. 99–506, § 103(d)(2)(C), substituted "individuals with handicaps" for "handicapped individuals".

1984—Subsec. (a). Pub. L. 98–221, § 104(b)(3)(A)–(D), substituted "the Chairman of the Office of Personnel Management" and "Education and Health and Human Services" for "the Chairman of the Civil Service Commission" and "Health, Education, and Welfare", respectively, in first sentence, "Secretary of Education and the Chairman of the Office of Personnel Management" for "Secretary of Health, Education, and Welfare and the Chairman of the Civil Service Commission" in second sentence, "Office of Personnel Management" for "Civil Service Commission" in four places, and "Office" for "Commission".

Subsec. (b). Pub. L. 98–221, § 104(b)(3)(C), (D), substituted "Office of Personnel Management" for "Civil Service Commission" and substituted "Office" for "Commission" in three places.

Subsec. (c). Pub. L. 98–221, § 104(b)(3)(C), substituted "Office of Personnel Management" for "Civil Service Commission".

Subsec. (d). Pub. L. 98–221, § 104(b)(3)(C), (E), substituted "Office of Personnel Management" for "Civil Service Commission" in two places and "the activities of the Office of Personnel Management" for "Civil Service Commission's activities".

Subsec. (f)(1). Pub. L. 98–221, § 104(b)(3)(F), substituted "Secretary of Education" for "Secretary of Health, Education, and Welfare".

EFFECTIVE DATE OF 1998 AMENDMENT

Amendment by section 341(c) of Pub. L. 105–220 effective Aug. 7, 1998, and applicable to and may be raised in any administrative or judicial claim or action brought before Aug. 7, 1998, but pending on such date, and any administrative or judicial claim or action brought after such date regardless of whether the claim or action arose prior to such date, if the claim or action was brought within the applicable statute of limitations, see section 341(d) of Pub. L. 105–220, set out as a note under section 633a of this title.

EFFECTIVE DATE OF 1992 AMENDMENT

Pub. L. 102–569, title I, § 138, Oct. 29, 1992, 106 Stat. 4397, as amended by Pub. L. 103–73, title I, § 102(3), Aug. 11, 1993, 107 Stat. 718, provided that:

"(a) EFFECTIVE DATE.—Except as provided in subsection (b), this title [enacting sections 718 to 718b, 725 to 728a, and 740 to 744 of this title, amending this section and sections 701, 705 to 707, 709, 711 to 715, 717, 720 to 724, 730 to 732, 740, 741, 750, 761a to 762, 770, 772 to 776, 777a, 777b, 777d to 777f, 780, 781, 783, 792 to 794, 795, 795d, 795e, and 795h of this title, repealing section 752 of this title, enacting provisions set out as notes under section 712 of this title, and amending provisions set out as a note under section 701 of this title] and the amendments made by this title shall take effect on the date of enactment of this Act [Oct. 29, 1992].

"(b) COMPLIANCE.—Each State agency subject to the provisions of title I of the Rehabilitation Act of 1973 [29 U.S.C. 720 et seq.] shall comply with the amendments made by this subtitle [subtitle B (§§ 121–138) of title I of Pub. L. 102–569, enacting sections 725 to 728a and 740 to 744 of this title, amending sections 705, 720 to 724, and 730 to 732 of this title, and repealing section 752 of this title], as soon as is practicable after the date of enactment of this Act [Oct. 29, 1992], consistent with the effective and efficient administration of the Rehabilitation Act of 1973 [29 U.S.C. 701 et seq.], but not later than October 1, 1993."

EFFECTIVE DATE OF 1986 AMENDMENT

Pub. L. 99–506, title X, § 1006, Oct. 21, 1986, 100 Stat. 1846, provided that: "Except as otherwise provided in this Act [see Short Title of 1986 Amendment note set out under section 701 of this title], this Act shall take effect on the date of its enactment [Oct. 21, 1986]."

TERMINATION OF REPORTING REQUIREMENTS

For termination, effective May 15, 2000, of provisions of law requiring submittal to Congress of any annual, semiannual, or other regular periodic report listed in House Document No. 103–7 (in which reports required under subsecs. (a) and (d) of this section are listed on page 188), see section 3003 of Pub. L. 104–66, as amended, set out as a note under section 1113 of Title 31, Money and Finance.

EXECUTIVE ORDER NO. 10640

Ex. Ord. No. 10640, Oct. 10, 1955, 20 F.R. 7717, formerly set out as a note under section 39 of this title, which related to President's Committee on Employment of the Physically Handicapped, was superseded by section 6(a) of Ex. Ord. No. 10994, Feb. 14, 1962, 27 F.R. 1447, which established President's Committee on Employment of the Handicapped.

EXECUTIVE ORDER NO. 10994

Ex. Ord. No. 10994, Feb. 14, 1962, 27 F.R. 1447, as amended by Ex. Ord. No. 11018, Apr. 27, 1962, 27 F.R. 4143, which established the President's Committee on Employment of the Handicapped, was superseded by Ex. Ord. No. 11480, Sept. 9, 1969, 34 F.R. 14273, formerly set out below.

EXECUTIVE ORDER NO. 11480

Ex. Ord. No. 11480, Sept. 9, 1969, 34 F.R. 14273, as amended by Ex. Ord. No. 12106, Dec. 26, 1978, 44 F.R. 1053; Ex. Ord. No. 12608, Sept. 9, 1987, 52 F.R. 34617, which established and provided for the functions of the President's Committee on Employment of the Handicapped, was superseded by Ex. Ord. No. 12640, May 10, 1988, 53 F.R. 16996, formerly set out below.

EX. ORD. NO. 11830. ENLARGING MEMBERSHIP OF INTERAGENCY COMMITTEE ON HANDICAPPED EMPLOYEES

Ex. Ord. No. 11830, Jan. 9, 1975, 40 F.R. 2411, as amended by Ex. Ord. No. 12106, Dec. 26, 1978, 44 F.R. 1053; Ex. Ord. No. 12450, Dec. 9, 1983, 48 F.R. 55409; Ex. Ord. No. 12672, Mar. 21, 1989, 54 F.R. 12167; Ex. Ord. No. 12704, § 1, Feb. 26, 1990, 55 F.R. 6969, provided:

By virtue of the authority vested in me by section 501(a) of the Rehabilitation Act of 1973 (Public Law 93–112; 87 Stat. 390) [subsec. (a) of this section], it is hereby ordered as follows:

SECTION 1. In accord with Section 501 of the Rehabilitation Act of 1973 (29 U.S.C. 791) and Section 4 of Reorganization Plan No. 1 of 1978 (43 FR 19808) [set out in the Appendix to Title 5, Government Organization and Employees], the Interagency Committee on Handicapped Employees is enlarged and composed of the following, or their designees whose positions are Executive level IV or higher:

(1) Secretary of Defense.
(2) Secretary of Labor.
(3) Secretary of Education, Co-Chairman.
(4) Director of the Office of Personnel Management.
(5) Administrator of Veterans Affairs.
(6) Administrator of General Services.
(7) Chairman of the Federal Communications Commission.
(8) Chairman of the Equal Employment Opportunity Commission, Co-Chairman.
(9) Secretary of Health and Human Services.
(10) Postmaster General of the United States Postal Service.
(11) Chairman of the President's Committee on Employment of People with Disabilities (Ex Officio).
(12) Such other members as the President may designate.

SEC. 2. The Interagency Committee on Handicapped Employees shall also be referred to as the Interagency Committee on Employment of People with Disabilities.

EXECUTIVE ORDER NO. 12640

Ex. Ord. No. 12640, May 10, 1988, 53 F.R. 16996, as amended by Ex. Ord. No. 12945, Jan. 20, 1995, 60 F.R. 4527, which established the President's Committee on Employment of People with Disabilities, the Executive Committee of the President's Committee on Employment of People with Disabilities, and the Advisory Council on Employment of People with Disabilities, and provided for the membership, functions, and administration of those bodies, and superseded Ex. Ord. No. 11480, was revoked by Ex. Ord. No. 13187, § 4(a), Jan. 10, 2001, 66 F.R. 3858, set out as a note under section 701 of this title.

EX. ORD. NO. 13163. INCREASING THE OPPORTUNITY FOR INDIVIDUALS WITH DISABILITIES TO BE EMPLOYED IN THE FEDERAL GOVERNMENT

Ex. Ord. No. 13163, July 26, 2000, 65 F.R. 46563, provided:

By the authority vested in me as President by the Constitution and the laws of the United States of America, and in order to promote an increase in the opportunities for individuals with disabilities to be employed at all levels and occupations of the Federal Government, and to support the goals articulated in section 501 of the Rehabilitation Act of 1973 (29 U.S.C. 791), it is hereby ordered as follows:

SECTION 1. *Increasing the Federal Employment Opportunities for Individuals with Disabilities.* (a) Recent evidence demonstrates that, throughout the United States, qualified persons with disabilities have been refused employment despite their availability and qualifications, and many qualified persons with disabilities are never made aware of available employment opportunities. Evidence also suggests that increased efforts at outreach, and increased understanding of the reasonable accommodations available for persons with disabilities, will permit persons with disabilities to compete for employment on a more level playing field.

(b) Based on current hiring patterns and anticipated increases from expanded outreach efforts and appropriate accommodations, the Federal Government, over the next 5 years, will be able to hire 100,000 qualified individuals with disabilities. In furtherance of such efforts, Federal agencies shall:

(1) Use available hiring authorities, consistent with statutes, regulations, and prior Executive orders and Presidential Memoranda;

(2) Expand their outreach efforts, using both traditional and nontraditional methods; and

(3) Increase their efforts to accommodate individuals with disabilities.

(c) As a model employer, the Federal Government will take the lead in educating the public about employment opportunities available for individuals with disabilities.

(d) This order does not require agencies to create new positions or to change existing qualification standards for any position.

SEC. 2. *Implementation.* Each Federal agency shall prepare a plan to increase the opportunities for individuals with disabilities to be employed in the agency. Each agency shall submit that plan to the Office of Personnel Management within 60 days from the date of this order.

SEC. 3. *Authority to Develop Guidance.* The Office of Personnel Management shall develop guidance on the provisions of this order to increase the opportunities for individuals with disabilities employed in the Federal Government.

SEC. 4. *Judicial Review.* This order is intended only to improve the internal management of the executive branch and does not create any right or benefit, substantive or procedural, enforceable at law or equity by a party against the United States, its agencies, its officers, its employees, or any person.

WILLIAM J. CLINTON.

EX. ORD. NO. 13164. REQUIRING FEDERAL AGENCIES TO ESTABLISH PROCEDURES TO FACILITATE THE PROVISION OF REASONABLE ACCOMMODATION

Ex. Ord. No. 13164, July 26, 2000, 65 F.R. 46565, provided:

By the authority vested in me as President by the Constitution and the laws of the United States of America, including the Rehabilitation Act of 1973 (29 U.S.C. 701 *et seq.*), as amended, and in order to promote a model Federal workplace that provides reasonable accommodation for (1) individuals with disabilities in the application process for Federal employment; (2) Federal employees with disabilities to perform the essential functions of a position; and (3) Federal employees with disabilities to enjoy benefits and privileges of employment equal to those enjoyed by employees without disabilities, it is hereby ordered as follows:

SECTION 1. *Establishment of Effective Written Procedures to Facilitate the Provision of Reasonable Accommodation.* (a) Each Federal agency shall establish effective written procedures for processing requests for reasonable accommodation by employees and applicants with disabilities. The written procedures may allow different components of an agency to tailor their procedures as necessary to ensure the expeditious processing of requests.

(b) As set forth in *Re-charting the Course: The First Report of the Presidential Task Force on Employment of Adults with Disabilities* (1998), effective written procedures for processing requests for reasonable accommodation should include the following:

(1) Explain that an employee or job applicant may initiate a request for reasonable accommodation orally or in writing. If the agency requires an applicant or employee to complete a reasonable accommodation request form for recordkeeping purposes, the form must be provided as an attachment to the agency's written procedures;

(2) Explain how the agency will process a request for reasonable accommodation, and from whom the individual will receive a final decision;

(3) Designate a time period during which reasonable accommodation requests will be granted or denied, absent extenuating circumstances. Time limits for decision making should be as short as reasonably possible;

(4) Explain the responsibility of the employee or applicant to provide appropriate medical information related to the functional impairment at issue and the requested accommodation where the disability and/or need for accommodation is not obvious;

(5) Explain the agency's right to request relevant supplemental medical information if the information submitted does not clearly explain the nature of the disability, or the need for the reasonable accommodation, or does not otherwise clarify how the requested accommodation will assist the employee to perform the essential functions of the job or to enjoy the benefits and privileges of the workplace;

(6) Explain the agency's right to have medical information reviewed by a medical expert of the agency's choosing at the agency's expense;

(7) Provide that reassignment will be considered as a reasonable accommodation if the agency determines that no other reasonable accommodation will permit the employee with a disability to perform the essential functions of his or her current position;

(8) Provide that reasonable accommodation denials be in writing and specify the reasons for denial;

(9) Ensure that agencies' systems of recordkeeping track the processing of requests for reasonable accommodation and maintain the confidentiality of medical information received in accordance with applicable law and regulations; and

(10) Encourage the use of informal dispute resolution processes to allow individuals with disabilities to obtain prompt reconsideration of denials of reasonable accommodation. Agencies must also inform individuals with disabilities that they have the right to file complaints in the Equal Employment Opportunity process and other statutory processes, as appropriate, if their requests for reasonable accommodation are denied.

SEC. 2. *Submission of Agency Reasonable Accommodation Procedures to the Equal Employment Opportunity Commission (EEOC).* Within 1 year from the date of this order, each agency shall submit its procedures to the EEOC. Each agency shall also submit to the EEOC any modifications to its reasonable accommodation procedures at the time that those modifications are adopted.

SEC. 3. *Collective Bargaining Obligations.* In adopting their reasonable accommodation procedures, agencies must honor their obligations to notify their collective bargaining representatives and bargain over such procedures to the extent required by law.

SEC. 4. *Implementation.* The EEOC shall issue guidance for the implementation of this order within 90 days from the date of this order.

SEC. 5. *Construction and Judicial Review.* (a) Nothing in this order limits the rights that individuals with disabilities may have under the Rehabilitation Act of 1973, as amended.

(b) This order is intended only to improve the internal management of the executive branch and does not create any right or benefit, substantive or procedural, enforceable at law or equity by a party against the United States, its agencies, its officers, its employees, or any person.

WILLIAM J. CLINTON.

§ 792. Architectural and Transportation Barriers Compliance Board

(a) Establishment; membership; chairperson; vice-chairperson; term of office; termination of membership; reappointment; compensation and travel expenses; bylaws; quorum requirements

(1) There is established within the Federal Government the Architectural and Transpor-

tation Barriers Compliance Board (hereinafter referred to as the "Access Board") which shall be composed as follows:

(A) Thirteen members shall be appointed by the President from among members of the general public of whom at least a majority shall be individuals with disabilities.

(B) The remaining members shall be the heads of each of the following departments or agencies (or their designees whose positions are executive level IV or higher):

(i) Department of Health and Human Services.

(ii) Department of Transportation.

(iii) Department of Housing and Urban Development.

(iv) Department of Labor.

(v) Department of the Interior.

(vi) Department of Defense.

(vii) Department of Justice.

(viii) General Services Administration.

(ix) Department of Veterans Affairs.

(x) United States Postal Service.

(xi) Department of Education.

(xii) Department of Commerce.

The chairperson and vice-chairperson of the Access Board shall be elected by majority vote of the members of the Access Board to serve for terms of one year. When the chairperson is a member of the general public, the vice-chairperson shall be a Federal official; and when the chairperson is a Federal official, the vice-chairperson shall be a member of the general public. Upon the expiration of the term as chairperson of a member who is a Federal official, the subsequent chairperson shall be a member of the general public; and vice versa.

(2)(A)(i) The term of office of each appointed member of the Access Board shall be 4 years, except as provided in clause (ii). Each year, the terms of office of at least three appointed members of the board[1] shall expire.

(ii)(I) One member appointed for a term beginning December 4, 1992 shall serve for a term of 3 years.

(II) One member appointed for a term beginning December 4, 1993 shall serve for a term of 2 years.

(III) One member appointed for a term beginning December 4, 1994 shall serve for a term of 1 year.

(IV) Members appointed for terms beginning before December 4, 1992 shall serve for terms of 3 years.

(B) A member whose term has expired may continue to serve until a successor has been appointed.

(C) A member appointed to fill a vacancy shall serve for the remainder of the term to which that member's predecessor was appointed.

(3) If any appointed member of the Access Board becomes a Federal employee, such member may continue as a member of the Access Board for not longer than the sixty-day period beginning on the date the member becomes a Federal employee.

(4) No individual appointed under paragraph (1)(A) of this subsection who has served as a member of the Access Board may be reappointed to the Access Board more than once unless such individual has not served on the Access Board for a period of two years prior to the effective date of such individual's appointment.

(5)(A) Members of the Access Board who are not regular full-time employees of the United States shall, while serving on the business of the Access Board, be entitled to receive compensation at rates fixed by the President, but not to exceed the daily equivalent of the rate of pay for level IV of the Executive Schedule under section 5315 of title 5, including travel time, for each day they are engaged in the performance of their duties as members of the Access Board; and shall be entitled to reimbursement for travel, subsistence, and other necessary expenses incurred by them in carrying out their duties under this section.

(B) Members of the Access Board who are employed by the Federal Government shall serve without compensation, but shall be reimbursed for travel, subsistence, and other necessary expenses incurred by them in carrying out their duties under this section.

(6)(A) The Access Board shall establish such bylaws and other rules as may be appropriate to enable the Access Board to carry out its functions under this chapter.

(B) The bylaws shall include quorum requirements. The quorum requirements shall provide that (i) a proxy may not be counted for purposes of establishing a quorum, and (ii) not less than half the members required for a quorum shall be members of the general public appointed under paragraph (1)(A).

(b) Functions

It shall be the function of the Access Board to—

(1) ensure compliance with the standards prescribed pursuant to the Act entitled "An Act to ensure that certain buildings financed with Federal funds are so designed and constructed as to be accessible to the physically handicapped", approved August 12, 1968 (commonly known as the Architectural Barriers Act of 1968; 42 U.S.C. 4151 et seq.) (including the application of such Act to the United States Postal Service), including enforcing all standards under such Act, and ensuring that all waivers and modifications to the standards are based on findings of fact and are not inconsistent with the provisions of this section;

(2) develop advisory information for, and provide appropriate technical assistance to, individuals or entities with rights or duties under regulations prescribed pursuant to this subchapter or titles II and III of the Americans with Disabilities Act of 1990 (42 U.S.C. 12131 et seq. and 12181 et seq.) with respect to overcoming architectural, transportation, and communication barriers;

(3) establish and maintain—

(A) minimum guidelines and requirements for the standards issued pursuant to the Act commonly known as the Architectural Barriers Act of 1968;

(B) minimum guidelines and requirements for the standards issued pursuant to titles II and III of the Americans with Disabilities Act of 1990;

[1] So in original. Probably should be "Access Board".

(C) guidelines for accessibility of telecommunications equipment and customer premises equipment under section 255 of title 47; and

(D) standards for accessible electronic and information technology under section 794d of this title;

(4) promote accessibility throughout all segments of society;

(5) investigate and examine alternative approaches to the architectural, transportation, communication, and attitudinal barriers confronting individuals with disabilities, particularly with respect to telecommunications devices, public buildings and monuments, parks and parklands, public transportation (including air, water, and surface transportation, whether interstate, foreign, intrastate, or local), and residential and institutional housing;

(6) determine what measures are being taken by Federal, State, and local governments and by other public or nonprofit agencies to eliminate the barriers described in paragraph (5);

(7) promote the use of the International Accessibility Symbol in all public facilities that are in compliance with the standards prescribed by the Administrator of General Services, the Secretary of Defense, and the Secretary of Housing and Urban Development pursuant to the Act commonly known as the Architectural Barriers Act of 1968;

(8) make to the President and to the Congress reports that shall describe in detail the results of its investigations under paragraphs (5) and (6);

(9) make to the President and to the Congress such recommendations for legislative and administrative changes as the Access Board determines to be necessary or desirable to eliminate the barriers described in paragraph (5);

(10) ensure that public conveyances, including rolling stock, are readily accessible to, and usable by, individuals with physical disabilities; and

(11) carry out the responsibilities specified for the Access Board in section 794d of this title.

(c) Additional functions; transportation barriers and housing needs; transportation and housing plans and proposals

The Access Board shall also (1)(A) determine how and to what extent transportation barriers impede the mobility of individuals with disabilities and aged individuals with disabilities and consider ways in which travel expenses in connection with transportation to and from work for individuals with disabilities can be met or subsidized when such individuals are unable to use mass transit systems or need special equipment in private transportation, and (B) consider the housing needs of individuals with disabilities; (2) determine what measures are being taken, especially by public and other nonprofit agencies and groups having an interest in and a capacity to deal with such problems, (A) to eliminate barriers from public transportation systems (including vehicles used in such systems), and to prevent their incorporation in new or expanded transportation systems, and (B) to make housing available and accessible to individuals with disabilities or to meet sheltered housing needs; and (3) prepare plans and proposals for such further actions as may be necessary to the goals of adequate transportation and housing for individuals with disabilities, including proposals for bringing together in a cooperative effort, agencies, organizations, and groups already working toward such goals or whose cooperation is essential to effective and comprehensive action.

(d) Electronic and information technology accessibility training

Beginning in fiscal year 2000, the Access Board, after consultation with the Secretary, representatives of such public and private entities as the Access Board determines to be appropriate (including the electronic and information technology industry), targeted individuals and entities (as defined in section 3002 of this title), and State information technology officers, shall provide training for Federal and State employees on any obligations related to section 794d of this title.

(e) Investigations; hearings; orders; administrative procedure applicable; final orders; judicial review; civil action; intervention

(1) The Access Board shall conduct investigations, hold public hearings, and issue such orders as it deems necessary to ensure compliance with the provisions of the Acts cited in subsection (b) of this section. Except as provided in paragraph (3) of subsection (f) of this section, the provisions of subchapter II of chapter 5, and chapter 7 of title 5 shall apply to procedures under this subsection, and an order of compliance issued by the Access Board shall be a final order for purposes of judicial review. Any such order affecting any Federal department, agency, or instrumentality of the United States shall be final and binding on such department, agency, or instrumentality. An order of compliance may include the withholding or suspension of Federal funds with respect to any building or public conveyance or rolling stock found not to be in compliance with standards enforced under this section. Pursuant to chapter 7 of title 5, any complainant or participant in a proceeding under this subsection may obtain review of a final order issued in such proceeding.

(2) The executive director is authorized, at the direction of the Access Board—

(A) to bring a civil action in any appropriate United States district court to enforce, in whole or in part, any final order of the Access Board under this subsection; and

(B) to intervene, appear, and participate, or to appear as amicus curiae, in any court of the United States or in any court of a State in civil actions that relate to this section or to the Architectural Barriers Act of 1968 [42 U.S.C. 4151 et seq.].

Except as provided in section 518(a) of title 28, relating to litigation before the Supreme Court, the executive director may appear for and represent the Access Board in any civil litigation brought under this section.

(f) Appointment of executive director, administrative law judges, and other personnel; provisions applicable to administrative law judges; authority and duties of executive director; finality of orders of compliance

(1) There shall be appointed by the Access Board an executive director and such other professional and clerical personnel as are necessary to carry out its functions under this chapter. The Access Board is authorized to appoint as many administrative law judges as are necessary for proceedings required to be conducted under this section. The provisions applicable to administrative law judges appointed under section 3105 of title 5 shall apply to administrative law judges appointed under this subsection.

(2) The Executive Director shall exercise general supervision over all personnel employed by the Access Board (other than administrative law judges and their assistants). The Executive Director shall have final authority on behalf of the Access Board, with respect to the investigation of alleged noncompliance and in the issuance of formal complaints before the Access Board, and shall have such other duties as the Access Board may prescribe.

(3) For the purpose of this section, an order of compliance issued by an administrative law judge shall be deemed to be an order of the Access Board and shall be the final order for the purpose of judicial review.

(g) Technical, administrative, or other assistance; appointment, compensation, and travel expenses of advisory and technical experts and consultants

(1)(A) In carrying out the technical assistance responsibilities of the Access Board under this section, the Board may enter into an interagency agreement with another Federal department or agency.

(B) Any funds appropriated to such a department or agency for the purpose of providing technical assistance may be transferred to the Access Board. Any funds appropriated to the Access Board for the purpose of providing such technical assistance may be transferred to such department or agency.

(C) The Access Board may arrange to carry out the technical assistance responsibilities of the Board under this section through such other departments and agencies for such periods as the Board determines to be appropriate.

(D) The Access Board shall establish a procedure to ensure separation of its compliance and technical assistance responsibilities under this section.

(2) The departments or agencies specified in subsection (a) of this section shall make available to the Access Board such technical, administrative, or other assistance as it may require to carry out its functions under this section, and the Access Board may appoint such other advisers, technical experts, and consultants as it deems necessary to assist it in carrying out its functions under this section. Special advisory and technical experts and consultants appointed pursuant to this paragraph shall, while performing their functions under this section, be entitled to receive compensation at rates fixed by the Chairperson,[2] but not exceeding the daily equivalent of the rate of pay for level 4 of the Senior Executive Service Schedule under section 5382 of title 5, including travel time, and while serving away from their homes or regular places of business they may be allowed travel expenses, including per diem in lieu of subsistence, as authorized by section 5703 of such title 5 for persons in the Government service employed intermittently.

(h) Omitted

(i) Grants and contracts to aid Access Board in carrying out its functions; acceptance of gifts, devises, and bequests of property

(1) The Access Board may make grants to, or enter into contracts with, public or private organizations to carry out its duties under subsections (b) and (c) of this section.

(2)(A) The Access Board may accept, hold, administer, and utilize gifts, devises, and bequests of property, both real and personal, for the purpose of aiding and facilitating the functions of the Access Board under paragraphs (2) and (4) of subsection (b) of this section. Gifts and bequests of money and proceeds from sales of other property received as gifts, devises, or bequests shall be deposited in the Treasury and shall be disbursed upon the order of the Chairperson.[2] Property accepted pursuant to this section, and the proceeds thereof, shall be used as nearly as possible in accordance with the terms of the gifts, devises, or bequests. For purposes of Federal income, estate, or gift taxes, property accepted under this section shall be considered as a gift, devise, or bequest to the United States.

(B) The Access Board shall publish regulations setting forth the criteria the Board will use in determining whether the acceptance of gifts, devises, and bequests of property, both real and personal, would reflect unfavorably upon the ability of the Board or any employee to carry out the responsibilities or official duties of the Board in a fair and objective manner, or would compromise the integrity of or the appearance of the integrity of a Government program or any official involved in that program.

(3) Omitted.

(j) Authorization of appropriations

There are authorized to be appropriated for the purpose of carrying out the duties and functions of the Access Board under this section such sums as may be necessary for each of the fiscal years 1999 through 2003.

(Pub. L. 93–112, title V, § 502, Sept. 26, 1973, 87 Stat. 391; Pub. L. 93–516, title I, §§ 110, 111(n)–(q), Dec. 7, 1974, 88 Stat. 1619, 1621, 1622; Pub. L. 93–651, title I, §§ 110, 111(n)–(q), Nov. 21, 1974, 89 Stat. 2–4, 2–6, 2–7; Pub. L. 94–230, §§ 10, 11(b)(13), Mar. 15, 1976, 90 Stat. 212, 214; Pub. L. 95–251, § 2(a)(8), Mar. 27, 1978, 92 Stat. 183; Pub. L. 95–602, title I, § 118, Nov. 6, 1978, 92 Stat. 2979; Pub. L. 96–374, title XIII, § 1321, Oct. 3, 1980, 94 Stat. 1499; Pub. L. 98–221, title I, § 151, Feb. 22, 1984, 98 Stat. 28; Pub. L. 99–506, title I, § 103(d)(2)(C), title VI, § 601, title X, § 1002(e)(2)(B)–(D), Oct. 21, 1986, 100 Stat. 1810, 1829, 1844; Pub. L. 100–630, title II,

[2] So in original. Probably should not be capitalized.

§206(b), Nov. 7, 1988, 102 Stat. 3311; Pub. L. 102–52, §6, June 6, 1991, 105 Stat. 262; Pub. L. 102–54, §13(k)(1)(A), June 13, 1991, 105 Stat. 276; Pub. L. 102–569, title I, §102(p)(30), title V, §504, Oct. 29, 1992, 106 Stat. 4360, 4424; Pub. L. 103–73, title I, §112(b), Aug. 11, 1993, 107 Stat. 727; Pub. L. 105–220, title IV, §408(a)(2), Aug. 7, 1998, 112 Stat. 1202; Pub. L. 105–394, title II, §203(a), Nov. 13, 1998, 112 Stat. 3653; Pub. L. 108–364, §3(b)(3), Oct. 25, 2004, 118 Stat. 1737.)

REFERENCES IN TEXT

Executive level IV, referred to in subsec. (a)(1)(B), is set out in section 5315 of Title 5, Government Organization and Employees.

The Act commonly known as the Architectural Barriers Act of 1968, referred to in subsecs. (b)(1), (3)(A), (7) and (e)(2)(B), is Pub. L. 90–480, Aug. 12, 1968, 82 Stat. 718, as amended, which is classified generally to chapter 51 (§4151 et seq.) of Title 42, The Public Health and Welfare. For complete classification of this Act to the Code, see Short Title note set out under section 4151 of Title 42 and Tables.

The Americans with Disabilities Act of 1990, referred to in subsec. (b)(2), (3)(B), is Pub. L. 101–336, July 26, 1990, 104 Stat. 327, as amended. Titles II and III of the Act are classified generally to subchapters II (§12131 et seq.) and III (§12181 et seq.), respectively, of chapter 126 of Title 42, The Public Health and Welfare. For complete classification of this Act to the Code, see Short Title note set out under section 12101 of Title 42 and Tables.

CODIFICATION

Subsecs. (h) and (i)(3) of this section, which required the Board to submit an annual report on its activities to Congress and, at the same time the Board transmits the report required under section 4157(b) of Title 42, The Public Health and Welfare, to transmit that report to the Committee on Education and the Workforce of the House of Representatives and the Committee on Labor and Human Resources of the Senate, terminated, effective May 15, 2000, pursuant to section 3003 of Pub. L. 104–66, as amended, set out as a note under section 1113 of Title 31, Money and Finance. See, also, items 4 to 6 on page 155 of House Document No. 103–7.

AMENDMENTS

2004—Subsec. (d). Pub. L. 108–364 substituted "targeted individuals and entities" for "targeted individuals".

1998—Subsec. (a)(1). Pub. L. 105–220, §408(a)(2)(A), substituted "chairperson and" for "Chairperson and" in concluding provisions.

Subsec. (b)(2). Pub. L. 105–220, §408(a)(2)(B)(i), substituted "information" for "guidelines".

Subsec. (b)(3). Pub. L. 105–220, §408(a)(2)(B)(ii), added par. (3) and struck out former par. (3) which read as follows: "establish and maintain minimum guidelines and requirements for the standards issued pursuant to the Act commonly known as the Architectural Barriers Act of 1968 and titles II and III of the Americans with Disabilities Act of 1990;".

Subsec. (b)(11). Pub. L. 105–220, §408(a)(2)(B)(iii)–(v), added par. (11).

Subsec. (d). Pub. L. 105–394, §203(a)(2), added subsec. (d). Former subsec. (d) redesignated (e).

Subsec. (d)(1). Pub. L. 105–220, §408(a)(2)(C), substituted "procedures under this subsection" for "procedures under this section".

Subsec. (e). Pub. L. 105–394, §203(a)(1), (3), redesignated subsec. (d) as (e) and substituted "subsection (f)" for "subsection (e)" in second sentence of par. (1). Former subsec. (e) redesignated (f).

Subsec. (f). Pub. L. 105–394, §203(a)(1), redesignated subsec. (e) as (f). Former subsec. (f) redesignated (g).

Subsec. (g). Pub. L. 105–394, §203(a)(1), redesignated subsec. (f) as (g). Former subsec. (g) redesignated (h).

Subsec. (g)(2). Pub. L. 105–220, §408(a)(2)(D), substituted "Committee on Education and the Workforce" for "Committee on Education and Labor".

Subsec. (h). Pub. L. 105–394, §203(a)(1), redesignated subsec. (g) as (h). Former subsec. (h) redesignated (i).

Subsec. (h)(2)(A). Pub. L. 105–220, §408(a)(2)(E), substituted "paragraphs (2) and (4)" for "paragraphs (5) and (7)".

Subsec. (i). Pub. L. 105–394, §203(a)(1), redesignated subsec. (h) as (i). Former subsec. (i) redesignated (j).

Pub. L. 105–220, §408(a)(2)(F), substituted "fiscal years 1999 through 2003" for "fiscal years 1993 through 1997".

Subsec. (j). Pub. L. 105–394, §203(a)(1), redesignated subsec. (i) as (j).

1993—Subsec. (a)(5)(A). Pub. L. 103–73 substituted "level IV of the Executive Schedule under section 5315" for "level 4 of the Senior Executive Service Schedule under section 5382".

1992—Pub. L. 102–569, §504(a)(2), (3), substituted "the Access Board" and "The Access Board" for "the Board" and "The Board", respectively, wherever appearing.

Subsec. (a)(1). Pub. L. 102–569, §504(a)(1), substituted "the 'Access Board'" for "the 'Board'" in introductory provisions.

Subsec. (a)(1)(A). Pub. L. 102–569, §504(b)(1)(A), substituted "Thirteen" for "Twelve" and "at least a majority" for "six".

Pub. L. 102–569, §102(p)(30), substituted "individuals with disabilities" for "individuals with handicaps".

Subsec. (a)(1)(B)(xii). Pub. L. 102–569, §504(b)(1)(B), added cl. (xii).

Subsec. (a)(2)(A). Pub. L. 102–569, §504(b)(2), designated existing provisions as cl. (i), substituted "4 years, except as provided in clause (ii)" for "three years" and "at least three" for "four", and added cl. (ii).

Subsec. (a)(3). Pub. L. 102–569, §504(b)(3), substituted "a Federal" for "such an" after "member becomes".

Subsec. (a)(5)(A). Pub. L. 102–569, §504(b)(4), substituted "the daily equivalent of the rate of pay for level 4 of the Senior Executive Service Schedule under section 5382" for "the daily rate prescribed for GS–18 under section 5332".

Subsec. (b). Pub. L. 102–569, §504(c), amended subsec. (b) generally, substituting present provisions for provisions which outlined eight specific functions of the Access Board.

Subsec. (c). Pub. L. 102–569, §102(p)(30), substituted "individuals with disabilities" for "individuals with handicaps" wherever appearing.

Subsec. (d)(1). Pub. L. 102–569, §504(d)(1), in first sentence, substituted "The Access Board shall conduct" for "In carrying out its functions under this chapter, the Access Board shall, directly or through grants to public or private nonprofit organizations or contracts with private nonprofit or forprofit organizations, carry out its functions under subsections (b) and (c) of this section, and shall conduct" and "to ensure compliance" for "to insure compliance".

Subsec. (d)(3). Pub. L. 102–569, §504(d)(2), struck out par. (3) which read as follows: "The Access Board, in consultation and coordination with other concerned Federal departments and agencies and agencies within the Department of Education, shall develop standards and provide appropriate technical assistance to any public or private activity, person, or entity affected by regulations prescribed pursuant to this subchapter with respect to overcoming architectural, transportation, and communication barriers. Any funds appropriated to any such department or agency for the purpose of providing such assistance may be transferred to the Access Board for the purpose of carrying out this paragraph. The Access Board may arrange to carry out its responsibilities under this paragraph through such other departments and agencies for such periods as the Access Board determines is appropriate. In carrying out its technical assistance responsibilities under this paragraph, the Access Board shall establish a procedure to insure separation of its compliance and technical assistance responsibilities under this section."

Subsec. (f). Pub. L. 102–569, §504(e), added par. (1), designated existing provisions as par. (2) and substituted "paragraph" for "subsection", "Chairperson" for "Secretary", and "the daily equivalent of the rate of pay for level 4 of the Senior Executive Service Schedule under section 5382" for "the daily pay rate for a person employed as a GS–18 under section 5332".

Subsec. (g). Pub. L. 102–569, §504(f), designated existing provisions as par. (1), substituted "paragraphs (8) and (9) of such subsection" for "clauses (5) and (6) of subsection (b) of this section", struck out at end "The Access Board shall prepare two final reports of its activities under subsection (c) of this section. One such report shall be on its activities in the field of transportation barriers facing individuals with disabilities, and the other such report shall be on its activities in the field of the housing needs of individuals with disabilities. The Access Board shall, not later than September 30, 1975, submit each such report, together with its recommendations, to the President and the Congress. The Access Board shall also prepare for such submission an interim report of its activities in each such field within 18 months after September 26, 1973. The Access Board shall prepare and submit two additional reports of its activities under subsection (c) of this section, one report on its activities in the field of transportation barriers facing individuals with disabilities and the other report on its activities in the field of the housing needs of individuals with disabilities. The two additional reports required by the previous sentence shall be submitted not later than February 1, 1988.", and added par. (2).

Pub. L. 102–569, §102(p)(30), substituted "individuals with disabilities" for "individuals with handicaps" wherever appearing.

Subsec. (h)(1). Pub. L. 102–569, §504(g)(1)–(3), redesignated par. (2) as (1), struck out at end "The Access Board may also make grants to any designated State unit for the purpose of conducting studies to provide the cost assessments required by paragraph (1). Before including in such report the findings of any study conducted for the Access Board under a grant or contract to provide the Access Board with such cost assessments, the Access Board shall take all necessary steps to validate the accuracy of any such findings.", and struck out former par. (1) which read as follows: "Within one year following November 6, 1978, the Access Board shall submit to the President and the Congress a report containing an assessment of the amounts required to be expended by States and by political subdivisions thereof to provide individuals with disabilities with full access to all programs and activities receiving Federal assistance."

Pub. L. 102–569, §102(p)(30), substituted "individuals with disabilities" for "individuals with handicaps" before "with full access".

Subsec. (h)(2). Pub. L. 102–569, §504(g)(4), which directed the addition of par. (2) "at the end" of subsec. (h), was executed by adding par. (2) before par. (3) to reflect the probable intent of Congress. Former par. (2) redesignated (1).

Subsec. (i). Pub. L. 102–569, §504(h), substituted "fiscal years 1993 through 1997." for "fiscal years 1987 through 1992, but in no event shall the amount appropriated for any one fiscal year exceed $3,000,000."

1991—Subsec. (a)(1)(B)(ix). Pub. L. 102–54 substituted "Department of Veterans Affairs" for "Veterans' Administration".

Subsec. (i). Pub. L. 102–52 substituted "1987 through 1992" for "1987, 1988, 1989, 1990, and 1991".

1988—Subsec. (a)(2). Pub. L. 100–630, §206(b)(1), amended par. (2) generally. Prior to amendment, par. (2) read as follows: "The term of office of each appointed member of the Board shall be three years; except that (i) the members first taking office shall serve, as designated by the President at the time of appointment, four for a term of one year, four for a term of two years, and three for a term of three years, (ii) a member whose term has expired may continue to serve until a successor has been appointed, and (iii) a member appointed to fill a vacancy shall serve for the remainder of the term to which that member's predecessor was appointed."

Subsec. (a)(3). Pub. L. 100–630, §206(b)(2), substituted "the member" for "he".

Subsec. (a)(5)(A). Pub. L. 100–630, §206(b)(3), substituted "travel time" for "traveltime".

Subsec. (b). Pub. L. 100–630, §206(b)(4)–(7), inserted a comma after "surface transportation" in cl. (2), and substituted "Administrator of General Services" for "Administrator of the General Services Administration" in cl. (4), "results of" for "results to" in cl. (5), and "individuals with physical handicaps" for "physically handicapped persons" in cl. (8).

Subsec. (c)(2)(A). Pub. L. 100–630, §206(b)(8), inserted a comma after "expanded transportation systems".

Subsec. (d)(2)((B). Pub. L. 100–630, §206(b)(9), substituted "that relate to" for "which related to".

Subsec. (f). Pub. L. 100–630, §206(b)(10), substituted "daily pay rate for" for "daily pay rate, for", "section 5332 of title 5" for "section 5332 of title 45", and "travel time" for "traveltime".

Subsec. (g). Pub. L. 100–630, §206(b)(11), substituted "transportation barriers facing individuals with handicaps" for "transportation barriers to individuals with handicaps" and for "transportation barriers of handicapped individuals" in fourth and seventh sentences, respectively, and "housing needs of individuals with handicaps" for "housing needs of handicapped individuals" in seventh sentence.

1986—Subsec. (a)(1)(A). Pub. L. 99–506, §§103(d)(2)(C), 601(a)(2), substituted "Twelve" for "Eleven", "six" for "five", and "individuals with handicaps" for "handicapped individuals".

Subsec. (a)(1)(B). Pub. L. 99–506, §601(a)(1), substituted provision that Chairperson and vice-chairperson of Board shall be elected by majority vote of members of Board to serve for terms of one year, for provision that President had to appoint first Chairman of such Board who was to serve for term of not more than two years, with subsequent Chairmen to be elected by majority vote of Board for term of one year, and inserted provisions that positions of Chairperson and vice-chairperson each be held alternately in succession by Federal official and by member of general public, and that when either office is held by member of general public, the other will be held by Federal official.

Subsec. (a)(2)(ii), (iii). Pub. L. 99–506, §601(a)(3), added cls. (ii) and (iii), and struck out former cl. (ii) which read as follows: "any member appointed to fill a vacancy shall serve for the remainder of the term for which his predecessor was appointed".

Subsec. (a)(6). Pub. L. 99–506, §601(a)(4), added par. (6).

Subsecs. (b)(2), (c). Pub. L. 99–506, §103(d)(2)(C), substituted "individuals with handicaps" for "handicapped individuals" wherever appearing.

Subsec. (d)(2)(A). Pub. L. 99–506, §1002(e)(2)(B), substituted "any final order" for "any, final order".

Subsec. (d)(3). Pub. L. 99–506, §1002(e)(2)(C), substituted "Department of Education" for "Department of Health, Education, and Welfare" and "with respect to overcoming" for "with respect overcoming to".

Subsec. (e)(2). Pub. L. 99–506, §1002(e)(2)(D), substituted "alleged noncompliance and in" for "alleged noncompliance in".

Subsec. (g). Pub. L. 99–506, §601(b), inserted provisions requiring the Board to submit, not later than Feb. 1, 1988, two additional reports on its activities under subsec. (c), one report to deal with its activities relating to transportation barriers to handicapped individuals, the other to deal with activities relating to the housing needs of handicapped individuals.

Pub. L. 99–506, §103(d)(2)(C), substituted "individuals with handicaps" for "handicapped individuals" wherever appearing.

Subsec. (h)(1). Pub. L. 99–506, §103(d)(2)(C), substituted reference to individuals with handicaps for reference to handicapped individuals.

Subsec. (i). Pub. L. 99–506, §601(c), which directed the substitution of "of the fiscal years 1987, 1988, 1989, 1990, and 1991," for "fiscal year ending before October 1,

1986," was executed by making the substitution for "fiscal year ending before October 1, 1986.," as the probable intent of Congress. See 1984 Amendment note below.

1984—Subsec. (i). Pub. L. 98–221 substituted "October 1, 1986." for "October 1, 1982".

1980—Subsec. (a)(1)(B)(i). Pub. L. 96–374, §1321(a)(1), substituted "Department of Health and Human Services" for "Department of Health, Education, and Welfare".

Subsec. (a)(1)(B)(xi). Pub. L. 96–374, §1321(a)(2), added cl. (xi).

Subsec. (h)(3). Pub. L. 96–374, §1321(b), added par. (3).

1978—Subsec. (a). Pub. L. 95–602, §118(a), substituted provision permitting President to appoint eleven members of Board from general public of whom five are to be handicapped, adding head of the Department of Justice as a Board member, authorizing President to appoint the first chairman, and providing for the term of office, reappointment, and compensation of Board members for provision restricting Board membership to head of Department of Health, Education, and Welfare, Department of Transportation, Department of Housing and Urban Development, Department of Labor, Department of the Interior, Department of Defense, General Services Administration, United States Postal Service, and Veterans' Administration, appointing Secretary of Health, Education, and Welfare as chairman, and authorizing appointment of a Consumer Advisory Panel, a majority of members of which were to be handicapped, to provide guidance, advice, and recommendations to Board.

Subsec. (b)(1). Pub. L. 95–602, §118(b)(1), substituted provision requiring Board to insure compliance with standards of Architectural Barriers Act of 1968, including application to United States Postal Service, and to insure all waivers and modifications of standards are based on findings of fact and are not inconsistent with that Act or this section for provision requiring Board to insure compliance with the standards prescribed by General Services Administration, Department of Defense, and Department of Housing and Urban Development pursuant to Architectural Barriers Act of 1968.

Subsec. (b)(2). Pub. L. 95–602, §118(b)(2), inserted "communication," before "and attitudinal" and "telecommunication devices," before "public buildings".

Subsec. (b)(7), (8). Pub. L. 95–602, §118(b)(3), added pars. (7) and (8).

Subsec. (d). Pub. L. 95–602, §118(c), designated existing provision as par. (1), substituted "public or private nonprofit organizations or contracts with private nonprofit or forprofit organizations" for "or contracts with public or private nonprofit organizations", "Except as provided in paragraph (3) of subsection (e) of this section, provisions" for "The provisions", "building or public conveyance or rolling stock found" for "building found", and "enforced under this section" for "prescribed pursuant to the Acts cited in subsection (b) of this section", inserted provision permitting a complainant or participant in a proceeding under this subsection to obtain review of a final order pursuant to chapter 7 of title 5, and added pars. (2) and (3).

Subsec. (e). Pub. L. 95–602, §118(d), designated existing provisions as par. (1) and added pars. (2) and (3).

Pub. L. 95–251 substituted "administrative law judges" for "hearing examiners" wherever appearing. Such substitution was made in pars. (2) and (3) as the probable intent of Congress in view of the amendment to subsec. (e) by section 2(a)(8) of Pub. L. 95–251 (although prior in time to the amendment by Pub. L. 95–602) requiring such substitution wherever appearing in text.

Subsec. (h). Pub. L. 95–602, §118(e), added subsec. (h). Former subsec. (h), which authorized appropriations for carrying out duties and functions of the Board of $1,000,000 for each of fiscal years ending June 30, 1974, and June 30, 1975, $1,500,000 for fiscal year ending June 30, 1976, and $1,500,000 for each of fiscal years ending Sept. 30, 1977 and Sept. 30, 1978, was struck out.

Subsec. (i). Pub. L. 95–602, §118(e), added subsec. (i).

1976—Subsec. (h). Pub. L. 94–230, §10, authorized appropriation of $1,500,000 for fiscal year ending Sept. 30, 1977.

Pub. L. 94–230, §11(b)(13), authorized appropriation of $1,500,000 for fiscal year ending Sept. 30, 1978.

1974—Subsec. (a). Pub. L. 93–516, §111(n), redesignated cls. (6), (7), and (8), as cls. (7), (8), and (9), added cl. (6), and following designated clauses, inserted provisions that Secretary of Health, Education, and Welfare shall be Chairman of Board, and that Board shall appoint, upon recommendation of Secretary, a Consumer Advisory Panel, a majority of members of which shall be handicapped individuals, to provide guidance, advice, and recommendations to Board in carrying out its functions.

Pub. L. 93–651, §111(n), amended subsec. (a) in exactly the same manner as it was amended by Pub. L. 93–516.

Subsec. (d). Pub. L. 93–516, §111(*o*), substituted "this chapter, the Board shall, directly or through grants to or contracts with public or private nonprofit organizations, carrying out its functions under subsections (b) and (c) of this section, and shall conduct" for "this section, the Board shall conduct", and inserted provisions that any such order affecting any Federal department, agency, or instrumentality of the United States shall be final and binding on such department, agency, or instrumentality, and that an order of compliance may include the withholding or suspension of Federal funds with respect to any building found not to be in compliance with standards prescribed pursuant to the Acts referred to in subsec. (b) of this section.

Pub. L. 93–651, 111(*o*), amended subsec. (d) in exactly the same manner as it was amended by Pub. L. 93–516.

Subsec. (e). Pub. L. 93–516, §111(p), inserted provisions relating to appointment of an executive director and other professional and clerical personnel.

Pub. L. 93–651, §111(p), amended subsec. (e) in exactly the same manner as it was amended by Pub. L. 93–516.

Subsec. (g). Pub. L. 93–516, §111(q), substituted "not later than September 30, 1975" for "prior to January 1, 1975".

Pub. L. 93–651, §111(q), amended subsec. (g) in exactly the same manner as it was amended by Pub. L. 93–516.

Subsec. (h). Pub. L. 93–516, §110, authorized appropriation of $1,500,000 for fiscal year ending June 30, 1976.

Pub. L. 93–651, §110, amended subsec. (h) in exactly the same manner as it was amended by Pub. L. 93–516.

Effective Date of 1980 Amendment

Amendment by Pub. L. 96–374 effective Oct. 1, 1980, see section 1393(a) of Pub. L. 96–374, set out as a note under section 1001 of Title 20, Education.

Extension of Vocational Rehabilitation Programs Through Fiscal Year Ending September 30, 1978; Effective Date of 1976 Amendment

For contingency provisions relating to the extensions of program authorizations and to the effective date of such extensions, see section 11(a), (b)(1), and (c) of Pub. L. 94–230, set out as a note under section 720 of this title.

Termination of Advisory Panels

Advisory panels established after Jan. 5, 1973, to terminate not later than the expiration of the 2-year period beginning on the date of their establishment, unless, in the case of a panel established by the President or an officer of the Federal Government, such panel is renewed by appropriate action prior to the expiration of such 2-year period, or in the case of a panel established by the Congress, its duration is otherwise provided for by law. See sections 3(2) and 14 of Pub. L. 92–463, Oct. 6, 1972, 86 Stat. 770, 776, set out in the Appendix to Title 5, Government Organization and Employees.

§ 793. Employment under Federal contracts

(a) Amount of contracts or subcontracts; provision for employment and advancement of qualified individuals with disabilities; regulations

Any contract in excess of $10,000 entered into by any Federal department or agency for the procurement of personal property and nonpersonal services (including construction) for the United States shall contain a provision requiring that the party contracting with the United States shall take affirmative action to employ and advance in employment qualified individuals with disabilities. The provisions of this section shall apply to any subcontract in excess of $10,000 entered into by a prime contractor in carrying out any contract for the procurement of personal property and nonpersonal services (including construction) for the United States. The President shall implement the provisions of this section by promulgating regulations within ninety days after September 26, 1973.

(b) Administrative enforcement; complaints; investigations; departmental action

If any individual with a disability believes any contractor has failed or refused to comply with the provisions of a contract with the United States, relating to employment of individuals with disabilities, such individual may file a complaint with the Department of Labor. The Department shall promptly investigate such complaint and shall take such action thereon as the facts and circumstances warrant, consistent with the terms of such contract and the laws and regulations applicable thereto.

(c) Waiver by President; national interest special circumstances for waiver of particular agreements; waiver by Secretary of Labor of affirmative action requirements

(1) The requirements of this section may be waived, in whole or in part, by the President with respect to a particular contract or subcontract, in accordance with guidelines set forth in regulations which the President shall prescribe, when the President determines that special circumstances in the national interest so require and states in writing the reasons for such determination.

(2)(A) The Secretary of Labor may waive the requirements of the affirmative action clause required by regulations promulgated under subsection (a) of this section with respect to any of a prime contractor's or subcontractor's facilities that are found to be in all respects separate and distinct from activities of the prime contractor or subcontractor related to the performance of the contract or subcontract, if the Secretary of Labor also finds that such a waiver will not interfere with or impede the effectuation of this chapter.

(B) Such waivers shall be considered only upon the request of the contractor or subcontractor. The Secretary of Labor shall promulgate regulations that set forth the standards used for granting such a waiver.

(d) Standards used in determining violation of section

The standards used to determine whether this section has been violated in a complaint alleging nonaffirmative action employment discrimination under this section shall be the standards applied under title I of the Americans with Disabilities Act of 1990 (42 U.S.C. 12111 et seq.) and the provisions of sections 501 through 504, and 510,[1] of the Americans with Disabilities Act of 1990 (42 U.S.C. 12201–12204 and 12210), as such sections relate to employment.

(e) Avoidance of duplicative efforts and inconsistencies

The Secretary shall develop procedures to ensure that administrative complaints filed under this section and under the Americans with Disabilities Act of 1990 [42 U.S.C. 12101 et seq.] are dealt with in a manner that avoids duplication of effort and prevents imposition of inconsistent or conflicting standards for the same requirements under this section and the Americans with Disabilities Act of 1990.

(Pub. L. 93–112, title V, § 503, Sept. 26, 1973, 87 Stat. 393; Pub. L. 95–602, title I, § 122(d)(1), Nov. 6, 1978, 92 Stat. 2987; Pub. L. 99–506, title I, § 103(d)(2)(B), (C), title X, §§ 1001(f)(2), (3), 1002(e)(3), Oct. 21, 1986, 100 Stat. 1810, 1843, 1844; Pub. L. 100–630, title II, § 206(c), Nov. 7, 1988, 102 Stat. 3312; Pub. L. 102–569, title I, § 102(p)(31), title V, § 505, Oct. 29, 1992, 106 Stat. 4360, 4427.)

References in Text

The Americans with Disabilities Act of 1990, referred to in subsecs. (d) and (e), is Pub. L. 101–336, July 26, 1990, 104 Stat. 327, which is classified principally to chapter 126 (§ 12101 et seq.) of Title 42, The Public Health and Welfare. Title I of the Act is classified generally to subchapter I (§ 12111 et seq.) of chapter 126 of Title 42. Section 510 of the Act was renumbered section 511 by Pub. L. 110–325, § 6(a)(2), Sept. 25, 2008, 122 Stat. 3558. For complete classification of this Act to the Code, see Short Title note set out under section 12101 of Title 42 and Tables.

Amendments

1992—Subsec. (a). Pub. L. 102–569, §§ 102(p)(31)(A), 505(a), substituted "$10,000" for "$2,500" in two places, struck out ", in employing persons to carry out such contract," after "contain a provision requiring that", and substituted "individuals with disabilities" for "individuals with handicaps as defined in section 706(8) of this title".

Subsec. (b). Pub. L. 102–569, § 102(p)(31)(B), substituted "individual with a disability" for "individual with handicaps" and "individuals with disabilities" for "individuals with handicaps".

Subsec. (c). Pub. L. 102–569, § 505(b), designated existing provisions as par. (1) and added par. (2).

Subsecs. (d), (e). Pub. L. 102–569, § 505(c), added subsecs. (d) and (e).

1988—Subsec. (a). Pub. L. 100–630, § 206(c)(1), inserted a comma after "to carry out such contract".

Subsec. (b). Pub. L. 100–630, § 206(c)(2), substituted "refused" for "refuses".

Subsec. (c). Pub. L. 100–630, § 206(c)(3), substituted "which the President" for "which The President" and "when the President" for "when The President".

1986—Subsec. (a). Pub. L. 99–506, §§ 103(d)(2)(C), 1002(e)(3), substituted "individuals with handicaps" for "handicapped individuals" and "section 706(8) of this title" for "section 706(7) of this title".

Subsec. (b). Pub. L. 99–506, §§ 103(d)(2)(B), (C), 1001(f)(2), substituted "individual with handicaps" for "handicapped individual", "individuals with handicaps" for "handicapped individuals", and "a contract" for "his contract".

---

[1] See References in Text note below.

Subsec. (c). Pub. L. 99–506, § 1001(f)(3), substituted "The President" for "he" in two places and substituted "the reasons" for "his reasons".

1978—Subsec. (a). Pub. L. 95–602 substituted "section 706(7) of this title" for "section 706(6) of this title".

§ 794. Nondiscrimination under Federal grants and programs

(a) Promulgation of rules and regulations

No otherwise qualified individual with a disability in the United States, as defined in section 705(20) of this title, shall, solely by reason of her or his disability, be excluded from the participation in, be denied the benefits of, or be subjected to discrimination under any program or activity receiving Federal financial assistance or under any program or activity conducted by any Executive agency or by the United States Postal Service. The head of each such agency shall promulgate such regulations as may be necessary to carry out the amendments to this section made by the Rehabilitation, Comprehensive Services, and Developmental Disabilities Act of 1978. Copies of any proposed regulation shall be submitted to appropriate authorizing committees of the Congress, and such regulation may take effect no earlier than the thirtieth day after the date on which such regulation is so submitted to such committees.

(b) "Program or activity" defined

For the purposes of this section, the term "program or activity" means all of the operations of—

(1)(A) a department, agency, special purpose district, or other instrumentality of a State or of a local government; or

(B) the entity of such State or local government that distributes such assistance and each such department or agency (and each other State or local government entity) to which the assistance is extended, in the case of assistance to a State or local government;

(2)(A) a college, university, or other postsecondary institution, or a public system of higher education; or

(B) a local educational agency (as defined in section 7801 of title 20), system of vocational education, or other school system;

(3)(A) an entire corporation, partnership, or other private organization, or an entire sole proprietorship—

(i) if assistance is extended to such corporation, partnership, private organization, or sole proprietorship as a whole; or

(ii) which is principally engaged in the business of providing education, health care, housing, social services, or parks and recreation; or

(B) the entire plant or other comparable, geographically separate facility to which Federal financial assistance is extended, in the case of any other corporation, partnership, private organization, or sole proprietorship; or

(4) any other entity which is established by two or more of the entities described in paragraph (1), (2), or (3);

any part of which is extended Federal financial assistance.

(c) Significant structural alterations by small providers

Small providers are not required by subsection (a) of this section to make significant structural alterations to their existing facilities for the purpose of assuring program accessibility, if alternative means of providing the services are available. The terms used in this subsection shall be construed with reference to the regulations existing on March 22, 1988.

(d) Standards used in determining violation of section

The standards used to determine whether this section has been violated in a complaint alleging employment discrimination under this section shall be the standards applied under title I of the Americans with Disabilities Act of 1990 (42 U.S.C. 12111 et seq.) and the provisions of sections 501 through 504, and 510,[1] of the Americans with Disabilities Act of 1990 (42 U.S.C. 12201–12204 and 12210), as such sections relate to employment.

(Pub. L. 93–112, title V, § 504, Sept. 26, 1973, 87 Stat. 394; Pub. L. 95–602, title I, §§ 119, 122(d)(2), Nov. 6, 1978, 92 Stat. 2982, 2987; Pub. L. 99–506, title I, § 103(d)(2)(B), title X, § 1002(e)(4), Oct. 21, 1986, 100 Stat. 1810, 1844; Pub. L. 100–259, § 4, Mar. 22, 1988, 102 Stat. 29; Pub. L. 100–630, title II, § 206(d), Nov. 7, 1988, 102 Stat. 3312; Pub. L. 102–569, title I, § 102(p)(32), title V, § 506, Oct. 29, 1992, 106 Stat. 4360, 4428; Pub. L. 103–382, title III, § 394(i)(2), Oct. 20, 1994, 108 Stat. 4029; Pub. L. 105–220, title IV, § 408(a)(3), Aug. 7, 1998, 112 Stat. 1203; Pub. L. 107–110, title X, § 1076(u)(2), Jan. 8, 2002, 115 Stat. 2093.)

REFERENCES IN TEXT

The amendments to this section made by the Rehabilitation, Comprehensive Services, and Developmental Disabilities Act of 1978, referred to in subsec. (a), mean the amendments made by Pub. L. 95–602. See 1978 Amendments note below.

The Americans with Disabilities Act of 1990, referred to in subsec. (d), is Pub. L. 101–336, July 26, 1990, 104 Stat. 327. Title I of the Act is classified generally to subchapter I (§ 12111 et seq.) of chapter 126 of Title 42, The Public Health and Welfare. Section 510 of the Act was renumbered section 511 by Pub. L. 110–325, § 6(a)(2), Sept. 25, 2008, 122 Stat. 3558. For complete classification of this Act to the Code, see Short Title note set out under section 12101 of Title 42 and Tables.

AMENDMENTS

2002—Subsec. (b)(2)(B). Pub. L. 107–110 substituted "section 7801 of title 20" for "section 8801 of title 20".

1998—Subsec. (a). Pub. L. 105–220 substituted "section 705(20)" for "section 706(8)".

1994—Subsec. (b)(2)(B). Pub. L. 103–382 substituted "section 8801 of title 20" for "section 2891(12) of title 20".

1992—Subsec. (a). Pub. L. 102–569, § 102(p)(32), substituted "a disability" for "handicaps" and "disability" for "handicap" in first sentence.

Subsec. (d). Pub. L. 102–569, § 506, added subsec. (d).

1988—Subsec. (a). Pub. L. 100–630, § 206(d)(1), substituted "her or his handicap" for "his handicap".

Pub. L. 100–259, § 4(1), designated existing provisions as subsec. (a).

Subsec. (b). Pub. L. 100–259, § 4(2), added subsec. (b).

Subsec. (b)(2)(B). Pub. L. 100–630, § 206(d)(2), substituted "section 2891(12) of title 20" for "section 2854(a)(10) of title 20".

[1] See References in Text note below.

Subsec. (c). Pub. L. 100–259, §4(2), added subsec. (c).

1986—Pub. L. 99–506 substituted "individual with handicaps" for "handicapped individual" and "section 706(8) of this title" for "section 706(7) of this title".

1978—Pub. L. 95–602 substituted "section 706(7) of this title" for "section 706(6) of this title" and inserted provision prohibiting discrimination under any program or activity conducted by any Executive agency or by the United States Postal Service and requiring the heads of these agencies to promulgate regulations prohibiting discrimination.

EFFECTIVE DATE OF 2002 AMENDMENT

Amendment by Pub. L. 107–110 effective Jan. 8, 2002, except with respect to certain noncompetitive programs and competitive programs, see section 5 of Pub. L. 107–110, set out as an Effective Date note under section 6301 of Title 20, Education.

EXCLUSION FROM COVERAGE

Amendment by Pub. L. 100–259 not to be construed to extend application of this chapter to ultimate beneficiaries of Federal financial assistance excluded from coverage before Mar. 22, 1988, see section 7 of Pub. L. 100–259, set out as a Construction note under section 1687 of Title 20, Education.

ABORTION NEUTRALITY

Amendment by Pub. L. 100–259 not to be construed to force or require any individual or hospital or any other institution, program, or activity receiving Federal funds to perform or pay for an abortion, see section 8 of Pub. L. 100–259, set out as a note under section 1688 of Title 20, Education.

CONSTRUCTION OF PROHIBITION AGAINST DISCRIMINATION UNDER FEDERAL GRANTS

Rights or protections of this section not affected by any provision of Pub. L. 98–457, see section 127 of Pub. L. 98–457, set out as a note under section 5101 of Title 42, The Public Health and Welfare.

COORDINATION OF IMPLEMENTATION AND ENFORCEMENT OF PROVISIONS

For provisions relating to the coordination of implementation and enforcement of the provisions of this section by the Attorney General, see section 1–201 of Ex. Ord. No. 12250, Nov. 2, 1980, 45 F.R. 72995, set out as a note under section 2000d–1 of Title 42, The Public Health and Welfare.

EXECUTIVE ORDER NO. 11914

Ex. Ord. No. 11914, Apr. 28, 1976, 41 F.R. 17871, which related to nondiscrimination in federally assisted programs, was revoked by Ex. Ord. No. 12250, Nov. 2, 1980, 45 F.R. 72995, set out as a note under section 2000d–1 of Title 42, The Public Health and Welfare.

§794a. Remedies and attorney fees

(a)(1) The remedies, procedures, and rights set forth in section 717 of the Civil Rights Act of 1964 (42 U.S.C. 2000e–16), including the application of sections 706(f) through 706(k) (42 U.S.C. 2000e–5(f) through (k)), shall be available, with respect to any complaint under section 791 of this title, to any employee or applicant for employment aggrieved by the final disposition of such complaint, or by the failure to take final action on such complaint. In fashioning an equitable or affirmative action remedy under such section, a court may take into account the reasonableness of the cost of any necessary work place accommodation, and the availability of alternatives therefor or other appropriate relief in order to achieve an equitable and appropriate remedy.

(2) The remedies, procedures, and rights set forth in title VI of the Civil Rights Act of 1964 [42 U.S.C. 2000d et seq.] shall be available to any person aggrieved by any act or failure to act by any recipient of Federal assistance or Federal provider of such assistance under section 794 of this title.

(b) In any action or proceeding to enforce or charge a violation of a provision of this subchapter, the court, in its discretion, may allow the prevailing party, other than the United States, a reasonable attorney's fee as part of the costs.

(Pub. L. 93–112, title V, §505, as added Pub. L. 95–602, title I, §120(a), Nov. 6, 1978, 92 Stat. 2982.)

REFERENCES IN TEXT

The Civil Rights Act of 1964, referred to in subsec. (a)(2), is Pub. L. 88–352, July 2, 1964, 78 Stat. 241, as amended. Title VI of the Civil Rights Act of 1964 is classified generally to subchapter V (§2000d et seq.) of chapter 21 of Title 42, The Public Health and Welfare. For complete classification of this Act to the Code, see Short Title note set out under section 2000a of Title 42 and Tables.

§794b. Removal of architectural, transportation, or communication barriers; technical and financial assistance; compensation of experts or consultants; authorization of appropriations

(a) The Secretary may provide directly or by contract with State vocational rehabilitation agencies or experts or consultants or groups thereof, technical assistance—

(1) to persons operating community rehabilitation programs; and

(2) with the concurrence of the Access Board established by section 792 of this title, to any public or nonprofit agency, institution, or organization;

for the purpose of assisting such persons or entities in removing architectural, transportation, or communication barriers. Any concurrence of the Access Board under paragraph (2) shall reflect its consideration of cost studies carried out by States.

(b) Any such experts or consultants, while serving pursuant to such contracts, shall be entitled to receive compensation at rates fixed by the Secretary, but not exceeding the daily equivalent of the rate of pay for level 4 of the Senior Executive Service Schedule under section 5382 of title 5, including travel time, and while so serving away from their homes or regular places of business, they may be allowed travel expenses, including per diem in lieu of subsistence, as authorized by section 5703 of title 5 for persons in the Government service employed intermittently.

(c) The Secretary, with the concurrence of the Access Board and the President, may provide, directly or by contract, financial assistance to any public or nonprofit agency, institution, or organization for the purpose of removing architectural, transportation, and communication barriers. No assistance may be provided under this subsection until a study demonstrating the need for such assistance has been conducted and submitted under section 792(i)(1) of this title.

(d) In order to carry out this section, there are authorized to be appropriated such sums as may be necessary.

(Pub. L. 93–112, title V, § 506, as added Pub. L. 95–602, title I, § 120(a), Nov. 6, 1978, 92 Stat. 2983; amended Pub. L. 100–630, title II, § 206(e), Nov. 7, 1988, 102 Stat. 3312; Pub. L. 102–569, title V, § 507, Oct. 29, 1992, 106 Stat. 4428; Pub. L. 105–220, title IV, § 408(a)(4), Aug. 7, 1998, 112 Stat. 1203; Pub. L. 105–394, title II, § 203(b), Nov. 13, 1998, 112 Stat. 3653.)

AMENDMENTS

1998—Subsec. (a). Pub. L. 105–220, § 408(a)(4)(A), in concluding provisions, inserted last sentence and struck out former last sentence which read as follows: "Any concurrence of the Access Board under this paragraph shall reflect its consideration of the cost studies carried out by States under section 792(c)(1) of this title."

Subsec. (c). Pub. L. 105–394 substituted "792(i)(1)" for "792(h)(1)".

Pub. L. 105–220, § 408(a)(4)(B), substituted "provided under this subsection" for "provided under this paragraph".

1992—Subsec. (a). Pub. L. 102–569, § 507(a), (b), substituted "community rehabilitation programs" for "rehabilitation facilities" in par. (1) and inserted "Access" before "Board" in par. (2) and concluding provisions.

Subsec. (b). Pub. L. 102–569, § 507(c), substituted "the rate of pay for level 4 of the Senior Executive Service Schedule under section 5382" for "the rate of basic pay payable for grade GS–18 of the General Schedule, under section 5332".

Subsec. (c). Pub. L. 102–569, § 507(a), (d), inserted "Access" before "Board" and substituted "792(h)(1)" for "792(h)(2)".

1988—Subsec. (a). Pub. L. 100–630, § 206(e)(1), (2), redesignated former par. (1) as subsec. (a) and former subpars. (A) and (B) as pars. (1) and (2), respectively.

Subsec. (b). Pub. L. 100–630, § 206(e)(1), (3), redesignated former par. (2) as subsec. (b) and substituted "travel time" for "traveltime".

Subsec. (c). Pub. L. 100–630, § 206(e)(1), (4), redesignated former par. (3) as subsec. (c) and inserted a comma after "the President".

Subsec. (d). Pub. L. 100–630, § 206(e)(1), redesignated former par. (4) as subsec. (d).

§ 794c. Interagency Disability Coordinating Council

(a) Establishment

There is hereby established an Interagency Disability Coordinating Council (hereafter in this section referred to as the "Council") composed of the Secretary of Education, the Secretary of Health and Human Services, the Secretary of Labor, the Secretary of Housing and Urban Development, the Secretary of Transportation, the Assistant Secretary of the Interior for Indian Affairs, the Attorney General, the Director of the Office of Personnel Management, the Chairperson of the Equal Employment Opportunity Commission, the Chairperson of the Architectural and Transportation Barriers Compliance Board, and such other officials as may be designated by the President.

(b) Duties

The Council shall—

(1) have the responsibility for developing and implementing agreements, policies, and practices designed to maximize effort, promote efficiency, and eliminate conflict, competition, duplication, and inconsistencies among the operations, functions, and jurisdictions of the various departments, agencies, and branches of the Federal Government responsible for the implementation and enforcement of the provisions of this subchapter, and the regulations prescribed thereunder;

(2) be responsible for developing and implementing agreements, policies, and practices designed to coordinate operations, functions, and jurisdictions of the various departments and agencies of the Federal Government responsible for promoting the full integration into society, independence, and productivity of individuals with disabilities; and

(3) carry out such studies and other activities, subject to the availability of resources, with advice from the National Council on Disability, in order to identify methods for overcoming barriers to integration into society, independence, and productivity of individuals with disabilities.

(c) Report

On or before July 1 of each year, the Interagency Disability Coordinating Council shall prepare and submit to the President and to the Congress a report of the activities of the Council designed to promote and meet the employment needs of individuals with disabilities, together with such recommendations for legislative and administrative changes as the Council concludes are desirable to further promote this section, along with any comments submitted by the National Council on Disability as to the effectiveness of such activities and recommendations in meeting the needs of individuals with disabilities. Nothing in this section shall impair any responsibilities assigned by any Executive order to any Federal department, agency, or instrumentality to act as a lead Federal agency with respect to any provisions of this subchapter.

(Pub. L. 93–112, title V, § 507, as added Pub. L. 95–602, title I, § 120(a), Nov. 6, 1978, 92 Stat. 2983; amended Pub. L. 96–88, title V, § 508(m)(2), Oct. 17, 1979, 93 Stat. 694; Pub. L. 98–221, title I, § 104(b)(4), Feb. 22, 1984, 98 Stat. 18; Pub. L. 99–506, title VI, § 602, title X, § 1001(f)(4), Oct. 21, 1986, 100 Stat. 1830, 1843; Pub. L. 102–569, title V, § 508(a), Oct. 29, 1992, 106 Stat. 4429.)

AMENDMENTS

1992—Pub. L. 102–569 amended section generally, changing Council name from Interagency Coordinating Council to Interagency Disability Coordinating Council, including as members Secretary of Housing and Urban Development, Secretary of Transportation, and such other officials as designated by the President, requiring Council to be responsible for developing and implementing policies and practices to eliminate inconsistencies among Federal departments and agencies responsible for enforcement of provisions of this subchapter and to carry out such studies and other activities, with advice from the National Council on Disability, to identify methods for overcoming barriers to integration into society, independence, and productivity of individuals with disabilities, and directing in annual report inclusion of any comments submitted by National Council on Disability as to effectiveness of activities and recommendations in meeting needs of individuals with disabilities.

1986—Pub. L. 99–506, § 602, inserted reference to Assistant Secretary of the Interior for Indian Affairs.

Pub. L. 99–506, § 1001(f)(4), which directed the substitution of "Chairperson" for "Chairman" was executed by substituting "Chairperson of the Architectural and Transportation Barriers Compliance Board" for "Chairman of the Architectural and Transportation Barriers Compliance Board" to reflect the probable intent of Congress.

1984—Pub. L. 98–221 substituted "Chairman of the Office of Personnel Management" for "Chairman of the United States Civil Service Commission" and purported to substitute "Secretary of Education, the Secretary of Health and Human Services," for "Secretary of Health, Education, and Welfare" which amendment could not be executed in view of the previous amendment by Pub. L. 96–88. See 1979 Amendment note below.

1979—Pub. L. 96–88 substituted requirement that the Secretaries of Education and Health and Human Services be members of the Council for requirement that the Secretary of Health, Education, and Welfare be a member.

EFFECTIVE DATE OF 1979 AMENDMENT

Amendment by Pub. L. 96–88 effective May 4, 1980, with specified exceptions, see section 601 of Pub. L. 96–88, set out as an Effective Date note under section 3401 of Title 20, Education.

TERMINATION OF REPORTING REQUIREMENTS

For termination, effective May 15, 2000, of provisions in subsec. (c) of this section relating to requirement that the Council submit an annual report of activities to Congress, see section 3003 of Pub. L. 104–66, as amended, set out as a note under section 1113 of Title 31, Money and Finance, and page 175 of House Document No. 103–7.

§ 794d. Electronic and information technology

(a) Requirements for Federal departments and agencies

(1) Accessibility

(A) Development, procurement, maintenance, or use of electronic and information technology

When developing, procuring, maintaining, or using electronic and information technology, each Federal department or agency, including the United States Postal Service, shall ensure, unless an undue burden would be imposed on the department or agency, that the electronic and information technology allows, regardless of the type of medium of the technology—

(i) individuals with disabilities who are Federal employees to have access to and use of information and data that is comparable to the access to and use of the information and data by Federal employees who are not individuals with disabilities; and

(ii) individuals with disabilities who are members of the public seeking information or services from a Federal department or agency to have access to and use of information and data that is comparable to the access to and use of the information and data by such members of the public who are not individuals with disabilities.

(B) Alternative means efforts

When development, procurement, maintenance, or use of electronic and information technology that meets the standards published by the Access Board under paragraph (2) would impose an undue burden, the Federal department or agency shall provide individuals with disabilities covered by paragraph (1) with the information and data involved by an alternative means of access that allows the individual to use the information and data.

(2) Electronic and information technology standards

(A) In general

Not later than 18 months after August 7, 1998, the Architectural and Transportation Barriers Compliance Board (referred to in this section as the "Access Board"), after consultation with the Secretary of Education, the Administrator of General Services, the Secretary of Commerce, the Chairman of the Federal Communications Commission, the Secretary of Defense, and the head of any other Federal department or agency that the Access Board determines to be appropriate, including consultation on relevant research findings, and after consultation with the electronic and information technology industry and appropriate public or nonprofit agencies or organizations, including organizations representing individuals with disabilities, shall issue and publish standards setting forth—

(i) for purposes of this section, a definition of electronic and information technology that is consistent with the definition of information technology specified in section 11101(6) of title 40; and

(ii) the technical and functional performance criteria necessary to implement the requirements set forth in paragraph (1).

(B) Review and amendment

The Access Board shall periodically review and, as appropriate, amend the standards required under subparagraph (A) to reflect technological advances or changes in electronic and information technology.

(3) Incorporation of standards

Not later than 6 months after the Access Board publishes the standards required under paragraph (2), the Federal Acquisition Regulatory Council shall revise the Federal Acquisition Regulation and each Federal department or agency shall revise the Federal procurement policies and directives under the control of the department or agency to incorporate those standards. Not later than 6 months after the Access Board revises any standards required under paragraph (2), the Council shall revise the Federal Acquisition Regulation and each appropriate Federal department or agency shall revise the procurement policies and directives, as necessary, to incorporate the revisions.

(4) Acquisition planning

In the event that a Federal department or agency determines that compliance with the standards issued by the Access Board under paragraph (2) relating to procurement imposes an undue burden, the documentation by the department or agency supporting the procurement shall explain why compliance creates an undue burden.

(5) Exemption for national security systems

This section shall not apply to national security systems, as that term is defined in section 11103(a) of title 40.

(6) Construction

(A) Equipment

In a case in which the Federal Government provides access to the public to information or data through electronic and information technology, nothing in this section shall be construed to require a Federal department or agency—

(i) to make equipment owned by the Federal Government available for access and use by individuals with disabilities covered by paragraph (1) at a location other than that where the electronic and information technology is provided to the public; or

(ii) to purchase equipment for access and use by individuals with disabilities covered by paragraph (1) at a location other than that where the electronic and information technology is provided to the public.

(B) Software and peripheral devices

Except as required to comply with standards issued by the Access Board under paragraph (2), nothing in paragraph (1) requires the installation of specific accessibility-related software or the attachment of a specific accessibility-related peripheral device at a workstation of a Federal employee who is not an individual with a disability.

(b) Technical assistance

The Administrator of General Services and the Access Board shall provide technical assistance to individuals and Federal departments and agencies concerning the requirements of this section.

(c) Agency evaluations

Not later than 6 months after August 7, 1998, the head of each Federal department or agency shall evaluate the extent to which the electronic and information technology of the department or agency is accessible to and usable by individuals with disabilities described in subsection (a)(1) of this section, compared to the access to and use of the technology by individuals described in such subsection who are not individuals with disabilities, and submit a report containing the evaluation to the Attorney General.

(d) Reports

(1) Interim report

Not later than 18 months after August 7, 1998, the Attorney General shall prepare and submit to the President a report containing information on and recommendations regarding the extent to which the electronic and information technology of the Federal Government is accessible to and usable by individuals with disabilities described in subsection (a)(1) of this section.

(2) Biennial reports

Not later than 3 years after August 7, 1998, and every 2 years thereafter, the Attorney General shall prepare and submit to the President and Congress a report containing information on and recommendations regarding the state of Federal department and agency compliance with the requirements of this section, including actions regarding individual complaints under subsection (f) of this section.

(e) Cooperation

Each head of a Federal department or agency (including the Access Board, the Equal Employment Opportunity Commission, and the General Services Administration) shall provide to the Attorney General such information as the Attorney General determines is necessary to conduct the evaluations under subsection (c) of this section and prepare the reports under subsection (d) of this section.

(f) Enforcement

(1) General

(A) Complaints

Effective 6 months after the date of publication by the Access Board of final standards described in subsection (a)(2) of this section, any individual with a disability may file a complaint alleging that a Federal department or agency fails to comply with subsection (a)(1) of this section in providing electronic and information technology.

(B) Application

This subsection shall apply only to electronic and information technology that is procured by a Federal department or agency not less than 6 months after the date of publication by the Access Board of final standards described in subsection (a)(2) of this section.

(2) Administrative complaints

Complaints filed under paragraph (1) shall be filed with the Federal department or agency alleged to be in noncompliance. The Federal department or agency receiving the complaint shall apply the complaint procedures established to implement section 794 of this title for resolving allegations of discrimination in a federally conducted program or activity.

(3) Civil actions

The remedies, procedures, and rights set forth in sections 794a(a)(2) and 794a(b) of this title shall be the remedies, procedures, and rights available to any individual with a disability filing a complaint under paragraph (1).

(g) Application to other Federal laws

This section shall not be construed to limit any right, remedy, or procedure otherwise available under any provision of Federal law (including sections 791 through 794a of this title) that provides greater or equal protection for the rights of individuals with disabilities than this section.

(Pub. L. 93–112, title V, § 508, as added Pub. L. 99–506, title VI, § 603(a), Oct. 21, 1986, 100 Stat. 1830; amended Pub. L. 100–630, title II, § 206(f), Nov. 7, 1988, 102 Stat. 3312; Pub. L. 102–569, title V, § 509(a), Oct. 29, 1992, 106 Stat. 4430; Pub. L. 105–220, title IV, § 408(b), Aug. 7, 1998, 112 Stat. 1203; Pub. L. 106–246, div. B, title II, § 2405, July 13, 2000, 114 Stat. 555.)

CODIFICATION

"Section 11101(6) of title 40" substituted in subsec. (a)(2)(A)(i) for "section 5002(3) of the Clinger-Cohen Act of 1996 (40 U.S.C. 1401(3))" and "section 11103(a) of title 40" substituted in subsec. (a)(5) for "section 5142 of the Clinger-Cohen Act of 1996 (40 U.S.C. 1452)" on authority of Pub. L. 107–217, § 5(c), Aug. 21, 2002, 116 Stat. 1303, the first section of which enacted Title 40, Public Buildings, Property, and Works.

AMENDMENTS

2000—Subsec. (f)(1)(A). Pub. L. 106–246, § 2405(1), substituted "Effective 6 months after the date of publication by the Access Board of final standards described in subsection (a)(2) of this section," for "Effective 2 years after August 7, 1998,".

Subsec. (f)(1)(B). Pub. L. 106–246, § 2405(2), substituted "6 months after the date of publication by the Access Board of final standards described in subsection (a)(2) of this section." for "2 years after August 7, 1998."

1998—Pub. L. 105–220 amended section catchline and text generally. Prior to amendment, text consisted of subsecs. (a) and (b) relating to electronic and information technology accessibility guidelines.

1992—Pub. L. 102–569 amended section generally, substituting present provisions for provisions relating to electronic equipment accessibility guidelines, in consultation with electronic industry, designed to insure individuals with handicaps use of electronic office equipment with or without special peripherals, requiring the Administrator of General Services to adopt guidelines for electronic equipment accessibility established under this section for Federal procurement of electronic equipment, and defining term "special peripherals".

1988—Subsec. (a)(1). Pub. L. 100–630, § 206(f)(1), inserted "the Director of" before "the National Institute", struck out "the" before "General Services", and substituted "individuals with handicaps" for "handicapped individuals".

Subsec. (a)(3). Pub. L. 100–630, § 206(f)(2), inserted "by the Director of the National Institute on Disability and Rehabilitation Research and the Administrator of General Services in consultation with the electronics industry and the Interagency Committee for Computer Support of Handicapped Employees" after "revised".

Subsec. (c). Pub. L. 100–630, § 206(f)(3), substituted "an individual with handicaps" for "a handicapped individual".

§ 794e. Protection and advocacy of individual rights

(a) Purpose and construction

(1) Purpose

The purpose of this section is to support a system in each State to protect the legal and human rights of individuals with disabilities who—

(A) need services that are beyond the scope of services authorized to be provided by the client assistance program under section 732 of this title; and

(B)(i) are ineligible for protection and advocacy programs under subtitle C of the Developmental Disabilities Assistance and Bill of Rights Act of 2000 [42 U.S.C. 15041 et seq.] because the individuals do not have a developmental disability, as defined in section 102 of such Act [42 U.S.C. 15002]; and

(ii) are ineligible for services under the Protection and Advocacy for Mentally Ill Individuals Act of 1986[1] (42 U.S.C. 10801 et seq.) because the individuals are not individuals with mental illness, as defined in section 102 of such Act (42 U.S.C. 10802).

[1] See References in Text note below.

(2) Construction

This section shall not be construed to require the provision of protection and advocacy services that can be provided under the Assistive Technology Act of 1998 [29 U.S.C. 3001 et seq.].

(b) Appropriations less than $5,500,000

For any fiscal year in which the amount appropriated to carry out this section is less than $5,500,000, the Commissioner may make grants from such amount to eligible systems within States to plan for, develop outreach strategies for, and carry out protection and advocacy programs authorized under this section for individuals with disabilities who meet the requirements of subparagraphs (A) and (B) of subsection (a)(1) of this section.

(c) Appropriations of $5,500,000 or more

(1) Reservations

(A) Technical assistance

For any fiscal year in which the amount appropriated to carry out this section equals or exceeds $5,500,000, the Commissioner shall set aside not less than 1.8 percent and not more than 2.2 percent of the amount to provide training and technical assistance to the systems established under this section.

(B) Grant for the eligible system serving the American Indian consortium

For any fiscal year in which the amount appropriated to carry out this section equals or exceeds $10,500,000, the Commissioner shall reserve a portion, and use the portion to make a grant for the eligible system serving the American Indian consortium. The Commission shall make the grant in an amount of not less than $50,000 for the fiscal year.

(2) Allotments

For any such fiscal year, after the reservations required by paragraph (1) have been made, the Commissioner shall make allotments from the remainder of such amount in accordance with paragraph (3) to eligible systems within States to enable such systems to carry out protection and advocacy programs authorized under this section for individuals referred to in subsection (b) of this section.

(3) Systems within States

(A) Population basis

Except as provided in subparagraph (B), from such remainder for each such fiscal year, the Commissioner shall make an allotment to the eligible system within a State of an amount bearing the same ratio to such remainder as the population of the State bears to the population of all States.

(B) Minimums

Subject to the availability of appropriations to carry out this section, and except as provided in paragraph (4), the allotment to any system under subparagraph (A) shall be not less than $100,000 or ⅓ of 1 percent of the remainder for the fiscal year for which the allotment is made, whichever is greater, and the allotment to any system under this section for any fiscal year that is less than $100,000 or 1/3 of 1 percent of such remainder shall be increased to the greater of the two amounts.

(4) Systems within other jurisdictions

(A) In general

For the purposes of paragraph (3)(B), Guam, American Samoa, the United States Virgin Islands, and the Commonwealth of the Northern Mariana Islands shall not be considered to be States.

(B) Allotment

The eligible system within a jurisdiction described in subparagraph (A) shall be allotted under paragraph (3)(A) not less than $50,000 for the fiscal year for which the allotment is made.

(5) Adjustment for inflation

For any fiscal year, beginning in fiscal year 1999, in which the total amount appropriated to carry out this section exceeds the total amount appropriated to carry out this section for the preceding fiscal year, the Commissioner shall increase each of the minimum grants or allotments under paragraphs (1)(B), (3)(B), and (4)(B) by a percentage that shall not exceed the percentage increase in the total amount appropriated to carry out this section between the preceding fiscal year and the fiscal year involved.

(d) Proportional reduction

To provide minimum allotments to systems within States (as increased under subsection (c)(5) of this section) under subsection (c)(3)(B) of this section, or to provide minimum allotments to systems within States (as increased under subsection (c)(5) of this section) under subsection (c)(4)(B) of this section, the Commissioner shall proportionately reduce the allotments of the remaining systems within States under subsection (c)(3) of this section, with such adjustments as may be necessary to prevent the allotment of any such remaining system within a State from being reduced to less than the minimum allotment for a system within a State (as increased under subsection (c)(5) of this section) under subsection (c)(3)(B) of this section, or the minimum allotment for a State (as increased under subsection (c)(5) of this section) under subsection (c)(4)(B) of this section, as appropriate.

(e) Reallotment

Whenever the Commissioner determines that any amount of an allotment to a system within a State for any fiscal year described in subsection (c)(1) of this section will not be expended by such system in carrying out the provisions of this section, the Commissioner shall make such amount available for carrying out the provisions of this section to one or more of the systems that the Commissioner determines will be able to use additional amounts during such year for carrying out such provisions. Any amount made available to a system for any fiscal year pursuant to the preceding sentence shall, for the purposes of this section, be regarded as an increase in the allotment of the system (as determined under the preceding provisions of this section) for such year.

(f) Application

In order to receive assistance under this section, an eligible system shall submit an application to the Commissioner, at such time, in such form and manner, and containing such information and assurances as the Commissioner determines necessary to meet the requirements of this section, including assurances that the eligible system will—

(1) have in effect a system to protect and advocate the rights of individuals with disabilities;

(2) have the same general authorities, including access to records and program income, as are set forth in subtitle C of the Developmental Disabilities Assistance and Bill of Rights Act of 2000 [42 U.S.C. 15041 et seq.];

(3) have the authority to pursue legal, administrative, and other appropriate remedies or approaches to ensure the protection of, and advocacy for, the rights of such individuals within the State or the American Indian consortium who are individuals described in subsection (a)(1) of this section;

(4) provide information on and make referrals to programs and services addressing the needs of individuals with disabilities in the State or the American Indian consortium;

(5) develop a statement of objectives and priorities on an annual basis, and provide to the public, including individuals with disabilities and, as appropriate, the individuals' representatives, an opportunity to comment on the objectives and priorities established by, and activities of, the system including—

(A) the objectives and priorities for the activities of the system for each year and the rationale for the establishment of such objectives and priorities; and

(B) the coordination of programs provided through the system under this section with the advocacy programs of the client assistance program under section 732 of this title, the State long-term care ombudsman program established under the Older Americans Act of 1965 (42 U.S.C. 3001 et seq.), the Developmental Disabilities Assistance and Bill of Rights Act of 2000 [42 U.S.C. 15001 et seq.], and the Protection and Advocacy for Mentally Ill Individuals Act of 1986[2] (42 U.S.C. 10801 et seq.);

(6) establish a grievance procedure for clients or prospective clients of the system to ensure that individuals with disabilities are afforded equal opportunity to access the services of the system; and

(7) provide assurances to the Commissioner that funds made available under this section will be used to supplement and not supplant the non-Federal funds that would otherwise be made available for the purpose for which Federal funds are provided.

(g) Carryover and direct payment

(1) Direct payment

Notwithstanding any other provision of law, the Commissioner shall pay directly to any

[2] See References in Text note below.

system that complies with the provisions of this section, the amount of the allotment of the State or the grant for the eligible system that serves the American Indian consortium involved under this section, unless the State or American Indian consortium provides otherwise.

(2) Carryover

Any amount paid to an eligible system that serves a State or American Indian consortium for a fiscal year that remains unobligated at the end of such year shall remain available to such system that serves the State or American Indian consortium for obligation during the next fiscal year for the purposes for which such amount was paid.

(h) Limitation on disclosure requirements

For purposes of any audit, report, or evaluation of the performance of the program established under this section, the Commissioner shall not require such a program to disclose the identity of, or any other personally identifiable information related to, any individual requesting assistance under such program.

(i) Administrative cost

In any State in which an eligible system is located within a State agency, a State may use a portion of any allotment under subsection (c) of this section for the cost of the administration of the system required by this section. Such portion may not exceed 5 percent of the allotment.

(j) Delegation

The Commissioner may delegate the administration of this program to the Commissioner of the Administration on Developmental Disabilities within the Department of Health and Human Services.

(k) Report

The Commissioner shall annually prepare and submit to the Committee on Education and the Workforce of the House of Representatives and the Committee on Labor and Human Resources of the Senate a report describing the types of services and activities being undertaken by programs funded under this section, the total number of individuals served under this section, the types of disabilities represented by such individuals, and the types of issues being addressed on behalf of such individuals.

(*l*) Authorization of appropriations

There are authorized to be appropriated to carry out this section such sums as may be necessary for each of the fiscal years 1999 through 2003.

(m) Definitions

As used in this section:

(1) Eligible system

The term "eligible system" means a protection and advocacy system that is established under subtitle C of the Developmental Disabilities Assistance and Bill of Rights Act of 2000 [42 U.S.C. 15041 et seq.] and that meets the requirements of subsection (f) of this section.

(2) American Indian consortium

The term "American Indian consortium" means a consortium established as described in section 142[2] of the Developmental Disabilities Assistance and Bill of Rights Act (42 U.S.C. 6042).

(Pub. L. 93–112, title V, §509, as added Pub. L. 102–569, title V, §510(a), Oct. 29, 1992, 106 Stat. 4430; amended Pub. L. 103–73, title I, §112(c), Aug. 11, 1993, 107 Stat. 727; Pub. L. 105–12, §9(n), Apr. 30, 1997, 111 Stat. 28; Pub. L. 105–220, title IV, §408(c), Aug. 7, 1998, 112 Stat. 1206; Pub. L. 105–394, title IV, §402(c), Nov. 13, 1998, 112 Stat. 3662; Pub. L. 106–402, title IV, §401(b)(3)(C), (D), Oct. 30, 2000, 114 Stat. 1738.)

REFERENCES IN TEXT

The Developmental Disabilities Assistance and Bill of Rights Act of 2000, referred to in subsecs. (a)(1)(B)(i), (f)(2), (5)(B), and (m)(1), is Pub. L. 106–402, Oct. 30, 2000, 114 Stat. 1677, which is classified principally to chapter 144 (§15001 et seq.) of Title 42, The Public Health and Welfare. Subtitle C of the Act probably means subtitle C of title I of the Act which is classified generally to part C (§15041 et seq.) of subchapter I of chapter 144 of Title 42. For complete classification of this Act to the Code, see Short Title note set out under section 15001 of Title 42 and Tables.

The Protection and Advocacy for Mentally Ill Individuals Act of 1986, referred to in subsecs. (a)(1)(B)(ii) and (f)(5)(B), was Pub. L. 99–319, May 23, 1986, 100 Stat. 478, as amended. Pub. L. 99–319 was renamed the Protection and Advocacy for Individuals with Mental Illness Act by Pub. L. 106–310, div. B, title XXXII, §3206(a), Oct. 17, 2000, 114 Stat. 1193, and is classified generally to chapter 114 (§10801 et seq.) of Title 42, The Public Health and Welfare. For complete classification of this Act to the Code, see Short Title note set out under section 10801 of Title 42 and Tables.

The Assistive Technology Act of 1998, referred to in subsec. (a)(2), is Pub. L. 105–394, Nov. 13, 1998, 112 Stat. 3627, which is classified principally to chapter 31 (§3001 et seq.) of this title. For complete classification of this Act to the Code, see Short Title note set out under section 3001 of this title and Tables.

The Older Americans Act of 1965, referred to in subsec. (f)(5)(B), is Pub. L. 89–73, July 14, 1965, 79 Stat. 218, as amended, which is classified generally to chapter 35 (§3001 et seq.) of Title 42, The Public Health and Welfare. For complete classification of this Act to the Code, see Short Title note set out under section 3001 of Title 42 and Tables.

Section 142 of the Developmental Disabilities Assistance and Bill of Rights Act (42 U.S.C. 6042), referred to in subsec. (m)(2), was repealed by Pub. L. 106–402, title IV, §401(a), Oct. 30, 2000, 114 Stat. 1737.

AMENDMENTS

2000—Subsecs. (a)(1)(B)(i), (f)(2). Pub. L. 106–402, §401(b)(3)(C), substituted "subtitle C of the Developmental Disabilities Assistance and Bill of Rights Act of 2000" for "part C of the Developmental Disabilities Assistance and Bill of Rights Act (42 U.S.C. 6041 et seq.)".

Subsec. (f)(5)(B). Pub. L. 106–402, §401(b)(3)(D), substituted "Developmental Disabilities Assistance and Bill of Rights Act of 2000" for "Developmental Disabilities Assistance and Bill of Rights Act (42 U.S.C. 6000 et seq.)".

Subsec. (m)(1). Pub. L. 106–402, §401(b)(3)(C), substituted "subtitle C of the Developmental Disabilities Assistance and Bill of Rights Act of 2000" for "part C of the Developmental Disabilities Assistance and Bill of Rights Act (42 U.S.C. 6041 et seq.)".

1998—Pub. L. 105–220 amended section catchline and text generally. Prior to amendment, text consisted of subsecs. (a) to (n) relating to protection and advocacy of individual rights.

Subsec. (a)(2). Pub. L. 105–394 substituted "the Assistive Technology Act of 1998" for "the Technology-Related Assistance for Individuals With Disabilities Act of 1988 (42 U.S.C. 2201 et seq.)".

1997—Subsec. (f)(8). Pub. L. 105–12 added par. (8).

1993—Subsec. (a)(1). Pub. L. 103–73, §112(c)(1), added par. (1) and struck out former par. (1) which read as follows: "are ineligible for client assistance programs under section 732 of this title; and".

Subsec. (b). Pub. L. 103–73, §112(c)(2), added subsec. (b) and struck out heading and text of former subsec. (b). Text read as follows:

"(1) ALLOTMENTS.—For any fiscal year in which the amount appropriated to carry out this section is less than $5,500,000, the Commissioner may make grants from such amount to eligible systems within States to plan for, develop outreach strategies for, and carry out protection and advocacy programs authorized under this section for individuals with disabilities who meet the requirements of paragraphs (1) and (2) of subsection (a) of this section.

"(2) OTHER JURISDICTIONS.—For the purposes of this subsection, Guam, American Samoa, the United States Virgin Islands, the Commonwealth of the Northern Mariana Islands, and the Republic of Palau shall not be considered to be States."

Subsec. (c)(4)(A). Pub. L. 103–73, §112(c)(3)(A)(i), substituted "paragraph (3)(B)" for "this subsection".

Subsec. (c)(4)(B). Pub. L. 103–73, §112(c)(3)(A)(ii), substituted "allotted under paragraph (3)(A)" for "allotted".

Subsec. (c)(5). Pub. L. 103–73, §112(c)(3)(B), added par. (5) and struck out heading and text of former par. (5). Text read as follows:

"(A) STATES.—For purposes of determining the minimum amount of an allotment under paragraph (3)(B), the amount $100,000 shall, in the case of such allotments for fiscal year 1994 and subsequent fiscal years, be increased to the extent necessary to offset the effects of inflation occurring since October 1992, as measured by the percentage increase in the Consumer Price Index For All Urban Consumers (U.S. city average) during the period ending on April 1 of the fiscal year preceding the fiscal year for which the allotment is to be made.

"(B) CERTAIN TERRITORIES.—For purposes of determining the minimum amount of an allotment under paragraph (4)(B), the amount $50,000 shall, in the case of such allotments for fiscal year 1994 and subsequent fiscal years, be increased to the extent necessary to offset the effects of inflation occurring since October 1992, as measured by the percentage increase in the Consumer Price Index For All Urban Consumers (U.S. city average) during the period ending on April 1 of the fiscal year preceding the fiscal year for which the allotment is to be made."

Subsec. (d). Pub. L. 103–73, §112(c)(4), added subsec. (d) and struck out heading and text of former subsec. (d). Text read as follows: "Amounts necessary to provide allotments to systems within States in accordance with subsection (c)(3)(B) of this section as increased under subsection (c)(5) of this section, or to provide allotments in accordance with subsection (c)(4)(B) of this section as increased in accordance with subsection (c)(5) of this section, shall be derived by proportionately reducing the allotments of the remaining systems within States under subsection (c)(3) of this section, but with such adjustments as may be necessary to prevent the allotment of any such remaining systems within States from being thereby reduced to less than the greater of $100,000 or one-third of one percent of the sums made available for purposes of this section for the fiscal year for which the allotment is made, as increased in accordance with subsection (c)(5) of this section."

Subsec. (i). Pub. L. 103–73, §112(c)(6), which directed the amendment of this section "in subsection (i), to read as follows:", was executed by adding subsec. (i). Former subsec. (i) redesignated (n).

Subsec. (j). Pub. L. 103–73, §112(c)(7), added subsec. (j) and struck out heading and text of former subsec. (j). Text read as follows: "An eligible system may not use more than 5 percent of any allotment under subsection (c) of this section for the cost of administration of the system required by this section."

Subsec. (n). Pub. L. 103–73, §112(c)(5), redesignated subsec. (i) as (n).

CHANGE OF NAME

Committee on Education and the Workforce of House of Representatives changed to Committee on Education and Labor of House of Representatives by House Resolution No. 6, One Hundred Tenth Congress, Jan. 5, 2007.

Committee on Labor and Human Resources of Senate changed to Committee on Health, Education, Labor, and Pensions of Senate by Senate Resolution No. 20, One Hundred Sixth Congress, Jan. 19, 1999.

EFFECTIVE DATE OF 1997 AMENDMENT

Amendment by Pub. L. 105–12 effective Apr. 30, 1997, applicable to Federal payments made pursuant to obligations incurred after Apr. 30, 1997, for items and services provided on or after such date, and also applicable with respect to contracts entered into, renewed, or extended after Apr. 30, 1997, as well as contracts entered into before Apr. 30, 1997, to the extent permitted under such contracts, see section 11 of Pub. L. 105–12, set out as an Effective Date note under section 14401 of Title 42, The Public Health and Welfare.

SUBCHAPTER VI—EMPLOYMENT OPPORTUNITIES FOR INDIVIDUALS WITH DISABILITIES

CODIFICATION

Title VI of the Rehabilitation Act of 1973, comprising this subchapter, was originally added to Pub. L. 93–112 by Pub. L. 95–602, title II, §201, Nov. 6, 1978, 92 Stat. 2989, and amended by Pub. L. 98–221, Feb. 22, 1984, 98 Stat. 17; Pub. L. 99–506, Oct. 21, 1986, 100 Stat. 1807; Pub. L. 100–630, Nov. 7, 1988, 102 Stat. 3289; Pub. L. 102–52, June 6, 1991, 105 Stat. 260; Pub. L. 102–119, Oct. 7, 1991, 105 Stat. 587; Pub. L. 102–569, Oct. 29, 1992, 106 Stat. 4344; Pub. L. 103–73, Aug. 11, 1993, 107 Stat. 718. Title VI is shown herein, however, as having been added by Pub. L. 105–220, title IV, §409, Aug. 7, 1998, 112 Stat. 1210, without reference to those intervening amendments because of the extensive revision of title VI by Pub. L. 105–220.

PART A—PROJECTS WITH INDUSTRY

§795. Projects With Industry

(a) Purpose; award of grants; eligibility; agreements; evaluation; technical assistance

(1) The purpose of this part is to create and expand job and career opportunities for individuals with disabilities in the competitive labor market by engaging the talent and leadership of private industry as partners in the rehabilitation process, to identify competitive job and career opportunities and the skills needed to perform such jobs, to create practical job and career readiness and training programs, and to provide job placements and career advancement.

(2) The Commissioner, in consultation with the Secretary of Labor and with designated State units, may award grants to individual employers, community rehabilitation program providers, labor unions, trade associations, Indian tribes, tribal organizations, designated State units, and other entities to establish jointly financed Projects With Industry to create and expand job and career opportunities for individuals with disabilities, which projects shall—

(A) provide for the establishment of business advisory councils, that shall—

(i) be comprised of—

(I) representatives of private industry, business concerns, and organized labor;

(II) individuals with disabilities and representatives of individuals with disabilities; and

(III) a representative of the appropriate designated State unit;

(ii) identify job and career availability within the community, consistent with the current and projected local employment opportunities identified by the local workforce investment board for the community under section 2833(b)(1)(B) of this title;

(iii) identify the skills necessary to perform the jobs and careers identified; and

(iv) prescribe training programs designed to develop appropriate job and career skills, or job placement programs designed to identify and develop job placement and career advancement opportunities, for individuals with disabilities in fields related to the job and career availability identified under clause (ii);

(B) provide job development, job placement, and career advancement services;

(C) to the extent appropriate, provide for—

(i) training in realistic work settings in order to prepare individuals with disabilities for employment and career advancement in the competitive market; and

(ii) to the extent practicable, the modification of any facilities or equipment of the employer involved that are used primarily by individuals with disabilities, except that a project shall not be required to provide for such modification if the modification is required as a reasonable accommodation under the Americans with Disabilities Act of 1990 (42 U.S.C. 12101 et seq.); and

(D) provide individuals with disabilities with such support services as may be required in order to maintain the employment and career advancement for which the individuals have received training under this part.

(3)(A) An individual shall be eligible for services described in paragraph (2) if the individual is determined to be an individual described in section 722(a)(1) of this title, and if the determination is made in a manner consistent with section 722(a) of this title.

(B) Such a determination may be made by the recipient of a grant under this part, to the extent the determination is appropriate and available and consistent with the requirements of section 722(a) of this title.

(4) The Commissioner shall enter into an agreement with the grant recipient regarding the establishment of the project. Any agreement shall be jointly developed by the Commissioner, the grant recipient, and, to the extent practicable, the appropriate designated State unit and the individuals with disabilities (or the individuals' representatives) involved. Such agreements shall specify the terms of training and employment under the project, provide for the payment by the Commissioner of part of the costs of the project (in accordance with subsection (c) of this section), and contain the items required under subsection (b) of this section and such other provisions as the parties to the agreement consider to be appropriate.

(5) Any agreement shall include a description of a plan to annually conduct a review and evaluation of the operation of the project in accordance with standards developed by the Commissioner under subsection (d) of this section, and, in conducting the review and evaluation, to collect data and information of the type described in subparagraphs (A) through (C) of section 721(a)(10) of this title, as determined to be appropriate by the Commissioner.

(6) The Commissioner may include, as part of agreements with grant recipients, authority for such grant recipients to provide technical assistance to—

(A) assist employers in hiring individuals with disabilities; or

(B) improve or develop relationships between—

(i) grant recipients or prospective grant recipients; and

(ii) employers or organized labor; or

(C) assist employers in understanding and meeting the requirements of the Americans with Disabilities Act of 1990 (42 U.S.C. 12101 et seq.) as the Act relates to employment of individuals with disabilities.

(b) Requirements for payment

No payment shall be made by the Commissioner under any agreement with a grant recipient entered into under subsection (a) of this section unless such agreement—

(1) provides an assurance that individuals with disabilities placed under such agreement shall receive at least the applicable minimum wage;

(2) provides an assurance that any individual with a disability placed under this part shall be afforded terms and benefits of employment equal to terms and benefits that are afforded to the similarly situated nondisabled co-workers of the individual, and that such individuals with disabilities shall not be segregated from their co-workers; and

(3) provides an assurance that an annual evaluation report containing information specified under subsection (a)(5) of this section shall be submitted as determined to be appropriate by the Commissioner.

(c) Amount of payments

Payments under this section with respect to any project may not exceed 80 per centum of the costs of the project.

(d) Standards for evaluation; recommendations

(1) The Commissioner shall develop standards for the evaluation described in subsection (a)(5) of this section and shall review and revise the evaluation standards as necessary, subject to paragraph (2).

(2) In revising the standards for evaluation to be used by the grant recipients, the Commissioner shall obtain and consider recommendations for such standards from State vocational rehabilitation agencies, current and former grant recipients, professional organizations representing business and industry, organizations representing individuals with disabilities, individuals served by grant recipients, organizations representing community rehabilitation program providers, and labor organizations.

(e) Period of grant; renewal; award on competitive basis; equitable distribution

(1)(A) A grant may be awarded under this section for a period of up to 5 years and such grant may be renewed.

(B) Grants under this section shall be awarded on a competitive basis. To be eligible to receive such a grant, a prospective grant recipient shall submit an application to the Commissioner at such time, in such manner, and containing such information as the Commissioner may require.

(2) The Commissioner shall, to the extent practicable, ensure an equitable distribution of payments made under this section among the States. To the extent funds are available, the Commissioner shall award grants under this section to new projects that will serve individuals with disabilities in States, portions of States, Indian tribes, or tribal organizations, that are currently unserved or underserved by projects.

(f) Indicators for compliance with evaluation standards; annual reports; onsite compliance reviews; analysis included in reports to Congress

(1) The Commissioner shall, as necessary, develop and publish in the Federal Register, in final form, indicators of what constitutes minimum compliance consistent with the evaluation standards under subsection (d)(1) of this section.

(2) Each grant recipient shall report to the Commissioner at the end of each project year the extent to which the grant recipient is in compliance with the evaluation standards.

(3)(A) The Commissioner shall annually conduct onsite compliance reviews of at least 15 percent of grant recipients. The Commissioner shall select grant recipients for review on a random basis.

(B) The Commissioner shall use the indicators in determining compliance with the evaluation standards.

(C) The Commissioner shall ensure that at least one member of a team conducting such a review shall be an individual who—

(i) is not an employee of the Federal Government; and

(ii) has experience or expertise in conducting projects.

(D) The Commissioner shall ensure that—

(i) a representative of the appropriate designated State unit shall participate in the review; and

(ii) no person shall participate in the review of a grant recipient if—

(I) the grant recipient provides any direct financial benefit to the reviewer; or

(II) participation in the review would give the appearance of a conflict of interest.

(4) In making a determination concerning any subsequent grant under this section, the Commissioner shall consider the past performance of the applicant, if applicable. The Commissioner shall use compliance indicators developed under this subsection that are consistent with program evaluation standards developed under subsection (d) of this section to assess minimum project performance for purposes of making continuation awards in the third, fourth, and fifth years.

(5) Each fiscal year the Commissioner shall include in the annual report to Congress required by section 710 of this title an analysis of the extent to which grant recipients have complied with the evaluation standards. The Commissioner may identify individual grant recipients in the analysis. In addition, the Commissioner shall report the results of onsite compliance reviews, identifying individual grant recipients.

(g) Technical assistance to entities conducting or planning projects

The Commissioner may provide, directly or by way of grant, contract, or cooperative agreement, technical assistance to—

(1) entities conducting projects for the purpose of assisting such entities in—

(A) the improvement of or the development of relationships with private industry or labor; or

(B) the improvement of relationships with State vocational rehabilitation agencies; and

(2) entities planning the development of new projects.

(h) Definitions

As used in this section:

(1) The term "agreement" means an agreement described in subsection (a)(4) of this section.

(2) The term "project" means a Project With Industry established under subsection (a)(2) of this section.

(3) The term "grant recipient" means a recipient of a grant under subsection (a)(2) of this section.

(Pub. L. 93–112, title VI, §611, as added Pub. L. 105–220, title IV, §409, Aug. 7, 1998, 112 Stat. 1210.)

REFERENCES IN TEXT

The Americans with Disabilities Act of 1990, referred to in subsec. (a)(2)(C)(ii), (6)(C), is Pub. L. 101–336, July 26, 1990, 104 Stat. 327, as amended, which is classified principally to chapter 126 (§12101 et seq.) of Title 42, The Public Health and Welfare. For complete classification of this Act to the Code, see Short Title note set out under section 12101 of Title 42 and Tables.

PRIOR PROVISIONS

Provisions similar to this section were contained in section 795g of this title prior to the general amendment of this subchapter by Pub. L. 105–220.

A prior section 795, Pub. L. 93–112, title VI, §611, as added Pub. L. 95–602, title II, §201, Nov. 6, 1978, 92 Stat. 2989; amended Pub. L. 99–506, title I, §103(d)(2)(C), title X, §1002(f), Oct. 21, 1986, 100 Stat. 1810, 1844; Pub. L. 102–569, title I, §102(p)(36), title VI, §601, Oct. 29, 1992, 106 Stat. 4360, 4434, authorized community service employment pilot programs for individuals with disabilities, prior to the general amendment of this subchapter by Pub. L. 105–220.

SHORT TITLE

For short title of this subchapter as the "Employment Opportunities for Individuals With Disabilities Act", see section 601 of Pub. L. 93–112, as amended, set out as a note under section 701 of this title.

§795a. Authorization of appropriations

There are authorized to be appropriated to carry out the provisions of this part, such sums as may be necessary for each of fiscal years 1999 through 2003.

(Pub. L. 93–112, title VI, § 612, as added Pub. L. 105–220, title IV, § 409, Aug. 7, 1998, 112 Stat. 1214.)

PRIOR PROVISIONS

Provisions similar to this section were contained in section 795i of this title prior to the general amendment of this subchapter by Pub. L. 105–220.

Prior sections 795a to 795f were omitted in the general amendment of this subchapter by Pub. L. 105–220.

Section 795a, Pub. L. 93–112, title VI, § 612, as added Pub. L. 95–602, title II, § 201, Nov. 6, 1978, 92 Stat. 2991; amended Pub. L. 98–221, title I, § 165, Feb. 22, 1984, 98 Stat. 30; Pub. L. 100–630, title II, § 207(a), Nov. 7, 1988, 102 Stat. 3313, related to administration of community service employment pilot programs for individuals with disabilities.

Section 795b, Pub. L. 93–112, title VI, § 613, as added Pub. L. 95–602, title II, § 201, Nov. 6, 1978, 92 Stat. 2991; amended Pub. L. 102–569, title VI, § 602, Oct. 29, 1992, 106 Stat. 4434, related to employment.

Section 795c, Pub. L. 93–112, title VI, § 614, as added Pub. L. 95–602, title II, § 201, Nov. 6, 1978, 92 Stat. 2992; amended Pub. L. 98–221, title I, § 104(b)(5), Feb. 22, 1984, 98 Stat. 18, related to interagency cooperation.

Section 795d, Pub. L. 93–112, title VI, § 615, as added Pub. L. 95–602, title II, § 201, Nov. 6, 1978, 92 Stat. 2992; amended Pub. L. 99–506, title I, § 103(d)(2)(C), title VII, § 701, Oct. 21, 1986, 100 Stat. 1810, 1831; Pub. L. 102–569, title I, § 102(p)(37), Oct. 29, 1992, 106 Stat. 4360, related to award of grants or contracts.

Section 795e, Pub. L. 93–112, title VI, § 616, as added Pub. L. 95–602, title II, § 201, Nov. 6, 1978, 92 Stat. 2993; amended Pub. L. 99–506, title I, § 103(d)(2)(C), Oct. 21, 1986, 100 Stat. 1810; Pub. L. 102–569, title I, § 102(p)(38), title VI, § 603, Oct. 29, 1992, 106 Stat. 4361, 4434, defined terms "community service" and "pilot program".

Section 795f, Pub. L. 93–112, title VI, § 617, as added Pub. L. 95–602, title II, § 201, Nov. 6, 1978, 92 Stat. 2993; amended Pub. L. 98–221, title I, § 161, Feb. 22, 1984, 98 Stat. 29; Pub. L. 99–506, title VII, § 702, Oct. 21, 1986, 100 Stat. 1831; Pub. L. 102–52, § 7(a), June 6, 1991, 105 Stat. 262; Pub. L. 102–569, title VI, § 604, Oct. 29, 1992, 106 Stat. 4434, authorized appropriations.

PART B—SUPPORTED EMPLOYMENT SERVICES FOR INDIVIDUALS WITH THE MOST SIGNIFICANT DISABILITIES

§ 795g. Purpose

It is the purpose of this part to authorize allotments, in addition to grants for vocational rehabilitation services under subchapter I of this chapter, to assist States in developing collaborative programs with appropriate entities to provide supported employment services for individuals with the most significant disabilities to enable such individuals to achieve the employment outcome of supported employment.

(Pub. L. 93–112, title VI, § 621, as added Pub. L. 105–220, title IV, § 409, Aug. 7, 1998, 112 Stat. 1214; amended Pub. L. 105–277, div. A, § 101(f) [title VIII, § 402(b)(12)], Oct. 21, 1998, 112 Stat. 2681–337, 2681–414.)

PRIOR PROVISIONS

Provisions similar to this section were contained in section 795j of this title prior to the general amendment of this subchapter by Pub. L. 105–220.

A prior section 795g, Pub. L. 93–112, title VI, § 621, as added Pub. L. 95–602, title II, § 201, Nov. 6, 1978, 92 Stat. 2993; amended Pub. L. 98–221, title I, §§ 162, 163, Feb. 22, 1984, 98 Stat. 29, 30; Pub. L. 99–506, title I, § 103(d)(2)(B), (C), title VII, § 703(a)(1)–(3), (b)–(d), Oct. 21, 1986, 100 Stat. 1810, 1831, 1832; Pub. L. 100–630, title II, § 207(b), Nov. 7, 1988, 102 Stat. 3313; Pub. L. 102–569, title VI, § 611, Oct. 29, 1992, 106 Stat. 4434, related to Projects With Industry, prior to the general amendment of this subchapter by Pub. L. 105–220. See section 795 of this title.

AMENDMENTS

1998—Pub. L. 105–277 made technical amendment to section designation and catchline in original.

§ 795h. Allotments

(a) In general

(1) States

The Secretary shall allot the sums appropriated for each fiscal year to carry out this part among the States on the basis of relative population of each State, except that—

(A) no State shall receive less than $250,000, or ⅓ of 1 percent of the sums appropriated for the fiscal year for which the allotment is made, whichever is greater; and

(B) if the sums appropriated to carry out this part for the fiscal year exceed by $1,000,000 or more the sums appropriated to carry out this part in fiscal year 1992, no State shall receive less than $300,000, or ⅓ of 1 percent of the sums appropriated for the fiscal year for which the allotment is made, whichever is greater.

(2) Certain territories

(A) In general

For the purposes of this subsection, Guam, American Samoa, the United States Virgin Islands, and the Commonwealth of the Northern Mariana Islands shall not be considered to be States.

(B) Allotment

Each jurisdiction described in subparagraph (A) shall be allotted not less than one-eighth of one percent of the amounts appropriated for the fiscal year for which the allotment is made.

(b) Reallotment

Whenever the Commissioner determines that any amount of an allotment to a State for any fiscal year will not be expended by such State for carrying out the provisions of this part, the Commissioner shall make such amount available for carrying out the provisions of this part to one or more of the States that the Commissioner determines will be able to use additional amounts during such year for carrying out such provisions. Any amount made available to a State for any fiscal year pursuant to the preceding sentence shall, for the purposes of this section, be regarded as an increase in the allotment of the State (as determined under the preceding provisions of this section) for such year.

(Pub. L. 93–112, title VI, § 622, as added Pub. L. 105–220, title IV, § 409, Aug. 7, 1998, 112 Stat. 1214; amended Pub. L. 105–277, div. A, § 101(f) [title VIII, § 402(b)(13)], Oct. 21, 1998, 112 Stat. 2681–337, 2681–414.)

PRIOR PROVISIONS

Provisions similar to this section were contained in section 795k of this title prior to the general amendment of this subchapter by Pub. L. 105–220.

A prior section 795h, Pub. L. 93–112, title VI, § 622, as added Pub. L. 95–602, title II, § 201, Nov. 6, 1978, 92 Stat. 2994, and amended, which related to business opportunities for individuals with disabilities and promulgation of regulations, was renumbered section 641 of Pub. L. 93–112, by Pub. L. 102–569, title VI, §612(a)(2), (3), Oct. 29, 1992, 106 Stat. 4438, and transferred to section 795r of this title, prior to the general amendment of this subchapter by Pub. L. 105–220.

AMENDMENTS

1998—Pub. L. 105–277 made technical amendment in original to section designation and catchline.

§ 795i. Availability of services

Funds provided under this part may be used to provide supported employment services to individuals who are eligible under this part. Funds provided under this part, or subchapter I of this chapter, may not be used to provide extended services to individuals who are eligible under this part or subchapter I of this chapter.

(Pub. L. 93–112, title VI, §623, as added Pub. L. 105–220, title IV, §409, Aug. 7, 1998, 112 Stat. 1215; amended Pub. L. 105–277, div. A, §101(f) [title VIII, §402(b)(14)], Oct. 21, 1998, 112 Stat. 2681–337, 2681–414.)

PRIOR PROVISIONS

Provisions similar to this section were contained in section 795*l* of this title prior to the general amendment of this subchapter by Pub. L. 105–220.

A prior section 795i, Pub. L. 93–112, title VI, §622, formerly §623, as added Pub. L. 95–602, title II, §201, Nov. 6, 1978, 92 Stat. 2994; amended Pub. L. 98–221, title I, §164, Feb. 22, 1984, 98 Stat. 30; Pub. L. 99–506, title VII, §704, Oct. 21, 1986, 100 Stat. 1834; Pub. L. 100–630, title II, §207(d), Nov. 7, 1988, 102 Stat. 3313; Pub. L. 102–52, §7(b), June 6, 1991, 105 Stat. 262; renumbered §622 and amended Pub. L. 102–569, title VI, §613(a), Oct. 29, 1992, 106 Stat. 4439, authorized appropriations, prior to the general amendment of this subchapter by Pub. L. 105–220. See section 795a of this title.

AMENDMENTS

1998—Pub. L. 105–277 made technical amendment to section designation and catchline in original.

§ 795j. Eligibility

An individual shall be eligible under this part to receive supported employment services authorized under this chapter if—

(1) the individual is eligible for vocational rehabilitation services;

(2) the individual is determined to be an individual with a most significant disability; and

(3) a comprehensive assessment of rehabilitation needs of the individual described in section 705(2)(B) of this title, including an evaluation of rehabilitation, career, and job needs, identifies supported employment as the appropriate employment outcome for the individual.

(Pub. L. 93–112, title VI, §624, as added Pub. L. 105–220, title IV, §409, Aug. 7, 1998, 112 Stat. 1215; amended Pub. L. 105–277, div. A, §101(f) [title VIII, §402(b)(15)], Oct. 21, 1998, 112 Stat. 2681–337, 2681–414.)

PRIOR PROVISIONS

Provisions similar to this section were contained in section 795m of this title prior to the general amendment of this subchapter by Pub. L. 105–220.

A prior section 795j, Pub. L. 93–112, title VI, §631, as added Pub. L. 102–569, title VI, §621(a), Oct. 29, 1992, 106 Stat. 4439, stated purpose of program for supported employment services for individuals with severe disabilities, prior to the general amendment of this subchapter by Pub. L. 105–220. See section 795g of this title.

Another prior section 795j, Pub. L. 93–112, title VI, §631, as added Pub. L. 99–506, title VII, §704(a)(1), Oct. 21, 1986, 100 Stat. 1834, outlined the purpose of former part C of this subchapter, prior to repeal by Pub. L. 102–569, §621(a).

AMENDMENTS

1998—Pub. L. 105–277 made technical amendment to section designation and catchline in original.

§ 795k. State plan

(a) State plan supplements

To be eligible for an allotment under this part, a State shall submit to the Commissioner, as part of the State plan under section 721 of this title, a State plan supplement for providing supported employment services authorized under this chapter to individuals who are eligible under this chapter to receive the services. Each State shall make such annual revisions in the plan supplement as may be necessary.

(b) Contents

Each such plan supplement shall—

(1) designate each designated State agency as the agency to administer the program assisted under this part;

(2) summarize the results of the comprehensive, statewide assessment conducted under section 721(a)(15)(A)(i) of this title, with respect to the rehabilitation needs of individuals with significant disabilities and the need for supported employment services, including needs related to coordination;

(3) describe the quality, scope, and extent of supported employment services authorized under this chapter to be provided to individuals who are eligible under this chapter to receive the services and specify the goals and plans of the State with respect to the distribution of funds received under section 795h of this title;

(4) demonstrate evidence of the efforts of the designated State agency to identify and make arrangements (including entering into cooperative agreements) with other State agencies and other appropriate entities to assist in the provision of supported employment services;

(5) demonstrate evidence of the efforts of the designated State agency to identify and make arrangements (including entering into cooperative agreements) with other public or nonprofit agencies or organizations within the State, employers, natural supports, and other entities with respect to the provision of extended services;

(6) provide assurances that—

(A) funds made available under this part will only be used to provide supported employment services authorized under this chapter to individuals who are eligible under this part to receive the services;

(B) the comprehensive assessments of individuals with significant disabilities conducted under section 722(b)(1) of this title and funded under subchapter I of this chapter will include consideration of supported employment as an appropriate employment outcome;

(C) an individualized plan for employment, as required by section 722 of this title, will be developed and updated using funds under subchapter I of this chapter in order to—

(i) specify the supported employment services to be provided;

(ii) specify the expected extended services needed; and

(iii) identify the source of extended services, which may include natural supports, or to the extent that it is not possible to identify the source of extended services at the time the individualized plan for employment is developed, a statement describing the basis for concluding that there is a reasonable expectation that such sources will become available;

(D) the State will use funds provided under this part only to supplement, and not supplant, the funds provided under subchapter I of this chapter, in providing supported employment services specified in the individualized plan for employment;

(E) services provided under an individualized plan for employment will be coordinated with services provided under other individualized plans established under other Federal or State programs;

(F) to the extent jobs skills training is provided, the training will be provided on site; and

(G) supported employment services will include placement in an integrated setting for the maximum number of hours possible based on the unique strengths, resources, priorities, concerns, abilities, capabilities, interests, and informed choice of individuals with the most significant disabilities;

(7) provide assurances that the State agencies designated under paragraph (1) will expend not more than 5 percent of the allotment of the State under this part for administrative costs of carrying out this part; and

(8) contain such other information and be submitted in such manner as the Commissioner may require.

(Pub. L. 93–112, title VI, § 625, as added Pub. L. 105–220, title IV, § 409, Aug. 7, 1998, 112 Stat. 1215; amended Pub. L. 105–277, div. A, § 101(f) [title VIII, § 402(b)(16)], Oct. 21, 1998, 112 Stat. 2681–337, 2681–414.)

PRIOR PROVISIONS

Provisions similar to this section were contained in section 795n of this title prior to the general amendment of this subchapter by Pub. L. 105–220.

A prior section 795k, Pub. L. 93–112, title VI, § 632, as added Pub. L. 102–569, title VI, § 621(a), Oct. 29, 1992, 106 Stat. 4439, related to allotments, prior to the general amendment of this subchapter by Pub. L. 105–220. See section 795h of this title.

Another prior section 795k, Pub. L. 93–112, title VI, § 632, as added Pub. L. 99–506, title VII, § 704(a)(1), Oct. 21, 1986, 100 Stat. 1834, related to eligibility for services under former part C of this subchapter, prior to repeal by Pub. L. 102–569, § 621(a).

AMENDMENTS

1998—Pub. L. 105–277 made technical amendment in original to section designation and catchline.

§ 795*l*. Restriction

Each State agency designated under section 795k(b)(1) of this title shall collect the information required by section 721(a)(10) of this title separately for eligible individuals receiving supported employment services under this part and for eligible individuals receiving supported employment services under subchapter I of this chapter.

(Pub. L. 93–112, title VI, § 626, as added Pub. L. 105–220, title IV, § 409, Aug. 7, 1998, 112 Stat. 1216; amended Pub. L. 105–277, div. A, § 101(f) [title VIII, § 402(b)(17)], Oct. 21, 1998, 112 Stat. 2681–337, 2681–414.)

PRIOR PROVISIONS

Provisions similar to this section were contained in section 795*o* of this title prior to the general amendment of this subchapter by Pub. L. 105–220.

A prior section 795*l*, Pub. L. 93–112, title VI, § 633, as added Pub. L. 102–569, title VI, § 621(a), Oct. 29, 1992, 106 Stat. 4440; amended Pub. L. 103–73, title I, § 113, Aug. 11, 1993, 107 Stat. 728, related to availability of services, prior to the general amendment of this subchapter by Pub. L. 105–220. See section 795i of this title.

Another prior section 795*l*, Pub. L. 93–112, title VI, § 633, as added Pub. L. 99–506, title VII, § 704(a)(1), Oct. 21, 1986, 100 Stat. 1834; amended Pub. L. 100–630, title II, § 207(e), Nov. 7, 1988, 102 Stat. 3313, provided for allotments to States, unused funds, and planning grants, prior to repeal by Pub. L. 102–569, § 621(a).

AMENDMENTS

1998—Pub. L. 105–277 made technical amendment to section designation and catchline in original.

§ 795m. Savings provision

(a) Supported employment services

Nothing in this chapter shall be construed to prohibit a State from providing supported employment services in accordance with the State plan submitted under section 721 of this title by using funds made available through a State allotment under section 730 of this title.

(b) Postemployment services

Nothing in this part shall be construed to prohibit a State from providing discrete postemployment services in accordance with the State plan submitted under section 721 of this title by using funds made available through a State allotment under section 730 of this title to an individual who is eligible under this part.

(Pub. L. 93–112, title VI, § 627, as added Pub. L. 105–220, title IV, § 409, Aug. 7, 1998, 112 Stat. 1216; amended Pub. L. 105–277, div. A, § 101(f) [title VIII, § 402(b)(18)], Oct. 21, 1998, 112 Stat. 2681–337, 2681–414.)

PRIOR PROVISIONS

Provisions similar to this section were contained in section 795p of this title prior to the general amendment of this subchapter by Pub. L. 105–220.

A prior section 795m, Pub. L. 93–112, title VI, § 634, as added Pub. L. 102–569, title VI, § 621(a), Oct. 29, 1992, 106 Stat. 4440, related to eligibility for services, prior to the general amendment of this subchapter by Pub. L. 105–220. See section 795j of this title.

Another prior section 795m, Pub. L. 93–112, title VI, § 634, as added Pub. L. 99–506, title VII, § 704(a)(1), Oct. 21, 1986, 100 Stat. 1835; amended Pub. L. 100–630, title II, § 207(f), Nov. 7, 1988, 102 Stat. 3313; Pub. L. 102–119,

§26(e), Oct. 7, 1991, 105 Stat. 607, provided for submission of State plans for assistance under former part C of this subchapter, prior to repeal by Pub. L. 102–569, §621(a).

AMENDMENTS

1998—Pub. L. 105–277 made technical amendment in original to section designation and catchline.

§795n. Authorization of appropriations

There are authorized to be appropriated to carry out this part such sums as may be necessary for each of fiscal years 1999 through 2003.

(Pub. L. 93–112, title VI, §628, as added Pub. L. 105–220, title IV, §409, Aug. 7, 1998, 112 Stat. 1217; amended Pub. L. 105–277, div. A, §101(f) [title VIII, §402(b)(19)], Oct. 21, 1998, 112 Stat. 2681–337, 2681–414.)

PRIOR PROVISIONS

Provisions similar to this section were contained in section 795q of this title prior to the general amendment of this subchapter by Pub. L. 105–220.

Prior sections 795n to 795r were omitted in the general amendment of this subchapter by Pub. L. 105–220.

Section 795n, Pub. L. 93–112, title VI, §635, as added Pub. L. 102–569, title VI, §621(a), Oct. 29, 1992, 106 Stat. 4440, related to State plans. See section 795k of this title.

Another prior section 795n, Pub. L. 93–112, title VI, §635, as added Pub. L. 99–506, title VII, §704(a)(1), Oct. 21, 1986, 100 Stat. 1836; amended Pub. L. 100–630, title II, §207(g), Nov. 7, 1988, 102 Stat. 3314, related to availability and comparability of services under former part C of this subchapter, prior to repeal by Pub. L. 102–569, §621(a).

Section 795*o*, Pub. L. 93–112, title VI, §636, as added Pub. L. 102–569, title VI, §621(a), Oct. 29, 1992, 106 Stat. 4442, related to collection of client information. See section 795*l* of this title.

Another prior section 795*o*, Pub. L. 93–112, title VI, §636, as added Pub. L. 99–506, title VII, §704(a)(1), Oct. 21, 1986, 100 Stat. 1836, related to collection of client information, prior to repeal by Pub. L. 102–569, §621(a).

Section 795p, Pub. L. 93–112, title VI, §637, as added Pub. L. 102–569, title VI, §621(a), Oct. 29, 1992, 106 Stat. 4442, contained savings provision. See section 795m of this title.

Another prior section 795p, Pub. L. 93–112, title VI, §637, as added Pub. L. 99–506, title VII, §704(a)(1), Oct. 21, 1986, 100 Stat. 1837, contained a savings provision not prohibiting a State from carrying out post-employment services leading to supported employment, prior to repeal by Pub. L. 102–569, §621(a).

Section 795q, Pub. L. 93–112, title VI, §638, as added Pub. L. 102–569, title VI, §621(a), Oct. 29, 1992, 106 Stat. 4442, authorized appropriations.

Another prior section 795q, Pub. L. 93–112, title VI, §638, as added Pub. L. 99–506, title VII, §704(a)(1), Oct. 21, 1986, 100 Stat. 1837; amended Pub. L. 100–630, title II, §207(h), Nov. 7, 1988, 102 Stat. 3314; Pub. L. 102–52, §7(c), June 6, 1991, 105 Stat. 262, authorized appropriations for fiscal years 1987 to 1992, prior to repeal by Pub. L. 102–569, §621(a).

Section 795r, Pub. L. 93–112, title VI, §641, formerly §622, as added Pub. L. 95–602, title II, §201, Nov. 6, 1978, 92 Stat. 2994; amended Pub. L. 99–506, title I, §103(d)(2)(C), Oct. 21, 1986, 100 Stat. 1810; Pub. L. 100–630, title II, §207(c), Nov. 7, 1988, 102 Stat. 3313; renumbered §641 and amended Pub. L. 102–569, title I, §102(p)(39), title VI, §612(a)(2), (3), (b), Oct. 29, 1992, 106 Stat. 4361, 4438, related to business opportunities for individuals with disabilities.

AMENDMENTS

1998—Pub. L. 105–277 made technical amendment to section designation and catchline in original.

SUBCHAPTER VII—INDEPENDENT LIVING SERVICES AND CENTERS FOR INDEPENDENT LIVING

CODIFICATION

Title VII of the Rehabilitation Act of 1973, comprising this subchapter, was originally added to Pub. L. 93–112 by Pub. L. 102–569, title VII, §701(2), Oct. 29, 1992, 106 Stat. 4443, and amended by Pub. L. 103–73, Aug. 11, 1993, 107 Stat. 718. Title VII is shown herein, however, as having been added by Pub. L. 105–220, title IV, §410, Aug. 7, 1998, 112 Stat. 1217, without reference to those intervening amendments because of the extensive revision of title VII by Pub. L. 105–220.

PART A—INDIVIDUALS WITH SIGNIFICANT DISABILITIES

SUBPART 1—GENERAL PROVISIONS

§796. Purpose

The purpose of this part is to promote a philosophy of independent living, including a philosophy of consumer control, peer support, self-help, self-determination, equal access, and individual and system advocacy, in order to maximize the leadership, empowerment, independence, and productivity of individuals with disabilities, and the integration and full inclusion of individuals with disabilities into the mainstream of American society, by—

(1) providing financial assistance to States for providing, expanding, and improving the provision of independent living services;

(2) providing financial assistance to develop and support statewide networks of centers for independent living; and

(3) providing financial assistance to States for improving working relationships among State independent living rehabilitation service programs, centers for independent living, Statewide Independent Living Councils established under section 796d of this title, State vocational rehabilitation programs receiving assistance under subchapter I of this chapter, State programs of supported employment services receiving assistance under part B of subchapter VI of this chapter, client assistance programs receiving assistance under section 732 of this title, programs funded under other subchapters of this chapter, programs funded under other Federal law, and programs funded through non-Federal sources.

(Pub. L. 93–112, title VII, §701, as added Pub. L. 105–220, title IV, §410, Aug. 7, 1998, 112 Stat. 1217.)

PRIOR PROVISIONS

A prior section 796, Pub. L. 93–112, title VII, §701, as added Pub. L. 102–569, title VII, §701(2), Oct. 29, 1992, 106 Stat. 4443; amended Pub. L. 103–73, title I, §114(a), Aug. 11, 1993, 107 Stat. 728, related to purpose of program to provide assistance for independent living for individuals with severe disabilities, prior to the general amendment of this subchapter by Pub. L. 105–220.

Another prior section 796, Pub. L. 93–112, title VII, §701, as added Pub. L. 95–602, title III, §301, Nov. 6, 1978, 92 Stat. 2995, provided Congressional statement of purpose of former subchapter VII, prior to repeal by Pub. L. 102–569, §701(1).

§796a. Definitions

As used in this part:

(1) Center for independent living

The term "center for independent living" means a consumer-controlled, community-based, cross-disability, nonresidential private nonprofit agency that—

(A) is designed and operated within a local community by individuals with disabilities; and

(B) provides an array of independent living services.

(2) Consumer control

The term "consumer control" means, with respect to a center for independent living, that the center vests power and authority in individuals with disabilities.

(Pub. L. 93–112, title VII, § 702, as added Pub. L. 105–220, title IV, § 410, Aug. 7, 1998, 112 Stat. 1218.)

PRIOR PROVISIONS

A prior section 796a, Pub. L. 93–112, title VII, § 702, as added Pub. L. 102–569, title VII, § 701(2), Oct. 29, 1992, 106 Stat. 4443, defined terms "center for independent living" and "consumer control", prior to the general amendment of this subchapter by Pub. L. 105–220.

Another prior section 796a, Pub. L. 93–112, title VII, § 702, as added Pub. L. 95–602, title III, § 301, Nov. 6, 1978, 92 Stat. 2995; amended Pub. L. 99–506, title I, § 103(d)(2)(A), (C), title VIII, § 801, title X, §§ 1001(g)(1), 1002(h), Oct. 21, 1986, 100 Stat. 1810, 1837, 1843, 1844; Pub. L. 100–630, title II, § 208(a), Nov. 7, 1988, 102 Stat. 3314, provided eligibility requirements and definition of "comprehensive services for independent living", prior to repeal by Pub. L. 102–569, § 701(1).

§ 796b. Eligibility for receipt of services

Services may be provided under this part to any individual with a significant disability, as defined in section 705(21)(B) of this title.

(Pub. L. 93–112, title VII, § 703, as added Pub. L. 105–220, title IV, § 410, Aug. 7, 1998, 112 Stat. 1218.)

PRIOR PROVISIONS

A prior section 796b, Pub. L. 93–112, title VII, § 703, as added Pub. L. 102–569, title VII, § 701(2), Oct. 29, 1992, 106 Stat. 4444, related to eligibility for receipt of services, prior to the general amendment of this subchapter by Pub. L. 105–220.

Another prior section 796b, Pub. L. 93–112, title VII, § 703, as added Pub. L. 95–602, title III, § 301, Nov. 6, 1978, 92 Stat. 2996; amended Pub. L. 99–506, title X, § 1001(g)(2), Oct. 21, 1986, 100 Stat. 1843; Pub. L. 100–630, title II, § 208(b), Nov. 7, 1988, 102 Stat. 3314, related to State allotments for comprehensive services for independent living, prior to repeal by Pub. L. 102–569, § 701(1).

§ 796c. State plan

(a) In general

(1) Requirement

To be eligible to receive financial assistance under this part, a State shall submit to the Commissioner, and obtain approval of, a State plan containing such provisions as the Commissioner may require, including, at a minimum, the provisions required in this section.

(2) Joint development

The plan under paragraph (1) shall be jointly developed and signed by—

(A) the director of the designated State unit; and

(B) the chairperson of the Statewide Independent Living Council, acting on behalf of and at the direction of the Council.

(3) Periodic review and revision

The plan shall provide for the review and revision of the plan, not less than once every 3 years, to ensure the existence of appropriate planning, financial support and coordination, and other assistance to appropriately address, on a statewide and comprehensive basis, needs in the State for—

(A) the provision of State independent living services;

(B) the development and support of a statewide network of centers for independent living; and

(C) working relationships between—

(i) programs providing independent living services and independent living centers; and

(ii) the vocational rehabilitation program established under subchapter I of this chapter, and other programs providing services for individuals with disabilities.

(4) Date of submission

The State shall submit the plan to the Commissioner 90 days before the completion date of the preceding plan. If a State fails to submit such a plan that complies with the requirements of this section, the Commissioner may withhold financial assistance under this part until such time as the State submits such a plan.

(b) Statewide Independent Living Council

The plan shall provide for the establishment of a Statewide Independent Living Council in accordance with section 796d of this title.

(c) Designation of State unit

The plan shall designate the designated State unit of such State as the agency that, on behalf of the State, shall—

(1) receive, account for, and disburse funds received by the State under this part based on the plan;

(2) provide administrative support services for a program under subpart 2, and a program under subpart 3 in a case in which the program is administered by the State under section 796f–2 of this title;

(3) keep such records and afford such access to such records as the Commissioner finds to be necessary with respect to the programs; and

(4) submit such additional information or provide such assurances as the Commissioner may require with respect to the programs.

(d) Objectives

The plan shall—

(1) specify the objectives to be achieved under the plan and establish timelines for the achievement of the objectives; and

(2) explain how such objectives are consistent with and further the purpose of this part.

(e) Independent living services

The plan shall provide that the State will provide independent living services under this part to individuals with significant disabilities, and will provide the services to such an individual in accordance with an independent living plan mutually agreed upon by an appropriate staff member of the service provider and the individual, unless the individual signs a waiver stating that such a plan is unnecessary.

(f) Scope and arrangements

The plan shall describe the extent and scope of independent living services to be provided under this part to meet such objectives. If the State makes arrangements, by grant or contract, for providing such services, such arrangements shall be described in the plan.

(g) Network

The plan shall set forth a design for the establishment of a statewide network of centers for independent living that comply with the standards and assurances set forth in section 796f–4 of this title.

(h) Centers

In States in which State funding for centers for independent living equals or exceeds the amount of funds allotted to the State under subpart 3, as provided in section 796f–2 of this title, the plan shall include policies, practices, and procedures governing the awarding of grants to centers for independent living and oversight of such centers consistent with section 796f–2 of this title.

(i) Cooperation, coordination, and working relationships among various entities

The plan shall set forth the steps that will be taken to maximize the cooperation, coordination, and working relationships among—

(1) the independent living rehabilitation service program, the Statewide Independent Living Council, and centers for independent living; and

(2) the designated State unit, other State agencies represented on such Council, other councils that address the needs of specific disability populations and issues, and other public and private entities determined to be appropriate by the Council.

(j) Coordination of services

The plan shall describe how services funded under this part will be coordinated with, and complement, other services, in order to avoid unnecessary duplication with other Federal, State, and local programs.

(k) Coordination between Federal and State sources

The plan shall describe efforts to coordinate Federal and State funding for centers for independent living and independent living services.

***(l)* Outreach**

With respect to services and centers funded under this part, the plan shall set forth steps to be taken regarding outreach to populations that are unserved or underserved by programs under this subchapter, including minority groups and urban and rural populations.

(m) Requirements

The plan shall provide satisfactory assurances that all recipients of financial assistance under this part will—

(1) notify all individuals seeking or receiving services under this part about the availability of the client assistance program under section 732 of this title, the purposes of the services provided under such program, and how to contact such program;

(2) take affirmative action to employ and advance in employment qualified individuals with disabilities on the same terms and conditions required with respect to the employment of such individuals under the provisions of section 793 of this title;

(3) adopt such fiscal control and fund accounting procedures as may be necessary to ensure the proper disbursement of and accounting for funds paid to the State under this part;

(4)(A) maintain records that fully disclose—

(i) the amount and disposition by such recipient of the proceeds of such financial assistance;

(ii) the total cost of the project or undertaking in connection with which such financial assistance is given or used; and

(iii) the amount of that portion of the cost of the project or undertaking supplied by other sources;

(B) maintain such other records as the Commissioner determines to be appropriate to facilitate an effective audit;

(C) afford such access to records maintained under subparagraphs (A) and (B) as the Commissioner determines to be appropriate; and

(D) submit such reports with respect to such records as the Commissioner determines to be appropriate;

(5) provide access to the Commissioner and the Comptroller General or any of their duly authorized representatives, for the purpose of conducting audits and examinations, of any books, documents, papers, and records of the recipients that are pertinent to the financial assistance received under this part; and

(6) provide for public hearings regarding the contents of the plan during both the formulation and review of the plan.

(n) Evaluation

The plan shall establish a method for the periodic evaluation of the effectiveness of the plan in meeting the objectives established in subsection (d) of this section, including evaluation of satisfaction by individuals with disabilities.

(Pub. L. 93–112, title VII, §704, as added Pub. L. 105–220, title IV, §410, Aug. 7, 1998, 112 Stat. 1218.)

PRIOR PROVISIONS

A prior section 796c, Pub. L. 93–112, title VII, §704, as added Pub. L. 102–569, title VII, §701(2), Oct. 29, 1992, 106 Stat. 4444; amended Pub. L. 103–73, title I, §114(b), Aug. 11, 1993, 107 Stat. 728, related to State plans, prior to the general amendment of this subchapter by Pub. L. 105–220.

Another prior section 796c, Pub. L. 93–112, title VII, §701, as added Pub. L. 95–602, title III, §301, Nov. 6, 1978, 92 Stat. 2997; amended Pub. L. 100–630, title II, §208(c), Nov. 7, 1988, 102 Stat. 3314, related to payments to States from allotments to pay Federal share of expenditures, prior to repeal by Pub. L. 102–569, §701(1).

§796d. Statewide Independent Living Council

(a) Establishment

To be eligible to receive financial assistance under this part, each State shall establish a

Statewide Independent Living Council (referred to in this section as the "Council"). The Council shall not be established as an entity within a State agency.

(b) Composition and appointment

(1) Appointment

Members of the Council shall be appointed by the Governor or, in the case of a State that, under State law, vests authority for the administration of the activities carried out under this chapter in an entity other than the Governor (such as one or more houses of the State legislature or an independent board), the chief officer of that entity. The appointing authority shall select members after soliciting recommendations from representatives of organizations representing a broad range of individuals with disabilities and organizations interested in individuals with disabilities.

(2) Composition

The Council shall include—

(A) at least one director of a center for independent living chosen by the directors of centers for independent living within the State;

(B) as ex officio, nonvoting members—

(i) a representative from the designated State unit; and

(ii) representatives from other State agencies that provide services for individuals with disabilities; and

(C) in a State in which one or more projects are carried out under section 741 of this title, at least one representative of the directors of the projects.

(3) Additional members

The Council may include—

(A) other representatives from centers for independent living;

(B) parents and guardians of individuals with disabilities;

(C) advocates of and for individuals with disabilities;

(D) representatives from private businesses;

(E) representatives from organizations that provide services for individuals with disabilities; and

(F) other appropriate individuals.

(4) Qualifications

(A) In general

The Council shall be composed of members—

(i) who provide statewide representation;

(ii) who represent a broad range of individuals with disabilities from diverse backgrounds;

(iii) who are knowledgeable about centers for independent living and independent living services; and

(iv) a majority of whom are persons who are—

(I) individuals with disabilities described in section 705(20)(B) of this title; and

(II) not employed by any State agency or center for independent living.

(B) Voting members

A majority of the voting members of the Council shall be—

(i) individuals with disabilities described in section 705(20)(B) of this title; and

(ii) not employed by any State agency or center for independent living.

(5) Chairperson

(A) In general

Except as provided in subparagraph (B), the Council shall select a chairperson from among the voting membership of the Council.

(B) Designation by chief executive officer

In States in which the Governor does not have veto power pursuant to State law, the appointing authority described in paragraph (3) shall designate a voting member of the Council to serve as the chairperson of the Council or shall require the Council to so designate such a voting member.

(6) Terms of appointment

(A) Length of term

Each member of the Council shall serve for a term of 3 years, except that—

(i) a member appointed to fill a vacancy occurring prior to the expiration of the term for which a predecessor was appointed, shall be appointed for the remainder of such term; and

(ii) the terms of service of the members initially appointed shall be (as specified by the appointing authority described in paragraph (3)) for such fewer number of years as will provide for the expiration of terms on a staggered basis.

(B) Number of terms

No member of the Council may serve more than two consecutive full terms.

(7) Vacancies

(A) In general

Except as provided in subparagraph (B), any vacancy occurring in the membership of the Council shall be filled in the same manner as the original appointment. The vacancy shall not affect the power of the remaining members to execute the duties of the Council.

(B) Delegation

The appointing authority described in paragraph (3) may delegate the authority to fill such a vacancy to the remaining voting members of the Council after making the original appointment.

(c) Duties

The Council shall—

(1) jointly develop and sign (in conjunction with the designated State unit) the State plan required in section 796c of this title;

(2) monitor, review, and evaluate the implementation of the State plan;

(3) coordinate activities with the State Rehabilitation Council established under section 725 of this title, if the State has such a Council, or the commission described in section

721(a)(21)(A) of this title, if the State has such a commission, and councils that address the needs of specific disability populations and issues under other Federal law;

(4) ensure that all regularly scheduled meetings of the Statewide Independent Living Council are open to the public and sufficient advance notice is provided; and

(5) submit to the Commissioner such periodic reports as the Commissioner may reasonably request, and keep such records, and afford such access to such records, as the Commissioner finds necessary to verify such reports.

(d) Hearings and forums

The Council is authorized to hold such hearings and forums as the Council may determine to be necessary to carry out the duties of the Council.

(e) Plan

(1) In general

The Council shall prepare, in conjunction with the designated State unit, a plan for the provision of such resources, including such staff and personnel, as may be necessary and sufficient to carry out the functions of the Council under this section, with funds made available under this part, and under section 730 of this title (consistent with section 721(a)(18) of this title), and from other public and private sources. The resource plan shall, to the maximum extent possible, rely on the use of resources in existence during the period of implementation of the plan.

(2) Supervision and evaluation

Each Council shall, consistent with State law, supervise and evaluate such staff and other personnel as may be necessary to carry out the functions of the Council under this section.

(3) Conflict of interest

While assisting the Council in carrying out its duties, staff and other personnel shall not be assigned duties by the designated State agency or any other agency or office of the State, that would create a conflict of interest.

(f) Compensation and expenses

The Council may use such resources to reimburse members of the Council for reasonable and necessary expenses of attending Council meetings and performing Council duties (including child care and personal assistance services), and to pay compensation to a member of the Council, if such member is not employed or must forfeit wages from other employment, for each day the member is engaged in performing Council duties.

(Pub. L. 93–112, title VII, § 705, as added Pub. L. 105–220, title IV, § 410, Aug. 7, 1998, 112 Stat. 1220; amended Pub. L. 105–277, div. A, § 101(f) [title VIII, § 402(c)(7)], Oct. 21, 1998, 112 Stat. 2681–337, 2681–416.)

PRIOR PROVISIONS

A prior section 796d, Pub. L. 93–112, title VII, § 705, as added Pub. L. 102–569, title VII, § 701(2), Oct. 29, 1992, 106 Stat. 4446; amended Pub. L. 103–73, title I, § 114(c), Aug. 11, 1993, 107 Stat. 728, related to Statewide Independent Living Councils, prior to the general amendment of this subchapter by Pub. L. 105–220.

Another prior section 796d, Pub. L. 93–112, title VII, § 705, as added Pub. L. 95–602, title III, § 301, Nov. 6, 1978, 92 Stat. 2997; amended Pub. L. 99–506, title I, § 103(d)(2)(B), (C), (h)(2), title VIII, § 802, title X, § 1001(g)(3), Oct. 21, 1986, 100 Stat. 1810, 1811, 1837, 1843; Pub. L. 100–630, title II, § 208(d), Nov. 7, 1988, 102 Stat. 3314; Pub. L. 102–119, § 26(e), Oct. 7, 1991, 105 Stat. 607, related to State plans for providing comprehensive services for independent living, prior to repeal by Pub. L. 102–569, § 701(1).

AMENDMENTS

1998—Subsec. (b)(1). Pub. L. 105–277, § 101(f) [title VIII, § 402(c)(7)(A)], in first sentence, substituted "by the Governor or, in the case of a State that, under State law, vests authority for the administration of the activities carried out under this chapter in an entity other than the Governor (such as one or more houses of the State legislature or an independent board), the chief officer of that entity" for "by the Governor" and, in second sentence, substituted "The appointing authority" for "The Governor".

Subsec. (b)(5)(B). Pub. L. 105–277, § 101(f) [title VIII, § 402(c)(7)(B)], substituted "chief executive officer" for "Governor" in heading and "appointing authority described in paragraph (3) shall" for "Governor shall" in text.

Subsec. (b)(6)(A)(ii), (7)(B). Pub. L. 105–277, § 101(f) [title VIII, § 402(c)(7)(C)], substituted "appointing authority described in paragraph (3)" for "Governor".

§ 796d–1. Responsibilities of Commissioner

(a) Approval of State plans

(1) In general

The Commissioner shall approve any State plan submitted under section 796c of this title that the Commissioner determines meets the requirements of section 796c of this title, and shall disapprove any such plan that does not meet such requirements, as soon as practicable after receiving the plan. Prior to such disapproval, the Commissioner shall notify the State of the intention to disapprove the plan, and shall afford such State reasonable notice and opportunity for a hearing.

(2) Procedures

(A) In general

Except as provided in subparagraph (B), the provisions of subsections (c) and (d) of section 727 of this title shall apply to any State plan submitted to the Commissioner under section 796c of this title.

(B) Application

For purposes of the application described in subparagraph (A), all references in such provisions—

(i) to the Secretary shall be deemed to be references to the Commissioner; and

(ii) to section 721 of this title shall be deemed to be references to section 796c of this title.

(b) Indicators

Not later than October 1, 1993, the Commissioner shall develop and publish in the Federal Register indicators of minimum compliance consistent with the standards set forth in section 796f–4 of this title.

(c) Onsite compliance reviews

(1) Reviews

The Commissioner shall annually conduct onsite compliance reviews of at least 15 percent of the centers for independent living that receive funds under section 796f–1 of this title and shall periodically conduct such a review of each such center. The Commissioner shall annually conduct onsite compliance reviews of at least one-third of the designated State units that receive funding under section 796f–2 of this title, and, to the extent necessary to determine the compliance of such a State unit with subsections (f) and (g) of section 796f–2 of this title, centers that receive funding under section 796f–2 of this title in such State. The Commissioner shall select the centers and State units described in this paragraph for review on a random basis.

(2) Qualifications of employees conducting reviews

The Commissioner shall—

(A) to the maximum extent practicable, carry out such a review by using employees of the Department who are knowledgeable about the provision of independent living services;

(B) ensure that the employee of the Department with responsibility for supervising such a review shall have such knowledge; and

(C) ensure that at least one member of a team conducting such a review shall be an individual who—

(i) is not a government employee; and

(ii) has experience in the operation of centers for independent living.

(d) Reports

The Commissioner shall include, in the annual report required under section 710 of this title, information on the extent to which centers for independent living receiving funds under subpart 3 have complied with the standards and assurances set forth in section 796f–4 of this title. The Commissioner may identify individual centers for independent living in the analysis. The Commissioner shall report the results of onsite compliance reviews, identifying individual centers for independent living and other recipients of assistance under this part.

(Pub. L. 93–112, title VII, § 706, as added Pub. L. 105–220, title IV, § 410, Aug. 7, 1998, 112 Stat. 1223.)

PRIOR PROVISIONS

A prior section 796d–1, Pub. L. 93–112, title VII, § 706, as added Pub. L. 102–569, title VII, § 701(2), Oct. 29, 1992, 106 Stat. 4448; amended Pub. L. 103–73, title I, § 114(d), Aug. 11, 1993, 107 Stat. 729, related to responsibilities of Commissioner, prior to the general amendment of this subchapter by Pub. L. 105–220.

Another prior section 796d–1, Pub. L. 93–112, title VII, § 706, as added Pub. L. 99–506, title VIII, § 803(a), Oct. 21, 1986, 100 Stat. 1837; amended Pub. L. 100–630, title II, § 208(e), Nov. 7, 1988, 102 Stat. 3314, provided for a State Independent Living Council, prior to repeal by Pub. L. 102–569, § 701(1).

SUBPART 2—INDEPENDENT LIVING SERVICES

§ 796e. Allotments

(a) In general

(1) States

(A) Population basis

Except as provided in subparagraphs (B) and (C), from sums appropriated for each fiscal year to carry out this subpart, the Commissioner shall make an allotment to each State whose State plan has been approved under section 796d–1 of this title of an amount bearing the same ratio to such sums as the population of the State bears to the population of all States.

(B) Maintenance of 1992 amounts

Subject to the availability of appropriations to carry out this subpart, the amount of any allotment made under subparagraph (A) to a State for a fiscal year shall not be less than the amount of an allotment made to the State for fiscal year 1992 under part A of this subchapter, as in effect on the day before October 29, 1992.

(C) Minimums

Subject to the availability of appropriations to carry out this subpart, and except as provided in subparagraph (B), the allotment to any State under subparagraph (A) shall be not less than $275,000 or ⅓ of 1 percent of the sums made available for the fiscal year for which the allotment is made, whichever is greater, and the allotment of any State under this section for any fiscal year that is less than $275,000 or ⅓ of 1 percent of such sums shall be increased to the greater of the two amounts.

(2) Certain territories

(A) In general

For the purposes of paragraph (1)(C), Guam, American Samoa, the United States Virgin Islands, and the Commonwealth of the Northern Mariana Islands shall not be considered to be States.

(B) Allotment

Each jurisdiction described in subparagraph (A) shall be allotted under paragraph (1)(A) not less than ⅛ of 1 percent of the amounts made available for purposes of this subpart for the fiscal year for which the allotment is made.

(3) Adjustment for inflation

For any fiscal year, beginning in fiscal year 1999, in which the total amount appropriated to carry out this subpart exceeds the total amount appropriated to carry out this subpart for the preceding fiscal year, the Commissioner shall increase the minimum allotment under paragraph (1)(C) by a percentage that shall not exceed the percentage increase in the total amount appropriated to carry out this subpart between the preceding fiscal year and the fiscal year involved.

(b) Proportional reduction

To provide allotments to States in accordance with subsection (a)(1)(B) of this section, to provide minimum allotments to States (as increased under subsection (a)(3) of this section) under subsection (a)(1)(C) of this section, or to provide minimum allotments to States under subsection (a)(2)(B) of this section, the Commissioner shall proportionately reduce the allotments of the remaining States under subsection (a)(1)(A) of this section, with such adjustments as may be necessary to prevent the allotment of any such remaining State from being reduced to less than the amount required by subsection (a)(1)(B) of this section.

(c) Reallotment

Whenever the Commissioner determines that any amount of an allotment to a State for any fiscal year will not be expended by such State in carrying out the provisions of this subpart, the Commissioner shall make such amount available for carrying out the provisions of this subpart to one or more of the States that the Commissioner determines will be able to use additional amounts during such year for carrying out such provisions. Any amount made available to a State for any fiscal year pursuant to the preceding sentence shall, for the purposes of this section, be regarded as an increase in the allotment of the State (as determined under the preceding provisions of this section) for such year.

(Pub. L. 93–112, title VII, § 711, as added Pub. L. 105–220, title IV, § 410, Aug. 7, 1998, 112 Stat. 1224.)

REFERENCES IN TEXT

Part A of this subchapter, as in effect on the day before October 29, 1992, referred to in subsec. (a)(1)(B), means former part A (§ 796 et seq.) which was included in the repeal of subchapter VII of this chapter by Pub. L. 102–569, title VII, § 701(1), Oct. 29, 1992, 106 Stat. 4443.

PRIOR PROVISIONS

A prior section 796e, Pub. L. 93–112, title VII, § 711, as added Pub. L. 102–569, title VII, § 701(2), Oct. 29, 1992, 106 Stat. 4450; amended Pub. L. 103–73, title I, § 114(e), Aug. 11, 1993, 107 Stat. 729, related to allotments to provide independent living services, prior to the general amendment of this subchapter by Pub. L. 105–220.

Another prior section 796e, Pub. L. 93–112, title VII, § 711, as added Pub. L. 95–602, title III, § 301, Nov. 6, 1978, 92 Stat. 2998; amended Pub. L. 98–221, title I, § 171, Feb. 22, 1984, 98 Stat. 30; Pub. L. 99–506, title I, § 103(d)(2)(C), title VIII, §§ 804(a)(1), (b), (c), 805, Oct. 21, 1986, 100 Stat. 1810, 1838, 1839; Pub. L. 100–630, title II, § 208(f), Nov. 7, 1988, 102 Stat. 3314, related to establishment and operation of independent living centers, prior to repeal by Pub. L. 102–569, § 701(1).

§ 796e–1. Payments to States from allotments

(a) Payments

From the allotment of each State for a fiscal year under section 796e of this title, the State shall be paid the Federal share of the expenditures incurred during such year under its State plan approved under section 796d–1 of this title. Such payments may be made (after necessary adjustments on account of previously made overpayments or underpayments) in advance or by way of reimbursement, and in such installments and on such conditions as the Commissioner may determine.

(b) Federal share

(1) In general

The Federal share with respect to any State for any fiscal year shall be 90 percent of the expenditures incurred by the State during such year under its State plan approved under section 796d–1 of this title.

(2) Non-Federal share

The non-Federal share of the cost of any project that receives assistance through an allotment under this subpart may be provided in cash or in kind, fairly evaluated, including plant, equipment, or services.

(Pub. L. 93–112, title VII, § 712, as added Pub. L. 105–220, title IV, § 410, Aug. 7, 1998, 112 Stat. 1225.)

PRIOR PROVISIONS

A prior section 796e–1, Pub. L. 93–112, title VII, § 712, as added Pub. L. 102–569, title VII, § 701(2), Oct. 29, 1992, 106 Stat. 4451; amended Pub. L. 103–73, title I, § 114(f), Aug. 11, 1993, 107 Stat. 730, related to payments to States from allotments, prior to the general amendment of this subchapter by Pub. L. 105–220.

§ 796e–2. Authorized uses of funds

The State may use funds received under this subpart to provide the resources described in section 796d(e) of this title, relating to the Statewide Independent Living Council, and may use funds received under this subpart—

(1) to provide independent living services to individuals with significant disabilities;

(2) to demonstrate ways to expand and improve independent living services;

(3) to support the operation of centers for independent living that are in compliance with the standards and assurances set forth in subsections (b) and (c) of section 796f–4 of this title;

(4) to support activities to increase the capacities of public or nonprofit agencies and organizations and other entities to develop comprehensive approaches or systems for providing independent living services;

(5) to conduct studies and analyses, gather information, develop model policies and procedures, and present information, approaches, strategies, findings, conclusions, and recommendations to Federal, State, and local policymakers in order to enhance independent living services for individuals with disabilities;

(6) to train individuals with disabilities and individuals providing services to individuals with disabilities and other persons regarding the independent living philosophy; and

(7) to provide outreach to populations that are unserved or underserved by programs under this subchapter, including minority groups and urban and rural populations.

(Pub. L. 93–112, title VII, § 713, as added Pub. L. 105–220, title IV, § 410, Aug. 7, 1998, 112 Stat. 1226.)

PRIOR PROVISIONS

A prior section 796e–2, Pub. L. 93–112, title VII, § 713, as added Pub. L. 102–569, title VII, § 701(2), Oct. 29, 1992, 106 Stat. 4451; amended Pub. L. 103–73, title I, § 114(g), Aug. 11, 1993, 107 Stat. 730, related to authorized uses of funds, prior to the general amendment of this subchapter by Pub. L. 105–220.

§ 796e–3. Authorization of appropriations

There are authorized to be appropriated to carry out this subpart such sums as may be necessary for each of the fiscal years 1999 through 2003.

(Pub. L. 93–112, title VII, § 714, as added Pub. L. 105–220, title IV, § 410, Aug. 7, 1998, 112 Stat. 1226.)

PRIOR PROVISIONS

A prior section 796e–3, Pub. L. 93–112, title VII, § 714, as added Pub. L. 102–569, title VII, § 701(2), Oct. 29, 1992,

106 Stat. 4452, authorized appropriations, prior to the general amendment of this subchapter by Pub. L. 105–220.

SUBPART 3—CENTERS FOR INDEPENDENT LIVING

§ 796f. Program authorization

(a) In general

From the funds appropriated for fiscal year 1999 and for each subsequent fiscal year to carry out this subpart, the Commissioner shall allot such sums as may be necessary to States and other entities in accordance with subsections (b) through (d) of this section.

(b) Training

(1) Grants; contracts; other arrangements

For any fiscal year in which the funds appropriated to carry out this subpart exceed the funds appropriated to carry out this subpart for fiscal year 1993, the Commissioner shall first reserve from such excess, to provide training and technical assistance to eligible agencies, centers for independent living, and Statewide Independent Living Councils for such fiscal year, not less than 1.8 percent, and not more than 2 percent, of the funds appropriated to carry out this subpart for the fiscal year involved.

(2) Allocation

From the funds reserved under paragraph (1), the Commissioner shall make grants to, and enter into contracts and other arrangements with, entities that have experience in the operation of centers for independent living to provide such training and technical assistance with respect to planning, developing, conducting, administering, and evaluating centers for independent living.

(3) Funding priorities

The Commissioner shall conduct a survey of Statewide Independent Living Councils and centers for independent living regarding training and technical assistance needs in order to determine funding priorities for such grants, contracts, and other arrangements.

(4) Review

To be eligible to receive a grant or enter into a contract or other arrangement under this subsection, such an entity shall submit an application to the Commissioner at such time, in such manner, and containing a proposal to provide such training and technical assistance, and containing such additional information as the Commissioner may require. The Commissioner shall provide for peer review of grant applications by panels that include persons who are not government employees and who have experience in the operation of centers for independent living.

(5) Prohibition on combined funds

No funds reserved by the Commissioner under this subsection may be combined with funds appropriated under any other Act or part of this chapter if the purpose of combining funds is to make a single discretionary grant or a single discretionary payment, unless such funds appropriated under this part are separately identified in such grant or payment and are used for the purposes of this part.

(c) In general

(1) States

(A) Population basis

After the reservation required by subsection (b) of this section has been made, and except as provided in subparagraphs (B) and (C), from the remainder of the amounts appropriated for each such fiscal year to carry out this subpart, the Commissioner shall make an allotment to each State whose State plan has been approved under section 796d–1 of this title of an amount bearing the same ratio to such remainder as the population of the State bears to the population of all States.

(B) Maintenance of 1992 amounts

Subject to the availability of appropriations to carry out this subpart, the amount of any allotment made under subparagraph (A) to a State for a fiscal year shall not be less than the amount of financial assistance received by centers for independent living in the State for fiscal year 1992 under part B of this subchapter, as in effect on the day before October 29, 1992.

(C) Minimums

Subject to the availability of appropriations to carry out this subpart and except as provided in subparagraph (B), for a fiscal year in which the amounts appropriated to carry out this subpart exceed the amounts appropriated for fiscal year 1992 to carry out part B of this subchapter, as in effect on the day before October 29, 1992—

(i) if such excess is not less than $8,000,000, the allotment to any State under subparagraph (A) shall be not less than $450,000 or ⅓ of 1 percent of the sums made available for the fiscal year for which the allotment is made, whichever is greater, and the allotment of any State under this section for any fiscal year that is less than $450,000 or ⅓ of 1 percent of such sums shall be increased to the greater of the 2 amounts;

(ii) if such excess is not less than $4,000,000 and is less than $8,000,000, the allotment to any State under subparagraph (A) shall be not less than $400,000 or ⅓ of 1 percent of the sums made available for the fiscal year for which the allotment is made, whichever is greater, and the allotment of any State under this section for any fiscal year that is less than $400,000 or ⅓ of 1 percent of such sums shall be increased to the greater of the 2 amounts; and

(iii) if such excess is less than $4,000,000, the allotment to any State under subparagraph (A) shall approach, as nearly as possible, the greater of the 2 amounts described in clause (ii).

(2) Certain territories

(A) In general

For the purposes of paragraph (1)(C), Guam, American Samoa, the United States

Virgin Islands, and the Commonwealth of the Northern Mariana Islands shall not be considered to be States.

(B) Allotment

Each jurisdiction described in subparagraph (A) shall be allotted under paragraph (1)(A) not less than 1/8 of 1 percent of the remainder for the fiscal year for which the allotment is made.

(3) Adjustment for inflation

For any fiscal year, beginning in fiscal year 1999, in which the total amount appropriated to carry out this subpart exceeds the total amount appropriated to carry out this subpart for the preceding fiscal year, the Commissioner shall increase the minimum allotment under paragraph (1)(C) by a percentage that shall not exceed the percentage increase in the total amount appropriated to carry out this subpart between the preceding fiscal year and the fiscal year involved.

(4) Proportional reduction

To provide allotments to States in accordance with paragraph (1)(B), to provide minimum allotments to States (as increased under paragraph (3)) under paragraph (1)(C), or to provide minimum allotments to States under paragraph (2)(B), the Commissioner shall proportionately reduce the allotments of the remaining States under paragraph (1)(A), with such adjustments as may be necessary to prevent the allotment of any such remaining State from being reduced to less than the amount required by paragraph (1)(B).

(d) Reallotment

Whenever the Commissioner determines that any amount of an allotment to a State for any fiscal year will not be expended by such State for carrying out the provisions of this subpart, the Commissioner shall make such amount available for carrying out the provisions of this subpart to one or more of the States that the Commissioner determines will be able to use additional amounts during such year for carrying out such provisions. Any amount made available to a State for any fiscal year pursuant to the preceding sentence shall, for the purposes of this section, be regarded as an increase in the allotment of the State (as determined under the preceding provisions of this section) for such year.

(Pub. L. 93–112, title VII, § 721, as added Pub. L. 105–220, title IV, § 410, Aug. 7, 1998, 112 Stat. 1226.)

REFERENCES IN TEXT

Part B of this subchapter, as in effect on the day before October 29, 1992, referred to in subsec. (c)(1)(B), (C), means former part B (§ 796e) which was included in the repeal of subchapter VII of this chapter by Pub. L. 102–569, title VII, § 701(1), Oct. 29, 1992, 106 Stat. 4443.

PRIOR PROVISIONS

A prior section 796f, Pub. L. 93–112, title VII, § 721, as added Pub. L. 102–569, title VII, § 701(2), Oct. 29, 1992, 106 Stat. 4452; amended Pub. L. 103–73, title I, § 114(h), Aug. 11, 1993, 107 Stat. 730, authorized program to assist centers for independent living, prior to the general amendment of this subchapter by Pub. L. 105–220.

Another prior section 796f, Pub. L. 93–112, title VII, § 721, as added Pub. L. 95–602, title III, § 301, Nov. 6, 1978, 92 Stat. 2999; amended Pub. L. 99–506, title X, § 1001(g)(4), Oct. 21, 1986, 100 Stat. 1843; Pub. L. 100–630, title II, § 208(g), Nov. 7, 1988, 102 Stat. 3314, related to establishment of independent living service programs for older blind individuals, prior to repeal by Pub. L. 102–569, § 701(1).

§ 796f–1. Grants to centers for independent living in States in which Federal funding exceeds State funding

(a) Establishment

(1) In general

Unless the director of a designated State unit awards grants under section 796f–2 of this title to eligible agencies in a State for a fiscal year, the Commissioner shall award grants under this section to such eligible agencies for such fiscal year from the amount of funds allotted to the State under subsection (c) or (d) of section 796f of this title for such year.

(2) Grants

The Commissioner shall award such grants, from the amount of funds so allotted, to such eligible agencies for the planning, conduct, administration, and evaluation of centers for independent living that comply with the standards and assurances set forth in section 796f–4 of this title.

(b) Eligible agencies

In any State in which the Commissioner has approved the State plan required by section 796c of this title, the Commissioner may make a grant under this section to any eligible agency that—

(1) has the power and authority to carry out the purpose of this subpart and perform the functions set forth in section 796f–4 of this title within a community and to receive and administer funds under this subpart, funds and contributions from private or public sources that may be used in support of a center for independent living, and funds from other public and private programs;

(2) is determined by the Commissioner to be able to plan, conduct, administer, and evaluate a center for independent living consistent with the standards and assurances set forth in section 796f–4 of this title; and

(3) submits an application to the Commissioner at such time, in such manner, and containing such information as the Commissioner may require.

(c) Existing eligible agencies

In the administration of the provisions of this section, the Commissioner shall award grants to any eligible agency that has been awarded a grant under this subpart by September 30, 1997, unless the Commissioner makes a finding that the agency involved fails to meet program and fiscal standards and assurances set forth in section 796f–4 of this title.

(d) New centers for independent living

(1) In general

If there is no center for independent living serving a region of the State or a region is underserved, and the increase in the allotment of the State is sufficient to support an additional center for independent living in the State, the

Commissioner may award a grant under this section to the most qualified applicant proposing to serve such region, consistent with the provisions in the State plan setting forth the design of the State for establishing a statewide network of centers for independent living.

(2) Selection

In selecting from among applicants for a grant under this section for a new center for independent living, the Commissioner—

(A) shall consider comments regarding the application, if any, by the Statewide Independent Living Council in the State in which the applicant is located;

(B) shall consider the ability of each such applicant to operate a center for independent living based on—

(i) evidence of the need for such a center;

(ii) any past performance of such applicant in providing services comparable to independent living services;

(iii) the plan for satisfying or demonstrated success in satisfying the standards and the assurances set forth in section 796f–4 of this title;

(iv) the quality of key personnel and the involvement of individuals with significant disabilities;

(v) budgets and cost-effectiveness;

(vi) an evaluation plan; and

(vii) the ability of such applicant to carry out the plans; and

(C) shall give priority to applications from applicants proposing to serve geographic areas within each State that are currently unserved or underserved by independent living programs, consistent with the provisions of the State plan submitted under section 796c of this title regarding establishment of a statewide network of centers for independent living.

(3) Current centers

Notwithstanding paragraphs (1) and (2), a center for independent living that receives assistance under subpart 2 for a fiscal year shall be eligible for a grant for the subsequent fiscal year under this subsection.

(e) Order of priorities

The Commissioner shall be guided by the following order of priorities in allocating funds among centers for independent living within a State, to the extent funds are available:

(1) The Commissioner shall support existing centers for independent living, as described in subsection (c) of this section, that comply with the standards and assurances set forth in section 796f–4 of this title, at the level of funding for the previous year.

(2) The Commissioner shall provide for a cost-of-living increase for such existing centers for independent living.

(3) The Commissioner shall fund new centers for independent living, as described in subsection (d) of this section, that comply with the standards and assurances set forth in section 796f–4 of this title.

(f) Nonresidential agencies

A center that provides or manages residential housing after October 1, 1994, shall not be considered to be an eligible agency under this section.

(g) Review

(1) In general

The Commissioner shall periodically review each center receiving funds under this section to determine whether such center is in compliance with the standards and assurances set forth in section 796f–4 of this title. If the Commissioner determines that any center receiving funds under this section is not in compliance with the standards and assurances set forth in section 796f–4 of this title, the Commissioner shall immediately notify such center that it is out of compliance.

(2) Enforcement

The Commissioner shall terminate all funds under this section to such center 90 days after the date of such notification unless the center submits a plan to achieve compliance within 90 days of such notification and such plan is approved by the Commissioner.

(Pub. L. 93–112, title VII, § 722, as added Pub. L. 105–220, title IV, § 410, Aug. 7, 1998, 112 Stat. 1229.)

REFERENCES IN TEXT

This subpart, referred to in subsec. (c), means subpart 3 (§ 796f et seq.) of part A of this subchapter, prior to the general amendment of this subchapter by Pub. L. 105–220, title IV, § 410, Aug. 7, 1998, 112 Stat. 1217.

PRIOR PROVISIONS

A prior section 796f–1, Pub. L. 93–112, title VII, § 722, as added Pub. L. 102–569, title VII, § 701(2), Oct. 29, 1992, 106 Stat. 4456; amended Pub. L. 103–73, title I, § 114(i), Aug. 11, 1993, 107 Stat. 731, related to grants to centers for independent living in States in which Federal funding exceeds State funding, prior to the general amendment of this subchapter by Pub. L. 105–220.

§ 796f–2. Grants to centers for independent living in States in which State funding equals or exceeds Federal funding

(a) Establishment

(1) In general

(A) Initial year

(i) Determination

The director of a designated State unit, as provided in paragraph (2), or the Commissioner, as provided in paragraph (3), shall award grants under this section for an initial fiscal year if the Commissioner determines that the amount of State funds that were earmarked by a State for a preceding fiscal year to support the general operation of centers for independent living meeting the requirements of this subpart equaled or exceeded the amount of funds allotted to the State under subsection (c) or (d) of section 796f of this title for such year.

(ii) Grants

The director or the Commissioner, as appropriate, shall award such grants, from the amount of funds so allotted for the initial fiscal year, to eligible agencies in the State for the planning, conduct, administration, and evaluation of centers for independent living that comply with the standards and assurances set forth in section 796f–4 of this title.

(iii) Regulation

The Commissioner shall by regulation specify the preceding fiscal year with respect to which the Commissioner will make the determinations described in clause (i) and subparagraph (B), making such adjustments as may be necessary to accommodate State funding cycles such as 2-year funding cycles or State fiscal years that do not coincide with the Federal fiscal year.

(B) Subsequent years

For each year subsequent to the initial fiscal year described in subparagraph (A), the director of the designated State unit shall continue to have the authority to award such grants under this section if the Commissioner determines that the State continues to earmark the amount of State funds described in subparagraph (A)(i). If the State does not continue to earmark such an amount for a fiscal year, the State shall be ineligible to make grants under this section after a final year following such fiscal year, as defined in accordance with regulations established by the Commissioner, and for each subsequent fiscal year.

(2) Grants by designated State units

In order for the designated State unit to be eligible to award the grants described in paragraph (1) and carry out this section for a fiscal year with respect to a State, the designated State agency shall submit an application to the Commissioner at such time, and in such manner as the Commissioner may require, including information about the amount of State funds described in paragraph (1) for the preceding fiscal year. If the Commissioner makes a determination described in subparagraph (A)(i) or (B), as appropriate, of paragraph (1), the Commissioner shall approve the application and designate the director of the designated State unit to award the grant and carry out this section.

(3) Grants by Commissioner

If the designated State agency of a State described in paragraph (1) does not submit and obtain approval of an application under paragraph (2), the Commissioner shall award the grant described in paragraph (1) to eligible agencies in the State in accordance with section 796f–1 of this title.

(b) Eligible agencies

In any State in which the Commissioner has approved the State plan required by section 796c of this title, the director of the designated State unit may award a grant under this section to any eligible agency that—

(1) has the power and authority to carry out the purpose of this subpart and perform the functions set forth in section 796f–4 of this title within a community and to receive and administer funds under this subpart, funds and contributions from private or public sources that may be used in support of a center for independent living, and funds from other public and private programs;

(2) is determined by the director to be able to plan, conduct, administer, and evaluate a center for independent living, consistent with the standards and assurances set forth in section 796f–4 of this title; and

(3) submits an application to the director at such time, in such manner, and containing such information as the head of the designated State unit may require.

(c) Existing eligible agencies

In the administration of the provisions of this section, the director of the designated State unit shall award grants under this section to any eligible agency that has been awarded a grant under this subpart by September 30, 1997, unless the director makes a finding that the agency involved fails to comply with the standards and assurances set forth in section 796f–4 of this title.

(d) New centers for independent living

(1) In general

If there is no center for independent living serving a region of the State or the region is unserved or underserved, and the increase in the allotment of the State is sufficient to support an additional center for independent living in the State, the director of the designated State unit may award a grant under this section from among eligible agencies, consistent with the provisions of the State plan under section 796c of this title setting forth the design of the State for establishing a statewide network of centers for independent living.

(2) Selection

In selecting from among eligible agencies in awarding a grant under this subpart for a new center for independent living—

(A) the director of the designated State unit and the chairperson of, or other individual designated by, the Statewide Independent Living Council acting on behalf of and at the direction of the Council, shall jointly appoint a peer review committee that shall rank applications in accordance with the standards and assurances set forth in section 796f–4 of this title and criteria jointly established by such director and such chairperson or individual;

(B) the peer review committee shall consider the ability of each such applicant to operate a center for independent living, and shall recommend an applicant to receive a grant under this section, based on—

(i) evidence of the need for a center for independent living, consistent with the State plan;

(ii) any past performance of such applicant in providing services comparable to independent living services;

(iii) the plan for complying with, or demonstrated success in complying with, the standards and the assurances set forth in section 796f–4 of this title;

(iv) the quality of key personnel of the applicant and the involvement of individuals with significant disabilities by the applicant;

(v) the budgets and cost-effectiveness of the applicant;

(vi) the evaluation plan of the applicant; and

(vii) the ability of such applicant to carry out the plans; and

(C) the director of the designated State unit shall award the grant on the basis of the recommendations of the peer review committee if the actions of the committee are consistent with Federal and State law.

(3) Current centers

Notwithstanding paragraphs (1) and (2), a center for independent living that receives assistance under subpart 2 for a fiscal year shall be eligible for a grant for the subsequent fiscal year under this subsection.

(e) Order of priorities

Unless the director of the designated State unit and the chairperson of the Council or other individual designated by the Council acting on behalf of and at the direction of the Council jointly agree on another order of priority, the director shall be guided by the following order of priorities in allocating funds among centers for independent living within a State, to the extent funds are available:

(1) The director of the designated State unit shall support existing centers for independent living, as described in subsection (c) of this section, that comply with the standards and assurances set forth in section 796f–4 of this title, at the level of funding for the previous year.

(2) The director of the designated State unit shall provide for a cost-of-living increase for such existing centers for independent living.

(3) The director of the designated State unit shall fund new centers for independent living, as described in subsection (d) of this section, that comply with the standards and assurances set forth in section 796f–4 of this title.

(f) Nonresidential agencies

A center that provides or manages residential housing after October 1, 1994, shall not be considered to be an eligible agency under this section.

(g) Review

(1) In general

The director of the designated State unit shall periodically review each center receiving funds under this section to determine whether such center is in compliance with the standards and assurances set forth in section 796f–4 of this title. If the director of the designated State unit determines that any center receiving funds under this section is not in compliance with the standards and assurances set forth in section 796f–4 of this title, the director of the designated State unit shall immediately notify such center that it is out of compliance.

(2) Enforcement

The director of the designated State unit shall terminate all funds under this section to such center 90 days after—

(A) the date of such notification; or

(B) in the case of a center that requests an appeal under subsection (i) of this section, the date of any final decision under subsection (i) of this section,

unless the center submits a plan to achieve compliance within 90 days and such plan is approved by the director, or if appealed, by the Commissioner.

(h) Onsite compliance review

The director of the designated State unit shall annually conduct onsite compliance reviews of at least 15 percent of the centers for independent living that receive funding under this section in the State. Each team that conducts onsite compliance review of centers for independent living shall include at least one person who is not an employee of the designated State agency, who has experience in the operation of centers for independent living, and who is jointly selected by the director of the designated State unit and the chairperson of or other individual designated by the Council acting on behalf of and at the direction of the Council. A copy of this review shall be provided to the Commissioner.

(i) Adverse actions

If the director of the designated State unit proposes to take a significant adverse action against a center for independent living, the center may seek mediation and conciliation to be provided by an individual or individuals who are free of conflicts of interest identified by the chairperson of or other individual designated by the Council. If the issue is not resolved through the mediation and conciliation, the center may appeal the proposed adverse action to the Commissioner for a final decision.

(Pub. L. 93–112, title VII, § 723, as added Pub. L. 105–220, title IV, § 410, Aug. 7, 1998, 112 Stat. 1231.)

REFERENCES IN TEXT

This subpart, referred to in subsec. (c), means subpart 3 (§ 796f et seq.) of part A of this subchapter, prior to the general amendment of this subchapter by Pub. L. 105–220, title IV, § 410, Aug. 7, 1998, 112 Stat. 1217.

PRIOR PROVISIONS

A prior section 796f–2, Pub. L. 93–112, title VII, § 723, as added Pub. L. 102–569, title VII, § 701(2), Oct. 29, 1992, 106 Stat. 4458; amended Pub. L. 103–73, title I, § 114(j), Aug. 11, 1993, 107 Stat. 731, related to grants to centers for independent living in States in which State funding equals or exceeds Federal funding, prior to the general amendment of this subchapter by Pub. L. 105–220.

§ 796f–3. Centers operated by State agencies

A State that receives assistance for fiscal year 1993 with respect to a center in accordance with subsection (a) of this section (as in effect on the day before August 7, 1998) may continue to receive assistance under this subpart for fiscal year 1994 or a succeeding fiscal year if, for such fiscal year—

(1) no nonprofit private agency—

(A) submits an acceptable application to operate a center for independent living for the fiscal year before a date specified by the Commissioner; and

(B) obtains approval of the application under section 796f–1 or 796f–2 of this title; or

(2) after funding all applications so submitted and approved, the Commissioner deter-

mines that funds remain available to provide such assistance.

(Pub. L. 93–112, title VII, § 724, as added Pub. L. 105–220, title IV, § 410, Aug. 7, 1998, 112 Stat. 1234.)

PRIOR PROVISIONS

A prior section 796f–3, Pub. L. 93–112, title VII, § 724, as added Pub. L. 102–569, title VII, § 701(2), Oct. 29, 1992, 106 Stat. 4461; amended Pub. L. 103–73, title I, § 114(k), Aug. 11, 1993, 107 Stat. 731, related to centers operated by State agencies, prior to the general amendment of this subchapter by Pub. L. 105–220.

§ 796f–4. Standards and assurances for centers for independent living

(a) In general

Each center for independent living that receives assistance under this subpart shall comply with the standards set out in subsection (b) of this section and provide and comply with the assurances set out in subsection (c) of this section in order to ensure that all programs and activities under this subpart are planned, conducted, administered, and evaluated in a manner consistent with the purposes of this part and the objective of providing assistance effectively and efficiently.

(b) Standards

(1) Philosophy

The center shall promote and practice the independent living philosophy of—

(A) consumer control of the center regarding decisionmaking, service delivery, management, and establishment of the policy and direction of the center;

(B) self-help and self-advocacy;

(C) development of peer relationships and peer role models; and

(D) equal access of individuals with significant disabilities to society and to all services, programs, activities, resources, and facilities, whether public or private and regardless of the funding source.

(2) Provision of services

The center shall provide services to individuals with a range of significant disabilities. The center shall provide services on a cross-disability basis (for individuals with all different types of significant disabilities, including individuals with significant disabilities who are members of populations that are unserved or underserved by programs under this subchapter). Eligibility for services at any center for independent living shall be determined by the center, and shall not be based on the presence of any one or more specific significant disabilities.

(3) Independent living goals

The center shall facilitate the development and achievement of independent living goals selected by individuals with significant disabilities who seek such assistance by the center.

(4) Community options

The center shall work to increase the availability and improve the quality of community options for independent living in order to facilitate the development and achievement of independent living goals by individuals with significant disabilities.

(5) Independent living core services

The center shall provide independent living core services and, as appropriate, a combination of any other independent living services.

(6) Activities to increase community capacity

The center shall conduct activities to increase the capacity of communities within the service area of the center to meet the needs of individuals with significant disabilities.

(7) Resource development activities

The center shall conduct resource development activities to obtain funding from sources other than this part.

(c) Assurances

The eligible agency shall provide at such time and in such manner as the Commissioner may require, such satisfactory assurances as the Commissioner may require, including satisfactory assurances that—

(1) the applicant is an eligible agency;

(2) the center will be designed and operated within local communities by individuals with disabilities, including an assurance that the center will have a Board that is the principal governing body of the center and a majority of which shall be composed of individuals with significant disabilities;

(3) the applicant will comply with the standards set forth in subsection (b) of this section;

(4) the applicant will establish clear priorities through annual and 3-year program and financial planning objectives for the center, including overall goals or a mission for the center, a work plan for achieving the goals or mission, specific objectives, service priorities, and types of services to be provided, and a description that shall demonstrate how the proposed activities of the applicant are consistent with the most recent 3-year State plan under section 796c of this title;

(5) the applicant will use sound organizational and personnel assignment practices, including taking affirmative action to employ and advance in employment qualified individuals with significant disabilities on the same terms and conditions required with respect to the employment of individuals with disabilities under section 793 of this title;

(6) the applicant will ensure that the majority of the staff, and individuals in decision-making positions, of the applicant are individuals with disabilities;

(7) the applicant will practice sound fiscal management;

(8) the applicant will conduct annual self-evaluations, prepare an annual report, and maintain records adequate to measure performance with respect to the standards, containing information regarding, at a minimum—

(A) the extent to which the center is in compliance with the standards;

(B) the number and types of individuals with significant disabilities receiving services through the center;

(C) the types of services provided through the center and the number of individuals with significant disabilities receiving each type of service;

(D) the sources and amounts of funding for the operation of the center;

(E) the number of individuals with significant disabilities who are employed by, and the number who are in management and decisionmaking positions in, the center; and

(F) a comparison, when appropriate, of the activities of the center in prior years with the activities of the center in the most recent year;

(9) individuals with significant disabilities who are seeking or receiving services at the center will be notified by the center of the existence of, the availability of, and how to contact, the client assistance program;

(10) aggressive outreach regarding services provided through the center will be conducted in an effort to reach populations of individuals with significant disabilities that are unserved or underserved by programs under this subchapter, especially minority groups and urban and rural populations;

(11) staff at centers for independent living will receive training on how to serve such unserved and underserved populations, including minority groups and urban and rural populations;

(12) the center will submit to the Statewide Independent Living Council a copy of its approved grant application and the annual report required under paragraph (8);

(13) the center will prepare and submit a report to the designated State unit or the Commissioner, as the case may be, at the end of each fiscal year that contains the information described in paragraph (8) and information regarding the extent to which the center is in compliance with the standards set forth in subsection (b) of this section; and

(14) an independent living plan described in section 796c(e) of this title will be developed unless the individual who would receive services under the plan signs a waiver stating that such a plan is unnecessary.

(Pub. L. 93–112, title VII, § 725, as added Pub. L. 105–220, title IV, § 410, Aug. 7, 1998, 112 Stat. 1234; amended Pub. L. 105–332, § 5(c), Oct. 31, 1998, 112 Stat. 3127.)

PRIOR PROVISIONS

A prior section 796f–4, Pub. L. 93–112, title VII, § 725, as added Pub. L. 102–569, title VII, § 701(2), Oct. 29, 1992, 106 Stat. 4462; amended Pub. L. 103–73, title I, § 114(*l*), Aug. 11, 1993, 107 Stat. 731, related to standards and assurances for centers for independent living, prior to the general amendment of this subchapter by Pub. L. 105–220.

AMENDMENTS

1998—Subsec. (c)(7). Pub. L. 105–332 substituted "management;" for "management, including making arrangements for an annual independent fiscal audit, notwithstanding section 7502(a)(2)(A) of title 31;".

§ 796f–5. "Eligible agency" defined

As used in this subpart, the term "eligible agency" means a consumer-controlled, community-based, cross-disability, nonresidential private nonprofit agency.

(Pub. L. 93–112, title VII, § 726, as added Pub. L. 105–220, title IV, § 410, Aug. 7, 1998, 112 Stat. 1237.)

PRIOR PROVISIONS

A prior section 796f–5, Pub. L. 93–112, title VII, § 726, as added Pub. L. 102–569, title VII, § 701(2), Oct. 29, 1992, 106 Stat. 4464, defined "eligible agency", prior to the general amendment of this subchapter by Pub. L. 105–220.

§ 796f–6. Authorization of appropriations

There are authorized to be appropriated to carry out this subpart such sums as may be necessary for each of the fiscal years 1999 through 2003.

(Pub. L. 93–112, title VII, § 727, as added Pub. L. 105–220, title IV, § 410, Aug. 7, 1998, 112 Stat. 1237.)

PRIOR PROVISIONS

A prior section 796f–6, Pub. L. 93–112, title VII, § 727, as added Pub. L. 102–569, title VII, § 701(2), Oct. 29, 1992, 106 Stat. 4464, authorized appropriations, prior to the general amendment of this subchapter by Pub. L. 105–220.

Prior sections 796g to 796i were repealed by Pub. L. 102–569, title VII, § 701(1), Oct. 29, 1992, 106 Stat. 4443.

Section 796g, Pub. L. 93–112, title VII, § 731, as added Pub. L. 95–602, title III, § 301, Nov. 6, 1978, 92 Stat. 3000; amended Pub. L. 99–506, title I, § 103(h)(2), Oct. 21, 1986, 100 Stat. 1811; Pub. L. 100–630, title II, § 208(h), Nov. 7, 1988, 102 Stat. 3314, provided for grants to States to establish systems to protect and advocate for rights of individuals with severe handicaps.

Section 796h, Pub. L. 93–112, title VII, § 732, as added Pub. L. 95–602, title III, § 301, Nov. 6, 1978, 92 Stat. 3000; amended Pub. L. 99–506, title I, § 103(d)(2)(C), Oct. 21, 1986, 100 Stat. 1810, related to affirmative action on part of recipients of assistance to employ and advance in employment qualified individuals with handicaps.

Section 796i, Pub. L. 93–112, title VII, § 741, formerly § 731, as added Pub. L. 95–602, title III, § 301, Nov. 6, 1978, 92 Stat. 3001; renumbered § 741 and amended Pub. L. 98–221, title I, § 172(a)(1), (b), Feb. 22, 1984, 98 Stat. 32; Pub. L. 99–506, title VIII, § 806, Oct. 21, 1986, 100 Stat. 1840; Pub. L. 100–630, title II, § 208(i), Nov. 7, 1988, 102 Stat. 3315; Pub. L. 102–52, § 8, June 6, 1991, 105 Stat. 262, provided for appropriations.

PART B—INDEPENDENT LIVING SERVICES FOR OLDER INDIVIDUALS WHO ARE BLIND

§ 796j. "Older individual who is blind" defined

For purposes of this part, the term "older individual who is blind" means an individual age 55 or older whose significant visual impairment makes competitive employment extremely difficult to attain but for whom independent living goals are feasible.

(Pub. L. 93–112, title VII, § 751, as added Pub. L. 105–220, title IV, § 410, Aug. 7, 1998, 112 Stat. 1237.)

PRIOR PROVISIONS

A prior section 796j, Pub. L. 93–112, title VII, § 751, as added Pub. L. 102–569, title VII, § 703(a), Oct. 29, 1992, 106 Stat. 4464, defined "older individual who is blind", prior to the general amendment of this subchapter by Pub. L. 105–220.

§ 796k. Program of grants

(a) In general

(1) Authority for grants

Subject to subsections (b) and (c) of this section, the Commissioner may make grants to

States for the purpose of providing the services described in subsection (d) of this section to older individuals who are blind.

(2) Designated State agency

The Commissioner may not make a grant under this subsection unless the State involved agrees that the grant will be administered solely by the agency described in section 721(a)(2)(A)(i) of this title.

(b) Contingent competitive grants

Beginning with fiscal year 1993, in the case of any fiscal year for which the amount appropriated under section 796*l* of this title is less than $13,000,000, grants made under subsection (a) of this section shall be—

(1) discretionary grants made on a competitive basis to States; or

(2) grants made on a noncompetitive basis to pay for the continuation costs of activities for which a grant was awarded—

(A) under this part; or

(B) under part C of this subchapter, as in effect on the day before October 29, 1992.

(c) Contingent formula grants

(1) In general

In the case of any fiscal year for which the amount appropriated under section 796*l* of this title is equal to or greater than $13,000,000, grants under subsection (a) of this section shall be made only to States and shall be made only from allotments under paragraph (2).

(2) Allotments

For grants under subsection (a) of this section for a fiscal year described in paragraph (1), the Commissioner shall make an allotment to each State in an amount determined in accordance with subsection (j) of this section, and shall make a grant to the State of the allotment made for the State if the State submits to the Commissioner an application in accordance with subsection (i) of this section.

(d) Services generally

The Commissioner may not make a grant under subsection (a) of this section unless the State involved agrees that the grant will be expended only for purposes of—

(1) providing independent living services to older individuals who are blind;

(2) conducting activities that will improve or expand services for such individuals; and

(3) conducting activities to help improve public understanding of the problems of such individuals.

(e) Independent living services

Independent living services for purposes of subsection (d)(1) of this section include—

(1) services to help correct blindness, such as—

(A) outreach services;

(B) visual screening;

(C) surgical or therapeutic treatment to prevent, correct, or modify disabling eye conditions; and

(D) hospitalization related to such services;

(2) the provision of eyeglasses and other visual aids;

(3) the provision of services and equipment to assist an older individual who is blind to become more mobile and more self-sufficient;

(4) mobility training, braille instruction, and other services and equipment to help an older individual who is blind adjust to blindness;

(5) guide services, reader services, and transportation;

(6) any other appropriate service designed to assist an older individual who is blind in coping with daily living activities, including supportive services and rehabilitation teaching services;

(7) independent living skills training, information and referral services, peer counseling, and individual advocacy training; and

(8) other independent living services.

(f) Matching funds

(1) In general

The Commissioner may not make a grant under subsection (a) of this section unless the State involved agrees, with respect to the costs of the program to be carried out by the State pursuant to such subsection, to make available (directly or through donations from public or private entities) non-Federal contributions toward such costs in an amount that is not less than $1 for each $9 of Federal funds provided in the grant.

(2) Determination of amount contributed

Non-Federal contributions required in paragraph (1) may be in cash or in kind, fairly evaluated, including plant, equipment, or services. Amounts provided by the Federal Government, or services assisted or subsidized to any significant extent by the Federal Government, may not be included in determining the amount of such non-Federal contributions.

(g) Certain expenditures of grants

A State may expend a grant under subsection (a) of this section to carry out the purposes specified in subsection (d) of this section through grants to public and nonprofit private agencies or organizations.

(h) Requirement regarding State plan

The Commissioner may not make a grant under subsection (a) of this section unless the State involved agrees that, in carrying out subsection (d)(1) of this section, the State will seek to incorporate into the State plan under section 796c of this title any new methods and approaches relating to independent living services for older individuals who are blind.

(i) Application for grant

(1) In general

The Commissioner may not make a grant under subsection (a) of this section unless an application for the grant is submitted to the Commissioner and the application is in such form, is made in such manner, and contains such agreements, assurances, and information as the Commissioner determines to be necessary to carry out this section (including agreements, assurances, and information with respect to any grants under subsection (j)(4) of this section).

(2) Contents

An application for a grant under this section shall contain—

(A) an assurance that the agency described in subsection (a)(2) of this section will prepare and submit to the Commissioner a report, at the end of each fiscal year, with respect to each project or program the agency operates or administers under this section, whether directly or through a grant or contract, which report shall contain, at a minimum, information on—

(i) the number and types of older individuals who are blind and are receiving services;

(ii) the types of services provided and the number of older individuals who are blind and are receiving each type of service;

(iii) the sources and amounts of funding for the operation of each project or program;

(iv) the amounts and percentages of resources committed to each type of service provided;

(v) data on actions taken to employ, and advance in employment, qualified individuals with significant disabilities, including older individuals who are blind; and

(vi) a comparison, if appropriate, of prior year activities with the activities of the most recent year;

(B) an assurance that the agency will—

(i) provide services that contribute to the maintenance of, or the increased independence of, older individuals who are blind; and

(ii) engage in—

(I) capacity-building activities, including collaboration with other agencies and organizations;

(II) activities to promote community awareness, involvement, and assistance; and

(III) outreach efforts; and

(C) an assurance that the application is consistent with the State plan for providing independent living services required by section 796c of this title.

(j) Amount of formula grant

(1) In general

Subject to the availability of appropriations, the amount of an allotment under subsection (a) of this section for a State for a fiscal year shall be the greater of—

(A) the amount determined under paragraph (2); or

(B) the amount determined under paragraph (3).

(2) Minimum allotment

(A) States

In the case of the several States, the District of Columbia, and the Commonwealth of Puerto Rico, the amount referred to in subparagraph (A) of paragraph (1) for a fiscal year is the greater of—

(i) $225,000; or

(ii) an amount equal to ⅓ of 1 percent of the amount appropriated under section 796*l* of this title for the fiscal year and available for allotments under subsection (a) of this section.

(B) Certain territories

In the case of Guam, American Samoa, the United States Virgin Islands, and the Commonwealth of the Northern Mariana Islands, the amount referred to in subparagraph (A) of paragraph (1) for a fiscal year is $40,000.

(3) Formula

The amount referred to in subparagraph (B) of paragraph (1) for a State for a fiscal year is the product of—

(A) the amount appropriated under section 796*l* of this title and available for allotments under subsection (a) of this section; and

(B) a percentage equal to the quotient of—

(i) an amount equal to the number of individuals residing in the State who are not less than 55 years of age; divided by

(ii) an amount equal to the number of individuals residing in the United States who are not less than 55 years of age.

(4) Disposition of certain amounts

(A) Grants

From the amounts specified in subparagraph (B), the Commissioner may make grants to States whose population of older individuals who are blind has a substantial need for the services specified in subsection (d) of this section relative to the populations in other States of older individuals who are blind.

(B) Amounts

The amounts referred to in subparagraph (A) are any amounts that are not paid to States under subsection (a) of this section as a result of—

(i) the failure of any State to submit an application under subsection (i) of this section;

(ii) the failure of any State to prepare within a reasonable period of time such application in compliance with such subsection; or

(iii) any State informing the Commissioner that the State does not intend to expend the full amount of the allotment made for the State under subsection (a) of this section.

(C) Conditions

The Commissioner may not make a grant under subparagraph (A) unless the State involved agrees that the grant is subject to the same conditions as grants made under subsection (a) of this section.

(Pub. L. 93–112, title VII, § 752, as added Pub. L. 105–220, title IV, § 410, Aug. 7, 1998, 112 Stat. 1237.)

REFERENCES IN TEXT

Part C of this subchapter, as in effect on the day before October 29, 1992, referred to in subsec. (b)(2)(B), means former part C (§ 796f) which was included in the repeal of subchapter VII of this chapter by Pub. L. 102–569, title VII, § 701(1), Oct. 29, 1992, 106 Stat. 4443.

PRIOR PROVISIONS

A prior section 796k, Pub. L. 93–112, title VII, § 752, as added Pub. L. 102–569, title VII, § 703(a), Oct. 29, 1992, 106

Stat. 4465; amended Pub. L. 103–73, title I, § 114(m), Aug. 11, 1993, 107 Stat. 732, authorized grants to provide independent living services for older individuals who are blind, prior to the general amendment of this subchapter by Pub. L. 105–220.

§ 796*l*. Authorization of appropriations

There are authorized to be appropriated to carry out this part such sums as may be necessary for each of the fiscal years 1999 through 2003.

(Pub. L. 93–112, title VII, § 753, as added Pub. L. 105–220, title IV, § 410, Aug. 7, 1998, 112 Stat. 1241.)

PRIOR PROVISIONS

A prior section 796*l*, Pub. L. 93–112, title VII, § 753, as added Pub. L. 102–569, title VII, § 703(a), Oct. 29, 1992, 106 Stat. 4468, authorized appropriations, prior to the general amendment of this subchapter by Pub. L. 105–220.

SUBCHAPTER VIII—SPECIAL DEMONSTRATIONS AND TRAINING PROJECTS

§§ 797 to 797b. Repealed. Pub. L. 105–220, title IV, § 411, Aug. 7, 1998, 112 Stat. 1241

Section 797, Pub. L. 93–112, title VIII, § 801, as added Pub. L. 102–569, title VIII, § 801(a), Oct. 29, 1992, 106 Stat. 4469, authorized appropriations.

Section 797a, Pub. L. 93–112, title VIII, § 802, as added Pub. L. 102–569, title VIII, § 801(a), Oct. 29, 1992, 106 Stat. 4469, authorized grants for various demonstration projects.

Section 797b, Pub. L. 93–112, title VIII, § 803, as added Pub. L. 102–569, title VIII, § 801(a), Oct. 29, 1992, 106 Stat. 4478, authorized grants for training projects.

CHAPTER 17—COMPREHENSIVE EMPLOYMENT AND TRAINING PROGRAMS

CODIFICATION

The Comprehensive Employment and Training Act of 1973, Pub. L. 93–203, Dec. 28, 1973, 87 Stat. 839, as amended by Pub. L. 93–567, Dec. 31, 1974, 88 Stat. 1845; Pub. L. 94–444, Oct. 1, 1976, 90 Stat. 1476; Pub. L. 94–482, Oct. 12, 1976, 90 Stat. 2081; Pub. L. 95–40, June 3, 1977, 91 Stat. 203; Pub. L. 95–44, June 15, 1977, 91 Stat. 220; Pub. L. 95–93, Aug. 5, 1977, 91 Stat. 627, comprised this chapter prior to its complete revision by Pub. L. 95–524, Oct. 27, 1978, 92 Stat. 1909. The Act, Pub. L. 93–203, as amended generally by Pub. L. 95–524, § 2, Oct. 27, 1978, 92 Stat. 1909, was known as the Comprehensive Employment and Training Act, and was set out as having been added by Pub. L. 95–524 without reference to the intervening amendments in view of the extensive revision of the Act's provisions by Pub. L. 95–524.

§§ 801, 802. Repealed. Pub. L. 97–300, title I, § 184(a)(1), Oct. 13, 1982, 96 Stat. 1357

Section 801, Pub. L. 93–203, § 2, as added Pub. L. 95–524, § 2, Oct. 27, 1978, 92 Stat. 1912, set out Congressional statement of purpose in enacting this chapter.

A prior section 801, Pub. L. 93–203, § 2, Dec. 28, 1973, 87 Stat. 839, provided for a Congressional statement of purpose for this chapter, prior to the general revision of Pub. L. 93–203 by Pub. L. 95–524.

Section 802, Pub. L. 93–203, § 3, as added Pub. L. 95–524, § 2, Oct. 27, 1978, 92 Stat. 1912, provided definitions for this chapter.

A prior section 802, Pub. L. 93–203, § 4, Dec. 28, 1973, 87 Stat. 839; Pub. L. 95–44, § 2(a), June 15, 1977, 91 Stat. 220; Pub. L. 95–93, title III, § 302, Aug. 5, 1977, 91 Stat. 650, authorized appropriations for this chapter, prior to the general revision of Pub. L. 93–203 by Pub. L. 95–524.

A prior section 3 of Pub. L. 93–203, Dec. 28, 1973, 87 Stat. 839, provided for transitional provisions and was set out as a note under section 801 of this title, prior to the general revision of Pub. L. 93–203 by Pub. L. 95–524.

Provisions similar to those comprising this section were contained in former section 981 of this title prior to the general revision of Pub. L. 93–203 by Pub. L. 95–524.

A prior section 803, Pub. L. 95–93, title III, § 305, Aug. 5, 1977, 91 Stat. 651, providing for increased participation of veterans in public service employment programs and job training opportunities, was omitted because it was limited to fiscal years 1977 and 1978.

EFFECTIVE DATE OF REPEAL

Pub. L. 97–300, title I, § 184(a), Oct. 13, 1982, 96 Stat. 1357, which provided for the repeal of the Comprehensive Employment and Training Act, this chapter, effective Oct. 13, 1982, was itself repealed by Pub. L. 105–220, title I, § 199(b)(2), (c)(2)(B), Aug. 7, 1998, 112 Stat. 1059, eff. July 1, 2000.

SUBCHAPTER I—ADMINISTRATIVE PROVISIONS

PART A—ORGANIZATIONAL PROVISIONS

§§ 811 to 822. Repealed. Pub. L. 97–300, title I, § 184(a)(1), Oct. 13, 1982, 96 Stat. 1357

Section 811, Pub. L. 93–203, title I, § 101, as added Pub. L. 95–524, § 2, Oct. 27, 1978, 92 Stat. 1917, related to prime sponsors under this chapter.

A prior section 811, Pub. L. 93–203, title I, § 101, Dec. 28, 1973, 87 Stat. 840, provided description of a program to provide comprehensive manpower services, prior to the general revision of Pub. L. 93–203 by Pub. L. 95–524.

Provisions similar to those comprising this section were contained in former section 812 of this title prior to the general revision of Pub. L. 93–203 by Pub. L. 95–524.

Section 812, Pub. L. 93–203, title I, § 102, as added Pub. L. 95–524, § 2, Oct. 27, 1978, 92 Stat. 1918, related to authority of Secretary to provide services.

A prior section 812, Pub. L. 93–203, title I, § 102, Dec. 28, 1973, 87 Stat. 841, related to prime sponsors, prior to the general revision of Pub. L. 93–203, by Pub. L. 95–524.

Provisions similar to those comprising this section were contained in former section 820 of this title prior to the general revision of Pub. L. 93–203 by Pub. L. 95–524.

Section 813, Pub. L. 93–203, title I, § 103, as added Pub. L. 95–524, § 2, Oct. 27, 1978, 92 Stat. 1918, related to submission and contents of a comprehensive employment and training plan.

A prior section 813, Pub. L. 93–203, title I, § 103, Dec. 28, 1973, 87 Stat. 842, provided for allocation of funds with respect to comprehensive manpower services program, prior to the general revision of Pub. L. 93–203 by Pub. L. 95–524.

Provisions similar to those comprising this section were contained in former section 815 of this title prior to the general revision of Pub. L. 93–203 by Pub. L. 95–524.

Section 814, Pub. L. 93–203, title I, § 104, as added Pub. L. 95–524, § 2, Oct. 27, 1978, 92 Stat. 1922, related to review of comprehensive employment and training plans.

A prior section 814, Pub. L. 93–203, title I, § 104, Dec. 28, 1973, 87 Stat. 843, related to establishment of prime sponsor's planning councils, prior to the general revision of Pub. L. 93–203 by Pub. L. 95–524.

Provisions similar to those comprising this section were contained in former section 818 of this title prior to the general revision of Pub. L. 93–203 by Pub. L. 95–524.

Section 815, Pub. L. 93–203, title I, § 105, as added Pub. L. 95–524, § 2, Oct. 27, 1978, 92 Stat. 1925, related to Governor's coordination and special services plan.

A prior section 815, Pub. L. 93–203, title I, § 105, Dec. 28, 1973, 87 Stat. 843; Pub. L. 94–444, § 12(b)(1), Oct. 1, 1976, 90 Stat. 1483, related to conditions for receipt of financial assistance, prior to the general revision of Pub. L. 93–203 by Pub. L. 95–524.

Provisions similar to those comprising this section were contained in former section 816 of this title prior to the general revision of Pub. L. 93–203, by Pub. L. 95–524.

Section 816, Pub. L. 93–203, title I, § 106, as added Pub. L. 95–524, § 2, Oct. 27, 1978, 92 Stat. 1926, related to complaints and sanctions against prime sponsors under this chapter.

A prior section 816, Pub. L. 93–203, title I, § 106, Dec. 28, 1973, 87 Stat. 845; Pub. L. 94–444, § 12(b)(2), Oct. 1, 1976, 90 Stat. 1483, provided for special provisions relating to State prime sponsors, prior to the general revision of Pub. L. 93–203 by Pub. L. 95–524.

Provisions similar to those comprising this section were contained in former section 818 of this title prior to the general revision of Pub. L. 93–203 by Pub. L. 95–524.

Section 817, Pub. L. 93–203, title I, § 107, as added Pub. L. 95–524, § 2, Oct. 27, 1978, 92 Stat. 1929, related to judicial review under this chapter.

A prior section 817, Pub. L. 93–203, title I, § 107, Dec. 28, 1973, 87 Stat. 846; Pub. L. 94–482, title II, § 203(a), Oct. 12, 1976, 90 Stat. 2213; Pub. L. 95–40, § 1(28)(A), June 3, 1977, 91 Stat. 207, related to establishment of a State Manpower Services Council, prior to the general revision of Pub. L. 93–203 by Pub. L. 95–524.

Provisions similar to those comprising this section were contained in former section 819 of this title prior to the general revision of Pub. L. 93–203 by Pub. L. 95–524.

Section 818, Pub. L. 93–203, title I, § 108, as added Pub. L. 95–524, § 2, Oct. 27, 1978, 92 Stat. 1929, authorized the Secretary to reallocate funds under this chapter.

A prior section 818, Pub. L. 93–203, title I, § 108, Dec. 28, 1973, 87 Stat. 847; Pub. L. 93–567, title I, § 101, Dec. 31, 1974, 88 Stat. 1845, provided for review of comprehensive manpower plans, prior to the general revision of Pub. L. 93–203 by Pub. L. 95–524.

Provisions similar to those comprising this section were contained in former section 813 of this title prior to the general revision of Pub. L. 93–203 by Pub. L. 95–524.

Section 819, Pub. L. 93–203, title I, § 109, as added Pub. L. 95–524, § 2, Oct. 27, 1978, 92 Stat. 1930, related to prime sponsor's planning councils.

A prior section 819, Pub. L. 93–203, title I, § 109, Dec. 28, 1973, 87 Stat. 848, provided for judicial review with respect to comprehensive manpower plans, prior to the general revision of Pub. L. 93–203 by Pub. L. 95–524.

Provisions similar to those comprising this section were contained in former section 814 of this title prior to the general revision of Pub. L. 93–203 by Pub. L. 95–524.

Section 820, Pub. L. 93–203, title I, § 110, as added Pub. L. 95–524, § 2, Oct. 27, 1978, 92 Stat. 1930, related to State employment and training councils.

A prior section 820, Pub. L. 93–203, title I, Dec. 28, 1973, 87 Stat. 848, related to authority of the Secretary to provide services, prior to the general revision of Pub. L. 93–203 by Pub. L. 95–524.

Provisions similar to those comprising this section were contained in former section 817 of this title prior to the general revision of Pub. L. 93–203 by Pub. L. 95–524.

Section 821, Pub. L. 93–203, title I, § 111, as added Pub. L. 95–524, § 2, Oct. 27, 1978, 92 Stat. 1932, related to consultation by the Secretary with various Federal and State agencies regarding education and health and welfare services and supporting programs.

A prior section 821, Pub. L. 93–203, title I, § 111, Dec. 28, 1973, 87 Stat. 849, provided for allowances for individuals receiving training or education with respect to comprehensive manpower services, prior to the general revision of Pub. L. 93–203 by Pub. L. 95–524.

Provisions similar to those comprising this section were contained in former section 875 of this title prior to the general revision of Pub. L. 93–203 by Pub. L. 95–524.

Section 822, Pub. L. 93–203, title I, § 112, as added Pub. L. 95–524, § 2, Oct. 27, 1978, 92 Stat. 1932; amended Pub. L. 96–583, § 1, Dec. 23, 1980, 94 Stat. 3375; Pub. L. 97–14, § 2, June 16, 1981, 95 Stat. 98; Pub. L. 97–35, title VII, § 701(a), Aug. 13, 1981, 95 Stat. 519, provided authorization of appropriations for carrying out this chapter.

A prior section 822, Pub. L. 93–203, title I, § 112, Dec. 28, 1973, 87 Stat. 850, provided for supplemental vocational education assistance, prior to the general revision of Pub. L. 93–203 by Pub. L. 95–524.

Provisions similar to those comprising this section were contained in former section 802 of this title prior to the general revision of Pub. L. 93–203 by Pub. L. 95–524.

PART B—GENERAL PROVISIONS

§§ 823 to 829. Repealed. Pub. L. 97–300, title I, § 184(a)(1), Oct. 13, 1982, 96 Stat. 1357

Section 823, Pub. L. 93–203, title I, § 121, as added Pub. L. 95–524, § 2, Oct. 27, 1978, 92 Stat. 1934, related to conditions applicable to all programs under this chapter.

Provisions similar to those comprising this section were contained in former section 983 of this title prior to the general revision of Pub. L. 93–203 by Pub. L. 95–524.

Section 824, Pub. L. 93–203, title I, § 122, as added Pub. L. 95–524, § 2, Oct. 27, 1978, 92 Stat. 1938, and amended Pub. L. 96–583, § 3(a), Dec. 23, 1980, 94 Stat. 3376, related to special conditions applicable to public service employment.

Provisions similar to those comprising this section were contained in former section 848 of this title prior to the general revision of Pub. L. 93–203 by Pub. L. 95–524.

Section 825, Pub. L. 93–203, title I, § 123, as added Pub. L. 95–524, § 2, Oct. 27, 1978, 92 Stat. 1941, set out various administrative provisions applicable to this chapter.

Provisions similar to those comprising this section were contained in former sections 813 and 984 of this title prior to the general revision of Pub. L. 93–203 by Pub. L. 95–524.

Section 826, Pub. L. 93–203, title I, § 124, as added Pub. L. 95–524, § 2, Oct. 27, 1978, 92 Stat. 1943, related to wages and allowances applicable to all activities financed under this chapter.

Provisions similar to those comprising this section were contained in former section 821 of this title prior to the general revision of Pub. L. 93–203 by Pub. L. 95–524.

Section 827, Pub. L. 93–203, title I, § 125, as added Pub. L. 95–524, § 2, Oct. 27, 1978, 92 Stat. 1944, related to labor standards for all laborers and mechanics employed on works that are federally assisted under this chapter.

Provisions similar to those comprising this section were contained in former section 986 of this title prior to the general revision of Pub. L. 93–203 by Pub. L. 95–524.

Section 828, Pub. L. 93–203, title I, § 126, as added Pub. L. 95–524, § 2, Oct. 27, 1978, 92 Stat. 1944, related to various powers of the Secretary under this chapter.

Provisions similar to those comprising this section were contained in former section 982 of this title prior to the general revision of Pub. L. 93–203 by Pub. L. 95–524.

Section 829, Pub. L. 93–203, title I, § 127, as added Pub. L. 95–524, § 2, Oct. 27, 1978, 92 Stat. 1945; amended Pub. L. 96–88, title V, § 508(h)(2), Oct. 17, 1979, 93 Stat. 693, related to various reports to be made by Federal agencies regarding programs, activities, etc., under this chapter.

Provisions similar to those comprising this section were contained in former sections 849 and 985 of this title prior to the general revision of Pub. L. 93–203 by Pub. L. 95–524.

§ 829a. Repealed. Pub. L. 97–300, title I, § 184(a)(2), Oct. 13, 1982, 96 Stat. 1358

Section, Pub. L. 95–524, § 5(b), Oct. 27, 1978, 92 Stat. 2019, related to development of methods to ascertain energy development and conservation employment impact data, and the presentation of best available data to the Secretary of Energy, Secretary of Housing and Urban Development, Director of the Office of Management and Budget, and committees of Congress.

§§830 to 837. Repealed. Pub. L. 97–300, title I, §184(a)(1), Oct. 13, 1982, 96 Stat. 1357

Section 830, Pub. L. 93–203, title I, §128, as added Pub. L. 95–524, §2, Oct. 27, 1978, 92 Stat. 1947, authorized the Secretary to accept and utilize services and property in the furtherance of the purposes of this chapter.

Provisions similar to those comprising this section were contained in former section 987 of this title prior to the general revision of Pub. L. 93–203 by Pub. L. 95–524.

Section 831, Pub. L. 93–203, title I, §129, as added Pub. L. 95–524, §2, Oct. 27, 1978, 92 Stat. 1947, provided the Secretary with additional authorization to utilize various services and facilities of Federal, State, and local agencies and public and private organizations in the performance of functions under this chapter.

Provisions similar to those comprising this section were contained in former section 988 of this title prior to the general revision of Pub. L. 93–203 by Pub. L. 95–524.

Section 832, Pub. L. 93–203, title I, §130, as added Pub. L. 95–524, §2, Oct. 27, 1978, 92 Stat. 1948, related to interstate agreements to facilitate compliance with the provisions of this chapter.

Provisions similar to those comprising this section were contained in former section 989 of this title prior to the general revision of Pub. L. 93–203 by Pub. L. 95–524.

Section 833, Pub. L. 93–203, title I, §131, as added Pub. L. 95–524, §2, Oct. 27, 1978, 92 Stat. 1948, prohibited financial assistance for programs under this chapter involving political activities.

Provisions similar to those comprising this section were contained in former section 990 of this title prior to the general revision of Pub. L. 93–203 by Pub. L. 95–524.

Section 834, Pub. L. 93–203, title I, §132, as added Pub. L. 95–524, §2, Oct. 27, 1978, 92 Stat. 1948, related to prohibition of, and sanctions against, discrimination under this chapter.

Provisions similar to those comprising this section were contained in former section 991 of this title prior to the general revision of Pub. L. 93–203 by Pub. L. 95–524.

Section 835, Pub. L. 93–203, title I, §133, as added Pub. L. 95–524, §2, Oct. 27, 1978, 92 Stat. 1949, related to records, audits, and investigations of recipients of funds under this chapter.

Provisions similar to those comprising this section were contained in former section 992 of this title prior to the general revision of Pub. L. 93–203 by Pub. L. 95–524.

Section 836, Pub. L. 93–203, title I, §134, as added Pub. L. 95–524, §2, Oct. 27, 1978, 92 Stat. 1949, related to bonding of those who handle funds or other financial assistance received under this chapter.

Section 837, Pub. L. 93–203, title I, §135, as added Pub. L. 95–524, §2, Oct. 27, 1978, 92 Stat. 1950, related to establishment of an Office of Management Assistance, the assignment of accountants, management specialists, and other professionals to such office, and reimbursement for services of such office.

SUBCHAPTER II—COMPREHENSIVE EMPLOYMENT AND TRAINING SERVICES

Part A—Financial Assistance Provisions

§§841 to 845. Repealed. Pub. L. 97–300, title I, §184(a)(1), Oct. 13, 1982, 96 Stat. 1357

Section 841, Pub. L. 93–203, title II, §201, as added Pub. L. 95–524, §2, Oct. 27, 1978, 92 Stat. 1950, set out the Congressional statement of purpose in enacting provisions relating to comprehensive employment and training services.

A prior section 841, Pub. L. 93–203, title II, §201, Dec. 28, 1973, 87 Stat. 850; Pub. L. 93–567, title I, §106(a), Dec. 31, 1974, 88 Stat. 1849, provided for a Congressional statement of purpose with respect to a public service employment program, prior to the general revision of Pub. L. 93–203 by Pub. L. 95–524.

Provisions similar to those comprising this section were contained in former section 811 of this title prior to the general revision of Pub. L. 93–203 by Pub. L. 95–524.

Section 842, Pub. L. 93–203, title II, §202, as added Pub. L. 95–524, §2, Oct. 27, 1978, 92 Stat. 1950; amended Pub. L. 96–583, §3(b), Dec. 23, 1980, 94 Stat. 3376; Pub. L. 97–35, title VII, §701(b), (c), Aug. 13, 1981, 95 Stat. 520, related to allocation of funds for comprehensive employment and training services.

A prior section 842, Pub. L. 93–203, title II, §202, Dec. 28, 1973, 87 Stat. 850; Pub. L. 93–567, title I, §106(b), Dec. 31, 1974, 88 Stat. 1849, Pub. L. 94–444, §14(a), Oct 1, 1976, 90 Stat. 1487, related to an allocation of funds with regard to the public service employment programs, prior to the general revision of Pub. L. 93–203 by Pub. L. 95–524.

Provisions similar to those comprising this section were contained in former section 813 of this title prior to the general revision of Pub. L. 93–203 by Pub. L. 95–524.

Section 843, Pub. L. 93–203, title II, §203, as added Pub. L. 95–524, §2, Oct. 27, 1978, 92 Stat. 1953, related to conditions for the receipt of financial assistance for comprehensive employment and training services.

A prior section 843, Pub. L. 93–203, title II, §203, Dec. 28, 1973, 87 Stat. 850; Pub. L. 94–444, §3(a)(1), Oct. 1, 1976, 90 Stat. 1476, related to availability of financial assistance, prior to the general revision of Pub. L. 93–203 by Pub. L. 95–524.

Provisions similar to those comprising this section were contained in former section 815 of this title prior to the general revision of Pub. L. 93–203 by Pub. L. 95–524.

Section 844, Pub. L. 93–203, title II, §204, as added Pub. L. 95–524, §2, Oct. 27, 1978, 92 Stat. 1953, related to supplemental vocational education assistance.

A prior section 844, Pub. L. 93–203, title II, §204, Dec. 28, 1973, 87 Stat. 850; Pub. L. 93–567, title I, §106 (c), (d), Dec. 31, 1974, 88 Stat. 1849, related to eligible applicants, prior to the general revision of Pub. L. 93–203 by Pub. L. 95–524.

Provisions similar to those comprising this section were contained in former section 822 of this title prior to the general revision of Pub. L. 93–203 by Pub. L. 95–524.

Section 845, Pub. L. 93–203, title II, §205, as added Pub. L. 95–524, §2, Oct. 27, 1978, 92 Stat. 1954, related to participant assessment in comprehensive employment and training services programs.

A prior section 845, Pub. L. 93–203, title II, §205, Dec. 28, 1973, 87 Stat. 851; Pub. L. 93–567, title I, §106 (e), (f), Dec. 31, 1974, 88 Stat. 1849; Pub. L. 94–444, §7, Oct. 1, 1976, 90 Stat. 1482; Pub. L. 95–93, title III, §306(a), Aug. 5, 1977, 91 Stat. 651, related to applications for financial assistance, prior to the general revision of Pub. L. 93–203 by Pub. L. 95–524.

Part B—Services for the Economically Disadvantaged

§§846 to 851. Repealed. Pub. L. 97–300, title I, §184(a)(1), Oct. 13, 1982, 96 Stat. 1357

Section 846, Pub. L. 93–203, title II, §211, as added Pub. L. 95–524, §2, Oct. 27, 1978, 92 Stat. 1954, described types of comprehensive employment and training services programs.

A prior section 846, Pub. L. 93–203, title II, §206, Dec. 28, 1973, 87 Stat. 854, related to approval of applications for financial assistance, prior to the general revision of Pub. L. 93–203 by Pub. L. 95–524.

A prior section 211 of Pub. L. 93–203, title II, Dec. 28, 1973, 87 Stat. 857; Pub. L. 93–567, title I, §103, Dec. 31, 1974, 88 Stat. 1847, related to a determination of areas of substantial unemployment which was formerly classified to section 851 of this title, prior to the general revision of Pub. L. 93–203 by Pub. L. 95–524.

Provisions similar to those comprising this section were contained in former section 811 of this title prior to the general revision of Pub. L. 93–203 by Pub. L. 95–524.

Section 847, Pub. L. 93–203, title II, §212, as added Pub. L. 95–524, §2, Oct. 27, 1978, 92 Stat. 1955, related to limitations on use of funds under comprehensive employment and training services programs.

A prior section 847, Pub. L. 93–203, title II, §207, Dec. 28, 1973, 87 Stat. 854, related to special responsibilities of Secretary, prior to the general revision of Pub. L. 93–203 by Pub. L. 95–524.

Section 848, Pub. L. 93–203, title II, §213, as added Pub. L. 95–524, §2, Oct. 27, 1978, 92 Stat. 1955, related to eligibility for participation in a program for services for economically disadvantaged.

A prior section 848, Pub. L. 93–203, title II, §208, Dec. 28, 1973, 87 Stat. 855, related to special conditions for providing financial assistance for public service employment programs, prior to the general revision of Pub. L. 93–203 by Pub. L. 95–524.

Section 849, Pub. L. 93–203, title II, §214, as added Pub. L. 95–524, §2, Oct. 27, 1978, 92 Stat. 1955, provided for services for youth.

A prior section 849, Pub. L. 93–203, title II, §209, Dec. 28, 1973, 87 Stat. 856; Pub. L. 93–567, title I, §105, Dec. 31, 1974, 88 Stat. 1848, provided for a special report to Congress with respect to activities concerning public service employment program, prior to the general revision of this Pub. L. 93–203 by Pub. L. 95–524.

Section 850, Pub. L. 93–203, title II, §215, as added Pub. L. 95–524, §2, Oct. 27, 1978, 92 Stat. 1956, related to services for older workers.

A prior section 850, Pub. L. 93–203, title II, §210, Dec. 28, 1973, 87 Stat. 857; Pub. L. 93–567, title I, §106(g), Dec. 31, 1974, 88 Stat. 1849, related to utilization of funds for public service employment programs, prior to the general revision of Pub. L. 93–203 by Pub. L. 95–524.

Section 851, Pub. L. 93–203, title II, §216, as added Pub. L. 95–524, §2, Oct. 27, 1978, 92 Stat. 1956, related to services for public assistance recipients.

A prior section 851, Pub. L. 93–203, title II, §211, Dec. 28, 1973, 87 Stat. 857; Pub. L. 93–567, title I, §103, Dec. 31, 1974, 88 Stat. 1847, related to determinations by Secretary of areas of substantial unemployment, prior to the general revision of Pub. L. 93–203 by Pub. L. 95–524.

PART C—UPGRADING AND RETRAINING

§852. Repealed. Pub. L. 97–300, title I, §184(a)(1), Oct. 13, 1982, 96 Stat. 1357

Section, Pub. L. 93–203, title II, §221, as added Pub. L. 95–524, §2, Oct. 27, 1978, 92 Stat. 1956, related to occupational upgrading and retraining programs.

PART D—TRANSITIONAL EMPLOYMENT OPPORTUNITIES FOR THE ECONOMICALLY DISADVANTAGED

§§853 to 859. Repealed, Pub. L. 97–300, title I, §184(a)(1), Oct. 13, 1982, 96 Stat. 1357

Section 853, Pub. L. 93–203, title II, §231, as added Pub. L. 95–524, §2, Oct. 27, 1978, 92 Stat. 1957, set out the Congressional statement of purpose for transitional employment opportunities for the economically disadvantaged.

Section 854, Pub. L. 93–203, title II, §232, as added Pub. L. 95–524, §2, Oct. 27, 1978, 92 Stat. 1958, related to financial assistance to prime sponsors for transitional public service employment for economically disadvantaged persons who are unemployed.

Section 855, Pub. L. 93–203, title II, §233, as added Pub. L. 95–524, §2, Oct. 27, 1978, 92 Stat. 1958; amended Pub. L. 96–583, §3(b), Dec. 23, 1980, 94 Stat. 3376, related to allocation of funds for carrying out of transitional employment opportunities for the economically disadvantaged.

Section 856, Pub. L. 93–203, title II, §234, as added Pub. L. 95–524, §2, Oct. 27, 1978, 92 Stat. 1959, related to expenditure of funds by prime sponsors for purposes of transitional employment opportunities for economically disadvantaged.

Section 857, Pub. L. 93–203, title II, §235, as added Pub. L. 95–524, §2, Oct. 27, 1978, 92 Stat. 1959, related to applicability of section 966 of this title to transitional employment opportunities for economically disadvantaged.

Section 858, Pub. L. 93–203, title II, §236, as added Pub. L. 95–524, §2, Oct. 27, 1978, 92 Stat. 1959, related to eligibility for transitional employment opportunities for economically disadvantaged.

Section 859, Pub. L. 93–203, title II, §237, as added Pub. L. 95–524, §2, Oct. 27, 1978, 92 Stat. 1960, related to payment of wages to economically disadvantaged individuals employed in transitional public service employment.

SUBCHAPTER III—SPECIAL FEDERAL RESPONSIBILITIES

PART A—SPECIAL NATIONAL PROGRAMS AND ACTIVITIES

§§871 to 878. Repealed. Pub. L. 97–300, title I, §184(a)(1), Oct. 13, 1982, 96 Stat. 1357

Section 871, Pub. L. 93–203, title III, §301, as added Pub. L. 95–524, §2, Oct. 27, 1978, 92 Stat. 1960, related to special programs and activities.

A prior section 871, Pub. L. 93–203, title III, §301, Dec. 28, 1973, 87 Stat. 857, provided for additional manpower services, prior to the general revision of Pub. L. 93–203 by Pub. L. 95–524.

Section 872, Pub. L. 93–203, title III, §302, as added Pub. L. 95–524, §2, Oct. 27, 1978, 92 Stat. 1962, related to Native American employment and training programs.

A prior section 872, Pub. L. 93–203, title III, §302, Dec. 28, 1973, 87 Stat. 858; Pub. L. 95–93, title III, §303(a)–(d), Aug. 5, 1977, 91 Stat. 650, related to Native American employment and training programs, prior to the general revision of Pub. L. 93–203 by Pub. L. 95–524.

Section 873, Pub. L. 93–203, title III, §303, as added Pub. L. 95–524, §2, Oct. 27, 1978, 92 Stat. 1964; amended Pub. L. 96–88, title V, §508(h)(3), Oct. 17, 1979, 93 Stat. 693, related to migrant and seasonal farmworker employment and training programs.

A prior section 873, Pub. L. 93–203, title III, §303, Dec. 28, 1973, 87 Stat. 859, related to migrant and seasonal farmworker manpower programs, prior to the general revision of Pub. L. 93–203 by Pub. L. 95–524.

Section 874, Pub. L. 93–203, title III, §304, as added Pub. L. 95–524, §2, Oct. 27, 1978, 92 Stat. 1965, related to job search and relocation assistance.

A prior section 874, Pub. L. 93–203, title III, §304, Dec. 28, 1973, 87 Stat. 859, provided for youth programs and other special programs, prior to the general revision of Pub. L. 93–203 by Pub. L. 95–524.

Section 875, Pub. L. 93–203, title III, §305, as added Pub. L. 95–524, §2, Oct. 27, 1978, 92 Stat. 1965; amended Pub. L. 96–583, §3(d), Dec. 23, 1980, 94 Stat. 3376, related to veterans information and outreach.

A prior section 875, Pub. L. 93–203, title III, §306, Dec. 28, 1973, 87 Stat. 860, related to a consultation with Secretary of Health, Education, and Welfare, prior to the general revision of Pub. L. 93–203 by Pub. L. 95–524.

Provisions similar to those comprising this section were contained in former section 803 of this title prior to the general revision of Pub. L. 93–203 by Pub. L. 95–524.

Section 876, Pub. L. 93–203, title III, §306, as added Pub. L. 95–524, §2, Oct. 27, 1978, 92 Stat. 1965, related to programs for the handicapped.

A prior section 306 of Pub. L. 93–203, title III, Dec. 28, 1973, 87 Stat. 860, related to a consultation with Secretary of Health, Education, and Welfare, was classified to former section 875 of this title prior to the general revision of Pub. L. 93–203 by Pub. L. 95–524.

Section 877, Pub. L. 93–203, title III, § 307, as added Pub. L. 95–524, § 2, Oct. 27, 1978, 92 Stat. 1966, related to partnership programs between prime sponsors and employment security agencies.

Section 878, Pub. L. 93–203, title III, § 308, as added Pub. L. 95–524, § 2, Oct. 27, 1978, 92 Stat. 1966, related to projects for middle-aged and older workers.

PART B—RESEARCH, TRAINING, AND EVALUATION

§§ 879 to 886. Repealed. Pub. L. 97–300, title I, § 184(a)(1), Oct. 13, 1982, 96 Stat. 1357

Section 879, Pub. L. 93–203, title III, § 311, as added Pub. L. 95–524, § 2, Oct. 27, 1978, 92 Stat. 1968; amended Pub. L. 96–88, title V, § 508(h)(4), Oct. 17, 1979, 93 Stat. 693; Pub. L. 96–583, § 3(c), Dec. 23, 1980, 94 Stat. 3376, related to establishment of various employment and training research programs.

A prior section 311 of Pub. L. 93–203, title III, Dec. 28, 1973, 87 Stat. 860; Pub. L. 94–444, § 10, Oct. 1, 1976, 90 Stat. 1483, which related to establishment of a comprehensive program of manpower research, was classified to former section 881 of this title prior to the general revision of Pub. L. 93–203 by Pub. L. 95–524.

Section 880, Pub. L. 93–203, title III, § 312, as added Pub. L. 95–524, § 2, Oct. 27, 1978, 92 Stat. 1970, provided for a labor market information and job bank program.

A prior section 312 of Pub. L. 93–203, title III, Dec. 28, 1973, 87 Stat. 861, which related to development of a system of labor market information and establishment of a job bank program, was classified to former section 882 of this title prior to the general revision of Pub. L. 93–203 by Pub. L. 95–524.

Section 881, Pub. L. 93–203, title III, § 313, as added Pub. L. 95–524, § 2, Oct. 27, 1978, 92 Stat. 1971, related to evaluation of all programs and activities under this chapter.

A prior section 881, Pub. L. 93–203, title III, § 311, Dec. 28, 1973, 87 Stat. 860; Pub. L. 94–444, § 10, Oct. 1, 1976, 90 Stat. 1483, related to establishment of a comprehensive program of manpower research, prior to the general revision of Pub. L. 93–203 by Pub. L. 95–524.

A prior section 313 of Pub. L. 93–203, title III, Dec. 28, 1973, 87 Stat. 862, which related to an evaluation of the programs and activities conducted under this chapter, was classified to section 883 of this title prior to the general revision of Pub. L. 93–203 by Pub. L. 95–524.

Section 882, Pub. L. 93–203, title III, § 314, as added Pub. L. 95–524, § 2, Oct. 27, 1978, 92 Stat. 1972; amended Pub. L. 96–88, title V, § 508(h)(5), Oct. 17, 1979, 93 Stat. 693, provided for training and technical assistance with respect to programs under this chapter.

A prior section 882, Pub. L. 93–203, title III, § 312, Dec. 28, 1973, 87 Stat. 861, related to development of a system of labor market information and establishment of a job bank program, prior to the general revision of Pub. L. 93–203 by Pub. L. 95–524.

A prior section 314 of Pub. L. 93–203, title III, Dec. 28, 1973, 87 Stat. 863, which related to a continuous study with respect to the removal of artificial barriers to employment and advancement, was classified to former section 884 of this title prior to the general revision of Pub. L. 93–203 by Pub. L. 95–524.

Provisions similar to those comprising this section were contained in former section 885 of this title prior to the general revision of Pub. L. 93–203 by Pub. L. 95–524.

Section 883, Pub. L. 93–203, title III, § 315, as added Pub. L. 95–524, § 2, Oct. 27, 1978, 92 Stat. 1972, related to National Occupational Information Coordinating Committee.

A prior section 883, Pub. L. 93–203, title III, § 313, Dec. 28, 1973, 87 Stat. 862, related to evaluation of programs and activities conducted under this chapter, prior to the general revision of Pub. L. 93–203 by Pub. L. 95–524.

A prior section 315 of Pub. L. 93–203, title III, Dec. 28, 1973, 87 Stat. 863, which related to training and technical assistance, was classified to former section 885 of this title prior to the general revision of Pub. L. 93–203 by Pub. L. 95–524.

Section 884, Pub. L. 93–203, title III, § 316, as added Pub. L. 95–524, § 2, Oct. 27, 1978, 92 Stat. 1973, related to evaluation of a prime sponsor's employment and training services program and to the awarding of incentive grants to such sponsors.

A prior section 884, Pub. L. 93–203, title III, § 314, Dec. 28, 1973, 87 Stat. 863, related to a continuous study with respect to the removal of artificial barriers to employment and advancement, prior to the general revision of Pub. L. 93–203 by Pub. L. 95–524.

Section 885, Pub. L. 93–203, title III, § 317, as added Pub. L. 95–524, § 2, Oct. 27, 1978, 92 Stat. 1973, related to voucher demonstration projects.

A prior section 885, Pub. L. 93–203, title III, § 315, Dec. 28, 1973, 87 Stat. 863, related to training and technical assistance, prior to the general revision of Pub. L. 93–203 by Pub. L. 95–524.

Section 886, Pub. L. 93–203, title III, § 318, as added Pub. L. 95–524, § 2, Oct. 27, 1978, 92 Stat. 1974, related to employment and training activities to stimulate local private economic development.

SUBCHAPTER IV—YOUTH PROGRAMS

§§ 891 to 892a. Repealed. Pub. L. 97–300, title I, § 184(a)(1), Oct. 13, 1982, 96 Stat. 1357

Section 891, Pub. L. 93–203, title IV, § 401, as added Pub. L. 95–524, § 2, Oct. 27, 1978, 92 Stat. 1974, set out Congressional declaration of purpose for youth employment and training programs.

A prior section 891, Pub. L. 93–203, title III, § 321, as added Pub. L. 95–93, title II, § 201, Aug. 5, 1977, 91 Stat. 632, provided for a Congressional declaration of purpose with respect to youth employment, training and demonstration programs, prior to the general revision of Pub. L. 93–203 by Pub. L. 95–524.

A prior section 401 of Pub. L. 93–203, title IV, Dec. 28, 1973, 87 Stat. 863, which provided for a congressional statement of purpose with respect to the Job Corps program, was classified to former section 911 of this title prior to the general revision of Pub. L. 93–203 by Pub. L. 95–524.

Provisions similar to those comprising this section were contained in former section 874 of this title prior to the general revision of Pub. L. 93–203 by Pub. L. 95–524.

Section 892, Pub. L. 93–203, title IV, § 402, as added Pub. L. 95–524, § 2, Oct. 27, 1978, 92 Stat. 1974, provided definitions of "eligible youth" under various youth programs.

A prior section 892, Pub. L. 93–203, title III, § 325, as added Pub. L. 95–93, title II, § 201, Aug. 5, 1977, 91 Stat. 632, related to authorization of youth incentive entitlement pilot projects, prior to the general revision of Pub. L. 93–203 by Pub. L. 95–524.

A prior section 402 of Pub. L. 93–203, title IV, Dec. 28, 1973, 87 Stat. 864, related to establishment of a Job Corps and was classified to former section 912 of this title prior to the general revision of Pub. L. 93–203 by Pub. L. 95–524.

Section 892a, Pub. L. 93–203, title IV, § 403, as added Pub. L. 97–35, title VII, § 701(e)(1), Aug. 13, 1981, 95 Stat. 520, related to transferability of funds for youth programs.

A prior section 892a, Pub. L. 93–203, title III, § 326, as added Pub. L. 95–93, title II, § 201, Aug. 5, 1977, 91 Stat. 633, related to guarantees of employment opportunities, prior to the general revision of Pub. L. 93–203 by Pub. L. 95–524.

Sections 892b to 892d of this title were eliminated in the general revision of Pub. L. 93–203 by Pub. L. 95–524.

Section 892b, Pub. L. 93–203, title III, § 327, as added Pub. L. 95–93, title II, § 201, Aug. 5, 1977, 91 Stat. 633, related to selection of prime sponsors.

Section 892c, Pub. L. 93–203, title III, § 328, as added Pub. L. 95–93, title II, § 201, Aug. 5, 1977, 91 Stat. 635, related to special provisions for development of a participants role as a member of the community and for restrictions on use of funds.

Section 892d, Pub. L. 93-203, title III, §329, as added Pub. L. 95-93, title II, §201, Aug. 5, 1977, 91 Stat. 635, related to reports to Congress.

PART A—YOUTH EMPLOYMENT DEMONSTRATION PROGRAMS

§893. Repealed. Pub. L. 97-300, title I, §184(a)(1), Oct. 13, 1982, 96 Stat. 1357

Section 893, Pub. L. 93-203, title IV, §411, as added Pub. L. 95-524, §2, Oct. 27, 1978, 92 Stat. 1974, set out Congressional statement of purpose for youth employment demonstration programs.

A prior section 893, Pub. L. 93-203, title III, §331, added Pub. L. 95-93, title II, §201, Aug. 5, 1977, 91 Stat. 636, provided for a Congressional declaration of purpose with respect to a program of community conservation and improvement projects, prior to the general revision of Pub. L. 93-203 by Pub. L. 95-524.

A prior section 411 of Pub. L. 93-203, title IV, Dec. 28, 1973, 87 Stat. 868, which related to activities designed to establish a mutually beneficial relationship between Job Corps centers and nearby communities, was classified to former section 921 of this title prior to the general revision of Pub. L. 93-203 by Pub. L. 95-524.

Provisions similar to those comprising this section were contained in former section 891 of this title prior to the general revision of Pub. L. 93-203 by Pub. L. 95-524.

Sections 893a to 893g of this title were eliminated in the general revision of Pub. L. 93-203 by Pub. L. 95-524.

Section 893a, Pub. L. 93-203, title III, §332, as added Pub. L. 95-93, title II, §201, Aug. 5, 1977, 91 Stat. 636, defined terms used in provisions covering youth community conservation and improvement projects.

Section 893b, Pub. L. 93-203, title III, §333, as added Pub. L. 95-93, title II, §201, Aug. 5, 1977, 91 Stat. 636, related to allocation of funds with respect to youth community conservation and improvement projects.

Section 893c, Pub. L. 93-203, title III, §334, as added Pub. L. 95-93, title II, §201, Aug. 5, 1977, 91 Stat. 637, authorized Secretary to enter into agreements with eligible applicants to pay the costs of community conservation and improvement youth employment projects.

Section 893d, Pub. L. 93-203, title III, §335, as added Pub. L. 95-93, title II, §201, Aug. 5, 1977, 91 Stat. 637, related to applications for community conservation and improvement youth employment projects.

Section 893e, Pub. L. 93-203, title III, §336, as added Pub. L. 95-93, title II, §201, Aug. 5, 1977, 91 Stat. 637, related to submittal of proposed agreements to Secretary.

Section 893f, Pub. L. 93-203, title III, §337, as added Pub. L. 95-93, title II, §201, Aug. 5, 1977, 91 Stat. 638, related to authority of Secretary to approve or deny project applications.

Section 893g, Pub. L. 93-203, title III, §338, as added Pub. L. 95-93, title II, §201, Aug. 5, 1977, 91 Stat. 639, related to a work limitation with respect to eligible youths involved in community conservation and improvement projects.

SUBPART 1—YOUTH INCENTIVE ENTITLEMENT PILOT PROJECTS

§§894 to 898. Repealed. Pub. L. 97-300, title I, §184(a)(1), Oct. 13, 1982, 96 Stat. 1357

Section 894, Pub. L. 93-203, title IV, §416, as added Pub. L. 95-524, §2, Oct. 27, 1978, 92 Stat. 1975, authorized youth incentive entitlement pilot projects.

A prior section 894, Pub. L. 93-203, title III, §341, as added Pub. L. 95-93, title II, §201, Aug. 5, 1977, 91 Stat. 639, provided for a Congressional declaration of purpose with respect to youth employment and training programs, prior to the general revision of Pub. L. 93-203 by Pub. L. 95-524.

A prior section 416 of Pub. L. 93-203, title IV, Dec. 28, 1973, 87 Stat. 872, which related to the Federal status of enrollees in the Job Corps, was classified to former section 926 of this title prior to the general revision of Pub. L. 93-203 by Pub. L. 95-524.

Provisions similar to those comprising this section were contained in former section 892 of this title prior to the general revision of Pub. L. 93-203, by Pub. L. 95-524.

Sections 894a to 894g of this title were eliminated in the general revision of Pub. L. 93-203 by Pub. L. 95-524.

Section 894a, Pub. L. 93-203, title III, §342, as added Pub. L. 95-93, title II, §201, Aug. 5, 1977, 91 Stat. 639, related to programs authorized for youth employment and training.

Section 894b, Pub. L. 93-203, title III, §343, as added Pub. L. 95-93, title II, §201, Aug. 5, 1977, 91 Stat. 640, related to allocation of funds with respect to youth employment and training programs.

Section 894c, Pub. L. 93-203, title III, §344, as added Pub. L. 95-93, title II, §201, Aug. 5, 1977, 91 Stat. 642, related to eligible applicants for purposes of the youth employment and training programs.

Section 894d, Pub. L. 93-203, title III, §345, as added Pub. L. 95-93, title II, §201, Aug. 5, 1977, 91 Stat. 642, related to eligible participants for programs for employment and training of youth.

Section 894e, Pub. L. 93-203, title III, §346, as added Pub. L. 95-93, title II, §201, Aug. 5, 1977, 91 Stat. 642, related to conditions for receipt of financial assistance for programs authorized under former section 894a of this title.

Section 894f, Pub. L. 93-203, title III, §347, as added Pub. L. 95-93, title II, §201, Aug. 5, 1977, 91 Stat. 645, related to a review of plans by the Secretary.

Section 894g, Pub. L. 93-203, title III, §348, as added Pub. L. 95-93, title II, §201, Aug. 5, 1977, 91 Stat. 645, related to discretionary projects of Secretary dealing with unemployment problems of youth.

Section 895, Pub. L. 93-203, title IV, §417, as added Pub. L. 95-524, §2, Oct. 27, 1978, 92 Stat. 1975, related to employment guarantees under youth incentive entitlement pilot projects.

A prior section 895, Pub. L. 93-203, title III, §351, as added Pub. L. 95-93, title II, §201, Aug. 5, 1977, 91 Stat. 646, provided for authorization of appropriations and distribution of funds with respect to youth employment demonstration programs, prior to the general revision of Pub. L. 93-203 by Pub. L. 95-524.

A prior section 417 of Pub. L. 93-203, title IV, Dec. 28, 1973, 87 Stat. 873, which related to special limitations with respect to the Job Corps, was classified to former section 927 of this title prior to the general revision of Pub. L. 93-203 by Pub. L. 95-524.

Provisions similar to those comprising this section were contained in former section 892a of this title prior to the general revision of Pub. L. 93-203 by Pub. L. 95-524.

Sections 895a to 895f of this title were eliminated in the general revision of Pub. L. 93-203 by Pub. L. 95-524.

Section 895a, Pub. L. 93-203, title III, §352, as added Pub. L. 95-93, title II, §201, Aug. 5, 1977, 91 Stat. 646, related to rates of pay.

Section 895b, Pub. L. 93-203, title III, §353, as added Pub. L. 95-93, title II, §201, Aug. 5, 1977, 91 Stat. 647, related to special conditions with respect to financial assistance to youth employment, training, and demonstration programs.

Section 895c, Pub. L. 93-203, title III, §354, as added Pub. L. 95-93, title II, §201, Aug. 5, 1977, 91 Stat. 648, related to special provisions for youth community conservation and improvement projects and for youth employment and training programs.

Section 895d, Pub. L. 93-203, title III, §355, as added Pub. L. 95-93, title II, §201, Aug. 5, 1977, 91 Stat. 649, related to grant or award of academic credit and counseling and placement services.

Section 895e, Pub. L. 93-203, title III, §356, as added Pub. L. 95-93, title II, §201, Aug. 5, 1977, 91 Stat. 649, related to affect of earnings received under the youth employment, training, and demonstration programs in determination of need under other programs.

Section 895f, Pub. L. 93–203, title III, §357, as added Pub. L. 95–93, title II, §201, Aug. 5, 1977, 91 Stat. 649, related to general provisions.

Section 896, Pub. L. 93–203, title IV, §418, as added Pub. L. 95–524, §2, Oct. 27, 1978, 92 Stat. 1976, related to selection of prime sponsors to operate youth incentive entitlement projects.

A prior section 418 of Pub. L. 93–203, title IV, Dec. 28, 1973, 87 Stat. 873, related to prohibitions respecting political discrimination and political activity, was classified to former section 928 of this title prior to the general revision of Pub. L. 93–203 by Pub. L. 95–524.

Provisions similar to those comprising this section were contained in former section 892b of this title prior to the general revision of Pub. L. 93–203 by Pub. L. 95–524.

Section 897, Pub. L. 93–203, title IV, §419, as added Pub. L. 95–524, §2, Oct. 27, 1978, 92 Stat. 1978, related to special provisions for development of participant's role as a member of the community and for restrictions on use of funds for youth incentive entitlement projects.

A prior section 419 of Pub. L. 93–203, title IV, Dec. 28, 1973, 87 Stat. 873; Pub. L. 93–567, title I, §101, Dec. 31, 1974, 88 Stat. 1845, which provided for administrative provisions, was classified to former section 929 of this title prior to the general revision of Pub. L. 93–203 by Pub. L. 95–524.

Provisions similar to those comprising this section were contained in former section 892c of this title prior to the general revision of Pub. L. 93–203 by Pub. L. 95–524.

Section 898, Pub. L. 93–203, title IV, §420, as added Pub. L. 95–524, §2, Oct. 27, 1978, 92 Stat. 1978, related to reports by the Secretary to Congress regarding youth incentive entitlement projects.

Provisions similar to those comprising this section were contained in former section 892d of this title prior to the general revision of Pub. L. 93–203 by Pub. L. 95–524.

SUBPART 2—YOUTH COMMUNITY CONSERVATION AND IMPROVEMENT PROJECTS

§§899 to 906. Repealed. Pub. L. 97–300, title I, §184(a)(1), Oct. 13, 1982, 96 Stat. 1357

Section 899, Pub. L. 93–203, title IV, §421, as added Pub. L. 95–524, §2, Oct. 27, 1978, 92 Stat. 1979, set out Congressional statement of purpose for youth community conservation and improvement projects.

Provisions similar to those comprising this section were contained in former section 893 of this title prior to the general revision of Pub. L. 93–203 by Pub. L. 95–524.

Section 900, Pub. L. 93–203, title IV, §422, as added Pub. L. 95–524, §2, Oct. 27, 1978, 92 Stat. 1979, provided definitions applicable to youth community conservation and improvement projects.

Provisions similar to those comprising this section were contained in former section 893a of this title prior to the general revision of Pub. L. 93–203 by Pub. L. 95–524.

Section 901, Pub. L. 93–203, title IV, §423, as added Pub. L. 95–524, §2, Oct. 27, 1978, 92 Stat. 1979, related to allocation of funds regarding youth community conservation projects.

Provisions similar to those comprising this section were contained in former section 893b of this title prior to the general revision of Pub. L. 93–203 by Pub. L. 95–524.

Section 902, Pub. L. 93–203, title IV, §424, as added Pub. L. 95–524, §2, Oct. 27, 1978, 92 Stat. 1980, authorized Secretary to enter into agreements with eligible applicants to pay the costs of community conversation and improvement youth employment projects.

Provisions similar to those comprising this section were contained in former section 893c of this title prior to the general revision of Pub. L. 93–203 by Pub. L. 95–524.

Section 903, Pub. L. 93–203, title IV, §425, as added Pub. L. 95–524, §2, Oct. 27, 1978, 92 Stat. 1980, related to applications for youth community conservation and improvement projects.

Provisions similar to those comprising this section were contained in former section 893d of this title prior to the general revision of Pub. L. 93–203 by Pub. L. 95–524.

Section 904, Pub. L. 93–203, title IV, §426, as added Pub. L. 95–524, §2, Oct. 27, 1978, 92 Stat. 1980, related to proposed agreements for funding submitted to Secretary by eligible applicants.

Provisions similar to those comprising this section were contained in former section 893e of this title prior to the general revision of Pub. L. 93–203 by Pub. L. 95–524.

Section 905, Pub. L. 93–203, title IV, §427, as added Pub. L. 95–524, §2, Oct. 27, 1978, 92 Stat. 1981, related to approval or denial of youth community conservation and improvement project applications submitted with an opposed agreement.

Provisions similar to those comprising this section were contained in former section 893f of this title prior to the general revision of Pub. L. 93–203 by Pub. L. 95–524.

Section 906, Pub. L. 93–203, title IV, §428, as added Pub. L. 95–524, §2, Oct. 27, 1978, 92 Stat. 1981, set out work limitations under youth community conservation and improvement projects.

Provisions similar to those comprising this section were contained in former section 893g of this title prior to the general revision of Pub. L. 93–203 by Pub. L. 95–524.

SUBPART 3—YOUTH EMPLOYMENT AND TRAINING PROGRAMS

§§907 to 915. Repealed. Pub. L. 97–300, title I, §184(a)(1), Oct. 13, 1982, 96 Stat. 1357

Section 907, Pub. L. 93–203, title IV, §431, as added Pub. L. 95–524, §2, Oct. 27, 1978, 92 Stat. 1982, set out Congressional statement of purpose for youth employment and training programs.

Provisions similar to those comprising this section were contained in former section 894 of this title prior to the general revision of Pub. L. 93–203 by Pub. L. 95–524.

Section 908, Pub. L. 93–203, title IV, §432, as added Pub. L. 95–524, §2, Oct. 27, 1978, 92 Stat. 1982, related to youth employment and training programs eligible to receive financial assistance.

Provisions similar to those comprising this section were contained in former section 894a of this title prior to the general revision of Pub. L. 93–203 by Pub. L. 95–524.

Section 909, Pub. L. 93–203, title IV, §433, as added Pub. L. 95–524, §2, Oct. 27, 1978, 92 Stat. 1983; amended Pub. L. 97–35, title VII, §701(d)(1), Aug. 13, 1981, 95 Stat. 520, related to allocation of funds for youth employment and training programs.

Provisions similar to those comprising this section were contained in former section 894b of this title prior to the general revision of Pub. L. 93–203 by Pub. L. 95–524.

Section 910, Pub. L. 93–203, title IV, §434, as added Pub. L. 95–524, §2, Oct. 27, 1978, 92 Stat. 1985, related to eligible applicants for youth employment and training programs.

Provisions similar to those comprising this section were contained in former section 894c of this title prior to the general revision of Pub. L. 93–203 by Pub. L. 95–524.

Section 911, Pub. L. 93–203, title IV, §435, as added Pub. L. 95–524, §2, Oct. 27, 1978, 92 Stat. 1985, related to eligible participants for youth employment and training programs.

A prior section 911, Pub. L. 93–203, title IV, §401, Dec. 28, 1973, 87 Stat. 863, provided for a congressional statement of purpose with regard to the Job Corps, prior to the general revision of Pub. L. 93–203 by Pub. L. 95–524.

Provisions similar to those comprising this section were contained in former section 894d of this title prior to the general revision of Pub. L. 93–203 by Pub. L. 95–524.

Section 912, Pub. L. 93–203, title IV, §436, as added Pub. L. 95–524, §2, Oct. 27, 1978, 92 Stat. 1985; amended Pub. L. 97–35, title VII, §701(d)(2), Aug. 13, 1981, 95 Stat. 520, related to conditions for receipt of financial assistance for youth employment and training programs.

A prior section 912, Pub. L. 93–203, title IV, §402, Dec. 28, 1973, 87 Stat. 864, related to establishment of the Job Corps, prior to the general revision of Pub. L. 93–203 by Pub. L. 95–524.

Provisions similar to those comprising this section were contained in former section 894e of this title prior to the general revision of Pub. L. 93–203 by Pub. L. 95–524.

Section 913, Pub. L. 93–203, title IV, §437, as added Pub. L. 95–524, §2, Oct. 27, 1978, 92 Stat. 1987, related to review of youth employment and training plans by Secretary.

A prior section 913, Pub. L. 93–203, title IV, §403, Dec. 28, 1973, 87 Stat. 864, related to eligibility for enrollment in the Job Corps, prior to the general revision of Pub. L. 93–203 by Pub. L. 95–524.

Provisions similar to those comprising this section were contained in former section 894f of this title prior to the general revision of Pub. L. 93–203 by Pub. L. 95–524.

Section 914, Pub. L. 93–203, title IV, §438, as added Pub. L. 95–524, §2, Oct. 27, 1978, 92 Stat. 1987; amended Pub. L. 96–88, title V, §508(h)(6), Oct. 17, 1979, 93 Stat. 693, related to Secretary's discretionary youth employment and training projects.

A prior section 914, Pub. L. 93–203, title IV, §404, Dec. 28, 1973, 87 Stat. 864, related to screening and selection of applicants, prior to the general revision of Pub. L. 93–203 by Pub. L. 95–524.

Provisions similar to those comprising this section were contained in former section 894g of this title prior to the general revision of Pub. L. 93–203 by Pub. L. 95–524.

Section 915, Pub. L. 93–203, title IV, §439, as added Pub. L. 95–524, §2, Oct. 27, 1978, 92 Stat. 1988, related to youth employment incentive and social bonus program.

A prior section 915, Pub. L. 93–203, title IV, §405, Dec. 28, 1973, 87 Stat. 865, related to special limitations on screening and selection of applicants, prior to the general revision of Pub. L. 93–203 by Pub. L. 95–524.

SUBPART 4—GENERAL PROVISIONS

§916. Repealed. Pub. L. 97–14, §3, June 16, 1981, 95 Stat. 98

Section, Pub. L. 93–203, title IV, §441, as added Pub. L. 95–524, §2, Oct. 27, 1978, 92 Stat. 1989, provided that, of the sums available for carrying out the provisions of this part, 15 percent would be available for subpart 1, 15 percent would be available for subpart 2, and 70 percent would be available for subpart 3.

A prior section 916, Pub. L. 93–203, title IV, §406, Dec. 28, 1973, 87 Stat. 865, related to enrollment and assignment in the Job Corps, prior to the general revision of Pub. L. 93–203 by Pub. L. 95–524.

Provisions similar to those comprising this section were contained in former section 895 of this title prior to the general revision of Pub. L. 93–203 by Pub. L. 95–524.

§§917 to 922. Repealed. Pub. L. 97–300, title I, §184(a)(1), Oct. 13, 1982, 96 Stat. 1357

Section 917, Pub. L. 93–203, title IV, §442, as added Pub. L. 95–524, §2, Oct. 27, 1978, 92 Stat. 1989, related to rates of pay under youth employment demonstration programs.

A prior section 917, Pub. L. 93–203, title IV, §407, Dec. 28, 1973, 87 Stat. 866, related to establishment and operation of Job Corps centers, prior to the general revision of Pub. L. 93–203 by Pub. L. 95–524.

Provisions similar to those comprising this section were contained in former section 895a of this title prior to the general revision of Pub. L. 93–203 by Pub. L. 95–524.

Section 918, Pub. L. 93–203, title IV, §443, as added Pub. L. 95–524, §2, Oct. 27, 1978, 92 Stat. 1990, related to special conditions for financial assistance for youth employment demonstration programs.

A prior section 918, Pub. L. 93–203, title IV, §408, Dec. 28, 1973, 87 Stat. 866, related to activities of the program, prior to the general revision of Pub. L. 93–203 by Pub. L. 95–524.

Provisions similar to those comprising this section were contained in former section 895b of this title prior to the general revision of Pub. L. 93–203 by Pub. L. 95–524.

Section 919, Pub. L. 93–203, title IV, §444, as added Pub. L. 95–524, §2, Oct. 27, 1978, 92 Stat. 1991, related to special provisions for youth community conservation and improvement projects and youth employment and training programs.

A prior section 919, Pub. L. 93–203, title IV, §409, Dec. 28, 1973, 87 Stat. 867, provided for allowances and support for the enrollees, prior to the general revision of Pub. L. 93–203 by Pub. L. 95–524.

Provisions similar to those comprising this section were contained in former section 895c of this title prior to the general revision of Pub. L. 93–203 by Pub. L. 95–524.

Section 920, Pub. L. 93–203, title IV, §445, as added Pub. L. 95–524, §2, Oct. 27, 1978, 92 Stat. 1992, related to academic credit and counseling and placement services.

A prior section 920, Pub. L. 93–203, title IV, §410, Dec. 28, 1973, 87 Stat. 868, related to Job Corps centers standards of conduct and deportment, prior to the general revision of Pub. L. 93–203 by Pub. L. 95–524.

Provisions similar to those comprising this section were contained in former section 895d of this title prior to the general revision of Pub. L. 93–203 by Pub. L. 95–524.

Section 921, Pub. L. 93–203, title IV, §446, as added Pub. L. 95–524, §2, Oct. 27, 1978, 92 Stat. 1992, provided that the earnings and allowances received by any youth under a youth employment demonstration program would be disregarded in determining the eligibility of the youth's family for, and the amount of, any benefits based on need under any Federal or federally assisted program.

A prior section 921, Pub. L. 93–203, title IV, §411, Dec. 28, 1973, 87 Stat. 868, related to activities designed to establish a mutually beneficial relationship between Job Corps centers and nearby communities, prior to the general revision of Pub. L. 93–203 by Pub. L. 95–524.

Provisions similar to those comprising this section were contained in former section 895e of this title prior to the general revision of Pub. L. 93–203 by Pub. L. 95–524.

Section 922, Pub. L. 93–203, title IV, §447, as added Pub. L. 95–524, §2, Oct. 27, 1978, 92 Stat. 1992, related to applicability of subchapter I of this chapter to youth employment demonstration programs.

A prior section 922, Pub. L. 93–203, title IV, §412, Dec. 28, 1973, 87 Stat. 869, related to counseling and job placement, prior to the general revision of Pub. L. 93–203 by Pub. L. 95–524.

Provisions similar to those comprising this section were contained in former section 895f of this title prior to the general revision of Pub. L. 93–203 by Pub. L. 95–524.

PART B—JOB CORPS

§§923 to 941a. Repealed. Pub. L. 97–300, title I, §184(a)(1), Oct. 13, 1982, 96 Stat. 1357

Section 923, Pub. L. 93–203, title IV, §450, as added Pub. L. 95–524, §2, Oct. 27, 1978, 92 Stat. 1992, set out Congressional statement of purpose for establishment of the Job Corps.

A prior section 923, Pub. L. 93–203, title IV, §413, Dec. 28, 1973, 87 Stat. 870, related to an evaluation of experimental and developmental projects, prior to the general revision of Pub. L. 93–203 by Pub. L. 95–524.

Provisions similar to those comprising this section were contained in former section 911 of this title prior to the general revision of Pub. L. 93–203 by Pub. L. 95–524.

Section 924, Pub. L. 93–203, title IV, § 451, as added Pub. L. 95–524, § 2, Oct. 27, 1978, 92 Stat. 1993, related to establishment of a Job Corps.

A prior section 924, Pub. L. 93–203, title IV, § 414, Dec. 28, 1973, 87 Stat. 871, related to use of advisory boards and committees by Secretary, prior to the general revision of Pub. L. 93–203 by Pub. L. 95–524.

Provisions similar to those comprising this section were contained in former section 912 of this title prior to the general revision of Pub. L. 93–203 by Pub. L. 95–524.

Section 925, Pub. L. 93–203, title IV, § 452, as added Pub. L. 95–524, § 2, Oct. 27, 1978, 92 Stat. 1993, related to individuals eligible to enroll in Job Corps.

A prior section 925, Pub. L. 93–203, title IV, § 415, Dec. 28, 1973, 87 Stat. 871, related to action by Secretary to facilitate participation by the States in the Job Corps program, prior to the general revision of Pub. L. 93–203 by Pub. L. 95–524.

Provisions similar to those comprising this section were contained in former section 913 of this title prior to the general revision of Pub. L. 93–203 by Pub. L. 95–524.

Section 926, Pub. L. 93–203, title IV, § 453, as added Pub. L. 95–524, § 2, Oct. 27, 1978, 92 Stat. 1993, related to screening and selection of applicants for Job Corps.

A prior section 926, Pub. L. 93–203, title IV, § 416, Dec. 28, 1973, 87 Stat. 872, related to applicability of certain Federal laws to the Job Corps program, prior to the general revision of Pub. L. 93–203 by Pub. L. 95–524.

Provisions similar to those comprising this section were contained in former section 914 of this title prior to the general revision of Pub. L. 93–203 by Pub. L. 95–524.

Section 927, Pub. L. 93–203, title IV, § 454, as added Pub. L. 95–524, § 2, Oct. 27, 1978, 92 Stat. 1994, related to special limitations on selection of enrollees in Job Corps.

A prior section 927, Pub. L. 93–203, title IV, § 417, Dec. 28, 1973, 87 Stat. 873, related to special limitations with regard to the Job Corps program, prior to the general revision of Pub. L. 93–203 by Pub. L. 95–524.

Provisions similar to those comprising this section were contained in former section 915 of this title prior to the general revision of Pub. L. 93–203 by Pub. L. 95–524.

Section 928, Pub. L. 93–203, title IV, § 455, as added Pub. L. 95–524, § 2, Oct. 27, 1978, 92 Stat. 1994, related to enrollment and assignment of enrollees in Job Corps.

A prior section 928, Pub. L. 93–203, title IV, § 418, Dec. 28, 1973, 87 Stat. 873, related to prohibitions concerning political discrimination and political activity, prior to the general revision of Pub. L. 93–203 by Pub. L. 95–524.

Provisions similar to those comprising this section were contained in former section 916 of this title prior to the general revision of Pub. L. 93–203 by Pub. L. 95–524.

Section 929, Pub. L. 93–203, title IV, § 456, as added Pub. L. 95–524, § 2, Oct. 27, 1978, 92 Stat. 1994, related to establishment of Job Corps centers.

A prior section 929, Pub. L. 93–203, title IV, § 419, Dec. 28, 1973, 87 Stat. 873; Pub. L. 93–567, title I, § 101, Dec. 31, 1974, 88 Stat. 1845, related to administrative provisions with regard to the Job Corps program, prior to the general revision of Pub. L. 93–203 by Pub. L. 95–524.

Provisions similar to those comprising this section were contained in former section 917 of this title prior to the general revision of Pub. L. 93–203 by Pub. L. 95–524.

Section 930, Pub. L. 93–203, title IV, § 457, as added Pub. L. 95–524, § 2, Oct. 27, 1978, 92 Stat. 1995; amended Pub. L. 96–583, § 3(c), Dec. 23, 1980, 94 Stat. 3376, related to various Job Corps activities.

Provisions similar to those comprising this section were contained in former section 918 of this title prior to the general revision of Pub. L. 93–203 by Pub. L. 95–524.

Section 931, Pub. L. 93–203, title IV, § 458, as added Pub. L. 95–524, § 2, Oct. 27, 1978, 92 Stat. 1995, related to allowances and support for enrollees of the Job Corps.

Provisions similar to those comprising this section were contained in former section 919 of this title prior to the general revision of Pub. L. 93–203 by Pub. L. 95–524.

Section 932, Pub. L. 93–203, title IV, § 459, as added Pub. L. 95–524, § 2, Oct. 27, 1978, 92 Stat. 1996, related to standards of conduct in Job Corps.

Provisions similar to those comprising this section were contained in former section 920 of this title prior to the general revision of Pub. L. 93–203 by Pub. L. 95–524.

Section 933, Pub. L. 93–203, title IV, § 460, as added Pub. L. 95–524, § 2, Oct. 27, 1978, 92 Stat. 1997, related to community participation, including community advisory councils, with regard to Job Corps.

Provisions similar to those comprising this section were contained in former section 921 of this title prior to the general revision of Pub. L. 93–203 by Pub. L. 95–524.

Section 934, Pub. L. 93–203, title IV, § 461, as added Pub. L. 95–524, § 2, Oct. 27, 1978, 92 Stat. 1997, related to counseling and job placement for enrollees of Job Corps.

Provisions similar to those comprising this section were contained in former section 922 of this title prior to the general revision of Pub. L. 93–203 by Pub. L. 95–524.

Section 935, Pub. L. 93–203, title IV, § 462, as added Pub. L. 95–524, § 2, Oct. 27, 1978, 92 Stat. 1998; amended Pub. L. 96–583, § 3(c), Dec. 23, 1980, 94 Stat. 3376, related to experimental and developmental projects in furtherance of Job Corps program.

Provisions similar to those comprising this section were contained in former section 923 of this title prior to the general revision of Pub. L. 93–203 by Pub. L. 95–524.

Section 936, Pub. L. 93–203, title IV, § 463, as added Pub. L. 95–524, § 2, Oct. 27, 1978, 92 Stat. 1998, related to advisory boards and committees in connection with the operation of Job Corps.

Provisions similar to those comprising this section were contained in former section 924 of this title prior to the general revision of Pub. L. 93–203 by Pub. L. 95–524.

Section 937, Pub. L. 93–203, title IV, § 464, as added Pub. L. 95–524, § 2, Oct. 27, 1978, 92 Stat. 1999, related to participation of States in Job Corps program.

Provisions similar to those comprising this section were contained in former section 925 of this title prior to the general revision of Pub. L. 93–203 by Pub. L. 95–524.

Section 938, Pub. L. 93–203, title IV, § 465, as added Pub. L. 95–524, § 2, Oct. 27, 1978, 92 Stat. 1999, related to application of provisions of Federal law to enrollees in Job Corps.

Provisions similar to those comprising this section were contained in former section 926 of this title prior to the general revision of Pub. L. 93–203 by Pub. L. 95–524.

Section 939, Pub. L. 93–203, title IV, § 466, as added Pub. L. 95–524, § 2, Oct. 27, 1978, 92 Stat. 2000, related to ratio of women enrollees in Job Corps, acquisition as property of United States of all studies, evaluations, and proposals produced with Federal funds in course of Job Corps program, and transactions conducted by private for-profit contractors for Job Corps centers.

Provisions similar to those comprising this section were contained in former section 927 of this title prior to the general revision of Pub. L. 93–203 by Pub. L. 95–524.

Section 940, Pub. L. 93–203, title IV, § 467, as added Pub. L. 95–524, § 2, Oct. 27, 1978, 92 Stat. 2000, set out administrative provisions in connection with Job Corps program.

Provisions similar to those comprising this section were contained in former section 929 of this title prior to the general revision of Pub. L. 93–203 by Pub. L. 95–524.

Section 941, Pub. L. 93–203, title IV, § 468, as added Pub. L. 95–524, § 2, Oct. 27, 1978, 92 Stat. 2001, related to utilization of funds for Job Corps program.

Section 941a, Pub. L. 93–203, title IV, § 469, as added Pub. L. 96–341, § 1, Sept. 8, 1980, 94 Stat. 1076, related to Earle C. Clements Job Corps Center.

PART C—SUMMER YOUTH PROGRAM

§§ 942 to 945. Repealed. Pub. L. 97–300, title I, § 184(a)(1), Oct. 13, 1982, 96 Stat. 1357

Section 942, Pub. L. 93–203, title IV, § 481, as added Pub. L. 95–524, § 2, Oct. 27, 1978, 92 Stat. 2001, related to establishment of summer youth programs.

Section 943, Pub. L. 93–203, title IV, § 482, as added Pub. L. 95–524, § 2, Oct. 27, 1978, 92 Stat. 2001, related to prime sponsors eligible for assistance under summer youth programs.

Section 944, Pub. L. 93–203, title IV, § 483, as added Pub. L. 95–524, § 2, Oct. 27, 1978, 92 Stat. 2001, related to financial assistance under summer youth programs.

Section 945, Pub. L. 93–203, title IV, § 484, as added Pub. L. 95–524, § 2, Oct. 27, 1978, 92 Stat. 2002, related to Secretarial authority over summer youth programs.

SUBCHAPTER V—NATIONAL COMMISSION FOR EMPLOYMENT POLICY

§§ 951 to 955. Repealed. Pub. L. 97–300, title I, § 184(a)(1), Oct. 13, 1982, 96 Stat. 1357

Section 951, Pub. L. 93–203, title V, § 501, as added Pub. L. 95–524, § 2, Oct. 27, 1978, 92 Stat. 2002, set out Congressional statement of purpose for establishment of a National Commission for Employment Policy.

A prior section 951, Pub. L. 93–203, title V, § 501, Dec. 28, 1973, 87 Stat. 874, provided for Congressional findings and declaration of purpose with regard to National Commission for Manpower Policy, prior to the general revision of Pub. L. 93–203 by Pub. L. 95–524.

Section 952, Pub. L. 93–203, title V, § 502, as added Pub. L. 95–524, § 2, Oct. 27, 1978, 92 Stat. 2002; amended Pub. L. 96–88, title V, § 508(h)(7), Oct. 17, 1979, 93 Stat. 693, related to establishment of National Commission for Employment Policy.

A prior section 952, Pub. L. 93–203, title V, § 502, Dec. 28, 1973, 87 Stat. 874; Pub. L. 94–482, title II, § 203(b)(1), Oct. 12, 1976, 90 Stat. 2214, related to establishment of National Commission for Manpower Policy, prior to the general revision of Pub. L. 95–203 by Pub. L. 95–524.

Section 953, Pub. L. 93–203, title V, § 503, as added Pub. L. 95–524, § 2, Oct. 27, 1978, 92 Stat. 2003, related to functions of National Commission for Employment Policy.

A prior section 953, Pub. L. 93–203, title V, § 503, Dec. 28, 1973, 87 Stat. 875; Pub. L. 94–482, title II, § 203(b)(2), Oct. 12, 1976, 90 Stat. 2214; Pub. L. 95–40, § 1(28)(B), June 3, 1977, 91 Stat. 207, related to functions of National Commission for Manpower Policy, prior to the general revision of Pub. L. 93–203 by Pub. L. 95–524.

Section 954, Pub. L. 93–203, title V, § 504, as added Pub. L. 95–524, § 2, Oct. 27, 1978, 92 Stat. 2004, set out administrative provisions relating to powers of Chairman of the National Commission for Employment Policy.

A prior section 954, Pub. L. 93–203, title V, § 504, Dec. 28, 1973, 87 Stat. 875, related to a study of utilization and interrelation of programs of manpower training with closely associated programs, prior to the general revision of Pub. L. 93–203 by Pub. L. 95–524.

Section 955, Pub. L. 93–203, title V, § 505, as added Pub. L. 95–524, § 2, Oct. 27, 1978, 92 Stat. 2005, related to reports made by Commission to President, Congress, and Federal departments and agencies.

A prior section 955, Pub. L. 93–203, title V, § 505, Dec. 28, 1973, 87 Stat. 875, related to reports to President and Congress, prior to the general revision of Pub. L. 93–203 by Pub. L. 95–524.

Section 956, Pub. L. 93–203, title V, § 506, Dec. 28, 1973, 87 Stat. 876, related to a study by Secretary concerning the impact of energy shortages upon manpower needs, prior to the general revision of Pub. L. 93–203 by Pub. L. 95–524.

COMMISSION AUTHORIZED UNTIL SEPTEMBER 30, 1983

Commission established by former sections 951 to 955 of this title continued until Sept. 30, 1983, and on that date the personnel, property, and records of that Commission transferred by former section 1591(b) of this title to the Commission established by former section 1771 et seq. of this title.

SUBCHAPTER VI—COUNTERCYCLICAL PUBLIC SERVICE EMPLOYMENT PROGRAM

§§ 961 to 970. Repealed. Pub. L. 97–300, title I, § 184(a)(1), Oct. 13, 1982, 96 Stat. 1357

Section 961, Pub. L. 93–203, title VI, § 601, as added Pub. L. 95–524, § 2, Oct. 27, 1978, 92 Stat. 2005, set out Congressional statement of purpose for a countercyclical public service employment program.

A prior section 961, Pub. L. 93–203, title VI, 601, as added Pub. L. 93–567, title I, § 101, Dec. 31, 1974, 88 Stat. 1845; amended Pub. L. 94–444, § 2, Oct. 1, 1976, 90 Stat. 1476; Pub. L. 95–44, § 2(b), June 15, 1977, 91 Stat. 220, authorized appropriations for emergency job programs, prior to the general revision of Pub. L. 93–203 by Pub. L. 95–524.

Section 962, Pub. L. 93–203, title VI, § 602, as added Pub. L. 95–524, § 2, Oct. 27, 1978, 92 Stat. 2006, related to reports on appropriations submitted by President to Congress.

A prior section 962, Pub. L. 93–203, title VI, § 602, as added Pub. L. 93–567, title I, § 101, Dec. 31, 1974, 88 Stat. 1845; amended Pub. L. 94–444, §§ 3(a)(2), 8(a), Oct. 1, 1976, 90 Stat. 1476, 1482; Pub. L. 95–93, title III, § 306(b), Aug. 5, 1977, 91 Stat. 651, related to availability of financial assistance for emergency job programs, prior to the general revision of Pub. L. 93–203 by Pub. L. 95–524.

Section 963, Pub. L. 93–203, title VI, § 603, as added Pub. L. 95–524, § 2, Oct. 27, 1978, 92 Stat. 2006, related to financial assistance for public service employment programs.

A prior section 963, Pub. L. 93–203, title VI, § 603, as added Pub. L. 93–567, title I, § 101, Dec. 31, 1974, 88 Stat. 1846; amended Pub. L. 94–444, §§ 4(b), 8(b), (c), 14(b), Oct. 1, 1976, 90 Stat. 1477, 1482, 1487, related to allotment of funds with regard to emergency job programs, prior to the general revision of Pub. L. 93–203 by Pub. L. 95–524.

Provisions similar to those comprising this section were contained in former section 962 of this title prior to the general revision of Pub. L. 93–203 by Pub. L. 95–524.

Section 964, Pub. L. 93–203, title VI, § 604, as added Pub. L. 95–524, § 2, Oct. 27, 1978, 92 Stat. 2007; amended Pub. L. 96–583, § 3(b), Dec. 23, 1980, 94 Stat. 3376, related to allocation of funds with regard to public service employment programs.

A prior section 964, Pub. L. 93–203, title VI, § 604, as added Pub. L. 93–567, title I, § 101, Dec. 31, 1974, 88 Stat. 1846, related to special provision for areas of excessively high unemployment and for expansion of job opportunities, prior to the general revision of Pub. L. 93–203 by Pub. L. 95–524.

Provisions similar to those comprising this section were contained in former section 963 of this title prior to the general revision of Pub. L. 93–203 by Pub. L. 95–524.

Section 965, Pub. L. 93–203, title VI, § 605, as added Pub. L. 95–524, § 2, Oct. 27, 1978, 92 Stat. 2008, related to expenditure of funds with regard to a public service employment program.

A prior section 965, Pub. L. 93–203, title VI, § 605, as added Pub. L. 93–567, title I, § 101, Dec. 31, 1974, 88 Stat. 1847; amended Pub. L. 94–444, § 5(b)(3), (d), Oct. 1, 1976, 90 Stat. 1480, related to expenditure of funds with regard to emergency job programs, prior to the general revision of Pub. L. 93–203 by Pub. L. 95–524.

Section 966, Pub. L. 93–203, title VI, § 606, as added Pub. L. 95–524, § 2, Oct. 27, 1978, 92 Stat. 2008, related to prime sponsors and Native American entities qualified to receive financial assistance and program agents.

A prior section 966, Pub. L. 93–203, title VI, §606, as added Pub. L. 93–567, title I, §101, Dec. 31, 1974, 88 Stat. 1847; amended Pub. L. 94–444, §5(b)(2), Oct. 1, 1976, 90 Stat. 1479, provided for reallocation of funds by Secretary, prior to the general revision of Pub. L. 93–203 by Pub. L. 95–524.

Section 967, Pub. L. 93–203, title VI, §607, as added Pub. L. 95–524, §2, Oct. 27, 1978, 92 Stat. 2009, related to eligibility for employment under a public service employment program.

A prior section 967, Pub. L. 93–203, title VI, §607, as added Pub. L. 94–444, §5(a), Oct. 1, 1976, 90 Stat. 1477; amended Pub. L. 95–44, §2(c), June 15, 1977, 91 Stat. 220, related to reservation of funds for certain public service jobholders, prior to the general revision of Pub. L. 93–203 by Pub. L. 95–524.

Provisions similar to those comprising this section were contained in former section 968 of this title prior to the general revision of Pub. L. 93–203 by Pub. L. 95–524.

Section 968, Pub. L. 93–203, title VI, §608, as added Pub. L. 95–524, §2, Oct. 27, 1978, 92 Stat. 2009, related to payment of wages to those employed under a public service employment program.

A prior section 968, Pub. L. 93–203, title VI, §608, as added Pub. L. 94–444, §5(a), Oct. 1, 1976, 90 Stat. 1478; amended Pub. L. 95–93, title III, §307, Aug. 5, 1977, 91 Stat. 652, related to eligibility of long-term unemployed low-income persons, prior to the general revision of Pub. L. 93–203 by Pub. L. 95–524.

Section 969, Pub. L. 93–203, title VI, §609, as added Pub. L. 95–524, §2, Oct. 27, 1978, 92 Stat. 2009, related to wage supplementation for public service employees receiving financial assistance under public service employment programs.

A prior section 969, Pub. L. 93–203, title VI, §609, as added Pub. L. 94–444, §5(a), Oct. 1, 1976, 90 Stat. 1479, related to approval of project applications, prior to the general revision of Pub. L. 93–203 by Pub. L. 95–524.

Section 970, Pub. L. 93–203, title VI, §610, as added Pub. L. 95–524, §2, Oct. 27, 1978, 92 Stat. 2009, related to utilization of funds available under public service employment programs.

SUBCHAPTER VII—PRIVATE SECTOR OPPORTUNITIES FOR THE ECONOMICALLY DISADVANTAGED

§§981 to 986. Repealed. Pub. L. 97–300, title I, §184(a)(1), Oct. 13, 1982, 96 Stat. 1357

Section 981, Pub. L. 93–203, title VII, §701, as added Pub. L. 95–524, §2, Oct. 27, 1978, 92 Stat. 2010; amended Pub. L. 96–583, §2(1), Dec. 23, 1980, 94 Stat. 3375, set out Congressional statement of purpose for increase of private sector opportunities for the economically disadvantaged.

A prior section 981, Pub. L. 93–203, title VII, §701, formerly title VI, §601, Dec. 28, 1973, 87 Stat. 876; renumbered title VII, §701, and amended Pub. L. 93–567, title I, §§101, 107(a)–(c), Dec. 31, 1974, 88 Stat. 1845, 1849; Pub. L. 94–444, §5(b)(1), Oct. 1, 1976, 90 Stat. 1479; Pub. L. 95–93, title III, §303(e), Aug. 5, 1977, 91 Stat. 650, defined terms for use in this chapter, prior to the general revision of Pub. L. 93–203 by Pub. L. 95–524.

Section 982, Pub. L. 93–203, title VII, §702, as added Pub. L. 95–524, §2, Oct. 27, 1978, 92 Stat. 2010; amended Pub. L. 96–583, §2(2), Dec. 23, 1980, 94 Stat. 3375; Pub. L. 97–35, title VII, §701(f), Aug. 13, 1981, 95 Stat. 521, related to financial assistance to prime sponsors for increase of private sector opportunities for economically disadvantaged.

A prior section 982, Pub. L. 93–203, title VII, §702, formerly title VI, §602, Dec. 28, 1973, 87 Stat. 877; renumbered title VII, §702, Pub. L. 93–567, title I, §101, Dec. 31, 1974, 88 Stat. 1845; amended Pub. L. 94–444, §5(c), Oct. 1, 1976, 90 Stat. 1480, related to legal authority of Secretary under this chapter, prior to the general revision of Pub. L. 93–203 by Pub. L. 95–524.

Section 983, Pub. L. 93–203, title VII, §703, as added Pub. L. 95–524, §2, Oct. 27, 1978, 92 Stat. 2010; amended Pub. L. 96–583, §2(3), Dec. 23, 1980, 94 Stat. 3375, related to conditions for receipt of financial assistance for increase of private sector opportunities for economically disadvantaged.

A prior section 983, Pub. L. 93–203, title VII, §703, formerly title VI, §603, Dec. 28, 1973, 87 Stat. 878; renumbered title VII, §703, and amended Pub. L. 93–567, title I, §§101, 107(d), Dec. 31, 1974, 88 Stat. 1845, 1849, related to conditions applicable to all programs, prior to the general revision of Pub. L. 93–203 by Pub. L. 95–524.

Section 984, Pub. L. 93–203, title VII, §704, as added Pub. L. 95–524, §2, Oct. 27, 1978, 92 Stat. 2011; amended Pub. L. 96–583, §2(4), (5), Dec. 23, 1980, 94 Stat. 3375, related to private industry councils.

A prior section 984, Pub. L. 93–203, title VII, §704, formerly title VI, §604, Dec. 28, 1973, 87 Stat. 879; renumbered title VII, §704, Pub. L. 93–567, title I, §101, Dec. 31, 1974, 88 Stat. 1845, and amended Pub. L. 94–444, §§3(b), 9, 11, Oct. 1, 1976, 90 Stat. 1476, 1482, 1483, related to special provisions applicable to this chapter, prior to the general revision of Pub. L. 93–203 by Pub. L. 95–524.

Section 985, Pub. L. 93–203, title VII, §705, as added Pub. L. 95–524, §2, Oct. 27, 1978, 92 Stat. 2012; amended Pub. L. 96–583, §2(6)–(9), Dec. 23, 1980, 94 Stat. 3375, 3376, related to private sector initiatives by prime sponsors.

A prior section 985, Pub. L. 93–203, title VII, §705, formerly title VI, §605, Dec. 28, 1973, 87 Stat. 879; renumbered title VII, §705, Pub. L. 93–567, title I, §101, Dec. 31, 1974, 88 Stat. 1845, provided for reports to President and Congress, prior to the general revision of Pub. L. 93–203 by Pub. L. 95–524.

Section 986, Pub. L. 93–203, title VII, §706, as added Pub. L. 95–524, §2, Oct. 27, 1978, 92 Stat. 2013, related to a report to Congress and dissemination of information to prime sponsors.

A prior section 986, Pub. L. 93–203, title VII, §706, formerly title VI, §606, Dec. 28, 1973, 87 Stat. 880; renumbered title VII, §706, Pub. L. 93–567, title I, §101, Dec. 31, 1974, 88 Stat. 1845, related to labor standards, prior to the general revision of Pub. L. 93–203 by Pub. L. 95–524.

Sections 987 to 990 of this title were eliminated in the general revision of Pub. L. 93–203 by Pub. L. 95–524.

Section 987, Pub. L. 93–203, title VII, §707, formerly title VI, §607, Dec. 28, 1973, 87 Stat. 880; renumbered title VII, §707, Pub. L. 93–567, title I, §101, Dec. 31, 1974, 88 Stat. 1845, related to authority of Secretary to accept gifts in name of Department.

Section 988, Pub. L. 93–203, title VII, §708, formerly title VI, §608, Dec. 28, 1973, 87 Stat. 881; renumbered title VII, §708, Pub. L. 93–567, title I, §101, Dec. 31, 1974, 88 Stat. 1845, related to use of the services and facilities of departments, agencies, and establishments of the United States by Secretary.

Section 989, Pub. L. 93–203, title VII, §709, formerly title VI, §609, Dec. 28, 1973, 87 Stat. 881; renumbered title VII, §709, Pub. L. 93–567, title I, §101, Dec. 31, 1974, 88 Stat. 1845, related to interstate agreements.

Section 990, Pub. L. 93–203, title VII, §710, formerly title VI, §610, Dec. 28, 1973, 87 Stat. 881; renumbered title VII, §710, Pub. L. 93–567, title I, §101, Dec. 31, 1974, 88 Stat. 1845, related to prohibition concerning political activities.

SUBCHAPTER VIII—YOUNG ADULT CONSERVATION CORPS

§§991 to 999. Repealed. Pub. L. 97–300, title I, §184(a)(1), Oct. 13, 1982, 96 Stat. 1357

Section 991, Pub. L. 93–203, title VIII, §801, as added Pub. L. 95–524, §2, Oct. 27, 1978, 92 Stat. 2013, set out Congressional statement of purpose for Young Adult Conservation Corps.

A prior section 991, Pub. L. 93–203, title VII, §712, formerly title VI, §612, Dec. 28, 1973, 87 Stat. 882; renumbered title VII, §712, Pub. L. 93–567, title I, §101, Dec. 31, 1974, 88 Stat. 1845, related to prohibition concerning discrimination, prior to the general revision of Pub. L. 93–203 by Pub. L. 95–524.

A prior section 801 of Pub. L. 93–203, title VIII, as added Pub. L. 95–93, title I, §101, Aug. 5, 1977, 91 Stat. 627, which provided for Congressional declaration of purpose with regard to Young Adult Conservation Corps, was formerly classified to section 993 of this title prior to the general revision of Pub. L. 93–203 by Pub. L. 95–524.

Section 992, Pub. L. 93–203, title VIII, §802, as added Pub. L. 95–524, §2, Oct. 27, 1978, 92 Stat. 2013, related to establishment of Young Adult Conservation Corps.

A prior section 992, Pub. L. 93–203, title VII, §713, formerly title VI, §613, Dec. 28, 1973, 87 Stat. 882; renumbered title VII, §713, Pub. L. 93–567, title I, §101, Dec. 31, 1974, 88 Stat. 1845, related to records, audits, and reports, prior to the general revision of Pub. L. 93–203 by Pub. L. 95–524.

A prior section 802 of Pub. L. 93–203, title VIII, as added Pub. L. 95–93, title I, §101, Aug. 5, 1977, 91 Stat. 627, which provided for establishment of Young Adult Conservation Corps, was formerly classified to section 993a of this title prior to the general revision of Pub. L. 93–203 by Pub. L. 95–524.

Section 993, Pub. L. 93–203, title VIII, §803, as added Pub. L. 95–524, §2, Oct. 27, 1978, 92 Stat. 2013, related to enrollees of Young Adult Conservation Corps.

A prior section 993, Pub. L. 93–203, title VIII, §801, as added Pub. L. 95–93, title I, §101, Aug. 5, 1977, 91 Stat. 627, provided for a Congressional declaration of purpose with regard to Young Adult Conservation Corps, prior to the general revision of Pub. L. 93–203 by Pub. L. 95–524.

A prior section 803 of Pub. L. 93–203, title VIII, as added Pub. L. 95–93, title I, §101, Aug. 5, 1977, 91 Stat. 627, which related to selection of enrollees, was formerly classified to section 993b of this title prior to the general revision of Pub. L. 93–203 by Pub. L. 95–524.

Sections 993a to 993i of this title were eliminated in the general revision of Pub. L. 93–203 by Pub. L. 95–524.

Section 993a, Pub. L. 93–203, title VIII, §802, as added Pub. L. 95–93, title I, §101, Aug. 5, 1977, 91 Stat. 627, related to establishment of Young Adult Conservation Corps.

Section 993b, Pub. L. 93–203, title VIII, §803, as added Pub. L. 95–93, title I, §101, Aug. 5, 1977, 91 Stat. 627, related to selection of enrollees of Young Adult Conservation Corps.

Section 993c, Pub. L. 93–203, title VIII, §804, as added Pub. L. 95–93, title I, §101, Aug. 5, 1977, 91 Stat. 628, related to activities of Young Adult Conservation Corps.

Section 993d, Pub. L. 93–203, title VIII, §805, as added Pub. L. 95–93, title I, §101, Aug. 5, 1977, 91 Stat. 629, related to conditions applicable to Young Adult Conservation Corps enrollees.

Section 993e, Pub. L. 93–203, title VIII, §806, as added Pub. L. 95–93, title I, §101, Aug. 5, 1977, 91 Stat. 630, related to State and local programs.

Section 993f, Pub. L. 93–203, title VIII, §807, as added Pub. L. 95–93, title I, §101, Aug. 5, 1977, 91 Stat. 631, related to an annual report to President and Congress.

Section 993g, Pub. L. 93–203, title VIII, §808, as added Pub. L. 95–93, title I, §101, Aug. 5, 1977, 91 Stat. 631, related to prohibition concerning discrimination.

Section 993h, Pub. L. 93–203, title VIII, §809, as added Pub. L. 95–93, title I, §101, Aug. 5, 1977, 91 Stat. 631, related to transfer of funds pursuant to an interagency agreement.

Section 993i, Pub. L. 93–203, title VIII, §810, as added Pub. L. 95–93, title I, §101, Aug. 5, 1977, 91 Stat. 631, related to authorization of appropriations for Young Adult Conservation Corps program.

Section 994, Pub. L. 93–203, title VIII, §804, as added Pub. L. 95–524, §2, Oct. 27, 1978, 92 Stat. 2014, related to activities of Young Adult Conservation Corps.

A prior section 804 of Pub. L. 93–203, title VIII, as added Pub. L. 95–93, title I, §101, Aug. 5, 1977, 91 Stat. 628, which related to activities of Young Adult Conservation Corps, was formerly classified to section 993c of this title prior to the general revision of Pub. L. 93–203 by Pub. L. 95–524.

Section 995, Pub. L. 93–203, title VIII, §805, as added Pub. L. 95–524, §2, Oct. 27, 1978, 92 Stat. 2015, related to conditions applicable to enrollees of Young Adult Conservation Corps.

A prior section 805 of Pub. L. 93–203, title VIII, as added Pub. L. 95–93, title I, §101, Aug. 5, 1977, 91 Stat. 629, which related to conditions applicable to Young Adult Conservation Corps enrollees, was formerly classified to section 993d of this title prior to the general revision of Pub. L. 93–203 by Pub. L. 95–524.

Section 996, Pub. L. 93–203, title VIII, §806, as added Pub. L. 95–524, §2, Oct. 27, 1978, 92 Stat. 2016, related to State and local programs in connection with Young Adult Conservation Corps.

A prior section 806 of Pub. L. 93–203, title VIII, as added Pub. L. 95–93, title I, §101, Aug. 5, 1977, 91 Stat. 630, which related to State and local programs, was formerly classified to section 993e of this title prior to the general revision of Pub. L. 93–203 by Pub. L. 95–524.

Section 997, Pub. L. 93–203, title VIII, §807, as added Pub. L. 95–524, §2, Oct. 27, 1978, 92 Stat. 2017, related to an annual report to President and Congress.

A prior section 807 of Pub. L. 93–203, title VIII, as added Pub. L. 95–93, title I, §101, Aug. 5, 1977, 91 Stat. 631, which related to an annual report to President and Congress, was formerly classified to section 993f of this title prior to the general revision of Pub. L. 93–203 by Pub. L. 95–524.

Section 998, Pub. L. 93–203, title VIII, §808, as added Pub. L. 95–524, §2, Oct. 27, 1978, 92 Stat. 2017, related to prohibition of discrimination.

A prior section 808 of Pub. L. 93–203, title VIII, as added Pub. L. 95–93, title I, §101, Aug. 5, 1977, 91 Stat. 631, which related to a prohibition concerning discrimination, was formerly classified to section 993g of this title prior to the general revision of Pub. L. 93–203 by Pub. L. 95–524.

Section 999, Pub. L. 93–203, title VIII, §809, as added Pub. L. 95–524, §2, Oct. 27, 1978, 92 Stat. 2017, related to transfer of funds pursuant to interagency agreement.

A prior section 809 of Pub. L. 93–203, title VIII, as added Pub. L. 95–93, title I, §101, Aug. 5, 1977, 91 Stat. 631, which related to a transfer of funds pursuant to an interagency agreement, was formerly classified to section 993h of this title prior to the general revision of Pub. L. 93–203 by Pub. L. 95–524.

CHAPTER 18—EMPLOYEE RETIREMENT INCOME SECURITY PROGRAM

SUBCHAPTER I—PROTECTION OF EMPLOYEE BENEFIT RIGHTS

SUBTITLE A—GENERAL PROVISIONS

SUBTITLE B—REGULATORY PROVISIONS

PART 1—REPORTING AND DISCLOSURE

PART 2—PARTICIPATION AND VESTING

SUBCHAPTER I—PROTECTION OF EMPLOYEE BENEFIT RIGHTS

SUBTITLE A—GENERAL PROVISIONS

§ 1001. Congressional findings and declaration of policy

(a) Benefit plans as affecting interstate commerce and the Federal taxing power

The Congress finds that the growth in size, scope, and numbers of employee benefit plans in recent years has been rapid and substantial;

that the operational scope and economic impact of such plans is increasingly interstate; that the continued well-being and security of millions of employees and their dependents are directly affected by these plans; that they are affected with a national public interest; that they have become an important factor affecting the stability of employment and the successful development of industrial relations; that they have become an important factor in commerce because of the interstate character of their activities, and of the activities of their participants, and the employers, employee organizations, and other entities by which they are established or maintained; that a large volume of the activities of such plans are carried on by means of the mails and instrumentalities of interstate commerce; that owing to the lack of employee information and adequate safeguards concerning their operation, it is desirable in the interests of employees and their beneficiaries, and to provide for the general welfare and the free flow of commerce, that disclosure be made and safeguards be provided with respect to the establishment, operation, and administration of such plans; that they substantially affect the revenues of the United States because they are afforded preferential Federal tax treatment; that despite the enormous growth in such plans many employees with long years of employment are losing anticipated retirement benefits owing to the lack of vesting provisions in such plans; that owing to the inadequacy of current minimum standards, the soundness and stability of plans with respect to adequate funds to pay promised benefits may be endangered; that owing to the termination of plans before requisite funds have been accumulated, employees and their beneficiaries have been deprived of anticipated benefits; and that it is therefore desirable in the interests of employees and their beneficiaries, for the protection of the revenue of the United States, and to provide for the free flow of commerce, that minimum standards be provided assuring the equitable character of such plans and their financial soundness.

(b) Protection of interstate commerce and beneficiaries by requiring disclosure and reporting, setting standards of conduct, etc., for fiduciaries

It is hereby declared to be the policy of this chapter to protect interstate commerce and the interests of participants in employee benefit plans and their beneficiaries, by requiring the disclosure and reporting to participants and beneficiaries of financial and other information with respect thereto, by establishing standards of conduct, responsibility, and obligation for fiduciaries of employee benefit plans, and by providing for appropriate remedies, sanctions, and ready access to the Federal courts.

(c) Protection of interstate commerce, the Federal taxing power, and beneficiaries by vesting of accrued benefits, setting minimum standards of funding, requiring termination insurance

It is hereby further declared to be the policy of this chapter to protect interstate commerce, the Federal taxing power, and the interests of participants in private pension plans and their beneficiaries by improving the equitable character and the soundness of such plans by requiring them to vest the accrued benefits of employees with significant periods of service, to meet minimum standards of funding, and by requiring plan termination insurance.

(Pub. L. 93–406, title I, §2, Sept. 2, 1974, 88 Stat. 832.)

REFERENCES IN TEXT

This chapter, referred to in subsecs. (b) and (c), was in the original "this Act", meaning Pub. L. 93–406, known as the Employee Retirement Income Security Act of 1974. Titles I, III, and IV of such Act are classified principally to this chapter. For complete classification of this Act to the Code, see Short Title note set out below and Tables.

EFFECTIVE DATE OF 1984 AMENDMENTS; TRANSITIONAL RULES

Pub. L. 98–397, title III, §§302, 303, Aug. 23, 1984, 98 Stat. 1451, 1452, as amended by Pub. L. 99–514, §2, title XI, §1145(c), title XVIII, §1898(g), (h)(1)(A), (2), (3), Oct. 22, 1986, 100 Stat. 2095, 2491, 2956, 2957; Pub. L. 101–239, title VII, §7861(d)(1), Dec. 19, 1989, 103 Stat. 2431, provided that:

"SEC. 302. GENERAL EFFECTIVE DATES.

"(a) IN GENERAL.—Except as otherwise provided in this section or section 303, the amendments made by this Act [see Short Title of 1984 Amendments note below] shall apply to plan years beginning after December 31, 1984.

"(b) SPECIAL RULE FOR COLLECTIVE BARGAINING AGREEMENTS.—In the case of a plan maintained pursuant to 1 or more collective bargaining agreements between employee representatives and 1 or more employers ratified before the date of the enactment of this Act [Aug. 23, 1984], except as provided in subsection (d) or section 303, the amendments made by this Act shall not apply to plan years beginning before the earlier of—

"(1) the date on which the last of the collective bargaining agreements relating to the plan terminates (determined without regard to any extension thereof agreed to after the date of the enactment of this Act [Aug. 23, 1984]), or

"(2) July 1, 1988.

For purposes of paragraph (1), any plan amendment made pursuant to a collective bargaining agreement relating to the plan which amends the plan solely to conform to any requirement added by title I or II [of Pub. L. 98–397] shall not be treated as a termination of such collective bargaining agreement.

"(c) NOTICE REQUIREMENT.—The amendments made by section 207 [amending sections 402 and 6652 of Title 26, Internal Revenue Code] shall apply to distributions after December 31, 1984.

"(d) SPECIAL RULES FOR TREATMENT OF PLAN AMENDMENTS.—

"(1) IN GENERAL.—Except as provided in paragraph (2), the amendments made by section 301 [amending section 1054 of this title and sections 401 and 411 of Title 26] shall apply to plan amendments made after July 30, 1984.

"(2) SPECIAL RULE FOR COLLECTIVE BARGAINING AGREEMENTS.—In the case of a plan maintained pursuant to 1 or more collective bargaining agreements entered into before January 1, 1985, which are—

"(A) between employee representatives and 1 or more employers, and

"(B) successor agreements to 1 or more collective bargaining agreements which terminate after July 30, 1984, and before January 1, 1985,

the amendments made by section 301 shall not apply to plan amendments adopted before April 1, 1985, pursuant to such successor agreements (without regard to any modification or reopening after December 31, 1984).

"SEC. 303. TRANSITIONAL RULES.

"(a) AMENDMENTS RELATING TO VESTING RULES; BREAKS IN SERVICE; MATERNITY OR PATERNITY LEAVE.—

"(1) MINIMUM AGE FOR VESTING.—The amendments made by sections 102(b) and 202(b) [amending section 1053 of this title and section 411 of Title 26, Internal Revenue Code] shall apply in the case of participants who have at least 1 hour of service under the plan on or after the first day of the first plan year to which the amendments made by this Act [see Short Title of 1984 Amendments note below] apply.

"(2) BREAK IN SERVICE RULES.—If, as of the day before the first day of the first plan year to which the amendments made by this Act apply, section 202(a) or (b) or 203(b) of the Employee Retirement Income Security Act of 1974 [section 1052(a) or (b) or section 1053(b) of this title] or section 410(a) or 411(a) of the Internal Revenue Code of 1986 [section 410(a) or section 411(a) of Title 26] (as in effect on the day before the date of the enactment of this Act [Aug. 23, 1984]) would not require any service to be taken into account, nothing in the amendments made by subsections (c) and (d) of section 102 of this Act [amending sections 1052 and 1053 of this title] and subsections (c) and (d) of section 202 of this Act [amending sections 410 and 411 of Title 26] shall be construed as requiring such service to be taken into account under such section 202(a) or (b), 203(b), 410(a), or 411(a); as the case may be.

"(3) MATERNITY OR PATERNITY LEAVE.—The amendments made by sections 102(e) and 202(e) [amending sections 1052 to 1054 of this title and sections 410 and 411 of Title 26] shall apply in the case of absences from work which begin on or after the first day of the first plan year to which the amendments made by this Act apply.

"(b) SPECIAL RULE FOR AMENDMENTS RELATING TO MATERNITY OR PATERNITY ABSENCES.—If a plan is administered in a manner which would meet the amendments made by sections 102(e) and 202(e) [amending sections 1052 to 1054 of this title and sections 410 and 411 of Title 26] (relating to certain maternity or paternity absences not treated as breaks in service), such plan need not be amended to meet such requirements until the earlier of—

"(1) the date on which such plan is first otherwise amended after the date of the enactment of this Act [Aug. 23, 1984], or

"(2) the beginning of the first plan year beginning after December 31, 1986.

"(c) REQUIREMENT OF JOINT AND SURVIVOR ANNUITY AND PRERETIREMENT SURVIVOR ANNUITY.—

"(1) REQUIREMENT THAT PARTICIPANT HAVE AT LEAST 1 HOUR OF SERVICE OR PAID LEAVE ON OR AFTER DATE OF ENACTMENT.—The amendments made by sections 103 and 203 [amending section 1055 of this title and section 401 of Title 26 and enacting section 417 of Title 26] shall apply only in the case of participants who have at least 1 hour of service under the plan on or after the date of the enactment of this Act [Aug. 23, 1984] or have at least 1 hour of paid leave on or after such date of enactment.

"(2) REQUIREMENT THAT PRERETIREMENT SURVIVOR ANNUITY BE PROVIDED IN CASE OF CERTAIN PARTICIPANTS DYING ON OR AFTER DATE OF ENACTMENT.—In the case of any participant—

"(A) who has at least 1 hour of service under the plan on or after the date of the enactment of this Act [Aug. 23, 1984] or has at least 1 hour of paid leave on or after such date of enactment,

"(B) who dies before the annuity starting date, and

"(C) who dies on or after the date of the enactment of this Act [Aug. 23, 1984] and before the first day of the first plan year to which the amendments made by this Act apply,

the amendments made by sections 103 and 203 shall be treated as in effect as of the time of such participant's death. In the case of a profit-sharing or stock bonus plan to which this paragraph applies, the plan shall be treated as meeting the requirements of the amendments made by sections 103 and 203 with respect to any participant if the plan made a distribution in a form other than a life annuity to the surviving spouse of the participant of such participant's nonforfeitable benefit.

"(3) SPOUSAL CONSENT REQUIRED FOR CERTAIN ELECTIONS AFTER DECEMBER 31, 1984.—Any election after December 31, 1984, and before the first day of the first plan year to which the amendments made by this Act apply not to take a joint and survivor annuity shall not be effective unless the requirements of section 205(c)(2) of the Employee Retirement Income Security Act of 1974 [section 1055(c)(2) of this title] (as amended by section 103 of this Act) and section 417(a)(2) of the Internal Revenue Code of 1986 [section 417(a)(2) of Title 26] (as added by section 203 of this Act) are met with respect to such election.

"(4) ELIMINATION OF DOUBLE DEATH BENEFITS.—

"(A) IN GENERAL.—In the case of a participant described in paragraph (2), death benefits (other than a qualified joint and survivor annuity or a qualified preretirement survivor annuity) payable to any beneficiary shall be reduced by the amount payable to the surviving spouse of such participant by reason of paragraph (2). The reduction under the preceding sentence shall be made on the basis of the respective present values (as of the date of the participant's death) of such death benefits and the amount so payable to the surviving spouse.

"(B) SPOUSE MAY WAIVE PROVISIONS OF PARAGRAPH (2).—In the case of any participant described in paragraph (2), the surviving spouse of such participant may waive the provisions of paragraph (2). Such waiver shall be made on or before the close of the second plan year to which the amendments made by section 103 of this Act [amending section 1055 of this title] apply. Such a waiver shall not be treated as a transfer of property for purposes of chapter 12 of the Internal Revenue Code of 1986 and shall not be treated as an assignment or alienation for purposes of section 401(a)(13) of the Internal Revenue Code of 1986 [section 401(a)(13) of Title 26] or section 206(d) of the Employee Retirement Income Security Act of 1974 [section 1056 of this title].

"(d) AMENDMENTS RELATING TO ASSIGNMENTS IN DIVORCE, ETC., PROCEEDINGS.—The amendments made by sections 104 and 204 [amending sections 1056 and 1144 of this title and sections 72, 401, 402 and 414 of Title 26] shall take effect on January 1, 1985, except that in the case of a domestic relations order entered before such date, the plan administrator—

"(1) shall treat such order as a qualified domestic relations order if such administrator is paying benefits pursuant to such order on such date, and

"(2) may treat any other such order entered before such date as a qualified domestic relations order even if such order does not meet the requirements of such amendments.

"(e) TREATMENT OF CERTAIN PARTICIPANTS WHO SEPARATE FROM SERVICE BEFORE DATE OF ENACTMENT.—

"(1) JOINT AND SURVIVOR ANNUITY PROVISIONS OF EMPLOYEE RETIREMENT INCOME SECURITY ACT OF 1974 APPLY TO CERTAIN PARTICIPANTS.—If—

"(A) a participant had at least 1 hour of service under the plan on or after September 2, 1974,

"(B) section 205 of the Employee Retirement Income Security Act of 1974 [section 1055 of this title] and section 401(a)(11) of the Internal Revenue Code of 1986 [section 401(a)(11) of Title 26] (as in effect on the day before the date of the enactment of this Act [Aug. 23, 1984]) would not (but for this paragraph) apply to such participant,

"(C) the amendments made by sections 103 and 203 [amending section 1055 of this title and section 401 of Title 26 and enacting section 417 of Title 26] of this Act do not apply to such participant, and

"(D) as of the date of the enactment of this Act [Aug. 23, 1984], the participant's annuity starting date has not occurred and the participant is alive, then such participant may elect to have section 205 of the Employee Retirement Income Security Act of 1974 [section 1055 of this title] and section 401(a)(11) of the Internal Revenue Code of 1986 [section 401(a)(11) of Title 26] (as in effect on the day before the date of the enactment of this Act) apply.

"(2) TREATMENT OF CERTAIN PARTICIPANTS WHO PERFORM SERVICE ON OR AFTER JANUARY 1, 1976.—If—

"(A) a participant had at least 1 hour of service in any plan year beginning on or after January 1, 1976,

"(B) the amendments made by sections 103 and 203 [amending section 1055 of this title and section 401 of Title 26 and enacting section 417 of Title 26] would not (but for this paragraph) apply to such participant,

"(C) when such participant separated from service, such participant had at least 10 years of service under the plan and had a nonforfeitable right to all (or any portion) of such participant's accrued benefit derived from employer contributions, and

"(D) as of the date of the enactment of this Act [Aug. 23, 1984], such participant's annuity starting date has not occurred and such participant is alive,

then such participant may elect to have the qualified preretirement survivor annuity requirements of the amendments made by sections 103 and 203 apply.

"(3) PERIOD DURING WHICH ELECTION MAY BE MADE.—An election under paragraph (1) or (2) may be made by any participant during the period—

"(A) beginning on the date of the enactment of this Act [Aug. 23, 1984], and

"(B) ending on the earlier of the participant's annuity starting date or the date of the participant's death.

"(4) REQUIREMENT OF NOTICE.—

"(A) IN GENERAL.—

"(i) TIME AND MANNER.—Every plan shall give notice of the provisions of this subsection at such time or times and in such manner or manners as the Secretary of the Treasury may prescribe.

"(ii) PENALTY.—If any plan fails to meet the requirements of clause (i), such plan shall pay a civil penalty to the Secretary of the Treasury equal to $1 per participant for each day during the period beginning with the first day on which such failure occurs and ending on the day before notice is given by the plan; except that the amount of such penalty imposed on any plan shall not exceed $2,500.

"(B) RESPONSIBILITIES OF SECRETARY OF LABOR.—The Secretary of Labor shall take such steps (by public announcements and otherwise) as may be necessary or appropriate to bring to public attention the provisions of this subsection.

"(f) The amendments made by section 301 of this Act [amending section 1054 of this title and sections 401 and 411 of Title 26] shall not apply to the termination of a defined benefit plan if such termination—

"(1) is pursuant to a resolution directing the termination of such plan which was adopted by the Board of Directors of a corporation on July 17, 1984, and

"(2) occurred on November 30, 1984."

[Amendment by section 1145(c) of Pub. L. 99–514 applicable as if included in the amendments made by the Retirement Equity Act of 1984, Pub. L. 98–397, see section 1145(d) of Pub. L. 99–514, set out as a note under section 401 of Title 26.]

[Amendment by section 1898(g), (h)(1)(A), (2), (3) of Pub. L. 99–514 effective as if included in the provision of the Retirement Equity Act of 1984, Pub. L. 98–397, to which such amendment relates, except as otherwise provided, see section 1898(j) of Pub. L. 99–514, set out as a note under section 401 of Title 26.]

SHORT TITLE OF 2008 AMENDMENT

Pub. L. 110–458, § 1(a), Dec. 23, 2008, 122 Stat. 5092, provided that: "This Act [see Tables for classification] may be cited as the 'Worker, Retiree, and Employer Recovery Act of 2008'."

SHORT TITLE OF 2006 AMENDMENT

Pub. L. 109–280, § 1(a), Aug. 17, 2006, 120 Stat. 780, provided that: "This Act [see Tables for classification] may be cited as the 'Pension Protection Act of 2006'."

SHORT TITLE OF 2004 AMENDMENT

Pub. L. 108–218, § 1, Apr. 10, 2004, 118 Stat. 596, provided that: "This Act [see Tables for classification] may be cited as the 'Pension Funding Equity Act of 2004'."

SHORT TITLE OF 1997 AMENDMENT

Pub. L. 105–92, § 1, Nov. 19, 1997, 111 Stat. 2139, provided that: "This Act [enacting sections 1146 and 1147 of this title and provisions set out as a note under section 1146 of this title] may be cited as the 'Savings Are Vital to Everyone's Retirement Act of 1997'."

SHORT TITLE OF 1994 AMENDMENT

Pub. L. 103–401, § 1, Oct. 22, 1994, 108 Stat. 4172, provided that: "This Act [amending section 1132 of this title and enacting provisions set out as notes under section 1132 of this title] may be cited as the 'Pension Annuitants Protection Act of 1994'."

SHORT TITLE OF 1991 AMENDMENT

Pub. L. 102–89, § 1, Aug. 14, 1991, 105 Stat. 446, provided that: "This Act [amending section 1002 of this title and enacting provisions set out as a note under section 1002 of this title] may be cited as the 'Rural Telephone Cooperative Associations ERISA Amendments Act of 1991'."

SHORT TITLE OF 1986 AMENDMENT

Pub. L. 99–272, title XI, § 11001, Apr. 7, 1986, 100 Stat. 237, provided that: "This title [enacting sections 1001b, 1085a, 1143a, 1349, 1369, and 1370 of this title, amending sections 1002, 1023, 1024, 1054, 1061, 1083, 1084, 1086, 1301, 1303, 1305, 1306, 1322, 1322a, 1341, 1342, 1344, 1347, 1348, 1362 to 1364, and 1366 to 1368 of this title, and sections 402, 404, 412, and 501 of Title 26, Internal Revenue Code, repealing section 1304 of this title, and enacting provisions set out as notes under sections 1023, 1054, 1085a, 1135, 1143a, 1303, 1306, 1341, 1362, and 1369 of this title and section 404 of Title 26] may be cited as 'Single-Employer Pension Plan Amendments Act of 1986'."

SHORT TITLE OF 1984 AMENDMENT

Pub. L. 98–397, § 1, Aug. 23, 1984, 98 Stat. 1426, provided that: "This Act [enacting section 417 of Title 26, Internal Revenue Code, amending sections 1025, 1052 to 1056, and 1144 of this title and sections 72, 401, 402, 410, 411, 414, 6057, and 6652 of Title 26, and enacting provisions set out as notes under this section] may be cited as the 'Retirement Equity Act of 1984'."

SHORT TITLE OF 1980 AMENDMENT

Pub. L. 96–364, § 1, Sept. 26, 1980, 94 Stat. 1208, provided that: "This Act [enacting sections 1001a, 1145, 1322a, 1322b, 1323, 1341a, 1381 to 1405, 1411 to 1415, 1421 to 1426, 1431, 1441, and 1451 to 1453 of this title and sections 418 to 418E of Title 26, Internal Revenue Code, amending sections 1002, 1023, 1051, 1053, 1058, 1081, 1082, 1103, 1104, 1108, 1132, 1202, 1301 to 1303, 1305 to 1307, 1321, 1322, 1341, 1342, 1344, 1346, 1348, 1361 to 1366, and 1461 of this title, section 8521 of Title 5, Government Organization and Employees, and sections 194, 401, 404, 411 to 414, 501, 3304, 4971 and 4975 of Title 26, repealing former section 1323 of this title, and enacting provisions set out as notes under this section, sections 1001a, 1302, 1306, 1381, 1385, 1426 and 1461 of this title, section 8521 of Title 5, and sections 401, 404, 414, 418, and 3304 of Title 26] may be cited as the 'Multiemployer Pension Plan Amendments Act of 1980'."

SHORT TITLE

Section 1 of Pub. L. 93–406 provided that: "This Act [enacting this chapter, sections 408 to 415, 4971 to 4975,

6057 to 6059, 6692, and 6693 of Title 26, Internal Revenue Code, section 1037 of former Title 31, Money and Finance, and section 1320b–1 of Title 42, The Public Health and Welfare, amending section 441 of this title, sections 5108 and 5109 of Title 5, Government Organization and Employees, sections 664, 1027, and 1954 of Title 18, Crimes and Criminal Procedure, sections 37, 46, 56, 62, 72, 101, 122, 219, 220, 275, 401, 402, 403, 404, 405, 406, 407, 503, 801, 805, 871, 901, 1304, 1348, 1379, 2039, 3401, 6033, 6047, 6051, 6103, 6104, 6161, 6201, 6204, 6211, 6212, 6213, 6214, 6344, 6501, 6503, 6511, 6512, 6601, 6652, 6653, 6659, 6676, 6677, 6679, 6682, 6688, 6690, 6861, 6862, 7422, 7451, 7459, 7482, 7701, and 7802, of Title 26, and section 846 of former Title 31, repealing sections 301 to 309 of this title, and enacting provisions set out as notes under sections 72, 122, 219, 401, 402, 403, 404, 410, 411, 412, 415, 501, 4973, 4975, 6057, 6059, 6103, 6104, 7476, and 7802 of Title 26] may be cited as the 'Employee Retirement Income Security Act of 1974'."

COORDINATION OF INTERNAL REVENUE CODE OF 1986 WITH EMPLOYEE RETIREMENT INCOME SECURITY ACT OF 1974

This subchapter and subchapter III of this chapter not applicable in interpreting Internal Revenue Code of 1986, except to the extent specifically provided in such Code, or as determined by the Secretary of the Treasury, see section 9343(a) of Pub. L. 100–203, set out as a note under section 401 of Title 26, Internal Revenue Code.

STUDY BY COMPTROLLER GENERAL OF THE UNITED STATES OF EFFECT OF PENSION RULES ON WOMEN

Pub. L. 98–397, title III, § 304, Aug. 23, 1984, 98 Stat. 1454, directed Comptroller General to conduct detailed study of effect on women of participation, vesting, funding, integration, survivorship features, and other relevant plan and Federal pension rules and, not later than Jan. 1, 1990, submit a report on the study to Congress.

STUDY BY GENERAL ACCOUNTING OFFICE REGARDING RESULTS OF MULTIEMPLOYER PENSION PLAN AMENDMENTS ACT OF 1980; PROCEDURES APPLICABLE

Pub. L. 96–364, title IV, § 413, Sept. 26, 1980, 94 Stat. 1309, directed Comptroller General to conduct a study of effects of amendments made by Pub. L. 99–364 on: participants, beneficiaries, employers, employee organizations, and other parties, and the self-sufficiency of the fund established under section 1305 of this title with respect to benefits guaranteed under section 1322a of this title, taking into account financial conditions of multiemployer plans and employers and to report to Congress no later than June 30, 1985, results of study including his recommendations with respect thereto.

PRESIDENT'S COMMISSION ON PENSION POLICY; EXTENSION OF TERM; CONTINUATION OF EFFORT

Pub. L. 96–14, May 24, 1979, 93 Stat. 29, known as the Pension Policy Commission Act, authorized the President's Commission on Pension Policy established by Ex. Ord. No. 12071 to continue in operation for two years following May 24, 1979, and set forth membership, compensation, implementation, and reporting requirements, with the Commission to cease to exist ninety days after submission of the final report.

REORGANIZATION PLAN NO. 4 OF 1978

43 F.R. 47713, 92 Stat. 3790, as amended Pub. L. 99–514, § 2, Oct. 22, 1986, 100 Stat. 2095; Pub. L. 109–280, title I, § 107(c), Aug. 17, 2006, 120 Stat. 820

Prepared by the President and transmitted to the Senate and the House of Representatives in Congress assembled, August 10, 1978, pursuant to the provisions of Chapter 9 of Title 5 of the United States Code.[1]

[1] As amended September 20, 1978.

EMPLOYEE RETIREMENT INCOME SECURITY ACT TRANSFERS

SECTION 101. TRANSFER TO THE SECRETARY OF THE TREASURY

Except as otherwise provided in Sections 104 and 106 of this Plan, all authority of the Secretary of Labor to issue the following described documents pursuant to the statutes hereinafter specified is hereby transferred to the Secretary of the Treasury:

(a) regulations, rulings, opinions, variances and waivers under Parts 2 [29 U.S.C. 1051 et seq.] and 3 [29 U.S.C. 1081 et seq.] of Subtitle B of Title I and subsection 1012(c) [set out as a note under 26 U.S.C. 411] of Title II of the Employee Retirement Income Security Act of 1974 (29 U.S.C. 1001 note) (hereinafter referred to as "ERISA"),

EXCEPT for sections and subsections 201, 203(a)(3)(B), 209, and 301(a) of ERISA; [29 U.S.C. 1051, 1053(a)(3)(B), 1059, and 1081(a)];

(b) such regulations, rulings, and opinions which are granted to the Secretary of Labor under Sections 404, 410, 411, 412, and 413 of the Internal Revenue Code of 1986, as amended [26 U.S.C. 404, 410, 411, 412, and 413], (hereinafter referred to as the "Code").

EXCEPT for subsection 411(a)(3)(B) of the Code [26 U.S.C. 411(a)(3)(B)] and the definitions of "collectively bargained plan" and "collective bargaining agreement" contained in subsections 404 (a)(1)(B) and (a)(1)(C), 410 (b)(2)(A) and (b)(2)(B), and 413(a)(1) of the Code [26 U.S.C. 404(a)(1)(B) and (a)(1)(C), 410 (b)(2)(A) and (b)(2)(B), and 413(a)(1)]; and

(c) regulations, rulings, and opinions under subsections 3(19), 3(22), 3(23), 3(24), 3(25), 3(27), 3(28), 3(29), 3(30), and 3(31) of Subtitle A of Title I of ERISA [29 U.S.C. 1002(19), (22), (23), (24), (25), (27), (28), (29), (30), and (31)]. [As amended Pub. L. 99–514, § 2, Oct. 22, 1986, 100 Stat. 2095.]

SEC. 102. TRANSFER TO THE SECRETARY OF LABOR

Except as otherwise provided in Section 105 of this Plan, all authority of the Secretary of the Treasury to issue the following described documents pursuant to the statutes hereinafter specified is hereby transferred to the Secretary of Labor;

(a) regulations, rulings, opinions, and exemptions under section 4975 of the Code [26 U.S.C. 4975],

EXCEPT for (i) subsections 4975(a), (b), (c)(3), (d)(3), (c)(1), and (e)(7) of the Code [26 U.S.C. 4975(a), (b), (c)(3), (d)(3), (e)(1), and (e)(7)]; (ii) to the extent necessary for the continued enforcement of subsections 4975(a) and (b) [26 U.S.C. 4975(a) and (b)] by the Secretary of the Treasury, subsections 4975(f)(1), (f)(2), (f)(4), (f)(5) and (f)(6) of the Code [26 U.S.C. 4975(f)(1), (f)(2), (f)(4), (f)(5) and (f)(6)]; and (iii) exemptions with respect to transactions that are exempted by subsection 404(c) of ERISA [29 U.S.C. 1104(c)] from the provisions of Part 4 of Subtitle B of Title I of ERISA [29 U.S.C. 1101 et seq.]; and

(b) regulations, rulings, and opinions under subsection 2003(c) of ERISA [set out as a note under 29 U.S.C. 4975].

EXCEPT for subsection 2003(c)(1)(B) [set out in the note under 26 U.S.C. 4975].

SEC. 103. COORDINATION CONCERNING CERTAIN FIDUCIARY ACTIONS

In the case of fiduciary actions which are subject to Part 4 of Subtitle B of Title I of ERISA [29 U.S.C. 1101 et seq.], the Secretary of the Treasury shall notify the Secretary of Labor prior to the time of commencing any proceeding to determine whether the action violates the exclusive benefit rule of subsection 401(a) of the Code [26 U.S.C. 401(a)], but not later than prior to issuing a preliminary notice of intent to disqualify under that rule, and the Secretary of the Treasury shall not issue a determination that a plan or trust does not satisfy the requirements of subsection 401(a) by reason of the exclusive benefit rule of subsection 401(a), unless within 90 days after the date on which the Secretary of the Treasury notifies the Secretary of Labor of pending action, the Secretary of Labor certifies that he has no objection to the disqualification or the Secretary of Labor fails to respond to the Secretary of the Treasury. The requirements of this paragraph do not apply in the case of any termination or jeopardy assessment under sections 6851 or 6861 of the Code [26 U.S.C. 6851 or 6861] that has been approved in advance by the Commissioner of Internal Revenue, or, as delegated, the Assistant Commissioner for Employee Plans and Exempt Organizations.

SEC. 104. ENFORCEMENT BY THE SECRETARY OF LABOR

The transfers provided for in Section 101 of this Plan shall not affect the ability of the Secretary of Labor, subject to the provisions of Title III of ERISA [29 U.S.C. 1201 et seq.] relating to jurisdiction, administration, and enforcement, to engage in enforcement under Section 502 of ERISA [29 U.S.C. 1132] or to exercise the authority set forth under Title III of ERISA, including the ability to make interpretations necessary to engage in such enforcement or to exercise such authority. However, in bringing such actions and in exercising such authority with respect to Parts 2 [29 U.S.C. 1051 et seq.] and 3 [29 U.S.C. 1081 et seq.] of Subtitle B of Title I of ERISA and any definitions for which the authority of the Secretary of Labor is transferred to the Secretary of the Treasury as provided in Section 101 of this Plan, the Secretary of Labor shall be bound by the regulations, rulings, opinions, variances, and waivers issued by the Secretary of the Treasury.

SEC. 105. ENFORCEMENT BY THE SECRETARY OF THE TREASURY

The transfers provided for in Section 102 of this Plan shall not affect the ability of the Secretary of the Treasury, subject to the provisions of Title III of ERISA [29 U.S.C. 1201 et seq.] relating to jurisdiction, administration, and enforcement, (a) to audit plans and employers and to enforce the excise tax provisions of subsections 4975(a) and 4975(b) of the Code [26 U.S.C. 4975(a) and (b)], to exercise the authority set forth in subsections 502(b)(1) and 502(h) of ERISA [29 U.S.C. 1132(b)(1) and (h)], or to exercise the authority set forth in Title III of ERISA, including the ability to make interpretations necessary to audit, to enforce such taxes, and to exercise such authority; and (b) consistent with the coordination requirements under Section 103 of this Plan, to disqualify, under section 401 of the Code [26 U.S.C. 401], a plan subject to Part 4 of Subtitle B of Title I of ERISA [29 U.S.C. 1101 et seq.], including the ability to make the interpretations necessary to make such disqualification. However, in enforcing such excise taxes and, to the extent applicable, in disqualifying such plans the Secretary of the Treasury shall be bound by the regulations, rulings, opinions, and exemptions issued by the Secretary of Labor pursuant to the authority transferred to the Secretary of Labor as provided in Section 102 of this Plan.

SEC. 106. COORDINATION FOR SECTION 101 TRANSFER

(a) The Secretary of the Treasury shall not exercise the functions transferred pursuant to Section 101 of this Plan to issue in proposed or final form any of the documents described in subsection (b) of this Section in any case in which such documents would significantly impact on or substantially affect collectively bargained plans unless, within 100 calendar days after the Secretary of the Treasury notifies the Secretary of Labor of such proposed action, the Secretary of Labor certifies that he has no objection or he fails to respond to the Secretary of the Treasury. The fact of such a notification, except for such notification for documents described in subsection (b)(iv) of this Section, from the Secretary of the Treasury to the Secretary of Labor shall be announced by the Secretary of Labor to the public within ten days following the date of receipt of the notification by the Secretary of Labor.

(b) The documents to which this Section applies are:

(i) amendments to regulations issued pursuant to subsections 202(a)(3), 203(b)(2) and (3)(A), 204(b)(3)(A), (C), and (E), and 210(a)(2) of ERISA [29 U.S.C. 1052(a)(3), 1053(b)(2) and (3)(A), 1054(b)(3)(A), (C), and (E), and 1060(a)(2)], and subsections 410(a)(3) and 411(a)(5), (6)(A), and (b)(3)(A), (C), and (E), 413(b)(4) and (c)(3) and 414(f) of the Code [26 U.S.C. 410(a)(3) and 411(a)(5), (6)(A), and (b)(3)(A), (C), and (E), 413 (b)(4) and (c)(3) and 414(f)];

(ii) regulations issued pursuant to subsections 204(b)(3)(D), 302(d)(2), and 304(d)(1), (d)(2), and (e)(2)(A) of ERISA [29 U.S.C. 1054(b)(3)(D), 1082(d)(2), and 1084(d)(1), (d)(2), and (e)(2)(A)], and subsections 411(b)(3)(D), [former] 412(c)(2) and 431(d)(1), (d)(2), and (e)(2)(A) of the Code [26 U.S.C. 411(b)(3)(D), [former] 412(c)(2) and 431(d)(1), (d)(2), and (e)(2)(A)]; and [As amended Pub. L. 109–280, title I, §107(c), Aug. 17, 2006, 120 Stat. 820.]

(iii) revenue rulings (within the meaning of 26 CFR Section 601.201(a)(6)), revenue procedures, and similar publications, if the rulings, procedures and publications are issued under one of the statutory provisions listed in (i) and (ii) of this subsection; and

(iv) rulings (within the meaning of 26 CFR Section 601.201(a)(2)) issued prior to the issuance of a published regulation under one of the statutory provisions listed in (i) and (ii) of this subsection and not issued under a published Revenue Ruling.

(c) For those documents described in subsections (b)(i), (b)(ii) and (b)(iii) of this Section, the Secretary of Labor may request the Secretary of the Treasury to initiate the actions described in this Section 106 of this Plan.

SEC. 107. EVALUATION

On or before January 31, 1980, the President will submit to both Houses of the Congress an evaluation of the extent to which this Reorganization Plan has alleviated the problems associated with the present administrative structure under ERISA, accompanied by specific legislative recommendations for a long-term administrative structure under ERISA.

SEC. 108. INCIDENTAL TRANSFERS

So much of the personnel, property, records, and unexpended balances of appropriations, allocations and other funds employed, used, held, available, or to be made available in connection with the functions transferred under this Plan, as the Director of the Office of Management and Budget shall determine, shall be transferred to the appropriate agency, or component at such time or times as the Director of the Office of Management and Budget shall provide, except that no such unexpended balances transferred shall be used for purposes other than those for which the appropriation was originally made. The Director of the Office of Management and Budget shall provide for terminating the affairs of any agencies abolished herein and for such further measures and dispositions as such Director deems necessary to effectuate the purposes of this Reorganization Plan.

SEC. 109. EFFECTIVE DATE

The provisions of this Reorganization Plan shall become effective at such time or times, on or before April 30, 1979, as the President shall specify, but not sooner than the earliest time allowable under Section 906 of Title 5, United States Code.

[Amendment by section 107(c) of Pub. L. 109–280 applicable to plan years beginning after 2007, see section 107(e) of Pub. L. 109–280, set out as a note under section 1021 of this title.]

[For special rules on applicability of amendments by subtitles A (§§101–107) and B (§§111–116) of title I of Pub. L. 109–280 to certain eligible cooperative plans, PBGC settlement plans, and eligible government contractor plans, see sections 104, 105, and 106 of Pub. L. 109–280, set out as notes under section 401 of Title 26, Internal Revenue Code.]

MESSAGE OF THE PRESIDENT

To the Congress of the United States:

Today I am submitting to the Congress my fourth Reorganization Plan for 1978. This proposal is designed to simplify and improve the unnecessarily complex administrative requirements of the Employee Retirement Income Security Act of 1974 (ERISA) [see Short Title note set out under this section]. The new plan will eliminate overlap and duplication in the administration of ERISA and help us achieve our goal of well regulated private pension plans.

ERISA was an essential step in the protection of worker pension rights. Its administrative provisions, however, have resulted in bureaucratic confusion and have been justifiably criticized by employers and unions alike. The biggest problem has been overlapping jurisdictional authority. Under current ERISA provisions, the Departments of Treasury and Labor both have authority to issue regulations and decisions.

This dual jurisdiction has delayed a good many important rulings and, more importantly, produced bureaucratic runarounds and burdensome reporting requirements.

The new plan will significantly reduce these problems. In addition, both Departments are trying to cut red tape and paperwork, to eliminate unnecessary reporting requirements, and to streamline forms wherever possible.

Both Departments have already made considerable progress, and both will continue the effort to simplify their rules and their forms.

The Reorganization Plan is the most significant result of their joint effort to modify and simplify ERISA. It will eliminate most of the jurisdictional overlap between Treasury and Labor by making the following changes:

1) Treasury will have statutory authority for minimum standards. The new plan puts all responsibility for funding, participation, and vesting of benefit rights in the Department of Treasury. These standards are necessary to ensure that employee benefit plans are adequately funded and that all beneficiary rights are protected. Treasury is the most appropriate Department to administer these provisions; however, Labor will continue to have veto power over Treasury decisions that significantly affect collectively bargained plans.

2) Labor will have statutory authority for fiduciary obligations. ERISA prohibits transactions in which self-interest or conflict of interest could occur, but allows certain exemptions from these prohibitions. Labor will be responsible for overseeing fiduciary conduct under these provisions.

3) Both Departments will retain enforcement powers. The Reorganization Plan will continue Treasury's authority to audit plans and levy tax penalties for any deviation from standards. The plan will also continue Labor's authority to bring civil action against plans and fiduciaries. These provisions are retained in order to keep the special expertise of each Department available. New coordination between the Departments will eliminate duplicative investigations of alleged violations.

This reorganization will make an immediate improvement in ERISA's administration. It will eliminate almost all of the dual and overlapping authority in the two departments and dramatically cut the time required to process applications for exemptions from prohibited transactions.

This plan is an interim arrangement. After the Departments have had a chance to administer ERISA under this new plan, the Office of Management and Budget and the Departments will jointly evaluate that experience. Based on that evaluation, early in 1980, the Administration will make appropriate legislative proposals to establish a long-term administrative structure for ERISA.

Each provision in this reorganization will accomplish one or more of the purposes in Title 5 of U.S.C. 901(a). There will be no change in expenditure or personnel levels, although a small number of people will be transferred from the Department of Treasury to the Department of Labor.

We all recognize that the administration of ERISA has been unduly burdensome. I am confident that this reorganization will significantly relieve much of that burden.

This plan is the culmination of our effort to streamline ERISA. It provides an administrative arrangement that will work.

ERISA has been a symbol of unnecessarily complex government regulation. I hope this new step will become equally symbolic of my Administration's commitment to making government more effective and less intrusive in the lives of our people.

JIMMY CARTER.

THE WHITE HOUSE, August 10, 1978.

EXECUTIVE ORDER NO. 12071

Ex. Ord. No. 12071, July 12, 1978, 43 F.R. 30259, which established the President's Commission on Pension Policy and provided for its membership, functions, etc., was revoked by Ex. Ord. No. 12379, §1, Aug. 17, 1982, 47 F.R. 36099, set out as a note under section 14 of the Federal Advisory Committee Act in the Appendix to Title 5, Government Organization and Employees.

EX. ORD. NO. 12108. EFFECTIVE DATE OF ERISA TRANSFERS

Ex. Ord. No. 12108, Dec. 28, 1978, 44 F.R. 1065, provided:

By the authority vested in me as President of the United States of America by Section 109 of Reorganization Plan No. 4 of 1978 (43 F.R. 47713) [set out above], it is hereby ordered that the provisions of Reorganization Plan No. 4 of 1978 shall be effective on Sunday, December 31, 1978.

JIMMY CARTER.

EXECUTIVE ORDER NO. 12262

Ex. Ord. No. 12262, Jan. 7, 1981, 46 F.R. 2313, which established the Interagency Employee Benefit Council and provided for its membership, functions, etc., was revoked by Ex. Ord. No. 12379, §9, Aug. 17, 1982, 47 F.R. 36099, set out as a note under section 14 of the Federal Advisory Committee Act in the Appendix to Title 5, Government Organization and Employees.

§1001a. Additional Congressional findings and declaration of policy

(a) Effects of multiemployer pension plans

The Congress finds that—

(1) multiemployer pension plans have a substantial impact on interstate commerce and are affected with a national public interest;

(2) multiemployer pension plans have accounted for a substantial portion of the increase in private pension plan coverage over the past three decades;

(3) the continued well-being and security of millions of employees, retirees, and their dependents are directly affected by multiemployer pension plans; and

(4)(A) withdrawals of contributing employers from a multiemployer pension plan frequently result in substantially increased funding obligations for employers who continue to contribute to the plan, adversely affecting the plan, its participants and beneficiaries, and labor-management relations, and

(B) in a declining industry, the incidence of employer withdrawals is higher and the adverse effects described in subparagraph (A) are exacerbated.

(b) Modification of multiemployer plan termination insurance provisions and replacement of program

The Congress further finds that—

(1) it is desirable to modify the current multiemployer plan termination insurance provisions in order to increase the likelihood of protecting plan participants against benefit losses; and

(2) it is desirable to replace the termination insurance program for multiemployer pension plans with an insolvency-based benefit protection program that will enhance the financial soundness of such plans, place primary emphasis on plan continuation, and contain program costs within reasonable limits.

(c) Policy

It is hereby declared to be the policy of this Act—

(1) to foster and facilitate interstate commerce,

(2) to alleviate certain problems which tend to discourage the maintenance and growth of multiemployer pension plans,

(3) to provide reasonable protection for the interests of participants and beneficiaries of financially distressed multiemployer pension plans, and

(4) to provide a financially self-sufficient program for the guarantee of employee benefits under multiemployer plans.

(Pub. L. 96–364, § 3, Sept. 26, 1980, 94 Stat. 1209.)

REFERENCES IN TEXT

This Act, referred to in subsec. (c), is Pub. L. 96–364, Sept. 26, 1980, 94 Stat. 1208, known as the Multiemployer Pension Plan Amendments Act of 1980. For complete classification of this Act to the Code, see Short Title of 1980 Amendment note set out under section 1001 of this title and Tables.

CODIFICATION

Section was enacted as part of the Multiemployer Pension Plan Amendments Act of 1980, and not as part of the Employee Retirement Income Security Act of 1974 which comprises this chapter.

EFFECTIVE DATE

Section effective Sept. 26, 1980, see section 1461(e)(1) of this title.

STUDY AND REPORT RESPECTING COLLECTIVE BARGAINING FOR CONTRIBUTIONS TO, AND BENEFITS FROM, MULTIEMPLOYER PLANS

Section 412(b) of Pub. L. 96–364 directed Secretary of Labor to study feasibility of requiring collective bargaining on both issues of contributions to, and benefits from, multiemployer plans, and submit a report on the study to Congress within 3 years of Sept. 26, 1980.

§ 1001b. Findings and declaration of policy

(a) Findings

The Congress finds that—

(1) single-employer defined benefit pension plans have a substantial impact on interstate commerce and are affected with a national interest;

(2) the continued well-being and retirement income security of millions of workers, retirees, and their dependents are directly affected by such plans;

(3) the existence of a sound termination insurance system is fundamental to the retirement income security of participants and beneficiaries of such plans; and

(4) the current termination insurance system in some instances encourages employers to terminate pension plans, evade their obligations to pay benefits, and shift unfunded pension liabilities onto the termination insurance system and the other premium-payers.

(b) Additional findings

The Congress further finds that modification of the current termination insurance system and an increase in the insurance premium for single-employer defined benefit pension plans—

(1) is desirable to increase the likelihood that full benefits will be paid to participants and beneficiaries of such plans;

(2) is desirable to provide for the transfer of liabilities to the termination insurance system only in cases of severe hardship;

(3) is necessary to maintain the premium costs of such system at a reasonable level; and

(4) is necessary to finance properly current funding deficiencies and future obligations of the single-employer pension plan termination insurance system.

(c) Declaration of policy

It is hereby declared to be the policy of this title—

(1) to foster and facilitate interstate commerce;

(2) to encourage the maintenance and growth of single-employer defined benefit pension plans;

(3) to increase the likelihood that participants and beneficiaries under single-employer defined benefit pension plans will receive their full benefits;

(4) to provide for the transfer of unfunded pension liabilities onto the single-employer pension plan termination insurance system only in cases of severe hardship;

(5) to maintain the premium costs of such system at a reasonable level; and

(6) to assure the prudent financing of current funding deficiencies and future obligations of the single-employer pension plan termination insurance system by increasing termination insurance premiums.

(Pub. L. 99–272, title XI, § 11002, Apr. 7, 1986, 100 Stat. 237.)

REFERENCES IN TEXT

This title, referred to in subsec. (c), is title XI of Pub. L. 99–272, Apr. 7, 1986, 100 Stat. 237, known as the Single-Employer Pension Plan Amendments Act of 1986. For complete classification of this Act to the Code, see Short Title of 1986 Amendment note set out under section 1001 of this title and Tables.

CODIFICATION

Section was enacted as part of the Single-Employer Pension Plan Amendments Act of 1986, and not as part of the Employee Retirement Income Security Act of 1974 which comprises this chapter.

EFFECTIVE DATE

Section effective Jan. 1, 1986, with certain exceptions, see section 11019 of Pub. L. 99–272, set out as an Effective Date of 1986 Amendment note under section 1341 of this title.

§ 1002. Definitions

For purposes of this subchapter:

(1) The terms "employee welfare benefit plan" and "welfare plan" mean any plan, fund, or program which was heretofore or is hereafter established or maintained by an employer or by an employee organization, or by both, to the extent that such plan, fund, or program was established or is maintained for the purpose of providing for its participants or their beneficiaries, through the purchase of insurance or otherwise, (A) medical, surgical, or hospital care or benefits, or benefits in the event of sickness, accident, disability, death or unemployment, or vacation benefits, apprenticeship or other training programs, or day care centers, scholarship funds, or prepaid legal services, or (B) any benefit described in section 186(c) of this title (other than pensions on retirement or death, and insurance to provide such pensions).

(2)(A) Except as provided in subparagraph (B), the terms "employee pension benefit plan" and "pension plan" mean any plan, fund, or program which was heretofore or is hereafter established or maintained by an employer or by an employee organization, or by both, to the extent that by its express terms or as a result of surrounding circumstances such plan, fund, or program—

(i) provides retirement income to employees, or

(ii) results in a deferral of income by employees for periods extending to the termination of covered employment or beyond,

regardless of the method of calculating the contributions made to the plan, the method of calculating the benefits under the plan or the method of distributing benefits from the plan. A distribution from a plan, fund, or program shall not be treated as made in a form other than retirement income or as a distribution prior to termination of covered employment solely because such distribution is made to an employee who has attained age 62 and who is not separated from employment at the time of such distribution.

(B) The Secretary may by regulation prescribe rules consistent with the standards and purposes of this chapter providing one or more exempt categories under which—

(i) severance pay arrangements, and

(ii) supplemental retirement income payments, under which the pension benefits of retirees or their beneficiaries are supplemented to take into account some portion or all of the increases in the cost of living (as determined by the Secretary of Labor) since retirement,

shall, for purposes of this subchapter, be treated as welfare plans rather than pension plans. In the case of any arrangement or payment a principal effect of which is the evasion of the standards or purposes of this chapter applicable to pension plans, such arrangement or payment shall be treated as a pension plan. An applicable voluntary early retirement incentive plan (as defined in section 457(e)(11)(D)(ii) of title 26) making payments or supplements described in section 457(e)(11)(D)(i) of title 26, and an applicable employment retention plan (as defined in section 457(f)(4)(C) of title 26) making payments of benefits described in section 457(f)(4)(A) of title 26, shall, for purposes of this subchapter, be treated as a welfare plan (and not a pension plan) with respect to such payments and supplements.

(3) The term "employee benefit plan" or "plan" means an employee welfare benefit plan or an employee pension benefit plan or a plan which is both an employee welfare benefit plan and an employee pension benefit plan.

(4) The term "employee organization" means any labor union or any organization of any kind, or any agency or employee representation committee, association, group, or plan, in which employees participate and which exists for the purpose, in whole or in part, of dealing with employers concerning an employee benefit plan, or other matters incidental to employment relationships; or any employees' beneficiary association organized for the purpose in whole or in part, of establishing such a plan.

(5) The term "employer" means any person acting directly as an employer, or indirectly in the interest of an employer, in relation to an employee benefit plan; and includes a group or association of employers acting for an employer in such capacity.

(6) The term "employee" means any individual employed by an employer.

(7) The term "participant" means any employee or former employee of an employer, or any member or former member of an employee organization, who is or may become eligible to receive a benefit of any type from an employee benefit plan which covers employees of such employer or members of such organization, or whose beneficiaries may be eligible to receive any such benefit.

(8) The term "beneficiary" means a person designated by a participant, or by the terms of an employee benefit plan, who is or may become entitled to a benefit thereunder.

(9) The term "person" means an individual, partnership, joint venture, corporation, mutual company, joint-stock company, trust, estate, unincorporated organization, association, or employee organization.

(10) The term "State" includes any State of the United States, the District of Columbia, Puerto Rico, the Virgin Islands, American Samoa, Guam, Wake Island, and the Canal Zone. The term "United States" when used in the geographic sense means the States and the Outer Continental Shelf lands defined in the Outer Continental Shelf Lands Act (43 U.S.C. 1331–1343).

(11) The term "commerce" means trade, traffic, commerce, transportation, or communication between any State and any place outside thereof.

(12) The term "industry or activity affecting commerce" means any activity, business, or industry in commerce or in which a labor dispute would hinder or obstruct commerce or the free flow of commerce, and includes any activity or industry "affecting commerce" within the meaning of the Labor Management Relations Act, 1947 [29 U.S.C. 141 et seq.], or the Railway Labor Act [45 U.S.C. 151 et seq.].

(13) The term "Secretary" means the Secretary of Labor.

(14) The term "party in interest" means, as to an employee benefit plan—

(A) any fiduciary (including, but not limited to, any administrator, officer, trustee, or custodian), counsel, or employee of such employee benefit plan;

(B) a person providing services to such plan;

(C) an employer any of whose employees are covered by such plan;

(D) an employee organization any of whose members are covered by such plan;

(E) an owner, direct or indirect, of 50 percent or more of—

(i) the combined voting power of all classes of stock entitled to vote or the total value of shares of all classes of stock of a corporation.[1]

(ii) the capital interest or the profits interest of a partnership, or

(iii) the beneficial interest of a trust or unincorporated enterprise,

which is an employer or an employee organization described in subparagraph (C) or (D);

(F) a relative (as defined in paragraph (15)) of any individual described in subparagraph (A), (B), (C), or (E);

(G) a corporation, partnership, or trust or estate of which (or in which) 50 percent or more of—

(i) the combined voting power of all classes of stock entitled to vote or the total value of shares of all classes of stock of such corporation,

(ii) the capital interest or profits interest of such partnership, or

(iii) the beneficial interest of such trust or estate,

is owned directly or indirectly, or held by persons described in subparagraph (A), (B), (C), (D), or (E);

(H) an employee, officer, director (or an individual having powers or responsibilities similar to those of officers or directors), or a 10 percent or more shareholder directly or indirectly, of a person described in subparagraph (B), (C), (D), (E), or (G), or of the employee benefit plan; or

(I) a 10 percent or more (directly or indirectly in capital or profits) partner or joint venturer of a person described in subparagraph (B), (C), (D), (E), or (G).

The Secretary, after consultation and coordination with the Secretary of the Treasury, may by regulation prescribe a percentage lower than 50 percent for subparagraph (E) and (G) and lower than 10 percent for subparagraph (H) or (I). The Secretary may prescribe regulations for determining the ownership (direct or indirect) of profits and beneficial interests, and the manner in which indirect stockholdings are taken into account. Any person who is a party in interest with respect to a plan to which a trust described in section 501(c)(22) of title 26 is permitted to make payments under section 1403 of this title shall be treated as a party in interest with respect to such trust.

(15) The term "relative" means a spouse, ancestor, lineal descendant, or spouse of a lineal descendant.

(16)(A) The term "administrator" means—

(i) the person specifically so designated by the terms of the instrument under which the plan is operated;

(ii) if an administrator is not so designated, the plan sponsor; or

(iii) in the case of a plan for which an administrator is not designated and a plan sponsor cannot be identified, such other person as the Secretary may by regulation prescribe.

(B) The term "plan sponsor" means (i) the employer in the case of an employee benefit plan established or maintained by a single employer, (ii) the employee organization in the case of a plan established or maintained by an employee organization, or (iii) in the case of a plan established or maintained by two or more employers or jointly by one or more employers and one or more employee organizations, the association, committee, joint board of trustees, or other similar group of representatives of the parties who establish or maintain the plan.

(17) The term "separate account" means an account established or maintained by an insurance company under which income, gains, and losses, whether or not realized, from assets allocated to such account, are, in accordance with the applicable contract, credited to or charged against such account without regard to other income, gains, or losses of the insurance company.

(18) The term "adequate consideration" when used in part 4 of subtitle B of this subchapter means (A) in the case of a security for which there is a generally recognized market, either (i) the price of the security prevailing on a national securities exchange which is registered under section 78f of title 15, or (ii) if the security is not traded on such a national securities exchange, a price not less favorable to the plan than the offering price for the security as established by the current bid and asked prices quoted by persons independent of the issuer and of any party in interest; and (B) in the case of an asset other than a security for which there is a generally recognized market, the fair market value of the asset as determined in good faith by the trustee or named fiduciary pursuant to the terms of the plan and in accordance with regulations promulgated by the Secretary.

(19) The term "nonforfeitable" when used with respect to a pension benefit or right means a claim obtained by a participant or his beneficiary to that part of an immediate or deferred benefit under a pension plan which arises from the participant's service, which is unconditional, and which is legally enforceable against the plan. For purposes of this paragraph, a right to an accrued benefit derived from employer contributions shall not be treated as forfeitable merely because the plan contains a provision described in section 1053(a)(3) of this title.

(20) The term "security" has the same meaning as such term has under section 77b(1)[2] of title 15.

(21)(A) Except as otherwise provided in subparagraph (B), a person is a fiduciary with respect to a plan to the extent (i) he exercises any discretionary authority or discretionary control

[1] So in original. The period probably should be a comma.

[2] See References in Text note below.

respecting management of such plan or exercises any authority or control respecting management or disposition of its assets, (ii) he renders investment advice for a fee or other compensation, direct or indirect, with respect to any moneys or other property of such plan, or has any authority or responsibility to do so, or (iii) he has any discretionary authority or discretionary responsibility in the administration of such plan. Such term includes any person designated under section 1105(c)(1)(B) of this title.

(B) If any money or other property of an employee benefit plan is invested in securities issued by an investment company registered under the Investment Company Act of 1940 [15 U.S.C. 80a-1 et seq.], such investment shall not by itself cause such investment company or such investment company's investment adviser or principal underwriter to be deemed to be a fiduciary or a party in interest as those terms are defined in this subchapter, except insofar as such investment company or its investment adviser or principal underwriter acts in connection with an employee benefit plan covering employees of the investment company, the investment adviser, or its principal underwriter. Nothing contained in this subparagraph shall limit the duties imposed on such investment company, investment adviser, or principal underwriter by any other law.

(22) The term "normal retirement benefit" means the greater of the early retirement benefit under the plan, or the benefit under the plan commencing at normal retirement age. The normal retirement benefit shall be determined without regard to—

(A) medical benefits, and

(B) disability benefits not in excess of the qualified disability benefit.

For purposes of this paragraph, a qualified disability benefit is a disability benefit provided by a plan which does not exceed the benefit which would be provided for the participant if he separated from the service at normal retirement age. For purposes of this paragraph, the early retirement benefit under a plan shall be determined without regard to any benefit under the plan which the Secretary of the Treasury finds to be a benefit described in section 1054(b)(1)(G) of this title.

(23) The term "accrued benefit" means—

(A) in the case of a defined benefit plan, the individual's accrued benefit determined under the plan and, except as provided in section 1054(c)(3) of this title, expressed in the form of an annual benefit commencing at normal retirement age, or

(B) in the case of a plan which is an individual account plan, the balance of the individual's account.

The accrued benefit of an employee shall not be less than the amount determined under section 1054(c)(2)(B) of this title with respect to the employee's accumulated contribution.

(24) The term "normal retirement age" means the earlier of—

(A) the time a plan participant attains normal retirement age under the plan, or

(B) the later of—

(i) the time a plan participant attains age 65, or

(ii) the 5th anniversary of the time a plan participant commenced participation in the plan.

(25) The term "vested liabilities" means the present value of the immediate or deferred benefits available at normal retirement age for participants and their beneficiaries which are nonforfeitable.

(26) The term "current value" means fair market value where available and otherwise the fair value as determined in good faith by a trustee or a named fiduciary (as defined in section 1102(a)(2) of this title) pursuant to the terms of the plan and in accordance with regulations of the Secretary, assuming an orderly liquidation at the time of such determination.

(27) The term "present value", with respect to a liability, means the value adjusted to reflect anticipated events. Such adjustments shall conform to such regulations as the Secretary of the Treasury may prescribe.

(28) The term "normal service cost" or "normal cost" means the annual cost of future pension benefits and administrative expenses assigned, under an actuarial cost method, to years subsequent to a particular valuation date of a pension plan. The Secretary of the Treasury may prescribe regulations to carry out this paragraph.

(29) The term "accrued liability" means the excess of the present value, as of a particular valuation date of a pension plan, of the projected future benefit costs and administrative expenses for all plan participants and beneficiaries over the present value of future contributions for the normal cost of all applicable plan participants and beneficiaries. The Secretary of the Treasury may prescribe regulations to carry out this paragraph.

(30) The term "unfunded accrued liability" means the excess of the accrued liability, under an actuarial cost method which so provides, over the present value of the assets of a pension plan. The Secretary of the Treasury may prescribe regulations to carry out this paragraph.

(31) The term "advance funding actuarial cost method" or "actuarial cost method" means a recognized actuarial technique utilized for establishing the amount and incidence of the annual actuarial cost of pension plan benefits and expenses. Acceptable actuarial cost methods shall include the accrued benefit cost method (unit credit method), the entry age normal cost method, the individual level premium cost method, the aggregate cost method, the attained age normal cost method, and the frozen initial liability cost method. The terminal funding cost method and the current funding (pay-as-you-go) cost method are not acceptable actuarial cost methods. The Secretary of the Treasury shall issue regulations to further define acceptable actuarial cost methods.

(32) The term "governmental plan" means a plan established or maintained for its employees by the Government of the United States, by the government of any State or political subdivision thereof, or by any agency or instrumentality of any of the foregoing. The term "governmental plan" also includes any plan to which the Railroad Retirement Act of 1935, or 1937 [45 U.S.C. 231 et seq.] applies, and which is financed by

contributions required under that Act and any plan of an international organization which is exempt from taxation under the provisions of the International Organizations Immunities Act [22 U.S.C. 288 et seq.]. The term "governmental plan" includes a plan which is established and maintained by an Indian tribal government (as defined in section 7701(a)(40) of title 26), a subdivision of an Indian tribal government (determined in accordance with section 7871(d) of title 26), or an agency or instrumentality of either, and all of the participants of which are employees of such entity substantially all of whose services as such an employee are in the performance of essential governmental functions but not in the performance of commercial activities (whether or not an essential government function)[3]

(33)(A) The term "church plan" means a plan established and maintained (to the extent required in clause (ii) of subparagraph (B)) for its employees (or their beneficiaries) by a church or by a convention or association of churches which is exempt from tax under section 501 of title 26.

(B) The term "church plan" does not include a plan—

(i) which is established and maintained primarily for the benefit of employees (or their beneficiaries) of such church or convention or association of churches who are employed in connection with one or more unrelated trades or businesses (within the meaning of section 513 of title 26), or

(ii) if less than substantially all of the individuals included in the plan are individuals described in subparagraph (A) or in clause (ii) of subparagraph (C) (or their beneficiaries).

(C) For purposes of this paragraph—

(i) A plan established and maintained for its employees (or their beneficiaries) by a church or by a convention or association of churches includes a plan maintained by an organization, whether a civil law corporation or otherwise, the principal purpose or function of which is the administration or funding of a plan or program for the provision of retirement benefits or welfare benefits, or both, for the employees of a church or a convention or association of churches, if such organization is controlled by or associated with a church or a convention or association of churches.

(ii) The term employee of a church or a convention or association of churches includes—

(I) a duly ordained, commissioned, or licensed minister of a church in the exercise of his ministry, regardless of the source of his compensation;

(II) an employee of an organization, whether a civil law corporation or otherwise, which is exempt from tax under section 501 of title 26 and which is controlled by or associated with a church or a convention or association of churches; and

(III) an individual described in clause (v).

(iii) A church or a convention or association of churches which is exempt from tax under section 501 of title 26 shall be deemed the employer of any individual included as an employee under clause (ii).

(iv) An organization, whether a civil law corporation or otherwise, is associated with a church or a convention or association of churches if it shares common religious bonds and convictions with that church or convention or association of churches.

(v) If an employee who is included in a church plan separates from the service of a church or a convention or association of churches or an organization, whether a civil law corporation or otherwise, which is exempt from tax under section 501 of title 26 and which is controlled by or associated with a church or a convention or association of churches, the church plan shall not fail to meet the requirements of this paragraph merely because the plan—

(I) retains the employee's accrued benefit or account for the payment of benefits to the employee or his beneficiaries pursuant to the terms of the plan; or

(II) receives contributions on the employee's behalf after the employee's separation from such service, but only for a period of 5 years after such separation, unless the employee is disabled (within the meaning of the disability provisions of the church plan or, if there are no such provisions in the church plan, within the meaning of section 72(m)(7) of title 26) at the time of such separation from service.

(D)(i) If a plan established and maintained for its employees (or their beneficiaries) by a church or by a convention or association of churches which is exempt from tax under section 501 of title 26 fails to meet one or more of the requirements of this paragraph and corrects its failure to meet such requirements within the correction period, the plan shall be deemed to meet the requirements of this paragraph for the year in which the correction was made and for all prior years.

(ii) If a correction is not made within the correction period, the plan shall be deemed not to meet the requirements of this paragraph beginning with the date on which the earliest failure to meet one or more of such requirements occurred.

(iii) For purposes of this subparagraph, the term "correction period" means—

(I) the period ending 270 days after the date of mailing by the Secretary of the Treasury of a notice of default with respect to the plan's failure to meet one or more of the requirements of this paragraph; or

(II) any period set by a court of competent jurisdiction after a final determination that the plan fails to meet such requirements, or, if the court does not specify such period, any reasonable period determined by the Secretary of the Treasury on the basis of all the facts and circumstances, but in any event not less than 270 days after the determination has become final; or

(III) any additional period which the Secretary of the Treasury determines is reasonable or necessary for the correction of the default,

whichever has the latest ending date.

[3] So in original. Probably should be followed by a period.

(34) The term "individual account plan" or "defined contribution plan" means a pension plan which provides for an individual account for each participant and for benefits based solely upon the amount contributed to the participant's account, and any income, expenses, gains and losses, and any forfeitures of accounts of other participants which may be allocated to such participant's account.

(35) The term "defined benefit plan" means a pension plan other than an individual account plan; except that a pension plan which is not an individual account plan and which provides a benefit derived from employer contributions which is based partly on the balance of the separate account of a participant—

(A) for the purposes of section 1052 of this title, shall be treated as an individual account plan, and

(B) for the purposes of paragraph (23) of this section and section 1054 of this title, shall be treated as an individual account plan to the extent benefits are based upon the separate account of a participant and as a defined benefit plan with respect to the remaining portion of benefits under the plan.

(36) The term "excess benefit plan" means a plan maintained by an employer solely for the purpose of providing benefits for certain employees in excess of the limitations on contributions and benefits imposed by section 415 of title 26 on plans to which that section applies without regard to whether the plan is funded. To the extent that a separable part of a plan (as determined by the Secretary of Labor) maintained by an employer is maintained for such purpose, that part shall be treated as a separate plan which is an excess benefit plan.

(37)(A) The term "multiemployer plan" means a plan—

(i) to which more than one employer is required to contribute,

(ii) which is maintained pursuant to one or more collective bargaining agreements between one or more employee organizations and more than one employer, and

(iii) which satisfies such other requirements as the Secretary may prescribe by regulation.

(B) For purposes of this paragraph, all trades or businesses (whether or not incorporated) which are under common control within the meaning of section 1301(b)(1) of this title are considered a single employer.

(C) Notwithstanding subparagraph (A), a plan is a multiemployer plan on and after its termination date if the plan was a multiemployer plan under this paragraph for the plan year preceding its termination date.

(D) For purposes of this subchapter, notwithstanding the preceding provisions of this paragraph, for any plan year which began before September 26, 1980, the term "multiemployer plan" means a plan described in this paragraph (37) as in effect immediately before such date.

(E) Within one year after September 26, 1980, a multiemployer plan may irrevocably elect, pursuant to procedures established by the corporation and subject to the provisions of sections 1453(b) and (c) of this title, that the plan shall not be treated as a multiemployer plan for all purposes under this chapter or the Internal Revenue Code of 1954 if for each of the last 3 plan years ending prior to the effective date of the Multiemployer Pension Plan Amendments Act of 1980—

(i) the plan was not a multiemployer plan because the plan was not a plan described in subparagraph (A)(iii) of this paragraph and section 414(f)(1)(C) of title 26 (as such provisions were in effect on the day before September 26, 1980); and

(ii) the plan had been identified as a plan that was not a multiemployer plan in substantially all its filings with the corporation, the Secretary of Labor and the Secretary of the Treasury.

(F)(i) For purposes of this subchapter a qualified football coaches plan—

(I) shall be treated as a multiemployer plan to the extent not inconsistent with the purposes of this subparagraph; and

(II) notwithstanding section 401(k)(4)(B) of title 26, may include a qualified cash and deferred arrangement.

(ii) For purposes of this subparagraph, the term "qualified football coaches plan" means any defined contribution plan which is established and maintained by an organization—

(I) which is described in section 501(c) of title 26;

(II) the membership of which consists entirely of individuals who primarily coach football as full-time employees of 4-year colleges or universities described in section 170(b)(1)(A)(ii) of title 26; and

(III) which was in existence on September 18, 1986.

(G)(i) Within 1 year after August 17, 2006—

(I) an election under subparagraph (E) may be revoked, pursuant to procedures prescribed by the Pension Benefit Guaranty Corporation, if, for each of the 3 plan years prior to August 17, 2006, the plan would have been a multiemployer plan but for the election under subparagraph (E), and

(II) a plan that meets the criteria in clauses (i) and (ii) of subparagraph (A) of this paragraph or that is described in clause (vi) may, pursuant to procedures prescribed by the Pension Benefit Guaranty Corporation, elect to be a multiemployer plan, if—

(aa) for each of the 3 plan years immediately preceding the first plan year for which the election under this paragraph is effective with respect to the plan, the plan has met those criteria or is so described,

(bb) substantially all of the plan's employer contributions for each of those plan years were made or required to be made by organizations that were exempt from tax under section 501 of title 26, and

(cc) the plan was established prior to September 2, 1974.

(ii) An election under this subparagraph shall be effective for all purposes under this chapter and under title 26, starting with any plan year beginning on or after January 1, 1999, and ending before January 1, 2008, as designated by the plan in the election made under clause (i)(II).

(iii) Once made, an election under this subparagraph shall be irrevocable, except that a plan described in clause (i)(II) shall cease to be a multiemployer plan as of the plan year beginning immediately after the first plan year for which the majority of its employer contributions were made or required to be made by organizations that were not exempt from tax under section 501 of title 26.

(iv) The fact that a plan makes an election under clause (i)(II) does not imply that the plan was not a multiemployer plan prior to the date of the election or would not be a multiemployer plan without regard to the election.

(v)(I) No later than 30 days before an election is made under this subparagraph, the plan administrator shall provide notice of the pending election to each plan participant and beneficiary, each labor organization representing such participants or beneficiaries, and each employer that has an obligation to contribute to the plan, describing the principal differences between the guarantee programs under subchapter III and the benefit restrictions under this subchapter for single employer and multiemployer plans, along with such other information as the plan administrator chooses to include.

(II) Within 180 days after August 17, 2006, the Secretary shall prescribe a model notice under this clause.

(III) A plan administrator's failure to provide the notice required under this subparagraph shall be treated for purposes of section 1132(c)(2) of this title as a failure or refusal by the plan administrator to file the annual report required to be filed with the Secretary under section 1021(b)(1) of this title.

(vi) A plan is described in this clause if it is a plan sponsored by an organization which is described in section 501(c)(5) of title 26 and exempt from tax under section 501(a) of such title and which was established in Chicago, Illinois, on August 12, 1881.

(vii) For purposes of this chapter and title 26, a plan making an election under this subparagraph shall be treated as maintained pursuant to a collective bargaining agreement if a collective bargaining agreement, expressly or otherwise, provides for or permits employer contributions to the plan by one or more employers that are signatory to such agreement, or participation in the plan by one or more employees of an employer that is signatory to such agreement, regardless of whether the plan was created, established, or maintained for such employees by virtue of another document that is not a collective bargaining agreement.

(38) The term "investment manager" means any fiduciary (other than a trustee or named fiduciary, as defined in section 1102(a)(2) of this title)—

(A) who has the power to manage, acquire, or dispose of any asset of a plan;

(B) who (i) is registered as an investment adviser under the Investment Advisers Act of 1940 [15 U.S.C. 80b–1 et seq.]; (ii) is not registered as an investment adviser under such Act by reason of paragraph (1) of section 203A(a) of such Act [15 U.S.C. 80b–3a(a)], is registered as an investment adviser under the laws of the State (referred to in such paragraph (1)) in which it maintains its principal office and place of business, and, at the time the fiduciary last filed the registration form most recently filed by the fiduciary with such State in order to maintain the fiduciary's registration under the laws of such State, also filed a copy of such form with the Secretary; (iii) is a bank, as defined in that Act; or (iv) is an insurance company qualified to perform services described in subparagraph (A) under the laws of more than one State; and

(C) has acknowledged in writing that he is a fiduciary with respect to the plan.

(39) The terms "plan year" and "fiscal year of the plan" mean, with respect to a plan, the calendar, policy, or fiscal year on which the records of the plan are kept.

(40)(A) The term "multiple employer welfare arrangement" means an employee welfare benefit plan, or any other arrangement (other than an employee welfare benefit plan), which is established or maintained for the purpose of offering or providing any benefit described in paragraph (1) to the employees of two or more employers (including one or more self-employed individuals), or to their beneficiaries, except that such term does not include any such plan or other arrangement which is established or maintained—

(i) under or pursuant to one or more agreements which the Secretary finds to be collective bargaining agreements,

(ii) by a rural electric cooperative, or

(iii) by a rural telephone cooperative association.

(B) For purposes of this paragraph—

(i) two or more trades or businesses, whether or not incorporated, shall be deemed a single employer if such trades or businesses are within the same control group,

(ii) the term "control group" means a group of trades or businesses under common control,

(iii) the determination of whether a trade or business is under "common control" with another trade or business shall be determined under regulations of the Secretary applying principles similar to the principles applied in determining whether employees of two or more trades or businesses are treated as employed by a single employer under section 1301(b) of this title, except that, for purposes of this paragraph, common control shall not be based on an interest of less than 25 percent,

(iv) the term "rural electric cooperative" means—

(I) any organization which is exempt from tax under section 501(a) of title 26 and which is engaged primarily in providing electric service on a mutual or cooperative basis, and

(II) any organization described in paragraph (4) or (6) of section 501(c) of title 26 which is exempt from tax under section 501(a) of title 26 and at least 80 percent of the members of which are organizations described in subclause (I), and

(v) the term "rural telephone cooperative association" means an organization described in paragraph (4) or (6) of section 501(c) of title 26 which is exempt from tax under section 501(a) of title 26 and at least 80 percent of the members of which are organizations engaged primarily in providing telephone service to rural areas of the United States on a mutual, cooperative, or other basis.

(41)[4] SINGLE-EMPLOYER PLAN.—The term "single-employer plan" means an employee benefit plan other than a multiemployer plan.

(41)[4] The term "single-employer plan" means a plan which is not a multiemployer plan.

(42) the term "plan assets" means plan assets as defined by such regulations as the Secretary may prescribe, except that under such regulations the assets of any entity shall not be treated as plan assets if, immediately after the most recent acquisition of any equity interest in the entity, less than 25 percent of the total value of each class of equity interest in the entity is held by benefit plan investors. For purposes of determinations pursuant to this paragraph, the value of any equity interest held by a person (other than such a benefit plan investor) who has discretionary authority or control with respect to the assets of the entity or any person who provides investment advice for a fee (direct or indirect) with respect to such assets, or any affiliate of such a person, shall be disregarded for purposes of calculating the 25 percent threshold. An entity shall be considered to hold plan assets only to the extent of the percentage of the equity interest held by benefit plan investors. For purposes of this paragraph, the term "benefit plan investor" means an employee benefit plan subject to part 4,[5] any plan to which section 4975 of title 26 applies, and any entity whose underlying assets include plan assets by reason of a plan's investment in such entity.

(Pub. L. 93–406, title I, §3, Sept. 2, 1974, 88 Stat. 833; Pub. L. 96–364, title III, §§302, 305, title IV, §§407(a), 409, Sept. 26, 1980, 94 Stat. 1291, 1294, 1303, 1307; Pub. L. 97–473, title III, §302(a), Jan. 14, 1983, 96 Stat. 2612; Pub. L. 99–272, title XI, §11016(c)(1), Apr. 7, 1986, 100 Stat. 273; Pub. L. 99–509, title IX, §9203(b)(1), Oct. 21, 1986, 100 Stat. 1979; Pub. L. 99–514, title XVIII, §1879(u)(3), Oct. 22, 1986, 100 Stat. 2913; Pub. L. 100–202, §136(a), Dec. 22, 1987, 101 Stat. 1329–441; Pub. L. 101–239, title VII, §§7871(b)(2), 7881(m)(2)(D), 7891(a)(1), 7893(a), 7894(a)(1)(A), (2)(A), (3), (4), Dec. 19, 1989, 103 Stat. 2435, 2444, 2445, 2447, 2448; Pub. L. 101–508, title XII, §12002(b)(2)(C), Nov. 5, 1990, 104 Stat. 1388–566; Pub. L. 102–89, §2, Aug. 14, 1991, 105 Stat. 446; Pub. L. 104–290, title III, §308(b)(1), Oct. 11, 1996, 110 Stat. 3440; Pub. L. 105–72, §1(a), Nov. 10, 1997, 111 Stat. 1457; Pub. L. 109–280, title VI, §611(f), title IX, §§905(a), 906(a)(2)(A), title XI, §§1104(c), 1106(a), Aug. 17, 2006, 120 Stat. 972, 1050, 1051, 1060; Pub. L. 110–28, title VI, §6611(a)(1), (b)(1), May 25, 2007, 121 Stat. 179, 180; Pub. L. 110–458, title I, §111(c), Dec. 23, 2008, 122 Stat. 5113.)

REFERENCES IN TEXT

This chapter, referred to in pars. (2)(B) and (37)(E), (G)(ii), (vii), was in the original "this Act", meaning Pub. L. 93–406, known as the Employee Retirement Income Security Act of 1974. Titles I, III, and IV of such Act are classified principally to this chapter. For complete classification of this Act to the Code, see Short Title note set out under section 1001 of this title and Tables.

The Outer Continental Shelf Lands Act, referred to in par. (10), is act Aug. 7, 1953, ch. 345, 67 Stat. 462, as amended, which is classified generally to subchapter III (§1331 et seq.) of chapter 29 of Title 43, Public Lands. For complete classification of this Act to the Code, see Short Title note set out under section 1331 of Title 43 and Tables.

The Labor Management Relations Act, 1947, referred to in par. (12), is act June 23, 1947, ch. 120, 61 Stat. 136, as amended, which is classified principally to chapter 7 (§141 et seq.) of this title. For complete classification of this Act to the Code, see section 141 of this title and Tables.

The Railway Labor Act, referred to in par. (12), is act May 20, 1926, ch. 347, 44 Stat. 577, as amended, which is classified principally to chapter 8 (§151 et seq.) of Title 45, Railroads. For complete classification of this Act to the Code, see section 151 of Title 45 and Tables.

Section 77b(1) of title 15, referred to in par. (20), was redesignated section 77b(a)(1) of title 15 by Pub. L. 104–290, title I, §106(a)(1), Oct. 11, 1996, 110 Stat. 3424.

The Investment Company Act of 1940, referred to in par. (21)(B), is title I of act Aug. 22, 1940, ch. 686, 54 Stat. 789, as amended, which is classified generally to subchapter I (§80a–1 et seq.) of chapter 2D of Title 15, Commerce and Trade. For complete classification of this Act to the Code, see section 80a–51 of Title 15 and Tables.

The Railroad Retirement Act of 1935 or 1937, referred to in par. (32), means act Aug. 29, 1935, ch. 812, 49 Stat. 967, as amended, known as the Railroad Retirement Act of 1935. The Railroad Retirement Act of 1935 was amended generally by act June 24, 1937, ch. 382, part I, 50 Stat. 307, and was known as the Railroad Retirement Act of 1937. The Railroad Retirement Act of 1937 was amended generally and redesignated the Railroad Retirement Act of 1974 by Pub. L. 93–445, title I, Oct. 16, 1974, 88 Stat. 1305 and is classified generally to subchapter IV (§231 et seq.) of chapter 9 of Title 45, Railroads. For complete classification of this Act to the Code, see Tables.

The International Organizations Immunities Act, referred to in par. (32), is title I of act Dec. 29, 1945, ch. 652, 59 Stat. 669, as amended, which is classified principally to subchapter XVIII (§288 et seq.) of chapter 7 of Title 22, Foreign Relations and Intercourse. For complete classification of this Act to the Code, see Short Title note set out under section 288 of Title 22 and Tables.

Sections 1453(b) and (c) of this title, referred to in par. (37)(E), was in the original "sections 4403(b) and (c)", meaning sections 4403(b) and (c) of the Employee Retirement Income Security Act of 1974, which was translated as section 1453(b) and (c) of this title as the probable intent of Congress, in view of the Employee Retirement Income Security Act of 1974 not containing a section 4403 and the subject matter of section 4303 of the Act which is classified to section 1453(b) and (c) of this title.

The Internal Revenue Code of 1954, referred to in par. (37)(E), was redesignated the Internal Revenue Code of 1986 by Pub. L. 99–514, §2, Oct. 22, 1986, 100 Stat. 2095, and is classified to Title 26, Internal Revenue Code.

For the effective date of the Multiemployer Pension Plan Amendments Act of 1980, referred to in par. (37)(E), see section 1461(e) of this title.

The Investment Advisers Act of 1940, referred to in par. (38)(B), is title II of act Aug. 22, 1940, ch. 686, 54 Stat. 847, as amended, which is classified generally to subchapter II (§80b–1 et seq.) of chapter 2D of Title 15, Commerce and Trade. For complete classification of this Act to the Code, see section 80b–20 of Title 15 and Tables.

AMENDMENTS

2008—Par. (37)(G). Pub. L. 110–458 substituted "subparagraph" for "paragraph" in cls. (ii), (iii), and (v)(I),

[4] So in original. Two pars. (41) have been enacted.

[5] So in original. Probably should be "part 4 of subtitle B,".

"clause (i)(II)" for "subclause (i)(II)" in cl. (iii), "clause" for "subparagraph" in cl. (v)(II), and "section 1021(b)(1)" for "section 1021(b)(4)" in cl. (v)(III).

2007—Par. (37)(G)(i)(II)(aa). Pub. L. 110–28, §6611(a)(1)(A), substituted "for each of the 3 plan years immediately preceding the first plan year for which the election under this paragraph is effective with respect to the plan," for "for each of the 3 plan years immediately before August 17, 2006,".

Par. (37)(G)(ii). Pub. L. 110–28, §6611(a)(1)(B), substituted "starting with any plan year beginning on or after January 1, 1999, and ending before January 1, 2008, as designated by the plan in the election made under clause (i)(II)" for "starting with the first plan year ending after August 17, 2006".

Par. (37)(G)(vi). Pub. L. 110–28, §6611(b)(1), substituted "if it is a plan sponsored by an organization which is described in section 501(c)(5) of title 26 and exempt from tax under section 501(a) of such title and which was established in Chicago, Illinois, on August 12, 1881." for "if it is a plan—

"(I) that was established in Chicago, Illinois, on August 12, 1881; and

"(II) sponsored by an organization described in section 501(c)(5) of title 26 and exempt from tax under section 501(a) of title 26."

Par. (37)(G)(vii). Pub. L. 110–28, §6611(a)(1)(C), added cl. (vii).

2006—Par. (2)(A). Pub. L. 109–280, §905(a), inserted at end "A distribution from a plan, fund, or program shall not be treated as made in a form other than retirement income or as a distribution prior to termination of covered employment solely because such distribution is made to an employee who has attained age 62 and who is not separated from employment at the time of such distribution."

Par. (2)(B). Pub. L. 109–280, §1104(c), inserted at end "An applicable voluntary early retirement incentive plan (as defined in section 457(e)(11)(D)(ii) of title 26) making payments or supplements described in section 457(e)(11)(D)(i) of title 26, and an applicable employment retention plan (as defined in section 457(f)(4)(C) of title 26) making payments of benefits described in section 457(f)(4)(A) of title 26, shall, for purposes of this subchapter, be treated as a welfare plan (and not a pension plan) with respect to such payments and supplements."

Par. (32). Pub. L. 109–280, §906(a)(2)(A), inserted at end "The term 'governmental plan' includes a plan which is established and maintained by an Indian tribal government (as defined in section 7701(a)(40) of title 26), a subdivision of an Indian tribal government (determined in accordance with section 7871(d) of title 26), or an agency or instrumentality of either, and all of the participants of which are employees of such entity substantially all of whose services as such an employee are in the performance of essential governmental functions but not in the performance of commercial activities (whether or not an essential government function)".

Par. (37)(G). Pub. L. 109–280, §1106(a), added subpar. (G).

Par. (42). Pub. L. 109–280, §611(f), added par. (42).

1997—Par. (38)(B). Pub. L. 105–72 added introductory provisions and cls. (i) and (ii), redesignated former cls. (ii) and (iii) as (iii) and (iv), respectively, and struck out former introductory provisions and cl. (i) which read as follows: "who is (i) registered as an investment adviser under the Investment Advisers Act of 1940 or under the laws of any State;".

1996—Par. (38)(B). Pub. L. 104–290 temporarily inserted "or under the laws of any State" before "; (ii) is a bank,". See Effective and Termination Dates of 1996 Amendment note below.

1991—Par. (40)(A)(iii), (B)(v). Pub. L. 102–89 added cl. (iii) at end of subpar. (A) and cl. (v) at end of subpar. (B).

1990—Par. (41). Pub. L. 101–508 added par. (41) which read as follows: "The term 'single-employer plan' means a plan which is not a multiemployer plan."

1989—Pars. (14), (33), (36), (40)(B)(iv). Pub. L. 101–239, §7891(a)(1), substituted "Internal Revenue Code of 1986" for "Internal Revenue Code of 1954", which for purposes of codification was translated as "title 26" thus requiring no change in text.

Par. (23). Pub. L. 101–239, §7881(m)(2)(D), inserted at end "The accrued benefit of an employee shall not be less than the amount determined under section 1054(c)(2)(B) of this title with respect to the employee's accumulated contribution."

Par. (24)(B). Pub. L. 101–239, §7871(b)(2), amended subpar. (B) generally. Prior to amendment, subpar. (B) read as follows: "the latest of—

"(i) the time a plan participant attains age 65,

"(ii) in the case of a plan participant who commences participation in the plan within 5 years before attaining normal retirement age under the plan, the 5th anniversary of the time the plan participant commences participation in the plan, or

"(iii) in the case of a plan participant not described in clause (ii), the 10th anniversary of the time the plan participant commences participation in the plan."

Par. (33)(D)(iii). Pub. L. 101–239, §7894(a)(1)(A), substituted "Secretary of the Treasury" for "Secretary" in subcls. (I) to (III).

Par. (37)(B). Pub. L. 101–239, §7893(a), substituted "section 1301(b)(1)" for "section 1301(c)(1)".

Par. (37)(F)(i)(II). Pub. L. 101–239, §7894(a)(2)(A)(i), substituted "the Internal Revenue Code of 1986" for "such Code", which for purposes of codification was translated as "title 26" thus requiring no change in text.

Par. (37)(F)(ii). Pub. L. 101–239, §7894(a)(2)(A)(ii), (iii), inserted "of such Code" after "section 501(c)" in subcl. (I) and after "section 170(b)(1)(A)(ii)" in subcl. (II), which for purposes of codification was translated as "of title 26" thus requiring no change in text.

Par. (39). Pub. L. 101–239, §7894(a)(3), substituted "mean, with respect to a plan, the calendar" for "mean with respect to a plan, calendar".

Par. (41). Pub. L. 101–239, §7894(a)(4), added par. (41).

1987—Par. (37)(F). Pub. L. 100–202 added subpar. (F).

1986—Par. (24)(B). Pub. L. 99–509 amended subpar. (B) generally. Prior to amendment, subpar. (B) read as follows: "the later of—

"(i) the time a plan participant attains age 65, or

"(ii) the 10th anniversary of the time a plan participant commenced participation in the plan."

Par. (37)(A). Pub. L. 99–514 repealed the amendment made by Pub. L. 99–272. See note below.

Pub. L. 99–272, which, eff. Jan. 1, 1986, directed the substitution of "means a pension plan" for "means a plan" was repealed by Pub. L. 99–514, eff. Jan. 1, 1986.

1983—Par. (40). Pub. L. 97–473 added par. (40).

1980—Par. (2). Pub. L. 96–364, §409, redesignated existing provisions as subpar. (A), inserted exception for subpar. (B), substituted "(i)" for "(A)" and "(ii)" for "(B)", and added subpar. (B).

Par. (14). Pub. L. 96–364, §305, inserted provisions respecting a trust described in section 501(c)(22) of title 26.

Par. (33). Pub. L. 96–364, §407(a), substituted provisions defining "church plan" as a plan established and maintained (to the extent required in cl. (ii) of subpar. (B)) for employees or beneficiaries by a church, etc., exempt from tax under section 501 of title 26, for provisions defining "church plan" as a plan established and maintained for employees by a church, etc., exempt from tax under section 501 of title 26, or a plan in existence on Jan. 1, 1974, established and maintained by a church, etc., for employees and employees of agencies of the church, etc.

Par. (37). Pub. L. 96–364, §302(a), substantially revised definition of term "multiemployer plan" by, among other changes, restructuring subpar. (A), resulting in elimination of provisions covering amount of contributions and payment of benefits, and subpar. (B), resulting in elimination of provisions reworking amount of contributions for subsequent plan years, and added subpars. (C) to (E).

EFFECTIVE DATE OF 2008 AMENDMENT

Amendment by Pub. L. 110–458 effective as if included in the provisions of Pub. L. 109–280 to which the amendment relates, except as otherwise provided, see section 112 of Pub. L. 110–458, set out as a note under section 72 of Title 26, Internal Revenue Code.

EFFECTIVE DATE OF 2007 AMENDMENT

Amendment by Pub. L. 110–28 effective as if included in section 1106 of the Pension Protection Act of 2006, Pub. L. 109–280, see section 6611(c) of Pub. L. 110–28, set out as a note under section 414 of Title 26, Internal Revenue Code.

EFFECTIVE DATE OF 2006 AMENDMENT

Amendment by section 611(f) of Pub. L. 109–280 applicable to transactions occurring after Aug. 17, 2006, see section 611(h)(1) of Pub. L. 109–280, set out as a note under section 4975 of Title 26, Internal Revenue Code.

Amendment by section 905(a) of Pub. L. 109–280 applicable to distributions in plan years beginning after Dec. 31, 2006, see section 905(c) of Pub. L. 109–280, set out as a note under section 401 of Title 26, Internal Revenue Code.

Amendment by section 906(a)(2)(A) of Pub. L. 109–280 applicable to any year beginning on or after Aug. 17, 2006, see section 906(c) of Pub. L. 109–280, set out as a note under section 414 of Title 26, Internal Revenue Code.

Amendment by section 1104(c) of Pub. L. 109–280 effective Aug. 17, 2006, and applicable to plan years ending after such date, see section 1104(d)(1), (3) of Pub. L. 109–280, set out as a note under section 457 of Title 26, Internal Revenue Code.

EFFECTIVE DATE OF 1997 AMENDMENT

Section 1(c) of Pub. L. 105–72 provided that: "The amendments made by subsection (a) [amending this section] shall take effect on July 8, 1997, except that the requirement of section 3(38)(B)(ii) of the Employee Retirement Income Security Act of 1974 [section 1002(38)(B)(ii) of this title] (as amended by this Act) for filing with the Secretary of Labor of a copy of a registration form which has been filed with a State before the date of the enactment of this Act [Nov. 10, 1997], or is to be filed with a State during the 1-year period beginning with such date, shall be treated as satisfied upon the filing of such a copy with the Secretary at any time during such 1-year period. This section shall supersede section 308(b) of the National Securities Markets Improvement Act of 1996 [Pub. L. 104–290, amending this section and enacting provisions set out as an Effective and Termination Dates of 1996 Amendment note below] (and the amendment made thereby)."

EFFECTIVE AND TERMINATION DATES OF 1996 AMENDMENT

Amendment by Pub. L. 104–290 effective 270 days after Oct. 11, 1996, see section 308(a) of Pub. L. 104–290, as amended, set out as a note under section 80b–2 of Title 15, Commerce and Trade.

Section 308(b)(2) of Pub. L. 104–290 which provided that the amendment made by paragraph (1), amending this section, ceased to be effective 2 years after Oct. 11, 1996, was superseded by section 1(c) of Pub. L. 105–72, set out as an Effective Date of 1997 Amendment note above.

EFFECTIVE DATE OF 1991 AMENDMENT

Section 3 of Pub. L. 102–89 provided that: "The amendments made by section 2 [amending this section] shall take effect on the date of the enactment of this Act [Aug. 14, 1991]."

EFFECTIVE DATE OF 1990 AMENDMENT

Amendment by Pub. L. 101–508 applicable to reversions occurring after Sept. 30, 1990, but not applicable to any reversion after Sept. 30, 1990, if (1) in the case of plans subject to subchapter III of this chapter, notice of intent to terminate under such subchapter was provided to participants (or if no participants, to Pension Benefit Guaranty Corporation) before Oct. 1, 1990, (2) in the case of plans subject to subchapter I of this chapter (and not subchapter III), notice of intent to reduce future accruals under section 1054(h) of this title was provided to participants in connection with termination before Oct. 1, 1990, (3) in the case of plans not subject to subchapter I or III of this chapter, a request for a determination letter with respect to termination was filed with Secretary of the Treasury or Secretary's delegate before Oct. 1, 1990, or (4) in the case of plans not subject to subchapter I or III of this chapter and having only one participant, a resolution terminating the plan was adopted by employer before Oct. 1, 1990, see section 12003 of Pub. L. 101–508, set out as a note under section 4980 of Title 26, Internal Revenue Code.

EFFECTIVE DATE OF 1989 AMENDMENT

Amendment by section 7871(b)(2) of Pub. L. 101–239 effective as if included in the amendments made by section 9203 of Pub. L. 99–509, see section 7871(b)(3) of Pub. L. 101–239, set out as a note under section 411 of Title 26, Internal Revenue Code.

Amendment by section 7881(m)(2)(D) of Pub. L. 101–239 effective, except as otherwise provided, as if included in the provision of the Pension Protection Act, Pub. L. 100–203, §§9302–9346, to which such amendment relates, see section 7882 of Pub. L. 101–239, set out as a note under section 401 of Title 26.

Section 7891(f) of Pub. L. 101–239 provided that: "Except as otherwise provided in this section, any amendment made by this section [amending this section, sections 1003, 1025, 1051 to 1056, 1060, 1061, 1081 to 1084, 1085a, 1101, 1103, 1107, 1108, 1132, 1134, 1137, 1161, 1166, 1167, 1201 to 1203, 1222, 1301, 1302, 1307, 1309, 1321 to 1322a, 1342 to 1345, 1362, 1368, 1384, 1385, 1390, 1391, 1393, 1403, 1421, 1423, 1425, and 1453 of this title, and section 4980B of Title 26] shall take effect as if included in the provision of the Reform Act [probably means Tax Reform Act of 1986, Pub. L. 99–514] to which such amendment relates."

Section 7893(h) of Pub. L. 101–239 provided that: "Any amendment made by this section [amending this section and sections 1322a, 1341, 1342, 1347, 1366, 1367, and 1398 of this title] shall take effect as if included in the provision of the Single-Employer Pension Plan Amendments Act of 1986 [Pub. L. 99–272, title XI] to which such amendment relates."

Section 7894(a)(1)(B) of Pub. L. 101–239 provided that: "The amendments made by subparagraph (A) [amending this section] shall take effect as if included in section 407 of the Multiemployer Pension Plan Amendments Act of 1980 [Pub. L. 96–364]."

Section 7894(a)(2)(B) of Pub. L. 101–239 provided that: "The amendment made by this paragraph [amending this section] shall take effect as if included in section 136 of Public Law 100–202."

Section 7894(i) of Pub. L. 101–239 provided that: "Except as otherwise provided in this section, any amendment made by this section [amending this section and sections 1021, 1024 to 1026, 1028, 1031, 1051 to 1056, 1060, 1061, 1081, 1082, 1084, 1086, 1103, 1107, 1108, 1113, 1114, 1132, 1144, 1321 to 1322a, 1344, 1368, and 1461 of this title] shall take effect as if originally included in the provision of the Employee Retirement Income Security Act of 1974 [Pub. L. 93–406] to which such amendment relates."

EFFECTIVE DATE OF 1987 AMENDMENT

Section 136(b) of Pub. L. 100–202 provided that: "The amendment made by this section [amending this section] shall apply to years beginning after the date of the enactment of this joint resolution [Dec. 22, 1987]."

EFFECTIVE DATE OF 1986 AMENDMENTS

Amendment by section 1879(u)(3) of Pub. L. 99–514 effective as if such provisions were included in the enactment of the Single-Employer Pension Plan Amendments Act of 1986 [Pub. L. 99–272], see section 1879(u)(4)(A) of Pub. L. 99–514, set out as a note under section 1054 of this title.

Amendment by Pub. L. 99–509 applicable only with respect to plan years beginning on or after Jan. 1, 1988, and only with respect to service performed on or after such date, see section 9204 of Pub. L. 99–509, set out as an Effective and Termination Dates of 1986 Amendments note under section 623 of this title.

Amendment by Pub. L. 99–272 effective Jan. 1, 1986, with certain exceptions, see section 11019 of Pub. L. 99–272, set out as a note under section 1341 of this title.

EFFECTIVE DATE OF 1983 AMENDMENT

Section 302(c) of Pub. L. 97–473 provided that: "The amendments made by this section [amending this section and section 1144 of this title] shall take effect on the date of the enactment of this Act [Jan. 14, 1983]."

EFFECTIVE DATE OF 1980 AMENDMENT

Amendment of pars. (2), (14), and (37), by Pub. L. 96–364 effective Sept. 26, 1980, except as specifically provided, see section 1461(e) of this title.

Amendment of par. (33) by Pub. L. 96–364 effective Jan. 1, 1974, see section 407(c) of Pub. L. 96–364, set out as a note under section 414 of Title 26, Internal Revenue Code.

REGULATIONS

Secretary of Labor, Secretary of the Treasury, and Equal Employment Opportunity Commission each to issue before Feb. 1, 1988, final regulations to carry out amendments made by Pub. L. 99–509, see section 9204 of Pub. L. 99–509, set out as an Effective and Termination Dates of 1986 Amendment note under section 623 of this title.

AVAILABILITY OF DOCUMENTS VIA FILING DEPOSITORY

Section 1(b) of Pub. L. 105–72 provided that: "A fiduciary shall be treated as meeting the requirements of section 3(38)(B)(ii) of the Employee Retirement Income Security Act of 1974 [29 U.S.C. 1002(38)(B)(ii)] (as amended by subsection (a)) relating to provision to the Secretary of Labor of a copy of the form referred to therein, if a copy of such form (or substantially similar information) is available to the Secretary of Labor from a centralized electronic or other record-keeping database."

PLAN AMENDMENTS NOT REQUIRED UNTIL JANUARY 1, 1989

For provisions directing that if any amendments made by subtitle A or subtitle C of title XI [§§ 1101–1147 and 1171–1177] or title XVIII [§§ 1800–1899A] of Pub. L. 99–514 require an amendment to any plan, such plan amendment shall not be required to be made before the first plan year beginning on or after Jan. 1, 1989, see section 1140 of Pub. L. 99–514, as amended, set out as a note under section 401 of Title 26, Internal Revenue Code.

For provisions directing that if any amendments made by Pub. L. 99–509 require an amendment to any plan, such plan amendment shall not be required to be made before the first plan year beginning on or after Jan. 1, 1989, see section 9204 of Pub. L. 99–509, set out as an Effective and Termination Dates of 1986 Amendment note under section 623 of this title.

§ 1003. Coverage

(a) In general

Except as provided in subsection (b) or (c) of this section and in sections 1051, 1081, and 1101 of this title, this subchapter shall apply to any employee benefit plan if it is established or maintained—

(1) by any employer engaged in commerce or in any industry or activity affecting commerce; or

(2) by any employee organization or organizations representing employees engaged in commerce or in any industry or activity affecting commerce; or

(3) by both.

(b) Exceptions for certain plans

The provisions of this subchapter shall not apply to any employee benefit plan if—

(1) such plan is a governmental plan (as defined in section 1002(32) of this title);

(2) such plan is a church plan (as defined in section 1002(33) of this title) with respect to which no election has been made under section 410(d) of title 26;

(3) such plan is maintained solely for the purpose of complying with applicable workmen's compensation laws or unemployment compensation or disability insurance laws;

(4) such plan is maintained outside of the United States primarily for the benefit of persons substantially all of whom are nonresident aliens; or

(5) such plan is an excess benefit plan (as defined in section 1002(36) of this title) and is unfunded.

The provisions of part 7 of subtitle B of this subchapter shall not apply to a health insurance issuer (as defined in section 1191b(b)(2) of this title) solely by reason of health insurance coverage (as defined in section 1191b(b)(1) of this title) provided by such issuer in connection with a group health plan (as defined in section 1191b(a)(1) of this title) if the provisions of this subchapter do not apply to such group health plan.

(c) Voluntary employee contributions to accounts and annuities

If a pension plan allows an employee to elect to make voluntary employee contributions to accounts and annuities as provided in section 408(q) of title 26, such accounts and annuities (and contributions thereto) shall not be treated as part of such plan (or as a separate pension plan) for purposes of any provision of this subchapter other than section 1103(c), 1104, or 1105 of this title (relating to exclusive benefit, and fiduciary and co-fiduciary responsibilities) and part 5 of subtitle B of this subchapter[1] (relating to administration and enforcement). Such provisions shall apply to such accounts and annuities in a manner similar to their application to a simplified employee pension under section 408(k) of title 26.

(Pub. L. 93–406, title I, § 4, Sept. 2, 1974, 88 Stat. 839; Pub. L. 101–239, title VII, § 7891(a)(1), Dec. 19, 1989, 103 Stat. 2445; Pub. L. 104–191, title I, § 101(d), Aug. 21, 1996, 110 Stat. 1952; Pub. L. 104–204, title VI, § 603(b)(3)(A), Sept. 26, 1996, 110 Stat. 2938; Pub. L. 107–16, title VI, § 602(b), June 7, 2001, 115 Stat. 96; Pub. L. 107–147, title IV, § 411(i)(2), Mar. 9, 2002, 116 Stat. 47.)

REFERENCES IN TEXT

Part 5 of subtitle B of this subchapter, referred to in subsec. (c), was in the original a reference to "part 5" and was translated as meaning part 5 of subtitle B of title I of Pub. L. 93–406, to reflect the probable intent of Congress.

AMENDMENTS

2002—Subsec. (c). Pub. L. 107–147 inserted "and part 5 of subtitle B of this subchapter (relating to administra-

[1] See References in Text note below.

tion and enforcement)" after "co-fiduciary responsibilities)" and "Such provisions shall apply to such accounts and annuities in a manner similar to their application to a simplified employee pension under section 408(k) of title 26." at end.

2001—Subsec. (a). Pub. L. 107–16, §602(b)(2), inserted "or (c)" after "subsection (b)" in introductory provisions.

Subsec. (c). Pub. L. 107–16, §602(b)(1), added subsec. (c).

1996—Subsec. (b). Pub. L. 104–204, in concluding provisions, made technical amendment to references in original act which appear in text as references to section 1191b of this title.

Pub. L. 104–191 inserted at end "The provisions of part 7 of subtitle B of this subchapter shall not apply to a health insurance issuer (as defined in section 1191b(b)(2) of this title) solely by reason of health insurance coverage (as defined in section 1191b(b)(1) of this title) provided by such issuer in connection with a group health plan (as defined in section 1191b(a)(1) of this title) if the provisions of this subchapter do not apply to such group health plan."

1989—Subsec. (b)(2). Pub. L. 101–239 substituted "Internal Revenue Code of 1986" for "Internal Revenue Code of 1954", which for purposes of codification was translated as "title 26" thus requiring no change in text.

EFFECTIVE DATE OF 2002 AMENDMENT

Amendment by Pub. L. 107–147 effective as if included in the provisions of the Economic Growth and Tax Relief Reconciliation Act of 2001, Pub. L. 107–16, to which such amendment relates, see section 411(x) of Pub. L. 107–147, set out as a note under section 25B of Title 26, Internal Revenue Code.

EFFECTIVE DATE OF 2001 AMENDMENT

Amendment by Pub. L. 107–16 applicable to plan years beginning after Dec. 31, 2002, see section 602(c) of Pub. L. 107–16, set out as a note under section 408 of Title 26, Internal Revenue Code.

EFFECTIVE DATE OF 1996 AMENDMENTS

Section 603(c) of Pub. L. 104–204 provided that: "The amendments made by this section [enacting section 1185 of this title and amending this section and sections 1021, 1022, 1024, 1132, 1136, 1144, 1181, 1191, and 1191a of this title] shall apply with respect to group health plans for plan years beginning on or after January 1, 1998."

Amendment by Pub. L. 104–191 applicable with respect to group health plans for plan years beginning after June 30, 1997, except as otherwise provided, see section 101(g) of Pub. L. 104–191, set out as an Effective Date note under section 1181 of this title.

EFFECTIVE DATE OF 1989 AMENDMENT

Amendment by Pub. L. 101–239 effective, except as otherwise provided, as if included in the provision of the Tax Reform Act of 1986, Pub. L. 99–514, to which such amendment relates, see section 7891(f) of Pub. L. 101–239, set out as a note under section 1002 of this title.

SUBTITLE B—REGULATORY PROVISIONS

PART 1—REPORTING AND DISCLOSURE

§1021. Duty of disclosure and reporting

(a) Summary plan description and information to be furnished to participants and beneficiaries

The administrator of each employee benefit plan shall cause to be furnished in accordance with section 1024(b) of this title to each participant covered under the plan and to each beneficiary who is receiving benefits under the plan—

(1) a summary plan description described in section 1022(a)(1)[1] of this title; and

(2) the information described in subsection (f) and sections 1024(b)(3) and 1025(a) and (c) of this title.

(b) Reports to be filed with Secretary of Labor

The administrator shall, in accordance with section 1024(a) of this title, file with the Secretary—

(1) the annual report containing the information required by section 1023 of this title; and

(2) terminal and supplementary reports as required by subsection (c) of this section.

(c) Terminal and supplementary reports

(1) Each administrator of an employee pension benefit plan which is winding up its affairs (without regard to the number of participants remaining in the plan) shall, in accordance with regulations prescribed by the Secretary, file such terminal reports as the Secretary may consider necessary. A copy of such report shall also be filed with the Pension Benefit Guaranty Corporation.

(2) The Secretary may require terminal reports to be filed with regard to any employee welfare benefit plan which is winding up its affairs in accordance with regulations promulgated by the Secretary.

(3) The Secretary may require that a plan described in paragraph (1) or (2) file a supplementary or terminal report with the annual report in the year such plan is terminated and that a copy of such supplementary or terminal report in the case of a plan described in paragraph (1) be also filed with the Pension Benefit Guaranty Corporation.

(d) Notice of failure to meet minimum funding standards

(1) In general

If an employer maintaining a plan other than a multiemployer plan fails to make a required installment or other payment required to meet the minimum funding standard under section 1082 of this title to a plan before the 60th day following the due date for such installment or other payment, the employer shall notify each participant and beneficiary (including an alternate payee as defined in section 1056(d)(3)(K) of this title) of such plan of such failure. Such notice shall be made at such time and in such manner as the Secretary may prescribe.

(2) Subsection not to apply if waiver pending

This subsection shall not apply to any failure if the employer has filed a waiver request under section 1083 of this title with respect to the plan year to which the required installment relates, except that if the waiver request is denied, notice under paragraph (1) shall be provided within 60 days after the date of such denial.

(3) Definitions

For purposes of this subsection, the terms "required installment" and "due date" have

[1] See References in Text note below.

the same meanings given such terms by section 1083(j) of this title.

(e) Notice of transfer of excess pension assets to health benefits accounts

(1) Notice to participants

Not later than 60 days before the date of a qualified transfer by an employee pension benefit plan of excess pension assets to a health benefits account, the administrator of the plan shall notify (in such manner as the Secretary may prescribe) each participant and beneficiary under the plan of such transfer. Such notice shall include information with respect to the amount of excess pension assets, the portion to be transferred, the amount of health benefits liabilities expected to be provided with the assets transferred, and the amount of pension benefits of the participant which will be nonforfeitable immediately after the transfer.

(2) Notice to Secretaries, administrator, and employee organizations

(A) In general

Not later than 60 days before the date of any qualified transfer by an employee pension benefit plan of excess pension assets to a health benefits account, the employer maintaining the plan from which the transfer is made shall provide the Secretary, the Secretary of the Treasury, the administrator, and each employee organization representing participants in the plan a written notice of such transfer. A copy of any such notice shall be available for inspection in the principal office of the administrator.

(B) Information relating to transfer

Such notice shall identify the plan from which the transfer is made, the amount of the transfer, a detailed accounting of assets projected to be held by the plan immediately before and immediately after the transfer, and the current liabilities under the plan at the time of the transfer.

(C) Authority for additional reporting requirements

The Secretary may prescribe such additional reporting requirements as may be necessary to carry out the purposes of this section.

(3) Definitions

For purposes of paragraph (1), any term used in such paragraph which is also used in section 420 of title 26 (as in effect on August 17, 2006) shall have the same meaning as when used in such section.

(f) Defined benefit plan funding notices

(1) In general

The administrator of a defined benefit plan to which subchapter III applies shall for each plan year provide a plan funding notice to the Pension Benefit Guaranty Corporation, to each plan participant and beneficiary, to each labor organization representing such participants or beneficiaries, and, in the case of a multiemployer plan, to each employer that has an obligation to contribute to the plan.

(2) Information contained in notices

(A) Identifying information

Each notice required under paragraph (1) shall contain identifying information, including the name of the plan, the address and phone number of the plan administrator and the plan's principal administrative officer, each plan sponsor's employer identification number, and the plan number of the plan.

(B) Specific information

A plan funding notice under paragraph (1) shall include—

(i)(I) in the case of a single-employer plan, a statement as to whether the plan's funding target attainment percentage (as defined in section 1083(d)(2) of this title) for the plan year to which the notice relates, and for the 2 preceding plan years, is at least 100 percent (and, if not, the actual percentages), or

(II) in the case of a multiemployer plan, a statement as to whether the plan's funded percentage (as defined in section 1085(i) of this title) for the plan year to which the notice relates, and for the 2 preceding plan years, is at least 100 percent (and, if not, the actual percentages),

(ii)(I) in the case of a single-employer plan, a statement of—

(aa) the total assets (separately stating the prefunding balance and the funding standard carryover balance) and liabilities of the plan, determined in the same manner as under section 1083 of this title, for the plan year to which the notice relates and for the 2 preceding plan years, as reported in the annual report for each such plan year, and

(bb) the value of the plan's assets and liabilities for the plan year to which the notice relates as of the last day of the plan year to which the notice relates determined using the asset valuation under subclause (II) of section 1306(a)(3)(E)(iii) of this title and the interest rate under section 1306(a)(3)(E)(iv) of this title, and

(II) in the case of a multiemployer plan, a statement, for the plan year to which the notice relates and the preceding 2 plan years, of the value of the plan assets (determined both in the same manner as under section 1084 of this title and under the rules of subclause (I)(bb)) and the value of the plan liabilities (determined in the same manner as under section 1084 of this title except that the method specified in section 1085(i)(8) of this title shall be used),

(iii) a statement of the number of participants who are—

(I) retired or separated from service and are receiving benefits,

(II) retired or separated participants entitled to future benefits, and

(III) active participants under the plan,

(iv) a statement setting forth the funding policy of the plan and the asset allocation of investments under the plan (expressed as percentages of total assets) as of the end of the plan year to which the notice relates,

(v) in the case of a multiemployer plan, whether the plan was in critical or endangered status under section 1085 of this title for such plan year and, if so—

(I) a statement describing how a person may obtain a copy of the plan's funding improvement or rehabilitation plan, as appropriate, adopted under section 1085 of this title and the actuarial and financial data that demonstrate any action taken by the plan toward fiscal improvement, and

(II) a summary of any funding improvement plan, rehabilitation plan, or modification thereof adopted under section 1085 of this title during the plan year to which the notice relates,

(vi) in the case of any plan amendment, scheduled benefit increase or reduction, or other known event taking effect in the current plan year and having a material effect on plan liabilities or assets for the year (as defined in regulations by the Secretary), an explanation of the amendment, schedule increase or reduction, or event, and a projection to the end of such plan year of the effect of the amendment, scheduled increase or reduction, or event on plan liabilities,

(vii)(I) in the case of a single-employer plan, a summary of the rules governing termination of single-employer plans under subtitle C of subchapter III, or

(II) in the case of a multiemployer plan, a summary of the rules governing reorganization or insolvency, including the limitations on benefit payments,

(viii) a general description of the benefits under the plan which are eligible to be guaranteed by the Pension Benefit Guaranty Corporation, along with an explanation of the limitations on the guarantee and the circumstances under which such limitations apply,

(ix) a statement that a person may obtain a copy of the annual report of the plan filed under section 1024(a) of this title upon request, through the Internet website of the Department of Labor, or through an Intranet website maintained by the applicable plan sponsor (or plan administrator on behalf of the plan sponsor), and

(x) if applicable, a statement that each contributing sponsor, and each member of the contributing sponsor's controlled group, of the single-employer plan was required to provide the information under section 1310 of this title for the plan year to which the notice relates.

(C) Other information

Each notice under paragraph (1) shall include—

(i) in the case of a multiemployer plan, a statement that the plan administrator shall provide, upon written request, to any labor organization representing plan participants and beneficiaries and any employer that has an obligation to contribute to the plan, a copy of the annual report filed with the Secretary under section 1024(a) of this title, and

(ii) any additional information which the plan administrator elects to include to the extent not inconsistent with regulations prescribed by the Secretary.

(3) Time for providing notice

(A) In general

Any notice under paragraph (1) shall be provided not later than 120 days after the end of the plan year to which the notice relates.

(B) Exception for small plans

In the case of a small plan (as such term is used under section 1083(g)(2)(B) of this title) any notice under paragraph (1) shall be provided upon filing of the annual report under section 1024(a) of this title.

(4) Form and manner

Any notice under paragraph (1)—

(A) shall be provided in a form and manner prescribed in regulations of the Secretary,

(B) shall be written in a manner so as to be understood by the average plan participant, and

(C) may be provided in written, electronic, or other appropriate form to the extent such form is reasonably accessible to persons to whom the notice is required to be provided.

(g) Reporting by certain arrangements

The Secretary may, by regulation, require multiple employer welfare arrangements providing benefits consisting of medical care (within the meaning of section 1191b(a)(2) of this title) which are not group health plans to report, not more frequently than annually, in such form and such manner as the Secretary may require for the purpose of determining the extent to which the requirements of part 7 are being carried out in connection with such benefits.

(h) Simple retirement accounts

(1) No employer reports

Except as provided in this subsection, no report shall be required under this section by an employer maintaining a qualified salary reduction arrangement under section 408(p) of title 26.

(2) Summary description

The trustee of any simple retirement account established pursuant to a qualified salary reduction arrangement under section 408(p) of title 26 shall provide to the employer maintaining the arrangement each year a description containing the following information:

(A) The name and address of the employer and the trustee.

(B) The requirements for eligibility for participation.

(C) The benefits provided with respect to the arrangement.

(D) The time and method of making elections with respect to the arrangement.

(E) The procedures for, and effects of, withdrawals (including rollovers) from the arrangement.

(3) Employee notification

The employer shall notify each employee immediately before the period for which an election described in section 408(p)(5)(C) of title 26 may be made of the employee's opportunity to make such election. Such notice shall include a copy of the description described in paragraph (2).

(i) Notice of blackout periods to participant or beneficiary under individual account plan

(1) Duties of plan administrator

In advance of the commencement of any blackout period with respect to an individual account plan, the plan administrator shall notify the plan participants and beneficiaries who are affected by such action in accordance with this subsection.

(2) Notice requirements

(A) In general

The notices described in paragraph (1) shall be written in a manner calculated to be understood by the average plan participant and shall include—

(i) the reasons for the blackout period,

(ii) an identification of the investments and other rights affected,

(iii) the expected beginning date and length of the blackout period,

(iv) in the case of investments affected, a statement that the participant or beneficiary should evaluate the appropriateness of their current investment decisions in light of their inability to direct or diversify assets credited to their accounts during the blackout period, and

(v) such other matters as the Secretary may require by regulation.

(B) Notice to participants and beneficiaries

Except as otherwise provided in this subsection, notices described in paragraph (1) shall be furnished to all participants and beneficiaries under the plan to whom the blackout period applies at least 30 days in advance of the blackout period.

(C) Exception to 30-day notice requirement

In any case in which—

(i) a deferral of the blackout period would violate the requirements of subparagraph (A) or (B) of section 1104(a)(1) of this title, and a fiduciary of the plan reasonably so determines in writing, or

(ii) the inability to provide the 30-day advance notice is due to events that were unforeseeable or circumstances beyond the reasonable control of the plan administrator, and a fiduciary of the plan reasonably so determines in writing,

subparagraph (B) shall not apply, and the notice shall be furnished to all participants and beneficiaries under the plan to whom the blackout period applies as soon as reasonably possible under the circumstances unless such a notice in advance of the termination of the blackout period is impracticable.

(D) Written notice

The notice required to be provided under this subsection shall be in writing, except that such notice may be in electronic or other form to the extent that such form is reasonably accessible to the recipient.

(E) Notice to issuers of employer securities subject to blackout period

In the case of any blackout period in connection with an individual account plan, the plan administrator shall provide timely notice of such blackout period to the issuer of any employer securities subject to such blackout period.

(3) Exception for blackout periods with limited applicability

In any case in which the blackout period applies only to 1 or more participants or beneficiaries in connection with a merger, acquisition, divestiture, or similar transaction involving the plan or plan sponsor and occurs solely in connection with becoming or ceasing to be a participant or beneficiary under the plan by reason of such merger, acquisition, divestiture, or transaction, the requirement of this subsection that the notice be provided to all participants and beneficiaries shall be treated as met if the notice required under paragraph (1) is provided to such participants or beneficiaries to whom the blackout period applies as soon as reasonably practicable.

(4) Changes in length of blackout period

If, following the furnishing of the notice pursuant to this subsection, there is a change in the beginning date or length of the blackout period (specified in such notice pursuant to paragraph (2)(A)(iii)), the administrator shall provide affected participants and beneficiaries notice of the change as soon as reasonably practicable. In relation to the extended blackout period, such notice shall meet the requirements of paragraph (2)(D) and shall specify any material change in the matters referred to in clauses (i) through (v) of paragraph (2)(A).

(5) Regulatory exceptions

The Secretary may provide by regulation for additional exceptions to the requirements of this subsection which the Secretary determines are in the interests of participants and beneficiaries.

(6) Guidance and model notices

The Secretary shall issue guidance and model notices which meet the requirements of this subsection.

(7) Blackout period

For purposes of this subsection—

(A) In general

The term "blackout period" means, in connection with an individual account plan, any period for which any ability of participants or beneficiaries under the plan, which is otherwise available under the terms of such plan, to direct or diversify assets credited to their accounts, to obtain loans from the plan, or to obtain distributions from the plan is temporarily suspended, limited, or restricted, if such suspension, limitation, or restriction is for any period of more than 3 consecutive business days.

(B) Exclusions

The term "blackout period" does not include a suspension, limitation, or restriction—

(i) which occurs by reason of the application of the securities laws (as defined in section 78c(a)(47) of title 15),

(ii) which is a change to the plan which provides for a regularly scheduled suspension, limitation, or restriction which is disclosed to participants or beneficiaries through any summary of material modifications, any materials describing specific investment alternatives under the plan, or any changes thereto, or

(iii) which applies only to 1 or more individuals, each of whom is the participant, an alternate payee (as defined in section 1056(d)(3)(K) of this title), or any other beneficiary pursuant to a qualified domestic relations order (as defined in section 1056(d)(3)(B)(i) of this title).

(8) Individual account plan

(A) In general

For purposes of this subsection, the term "individual account plan" shall have the meaning provided such term in section 1002(34) of this title, except that such term shall not include a one-participant retirement plan.

(B) One-participant retirement plan

For purposes of subparagraph (A), the term "one-participant retirement plan" means a retirement plan that on the first day of the plan year—

(i) covered only one individual (or the individual and the individual's spouse) and the individual (or the individual and the individual's spouse) owned 100 percent of the plan sponsor (whether or not incorporated), or

(ii) covered only one or more partners (or partners and their spouses) in the plan sponsor.

(j) Notice of funding-based limitation on certain forms of distribution

The plan administrator of a single-employer plan shall provide a written notice to plan participants and beneficiaries within 30 days—

(1) after the plan has become subject to a restriction described in paragraph (1) or (3) of section 1056(g) of this title),[2]

(2) in the case of a plan to which section 1056(g)(4) of this title applies, after the valuation date for the plan year described in section 1056(g)(4)(A) of this title for which the plan's adjusted funding target attainment percentage for the plan year is less than 60 percent (or, if earlier, the date such percentage is deemed to be less than 60 percent under section 1056(g)(7) of this title), and

(3) at such other time as may be determined by the Secretary of the Treasury.

The notice required to be provided under this subsection shall be in writing, except that such notice may be in electronic or other form to the extent that such form is reasonably accessible to the recipient. The Secretary of the Treasury, in consultation with the Secretary, shall have the authority to prescribe rules applicable to the notices required under this subsection.

(k) Multiemployer plan information made available on request

(1) In general

Each administrator of a multiemployer plan shall, upon written request, furnish to any plan participant or beneficiary, employee representative, or any employer that has an obligation to contribute to the plan—

(A) a copy of any periodic actuarial report (including any sensitivity testing) received by the plan for any plan year which has been in the plan's possession for at least 30 days,

(B) a copy of any quarterly, semi-annual, or annual financial report prepared for the plan by any plan investment manager or advisor or other fiduciary which has been in the plan's possession for at least 30 days, and

(C) a copy of any application filed with the Secretary of the Treasury requesting an extension under section 1084 of this title or section 431(d) of title 26 and the determination of such Secretary pursuant to such application.

(2) Compliance

Information required to be provided under paragraph (1)—

(A) shall be provided to the requesting participant, beneficiary, or employer within 30 days after the request in a form and manner prescribed in regulations of the Secretary,

(B) may be provided in written, electronic, or other appropriate form to the extent such form is reasonably accessible to persons to whom the information is required to be provided, and

(C) shall not—

(i) include any individually identifiable information regarding any plan participant, beneficiary, employee, fiduciary, or contributing employer, or

(ii) reveal any proprietary information regarding the plan, any contributing employer, or entity providing services to the plan.

Subparagraph (C)(i) shall not apply to individually identifiable information with respect to any plan investment manager or adviser, or with respect to any other person (other than an employee of the plan) preparing a financial report required to be included under paragraph (1)(B).

(3) Limitations

In no case shall a participant, beneficiary, or employer be entitled under this subsection to receive more than one copy of any report or application described in paragraph (1) during any one 12-month period. The administrator may make a reasonable charge to cover copying, mailing, and other costs of furnishing copies of information pursuant to paragraph (1).

[2] So in original. The closing parenthesis probably should not appear.

The Secretary may by regulations prescribe the maximum amount which will constitute a reasonable charge under the preceding sentence.

(*l*) Notice of potential withdrawal liability

(1) In general

The plan sponsor or administrator of a multiemployer plan shall, upon written request, furnish to any employer who has an obligation to contribute to the plan a notice of—

(A) the estimated amount which would be the amount of such employer's withdrawal liability under part 1 of subtitle E of subchapter III if such employer withdrew on the last day of the plan year preceding the date of the request, and

(B) an explanation of how such estimated liability amount was determined, including the actuarial assumptions and methods used to determine the value of the plan liabilities and assets, the data regarding employer contributions, unfunded vested benefits, annual changes in the plan's unfunded vested benefits, and the application of any relevant limitations on the estimated withdrawal liability.

For purposes of subparagraph (B), the term "employer contribution" means, in connection with a participant, a contribution made by an employer as an employer of such participant.

(2) Compliance

Any notice required to be provided under paragraph (1)—

(A) shall be provided in a form and manner prescribed in regulations of the Secretary to the requesting employer within—

(i) 180 days after the request, or

(ii) subject to regulations of the Secretary, such longer time as may be necessary in the case of a plan that determines withdrawal liability based on any method described under paragraph (4) or (5) of section 1391(c) of this title; and

(B) may be provided in written, electronic, or other appropriate form to the extent such form is reasonably accessible to employers to whom the information is required to be provided.

(3) Limitations

In no case shall an employer be entitled under this subsection to receive more than one notice described in paragraph (1) during any one 12-month period. The person required to provide such notice may make a reasonable charge to cover copying, mailing, and other costs of furnishing such notice pursuant to paragraph (1). The Secretary may by regulations prescribe the maximum amount which will constitute a reasonable charge under the preceding sentence.

(m) Notice of right to divest

Not later than 30 days before the first date on which an applicable individual of an applicable individual account plan is eligible to exercise the right under section 1054(j) of this title to direct the proceeds from the divestment of employer securities with respect to any type of contribution, the administrator shall provide to such individual a notice—

(1) setting forth such right under such section, and

(2) describing the importance of diversifying the investment of retirement account assets.

The notice required by this subsection shall be written in a manner calculated to be understood by the average plan participant and may be delivered in written, electronic, or other appropriate form to the extent that such form is reasonably accessible to the recipient.

(n) Cross reference

For regulations relating to coordination of reports to the Secretaries of Labor and the Treasury, see section 1204 of this title.

(Pub. L. 93–406, title I, §101, Sept. 2, 1974, 88 Stat. 840; Pub. L. 100–203, title IX, §9304(d), Dec. 22, 1987, 101 Stat. 1330–348; Pub. L. 101–239, title VII, §§7881(b)(5)(A), 7894(b)(2), Dec. 19, 1989, 103 Stat. 2438, 2448; Pub. L. 101–508, title XII, §12012(d)(1), Nov. 5, 1990, 104 Stat. 1388–572; Pub. L. 103–66, title IV, §4301(b)(1), Aug. 10, 1993, 107 Stat. 375; Pub. L. 103–465, title VII, §731(c)(4)(A), Dec. 8, 1994, 108 Stat. 5004; Pub. L. 104–188, title I, §1421(d)(1), Aug. 20, 1996, 110 Stat. 1799; Pub. L. 104–191, title I, §101(e)(1), Aug. 21, 1996, 110 Stat. 1952; Pub. L. 104–204, title VI, §603(b)(3)(B), Sept. 26, 1996, 110 Stat. 2938; Pub. L. 105–34, title XV, §1503(a), Aug. 5, 1997, 111 Stat. 1061; Pub. L. 105–200, title IV, §401(h)(1)(A), July 16, 1998, 112 Stat. 668; Pub. L. 106–170, title V, §535(a)(2)(A), Dec. 17, 1999, 113 Stat. 1934; Pub. L. 107–204, title III, §306(b)(1), July 30, 2002, 116 Stat. 780; Pub. L. 108–218, title I, §103(a), title II, §204(b)(1), Apr. 10, 2004, 118 Stat. 602, 609; Pub. L. 108–357, title VII, §709(a)(1), Oct. 22, 2004, 118 Stat. 1551; Pub. L. 109–280, title I, §§103(b)(1), 107(a)(1), (11), title V, §§501(a), 502(a)(1), (b)(1), 503(c)(2), 507(a), 509(a), Aug. 17, 2006, 120 Stat. 815, 818, 819, 936, 939, 940, 944, 948, 952; Pub. L. 110–458, title I, §§101(c)(1)(A), 105(a), (b)(1), (g), Dec. 23, 2008, 122 Stat. 5097, 5104, 5105.)

References in Text

Section 1022(a)(1) of this title, referred to in subsec. (a)(1), was redesignated section 1022(a) of this title by Pub. L. 105–34, title XV, §1503(b)(1)(B), Aug. 5, 1997, 111 Stat. 1061.

Amendments

2008—Subsec. (f)(2)(B)(ii)(I)(aa). Pub. L. 110–458, §105(a)(1), substituted "to which the notice relates" for "for which the latest annual report filed under section 1024(a) of this title was filed".

Subsec. (f)(2)(B)(ii)(II). Pub. L. 110–458, §105(a)(2), added subcl. (II) and struck out former subcl. (II) which read as follows: "in the case of a multiemployer plan, a statement of the value of the plan's assets and liabilities for the plan year to which the notice relates as the last day of such plan year and the preceding 2 plan years,".

Subsec. (i)(8)(B). Pub. L. 110–458, §105(g), amended subpar. (B) generally. Prior to amendment, text read as follows: "For purposes of subparagraph (A), the term 'one-participant retirement plan' means a retirement plan that—

"(i) on the first day of the plan year—

"(I) covered only one individual (or the individual and the individual's spouse) and the individual (or the individual and the individual's spouse) owned 100 percent of the plan sponsor (whether or not incorporated), or

"(II) covered only one or more partners (or partners and their spouses) in the plan sponsor, and

"(ii) does not cover a business that leases employees."

Subsec. (j). Pub. L. 110–458, §101(c)(1)(A), substituted "section 1056(g)(4)(A)" for "section 1056(g)(4)(B)" in par. (2) and inserted "The Secretary of the Treasury, in consultation with the Secretary, shall have the authority to prescribe rules applicable to the notices required under this subsection." in concluding provisions.

Subsec. (k)(2). Pub. L. 110–458, §105(b)(1), inserted concluding provisions.

2006—Subsec. (a)(2). Pub. L. 109–280, §503(c)(2), inserted "subsection (f) and" after "described in".

Subsec. (d)(3). Pub. L. 109–280, §107(a)(1), substituted "1083(j)" for "1082(e)".

Subsec. (e)(3). Pub. L. 109–280, §107(a)(11), substituted "August 17, 2006" for "October 22, 2004".

Subsec. (f). Pub. L. 109–280, §501(a), amended heading and text of subsec. (f) generally, substituting provisions relating to defined benefit plan funding notices for provisions relating to multiemployer defined benefit plan funding notices.

Subsec. (i)(8)(B). Pub. L. 109–280, §509(a), added cl. (i), redesignated cl. (v) as (ii), and struck out former cls. (i) to (iv) which read as follows:

"(i) on the first day of the plan year—

"(I) covered only the employer (and the employer's spouse) and the employer owned the entire business (whether or not incorporated), or

"(II) covered only one or more partners (and their spouses) in a business partnership (including partners in an S or C corporation (as defined in section 1361(a) of title 26)),

"(ii) meets the minimum coverage requirements of section 410(b) of title 26 (as in effect on July 30, 2002) without being combined with any other plan of the business that covers the employees of the business,

"(iii) does not provide benefits to anyone except the employer (and the employer's spouse) or the partners (and their spouses),

"(iv) does not cover a business that is a member of an affiliated service group, a controlled group of corporations, or a group of businesses under common control, and".

Subsec. (j). Pub. L. 109–280, §103(b)(1)(B), added subsec. (j). Former subsec. (j) redesignated (k).

Subsec. (k). Pub. L. 109–280, §502(a)(1)(B), added subsec. (k). Former subsec. (k) redesignated (*l*).

Pub. L. 109–280, §103(b)(1)(A), redesignated subsec. (j) as (k).

Subsec. (*l*). Pub. L. 109–280, §502(b)(1)(B), added subsec. (*l*). Former subsec. (*l*) redesignated (m).

Pub. L. 109–280, §502(a)(1)(A), redesignated subsec. (k) as (*l*).

Subsec. (m). Pub. L. 109–280, §507(a), added subsec. (m). Former subsec. (m) redesignated (n).

Pub. L. 109–280, §502(b)(1)(A), redesignated subsec. (*l*) as (m).

Subsec. (n). Pub. L. 109–280, §507(a), redesignated subsec. (m) as (n).

2004—Subsec. (e)(3). Pub. L. 108–357 substituted "October 22, 2004" for "April 10, 2004".

Pub. L. 108–218, §204(b)(1), substituted "April 10, 2004" for "December 17, 1999".

Subsec. (f). Pub. L. 108–218, §103(a), added subsec. (f).

2002—Subsecs. (h) to (j). Pub. L. 107–204 added subsec. (i) and redesignated subsec. (h) relating to cross reference as (j).

1999—Subsec. (e)(3). Pub. L. 106–170 substituted "December 17, 1999" for "January 1, 1995".

1998—Subsec. (f). Pub. L. 105–200 struck out subsec. (f) relating to information necessary to comply with Medicare and Medicaid Coverage Data Bank requirements.

1997—Subsec. (b). Pub. L. 105–34 redesignated pars. (4) and (5) as (1) and (2), respectively, and struck out former pars. (1) to (3), which read as follows:

"(1) the summary plan description described in section 1022(a)(1) of this title;

"(2) a plan description containing the matter required in section 1022(b) of this title;

"(3) modifications and changes referred to in section 1022(a)(2) of this title;".

1996—Subsec. (g). Pub. L. 104–204 made technical amendment to reference in original act which appears in text as reference to section 1191b of this title.

Pub. L. 104–191, §101(e)(1)(B), added subsec. (g). Former subsec. (g) redesignated (h).

Pub. L. 104–188 added subsec. (g). Former subsec. (g) redesignated (h).

Subsec. (h). Pub. L. 104–191, §101(e)(1)(A), redesignated subsec. (g), relating to simple retirement accounts, as (h).

Pub. L. 104–188, §1421(d)(1), redesignated subsec. (g), relating to cross references, as (h).

1994—Subsec. (e)(3). Pub. L. 103–465 substituted "1995" for "1991".

1993—Subsecs. (f), (g). Pub. L. 103–66 added subsec. (f) and redesignated former subsec. (f) as (g).

1990—Subsecs. (e), (f). Pub. L. 101–508 added subsec. (e) and redesignated former subsec. (e) as (f).

1989—Subsec. (a)(2). Pub. L. 101–239, §7894(b)(2), substituted "sections" for "section".

Subsec. (d)(1). Pub. L. 101–239, §7881(b)(5)(A), substituted "an employer maintaining a plan" for "an employer of a plan".

1987—Subsecs. (d), (e). Pub. L. 100–203 added subsec. (d) and redesignated former subsec. (d) as (e).

Effective Date of 2008 Amendment

Amendment by Pub. L. 110–458 effective as if included in the provisions of Pub. L. 109–280 to which the amendment relates, except as otherwise provided, see section 112 of Pub. L. 110–458, set out as a note under section 72 Title 26, Internal Revenue Code.

Effective Date of 2006 Amendment

Pub. L. 109–280, title I, §103(c), Aug. 17, 2006, 120 Stat. 816, as amended by Pub. L. 110–458, title I, §101(c)(3), Dec. 23, 2008, 122 Stat. 5098, provided that:

"(1) In general.—The amendments made by this section [amending this section and sections 1056 and 1132 of this title] shall apply to plan years beginning after December 31, 2007.

"(2) Collective bargaining exception.—In the case of a plan maintained pursuant to 1 or more collective bargaining agreements between employee representatives and 1 or more employers ratified before January 1, 2008, the amendments made by this section shall not apply to plan years beginning before the earlier of—

"(A) the later of—

"(i) the date on which the last collective bargaining agreement relating to the plan terminates (determined without regard to any extension thereof agreed to after the date of the enactment of this Act [Aug. 17, 2006]), or

"(ii) the first day of the first plan year to which the amendments made by this section would (but for this paragraph) apply, or

"(B) January 1, 2010.

For purposes of subparagraph (A)(i), any plan amendment made pursuant to a collective bargaining agreement relating to the plan which amends the plan solely to conform to any requirement added by this section shall not be treated as a termination of such collective bargaining agreement."

Pub. L. 109–280, title I, §107(e), Aug. 17, 2006, 120 Stat. 820, provided that: "The amendments made by this section [amending this section, sections 1023, 1053, 1054, 1056, 1103, 1108, 1301, 1303, 1310, 1362, 1371, and 1423 of this title, and Reorganization Plan No. 4 of 1978, set out as a note under section 1001 of this title and in the Appendix to Title 5, Government Organization and Employees, and repealing section 1057 of this title] shall apply to plan years beginning after 2007."

Pub. L. 109–280, title V, §501(d), Aug. 17, 2006, 120 Stat. 939, provided that:

"(1) In general.—The amendments made by this section [amending this section and repealing section 1311 of this title] shall apply to plan years beginning after

December 31, 2007, except that the amendment made by subsection (b) [repealing section 1311 of this title] shall apply to plan years beginning after December 31, 2006.

"(2) TRANSITION RULE.—Any requirement under section 101(f) of the Employee Retirement Income Security Act of 1974 [29 U.S.C. 1021(f)] (as amended by this section) to report the funding target attainment percentage or funded percentage of a plan with respect to any plan year beginning before January 1, 2008, shall be treated as met if the plan reports—

"(A) in the case of a plan year beginning in 2006, the funded current liability percentage (as defined in section 302(d)(8) of such Act [29 U.S.C. 1082(d)(8)]) of the plan for such plan year, and

"(B) in the case of a plan year beginning in 2007, the funding target attainment percentage or funded percentage as determined using such methods of estimation as the Secretary of the Treasury may provide."

Amendment by section 502(a)(1), (b)(1) of Pub. L. 109–280 applicable to plan years beginning after Dec. 31, 2007, see section 502(d) of Pub. L. 109–280, set out as a note under section 4980F of Title 26, Internal Revenue Code.

Pub. L. 109–280, title V, §503(f), Aug. 17, 2006, 120 Stat. 945, provided that: "The amendments made by this section [amending this section and sections 1023 and 1024 of this title] shall apply to plan years beginning after December 31, 2007."

Pub. L. 109–280, title V, §507(d), Aug. 17, 2006, 120 Stat. 949, provided that:

"(1) IN GENERAL.—The amendments made by this section [amending this section and section 1132 of this title] shall apply to plan years beginning after December 31, 2006.

"(2) TRANSITION RULE.—If notice under section 101(m) of the Employee Retirement Income Security Act of 1974 [29 U.S.C. 1021(m)] (as added by this section) would otherwise be required to be provided before the 90th day after the date of the enactment of this Act [Aug. 17, 2006], such notice shall not be required to be provided until such 90th day."

Pub. L. 109–280, title V, §509(b), Aug. 17, 2006, 120 Stat. 952, provided that: "The amendments made by this subsection [probably means this section, amending this section] shall take effect as if included in the provisions of section 306 of Public Law 107–204 (116 Stat. 745 et seq.)."

EFFECTIVE DATE OF 2004 AMENDMENT

Pub. L. 108–218, title I, §103(d), Apr. 10, 2004, 118 Stat. 604, provided that: "The amendments made by this section [amending this section and section 1132 of this title] shall apply to plan years beginning after December 31, 2004."

EFFECTIVE DATE OF 2002 AMENDMENT

Amendment by Pub. L. 107–204 effective 180 days after July 30, 2002, see section 7244(c) of Title 15, Commerce and Trade.

EFFECTIVE DATE OF 1999 AMENDMENT

Amendment by Pub. L. 106–170 applicable to qualified transfers occurring after Dec. 17, 1999, see section 535(c)(1) of Pub. L. 106–170, set out as a note under section 420 of Title 26, Internal Revenue Code.

EFFECTIVE DATE OF 1998 AMENDMENT

Pub. L. 105–200, title IV, §401(h)(1)(B), July 16, 1998, 112 Stat. 668, provided that: "The amendment made by subparagraph (A) [amending this section] shall take effect as if included in the enactment of the Act entitled 'An Act to repeal the Medicare and Medicaid Coverage Data Bank', approved October 2, 1996 (Public Law 104–226; 110 Stat. 3033)."

EFFECTIVE DATE OF 1996 AMENDMENTS

Amendment by Pub. L. 104–204 applicable with respect to group health plans for plan years beginning on or after Jan. 1, 1998, see section 603(c) of Pub. L. 104–204 set out as a note under section 1003 of this title.

Amendment of Pub. L. 104–191 applicable with respect to group health plans for plan years beginning after June 30, 1997, except as otherwise provided, see section 101(g) of Pub. L. 104–191, set out as an Effective Date note under section 1181 of this title.

Amendment by Pub. L. 104–188 applicable to taxable years beginning after Dec. 31, 1996, see section 1421(e) of Pub. L. 104–188, set out as a note under section 72 of Title 26, Internal Revenue Code.

EFFECTIVE DATE OF 1993 AMENDMENT

Section 4301(d) of Pub. L. 103–66 provided that:

"(1) IN GENERAL.—The amendments made by this section [enacting section 1169 of this title and amending this section and sections 1132 and 1144 of this title] shall take effect on the date of the enactment of this Act [Aug. 10, 1993].

"(2) PLAN AMENDMENTS NOT REQUIRED UNTIL JANUARY 1, 1994.—Any amendment to a plan required to be made by an amendment made by this section shall not be required to be made before the first plan year beginning on or after January 1, 1994, if—

"(A) during the period after the date before the date of the enactment of this Act and before such first plan year, the plan is operated in accordance with the requirements of the amendments made by this section, and

"(B) such plan amendment applies retroactively to the period after the date before the date of the enactment of this Act and before such first plan year.

A plan shall not be treated as failing to be operated in accordance with the provisions of the plan merely because it operates in accordance with this paragraph."

EFFECTIVE DATE OF 1990 AMENDMENT

Section 12012(e) of Pub. L. 101–508 provided that: "The amendments made by this section [amending this section and sections 1082, 1103, 1108, and 1132 of this title] shall apply to qualified transfers under section 420 of the Internal Revenue Code of 1986 [26 U.S.C. 420] made after the date of the enactment of this Act [Nov. 5, 1990]."

EFFECTIVE DATE OF 1989 AMENDMENT

Amendment by section 7881(b)(5)(A) of Pub. L. 101–239 effective, except as otherwise provided, as if included in the provision of the Pension Protection Act, Pub. L. 100–203, §§9302–9346, to which such amendment relates, see section 7882 of Pub. L. 101–239, set out as a note under section 401 of Title 26, Internal Revenue Code.

Amendment by section 7894(b)(2) of Pub. L. 101–239 effective, except as otherwise provided, as if originally included in the provision of the Employee Retirement Income Security Act of 1974, Pub. L. 93–406, to which such amendment relates, see section 7894(i) of Pub. L. 101–239, set out as a note under section 1002 of this title.

EFFECTIVE DATE OF 1987 AMENDMENT

Section 9304(d) of Pub. L. 100–203, as amended by Pub. L. 101–239, title VII, §7881(b)(5)(C), Dec. 19, 1989, 103 Stat. 2438, provided that the amendment made by that section is effective with respect to plan years beginning after Dec. 31, 1987.

REGULATIONS

Pub. L. 109–280, title V, §502(a)(3), Aug. 17, 2006, 120 Stat. 940, provided that: "The Secretary shall prescribe regulations under section 101(k)(2) of the Employee Retirement Income Security Act of 1974 [29 U.S.C. 1021(k)(2)] (as added by paragraph (1)) not later than 1 year after the date of the enactment of this Act [Aug. 17, 2006]."

Pub. L. 108–218, title I, §103(c), Apr. 10, 2004, 118 Stat. 604, provided that: "The Secretary of Labor shall, not later than 1 year after the date of the enactment of this Act [Apr. 10, 2004], issue regulations (including a model notice) necessary to implement the amendments made by this section [amending this section and section 1132 of this title]."

Secretary authorized, effective Sept. 2, 1974, to promulgate regulations wherever provisions of this subchapter call for the promulgation of regulations, see section 1031 of this title.

APPLICABILITY OF AMENDMENTS BY SUBTITLES A AND B OF TITLE I OF PUB. L. 109–280

For special rules on applicability of amendments by subtitles A (§§101–107) and B (§§111–116) of title I of Pub. L. 109–280 to certain eligible cooperative plans, PBGC settlement plans, and eligible government contractor plans, see sections 104, 105, and 106 of Pub. L. 109–280, set out as notes under section 401 of Title 26, Internal Revenue Code.

MODEL NOTICES AND FORMS

Pub. L. 109–280, title V, §501(c), Aug. 17, 2006, 120 Stat. 939, provided that: "Not later than 1 year after the date of the enactment of this Act [Aug. 17, 2006], the Secretary of Labor shall publish a model version of the notice required by section 101(f) of the Employee Retirement Income Security Act of 1974 [29 U.S.C. 1021(f)]. The Secretary of Labor may promulgate any interim final rules as the Secretary determines appropriate to carry out the provisions of this subsection."

Pub. L. 109–280, title V, §503(e), Aug. 17, 2006, 120 Stat. 945, as amended by Pub. L. 110–458, title I, §105(c)(2), Dec. 23, 2008, 122 Stat. 5105, provided that: "Not later than 1 year after the date of the enactment of this Act [Aug. 17, 2006], the Secretary of Labor shall publish a model form for providing the statements, schedules, and other material required to be provided under section 104(d) of the Employee Retirement Income Security Act of 1974 [29 U.S.C. 1024(d)], as amended by this section. The Secretary of Labor may promulgate any interim final rules as the Secretary determines appropriate to carry out the provisions of this subsection."

Pub. L. 109–280, title V, §507(c), Aug. 17, 2006, 120 Stat. 949, provided that: "The Secretary of the Treasury shall, within 180 days after the date of the enactment of this subsection [Aug. 17, 2006], prescribe a model notice for purposes of satisfying the requirements of the amendments made by this section [amending this section and section 1132 of this title]."

PLAN AMENDMENTS NOT REQUIRED UNTIL JULY 30, 2002

For provisions directing that if any amendment made by section 306(b) of Pub. L. 107–204 requires an amendment to any plan, such plan amendment shall not be required to be made before the first plan year beginning on or after July 30, 2002, see section 7244(b)(3) of Title 15, Commerce and Trade.

PLAN AMENDMENTS NOT REQUIRED UNTIL JANUARY 1, 1998

For provisions directing that if any amendments made by subtitle D [§§1401–1465] of title I of Pub. L. 104–188 require an amendment to any plan or annuity contract, such amendment shall not be required to be made before the first day of the first plan year beginning on or after Jan. 1, 1998, see section 1465 of Pub. L. 104–188, set out as a note under section 401 of Title 26, Internal Revenue Code.

§1022. Summary plan description

(a) A summary plan description of any employee benefit plan shall be furnished to participants and beneficiaries as provided in section 1024(b) of this title. The summary plan description shall include the information described in subsection (b) of this section, shall be written in a manner calculated to be understood by the average plan participant, and shall be sufficiently accurate and comprehensive to reasonably apprise such participants and beneficiaries of their rights and obligations under the plan. A summary of any material modification in the terms of the plan and any change in the information required under subsection (b) of this section shall be written in a manner calculated to be understood by the average plan participant and shall be furnished in accordance with section 1024(b)(1) of this title.

(b) The summary plan description shall contain the following information: The name and type of administration of the plan; in the case of a group health plan (as defined in section 1191b(a)(1) of this title), whether a health insurance issuer (as defined in section 1191b(b)(2) of this title) is responsible for the financing or administration (including payment of claims) of the plan and (if so) the name and address of such issuer; the name and address of the person designated as agent for the service of legal process, if such person is not the administrator; the name and address of the administrator; names, titles, and addresses of any trustee or trustees (if they are persons different from the administrator); a description of the relevant provisions of any applicable collective bargaining agreement; the plan's requirements respecting eligibility for participation and benefits; a description of the provisions providing for nonforfeitable pension benefits; circumstances which may result in disqualification, ineligibility, or denial or loss of benefits; the source of financing of the plan and the identity of any organization through which benefits are provided; the date of the end of the plan year and whether the records of the plan are kept on a calendar, policy, or fiscal year basis; the procedures to be followed in presenting claims for benefits under the plan including the office at the Department of Labor through which participants and beneficiaries may seek assistance or information regarding their rights under this chapter and the Health Insurance Portability and Accountability Act of 1996 with respect to health benefits that are offered through a group health plan (as defined in section 1191b(a)(1) of this title) and the remedies available under the plan for the redress of claims which are denied in whole or in part (including procedures required under section 1133 of this title).

(Pub. L. 93–406, title I, §102, Sept. 2, 1974, 88 Stat. 841; Pub. L. 104–191, title I, §101(c)(2), Aug. 21, 1996, 110 Stat. 1951; Pub. L. 104–204, title VI, §603(b)(3)(C), Sept. 26, 1996, 110 Stat. 2938; Pub. L. 105–34, title XV, §1503(b), Aug. 5, 1997, 111 Stat. 1061.)

REFERENCES IN TEXT

This chapter, referred to in subsec. (b), was in the original "this Act", meaning Pub. L. 93–406, known as the Employee Retirement Income Security Act of 1974. Titles I, III, and IV of such Act are classified principally to this chapter. For complete classification of this Act to the Code, see Short Title note set out under section 1001 of this title and Tables.

The Health Insurance Portability and Accountability Act of 1996, referred to in subsec. (b), is Pub. L. 104–191, Aug. 21, 1996, 110 Stat. 1936. For complete classification of this Act to the Code, see Short Title of 1996 Amendment note set out under section 201 of Title 42, The Public Health and Welfare, and Tables.

AMENDMENTS

1997—Pub. L. 105–34, § 1503(b)(2)(B), substituted "Summary plan description" for "Plan description and summary plan description" in section catchline.

Subsec. (a). Pub. L. 105–34, § 1503(b)(1), struck out "(1)" after subsec. designation and struck out par. (2) which read as follows: "A plan description (containing the information required by subsection (b) of this section) of any employee benefit plan shall be prepared on forms prescribed by the Secretary, and shall be filed with the Secretary as required by section 1024(a)(1) of this title. Any material modification in the terms of the plan and any change in the information described in subsection (b) of this section shall be filed in accordance with section 1024(a)(1)(D) of this title."

Subsec. (b). Pub. L. 105–34, § 1503(b)(2)(A), substituted "The summary plan description shall contain" for "The plan description and summary plan description shall contain".

1996—Subsec. (b). Pub. L. 104–204 made technical amendment to references in original act which appear in text as references to section 1191b of this title.

Pub. L. 104–191 inserted "in the case of a group health plan (as defined in section 1191b(a)(1) of this title), whether a health insurance issuer (as defined in section 1191b(b)(2) of this title) is responsible for the financing or administration (including payment of claims) of the plan and (if so) the name and address of such issuer;" after "type of administration of the plan;" and "including the office at the Department of Labor through which participants and beneficiaries may seek assistance or information regarding their rights under this chapter and the Health Insurance Portability and Accountability Act of 1996 with respect to health benefits that are offered through a group health plan (as defined in section 1191b(a)(1) of this title)" after "presenting claims for benefits under the plan".

EFFECTIVE DATE OF 1996 AMENDMENTS

Amendment by Pub. L. 104–204 applicable with respect to group health plans for plan years beginning on or after Jan. 1, 1998, see section 603(c) of Pub. L. 104–204 set out as a note under section 1003 of this title.

Amendment by Pub. L. 104–191 applicable with respect to group health plans for plan years beginning after June 30, 1997, except as otherwise provided, see section 101(g) of Pub. L. 104–191, set out as an Effective Date note under section 1181 of this title.

REGULATIONS

Secretary authorized, effective Sept. 2, 1974, to promulgate regulations wherever provisions of this subchapter call for the promulgation of regulations, see section 1031 of this title.

§ 1023. Annual reports

(a) Publication and filing

(1)(A) An annual report shall be published with respect to every employee benefit plan to which this part applies. Such report shall be filed with the Secretary in accordance with section 1024(a) of this title, and shall be made available and furnished to participants in accordance with section 1024(b) of this title.

(B) The annual report shall include the information described in subsections (b) and (c) and where applicable subsections (d), (e), and (f) and shall also include—

(i) a financial statement and opinion, as required by paragraph (3) of this subsection, and

(ii) an actuarial statement and opinion, as required by paragraph (4) of this subsection.

(2) If some or all of the information necessary to enable the administrator to comply with the requirements of this subchapter is maintained by—

(A) an insurance carrier or other organization which provides some or all of the benefits under the plan, or holds assets of the plan in a separate account,

(B) a bank or similar institution which holds some or all of the assets of the plan in a common or collective trust or a separate trust, or custodial account, or

(C) a plan sponsor as defined in section 1002(16)(B) of this title,

such carrier, organization, bank, institution, or plan sponsor shall transmit and certify the accuracy of such information to the administrator within 120 days after the end of the plan year (or such other date as may be prescribed under regulations of the Secretary).

(3)(A) Except as provided in subparagraph (C), the administrator of an employee benefit plan shall engage, on behalf of all plan participants, an independent qualified public accountant, who shall conduct such an examination of any financial statements of the plan, and of other books and records of the plan, as the accountant may deem necessary to enable the accountant to form an opinion as to whether the financial statements and schedules required to be included in the annual reports by subsection (b) of this section are presented fairly in conformity with generally accepted accounting principles applied on a basis consistent with that of the preceding year. Such examination shall be conducted in accordance with generally accepted auditing standards, and shall involve such tests of the books and records of the plan as are considered necessary by the independent qualified public accountant. The independent qualified public accountant shall also offer his opinion as to whether the separate schedules specified in subsection (b)(3) of this section and the summary material required under section 1024(b)(3) of this title present fairly, and in all material respects the information contained therein when considered in conjunction with the financial statements taken as a whole. The opinion by the independent qualified public accountant shall be made a part of the annual report. In a case where a plan is not required to file an annual report, the requirements of this paragraph shall not apply. In a case where by reason of section 1024(a)(2) of this title a plan is required only to file a simplified annual report, the Secretary may waive the requirements of this paragraph.

(B) In offering his opinion under this section the accountant may rely on the correctness of any actuarial matter certified to by an enrolled actuary, if he so states his reliance.

(C) The opinion required by subparagraph (A) need not be expressed as to any statements required by subsection (b)(3)(G) of this section prepared by a bank or similar institution or insurance carrier regulated and supervised and subject to periodic examination by a State or Federal agency if such statements are certified by the bank, similar institution, or insurance carrier as accurate and are made a part of the annual report.

(D) For purposes of this subchapter, the term "qualified public accountant" means—

(i) a person who is a certified public accountant, certified by a regulatory authority of a State;

(ii) a person who is a licensed public accountant licensed by a regulatory authority of a State; or

(iii) a person certified by the Secretary as a qualified public accountant in accordance with regulations published by him for a person who practices in States where there is no certification or licensing procedure for accountants.

(4)(A) The administrator of an employee pension benefit plan subject to the reporting requirement of subsection (d) of this section shall engage, on behalf of all plan participants, an enrolled actuary who shall be responsible for the preparation of the materials comprising the actuarial statement required under subsection (d) of this section. In a case where a plan is not required to file an annual report, the requirement of this paragraph shall not apply, and, in a case where by reason of section 1024(a)(2) of this title, a plan is required only to file a simplified report, the Secretary may waive the requirement of this paragraph.

(B) The enrolled actuary shall utilize such assumptions and techniques as are necessary to enable him to form an opinion as to whether the contents of the matters reported under subsection (d) of this section—

(i) are in the aggregate reasonably related to the experience of the plan and to reasonable expectations; and

(ii) represent his best estimate of anticipated experience under the plan.

The opinion by the enrolled actuary shall be made with respect to, and shall be made a part of, each annual report.

(C) For purposes of this subchapter, the term "enrolled actuary" means an actuary enrolled under subtitle C of subchapter II of this chapter.

(D) In making a certification under this section the enrolled actuary may rely on the correctness of any accounting matter under subsection (b) of this section to which any qualified public accountant has expressed an opinion, if he so states his reliance.

(b) Financial statement

An annual report under this section shall include a financial statement containing the following information:

(1) With respect to an employee welfare benefit plan: a statement of assets and liabilities; a statement of changes in fund balance; and a statement of changes in financial position. In the notes to financial statements, disclosures concerning the following items shall be considered by the accountant: a description of the plan including any significant changes in the plan made during the period and the impact of such changes on benefits; a description of material lease commitments, other commitments, and contingent liabilities; a description of agreements and transactions with persons known to be parties in interest; a general description of priorities upon termination of the plan; information concerning whether or not a tax ruling or determination letter has been obtained; and any other matters necessary to fully and fairly present the financial statements of the plan.

(2) With respect to an employee pension benefit plan: a statement of assets and liabilities, and a statement of changes in net assets available for plan benefits which shall include details of revenues and expenses and other changes aggregated by general source and application. In the notes to financial statements, disclosures concerning the following items shall be considered by the accountant: a description of the plan including any significant changes in the plan made during the period and the impact of such changes on benefits; the funding policy (including policy with respect to prior service cost), and any changes in such policies during the year; a description of any significant changes in plan benefits made during the period; a description of material lease commitments, other commitments, and contingent liabilities; a description of agreements and transactions with persons known to be parties in interest; a general description of priorities upon termination of the plan; information concerning whether or not a tax ruling or determination letter has been obtained; and any other matters necessary to fully and fairly present the financial statements of such pension plan.

(3) With respect to all employee benefit plans, the statement required under paragraph (1) or (2) shall have attached the following information in separate schedules:

(A) a statement of the assets and liabilities of the plan aggregated by categories and valued at their current value, and the same data displayed in comparative form for the end of the previous fiscal year of the plan;

(B) a statement of receipts and disbursements during the preceding twelve-month period aggregated by general sources and applications;

(C) a schedule of all assets held for investment purposes aggregated and identified by issuer, borrower, or lessor, or similar party to the transaction (including a notation as to whether such party is known to be a party in interest), maturity date, rate of interest, collateral, par or maturity value, cost, and current value;

(D) a schedule of each transaction involving a person known to be party in interest, the identity of such party in interest and his relationship or that of any other party in interest to the plan, a description of each asset to which the transaction relates; the purchase or selling price in case of a sale or purchase, the rental in case of a lease, or the interest rate and maturity date in case of a loan; expense incurred in connection with the transaction; the cost of the asset, the current value of the asset, and the net gain (or loss) on each transaction;

(E) a schedule of all loans or fixed income obligations which were in default as of the close of the plan's fiscal year or were classified during the year as uncollectable and the following information with respect to each loan on such schedule (including a notation as to whether parties involved are known to be parties in interest): the original principal amount of the loan, the amount of principal and interest received during the reporting year, the unpaid balance, the identity and address of the obligor, a detailed description of the loan (including date of making and maturity, interest rate, the type and value of collateral, and other material terms), the amount of principal and interest overdue (if any) and an explanation thereof;

(F) a list of all leases which were in default or were classified during the year as uncollectable; and the following information with respect to each lease on such schedule (including a notation as to whether parties involved are known to be parties in interest): the type of property leased (and, in the case of fixed assets such as land, buildings, leasehold, and so forth, the location of the property), the identity of the lessor or lessee from or to whom the plan is leasing, the relationship of such lessors and lessees, if any, to the plan, the employer, employee organization, or any other party in interest, the terms of the lease regarding rent, taxes, insurance, repairs, expenses, and renewal options; the date the leased property was purchased and its cost, the date the property was leased and its approximate value at such date, the gross rental receipts during the reporting period, expenses paid for the leased property during the reporting period, the net receipts from the lease, the amounts in arrears, and a statement as to what steps have been taken to collect amounts due or otherwise remedy the default;

(G) if some or all of the assets of a plan or plans are held in a common or collective trust maintained by a bank or similar institution or in a separate account maintained by an insurance carrier or a separate trust maintained by a bank as trustee, the report shall include the most recent annual statement of assets and liabilities of such common or collective trust, and in the case of a separate account or a separate trust, such other information as is required by the administrator in order to comply with this subsection; and

(H) a schedule of each reportable transaction, the name of each party to the transaction (except that, in the case of an acquisition or sale of a security on the market, the report need not identify the person from whom the security was acquired or to whom it was sold) and a description of each asset to which the transaction applies; the purchase or selling price in case of a sale or purchase, the rental in case of a lease, or the interest rate and maturity date in case of a loan; expenses incurred in connection with the transaction; the cost of the asset, the current value of the asset, and the net gain (or loss) on each transaction. For purposes of the preceding sentence, the term "reportable transaction" means a transaction to which the plan is a party if such transaction is—

(i) a transaction involving an amount in excess of 3 percent of the current value of the assets of the plan;

(ii) any transaction (other than a transaction respecting a security) which is part of a series of transactions with or in conjunction with a person in a plan year, if the aggregate amount of such transactions exceeds 3 percent of the current value of the assets of the plan;

(iii) a transaction which is part of a series of transactions respecting one or more securities of the same issuer, if the aggregate amount of such transactions in the plan year exceeds 3 percent of the current value of the assets of the plan; or

(iv) a transaction with or in conjunction with a person respecting a security, if any other transaction with or in conjunction with such person in the plan year respecting a security is required to be reported by reason of clause (i).

(4) The Secretary may, by regulation, relieve any plan from filing a copy of a statement of assets and liabilities (or other information) described in paragraph (3)(G) if such statement and other information is filed with the Secretary by the bank or insurance carrier which maintains the common or collective trust or separate account.

(c) Information to be furnished by administrator

The administrator shall furnish as a part of a report under this section the following information:

(1) The number of employees covered by the plan.

(2) The name and address of each fiduciary.

(3) Except in the case of a person whose compensation is minimal (determined under regulations of the Secretary) and who performs solely ministerial duties (determined under such regulations), the name of each person (including but not limited to, any consultant, broker, trustee, accountant, insurance carrier, actuary, administrator, investment manager, or custodian who rendered services to the plan or who had transactions with the plan) who received directly or indirectly compensation from the plan during the preceding year for services rendered to the plan or its participants, the amount of such compensation, the nature of his services to the plan or its participants, his relationship to the employer of the employees covered by the plan, or the employee organization, and any other office, position, or employment he holds with any party in interest.

(4) An explanation of the reason for any change in appointment of trustee, accountant, insurance carrier, enrolled actuary, administrator, investment manager, or custodian.

(5) Such financial and actuarial information including but not limited to the material described in subsections (b) and (d) of this section as the Secretary may find necessary or appropriate.

(d) Actuarial statement

With respect to an employee pension benefit plan (other than (A) a profit sharing, savings, or other plan, which is an individual account plan, (B) a plan described in section 1081(b) of this title, or (C) a plan described both in section 1321(b) of this title and in paragraph (1), (2), (3), (4), (5), (6), or (7) of section 1081(a) of this title) an annual report under this section for a plan year shall include a complete actuarial statement applicable to the plan year which shall include the following:

(1) The date of the plan year, and the date of the actuarial valuation applicable to the plan year for which the report is filed.

(2) The date and amount of the contribution (or contributions) received by the plan for the plan year for which the report is filed and contributions for prior plan years not previously reported.

(3) The following information applicable to the plan year for which the report is filed: the normal costs or target normal costs, the accrued liabilities or funding target, an identification of benefits not included in the calculation; a statement of the other facts and actuarial assumptions and methods used to determine costs, and a justification for any change in actuarial assumptions or cost methods; and the minimum contribution required under section 1082 of this title.

(4) The number of participants and beneficiaries, both retired and nonretired, covered by the plan.

(5) The current value of the assets accumulated in the plan, and the present value of the assets of the plan used by the actuary in any computation of the amount of contributions to the plan required under section 1082 of this title and a statement explaining the basis of such valuation of present value of assets.

(6) Information required in regulations of the Pension Benefit Guaranty Corporation with respect to:

(A) the current value of the assets of the plan,

(B) the present value of all nonforfeitable benefits for participants and beneficiaries receiving payments under the plan,

(C) the present value of all nonforfeitable benefits for all other participants and beneficiaries,

(D) the present value of all accrued benefits which are not nonforfeitable (including a separate accounting of such benefits which are benefit commitments, as defined in section 1301(a)(16) of this title), and

(E) the actuarial assumptions and techniques used in determining the values described in subparagraphs (A) through (D).

(7) A certification of the contribution necessary to reduce the minimum required contribution determined under section 1083 of this title, or the accumulated funding deficiency determined under section 1084 of this title, to zero.

(8) A statement by the enrolled actuary—

(A) that to the best of his knowledge the report is complete and accurate, and

(B) the applicable requirements of sections 1083(h) and 1084(c)(3) of this title (relating to reasonable actuarial assumptions and methods) have been complied with.

(9) A copy of the opinion required by subsection (a)(4) of this section.

(10) A statement by the actuary which discloses—

(A) any event which the actuary has not taken into account, and

(B) any trend which, for purposes of the actuarial assumptions used, was not assumed to continue in the future,

but only if, to the best of the actuary's knowledge, such event or trend may require a material increase in plan costs or required contribution rates.

(11) If the current value of the assets of the plan is less than 70 percent of—

(A) in the case of a single-employer plan, the funding target (as defined in section 1083(d)(1) of this title) of the plan, or

(B) in the case of a multiemployer plan, the current liability (as defined in section 1084(c)(6)(D) of this title) under the plan,

the percentage which such value is of the amount described in subparagraph (A) or (B).

(12) A statement explaining the actuarial assumptions and methods used in projecting future retirements and forms of benefit distributions under the plan.

(13) Such other information regarding the plan as the Secretary may by regulation require.

(14) Such other information as may be necessary to fully and fairly disclose the actuarial position of the plan.

Such actuary shall make an actuarial valuation of the plan for every third plan year, unless he determines that a more frequent valuation is necessary to support his opinion under subsection (a)(4) of this section.

(e) Statement from insurance company, insurance service, or other similar organizations which sell or guarantee plan benefits

If some or all of the benefits under the plan are purchased from and guaranteed by an insurance company, insurance service, or other similar organization, a report under this section shall include a statement from such insurance company, service, or other similar organization covering the plan year and enumerating—

(1) the premium rate or subscription charge and the total premium or subscription charges paid to each such carrier, insurance service, or other similar organization and the approximate number of persons covered by each class of such benefits; and

(2) the total amount of premiums received, the approximate number of persons covered by each class of benefits, and the total claims paid by such company, service, or other organization; dividends or retroactive rate adjustments, commissions, and administrative service or other fees or other specific acquisition costs paid by such company, service, or other organization; any amounts held to provide benefits after retirement; the remainder of such premiums; and the names and addresses of the brokers, agents, or other persons to whom commissions or fees were paid, the amount paid to each, and for what purpose. If any such company, service, or other organization does not maintain separate experience records covering the specific groups it serves, the report shall include in lieu of the information required by the foregoing provisions of this paragraph (A) a statement as to the basis of its premium rate or subscription charge, the total amount of premiums or subscription charges received from the plan, and a copy of the financial report of the company, service, or other organization and (B) if such company, service, or organization incurs specific costs in connection with the acquisition or retention of any particular plan or plans, a detailed statement of such costs.

(f) Additional information with respect to defined benefit plans

(1) Liabilities under 2 or more plans

(A) In general

In any case in which any liabilities to participants or their beneficiaries under a defined benefit plan as of the end of a plan year consist (in whole or in part) of liabilities to such participants and beneficiaries under 2 or more pension plans as of immediately before such plan year, an annual report under this section for such plan year shall include the funded percentage of each of such 2 or more pension plans as of the last day of such plan year and the funded percentage of the plan with respect to which the annual report is filed as of the last day of such plan year.

(B) Funded percentage

For purposes of this paragraph, the term "funded percentage"—

(i) in the case of a single-employer plan, means the funding target attainment percentage, as defined in section 1083(d)(2) of this title, and

(ii) in the case of a multiemployer plan, has the meaning given such term in section 1085(i)(2) of this title.

(2) Additional information for multiemployer plans

With respect to any defined benefit plan which is a multiemployer plan, an annual report under this section for a plan year shall include, in addition to the information required under paragraph (1), the following, as of the end of the plan year to which the report relates:

(A) The number of employers obligated to contribute to the plan.

(B) A list of the employers that contributed more than 5 percent of the total contributions to the plan during such plan year.

(C) The number of participants under the plan on whose behalf no contributions were made by an employer as an employer of the participant for such plan year and for each of the 2 preceding plan years.

(D) The ratios of—

(i) the number of participants under the plan on whose behalf no employer had an obligation to make an employer contribution during the plan year, to

(ii) the number of participants under the plan on whose behalf no employer had an obligation to make an employer contribution during each of the 2 preceding plan years.

(E) Whether the plan received an amortization extension under section 1084(d) of this title or section 431(d) of title 26 for such plan year and, if so, the amount of the difference between the minimum required contribution for the year and the minimum required contribution which would have been required without regard to the extension, and the period of such extension.

(F) Whether the plan used the shortfall funding method (as such term is used in section 1085 of this title) for such plan year and, if so, the amount of the difference between the minimum required contribution for the year and the minimum required contribution which would have been required without regard to the use of such method, and the period of use of such method.

(G) Whether the plan was in critical or endangered status under section 1085 of this title for such plan year, and if so, a summary of any funding improvement or rehabilitation plan (or modification thereto) adopted during the plan year, and the funded percentage of the plan.

(H) The number of employers that withdrew from the plan during the preceding plan year and the aggregate amount of withdrawal liability assessed, or estimated to be assessed, against such withdrawn employers.

(I) In the case of a multiemployer plan that has merged with another plan or to which assets and liabilities have been transferred, the actuarial valuation of the assets and liabilities of each affected plan during the year preceding the effective date of the merger or transfer, based upon the most recent data available as of the day before the first day of the plan year, or other valuation method performed under standards and procedures as the Secretary may prescribe by regulation.

(Pub. L. 93–406, title I, §103, Sept. 2, 1974, 88 Stat. 841; Pub. L. 96–364, title III, §307, Sept. 26, 1980, 94 Stat. 1295; Pub. L. 99–272, title XI, §11016(b)(1), Apr. 7, 1986, 100 Stat. 272; Pub. L. 100–203, title IX, §9342(a)(1), Dec. 22, 1987, 101 Stat. 1330–371; Pub. L. 101–239, title VII, §7881(j)(1), Dec. 19, 1989, 103 Stat. 2442; Pub. L. 109–280, title I, §107(a)(2), (3), title V, §503(a)(1), (b), Aug. 17, 2006, 120 Stat. 818, 942, 943; Pub. L. 110–458, title I, §101(d)(1)(A), Dec. 23, 2008, 122 Stat. 5098.)

AMENDMENTS

2008—Subsec. (d)(3). Pub. L. 110–458, §101(d)(1)(A)(i), substituted "the normal costs or target normal costs, the accrued liabilities or funding target" for "the normal costs, the accrued liabilities".

Subsec. (d)(7). Pub. L. 110–458, §101(d)(1)(A)(ii), added par. (7) and struck out former par. (7) which read as follows: "A certification of the contribution necessary to reduce the accumulated funding deficiency to zero."

2006—Subsec. (a)(1)(B). Pub. L. 109–280, §503(a)(1)(A), substituted "subsections (d), (e), and (f)" for "subsections (d) and (e)" in introductory provisions.

Subsec. (d)(8)(B). Pub. L. 109–280, §107(a)(2), substituted "the applicable requirements of sections 1083(h) and 1084(c)(3)" for "the requirements of section 1082(c)(3)".

Subsec. (d)(11). Pub. L. 109–280, §107(a)(3), added par. (11) and struck out former par. (11) which read as follows: "If the current value of the assets of the plan is less than 70 percent of the current liability under the plan (within the meaning of section 1082(d)(7) of this title), the percentage which such value is of such liability.."

Subsec. (d)(12) to (14). Pub. L. 109–280, §503(b), added par. (12) and redesignated former pars. (12) and (13) as (13) and (14), respectively.

Subsec. (f). Pub. L. 109–280, §503(a)(1)(B), added subsec. (f).

1989—Subsec. (d)(11). Pub. L. 101–239 substituted "70 percent" for "60 percent" and "the percentage which such value is of such liability." for "such percentage".

1987—Subsec. (d)(11) to (13). Pub. L. 100–203 added par. (11) and redesignated former pars. (11) and (12) as (12) and (13), respectively.

1986—Subsec. (d)(6). Pub. L. 99–272 amended par. (6) generally. Prior to amendment, par. (6) read as follows: "The present value of all of the plan's liabilities for nonforfeitable pension benefits allocated by the termination priority categories as set forth in section 1344 of this title, and the actuarial assumptions used in these computations. The Secretary shall establish regulations defining (for purposes of this section) 'termination priority categories' and acceptable methods, including approximate methods, for allocating the plan's liabilities to such termination priority categories."

1980—Subsec. (d)(10) to (12). Pub. L. 96–364 added par. (10) and redesignated former pars. (10) and (11) as (11) and (12), respectively.

EFFECTIVE DATE OF 2008 AMENDMENT

Amendment by Pub. L. 110–458 effective as if included in the provisions of Pub. L. 109–280 to which the amendment relates, except as otherwise provided, see section 112 of Pub. L. 110–458, set out as a note under section 72 of Title 26, Internal Revenue Code.

EFFECTIVE DATE OF 2006 AMENDMENT

Amendment by section 107(a)(2), (3) of Pub. L. 109–280 applicable to plan years beginning after 2007, see section 107(e) of Pub. L. 109–280, set out as a note under section 1021 of this title.

Amendment by section 503(a)(1), (b) of Pub. L. 109–280 applicable to plan years beginning after Dec. 31, 2007, see section 503(f) of Pub. L. 109–280, set out as a note under section 1021 of this title.

EFFECTIVE DATE OF 1989 AMENDMENT

Amendment by Pub. L. 101–239 effective, except as otherwise provided, as if included in the provision of the Pension Protection Act, Pub. L. 100–203, §§9302–9346, to which such amendment relates, see section 7882 of Pub. L. 101–239, set out as a note under section 401 of Title 26, Internal Revenue Code.

EFFECTIVE DATE OF 1987 AMENDMENT

Amendment by Pub. L. 100–203 applicable with respect to reports required to be filed after Dec. 31, 1987, see section 9342(d)(1) of Pub. L. 100–203, set out as a note under section 1132 of this title.

EFFECTIVE DATE OF 1986 AMENDMENT

Amendment by Pub. L. 99–272 effective Jan. 1, 1986, with certain exceptions, see section 11019 of Pub. L. 99–272, set out as a note under section 1341 of this title.

EFFECTIVE DATE OF 1980 AMENDMENT

Amendment by Pub. L. 96–364 effective Sept. 26, 1980, except as specifically provided, see section 1461(e) of this title.

REGULATIONS

Secretary authorized, effective Sept. 2, 1974, to promulgate regulations wherever provisions of this subchapter call for the promulgation of regulations, see section 1031 of this title.

APPLICABILITY OF AMENDMENTS BY SUBTITLES A AND B OF TITLE I OF PUB. L. 109–280

For special rules on applicability of amendments by subtitles A (§§101–107) and B (§§111–116) of title I of Pub. L. 109–280 to certain eligible cooperative plans, PBGC settlement plans, and eligible government contractor plans, see sections 104, 105, and 106 of Pub. L. 109–280, set out as notes under section 401 of Title 26, Internal Revenue Code.

GUIDANCE BY SECRETARY OF LABOR

Pub. L. 109–280, title V, §503(a)(2), Aug. 17, 2006, 120 Stat. 943, provided that: "Not later than 1 year after the date of enactment of this Act [Aug. 17, 2006], the Secretary of Labor shall publish guidance to assist multiemployer defined benefit plans to—

"(A) identify and enumerate plan participants for whom there is no employer with an obligation to make an employer contribution under the plan; and

"(B) report such information under section 103(f)(2)(D) of the Employee Retirement Income Security Act of 1974 [29 U.S.C. 1023(f)(2)(D)] (as added by this section)."

TRANSITION RULES

Section 11016(b)(3) of Pub. L. 99–272 provided that: "Any regulations, modifications, or waivers which have been issued by the Secretary of Labor with respect to section 103(d)(6) of the Employee Retirement Income Security Act of 1974 [29 U.S.C. 1023(d)(6)] (as in effect immediately before the date of the enactment of this Act [Apr. 7, 1986]) shall remain in full force and effect until modified by any regulations with respect to such section 103(d)(6) prescribed by the Pension Benefit Guaranty Corporation."

CONSOLIDATION OF ACTUARIAL REPORTS

Secretary of the Treasury and Secretary of Labor to take such steps as may be necessary to assure coordination to the maximum extent feasible between the actuarial reports required by subsec. (d) of this section and section 6059 of Title 26, Internal Revenue Code, see section 1033(c) of Pub. L. 93–406, set out as a note under section 6059 of Title 26.

§1024. Filing with Secretary and furnishing information to participants and certain employers

(a) Filing of annual report with Secretary

(1) The administrator of any employee benefit plan subject to this part shall file with the Secretary the annual report for a plan year within 210 days after the close of such year (or within such time as may be required by regulations promulgated by the Secretary in order to reduce duplicative filing). The Secretary shall make copies of such annual reports available for inspection in the public document room of the Department of Labor.

(2)(A) With respect to annual reports required to be filed with the Secretary under this part, he may by regulation prescribe simplified annual reports for any pension plan which covers less than 100 participants.

(B) Nothing contained in this paragraph shall preclude the Secretary from requiring any information or data from any such plan to which this part applies where he finds such data or information is necessary to carry out the purposes of this subchapter nor shall the Secretary be precluded from revoking provisions for simplified reports for any such plan if he finds it necessary to do so in order to carry out the objectives of this subchapter.

(3) The Secretary may by regulation exempt any welfare benefit plan from all or part of the reporting and disclosure requirements of this subchapter, or may provide for simplified reporting and disclosure if he finds that such requirements are inappropriate as applied to welfare benefit plans.

(4) The Secretary may reject any filing under this section—

(A) if he determines that such filing is incomplete for purposes of this part; or

(B) if he determines that there is any material qualification by an accountant or actuary contained in an opinion submitted pursuant to section 1023(a)(3)(A) or section 1023(a)(4)(B) of this title.

(5) If the Secretary rejects a filing of a report under paragraph (4) and if a revised filing satisfactory to the Secretary is not submitted within 45 days after the Secretary makes his determination under paragraph (4) to reject the filing, and if the Secretary deems it in the best interest of the participants, he may take any one or more of the following actions—

(A) retain an independent qualified public accountant (as defined in section 1023(a)(3)(D) of this title) on behalf of the participants to perform an audit,

(B) retain an enrolled actuary (as defined in section 1023(a)(4)(C) of this title) on behalf of the plan participants, to prepare an actuarial statement,

(C) bring a civil action for such legal or equitable relief as may be appropriate to enforce the provisions of this part, or

(D) take any other action authorized by this subchapter.

The administrator shall permit such accountant or actuary to inspect whatever books and records of the plan are necessary for such audit. The plan shall be liable to the Secretary for the expenses for such audit or report, and the Secretary may bring an action against the plan in any court of competent jurisdiction to recover such expenses.

(6) The administrator of any employee benefit plan subject to this part shall furnish to the Secretary, upon request, any documents relating to the employee benefit plan, including but not limited to, the latest summary plan description (including any summaries of plan changes not contained in the summary plan description), and the bargaining agreement, trust agreement, contract, or other instrument under which the plan is established or operated.

(b) Publication of summary plan description and annual report to participants and beneficiaries of plan

Publication of the summary plan descriptions and annual reports shall be made to participants and beneficiaries of the particular plan as follows:

(1) The administrator shall furnish to each participant, and each beneficiary receiving benefits under the plan, a copy of the summary plan description, and all modifications and changes referred to in section 1022(a) of this title—

(A) within 90 days after he becomes a participant, or (in the case of a beneficiary) within 90 days after he first receives benefits, or

(B) if later, within 120 days after the plan becomes subject to this part.

The administrator shall furnish to each participant, and each beneficiary receiving benefits under the plan, every fifth year after the plan becomes subject to this part an updated summary plan description described in section 1022 of this title which integrates all plan amendments made within such five-year period, except that in a case where no amendments have been made to a plan during such five-year period this sentence shall not apply. Notwithstanding the foregoing, the administrator shall furnish to each participant, and to each beneficiary receiving benefits under the plan, the summary plan description described in section 1022 of this title every tenth year after the plan becomes subject to this part. If there is a modification or change described in section 1022(a) of this title (other than a material reduction in covered services or benefits provided in the case of a group health plan (as defined in section 1191b(a)(1) of this title)), a summary description of such modification or change shall be furnished not later than 210 days after the end of the plan year in which the change is adopted to each participant, and to each beneficiary who is receiving benefits under the plan. If there is a modification or change described in section 1022(a) of this title that is a material reduction in covered services or benefits provided under a group health plan (as defined in section 1191b(a)(1) of this title), a summary description of such modification or change shall be furnished to participants and beneficiaries not later than 60 days after the date of the adoption of the modification or change. In the alternative, the plan sponsors may provide such description at regular intervals of not more than 90 days. The Secretary shall issue regulations within 180 days after August 21, 1996, providing alternative mechanisms to delivery by mail through which group health plans (as so defined) may notify participants and beneficiaries of material reductions in covered services or benefits.

(2) The administrator shall make copies of the latest updated summary plan description and the latest annual report and the bargaining agreement, trust agreement, contract, or other instruments under which the plan was established or is operated available for examination by any plan participant or beneficiary in the principal office of the administrator and in such other places as may be necessary to make available all pertinent information to all participants (including such places as the Secretary may prescribe by regulations).

(3) Within 210 days after the close of the fiscal year of the plan, the administrator (other than an administrator of a defined benefit plan to which the requirements of section 1021(f) of this title applies)[1] shall furnish to each participant, and to each beneficiary receiving benefits under the plan, a copy of the statements and schedules, for such fiscal year, described in subparagraphs (A) and (B) of section 1023(b)(3) of this title and such other material (including the percentage determined under section 1023(d)(11) of this title) as is necessary to fairly summarize the latest annual report.

(4) The administrator shall, upon written request of any participant or beneficiary, furnish a copy of the latest updated summary,[2] plan description, and the latest annual report, any terminal report, the bargaining agreement, trust agreement, contract, or other instruments under which the plan is established or operated. The administrator may make a reasonable charge to cover the cost of furnishing such complete copies. The Secretary may by regulation prescribe the maximum amount which will constitute a reasonable charge under the preceding sentence.

(5) Identification and basic plan information and actuarial information included in the an-

[1] So in original. Probably should be "apply)".

[2] So in original. Comma probably should not appear.

nual report for any plan year shall be filed with the Secretary in an electronic format which accommodates display on the Internet, in accordance with regulations which shall be prescribed by the Secretary. The Secretary shall provide for display of such information included in the annual report, within 90 days after the date of the filing of the annual report, on an Internet website maintained by the Secretary and other appropriate media. Such information shall also be displayed on any Intranet website maintained by the plan sponsor (or by the plan administrator on behalf of the plan sponsor) for the purpose of communicating with employees and not the public, in accordance with regulations which shall be prescribed by the Secretary.

(c) Statement of rights

The Secretary may by regulation require that the administrator of any employee benefit plan furnish to each participant and to each beneficiary receiving benefits under the plan a statement of the rights of participants and beneficiaries under this subchapter.

(d) Furnishing summary plan information to employers and employee representatives of multiemployer plans

(1) In general

With respect to a multiemployer plan subject to this section, within 30 days after the due date under subsection (a)(1) for the filing of the annual report for the fiscal year of the plan, the administrators shall furnish to each employee organization and to each employer with an obligation to contribute to the plan a report that contains—

(A) a description of the contribution schedules and benefit formulas under the plan, and any modification to such schedules and formulas, during such plan year;

(B) the number of employers obligated to contribute to the plan;

(C) a list of the employers that contributed more than 5 percent of the total contributions to the plan during such plan year;

(D) the number of participants under the plan on whose behalf no contributions were made by an employer as an employer of the participant for such plan year and for each of the 2 preceding plan years;

(E) whether the plan was in critical or endangered status under section 1085 of this title for such plan year and, if so, include—

(i) a list of the actions taken by the plan to improve its funding status; and

(ii) a statement describing how a person may obtain a copy of the plan's funding improvement or rehabilitation plan, as applicable, adopted under section 1085 of this title and the actuarial and financial data that demonstrate any action taken by the plan toward fiscal improvement;

(F) the number of employers that withdrew from the plan during the preceding plan year and the aggregate amount of withdrawal liability assessed, or estimated to be assessed, against such withdrawn employers, as reported on the annual report for the plan year to which the report under this subsection relates;

(G) in the case of a multiemployer plan that has merged with another plan or to which assets and liabilities have been transferred, the actuarial valuation of the assets and liabilities of each affected plan during the year preceding the effective date of the merger or transfer, based upon the most recent data available as of the day before the first day of the plan year, or other valuation method performed under standards and procedures as the Secretary may prescribe by regulation;

(H) a description as to whether the plan—

(i) sought or received an amortization extension under section 1084(d) of this title or section 431(d) of title 26 for such plan year; or

(ii) used the shortfall funding method (as such term is used in section 1085 of this title) for such plan year; and

(I) notification of the right under this section of the recipient to a copy of the annual report filed with the Secretary under subsection (a), summary plan description, summary of any material modification of the plan, upon written request, but that—

(i) in no case shall a recipient be entitled to receive more than one copy of any such document described during any one 12-month period; and

(ii) the administrator may make a reasonable charge to cover copying, mailing, and other costs of furnishing copies of information pursuant to this subparagraph.

(2) Effect of subsection

Nothing in this subsection waives any other provision under this subchapter requiring plan administrators to provide, upon request, information to employers that have an obligation to contribute under the plan.

(e) Cross references

For regulations respecting coordination of reports to the Secretaries of Labor and the Treasury, see section 1204 of this title.

(Pub. L. 93–406, title I, § 104, Sept. 2, 1974, 88 Stat. 847; Pub. L. 99–272, title XI, § 11016(b)(2), Apr. 7, 1986, 100 Stat. 273; Pub. L. 100–203, title IX, § 9342(a)(2), Dec. 22, 1987, 101 Stat. 1330–371; Pub. L. 101–239, title VII, § 7894(b)(3), (4), Dec. 19, 1989, 103 Stat. 2448; Pub. L. 104–191, title I, § 101(c)(1), Aug. 21, 1996, 110 Stat. 1951; Pub. L. 104–204, title VI, § 603(b)(3)(D), Sept. 26, 1996, 110 Stat. 2938; Pub. L. 105–34, title XV, § 1503(c)(1), (2)(A), (d)(1)–(3), Aug. 5, 1997, 111 Stat. 1062; Pub. L. 109–280, title V, §§ 503(c)(1), (d), 504(a), Aug. 17, 2006, 120 Stat. 943–945; Pub. L. 110–458, title I, § 105(c)(1), Dec. 23, 2008, 122 Stat. 5105.)

AMENDMENTS

2008—Subsec. (b)(3). Pub. L. 110–458, § 105(c)(1)(A)(ii), which directed substitution of "the administrator" for "the administrators" in par. (3), could not be executed because the words "the administrators" did not appear.

Pub. L. 110–458, § 105(c)(1)(A)(i), substituted "section 1021(f)" for "section 1023(f)".

Subsec. (d)(1)(E)(ii). Pub. L. 110–458, § 105(c)(1)(B), inserted "funding" after "plan's".

2006—Pub. L. 109–280, § 503(d)(1), substituted "participants and certain employers" for "participants" in section catchline.

Subsec. (b)(3). Pub. L. 109–280, § 503(c)(1), which directed amendment of par. (3) by inserting "(other than an administrator of a defined benefit plan to which the requirements of section 1023(f) of this title applies)" after "the administrators", was executed by making the insertion after "the administrator", to reflect the probable intent of Congress.

Subsec. (b)(5). Pub. L. 109–280, § 504(a), added par. (5).

Subsecs. (d), (e). Pub. L. 109–280, § 503(d)(2), (3), added subsec. (d) and redesignated former subsec. (d) as (e).

1997—Subsec. (a)(1). Pub. L. 105–34, § 1503(c)(1), amended par. (1) generally, substituting present provisions for provisions requiring filing of annual report, plan description, summary plan description, as well as modifications and changes in plan descriptions.

Subsec. (a)(6). Pub. L. 105–34, § 1503(c)(2)(A), added par. (6).

Subsec. (b)(1). Pub. L. 105–34, § 1503(d)(1), substituted "section 1022(a) of this title" for "section 1022(a)(1) of this title" wherever appearing.

Subsec. (b)(2). Pub. L. 105–34, § 1503(d)(2), substituted "the latest updated summary plan description and" for "the plan description and".

Subsec. (b)(4). Pub. L. 105–34, § 1503(d)(3), struck out "plan description" before ", plan description, and the latest annual report".

1996—Subsec. (b)(1). Pub. L. 104–204 made technical amendment to references in original act which appear in text as references to section 1191b of this title.

Pub. L. 104–191, in closing provisions, substituted "1022(a)(1) of this title (other than a material reduction in covered services or benefits provided in the case of a group health plan (as defined in section 1191b(a)(1) of this title))," for "1022(a)(1) of this title," and inserted at end "If there is a modification or change described in section 1022(a)(1) of this title that is a material reduction in covered services or benefits provided under a group health plan (as defined in section 1191b(a)(1) of this title), a summary description of such modification or change shall be furnished to participants and beneficiaries not later than 60 days after the date of the adoption of the modification or change. In the alternative, the plan sponsors may provide such description at regular intervals of not more than 90 days. The Secretary shall issue regulations within 180 days after August 21, 1996, providing alternative mechanisms to delivery by mail through which group health plans (as so defined) may notify participants and beneficiaries of material reductions in covered services or benefits."

1989—Subsec. (a)(5)(B). Pub. L. 101–239, § 7894(b)(3), substituted a comma for period at end.

Subsec. (b)(1). Pub. L. 101–239, § 7894(b)(4), struck out comma after "summary".

1987—Subsec. (b)(3). Pub. L. 100–203 inserted "(including the percentage determined under section 1023(d)(11) of this title)" after "material".

1986—Subsec. (a)(2)(A). Pub. L. 99–272 struck out provision permitting the Secretary to waive or modify the requirements of section 1023(d)(6) of this title if he found that the interests of the plan participants were not harmed and the expense of compliance was not justified by the needs of the participants, the Pension Benefit Guaranty Corporation, and the Department of Labor for some portion or all of the information otherwise required under section 1023(d)(6) of this title.

EFFECTIVE DATE OF 2008 AMENDMENT

Amendment by Pub. L. 110–458 effective as if included in the provisions of Pub. L. 109–280 to which the amendment relates, except as otherwise provided, see section 112 of Pub. L. 110–458, set out as a note under section 72 of Title 26, Internal Revenue Code.

EFFECTIVE DATE OF 2006 AMENDMENT

Amendment by section 503(c)(1), (d) of Pub. L. 109–280 applicable to plan years beginning after Dec. 31, 2007, see section 503(f) of Pub. L. 109–280, set out as a note under section 1021 of this title.

Pub. L. 109–280, title V, § 504(b), Aug. 17, 2006, 120 Stat. 945, provided that: "The amendment made by this section [amending this section] shall apply to plan years beginning after December 31, 2007."

EFFECTIVE DATE OF 1996 AMENDMENTS

Amendment by Pub. L. 104–204 applicable with respect to group health plans for plan years beginning on or after Jan. 1, 1998, see section 603(c) of Pub. L. 104–204 set out as a note under section 1003 of this title.

Amendment by Pub. L. 104–191 applicable with respect to group health plans for plan years beginning after June 30, 1997, except as otherwise provided, see section 101(g) of Pub. L. 104–191, set out as an Effective Date note under section 1181 of this title.

EFFECTIVE DATE OF 1989 AMENDMENT

Amendment by Pub. L. 101–239 effective, except as otherwise provided, as if originally included in the provision of the Employee Retirement Income Security Act of 1974, Pub. L. 93–406, to which such amendment relates, see section 7894(i) of Pub. L. 101–239, set out as a note under section 1002 of this title.

EFFECTIVE DATE OF 1987 AMENDMENT

Amendment by Pub. L. 100–203 applicable with respect to reports required to be filed after Dec. 31, 1987, see section 9342(d)(1) of Pub. L. 100–203, set out as a note under section 1132 of this title.

EFFECTIVE DATE OF 1986 AMENDMENT

Amendment by Pub. L. 99–272 effective Jan. 1, 1986, with certain exceptions, see section 11019 of Pub. L. 99–272, set out as a note under section 1341 of this title.

REGULATIONS

Secretary authorized, effective Sept. 2, 1974, to promulgate regulations wherever provisions of this subchapter call for the promulgation of regulations, see section 1031 of this title.

MODEL NOTICES AND FORMS

For provisions requiring the Secretary of Labor to publish a model form for providing the statements, schedules, and other material required to be provided under subsec. (d) of this section, see section 503(e) of Pub. L. 109–280, set out as a note under section 1021 of this title.

§ 1025. Reporting of participant's benefit rights

(a) Requirements to provide pension benefit statements

(1) Requirements

(A) Individual account plan

The administrator of an individual account plan (other than a one-participant retirement plan described in section 1021(i)(8)(B) of this title) shall furnish a pension benefit statement—

(i) at least once each calendar quarter to a participant or beneficiary who has the right to direct the investment of assets in his or her account under the plan,

(ii) at least once each calendar year to a participant or beneficiary who has his or her own account under the plan but does not have the right to direct the investment of assets in that account, and

(iii) upon written request to a plan beneficiary not described in clause (i) or (ii).

(B) Defined benefit plan

The administrator of a defined benefit plan (other than a one-participant retirement plan described in section 1021(i)(8)(B) of this title) shall furnish a pension benefit statement—

(i) at least once every 3 years to each participant with a nonforfeitable accrued benefit and who is employed by the employer maintaining the plan at the time the statement is to be furnished, and

(ii) to a participant or beneficiary of the plan upon written request.

Information furnished under clause (i) to a participant may be based on reasonable estimates determined under regulations prescribed by the Secretary, in consultation with the Pension Benefit Guaranty Corporation.

(2) Statements

(A) In general

A pension benefit statement under paragraph (1)—

(i) shall indicate, on the basis of the latest available information—

(I) the total benefits accrued, and

(II) the nonforfeitable pension benefits, if any, which have accrued, or the earliest date on which benefits will become nonforfeitable,

(ii) shall include an explanation of any permitted disparity under section 401(*l*) of title 26 or any floor-offset arrangement that may be applied in determining any accrued benefits described in clause (i),

(iii) shall be written in a manner calculated to be understood by the average plan participant, and

(iv) may be delivered in written, electronic, or other appropriate form to the extent such form is reasonably accessible to the participant or beneficiary.

(B) Additional information

In the case of an individual account plan, any pension benefit statement under clause (i) or (ii) of paragraph (1)(A) shall include—

(i) the value of each investment to which assets in the individual account have been allocated, determined as of the most recent valuation date under the plan, including the value of any assets held in the form of employer securities, without regard to whether such securities were contributed by the plan sponsor or acquired at the direction of the plan or of the participant or beneficiary, and

(ii) in the case of a pension benefit statement under paragraph (1)(A)(i)—

(I) an explanation of any limitations or restrictions on any right of the participant or beneficiary under the plan to direct an investment,

(II) an explanation, written in a manner calculated to be understood by the average plan participant, of the importance, for the long-term retirement security of participants and beneficiaries, of a well-balanced and diversified investment portfolio, including a statement of the risk that holding more than 20 percent of a portfolio in the security of one entity (such as employer securities) may not be adequately diversified, and

(III) a notice directing the participant or beneficiary to the Internet website of the Department of Labor for sources of information on individual investing and diversification.

(C) Alternative notice

The requirements of subparagraph (A)(i)(II) are met if, at least annually and in accordance with requirements of the Secretary, the plan—

(i) updates the information described in such paragraph which is provided in the pension benefit statement, or

(ii) provides in a separate statement such information as is necessary to enable a participant or beneficiary to determine their nonforfeitable vested benefits.

(3) Defined benefit plans

(A) Alternative notice

In the case of a defined benefit plan, the requirements of paragraph (1)(B)(i) shall be treated as met with respect to a participant if at least once each year the administrator provides to the participant notice of the availability of the pension benefit statement and the ways in which the participant may obtain such statement. Such notice may be delivered in written, electronic, or other appropriate form to the extent such form is reasonably accessible to the participant.

(B) Years in which no benefits accrue

The Secretary may provide that years in which no employee or former employee benefits (within the meaning of section 410(b) of title 26) under the plan need not be taken into account in determining the 3-year period under paragraph (1)(B)(i).

(b) Limitation on number of statements

In no case shall a participant or beneficiary of a plan be entitled to more than 1 statement described in subparagraph (A)(iii) or (B)(ii) of subsection (a)(1), whichever is applicable, in any 12-month period.

(c) Individual statement furnished by administrator to participants setting forth information in administrator's Internal Revenue registration statement and notification of forfeitable benefits

Each administrator required to register under section 6057 of title 26 shall, before the expiration of the time prescribed for such registration, furnish to each participant described in subsection (a)(2)(C) of such section, an individual statement setting forth the information with respect to such participant required to be contained in the registration statement required by section 6057(a)(2) of title 26. Such statement shall also include a notice to the participant of any benefits which are forfeitable if the participant dies before a certain date.

(Pub. L. 93–406, title I, § 105, Sept. 2, 1974, 88 Stat. 849; Pub. L. 98–397, title I, § 106, Aug. 23, 1984, 98 Stat. 1436; Pub. L. 101–239, title VII, §§ 7891(a)(1), 7894(b)(5), Dec. 19, 1989, 103 Stat. 2445, 2448; Pub. L. 109–280, title V, § 508(a)(1)–(2)(B), Aug. 17, 2006, 120 Stat. 949, 951.)

AMENDMENTS

2006—Subsec. (a). Pub. L. 109–280, § 508(a)(1), amended heading and text of subsec. (a) generally. Prior to amendment, text read as follows: "Each administrator of an employee pension benefit plan shall furnish to any plan participant or beneficiary who so requests in writing, a statement indicating, on the basis of the latest available information—

"(1) the total benefits accrued, and

"(2) the nonforfeitable pension benefits, if any, which have accrued, or the earliest date on which benefits will become nonforfeitable."

Subsec. (b). Pub. L. 109–280, §508(a)(2)(B), amended heading and text of subsec. (b) generally. Prior to amendment, text read as follows: "In no case shall a participant or beneficiary be entitled under this section to receive more than one report described in subsection (a) of this section during any one 12-month period."

Subsec. (d). Pub. L. 109–280, §508(a)(2)(A), struck out heading and text of subsec. (d). Text read as follows: "Subsection (a) of this section shall apply to a plan to which more than one unaffiliated employer is required to contribute only to the extent provided in regulations prescribed by the Secretary in coordination with the Secretary of the Treasury."

1989—Subsec. (b). Pub. L. 101–239, §7894(b)(5), substituted "12-month" for "12 month".

Subsec. (c). Pub. L. 101–239, §7891(a)(1), substituted "Internal Revenue Code of 1986" for "Internal Revenue Code of 1954", which for purposes of codification was translated as "title 26" thus requiring no change in text.

1984—Subsec. (c). Pub. L. 98–397 inserted at end "Such statement shall also include a notice to the participant of any benefits which are forfeitable if the participant dies before a certain date."

EFFECTIVE DATE OF 2006 AMENDMENT

Pub. L. 109–280, title V, §508(c), Aug. 17, 2006, 120 Stat. 952, provided that:

"(1) IN GENERAL.—The amendments made by this section [amending this section and section 1132 of this title] shall apply to plan years beginning after December 31, 2006.

"(2) SPECIAL RULE FOR COLLECTIVELY BARGAINED AGREEMENTS.—In the case of a plan maintained pursuant to 1 or more collective bargaining agreements between employee representatives and 1 or more employers ratified on or before the date of the enactment of this Act [Aug. 17, 2006], paragraph (1) shall be applied to benefits pursuant to, and individuals covered by, any such agreement by substituting for 'December 31, 2006' the earlier of—

"(A) the later of—

"(i) December 31, 2007, or

"(ii) the date on which the last of such collective bargaining agreements terminates (determined without regard to any extension thereof after such date of enactment), or

"(B) December 31, 2008."

EFFECTIVE DATE OF 1989 AMENDMENT

Amendment by section 7891(a)(1) of Pub. L. 101–239 effective, except as otherwise provided, as if included in the provision of the Tax Reform Act of 1986, Pub. L. 99–514, to which such amendment relates, see section 7891(f) of Pub. L. 101–239, set out as a note under section 1002 of this title.

Amendment by section 7894(b)(5) of Pub. L. 101–239 effective, except as otherwise provided, as if originally included in the provision of the Employee Retirement Income Security Act of 1974, Pub. L. 93–406, to which such amendment relates, see section 7894(i) of Pub. L. 101–239, set out as a note under section 1002 of this title.

EFFECTIVE DATE OF 1984 AMENDMENT

Amendment by Pub. L. 98–397 applicable to plan years beginning after Dec. 31, 1984, except as otherwise provided, see sections 302 and 303 of Pub. L. 98–397, set out as a note under section 1001 of this title.

REGULATIONS

Secretary of Labor authorized, effective Sept. 2, 1974, to promulgate regulations wherever provisions of this subchapter call for the promulgation of regulations by him, see section 1031 of this title.

MODEL STATEMENTS

Pub. L. 109–280, title V, §508(b), Aug. 17, 2006, 120 Stat. 951, provided that:

"(1) IN GENERAL.—The Secretary of Labor shall, within 1 year after the date of the enactment of this section [Aug. 17, 2006], develop 1 or more model benefit statements that are written in a manner calculated to be understood by the average plan participant and that may be used by plan administrators in complying with the requirements of section 105 of the Employee Retirement Income Security Act of 1974 [29 U.S.C. 1025].

"(2) INTERIM FINAL RULES.—The Secretary of Labor may promulgate any interim final rules as the Secretary determines appropriate to carry out the provisions of this subsection."

§1026. Reports made public information

(a) Except as provided in subsection (b) of this section, the contents of the annual reports, statements, and other documents filed with the Secretary pursuant to this part shall be public information and the Secretary shall make any such information and data available for inspection in the public document room of the Department of Labor. The Secretary may use the information and data for statistical and research purposes, and compile and publish such studies, analyses, reports, and surveys based thereon as he may deem appropriate.

(b) Information described in sections 1025(a) and 1025(c) of this title with respect to a participant may be disclosed only to the extent that information respecting that participant's benefits under title II of the Social Security Act [42 U.S.C. 401 et seq.] may be disclosed under such Act.

(Pub. L. 93–406, title I, §106, Sept. 2, 1974, 88 Stat. 850; Pub. L. 101–239, title VII, §7894(b)(6), Dec. 19, 1989, 103 Stat. 2448; Pub. L. 105–34, title XV, §1503(d)(4), Aug. 5, 1997, 111 Stat. 1062.)

REFERENCES IN TEXT

The Social Security Act, referred to in subsec. (b), is act Aug. 14, 1935, ch. 531, 49 Stat. 620, as amended. Title II of the Social Security Act is classified generally to subchapter II (§401 et seq.) of chapter 7 of Title 42, The Public Health and Welfare. For complete classification of this Act to the Code, see section 1305 of Title 42 and Tables.

AMENDMENTS

1997—Subsec. (a). Pub. L. 105–34 struck out "descriptions," before "annual reports,".

1989—Subsec. (b). Pub. L. 101–239 substituted "sections" for "section".

EFFECTIVE DATE OF 1989 AMENDMENT

Amendment by Pub. L. 101–239 effective, except as otherwise provided, as if originally included in the provision of the Employee Retirement Income Security Act of 1974, Pub. L. 93–406, to which such amendment relates, see section 7894(i) of Pub. L. 101–239, set out as a note under section 1002 of this title.

§1027. Retention of records

Every person subject to a requirement to file any report or to certify any information therefor under this subchapter or who would be subject to such a requirement but for an exemption or simplified reporting requirement under section 1024(a)(2) or (3) of this title shall maintain records on the matters of which disclosure is required which will provide in sufficient detail the necessary basic information and data from which the documents thus required may be verified, explained, or clarified, and checked for accuracy and completeness, and shall include vouchers, worksheets, receipts, and applicable resolutions, and shall keep such records available for examination for a period of not less than six years after the filing date of the documents based on the information which they contain, or six years after the date on which such documents would have been filed but for an exemption or simplified reporting requirement under section 1024(a)(2) or (3) of this title.

(Pub. L. 93–406, title I, §107, Sept. 2, 1974, 88 Stat. 850; Pub. L. 105–34, title XV, §1503(d)(5), Aug. 5, 1997, 111 Stat. 1062.)

AMENDMENTS

1997—Pub. L. 105–34 struck out "description or" after "requirement to file any".

§1028. Reliance on administrative interpretations

In any criminal proceeding under section 1131 of this title, based on any act or omission in alleged violation of this part or section 1112 of this title, no person shall be subject to any liability or punishment for or on account of the failure of such person to (1) comply with this part or section 1112 of this title, if he pleads and proves that the act or omission complained of was in good faith, in conformity with, and in reliance on any regulation or written ruling of the Secretary, or (2) publish and file any information required by any provision of this part if he pleads and proves that he published and filed such information in good faith, and in conformity with any regulation or written ruling of the Secretary issued under this part regarding the filing of such reports. Such a defense, if established, shall be a bar to the action or proceeding, notwithstanding that (A) after such act or omission, such interpretation or opinion is modified or rescinded or is determined by judicial authority to be invalid or of no legal effect, or (B) after publishing or filing the annual reports and other reports required by this subchapter, such publication or filing is determined by judicial authority not to be in conformity with the requirements of this part.

(Pub. L. 93–406, title I, §108, Sept. 2, 1974, 88 Stat. 850; Pub. L. 101–239, title VII, §7894(b)(7), Dec. 19, 1989, 103 Stat. 2448; Pub. L. 105–34, title XV, §1503(d)(6), Aug. 5, 1997, 111 Stat. 1062.)

AMENDMENTS

1997—Pub. L. 105–34, which directed the amendment of cl. (2)(B) by substituting "annual reports" for "plan descriptions, annual reports,", was executed by making the substitution for "plan description, annual reports," to reflect the probable intent of Congress.

1989—Pub. L. 101–239 substituted "act or omission" for "act of omission" before "complained of".

EFFECTIVE DATE OF 1989 AMENDMENT

Amendment by Pub. L. 101–239 effective, except as otherwise provided, as if originally included in the provision of the Employee Retirement Income Security Act of 1974, Pub. L. 93–406, to which such amendment relates, see section 7894(i) of Pub. L. 101–239, set out as a note under section 1002 of this title.

REGULATIONS

Secretary authorized, effective Sept. 2, 1974, to promulgate regulations wherever provisions of this subchapter call for the promulgation of regulations, see section 1031 of this title.

§1029. Forms

(a) Information required on forms

Except as provided in subsection (b) of this section, the Secretary may require that any information required under this subchapter to be submitted to him, including but not limited to the information required to be filed by the administrator pursuant to section 1023(b)(3) and (c) of this title, must be submitted on such forms as he may prescribe.

(b) Information not required on forms

The financial statement and opinion required to be prepared by an independent qualified public accountant pursuant to section 1023(a)(3)(A) of this title, the actuarial statement required to be prepared by an enrolled actuary pursuant to section 1023(a)(4)(A) of this title and the summary plan description required by section 1022(a) of this title shall not be required to be submitted on forms.

(c) Format and content of summary plan description, annual report, etc., required to be furnished to plan participants and beneficiaries

The Secretary may prescribe the format and content of the summary plan description, the summary of the annual report described in section 1024(b)(3) of this title and any other report, statements or documents (other than the bargaining agreement, trust agreement, contract, or other instrument under which the plan is established or operated), which are required to be furnished or made available to plan participants and beneficiaries receiving benefits under the plan.

(Pub. L. 93–406, title I, §109, Sept. 2, 1974, 88 Stat. 850.)

REGULATIONS

Secretary authorized, effective Sept. 2, 1974, to promulgate regulations wherever provisions of this subchapter call for the promulgation of regulations, see section 1031 of this title.

§1030. Alternative methods of compliance

(a) The Secretary on his own motion or after having received the petition of an administrator may prescribe an alternative method for satisfying any requirement of this part with respect to any pension plan, or class of pension plans, subject to such requirement if he determines—

(1) that the use of such alternative method is consistent with the purposes of this subchapter and that it provides adequate disclosure to the participants and beneficiaries in the plan, and adequate reporting to the Secretary,

(2) that the application of such requirement of this part would—

(A) increase the costs to the plan, or

(B) impose unreasonable administrative burdens with respect to the operation of the plan, having regard to the particular characteristics of the plan or the type of plan involved; and

(3) that the application of this part would be adverse to the interests of plan participants in the aggregate.

(b) An alternative method may be prescribed under subsection (a) of this section by regulation or otherwise. If an alternative method is prescribed other than by regulation, the Secretary shall provide notice and an opportunity for interested persons to present their views, and shall publish in the Federal Register the provisions of such alternative method.

(Pub. L. 93–406, title I, §110, Sept. 2, 1974, 88 Stat. 851.)

REGULATIONS

Secretary authorized, effective Sept. 2, 1974, to promulgate regulations wherever provisions of this subchapter call for the promulgation of regulations, see section 1031 of this title.

§ 1031. Repeal and effective date

(a)(1) The Welfare and Pension Plans Disclosure Act [29 U.S.C. 301 et seq.] is repealed except that such Act shall continue to apply to any conduct and events which occurred before the effective date of this part.

(2)(A) Section 664 of title 18 is amended by striking out "any such plan subject to the provisions of the Welfare and Pension Plans Disclosure Act" and inserting in lieu thereof "any employee benefit plan subject to any provisions of title I of the Employee Retirement Income Security Act of 1974".

(B)(i) Section 1027 of such title 18 is amended by striking out "Welfare and Pension Plans Disclosure Act" and inserting in lieu thereof "title I of the Employee Retirement Income Security Act of 1974", and by striking out "Act" each place it appears and inserting in lieu thereof "title".

(ii) The heading for such section is amended by striking out "WELFARE AND PENSION PLANS DISCLOSURE ACT" and inserting in lieu thereof "EMPLOYEE RETIREMENT INCOME SECURITY ACT OF 1974".

(iii) The table of sections of chapter 47 of such title 18 is amended by striking out "Welfare and Pension Plans Disclosure Act" in the item relating to section 1027 and inserting in lieu thereof "Employee Retirement Income Security Act of 1974".

(C) Section 1954 of such title 18 is amended by striking out "any plan subject to the provisions of the Welfare and Pension Plans Disclosure Act as amended" and inserting in lieu thereof "any employee welfare benefit plan or employee pension benefit plan, respectively, subject to any provision of title I of the Employee Retirement Income Security Act of 1974"; and by striking out "sections 3(3) and 5(b)(1) and (2) of the Welfare and Pension Plans Disclosure Act, as amended" and inserting in lieu thereof "sections 3(4) and (3)(16)[1] of the Employee Retirement Income Security Act of 1974".

(D) Section 211 of the Labor-Management Reporting and Disclosure Act of 1959 (29 U.S.C. 441) is amended by striking out "Welfare and Pension Plans Disclosure Act" and inserting in lieu thereof "Employee Retirement Income Security Act of 1974".

(b)(1) Except as provided in paragraph (2), this part (including the amendments and repeals made by subsection (a) of this section) shall take effect on January 1, 1975.

(2) In the case of a plan which has a plan year which begins before January 1, 1975, and ends after December 31, 1974, the Secretary may postpone by regulation the effective date of the repeal of any provision of the Welfare and Pension Plans Disclosure Act (and of any amendment made by subsection (a)(2) of this section) and the effective date of any provision of this part, until the beginning of the first plan year of such plan which begins after January 1, 1975.

(c) The provisions of this subchapter authorizing the Secretary to promulgate regulations shall take effect on September 2, 1974.

(d) Subsections (b) and (c) of this section shall not apply with respect to amendments made to this part in provisions enacted after September 2, 1974.

(Pub. L. 93–406, title I, §111, Sept. 2, 1974, 88 Stat. 851; Pub. L. 101–239, title VII, §7894(h)(1), Dec. 19, 1989, 103 Stat. 2451.)

REFERENCES IN TEXT

The Welfare and Pension Plans Disclosure Act, referred to in subsecs. (a) and (b)(2), is Pub. L. 85–836, Aug. 28, 1958, 72 Stat. 997, as amended, which was classified generally to chapter 10 (§301 et seq.) of this title. For complete classification of this Act to the Code, see Short Title note set out under section 301 of this title and Tables.

Title I of the Employee Retirement Income Security Act of 1974, referred to in subsec. (a)(2)(A) to (C), means title I of Pub. L. 93–406, which enacted this subchapter, amended section 441 of this title, section 5108 of Title 5, Government Organization and Employees, and sections 664, 1027, and 1954 of Title 18, Crimes and Criminal Procedure, and repealed sections 301 to 309 of this title.

The Employee Retirement Income Security Act of 1974, referred to in subsec. (a)(2)(B)(ii), (iii), (D), is Pub. L. 93–406, Sept. 2, 1974, 88 Stat. 829, as amended. Titles I, III, and IV of such act are classified principally to this chapter. For complete classification of this Act to the Code, see Short Title note set out under section 1001 of this title and Tables.

AMENDMENTS

1989—Subsec. (d). Pub. L. 101–239 added subsec. (d).

EFFECTIVE DATE OF 1989 AMENDMENT

Amendment by Pub. L. 101–239 effective, except as otherwise provided, as if originally included in the provision of the Employee Retirement Income Security Act of 1974, Pub. L. 93–406, to which such amendment relates, see section 7894(i) of Pub. L. 101–239, set out as a note under section 1002 of this title.

PART 2—PARTICIPATION AND VESTING

§ 1051. Coverage

This part shall apply to any employee benefit plan described in section 1003(a) of this title (and not exempted under section 1003(b) of this title) other than—

(1) an employee welfare benefit plan;

(2) a plan which is unfunded and is maintained by an employer primarily for the purpose of providing deferred compensation for a

[1] So in original. Probably should be "3(16)".

select group of management or highly compensated employees;

(3)(A) a plan established and maintained by a society, order, or association described in section 501(c)(8) or (9) of title 26, if no part of the contributions to or under such plan are made by employers of participants in such plan, or

(B) a trust described in section 501(c)(18) of title 26;

(4) a plan which is established and maintained by a labor organization described in section 501(c)(5) of title 26 and which does not at any time after September 2, 1974, provide for employer contributions;

(5) any agreement providing payments to a retired partner or a deceased partner's successor in interest, as described in section 736 of title 26;

(6) an individual retirement account or annuity described in section 408 of title 26, or a retirement bond described in section 409 of title 26 (as effective for obligations issued before January 1, 1984);

(7) an excess benefit plan; or

(8) any plan, fund or program under which an employer, all of whose stock is directly or indirectly owned by employees, former employees or their beneficiaries, proposes through an unfunded arrangement to compensate retired employees for benefits which were forfeited by such employees under a pension plan maintained by a former employer prior to the date such pension plan became subject to this chapter.

(Pub. L. 93–406, title I, §201, Sept. 2, 1974, 88 Stat. 852; Pub. L. 96–364, title IV, §411(a), Sept. 26, 1980, 94 Stat. 1308; Pub. L. 101–239, title VII, §§7891(a)(1), 7894(c)(1)(A), (11)(A), Dec. 19, 1989, 103 Stat. 2445, 2448, 2449.)

REFERENCES IN TEXT

Section 409 of title 26, referred to in par. (6), means section 409 of Title 26, Internal Revenue Code, prior to its repeal by Pub. L. 98–369, div. A, title IV, §491(b), July 18, 1984, 98 Stat. 848, applicable to obligations issued after Dec. 31, 1983.

This chapter, referred to in par. (8), was in the original "this Act", meaning Pub. L. 93–406, known as the Employee Retirement Income Security Act of 1974. Titles I, III, and IV of such Act are classified principally to this chapter. For complete classification of this Act to the Code, see Short Title note set out under section 1001 of this title and Tables.

AMENDMENTS

1989—Pars. (3)(A), (4), (5). Pub. L. 101–239, §7891(a)(1), substituted "Internal Revenue Code of 1986" for "Internal Revenue Code of 1954", which for purposes of codification was translated as "title 26" thus requiring no change in text.

Par. (6). Pub. L. 101–239, §7891(a)(1), substituted "section 408 of the Internal Revenue Code of 1986" for "section 408 of the Internal Revenue Code of 1954", which for purposes of codification was translated as "section 408 of title 26" thus requiring no change in text.

Pub. L. 101–239, §7894(c)(11)(A), substituted "section 409 of title 26 (as effective for obligations issued before January 1, 1984)" for "section 409 of title 26".

Pub. L. 101–239, §7894(c)(1)(A)(i), struck out "or" after semicolon at end.

Par. (7). Pub. L. 101–239, §7894(c)(1)(A)(ii), substituted "plan; or" for "plan."

Par. (8). Pub. L. 101–239, §7894(c)(1)(A)(iii), substituted "any plan" for "Any plan".

1980—Par. (8). Pub. L. 96–364 added par. (8).

EFFECTIVE DATE OF 1989 AMENDMENT

Amendment by section 7891(a)(1) of Pub. L. 101–239 effective, except as otherwise provided, as if included in the provision of the Tax Reform Act of 1986, Pub. L. 99–514, to which such amendment relates, see section 7891(f) of Pub. L. 101–239, set out as a note under section 1002 of this title.

Section 7894(c)(1)(B) of Pub. L. 101–239 provided that: "The amendments made by subparagraph (A) [amending this section] shall take effect as if included in section 411 of the Multiemployer Pension Plan Amendments Act of 1980 [Pub. L. 96–364]."

Section 7894(c)(11)(B) of Pub. L. 101–239 provided that: "The amendment made by subparagraph (A) [amending this section] shall take effect as if originally included in section 491(b) of Public Law 98–369."

EFFECTIVE DATE OF 1980 AMENDMENT

Amendment by Pub. L. 96–364 effective Sept. 26, 1980, except as specifically provided, see section 1461(e) of this title.

§1052. Minimum participation standards

(a)(1)(A) No pension plan may require, as a condition of participation in the plan, that an employee complete a period of service with the employer or employers maintaining the plan extending beyond the later of the following dates—

(i) the date on which the employee attains the age of 21; or

(ii) the date on which he completes 1 year of service.

(B)(i) In the case of any plan which provides that after not more than 2 years of service each participant has a right to 100 percent of his accrued benefit under the plan which is nonforfeitable at the time such benefit accrues, clause (ii) of subparagraph (A) shall be applied by substituting "2 years of service" for "1 year of service".

(ii) In the case of any plan maintained exclusively for employees of an educational organization (as defined in section 170(b)(1)(A)(ii) of title 26) by an employer which is exempt from tax under section 501(a) of title 26, which provides that each participant having at least 1 year of service has a right to 100 percent of his accrued benefit under the plan which is nonforfeitable at the time such benefit accrues, clause (i) of subparagraph (A) shall be applied by substituting "26" for "21". This clause shall not apply to any plan to which clause (i) applies.

(2) No pension plan may exclude from participation (on the basis of age) employees who have attained a specified age.

(3)(A) For purposes of this section, the term "year of service" means a 12-month period during which the employee has not less than 1,000 hours of service. For purposes of this paragraph, computation of any 12-month period shall be made with reference to the date on which the employee's employment commenced, except that, in accordance with regulations prescribed by the Secretary, such computation may be made by reference to the first day of a plan year in the case of an employee who does not complete 1,000 hours of service during the 12-month period beginning on the date his employment commenced.

(B) In the case of any seasonal industry where the customary period of employment is less than 1,000 hours during a calendar year, the term "year of service" shall be such period as may be determined under regulations prescribed by the Secretary.

(C) For purposes of this section, the term "hour of service" means a time of service determined under regulations prescribed by the Secretary.

(D) For purposes of this section, in the case of any maritime industry, 125 days of service shall be treated as 1,000 hours of service. The Secretary may prescribe regulations to carry out the purposes of this subparagraph.

(4) A plan shall be treated as not meeting the requirements of paragraph (1) unless it provides that any employee who has satisfied the minimum age and service requirements specified in such paragraph, and who is otherwise entitled to participate in the plan, commences participation in the plan no later than the earlier of—

(A) the first day of the first plan year beginning after the date on which such employee satisfied such requirements, or

(B) the date 6 months after the date on which he satisfied such requirements,

unless such employee was separated from the service before the date referred to in subparagraph (A) or (B), whichever is applicable.

(b)(1) Except as otherwise provided in paragraphs (2), (3), and (4), all years of service with the employer or employers maintaining the plan shall be taken into account in computing the period of service for purposes of subsection (a)(1) of this section.

(2) In the case of any employee who has any 1-year break in service (as defined in section 1053(b)(3)(A) of this title) under a plan to which the service requirements of clause (i) of subsection (a)(1)(B) of this section apply, if such employee has not satisfied such requirements, service before such break shall not be required to be taken into account.

(3) In computing an employee's period of service for purposes of subsection (a)(1) of this section in the case of any participant who has any 1-year break in service (as defined in section 1053(b)(3)(A) of this title), service before such break shall not be required to be taken into account under the plan until he has completed a year of service (as defined in subsection (a)(3) of this section) after his return.

(4)(A) For purposes of paragraph (1), in the case of a nonvested participant, years of service with the employer or employers maintaining the plan before any period of consecutive 1-year breaks in service shall not be required to be taken into account in computing the period of service if the number of consecutive 1-year breaks in service within such period equals or exceeds the greater of—

(i) 5, or

(ii) the aggregate number of years of service before such period.

(B) If any years of service are not required to be taken into account by reason of a period of breaks in service to which subparagraph (A) applies, such years of service shall not be taken into account in applying subparagraph (A) to a subsequent period of breaks in service.

(C) For purposes of subparagraph (A), the term "nonvested participant" means a participant who does not have any nonforfeitable right under the plan to an accrued benefit derived from employer contributions.

(5)(A) In the case of each individual who is absent from work for any period—

(i) by reason of the pregnancy of the individual,

(ii) by reason of the birth of a child of the individual,

(iii) by reason of the placement of a child with the individual in connection with the adoption of such child by such individual, or

(iv) for purposes of caring for such child for a period beginning immediately following such birth or placement,

the plan shall treat as hours of service, solely for purposes of determining under this subsection whether a 1-year break in service (as defined in section 1053(b)(3)(A) of this title) has occurred, the hours described in subparagraph (B).

(B) The hours described in this subparagraph are—

(i) the hours of service which otherwise would normally have been credited to such individual but for such absence, or

(ii) in any case in which the plan is unable to determine the hours described in clause (i), 8 hours of service per day of such absence,

except that the total number of hours treated as hours of service under this subparagraph by reason of any such pregnancy or placement shall not exceed 501 hours.

(C) The hours described in subparagraph (B) shall be treated as hours of service as provided in this paragraph—

(i) only in the year in which the absence from work begins, if a participant would be prevented from incurring a 1-year break in service in such year solely because the period of absence is treated as hours of service as provided in subparagraph (A); or

(ii) in any other case, in the immediately following year.

(D) For purposes of this paragraph, the term "year" means the period used in computations pursuant to subsection (a)(3)(A) of this section.

(E) A plan may provide that no credit will be given pursuant to this paragraph unless the individual furnishes to the plan administrator such timely information as the plan may reasonably require to establish—

(i) that the absence from work is for reasons referred to in subparagraph (A), and

(ii) the number of days for which there was such an absence.

(Pub. L. 93–406, title I, §202, Sept. 2, 1974, 88 Stat. 853; Pub. L. 98–397, title I, §102(a), (d)(1), (e)(1), Aug. 23, 1984, 98 Stat. 1426, 1427; Pub. L. 99–509, title IX, §9203(a)(1), Oct. 21, 1986, 100 Stat. 1979; Pub. L. 99–514, title XI, §1113(e)(3), Oct. 22, 1986, 100 Stat. 2448; Pub. L. 101–239, title VII, §§7861(a)(2), 7891(a)(1), 7892(a), 7894(c)(2), Dec. 19, 1989, 103 Stat. 2430, 2445, 2447, 2449.)

AMENDMENTS

1989—Subsec. (a)(1)(B)(i). Pub. L. 101–239, §7861(a)(2), made technical correction to directory language of Pub. L. 99–514. See 1986 Amendment note below.

Subsec. (a)(1)(B)(ii). Pub. L. 101–239, §7894(c)(2)(A), substituted "educational organization" for "educational institution".

Pub. L. 101–239, §7891(a)(1), substituted "Internal Revenue Code of 1986" for "Internal Revenue Code of 1954", which for purposes of codification was translated as "title 26" thus requiring no change in text.

Subsec. (a)(2). Pub. L. 101–239, §7892(a), struck out comma after "specified age".

Subsec. (b)(2). Pub. L. 101–239, §7894(c)(2)(B), substituted "a plan" for "the plan".

1986—Subsec. (a)(1)(B)(i). Pub. L. 99–514, as amended by Pub. L. 101–239, §7861(a)(2), substituted "2 years of service" for "3 years of service" in two places.

Subsec. (a)(2). Pub. L. 99–509 substituted a period for "unless—

"(A) the plan is a—

"(i) defined benefit plan, or

"(ii) target benefit plan (as defined under regulations prescribed by the Secretary of the Treasury), and

"(B) such employees begin employment with the employer after they have attained a specified age which is not more than 5 years before the normal retirement age under the plan."

1984—Subsec. (a)(1). Pub. L. 98–397, §102(a), substituted "21" for "25" in subpar. (A)(i) and "'26' for '21'" for "'30' for '25'" in subpar. (B)(ii).

Subsec. (b)(4). Pub. L. 98–397, §102(d)(1), amended par. (4) generally. Prior to amendment, par. (4) read as follows: "In the case of an employee who does not have any nonforfeitable right to an accrued benefit derived from employer contributions, years of service with the employer or employers maintaining the plan before a break in service shall not be required to be taken into account in computing the period of service for purposes of subsection (a)(1) of this section if the number of consecutive 1-year breaks in service equals or exceeds the aggregate number of such years of service before such break. Such aggregate number of years of service before such break shall be deemed not to include any years of service not required to be taken into account under this paragraph by reason of any prior break in service."

Subsec. (b)(5). Pub. L. 98–397, §102(e)(1), added par. (5).

EFFECTIVE DATE OF 1989 AMENDMENT

Amendment by section 7861(a)(2) of Pub. L. 101–239 effective as if included in the provision of the Tax Reform Act of 1986, Pub. L. 99–514, to which such amendment relates, see section 7863 of Pub. L. 101–239, set out as a note under section 106 of Title 26, Internal Revenue Code.

Amendment by section 7891(a)(1) of Pub. L. 101–239 effective, except as otherwise provided, as if included in the provision of the Tax Reform Act of 1986, Pub. L. 99–514, to which such amendment relates, see section 7891(f) of Pub. L. 101–239, set out as a note under section 1002 of this title.

Section 7892(c) of Pub. L. 101–239 provided that: "Any amendment made by this section [amending this section and section 1082 of this title] shall take effect as if included in the provision of the Omnibus Budget Reconciliation Act of 1987 [Pub. L. 100–203, probably should refer to Omnibus Budget Reconciliation Act of 1986, Pub. L. 99–509] or Pension Protection Act [Pub. L. 100–203, §§9302–9346, probably should refer to Omnibus Budget Reconciliation Act of 1987, Pub. L. 100–203] to which such amendment relates."

Amendment by section 7894(c)(2) of Pub. L. 101–239 effective, except as otherwise provided, as if originally included in the provision of the Employee Retirement Income Security Act of 1974, Pub. L. 93–406, to which such amendment relates, see section 7894(i) of Pub. L. 101–239, set out as a note under section 1002 of this title.

EFFECTIVE DATE OF 1986 AMENDMENTS

Amendment by section 1113(e)(3) of Pub. L. 99–514 applicable to plan years beginning after Dec. 31, 1988, with special rule for plans maintained pursuant to collective bargaining agreements ratified before Mar. 1, 1986, and not applicable to employees who do not have 1 hour of service in any plan year to which the amendment applies, see section 1113(f) of Pub. L. 99–514, as amended, set out as a note under section 411 of Title 26, Internal Revenue Code.

Amendment by Pub. L. 99–509 applicable only with respect to plan years beginning on or after Jan. 1, 1988, and only with respect to service performed on or after such date, see section 9204 of Pub. L. 99–509, set out as an Effective and Termination Dates of 1986 Amendments note under section 623 of this title.

EFFECTIVE DATE OF 1984 AMENDMENT

Amendment by Pub. L. 98–397 applicable to plan years beginning after Dec. 31, 1984, except as otherwise provided, see sections 302 and 303 of Pub. L. 98–397, set out as a note under section 1001 of this title.

REGULATIONS

Secretary of Labor, Secretary of the Treasury, and Equal Employment Opportunity Commission each to issue before Feb. 1, 1988, final regulations to carry out amendments made by Pub. L. 99–509, see section 9204 of Pub. L. 99–509, set out as an Effective and Termination Dates of 1986 Amendment note under section 623 of this title.

Secretary authorized, effective Sept. 2, 1974, to promulgate regulations wherever provisions of this subchapter call for the promulgation of regulations, see section 1031 of this title.

PLAN AMENDMENTS NOT REQUIRED UNTIL JANUARY 1, 1989

For provisions directing that if any amendments made by subtitle A or subtitle C of title XI [§§1101–1147 and 1171–1177] or title XVIII [§§1800–1899A] of Pub. L. 99–514 require an amendment to any plan, such plan amendment shall not be required to be made before the first plan year beginning on or after Jan. 1, 1989, see section 1140 of Pub. L. 99–514, as amended, set out as a note under section 401 of Title 26, Internal Revenue Code.

For provisions directing that if any amendments made by Pub. L. 99–509 require an amendment to any plan, such plan amendment shall not be required to be made before the first plan year beginning on or after Jan. 1, 1989, see section 9204 of Pub. L. 99–509, set out as an Effective and Termination Dates of 1986 Amendment note under section 623 of this title.

§1053. Minimum vesting standards

(a) Nonforfeitability requirements

Each pension plan shall provide that an employee's right to his normal retirement benefit is nonforfeitable upon the attainment of normal retirement age and in addition shall satisfy the requirements of paragraphs (1) and (2) of this subsection.

(1) A plan satisfies the requirements of this paragraph if an employee's rights in his accrued benefit derived from his own contributions are nonforfeitable.

(2)(A)(i) In the case of a defined benefit plan, a plan satisfies the requirements of this paragraph if it satisfies the requirements of clause (ii) or (iii).

(ii) A plan satisfies the requirements of this clause if an employee who has completed at least 5 years of service has a nonforfeitable right to 100 percent of the employee's accrued benefit derived from employer contributions.

(iii) A plan satisfies the requirements of this clause if an employee has a nonforfeitable right to a percentage of the employee's accrued benefit derived from employer contributions determined under the following table:

Years of service:	The nonforfeitable percentage is:
3	20
4	40
5	60
6	80
7 or more	100.

(B)(i) In the case of an individual account plan, a plan satisfies the requirements of this paragraph if it satisfies the requirements of clause (ii) or (iii).

(ii) A plan satisfies the requirements of this clause if an employee who has completed at least 3 years of service has a nonforfeitable right to 100 percent of the employee's accrued benefit derived from employer contributions.

(iii) A plan satisfies the requirements of this clause if an employee has a nonforfeitable right to a percentage of the employee's accrued benefit derived from employer contributions determined under the following table:

Years of service:	The nonforfeitable percentage is:
2	20
3	40
4	60
5	80
6 or more	100.

(3)(A) A right to an accrued benefit derived from employer contributions shall not be treated as forfeitable solely because the plan provides that it is not payable if the participant dies (except in the case of a survivor annuity which is payable as provided in section 1055 of this title).

(B) A right to an accrued benefit derived from employer contributions shall not be treated as forfeitable solely because the plan provides that the payment of benefits is suspended for such period as the employee is employed, subsequent to the commencement of payment of such benefits—

(i) in the case of a plan other than a multiemployer plan, by an employer who maintains the plan under which such benefits were being paid; and

(ii) in the case of a multiemployer plan, in the same industry, in the same trade or craft, and the same geographic area covered by the plan, as when such benefits commenced.

The Secretary shall prescribe such regulations as may be necessary to carry out the purposes of this subparagraph, including regulations with respect to the meaning of the term "employed".

(C) A right to an accrued benefit derived from employer contributions shall not be treated as forfeitable solely because plan amendments may be given retroactive application as provided in section 1002(d)(2) of this title.

(D)(i) A right to an accrued benefit derived from employer contributions shall not be treated as forfeitable solely because the plan provides that, in the case of a participant who does not have a nonforfeitable right to at least 50 percent of his accrued benefit derived from employer contributions, such accrued benefit may be forfeited on account of the withdrawal by the participant of any amount attributable to the benefit derived from mandatory contributions (as defined in the last sentence of section 1054(c)(2)(C) of this title) made by such participant.

(ii) Clause (i) shall not apply to a plan unless the plan provides that any accrued benefit forfeited under a plan provision described in such clause shall be restored upon repayment by the participant of the full amount of the withdrawal described in such clause plus, in the case of a defined benefit plan, interest. Such interest shall be computed on such amount at the rate determined for purposes of section 1054(c)(2)(C) of this title (if such subsection applies) on the date of such repayment (computed annually from the date of such withdrawal). The plan provision required under this clause may provide that such repayment must be made (I) in the case of a withdrawal on account of separation from service, before the earlier of 5 years after the first date on which the participant is subsequently re-employed by the employer, or the close of the first period of 5 consecutive 1-year breaks in service commencing after the withdrawal; or (II) in the case of any other withdrawal, 5 years after the date of the withdrawal.

(iii) In the case of accrued benefits derived from employer contributions which accrued before September 2, 1974, a right to such accrued benefit derived from employer contributions shall not be treated as forfeitable solely because the plan provides that an amount of such accrued benefit may be forfeited on account of the withdrawal by the participant of an amount attributable to the benefit derived from mandatory contributions, made by such participant before September 2, 1974, if such amount forfeited is proportional to such amount withdrawn. This clause shall not apply to any plan to which any mandatory contribution is made after September 2, 1974. The Secretary of the Treasury shall prescribe such regulations as may be necessary to carry out the purposes of this clause.

(iv) For purposes of this subparagraph, in the case of any class-year plan, a withdrawal of employee contributions shall be treated as a withdrawal of such contributions on a plan year by plan year basis in succeeding order of time.

(v) Cross reference.—

For nonforfeitability where the employee has a nonforfeitable right to at least 50 percent of his accrued benefit, see section 1056(c) of this title.

(E)(i) A right to an accrued benefit derived from employer contributions under a multiemployer plan shall not be treated as forfeitable solely because the plan provides that benefits accrued as a result of service with the participant's employer before the employer had an obligation to contribute under the plan may not be payable if the employer ceases contributions to the multiemployer plan.

(ii) A participant's right to an accrued benefit derived from employer contributions under a multiemployer plan shall not be treated as forfeitable solely because—

(I) the plan is amended to reduce benefits under section 1425 or 1441 of this title, or

(II) benefit payments under the plan may be suspended under section 1426 or 1441 of this title.

(F) A matching contribution (within the meaning of section 401(m) of title 26) shall not be treated as forfeitable merely because such contribution is forfeitable if the contribution to which the matching contribution relates is treated as an excess contribution under section 401(k)(8)(B) of title 26, an excess deferral under section 402(g)(2)(A) of title 26, an erroneous automatic contribution under section 414(w) of title 26, or an excess aggregate contribution under section 401(m)(6)(B) of title 26.

(b) Computation of period of service

(1) In computing the period of service under the plan for purposes of determining the nonforfeitable percentage under subsection (a)(2) of this section, all of an employee's years of service with the employer or employers maintaining the plan shall be taken into account, except that the following may be disregarded:

(A) years of service before age 18,[1]

(B) years of service during a period for which the employee declined to contribute to a plan requiring employee contributions,[1]

(C) years of service with an employer during any period for which the employer did not maintain the plan or a predecessor plan, defined by the Secretary of the Treasury;

(D) service not required to be taken into account under paragraph (3);

(E) years of service before January 1, 1971, unless the employee has had at least 3 years of service after December 31, 1970;

(F) years of service before this part first applies to the plan if such service would have been disregarded under the rules of the plan with regard to breaks in service, as in effect on the applicable date; and

(G) in the case of a multiemployer plan, years of service—

(i) with an employer after—

(I) a complete withdrawal of such employer from the plan (within the meaning of section 1383 of this title), or

(II) to the extent permitted by regulations prescribed by the Secretary of the Treasury, a partial withdrawal described in section 1385(b)(2)(A)(i) of this title in connection with the decertification of the collective bargaining representative; and

(ii) with any employer under the plan after the termination date of the plan under section 1348 of this title.

(2)(A) For purposes of this section, except as provided in subparagraph (C), the term "year of service" means a calendar year, plan year, or other 12-consecutive month period designated by the plan (and not prohibited under regulations prescribed by the Secretary) during which the participant has completed 1,000 hours of service.

(B) For purposes of this section, the term "hour of service" has the meaning provided by section 1052(a)(3)(C) of this title.

(C) In the case of any seasonal industry where the customary period of employment is less than 1,000 hours during a calendar year, the term "year of service" shall be such period as determined under regulations of the Secretary.

(D) For purposes of this section, in the case of any maritime industry, 125 days of service shall be treated as 1,000 hours of service. The Secretary may prescribe regulations to carry out the purposes of this subparagraph.

(3)(A) For purposes of this paragraph, the term "1-year break in service" means a calendar year, plan year, or other 12-consecutive-month period designated by the plan (and not prohibited under regulations prescribed by the Secretary) during which the participant has not completed more than 500 hours of service.

(B) For purposes of paragraph (1), in the case of any employee who has any 1-year break in service, years of service before such break shall not be required to be taken into account until he has completed a year of service after his return.

(C) For purposes of paragraph (1), in the case of any participant in an individual account plan or an insured defined benefit plan which satisfies the requirements of subsection 1054(b)(1)(F) of this title who has 5 consecutive 1-year breaks in service, years of service after such 5-year period shall not be required to be taken into account for purposes of determining the nonforfeitable percentage of his accrued benefit derived from employer contributions which accrued before such 5-year period.

(D)(i) For purposes of paragraph (1), in the case of a nonvested participant, years of service with the employer or employers maintaining the plan before any period of consecutive 1-year breaks in service shall not be required to be taken into account if the number of consecutive 1-year breaks in service within such period equals or exceeds the greater of—

(I) 5, or

(II) the aggregate number of years of service before such period.

(ii) If any years of service are not required to be taken into account by reason of a period of breaks in service to which clause (i) applies, such years of service shall not be taken into account in applying clause (i) to a subsequent period of breaks in service.

(iii) For purposes of clause (i), the term "nonvested participant" means a participant who does not have any nonforfeitable right under the plan to an accrued benefit derived from employer contributions.

(E)(i) In the case of each individual who is absent from work for any period—

(I) by reason of the pregnancy of the individual,

(II) by reason of the birth of a child of the individual,

(III) by reason of the placement of a child with the individual in connection with the adoption of such child by such individual, or

(IV) for purposes of caring for such child for a period beginning immediately following such birth or placement,

the plan shall treat as hours of service, solely for purposes of determining under this paragraph whether a 1-year break in service has occurred, the hours described in clause (ii).

[1] So in original. The comma probably should be a semicolon.

(ii) The hours described in this clause are—

(I) the hours of service which otherwise would normally have been credited to such individual but for such absence, or

(II) in any case in which the plan is unable to determine the hours described in subclause (I), 8 hours of service per day of absence,

except that the total number of hours treated as hours of service under this clause by reason of such pregnancy or placement shall not exceed 501 hours.

(iii) The hours described in clause (ii) shall be treated as hours of service as provided in this subparagraph—

(I) only in the year in which the absence from work begins, if a participant would be prevented from incurring a 1-year break in service in such year solely because the period of absence is treated as hours of service as provided in clause (i); or

(II) in any other case, in the immediately following year.

(iv) For purposes of this subparagraph, the term "year" means the period used in computations pursuant to paragraph (2).

(v) A plan may provide that no credit will be given pursuant to this subparagraph unless the individual furnishes to the plan administrator such timely information as the plan may reasonably require to establish—

(I) that the absence from work is for reasons referred to in clause (i), and

(II) the number of days for which there was such an absence.

(4) Cross references.—

(A) For definitions of "accrued benefit" and "normal retirement age", see sections 1002(23) and (24) of this title.

(B) For effect of certain cash out distributions, see section 1054(d)(1) of this title.

(c) Plan amendments altering vesting schedule

(1)(A) A plan amendment changing any vesting schedule under the plan shall be treated as not satisfying the requirements of subsection (a)(2) of this section if the nonforfeitable percentage of the accrued benefit derived from employer contributions (determined as of the later of the date such amendment is adopted, or the date such amendment becomes effective) of any employee who is a participant in the plan is less than such nonforfeitable percentage computed under the plan without regard to such amendment.

(B) A plan amendment changing any vesting schedule under the plan shall be treated as not satisfying the requirements of subsection (a)(2) of this section unless each participant having not less than 3 years of service is permitted to elect, within a reasonable period after adoption of such amendment, to have his nonforfeitable percentage computed under the plan without regard to such amendment.

(2) Subsection (a) of this section shall not apply to benefits which may not be provided for designated employees in the event of early termination of the plan under provisions of the plan adopted pursuant to regulations prescribed by the Secretary of the Treasury to preclude the discrimination prohibited by section 401(a)(4) of title 26.

(d) Nonforfeitable benefits after lesser period and in greater amounts than required

A pension plan may allow for nonforfeitable benefits after a lesser period and in greater amounts than are required by this part.

(e) Consent for distribution; present value; covered distributions

(1) If the present value of any nonforfeitable benefit with respect to a participant in a plan exceeds $5,000, the plan shall provide that such benefit may not be immediately distributed without the consent of the participant.

(2) For purposes of paragraph (1), the present value shall be calculated in accordance with section 1055(g)(3) of this title.

(3) This subsection shall not apply to any distribution of dividends to which section 404(k) of title 26 applies.

(4) A plan shall not fail to meet the requirements of this subsection if, under the terms of the plan, the present value of the nonforfeitable accrued benefit is determined without regard to that portion of such benefit which is attributable to rollover contributions (and earnings allocable thereto). For purposes of this subparagraph, the term "rollover contributions" means any rollover contribution under sections 402(c), 403(a)(4), 403(b)(8), 408(d)(3)(A)(ii), and 457(e)(16) of title 26.

(f) Special rules for plans computing accrued benefits by reference to hypothetical account balance or equivalent amounts

(1) In general

An applicable defined benefit plan shall not be treated as failing to meet—

(A) subject to paragraph (2), the requirements of subsection (a)(2), or

(B) the requirements of section 1054(c) or 1055(g) of this title, or the requirements of subsection (e), with respect to accrued benefits derived from employer contributions,

solely because the present value of the accrued benefit (or any portion thereof) of any participant is, under the terms of the plan, equal to the amount expressed as the balance in the hypothetical account described in paragraph (3) or as an accumulated percentage of the participant's final average compensation.

(2) 3-year vesting

In the case of an applicable defined benefit plan, such plan shall be treated as meeting the requirements of subsection (a)(2) only if an employee who has completed at least 3 years of service has a nonforfeitable right to 100 percent of the employee's accrued benefit derived from employer contributions.

(3) Applicable defined benefit plan and related rules

For purposes of this subsection—

(A) In general

The term "applicable defined benefit plan" means a defined benefit plan under which the accrued benefit (or any portion thereof) is calculated as the balance of a hypothetical account maintained for the participant or as an accumulated percentage of the participant's final average compensation.

(B) Regulations to include similar plans

The Secretary of the Treasury shall issue regulations which include in the definition of an applicable defined benefit plan any defined benefit plan (or any portion of such a plan) which has an effect similar to an applicable defined benefit plan.

(Pub. L. 93–406, title I, § 203, Sept. 2, 1974, 88 Stat. 854; Pub. L. 96–364, title III, § 303, Sept. 26, 1980, 94 Stat. 1292; Pub. L. 98–397, title I, §§ 102(b), (c), (d)(2), (e)(2), 105(a), Aug. 23, 1984, 98 Stat. 1426–1428, 1436; Pub. L. 99–514, title XI, §§ 1113(e)(1), (2), (4)(A), 1139(c)(1), title XVIII, § 1898(a)(1)(B), (4)(B)(i), (d)(1)(B), (2)(B), Oct. 22, 1986, 100 Stat. 2447, 2448, 2487, 2942, 2944, 2955; Pub. L. 101–239, title VII, §§ 7861(a)(1), (5)(B), (6)(B), 7862(d)(4), (5), (10), 7891(a)(1), (b)(1), (2), 7894(c)(3), Dec. 19, 1989, 103 Stat. 2430, 2434, 2445, 2449; Pub. L. 103–465, title VII, § 767(c)(1), Dec. 8, 1994, 108 Stat. 5039; Pub. L. 104–188, title I, § 1442(b), Aug. 20, 1996, 110 Stat. 1808; Pub. L. 105–34, title X, § 1071(b)(1), Aug. 5, 1997, 111 Stat. 948; Pub. L. 107–16, title VI, §§ 633(b), 648(a)(2), June 7, 2001, 115 Stat. 116, 127; Pub. L. 108–311, title IV, § 408(b)(8), Oct. 4, 2004, 118 Stat. 1193; Pub. L. 109–280, title I, § 107(a)(4), title VII, § 701(a)(2), title IX, §§ 902(d)(2)(E), 904(b), Aug. 17, 2006, 120 Stat. 819, 984, 1038, 1049; Pub. L. 110–458, title I, § 107(a)(1), Dec. 23, 2008, 122 Stat. 5107.)

AMENDMENTS

2008—Subsec. (f)(1)(B). Pub. L. 110–458 amended subpar. (B) generally. Prior to amendment, subpar. (B) read as follows: "the requirements of section 1054(c) of this title or section 1055(g) of this title with respect to contributions other than employee contributions,".

2006—Subsec. (a)(2). Pub. L. 109–280, § 904(b)(1), amended par. (2) generally, substituting provisions relating to satisfaction of requirements in the case of a defined benefit plan and in the case of an individual account plan for provisions relating to satisfaction of requirements if an employee who has completed at least 5 years of service has a nonforfeitable right to 100 percent of the employee's accrued benefit derived from employer contributions or if an employee has a nonforfeitable right to a percentage of such benefit based upon number of years of service.

Subsec. (a)(3)(C). Pub. L. 109–280, § 107(a)(4), substituted "1082(d)(2)" for "1082(c)(8)".

Subsec. (a)(3)(F). Pub. L. 109–280, § 902(d)(2)(E), inserted "an erroneous automatic contribution under section 414(w) of title 26," before "or an excess aggregate contribution".

Subsec. (a)(4). Pub. L. 109–280, § 904(b)(2), struck out par. (4), which related to application of par. (2) in the case of matching contributions, as defined in section 401(m)(4)(A) of title 26.

Subsec. (f). Pub. L. 109–280, § 701(a)(2), added subsec. (f).

2004—Subsec. (a)(4)(B). Pub. L. 108–311 substituted "6 or more" for "6" in table.

2001—Subsec. (a)(2). Pub. L. 107–16, § 633(b)(1), substituted "Except as provided in paragraph (4), a plan" for "A plan" in introductory provisions.

Subsec. (a)(4). Pub. L. 107–16, § 633(b)(2), added par. (4).

Subsec. (e)(4). Pub. L. 107–16, § 648(a)(2), added par. (4).

1997—Subsec. (e)(1). Pub. L. 105–34 substituted "$5,000" for "$3,500".

1996—Subsec. (a)(2). Pub. L. 104–188, § 1442(b)(1), substituted "subparagraph (A) or (B)" for "subparagraph (A), (B), or (C)" in introductory provisions.

Subsec. (a)(2)(C). Pub. L. 104–188, § 1442(b)(2), struck out subpar. (C) which read as follows: "A plan satisfies the requirements of this subparagraph if—

"(i) the plan is a multiemployer plan (within the meaning of section 1002(37)), and

"(ii) under the plan—

"(I) an employee who is covered pursuant to a collective bargaining agreement described in section 1002(37)(A)(ii) of this title and who has completed at least 10 years of service has a nonforfeitable right to 100 percent of the employee's accrued benefit derived from employer contributions, and

"(II) the requirements of subparagraph (A) or (B) are met with respect to employees not described in subclause (I)."

1994—Subsec. (e)(2). Pub. L. 103–465 amended par. (2) generally. Prior to amendment, par. (2) read as follows:

"(2)(A) For purposes of paragraph (1), the present value shall be calculated—

"(i) by using an interest rate no greater than the applicable interest rate if the vested accrued benefit (using such rate) is not in excess of $25,000, and

"(ii) by using an interest rate no greater than 120 percent of the applicable interest rate if the vested accrued benefit exceeds $25,000 (as determined under clause (i)).

In no event shall the present value determined under subclause (II) be less than $25,000.

"(B) For purposes of subparagraph (A), the term 'applicable interest rate' means the interest rate which would be used (as of the date of the distribution) by the Pension Benefit Guaranty Corporation for purposes of determining the present value of a lump sum distribution on plan termination."

1989—Subsec. (a)(2). Pub. L. 101–239, § 7861(a)(1)(A), substituted "satisfies the requirements" for "satisfies the following requirements" in introductory provisions.

Subsec. (a)(2)(C)(ii)(I). Pub. L. 101–239, § 7861(a)(1)(B), substituted "section 1002(37)(A)(ii) of this title" for "section 414(f)(1)(B)".

Subsec. (a)(3)(D)(v). Pub. L. 101–239, § 7894(c)(3), substituted "nonforfeitability" for "nonforfeitably".

Subsec. (a)(3)(F). Pub. L. 101–239, § 7861(a)(5)(B), added subpar. (F).

Subsec. (b)(1)(A). Pub. L. 101–239, § 7861(a)(6)(B), amended subpar. (A) generally. Prior to amendment, subpar. (A) read as follows: "years of service before age 18, except that in case of a plan which does not satisfy subparagraph (A) or (B) of subsection (a)(2) of this section, the plan may not disregard any such year of service during which the employee was a participant;".

Subsec. (c)(2). Pub. L. 101–239, § 7891(a)(1), substituted "Internal Revenue Code of 1986" for "Internal Revenue Code of 1954", which for purposes of codification was translated as "title 26" thus requiring no change in text.

Subsec. (e)(1). Pub. L. 101–239, § 7862(d)(10), which directed amendment of par. (1) by substituting "nonforfeitable benefit" for "vested accrued benefit", could not be executed because the language "vested accrued benefit" did not appear after the amendment by Pub. L. 101–239, § 7862(d)(5), see below.

Pub. L. 101–239, § 7862(d)(5), amended par. (1) generally. Prior to amendment, par. (1) read as follows: "If the present value of any vested accrued benefit exceeds $3,500, a pension plan shall provide that such benefit may not be immediately distributed without the consent of the participant."

Pub. L. 101–239, § 7862(d)(4), made technical correction to Pub. L. 99–514, § 1898(d)(1)(B), see 1986 Amendment note below.

Subsec. (e)(2). Pub. L. 101–239, § 7891(b)(1), (2), realigned margins of subpars. (A) and (B) and struck out subpar. (B) heading "Applicable interest rate".

Subsec. (e)(3). Pub. L. 101–239, § 7891(a)(1), substituted "Internal Revenue Code of 1986" for "Internal Revenue Code of 1954", which for purposes of codification was translated as "title 26" thus requiring no change in text.

1986—Subsec. (a)(2). Pub. L. 99–514, § 1113(e)(1), amended par. (2) generally, substituting provisions covering 5-year vesting, 3- to 7-year vesting, and multiemployer plans, for former provisions which covered 10-year vesting, 5- to 15-year vesting, and the "rule of 45" under which a plan satisfied the requirements of this paragraph if an employee who had completed at least 5 years of service and with respect to whom the sum of his age and years of service equalled or exceeded 45 had a right to a percentage of his accrued benefits derived from employer contributions.

Subsec. (a)(3)(D)(ii). Pub. L. 99–514, §1898(a)(4)(B)(i), inserted last sentence and struck out former last sentence which read as follows: "In the case of a defined contribution plan the plan provision required under this clause may provide that such repayment must be made before the participant has any 1-year break in service commencing after the withdrawal."

Subsec. (c)(1)(B). Pub. L. 99–514, §1113(e)(4)(A), substituted "3 years" for "5 years".

Subsec. (c)(3). Pub. L. 99–514, §1113(e)(2), struck out par. (3) which provided for class year vesting.

Pub. L. 99–514, §1898(a)(1)(B), amended par. (3) generally. Prior to amendment, par. (3) read as follows: "The requirements of subsection (a)(2) of this section shall be deemed to be satisfied in the case of a class year plan if such plan provides that 100 percent of each employee's right to or derived from the contributions of the employer on his behalf with respect to any plan year are nonforfeitable not later than the end of the 5th year following the plan year for which such contributions were made. For purposes of this part, the term 'class year plan' means a profit sharing, stock bonus, or money purchase plan which provides for the separate nonforfeitability of employees' rights to or derived from the contributions for each plan year."

Subsec. (e)(1). Pub. L. 99–514, §1898(d)(1)(B), as amended by Pub. L. 101–239, §7862(d)(4), amended par. (1) generally. Prior to amendment, par. (1) read as follows: "If the present value of any accrued benefit exceeds $3,500, such benefit shall not be treated as nonforfeitable if the plan provides that the present value of such benefit could be immediately distributed without the consent of the participant."

Subsec. (e)(2). Pub. L. 99–514, §1139(c)(1), amended par. (2) generally. Prior to amendment, par. (2) read as follows: "For purposes of paragraph (1), the present value shall be calculated by using an interest rate not greater than the interest rate which would be used (as of the date of the distribution) by the Pension Benefit Guaranty Corporation for purposes of determining the present value of a lump sum distribution on plan termination."

Pub. L. 99–514, §1898(d)(2)(B), added par. (3).

1984—Subsec. (b)(1)(A). Pub. L. 98–397, §102(b), substituted "18" for "22".

Subsec. (b)(3)(C). Pub. L. 98–397, §102(c), substituted "5 consecutive 1-year breaks in service" for "any 1-year break in service" and substituted "such 5-year period" for "such break" in two places.

Subsec. (b)(3)(D). Pub. L. 98–397, §102(d)(2), amended subpar. (D) generally. Prior to amendment, subpar. (D) read as follows: "For purposes of paragraph (1), in the case of a participant who, under the plan, does not have any nonforfeitable right to an accrued benefit derived from employer contributions, years of service before any 1-year break in service shall not be required to be taken into account if the number of consecutive 1-year breaks in service equals or exceeds the aggregate number of such years of service prior to such break. Such aggregate number of years of service before such break shall be deemed not to include any years of service not required to be taken into account under this subparagraph by reason of any prior break in service."

Subsec. (b)(3)(E). Pub. L. 98–397, §102(e)(2), added subpar. (E).

Subsec. (e). Pub. L. 98–397, §105(a), added subsec. (e).

1980—Subsec. (a)(3)(E). Pub. L. 96–364, §303(1), added subpar. (E).

Subsec. (b)(1)(G). Pub. L. 96–364, §303(2)–(4), added subpar. (G).

EFFECTIVE DATE OF 2008 AMENDMENT

Amendment by Pub. L. 110–458 effective as if included in the provisions of Pub. L. 109–280 to which the amendment relates, except as otherwise provided, see section 112 of Pub. L. 110–458, set out as a note under section 72 of Title 26, Internal Revenue Code.

EFFECTIVE DATE OF 2006 AMENDMENT

Amendment by section 107(a)(4) of Pub. L. 109–280 applicable to plan years beginning after 2007, see section 107(e) of Pub. L. 109–280, set out as a note under section 1021 of this title.

Amendment by section 701(a)(2) of Pub. L. 109–280 applicable to periods beginning on or after June 29, 2005, and to distributions made after Aug. 17, 2006, with provisions relating to vesting and interest credit requirements for plans in existence on June 29, 2005, special rule for collectively bargained plans, and provisions relating to conversions of plan amendments adopted after, and taking effect after, June 29, 2005, see section 701(e) of Pub. L. 109–280, set out as a note under section 411 of Title 26, Internal Revenue Code.

Amendment by section 902(d)(2)(E) of Pub. L. 109–280 applicable to plan years beginning after Dec. 31, 2007, see section 902(g) of Pub. L. 109–280, set out as a note under section 401 of Title 26, Internal Revenue Code.

Amendment by section 904(b) of Pub. L. 109–280 applicable to contributions for plan years beginning after Dec. 31, 2006, with provisions relating to collective bargaining agreements and amount of service required in any plan year and special rule for stock ownership plans, see section 904(c) of Pub. L. 109–280, set out as a note under section 411 of Title 26, Internal Revenue Code.

EFFECTIVE DATE OF 2001 AMENDMENT

Amendment by section 633(b) of Pub. L. 107–16 applicable to contributions for plan years beginning after Dec. 31, 2001, with exception in the case of a plan maintained pursuant to one or more collective bargaining agreements ratified by June 7, 2001, and service requirement with respect to any plan, see section 633(c) of Pub. L. 107–16, set out as a note under section 411 of Title 26, Internal Revenue Code.

Amendment by section 648(a)(2) of Pub. L. 107–16 applicable to distributions after Dec. 31, 2001, see section 648(c) of Pub. L. 107–16, set out as a note under section 411 of Title 26, Internal Revenue Code.

EFFECTIVE DATE OF 1997 AMENDMENT

Amendment by Pub. L. 105–34 applicable to plan years beginning after Aug. 5, 1997, see section 1071(c) of Pub. L. 105–34, set out as a note under section 411 of Title 26, Internal Revenue Code.

EFFECTIVE DATE OF 1996 AMENDMENT

Amendment by Pub. L. 104–188 applicable to plan years beginning on or after the earlier of (1) the later of (A) Jan. 1, 1997, or (B) the date on which the last of the collective bargaining agreements pursuant to which the plan is maintained terminates (determined without regard to any extension thereof after Aug. 20, 1996), or (2) Jan. 1, 1999, but such amendment not applicable to any individual who does not have more than 1 hour of service under the plan on or after the 1st day of the 1st plan year to which such amendment applies, see section 1442(c) of Pub. L. 104–188, set out as a note under section 411 of Title 26, Internal Revenue Code.

EFFECTIVE DATE OF 1994 AMENDMENT

Amendment by Pub. L. 103–465 applicable to plan years and limitation years beginning after Dec. 31, 1994, except that employer may elect to treat such amendment as effective on or after Dec. 8, 1994, with provisions relating to reduction of accrued benefits, exception, and timing of plan amendment, see section 767(d) of Pub. L. 103–465, as amended, set out as a note under section 411 of Title 26, Internal Revenue Code.

EFFECTIVE DATE OF 1989 AMENDMENT

Amendment by sections 7861(a)(1), (5)(B), (6)(B) and 7862(d)(4), (5), (10) of Pub. L. 101–239 effective as if included in the provision of the Tax Reform Act of 1986, Pub. L. 99–514, to which such amendment relates, see section 7863 of Pub. L. 101–239, set out as a note under section 106 of Title 26, Internal Revenue Code.

Amendment by section 7891(a)(1), (b)(1), (2) of Pub. L. 101–239 effective, except as otherwise provided, as if included in the provision of the Tax Reform Act of 1986, Pub. L. 99–514, to which such amendment relates, see section 7891(f) of Pub. L. 101–239, set out as a note under section 1002 of this title.

Amendment by section 7894(c)(3) of Pub. L. 101–239 effective, except as otherwise provided, as if originally included in the provision of the Employee Retirement Income Security Act of 1974, Pub. L. 93–406, to which such amendment relates, see section 7894(i) of Pub. L. 101–239, set out as a note under section 1002 of this title.

EFFECTIVE DATE OF 1986 AMENDMENT

Amendment by section 1113(e)(1), (2), (4)(A) of Pub. L. 99–514 applicable to plan years beginning after Dec. 31, 1988, with special rule for plans maintained pursuant to collective bargaining agreements ratified before Mar. 1, 1986, and not applicable to employees who do not have 1 hour of service in any plan year to which the amendment applies, see section 1113(f) of Pub. L. 99–514, as amended, set out as a note under section 411 of Title 26, Internal Revenue Code.

Amendment by section 1139(c)(1) of Pub. L. 99–514 applicable to distributions in plan years beginning after Dec. 31, 1984, except that such amendments shall not apply to any distributions in plan years beginning after Dec. 31, 1984, and before Jan. 1, 1987, if such distributions were made in accordance with the requirements of the regulations issued under the Retirement Equity Act of 1984, Pub. L. 98–397, with additional provisions relating to reductions in accrued benefits, see section 1139(d) of Pub. L. 99–514, set out as a note under section 411 of Title 26.

Amendment by section 1898(a)(1)(B) of Pub. L. 99–514 applicable to contributions made for plan years beginning after Oct. 22, 1986, except that in the case of a plan described in section 302(b) of Pub. L. 98–397, set out as a note under section 1001 of this title, such amendments shall not apply to any plan year to which amendments made by Pub. L. 98–397 do not apply by reason of such section 302(b), see section 1898(a)(1)(C) of Pub. L. 99–514, set out as a note under section 411 of Title 26.

Amendment by section 1898(a)(4)(B)(i), (d)(1)(B), (2)(B), of Pub. L. 99–514 effective as if included in the provision of the Retirement Equity Act of 1984, Pub. L. 98–397, to which such amendment relates, except as otherwise provided, see section 1898(j) of Pub. L. 99–514, set out as a note under section 401 of Title 26.

EFFECTIVE DATE OF 1984 AMENDMENT

Amendment by Pub. L. 98–397 applicable to plan years beginning after Dec. 31, 1984, except as otherwise provided, see sections 302 and 303 of Pub. L. 98–397, set out as a note under section 1001 of this title.

EFFECTIVE DATE OF 1980 AMENDMENT

Amendment by Pub. L. 96–364 effective Sept. 26, 1980, except as specifically provided, see section 1461(e) of this title.

REGULATIONS

Secretary of the Treasury or his delegate to issue before Feb. 1, 1988, final regulations to carry out amendments made by section 1113 of Pub. L. 99–514, see section 1141 of Pub. L. 99–514, set out as a note under section 401 of Title 26, Internal Revenue Code.

Secretary authorized, effective Sept. 2, 1974, to promulgate regulations wherever provisions of this subchapter call for the promulgation of regulations, see section 1031 of this title.

APPLICABILITY OF AMENDMENTS BY SUBTITLES A AND B OF TITLE I OF PUB. L. 109–280

For special rules on applicability of amendments by subtitles A (§§101–107) and B (§§111–116) of title I of Pub. L. 109–280 to certain eligible cooperative plans, PBGC settlement plans, and eligible government contractor plans, see sections 104, 105, and 106 of Pub. L. 109–280, set out as notes under section 401 of Title 26, Internal Revenue Code.

PLAN AMENDMENTS NOT REQUIRED UNTIL JANUARY 1, 1998

For provisions directing that if any amendments made by subtitle D [§§1401–1465] of title I of Pub. L. 104–188 require an amendment to any plan or annuity contract, such amendment shall not be required to be made before the first day of the first plan year beginning on or after Jan. 1, 1998, see section 1465 of Pub. L. 104–188, set out as a note under section 401 of Title 26, Internal Revenue Code.

PLAN AMENDMENTS NOT REQUIRED UNTIL JANUARY 1, 1989

For provisions directing that if any amendments made by subtitle A or subtitle C of title XI [§§1101–1147 and 1171–1177] or title XVIII [§§1800–1899A] of Pub. L. 99–514 require an amendment to any plan, such plan amendment shall not be required to be made before the first plan year beginning on or after Jan. 1, 1989, see section 1140 of Pub. L. 99–514, as amended, set out as a note under section 401 of Title 26, Internal Revenue Code.

§1054. Benefit accrual requirements

(a) Satisfaction of requirements by pension plans

Each pension plan shall satisfy the requirements of subsection (b)(3) of this section, and—

(1) in the case of a defined benefit plan, shall satisfy the requirements of subsection (b)(1) of this section; and

(2) in the case of a defined contribution plan, shall satisfy the requirements of subsection (b)(2) of this section.

(b) Enumeration of plan requirements

(1)(A) A defined benefit plan satisfies the requirements of this paragraph if the accrued benefit to which each participant is entitled upon his separation from the service is not less than—

(i) 3 percent of the normal retirement benefit to which he would be entitled at the normal retirement age if he commenced participation at the earliest possible entry age under the plan and served continuously until the earlier of age 65 or the normal retirement age specified under the plan, multiplied by

(ii) the number of years (not in excess of 33⅓) of his participation in the plan.

In the case of a plan providing retirement benefits based on compensation during any period, the normal retirement benefit to which a participant would be entitled shall be determined as if he continued to earn annually the average rate of compensation which he earned during consecutive years of service, not in excess of 10, for which his compensation was the highest. For purposes of this subparagraph, social security benefits and all other relevant factors used to compute benefits shall be treated as remaining constant as of the current year for all years after such current year.

(B) A defined benefit plan satisfies the requirements of this paragraph of a particular plan year if under the plan the accrued benefit payable at the normal retirement age is equal to the normal retirement benefit and the annual rate at which any individual who is or could be a participant can accrue the retirement benefits payable at normal retirement age under the plan for any later plan year is not more than 133⅓ percent of the annual rate at which he can accrue benefits for any plan year beginning on or after such particular plan year and before such later plan year. For purposes of this subparagraph—

(i) any amendment to the plan which is in effect for the current year shall be treated as in effect for all other plan years;

(ii) any change in an accrual rate which does not apply to any individual who is or could be a participant in the current year shall be disregarded;

(iii) the fact that benefits under the plan may be payable to certain employees before normal retirement age shall be disregarded; and

(iv) social security benefits and all other relevant factors used to compute benefits shall be treated as remaining constant as of the current year for all years after the current year.

(C) A defined benefit plan satisfies the requirements of this paragraph if the accrued benefit to which any participant is entitled upon his separation from the service is not less than a fraction of the annual benefit commencing at normal retirement age to which he would be entitled under the plan as in effect on the date of his separation if he continued to earn annually until normal retirement age the same rate of compensation upon which his normal retirement benefit would be computed under the plan, determined as if he had attained normal retirement age on the date any such determination is made (but taking into account no more than the 10 years of service immediately preceding his separation from service). Such fraction shall be a fraction, not exceeding 1, the numerator of which is the total number of his years of participation in the plan (as of the date of his separation from the service) and the denominator of which is the total number of years he would have participated in the plan if he separated from the service at the normal retirement age. For purposes of this subparagraph, social security benefits and all other relevant factors used to compute benefits shall be treated as remaining constant as of the current year for all years after such current year.

(D) Subparagraphs (A), (B), and (C) shall not apply with respect to years of participation before the first plan year to which this section applies but a defined benefit plan satisfies the requirements of this subparagraph with respect to such years of participation only if the accrued benefit of any participant with respect to such years of participation is not less than the greater of—

(i) his accrued benefit determined under the plan, as in effect from time to time prior to September 2, 1974, or

(ii) an accrued benefit which is not less than one-half of the accrued benefit to which such participant would have been entitled if subparagraph (A), (B), or (C) applied with respect to such years of participation.

(E) Notwithstanding subparagraphs (A), (B), and (C) of this paragraph, a plan shall not be treated as not satisfying the requirements of this paragraph solely because the accrual of benefits under the plan does not become effective until the employee has two continuous years of service. For purposes of this subparagraph, the term "year of service" has the meaning provided by section 1052(a)(3)(A) of this title.

(F) Notwithstanding subparagraphs (A), (B), and (C), a defined benefit plan satisfies the requirements of this paragraph if such plan

(i) is funded exclusively by the purchase of insurance contracts, and

(ii) satisfies the requirements of paragraphs (2) and (3) of section 1081(b) of this title (relating to certain insurance contract plans),

but only if an employee's accrued benefit as of any applicable date is not less than the cash surrender value his insurance contracts would have on such applicable date if the requirements of paragraphs (4), (5), and (6) of section 1081(b) of this title were satisfied.

(G) Notwithstanding the preceding subparagraphs, a defined benefit plan shall be treated as not satisfying the requirements of this paragraph if the participant's accrued benefit is reduced on account of any increase in his age or service. The preceding sentence shall not apply to benefits under the plan commencing before benefits payable under title II of the Social Security Act [42 U.S.C. 401 et seq.] which benefits under the plan—

(i) do not exceed social security benefits, and

(ii) terminate when such social security benefits commence.

(H)(i) Notwithstanding the preceding subparagraphs, a defined benefit plan shall be treated as not satisfying the requirements of this paragraph if, under the plan, an employee's benefit accrual is ceased, or the rate of an employee's benefit accrual is reduced, because of the attainment of any age.

(ii) A plan shall not be treated as failing to meet the requirements of this subparagraph solely because the plan imposes (without regard to age) a limitation on the amount of benefits that the plan provides or a limitation on the number of years of service or years of participation which are taken into account for purposes of determining benefit accrual under the plan.

(iii) In the case of any employee who, as of the end of any plan year under a defined benefit plan, has attained normal retirement age under such plan—

(I) if distribution of benefits under such plan with respect to such employee has commenced as of the end of such plan year, then any requirement of this subparagraph for continued accrual of benefits under such plan with respect to such employee during such plan year shall be treated as satisfied to the extent of the actuarial equivalent of in-service distribution of benefits, and

(II) if distribution of benefits under such plan with respect to such employee has not commenced as of the end of such year in accordance with section 1056(a)(3) of this title, and the payment of benefits under such plan with respect to such employee is not suspended during such plan year pursuant to section 1053(a)(3)(B) of this title, then any requirement of this subparagraph for continued accrual of benefits under such plan with respect to such employee during such plan year shall be treated as satisfied to the extent of any adjustment in the benefit payable under the plan during such plan year attributable to the delay in the distribution of benefits after the attainment of normal retirement age.

The preceding provisions of this clause shall apply in accordance with regulations of the Secretary of the Treasury. Such regulations may provide for the application of the preceding provisions of this clause, in the case of any such employee, with respect to any period of time within a plan year.

(iv) Clause (i) shall not apply with respect to any employee who is a highly compensated employee (within the meaning of section 414(q) of title 26) to the extent provided in regulations prescribed by the Secretary of the Treasury for purposes of precluding discrimination in favor of highly compensated employees within the meaning of subchapter D of chapter 1 of title 26.

(v) A plan shall not be treated as failing to meet the requirements of clause (i) solely because the subsidized portion of any early retirement benefit is disregarded in determining benefit accruals.

(vi) Any regulations prescribed by the Secretary of the Treasury pursuant to clause (v) of section 411(b)(1)(H) of title 26 shall apply with respect to the requirements of this subparagraph in the same manner and to the same extent as such regulations apply with respect to the requirements of such section 411(b)(1)(H).

(2)(A) A defined contribution plan satisfies the requirements of this paragraph if, under the plan, allocations to the employee's account are not ceased, and the rate at which amounts are allocated to the employee's account is not reduced, because of the attainment of any age.

(B) A plan shall not be treated as failing to meet the requirements of subparagraph (A) solely because the subsidized portion of any early retirement benefit is disregarded in determining benefit accruals.

(C) Any regulations prescribed by the Secretary of the Treasury pursuant to subparagraphs (B) and (C) of section 411(b)(2) of title 26 shall apply with respect to the requirements of this paragraph in the same manner and to the same extent as such regulations apply with respect to the requirements of such section 411(b)(2).

(3) A plan satisfies the requirements of this paragraph if—

(A) in the case of a defined benefit plan, the plan requires separate accounting for the portion of each employee's accrued benefit derived from any voluntary employee contributions permitted under the plan; and

(B) in the case of any plan which is not a defined benefit plan, the plan requires separate accounting for each employee's accrued benefit.

(4)(A) For purposes of determining an employee's accrued benefit, the term "year of participation" means a period of service (beginning at the earliest date on which the employee is a participant in the plan and which is included in a period of service required to be taken into account under section 1052(b) of this title, determined without regard to section 1052(b)(5) of this title) as determined under regulations prescribed by the Secretary which provide for the calculation of such period on any reasonable and consistent basis.

(B) For purposes of this paragraph, except as provided in subparagraph (C), in the case of any employee whose customary employment is less than full time, the calculation of such employee's service on any basis which provides less than a ratable portion of the accrued benefit to which he would be entitled under the plan if his customary employment were full time shall not be treated as made on a reasonable and consistent basis.

(C) For purposes of this paragraph, in the case of any employee whose service is less than 1,000 hours during any calendar year, plan year or other 12-consecutive-month period designated by the plan (and not prohibited under regulations prescribed by the Secretary) the calculation of his period of service shall not be treated as not made on a reasonable and consistent basis merely because such service is not taken into account.

(D) In the case of any seasonal industry where the customary period of employment is less than 1,000 hours during a calendar year, the term "year of participation" shall be such period as determined under regulations prescribed by the Secretary.

(E) For purposes of this subsection in the case of any maritime industry, 125 days of service shall be treated as a year of participation. The Secretary may prescribe regulations to carry out the purposes of this subparagraph.

(5) SPECIAL RULES RELATING TO AGE.—

(A) COMPARISON TO SIMILARLY SITUATED YOUNGER INDIVIDUAL.—

(i) IN GENERAL.—A plan shall not be treated as failing to meet the requirements of paragraph (1)(H)(i) if a participant's accrued benefit, as determined as of any date under the terms of the plan, would be equal to or greater than that of any similarly situated, younger individual who is or could be a participant.

(ii) SIMILARLY SITUATED.—For purposes of this subparagraph, a participant is similarly situated to any other individual if such participant is identical to such other individual in every respect (including period of service, compensation, position, date of hire, work history, and any other respect) except for age.

(iii) DISREGARD OF SUBSIDIZED EARLY RETIREMENT BENEFITS.—In determining the accrued benefit as of any date for purposes of this subparagraph, the subsidized portion of any early retirement benefit or retirement-type subsidy shall be disregarded.

(iv) ACCRUED BENEFIT.—For purposes of this subparagraph, the accrued benefit may, under the terms of the plan, be expressed as an annuity payable at normal retirement age, the balance of a hypothetical account, or the current value of the accumulated percentage of the employee's final average compensation.

(B) APPLICABLE DEFINED BENEFIT PLANS.—

(i) INTEREST CREDITS.—

(I) IN GENERAL.—An applicable defined benefit plan shall be treated as failing to meet the requirements of paragraph (1)(H) unless the terms of the plan provide that any interest credit (or an equivalent amount) for any plan year shall be at a rate which is not greater than a market rate of return. A plan shall not be treated as failing to meet the requirements of this subclause merely because the plan provides for a reasonable minimum guaranteed rate of return or for a rate of return that is equal to the greater of a fixed or variable rate of return.

(II) PRESERVATION OF CAPITAL.—An applicable defined benefit plan shall be treated as failing to meet the requirements of paragraph (1)(H) unless the plan provides that an interest credit (or equivalent amount) of less than zero shall in no event result in the account balance or similar amount being less than the aggregate amount of contributions credited to the account.

(III) MARKET RATE OF RETURN.—The Secretary of the Treasury may provide by regulation for rules governing the calculation of a market rate of return for purposes of subclause (I) and for permissible methods of crediting interest to the account (including fixed or variable interest rates) resulting in effective rates of return meeting the requirements of subclause (I).

(ii) SPECIAL RULE FOR PLAN CONVERSIONS.—If, after June 29, 2005, an applicable plan amendment is adopted, the plan shall be treated as failing to meet the requirements of paragraph (1)(H) unless the requirements of clause (iii) are met with respect to each individual who was a participant in the plan immediately before the adoption of the amendment.

(iii) RATE OF BENEFIT ACCRUAL.—Subject to clause (iv), the requirements of this clause are met with respect to any participant if the accrued benefit of the participant under the terms of the plan as in effect after the amendment is not less than the sum of—

(I) the participant's accrued benefit for years of service before the effective date of the amendment, determined under the terms of the plan as in effect before the amendment, plus

(II) the participant's accrued benefit for years of service after the effective date of the amendment, determined under the terms of the plan as in effect after the amendment.

(iv) SPECIAL RULES FOR EARLY RETIREMENT SUBSIDIES.—For purposes of clause (iii)(I), the plan shall credit the accumulation account or similar amount[1] with the amount of any early retirement benefit or retirement-type subsidy for the plan year in which the participant retires if, as of such time, the participant has met the age, years of service, and other requirements under the plan for entitlement to such benefit or subsidy.

(v) APPLICABLE PLAN AMENDMENT.—For purposes of this subparagraph—

(I) IN GENERAL.—The term "applicable plan amendment" means an amendment to a defined benefit plan which has the effect of converting the plan to an applicable defined benefit plan.

(II) SPECIAL RULE FOR COORDINATED BENEFITS.—If the benefits of 2 or more defined benefit plans established or maintained by an employer are coordinated in such a manner as to have the effect of the adoption of an amendment described in subclause (I), the sponsor of the defined benefit plan or plans providing for such coordination shall be treated as having adopted such a plan amendment as of the date such coordination begins.

(III) MULTIPLE AMENDMENTS.—The Secretary of the Treasury shall issue regulations to prevent the avoidance of the purposes of this subparagraph through the use of 2 or more plan amendments rather than a single amendment.

(IV) APPLICABLE DEFINED BENEFIT PLAN.—For purposes of this subparagraph, the term "applicable defined benefit plan" has the meaning given such term by section 1053(f)(3) of this title.

(vi) TERMINATION REQUIREMENTS.—An applicable defined benefit plan shall not be treated as meeting the requirements of clause (i) unless the plan provides that, upon the termination of the plan—

(I) if the interest credit rate (or an equivalent amount) under the plan is a variable rate, the rate of interest used to determine accrued benefits under the plan shall be equal to the average of the rates of interest used under the plan during the 5-year period ending on the termination date, and

(II) the interest rate and mortality table used to determine the amount of any benefit under the plan payable in the form of an annuity payable at normal retirement age shall be the rate and table specified under the plan for such purpose as of the termination date, except that if such interest rate is a variable rate, the interest rate shall be determined under the rules of subclause (I).

(C) CERTAIN OFFSETS PERMITTED.—A plan shall not be treated as failing to meet the requirements of paragraph (1)(H)(i) solely because the plan provides offsets against benefits under the plan to the extent such offsets are otherwise allowable in applying the requirements of section 401(a) of title 26.

(D) PERMITTED DISPARITIES IN PLAN CONTRIBUTIONS OR BENEFITS.—A plan shall not be treated as failing to meet the requirements of paragraph (1)(H) solely because the plan provides a disparity in contributions or benefits with respect to which the requirements of section 401(*l*) of title 26 are met.

(E) INDEXING PERMITTED.—

[1] So in original. Probably should be "similar account".

(i) IN GENERAL.—A plan shall not be treated as failing to meet the requirements of paragraph (1)(H) solely because the plan provides for indexing of accrued benefits under the plan.

(ii) PROTECTION AGAINST LOSS.—Except in the case of any benefit provided in the form of a variable annuity, clause (i) shall not apply with respect to any indexing which results in an accrued benefit less than the accrued benefit determined without regard to such indexing.

(iii) INDEXING.—For purposes of this subparagraph, the term "indexing" means, in connection with an accrued benefit, the periodic adjustment of the accrued benefit by means of the application of a recognized investment index or methodology.

(F) EARLY RETIREMENT BENEFIT OR RETIREMENT-TYPE SUBSIDY.—For purposes of this paragraph, the terms "early retirement benefit" and "retirement-type subsidy" have the meaning given such terms in subsection (g)(2)(A).

(G) BENEFIT ACCRUED TO DATE.—For purposes of this paragraph, any reference to the accrued benefit shall be a reference to such benefit accrued to date.

(c) Employee's accrued benefits derived from employer and employee contributions

(1) For purposes of this section and section 1053 of this title an employee's accrued benefit derived from employer contributions as of any applicable date is the excess (if any) of the accrued benefit for such employee as of such applicable date over the accrued benefit derived from contributions made by such employee as of such date.

(2)(A) In the case of a plan other than a defined benefit plan, the accrued benefit derived from contributions made by an employee as of any applicable date is—

(i) except as provided in clause (ii), the balance of the employee's separate account consisting only of his contributions and the income, expenses, gains, and losses attributable thereto, or

(ii) if a separate account is not maintained with respect to an employee's contributions under such a plan, the amount which bears the same ratio to his total accrued benefit as the total amount of the employee's contributions (less withdrawals) bears to the sum of such contributions and the contributions made on his behalf by the employer (less withdrawals).

(B) DEFINED BENEFIT PLANS.—In the case of a defined benefit plan, the accrued benefit derived from contributions made by an employee as of any applicable date is the amount equal to the employee's accumulated contributions expressed as an annual benefit commencing at normal retirement age, using an interest rate which would be used under the plan under section 1055(g)(3) of this title (as of the determination date).

(C) For purposes of this subsection, the term "accumulated contributions" means the total of—

(i) all mandatory contributions made by the employee,

(ii) interest (if any) under the plan to the end of the last plan year to which section 1053(a)(2) of this title does not apply (by reason of the applicable effective date), and

(iii) interest on the sum of the amounts determined under clauses (i) and (ii) compounded annually—

(I) at the rate of 120 percent of the Federal mid-term rate (as in effect under section 1274 of title 26 for the 1st month of a plan year for the period beginning with the 1st plan year to which subsection (a)(2) of this section applies by reason of the applicable effective date) and ending with the date on which the determination is being made, and

(II) at the interest rate which would be used under the plan under section 1055(g)(3) of this title (as of the determination date) for the period beginning with the determination date and ending on the date on which the employee attains normal retirement age.

For purposes of this subparagraph, the term "mandatory contributions" means amounts contributed to the plan by the employee which are required as a condition of employment, as a condition of participation in such plans, or as a condition of obtaining benefits under the plan attributable to employer contributions.

(D) The Secretary of the Treasury is authorized to adjust by regulation the conversion factor described in subparagraph (B) from time to time as he may deem necessary. No such adjustment shall be effective for a plan year beginning before the expiration of 1 year after such adjustment is determined and published.

(3) For purposes of this section, in the case of any defined benefit plan, if an employee's accrued benefit is to be determined as an amount other than an annual benefit commencing at normal retirement age, or if the accrued benefit derived from contributions made by an employee is to be determined with respect to a benefit other than an annual benefit in the form of a single life annuity (without ancillary benefits) commencing at normal retirement age, the employee's accrued benefit, or the accrued benefits derived from contributions made by an employee, as the case may be, shall be the actuarial equivalent of such benefit or amount determined under paragraph (1) or (2).

(4) In the case of a defined benefit plan which permits voluntary employee contributions, the portion of an employee's accrued benefit derived from such contributions shall be treated as an accrued benefit derived from employee contributions under a plan other than a defined benefit plan.

(d) Employee service which may be disregarded in determining employee's accrued benefits under plan

Notwithstanding section 1053(b)(1) of this title, for purposes of determining the employee's accrued benefit under the plan, the plan may disregard service performed by the employee with respect to which he has received—

(1) a distribution of the present value of his entire nonforfeitable benefit if such distribution was in an amount (not more than the dollar limit under section 1053(e)(1) of this title) permitted under regulations prescribed by the Secretary of the Treasury, or

(2) a distribution of the present value of his nonforfeitable benefit attributable to such service which he elected to receive.

Paragraph (1) shall apply only if such distribution was made on termination of the employee's participation in the plan. Paragraph (2) shall apply only if such distribution was made on termination of the employee's participation in the plan or under such other circumstances as may be provided under regulations prescribed by the Secretary of the Treasury.

(e) Opportunity to repay full amount of distributions which have been reduced through disregarded employee service

For purposes of determining the employee's accrued benefit, the plan shall not disregard service as provided in subsection (d) of this section unless the plan provides an opportunity for the participant to repay the full amount of a distribution described in subsection (d) of this section with, in the case of a defined benefit plan, interest at the rate determined for purposes of subsection (c)(2)(C) of this section and provides that upon such repayment the employee's accrued benefit shall be recomputed by taking into account service so disregarded. This subsection shall apply only in the case of a participant who—

(1) received such a distribution in any plan year to which this section applies which distribution was less than the present value of his accrued benefit,

(2) resumes employment covered under the plan, and

(3) repays the full amount of such distribution with, in the case of a defined benefit plan, interest at the rate determined for purposes of subsection (c)(2)(C) of this section.

The plan provision required under this subsection may provide that such repayment must be made (A) in the case of a withdrawal on account of separation from service, before the earlier of 5 years after the first date on which the participant is subsequently re-employed by the employer, or the close of the first period of 5 consecutive 1-year breaks in service commencing after the withdrawal; or (B) in the case of any other withdrawal, 5 years after the date of the withdrawal.

(f) Employer treated as maintaining a plan

For the purposes of this part, an employer shall be treated as maintaining a plan if any employee of such employer accrues benefits under such plan by reason of service with such employer.

(g) Decrease of accrued benefits through amendment of plan

(1) The accrued benefit of a participant under a plan may not be decreased by an amendment of the plan, other than an amendment described in section 1082(d)(2) or 1441 of this title.

(2) For purposes of paragraph (1), a plan amendment which has the effect of—

(A) eliminating or reducing an early retirement benefit or a retirement-type subsidy (as defined in regulations), or

(B) eliminating an optional form of benefit,

with respect to benefits attributable to service before the amendment shall be treated as reducing accrued benefits. In the case of a retirement-type subsidy, the preceding sentence shall apply only with respect to a participant who satisfies (either before or after the amendment) the pre-amendment conditions for the subsidy. The Secretary of the Treasury shall by regulations provide that this paragraph shall not apply to any plan amendment which reduces or eliminates benefits or subsidies which create significant burdens or complexities for the plan and plan participants, unless such amendment adversely affects the rights of any participant in a more than de minimis manner. The Secretary of the Treasury may by regulations provide that this subparagraph shall not apply to a plan amendment described in subparagraph (B) (other than a plan amendment having an effect described in subparagraph (A)).

(3) For purposes of this subsection, any—

(A) tax credit employee stock ownership plan (as defined in section 409(a) of title 26, or

(B) employee stock ownership plan (as defined in section 4975(e)(7) of title 26),

shall not be treated as failing to meet the requirements of this subsection merely because it modifies distribution options in a nondiscriminatory manner.

(4)(A) A defined contribution plan (in this subparagraph referred to as the "transferee plan") shall not be treated as failing to meet the requirements of this subsection merely because the transferee plan does not provide some or all of the forms of distribution previously available under another defined contribution plan (in this subparagraph referred to as the "transferor plan") to the extent that—

(i) the forms of distribution previously available under the transferor plan applied to the account of a participant or beneficiary under the transferor plan that was transferred from the transferor plan to the transferee plan pursuant to a direct transfer rather than pursuant to a distribution from the transferor plan;

(ii) the terms of both the transferor plan and the transferee plan authorize the transfer described in clause (i);

(iii) the transfer described in clause (i) was made pursuant to a voluntary election by the participant or beneficiary whose account was transferred to the transferee plan;

(iv) the election described in clause (iii) was made after the participant or beneficiary received a notice describing the consequences of making the election; and

(v) the transferee plan allows the participant or beneficiary described in clause (iii) to receive any distribution to which the participant or beneficiary is entitled under the transferee plan in the form of a single sum distribution.

(B) Subparagraph (A) shall apply to plan mergers and other transactions having the effect of a direct transfer, including consolidations of benefits attributable to different employers within a multiple employer plan.

(5) Except to the extent provided in regulations promulgated by the Secretary of the Treasury, a defined contribution plan shall not be treated as failing to meet the requirements of this subsection merely because of the elimi-

nation of a form of distribution previously available thereunder. This paragraph shall not apply to the elimination of a form of distribution with respect to any participant unless—

(A) a single sum payment is available to such participant at the same time or times as the form of distribution being eliminated; and

(B) such single sum payment is based on the same or greater portion of the participant's account as the form of distribution being eliminated.

(h) Notice of significant reduction in benefit accruals

(1) An applicable pension plan may not be amended so as to provide for a significant reduction in the rate of future benefit accrual unless the plan administrator provides the notice described in paragraph (2) to each applicable individual (and to each employee organization representing applicable individuals) and to each employer who has an obligation to contribute to the plan.

(2) The notice required by paragraph (1) shall be written in a manner calculated to be understood by the average plan participant and shall provide sufficient information (as determined in accordance with regulations prescribed by the Secretary of the Treasury) to allow applicable individuals to understand the effect of the plan amendment. The Secretary of the Treasury may provide a simplified form of notice for, or exempt from any notice requirement, a plan—

(A) which has fewer than 100 participants who have accrued a benefit under the plan, or

(B) which offers participants the option to choose between the new benefit formula and the old benefit formula.

(3) Except as provided in regulations prescribed by the Secretary of the Treasury, the notice required by paragraph (1) shall be provided within a reasonable time before the effective date of the plan amendment.

(4) Any notice under paragraph (1) may be provided to a person designated, in writing, by the person to which it would otherwise be provided.

(5) A plan shall not be treated as failing to meet the requirements of paragraph (1) merely because notice is provided before the adoption of the plan amendment if no material modification of the amendment occurs before the amendment is adopted.

(6)(A) In the case of any egregious failure to meet any requirement of this subsection with respect to any plan amendment, the provisions of the applicable pension plan shall be applied as if such plan amendment entitled all applicable individuals to the greater of—

(i) the benefits to which they would have been entitled without regard to such amendment, or

(ii) the benefits under the plan with regard to such amendment.

(B) For purposes of subparagraph (A), there is an egregious failure to meet the requirements of this subsection if such failure is within the control of the plan sponsor and is—

(i) an intentional failure (including any failure to promptly provide the required notice or information after the plan administrator discovers an unintentional failure to meet the requirements of this subsection),

(ii) a failure to provide most of the individuals with most of the information they are entitled to receive under this subsection, or

(iii) a failure which is determined to be egregious under regulations prescribed by the Secretary of the Treasury.

(7) The Secretary of the Treasury may by regulations allow any notice under this subsection to be provided by using new technologies.

(8) For purposes of this subsection—

(A) The term "applicable individual" means, with respect to any plan amendment—

(i) each participant in the plan; and

(ii) any beneficiary who is an alternate payee (within the meaning of section 1056(d)(3)(K) of this title) under an applicable qualified domestic relations order (within the meaning of section 1056(d)(3)(B)(i) of this title),

whose rate of future benefit accrual under the plan may reasonably be expected to be significantly reduced by such plan amendment.

(B) The term "applicable pension plan" means—

(i) any defined benefit plan; or

(ii) an individual account plan which is subject to the funding standards of section 412 of title 26.

(9) For purposes of this subsection, a plan amendment which eliminates or reduces any early retirement benefit or retirement-type subsidy (within the meaning of subsection (g)(2)(A) of this section) shall be treated as having the effect of reducing the rate of future benefit accrual.

(i) Prohibition on benefit increases where plan sponsor is in bankruptcy

(1) In the case of a plan described in paragraph (3) which is maintained by an employer that is a debtor in a case under title 11 or similar Federal or State law, no amendment of the plan which increases the liabilities of the plan by reason of—

(A) any increase in benefits,

(B) any change in the accrual of benefits, or

(C) any change in the rate at which benefits become nonforfeitable under the plan,

with respect to employees of the debtor, shall be effective prior to the effective date of such employer's plan of reorganization.

(2) Paragraph (1) shall not apply to any plan amendment that—

(A) the Secretary of the Treasury determines to be reasonable and that provides for only de minimis increases in the liabilities of the plan with respect to employees of the debtor,

(B) only repeals an amendment described in section 1082(d)(2) of this title,

(C) is required as a condition of qualification under part I of subchapter D of chapter 1 of title 26, or

(D) was adopted prior to, or pursuant to a collective bargaining agreement entered into prior to, the date on which the employer became a debtor in a case under title 11 or similar Federal or State law.

(3) This subsection shall apply only to plans (other than multiemployer plans) covered under section 1321 of this title for which the funding target attainment percentage (as defined in section 1083(d)(2) of this title) is less than 100 percent after taking into account the effect of the amendment.

(4) For purposes of this subsection, the term "employer" has the meaning set forth in section 1082(b)(1) of this title, without regard to section 1082(b)(2) of this title.

(j) Diversification requirements for certain individual account plans

(1) In general

An applicable individual account plan shall meet the diversification requirements of paragraphs (2), (3), and (4).

(2) Employee contributions and elective deferrals invested in employer securities

In the case of the portion of an applicable individual's account attributable to employee contributions and elective deferrals which is invested in employer securities, a plan meets the requirements of this paragraph if the applicable individual may elect to direct the plan to divest any such securities and to reinvest an equivalent amount in other investment options meeting the requirements of paragraph (4).

(3) Employer contributions invested in employer securities

In the case of the portion of the account attributable to employer contributions other than elective deferrals which is invested in employer securities, a plan meets the requirements of this paragraph if each applicable individual who—

(A) is a participant who has completed at least 3 years of service, or

(B) is a beneficiary of a participant described in subparagraph (A) or of a deceased participant,

may elect to direct the plan to divest any such securities and to reinvest an equivalent amount in other investment options meeting the requirements of paragraph (4).

(4) Investment options

(A) In general

The requirements of this paragraph are met if the plan offers not less than 3 investment options, other than employer securities, to which an applicable individual may direct the proceeds from the divestment of employer securities pursuant to this subsection, each of which is diversified and has materially different risk and return characteristics.

(B) Treatment of certain restrictions and conditions

(i) Time for making investment choices

A plan shall not be treated as failing to meet the requirements of this paragraph merely because the plan limits the time for divestment and reinvestment to periodic, reasonable opportunities occurring no less frequently than quarterly.

(ii) Certain restrictions and conditions not allowed

Except as provided in regulations, a plan shall not meet the requirements of this paragraph if the plan imposes restrictions or conditions with respect to the investment of employer securities which are not imposed on the investment of other assets of the plan. This subparagraph shall not apply to any restrictions or conditions imposed by reason of the application of securities laws.

(5) Applicable individual account plan

For purposes of this subsection—

(A) In general

The term "applicable individual account plan" means any individual account plan (as defined in section 1002(34) of this title) which holds any publicly traded employer securities.

(B) Exception for certain ESOPS

Such term does not include an employee stock ownership plan if—

(i) there are no contributions to such plan (or earnings thereunder) which are held within such plan and are subject to subsection (k) or (m) of section 401 of title 26, and

(ii) such plan is a separate plan (for purposes of section 414(*l*) of title 26) with respect to any other defined benefit plan or individual account plan maintained by the same employer or employers.

(C) Exception for one participant plans

Such term shall not include a one-participant retirement plan (as defined in section 1021(i)(8)(B) of this title).

(D) Certain plans treated as holding publicly traded employer securities

(i) In general

Except as provided in regulations or in clause (ii), a plan holding employer securities which are not publicly traded employer securities shall be treated as holding publicly traded employer securities if any employer corporation, or any member of a controlled group of corporations which includes such employer corporation, has issued a class of stock which is a publicly traded employer security.

(ii) Exception for certain controlled groups with publicly traded securities

Clause (i) shall not apply to a plan if—

(I) no employer corporation, or parent corporation of an employer corporation, has issued any publicly traded employer security, and

(II) no employer corporation, or parent corporation of an employer corporation, has issued any special class of stock which grants particular rights to, or bears particular risks for, the holder or issuer with respect to any corporation described in clause (i) which has issued any publicly traded employer security.

(iii) Definitions

For purposes of this subparagraph, the term—

(I) "controlled group of corporations" has the meaning given such term by section 1563(a) of title 26, except that "50 percent" shall be substituted for "80 percent" each place it appears,

(II) "employer corporation" means a corporation which is an employer maintaining the plan, and

(III) "parent corporation" has the meaning given such term by section 424(e) of title 26.

(6) Other definitions

For purposes of this paragraph—

(A) Applicable individual

The term "applicable individual" means—

(i) any participant in the plan, and

(ii) any beneficiary who has an account under the plan with respect to which the beneficiary is entitled to exercise the rights of a participant.

(B) Elective deferral

The term "elective deferral" means an employer contribution described in section 402(g)(3)(A) of title 26.

(C) Employer security

The term "employer security" has the meaning given such term by section 1107(d)(1) of this title.

(D) Employee stock ownership plan

The term "employee stock ownership plan" has the meaning given such term by section 4975(e)(7) of title 26.

(E) Publicly traded employer securities

The term "publicly traded employer securities" means employer securities which are readily tradable on an established securities market.

(F) Year of service

The term "year of service" has the meaning given such term by section 1053(b)(2) of this title.

(7) Transition rule for securities attributable to employer contributions

(A) Rules phased in over 3 years

(i) In general

In the case of the portion of an account to which paragraph (3) applies and which consists of employer securities acquired in a plan year beginning before January 1, 2007, paragraph (3) shall only apply to the applicable percentage of such securities. This subparagraph shall be applied separately with respect to each class of securities.

(ii) Exception for certain participants aged 55 or over

Clause (i) shall not apply to an applicable individual who is a participant who has attained age 55 and completed at least 3 years of service before the first plan year beginning after December 31, 2005.

(B) Applicable percentage

For purposes of subparagraph (A), the applicable percentage shall be determined as follows:

Plan year to which paragraph (3) applies:	The applicable percentage is:
1st	33
2d	66
3d	100.

(k) Cross reference

For special rules relating to plan provisions adopted to preclude discrimination, see section 1053(c)(2) of this title.

(Pub. L. 93–406, title I, §204, Sept. 2, 1974, 88 Stat. 858; Pub. L. 98–397, title I, §§102(e)(3), (f), 105(b), title III, §301(a)(2), Aug. 23, 1984, 98 Stat. 1429, 1436, 1451; Pub. L. 99–272, title XI, §11006(a), Apr. 7, 1986, 100 Stat. 243; Pub. L. 99–509, title IX, §9202(a), Oct. 21, 1986, 100 Stat. 1975; Pub. L. 99–514, title XI, §1113(e)(4)(B), title XVIII, §§1879(u)(1), 1898(a)(4)(B)(ii), (f)(1)(B), (2), Oct. 22, 1986, 100 Stat. 2448, 2913, 2944, 2956; Pub. L. 100–203, title IX, §9346(a), Dec. 22, 1987, 101 Stat. 1330–374; Pub. L. 101–239, title VII, §§7862(b)(1)(A), (2), 7871(a)(1), (3), 7881(m)(2)(A)–(C), 7891(a)(1), 7894(c)(4)–(6), Dec. 19, 1989, 103 Stat. 2432, 2434, 2435, 2444, 2445, 2449; Pub. L. 103–465, title VII, §766(a), Dec. 8, 1994, 108 Stat. 5036; Pub. L. 105–34, title X, §1071(b)(2), Aug. 5, 1997, 111 Stat. 948; Pub. L. 107–16, title VI, §§645(a)(2), (b)(2), 659(b), June 7, 2001, 115 Stat. 124, 125, 139; Pub. L. 107–147, title IV, §411(u)(2), Mar. 9, 2002, 116 Stat. 52; Pub. L. 109–280, title I, §107(a)(5)–(8), title V, §502(c)(1), title VII, §701(a)(1), title IX, §901(b)(1), Aug. 17, 2006, 120 Stat. 819, 941, 981, 1029; Pub. L. 110–458, title I, §107(a)(2), (3), Dec. 23, 2008, 122 Stat. 5107.)

REFERENCES IN TEXT

The Social Security Act, referred to in subsec. (b)(1)(G), is act Aug. 14, 1935, ch. 531, 49 Stat. 620, as amended. Title II of the Social Security Act is classified generally to subchapter II (§401 et seq.) of chapter 7 of Title 42, The Public Health and Welfare. For complete classification of this Act to the Code, see section 1305 of Title 42 and Tables.

AMENDMENTS

2008—Subsec. (b)(5)(A)(iii). Pub. L. 110–458, §107(a)(2)(A), substituted "subparagraph" for "clause".

Subsec. (b)(5)(B)(i)(II). Pub. L. 110–458, §107(a)(3), amended subcl. (II) generally. Prior to amendment, text read as follows: "An interest credit (or an equivalent amount) of less than zero shall in no event result in the account balance or similar amount being less than the aggregate amount of contributions credited to the account."

Subsec. (b)(5)(C). Pub. L. 110–458, §107(a)(2)(B), inserted "otherwise" before "allowable".

2006—Subsec. (b)(5). Pub. L. 109–280, §701(a)(1), added par. (5).

Subsec. (g)(1). Pub. L. 109–280, §107(a)(5), substituted "1082(d)(2)" for "1082(c)(8)".

Subsec. (h)(1). Pub. L. 109–280, §502(c)(1), inserted before period at end "and to each employer who has an obligation to contribute to the plan".

Subsec. (i)(2)(B). Pub. L. 109–280, §107(a)(6), substituted "1082(d)(2)" for "1082(c)(8)".

Subsec. (i)(3). Pub. L. 109–280, §107(a)(7), substituted "funding target attainment percentage (as defined in section 1083(d)(2) of this title)" for "funded current liability percentage (within the meaning of section 1082(d)(8) of this title)".

Subsec. (i)(4). Pub. L. 109–280, §107(a)(8), substituted "section 1082(b)(1) of this title, without regard to section 1082(b)(2) of this title" for "section 1082(c)(11)(A) of this title, without regard to section 1082(c)(11)(B) of this title".

Subsecs. (j), (k). Pub. L. 109–280, § 901(b)(1), added subsec. (j) and redesignated former subsec. (j) as (k).

2002—Subsec. (h)(9). Pub. L. 107–147 struck out "significantly" before "reduces" and before "reducing".

2001—Subsec. (g)(2). Pub. L. 107–16, § 645(b)(2), inserted after second sentence "The Secretary of the Treasury shall by regulations provide that this paragraph shall not apply to any plan amendment which reduces or eliminates benefits or subsidies which create significant burdens or complexities for the plan and plan participants, unless such amendment adversely affects the rights of any participant in a more than de minimis manner."

Subsec. (g)(4), (5). Pub. L. 107–16, § 645(a)(2), added pars. (4) and (5).

Subsec. (h). Pub. L. 107–16, § 659(b), amended subsec. (h) generally. Prior to amendment, subsec. (h) read as follows:

"(1) A plan described in paragraph (2) may not be amended so as to provide for a significant reduction in the rate of future benefit accrual, unless, after adoption of the plan amendment and not less than 15 days before the effective date of the plan amendment, the plan administrator provides a written notice, setting forth the plan amendment and its effective date, to—

"(A) each participant in the plan,

"(B) each beneficiary who is an alternate payee (within the meaning of section 1056(d)(3)(K) of this title) under an applicable qualified domestic relations order (within the meaning of section 1056(d)(3)(B)(i) of this title), and

"(C) each employee organization representing participants in the plan,

except that such notice shall instead be provided to a person designated, in writing, to receive such notice on behalf of any person referred to in subparagraph (A), (B), or (C).

"(2) A plan is described in this paragraph if such plan is—

"(A) a defined benefit plan, or

"(B) an individual account plan which is subject to the funding standards of section 1082 of this title."

1997—Subsec. (d)(1). Pub. L. 105–34 substituted "the dollar limit under section 1053(e)(1) of this title" for "$3,500".

1994—Subsecs. (i), (j). Pub. L. 103–465 added subsec. (i) and redesignated former subsec. (i) as (j).

1989—Subsec. (b)(1)(A). Pub. L. 101–239, § 7894(c)(4), substituted "subparagraph" for "suparagraph" in last sentence.

Subsec. (b)(1)(E). Pub. L. 101–239, § 7894(c)(5), substituted "term 'year of service'" for "term 'years of service'".

Subsec. (b)(2)(B). Pub. L. 101–239, § 7871(a)(1), redesignated subpar. (C) as (B) and struck out former subpar. (B) which read as follows: "Subparagraph (A) shall not apply with respect to any employee who is a highly compensated employee (within the meaning of section 414(q) of title 26) to the extent provided in regulations prescribed by the Secretary of the Treasury for purposes of precluding discrimination in favor of highly compensated employees within the meaning of subchapter D of chapter 1 of title 26."

Subsec. (b)(2)(C). Pub. L. 101–239, § 7871(a)(3), substituted "subparagraphs (B) and (C)" for "subparagraphs (C) and (D)".

Pub. L. 101–239, § 7871(a)(1), redesignated subpar. (D) as (C). Former subpar. (C) redesignated (B).

Subsec. (b)(2)(D). Pub. L. 101–239, § 7871(a)(1), redesignated subpar. (D) as (C).

Subsec. (c)(2)(B). Pub. L. 101–239, § 7881(m)(2)(B), inserted heading and amended text generally. Prior to amendment, text read as follows:

"(i) In the case of a defined benefit plan providing an annual benefit in the form of a single life annuity (without ancillary benefits) commencing at normal retirement age, the accrued benefit derived from contributions made by an employee as of any applicable date is the annual benefit equal to the employee's accumulated contributions multiplied by the appropriate conversion factor.

"(ii) For purposes of clause (i), the term 'appropriate conversion factor' means the factor necessary to convert an amount equal to the accumulated contributions to a single life annuity (without ancillary benefits) commencing at normal retirement age and shall be 10 percent for a normal retirement age of 65 years. For other normal retirement ages the conversion factor shall be determined in accordance with regulations prescribed by the Secretary of the Treasury or his delegate."

Subsec. (c)(2)(C)(iii). Pub. L. 101–239, § 7881(m)(2)(A), amended cl. (iii) generally. Prior to amendment, cl. (iii) read as follows: "interest on the sum of the amounts determined under clauses (i) and (ii) compounded annually at the rate of 120 percent of the Federal mid-term rate (as in effect under section 1274 of title 26 for the 1st month of a plan year) from the beginning of the first plan year to which section 1053(a)(2) of this title applies (by reason of the applicable effective date) to the date upon which the employee would attain normal retirement age."

Subsec. (c)(2)(E). Pub. L. 101–239, § 7881(m)(2)(C), struck out subpar. (E) which read as follows: "The accrued benefit derived from employee contributions shall not exceed the greater of—

"(i) the employee's accrued benefit under the plan, or

"(ii) the accrued benefit derived from employee contributions determined as though the amounts calculated under clauses (ii) and (iii) of subparagraph (C) were zero."

Subsec. (d). Pub. L. 101–239, § 7894(c)(6), removed the indentation of the term "Paragraph" where first appearing in concluding provisions.

Subsec. (g)(3)(A). Pub. L. 101–239, § 7891(a)(1), substituted "Internal Revenue Code of 1986" for "Internal Revenue Code of 1954", which for purposes of codification was translated as "title 26" thus requiring no change in text.

Subsec. (h). Pub. L. 101–239, § 7862(b)(1)(A), made technical correction to directory language of Pub. L. 99–514, § 1879(u)(1), see 1986 Amendment note below.

Subsec. (h)(2). Pub. L. 101–239, § 7862(b)(2), adjusted left-hand margin of introductory provisions to full measure.

1987—Subsec. (c)(2)(C)(iii). Pub. L. 100–203, § 9346(a)(1), substituted "120 percent of the Federal mid-term rate (as in effect under section 1274 of title 26 for the 1st month of a plan year)" for "5 percent per annum".

Subsec. (c)(2)(D). Pub. L. 100–203, § 9346(a)(2), struck out ", the rate of interest described in clause (iii) of subparagraph (C), or both," before "from time to time" in first sentence and struck out second sentence which read as follows: "The rate of interest shall bear the relationship to 5 percent which the Secretary of the Treasury determines to be comparable to the relationship which the long-term money rates and investment yields for the last period of 10 calendar years ending at least 12 months before the beginning of the plan year bear to the long-term money rates and investment yields for the 10-calendar year period 1964 through 1973."

1986—Subsec. (a). Pub. L. 99–509, § 9202(a)(1), amended subsec. (a) generally. Prior to amendment, subsec. (a) read as follows: "Each pension plan shall satisfy the requirements of subsection (b)(2) of this section, and in the case of a defined benefit plan shall also satisfy the requirements of subsection (b)(1) of this section."

Subsec. (b)(1)(H). Pub. L. 99–509, § 9202(a)(2), added subpar. (H).

Subsec. (b)(2) to (4). Pub. L. 99–509, § 9202(a)(3), added par. (2) and redesignated former pars. (2) and (3) as (3) and (4), respectively.

Subsec. (e). Pub. L. 99–514, § 1898(a)(4)(B)(ii), inserted last sentence and struck out former last sentence which read as follows: "In the case of a defined contribution plan, the plan provision required under this subsection may provide that such repayment must be made before the participant has 5 consecutive 1-year breaks in service commencing after such withdrawal".

Subsec. (g)(1). Pub. L. 99–514, § 1898(f)(2), inserted reference to section 1441.

Subsec. (g)(3). Pub. L. 99–514, § 1898(f)(1)(B), added par. (3).

Subsec. (h). Pub. L. 99–514, § 1879(u)(1), as amended by Pub. L. 101–239, § 7862(b)(1)(A), designated existing provisions as par. (1), substituted "plan described in paragraph (2)" for "single-employer plan", redesignated former pars. (1) to (3) as subpars. (A) to (C), respectively, substituted "subparagraph (A), (B), or (C)" for "paragraph (1), (2), or (3)" in concluding provisions, and added par. (2).

Pub. L. 99–272 added subsec. (h). Former subsec. (h) redesignated (i).

Subsec. (i). Pub. L. 99–514, § 1113(e)(4)(B), amended subsec. (i) generally, striking out reference to class year plans under section 1053(c)(3) of this title.

Pub. L. 99–272 redesignated former subsec. (h) as (i).

1984—Subsec. (b)(3)(A). Pub. L. 98–397, § 102(e)(3), inserted ", determined without regard to section 1052(b)(5) of this title" after "section 1052(b) of this title".

Subsec. (d)(1). Pub. L. 98–397, § 105(b), substituted "$3,500" for "$1,750".

Subsec. (e). Pub. L. 98–397, § 102(f), substituted "5 consecutive 1-year breaks in service" for "any 1-year break in service".

Subsec. (g). Pub. L. 98–397, § 301(a)(2), designated existing provisions as par. (1) and added par. (2).

Effective Date of 2008 Amendment

Amendment by Pub. L. 110–458 effective as if included in the provisions of Pub. L. 109–280 to which the amendment relates, except as otherwise provided, see section 112 of Pub. L. 110–458, set out as a note under section 72 of Title 26, Internal Revenue Code.

Effective Date of 2006 Amendment

Amendment by section 107(a)(5) to (8) of Pub. L. 109–280 applicable to plan years beginning after 2007, see section 107(e) of Pub. L. 109–280, set out as a note under section 1021 of this title.

Amendment by section 502(c)(1) of Pub. L. 109–280 applicable to plan years beginning after Dec. 31, 2007, see section 502(d) of Pub. L. 109–280, set out as a note under section 4980F of Title 26, Internal Revenue Code.

Amendment by section 701(a)(1) of Pub. L. 109–280 applicable to periods beginning on or after June 29, 2005, with provisions relating to vesting and interest credit requirements for plans in existence on June 29, 2005, special rule for collectively bargained plans, and provisions relating to conversions of plan amendments adopted after, and taking effect after, June 29, 2005, see section 701(e) of Pub. L. 109–280, set out as a note under section 411 of Title 26, Internal Revenue Code.

Amendment by section 901(b)(1) of Pub. L. 109–280 applicable to plan years beginning after Dec. 31, 2006, with special rules for collectively bargained agreements and certain employer securities held in an ESOP, see section 901(c) of Pub. L. 109–280, set out as a note under section 401 of Title 26, Internal Revenue Code.

Effective Date of 2002 Amendment

Amendment by Pub. L. 107–147 effective as if included in the provisions of the Economic Growth and Tax Relief Reconciliation Act of 2001, Pub. L. 107–16, to which such amendment relates, see section 411(x) of Pub. L. 107–147, set out as a note under section 25B of Title 26, Internal Revenue Code.

Effective Date of 2001 Amendment

Amendment by section 645(a)(2) of Pub. L. 107–16 applicable to years beginning after Dec. 31, 2001, see section 645(a)(3) of Pub. L. 107–16, set out as a note under section 411 of Title 26, Internal Revenue Code.

Amendment by section 659(b) of Pub. L. 107–16 applicable to plan amendments taking effect on or after June 7, 2001, with transition provisions and special notice rule, see section 659(c) of Pub. L. 107–16, set out as an Effective Date note under section 4980F of Title 26, Internal Revenue Code.

Effective Date of 1997 Amendment

Amendment by Pub. L. 105–34 applicable to plan years beginning after Aug. 5, 1997, see section 1071(c) of Pub. L. 105–34, set out as a note under section 411 of Title 26, Internal Revenue Code.

Effective Date of 1994 Amendment

Amendment by Pub. L. 103–465 applicable to plan amendments adopted on or after Dec. 8, 1994, see section 766(d) of Pub. L. 103–465, set out as a note under section 401 of Title 26, Internal Revenue Code.

Effective Date of 1989 Amendment

Amendment by section 7862(b)(1)(A), (2) of Pub. L. 101–239 effective as if included in the provision of the Tax Reform Act of 1986, Pub. L. 99–514, to which such amendment relates, see section 7863 of Pub. L. 101–239, set out as a note under section 106 of Title 26, Internal Revenue Code.

Amendment by section 7871(a)(1), (3) of Pub. L. 101–239 effective as if included in the amendments made by section 9202 of the Omnibus Budget Reconciliation Act of 1986, Pub. L. 99–509, see section 7871(a)(4) of Pub. L. 101–239, set out as a note under section 411 of Title 26.

Amendment by section 7881(m)(2)(A)–(C) of Pub. L. 101–239 effective, except as otherwise provided, as if included in the provision of the Pension Protection Act, Pub. L. 100–203, §§ 9302–9346, to which such amendment relates, see section 7882 of Pub. L. 101–239, set out as a note under section 401 of Title 26.

Amendment by section 7891(a)(1) of Pub. L. 101–239 effective, except as otherwise provided, as if included in the provision of the Tax Reform Act of 1986, Pub. L. 99–514, to which such amendment relates, see section 7891(f) of Pub. L. 101–239, set out as a note under section 1002 of this title.

Amendment by section 7894(c)(4)–(6) of Pub. L. 101–239 effective, except as otherwise provided, as if originally included in the provision of the Employee Retirement Income Security Act of 1974, Pub. L. 93–406, to which such amendment relates, see section 7894(i) of Pub. L. 101–239, set out as a note under section 1002 of this title.

Effective Date of 1987 Amendment

Section 9346(c) of Pub. L. 100–203 provided that:

"(1) In general.—The amendments made by this section [amending this section and section 411 of Title 26, Internal Revenue Code] shall apply to plan years beginning after December 31, 1987.

"(2) Plan amendments not required until January 1, 1989.—If any amendment made by this section requires an amendment to any plan, such plan amendment shall not be required to be made before the first plan year beginning on or after January 1, 1989, if—

"(A) during the period after such amendments made by this section take effect and before such first plan year, the plan is operated in accordance with the requirements of such amendments or in accordance with an amendment prescribed by the Secretary of the Treasury and adopted by the plan, and

"(B) such plan amendment applies retroactively to the period after such amendments take effect and such first plan year.

A plan shall not be treated as failing to provide definitely determinable benefits or contributions, or to be operated in accordance with the provisions of the plan, merely because it operates in accordance with this subsection."

Effective Date of 1986 Amendments

Amendment by section 1113(e)(4)(B) of Pub. L. 99–514 applicable to plan years beginning after Dec. 31, 1988, with special rule for plans maintained pursuant to collective bargaining agreements ratified before Mar. 1, 1986, and not applicable to employees who do not have 1 hour of service in any plan year to which the amendment applies, see section 1113(f) of Pub. L. 99–514, as amended, set out as a note under section 411 of Title 26, Internal Revenue Code.

Section 1879(u)(5), formerly section 1879(u)(4), of Pub. L. 99–514, as redesignated and amended by Pub. L. 101–239, title VII, § 7862(b)(1)(A), (B), Dec. 19, 1989, 103 Stat. 2432, provided that:

"(A) GENERAL RULE.—Except as provided in subparagraph (B), the preceding provisions of this subsection [amending this section and sections 1002 and 1349 of this title] shall be effective as if such provisions were included in the enactment of the Single-Employer Pension Plan Amendments Act of 1986 [Pub. L. 99–272, title XI].

"(B) SPECIAL RULE.—Subparagraph (B) of section 204(h)(2) of the Employee Retirement Income Security Act of 1974 (as amended by paragraph (1)) [29 U.S.C. 1054(h)(2)(B)] shall apply only with respect to plan amendments adopted on or after the date of the enactment of this Act [Oct. 22, 1986]."

Amendment by section 1898(a)(4)(B)(ii), (f)(1)(B), (2) of Pub. L. 99–514 effective as if included in the provision of the Retirement Equity Act of 1984, Pub. L. 98–397, to which such amendment relates, except as otherwise provided, see section 1898(j) of Pub. L. 99–514, set out as a note under section 401 of this title.

Amendment by Pub. L. 99–509 applicable only with respect to plan years beginning on or after Jan. 1, 1988, and only to employees who have 1 hour of service in any plan year to which amendment applies, with special rule for collectively bargained plans, see section 9204 of Pub. L. 99–509, set out as an Effective and Termination Dates of 1986 Amendments note under section 623 of this title.

Section 11006(b) of Pub. L. 99–272 provided that: "The amendments made by subsection (a) [amending this section] shall apply with respect to plan amendments adopted on or after January 1, 1986, except that, in the case of plan amendments adopted on or after January 1, 1986, and on or before the date of the enactment of this Act [Apr. 7, 1986], the requirements of section 204(h) of the Employee Retirement Income Security Act of 1974 [subsec. (h) of this section] (as added by this section) shall be treated as met if the written notice required under such section 204(h) is provided before 60 days after the date of the enactment of this Act."

EFFECTIVE DATE OF 1984 AMENDMENT

Amendment by sections 102(e)(3), (f), and 105(b) of Pub. L. 98–397 applicable to plan years beginning after Dec. 31, 1984, except as otherwise provided, see sections 302 and 303 of Pub. L. 98–397, set out as a note under section 1001 of this title.

Amendment by section 301(a)(2) of Pub. L. 98–397 not applicable to the termination of a certain defined benefit plan, see section 303(f) of Pub. L. 98–397.

REGULATIONS

Secretary of Labor, Secretary of the Treasury, and Equal Employment Opportunity Commission each to issue before Feb. 1, 1988, final regulations to carry out amendments made by Pub. L. 99–509, see section 9204 of Pub. L. 99–509, set out as an Effective and Termination Dates of 1986 Amendment note under section 623 of this title.

Secretary authorized, effective Sept. 2, 1974, to promulgate regulations wherever provisions of this subchapter call for the promulgation of regulations, see section 1031 of this title.

APPLICABILITY OF AMENDMENTS BY SUBTITLES A AND B OF TITLE I OF PUB. L. 109–280

For special rules on applicability of amendments by subtitles A (§§ 101–107) and B (§§ 111–116) of title I of Pub. L. 109–280 to certain eligible cooperative plans, PBGC settlement plans, and eligible government contractor plans, see sections 104, 105, and 106 of Pub. L. 109–280, set out as notes under section 401 of Title 26, Internal Revenue Code.

PLAN AMENDMENTS REFLECTING AMENDMENTS BY SECTION 7881(m) OF PUB. L. 101–239 NOT TREATED AS REDUCING ACCRUED BENEFIT

Section 7881(m)(3) of Pub. L. 101–239 provided that:"If—

"(A) during the period beginning December 22, 1987, and ending June 21, 1988, a plan was amended to reflect the amendments made by section 9346 of the Pension Protection Act [Pub. L. 100–203, amending this section and section 411 of Title 26, Internal Revenue Code], and

"(B) such plan is amended to reflect the amendments made by this subsection [amending this section, section 1002 of this title, and section 411 of Title 26],

any plan amendment described in subparagraph (B) shall not be treated as reducing accrued benefits for purposes of section 411(d)(6) of the Internal Revenue Code of 1986 [section 411(d)(6) of Title 26] or section 204(g) of ERISA [subsec. (g) of this section]."

PLAN AMENDMENTS NOT REQUIRED UNTIL JANUARY 1, 1989

For provisions directing that if any amendments made by subtitle A or subtitle C of title XI [§§ 1101–1147 and 1171–1177] or title XVIII [§§ 1800–1899A] of Pub. L. 99–514 require an amendment to any plan, such plan amendment shall not be required to be made before the first plan year beginning on or after Jan. 1, 1989, see section 1140 of Pub. L. 99–514, as amended, set out as a note under section 401 of Title 26, Internal Revenue Code.

For provisions directing that if any amendments made by Pub. L. 99–509 require an amendment to any plan, such plan amendment shall not be required to be made before the first plan year beginning on or after Jan. 1, 1989, see section 9204 of Pub. L. 99–509, set out as an Effective and Termination Dates of 1986 Amendment note under section 623 of this title.

§ 1055. Requirement of joint and survivor annuity and preretirement survivor annuity

(a) Required contents for applicable plans

Each pension plan to which this section applies shall provide that—

(1) in the case of a vested participant who does not die before the annuity starting date, the accrued benefit payable to such participant shall be provided in the form of a qualified joint and survivor annuity, and

(2) in the case of a vested participant who dies before the annuity starting date and who has a surviving spouse, a qualified preretirement survivor annuity shall be provided to the surviving spouse of such participant.

(b) Applicable plans

(1) This section shall apply to—

(A) any defined benefit plan,

(B) any individual account plan which is subject to the funding standards of section 1082 of this title, and

(C) any participant under any other individual account plan unless—

(i) such plan provides that the participant's nonforfeitable accrued benefit (reduced by any security interest held by the plan by reason of a loan outstanding to such participant) is payable in full, on the death of the participant, to the participant's surviving spouse (or, if there is no surviving spouse or the surviving spouse consents in the manner required under subsection (c)(2) of this section, to a designated beneficiary),

(ii) such participant does not elect the payment of benefits in the form of a life annuity, and

(iii) with respect to such participant, such plan is not a direct or indirect transferee (in a transfer after December 31, 1984) of a plan which is described in subparagraph (A) or (B) or to which this clause applied with respect to the participant.

Clause (iii) of subparagraph (C) shall apply only with respect to the transferred assets (and income therefrom) if the plan separately accounts for such assets and any income therefrom.

(2)(A) In the case of—

(i) a tax credit employee stock ownership plan (as defined in section 409(a) of title 26), or

(ii) an employee stock ownership plan (as defined in section 4975(e)(7) of title 26),

subsection (a) of this section shall not apply to that portion of the employee's accrued benefit to which the requirements of section 409(h) of title 26 apply.

(B) Subparagraph (A) shall not apply with respect to any participant unless the requirements of clause[1] (i), (ii), and (iii) of paragraph (1)(C) are met with respect to such participant.

(4)[2] This section shall not apply to a plan which the Secretary of the Treasury or his delegate has determined is a plan described in section 404(c) of title 26 (or a continuation thereof) in which participation is substantially limited to individuals who, before January 1, 1976, ceased employment covered by the plan.

(4)[2] A plan shall not be treated as failing to meet the requirements of paragraph (1)(C) or (2) merely because the plan provides that benefits will not be payable to the surviving spouse of the participant unless the participant and such spouse had been married throughout the 1-year period ending on the earlier of the participant's annuity starting date or the date of the participant's death.

(c) Plans meeting requirements of section

(1) A plan meets the requirements of this section only if—

(A) under the plan, each participant—

(i) may elect at any time during the applicable election period to waive the qualified joint and survivor annuity form of benefit or the qualified preretirement survivor annuity form of benefit (or both),

(ii) if the participant elects a waiver under clause (i), may elect the qualified optional survivor annuity at any time during the applicable election period, and

(iii) may revoke any such election at any time during the applicable election period, and

(B) the plan meets the requirements of paragraphs (2), (3), and (4).

(2) Each plan shall provide that an election under paragraph (1)(A)(i) shall not take effect unless—

(A)(i) the spouse of the participant consents in writing to such election, (ii) such election designates a beneficiary (or a form of benefits) which may not be changed without spousal consent (or the consent of the spouse expressly permits designations by the participant without any requirement of further consent by the spouse), and (iii) the spouse's consent acknowledges the effect of such election and is witnessed by a plan representative or a notary public, or

(B) it is established to the satisfaction of a plan representative that the consent required under subparagraph (A) may not be obtained because there is no spouse, because the spouse cannot be located, or because of such other circumstances as the Secretary of the Treasury may by regulations prescribe.

Any consent by a spouse (or establishment that the consent of a spouse may not be obtained) under the preceding sentence shall be effective only with respect to such spouse.

(3)(A) Each plan shall provide to each participant, within a reasonable period of time before the annuity starting date (and consistent with such regulations as the Secretary of the Treasury may prescribe) a written explanation of—

(i) the terms and conditions of the qualified joint and survivor annuity and of the qualified optional survivor annuity,

(ii) the participant's right to make, and the effect of, an election under paragraph (1) to waive the joint and survivor annuity form of benefit,

(iii) the rights of the participant's spouse under paragraph (2), and

(iv) the right to make, and the effect of, a revocation of an election under paragraph (1).

(B)(i) Each plan shall provide to each participant, within the applicable period with respect to such participant (and consistent with such regulations as the Secretary may prescribe), a written explanation with respect to the qualified preretirement survivor annuity comparable to that required under subparagraph (A).

(ii) For purposes of clause (i), the term "applicable period" means, with respect to a participant, whichever of the following periods ends last:

(I) The period beginning with the first day of the plan year in which the participant attains age 32 and ending with the close of the plan year preceding the plan year in which the participant attains age 35.

(II) A reasonable period after the individual becomes a participant.

(III) A reasonable period ending after paragraph (5) ceases to apply to the participant.

(IV) A reasonable period ending after this section applies to the participant.

In the case of a participant who separates from service before attaining age 35, the applicable period shall be a reasonable period after separation.

(4) Each plan shall provide that, if this section applies to a participant when part or all of the participant's accrued benefit is to be used as security for a loan, no portion of the participant's accrued benefit may be used as security for such loan unless—

---

[1] So in original. Probably should be "clauses".

[2] So in original. There are two pars. designated (4) and no par. (3).

(A) the spouse of the participant (if any) consents in writing to such use during the 90-day period ending on the date on which the loan is to be so secured, and

(B) requirements comparable to the requirements of paragraph (2) are met with respect to such consent.

(5)(A) The requirements of this subsection shall not apply with respect to the qualified joint and survivor annuity form of benefit or the qualified preretirement survivor annuity form of benefit, as the case may be, if such benefit may not be waived (or another beneficiary selected) and if the plan fully subsidizes the costs of such benefit.

(B) For purposes of subparagraph (A), a plan fully subsidizes the costs of a benefit if under the plan the failure to waive such benefit by a participant would not result in a decrease in any plan benefits with respect to such participant and would not result in increased contributions from such participant.

(6) If a plan fiduciary acts in accordance with part 4 of this subtitle in—

(A) relying on a consent or revocation referred to in paragraph (1)(A), or

(B) making a determination under paragraph (2),

then such consent, revocation, or determination shall be treated as valid for purposes of discharging the plan from liability to the extent of payments made pursuant to such Act.

(7) For purposes of this subsection, the term "applicable election period" means—

(A) in the case of an election to waive the qualified joint and survivor annuity form of benefit, the 180-day period ending on the annuity starting date, or

(B) in the case of an election to waive the qualified preretirement survivor annuity, the period which begins on the first day of the plan year in which the participant attains age 35 and ends on the date of the participant's death.

In the case of a participant who is separated from service, the applicable election period under subparagraph (B) with respect to benefits accrued before the date of such separation from service shall not begin later than such date.

(8) Notwithstanding any other provision of this subsection—

(A)(i) A plan may provide the written explanation described in paragraph (3)(A) after the annuity starting date. In any case to which this subparagraph applies, the applicable election period under paragraph (7) shall not end before the 30th day after the date on which such explanation is provided.

(ii) The Secretary of the Treasury may by regulations limit the application of clause (i), except that such regulations may not limit the period of time by which the annuity starting date precedes the provision of the written explanation other than by providing that the annuity starting date may not be earlier than termination of employment.

(B) A plan may permit a participant to elect (with any applicable spousal consent) to waive any requirement that the written explanation be provided at least 30 days before the annuity starting date (or to waive the 30-day requirement under subparagraph (A)) if the distribution commences more than 7 days after such explanation is provided.

(d)(1) "Qualified joint and survivor annuity" defined

For purposes of this section, the term "qualified joint and survivor annuity" means an annuity—

(A) for the life of the participant with a survivor annuity for the life of the spouse which is not less than 50 percent of (and is not greater than 100 percent of) the amount of the annuity which is payable during the joint lives of the participant and the spouse, and

(B) which is the actuarial equivalent of a single annuity for the life of the participant.

Such term also includes any annuity in a form having the effect of an annuity described in the preceding sentence.

(2)(A) For purposes of this section, the term "qualified optional survivor annuity" means an annuity—

(i) for the life of the participant with a survivor annuity for the life of the spouse which is equal to the applicable percentage of the amount of the annuity which is payable during the joint lives of the participant and the spouse, and

(ii) which is the actuarial equivalent of a single annuity for the life of the participant.

Such term also includes any annuity in a form having the effect of an annuity described in the preceding sentence.

(B)(i) For purposes of subparagraph (A), if the survivor annuity percentage—

(I) is less than 75 percent, the applicable percentage is 75 percent, and

(II) is greater than or equal to 75 percent, the applicable percentage is 50 percent.

(ii) For purposes of clause (i), the term "survivor annuity percentage" means the percentage which the survivor annuity under the plan's qualified joint and survivor annuity bears to the annuity payable during the joint lives of the participant and the spouse.

(e) "Qualified preretirement survivor annuity" defined

For purposes of this section—

(1) Except as provided in paragraph (2), the term "qualified preretirement survivor annuity" means a survivor annuity for the life of the surviving spouse of the participant if—

(A) the payments to the surviving spouse under such annuity are not less than the amounts which would be payable as a survivor annuity under the qualified joint and survivor annuity under the plan (or the actuarial equivalent thereof) if—

(i) in the case of a participant who dies after the date on which the participant attained the earliest retirement age, such participant had retired with an immediate qualified joint and survivor annuity on the day before the participant's date of death, or

(ii) in the case of a participant who dies on or before the date on which the participant would have attained the earliest retirement age, such participant had—

(I) separated from service on the date of death,

(II) survived to the earliest retirement age,

(III) retired with an immediate qualified joint and survivor annuity at the earliest retirement age, and

(IV) died on the day after the day on which such participant would have attained the earliest retirement age, and

(B) under the plan, the earliest period for which the surviving spouse may receive a payment under such annuity is not later than the month in which the participant would have attained the earliest retirement age under the plan.

In the case of an individual who separated from service before the date of such individual's death, subparagraph (A)(ii)(I) shall not apply.

(2) In the case of any individual account plan or participant described in subparagraph (B) or (C) of subsection (b)(1) of this section, the term "qualified preretirement survivor annuity" means an annuity for the life of the surviving spouse the actuarial equivalent of which is not less than 50 percent of the portion of the account balance of the participant (as of the date of death) to which the participant had a nonforfeitable right (within the meaning of section 1053 of this title).

(3) For purposes of paragraphs (1) and (2), any security interest held by the plan by reason of a loan outstanding to the participant shall be taken into account in determining the amount of the qualified preretirement survivor annuity.

(f) Marriage requirements for plan

(1) Except as provided in paragraph (2), a plan may provide that a qualified joint and survivor annuity (or a qualified preretirement survivor annuity) will not be provided unless the participant and spouse had been married throughout the 1-year period ending on the earlier of—

(A) the participant's annuity starting date, or

(B) the date of the participant's death.

(2) For purposes of paragraph (1), if—

(A) a participant marries within 1 year before the annuity starting date, and

(B) the participant and the participant's spouse in such marriage have been married for at least a 1-year period ending on or before the date of the participant's death,

such participant and such spouse shall be treated as having been married throughout the 1-year period ending on the participant's annuity starting date.

(g) Distribution of present value of annuity; written consent; determination of present value

(1) A plan may provide that the present value of a qualified joint and survivor annuity or a qualified preretirement survivor annuity will be immediately distributed if such value does not exceed the amount that can be distributed without the participant's consent under section 1053(e) of this title. No distribution may be made under the preceding sentence after the annuity starting date unless the participant and the spouse of the participant (or where the participant has died, the surviving spouse) consent in writing to such distribution.

(2) If—

(A) the present value of the qualified joint and survivor annuity or the qualified preretirement survivor annuity exceeds the amount that can be distributed without the participant's consent under section 1053(e) of this title, and

(B) the participant and the spouse of the participant (or where the participant has died, the surviving spouse) consent in writing to the distribution,

the plan may immediately distribute the present value of such annuity.

(3)(A) For purposes of paragraphs (1) and (2), the present value shall not be less than the present value calculated by using the applicable mortality table and the applicable interest rate.

(B) For purposes of subparagraph (A)—

(i) The term "applicable mortality table" means a mortality table, modified as appropriate by the Secretary of the Treasury, based on the mortality table specified for the plan year under subparagraph (A) of section 1083(h)(3) of this title (without regard to subparagraph (C) or (D) of such section).

(ii) The term "applicable interest rate" means the adjusted first, second, and third segment rates applied under rules similar to the rules of section 1083(h)(2)(C) of this title for the month before the date of the distribution or such other time as the Secretary of the Treasury may by regulations prescribe.

(iii) For purposes of clause (ii), the adjusted first, second, and third segment rates are the first, second, and third segment rates which would be determined under section 1083(h)(2)(C) of this title if—

(I) section 1083(h)(2)(D) of this title were applied by substituting the average yields for the month described in clause (ii) for the average yields for the 24-month period described in such section,

(II) section 1083(h)(2)(G)(i)(II) of this title were applied by substituting "section 1055(g)(3)(A)(ii)(II) of this title" for "section 1082(b)(5)(B)(ii)(II) of this title", and

(III) the applicable percentage under section 1083(h)(2)(G) of this title were determined in accordance with the following table:

In the case of plan years beginning in:	The applicable percentage is:
2008	20 percent
2009	40 percent
2010	60 percent
2011	80 percent.

(h) Definitions

For purposes of this section—

(1) The term "vested participant" means any participant who has a nonforfeitable right (within the meaning of section 1002(19) of this title) to any portion of such participant's accrued benefit.

(2)(A) The term "annuity starting date" means—

(i) the first day of the first period for which an amount is payable as an annuity, or

(ii) in the case of a benefit not payable in the form of an annuity, the first day on which all events have occurred which entitle the participant to such benefit.

(B) For purposes of subparagraph (A), the first day of the first period for which a benefit is to be received by reason of disability shall be treated as the annuity starting date only if such benefit is not an auxiliary benefit.

(3) The term "earliest retirement age" means the earliest date on which, under the plan, the participant could elect to receive retirement benefits.

(i) Increased costs from providing annuity

A plan may take into account in any equitable manner (as determined by the Secretary of the Treasury) any increased costs resulting from providing a qualified joint or survivor annuity or a qualified preretirement survivor annuity.

(j) Use of participant's accrued benefit as security for loan as not preventing distribution

If the use of any participant's accrued benefit (or any portion thereof) as security for a loan meets the requirements of subsection (c)(4) of this section, nothing in this section shall prevent any distribution required by reason of a failure to comply with the terms of such loan.

(k) Spousal consent

No consent of a spouse shall be effective for purposes of subsection (g)(1) or (g)(2) of this section (as the case may be) unless requirements comparable to the requirements for spousal consent to an election under subsection (c)(1)(A) of this section are met.

(*l*) Regulations; consultation of Secretary of the Treasury with Secretary of Labor

In prescribing regulations under this section, the Secretary of the Treasury shall consult with the Secretary of Labor.

(Pub. L. 93–406, title I, § 205, Sept. 2, 1974, 88 Stat. 862; Pub. L. 98–397, title I, § 103(a), Aug. 23, 1984, 98 Stat. 1429; Pub. L. 99–514, title XI, §§ 1139(c)(2), 1145(b), title XVIII, § 1898(b)(1)(B), (2)(B), (3)(B), (4)(B), (5)(B), (6)(B), (7)(B), (8)(B), (9)(B), (10)(B), (11)(B), (12)(B), (13)(B), (14)(B), Oct. 22, 1986, 100 Stat. 2488, 2491, 2945–2951; Pub. L. 101–239, title VII, §§ 7861(d)(2), 7862(d)(1)(B), (3), (6)–(9), 7891(a)(1), (b)(3), (c), (e), 7894(c)(7)(A), Dec. 19, 1989, 103 Stat. 2431, 2434, 2445, 2447, 2449; Pub. L. 103–465, title VII, § 767(c)(2), Dec. 8, 1994, 108 Stat. 5039; Pub. L. 104–188, title I, § 1451(b), Aug. 20, 1996, 110 Stat. 1815; Pub. L. 105–34, title X, § 1071(b)(2), title XVI, § 1601(d)(5), Aug. 5, 1997, 111 Stat. 948, 1089; Pub. L. 107–147, title IV, § 411(r)(2), Mar. 9, 2002, 116 Stat. 51; Pub. L. 109–280, title III, § 302(a), title X, § 1004(b), title XI, § 1102(a)(2)(A), Aug. 17, 2006, 120 Stat. 920, 1054, 1056; Pub. L. 110–458, title I, § 103(b)(1), Dec. 23, 2008, 122 Stat. 5103.)

AMENDMENTS

2008—Subsec. (g)(3)(B)(iii)(II). Pub. L. 110–458 substituted "section 1055(g)(3)(A)(ii)(II)" for "section 1055(g)(3)(B)(iii)(II)".

2006—Subsec. (c)(1)(A). Pub. L. 109–280, § 1004(b)(1), substituted comma for ", and" at end of cl. (i), added cl. (ii), and redesignated former cl. (ii) as (iii).

Subsec. (c)(3)(A)(i). Pub. L. 109–280, § 1004(b)(3), inserted "and of the qualified optional survivor annuity" before comma at end.

Subsec. (c)(7)(A). Pub. L. 109–280, § 1102(a)(2)(A), substituted "180-day" for "90-day".

Subsec. (d). Pub. L. 109–280, § 1004(b)(2), designated existing provisions as par. (1), redesignated former pars. (1) and (2) as subpars. (A) and (B), respectively, of par. (1), and added par. (2).

Subsec. (g)(3). Pub. L. 109–280, § 302(a), struck out heading and amended text of par. (3) generally. Prior to amendment, par. (3) stated general rule for determination of present value, defined "applicable mortality table" and "applicable interest rate", and set forth exception from general rule in the case of a distribution from a plan that was adopted and in effect prior to Dec. 8, 1994.

2002—Subsec. (g)(1). Pub. L. 107–147, § 411(r)(2)(A), substituted "exceed the amount that can be distributed without the participant's consent under section 1053(e) of this title" for "exceed the dollar limit under section 1053(e)(1) of this title".

Subsec. (g)(2)(A). Pub. L. 107–147, § 411(r)(2)(B), substituted "exceeds the amount that can be distributed without the participant's consent under section 1053(e) of this title" for "exceeds the dollar limit under section 1053(e)(1) of this title".

1997—Subsec. (c)(8)(A)(ii). Pub. L. 105–34, § 1601(d)(5), substituted "Secretary of the Treasury" for "Secretary".

Subsec. (g)(1), (2)(A). Pub. L. 105–34, § 1071(b)(2), substituted "the dollar limit under section 1053(e)(1) of this title" for "$3,500".

1996—Subsec. (c)(8). Pub. L. 104–188 added par. (8).

1994—Subsec. (g)(3). Pub. L. 103–465 amended par. (3) generally. Prior to amendment, par. (3) read as follows:

"(3)(A) For purposes of paragraphs (1) and (2), the present value shall be calculated—

"(i) by using an interest rate no greater than the applicable interest rate if the vested accrued benefit (using such rate) is not in excess of $25,000, and

"(ii) by using an interest rate no greater than 120 percent of the applicable interest rate if the vested accrued benefit exceeds $25,000 (as determined under clause (i)).

In no event shall the present value determined under subclause (II) be less than $25,000.

"(B) For purposes of subparagraph (A), the term 'applicable interest rate' means the interest rate which would be used (as of the date of the distribution) by the Pension Benefit Guaranty Corporation for purposes of determining the present value of a lump sum distribution on plan termination."

1989—Subsec. (b)(1)(C)(i). Pub. L. 101–239, § 7862(d)(7), made technical correction to directory language of Pub. L. 99–514, § 1898(b)(7)(B), see 1986 Amendment note below.

Subsec. (b)(2)(A)(i). Pub. L. 101–239, § 7891(a)(1), substituted "Internal Revenue Code of 1986" for "Internal Revenue Code of 1954", which for purposes of codification was translated as "title 26" thus requiring no change in text.

Subsec. (b)(3), (4). Pub. L. 101–239, § 7862(d)(9), amended directory language of Pub. L. 99–514, § 1898(b)(14)(B), see 1986 Amendment note below, and redesignated par. (3), as added by Pub. L. 99–514, § 1898(b)(14)(B), as par. (4).

Pub. L. 101–239, §§ 7861(d)(2), 7891(c), realigned margins of par. (3), as added by Pub. L. 99–514, § 1145(b), and redesignated such par. (3) as (4).

Subsec. (c)(3)(B)(ii). Pub. L. 101–239, § 7862(d)(1)(B), inserted at end "In the case of a participant who separates from service before attaining age 35, the applicable period shall be a reasonable period after separation."

Subsec. (c)(3)(B)(ii)(IV). Pub. L. 101–239, § 7862(d)(6), substituted "after this section" for "after section 1101(a)(11) of this title".

Subsec. (c)(3)(B)(ii)(V). Pub. L. 101–239, § 7862(d)(1)(B), struck out subcl. (V) which read as follows: "A reasonable period after separation from service in case of a participant who separates before attaining age 35."

Subsec. (c)(6). Pub. L. 101–239, §7894(c)(7)(A), substituted "such Act" for "such act".

Subsec. (e)(2). Pub. L. 101–239, §7862(d)(8), substituted "nonforfeitable right (within the meaning of section 1053 of this title)" for "nonforfeitable accrued benefit".

Subsec. (g)(3)(A). Pub. L. 101–239, §7891(b)(3), realigned margins of subpar. (A).

Subsec. (h)(1). Pub. L. 101–239, §§7862(d)(3)(A), 7891(e)(1), amended par. (1) identically, substituting "The term" for "the term" and "benefit." for "benefit,".

Subsec. (h)(3). Pub. L. 101–239, §§7862(d)(3)B), 7891(e)(2), amended par. (3) identically, substituting "The term" for "the term".

1986—Subsec. (a)(1). Pub. L. 99–514, §1898(b)(3)(B), substituted "who does not die before the annuity starting date" for "who retires under the plan".

Subsec. (b)(1). Pub. L. 99–514, §1898(b)(2)(B)(ii), inserted at end "Clause (iii) of subparagraph (C) shall apply only with respect to the transferred assets (and income therefrom) if the plan separately accounts for such assets and any income therefrom."

Subsec. (b)(1)(C)(i). Pub. L. 99–514, §1898(b)(13)(B), substituted "(c)(2)" for "(c)(2)(A)".

Pub. L. 99–514, §1898(b)(7)(B), as amended by Pub. L. 101–239, §7862(d)(7), inserted "(reduced by any security interest held by the plan by reason of a loan outstanding to such participant)".

Subsec. (b)(1)(C)(iii). Pub. L. 99–514, §1898(b)(2)(B)(i), substituted "a direct or indirect transferee (in a transfer after December 31, 1984)" for "a transferee".

Subsec. (b)(3). Pub. L. 99–514, §1898(b)(14)(B), as amended by Pub. L. 101–239, §7862(d)(9)(A), added par. (3) relating to treatment of plan as meeting requirements of par. (1)(C) or (2) of subsec. (b).

Pub. L. 99–514, §1145(b), added par. (3) relating to applicability of this section to plans described in section 404(c) of title 26.

Subsec. (c)(1)(B). Pub. L. 99–514, §1898(b)(4)(B)(i), substituted "paragraphs (2), (3), and (4)" for "paragraphs (2) and (3)".

Subsec. (c)(2)(A). Pub. L. 99–514, §1898(b)(6)(B), amended subpar. (A) generally. Prior to amendment, subpar. (A) read as follows: "the spouse of the participant consents in writing to such election, and the spouse's consent acknowledges the effect of such election and is witnessed by a plan representative or a notary public, or".

Subsec. (c)(3)(B). Pub. L. 99–514, §1898(b)(5)(B), amended subpar. (B) generally. Prior to amendment, subpar. (B) read as follows: "Each plan shall provide to each participant, within the period beginning with the first day of the plan year in which the participant attains age 32 and ending with the close of the plan year preceding the plan year in which the participant attains age 35 (and consistent with such regulations as the Secretary of the Treasury may prescribe), a written explanation with respect to the qualified preretirement survivor annuity comparable to that required under subparagraph (A)."

Subsec. (c)(4). Pub. L. 99–514, §1898(b)(4)(B)(ii), added par. (4). Former par. (4) redesignated (5).

Subsec. (c)(5). Pub. L. 99–514, §1898(b)(4)(B)(ii), redesignated par. (4) as (5). Former par. (5) redesignated (6).

Subsec. (c)(5)(A). Pub. L. 99–514, §1898(b)(11)(B), inserted "if such benefit may not be waived (or another beneficiary selected) and".

Subsec. (c)(6), (7). Pub. L. 99–514, §1898(b)(4)(B)(ii), redesignated pars. (5) and (6) as (6) and (7), respectively.

Subsec. (e)(1). Pub. L. 99–514, §1898(b)(1)(B), inserted at end "In the case of an individual who separated from service before the date of such individual's death, subparagraph (A)(ii)(I) shall not apply."

Subsec. (e)(2). Pub. L. 99–514, §1898(b)(9)(B)(i), substituted "the portion of the account balance of the participant (as of the date of death) to which the participant had a nonforfeitable accrued benefit" for "the account balance of the participant as of the date of death".

Subsec. (e)(3). Pub. L. 99–514, §1898(b)(9)(B)(ii), added par. (3).

Subsec. (g)(3). Pub. L. 99–514, §1139(c)(2), amended par. (3) generally. Prior to amendment, par. (3) read as follows: "For purposes of paragraphs (1) and (2), the present value of a qualified joint and survivor annuity or a qualified preretirement survivor annuity shall be determined as of the date of the distribution and by using an interest rate not greater than the interest rate which would be used (as of the date of the distribution) by the Pension Benefit Guaranty Corporation for purposes of determining the present value of a lump sum distribution on plan termination."

Subsec. (h)(1). Pub. L. 99–514, §1898(b)(8)(B), substituted "such participant's accrued benefit" for "the accrued benefit derived from employer contributions".

Subsec. (h)(2). Pub. L. 99–514, §1898(b)(12)(B), amended par. (2) generally. Prior to amendment, par. (2) read as follows: "the term 'annuity starting date' means the first day of the first period for which an amount is received as an annuity (whether by reason of retirement or disability), and".

Subsec. (j). Pub. L. 99–514, §1898(b)(4)(B)(iii), added subsec. (j). Former subsec. (j) redesignated (k).

Subsec. (k). Pub. L. 99–514, §1898(b)(10)(B), added subsec. (k). Former subsec. (k) redesignated (*l*).

Pub. L. 99–514, §1898(b)(4)(B)(iii), redesignated subsec. (j) as (k).

Subsec. (*l*). Pub. L. 99–514, §1898(b)(10)(B), redesignated subsec. (k) as (*l*).

1984—Subsec. (a). Pub. L. 98–397 substituted provisions relating to provisions to be included in applicable plans for former provisions relating to form of payment of annuity benefits.

Subsec. (b). Pub. L. 98–397 substituted provisions relating to applicable plans under this section for former provisions relating to plans providing for payment of benefits before normal retirement age.

Subsec. (c). Pub. L. 98–397 substituted provisions relating to conditions under which plans meet the requirements of this section for former provisions relating to election of qualified joint and survivor annuity form.

Subsec. (d). Pub. L. 98–397 substituted provisions defining "qualified joint and survivor annuity" for former provisions relating to the participant's spouse not being entitled to receive survivor annuity.

Subsec. (e). Pub. L. 98–397 substituted provisions defining "qualified preretirement survivor annuity" for former provisions relating to election to take annuity.

Subsec. (f). Pub. L. 98–397 substituted provisions to the effect that plans may provide that annuities will not be provided unless the participant and spouse had been married for a certain 1-year period, for former provisions relating to plan provisions which render election or revocation ineffective if participant dies within period of up to 2 years following the date of election or revocation.

Subsec. (g). Pub. L. 98–397 substituted provisions relating to plan provisions for immediate distribution of present value if such value does not exceed $3,500 and for written consent from the participant and spouse for former provisions setting forth definitions. See subsec. (h) of this section.

Subsec. (h). Pub. L. 98–397 substituted provisions setting forth definitions for former provisions relating to increased costs resulting from providing joint and survivor annuity benefits. See subsec. (i) of this section.

Subsec. (i). Pub. L. 98–397 substituted provisions relating to increased costs resulting from providing annuities under applicable plans for former provisions setting forth the effective date of this section.

Subsec. (j). Pub. L. 98–397 added subsec. (j).

Effective Date of 2008 Amendment

Amendment by Pub. L. 110–458 effective as if included in the provisions of Pub. L. 109–280 to which the amendment relates, except as otherwise provided, see section 112 of Pub. L. 110–458, set out as a note under section 72 of Title 26, Internal Revenue Code.

Effective Date of 2006 Amendment

Amendment by section 302(a) of Pub. L. 109–280 applicable with respect to plan years beginning after Dec. 31,

2007, see section 302(c) of Pub. L. 109–280, set out as a note under section 417 of Title 26, Internal Revenue Code.

Amendment by section 1004(b) of Pub. L. 109–280 applicable to plan years beginning after Dec. 31, 2007, with special rule for collectively bargained plans, see section 1004(c) of Pub. L. 109–280, set out as a note under section 417 of Title 26, Internal Revenue Code.

Amendments and modifications made or required by section 1102(a)(2)(A) of Pub. L. 109–280 applicable to years beginning after Dec. 31, 2006, see section 1102(a)(3) of Pub. L. 109–280, set out as a note under section 417 of Title 26, Internal Revenue Code.

EFFECTIVE DATE OF 2002 AMENDMENT

Amendment by Pub. L. 107–147 effective as if included in the provisions of the Economic Growth and Tax Relief Reconciliation Act of 2001, Pub. L. 107–16, to which such amendment relates, see section 411(x) of Pub. L. 107–147, set out as a note under section 25B of Title 26, Internal Revenue Code.

EFFECTIVE DATE OF 1997 AMENDMENT

Amendment by section 1071(b)(2) of Pub. L. 105–34 applicable to plan years beginning after Aug. 5, 1997, see section 1071(c) of Pub. L. 105–34, set out as a note under section 411 of Title 26, Internal Revenue Code.

Amendment by section 1601(d)(5) of Pub. L. 105–34 effective as if included in the provisions of the Small Business Job Protection Act of 1996, Pub. L. 104–188, to which it relates, see section 1601(j) of Pub. L. 105–34, set out as a note under section 23 of Title 26, Internal Revenue Code.

EFFECTIVE DATE OF 1996 AMENDMENT

Amendment by Pub. L. 104–188 applicable to plan years beginning after Dec. 31, 1996, see section 1451(c) of Pub. L. 104–188, set out as a note under section 417 of Title 26, Internal Revenue Code.

EFFECTIVE DATE OF 1994 AMENDMENT

Amendment by Pub. L. 103–465 applicable to plan years and limitation years beginning after Dec. 31, 1994, except that employer may elect to treat such amendment as effective on or after Dec. 8, 1994, with provisions relating to reduction of accrued benefits, exception, and timing of plan amendment, see section 767(d) of Pub. L. 103–465, as amended, set out as a note under section 411 of Title 26, Internal Revenue Code.

EFFECTIVE DATE OF 1989 AMENDMENT

Amendment by sections 7861(d)(2) and 7862(d)(1)(B), (3), (6)–(9) of Pub. L. 101–239 effective as if included in the provision of the Tax Reform Act of 1986, Pub. L. 99–514, to which such amendment relates, see section 7863 of Pub. L. 101–239, set out as a note under section 106 of Title 26, Internal Revenue Code.

Amendment by section 7891(a)(1), (b)(3), (c), (e) of Pub. L. 101–239 effective, except as otherwise provided, as if included in the provision of the Tax Reform Act of 1986, Pub. L. 99–514, to which such amendment relates, see section 7891(f) of Pub. L. 101–239, set out as a note under section 1002 of this title.

Section 7894(c)(7)(B) of Pub. L. 101–239 provided that: "The amendment made by subparagraph (A) [amending this section] shall take effect as if included in section 103 of the Retirement Equity Act of 1984 [Pub. L. 98–397] in reference to the new section 205(c)(5) of ERISA [subsec. (c)(5) of this section] as added by such section 3113."

EFFECTIVE DATE OF 1986 AMENDMENT

Amendment by section 1139(c)(2) of Pub. L. 99–514 applicable to distributions in plan years beginning after Dec. 31, 1984, except that such amendments shall not apply to any distributions in plan years beginning after Dec. 31, 1984, and before Jan. 1, 1987, if such distributions were made in accordance with the requirements of the regulations issued under the Retirement Equity Act of 1984, Pub. L. 98–397, with additional provisions relating to reductions in accrued benefits, see section 1139(d) of Pub. L. 99–514, set out as a note under section 411 of Title 26, Internal Revenue Code.

Amendment by section 1145(b) of Pub. L. 99–514 applicable as if included in the amendments made by the Retirement Equity Act of 1984, Pub. L. 98–397, see section 1145(d) of Pub. L. 99–514, set out as a note under section 401 of Title 26.

Amendment by section 1898(b)(4)(B) of Pub. L. 99–514 applicable with respect to loans made after Aug. 18, 1985, see section 1898(b)(4)(C) of Pub. L. 99–514, set out as a note under section 417 of Title 26.

Amendment by section 1898(b)(6)(B) of Pub. L. 99–514 applicable to plan years beginning after Oct. 22, 1986, see section 1898(b)(6)(C) of Pub. L. 99–514, set out as a note under section 417 of Title 26.

Amendment by section 1898(b)(8)(B) of Pub. L. 99–514 applicable to distributions after Oct. 22, 1986, see section 1898(b)(8)(C) of Pub. L. 99–514, as added, set out as a note under section 417 of Title 26.

Amendment by section 1898(b)(1)(B), (2)(B), (3)(B), (5)(B), (7)(B), (9)(B), (10)(B), (11)(B), (12)(B), (13)(B), (14)(B) of Pub. L. 99–514 effective as if included in the provision of the Retirement Equity Act of 1984, Pub. L. 98–397, to which such amendment relates, except as otherwise provided, see section 1898(j) of Pub. L. 99–514, set out as a note under section 401 of Title 26.

EFFECTIVE DATE OF 1984 AMENDMENT

Amendment by Pub. L. 98–397 applicable to plan years beginning after Dec. 31, 1984, except as otherwise provided, see sections 302 and 303 of Pub. L. 98–397, set out as a note under section 1001 of this title.

Nothing in amendment by Pub. L. 98–397 to prevent any distribution required by reason of failure to comply with terms of loan made on or before Aug. 18, 1985, and secured by portion of participant's accrued benefit, see section 1898(b)(4)(C)(ii) of Pub. L. 99–514, set out as an Effective Date of 1986 Amendment note under section 417 of Title 26, Internal Revenue Code.

PLAN AMENDMENTS NOT REQUIRED UNTIL JANUARY 1, 1998

For provisions directing that if any amendments made by subtitle D [§§ 1401–1465] of title I of Pub. L. 104–188 require an amendment to any plan or annuity contract, such amendment shall not be required to be made before the first day of the first plan year beginning on or after Jan. 1, 1998, see section 1465 of Pub. L. 104–188, set out as a note under section 401 of Title 26, Internal Revenue Code.

PLAN AMENDMENTS NOT REQUIRED UNTIL JANUARY 1, 1989

For provisions directing that if any amendments made by subtitle A or subtitle C of title XI [§§ 1101–1147 and 1171–1177] or title XVIII [§§ 1800–1899A] of Pub. L. 99–514 require an amendment to any plan, such plan amendment shall not be required to be made before the first plan year beginning on or after Jan. 1, 1989, see section 1140 of Pub. L. 99–514, as amended, set out as a note under section 401 of Title 26, Internal Revenue Code.

§ 1056. Form and payment of benefits

(a) Commencement date for payment of benefits

Each pension plan shall provide that unless the participant otherwise elects, the payment of benefits under the plan to the participant shall begin not later than the 60th day after the latest of the close of the plan year in which—

(1) occurs the date on which the participant attains the earlier of age 65 or the normal retirement age specified under the plan,

(2) occurs the 10th anniversary of the year in which the participant commenced participation in the plan, or

(3) the participant terminates his service with the employer.

In the case of a plan which provides for the payment of an early retirement benefit, such plan shall provide that a participant who satisfied the service requirements for such early retirement benefit, but separated from the service (with any nonforfeitable right to an accrued benefit) before satisfying the age requirement for such early retirement benefit, is entitled upon satisfaction of such age requirement to receive a benefit not less than the benefit to which he would be entitled at the normal retirement age, actuarially reduced under regulations prescribed by the Secretary of the Treasury.

(b) Decrease in plan benefits by reason of increases in benefit levels under Social Security Act or Railroad Retirement Act of 1937

If—

(1) a participant or beneficiary is receiving benefits under a pension plan, or

(2) a participant is separated from the service and has non-forfeitable rights to benefits,

a plan may not decrease benefits of such a participant by reason of any increase in the benefit levels payable under title II of the Social Security Act [42 U.S.C. 401 et seq.] or the Railroad Retirement Act of 1937 [45 U.S.C. 231 et seq.] or any increase in the wage base under such title II, if such increase takes place after September 2, 1974, or (if later) the earlier of the date of first entitlement of such benefits or the date of such separation.

(c) Forfeiture of accrued benefits derived from employer contributions

No pension plan may provide that any part of a participant's accrued benefit derived from employer contributions (whether or not otherwise nonforfeitable) is forfeitable solely because of withdrawal by such participant of any amount attributable to the benefit derived from contributions made by such participant. The preceding sentence shall not apply (1) to the accrued benefit of any participant unless, at the time of such withdrawal, such participant has a nonforfeitable right to at least 50 percent of such accrued benefit, or (2) to the extent that an accrued benefit is permitted to be forfeited in accordance with section 1053(a)(3)(D)(iii) of this title.

(d) Assignment or alienation of plan benefits

(1) Each pension plan shall provide that benefits provided under the plan may not be assigned or alienated.

(2) For the purposes of paragraph (1) of this subsection, there shall not be taken into account any voluntary and revocable assignment of not to exceed 10 percent of any benefit payment, or of any irrevocable assignment or alienation of benefits executed before September 2, 1974. The preceding sentence shall not apply to any assignment or alienation made for the purposes of defraying plan administration costs. For purposes of this paragraph a loan made to a participant or beneficiary shall not be treated as an assignment or alienation if such loan is secured by the participant's accrued non-forfeitable benefit and is exempt from the tax imposed by section 4975 of title 26 (relating to tax on prohibited transactions) by reason of section 4975(d)(1) of title 26.

(3)(A) Paragraph (1) shall apply to the creation, assignment, or recognition of a right to any benefit payable with respect to a participant pursuant to a domestic relations order, except that paragraph (1) shall not apply if the order is determined to be a qualified domestic relations order. Each pension plan shall provide for the payment of benefits in accordance with the applicable requirements of any qualified domestic relations order.

(B) For purposes of this paragraph—

(i) the term "qualified domestic relations order" means a domestic relations order—

(I) which creates or recognizes the existence of an alternate payee's right to, or assigns to an alternate payee the right to, receive all or a portion of the benefits payable with respect to a participant under a plan, and

(II) with respect to which the requirements of subparagraphs (C) and (D) are met, and

(ii) the term "domestic relations order" means any judgment, decree, or order (including approval of a property settlement agreement) which—

(I) relates to the provision of child support, alimony payments, or marital property rights to a spouse, former spouse, child, or other dependent of a participant, and

(II) is made pursuant to a State domestic relations law (including a community property law).

(C) A domestic relations order meets the requirements of this subparagraph only if such order clearly specifies—

(i) the name and the last known mailing address (if any) of the participant and the name and mailing address of each alternate payee covered by the order,

(ii) the amount or percentage of the participant's benefits to be paid by the plan to each such alternate payee, or the manner in which such amount or percentage is to be determined,

(iii) the number of payments or period to which such order applies, and

(iv) each plan to which such order applies.

(D) A domestic relations order meets the requirements of this subparagraph only if such order—

(i) does not require a plan to provide any type or form of benefit, or any option, not otherwise provided under the plan,

(ii) does not require the plan to provide increased benefits (determined on the basis of actuarial value), and

(iii) does not require the payment of benefits to an alternate payee which are required to be paid to another alternate payee under another order previously determined to be a qualified domestic relations order.

(E)(i) A domestic relations order shall not be treated as failing to meet the requirements of clause (i) of subparagraph (D) solely because such order requires that payment of benefits be made to an alternate payee—

(I) in the case of any payment before a participant has separated from service, on or after the date on which the participant attains (or would have attained) the earliest retirement age,

(II) as if the participant had retired on the date on which such payment is to begin under such order (but taking into account only the present value of benefits actually accrued and not taking into account the present value of any employer subsidy for early retirement), and

(III) in any form in which such benefits may be paid under the plan to the participant (other than in the form of a joint and survivor annuity with respect to the alternate payee and his or her subsequent spouse).

For purposes of subclause (II), the interest rate assumption used in determining the present value shall be the interest rate specified in the plan or, if no rate is specified, 5 percent.

(ii) For purposes of this subparagraph, the term "earliest retirement age" means the earlier of—

(I) the date on which the participant is entitled to a distribution under the plan, or

(II) the later of the date of the participant attains age 50 or the earliest date on which the participant could begin receiving benefits under the plan if the participant separated from service.

(F) To the extent provided in any qualified domestic relations order—

(i) the former spouse of a participant shall be treated as a surviving spouse of such participant for purposes of section 1055 of this title (and any spouse of the participant shall not be treated as a spouse of the participant for such purposes), and

(ii) if married for at least 1 year, the surviving former spouse shall be treated as meeting the requirements of section 1055(f) of this title.

(G)(i) In the case of any domestic relations order received by a plan—

(I) the plan administrator shall promptly notify the participant and each alternate payee of the receipt of such order and the plan's procedures for determining the qualified status of domestic relations orders, and

(II) within a reasonable period after receipt of such order, the plan administrator shall determine whether such order is a qualified domestic relations order and notify the participant and each alternate payee of such determination.

(ii) Each plan shall establish reasonable procedures to determine the qualified status of domestic relations orders and to administer distributions under such qualified orders. Such procedures—

(I) shall be in writing,

(II) shall provide for the notification of each person specified in a domestic relations order as entitled to payment of benefits under the plan (at the address included in the domestic relations order) of such procedures promptly upon receipt by the plan of the domestic relations order, and

(III) shall permit an alternate payee to designate a representative for receipt of copies of notices that are sent to the alternate payee with respect to a domestic relations order.

(H)(i) During any period in which the issue of whether a domestic relations order is a qualified domestic relations order is being determined (by the plan administrator, by a court of competent jurisdiction, or otherwise), the plan administrator shall separately account for the amounts (hereinafter in this subparagraph referred to as the "segregated amounts") which would have been payable to the alternate payee during such period if the order had been determined to be a qualified domestic relations order.

(ii) If within the 18-month period described in clause (v) the order (or modification thereof) is determined to be a qualified domestic relations order, the plan administrator shall pay the segregated amounts (including any interest thereon) to the person or persons entitled thereto.

(iii) If within the 18-month period described in clause (v)—

(I) it is determined that the order is not a qualified domestic relations order, or

(II) the issue as to whether such order is a qualified domestic relations order is not resolved,

then the plan administrator shall pay the segregated amounts (including any interest thereon) to the person or persons who would have been entitled to such amounts if there had been no order.

(iv) Any determination that an order is a qualified domestic relations order which is made after the close of the 18-month period described in clause (v) shall be applied prospectively only.

(v) For purposes of this subparagraph, the 18-month period described in this clause is the 18-month period beginning with the date on which the first payment would be required to be made under the domestic relations order.

(I) If a plan fiduciary acts in accordance with part 4 of this subtitle in—

(i) treating a domestic relations order as being (or not being) a qualified domestic relations order, or

(ii) taking action under subparagraph (H),

then the plan's obligation to the participant and each alternate payee shall be discharged to the extent of any payment made pursuant to such Act.

(J) A person who is an alternate payee under a qualified domestic relations order shall be considered for purposes of any provision of this chapter a beneficiary under the plan. Nothing in the preceding sentence shall permit a requirement under section 1301 of this title of the payment of more than 1 premium with respect to a participant for any period.

(K) The term "alternate payee" means any spouse, former spouse, child, or other dependent of a participant who is recognized by a domestic relations order as having a right to receive all, or a portion of, the benefits payable under a plan with respect to such participant.

(L) This paragraph shall not apply to any plan to which paragraph (1) does not apply.

(M) Payment of benefits by a pension plan in accordance with the applicable requirements of a qualified domestic relations order shall not be treated as garnishment for purposes of section 1673(a) of title 15.

(N) In prescribing regulations under this paragraph, the Secretary shall consult with the Secretary of the Treasury.

(4) Paragraph (1) shall not apply to any offset of a participant's benefits provided under an employee pension benefit plan against an amount that the participant is ordered or required to pay to the plan if—

(A) the order or requirement to pay arises—

(i) under a judgment of conviction for a crime involving such plan,

(ii) under a civil judgment (including a consent order or decree) entered by a court in an action brought in connection with a violation (or alleged violation) of part 4 of this subtitle, or

(iii) pursuant to a settlement agreement between the Secretary and the participant, or a settlement agreement between the Pension Benefit Guaranty Corporation and the participant, in connection with a violation (or alleged violation) of part 4 of this subtitle by a fiduciary or any other person,

(B) the judgment, order, decree, or settlement agreement expressly provides for the offset of all or part of the amount ordered or required to be paid to the plan against the participant's benefits provided under the plan, and

(C) in a case in which the survivor annuity requirements of section 1055 of this title apply with respect to distributions from the plan to the participant, if the participant has a spouse at the time at which the offset is to be made—

(i) either—

(I) such spouse has consented in writing to such offset and such consent is witnessed by a notary public or representative of the plan (or it is established to the satisfaction of a plan representative that such consent may not be obtained by reason of circumstances described in section 1055(c)(2)(B) of this title), or

(II) an election to waive the right of the spouse to a qualified joint and survivor annuity or a qualified preretirement survivor annuity is in effect in accordance with the requirements of section 1055(c) of this title,

(ii) such spouse is ordered or required in such judgment, order, decree, or settlement to pay an amount to the plan in connection with a violation of part 4 of this subtitle, or

(iii) in such judgment, order, decree, or settlement, such spouse retains the right to receive the survivor annuity under a qualified joint and survivor annuity provided pursuant to section 1055(a)(1) of this title and under a qualified preretirement survivor annuity provided pursuant to section 1055(a)(2) of this title, determined in accordance with paragraph (5).

A plan shall not be treated as failing to meet the requirements of section 1055 of this title solely by reason of an offset under this paragraph.

(5)(A) The survivor annuity described in paragraph (4)(C)(iii) shall be determined as if—

(i) the participant terminated employment on the date of the offset,

(ii) there was no offset,

(iii) the plan permitted commencement of benefits only on or after normal retirement age,

(iv) the plan provided only the minimum-required qualified joint and survivor annuity, and

(v) the amount of the qualified preretirement survivor annuity under the plan is equal to the amount of the survivor annuity payable under the minimum-required qualified joint and survivor annuity.

(B) For purposes of this paragraph, the term "minimum-required qualified joint and survivor annuity" means the qualified joint and survivor annuity which is the actuarial equivalent of the participant's accrued benefit (within the meaning of section 1002(23) of this title) and under which the survivor annuity is 50 percent of the amount of the annuity which is payable during the joint lives of the participant and the spouse.

(e) Limitation on distributions other than life annuities paid by plan

(1) In general

Notwithstanding any other provision of this part, the fiduciary of a pension plan that is subject to the additional funding requirements of section 1083(j)(4) of this title shall not permit a prohibited payment to be made from a plan during a period in which such plan has a liquidity shortfall (as defined in section 1083(j)(4)(E)(i) of this title).

(2) Prohibited payment

For purposes of paragraph (1), the term "prohibited payment" means—

(A) any payment, in excess of the monthly amount paid under a single life annuity (plus any social security supplements described in the last sentence of section 1054(b)(1)(G) of this title), to a participant or beneficiary whose annuity starting date (as defined in section 1055(h)(2) of this title), that occurs during the period referred to in paragraph (1),

(B) any payment for the purchase of an irrevocable commitment from an insurer to pay benefits, and

(C) any other payment specified by the Secretary of the Treasury by regulations.

(3) Period of shortfall

For purposes of this subsection, a plan has a liquidity shortfall during the period that there is an underpayment of an installment under section 1083(j)(3) of this title by reason of section 1083(j)(4)(A) of this title.

(4) Coordination with other provisions

Compliance with this subsection shall not constitute a violation of any other provision of this chapter.

(f) Missing participants in terminated plans

In the case of a plan covered by section 1350 of this title, upon termination of the plan, benefits of missing participants shall be treated in accordance with section 1350 of this title.

(g) Funding-based limits on benefits and benefit accruals under single-employer plans

(1) Funding-based limitation on shutdown benefits and other unpredictable contingent event benefits under single-employer plans

(A) In general

If a participant of a defined benefit plan which is a single-employer plan is entitled to an unpredictable contingent event benefit payable with respect to any event occurring during any plan year, the plan shall provide that such benefit may not be provided if the adjusted funding target attainment percentage for such plan year—

(i) is less than 60 percent, or

(ii) would be less than 60 percent taking into account such occurrence.

(B) Exemption

Subparagraph (A) shall cease to apply with respect to any plan year, effective as of the first day of the plan year, upon payment by the plan sponsor of a contribution (in addition to any minimum required contribution under section 1083 of this title) equal to—

(i) in the case of subparagraph (A)(i), the amount of the increase in the funding target of the plan (under section 1083 of this title) for the plan year attributable to the occurrence referred to in subparagraph (A), and

(ii) in the case of subparagraph (A)(ii), the amount sufficient to result in an adjusted funding target attainment percentage of 60 percent.

(C) Unpredictable contingent event benefit

For purposes of this paragraph, the term "unpredictable contingent event benefit" means any benefit payable solely by reason of—

(i) a plant shutdown (or similar event, as determined by the Secretary of the Treasury), or

(ii) an event other than the attainment of any age, performance of any service, receipt or derivation of any compensation, or occurrence of death or disability.

(2) Limitations on plan amendments increasing liability for benefits

(A) In general

No amendment to a defined benefit plan which is a single-employer plan which has the effect of increasing liabilities of the plan by reason of increases in benefits, establishment of new benefits, changing the rate of benefit accrual, or changing the rate at which benefits become nonforfeitable may take effect during any plan year if the adjusted funding target attainment percentage for such plan year is—

(i) less than 80 percent, or

(ii) would be less than 80 percent taking into account such amendment.

(B) Exemption

Subparagraph (A) shall cease to apply with respect to any plan year, effective as of the first day of the plan year (or if later, the effective date of the amendment), upon payment by the plan sponsor of a contribution (in addition to any minimum required contribution under section 1083 of this title) equal to—

(i) in the case of subparagraph (A)(i), the amount of the increase in the funding target of the plan (under section 1083 of this title) for the plan year attributable to the amendment, and

(ii) in the case of subparagraph (A)(ii), the amount sufficient to result in an adjusted funding target attainment percentage of 80 percent.

(C) Exception for certain benefit increases

Subparagraph (A) shall not apply to any amendment which provides for an increase in benefits under a formula which is not based on a participant's compensation, but only if the rate of such increase is not in excess of the contemporaneous rate of increase in average wages of participants covered by the amendment.

(3) Limitations on accelerated benefit distributions

(A) Funding percentage less than 60 percent

A defined benefit plan which is a single-employer plan shall provide that, in any case in which the plan's adjusted funding target attainment percentage for a plan year is less than 60 percent, the plan may not pay any prohibited payment after the valuation date for the plan year.

(B) Bankruptcy

A defined benefit plan which is a single-employer plan shall provide that, during any period in which the plan sponsor is a debtor in a case under title 11 or similar Federal or State law, the plan may not pay any prohibited payment. The preceding sentence shall not apply on or after the date on which the enrolled actuary of the plan certifies that the adjusted funding target attainment percentage of such plan is not less than 100 percent.

(C) Limited payment if percentage at least 60 percent but less than 80 percent

(i) In general

A defined benefit plan which is a single-employer plan shall provide that, in any case in which the plan's adjusted funding target attainment percentage for a plan year is 60 percent or greater but less than 80 percent, the plan may not pay any prohibited payment after the valuation date for the plan year to the extent the amount of the payment exceeds the lesser of—

(I) 50 percent of the amount of the payment which could be made without regard to this subsection, or

(II) the present value (determined under guidance prescribed by the Pension Benefit Guaranty Corporation, using the interest and mortality assumptions under section 1055(g) of this title) of the maximum guarantee with respect to the participant under section 1322 of this title.

(ii) One-time application

(I) In general

The plan shall also provide that only 1 prohibited payment meeting the requirements of clause (i) may be made with respect to any participant during any period of consecutive plan years to which the limitations under either subparagraph (A) or (B) or this subparagraph applies.

(II) Treatment of beneficiaries

For purposes of this clause, a participant and any beneficiary on his behalf (including an alternate payee, as defined in subsection (d)(3)(K)) shall be treated as 1 participant. If the accrued benefit of a participant is allocated to such an alternate payee and 1 or more other persons, the amount under clause (i) shall be allocated among such persons in the same manner as the accrued benefit is allocated unless the qualified domestic relations order (as defined in subsection (d)(3)(B)(i)) provides otherwise.

(D) Exception

This paragraph shall not apply to any plan for any plan year if the terms of such plan (as in effect for the period beginning on September 1, 2005, and ending with such plan year) provide for no benefit accruals with respect to any participant during such period.

(E) Prohibited payment

For purpose[1] of this paragraph, the term "prohibited payment" means—

(i) any payment, in excess of the monthly amount paid under a single life annuity (plus any social security supplements described in the last sentence of section 1054(b)(1)(G) of this title), to a participant or beneficiary whose annuity starting date (as defined in section 1055(h)(2) of this title) occurs during any period a limitation under subparagraph (A) or (B) is in effect,

(ii) any payment for the purchase of an irrevocable commitment from an insurer to pay benefits, and

(iii) any other payment specified by the Secretary of the Treasury by regulations.

Such term shall not include the payment of a benefit which under section 1053(e) of this title may be immediately distributed without the consent of the participant.

(4) Limitation on benefit accruals for plans with severe funding shortfalls

(A) In general

A defined benefit plan which is a single-employer plan shall provide that, in any case in which the plan's adjusted funding target attainment percentage for a plan year is less than 60 percent, benefit accruals under the plan shall cease as of the valuation date for the plan year.

(B) Exemption

Subparagraph (A) shall cease to apply with respect to any plan year, effective as of the first day of the plan year, upon payment by the plan sponsor of a contribution (in addition to any minimum required contribution under section 1083 of this title) equal to the amount sufficient to result in an adjusted funding target attainment percentage of 60 percent.

(5) Rules relating to contributions required to avoid benefit limitations

(A) Security may be provided

(i) In general

For purposes of this subsection, the adjusted funding target attainment percentage shall be determined by treating as an asset of the plan any security provided by a plan sponsor in a form meeting the requirements of clause (ii).

(ii) Form of security

The security required under clause (i) shall consist of—

(I) a bond issued by a corporate surety company that is an acceptable surety for purposes of section 1112 of this title,

(II) cash, or United States obligations which mature in 3 years or less, held in escrow by a bank or similar financial institution, or

(III) such other form of security as is satisfactory to the Secretary of the Treasury and the parties involved.

(iii) Enforcement

Any security provided under clause (i) may be perfected and enforced at any time after the earlier of—

(I) the date on which the plan terminates,

(II) if there is a failure to make a payment of the minimum required contribution for any plan year beginning after the security is provided, the due date for the payment under section 1083(j) of this title, or

(III) if the adjusted funding target attainment percentage is less than 60 percent for a consecutive period of 7 years, the valuation date for the last year in the period.

(iv) Release of security

The security shall be released (and any amounts thereunder shall be refunded together with any interest accrued thereon) at such time as the Secretary of the Treasury may prescribe in regulations, including regulations for partial releases of the security by reason of increases in the adjusted funding target attainment percentage.

(B) Prefunding balance or funding standard carryover balance may not be used

No prefunding balance or funding standard carryover balance under section 1083(f) of this title may be used under paragraph (1), (2), or (4) to satisfy any payment an employer may make under any such paragraph to avoid or terminate the application of any limitation under such paragraph.

[1] So in original. Probably should be "purposes".

(C) Deemed reduction of funding balances

(i) In general

Subject to clause (iii), in any case in which a benefit limitation under paragraph (1), (2), (3), or (4) would (but for this subparagraph and determined without regard to paragraph (1)(B), (2)(B), or (4)(B)) apply to such plan for the plan year, the plan sponsor of such plan shall be treated for purposes of this chapter as having made an election under section 1083(f) of this title to reduce the prefunding balance or funding standard carryover balance by such amount as is necessary for such benefit limitation to not apply to the plan for such plan year.

(ii) Exception for insufficient funding balances

Clause (i) shall not apply with respect to a benefit limitation for any plan year if the application of clause (i) would not result in the benefit limitation not applying for such plan year.

(iii) Restrictions of certain rules to collectively bargained plans

With respect to any benefit limitation under paragraph (1), (2), or (4), clause (i) shall only apply in the case of a plan maintained pursuant to 1 or more collective bargaining agreements between employee representatives and 1 or more employers.

(6) New plans

Paragraphs (1), (2), and (4) shall not apply to a plan for the first 5 plan years of the plan. For purposes of this paragraph, the reference in this paragraph to a plan shall include a reference to any predecessor plan.

(7) Presumed underfunding for purposes of benefit limitations

(A) Presumption of continued underfunding

In any case in which a benefit limitation under paragraph (1), (2), (3), or (4) has been applied to a plan with respect to the plan year preceding the current plan year, the adjusted funding target attainment percentage of the plan for the current plan year shall be presumed to be equal to the adjusted funding target attainment percentage of the plan for the preceding plan year until the enrolled actuary of the plan certifies the actual adjusted funding target attainment percentage of the plan for the current plan year.

(B) Presumption of underfunding after 10th month

In any case in which no certification of the adjusted funding target attainment percentage for the current plan year is made with respect to the plan before the first day of the 10th month of such year, for purposes of paragraphs (1), (2), (3), and (4), such first day shall be deemed, for purposes of such paragraph, to be the valuation date of the plan for the current plan year and the plan's adjusted funding target attainment percentage shall be conclusively presumed to be less than 60 percent as of such first day.

(C) Presumption of underfunding after 4th month for nearly underfunded plans

In any case in which—

(i) a benefit limitation under paragraph (1), (2), (3), or (4) did not apply to a plan with respect to the plan year preceding the current plan year, but the adjusted funding target attainment percentage of the plan for such preceding plan year was not more than 10 percentage points greater than the percentage which would have caused such paragraph to apply to the plan with respect to such preceding plan year, and

(ii) as of the first day of the 4th month of the current plan year, the enrolled actuary of the plan has not certified the actual adjusted funding target attainment percentage of the plan for the current plan year,

until the enrolled actuary so certifies, such first day shall be deemed, for purposes of such paragraph, to be the valuation date of the plan for the current plan year and the adjusted funding target attainment percentage of the plan as of such first day shall, for purposes of such paragraph, be presumed to be equal to 10 percentage points less than the adjusted funding target attainment percentage of the plan for such preceding plan year.

(8) Treatment of plan as of close of prohibited or cessation period

For purposes of applying this part—

(A) Operation of plan after period

Unless the plan provides otherwise, payments and accruals will resume effective as of the day following the close of the period for which any limitation of payment or accrual of benefits under paragraph (3) or (4) applies.

(B) Treatment of affected benefits

Nothing in this paragraph shall be construed as affecting the plan's treatment of benefits which would have been paid or accrued but for this subsection.

(9) Terms relating to funding target attainment percentage

For purposes of this subsection—

(A) In general

The term "funding target attainment percentage" has the same meaning given such term by section 1083(d)(2) of this title.

(B) Adjusted funding target attainment percentage

The term "adjusted funding target attainment percentage" means the funding target attainment percentage which is determined under subparagraph (A) by increasing each of the amounts under subparagraphs (A) and (B) of section 1083(d)(2) of this title by the aggregate amount of purchases of annuities for employees other than highly compensated employees (as defined in section 414(q) of title 26) which were made by the plan during the preceding 2 plan years.

(C) Application to plans which are fully funded without regard to reductions for funding balances

(i) In general

In the case of a plan for any plan year, if the funding target attainment percentage is 100 percent or more (determined without regard to the reduction in the value of assets under section 1083(f)(4) of this title), the funding target attainment percentage for purposes of subparagraphs (A) and (B) shall be determined without regard to such reduction.

(ii) Transition rule

Clause (i) shall be applied to plan years beginning after 2007 and before 2011 by substituting for "100 percent" the applicable percentage determined in accordance with the following table:

In the case of a plan year beginning in calendar year:	The applicable percentage is
2008	92
2009	94
2010	96.

(iii) Limitation

Clause (ii) shall not apply with respect to any plan year beginning after 2008 unless the funding target attainment percentage (determined without regard to the reduction in the value of assets under section 1083(f)(4) of this title) of the plan for each preceding plan year beginning after 2007 was not less than the applicable percentage with respect to such preceding plan year determined under clause (ii).

(10) Secretarial authority for plans with alternate valuation date

In the case of a plan which has designated a valuation date other than the first day of the plan year, the Secretary of the Treasury may prescribe rules for the application of this subsection which are necessary to reflect the alternate valuation date.

(11) Special rule for 2008

For purposes of this subsection, in the case of plan years beginning in 2008, the funding target attainment percentage for the preceding plan year may be determined using such methods of estimation as the Secretary of the Treasury may provide.

(Pub. L. 93–406, title I, §206, Sept. 2, 1974, 88 Stat. 864; Pub. L. 98–397, title I, §104(a), Aug. 23, 1984, 98 Stat. 1433; Pub. L. 99–514, title XVIII, §1898(c)(2)(B), (4)(B), (5), (6)(B), (7)(B), Oct. 22, 1986, 100 Stat. 2952–2954; Pub. L. 101–239, title VII, §§7891(a)(1), 7894(c)(8), (9)(A), Dec. 19, 1989, 103 Stat. 2445, 2449; Pub. L. 103–465, title VII, §§761(a)(9)(B)(i), 776(c)(2), Dec. 8, 1994, 108 Stat. 5033, 5048; Pub. L. 105–34, title XV, §1502(a), Aug. 5, 1997, 111 Stat. 1058; Pub. L. 109–280, title I, §§103(a), 107(a)(9), (10), title IV, §410(b), Aug. 17, 2006, 120 Stat. 809, 819, 935; Pub. L. 110–458, title I, §101(c)(1)(B)–(G), Dec. 23, 2008, 122 Stat. 5097.)

REFERENCES IN TEXT

The Social Security Act, referred to in subsec. (b), is act Aug. 14, 1935, ch. 531, 49 Stat. 620, as amended. Title II of the Social Security Act is classified generally to subchapter II (§401 et seq.) of chapter 7 of Title 42, The Public Health and Welfare. For complete classification of this Act to the Code, see section 1305 of Title 42 and Tables.

The Railroad Retirement Act of 1937, referred to in subsec. (b), is act Aug. 29, 1935, ch. 812, 49 Stat. 967, as amended generally by act June 24, 1937, ch. 382, part I, 50 Stat. 307, and which was classified principally to subchapter III (§228a et seq.) of chapter 9 of Title 45, Railroads. The Railroad Retirement Act of 1937 was amended generally and redesignated the Railroad Retirement Act of 1974 by Pub. L. 93–445, title I, Oct. 16, 1974, 88 Stat. 1305. The Railroad Retirement Act of 1974 is classified generally to subchapter IV (§231 et seq.) of chapter 9 of Title 45. For complete classification of these acts to the Code, see Tables.

This chapter, referred to in subsecs. (e)(4) and (g)(5)(C)(i), was in the original "this Act", meaning Pub. L. 93–406, known as the Employee Retirement Income Security Act of 1974. Titles I, III, and IV of such Act are classified principally to this chapter. For complete classification of this Act to the Code, see Short Title note set out under section 1001 of this title and Tables.

AMENDMENTS

2008—Subsec. (g)(1)(B)(ii). Pub. L. 110–458, §101(c)(1)(B), substituted "an adjusted funding" for "a funding".

Subsec. (g)(1)(C). Pub. L. 110–458, §101(c)(1)(C), inserted "benefit" after "event" in heading.

Subsec. (g)(3)(E). Pub. L. 110–458, §101(c)(1)(D), inserted concluding provisions.

Subsec. (g)(5)(A)(iv). Pub. L. 110–458, §101(c)(1)(E), inserted "adjusted" before "funding".

Subsec. (g)(9)(C). Pub. L. 110–458, §101(c)(1)(F), in cl. (i), struck out "without regard to this subparagraph and" before "without regard to the reduction" and, in cl. (iii), substituted "without regard to the reduction in the value of assets under section 1083(f)(4) of this title" for "without regard to this subparagraph" and inserted "beginning" before "after" in two places.

Subsec. (g)(10), (11). Pub. L. 110–458, §101(c)(1)(G), added par. (10) and redesignated former par. (10) as (11).

2006—Subsec. (e)(1). Pub. L. 109–280, §107(a)(9), substituted "1083(j)(4)" for "1082(d)" and "1083(j)(4)(E)(i)" for "1082(e)(5)".

Subsec. (e)(3). Pub. L. 109–280, §107(a)(10), substituted "section 1083(j)(3) of this title by reason of section 1083(j)(4)(A) of this title" for "section 1082(e) of this title by reason of paragraph (5)(A) thereof".

Subsec. (f). Pub. L. 109–280, §410(b), substituted "section 1350 of this title" for "subchapter III of this chapter, the plan shall provide that".

Subsec. (g). Pub. L. 109–280, §103(a), added subsec. (g).

1997—Subsec. (d)(4), (5). Pub. L. 105–34 added pars. (4) and (5).

1994—Subsec. (e). Pub. L. 103–465, §761(a)(9)(B)(i), added subsec. (e).

Subsec. (f). Pub. L. 103–465, §776(c)(2), added subsec. (f).

1989—Subsec. (a)(1). Pub. L. 101–239, §7894(c)(8), inserted "occurs" before "the date".

Subsec. (d)(2). Pub. L. 101–239, §7891(a)(1), substituted "Internal Revenue Code of 1986" for "Internal Revenue Code of 1954", which for purposes of codification was translated as "title 26" thus requiring no change in text.

Subsec. (d)(3)(I). Pub. L. 101–239, §7894(c)(9)(A), substituted "such Act" for "such act".

1986—Subsec. (d)(3)(E)(i). Pub. L. 99–514, §1898(c)(7)(B)(iii), substituted "A" for "In the case of any payment before a participant has separated from service, a" in introductory provisions and inserted "in the case of any payment before a participant has separated from service," in subcl. (I).

Subsec. (d)(3)(E)(ii). Pub. L. 99–514, §1898(c)(7)(B)(iv), amended cl. (ii) generally. Prior to amendment, cl. (ii) read as follows: "For purposes of this subparagraph, the term 'earliest retirement age' has the meaning given such term by section 1055(h)(3) of this section, except that in the case of any individual account plan, the earliest retirement age shall be the date which is 10 years before the normal retirement age."

Subsec. (d)(3)(F)(i). Pub. L. 99–514, § 1898(c)(6)(B), inserted "(and any spouse of the participant shall not be treated as a spouse of the participant for such purposes)".

Subsec. (d)(3)(F)(ii). Pub. L. 99–514, § 1898(c)(7)(B)(i), inserted "surviving" before "former spouse".

Subsec. (d)(3)(G)(i)(I). Pub. L. 99–514, § 1898(c)(7)(B)(ii), substituted "each" for "any other".

Subsec. (d)(3)(H)(i). Pub. L. 99–514, § 1898(c)(2)(B)(i), substituted "shall separately account for the amounts (hereinafter in this subparagraph referred to as the 'segregated amounts')" for "shall segregate in a separate account in the plan or in an escrow account the amounts".

Subsec. (d)(3)(H)(ii), (iii). Pub. L. 99–514, § 1898(c)(2)(B)(ii), (iii), substituted "the 18-month period described in clause (v)" for "18 months" and "including any interest" for "plus any interest".

Subsec. (d)(3)(H)(iv). Pub. L. 99–514, § 1898(c)(2)(B)(iv), inserted "described in clause (v)".

Subsec. (d)(3)(H)(v). Pub. L. 99–514, § 1898(c)(2)(B)(v), added cl. (v).

Subsec. (d)(3)(L). Pub. L. 99–514, § 1898(c)(4)(B), added subpar. (L) and redesignated former subpar. (L) as (N).

Subsec. (d)(3)(M). Pub. L. 99–514, § 1898(c)(5), added subpar. (M).

Subsec. (d)(3)(N). Pub. L. 99–514, § 1898(c)(4)(B), redesignated subpar. (L) as (N).

1984—Subsec. (d)(3). Pub. L. 98–397 added par. (3).

EFFECTIVE DATE OF 2008 AMENDMENT

Amendment by Pub. L. 110–458 effective as if included in the provisions of Pub. L. 109–280 to which the amendment relates, except as otherwise provided, see section 112 of Pub. L. 110–458, set out as a note under section 72 of Title 26, Internal Revenue Code.

EFFECTIVE DATE OF 2006 AMENDMENT

Amendment by section 103(a) of Pub. L. 109–280 applicable to plan years beginning after Dec. 31, 2007, with collective bargaining exception, see section 103(c) of Pub. L. 109–280, set out as a note under section 1021 of this title.

Amendment by section 107(a)(9), (10) of Pub. L. 109–280 applicable to plan years beginning after 2007, see section 107(e) of Pub. L. 109–280, set out as a note under section 1021 of this title.

Pub. L. 109–280, title IV, § 410(c), Aug. 17, 2006, 120 Stat. 935, provided that: "The amendments made by this section [amending this section and section 1350 of this title] shall apply to distributions made after final regulations implementing subsections (c) and (d) of section 4050 of the Employee Retirement Income Security Act of 1974 [29 U.S.C. 1350(c), (d)] (as added by subsection (a)), respectively, are prescribed."

EFFECTIVE DATE OF 1997 AMENDMENT

Amendment by Pub. L. 105–34 applicable to judgments, orders, and decrees issued, and settlement agreements entered into, on or after Aug. 5, 1997, see section 1502(c) of Pub. L. 105–34, set out as a note under section 401 of Title 26, Internal Revenue Code.

EFFECTIVE DATE OF 1994 AMENDMENT

Section 761(b) of Pub. L. 103–465 provided that:

"(1) IN GENERAL.—Except as provided in paragraph (2), the amendments made by this section [amending this section and sections 1082, 1132, and 1301 of this title] shall apply to plan years beginning after December 31, 1994.

"(2) CONTRIBUTING SPONSOR.—The amendment made by subsection (a)(11) [amending section 1301 of this title] shall be effective as if included in the Pension Protection Act [Pub. L. 100–203, title IX, subtitle D, part II, §§ 9302–9346]."

Section 776(e) of Pub. L. 103–465 provided that: "The provisions of this section [enacting section 1350 of this title and amending this section and sections 1303, 1305, and 1341 of this title and section 401 of Title 26, Internal Revenue Code] shall be effective with respect to distributions that occur in plan years commencing after final regulations implementing these provisions are prescribed by the Pension Benefit Guaranty Corporation." [Final implementing regulations were issued Nov. 22, 1995, effective for distributions in plan years beginning on or after Jan. 1, 1996. See 60 F.R. 61740.]

EFFECTIVE DATE OF 1989 AMENDMENT

Amendment by section 7891(a)(1) of Pub. L. 101–239 effective, except as otherwise provided, as if included in the provision of the Tax Reform Act of 1986, Pub. L. 99–514, to which such amendment relates, see section 7891(f) of Pub. L. 101–239, set out as a note under section 1002 of this title.

Amendment by section 7894(c)(8) of Pub. L. 101–239 effective, except as otherwise provided, as if originally included in the provision of the Employee Retirement Income Security Act of 1974, Pub. L. 93–406, to which such amendment relates, see section 7894(i) of Pub. L. 101–239, set out as a note under section 1002 of this title.

Section 7894(c)(9)(B) of Pub. L. 101–239 provided that: "The amendment made by subparagraph (A) [amending this section] shall take effect as if included in section 104 of the Retirement Equity Act of 1984 [Pub. L. 98–397]."

EFFECTIVE DATE OF 1986 AMENDMENT

Amendment by Pub. L. 99–514 effective as if included in the provision of the Retirement Equity Act of 1984, Pub. L. 98–397, to which such amendment relates, except as otherwise provided, see section 1898(j) of Pub. L. 99–514, set out as a note under section 401 of Title 26, Internal Revenue Code.

EFFECTIVE DATE OF 1984 AMENDMENT

Amendment by Pub. L. 98–397 effective Jan. 1, 1985, except as otherwise provided, see section 303(d) of Pub. L. 98–397, set out as a note under section 1001 of this title.

APPLICABILITY OF AMENDMENTS BY SUBTITLES A AND B OF TITLE I OF PUB. L. 109–280

For special rules on applicability of amendments by subtitles A (§§ 101–107) and B (§§ 111–116) of title I of Pub. L. 109–280 to certain eligible cooperative plans, PBGC settlement plans, and eligible government contractor plans, see sections 104, 105, and 106 of Pub. L. 109–280, set out as notes under section 401 of Title 26, Internal Revenue Code.

PLAN AMENDMENTS NOT REQUIRED UNTIL JANUARY 1, 1989

For provisions directing that if any amendments made by subtitle A or subtitle C of title XI [§§ 1101–1147 and 1171–1177] or title XVIII [§§ 1800–1899A] of Pub. L. 99–514 require an amendment to any plan, such plan amendment shall not be required to be made before the first plan year beginning on or after Jan. 1, 1989, see section 1140 of Pub. L. 99–514, as amended, set out as a note under section 401 of Title 26, Internal Revenue Code.

§ 1057. Repealed. Pub. L. 109–280, title I, § 107(d), Aug. 17, 2006, 120 Stat. 820

Section, Pub. L. 93–406, title I, § 207, Sept. 2, 1974, 88 Stat. 865, related to temporary variances from certain vesting requirements.

EFFECTIVE DATE OF REPEAL

Repeal applicable to plan years beginning after 2007, see section 107(e) of Pub. L. 109–280, set out as an Effective Date of 2006 Amendment note under section 1021 of this title.

§1058. Mergers and consolidations of plans or transfers of plan assets

A pension plan may not merge or consolidate with, or transfer its assets or liabilities to, any other plan after September 2, 1974, unless each participant in the plan would (if the plan then terminated) receive a benefit immediately after the merger, consolidation, or transfer which is equal to or greater than the benefit he would have been entitled to receive immediately before the merger, consolidation, or transfer (if the plan had then terminated). The preceding sentence shall not apply to any transaction to the extent that participants either before or after the transaction are covered under a multiemployer plan to which subchapter III of this chapter applies.

(Pub. L. 93–406, title I, §208, Sept. 2, 1974, 88 Stat. 865; Pub. L. 96–364, title IV, §402(b)(1), Sept. 26, 1980, 94 Stat. 1299.)

AMENDMENTS

1980—Pub. L. 96–364 substituted provisions respecting applicability of preceding sentence to transactions under a covered multiemployer plan to which subchapter III applies, for provisions relating to applicability of paragraph to a multiemployer plan only to extent determined by Corporation.

EFFECTIVE DATE OF 1980 AMENDMENT

Amendment by Pub. L. 96–364 effective Sept. 26, 1980, except as specifically provided, see section 1461(e) of this title.

§1059. Recordkeeping and reporting requirements

(a)(1) Except as provided by paragraph (2) every employer shall, in accordance with such regulations as the Secretary may prescribe, maintain records with respect to each of his employees sufficient to determine the benefits due or which may become due to such employees. The plan administrator shall make a report, in such manner and at such time as may be provided in regulations prescribed by the Secretary, to each employee who is a participant under the plan and who—

(A) requests such report, in such manner and at such time as may be provided in such regulations,

(B) terminates his service with the employer, or

(C) has a 1-year break in service (as defined in section 1053(b)(3)(A) of this title).

The employer shall furnish to the plan administrator the information necessary for the administrator to make the reports required by the preceding sentence. Not more than one report shall be required under subparagraph (A) in any 12-month period. Not more than one report shall be required under subparagraph (C) with respect to consecutive 1-year breaks in service. The report required under this paragraph shall be in the same form, and contain the same information, as periodic benefit statements under section 1025(a) of this title.

(2) If more than one employer adopts a plan, each such employer shall furnish to the plan administrator the information necessary for the administrator to maintain the records, and make the reports, required by paragraph (1). Such administrator shall maintain the records, and make the reports, required by paragraph (1).

(b) If any person who is required, under subsection (a) of this section, to furnish information or maintain records for any plan year fails to comply with such requirement, he shall pay to the Secretary a civil penalty of $10 for each employee with respect to whom such failure occurs, unless it is shown that such failure is due to reasonable cause.

(Pub. L. 93–406, title I, §209, Sept. 2, 1974, 88 Stat. 865; Pub. L. 110–458, title I, §105(f), Dec. 23, 2008, 122 Stat. 5105.)

AMENDMENTS

2008—Subsec. (a)(1). Pub. L. 110–458, §105(f)(1), in introductory provisions, substituted "such regulations as the Secretary may prescribe" for "regulations prescribed by the Secretary" and, in concluding provisions, inserted last sentence and struck out former last sentence which read as follows: "The report required under this paragraph shall be sufficient to inform the employee of his accrued benefits under the plan and the percentage of such benefits which are nonforfeitable under the plan."

Subsec. (a)(2). Pub. L. 110–458, §105(f)(2), added par. (2) and struck out former par. (2) which read as follows: "If more than one employer adopts a plan, each such employer shall, in accordance with regulations prescribed by the Secretary, furnish to the plan administrator the information necessary for the administrator to maintain the records and make the reports required by paragraph (1). Such administrator shall maintain the records and, to the extent provided under regulations prescribed by the Secretary, make the reports, required by paragraph (1)."

EFFECTIVE DATE OF 2008 AMENDMENT

Amendment by Pub. L. 110–458 effective as if included in the provisions of Pub. L. 109–280 to which the amendment relates, except as otherwise provided, see section 112 of Pub. L. 110–458, set out as a note under section 72 of Title 26, Internal Revenue Code.

REGULATIONS

Secretary authorized, effective Sept. 2, 1974, to promulgate regulations wherever provisions of this subchapter call for the promulgation of regulations, see section 1031 of this title.

§1060. Multiple employer plans

(a) Plan maintained by more than one employer

Notwithstanding any other provision of this part or part 3, the following provisions of this subsection shall apply to a plan maintained by more than one employer:

(1) Section 1052 of this title shall be applied as if all employees of each of the employers were employed by a single employer.

(2) Sections 1053 and 1054 of this title shall be applied as if all such employers constituted a single employer, except that the application of any rules with respect to breaks in service shall be made under regulations prescribed by the Secretary.

(3) The minimum funding standard provided by section 1082 of this title shall be determined as if all participants in the plan were employed by a single employer.

(b) Maintenance of plan of predecessor employer

For purposes of this part and part 3—

(1) in any case in which the employer maintains a plan of a predecessor employer, service

for such predecessor shall be treated as service for the employer, and

(2) in any case in which the employer maintains a plan which is not the plan maintained by a predecessor employer, service for such predecessor shall, to the extent provided in regulations prescribed by the Secretary of the Treasury, be treated as service for the employer.

(c) Plan maintained by controlled group of corporations

For purposes of sections 1052, 1053, and 1054 of this title, all employees of all corporations which are members of a controlled group of corporations (within the meaning of section 1563(a) of title 26, determined without regard to section 1563(a)(4) and (e)(3)(C) of title 26) shall be treated as employed by a single employer. With respect to a plan adopted by more than one such corporation, the minimum funding standard of section 1082 of this title shall be determined as if all such employers were a single employer, and allocated to each employer in accordance with regulations prescribed by the Secretary of the Treasury.

(d) Plan of trades or businesses under common control

For purposes of sections 1052, 1053, and 1054 of this title, under regulations prescribed by the Secretary of the Treasury, all employees of trades or businesses (whether or not incorporated) which are under common control shall be treated as employed by a single employer. The regulations prescribed under this subsection shall be based on principles similar to the principles which apply in the case of subsection (c) of this section.

(Pub. L. 93–406, title I, §210, Sept. 2, 1974, 88 Stat. 866; Pub. L. 101–239, title VII, §§7891(a)(1), 7894(c)(10), Dec. 19, 1989, 103 Stat. 2445, 2449; Pub. L. 109–280, title IX, §903(b)(1), (2)(A), Aug. 17, 2006, 120 Stat. 1044, 1048; Pub. L. 110–458, title I, §109(c)(2), Dec. 23, 2008, 122 Stat. 5111.)

AMENDMENT OF SECTION

Pub. L. 110–458, title I, §§109(c)(2), 112, Dec. 23, 2008, 122 Stat. 5111, 5113, provided that, effective as if included in the provisions of Pub. L. 109–280 to which the amendment relates, subsection (e) of this section is amended as follows:

(1) by adding at the end of paragraph (1) the following new sentence: "In the case of a termination of the defined benefit plan and the applicable defined contribution plan forming part of an eligible combined plan, the plan administrator shall terminate each such plan separately."; and

(2) by striking paragraph (3) and by redesignating paragraphs (4), (5), and (6) as paragraphs (3), (4), and (5), respectively.

Pub. L. 109–280, title IX, §903(b)(1), (2)(A), (c), Aug. 17, 2006, 120 Stat. 1044, 1048, provided that, applicable to plan years beginning after Dec. 31, 2009, this section is amended as follows:

(1) by amending the section catchline to read as follows: "Multiple employer plans and other special rules"; and

(2) by adding subsection (e) at the end to read as follows:

(e) Special rules for eligible combined defined benefit plans and qualified cash or deferred arrangements

(1) General rule

Except as provided in this subsection, this chapter shall be applied to any defined benefit plan or applicable individual account plan which are part of an eligible combined plan in the same manner as if each such plan were not a part of the eligible combined plan.

(2) Eligible combined plan

For purposes of this subsection—

(A) In general

The term "eligible combined plan" means a plan—

(i) which is maintained by an employer which, at the time the plan is established, is a small employer,

(ii) which consists of a defined benefit plan and an applicable individual account plan each of which qualifies under section 401(a) of title 26,

(iii) the assets of which are held in a single trust forming part of the plan and are clearly identified and allocated to the defined benefit plan and the applicable individual account plan to the extent necessary for the separate application of this chapter under paragraph (1), and

(iv) with respect to which the benefit, contribution, vesting, and nondiscrimination requirements of subparagraphs (B), (C), (D), (E), and (F) are met.

For purposes of this subparagraph, the term "small employer" has the meaning given such term by section 4980D(d)(2) of title 26, except that such section shall be applied by substituting "500" for "50" each place it appears.

(B) Benefit requirements

(i) In general

The benefit requirements of this subparagraph are met with respect to the defined benefit plan forming part of the eligible combined plan if the accrued benefit of each participant derived from employer contributions, when expressed as an annual retirement benefit, is not less than the applicable percentage of the participant's final average pay. For purposes of this clause, final average pay shall be determined using the period of consecutive years (not exceeding 5) during which the participant had the greatest aggregate compensation from the employer.

(ii) Applicable percentage

For purposes of clause (i), the applicable percentage is the lesser of—

(I) 1 percent multiplied by the number of years of service with the employer, or

(II) 20 percent.

(iii) Special rule for applicable defined benefit plans

If the defined benefit plan under clause (i) is an applicable defined benefit plan as defined in section 1053(f)(3)(B) of this title which meets the interest credit requirements of section 1054(b)(5)(B)(i) of this title, the plan shall be treated as meeting the requirements of clause (i) with respect to any plan year if each participant receives pay credit for the year which is not less than the percentage of compensation determined in accordance with the following table:

If the participant's age as of the beginning of the year is—	*The percentage is—*
30 or less	2
Over 30 but less than 40	4
40 or over but less than 50	6
50 or over	8.

(iv) Years of service

For purposes of this subparagraph, years of service shall be determined under the rules of paragraphs (1), (2), and (3) of section 1053(b) of this title, except that the plan may not disregard any year of service because of a participant making, or failing to make, any elective deferral with respect to the qualified cash or deferred arrangement to which subparagraph (C) applies.

(C) Contribution requirements

(i) In general

The contribution requirements of this subparagraph with respect to any applicable individual account plan forming part of an eligible combined plan are met if—

(I) the qualified cash or deferred arrangement included in such plan constitutes an automatic contribution arrangement, and

(II) the employer is required to make matching contributions on behalf of each employee eligible to participate in the arrangement in an amount equal to 50 percent of the elective contributions of the employee to the extent such elective contributions do not exceed 4 percent of compensation.

Rules similar to the rules of clauses (ii) and (iii) of section 401(k)(12)(B) of title 26 shall apply for purposes of this clause.

(ii) Nonelective contributions

An applicable individual account plan shall not be treated as failing to meet the requirements of clause (i) because the employer makes nonelective contributions under the plan but such contributions shall not be taken into account in determining whether the requirements of clause (i)(II) are met.

(D) Vesting requirements

The vesting requirements of this subparagraph are met if—

(i) in the case of a defined benefit plan forming part of an eligible combined plan an employee who has completed at least 3 years of service has a nonforfeitable right to 100 percent of the employee's accrued benefit under the plan derived from employer contributions, and

(ii) in the case of an applicable individual account plan forming part of eligible combined plan—

(I) an employee has a nonforfeitable right to any matching contribution made under the qualified cash or deferred arrangement included in such plan by an employer with respect to any elective contribution, including matching contributions in excess of the contributions required under subparagraph (C)(i)(II), and

(II) an employee who has completed at least 3 years of service has a nonforfeitable right to 100 percent of the employee's accrued benefit derived under the arrangement from nonelective contributions of the employer.

For purposes of this subparagraph, the rules of section 1053 of this title shall apply to the extent not inconsistent with this subparagraph.

(E) Uniform provision of contributions and benefits

In the case of a defined benefit plan or applicable individual account plan forming part of an eligible combined plan, the requirements of this subparagraph are met if all contributions and benefits under each such plan, and all rights and features under each such plan, must be provided uniformly to all participants.

(F) Requirements must be met without taking into account social security and similar contributions and benefits or other plans

(i) In general

The requirements of this subparagraph are met if the requirements of clauses (ii) and (iii) are met.

(ii) Social security and similar contributions

The requirements of this clause are met if—

(I) the requirements of subparagraphs (B) and (C) are met without regard to section 401(l) of title 26, and

(II) the requirements of sections 401(a)(4) and 410(b) of title 26 are met with respect to both the applicable defined contribution plan and defined benefit plan forming part of an eligible combined plan without regard to section 401(l) of title 26.

(iii) Other plans and arrangements

The requirements of this clause are met if the applicable defined contribution plan and defined benefit plan forming part of an eligible combined plan meet the requirements of sections 401(a)(4) and 410(b) of title 26 without being combined with any other plan.

(3) Nondiscrimination requirements for qualified cash or deferred arrangement

(A) In general

A qualified cash or deferred arrangement which is included in an applicable individual account plan forming part of an eligible combined plan shall be treated as meeting the requirements of section 401(k)(3)(A)(ii) of title 26 if the requirements of paragraph (2) are met with respect to such arrangement.

(B) Matching contributions

In applying section 401(m)(11) of title 26 to any matching contribution with respect to a contribution to which paragraph (2)(C) applies, the contribution requirement of paragraph (2)(C) and the notice requirements of paragraph (5)(B) shall be substituted for the requirements otherwise applicable under clauses (i) and (ii) of section 401(m)(11)(A) of title 26.

(4) Automatic contribution arrangement

For purposes of this subsection—

(A) In general

A qualified cash or deferred arrangement shall be treated as an automatic contribution arrangement if the arrangement—

(i) provides that each employee eligible to participate in the arrangement is treated as having elected to have the employer make elective contributions in an amount equal to 4 percent of the employee's compensation unless the employee specifically elects not to have such contributions made or to have such contributions made at a different rate, and

(ii) meets the notice requirements under subparagraph (B).

(B) Notice requirements

(i) In general

The requirements of this subparagraph are met if the requirements of clauses (ii) and (iii) are met.

(ii) Reasonable period to make election

The requirements of this clause are met if each employee to whom subparagraph (A)(i) applies—

(I) receives a notice explaining the employee's right under the arrangement to elect not to have elective contributions made on the employee's behalf or to have the contributions made at a different rate, and

(II) has a reasonable period of time after receipt of such notice and before the first elective contribution is made to make such election.

(iii) Annual notice of rights and obligations

The requirements of this clause are met if each employee eligible to participate in the arrangement is, within a reasonable period before any year, given notice of the employee's rights and obligations under the arrangement.

The requirements of this subparagraph shall not be treated as met unless the requirements of clauses (i) and (ii) of section 401(k)(12)(D) of title 26 are met with respect to the notices described in clauses (ii) and (iii) of this subparagraph.

(5) Coordination with other requirements

(A) Treatment of separate plans

The except clause in section 1002(35) of this title shall not apply to an eligible combined plan.

(B) Reporting

An eligible combined plan shall be treated as a single plan for purposes of section 1023 of this title.

(6) Applicable individual account plan

For purposes of this subsection—

(A) In general

The term "applicable individual account plan" means an individual account plan which includes a qualified cash or deferred arrangement.

(B) Qualified cash or deferred arrangement

The term "qualified cash or deferred arrangement" has the meaning given such term by section 401(k)(2) of title 26.

AMENDMENTS

1989—Subsec. (c). Pub. L. 101–239, §7894(c)(10), substituted "and (e)(3)(C) of such Code" for "and (e)(3)(C) of such code", which for purposes of codification was translated as "and (e)(3)(C) of title 26" thus requiring no change in text.

Pub. L. 101–239, §7891(a)(1), substituted "Internal Revenue Code of 1986" for "Internal Revenue Code of 1954", which for purposes of codification was translated as "title 26" thus requiring no change in text.

EFFECTIVE DATE OF 2008 AMENDMENT

Amendment by Pub. L. 110–458 effective as if included in the provisions of Pub. L. 109–280 to which the amendment relates, except as otherwise provided, see section 112 of Pub. L. 110–458, set out as a note under section 72 of Title 26, Internal Revenue Code.

EFFECTIVE DATE OF 2006 AMENDMENT

Amendment by Pub. L. 109–280 applicable to plan years beginning after Dec. 31, 2009, see section 903(c) of Pub. L. 109–280, set out as a note under section 414 of Title 26, Internal Revenue Code.

EFFECTIVE DATE OF 1989 AMENDMENT

Amendment by section 7891(a)(1) of Pub. L. 101–239 effective, except as otherwise provided, as if included in the provision of the Tax Reform Act of 1986, Pub. L. 99–514, to which such amendment relates, see section 7891(f) of Pub. L. 101–239, set out as a note under section 1002 of this title.

Amendment by section 7894(c)(10) of Pub. L. 101–239 effective, except as otherwise provided, as if originally included in the provision of the Employee Retirement Income Security Act of 1974, Pub. L. 93–406, to which such amendment relates, see section 7894(i) of Pub. L. 101–239, set out as a note under section 1002 of this title.

REGULATIONS

Secretary authorized, effective Sept. 2, 1974, to promulgate regulations wherever provisions of this subchapter call for the promulgation of regulations, see section 1031 of this title.

§1061. Effective dates

(a) Except as otherwise provided in this section, this part shall apply in the case of plan years beginning after September 2, 1974.

(b)(1) Except as otherwise provided in subsection (d) of this section, sections 1055, 1056(d) and 1058 of this title shall apply with respect to plan years beginning after December 31, 1975.

(2) Except as otherwise provided in subsections (c) and (d) of this section in the case of a plan in existence on January 1, 1974, this part shall apply in the case of plan years beginning after December 31, 1975.

(c)(1) In the case of a plan maintained on January 1, 1974, pursuant to one or more agreements which the Secretary finds to be collective bargaining agreements between employee organizations and one or more employers, no plan shall be treated as not meeting the requirements of sections 1054 and 1055 of this title by reason of a supplementary or special plan provision (within the meaning of paragraph (2)) for any plan year before the year which begins after the earlier of—

(A) the date on which the last of such agreements relating to the plan terminates (determined without regard to any extension thereof agreed to after September 2, 1974), or

(B) December 31, 1980.

For purposes of subparagraph (A) and section 1086(c)[1] of this title, any plan amendment made pursuant to a collective bargaining agreement relating to the plan which amends the plan solely to conform to any requirement contained in this chapter or title 26 shall not be treated as a termination of such collective bargaining agreement. This paragraph shall not apply unless the Secretary determines that the participation and vesting rules in effect on September 2, 1974, are not less favorable to participants, in the aggregate, than the rules provided under sections 1052, 1053, and 1054 of this title.

(2) For purposes of paragraph (1), the term "supplementary or special plan provision" means any plan provision which—

(A) provides supplementary benefits, not in excess of one-third of the basic benefit, in the form of an annuity for the life of the participant, or

(B) provides that, under a contractual agreement based on medical evidence as to the effects of working in an adverse environment for an extended period of time, a participant having 25 years of service is to be treated as having 30 years of service.

(3) This subsection shall apply with respect to a plan if (and only if) the application of this subsection results in a later effective date for this part than the effective date required by subsection (b) of this section.

(d) If the administrator of a plan elects under section 1017(d) of this Act to make applicable to a plan year and to all subsequent plan years the provisions of title 26 relating to participation, vesting, funding, and form of benefit, this part shall apply to the first plan year to which such election applies and to all subsequent plan years.

(e)(1) No pension plan to which section 1052 of this title applies may make effective any plan amendment with respect to breaks in service (which amendment is made or becomes effective after January 1, 1974, and before the date on which section 1052 of this title first becomes effective with respect to such plan) which provides that any employee's participation in the plan would commence at any date later than the later of—

(A) the date on which his participation would commence under the break in service rules of section 1052(b) of this title, or

(B) the date on which his participation would commence under the plan as in effect on January 1, 1974.

(2) No pension plan to which section 1053 of this title applies may make effective any plan amendment with respect to breaks in service (which amendment is made or becomes effective after January 1, 1974, and before the date on which section 1053 of this title first becomes effective with respect to such plan) if such amendment provides that the nonforfeitable benefit derived from employer contributions to which any employee would be entitled is less than the lesser of the nonforfeitable benefit derived from employer contributions to which he would be entitled under—

(A) the break in service rules of section 1052(b)(3) of this title, or

(B) the plan as in effect on January 1, 1974.

Subparagraph (B) shall not apply if the break in service rules under the plan would have been in violation of any law or rule of law in effect on January 1, 1974.

(f) The preceding provisions of this section shall not apply with respect to amendments made to this part in provisions enacted after September 2, 1974.

(Pub. L. 93–406, title I, § 211, Sept. 2, 1974, 88 Stat. 867; Pub. L. 99–272, title XI, § 11015(a)(1)(B), Apr. 7, 1986, 100 Stat. 265; Pub. L. 101–239, title VII, §§ 7891(a)(1), 7894(h)(2), Dec. 19, 1989, 103 Stat. 2445, 2451.)

REFERENCES IN TEXT

Section 1086(c) of this title, referred to in subsec. (c)(1), was in the original "section 307(c)", meaning section 307(c) of Pub. L. 93–406, the Employee Retirement Income Security Act of 1974. Section 307(c) was renumbered section 308(c) by Pub. L. 100–203, title IX, § 9341(b)(1), Dec. 22, 1987, 101 Stat. 1330–370.

This chapter, referred to in subsec. (c)(1), was in the original "this Act", meaning Pub. L. 93–406, known as the Employee Retirement Income Security Act of 1974. Titles I, III, and IV of such Act are classified principally to this chapter. For complete classification of this Act to the Code, see Short Title note set out under section 1001 of this title and Tables.

Section 1017(d) of this Act, referred to in subsec. (d), is section 1017 of Pub. L. 93–406, which is set out as an Effective Date; Transitional Rules note under section 410 of Title 26.

AMENDMENTS

1989—Subsecs. (c)(1), (d). Pub. L. 101–239, § 7891(a)(1), substituted "Internal Revenue Code of 1986" for "Internal Revenue Code of 1954", which for purposes of codification was translated as "title 26".

Subsec. (f). Pub. L. 101–239, § 7894(h)(2), added subsec. (f).

1986—Subsec. (c)(1). Pub. L. 99–272 made a technical amendment to the reference to section 1086(c) of this title to reflect the renumbering of the corresponding section of the original act.

EFFECTIVE DATE OF 1989 AMENDMENT

Amendment by section 7891(a)(1) of Pub. L. 101–239 effective, except as otherwise provided, as if included in the provision of the Tax Reform Act of 1986, Pub. L. 99–514, to which such amendment relates, see section 7891(f) of Pub. L. 101–239, set out as a note under section 1002 of this title.

Amendment by section 7894(h)(2) of Pub. L. 101–239 effective, except as otherwise provided, as if originally included in the provision of the Employee Retirement Income Security Act of 1974, Pub. L. 93–406, to which such amendment relates, see section 7894(i) of Pub. L. 101–239, set out as a note under section 1002 of this title.

EFFECTIVE DATE OF 1986 AMENDMENT

Amendment by Pub. L. 99–272 applicable with respect to applications for waivers, extensions, and modifications filed on or after Apr. 7, 1986, see section 11015(a)(3) of Pub. L. 99–272, set out as an Effective Date note under section 412 of Title 26, Internal Revenue Code.

PART 3—FUNDING

§ 1081. Coverage

(a) Plans excepted from applicability of this part

This part shall apply to any employee pension benefit plan described in section 1003(a) of this

[1] See References in Text note below.

title, (and not exempted under section 1003(b) of this title), other than—

(1) an employee welfare benefit plan;

(2) an insurance contract plan described in subsection (b) of this section;

(3) a plan which is unfunded and is maintained by an employer primarily for the purpose of providing deferred compensation for a select group of management or highly compensated employees;

(4)(A) a plan which is established and maintained by a society, order, or association described in section 501(c)(8) or (9) of title 26, if no part of the contributions to or under such plan are made by employers of participants in such plan; or

(B) a trust described in section 501(c)(18) of title 26;

(5) a plan which has not at any time after September 2, 1974, provided for employer contributions;

(6) an agreement providing payments to a retired partner or deceased partner or a deceased partner's successor in interest as described in section 736 of title 26;

(7) an individual retirement account or annuity as described in section 408(a) of title 26, or a retirement bond described in section 409 of title 26 (as effective for obligations issued before January 1, 1984);

(8) an individual account plan (other than a money purchase plan) and a defined benefit plan to the extent it is treated as an individual account plan (other than a money purchase plan) under section 1002(35)(B) of this title;

(9) an excess benefit plan; or

(10) any plan, fund or program under which an employer, all of whose stock is directly or indirectly owned by employees, former employees or their beneficiaries, proposes through an unfunded arrangement to compensate retired employees for benefits which were forfeited by such employees under a pension plan maintained by a former employer prior to the date such pension plan became subject to this chapter.

(b) "Insurance contract plan" defined

For the purposes of paragraph (2) of subsection (a) of this section a plan is an "insurance contract plan" if—

(1) the plan is funded exclusively by the purchase of individual insurance contracts,

(2) such contracts provide for level annual premium payments to be paid extending not later than the retirement age for each individual participating in the plan, and commencing with the date the individual became a participant in the plan (or, in the case of an increase in benefits, commencing at the time such increase became effective),

(3) benefits provided by the plan are equal to the benefits provided under each contract at normal retirement age under the plan and are guaranteed by an insurance carrier (licensed under the laws of a State to do business with the plan) to the extent premiums have been paid,

(4) premiums payable for the plan year, and all prior plan years under such contracts have been paid before lapse or there is reinstatement of the policy,

(5) no rights under such contracts have been subject to a security interest at any time during the plan year, and

(6) no policy loans are outstanding at any time during the plan year.

A plan funded exclusively by the purchase of group insurance contracts which is determined under regulations prescribed by the Secretary of the Treasury to have the same characteristics as contracts described in the preceding sentence shall be treated as a plan described in this subsection.

(c) Applicability of this part to terminated multiemployer plans

This part applies, with respect to a terminated multiemployer plan to which section 1321 of this title applies, until the last day of the plan year in which the plan terminates, within the meaning of section 1341a(a)(2) of this title.

(Pub. L. 93–406, title I, §301, Sept. 2, 1974, 88 Stat. 868; Pub. L. 96–364, title III, §304(a), title IV, §411(b), Sept. 26, 1980, 94 Stat. 1293, 1308; Pub. L. 101–239, title VII, §§7891(a)(1), 7894(d)(1)(A), (4)(A), Dec. 19, 1989, 103 Stat. 2445, 2449; Pub. L. 109–280, title II, §201(c)(1), Aug. 17, 2006, 120 Stat. 868.)

REFERENCES IN TEXT

Section 409 of title 26, referred to in subsec. (a)(7), means section 409 of Title 26, Internal Revenue Code, prior to its repeal by Pub. L. 98–369, div. A, title IV, §491(b), July 18, 1984, 98 Stat. 848, applicable to obligations issued after Dec. 31, 1983.

This chapter, referred to in subsec. (a)(10), was in the original "this Act", meaning Pub. L. 93–406, known as the Employee Retirement Income Security Act of 1974. Titles I, III, and IV of such Act are classified principally to this chapter. For complete classification of this Act to the Code, see Short Title note set out under section 1001 of this title and Tables.

AMENDMENTS

2006—Subsec. (d). Pub. L. 109–280 struck out heading and text of subsec. (d). Text read as follows: "Any amount of any financial assistance from the Pension Benefit Guaranty Corporation to any plan, and any repayment of such amount, shall be taken into account under this section in such manner as determined by the Secretary of the Treasury."

1989—Subsec. (a)(4)(A), (6). Pub. L. 101–239, §7891(a)(1), substituted "Internal Revenue Code of 1986" for "Internal Revenue Code of 1954", which for purposes of codification was translated as "title 26" thus requiring no change in text.

Subsec. (a)(7). Pub. L. 101–239, §7894(d)(4)(A), substituted "section 409 of title 26 (as effective for obligations issued before January 1, 1984)" for "section 409 of title 26".

Subsec. (a)(8). Pub. L. 101–239, §7894(d)(1)(A)(i), struck out "or" after semicolon at end.

Subsec. (a)(9). Pub. L. 101–239, §7894(d)(1)(A)(ii), substituted "; or" for period at end.

Subsec. (a)(10). Pub. L. 101–239, §7894(d)(1)(A)(iii), substituted "any" for "Any".

1980—Subsec. (a)(10). Pub. L. 96–364, §411(b), added par. (10).

Subsecs. (c), (d). Pub. L. 96–364, §304(a), added subsecs. (c) and (d).

EFFECTIVE DATE OF 2006 AMENDMENT

Pub. L. 109–280, title II, §201(d), Aug. 17, 2006, 120 Stat. 868, provided that:

"(1) IN GENERAL.—The amendments made by this section [enacting section 1084 of this title and amending this section] shall apply to plan years beginning after 2007.

"(2) SPECIAL RULE FOR CERTAIN AMORTIZATION EXTENSIONS.—If the Secretary of the Treasury grants an extension under section 304 of the Employee Retirement Income Security Act of 1974 [29 U.S.C. 1084] and section 412(e) of the Internal Revenue Code of 1986 [former 26 U.S.C. 412(e)] with respect to any application filed with the Secretary of the Treasury on or before June 30, 2005, the extension (and any modification thereof) shall be applied and administered under the rules of such sections as in effect before the enactment of this Act [Aug. 17, 2006], including the use of the rate of interest determined under section 6621(b) of such Code [26 U.S.C. 6621(b)]."

EFFECTIVE DATE OF 1989 AMENDMENT

Amendment by section 7891(a)(1) of Pub. L. 101–239 effective, except as otherwise provided, as if included in the provision of the Tax Reform Act of 1986, Pub. L. 99–514, to which such amendment relates, see section 7891(f) of Pub. L. 101–239, set out as a note under section 1002 of this title.

Section 7894(d)(1)(B) of Pub. L. 101–239 provided that: "The amendments made by subparagraph (A) [amending this section] shall take effect as if included in section 411 of the Multiemployer Pension Plan Amendments Act of 1980 [Pub. L. 96–364]."

Section 7894(d)(4)(B) of Pub. L. 101–239 provided that: "The amendment made by subparagraph (A) [amending this section] shall take effect as if originally included in section 491(b) of Public Law 98–369."

EFFECTIVE DATE OF 1980 AMENDMENT

Amendment by Pub. L. 96–364 effective Sept. 26, 1980, except as specifically provided, see section 1461(e) of this title.

REGULATIONS

Secretary authorized, effective Sept. 2, 1974, to promulgate regulations wherever provisions of this subchapter call for the promulgation of regulations, see section 1031 of this title.

SPECIAL RULE FOR CERTAIN BENEFITS FUNDED UNDER AN AGREEMENT APPROVED BY THE PENSION BENEFIT GUARANTY CORPORATION

For applicability of amendment by Pub. L. 109–280 to a multiemployer plan that is a party to an agreement that was approved by the Pension Benefit Guaranty Corporation prior to June 30, 2005, and that increases benefits and provides for certain withdrawal liability rules, see section 206 of Pub. L. 109–280, set out as a note under section 412 of Title 26, Internal Revenue Code.

§ 1082. Minimum funding standards

(a) Requirement to meet minimum funding standard

(1) In general

A plan to which this part applies shall satisfy the minimum funding standard applicable to the plan for any plan year.

(2) Minimum funding standard

For purposes of paragraph (1), a plan shall be treated as satisfying the minimum funding standard for a plan year if—

(A) in the case of a defined benefit plan which is a single-employer plan, the employer makes contributions to or under the plan for the plan year which, in the aggregate, are not less than the minimum required contribution determined under section 1083 of this title for the plan for the plan year,

(B) in the case of a money purchase plan which is a single-employer plan, the employer makes contributions to or under the plan for the plan year which are required under the terms of the plan, and

(C) in the case of a multiemployer plan, the employers make contributions to or under the plan for any plan year which, in the aggregate, are sufficient to ensure that the plan does not have an accumulated funding deficiency under section 1084 of this title as of the end of the plan year.

(b) Liability for contributions

(1) In general

Except as provided in paragraph (2), the amount of any contribution required by this section (including any required installments under paragraphs (3) and (4) of section 1083(j) of this title) shall be paid by the employer responsible for making contributions to or under the plan.

(2) Joint and several liability where employer member of controlled group

If the employer referred to in paragraph (1) is a member of a controlled group, each member of such group shall be jointly and severally liable for payment of such contributions.

(3) Multiemployer plans in critical status

Paragraph (1) shall not apply in the case of a multiemployer plan for any plan year in which the plan is in critical status pursuant to section 1085 of this title. This paragraph shall only apply if the plan sponsor adopts a rehabilitation plan in accordance with section 1085(e) of this title and complies with the terms of such rehabilitation plan (and any updates or modifications of the plan).

(c) Variance from minimum funding standards

(1) Waiver in case of business hardship

(A) In general

If—

(i) an employer is (or in the case of a multiemployer plan, 10 percent or more of the number of employers contributing to or under the plan are) unable to satisfy the minimum funding standard for a plan year without temporary substantial business hardship (substantial business hardship in the case of a multiemployer plan), and

(ii) application of the standard would be adverse to the interests of plan participants in the aggregate,

the Secretary of the Treasury may, subject to subparagraph (C), waive the requirements of subsection (a) for such year with respect to all or any portion of the minimum funding standard. The Secretary of the Treasury shall not waive the minimum funding standard with respect to a plan for more than 3 of any 15 (5 of any 15 in the case of a multiemployer plan) consecutive plan years.

(B) Effects of waiver

If a waiver is granted under subparagraph (A) for any plan year—

(i) in the case of a single-employer plan, the minimum required contribution under section 1083 of this title for the plan year shall be reduced by the amount of the waived funding deficiency and such amount shall be amortized as required under section 1083(e) of this title, and

(ii) in the case of a multiemployer plan, the funding standard account shall be credited under section 1084(b)(3)(C) of this title with the amount of the waived funding deficiency and such amount shall be amortized as required under section 1084(b)(2)(C) of this title.

(C) Waiver of amortized portion not allowed

The Secretary of the Treasury may not waive under subparagraph (A) any portion of the minimum funding standard under subsection (a) for a plan year which is attributable to any waived funding deficiency for any preceding plan year.

(2) Determination of business hardship

For purposes of this subsection, the factors taken into account in determining temporary substantial business hardship (substantial business hardship in the case of a multiemployer plan) shall include (but shall not be limited to) whether or not—

(A) the employer is operating at an economic loss,

(B) there is substantial unemployment or underemployment in the trade or business and in the industry concerned,

(C) the sales and profits of the industry concerned are depressed or declining, and

(D) it is reasonable to expect that the plan will be continued only if the waiver is granted.

(3) Waived funding deficiency

For purposes of this part, the term "waived funding deficiency" means the portion of the minimum funding standard under subsection (a) (determined without regard to the waiver) for a plan year waived by the Secretary of the Treasury and not satisfied by employer contributions.

(4) Security for waivers for single-employer plans, consultations

(A) Security may be required

(i) In general

Except as provided in subparagraph (C), the Secretary of the Treasury may require an employer maintaining a defined benefit plan which is a single-employer plan (within the meaning of section 1301(a)(15) of this title) to provide security to such plan as a condition for granting or modifying a waiver under paragraph (1).

(ii) Special rules

Any security provided under clause (i) may be perfected and enforced only by the Pension Benefit Guaranty Corporation, or at the direction of the Corporation, by a contributing sponsor (within the meaning of section 1301(a)(13) of this title), or a member of such sponsor's controlled group (within the meaning of section 1301(a)(14) of this title).

(B) Consultation with the Pension Benefit Guaranty Corporation

Except as provided in subparagraph (C), the Secretary of the Treasury shall, before granting or modifying a waiver under this subsection with respect to a plan described in subparagraph (A)(i)—

(i) provide the Pension Benefit Guaranty Corporation with—

(I) notice of the completed application for any waiver or modification, and

(II) an opportunity to comment on such application within 30 days after receipt of such notice, and

(ii) consider—

(I) any comments of the Corporation under clause (i)(II), and

(II) any views of any employee organization (within the meaning of section 1002(4) of this title) representing participants in the plan which are submitted in writing to the Secretary of the Treasury in connection with such application.

Information provided to the Corporation under this subparagraph shall be considered tax return information and subject to the safeguarding and reporting requirements of section 6103(p) of title 26.

(C) Exception for certain waivers

(i) In general

The preceding provisions of this paragraph shall not apply to any plan with respect to which the sum of—

(I) the aggregate unpaid minimum required contributions for the plan year and all preceding plan years, and

(II) the present value of all waiver amortization installments determined for the plan year and succeeding plan years under section 1083(e)(2) of this title,

is less than $1,000,000.

(ii) Treatment of waivers for which applications are pending

The amount described in clause (i)(I) shall include any increase in such amount which would result if all applications for waivers of the minimum funding standard under this subsection which are pending with respect to such plan were denied.

(iii) Unpaid minimum required contribution

For purposes of this subparagraph—

(I) In general

The term "unpaid minimum required contribution" means, with respect to any plan year, any minimum required contribution under section 1083 of this title for the plan year which is not paid on or before the due date (as determined under section 1083(j)(1) of this title) for the plan year.

(II) Ordering rule

For purposes of subclause (I), any payment to or under a plan for any plan year shall be allocated first to unpaid minimum required contributions for all preceding plan years on a first-in, first-out basis and then to the minimum required contribution under section 1083 of this title for the plan year.

(5) Special rules for single-employer plans

(A) Application must be submitted before date 2½ months after close of year

In the case of a single-employer plan, no waiver may be granted under this subsection with respect to any plan for any plan year unless an application therefor is submitted to the Secretary of the Treasury not later than the 15th day of the 3rd month beginning after the close of such plan year.

(B) Special rule if employer is member of controlled group

In the case of a single-employer plan, if an employer is a member of a controlled group, the temporary substantial business hardship requirements of paragraph (1) shall be treated as met only if such requirements are met—

(i) with respect to such employer, and

(ii) with respect to the controlled group of which such employer is a member (determined by treating all members of such group as a single employer).

The Secretary of the Treasury may provide that an analysis of a trade or business or industry of a member need not be conducted if such Secretary determines such analysis is not necessary because the taking into account of such member would not significantly affect the determination under this paragraph.

(6) Advance notice

(A) In general

The Secretary of the Treasury shall, before granting a waiver under this subsection, require each applicant to provide evidence satisfactory to such Secretary that the applicant has provided notice of the filing of the application for such waiver to each affected party (as defined in section 1301(a)(21) of this title). Such notice shall include a description of the extent to which the plan is funded for benefits which are guaranteed under subchapter III and for benefit liabilities.

(B) Consideration of relevant information

The Secretary of the Treasury shall consider any relevant information provided by a person to whom notice was given under subparagraph (A).

(7) Restriction on plan amendments

(A) In general

No amendment of a plan which increases the liabilities of the plan by reason of any increase in benefits, any change in the accrual of benefits, or any change in the rate at which benefits become nonforfeitable under the plan shall be adopted if a waiver under this subsection or an extension of time under section 1084(d) of this title is in effect with respect to the plan, or if a plan amendment described in subsection (d)(2) which reduces the accrued benefit of any participant has been made at any time in the preceding 12 months (24 months in the case of a multiemployer plan). If a plan is amended in violation of the preceding sentence, any such waiver, or extension of time, shall not apply to any plan year ending on or after the date on which such amendment is adopted.

(B) Exception

Subparagraph (A) shall not apply to any plan amendment which—

(i) the Secretary of the Treasury determines to be reasonable and which provides for only de minimis increases in the liabilities of the plan,

(ii) only repeals an amendment described in subsection (d)(2), or

(iii) is required as a condition of qualification under part I of subchapter D of chapter 1 of title 26.

(8) Cross reference

For corresponding duties of the Secretary of the Treasury with regard to implementation of title 26, see section 412(c) of title 26.

(d) Miscellaneous rules

(1) Change in method or year

If the funding method or a plan year for a plan is changed, the change shall take effect only if approved by the Secretary of the Treasury.

(2) Certain retroactive plan amendments

For purposes of this section, any amendment applying to a plan year which—

(A) is adopted after the close of such plan year but no later than 2½ months after the close of the plan year (or, in the case of a multiemployer plan, no later than 2 years after the close of such plan year),

(B) does not reduce the accrued benefit of any participant determined as of the beginning of the first plan year to which the amendment applies, and

(C) does not reduce the accrued benefit of any participant determined as of the time of adoption except to the extent required by the circumstances,

shall, at the election of the plan administrator, be deemed to have been made on the first day of such plan year. No amendment described in this paragraph which reduces the accrued benefits of any participant shall take effect unless the plan administrator files a notice with the Secretary of the Treasury notifying him of such amendment and such Secretary has approved such amendment, or within 90 days after the date on which such notice was filed, failed to disapprove such amendment. No amendment described in this subsection shall be approved by the Secretary of the Treasury unless such Secretary determines that such amendment is necessary because of a temporary substantial business hardship (as determined under subsection (c)(2)) or a substantial business hardship (as so determined) in the case of a multiemployer plan and that a waiver under subsection (c) (or, in the case of a multiemployer plan, any extension of the amortization period under section 1084(d) of this title) is unavailable or inadequate.

(3) Controlled group

For purposes of this section, the term "controlled group" means any group treated as a single employer under subsection (b), (c), (m), or (*o*) of section 414 of title 26.

(Pub. L. 93–406, title I, § 302, as added and amended Pub. L. 109–280, title I, § 101(b), title II, § 202(d), Aug. 17, 2006, 120 Stat. 784, 885; Pub. L. 110–458, title I, §§ 101(a)(1), 102(b)(1)(A), Dec. 23, 2008, 122 Stat. 5093, 5100.)

AMENDMENT OF SECTION

For termination of amendment by section 221(c) of Pub. L. 109–280, see Effective and Termination Dates of 2006 Amendment note below.

PRIOR PROVISIONS

A prior section 1082, Pub. L. 93–406, title I, § 302, Sept. 2, 1974, 88 Stat. 869; Pub. L. 96–364, title III, § 304(b), Sept. 26, 1980, 94 Stat. 1293; Pub. L. 100–203, title IX, §§ 9301(b), 9303(b), (d)(2), 9304(a)(2), (b)(2), (e)(2), 9305(b)(2), 9307(a)(2), (b)(2), (e)(2), Dec. 22, 1987, 101 Stat. 1330–332, 1330–337, 1330–342, 1330–344, 1330–346, 1330–349, 1330–352, 1330–356 to 1330–358; Pub. L. 100–647, title II, § 2005(a)(2)(B), (d)(2), Nov. 10, 1988, 102 Stat. 3610, 3612; Pub. L. 101–239, title VII, §§ 7881(a)(1)(B), (2)(B), (3)(B), (4)(B), (5)(B), (6)(B), (b)(1)(B), (2)(B), (3)(B), (4)(B), (6)(B)(i), (d)(1)(B), (2), (4), 7891(a)(1), 7892(b), 7894(d)(2), (5), Dec. 19, 1989, 103 Stat. 2435–2439, 2445, 2447, 2449, 2450; Pub. L. 101–508, title XII, § 12012(c), Nov. 5, 1990, 104 Stat. 1388–572; Pub. L. 103–465, title VII, §§ 761(a)(1)–(9)(A), (10), 762(a), 763(a), 764(a), 768(b), Dec. 8, 1994, 108 Stat. 5024–5031, 5033–5036, 5041; Pub. L. 105–34, title XV, § 1521(b), (c)(2), (3)(B), title XVI, § 1604(b)(2)(B), Aug. 5, 1997, 111 Stat. 1069, 1070, 1097; Pub. L. 107–16, title VI, §§ 651(b), 661(b), June 7, 2001, 115 Stat. 129, 142; Pub. L. 107–147, title IV, §§ 405(b), 411(v)(2), Mar. 9, 2002, 116 Stat. 42, 52; Pub. L. 108–218, title I, §§ 101(a)(1)–(3), 102(a), 104(a)(1), Apr. 10, 2004, 118 Stat. 596, 597, 599, 604; Pub. L. 109–135, title IV, § 412(x)(2), Dec. 21, 2005, 119 Stat. 2638; Pub. L. 109–280, title III, § 301(a)(1), (2), Aug. 17, 2006, 120 Stat. 919, related to minimum funding standards, prior to repeal by Pub. L. 109–280, title I, § 101(a), (d), Aug. 17, 2006, 120 Stat. 784, 789, applicable to plan years beginning after 2007.

AMENDMENTS

2008—Subsec. (b)(3). Pub. L. 110–458, § 102(b)(1)(A), substituted "the plan sponsor adopts" for "the plan adopts".

Subsec. (c)(1)(A)(i). Pub. L. 110–458, § 101(a)(1)(A), substituted "the plan are" for "the plan is".

Subsec. (c)(7)(A). Pub. L. 110–458, § 101(a)(1)(B), inserted "which reduces the accrued benefit of any participant" after "subsection (d)(2)".

Subsec. (d)(1). Pub. L. 110–458, § 101(a)(1)(C), struck out ", the valuation date," after "funding method".

2006—Subsec. (b)(3). Pub. L. 109–280, §§ 202(d), 221(c), temporarily added par. (3). See Effective and Termination Dates of 2006 Amendment note below.

EFFECTIVE DATE OF 2008 AMENDMENT

Amendment by Pub. L. 110–458 effective as if included in the provisions of Pub. L. 109–280 to which the amendment relates, except as otherwise provided, see section 112 of Pub. L. 110–458, set out as a note under section 72 of Title 26, Internal Revenue Code.

EFFECTIVE AND TERMINATION DATES OF 2006 AMENDMENT

Pub. L. 109–280, title II, § 202(f), Aug. 17, 2006, 120 Stat. 885, provided that:

"(1) IN GENERAL.—The amendments made by this section [enacting section 1085 of this title and amending this section and section 1132 of this title] shall apply with respect to plan years beginning after 2007.

"(2) SPECIAL RULE FOR CERTAIN NOTICES.—In any case in which a plan's actuary certifies that it is reasonably expected that a multiemployer plan will be in critical status under section 305(b)(3) of the Employee Retirement Income Security Act of 1974 [29 U.S.C. 1085(b)(3)], as added by this section, with respect to the first plan year beginning after 2007, the notice required under subparagraph (D) of such section may be provided at any time after the date of enactment [Aug. 17, 2006], so long as it is provided on or before the last date for providing the notice under such subparagraph.

"(3) SPECIAL RULE FOR CERTAIN RESTORED BENEFITS.—In the case of a multiemployer plan—

"(A) with respect to which benefits were reduced pursuant to a plan amendment adopted on or after January 1, 2002, and before June 30, 2005, and

"(B) which, pursuant to the plan document, the trust agreement, or a formal written communication from the plan sponsor to participants provided before June 30, 2005, provided for the restoration of such benefits,

the amendments made by this section shall not apply to such benefit restorations to the extent that any restriction on the providing or accrual of such benefits would otherwise apply by reason of such amendments."

Amendment by section 202(d) of Pub. L. 109–280 inapplicable to plan years beginning after Dec. 31, 2014, with exception for certain funding improvement and rehabilitation plans, see section 221(c) of Pub. L. 109–280, set out as a note under section 412 of Title 26, Internal Revenue Code.

EFFECTIVE DATE

Pub. L. 109–280, title I, § 101(d), Aug. 17, 2006, 120 Stat. 789, provided that: "The amendments made by this section [enacting this section and repealing former section 1082 of this title and sections 1083 to 1085, 1085a, 1085b, and 1086 of this title] shall apply to plan years beginning after 2007."

REGULATIONS

Secretary authorized, effective Sept. 2, 1974, to promulgate regulations wherever provisions of this subchapter call for the promulgation of regulations, see section 1031 of this title.

APPLICABILITY OF AMENDMENTS BY SUBTITLES A AND B OF TITLE I OF PUB. L. 109–280

For special rules on applicability of amendments by subtitles A (§§ 101–107) and B (§§ 111–116) of title I of Pub. L. 109–280 to certain eligible cooperative plans, PBGC settlement plans, and eligible government contractor plans, see sections 104, 105, and 106 of Pub. L. 109–280, set out as notes under section 401 of Title 26, Internal Revenue Code.

SPECIAL RULE FOR CERTAIN BENEFITS FUNDED UNDER AN AGREEMENT APPROVED BY THE PENSION BENEFIT GUARANTY CORPORATION

For applicability of amendment by section 202(d) of Pub. L. 109–280 to a multiemployer plan that is a party to an agreement that was approved by the Pension Benefit Guaranty Corporation prior to June 30, 2005, and that increases benefits and provides for certain withdrawal liability rules, see section 206 of Pub. L. 109–280, set out as a note under section 412 of Title 26, Internal Revenue Code.

§ 1083. Minimum funding standards for single-employer defined benefit pension plans

(a) Minimum required contribution

For purposes of this section and section 1082(a)(2)(A) of this title, except as provided in subsection (f), the term "minimum required contribution" means, with respect to any plan year of a single-employer plan—

(1) in any case in which the value of plan assets of the plan (as reduced under subsection (f)(4)(B)) is less than the funding target of the plan for the plan year, the sum of—

(A) the target normal cost of the plan for the plan year,

(B) the shortfall amortization charge (if any) for the plan for the plan year determined under subsection (c), and

(C) the waiver amortization charge (if any) for the plan for the plan year as determined under subsection (e); or

(2) in any case in which the value of plan assets of the plan (as reduced under subsection (f)(4)(B)) equals or exceeds the funding target of the plan for the plan year, the target normal cost of the plan for the plan year reduced (but not below zero) by such excess.

(b) Target normal cost

For purposes of this section:

(1) In general

Except as provided in subsection (i)(2) with respect to plans in at-risk status, the term "target normal cost" means, for any plan year, the excess of—

(A) the sum of—

(i) the present value of all benefits which are expected to accrue or to be earned under the plan during the plan year, plus

(ii) the amount of plan-related expenses expected to be paid from plan assets during the plan year, over

(B) the amount of mandatory employee contributions expected to be made during the plan year.

(2) Special rule for increase in compensation

For purposes of this subsection, if any benefit attributable to services performed in a preceding plan year is increased by reason of any increase in compensation during the current plan year, the increase in such benefit shall be treated as having accrued during the current plan year.

(c) Shortfall amortization charge

(1) In general

For purposes of this section, the shortfall amortization charge for a plan for any plan year is the aggregate total (not less than zero) of the shortfall amortization installments for such plan year with respect to the shortfall amortization bases for such plan year and each of the 6 preceding plan years.

(2) Shortfall amortization installment

For purposes of paragraph (1)—

(A) Determination

The shortfall amortization installments are the amounts necessary to amortize the shortfall amortization base of the plan for any plan year in level annual installments over the 7-plan-year period beginning with such plan year.

(B) Shortfall installment

The shortfall amortization installment for any plan year in the 7-plan-year period under subparagraph (A) with respect to any shortfall amortization base is the annual installment determined under subparagraph (A) for that year for that base.

(C) Segment rates

In determining any shortfall amortization installment under this paragraph, the plan sponsor shall use the segment rates determined under subparagraph (C) of subsection (h)(2), applied under rules similar to the rules of subparagraph (B) of subsection (h)(2).

(3) Shortfall amortization base

For purposes of this section, the shortfall amortization base of a plan for a plan year is—

(A) the funding shortfall of such plan for such plan year, minus

(B) the present value (determined using the segment rates determined under subparagraph (C) of subsection (h)(2), applied under rules similar to the rules of subparagraph (B) of subsection (h)(2)) of the aggregate total of the shortfall amortization installments and waiver amortization installments which have been determined for such plan year and any succeeding plan year with respect to the shortfall amortization bases and waiver amortization bases of the plan for any plan year preceding such plan year.

(4) Funding shortfall

For purposes of this section, the funding shortfall of a plan for any plan year is the excess (if any) of—

(A) the funding target of the plan for the plan year, over

(B) the value of plan assets of the plan (as reduced under subsection (f)(4)(B)) for the plan year which are held by the plan on the valuation date.

(5) Exemption from new shortfall amortization base

(A) In general

In any case in which the value of plan assets of the plan (as reduced under subsection (f)(4)(A)) is equal to or greater than the funding target of the plan for the plan year, the shortfall amortization base of the plan for such plan year shall be zero.

(B) Transition rule

(i) In general

Except as provided in clause (iii), in the case of plan years beginning after 2007 and before 2011, only the applicable percentage of the funding target shall be taken into account under paragraph (3)(A) in determining the funding shortfall for purposes of paragraph (3)(A) and subparagraph (A).

(ii) Applicable percentage

For purposes of subparagraph (A), the applicable percentage shall be determined in accordance with the following table:

In the case of a plan year beginning in calendar year:	The applicable percentage is
2008	92
2009	94
2010	96.

(iii) Transition relief not available for new or deficit reduction plans

Clause (i) shall not apply to a plan—

(I) which was not in effect for a plan year beginning in 2007, or

(II) which was in effect for a plan year beginning in 2007 and which was subject to section 1082(d) of this title (as in effect for plan years beginning in 2007) for such year, determined after the application of paragraphs (6) and (9) thereof.

(6) Early deemed amortization upon attainment of funding target

In any case in which the funding shortfall of a plan for a plan year is zero, for purposes of determining the shortfall amortization charge for such plan year and succeeding plan years, the shortfall amortization bases for all preceding plan years (and all shortfall amortization installments determined with respect to such bases) shall be reduced to zero.

(d) Rules relating to funding target

For purposes of this section—

(1) Funding target

Except as provided in subsection (i)(1) with respect to plans in at-risk status, the funding target of a plan for a plan year is the present value of all benefits accrued or earned under the plan as of the beginning of the plan year.

(2) Funding target attainment percentage

The "funding target attainment percentage" of a plan for a plan year is the ratio (expressed as a percentage) which—

(A) the value of plan assets for the plan year (as reduced under subsection (f)(4)(B)), bears to

(B) the funding target of the plan for the plan year (determined without regard to subsection (i)(1)).

(e) Waiver amortization charge

(1) Determination of waiver amortization charge

The waiver amortization charge (if any) for a plan for any plan year is the aggregate total of the waiver amortization installments for such plan year with respect to the waiver amortization bases for each of the 5 preceding plan years.

(2) Waiver amortization installment

For purposes of paragraph (1)—

(A) Determination

The waiver amortization installments are the amounts necessary to amortize the waiver amortization base of the plan for any plan year in level annual installments over a period of 5 plan years beginning with the succeeding plan year.

(B) Waiver installment

The waiver amortization installment for any plan year in the 5-year period under subparagraph (A) with respect to any waiver amortization base is the annual installment determined under subparagraph (A) for that year for that base.

(3) Interest rate

In determining any waiver amortization installment under this subsection, the plan sponsor shall use the segment rates determined under subparagraph (C) of subsection (h)(2), applied under rules similar to the rules of subparagraph (B) of subsection (h)(2).

(4) Waiver amortization base

The waiver amortization base of a plan for a plan year is the amount of the waived funding deficiency (if any) for such plan year under section 1082(c) of this title.

(5) Early deemed amortization upon attainment of funding target

In any case in which the funding shortfall of a plan for a plan year is zero, for purposes of determining the waiver amortization charge for such plan year and succeeding plan years, the waiver amortization bases for all preceding plan years (and all waiver amortization installments determined with respect to such bases) shall be reduced to zero.

(f) Reduction of minimum required contribution by prefunding balance and funding standard carryover balance

(1) Election to maintain balances

(A) Prefunding balance

The plan sponsor of a single-employer plan may elect to maintain a prefunding balance.

(B) Funding standard carryover balance

(i) In general

In the case of a single-employer plan described in clause (ii), the plan sponsor may elect to maintain a funding standard carryover balance, until such balance is reduced to zero.

(ii) Plans maintaining funding standard account in 2007

A plan is described in this clause if the plan—

(I) was in effect for a plan year beginning in 2007, and

(II) had a positive balance in the funding standard account under section 1082(b) of this title as in effect for such plan year and determined as of the end of such plan year.

(2) Application of balances

A prefunding balance and a funding standard carryover balance maintained pursuant to this paragraph—

(A) shall be available for crediting against the minimum required contribution, pursuant to an election under paragraph (3),

(B) shall be applied as a reduction in the amount treated as the value of plan assets for purposes of this section, to the extent provided in paragraph (4), and

(C) may be reduced at any time, pursuant to an election under paragraph (5).

(3) Election to apply balances against minimum required contribution

(A) In general

Except as provided in subparagraphs (B) and (C), in the case of any plan year in which the plan sponsor elects to credit against the minimum required contribution for the current plan year all or a portion of the prefunding balance or the funding standard carryover balance for the current plan year (not in excess of such minimum required contribution), the minimum required contribution for the plan year shall be reduced as of the first day of the plan year by the amount so credited by the plan sponsor. For purposes of the preceding sentence, the minimum required contribution shall be determined after taking into account any waiver under section 1082(c) of this title.

(B) Coordination with funding standard carryover balance

To the extent that any plan has a funding standard carryover balance greater than zero, no amount of the prefunding balance of such plan may be credited under this paragraph in reducing the minimum required contribution.

(C) Limitation for underfunded plans

The preceding provisions of this paragraph shall not apply for any plan year if the ratio (expressed as a percentage) which—

(i) the value of plan assets for the preceding plan year (as reduced under paragraph (4)(C)), bears to

(ii) the funding target of the plan for the preceding plan year (determined without regard to subsection (i)(1)),

is less than 80 percent. In the case of plan years beginning in 2008, the ratio under this subparagraph may be determined using such methods of estimation as the Secretary of the Treasury may prescribe.

(4) Effect of balances on amounts treated as value of plan assets

In the case of any plan maintaining a prefunding balance or a funding standard carryover balance pursuant to this subsection, the amount treated as the value of plan assets shall be deemed to be such amount, reduced as provided in the following subparagraphs:

(A) Applicability of shortfall amortization base

For purposes of subsection (c)(5), the value of plan assets is deemed to be such amount, reduced by the amount of the prefunding balance, but only if an election under paragraph (3) applying any portion of the prefunding balance in reducing the minimum required contribution is in effect for the plan year.

(B) Determination of excess assets, funding shortfall, and funding target attainment percentage

(i) In general

For purposes of subsections (a), (c)(4)(B), and (d)(2)(A), the value of plan assets is deemed to be such amount, reduced by the amount of the prefunding balance and the funding standard carryover balance.

(ii) Special rule for certain binding agreements with PBGC

For purposes of subsection (c)(4)(B), the value of plan assets shall not be deemed to be reduced for a plan year by the amount of the specified balance if, with respect to such balance, there is in effect for a plan year a binding written agreement with the Pension Benefit Guaranty Corporation which provides that such balance is not available to reduce the minimum required contribution for the plan year. For purposes of the preceding sentence, the term "specified balance" means the prefunding balance or the funding standard carryover balance, as the case may be.

(C) Availability of balances in plan year for crediting against minimum required contribution

For purposes of paragraph (3)(C)(i) of this subsection, the value of plan assets is deemed to be such amount, reduced by the amount of the prefunding balance.

(5) Election to reduce balance prior to determinations of value of plan assets and crediting against minimum required contribution

(A) In general

The plan sponsor may elect to reduce by any amount the balance of the prefunding balance and the funding standard carryover balance for any plan year (but not below zero). Such reduction shall be effective prior to any determination of the value of plan assets for such plan year under this section and application of the balance in reducing the minimum required contribution for such plan for such plan year pursuant to an election under paragraph (2).

(B) Coordination between prefunding balance and funding standard carryover balance

To the extent that any plan has a funding standard carryover balance greater than zero, no election may be made under subparagraph (A) with respect to the prefunding balance.

(6) Prefunding balance

(A) In general

A prefunding balance maintained by a plan shall consist of a beginning balance of zero, increased and decreased to the extent provided in subparagraphs (B) and (C), and adjusted further as provided in paragraph (8).

(B) Increases

(i) In general

As of the first day of each plan year beginning after 2008, the prefunding balance of a plan shall be increased by the amount elected by the plan sponsor for the plan year. Such amount shall not exceed the excess (if any) of—

(I) the aggregate total of employer contributions to the plan for the preceding plan year, over—

(II) the minimum required contribution for such preceding plan year.

(ii) Adjustments for interest

Any excess contributions under clause (i) shall be properly adjusted for interest accruing for the periods between the first day of the current plan year and the dates on which the excess contributions were made, determined by using the effective interest rate for the preceding plan year and by treating contributions as being first used to satisfy the minimum required contribution.

(iii) Certain contributions necessary to avoid benefit limitations disregarded

The excess described in clause (i) with respect to any preceding plan year shall be reduced (but not below zero) by the amount of contributions an employer would be required to make under paragraph (1), (2), or (4) of section 1056(g) of this title to avoid a benefit limitation which would otherwise be imposed under such paragraph for the preceding plan year. Any contribution which may be taken into account in satisfying the requirements of more than 1 of such paragraphs shall be taken into account only once for purposes of this clause.

(C) Decrease

The prefunding balance of a plan shall be decreased (but not below zero) by—

(i) as of the first day of each plan year after 2008, the amount of such balance credited under paragraph (2) (if any) in reducing the minimum required contribution of the plan for the preceding plan year, and

(ii) as of the time specified in paragraph (5)(A), any reduction in such balance elected under paragraph (5).

(7) Funding standard carryover balance

(A) In general

A funding standard carryover balance maintained by a plan shall consist of a beginning balance determined under subparagraph (B), decreased to the extent provided in subparagraph (C), and adjusted further as provided in paragraph (8).

(B) Beginning balance

The beginning balance of the funding standard carryover balance shall be the positive balance described in paragraph (1)(B)(ii)(II).

(C) Decreases

The funding standard carryover balance of a plan shall be decreased (but not below zero) by—

(i) as of the first day of each plan year after 2008, the amount of such balance credited under paragraph (2) (if any) in reducing the minimum required contribution of the plan for the preceding plan year, and

(ii) as of the time specified in paragraph (5)(A), any reduction in such balance elected under paragraph (5).

(8) Adjustments for investment experience

In determining the prefunding balance or the funding standard carryover balance of a plan as of the first day of the plan year, the plan sponsor shall, in accordance with regulations prescribed by the Secretary of the Treasury, adjust such balance to reflect the rate of return on plan assets for the preceding plan year. Notwithstanding subsection (g)(3), such rate of return shall be determined on the basis of fair market value and shall properly take into account, in accordance with such regulations, all contributions, distributions, and other plan payments made during such period.

(9) Elections

Elections under this subsection shall be made at such times, and in such form and manner, as shall be prescribed in regulations of the Secretary of the Treasury.

(g) Valuation of plan assets and liabilities

(1) Timing of determinations

Except as otherwise provided under this subsection, all determinations under this section for a plan year shall be made as of the valuation date of the plan for such plan year.

(2) Valuation date

For purposes of this section—

(A) In general

Except as provided in subparagraph (B), the valuation date of a plan for any plan year shall be the first day of the plan year.

(B) Exception for small plans

If, on each day during the preceding plan year, a plan had 100 or fewer participants, the plan may designate any day during the plan year as its valuation date for such plan year and succeeding plan years. For purposes of this subparagraph, all defined benefit plans which are single-employer plans and are maintained by the same employer (or any member of such employer's controlled group) shall be treated as 1 plan, but only participants with respect to such employer or member shall be taken into account.

(C) Application of certain rules in determination of plan size

For purposes of this paragraph—

(i) Plans not in existence in preceding year

In the case of the first plan year of any plan, subparagraph (B) shall apply to such plan by taking into account the number of participants that the plan is reasonably expected to have on days during such first plan year.

(ii) Predecessors

Any reference in subparagraph (B) to an employer shall include a reference to any predecessor of such employer.

(3) Determination of value of plan assets

For purposes of this section—

(A) In general

Except as provided in subparagraph (B), the value of plan assets shall be the fair market value of the assets.

(B) Averaging allowed

A plan may determine the value of plan assets on the basis of the averaging of fair market values, but only if such method—

(i) is permitted under regulations prescribed by the Secretary of the Treasury,

(ii) does not provide for averaging of such values over more than the period beginning on the last day of the 25th month preceding the month in which the valuation date occurs and ending on the valuation date (or a similar period in the case of a valuation date which is not the 1st day of a month), and

(iii) does not result in a determination of the value of plan assets which, at any time, is lower than 90 percent or greater than 110 percent of the fair market value of such assets at such time.

Any such averaging shall be adjusted for contributions, distributions, and expected earnings (as determined by the plan's actuary on the basis of an assumed earnings rate specified by the actuary but not in excess of the third segment rate applicable under subsection (h)(2)(C)(iii)), as specified by the Secretary of the Treasury.

(4) Accounting for contribution receipts

For purposes of determining the value of assets under paragraph (3)—

(A) Prior year contributions

If—

(i) an employer makes any contribution to the plan after the valuation date for the plan year in which the contribution is made, and

(ii) the contribution is for a preceding plan year,

the contribution shall be taken into account as an asset of the plan as of the valuation date, except that in the case of any plan year beginning after 2008, only the present value (determined as of the valuation date) of such contribution may be taken into account. For purposes of the preceding sentence, present value shall be determined using the effective interest rate for the preceding plan year to which the contribution is properly allocable.

(B) Special rule for current year contributions made before valuation date

If any contributions for any plan year are made to or under the plan during the plan year but before the valuation date for the plan year, the assets of the plan as of the valuation date shall not include—

(i) such contributions, and

(ii) interest on such contributions for the period between the date of the contributions and the valuation date, determined by using the effective interest rate for the plan year.

(h) Actuarial assumptions and methods

(1) In general

Subject to this subsection, the determination of any present value or other computation under this section shall be made on the basis of actuarial assumptions and methods—

(A) each of which is reasonable (taking into account the experience of the plan and reasonable expectations), and

(B) which, in combination, offer the actuary's best estimate of anticipated experience under the plan.

(2) Interest rates

(A) Effective interest rate

For purposes of this section, the term "effective interest rate" means, with respect to any plan for any plan year, the single rate of interest which, if used to determine the present value of the plan's accrued or earned benefits referred to in subsection (d)(1), would result in an amount equal to the funding target of the plan for such plan year.

(B) Interest rates for determining funding target

For purposes of determining the funding target and normal cost of a plan for any plan year, the interest rate used in determining the present value of the benefits of the plan shall be—

(i) in the case of benefits reasonably determined to be payable during the 5-year period beginning on the first day of the plan year, the first segment rate with respect to the applicable month,

(ii) in the case of benefits reasonably determined to be payable during the 15-year period beginning at the end of the period described in clause (i), the second segment rate with respect to the applicable month, and

(iii) in the case of benefits reasonably determined to be payable after the period described in clause (ii), the third segment rate with respect to the applicable month.

(C) Segment rates

For purposes of this paragraph—

(i) First segment rate

The term "first segment rate" means, with respect to any month, the single rate of interest which shall be determined by the Secretary of the Treasury for such month on the basis of the corporate bond yield curve for such month, taking into account only that portion of such yield curve which is based on bonds maturing during the 5-year period commencing with such month.

(ii) Second segment rate

The term "second segment rate" means, with respect to any month, the single rate of interest which shall be determined by the Secretary of the Treasury for such month on the basis of the corporate bond yield curve for such month, taking into account only that portion of such yield curve which is based on bonds maturing during the 15-year period beginning at the end of the period described in clause (i).

(iii) Third segment rate

The term "third segment rate" means, with respect to any month, the single rate of interest which shall be determined by the Secretary of the Treasury for such month on the basis of the corporate bond yield curve for such month, taking into account only that portion of such yield curve which is based on bonds maturing during periods beginning after the period described in clause (ii).

(D) Corporate bond yield curve

For purposes of this paragraph—

(i) In general

The term "corporate bond yield curve" means, with respect to any month, a yield curve which is prescribed by the Secretary of the Treasury for such month and which reflects the average, for the 24-month period ending with the month preceding such month, of monthly yields on investment grade corporate bonds with varying maturities and that are in the top 3 quality levels available.

(ii) Election to use yield curve

Solely for purposes of determining the minimum required contribution under this section, the plan sponsor may, in lieu of the segment rates determined under subparagraph (C), elect to use interest rates under the corporate bond yield curve. For purposes of the preceding sentence such curve shall be determined without regard to the 24-month averaging described in clause (i). Such election, once made, may be revoked only with the consent of the Secretary of the Treasury.

(E) Applicable month

For purposes of this paragraph, the term "applicable month" means, with respect to any plan for any plan year, the month which includes the valuation date of such plan for such plan year or, at the election of the plan sponsor, any of the 4 months which precede such month. Any election made under this subparagraph shall apply to the plan year for which the election is made and all succeeding plan years, unless the election is revoked with the consent of the Secretary of the Treasury.

(F) Publication requirements

The Secretary of the Treasury shall publish for each month the corporate bond yield curve (and the corporate bond yield curve reflecting the modification described in section 1055(g)(3)(B)(iii)(I) of this title for such month) and each of the rates determined under subparagraph (C) for such month. The Secretary of the Treasury shall also publish a description of the methodology used to determine such yield curve and such rates which is sufficiently detailed to enable plans to make reasonable projections regarding the yield curve and such rates for future months based on the plan's projection of future interest rates.

(G) Transition rule

(i) In general

Notwithstanding the preceding provisions of this paragraph, for plan years beginning in 2008 or 2009, the first, second, or third segment rate for a plan with respect to any month shall be equal to the sum of—

(I) the product of such rate for such month determined without regard to this subparagraph, multiplied by the applicable percentage, and

(II) the product of the rate determined under the rules of section 1082(b)(5)(B)(ii)(II) of this title (as in effect for plan years beginning in 2007), multiplied by a percentage equal to 100 percent minus the applicable percentage.

(ii) Applicable percentage

For purposes of clause (i), the applicable percentage is 33⅓ percent for plan years beginning in 2008 and 66⅔ percent for plan years beginning in 2009.

(iii) New plans ineligible

Clause (i) shall not apply to any plan if the first plan year of the plan begins after December 31, 2007.

(iv) Election

The plan sponsor may elect not to have this subparagraph apply. Such election, once made, may be revoked only with the consent of the Secretary of the Treasury.

(3) Mortality tables

(A) In general

Except as provided in subparagraph (C) or (D), the Secretary of the Treasury shall by regulation prescribe mortality tables to be used in determining any present value or making any computation under this section. Such tables shall be based on the actual experience of pension plans and projected trends in such experience. In prescribing such tables, the Secretary of the Treasury shall take into account results of available independent studies of mortality of individuals covered by pension plans.

(B) Periodic revision

The Secretary of the Treasury shall (at least every 10 years) make revisions in any table in effect under subparagraph (A) to reflect the actual experience of pension plans and projected trends in such experience.

(C) Substitute mortality table

(i) In general

Upon request by the plan sponsor and approval by the Secretary of the Treasury, a mortality table which meets the requirements of clause (iii) shall be used in determining any present value or making any computation under this section during the period of consecutive plan years (not to exceed 10) specified in the request.

(ii) Early termination of period

Notwithstanding clause (i), a mortality table described in clause (i) shall cease to be in effect as of the earliest of—

(I) the date on which there is a significant change in the participants in the plan by reason of a plan spinoff or merger or otherwise, or

(II) the date on which the plan actuary determines that such table does not meet the requirements of clause (iii).

(iii) Requirements

A mortality table meets the requirements of this clause if—

(I) there is a sufficient number of plan participants, and the pension plans have been maintained for a sufficient period of time, to have credible information necessary for purposes of subclause (II), and

(II) such table reflects the actual experience of the pension plans maintained by the sponsor and projected trends in general mortality experience.

(iv) All plans in controlled group must use separate table

Except as provided by the Secretary of the Treasury, a plan sponsor may not use a mortality table under this subparagraph for any plan maintained by the plan sponsor unless—

(I) a separate mortality table is established and used under this subparagraph for each other plan maintained by the plan sponsor and if the plan sponsor is a member of a controlled group, each member of the controlled group, and

(II) the requirements of clause (iii) are met separately with respect to the table so established for each such plan, determined by only taking into account the participants of such plan, the time such plan has been in existence, and the actual experience of such plan.

(v) Deadline for submission and disposition of application

(I) Submission

The plan sponsor shall submit a mortality table to the Secretary of the Treasury for approval under this subparagraph at least 7 months before the 1st day of the period described in clause (i).

(II) Disposition

Any mortality table submitted to the Secretary of the Treasury for approval under this subparagraph shall be treated as in effect as of the 1st day of the period described in clause (i) unless the Secretary of the Treasury, during the 180-day period beginning on the date of such submission, disapproves of such table and provides the reasons that such table fails to meet the requirements of clause (iii). The 180-day period shall be extended upon mutual agreement of the Secretary of the Treasury and the plan sponsor.

(D) Separate mortality tables for the disabled

Notwithstanding subparagraph (A)—

(i) In general

The Secretary of the Treasury shall establish mortality tables which may be used (in lieu of the tables under subparagraph (A)) under this subsection for individuals who are entitled to benefits under the plan on account of disability. The Secretary of the Treasury shall establish separate tables for individuals whose disabilities occur in plan years beginning before January 1, 1995, and for individuals whose disabilities occur in plan years beginning on or after such date.

(ii) Special rule for disabilities occurring after 1994

In the case of disabilities occurring in plan years beginning after December 31, 1994, the tables under clause (i) shall apply only with respect to individuals described in such subclause who are disabled within the meaning of title II of the Social Security Act [42 U.S.C. 401 et seq.] and the regulations thereunder.

(iii) Periodic revision

The Secretary of the Treasury shall (at least every 10 years) make revisions in any table in effect under clause (i) to reflect the actual experience of pension plans and projected trends in such experience.

(4) Probability of benefit payments in the form of lump sums or other optional forms

For purposes of determining any present value or making any computation under this section, there shall be taken into account—

(A) the probability that future benefit payments under the plan will be made in the form of optional forms of benefits provided under the plan (including lump sum distributions, determined on the basis of the plan's experience and other related assumptions), and

(B) any difference in the present value of such future benefit payments resulting from the use of actuarial assumptions, in determining benefit payments in any such optional form of benefits, which are different from those specified in this subsection.

(5) Approval of large changes in actuarial assumptions

(A) In general

No actuarial assumption used to determine the funding target for a plan to which this paragraph applies may be changed without the approval of the Secretary of the Treasury.

(B) Plans to which paragraph applies

This paragraph shall apply to a plan only if—

(i) the plan is a single-employer plan to which subchapter III applies,

(ii) the aggregate unfunded vested benefits as of the close of the preceding plan year (as determined under section 1306(a)(3)(E)(iii) of this title) of such plan and all other plans maintained by the contributing sponsors (as defined in section 1301(a)(13) of this title) and members of such sponsors' controlled groups (as defined in section 1301(a)(14) of this title) which are covered by subchapter III (disregarding plans with no unfunded vested benefits) exceed $50,000,000, and

(iii) the change in assumptions (determined after taking into account any changes in interest rate and mortality table) results in a decrease in the funding shortfall of the plan for the current plan year that exceeds $50,000,000, or that exceeds $5,000,000 and that is 5 percent or more of the funding target of the plan before such change.

(i) Special rules for at-risk plans

(1) Funding target for plans in at-risk status

(A) In general

In the case of a plan which is in at-risk status for a plan year, the funding target of the plan for the plan year shall be equal to the sum of—

(i) the present value of all benefits accrued or earned under the plan as of the beginning of the plan year, as determined by using the additional actuarial assumptions described in subparagraph (B), and

(ii) in the case of a plan which also has been in at-risk status for at least 2 of the 4 preceding plan years, a loading factor determined under subparagraph (C).

(B) Additional actuarial assumptions

The actuarial assumptions described in this subparagraph are as follows:

(i) All employees who are not otherwise assumed to retire as of the valuation date but who will be eligible to elect benefits during the plan year and the 10 succeeding plan years shall be assumed to retire at the earliest retirement date under the plan but not before the end of the plan year for which the at-risk funding target and at-risk target normal cost are being determined.

(ii) All employees shall be assumed to elect the retirement benefit available under the plan at the assumed retirement age (determined after application of clause (i)) which would result in the highest present value of benefits.

(C) Loading factor

The loading factor applied with respect to a plan under this paragraph for any plan year is the sum of—

(i) $700, times the number of participants in the plan, plus

(ii) 4 percent of the funding target (determined without regard to this paragraph) of the plan for the plan year.

(2) Target normal cost of at-risk plans

In the case of a plan which is in at-risk status for a plan year, the target normal cost of the plan for such plan year shall be equal to the sum of—

(A) the excess of—

(i) the sum of—

(I) the present value of all benefits which are expected to accrue or to be earned under the plan during the plan year, determined using the additional actuarial assumptions described in paragraph (1)(B), plus

(II) the amount of plan-related expenses expected to be paid from plan assets during the plan year, over

(ii) the amount of mandatory employee contributions expected to be made during the plan year, plus

(B) in the case of a plan which also has been in at-risk status for at least 2 of the 4 preceding plan years, a loading factor equal to 4 percent of the amount determined under subsection (b)(1)(A)(i) with respect to the plan for the plan year.

(3) Minimum amount

In no event shall—

(A) the at-risk funding target be less than the funding target, as determined without regard to this subsection, or

(B) the at-risk target normal cost be less than the target normal cost, as determined without regard to this subsection.

(4) Determination of at-risk status

For purposes of this subsection—

(A) In general

A plan is in at-risk status for a plan year if—

(i) the funding target attainment percentage for the preceding plan year (determined under this section without regard to this subsection) is less than 80 percent, and

(ii) the funding target attainment percentage for the preceding plan year (determined under this section by using the additional actuarial assumptions described in paragraph (1)(B) in computing the funding target) is less than 70 percent.

(B) Transition rule

In the case of plan years beginning in 2008, 2009, and 2010, subparagraph (A)(i) shall be applied by substituting the following percentages for "80 percent":

(i) 65 percent in the case of 2008.

(ii) 70 percent in the case of 2009.

(iii) 75 percent in the case of 2010.

In the case of plan years beginning in 2008, the funding target attainment percentage for the preceding plan year under subparagraph (A) may be determined using such methods of estimation as the Secretary of the Treasury may provide.

(C) Special rule for employees offered early retirement in 2006

(i) In general

For purposes of subparagraph (A)(ii), the additional actuarial assumptions described in paragraph (1)(B) shall not be taken into account with respect to any employee if—

(I) such employee is employed by a specified automobile manufacturer,

(II) such employee is offered a substantial amount of additional cash compensation, substantially enhanced retirement benefits under the plan, or materially reduced employment duties on the condition that by a specified date (not later than December 31, 2010) the employee retires (as defined under the terms of the plan),

(III) such offer is made during 2006 and pursuant to a bona fide retirement incentive program and requires, by the terms of the offer, that such offer can be accepted not later than a specified date (not later than December 31, 2006), and

(IV) such employee does not elect to accept such offer before the specified date on which the offer expires.

(ii) **Specified automobile manufacturer**

For purposes of clause (i), the term "specified automobile manufacturer" means—

(I) any manufacturer of automobiles, and

(II) any manufacturer of automobile parts which supplies such parts directly to a manufacturer of automobiles and which, after a transaction or series of transactions ending in 1999, ceased to be a member of a controlled group which included such manufacturer of automobiles.

(5) Transition between applicable funding targets and between applicable target normal costs

(A) In general

In any case in which a plan which is in at-risk status for a plan year has been in such status for a consecutive period of fewer than 5 plan years, the applicable amount of the funding target and of the target normal cost shall be, in lieu of the amount determined without regard to this paragraph, the sum of—

(i) the amount determined under this section without regard to this subsection, plus

(ii) the transition percentage for such plan year of the excess of the amount determined under this subsection (without regard to this paragraph) over the amount determined under this section without regard to this subsection.

(B) Transition percentage

For purposes of subparagraph (A), the transition percentage shall be determined in accordance with the following table:

If the consecutive number of years (including the plan year) the plan is in at-risk status is—	The transition percentage is—
1	20
2	40
3	60
4	80.

(C) Years before effective date

For purposes of this paragraph, plan years beginning before 2008 shall not be taken into account.

(6) Small plan exception

If, on each day during the preceding plan year, a plan had 500 or fewer participants, the plan shall not be treated as in at-risk status for the plan year. For purposes of this paragraph, all defined benefit plans (other than multiemployer plans) maintained by the same employer (or any member of such employer's controlled group) shall be treated as 1 plan, but only participants with respect to such employer or member shall be taken into account and the rules of subsection (g)(2)(C) shall apply.

(j) Payment of minimum required contributions

(1) In general

For purposes of this section, the due date for any payment of any minimum required contribution for any plan year shall be 8½ months after the close of the plan year.

(2) Interest

Any payment required under paragraph (1) for a plan year that is made on a date other than the valuation date for such plan year shall be adjusted for interest accruing for the period between the valuation date and the payment date, at the effective rate of interest for the plan for such plan year.

(3) Accelerated quarterly contribution schedule for underfunded plans

(A) Failure to timely make required installment

In any case in which the plan has a funding shortfall for the preceding plan year, the employer maintaining the plan shall make the required installments under this paragraph and if the employer fails to pay the full amount of a required installment for the plan year, then the amount of interest charged under paragraph (2) on the underpayment for the period of underpayment shall be determined by using a rate of interest equal to the rate otherwise used under paragraph (2) plus 5 percentage points. In the case of plan years beginning in 2008, the funding shortfall for the preceding plan year may be determined using such methods of estimation as the Secretary of the Treasury may provide.

(B) Amount of underpayment, period of underpayment

For purposes of subparagraph (A)—

(i) Amount

The amount of the underpayment shall be the excess of—

(I) the required installment, over

(II) the amount (if any) of the installment contributed to or under the plan on or before the due date for the installment.

(ii) Period of underpayment

The period for which any interest is charged under this paragraph with respect to any portion of the underpayment shall run from the due date for the installment to the date on which such portion is contributed to or under the plan.

(iii) Order of crediting contributions

For purposes of clause (i)(II), contributions shall be credited against unpaid required installments in the order in which such installments are required to be paid.

(C) Number of required installments; due dates

For purposes of this paragraph—

(i) Payable in 4 installments

There shall be 4 required installments for each plan year.

(ii) Time for payment of installments

The due dates for required installments are set forth in the following table:

In the case of the following required installment:	The due date is:
1st	April 15

2nd	July 15
3rd	October 15
4th	January 15 of the following year.

(D) Amount of required installment

For purposes of this paragraph—

(i) In general

The amount of any required installment shall be 25 percent of the required annual payment.

(ii) Required annual payment

For purposes of clause (i), the term "required annual payment" means the lesser of—

(I) 90 percent of the minimum required contribution (determined without regard to this subsection) to the plan for the plan year under this section, or

(II) 100 percent of the minimum required contribution (determined without regard to this subsection or to any waiver under section 1082(c) of this title) to the plan for the preceding plan year.

Subclause (II) shall not apply if the preceding plan year referred to in such clause was not a year of 12 months.

(E) Fiscal years, short years, and years with alternate valuation date

(i) Fiscal years

In applying this paragraph to a plan year beginning on any date other than January 1, there shall be substituted for the months specified in this paragraph, the months which correspond thereto.

(ii) Short plan year

This subparagraph shall be applied to plan years of less than 12 months in accordance with regulations prescribed by the Secretary of the Treasury.

(iii) Plan with alternate valuation date

The Secretary of the Treasury shall prescribe regulations for the application of this paragraph in the case of a plan which has a valuation date other than the first day of the plan year.

(4) Liquidity requirement in connection with quarterly contributions

(A) In general

A plan to which this paragraph applies shall be treated as failing to pay the full amount of any required installment under paragraph (3) to the extent that the value of the liquid assets paid in such installment is less than the liquidity shortfall (whether or not such liquidity shortfall exceeds the amount of such installment required to be paid but for this paragraph).

(B) Plans to which paragraph applies

This paragraph shall apply to a plan (other than a plan described in subsection (g)(2)(B)) which—

(i) is required to pay installments under paragraph (3) for a plan year, and

(ii) has a liquidity shortfall for any quarter during such plan year.

(C) Period of underpayment

For purposes of paragraph (3)(A), any portion of an installment that is treated as not paid under subparagraph (A) shall continue to be treated as unpaid until the close of the quarter in which the due date for such installment occurs.

(D) Limitation on increase

If the amount of any required installment is increased by reason of subparagraph (A), in no event shall such increase exceed the amount which, when added to prior installments for the plan year, is necessary to increase the funding target attainment percentage of the plan for the plan year (taking into account the expected increase in funding target due to benefits accruing or earned during the plan year) to 100 percent.

(E) Definitions

For purposes of this paragraph—

(i) Liquidity shortfall

The term "liquidity shortfall" means, with respect to any required installment, an amount equal to the excess (as of the last day of the quarter for which such installment is made) of—

(I) the base amount with respect to such quarter, over

(II) the value (as of such last day) of the plan's liquid assets.

(ii) Base amount

(I) In general

The term "base amount" means, with respect to any quarter, an amount equal to 3 times the sum of the adjusted disbursements from the plan for the 12 months ending on the last day of such quarter.

(II) Special rule

If the amount determined under subclause (I) exceeds an amount equal to 2 times the sum of the adjusted disbursements from the plan for the 36 months ending on the last day of the quarter and an enrolled actuary certifies to the satisfaction of the Secretary of the Treasury that such excess is the result of nonrecurring circumstances, the base amount with respect to such quarter shall be determined without regard to amounts related to those nonrecurring circumstances.

(iii) Disbursements from the plan

The term "disbursements from the plan" means all disbursements from the trust, including purchases of annuities, payments of single sums and other benefits, and administrative expenses.

(iv) Adjusted disbursements

The term "adjusted disbursements" means disbursements from the plan reduced by the product of—

(I) the plan's funding target attainment percentage for the plan year, and

(II) the sum of the purchases of annuities, payments of single sums, and such other disbursements as the Secretary of the Treasury shall provide in regulations.

(v) Liquid assets

The term "liquid assets" means cash, marketable securities, and such other assets as specified by the Secretary of the Treasury in regulations.

(vi) Quarter

The term "quarter" means, with respect to any required installment, the 3-month period preceding the month in which the due date for such installment occurs.

(F) Regulations

The Secretary of the Treasury may prescribe such regulations as are necessary to carry out this paragraph.

(k) Imposition of lien where failure to make required contributions

(1) In general

In the case of a plan to which this subsection applies (as provided under paragraph (2)), if—

(A) any person fails to make a contribution payment required by section 1082 of this title and this section before the due date for such payment, and

(B) the unpaid balance of such payment (including interest), when added to the aggregate unpaid balance of all preceding such payments for which payment was not made before the due date (including interest), exceeds $1,000,000,

then there shall be a lien in favor of the plan in the amount determined under paragraph (3) upon all property and rights to property, whether real or personal, belonging to such person and any other person who is a member of the same controlled group of which such person is a member.

(2) Plans to which subsection applies

This subsection shall apply to a single-employer plan covered under section 1321 of this title for any plan year for which the funding target attainment percentage (as defined in subsection (d)(2)) of such plan is less than 100 percent.

(3) Amount of lien

For purposes of paragraph (1), the amount of the lien shall be equal to the aggregate unpaid balance of contribution payments required under this section and section 1082 of this title for which payment has not been made before the due date.

(4) Notice of failure; lien

(A) Notice of failure

A person committing a failure described in paragraph (1) shall notify the Pension Benefit Guaranty Corporation of such failure within 10 days of the due date for the required contribution payment.

(B) Period of lien

The lien imposed by paragraph (1) shall arise on the due date for the required contribution payment and shall continue until the last day of the first plan year in which the plan ceases to be described in paragraph (1)(B). Such lien shall continue to run without regard to whether such plan continues to be described in paragraph (2) during the period referred to in the preceding sentence.

(C) Certain rules to apply

Any amount with respect to which a lien is imposed under paragraph (1) shall be treated as taxes due and owing the United States and rules similar to the rules of subsections (c), (d), and (e) of section 1368 of this title shall apply with respect to a lien imposed by subsection (a) and the amount with respect to such lien.

(5) Enforcement

Any lien created under paragraph (1) may be perfected and enforced only by the Pension Benefit Guaranty Corporation, or at the direction of the Pension Benefit Guaranty Corporation, by the contributing sponsor (or any member of the controlled group of the contributing sponsor).

(6) Definitions

For purposes of this subsection—

(A) Contribution payment

The term "contribution payment" means, in connection with a plan, a contribution payment required to be made to the plan, including any required installment under paragraphs (3) and (4) of subsection (j).

(B) Due date; required installment

The terms "due date" and "required installment" have the meanings given such terms by subsection (j).

(C) Controlled group

The term "controlled group" means any group treated as a single employer under subsections (b), (c), (m), and (*o*) of section 414 of title 26.

(*l*) Qualified transfers to health benefit accounts

In the case of a qualified transfer (as defined in section 420 of title 26), any assets so transferred shall not, for purposes of this section, be treated as assets in the plan.

(Pub. L. 93–406, title I, §303, as added Pub. L. 109–280, title I, §102(a), Aug. 17, 2006, 120 Stat. 789; amended Pub. L. 110–458, title I, §§101(b)(1), 121(a), title II, §202(a), Dec. 23, 2008, 122 Stat. 5093, 5113, 5117.)

REFERENCES IN TEXT

The Social Security Act, referred to in subsec. (h)(3)(D)(ii), is act Aug. 14, 1935, ch. 531, 49 Stat. 620. Title II of the Act is classified generally to subchapter II (§401 et seq.) of chapter 7 of Title 42, The Public Health and Welfare. For complete classification of this Act to the Code, see section 1305 of Title 42 and Tables.

PRIOR PROVISIONS

A prior section 1083, Pub. L. 93–406, title I, §303, Sept. 2, 1974, 88 Stat. 872; Pub. L. 99–272, title XI, §§11015(b)(1)(A), 11016(c)(2), Apr. 7, 1986, 100 Stat. 267, 273; Pub. L. 100–203, title IX, §9306(a)(2), (b)(2), (c)(2)(A), (d)(2), Dec. 22, 1987, 101 Stat. 1330–353 to 1330–355; Pub. L. 101–239, title VII, §§7881(b)(6)(B)(ii), (7), (8), (c)(2), 7891(a)(1), Dec. 19, 1989, 103 Stat. 2438, 2439, 2445, related to variance from minimum funding standard, prior to repeal by Pub. L. 109–280, title I, § 101(a), (d), Aug. 17, 2006, 120 Stat. 784, 789, applicable to plan years beginning after 2007.

AMENDMENTS

2008—Subsec. (b). Pub. L. 110–458, § 101(b)(1)(A), amended subsec. (b) generally. Prior to amendment, text read as follows: "For purposes of this section, except as provided in subsection (i)(2) with respect to plans in at-risk status, the term 'target normal cost' means, for any plan year, the present value of all benefits which are expected to accrue or to be earned under the plan during the plan year. For purposes of this subsection, if any benefit attributable to services performed in a preceding plan year is increased by reason of any increase in compensation during the current plan year, the increase in such benefit shall be treated as having accrued during the current plan year."

Subsec. (c)(5)(B)(i). Pub. L. 110–458, § 202(a)(2), added cl. (i) and struck out former cl. (i). Prior to amendment, text read as follows: "Except as provided in clauses (iii) and (iv), in the case of plan years beginning after 2007 and before 2011, only the applicable percentage of the funding target shall be taken into account under paragraph (3)(A) in determining the funding shortfall for the plan year for purposes of subparagraph (A)."

Subsec. (c)(5)(B)(iii). Pub. L. 110–458, § 202(a)(1), redesignated cl. (iv) as (iii) and struck out former cl. (iii). Prior to amendment, text read as follows: "Clause (i) shall not apply with respect to any plan year beginning after 2008 unless the shortfall amortization base for each of the preceding years beginning after 2007 was zero (determined after application of this subparagraph)."

Pub. L. 110–458, § 101(b)(1)(B), inserted "beginning" before "after 2008".

Subsec. (c)(5)(B)(iv). Pub. L. 110–458, § 202(a)(1), redesignated cl. (iv) as (iii).

Subsec. (c)(5)(B)(iv)(II). Pub. L. 110–458, § 101(b)(1)(C), inserted "for such year" after "beginning in 2007)".

Subsec. (f)(4)(A). Pub. L. 110–458, § 101(b)(1)(D), substituted "paragraph (3)" for "paragraph (2)".

Subsec. (g)(3)(B). Pub. L. 110–458, § 121(a), amended concluding provisions generally. Prior to amendment, concluding provisions read as follows: "Any such averaging shall be adjusted for contributions and distributions (as provided by the Secretary of the Treasury)."

Subsec. (h)(2)(F). Pub. L. 110–458, § 101(b)(1)(E), substituted "section 1055(g)(3)(B)(iii)(I) of this title for such month)" for "section 1055(g)(3)(B)(iii)(I) of this title) for such month" and "subparagraph (C)" for "subparagraph (B)".

Subsec. (i)(2)(A). Pub. L. 110–458, § 101(b)(1)(F)(i)(I), added subpar. (A) and struck out former subpar. (A) which read as follows: "the present value of all benefits which are expected to accrue or be earned under the plan during the plan year, determined using the additional actuarial assumptions described in paragraph (1)(B), plus".

Subsec. (i)(2)(B). Pub. L. 110–458, § 101(b)(1)(F)(i)(II), substituted "the amount determined under subsection (b)(1)(A)(i) with respect to the plan for the plan year" for "the target normal cost (determined without regard to this paragraph) of the plan for the plan year".

Subsec. (i)(4)(B). Pub. L. 110–458, § 101(b)(1)(F)(ii), substituted "subparagraph (A)" for "subparagraph (A)(ii)" in concluding provisions.

Subsec. (j)(3)(A). Pub. L. 110–458, § 101(b)(1)(G)(i), inserted last sentence.

Subsec. (j)(3)(E). Pub. L. 110–458, § 101(b)(1)(G)(ii), (iii), substituted ", short years, and years with alternate valuation date" for "and short years" in heading and added cl. (iii).

Subsec. (k)(6)(B). Pub. L. 110–458, § 101(b)(1)(H), struck out ", except that in the case of a payment other than a required installment, the due date shall be the date such payment is required to be made under this section" after "subsection (j)".

EFFECTIVE DATE OF 2008 AMENDMENT

Amendment by section 101(b)(1)(A), (F)(i) of Pub. L. 110–458 applicable to plan years beginning after Dec. 31, 2008, and applicable to a plan for the first plan year beginning after Dec. 31, 2007, under certain conditions, see section 101(b)(3) of Pub. L. 110–458, set out as a note under section 430 of Title 26, Internal Revenue Code.

Amendment by section 101(b)(1)(B)–(E), (F)(ii)–(H) of Pub. L. 110–458 effective as if included in the provisions of Pub. L. 109–280 to which the amendment relates, except as otherwise provided, see section 112 of Pub. L. 110–458, set out as a note under section 72 of Title 26, Internal Revenue Code.

Amendment by section 121(a) of Pub. L. 110–458 effective as if included in the provisions of Pub. L. 109–280 to which the amendment relates, see section 121(c) of Pub. L. 110–458, set out as a note under section 430 of Title 26, Internal Revenue Code.

Amendment by section 202(a) of Pub. L. 110–458 applicable as if included in the enactment of this section, see section 202(c) of Pub. L. 110–458, set out as a note under section 430 of Title 26, Internal Revenue Code.

EFFECTIVE DATE

Pub. L. 109–280, title I, § 102(c), Aug. 17, 2006, 120 Stat. 809, provided that: "The amendments made by this section [enacting this section] shall apply with respect to plan years beginning after 2007."

APPLICABILITY OF AMENDMENTS BY SUBTITLES A AND B OF TITLE I OF PUB. L. 109–280

For special rules on applicability of amendments by subtitles A (§§ 101–107) and B (§§ 111–116) of title I of Pub. L. 109–280 to certain eligible cooperative plans, PBGC settlement plans, and eligible government contractor plans, see sections 104, 105, and 106 of Pub. L. 109–280, set out as notes under section 401 of Title 26, Internal Revenue Code.

MODIFICATION OF TRANSITION RULE TO PENSION FUNDING REQUIREMENTS

For modification of transition rule to pension funding requirements in the case of a plan that was not required to pay a variable rate premium for the plan year beginning in 1996, has not, in any plan year beginning after 1995, merged with another plan (other than a plan sponsored by an employer that was in 1996 within the controlled group of the plan sponsor), and is sponsored by a company that is engaged primarily in the interurban or interstate passenger bus service, see section 115(a)–(c) of Pub. L. 109–280, set out as a note under section 430 of Title 26, Internal Revenue Code.

§ 1084. Minimum funding standards for multiemployer plans

(a) In general

For purposes of section 1082 of this title, the accumulated funding deficiency of a multiemployer plan for any plan year is—

(1) except as provided in paragraph (2), the amount, determined as of the end of the plan year, equal to the excess (if any) of the total charges to the funding standard account of the plan for all plan years (beginning with the first plan year for which this part applies to the plan) over the total credits to such account for such years, and

(2) if the multiemployer plan is in reorganization for any plan year, the accumulated funding deficiency of the plan determined under section 1423 of this title.

(b) Funding standard account

(1) Account required

Each multiemployer plan to which this part applies shall establish and maintain a funding standard account. Such account shall be credited and charged solely as provided in this section.

(2) Charges to account

For a plan year, the funding standard account shall be charged with the sum of—

(A) the normal cost of the plan for the plan year,

(B) the amounts necessary to amortize in equal annual installments (until fully amortized)—

(i) in the case of a plan which comes into existence on or after January 1, 2008, the unfunded past service liability under the plan on the first day of the first plan year to which this section applies, over a period of 15 plan years,

(ii) separately, with respect to each plan year, the net increase (if any) in unfunded past service liability under the plan arising from plan amendments adopted in such year, over a period of 15 plan years,

(iii) separately, with respect to each plan year, the net experience loss (if any) under the plan, over a period of 15 plan years, and

(iv) separately, with respect to each plan year, the net loss (if any) resulting from changes in actuarial assumptions used under the plan, over a period of 15 plan years,

(C) the amount necessary to amortize each waived funding deficiency (within the meaning of section 1082(c)(3) of this title) for each prior plan year in equal annual installments (until fully amortized) over a period of 15 plan years,

(D) the amount necessary to amortize in equal annual installments (until fully amortized) over a period of 5 plan years any amount credited to the funding standard account under section 1082(b)(3)(D) of this title (as in effect on the day before August 17, 2006), and

(E) the amount necessary to amortize in equal annual installments (until fully amortized) over a period of 20 years the contributions which would be required to be made under the plan but for the provisions of section 1082(c)(7)(A)(i)(I) of this title (as in effect on the day before August 17, 2006).

(3) Credits to account

For a plan year, the funding standard account shall be credited with the sum of—

(A) the amount considered contributed by the employer to or under the plan for the plan year,

(B) the amount necessary to amortize in equal annual installments (until fully amortized)—

(i) separately, with respect to each plan year, the net decrease (if any) in unfunded past service liability under the plan arising from plan amendments adopted in such year, over a period of 15 plan years,

(ii) separately, with respect to each plan year, the net experience gain (if any) under the plan, over a period of 15 plan years, and

(iii) separately, with respect to each plan year, the net gain (if any) resulting from changes in actuarial assumptions used under the plan, over a period of 15 plan years,

(C) the amount of the waived funding deficiency (within the meaning of section 1082(c)(3) of this title) for the plan year, and

(D) in the case of a plan year for which the accumulated funding deficiency is determined under the funding standard account if such plan year follows a plan year for which such deficiency was determined under the alternative minimum funding standard under section 1085 of this title (as in effect on the day before August 17, 2006), the excess (if any) of any debit balance in the funding standard account (determined without regard to this subparagraph) over any debit balance in the alternative minimum funding standard account.

(4) Special rule for amounts first amortized in plan years before 2008

In the case of any amount amortized under section 1082(b) of this title (as in effect on the day before August 17, 2006) over any period beginning with a plan year beginning before 2008, in lieu of the amortization described in paragraphs (2)(B) and (3)(B), such amount shall continue to be amortized under such section as so in effect.

(5) Combining and offsetting amounts to be amortized

Under regulations prescribed by the Secretary of the Treasury, amounts required to be amortized under paragraph (2) or paragraph (3), as the case may be—

(A) may be combined into one amount under such paragraph to be amortized over a period determined on the basis of the remaining amortization period for all items entering into such combined amount, and

(B) may be offset against amounts required to be amortized under the other such paragraph, with the resulting amount to be amortized over a period determined on the basis of the remaining amortization periods for all items entering into whichever of the two amounts being offset is the greater.

(6) Interest

The funding standard account (and items therein) shall be charged or credited (as determined under regulations prescribed by the Secretary of the Treasury) with interest at the appropriate rate consistent with the rate or rates of interest used under the plan to determine costs.

(7) Special rules relating to charges and credits to funding standard account

For purposes of this part—

(A) Withdrawal liability

Any amount received by a multiemployer plan in payment of all or part of an employer's withdrawal liability under part 1 of subtitle E of subchapter III shall be considered an amount contributed by the employer to or under the plan. The Secretary of the

Treasury may prescribe by regulation additional charges and credits to a multiemployer plan's funding standard account to the extent necessary to prevent withdrawal liability payments from being unduly reflected as advance funding for plan liabilities.

(B) Adjustments when a multiemployer plan leaves reorganization

If a multiemployer plan is not in reorganization in the plan year but was in reorganization in the immediately preceding plan year, any balance in the funding standard account at the close of such immediately preceding plan year—

(i) shall be eliminated by an offsetting credit or charge (as the case may be), but

(ii) shall be taken into account in subsequent plan years by being amortized in equal annual installments (until fully amortized) over 30 plan years.

The preceding sentence shall not apply to the extent of any accumulated funding deficiency under section 1423(a) of this title as of the end of the last plan year that the plan was in reorganization.

(C) Plan payments to supplemental program or withdrawal liability payment fund

Any amount paid by a plan during a plan year to the Pension Benefit Guaranty Corporation pursuant to section 1402 of this title or to a fund exempt under section 501(c)(22) of title 26 pursuant to section 1403 of this title shall reduce the amount of contributions considered received by the plan for the plan year.

(D) Interim withdrawal liability payments

Any amount paid by an employer pending a final determination of the employer's withdrawal liability under part 1 of subtitle E of subchapter III and subsequently refunded to the employer by the plan shall be charged to the funding standard account in accordance with regulations prescribed by the Secretary of the Treasury.

(E) Election for deferral of charge for portion of net experience loss

If an election is in effect under section 1082(b)(7)(F) of this title (as in effect on the day before August 17, 2006) for any plan year, the funding standard account shall be charged in the plan year to which the portion of the net experience loss deferred by such election was deferred with the amount so deferred (and paragraph (2)(B)(iii) shall not apply to the amount so charged).

(F) Financial assistance

Any amount of any financial assistance from the Pension Benefit Guaranty Corporation to any plan, and any repayment of such amount, shall be taken into account under this section and section 1082 of this title in such manner as is determined by the Secretary of the Treasury.

(G) Short-term benefits

To the extent that any plan amendment increases the unfunded past service liability under the plan by reason of an increase in benefits which are not payable as a life annuity but are payable under the terms of the plan for a period that does not exceed 14 years from the effective date of the amendment, paragraph (2)(B)(ii) shall be applied separately with respect to such increase in unfunded past service liability by substituting the number of years of the period during which such benefits are payable for "15".

(c) Additional rules

(1) Determinations to be made under funding method

For purposes of this part, normal costs, accrued liability, past service liabilities, and experience gains and losses shall be determined under the funding method used to determine costs under the plan.

(2) Valuation of assets

(A) In general

For purposes of this part, the value of the plan's assets shall be determined on the basis of any reasonable actuarial method of valuation which takes into account fair market value and which is permitted under regulations prescribed by the Secretary of the Treasury.

(B) Election with respect to bonds

The value of a bond or other evidence of indebtedness which is not in default as to principal or interest may, at the election of the plan administrator, be determined on an amortized basis running from initial cost at purchase to par value at maturity or earliest call date. Any election under this subparagraph shall be made at such time and in such manner as the Secretary of the Treasury shall by regulations provide, shall apply to all such evidences of indebtedness, and may be revoked only with the consent of such Secretary.

(3) Actuarial assumptions must be reasonable

For purposes of this section, all costs, liabilities, rates of interest, and other factors under the plan shall be determined on the basis of actuarial assumptions and methods—

(A) each of which is reasonable (taking into account the experience of the plan and reasonable expectations), and

(B) which, in combination, offer the actuary's best estimate of anticipated experience under the plan.

(4) Treatment of certain changes as experience gain or loss

For purposes of this section, if—

(A) a change in benefits under the Social Security Act [42 U.S.C. 301 et seq.] or in other retirement benefits created under Federal or State law, or

(B) a change in the definition of the term "wages" under section 3121 of title 26, or a change in the amount of such wages taken into account under regulations prescribed for purposes of section 401(a)(5) of title 26,

results in an increase or decrease in accrued liability under a plan, such increase or decrease shall be treated as an experience loss or gain.

(5) Full funding

If, as of the close of a plan year, a plan would (without regard to this paragraph) have an accumulated funding deficiency in excess of the full funding limitation—

(A) the funding standard account shall be credited with the amount of such excess, and

(B) all amounts described in subparagraphs (B), (C), and (D) of subsection (b) (2) and subparagraph (B) of subsection (b)(3) which are required to be amortized shall be considered fully amortized for purposes of such subparagraphs.

(6) Full-funding limitation

(A) In general

For purposes of paragraph (5), the term "full-funding limitation" means the excess (if any) of—

(i) the accrued liability (including normal cost) under the plan (determined under the entry age normal funding method if such accrued liability cannot be directly calculated under the funding method used for the plan), over

(ii) the lesser of—

(I) the fair market value of the plan's assets, or

(II) the value of such assets determined under paragraph (2).

(B) Minimum amount

(i) In general

In no event shall the full-funding limitation determined under subparagraph (A) be less than the excess (if any) of—

(I) 90 percent of the current liability of the plan (including the expected increase in current liability due to benefits accruing during the plan year), over

(II) the value of the plan's assets determined under paragraph (2).

(ii) Assets

For purposes of clause (i), assets shall not be reduced by any credit balance in the funding standard account.

(C) Full funding limitation

For purposes of this paragraph, unless otherwise provided by the plan, the accrued liability under a multiemployer plan shall not include benefits which are not nonforfeitable under the plan after the termination of the plan (taking into consideration section 411(d)(3) of title 26).

(D) Current liability

For purposes of this paragraph—

(i) In general

The term "current liability" means all liabilities to employees and their beneficiaries under the plan.

(ii) Treatment of unpredictable contingent event benefits

For purposes of clause (i), any benefit contingent on an event other than—

(I) age, service, compensation, death, or disability, or

(II) an event which is reasonably and reliably predictable (as determined by the Secretary of the Treasury),

shall not be taken into account until the event on which the benefit is contingent occurs.

(iii) Interest rate used

The rate of interest used to determine current liability under this paragraph shall be the rate of interest determined under subparagraph (E).

(iv) Mortality tables

(I) Commissioners' standard table

In the case of plan years beginning before the first plan year to which the first tables prescribed under subclause (II) apply, the mortality table used in determining current liability under this paragraph shall be the table prescribed by the Secretary of the Treasury which is based on the prevailing commissioners' standard table (described in section 807(d)(5)(A) of title 26) used to determine reserves for group annuity contracts issued on January 1, 1993.

(II) Secretarial authority

The Secretary of the Treasury may by regulation prescribe for plan years beginning after December 31, 1999, mortality tables to be used in determining current liability under this subsection. Such tables shall be based upon the actual experience of pension plans and projected trends in such experience. In prescribing such tables, such Secretary shall take into account results of available independent studies of mortality of individuals covered by pension plans.

(v) Separate mortality tables for the disabled

Notwithstanding clause (iv)—

(I) In general

The Secretary of the Treasury shall establish mortality tables which may be used (in lieu of the tables under clause (iv)) to determine current liability under this subsection for individuals who are entitled to benefits under the plan on account of disability. Such Secretary shall establish separate tables for individuals whose disabilities occur in plan years beginning before January 1, 1995, and for individuals whose disabilities occur in plan years beginning on or after such date.

(II) Special rule for disabilities occurring after 1994

In the case of disabilities occurring in plan years beginning after December 31, 1994, the tables under subclause (I) shall apply only with respect to individuals described in such subclause who are disabled within the meaning of title II of the Social Security Act [42 U.S.C. 401 et seq.] and the regulations thereunder.

(vi) Periodic review

The Secretary of the Treasury shall periodically (at least every 5 years) review any tables in effect under this subparagraph and shall, to the extent such Secretary determines necessary, by regulation update the tables to reflect the actual experience of pension plans and projected trends in such experience.

(E) Required change of interest rate

For purposes of determining a plan's current liability for purposes of this paragraph—

(i) In general

If any rate of interest used under the plan under subsection (b)(6) to determine cost is not within the permissible range, the plan shall establish a new rate of interest within the permissible range.

(ii) Permissible range

For purposes of this subparagraph—

(I) In general

Except as provided in subclause (II), the term "permissible range" means a rate of interest which is not more than 5 percent above, and not more than 10 percent below, the weighted average of the rates of interest on 30-year Treasury securities during the 4-year period ending on the last day before the beginning of the plan year.

(II) Secretarial authority

If the Secretary of the Treasury finds that the lowest rate of interest permissible under subclause (I) is unreasonably high, such Secretary may prescribe a lower rate of interest, except that such rate may not be less than 80 percent of the average rate determined under such subclause.

(iii) Assumptions

Notwithstanding paragraph (3)(A), the interest rate used under the plan shall be—

(I) determined without taking into account the experience of the plan and reasonable expectations, but

(II) consistent with the assumptions which reflect the purchase rates which would be used by insurance companies to satisfy the liabilities under the plan.

(7) Annual valuation

(A) In general

For purposes of this section, a determination of experience gains and losses and a valuation of the plan's liability shall be made not less frequently than once every year, except that such determination shall be made more frequently to the extent required in particular cases under regulations prescribed by the Secretary of the Treasury.

(B) Valuation date

(i) Current year

Except as provided in clause (ii), the valuation referred to in subparagraph (A) shall be made as of a date within the plan year to which the valuation refers or within one month prior to the beginning of such year.

(ii) Use of prior year valuation

The valuation referred to in subparagraph (A) may be made as of a date within the plan year prior to the year to which the valuation refers if, as of such date, the value of the assets of the plan are not less than 100 percent of the plan's current liability (as defined in paragraph (6)(D) without regard to clause (iv) thereof).

(iii) Adjustments

Information under clause (ii) shall, in accordance with regulations, be actuarially adjusted to reflect significant differences in participants.

(iv) Limitation

A change in funding method to use a prior year valuation, as provided in clause (ii), may not be made unless as of the valuation date within the prior plan year, the value of the assets of the plan are not less than 125 percent of the plan's current liability (as defined in paragraph (6)(D) without regard to clause (iv) thereof).

(8) Time when certain contributions deemed made

For purposes of this section, any contributions for a plan year made by an employer after the last day of such plan year, but not later than two and one-half months after such day, shall be deemed to have been made on such last day. For purposes of this subparagraph, such two and one-half month period may be extended for not more than six months under regulations prescribed by the Secretary of the Treasury.

(d) Extension of amortization periods for multiemployer plans

(1) Automatic extension upon application by certain plans

(A) In general

If the plan sponsor of a multiemployer plan—

(i) submits to the Secretary of the Treasury an application for an extension of the period of years required to amortize any unfunded liability described in any clause of subsection (b)(2)(B) or described in subsection (b)(4), and

(ii) includes with the application a certification by the plan's actuary described in subparagraph (B),

the Secretary of the Treasury shall extend the amortization period for the period of time (not in excess of 5 years) specified in the application. Such extension shall be in addition to any extension under paragraph (2).

(B) Criteria

A certification with respect to a multiemployer plan is described in this subparagraph if the plan's actuary certifies that, based on reasonable assumptions—

(i) absent the extension under subparagraph (A), the plan would have an accumulated funding deficiency in the current plan year or any of the 9 succeeding plan years,

(ii) the plan sponsor has adopted a plan to improve the plan's funding status,

(iii) the plan is projected to have sufficient assets to timely pay expected benefits and anticipated expenditures over the amortization period as extended, and

(iv) the notice required under paragraph (3)(A) has been provided.

(C) Termination

The preceding provisions of this paragraph shall not apply with respect to any application submitted after December 31, 2014.

(2) Alternative extension

(A) In general

If the plan sponsor of a multiemployer plan submits to the Secretary of the Treasury an application for an extension of the period of years required to amortize any unfunded liability described in any clause of subsection (b)(2)(B) or described in subsection (b)(4), the Secretary of the Treasury may extend the amortization period for a period of time (not in excess of 10 years reduced by the number of years of any extension under paragraph (1) with respect to such unfunded liability) if the Secretary of the Treasury makes the determination described in subparagraph (B). Such extension shall be in addition to any extension under paragraph (1).

(B) Determination

The Secretary of the Treasury may grant an extension under subparagraph (A) if such Secretary determines that—

(i) such extension would carry out the purposes of this chapter and would provide adequate protection for participants under the plan and their beneficiaries, and

(ii) the failure to permit such extension would—

(I) result in a substantial risk to the voluntary continuation of the plan, or a substantial curtailment of pension benefit levels or employee compensation, and

(II) be adverse to the interests of plan participants in the aggregate.

(C) Action by Secretary of the Treasury

The Secretary of the Treasury shall act upon any application for an extension under this paragraph within 180 days of the submission of such application. If such Secretary rejects the application for an extension under this paragraph, such Secretary shall provide notice to the plan detailing the specific reasons for the rejection, including references to the criteria set forth above.

(3) Advance notice

(A) In general

The Secretary of the Treasury shall, before granting an extension under this subsection, require each applicant to provide evidence satisfactory to such Secretary that the applicant has provided notice of the filing of the application for such extension to each affected party (as defined in section 1301(a)(21) of this title) with respect to the affected plan. Such notice shall include a description of the extent to which the plan is funded for benefits which are guaranteed under subchapter III and for benefit liabilities.

(B) Consideration of relevant information

The Secretary of the Treasury shall consider any relevant information provided by a person to whom notice was given under paragraph (1).

(Pub. L. 93–406, title I, § 304, as added Pub. L. 109–280, title II, § 201(a), Aug. 17, 2006, 120 Stat. 858.)

REFERENCES IN TEXT

The Social Security Act, referred to in subsec. (c)(4)(A), (6)(D)(v)(II), is act Aug. 14, 1935, ch. 531, 49 Stat. 620, which is classified generally to chapter 7 (§ 301 et seq.) of Title 42, The Public Health and Welfare. Title II of the Act is classified generally to subchapter II (§ 401 et seq.) of chapter 7 of Title 42. For complete classification of this Act to the Code, see section 1305 of Title 42 and Tables.

This chapter, referred to in subsec. (d)(2)(B)(i), was in the original "this Act", meaning Pub. L. 93–406, known as the Employee Retirement Income Security Act of 1974. Titles I, III, and IV of such Act are classified principally to this chapter. For complete classification of this Act to the Code, see Short Title note set out under section 1001 of this title and Tables.

PRIOR PROVISIONS

A prior section 1084, Pub. L. 93–406, title I, § 304, Sept. 2, 1974, 88 Stat. 873; Pub. L. 99–272, title XI, §§ 11015(b)(1)(B), 11016(c)(3), Apr. 7, 1986, 100 Stat. 267, 273; Pub. L. 100–203, title IX, § 9306(c)(2)(B), Dec. 22, 1987, 101 Stat. 1330–355; Pub. L. 101–239, title VII, §§ 7891(a)(1), 7894(d)(3), Dec. 19, 1989, 103 Stat. 2445, 2449, related to extension of amortization periods, prior to repeal by Pub. L. 109–280, title I, § 101(a), (d), Aug. 17, 2006, 120 Stat. 784, 789, applicable to plan years beginning after 2007.

EFFECTIVE DATE

Section applicable to plan years beginning after 2007, with special rule for certain amortization extensions, see section 201(d) of Pub. L. 109–280, set out as an Effective Date of 2006 Amendment note under section 1081 of this title.

SHORTFALL FUNDING METHOD

Pub. L. 109–280, title II, § 201(b), Aug. 17, 2006, 120 Stat. 867, as amended by Pub. L. 110–458, title I, § 102(a), Dec. 23, 2008, 122 Stat. 5100, provided that:

"(1) IN GENERAL.—A multiemployer plan meeting the criteria of paragraph (2) may adopt, use, or cease using, the shortfall funding method and such adoption, use, or cessation of use of such method, shall be deemed approved by the Secretary of the Treasury under section 302(d)(1) of the Employee Retirement Income Security Act of 1974 [29 U.S.C. 1082(d)(1)] and section 412(d)(1) of the Internal Revenue Code of 1986 [26 U.S.C. 412(d)(1)].

"(2) CRITERIA.—A multiemployer pension plan meets the criteria of this clause if—

"(A) the plan has not adopted, or ceased using, the shortfall funding method during the 5-year period ending on the day before the date the plan is to use the method under paragraph (1); and

"(B) the plan is not operating under an amortization period extension under section 304(d) of such Act [29 U.S.C. 1084(d)] and did not operate under such an extension during such 5-year period.

"(3) SHORTFALL FUNDING METHOD DEFINED.—For purposes of this subsection, the term 'shortfall funding method' means the shortfall funding method described in Treasury Regulations section 1.412(c)(1)–2 (26 CFR 1.412(c)(1)–2).

"(4) BENEFIT RESTRICTIONS TO APPLY.—The benefit restrictions under section 302(c)(7) of such Act [29 U.S.C. 1082(c)(7)] and section 412(c)(7) of such Code [26 U.S.C. 412(c)(7)] shall apply during any period a multiemployer plan is on the shortfall funding method pursuant to this subsection.

"(5) USE OF SHORTFALL METHOD NOT TO PRECLUDE OTHER OPTIONS.—Nothing in this subsection shall be construed to affect a multiemployer plan's ability to adopt the shortfall funding method with the Secretary's permission under otherwise applicable regulations or to affect a multiemployer plan's right to change funding methods, with or without the Secretary's consent, as provided in applicable rules and regulations."

[Pub. L. 109–280, § 201(b), set out above, applicable to plan years beginning after 2007, with special rule for certain amortization extensions, see section 201(d) of Pub. L. 109–280, set out as an Effective Date of 2006 Amendment note under section 1081 of this title.]

[Pub. L. 109–280, § 201(b), set out above, inapplicable to plan years beginning after Dec. 31, 2014, with exception for certain funding improvement and rehabilitation plans, see section 221(c) of Pub. L. 109–280, set out as an Effective and Termination Dates of 2006 Amendment note under section 412 of Title 26, Internal Revenue Code.]

SPECIAL RULE FOR CERTAIN BENEFITS FUNDED UNDER AN AGREEMENT APPROVED BY THE PENSION BENEFIT GUARANTY CORPORATION

For applicability of this section to a multiemployer plan that is a party to an agreement that was approved by the Pension Benefit Guaranty Corporation prior to June 30, 2005, and that increases benefits and provides for certain withdrawal liability rules, see section 206 of Pub. L. 109–280, set out as a note under section 412 of Title 26, Internal Revenue Code.

§ 1085. Additional funding rules for multiemployer plans in endangered status or critical status

(a) General rule

For purposes of this part, in the case of a multiemployer plan in effect on July 16, 2006—

(1) if the plan is in endangered status—

(A) the plan sponsor shall adopt and implement a funding improvement plan in accordance with the requirements of subsection (c), and

(B) the requirements of subsection (d) shall apply during the funding plan adoption period and the funding improvement period, and

(2) if the plan is in critical status—

(A) the plan sponsor shall adopt and implement a rehabilitation plan in accordance with the requirements of subsection (e), and

(B) the requirements of subsection (f) shall apply during the rehabilitation plan adoption period and the rehabilitation period.

(b) Determination of endangered and critical status

For purposes of this section—

(1) Endangered status

A multiemployer plan is in endangered status for a plan year if, as determined by the plan actuary under paragraph (3), the plan is not in critical status for the plan year and, as of the beginning of the plan year, either

(A) the plan's funded percentage for such plan year is less than 80 percent, or

(B) the plan has an accumulated funding deficiency for such plan year, or is projected to have such an accumulated funding deficiency for any of the 6 succeeding plan years, taking into account any extension of amortization periods under section 1084(d) of this title.

For purposes of this section, a plan shall be treated as in seriously endangered status for a plan year if the plan is described in both subparagraphs (A) and (B).

(2) Critical status

A multiemployer plan is in critical status for a plan year if, as determined by the plan actuary under paragraph (3), the plan is described in 1 or more of the following subparagraphs as of the beginning of the plan year:

(A) A plan is described in this subparagraph if—

(i) the funded percentage of the plan is less than 65 percent, and

(ii) the sum of—

(I) the fair market value of plan assets, plus

(II) the present value of the reasonably anticipated employer contributions for the current plan year and each of the 6 succeeding plan years, assuming that the terms of all collective bargaining agreements pursuant to which the plan is maintained for the current plan year continue in effect for succeeding plan years,

is less than the present value of all nonforfeitable benefits projected to be payable under the plan during the current plan year and each of the 6 succeeding plan years (plus administrative expenses for such plan years).

(B) A plan is described in this subparagraph if—

(i) the plan has an accumulated funding deficiency for the current plan year, not taking into account any extension of amortization periods under section 1084(d) of this title, or

(ii) the plan is projected to have an accumulated funding deficiency for any of the 3 succeeding plan years (4 succeeding plan years if the funded percentage of the plan is 65 percent or less), not taking into account any extension of amortization periods under section 1084(d) of this title.

(C) A plan is described in this subparagraph if—

(i)(I) the plan's normal cost for the current plan year, plus interest (determined at the rate used for determining costs under the plan) for the current plan year on the amount of unfunded benefit liabilities under the plan as of the last date of the preceding plan year, exceeds

(II) the present value of the reasonably anticipated employer and employee contributions for the current plan year,

(ii) the present value, as of the beginning of the current plan year, of nonforfeitable benefits of inactive participants is greater than the present value of nonforfeitable benefits of active participants, and

(iii) the plan has an accumulated funding deficiency for the current plan year, or is projected to have such a deficiency for any of the 4 succeeding plan years, not taking into account any extension of amortization periods under section 1084(d) of this title.

(D) A plan is described in this subparagraph if the sum of—

(i) the fair market value of plan assets, plus

(ii) the present value of the reasonably anticipated employer contributions for the current plan year and each of the 4 succeeding plan years, assuming that the terms of all collective bargaining agreements pursuant to which the plan is maintained for the current plan year continue in effect for succeeding plan years,

is less than the present value of all benefits projected to be payable under the plan during the current plan year and each of the 4 succeeding plan years (plus administrative expenses for such plan years).

(3) Annual certification by plan actuary

(A) In general

Not later than the 90th day of each plan year of a multiemployer plan, the plan actuary shall certify to the Secretary of the Treasury and to the plan sponsor—

(i) whether or not the plan is in endangered status for such plan year and whether or not the plan is or will be in critical status for such plan year, and

(ii) in the case of a plan which is in a funding improvement or rehabilitation period, whether or not the plan is making the scheduled progress in meeting the requirements of its funding improvement or rehabilitation plan.

(B) Actuarial projections of assets and liabilities

(i) In general

In making the determinations and projections under this subsection, the plan actuary shall make projections required for the current and succeeding plan years of the current value of the assets of the plan and the present value of all liabilities to participants and beneficiaries under the plan for the current plan year as of the beginning of such year. The actuary's projections shall be based on reasonable actuarial estimates, assumptions, and methods that, except as provided in clause (iii), offer the actuary's best estimate of anticipated experience under the plan. The projected present value of liabilities as of the beginning of such year shall be determined based on the most recent of either—

(I) the actuarial statement required under section 1023(d) of this title with respect to the most recently filed annual report, or

(II) the actuarial valuation for the preceding plan year.

(ii) Determinations of future contributions

Any actuarial projection of plan assets shall assume—

(I) reasonably anticipated employer contributions for the current and succeeding plan years, assuming that the terms of the one or more collective bargaining agreements pursuant to which the plan is maintained for the current plan year continue in effect for succeeding plan years, or

(II) that employer contributions for the most recent plan year will continue indefinitely, but only if the plan actuary determines there have been no significant demographic changes that would make such assumption unreasonable.

(iii) Projected industry activity

Any projection of activity in the industry or industries covered by the plan, including future covered employment and contribution levels, shall be based on information provided by the plan sponsor, which shall act reasonably and in good faith.

(C) Penalty for failure to secure timely actuarial certification

Any failure of the plan's actuary to certify the plan's status under this subsection by the date specified in subparagraph (A) shall be treated for purposes of section 1132(c)(2) of this title as a failure or refusal by the plan administrator to file the annual report required to be filed with the Secretary under section 1021(b)(1) of this title.

(D) Notice

(i) In general

In any case in which it is certified under subparagraph (A) that a multiemployer plan is or will be in endangered or critical status for a plan year, the plan sponsor shall, not later than 30 days after the date of the certification, provide notification of the endangered or critical status to the participants and beneficiaries, the bargaining parties, the Pension Benefit Guaranty Corporation, and the Secretary.

(ii) Plans in critical status

If it is certified under subparagraph (A) that a multiemployer plan is or will be in critical status, the plan sponsor shall include in the notice under clause (i) an explanation of the possibility that—

(I) adjustable benefits (as defined in subsection (e)(8)) may be reduced, and

(II) such reductions may apply to participants and beneficiaries whose benefit commencement date is on or after the date such notice is provided for the first plan year in which the plan is in critical status.

(iii) Model notice

The Secretary of the Treasury, in consultation with the Secretary[1] shall prescribe a model notice that a multiemployer plan may use to satisfy the requirements under clause (ii).

(c) Funding improvement plan must be adopted for multiemployer plans in endangered status

(1) In general

In any case in which a multiemployer plan is in endangered status for a plan year, the plan sponsor, in accordance with this subsection—

[1] So in original. Probably should be followed by a comma.

(A) shall adopt a funding improvement plan not later than 240 days following the required date for the actuarial certification of endangered status under subsection (b)(3)(A), and

(B) within 30 days after the adoption of the funding improvement plan—

(i) shall provide to the bargaining parties 1 or more schedules showing revised benefit structures, revised contribution structures, or both, which, if adopted, may reasonably be expected to enable the multiemployer plan to meet the applicable benchmarks in accordance with the funding improvement plan, including—

(I) one proposal for reductions in the amount of future benefit accruals necessary to achieve the applicable benchmarks, assuming no amendments increasing contributions under the plan (other than amendments increasing contributions necessary to achieve the applicable benchmarks after amendments have reduced future benefit accruals to the maximum extent permitted by law), and

(II) one proposal for increases in contributions under the plan necessary to achieve the applicable benchmarks, assuming no amendments reducing future benefit accruals under the plan, and

(ii) may, if the plan sponsor deems appropriate, prepare and provide the bargaining parties with additional information relating to contribution rates or benefit reductions, alternative schedules, or other information relevant to achieving the applicable benchmarks in accordance with the funding improvement plan.

For purposes of this section, the term "applicable benchmarks" means the requirements applicable to the multiemployer plan under paragraph (3) (as modified by paragraph (5)).

(2) Exception for years after process begins

Paragraph (1) shall not apply to a plan year if such year is in a funding plan adoption period or funding improvement period by reason of the plan being in endangered status for a preceding plan year. For purposes of this section, such preceding plan year shall be the initial determination year with respect to the funding improvement plan to which it relates.

(3) Funding improvement plan

For purposes of this section—

(A) In general

A funding improvement plan is a plan which consists of the actions, including options or a range of options to be proposed to the bargaining parties, formulated to provide, based on reasonably anticipated experience and reasonable actuarial assumptions, for the attainment by the plan during the funding improvement period of the following requirements:

(i) Increase in plan's funding percentage

The plan's funded percentage as of the close of the funding improvement period equals or exceeds a percentage equal to the sum of—

(I) such percentage as of the beginning of such period, plus

(II) 33 percent of the difference between 100 percent and the percentage under subclause (I).

(ii) Avoidance of accumulated funding deficiencies

No accumulated funding deficiency for any plan year during the funding improvement period (taking into account any extension of amortization periods under section 1084(d) of this title).

(B) Seriously endangered plans

In the case of a plan in seriously endangered status, except as provided in paragraph (5), subparagraph (A)(i)(II) shall be applied by substituting "20 percent" for "33 percent".

(4) Funding improvement period

For purposes of this section—

(A) In general

The funding improvement period for any funding improvement plan adopted pursuant to this subsection is the 10-year period beginning on the first day of the first plan year of the multiemployer plan beginning after the earlier of—

(i) the second anniversary of the date of the adoption of the funding improvement plan, or

(ii) the expiration of the collective bargaining agreements in effect on the due date for the actuarial certification of endangered status for the initial determination year under subsection (b)(3)(A) and covering, as of such due date, at least 75 percent of the active participants in such multiemployer plan.

(B) Seriously endangered plans

In the case of a plan in seriously endangered status, except as provided in paragraph (5), subparagraph (A) shall be applied by substituting "15-year period" for "10-year period".

(C) Coordination with changes in status

(i) Plans no longer in endangered status

If the plan's actuary certifies under subsection (b)(3)(A) for a plan year in any funding plan adoption period or funding improvement period that the plan is no longer in endangered status and is not in critical status, the funding plan adoption period or funding improvement period, whichever is applicable, shall end as of the close of the preceding plan year.

(ii) Plans in critical status

If the plan's actuary certifies under subsection (b)(3)(A) for a plan year in any funding plan adoption period or funding improvement period that the plan is in critical status, the funding plan adoption period or funding improvement period, whichever is applicable, shall end as of the close of the plan year preceding the first plan year in the rehabilitation period with respect to such status.

(D) Plans in endangered status at end of period

If the plan's actuary certifies under subsection (b)(3)(A) for the first plan year following the close of the period described in subparagraph (A) that the plan is in endangered status, the provisions of this subsection and subsection (d) shall be applied as if such first plan year were an initial determination year, except that the plan may not be amended in a manner inconsistent with the funding improvement plan in effect for the preceding plan year until a new funding improvement plan is adopted.

(5) Special rules for seriously endangered plans more than 70 percent funded

(A) In general

If the funded percentage of a plan in seriously endangered status was more than 70 percent as of the beginning of the initial determination year—

(i) paragraphs (3)(B) and (4)(B) shall apply only if the plan's actuary certifies, within 30 days after the certification under subsection (b)(3)(A) for the initial determination year, that, based on the terms of the plan and the collective bargaining agreements in effect at the time of such certification, the plan is not projected to meet the requirements of paragraph (3)(A) (without regard to paragraphs (3)(B) and (4)(B)), and

(ii) if there is a certification under clause (i), the plan may, in formulating its funding improvement plan, only take into account the rules of paragraph (3)(B) and (4)(B) for plan years in the funding improvement period beginning on or before the date on which the last of the collective bargaining agreements described in paragraph (4)(A)(ii) expires.

(B) Special rule after expiration of agreements

Notwithstanding subparagraph (A)(ii), if, for any plan year ending after the date described in subparagraph (A)(ii), the plan actuary certifies (at the time of the annual certification under subsection (b)(3)(A) for such plan year) that, based on the terms of the plan and collective bargaining agreements in effect at the time of that annual certification, the plan is not projected to be able to meet the requirements of paragraph (3)(A) (without regard to paragraphs (3)(B) and (4)(B)), paragraphs (3)(B) and (4)(B) shall continue to apply for such year.

(6) Updates to funding improvement plan and schedules

(A) Funding improvement plan

The plan sponsor shall annually update the funding improvement plan and shall file the update with the plan's annual report under section 1024 of this title.

(B) Schedules

The plan sponsor shall annually update any schedule of contribution rates provided under this subsection to reflect the experience of the plan.

(C) Duration of schedule

A schedule of contribution rates provided by the plan sponsor and relied upon by bargaining parties in negotiating a collective bargaining agreement shall remain in effect for the duration of that collective bargaining agreement.

(7) Imposition of default schedule where failure to adopt funding improvement plan

(A) In general

If—

(i) a collective bargaining agreement providing for contributions under a multiemployer plan that was in effect at the time the plan entered endangered status expires, and

(ii) after receiving one or more schedules from the plan sponsor under paragraph (1)(B), the bargaining parties with respect to such agreement fail to adopt a contribution schedule with terms consistent with the funding improvement plan and a schedule from the plan sponsor,

the plan sponsor shall implement the schedule described in paragraph (1)(B)(i)(I) beginning on the date specified in subparagraph (B).

(B) Date of implementation

The date specified in this subparagraph is the date which is 180 days after the date on which the collective bargaining agreement described in subparagraph (A) expires.

(C) Failure to make scheduled contributions

Any failure to make a contribution under a schedule of contribution rates provided under this paragraph shall be treated as a delinquent contribution under section 1145 of this title and shall be enforceable as such.

(8) Funding plan adoption period

For purposes of this section, the term "funding plan adoption period" means the period beginning on the date of the certification under subsection (b)(3)(A) for the initial determination year and ending on the day before the first day of the funding improvement period.

(d) Rules for operation of plan during adoption and improvement periods

(1) Special rules for plan adoption period

During the funding plan adoption period—

(A) the plan sponsor may not accept a collective bargaining agreement or participation agreement with respect to the multiemployer plan that provides for—

(i) a reduction in the level of contributions for any participants,

(ii) a suspension of contributions with respect to any period of service, or

(iii) any new direct or indirect exclusion of younger or newly hired employees from plan participation,

(B) no amendment of the plan which increases the liabilities of the plan by reason of any increase in benefits, any change in the accrual of benefits, or any change in the rate at which benefits become nonforfeitable under the plan may be adopted unless the amendment is required as a condition of qualification under part I of subchapter D of chapter 1 of title 26 or to comply with other applicable law, and

(C) in the case of a plan in seriously endangered status, the plan sponsor shall take all reasonable actions which are consistent with the terms of the plan and applicable law and which are expected, based on reasonable assumptions, to achieve—

(i) an increase in the plan's funded percentage, and

(ii) postponement of an accumulated funding deficiency for at least 1 additional plan year.

Actions under subparagraph (C) include applications for extensions of amortization periods under section 1084(d) of this title, use of the shortfall funding method in making funding standard account computations, amendments to the plan's benefit structure, reductions in future benefit accruals, and other reasonable actions consistent with the terms of the plan and applicable law.

(2) Compliance with funding improvement plan

(A) In general

A plan may not be amended after the date of the adoption of a funding improvement plan so as to be inconsistent with the funding improvement plan.

(B) No reduction in contributions

A plan sponsor may not during any funding improvement period accept a collective bargaining agreement or participation agreement with respect to the multiemployer plan that provides for—

(i) a reduction in the level of contributions for any participants,

(ii) a suspension of contributions with respect to any period of service, or

(iii) any new direct or indirect exclusion of younger or newly hired employees from plan participation.

(C) Special rules for benefit increases

A plan may not be amended after the date of the adoption of a funding improvement plan so as to increase benefits, including future benefit accruals, unless the plan actuary certifies that the benefit increase is consistent with the funding improvement plan and is paid for out of contributions not required by the funding improvement plan to meet the applicable benchmark in accordance with the schedule contemplated in the funding improvement plan.

(e) Rehabilitation plan must be adopted for multiemployer plans in critical status

(1) In general

In any case in which a multiemployer plan is in critical status for a plan year, the plan sponsor, in accordance with this subsection—

(A) shall adopt a rehabilitation plan not later than 240 days following the required date for the actuarial certification of critical status under subsection (b)(3)(A), and

(B) within 30 days after the adoption of the rehabilitation plan—

(i) shall provide to the bargaining parties 1 or more schedules showing revised benefit structures, revised contribution structures, or both, which, if adopted, may reasonably be expected to enable the multiemployer plan to emerge from critical status in accordance with the rehabilitation plan, and

(ii) may, if the plan sponsor deems appropriate, prepare and provide the bargaining parties with additional information relating to contribution rates or benefit reductions, alternative schedules, or other information relevant to emerging from critical status in accordance with the rehabilitation plan.

The schedule or schedules described in subparagraph (B)(i) shall reflect reductions in future benefit accruals and adjustable benefits, and increases in contributions, that the plan sponsor determines are reasonably necessary to emerge from critical status. One schedule shall be designated as the default schedule and such schedule shall assume that there are no increases in contributions under the plan other than the increases necessary to emerge from critical status after future benefit accruals and other benefits (other than benefits the reduction or elimination of which are not permitted under section 1054(g) of this title) have been reduced to the maximum extent permitted by law.

(2) Exception for years after process begins

Paragraph (1) shall not apply to a plan year if such year is in a rehabilitation plan adoption period or rehabilitation period by reason of the plan being in critical status for a preceding plan year. For purposes of this section, such preceding plan year shall be the initial critical year with respect to the rehabilitation plan to which it relates.

(3) Rehabilitation plan

For purposes of this section—

(A) In general

A rehabilitation plan is a plan which consists of—

(i) actions, including options or a range of options to be proposed to the bargaining parties, formulated, based on reasonably anticipated experience and reasonable actuarial assumptions, to enable the plan to cease to be in critical status by the end of the rehabilitation period and may include reductions in plan expenditures (including plan mergers and consolidations), reductions in future benefit accruals or increases in contributions, if agreed to by the bargaining parties, or any combination of such actions, or

(ii) if the plan sponsor determines that, based on reasonable actuarial assumptions and upon exhaustion of all reasonable measures, the plan can not reasonably be expected to emerge from critical status by the end of the rehabilitation period, reasonable measures to emerge from critical status at a later time or to forestall possible insolvency (within the meaning of section 1426 of this title).

A rehabilitation plan must provide annual standards for meeting the requirements of such rehabilitation plan. Such plan shall also include the schedules required to be provided under paragraph (1)(B)(i) and if clause (ii) applies, shall set forth the alternatives considered, explain why the plan is not reasonably expected to emerge from critical status by the end of the rehabilitation period, and specify when, if ever, the plan is expected to emerge from critical status in accordance with the rehabilitation plan.

(B) Updates to rehabilitation plan and schedules

(i) Rehabilitation plan

The plan sponsor shall annually update the rehabilitation plan and shall file the update with the plan's annual report under section 1024 of this title.

(ii) Schedules

The plan sponsor shall annually update any schedule of contribution rates provided under this subsection to reflect the experience of the plan.

(iii) Duration of schedule

A schedule of contribution rates provided by the plan sponsor and relied upon by bargaining parties in negotiating a collective bargaining agreement shall remain in effect for the duration of that collective bargaining agreement.

(C) Imposition of default schedule where failure to adopt rehabilitation plan

(i) In general

If—

(I) a collective bargaining agreement providing for contributions under a multiemployer plan that was in effect at the time the plan entered critical status expires, and

(II) after receiving one or more schedules from the plan sponsor under paragraph (1)(B), the bargaining parties with respect to such agreement fail to adopt a to adopt a[2] contribution schedule with terms consistent with the rehabilitation plan and a schedule from the plan sponsor under paragraph (1)(B)(i),

the plan sponsor shall implement the default schedule described in the last sentence of paragraph (1) beginning on the date specified in clause (ii).

(ii) Date of implementation

The date specified in this clause is the date which is 180 days after the date on which the collective bargaining agreement described in clause (i) expires.

(iii) Failure to make scheduled contributions

Any failure to make a contribution under a schedule of contribution rates provided under this subsection shall be treated as a delinquent contribution under section 1145 of this title and shall be enforceable as such.

(4) Rehabilitation period

For purposes of this section—

(A) In general

The rehabilitation period for a plan in critical status is the 10-year period beginning on the first day of the first plan year of the multiemployer plan following the earlier of—

(i) the second anniversary of the date of the adoption of the rehabilitation plan, or

(ii) the expiration of the collective bargaining agreements in effect on the due date for the actuarial certification of critical status for the initial critical year under subsection (a)(1) and covering, as of such date at least 75 percent of the active participants in such multiemployer plan.

If a plan emerges from critical status as provided under subparagraph (B) before the end of such 10-year period, the rehabilitation period shall end with the plan year preceding the plan year for which the determination under subparagraph (B) is made.

(B) Emergence

A plan in critical status shall remain in such status until a plan year for which the plan actuary certifies, in accordance with subsection (b)(3)(A), that the plan is not projected to have an accumulated funding deficiency for the plan year or any of the 9 succeeding plan years, without regard to the use of the shortfall method but taking into account any extension of amortization periods under section 1084(d) of this title.

(5) Rehabilitation plan adoption period

For purposes of this section, the term "rehabilitation plan adoption period" means the period beginning on the date of the certification under subsection (b)(3)(A) for the initial critical year and ending on the day before the first day of the rehabilitation period.

(6) Limitation on reduction in rates of future accruals

Any reduction in the rate of future accruals under the default schedule described in the last sentence of paragraph (1) shall not reduce the rate of future accruals below—

(A) a monthly benefit (payable as a single life annuity commencing at the participant's normal retirement age) equal to 1 percent of the contributions required to be made with respect to a participant, or the equivalent standard accrual rate for a participant or group of participants under the collective bargaining agreements in effect as of the first day of the initial critical year, or

(B) if lower, the accrual rate under the plan on such first day.

The equivalent standard accrual rate shall be determined by the plan sponsor based on the standard or average contribution base units which the plan sponsor determines to be representative for active participants and such

[2] So in original. See 2008 Amendment note below.

other factors as the plan sponsor determines to be relevant. Nothing in this paragraph shall be construed as limiting the ability of the plan sponsor to prepare and provide the bargaining parties with alternative schedules to the default schedule that establish lower or higher accrual and contribution rates than the rates otherwise described in this paragraph.

(7) Automatic employer surcharge

(A) Imposition of surcharge

Each employer otherwise obligated to make contributions for the initial critical year shall be obligated to pay to the plan for such year a surcharge equal to 5 percent of the contributions otherwise required under the applicable collective bargaining agreement (or other agreement pursuant to which the employer contributes). For each succeeding plan year in which the plan is in critical status for a consecutive period of years beginning with the initial critical year, the surcharge shall be 10 percent of the contributions otherwise so required.

(B) Enforcement of surcharge

The surcharges under subparagraph (A) shall be due and payable on the same schedule as the contributions on which the surcharges are based. Any failure to make a surcharge payment shall be treated as a delinquent contribution under section 1145 of this title and shall be enforceable as such.

(C) Surcharge to terminate upon collective bargaining agreement renegotiation

The surcharge under this paragraph shall cease to be effective with respect to employees covered by a collective bargaining agreement (or other agreement pursuant to which the employer contributes), beginning on the effective date of a collective bargaining agreement (or other such agreement) that includes terms consistent with a schedule presented by the plan sponsor under paragraph (1)(B)(i), as modified under subparagraph (B) of paragraph (3).

(D) Surcharge not to apply until employer receives notice

The surcharge under this paragraph shall not apply to an employer until 30 days after the employer has been notified by the plan sponsor that the plan is in critical status and that the surcharge is in effect.

(E) Surcharge not to generate increased benefit accruals

Notwithstanding any provision of a plan to the contrary, the amount of any surcharge under this paragraph shall not be the basis for any benefit accrual under the plan.

(8) Benefit adjustments

(A) Adjustable benefits

(i) In general

Notwithstanding section 1054(g) of this title, the plan sponsor shall, subject to the notice requirements in subparagraph (C), make any reductions to adjustable benefits which the plan sponsor deems appropriate, based upon the outcome of collective bargaining over the schedule or schedules provided under paragraph (1)(B)(i).

(ii) Exception for retirees

Except in the case of adjustable benefits described in clause (iv)(III), the plan sponsor of a plan in critical status shall not reduce adjustable benefits of any participant or beneficiary whose benefit commencement date is before the date on which the plan provides notice to the participant or beneficiary under subsection (b)(3)(D) for the initial critical year.

(iii) Plan sponsor flexibility

The plan sponsor shall include in the schedules provided to the bargaining parties an allowance for funding the benefits of participants with respect to whom contributions are not currently required to be made, and shall reduce their benefits to the extent permitted under this subchapter and considered appropriate by the plan sponsor based on the plan's then current overall funding status.

(iv) Adjustable benefit defined

For purposes of this paragraph, the term "adjustable benefit" means—

(I) benefits, rights, and features under the plan, including post-retirement death benefits, 60-month guarantees, disability benefits not yet in pay status, and similar benefits,

(II) any early retirement benefit or retirement-type subsidy (within the meaning of section 1054(g)(2)(A) of this title) and any benefit payment option (other than the qualified joint and survivor annuity), and

(III) benefit increases that would not be eligible for a guarantee under section 1322a of this title on the first day of initial critical year because the increases were adopted (or, if later, took effect) less than 60 months before such first day.

(B) Normal retirement benefits protected

Except as provided in subparagraph (A)(iv)(III), nothing in this paragraph shall be construed to permit a plan to reduce the level of a participant's accrued benefit payable at normal retirement age.

(C) Notice requirements

(i) In general

No reduction may be made to adjustable benefits under subparagraph (A) unless notice of such reduction has been given at least 30 days before the general effective date of such reduction for all participants and beneficiaries to—

(I) plan participants and beneficiaries,

(II) each employer who has an obligation to contribute (within the meaning of section 1392(a) of this title) under the plan, and

(III) each employee organization which, for purposes of collective bargaining, represents plan participants employed by such an employer.

(ii) Content of notice

The notice under clause (i) shall contain—

(I) sufficient information to enable participants and beneficiaries to understand the effect of any reduction on their benefits, including an estimate (on an annual or monthly basis) of any affected adjustable benefit that a participant or beneficiary would otherwise have been eligible for as of the general effective date described in clause (i), and

(II) information as to the rights and remedies of plan participants and beneficiaries as well as how to contact the Department of Labor for further information and assistance where appropriate.

(iii) Form and manner

Any notice under clause (i)—

(I) shall be provided in a form and manner prescribed in regulations of the Secretary of the Treasury, in consultation with the Secretary,

(II) shall be written in a manner so as to be understood by the average plan participant, and

(III) may be provided in written, electronic, or other appropriate form to the extent such form is reasonably accessible to persons to whom the notice is required to be provided.

The Secretary of the Treasury shall in the regulations prescribed under subclause (I) establish a model notice that a plan sponsor may use to meet the requirements of this subparagraph.

(9) Adjustments disregarded in withdrawal liability determination

(A) Benefit reductions

Any benefit reductions under this subsection shall be disregarded in determining a plan's unfunded vested benefits for purposes of determining an employer's withdrawal liability under section 1381 of this title.

(B) Surcharges

Any surcharges under paragraph (7) shall be disregarded in determining the allocation of unfunded vested benefits to an employer under section 1391 of this title, except for purposes of determining the unfunded vested benefits attributable to an employer under section 1391(c)(4) of this title or a comparable method approved under section 1391(c)(5) of this title.

(C) Simplified calculations

The Pension Benefit Guaranty Corporation shall prescribe simplified methods for the application of this paragraph in determining withdrawal liability.

(f) Rules for operation of plan during adoption and rehabilitation period

(1) Compliance with rehabilitation plan

(A) In general

A plan may not be amended after the date of the adoption of a rehabilitation plan under subsection (e) so as to be inconsistent with the rehabilitation plan.

(B) Special rules for benefit increases

A plan may not be amended after the date of the adoption of a rehabilitation plan under subsection (e) so as to increase benefits, including future benefit accruals, unless the plan actuary certifies that such increase is paid for out of additional contributions not contemplated by the rehabilitation plan, and, after taking into account the benefit increase, the multiemployer plan still is reasonably expected to emerge from critical status by the end of the rehabilitation period on the schedule contemplated in the rehabilitation plan.

(2) Restriction on lump sums and similar benefits

(A) In general

Effective on the date the notice of certification of the plan's critical status for the initial critical year under subsection (b)(3)(D) is sent, and notwithstanding section 1054(g) of this title, the plan shall not pay—

(i) any payment, in excess of the monthly amount paid under a single life annuity (plus any social security supplements described in the last sentence of section 1054(b)(1)(G) of this title), to a participant or beneficiary whose annuity starting date (as defined in section 1055(h)(2) of this title) occurs after the date such notice is sent,

(ii) any payment for the purchase of an irrevocable commitment from an insurer to pay benefits, and

(iii) any other payment specified by the Secretary of the Treasury by regulations.

(B) Exception

Subparagraph (A) shall not apply to a benefit which under section 1053(e) of this title may be immediately distributed without the consent of the participant or to any makeup payment in the case of a retroactive annuity starting date or any similar payment of benefits owed with respect to a prior period.

(3) Adjustments disregarded in withdrawal liability determination

Any benefit reductions under this subsection shall be disregarded in determining a plan's unfunded vested benefits for purposes of determining an employer's withdrawal liability under section 1381 of this title.

(4) Special rules for plan adoption period

During the rehabilitation plan adoption period—

(A) the plan sponsor may not accept a collective bargaining agreement or participation agreement with respect to the multiemployer plan that provides for—

(i) a reduction in the level of contributions for any participants,

(ii) a suspension of contributions with respect to any period of service, or

(iii) any new direct or indirect exclusion of younger or newly hired employees from plan participation, and

(B) no amendment of the plan which increases the liabilities of the plan by reason of any increase in benefits, any change in the accrual of benefits, or any change in the rate at which benefits become nonforfeitable under the plan may be adopted unless the amendment is required as a condition of qualification under part I of subchapter D of chapter 1 of title 26 or to comply with other applicable law.

(g) Expedited resolution of plan sponsor decisions

If, within 60 days of the due date for adoption of a funding improvement plan under subsection (c) or a rehabilitation plan under subsection (e), the plan sponsor of a plan in endangered status or a plan in critical status has not agreed on a funding improvement plan or rehabilitation plan, then any member of the board or group that constitutes the plan sponsor may require that the plan sponsor enter into an expedited dispute resolution procedure for the development and adoption of a funding improvement plan or rehabilitation plan.

(h) Nonbargained participation

(1) Both bargained and nonbargained employee-participants

In the case of an employer that contributes to a multiemployer plan with respect to both employees who are covered by one or more collective bargaining agreements and employees who are not so covered, if the plan is in endangered status or in critical status, benefits of and contributions for the nonbargained employees, including surcharges on those contributions, shall be determined as if those nonbargained employees were covered under the first to expire of the employer's collective bargaining agreements in effect when the plan entered endangered or critical status.

(2) Nonbargained employees only

In the case of an employer that contributes to a multiemployer plan only with respect to employees who are not covered by a collective bargaining agreement, this section shall be applied as if the employer were the bargaining party, and its participation agreement with the plan were a collective bargaining agreement with a term ending on the first day of the plan year beginning after the employer is provided the schedule or schedules described in subsections (c) and (e).

(i) Definitions; actuarial method

For purposes of this section—

(1) Bargaining party

The term "bargaining party" means—

(A)(i) except as provided in clause (ii), an employer who has an obligation to contribute under the plan; or

(ii) in the case of a plan described under section 404(c) of title 26, or a continuation of such a plan, the association of employers that is the employer settlor of the plan; and

(B) an employee organization which, for purposes of collective bargaining, represents plan participants employed by an employer who has an obligation to contribute under the plan.

(2) Funded percentage

The term "funded percentage" means the percentage equal to a fraction—

(A) the numerator of which is the value of the plan's assets, as determined under section 1084(c)(2) of this title, and

(B) the denominator of which is the accrued liability of the plan, determined using actuarial assumptions described in section 1084(c)(3) of this title.

(3) Accumulated funding deficiency

The term "accumulated funding deficiency" has the meaning given such term in section 1084(a) of this title.

(4) Active participant

The term "active participant" means, in connection with a multiemployer plan, a participant who is in covered service under the plan.

(5) Inactive participant

The term "inactive participant" means, in connection with a multiemployer plan, a participant, or the beneficiary or alternate payee of a participant, who—

(A) is not in covered service under the plan, and

(B) is in pay status under the plan or has a nonforfeitable right to benefits under the plan.

(6) Pay status

A person is in pay status under a multiemployer plan if—

(A) at any time during the current plan year, such person is a participant or beneficiary under the plan and is paid an early, late, normal, or disability retirement benefit under the plan (or a death benefit under the plan related to a retirement benefit), or

(B) to the extent provided in regulations of the Secretary of the Treasury, such person is entitled to such a benefit under the plan.

(7) Obligation to contribute

The term "obligation to contribute" has the meaning given such term under section 1392(a) of this title.

(8) Actuarial method

Notwithstanding any other provision of this section, the actuary's determinations with respect to a plan's normal cost, actuarial accrued liability, and improvements in a plan's funded percentage under this section shall be based upon the unit credit funding method (whether or not that method is used for the plan's actuarial valuation).

(9) Plan sponsor

In the case of a plan described under section 404(c) of title 26, or a continuation of such a plan, the term "plan sponsor" means the bargaining parties described under paragraph (1).

(10) Benefit commencement date

The term "benefit commencement date" means the annuity starting date (or in the case of a retroactive annuity starting date, the date on which benefit payments begin).

(Pub. L. 93–406, title I, § 305, as added Pub. L. 109–280, title II, § 202(a), Aug. 17, 2006, 120 Stat. 868; amended Pub. L. 110–458, title I, § 102(b)(1)(B)–(G), Dec. 23, 2008, 122 Stat. 5100, 5101.)

TERMINATION OF SECTION

For termination of section by section 221(c) of Pub. L. 109–280, see Effective and Termination Dates note below.

PRIOR PROVISIONS

A prior section 1085, Pub. L. 93–406, title I, §305, Sept. 2, 1974, 88 Stat. 873, related to alternative minimum funding standard, prior to repeal by Pub. L. 109–280, title I, §101(a), (d), Aug. 17, 2006, 120 Stat. 784, 789, applicable to plan years beginning after 2007.

AMENDMENTS

2008—Subsec. (b)(3)(C). Pub. L. 110–458, §102(b)(1)(B), substituted "section 1021(b)(1)" for "section 1021(b)(4)".

Subsec. (b)(3)(D)(iii). Pub. L. 110–458, §102(b)(1)(C), substituted "The Secretary of the Treasury, in consultation with the Secretary" for "The Secretary".

Subsec. (c)(7)(A)(ii). Pub. L. 110–458, §102(b)(1)(D)(i), substituted "to adopt a contribution schedule with terms consistent with the funding improvement plan and a schedule from the plan sponsor," for "to agree on changes to contribution or benefit schedules necessary to meet the applicable benchmarks in accordance with the funding improvement plan,".

Subsec. (c)(7)(B), (C). Pub. L. 110–458, §102(b)(1)(D)(ii), (iii), added subpars. (B) and (C) and struck out former subpar. (B). Prior to amendment, text read as follows: "The date specified in this subparagraph is the earlier of the date—

"(i) on which the Secretary certifies that the parties are at an impasse, or

"(ii) which is 180 days after the date on which the collective bargaining agreement described in subparagraph (A) expires."

Subsec. (e)(3)(C)(i)(II). Pub. L. 110–458, §102(b)(1)(E)(i)(I), substituted "to adopt a contribution schedule with terms consistent with the rehabilitation plan and a schedule from the plan sponsor under paragraph (1)(B)(i)," for "contribution or benefit schedules with terms consistent with the rehabilitation plan and the schedule from the plan sponsor under paragraph (1)(B)(i),".

Subsec. (e)(3)(C)(ii), (iii). Pub. L. 110–458, §102(b)(1)(E)(i)(II), (III), added cls. (ii) and (iii) and struck out former cl. (ii). Prior to amendment, text read as follows: "The date specified in this clause is the earlier of the date—

"(I) on which the Secretary certifies that the parties are at an impasse, or

"(II) which is 180 days after the date on which the collective bargaining agreement described in clause (i) expires."

Subsec. (e)(4)(A)(ii). Pub. L. 110–458, §102(b)(1)(E)(ii)(I), struck out "the date of" before "the due date".

Subsec. (e)(4)(B). Pub. L. 110–458, §102(b)(1)(E)(ii)(II), substituted "but taking" for "and taking".

Subsec. (e)(6). Pub. L. 110–458, §102(b)(1)(E)(iii), substituted "the last sentence of paragraph (1)" for "paragraph (1)(B)(i)" in introductory provisions and "establish" for "established" in concluding provisions.

Subsec. (e)(8)(C)(iii). Pub. L. 110–458, §102(b)(1)(E)(iv), substituted "the Secretary of the Treasury, in consultation with the Secretary" for "the Secretary" in subcl. (I) and "Secretary of the Treasury" for "Secretary" in concluding provisions.

Subsec. (e)(9)(B). Pub. L. 110–458, §102(b)(1)(E)(v), substituted "the allocation of unfunded vested benefits to an employer" for "an employer's withdrawal liability".

Subsec. (f)(2)(A)(i). Pub. L. 110–458, §102(b)(1)(F), inserted at end "to a participant or beneficiary whose annuity starting date (as defined in section 1055(h)(2) of this title) occurs after the date such notice is sent,".

Subsec. (g). Pub. L. 110–458, §102(b)(1)(G), inserted "under subsection (c)" before "or a rehabilitation plan under subsection (e)".

EFFECTIVE DATE OF 2008 AMENDMENT

Amendment by Pub. L. 110–458 effective as if included in the provisions of Pub. L. 109–280 to which the amendment relates, except as otherwise provided, see section 112 of Pub. L. 110–458, set out as a note under section 72 of Title 26, Internal Revenue Code.

EFFECTIVE AND TERMINATION DATES

Section applicable with respect to plan years beginning after 2007, with special rules for certain notices and certain restored benefits, see section 202(f) of Pub. L. 109–280, set out as an Effective and Termination Dates of 2006 Amendment note under section 1082 of this title.

Section inapplicable to plan years beginning after Dec. 31, 2014, with exception for certain funding improvement and rehabilitation plans, see section 221(c) of Pub. L. 109–280, set out as an Effective and Termination Dates of 2006 Amendment note under section 412 of Title 26, Internal Revenue Code.

TEMPORARY DELAY OF DESIGNATION OF MULTIEMPLOYER PLANS AS IN ENDANGERED OR CRITICAL STATUS

For provisions allowing election of delay of status designation of endangered or critical multiemployer plans for purposes of this section, see section 204 of Pub. L. 110–458, set out as a note under section 432 of Title 26, Internal Revenue Code.

TEMPORARY EXTENSION OF THE FUNDING IMPROVEMENT AND REHABILITATION PERIODS FOR MULTIEMPLOYER PENSION PLANS IN CRITICAL AND ENDANGERED STATUS FOR 2008 OR 2009

For provisions allowing election of extension of funding improvement period or rehabilitation period of endangered or critical multiemployer plans for purposes of this section, see section 205 of Pub. L. 110–458, set out as a note under section 432 of Title 26, Internal Revenue Code.

SPECIAL RULE FOR CERTAIN BENEFITS FUNDED UNDER AN AGREEMENT APPROVED BY THE PENSION BENEFIT GUARANTY CORPORATION

For applicability of this section to a multiemployer plan that is a party to an agreement that was approved by the Pension Benefit Guaranty Corporation prior to June 30, 2005, and that increases benefits and provides for certain withdrawal liability rules, see section 206 of Pub. L. 109–280, set out as a note under section 412 of Title 26, Internal Revenue Code.

§§ 1085a, 1085b, 1086. Repealed. Pub. L. 109–280, title I, § 101(a), Aug. 17, 2006, 120 Stat. 784

Section 1085a, Pub. L. 93–406, title I, §306, as added Pub. L. 99–272, title XI, §11015(a)(1)(A)(ii), Apr. 7, 1986, 100 Stat. 264; amended Pub. L. 100–203, title IX, §9306(e)(2), Dec. 22, 1987, 101 Stat. 1330–355; Pub. L. 101–239, title VII, §7891(a)(1), Dec. 19, 1989, 103 Stat. 2445, related to security for waivers of minimum funding standard and extensions of amortization period.

Section 1085b, Pub. L. 93–406, title I, §307, as added Pub. L. 100–203, title IX, §9341(b)(2), Dec. 22, 1987, 101 Stat. 1330–370; amended Pub. L. 101–239, title VII, §7881(i)(1)(B)–(3)(A), (4)(B), Dec. 19, 1989, 103 Stat. 2442, related to security required upon adoption of plan amendment resulting in significant underfunding.

Section 1086, Pub. L. 93–406, title I, §308, formerly §306, Sept. 2, 1974, 88 Stat. 874, renumbered §307, Pub. L. 99–272, title XI, §11015(a)(1)(A)(i), Apr. 7, 1986, 100 Stat. 264; renumbered §308, Pub. L. 100–203, title IX, §9341(b)(1), Dec. 22, 1987, 101 Stat. 1330–370; amended Pub. L. 101–239, title VII, §7894(h)(3), Dec. 19, 1989, 103 Stat. 2451, related to effective dates of part.

EFFECTIVE DATE OF REPEAL

Repeal applicable to plan years beginning after 2007, see section 101(d) of Pub. L. 109–280, set out as an Effective Date note under section 1082 of this title.

APPLICABILITY OF AMENDMENTS BY SUBTITLES A AND B OF TITLE I OF PUB. L. 109–280

For special rules on applicability of amendments by subtitles A (§§101–107) and B (§§111–116) of title I of Pub.

L. 109–280 to certain eligible cooperative plans, PBGC settlement plans, and eligible government contractor plans, see sections 104, 105, and 106 of Pub. L. 109–280, set out as notes under section 401 of Title 26, Internal Revenue Code.

PART 4—FIDUCIARY RESPONSIBILITY

§1101. Coverage

(a) Scope of coverage

This part shall apply to any employee benefit plan described in section 1003(a) of this title (and not exempted under section 1003(b) of this title), other than—

(1) a plan which is unfunded and is maintained by an employer primarily for the purpose of providing deferred compensation for a select group of management or highly compensated employees; or

(2) any agreement described in section 736 of title 26, which provides payments to a retired partner or deceased partner or a deceased partner's successor in interest.

(b) Securities or policies deemed to be included in plan assets

For purposes of this part:

(1) In the case of a plan which invests in any security issued by an investment company registered under the Investment Company Act of 1940 [15 U.S.C. 80a–1 et seq.], the assets of such plan shall be deemed to include such security but shall not, solely by reason of such investment, be deemed to include any assets of such investment company.

(2) In the case of a plan to which a guaranteed benefit policy is issued by an insurer, the assets of such plan shall be deemed to include such policy, but shall not, solely by reason of the issuance of such policy, be deemed to include any assets of such insurer. For purposes of this paragraph:

(A) The term "insurer" means an insurance company, insurance service, or insurance organization, qualified to do business in a State.

(B) The term "guaranteed benefit policy" means an insurance policy or contract to the extent that such policy or contract provides for benefits the amount of which is guaranteed by the insurer. Such term includes any surplus in a separate account, but excludes any other portion of a separate account.

(c) Clarification of application of ERISA to insurance company general accounts

(1)(A) Not later than June 30, 1997, the Secretary shall issue proposed regulations to provide guidance for the purpose of determining, in cases where an insurer issues 1 or more policies to or for the benefit of an employee benefit plan (and such policies are supported by assets of such insurer's general account), which assets held by the insurer (other than plan assets held in its separate accounts) constitute assets of the plan for purposes of this part and section 4975 of title 26 and to provide guidance with respect to the application of this subchapter to the general account assets of insurers.

(B) The proposed regulations under subparagraph (A) shall be subject to public notice and comment until September 30, 1997.

(C) The Secretary shall issue final regulations providing the guidance described in subparagraph (A) not later than December 31, 1997.

(D) Such regulations shall only apply with respect to policies which are issued by an insurer on or before December 31, 1998, to or for the benefit of an employee benefit plan which is supported by assets of such insurer's general account. With respect to policies issued on or before December 31, 1998, such regulations shall take effect at the end of the 18-month period following the date on which such regulations become final.

(2) The Secretary shall ensure that the regulations issued under paragraph (1)—

(A) are administratively feasible, and

(B) protect the interests and rights of the plan and of its participants and beneficiaries (including meeting the requirements of paragraph (3)).

(3) The regulations prescribed by the Secretary pursuant to paragraph (1) shall require, in connection with any policy issued by an insurer to or for the benefit of an employee benefit plan to the extent that the policy is not a guaranteed benefit policy (as defined in subsection (b)(2)(B) of this section)—

(A) that a plan fiduciary totally independent of the insurer authorize the purchase of such policy (unless such purchase is a transaction exempt under section 1108(b)(5) of this title),

(B) that the insurer describe (in such form and manner as shall be prescribed in such regulations), in annual reports and in policies issued to the policyholder after the date on which such regulations are issued in final form pursuant to paragraph (1)(C)—

(i) a description of the method by which any income and expenses of the insurer's general account are allocated to the policy during the term of the policy and upon the termination of the policy, and

(ii) for each report, the actual return to the plan under the policy and such other financial information as the Secretary may deem appropriate for the period covered by each such annual report,

(C) that the insurer disclose to the plan fiduciary the extent to which alternative arrangements supported by assets of separate accounts of the insurer (which generally hold plan assets) are available, whether there is a right under the policy to transfer funds to a separate account and the terms governing any such right, and the extent to which support by assets of the insurer's general account and support by assets of separate accounts of the insurer might pose differing risks to the plan, and

(D) that the insurer manage those assets of the insurer which are assets of such insurer's general account (irrespective of whether any such assets are plan assets) with the care, skill, prudence, and diligence under the circumstances then prevailing that a prudent man acting in a like capacity and familiar with such matters would use in the conduct of an enterprise of a like character and with like aims, taking into account all obligations supported by such enterprise.

(4) Compliance by the insurer with all requirements of the regulations issued by the Secretary pursuant to paragraph (1) shall be deemed compliance by such insurer with sections 1104, 1106, and 1107 of this title with respect to those assets of the insurer's general account which support a policy described in paragraph (3).

(5)(A) Subject to subparagraph (B), any regulations issued under paragraph (1) shall not take effect before the date on which such regulations become final.

(B) No person shall be subject to liability under this part or section 4975 of title 26 for conduct which occurred before the date which is 18 months following the date described in subparagraph (A) on the basis of a claim that the assets of an insurer (other than plan assets held in a separate account) constitute assets of the plan, except—

(i) as otherwise provided by the Secretary in regulations intended to prevent avoidance of the regulations issued under paragraph (1), or

(ii) as provided in an action brought by the Secretary pursuant to paragraph (2) or (5) of section 1132(a) of this title for a breach of fiduciary responsibilities which would also constitute a violation of Federal or State criminal law.

The Secretary shall bring a cause of action described in clause (ii) if a participant, beneficiary, or fiduciary demonstrates to the satisfaction of the Secretary that a breach described in clause (ii) has occurred.

(6) Nothing in this subsection shall preclude the application of any Federal criminal law.

(7) For purposes of this subsection, the term "policy" includes a contract.

(Pub. L. 93–406, title I, § 401, Sept. 2, 1974, 88 Stat. 874; Pub. L. 101–239, title VII, § 7891(a)(1), Dec. 19, 1989, 103 Stat. 2445; Pub. L. 104–188, title I, § 1460(a), Aug. 20, 1996, 110 Stat. 1820.)

REFERENCES IN TEXT

The Investment Company Act of 1940, referred to in subsec. (b)(1), is title I of act Aug. 22, 1940, ch. 686, 54 Stat. 789, as amended, which is classified generally to subchapter I (§ 80a–1 et seq.) of chapter 2D of Title 15, Commerce and Trade. For complete classification of this Act to the Code, see section 80a–51 of Title 15 and Tables.

AMENDMENTS

1996—Subsec. (c). Pub. L. 104–188 added subsec. (c).

1989—Subsec. (a)(2). Pub. L. 101–239 substituted "Internal Revenue Code of 1986" for "Internal Revenue Code of 1954", which for purposes of codification was translated as "title 26" thus requiring no change in text.

EFFECTIVE DATE OF 1996 AMENDMENT

Section 1460(b) of Pub. L. 104–188 provided that:

"(1) IN GENERAL.—Except as provided in paragraph (2), the amendment made by this section [amending this section] shall take effect on January 1, 1975.

"(2) CIVIL ACTIONS.—The amendment made by this section shall not apply to any civil action commenced before November 7, 1995."

EFFECTIVE DATE OF 1989 AMENDMENT

Amendment by Pub. L. 101–239 effective, except as otherwise provided, as if included in the provision of the Tax Reform Act of 1986, Pub. L. 99–514, to which such amendment relates, see section 7891(f) of Pub. L. 101–239, set out as a note under section 1002 of this title.

PLAN AMENDMENTS NOT REQUIRED UNTIL JANUARY 1, 1998

For provisions directing that if any amendments made by subtitle D [§§ 1401–1465] of title I of Pub. L. 104–188 require an amendment to any plan or annuity contract, such amendment shall not be required to be made before the first day of the first plan year beginning on or after Jan. 1, 1998, see section 1465 of Pub. L. 104–188, set out as a note under section 401 of Title 26, Internal Revenue Code.

§ 1102. Establishment of plan

(a) Named fiduciaries

(1) Every employee benefit plan shall be established and maintained pursuant to a written instrument. Such instrument shall provide for one or more named fiduciaries who jointly or severally shall have authority to control and manage the operation and administration of the plan.

(2) For purposes of this subchapter, the term "named fiduciary" means a fiduciary who is named in the plan instrument, or who, pursuant to a procedure specified in the plan, is identified as a fiduciary (A) by a person who is an employer or employee organization with respect to the plan or (B) by such an employer and such an employee organization acting jointly.

(b) Requisite features of plan

Every employee benefit plan shall—

(1) provide a procedure for establishing and carrying out a funding policy and method consistent with the objectives of the plan and the requirements of this subchapter,

(2) describe any procedure under the plan for the allocation of responsibilities for the operation and administration of the plan (including any procedure described in section 1105(c)(1) of this title),

(3) provide a procedure for amending such plan, and for identifying the persons who have authority to amend the plan, and

(4) specify the basis on which payments are made to and from the plan.

(c) Optional features of plan

Any employee benefit plan may provide—

(1) that any person or group of persons may serve in more than one fiduciary capacity with respect to the plan (including service both as trustee and administrator);

(2) that a named fiduciary, or a fiduciary designated by a named fiduciary pursuant to a plan procedure described in section 1105(c)(1) of this title, may employ one or more persons to render advice with regard to any responsibility such fiduciary has under the plan; or

(3) that a person who is a named fiduciary with respect to control or management of the assets of the plan may appoint an investment manager or managers to manage (including the power to acquire and dispose of) any assets of a plan.

(Pub. L. 93–406, title I, § 402, Sept. 2, 1974, 88 Stat. 875.)

§ 1103. Establishment of trust

(a) Benefit plan assets to be held in trust; authority of trustees

Except as provided in subsection (b) of this section, all assets of an employee benefit plan shall be held in trust by one or more trustees. Such trustee or trustees shall be either named in the trust instrument or in the plan instrument described in section 1102(a) of this title or appointed by a person who is a named fiduciary, and upon acceptance of being named or appointed, the trustee or trustees shall have exclusive authority and discretion to manage and control the assets of the plan, except to the extent that—

(1) the plan expressly provides that the trustee or trustees are subject to the direction of a named fiduciary who is not a trustee, in which case the trustees shall be subject to proper directions of such fiduciary which are made in accordance with the terms of the plan and which are not contrary to this chapter, or

(2) authority to manage, acquire, or dispose of assets of the plan is delegated to one or more investment managers pursuant to section 1102(c)(3) of this title.

(b) Exceptions

The requirements of subsection (a) of this section shall not apply—

(1) to any assets of a plan which consist of insurance contracts or policies issued by an insurance company qualified to do business in a State;

(2) to any assets of such an insurance company or any assets of a plan which are held by such an insurance company;

(3) to a plan—

(A) some or all of the participants of which are employees described in section 401(c)(1) of title 26; or

(B) which consists of one or more individual retirement accounts described in section 408 of title 26;

to the extent that such plan's assets are held in one or more custodial accounts which qualify under section 401(f) or 408(h) of title 26, whichever is applicable.

(4) to a plan which the Secretary exempts from the requirement of subsection (a) of this section and which is not subject to any of the following provisions of this chapter—

(A) part 2 of this subtitle,

(B) part 3 of this subtitle, or

(C) subchapter III of this chapter; or

(5) to a contract established and maintained under section 403(b) of title 26 to the extent that the assets of the contract are held in one or more custodial accounts pursuant to section 403(b)(7) of title 26.

(6) Any plan, fund or program under which an employer, all of whose stock is directly or indirectly owned by employees, former employees or their beneficiaries, proposes through an unfunded arrangement to compensate retired employees for benefits which were forfeited by such employees under a pension plan maintained by a former employer prior to the date such pension plan became subject to this chapter.

(c) Assets of plan not to inure to benefit of employer; allowable purposes of holding plan assets

(1) Except as provided in paragraph (2), (3), or (4) or subsection (d) of this section, or under sections 1342 and 1344 of this title (relating to termination of insured plans), or under section 420 of title 26 (as in effect on August 17, 2006), the assets of a plan shall never inure to the benefit of any employer and shall be held for the exclusive purposes of providing benefits to participants in the plan and their beneficiaries and defraying reasonable expenses of administering the plan.

(2)(A) In the case of a contribution, or a payment of withdrawal liability under part 1 of subtitle E of subchapter III of this chapter—

(i) if such contribution or payment is made by an employer to a plan (other than a multiemployer plan) by a mistake of fact, paragraph (1) shall not prohibit the return of such contribution to the employer within one year after the payment of the contribution, and

(ii) if such contribution or payment is made by an employer to a multiemployer plan by a mistake of fact or law (other than a mistake relating to whether the plan is described in section 401(a) of title 26 or the trust which is part of such plan is exempt from taxation under section 501(a) of title 26), paragraph (1) shall not prohibit the return of such contribution or payment to the employer within 6 months after the plan administrator determines that the contribution was made by such a mistake.

(B) If a contribution is conditioned on initial qualification of the plan under section 401 or 403(a) of title 26, and if the plan receives an adverse determination with respect to its initial qualification, then paragraph (1) shall not prohibit the return of such contribution to the employer within one year after such determination, but only if the application for the determination is made by the time prescribed by law for filing the employer's return for the taxable year in which such plan was adopted, or such later date as the Secretary of the Treasury may prescribe.

(C) If a contribution is conditioned upon the deductibility of the contribution under section 404 of title 26, then, to the extent the deduction is disallowed, paragraph (1) shall not prohibit the return to the employer of such contribution (to the extent disallowed) within one year after the disallowance of the deduction.

(3) In the case of a withdrawal liability payment which has been determined to be an overpayment, paragraph (1) shall not prohibit the return of such payment to the employer within 6 months after the date of such determination.

(d) Termination of plan

(1) Upon termination of a pension plan to which section 1321 of this title does not apply at the time of termination and to which this part applies (other than a plan to which no employer contributions have been made) the assets of the plan shall be allocated in accordance with the provisions of section 1344 of this title, except as otherwise provided in regulations of the Secretary.

(2) The assets of a welfare plan which terminates shall be distributed in accordance with the terms of the plan, except as otherwise provided in regulations of the Secretary.

(Pub. L. 93–406, title I, § 403, Sept. 2, 1974, 88 Stat. 876; Pub. L. 96–364, title III, § 310, title IV,

§§402(b)(2), 410(a), 411(c), Sept. 26, 1980, 94 Stat. 1296, 1299, 1308; Pub. L. 100–203, title IX, §9343(c), Dec. 22, 1987, 101 Stat. 1330–372; Pub. L. 101–239, title VII, §§7881(k), 7891(a)(1), 7894(e)(1)(A), (3), Dec. 19, 1989, 103 Stat. 2443, 2445, 2450; Pub. L. 101–508, title XII, §12012(a), Nov. 5, 1990, 104 Stat. 1388–571; Pub. L. 103–465, title VII, §731(c)(4)(B), Dec. 8, 1994, 108 Stat. 5004; Pub. L. 106–170, title V, §535(a)(2)(B), Dec. 17, 1999, 113 Stat. 1934; Pub. L. 108–218, title II, §204(b)(2), Apr. 10, 2004, 118 Stat. 609; Pub. L. 108–357, title VII, §709(a)(2), Oct. 22, 2004, 118 Stat. 1551; Pub. L. 109–280, title I, §107(a)(11), Aug. 17, 2006, 120 Stat. 819.)

REFERENCES IN TEXT

This chapter, referred to in subsecs. (a)(1) and (b)(4), (6), was in the original "this Act", meaning Pub. L. 93–406, known as the Employee Retirement Income Security Act of 1974. Titles I, III, and IV of such Act are classified principally to this chapter. For complete classification of this Act to the Code, see Short Title note set out under section 1001 of this title and Tables.

AMENDMENTS

2006—Subsec. (c)(1). Pub. L. 109–280 substituted "August 17, 2006" for "October 22, 2004".

2004—Subsec. (c)(1). Pub. L. 108–357 substituted "October 22, 2004" for "April 10, 2004".

Pub. L. 108–218 substituted "April 10, 2004" for "December 17, 1999".

1999—Subsec. (c)(1). Pub. L. 106–170 substituted "December 17, 1999" for "January 1, 1995".

1994—Subsec. (c)(1). Pub. L. 103–465 substituted "1995" for "1991".

1990—Subsec. (c)(1). Pub. L. 101–508 inserted ", or under section 420 of title 26 (as in effect on January 1, 1991)" after "insured plans".

1989—Subsecs. (b)(3), (5), (c)(2)(A)(ii), (C). Pub. L. 101–239, §7891(a)(1), substituted "Internal Revenue Code of 1986" for "Internal Revenue Code of 1954", which for purposes of codification was translated as "title 26" thus requiring no change in text.

Subsec. (b)(3). Pub. L. 101–239, §7894(e)(3), redesignated cls. (i) and (ii) as subpars. (A) and (B), respectively, struck out ", to the extent that such plan's assets are held in one or more custodial accounts which qualify under section 401(f) or 408(h) of title 26, whichever is applicable" before the semicolon in subpar. (B), and inserted concluding provision "to the extent that such plan's assets are held in one or more custodial accounts which qualify under section 401(f) or 408(h) of title 26, whichever is applicable."

Subsec. (c)(2)(A). Pub. L. 101–239, §7894(e)(1)(A), in introductory provisions, made technical amendment to reference to part 1 of subtitle E of subchapter III of this chapter to correct reference to corresponding part of original Act, requiring no change in text, and in cls. (i) and (ii), inserted "if such contribution or payment is" before "made by an employer".

Subsec. (c)(3), (4). Pub. L. 101–239, §7881(k), redesignated par. (4) as (3) and struck out former par. (3) which read as follows: "In the case of a contribution which would otherwise be an excess contribution (as defined in section 4979(c) of title 26) paragraph (1) shall not prohibit a correcting distribution with respect to such contribution from the plan to the employer to the extent permitted in such section to avoid payment of an excise tax on excess contributions under such section."

1987—Subsec. (c)(2)(B). Pub. L. 100–203, §9343(c)(1), amended subpar. (B) generally. Prior to amendment, subpar. (B) read as follows: "If a contribution is conditioned on qualification of the plan under section 401, 403(a), or 405(a) of title 26, and if the plan does not qualify, then paragraph (1) shall not prohibit the return of such contributions to the employer within one year after the date of denial of qualification of the plan."

Subsec. (c)(3). Pub. L. 100–203, §9343(c)(2), substituted "section 4979(c) of title 26" for "section 4972(b) of title 26".

1980—Subsec. (a)(1). Pub. L. 96–364, §402(b)(2), substituted "chapter" for "subchapter".

Subsec. (b)(6). Pub. L. 96–364, §411(c), added par. (6).

Subsec. (c)(1). Pub. L. 96–364, §310(1), inserted reference to par. (4).

Subsec. (c)(2)(A). Pub. L. 96–364, §410(a), substituted provisions relating to contributions or payments of withdrawal liability under part 1 of subtitle E of subchapter III of this chapter made by an employer to a plan by a mistake of fact, and by an employer to a multiemployer plan by a mistake of fact or law, for provisions relating to contributions made by an employer by a mistake of fact.

Subsec. (c)(4). Pub. L. 96–364, §310(2), added par. (4).

EFFECTIVE DATE OF 2006 AMENDMENT

Amendment by Pub. L. 109–280 applicable to plan years beginning after 2007, see section 107(e) of Pub. L. 109–280, set out as a note under section 1021 of this title.

EFFECTIVE DATE OF 1999 AMENDMENT

Amendment by Pub. L. 106–170 applicable to qualified transfers occurring after Dec. 17, 1999, see section 535(c)(1) of Pub. L. 106–170, set out as a note under section 420 of Title 26, Internal Revenue Code.

EFFECTIVE DATE OF 1990 AMENDMENT

Amendment by Pub. L. 101–508 applicable to qualified transfers under section 420 of title 26 made after Nov. 5, 1990, see section 12012(e) of Pub. L. 101–508, set out as a note under section 1021 of this title.

EFFECTIVE DATE OF 1989 AMENDMENT

Amendment by section 7881(k) of Pub. L. 101–239 effective, except as otherwise provided, as if included in the provision of the Pension Protection Act, Pub. L. 100–203, §§9302–9346, to which such amendment relates, see section 7882 of Pub. L. 101–239, set out as a note under section 401 of Title 26, Internal Revenue Code.

Amendment by section 7891(a)(1) of Pub. L. 101–239 effective, except as otherwise provided, as if included in the provision of the Tax Reform Act of 1986, Pub. L. 99–514, to which such amendment relates, see section 7891(f) of Pub. L. 101–239, set out as a note under section 1002 of this title.

Section 7894(e)(1)(B) of Pub. L. 101–239 provided that: "The amendments made by subparagraph (A) [amending this section] shall take effect as if included in section 410 of the Multiemployer Pension Plan Amendments Act of 1980 [Pub. L. 96–364]."

Amendment by section 7894(e)(3) of Pub. L. 101–239 effective, except as otherwise provided, as if originally included in the provision of the Employee Retirement Income Security Act of 1974, Pub. L. 93–406, to which such amendment relates, see section 7894(i) of Pub. L. 101–239, set out as a note under section 1002 of this title.

EFFECTIVE DATE OF 1980 AMENDMENT

Amendment by Pub. L. 96–364 effective Sept. 26, 1980, except as specifically provided, see section 1461(e) of this title.

Amendment by section 410(a) of Pub. L. 96–364 effective Jan. 1, 1975, except with respect to contributions received by a collectively bargained plan maintained by more than one employer before Sept. 26, 1980, see section 410(c) of Pub. L. 96–364, set out as a note under section 401 of Title 26, Internal Revenue Code.

REGULATIONS

Secretary authorized, effective Sept. 2, 1974, to promulgate regulations wherever provisions of this part call for the promulgation of regulations, see sections 1031 and 1114 of this title.

APPLICABILITY OF AMENDMENTS BY SUBTITLES A AND B OF TITLE I OF PUB. L. 109–280

For special rules on applicability of amendments by subtitles A (§§101–107) and B (§§111–116) of title I of Pub.

L. 109–280 to certain eligible cooperative plans, PBGC settlement plans, and eligible government contractor plans, see sections 104, 105, and 106 of Pub. L. 109–280, set out as notes under section 401 of Title 26, Internal Revenue Code.

§1104. Fiduciary duties

(a) Prudent man standard of care

(1) Subject to sections 1103(c) and (d), 1342, and 1344 of this title, a fiduciary shall discharge his duties with respect to a plan solely in the interest of the participants and beneficiaries and—

(A) for the exclusive purpose of:

(i) providing benefits to participants and their beneficiaries; and

(ii) defraying reasonable expenses of administering the plan;

(B) with the care, skill, prudence, and diligence under the circumstances then prevailing that a prudent man acting in a like capacity and familiar with such matters would use in the conduct of an enterprise of a like character and with like aims;

(C) by diversifying the investments of the plan so as to minimize the risk of large losses, unless under the circumstances it is clearly prudent not to do so; and

(D) in accordance with the documents and instruments governing the plan insofar as such documents and instruments are consistent with the provisions of this subchapter and subchapter III of this chapter.

(2) In the case of an eligible individual account plan (as defined in section 1107(d)(3) of this title), the diversification requirement of paragraph (1)(C) and the prudence requirement (only to the extent that it requires diversification) of paragraph (1)(B) is not violated by acquisition or holding of qualifying employer real property or qualifying employer securities (as defined in section 1107(d)(4) and (5) of this title).

(b) Indicia of ownership of assets outside jurisdiction of district courts

Except as authorized by the Secretary by regulations, no fiduciary may maintain the indicia of ownership of any assets of a plan outside the jurisdiction of the district courts of the United States.

(c) Control over assets by participant or beneficiary

(1)(A) In the case of a pension plan which provides for individual accounts and permits a participant or beneficiary to exercise control over the assets in his account, if a participant or beneficiary exercises control over the assets in his account (as determined under regulations of the Secretary)—

(i) such participant or beneficiary shall not be deemed to be a fiduciary by reason of such exercise, and

(ii) no person who is otherwise a fiduciary shall be liable under this part for any loss, or by reason of any breach, which results from such participant's or beneficiary's exercise of control, except that this clause shall not apply in connection with such participant or beneficiary for any blackout period during which the ability of such participant or beneficiary to direct the investment of the assets in his or her account is suspended by a plan sponsor or fiduciary.

(B) If a person referred to in subparagraph (A)(ii) meets the requirements of this subchapter in connection with authorizing and implementing the blackout period, any person who is otherwise a fiduciary shall not be liable under this subchapter for any loss occurring during such period.

(C) For purposes of this paragraph, the term "blackout period" has the meaning given such term by section 1021(i)(7) of this title.

(2) In the case of a simple retirement account established pursuant to a qualified salary reduction arrangement under section 408(p) of title 26, a participant or beneficiary shall, for purposes of paragraph (1), be treated as exercising control over the assets in the account upon the earliest of—

(A) an affirmative election among investment options with respect to the initial investment of any contribution,

(B) a rollover to any other simple retirement account or individual retirement plan, or

(C) one year after the simple retirement account is established.

No reports, other than those required under section 1021(g) of this title, shall be required with respect to a simple retirement account established pursuant to such a qualified salary reduction arrangement.

(3) In the case of a pension plan which makes a transfer to an individual retirement account or annuity of a designated trustee or issuer under section 401(a)(31)(B) of title 26, the participant or beneficiary shall, for purposes of paragraph (1), be treated as exercising control over the assets in the account or annuity upon—

(A) the earlier of—

(i) a rollover of all or a portion of the amount to another individual retirement account or annuity; or

(ii) one year after the transfer is made; or

(B) a transfer that is made in a manner consistent with guidance provided by the Secretary.

(4)(A) In any case in which a qualified change in investment options occurs in connection with an individual account plan, a participant or beneficiary shall not be treated for purposes of paragraph (1) as not exercising control over the assets in his account in connection with such change if the requirements of subparagraph (C) are met in connection with such change.

(B) For purposes of subparagraph (A), the term "qualified change in investment options" means, in connection with an individual account plan, a change in the investment options offered to the participant or beneficiary under the terms of the plan, under which—

(i) the account of the participant or beneficiary is reallocated among one or more remaining or new investment options which are offered in lieu of one or more investment options offered immediately prior to the effective date of the change, and

(ii) the stated characteristics of the remaining or new investment options provided under clause (i), including characteristics relating to risk and rate of return, are, as of immediately after the change, reasonably similar to those of the existing investment options as of immediately before the change.

(C) The requirements of this subparagraph are met in connection with a qualified change in investment options if—

(i) at least 30 days and no more than 60 days prior to the effective date of the change, the plan administrator furnishes written notice of the change to the participants and beneficiaries, including information comparing the existing and new investment options and an explanation that, in the absence of affirmative investment instructions from the participant or beneficiary to the contrary, the account of the participant or beneficiary will be invested in the manner described in subparagraph (B),

(ii) the participant or beneficiary has not provided to the plan administrator, in advance of the effective date of the change, affirmative investment instructions contrary to the change, and

(iii) the investments under the plan of the participant or beneficiary as in effect immediately prior to the effective date of the change were the product of the exercise by such participant or beneficiary of control over the assets of the account within the meaning of paragraph (1).

(5) DEFAULT INVESTMENT ARRANGEMENTS.—

(A) IN GENERAL.—For purposes of paragraph (1), a participant or beneficiary in an individual account plan meeting the notice requirements of subparagraph (B) shall be treated as exercising control over the assets in the account with respect to the amount of contributions and earnings which, in the absence of an investment election by the participant or beneficiary, are invested by the plan in accordance with regulations prescribed by the Secretary. The regulations under this subparagraph shall provide guidance on the appropriateness of designating default investments that include a mix of asset classes consistent with capital preservation or long-term capital appreciation, or a blend of both.

(B) NOTICE REQUIREMENTS.—

(i) IN GENERAL.—The requirements of this subparagraph are met if each participant or beneficiary—

(I) receives, within a reasonable period of time before each plan year, a notice explaining the employee's right under the plan to designate how contributions and earnings will be invested and explaining how, in the absence of any investment election by the participant or beneficiary, such contributions and earnings will be invested, and

(II) has a reasonable period of time after receipt of such notice and before the beginning of the plan year to make such designation.

(ii) FORM OF NOTICE.—The requirements of clauses (i) and (ii) of section 401(k)(12)(D) of title 26 shall apply with respect to the notices described in this subparagraph.

(d) Plan terminations

(1) If, in connection with the termination of a pension plan which is a single-employer plan, there is an election to establish or maintain a qualified replacement plan, or to increase benefits, as provided under section 4980(d) of title 26, a fiduciary shall discharge the fiduciary's duties under this subchapter and subchapter III of this chapter in accordance with the following requirements:

(A) In the case of a fiduciary of the terminated plan, any requirement—

(i) under section 4980(d)(2)(B) of title 26 with respect to the transfer of assets from the terminated plan to a qualified replacement plan, and

(ii) under section 4980(d)(2)(B)(ii) or 4980(d)(3) of title 26 with respect to any increase in benefits under the terminated plan.

(B) In the case of a fiduciary of a qualified replacement plan, any requirement—

(i) under section 4980(d)(2)(A) of title 26 with respect to participation in the qualified replacement plan of active participants in the terminated plan,

(ii) under section 4980(d)(2)(B) of title 26 with respect to the receipt of assets from the terminated plan, and

(iii) under section 4980(d)(2)(C) of title 26 with respect to the allocation of assets to participants of the qualified replacement plan.

(2) For purposes of this subsection—

(A) any term used in this subsection which is also used in section 4980(d) of title 26 shall have the same meaning as when used in such section, and

(B) any reference in this subsection to title 26 shall be a reference to title 26 as in effect immediately after the enactment of the Omnibus Budget Reconciliation Act of 1990.

(Pub. L. 93–406, title I, §404, Sept. 2, 1974, 88 Stat. 877; Pub. L. 96–364, title III, §309, Sept. 26, 1980, 94 Stat. 1296; Pub. L. 101–508, title XII, §12002(b)(1), (2)(A), Nov. 5, 1990, 104 Stat. 1388–565, 1388–566; Pub. L. 104–188, title I, §1421(d)(2), Aug. 20, 1996, 110 Stat. 1799; Pub. L. 107–16, title VI, §657(c)(1), June 7, 2001, 115 Stat. 136; Pub. L. 107–147, title IV, §411(t), Mar. 9, 2002, 116 Stat. 51; Pub. L. 109–280, title VI, §§621(a), 624(a), Aug. 17, 2006, 120 Stat. 978, 980; Pub. L. 110–458, title I, §106(d), Dec. 23, 2008, 122 Stat. 5107.)

REFERENCES IN TEXT

The enactment of the Omnibus Budget Reconciliation Act of 1990, referred to in subsec. (d)(2)(B), is the enactment of Pub. L. 101–508, which was approved Nov. 5, 1990.

AMENDMENTS

2008—Subsec. (c)(5). Pub. L. 110–458 substituted "participant or beneficiary" for "participant" wherever appearing.

2006—Subsec. (c)(1). Pub. L. 109–280, §621(a)(1), designated existing provisions as subpar. (A), redesignated former subpars. (A) and (B) as cls. (i) and (ii), respectively, of subpar. (A), in cl. (ii), inserted ", except that this clause shall not apply in connection with such participant or beneficiary for any blackout period during which the ability of such participant or beneficiary to direct the investment of the assets in his or her account is suspended by a plan sponsor or fiduciary" before period at end, and added subpars. (B) and (C).

Subsec. (c)(4). Pub. L. 109–280, §621(a)(2), added par. (4).

Subsec. (c)(5). Pub. L. 109–280, § 624(a), added par. (5).

2002—Subsec. (c)(3)(A). Pub. L. 107–147, § 411(t)(1), struck out "the earlier of" after "the earlier of" in introductory provisions.

Subsec. (c)(3)(B). Pub. L. 107–147, § 411(t)(2), substituted "a transfer that" for "if the transfer".

2001—Subsec. (c)(3). Pub. L. 107–16 added par. (3).

1996—Subsec. (c). Pub. L. 104–188 designated existing provisions as par. (1), redesignated former pars. (1) and (2) as subpars. (A) and (B), respectively, and added par. (2).

1990—Subsec. (a)(1)(D). Pub. L. 101–508, § 12002(b)(2)(A), substituted "and subchapter III" for "or subchapter III".

Subsec. (d). Pub. L. 101–508, § 12002(b)(1), added subsec. (d).

1980—Subsec. (a)(1)(D). Pub. L. 96–364 inserted reference to subchapter III of this chapter.

EFFECTIVE DATE OF 2008 AMENDMENT

Amendment by Pub. L. 110–458 effective as if included in the provisions of Pub. L. 109–280 to which the amendment relates, except as otherwise provided, see section 112 of Pub. L. 110–458, set out as a note under section 72 of Title 26, Internal Revenue Code.

EFFECTIVE DATE OF 2006 AMENDMENT

Pub. L. 109–280, title VI, § 621(b), Aug. 17, 2006, 120 Stat. 979, provided that:

"(1) IN GENERAL.—The amendments made by this section [amending this section] shall apply to plan years beginning after December 31, 2007.

"(2) SPECIAL RULE FOR COLLECTIVELY BARGAINED AGREEMENTS.—In the case of a plan maintained pursuant to 1 or more collective bargaining agreements between employee representatives and 1 or more employers ratified on or before the date of the enactment of this Act [Aug. 17, 2006], paragraph (1) shall be applied to benefits pursuant to, and individuals covered by, any such agreement by substituting for 'December 31, 2007' the earlier of—

"(A) the later of—

"(i) December 31, 2008, or

"(ii) the date on which the last of such collective bargaining agreements terminates (determined without regard to any extension thereof after such date of enactment), or

"(B) December 31, 2009."

Pub. L. 109–280, title VI, § 624(b), Aug. 17, 2006, 120 Stat. 980, provided that:

"(1) IN GENERAL.—The amendments made by this section [amending this section] shall apply to plan years beginning after December 31, 2006.

"(2) REGULATIONS.—Final regulations under section 404(c)(5)(A) of the Employee Retirement Income Security Act of 1974 [29 U.S.C. 1104(c)(5)(A)] (as added by this section) shall be issued no later than 6 months after the date of the enactment of this Act [Aug. 17, 2006]."

EFFECTIVE DATE OF 2002 AMENDMENT

Amendment by Pub. L. 107–147 effective as if included in the provisions of the Economic Growth and Tax Relief Reconciliation Act of 2001, Pub. L. 107–16, to which such amendment relates, see section 411(x) of Pub. L. 107–147, set out as a note under section 25B of Title 26, Internal Revenue Code.

EFFECTIVE DATE OF 2001 AMENDMENT

Amendment by Pub. L. 107–16 applicable to distributions made after Mar. 28, 2005, see section 657(d) of Pub. L. 107–16, set out as a note under section 401 of Title 26, Internal Revenue Code.

EFFECTIVE DATE OF 1996 AMENDMENT

Amendment by Pub. L. 104–188 applicable to taxable years beginning after Dec. 31, 1996, see section 1421(e) of Pub. L. 104–188, set out as a note under section 72 of Title 26, Internal Revenue Code.

EFFECTIVE DATE OF 1990 AMENDMENT

Amendment by Pub. L. 101–508 applicable to reversions occurring after Sept. 30, 1990, but not applicable to any reversion after Sept. 30, 1990, if (1) in the case of plans subject to subchapter III of this chapter, notice of intent to terminate under such subchapter was provided to participants (or if no participants, to Pension Benefit Guaranty Corporation) before Oct. 1, 1990, (2) in the case of plans subject to subchapter I of this chapter (and not subchapter III), notice of intent to reduce future accruals under section 1054(h) of this title was provided to participants in connection with termination before Oct. 1, 1990, (3) in the case of plans not subject to subchapter I or III of this chapter, a request for a determination letter with respect to termination was filed with Secretary of the Treasury or Secretary's delegate before Oct. 1, 1990, or (4) in the case of plans not subject to subchapter I or III of this chapter and having only one participant, a resolution terminating the plan was adopted by employer before Oct. 1, 1990, see section 12003 of Pub. L. 101–508, set out as a note under section 4980 of Title 26, Internal Revenue Code.

EFFECTIVE DATE OF 1980 AMENDMENT

Amendment by Pub. L. 96–364 effective Sept. 26, 1980, except as specifically provided, see section 1461(e) of this title.

REGULATIONS

Pub. L. 109–280, title VI, § 625, Aug. 17, 2006, 120 Stat. 980, provided that:

"(a) IN GENERAL.—Not later than 1 year after the date of the enactment of this Act [Aug. 17, 2006], the Secretary of Labor shall issue final regulations clarifying that the selection of an annuity contract as an optional form of distribution from an individual account plan to a participant or beneficiary—

"(1) is not subject to the safest available annuity standard under Interpretive Bulletin 95–1 (29 CFR 2509.95–1), and

"(2) is subject to all otherwise applicable fiduciary standards.

"(b) EFFECTIVE DATE.—This section shall take effect on the date of enactment of this Act [Aug. 17, 2006]."

Secretary authorized, effective Sept. 2, 1974, to promulgate regulations wherever provisions of this part call for the promulgation of regulations, see sections 1031 and 1114 of this title.

PLAN AMENDMENTS NOT REQUIRED UNTIL JANUARY 1, 1998

For provisions directing that if any amendments made by subtitle D [§§ 1401–1465] of title I of Pub. L. 104–188 require an amendment to any plan or annuity contract, such amendment shall not be required to be made before the first day of the first plan year beginning on or after Jan. 1, 1998, see section 1465 of Pub. L. 104–188, set out as a note under section 401 of Title 26, Internal Revenue Code.

§ 1105. Liability for breach of co-fiduciary

(a) Circumstances giving rise to liability

In addition to any liability which he may have under any other provisions of this part, a fiduciary with respect to a plan shall be liable for a breach of fiduciary responsibility of another fiduciary with respect to the same plan in the following circumstances:

(1) if he participates knowingly in, or knowingly undertakes to conceal, an act or omission of such other fiduciary, knowing such act or omission is a breach;

(2) if, by his failure to comply with section 1104(a)(1) of this title in the administration of his specific responsibilities which give rise to his status as a fiduciary, he has enabled such other fiduciary to commit a breach; or

(3) if he has knowledge of a breach by such other fiduciary, unless he makes reasonable

efforts under the circumstances to remedy the breach.

(b) Assets held by two or more trustees

(1) Except as otherwise provided in subsection (d) of this section and in section 1103(a)(1) and (2) of this title, if the assets of a plan are held by two or more trustees—

(A) each shall use reasonable care to prevent a co-trustee from committing a breach; and

(B) they shall jointly manage and control the assets of the plan, except that nothing in this subparagraph (B) shall preclude any agreement, authorized by the trust instrument, allocating specific responsibilities, obligations, or duties among trustees, in which event a trustee to whom certain responsibilities, obligations, or duties have not been allocated shall not be liable by reason of this subparagraph (B) either individually or as a trustee for any loss resulting to the plan arising from the acts or omissions on the part of another trustee to whom such responsibilities, obligations, or duties have been allocated.

(2) Nothing in this subsection shall limit any liability that a fiduciary may have under subsection (a) of this section or any other provision of this part.

(3)(A) In the case of a plan the assets of which are held in more than one trust, a trustee shall not be liable under paragraph (1) except with respect to an act or omission of a trustee of a trust of which he is a trustee.

(B) No trustee shall be liable under this subsection for following instructions referred to in section 1103(a)(1) of this title.

(c) Allocation of fiduciary responsibility; designated persons to carry out fiduciary responsibilities

(1) The instrument under which a plan is maintained may expressly provide for procedures (A) for allocating fiduciary responsibilities (other than trustee responsibilities) among named fiduciaries, and (B) for named fiduciaries to designate persons other than named fiduciaries to carry out fiduciary responsibilities (other than trustee responsibilities) under the plan.

(2) If a plan expressly provides for a procedure described in paragraph (1), and pursuant to such procedure any fiduciary responsibility of a named fiduciary is allocated to any person, or a person is designated to carry out any such responsibility, then such named fiduciary shall not be liable for an act or omission of such person in carrying out such responsibility except to the extent that—

(A) the named fiduciary violated section 1104(a)(1) of this title—

(i) with respect to such allocation or designation,

(ii) with respect to the establishment or implementation of the procedure under paragraph (1), or

(iii) in continuing the allocation or designation; or

(B) the named fiduciary would otherwise be liable in accordance with subsection (a) of this section.

(3) For purposes of this subsection, the term "trustee responsibility" means any responsibility provided in the plan's trust instrument (if any) to manage or control the assets of the plan, other than a power under the trust instrument of a named fiduciary to appoint an investment manager in accordance with section 1102(c)(3) of this title.

(d) Investment managers

(1) If an investment manager or managers have been appointed under section 1102(c)(3) of this title, then, notwithstanding subsections (a)(2) and (3) and subsection (b) of this section, no trustee shall be liable for the acts or omissions of such investment manager or managers, or be under an obligation to invest or otherwise manage any asset of the plan which is subject to the management of such investment manager.

(2) Nothing in this subsection shall relieve any trustee of any liability under this part for any act of such trustee.

(Pub. L. 93–406, title I, §405, Sept. 2, 1974, 88 Stat. 878.)

§1106. Prohibited transactions

(a) Transactions between plan and party in interest

Except as provided in section 1108 of this title:

(1) A fiduciary with respect to a plan shall not cause the plan to engage in a transaction, if he knows or should know that such transaction constitutes a direct or indirect—

(A) sale or exchange, or leasing, of any property between the plan and a party in interest;

(B) lending of money or other extension of credit between the plan and a party in interest;

(C) furnishing of goods, services, or facilities between the plan and a party in interest;

(D) transfer to, or use by or for the benefit of a party in interest, of any assets of the plan; or

(E) acquisition, on behalf of the plan, of any employer security or employer real property in violation of section 1107(a) of this title.

(2) No fiduciary who has authority or discretion to control or manage the assets of a plan shall permit the plan to hold any employer security or employer real property if he knows or should know that holding such security or real property violates section 1107(a) of this title.

(b) Transactions between plan and fiduciary

A fiduciary with respect to a plan shall not—

(1) deal with the assets of the plan in his own interest or for his own account,

(2) in his individual or in any other capacity act in any transaction involving the plan on behalf of a party (or represent a party) whose interests are adverse to the interests of the plan or the interests of its participants or beneficiaries, or

(3) receive any consideration for his own personal account from any party dealing with such plan in connection with a transaction involving the assets of the plan.

(c) Transfer of real or personal property to plan by party in interest

A transfer of real or personal property by a party in interest to a plan shall be treated as a sale or exchange if the property is subject to a mortgage or similar lien which the plan assumes or if it is subject to a mortgage or similar lien which a party-in-interest placed on the property within the 10-year period ending on the date of the transfer.

(Pub. L. 93–406, title I, §406, Sept. 2, 1974, 88 Stat. 879.)

§1107. Limitation with respect to acquisition and holding of employer securities and employer real property by certain plans

(a) Percentage limitation

Except as otherwise provided in this section and section 1114 of this title:

(1) A plan may not acquire or hold—

(A) any employer security which is not a qualifying employer security, or

(B) any employer real property which is not qualifying employer real property.

(2) A plan may not acquire any qualifying employer security or qualifying employer real property, if immediately after such acquisition the aggregate fair market value of employer securities and employer real property held by the plan exceeds 10 percent of the fair market value of the assets of the plan.

(3)(A) After December 31, 1984, a plan may not hold any qualifying employer securities or qualifying employer real property (or both) to the extent that the aggregate fair market value of such securities and property determined on December 31, 1984, exceeds 10 percent of the greater of—

(i) the fair market value of the assets of the plan, determined on December 31, 1984, or

(ii) the fair market value of the assets of the plan determined on January 1, 1975.

(B) Subparagraph (A) of this paragraph shall not apply to any plan which on any date after December 31, 1974; and before January 1, 1985, did not hold employer securities or employer real property (or both) the aggregate fair market value of which determined on such date exceeded 10 percent of the greater of

(i) the fair market value of the assets of the plan, determined on such date, or

(ii) the fair market value of the assets of the plan determined on January 1, 1975.

(4)(A) After December 31, 1979, a plan may not hold any employer securities or employer real property in excess of the amount specified in regulations under subparagraph (B). This subparagraph shall not apply to a plan after the earliest date after December 31, 1974, on which it complies with such regulations.

(B) Not later than December 31, 1976, the Secretary shall prescribe regulations which shall have the effect of requiring that a plan divest itself of 50 percent of the holdings of employer securities and employer real property which the plan would be required to divest before January 1, 1985, under paragraph (2) or subsection (c) of this section (whichever is applicable).

(b) Exception

(1) Subsection (a) of this section shall not apply to any acquisition or holding of qualifying employer securities or qualifying employer real property by an eligible individual account plan.

(2)(A) If this paragraph applies to an eligible individual account plan, the portion of such plan which consists of applicable elective deferrals (and earnings allocable thereto) shall be treated as a separate plan—

(i) which is not an eligible individual account plan, and

(ii) to which the requirements of this section apply.

(B)(i) This paragraph shall apply to any eligible individual account plan if any portion of the plan's applicable elective deferrals (or earnings allocable thereto) are required to be invested in qualifying employer securities or qualifying employer real property or both—

(I) pursuant to the terms of the plan, or

(II) at the direction of a person other than the participant on whose behalf such elective deferrals are made to the plan (or a beneficiary).

(ii) This paragraph shall not apply to an individual account plan for a plan year if, on the last day of the preceding plan year, the fair market value of the assets of all individual account plans maintained by the employer equals not more than 10 percent of the fair market value of the assets of all pension plans (other than multiemployer plans) maintained by the employer.

(iii) This paragraph shall not apply to an individual account plan that is an employee stock ownership plan as defined in section 4975(e)(7) of title 26.

(iv) This paragraph shall not apply to an individual account plan if, pursuant to the terms of the plan, the portion of any employee's applicable elective deferrals which is required to be invested in qualifying employer securities and qualifying employer real property for any year may not exceed 1 percent of the employee's compensation which is taken into account under the plan in determining the maximum amount of the employee's applicable elective deferrals for such year.

(C) For purposes of this paragraph, the term "applicable elective deferral" means any elective deferral (as defined in section 402(g)(3)(A) of title 26) which is made pursuant to a qualified cash or deferred arrangement as defined in section 401(k) of title 26.

(3) CROSS REFERENCES.—

(A) For exemption from diversification requirements for holding of qualifying employer securities and qualifying employer real property by eligible individual account plans, see section 1104(a)(2) of this title.

(B) For exemption from prohibited transactions for certain acquisitions of qualifying employer securities and qualifying employer real property which are not in violation of 10 percent limitation, see section 1108(e) of this title.

(C) For transitional rules respecting securities or real property subject to binding contracts in effect on June 30, 1974, see section 1114(c) of this title.

(D) For diversification requirements for qualifying employer securities held in certain individual account plans, see section 1054(j) of this title.

(c) Election

(1) A plan which makes the election, under paragraph (3) shall be treated as satisfying the requirement of subsection (a)(3) of this section if and only if employer securities held on any date after December 31, 1974 and before January 1, 1985 have a fair market value, determined as of December 31, 1974, not in excess of 10 percent of the lesser of—

(A) the fair market value of the assets of the plan determined on such date (disregarding any portion of the fair market value of employer securities which is attributable to appreciation of such securities after December 31, 1974) but not less than the fair market value of plan assets on January 1, 1975, or

(B) an amount equal to the sum of (i) the total amount of the contributions to the plan received after December 31, 1974, and prior to such date, plus (ii) the fair market value of the assets of the plan, determined on January 1, 1975.

(2) For purposes of this subsection, in the case of an employer security held by a plan after January 1, 1975, the ownership of which is derived from ownership of employer securities held by the plan on January 1, 1975, or from the exercise of rights derived from such ownership, the value of such security held after January 1, 1975, shall be based on the value as of January 1, 1975, of the security from which ownership was derived. The Secretary shall prescribe regulations to carry out this paragraph.

(3) An election under this paragraph may not be made after December 31, 1975. Such an election shall be made in accordance with regulations prescribed by the Secretary, and shall be irrevocable. A plan may make an election under this paragraph only if on January 1, 1975, the plan holds no employer real property. After such election and before January 1, 1985 the plan may not acquire any employer real property.

(d) Definitions

For purposes of this section—

(1) The term "employer security" means a security issued by an employer of employees covered by the plan, or by an affiliate of such employer. A contract to which section 1108(b)(5) of this title applies shall not be treated as a security for purposes of this section.

(2) The term "employer real property" means real property (and related personal property) which is leased to an employer of employees covered by the plan, or to an affiliate of such employer. For purposes of determining the time at which a plan acquires employer real property for purposes of this section, such property shall be deemed to be acquired by the plan on the date on which the plan acquires the property or on the date on which the lease to the employer (or affiliate) is entered into, whichever is later.

(3)(A) The term "eligible individual account plan" means an individual account plan which is (i) a profit-sharing, stock bonus, thrift, or savings plan; (ii) an employee stock ownership plan; or (iii) a money purchase plan which was in existence on September 2, 1974, and which on such date invested primarily in qualifying employer securities. Such term excludes an individual retirement account or annuity described in section 408 of title 26.

(B) Notwithstanding subparagraph (A), a plan shall be treated as an eligible individual account plan with respect to the acquisition or holding of qualifying employer real property or qualifying employer securities only if such plan explicitly provides for acquisition and holding of qualifying employer securities or qualifying employer real property (as the case may be). In the case of a plan in existence on September 2, 1974, this subparagraph shall not take effect until January 1, 1976.

(C) The term "eligible individual account plan" does not include any individual account plan the benefits of which are taken into account in determining the benefits payable to a participant under any defined benefit plan.

(4) The term "qualifying employer real property" means parcels of employer real property—

(A) if a substantial number of the parcels are dispersed geographically;

(B) if each parcel of real property and the improvements thereon are suitable (or adaptable without excessive cost) for more than one use;

(C) even if all of such real property is leased to one lessee (which may be an employer, or an affiliate of an employer); and

(D) if the acquisition and retention of such property comply with the provisions of this part (other than section 1104(a)(1)(B) of this title to the extent it requires diversification, and sections 1104(a)(1)(C), 1106 of this title, and subsection (a) of this section).

(5) The term "qualifying employer security" means an employer security which is—

(A) stock,

(B) a marketable obligation (as defined in subsection (e) of this section), or

(C) an interest in a publicly traded partnership (as defined in section 7704(b) of title 26), but only if such partnership is an existing partnership as defined in section 10211(c)(2)(A) of the Revenue Act of 1987 (Public Law 100–203).

After December 17, 1987, in the case of a plan other than an eligible individual account plan, an employer security described in subparagraph (A) or (C) shall be considered a qualifying employer security only if such employer security satisfies the requirements of subsection (f)(1) of this section.

(6) The term "employee stock ownership plan" means an individual account plan—

(A) which is a stock bonus plan which is qualified, or a stock bonus plan and money purchase plan both of which are qualified, under section 401 of title 26, and which is designed to invest primarily in qualifying employer securities, and

(B) which meets such other requirements as the Secretary of the Treasury may prescribe by regulation.

(7) A corporation is an affiliate of an employer if it is a member of any controlled group of corporations (as defined in section 1563(a) of title 26, except that "applicable per-

centage" shall be substituted for "80 percent" wherever the latter percentage appears in such section) of which the employer who maintains the plan is a member. For purposes of the preceding sentence, the term "applicable percentage" means 50 percent, or such lower percentage as the Secretary may prescribe by regulation. A person other than a corporation shall be treated as an affiliate of an employer to the extent provided in regulations of the Secretary. An employer which is a person other than a corporation shall be treated as affiliated with another person to the extent provided by regulations of the Secretary. Regulations under this paragraph shall be prescribed only after consultation and coordination with the Secretary of the Treasury.

(8) The Secretary may prescribe regulations specifying the extent to which conversions, splits, the exercise of rights, and similar transactions are not treated as acquisitions.

(9) For purposes of this section, an arrangement which consists of a defined benefit plan and an individual account plan shall be treated as 1 plan if the benefits of such individual account plan are taken into account in determining the benefits payable under such defined benefit plan.

(e) Marketable obligations

For purposes of subsection (d)(5) of this section, the term "marketable obligation" means a bond, debenture, note, or certificate, or other evidence of indebtedness (hereinafter in this subsection referred to as "obligation") if—

(1) such obligation is acquired—

(A) on the market, either (i) at the price of the obligation prevailing on a national securities exchange which is registered with the Securities and Exchange Commission, or (ii) if the obligation is not traded on such a national securities exchange, at a price not less favorable to the plan than the offering price for the obligation as established by current bid and asked prices quoted by persons independent of the issuer;

(B) from an underwriter, at a price (i) not in excess of the public offering price for the obligation as set forth in a prospectus or offering circular filed with the Securities and Exchange Commission, and (ii) at which a substantial portion of the same issue is acquired by persons independent of the issuer; or

(C) directly from the issuer, at a price not less favorable to the plan than the price paid currently for a substantial portion of the same issue by persons independent of the issuer;

(2) immediately following acquisition of such obligation—

(A) not more than 25 percent of the aggregate amount of obligations issued in such issue and outstanding at the time of acquisition is held by the plan, and

(B) at least 50 percent of the aggregate amount referred to in subparagraph (A) is held by persons independent of the issuer; and

(3) immediately following acquisition of the obligation, not more than 25 percent of the assets of the plan is invested in obligations of the employer or an affiliate of the employer.

(f) Maximum percentage of stock held by plan; time of holding or acquisition; necessity of legally binding contract

(1) Stock satisfies the requirements of this paragraph if, immediately following the acquisition of such stock—

(A) no more than 25 percent of the aggregate amount of stock of the same class issued and outstanding at the time of acquisition is held by the plan, and

(B) at least 50 percent of the aggregate amount referred to in subparagraph (A) is held by persons independent of the issuer.

(2) Until January 1, 1993, a plan shall not be treated as violating subsection (a) of this section solely by holding stock which fails to satisfy the requirements of paragraph (1) if such stock—

(A) has been so held since December 17, 1987, or

(B) was acquired after December 17, 1987, pursuant to a legally binding contract in effect on December 17, 1987, and has been so held at all times after the acquisition.

(Pub. L. 93–406, title I, §407, Sept. 2, 1974, 88 Stat. 880; Pub. L. 100–203, title IX, §9345(a)(1), (2), (b), Dec. 22, 1987, 101 Stat. 1330–373; Pub. L. 101–239, title VII, §§7881(*l*)(1)–(4), 7891(a)(1), 7894(e)(2), Dec. 19, 1989, 103 Stat. 2443, 2445, 2450; Pub. L. 101–540, §1, Nov. 8, 1990, 104 Stat. 2379; Pub. L. 105–34, title XV, §1524(a), Aug. 5, 1997, 111 Stat. 1071; Pub. L. 109–280, title IX, §901(b)(2), Aug. 17, 2006, 120 Stat. 1032.)

REFERENCES IN TEXT

Section 10211(c)(2)(A) of the Revenue Act of 1987 (Public Law 100–203), referred to in subsec. (d)(5)(C), is set out as a note under section 7704 of Title 26, Internal Revenue Code.

AMENDMENTS

2006—Subsec. (b)(3)(D). Pub. L. 109–280 added subpar. (D).

1997—Subsec. (b)(2), (3). Pub. L. 105–34 added par. (2) and redesignated former par. (2) as (3).

1990—Subsec. (d)(5). Pub. L. 101–540 amended par. (5) generally. Prior to amendment, par. (5) read as follows: "The term 'qualifying employer security' means an employer security which is stock or a marketable obligation (as defined in subsection (e) of this section). After December 17, 1987, in the case of a plan other than an eligible individual account plan, stock shall be considered a qualifying employer security only if such stock satisfies the requirements of subsection (f)(1) of this section."

1989—Subsec. (d)(3)(A), (6)(A), (7). Pub. L. 101–239, §7891(a)(1), substituted "Internal Revenue Code of 1986" for "Internal Revenue Code of 1954", which for purposes of codification was translated as "title 26" thus requiring no change in text.

Subsec. (d)(3)(C). Pub. L. 101–239, §7881(*l*)(1), realigned margin.

Subsec. (d)(6)(A). Pub. L. 101–239, §7894(e)(2), substituted "money purchase plan" for "money purchase" and "employer securities" for "employee securities".

Subsec. (d)(9). Pub. L. 101–239, §7881(*l*)(2), substituted "such individual account plan" for "such arrangement" and realigned margin.

Subsec. (f)(1). Pub. L. 101–239, §7881(*l*)(3)(A), (4), substituted "paragraph" for "subsection" and "if, immediately following the acquisition of such stock" for "if".

Subsec. (f)(3). Pub. L. 101–239, §7881(*l*)(3)(B), struck out par. (3) which read as follows: "After December 17, 1987, no plan may acquire stock which does not satisfy the requirements of paragraph (1) unless the acquisition is made pursuant to a legally binding contract in effect on such date."

1987—Subsec. (d)(3)(C). Pub. L. 100–203, §9345(a)(1), added subpar. (C).

Subsec. (d)(5). Pub. L. 100–203, §9345(b)(1), inserted at end "After December 17, 1987, in the case of a plan other than an eligible individual account plan, stock shall be considered a qualifying employer security only if such stock satisfies the requirements of subsection (f)(1) of this section."

Subsec. (d)(9). Pub. L. 100–203, §9345(a)(2), added par. (9).

Subsec. (f). Pub. L. 100–203, §9345(b)(2), added subsec. (f).

EFFECTIVE DATE OF 2006 AMENDMENT

Amendment by Pub. L. 109–280 applicable to plan years beginning after Dec. 31, 2006, with special rules for collectively bargained agreements and certain employer securities held in an ESOP, see section 901(c) of Pub. L. 109–280, set out as a note under section 401 of Title 26, Internal Revenue Code.

EFFECTIVE DATE OF 1997 AMENDMENT

Section 1524(b) of Pub. L. 105–34, as amended by Pub. L. 107–16, title VI, §655(a), June 7, 2001, 115 Stat. 131, provided that:

"(1) IN GENERAL.—Except as provided in paragraph (2), the amendments made by this section [amending this section] shall apply to elective deferrals for plan years beginning after December 31, 1998.

"(2) NONAPPLICATION TO PREVIOUSLY ACQUIRED PROPERTY.—The amendments made by this section shall not apply to any elective deferral which is invested in assets consisting of qualifying employer securities, qualifying employer real property, or both, if such assets were acquired before January 1, 1999."

[Pub. L. 107–16, title VI, §655(b), June 7, 2001, 115 Stat. 131, provided that: "The amendment made by this section [amending section 1524(b) of Pub. L. 105–34, set out above] shall apply as if included in the provision of the Taxpayer Relief Act of 1997 [Pub. L. 105–34] to which it relates."]

EFFECTIVE DATE OF 1990 AMENDMENT

Section 2 of Pub. L. 101–540 provided that: "The amendment made by section 1 [amending this section] shall apply to interests in publicly traded partnerships acquired before, on, or after January 1, 1987."

EFFECTIVE DATE OF 1989 AMENDMENT

Amendment by section 7881(*l*)(1)–(4) of Pub. L. 101–239 effective, except as otherwise provided, as if included in the provision of the Pension Protection Act, Pub. L. 100–203, §§9302–9346, to which such amendment relates, see section 7882 of Pub. L. 101–239, set out as a note under section 401 of Title 26, Internal Revenue Code.

Amendment by section 7891(a)(1) of Pub. L. 101–239 effective, except as otherwise provided, as if included in the provision of the Tax Reform Act of 1986, Pub. L. 99–514, to which such amendment relates, see section 7891(f) of Pub. L. 101–239, set out as a note under section 1002 of this title.

Amendment by section 7894(e)(2) of Pub. L. 101–239 effective, except as otherwise provided, as if originally included in the provision of the Employee Retirement Income Security Act of 1974, Pub. L. 93–406, to which such amendment relates, see section 7894(i) of Pub. L. 101–239, set out as a note under section 1002 of this title.

EFFECTIVE DATE OF 1987 AMENDMENT

Section 9345(a)(3) of Pub. L. 100–203 provided that: "The amendments made by this subsection [amending this section] shall apply with respect to arrangements established after December 17, 1987."

REGULATIONS

Secretary authorized, effective Sept. 2, 1974, to promulgate regulations wherever provisions of this part call for the promulgation of regulations, see sections 1031 and 1114 of this title.

§1108. Exemptions from prohibited transactions

(a) Grant of exemptions

The Secretary shall establish an exemption procedure for purposes of this subsection. Pursuant to such procedure, he may grant a conditional or unconditional exemption of any fiduciary or transaction, or class of fiduciaries or transactions, from all or part of the restrictions imposed by sections 1106 and 1107(a) of this title. Action under this subsection may be taken only after consultation and coordination with the Secretary of the Treasury. An exemption granted under this section shall not relieve a fiduciary from any other applicable provision of this chapter. The Secretary may not grant an exemption under this subsection unless he finds that such exemption is—

(1) administratively feasible,

(2) in the interests of the plan and of its participants and beneficiaries, and

(3) protective of the rights of participants and beneficiaries of such plan.

Before granting an exemption under this subsection from section 1106(a) or 1107(a) of this title, the Secretary shall publish notice in the Federal Register of the pendency of the exemption, shall require that adequate notice be given to interested persons, and shall afford interested persons opportunity to present views. The Secretary may not grant an exemption under this subsection from section 1106(b) of this title unless he affords an opportunity for a hearing and makes a determination on the record with respect to the findings required by paragraphs (1), (2), and (3) of this subsection.

(b) Enumeration of transactions exempted from section 1106 prohibitions

The prohibitions provided in section 1106 of this title shall not apply to any of the following transactions:

(1) Any loans made by the plan to parties in interest who are participants or beneficiaries of the plan if such loans (A) are available to all such participants and beneficiaries on a reasonably equivalent basis, (B) are not made available to highly compensated employees (within the meaning of section 414(q) of title 26) in an amount greater than the amount made available to other employees, (C) are made in accordance with specific provisions regarding such loans set forth in the plan, (D) bear a reasonable rate of interest, and (E) are adequately secured. A loan made by a plan shall not fail to meet the requirements of the preceding sentence by reason of a loan repayment suspension described under section 414(u)(4) of title 26.

(2) Contracting or making reasonable arrangements with a party in interest for office space, or legal, accounting, or other services necessary for the establishment or operation of the plan, if no more than reasonable compensation is paid therefor.

(3) A loan to an employee stock ownership plan (as defined in section 1107(d)(6) of this title), if—

(A) such loan is primarily for the benefit of participants and beneficiaries of the plan, and

(B) such loan is at an interest rate which is not in excess of a reasonable rate.

If the plan gives collateral to a party in interest for such loan, such collateral may consist only of qualifying employer securities (as defined in section 1107(d)(5) of this title).

(4) The investment of all or part of a plan's assets in deposits which bear a reasonable interest rate in a bank or similar financial institution supervised by the United States or a State, if such bank or other institution is a fiduciary of such plan and if—

(A) the plan covers only employees of such bank or other institution and employees of affiliates of such bank or other institution, or

(B) such investment is expressly authorized by a provision of the plan or by a fiduciary (other than such bank or institution or affiliate thereof) who is expressly empowered by the plan to so instruct the trustee with respect to such investment.

(5) Any contract for life insurance, health insurance, or annuities with one or more insurers which are qualified to do business in a State, if the plan pays no more than adequate consideration, and if each such insurer or insurers is—

(A) the employer maintaining the plan, or

(B) a party in interest which is wholly owned (directly or indirectly) by the employer maintaining the plan, or by any person which is a party in interest with respect to the plan, but only if the total premiums and annuity considerations written by such insurers for life insurance, health insurance, or annuities for all plans (and their employers) with respect to which such insurers are parties in interest (not including premiums or annuity considerations written by the employer maintaining the plan) do not exceed 5 percent of the total premiums and annuity considerations written for all lines of insurance in that year by such insurers (not including premiums or annuity considerations written by the employer maintaining the plan).

(6) The providing of any ancillary service by a bank or similar financial institution supervised by the United States or a State, if such bank or other institution is a fiduciary of such plan, and if—

(A) such bank or similar financial institution has adopted adequate internal safeguards which assure that the providing of such ancillary service is consistent with sound banking and financial practice, as determined by Federal or State supervisory authority, and

(B) the extent to which such ancillary service is provided is subject to specific guidelines issued by such bank or similar financial institution (as determined by the Secretary after consultation with Federal and State supervisory authority), and adherence to such guidelines would reasonably preclude such bank or similar financial institution from providing such ancillary service (i) in an excessive or unreasonable manner, and (ii) in a manner that would be inconsistent with the best interests of participants and beneficiaries of employee benefit plans.

Such ancillary services shall not be provided at more than reasonable compensation.

(7) The exercise of a privilege to convert securities, to the extent provided in regulations of the Secretary, but only if the plan receives no less than adequate consideration pursuant to such conversion.

(8) Any transaction between a plan and (i) a common or collective trust fund or pooled investment fund maintained by a party in interest which is a bank or trust company supervised by a State or Federal agency or (ii) a pooled investment fund of an insurance company qualified to do business in a State, if—

(A) the transaction is a sale or purchase of an interest in the fund,

(B) the bank, trust company, or insurance company receives not more than reasonable compensation, and

(C) such transaction is expressly permitted by the instrument under which the plan is maintained, or by a fiduciary (other than the bank, trust company, or insurance company, or an affiliate thereof) who has authority to manage and control the assets of the plan.

(9) The making by a fiduciary of a distribution of the assets of the plan in accordance with the terms of the plan if such assets are distributed in the same manner as provided under section 1344 of this title (relating to allocation of assets).

(10) Any transaction required or permitted under part 1 of subtitle E of subchapter III of this chapter.

(11) A merger of multiemployer plans, or the transfer of assets or liabilities between multiemployer plans, determined by the Pension Benefit Guaranty Corporation to meet the requirements of section 1411 of this title.

(12) The sale by a plan to a party in interest on or after December 18, 1987, of any stock, if—

(A) the requirements of paragraphs (1) and (2) of subsection (e) of this section are met with respect to such stock,

(B) on the later of the date on which the stock was acquired by the plan, or January 1, 1975, such stock constituted a qualifying employer security (as defined in section 1107(d)(5) of this title as then in effect), and

(C) such stock does not constitute a qualifying employer security (as defined in section 1107(d)(5) of this title as in effect at the time of the sale).

(13) Any transfer made before January 1, 2014, of excess pension assets from a defined benefit plan to a retiree health account in a qualified transfer permitted under section 420 of title 26 (as in effect on August 17, 2006).

(14) Any transaction in connection with the provision of investment advice described in

section 1002(21)(A)(ii) of this title to a participant or beneficiary of an individual account plan that permits such participant or beneficiary to direct the investment of assets in their individual account, if—

(A) the transaction is—

(i) the provision of the investment advice to the participant or beneficiary of the plan with respect to a security or other property available as an investment under the plan,

(ii) the acquisition, holding, or sale of a security or other property available as an investment under the plan pursuant to the investment advice, or

(iii) the direct or indirect receipt of fees or other compensation by the fiduciary adviser or an affiliate thereof (or any employee, agent, or registered representative of the fiduciary adviser or affiliate) in connection with the provision of the advice or in connection with an acquisition, holding, or sale of a security or other property available as an investment under the plan pursuant to the investment advice; and

(B) the requirements of subsection (g) are met.

(15)(A) Any transaction involving the purchase or sale of securities, or other property (as determined by the Secretary), between a plan and a party in interest (other than a fiduciary described in section 1002(21)(A) of this title) with respect to a plan if—

(i) the transaction involves a block trade,

(ii) at the time of the transaction, the interest of the plan (together with the interests of any other plans maintained by the same plan sponsor), does not exceed 10 percent of the aggregate size of the block trade,

(iii) the terms of the transaction, including the price, are at least as favorable to the plan as an arm's length[1] transaction, and

(iv) the compensation associated with the purchase and sale is not greater than the compensation associated with an arm's length[1] transaction with an unrelated party.

(B) For purposes of this paragraph, the term "block trade" means any trade of at least 10,000 shares or with a market value of at least $200,000 which will be allocated across two or more unrelated client accounts of a fiduciary.

(16) Any transaction involving the purchase or sale of securities, or other property (as determined by the Secretary), between a plan and a party in interest if—

(A) the transaction is executed through an electronic communication network, alternative trading system, or similar execution system or trading venue subject to regulation and oversight by—

(i) the applicable Federal regulating entity, or

(ii) such foreign regulatory entity as the Secretary may determine by regulation,

(B) either—

(i) the transaction is effected pursuant to rules designed to match purchases and sales at the best price available through the execution system in accordance with applicable rules of the Securities and Exchange Commission or other relevant governmental authority, or

(ii) neither the execution system nor the parties to the transaction take into account the identity of the parties in the execution of trades,

(C) the price and compensation associated with the purchase and sale are not greater than the price and compensation associated with an arm's length[1] transaction with an unrelated party,

(D) if the party in interest has an ownership interest in the system or venue described in subparagraph (A), the system or venue has been authorized by the plan sponsor or other independent fiduciary for transactions described in this paragraph, and

(E) not less than 30 days prior to the initial transaction described in this paragraph executed through any system or venue described in subparagraph (A), a plan fiduciary is provided written or electronic notice of the execution of such transaction through such system or venue.

(17)(A) Transactions described in subparagraphs (A), (B), and (D) of section 1106(a)(1) of this title between a plan and a person that is a party in interest other than a fiduciary (or an affiliate) who has or exercises any discretionary authority or control with respect to the investment of the plan assets involved in the transaction or renders investment advice (within the meaning of section 1002(21)(A)(ii) of this title) with respect to those assets, solely by reason of providing services to the plan or solely by reason of a relationship to such a service provider described in subparagraph (F), (G), (H), or (I) of section 1002(14) of this title, or both, but only if in connection with such transaction the plan receives no less, nor pays no more, than adequate consideration.

(B) For purposes of this paragraph, the term "adequate consideration" means—

(i) in the case of a security for which there is a generally recognized market—

(I) the price of the security prevailing on a national securities exchange which is registered under section 6 of the Securities Exchange Act of 1934 [15 U.S.C. 78f], taking into account factors such as the size of the transaction and marketability of the security, or

(II) if the security is not traded on such a national securities exchange, a price not less favorable to the plan than the offering price for the security as established by the current bid and asked prices quoted by persons independent of the issuer and of the party in interest, taking into account factors such as the size of the transaction and marketability of the security, and

(ii) in the case of an asset other than a security for which there is a generally recognized market, the fair market value of the asset as determined in good faith by a fiduciary or fiduciaries in accordance with regulations prescribed by the Secretary.

[1] So in original. Probably should be "arm's-length".

(18) FOREIGN EXCHANGE TRANSACTIONS.—Any foreign exchange transactions, between a bank or broker-dealer (or any affiliate of either), and a plan (as defined in section 1002(3) of this title) with respect to which such bank or broker-dealer (or affiliate) is a trustee, custodian, fiduciary, or other party in interest, if—

(A) the transaction is in connection with the purchase, holding, or sale of securities or other investment assets (other than a foreign exchange transaction unrelated to any other investment in securities or other investment assets),

(B) at the time the foreign exchange transaction is entered into, the terms of the transaction are not less favorable to the plan than the terms generally available in comparable arm's length[1] foreign exchange transactions between unrelated parties, or the terms afforded by the bank or broker-dealer (or any affiliate of either) in comparable arm's-length foreign exchange transactions involving unrelated parties,

(C) the exchange rate used by such bank or broker-dealer (or affiliate) for a particular foreign exchange transaction does not deviate by more than 3 percent from the interbank bid and asked rates for transactions of comparable size and maturity at the time of the transaction as displayed on an independent service that reports rates of exchange in the foreign currency market for such currency, and

(D) the bank or broker-dealer (or any affiliate of either) does not have investment discretion, or provide investment advice, with respect to the transaction.

(19) CROSS TRADING.—Any transaction described in sections 1106(a)(1)(A) and 1106(b)(2) of this title involving the purchase and sale of a security between a plan and any other account managed by the same investment manager, if—

(A) the transaction is a purchase or sale, for no consideration other than cash payment against prompt delivery of a security for which market quotations are readily available,

(B) the transaction is effected at the independent current market price of the security (within the meaning of section 270.17a–7(b) of title 17, Code of Federal Regulations),

(C) no brokerage commission, fee (except for customary transfer fees, the fact of which is disclosed pursuant to subparagraph (D)), or other remuneration is paid in connection with the transaction,

(D) a fiduciary (other than the investment manager engaging in the cross-trades or any affiliate) for each plan participating in the transaction authorizes in advance of any cross-trades (in a document that is separate from any other written agreement of the parties) the investment manager to engage in cross trades at the investment manager's discretion, after such fiduciary has received disclosure regarding the conditions under which cross trades may take place (but only if such disclosure is separate from any other agreement or disclosure involving the asset management relationship), including the written policies and procedures of the investment manager described in subparagraph (H),

(E) each plan participating in the transaction has assets of at least $100,000,000, except that if the assets of a plan are invested in a master trust containing the assets of plans maintained by employers in the same controlled group (as defined in section 1107(d)(7) of this title), the master trust has assets of at least $100,000,000,

(F) the investment manager provides to the plan fiduciary who authorized cross trading under subparagraph (D) a quarterly report detailing all cross trades executed by the investment manager in which the plan participated during such quarter, including the following information, as applicable: (i) the identity of each security bought or sold; (ii) the number of shares or units traded; (iii) the parties involved in the cross-trade; and (iv) trade price and the method used to establish the trade price,

(G) the investment manager does not base its fee schedule on the plan's consent to cross trading, and no other service (other than the investment opportunities and cost savings available through a cross trade) is conditioned on the plan's consent to cross trading,

(H) the investment manager has adopted, and cross-trades are effected in accordance with, written cross-trading policies and procedures that are fair and equitable to all accounts participating in the cross-trading program, and that include a description of the manager's pricing policies and procedures, and the manager's policies and procedures for allocating cross trades in an objective manner among accounts participating in the cross-trading program, and

(I) the investment manager has designated an individual responsible for periodically reviewing such purchases and sales to ensure compliance with the written policies and procedures described in subparagraph (H), and following such review, the individual shall issue an annual written report no later than 90 days following the period to which it relates signed under penalty of perjury to the plan fiduciary who authorized cross trading under subparagraph (D) describing the steps performed during the course of the review, the level of compliance, and any specific instances of non-compliance.

The written report under subparagraph (I) shall also notify the plan fiduciary of the plan's right to terminate participation in the investment manager's cross-trading program at any time.

(20)(A) Except as provided in subparagraphs (B) and (C), a transaction described in section 1106(a) of this title in connection with the acquisition, holding, or disposition of any security or commodity, if the transaction is corrected before the end of the correction period.

(B) Subparagraph (A) does not apply to any transaction between a plan and a plan sponsor or its affiliates that involves the acquisition or sale of an employer security (as defined in section 1107(d)(1) of this title) or the acquisition, sale, or lease of employer real property (as defined in section 1107(d)(2) of this title).

(C) In the case of any fiduciary or other party in interest (or any other person knowingly participating in such transaction), subparagraph (A) does not apply to any transaction if, at the time the transaction occurs, such fiduciary or party in interest (or other person) knew (or reasonably should have known) that the transaction would (without regard to this paragraph) constitute a violation of section 1106(a) of this title.

(D) For purposes of this paragraph, the term "correction period" means, in connection with a fiduciary or party in interest (or other person knowingly participating in the transaction), the 14-day period beginning on the date on which such fiduciary or party in interest (or other person) discovers, or reasonably should have discovered, that the transaction would (without regard to this paragraph) constitute a violation of section 1106(a) of this title.

(E) For purposes of this paragraph—

(i) The term "security" has the meaning given such term by section 475(c)(2) of title 26 (without regard to subparagraph (F)(iii) and the last sentence thereof).

(ii) The term "commodity" has the meaning given such term by section 475(e)(2) of title 26 (without regard to subparagraph (D)(iii) thereof).

(iii) The term "correct" means, with respect to a transaction—

(I) to undo the transaction to the extent possible and in any case to make good to the plan or affected account any losses resulting from the transaction, and

(II) to restore to the plan or affected account any profits made through the use of assets of the plan.

(c) Fiduciary benefits and compensation not prohibited by section 1106

Nothing in section 1106 of this title shall be construed to prohibit any fiduciary from—

(1) receiving any benefit to which he may be entitled as a participant or beneficiary in the plan, so long as the benefit is computed and paid on a basis which is consistent with the terms of the plan as applied to all other participants and beneficiaries;

(2) receiving any reasonable compensation for services rendered, or for the reimbursement of expenses properly and actually incurred, in the performance of his duties with the plan; except that no person so serving who already receives full time pay from an employer or an association of employers, whose employees are participants in the plan, or from an employee organization whose members are participants in such plan shall receive compensation from such plan, except for reimbursement of expenses properly and actually incurred; or

(3) serving as a fiduciary in addition to being an officer, employee, agent, or other representative of a party in interest.

(d) Owner-employees; family members; shareholder employees

(1) Section 1107(b) of this title and subsections (b), (c), and (e) of this section shall not apply to a transaction in which a plan directly or indirectly—

(A) lends any part of the corpus or income of the plan to,

(B) pays any compensation for personal services rendered to the plan to, or

(C) acquires for the plan any property from, or sells any property to,

any person who is with respect to the plan an owner-employee (as defined in section 401(c)(3) of title 26), a member of the family (as defined in section 267(c)(4) of such title) of any such owner-employee, or any corporation in which any such owner-employee owns, directly or indirectly, 50 percent or more of the total combined voting power of all classes of stock entitled to vote or 50 percent or more of the total value of shares of all classes of stock of the corporation.

(2)(A) For purposes of paragraph (1), the following shall be treated as owner-employees:

(i) A shareholder-employee.

(ii) A participant or beneficiary of an individual retirement plan (as defined in section 7701(a)(37) of title 26).

(iii) An employer or association of employees which establishes such an individual retirement plan under section 408(c) of such title.

(B) Paragraph (1)(C) shall not apply to a transaction which consists of a sale of employer securities to an employee stock ownership plan (as defined in section 1107(d)(6) of this title) by a shareholder-employee, a member of the family (as defined in section 267(c)(4) of such title) of any such owner-employee, or a corporation in which such a shareholder-employee owns stock representing a 50 percent or greater interest described in paragraph (1).

(C) For purposes of paragraph (1)(A), the term "owner-employee" shall only include a person described in clause (ii) or (iii) of subparagraph (A).

(3) For purposes of paragraph (2), the term "shareholder-employee" means an employee or officer of an S corporation (as defined in section 1361(a)(1) of such title) who owns (or is considered as owning within the meaning of section 318(a)(1) of such title) more than 5 percent of the outstanding stock of the corporation on any day during the taxable year of such corporation.

(e) Acquisition or sale by plan of qualifying employer securities; acquisition, sale, or lease by plan of qualifying employer real property

Sections 1106 and 1107 of this title shall not apply to the acquisition or sale by a plan of qualifying employer securities (as defined in section 1107(d)(5) of this title) or acquisition, sale or lease by a plan of qualifying employer real property (as defined in section 1107(d)(4) of this title)—

(1) if such acquisition, sale, or lease is for adequate consideration (or in the case of a marketable obligation, at a price not less favorable to the plan than the price determined under section 1107(e)(1) of this title),

(2) if no commission is charged with respect thereto, and

(3) if—

(A) the plan is an eligible individual account plan (as defined in section 1107(d)(3) of this title), or

(B) in the case of an acquisition or lease of qualifying employer real property by a plan which is not an eligible individual account plan, or of an acquisition of qualifying employer securities by such a plan, the lease or acquisition is not prohibited by section 1107(a) of this title.

(f) Applicability of statutory prohibitions to mergers or transfers

Section 1106(b)(2) of this title shall not apply to any merger or transfer described in subsection (b)(11) of this section.

(g) Provision of investment advice to participant and beneficiaries

(1) In general

The prohibitions provided in section 1106 of this title shall not apply to transactions described in subsection (b)(14) if the investment advice provided by a fiduciary adviser is provided under an eligible investment advice arrangement.

(2) Eligible investment advice arrangement

For purposes of this subsection, the term "eligible investment advice arrangement" means an arrangement—

(A) which either—

(i) provides that any fees (including any commission or other compensation) received by the fiduciary adviser for investment advice or with respect to the sale, holding, or acquisition of any security or other property for purposes of investment of plan assets do not vary depending on the basis of any investment option selected, or

(ii) uses a computer model under an investment advice program meeting the requirements of paragraph (3) in connection with the provision of investment advice by a fiduciary adviser to a participant or beneficiary, and

(B) with respect to which the requirements of paragraph (4), (5), (6), (7), (8), and (9) are met.

(3) Investment advice program using computer model

(A) In general

An investment advice program meets the requirements of this paragraph if the requirements of subparagraphs (B), (C), and (D) are met.

(B) Computer model

The requirements of this subparagraph are met if the investment advice provided under the investment advice program is provided pursuant to a computer model that—

(i) applies generally accepted investment theories that take into account the historic returns of different asset classes over defined periods of time,

(ii) utilizes relevant information about the participant, which may include age, life expectancy, retirement age, risk tolerance, other assets or sources of income, and preferences as to certain types of investments,

(iii) utilizes prescribed objective criteria to provide asset allocation portfolios comprised of investment options available under the plan,

(iv) operates in a manner that is not biased in favor of investments offered by the fiduciary adviser or a person with a material affiliation or contractual relationship with the fiduciary adviser, and

(v) takes into account all investment options under the plan in specifying how a participant's account balance should be invested and is not inappropriately weighted with respect to any investment option.

(C) Certification

(i) In general

The requirements of this subparagraph are met with respect to any investment advice program if an eligible investment expert certifies, prior to the utilization of the computer model and in accordance with rules prescribed by the Secretary, that the computer model meets the requirements of subparagraph (B).

(ii) Renewal of certifications

If, as determined under regulations prescribed by the Secretary, there are material modifications to a computer model, the requirements of this subparagraph are met only if a certification described in clause (i) is obtained with respect to the computer model as so modified.

(iii) Eligible investment expert

The term "eligible investment expert" means any person—

(I) which meets such requirements as the Secretary may provide, and

(II) does not bear any material affiliation or contractual relationship with any investment adviser or a related person thereof (or any employee, agent, or registered representative of the investment adviser or related person).

(D) Exclusivity of recommendation

The requirements of this subparagraph are met with respect to any investment advice program if—

(i) the only investment advice provided under the program is the advice generated by the computer model described in subparagraph (B), and

(ii) any transaction described in subsection (b)(14)(A)(ii) occurs solely at the direction of the participant or beneficiary.

Nothing in the preceding sentence shall preclude the participant or beneficiary from requesting investment advice other than that described in subparagraph (A), but only if such request has not been solicited by any person connected with carrying out the arrangement.

(4) Express authorization by separate fiduciary

The requirements of this paragraph are met with respect to an arrangement if the arrangement is expressly authorized by a plan fiduciary other than the person offering the investment advice program, any person providing investment options under the plan, or any affiliate of either.

(5) Annual audit

The requirements of this paragraph are met if an independent auditor, who has appropriate technical training or experience and proficiency and so represents in writing—

(A) conducts an annual audit of the arrangement for compliance with the requirements of this subsection, and

(B) following completion of the annual audit, issues a written report to the fiduciary who authorized use of the arrangement which presents its specific findings regarding compliance of the arrangement with the requirements of this subsection.

For purposes of this paragraph, an auditor is considered independent if it is not related to the person offering the arrangement to the plan and is not related to any person providing investment options under the plan.

(6) Disclosure

The requirements of this paragraph are met if—

(A) the fiduciary adviser provides to a participant or a beneficiary before the initial provision of the investment advice with regard to any security or other property offered as an investment option, a written notification (which may consist of notification by means of electronic communication)—

(i) of the role of any party that has a material affiliation or contractual relationship with the fiduciary adviser in the development of the investment advice program and in the selection of investment options available under the plan,

(ii) of the past performance and historical rates of return of the investment options available under the plan,

(iii) of all fees or other compensation relating to the advice that the fiduciary adviser or any affiliate thereof is to receive (including compensation provided by any third party) in connection with the provision of the advice or in connection with the sale, acquisition, or holding of the security or other property,

(iv) of any material affiliation or contractual relationship of the fiduciary adviser or affiliates thereof in the security or other property,

(v)[2] the manner, and under what circumstances, any participant or beneficiary information provided under the arrangement will be used or disclosed,

(vi) of the types of services provided by the fiduciary adviser in connection with the provision of investment advice by the fiduciary adviser,

(vii) that the adviser is acting as a fiduciary of the plan in connection with the provision of the advice, and

(viii) that a recipient of the advice may separately arrange for the provision of advice by another adviser, that could have no material affiliation with and receive no fees or other compensation in connection with the security or other property, and

(B) at all times during the provision of advisory services to the participant or beneficiary, the fiduciary adviser—

(i) maintains the information described in subparagraph (A) in accurate form and in the manner described in paragraph (8),

(ii) provides, without charge, accurate information to the recipient of the advice no less frequently than annually,

(iii) provides, without charge, accurate information to the recipient of the advice upon request of the recipient, and

(iv) provides, without charge, accurate information to the recipient of the advice concerning any material change to the information required to be provided to the recipient of the advice at a time reasonably contemporaneous to the change in information.

(7) Other conditions

The requirements of this paragraph are met if—

(A) the fiduciary adviser provides appropriate disclosure, in connection with the sale, acquisition, or holding of the security or other property, in accordance with all applicable securities laws,

(B) the sale, acquisition, or holding occurs solely at the direction of the recipient of the advice,

(C) the compensation received by the fiduciary adviser and affiliates thereof in connection with the sale, acquisition, or holding of the security or other property is reasonable, and

(D) the terms of the sale, acquisition, or holding of the security or other property are at least as favorable to the plan as an arm's length[1] transaction would be.

(8) Standards for presentation of information

(A) In general

The requirements of this paragraph are met if the notification required to be provided to participants and beneficiaries under paragraph (6)(A) is written in a clear and conspicuous manner and in a manner calculated to be understood by the average plan participant and is sufficiently accurate and comprehensive to reasonably apprise such participants and beneficiaries of the information required to be provided in the notification.

(B) Model form for disclosure of fees and other compensation

The Secretary shall issue a model form for the disclosure of fees and other compensation required in paragraph (6)(A)(iii) which meets the requirements of subparagraph (A).

(9) Maintenance for 6 years of evidence of compliance

The requirements of this paragraph are met if a fiduciary adviser who has provided advice referred to in paragraph (1) maintains, for a period of not less than 6 years after the provision of the advice, any records necessary for determining whether the requirements of the preceding provisions of this subsection and of subsection (b)(14) have been met. A trans-

[2] So in original. The word "of" probably should appear.

action prohibited under section 1106 of this title shall not be considered to have occurred solely because the records are lost or destroyed prior to the end of the 6-year period due to circumstances beyond the control of the fiduciary adviser.

(10) Exemption for plan sponsor and certain other fiduciaries

(A) In general

Subject to subparagraph (B), a plan sponsor or other person who is a fiduciary (other than a fiduciary adviser) shall not be treated as failing to meet the requirements of this part solely by reason of the provision of investment advice referred to in section 1002(21)(A)(ii) of this title (or solely by reason of contracting for or otherwise arranging for the provision of the advice), if—

(i) the advice is provided by a fiduciary adviser pursuant to an eligible investment advice arrangement between the plan sponsor or other fiduciary and the fiduciary adviser for the provision by the fiduciary adviser of investment advice referred to in such section,

(ii) the terms of the eligible investment advice arrangement require compliance by the fiduciary adviser with the requirements of this subsection, and

(iii) the terms of the eligible investment advice arrangement include a written acknowledgment by the fiduciary adviser that the fiduciary adviser is a fiduciary of the plan with respect to the provision of the advice.

(B) Continued duty of prudent selection of adviser and periodic review

Nothing in subparagraph (A) shall be construed to exempt a plan sponsor or other person who is a fiduciary from any requirement of this part for the prudent selection and periodic review of a fiduciary adviser with whom the plan sponsor or other person enters into an eligible investment advice arrangement for the provision of investment advice referred to in section 1002(21)(A)(ii) of this title. The plan sponsor or other person who is a fiduciary has no duty under this part to monitor the specific investment advice given by the fiduciary adviser to any particular recipient of the advice.

(C) Availability of plan assets for payment for advice

Nothing in this part shall be construed to preclude the use of plan assets to pay for reasonable expenses in providing investment advice referred to in section 1002(21)(A)(ii) of this title.

(11) Definitions

For purposes of this subsection and subsection (b)(14)—

(A) Fiduciary adviser

The term "fiduciary adviser" means, with respect to a plan, a person who is a fiduciary of the plan by reason of the provision of investment advice referred to in section 1002(21)(A)(ii) of this title by the person to a participant or beneficiary of the plan and who is—

(i) registered as an investment adviser under the Investment Advisers Act of 1940 (15 U.S.C. 80b–1 et seq.) or under the laws of the State in which the fiduciary maintains its principal office and place of business,

(ii) a bank or similar financial institution referred to in subsection (b)(4) or a savings association (as defined in section 1813(b)(1) of title 12), but only if the advice is provided through a trust department of the bank or similar financial institution or savings association which is subject to periodic examination and review by Federal or State banking authorities,

(iii) an insurance company qualified to do business under the laws of a State,

(iv) a person registered as a broker or dealer under the Securities Exchange Act of 1934 (15 U.S.C. 78a et seq.),

(v) an affiliate of a person described in any of clauses (i) through (iv), or

(vi) an employee, agent, or registered representative of a person described in clauses (i) through (v) who satisfies the requirements of applicable insurance, banking, and securities laws relating to the provision of the advice.

For purposes of this part, a person who develops the computer model described in paragraph (3)(B) or markets the investment advice program or computer model shall be treated as a person who is a fiduciary of the plan by reason of the provision of investment advice referred to in section 1002(21)(A)(ii) of this title to a participant or beneficiary and shall be treated as a fiduciary adviser for purposes of this subsection and subsection (b)(14), except that the Secretary may prescribe rules under which only 1 fiduciary adviser may elect to be treated as a fiduciary with respect to the plan.

(B) Affiliate

The term "affiliate" of another entity means an affiliated person of the entity (as defined in section 80a–2(a)(3) of title 15).

(C) Registered representative

The term "registered representative" of another entity means a person described in section 3(a)(18) of the Securities Exchange Act of 1934 (15 U.S.C. 78c(a)(18)) (substituting the entity for the broker or dealer referred to in such section) or a person described in section 202(a)(17) of the Investment Advisers Act of 1940 (15 U.S.C. 80b–2(a)(17)) (substituting the entity for the investment adviser referred to in such section).

(Pub. L. 93–406, title I, §408, Sept. 2, 1974, 88 Stat. 883; Pub. L. 96–364, title III, §308, Sept. 26, 1980, 94 Stat. 1295; Pub. L. 97–354, §5(a)(43), Oct. 19, 1982, 96 Stat. 1697; Pub. L. 99–514, title XI, §1114(b)(15)(B), title XVIII, §1898(i)(1), Oct. 22, 1986, 100 Stat. 2452, 2957; Pub. L. 101–239, title VII, §§7881(*l*)(5), 7891, 7894(e)(4)(A), Dec. 19, 1989, 103 Stat. 2443, 2445, 2450; Pub. L. 101–508, title XII, §12012(b), Nov. 5, 1990, 104 Stat. 1388–571; Pub. L. 103–465, title VII, §731(c)(4)(C), Dec. 8,

1994, 108 Stat. 5004; Pub. L. 104–188, title I, §1704(n)(2), Aug. 20, 1996, 110 Stat. 1886; Pub. L. 105–34, title XV, §1506(b)(2), Aug. 5, 1997, 111 Stat. 1066; Pub. L. 106–170, title V, §535(a)(2)(C), Dec. 17, 1999, 113 Stat. 1934; Pub. L. 107–16, title VI, §612(b), June 7, 2001, 115 Stat. 100; Pub. L. 108–218, title II, §204(b)(3), Apr. 10, 2004, 118 Stat. 609; Pub. L. 108–357, title VII, §709(a)(3), Oct. 22, 2004, 118 Stat. 1551; Pub. L. 109–280, title I, §107(a)(11), title VI, §§601(a)(1), (2), 611(a)(1), (c)(1), (d)(1), (e)(1), (g)(1), 612(a), Aug. 17, 2006, 120 Stat. 819, 952, 953, 967–969, 971, 972, 975; Pub. L. 110–458, title I, §106(a)(1), (b)(1), Dec. 23, 2008, 122 Stat. 5106.)

REFERENCES IN TEXT

This chapter, referred to in subsec. (a), was in the original "this Act", meaning Pub. L. 93–406, known as the Employee Retirement Income Security Act of 1974. Titles I, III, and IV of such Act are classified principally to this chapter. For complete classification of this Act to the Code, see Short Title note set out under section 1001 of this title and Tables.

The Investment Advisers Act of 1940, referred to in subsec. (g)(11)(A)(i), is title II of act Aug. 22, 1940, ch. 686, 54 Stat. 847, as amended, which is classified generally to subchapter II (§80b–1 et seq.) of chapter 2D of Title 15, Commerce and Trade. For complete classification of this Act to the Code, see section 80b–20 of Title 15 and Tables.

The Securities Exchange Act of 1934, referred to in subsec. (g)(11)(A)(iv), is act June 6, 1934, ch. 404, 48 Stat. 881, as amended, which is classified principally to chapter 2B (§78a et seq.) of Title 15, Commerce and Trade. For complete classification of this Act to the Code, see section 78a of Title 15 and Tables.

AMENDMENTS

2008—Subsec. (b)(18)(C). Pub. L. 110–458, §106(b)(1), struck out "or less" after "deviate by more".

Subsec. (g)(3)(D)(ii). Pub. L. 110–458, §106(a)(1)(A), substituted "subsection (b)(14)(A)(ii)" for "subsection (b)(14)(B)(ii)".

Subsec. (g)(6)(A)(i). Pub. L. 110–458, §106(a)(1)(B), substituted "fiduciary adviser" for "financial adviser".

Subsec. (g)(11)(A). Pub. L. 110–458, §106(a)(1)(C), substituted "a participant" for "the participant" in introductory and concluding provisions and "subsection (b)(4)" for "section 1108(b)(4) of this title" in cl. (ii).

2006—Subsec. (b)(13). Pub. L. 109–280, §107(a)(11), substituted "August 17, 2006" for "October 22, 2004".

Subsec. (b)(14). Pub. L. 109–280, §601(a)(1), added par. (14).

Subsec. (b)(15) to (19). Pub. L. 109–280, §611(a)(1), (c)(1), (d)(1), (e)(1), (g)(1), added pars. (15) to (19).

Subsec. (b)(20). Pub. L. 109–280, §612(a), added par. (20).

Subsec. (g). Pub. L. 109–280, §601(a)(2), added subsec. (g).

2004—Subsec. (b)(13). Pub. L. 108–357 substituted "October 22, 2004" for "April 10, 2004".

Pub. L. 108–218 substituted "January 1, 2014" for "January 1, 2006" and "April 10, 2004" for "December 17, 1999".

2001—Subsec. (d)(2)(C). Pub. L. 107–16 added subpar. (C).

1999—Subsec. (b)(13). Pub. L. 106–170 substituted "made before January 1, 2006" for "in a taxable year beginning before January 1, 2001" and "December 17, 1999" for "January 1, 1995".

1997—Subsec. (d). Pub. L. 105–34 amended subsec. (d) generally, substituting present provisions for provisions exempting transactions involving an owner-employee, a member of the family, or a corporation controlled by any such owner-employee through the ownership, directly or indirectly, of 50 percent or more of the total combined voting power of all classes of stock entitled to vote or 50 percent or more of the total value of shares of all classes of stock of the corporation.

1996—Subsec. (b)(1). Pub. L. 104–188 inserted at end "A loan made by a plan shall not fail to meet the requirements of the preceding sentence by reason of a loan repayment suspension described under section 414(u)(4) of title 26."

1994—Subsec. (b)(13). Pub. L. 103–465 substituted "2001" for "1996" and "1995" for "1991".

1990—Subsec. (b)(13). Pub. L. 101–508 added par. (13).

1989—Subsec. (b)(12). Pub. L. 101–239, §7881(*l*)(5), added par. (12).

Subsec. (d). Pub. L. 101–239, §7891(a)(1), in last sentence, substituted "section 401(c)(3) of the Internal Revenue Code of 1986" for "section 401(c)(3) of the Internal Revenue Code of 1954", which for purposes of codification was translated as "section 401(c)(3) of title 26" thus requiring no change in text.

Pub. L. 101–239, §7891(a)(2), in last sentence, substituted "section 408 of the Internal Revenue Code of 1986" for "section 408 of the Internal Revenue Code of 1954" and "section 408(c) of the Internal Revenue Code of 1986" for "section 408(c) of such Code" which for purposes of codification were translated as "section 408 of title 26" and "section 408(c) of title 26", respectively, thus requiring no change in text.

Pub. L. 101–239, §7894(e)(4)(A), in last sentence, substituted "individual retirement account or individual retirement annuity described in section 408 of title 26 or a retirement bond described in section 409 of title 26 (as effective for obligations issued before January 1, 1984)" for "individual retirement account, individual retirement annuity, or an individual retirement bond (as defined in section 408 or 409 of title 26)" and "section 408(c) of such Code" for "section 408(c) of such code", which for purposes of codification was translated as "section 408(c) of title 26" thus requiring no change in text.

1986—Subsec. (b)(1)(B). Pub. L. 99–514, §1114(b)(15)(B), substituted "highly compensated employees (within the meaning of section 414(q) of title 26)" for "highly compensated employees, officers, or shareholders".

Subsec. (d). Pub. L. 99–514, §1898(i)(1), struck out "(a)," before "(b)," in introductory provisions.

1982—Subsec. (d). Pub. L. 97–354 substituted "section 1379 of title 26 as in effect on the day before the date of the enactment of the Subchapter S Revision Act of 1982" for "section 1379 of title 26".

1980—Subsec. (b)(10), (11). Pub. L. 96–364, §308(a), added pars. (10) and (11).

Subsec. (f). Pub. L. 96–364, §308(b), added subsec. (f).

EFFECTIVE DATE OF 2008 AMENDMENT

Amendment by Pub. L. 110–458 effective as if included in the provisions of Pub. L. 109–280 to which the amendment relates, except as otherwise provided, see section 112 of Pub. L. 110–458, set out as a note under section 72 of Title 26, Internal Revenue Code.

EFFECTIVE DATE OF 2006 AMENDMENT

Amendment by section 107(a)(11) of Pub. L. 109–280 applicable to plan years beginning after 2007, see section 107(e) of Pub. L. 109–280, set out as a note under section 1021 of this title.

Pub. L. 109–280, title VI, §601(a)(3), Aug. 17, 2006, 120 Stat. 958, provided that: "The amendments made by this subsection [amending this section] shall apply with respect to advice referred to in section 3(21)(A)(ii) of the Employee Retirement Income Security Act of 1974 [29 U.S.C. 1002(21)(A)(ii)] provided after December 31, 2006."

Amendment by section 611(a)(1), (c)(1), (d)(1), (e)(1), (g)(1) of Pub. L. 109–280 applicable to transactions occurring after Aug. 17, 2006, see section 611(h)(1) of Pub. L. 109–280, set out as a note under section 4975 of Title 26, Internal Revenue Code.

Amendment by section 612(a) of Pub. L. 109–280 applicable to any transaction which the fiduciary or disqualified person discovers, or reasonably should have discovered, after Aug. 17, 2006, constitutes a prohibited transaction, see section 612(c) of Pub. L. 109–280, set out as a note under section 4975 of Title 26, Internal Revenue Code.

EFFECTIVE DATE OF 2001 AMENDMENT

Amendment by Pub. L. 107–16 applicable to years beginning after Dec. 31, 2001, see section 612(c) of Pub. L. 107–16, set out as a note under section 4975 of Title 26, Internal Revenue Code.

EFFECTIVE DATE OF 1999 AMENDMENT

Amendment by Pub. L. 106–170 applicable to qualified transfers occurring after Dec. 17, 1999, see section 535(c)(1) of Pub. L. 106–170, set out as a note under section 420 of Title 26, Internal Revenue Code.

EFFECTIVE DATE OF 1997 AMENDMENT

Amendment by Pub. L. 105–34 applicable to taxable years beginning after Dec. 31, 1997, see section 1506(c) of Pub. L. 105–34, set out as a note under section 409 of Title 26, Internal Revenue Code.

EFFECTIVE DATE OF 1996 AMENDMENT

Amendment by Pub. L. 104–188 effective as of Dec. 12, 1994, see section 1704(n)(3) of Pub. L. 104–188, set out as a note under section 414 of Title 26, Internal Revenue Code.

EFFECTIVE DATE OF 1990 AMENDMENT

Amendment by Pub. L. 101–508 applicable to qualified transfers under section 420 of title 26 made after Nov. 5, 1990, see section 12012(e) of Pub. L. 101–508, set out as a note under section 1021 of this title.

EFFECTIVE DATE OF 1989 AMENDMENT

Amendment by section 7881(*l*)(5) of Pub. L. 101–239 effective, except as otherwise provided, as if included in the provision of the Pension Protection Act, Pub. L. 100–203, §§9302–9346, to which such amendment relates, see section 7882 of Pub. L. 101–239, set out as a note under section 401 of Title 26, Internal Revenue Code.

Amendment by section 7891(a) of Pub. L. 101–239 effective, except as otherwise provided, as if included in the provision of the Tax Reform Act of 1986, Pub. L. 99–514, to which such amendment relates, see section 7891(f) of Pub. L. 101–239, set out as a note under section 1002 of this title.

Section 7894(e)(4)(B) of Pub. L. 101–239 provided that: "The amendments made by subparagraph (A) [amending this section] shall take effect as if originally included in section 491(b) of the Deficit Reduction Act of 1984 [Pub. L. 98–369]."

EFFECTIVE DATE OF 1986 AMENDMENT

Amendment by section 1114(b)(15)(B) of Pub. L. 99–514 applicable to years beginning after Dec. 31, 1988, see section 1114(c)(3) of Pub. L. 99–514, set out as a note under section 414 of Title 26, Internal Revenue Code.

Section 1898(i)(2) of Pub. L. 99–514 provided that: "The amendment made by paragraph (1) [amending this section] shall apply to transactions after the date of the enactment of this Act [Oct. 22, 1986]."

EFFECTIVE DATE OF 1982 AMENDMENT

Amendment by Pub. L. 97–354 applicable to taxable years beginning after Dec. 31, 1982, see section 6(a) of Pub. L. 97–354, set out as a note under section 1361 of Title 26, Internal Revenue Code.

EFFECTIVE DATE OF 1980 AMENDMENT

Amendment by Pub. L. 96–364 effective Sept. 26, 1980, except as specifically provided, see section 1461(e) of this title.

REGULATIONS

Pub. L. 109–280, title VI, §611(g)(3), Aug. 17, 2006, 120 Stat. 975, provided that: "No later than 180 days after the date of the enactment of this Act [Aug. 17, 2006], the Secretary of Labor, after consultation with the Securities and Exchange Commission, shall issue regulations regarding the content of policies and procedures required to be adopted by an investment manager under section 408(b)(19) of the Employee Retirement Income Security Act of 1974 [29 U.S.C. 1108(b)(19)]."

Secretary of the Treasury or his delegate to issue before Feb. 1, 1988, final regulations to carry out amendments made by section 1114 of Pub. L. 99–514, see section 1141 of Pub. L. 99–514, set out as a note under section 401 of Title 26, Internal Revenue Code.

Secretary authorized, effective Sept. 2, 1974, to promulgate regulations wherever provisions of this part call for the promulgation of regulations, see sections 1031 and 1114 of this title.

APPLICABILITY OF AMENDMENTS BY SUBTITLES A AND B OF TITLE I OF PUB. L. 109–280

For special rules on applicability of amendments by subtitles A (§§101–107) and B (§§111–116) of title I of Pub. L. 109–280 to certain eligible cooperative plans, PBGC settlement plans, and eligible government contractor plans, see sections 104, 105, and 106 of Pub. L. 109–280, set out as notes under section 401 of Title 26, Internal Revenue Code.

COORDINATION OF 2006 AMENDMENT WITH EXISTING EXEMPTIONS

Any exemption under subsec. (b) of this section provided by amendment by section 601(a)(1), (2) of Pub. L. 109–280 not to alter existing individual or class exemptions provided by statute or administrative action, see section 601(c) of Pub. L. 109–280, set out as a note under section 4975 of Title 26, Internal Revenue Code.

PLAN AMENDMENTS NOT REQUIRED UNTIL JANUARY 1, 1989

For provisions directing that if any amendments made by subtitle A or subtitle C of title XI [§§1101–1147 and 1171–1177] or title XVIII [§§1800–1899A] of Pub. L. 99–514 require an amendment to any plan, such plan amendment shall not be required to be made before the first plan year beginning on or after Jan. 1, 1989, see section 1140 of Pub. L. 99–514, as amended, set out as a note under section 401 of Title 26, Internal Revenue Code.

§1109. Liability for breach of fiduciary duty

(a) Any person who is a fiduciary with respect to a plan who breaches any of the responsibilities, obligations, or duties imposed upon fiduciaries by this subchapter shall be personally liable to make good to such plan any losses to the plan resulting from each such breach, and to restore to such plan any profits of such fiduciary which have been made through use of assets of the plan by the fiduciary, and shall be subject to such other equitable or remedial relief as the court may deem appropriate, including removal of such fiduciary. A fiduciary may also be removed for a violation of section 1111 of this title.

(b) No fiduciary shall be liable with respect to a breach of fiduciary duty under this subchapter if such breach was committed before he became a fiduciary or after he ceased to be a fiduciary.

(Pub. L. 93–406, title I, §409, Sept. 2, 1974, 88 Stat. 886.)

§1110. Exculpatory provisions; insurance

(a) Except as provided in sections 1105(b)(1) and 1105(d) of this title, any provision in an agreement or instrument which purports to relieve a fiduciary from responsibility or liability for any responsibility, obligation, or duty under this part shall be void as against public policy.

(b) Nothing in this subpart[1] shall preclude—

(1) a plan from purchasing insurance for its fiduciaries or for itself to cover liability or losses occurring by reason of the act or omission of a fiduciary, if such insurance permits recourse by the insurer against the fiduciary in the case of a breach of a fiduciary obligation by such fiduciary;

(2) a fiduciary from purchasing insurance to cover liability under this part from and for his own account; or

(3) an employer or an employee organization from purchasing insurance to cover potential liability of one or more persons who serve in a fiduciary capacity with regard to an employee benefit plan.

(Pub. L. 93–406, title I, §410, Sept. 2, 1974, 88 Stat. 886.)

§1111. Persons prohibited from holding certain positions

(a) Conviction or imprisonment

No person who has been convicted of, or has been imprisoned as a result of his conviction of, robbery, bribery, extortion, embezzlement, fraud, grand larceny, burglary, arson, a felony violation of Federal or State law involving substances defined in section 802(6) of title 21, murder, rape, kidnaping, perjury, assault with intent to kill, any crime described in section 80a–9(a)(1) of title 15, a violation of any provision of this chapter, a violation of section 186 of this title, a violation of chapter 63 of title 18, a violation of section 874, 1027, 1503, 1505, 1506, 1510, 1951, or 1954 of title 18, a violation of the Labor-Management Reporting and Disclosure Act of 1959 (29 U.S.C. 401), any felony involving abuse or misuse of such person's position or employment in a labor organization or employee benefit plan to seek or obtain an illegal gain at the expense of the members of the labor organization or the beneficiaries of the employee benefit plan, or conspiracy to commit any such crimes or attempt to commit any such crimes, or a crime in which any of the foregoing crimes is an element, shall serve or be permitted to serve—

(1) as an administrator, fiduciary, officer, trustee, custodian, counsel, agent, employee, or representative in any capacity of any employee benefit plan,

(2) as a consultant or adviser to an employee benefit plan, including but not limited to any entity whose activities are in whole or substantial part devoted to providing goods or services to any employee benefit plan, or

(3) in any capacity that involves decision-making authority or custody or control of the moneys, funds, assets, or property of any employee benefit plan,

during or for the period of thirteen years after such conviction or after the end of such imprisonment, whichever is later, unless the sentencing court on the motion of the person convicted sets a lesser period of at least three years after such conviction or after the end of such imprisonment, whichever is later, or unless prior to the end of such period, in the case of a person so convicted or imprisoned (A) his citizenship rights, having been revoked as a result of such conviction, have been fully restored, or (B) if the offense is a Federal offense, the sentencing judge or, if the offense is a State or local offense, the United States district court for the district in which the offense was committed, pursuant to sentencing guidelines and policy statements under section 994(a) of title 28, determines that such person's service in any capacity referred to in paragraphs (1) through (3) would not be contrary to the purposes of this subchapter. Prior to making any such determination the court shall hold a hearing and shall give notice to[1] such proceeding by certified mail to the Secretary of Labor and to State, county, and Federal prosecuting officials in the jurisdiction or jurisdictions in which such person was convicted. The court's determination in any such proceeding shall be final. No person shall knowingly hire, retain, employ, or otherwise place any other person to serve in any capacity in violation of this subsection. Notwithstanding the preceding provisions of this subsection, no corporation or partnership will be precluded from acting as an administrator, fiduciary, officer, trustee, custodian, counsel, agent, or employee of any employee benefit plan or as a consultant to any employee benefit plan without a notice, hearing, and determination by such court that such service would be inconsistent with the intention of this section.

(b) Penalty

Any person who intentionally violates this section shall be fined not more than $10,000 or imprisoned for not more than five years, or both.

(c) Definitions

For the purpose of this section—

(1) A person shall be deemed to have been "convicted" and under the disability of "conviction" from the date of the judgment of the trial court, regardless of whether that judgment remains under appeal.

(2) The term "consultant" means any person who, for compensation, advises, or represents an employee benefit plan or who provides other assistance to such plan, concerning the establishment or operation of such plan.

(3) A period of parole or supervised release shall not be considered as part of a period of imprisonment.

(d) Salary of person barred from employee benefit plan office during appeal of conviction

Whenever any person—

(1) by operation of this section, has been barred from office or other position in an employee benefit plan as a result of a conviction, and

(2) has filed an appeal of that conviction,

any salary which would be otherwise due such person by virtue of such office or position, shall be placed in escrow by the individual or organization responsible for payment of such salary.

[1] So in original. This part does not contain subparts.

[1] So in original. Probably should be "of".

Payment of such salary into escrow shall continue for the duration of the appeal or for the period of time during which such salary would be otherwise due, whichever period is shorter. Upon the final reversal of such person's conviction on appeal, the amounts in escrow shall be paid to such person. Upon the final sustaining of that person's conviction on appeal, the amounts in escrow shall be returned to the individual or organization responsible for payments of those amounts. Upon final reversal of such person's conviction, such person shall no longer be barred by this statute[2] from assuming any position from which such person was previously barred.

(Pub. L. 93–406, title I, § 411, Sept. 2, 1974, 88 Stat. 887; Pub. L. 98–473, title II, §§ 229, 230, 802, Oct. 12, 1984, 98 Stat. 2031, 2131; Pub. L. 100–182, § 15(b), Dec. 7, 1987, 101 Stat. 1269.)

REFERENCES IN TEXT

This chapter, referred to in subsec. (a), was in the original "this Act", meaning Pub. L. 93–406, known as the Employee Retirement Income Security Act of 1974. Titles I, III, and IV of such Act are classified principally to this chapter. For complete classification of this Act to the Code, see Short Title note set out under section 1001 of this title and Tables.

The Labor-Management Reporting and Disclosure Act of 1959, referred to in subsec. (a), is Pub. L. 86–257, Sept. 14, 1959, 73 Stat. 519, as amended, which is classified principally to chapter 11 (§ 401 et seq.) of this title. For complete classification of this Act to the Code, see Short Title note set out under section 401 of this title, and Tables.

AMENDMENTS

1987—Subsec. (a). Pub. L. 100–182, in concluding provisions, substituted "if the offense is a Federal offense, the sentencing judge or, if the offense is a State or local offense, the United States district court for the district in which the offense was committed, pursuant to sentencing guidelines and policy statements under section 994(a) of title 28," for "the United States Parole Commission", "court shall" for "Commission shall", "court's" for "Commission's", "such court" for "such Parole Commission", and "a hearing" for "an administrative hearing".

1984—Subsec. (a). Pub. L. 98–473, § 229, which directed substitution of "if the offense is a Federal offense, the sentencing judge or, if the offense is a State or local offense, on motion of the United States Department of Justice, the district court of the United States for the district in which the offense was committed, pursuant to sentencing guidelines and policy statements issued pursuant to section 994(a) of title 28," for "the Board of Parole of the United States Justice Department", "court" and "court's" for "Board" and "Board's", respectively, and "a" for "an administrative", was (except for the last substitution) incapable of execution in view of the previous amendment by section 802 of Pub. L. 98–473 which became effective prior to the effective date of the amendment by section 229. See note below.

Pub. L. 98–473, § 802(a), in amending provisions after "the Labor-Management Reporting and Disclosure Act of 1959 (29 U.S.C. 401)," generally, inserted provisions relating to abuse or misuse of employment in a labor organization or employee benefit plan, in cl. (1) substituted "employee, or representative in any capacity" for "or employee", in cl. (2) substituted "consultant or adviser to an" for "consultant to any", added cl. (3), substituted "the period of thirteen years" for "five years", "unless the sentencing court on the motion of the person convicted sets a lesser period of at least three years after such conviction or after the end of such imprisonment, whichever is later, or unless prior to the end of such period," for "unless prior to the end of such five-year period,", in cl. (B) substituted "the United States Parole Commission" for "the Board of Parole of the United States Department of Justice" and "paragraphs (1) through (3)" for "paragraph (1) or (2)", and in provisions following cl. (B) substituted "Commission" and "Commission's" for "Board" and "Board's", respectively, inserted provision of notice to the Secretary of Labor, and substituted "hire, retain, employ, or otherwise place any other person to serve in any capacity" for "permit any other person to serve in any capacity referred to in paragraph (1) or (2)" and "Parole Commission" for "Board of Parole".

Subsec. (b). Pub. L. 98–473, § 802(b), substituted "five years" for "one year".

Subsec. (c)(1). Pub. L. 98–473, § 802(c), substituted ", regardless of whether that judgment remains under appeal" for "or the date of the final sustaining of such judgment on appeal, whichever is the later event".

Subsec. (c)(3). Pub. L. 98–473, § 230, inserted "or supervised release" after "parole".

Subsec. (d). Pub. L. 98–473, § 802(d), added subsec. (d).

EFFECTIVE DATE OF 1987 AMENDMENT

Amendment by Pub. L. 100–182 applicable with respect to offenses committed after Dec. 7, 1987, see section 26 of Pub. L. 100–182, set out as a note under section 3006A of Title 18, Crimes and Criminal Procedure.

EFFECTIVE DATE OF 1984 AMENDMENT

Amendments by sections 229 and 230 of Pub. L. 98–473 effective Nov. 1, 1987, and applicable only to offenses committed after the taking effect of such amendments, see section 235(a)(1) of Pub. L. 98–473, set out as an Effective Date note under section 3551 of Title 18, Crimes and Criminal Procedure.

Amendment by section 802 of Pub. L. 98–473 effective with respect to any judgment of conviction entered by the trial court after Oct. 12, 1984, except as otherwise provided, see section 804 of Pub. L. 98–473, set out as a note under section 504 of this title.

§ 1112. Bonding

(a) Requisite bonding of plan officials

Every fiduciary of an employee benefit plan and every person who handles funds or other property of such a plan (hereafter in this section referred to as "plan official") shall be bonded as provided in this section; except that—

(1) where such plan is one under which the only assets from which benefits are paid are the general assets of a union or of an employer, the administrator, officers, and employees of such plan shall be exempt from the bonding requirements of this section,

(2) no bond shall be required of any entity which is registered as a broker or a dealer under section 78*o*(b) of title 15 if the broker or dealer is subject to the fidelity bond requirements of a self-regulatory organization (within the meaning of section 78c(a)(26) of title 15).[1]

(3) no bond shall be required of a fiduciary (or of any director, officer, or employee of such fiduciary) if such fiduciary—

(A) is a corporation organized and doing business under the laws of the United States or of any State;

(B) is authorized under such laws to exercise trust powers or to conduct an insurance business;

(C) is subject to supervision or examination by Federal or State authority; and

[2] So in original. Probably should be "section".

[1] So in original. The period probably should be ", and".

(D) has at all times a combined capital and surplus in excess of such a minimum amount as may be established by regulations issued by the Secretary, which amount shall be at least $1,000,000. Paragraph (2) shall apply to a bank or other financial institution which is authorized to exercise trust powers and the deposits of which are not insured by the Federal Deposit Insurance Corporation, only if such bank or institution meets bonding or similar requirements under State law which the Secretary determines are at least equivalent to those imposed on banks by Federal law.

The amount of such bond shall be fixed at the beginning of each fiscal year of the plan. Such amount shall be not less than 10 per centum of the amount of funds handled. In no case shall such bond be less than $1,000 nor more than $500,000, except that the Secretary, after due notice and opportunity for hearing to all interested parties, and after consideration of the record, may prescribe an amount in excess of $500,000, subject to the 10 per centum limitation of the preceding sentence. For purposes of fixing the amount of such bond, the amount of funds handled shall be determined by the funds handled by the person, group, or class to be covered by such bond and by their predecessor or predecessors, if any, during the preceding reporting year, or if the plan has no preceding reporting year, the amount of funds to be handled during the current reporting year by such person, group, or class, estimated as provided in regulations of the Secretary. Such bond shall provide protection to the plan against loss by reason of acts of fraud or dishonesty on the part of the plan official, directly or through connivance with others. Any bond shall have as surety thereon a corporate surety company which is an acceptable surety on Federal bonds under authority granted by the Secretary of the Treasury pursuant to sections 9304–9308 of title 31. Any bond shall be in a form or of a type approved by the Secretary, including individual bonds or schedule or blanket forms of bonds which cover a group or class. In the case of a plan that holds employer securities (within the meaning of section 1107(d)(1) of this title), this subsection shall be applied by substituting "$1,000,000" for "$500,000" each place it appears.

(b) Unlawful acts

It shall be unlawful for any plan official to whom subsection (a) of this section applies, to receive, handle, disburse, or otherwise exercise custody or control of any of the funds or other property of any employee benefit plan, without being bonded as required by subsection (a) of this section and it shall be unlawful for any plan official of such plan, or any other person having authority to direct the performance of such functions, to permit such functions, or any of them, to be performed by any plan official, with respect to whom the requirements of subsection (a) of this section have not been met.

(c) Conflict of interest prohibited in procuring bonds

It shall be unlawful for any person to procure any bond required by subsection (a) of this section from any surety or other company or through any agent or broker in whose business operations such plan or any party in interest in such plan has any control or significant financial interest, direct or indirect.

(d) Exclusiveness of statutory basis for bonding requirement for persons handling funds or other property of employee benefit plans

Nothing in any other provision of law shall require any person, required to be bonded as provided in subsection (a) of this section because he handles funds or other property of an employee benefit plan, to be bonded insofar as the handling by such person of the funds or other property of such plan is concerned.

(e) Regulations

The Secretary shall prescribe such regulations as may be necessary to carry out the provisions of this section including exempting a plan from the requirements of this section where he finds that (1) other bonding arrangements or (2) the overall financial condition of the plan would be adequate to protect the interests of the beneficiaries and participants. When, in the opinion of the Secretary, the administrator of a plan offers adequate evidence of the financial responsibility of the plan, or that other bonding arrangements would provide adequate protection of the beneficiaries and participants, he may exempt such plan from the requirements of this section.

(Pub. L. 93–406, title I, §412, Sept. 2, 1974, 88 Stat. 888; Pub. L. 109–280, title VI, §§611(b), 622(a), Aug. 17, 2006, 120 Stat. 968, 979.)

CODIFICATION

In subsec. (a), "sections 9304–9308 of title 31" substituted for "sections 6 through 13 of title 6, United States Code" on authority of Pub. L. 97–258, §4(b), Sept. 13, 1982, 96 Stat. 1067, the first section of which enacted Title 31, Money and Finance.

AMENDMENTS

2006—Subsec. (a). Pub. L. 109–280, §622(a), inserted at end of concluding provisions "In the case of a plan that holds employer securities (within the meaning of section 1107(d)(1) of this title), this subsection shall be applied by substituting '$1,000,000' for '$500,000' each place it appears."

Subsec. (a)(2), (3). Pub. L. 109–280, §611(b), added par. (2) and redesignated former par. (2) as (3).

EFFECTIVE DATE OF 2006 AMENDMENT

Amendment by section 611(b) of Pub. L. 109–280 applicable to plan years beginning after Aug. 17, 2006, see section 611(h)(2) of Pub. L. 109–280, set out as a note under section 4975 of Title 26, Internal Revenue Code.

Pub. L. 109–280, title VI, §622(b), Aug. 17, 2006, 120 Stat. 979, provided that: "The amendment made by this section [amending this section] shall apply to plan years beginning after December 31, 2007."

REGULATIONS

Secretary authorized, effective Sept. 2, 1974, to promulgate regulations wherever provisions of this part call for the promulgation of regulations, see sections 1031 and 1114 of this title.

§1113. Limitation of actions

No action may be commenced under this subchapter with respect to a fiduciary's breach of any responsibility, duty, or obligation under this part, or with respect to a violation of this part, after the earlier of—

(1) six years after (A) the date of the last action which constituted a part of the breach or violation, or (B) in the case of an omission the latest date on which the fiduciary could have cured the breach or violation, or

(2) three years after the earliest date on which the plaintiff had actual knowledge of the breach or violation;

except that in the case of fraud or concealment, such action may be commenced not later than six years after the date of discovery of such breach or violation.

(Pub. L. 93–406, title I, §413, Sept. 2, 1974, 88 Stat. 889; Pub. L. 100–203, title IX, §9342(b), Dec. 22, 1987, 101 Stat. 1330–371; Pub. L. 101–239, title VII, §§7881(j)(4), 7894(e)(5), Dec. 19, 1989, 103 Stat. 2443, 2450.)

AMENDMENTS

1989—Pub. L. 101–239, §7894(e)(5), struck out "(a)" before "No action".

Par. (2). Pub. L. 101–239, §7881(j)(4), struck out comma after "violation".

1987—Subsec. (a)(2). Pub. L. 100–203 struck out "(A)" after "date" and struck out "or (B) on which a report from which he could reasonably be expected to have obtained knowledge of such breach or violation was filed with the Secretary under this subchapter".

EFFECTIVE DATE OF 1989 AMENDMENT

Amendment by section 7881(j)(4) of Pub. L. 101–239 effective, except as otherwise provided, as if included in the provision of the Pension Protection Act, Pub. L. 100–203, §§9302–9346, to which such amendment relates, see section 7882 of Pub. L. 101–239, set out as a note under section 401 of Title 26, Internal Revenue Code.

Amendment by section 7894(e)(5) of Pub. L. 101–239 effective, except as otherwise provided, as if originally included in the provision of the Employee Retirement Income Security Act of 1974, Pub. L. 93–406, to which such amendment relates, see section 7894(i) of Pub. L. 101–239, set out as a note under section 1002 of this title.

EFFECTIVE DATE OF 1987 AMENDMENT

Amendment by Pub. L. 100–203 applicable with respect to reports required to be filed after Dec. 31, 1987, see section 9342(d)(1) of Pub. L. 100–203, set out as a note under section 1132 of this title.

§1114. Effective date

(a) Except as provided in subsections (b), (c), and (d) of this section, this part shall take effect on January 1, 1975.

(b)(1) The provisions of this part authorizing the Secretary to promulgate regulations shall take effect on September 2, 1974.

(2) Upon application of a plan, the Secretary may postpone until not later than January 1, 1976, the applicability of any provision of sections 1102, 1103 (other than 1103(c)), 1105 (other than 1105(a) and (d)), and 1110(a) of this title, as it applies to any plan in existence on September 2, 1974, if he determines such postponement is (A) necessary to amend the instrument establishing the plan under which the plan is maintained and (B) not adverse to the interest of participants and beneficiaries.

(3) This part shall take effect on September 2, 1974, with respect to a plan which terminates after June 30, 1974, and before January 1, 1975, and to which at the time of termination section 1321 of this title applies.

(c) Sections 1106 and 1107(a) of this title (relating to prohibited transactions) shall not apply—

(1) until June 30, 1984, to a loan of money or other extension of credit between a plan and a party in interest under a binding contract in effect on July 1, 1974 (or pursuant to renewals of such a contract), if such loan or other extension of credit remains at least as favorable to the plan as an arm's-length transaction with an unrelated party would be, and if the execution of the contract, the making of the loan, or the extension of credit was not, at the time of such execution, making, or extension, a prohibited transaction (within the meaning of section 503(b) of title 26 or the corresponding provisions of prior law);

(2) until June 30, 1984, to a lease or joint use of property involving the plan and a party in interest pursuant to a binding contract in effect on July 1, 1974 (or pursuant to renewals of such a contract), if such lease or joint use remains at least as favorable to the plan as an arm's-length transaction with an unrelated party would be and if the execution of the contract was not, at the time of such execution, a prohibited transaction (within the meaning of section 503(b) of title 26 or the corresponding provisions of prior law);

(3) until June 30, 1984, to the sale, exchange or other disposition of property described in paragraph (2) between a plan and a party in interest if—

(A) in the case of a sale, exchange, or other disposition of the property by the plan to the party in interest, the plan receives an amount which is not less than the fair market value of the property at the time of such disposition; and

(B) in the case of the acquisition of the property by the plan, the plan pays an amount which is not in excess of the fair market value of the property at the time of such acquisition;

(4) until June 30, 1977, to the provision of services, to which paragraphs (1), (2), and (3) do not apply between a plan and a party in interest—

(A) under a binding contract in effect on July 1, 1974 (or pursuant to renewals of such contract), or

(B) if the party in interest ordinarily and customarily furnished such services on June 30, 1974, if such provision of services remains at least as favorable to the plan as an arm's-length transaction with an unrelated party would be and if such provision of services was not, at the time of such provision, a prohibited transaction (within the meaning of section 503(b) of title 26) or the corresponding provisions of prior law; or

(5) the sale, exchange, or other disposition of property which is owned by a plan on June 30, 1974, and all times thereafter, to a party in interest, if such plan is required to dispose of such property in order to comply with the provisions of section 1107(a) of this title (relating to the prohibition against holding excess employer securities and employer real property), and if the plan receives not less than adequate consideration.

(d) Any election, or failure to elect, by a disqualified person under section 2003(c)(1)(B) of this Act shall be treated for purposes of this part (but not for purposes of section 1144 of this title) as an act or omission occurring before the effective date of this part.

(e) The preceding provisions of this section shall not apply with respect to amendments made to this part in provisions enacted after September 2, 1974.

(Pub. L. 93–406, title I, §414, Sept. 2, 1974, 88 Stat. 889; Pub. L. 101–239, title VII, §7894(e)(6), (h)(4), Dec. 19, 1989, 103 Stat. 2450, 2451.)

REFERENCES IN TEXT

Section 2003(c)(1)(B) of this Act, referred to in subsec. (d), is section 2003(c)(1)(B) of Pub. L. 93–406, which is set out as an Effective Date; Savings Provisions note under section 4975 of Title 26, Internal Revenue Code.

AMENDMENTS

1989—Subsec. (c)(2). Pub. L. 101–239, §7894(e)(6), substituted "Internal Revenue Code of 1986" for "Internal Revenue Code of 1954", which for purposes of codification was translated as "title 26" thus requiring no change in text, and substituted "or the corresponding provisions of prior law)" for ") or the corresponding provisions of prior law".

Subsec. (e). Pub. L. 101–239, §7894(h)(4), added subsec. (e).

EFFECTIVE DATE OF 1989 AMENDMENT

Amendment by Pub. L. 101–239 effective, except as otherwise provided, as if originally included in the provision of the Employee Retirement Income Security Act of 1974, Pub. L. 93–406, to which such amendment relates, see section 7894(i) of Pub. L. 101–239, set out as a note under section 1002 of this title.

PART 5—ADMINISTRATION AND ENFORCEMENT

§1131. Criminal penalties

Any person who willfully violates any provision of part 1 of this subtitle, or any regulation or order issued under any such provision, shall upon conviction be fined not more than $100,000 or imprisoned not more than 10 years, or both; except that in the case of such violation by a person not an individual, the fine imposed upon such person shall be a fine not exceeding $500,000.

(Pub. L. 93–406, title I, §501, Sept. 2, 1974, 88 Stat. 891; Pub. L. 107–204, title IX, §904, July 30, 2002, 116 Stat. 805.)

AMENDMENTS

2002—Pub. L. 107–204 substituted "$100,000" for "$5,000", "10 years" for "one year", and "$500,000" for "$100,000".

REGULATIONS

Secretary authorized, effective Sept. 2, 1974, to promulgate regulations wherever provisions of this subchapter call for the promulgation of regulations, see section 1031 of this title.

§1132. Civil enforcement

(a) Persons empowered to bring a civil action

A civil action may be brought—

(1) by a participant or beneficiary—

(A) for the relief provided for in subsection (c) of this section, or

(B) to recover benefits due to him under the terms of his plan, to enforce his rights under the terms of the plan, or to clarify his rights to future benefits under the terms of the plan;

(2) by the Secretary, or by a participant, beneficiary or fiduciary for appropriate relief under section 1109 of this title;

(3) by a participant, beneficiary, or fiduciary (A) to enjoin any act or practice which violates any provision of this subchapter or the terms of the plan, or (B) to obtain other appropriate equitable relief (i) to redress such violations or (ii) to enforce any provisions of this subchapter or the terms of the plan;

(4) by the Secretary, or by a participant, or beneficiary for appropriate relief in the case of a violation of 1025(c) of this title;

(5) except as otherwise provided in subsection (b) of this section, by the Secretary (A) to enjoin any act or practice which violates any provision of this subchapter, or (B) to obtain other appropriate equitable relief (i) to redress such violation or (ii) to enforce any provision of this subchapter;

(6) by the Secretary to collect any civil penalty under paragraph (2), (4), (5), (6), (7), (8), or (9) of subsection (c) of this section or under subsection (i) or (*l*) of this section;

(7) by a State to enforce compliance with a qualified medical child support order (as defined in section 1169(a)(2)(A) of this title);

(8) by the Secretary, or by an employer or other person referred to in section 1021(f)(1) of this title, (A) to enjoin any act or practice which violates subsection (f) of section 1021 of this title, or (B) to obtain appropriate equitable relief (i) to redress such violation or (ii) to enforce such subsection;

(9) in the event that the purchase of an insurance contract or insurance annuity in connection with termination of an individual's status as a participant covered under a pension plan with respect to all or any portion of the participant's pension benefit under such plan constitutes a violation of part 4 of this title[1] or the terms of the plan, by the Secretary, by any individual who was a participant or beneficiary at the time of the alleged violation, or by a fiduciary, to obtain appropriate relief, including the posting of security if necessary, to assure receipt by the participant or beneficiary of the amounts provided or to be provided by such insurance contract or annuity, plus reasonable prejudgment interest on such amounts; or

(10) in the case of a multiemployer plan that has been certified by the actuary to be in endangered or critical status under section 1085 of this title, if the plan sponsor—

(A) has not adopted a funding improvement or rehabilitation plan under that section by the deadline established in such section, or

(B) fails to update or comply with the terms of the funding improvement or rehabilitation plan in accordance with the requirements of such section,

by an employer that has an obligation to contribute with respect to the multiemployer

[1] So in original. Probably should be "subtitle".

plan or an employee organization that represents active participants in the multiemployer plan, for an order compelling the plan sponsor to adopt a funding improvement or rehabilitation plan or to update or comply with the terms of the funding improvement or rehabilitation plan in accordance with the requirements of such section and the funding improvement or rehabilitation plan.

(b) Plans qualified under Internal Revenue Code; maintenance of actions involving delinquent contributions

(1) In the case of a plan which is qualified under section 401(a), 403(a), or 405(a)[2] of title 26 (or with respect to which an application to so qualify has been filed and has not been finally determined) the Secretary may exercise his authority under subsection (a)(5) of this section with respect to a violation of, or the enforcement of, parts 2 and 3 of this subtitle (relating to participation, vesting, and funding), only if—

(A) requested by the Secretary of the Treasury, or

(B) one or more participants, beneficiaries, or fiduciaries, of such plan request in writing (in such manner as the Secretary shall prescribe by regulation) that he exercise such authority on their behalf. In the case of such a request under this paragraph he may exercise such authority only if he determines that such violation affects, or such enforcement is necessary to protect, claims of participants or beneficiaries to benefits under the plan.

(2) The Secretary shall not initiate an action to enforce section 1145 of this title.

(3) Except as provided in subsections (c)(9) and (a)(6) (with respect to collecting civil penalties under subsection (c)(9)), the Secretary is not authorized to enforce under this part any requirement of part 7 against a health insurance issuer offering health insurance coverage in connection with a group health plan (as defined in section 1191b(a)(1) of this title). Nothing in this paragraph shall affect the authority of the Secretary to issue regulations to carry out such part.

(c) Administrator's refusal to supply requested information; penalty for failure to provide annual report in complete form

(1) Any administrator (A) who fails to meet the requirements of paragraph (1) or (4) of section 1166[2] of this title, section 1021(e)(1) of this title, section 1021(f) of this title, or section 1025(a) of this title with respect to a participant or beneficiary, or (B) who fails or refuses to comply with a request for any information which such administrator is required by this subchapter to furnish to a participant or beneficiary (unless such failure or refusal results from matters reasonably beyond the control of the administrator) by mailing the material requested to the last known address of the requesting participant or beneficiary within 30 days after such request may in the court's discretion be personally liable to such participant or beneficiary in the amount of up to $100 a day from the date of such failure or refusal, and the court may in its discretion order such other relief as it deems proper. For purposes of this paragraph, each violation described in subparagraph (A) with respect to any single participant, and each violation described in subparagraph (B) with respect to any single participant or beneficiary, shall be treated as a separate violation.

(2) The Secretary may assess a civil penalty against any plan administrator of up to $1,000 a day from the date of such plan administrator's failure or refusal to file the annual report required to be filed with the Secretary under section 1021(b)(1) of this title. For purposes of this paragraph, an annual report that has been rejected under section 1024(a)(4) of this title for failure to provide material information shall not be treated as having been filed with the Secretary.

(3) Any employer maintaining a plan who fails to meet the notice requirement of section 1021(d) of this title with respect to any participant or beneficiary or who fails to meet the requirements of section 1021(e)(2) of this title with respect to any person or who fails to meet the requirements of section 1082(d)(12)(E)[2] of this title with respect to any person may in the court's discretion be liable to such participant or beneficiary or to such person in the amount of up to $100 a day from the date of such failure, and the court may in its discretion order such other relief as it deems proper.

(4) The Secretary may assess a civil penalty of not more than $1,000 a day for each violation by any person of subsection (j), (k), or (*l*) of section 1021 of this title or section 1144(e)(3) of this title.

(5) The Secretary may assess a civil penalty against any person of up to $1,000 a day from the date of the person's failure or refusal to file the information required to be filed by such person with the Secretary under regulations prescribed pursuant to section 1021(g) of this title.

(6) If, within 30 days of a request by the Secretary to a plan administrator for documents under section 1024(a)(6) of this title, the plan administrator fails to furnish the material requested to the Secretary, the Secretary may assess a civil penalty against the plan administrator of up to $100 a day from the date of such failure (but in no event in excess of $1,000 per request). No penalty shall be imposed under this paragraph for any failure resulting from matters reasonably beyond the control of the plan administrator.

(7) The Secretary may assess a civil penalty against a plan administrator of up to $100 a day from the date of the plan administrator's failure or refusal to provide notice to participants and beneficiaries in accordance with subsection (i) or (m) of section 1021 of this title. For purposes of this paragraph, each violation with respect to any single participant or beneficiary shall be treated as a separate violation.

(8) The Secretary may assess against any plan sponsor of a multiemployer plan a civil penalty of not more than $1,100 per day—

(A) for each violation by such sponsor of the requirement under section 1085 of this title to adopt by the deadline established in that section a funding improvement plan or rehabilitation plan with respect to a multiemployer plan which is in endangered or critical status, or

[2] See References in Text note below.

(B) in the case of a plan in endangered status which is not in seriously endangered status, for failure by the plan to meet the applicable benchmarks under section 1085 of this title by the end of the funding improvement period with respect to the plan.

(9) SECRETARIAL ENFORCEMENT AUTHORITY RELATING TO USE OF GENETIC INFORMATION.—

(A) GENERAL RULE.—The Secretary may impose a penalty against any plan sponsor of a group health plan, or any health insurance issuer offering health insurance coverage in connection with the plan, for any failure by such sponsor or issuer to meet the requirements of subsection (a)(1)(F), (b)(3), (c), or (d) of section 1182 of this title or section 1181 or 1182(b)(1) of this title with respect to genetic information, in connection with the plan.

(B) AMOUNT.—

(i) IN GENERAL.—The amount of the penalty imposed by subparagraph (A) shall be $100 for each day in the noncompliance period with respect to each participant or beneficiary to whom such failure relates.

(ii) NONCOMPLIANCE PERIOD.—For purposes of this paragraph, the term "noncompliance period" means, with respect to any failure, the period—

(I) beginning on the date such failure first occurs; and

(II) ending on the date the failure is corrected.

(C) MINIMUM PENALTIES WHERE FAILURE DISCOVERED.—Notwithstanding clauses (i) and (ii) of subparagraph (D):

(i) IN GENERAL.—In the case of 1 or more failures with respect to a participant or beneficiary—

(I) which are not corrected before the date on which the plan receives a notice from the Secretary of such violation; and

(II) which occurred or continued during the period involved;

the amount of penalty imposed by subparagraph (A) by reason of such failures with respect to such participant or beneficiary shall not be less than $2,500.

(ii) HIGHER MINIMUM PENALTY WHERE VIOLATIONS ARE MORE THAN DE MINIMIS.—To the extent violations for which any person is liable under this paragraph for any year are more than de minimis, clause (i) shall be applied by substituting "$15,000" for "$2,500" with respect to such person.

(D) LIMITATIONS.—

(i) PENALTY NOT TO APPLY WHERE FAILURE NOT DISCOVERED EXERCISING REASONABLE DILIGENCE.—No penalty shall be imposed by subparagraph (A) on any failure during any period for which it is established to the satisfaction of the Secretary that the person otherwise liable for such penalty did not know, and exercising reasonable diligence would not have known, that such failure existed.

(ii) PENALTY NOT TO APPLY TO FAILURES CORRECTED WITHIN CERTAIN PERIODS.—No penalty shall be imposed by subparagraph (A) on any failure if—

(I) such failure was due to reasonable cause and not to willful neglect; and

(II) such failure is corrected during the 30-day period beginning on the first date the person otherwise liable for such penalty knew, or exercising reasonable diligence would have known, that such failure existed.

(iii) OVERALL LIMITATION FOR UNINTENTIONAL FAILURES.—In the case of failures which are due to reasonable cause and not to willful neglect, the penalty imposed by subparagraph (A) for failures shall not exceed the amount equal to the lesser of—

(I) 10 percent of the aggregate amount paid or incurred by the plan sponsor (or predecessor plan sponsor) during the preceding taxable year for group health plans; or

(II) $500,000.

(E) WAIVER BY SECRETARY.—In the case of a failure which is due to reasonable cause and not to willful neglect, the Secretary may waive part or all of the penalty imposed by subparagraph (A) to the extent that the payment of such penalty would be excessive relative to the failure involved.

(F) DEFINITIONS.—Terms used in this paragraph which are defined in section 1191b of this title shall have the meanings provided such terms in such section.

(10) The Secretary and the Secretary of Health and Human Services shall maintain such ongoing consultation as may be necessary and appropriate to coordinate enforcement under this subsection with enforcement under section 1320b–14(c)(8)[2] of title 42.

(d) Status of employee benefit plan as entity

(1) An employee benefit plan may sue or be sued under this subchapter as an entity. Service of summons, subpena, or other legal process of a court upon a trustee or an administrator of an employee benefit plan in his capacity as such shall constitute service upon the employee benefit plan. In a case where a plan has not designated in the summary plan description of the plan an individual as agent for the service of legal process, service upon the Secretary shall constitute such service. The Secretary, not later than 15 days after receipt of service under the preceding sentence, shall notify the administrator or any trustee of the plan of receipt of such service.

(2) Any money judgment under this subchapter against an employee benefit plan shall be enforceable only against the plan as an entity and shall not be enforceable against any other person unless liability against such person is established in his individual capacity under this subchapter.

(e) Jurisdiction

(1) Except for actions under subsection (a)(1)(B) of this section, the district courts of the United States shall have exclusive jurisdiction of civil actions under this subchapter brought by the Secretary or by a participant, beneficiary, fiduciary, or any person referred to in section 1021(f)(1) of this title. State courts of

competent jurisdiction and district courts of the United States shall have concurrent jurisdiction of actions under paragraphs (1)(B) and (7) of subsection (a) of this section.

(2) Where an action under this subchapter is brought in a district court of the United States, it may be brought in the district where the plan is administered, where the breach took place, or where a defendant resides or may be found, and process may be served in any other district where a defendant resides or may be found.

(f) Amount in controversy; citizenship of parties

The district courts of the United States shall have jurisdiction, without respect to the amount in controversy or the citizenship of the parties, to grant the relief provided for in subsection (a) of this section in any action.

(g) Attorney's fees and costs; awards in actions involving delinquent contributions

(1) In any action under this subchapter (other than an action described in paragraph (2)) by a participant, beneficiary, or fiduciary, the court in its discretion may allow a reasonable attorney's fee and costs of action to either party.

(2) In any action under this subchapter by a fiduciary for or on behalf of a plan to enforce section 1145 of this title in which a judgment in favor of the plan is awarded, the court shall award the plan—

(A) the unpaid contributions,

(B) interest on the unpaid contributions,

(C) an amount equal to the greater of—

(i) interest on the unpaid contributions, or

(ii) liquidated damages provided for under the plan in an amount not in excess of 20 percent (or such higher percentage as may be permitted under Federal or State law) of the amount determined by the court under subparagraph (A),

(D) reasonable attorney's fees and costs of the action, to be paid by the defendant, and

(E) such other legal or equitable relief as the court deems appropriate.

For purposes of this paragraph, interest on unpaid contributions shall be determined by using the rate provided under the plan, or, if none, the rate prescribed under section 6621 of title 26.

(h) Service upon Secretary of Labor and Secretary of the Treasury

A copy of the complaint in any action under this subchapter by a participant, beneficiary, or fiduciary (other than an action brought by one or more participants or beneficiaries under subsection (a)(1)(B) of this section which is solely for the purpose of recovering benefits due such participants under the terms of the plan) shall be served upon the Secretary and the Secretary of the Treasury by certified mail. Either Secretary shall have the right in his discretion to intervene in any action, except that the Secretary of the Treasury may not intervene in any action under part 4 of this subtitle. If the Secretary brings an action under subsection (a) of this section on behalf of a participant or beneficiary, he shall notify the Secretary of the Treasury.

(i) Administrative assessment of civil penalty

In the case of a transaction prohibited by section 1106 of this title by a party in interest with respect to a plan to which this part applies, the Secretary may assess a civil penalty against such party in interest. The amount of such penalty may not exceed 5 percent of the amount involved in each such transaction (as defined in section 4975(f)(4) of title 26) for each year or part thereof during which the prohibited transaction continues, except that, if the transaction is not corrected (in such manner as the Secretary shall prescribe in regulations which shall be consistent with section 4975(f)(5) of title 26) within 90 days after notice from the Secretary (or such longer period as the Secretary may permit), such penalty may be in an amount not more than 100 percent of the amount involved. This subsection shall not apply to a transaction with respect to a plan described in section 4975(e)(1) of title 26.

(j) Direction and control of litigation by Attorney General

In all civil actions under this subchapter, attorneys appointed by the Secretary may represent the Secretary (except as provided in section 518(a) of title 28), but all such litigation shall be subject to the direction and control of the Attorney General.

(k) Jurisdiction of actions against the Secretary of Labor

Suits by an administrator, fiduciary, participant, or beneficiary of an employee benefit plan to review a final order of the Secretary, to restrain the Secretary from taking any action contrary to the provisions of this chapter, or to compel him to take action required under this subchapter, may be brought in the district court of the United States for the district where the plan has its principal office, or in the United States District Court for the District of Columbia.

(*l*) Civil penalties on violations by fiduciaries

(1) In the case of—

(A) any breach of fiduciary responsibility under (or other violation of) part 4 of this subtitle by a fiduciary, or

(B) any knowing participation in such a breach or violation by any other person,

the Secretary shall assess a civil penalty against such fiduciary or other person in an amount equal to 20 percent of the applicable recovery amount.

(2) For purposes of paragraph (1), the term "applicable recovery amount" means any amount which is recovered from a fiduciary or other person with respect to a breach or violation described in paragraph (1)—

(A) pursuant to any settlement agreement with the Secretary, or

(B) ordered by a court to be paid by such fiduciary or other person to a plan or its participants and beneficiaries in a judicial proceeding instituted by the Secretary under subsection (a)(2) or (a)(5) of this section.

(3) The Secretary may, in the Secretary's sole discretion, waive or reduce the penalty under paragraph (1) if the Secretary determines in writing that—

(A) the fiduciary or other person acted reasonably and in good faith, or

(B) it is reasonable to expect that the fiduciary or other person will not be able to restore all losses to the plan (or to provide the relief ordered pursuant to subsection (a)(9) of this section) without severe financial hardship unless such waiver or reduction is granted.

(4) The penalty imposed on a fiduciary or other person under this subsection with respect to any transaction shall be reduced by the amount of any penalty or tax imposed on such fiduciary or other person with respect to such transaction under subsection (i) of this section and section 4975 of title 26.

(m) Penalty for improper distribution

In the case of a distribution to a pension plan participant or beneficiary in violation of section 1056(e) of this title by a plan fiduciary, the Secretary shall assess a penalty against such fiduciary in an amount equal to the value of the distribution. Such penalty shall not exceed $10,000 for each such distribution.

(Pub. L. 93–406, title I, §502, Sept. 2, 1974, 88 Stat. 891; Pub. L. 96–364, title III, §306(b), Sept. 26, 1980, 94 Stat. 1295; Pub. L. 99–272, title X, §10002(b), Apr. 7, 1986, 100 Stat. 231; Pub. L. 100–203, title IX, §§9342(c), 9344, Dec. 22, 1987, 101 Stat. 1330–372, 1330–373; Pub. L. 101–239, title II, §2101(a), (b), title VII, §§7881(b)(5)(B), (j)(2), (3), 7891(a)(1), 7894(f)(1), Dec. 19, 1989, 103 Stat. 2123, 2438, 2442, 2445, 2450; Pub. L. 101–508, title XII, §12012(d)(2), Nov. 5, 1990, 104 Stat. 1388–573; Pub. L. 103–66, title IV, §4301(c)(1)–(3), Aug. 10, 1993, 107 Stat. 376; Pub. L. 103–401, §§2, 3, Oct. 22, 1994, 108 Stat. 4172; Pub. L. 103–465, title VII, §761(a)(9)(B)(ii), Dec. 8, 1994, 108 Stat. 5033; Pub. L. 104–191, title I, §101(b), (e)(2), Aug. 21, 1996, 110 Stat. 1951, 1952; Pub. L. 104–204, title VI, §603(b)(3)(E), Sept. 26, 1996, 110 Stat. 2938; Pub. L. 105–34, title XV, §1503(c)(2)(B), (d)(7), Aug. 5, 1997, 111 Stat. 1062; Pub. L. 107–204, title III, §306(b)(3), July 30, 2002, 116 Stat. 783; Pub. L. 108–218, title I, §§102(d), 103(b), 104(a)(2), Apr. 10, 2004, 118 Stat. 602, 603, 606; Pub. L. 109–280, title I, §103(b)(2), title II, §202(b), (c), title V, §§502(a)(2), (b)(2), 507(b), 508(a)(2)(C), title IX, §902(f)(2), Aug. 17, 2006, 120 Stat. 816, 884, 885, 940, 941, 949, 951, 1039; Pub. L. 110–233, title I, §101(e), May 21, 2008, 122 Stat. 886; Pub. L. 110–458, title I, §§101(c)(1)(H), 102(b)(1)(H), (I), Dec. 23, 2008, 122 Stat. 5097, 5101.)

AMENDMENT OF SECTION

For termination of amendment by section 221(c) of Pub. L. 109–280, see Effective and Termination Dates of 2006 Amendment note below.

REFERENCES IN TEXT

Section 405(a) of title 26, referred to in subsec. (b)(1), was repealed by Pub. L. 98–369, div. A, title IV, §491(a), July 18, 1984, 98 Stat. 848.

Paragraphs (1) and (4) of section 1166 of this title, referred to in subsec. (c)(1), were redesignated as pars. (1) and (4) of section 1166(a) of this title by Pub. L. 101–239, title VII, §7891(d)(1)(A)(ii)(I), Dec. 19, 1989, 103 Stat. 2445.

Section 1082 of this title, referred to in subsec. (c)(3), was repealed and a new section 1082 was enacted by Pub. L. 109–280, title I, §101(a), (b), Aug. 17, 2006, 120 Stat. 784, and, as so enacted, section 1082 of this title no longer contains a subsec. (d)(12)(E).

Section 1320b–14 of title 42, referred to in subsec. (c)(10), was repealed by Pub. L. 104–226, §1(a), Oct. 2, 1996, 110 Stat. 3033, and a new section 1320b–14 of title 42, which does not contain a subsec. (c)(8), was enacted by Pub. L. 106–554, §1(a)(6) [title IX, §911(a)(1)], Dec. 21, 2000, 114 Stat. 2763, 2763A–583.

This chapter, referred to in subsec. (k), was in the original "this Act", meaning Pub. L. 93–406, known as the Employee Retirement Income Security Act of 1974. Titles I, III, and IV of such Act are classified principally to this chapter. For complete classification of this Act to the Code, see Short Title note set out under section 1001 of this title and Tables.

CODIFICATION

Another section 306(b)(3) of Pub. L. 107–204 is classified to section 7244(b)(3) of Title 15, Commerce and Trade.

AMENDMENTS

2008—Subsec. (a)(6). Pub. L. 110–233, §101(e)(1), substituted "(7), (8), or (9)" for "(7), or (8)".

Subsec. (b)(3). Pub. L. 110–233, §101(e)(2), substituted "Except as provided in subsections (c)(9) and (a)(6) (with respect to collecting civil penalties under subsection (c)(9)), the Secretary" for "The Secretary".

Subsec. (c)(2). Pub. L. 110–458, §102(b)(1)(H), substituted "1021(b)(1)" for "1021(b)(4)".

Subsec. (c)(4). Pub. L. 110–458, §101(c)(1)(H), substituted "by any person of subsection (j), (k), or (*l*) of section 1021 of this title or section 1144(e)(3) of this title." for "by any person of subsection (j), (k), or (*l*) of section 1021 of this title, section 1082(b)(7)(F)(vi) of this title, or section 1144(e)(3) of this title."

Subsec. (c)(8)(A). Pub. L. 110–458, §102(b)(1)(I), inserted "plan" after "multiemployer".

Subsec. (c)(9), (10). Pub. L. 110–233, §101(e)(3), added par. (9) and redesignated former par. (9) as (10).

2006—Subsec. (a)(6). Pub. L. 109–280, §§202(b)(1), 221(c), temporarily substituted "(6), (7), or (8)" for "(6), or (7)". See Effective and Termination Dates of 2006 Amendment note below.

Subsec. (a)(8) to (10). Pub. L. 109–280, §§202(c), 221(c), temporarily amended subsec. (a) by striking out "or" at end of par. (8), substituting "; or" for period at end of par. (9), and adding par. (10). See Effective and Termination Dates of 2006 Amendment note below.

Subsec. (c)(1). Pub. L. 109–280, §508(a)(2)(C), substituted "section 1021(f) of this title, or section 1025(a) of this title" for "or section 1021(f) of this title".

Subsec. (c)(4). Pub. L. 109–280, §902(f)(2), which directed amendment of par. (4) by substituting ", section 1082(b)(7)(F)(vi) of this title, or section 1144(e)(3) of this title" for "or section 1082(b)(7)(F)(vi) of this title", was executed by making the substitution for "or 1082(b)(7)(F)(iv) of this title", to reflect the probable intent of Congress.

Pub. L. 109–280, §502(b)(2), which directed amendment of par. (4) by substituting "subsection (j), (k), or (*l*) of section 1021 of this title" for "section 1021(j) or (k) of this title", was executed by making the substitution for "subsection (j) or (k) of section 1021 of this title", to reflect the probable intent of Congress.

Pub. L. 109–280, §502(a)(2), substituted "subsection (j) or (k) of section 1021 of this title" for "section 1021(j)".

Pub. L. 109–280, §103(b)(2), which directed amendment of par. (4) by substituting "section 1021(j) or 1082(b)(7)(F)(iv) of this title" for "section 1082(b)(7)(F)(iv) of this title", was executed by making the substitution for "section 1082(b)(7)(F)(vi) of this title", to reflect the probable intent of Congress.

Subsec. (c)(7). Pub. L. 109–280, §507(b), substituted "subsection (i) or (m) of section 1021" for "section 1021(i)".

Subsec. (c)(8), (9). Pub. L. 109–280, §§202(b)(2), (3), 221(c), temporarily added par. (8) and redesignated former par. (8) as (9). See Effective and Termination Dates of 2006 Amendment note below.

2004—Subsec. (c)(1). Pub. L. 108–218, §103(b), substituted ", section 1021(e)(1) of this title, or section 1021(f) of this title" for "or section 1021(e)(1) of this title".

Subsec. (c)(3). Pub. L. 108–218, § 102(d), inserted "or who fails to meet the requirements of section 1082(d)(12)(E) of this title with respect to any person" after "1021(e)(2) of this title with respect to any person".

Subsec. (c)(4). Pub. L. 108–218, § 104(a)(2), amended par. (4) generally. Prior to amendment, par. (4) read as follows: "The Secretary may assess a civil penalty of not more than $1,000 for each violation by any person of section 1021(f)(1) of this title."

2002—Subsec. (a)(6). Pub. L. 107–204, § 306(b)(3)(A), substituted "(5), (6), or (7)" for "(5), or (6)".

Subsec. (c)(7), (8). Pub. L. 107–204, § 306(b)(3)(B), (C), added par. (7) and redesignated former par. (7) as (8).

1997—Subsec. (a)(6). Pub. L. 105–34, § 1503(d)(7), substituted "(5), or (6)" for "or (5)".

Subsec. (c)(6), (7). Pub. L. 105–34, § 1503(c)(2)(B), added par. (6) and redesignated former par. (6) as (7).

1996—Subsec. (a)(6). Pub. L. 104–191, § 101(e)(2)(A)(i), substituted "under paragraph (2), (4), or (5) of subsection (c) of this section or under subsection (i) or (*l*) of this section" for "under subsection (c)(2) or (i) or (*l*) of this section".

Subsec. (b)(3). Pub. L. 104–204 made technical amendment to reference in original act which appears in text as reference to section 1191b of this title.

Pub. L. 104–191, § 101(b), added par. (3).

Subsec. (c)(1). Pub. L. 104–191, § 101(e)(2)(B), inserted at end "For purposes of this paragraph, each violation described in subparagraph (A) with respect to any single participant, and each violation described in subparagraph (B) with respect to any single participant or beneficiary, shall be treated as a separate violation."

Subsec. (c)(4) to (6). Pub. L. 104–191, § 101(e)(2)(A)(ii), struck out "For purposes of this paragraph, each violation described in subparagraph (A) with respect to any single participant, and each violation described in subparagraph (B) with respect to any single participant or beneficiary, shall be treated as a separate violation. The Secretary and" after "section 1021(f)(1) of this title.", redesignated "the Secretary of Health and Human Services shall maintain such ongoing consultation as may be necessary and appropriate to coordinate enforcement under this subsection with enforcement under section 1320b–14(c)(8) of title 42." as par. (6) and inserted "The Secretary and" before "the Secretary of Health and Human Services", and added par. (5).

1994—Subsec. (a)(9). Pub. L. 103–401, § 2, added par. (9).

Subsec. (*l*)(3)(B). Pub. L. 103–401, § 3, inserted "(or to provide the relief ordered pursuant to subsection (a)(9) of this section)" after "to restore all losses to the plan".

Subsec. (m). Pub. L. 103–465 added subsec. (m).

1993—Subsec. (a)(7), (8). Pub. L. 103–66, § 4301(c)(1), added pars. (7) and (8).

Subsec. (c)(4). Pub. L. 103–66, § 4301(c)(2), added par. (4).

Subsec. (e)(1). Pub. L. 103–66, § 4301(c)(3), substituted in first sentence "fiduciary, or any person referred to in section 1021(f)(1) of this title" for "or fiduciary" and in second sentence "paragraphs (1)(B) and (7) of subsection (a)" for "subsection (a)(1)(B)".

1990—Subsec. (c)(1). Pub. L. 101–508, § 12012(d)(2)(A), inserted "or section 1021(e)(1) of this title" after "section 1166 of this title".

Subsec. (c)(3). Pub. L. 101–508, § 12012(d)(2)(B), inserted "or who fails to meet the requirements of section 1021(e)(2) of this title with respect to any person" after first reference to "beneficiary" and "or to such person" after second reference to "beneficiary".

1989—Subsec. (a)(6). Pub. L. 101–239, § 7881(j)(2), substituted "subsection (c)(2) or (i)" for "subsection (i)".

Pub. L. 101–239, § 2101(b), inserted "or (*l*)" after "subsection (i)".

Subsec. (b)(1). Pub. L. 101–239, § 7894(f)(1), substituted "respect" for "respct" before "to a violation" in introductory provisions.

Pub. L. 101–239, § 7891(a)(1), substituted "Internal Revenue Code of 1986" for "Internal Revenue Code of 1954", which for purposes of codification was translated as "title 26" thus requiring no change in text.

Subsec. (c)(2). Pub. L. 101–239, § 7881(j)(3), inserted "against any plan administrator" after "civil penalty" and substituted "such plan administrator's" for "a plan administrator's".

Subsec. (c)(3). Pub. L. 101–239, § 7881(b)(5)(B), added par. (3).

Subsec. (g)(2). Pub. L. 101–239, § 7891(a)(1), substituted "Internal Revenue Code of 1986" for "Internal Revenue Code of 1954", which for purposes of codification was translated as "title 26" thus requiring no change in text.

Subsec. (*l*). Pub. L. 101–239, § 2101(a), added subsec. (*l*).

1987—Subsec. (c). Pub. L. 100–203, § 9342(c), designated existing provision as par. (1), redesignated as cls. (A) and (B) former cls. (1) and (2), and added par. (2).

Subsec. (i). Pub. L. 100–203, § 9344, amended second sentence generally. Prior to amendment, second sentence read as follows: "The amount of such penalty may not exceed 5 percent of the amount involved (as defined in section 4975(f)(4) of title 26); except that if the transaction is not corrected (in such manner as the Secretary shall prescribe by regulation, which regulations shall be consistent with section 4975(f)(5) of title 26) within 90 days after notice from the Secretary (or such longer period as the Secretary may permit), such penalty may be in an amount not more than 100 percent of the amount involved."

1986—Subsec. (c). Pub. L. 99–272 inserted "(1) who fails to meet the requirements of paragraph (1) or (4) of section 1166 of this title with respect to a participant or beneficiary, or (2)".

1980—Subsec. (b). Pub. L. 96–364, § 306(b)(1), redesignated existing provisions as par. (1)(A) and (B) and added par. (2).

Subsec. (g). Pub. L. 96–364, § 306(b)(2), redesignated existing provisions as par. (1), inserted exception for actions under paragraph (2), and added par. (2).

Effective Date of 2008 Amendment

Amendment by Pub. L. 110–458 effective as if included in the provisions of Pub. L. 109–280 to which the amendment relates, except as otherwise provided, see section 112 of Pub. L. 110–458, set out as a note under section 72 of Title 26, Internal Revenue Code.

Pub. L. 110–233, title I, § 101(f)(2), May 21, 2008, 122 Stat. 888, provided that: "The amendments made by this section [amending this section and sections 1182 and 1191b of this title] shall apply with respect to group health plans for plan years beginning after the date that is 1 year after the date of enactment of this Act [May 21, 2008]."

Effective and Termination Dates of 2006 Amendment

Amendment by section 103(b)(2) of Pub. L. 109–280 applicable to plan years beginning after Dec. 31, 2007, with collective bargaining exception, see section 103(c) of Pub. L. 109–280, set out as an Effective Date of 2006 Amendment note under section 1021 of this title.

Amendment by section 202(b), (c) of Pub. L. 109–280 applicable with respect to plan years beginning after 2007, with special rules for certain notices and certain restored benefits, see section 202(f) of Pub. L. 109–280, set out as a note under section 1082 of this title.

Amendment by section 202(b), (c) of Pub. L. 109–280 inapplicable to plan years beginning after Dec. 31, 2014, with exception for certain funding improvement and rehabilitation plans, see section 221(c) of Pub. L. 109–280, set out as a note under section 412 of Title 26, Internal Revenue Code.

Amendment by section 502(a)(2), (b)(2) of Pub. L. 109–280 applicable to plan years beginning after Dec. 31, 2007, see section 502(d) of Pub. L. 109–280, set out as an Effective Date of 2006 Amendment note under section 4980F of Title 26, Internal Revenue Code.

Amendment by section 507(b) of Pub. L. 109–280 applicable to plan years beginning after Dec. 31, 2006, see section 507(d)(1) of Pub. L. 109–280, set out as an Effective Date of 2006 Amendment note under section 1021 of this title.

Amendment by section 508(a)(2)(C) of Pub. L. 109–280 applicable to plan years beginning after Dec. 31, 2006, with special rule for collectively bargained agreements that were ratified on or before such date, see section 508(c) of Pub. L. 109–280, set out as an Effective Date of 2006 Amendment note under section 1025 of this title.

Amendment by section 902(f)(2) effective Aug. 17, 2006, see section 902(g) of Pub. L. 109–280, set out as an Effective Date of 2006 Amendment note under section 401 of Title 26, Internal Revenue Code.

EFFECTIVE DATE OF 2004 AMENDMENT

Amendment by section 103(b) of Pub. L. 108–218 applicable to plan years beginning after Dec. 31, 2004, see section 103(d) of Pub. L. 108–218, set out as a note under section 1021 of this title.

EFFECTIVE DATE OF 2002 AMENDMENT

Amendment by Pub. L. 107–204 effective 180 days after July 30, 2002, see section 7244(c) of Title 15, Commerce and Trade.

EFFECTIVE DATE OF 1996 AMENDMENTS

Amendment by Pub. L. 104–204 applicable with respect to group health plans for plan years beginning on or after Jan. 1, 1998, see section 603(c) of Pub. L. 104–204 set out as a note under section 1003 of this title.

Amendment by Pub. L. 104–191 applicable with respect to group health plans for plan years beginning after June 30, 1997, except as otherwise provided, see section 101(g) of Pub. L. 104–191, set out as a note under section 1181 of this title.

EFFECTIVE DATE OF 1994 AMENDMENTS

Amendment by Pub. L. 103–465 applicable to plan years beginning after Dec. 31, 1994, see section 761(b)(1) of Pub. L. 103–465, set out as a note under section 1056 of this title.

Section 5 of Pub. L. 103–401 provided that: "The amendments made by this Act [amending this section] shall apply to any legal proceeding pending, or brought, on or after May 31, 1993."

EFFECTIVE DATE OF 1990 AMENDMENT

Amendment by Pub. L. 101–508 applicable to qualified transfers under section 420 of title 26 made after Nov. 5, 1990, see section 12012(e) of Pub. L. 101–508, set out as a note under section 1021 of this title.

EFFECTIVE DATE OF 1989 AMENDMENT

Section 2101(c) of Pub. L. 101–239 provided that: "The amendments made by this section [amending this section] shall apply to any breach of fiduciary responsibility or other violation occurring on or after the date of the enactment of this Act [Dec. 19, 1989]."

Amendment by section 7881(b)(5)(B), (j)(2), (3) of Pub. L. 101–239 effective, except as otherwise provided, as if included in the provision of the Pension Protection Act, Pub. L. 100–203, §§9302–9346, to which such amendment relates, see section 7882 of Pub. L. 101–239, set out as a note under section 401 of Title 26, Internal Revenue Code.

Amendment by section 7891(a)(1) of Pub. L. 101–239 effective, except as otherwise provided, as if included in the provision of the Tax Reform Act of 1986, Pub. L. 99–514, to which such amendment relates, see section 7891(f) of Pub. L. 101–239, set out as a note under section 1002 of this title.

Amendment by section 7894(f)(1) of Pub. L. 101–239 effective, except as otherwise provided, as if originally included in the provision of the Employee Retirement Income Security Act of 1974, Pub. L. 93–406, to which such amendment relates, see section 7894(i) of Pub. L. 101–239, set out as a note under section 1002 of this title.

EFFECTIVE DATE OF 1987 AMENDMENT

Section 9342(d) of Pub. L. 100–203 provided that:

"(1) IN GENERAL.—The amendments made by this section [amending this section and sections 1023, 1024, and 1113 of this title] shall apply with respect to reports required to be filed after December 31, 1987.

"(2) REGULATIONS.—The Secretary of Labor shall issue the regulations required to carry out the amendments made by subsection (c) [amending this section] not later than January 1, 1989."

EFFECTIVE DATE OF 1986 AMENDMENT

Amendment by Pub. L. 99–272 applicable to plan years beginning on or after July 1, 1986, with special rule for collective bargaining agreements, see section 10002(d) of Pub. L. 99–272, set out as an Effective Date note under section 1161 of this title.

EFFECTIVE DATE OF 1980 AMENDMENT

Amendment by Pub. L. 96–364 effective Sept. 26, 1980, except as specifically provided, see section 1461(e) of this title.

REGULATIONS

Pub. L. 110–233, title I, §101(f)(1), May 21, 2008, 122 Stat. 888, provided that: "The Secretary of Labor shall issue final regulations not later than 12 months after the date of enactment of this Act [May 21, 2008] to carry out the amendments made by this section [amending this section and sections 1182 and 1191b of this title]."

Secretary authorized, effective Sept. 2, 1974, to promulgate regulations wherever provisions of this subchapter call for the promulgation of regulations, see section 1031 of this title.

APPLICABILITY OF AMENDMENTS BY SUBTITLES A AND B OF TITLE I OF PUB. L. 109–280

For special rules on applicability of amendments by subtitles A (§§101–107) and B (§§111–116) of title I of Pub. L. 109–280 to certain eligible cooperative plans, PBGC settlement plans, and eligible government contractor plans, see sections 104, 105, and 106 of Pub. L. 109–280, set out as notes under section 401 of Title 26, Internal Revenue Code.

SPECIAL RULE FOR CERTAIN BENEFITS FUNDED UNDER AN AGREEMENT APPROVED BY THE PENSION BENEFIT GUARANTY CORPORATION

For applicability of amendment by section 202(b), (c) of Pub. L. 109–280 to a multiemployer plan that is a party to an agreement that was approved by the Pension Benefit Guaranty Corporation prior to June 30, 2005, and that increases benefits and provides for certain withdrawal liability rules, see section 206 of Pub. L. 109–280, set out as a note under section 412 of Title 26, Internal Revenue Code.

EFFECT OF PUB. L. 103–401 ON OTHER PROVISIONS

Section 4 of Pub. L. 103–401 provided that: "Nothing in this Act [amending this section and enacting provisions set out as notes under this section and section 1001 of this title] shall be construed to limit the legal standing of individuals to bring a civil action as participants or beneficiaries under section 502(a) of the Employee Retirement Income Security Act of 1974 (29 U.S.C. 1132(a)), and nothing in this Act shall affect the responsibilities, obligations, or duties imposed upon fiduciaries by title I of the Employee Retirement Income Security Act of 1974 [this subchapter]."

PLAN AMENDMENTS NOT REQUIRED UNTIL JULY 30, 2002

For provisions directing that if any amendment made by section 306(b) of Pub. L. 107–204 requires an amendment to any plan, such plan amendment shall not be required to be made before the first plan year beginning on or after July 30, 2002, see section 7244(b)(3) of Title 15, Commerce and Trade.

PLAN AMENDMENTS NOT REQUIRED UNTIL JANUARY 1, 1994

For provisions setting forth circumstances under which any amendment to a plan required to be made by an amendment made by section 4301 of Pub. L. 103–66 shall not be required to be made before the first plan year beginning on or after Jan. 1, 1994, see section 4301(d) of Pub. L. 103–66, set out as an Effective Date of 1993 Amendment note under section 1021 of this title.

§1133. Claims procedure

In accordance with regulations of the Secretary, every employee benefit plan shall—

(1) provide adequate notice in writing to any participant or beneficiary whose claim for benefits under the plan has been denied, setting forth the specific reasons for such denial, written in a manner calculated to be understood by the participant, and

(2) afford a reasonable opportunity to any participant whose claim for benefits has been denied for a full and fair review by the appropriate named fiduciary of the decision denying the claim.

(Pub. L. 93–406, title I, §503, Sept. 2, 1974, 88 Stat. 893.)

REGULATIONS

Secretary authorized, effective Sept. 2, 1974, to promulgate regulations wherever provisions of this subchapter call for the promulgation of regulations, see section 1031 of this title.

§1134. Investigative authority

(a) Investigation and submission of reports, books, etc.

The Secretary shall have the power, in order to determine whether any person has violated or is about to violate any provision of this subchapter or any regulation or order thereunder—

(1) to make an investigation, and in connection therewith to require the submission of reports, books, and records, and the filing of data in support of any information required to be filed with the Secretary under this subchapter, and

(2) to enter such places, inspect such books and records and question such persons as he may deem necessary to enable him to determine the facts relative to such investigation, if he has reasonable cause to believe there may exist a violation of this subchapter or any rule or regulation issued thereunder or if the entry is pursuant to an agreement with the plan.

The Secretary may make available to any person actually affected by any matter which is the subject of an investigation under this section, and to any department or agency of the United States, information concerning any matter which may be the subject of such investigation; except that any information obtained by the Secretary pursuant to section 6103(g) of title 26 shall be made available only in accordance with regulations prescribed by the Secretary of the Treasury.

(b) Frequency of submission of books and records

The Secretary may not under the authority of this section require any plan to submit to the Secretary any books or records of the plan more than once in any 12 month period, unless the Secretary has reasonable cause to believe there may exist a violation of this subchapter or any regulation or order thereunder.

(c) Other provisions applicable relating to attendance of witnesses and production of books, records, etc.

For the purposes of any investigation provided for in this subchapter, the provisions of sections 49 and 50 of title 15 (relating to the attendance of witnesses and the production of books, records, and documents) are hereby made applicable (without regard to any limitation in such sections respecting persons, partnerships, banks, or common carriers) to the jurisdiction, powers, and duties of the Secretary or any officers designated by him. To the extent he considers appropriate, the Secretary may delegate his investigative functions under this section with respect to insured banks acting as fiduciaries of employee benefit plans to the appropriate Federal banking agency (as defined in section 1813(q) of title 12).

(Pub. L. 93–406, title I, §504, Sept. 2, 1974, 88 Stat. 893; Pub. L. 101–239, title VII, §7891(a)(1), Dec. 19, 1989, 103 Stat. 2445.)

AMENDMENTS

1989—Subsec. (a). Pub. L. 101–239 substituted "Internal Revenue Code of 1986" for "Internal Revenue Code of 1954", which for purposes of codification was translated as "title 26" thus requiring no change in text.

EFFECTIVE DATE OF 1989 AMENDMENT

Amendment by Pub. L. 101–239 effective, except as otherwise provided, as if included in the provision of the Tax Reform Act of 1986, Pub. L. 99–514, to which such amendment relates, see section 7891(f) of Pub. L. 101–239, set out as a note under section 1002 of this title.

REGULATIONS

Secretary authorized, effective Sept. 2, 1974, to promulgate regulations wherever provisions of this subchapter call for the promulgation of regulations, see section 1031 of this title.

§1135. Regulations

Subject to subchapter II of this chapter and section 1029 of this title, the Secretary may prescribe such regulations as he finds necessary or appropriate to carry out the provisions of this subchapter. Among other things, such regulations may define accounting, technical and trade terms used in such provisions; may prescribe forms; and may provide for the keeping of books and records, and for the inspection of such books and records (subject to section 1134(a) and (b) of this title).

(Pub. L. 93–406, title I, §505, Sept. 2, 1974, 88 Stat. 894.)

REGULATIONS

Pub. L. 99–272, title XI, §11018, Apr. 7, 1986, 100 Stat. 277, provided that:

"(a) REGULATORY TREATMENT OF ASSETS OF REAL ESTATE ENTITIES.—

"(1) IN GENERAL.—Except as a defense, no rule or regulation adopted pursuant to the Secretary's proposed regulation defining 'plan assets' for purposes of the Employee Retirement Income Security Act of 1974 [29 U.S.C. 1001 et seq.] (50 Fed. Reg. 961, January 8, 1985, as modified by 50 Fed. Reg. 6361, February 15, 1985), or any reproposal thereof prior to the adoption of the regulations required to be issued in accordance with subsection (d), shall apply to any asset of a real estate entity in which a plan, account, or arrangement subject to such Act invests if—

"(A) any interest in the entity is first offered to a plan, account, or arrangement subject to such Act investing in the entity (hereinafter in this section referred to as a 'plan investor') on or before the date which is 120 days after the date of publication of such rule or regulation as a final rule or regulation;

"(B) no plan investor acquires an interest in the entity from an issuer or underwriter at any time on or after the date which is 270 days after the date of publication of such rule or regulation as a final rule or regulation (except pursuant to a contract or subscription binding on the plan investor and entered into, or tendered, before the expiration of such 270-day period, or pursuant to the exercise, on or before December 31, 1990, of a warrant which was the subject of an effective registration under the Securities Act of 1933 (15 U.S.C. 77q et seq.) [15 U.S.C. 77a et seq.] prior to the date of the enactment of this section [Apr. 7, 1986]); and

"(C) every interest in the entity acquired by a plan investor (or contracted for or subscribed to by a plan investor) before the expiration of such 270-day period is a security—

"(i) which is part of an issue or class of securities which upon such acquisition or at any time during the offering period is held by 100 or more persons;

"(ii) the economic rights of ownership in respect of which are freely transferable;

"(iii) which is registered under the Securities Act of 1933; and

"(iv) which is part of an issue or class of securities which is registered under the Securities Exchange Act of 1934 (15 U.S.C. 78a et seq.) (or is so registered within three years of the effective date of the registration statement of such securities for purposes of the Securities Act of 1933: *Provided*, That the issuer provides plan investors with such reports with respect to the offering period as are required with respect to such period by the Securities and Exchange Commission under such Acts and the rules and regulations promulgated thereunder).

In the case of partnerships organized prior to enactment of this section, the requirements of subparagraphs (iii) and (iv) shall not apply to initial limited partnership interests in an entity otherwise described above: *Provided*, That such entity was the subject of an effective registration under the Securities Act of 1933 prior to the date of the enactment of this section, such interests were issued solely for partnership organizational purposes in compliance with State limited partnership laws, and such interest has a value as of the date of issue of less than $20,000 and represents less than one percent of the total interests outstanding as of the completion of the offering period.

"(2) MAINTENANCE OF CURRENT REGULATORY TREATMENT.—No asset of any real estate entity described in paragraph (1) shall be treated as an asset of any plan investor for any purpose of the Employee Retirement Income Security Act of 1974 [29 U.S.C. 1001 et seq.] if the assets of such entity would not have been assets of such plan investor under the provisions of—

"(A) Interpretive Bulletin 75–2 (29 CFR 2509.750–2); or

"(B) the regulations proposed by the Secretary of Labor and published—

"(i) on August 28, 1979, at 44 Fed. Reg. 50363;

"(ii) on June 6, 1980, at 45 Fed. Reg. 38084;

"(iii) on January 8, 1985, at 50 Fed. Reg. 961; or

"(iv) on February 15, 1985, at 50 Fed. Reg. 6361,

without regard to any limitation of any effective date proposed therein.

"(b) DEFINITIONS AND SPECIAL RULES.—For purposes of this section—

"(1) The term 'real estate entity' means an entity which, at any time within two years after the closing of its offering period has invested or has contracted to invest at least 75 percent of the value of its net assets available for investment in direct or indirect ownership of 'real estate assets' or 'interests in real property'.

"(2) The term 'real estate asset' means real property (including an interest in real property) and any share of stock or beneficial interest, partnership interest, depository receipt, or any other interest in any other real estate entity.

"(3) The term 'interest in real property' includes, directly or indirectly, the following:

"(A) the ownership or co-ownership of land or improvements thereon;

"(B) any mortgage (including an interest in or co-ownership of any mortgage, leasehold mortgage, pool of mortgages, deed of trust, or similar instrument) on land or improvements thereon,

"(C) any leasehold of land or improvements thereon; and

"(D) any option to acquire any of the foregoing, but does not include any mineral, oil, or gas royalty interest.

"(4) Whether the economic rights of ownership with respect to a security are 'freely transferable' shall be determined based upon all the facts and circumstances, but ordinarily none of the following, alone or in any combination, shall cause the economic rights of ownership to be considered not freely transferable—

"(A) any requirement that not less than a minimum number of shares or units of such security be transferred or assigned by any investor: *Provided*, That such requirement does not prevent transfer of all of the then remaining shares or units held by an investor;

"(B) any prohibition against transfer or assignment of such security or rights in respect thereof to an ineligible or unsuitable investor;

"(C) any restriction on or prohibition against any transfer or assignment which would either result in a termination or reclassification of the entity for Federal or State tax purposes or which would violate any State or Federal statute, regulation, court order, judicial decree, or rule of law;

"(D) any requirement that reasonable transfer or administrative fees be paid in connection with a transfer or assignment;

"(E) any requirement that advance notice of a transfer or assignment be given to the entity and any requirement regarding execution of documentation evidencing such transfer or assignment (including documentation setting forth representations from either or both of the transferor or transferee as to compliance with any restriction or requirement described in this section or requiring compliance with the entity's governing instruments);

"(F) any restriction on substitution of an assignee as a limited partner of a partnership, including a general partner consent requirement: *Provided*, That the economic benefits of ownership of the assignor may be transferred or assigned without regard to such restriction or consent (other than compliance with any other restriction described in this section);

"(G) any administrative procedure which establishes an effective date, or an event such as the completion of the offering, prior to which a transfer or assignment will not be effective; and

"(H) any limitation or restriction on transfer or assignment which is not created or imposed by the issuer or any person acting for or on behalf of such issuer.

"(c) NO EFFECT ON SECRETARY'S AUTHORITY OTHER THAN AS PROVIDED.—Except as provided in subsection (a), nothing in this section shall limit the authority of the Secretary of Labor to issue regulations or otherwise interpret section 3(21) of the Employee Retirement Income Security Act of 1974 [29 U.S.C. 1002(21)].

"(d) TIME LIMIT FOR FINAL REGULATIONS.—The Secretary of Labor shall adopt final regulations defining 'plan assets' by December 31, 1986.

"(e) EFFECTIVE DATE.—The preceding provisions of this section shall take effect on the date of the enactment of this Act [Apr. 7, 1986]."

Secretary authorized, effective Sept. 2, 1974, to promulgate regulations wherever provisions of this subchapter call for the promulgation of regulations, see section 1031 of this title.

§1136. Coordination and responsibility of agencies enforcing this subchapter and related Federal laws

(a) Coordination with other agencies and departments

In order to avoid unnecessary expense and duplication of functions among Government agencies, the Secretary may make such arrangements or agreements for cooperation or mutual assistance in the performance of his functions under this subchapter and the functions of any such agency as he may find to be practicable and consistent with law. The Secretary may utilize, on a reimbursable or other basis, the facilities or services of any department, agency, or establishment of the United States or of any State or political subdivision of a State, including the services of any of its employees, with the lawful consent of such department, agency, or establishment; and each department, agency, or establishment of the United States is authorized and directed to cooperate with the Secretary and, to the extent permitted by law, to provide such information and facilities as he may request for his assistance in the performance of his functions under this subchapter. The Attorney General or his representative shall receive from the Secretary for appropriate action such evidence developed in the performance of his functions under this subchapter as may be found to warrant consideration for criminal prosecution under the provisions of this subchapter or other Federal law.

(b) Responsibility for detecting and investigating civil and criminal violations of this subchapter and related Federal laws

The Secretary shall have the responsibility and authority to detect and investigate and refer, where appropriate, civil and criminal violations related to the provisions of this subchapter and other related Federal laws, including the detection, investigation, and appropriate referrals of related violations of title 18. Nothing in this subsection shall be construed to preclude other appropriate Federal agencies from detecting and investigating civil and criminal violations of this subchapter and other related Federal laws.

(c) Coordination of enforcement with States with respect to certain arrangements

A State may enter into an agreement with the Secretary for delegation to the State of some or all of the Secretary's authority under sections 1132 and 1134 of this title to enforce the requirements under part 7 in connection with multiple employer welfare arrangements, providing medical care (within the meaning of section 1191b(a)(2) of this title), which are not group health plans.

(Pub. L. 93–406, title I, §506, Sept. 2, 1974, 88 Stat. 894; Pub. L. 98–473, title II, §805, Oct. 12, 1984, 98 Stat. 2134; Pub. L. 104–191, title I, §101(e)(3), Aug. 21, 1996, 110 Stat. 1953; Pub. L. 104–204, title VI, §603(b)(3)(F), Sept. 26, 1996, 110 Stat. 2938.)

AMENDMENTS

1996—Subsec. (c). Pub. L. 104–204 made technical amendment to reference in original act which appears in text as reference to section 1191b of this title.

Pub. L. 104–191 added subsec. (c).

1984—Pub. L. 98–473 designated existing provisions as subsec. (a), added subsec. (b), and amended section catchline.

EFFECTIVE DATE OF 1996 AMENDMENTS

Amendment by Pub. L. 104–204 applicable with respect to group health plans for plan years beginning on or after Jan. 1, 1998, see section 603(c) of Pub. L. 104–204 set out as a note under section 1003 of this title.

Amendment by Pub. L. 104–191 applicable with respect to group health plans for plan years beginning after June 30, 1997, except as otherwise provided, see section 101(g) of Pub. L. 104–191, set out as a note under section 1181 of this title.

REGULATIONS

Secretary authorized, effective Sept. 2, 1974, to promulgate regulations wherever provisions of this subchapter call for the promulgation of regulations, see section 1031 of this title.

RELATION OF SUBTITLE E OF TITLE II OF PUB. L. 104–191 TO ERISA AUTHORITY

Section 250 of title II of Pub. L. 104–191 provided that: "Nothing in this subtitle [subtitle E (§§241–250) of title II of Pub. L. 104–191, enacting sections 24, 669, 1035, 1347, 1518, and 3486 of Title 18, Crimes and Criminal Procedure, amending sections 982, 1345, 1510, and 1956 of Title 18, and enacting provisions set out as notes under section 1395i of Title 42, The Public Health and Welfare] shall be construed as affecting the authority of the Secretary of Labor under section 506(b) of the Employee Retirement Income Security Act of 1974 [29 U.S.C. 1136(b)], including the Secretary's authority with respect to violations of title 18, United States Code (as amended by this subtitle)."

§1137. Administration

(a) Subchapter II of chapter 5, and chapter 7, of title 5 (relating to administrative procedure), shall be applicable to this subchapter.

(b) Omitted.

(c) No employee of the Department of Labor or the Department of the Treasury shall administer or enforce this subchapter or title 26 with respect to any employee benefit plan under which he is a participant or beneficiary, any employee organization of which he is a member, or any employer organization in which he has an interest. This subsection does not apply to an employee benefit plan which covers only employees of the United States.

(Pub. L. 93–406, title I, §507, Sept. 2, 1974, 88 Stat. 894; Pub. L. 101–239, title VII, §7891(a), Dec. 19, 1989, 103 Stat. 2445.)

CODIFICATION

Subsec. (b) of this section amended section 5108 of Title 5, Government Organization and Employees.

AMENDMENTS

1989—Subsec. (c). Pub. L. 101–239 substituted "Internal Revenue Code of 1986" for "Internal Revenue Code of 1954", which for purposes of codification was translated as "title 26" thus requiring no change in text.

EFFECTIVE DATE OF 1989 AMENDMENT

Amendment by Pub. L. 101–239 effective, except as otherwise provided, as if included in the provision of the Tax Reform Act of 1986, Pub. L. 99–514, to which such amendment relates, see section 7891(f) of Pub. L. 101–239, set out as a note under section 1002 of this title.

REGULATIONS

Secretary authorized, effective Sept. 2, 1974, to promulgate regulations wherever provisions of this subchapter call for the promulgation of regulations, see section 1031 of this title.

§1138. Appropriations

There are hereby authorized to be appropriated such sums as may be necessary to enable the Secretary to carry out his functions and duties under this chapter.

(Pub. L. 93–406, title I, §508, Sept. 2, 1974, 88 Stat. 895.)

REFERENCES IN TEXT

This chapter, referred to in text, was in the original "this Act", meaning Pub. L. 93–406, known as the Employee Retirement Income Security Act of 1974. Titles I, III, and IV of such Act are classified principally to this chapter. For complete classification of this Act to the Code, see Short Title note set out under section 1001 of this title and Tables.

REGULATIONS

Secretary authorized, effective Sept. 2, 1974, to promulgate regulations wherever provisions of this subchapter call for the promulgation of regulations, see section 1031 of this title.

§1139. Separability

If any provision of this chapter, or the application of such provision to any person or circumstances, shall be held invalid, the remainder of this chapter, or the application of such provision to persons or circumstances other than those as to which it is held invalid, shall not be affected thereby.

(Pub. L. 93–406, title I, §509, Sept. 2, 1974, 88 Stat. 895.)

REFERENCES IN TEXT

This chapter, referred to in text, was in the original "this Act", meaning Pub. L. 93–406, known as the Employee Retirement Income Security Act of 1974. Titles I, III, and IV of such Act are classified principally to this chapter. For complete classification of this Act to the Code, see Short Title note set out under section 1001 of this title and Tables.

REGULATIONS

Secretary authorized, effective Sept. 2, 1974, to promulgate regulations wherever provisions of this subchapter call for the promulgation of regulations, see section 1031 of this title.

§1140. Interference with protected rights

It shall be unlawful for any person to discharge, fine, suspend, expel, discipline, or discriminate against a participant or beneficiary for exercising any right to which he is entitled under the provisions of an employee benefit plan, this subchapter, section 1201 of this title, or the Welfare and Pension Plans Disclosure Act [29 U.S.C. 301 et seq.], or for the purpose of interfering with the attainment of any right to which such participant may become entitled under the plan, this subchapter, or the Welfare and Pension Plans Disclosure Act. It shall be unlawful for any person to discharge, fine, suspend, expel, or discriminate against any person because he has given information or has testified or is about to testify in any inquiry or proceeding relating to this chapter or the Welfare and Pension Plans Disclosure Act. In the case of a multiemployer plan, it shall be unlawful for the plan sponsor or any other person to discriminate against any contributing employer for exercising rights under this chapter or for giving information or testifying in any inquiry or proceeding relating to this chapter before Congress. The provisions of section 1132 of this title shall be applicable in the enforcement of this section.

(Pub. L. 93–406, title I, §510, Sept. 2, 1974, 88 Stat. 895; Pub. L. 109–280, title II, §205, Aug. 17, 2006, 120 Stat. 889.)

REFERENCES IN TEXT

The Welfare and Pension Plans Disclosure Act, referred to in text, is Pub. L. 85–836, Aug. 28, 1958, 72 Stat. 997, as amended, which was classified generally to chapter 10 (§301 et seq.) of this title, and was repealed by Pub. L. 93–406, title I, §111(a)(1), Sept. 2, 1974, 88 Stat. 851 (Employee Retirement Income Security Act of 1974), effective Jan. 1, 1975. Such section 111(a)(1) also provided that the Welfare and Pension Plans Disclosure Act should continue to apply to any conduct and events which occurred before Jan. 1, 1975 (see section 1031 of this title). For complete classification of the Welfare and Pension Plans Disclosure Act to the Code prior to such repeal, see Tables.

This chapter, referred to in text, was in the original "this Act", meaning Pub. L. 93–406, known as the Employee Retirement Income Security Act of 1974. Titles I, III, and IV of such Act are classified principally to this chapter. For complete classification of this Act to the Code, see Short Title note set out under section 1001 of this title and Tables.

AMENDMENTS

2006—Pub. L. 109–280 inserted before last sentence "In the case of a multiemployer plan, it shall be unlawful for the plan sponsor or any other person to discriminate against any contributing employer for exercising rights under this chapter or for giving information or testifying in any inquiry or proceeding relating to this chapter before Congress."

REGULATIONS

Secretary authorized, effective Sept. 2, 1974, to promulgate regulations wherever provisions of this subchapter call for the promulgation of regulations, see section 1031 of this title.

§1141. Coercive interference

It shall be unlawful for any person through the use of fraud, force, violence, or threat of the use of force or violence, to restrain, coerce, intimidate, or attempt to restrain, coerce, or intimidate any participant or beneficiary for the purpose of interfering with or preventing the exercise of any right to which he is or may become entitled under the plan, this subchapter, section 1201 of this title, or the Welfare and Pension Plans Disclosure Act [29 U.S.C. 301 et seq.]. Any person who willfully violates this section shall be fined $100,000 or imprisoned for not more than 10 years, or both.

(Pub. L. 93–406, title I, §511, Sept. 2, 1974, 88 Stat. 895; Pub. L. 109–280, title VI, §623(a), Aug. 17, 2006, 120 Stat. 979.)

REFERENCES IN TEXT

The Welfare and Pension Plans Disclosure Act, referred to in text, is Pub. L. 85–836, Aug. 28, 1958, 72 Stat. 997, as amended, which was classified generally to chapter 10 (§301 et seq.) of this title, and was repealed by Pub. L. 93–406, title I, §111(a)(1), Sept. 2, 1974, 88 Stat. 851 (Employee Retirement Income Security Act of 1974), effective Jan. 1, 1975. Such section 111(a)(1) also provided that the Welfare and Pension Plans Disclosure Act should continue to apply to any conduct and events which occurred before Jan. 1, 1975 (see section 1031 of this title). For complete classification of the Welfare and Pension Plans Disclosure Act to the Code prior to such repeal, see Tables.

AMENDMENTS

2006—Pub. L. 109–280 substituted "$100,000" for "$10,000" and "10 years" for "one year".

EFFECTIVE DATE OF 2006 AMENDMENT

Pub. L. 109–280, title VI, §623(b), Aug. 17, 2006, 120 Stat. 979, provided that: "The amendments made by this section [amending this section] shall apply to violations occurring on and after the date of the enactment of this Act [Aug. 17, 2006]."

REGULATIONS

Secretary authorized, effective Sept. 2, 1974, to promulgate regulations wherever provisions of this subchapter call for the promulgation of regulations, see section 1031 of this title.

§1142. Advisory Council on Employee Welfare and Pension Benefit Plans

(a) Establishment; membership; terms; appointment and reappointment; vacancies; quorum

(1) There is hereby established an Advisory Council on Employee Welfare and Pension Benefit Plans (hereinafter in this section referred to as the "Council") consisting of fifteen members appointed by the Secretary. Not more than eight members of the Council shall be members of the same political party.

(2) Members shall be persons qualified to appraise the programs instituted under this chapter.

(3) Of the members appointed, three shall be representatives of employee organizations (at least one of whom shall be representative of any organization members of which are participants in a multiemployer plan); three shall be representatives of employers (at least one of whom shall be representative of employers maintaining or contributing to multi-employer plans); three representatives shall be appointed from the general public, one of whom shall be a person representing those receiving benefits from a pension plan; and there shall be one representative each from the fields of insurance, corporate trust, actuarial counseling, investment counseling, investment management, and the accounting field.

(4) Members shall serve for terms of three years except that of those first appointed, five shall be appointed for terms of one year, five shall be appointed for terms of two years, and five shall be appointed for terms of three years. A member may be reappointed. A member appointed to fill a vacancy shall be appointed only for the remainder of such term. A majority of members shall constitute a quorum and action shall be taken only by a majority vote of those present and voting.

(b) Duties and functions

It shall be the duty of the Council to advise the Secretary with respect to the carrying out of his functions under this chapter and to submit to the Secretary recommendations with respect thereto. The Council shall meet at least four times each year and at such other times as the Secretary requests. In his annual report submitted pursuant to section 1143(b)[1] of this title, the Secretary shall include each recommendation which he has received from the Council during the preceding calendar year.

(c) Executive secretary; secretarial and clerical services

The Secretary shall furnish to the Council an executive secretary and such secretarial, clerical, and other services as are deemed necessary to conduct its business. The Secretary may call upon other agencies of the Government for statistical data, reports, and other information which will assist the Council in the performance of its duties.

(d) Compensation

(1) Members of the Council shall each be entitled to receive the daily equivalent of the annual rate of basic pay in effect for grade GS–18 of the General Schedule for each day (including travel time) during which they are engaged in the actual performance of duties vested in the Council.

(2) While away from their homes or regular places of business in the performance of services for Council, members of the Council shall be allowed travel expenses, including per diem in lieu of subsistence, in the same manner as persons employed intermittently in the Government service are allowed expenses under section 5703(b) of title 5.[1]

(e) Termination

Section 14(a) of the Federal Advisory Committee Act (relating to termination) shall not apply to the Council.

(Pub. L. 93–406, title I, §512, Sept. 2, 1974, 88 Stat. 895.)

REFERENCES IN TEXT

This chapter, referred to in subsecs. (a)(2), (b), was in the original "this Act", meaning Pub. L. 93–406, known as the Employee Retirement Income Security Act of 1974. Titles I, III, and IV of such Act are classified principally to this chapter. For complete classification of this Act to the Code, see Short Title note set out under section 1001 of this title and Tables.

Section 1143(b) of this title, referred to in subsec. (b), was omitted from the Code.

Section 5703 of title 5, referred to in subsec. (d)(2), was amended generally by Pub. L. 94–22, §4, May 19, 1975, 89 Stat. 85, and, as so amended, does not contain a subsec. (b).

Section 14(a) of the Federal Advisory Committee Act, referred to in subsec. (e), is section 14(a) of Pub. L. 92–463, which is set out in the Appendix to Title 5, Government Organization and Employees.

[1] See References in Text note below.

REGULATIONS

Secretary authorized, effective Sept. 2, 1974, to promulgate regulations wherever provisions of this subchapter call for the promulgation of regulations, see section 1031 of this title.

REFERENCES IN OTHER LAWS TO GS-16, 17, OR 18 PAY RATES

References in laws to the rates of pay for GS-16, 17, or 18, or to maximum rates of pay under the General Schedule, to be considered references to rates payable under specified sections of Title 5, Government Organization and Employees, see section 529 [title I, § 101(c)(1)] of Pub. L. 101–509, set out in a note under section 5376 of Title 5.

§ 1143. Research, studies, and reports

(a) Authorization to undertake research and surveys

(1) The Secretary is authorized to undertake research and surveys and in connection therewith to collect, compile, analyze and publish data, information, and statistics relating to employee benefit plans, including retirement, deferred compensation, and welfare plans, and types of plans not subject to this chapter.

(2) The Secretary is authorized and directed to undertake research studies relating to pension plans, including but not limited to (A) the effects of this subchapter upon the provisions and costs of pension plans, (B) the role of private pensions in meeting the economic security needs of the Nation, and (C) the operation of private pension plans including types and levels of benefits, degree of reciprocity or portability, and financial and actuarial characteristics and practices, and methods of encouraging the growth of the private pension system.

(3) The Secretary may, as he deems appropriate or necessary, undertake other studies relating to employee benefit plans, the matters regulated by this subchapter, and the enforcement procedures provided for under this subchapter.

(4) The research, surveys, studies, and publications referred to in this subsection may be conducted directly, or indirectly through grant or contract arrangements.

(b) Omitted

(c) Cooperation with Congress

The Secretary is authorized and directed to cooperate with the Congress and its appropriate committees, subcommittees, and staff in supplying data and any other information, and personnel and services, required by the Congress in any study, examination, or report by the Congress relating to pension benefit plans established or maintained by States or their political subdivisions.

(Pub. L. 93–406, title I, § 513, Sept. 2, 1974, 88 Stat. 896.)

REFERENCES IN TEXT

This chapter, referred to in subsec. (a)(1), was in the original "this Act", meaning Pub. L. 93–406, known as the Employee Retirement Income Security Act of 1974. Titles I, III, and IV of such Act are classified principally to this chapter. For complete classification of this Act to the Code, see Short Title note set out under section 1001 of this title and Tables.

CODIFICATION

Subsec. (b) of this section, which required the Secretary to submit annually a report to Congress on the administration of this subchapter, terminated, effective May 15, 2000, pursuant to section 3003 of Pub. L. 104–66, as amended, set out as a note under section 1113 of Title 31, Money and Finance. See, also, page 123 of House Document No. 103–7.

REGULATIONS

Secretary authorized, effective Sept. 2, 1974, to promulgate regulations wherever provisions of this subchapter call for the promulgation of regulations, see section 1031 of this title.

§ 1143a. Studies by Comptroller General

(1) In general

The Comptroller General of the United States may, pursuant to the request of any Member of Congress, study employee benefit plans, including the effects of such plans on employees, participants, and their beneficiaries.

(2) Access to books, documents, etc.

For the purpose of conducting studies under this section, the Comptroller General, or any of his duly authorized representatives, shall have access to and the right to examine and copy any books, documents, papers, records, or other recorded information—

(A) within the possession or control of the administrator, sponsor, or employer of and persons providing services to any employee benefit plan, and

(B) which the Comptroller General or his representative finds, in his own judgment, pertinent to such study.

The Comptroller General shall not disclose the identity of any individual or employer in making any information obtained under this section available to the public.

(3) Definitions

For purposes of this section, the terms "employee benefit plan", "participant", "administrator", "beneficiary", "plan sponsor", "employee", and "employer" are defined in section 1002 of this title.

(4) Effective date

The preceding provisions of this section shall be effective on April 7, 1986.

(Pub. L. 99–272, title XI, § 11016(d), Apr. 7, 1986, 100 Stat. 275.)

CODIFICATION

Section was enacted as part of the Single-Employer Pension Plan Amendments Act of 1986, and also as part of the Consolidated Omnibus Budget Reconciliation Act of 1985, and not as part of the Employee Retirement Income Security Act of 1974 which comprises this chapter.

§ 1144. Other laws

(a) Supersedure; effective date

Except as provided in subsection (b) of this section, the provisions of this subchapter and subchapter III of this chapter shall supersede any and all State laws insofar as they may now or hereafter relate to any employee benefit plan described in section 1003(a) of this title and not exempt under section 1003(b) of this title. This section shall take effect on January 1, 1975.

(b) Construction and application

(1) This section shall not apply with respect to any cause of action which arose, or any act or omission which occurred, before January 1, 1975.

(2)(A) Except as provided in subparagraph (B), nothing in this subchapter shall be construed to exempt or relieve any person from any law of any State which regulates insurance, banking, or securities.

(B) Neither an employee benefit plan described in section 1003(a) of this title, which is not exempt under section 1003(b) of this title (other than a plan established primarily for the purpose of providing death benefits), nor any trust established under such a plan, shall be deemed to be an insurance company or other insurer, bank, trust company, or investment company or to be engaged in the business of insurance or banking for purposes of any law of any State purporting to regulate insurance companies, insurance contracts, banks, trust companies, or investment companies.

(3) Nothing in this section shall be construed to prohibit use by the Secretary of services or facilities of a State agency as permitted under section 1136 of this title.

(4) Subsection (a) of this section shall not apply to any generally applicable criminal law of a State.

(5)(A) Except as provided in subparagraph (B), subsection (a) of this section shall not apply to the Hawaii Prepaid Health Care Act (Haw. Rev. Stat. §§393–1 through 393–51).

(B) Nothing in subparagraph (A) shall be construed to exempt from subsection (a) of this section—

(i) any State tax law relating to employee benefit plans, or

(ii) any amendment of the Hawaii Prepaid Health Care Act enacted after September 2, 1974, to the extent it provides for more than the effective administration of such Act as in effect on such date.

(C) Notwithstanding subparagraph (A), parts 1 and 4 of this subtitle, and the preceding sections of this part to the extent they govern matters which are governed by the provisions of such parts 1 and 4, shall supersede the Hawaii Prepaid Health Care Act (as in effect on or after January 14, 1983), but the Secretary may enter into cooperative arrangements under this paragraph and section 1136 of this title with officials of the State of Hawaii to assist them in effectuating the policies of provisions of such Act which are superseded by such parts 1 and 4 and the preceding sections of this part.

(6)(A) Notwithstanding any other provision of this section—

(i) in the case of an employee welfare benefit plan which is a multiple employer welfare arrangement and is fully insured (or which is a multiple employer welfare arrangement subject to an exemption under subparagraph (B)), any law of any State which regulates insurance may apply to such arrangement to the extent that such law provides—

(I) standards, requiring the maintenance of specified levels of reserves and specified levels of contributions, which any such plan, or any trust established under such a plan, must meet in order to be considered under such law able to pay benefits in full when due, and

(II) provisions to enforce such standards, and

(ii) in the case of any other employee welfare benefit plan which is a multiple employer welfare arrangement, in addition to this subchapter, any law of any State which regulates insurance may apply to the extent not inconsistent with the preceding sections of this subchapter.

(B) The Secretary may, under regulations which may be prescribed by the Secretary, exempt from subparagraph (A)(ii), individually or by class, multiple employer welfare arrangements which are not fully insured. Any such exemption may be granted with respect to any arrangement or class of arrangements only if such arrangement or each arrangement which is a member of such class meets the requirements of section 1002(1) and section 1003 of this title necessary to be considered an employee welfare benefit plan to which this subchapter applies.

(C) Nothing in subparagraph (A) shall affect the manner or extent to which the provisions of this subchapter apply to an employee welfare benefit plan which is not a multiple employer welfare arrangement and which is a plan, fund, or program participating in, subscribing to, or otherwise using a multiple employer welfare arrangement to fund or administer benefits to such plan's participants and beneficiaries.

(D) For purposes of this paragraph, a multiple employer welfare arrangement shall be considered fully insured only if the terms of the arrangement provide for benefits the amount of all of which the Secretary determines are guaranteed under a contract, or policy of insurance, issued by an insurance company, insurance service, or insurance organization, qualified to conduct business in a State.

(7) Subsection (a) of this section shall not apply to qualified domestic relations orders (within the meaning of section 1056(d)(3)(B)(i) of this title), qualified medical child support orders (within the meaning of section 1169(a)(2)(A) of this title), and the provisions of law referred to in section 1169(a)(2)(B)(ii) of this title to the extent they apply to qualified medical child support orders.

(8) Subsection (a) of this section shall not be construed to preclude any State cause of action—

(A) with respect to which the State exercises its acquired rights under section 1169(b)(3) of this title with respect to a group health plan (as defined in section 1167(1) of this title), or

(B) for recoupment of payment with respect to items or services pursuant to a State plan for medical assistance approved under title XIX of the Social Security Act [42 U.S.C. 1396 et seq.] which would not have been payable if such acquired rights had been executed before payment with respect to such items or services by the group health plan.

(9) For additional provisions relating to group health plans, see section 1191 of this title.

(c) Definitions

For purposes of this section:

(1) The term "State law" includes all laws, decisions, rules, regulations, or other State action having the effect of law, of any State. A law of the United States applicable only to the District of Columbia shall be treated as a State law rather than a law of the United States.

(2) The term "State" includes a State, any political subdivisions thereof, or any agency or instrumentality of either, which purports to regulate, directly or indirectly, the terms and conditions of employee benefit plans covered by this subchapter.

(d) Alteration, amendment, modification, invalidation, impairment, or supersedure of any law of the United States prohibited

Nothing in this subchapter shall be construed to alter, amend, modify, invalidate, impair, or supersede any law of the United States (except as provided in sections 1031 and 1137(b) of this title) or any rule or regulation issued under any such law.

(e) Automatic contribution arrangements

(1) Notwithstanding any other provision of this section, this subchapter shall supersede any law of a State which would directly or indirectly prohibit or restrict the inclusion in any plan of an automatic contribution arrangement. The Secretary may prescribe regulations which would establish minimum standards that such an arrangement would be required to satisfy in order for this subsection to apply in the case of such arrangement.

(2) For purposes of this subsection, the term "automatic contribution arrangement" means an arrangement—

(A) under which a participant may elect to have the plan sponsor make payments as contributions under the plan on behalf of the participant, or to the participant directly in cash,

(B) under which a participant is treated as having elected to have the plan sponsor make such contributions in an amount equal to a uniform percentage of compensation provided under the plan until the participant specifically elects not to have such contributions made (or specifically elects to have such contributions made at a different percentage), and

(C) under which such contributions are invested in accordance with regulations prescribed by the Secretary under section 1104(c)(5) of this title.

(3)(A) The plan administrator of an automatic contribution arrangement shall, within a reasonable period before such plan year, provide to each participant to whom the arrangement applies for such plan year notice of the participant's rights and obligations under the arrangement which—

(i) is sufficiently accurate and comprehensive to apprise the participant of such rights and obligations, and

(ii) is written in a manner calculated to be understood by the average participant to whom the arrangement applies.

(B) A notice shall not be treated as meeting the requirements of subparagraph (A) with respect to a participant unless—

(i) the notice includes an explanation of the participant's right under the arrangement not to have elective contributions made on the participant's behalf (or to elect to have such contributions made at a different percentage),

(ii) the participant has a reasonable period of time, after receipt of the notice described in clause (i) and before the first elective contribution is made, to make such election, and

(iii) the notice explains how contributions made under the arrangement will be invested in the absence of any investment election by the participant.

(Pub. L. 93–406, title I, §514, Sept. 2, 1974, 88 Stat. 897; Pub. L. 97–473, title III, §§301(a), 302(b), Jan. 14, 1983, 96 Stat. 2611, 2613; Pub. L. 98–397, title I, §104(b), Aug. 23, 1984, 98 Stat. 1436; Pub. L. 99–272, title IX, §9503(d)(1), Apr. 7, 1986, 100 Stat. 207; Pub. L. 101–239, title VII, §7894(f)(2)(A), (3)(A), Dec. 19, 1989, 103 Stat. 2450, 2451; Pub. L. 103–66, title IV, §4301(c)(4), Aug. 10, 1993, 107 Stat. 377; Pub. L. 104–191, title I, §101(f)(1), Aug. 21, 1996, 110 Stat. 1953; Pub. L. 104–204, title VI, §603(b)(3)(G), Sept. 26, 1996, 110 Stat. 2938; Pub. L. 105–200, title IV, §401(h)(2)(A)(i), (ii), July 16, 1998, 112 Stat. 668; Pub. L. 109–280, title IX, §902(f)(1), Aug. 17, 2006, 120 Stat. 1039.)

REFERENCES IN TEXT

The Social Security Act, referred to in subsec. (b)(8)(B), is act Aug. 14, 1935, ch. 531, 49 Stat. 620, as amended. Title XIX of the Social Security Act is classified generally to subchapter XIX (§1396 et seq.) of chapter 7 of Title 42, The Public Health and Welfare. For complete classification of this Act to the Code, see section 1305 of Title 42 and Tables.

AMENDMENTS

2006—Subsec. (e). Pub. L. 109–280 added subsec. (e).

1998—Subsec. (b)(7). Pub. L. 105–200, §401(h)(2)(A)(ii), substituted "they apply to" for "enforced by".

Pub. L. 105–200, §401(h)(2)(A)(i), amended directory language of Pub. L. 103–66, §4301(c)(4)(A). See 1993 Amendment note below.

1996—Subsec. (b)(9). Pub. L. 104–204 made technical amendment to reference in original act which appears in text as reference to section 1191 of this title.

Pub. L. 104–191 added par. (9).

1993—Subsec. (b)(7). Pub. L. 103–66, §4301(c)(4)(A), as amended by Pub. L. 105–200, §401(h)(1)(A)(i), inserted ", qualified medical child support orders (within the meaning of section 1169(a)(2)(A) of this title), and the provisions of law referred to in section 1169(a)(2)(B)(ii) of this title to the extent enforced by qualified medical child support orders" before period at end.

Subsec. (b)(8). Pub. L. 103–66, §4301(c)(4)(B), added par. (8) and struck out former par. (8) which read as follows: "Subsection (a) of this section shall not apply to any State law mandating that an employee benefit plan not include any provision which has the effect of limiting or excluding coverage or payment for any health care for an individual who would otherwise be covered or entitled to benefits or services under the terms of the employee benefit plan, because that individual is provided, or is eligible for, benefits or services pursuant to a plan under title XIX of the Social Security Act, to the extent such law is necessary for the State to be eligible to receive reimbursement under title XIX of that Act."

1989—Subsec. (b)(5)(C). Pub. L. 101–239, §7894(f)(2)(A), substituted "by such parts 1 and 4 and the preceding sections of this part" for "by such parts".

Subsec. (b)(6)(B). Pub. L. 101–239, §7894(f)(3)(A), substituted "section 1002(1)" for "section 1002(*l*)".

1986—Subsec. (b)(8). Pub. L. 99–272 added par. (8).

1984—Subsec. (b)(7). Pub. L. 98–397 added par. (7).

1983—Subsec. (b)(5). Pub. L. 97–473, §301(a), added par. (5).

Subsec. (b)(6). Pub. L. 97–473, §302(b), added par. (6).

EFFECTIVE DATE OF 1998 AMENDMENT

Pub. L. 105–200, title IV, §401(h)(2)(C), July 16, 1998, 112 Stat. 668, provided that: "The amendments made by subparagraph (A) [amending this section and section 1169 of this title] shall be effective as if included in the enactment of section 4301(c)(4)(A) of the Omnibus Budget Reconciliation Act of 1993 [Pub. L. 103–66]."

EFFECTIVE DATE OF 1996 AMENDMENTS

Amendment by Pub. L. 104–204 applicable with respect to group health plans for plan years beginning on or after Jan. 1, 1998, see section 603(c) of Pub. L. 104–204, set out as a note under section 1003 of this title.

Amendment by Pub. L. 104–191 applicable with respect to group health plans for plan years beginning after June 30, 1997, except as otherwise provided, see section 101(g) of Pub. L. 104–191, set out as a note under section 1181 of this title.

EFFECTIVE DATE OF 1989 AMENDMENT

Section 7894(f)(2)(B) of Pub. L. 101–239 provided that: "The amendment made by this paragraph [amending this section] shall take effect as if included in section 301 of Public Law 97–473."

Section 7894(f)(3)(B) of Pub. L. 101–239 provided that: "The amendments made by this paragraph [amending this section] shall take effect as if included in section 302 of Public Law 97–473."

EFFECTIVE DATE OF 1986 AMENDMENT

Section 9503(d)(2) of Pub. L. 99–272 provided that:

"(2)(A) Except as provided in subparagraph (B), the amendment made by paragraph (1) [amending this section] shall become effective on October 1, 1986.

"(B) In the case of a plan maintained pursuant to one or more collective bargaining agreements between employee representatives and one or more employers ratified on or before the date of the enactment of this Act [Apr. 7, 1986], the amendment made by paragraph (1) shall become effective on the later of—

"(i) October 1, 1986; or

"(ii) the earlier of—

"(I) the date on which the last of the collective bargaining agreements under which the plan is maintained, which were in effect on the date of the enactment of this Act, terminates (determined without regard to any extension thereof agreed to after the date of the enactment of this Act); or

"(II) three years after the date of the enactment of this Act."

EFFECTIVE DATE OF 1984 AMENDMENT

Amendment by Pub. L. 98–397 effective Jan. 1, 1985, except as otherwise provided, see section 303(d) of Pub. L. 98–397, set out as a note under section 1001 of this title.

EFFECTIVE DATE OF 1983 AMENDMENT

Section 301(c) of Pub. L. 97–473 provided that: "The amendment made by this section [amending this section] shall take effect on the date of the enactment of this Act [Jan. 14, 1983]."

Amendment by section 302(b) of Pub. L. 97–473 effective Jan. 14, 1983, see section 302(c) of Pub. L. 97–473, set out as a note under section 1002 of this title.

REGULATIONS

Secretary authorized, effective Sept. 2, 1974, to promulgate regulations wherever provisions of this subchapter call for the promulgation of regulations, see section 1031 of this title.

PLAN AMENDMENTS NOT REQUIRED UNTIL JANUARY 1, 1994

For provisions setting forth circumstances under which any amendment to a plan required to be made by an amendment made by section 4301 of Pub. L. 103–66 shall not be required to be made before the first plan year beginning on or after Jan. 1, 1994, see section 4301(d) of Pub. L. 103–66, set out as an Effective Date of 1993 Amendment note under section 1021 of this title.

TREATMENT OF OTHER STATE LAWS

Section 301(b) of Pub. L. 97–473 provided that: "The amendment made by this section [amending this section] shall not be considered a precedent with respect to extending such amendment to any other State law."

§1144a. Clarification of church welfare plan status under State insurance law

(a) In general

For purposes of determining the status of a church plan that is a welfare plan under provisions of a State insurance law described in subsection (b) of this section, such a church plan (and any trust under such plan) shall be deemed to be a plan sponsored by a single employer that reimburses costs from general church assets, or purchases insurance coverage with general church assets, or both.

(b) State insurance law

A State insurance law described in this subsection is a law that—

(1) requires a church plan, or an organization described in section 414(e)(3)(A) of title 26 and section 1002(33)(C)(i) of this title to the extent that it is administering or funding such a plan, to be licensed; or

(2) relates solely to the solvency or insolvency of a church plan (including participation in State guaranty funds and associations).

(c) Definitions

For purposes of this section:

(1) Church plan

The term "church plan" has the meaning given such term by section 414(e) of title 26 and section 1002(33) of this title.

(2) Reimburses costs from general church assets

The term "reimburses costs from general church assets" means engaging in an activity that is not the spreading of risk solely for the purposes of the provisions of State insurance laws described in subsection (b) of this section.

(3) Welfare plan

The term "welfare plan"—

(A) means any church plan to the extent that such plan provides medical, surgical, or hospital care or benefits, or benefits in the event of sickness, accident, disability, death or unemployment, or vacation benefits, apprenticeship or other training programs, or day care centers, scholarship funds, or prepaid legal services; and

(B) does not include any entity, such as a health insurance issuer described in section 9832(b)(2) of title 26 or a health maintenance organization described in section 9832(b)(3) of title 26, or any other organization that does business with the church plan or organization sponsoring or maintaining such a plan.

(d) Enforcement authority

Notwithstanding any other provision of this section, for purposes of enforcing provisions of

State insurance laws that apply to a church plan that is a welfare plan, the church plan shall be subject to State enforcement as if the church plan were an insurer licensed by the State.

(e) Application of section

Except as provided in subsection (d) of this section, the application of this section is limited to determining the status of a church plan that is a welfare plan under the provisions of State insurance laws described in subsection (b) of this section. This section shall not otherwise be construed to recharacterize the status, or modify or affect the rights, of any plan participant or beneficiary, including participants or beneficiaries who make plan contributions.

(Pub. L. 106–244, §2, July 10, 2000, 114 Stat. 499.)

CODIFICATION

Section was not enacted as part of the Employee Retirement Income Security Act of 1974 which comprises this chapter.

PURPOSE

Pub. L. 106–244, §1, July 10, 2000, 114 Stat. 499, provided that: "The purpose of this Act [enacting this section] is only to clarify the application to a church plan that is a welfare plan of State insurance laws that require or solely relate to licensing, solvency, insolvency, or the status of such plan as a single employer plan."

§1145. Delinquent contributions

Every employer who is obligated to make contributions to a multiemployer plan under the terms of the plan or under the terms of a collectively bargained agreement shall, to the extent not inconsistent with law, make such contributions in accordance with the terms and conditions of such plan or such agreement.

(Pub. L. 93–406, title I, §515, as added Pub. L. 96–364, title III, §306(a), Sept. 26, 1980, 94 Stat. 1295.)

EFFECTIVE DATE

Section effective Sept. 26, 1980, except as specifically provided, see section 1461(e) of this title.

§1146. Outreach to promote retirement income savings

(a) In general

The Secretary shall maintain an ongoing program of outreach to the public designed to effectively promote retirement income savings by the public.

(b) Methods

The Secretary shall carry out the requirements of subsection (a) of this section by means which shall ensure effective communication to the public, including publication of public service announcements, public meetings, creation of educational materials, and establishment of a site on the Internet.

(c) Information to be made available

The information to be made available by the Secretary as part of the program of outreach required under subsection (a) of this section shall include the following:

(1) a description of the vehicles currently available to individuals and employers for creating and maintaining retirement income savings, specifically including information explaining to employers, in simple terms, the characteristics and operation of the different retirement savings vehicles, including the steps to establish each such vehicle; and

(2) information regarding matters relevant to establishing retirement income savings, such as—

(A) the forms of retirement income savings;

(B) the concept of compound interest;

(C) the importance of commencing savings early in life;

(D) savings principles;

(E) the importance of prudence and diversification in investing;

(F) the importance of the timing of investments; and

(G) the impact on retirement savings of life's uncertainties, such as living beyond one's life expectancy.

(d) Establishment of site on Internet

The Secretary shall establish a permanent site on the Internet concerning retirement income savings. The site shall contain at least the following information:

(1) a means for individuals to calculate their estimated retirement savings needs, based on their retirement income goal as a percentage of their preretirement income;

(2) a description in simple terms of the common types of retirement income savings arrangements available to both individuals and employers (specifically including small employers), including information on the amount of money that can be placed into a given vehicle, the tax treatment of the money, the amount of accumulation possible through different typical investment options and interest rate projections, and a directory of resources of more descriptive information;

(3) materials explaining to employers in simple terms, the characteristics and operation of the different retirement savings arrangements for their workers and what the basic legal requirements are under this chapter and title 26, including the steps to establish each such arrangement;

(4) copies of all educational materials developed by the Department of Labor, and by other Federal agencies in consultation with such Department, to promote retirement income savings by workers and employers; and

(5) links to other sites maintained on the Internet by governmental agencies and nonprofit organizations that provide additional detail on retirement income savings arrangements and related topics on savings or investing.

(e) Coordination

The Secretary shall coordinate the outreach program under this section with similar efforts undertaken by other public and private entities.

(Pub. L. 93–406, title I, §516, as added Pub. L. 105–92, §3(a), Nov. 19, 1997, 111 Stat. 2139.)

REFERENCES IN TEXT

This chapter, referred to in subsec. (d)(3), was in the original "this Act", meaning Pub. L. 93–406, known as the Employee Retirement Income Security Act of 1974. Titles I, III, and IV of such Act are classified principally to this chapter. For complete classification of this Act to the Code, see Short Title note set out under section 1001 of this title and Tables.

FINDINGS AND PURPOSE

Section 2 of Pub. L. 105–92 provided that:

"(a) FINDINGS.—The Congress finds as follows:

"(1) The impending retirement of the baby boom generation will severely strain our already overburdened entitlement system, necessitating increased reliance on pension and other personal savings.

"(2) Studies have found that less than a third of Americans have even tried to calculate how much they will need to have saved by retirement, and that less than 20 percent are very confident they will have enough money to live comfortably throughout their retirement.

"(3) A leading obstacle to expanding retirement savings is the simple fact that far too many Americans—particularly the young—are either unaware of, or without the knowledge and resources necessary to take advantage of, the extensive benefits offered by our retirement savings system.

"(b) PURPOSE.—It is the purpose of this Act [see Short Title of 1997 Amendment note, set out under section 1001 of this title]—

"(1) to advance the public's knowledge and understanding of retirement savings and its critical importance to the future well-being of American workers and their families;

"(2) to provide for a periodic, bipartisan national retirement savings summit in conjunction with the White House to elevate the issue of savings to national prominence; and

"(3) to initiate the development of a broad-based, public education program to encourage and enhance individual commitment to a personal retirement savings strategy."

§1147. National Summit on Retirement Savings

(a) Authority to call Summit

Not later than July 15, 1998, the President shall convene a National Summit on Retirement Income Savings at the White House, to be co-hosted by the President and the Speaker and the Minority Leader of the House of Representatives and the Majority Leader and Minority Leader of the Senate. Such a National Summit shall be convened thereafter in 2001 and 2005 on or after September 1 of each year involved. Such a National Summit shall—

(1) advance the public's knowledge and understanding of retirement savings and its critical importance to the future well-being of American workers and their families;

(2) facilitate the development of a broad-based, public education program to encourage and enhance individual commitment to a personal retirement savings strategy;

(3) develop recommendations for additional research, reforms, and actions in the field of private pensions and individual retirement savings; and

(4) disseminate the report of, and information obtained by, the National Summit and exhibit materials and works of the National Summit.

(b) Planning and direction

The National Summit shall be planned and conducted under the direction of the Secretary, in consultation with, and with the assistance of, the heads of such other Federal departments and agencies as the President may designate. Such assistance may include the assignment of personnel. The Secretary shall, in planning and conducting the National Summit, consult with the congressional leaders specified in subsection (e)(2) of this section. The Secretary shall also, in carrying out the Secretary's duties under this subsection, consult and coordinate with at least one organization made up of private sector businesses and associations partnered with Government entities to promote long-term financial security in retirement through savings.

(c) Purpose of National Summit

The purpose of the National Summit shall be—

(1) to increase the public awareness of the value of personal savings for retirement;

(2) to advance the public's knowledge and understanding of retirement savings and its critical importance to the future well-being of American workers and their families;

(3) to facilitate the development of a broad-based, public education program to encourage and enhance individual commitment to a personal retirement savings strategy;

(4) to identify the problems workers have in setting aside adequate savings for retirement;

(5) to identify the barriers which employers, especially small employers, face in assisting their workers in accumulating retirement savings;

(6) to examine the impact and effectiveness of individual employers to promote personal savings for retirement among their workers and to promote participation in company savings options;

(7) to examine the impact and effectiveness of government programs at the Federal, State, and local levels to educate the public about, and to encourage, retirement income savings;

(8) to develop such specific and comprehensive recommendations for the legislative and executive branches of the Government and for private sector action as may be appropriate for promoting private pensions and individual retirement savings; and

(9) to develop recommendations for the coordination of Federal, State, and local retirement income savings initiatives among the Federal, State, and local levels of government and for the coordination of such initiatives.

(d) Scope of National Summit

The scope of the National Summit shall consist of issues relating to individual and employer-based retirement savings and shall not include issues relating to the old-age, survivors, and disability insurance program under title II of the Social Security Act [42 U.S.C. 401 et seq.].

(e) National Summit participants

(1) In general

To carry out the purposes of the National Summit, the National Summit shall bring together—

(A) professionals and other individuals working in the fields of employee benefits and retirement savings;

(B) Members of Congress and officials in the executive branch;

(C) representatives of State and local governments;

(D) representatives of private sector institutions, including individual employers, concerned about promoting the issue of retirement savings and facilitating savings among American workers; and

(E) representatives of the general public.

(2) Statutorily required participation

The participants in the National Summit shall include the following individuals or their designees:

(A) the Speaker and the Minority Leader of the House of Representatives;

(B) the Majority Leader and the Minority Leader of the Senate;

(C) the Chairman and ranking Member of the Committee on Education and the Workforce of the House of Representatives;

(D) the Chairman and ranking Member of the Committee on Labor and Human Resources of the Senate;

(E) the Chairman and ranking Member of the Special Committee on Aging of the Senate;

(F) the Chairman and ranking Member of the Subcommittees on Labor, Health and Human Services, and Education of the Senate and House of Representatives; and

(G) the parties referred to in subsection (b) of this section.

(3) Additional participants

(A) In general

There shall be not more than 200 additional participants. Of such additional participants—

(i) one-half shall be appointed by the President, in consultation with the elected leaders of the President's party in Congress (either the Speaker of the House of Representatives or the Minority Leader of the House of Representatives, and either the Majority Leader or the Minority Leader of the Senate;[1] and

(ii) one-half shall be appointed by the elected leaders of Congress of the party to which the President does not belong (one-half of that allotment to be appointed by either the Speaker of the House of Representatives or the Minority Leader of the House of Representatives, and one-half of that allotment to be appointed by either the Majority Leader or the Minority Leader of the Senate).

(B) Appointment requirements

The additional participants described in subparagraph (A) shall be—

(i) appointed not later than January 31, 1998;

(ii) selected without regard to political affiliation or past partisan activity; and

(iii) representative of the diversity of thought in the fields of employee benefits and retirement income savings.

(4) Presiding officers

The National Summit shall be presided over equally by representatives of the executive and legislative branches.

(f) National Summit administration

(1) Administration

In administering this section, the Secretary shall—

(A) request the cooperation and assistance of such other Federal departments and agencies and other parties referred to in subsection (b) of this section as may be appropriate in the carrying out of this section;

(B) furnish all reasonable assistance to State agencies, area agencies, and other appropriate organizations to enable them to organize and conduct conferences in conjunction with the National Summit;

(C) make available for public comment a proposed agenda for the National Summit that reflects to the greatest extent possible the purposes for the National Summit set out in this section;

(D) prepare and make available background materials for the use of participants in the National Summit that the Secretary considers necessary; and

(E) appoint and fix the pay of such additional personnel as may be necessary to carry out the provisions of this section without regard to provisions of title 5 governing appointments in the competitive service, and without regard to chapter 51 and subchapter III of chapter 53 of such title relating to classification and General Schedule pay rates.

(2) Duties

The Secretary shall, in carrying out the responsibilities and functions of the Secretary under this section, and as part of the National Summit, ensure that—

(A) the National Summit shall be conducted in a manner that ensures broad participation of Federal, State, and local agencies and private organizations, professionals, and others involved in retirement income savings and provides a strong basis for assistance to be provided under paragraph (1)(B);

(B) the agenda prepared under paragraph (1)(C) for the National Summit is published in the Federal Register; and

(C) the personnel appointed under paragraph (1)(E) shall be fairly balanced in terms of points of views represented and shall be appointed without regard to political affiliation or previous partisan activities.

(3) Nonapplication of FACA

The provisions of the Federal Advisory Committee Act (5 U.S.C. App.) shall not apply to the National Summit.

(g) Report

The Secretary shall prepare a report describing the activities of the National Summit and shall submit the report to the President, the Speaker and Minority Leader of the House of Representatives, the Majority and Minority Leaders of the Senate, and the chief executive officers of the States not later than 90 days after the date on which the National Summit is adjourned.

(h) "State" defined

For purposes of this section, the term "State" means a State, the District of Columbia, the

[1] So in original. A closing parenthesis probably should precede the semicolon.

Commonwealth of Puerto Rico, the Commonwealth of the Northern Mariana Islands, Guam, the Virgin Islands, American Samoa, and any other territory or possession of the United States.

(i) Authorization of appropriations

(1) In general

There is authorized to be appropriated for fiscal years beginning on or after October 1, 1997, such sums as are necessary to carry out this section.

(2) Authorization to accept private contributions

In order to facilitate the National Summit as a public-private partnership, the Secretary may accept private contributions, in the form of money, supplies, or services, to defray the costs of the National Summit.

(j) Financial obligation for fiscal year 1998

The financial obligation for the Department of Labor for fiscal year 1998 shall not exceed the lesser of—

(1) one-half of the costs of the National Summit; or

(2) $250,000.

The private sector organization described in subsection (b) of this section and contracted with by the Secretary shall be obligated for the balance of the cost of the National Summit.

(k) Contracts

The Secretary may enter into contracts to carry out the Secretary's responsibilities under this section. The Secretary shall enter into a contract on a sole-source basis to ensure the timely completion of the National Summit in fiscal year 1998.

(Pub. L. 93–406, title I, §517, as added Pub. L. 105–92, §4(a), Nov. 19, 1997, 111 Stat. 2141.)

REFERENCES IN TEXT

The Social Security Act, referred to in subsec. (d), is act Aug. 14, 1935, ch. 531, 49 Stat. 620, as amended. Title II of the Act is classified generally to subchapter II (§401 et seq.) of chapter 7 of Title 42, The Public Health and Welfare. For complete classification of this Act to the Code, see section 1305 of Title 42 and Tables.

The provisions of title 5 governing appointments in the competitive service, referred to in subsec. (f)(1)(E), are classified generally to section 3301 et seq. of Title 5, Government Organization and Employees.

The Federal Advisory Committee Act, referred to in subsec. (f)(3), is Pub. L. 92–463, Oct. 6, 1972, 86 Stat. 770, as amended, which is set out in the Appendix to Title 5, Government Organization and Employees.

CHANGE OF NAME

Committee on Education and the Workforce of House of Representatives changed to Committee on Education and Labor of House of Representatives by House Resolution No. 6, One Hundred Tenth Congress, Jan. 5, 2007.

Committee on Labor and Human Resources of Senate changed to Committee on Health, Education, Labor, and Pensions of Senate by Senate Resolution No. 20, One Hundred Sixth Congress, Jan. 19, 1999.

§1148. Authority to postpone certain deadlines by reason of Presidentially declared disaster or terroristic or military actions

In the case of a pension or other employee benefit plan, or any sponsor, administrator, participant, beneficiary, or other person with respect to such plan, affected by a Presidentially declared disaster (as defined in section 1033(h)(3) of title 26) or a terroristic or military action (as defined in section 692(c)(2) of such title), the Secretary may, notwithstanding any other provision of law, prescribe, by notice or otherwise, a period of up to 1 year which may be disregarded in determining the date by which any action is required or permitted to be completed under this chapter. No plan shall be treated as failing to be operated in accordance with the terms of the plan solely as the result of disregarding any period by reason of the preceding sentence.

(Pub. L. 93–406, title I, §518, as added Pub. L. 107–134, title I, §112(c)(1), Jan. 23, 2002, 115 Stat. 2434.)

REFERENCES IN TEXT

This chapter, referred to in text, was in the original "this Act", meaning Pub. L. 93–406, known as the Employee Retirement Income Security Act of 1974. Titles I, III, and IV of such Act are classified principally to this chapter. For complete classification of this Act to the Code, see Short Title note set out under section 1001 of this title and Tables.

EFFECTIVE DATE

Section applicable to disasters and terroristic or military actions occurring on or after Sept. 11, 2001, with respect to any action of the Secretary of the Treasury, the Secretary of Labor, or the Pension Benefit Guaranty Corporation occurring on or after Jan. 23, 2002, see section 112(f) of Pub. L. 107–134, set out as an Effective Date of 2002 Amendment note under section 6081 of Title 26, Internal Revenue Code.

PART 6—CONTINUATION COVERAGE AND ADDITIONAL STANDARDS FOR GROUP HEALTH PLANS

§1161. Plans must provide continuation coverage to certain individuals

(a) In general

The plan sponsor of each group health plan shall provide, in accordance with this part, that each qualified beneficiary who would lose coverage under the plan as a result of a qualifying event is entitled, under the plan, to elect, within the election period, continuation coverage under the plan.

(b) Exception for certain plans

Subsection (a) of this section shall not apply to any group health plan for any calendar year if all employers maintaining such plan normally employed fewer than 20 employees on a typical business day during the preceding calendar year.

(Pub. L. 93–406, title I, §601, as added Pub. L. 99–272, title X, §10002(a), Apr. 7, 1986, 100 Stat. 227; amended Pub. L. 101–239, title VII, §§7862(c)(1)(B), 7891(a)(1), Dec. 19, 1989, 103 Stat. 2432, 2445.)

AMENDMENTS

1989—Subsec. (b). Pub. L. 101–239 struck out at end "Under regulations, rules similar to the rules of subsections (a) and (b) of section 52 of title 26 (relating to employers under common control) shall apply for purposes of this subsection."

Pub. L. 101–239, §7891(a)(1), substituted "Internal Revenue Code of 1986" for "Internal Revenue Code of 1954", which for purposes of codification was translated as "title 26" thus requiring no change in text.

EFFECTIVE DATE OF 1989 AMENDMENT

Amendment by section 7862(c)(1)(B) of Pub. L. 101–239 applicable to years beginning after Dec. 31, 1986, see section 7862(c)(1)(C) of Pub. L. 101–239, set out as a note under section 106 of Title 26, Internal Revenue Code.

Amendment by section 7891(a)(1) of Pub. L. 101–239 effective, except as otherwise provided, as if included in the provision of the Tax Reform Act of 1986, Pub. L. 99–514, to which such amendment relates, see section 7891(f) of Pub. L. 101–239, set out as a note under section 1002 of this title.

EFFECTIVE DATE

Section 10002(d) of Pub. L. 99–272 provided that:

"(1) GENERAL RULE.—The amendments made by this section [enacting this part and amending section 1132 of this title] shall apply to plan years beginning on or after July 1, 1986.

"(2) SPECIAL RULE FOR COLLECTIVE BARGAINING AGREEMENTS.—In the case of a group health plan maintained pursuant to one or more collective bargaining agreements between employee representatives and one or more employers ratified before the date of the enactment of this Act [Apr. 7, 1986], the amendments made by this section shall not apply to plan years beginning before the later of—

"(A) the date on which the last of the collective bargaining agreements relating to the plan terminates (determined without regard to any extension thereof agreed to after the date of the enactment of this Act), or

"(B) January 1, 1987.

For purposes of subparagraph (A), any plan amendment made pursuant to a collective bargaining agreement relating to the plan which amends the plan solely to conform to any requirement added by this section shall not be treated as a termination of such collective bargaining agreement."

§1162. Continuation coverage

For purposes of section 1161 of this title, the term "continuation coverage" means coverage under the plan which meets the following requirements:

(1) Type of benefit coverage

The coverage must consist of coverage which, as of the time the coverage is being provided, is identical to the coverage provided under the plan to similarly situated beneficiaries under the plan with respect to whom a qualifying event has not occurred. If coverage is modified under the plan for any group of similarly situated beneficiaries, such coverage shall also be modified in the same manner for all individuals who are qualified beneficiaries under the plan pursuant to this part in connection with such group.

(2) Period of coverage

The coverage must extend for at least the period beginning on the date of the qualifying event and ending not earlier than the earliest of the following:

(A) Maximum required period

(i) General rule for terminations and reduced hours

In the case of a qualifying event described in section 1163(2) of this title, except as provided in clause (ii), the date which is 18 months after the date of the qualifying event.

(ii) Special rule for multiple qualifying events

If a qualifying event (other than a qualifying event described in section 1163(6) of this title) occurs during the 18 months after the date of a qualifying event described in section 1163(2) of this title, the date which is 36 months after the date of the qualifying event described in section 1163(2) of this title.

(iii) Special rule for certain bankruptcy proceedings

In the case of a qualifying event described in section 1163(6) of this title (relating to bankruptcy proceedings), the date of the death of the covered employee or qualified beneficiary (described in section 1167(3)(C)(iii) of this title), or in the case of the surviving spouse or dependent children of the covered employee, 36 months after the date of the death of the covered employee.

(iv) General rule for other qualifying events

In the case of a qualifying event not described in section 1163(2) or 1163(6) of this title, the date which is 36 months after the date of the qualifying event.

(v) Medicare entitlement followed by qualifying event

In the case of a qualifying event described in section 1163(2) of this title that occurs less than 18 months after the date the covered employee became entitled to benefits under title XVIII of the Social Security Act [42 U.S.C. 1395 et seq.], the period of coverage for qualified beneficiaries other than the covered employee shall not terminate under this subparagraph before the close of the 36-month period beginning on the date the covered employee became so entitled.

In the case of a qualified beneficiary who is determined, under title II or XVI of the Social Security Act [42 U.S.C. 401 et seq., 1381 et seq.], to have been disabled at any time during the first 60 days of continuation coverage under this part, any reference in clause (i) or (ii) to 18 months is deemed a reference to 29 months (with respect to all qualified beneficiaries), but only if the qualified beneficiary has provided notice of such determination under section 1166(3)[1] of this title before the end of such 18 months.

(B) End of plan

The date on which the employer ceases to provide any group health plan to any employee.

(C) Failure to pay premium

The date on which coverage ceases under the plan by reason of a failure to make timely payment of any premium required under the plan with respect to the qualified beneficiary. The payment of any premium (other than any payment referred to in the last

[1] See References in Text note below.

sentence of paragraph (3)) shall be considered to be timely if made within 30 days after the date due or within such longer period as applies to or under the plan.

(D) Group health plan coverage or medicare entitlement

The date on which the qualified beneficiary first becomes, after the date of the election—

(i) covered under any other group health plan (as an employee or otherwise) which does not contain any exclusion or limitation with respect to any preexisting condition of such beneficiary (other than such an exclusion or limitation which does not apply to (or is satisfied by) such beneficiary by reason of chapter 100 of title 26, part 7 of this subtitle, or title XXVII of the Public Health Service Act [42 U.S.C. 300gg et seq.]), or

(ii) in the case of a qualified beneficiary other than a qualified beneficiary described in section 1167(3)(C) of this title, entitled to benefits under title XVIII of the Social Security Act [42 U.S.C. 1395 et seq.].

(E) Termination of extended coverage for disability

In the case of a qualified beneficiary who is disabled at any time during the first 60 days of continuation coverage under this part, the month that begins more than 30 days after the date of the final determination under title II or XVI of the Social Security Act [42 U.S.C. 401 et seq., 1381 et seq.] that the qualified beneficiary is no longer disabled.

(3) Premium requirements

The plan may require payment of a premium for any period of continuation coverage, except that such premium—

(A) shall not exceed 102 percent of the applicable premium for such period, and

(B) may, at the election of the payor, be made in monthly installments.

In no event may the plan require the payment of any premium before the day which is 45 days after the day on which the qualified beneficiary made the initial election for continuation coverage. In the case of an individual described in the last sentence of paragraph (2)(A), any reference in subparagraph (A) of this paragraph to "102 percent" is deemed a reference to "150 percent" for any month after the 18th month of continuation coverage described in clause (i) or (ii) of paragraph (2)(A).

(4) No requirement of insurability

The coverage may not be conditioned upon, or discriminate on the basis of lack of, evidence of insurability.

(5) Conversion option

In the case of a qualified beneficiary whose period of continuation coverage expires under paragraph (2)(A), the plan must, during the 180-day period ending on such expiration date, provide to the qualified beneficiary the option of enrollment under a conversion health plan otherwise generally available under the plan.

(Pub. L. 93–406, title I, §602, as added Pub. L. 99–272, title X, §10002(a), Apr. 7, 1986, 100 Stat. 228; amended Pub. L. 99–509, title IX, §9501(b)(1)(B), (2)(B), Oct. 21, 1986, 100 Stat. 2076, 2077; Pub. L. 99–514, title XVIII, §1895(d)(1)(B), (2)(B), (3)(B), (4)(B), Oct. 22, 1986, 100 Stat. 2936–2938; Pub. L. 101–239, title VI, §6703(a), (b), title VII, §§7862(c)(3)(B), (4)(A), (5)(B), 7871(c), Dec. 19, 1989, 103 Stat. 2296, 2432, 2433, 2435; Pub. L. 104–188, title I, §1704(g)(1)(B), Aug. 20, 1996, 110 Stat. 1880; Pub. L. 104–191, title IV, §421(b)(1), Aug. 21, 1996, 110 Stat. 2088.)

REFERENCES IN TEXT

The Social Security Act, referred to in par. (2)(A), (D)(ii), (E), is act Aug. 14, 1935, ch. 531, 49 Stat. 620, as amended. Titles II, XVI, and XVIII of the Social Security Act are classified generally to subchapters II (§401 et seq.), XVI (§1381 et seq.), and XVIII (§1395 et seq.), respectively, of chapter 7 of Title 42, The Public Health and Welfare. For complete classification of this Act to the Code, see section 1305 of Title 42 and Tables.

Section 1166(3) of this title, referred to in par. (2)(A), was redesignated as section 1166(a)(3) of this title by Pub. L. 101–239, title VII, §7891(d)(1)(A)(ii)(I), Dec. 19, 1989, 103 Stat. 2445.

The Public Health Service Act, referred to in par. (2)(D)(i), is act July 1, 1944, ch. 373, 58 Stat. 682, as amended. Title XXVII of the Act is classified generally to subchapter XXV (§300gg et seq.) of chapter 6A of Title 42, The Public Health and Welfare. For complete classification of this Act to the Code, see Short Title note set out under section 201 of Title 42 and Tables.

AMENDMENTS

1996—Par. (2)(A). Pub. L. 104–191, §421(b)(1)(A), in closing provisions, substituted "In the case of a qualified beneficiary" for "In the case of an individual" and "at any time during the first 60 days of continuation coverage under this part" for "at the time of a qualifying event described in section 1163(2) of this title", struck out "with respect to such event" after "(ii) to 18 months", and inserted "(with respect to all qualified beneficiaries)" after "29 months".

Par. (2)(A)(v). Pub. L. 104–188 amended cl. (v) generally. Prior to amendment, cl. (v) read as follows:

"(v) QUALIFYING EVENT INVOLVING MEDICARE ENTITLEMENT.—In the case of an event described in section 1163(4) of this title (without regard to whether such event is a qualifying event), the period of coverage for qualified beneficiaries other than the covered employee for such event or any subsequent qualifying event shall not terminate before the close of the 36-month period beginning on the date the covered employee becomes entitled to benefits under title XVIII of the Social Security Act."

Par. (2)(D)(i). Pub. L. 104–191, §421(b)(1)(B), inserted "(other than such an exclusion or limitation which does not apply to (or is satisfied by) such beneficiary by reason of chapter 100 of title 26, part 7 of this subtitle, or title XXVII of the Public Health Service Act [42 U.S.C. 300gg et seq.])" before ", or" at end.

Par. (2)(E). Pub. L. 104–191, §421(b)(1)(C), substituted "at any time during the first 60 days of continuation coverage under this part" for "at the time of a qualifying event described in section 1163(2) of this title".

1989—Par. (2)(A). Pub. L. 101–239, §6703(a)(1), inserted after and below cl. (iv) "In the case of an individual who is determined, under title II or XVI of the Social Security Act, to have been disabled at the time of a qualifying event described in section 1163(2) of this title, any reference in clause (i) or (ii) to 18 months with respect to such event is deemed a reference to 29 months, but only if the qualified beneficiary has provided notice of such determination under section 1166(3) of this title before the end of such 18 months."

Par. (2)(A)(iii). Pub. L. 101–239, §7871(c), substituted "described in section 1163(6)" for "described in 1163(6)".

Par. (2)(A)(v). Pub. L. 101–239, § 7862(c)(5)(B), which directed the insertion of cl. (v) "at the end" of par. (2)(A), was executed by inserting cl. (v) after cl. (iv), to reflect the probable intent of Congress.

Par. (2)(D). Pub. L. 101–239, § 7862(c)(3)(B), substituted "entitlement" for "eligibility" in heading and inserted "which does not contain any exclusion or limitation with respect to any preexisting condition of such beneficiary" after "or otherwise)" in cl. (i).

Par. (2)(E). Pub. L. 101–239, § 6703(a)(2), added subpar. (E).

Par. (3). Pub. L. 101–239, § 7862(c)(4)(A), which directed substitution of "In no event may the plan require the payment of any premium before the day which is 45 days after the day on which the qualified beneficiary made the initial election for continuation coverage." for last sentence of par. (3), was executed by making the substitution for the following sentence: "If an election is made after the qualifying event, the plan shall permit payment for continuation coverage during the period preceding the election to be made within 45 days of the date of the election.", notwithstanding the sentence added at the end of par. (3) by Pub. L. 101–239, § 6703(b).

Pub. L. 101–239, § 6703(b), inserted at end "In the case of an individual described in the last sentence of paragraph (2)(A), any reference in subparagraph (A) of this paragraph to '102 percent' is deemed a reference to '150 percent' for any month after the 18th month of continuation coverage described in clause (i) or (ii) of paragraph (2)(A)."

1986—Par. (1). Pub. L. 99–514, § 1895(d)(1)(B), inserted "If coverage is modified under the plan for any group of similarly situated beneficiaries, such coverage shall also be modified in the same manner for all individuals who are qualified beneficiaries under the plan pursuant to this part in connection with such group."

Par. (2)(A). Pub. L. 99–514, § 1895(d)(2)(B), amended subpar. (A) generally. Prior to amendment, subpar. (A) read as follows:

"(A) MAXIMUM PERIOD.—In the case of—

"(i) a qualifying event described in section 1163(2) of this title (relating to terminations and reduced hours), the date which is 18 months after the date of the qualifying event, and

"(ii) any qualifying event not described in clause (i), the date which is 36 months after the date of the qualifying event."

Par. (2)(A)(ii). Pub. L. 99–509, § 9501(b)(1)(B)(i), inserted "(other than a qualifying event described in section 1163(6) of this title)".

Par. (2)(A)(iii). Pub. L. 99–509, § 9501(b)(1)(B)(iv), added cl. (iii). Former cl. (iii) redesignated (iv).

Par. (2)(A)(iv). Pub. L. 99–509, § 9501(b)(1)(B)(ii), (iii), redesignated cl. (iii) as (iv) and inserted "or 1163(6)".

Par. (2)(C). Pub. L. 99–514, § 1895(d)(3)(B), inserted "The payment of any premium (other than any payment referred to in the last sentence of paragraph (3)) shall be considered to be timely if made within 30 days after the date due or within such longer period as applies to or under the plan."

Par. (2)(D). Pub. L. 99–514, § 1895(d)(4)(B)(ii), (iii), substituted "Group health plan coverage or medicare eligibility" for "Reemployment or medicare eligibility" as heading and substituted "covered under any other group health plan (as an employee or otherwise)" for "a covered employee under any other group health plan" in cl. (i).

Par. (2)(D)(ii). Pub. L. 99–509, § 9501(b)(2)(B), inserted "in the case of a qualified beneficiary other than a qualified beneficiary described in section 1167(3)(C) of this title" before "entitled".

Par. (2)(E). Pub. L. 99–514, § 1895(d)(4)(B)(i), struck out subpar. (E), remarriage of spouse, which read as follows: "In the case of an individual who is a qualified beneficiary by reason of being the spouse of a covered employee, the date on which the beneficiary remarries and becomes covered under a group health plan."

EFFECTIVE DATE OF 1996 AMENDMENTS

Amendment by Pub. L. 104–191 effective Jan. 1, 1997, regardless of whether qualifying event occurred before, on, or after such date, see section 421(d) of Pub. L. 104–191 set out as a note under section 4980B of Title 26, Internal Revenue Code.

Amendment by Pub. L. 104–188 applicable to plan years beginning after Dec. 31, 1989, see section 1704(g)(2) of Pub. L. 104–188, set out as a note under section 4980B of Title 26.

EFFECTIVE DATE OF 1989 AMENDMENT

Section 6703(d) of Pub. L. 101–239 provided that: "The amendments made by this section [amending this section and section 1166 of this title] shall apply to plan years beginning on or after the date of the enactment of this Act [Dec. 19, 1989], regardless of whether the qualifying event occurred before, on, or after such date."

Amendment by section 7862(c)(3)(B) of Pub. L. 101–239 applicable to (i) qualifying events occurring after Dec. 31, 1989, and (ii) in the case of qualified beneficiaries who elected continuation coverage after Dec. 31, 1988, the period for which the required premium was paid (or was attempted to be paid but was rejected as such), see section 7862(c)(3)(D) of Pub. L. 101–239, set out as a note under section 162 of Title 26, Internal Revenue Code.

Amendment by section 7862(c)(4)(A) of Pub. L. 101–239 applicable to plan years beginning after Dec. 31, 1989, see section 7862(c)(4)(C) of Pub. L. 101–239, set out as a note under section 4980B of Title 26.

Amendment by section 7862(c)(5)(B) of Pub. L. 101–239 applicable to plan years beginning after Dec. 31, 1989, see section 7862(c)(5)(C) of Pub. L. 101–239, set out as a note under section 4980B of Title 26.

EFFECTIVE DATE OF 1986 AMENDMENTS

Amendment by Pub. L. 99–514 effective, except as otherwise provided, as if included in enactment of the Consolidated Omnibus Budget Reconciliation Act of 1985, Pub. L. 99–272, see section 1895(e) of Pub. L. 99–514, set out as a note under section 162 of Title 26, Internal Revenue Code.

Amendment by Pub. L. 99–509 effective, except as otherwise provided, as if included in title X of the Consolidated Omnibus Budget Reconciliation Act of 1985, Pub. L. 99–272, see section 9501(e) of Pub. L. 99–509, set out as a note under section 162 of Title 26.

PLAN AMENDMENTS NOT REQUIRED UNTIL JANUARY 1, 1989

For provisions directing that if any amendments made by subtitle A or subtitle C of title XI [§§ 1101–1147 and 1171–1177] or title XVIII [§§ 1800–1899A] of Pub. L. 99–514 require an amendment to any plan, such plan amendment shall not be required to be made before the first plan year beginning on or after Jan. 1, 1989, see section 1140 of Pub. L. 99–514, as amended, set out as a note under section 401 of Title 26, Internal Revenue Code.

§ 1163. Qualifying event

For purposes of this part, the term "qualifying event" means, with respect to any covered employee, any of the following events which, but for the continuation coverage required under this part, would result in the loss of coverage of a qualified beneficiary:

(1) The death of the covered employee.

(2) The termination (other than by reason of such employee's gross misconduct), or reduction of hours, of the covered employee's employment.

(3) The divorce or legal separation of the covered employee from the employee's spouse.

(4) The covered employee becoming entitled to benefits under title XVIII of the Social Security Act [42 U.S.C. 1395 et seq.].

(5) A dependent child ceasing to be a dependent child under the generally applicable requirements of the plan.

(6) A proceeding in a case under title 11, commencing on or after July 1, 1986, with respect to the employer from whose employment the covered employee retired at any time.

In the case of an event described in paragraph (6), a loss of coverage includes a substantial elimination of coverage with respect to a qualified beneficiary described in section 1167(3)(C) of this title within one year before or after the date of commencement of the proceeding.

(Pub. L. 93–406, title I, § 603, as added Pub. L. 99–272, title X, § 10002(a), Apr. 7, 1986, 100 Stat. 229; amended Pub. L. 99–509, title IX, § 9501(a)(2), Oct. 21, 1986, 100 Stat. 2076.)

REFERENCES IN TEXT

The Social Security Act, referred to in par. (4), is act Aug. 14, 1935, ch. 531, 49 Stat. 620, as amended. Title XVIII of the Social Security Act is classified generally to subchapter XVIII (§ 1395 et seq.) of chapter 7 of Title 42, The Public Health and Welfare. For complete classification of this Act to the Code, see section 1305 of Title 42 and Tables.

AMENDMENTS

1986—Pub. L. 99–509 added par. (6) and last sentence.

EFFECTIVE DATE OF 1986 AMENDMENT

Amendment by Pub. L. 99–509 effective, except as otherwise provided, as if included in title X of the Consolidated Omnibus Budget Reconciliation Act of 1985, Pub. L. 99–272, see section 9501(e) of Pub. L. 99–509, set out as a note under section 162 of Title 26, Internal Revenue Code.

§ 1164. Applicable premium

For purposes of this part—

(1) In general

The term "applicable premium" means, with respect to any period of continuation coverage of qualified beneficiaries, the cost to the plan for such period of the coverage for similarly situated beneficiaries with respect to whom a qualifying event has not occurred (without regard to whether such cost is paid by the employer or employee).

(2) Special rule for self-insured plans

To the extent that a plan is a self-insured plan—

(A) In general

Except as provided in subparagraph (B), the applicable premium for any period of continuation coverage of qualified beneficiaries shall be equal to a reasonable estimate of the cost of providing coverage for such period for similarly situated beneficiaries which—

(i) is determined on an actuarial basis, and

(ii) takes into account such factors as the Secretary may prescribe in regulations.

(B) Determination on basis of past cost

If an administrator elects to have this subparagraph apply, the applicable premium for any period of continuation coverage of qualified beneficiaries shall be equal to—

(i) the cost to the plan for similarly situated beneficiaries for the same period occurring during the preceding determination period under paragraph (3), adjusted by

(ii) the percentage increase or decrease in the implicit price deflator of the gross national product (calculated by the Department of Commerce and published in the Survey of Current Business) for the 12-month period ending on the last day of the sixth month of such preceding determination period.

(C) Subparagraph (B) not to apply where significant change

An administrator may not elect to have subparagraph (B) apply in any case in which there is any significant difference, between the determination period and the preceding determination period, in coverage under, or in employees covered by, the plan. The determination under the preceding sentence for any determination period shall be made at the same time as the determination under paragraph (3).

(3) Determination period

The determination of any applicable premium shall be made for a period of 12 months and shall be made before the beginning of such period.

(Pub. L. 93–406, title I, § 604, as added Pub. L. 99–272, title X, § 10002(a), Apr. 7, 1986, 100 Stat. 229.)

§ 1165. Election

(a) In general

For purposes of this part—

(1) Election period

The term "election period" means the period which—

(A) begins not later than the date on which coverage terminates under the plan by reason of a qualifying event,

(B) is of at least 60 days' duration, and

(C) ends not earlier than 60 days after the later of—

(i) the date described in subparagraph (A), or

(ii) in the case of any qualified beneficiary who receives notice under section 1166(4)[1] of this title, the date of such notice.

(2) Effect of election on other beneficiaries

Except as otherwise specified in an election, any election of continuation coverage by a qualified beneficiary described in subparagraph (A)(i) or (B) of section 1167(3) of this title shall be deemed to include an election of continuation coverage on behalf of any other qualified beneficiary who would lose coverage under the plan by reason of the qualifying event. If there is a choice among types of coverage under the plan, each qualified beneficiary is entitled to make a separate selection among such types of coverage.

---

[1] See References in Text note below.

(b) Temporary extension of COBRA election period for certain individuals

(1) In general

In the case of a nonelecting TAA-eligible individual and notwithstanding subsection (a) of this section, such individual may elect continuation coverage under this part during the 60-day period that begins on the first day of the month in which the individual becomes a TAA-eligible individual, but only if such election is made not later than 6 months after the date of the TAA-related loss of coverage.

(2) Commencement of coverage; no reach-back

Any continuation coverage elected by a TAA-eligible individual under paragraph (1) shall commence at the beginning of the 60-day election period described in such paragraph and shall not include any period prior to such 60-day election period.

(3) Preexisting conditions

With respect to an individual who elects continuation coverage pursuant to paragraph (1), the period—

(A) beginning on the date of the TAA-related loss of coverage, and

(B) ending on the first day of the 60-day election period described in paragraph (1),

shall be disregarded for purposes of determining the 63-day periods referred to in section 1181(c)(2) of this title, section 300gg(c)(2) of title 42, and section 9801(c)(2) of title 26.

(4) Definitions

For purposes of this subsection:

(A) Nonelecting TAA-eligible individual

The term "nonelecting TAA-eligible individual" means a TAA-eligible individual who—

(i) has a TAA-related loss of coverage; and

(ii) did not elect continuation coverage under this part during the TAA-related election period.

(B) TAA-eligible individual

The term "TAA-eligible individual" means—

(i) an eligible TAA recipient (as defined in paragraph (2) of section 35(c) of title 26), and

(ii) an eligible alternative TAA recipient (as defined in paragraph (3) of such section).

(C) TAA-related election period

The term "TAA-related election period" means, with respect to a TAA-related loss of coverage, the 60-day election period under this part which is a direct consequence of such loss.

(D) TAA-related loss of coverage

The term "TAA-related loss of coverage" means, with respect to an individual whose separation from employment gives rise to being an TAA-eligible individual, the loss of health benefits coverage associated with such separation.

(Pub. L. 93–406, title I, §605, as added Pub. L. 99–272, title X, §10002(a), Apr. 7, 1986, 100 Stat. 230; amended Pub. L. 99–514, title XVIII, §1895(d)(5)(B), Oct. 22, 1986, 100 Stat. 2939; Pub. L. 107–210, div. A, title II, §203(e)(1), Aug. 6, 2002, 116 Stat. 969.)

REFERENCES IN TEXT

Section 1166(4) of this title, referred to in subsec. (a)(1)(C)(ii), was redesignated as section 1166(a)(4) of this title by Pub. L. 101–239, title VII, §7891(d)(1)(A)(ii)(I), Dec. 19, 1989, 103 Stat. 2445.

AMENDMENTS

2002—Pub. L. 107–210 designated existing provisions as subsec. (a), inserted heading, and added subsec. (b).

1986—Par. (2). Pub. L. 99–514 inserted "of continuation coverage" after "any election" and inserted at end "If there is a choice among types of coverage under the plan, each qualified beneficiary is entitled to make a separate selection among such types of coverage."

EFFECTIVE DATE OF 2002 AMENDMENT

Amendment by Pub. L. 107–210 applicable to petitions for certification filed under part 2 or 3 of subchapter II of chapter 12 of Title 19, Customs Duties, on or after the date that is 90 days after Aug. 6, 2002, except as otherwise provided, see section 151 of Pub. L. 107–210, set out as a note preceding section 2271 of Title 19.

EFFECTIVE DATE OF 1986 AMENDMENT

Amendment by Pub. L. 99–514 effective, except as otherwise provided, as if included in enactment of the Consolidated Omnibus Budget Reconciliation Act of 1985, Pub. L. 99–272, see section 1895(e) of Pub. L. 99–514, set out as a note under section 162 of Title 26, Internal Revenue Code.

CONSTRUCTION OF 2002 AMENDMENT

Nothing in amendment by Pub. L. 107–210, other than provisions relating to COBRA continuation coverage and reporting requirements, to be construed as creating new mandate on any party regarding health insurance coverage, see section 203(f) of Pub. L. 107–210, set out as a note under section 2918 of this title.

PLAN AMENDMENTS NOT REQUIRED UNTIL JANUARY 1, 1989

For provisions directing that if any amendments made by subtitle A or subtitle C of title XI [§§1101–1147 and 1171–1177] or title XVIII [§§1800–1899A] of Pub. L. 99–514 require an amendment to any plan, such plan amendment shall not be required to be made before the first plan year beginning on or after Jan. 1, 1989, see section 1140 of Pub. L. 99–514, as amended, set out as a note under section 401 of Title 26, Internal Revenue Code.

§1166. Notice requirements

(a) In general

In accordance with regulations prescribed by the Secretary—

(1) the group health plan shall provide, at the time of commencement of coverage under the plan, written notice to each covered employee and spouse of the employee (if any) of the rights provided under this subsection,

(2) the employer of an employee under a plan must notify the administrator of a qualifying event described in paragraph (1), (2), (4), or (6) of section 1163 of this title within 30 days (or, in the case of a group health plan which is a multiemployer plan, such longer period of time as may be provided in the terms of the plan) of the date of the qualifying event,

(3) each covered employee or qualified beneficiary is responsible for notifying the admin-

istrator of the occurrence of any qualifying event described in paragraph (3) or (5) of section 1163 of this title within 60 days after the date of the qualifying event and each qualified beneficiary who is determined, under title II or XVI of the Social Security Act [42 U.S.C. 401 et seq., 1381 et seq.], to have been disabled at any time during the first 60 days of continuation coverage under this part is responsible for notifying the plan administrator of such determination within 60 days after the date of the determination and for notifying the plan administrator within 30 days after the date of any final determination under such title or titles that the qualified beneficiary is no longer disabled, and

(4) the administrator shall notify—

(A) in the case of a qualifying event described in paragraph (1), (2), (4), or (6) of section 1163 of this title, any qualified beneficiary with respect to such event, and

(B) in the case of a qualifying event described in paragraph (3) or (5) of section 1163 of this title where the covered employee notifies the administrator under paragraph (3), any qualified beneficiary with respect to such event,

of such beneficiary's rights under this subsection.

(b) Alternative means of compliance with requirements for notification of multiemployer plans by employers

The requirements of subsection (a)(2) of this section shall be considered satisfied in the case of a multiemployer plan in connection with a qualifying event described in paragraph (2) of section 1163 of this title if the plan provides that the determination of the occurrence of such qualifying event will be made by the plan administrator.

(c) Rules relating to notification of qualified beneficiaries by plan administrator

For purposes of subsection (a)(4) of this section, any notification shall be made within 14 days (or, in the case of a group health plan which is a multiemployer plan, such longer period of time as may be provided in the terms of the plan) of the date on which the administrator is notified under paragraph (2) or (3), whichever is applicable, and any such notification to an individual who is a qualified beneficiary as the spouse of the covered employee shall be treated as notification to all other qualified beneficiaries residing with such spouse at the time such notification is made.

(Pub. L. 93–406, title I, § 606, as added Pub. L. 99–272, title X, § 10002(a), Apr. 7, 1986, 100 Stat. 230; amended Pub. L. 99–509, title IX, § 9501(d)(2), Oct. 21, 1986, 100 Stat. 2077; Pub. L. 99–514, title XVIII, § 1895(d)(6)(B), Oct. 22, 1986, 100 Stat. 2939; Pub. L. 101–239, title VI, § 6703(c), title VII, § 7891(d)(1)(A), Dec. 19, 1989, 103 Stat. 2296, 2445; Pub. L. 104–191, title IV, § 421(b)(2), Aug. 21, 1996, 110 Stat. 2088.)

REFERENCES IN TEXT

The Social Security Act, referred to in subsec. (a)(3), is act Aug. 14, 1935, ch. 531, 49 Stat. 620, as amended. Titles II and XVI of the Social Security Act are classified generally to subchapters II (§ 401 et seq.) and XVI (§ 1381 et seq.), respectively, of chapter 7 of Title 42, The Public Health and Welfare. For complete classification of this Act to the Code, see section 1305 of Title 42 and Tables.

AMENDMENTS

1996—Subsec. (a)(3). Pub. L. 104–191 substituted "at any time during the first 60 days of continuation coverage under this part" for "at the time of a qualifying event described in section 1163(2) of this title".

1989—Pub. L. 101–239, § 7891(d)(1)(A)(ii), designated first sentence as subsec. (a), added subsec. (b), designated second sentence as subsec. (c), and substituted "For purposes of subsection (a)(4) of this section" for "For purposes of paragraph (4)".

Pub. L. 101–239, § 7891(d)(1)(A)(i)(II), inserted in last sentence "(or, in the case of a group health plan which is a multiemployer plan, such longer period of time as may be provided in the terms of the plan)" after "14 days".

Pub. L. 101–239, § 7891(d)(1)(A)(i)(I), inserted "(or, in the case of a group health plan which is a multiemployer plan, such longer period of time as may be provided in the terms of the plan)" after "30 days" in par. (2).

Pub. L. 101–239, § 6703(c), inserted "and each qualified beneficiary who is determined, under title II or XVI of the Social Security Act, to have been disabled at the time of a qualifying event described in section 1163(2) of this title is responsible for notifying the plan administrator of such determination within 60 days after the date of the determination and for notifying the plan administrator within 30 days after the date of any final determination under such title or titles that the qualified beneficiary is no longer disabled" before comma in par. (3).

1986—Par. (2). Pub. L. 99–509 substituted "(4), or (6)" for "or (4)".

Par. (3). Pub. L. 99–514 inserted "within 60 days after the date of the qualifying event".

Par. (4)(A). Pub. L. 99–509 substituted "(4), or (6)" for "or (4)".

EFFECTIVE DATE OF 1996 AMENDMENT

Amendment by Pub. L. 104–191 effective Jan. 1, 1997, regardless of whether qualifying event occurred before, on, or after such date, see section 421(d) of Pub. L. 104–191 set out as a note under section 4980B of Title 26, Internal Revenue Code.

EFFECTIVE DATE OF 1989 AMENDMENT

Amendment by section 6703(c) of Pub. L. 101–239 applicable to plan years beginning on or after Dec. 19, 1989, regardless of whether the qualifying event occurred before, on, or after such date, see section 6703(d) of Pub. L. 101–239, set out as a note under section 1162 of this title.

Amendment by section 7891(d)(1)(A) of Pub. L. 101–239 applicable with respect to plan years beginning on or after Jan. 1, 1990, see section 7891(d)(1)(C) of Pub. L. 101–239, set out as a note under section 4980B of Title 26, Internal Revenue Code.

EFFECTIVE DATE OF 1986 AMENDMENTS

Amendment by Pub. L. 99–514 applicable only with respect to qualifying events occurring after Oct. 22, 1986, see section 1895(d)(6)(D) of Pub. L. 99–514, set out as a note under section 162 of Title 26, Internal Revenue Code.

Amendment by Pub. L. 99–509 effective, except as otherwise provided, as if included in title X of the Consolidated Omnibus Budget Reconciliation Act of 1985, Pub. L. 99–272, see section 9501(e) of Pub. L. 99–509, set out as a note under section 162 of Title 26.

PLAN AMENDMENTS NOT REQUIRED UNTIL JANUARY 1, 1989

For provisions directing that if any amendments made by subtitle A or subtitle C of title XI [§§ 1101–1147 and 1171–1177] or title XVIII [§§1800–1899A] of Pub. L. 99–514 require an amendment to any plan, such plan amendment shall not be required to be made before the first plan year beginning on or after Jan. 1, 1989, see section 1140 of Pub. L. 99–514, as amended, set out as a note under section 401 of Title 26, Internal Revenue Code.

NOTIFICATION TO COVERED EMPLOYEES

Section 10002(e) of Pub. L. 99–272 provided that: "At the time that the amendments made by this section [enacting this part and amending section 1132 of this title] apply to a group health plan (within the meaning of section 607(1) of the Employee Retirement Income Security Act of 1974 [29 U.S.C. 1167(1)]), the plan shall notify each covered employee, and spouse of the employee (if any), who is covered under the plan at that time of the continuation coverage required under part 6 of subtitle B of title I of such Act [this part]. The notice furnished under this subsection is in lieu of notice that may otherwise be required under section 606(1) of such Act [29 U.S.C. 1166(1)] with respect to such individuals."

§1167. Definitions and special rules

For purposes of this part—

(1) Group health plan

The term "group health plan" means an employee welfare benefit plan providing medical care (as defined in section 213(d) of title 26) to participants or beneficiaries directly or through insurance, reimbursement, or otherwise. Such term shall not include any plan substantially all of the coverage under which is for qualified long-term care services (as defined in section 7702B(c) of title 26).

(2) Covered employee

The term "covered employee" means an individual who is (or was) provided coverage under a group health plan by virtue of the performance of services by the individual for 1 or more persons maintaining the plan (including as an employee defined in section 401(c)(1) of title 26).

(3) Qualified beneficiary

(A) In general

The term "qualified beneficiary" means, with respect to a covered employee under a group health plan, any other individual who, on the day before the qualifying event for that employee, is a beneficiary under the plan—

(i) as the spouse of the covered employee, or

(ii) as the dependent child of the employee.

Such term shall also include a child who is born to or placed for adoption with the covered employee during the period of continuation coverage under this part.

(B) Special rule for terminations and reduced employment

In the case of a qualifying event described in section 1163(2) of this title, the term "qualified beneficiary" includes the covered employee.

(C) Special rule for retirees and widows

In the case of a qualifying event described in section 1163(6) of this title, the term "qualified beneficiary" includes a covered employee who had retired on or before the date of substantial elimination of coverage and any other individual who, on the day before such qualifying event, is a beneficiary under the plan—

(i) as the spouse of the covered employee,

(ii) as the dependent child of the employee, or

(iii) as the surviving spouse of the covered employee.

(4) Employer

Subsection (n) (relating to leased employees) and subsection (t) (relating to application of controlled group rules to certain employee benefits) of section 414 of title 26 shall apply for purposes of this part in the same manner and to the same extent as such subsections apply for purposes of section 106 of title 26. Any regulations prescribed by the Secretary pursuant to the preceding sentence shall be consistent and coextensive with any regulations prescribed for similar purposes by the Secretary of the Treasury (or such Secretary's delegate) under such subsections.

(5) Optional extension of required periods

A group health plan shall not be treated as failing to meet the requirements of this part solely because the plan provides both—

(A) that the period of extended coverage referred to in section 1162(2) of this title commences with the date of the loss of coverage, and

(B) that the applicable notice period provided under section 1166(a)(2) of this title commences with the date of the loss of coverage.

(Pub. L. 93–406, title I, §607, as added Pub. L. 99–272, title X, §10002(a), Apr. 7, 1986, 100 Stat. 231; amended Pub. L. 99–509, title IX, §9501(c)(2), Oct. 21, 1986, 100 Stat. 2077; Pub. L. 99–514, title XVIII, §1895(d)(8), (9)(A), Oct. 22, 1986, 100 Stat. 2940; Pub. L. 100–647, title III, §3011(b)(6), Nov. 10, 1988, 102 Stat. 3625; Pub. L. 101–239, title VII, §§7862(c)(2)(A), (6)(A), 7891(a)(1), (d)(2)(B)(i), Dec. 19, 1989, 103 Stat. 2432, 2433, 2445, 2446; Pub. L. 104–191, title III, §321(d)(2), title IV, §421(b)(3), Aug. 21, 1996, 110 Stat. 2058, 2088.)

AMENDMENTS

1996—Par. (1). Pub. L. 104–191, §321(d)(2), inserted at end "Such term shall not include any plan substantially all of the coverage under which is for qualified long-term care services (as defined in section 7702B(c) of title 26)."

Par. (3)(A). Pub. L. 104–191, §421(b)(3), inserted at end "Such term shall also include a child who is born to or placed for adoption with the covered employee during the period of continuation coverage under this part."

1989—Pub. L. 101–239, §7891(d)(2)(B)(i)(I), inserted "and special rules" after "Definitions" in section catchline.

Par. (1). Pub. L. 101–239, §7862(c)(6)(A), repealed Pub. L. 100–647, §3011(b)(6), see 1988 Amendment note below.

Pub. L. 101–239, §7891(a)(1), substituted "Internal Revenue Code of 1986" for "Internal Revenue Code of 1954", which for purposes of codification was translated as "title 26" thus requiring no change in text.

Par. (2). Pub. L. 101–239, §7862(c)(2)(A), substituted "the performance of services by the individual for 1 or more persons maintaining the plan (including as an employee defined in section 401(c)(1) of title 26)" for "the individual's employment or previous employment with an employer".

Par. (5). Pub. L. 101–239, § 7891(d)(2)(B)(i)(II), added par. (5).

1988—Par. (1). Pub. L. 100–647, § 3011(b)(6), which directed amendment of par. (1) by substituting "section 162(i)(2) of title 26" for "section 162(i)(3) of title 26", was repealed by Pub. L. 101–239, § 7862(c)(6)(A).

Pub. L. 99–514, § 1895(d)(8), amended par. (1) generally. Prior to amendment, par. (1) read as follows: "The term 'group health plan' means an employee welfare benefit plan that is a group health plan (within the meaning of section 162(i)(3) of title 26)."

Par. (3)(C). Pub. L. 99–509 added subpar. (C).

Par. (4). Pub. L. 99–514, § 1895(d)(9)(A), added par. (4).

EFFECTIVE DATE OF 1996 AMENDMENT

Amendment by section 321(d)(2) of Pub. L. 104–191 applicable to contracts issued after Dec. 31, 1996, see section 321(f) of Pub. L. 104–191, set out as an Effective Date note under section 7702B of Title 26, Internal Revenue Code.

Amendment by section 421(b)(3) of Pub. L. 104–191 effective Jan. 1, 1997, regardless of whether qualifying event occurred before, on, or after such date, see section 421(d) of Pub. L. 104–191 set out as a note under section 4980B of Title 26.

EFFECTIVE DATE OF 1989 AMENDMENT

Amendment by section 7862(c)(2)(A) of Pub. L. 101–239 applicable to plan years beginning after Dec. 31, 1989, see section 7862(c)(2)(C) of Pub. L. 101–239, set out as a note under section 4980B of Title 26, Internal Revenue Code.

Section 7862(c)(6)(B) of Pub. L. 101–239 provided that: "Subparagraph (A) [repealing section 3011(b)(6) of Pub. L. 100–647, which amended this section] shall be effective as if included in the enactment of section 3011(b) of the Technical and Miscellaneous Revenue Act of 1988 [Pub. L. 100–647]."

Amendment by section 7891(a)(1) of Pub. L. 101–239 effective, except as otherwise provided, as if included in the provision of the Tax Reform Act of 1986, Pub. L. 99–514, to which such amendment relates, see section 7891(f) of Pub. L. 101–239, set out as a note under section 1002 of this title.

Amendment by section 7891(d)(2)(B)(i) of Pub. L. 101–239 applicable with respect to plan years beginning on or after Jan. 1, 1990, see section 7891(d)(2)(C) of Pub. L. 101–239, set out as a note under section 4980B of Title 26, Internal Revenue Code.

EFFECTIVE DATE OF 1988 AMENDMENT

Amendment by Pub. L. 100–647 applicable to taxable years beginning after Dec. 31, 1988, but not applicable to any plan for any plan year to which section 162(k) of Title 26, Internal Revenue Code (as in effect on the day before Nov. 10, 1988) did not apply by reason of section 10001(e)(2) of Pub. L. 99–272, see section 3011(d) of Pub. L. 100–647, set out as a note under section 162 of Title 26.

EFFECTIVE DATE OF 1986 AMENDMENTS

Section 1895(d)(9)(B) of Pub. L. 99–514 provided that: "The amendment made by subparagraph (A) [amending this section] shall take effect in the same manner and to the same extent as the amendments made by subsections (e) and (i) of section 1151 of this Act [amending sections 132 and 414 of Title 26, Internal Revenue Code, see section 1151(k) of Pub. L. 99–514, set out as an Effective Date note under section 89 of Title 26]."

Amendment by section 1895(d)(8) of Pub. L. 99–514 effective, except as otherwise provided, as if included in enactment of the Consolidated Omnibus Budget Reconciliation Act of 1985, Pub. L. 99–272, see section 1895(e) of Pub. L. 99–514, set out as a note under section 162 of Title 26.

Amendment by Pub. L. 99–509 effective, except as otherwise provided, as if included in title X of the Consolidated Omnibus Budget Reconciliation Act of 1985, Pub. L. 99–272, see section 9501(e) of Pub. L. 99–509, set out as a note under section 162 of Title 26.

PLAN AMENDMENTS NOT REQUIRED UNTIL JANUARY 1, 1989

For provisions directing that if any amendments made by subtitle A or subtitle C of title XI [§§ 1101–1147 and 1171–1177] or title XVIII [§§ 1800–1899A] of Pub. L. 99–514 require an amendment to any plan, such plan amendment shall not be required to be made before the first plan year beginning on or after Jan. 1, 1989, see section 1140 of Pub. L. 99–514, as amended, set out as a note under section 401 of Title 26, Internal Revenue Code.

§ 1168. Regulations

The Secretary may prescribe regulations to carry out the provisions of this part.

(Pub. L. 93–406, title I, § 608, as added Pub. L. 99–272, title X, § 10002(a), Apr. 7, 1986, 100 Stat. 231.)

§ 1169. Additional standards for group health plans

(a) Group health plan coverage pursuant to medical child support orders

(1) In general

Each group health plan shall provide benefits in accordance with the applicable requirements of any qualified medical child support order. A qualified medical child support order with respect to any participant or beneficiary shall be deemed to apply to each group health plan which has received such order, from which the participant or beneficiary is eligible to receive benefits, and with respect to which the requirements of paragraph (4) are met.

(2) Definitions

For purposes of this subsection—

(A) Qualified medical child support order

The term "qualified medical child support order" means a medical child support order—

(i) which creates or recognizes the existence of an alternate recipient's right to, or assigns to an alternate recipient the right to, receive benefits for which a participant or beneficiary is eligible under a group health plan, and

(ii) with respect to which the requirements of paragraphs (3) and (4) are met.

(B) Medical child support order

The term "medical child support order" means any judgment, decree, or order (including approval of a settlement agreement) which—

(i) provides for child support with respect to a child of a participant under a group health plan or provides for health benefit coverage to such a child, is made pursuant to a State domestic relations law (including a community property law), and relates to benefits under such plan, or

(ii) is made pursuant to a law relating to medical child support described in section 1908 of the Social Security Act [42 U.S.C. 1396g–1] (as added by section 13822[1] of the

[1] So in original. Probably should be section "13623".

Omnibus Budget Reconciliation Act of 1993) with respect to a group health plan,

if such judgment, decree, or order (I) is issued by a court of competent jurisdiction or (II) is issued through an administrative process established under State law and has the force and effect of law under applicable State law. For purposes of this subparagraph, an administrative notice which is issued pursuant to an administrative process referred to in subclause (II) of the preceding sentence and which has the effect of an order described in clause (i) or (ii) of the preceding sentence shall be treated as such an order.

(C) Alternate recipient

The term "alternate recipient" means any child of a participant who is recognized under a medical child support order as having a right to enrollment under a group health plan with respect to such participant.

(D) Child

The term "child" includes any child adopted by, or placed for adoption with, a participant of a group health plan.

(3) Information to be included in qualified order

A medical child support order meets the requirements of this paragraph only if such order clearly specifies—

(A) the name and the last known mailing address (if any) of the participant and the name and mailing address of each alternate recipient covered by the order, except that, to the extent provided in the order, the name and mailing address of an official of a State or a political subdivision thereof may be substituted for the mailing address of any such alternate recipient,

(B) a reasonable description of the type of coverage to be provided to each such alternate recipient, or the manner in which such type of coverage is to be determined, and

(C) the period to which such order applies.

(4) Restriction on new types or forms of benefits

A medical child support order meets the requirements of this paragraph only if such order does not require a plan to provide any type or form of benefit, or any option, not otherwise provided under the plan, except to the extent necessary to meet the requirements of a law relating to medical child support described in section 1908 of the Social Security Act [42 U.S.C. 1396g–1] (as added by section 13822[1] of the Omnibus Budget Reconciliation Act of 1993).

(5) Procedural requirements

(A) Timely notifications and determinations

In the case of any medical child support order received by a group health plan—

(i) the plan administrator shall promptly notify the participant and each alternate recipient of the receipt of such order and the plan's procedures for determining whether medical child support orders are qualified medical child support orders, and

(ii) within a reasonable period after receipt of such order, the plan administrator shall determine whether such order is a qualified medical child support order and notify the participant and each alternate recipient of such determination.

(B) Establishment of procedures for determining qualified status of orders

Each group health plan shall establish reasonable procedures to determine whether medical child support orders are qualified medical child support orders and to administer the provision of benefits under such qualified orders. Such procedures—

(i) shall be in writing,

(ii) shall provide for the notification of each person specified in a medical child support order as eligible to receive benefits under the plan (at the address included in the medical child support order) of such procedures promptly upon receipt by the plan of the medical child support order, and

(iii) shall permit an alternate recipient to designate a representative for receipt of copies of notices that are sent to the alternate recipient with respect to a medical child support order.

(C) National Medical Support Notice deemed to be a qualified medical child support order

(i) In general

If the plan administrator of a group health plan which is maintained by the employer of a noncustodial parent of a child or to which such an employer contributes receives an appropriately completed National Medical Support Notice promulgated pursuant to section 401(b) of the Child Support Performance and Incentive Act of 1998 in the case of such child, and the Notice meets the requirements of paragraphs (3) and (4), the Notice shall be deemed to be a qualified medical child support order in the case of such child.

(ii) Enrollment of child in plan

In any case in which an appropriately completed National Medical Support Notice is issued in the case of a child of a participant under a group health plan who is a noncustodial parent of the child, and the Notice is deemed under clause (i) to be a qualified medical child support order, the plan administrator, within 40 business days after the date of the Notice, shall—

(I) notify the State agency issuing the Notice with respect to such child whether coverage of the child is available under the terms of the plan and, if so, whether such child is covered under the plan and either the effective date of the coverage or, if necessary, any steps to be taken by the custodial parent (or by the official of a State or political subdivision thereof substituted for the name of such child pursuant to paragraph (3)(A)) to effectuate the coverage; and

(II) provide to the custodial parent (or such substituted official) a description of the coverage available and any forms or documents necessary to effectuate such coverage.

(iii) **Rule of construction**

Nothing in this subparagraph shall be construed as requiring a group health plan, upon receipt of a National Medical Support Notice, to provide benefits under the plan (or eligibility for such benefits) in addition to benefits (or eligibility for benefits) provided under the terms of the plan as of immediately before receipt of such Notice.

(6) Actions taken by fiduciaries

If a plan fiduciary acts in accordance with part 4 of this subtitle in treating a medical child support order as being (or not being) a qualified medical child support order, then the plan's obligation to the participant and each alternate recipient shall be discharged to the extent of any payment made pursuant to such act of the fiduciary.

(7) Treatment of alternate recipients

(A) Treatment as beneficiary generally

A person who is an alternate recipient under a qualified medical child support order shall be considered a beneficiary under the plan for purposes of any provision of this chapter.

(B) Treatment as participant for purposes of reporting and disclosure requirements

A person who is an alternate recipient under any medical child support order shall be considered a participant under the plan for purposes of the reporting and disclosure requirements of part 1 of this subtitle.

(8) Direct provision of benefits provided to alternate recipients

Any payment for benefits made by a group health plan pursuant to a medical child support order in reimbursement for expenses paid by an alternate recipient or an alternate recipient's custodial parent or legal guardian shall be made to the alternate recipient or the alternate recipient's custodial parent or legal guardian.

(9) Payment to State official treated as satisfaction of plan's obligation to make payment to alternate recipient

Payment of benefits by a group health plan to an official of a State or a political subdivision thereof whose name and address have been substituted for the address of an alternate recipient in a qualified medical child support order, pursuant to paragraph (3)(A), shall be treated, for purposes of this subchapter, as payment of benefits to the alternate recipient.

(b) Rights of States with respect to group health plans where participants or beneficiaries thereunder are eligible for medicaid benefits

(1) Compliance by plans with assignment of rights

A group health plan shall provide that payment for benefits with respect to a participant under the plan will be made in accordance with any assignment of rights made by or on behalf of such participant or a beneficiary of the participant as required by a State plan for medical assistance approved under title XIX of the Social Security Act [42 U.S.C. 1396 et seq.] pursuant to section 1912(a)(1)(A) of such Act [42 U.S.C. 1396k(a)(1)(A)] (as in effect on August 10, 1993).

(2) Enrollment and provision of benefits without regard to medicaid eligibility

A group health plan shall provide that, in enrolling an individual as a participant or beneficiary or in determining or making any payments for benefits of an individual as a participant or beneficiary, the fact that the individual is eligible for or is provided medical assistance under a State plan for medical assistance approved under title XIX of the Social Security Act [42 U.S.C. 1396 et seq.] will not be taken into account.

(3) Acquisition by States of rights of third parties

A group health plan shall provide that, to the extent that payment has been made under a State plan for medical assistance approved under title XIX of the Social Security Act [42 U.S.C. 1396 et seq.] in any case in which a group health plan has a legal liability to make payment for items or services constituting such assistance, payment for benefits under the plan will be made in accordance with any State law which provides that the State has acquired the rights with respect to a participant to such payment for such items or services.

(c) Group health plan coverage of dependent children in cases of adoption

(1) Coverage effective upon placement for adoption

In any case in which a group health plan provides coverage for dependent children of participants or beneficiaries, such plan shall provide benefits to dependent children placed with participants or beneficiaries for adoption under the same terms and conditions as apply in the case of dependent children who are natural children of participants or beneficiaries under the plan, irrespective of whether the adoption has become final.

(2) Restrictions based on preexisting conditions at time of placement for adoption prohibited

A group health plan may not restrict coverage under the plan of any dependent child adopted by a participant or beneficiary, or placed with a participant or beneficiary for adoption, solely on the basis of a preexisting condition of such child at the time that such child would otherwise become eligible for coverage under the plan, if the adoption or placement for adoption occurs while the participant or beneficiary is eligible for coverage under the plan.

(3) Definitions

For purposes of this subsection—

(A) Child

The term "child" means, in connection with any adoption, or placement for adoption, of the child, an individual who has not attained age 18 as of the date of such adoption or placement for adoption.

(B) Placement for adoption

The term "placement", or being "placed", for adoption, in connection with any placement for adoption of a child with any person, means the assumption and retention by such person of a legal obligation for total or partial support of such child in anticipation of adoption of such child. The child's placement with such person terminates upon the termination of such legal obligation.

(d) Continued coverage of costs of a pediatric vaccine under group health plans

A group health plan may not reduce its coverage of the costs of pediatric vaccines (as defined under section 1928(h)(6) of the Social Security Act [42 U.S.C. 1396s(h)(6)] as amended by section 13830[2] of the Omnibus Budget Reconciliation Act of 1993) below the coverage it provided as of May 1, 1993.

(e) Regulations

Any regulations prescribed under this section shall be prescribed by the Secretary of Labor, in consultation with the Secretary of Health and Human Services.

(Pub. L. 93–406, title I, § 609, as added Pub. L. 103–66, title IV, § 4301(a), Aug. 10, 1993, 107 Stat. 371; amended Pub. L. 104–193, title III, § 381(a), Aug. 22, 1996, 110 Stat. 2257; Pub. L. 105–33, title V, §§ 5611(a), (b), 5612(a), 5613(a), (b), Aug. 5, 1997, 111 Stat. 647, 648; Pub. L. 105–200, title IV, § 401(d), (h)(2)(A)(iii), (B), (3)(A), July 16, 1998, 112 Stat. 662, 668.)

REFERENCES IN TEXT

Section 401(b) of the Child Support Performance and Incentive Act of 1998, referred to in subsec. (a)(5)(C)(i), is section 401(b) of Pub. L. 105–200, which is set out as a note under section 651 of Title 42, The Public Health and Welfare.

This chapter, referred to in subsec. (a)(7)(A), was in the original "this Act", meaning Pub. L. 93–406, known as the Employee Retirement Income Security Act of 1974. Titles I, III, and IV of such Act are classified principally to this chapter. For complete classification of this Act to the Code, see Short Title note set out under section 1001 of this title and Tables.

The Social Security Act, referred to in subsec. (b), is act Aug. 14, 1935, ch. 531, 49 Stat. 620, as amended. Title XIX of the Act is classified generally to subchapter XIX (§ 1396 et seq.) of chapter 7 of Title 42, The Public Health and Welfare. For complete classification of this Act to the Code, see section 1305 of Title 42 and Tables.

AMENDMENTS

1998—Subsec. (a)(2)(B)(ii). Pub. L. 105–200, § 401(h)(2)(A)(iii), substituted "is made pursuant to" for "enforces".

Subsec. (a)(2)(D). Pub. L. 105–200, § 401(h)(2)(B), added subpar. (D).

Subsec. (a)(5)(C). Pub. L. 105–200, § 401(d), added subpar. (C).

Subsec. (a)(9). Pub. L. 105–200, § 401(h)(3)(A), substituted "the address of an alternate recipient" for "the name and address of an alternate recipient".

1997—Subsec. (a)(1). Pub. L. 105–33, § 5613(b), inserted at end "A qualified medical child support order with respect to any participant or beneficiary shall be deemed to apply to each group health plan which has received such order, from which the participant or beneficiary is eligible to receive benefits, and with respect to which the requirements of paragraph (4) are met."

Subsec. (a)(2)(B). Pub. L. 105–33, § 5612(a), inserted at end of concluding provisions "For purposes of this subparagraph, an administrative notice which is issued pursuant to an administrative process referred to in subclause (II) of the preceding sentence and which has the effect of an order described in clause (i) or (ii) of the preceding sentence shall be treated as such an order."

Subsec. (a)(3)(A). Pub. L. 105–33, § 5611(a), inserted at end "except that, to the extent provided in the order, the name and mailing address of an official of a State or a political subdivision thereof may be substituted for the mailing address of any such alternate recipient,".

Subsec. (a)(3)(B). Pub. L. 105–33, § 5613(a)(1), (2), struck out "by the plan" after "to be provided" and inserted "and" at end.

Subsec. (a)(3)(C). Pub. L. 105–33, § 5613(a)(3), substituted a period for ", and" at end.

Subsec. (a)(3)(D). Pub. L. 105–33, § 5613(a)(4), struck out subpar. (D) which read as follows: "each plan to which such order applies."

Subsec. (a)(9). Pub. L. 105–33, § 5611(b), added par. (9).

1996—Subsec. (a)(2)(B). Pub. L. 104–193 substituted "which—" for "issued by a court of competent jurisdiction which—" in introductory provisions, substituted a comma for a period at end of cl. (ii), and inserted concluding provisions after cl. (ii).

EFFECTIVE DATE OF 1998 AMENDMENT

Amendment by section 401(h)(2)(A)(iii) of Pub. L. 105–200 effective as if included in the enactment of section 4301(c)(4)(A) of the Omnibus Budget Reconciliation Act of 1993, Pub. L. 103–66, see section 401(h)(2)(C) of Pub. L. 105–200, set out as a note under section 1144 of this title.

Pub. L. 105–200, title IV, § 401(h)(3)(B), July 16, 1998, 112 Stat. 668, provided that: "The amendment made by subparagraph (A) [amending this section] shall be effective as if included in the enactment of section 5611(b) of the Balanced Budget Act of 1997 [Pub. L. 105–33]."

EFFECTIVE DATE OF 1997 AMENDMENT

Section 5611(c) of Pub. L. 105–33 provided that: "The amendments made by this section [amending this section] shall apply with respect to medical child support orders issued on or after the date of the enactment of this Act [Aug. 5, 1997]."

Section 5612(b) of Pub. L. 105–33 provided that: "The amendment made by this section [amending this section] shall be effective as if included in the enactment of section 381 of the Personal Responsibility and Work Opportunity Reconciliation Act of 1996 (Public Law 104–193; 110 Stat. 2257)."

Section 5613(c) of Pub. L. 105–33 provided that: "The amendments made by this section [amending this section] shall apply with respect to medical child support orders issued on or after the date of the enactment of this Act [Aug. 5, 1997]."

EFFECTIVE DATE OF 1996 AMENDMENT

Section 381(b) of Pub. L. 104–193 provided that:

"(1) IN GENERAL.—The amendments made by this section [amending this section] shall take effect on the date of the enactment of this Act [Aug. 22, 1996].

"(2) PLAN AMENDMENTS NOT REQUIRED UNTIL JANUARY 1, 1997.—Any amendment to a plan required to be made by an amendment made by this section shall not be required to be made before the 1st plan year beginning on or after January 1, 1997, if—

"(A) during the period after the date before the date of the enactment of this Act and before such 1st plan year, the plan is operated in accordance with the requirements of the amendments made by this section; and

"(B) such plan amendment applies retroactively to the period after the date before the date of the enactment of this Act and before such 1st plan year.

A plan shall not be treated as failing to be operated in accordance with the provisions of the plan merely because it operates in accordance with this paragraph."

[2] So in original. Probably should be section "13631".

[For provisions relating to effective date of title III of Pub. L. 104–193, see section 395(a)–(c) of Pub. L. 104–193, set out as a note under section 654 of Title 42, The Public Health and Welfare.]

NATIONAL MEDICAL SUPPORT NOTICES FOR HEALTH PLANS; QUALIFIED MEDICAL CHILD SUPPORT ORDERS

Pub. L. 105–200, title IV, §401(e)–(g), July 16, 1998, 112 Stat. 663–668, as amended by Pub. L. 109–171, title VII, §7307(a)(2)(B), (C), Feb. 8, 2006, 120 Stat. 146, provided that:

"(e) NATIONAL MEDICAL SUPPORT NOTICES FOR STATE OR LOCAL GOVERNMENTAL GROUP HEALTH PLANS.—

"(1) IN GENERAL.—Each State or local governmental group health plan shall provide benefits in accordance with the applicable requirements of any National Medical Support Notice.

"(2) ENROLLMENT OF CHILD IN PLAN.—In any case in which an appropriately completed National Medical Support Notice is issued in the case of a child of a participant under a State or local governmental group health plan, the plan administrator, within 40 business days after the date of the Notice, shall—

"(A) notify the State agency issuing the Notice with respect to such child whether coverage of the child is available under the terms of the plan and, if so, whether such child is covered under the plan and either the effective date of the coverage or any steps necessary to be taken by the custodial parent (or by any official of a State or political subdivision thereof substituted in the Notice for the name of such child in accordance with procedures appliable [sic] under subsection (b)(2) of this section [section 401(b)(2) of Pub. L. 105–200, 42 U.S.C. 651 note]) to effectuate the coverage; and

"(B) provide to the custodial parent (or such substituted official) a description of the coverage available and any forms or documents necessary to effectuate such coverage.

"(3) RULE OF CONSTRUCTION.—Nothing in this subsection shall be construed as requiring a State or local governmental group health plan, upon receipt of a National Medical Support Notice, to provide benefits under the plan (or eligibility for such benefits) in addition to benefits (or eligibility for benefits) provided under the terms of the plan as of immediately before receipt of such Notice.

"(4) DEFINITIONS.—For purposes of this subsection—

"(A) STATE OR LOCAL GOVERNMENTAL GROUP HEALTH PLAN.—The term 'State or local governmental group health plan' means a group health plan which is established or maintained for its employees by the government of any State, any political subdivision of a State, or any agency or instrumentality of either of the foregoing.

"(B) ALTERNATE RECIPIENT.—The term 'alternate recipient' means any child of a participant who is recognized under a National Medical Support Notice as having a right to enrollment under a State or local governmental group health plan with respect to such participant.

"(C) GROUP HEALTH PLAN.—The term 'group health plan' has the meaning provided in section 607(1) of the Employee Retirement Income Security Act of 1974 [29 U.S.C. 1167(1)].

"(D) STATE.—The term 'State' includes the District of Columbia, the Commonwealth of Puerto Rico, the Virgin Islands, Guam, and American Samoa.

"(E) OTHER TERMS.—The terms 'participant' and 'administrator' shall have the meanings provided such terms, respectively, by paragraphs (7) and (16) of section 3 of the Employee Retirement Income Security Act of 1974 [29 U.S.C. 1002].

"(5) EFFECTIVE DATE.—The provisions of this subsection shall take effect on the date of the issuance of interim regulations pursuant to subsection (b)(4) of this section [section 401(b)(4) of Pub. L. 105–200, 42 U.S.C. 651 note].

"(f) QUALIFIED MEDICAL CHILD SUPPORT ORDERS AND NATIONAL MEDICAL SUPPORT NOTICES FOR CHURCH PLANS.—

"(1) IN GENERAL.—Each church group health plan shall provide benefits in accordance with the applicable requirements of any qualified medical child support order. A qualified medical child support order with respect to any participant or beneficiary shall be deemed to apply to each such group health plan which has received such order, from which the participant or beneficiary is eligible to receive benefits, and with respect to which the requirements of paragraph (4) are met.

"(2) DEFINITIONS.—For purposes of this subsection—

"(A) CHURCH GROUP HEALTH PLAN.—The term 'church group health plan' means a group health plan which is a church plan.

"(B) QUALIFIED MEDICAL CHILD SUPPORT ORDER.—The term 'qualified medical child support order' means a medical child support order—

"(i) which creates or recognizes the existence of an alternate recipient's right to, or assigns to an alternate recipient the right to, receive benefits for which a participant or beneficiary is eligible under a church group health plan; and

"(ii) with respect to which the requirements of paragraphs (3) and (4) are met.

"(C) MEDICAL CHILD SUPPORT ORDER.—The term 'medical child support order' means any judgment, decree, or order (including approval of a settlement agreement) which—

"(i) provides for child support with respect to a child of a participant under a church group health plan or provides for health benefit coverage to such a child, is made pursuant to a State domestic relations law (including a community property law), and relates to benefits under such plan; or

"(ii) is made pursuant to a law relating to medical child support described in section 1908 of the Social Security Act [42 U.S.C. 1396g–1] (as added by section 13822 [13623] of the Omnibus Budget Reconciliation Act of 1993 [Pub. L. 103–66]) with respect to a church group health plan,

if such judgment, decree, or order: (I) is issued by a court of competent jurisdiction; or (II) is issued through an administrative process established under State law and has the force and effect of law under applicable State law. For purposes of this paragraph, an administrative notice which is issued pursuant to an administrative process referred to in subclause (II) of the preceding sentence and which has the effect of an order described in clause (i) or (ii) of the preceding sentence shall be treated as such an order.

"(D) ALTERNATE RECIPIENT.—The term 'alternate recipient' means any child of a participant who is recognized under a medical child support order as having a right to enrollment under a church group health plan with respect to such participant.

"(E) GROUP HEALTH PLAN.—The term 'group health plan' has the meaning provided in section 607(1) of the Employee Retirement Income Security Act of 1974 [29 U.S.C. 1167(1)].

"(F) STATE.—The term 'State' includes the District of Columbia, the Commonwealth of Puerto Rico, the Virgin Islands, Guam, and American Samoa.

"(G) OTHER TERMS.—The terms 'participant', 'beneficiary', 'administrator', and 'church plan' shall have the meanings provided such terms, respectively, by paragraphs (7), (8), (16), and (33) of section 3 of the Employee Retirement Income Security Act of 1974 [29 U.S.C. 1102].

"(3) INFORMATION TO BE INCLUDED IN QUALIFIED ORDER.—A medical child support order meets the requirements of this paragraph only if such order clearly specifies—

"(A) the name and the last known mailing address (if any) of the participant and the name and mailing address of each alternate recipient covered by the order, except that, to the extent provided in the order, the name and mailing address of an official of a State or a political subdivision thereof may be substituted for the mailing address of any such alternate recipient;

"(B) a reasonable description of the type of coverage to be provided to each such alternate recipient, or the manner in which such type of coverage is to be determined; and

"(C) the period to which such order applies.

"(4) RESTRICTION ON NEW TYPES OR FORMS OF BENEFITS.—A medical child support order meets the requirements of this paragraph only if such order does not require a church group health plan to provide any type or form of benefit, or any option, not otherwise provided under the plan, except to the extent necessary to meet the requirements of a law relating to medical child support described in section 1908 of the Social Security Act [42 U.S.C. 1396g–1] (as added by section 13822 [13623] of the Omnibus Budget Reconciliation Act of 1993 [Pub. L. 103–66]).

"(5) PROCEDURAL REQUIREMENTS.—

"(A) TIMELY NOTIFICATIONS AND DETERMINATIONS.—In the case of any medical child support order received by a church group health plan—

"(i) the plan administrator shall promptly notify the participant and each alternate recipient of the receipt of such order and the plan's procedures for determining whether medical child support orders are qualified medical child support orders; and

"(ii) within a reasonable period after receipt of such order, the plan administrator shall determine whether such order is a qualified medical child support order and notify the participant and each alternate recipient of such determination.

"(B) ESTABLISHMENT OF PROCEDURES FOR DETERMINING QUALIFIED STATUS OF ORDERS.—Each church group health plan shall establish reasonable procedures to determine whether medical child support orders are qualified medical child support orders and to administer the provision of benefits under such qualified orders. Such procedures—

"(i) shall be in writing;

"(ii) shall provide for the notification of each person specified in a medical child support order as eligible to receive benefits under the plan (at the address included in the medical child support order) of such procedures promptly upon receipt by the plan of the medical child support order; and

"(iii) shall permit an alternate recipient to designate a representative for receipt of copies of notices that are sent to the alternate recipient with respect to a medical child support order.

"(C) NATIONAL MEDICAL SUPPORT NOTICE DEEMED TO BE A QUALIFIED MEDICAL CHILD SUPPORT ORDER.—

"(i) IN GENERAL.—If the plan administrator of any church group health plan which is maintained by the employer of a parent of a child or to which such an employer contributes receives an appropriately completed National Medical Support Notice promulgated pursuant to subsection (b) of this section [section 401(b) of Pub. L. 105–200, 42 U.S.C. 651 note] in the case of such child, and the Notice meets the requirements of paragraphs (3) and (4) of this subsection, the Notice shall be deemed to be a qualified medical child support order in the case of such child.

"(ii) ENROLLMENT OF CHILD IN PLAN.—In any case in which an appropriately completed National Medical Support Notice is issued in the case of a child of a participant under a church group health plan who is a parent of the child, and the Notice is deemed under clause (i) to be a qualified medical child support order, the plan administrator, within 40 business days after the date of the Notice, shall—

"(I) notify the State agency issuing the Notice with respect to such child whether coverage of the child is available under the terms of the plan and, if so, whether such child is covered under the plan and either the effective date of the coverage or any steps necessary to be taken by the custodial parent (or by the official of a State or political subdivision thereof substituted for the name of such child pursuant to paragraph (3)(A)) to effectuate the coverage; and

"(II) provide to the custodial parent (or such substituted official) a description of the coverage available and any forms or documents necessary to effectuate such coverage.

"(iii) RULE OF CONSTRUCTION.—Nothing in this subparagraph shall be construed as requiring a church group health plan, upon receipt of a National Medical Support Notice, to provide benefits under the plan (or eligibility for such benefits) in addition to benefits (or eligibility for benefits) provided under the terms of the plan as of immediately before receipt of such Notice.

"(6) DIRECT PROVISION OF BENEFITS PROVIDED TO ALTERNATE RECIPIENTS.—Any payment for benefits made by a church group health plan pursuant to a medical child support order in reimbursement for expenses paid by an alternate recipient or an alternate recipient's custodial parent or legal guardian shall be made to the alternate recipient or the alternate recipient's custodial parent or legal guardian.

"(7) PAYMENT TO STATE OFFICIAL TREATED AS SATISFACTION OF PLAN'S OBLIGATION TO MAKE PAYMENT TO ALTERNATE RECIPIENT.—Payment of benefits by a church group health plan to an official of a State or a political subdivision thereof whose name and address have been substituted for the address of an alternate recipient in a medical child support order, pursuant to paragraph (3)(A), shall be treated, for purposes of this subsection and part D of title IV of the Social Security Act [42 U.S.C. 651 et seq.], as payment of benefits to the alternate recipient.

"(8) EFFECTIVE DATE.—The provisions of this subsection shall take effect on the date of the issuance of interim regulations pursuant to subsection (b)(4) of this section [section 401(b)(4) of Pub. L. 105–200, 42 U.S.C. 651 note].

"(g) REPORT AND RECOMMENDATIONS REGARDING THE ENFORCEMENT OF QUALIFIED MEDICAL CHILD SUPPORT ORDERS.—Not later than 8 months after the issuance of the report to the Congress pursuant to subsection (a)(5) [section 401(a)(5) of Pub. L. 105–200, 42 U.S.C. 651 note], the Secretary of Health and Human Services and the Secretary of Labor shall jointly submit to each House of the Congress a report containing recommendations for appropriate legislation to improve the effectiveness of, and enforcement of, qualified medical child support orders under the provisions of subsection (f) of this section and section 609(a) of the Employee Retirement Income Security Act of 1974 (29 U.S.C. 1169(a))."

PLAN AMENDMENTS NOT REQUIRED UNTIL JANUARY 1, 1994

For provisions setting forth circumstances under which any amendment to a plan required to be made by an amendment made by section 4301(d) of Pub. L. 103–66 shall not be required to be made before the first plan year beginning on or after Jan. 1, 1994, see section 4301(d) of Pub. L. 103–66, set out as an Effective Date of 1993 Amendment note under section 1021 of this title.

PART 7—GROUP HEALTH PLAN REQUIREMENTS

Subpart A—Requirements Relating to Portability, Access, and Renewability

§ 1181. Increased portability through limitation on preexisting condition exclusions

(a) Limitation on preexisting condition exclusion period; crediting for periods of previous coverage

Subject to subsection (d) of this section, a group health plan, and a health insurance issuer offering group health insurance coverage, may, with respect to a participant or beneficiary, impose a preexisting condition exclusion only if—

(1) such exclusion relates to a condition (whether physical or mental), regardless of the cause of the condition, for which medical advice, diagnosis, care, or treatment was recommended or received within the 6-month period ending on the enrollment date;

(2) such exclusion extends for a period of not more than 12 months (or 18 months in the case of a late enrollee) after the enrollment date; and

(3) the period of any such preexisting condition exclusion is reduced by the aggregate of the periods of creditable coverage (if any, as defined in subsection (c)(1) of this section) applicable to the participant or beneficiary as of the enrollment date.

(b) Definitions

For purposes of this part—

(1) Preexisting condition exclusion

(A) In general

The term "preexisting condition exclusion" means, with respect to coverage, a limitation or exclusion of benefits relating to a condition based on the fact that the condition was present before the date of enrollment for such coverage, whether or not any medical advice, diagnosis, care, or treatment was recommended or received before such date.

(B) Treatment of genetic information

Genetic information shall not be treated as a condition described in subsection (a)(1) of this section in the absence of a diagnosis of the condition related to such information.

(2) Enrollment date

The term "enrollment date" means, with respect to an individual covered under a group health plan or health insurance coverage, the date of enrollment of the individual in the plan or coverage or, if earlier, the first day of the waiting period for such enrollment.

(3) Late enrollee

The term "late enrollee" means, with respect to coverage under a group health plan, a participant or beneficiary who enrolls under the plan other than during—

(A) the first period in which the individual is eligible to enroll under the plan, or

(B) a special enrollment period under subsection (f) of this section.

(4) Waiting period

The term "waiting period" means, with respect to a group health plan and an individual who is a potential participant or beneficiary in the plan, the period that must pass with respect to the individual before the individual is eligible to be covered for benefits under the terms of the plan.

(c) Rules relating to crediting previous coverage

(1) "Creditable coverage" defined

For purposes of this part, the term "creditable coverage" means, with respect to an individual, coverage of the individual under any of the following:

(A) A group health plan.

(B) Health insurance coverage.

(C) Part A or part B of title XVIII of the Social Security Act [42 U.S.C. 1395c et seq.; 1395j et seq.].

(D) Title XIX of the Social Security Act [42 U.S.C. 1396 et seq.], other than coverage consisting solely of benefits under section 1928 [42 U.S.C. 1396s].

(E) Chapter 55 of title 10.

(F) A medical care program of the Indian Health Service or of a tribal organization.

(G) A State health benefits risk pool.

(H) A health plan offered under chapter 89 of title 5.

(I) A public health plan (as defined in regulations).

(J) A health benefit plan under section 2504(e) of title 22.

Such term does not include coverage consisting solely of coverage of excepted benefits (as defined in section 1191b(c) of this title).

(2) Not counting periods before significant breaks in coverage

(A) In general

A period of creditable coverage shall not be counted, with respect to enrollment of an individual under a group health plan, if, after such period and before the enrollment date, there was a 63-day period during all of which the individual was not covered under any creditable coverage.

(B) Waiting period not treated as a break in coverage

For purposes of subparagraph (A) and subsection (d)(4) of this section, any period that an individual is in a waiting period for any coverage under a group health plan (or for group health insurance coverage) or is in an affiliation period (as defined in subsection (g)(2) of this section) shall not be taken into account in determining the continuous period under subparagraph (A).

(3) Method of crediting coverage

(A) Standard method

Except as otherwise provided under subparagraph (B), for purposes of applying subsection (a)(3) of this section, a group health plan, and a health insurance issuer offering group health insurance coverage, shall count a period of creditable coverage without regard to the specific benefits covered during the period.

(B) Election of alternative method

A group health plan, or a health insurance issuer offering group health insurance coverage, may elect to apply subsection (a)(3) of this section based on coverage of benefits within each of several classes or categories of benefits specified in regulations rather than as provided under subparagraph (A). Such election shall be made on a uniform basis for all participants and beneficiaries. Under such election a group health plan or issuer shall count a period of creditable coverage with respect to any class or category of benefits if any level of benefits is covered within such class or category.

(C) Plan notice

In the case of an election with respect to a group health plan under subparagraph (B) (whether or not health insurance coverage is provided in connection with such plan), the plan shall—

(i) prominently state in any disclosure statements concerning the plan, and state to each enrollee at the time of enrollment under the plan, that the plan has made such election, and

(ii) include in such statements a description of the effect of this election.

(4) Establishment of period

Periods of creditable coverage with respect to an individual shall be established through presentation of certifications described in subsection (e) of this section or in such other manner as may be specified in regulations.

(d) Exceptions

(1) Exclusion not applicable to certain newborns

Subject to paragraph (4), a group health plan, and a health insurance issuer offering group health insurance coverage, may not impose any preexisting condition exclusion in the case of an individual who, as of the last day of the 30-day period beginning with the date of birth, is covered under creditable coverage.

(2) Exclusion not applicable to certain adopted children

Subject to paragraph (4), a group health plan, and a health insurance issuer offering group health insurance coverage, may not impose any preexisting condition exclusion in the case of a child who is adopted or placed for adoption before attaining 18 years of age and who, as of the last day of the 30-day period beginning on the date of the adoption or placement for adoption, is covered under creditable coverage. The previous sentence shall not apply to coverage before the date of such adoption or placement for adoption.

(3) Exclusion not applicable to pregnancy

A group health plan, and health insurance issuer offering group health insurance coverage, may not impose any preexisting condition exclusion relating to pregnancy as a preexisting condition.

(4) Loss if break in coverage

Paragraphs (1) and (2) shall no longer apply to an individual after the end of the first 63-day period during all of which the individual was not covered under any creditable coverage.

(e) Certifications and disclosure of coverage

(1) Requirement for certification of period of creditable coverage

(A) In general

A group health plan, and a health insurance issuer offering group health insurance coverage, shall provide the certification described in subparagraph (B)—

(i) at the time an individual ceases to be covered under the plan or otherwise becomes covered under a COBRA continuation provision,

(ii) in the case of an individual becoming covered under such a provision, at the time the individual ceases to be covered under such provision, and

(iii) on the request on behalf of an individual made not later than 24 months after the date of cessation of the coverage described in clause (i) or (ii), whichever is later.

The certification under clause (i) may be provided, to the extent practicable, at a time consistent with notices required under any applicable COBRA continuation provision.

(B) Certification

The certification described in this subparagraph is a written certification of—

(i) the period of creditable coverage of the individual under such plan and the coverage (if any) under such COBRA continuation provision, and

(ii) the waiting period (if any) (and affiliation period, if applicable) imposed with respect to the individual for any coverage under such plan.

(C) Issuer compliance

To the extent that medical care under a group health plan consists of group health insurance coverage, the plan is deemed to have satisfied the certification requirement under this paragraph if the health insurance issuer offering the coverage provides for such certification in accordance with this paragraph.

(2) Disclosure of information on previous benefits

In the case of an election described in subsection (c)(3)(B) of this section by a group health plan or health insurance issuer, if the plan or issuer enrolls an individual for coverage under the plan and the individual provides a certification of coverage of the individual under paragraph (1)—

(A) upon request of such plan or issuer, the entity which issued the certification provided by the individual shall promptly disclose to such requesting plan or issuer information on coverage of classes and categories of health benefits available under such entity's plan or coverage, and

(B) such entity may charge the requesting plan or issuer for the reasonable cost of disclosing such information.

(3) Regulations

The Secretary shall establish rules to prevent an entity's failure to provide information under paragraph (1) or (2) with respect to previous coverage of an individual from adversely affecting any subsequent coverage of the individual under another group health plan or health insurance coverage.

(f) Special enrollment periods

(1) Individuals losing other coverage

A group health plan, and a health insurance issuer offering group health insurance coverage in connection with a group health plan, shall permit an employee who is eligible, but not enrolled, for coverage under the terms of the plan (or a dependent of such an employee if the dependent is eligible, but not enrolled, for coverage under such terms) to enroll for coverage under the terms of the plan if each of the following conditions is met:

(A) The employee or dependent was covered under a group health plan or had health insurance coverage at the time coverage was previously offered to the employee or dependent.

(B) The employee stated in writing at such time that coverage under a group health plan or health insurance coverage was the reason for declining enrollment, but only if the plan sponsor or issuer (if applicable) required such a statement at such time and provided the employee with notice of such requirement (and the consequences of such requirement) at such time.

(C) The employee's or dependent's coverage described in subparagraph (A)—

(i) was under a COBRA continuation provision and the coverage under such provision was exhausted; or

(ii) was not under such a provision and either the coverage was terminated as a result of loss of eligibility for the coverage (including as a result of legal separation, divorce, death, termination of employment, or reduction in the number of hours of employment) or employer contributions toward such coverage were terminated.

(D) Under the terms of the plan, the employee requests such enrollment not later than 30 days after the date of exhaustion of coverage described in subparagraph (C)(i) or termination of coverage or employer contribution described in subparagraph (C)(ii).

(2) For dependent beneficiaries

(A) In general

If—

(i) a group health plan makes coverage available with respect to a dependent of an individual,

(ii) the individual is a participant under the plan (or has met any waiting period applicable to becoming a participant under the plan and is eligible to be enrolled under the plan but for a failure to enroll during a previous enrollment period), and

(iii) a person becomes such a dependent of the individual through marriage, birth, or adoption or placement for adoption,

the group health plan shall provide for a dependent special enrollment period described in subparagraph (B) during which the person (or, if not otherwise enrolled, the individual) may be enrolled under the plan as a dependent of the individual, and in the case of the birth or adoption of a child, the spouse of the individual may be enrolled as a dependent of the individual if such spouse is otherwise eligible for coverage.

(B) Dependent special enrollment period

A dependent special enrollment period under this subparagraph shall be a period of not less than 30 days and shall begin on the later of—

(i) the date dependent coverage is made available, or

(ii) the date of the marriage, birth, or adoption or placement for adoption (as the case may be) described in subparagraph (A)(iii).

(C) No waiting period

If an individual seeks to enroll a dependent during the first 30 days of such a dependent special enrollment period, the coverage of the dependent shall become effective—

(i) in the case of marriage, not later than the first day of the first month beginning after the date the completed request for enrollment is received;

(ii) in the case of a dependent's birth, as of the date of such birth; or

(iii) in the case of a dependent's adoption or placement for adoption, the date of such adoption or placement for adoption.

(g) Use of affiliation period by HMOs as alternative to preexisting condition exclusion

(1) In general

In the case of a group health plan that offers medical care through health insurance coverage offered by a health maintenance organization, the plan may provide for an affiliation period with respect to coverage through the organization only if—

(A) no preexisting condition exclusion is imposed with respect to coverage through the organization,

(B) the period is applied uniformly without regard to any health status-related factors, and

(C) such period does not exceed 2 months (or 3 months in the case of a late enrollee).

(2) Affiliation period

(A) Defined

For purposes of this part, the term "affiliation period" means a period which, under the terms of the health insurance coverage offered by the health maintenance organization, must expire before the health insurance coverage becomes effective. The organization is not required to provide health care services or benefits during such period and no premium shall be charged to the participant or beneficiary for any coverage during the period.

(B) Beginning

Such period shall begin on the enrollment date.

(C) Runs concurrently with waiting periods

An affiliation period under a plan shall run concurrently with any waiting period under the plan.

(3) Alternative methods

A health maintenance organization described in paragraph (1) may use alternative methods, from those described in such paragraph, to address adverse selection as approved by the State insurance commissioner or official or officials designated by the State to enforce the requirements of part A of title XXVII of the Public Health Service Act [42 U.S.C. 300gg et seq.] for the State involved with respect to such issuer.

(Pub. L. 93–406, title I, §701, as added Pub. L. 104–191, title I, §101(a), Aug. 21, 1996, 110 Stat. 1939; amended Pub. L. 104–204, title VI, §603(b)(3)(H), Sept. 26, 1996, 110 Stat. 2938.)

REFERENCES IN TEXT

The Social Security Act, referred to in subsec. (c)(1)(C), (D), is act Aug. 14, 1935, ch. 531, 49 Stat. 620, as amended. Parts A and B of title XVIII of the Act are classified generally to parts A (§1395c et seq.) and B (§1395j et seq.) of subchapter XVIII of chapter 7 of Title 42, The Public Health and Welfare. Title XIX of the Act is classified generally to subchapter XIX (§1396 et seq.) of chapter 7 of Title 42. For complete classification of this Act to the Code, see section 1305 of Title 42 and Tables.

The Public Health Service Act, referred to in subsec. (g)(3), is act July 1, 1944, ch. 373, 58 Stat. 682, as amended. Part A of title XXVII of the Act is classified generally to part A (§300gg et seq.) of subchapter XXV of chapter 6A of Title 42. For complete classification of this Act to the Code, see Short Title note set out under section 201 of Title 42 and Tables.

AMENDMENTS

1996—Subsec. (c)(1). Pub. L. 104–204 made technical amendment to reference in original act which appears in text as reference to section 1191b of this title.

EFFECTIVE DATE OF 1996 AMENDMENT

Amendment by Pub. L. 104–204 applicable with respect to group health plans for plan years beginning on and after Jan. 1, 1998, see section 603(c) of Pub. L. 104–204, set out as a note under section 1003 of this title.

EFFECTIVE DATE

Section 101(g) of Pub. L. 104–191 provided that:

"(1) IN GENERAL.—Except as provided in this section, this section [enacting this part and amending sections 1003, 1021, 1022, 1024, 1132, 1136, and 1144 of this title] (and the amendments made by this section) shall apply with respect to group health plans for plan years beginning after June 30, 1997.

"(2) DETERMINATION OF CREDITABLE COVERAGE.—

"(A) PERIOD OF COVERAGE.—

"(i) IN GENERAL.—Subject to clause (ii), no period before July 1, 1996, shall be taken into account under part 7 of subtitle B of title I of the Employee Retirement Income Security Act of 1974 (as added by this section) [this part] in determining creditable coverage.

"(ii) SPECIAL RULE FOR CERTAIN PERIODS.—The Secretary of Labor, consistent with section 104 [42 U.S.C. 300gg–92 note], shall provide for a process whereby individuals who need to establish creditable coverage for periods before July 1, 1996, and who would have such coverage credited but for clause (i) may be given credit for creditable coverage for such periods through the presentation of documents or other means.

"(B) CERTIFICATIONS, ETC.—

"(i) IN GENERAL.—Subject to clauses (ii) and (iii), subsection (e) of section 701 of the Employee Retirement Income Security Act of 1974 [29 U.S.C. 1181(e)](as added by this section) shall apply to events occurring after June 30, 1996.

"(ii) NO CERTIFICATION REQUIRED TO BE PROVIDED BEFORE JUNE 1, 1997.—In no case is a certification required to be provided under such subsection before June 1, 1997.

"(iii) CERTIFICATION ONLY ON WRITTEN REQUEST FOR EVENTS OCCURRING BEFORE OCTOBER 1, 1996.—In the case of an event occurring after June 30, 1996, and before October 1, 1996, a certification is not required to be provided under such subsection unless an individual (with respect to whom the certification is otherwise required to be made) requests such certification in writing.

"(C) TRANSITIONAL RULE.—In the case of an individual who seeks to establish creditable coverage for any period for which certification is not required because it relates to an event occurring before June 30, 1996—

"(i) the individual may present other credible evidence of such coverage in order to establish the period of creditable coverage; and

"(ii) a group health plan and a health insurance issuer shall not be subject to any penalty or enforcement action with respect to the plan's or issuer's crediting (or not crediting) such coverage if the plan or issuer has sought to comply in good faith with the applicable requirements under the amendments made by this section [enacting this part and amending sections 1003, 1021, 1022, 1024, 1132, 1136, and 1144 of this title].

"(3) SPECIAL RULE FOR COLLECTIVE BARGAINING AGREEMENTS.—Except as provided in paragraph (2), in the case of a group health plan maintained pursuant to one or more collective bargaining agreements between employee representatives and one or more employers ratified before the date of the enactment of this Act [Aug. 21, 1996], part 7 of subtitle B of title I of Employee Retirement Income Security Act of 1974 [this part] (other than section 701(e) thereof [29 U.S.C. 1181(e)]) shall not apply to plan years beginning before the later of—

"(A) the date on which the last of the collective bargaining agreements relating to the plan terminates (determined without regard to any extension thereof agreed to after the date of the enactment of this Act), or

"(B) July 1, 1997.

For purposes of subparagraph (A), any plan amendment made pursuant to a collective bargaining agreement relating to the plan which amends the plan solely to conform to any requirement of such part shall not be treated as a termination of such collective bargaining agreement.

"(4) TIMELY REGULATIONS.—The Secretary of Labor, consistent with section 104 [42 U.S.C. 300gg–92 note], shall first issue by not later than April 1, 1997, such regulations as may be necessary to carry out the amendments made by this section.

"(5) LIMITATION ON ACTIONS.—No enforcement action shall be taken, pursuant to the amendments made by this section, against a group health plan or health insurance issuer with respect to a violation of a requirement imposed by such amendments before January 1, 1998, or, if later, the date of issuance of regulations referred to in paragraph (4), if the plan or issuer has sought to comply in good faith with such requirements."

§1182. Prohibiting discrimination against individual participants and beneficiaries based on health status

(a) In eligibility to enroll

(1) In general

Subject to paragraph (2), a group health plan, and a health insurance issuer offering group health insurance coverage in connection with a group health plan, may not establish rules for eligibility (including continued eligibility) of any individual to enroll under the terms of the plan based on any of the following health status-related factors in relation to the individual or a dependent of the individual:

(A) Health status.

(B) Medical condition (including both physical and mental illnesses).

(C) Claims experience.
(D) Receipt of health care.
(E) Medical history.
(F) Genetic information.
(G) Evidence of insurability (including conditions arising out of acts of domestic violence).
(H) Disability.

(2) No application to benefits or exclusions

To the extent consistent with section 1181 of this title, paragraph (1) shall not be construed—

(A) to require a group health plan, or group health insurance coverage, to provide particular benefits other than those provided under the terms of such plan or coverage, or

(B) to prevent such a plan or coverage from establishing limitations or restrictions on the amount, level, extent, or nature of the benefits or coverage for similarly situated individuals enrolled in the plan or coverage.

(3) Construction

For purposes of paragraph (1), rules for eligibility to enroll under a plan include rules defining any applicable waiting periods for such enrollment.

(b) In premium contributions

(1) In general

A group health plan, and a health insurance issuer offering health insurance coverage in connection with a group health plan, may not require any individual (as a condition of enrollment or continued enrollment under the plan) to pay a premium or contribution which is greater than such premium or contribution for a similarly situated individual enrolled in the plan on the basis of any health status-related factor in relation to the individual or to an individual enrolled under the plan as a dependent of the individual.

(2) Construction

Nothing in paragraph (1) shall be construed—

(A) to restrict the amount that an employer may be charged for coverage under a group health plan except as provided in paragraph (3); or

(B) to prevent a group health plan, and a health insurance issuer offering group health insurance coverage, from establishing premium discounts or rebates or modifying otherwise applicable copayments or deductibles in return for adherence to programs of health promotion and disease prevention.

(3) No group-based discrimination on basis of genetic information

(A) In general

For purposes of this section, a group health plan, and a health insurance issuer offering group health insurance coverage in connection with a group health plan, may not adjust premium or contribution amounts for the group covered under such plan on the basis of genetic information.

(B) Rule of construction

Nothing in subparagraph (A) or in paragraphs (1) and (2) of subsection (d) shall be construed to limit the ability of a health insurance issuer offering health insurance coverage in connection with a group health plan to increase the premium for an employer based on the manifestation of a disease or disorder of an individual who is enrolled in the plan. In such case, the manifestation of a disease or disorder in one individual cannot also be used as genetic information about other group members and to further increase the premium for the employer.

(c) Genetic testing

(1) Limitation on requesting or requiring genetic testing

A group health plan, and a health insurance issuer offering health insurance coverage in connection with a group health plan, shall not request or require an individual or a family member of such individual to undergo a genetic test.

(2) Rule of construction

Paragraph (1) shall not be construed to limit the authority of a health care professional who is providing health care services to an individual to request that such individual undergo a genetic test.

(3) Rule of construction regarding payment

(A) In general

Nothing in paragraph (1) shall be construed to preclude a group health plan, or a health insurance issuer offering health insurance coverage in connection with a group health plan, from obtaining and using the results of a genetic test in making a determination regarding payment (as such term is defined for the purposes of applying the regulations promulgated by the Secretary of Health and Human Services under part C of title XI of the Social Security Act [42 U.S.C. 1320d et seq.] and section 264 of the Health Insurance Portability and Accountability Act of 1996, as may be revised from time to time) consistent with subsection (a).

(B) Limitation

For purposes of subparagraph (A), a group health plan, or a health insurance issuer offering health insurance coverage in connection with a group health plan, may request only the minimum amount of information necessary to accomplish the intended purpose.

(4) Research exception

Notwithstanding paragraph (1), a group health plan, or a health insurance issuer offering health insurance coverage in connection with a group health plan, may request, but not require, that a participant or beneficiary undergo a genetic test if each of the following conditions is met:

(A) The request is made, in writing, pursuant to research that complies with part 46 of title 45, Code of Federal Regulations, or equivalent Federal regulations, and any applicable State or local law or regulations for the protection of human subjects in research.

(B) The plan or issuer clearly indicates to each participant or beneficiary, or in the case of a minor child, to the legal guardian of such beneficiary, to whom the request is made that—

(i) compliance with the request is voluntary; and

(ii) non-compliance will have no effect on enrollment status or premium or contribution amounts.

(C) No genetic information collected or acquired under this paragraph shall be used for underwriting purposes.

(D) The plan or issuer notifies the Secretary in writing that the plan or issuer is conducting activities pursuant to the exception provided for under this paragraph, including a description of the activities conducted.

(E) The plan or issuer complies with such other conditions as the Secretary may by regulation require for activities conducted under this paragraph.

(d) Prohibition on collection of genetic information

(1) In general

A group health plan, and a health insurance issuer offering health insurance coverage in connection with a group health plan, shall not request, require, or purchase genetic information for underwriting purposes (as defined in section 1191b of this title).

(2) Prohibition on collection of genetic information prior to enrollment

A group health plan, and a health insurance issuer offering health insurance coverage in connection with a group health plan, shall not request, require, or purchase genetic information with respect to any individual prior to such individual's enrollment under the plan or coverage in connection with such enrollment.

(3) Incidental collection

If a group health plan, or a health insurance issuer offering health insurance coverage in connection with a group health plan, obtains genetic information incidental to the requesting, requiring, or purchasing of other information concerning any individual, such request, requirement, or purchase shall not be considered a violation of paragraph (2) if such request, requirement, or purchase is not in violation of paragraph (1).

(e) Application to all plans

The provisions of subsections (a)(1)(F), (b)(3), (c), and (d), and subsection (b)(1) and section 1181 of this title with respect to genetic information, shall apply to group health plans and health insurance issuers without regard to section 1191a(a) of this title.

(f) Genetic information of a fetus or embryo

Any reference in this part to genetic information concerning an individual or family member of an individual shall—

(1) with respect to such an individual or family member of an individual who is a pregnant woman, include genetic information of any fetus carried by such pregnant woman; and

(2) with respect to an individual or family member utilizing an assisted reproductive technology, include genetic information of any embryo legally held by the individual or family member.

(Pub. L. 93–406, title I, §702, as added Pub. L. 104–191, title I, §101(a), Aug. 21, 1996, 110 Stat. 1945; amended Pub. L. 110–233, title I, §101(a)–(c), May 21, 2008, 122 Stat. 883, 885.)

REFERENCES IN TEXT

The Social Security Act, referred to in subsec. (c)(3)(A), is act Aug. 14, 1935, ch. 531, 49 Stat. 620. Part C of title XI of the Act is classified generally to part C (§1320d et seq.) of subchapter XI of chapter 7 of Title 42, The Public Health and Welfare. For complete classification of this Act to the Code, see section 1305 of Title 42 and Tables.

Section 264 of the Health Insurance Portability and Accountability Act of 1996, referred to in subsec. (c)(3)(A), is section 264 of Pub. L. 104–191, which is set out as a note under section 1320d–2 of Title 42, The Public Health and Welfare.

AMENDMENTS

2008—Subsec. (b)(2)(A). Pub. L. 110–233, §101(a)(1), inserted "except as provided in paragraph (3)" before semicolon.

Subsec. (b)(3). Pub. L. 110–233, §101(a)(2), added par. (3).

Subsecs. (c) to (e). Pub. L. 110–233, §101(b), added subsecs. (c) to (e).

Subsec. (f). Pub. L. 110–233, §101(c), added subsec. (f).

EFFECTIVE DATE OF 2008 AMENDMENT

Amendment by Pub. L. 110–233 applicable with respect to group health plans for plan years beginning after the date that is one year after May 21, 2008, see section 101(f)(2) of Pub. L. 110–233, set out as a note under section 1132 of this title.

§1183. Guaranteed renewability in multiemployer plans and multiple employer welfare arrangements

A group health plan which is a multiemployer plan or which is a multiple employer welfare arrangement may not deny an employer whose employees are covered under such a plan continued access to the same or different coverage under the terms of such a plan, other than—

(1) for nonpayment of contributions;

(2) for fraud or other intentional misrepresentation of material fact by the employer;

(3) for noncompliance with material plan provisions;

(4) because the plan is ceasing to offer any coverage in a geographic area;

(5) in the case of a plan that offers benefits through a network plan, there is no longer any individual enrolled through the employer who lives, resides, or works in the service area of the network plan and the plan applies this paragraph uniformly without regard to the claims experience of employers or any health status-related factor in relation to such individuals or their dependents; and

(6) for failure to meet the terms of an applicable collective bargaining agreement, to renew a collective bargaining or other agreement requiring or authorizing contributions to the plan, or to employ employees covered by such an agreement.

(Pub. L. 93–406, title I, §703, as added Pub. L. 104–191, title I, §101(a), Aug. 21, 1996, 110 Stat. 1946.)

Subpart B—Other Requirements

§1185. Standards relating to benefits for mothers and newborns

(a) Requirements for minimum hospital stay following birth

(1) In general

A group health plan, and a health insurance issuer offering group health insurance coverage, may not—

(A) except as provided in paragraph (2)—

(i) restrict benefits for any hospital length of stay in connection with childbirth for the mother or newborn child, following a normal vaginal delivery, to less than 48 hours, or

(ii) restrict benefits for any hospital length of stay in connection with childbirth for the mother or newborn child, following a cesarean section, to less than 96 hours; or

(B) require that a provider obtain authorization from the plan or the issuer for prescribing any length of stay required under subparagraph (A) (without regard to paragraph (2)).

(2) Exception

Paragraph (1)(A) shall not apply in connection with any group health plan or health insurance issuer in any case in which the decision to discharge the mother or her newborn child prior to the expiration of the minimum length of stay otherwise required under paragraph (1)(A) is made by an attending provider in consultation with the mother.

(b) Prohibitions

A group health plan, and a health insurance issuer offering group health insurance coverage in connection with a group health plan, may not—

(1) deny to the mother or her newborn child eligibility, or continued eligibility, to enroll or to renew coverage under the terms of the plan, solely for the purpose of avoiding the requirements of this section;

(2) provide monetary payments or rebates to mothers to encourage such mothers to accept less than the minimum protections available under this section;

(3) penalize or otherwise reduce or limit the reimbursement of an attending provider because such provider provided care to an individual participant or beneficiary in accordance with this section;

(4) provide incentives (monetary or otherwise) to an attending provider to induce such provider to provide care to an individual participant or beneficiary in a manner inconsistent with this section; or

(5) subject to subsection (c)(3) of this section, restrict benefits for any portion of a period within a hospital length of stay required under subsection (a) of this section in a manner which is less favorable than the benefits provided for any preceding portion of such stay.

(c) Rules of construction

(1) Nothing in this section shall be construed to require a mother who is a participant or beneficiary—

(A) to give birth in a hospital; or

(B) to stay in the hospital for a fixed period of time following the birth of her child.

(2) This section shall not apply with respect to any group health plan, or any group health insurance coverage offered by a health insurance issuer, which does not provide benefits for hospital lengths of stay in connection with childbirth for a mother or her newborn child.

(3) Nothing in this section shall be construed as preventing a group health plan or issuer from imposing deductibles, coinsurance, or other cost-sharing in relation to benefits for hospital lengths of stay in connection with childbirth for a mother or newborn child under the plan (or under health insurance coverage offered in connection with a group health plan), except that such coinsurance or other cost-sharing for any portion of a period within a hospital length of stay required under subsection (a) of this section may not be greater than such coinsurance or cost-sharing for any preceding portion of such stay.

(d) Notice under group health plan

The imposition of the requirements of this section shall be treated as a material modification in the terms of the plan described in section 1022(a)(1)[1] of this title, for purposes of assuring notice of such requirements under the plan; except that the summary description required to be provided under the last sentence of section 1024(b)(1) of this title with respect to such modification shall be provided by not later than 60 days after the first day of the first plan year in which such requirements apply.

(e) Level and type of reimbursements

Nothing in this section shall be construed to prevent a group health plan or a health insurance issuer offering group health insurance coverage from negotiating the level and type of reimbursement with a provider for care provided in accordance with this section.

(f) Preemption; exception for health insurance coverage in certain States

(1) In general

The requirements of this section shall not apply with respect to health insurance coverage if there is a State law (as defined in section 1191(d)(1) of this title) for a State that regulates such coverage that is described in any of the following subparagraphs:

(A) Such State law requires such coverage to provide for at least a 48-hour hospital length of stay following a normal vaginal delivery and at least a 96-hour hospital length of stay following a cesarean section.

(B) Such State law requires such coverage to provide for maternity and pediatric care in accordance with guidelines established by the American College of Obstetricians and Gynecologists, the American Academy of Pediatrics, or other established professional medical associations.

(C) Such State law requires, in connection with such coverage for maternity care, that the hospital length of stay for such care is

[1] See References in Text note below.

left to the decision of (or required to be made by) the attending provider in consultation with the mother.

(2) Construction

Section 1191(a)(1) of this title shall not be construed as superseding a State law described in paragraph (1).

(Pub. L. 93–406, title I, §711, as added Pub. L. 104–204, title VI, §603(a)(5), Sept. 26, 1996, 110 Stat. 2935.)

REFERENCES IN TEXT

Section 1022(a)(1) of this title, referred to in subsec. (d), was redesignated section 1022(a) of this title by Pub. L. 105–34, title XV, §1503(b)(1)(B), Aug. 5, 1997, 111 Stat. 1061.

EFFECTIVE DATE

Section applicable with respect to group health plans for plan years beginning on and after Jan. 1, 1998, see section 603(c) of Pub. L. 104–204, set out as an Effective Date of 1996 Amendment note under section 1003 of this title.

§1185a. Parity in mental health and substance use disorder benefits

(a) In general

(1) Aggregate lifetime limits

In the case of a group health plan (or health insurance coverage offered in connection with such a plan) that provides both medical and surgical benefits and mental health or substance use disorder benefits—

(A) No lifetime limit

If the plan or coverage does not include an aggregate lifetime limit on substantially all medical and surgical benefits, the plan or coverage may not impose any aggregate lifetime limit on mental health or substance use disorder benefits.

(B) Lifetime limit

If the plan or coverage includes an aggregate lifetime limit on substantially all medical and surgical benefits (in this paragraph referred to as the "applicable lifetime limit"), the plan or coverage shall either—

(i) apply the applicable lifetime limit both to the medical and surgical benefits to which it otherwise would apply and to mental health and substance use disorder benefits and not distinguish in the application of such limit between such medical and surgical benefits and mental health and substance use disorder benefits; or

(ii) not include any aggregate lifetime limit on mental health or substance use disorder benefits that is less than the applicable lifetime limit.

(C) Rule in case of different limits

In the case of a plan or coverage that is not described in subparagraph (A) or (B) and that includes no or different aggregate lifetime limits on different categories of medical and surgical benefits, the Secretary shall establish rules under which subparagraph (B) is applied to such plan or coverage with respect to mental health and substance use disorder benefits by substituting for the applicable lifetime limit an average aggregate lifetime limit that is computed taking into account the weighted average of the aggregate lifetime limits applicable to such categories.

(2) Annual limits

In the case of a group health plan (or health insurance coverage offered in connection with such a plan) that provides both medical and surgical benefits and mental health or substance use disorder benefits—

(A) No annual limit

If the plan or coverage does not include an annual limit on substantially all medical and surgical benefits, the plan or coverage may not impose any annual limit on mental health or substance use disorder benefits.

(B) Annual limit

If the plan or coverage includes an annual limit on substantially all medical and surgical benefits (in this paragraph referred to as the "applicable annual limit"), the plan or coverage shall either—

(i) apply the applicable annual limit both to medical and surgical benefits to which it otherwise would apply and to mental health and substance use disorder benefits and not distinguish in the application of such limit between such medical and surgical benefits and mental health and substance use disorder benefits; or

(ii) not include any annual limit on mental health or substance use disorder benefits that is less than the applicable annual limit.

(C) Rule in case of different limits

In the case of a plan or coverage that is not described in subparagraph (A) or (B) and that includes no or different annual limits on different categories of medical and surgical benefits, the Secretary shall establish rules under which subparagraph (B) is applied to such plan or coverage with respect to mental health and substance use disorder benefits by substituting for the applicable annual limit an average annual limit that is computed taking into account the weighted average of the annual limits applicable to such categories.

(3) Financial requirements and treatment limitations

(A) In general

In the case of a group health plan (or health insurance coverage offered in connection with such a plan) that provides both medical and surgical benefits and mental health or substance use disorder benefits, such plan or coverage shall ensure that—

(i) the financial requirements applicable to such mental health or substance use disorder benefits are no more restrictive than the predominant financial requirements applied to substantially all medical and surgical benefits covered by the plan (or coverage), and there are no separate cost sharing requirements that are applicable only with respect to mental health or substance use disorder benefits; and

(ii) the treatment limitations applicable to such mental health or substance use disorder benefits are no more restrictive than the predominant treatment limitations applied to substantially all medical and surgical benefits covered by the plan (or coverage) and there are no separate treatment limitations that are applicable only with respect to mental health or substance use disorder benefits.

(B) Definitions

In this paragraph:

(i) Financial requirement

The term "financial requirement" includes deductibles, copayments, coinsurance, and out-of-pocket expenses, but excludes an aggregate lifetime limit and an annual limit subject to paragraphs (1) and (2),[1]

(ii) Predominant

A financial requirement or treatment limit is considered to be predominant if it is the most common or frequent of such type of limit or requirement.

(iii) Treatment limitation

The term "treatment limitation" includes limits on the frequency of treatment, number of visits, days of coverage, or other similar limits on the scope or duration of treatment.

(4) Availability of plan information

The criteria for medical necessity determinations made under the plan with respect to mental health or substance use disorder benefits (or the health insurance coverage offered in connection with the plan with respect to such benefits) shall be made available by the plan administrator (or the health insurance issuer offering such coverage) in accordance with regulations to any current or potential participant, beneficiary, or contracting provider upon request. The reason for any denial under the plan (or coverage) of reimbursement or payment for services with respect to mental health or substance use disorder benefits in the case of any participant or beneficiary shall, on request or as otherwise required, be made available by the plan administrator (or the health insurance issuer offering such coverage) to the participant or beneficiary in accordance with regulations.

(5) Out-of-network providers

In the case of a plan or coverage that provides both medical and surgical benefits and mental health or substance use disorder benefits, if the plan or coverage provides coverage for medical or surgical benefits provided by out-of-network providers, the plan or coverage shall provide coverage for mental health or substance use disorder benefits provided by out-of-network providers in a manner that is consistent with the requirements of this section.

(b) Construction

Nothing in this section shall be construed—

(1) as requiring a group health plan (or health insurance coverage offered in connection with such a plan) to provide any mental health or substance use disorder benefits; or

(2) in the case of a group health plan (or health insurance coverage offered in connection with such a plan) that provides mental health or substance use disorder benefits, as affecting the terms and conditions of the plan or coverage relating to such benefits under the plan or coverage, except as provided in subsection (a).

(c) Exemptions

(1) Small employer exemption

(A) In general

This section shall not apply to any group health plan (and group health insurance coverage offered in connection with a group health plan) for any plan year of a small employer.

(B) Small employer

For purposes of subparagraph (A), the term "small employer" means, in connection with a group health plan with respect to a calendar year and a plan year, an employer who employed an average of at least 2 (or 1 in the case of an employer residing in a State that permits small groups to include a single individual) but not more than 50 employees on business days during the preceding calendar year.

(C) Application of certain rules in determination of employer size

For purposes of this paragraph—

(i) Application of aggregation rule for employers

Rules similar to the rules under subsections (b), (c), (m), and (*o*) of section 414 of title 26 shall apply for purposes of treating persons as a single employer.

(ii) Employers not in existence in preceding year

In the case of an employer which was not in existence throughout the preceding calendar year, the determination of whether such employer is a small employer shall be based on the average number of employees that it is reasonably expected such employer will employ on business days in the current calendar year.

(iii) Predecessors

Any reference in this paragraph to an employer shall include a reference to any predecessor of such employer.

(2) Cost exemption

(A) In general

With respect to a group health plan (or health insurance coverage offered in connection with such a plan), if the application of this section to such plan (or coverage) results in an increase for the plan year involved of the actual total costs of coverage with respect to medical and surgical benefits and mental health and substance use disorder benefits under the plan (as determined

[1] So in original. The comma probably should be a period.

and certified under subparagraph (C)) by an amount that exceeds the applicable percentage described in subparagraph (B) of the actual total plan costs, the provisions of this section shall not apply to such plan (or coverage) during the following plan year, and such exemption shall apply to the plan (or coverage) for 1 plan year. An employer may elect to continue to apply mental health and substance use disorder parity pursuant to this section with respect to the group health plan (or coverage) involved regardless of any increase in total costs.

(B) Applicable percentage

With respect to a plan (or coverage), the applicable percentage described in this subparagraph shall be—

(i) 2 percent in the case of the first plan year in which this section is applied; and

(ii) 1 percent in the case of each subsequent plan year.

(C) Determinations by actuaries

Determinations as to increases in actual costs under a plan (or coverage) for purposes of this section shall be made and certified by a qualified and licensed actuary who is a member in good standing of the American Academy of Actuaries. All such determinations shall be in a written report prepared by the actuary. The report, and all underlying documentation relied upon by the actuary, shall be maintained by the group health plan or health insurance issuer for a period of 6 years following the notification made under subparagraph (E).

(D) 6-month determinations

If a group health plan (or a health insurance issuer offering coverage in connection with a group health plan) seeks an exemption under this paragraph, determinations under subparagraph (A) shall be made after such plan (or coverage) has complied with this section for the first 6 months of the plan year involved.

(E) Notification

(i) In general

A group health plan (or a health insurance issuer offering coverage in connection with a group health plan) that, based upon a certification described under subparagraph (C), qualifies for an exemption under this paragraph, and elects to implement the exemption, shall promptly notify the Secretary, the appropriate State agencies, and participants and beneficiaries in the plan of such election.

(ii) Requirement

A notification to the Secretary under clause (i) shall include—

(I) a description of the number of covered lives under the plan (or coverage) involved at the time of the notification, and as applicable, at the time of any prior election of the cost-exemption under this paragraph by such plan (or coverage);

(II) for both the plan year upon which a cost exemption is sought and the year prior, a description of the actual total costs of coverage with respect to medical and surgical benefits and mental health and substance use disorder benefits under the plan; and

(III) for both the plan year upon which a cost exemption is sought and the year prior, the actual total costs of coverage with respect to mental health and substance use disorder benefits under the plan.

(iii) Confidentiality

A notification to the Secretary under clause (i) shall be confidential. The Secretary shall make available, upon request and on not more than an annual basis, an anonymous itemization of such notifications, that includes—

(I) a breakdown of States by the size and type of employers submitting such notification; and

(II) a summary of the data received under clause (ii).

(F) Audits by appropriate agencies

To determine compliance with this paragraph, the Secretary may audit the books and records of a group health plan or health insurance issuer relating to an exemption, including any actuarial reports prepared pursuant to subparagraph (C), during the 6 year period following the notification of such exemption under subparagraph (E). A State agency receiving a notification under subparagraph (E) may also conduct such an audit with respect to an exemption covered by such notification.

(d) Separate application to each option offered

In the case of a group health plan that offers a participant or beneficiary two or more benefit package options under the plan, the requirements of this section shall be applied separately with respect to each such option.

(e) Definitions

For purposes of this section—

(1) Aggregate lifetime limit

The term "aggregate lifetime limit" means, with respect to benefits under a group health plan or health insurance coverage, a dollar limitation on the total amount that may be paid with respect to such benefits under the plan or health insurance coverage with respect to an individual or other coverage unit.

(2) Annual limit

The term "annual limit" means, with respect to benefits under a group health plan or health insurance coverage, a dollar limitation on the total amount of benefits that may be paid with respect to such benefits in a 12-month period under the plan or health insurance coverage with respect to an individual or other coverage unit.

(3) Medical or surgical benefits

The term "medical or surgical benefits" means benefits with respect to medical or surgical services, as defined under the terms of the plan or coverage (as the case may be), but does not include mental health or substance use disorder benefits.

(4) Mental health benefits

The term "mental health benefits" means benefits with respect to services for mental health conditions, as defined under the terms of the plan and in accordance with applicable Federal and State law.

(5) Substance use disorder benefits

The term "substance use disorder benefits" means benefits with respect to services for substance use disorders, as defined under the terms of the plan and in accordance with applicable Federal and State law.

(f) Secretary report

The Secretary shall, by January 1, 2012, and every two years thereafter, submit to the appropriate committees of Congress a report on compliance of group health plans (and health insurance coverage offered in connection with such plans) with the requirements of this section. Such report shall include the results of any surveys or audits on compliance of group health plans (and health insurance coverage offered in connection with such plans) with such requirements and an analysis of the reasons for any failures to comply.

(g) Notice and assistance

The Secretary, in cooperation with the Secretaries of Health and Human Services and Treasury, as appropriate, shall publish and widely disseminate guidance and information for group health plans, participants and beneficiaries, applicable State and local regulatory bodies, and the National Association of Insurance Commissioners concerning the requirements of this section and shall provide assistance concerning such requirements and the continued operation of applicable State law. Such guidance and information shall inform participants and beneficiaries of how they may obtain assistance under this section, including, where appropriate, assistance from State consumer and insurance agencies.

(Pub. L. 93–406, title I, §712, as added Pub. L. 104–204, title VII, §702(a), Sept. 26, 1996, 110 Stat. 2944; amended Pub. L. 107–116, title VII, §701(a), Jan. 10, 2002, 115 Stat. 2228; Pub. L. 107–313, §2(a), Dec. 2, 2002, 116 Stat. 2457; Pub. L. 108–197, §2(a), Dec. 19, 2003, 117 Stat. 2898; Pub. L. 108–311, title III, §302(b), Oct. 4, 2004, 118 Stat. 1178; Pub. L. 109–151, §1(a), Dec. 30, 2005, 119 Stat. 2886; Pub. L. 109–432, div. A, title I, §115(b), Dec. 20, 2006, 120 Stat. 2941; Pub. L. 110–245, title IV, §401(b), June 17, 2008, 122 Stat. 1649; Pub. L. 110–343, div. C, title V, §512(a), (g)(1)(A), Oct. 3, 2008, 122 Stat. 3881, 3892.)

AMENDMENTS

2008—Pub. L. 110–343, §512(g)(1)(A), amended section catchline generally. Prior to amendment, catchline read as follows: "Parity in application of certain limits to mental health benefits".

Subsec. (a)(1), (2). Pub. L. 110–343, §512(a)(8), substituted "mental health or substance use disorder benefits" for "mental health benefits" wherever appearing in pars. (1)(introductory provisions), (A), and (B)(ii) and (2)(introductory provisions), (A), and (B)(ii).

Pub. L. 110–343, §512(a)(7), substituted "mental health and substance use disorder benefits" for "mental health benefits" wherever appearing in pars. (1)(B)(i) and (C) and (2)(B)(i) and (C).

Subsec. (a)(3) to (5). Pub. L. 110–343, §512(a)(1), added pars. (3) to (5).

Subsec. (b)(1). Pub. L. 110–343, §512(a)(8), substituted "mental health or substance use disorder benefits" for "mental health benefits".

Subsec. (b)(2). Pub. L. 110–343, §512(a)(2), amended par. (2) generally. Prior to amendment, par. (2) read as follows: "in the case of a group health plan (or health insurance coverage offered in connection with such a plan) that provides mental health benefits, as affecting the terms and conditions (including cost sharing, limits on numbers of visits or days of coverage, and requirements relating to medical necessity) relating to the amount, duration, or scope of mental health benefits under the plan or coverage, except as specifically provided in subsection (a) of this section (in regard to parity in the imposition of aggregate lifetime limits and annual limits for mental health benefits)."

Subsec. (c)(1)(B). Pub. L. 110–343, §512(a)(3)(A), inserted "(or 1 in the case of an employer residing in a State that permits small groups to include a single individual)" after "of at least 2" and struck out "and who employs at least 2 employees on the first day of the plan year" after "preceding calendar year".

Subsec. (c)(2). Pub. L. 110–343, §512(a)(3)(B), added par. (2) and struck out former par. (2). Prior to amendment, text read as follows: "This section shall not apply with respect to a group health plan (or health insurance coverage offered in connection with a group health plan) if the application of this section to such plan (or to such coverage) results in an increase in the cost under the plan (or for such coverage) of at least 1 percent."

Subsec. (e)(3). Pub. L. 110–343, §512(a)(8), substituted "mental health or substance use disorder benefits" for "mental health benefits".

Subsec. (e)(4). Pub. L. 110–343, §512(a)(8), which directed amendment of this section by substituting "mental health or substance use disorder benefits" for "mental health benefits" wherever appearing (except in provisions amended by Pub. L. 110–343, §512(a)(7)), was not executed to par. (4) as added by Pub. L. 110–343, §512(a)(4), to reflect the probable intent of Congress. See below.

Pub. L. 110–343, §512(a)(4), added par. (4) and struck out former par. (4). Text read as follows: "The term 'mental health benefits' means benefits with respect to mental health services, as defined under the terms of the plan or coverage (as the case may be), but does not include benefits with respect to treatment of substance abuse or chemical dependency."

Subsec. (e)(5). Pub. L. 110–343, §512(a)(4), added par. (5).

Subsec. (f). Pub. L. 110–343, §512(a)(6), added subsec. (f).

Pub. L. 110–343, §512(a)(5), struck out subsec. (f). Text read as follows: "This section shall not apply to benefits for services furnished—

"(1) on or after January 1, 2008, and before June 17, 2008, and

"(2) after December 31, 2008.."

Pub. L. 110–245 substituted "services furnished—" for "services furnished after December 31, 2007" and added pars. (1) and (2).

Subsec. (g). Pub. L. 110–343, §512(a)(6), added subsec. (g).

2006—Subsec. (f). Pub. L. 109–432 substituted "2007" for "2006".

2005—Subsec. (f). Pub. L. 109–151 substituted "December 31, 2006" for "December 31, 2005".

2004—Subsec. (f). Pub. L. 108–311 substituted "after December 31, 2005" for "on or after December 31, 2004".

2003—Subsec. (f). Pub. L. 108–197 substituted "December 31, 2004" for "December 31, 2003".

2002—Subsec. (f). Pub. L. 107–313 substituted "December 31, 2003" for "December 31, 2002".

Pub. L. 107–116 substituted "December 31, 2002" for "September 30, 2001".

EFFECTIVE DATE OF 2008 AMENDMENT

Amendment by Pub. L. 110–343 applicable with respect to group health plans for plan years beginning after the date that is 1 year after Oct. 3, 2008, except that amendment by section 512(a)(5) of Pub. L. 110–343 effective Jan. 1, 2009, with special rule for collective bargaining agreements, see section 512(e) of Pub. L. 110–343, set out as a note under section 300gg–5 of Title 42, The Public Health and Welfare.

EFFECTIVE DATE

Section 702(c) of Pub. L. 104–204 provided that: "The amendments made by this section [enacting this section] shall apply with respect to group health plans for plan years beginning on or after January 1, 1998."

§ 1185b. Required coverage for reconstructive surgery following mastectomies

(a) In general

A group health plan, and a health insurance issuer providing health insurance coverage in connection with a group health plan, that provides medical and surgical benefits with respect to a mastectomy shall provide, in a case of a participant or beneficiary who is receiving benefits in connection with a mastectomy and who elects breast reconstruction in connection with such mastectomy, coverage for—

(1) all stages of reconstruction of the breast on which the mastectomy has been performed;

(2) surgery and reconstruction of the other breast to produce a symmetrical appearance; and

(3) prostheses and physical complications of mastectomy, including lymphedemas;

in a manner determined in consultation with the attending physician and the patient. Such coverage may be subject to annual deductibles and coinsurance provisions as may be deemed appropriate and as are consistent with those established for other benefits under the plan or coverage. Written notice of the availability of such coverage shall be delivered to the participant upon enrollment and annually thereafter.

(b) Notice

A group health plan, and a health insurance issuer providing health insurance coverage in connection with a group health plan shall provide notice to each participant and beneficiary under such plan regarding the coverage required by this section in accordance with regulations promulgated by the Secretary. Such notice shall be in writing and prominently positioned in any literature or correspondence made available or distributed by the plan or issuer and shall be transmitted—

(1) in the next mailing made by the plan or issuer to the participant or beneficiary;

(2) as part of any yearly informational packet sent to the participant or beneficiary; or

(3) not later than January 1, 1999;

whichever is earlier.

(c) Prohibitions

A group health plan, and a health insurance issuer offering group health insurance coverage in connection with a group health plan, may not—

(1) deny to a patient eligibility, or continued eligibility, to enroll or to renew coverage under the terms of the plan, solely for the purpose of avoiding the requirements of this section; and

(2) penalize or otherwise reduce or limit the reimbursement of an attending provider, or provide incentives (monetary or otherwise) to an attending provider, to induce such provider to provide care to an individual participant or beneficiary in a manner inconsistent with this section.

(d) Rule of construction

Nothing in this section shall be construed to prevent a group health plan or a health insurance issuer offering group health insurance coverage from negotiating the level and type of reimbursement with a provider for care provided in accordance with this section.

(e) Preemption, relation to State laws

(1) In general

Nothing in this section shall be construed to preempt any State law in effect on October 21, 1998, with respect to health insurance coverage that requires coverage of at least the coverage of reconstructive breast surgery otherwise required under this section.

(2) ERISA

Nothing in this section shall be construed to affect or modify the provisions of section 1144 of this title with respect to group health plans.

(Pub. L. 93–406, title I, § 713, as added Pub. L. 105–277, div. A, § 101(f) [title IX, § 902(a)], Oct. 21, 1998, 112 Stat. 2681–337, 2681–436.)

EFFECTIVE DATE

Pub. L. 105–277, div. A, § 101(f) [title IX, § 902(c)], Oct. 21, 1998, 112 Stat. 2681–337, 2681–438, provided that:

"(1) IN GENERAL.—The amendments made by this section [enacting this section] shall apply with respect to plan years beginning on or after the date of enactment of this Act [Oct. 21, 1998].

"(2) SPECIAL RULE FOR COLLECTIVE BARGAINING AGREEMENTS.—In the case of a group health plan maintained pursuant to 1 or more collective bargaining agreements between employee representatives and 1 or more employers, any plan amendment made pursuant to a collective bargaining agreement relating to the plan which amends the plan solely to conform to any requirement added by this section shall not be treated as a termination of such collective bargaining agreement."

§ 1185c. Coverage of dependent students on medically necessary leave of absence

(a) Medically necessary leave of absence

In this section, the term "medically necessary leave of absence" means, with respect to a dependent child described in subsection (b)(2) in connection with a group health plan or health insurance coverage offered in connection with such plan, a leave of absence of such child from a postsecondary educational institution (including an institution of higher education as defined in section 1002 of title 20), or any other change in enrollment of such child at such an institution, that—

(1) commences while such child is suffering from a serious illness or injury;

(2) is medically necessary; and

(3) causes such child to lose student status for purposes of coverage under the terms of the plan or coverage.

(b) Requirement to continue coverage

(1) In general

In the case of a dependent child described in paragraph (2), a group health plan, or a health insurance issuer that provides health insurance coverage in connection with a group health plan, shall not terminate coverage of such child under such plan or health insurance coverage due to a medically necessary leave of absence before the date that is the earlier of—

(A) the date that is 1 year after the first day of the medically necessary leave of absence; or

(B) the date on which such coverage would otherwise terminate under the terms of the plan or health insurance coverage.

(2) Dependent child described

A dependent child described in this paragraph is, with respect to a group health plan or health insurance coverage offered in connection with the plan, a beneficiary under the plan who—

(A) is a dependent child, under the terms of the plan or coverage, of a participant or beneficiary under the plan or coverage; and

(B) was enrolled in the plan or coverage, on the basis of being a student at a postsecondary educational institution (as described in subsection (a)), immediately before the first day of the medically necessary leave of absence involved.

(3) Certification by physician

Paragraph (1) shall apply to a group health plan or health insurance coverage offered by an issuer in connection with such plan only if the plan or issuer of the coverage has received written certification by a treating physician of the dependent child which states that the child is suffering from a serious illness or injury and that the leave of absence (or other change of enrollment) described in subsection (a) is medically necessary.

(c) Notice

A group health plan, and a health insurance issuer providing health insurance coverage in connection with a group health plan, shall include, with any notice regarding a requirement for certification of student status for coverage under the plan or coverage, a description of the terms of this section for continued coverage during medically necessary leaves of absence. Such description shall be in language which is understandable to the typical plan participant.

(d) No change in benefits

A dependent child whose benefits are continued under this section shall be entitled to the same benefits as if (during the medically necessary leave of absence) the child continued to be a covered student at the institution of higher education and was not on a medically necessary leave of absence.

(e) Continued application in case of changed coverage

If—

(1) a dependent child of a participant or beneficiary is in a period of coverage under a group health plan or health insurance coverage offered in connection with such a plan, pursuant to a medically necessary leave of absence of the child described in subsection (b);

(2) the manner in which the participant or beneficiary is covered under the plan changes, whether through a change in health insurance coverage or health insurance issuer, a change between health insurance coverage and self-insured coverage, or otherwise; and

(3) the coverage as so changed continues to provide coverage of beneficiaries as dependent children,

this section shall apply to coverage of the child under the changed coverage for the remainder of the period of the medically necessary leave of absence of the dependent child under the plan in the same manner as it would have applied if the changed coverage had been the previous coverage.

(Pub. L. 93–406, title I, §714, as added Pub. L. 110–381, §2(a)(1), Oct. 9, 2008, 122 Stat. 4081.)

EFFECTIVE DATE

Section applicable with respect to plan years beginning on or after the date that is one year after Oct. 9, 2008, and to medically necessary leaves of absence beginning during such plan years, see section 2(d) of Pub. L. 110–381, set out as a note under section 9813 of Title 26, Internal Revenue Code.

Subpart C—General Provisions

§1191. Preemption; State flexibility; construction

(a) Continued applicability of State law with respect to health insurance issuers

(1) In general

Subject to paragraph (2) and except as provided in subsection (b) of this section, this part shall not be construed to supersede any provision of State law which establishes, implements, or continues in effect any standard or requirement solely relating to health insurance issuers in connection with group health insurance coverage except to the extent that such standard or requirement prevents the application of a requirement of this part.

(2) Continued preemption with respect to group health plans

Nothing in this part shall be construed to affect or modify the provisions of section 1144 of this title with respect to group health plans.

(b) Special rules in case of portability requirements

(1) In general

Subject to paragraph (2), the provisions of this part relating to health insurance coverage offered by a health insurance issuer supersede any provision of State law which establishes, implements, or continues in effect a standard or requirement applicable to imposition of a preexisting condition exclusion specifically governed by section 1181 of this title which differs from the standards or requirements specified in such section.

(2) Exceptions

Only in relation to health insurance coverage offered by a health insurance issuer, the provisions of this part do not supersede any provision of State law to the extent that such provision—

(A) substitutes for the reference to "6-month period" in section 1181(a)(1) of this title a reference to any shorter period of time;

(B) substitutes for the reference to "12 months" and "18 months" in section 1181(a)(2) of this title a reference to any shorter period of time;

(C) substitutes for the references to "63 days" in sections 1181(c)(2)(A) and (d)(4)(A) of this title a reference to any greater number of days;

(D) substitutes for the reference to "30-day period" in sections 1181(b)(2) and (d)(1) of this title a reference to any greater period;

(E) prohibits the imposition of any preexisting condition exclusion in cases not described in section 1181(d) of this title or expands the exceptions described in such section;

(F) requires special enrollment periods in addition to those required under section 1181(f) of this title; or

(G) reduces the maximum period permitted in an affiliation period under section 1181(g)(1)(B) of this title.

(c) Rules of construction

Except as provided in section 1185 of this title, nothing in this part shall be construed as requiring a group health plan or health insurance coverage to provide specific benefits under the terms of such plan or coverage.

(d) Definitions

For purposes of this section—

(1) State law

The term "State law" includes all laws, decisions, rules, regulations, or other State action having the effect of law, of any State. A law of the United States applicable only to the District of Columbia shall be treated as a State law rather than a law of the United States.

(2) State

The term "State" includes a State, the Northern Mariana Islands, any political subdivisions of a State or such Islands, or any agency or instrumentality of either.

(Pub. L. 93–406, title I, §731, formerly §704, as added Pub. L. 104–191, title I, §101(a), Aug. 21, 1996, 110 Stat. 1946; renumbered §731 and amended Pub. L. 104–204, title VI, §603(a)(3), (b)(1), Sept. 26, 1996, 110 Stat. 2935, 2937.)

AMENDMENTS

1996—Subsec. (c). Pub. L. 104–204, §603(b)(1), substituted "Except as provided in section 1185 of this title, nothing" for "Nothing".

EFFECTIVE DATE OF 1996 AMENDMENT

Amendment by Pub. L. 104–204 applicable with respect to group health plans for plan years beginning on and after Jan. 1, 1998, see section 603(c) of Pub. L. 104–204, set out as a note under section 1003 of this title.

EFFECTIVE DATE

Section applicable with respect to group health plans for plan years beginning after June 30, 1997, except as otherwise provided, see section 101(g) of Pub. L. 104–191, set out as a note under section 1181 of this title.

§1191a. Special rules relating to group health plans

(a) General exception for certain small group health plans

The requirements of this part (other than section 1185 of this title) shall not apply to any group health plan (and group health insurance coverage offered in connection with a group health plan) for any plan year if, on the first day of such plan year, such plan has less than 2 participants who are current employees.

(b) Exception for certain benefits

The requirements of this part shall not apply to any group health plan (and group health insurance coverage) in relation to its provision of excepted benefits described in section 1191b(c)(1) of this title.

(c) Exception for certain benefits if certain conditions met

(1) Limited, excepted benefits

The requirements of this part shall not apply to any group health plan (and group health insurance coverage offered in connection with a group health plan) in relation to its provision of excepted benefits described in section 1191b(c)(2) of this title if the benefits—

(A) are provided under a separate policy, certificate, or contract of insurance; or

(B) are otherwise not an integral part of the plan.

(2) Noncoordinated, excepted benefits

The requirements of this part shall not apply to any group health plan (and group health insurance coverage offered in connection with a group health plan) in relation to its provision of excepted benefits described in section 1191b(c)(3) of this title if all of the following conditions are met:

(A) The benefits are provided under a separate policy, certificate, or contract of insurance.

(B) There is no coordination between the provision of such benefits and any exclusion of benefits under any group health plan maintained by the same plan sponsor.

(C) Such benefits are paid with respect to an event without regard to whether benefits are provided with respect to such an event under any group health plan maintained by the same plan sponsor.

(3) Supplemental excepted benefits

The requirements of this part shall not apply to any group health plan (and group health insurance coverage) in relation to its provision of excepted benefits described in section 1191b(c)(4) of this title if the benefits are provided under a separate policy, certificate, or contract of insurance.

(d) Treatment of partnerships

For purposes of this part—

(1) Treatment as a group health plan

Any plan, fund, or program which would not be (but for this subsection) an employee welfare benefit plan and which is established or maintained by a partnership, to the extent that such plan, fund, or program provides medical care (including items and services paid for as medical care) to present or former partners in the partnership or to their dependents (as defined under the terms of the plan, fund, or program), directly or through insurance, reimbursement, or otherwise, shall be treated (subject to paragraph (2)) as an employee welfare benefit plan which is a group health plan.

(2) Employer

In the case of a group health plan, the term "employer" also includes the partnership in relation to any partner.

(3) Participants of group health plans

In the case of a group health plan, the term "participant" also includes—

(A) in connection with a group health plan maintained by a partnership, an individual who is a partner in relation to the partnership, or

(B) in connection with a group health plan maintained by a self-employed individual (under which one or more employees are participants), the self-employed individual,

if such individual is, or may become, eligible to receive a benefit under the plan or such individual's beneficiaries may be eligible to receive any such benefit.

(Pub. L. 93–406, title I, §732, formerly §705, as added Pub. L. 104–191, title I, §101(a), Aug. 21, 1996, 110 Stat. 1948; renumbered §732 and amended Pub. L. 104–204, title VI, §603(a)(3), (b)(2), (3)(I)–(L), Sept. 26, 1996, 110 Stat. 2935, 2937, 2938.)

AMENDMENTS

1996—Subsec. (a). Pub. L. 104–204, §603(b)(2), inserted "(other than section 1185 of this title)" after "part".

Subsecs. (b), (c)(1) to (3). Pub. L. 104–204, §603(b)(3)(I)–(L), made technical amendment to references in original act which appear in text as references to section 1191b of this title.

EFFECTIVE DATE OF 1996 AMENDMENT

Amendment by Pub. L. 104–204 applicable with respect to group health plans for plan years beginning on and after Jan. 1, 1998, see section 603(c) of Pub. L. 104–204, set out as a note under section 1003 of this title.

EFFECTIVE DATE

Section applicable with respect to group health plans for plan years beginning after June 30, 1997, except as otherwise provided, see section 101(g) of Pub. L. 104–191, set out as a note under section 1181 of this title.

§ 1191b. Definitions

(a) Group health plan

For purposes of this part—

(1) In general

The term "group health plan" means an employee welfare benefit plan to the extent that the plan provides medical care (as defined in paragraph (2) and including items and services paid for as medical care) to employees or their dependents (as defined under the terms of the plan) directly or through insurance, reimbursement, or otherwise.

(2) Medical care

The term "medical care" means amounts paid for—

(A) the diagnosis, cure, mitigation, treatment, or prevention of disease, or amounts paid for the purpose of affecting any structure or function of the body,

(B) amounts paid for transportation primarily for and essential to medical care referred to in subparagraph (A), and

(C) amounts paid for insurance covering medical care referred to in subparagraphs (A) and (B).

(b) Definitions relating to health insurance

For purposes of this part—

(1) Health insurance coverage

The term "health insurance coverage" means benefits consisting of medical care (provided directly, through insurance or reimbursement, or otherwise and including items and services paid for as medical care) under any hospital or medical service policy or certificate, hospital or medical service plan contract, or health maintenance organization contract offered by a health insurance issuer.

(2) Health insurance issuer

The term "health insurance issuer" means an insurance company, insurance service, or insurance organization (including a health maintenance organization, as defined in paragraph (3)) which is licensed to engage in the business of insurance in a State and which is subject to State law which regulates insurance (within the meaning of section 1144(b)(2) of this title). Such term does not include a group health plan.

(3) Health maintenance organization

The term "health maintenance organization" means—

(A) a federally qualified health maintenance organization (as defined in section 1301(a) of the Public Health Service Act (42 U.S.C. 300e(a))),

(B) an organization recognized under State law as a health maintenance organization, or

(C) a similar organization regulated under State law for solvency in the same manner and to the same extent as such a health maintenance organization.

(4) Group health insurance coverage

The term "group health insurance coverage" means, in connection with a group health plan, health insurance coverage offered in connection with such plan.

(c) Excepted benefits

For purposes of this part, the term "excepted benefits" means benefits under one or more (or any combination thereof) of the following:

(1) Benefits not subject to requirements

(A) Coverage only for accident, or disability income insurance, or any combination thereof.

(B) Coverage issued as a supplement to liability insurance.

(C) Liability insurance, including general liability insurance and automobile liability insurance.

(D) Workers' compensation or similar insurance.

(E) Automobile medical payment insurance.

(F) Credit-only insurance.

(G) Coverage for on-site medical clinics.

(H) Other similar insurance coverage, specified in regulations, under which benefits for medical care are secondary or incidental to other insurance benefits.

(2) Benefits not subject to requirements if offered separately

(A) Limited scope dental or vision benefits.

(B) Benefits for long-term care, nursing home care, home health care, community-based care, or any combination thereof.

(C) Such other similar, limited benefits as are specified in regulations.

(3) Benefits not subject to requirements if offered as independent, noncoordinated benefits

(A) Coverage only for a specified disease or illness.

(B) Hospital indemnity or other fixed indemnity insurance.

(4) Benefits not subject to requirements if offered as separate insurance policy

Medicare supplemental health insurance (as defined under section 1395ss(g)(1) of title 42), coverage supplemental to the coverage provided under chapter 55 of title 10, and similar supplemental coverage provided to coverage under a group health plan.

(d) Other definitions

For purposes of this part—

(1) COBRA continuation provision

The term "COBRA continuation provision" means any of the following:

(A) Part 6 of this subtitle.

(B) Section 4980B of title 26, other than subsection (f)(1) of such section insofar as it relates to pediatric vaccines.

(C) Title XXII of the Public Health Service Act [42 U.S.C. 300bb-1 et seq.].

(2) Health status-related factor

The term "health status-related factor" means any of the factors described in section 1182(a)(1) of this title.

(3) Network plan

The term "network plan" means health insurance coverage offered by a health insurance issuer under which the financing and delivery of medical care (including items and services paid for as medical care) are provided, in whole or in part, through a defined set of providers under contract with the issuer.

(4) Placed for adoption

The term "placement", or being "placed", for adoption, has the meaning given such term in section 1169(c)(3)(B) of this title.

(5) Family member

The term "family member" means, with respect to an individual—

(A) a dependent (as such term is used for purposes of section 1181(f)(2) of this title) of such individual, and

(B) any other individual who is a first-degree, second-degree, third-degree, or fourth-degree relative of such individual or of an individual described in subparagraph (A).

(6) Genetic information

(A) In general

The term "genetic information" means, with respect to any individual, information about—

(i) such individual's genetic tests,

(ii) the genetic tests of family members of such individual, and

(iii) the manifestation of a disease or disorder in family members of such individual.

(B) Inclusion of genetic services and participation in genetic research

Such term includes, with respect to any individual, any request for, or receipt of, genetic services, or participation in clinical research which includes genetic services, by such individual or any family member of such individual.

(C) Exclusions

The term "genetic information" shall not include information about the sex or age of any individual.

(7) Genetic test

(A) In general

The term "genetic test" means an analysis of human DNA, RNA, chromosomes, proteins, or metabolites, that detects genotypes, mutations, or chromosomal changes.

(B) Exceptions

The term "genetic test" does not mean—

(i) an analysis of proteins or metabolites that does not detect genotypes, mutations, or chromosomal changes; or

(ii) an analysis of proteins or metabolites that is directly related to a manifested disease, disorder, or pathological condition that could reasonably be detected by a health care professional with appropriate training and expertise in the field of medicine involved.

(8) Genetic services

The term "genetic services" means—

(A) a genetic test;

(B) genetic counseling (including obtaining, interpreting, or assessing genetic information); or

(C) genetic education.

(9) Underwriting purposes

The term "underwriting purposes" means, with respect to any group health plan, or health insurance coverage offered in connection with a group health plan—

(A) rules for, or determination of, eligibility (including enrollment and continued eligibility) for benefits under the plan or coverage;

(B) the computation of premium or contribution amounts under the plan or coverage;

(C) the application of any pre-existing condition exclusion under the plan or coverage; and

(D) other activities related to the creation, renewal, or replacement of a contract of health insurance or health benefits.

(Pub. L. 93–406, title I, § 733, formerly § 706, as added Pub. L. 104–191, title I, § 101(a), Aug. 21, 1996, 110 Stat. 1949; renumbered § 733, Pub. L. 104–204, title VI, § 603(a)(3), Sept. 26, 1996, 110 Stat. 2935; amended Pub. L. 110–233, title I, § 101(d), May 21, 2008, 122 Stat. 885.)

REFERENCES IN TEXT

The Public Health Service Act, referred to in subsec. (d)(1)(C), is act July 1, 1944, ch. 373, 58 Stat. 682, as amended. Title XXII of the Act is classified generally to subchapter XX (§ 300bb–1 et seq.) of chapter 6A of Title 42, The Public Health and Welfare. For complete classification of this Act to the Code, see Short Title note set out under section 201 of Title 42 and Tables.

AMENDMENTS

2008—Subsec. (d)(5) to (9). Pub. L. 110–233 added pars. (5) to (9).

EFFECTIVE DATE OF 2008 AMENDMENT

Amendment by Pub. L. 110–233 applicable with respect to group health plans for plan years beginning after the date that is one year after May 21, 2008, see section 101(f)(2) of Pub. L. 110–233, set out as a note under section 1132 of this title.

EFFECTIVE DATE

Section applicable with respect to group health plans for plan years beginning after June 30, 1997, except as otherwise provided, see section 101(g) of Pub. L. 104–191, set out as a note under section 1181 of this title.

§ 1191c. Regulations

The Secretary, consistent with section 104 of the Health Care Portability and Accountability Act of 1996, may promulgate such regulations as may be necessary or appropriate to carry out the provisions of this part. The Secretary may promulgate any interim final rules as the Secretary determines are appropriate to carry out this part.

(Pub. L. 93–406, title I, § 734, formerly § 707, as added Pub. L. 104–191, title I, § 101(a), Aug. 21, 1996, 110 Stat. 1951; renumbered § 734, Pub. L. 104–204, title VI, § 603(a)(3), Sept. 26, 1996, 110 Stat. 2935.)

REFERENCES IN TEXT

Section 104 of the Health Care Portability and Accountability Act of 1996, referred to in text, probably means section 104 of the Health Insurance Portability and Accountability Act of 1996, Pub. L. 104–191, which is set out as a note under section 300gg–92 of Title 42, The Public Health and Welfare.

EFFECTIVE DATE

Section applicable with respect to group health plans for plan years beginning after June 30, 1997, except as otherwise provided, see section 101(g) of Pub. L. 104–191, set out as a note under section 1181 of this title.

SUBCHAPTER II—JURISDICTION, ADMINISTRATION, ENFORCEMENT; JOINT PENSION TASK FORCE, ETC.

SUBTITLE A—JURISDICTION, ADMINISTRATION, AND ENFORCEMENT

§ 1201. Procedures in connection with the issuance of certain determination letters by the Secretary of the Treasury covering qualifications under Internal Revenue Code

(a) Additional material required of applicants

Before issuing an advance determination of whether a pension, profit-sharing, or stock bonus plan, a trust which is a part of such a plan, or an annuity or bond purchase plan meets the requirements of part I of subchapter D of chapter 1 of title 26, the Secretary of the Treasury shall require the person applying for the determination to provide, in addition to any material and information necessary for such determination, such other material and information as may reasonably be made available at the time such application is made as the Secretary of Labor may require under subchapter I of this chapter for the administration of that subchapter. The Secretary of the Treasury shall also require that the applicant provide evidence satisfactory to the Secretary that the applicant has notified each employee who qualifies as an interested party (within the meaning of regulations prescribed under section 7476(b)(1) of title 26 (relating to declaratory judgments in connection with the qualification of certain retirement plans)) of the application for a determination.

(b) Opportunity to comment on application

(1) Whenever an application is made to the Secretary of the Treasury for a determination of whether a pension, profit-sharing, or stock bonus plan, a trust which is a part of such a plan, or an annuity or bond purchase plan meets the requirements of part I of subchapter D of chapter 1 of title 26, the Secretary shall upon request afford an opportunity to comment on the application at any time within 45 days after receipt thereof to—

(A) any employee or class of employee qualifying as an interested party within the meaning of the regulations referred to in subsection (a) of this section.[1]

(B) the Secretary of Labor, and

(C) the Pension Benefit Guaranty Corporation.

(2) The Secretary of Labor may not request an opportunity to comment upon such an application unless he has been requested in writing to do so by the Pension Benefit Guaranty Corporation or by the lesser of—

(A) 10 employees, or

(B) 10 percent of the employees

who qualify as interested parties within the meaning of the regulations referred to in subsection (a) of this section. Upon receiving such a request, the Secretary of Labor shall furnish a copy of the request to the Secretary of the Treasury within 5 days (excluding Saturdays, Sundays, and legal public holidays (as set forth in section 6103 of title 5)).

[1] So in original. The period probably should be a comma.

(3) Upon receiving such a request from the Secretary of Labor, the Secretary of the Treasury shall furnish to the Secretary of Labor such information held by the Secretary of the Treasury relating to the application as the Secretary of Labor may request.

(4) The Secretary of Labor shall, within 30 days after receiving a request from the Pension Benefit Guaranty Corporation or from the necessary number of employees who qualify as interested parties, notify the Secretary of the Treasury, the Pension Benefit Guaranty Corporation, and such employees with respect to whether he is going to comment on the application to which the request relates and with respect to any matters raised in such request on which he is not going to comment. If the Secretary of Labor indicates in the notice required under the preceding sentence that he is not going to comment on all or part of the matters raised in such request, the Secretary of the Treasury shall afford the corporation, and such employees, an opportunity to comment on the application with respect to any matter on which the Secretary of Labor has declined to comment.

(c) Intervention by Pension Benefit Guaranty Corporation or Secretary of Labor into declaratory judgment action under section 7476 of title 26, action by Corporation authorized

The Pension Benefit Guaranty Corporation and, upon petition of a group of employees referred to in subsection (b)(2) of this section, the Secretary of Labor, may intervene in any action brought for declaratory judgment under section 7476 of title 26 in accordance with the provisions of such section. The Pension Benefit Guaranty Corporation is permitted to bring an action under such section 7476 under such rules as may be prescribed by the United States Tax Court.

(d) Notification and information by Secretary of the Treasury to Secretary of Labor upon issuance by Secretary of the Treasury of a determination letter to applicant

If the Secretary of the Treasury determines that a plan or trust to which this section applies meets the applicable requirements of part I of subchapter D of chapter 1 of title 26 and issues a determination letter to the applicant, the Secretary shall notify the Secretary of Labor of his determination and furnish such information and material relating to the application and determination held by the Secretary of the Treasury as the Secretary of Labor may request for the proper administration of subchapter I of this chapter. The Secretary of Labor shall accept the determination of the Secretary of the Treasury as prima facie evidence of initial compliance by the plan with the standards of parts 2, 3, and 4 of subtitle B of subchapter I of this chapter. The determination of the Secretary of the Treasury shall not be prima facie evidence on issues relating solely to part 4 of subtitle B of subchapter I of this chapter. If an application for such a determination is withdrawn, or if the Secretary of the Treasury issues a determination that the plan or trust does not meet the requirements of such part I, the Secretary shall notify the Secretary of Labor of the withdrawal or determination.

(e) Effective date

This section does not apply with respect to an application for any plan received by the Secretary of the Treasury before the date on which section 410 of title 26 applies to the plan, or on which such section will apply if the plan is determined by the Secretary to be a qualified plan.

(Pub. L. 93–406, title III, §3001, Sept. 2, 1974, 88 Stat. 995; Pub. L. 100–203, title IX, §9343(b), Dec. 22, 1987, 101 Stat. 1330–372; Pub. L. 101–239, title VII, §7891(a)(1), Dec. 19, 1989, 103 Stat. 2445.)

AMENDMENTS

1989—Subsecs. (a), (b)(1), (c) to (e). Pub. L. 101–239 substituted "Internal Revenue Code of 1986" for "Internal Revenue Code of 1954", which for purposes of codification was translated as "title 26" thus requiring no change in text.

1987—Subsec. (d). Pub. L. 100–203 inserted after second sentence "The determination of the Secretary of the Treasury shall not be prima facie evidence on issues relating solely to part 4 of subtitle B of subchapter I of this chapter."

EFFECTIVE DATE OF 1989 AMENDMENT

Amendment by Pub. L. 101–239 effective, except as otherwise provided, as if included in the provision of the Tax Reform Act of 1986, Pub. L. 99–514, to which such amendment relates, see section 7891(f) of Pub. L. 101–239, set out as a note under section 1002 of this title.

§1202. Procedures with respect to continued compliance with Internal Revenue requirements relating to participation, vesting, and funding standards

(a) Notification by Secretary of the Treasury to Secretary of Labor of issuance of a preliminary notice of intent to disqualify or of commencement of proceedings to determine satisfaction of requirements

In carrying out the provisions of part I of subchapter D of chapter 1 of title 26 with respect to whether a plan or a trust meets the requirements of section 410(a) or 411 of title 26 (relating to minimum participation standards and minimum vesting standards, respectively), the Secretary of the Treasury shall notify the Secretary of Labor when the Secretary of the Treasury issues a preliminary notice of intent to disqualify related to the plan or trust or, if earlier, at the time of commencing any proceeding to determine whether the plan or trust satisfies such requirements. Unless the Secretary of the Treasury finds that the collection of a tax imposed under title 26 is in jeopardy, the Secretary of the Treasury shall not issue a determination that the plan or trust does not satisfy the requirements of such section until the expiration of a period of 60 days after the date on which he notifies the Secretary of Labor of such review. The Secretary of the Treasury, in his discretion, may extend the 60-day period referred to in the preceding sentence if he determines that such an extension would enable the Secretary of Labor to obtain compliance with such requirements by the plan within the extension period. Except as otherwise provided in this chapter, the Secretary of Labor shall not generally apply part 2 of subtitle B of subchapter I of this chapter to any plan or trust subject to sections 410(a) and 411 of title 26, but shall refer alleged general violations of the vesting or participation standards to the Secretary of the Treasury. (The preceding sentence shall not apply to matters relating to individuals benefits.)

(b) Notification to Secretary of Labor before Secretary of the Treasury sends notice of deficiency under section 4971 of title 26; waiver of imposition of tax; requests for investigation; consultation

Unless the Secretary of the Treasury finds that the collection of a tax is in jeopardy, in carrying out the provisions of section 4971 of title 26 (relating to taxes on the failure to meet minimum funding standards), the Secretary of the Treasury shall notify the Secretary of Labor before sending a notice of deficiency with respect to any tax imposed under that section on an employer, and, in accordance with the provisions of subsection (d) of that section, afford the Secretary of Labor an opportunity to comment on the imposition of the tax in the case. The Secretary of the Treasury may waive the imposition of the tax imposed under section 4971(b) of title 26 in appropriate cases. Upon receiving a written request from the Secretary of Labor or from the Pension Benefit Guaranty Corporation, the Secretary of the Treasury shall cause an investigation to be commenced expeditiously with respect to whether the tax imposed under section 4971 of title 26 should be applied with respect to any employer to which the request relates. The Secretary of the Treasury and the Secretary of Labor shall consult with each other from time to time with respect to the provisions of section 412 of title 26 (relating to minimum funding standards) and with respect to the funding standards applicable under subchapter I of this chapter in order to coordinate the rules applicable under such standards.

(c) Extended application of regulations prescribed by Secretary of the Treasury relating to minimum participation standards, minimum vesting standards, and minimum funding standards

Regulations prescribed by the Secretary of the Treasury under sections 410(a), 411, and 412 of title 26 (relating to minimum participation standards, minimum vesting standards, and minimum funding standards, respectively) shall also apply to the minimum participation, vesting, and funding standards set forth in parts 2 and 3 of subtitle B of subchapter I of this chapter. Except as otherwise expressly provided in this chapter, the Secretary of Labor shall not prescribe other regulations under such parts, or apply the regulations prescribed by the Secretary of the Treasury under sections 410(a), 411, 412 of title 26 and applicable to the minimum participation, vesting, and funding standards under such parts in a manner inconsistent with the way such regulations apply under sections 410(a), 411, and 412 of title 26.

(d) Opportunity afforded Secretary of the Treasury to intervene in cases involving construction or application of minimum standards; review of briefs filed by Pension Benefit Guaranty Corporation or Secretary of Labor

The Secretary of Labor and the Pension Benefit Guaranty Corporation, before filing briefs in any case involving the construction or application of minimum participation standards, minimum vesting standards, or minimum funding standards under subchapter I of this chapter shall afford the Secretary of the Treasury a reasonable opportunity to review any such brief. The Secretary of the Treasury shall have the right to intervene in any such case.

(e) Consultative requirements respecting promulgation of proposed or final regulations

The Secretary of the Treasury shall consult with the Pension Benefit Guaranty Corporation with respect to any proposed or final regulation authorized by subpart C of part I of subchapter D of chapter 1 of title 26, or by sections 1421 through 1426 of this title, before publishing any such proposed or final regulation.

(Pub. L. 93–406, title III, §3002, Sept. 2, 1974, 88 Stat. 996; Pub. L. 96–364, title IV, §402(b)(3), Sept. 26, 1980, 94 Stat. 1299; Pub. L. 101–239, title VII, §7891(a)(1), Dec. 19, 1989, 103 Stat. 2445.)

REFERENCES IN TEXT

This chapter, referred to in subsecs. (a), (c), was in the original "this Act", meaning Pub. L. 93–406, known as the Employee Retirement Income Security Act of 1974. Titles I, III, and IV of such Act are classified principally to this chapter. For complete classification of this Act to the Code, see Short Title note set out under section 1001 of this title and Tables.

Subpart C of part I of subchapter D of chapter 1 of title 26, referred to in subsec. (e), commences with section 418 of Title 26, Internal Revenue Code.

AMENDMENTS

1989—Subsecs. (a) to (c), (e). Pub. L. 101–239 substituted "Internal Revenue Code of 1986" for "Internal Revenue Code of 1954" wherever appearing, which for purposes of codification was translated as "title 26".

1980—Subsec. (e). Pub. L. 96–364 added subsec. (e).

EFFECTIVE DATE OF 1989 AMENDMENT

Amendment by Pub. L. 101–239 effective, except as otherwise provided, as if included in the provision of the Tax Reform Act of 1986, Pub. L. 99–514, to which such amendment relates, see section 7891(f) of Pub. L. 101–239, set out as a note under section 1002 of this title.

EFFECTIVE DATE OF 1980 AMENDMENT

Amendment by Pub. L. 96–364 effective Sept. 26, 1980, except as specifically provided, see section 1461(e) of this title.

§1202a. Employee plans compliance resolution system

(a) In general

The Secretary of the Treasury shall have full authority to establish and implement the Employee Plans Compliance Resolution System (or any successor program) and any other employee plans correction policies, including the authority to waive income, excise, or other taxes to ensure that any tax, penalty, or sanction is not excessive and bears a reasonable relationship to the nature, extent, and severity of the failure.

(b) Improvements

The Secretary of the Treasury shall continue to update and improve the Employee Plans Compliance Resolution System (or any successor program), giving special attention to—

(1) increasing the awareness and knowledge of small employers concerning the availability and use of the program;

(2) taking into account special concerns and circumstances that small employers face with respect to compliance and correction of compliance failures;

(3) extending the duration of the self-correction period under the Self-Correction Program for significant compliance failures;

(4) expanding the availability to correct insignificant compliance failures under the Self-Correction Program during audit; and

(5) assuring that any tax, penalty, or sanction that is imposed by reason of a compliance failure is not excessive and bears a reasonable relationship to the nature, extent, and severity of the failure.

(Pub. L. 109–280, title XI, §1101, Aug. 17, 2006, 120 Stat. 1055.)

CODIFICATION

Section was enacted as part of the Pension Protection Act of 2006, and not as part of the Employee Retirement Income Security Act of 1974 which comprises this chapter.

§1203. Procedures in connection with prohibited transactions

(a) Notification to Secretary of Labor; opportunity to comment on imposition of tax under section 4975 of title 26; waiver; requests for investigations

Unless the Secretary of the Treasury finds that the collection of a tax is in jeopardy, in carrying out the provisions of section 4975 of title 26 (relating to tax on prohibited transactions) the Secretary of the Treasury shall, in accordance with the provisions of subsection (h) of such section, notify the Secretary of Labor before sending a notice of deficiency with respect to the tax imposed by subsection (a) or (b) of such section, and, in accordance with the provisions of subsection (h) of such section, afford the Secretary an opportunity to comment on the imposition of the tax in any case. The Secretary of the Treasury shall have authority to waive the imposition of the tax imposed under section 4975(b) in appropriate cases. Upon receiving a written request from the Secretary of Labor or from the Pension Benefit Guaranty Corporation, the Secretary of the Treasury shall cause an investigation to be carried out with respect to whether the tax imposed by section 4975 of title 26 should be applied to any person referred to in the request.

(b) Consultation

The Secretary of the Treasury and the Secretary of Labor shall consult with each other from time to time with respect to the provisions of section 4975 of title 26 (relating to tax on prohibited transactions) and with respect to the provisions of subchapter I of this chapter relating to prohibited transactions and exemptions therefrom in order to coordinate the rules applicable under such standards.

(c) Transmission of information to Secretary of the Treasury

Whenever the Secretary of Labor obtains information indicating that a party-in-interest or disqualified person is violating section 1106 of this title, he shall transmit such information to the Secretary of the Treasury.

(Pub. L. 93–406, title III, §3003, Sept. 2, 1974, 88 Stat. 998; Pub. L. 101–239, title VII, §7891(a)(1), Dec. 19, 1989, 103 Stat. 2445.)

AMENDMENTS

1989—Subsecs. (a), (b). Pub. L. 101–239 substituted "Internal Revenue Code of 1986" for "Internal Revenue Code of 1954", which for purposes of codification was translated as "title 26" thus requiring no change in text.

EFFECTIVE DATE OF 1989 AMENDMENT

Amendment by Pub. L. 101–239 effective, except as otherwise provided, as if included in the provision of the Tax Reform Act of 1986, Pub. L. 99–514, to which such amendment relates, see section 7891(f) of Pub. L. 101–239, set out as a note under section 1002 of this title.

§1204. Coordination between the Department of the Treasury and the Department of Labor

(a) Whenever in this chapter or in any provision of law amended by this chapter the Secretary of the Treasury and the Secretary of Labor are required to carry out provisions relating to the same subject matter (as determined by them) they shall consult with each other and shall develop rules, regulations, practices, and forms which, to the extent appropriate for the efficient administration of such provisions, are designed to reduce duplication of effort, duplication of reporting, conflicting or overlapping requirements, and the burden of compliance with such provisions by plan administrators, employers, and participants and beneficiaries.

(b) In order to avoid unnecessary expense and duplication of functions among Government agencies, the Secretary of the Treasury and the Secretary of Labor may make such arrangements or agreements for cooperation or mutual assistance in the performance of their functions under this chapter, and the functions of any such agencies as they find to be practicable and consistent with law. The Secretary of the Treasury and the Secretary of Labor may utilize, on a reimbursable or other basis, the facilities or services, of any department, agency, or establishment of the United States or of any State or political subdivision of a State, including the services, of any of its employees, with the lawful consent of such department, agency, or establishment; and each department, agency, or establishment of the United States is authorized and directed to cooperate with the Secretary of the Treasury and the Secretary of Labor and, to the extent permitted by law, to provide such information and facilities as they may request for their assistance in the performance of their functions under this chapter. The Attorney General or his representative shall receive from the Secretary of the Treasury and the Secretary of Labor for appropriate action such evidence developed in the performance of their functions under this chapter as may be found to warrant consideration for criminal prosecution under the provisions of this subchapter or other Federal law.

(Pub. L. 93–406, title III, §3004, Sept. 2, 1974, 88 Stat. 998.)

REFERENCES IN TEXT

This chapter, referred to in text, was in the original "this Act", meaning Pub. L. 93–406, known as the Employee Retirement Income Security Act of 1974. Titles I, III, and IV of such Act are classified principally to this chapter. For complete classification of this Act to the Code, see Short Title note set out under section 1001 of this title and Tables.

SUBTITLE B—JOINT PENSION, PROFIT-SHARING, AND EMPLOYEE STOCK OWNERSHIP PLAN TASK FORCE; STUDIES

PART 1—JOINT PENSION, PROFIT-SHARING, AND EMPLOYEE STOCK OWNERSHIP PLAN TASK FORCE

§1221. Establishment

The staffs of the Committee on Ways and Means and the Committee on Education and Labor of the House of Representatives, the Joint Committee on Taxation, and the Committee on Finance and the Committee on Labor and Public Welfare of the Senate shall carry out the duties assigned under this subchapter to the Joint Pension, Profit-Sharing, and Employee Stock Ownership Plan Task Force. By agreement among the chairmen of such Committees, the Joint Pension, Profit-Sharing, and Employee Stock Ownership Plan Task Force shall be furnished with office space, clerical personnel, and such supplies and equipment as may be necessary for the Joint Pension, Profit-Sharing, and Employee Stock Ownership Plan Task Force to carry out its duties under this subchapter.

(Pub. L. 93–406, title III, §3021, Sept. 2, 1974, 88 Stat. 999; Pub. L. 94–455, title VIII, §803(i)(2)(A)(iii), title XIX, §1907(a)(5), Oct. 4, 1976, 90 Stat. 1591, 1836.)

AMENDMENTS

1976—Pub. L. 94–455, §803(i)(2)(A)(iii), substituted "Joint Pension, Profit-Sharing, and Employee Stock Ownership Plan Task Force" for "Joint Pension Task Force" wherever appearing.

CHANGE OF NAME

"Joint Committee on Taxation" substituted for "Joint Committee on Internal Revenue Taxation" on authority of section 1907(a)(5) of Pub. L. 94–455.

Committee on Labor and Public Welfare of Senate abolished and replaced by Committee on Human Resources of Senate, effective Feb. 11, 1977. See Rule XXV of Standing Rules of Senate, as amended by Senate Resolution No. 4 (popularly cited as the "Committee System Reorganization Amendments of 1977"), approved Feb. 4, 1977. Committee on Human Resources of Senate changed to Committee on Labor and Human Resources of Senate, effective Mar. 7, 1979, by Senate Resolution No. 30, 96th Congress. See, also, Rule XXV of Standing Rules of Senate adopted Nov. 14, 1979. Committee on Labor and Human Resources of Senate changed to Committee on Health, Education, Labor, and Pensions of Senate by Senate Resolution No. 20, One Hundred Sixth Congress, Jan. 19, 1999.

§1222. Duties

(a) The Joint Pension, Profit-Sharing, and Employee Stock Ownership Plan Task Force shall, within 24 months after September 2, 1974, make a full study and review of—

(1) the effect of the requirements of section 411 of title 26 and of section 1053 of this title to determine the extent of discrimination, if any, among employees in various age groups resulting from the application of such requirements;

(2) means of providing for the portability of pension rights among different pension plans;

(3) the appropriate treatment under subchapter III of this chapter (relating to termination insurance) of plans established and maintained by small employers;

(4) the broadening of stock ownership, particularly with regard to employee stock ownership plans (as defined in section 4975(e)(7) of title 26 and section 1107(d)(6) of this title) and all other alternative methods for broadening stock ownership to the American labor force and others;

(5) the effects and desirability of the Federal preemption of State and local law with respect to matters relating to pension and similar plans; and

(6) such other matter as any of the committees referred to in section 1221 of this title may refer to it.

(b) The Joint Pension, Profit-Sharing, and Employee Stock Ownership Plan Task Force shall report the results of its study and review to each of the committees referred to in section 1221 of this title.

(Pub. L. 93–406, title III, §3022, Sept. 2, 1974, 88 Stat. 999; Pub. L. 94–455, title VIII, §803(i)(1), (2)(A)(iii), Oct. 4, 1976, 90 Stat. 1590, 1591; Pub. L. 101–239, title VII, §7891(a)(1), Dec. 19, 1989, 103 Stat. 2445.)

AMENDMENTS

1989—Subsec. (a)(1), (4). Pub. L. 101–239 substituted "Internal Revenue Code of 1986" for "Internal Revenue Code of 1954", which for purposes of codification was translated as "title 26" thus requiring no change in text.

1976—Subsec. (a). Pub. L. 94–455, §803(i)(1), (2)(A)(iii), substituted "Joint Pension, Profit-Sharing, and Employee Stock Ownership Plan Task Force" for "Joint Pension Task Force" in provision preceding par. (1), redesignated pars. (4) and (5) as (5) and (6), respectively, and added par. (4).

Subsec. (b). Pub. L. 94–455, §803(i)(2)(A)(iii), substituted "Joint Pension, Profit-Sharing, and Employee Stock Ownership Plan Task Force" for "Joint Pension Task Force".

EFFECTIVE DATE OF 1989 AMENDMENT

Amendment by Pub. L. 101–239 effective, except as otherwise provided, as if included in the provision of the Tax Reform Act of 1986, Pub. L. 99–514, to which such amendment relates, see section 7891(f) of Pub. L. 101–239, set out as a note under section 1002 of this title.

PART 2—OTHER STUDIES

§1231. Congressional study

(a) The Committee on Education and Labor and the Committee on Ways and Means of the House of Representatives and the Committee on Finance and the Committee on Labor and Public Welfare of the Senate shall study retirement plans established and maintained or financed (directly or indirectly) by the Government of the United States, by any State (including the District of Columbia) or political subdivision thereof, or by any agency or instrumentality of any of the foregoing. Such study shall include an analysis of—

(1) the adequacy of existing levels of participation, vesting, and financing arrangements,

(2) existing fiduciary standards, and

(3) the necessity for Federal legislation and standards with respect to such plans.

In determining whether any such plan is adequately financed, each committee shall consider the necessity for minimum funding standards, as well as the taxing power of the government maintaining the plan.

(b) Not later than December 31, 1976, the Committee on Education and Labor and the Committee on Ways and Means shall each submit to the House of Representatives the results of the studies conducted under this section, together with such recommendations as they deem appropriate. The Committee on Finance and the Committee on Labor and Public Welfare shall each submit to the Senate the results of the studies conducted under this section together with such recommendations as they deem appropriate not later than such date.

(Pub. L. 93–406, title III, §3031, Sept. 2, 1974, 88 Stat. 999.)

CHANGE OF NAME

Committee on Labor and Public Welfare of Senate abolished and replaced by Committee on Human Resources of Senate, effective Feb. 11, 1977. See Rule XXV of Standing Rules of Senate, as amended by Senate Resolution No. 4 (popularly cited as the "Committee System Reorganization Amendments of 1977"), approved Feb. 4, 1977. Committee on Human Resources of Senate changed to Committee on Labor and Human Resources of Senate, effective Mar. 7, 1979, by Senate Resolution No. 30, 96th Congress. See, also, Rule XXV of Standing Rules of Senate adopted Nov. 14, 1979. Committee on Labor and Human Resources of Senate changed to Committee on Health, Education, Labor, and Pensions of Senate by Senate Resolution No. 20, One Hundred Sixth Congress, Jan. 19, 1999.

§1232. Protection for employees under Federal procurement, construction, and research contracts and grants

(a) Study and investigation by Secretary of Labor

The Secretary of Labor shall, during the 2-year period beginning on September 2, 1974, conduct a full and complete study and investigation of the steps necessary to be taken to insure that professional, scientific, and technical personnel and others working in associated occupations employed under Federal procurement, construction, or research contracts or grants will, to the extent feasible, be protected against forfeitures of pension or retirement rights or benefits, otherwise provided, as a consequence of job transfers or loss of employment resulting from terminations or modifications of Federal contracts, grants, or procurement policies. The Secretary of Labor shall report the results of his study and investigation to the Congress within 2 years after September 2, 1974. The Secretary of Labor is authorized, to the extent provided by law, to obtain the services of private research institutions and such other persons by contract or other arrangement as he determines necessary in carrying out the provisions of this section.

(b) Consultation

In the course of conducting the study and investigation described in subsection (a) of this section, and in developing the regulations referred to in subsection (c) of this section, the Secretary of Labor shall consult—

(1) with appropriate professional societies, business organizations, and labor organizations, and

(2) with the heads of interested Federal departments and agencies.

(c) Regulations

Within 1 year after the date on which he submits his report to the Congress under subsection (a) of this section, the Secretary of Labor shall, if he determines it to be feasible, develop regulations, which will provide the protection of pension and retirement rights and benefits referred to in subsection (a) of this section.

(d) Congressional review of regulations; resolution of disapproval

(1) Any regulations developed pursuant to subsection (c) of this section shall take effect if, and only if—

(A) the Secretary of Labor, not later than the day which is 3 years after September 2, 1974, delivers a copy of such regulations to the House of Representatives and a copy to the Senate, and

(B) before the close of the 120-day period which begins on the day on which the copies of such regulations are delivered to the House of Representatives and to the Senate, neither the House of Representatives nor the Senate adopts, by an affirmative vote of a majority of those present and voting in that House, a resolution of disapproval.

(2) For purposes of this subsection, the term "resolution of disapproval" means only a resolution of either House of Congress, the matter after the resolving clause of which is as follows: "That the ___ does not favor the taking effect of the regulations transmitted to the Congress by the Secretary of Labor on ___", the first blank space therein being filled with the name of the resolving House and the second blank space therein being filled with the day and year.

(3) A resolution of disapproval in the House of Representatives shall be referred to the Committee on Education and Labor. A resolution of disapproval in the Senate shall be referred to the Committee on Labor and Public Welfare.

(4)(A) If the committee to which a resolution of disapproval has been referred has not reported it at the end of 7 calendar days after its introduction, it is in order to move either to discharge the committee from further consideration of the resolution or to discharge the committee from further consideration of any other resolution of disapproval which has been referred to the committee.

(B) A motion to discharge may be made only by an individual favoring the resolution, is highly privileged (except that it may not be made after the committee has reported a resolution of disapproval), and debate thereon shall be limited to not more than 1 hour, to be divided equally between those favoring and those opposing the resolution. An amendment to the motion is not in order, and it is not in order to move to reconsider the vote by which the motion is agreed to or disagreed to.

(C) If the motion to discharge is agreed to or disagreed to, the motion may not be renewed, nor may another motion to discharge the committee be made with respect to any other resolution of disapproval.

(5)(A) When the committee has reported, or has been discharged from further consideration of, a resolution of disapproval, it is at any time thereafter in order (even though a previous motion to the same effect has been disagreed to) to move to proceed to the consideration of the resolution. The motion is highly privileged and is not debatable. An amendment to the motion is not in order, and it is not in order to move to reconsider the vote by which the motion is agreed to or disagreed to.

(B) Debate on the resolution of disapproval shall be limited to not more than 10 hours, which shall be divided equally between those favoring and those opposing the resolution. A motion further to limit debate is not debatable. An amendment to, or motion to recommit, the resolution is not in order, and it is not in order to move to reconsider the vote by which the resolution is agreed to or disagreed to.

(6)(A) Motions to postpone, made with respect to the discharge from committee or the consideration of a resolution of disapproval, and motions to proceed to the consideration of other business, shall be decided without debate.

(B) Appeals from the decisions of the Chair relating to the application of the rules of the House of Representatives or the Senate, as the case may be, to the procedure relating to any resolution of disapproval shall be decided without debate.

(7) Whenever the Secretary of Labor transmits copies of the regulations to the Congress, a copy of such regulations shall be delivered to each House of Congress on the same day and shall be delivered to the Clerk of the House of Representatives if the House is not in session and to the Secretary of the Senate if the Senate is not in session.

(8) The 120 day period referred to in paragraph (1) shall be computed by excluding—

(A) the days on which either House is not in session because of an adjournment of more than 3 days to a day certain or an adjournment of the Congress sine die, and

(B) any Saturday and Sunday, not excluded under subparagraph (A), when either House is not in session.

(9) This subsection is enacted by the Congress—

(A) as an exercise of the rulemaking power of the House of Representatives and the Senate, respectively, and as such they are deemed a part of the rules of each House, respectively, but applicable only with respect to the procedure to be followed in that House in the case of resolutions of disapproval described in paragraph (2); and they supersede other rules only to the extent that they are inconsistent therewith; and

(B) with full recognition of the constitutional right of either House to change the rules (so far as relating to the procedures of that House) at any time, in the same manner and to the same extent as in the case of any other rule of that House.

(Pub. L. 93–406, title III, §3032, Sept. 2, 1974, 88 Stat. 1000.)

CHANGE OF NAME

Committee on Labor and Public Welfare of Senate abolished and replaced by Committee on Human Resources of Senate, effective Feb. 11, 1977. See Rule XXV of Standing Rules of Senate, as amended by Senate Resolution No. 4 (popularly cited as the "Committee System Reorganization Amendments of 1977"), approved Feb. 4, 1977. Committee on Human Resources of Senate changed to Committee on Labor and Human Resources of Senate, effective Mar. 7, 1979, by Senate Resolution No. 30, 96th Congress. See, also, Rule XXV of Standing Rules of Senate adopted Nov. 14, 1979. Committee on Labor and Human Resources of Senate changed to Committee on Health, Education, Labor, and Pensions of Senate by Senate Resolution No. 20, One Hundred Sixth Congress, Jan. 19, 1999.

SUBTITLE C—ENROLLMENT OF ACTUARIES

§1241. Joint Board for the Enrollment of Actuaries

The Secretary of Labor and the Secretary of the Treasury shall, not later than the last day of the first calendar month beginning after September 2, 1974, establish a Joint Board for the Enrollment of Actuaries (hereinafter in this part referred to as the "Joint Board").

(Pub. L. 93–406, title III, §3041, Sept. 2, 1974, 88 Stat. 1002.)

§1242. Enrollment by Board; standards and qualifications; suspension or termination of enrollment

(a) The Joint Board shall, by regulations, establish reasonable standards and qualifications for persons performing actuarial services with respect to plans in which this chapter applies and, upon application by any individual, shall enroll such individual if the Joint Board finds that such individual satisfies such standards and qualifications. With respect to individuals applying for enrollment before January 1, 1976, such standards and qualifications shall include a requirement for an appropriate period of responsible actuarial experience relating to pension plans. With respect to individuals applying for enrollment on or after January 1, 1976, such standards and qualifications shall include—

(1) education and training in actuarial mathematics and methodology, as evidenced by—

(A) a degree in actuarial mathematics or its equivalent from an accredited college or university,

(B) successful completion of an examination in actuarial mathematics and methodology to be given by the Joint Board, or

(C) successful completion of other actuarial examinations deemed adequate by the Joint Board, and

(2) an appropriate period of responsible actuarial experience.

Notwithstanding the preceding provisions of this subsection, the Joint Board may provide for the temporary enrollment for the period ending January 1, 1976, of actuaries under such interim standards as it deems adequate.

(b) The Joint Board may, after notice and an opportunity for a hearing, suspend or terminate the enrollment of an individual under this section if the Joint Board finds that such individual—

(1) has failed to discharge his duties under this chapter, or

(2) does not satisfy the requirements for enrollment as in effect at the time of his enrollment.

The Joint Board may also, after notice and opportunity for hearing, suspend or terminate the temporary enrollment of an individual who fails to discharge his duties under this chapter or who does not satisfy the interim enrollment standards.

(Pub. L. 93–406, title III, § 3042, Sept. 2, 1974, 88 Stat. 1002.)

REFERENCES IN TEXT

This chapter, referred to in subsecs. (a) and (b), was in the original "this Act", meaning Pub. L. 93–406, known as the Employee Retirement Income Security Act of 1974. Titles I, III, and IV of such Act are classified principally to this chapter. For complete classification of this Act to the Code, see Short Title note set out under section 1001 of this title and Tables.

SUBCHAPTER III—PLAN TERMINATION INSURANCE

SUBTITLE A—PENSION BENEFIT GUARANTY CORPORATION

§ 1301. Definitions

(a) For purposes of this subchapter, the term—

(1) "administrator" means the person or persons described in paragraph (16) of section 1002 of this title;

(2) "substantial employer", for any plan year of a single-employer plan, means one or more persons—

(A) who are contributing sponsors of the plan in such plan year,

(B) who, at any time during such plan year, are members of the same controlled group, and

(C) whose required contributions to the plan for each plan year constituting one of—

(i) the two immediately preceding plan years, or

(ii) the first two of the three immediately preceding plan years,

total an amount greater than or equal to 10 percent of all contributions required to be paid to or under the plan for such plan year;

(3) "multiemployer plan" means a plan—

(A) to which more than one employer is required to contribute,

(B) which is maintained pursuant to one or more collective bargaining agreements between one or more employee organizations and more than one employer, and

(C) which satisfies such other requirements as the Secretary of Labor may prescribe by regulation,

except that, in applying this paragraph—

(i) a plan shall be considered a multiemployer plan on and after its termination date if the plan was a multiemployer plan under this paragraph for the plan year preceding such termination, and

(ii) for any plan year which began before September 26, 1980, the term "multiemployer plan" means a plan described in section 414(f) of title 26 as in effect immediately before such date;

(4) "corporation", except where the context clearly requires otherwise, means the Pension Benefit Guaranty Corporation established under section 1302 of this title;

(5) "fund" means the appropriate fund established under section 1305 of this title;

(6) "basic benefits" means benefits guaranteed under section 1322 of this title (other than under section 1322(c)[1] of this title), or under section 1322a of this title (other than under section 1322a(g) of this title);

(7) "non-basic benefits" means benefits guaranteed under section 1322(c)[1] of this title or 1322a(g) of this title;

(8) "nonforfeitable benefit" means, with respect to a plan, a benefit for which a participant has satisfied the conditions for entitlement under the plan or the requirements of this chapter (other than submission of a formal application, retirement, completion of a required waiting period, or death in the case of a benefit which returns all or a portion of a participant's accumulated mandatory employee contributions upon the participant's death), whether or not the benefit may subsequently be reduced or suspended by a plan amendment, an occurrence of any condition, or operation of this chapter or title 26;

(9) "reorganization index" means the amount determined under section 1421(b) of this title;

(10) "plan sponsor" means, with respect to a multiemployer plan—

(A) the plan's joint board of trustees, or

(B) if the plan has no joint board of trustees, the plan administrator;

(11) "contribution base unit" means a unit with respect to which an employer has an obligation to contribute under a multiemployer plan, as defined in regulations prescribed by the Secretary of the Treasury;

(12) "outstanding claim for withdrawal liability" means a plan's claim for the unpaid balance of the liability determined under part 1 of subtitle E of this subchapter for which demand has been made, valued in accordance with regulations prescribed by the corporation;

(13) "contributing sponsor", of a single-employer plan, means a person described in section 1082(b)(1) of this title (without regard to section 1082(b)(2) of this title) or section 412(b)(1) of title 26 (without regard to section 412(b)(2) of such title).[2]

(14) in the case of a single-employer plan—

(A) "controlled group" means, in connection with any person, a group consisting of such person and all other persons under common control with such person;

(B) the determination of whether two or more persons are under "common control" shall be made under regulations of the cor-

[1] See References in Text note below.

[2] So in original. The period probably should be a semicolon.

poration which are consistent and coextensive with regulations prescribed for similar purposes by the Secretary of the Treasury under subsections (b) and (c) of section 414 of title 26; and

(C)(i) notwithstanding any other provision of this subchapter, during any period in which an individual possesses, directly or indirectly, the power to direct or cause the direction of the management and policies of an affected air carrier of which he was an accountable owner, whether through the ownership of voting securities, by contract, or otherwise, the affected air carrier shall be considered to be under common control not only with those persons described in subparagraph (B), but also with all related persons; and

(ii) for purposes of this subparagraph, the term—

(I) "affected air carrier" means an air carrier, as defined in section 40102(a)(2) of title 49, that holds a certificate of public convenience and necessity under section 41102 of title 49 for route number 147, as of November 12, 1991;

(II) "related person" means any person which was under common control (as determined under subparagraph (B)) with an affected air carrier on October 10, 1991, or any successor to such related person;

(III) "accountable owner" means any individual who on October 10, 1991, owned directly or indirectly through the application of section 318 of title 26 more than 50 percent of the total voting power of the stock of an affected air carrier;

(IV) "successor" means any person that acquires, directly or indirectly through the application of section 318 of title 26, more than 50 percent of the total voting power of the stock of a related person, more than 50 percent of the total value of the securities (as defined in section 1002(20) of this title) of the related person, more than 50 percent of the total value of the assets of the related person, or any person into which such related person shall be merged or consolidated; and

(V) "individual" means a living human being;

(15) "single-employer plan" means any defined benefit plan (as defined in section 1002(35) of this title) which is not a multiemployer plan;

(16) "benefit liabilities" means the benefits of employees and their beneficiaries under the plan (within the meaning of section 401(a)(2) of title 26);

(17) "amount of unfunded guaranteed benefits", of a participant or beneficiary as of any date under a single-employer plan, means an amount equal to the excess of—

(A) the actuarial present value (determined as of such date on the basis of assumptions prescribed by the corporation for purposes of section 1344 of this title) of the benefits of the participant or beneficiary under the plan which are guaranteed under section 1322 of this title, over

(B) the current value (as of such date) of the assets of the plan which are required to be allocated to those benefits under section 1344 of this title;

(18) "amount of unfunded benefit liabilities" means, as of any date, the excess (if any) of—

(A) the value of the benefit liabilities under the plan (determined as of such date on the basis of assumptions prescribed by the corporation for purposes of section 1344 of this title), over

(B) the current value (as of such date) of the assets of the plan;

(19) "outstanding amount of benefit liabilities" means, with respect to any plan, the excess (if any) of—

(A) the value of the benefit liabilities under the plan (determined as of the termination date on the basis of assumptions prescribed by the corporation for purposes of section 1344 of this title), over

(B) the value of the benefit liabilities which would be so determined by only taking into account benefits which are guaranteed under section 1322 of this title or to which assets of the plan are allocated under section 1344 of this title;

(20) "person" has the meaning set forth in section 1002(9) of this title;

(21) "affected party" means, with respect to a plan—

(A) each participant in the plan,

(B) each beneficiary under the plan who is a beneficiary of a deceased participant or who is an alternate payee (within the meaning of section 1056(d)(3)(K) of this title) under an applicable qualified domestic relations order (within the meaning of section 1056(d)(3)(B)(i) of this title),

(C) each employee organization representing participants in the plan, and

(D) the corporation,

except that, in connection with any notice required to be provided to the affected party, if an affected party has designated, in writing, a person to receive such notice on behalf of the affected party, any reference to the affected party shall be construed to refer to such person.

(b)(1) An individual who owns the entire interest in an unincorporated trade or business is treated as his own employer, and a partnership is treated as the employer of each partner who is an employee within the meaning of section 401(c)(1) of title 26. For purposes of this subchapter, under regulations prescribed by the corporation, all employees of trades or businesses (whether or not incorporated) which are under common control shall be treated as employed by a single employer and all such trades and businesses as a single employer. The regulations prescribed under the preceding sentence shall be consistent and coextensive with regulations prescribed for similar purposes by the Secretary of the Treasury under section 414(c) of title 26.

(2) For purposes of subtitle E of this subchapter—

(A) except as otherwise provided in subtitle E of this subchapter, contributions or other payments shall be considered made under a plan for a plan year if they are made within the period prescribed under section 412(c)(10)[3] of title 26 (determined, in the case of a terminated plan, as if the plan had continued beyond the termination date), and

(B) the term "Secretary of the Treasury" means the Secretary of the Treasury or such Secretary's delegate.

(Pub. L. 93–406, title IV, § 4001, Sept. 2, 1974, 88 Stat. 1003; Pub. L. 96–364, title IV, § 402(a)(1), Sept. 26, 1980, 94 Stat. 1296; Pub. L. 99–272, title XI, § 11004, Apr. 7, 1986, 100 Stat. 238; Pub. L. 100–203, title IX, §§ 9312(b)(4), (5), 9313(a)(2)(F), Dec. 22, 1987, 101 Stat. 1330–363, 1330–365; Pub. L. 101–239, title VII, § 7891(a)(1), Dec. 19, 1989, 103 Stat. 2445; Pub. L. 102–229, title II, § 214, Dec. 12, 1991, 105 Stat. 1718; Pub. L. 103–465, title VII, § 761(a)(11), Dec. 8, 1994, 108 Stat. 5034; Pub. L. 109–280, title I, § 107(b)(1), Aug. 17, 2006, 120 Stat. 819.)

REFERENCES IN TEXT

Section 1322(c) of this title, referred to in subsec. (a)(6), (7), was redesignated section 1322(d) of this title by Pub. L. 100–203, title IX, § 9312(b)(3)(A)(i), Dec. 22, 1987, 101 Stat. 1330–362.

This chapter, referred to in subsec. (a)(8), was in the original "this Act", meaning Pub. L. 93–406, known as the Employee Retirement Income Security Act of 1974. Titles I, III, and IV of such Act are classified principally to this chapter. For complete classification of this Act to the Code, see Short Title note set out under section 1001 of this title and Tables.

Section 412, referred to in subsec. (b)(2)(A), was amended generally by Pub. L. 109–280, title I, § 111(a), Aug. 17, 2006, 120 Stat. 820, and as so amended, no longer contains a subsec. (c)(10).

CODIFICATION

In subsec. (a)(14)(C)(ii)(I), "section 40102(a)(2) of title 49" substituted for "section 101(3) of the Federal Aviation Act of 1958" and "section 41102 of title 49" substituted for "section 401 of such Act" on authority of Pub. L. 103–272, § 6(b), July 5, 1994, 108 Stat. 1378, the first section of which enacted subtitles II, III, and V to X of Title 49, Transportation.

AMENDMENTS

2006—Subsec. (a)(13). Pub. L. 109–280 substituted "1082(b)(1)" for "1082(c)(11)(A)", "1082(b)(2)" for "1082(c)(11)(B)", "412(b)(1)" for "412(c)(11)(A)", and "412(b)(2)" for "412(c)(11)(B)".

1994—Subsec. (a)(13). Pub. L. 103–465 substituted "means a person described in section 1082(c)(11)(A) of this title (without regard to section 1082(c)(11)(B) of this title) or section 412(c)(11)(A) of title 26 (without regard to section 412(c)(11)(B) of such title)." for "means a person—

"(A) who is responsible, in connection with such plan, for meeting the funding requirements under section 1082 of this title or section 412 of title 26, or

"(B) who is a member of the controlled group of a person described in subparagraph (A), has been responsible for meeting such funding requirements, and has employed a significant number (as may be defined in regulations of the corporation) of participants under such plan while such person was so responsible;".

1991—Subsec. (a)(14)(C). Pub. L. 102–229, which directed the amendment of section 4001(a)(14) of the Employment Retirement Income Security Act of 1974 by adding subpar. (C), was executed to section 4001(a)(14) of the Employee Retirement Income Security Act of 1974, which is classified to this section, to reflect the probable intent of Congress.

1989—Subsecs. (a)(8), (13)(A), (14)(B), (b)(1), (2)(A). Pub. L. 101–239 substituted "Internal Revenue Code of 1986" for "Internal Revenue Code of 1954", which for purposes of codification was translated as "title 26" thus requiring no change in text.

1987—Subsec. (a)(16). Pub. L. 100–203, § 9312(b)(4), amended par. (16) generally. Prior to amendment, par. (16) read as follows: "'benefit commitments', to a participant or beneficiary as of any date under a single-employer plan, means all benefits provided by the plan with respect to the participant or beneficiary which—

"(A) are guaranteed under section 1322 of this title,

"(B) would be guaranteed under section 1322 of this title, but for the operation of subsection 1322(b) of this title, or

"(C) constitute—

"(i) early retirement supplements or subsidies, or

"(ii) plant closing benefits,

irrespective of whether any such supplements, subsidies, or benefits are benefits guaranteed under section 1322 of this title, if the participant or beneficiary has satisfied, as of such date, all of the conditions required of him or her under the provisions of the plan to establish entitlement to the benefits, except for the submission of a formal application, retirement, completion of a required waiting period subsequent to application for benefits, or designation of a beneficiary;".

Subsec. (a)(18). Pub. L. 100–203, § 9313(a)(2)(F), amended par. (18) generally. Prior to amendment, par. (18) read as follows: "'amount of unfunded benefit commitments', of a participant or beneficiary as of any date under a single-employer plan, means an amount equal to the excess of—

"(A) the actuarial present value (determined as of such date on the basis of assumptions prescribed by the corporation for purposes of section 1344 of this title) of the benefit commitments to the participant or beneficiary under the plan, over

"(B) the current value (as of such date) of the assets of the plan which are required to be allocated to those benefit commitments under section 1344 of this title;".

Subsec. (a)(19). Pub. L. 100–203, § 9312(b)(5), amended par. (19) generally. Prior to amendment, par. (19) read as follows: "'outstanding amount of benefit commitments', of a participant or beneficiary under a terminated single-employer plan, means the excess of—

"(A) the actuarial present value (determined as of the termination date on the basis of assumptions prescribed by the corporation for purposes of section 1344 of this title) of the benefit commitments to such participant or beneficiary under the plan, over

"(B) the actuarial present value (determined as of such date on the basis of assumptions prescribed by the corporation for purposes of section 1344 of this title) of the benefits of such participant or beneficiary which are guaranteed under section 1322 of this title or to which assets of the plan are required to be allocated under section 1344 of this title;".

1986—Subsec. (a)(2). Pub. L. 99–272, § 11004(a)(1), amended par. (2) generally, substituting provisions defining "substantial employer" for any plan year of a single-employer plan for provisions defining "substantial employer" for any plan year as an employer, treating employers who are members of the same affiliated group as one employer, who has made contributions to or under a plan under which more than one employer, other than a multi-employer plan, makes contributions for each of the two immediately preceding plan years or the second and third preceding plan years equaling or exceeding 10 percent of all employer contributions paid to or under that plan for such year.

Subsec. (a)(13). Pub. L. 99–272, § 11004(a)(2)–(4), added par. (13).

Subsec. (a)(14). Pub. L. 99–272, § 11004(a)(2)–(4), added par. (14).

Subsec. (a)(15) to (21). Pub. L. 99–272, § 11004(a)(2)–(4), added pars. (15) to (21).

Subsec. (b). Pub. L. 99–272, § 11004(b), designated existing provisions as par. (1), added par. (2), and struck out

[3] See References in Text note below.

amendments by Pub. L. 96–364, §402(a)(1)(F), which had been executed by designating existing provisions as par. (1) and adding pars. (2) to (4). See 1980 Amendment note below. For successor provisions to former pars. (2), (3), and (4), see subsecs. (a)(15), (b)(2)(A), and (b)(2)(B), respectively.

1980—Subsec. (a)(2). Pub. L. 96–364, §402(a)(1)(A), inserted provision excepting multiemployer plan.

Subsec. (a)(3). Pub. L. 96–364, §402(a)(1)(B), substantially revised definition of term "multiemployer plan" by, among other changes, adding subpars. (A) to (C) and cl. (i), and restating existing provisions as cl. (ii) with respect to plan years beginning before Sept. 26, 1980.

Subsec. (a)(6). Pub. L. 96–364, §402(a)(1)(C), inserted references to section 1322a of this title.

Subsec. (a)(7). Pub. L. 96–364, §402(a)(1)(D), inserted reference to section 1322a(g) of this title.

Subsec. (a)(8) to (12). Pub. L. 96–364, §402(a)(1)(E), added pars. (8) to (12).

Subsec. (b). Pub. L. 96–364, §402(a)(1)(F), which was executed by designating existing provisions as par. (1) and adding pars. (2) to (4), notwithstanding directory language that pars. (2) to (4) be added at end of subsec. (c)(1) as redesignated, was struck out by Pub. L. 99–272, §11004(b). See 1986 Amendment note above.

Effective Date of 2006 Amendment

Amendment by Pub. L. 109–280 applicable to plan years beginning after 2007, see section 107(e) of Pub. L. 109–280, set out as a note under section 1021 of this title.

Effective Date of 1994 Amendment

Amendment by Pub. L. 103–465 effective as if included in the Pension Protection Act, Pub. L. 100–203, §§9302–9346, see section 761(b)(2) of Pub. L. 103–465, set out as a note under section 1056 of this title.

Effective Date of 1989 Amendment

Amendment by Pub. L. 101–239 effective, except as otherwise provided, as if included in the provision of the Tax Reform Act of 1986, Pub. L. 99–514, to which such amendment relates, see section 7891(f) of Pub. L. 101–239, set out as a note under section 1002 of this title.

Effective Date of 1987 Amendment

Section 9312(d)(1) of Pub. L. 100–203, as amended by Pub. L. 101–239, title VII, §7881(f)(9), Dec. 19, 1989, 103 Stat. 2440, provided that: "The amendments made by this section [amending this section and sections 1305, 1322, 1341, 1342, 1349, 1362, 1364, and 1368 of this title and repealing section 1349 of this title] shall apply with respect to—

"(A) plan terminations under section 4041 of ERISA [29 U.S.C. 1341] with respect to which notices of intent to terminate are provided under section 4041(a)(2) of ERISA after December 17, 1987, and

"(B) plan terminations with respect to which proceedings are instituted by the Pension Benefit Guaranty Corporation under section 4042 of ERISA [29 U.S.C. 1342] after December 17, 1987."

Section 9313(c) of Pub. L. 100–203 provided that: "The amendments made by this section [amending this section and sections 1341 and 1367 of this title] shall apply with respect to plan terminations under section 4041 of ERISA [29 U.S.C. 1341] with respect to which notices of intent to terminate are provided under section 4041(a)(2) of ERISA after December 17, 1987."

Effective Date of 1986 Amendment

Amendment by Pub. L. 99–272 effective Jan. 1, 1986, with certain exceptions, see section 11019 of Pub. L. 99–272, set out as a note under section 1341 of this title.

Effective Date of 1980 Amendment

Amendment by Pub. L. 96–364 effective Sept. 26, 1980, except as specifically provided, see section 1461(e) of this title.

Applicability of Amendments by Subtitles A and B of Title I of Pub. L. 109–280

For special rules on applicability of amendments by subtitles A (§§101–107) and B (§§111–116) of title I of Pub. L. 109–280 to certain eligible cooperative plans, PBGC settlement plans, and eligible government contractor plans, see sections 104, 105, and 106 of Pub. L. 109–280, set out as notes under section 401 of Title 26, Internal Revenue Code.

Coordination of Internal Revenue Code of 1986 With Employee Retirement Income Security Act of 1974

This subchapter not applicable in interpreting Internal Revenue Code of 1986, except to the extent specifically provided in such Code, or as determined by the Secretary of the Treasury, see section 9343(a) of Pub. L. 100–203, set out as a note under section 401 of Title 26, Internal Revenue Code.

§1302. Pension Benefit Guaranty Corporation

(a) Establishment within Department of Labor

There is established within the Department of Labor a body corporate to be known as the Pension Benefit Guaranty Corporation. In carrying out its functions under this subchapter, the corporation shall be administered by a Director, who shall be appointed by the President, by and with the advice and consent of the Senate, and who shall act in accordance with the policies established by the board. The purposes of this subchapter, which are to be carried out by the corporation, are—

(1) to encourage the continuation and maintenance of voluntary private pension plans for the benefit of their participants,

(2) to provide for the timely and uninterrupted payment of pension benefits to participants and beneficiaries under plans to which this subchapter applies, and

(3) to maintain premiums established by the corporation under section 1306 of this title at the lowest level consistent with carrying out its obligations under this subchapter.

(b) Powers of corporation

To carry out the purposes of this subchapter, the corporation has the powers conferred on a nonprofit corporation under the District of Columbia Nonprofit Corporation Act and, in addition to any specific power granted to the corporation elsewhere in this subchapter or under that Act, the corporation has the power—

(1) to sue and be sued, complain and defend, in its corporate name and through its own counsel, in any court, State or Federal;

(2) to adopt, alter, and use a corporate seal, which shall be judicially noticed;

(3) to adopt, amend, and repeal, by the board of directors, bylaws, rules, and regulations relating to the conduct of its business and the exercise of all other rights and powers granted to it by this chapter and such other bylaws, rules, and regulations as may be necessary to carry out the purposes of this subchapter;

(4) to conduct its business (including the carrying on of operations and the maintenance of offices) and to exercise all other rights and powers granted to it by this chapter in any State or other jurisdiction without regard to qualification, licensing, or other requirements imposed by law in such State or other jurisdiction;

(5) to lease, purchase, accept gifts or donations of, or otherwise to acquire, to own, hold, improve, use, or otherwise deal in or with, and to sell, convey, mortgage, pledge, lease, exchange, or otherwise dispose of, any property, real, personal, or mixed, or any interest therein wherever situated;

(6) to appoint and fix the compensation of such officers, attorneys, employees, and agents as may be required, to determine their qualifications, to define their duties, and, to the extent desired by the corporation, require bonds for them and fix the penalty thereof, and to appoint and fix the compensation of experts and consultants in accordance with the provisions of section 3109 of title 5;

(7) to utilize the personnel and facilities of any other agency or department of the United States Government, with or without reimbursement, with the consent of the head of such agency or department; and

(8) to enter into contracts, to execute instruments, to incur liabilities, and to do any and all other acts and things as may be necessary or incidental to the conduct of its business and the exercise of all other rights and powers granted to the corporation by this chapter.

(c) Omitted

(d) Board of directors; compensation; reimbursement for expenses

The board of directors of the corporation consists of the Secretary of the Treasury, the Secretary of Labor, and the Secretary of Commerce. Members of the Board shall serve without compensation, but shall be reimbursed for travel, subsistence, and other necessary expenses incurred in the performance of their duties as members of the board. The Secretary of Labor is the chairman of the board of directors.

(e) Meetings

The board of directors shall meet at the call of its chairman, or as otherwise provided by the bylaws of the corporation.

(f) Adoption of bylaws; amendment, alteration; publication in the Federal Register

As soon as practicable, but not later than 180 days after September 2, 1974, the board of directors shall adopt initial bylaws and rules relating to the conduct of the business of the corporation. Thereafter, the board of directors may alter, supplement, or repeal any existing bylaw or rule, and may adopt additional bylaws and rules from time to time as may be necessary. The chairman of the board shall cause a copy of the bylaws of the corporation to be published in the Federal Register not less often than once each year.

(g) Exemption from taxation

(1) The corporation, its property, its franchise, capital, reserves, surplus, and its income (including, but not limited to, any income of any fund established under section 1305 of this title), shall be exempt from all taxation now or hereafter imposed by the United States (other than taxes imposed under chapter 21 of title 26, relating to Federal Insurance Contributions Act [26 U.S.C. 3101 et seq.], and chapter 23 of title 26, relating to Federal Unemployment Tax Act [26 U.S.C. 3301 et seq.]), or by any State or local taxing authority, except that any real property and any tangible personal property (other than cash and securities) of the corporation shall be subject to State and local taxation to the same extent according to its value as other real and tangible personal property is taxed.

(2) The receipts and disbursements of the corporation in the discharge of its functions shall be included in the totals of the budget of the United States Government. The United States is not liable for any obligation or liability incurred by the corporation.

(3) Omitted.

(h) Advisory committee to corporation

(1) There is established an advisory committee to the corporation, for the purpose of advising the corporation as to its policies and procedures relating to (A) the appointment of trustees in termination proceedings, (B) investment of moneys, (C) whether plans being terminated should be liquidated immediately or continued in operation under a trustee, and (D) such other issues as the corporation may request from time to time. The advisory committee may also recommend persons for appointment as trustees in termination proceedings, make recommendations with respect to the investment of moneys in the funds, and advise the corporation as to whether a plan subject to being terminated should be liquidated immediately or continued in operation under a trustee.

(2) The advisory committee consists of seven members appointed, from among individuals recommended by the board of directors, by the President. Of the seven members, two shall represent the interests of employee organizations, two shall represent the interests of employers who maintain pension plans, and three shall represent the interests of the general public. The President shall designate one member as chairman at the time of the appointment of that member.

(3) Members shall serve for terms of 3 years each, except that, of the members first appointed, one of the members representing the interests of employee organizations, one of the members representing the interests of employers, and one of the members representing the interests of the general public shall be appointed for terms of 2 years each, one of the members representing the interests of the general public shall be appointed for a term of 1 year, and the other members shall be appointed to full 3-year terms. The advisory committee shall meet at least six times each year and at such other times as may be determined by the chairman or requested by any three members of the advisory committee.

(4) Members shall be chosen on the basis of their experience with employee organizations, with employers who maintain pension plans, with the administration of pension plans, or otherwise on account of outstanding demonstrated ability in related fields. Of the members serving on the advisory committee at any time, no more than four shall be affiliated with the same political party.

(5) An individual appointed to fill a vacancy occurring other than by the expiration of a term

of office shall be appointed only for the unexpired term of the member he succeeds. Any vacancy occurring in the office of a member of the advisory committee shall be filled in the manner in which that office was originally filled.

(6) The advisory committee shall appoint and fix the compensation of such employees as it determines necessary to discharge its duties, including experts and consultants in accordance with the provisions of section 3109 of title 5. The corporation shall furnish to the advisory committee such professional, secretarial, and other services as the committee may request.

(7) Members of the advisory committee shall, for each day (including traveltime) during which they are attending meetings or conferences of the committee or otherwise engaged in the business of the committee, be compensated at a rate fixed by the corporation which is not in excess of the daily equivalent of the annual rate of basic pay in effect for grade GS–18 of the General Schedule, and while away from their homes or regular places of business they may be allowed travel expenses, including per diem in lieu of subsistence, as authorized by section 5703 of title 5.

(8) The Federal Advisory Committee Act does not apply to the advisory committee established by this subsection.

(i) Special rules regarding disasters, etc.

In the case of a pension or other employee benefit plan, or any sponsor, administrator, participant, beneficiary, or other person with respect to such plan, affected by a Presidentially declared disaster (as defined in section 1033(h)(3) of title 26) or a terroristic or military action (as defined in section 692(c)(2) of such title), the corporation may, notwithstanding any other provision of law, prescribe, by notice or otherwise, a period of up to 1 year which may be disregarded in determining the date by which any action is required or permitted to be completed under this chapter. No plan shall be treated as failing to be operated in accordance with the terms of the plan solely as the result of disregarding any period by reason of the preceding sentence.

(Pub. L. 93–406, title IV, § 4002, Sept. 2, 1974, 88 Stat. 1004; Pub. L. 94–455, title XV, § 1510(a), Oct. 4, 1976, 90 Stat. 1741; Pub. L. 96–364, title IV, §§ 403(*l*), 406(a), Sept. 26, 1980, 94 Stat. 1302, 1303; Pub. L. 101–239, title VII, § 7891(a)(1), Dec. 19, 1989, 103 Stat. 2445; Pub. L. 107–134, title I, § 112(c)(2), Jan. 23, 2002, 115 Stat. 2434; Pub. L. 109–280, title IV, § 411(a)(1), Aug. 17, 2006, 120 Stat. 935.)

REFERENCES IN TEXT

The District of Columbia Nonprofit Corporation Act, referred to in subsec. (b), is Pub. L. 87–569, Aug. 6, 1962, 76 Stat. 265, as amended, which is not classified to the Code.

This chapter, referred to in subsecs. (b)(3), (4), (8) and (i), was in original "this Act", meaning Pub. L. 93–406, known as the Employee Retirement Income Security Act of 1974. Titles I, III, and IV of such Act are classified principally to this chapter. For complete classification of this Act to the Code, see Short Title note set out under section 1001 of this title and Tables.

The Federal Insurance Contributions Act, referred to in subsec. (g)(1), is act Aug. 16, 1954, ch. 736, §§ 3101, 3102, 3111, 3112, 3121 to 3128, 68A Stat. 415, as amended, which is classified generally to chapter 21 (§ 3101 et seq.) of Title 26, Internal Revenue Code. For complete classification of this Act to the Code, see section 3128 of Title 26 and Tables.

The Federal Unemployment Tax Act, referred to in subsec. (g)(1), is act Aug. 16, 1954, ch. 736, §§ 3301 to 3311, 68A Stat. 454, as amended, which is classified generally to chapter 23 (§ 3301 et seq.) of Title 26. For complete classification of this Act to the Code, see section 3311 of Title 26 and Tables.

The Federal Advisory Committee Act, referred to in subsec. (h)(8), is Pub. L. 92–463, Oct. 6, 1972, 86 Stat. 770, as amended, which is set out in the Appendix to Title 5, Government Organization and Employees.

CODIFICATION

Subsec. (c) amended section 5108 of Title 5, Government Organization and Employees, and subsec. (g)(3) amended section 846 of former Title 31, Money and Finance.

AMENDMENTS

2006—Subsec. (a). Pub. L. 109–280 in introductory provisions substituted "In carrying out its functions under this subchapter, the corporation shall be administered by a Director, who shall be appointed by the President, by and with the advice and consent of the Senate, and who shall act in accordance with the policies established by the board" for "In carrying out its functions under this subchapter, the corporation shall be administered by the chairman of the board of directors in accordance with policies established by the board".

2002—Subsec. (i). Pub. L. 107–134 added subsec. (i).

1989—Subsec. (g)(1). Pub. L. 101–239 substituted "Internal Revenue Code of 1986" for "Internal Revenue Code of 1954", which for purposes of codification was translated as "title 26" thus requiring no change in text.

1980—Subsec. (b)(3). Pub. L. 96–364, § 403(*l*), inserted provisions respecting bylaws, etc., to carry out this subchapter.

Subsec. (g)(2). Pub. L. 96–364, § 406(a), substituted provisions relating to inclusion of receipts and disbursements in United States budget totals and nonliability of United States for obligation or liability of corporation, for provisions relating to noninclusion of receipts and disbursements in United States budget totals, exemption from limitations with respect to budget outlays, and restrictions on liability for obligation or liability incurred by the corporation.

1976—Subsec. (g)(1). Pub. L. 94–455 exempted corporation from all taxation now or hereafter imposed by United States (other than taxes imposed under chapter 21 of title 26, relating to Federal Insurance Contributions Act, and chapter 23 of title 26, relating to Federal Unemployment Tax Act).

EFFECTIVE DATE OF 2002 AMENDMENT

Amendment by Pub. L. 107–134 applicable to disasters and terroristic or military actions occurring on or after Sept. 11, 2001, with respect to any action of the Secretary of the Treasury, the Secretary of Labor, or the Pension Benefit Guaranty Corporation occurring on or after Jan. 23, 2002, see section 112(f) of Pub. L. 107–134, set out as a note under section 6081 of Title 26, Internal Revenue Code.

EFFECTIVE DATE OF 1989 AMENDMENT

Amendment by Pub. L. 101–239 effective, except as otherwise provided, as if included in the provision of the Tax Reform Act of 1986, Pub. L. 99–514, to which such amendment relates, see section 7891(f) of Pub. L. 101–239, set out as a note under section 1002 of this title.

EFFECTIVE DATE OF 1980 AMENDMENT

Amendment by Pub. L. 96–364 effective Sept. 26, 1980, except as specifically provided, see section 1461(e) of this title.

Section 406(b) of Pub. L. 96–364 provided that: "The amendment made by subsection (a) [amending this section] shall apply to fiscal years beginning after September 30, 1980."

EFFECTIVE DATE OF 1976 AMENDMENT

Section 1510(b) of Pub. L. 94–455 provided that: "The amendment made by subsection (a) [amending this section] shall take effect on September 2, 1974."

TRANSITION

Pub. L. 109–280, title IV, § 411(d), Aug. 17, 2006, 120 Stat. 936, provided that: "The term of the individual serving as Executive Director of the Pension Benefit Guaranty Corporation on the date of enactment of this Act [Aug. 17, 2006] shall expire on such date of enactment. Such individual, or any other individual, may serve as interim Director of such Corporation until an individual is appointed as Director of such Corporation under section 4002 of the Employee Retirement Income Security Act of 1974 (29 U.S.C. 1302) (as amended by this Act)."

REFERENCES IN OTHER LAWS TO GS–16, 17, OR 18 PAY RATES

References in laws to the rates of pay for GS–16, 17, or 18, or to maximum rates of pay under the General Schedule, to be considered references to rates payable under specified sections of Title 5, Government Organization and Employees, see section 529 [title I, § 101(c)(1)] of Pub. L. 101–509, set out in a note under section 5376 of Title 5.

§ 1303. Operation of corporation

(a) Investigatory authority; audit of statistically significant number of terminating plans

The corporation may make such investigations as it deems necessary to enforce any provision of this subchapter or any rule or regulation thereunder, and may require or permit any person to file with it a statement in writing, under oath or otherwise as the corporation shall determine, as to all the facts and circumstances concerning the matter to be investigated. The corporation shall annually audit a statistically significant number of plans terminating under section 1341(b) of this title to determine whether participants and beneficiaries have received their benefit commitments and whether section 1350(a) of this title has been satisfied. Each audit shall include a statistically significant number of participants and beneficiaries.

(b) Discovery powers vested in board members or officers designated by the chairman

For the purpose of any such investigation, or any other proceeding under this subchapter, the Director, any member of the board of directors of the corporation, or any officer designated by the Director or chairman, may administer oaths and affirmations, subpena witnesses, compel their attendance, take evidence, and require the production of any books, papers, correspondence, memoranda, or other records which the corporation deems relevant or material to the inquiry.

(c) Contempt

In the case of contumacy by, or refusal to obey a subpena issued to, any person, the corporation may invoke the aid of any court of the United States within the jurisdiction of which such investigation or proceeding is carried on, or where such person resides or carries on business, in requiring the attendance and testimony of witnesses and the production of books, papers, correspondence, memoranda, and other records. The court may issue an order requiring such person to appear before the corporation, or member or officer designated by the corporation, and to produce records or to give testimony related to the matter under investigation or in question. Any failure to obey such order of the court may be punished by the court as a contempt thereof. All process in any such case may be served in the judicial district in which such person is an inhabitant or may be found.

(d) Cooperation with other governmental agencies

In order to avoid unnecessary expense and duplication of functions among government agencies, the corporation may make such arrangements or agreements for cooperation or mutual assistance in the performance of its functions under this subchapter as is practicable and consistent with law. The corporation may utilize the facilities or services of any department, agency, or establishment of the United States or of any State or political subdivision of a State, including the services of any of its employees, with the lawful consent of such department, agency, or establishment. The head of each department, agency, or establishment of the United States shall cooperate with the corporation and, to the extent permitted by law, provide such information and facilities as it may request for its assistance in the performance of its functions under this subchapter. The Attorney General or his representative shall receive from the corporation for appropriate action such evidence developed in the performance of its functions under this subchapter as may be found to warrant consideration for criminal prosecution under the provisions of this or any other Federal law.

(e) Civil actions by corporation; jurisdiction; process; expeditious handling of case; costs; limitation on actions

(1) Civil actions may be brought by the corporation for appropriate relief, legal or equitable or both, to enforce (A) the provisions of this subchapter, and (B) in the case of a plan which is covered under this subchapter (other than a multiemployer plan) and for which the conditions for imposition of a lien described in section 1083(k)(1)(A) and (B) of this title or section 430(k)(1)(A) and (B) of title 26 have been met, section 1082 of this title and section 412 of title 26.

(2) Except as otherwise provided in this subchapter, where such an action is brought in a district court of the United States, it may be brought in the district where the plan is administered, where the violation took place, or where a defendant resides or may be found, and process may be served in any other district where a defendant resides or may be found.

(3) The district courts of the United States shall have jurisdiction of actions brought by the corporation under this subchapter without regard to the amount in controversy in any such action.

(4) Repealed. Pub. L. 98–620, title IV, § 402(33), Nov. 8, 1984, 98 Stat. 3360.

(5) In any action brought under this subchapter, whether to collect premiums, penalties, and interest under section 1307 of this title or for any other purpose, the court may award to the corporation all or a portion of the costs of litigation incurred by the corporation in connection with such action.

(6)(A) Except as provided in subparagraph (C), an action under this subsection may not be brought after the later of—

(i) 6 years after the date on which the cause of action arose, or

(ii) 3 years after the applicable date specified in subparagraph (B).

(B)(i) Except as provided in clause (ii), the applicable date specified in this subparagraph is the earliest date on which the corporation acquired or should have acquired actual knowledge of the existence of such cause of action.

(ii) If the corporation brings the action as a trustee, the applicable date specified in this subparagraph is the date on which the corporation became a trustee with respect to the plan if such date is later than the date described in clause (i).

(C) In the case of fraud or concealment, the period described in subparagraph (A)(ii) shall be extended to 6 years after the applicable date specified in subparagraph (B).

(f) Civil actions against corporation; appropriate court; award of costs and expenses; limitation on actions; jurisdiction; removal of actions

(1) Except with respect to withdrawal liability disputes under part 1 of subtitle E of this subchapter, any person who is a fiduciary, employer, contributing sponsor, member of a contributing sponsor's controlled group, participant, or beneficiary, and is adversely affected by any action of the corporation with respect to a plan in which such person has an interest, or who is an employee organization representing such a participant or beneficiary so adversely affected for purposes of collective bargaining with respect to such plan, may bring an action against the corporation for appropriate equitable relief in the appropriate court.

(2) For purposes of this subsection, the term "appropriate court" means—

(A) the United States district court before which proceedings under section 1341 or 1342 of this title are being conducted,

(B) if no such proceedings are being conducted, the United States district court for the judicial district in which the plan has its principal office, or

(C) the United States District Court for the District of Columbia.

(3) In any action brought under this subsection, the court may award all or a portion of the costs and expenses incurred in connection with such action to any party who prevails or substantially prevails in such action.

(4) This subsection shall be the exclusive means for bringing actions against the corporation under this subchapter, including actions against the corporation in its capacity as a trustee under section 1342 or 1349[1] of this title.

[1] See References in Text note below.

(5)(A) Except as provided in subparagraph (C), an action under this subsection may not be brought after the later of—

(i) 6 years after the date on which the cause of action arose, or

(ii) 3 years after the applicable date specified in subparagraph (B).

(B)(i) Except as provided in clause (ii), the applicable date specified in this subparagraph is the earliest date on which the plaintiff acquired or should have acquired actual knowledge of the existence of such cause of action.

(ii) In the case of a plaintiff who is a fiduciary bringing the action in the exercise of fiduciary duties, the applicable date specified in this subparagraph is the date on which the plaintiff became a fiduciary with respect to the plan if such date is later than the date specified in clause (i).

(C) In the case of fraud or concealment, the period described in subparagraph (A)(ii) shall be extended to 6 years after the applicable date specified in subparagraph (B).

(6) The district courts of the United States have jurisdiction of actions brought under this subsection without regard to the amount in controversy.

(7) In any suit, action, or proceeding in which the corporation is a party, or intervenes under section 1451 of this title, in any State court, the corporation may, without bond or security, remove such suit, action, or proceeding from the State court to the United States district court for the district or division in which such suit, action, or proceeding is pending by following any procedure for removal now or hereafter in effect.

(Pub. L. 93–406, title IV, § 4003, Sept. 2, 1974, 88 Stat. 1006; Pub. L. 96–364, title IV, §§ 402(a)(2), 403(k), Sept. 26, 1980, 94 Stat. 1297, 1302; Pub. L. 98–620, title IV, § 402(33), Nov. 8, 1984, 98 Stat. 3360; Pub. L. 99–272, title XI, §§ 11014(b)(1), (2), 11016(c)(5), Apr. 7, 1986, 100 Stat. 262, 264, 274; Pub. L. 103–465, title VII, §§ 773(a), 776(b)(1), Dec. 8, 1994, 108 Stat. 5044, 5048; Pub. L. 109–280, title I, § 107(b)(2), title IV, § 411(a)(2), Aug. 17, 2006, 120 Stat. 819, 935.)

REFERENCES IN TEXT

Section 1349 of this title, referred to in subsec. (f)(4), was repealed by Pub. L. 100–203, title IX, § 9312(a), Dec. 22, 1987, 101 Stat. 1330–361.

AMENDMENTS

2006—Subsec. (b). Pub. L. 109–280, § 411(a)(2), substituted "under this subchapter, the Director, any member" for "under this subchapter, any member" and "designated by the Director or chairman" for "designated by the chairman".

Subsec. (e)(1). Pub. L. 109–280, § 107(b)(2), substituted "1083(k)(1)(A) and (B)" for "1082(f)(1)(A) and (B)" and "430(k)(1)(A) and (B)" for "412(n)(1)(A) and (B)".

1994—Subsec. (a). Pub. L. 103–465, § 776(b)(1), inserted "and whether section 1350(a) of this title has been satisfied" before period at end of second sentence.

Subsec. (e)(1). Pub. L. 103–465, § 773(a), inserted "(A)" after "enforce" and substituted ", and" and cl. (B) for period at end.

1986—Subsec. (a). Pub. L. 99–272, § 11016(c)(5), inserted provisions directing the corporation to audit annually a statistically significant number of plans terminating under section 1341(b) of this title to determine whether participants and beneficiaries have received their benefit commitments and to include a statistically significant number of participants and beneficiaries in each audit.

Subsec. (e)(6). Pub. L. 99–272, §11014(b)(2), added par. (6).

Subsec. (f). Pub. L. 99–272, §11014(b)(1), amended subsec. (f) generally. Prior to amendment, subsec. (f) read as follows: "Except as provided in section 1451(a)(2) of this title, any participant, beneficiary, plan administrator, or employee adversely affected by any action of the corporation, or by a receiver or trustee appointed by the corporation, with respect to a plan in which such participant, beneficiary, plan administrator or employer has an interest, may bring an action against the corporation, receiver, or trustee in the appropriate court. For purposes of this subsection the term 'appropriate court' means the United States district court before which proceedings under section 1341 or 1342 of this title are being conducted, or if no such proceedings are being conducted the United States district court for the district in which the plan has its principal office, or the United States district court for the District of Columbia. The district courts of the United States have jurisdiction of actions brought under this subsection without regard to the amount in controversy. In any suit, action, or proceeding in which the corporation is a party, or intervenes under section 1451 of this title, in any State court, the corporation may, without bond or security, remove such suit, action, or proceeding from the State court to the United States District Court for the district or division embracing the place where the same is pending by following any procedure for removal now or hereafter in effect."

1984—Subsec. (e)(4). Pub. L. 98–620 struck out par. (4) which provided that upon application by the corporation to a court of the United States for expedited handling of any case in which the corporation was a party, it was the duty of that court to assign such case for hearing at the earliest practical date and to cause such case to be in every way expedited.

1980—Subsec. (a). Pub. L. 96–364, §402(a)(2)(A), substituted "enforce" for "determine whether any person has violated or is about to violate".

Subsec. (e)(1). Pub. L. 96–364, §402(a)(2)(B), substituted "enforce" for "redress violations of".

Subsec. (f). Pub. L. 96–364, §§402(a)(2)(C), 403(k), substituted "Except as provided in section 1451(a)(2) of the title, any" for "Any" and inserted provisions relating to removal of actions.

EFFECTIVE DATE OF 2006 AMENDMENT

Amendment by section 107(b)(2) of Pub. L. 109–280 applicable to plan years beginning after 2007, see section 107(e) of Pub. L. 109–280, set out as a note under section 1021 of this title.

EFFECTIVE DATE OF 1994 AMENDMENT

Section 773(b) of Pub. L. 103–465 provided that: "The amendments made by this section [amending this section] shall be effective for installments and other payments required under section 302 of the Employee Retirement Income Security Act of 1974 [29 U.S.C. 1082] or section 412 of the Internal Revenue Code of 1986 [26 U.S.C. 412] that become due on or after the date of the enactment of this Act [Dec. 8, 1994]."

Amendment by section 776(b)(1) of Pub. L. 103–465 effective with respect to distributions that occur in plan years commencing on or after Jan. 1, 1996, see section 776(e) of Pub. L. 103–465, set out as a note under section 1056 of this title.

EFFECTIVE DATE OF 1986 AMENDMENT

Section 11014(b)(3) of Pub. L. 99–272 provided that: "The amendments made by this subsection [amending this section] shall apply with respect to actions filed after the date of the enactment of this Act [Apr. 7, 1986]."

Amendment by section 11016(c)(5) of Pub. L. 99–272 effective Jan. 1, 1986, with certain exceptions, see section 11019 of Pub. L. 99–272, set out as a note under section 1341 of this title.

EFFECTIVE DATE OF 1984 AMENDMENT

Amendment by Pub. L. 98–620 not applicable to cases pending on Nov. 8, 1984, see section 403 of Pub. L. 98–620, set out as a note under section 1657 of Title 28, Judiciary and Judicial Procedure.

EFFECTIVE DATE OF 1980 AMENDMENT

Amendment by Pub. L. 96–364 effective Sept. 26, 1980, except as specifically provided, see section 1461(e) of this title.

APPLICABILITY OF AMENDMENTS BY SUBTITLES A AND B OF TITLE I OF PUB. L. 109–280

For special rules on applicability of amendments by subtitles A (§§101–107) and B (§§111–116) of title I of Pub. L. 109–280 to certain eligible cooperative plans, PBGC settlement plans, and eligible government contractor plans, see sections 104, 105, and 106 of Pub. L. 109–280, set out as notes under section 401 of Title 26, Internal Revenue Code.

§1304. Repealed. Pub. L. 99–272, title XI, §11016(c)(6), Apr. 7, 1986, 100 Stat. 274

Section, Pub. L. 93–406, title IV, §4004, Sept. 2, 1974, 88 Stat. 1008, related to appointment, within 270 days after Sept. 2, 1974, and powers and functions of a receiver to assume control of terminated plan and its assets.

EFFECTIVE DATE OF REPEAL

Repeal effective Jan. 1, 1986, with certain exceptions, see section 11019 of Pub. L. 99–272, set out as an Effective Date of 1986 Amendment note under section 1341 of this title.

§1305. Pension benefit guaranty funds

(a) Establishment of four revolving funds on books of Treasury of the United States

There are established on the books of the Treasury of the United States for revolving funds to be used by the corporation in carrying out its duties under this subchapter. One of the funds shall be used with respect to basic benefits guaranteed under section 1322 of this title, one of the funds shall be used with respect to basic benefits guaranteed under section 1322a of this title, one of the funds shall be used with respect to nonbasic benefits guaranteed under section 1322 of this title (if any), and the remaining fund shall be used with respect to nonbasic benefits guaranteed under section 1322a of this title (if any), other than subsection (g)(2) thereof (if any). Whenever in this subchapter reference is made to the term "fund" the reference shall be considered to refer to the appropriate fund established under this subsection.

(b) Credits to funds; availability of funds; investment of moneys in excess of current needs

(1) Each fund established under this section shall be credited with the appropriate portion of—

(A) funds borrowed under subsection (c) of this section,

(B) premiums, penalties, interest, and charges collected under this subchapter,

(C) the value of the assets of a plan administered under section 1342 of this title by a trustee to the extent that they exceed the liabilities of such plan,

(D) the amount of any employer liability payments under subtitle D of this subchapter, to the extent that such payments exceed liabilities of the plan (taking into account all other plan assets),

(E) earnings on investments of the fund or on assets credited to the fund under this subsection,

(F) attorney's fees awarded to the corporation, and

(G) receipts from any other operations under this subchapter.

(2) Subject to the provisions of subsection (a) of this section, each fund shall be available—

(A) for making such payments as the corporation determines are necessary to pay benefits guaranteed under section 1322 or 1322a of this title or benefits payable under section 1350 of this title,

(B) to purchase assets from a plan being terminated by the corporation when the corporation determines such purchase will best protect the interests of the corporation, participants in the plan being terminated, and other insured plans,

(C) to repay to the Secretary of the Treasury such sums as may be borrowed (together with interest thereon) under subsection (c) of this section,

(D) to pay the operational and administrative expenses of the corporation, including reimbursement of the expenses incurred by the Department of the Treasury in maintaining the funds, and the Comptroller General in auditing the corporation, and

(E) to pay to participants and beneficiaries the estimated amount of benefits which are guaranteed by the corporation under this subchapter and the estimated amount of other benefits to which plan assets are allocated under section 1344 of this title, under single-employer plans which are unable to pay benefits when due or which are abandoned.

(3) Whenever the corporation determines that the moneys of any fund are in excess of current needs, it may request the investment of such amounts as it determines advisable by the Secretary of the Treasury in obligations issued or guaranteed by the United States but, until all borrowings under subsection (c) of this section have been repaid, the obligations in which such excess moneys are invested may not yield a rate of return in excess of the rate of interest payable on such borrowings.

(c) Authority to issue notes or other obligations; purchase by Secretary of the Treasury as public debt transaction

The corporation is authorized to issue to the Secretary of the Treasury notes or other obligations in an aggregate amount of not to exceed $100,000,000, in such forms and denominations, bearing such maturities, and subject to such terms and conditions as may be prescribed by the Secretary of the Treasury. Such notes or other obligations shall bear interest at a rate determined by the Secretary of the Treasury, taking into consideration the current average market yield on outstanding marketable obligations of the United States of comparable maturities during the month preceding the issuance of such notes or other obligations of the corporation. The Secretary of the Treasury is authorized and directed to purchase any notes or other obligations issued by the corporation under this subsection, and for that purpose he is authorized to use as a public debt transaction the proceeds from the sale of any securities issued under chapter 31 of title 31, and the purposes for which securities may be issued under that chapter, are extended to include any purchase of such notes and obligations. The Secretary of the Treasury may at any time sell any of the notes or other obligations acquired by him under this subsection. All redemptions, purchases, and sales by the Secretary of the Treasury of such notes or other obligations shall be treated as public debt transactions of the United States.

(d) Establishment of fifth fund; purpose, availability, etc.

(1) A fifth fund shall be established for the reimbursement of uncollectible withdrawal liability under section 1402 of this title, and shall be credited with the appropriate—

(A) premiums, penalties, and interest charges collected under this subchapter, and

(B) earnings on investments of the fund or on assets credited to the fund.

The fund shall be available to make payments pursuant to the supplemental program established under section 1402 of this title, including those expenses and other charges determined to be appropriate by the corporation.

(2) The corporation may invest amounts of the fund in such obligations as the corporation considers appropriate.

(e) Establishment of sixth fund; purpose, availability, etc.

(1) A sixth fund shall be established for the supplemental benefit guarantee program provided under section 1322a(g)(2) of this title.

(2) Such fund shall be credited with the appropriate—

(A) premiums, penalties, and interest charges collected under section 1322a(g)(2) of this title, and

(B) earnings on investments of the fund or on assets credited to the fund.

The fund shall be available for making payments pursuant to the supplemental benefit guarantee program established under section 1322a(g)(2) of this title, including those expenses and other charges determined to be appropriate by the corporation.

(3) The corporation may invest amounts of the fund in such obligations as the corporation considers appropriate.

(f) Deposit of premiums into separate revolving fund

(1) A seventh fund shall be established and credited with—

(A) premiums, penalties, and interest charges collected under section 1306(a)(3)(A)(i) of this title (not described in subparagraph (B)) to the extent attributable to the amount of the premium in excess of $8.50,

(B) premiums, penalties, and interest charges collected under section 1306(a)(3)(E) of this title, and

(C) earnings on investments of the fund or on assets credited to the fund.

(2) Amounts in the fund shall be available for transfer to other funds established under this section with respect to a single-employer plan but shall not be available to pay—

(A) administrative costs of the corporation, or

(B) benefits under any plan which was terminated before October 1, 1988,

unless no other amounts are available for such payment.

(3) The corporation may invest amounts of the fund in such obligations as the corporation considers appropriate.

(g) Other use of funds; deposits of repayments

(1) Amounts in any fund established under this section may be used only for the purposes for which such fund was established and may not be used to make loans to (or on behalf of) any other fund or to finance any other activity of the corporation.

(2) None of the funds borrowed under subsection (c) of this section may be used to make loans to (or on behalf of) any fund other than a fund described in the second sentence of subsection (a) of this section.

(3) Any repayment to the corporation of any amount paid out of any fund in connection with a multiemployer plan shall be deposited in such fund.

(h) Voting by corporation of stock paid as liability

Any stock in a person liable to the corporation under this subchapter which is paid to the corporation by such person or a member of such person's controlled group in satisfaction of such person's liability under this subchapter may be voted only by the custodial trustees or outside money managers of the corporation.

(Pub. L. 93–406, title IV, §4005, Sept. 2, 1974, 88 Stat. 1009; Pub. L. 96–364, title IV, §403(a), Sept. 26, 1980, 94 Stat. 1300; Pub. L. 99–272, title XI, §11016(a)(1), (2), (c)(7), Apr. 7, 1986, 100 Stat. 268, 274; Pub. L. 100–203, title IX, §§9312(c)(4), 9331(d), Dec. 22, 1987, 101 Stat. 1330–364, 1330–368; Pub. L. 103–465, title VII, §776(b)(2), Dec. 8, 1994, 108 Stat. 5048.)

CODIFICATION

In subsec. (c), "chapter 31 of title 31" and "that chapter" substituted for "the Second Liberty Bond Act, as amended" and "that Act, as amended,", respectively, on authority of Pub. L. 97–258, §4(b), Sept. 13, 1982, 96 Stat. 1067, the first section of which enacted Title 31, Money and Finance.

AMENDMENTS

1994—Subsec. (b)(2)(A). Pub. L. 103–465, which directed the amendment of subpar. (A) by inserting "or benefits payable under section 1350 of this title" after "section 1322a of this title", was executed by making the insertion after "section 1322 or 1322a of this title" to reflect the probable intent of Congress.

1987—Subsec. (f). Pub. L. 100–203, §9331(d), added subsec. (f). Former subsec. (f) redesignated (g).

Subsec. (g). Pub. L. 100–203, §9331(d), redesignated former subsec. (f) as (g). Former subsec. (g) redesignated (h).

Pub. L. 100–203, §9312(c)(4), struck out "or fiduciaries with respect to trusts to which the requirements of section 1349 of this title apply" after "money managers of the corporation".

Subsec. (h). Pub. L. 100–203, §9331(d), redesignated former subsec. (g) as (h).

1986—Subsec. (b)(1)(F), (G). Pub. L. 99–272, §11016(a)(2), added subpar. (F) and redesignated former subpar. (F) as (G).

Subsec. (b)(2)(E). Pub. L. 99–272, §11016(a)(1), added subpar. (E).

Subsec. (g). Pub. L. 99–272, §11016(c)(7), added subsec. (g).

1980—Subsec. (a). Pub. L. 96–364, §403(a)(1), substituted provisions respecting benefits guaranteed under sections 1322 and 1322a of this title, for provisions respecting benefits guaranteed under sections 1322 and 1323 of this title.

Subsec. (b)(2). Pub. L. 96–364, §403(a)(2), (3), in subpar. (A) inserted reference to section 1322a of this title, struck out subpar. (B) relating to payments under section 1323 of this title, and redesignated former subpars. (C) to (E) as (B) to (D), respectively.

Subsecs. (d) to (f). Pub. L. 96–364, §403(a)(4), added subsecs. (d) to (f).

EFFECTIVE DATE OF 1994 AMENDMENT

Amendment by Pub. L. 103–465 effective with respect to distributions that occur in plan years commencing on or after Jan. 1, 1996, see section 776(e) of Pub. L. 103–465, set out as a note under section 1056 of this title.

EFFECTIVE DATE OF 1987 AMENDMENT

Amendment by section 9312(c)(4) of Pub. L. 100–203 applicable with respect to plan terminations under section 1341 of this title with respect to which notices of intent to terminate are provided under section 1341(a)(2) of this title after Dec. 17, 1987, and plan terminations with respect to which proceedings are instituted by the Pension Benefit Guaranty Corporation under section 1342 of this title after that date, see section 9312(d)(1) of Pub. L. 100–203, as amended, set out as a note under section 1301 of this title.

Section 9331(f) of Pub. L. 100–203 provided that:

"(1) IN GENERAL.—The amendments made by this section [amending this section and sections 1306 and 1307 of this title] shall apply to plan years beginning after December 31, 1987.

"(2) SEPARATE ACCOUNTING.—The amendments made by subsection (d) [amending this section] shall apply to fiscal years beginning after September 30, 1988."

EFFECTIVE DATE OF 1986 AMENDMENT

Amendment by Pub. L. 99–272 effective Jan. 1, 1986, with certain exceptions, see section 11019 of Pub. L. 99–272, set out as a note under section 1341 of this title.

EFFECTIVE DATE OF 1980 AMENDMENT

Amendment by Pub. L. 96–364 effective Sept. 26, 1980, except as specifically provided, see section 1461(e) of this title.

§1306. Premium rates

(a) Schedules for premium rates and bases for application; establishment, coverage, etc.

(1) The corporation shall prescribe such schedules of premium rates and bases for the application of those rates as may be necessary to provide sufficient revenue to the fund for the corporation to carry out its functions under this subchapter. The premium rates charged by the corporation for any period shall be uniform for all plans, other than multiemployer plans, insured by the corporation with respect to basic benefits guaranteed by it under section 1322 of this title, and shall be uniform for all multiemployer plans with respect to basic benefits guaranteed by it under section 1322a of this title.

(2) The corporation shall maintain separate schedules of premium rates, and bases for the application of those rates, for—

(A) basic benefits guaranteed by it under section 1322 of this title for single-employer plans,

(B) basic benefits guaranteed by it under section 1322a of this title for multiemployer plans,

(C) nonbasic benefits guaranteed by it under section 1322 of this title for single-employer plans,

(D) nonbasic benefits guaranteed by it under section 1322a of this title for multiemployer plans, and

(E) reimbursements of uncollectible withdrawal liability under section 1402 of this title.

The corporation may revise such schedules whenever it determines that revised schedules are necessary. Except as provided in section 1322a(f) of this title, in order to place a revised schedule described in subparagraph (A) or (B) in effect, the corporation shall proceed in accordance with subsection (b)(1) of this section, and such schedule shall apply only to plan years beginning more than 30 days after the date on which a joint resolution approving such revised schedule is enacted.

(3)(A) Except as provided in subparagraph (C), the annual premium rate payable to the corporation by all plans for basic benefits guaranteed under this subchapter is—

(i) in the case of a single-employer plan, for plan years beginning after December 31, 2005, an amount equal to the sum of $30 plus the additional premium (if any) determined under subparagraph (E) for each individual who is a participant in such plan during the plan year;[1]

(ii) in the case of a multiemployer plan, for the plan year within which the date of enactment of the Multiemployer Pension Plan Amendments Act of 1980 falls, an amount for each individual who is a participant in such plan for such plan year equal to the sum of—

(I) 50 cents, multiplied by a fraction the numerator of which is the number of months in such year ending on or before such date and the denominator of which is 12, and

(II) $1.00, multiplied by a fraction equal to 1 minus the fraction determined under clause (i),

(iii) in the case of a multiemployer plan, for plan years beginning after September 26, 1980, and before January 1, 2006, an amount equal to—

(I) $1.40 for each participant, for the first, second, third, and fourth plan years,

(II) $1.80 for each participant, for the fifth and sixth plan years,

(III) $2.20 for each participant, for the seventh and eighth plan years, and

(IV) $2.60 for each participant, for the ninth plan year, and for each succeeding plan year, or

(iv) in the case of a multiemployer plan, for plan years beginning after December 31, 2005, $8.00 for each individual who is a participant in such plan during the applicable plan year.

(B) The corporation may prescribe by regulation the extent to which the rate described in subparagraph (A)(i) applies more than once for any plan year to an individual participating in more than one plan maintained by the same employer, and the corporation may prescribe regulations under which the rate described in clause (iii) or (iv) of subparagraph (A) will not apply to the same participant in any multiemployer plan more than once for any plan year.

(C)(i) If the sum of—

(I) the amounts in any fund for basic benefits guaranteed for multiemployer plans, and

(II) the value of any assets held by the corporation for payment of basic benefits guaranteed for multiemployer plans,

is for any calendar year less than 2 times the amount of basic benefits guaranteed by the corporation under this subchapter for multiemployer plans which were paid out of any such fund or assets during the preceding calendar year, the annual premium rates under subparagraph (A) shall be increased to the next highest premium level necessary to insure that such sum will be at least 2 times greater than such amount during the following calendar year.

(ii) If the board of directors of the corporation determines that an increase in the premium rates under subparagraph (A) is necessary to provide assistance to plans which are receiving assistance under section 1431 of this title and to plans the board finds are reasonably likely to require such assistance, the board may order such increase in the premium rates.

(iii) The maximum annual premium rate which may be established under this subparagraph is $2.60 for each participant.

(iv) The provisions of this subparagraph shall not apply if the annual premium rate is increased to a level in excess of $2.60 per participant under any other provisions of this subchapter.

(D)(i) Not later than 120 days before the date on which an increase under subparagraph (C)(ii) is to become effective, the corporation shall publish in the Federal Register a notice of the determination described in subparagraph (C)(ii), the basis for the determination, the amount of the increase in the premium, and the anticipated increase in premium income that would result from the increase in the premium rate. The notice shall invite public comment, and shall provide for a public hearing if one is requested. Any such hearing shall be commenced not later than 60 days before the date on which the increase is to become effective.

(ii) The board of directors shall review the hearing record established under clause (i) and shall, not later than 30 days before the date on which the increase is to become effective, determine (after consideration of the comments received) whether the amount of the increase should be changed and shall publish its determination in the Federal Register.

(E)(i) Except as provided in subparagraph (H), the additional premium determined under this subparagraph with respect to any plan for any plan year shall be an amount equal to the amount determined under clause (ii) divided by the number of participants in such plan as of the close of the preceding plan year.

(ii) The amount determined under this clause for any plan year shall be an amount equal to

[1] So in original. The semicolon probably should be a comma.

$9.00 for each $1,000 (or fraction thereof) of unfunded vested benefits under the plan as of the close of the preceding plan year.

(iii) For purposes of clause (ii), the term "unfunded vested benefits" means, for a plan year, the excess (if any) of—

(I) the funding target of the plan as determined under section 1083(d) of this title for the plan year by only taking into account vested benefits and by using the interest rate described in clause (iv), over

(II) the fair market value of plan assets for the plan year which are held by the plan on the valuation date.

(iv) The interest rate used in valuing benefits for purposes of subclause (I) of clause (iii) shall be equal to the first, second, or third segment rate for the month preceding the month in which the plan year begins, which would be determined under section 1083(h)(2)(C) of this title if section 1083(h)(2)(D) of this title were applied by using the monthly yields for the month preceding the month in which the plan year begins on investment grade corporate bonds with varying maturities and in the top 3 quality levels rather than the average of such yields for a 24-month period.

(F) For each plan year beginning in a calendar year after 2006, there shall be substituted for the premium rate specified in clause (i) of subparagraph (A) an amount equal to the greater of—

(i) the product derived by multiplying the premium rate specified in clause (i) of subparagraph (A) by the ratio of—

(I) the national average wage index (as defined in section 409(k)(1) of title 42) for the first of the 2 calendar years preceding the calendar year in which such plan year begins, to

(II) the national average wage index (as so defined) for 2004; and

(ii) the premium rate in effect under clause (i) of subparagraph (A) for plan years beginning in the preceding calendar year.

If the amount determined under this subparagraph is not a multiple of $1, such product shall be rounded to the nearest multiple of $1.

(G) For each plan year beginning in a calendar year after 2006, there shall be substituted for the premium rate specified in clause (iv) of subparagraph (A) an amount equal to the greater of—

(i) the product derived by multiplying the premium rate specified in clause (iv) of subparagraph (A) by the ratio of—

(I) the national average wage index (as defined in section 409(k)(1) of title 42) for the first of the 2 calendar years preceding the calendar year in which such plan year begins, to

(II) the national average wage index (as so defined) for 2004; and

(ii) the premium rate in effect under clause (iv) of subparagraph (A) for plan years beginning in the preceding calendar year.

If the amount determined under this subparagraph is not a multiple of $1, such product shall be rounded to the nearest multiple of $1.

(H)(i) In the case of an employer who has 25 or fewer employees on the first day of the plan year, the additional premium determined under subparagraph (E) for each participant shall not exceed $5 multiplied by the number of participants in the plan as of the close of the preceding plan year.

(ii) For purposes of clause (i), whether an employer has 25 or fewer employees on the first day of the plan year is determined by taking into consideration all of the employees of all members of the contributing sponsor's controlled group. In the case of a plan maintained by two or more contributing sponsors, the employees of all contributing sponsors and their controlled groups shall be aggregated for purposes of determining whether the 25-or-fewer-employees limitation has been satisfied.

(4) The corporation may prescribe, subject to the enactment of a joint resolution in accordance with this section or section 1322a(f) of this title, alternative schedules of premium rates, and bases for the application of those rates, for basic benefits guaranteed by it under sections 1322 and 1322a of this title based, in whole or in part, on the risks insured by the corporation in each plan.

(5)(A) In carrying out its authority under paragraph (1) to establish schedules of premium rates, and bases for the application of those rates, for nonbasic benefits guaranteed under sections 1322 and 1322a of this title the premium rates charged by the corporation for any period for nonbasic benefits guaranteed shall—

(i) be uniform by category of nonbasic benefits guaranteed,

(ii) be based on the risks insured in each category, and

(iii) reflect the experience of the corporation (including experience which may be reasonably anticipated) in guaranteeing such benefits.

(B) Notwithstanding subparagraph (A), premium rates charged to any multiemployer plan by the corporation for any period for supplemental guarantees under section 1322a(g)(2) of this title may reflect any reasonable considerations which the corporation determines to be appropriate.

(6)(A) In carrying out its authority under paragraph (1) to establish premium rates and bases for basic benefits guaranteed under section 1322 of this title with respect to single-employer plans, the corporation shall establish such rates and bases in coverage schedules in accordance with the provisions of this paragraph.

(B) The corporation may establish annual premiums for single-employer plans composed of the sum of—

(i) a charge based on a rate applicable to the excess, if any, of the present value of the basic benefits of the plan which are guaranteed over the value of the assets of the plan, not in excess of 0.1 percent, and

(ii) an additional charge based on a rate applicable to the present value of the basic benefits of the plan which are guaranteed.

The rate for the additional charge referred to in clause (ii) shall be set by the corporation for every year at a level which the corporation estimates will yield total revenue approximately equal to the total revenue to be derived by the corporation from the charges referred to in clause (i) of this subparagraph.

(C) The corporation may establish annual premiums for single-employer plans based on—

(i) the number of participants in a plan, but such premium rates shall not exceed the rates described in paragraph (3),

(ii) unfunded basic benefits guaranteed under this subchapter, but such premium rates shall not exceed the limitations applicable to charges referred to in subparagraph (B)(i), or

(iii) total guaranteed basic benefits, but such premium rates shall not exceed the rates for additional charges referred to in subparagraph (B)(ii).

If the corporation uses two or more of the rate bases described in this subparagraph, the premium rates shall be designed to produce approximately equal amounts of aggregate premium revenue from each of the rate bases used.

(D) For purposes of this paragraph, the corporation shall by regulation define the terms "value of assets" and "present value of the benefits of the plan which are guaranteed" in a manner consistent with the purposes of this subchapter and the provisions of this section.

(7) PREMIUM RATE FOR CERTAIN TERMINATED SINGLE-EMPLOYER PLANS.—

(A) IN GENERAL.—If there is a termination of a single-employer plan under clause (ii) or (iii) of section 1341(c)(2)(B) of this title or section 1342 of this title, there shall be payable to the corporation, with respect to each applicable 12-month period, a premium at a rate equal to $1,250 multiplied by the number of individuals who were participants in the plan immediately before the termination date. Such premium shall be in addition to any other premium under this section.

(B) SPECIAL RULE FOR PLANS TERMINATED IN BANKRUPTCY REORGANIZATION.—In the case of a single-employer plan terminated under section 1341(c)(2)(B)(ii) of this title or under section 1342 of this title during pendency of any bankruptcy reorganization proceeding under chapter 11 of title 11 or under any similar law of a State or a political subdivision of a State (or a case described in section 1341(c)(2)(B)(i) of this title filed by or against such person has been converted, as of such date, to such a case in which reorganization is sought), subparagraph (A) shall not apply to such plan until the date of the discharge or dismissal of such person in such case.

(C) APPLICABLE 12-MONTH PERIOD.—For purposes of subparagraph (A)—

(i) IN GENERAL.—The term "applicable 12-month period" means—

(I) the 12-month period beginning with the first month following the month in which the termination date occurs, and

(II) each of the first two 12-month periods immediately following the period described in subclause (I).

(ii) PLANS TERMINATED IN BANKRUPTCY REORGANIZATION.—In any case in which the requirements of subparagraph (B) are met in connection with the termination of the plan with respect to 1 or more persons described in such subparagraph, the 12-month period described in clause (i)(I) shall be the 12-month period beginning with the first month following the month which includes the earliest date as of which each such person is discharged or dismissed in the case described in such clause in connection with such person.

(D) COORDINATION WITH SECTION 1307.—

(i) Notwithstanding section 1307 of this title—

(I) premiums under this paragraph shall be due within 30 days after the beginning of any applicable 12-month period, and

(II) the designated payor shall be the person who is the contributing sponsor as of immediately before the termination date.

(ii) The fifth sentence of section 1307(a) of this title shall not apply in connection with premiums determined under this paragraph.

(b) Revised schedule; Congressional procedures applicable

(1) In order to place a revised schedule (other than a schedule described in subsection (a)(2)(C), (D), or (E) of this section) in effect, the corporation shall transmit the proposed schedule, its proposed effective date, and the reasons for its proposal to the Committee on Ways and Means and the Committee on Education and Labor of the House of Representatives, and to the Committee on Finance and the Committee on Labor and Human Resources of the Senate.

(2) The succeeding paragraphs of this subsection are enacted by Congress as an exercise of the rulemaking power of the Senate and the House of Representatives, respectively, and as such they shall be deemed a part of the rules of each House, respectively, but applicable only with respect to the procedure to be followed in that House in the case of resolutions described in paragraph (3). They shall supersede other rules only to the extent that they are inconsistent therewith. They are enacted with full recognition of the constitutional right of either House to change the rules (so far as relating to the procedure of that House) at any time, in the same manner and to the same extent as in the case of any rule of that House.

(3) For the purpose of the succeeding paragraphs of this subsection, "resolution" means only a joint resolution, the matter after the resolving clause of which is as follows: "The proposed revised schedule transmitted to Congress by the Pension Benefit Guaranty Corporation on ____ is hereby approved.", the blank space therein being filled with the date on which the corporation's message proposing the rate was delivered.

(4) A resolution shall be referred to the Committee on Ways and Means and the Committee on Education and Labor of the House of Representatives and to the Committee on Finance and the Committee on Labor and Human Resources of the Senate.

(5) If a committee to which has been referred a resolution has not reported it before the expiration of 10 calendar days after its introduction, it shall then (but not before) be in order to move to discharge the committee from further consid-

eration of that resolution, or to discharge the committee from further consideration of any other resolution with respect to the proposed adjustment which has been referred to the committee. The motion to discharge may be made only by a person favoring the resolution, shall be highly privileged (except that it may not be made after the committee has reported a resolution with respect to the same proposed rate), and debate thereon shall be limited to not more than 1 hour, to be divided equally between those favoring and those opposing the resolution. An amendment to the motion is not in order, and it is not in order to move to reconsider the vote by which the motion is agreed to or disagreed to. If the motion to discharge is agreed to or disagreed to, the motion may not be renewed, nor may another motion to discharge the committee be made with respect to any other resolution with respect to the same proposed rate.

(6) When a committee has reported, or has been discharged from further consideration of a resolution, it is at any time thereafter in order (even though a previous motion to the same effect has been disagreed to) to move to proceed to the consideration of the resolution. The motion is highly privileged and is not debatable. An amendment to the motion is not in order, and it is not in order to move to reconsider the vote by which the motion is agreed to or disagreed to. Debate on the resolution shall be limited to not more than 10 hours, which shall be divided equally between those favoring and those opposing the resolution. A motion further to limit debate is not debatable. An amendment to, or motion to recommit, the resolution is not in order, and it is not in order to move to reconsider the vote by which the resolution is agreed to or disagreed to.

(7) Motions to postpone, made with respect to the discharge from committee, or the consideration of, a resolution and motions to proceed to the consideration of other business shall be decided without debate. Appeals from the decisions of the Chair relating to the application of the rules of the Senate or the House of Representatives, as the case may be, to the procedure relating to a resolution shall be decided without debate.

(c) Rates for plans for basic benefits

(1) Except as provided in subsection (a)(3) of this section, and subject to paragraph (2), the rate for all plans for basic benefits guaranteed under this subchapter with respect to plan years ending after September 2, 1974, is—

(A) in the case of each plan which was not a multiemployer plan in a plan year—

(i) with respect to each plan year beginning before January 1, 1978, an amount equal to $1 for each individual who was a participant in such plan during the plan year,

(ii) with respect to each plan year beginning after December 31, 1977, and before January 1, 1986, an amount equal to $2.60 for each individual who was a participant in such plan during the plan year, and[2]

(iii) with respect to each plan year beginning after December 31, 1985, and before January 1, 1988, an amount equal to $8.50 for each individual who was a participant in such plan during the plan year, and

(iv) with respect to each plan year beginning after December 31, 1987, and before January 1, 1991, an amount equal to $16 for each individual who was a participant in such plan during the plan year, and

(B) in the case of each plan which was a multiemployer plan in a plan year, an amount equal to 50 cents for each individual who was a participant in such plan during the plan year.

(2) The rate applicable under this subsection for the plan year preceding September 1, 1975, is the product of—

(A) the rate described in the preceding sentence; and

(B) a fraction—

(i) the numerator of which is the number of calendar months in the plan year which ends after September 2, 1974, and before the date on which the new plan year commences, and

(ii) the denominator of which is 12.

(Pub. L. 93–406, title IV, § 4006, Sept. 2, 1974, 88 Stat. 1010; Pub. L. 96–364, title I, § 105, Sept. 26, 1980, 94 Stat. 1264; Pub. L. 99–272, title XI, § 11005(a)–(c)(3), Apr. 7, 1986, 100 Stat. 240–242; Pub. L. 100–203, title IX, § 9331(a), (b), (e), Dec. 22, 1987, 101 Stat. 1330–367, 1330–368; Pub. L. 101–239, title VII, § 7881(h), Dec. 19, 1989, 103 Stat. 2442; Pub. L. 101–508, title XII, § 12021(a), (b), Nov. 5, 1990, 104 Stat. 1388–573; Pub. L. 103–465, title VII, § 774(a)(1), (b)(1), (2), Dec. 8, 1994, 108 Stat. 5045, 5046; Pub. L. 107–147, title IV, § 405(c), Mar. 9, 2002, 116 Stat. 43; Pub. L. 108–218, title I, § 101(a)(4), Apr. 10, 2004, 118 Stat. 597; Pub. L. 108–311, title IV, § 403(d), Oct. 4, 2004, 118 Stat. 1187; Pub. L. 109–171, title VIII, § 8101(a)–(c), Feb. 8, 2006, 120 Stat. 180–182; Pub. L. 109–280, title III, § 301(a)(3), title IV, §§ 401(a)(1), (b)(1), (2)(A), 405(a), Aug. 17, 2006, 120 Stat. 919, 922, 928; Pub. L. 110–458, title I, § 104(a), Dec. 23, 2008, 122 Stat. 5104.)

REFERENCES IN TEXT

The plan year within which the date of enactment of the Multiemployer Pension Plan Amendments Act of 1980 falls, referred to in subsec. (a)(3)(A)(ii), refers to the plan year within which the date of the enactment of Pub. L. 96–364 falls, such enactment being approved Sept. 26, 1980.

AMENDMENTS

2008—Subsec. (a)(3)(A)(i). Pub. L. 110–458 substituted "2005" for "1990".

2006—Subsec. (a)(3)(A)(i). Pub. L. 109–171, § 8101(a)(1)(A), substituted "$30" for "$19".

Subsec. (a)(3)(A)(iii). Pub. L. 109–171, § 8101(a)(2)(A)(i)(I), inserted "and before January 1, 2006," after "September 26, 1980," in introductory provisions.

Subsec. (a)(3)(A)(iv). Pub. L. 109–171, § 8101(a)(2)(A)(i)(II), (ii), added cl. (iv).

Subsec. (a)(3)(B). Pub. L. 109–171, § 8101(c), substituted "clause (iii) or (iv) of subparagraph (A)" for "subparagraph (A)(iii)".

Subsec. (a)(3)(E)(i). Pub. L. 109–280, § 405(a)(1), substituted "Except as provided in subparagraph (H), the additional" for "The additional".

Subsec. (a)(3)(E)(iii). Pub. L. 109–280, § 401(a)(1), added cl. (iii) and struck out former cl. (iii), which defined

[2] So in original. The word "and" probably should not appear.

"unfunded vested benefits" for purposes of clause (ii) and set forth provisions relating to the interest rate used in valuing vested benefits, the value of the plan's assets in the case of any plan year for which the applicable percentage is 100 percent, the applicable percentage in the case of plan years beginning after Dec. 31, 2001, and before Jan. 1, 2004, and the annual yield taken into account in the case of plan years beginning after Dec. 31, 2003, and before Jan. 1, 2008.

Subsec. (a)(3)(E)(iii)(V). Pub. L. 109–280, §301(a)(3), substituted "2008" for "2006".

Subsec. (a)(3)(E)(iv). Pub. L. 109–280, §401(a)(1), added cl. (iv) and struck out former cl. (iv) which read as follows: "No premium shall be determined under this subparagraph for any plan year if, as of the close of the preceding plan year, contributions to the plan for the preceding plan year were not less than the full funding limitation for the preceding plan year under section 412(c)(7) of title 26."

Subsec. (a)(3)(F). Pub. L. 109–171, §8101(a)(1)(B), added subpar. (F).

Subsec. (a)(3)(G). Pub. L. 109–171, §8101(a)(2)(B), added subpar. (G).

Subsec. (a)(3)(H). Pub. L. 109–280, §405(a)(2), added subpar. (H).

Subsec. (a)(7). Pub. L. 109–171, §8101(b), added par. (7).

Subsec. (a)(7)(C)(ii). Pub. L. 109–280, §401(b)(2)(A), substituted "subparagraph (B)" for "subparagraph (B)(i)(I)".

Subsec. (a)(7)(E). Pub. L. 109–280, §401(b)(1), struck out heading and text of subpar. (E). Text read as follows: "Subparagraph (A) shall not apply with respect to any plan terminated after December 31, 2010."

2004–Subsec. (a)(3)(E)(iii)(IV). Pub. L. 108–311, in last sentence, inserted "or this subparagraph" after "this clause" in two places and inserted "(other than sections 1305, 1310, 1311, and 1343 of this title)" after "subsections".

Subsec. (a)(3)(E)(iii)(V). Pub. L. 108–218 added subcl. (V).

2002—Subsec. (a)(3)(E)(iii)(IV). Pub. L. 107–147 added subcl. (IV).

1994—Subsec. (a)(3)(E)(iii). Pub. L. 103–465, §774(b)(1), (2), in subcl. (I), inserted "or (III)" after "subclause (II)", in subcl. (II), substituted "equal to the applicable percentage" for "equal to 80 percent" and inserted at end "For purposes of this subclause, the applicable percentage is 80 percent for plan years beginning before July 1, 1997, 85 percent for plan years beginning after June 30, 1997, and before the 1st plan year to which the first tables prescribed under section 1082(d)(7)(C)(ii)(II) of this title apply, and 100 percent for such 1st plan year and subsequent plan years.", and added subcl. (III).

Subsec. (a)(3)(E)(iv), (v). Pub. L. 103–465, §774(a)(1), redesignated cl. (v) as (iv) and struck out former cl. (iv) which read as follows:

"(iv)(I) Except as provided in this clause, the aggregate increase in the premium payable with respect to any participant by reason of this subparagraph shall not exceed $53.

"(II) If an employer made contributions to a plan during 1 or more of the 5 plan years preceding the 1st plan year to which this subparagraph applies in an amount not less than the maximum amount allowable as a deduction with respect to such contributions under section 404 of title 26, the dollar amount in effect under subclause (I) for the 1st 5 plan years to which this subparagraph applies shall be reduced by $3 for each plan year for which such contributions were made in such amount."

1990—Subsec. (a)(3)(A)(i). Pub. L. 101–508, §12021(a)(1), substituted "for plan years beginning after December 31, 1990, an amount equal to the sum of $19" for "for plan years beginning after December 31, 1987, an amount equal to the sum of $16".

Subsec. (a)(3)(E)(ii). Pub. L. 101–508, §12021(b)(1), substituted "$9.00" for "$6.00".

Subsec. (a)(3)(E)(iv)(I). Pub. L. 101–508, §12021(b)(2), substituted "$53" for "$34".

Subsec. (c)(1)(A)(iv). Pub. L. 101–508, §12021(a)(2), added cl. (iv).

1989—Subsec. (a)(3)(E)(v). Pub. L. 101–239, §7881(h)(1), added cl. (v).

Subsec. (c)(1)(A)(iii). Pub. L. 101–239, §7881(h)(2), realigned margin.

1987—Subsec. (a)(3)(A)(i). Pub. L. 100–203, §9331(a), substituted "for plan years beginning after December 31, 1987, an amount equal to the sum of $16 plus the additional premium (if any) determined under subparagraph (E)" for "for plan years beginning after December 31, 1985, an amount equal to $8.50".

Subsec. (a)(3)(E). Pub. L. 100–203, §9331(b), added subpar. (E).

Subsec. (c)(1)(A). Pub. L. 100–203, §9331(e), struck out "and" at end of cl. (i), inserted "and before January 1, 1986," in cl. (ii), and added cl. (iii).

1986—Subsec. (a)(1). Pub. L. 99–272, §11005(b)(1), struck out provision that in establishing annual premiums with respect to plans, other than multiemployer plans, pars. (5) and (6) of this subsection, as in effect before Sept. 26, 1980, would continue to apply.

Subsec. (a)(2). Pub. L. 99–272, §11005(c)(1), substituted "a joint resolution approving such revised schedule is enacted" for "the Congress approves such revised schedule by a concurrent resolution".

Subsec. (a)(3)(A)(i). Pub. L. 99–272, §11005(a)(1), substituted "December 31, 1985, an amount equal to $8.50" for "December 31, 1977, an amount equal to $2.60".

Subsec. (a)(4). Pub. L. 99–272, §11005(c)(2), substituted "the enactment of a joint resolution" for "approval by the Congress".

Subsec. (a)(6). Pub. L. 99–272, §11005(b)(2), added par. (6).

Subsec. (b)(3). Pub. L. 99–272, §11005(c)(3), substituted "joint" for "concurrent" and "The" for "That the Congress favors the" and inserted "is hereby approved".

Subsec. (c)(1)(A). Pub. L. 99–272, §11005(a)(2), amended subpar. (A) generally. Prior to amendment, subpar. (A) read as follows: "in the case of each plan which was not a multiemployer plan in a plan year, an amount equal to $1 for each individual who was a participant in such plan during the plan year, and".

1980—Subsec. (a). Pub. L. 96–364, §105(a), substituted provisions setting forth authority of corporation to prescribe schedules of premium rates and bases for the application of such rates and provisions respecting contents, coverages, alternate schedules, etc., of schedules and application bases, for provisions setting forth authority of corporation to prescribe insurance premium rates and coverage schedules for the application of such rates and provisions respecting contents, coverages, rates, etc., of schedules and premium rates.

Subsec. (b). Pub. L. 96–364, §105(b), in par. (1) substituted "(C), (D), or (E)" for "(B) or (C)", "revised schedule" for "revised coverage schedule", and "Human Resources" for "Public Welfare", in par. (3) substituted "revised schedule" for "revised coverage schedule", and in par. (4) substituted "Human Resources" for "Public Welfare".

Subsec. (c). Pub. L. 96–364, §105(c), added subsec. (c).

CHANGE OF NAME

Committee on Labor and Human Resources of Senate changed to Committee on Health, Education, Labor, and Pensions of Senate by Senate Resolution No. 20, One Hundred Sixth Congress, Jan. 19, 1999.

EFFECTIVE DATE OF 2008 AMENDMENT

Amendment by Pub. L. 110–458 effective as if included in the provisions of Pub. L. 109–280 to which the amendment relates, except as otherwise provided, see section 112 of Pub. L. 110–458, set out as a note under section 72 of Title 26, Internal Revenue Code.

EFFECTIVE DATE OF 2006 AMENDMENT

Pub. L. 109–280, title IV, §401(a)(2), Aug. 17, 2006, 120 Stat. 922, provided that: "The amendments made by paragraph (1) [amending this section] shall apply with respect to plan years beginning after 2007."

Pub. L. 109–280, title IV, §401(b)(2)(B), Aug. 17, 2006, 120 Stat. 922, provided that: "The amendment made by this paragraph [amending this section] shall take effect as if included in the provision of the Deficit Reduction Act of 2005 [Pub. L. 109–171] to which it relates."

Pub. L. 109–280, title IV, §405(b), Aug. 17, 2006, 120 Stat. 929, provided that: "The amendment made by this section [amending this section] shall apply to plan years beginning after December 31, 2006."

Pub. L. 109–171, title VIII, §8101(d), Feb. 8, 2006, 120 Stat. 182, provided that:

"(1) IN GENERAL.—Except as otherwise provided in this subsection, the amendments made by this section [amending this section] shall apply to plan years beginning after December 31, 2005.

"(2) PREMIUM RATE FOR CERTAIN TERMINATED SINGLE-EMPLOYER PLANS.—

"(A) IN GENERAL.—Except as provided in subparagraph (B), the amendment made by subsection (b) [amending this section] shall apply to plans terminated after December 31, 2005.

"(B) SPECIAL RULE FOR PLANS TERMINATED IN BANKRUPTCY.—The amendment made by subsection (b) shall not apply to a termination of a single-employer plan that is terminated during the pendency of any bankruptcy reorganization proceeding under chapter 11 of title 11, United States Code (or under any similar law of a State or political subdivision of a State), if the proceeding is pursuant to a bankruptcy filing occurring before October 18, 2005."

EFFECTIVE DATE OF 2004 AMENDMENTS

Amendment by Pub. L. 108–311 effective as if included in the provisions of the Job Creation and Worker Assistance Act of 2002, Pub. L. 107–147, to which such amendment relates, see section 403(f) of Pub. L. 108–311, set out as a note under section 56 of Title 26, Internal Revenue Code.

Amendment by Pub. L. 108–218 applicable, except as otherwise provided, to plan years beginning after Dec. 31, 2003, see section 101(d) of Pub. L. 108–218, set out as a note under section 404 of Title 26, Internal Revenue Code.

EFFECTIVE DATE OF 1994 AMENDMENT

Section 774(a)(2) of Pub. L. 103–465 provided that:

"(A) IN GENERAL.—The amendments made by this subsection [amending this section] shall be effective for plan years beginning on or after July 1, 1994.

"(B) TRANSITION RULE.—In the case of plan years beginning on or after July 1, 1994, and before July 1, 1996, the additional premium payable with respect to any participant by reason of the amendments made by this section shall not exceed the sum of—

"(i) $53, and

"(ii) the product derived by multiplying—

"(I) the excess (if any) of the amount determined under clause (i) of section 4006(a)(3)(E) of the Employee Retirement Income Security Act of 1974 [subsec. (a)(3)(E) of this section], over $53, by

"(II) the applicable percentage.

For purposes of this subparagraph, the applicable percentage shall be the percentage specified in the following table:

For the plan year beginning: on or after	but before	The applicable percentage is:
July 1, 1994	July 1, 1995	20 percent
July 1, 1995	July 1, 1996	60 percent."

Section 774(b)(3) of Pub. L. 103–465 provided that: "The amendments made by this subsection [amending this section] shall apply to plan years beginning after the date of the enactment of this Act [Dec. 8, 1994]."

EFFECTIVE DATE OF 1990 AMENDMENT

Section 12021(c) of Pub. L. 101–508 provided that: "The amendments made by this section [amending this section] shall apply to plan years beginning after December 31, 1990."

EFFECTIVE DATE OF 1989 AMENDMENT

Amendment by Pub. L. 101–239 effective, except as otherwise provided, as if included in the provision of the Pension Protection Act, Pub. L. 100–203, §§9302–9346, to which such amendment relates, see section 7882 of Pub. L. 101–239, set out as a note under section 401 of Title 26, Internal Revenue Code.

EFFECTIVE DATE OF 1987 AMENDMENT

Amendment by Pub. L. 100–203 applicable to plan years beginning after Dec. 31, 1987, see section 9331(f)(1) of Pub. L. 100–203, set out as a note under section 1305 of this title.

EFFECTIVE DATE OF 1986 AMENDMENT

Section 11005(d) of Pub. L. 99–272 provided that:

"(1) GENERAL RULE.—Except as provided in paragraph (2), the amendments made by this section [amending this section and section 1322a of this title] shall be effective for plan years commencing after December 31, 1985.

"(2) SPECIAL RULE.—The amendments made by subsection (b) [amending this section] shall be effective as of the date of the enactment of the Multiemployer Pension Plan Amendments Act of 1980 [Sept. 26, 1980]."

EFFECTIVE DATE OF 1980 AMENDMENT

Amendment by Pub. L. 96–364 effective Sept. 26, 1980, except as specifically provided, see section 1461(e) of this title.

MODIFICATION OF TRANSITION RULE TO PENSION FUNDING REQUIREMENTS

For modification of transition rule to pension funding requirements in the case of a plan that was not required to pay a variable rate premium for the plan year beginning in 1996, has not, in any plan year beginning after 1995, merged with another plan (other than a plan sponsored by an employer that was in 1996 within the controlled group of the plan sponsor), and is sponsored by a company that is engaged primarily in the interurban or interstate passenger bus service, see section 115(a)–(c) of Pub. L. 109–280, set out as a note under section 430 of Title 26, Internal Revenue Code.

APPLICABILITY OF THIS SECTION TO CERTAIN PLANS MAINTAINED BY COMMERCIAL AIRLINES

For special rules on applicability of this section to certain plans maintained by commercial airlines, see section 402 of Pub. L. 109–280, set out as a note under section 430 of Title 26, Internal Revenue Code.

TRANSITIONAL RULE

Section 774(c) of Pub. L. 103–465 provided that: "In the case of a regulated public utility described in section 7701(a)(33)(A)(i) of the Internal Revenue Code of 1986 [26 U.S.C. 7701(a)(33)(A)(i)], the amendments made by this section [amending this section] shall not apply to plan years beginning before the earlier of—

"(1) January 1, 1998, or

"(2) the date the regulated public utility begins to collect from utility customers rates that reflect the costs incurred or projected to be incurred for additional premiums under section 4006(a)(3)(E) of the Employee Retirement Income Security Act of 1974 [subsec. (a)(3)(E) of this section] pursuant to final and nonappealable determinations by all public utility commissions (or other authorities having jurisdiction over the rates and terms of service by the regulated public utility) that the costs are just and reasonable and recoverable from customers of the regulated public utility."

Section 11005(e) of Pub. L. 99–272 provided that:

"(1) NOTICE OF PREMIUM INCREASE.—Not later than 30 days after the date of the enactment of this Act [Apr.

7, 1986], the Pension Benefit Guaranty Corporation shall send a notice to the plan administrator of each single-employer plan affected by the premium increase established by the amendment made by subsection (a)(1) [amending this section]. Such notice shall describe such increase and the requirements of this subsection.

"(2) DUE DATE FOR UNPAID PREMIUMS.—With respect to any plan year beginning during the period beginning on January 1, 1986, and ending 30 days after the date of the enactment of this Act, any unpaid amount of such premium increase shall be due and payable no later than the earlier of 60 days after the date of the enactment of this Act or 30 days after the date on which the notice required by paragraph (1) is sent, except that in no event shall the amount of the premium increase established under the amendment made by subsection (a)(1) be due and payable for a plan year earlier than the date on which premiums for the plan would have been due for such plan year had this Act [probably means the Single-Employee Pension Plan Amendments Act of 1986, title XI of Pub. L. 99–272, see Short Title of 1986 Amendment note set out under section 1001 of this title] not been enacted.

"(3) ENFORCEMENT.—For purposes of enforcement, the requirements of paragraphs (1) and (2) shall be considered to be requirements of sections 4006 and 4007 of the Employee Retirement Income Security Act of 1974 (29 U.S.C. 1306 and 1307)."

SINGLE-EMPLOYER PENSION PLAN TERMINATION INSURANCE PREMIUM STUDY

Section 11017(a) of Pub. L. 99–272 directed Pension Benefit Guaranty Corporation to conduct a study of, and submit to an advisory council not later than one year after Apr. 7, 1986, a report on the premiums established under the single-employer pension plan termination insurance program under this subchapter, including (1) the long-term stability of the program, (2) alternatives with respect to proposals for changes in the premium levels under such program, (3) methods currently used in projecting future costs, (4) alternative methods of projecting such future costs, (5) methods currently used in determining premiums needed to allocate and adequately fund such future costs, along with any alternative methods of making such premium determinations, and (6) alternative premium bases upon which some or all of such projected future costs would be allocated on an exposure-related or risk-related computation; and further provided for submission of the advisory council's report to Congress 180 days after submission of the Corporation's report to the advisory council, as well as the cooperation and consultation with other Federal agencies in compilation of reports.

STUDIES AND REPORTS RESPECTING GRADUATED PREMIUM RATE SCHEDULES AND UNION MANDATED WITHDRAWALS FROM MULTIEMPLOYER PENSION PLANS

Section 412(a) of Pub. L. 96–364 directed Pension Benefit Guaranty Corporation to conduct a separate study with respect to advantages and disadvantages of establishing a graduated premium rate schedule under this section which is based on risk, and necessity of adopting special rules in cases of union-mandated withdrawal from multiemployer pension plans, and to report to Congress the results of the studies conducted, including its recommendations with respect thereto.

§1307. Payment of premiums

(a) Premiums payable when due; accrual; waiver or reduction

The designated payor of each plan shall pay the premiums imposed by the corporation under this subchapter with respect to that plan when they are due. Premiums under this subchapter are payable at the time, and on an estimated, advance, or other basis, as determined by the corporation. Premiums imposed by this subchapter on September 2, 1974 (applicable to that portion of any plan year during which such date occurs) are due within 30 days after such date. Premiums imposed by this subchapter on the first plan year commencing after September 2, 1974, are due within 30 days after such plan year commences. Premiums shall continue to accrue until a plan's assets are distributed pursuant to a termination procedure, or until a trustee is appointed pursuant to section 1342 of this title, whichever is earlier. The corporation may waive or reduce premiums for a multiemployer plan for any plan year during which such plan receives financial assistance from the corporation under section 1431 of this title, except that any amount so waived or reduced shall be treated as financial assistance under such section.

(b) Late payment charge; waiver; interest on overpayment

(1) If any basic benefit premium is not paid when it is due the corporation is authorized to assess a late payment charge of not more than 100 percent of the premium payment which was not timely paid. The preceding sentence shall not apply to any payment of premium made within 60 days after the date on which payment is due, if before such date, the designated payor obtains a waiver from the corporation based upon a showing of substantial hardship arising from the timely payment of the premium. The corporation is authorized to grant a waiver under this subsection upon application made by the designated payor, but the corporation may not grant a waiver if it appears that the designated payor will be unable to pay the premium within 60 days after the date on which it is due. If any premium is not paid by the last date prescribed for a payment, interest on the amount of such premium at the rate imposed under section 6601(a) of title 26 (relating to interest on underpayment, nonpayment, or extensions of time for payment of tax) shall be paid for the period from such last date to the date paid.

(2) The corporation is authorized to pay, subject to regulations prescribed by the corporation, interest on the amount of any overpayment of premium refunded to a designated payor. Interest under this paragraph shall be calculated at the same rate and in the same manner as interest is calculated for underpayments under paragraph (1).

(c) Civil action to recover premium penalty and interest

If any designated payor fails to pay a premium when due, the corporation is authorized to bring a civil action in any district court of the United States within the jurisdiction of which the plan assets are located, the plan is administered, or in which a defendant resides or is found for the recovery of the amount of the premium penalty, and interest, and process may be served in any other district. The district courts of the United States shall have jurisdiction over actions brought under this subsection by the corporation without regard to the amount in controversy.

(d) Basic benefits guarantee not stopped by designated payor's failure to pay premiums when due

The corporation shall not cease to guarantee basic benefits on account of the failure of a designated payor to pay any premium when due.

(e) Designated payor

(1) For purposes of this section, the term "designated payor" means—

(A) the contributing sponsor or plan administrator in the case of a single-employer plan, and

(B) the plan administrator in the case of a multiemployer plan.

(2) If the contributing sponsor of any single-employer plan is a member of a controlled group, each member of such group shall be jointly and severally liable for any premiums required to be paid by such contributing sponsor. For purposes of the preceding sentence, the term "controlled group" means any group treated as a single employer under subsection (b), (c), (m), or (*o*) of section 414 of title 26.

(Pub. L. 93–406, title IV, § 4007, Sept. 2, 1974, 88 Stat. 1013; Pub. L. 96–364, title IV, §§ 402(a)(3), 403(b), Sept. 26, 1980, 94 Stat. 1298, 1300; Pub. L. 100–203, title IX, § 9331(c), Dec. 22, 1987, 101 Stat. 1330–368; Pub. L. 101–239, title VII, § 7891(a)(1), Dec. 19, 1989, 103 Stat. 2445; Pub. L. 109–280, title IV, § 406(a), Aug. 17, 2006, 120 Stat. 929.)

AMENDMENTS

2006—Subsec. (b). Pub. L. 109–280 designated existing provisions as par. (1) and added par. (2).

1989—Subsec. (b). Pub. L. 101–239 substituted "Internal Revenue Code of 1986" for "Internal Revenue Code of 1954", which for purposes of codification was translated as "title 26" thus requiring no change in text.

1987—Subsecs. (a) to (d). Pub. L. 100–203, § 9331(c)(1), substituted "designated payor" for "plan administrator" wherever appearing.

Subsec. (e). Pub. L. 100–203, § 9331(c)(2), added subsec. (e).

1980—Subsec. (a). Pub. L. 96–364 inserted provisions relating to waiver or reduction of premiums, and struck out provisions relating to payment of premiums under statutory requirements respecting contingent liability coverage.

EFFECTIVE DATE OF 2006 AMENDMENT

Pub. L. 109–280, title IV, § 406(b), Aug. 17, 2006, 120 Stat. 929, provided that: "The amendments made by subsection (a) [amending this section] shall apply to interest accruing for periods beginning not earlier than the date of the enactment of this Act [Aug. 17, 2006]."

EFFECTIVE DATE OF 1989 AMENDMENT

Amendment by Pub. L. 101–239 effective, except as otherwise provided, as if included in the provision of the Tax Reform Act of 1986, Pub. L. 99–514, to which such amendment relates, see section 7891(f) of Pub. L. 101–239, set out as a note under section 1002 of this title.

EFFECTIVE DATE OF 1987 AMENDMENT

Amendment by Pub. L. 100–203 applicable to plan years beginning after Dec. 31, 1987, see section 9331(f)(1) of Pub. L. 100–203, set out as a note under section 1305 of this title.

EFFECTIVE DATE OF 1980 AMENDMENT

Amendment by Pub. L. 96–364 effective Sept. 26, 1980, except as specifically provided, see section 1461(e) of this title.

§ 1308. Annual report by the corporation

(a) As soon as practicable after the close of each fiscal year the corporation shall transmit to the President and the Congress a report relative to the conduct of its business under this subchapter for that fiscal year. The report shall include financial statements setting forth the finances of the corporation at the end of such fiscal year and the result of its operations (including the source and application of its funds) for the fiscal year and shall include an actuarial evaluation of the expected operations and status of the funds established under section 1305 of this title for the next five years (including a detailed statement of the actuarial assumptions and methods used in making such evaluation).

(b) The report under subsection (a) shall include—

(1) a summary of the Pension Insurance Modeling System microsimulation model, including the specific simulation parameters, specific initial values, temporal parameters, and policy parameters used to calculate the financial statements for the corporation;

(2) a comparison of—

(A) the average return on investments earned with respect to assets invested by the corporation for the year to which the report relates; and

(B) an amount equal to 60 percent of the average return on investment for such year in the Standard & Poor's 500 Index, plus 40 percent of the average return on investment for such year in the Lehman Aggregate Bond Index (or in a similar fixed income index); and

(3) a statement regarding the deficit or surplus for such year that the corporation would have had if the corporation had earned the return described in paragraph (2)(B) with respect to assets invested by the corporation.

(Pub. L. 93–406, title IV, § 4008, Sept. 2, 1974, 88 Stat. 1014; Pub. L. 109–280, title IV, § 412, Aug. 17, 2006, 120 Stat. 936.)

AMENDMENTS

2006—Pub. L. 109–280 designated existing provisions as subsec. (a) and added subsec. (b).

§ 1309. Portability assistance

The corporation shall provide advice and assistance to individuals with respect to evaluating the economic desirability of establishing individual retirement accounts or other forms of individual retirement savings for which a deduction is allowable under section 219 of title 26 and with respect to evaluating the desirability, in particular cases, of transferring amounts representing an employee's interest in a qualified plan to such an account upon the employee's separation from service with an employer.

(Pub. L. 93–406, title IV, § 4009, Sept. 2, 1974, 88 Stat. 1014; Pub. L. 101–239, title VII, § 7891(a)(1), Dec. 19, 1989, 103 Stat. 2445.)

AMENDMENTS

1989—Pub. L. 101–239 substituted "Internal Revenue Code of 1986" for "Internal Revenue Code of 1954", which for purposes of codification was translated as "title 26" thus requiring no change in text.

EFFECTIVE DATE OF 1989 AMENDMENT

Amendment by Pub. L. 101–239 effective, except as otherwise provided, as if included in the provision of the Tax Reform Act of 1986, Pub. L. 99–514, to which such amendment relates, see section 7891(f) of Pub. L. 101–239, set out as a note under section 1002 of this title.

§ 1310. Authority to require certain information

(a) Information required

Each person described in subsection (b) of this section shall provide the corporation annually, on or before a date specified by the corporation in regulations, with—

(1) such records, documents, or other information that the corporation specifies in regulations as necessary to determine the liabilities and assets of plans covered by this subchapter; and

(2) copies of such person's audited (or, if unavailable, unaudited) financial statements, and such other financial information as the corporation may prescribe in regulations.

(b) Persons required to provide information

The persons covered by subsection (a) of this section are each contributing sponsor, and each member of a contributing sponsor's controlled group, of a single-employer plan covered by this subchapter, if—

(1) the funding target attainment percentage (as defined in subsection (d)) at the end of the preceding plan year of a plan maintained by the contributing sponsor or any member of its controlled group is less than 80 percent;

(2) the conditions for imposition of a lien described in section 1083(k)(1)(A) and (B) of this title or section 430(k)(1)(A) and (B) of title 26 have been met with respect to any plan maintained by the contributing sponsor or any member of its controlled group; or

(3) minimum funding waivers in excess of $1,000,000 have been granted with respect to any plan maintained by the contributing sponsor or any member of its controlled group, and any portion thereof is still outstanding.

(c) Information exempt from disclosure requirements

Any information or documentary material submitted to the corporation pursuant to this section shall be exempt from disclosure under section 552 of title 5, and no such information or documentary material may be made public, except as may be relevant to any administrative or judicial action or proceeding. Nothing in this section is intended to prevent disclosure to either body of Congress or to any duly authorized committee or subcommittee of the Congress.

(d) Additional information required

(1) In general

The information submitted to the corporation under subsection (a) shall include—

(A) the amount of benefit liabilities under the plan determined using the assumptions used by the corporation in determining liabilities;

(B) the funding target of the plan determined as if the plan has been in at-risk status for at least 5 plan years; and

(C) the funding target attainment percentage of the plan.

(2) Definitions

For purposes of this subsection:

(A) Funding target

The term "funding target" has the meaning provided under section 1083(d)(1) of this title.

(B) Funding target attainment percentage

The term "funding target attainment percentage" has the meaning provided under section 1083(d)(2) of this title.

(C) At-risk status

The term "at-risk status" has the meaning provided in section 1083(i)(4) of this title.

(e) Notice to Congress

The corporation shall, on an annual basis, submit to the Committee on Health, Education, Labor, and Pensions and the Committee on Finance of the Senate and the Committee on Education and the Workforce and the Committee on Ways and Means of the House of Representatives, a summary report in the aggregate of the information submitted to the corporation under this section.

(Pub. L. 93–406, title IV, § 4010, as added Pub. L. 103–465, title VII, § 772(a), Dec. 8, 1994, 108 Stat. 5044; amended Pub. L. 109–280, title I, § 107(b)(3), title V, § 505(a), (b), Aug. 17, 2006, 120 Stat. 819, 946; Pub. L. 110–458, title I, § 105(d), Dec. 23, 2008, 122 Stat. 5105.)

AMENDMENTS

2008—Subsec. (d)(2)(B). Pub. L. 110–458 substituted "section 1083(d)(2)" for "section 1082(d)(2)".

2006—Subsec. (b)(1). Pub. L. 109–280, § 505(a), added par. (1) and struck out former par. (1) which read as follows: "the aggregate unfunded vested benefits at the end of the preceding plan year (as determined under section 1306(a)(3)(E)(iii) of this title) of plans maintained by the contributing sponsor and the members of its controlled group exceed $50,000,000 (disregarding plans with no unfunded vested benefits);".

Subsec. (b)(2). Pub. L. 109–280, § 107(b)(3), substituted "1083(k)(1)(A) and (B)" for "1082(f)(1)(A) and (B)" and "430(k)(1)(A) and (B)" for "412(n)(1)(A) and (B)".

Subsecs. (d), (e). Pub. L. 109–280, § 505(b), added subsecs. (d) and (e).

CHANGE OF NAME

Committee on Education and the Workforce of House of Representatives changed to Committee on Education and Labor of House of Representatives by House Resolution No. 6, One Hundred Tenth Congress, Jan. 5, 2007.

EFFECTIVE DATE OF 2008 AMENDMENT

Amendment by Pub. L. 110–458 effective as if included in the provisions of Pub. L. 109–280 to which the amendment relates, except as otherwise provided, see section 112 of Pub. L. 110–458, set out as a note under section 72 of Title 26, Internal Revenue Code.

EFFECTIVE DATE OF 2006 AMENDMENT

Amendment by section 107(b)(3) of Pub. L. 109–280 applicable to plan years beginning after 2007, see section 107(e) of Pub. L. 109–280, set out as a note under section 1021 of this title.

Pub. L. 109–280, title V, § 505(c), Aug. 17, 2006, 120 Stat. 946, provided that: "The amendments made by this section [amending this section] shall apply with respect to years beginning after 2007."

EFFECTIVE DATE

Section 772(c) of Pub. L. 103–465 provided that: "The amendments made by this section [enacting this section] shall be effective on the date of enactment of this Act [Dec. 8, 1994].''

APPLICABILITY OF AMENDMENTS BY SUBTITLES A AND B OF TITLE I OF PUB. L. 109–280

For special rules on applicability of amendments by subtitles A (§§101–107) and B (§§111–116) of title I of Pub. L. 109–280 to certain eligible cooperative plans, PBGC settlement plans, and eligible government contractor plans, see sections 104, 105, and 106 of Pub. L. 109–280, set out as notes under section 401 of Title 26, Internal Revenue Code.

§1311. Repealed. Pub. L. 109–280, title V, §501(b)(1), Aug. 17, 2006, 120 Stat. 939

Section, Pub. L. 93–406, title IV, §4011, as added Pub. L. 103–465, title VII, §775(a), Dec. 8, 1994, 108 Stat. 5046, related to notice to participants of plan's funding status and limitations on corporation's guaranty.

EFFECTIVE DATE OF REPEAL

Repeal applicable to plan years beginning after Dec. 31, 2006, see section 501(d)(1) of Pub. L. 109–280, set out as an Effective Date of 2006 Amendment note under section 1021 of this title.

SUBTITLE B—COVERAGE

§1321. Coverage

(a) Plans covered

Except as provided in subsection (b) of this section, this subchapter applies to any plan (including a successor plan) which, for a plan year—

(1) is an employee pension benefit plan (as defined in paragraph (2) of section 1002 of this title) established or maintained—

(A) by an employer engaged in commerce or in any industry or activity affecting commerce, or

(B) by any employee organization, or organization representing employees, engaged in commerce or in any industry or activity affecting commerce, or

(C) by both,

which has, in practice, met the requirements of part I of subchapter D of chapter 1 of title 26 (as in effect for the preceding 5 plan years of the plan) applicable to the plans described in paragraph (2) for the preceding 5 plan years; or

(2) is, or has been determined by the Secretary of the Treasury to be, a plan described in section 401(a) of title 26, or which meets, or has been determined by the Secretary of the Treasury to meet, the requirements of section 404(a)(2) of title 26.

For purposes of this subchapter, a successor plan is considered to be a continuation of a predecessor plan. For this purpose, unless otherwise specifically indicated in this subchapter, a successor plan is a plan which covers a group of employees which includes substantially the same employees as a previously established plan, and provides substantially the same benefits as that plan provided.

(b) Plans not covered

This section does not apply to any plan—

(1) which is an individual account plan, as defined in paragraph (34) of section 1002 of this title,[1]

(2) established and maintained for its employees by the Government of the United States, by the government of any State or political subdivision thereof, or by any agency or instrumentality of any of the foregoing, or to which the Railroad Retirement Act of 1935 or 1937 [45 U.S.C. 231 et seq.] applies and which is financed by contributions required under that Act, or which is described in the last sentence of section 1002(32) of this title[2]

(3) which is a church plan as defined in section 414(e) of title 26, unless that plan has made an election under section 410(d) of title 26, and has notified the corporation in accordance with procedures prescribed by the corporation, that it wishes to have the provisions of this part apply to it,[1]

(4)(A) established and maintained by a society, order, or association described in section 501(c)(8) or (9) of title 26, if no part of the contributions to or under the plan is made by employers of participants in the plan, or

(B) of which a trust described in section 501(c)(18) of title 26 is a part;

(5) which has not at any time after September 2, 1974, provided for employer contributions;

(6) which is unfunded and which is maintained by an employer primarily for the purpose of providing deferred compensation for a select group of management or highly compensated employees;

(7) which is established and maintained outside of the United States primarily for the benefit of individuals substantially all of whom are nonresident aliens;

(8) which is maintained by an employer solely for the purpose of providing benefits for certain employees in excess of the limitations on contributions and benefits imposed by section 415 of title 26 on plans to which that section applies, without regard to whether the plan is funded, and, to the extent that a separable part of a plan (as determined by the corporation) maintained by an employer is maintained for such purpose, that part shall be treated for purposes of this subchapter, as a separate plan which is an excess benefit plan;

(9) which is established and maintained exclusively for substantial owners;

(10) of an international organization which is exempt from taxation under the International Organizations Immunities Act [22 U.S.C. 288 et seq.];

(11) maintained solely for the purpose of complying with applicable workmen's compensation laws or unemployment compensation or disability insurance laws;

(12) which is a defined benefit plan, to the extent that it is treated as an individual account plan under paragraph (35)(B) of section 1002 of this title; or

(13) established and maintained by a professional service employer which does not at any time after September 2, 1974, have more than 25 active participants in the plan.

(c) Definitions

(1) For purposes of subsection (b)(1) of this section, the term ''individual account plan'' does

[1] So in original. The comma probably should be a semicolon.

[2] So in original. A semicolon probably should appear.

not include a plan under which a fixed benefit is promised if the employer or his representative participated in the determination of that benefit.

(2) For purposes of this paragraph and for purposes of subsection (b)(13) of this section—

(A) the term "professional service employer" means any proprietorship, partnership, corporation, or other association or organization (i) owned or controlled by professional individuals or by executors or administrators of professional individuals, (ii) the principal business of which is the performance of professional services, and

(B) the term "professional individuals" includes but is not limited to, physicians, dentists, chiropractors, osteopaths, optometrists, other licensed practitioners of the healing arts, attorneys at law, public accountants, public engineers, architects, draftsmen, actuaries, psychologists, social or physical scientists, and performing artists.

(3) In the case of a plan established and maintained by more than one professional service employer, the plan shall not be treated as a plan described in subsection (b)(13) of this section if, at any time after September 2, 1974, the plan has more than 25 active participants.

(d) Substantial owner defined

For purposes of subsection (b)(9), the term "substantial owner" means an individual who, at any time during the 60-month period ending on the date the determination is being made—

(1) owns the entire interest in an unincorporated trade or business,

(2) in the case of a partnership, is a partner who owns, directly or indirectly, more than 10 percent of either the capital interest or the profits interest in such partnership, or

(3) in the case of a corporation, owns, directly or indirectly, more than 10 percent in value of either the voting stock of that corporation or all the stock of that corporation.

For purposes of paragraph (3), the constructive ownership rules of section 1563(e) of title 26 (other than paragraph (3)(C) thereof) shall apply, including the application of such rules under section 414(c) of title 26.

(Pub. L. 93–406, title IV, § 4021, Sept. 2, 1974, 88 Stat. 1014; Pub. L. 96–364, title IV, § 402(a)(4), Sept. 26, 1980, 94 Stat. 1298; Pub. L. 101–239, title VII, §§ 7891(a)(1), 7894(g)(3)(A), Dec. 19, 1989, 103 Stat. 2445, 2451; Pub. L. 109–280, title IV, § 407(c)(1), title IX, § 906(a)(2)(B), (b)(2), Aug. 17, 2006, 120 Stat. 930, 1051, 1052; Pub. L. 110–458, title I, § 109(d)(2), Dec. 23, 2008, 122 Stat. 5112.)

REFERENCES IN TEXT

The Railroad Retirement Act of 1935 or 1937, referred to in subsec. (b)(2), means act Aug. 29, 1935, ch. 812, 49 Stat. 967, known as the Railroad Retirement Act of 1935. The Railroad Retirement Act of 1935 was amended generally by act June 24, 1937, ch. 382, part I, 50 Stat. 307, and was known as the Railroad Retirement Act of 1937. The Railroad Retirement Act of 1937 was amended generally and redesignated the Railroad Retirement Act of 1974 by Pub. L. 93–445, title I, Oct. 16, 1974, 88 Stat. 1305, and is classified generally to subchapter IV (§ 231 et seq.) of chapter 9 of Title 45, Railroads. For complete classification of this Act to the Code, see Tables.

The International Organizations Immunities Act, referred to in subsec. (b)(10), is title I of act Dec. 29, 1945, ch. 652, 59 Stat. 669, as amended, which is classified principally to subchapter XVIII (§ 288 et seq.) of chapter 7 of Title 22, Foreign Relations and Intercourse. For complete classification of this Act to the Code, see Short Title note set out under section 288 of Title 22 and Tables.

AMENDMENTS

2008—Subsec. (b)(14). Pub. L. 110–458 struck out par. (14) which read as follows: "established and maintained by an Indian tribal government (as defined in section 7701(a)(40) of title 26), a subdivision of an Indian tribal government (determined in accordance with section 7871(d) of title 26), or an agency or instrumentality of either, and all of the participants of which are employees of such entity substantially all of whose services as such an employee are in the performance of essential governmental functions but not in the performance of commercial activities (whether or not an essential government function)."

2006—Subsec. (b)(2). Pub. L. 109–280, § 906(a)(2)(B), inserted "or which is described in the last sentence of section 1002(32) of this title" at end.

Subsec. (b)(9). Pub. L. 109–280, § 407(c)(1)(A), struck out "as defined in section 1322(b)(6) of this title" before semicolon at end.

Subsec. (b)(14). Pub. L. 109–280, § 906(b)(2), added par. (14).

Subsec. (d). Pub. L. 109–280, § 407(c)(1)(B), added subsec. (d).

1989—Subsec. (a). Pub. L. 101–239, § 7894(g)(3)(A), substituted "this subchapter applies" for "this section applies" in introductory provisions.

Subsecs. (a)(1), (2), (b)(3), (4)(A), (8). Pub. L. 101–239, § 7891(a)(1), substituted "Internal Revenue Code of 1986" for "Internal Revenue Code of 1954", which for purposes of codification was translated as "title 26" thus requiring no change in text.

1980—Subsec. (a). Pub. L. 96–364 inserted "unless otherwise specifically indicated in this subchapter," after "For this purpose,".

EFFECTIVE DATE OF 2008 AMENDMENT

Amendment by Pub. L. 110–458 effective as if included in the provisions of Pub. L. 109–280 to which the amendment relates, except as otherwise provided, see section 112 of Pub. L. 110–458, set out as a note under section 72 of Title 26, Internal Revenue Code.

EFFECTIVE DATE OF 2006 AMENDMENT

Pub. L. 109–280, title IV, § 407(d), Aug. 17, 2006, 120 Stat. 931, provided that:

"(1) IN GENERAL.—Except as provided in paragraph (2), the amendments made by this section [amending this section and sections 1322, 1343, and 1344 of this title] shall apply to plan terminations—

"(A) under section 4041(c) of the Employee Retirement Income Security Act of 1974 (29 U.S.C. 1341(c)) with respect to which notices of intent to terminate are provided under section 4041(a)(2) of such Act (29 U.S.C. 1341(a)(2)) after December 31, 2005, and

"(B) under section 4042 of such Act (29 U.S.C. 1342) with respect to which notices of determination are provided under such section after such date.

"(2) CONFORMING AMENDMENTS.—The amendments made by subsection (c) [amending this section and section 1343 of this title] shall take effect on January 1, 2006."

Amendment by section 906(a)(2)(B), (b)(2) of Pub. L. 109–280 applicable to any year beginning on or after Aug. 17, 2006, see section 906(c) of Pub. L. 109–280, set out as a note under section 414 of Title 26, Internal Revenue Code.

EFFECTIVE DATE OF 1989 AMENDMENT

Amendment by section 7891(a)(1) of Pub. L. 101–239 effective, except as otherwise provided, as if included in the provision of the Tax Reform Act of 1986, Pub. L. 99–514, to which such amendment relates, see section 7891(f) of Pub. L. 101–239, set out as a note under section 1002 of this title.

Amendment by section 7894(g)(3)(A) of Pub. L. 101–239 effective, except as otherwise provided, as if originally included in the provision of the Employee Retirement Income Security Act of 1974, Pub. L. 93–406, to which such amendment relates, see section 7894(i) of Pub. L. 101–239, set out as a note under section 1002 of this title.

EFFECTIVE DATE OF 1980 AMENDMENT

Amendment by Pub. L. 96–364 effective Sept. 26, 1980, except as specifically provided, see section 1461(e) of this title.

§ 1322. Single-employer plan benefits guaranteed

(a) Nonforfeitable benefits

Subject to the limitations contained in subsection (b) of this section, the corporation shall guarantee, in accordance with this section, the payment of all nonforfeitable benefits (other than benefits becoming nonforfeitable solely on account of the termination of a plan) under a single-employer plan which terminates at a time when this subchapter applies to it.

(b) Exceptions

(1) Except to the extent provided in paragraph (7)—

(A) no benefits provided by a plan which has been in effect for less than 60 months at the time the plan terminates shall be guaranteed under this section, and

(B) any increase in the amount of benefits under a plan resulting from a plan amendment which was made, or became effective, whichever is later, within 60 months before the date on which the plan terminates shall be disregarded.

(2) For purposes of this subsection, the time a successor plan (within the meaning of section 1321(a) of this title) has been in effect includes the time a previously established plan (within the meaning of section 1321(a) of this title) was in effect. For purposes of determining what benefits are guaranteed under this section in the case of a plan to which section 1321 of this title does not apply on September 3, 1974, the 60-month period referred to in paragraph (1) shall be computed beginning on the first date on which such section does apply to the plan.

(3) The amount of monthly benefits described in subsection (a) of this section provided by a plan, which are guaranteed under this section with respect to a participant, shall not have an actuarial value which exceeds the actuarial value of a monthly benefit in the form of a life annuity commencing at age 65 equal to the lesser of—

(A) his average monthly gross income from his employer during the 5 consecutive calendar year period (or, if less, during the number of calendar years in such period in which he actively participates in the plan) during which his gross income from that employer was greater than during any other such period with that employer determined by dividing 1/12 of the sum of all such gross income by the number of such calendar years in which he had such gross income, or

(B) $750 multiplied by a fraction, the numerator of which is the contribution and benefit base (determined under section 230 of the Social Security Act [42 U.S.C. 430]) in effect at the time the plan terminates and the denominator of which is such contribution and benefit base in effect in calendar year 1974.

The provisions of this paragraph do not apply to non-basic benefits. The maximum guaranteed monthly benefit shall not be reduced solely on account of the age of a participant in the case of a benefit payable by reason of disability that occurred on or before the termination date, if the participant demonstrates to the satisfaction of the corporation that the Social Security Administration has determined that the participant satisfies the definition of disability under title II or XVI of the Social Security Act [42 U.S.C. 401 et seq.; 1381 et seq.], and the regulations thereunder. If a benefit payable by reason of disability is converted to an early or normal retirement benefit for reasons other than a change in the health of the participant, such early or normal retirement benefit shall be treated as a continuation of the benefit payable by reason of disability and this subparagraph shall continue to apply.

(4)(A) The actuarial value of a benefit, for purposes of this subsection, shall be determined in accordance with regulations prescribed by the corporation.

(B) For purposes of paragraph (3)—

(i) the term "gross income" means "earned income" within the meaning of section 911(b) of title 26 (determined without regard to any community property laws),

(ii) in the case of a participant in a plan under which contributions are made by more than one employer, amounts received as gross income from any employer under that plan shall be aggregated with amounts received from any other employer under that plan during the same period, and

(iii) any non-basic benefit shall be disregarded.

(5)(A) For purposes of this paragraph, the term "majority owner" means an individual who, at any time during the 60-month period ending on the date the determination is being made—

(i) owns the entire interest in an unincorporated trade or business,

(ii) in the case of a partnership, is a partner who owns, directly or indirectly, 50 percent or more of either the capital interest or the profits interest in such partnership, or

(iii) in the case of a corporation, owns, directly or indirectly, 50 percent or more in value of either the voting stock of that corporation or all the stock of that corporation.

For purposes of clause (iii), the constructive ownership rules of section 1563(e) of title 26 (other than paragraph (3)(C) thereof) shall apply, including the application of such rules under section 414(c) of title 26.

(B) In the case of a participant who is a majority owner, the amount of benefits guaranteed under this section shall equal the product of—

(i) a fraction (not to exceed 1) the numerator of which is the number of years from the later of the effective date or the adoption date of the plan to the termination date, and the denominator of which is 10, and

(ii) the amount of benefits that would be guaranteed under this section if the participant were not a majority owner.

(6)(A) No benefits accrued under a plan after the date on which the Secretary of the Treasury issues notice that he has determined that any trust which is a part of a plan does not meet the requirements of section 401(a) of title 26, or that the plan does not meet the requirements of section 404(a)(2) of title 26, are guaranteed under this section unless such determination is erroneous. This subparagraph does not apply if the Secretary subsequently issues a notice that such trust meets the requirements of section 401(a) of title 26 or that the plan meets the requirements of section 404(a)(2) of title 26 and if the Secretary determines that the trust or plan has taken action necessary to meet such requirements during the period between the issuance of the notice referred to in the preceding sentence and the issuance of the notice referred to in this sentence.

(B) No benefits accrued under a plan after the date on which an amendment of the plan is adopted which causes the Secretary of the Treasury to determine that any trust under the plan has ceased to meet the requirements of section 401(a) of title 26 or that the plan has ceased to meet the requirements of section 404(a)(2) of title 26, are guaranteed under this section unless such determination is erroneous. This subparagraph shall not apply if the amendment is revoked as of the date it was first effective or amended to comply with such requirements.

(7) Benefits described in paragraph (1) are guaranteed only to the extent of the greater of—

(A) 20 percent of the amount which, but for the fact that the plan or amendment has not been in effect for 60 months or more, would be guaranteed under this section, or

(B) $20 per month,

multiplied by the number of years (but not more than 5) the plan or amendment, as the case may be, has been in effect. In determining how many years a plan or amendment has been in effect for purposes of this paragraph, the first 12 months beginning with the date on which the plan or amendment is made or first becomes effective (whichever is later) constitutes one year, and each consecutive period of 12 months thereafter constitutes an additional year. This paragraph does not apply to benefits payable under a plan unless the corporation finds substantial evidence that the plan was terminated for a reasonable business purpose and not for the purpose of obtaining the payment of benefits by the corporation under this subchapter.

(8) If an unpredictable contingent event benefit (as defined in section 1056(g)(1) of this title) is payable by reason of the occurrence of any event, this section shall be applied as if a plan amendment had been adopted on the date such event occurred.

(c) Payment by corporation to participants and beneficiaries of recovery percentage of outstanding amount of benefit liabilities

(1) In addition to benefits paid under the preceding provisions of this section with respect to a terminated plan, the corporation shall pay the portion of the amount determined under paragraph (2) which is allocated with respect to each participant under section 1344(a) of this title. Such payment shall be made to such participant or to such participant's beneficiaries (including alternate payees, within the meaning of section 1056(d)(3)(K) of this title).

(2) The amount determined under this paragraph is an amount equal to the product derived by multiplying—

(A) the outstanding amount of benefit liabilities under the plan (including interest calculated from the termination date), by

(B) the applicable recovery ratio.

(3)(A) IN GENERAL.—Except as provided in subparagraph (C), the term "recovery ratio" means the ratio which—

(i) the sum of the values of all recoveries under section 1362, 1363, or 1364 of this title, determined by the corporation in connection with plan terminations described under subparagraph (B), bears to

(ii) the sum of all unfunded benefit liabilities under such plans as of the termination date in connection with any such prior termination.

(B) A plan termination described in this subparagraph is a termination with respect to which—

(i) the corporation has determined the value of recoveries under section 1362, 1363, or 1364 of this title, and

(ii) notices of intent to terminate were provided (or in the case of a termination by the corporation, a notice of determination under section 1342 of this title was issued) during the 5-Federal fiscal year period ending with the third fiscal year preceding the fiscal year in which occurs the date of the notice of intent to terminate (or the notice of determination under section 1342 of this title) with respect to the plan termination for which the recovery ratio is being determined.

(C) In the case of a terminated plan with respect to which the outstanding amount of benefit liabilities exceeds $20,000,000, for purposes of this section, the term "recovery ratio" means, with respect to the termination of such plan, the ratio of—

(i) the value of the recoveries of the corporation under section 1362, 1363, or 1364 of this title in connection with such plan, to

(ii) the amount of unfunded benefit liabilities under such plan as of the termination date.

(4) Determinations under this subsection shall be made by the corporation. Such determinations shall be binding unless shown by clear and convincing evidence to be unreasonable.

(d) Authorization to guarantee other classes of benefits

The corporation is authorized to guarantee the payment of such other classes of benefits and to establish the terms and conditions under which such other classes of benefits are guaranteed as it determines to be appropriate.

(e) Nonforfeitability of preretirement survivor annuity

For purposes of subsection (a) of this section, a qualified preretirement survivor annuity (as defined in section 1055(e)(1) of this title) with respect to a participant under a terminated single-employer plan shall not be treated as forfeitable solely because the participant has not died as of the termination date.

(f) Effective date of plan amendments

For purposes of this section, the effective date of a plan amendment described in section 1054(i)(1) of this title shall be the effective date of the plan of reorganization of the employer described in section 1054(i)(1) of this title or, if later, the effective date stated in such amendment.

(g) Bankruptcy filing substituted for termination date

If a contributing sponsor of a plan has filed or has had filed against such person a petition seeking liquidation or reorganization in a case under title 11 or under any similar Federal law or law of a State or political subdivision, and the case has not been dismissed as of the termination date of the plan, then this section shall be applied by treating the date such petition was filed as the termination date of the plan.

(h) Special rule for plans electing certain funding requirements

If any plan makes an election under section 402(a)(1) of the Pension Protection Act of 2006 and is terminated effective before the end of the 10-year period beginning on the first day of the first applicable plan year—

(1) this section shall be applied—

(A) by treating the first day of the first applicable plan year as the termination date of the plan, and

(B) by determining the amount of guaranteed benefits on the basis of plan assets and liabilities as of such assumed termination date, and

(2) notwithstanding section 1344(a) of this title, plan assets shall first be allocated to pay the amount, if any, by which—

(A) the amount of guaranteed benefits under this section (determined without regard to paragraph (1) and on the basis of plan assets and liabilities as of the actual date of plan termination), exceeds

(B) the amount determined under paragraph (1).

(Pub. L. 93–406, title IV, §4022, Sept. 2, 1974, 88 Stat. 1016; Pub. L. 96–364, title IV, §403(c), Sept. 26, 1980, 94 Stat. 1301; Pub. L. 99–272, title XI, §11016(c)(8), (9), Apr. 7, 1986, 100 Stat. 274; Pub. L. 100–203, title IX, §9312(b)(3)(A), Dec. 22, 1987, 101 Stat. 1330–362; Pub. L. 101–239, title VII, §§7881(f)(4), (5), (11), 7891(a)(1), 7894(g)(1), (3)(B), Dec. 19, 1989, 103 Stat. 2440, 2441, 2445, 2451; Pub. L. 103–465, title VII, §§766(c), 777(a), Dec. 8, 1994, 108 Stat. 5037, 5049; Pub. L. 109–280, title IV, §§402(g)(2)(A), 403(a), 404(a), 407(a), 408(a), (b)(1), Aug. 17, 2006, 120 Stat. 926, 928, 929, 931.)

REFERENCES IN TEXT

The Social Security Act, referred to in subsec. (b)(3), is act Aug. 14, 1935, ch. 531, 49 Stat. 620, as amended. Titles II, and XVI of the Act are classified generally to subchapters II (§401 et seq.) and XVI (§1381 et seq.), respectively, of chapter 7 of Title 42, The Public Health and Welfare. For complete classification of this Act to the Code, see section 1305 of Title 42 and Tables.

Section 402(a)(1) of the Pension Protection Act of 2006, referred to in subsec. (h), is section 402(a)(1) of Pub. L. 109–280, which is set out as a note under section 430 of Title 26, Internal Revenue Code.

AMENDMENTS

2006—Subsec. (b)(5). Pub. L. 109–280, §407(a), amended par. (5) generally. Prior to amendment, par. (5) related to the amount of benefits guaranteed under this section in the case of a participant in a plan who was covered by the plan as a substantial owner.

Subsec. (b)(8). Pub. L. 109–280, §403(a), added par. (8).

Subsec. (c)(3)(A). Pub. L. 109–280, §408(b)(1), amended subpar. (A) generally. Prior to amendment, subpar. (A) read as follows: "Except as provided in subparagraph (C), for purposes of this subsection, the term 'recovery ratio' means the average ratio, with respect to prior plan terminations described in subparagraph (B), of—

"(i) the value of the recovery of the corporation under section 1362, 1363, or 1364 of this title in connection with such prior terminations, to

"(ii) the amount of unfunded benefit liabilities under such plans as of the termination date in connection with such prior terminations."

Subsec. (c)(3)(B)(ii). Pub. L. 109–280, §408(a), amended cl. (ii) generally. Prior to amendment, cl. (ii) read as follows: "notices of intent to terminate were provided after December 17, 1987, and during the 5-Federal fiscal year period ending with the fiscal year preceding the fiscal year in which occurs the date of the notice of intent to terminate with respect to the plan termination for which the recovery ratio is being determined."

Subsec. (g). Pub. L. 109–280, §404(a), which directed amendment of this section, as amended by Pub. L. 109–280, by adding subsec. (g) at the end, was executed by adding subsec. (g) after subsec. (f) and before subsec. (h) to reflect the probable intent of Congress.

Subsec. (h). Pub. L. 109–280, §402(g)(2)(A), added subsec. (h).

1994—Subsec. (b)(3). Pub. L. 103–465, §777(a), inserted at end "The maximum guaranteed monthly benefit shall not be reduced solely on account of the age of a participant in the case of a benefit payable by reason of disability that occurred on or before the termination date, if the participant demonstrates to the satisfaction of the corporation that the Social Security Administration has determined that the participant satisfies the definition of disability under title II or XVI of the Social Security Act, and the regulations thereunder. If a benefit payable by reason of disability is converted to an early or normal retirement benefit for reasons other than a change in the health of the participant, such early or normal retirement benefit shall be treated as a continuation of the benefit payable by reason of disability and this subparagraph shall continue to apply."

Subsec. (f). Pub. L. 103–465, §766(c), added subsec. (f).

1989—Subsec. (a). Pub. L. 101–239, §7894(g)(3)(B), substituted "this subchapter" for "section 1321 of this title".

Subsec. (b)(2). Pub. L. 101–239, §7894(g)(1), substituted "60-month" for "60 month".

Subsec. (b)(4)(B)(i), (5)(A), (6). Pub. L. 101–239, §7891(a)(1), substituted "Internal Revenue Code of 1986" for "Internal Revenue Code of 1954", which for purposes of codification was translated as "title 26" thus requiring no change in text.

Subsec. (c)(1). Pub. L. 101–239, §7881(f)(11), substituted "under section 1344(a) of this title. Such payment shall be made to such participant" for "under section 1344(a) of this title, to such participant".

Pub. L. 101–239, §7881(f)(4), struck out "(in the case of a deceased participant)" before "to such participant's beneficiaries".

Subsec. (c)(3)(B)(ii). Pub. L. 101–239, §7881(f)(5), inserted before period at end ", and during the 5-Federal fiscal year period ending with the fiscal year preceding the fiscal year in which occurs the date of the notice of intent to terminate with respect to the plan termination for which the recovery ratio is being determined".

1987—Subsecs. (c) to (e). Pub. L. 100–203 added subsec. (c) and redesignated former subsecs. (c) and (d) as (d) and (e), respectively.

Subsec. (b)(7). Pub. L. 99–272, §11016(c)(8), in provisions following subpar. (B) substituted "12 months beginning with" for "12 months following".

Subsec. (d). Pub. L. 99–272, §11016(c)(9), added subsec. (d).

1980—Subsec. (a). Pub. L. 96–364, §403(c)(2), inserted ", in accordance with this section," after "guarantee" and "single-employer" before "plan which", and struck out "the terms of" after "under".

Subsec. (b). Pub. L. 96–364, §403(c)(3), (4), in par. (1) substituted "(7)" for "(8)", struck out par. (5) relating to receipt of a life annuity commencing at age 65, and redesignated pars. (6) to (8) as (5) to (7), respectively.

EFFECTIVE DATE OF 2006 AMENDMENT

Amendment by section 402(g)(2)(A) of Pub. L. 109–280 applicable to plan years ending after Aug. 17, 2006, see section 402(j) of Pub. L. 109–280, set out as a Special Funding Rules for Certain Plans Maintained by Commercial Airlines note under section 430 of Title 26, Internal Revenue Code.

Pub. L. 109–280, title IV, §403(b), Aug. 17, 2006, 120 Stat. 928, provided that: "The amendment made by this section [amending this section] shall apply to benefits that become payable as a result of an event which occurs after July 26, 2005."

Pub. L. 109–280, title IV, §404(c), Aug. 17, 2006, 120 Stat. 928, provided that: "The amendments made this section [amending this section and section 1344 of this title] shall apply with respect to proceedings initiated under title 11, United States Code, or under any similar Federal law or law of a State or political subdivision, on or after the date that is 30 days after the date of enactment of this Act [Aug. 17, 2006]."

Amendment by section 407(a) of Pub. L. 109–280 applicable to plan terminations under section 1341(c) of this title with respect to which notices of intent to terminate are provided under section 1341(a)(2) of this title after Dec. 31, 2005, and under section 1342 of this title with respect to which notices of determination are provided under such section after such date, see section 407(d)(1) of Pub. L. 109–280, set out as a note under section 1321 of this title.

Pub. L. 109–280, title IV, §408(c), Aug. 17, 2006, 120 Stat. 932, provided that: "The amendments made by this section [amending this section and section 1344 of this title] shall apply for any termination for which notices of intent to terminate are provided (or in the case of a termination by the corporation, a notice of determination under section 4042 under the Employee Retirement Income Security Act of 1974 [29 U.S.C. 1342] is issued) on or after the date which is 30 days after the date of enactment of this section [Aug. 17, 2006]."

EFFECTIVE DATE OF 1994 AMENDMENT

Amendment by section 766(c) of Pub. L. 103–465 applicable to plan amendments adopted on or after Dec. 8, 1994, see section 766(d) of Pub. L. 103–465, set out as a note under section 401 of Title 26, Internal Revenue Code.

Section 777(b) of Pub. L. 103–465 provided that: "The amendment made by this section [amending this section] shall be effective for plan terminations under section 4041(c) of the Employee Retirement Income Security Act of 1974 [29 U.S.C. 1341(c)] with respect to which notices of intent to terminate are provided under section 4041(a)(2) of such Act [29 U.S.C. 1342], or under section 4042 of such Act with respect to which proceedings are instituted by the corporation, on or after the date of enactment of this Act [Dec. 8, 1994]."

EFFECTIVE DATE OF 1989 AMENDMENT

Amendment by section 7881(f)(4), (5), (11) of Pub. L. 101–239 effective, except as otherwise provided, as if included in the provision of the Pension Protection Act, Pub. L. 100–203, §§9302–9346, to which such amendment relates, see section 7882 of Pub. L. 101–239, set out as a note under section 401 of Title 26, Internal Revenue Code.

Amendment by section 7891(a)(1) of Pub. L. 101–239 effective, except as otherwise provided, as if included in the provision of the Tax Reform Act of 1986, Pub. L. 99–514, to which such amendment relates, see section 7891(f) of Pub. L. 101–239, set out as a note under section 1002 of this title.

Amendment by section 7894(g)(1), (3)(B) of Pub. L. 101–239 effective, except as otherwise provided, as if originally included in the provision of the Employee Retirement Income Security Act of 1974, Pub. L. 93–406, to which such amendment relates, see section 7894(i) of Pub. L. 101–239, set out as a note under section 1002 of this title.

EFFECTIVE DATE OF 1987 AMENDMENT

Amendment by Pub. L. 100–203 applicable with respect to plan terminations under section 1341 of this title with respect to which notices of intent to terminate are provided under section 1341(a)(2) of this title after Dec. 17, 1987, and plan terminations with respect to which proceedings are instituted by the Pension Benefit Guaranty Corporation under section 1342 of this title after that date, see section 9312(d)(1) of Pub. L. 100–203, as amended, set out as a note under section 1301 of this title.

EFFECTIVE DATE OF 1986 AMENDMENT

Amendment by Pub. L. 99–272 effective Jan. 1, 1986, with certain exceptions, see section 11019 of Pub. L. 99–272, set out as a note under section 1341 of this title.

EFFECTIVE DATE OF 1980 AMENDMENT

Amendment by Pub. L. 96–364 effective Sept. 26, 1980, except as specifically provided, see section 1461(e) of this title.

TRANSITIONAL RULE REGARDING AMENDMENTS BY SECTION 9312 OF PUB. L. 100–203

Section 9312(b)(3)(B) of Pub. L. 100–203, as amended by Pub. L. 101–239, title VII, §7881(f)(1), (6), Dec. 19, 1989, 103 Stat. 2440, provided that:

"(i) IN GENERAL.—In the case of any plan termination to which the amendments made by this section [amending sections 1301, 1305, 1322, 1341, 1342, 1349, 1362, 1364, and 1368 of this title and repealing section 1349 of this title] apply and with respect to which notices of intent to terminate were provided on or before December 17, 1990—

"(I) subparagraph (A) of section 4022(c)(3) of ERISA [29 U.S.C. 1322(c)(3)(A)] (as amended by this paragraph) shall not apply, and

"(II) subparagraph (C) of section 4022(c)(3) of ERISA (as so amended) shall apply irrespective of the outstanding amount of benefit liabilities under the plan.

"(ii) [Repealed. Pub. L. 101–239, title VII, §7881(f)(6), Dec. 19, 1989, 103 Stat. 2440.]"

§1322a. Multiemployer plan benefits guaranteed

(a) Benefits of covered plans subject to guarantee

The corporation shall guarantee, in accordance with this section, the payment of all nonforfeitable benefits (other than benefits becoming nonforfeitable solely on account of the termination of a plan) under a multiemployer plan—

(1) to which this subchapter applies, and

(2) which is insolvent under section 1426(b) or 1441(d)(2) of this title.

(b) Benefits or benefit increases not eligible for guarantee

(1)(A) For purposes of this section, a benefit or benefit increase which has been in effect under a plan for less than 60 months is not eligible for the corporation's guarantee. For purposes of this paragraph, any month of any plan year during which the plan was insolvent or terminated (within the meaning of section 1341a(a)(2) of this title) shall not be taken into account.

(B) For purposes of this section, a benefit or benefit increase which has been in effect under a plan for less than 60 months before the first day of the plan year for which an amendment reducing the benefit or the benefit increase is taken into account under section 1425(a)(2) of this title in determining the minimum contribution requirement for the plan year under section 1423(b) of this title is not eligible for the corporation's guarantee.

(2) For purposes of this section—

(A) the date on which a benefit or a benefit increase under a plan is first in effect is the later of—

(i) the date on which the documents establishing or increasing the benefit were executed, or

(ii) the effective date of the benefit or benefit increase;

(B) the period of time for which a benefit or a benefit increase has been in effect under a successor plan includes the period of time for which the benefit or benefit increase was in effect under a previously established plan; and

(C) in the case of a plan to which section 1321 of this title did not apply on September 3, 1974, the time periods referred to in this section are computed beginning on the date on which section 1321 of this title first applies to the plan.

(c) Determinations respecting amount of guarantee

(1) Except as provided in subsection (g) of this section, the monthly benefit of a participant or a beneficiary which is guaranteed under this section by the corporation with respect to a plan is the product of—

(A) 100 percent of the accrual rate up to $11, plus 75 percent of the lesser of—

(i) $33, or

(ii) the accrual rate, if any, in excess of $11, and

(B) the number of the participant's years of credited service.

(2) For purposes of this section, the accrual rate is—

(A) the monthly benefit of the participant or beneficiary which is described in subsection (a) of this section and which is eligible for the corporation's guarantee under subsection (b) of this section, except that such benefit shall be—

(i) no greater than the monthly benefit which would be payable under the plan at normal retirement age in the form of a single life annuity, and

(ii) determined without regard to any reduction under section 411(a)(3)(E) of title 26; divided by

(B) the participant's years of credited service.

(3) For purposes of this subsection—

(A) a year of credited service is a year in which the participant completed—

(i) a full year of participation in the plan, or

(ii) any period of service before participation which is credited for purposes of benefit accrual as the equivalent of a full year of participation;

(B) any year for which the participant is credited for purposes of benefit accrual with a fraction of the equivalent of a full year of participation shall be counted as such a fraction of a year of credited service; and

(C) years of credited service shall be determined by including service which may otherwise be disregarded by the plan under section 411(a)(3)(E) of title 26.

(d) Amount of guarantee of reduced benefit

In the case of a benefit which has been reduced under section 411(a)(3)(E) of title 26, the corporation shall guarantee the lesser of—

(1) the reduced benefit, or

(2) the amount determined under subsection (c) of this section.

(e) Ineligibility of benefits for guarantee

The corporation shall not guarantee benefits under a multiemployer plan which, under section 1322(b)(6) of this title, would not be guaranteed under a single-employer plan.

(f) Study, report, etc., respecting premium increase in existing basic-benefit guarantee levels; Congressional procedures applicable for revision of schedules

(1) No later than 5 years after September 26, 1980, and at least every fifth year thereafter, the corporation shall—

(A) conduct a study to determine—

(i) the premiums needed to maintain the basic-benefit guarantee levels for multiemployer plans described in subsection (c) of this section, and

(ii) whether the basic-benefit guarantee levels for multiemployer plans may be increased without increasing the basic-benefit premiums for multiemployer plans under this subchapter; and

(B) report such determinations to the Committee on Ways and Means and the Committee on Education and Labor of the House of Representatives and to the Committee on Finance and the Committee on Labor and Human Resources of the Senate.

(2)(A) If the last report described in paragraph (1) indicates that a premium increase is necessary to support the existing basic-benefit guarantee levels for multiemployer plans, the corporation shall transmit to the Committee on Ways and Means and the Committee on Education and Labor of the House of Representatives and to the Committee on Finance and the Committee on Labor and Human Resources of the Senate by March 31 of any calendar year in which congressional action under this subsection is requested—

(i) a revised schedule of basic-benefit guarantees for multiemployer plans which would be necessary in the absence of an increase in premiums approved in accordance with section 1306(b) of this title,

(ii) a revised schedule of basic-benefit premiums for multiemployer plans which is necessary to support the existing basic-benefit guarantees for such plans, and

(iii) a revised schedule of basic-benefit guarantees for multiemployer plans for which the schedule of premiums necessary is higher than the existing premium schedule for such plans but lower than the revised schedule of premiums for such plans specified in clause (ii), together with such schedule of premiums.

(B) The revised schedule of increased premiums referred to in subparagraph (A)(ii) or (A)(iii) shall go into effect as approved by the enactment of a joint resolution.

(C) If an increase in premiums is not so enacted, the revised guarantee schedule described in subparagraph (A)(i) shall go into effect on the first day of the second calendar year following the year in which such revised guarantee schedule was submitted to the Congress.

(3)(A) If the last report described in paragraph (1) indicates that basic-benefit guarantees for multiemployer plans can be increased without increasing the basic-benefit premiums for multiemployer plans under this subchapter, the corporation shall submit to the Committee on Ways and Means and the Committee on Education and Labor of the House of Representatives and to the Committee on Finance and the Committee on Labor and Human Resources of the Senate by March 31 of the calendar year in which congressional action under this paragraph is requested—

(i) a revised schedule of increases in the basic-benefit guarantees which can be supported by the existing schedule of basic-benefit premiums for multiemployer plans, and

(ii) a revised schedule of basic-benefit premiums sufficient to support the existing basic-benefit guarantees.

(B) The revised schedules referred to in subparagraph (A)(i) or subparagraph (A)(ii) shall go into effect as approved by the enactment of a joint resolution.

(4)(A) The succeeding subparagraphs of this paragraph are enacted by the Congress as an exercise of the rulemaking power of the Senate and the House of Representatives, respectively, and as such they shall be deemed a part of the rules of each House, respectively, but applicable only with respect to the procedure to be followed in that House in the case of joint resolutions (as defined in subparagraph (B)). Such subparagraphs shall supersede other rules only to the extent that they are inconsistent therewith. They are enacted with full recognition of the constitutional right of either House to change the rules (so far as relating to the procedure of that House) at any time, in the same manner, and to the same extent as in the case of any rule of that House.

(B) For purposes of this subsection, "joint resolution" means only a joint resolution, the matter after the resolving clause of which is as follows: "The proposed schedule described in ______ transmitted to the Congress by the Pension Benefit Guaranty Corporation on ______ is hereby approved.", the first blank space therein being filled with "section 4022A(f)(2)(A)(ii) of the Employee Retirement Income Security Act of 1974", "section 4022A(f)(2)(A)(iii) of the Employee Retirement Income Security Act of 1974", "section 4022A(f)(3)(A)(i) of the Employee Retirement Income Security Act of 1974", or "section 4022A(f)(3)(A)(ii) of the Employee Retirement Income Security Act of 1974" (whichever is applicable), and the second blank space therein being filled with the date on which the corporation's message proposing the revision was submitted.

(C) The procedure for disposition of a joint resolution shall be the procedure described in section 1306(b)(4) through (7) of this title.

(g) Guarantee of payment of other classes of benefits and establishment of terms and conditions of guarantee; promulgation of regulations for establishment of supplemental program to guarantee benefits otherwise ineligible; status of benefits; applicability of revised schedule of premiums

(1) The corporation may guarantee the payment of such other classes of benefits under multiemployer plans, and establish the terms and conditions under which those other classes of benefits are guaranteed, as it determines to be appropriate.

(2)(A) The corporation shall prescribe regulations to establish a supplemental program to guarantee benefits under multiemployer plans which would be guaranteed under this section but for the limitations in subsection (c) of this section. Such regulations shall be proposed by the corporation no later than the end of the 18th calendar month following September 26, 1980. The regulations shall make coverage under the supplemental program available no later than January 1, 1983. Any election to participate in the supplemental program shall be on a voluntary basis, and a plan electing such coverage shall continue to pay the premiums required under section 1306(a)(2)(B) of this title to the revolving fund used pursuant to section 1305 of this title in connection with benefits otherwise guaranteed under this section. Any such election shall be irrevocable, except to the extent otherwise provided by regulations prescribed by the corporation.

(B) The regulations prescribed under this paragraph shall provide—

(i) that a plan must elect coverage under the supplemental program within the time permitted by the regulations;

(ii) unless the corporation determines otherwise, that a plan may not elect supplemental coverage unless the value of the assets of the plan as of the end of the plan year preceding the plan year in which the election must be made is an amount equal to 15 times the total amount of the benefit payments made under the plan for that year; and

(iii) such other reasonable terms and conditions for supplemental coverage, including funding standards and any other reasonable limitations with respect to plans or benefits covered or to means of program financing, as the corporation determines are necessary and appropriate for a feasible supplemental program consistent with the purposes of this subchapter.

(3) Any benefits guaranteed under this subsection shall be considered nonbasic benefits for purposes of this subchapter.

(4)(A) No revised schedule of premiums under this subsection, after the initial schedule, shall go into effect unless—

(i) the revised schedule is submitted to the Congress, and

(ii) a joint resolution described in subparagraph (B) is not enacted before the close of the 60th legislative day after such schedule is submitted to the Congress.

(B) For purposes of subparagraph (A), a joint resolution described in this subparagraph is a joint resolution the matter after the resolving clause of which is as follows: "The revised premium schedule transmitted to the Congress by the Pension Benefit Guaranty Corporation under section 4022A(g)(4) of the Employee Retirement Income Security Act of 1974 on   is hereby disapproved.", the blank space therein being filled with the date on which the revised schedule was submitted.

(C) For purposes of subparagraph (A), the term "legislative day" means any calendar day other than a day on which either House is not in session because of a sine die adjournment or an adjournment of more than 3 days to a day certain.

(D) The procedure for disposition of a joint resolution described in subparagraph (B) shall be the procedure described in paragraphs (4) through (7) of section 1306(b) of this title.

(5) Regulations prescribed by the corporation to carry out the provisions of this subsection, may, to the extent provided therein, supersede the requirements of sections 1426, 1431, and 1441 of this title, and the requirements of section 418E of title 26, but only with respect to benefits guaranteed under this subsection.

(h) Applicability to nonforfeitable benefits accrued as of July 30, 1980; manner and extent of guarantee

(1) Except as provided in paragraph (3), subsections (b) and (c) of this section shall not apply with respect to the nonforfeitable benefits accrued as of July 29, 1980, with respect to a participant or beneficiary under a multiemployer plan—

(1) who is in pay status on July 29, 1980, or

(2) who is within 36 months of the normal retirement age and has a nonforfeitable right to a pension as of that date.

(2) The benefits described in paragraph (1) shall be guaranteed by the corporation in the same manner and to the same extent as benefits are guaranteed by the corporation under section 1322 of this title (without regard to this section).

(3) This subsection does not apply with respect to a plan for plan years following a plan year—

(A) in which the plan has terminated within the meaning of section 1341a(a)(2) of this title, or

(B) in which it is determined by the corporation that substantially all the employers have withdrawn from the plan pursuant to an agreement or arrangement to withdraw.

(Pub. L. 93–406, title IV, § 4022A, as added Pub. L. 96–364, title I, § 102, Sept. 26, 1980, 94 Stat. 1210; amended Pub. L. 99–272, title XI, § 11005(c)(4)–(12), Apr. 7, 1986, 100 Stat. 242; Pub. L. 101–239, title VII, §§ 7891(a)(1), 7893(b), 7894(g)(3)(C)(i), Dec. 19, 1989, 103 Stat. 2445, 2447, 2451; Pub. L. 106–554, § 1(a)(6) [title IX, § 951(a)], Dec. 21, 2000, 114 Stat. 2763, 2763A–586.)

REFERENCES IN TEXT

Section 4022A(f)(2)(A)(ii), (iii), (3)(A)(i), and (ii) of the Employee Retirement Income Security Act of 1974, referred to in subsec. (f)(4)(B), is classified to subsec. (f)(2)(A)(ii), (iii), (3)(A)(i) and (ii) of this section.

Section 4022A(g)(4) of the Employee Retirement Income Security Act of 1974, referred to in subsec. (g)(4)(B), is classified to subsec. (g)(4) of this section.

AMENDMENTS

2000—Subsec. (c)(1)(A). Pub. L. 106–554, § 1(a)(6) [title IX, § 951(a)(1)], substituted "$11" for "$5" in two places.

Subsec. (c)(1)(A)(i). Pub. L. 106–554, § 1(a)(6) [title IX, § 951(a)(2)], substituted "$33" for "$15".

Subsec. (c)(2) to (6). Pub. L. 106–554, § 1(a)(6) [title IX, § 951(a)(3)], redesignated pars. (3) and (4) as (2) and (3), respectively, and struck out former pars. (2), (5), and (6). Prior to amendment, par. (2) modified the amount of benefits guaranteed under par. (1) with respect to plans described in par. (5)(A), par. (5) described certain plans for which the first plan year in which the plan was insolvent and in which benefits were required to be suspended or reduced to a certain level began before the year 2000, and par. (6) provided that par. (2) did not apply to a plan described in par. (5)(A) if the value of the assets of the plan was at least a specified amount for a specified period of time.

1989—Subsec. (a)(1). Pub. L. 101–239, § 7894(g)(3)(C)(i), substituted "this subchapter" for "section 1321 of this title".

Subsecs. (c)(3)(A)(ii), (4)(C), (5)(A)(ii), (6), (d), (g)(5). Pub. L. 101–239, § 7891(a)(1), substituted "Internal Revenue Code of 1986" for "Internal Revenue Code of 1954", which for purposes of codification was translated as "title 26" thus requiring no change in text.

Subsec. (f)(2)(B). Pub. L. 101–239, § 7893(b), substituted "the enactment" for "the the enactment".

1986—Subsec. (f)(2)(B). Pub. L. 99–272, § 11005(c)(4), substituted "the enactment of a joint resolution" for "Congress by concurrent resolution".

Subsec. (f)(2)(C). Pub. L. 99–272, § 11005(c)(5), substituted "so enacted" for "approved".

Subsec. (f)(3)(B). Pub. L. 99–272, § 11005(c)(6), substituted "enactment of a joint resolution" for "Congress by concurrent resolution".

Subsec. (f)(4)(A). Pub. L. 99–272, § 11005(c)(7), substituted "joint" for "concurrent".

Subsec. (f)(4)(B). Pub. L. 99–272, § 11005(c)(8), substituted "joint" for "concurrent" in two places and "The" for "That the Congress favors the" and inserted "is hereby approved".

Subsec. (f)(4)(C). Pub. L. 99–272, § 11005(c)(9), substituted "joint" for "concurrent".

Subsec. (g)(4)(A)(ii). Pub. L. 99–272, § 11005(c)(10), substituted "joint" for "concurrent" and "enacted" for "adopted".

Subsec. (g)(4)(B). Pub. L. 99–272, § 11005(c)(11), substituted "joint" for "concurrent" in two places and "The" for "That the Congress disapproves the" and inserted "is hereby disapproved".

Subsec. (g)(4)(D). Pub. L. 99–272, § 11005(c)(12), substituted "joint" for "concurrent".

CHANGE OF NAME

Committee on Labor and Human Resources of Senate changed to Committee on Health, Education, Labor, and Pensions of Senate by Senate Resolution No. 20, One Hundred Sixth Congress, Jan. 19, 1999.

EFFECTIVE DATE OF 2000 AMENDMENT

Pub. L. 106–554, § 1(a)(6) [title IX, § 951(b)], Dec. 21, 2000, 114 Stat. 2763, 2763A–586, provided that: "The amendments made by this section [amending this section] shall apply to any multiemployer plan that has not received financial assistance (within the meaning of section 4261 of the Employee Retirement Income Security Act of 1974 [29 U.S.C. 1431]) within the 1-year period ending on the date of the enactment of this Act [Dec. 21, 2000]."

EFFECTIVE DATE OF 1989 AMENDMENT

Amendment by section 7891(a)(1) of Pub. L. 101–239 effective, except as otherwise provided, as if included in the provision of the Tax Reform Act of 1986, Pub. L. 99–514, to which such amendment relates, see section 7891(f) of Pub. L. 101–239, set out as a note under section 1002 of this title.

Amendment by section 7893(b) of Pub. L. 101–239 effective as if included in the provision of the Single-Employer Pension Plan Amendments Act of 1986, Pub. L. 99–272, title XI, to which such amendment relates, see section 7893(h) of Pub. L. 101–239, set out as a note under section 1002 of this title.

Section 7894(g)(3)(C)(ii) of Pub. L. 101–239 provided that: "The amendment made by clause (i) [amending this section] shall take effect as if originally included in section 102 of the Multiemployer Pension Plan Amendments Act of 1980 [Pub. L. 96–364]."

EFFECTIVE DATE OF 1986 AMENDMENT

Amendment by Pub. L. 99–272 effective for plan years commencing after Dec. 31, 1985, see section 11005(d)(1) of Pub. L. 99–272, set out as a note under section 1306 of this title.

EFFECTIVE DATE

Section effective Sept. 26, 1980, except as specifically provided, see section 1461(e) of this title.

§ 1322b. Aggregate limit on benefits guaranteed; criteria applicable

(a) Notwithstanding sections 1322 and 1322a of this title, no person shall receive from the corporation pursuant to a guarantee by the corporation of basic benefits with respect to a participant under all multiemployer and single employer plans an amount, or amounts, with an actuarial value which exceeds the actuarial value of a monthly benefit in the form of a life annuity commencing at age 65 equal to the amount determined under section 1322(b)(3)(B) of this title as of the date of the last plan termination.

(b) For purposes of this section—

(1) the receipt of benefits under a multiemployer plan receiving financial assistance from the corporation shall be considered the receipt of amounts from the corporation pursuant to a guarantee by the corporation of basic benefits except to the extent provided in regulations prescribed by the corporation, and

(2) the date on which a multiemployer plan, whether or not terminated, begins receiving financial assistance from the corporation shall be considered a date of plan termination.

(Pub. L. 93–406, title IV, § 4022B, as added Pub. L. 96–364, title I, § 102, Sept. 26, 1980, 94 Stat. 1215.)

EFFECTIVE DATE

Section effective Sept. 26, 1980, except as specifically provided, see section 1461(e) of this title.

§ 1323. Plan fiduciaries

Notwithstanding any other provision of this chapter, a fiduciary of a plan to which section 1321 of this title applies is not in violation of the fiduciary's duties as a result of any act or of any withholding of action required by this subchapter.

(Pub. L. 93–406, title IV, § 4023, as added Pub. L. 96–364, title IV, § 402(a)(5), Sept. 26, 1980, 94 Stat. 1298.)

REFERENCES IN TEXT

This chapter, referred to in text, was in the original "this Act", meaning Pub. L. 93–406, known as the Employee Retirement Income Security Act of 1974. Titles I, III, and IV of such Act are classified principally to this chapter. For complete classification of this Act to the Code, see Short Title note set out under section 1001 of the title and Tables.

PRIOR PROVISIONS

A prior section 1323, Pub. L. 93–406, title IV, § 4023, Sept. 2, 1974, 88 Stat. 1019, related to contingent liability coverage, prior to repeal by Pub. L. 96–364, title I, § 107, Sept. 26, 1980, 94 Stat. 1267.

EFFECTIVE DATE

Section effective Sept. 26, 1980, except as specifically provided, see section 1461(e) of this title.

SUBTITLE C—TERMINATIONS

§ 1341. Termination of single-employer plans

(a) General rules governing single-employer plan terminations

(1) Exclusive means of plan termination

Except in the case of a termination for which proceedings are otherwise instituted by the corporation as provided in section 1342 of this title, a single-employer plan may be terminated only in a standard termination under subsection (b) of this section or a distress termination under subsection (c) of this section.

(2) 60-day notice of intent to terminate

Not less than 60 days before the proposed termination date of a standard termination under subsection (b) of this section or a distress termination under subsection (c) of this section, the plan administrator shall provide to each affected party (other than the corporation in the case of a standard termination) a written notice of intent to terminate stating that such termination is intended and the proposed termination date. The written notice shall include any related additional information required in regulations of the corporation.

(3) Adherence to collective bargaining agreements

The corporation shall not proceed with a termination of a plan under this section if the termination would violate the terms and conditions of an existing collective bargaining agreement. Nothing in the preceding sentence shall be construed as limiting the authority of the corporation to institute proceedings to involuntarily terminate a plan under section 1342 of this title.

(b) Standard termination of single-employer plans

(1) General requirements

A single-employer plan may terminate under a standard termination only if—

(A) the plan administrator provides the 60-day advance notice of intent to terminate to affected parties required under subsection (a)(2) of this section,

(B) the requirements of subparagraphs (A) and (B) of paragraph (2) are met,

(C) the corporation does not issue a notice of noncompliance under subparagraph (C) of paragraph (2), and

(D) when the final distribution of assets occurs, the plan is sufficient for benefit liabilities (determined as of the termination date).

(2) Termination procedure

(A) Notice to the corporation

As soon as practicable after the date on which the notice of intent to terminate is provided pursuant to subsection (a)(2) of this section, the plan administrator shall send a notice to the corporation setting forth—

(i) certification by an enrolled actuary—

(I) of the projected amount of the assets of the plan (as of a proposed date of final distribution of assets),

(II) of the actuarial present value (as of such date) of the benefit liabilities (determined as of the proposed termination date) under the plan, and

(III) that the plan is projected to be sufficient (as of such proposed date of final distribution) for such benefit liabilities,

(ii) such information as the corporation may prescribe in regulations as necessary to enable the corporation to make determinations under subparagraph (C), and

(iii) certification by the plan administrator that—

(I) the information on which the enrolled actuary based the certification under clause (i) is accurate and complete, and

(II) the information provided to the corporation under clause (ii) is accurate and complete.

Clause (i) and clause (iii)(I) shall not apply to a plan described in section 412(i)[1] of title 26.

(B) Notice to participants and beneficiaries of benefit commitments[2]

No later than the date on which a notice is sent by the plan administrator under subparagraph (A), the plan administrator shall send a notice to each person who is a participant or beneficiary under the plan—

(i) specifying the amount of the benefit liabilities (if any) attributable to such person as of the proposed termination date and the benefit form on the basis of which such amount is determined, and

(ii) including the following information used in determining such benefit liabilities:

(I) the length of service,

(II) the age of the participant or beneficiary,

(III) wages,

(IV) the assumptions, including the interest rate, and

(V) such other information as the corporation may require.

Such notice shall be written in such manner as is likely to be understood by the participant or beneficiary and as may be prescribed in regulations of the corporation.

(C) Notice from the corporation of noncompliance

(i) In general

Within 60 days after receipt of the notice under subparagraph (A), the corporation shall issue a notice of noncompliance to the plan administrator if—

(I) it determines, based on the notice sent under paragraph (2)(A) of subsection (b) of this section, that there is reason to believe that the plan is not sufficient for benefit liabilities,

(II) it otherwise determines, on the basis of information provided by affected parties or otherwise obtained by the corporation, that there is reason to believe that the plan is not sufficient for benefit liabilities, or

(III) it determines that any other requirement of subparagraph (A) or (B) of this paragraph or of subsection (a)(2) of this section has not been met, unless it further determines that the issuance of such notice would be inconsistent with the interests of participants and beneficiaries.

(ii) Extension

The corporation and the plan administrator may agree to extend the 60-day period referred to in clause (i) by a written agreement signed by the corporation and the plan administrator before the expiration of the 60-day period. The 60-day period shall be extended as provided in the agreement and may be further extended by subsequent written agreements signed by the corporation and the plan administrator made before the expiration of a previously agreed upon extension of the 60-day period. Any extension may be made upon such terms and conditions (including the payment of benefits) as are agreed upon by the corporation and the plan administrator.

(D) Final distribution of assets in absence of notice of noncompliance

The plan administrator shall commence the final distribution of assets pursuant to the standard termination of the plan as soon as practicable after the expiration of the 60-day (or extended) period referred to in subparagraph (C), but such final distribution may occur only if—

(i) the plan administrator has not received during such period a notice of noncompliance from the corporation under subparagraph (C), and

(ii) when such final distribution occurs, the plan is sufficient for benefit liabilities (determined as of the termination date).

(3) Methods of final distribution of assets

(A) In general

In connection with any final distribution of assets pursuant to the standard termination of the plan under this subsection, the plan administrator shall distribute the assets in accordance with section 1344 of this title. In distributing such assets, the plan administrator shall—

---

[1] See References in Text note below.

[2] So in original. Probably should be "benefit liabilities".

(i) purchase irrevocable commitments from an insurer to provide all benefit liabilities under the plan, or

(ii) in accordance with the provisions of the plan and any applicable regulations, otherwise fully provide all benefit liabilities under the plan. A transfer of assets to the corporation in accordance with section 1350 of this title on behalf of a missing participant shall satisfy this subparagraph with respect to such participant.

(B) Certification to the corporation of final distribution of assets

Within 30 days after the final distribution of assets is completed pursuant to the standard termination of the plan under this subsection, the plan administrator shall send a notice to the corporation certifying that the assets of the plan have been distributed in accordance with the provisions of subparagraph (A) so as to pay all benefit liabilities under the plan.

(4) Continuing authority

Nothing in this section shall be construed to preclude the continued exercise by the corporation, after the termination date of a plan terminated in a standard termination under this subsection, of its authority under section 1303 of this title with respect to matters relating to the termination. A certification under paragraph (3)(B) shall not affect the corporation's obligations under section 1322 of this title.

(5) Special rule for certain plans where cessation or change in membership of a controlled group

(A) In general

Except as provided in subparagraphs (B) and (D), if—

(i) there is[3] transaction or series of transactions which result in a person ceasing to be a member of a controlled group, and

(ii) such person immediately before the transaction or series of transactions maintained a single-employer plan which is a defined benefit plan which is fully funded,

then the interest rate used in determining whether the plan is sufficient for benefit liabilities or to otherwise assess plan liabilities for purposes of this subsection or section 1342(a)(4) of this title shall be not less than the interest rate used in determining whether the plan is fully funded.

(B) Limitations

Subparagraph (A) shall not apply to any transaction or series of transactions unless—

(i) any employer maintaining the plan immediately before or after such transaction or series of transactions—

(I) has an outstanding senior unsecured debt instrument which is rated investment grade by each of the nationally recognized statistical rating organizations for corporate bonds that has issued a credit rating for such instrument, or

(II) if no such debt instrument of such employer has been rated by such an organization but 1 or more of such organizations has made an issuer credit rating for such employer, all such organizations which have so rated the employer have rated such employer investment grade, and

(ii) the employer maintaining the plan after the transaction or series of transactions employs at least 20 percent of the employees located in the United States who were employed by such employer immediately before the transaction or series of transactions.

(C) Fully funded

For purposes of subparagraph (A), a plan shall be treated as fully funded with respect to any transaction or series of transactions if—

(i) in the case of a transaction or series of transactions which occur in a plan year beginning before January 1, 2008, the funded current liability percentage determined under section 1082(d) of this title for the plan year is at least 100 percent, and

(ii) in the case of a transaction or series of transactions which occur in a plan year beginning on or after such date, the funding target attainment percentage determined under section 1083 of this title is, as of the valuation date for such plan year, at least 100 percent.

(D) 2 year limitation

Subparagraph (A) shall not apply to any transaction or series of transactions if the plan referred to in subparagraph (A)(ii) is terminated under subsection (c) or section 1342 of this title after the close of the 2-year period beginning on the date on which the first such transaction occurs.

(c) Distress termination of single-employer plans

(1) In general

A single-employer plan may terminate under a distress termination only if—

(A) the plan administrator provides the 60-day advance notice of intent to terminate to affected parties required under subsection (a)(2) of this section,

(B) the requirements of subparagraph (A) of paragraph (2) are met, and

(C) the corporation determines that the requirements of subparagraphs (B) and (D) of paragraph (2) are met.

(2) Termination requirements

(A) Information submitted to the corporation

As soon as practicable after the date on which the notice of intent to terminate is provided pursuant to subsection (a)(2) of this section, the plan administrator shall provide the corporation, in such form as may be prescribed by the corporation in regulations, the following information:

(i) such information as the corporation may prescribe by regulation as necessary to make determinations under subparagraph (B) and paragraph (3);

[3] So in original. The word "a" probably should appear.

(ii) unless the corporation determines the information is not necessary for purposes of paragraph (3)(A) or section 1362 of this title, certification by an enrolled actuary of—

(I) the amount (as of the proposed termination date and, if applicable, the proposed distribution date) of the current value of the assets of the plan,

(II) the actuarial present value (as of such dates) of the benefit liabilities under the plan,

(III) whether the plan is sufficient for benefit liabilities as of such dates,

(IV) the actuarial present value (as of such dates) of benefits under the plan guaranteed under section 1322 of this title, and

(V) whether the plan is sufficient for guaranteed benefits as of such dates;

(iii) in any case in which the plan is not sufficient for benefit liabilities as of such date—

(I) the name and address of each participant and beneficiary under the plan as of such date, and

(II) such other information as shall be prescribed by the corporation by regulation as necessary to enable the corporation to be able to make payments to participants and beneficiaries as required under section 1322(c) of this title; and

(iv) certification by the plan administrator that—

(I) the information on which the enrolled actuary based the certifications under clause (ii) is accurate and complete, and

(II) the information provided to the corporation under clauses (i) and (iii) is accurate and complete.

Clause (ii) and clause (iv)(I) shall not apply to a plan described in section 412(i)[1] of title 26.

(B) Determination by the corporation of necessary distress criteria

Upon receipt of the notice of intent to terminate required under subsection (a)(2) of this section and the information required under subparagraph (A), the corporation shall determine whether the requirements of this subparagraph are met as provided in clause (i), (ii), or (iii). The requirements of this subparagraph are met if each person who is (as of the proposed termination date) a contributing sponsor of such plan or a member of such sponsor's controlled group meets the requirements of any of the following clauses:

(i) Liquidation in bankruptcy or insolvency proceedings

The requirements of this clause are met by a person if—

(I) such person has filed or has had filed against such person, as of the proposed termination date, a petition seeking liquidation in a case under title 11 or under any similar Federal law or law of a State or political subdivision of a State (or a case described in clause (ii) filed by or against such person has been converted, as of such date, to a case in which liquidation is sought), and

(II) such case has not, as of the proposed termination date, been dismissed.

(ii) Reorganization in bankruptcy or insolvency proceedings

The requirements of this clause are met by a person if—

(I) such person has filed, or has had filed against such person, as of the proposed termination date, a petition seeking reorganization in a case under title 11 or under any similar law of a State or political subdivision of a State (or a case described in clause (i) filed by or against such person has been converted, as of such date, to such a case in which reorganization is sought),

(II) such case has not, as of the proposed termination date, been dismissed,

(III) such person timely submits to the corporation any request for the approval of the bankruptcy court (or other appropriate court in a case under such similar law of a State or political subdivision) of the plan termination, and

(IV) the bankruptcy court (or such other appropriate court) determines that, unless the plan is terminated, such person will be unable to pay all its debts pursuant to a plan of reorganization and will be unable to continue in business outside the chapter 11 reorganization process and approves the termination.

(iii) Termination required to enable payment of debts while staying in business or to avoid unreasonably burdensome pension costs caused by declining workforce

The requirements of this clause are met by a person if such person demonstrates to the satisfaction of the corporation that—

(I) unless a distress termination occurs, such person will be unable to pay such person's debts when due and will be unable to continue in business, or

(II) the costs of providing pension coverage have become unreasonably burdensome to such person, solely as a result of a decline of such person's workforce covered as participants under all single-employer plans of which such person is a contributing sponsor.

(C) Notification of determinations by the corporation

The corporation shall notify the plan administrator as soon as practicable of its determinations made pursuant to subparagraph (B).

(D) Disclosure of termination information

(i) In general

A plan administrator that has filed a notice of intent to terminate under subsection (a)(2) shall provide to an affected party any information provided to the corporation under subparagraph (A) or the regulations under subsection (a)(2) not later than 15 days after—

(I) receipt of a request from the affected party for the information; or

(II) the provision of new information to the corporation relating to a previous request.

(ii) Confidentiality

(I) In general

The plan administrator shall not provide information under clause (i) in a form that includes any information that may directly or indirectly be associated with, or otherwise identify, an individual participant or beneficiary.

(II) Limitation

A court may limit disclosure under this subparagraph of confidential information described in section 552(b) of title 5 to any authorized representative of the participants or beneficiaries that agrees to ensure the confidentiality of such information.

(iii) Form and manner of information; charges

(I) Form and manner

The corporation may prescribe the form and manner of the provision of information under this subparagraph, which shall include delivery in written, electronic, or other appropriate form to the extent that such form is reasonably accessible to individuals to whom the information is required to be provided.

(II) Reasonable charges

A plan administrator may charge a reasonable fee for any information provided under this subparagraph in other than electronic form.

(iv) Authorized representative

For purposes of this subparagraph, the term "authorized representative" means any employee organization representing participants in the pension plan.

(3) Termination procedure

(A) Determinations by the corporation relating to plan sufficiency for guaranteed benefits and for benefit liabilities

If the corporation determines that the requirements for a distress termination set forth in paragraphs (1) and (2) are met, the corporation shall—

(i) determine that the plan is sufficient for guaranteed benefits (as of the termination date) or that the corporation is unable to make such determination on the basis of information made available to the corporation,

(ii) determine that the plan is sufficient for benefit liabilities (as of the termination date) or that the corporation is unable to make such determination on the basis of information made available to the corporation, and

(iii) notify the plan administrator of the determinations made pursuant to this subparagraph as soon as practicable.

(B) Implementation of termination

After the corporation notifies the plan administrator of its determinations under subparagraph (A), the termination of the plan shall be carried out as soon as practicable, as provided in clause (i), (ii), or (iii).

(i) Cases of sufficiency for benefit liabilities

In any case in which the corporation determines that the plan is sufficient for benefit liabilities, the plan administrator shall proceed to distribute the plan's assets, and make certification to the corporation with respect to such distribution, in the manner described in subsection (b)(3) of this section, and shall take such other actions as may be appropriate to carry out the termination of the plan.

(ii) Cases of sufficiency for guaranteed benefits without a finding of sufficiency for benefit liabilities

In any case in which the corporation determines that the plan is sufficient for guaranteed benefits, but further determines that it is unable to determine that the plan is sufficient for benefit liabilities on the basis of the information made available to it, the plan administrator shall proceed to distribute the plan's assets in the manner described in subsection (b)(3) of this section, make certification to the corporation that the distribution has occurred, and take such actions as may be appropriate to carry out the termination of the plan.

(iii) Cases without any finding of sufficiency

In any case in which the corporation determines that it is unable to determine that the plan is sufficient for guaranteed benefits on the basis of the information made available to it, the corporation shall commence proceedings in accordance with section 1342 of this title.

(C) Finding after authorized commencement of termination that plan is unable to pay benefits

(i) Finding with respect to benefit liabilities which are not guaranteed benefits

If, after the plan administrator has begun to terminate the plan as authorized under subparagraph (B)(i), the plan administrator finds that the plan is unable, or will be unable, to pay benefit liabilities which are not benefits guaranteed by the corporation under section 1322 of this title, the plan administrator shall notify the corporation of such finding as soon as practicable thereafter.

(ii) Finding with respect to guaranteed benefits

If, after the plan administrator has begun to terminate the plan as authorized by subparagraph (B)(i) or (ii), the plan administrator finds that the plan is unable, or will be unable, to pay all benefits under the plan which are guaranteed by the corporation under section 1322 of this title, the plan administrator shall notify the corporation of such finding as soon as practicable thereafter. If the corporation concurs in the finding of the plan administrator (or the corporation itself makes such a finding), the corporation shall institute appropriate proceedings under section 1342 of this title.

(D) Administration of the plan during interim period

(i) In general

The plan administrator shall—

(I) meet the requirements of clause (ii) for the period commencing on the date on which the plan administrator provides a notice of distress termination to the corporation under subsection (a)(2) of this section and ending on the date on which the plan administrator receives notification from the corporation of its determinations under subparagraph (A), and

(II) meet the requirements of clause (ii) commencing on the date on which the plan administrator or the corporation makes a finding under subparagraph (C)(ii).

(ii) Requirements

The requirements of this clause are met by the plan administrator if the plan administrator—

(I) refrains from distributing assets or taking any other actions to carry out the proposed termination under this subsection,

(II) pays benefits attributable to employer contributions, other than death benefits, only in the form of an annuity,

(III) does not use plan assets to purchase irrevocable commitments to provide benefits from an insurer, and

(IV) continues to pay all benefit liabilities under the plan, but, commencing on the proposed termination date, limits the payment of benefits under the plan to those benefits which are guaranteed by the corporation under section 1322 of this title or to which assets are required to be allocated under section 1344 of this title.

In the event the plan administrator is later determined not to have met the requirements for distress termination, any benefits which are not paid solely by reason of compliance with subclause (IV) shall be due and payable immediately (together with interest, at a reasonable rate, in accordance with regulations of the corporation).

(d) Sufficiency

For purposes of this section—

(1) Sufficiency for benefit liabilities

A single-employer plan is sufficient for benefit liabilities if there is no amount of unfunded benefit liabilities under the plan.

(2) Sufficiency for guaranteed benefits

A single-employer plan is sufficient for guaranteed benefits if there is no amount of unfunded guaranteed benefits under the plan.

(e) Limitation on the conversion of a defined benefit plan to a defined contribution plan

The adoption of an amendment to a plan which causes the plan to become a plan described in section 1321(b)(1) of this title constitutes a termination of the plan. Such an amendment may take effect only after the plan satisfies the requirements for standard termination under subsection (b) of this section or distress termination under subsection (c) of this section.

(Pub. L. 93–406, title IV, § 4041, Sept. 2, 1974, 88 Stat. 1020; Pub. L. 96–364, title IV, § 403(d), Sept. 26, 1980, 94 Stat. 1301; Pub. L. 99–272, title XI, §§ 11007, 11008(a), (b), 11009, Apr. 7, 1986, 100 Stat. 244, 247, 248; Pub. L. 100–203, title IX, §§ 9312(c)(1), (2), 9313(a)(1)–(2)(E), (b)(1)–(5), 9314(a), Dec. 22, 1987, 101 Stat. 1330–363 to 1330–366; Pub. L. 101–239, title VII, §§ 7881(f)(7), (g)(1)–(6), 7893(c), (d), Dec. 19, 1989, 103 Stat. 2440, 2441, 2447; Pub. L. 103–465, title VII, §§ 776(b)(3), 778(a)(1), (b)(1), Dec. 8, 1994, 108 Stat. 5048–5050; Pub. L. 109–280, title IV, § 409(a), title V, § 506(a), Aug. 17, 2006, 120 Stat. 933, 946; Pub. L. 110–458, title I, §§ 104(d), 105(e)(1), Dec. 23, 2008, 122 Stat. 5104, 5105.)

REFERENCES IN TEXT

Section 412, referred to in subsecs. (b)(2)(A) and (c)(2)(A), was amended generally by Pub. L. 109–280, title I, § 111(a), Aug. 17, 2006, 120 Stat. 820, and as so amended, no longer contains a subsec. (i).

Chapter 11, referred to in subsec. (c)(2)(B)(ii)(IV), probably means chapter 11 of Title 11, Bankruptcy.

AMENDMENTS

2008—Subsec. (b)(5)(A). Pub. L. 110–458, § 104(d), substituted "subparagraphs (B) and (D)" for "subparagraph (B)" in introductory provisions.

Subsec. (c)(2)(D)(i). Pub. L. 110–458, § 105(e)(1), substituted "subparagraph (A) or the regulations under subsection (a)(2)" for "subsection (a)(2)".

2006—Subsec. (b)(5). Pub. L. 109–280, § 409(a), added par. (5).

Subsec. (c)(1)(C). Pub. L. 109–280, § 506(a)(2), substituted "subparagraphs (B) and (D)" for "subparagraph (B)".

Subsec. (c)(2)(D). Pub. L. 109–280, § 506(a)(1), added subpar. (D).

1994—Subsec. (b)(2)(C)(i)(I). Pub. L. 103–465, § 778(a)(1)(A), added subcl. (I) and struck out former subcl. (I) which read as follows: "It has reason to believe that any requirement of subsection (a)(2) of this section or subparagraph (A) or (B) has not been met, or".

Subsec. (b)(2)(C)(i)(III). Pub. L. 103–465, § 778(a)(1)(B), (C), added subcl. (III).

Subsec. (b)(3)(A)(ii). Pub. L. 103–465, § 776(b)(3), inserted at end "A transfer of assets to the corporation in accordance with section 1350 of this title on behalf of a missing participant shall satisfy this subparagraph with respect to such participant."

Subsec. (c)(2)(B)(i)(I). Pub. L. 103–465, § 778(b)(1), inserted "Federal law or" after "under any similar".

1989—Subsec. (b)(2)(A). Pub. L. 101–239, § 7881(g)(6), realigned margin of last sentence.

Subsec. (b)(2)(B). Pub. L. 101–239, § 7893(c), realigned margin of last sentence.

Subsec. (b)(3)(B). Pub. L. 101–239, § 7881(g)(4), inserted period at end.

Subsec. (c)(2)(A)(ii). Pub. L. 101–239, § 7881(g)(3), in introductory provisions, inserted "unless the corporation determines the information is not necessary for purposes of paragraph (3)(A) or section 1362 of this title," before "certification", in subcl. (I), inserted "and, if applicable, the proposed distribution date" after "termination date", and in subcls. (II) to (V), substituted "dates" for "date".

Subsec. (c)(2)(A)(iii)(II). Pub. L. 101–239, § 7881(f)(7)(A), (B), struck out "(or its designee under section 1349(b) of this title)" before "to be able" and substituted "section 1322(c) of this title" for "section 1349 of this title".

Subsec. (c)(2)(B). Pub. L. 101–239, § 7881(g)(2), substituted "(as of the proposed termination date)" for "(as of the termination date)".

Subsec. (c)(2)(B)(i), (ii). Pub. L. 101–239, § 7881(g)(5), made clarifying amendment to directory language of Pub. L. 100–203, § 9313(b)(3), see 1987 Amendment note below.

Subsec. (c)(3)(C)(i). Pub. L. 101–239, § 7881(f)(7)(C), struck out at end "If the corporation concurs in the finding of the plan administrator (or the corporation itself makes such a finding) the corporation shall take the actions set forth in subparagraph (B)(ii)(II) relating to the trust established for purposes of section 1349 of this title."

Subsec. (c)(3)(D). Pub. L. 101–239, § 7893(d)(1), realigned margins.

Subsec. (c)(3)(D)(ii)(I). Pub. L. 101–239, § 7893(d)(2), substituted "under this subsection" for "of this subsection".

Subsec. (d)(1). Pub. L. 101–239, § 7881(g)(1), substituted "sufficient for benefit liabilities" for "sufficient for benefit commitments".

1987—Subsec. (b)(1)(D). Pub. L. 100–203, § 9313(a)(1), amended subpar. (D) generally. Prior to amendment, subpar. (D) read as follows: "when the final distribution of assets occurs, the plan is sufficient for benefit commitments (determined as of the termination date)."

Subsec. (b)(2)(A). Pub. L. 100–203, § 9314(a)(1)(B), inserted at end "Clause (i) and clause (iii)(I) shall not apply to a plan described in section 412(i) of title 26."

Subsec. (b)(2)(A)(i). Pub. L. 100–203, § 9313(a)(2)(A), substituted "benefit liabilities" for "benefit commitments" in subcls. (II) and (III).

Subsec. (b)(2)(A)(iii). Pub. L. 100–203, § 9314(a)(1)(A), added cl. (iii) and struck out former cl. (iii) which read as follows: "certification by the plan administrator that the information on which the enrolled actuary based the certification under clause (i) and the information provided to the corporation under clause (ii) are accurate and complete."

Subsec. (b)(2)(B). Pub. L. 100–203, § 9313(a)(2)(B), substituted "the amount of the benefit liabilities (if any) attributable to such person" for "the amount of such person's benefit commitments (if any)" in cl. (i), and "such benefit liabilities" for "such benefit commitments" in cl. (ii).

Subsec. (b)(2)(C)(i)(II), (D)(ii). Pub. L. 100–203, § 9313(a)(2)(A), substituted "benefit liabilities" for "benefit commitments".

Subsec. (b)(3)(A)(i). Pub. L. 100–203, § 9313(a)(2)(C)(i), added cl. (i) and struck out former cl. (i) which read as follows: "purchase irrevocable commitments from an insurer to provide the benefit liabilities under the plan and all other benefits (if any) under the plan to which assets are required to be allocated under section 1344 of this title, or".

Pub. L. 100–203, § 9313(a)(2)(A), substituted "benefit liabilities" for "benefit commitments".

Subsec. (b)(3)(A)(ii). Pub. L. 100–203, § 9313(a)(2)(C)(i), added cl. (ii) and struck out former cl. (ii) which read as follows: "in accordance with the provisions of the plan and any applicable regulations of the corporation, otherwise fully provide the benefit liabilities under the plan and all other benefits (if any) under the plan to which assets are required to be allocated under section 1344 of this title."

Pub. L. 100–203, § 9313(a)(2)(A), substituted "benefit liabilities" for "benefit commitments".

Subsec. (b)(3)(B). Pub. L. 100–203, § 9313(a)(2)(C)(ii), substituted "so as to pay all benefit liabilities under the plan" for "so as to pay the benefit liabilities under the plan and all other benefits under the plan to which assets are required to be allocated under section 1344 of this title."

Pub. L. 100–203, § 9313(a)(2)(A), substituted "benefit liabilities" for "benefit commitments".

Subsec. (c)(2)(A). Pub. L. 100–203, § 9314(a)(1)(B), inserted at end "Clause (ii) and clause (iv)(I) shall not apply to a plan described in section 412(i) of title 26."

Subsec. (c)(2)(A)(ii). Pub. L. 100–203, § 9313(a)(2)(D), substituted "benefit liabilities" for "benefit commitments" in subcls. (II) and (III).

Subsec. (c)(2)(A)(iii). Pub. L. 100–203, § 9313(a)(2)(D), substituted "benefit liabilities" for "benefit commitments" in introductory provision.

Subsec. (c)(2)(A)(iv). Pub. L. 100–203, § 9314(a)(2)(A), added cl. (iv) and struck out former cl. (iv) which read as follows: "certification by the plan administrator that the information on which the enrolled actuary based the certifications under clause (ii) and the information provided to the corporation under clauses (i) and (iii) are accurate and complete."

Subsec. (c)(2)(B). Pub. L. 100–203, § 9313(b)(1)(A), substituted "a member" for "a substantial member" in introductory provisions.

Subsec. (c)(2)(B)(i). Pub. L. 100–203, § 9313(b)(3), as amended by Pub. L. 101–239, § 7881(g)(5), substituted "proposed termination date" for "termination date" in subcls. (I) and (II).

Pub. L. 100–203, § 9313(b)(4), inserted "(or a case described in clause (ii) filed by or against such person has been converted, as of such date, to a case in which liquidation is sought)" in subcl. (I).

Subsec. (c)(2)(B)(ii)(I). Pub. L. 100–203, § 9313(b)(3), as amended by Pub. L. 101–239, § 7881(g)(5), substituted "proposed termination date" for "termination date".

Subsec. (c)(2)(B)(ii)(II). Pub. L. 100–203 § 9313(b)(5)(A), struck out "and" at end.

Pub. L. 100–203, § 9313(b)(3), as amended by Pub. L. 101–239, § 7881(g)(5), substituted "proposed termination date" for "termination date".

Subsec. (c)(2)(B)(ii)(III). Pub. L. 100–203, § 9313(b)(5)(C), added subcl. (III). Former subcl. (III) redesignated (IV).

Subsec. (c)(2)(B)(ii)(IV). Pub. L. 100–203, § 9313(b)(2), (5)(B), (D), redesignated former subcl. (III) as (IV) and substituted "(or such other appropriate court) determines that, unless the plan is terminated, such person will be unable to pay all its debts pursuant to a plan of reorganization and will be unable to continue in business outside the chapter 11 reorganization process and approves the termination" for "(or other appropriate court in a case under such similar law of a State or political subdivision) approves the termination".

Subsec. (c)(2)(C), (D). Pub. L. 100–203, § 9313(b)(1)(B), redesignated former subpar. (D) as (C) and struck out former subpar. (C) which read as follows: "For purposes of subparagraph (B), the term 'substantial member' of a controlled group means a person whose assets comprise 5 percent or more of the total assets of the controlled group as a whole."

Subsec. (c)(3)(A). Pub. L. 100–203, § 9313(a)(2)(D), substituted "benefit liabilities" for "benefit commitments" in heading and in cl. (ii).

Subsec. (c)(3)(B)(i). Pub. L. 100–203, § 9313(a)(2)(D), substituted in heading and text "benefit liabilities" for "benefit commitments".

Subsec. (c)(3)(B)(ii). Pub. L. 100–203, § 9313(a)(2)(D), substituted in heading and text "benefit liabilities" for "benefit commitments".

Pub. L. 100–203, § 9312(c)(1), struck out former subcl. (I) designation and substituted comma for dash before "the plan administrator", substituted period for ", and" after "termination of the plan", and struck out former subcl. (II) which read as follows: "the corporation shall establish a separate trust in connection with the plan for purposes of section 1349 of this title."

Subsec. (c)(3)(B)(iii). Pub. L. 100–203, § 9312(c)(2), struck out former subcl. (I) designation and substituted comma for dash before "the corporation shall commence", substituted period for ", and" after "section

1342 of this title", and struck out former subcl. (II) which read as follows: "the corporation shall establish a separate trust in connection with the plan for purposes of section 1349 of this title unless the corporation determines that all benefit commitments under the plan are benefits guaranteed by the corporation under section 1322 of this title."

Subsec. (c)(3)(C)(i). Pub. L. 100–203, §9313(a)(2)(D), substituted in heading and text "benefit liabilities" for "benefit commitments".

Subsec. (c)(3)(D)(ii)(IV). Pub. L. 100–203, §9313(a)(2)(D), substituted "benefit liabilities" for "benefit commitments".

Subsec. (d)(1). Pub. L. 100–203, §9313(a)(2)(E), substituted in text, "no amount of unfunded benefit liabilities" for "no amount of unfunded benefit commitments" and in heading, "benefit liabilities" for "benefit commitments".

1986—Subsec. (a). Pub. L. 99–272, §11007(a), added subsec. (a) relating to general rules governing single-employer plan terminations and struck out former subsec. (a) relating to filing of notice that the plan is to be terminated.

Subsec. (b). Pub. L. 99–272, §§11007(a), 11008(a), added subsec. (b) relating to standard termination of single-employer plans and struck out former subsec. (b) relating to notice of sufficiency of plan assets.

Subsec. (c). Pub. L. 99–272, §§11007(a), 11009(a), added subsec. (c) relating to distress termination of single-employer plans and struck out former subsec. (c) relating to a finding and notice of inability to determine that the assets of a plan are sufficient.

Subsec. (d). Pub. L. 99–272, §11007(b), amended subsec. (d) generally, substituting provisions relating to sufficiency for benefit commitments and for guaranteed benefits, for provisions relating to an extension of the 90-day period upon written agreement.

Subsec. (e). Pub. L. 99–272, §11009(b), redesignated subsec. (f) as (e) and struck out former subsec. (e) which related to notification and appropriate proceedings upon a finding after authorized commencement of termination that the plan is unable to pay basic benefits when due.

Subsec. (f). Pub. L. 99–272, §11009(b)(2), redesignated subsec. (f) as (e).

Pub. L. 99–272, §11008(b), amended subsec. (f) generally, substituting provisions relating to limitation on the conversion of a defined benefit plan to a defined contribution plan, for provisions relating to amendment of a plan with respect to which basic benefits are guaranteed.

1980—Subsec. (a). Pub. L. 96–364, §403(d)(2), inserted "single-employer" after "termination of a".

Subsec. (g). Pub. L. 96–364, §403(d)(3), struck out subsec. (g) which related to petition to the appropriate court for appointment of a trustee.

EFFECTIVE DATE OF 2008 AMENDMENT

Amendment by Pub. L. 110–458 effective as if included in the provisions of Pub. L. 109–280 to which the amendment relates, except as otherwise provided, see section 112 of Pub. L. 110–458, set out as a note under section 72 of Title 26, Internal Revenue Code.

EFFECTIVE DATE OF 2006 AMENDMENT

Pub. L. 109–280, title IV, §409(b), Aug. 17, 2006, 120 Stat. 934, provided that: "The amendments made by this section [amending this section] shall apply to any transaction or series of transactions occurring on and after the date of the enactment of this Act [Aug. 17, 2006]."

Pub. L. 109–280, title V, §506(c), Aug. 17, 2006, 120 Stat. 948, provided that:

"(1) IN GENERAL.—The amendments made by this section [amending this section and section 1342 of this title] shall apply to any plan termination under title IV of the Employee Retirement Income Security Act of 1974 (29 U.S.C. 1301 et seq.) with respect to which the notice of intent to terminate (or in the case of a termination by the Pension Benefit Guaranty Corporation, a notice of determination under section 4042 of such Act (29 U.S.C. 1342)) occurs after the date of enactment of this Act [Aug. 17, 2006].

"(2) TRANSITION RULE.—If notice under section 4041(c)(2)(D) or 4042(c)(3) of the Employee Retirement Income Security Act of 1974 [29 U.S.C. 1341(c)(2)(D), 1342(c)(3)] (as added by this section) would otherwise be required to be provided before the 90th day after the date of the enactment of this Act [Aug. 17, 2006], such notice shall not be required to be provided until such 90th day."

EFFECTIVE DATE OF 1994 AMENDMENT

Amendment by section 776(b)(3) of Pub. L. 103–465 effective with respect to distributions that occur in plan years commencing on or after Jan. 1, 1996, see section 776(e) of Pub. L. 103–465, set out as a note under section 1056 of this title.

Section 778(a)(2) of Pub. L. 103–465 provided that: "The amendments made by this subsection [amending this section] shall apply to any plan termination under section 4041(b) of the Employee Retirement Income Security Act of 1974 [subsec. (b) of this section] with respect to which the Pension Benefit Guaranty Corporation has not, as of the date of enactment of this Act [Dec. 8, 1994], issued a notice of noncompliance that has become final, or otherwise issued a final determination that the plan termination is nullified."

Section 778(b)(2) of Pub. L. 103–465 provided that: "The amendment made by this subsection [amending this section] shall be effective as if included in the Single-Employer Pension Plan Amendments Act of 1986 [Pub. L. 99–272, title XI]."

EFFECTIVE DATE OF 1989 AMENDMENT

Amendment by section 7881(f)(7), (g)(1)–(6) of Pub. L. 101–239 effective, except as otherwise provided, as if included in the provision of the Pension Protection Act, Pub. L. 100–203, §§9302–9346, to which such amendment relates, see section 7882 of Pub. L. 101–239, set out as a note under section 401 of Title 26, Internal Revenue Code.

Amendment by section 7893(c), (d) of Pub. L. 101–239 effective as if included in the provision of the Single-Employer Pension Plan Amendments Act of 1986, Pub. L. 99–272, title XI, to which such amendment relates, see section 7893(h) of Pub. L. 101–239, set out as a note under section 1002 of this title.

EFFECTIVE DATE OF 1987 AMENDMENT

Amendment by section 9312(c)(1), (2) of Pub. L. 100–203 applicable with respect to plan terminations under section 1341 of this title with respect to which notices of intent to terminate are provided under section 1341(a)(2) of this title after Dec. 17, 1987, and plan terminations with respect to which proceedings are instituted by the Pension Benefit Guaranty Corporation under section 1342 of this title after that date, see section 9312(d)(1) of Pub. L. 100–203, as amended, set out as a note under section 1301 of this title.

Amendment by section 9313(a)(1)–(2)(E), (b)(1)–(5) of Pub. L. 100–203 applicable with respect to plan terminations under section 1341 of this title with respect to which notices of intent to terminate are provided under section 1341(a)(2) of this title after Dec. 17, 1987, see section 9313(c) of Pub. L. 100–203, set out as a note under section 1301 of this title.

EFFECTIVE DATE OF 1986 AMENDMENT

Section 11019 of title XI of Pub. L. 99–272 provided that:

"(a) IN GENERAL.—Except as otherwise provided in this title, the amendments made by this title [see Short Title of 1986 Amendment note set out under section 1001 of this title] shall be effective as of January 1, 1986, except that such amendments shall not apply with respect to terminations for which—

"(1) notices of intent to terminate were filed with the Pension Benefit Guaranty Corporation under section 4041 of the Employee Retirement Income Security Act of 1974 [29 U.S.C. 1341] before such date, or

"(2) proceedings were commenced under section 4042 of such Act [29 U.S.C. 1342] before such date.

"(b) TRANSITIONAL RULES.—

"(1) IN GENERAL.—In the case of a single-employer plan termination for which a notice of intent to terminate was filed with the Pension Benefit Guaranty Corporation under section 4041 of the Employee Retirement Income Security Act of 1974 (as in effect before the amendments made by this title) [29 U.S.C. 1341] on or after January 1, 1986, but before the date of the enactment of this Act [Apr. 7, 1986], the amendments made by this title [see Short Title of 1986 Amendment note set out under section 1001 of this title] shall apply with respect to such termination, as modified by paragraphs (2) and (3).

"(2) DEEMED COMPLIANCE WITH NOTICE REQUIREMENTS.—The requirements of subsections (a)(2), (b)(1)(A), and (c)(1)(A) of section 4041 of the Employee Retirement Income Security Act of 1974 (as amended by this title) [29 U.S.C. 1341] shall be considered to have been met with respect to a termination described in paragraph (1) if—

"(A) the plan administrator provided notice to the participants in the plan regarding the termination in compliance with applicable regulations of the Pension Benefit Guaranty Corporation as in effect on the date of the notice, and

"(B) the notice of intent to terminate provided to the Pension Benefit Guaranty Corporation in connection with the termination was filed with the Corporation not less than 10 days before the proposed date of termination specified in the notice.

For purposes of section 4041 of such Act (as amended by this title), the proposed date of termination specified in the notice of intent to terminate referred to in subparagraph (B) shall be considered the proposed termination date.

"(3) SPECIAL TERMINATION PROCEDURES.—

"(A) IN GENERAL.—This paragraph shall apply with respect to any termination described in paragraph (1) if, within 90 days after the date of enactment of this Act [Apr. 7, 1986], the plan administrator notifies the Corporation in writing—

"(i) that the plan administrator wishes the termination to proceed as a standard termination under section 4041(b) of the Employee Retirement Income Security Act of 1974 (as amended by this title) [29 U.S.C. 1341(b)] in accordance with subparagraph (B),

"(ii) that the plan administrator wishes the termination to proceed as a distress termination under section 4041(c) of such Act (as amended by this title) in accordance with subparagraph (C), or

"(iii) that the plan administrator wishes to stop the termination proceedings in accordance with subparagraph (D).

"(B) TERMINATIONS PROCEEDING AS STANDARD TERMINATION.—

"(i) TERMINATIONS FOR WHICH SUFFICIENCY NOTICES HAVE NOT BEEN ISSUED.—

"(I) IN GENERAL.—In the case of a plan termination described in paragraph (1) with respect to which the Corporation has been provided the notification described in subparagraph (A)(i) and with respect to which a notice of sufficiency has not been issued by the Corporation before the date of the enactment of this Act, if, during the 90-day period commencing on the date of the notice required in subclause (II), all benefit commitments under the plan have been satisfied, the termination shall be treated as a standard termination under section 4041(b) of such Act (as amended by this title).

"(II) SPECIAL NOTICE REGARDING SUFFICIENCY FOR TERMINATIONS FOR WHICH NOTICES OF SUFFICIENCY HAVE NOT BEEN ISSUED AS OF DATE OF ENACTMENT.—In the case of a plan termination described in paragraph (1) with respect to which the Corporation has been provided the notification described in subparagraph (A)(i) and with respect to which a notice of sufficiency has not been issued by the Corporation before the date of the enactment of this Act, the Corporation shall make the determinations described in section 4041(c)(3)(A)(i) and (ii) (as amended by this title) and notify the plan administrator of such determinations as provided in section 4041(c)(3)(A)(iii) (as amended by this title).

"(ii) TERMINATIONS FOR WHICH NOTICES OF SUFFICIENCY HAVE BEEN ISSUED.—In the case of a plan termination described in paragraph (1) with respect to which the Corporation has been provided the notification described in subparagraph (A)(i) and with respect to which a notice of sufficiency has been issued by the Corporation before the date of the enactment of this Act, clause (i)(I) shall apply, except that the 90-day period referred to in clause (i)(I) shall begin on the date of the enactment of this Act.

"(C) TERMINATIONS PROCEEDING AS DISTRESS TERMINATION.—In the case of a plan termination described in paragraph (1) with respect to which the Corporation has been provided the notification described in subparagraph (A)(ii), if the requirements of section 4041(c)(2)(B) of such Act (as amended by this title) are met, the termination shall be treated as a distress termination under section 4041(c) of such Act (as amended by this title).

"(D) TERMINATION OF PROCEEDINGS BY PLAN ADMINISTRATOR.—

"(i) IN GENERAL.—Except as provided in clause (ii), in the case of a plan termination described in paragraph (1) with respect to which the Corporation has been provided the notification described in subparagraph (A)(iii), the termination shall not take effect.

"(ii) TERMINATIONS WITH RESPECT TO WHICH FINAL DISTRIBUTION OF ASSETS HAS COMMENCED.—Clause (i) shall not apply with respect to a termination with respect to which the final distribution of assets has commenced before the date of the enactment of this Act unless, within 90 days after the date of the enactment of this Act, the plan has been restored in accordance with procedures issued by the Corporation pursuant to subsection (c).

"(E) AUTHORITY OF CORPORATION TO EXTEND 90-DAY PERIODS TO PERMIT STANDARD TERMINATION.—The Corporation may, on a case-by-case basis in accordance with subsection (c), provide for extensions of the applicable 90-day period referred to in clause (i) or (ii) of subparagraph (B) if it is demonstrated to the satisfaction of the Corporation that—

"(i) the plan could not otherwise, pursuant to the preceding provisions of this paragraph, terminate in a termination treated as a standard termination under section 4041(b) of the Employee Retirement Income Security Act of 1974 (as amended by this title), and

"(ii) the extension would result in a greater likelihood that benefit commitments under the plan would be paid in full,

except that any such period may not be so extended beyond one year after the date of the enactment of this Act.

"(c) AUTHORITY TO PRESCRIBE TEMPORARY PROCEDURES.—The Pension Benefit Guaranty Corporation may prescribe temporary procedures for purposes of carrying out the amendments made by this title [see Short Title of 1986 Amendment note set out under section 1001 of this title] during the 180-day period beginning on the date described in subsection (a)."

EFFECTIVE DATE OF 1980 AMENDMENT

Amendment by Pub. L. 96–364 effective Sept. 26, 1980, except as specifically provided, see section 1461(e) of this title.

60-DAY EXTENSION BY PENSION BENEFIT GUARANTY CORPORATION FOR NOTICE OF NONCOMPLIANCE

Section 11008(c) of Pub. L. 99–272 provided that: "In the case of a standard termination of a plan under section 4041(b) of the Employee Retirement Income Security Act of 1974 (as amended by this section) [29 U.S.C. 1341(b)] with respect to which a notice of intent to terminate is filed before 120 days after the date of the enactment of this Act [Apr. 7, 1986], the Pension Benefit Guaranty Corporation may, without the consent of the plan administrator, extend the 60-day period under section 4041(b)(2)(C)(i) of such Act (as so amended) for a period not to exceed 60 days."

SPECIAL TEMPORARY RULE FOR TERMINATION OF SINGLE-EMPLOYER PLAN

Section 11008(d) of Pub. L. 99–272 provided that:

"(1) REQUIREMENTS TO BE MET BEFORE FINAL DISTRIBUTION OF ASSETS.—In the case of the termination of a single-employer plan described in paragraph (2) with respect to which the amount payable to the employer pursuant to section 4044(d) [29 U.S.C. 1344(d)] exceeds $1,000,000 (determined as of the proposed date of final distribution of assets), the final distribution of assets pursuant to such termination may not occur unless the Pension Benefit Guaranty Corporation—

"(A) determines that the assets of the plan are sufficient for benefit commitments (within the meaning of section 4041(d)(1) of the Employee Retirement Income Security Act of 1974 (as amended by section 11007) [29 U.S.C. 1341(d)(1)]) under the plan, and

"(B) issues to the plan administrator a written notice setting forth the determination described in subparagraph (A).

"(2) PLANS TO WHICH SUBSECTION APPLIES.—A single-employer plan is described in this paragraph if—

"(A) the plan administrator has filed a notice of intent to terminate with the Pension Benefit Guaranty Corporation, and—

"(i) the filing was made before January 1, 1986, and the Corporation has not issued a notice of sufficiency for such plan before the date of the enactment of this Act [Apr. 7, 1986], or

"(ii) the filing is made on or after January 1, 1986, and before 60 days after the date of the enactment of this Act and the Corporation has not issued a notice of sufficiency for such plan before the date of the enactment of this Act, and

"(B) of the persons who are (as of the termination date) participants in the plan, the lesser of 10 percent or 200 have filed complaints with the Corporation regarding such termination—

"(i) in the case of plans described in subparagraph (A)(i), before 15 days after the date of the enactment of this Act, or

"(ii) in any other case, before the later of 15 days after the date of the enactment of this Act or 45 days after the date of the filing of such notice.

"(3) CONSIDERATION OF COMPLAINTS.—The Corporation shall consider and respond to such complaints not later than 90 days after the date on which the Corporation makes the determination described in paragraph (1)(A). The Corporation may hold informal hearings to expedite consideration of such complaints. Any such hearing shall be exempt from the requirements of chapter 5 of title 5, United States Code.

"(4) DELAY ON ISSUANCE OF NOTICE.—

"(A) GENERAL RULE.—Except as provided in subparagraph (B), the Corporation shall not issue any notice described in paragraph (1)(B) until 90 days after the date on which the Corporation makes the determination described in paragraph (1)(A).

"(B) EXCEPTION IN CASES OF SUBSTANTIAL BUSINESS HARDSHIP.—Except in the case of an acquisition, takeover, or leveraged buyout, the preceding provisions of this subsection shall not apply if the contributing sponsor demonstrates to the satisfaction of the Corporation that the contributing sponsor is experiencing substantial business hardship. For purposes of this subparagraph, a contributing sponsor shall be considered as experiencing substantial business hardship if the contributing sponsor has been operating, and can demonstrate that the contributing sponsor will continue to operate, at an economic loss."

§1341a. Termination of multiemployer plans

(a) Determinative factors

Termination of a multiemployer plan under this section occurs as a result of—

(1) the adoption after September 26, 1980, of a plan amendment which provides that participants will receive no credit for any purpose under the plan for service with any employer after the date specified by such amendment;

(2) the withdrawal of every employer from the plan, within the meaning of section 1383 of this title, or the cessation of the obligation of all employers to contribute under the plan; or

(3) the adoption of an amendment to the plan which causes the plan to become a plan described in section 1321(b)(1) of this title.

(b) Date of termination

(1) The date on which a plan terminates under paragraph (1) or (3) of subsection (a) of this section is the later of—

(A) the date on which the amendment is adopted, or

(B) the date on which the amendment takes effect.

(2) The date on which a plan terminates under paragraph (2) of subsection (a) of this section is the earlier of—

(A) the date on which the last employer withdraws, or

(B) the first day of the first plan year for which no employer contributions were required under the plan.

(c) Duties of plan sponsor of amended plan

Except as provided in subsection (f)(1) of this section, the plan sponsor of a plan which terminates under paragraph (2) of subsection (a) of this section shall—

(1) limit the payment of benefits to benefits which are nonforfeitable under the plan as of the date of the termination, and

(2) pay benefits attributable to employer contributions, other than death benefits, only in the form of an annuity, unless the plan assets are distributed in full satisfaction of all nonforfeitable benefits under the plan.

(d) Duties of plan sponsor of nonoperative plan

The plan sponsor of a plan which terminates under paragraph (2) of subsection (a) of this section shall reduce benefits and suspend benefit payments in accordance with section 1441 of this title.

(e) Amount of contribution of employer under amended plan for each plan year subsequent to plan termination date

In the case of a plan which terminates under paragraph (1) or (3) of subsection (a) of this section, the rate of an employer's contributions under the plan for each plan year beginning on or after the plan termination date shall equal or exceed the highest rate of employer contributions at which the employer had an obligation to contribute under the plan in the 5 preceding plan years ending on or before the plan termination date, unless the corporation approves a reduction in the rate based on a finding that the plan is or soon will be fully funded.

(f) Payment of benefits; reporting requirements for terminated plans and rules and standards for administration of such plans

(1) The plan sponsor of a terminated plan may authorize the payment other than in the form of an annuity of a participant's entire nonforfeitable benefit attributable to employer contributions, other than a death benefit, if the value of the entire nonforfeitable benefit does not exceed $1,750. The corporation may authorize the payment of benefits under the terms of a terminated plan other than nonforfeitable benefits, or the payment other than in the form of an annuity of benefits having a value greater than $1,750, if the corporation determines that such payment is not adverse to the interest of the plan's participants and beneficiaries generally and does not unreasonably increase the corporation's risk of loss with respect to the plan.

(2) The corporation may prescribe reporting requirements for terminated plans, and rules and standards for the administration of such plans, which the corporation considers appropriate to protect the interests of plan participants and beneficiaries or to prevent unreasonable loss to the corporation.

(Pub. L. 93–406, title IV, § 4041A, as added Pub. L. 96–364, title I, § 103, Sept. 26, 1980, 94 Stat. 1216.)

EFFECTIVE DATE

Section effective Sept. 26, 1980, except as specifically provided, see section 1461(e) of this title.

§ 1342. Institution of termination proceedings by the corporation

(a) Authority to institute proceedings to terminate a plan

The corporation may institute proceedings under this section to terminate a plan whenever it determines that—

(1) the plan has not met the minimum funding standard required under section 412 of title 26, or has been notified by the Secretary of the Treasury that a notice of deficiency under section 6212 of title 26 has been mailed with respect to the tax imposed under section 4971(a) of title 26,

(2) the plan will be unable to pay benefits when due,

(3) the reportable event described in section 1343(c)(7) of this title has occurred, or

(4) the possible long-run loss of the corporation with respect to the plan may reasonably be expected to increase unreasonably if the plan is not terminated.

The corporation shall as soon as practicable institute proceedings under this section to terminate a single-employer plan whenever the corporation determines that the plan does not have assets available to pay benefits which are currently due under the terms of the plan. The corporation may prescribe a simplified procedure to follow in terminating small plans as long as that procedure includes substantial safeguards for the rights of the participants and beneficiaries under the plans, and for the employers who maintain such plans (including the requirement for a court decree under subsection (c) of this section). Notwithstanding any other provision of this subchapter, the corporation is authorized to pool assets of terminated plans for purposes of administration, investment, payment of liabilities of all such terminated plans, and such other purposes as it determines to be appropriate in the administration of this subchapter.

(b) Appointment of trustee

(1) Whenever the corporation makes a determination under subsection (a) of this section with respect to a plan or is required under subsection (a) of this section to institute proceedings under this section, it may, upon notice to the plan, apply to the appropriate United States district court for the appointment of a trustee to administer the plan with respect to which the determination is made pending the issuance of a decree under subsection (c) of this section ordering the termination of the plan. If within 3 business days after the filing of an application under this subsection, or such other period as the court may order, the administrator of the plan consents to the appointment of a trustee, or fails to show why a trustee should not be appointed, the court may grant the application and appoint a trustee to administer the plan in accordance with its terms until the corporation determines that the plan should be terminated or that termination is unnecessary. The corporation may request that it be appointed as trustee of a plan in any case.

(2) Notwithstanding any other provision of this subchapter—

(A) upon the petition of a plan administrator or the corporation, the appropriate United States district court may appoint a trustee in accordance with the provisions of this section if the interests of the plan participants would be better served by the appointment of the trustee, and

(B) upon the petition of the corporation, the appropriate United States district court shall appoint a trustee proposed by the corporation for a multiemployer plan which is in reorganization or to which section 1341a(d) of this title applies, unless such appointment would be adverse to the interests of the plan participants and beneficiaries in the aggregate.

(3) The corporation and plan administrator may agree to the appointment of a trustee without proceeding in accordance with the requirements of paragraphs (1) and (2).

(c) Adjudication that plan must be terminated

(1) If the corporation is required under subsection (a) of this section to commence proceedings under this section with respect to a plan or, after issuing a notice under this section to a plan administrator, has determined that the plan should be terminated, it may, upon notice to the plan administrator, apply to the appropriate United States district court for a decree adjudicating that the plan must be terminated in order to protect the interests of the participants or to avoid any unreasonable deterioration of the financial condition of the plan or any

unreasonable increase in the liability of the fund. If the trustee appointed under subsection (b) of this section disagrees with the determination of the corporation under the preceding sentence he may intervene in the proceeding relating to the application for the decree, or make application for such decree himself. Upon granting a decree for which the corporation or trustee has applied under this subsection the court shall authorize the trustee appointed under subsection (b) of this section (or appoint a trustee if one has not been appointed under such subsection and authorize him) to terminate the plan in accordance with the provisions of this subtitle. If the corporation and the plan administrator agree that a plan should be terminated and agree to the appointment of a trustee without proceeding in accordance with the requirements of this subsection (other than this sentence) the trustee shall have the power described in subsection (d)(1) of this section and, in addition to any other duties imposed on the trustee under law or by agreement between the corporation and the plan administrator, the trustee is subject to the duties described in subsection (d)(3) of this section. Whenever a trustee appointed under this subchapter is operating a plan with discretion as to the date upon which final distribution of the assets is to be commenced, the trustee shall notify the corporation at least 10 days before the date on which he proposes to commence such distribution.

(2) In the case of a proceeding initiated under this section, the plan administrator shall provide the corporation, upon the request of the corporation, the information described in clauses (ii), (iii), and (iv) of section 1341(c)(2)(A) of this title.

(3) DISCLOSURE OF TERMINATION INFORMATION.—

(A) IN GENERAL.—

(i) INFORMATION FROM PLAN SPONSOR OR ADMINISTRATOR.—A plan sponsor or plan administrator of a single-employer plan that has received a notice from the corporation of a determination that the plan should be terminated under this section shall provide to an affected party any information provided to the corporation in connection with the plan termination.

(ii) INFORMATION FROM CORPORATION.—The corporation shall provide a copy of the administrative record, including the trusteeship decision record of a termination of a plan described under clause (i).

(B) TIMING OF DISCLOSURE.—The plan sponsor, plan administrator, or the corporation, as applicable, shall provide the information described in subparagraph (A) not later than 15 days after—

(i) receipt of a request from an affected party for such information; or

(ii) in the case of information described under subparagraph (A)(i), the provision of any new information to the corporation relating to a previous request by an affected party.

(C) CONFIDENTIALITY.—

(i) IN GENERAL.—The plan administrator, the plan sponsor, or the corporation shall not provide information under subparagraph (A) in a form which includes any information that may directly or indirectly be associated with, or otherwise identify, an individual participant or beneficiary.

(ii) LIMITATION.—A court may limit disclosure under this paragraph of confidential information described in section 552(b) of title 5 to authorized representatives (within the meaning of section 1341(c)(2)(D)(iv) of this title) of the participants or beneficiaries that agree to ensure the confidentiality of such information.

(D) FORM AND MANNER OF INFORMATION; CHARGES.—

(i) FORM AND MANNER.—The corporation may prescribe the form and manner of the provision of information under this paragraph, which shall include delivery in written, electronic, or other appropriate form to the extent that such form is reasonably accessible to individuals to whom the information is required to be provided.

(ii) REASONABLE CHARGES.—A plan sponsor may charge a reasonable fee for any information provided under this paragraph in other than electronic form.

(d) Powers of trustee

(1)(A) A trustee appointed under subsection (b) of this section shall have the power—

(i) to do any act authorized by the plan or this subchapter to be done by the plan administrator or any trustee of the plan;

(ii) to require the transfer of all (or any part) of the assets and records of the plan to himself as trustee;

(iii) to invest any assets of the plan which he holds in accordance with the provisions of the plan, regulations of the corporation, and applicable rules of law;

(iv) to limit payment of benefits under the plan to basic benefits or to continue payment of some or all of the benefits which were being paid prior to his appointment;

(v) in the case of a multiemployer plan, to reduce benefits or suspend benefit payments under the plan, give appropriate notices, amend the plan, and perform other acts required or authorized by subtitle (E) of this subchapter to be performed by the plan sponsor or administrator;

(vi) to do such other acts as he deems necessary to continue operation of the plan without increasing the potential liability of the corporation, if such acts may be done under the provisions of the plan; and

(vii) to require the plan sponsor, the plan administrator, any contributing or withdrawn employer, and any employee organization representing plan participants to furnish any information with respect to the plan which the trustee may reasonably need in order to administer the plan.

If the court to which application is made under subsection (c) of this section dismisses the application with prejudice, or if the corporation fails to apply for a decree under subsection (c) of this section, within 30 days after the date on which the trustee is appointed under subsection (b) of this section, the trustee shall transfer all assets and records of the plan held by him to the plan administrator within 3 business days after such dismissal or the expiration of such 30-day period, and shall not be liable to the plan or any other person for his acts as trustee except for willful misconduct, or for conduct in violation of the provisions of part 4 of subtitle B of subchapter I of this chapter (except as provided in subsection (d)(1)(A)(v) of this section). The 30-day period referred to in this subparagraph may be extended as provided by agreement between the plan administrator and the corporation or by court order obtained by the corporation.

(B) If the court to which an application is made under subsection (c) of this section issues the decree requested in such application, in addition to the powers described in subparagraph (A), the trustee shall have the power—

(i) to pay benefits under the plan in accordance with the requirements of this subchapter;

(ii) to collect for the plan any amounts due the plan, including but not limited to the power to collect from the persons obligated to meet the requirements of section 1082 of this title or the terms of the plan;

(iii) to receive any payment made by the corporation to the plan under this subchapter;

(iv) to commence, prosecute, or defend on behalf of the plan any suit or proceeding involving the plan;

(v) to issue, publish, or file such notices, statements, and reports as may be required by the corporation or any order of the court;

(vi) to liquidate the plan assets;

(vii) to recover payments under section 1345(a) of this title; and

(viii) to do such other acts as may be necessary to comply with this subchapter or any order of the court and to protect the interests of plan participants and beneficiaries.

(2) As soon as practicable after his appointment, the trustee shall give notice to interested parties of the institution of proceedings under this subchapter to determine whether the plan should be terminated or to terminate the plan, whichever is applicable. For purposes of this paragraph, the term "interested party" means—

(A) the plan administrator,

(B) each participant in the plan and each beneficiary of a deceased participant,

(C) each employer who may be subject to liability under section 1362, 1363, or 1364 of this title,

(D) each employer who is or may be liable to the plan under section[1] part 1 of subtitle E of this subchapter,

(E) each employer who has an obligation to contribute, within the meaning of section 1392(a) of this title, under a multiemployer plan, and

(F) each employee organization which, for purposes of collective bargaining, represents plan participants employed by an employer described in subparagraph (C), (D), or (E).

(3) Except to the extent inconsistent with the provisions of this chapter, or as may be otherwise ordered by the court, a trustee appointed under this section shall be subject to the same duties as those of a trustee under section 704 of title 11, and shall be, with respect to the plan, a fiduciary within the meaning of paragraph (21) of section 1002 of this title and under section 4975(e) of title 26 (except to the extent that the provisions of this subchapter are inconsistent with the requirements applicable under part 4 of subtitle B of subchapter I of this chapter and of such section 4975).

(e) Filing of application notwithstanding pendency of other proceedings

An application by the corporation under this section may be filed notwithstanding the pendency in the same or any other court of any bankruptcy, mortgage foreclosure, or equity receivership proceeding, or any proceeding to reorganize, conserve, or liquidate such plan or its property, or any proceeding to enforce a lien against property of the plan.

(f) Exclusive jurisdiction; stay of other proceedings

Upon the filing of an application for the appointment of a trustee or the issuance of a decree under this section, the court to which an application is made shall have exclusive jurisdiction of the plan involved and its property wherever located with the powers, to the extent consistent with the purposes of this section, of a court of the United States having jurisdiction over cases under chapter 11 of title 11. Pending an adjudication under subsection (c) of this section such court shall stay, and upon appointment by it of a trustee, as provided in this section such court shall continue the stay of, any pending mortgage foreclosure, equity receivership, or other proceeding to reorganize, conserve, or liquidate the plan or its property and any other suit against any receiver, conservator, or trustee of the plan or its property. Pending such adjudication and upon the appointment by it of such trustee, the court may stay any proceeding to enforce a lien against property of the plan or any other suit against the plan.

(g) Venue

An action under this subsection may be brought in the judicial district where the plan administrator resides or does business or where any asset of the plan is situated. A district court in which such action is brought may issue process with respect to such action in any other judicial district.

(h) Compensation of trustee and professional service personnel appointed or retained by trustee

(1) The amount of compensation paid to each trustee appointed under the provisions of this subchapter shall require the prior approval of the corporation, and, in the case of a trustee appointed by a court, the consent of that court.

(2) Trustees shall appoint, retain, and compensate accountants, actuaries, and other professional service personnel in accordance with regulations prescribed by the corporation.

(Pub. L. 93–406, title IV, § 4042, Sept. 2, 1974, 88 Stat. 1021; Pub. L. 95–598, title III, § 321(a), Nov. 6, 1978, 92 Stat. 2678; Pub. L. 96–364, title IV, § 402(a)(6), Sept. 26, 1980, 94 Stat. 1298; Pub. L. 99–272, title XI, §§ 11010, 11016(c)(10), (11), Apr. 7,

[1] So in original.

1986, 100 Stat. 253, 274; Pub. L. 100–203, title IX, §§ 9312(c)(3), 9314(b), 9314(b), Dec. 22, 1987, 101 Stat. 1330–363, 1330–366, 1330–367; Pub. L. 101–239, title VII, §§ 7881(g)(7), 7891(a)(1), 7893(e), Dec. 19, 1989, 103 Stat. 2441, 2445, 2447; Pub. L. 103–465, title VII, § 771(e)(2), Dec. 8, 1994, 108 Stat. 5043; Pub. L. 109–280, title V, § 506(b), Aug. 17, 2006, 120 Stat. 947; Pub. L. 110–458, title I, § 105(e)(2), Dec. 23, 2008, 122 Stat. 5105.)

REFERENCES IN TEXT

This chapter, referred to in subsec. (d)(3), was in the original "this Act", meaning Pub. L. 93–406, known as the Employee Retirement Income Security Act of 1974. Titles I, III, and IV of such Act are classified principally to this chapter. For complete classification of this Act to the Code, see Short Title note set out under section 1001 of this title and Tables.

AMENDMENTS

2008—Subsec. (c)(3)(C)(i). Pub. L. 110–458 substituted ", the plan sponsor, or the corporation" for "and plan sponsor" and "subparagraph (A)" for "subparagraph (A)(i)".

2006—Subsec. (c). Pub. L. 109–280 designated first par. as par. (1), redesignated par. (3) as (2), and added a new par. (3).

1994—Subsec. (a)(3). Pub. L. 103–465 substituted "1343(c)(7)" for "1343(b)(7)".

1989—Subsec. (a). Pub. L. 101–239, § 7893(e), inserted period after "terms of the plan" at end of second sentence.

Pub. L. 101–239, § 7881(g)(7), made technical correction to directory language of Pub. L. 100–203, § 9314(b), see 1987 Amendment note below.

Subsecs. (a)(1), (d)(3). Pub. L. 101–239, § 7891(a)(1), substituted "Internal Revenue Code of 1986" for "Internal Revenue Code of 1954", which for purposes of codification was translated as "title 26" thus requiring no change in text.

1987—Subsec. (a). Pub. L. 100–203, § 9314(b), as amended by Pub. L. 101–239, § 7881(g)(7), amended last sentence generally. Prior to amendment, last sentence read as follows: "The corporation is authorized to pool the assets of terminated plans for purposes of administration and such other purposes, not inconsistent with its duties to the plan participants and the employer maintaining the plan under this subchapter, as it determines to be required for the efficient administration of this subchapter." Another section 9314(b) of Pub. L. 100–203 amended subsec. (c) of this section, see below.

Subsec. (c)(3). Pub. L. 100–203, § 9314(b), added par. (3). Another section 9314(b) of Pub. L. 100–203 amended subsec. (a) of this section, see above.

Subsec. (i). Pub. L. 100–203, § 9312(c)(3), struck out subsec. (i) which read as follows: "In any case in which a plan is terminated under this section in a termination proceeding initiated by the corporation pursuant to subsection (a) of this section, the corporation shall establish a separate trust in connection with the plan for purposes of section 1349 of this title, unless the corporation determines that all benefit commitments under the plan are benefits guaranteed by the corporation under section 1322 of this title or that there is no amount of unfunded benefit commitments under the plan."

1986—Pub. L. 99–272, § 11010(c), substituted "Institution of termination proceedings by the corporation" for "Termination by corporation" in section catchline.

Subsec. (a). Pub. L. 99–272, § 11010(a)(1)(B), in provision following par. (4) inserted provision that the corporation as soon as practicable institute proceedings under this section to terminate a single-employer plan whenever the corporation determines that the plan does not have assets available to pay benefits currently due under the terms of the plan.

Subsec. (a)(2). Pub. L. 99–272, § 11010(a)(1)(A), substituted "will be" for "is".

Subsec. (b)(1). Pub. L. 99–272, § 11010(a)(2)(A), inserted "or is required under subsection (a) of this section to institute proceedings under this section,".

Subsec. (c). Pub. L. 99–272, § 11010(a)(2)(B), substituted "is required under subsection (a) of this section to commence proceedings under this section with respect to a plan or, after issuing a notice under this section to a plan administrator," for "has issued a notice under this section to a plan administrator and (whether or not a trustee has been appointed under subsection (b) of this section)".

Subsec. (d)(1)(B)(ii). Pub. L. 99–272, § 11016(c)(10), inserted ", including but not limited to the power to collect from the persons obligated to meet the requirements of section 1082 of this title or the terms of the plan".

Subsec. (d)(3). Pub. L. 99–272, § 11016(c)(11), substituted "those of a trustee under section 704 of title 11" for "a trustee appointed under section 75 of title 11".

Subsec. (i). Pub. L. 99–272, § 11010(b), added subsec. (i).

1980—Subsec. (a). Pub. L. 96–364, § 402(a)(6)(A), substituted "terminated plans" for "such small plans".

Subsec. (b). Pub. L. 96–364, § 402(a)(6)(B), redesignated existing provisions as par. (1) and added pars. (2) and (3).

Subsec. (c). Pub. L. 96–364, § 402(a)(6)(C), (D), substituted "unreasonable" for "further" wherever appearing, and "of the participants or" for "of the participants and".

Subsec. (d)(1)(A). Pub. L. 96–364, § 402(a)(6)(E), added cls. (v) and (vii) and redesignated former cl. (v) as (vi).

Subsec. (d)(1)(B). Pub. L. 96–364, § 402(a)(6)(F), (G), in cl. (i) substituted "requirements of this subchapter" for "allocation requirements of section 1344 of this title", and in cl. (iv) struck out exception respecting adverse party status of corporation.

Subsec. (d)(2)(D) to (F). Pub. L. 96–364, § 402(a)(6)(H)–(J), added subpars. (D) to (F).

1978—Subsec. (f). Pub. L. 95–598 substituted "of a court of the United States having jurisdiction over cases under chapter 11 of title 11" for "of a court of bankruptcy and of a court in a proceeding under chapter X of the Bankruptcy Act" in first sentence and struck out "bankruptcy," before "mortgage foreclosure" in second sentence.

EFFECTIVE DATE OF 2008 AMENDMENT

Amendment by Pub. L. 110–458 effective as if included in the provisions of Pub. L. 109–280 to which the amendment relates, except as otherwise provided, see section 112 of Pub. L. 110–458, set out as a note under section 72 of Title 26, Internal Revenue Code.

EFFECTIVE DATE OF 2006 AMENDMENT

Amendment by Pub. L. 109–280 applicable to any plan termination under this subchapter with respect to which the notice of intent to terminate, or in the case of a termination by the Pension Benefit Guaranty Corporation, a notice of determination under this section occurs after Aug. 17, 2006, with transition rule, see section 506(c) of Pub. L. 109–280, set out as a note under section 1341 of this title.

EFFECTIVE DATE OF 1994 AMENDMENT

Section 771(f) of Pub. L. 103–465 provided that: "The amendments made by this section [amending this section and section 1343 of this title] shall be effective for events occurring 60 days or more after the date of enactment of this Act [Dec. 8, 1994]."

EFFECTIVE DATE OF 1989 AMENDMENT

Amendment by section 7881(g)(7) of Pub. L. 101–239 effective, except as otherwise provided, as if included in the provision of the Pension Protection Act, Pub. L. 100–203, §§ 9302–9346, to which such amendment relates, see section 7882 of Pub. L. 101–239, set out as a note under section 401 of Title 26, Internal Revenue Code.

Amendment by section 7891(a)(1) of Pub. L. 101–239 effective, except as otherwise provided, as if included in the provision of the Tax Reform Act of 1986, Pub. L. 99–514, to which such amendment relates, see section 7891(f) of Pub. L. 101–239, set out as a note under section 1002 of this title.

Amendment by section 7893(e) of Pub. L. 101–239 effective as if included in the provision of the Single-Employer Pension Plan Amendments Act of 1986, Pub. L. 99–272, title XI, to which such amendment relates, see section 7893(h) of Pub. L. 101–239, set out as a note under section 1002 of this title.

EFFECTIVE DATE OF 1987 AMENDMENT

Amendment by section 9312(c)(3) of Pub. L. 100–203 applicable with respect to plan terminations under section 1341 of this title with respect to which notices of intent to terminate are provided under section 1341(a)(2) of this title after Dec. 17, 1987, and plan terminations with respect to which proceedings are instituted by the Pension Benefit Guaranty Corporation under this section after that date, see section 9312(d)(1) of Pub. L. 100–203, as amended, set out as a note under section 1301 of this title.

EFFECTIVE DATE OF 1986 AMENDMENT

Amendment by Pub. L. 99–272 effective Jan. 1, 1986, with certain exceptions, see section 11019 of Pub. L. 99–272, set out as a note under section 1341 of this title.

EFFECTIVE DATE OF 1980 AMENDMENT

Amendment by Pub. L. 96–364 effective Sept. 26, 1980, except as specifically provided, see section 1461(e) of this title.

EFFECTIVE DATE OF 1978 AMENDMENT

Amendment by Pub. L. 95–598 effective Oct. 1, 1979, see section 402(a) of Pub. L. 95–598, set out as an Effective Date note preceding section 101 of Title 11, Bankruptcy.

§ 1343. Reportable events

(a) Notification that event has occurred

Within 30 days after the plan administrator or the contributing sponsor knows or has reason to know that a reportable event described in subsection (c) of this section has occurred, he shall notify the corporation that such event has occurred, unless a notice otherwise required under this subsection has already been provided with respect to such event. The corporation is authorized to waive the requirement of the preceding sentence with respect to any or all reportable events with respect to any plan, and to require the notification to be made by including the event in the annual report made by the plan.

(b) Notification that event is about to occur

(1) The requirements of this subsection shall be applicable to a contributing sponsor if, as of the close of the preceding plan year—

(A) the aggregate unfunded vested benefits (as determined under section 1306(a)(3)(E)(iii) of this title) of plans subject to this subchapter which are maintained by such sponsor and members of such sponsor's controlled groups (disregarding plans with no unfunded vested benefits) exceed $50,000,000, and

(B) the funded vested benefit percentage for such plans is less than 90 percent.

For purposes of subparagraph (B), the funded vested benefit percentage means the percentage which the aggregate value of the assets of such plans bears to the aggregate vested benefits of such plans (determined in accordance with section 1306(a)(3)(E)(iii) of this title).

(2) This subsection shall not apply to an event if the contributing sponsor, or the member of the contributing sponsor's controlled group to which the event relates, is—

(A) a person subject to the reporting requirements of section 13 or 15(d) of the Securities Exchange Act of 1934 [15 U.S.C. 78m, 78*o*(d)], or

(B) a subsidiary (as defined for purposes of such Act [15 U.S.C. 78a et seq.]) of a person subject to such reporting requirements.

(3) No later than 30 days prior to the effective date of an event described in paragraph (9), (10), (11), (12), or (13) of subsection (c) of this section, a contributing sponsor to which the requirements of this subsection apply shall notify the corporation that the event is about to occur.

(4) The corporation may waive the requirement of this subsection with respect to any or all reportable events with respect to any contributing sponsor.

(c) Enumeration of reportable events

For purposes of this section a reportable event occurs—

(1) when the Secretary of the Treasury issues notice that a plan has ceased to be a plan described in section 1321(a)(2) of this title, or when the Secretary of Labor determines the plan is not in compliance with subchapter I of this chapter;

(2) when an amendment of the plan is adopted if, under the amendment, the benefit payable with respect to any participant may be decreased;

(3) when the number of active participants is less than 80 percent of the number of such participants at the beginning of the plan year, or is less than 75 percent of the number of such participants at the beginning of the previous plan year;

(4) when the Secretary of the Treasury determines that there has been a termination or partial termination of the plan within the meaning of section 411(d)(3) of title 26, but the occurrence of such a termination or partial termination does not, by itself, constitute or require a termination of a plan under this subchapter;

(5) when the plan fails to meet the minimum funding standards under section 412 of title 26 (without regard to whether the plan is a plan described in section 1321(a)(2) of this title) or under section 1082 of this title;

(6) when the plan is unable to pay benefits thereunder when due;

(7) when there is a distribution under the plan to a participant who is a substantial owner as defined in section 1321(d) of this title if—

(A) such distribution has a value of $10,000 or more;

(B) such distribution is not made by reason of the death of the participant; and

(C) immediately after the distribution, the plan has nonforfeitable benefits which are not funded;

(8) when a plan merges, consolidates, or transfers its assets under section 1058 of this title, or when an alternative method of compliance is prescribed by the Secretary of Labor under section 1030 of this title;

(9) when, as a result of an event, a person ceases to be a member of the controlled group;

(10) when a contributing sponsor or a member of a contributing sponsor's controlled group liquidates in a case under title 11, or under any similar Federal law or law of a State or political subdivision of a State;

(11) when a contributing sponsor or a member of a contributing sponsor's controlled group declares an extraordinary dividend (as defined in section 1059(c) of title 26) or redeems, in any 12-month period, an aggregate of 10 percent or more of the total combined voting power of all classes of stock entitled to vote, or an aggregate of 10 percent or more of the total value of shares of all classes of stock, of a contributing sponsor and all members of its controlled group;

(12) when, in any 12-month period, an aggregate of 3 percent or more of the benefit liabilities of a plan covered by this subchapter and maintained by a contributing sponsor or a member of its controlled group are transferred to a person that is not a member of the controlled group or to a plan or plans maintained by a person or persons that are not such a contributing sponsor or a member of its controlled group; or

(13) when any other event occurs that may be indicative of a need to terminate the plan and that is prescribed by the corporation in regulations.

For purposes of paragraph (7), all distributions to a participant within any 24-month period are treated as a single distribution.

(d) Notification to corporation by Secretary of the Treasury

The Secretary of the Treasury shall notify the corporation—

(1) whenever a reportable event described in paragraph (1), (4), or (5) of subsection (c) of this section occurs, or

(2) whenever any other event occurs which the Secretary of the Treasury believes indicates that the plan may not be sound.

(e) Notification to corporation by Secretary of Labor

The Secretary of Labor shall notify the corporation—

(1) whenever a reportable event described in paragraph (1), (5), or (8) of subsection (c) of this section occurs, or

(2) whenever any other event occurs which the Secretary of Labor believes indicates that the plan may not be sound.

(f) Disclosure exemption

Any information or documentary material submitted to the corporation pursuant to this section shall be exempt from disclosure under section 552 of title 5, and no such information or documentary material may be made public, except as may be relevant to any administrative or judicial action or proceeding. Nothing in this section is intended to prevent disclosure to either body of Congress or to any duly authorized committee or subcommittee of the Congress.

(Pub. L. 93–406, title IV, §4043, Sept. 2, 1974, 88 Stat. 1024; Pub. L. 101–239, title VII, §7891(a), Dec. 19, 1989, 103 Stat. 2445; Pub. L. 103–465, title VII, §771(a)–(e)(1), Dec. 8, 1994, 108 Stat. 5042, 5043; Pub. L. 109–280, title IV, §407(c)(2), Aug. 17, 2006, 120 Stat. 930.)

REFERENCES IN TEXT

The Securities Exchange Act of 1934, referred to in subsec. (b)(2)(B), is act June 6, 1934, ch. 404, 48 Stat. 881, as amended, which is classified principally to chapter 2B (§78a et seq.) of Title 15, Commerce and Trade. For complete classification of this Act to the Code, see section 78a of Title 15 and Tables.

AMENDMENTS

2006—Subsec. (c)(7). Pub. L. 109–280 substituted "1321(d)" for "1322(b)(6)" in introductory provisions.

1994—Subsec. (a). Pub. L. 103–465, §771(a), (e)(1), in first sentence, inserted "or the contributing sponsor" after "administrator", substituted "subsection (c)" for "subsection (b)", and inserted before period at end ", unless a notice otherwise required under this subsection has already been provided with respect to such event", and struck out last sentence which read as follows: "Whenever an employer making contributions under a plan to which section 1321 of this title applies knows or has reason to know that a reportable event has occurred he shall notify the plan administrator immediately."

Subsec. (b). Pub. L. 103–465, §771(b), added subsec. (b). Former subsec. (b) redesignated (c).

Subsec. (c). Pub. L. 103–465, §771(b), redesignated subsec. (b) as (c). Former subsec. (c) redesignated (d).

Subsec. (c)(8) to (13). Pub. L. 103–465, §771(c), struck out "or" at end of par. (8), added pars. (9) to (13), and struck out former par. (9) which read as follows: "when any other event occurs which the corporation determines may be indicative of a need to terminate the plan.".

Subsecs. (d), (e). Pub. L. 103–465, §771(b), (e)(1), redesignated subsecs. (c) and (d) as (d) and (e), respectively, and substituted "subsection (c)" for "subsection (b)" in par. (1) of each subsec.

Subsec. (f). Pub. L. 103–465, §771(d), added subsec. (f).

1989—Subsec. (b)(4). Pub. L. 101–239 substituted "Internal Revenue Code of 1986" for "Internal Revenue Code of 1954", which for purposes of codification was translated as "title 26" thus requiring no change in text.

EFFECTIVE DATE OF 2006 AMENDMENT

Amendment by Pub. L. 109–280 effective Jan. 1, 2006, see section 407(d)(2) of Pub. L. 109–280, set out as a note under section 1321 of this title.

EFFECTIVE DATE OF 1994 AMENDMENT

Amendment by Pub. L. 103–465 effective for events occurring 60 days or more after Dec. 8, 1994, see section 771(f) of Pub. L. 103–465, set out as a note under section 1342 of this title.

EFFECTIVE DATE OF 1989 AMENDMENT

Amendment by Pub. L. 101–239 effective, except as otherwise provided, as if included in the provision of the Tax Reform Act of 1986, Pub. L. 99–514, to which such amendment relates, see section 7891(f) of Pub. L. 101–239, set out as a note under section 1002 of this title.

§1344. Allocation of assets

(a) Order of priority of participants and beneficiaries

In the case of the termination of a single-employer plan, the plan administrator shall allocate the assets of the plan (available to provide benefits) among the participants and beneficiaries of the plan in the following order:

(1) First, to that portion of each individual's accrued benefit which is derived from the par-

ticipant's contributions to the plan which were not mandatory contributions.

(2) Second, to that portion of each individual's accrued benefit which is derived from the participant's mandatory contributions.

(3) Third, in the case of benefits payable as an annuity—

(A) in the case of the benefit of a participant or beneficiary which was in pay status as of the beginning of the 3-year period ending on the termination date of the plan, to each such benefit, based on the provisions of the plan (as in effect during the 5-year period ending on such date) under which such benefit would be the least,

(B) in the case of a participant's or beneficiary's benefit (other than a benefit described in subparagraph (A)) which would have been in pay status as of the beginning of such 3-year period if the participant had retired prior to the beginning of the 3-year period and if his benefits had commenced (in the normal form of annuity under the plan) as of the beginning of such period, to each such benefit based on the provisions of the plan (as in effect during the 5-year period ending on such date) under which such benefit would be the least.

For purposes of subparagraph (A), the lowest benefit in pay status during a 3-year period shall be considered the benefit in pay status for such period.

(4) Fourth—

(A) to all other benefits (if any) of individuals under the plan guaranteed under this subchapter (determined without regard to section 1322b(a) of this title), and

(B) to the additional benefits (if any) which would be determined under subparagraph (A) if section 1322(b)(5)(B) of this title did not apply.

For purposes of this paragraph, section 1321 of this title shall be applied without regard to subsection (c) thereof.

(5) Fifth, to all other nonforfeitable benefits under the plan.

(6) Sixth, to all other benefits under the plan.

(b) Adjustment of allocations; reallocations; mandatory contributions; establishment of subclasses and categories

For purposes of subsection (a) of this section—

(1) The amount allocated under any paragraph of subsection (a) of this section with respect to any benefit shall be properly adjusted for any allocation of assets with respect to that benefit under a prior paragraph of subsection (a) of this section.

(2) If the assets available for allocation under any paragraph of subsection (a) of this section (other than paragraphs (4), (5), and (6)) are insufficient to satisfy in full the benefits of all individuals which are described in that paragraph, the assets shall be allocated pro rata among such individuals on the basis of the present value (as of the termination date) of their respective benefits described in that paragraph.

(3) If assets available for allocation under paragraph (4) of subsection (a) are insufficient to satisfy in full the benefits of all individuals who are described in that paragraph, the assets shall be allocated first to benefits described in subparagraph (A) of that paragraph. Any remaining assets shall then be allocated to benefits described in subparagraph (B) of that paragraph. If assets allocated to such subparagraph (B) are insufficient to satisfy in full the benefits described in that subparagraph, the assets shall be allocated pro rata among individuals on the basis of the present value (as of the termination date) of their respective benefits described in that subparagraph.

(4) This paragraph applies if the assets available for allocation under paragraph (5) of subsection (a) of this section are not sufficient to satisfy in full the benefits of individuals described in that paragraph.

(A) If this paragraph applies, except as provided in subparagraph (B), the assets shall be allocated to the benefits of individuals described in such paragraph (5) on the basis of the benefits of individuals which would have been described in such paragraph (5) under the plan as in effect at the beginning of the 5-year period ending on the date of plan termination.

(B) If the assets available for allocation under subparagraph (A) are sufficient to satisfy in full the benefits described in such subparagraph (without regard to this subparagraph), then for purposes of subparagraph (A), benefits of individuals described in such subparagraph shall be determined on the basis of the plan as amended by the most recent plan amendment effective during such 5-year period under which the assets available for allocation are sufficient to satisfy in full the benefits of individuals described in subparagraph (A) and any assets remaining to be allocated under such subparagraph shall be allocated under subparagraph (A) on the basis of the plan as amended by the next succeeding plan amendment effective during such period.

(5) If the Secretary of the Treasury determines that the allocation made pursuant to this section (without regard to this paragraph) results in discrimination prohibited by section 401(a)(4) of title 26 then, if required to prevent the disqualification of the plan (or any trust under the plan) under section 401(a) or 403(a) of title 26, the assets allocated under subsections (a)(4)(B), (a)(5), and (a)(6) of this section shall be reallocated to the extent necessary to avoid such discrimination.

(6) The term "mandatory contributions" means amounts contributed to the plan by a participant which are required as a condition of employment, as a condition of participation in such plan, or as a condition of obtaining benefits under the plan attributable to employer contributions. For this purpose, the total amount of mandatory contributions of a participant is the amount of such contributions reduced (but not below zero) by the sum of the amounts paid or distributed to him under the plan before its termination.

(7) A plan may establish subclasses and categories within the classes described in paragraphs (1) through (6) of subsection (a) of this

section in accordance with regulations prescribed by the corporation.

(c) Increase or decrease in value of assets

Any increase or decrease in the value of the assets of a single-employer plan occurring during the period beginning on the later of (1) the date a trustee is appointed under section 1342(b) of this title or (2) the date on which the plan is terminated is to be allocated between the plan and the corporation in the manner determined by the court (in the case of a court-appointed trustee) or as agreed upon by the corporation and the plan administrator in any other case. Any increase or decrease in the value of the assets of a single-employer plan occurring after the date on which the plan is terminated shall be credited to, or suffered by, the corporation.

(d) Distribution of residual assets; restrictions on reversions pursuant to recently amended plans; assets attributable to employee contributions; calculation of remaining assets

(1) Subject to paragraph (3), any residual assets of a single-employer plan may be distributed to the employer if—

(A) all liabilities of the plan to participants and their beneficiaries have been satisfied,

(B) the distribution does not contravene any provision of law, and

(C) the plan provides for such a distribution in these circumstances.

(2)(A) In determining the extent to which a plan provides for the distribution of plan assets to the employer for purposes of paragraph (1)(C), any such provision, and any amendment increasing the amount which may be distributed to the employer, shall not be treated as effective before the end of the fifth calendar year following the date of the adoption of such provision or amendment.

(B) A distribution to the employer from a plan shall not be treated as failing to satisfy the requirements of this paragraph if the plan has been in effect for fewer than 5 years and the plan has provided for such a distribution since the effective date of the plan.

(C) Except as otherwise provided in regulations of the Secretary of the Treasury, in any case in which a transaction described in section 1058 of this title occurs, subparagraph (A) shall continue to apply separately with respect to the amount of any assets transferred in such transaction.

(D) For purposes of this subsection, the term "employer" includes any member of the controlled group of which the employer is a member. For purposes of the preceding sentence, the term "controlled group" means any group treated as a single employer under subsection (b), (c), (m) or (*o*) of section 414 of title 26.

(3)(A) Before any distribution from a plan pursuant to paragraph (1), if any assets of the plan attributable to employee contributions remain after satisfaction of all liabilities described in subsection (a) of this section, such remaining assets shall be equitably distributed to the participants who made such contributions or their beneficiaries (including alternate payees, within the meaning of section 1056(d)(3)(K) of this title).

(B) For purposes of subparagraph (A), the portion of the remaining assets which are attributable to employee contributions shall be an amount equal to the product derived by multiplying—

(i) the market value of the total remaining assets, by

(ii) a fraction—

(I) the numerator of which is the present value of all portions of the accrued benefits with respect to participants which are derived from participants' mandatory contributions (referred to in subsection (a)(2) of this section), and

(II) the denominator of which is the present value of all benefits with respect to which assets are allocated under paragraphs (2) through (6) of subsection (a) of this section.

(C) For purposes of this paragraph, each person who is, as of the termination date—

(i) a participant under the plan, or

(ii) an individual who has received, during the 3-year period ending with the termination date, a distribution from the plan of such individual's entire nonforfeitable benefit in the form of a single sum distribution in accordance with section 1053(e) of this title or in the form of irrevocable commitments purchased by the plan from an insurer to provide such nonforfeitable benefit,

shall be treated as a participant with respect to the termination, if all or part of the nonforfeitable benefit with respect to such person is or was attributable to participants' mandatory contributions (referred to in subsection (a)(2) of this section).

(4) Nothing in this subsection shall be construed to limit the requirements of section 4980(d) of title 26 (as in effect immediately after the enactment of the Omnibus Budget Reconciliation Act of 1990) or section 1104(d) of this title with respect to any distribution of residual assets of a single-employer plan to the employer.

(e) Bankruptcy filing substituted for termination date

If a contributing sponsor of a plan has filed or has had filed against such person a petition seeking liquidation or reorganization in a case under title 11 or under any similar Federal law or law of a State or political subdivision, and the case has not been dismissed as of the termination date of the plan, then subsection (a)(3) shall be applied by treating the date such petition was filed as the termination date of the plan.

(f) Valuation of section 1362(c) liability for determining amounts payable by corporation to participants and beneficiaries

(1) In general

In the case of a terminated plan, the value of the recovery of liability under section 1362(c) of this title allocable as a plan asset under this section for purposes of determining the amount of benefits payable by the corporation shall be determined by multiplying—

(A) the amount of liability under section 1362(c) of this title as of the termination date of the plan, by

(B) the applicable section 1362(c) recovery ratio.

(2) Section 1362(c) recovery ratio

For purposes of this subsection—

(A) In general

Except as provided in subparagraph (C), the term "section 1362(c) recovery ratio" means the ratio which—

(i) the sum of the values of all recoveries under section 1362(c) of this title determined by the corporation in connection with plan terminations described under subparagraph (B), bears to

(ii) the sum of all the amounts of liability under section 1362(c) of this title with respect to such plans as of the termination date in connection with any such prior termination.

(B) Prior terminations

A plan termination described in this subparagraph is a termination with respect to which—

(i) the value of recoveries under section 1362(c) of this title have been determined by the corporation, and

(ii) notices of intent to terminate were provided (or in the case of a termination by the corporation, a notice of determination under section 1342 of this title was issued) during the 5-Federal fiscal year period ending with the third fiscal year preceding the fiscal year in which occurs the date of the notice of intent to terminate (or the notice of determination under section 1342 of this title) with respect to the plan termination for which the recovery ratio is being determined.

(C) Exception

In the case of a terminated plan with respect to which the outstanding amount of benefit liabilities exceeds $20,000,000, the term "section 1362(c) recovery ratio" means, with respect to the termination of such plan, the ratio of—

(i) the value of the recoveries on behalf of the plan under section 1362(c) of this title, to

(ii) the amount of the liability owed under section 1362(c) of this title as of the date of plan termination to the trustee appointed under section 1342(b) or (c) of this title.

(3) Subsection not to apply

This subsection shall not apply with respect to the determination of—

(A) whether the amount of outstanding benefit liabilities exceeds $20,000,000, or

(B) the amount of any liability under section 1362 of this title to the corporation or the trustee appointed under section 1342(b) or (c) of this title.

(4) Determinations

Determinations under this subsection shall be made by the corporation. Such determinations shall be binding unless shown by clear and convincing evidence to be unreasonable.

(Pub. L. 93–406, title IV, § 4044, Sept. 2, 1974, 88 Stat. 1025; Pub. L. 96–364, title IV, § 402(a)(7), Sept. 26, 1980, 94 Stat. 1299; Pub. L. 99–272, title XI, § 11016(c)(12), (13), Apr. 7, 1986, 100 Stat. 274; Pub. L. 100–203, title IX, § 9311(a)(1), (b), (c), Dec. 22, 1987, 101 Stat. 1330–359, 1330–360; Pub. L. 101–239, title VII, §§ 7881(e)(3), 7891(a)(1), 7894(g)(2), Dec. 19, 1989, 103 Stat. 2440, 2445, 2451; Pub. L. 101–508, title XII, § 12002(b)(2)(B), Nov. 5, 1990, 104 Stat. 1388–566; Pub. L. 109–280, title IV, §§ 404(b), 407(b), 408(b)(2), Aug. 17, 2006, 120 Stat. 928, 930, 931; Pub. L. 110–458, title I, § 104(c), Dec. 23, 2008, 122 Stat. 5104.)

REFERENCES IN TEXT

The enactment of the Omnibus Budget Reconciliation Act of 1990, referred to in subsec. (d)(4), is the enactment of Pub. L. 101–508, which was approved Nov. 5, 1990.

AMENDMENTS

2008—Subsecs. (e), (f). Pub. L. 110–458 redesignated subsec. (e) relating to valuation of section 1362(c) liability for determining amounts payable by corporation to participants and beneficiaries as (f).

2006—Subsec. (a)(4)(B). Pub. L. 109–280, § 407(b)(1), substituted "1322(b)(5)(B)" for "1322(b)(5)".

Subsec. (b)(2). Pub. L. 109–280, § 407(b)(2)(A), substituted "(4), (5)," for "(5)".

Subsec. (b)(3) to (7). Pub. L. 109–280, § 407(b)(2)(B), added par. (3) and redesignated former pars. (3) to (6) as (4) to (7), respectively.

Subsec. (e). Pub. L. 109–280, § 408(b)(2), added subsec. (e) relating to valuation of section 1362(c) liability for determining amounts payable by corporation to participants and beneficiaries.

Pub. L. 109–280, § 404(b), added subsec. (e) relating to substitution of bankruptcy filing date for termination date.

1990—Subsec. (d)(4). Pub. L. 101–508 added par. (4).

1989—Subsec. (a)(1). Pub. L. 101–239, § 7894(g)(2), substituted "accrued" for "accured".

Subsec. (b)(4). Pub. L. 101–239, § 7891(a)(1), substituted "Internal Revenue Code of 1986" for "Internal Revenue Code of 1954", which for purposes of codification was translated as "title 26" thus requiring no change in text.

Subsec. (d)(3). Pub. L. 101–239, § 7881(e)(3), made technical correction to directory language of Pub. L. 100–203, § 9311(b)(2), see 1987 Amendment note below.

1987—Subsec. (b)(4). Pub. L. 100–203, § 9311(c), struck out reference to section 405(a) of title 26.

Subsec. (d)(1). Pub. L. 100–203, § 9311(b)(1), substituted "Subject to paragraph (3), any" for "Any".

Subsec. (d)(2). Pub. L. 100–203, § 9311(a)(1)(B), added par. (2). Former par. (2) redesignated (3).

Subsec. (d)(3). Pub. L. 100–203, § 9311(b)(2), as amended by Pub. L. 101–239, § 7881(e)(3), added par. (3), and struck out former par. (3) which read as follows: "Notwithstanding the provisions of paragraph (1), if any assets of the plan attributable to employee contributions, remain after all liabilities of the plan to participants and their beneficiaries have been satisfied, such assets shall be equitably distributed to the employees who made such contributions (or their beneficiaries) in accordance with their rate of contributions."

Pub. L. 100–203, § 9311(a)(1)(A), redesignated former par. (2) as (3).

1986—Subsec. (a). Pub. L. 99–272, § 11016(c)(12), in provision preceding par. (1) struck out "defined benefit" after "single-employer".

Subsec. (a)(4)(A). Pub. L. 99–272, § 11016(c)(13)(A), substituted "section 1322b(a)" for "section 1322(b)(5)".

Subsec. (a)(4)(B). Pub. L. 99–272, § 11016(c)(13)(B), substituted "section 1322(b)(5)" for "section 1322(b)(6)".

1980—Subsec. (a). Pub. L. 96–364, § 402(a)(7)(A), inserted "single-employer" before "defined benefit".

Subsec. (c). Pub. L. 96–364, § 402(a)(7)(B), inserted "single-employer" before "plan occurring" wherever appearing.

Subsec. (d)(1). Pub. L. 96–364, § 402(a)(7)(C), inserted "single-employer" after "assets of a".

EFFECTIVE DATE OF 2008 AMENDMENT

Amendment by Pub. L. 110–458 effective as if included in the provisions of Pub. L. 109–280 to which the amendment relates, except as otherwise provided, see section 112 of Pub. L. 110–458, set out as a note under section 72 of Title 26, Internal Revenue Code.

EFFECTIVE DATE OF 2006 AMENDMENT

Amendment by section 404(b) of Pub. L. 109–280 applicable with respect to proceedings initiated under Title 11, Bankruptcy, or under any similar Federal law or law of a State or political subdivision, on or after the date that is 30 days after Aug. 17, 2006, see section 404(c) of Pub. L. 109–280, set out as a note under section 1322 of this title.

Amendment by section 407(b) of Pub. L. 109–280 applicable to plan terminations under section 1341(c) of this title with respect to which notices of intent to terminate are provided under section 1341(a)(2) of this title after Dec. 31, 2005, and under section 1342 of this title with respect to which notices of determination are provided under such section after such date, see section 407(d)(1) of Pub. L. 109–280, set out as a note under section 1321 of this title.

Amendment by section 408(b)(2) of Pub. L. 109–280 applicable for any termination for which notices of intent to terminate are provided, or in the case of a termination by the corporation, a notice of determination under section 1342 of this title is issued, on or after the date which is 30 days after Aug. 17, 2006, see section 408(c) of Pub. L. 109–280, set out as a note under section 1322 of this title.

EFFECTIVE DATE OF 1990 AMENDMENT

Amendment by Pub. L. 101–508 applicable to reversions occurring after Sept. 30, 1990, but not applicable to any reversion after Sept. 30, 1990, if (1) in the case of plans subject to subchapter III of this chapter, notice of intent to terminate under such subchapter was provided to participants (or if no participants, to Pension Benefit Guaranty Corporation) before Oct. 1, 1990, (2) in the case of plans subject to subchapter I of this chapter (and not subchapter III), notice of intent to reduce future accruals under section 1054(h) of this title was provided to participants in connection with termination before Oct. 1, 1990, (3) in the case of plans not subject to subchapter I or III of this chapter, a request for a determination letter with respect to termination was filed with Secretary of the Treasury or Secretary's delegate before Oct. 1, 1990, or (4) in the case of plans not subject to subchapter I or III of this chapter and having only one participant, a resolution terminating the plan was adopted by employer before Oct. 1, 1990, see section 12003 of Pub. L. 101–508, set out as a note under section 4980 of Title 26, Internal Revenue Code.

EFFECTIVE DATE OF 1989 AMENDMENT

Amendment by section 7881(e)(3) of Pub. L. 101–239 effective, except as otherwise provided, as if included in the provision of the Pension Protection Act, Pub. L. 100–203, §§9302–9346, to which such amendment relates, see section 7882 of Pub. L. 101–239, set out as a note under section 401 of Title 26, Internal Revenue Code.

Amendment by section 7891(a)(1) of Pub. L. 101–239 effective, except as otherwise provided, as if included in the provision of the Tax Reform Act of 1986, Pub. L. 99–514, to which such amendment relates, see section 7891(f) of Pub. L. 101–239, set out as a note under section 1002 of this title.

Amendment by section 7894(g)(2) of Pub. L. 101–239 effective, except as otherwise provided, as if originally included in the provision of the Employee Retirement Income Security Act of 1974, Pub. L. 93–406, to which such amendment relates, see section 7894(i) of Pub. L. 101–239, set out as a note under section 1002 of this title.

EFFECTIVE DATE OF 1987 AMENDMENT

Section 9311(d) of Pub. L. 100–203, as amended by Pub. L. 101–239, title VII, §7881(e)(2), Dec. 19, 1989, 103 Stat. 2439, provided that: "The amendments made by this section [amending this section] shall apply with respect to—

"(1) plan terminations under section 4041 of ERISA [29 U.S.C. 1341] with respect to which notices of intent to terminate are provided under section 4041(a)(2) of ERISA after December 17, 1987, and

"(2) plan terminations with respect to which proceedings are instituted by the Pension Benefit Guaranty Corporation under section 4042 of ERISA [29 U.S.C. 1342] after December 17, 1987.

Except as provided in subsection (a)(2) [set out below], the amendments made by subsection (a) [amending this section] shall apply to any provision of the plan or plan amendment adopted after December 17, 1987."

EFFECTIVE DATE OF 1986 AMENDMENT

Amendment by Pub. L. 99–272 effective Jan. 1, 1986, with certain exceptions, see section 11019 of Pub. L. 99–272, set out as a note under section 1341 of this title.

EFFECTIVE DATE OF 1980 AMENDMENT

Amendment by Pub. L. 96–364 effective Sept. 26, 1980, except as specifically provided, see section 1461(e) of this title.

TRANSITIONAL RULE RELATING TO RESTRICTIONS ON EMPLOYER REVERSIONS UPON PLAN TERMINATION PURSUANT TO RECENTLY AMENDED PLANS

Section 9311(a)(2) of Pub. L. 100–203, as amended by Pub. L. 101–239, title VII, §7881(e)(1), (4), Dec. 19, 1989, 103 Stat. 2439, 2440, provided that: "The amendments made by paragraph (1) [amending this section] shall apply, in the case of plans which, as of December 17, 1987, have no provision relating to the distribution of residual plan assets upon termination, only with respect to plan amendments providing for the distribution of plan assets to the employer which are adopted after December 17, 1988."

SPECIAL TEMPORARY RULE FOR TERMINATION OF SINGLE-EMPLOYER PLAN

For special temporary rule relating to requirements to be met before the final distribution of assets in the case of the termination of certain single-employer plans with respect to which the amount payable to the employer pursuant to subsec. (d) of this section exceeds $1,000,000, see section 11008(d) of Pub. L. 99–272, set out as a note under section 1341 of this title.

§1345. Recapture of payments

(a) Authorization to recover benefits

Except as provided in subsection (c) of this section, the trustee is authorized to recover for the benefit of a plan from a participant the recoverable amount (as defined in subsection (b) of this section) of all payments from the plan to him which commenced within the 3-year period immediately preceding the time the plan is terminated.

(b) Recoverable amount

For purposes of subsection (a) of this section the recoverable amount is the excess of the amount determined under paragraph (1) over the amount determined under paragraph (2).

(1) The amount determined under this paragraph is the sum of the amount of the actual payments received by the participant within the 3-year period.

(2) The amount determined under this paragraph is the sum of—

(A) the sum of the amount such participant would have received during each consecutive 12-month period within the 3 years if the participant received the benefit in the form described in paragraph (3),

(B) the sum for each of the consecutive 12-month periods of the lesser of—

(i) the excess, if any, of $10,000 over the benefit in the form described in paragraph (3), or

(ii) the excess of the actual payment, if any, over the benefit in the form described in paragraph (3), and

(C) the present value at the time of termination of the participant's future benefits guaranteed under this subchapter as if the benefits commenced in the form described in paragraph (3).

(3) The form of benefit for purposes of this subsection shall be the monthly benefit the participant would have received during the consecutive 12-month period, if he had elected at the time of the first payment made during the 3-year period, to receive his interest in the plan as a monthly benefit in the form of a life annuity commencing at the time of such first payment.

(c) Payments made on or after death or disability of participant; waiver of recovery in case of hardship

(1) In the event of a distribution described in section 1343(b)(7)[1] of this title the 3-year period referred to in subsection (b) of this section shall not end sooner than the date on which the corporation is notified of the distribution.

(2) The trustee shall not recover any payment made from a plan after or on account of the death of a participant, or to a participant who is disabled (within the meaning of section 72(m)(7) of title 26).

(3) The corporation is authorized to waive, in whole or in part, the recovery of any amount which the trustee is authorized to recover for the benefit of a plan under this section in any case in which it determines that substantial economic hardship would result to the participant or his beneficiaries from whom such amount is recoverable.

(Pub. L. 93–406, title IV, § 4045, Sept. 2, 1974, 88 Stat. 1027; Pub. L. 101–239, title VII, § 7891(a)(1), Dec. 19, 1989, 103 Stat. 2445.)

REFERENCES IN TEXT

Section 1343(b)(7) of this title, referred to in subsec. (c)(1), was redesignated section 1343(c)(7) of this title by Pub. L. 103–465, title VII, § 771(b), Dec. 8, 1994, 108 Stat. 5042.

AMENDMENTS

1989—Subsec. (c)(2). Pub. L. 101–239 substituted "Internal Revenue Code of 1986" for "Internal Revenue Code of 1954", which for purposes of codification was translated as "title 26" thus requiring no change in text.

EFFECTIVE DATE OF 1989 AMENDMENT

Amendment by Pub. L. 101–239 effective, except as otherwise provided, as if included in the provision of the Tax Reform Act of 1986, Pub. L. 99–514, to which such amendment relates, see section 7891(f) of Pub. L. 101–239, set out as a note under section 1002 of this title.

[1] See References in Text note below.

§ 1346. Reports to trustee

The corporation and the plan administrator of any plan to be terminated under this subtitle shall furnish to the trustee such information as the corporation or the plan administrator has and, to the extent practicable, can obtain regarding—

(1) the amount of benefits payable with respect to each participant under a plan to be terminated,

(2) the amount of basic benefits guaranteed under section 1322 or 1322a of this title which are payable with respect to each participant in the plan,

(3) the present value, as of the time of termination, of the aggregate amount of basic benefits payable under section 1322 or 1322a of this title (determined without regard to section 1322b of this title),

(4) the fair market value of the assets of the plan at the time of termination,

(5) the computations under section 1344 of this title, and all actuarial assumptions under which the items described in paragraphs (1) through (4) were computed, and

(6) any other information with respect to the plan the trustee may require in order to terminate the plan.

(Pub. L. 93–406, title IV, § 4046, Sept. 2, 1974, 88 Stat. 1028; Pub. L. 96–364, title IV, § 403(e), Sept. 26, 1980, 94 Stat. 1301.)

AMENDMENTS

1980—Par. (2). Pub. L. 96–364, § 403(e)(1), inserted "basic" before "benefits" and "or 1322a" after "1322".

Par. (3). Pub. L. 96–364, § 403(e), inserted "basic" before "benefits" and "or 1322a" after "1322", and substituted "1322b" for "1322(b)(5)".

EFFECTIVE DATE OF 1980 AMENDMENT

Amendment by Pub. L. 96–364 effective Sept. 26, 1980, except as specifically provided, see section 1461(e) of this title.

§ 1347. Restoration of plans

Whenever the corporation determines that a plan which is to be terminated under section 1341 or 1342 of this title, or which is in the process of being terminated under section 1341 or 1342 of this title, should not be terminated under section 1341 or 1342 of this title as a result of such circumstances as the corporation determines to be relevant, the corporation is authorized to cease any activities undertaken to terminate the plan, and to take whatever action is necessary and within its power to restore the plan to its status prior to the determination that the plan was to be terminated under section 1341 or 1342 of this title. In the case of a plan which has been terminated under section 1341 or 1342 of this title the corporation is authorized in any such case in which the corporation determines such action to be appropriate and consistent with its duties under this subchapter, to take such action as may be necessary to restore the plan to its pretermination status, including, but not limited to, the transfer to the employer or a plan administrator of control of part or all of the remaining assets and liabilities of the plan.

(Pub. L. 93–406, title IV, § 4047, Sept. 2, 1974, 88 Stat. 1028; Pub. L. 99–272, title XI, § 11016(a)(3),

Apr. 7, 1986, 100 Stat. 268; Pub. L. 101–239, title VII, §7893(g)(1), Dec. 19, 1989, 103 Stat. 2447.)

AMENDMENTS

1989—Pub. L. 101–239 struck out "under this subtitle" before "should not be terminated".

1986—Pub. L. 99–272 inserted "under section 1341 or 1342 of this title" after "terminated" in four places and substituted "section 1341 or 1342 of this title the corporation" for "section 1342 of this title the corporation".

EFFECTIVE DATE OF 1989 AMENDMENT

Amendment by Pub. L. 101–239 effective as if included in the provision of the Single-Employer Pension Plan Amendments Act of 1986, Pub. L. 99–272, title XI, to which such amendment relates, see section 7893(h) of Pub. L. 101–239, set out as a note under section 1002 of this title.

EFFECTIVE DATE OF 1986 AMENDMENT

Amendment by Pub. L. 99–272 effective Jan. 1, 1986, with certain exceptions, see section 11019 of Pub. L. 99–272, set out as a note under section 1341 of this title.

§1348. Termination date

(a) For purposes of this subchapter the termination date of a single-employer plan is—

(1) in the case of a plan terminated in a standard termination in accordance with the provisions of section 1341(b) of this title, the termination date proposed in the notice provided under section 1341(a)(2) of this title,

(2) in the case of a plan terminated in a distress termination in accordance with the provisions of section 1341(c) of this title, the date established by the plan administrator and agreed to by the corporation,

(3) in the case of a plan terminated in accordance with the provisions of section 1342 of this title, the date established by the corporation and agreed to by the plan administrator, or

(4) in the case of a plan terminated under section 1341(c) or 1342 of this title in any case in which no agreement is reached between the plan administrator and the corporation (or the trustee), the date established by the court.

(b) For purposes of this subchapter, the date of termination of a multiemployer plan is—

(1) in the case of a plan terminated in accordance with the provisions of section 1341a of this title, the date determined under subsection (b) of that section; or

(2) in the case of a plan terminated in accordance with the provisions of section 1342 of this title, the date agreed to between the plan administrator and the corporation (or the trustee appointed under section 1342(b)(2) of this title, if any), or, if no agreement is reached, the date established by the court.

(Pub. L. 93–406, title IV, §4048, Sept. 2, 1974, 88 Stat. 1028; Pub. L. 96–364, title IV, §402(a)(8), Sept. 26, 1980, 94 Stat. 1299; Pub. L. 99–272, title XI, §11016(a)(4), Apr. 7, 1986, 100 Stat. 268.)

AMENDMENTS

1986—Subsec. (a). Pub. L. 99–272 in provisions preceding par. (1) substituted "termination date" for "date of termination", redesignated pars. (1) to (3) as (2) to (4), respectively, added par. (1), in par. (2), as so redesignated, inserted "in a distress termination" after "terminated" and substituted "section 1341(c)" for "section 1341", and in par. (4), as so redesignated, substituted "under section 1341(c) or 1342 of this title" for "in accordance with the provisions of either section".

1980—Subsec. (a). Pub. L. 96–364, §402(a)(8)(A), (B), designated existing provisions as subsec. (a), and inserted applicability to a single-employer plan.

Subsec. (b). Pub. L. 96–364, §402(a)(8)(C), added subsec. (b).

EFFECTIVE DATE OF 1986 AMENDMENT

Amendment by Pub. L. 99–272 effective Jan. 1, 1986, with certain exceptions, see section 11019 of Pub. L. 99–272, set out as a note under section 1341 of this title.

EFFECTIVE DATE OF 1980 AMENDMENT

Amendment by Pub. L. 96–364 effective Sept. 26, 1980, except as specifically provided, see section 1461(e) of this title.

§1349. Repealed. Pub. L. 100–203, title IX, §9312(a), Dec. 22, 1987, 101 Stat. 1330–361

Section, Pub. L. 93–406, title IV, §4049, as added Pub. L. 99–272, title XI, §11012(a), Apr. 7, 1986, 100 Stat. 258; amended Pub. L. 99–514, title XVIII, §1879(u)(2), Oct. 22, 1986, 100 Stat. 2913; Pub. L. 100–203, title IX, §9312(d)(2), Dec. 22, 1987, 101 Stat. 1330–364, related to distribution of liability payments to participants and beneficiaries.

EFFECTIVE DATE OF REPEAL

Repeal applicable with respect to plan terminations under section 1341 of this title with respect to which notices of intent to terminate are provided under section 1341(a)(2) of this title after Dec. 17, 1987, and plan terminations with respect to which proceedings are instituted by the Pension Benefit Guaranty Corporation under section 1342 of this title after that date, see section 9312(d)(1) of Pub. L. 100–203, as amended, set out as an Effective Date of 1987 Amendment note under section 1301 of this title.

§1350. Missing participants

(a) General rule

(1) Payment to the corporation

A plan administrator satisfies section 1341(b)(3)(A) of this title in the case of a missing participant only if the plan administrator—

(A) transfers the participant's designated benefit to the corporation or purchases an irrevocable commitment from an insurer in accordance with clause (i) of section 1341(b)(3)(A) of this title, and

(B) provides the corporation such information and certifications with respect to such designated benefits or irrevocable commitments as the corporation shall specify.

(2) Treatment of transferred assets

A transfer to the corporation under this section shall be treated as a transfer of assets from a terminated plan to the corporation as trustee, and shall be held with assets of terminated plans for which the corporation is trustee under section 1342 of this title, subject to the rules set forth in that section.

(3) Payment by the corporation

After a missing participant whose designated benefit was transferred to the corporation is located—

(A) in any case in which the plan could have distributed the benefit of the missing participant in a single sum without participant or spousal consent under section 1055(g) of this title, the corporation shall pay the participant or beneficiary a single sum benefit equal to the designated benefit paid the corporation plus interest as specified by the corporation, and

(B) in any other case, the corporation shall pay a benefit based on the designated benefit and the assumptions prescribed by the corporation at the time that the corporation received the designated benefit.

The corporation shall make payments under subparagraph (B) available in the same forms and at the same times as a guaranteed benefit under section 1322 of this title would be available to be paid, except that the corporation may make a benefit available in the form of a single sum if the plan provided a single sum benefit (other than a single sum described in subsection (b)(2)(A) of this section).

(b) Definitions

For purposes of this section—

(1) Missing participant

The term "missing participant" means a participant or beneficiary under a terminating plan whom the plan administrator cannot locate after a diligent search.

(2) Designated benefit

The term "designated benefit" means the single sum benefit the participant would receive—

(A) under the plan's assumptions, in the case of a distribution that can be made without participant or spousal consent under section 1055(g) of this title;

(B) under the assumptions of the corporation in effect on the date that the designated benefit is transferred to the corporation, in the case of a plan that does not pay any single sums other than those described in subparagraph (A); or

(C) under the assumptions of the corporation or of the plan, whichever provides the higher single sum, in the case of a plan that pays a single sum other than those described in subparagraph (A).

(c) Multiemployer plans

The corporation shall prescribe rules similar to the rules in subsection (a) for multiemployer plans covered by this subchapter that terminate under section 1341a of this title.

(d) Plans not otherwise subject to subchapter

(1) Transfer to corporation

The plan administrator of a plan described in paragraph (4) may elect to transfer a missing participant's benefits to the corporation upon termination of the plan.

(2) Information to the corporation

To the extent provided in regulations, the plan administrator of a plan described in paragraph (4) shall, upon termination of the plan, provide the corporation information with respect to benefits of a missing participant if the plan transfers such benefits—

(A) to the corporation, or

(B) to an entity other than the corporation or a plan described in paragraph (4)(B)(ii).

(3) Payment by the corporation

If benefits of a missing participant were transferred to the corporation under paragraph (1), the corporation shall, upon location of the participant or beneficiary, pay to the participant or beneficiary the amount transferred (or the appropriate survivor benefit) either—

(A) in a single sum (plus interest), or

(B) in such other form as is specified in regulations of the corporation.

(4) Plans described

A plan is described in this paragraph if—

(A) the plan is a pension plan (within the meaning of section 1002(2) of this title)—

(i) to which the provisions of this section do not apply (without regard to this subsection),

(ii) which is not a plan described in paragraph (2), (3), (4), (6), (7), (8), (9), (10), or (11) of section 1321(b) of this title, and

(iii) which,[1] was a plan described in section 401(a) of title 26 which includes a trust exempt from tax under section 501(a) of such title, and

(B) at the time the assets are to be distributed upon termination, the plan—

(i) has missing participants, and

(ii) has not provided for the transfer of assets to pay the benefits of all missing participants to another pension plan (within the meaning of section 1002(2) of this title).

(5) Certain provisions not to apply

Subsections (a)(1) and (a)(3) shall not apply to a plan described in paragraph (4).

(e) Regulatory authority

The corporation shall prescribe such regulations as are necessary to carry out the purposes of this section, including rules relating to what will be considered a diligent search, the amount payable to the corporation, and the amount to be paid by the corporation.

(Pub. L. 93–406, title IV, § 4050, as added Pub. L. 103–465, title VII, § 776(a), Dec. 8, 1994, 108 Stat. 5047; amended Pub. L. 109–280, title IV, § 410(a), Aug. 17, 2006, 120 Stat. 934; Pub. L. 110–458, title I, § 104(e), Dec. 23, 2008, 122 Stat. 5104.)

AMENDMENTS

2008—Subsec. (d)(4)(A)(ii), (iii). Pub. L. 110–458 added cls. (ii) and (iii) and struck out former cl. (ii) which read as follows: "which is not a plan described in paragraphs (2) through (11) of section 1321(b) of this title, and".

2006—Subsecs. (c) to (e). Pub. L. 109–280 added subsecs. (c) and (d) and redesignated former subsec. (c) as (e).

EFFECTIVE DATE OF 2008 AMENDMENT

Amendment by Pub. L. 110–458 effective as if included in the provisions of Pub. L. 109–280 to which the amendment relates, except as otherwise provided, see section 112 of Pub. L. 110–458, set out as a note under section 72 of Title 26, Internal Revenue Code.

EFFECTIVE DATE OF 2006 AMENDMENT

Amendment by Pub. L. 109–280 applicable to distributions made after final regulations implementing sub-

[1] So in original. The comma probably should not appear.

sections (c) and (d) of this section are prescribed, see section 410(c) of Pub. L. 109–280, set out as a note under section 1056 of this title.

EFFECTIVE DATE

Section effective with respect to distributions that occur in plan years commencing on or after Jan. 1, 1996, see section 776(e) of Pub. L. 103–465, set out as an Effective Date of 1994 Amendment note under section 1056 of this title.

SUBTITLE D—LIABILITY

§ 1361. Amounts payable by corporation

The corporation shall pay benefits under a single-employer plan terminated under this subchapter subject to the limitations and requirements of subtitle B of this subchapter. The corporation shall provide financial assistance to pay benefits under a multiemployer plan which is insolvent under section 1426 or 1441(d)(2)(A) of this title, subject to the limitations and requirements of subtitles B, C, and E of this subchapter. Amounts guaranteed by the corporation under sections 1322 and 1322a of this title shall be paid by the corporation only out of the appropriate fund. The corporation shall make payments under the supplemental program to reimburse multiemployer plans for uncollectible withdrawal liability only out of the fund established under section 1305(e) of this title.

(Pub. L. 93–406, title IV, § 4061, Sept. 2, 1974, 88 Stat. 1029; Pub. L. 96–364, title IV, § 403(f), Sept. 26, 1980, 94 Stat. 1301.)

AMENDMENTS

1980—Pub. L. 96–364 substituted provisions relating to payment of benefits under a single-employer plan terminated under this subchapter subject to limitations and requirements of subtitle B of this subchapter for provisions relating to payment of benefits under a plan terminated under this subchapter subject to limitations and requirements of subtitle B of this subchapter.

EFFECTIVE DATE OF 1980 AMENDMENT

Amendment by Pub. L. 96–364 effective Sept. 26, 1980, except as specifically provided, see section 1461(e) of this title.

§ 1362. Liability for termination of single-employer plans under a distress termination or a termination by corporation

(a) In general

In any case in which a single-employer plan is terminated in a distress termination under section 1341(c) of this title or a termination otherwise instituted by the corporation under section 1342 of this title, any person who is, on the termination date, a contributing sponsor of the plan or a member of such a contributing sponsor's controlled group shall incur liability under this section. The liability under this section of all such persons shall be joint and several. The liability under this section consists of—

(1) liability to the corporation, to the extent provided in subsection (b) of this section, and

(2) liability to the trustee appointed under subsection (b) or (c) of section 1342 of this title, to the extent provided in subsection (c) of this section.

(b) Liability to corporation

(1) Amount of liability

(A) In general

Except as provided in subparagraph (B), the liability to the corporation of a person described in subsection (a) of this section shall be the total amount of the unfunded benefit liabilities (as of the termination date) to all participants and beneficiaries under the plan, together with interest (at a reasonable rate) calculated from the termination date in accordance with regulations prescribed by the corporation.

(B) Special rule in case of subsequent insufficiency

For purposes of subparagraph (A), in any case described in section 1341(c)(3)(C)(ii) of this title, actuarial present values shall be determined as of the date of the notice to the corporation (or the finding by the corporation) described in such section.

(2) Payment of liability

(A) In general

Except as provided in subparagraph (B), the liability to the corporation under this subsection shall be due and payable to the corporation as of the termination date, in cash or securities acceptable to the corporation.

(B) Special rule

Payment of so much of the liability under paragraph (1)(A) as exceeds 30 percent of the collective net worth of all persons described in subsection (a) of this section (including interest) shall be made under commercially reasonable terms prescribed by the corporation. The parties involved shall make a reasonable effort to reach agreement on such commercially reasonable terms. Any such terms prescribed by the corporation shall provide for deferral of 50 percent of any amount of liability otherwise payable for any year under this subparagraph if a person subject to such liability demonstrates to the satisfaction of the corporation that no person subject to such liability has any individual pre-tax profits for such person's fiscal year ending during such year.

(3) Alternative arrangements

The corporation and any person liable under this section may agree to alternative arrangements for the satisfaction of liability to the corporation under this subsection.

(c) Liability to section 1342 trustee

A person described in subsection (a) of this section shall be subject to liability under this subsection to the trustee appointed under subsection (b) or (c) of section 1342 of this title. The liability of such person under this subsection shall consist of—

(1) the sum of the shortfall amortization charge (within the meaning of section 1083(c)(1) of this title and 430(d)(1)[1] of title 26) with respect to the plan (if any) for the plan

[1] So in original. Probably should be preceded by "section".

year in which the termination date occurs, plus the aggregate total of shortfall amortization installments (if any) determined for succeeding plan years under section 1083(c)(2) of this title and section 430(d)(2) of title 26 (which, for purposes of this subparagraph, shall include any increase in such sum which would result if all applications for waivers of the minimum funding standard under section 1082(c) of this title and section 412(c) of title 26 which are pending with respect to such plan were denied and if no additional contributions (other than those already made by the termination date) were made for the plan year in which the termination date occurs or for any previous plan year), and

(2) the sum of the waiver amortization charge (within the meaning of section 1083(e)(1) of this title and 430(e)(1)[1] of title 26) with respect to the plan (if any) for the plan year in which the termination date occurs, plus the aggregate total of waiver amortization installments (if any) determined for succeeding plan years under section 1083(e)(2) of this title and section 430(e)(2) of title 26,

together with interest (at a reasonable rate) calculated from the termination date in accordance with regulations prescribed by the corporation. The liability under this subsection shall be due and payable to such trustee as of the termination date, in cash or securities acceptable to such trustee.

(d) Definitions

(1) Collective net worth of persons subject to liability

(A) In general

The collective net worth of persons subject to liability in connection with a plan termination consists of the sum of the individual net worths of all persons who—

(i) have individual net worths which are greater than zero, and

(ii) are (as of the termination date) contributing sponsors of the terminated plan or members of their controlled groups.

(B) Determination of net worth

For purposes of this paragraph, the net worth of a person is—

(i) determined on whatever basis best reflects, in the determination of the corporation, the current status of the person's operations and prospects at the time chosen for determining the net worth of the person, and

(ii) increased by the amount of any transfers of assets made by the person which are determined by the corporation to be improper under the circumstances, including any such transfers which would be inappropriate under title 11 if the person were a debtor in a case under chapter 7 of such title.

(C) Timing of determination

For purposes of this paragraph, determinations of net worth shall be made as of a day chosen by the corporation (during the 120-day period ending with the termination date) and shall be computed without regard to any liability under this section.

(2) Pre-tax profits

The term "pre-tax profits" means—

(A) except as provided in subparagraph (B), for any fiscal year of any person, such person's consolidated net income (excluding any extraordinary charges to income and including any extraordinary credits to income) for such fiscal year, as shown on audited financial statements prepared in accordance with generally accepted accounting principles, or

(B) for any fiscal year of an organization described in section 501(c) of title 26, the excess of income over expenses (as such terms are defined for such organizations under generally accepted accounting principles),

before provision for or deduction of Federal or other income tax, any contribution to any single-employer plan of which such person is a contributing sponsor at any time during the period beginning on the termination date and ending with the end of such fiscal year, and any amounts required to be paid for such fiscal year under this section. The corporation may by regulation require such information to be filed on such forms as may be necessary to determine the existence and amount of such pre-tax profits.

(e) Treatment of substantial cessation of operations

If an employer ceases operations at a facility in any location and, as a result of such cessation of operations, more than 20 percent of the total number of his employees who are participants under a plan established and maintained by him are separated from employment, the employer shall be treated with respect to that plan as if he were a substantial employer under a plan under which more than one employer makes contributions and the provisions of sections 1363, 1364, and 1365 of this title shall apply.

(Pub. L. 93–406, title IV, § 4062, Sept. 2, 1974, 88 Stat. 1029; Pub. L. 95–598, title III, § 321(b), Nov. 6, 1978, 92 Stat. 2678; Pub. L. 96–364, title IV, § 403(g), Sept. 26, 1980, 94 Stat. 1301; Pub. L. 99–272, title XI, § 11011(a), (b), Apr. 7, 1986, 100 Stat. 253, 257; Pub. L. 100–203, title IX, § 9312(b)(1), (2)(A), (B)(ii), Dec. 22, 1987, 101 Stat. 1330–361; Pub. L. 101–239, title VII, §§ 7881(f)(2), (10)(A), (B), 7891(a)(1), Dec. 19, 1989, 103 Stat. 2440, 2441, 2445; Pub. L. 109–280, title I, § 107(b)(4), Aug. 17, 2006, 120 Stat. 819.)

AMENDMENTS

2006—Subsec. (c)(1) to (3). Pub. L. 109–280 added pars. (1) and (2) and struck out former pars. (1) to (3) which read as follows:

"(1) the outstanding balance of the accumulated funding deficiencies (within the meaning of section 1082(a)(2) of this title and section 412(a) of title 26) of the plan (if any) (which, for purposes of this subparagraph, shall include the amount of any increase in such accumulated funding deficiencies of the plan which would result if all pending applications for waivers of the minimum funding standard under section 1083 of this title or section 412(d) of title 26 and for extensions of the amortization period under section 1084 of this title or section 412(e) of title 26 with respect to such plan were denied and if no additional contributions (other than those already made by the termination date) were made for the plan year in which the termination date occurs or for any previous plan year),

"(2) the outstanding balance of the amount of waived funding deficiencies of the plan waived before such date under section 1083 of this title or section 412(d) of title 26 (if any), and

"(3) the outstanding balance of the amount of decreases in the minimum funding standard allowed before such date under section 1084 of this title or section 412(e) of title 26 (if any),".

1989—Subsec. (a). Pub. L. 101–239, § 7881(f)(2), inserted "and" at end of par. (1), redesignated par. (3) as (2), substituted "subsection (c)" for "subsection (d)", and struck out former par. (2) which read as follows: "liability to the trust established pursuant to section 1341(c)(3)(B)(ii) or (iii) of this title or section 1342(i) of this title, to the extent provided in subsection (c) of this section, and".

Subsec. (b)(2)(B). Pub. L. 101–239, § 7881(f)(10)(A), substituted "so much of the liability under paragraph (1)(A) as exceeds 30 percent of the collective net worth of all persons described in subsection (a) of this section (including interest)" for "the liability under paragraph (1)(A)(ii)".

Subsecs. (c)(1), (d)(2)(B). Pub. L. 101–239, § 7891(a)(1), substituted "Internal Revenue Code of 1986" for "Internal Revenue Code of 1954", which for purposes of codification was translated as "title 26" thus requiring no change in text.

Subsec. (d)(3). Pub. L. 101–239, § 7881(f)(10)(B), amended Pub. L. 100–203, § 9312(b)(2)(B)(ii), see 1987 Amendment note below.

1987—Subsec. (b)(1)(A). Pub. L. 100–203, § 9312(b)(2)(A), amended subpar. (A) generally. Prior to amendment, subpar. (A) read as follows: "Except as provided in subparagraph (B), the liability to the corporation of a person described in subsection (a) of this section shall consist of the sum of—

"(i) the lesser of—

"(I) the total amount of unfunded guaranteed benefits (as of the termination date) of all participants and beneficiaries under the plan, or

"(II) 30 percent of the collective net worth of all persons described in subsection (a) of this section, and

"(ii) the excess (if any) of—

"(I) 75 percent of the amount described in clause (i)(I), over

"(II) the amount described in clause (i)(II),

together with interest (at a reasonable rate) calculated from the termination date in accordance with regulations prescribed by the corporation."

Subsec. (c). Pub. L. 100–203, § 9312(b)(1), redesignated subsec. (d) as (c) and struck out former subsec. (c) which related to liability to section 1349 trust.

Subsec. (d). Pub. L. 100–203, § 9312(b)(1)(B), redesignated subsec. (e) as (d). Former subsec. (d) redesignated (c).

Subsec. (d)(3). Pub. L. 100–203, § 9312(b)(2)(B)(ii), as amended by Pub. L. 101–239, § 7881(f)(10)(B), struck out par. (3) which read as follows: "The liability payment years in connection with a terminated plan consist of the consecutive one-year periods following the last plan year preceding the termination date, excluding the first such year in any case in which the first such year ends less than 180 days after the termination date."

Subsecs. (e), (f). Pub. L. 100–203, § 9312(b)(1)(B), redesignated subsec. (f) as (e). Former subsec. (e) redesignated (d).

1986—Pub. L. 99–272, § 11011(a)(2), substituted "Liability for termination of single-employer plans under a distress termination or a termination by the corporation" for "Liability of employer" in section catchline.

Subsec. (a). Pub. L. 99–272, § 11011(a)(2), added subsec. (a) specifying persons liable and the nature and extent of liability and struck out former subsec. (a) specifying employers covered.

Subsec. (b). Pub. L. 99–272, § 11011(a)(2), added subsec. (b) relating to liability to corporation and struck out former subsec. (b) relating to amount of liability.

Subsec. (c). Pub. L. 99–272, § 11011(a)(2), added subsec. (c) relating to liability to section 1349 trust and struck out former subsec. (c) relating to method of determining net worth of employer.

Subsec. (d). Pub. L. 99–272, § 11011(a)(2), added subsec. (d) relating to liability to section 1342 trustee and struck out former subsec. (d) relating to corporate reorganizations.

Subsec. (e). Pub. L. 99–272, § 11011(a), added subsec. (e) and redesignated former subsec. (e) as (f).

Subsec. (f). Pub. L. 99–272, § 11011(a)(1), (b), redesignated former subsec. (e) as (f), and substituted in heading "Treatment of substantial cessation of operations" for "Cessation of operations at one facility".

1980—Subsec. (a). Pub. L. 96–364 substituted "single-employee plan" for "plan (other than a multiemployer plan)".

1978—Subsec. (c)(2). Pub. L. 95–598 substituted "title 11" and "a debtor in a case under chapter 7 of such title" for "the Bankruptcy Act" and "the subject of a proceeding under that Act", respectively.

Effective Date of 2006 Amendment

Amendment by Pub. L. 109–280 applicable to plan years beginning after 2007, see section 107(e) of Pub. L. 109–280, set out as a note under section 1021 of this title.

Effective Date of 1989 Amendment

Amendment by section 7881(f)(2), (10)(A), (B) of Pub. L. 101–239 effective, except as otherwise provided, as if included in the provision of the Pension Protection Act, Pub. L. 100–203, §§ 9302–9346, to which such amendment relates, see section 7882 of Pub. L. 101–239, set out as a note under section 401 of Title 26, Internal Revenue Code.

Amendment by section 7891(a)(1) of Pub. L. 101–239 effective, except as otherwise provided, as if included in the provision of the Tax Reform Act of 1986, Pub. L. 99–514, to which such amendment relates, see section 7891(f) of Pub. L. 101–239, set out as a note under section 1002 of this title.

Effective Date of 1987 Amendment

Amendment by Pub. L. 100–203 applicable with respect to plan terminations under section 1341 of this title with respect to which notices of intent to terminate are provided under section 1341(a)(2) of this title after Dec. 17, 1987, and plan terminations with respect to which proceedings are instituted by the Pension Benefit Guaranty Corporation under section 1342 of this title after that date, see section 9312(d)(1) of Pub. L. 100–203, as amended, set out as a note under section 1301 of this title.

Effective Date of 1986 Amendment

Amendment by Pub. L. 99–272 effective Jan. 1, 1986, with certain exceptions, see section 11019 of Pub. L. 99–272, set out as a note under section 1341 of this title.

Effective Date of 1980 Amendment

Amendment by Pub. L. 96–364 effective Sept. 26, 1980, except as specifically provided, see section 1461(e) of this title.

Effective Date of 1978 Amendment

Amendment by Pub. L. 95–598 effective Oct. 1, 1979, see section 402(a) of Pub. L. 95–598, set out as an Effective Date note preceding section 101 of Title 11, Bankruptcy.

Applicability of Amendments by Subtitles A and B of Title I of Pub. L. 109–280

For special rules on applicability of amendments by subtitles A (§§ 101–107) and B (§§ 111–116) of title I of Pub. L. 109–280 to certain eligible cooperative plans, PBGC settlement plans, and eligible government contractor plans, see sections 104, 105, and 106 of Pub. L. 109–280, set out as notes under section 401 of Title 26, Internal Revenue Code.

Special Delayed Payment Rule

Pub. L. 99–272, title XI, § 11012(d), Apr. 7, 1986, 100 Stat. 260, provided that: "In the case of a distress termination under section 4041(c) of the Employee Retirement Income Security Act of 1974 (as amended by section 11009) [29 U.S.C. 1341(c)] pursuant to a notice of intent to terminate filed before January 1, 1987, no payment of liability otherwise payable as provided in section 4062(c)(2)(B) of such Act [former 29 U.S.C. 1362(c)(2)(B)] (as amended by this section [Act]) shall be required to be made before January 1, 1989."

§1363. Liability of substantial employer for withdrawal from single-employer plans under multiple controlled groups

(a) Single-employer plans with two or more contributing sponsors

Except as provided in subsection (d) of this section, the plan administrator of a single-employer plan which has two or more contributing sponsors at least two of whom are not under common control—

(1) shall notify the corporation of the withdrawal during a plan year of a substantial employer for such plan year from the plan, within 60 days after such withdrawal, and

(2) request that the corporation determine the liability of all persons with respect to the withdrawal of the substantial employer.

The corporation shall, as soon as practicable thereafter, determine whether there is liability resulting from the withdrawal of the substantial employer and notify the liable persons of such liability.

(b) Computation of liability

Except as provided in subsection (c) of this section, any one or more contributing sponsors who withdraw, during a plan year for which they constitute a substantial employer, from a single-employer plan which has two or more contributing sponsors at least two of whom are not under common control, shall, upon notification of such contributing sponsors by the corporation as provided by subsection (a) of this section, be liable, together with the members of their controlled groups, to the corporation in accordance with the provisions of section 1362 of this title and this section. The amount of liability shall be computed on the basis of an amount determined by the corporation to be the amount described in section 1362 of this title for the entire plan, as if the plan had been terminated by the corporation on the date of the withdrawal referred to in subsection (a)(1) of this section multiplied by a fraction—

(1) the numerator of which is the total amount required to be contributed to the plan by such contributing sponsors for the last 5 years ending prior to the withdrawal, and

(2) the denominator of which is the total amount required to be contributed to the plan by all contributing sponsors for such last 5 years.

In addition to and in lieu of the manner prescribed in the preceding sentence, the corporation may also determine such liability on any other equitable basis prescribed by the corporation in regulations. Any amount collected by the corporation under this subsection shall be held in escrow subject to disposition in accordance with the provisions of paragraphs (2) and (3) of subsection (c) of this section.

(c) Bond in lieu of payment of liability; 5-year termination period

(1) In lieu of payment of a contributing sponsor's liability under this section, the contributing sponsor may be required to furnish a bond to the corporation in an amount not exceeding 150 percent of his liability to insure payment of his liability under this section. The bond shall have as surety thereon a corporate surety company which is an acceptable surety on Federal bonds under authority granted by the Secretary of the Treasury under sections 9304–9308 of title 31. Any such bond shall be in a form or of a type approved by the Secretary including individual bonds or schedule or blanket forms of bonds which cover a group or class.

(2) If the plan is not terminated under section 1341(c) or 1342 of this title within the 5-year period commencing on the day of withdrawal, the liability is abated and any payment held in escrow shall be refunded without interest (or the bond cancelled) in accordance with bylaws or rules prescribed by the corporation.

(3) If the plan terminates under section 1341(c) or 1342 of this title within the 5-year period commencing on the day of withdrawal, the corporation shall—

(A) demand payment or realize on the bond and hold such amount in escrow for the benefit of the plan;

(B) treat any escrowed payments under this section as if they were plan assets and apply them in a manner consistent with this subtitle; and

(C) refund any amount to the contributing sponsor which is not required to meet any obligation of the corporation with respect to the plan.

(d) Alternate appropriate procedure

The provisions of this subsection apply in the case of a withdrawal described in subsection (a) of this section, and the provisions of subsections (b) and (c) of this section shall not apply, if the corporation determines that the procedure provided for under this subsection is consistent with the purposes of this section and section 1364 of this title and is more appropriate in the particular case. Upon a showing by the plan administrator of the plan that the withdrawal from the plan by one or more contributing sponsors has resulted, or will result, in a significant reduction in the amount of aggregate contributions to or under the plan, the corporation may—

(1) require the plan fund to be equitably allocated between those participants no longer working in covered service under the plan as a result of the withdrawal, and those participants who remain in covered service under the plan;

(2) treat that portion of the plan funds allocable under paragraph (1) to participants no longer in covered service as a plan terminated under section 1342 of this title; and

(3) treat that portion of the plan fund allocable to participants remaining in covered service as a separate plan.

(e) Indemnity agreement

The corporation is authorized to waive the application of the provisions of subsections (b), (c), and (d) of this section whenever it determines that there is an indemnity agreement in effect among contributing sponsors under the plan which is adequate to satisfy the purposes of this section and of section 1364 of this title.

(Pub. L. 93–406, title IV, §4063, Sept. 2, 1974, 88 Stat. 1030; Pub. L. 96–364, title IV, §403(h), Sept. 26, 1980, 94 Stat. 1301; Pub. L. 99–272, title XI, §11016(a)(5)(A), Apr. 7, 1986, 100 Stat. 268.)

CODIFICATION

In subsec. (c)(1), "sections 9304–9308 of title 31" substituted for "sections 6 through 13 of title 6, United States Code" on authority of Pub. L. 97–258, §4(b), Sept. 13, 1982, 96 Stat. 1067, the first section of which enacted Title 31, Money and Finance.

AMENDMENTS

1986—Pub. L. 99–272, §11016(a)(5)(A)(vi), inserted "from single-employer plans under multiple controlled groups" in section catchline.

Subsec. (a). Pub. L. 99–272, §11016(a)(5)(A)(i), in introductory par., substituted "single-employer plan which has two or more contributing sponsors at least two of whom are not under common control" for "plan under which more than one employer makes contributions (other than a multiemployer plan)", in par. (1), substituted "withdrawal during a plan year of a substantial employer for such plan year" for "withdrawal of a substantial employer", in par. (2), substituted "of all persons with respect to the withdrawal of the substantial employer" for "of such employer under this subtitle with respect to such withdrawal", and in concluding provision substituted "whether there is liability resulting from the withdrawal of the substantial employer" for "whether such employer is liable for any amount under this subtitle with respect to the withdrawal" and "notify the liable persons" for "notify such employer".

Subsec. (b). Pub. L. 99–272, §11016(a)(5)(A)(ii), in introductory par., substituted "any one or more contributing sponsors who withdraw, during a plan year for which they constitute a substantial employer, from a single-employer plan which has two or more contributing sponsors at least two of whom are not under common control, shall, upon notification of such contributing sponsors by the corporation as provided by subsection (a) of this section, be liable, together with the members of their controlled groups," for "an employer who withdraws from a plan to which section 1321 of this title applies, during a plan year for which he was a substantial employer, and who is notified by the corporation as provided by subsection (a) of this section, shall be liable", "amount of liability" for "amount of such employer's liability", and "the withdrawal referred to in subsection (a)(1) of this section" for "the employer's withdrawal", in par. (1), substituted "such contributing sponsors" for "such employer", in par. (2), substituted "all contributing sponsors" for "all employers", and in concluding provision substituted "such liability" for "the liability of each such employer".

Subsec. (c)(1). Pub. L. 99–272, §11016(a)(5)(A)(iii)(I), substituted "of a contributing sponsor's liability under this section, the contributing sponsor" for "of his liability under this section the employer".

Subsec. (c)(2). Pub. L. 99–272, §11016(a)(5)(A)(iii)(II), inserted "under section 1341(c) or 1342 of this title" and substituted "liability is" for "liability of such employer is" and "(or the bond cancelled)" for "to the employer (or his bond cancelled)".

Subsec. (c)(3). Pub. L. 99–272, §11016(a)(5)(A)(iii)(III), in introductory par., inserted "under section 1341(c) or 1342 of this title" and, in subpar. (C), substituted "contributing sponsor" for "employer".

Subsec. (d). Pub. L. 99–272, §11016(a)(5)(A)(iv), in introductory par., substituted "of the plan that the withdrawal from the plan by one or more contributing sponsors" for "of a plan (other than a multiemployer plan) that the withdrawal from the plan by any employer or employers" and struck out "by employers" after "contributions to or under the plan", in par. (1), substituted "the withdrawal" for "their employer's withdrawal", and in par. (2), substituted "plan terminated under section 1342 of this title" for "termination".

Subsec. (e). Pub. L. 99–272, §11016(a)(5)(A)(v), struck out "to any employer or plan administrator" before "whenever it determines" and substituted "contributing sponsors" for "all other employers".

1980—Subsecs. (a), (d). Pub. L. 96–364 inserted provisions excepting a multiemployer plan.

EFFECTIVE DATE OF 1986 AMENDMENT

Amendment by Pub. L. 99–272 effective Jan. 1, 1986, with certain exceptions, see section 11019 of Pub. L. 99–272, set out as a note under section 1341 of this title.

EFFECTIVE DATE OF 1980 AMENDMENT

Amendment by Pub. L. 96–364 effective Sept. 26, 1980, except as specifically provided, see section 1461(e) of this title.

§1364. Liability on termination of single-employer plans under multiple controlled groups

(a) This section applies to all contributing sponsors of a single-employer plan which has two or more contributing sponsors at least two of whom are not under common control at the time such plan is terminated under section 1341(c) or 1342 of this title, or who, at any time within the 5 plan years preceding the date of termination, made contributions under the plan.

(b) The corporation shall determine the liability with respect to each contributing sponsor and each member of its controlled group in a manner consistent with section 1362 of this title, except that the amount of liability determined under section 1362(b)(1) of this title with respect to the entire plan shall be allocated to each controlled group by multiplying such amount by a fraction—

(1) the numerator of which is the amount required to be contributed to the plan for the last 5 plan years ending prior to the termination date by persons in such controlled group as contributing sponsors, and

(2) the denominator of which is the total amount required to be contributed to the plan for such last 5 plan years by all persons as contributing sponsors,

and section 1368(a) of this title shall be applied separately with respect to each controlled group. The corporation may also determine the liability of each such contributing sponsor and member of its controlled group on any other equitable basis prescribed by the corporation in regulations.

(Pub. L. 93–406, title IV, §4064, Sept. 2, 1974, 88 Stat. 1031; Pub. L. 96–364, title IV, §403(i), Sept. 26, 1980, 94 Stat. 1301; Pub. L. 99–272, title XI, §11016(a)(5)(B), Apr. 7, 1986, 100 Stat. 270; Pub. L. 100–203, title IX, §9312(b)(2)(C)(i), Dec. 22, 1987, 101 Stat. 1330–361; Pub. L. 101–239, title VII, §7881(f)(3)(A), Dec. 19, 1989, 103 Stat. 2440.)

AMENDMENTS

1989—Subsec. (b). Pub. L. 101–239 substituted "section 1368(a)" for "clauses (i)(II) and (ii) of section 1362(b)(1)(A)".

1987—Subsec. (b). Pub. L. 100–203 amended first sentence generally. Prior to amendment, first sentence read as follows: "The corporation shall determine the liability with respect to each contributing sponsor and each member of its controlled group in a manner consistent with section 1362 of this title, except that—

"(1) the amount of the liability determined under section 1362(b)(1) of this title with respect to the entire plan—

"(A) shall be determined without regard to clauses (i)(II) and (ii) of section 1362(b)(1)(A) of this title, and

"(B) shall be allocated to each controlled group by multiplying such amount by a fraction—

"(i) the numerator of which is the amount required to be contributed to the plan for the last 5 plan years ending prior to the termination date by persons in such controlled group as contributing sponsors, and

"(ii) the denominator of which is the total amount required to be contributed to the plan for such last 5 plan years by all persons as contributing sponsors,

and clauses (i)(II) and (ii) of section 1362(b)(1)(A) of this title shall be applied separately with respect to each such controlled group, and

"(2) the amount of the liability determined under section 1362(c)(1) of this title with respect to the entire plan shall be allocated to each controlled group by multiplying such amount by the fraction described in paragraph (1)(B) in connection with such controlled group."

1986—Pub. L. 99–272, §11016(a)(5)(B)(iii), substituted "on termination of single-employer plans under multiple controlled groups" for "of employers on termination of plan maintained by more than one employer" in section catchline.

Subsec. (a). Pub. L. 99–272, §11016(a)(5)(B)(i), substituted "all contributing sponsors of a single-employer plan which has two or more contributing sponsors at least two of whom are not under common control" for "all employers who maintain a plan under which more than one employer makes contributions (other than a multiemployer plan)" and inserted "under section 1341(c) or 1342 of this title" after "terminated".

Subsec. (b). Pub. L. 99–272, §11016(a)(5)(B)(ii), amended subsec. (b) generally, substituting reference to each contributing sponsor and each member of its controlled group for reference to each employer of a plan maintained by more than one employer and inserted provisions that liability determined under section 1362(b)(1) of this title with respect to the entire plan be determined without regard to cls. (i)(II) and (ii) of section 1362(b)(1)(A) of this title and that the amount of liability determined under section 1362(c)(1) of this title with respect to the entire plan be allocated to each controlled group by multiplying such amount by the fraction described in par. (1)(B) in connection with such controlled group.

1980—Subsec. (a). Pub. L. 96–364 inserted provisions excepting a multiemployer plan.

EFFECTIVE DATE OF 1989 AMENDMENT

Amendment by Pub. L. 101–239 effective, except as otherwise provided, as if included in the provision of the Pension Protection Act, Pub. L. 100–203, §§9302–9346, to which such amendment relates, see section 7882 of Pub. L. 101–239, set out as a note under section 401 of Title 26, Internal Revenue Code.

EFFECTIVE DATE OF 1987 AMENDMENT

Amendment by Pub. L. 100–203 applicable with respect to plan terminations under section 1341 of this title with respect to which notices of intent to terminate are provided under section 1341(a)(2) of this title after Dec. 17, 1987, and plan terminations with respect to which proceedings are instituted by the Pension Benefit Guaranty Corporation under section 1342 of this title after that date, see section 9312(d)(1) of Pub. L. 100–203, as amended, set out as a note under section 1301 of this title.

EFFECTIVE DATE OF 1986 AMENDMENT

Amendment by Pub. L. 99–272 effective Jan. 1, 1986, with certain exceptions, see section 11019 of Pub. L. 99–272, set out as a note under section 1341 of this title.

EFFECTIVE DATE OF 1980 AMENDMENT

Amendment by Pub. L. 96–364 effective Sept. 26, 1980, except as specifically provided, see section 1461(e) of this title.

§ 1365. Annual report of plan administrator

For each plan year for which section 1321 of this title applies to a plan, the plan administrator shall file with the corporation, on a form prescribed by the corporation, an annual report which identifies the plan and plan administrator and which includes—

(1) a copy of each notification required under section 1363 of this title with respect to such year,

(2) a statement disclosing whether any reportable event (described in section 1343(b)[1] of this title) occurred during the plan year except to the extent the corporation waives such requirement, and

(3) in the case of a multiemployer plan, information with respect to such plan which the corporation determines is necessary for the enforcement of subtitle E of this subchapter and requires by regulation, which may include—

(A) a statement certified by the plan's enrolled actuary of—

(i) the value of all vested benefits under the plan as of the end of the plan year, and

(ii) the value of the plan's assets as of the end of the plan year;

(B) a statement certified by the plan sponsor of each claim for outstanding withdrawal liability (within the meaning of section 1301(a)(12) of this title) and its value as of the end of that plan year and as of the end of the preceding plan year; and

(C) the number of employers having an obligation to contribute to the plan and the number of employers required to make withdrawal liability payments.

The report shall be filed within 6 months after the close of the plan year to which it relates. The corporation shall cooperate with the Secretary of the Treasury and the Secretary of Labor in an endeavor to coordinate the timing and content, and possibly obtain the combination, of reports under this section with reports required to be made by plan administrators to such Secretaries.

(Pub. L. 93–406, title IV, §4065, Sept. 2, 1974, 88 Stat. 1032; Pub. L. 96–364, title I, §106, Sept. 26, 1980, 94 Stat. 1266.)

REFERENCES IN TEXT

Section 1343(b) of this title, referred to in par. (2), was redesignated section 1343(c) of this title and a new section 1343(b) was added by Pub. L. 103–465, title VII, §771(b), Dec. 8, 1994, 108 Stat. 5042.

AMENDMENTS

1980—Pub. L. 96–364 inserted provisions in par. (2) respecting waiver by corporation and added par. (3).

[1] See References in Text note below.

EFFECTIVE DATE OF 1980 AMENDMENT

Amendment by Pub. L. 96–364 effective Sept. 26, 1980, except as specifically provided, see section 1461(e) of this title.

§1366. Annual notification to substantial employers

The plan administrator of each single-employer plan which has at least two contributing sponsors at least two of whom are not under common control shall notify, within 6 months after the close of each plan year, any contributing sponsor of the plan who is described in section 1301(a)(2) of this title that such contributing sponsor (alone or together with members of such contributing sponsor's controlled group) constitutes a substantial employer for that year.

(Pub. L. 93–406, title IV, §4066, Sept. 2, 1974, 88 Stat. 1032; Pub. L. 96–364, title IV, §403(j), Sept. 26, 1980, 94 Stat. 1301; Pub. L. 99–272, title XI, §11016(a)(5)(C), Apr. 7, 1986, 100 Stat. 271; Pub. L. 101–239, title VII, §7893(g)(2), Dec. 19, 1989, 103 Stat. 2447.)

AMENDMENTS

1989—Pub. L. 101–239 inserted "any" before "contributing sponsor of the plan".

1986—Pub. L. 99–272 substituted "each single-employer plan which has at least two contributing sponsors at least two of whom are not under common control" for "each plan under which contributions are made by more than one employer (other than a multiemployer plan)", "contributing sponsor of the plan" for "any employer making contributions under that plan", and "that such contributing sponsor (alone or together with members of such contributing sponsor's controlled group) constitutes a substantial employer" for "that he is a substantial employer".

1980—Pub. L. 96–364 inserted provisions excepting a multiemployer plan.

EFFECTIVE DATE OF 1989 AMENDMENT

Amendment by Pub. L. 101–239 effective as if included in the provision of the Single-Employer Pension Plan Amendments Act of 1986, Pub. L. 99–272, title XI, to which such amendment relates, see section 7893(h) of Pub. L. 101–239, set out as a note under section 1002 of this title.

EFFECTIVE DATE OF 1986 AMENDMENT

Amendment by Pub. L. 99–272 effective Jan. 1, 1986, with certain exceptions, see section 11019 of Pub. L. 99–272, set out as a note under section 1341 of this title.

EFFECTIVE DATE OF 1980 AMENDMENT

Amendment by Pub. L. 96–364 effective Sept. 26, 1980, except as specifically provided, see section 1461(e) of this title.

§1367. Recovery of liability for plan termination

The corporation is authorized to make arrangements with contributing sponsors and members of their controlled groups who are or may become liable under section 1362, 1363, or 1364 of this title for payment of their liability, including arrangements for deferred payment of amounts of liability to the corporation accruing as of the termination date on such terms and for such periods as the corporation deems equitable and appropriate.

(Pub. L. 93–406, title IV, §4067, Sept. 2, 1974, 88 Stat. 1032; Pub. L. 99–272, title XI, §11016(a)(6)(A), Apr. 7, 1986, 100 Stat. 271; Pub. L. 100–203, title IX, §9313(b)(6), Dec. 22, 1987, 101 Stat. 1330–366; Pub. L. 101–239, title VII, §7893(g)(3), Dec. 19, 1989, 103 Stat. 2448.)

AMENDMENTS

1989—Pub. L. 101–239 amended directory language of Pub. L. 99–272, §11016(a)(6)(A)(ii), see 1986 Amendment note below.

1987—Pub. L. 100–203 inserted "or may become" after "who are".

1986—Pub. L. 99–272, §11016(a)(6)(A)(i), (iii), substituted "of liability" for "of employer liability" in section catchline and inserted "of amounts of liability to the corporation accruing as of the termination date" in text.

Pub. L. 99–272, §11016(a)(6)(A)(ii), as amended by Pub. L. 101–239, substituted "contributing sponsors and members of their controlled groups" for "employers".

EFFECTIVE DATE OF 1989 AMENDMENT

Amendment by Pub. L. 101–239 effective as if included in the provision of the Single-Employer Pension Plan Amendments Act of 1986, Pub. L. 99–272, title XI, to which such amendment relates, see section 7893(h) of Pub. L. 101–239, set out as a note under section 1002 of this title.

EFFECTIVE DATE OF 1987 AMENDMENT

Amendment by Pub. L. 100–203 applicable with respect to plan terminations under section 1341 of this title with respect to which notices of intent to terminate are provided under section 1341(a)(2) of this title after Dec. 17, 1987, see section 9313(c) of Pub. L. 100–203, set out as a note under section 1301 of this title.

EFFECTIVE DATE OF 1986 AMENDMENT

Amendment by Pub. L. 99–272 effective Jan. 1, 1986, with certain exceptions, see section 11019 of Pub. L. 99–272, set out as a note under section 1341 of this title.

§1368. Lien for liability

(a) Creation of lien

If any person liable to the corporation under section 1362, 1363, or 1364 of this title neglects or refuses to pay, after demand, the amount of such liability (including interest), there shall be a lien in favor of the corporation in the amount of such liability (including interest) upon all property and rights to property, whether real or personal, belonging to such person, except that such lien may not be in an amount in excess of 30 percent of the collective net worth of all persons described in section 1362(a) of this title[1]

(b) Term of lien

The lien imposed by subsection (a) of this section arises on the date of termination of a plan, and continues until the liability imposed under section 1362, 1363, or 1364 of this title is satisfied or becomes unenforceable by reason of lapse of time.

(c) Priority

(1) Except as otherwise provided under this section, the priority of a lien imposed under subsection (a) of this section shall be determined in the same manner as under section 6323 of title 26 (as in effect on April 7, 1986). Such section 6323 shall be applied for purposes of this section by disregarding subsection (g)(4) and by substituting—

[1] So in original. Probably should be followed by a period.

(A) "lien imposed by section 4068 of the Employee Retirement Income Security Act of 1974 [29 U.S.C. 1368]" for "lien imposed by section 6321" each place it appears in subsections (a), (b), (c)(1), (c)(4)(B), (d), (e), and (h)(5);

(B) "the corporation" for "the Secretary" in subsections (a) and (b)(9)(C);

(C) "the payment of the amount on which the section 4068(a) lien is based" for "the collection of any tax under this title" in subsection (b)(3);

(D) "a person whose property is subject to the lien" for "the taxpayer" in subsections (b)(8), (c)(2)(A)(i) (the first place it appears), (c)(2)(A)(ii), (c)(2)(B), (c)(4)(B), and (c)(4)(C) (in the matter preceding clause (i));

(E) "such person" for "the taxpayer" in subsections (c)(2)(A)(i) (the second place it appears) and (c)(4)(C)(ii);

(F) "payment of the loan value of the amount on which the lien is based is made to the corporation" for "satisfaction of a levy pursuant to section 6332(b)" in subsection (b)(9)(C);

(G) "section 4068(a) lien" for "tax lien" each place it appears in subsections (c)(1), (c)(2)(A), (c)(2)(B), (c)(3)(B)(iii), (c)(4)(B), (d), and (h)(5); and

(H) "the date on which the lien is first filed" for "the date of the assessment of the tax" in subsection (g)(3)(A).

(2) In a case under title 11 or in insolvency proceedings, the lien imposed under subsection (a) of this section shall be treated in the same manner as a tax due and owing to the United States for purposes of title 11 or section 3713 of title 31.

(3) For purposes of applying section 6323(a) of title 26 to determine the priority between the lien imposed under subsection (a) of this section and a Federal tax lien, each lien shall be treated as a judgment lien arising as of the time notice of such lien is filed.

(4) For purposes of this subsection, notice of the lien imposed by subsection (a) of this section shall be filed in the same manner as under section 6323(f) and (g) of title 26.

(d) Civil action; limitation period

(1) In any case where there has been a refusal or neglect to pay the liability imposed under section 1362, 1363, or 1364 of this title, the corporation may bring civil action in a district court of the United States to enforce the lien of the corporation under this section with respect to such liability or to subject any property, of whatever nature, of the liable person, or in which he has any right, title, or interest to the payment of such liability.

(2) The liability imposed by section 1362, 1363, or 1364 of this title may be collected by a proceeding in court if the proceeding is commenced within 6 years after the date upon which the plan was terminated or prior to the expiration of any period for collection agreed upon in writing by the corporation and the liable person before the expiration of such 6-year period. The period of limitations provided under this paragraph shall be suspended for the period the assets of the liable person are in the control or custody of any court of the United States, or of any State, or of the District of Columbia, and for 6 months thereafter, and for any period during which the liable person is outside the United States if such period of absence is for a continuous period of at least 6 months.

(e) Release or subordination

If the corporation determines that release of the lien or subordination of the lien to any other creditor of the liable person would not adversely affect the collection of the liability imposed under section 1362, 1363, or 1364 of this title, or that the amount realizable by the corporation from the property to which the lien attaches will ultimately be increased by such release or subordination, and that the ultimate collection of the liability will be facilitated by such release or subordination, the corporation may issue a certificate of release or subordination of the lien with respect to such property, or any part thereof.

(f) Definitions

For purposes of this section—

(1) The collective net worth of persons subject to liability in connection with a plan termination shall be determined as provided in section 1362(d)(1) of this title.

(2) The term "pre-tax profits" has the meaning provided in section 1362(d)(2) of this title.

(Pub. L. 93–406, title IV, § 4068, Sept. 2, 1974, 88 Stat. 1032; Pub. L. 95–598, title III, § 321(c), Nov. 6, 1978, 92 Stat. 2678; Pub. L. 99–272, title XI, § 11016(a)(6)(B), (c)(14), Apr. 7, 1986, 100 Stat. 271, 275; Pub. L. 100–203, title IX, § 9312(b)(2)(B)(i), (C)(ii), Dec. 22, 1987, 101 Stat. 1330–361, 1330–362; Pub. L. 101–239, title VII, §§ 7881(f)(3)(B), (10)(C), (12), 7891(a)(1), 7894(g)(4)(A), Dec. 19, 1989, 103 Stat. 2440, 2441, 2445, 2451.)

CODIFICATION

A former subsec. (f) of this section was originally subsec. (e) of section 1362 of this title and was redesignated as subsec. (f) of this section by Pub. L. 100–203, § 9312(b)(2)(B)(ii). Subsequently, Pub. L. 100–203, § 9312(b)(2)(B)(ii), was amended generally by Pub. L. 101–239, § 7881(f)(10)(B), and, as so amended, no longer contains language redesignating subsec. (e) of section 1362 as subsec. (f) of this section. As a result of that amendment, the transfer of subsec. (e) of section 1362 to subsec. (f) of this section was rescinded.

AMENDMENTS

1989—Subsec. (a). Pub. L. 101–239, § 7881(f)(12), struck out "to the extent such amount does not exceed 30 percent of the collective net worth of all persons described in section 1362(a) of this title" after "the amount of such liability" and substituted "in the amount of such liability (including interest) upon all property and rights to property, whether real or personal, belonging to such person, except that such lien may not be in an amount in excess of 30 percent of the collective net worth of all persons described in section 1362(a) of this title" for "to the extent such amount does not exceed 30 percent of the collective net worth of all persons described in section 1362(a) of this title upon all property and rights to property, whether real or personal, belonging to such person."

Pub. L. 101–239, § 7881(f)(3)(B), struck out at end "The preceding provisions of this subsection shall be applied in a manner consistent with the provisions of section 1364(d) of this title relating to treatment of multiple controlled groups."

Subsec. (c). Pub. L. 101–239, § 7891(a)(1), in pars. (1), (3), and (4), substituted "Internal Revenue Code of 1986" for

"Internal Revenue Code of 1954", which for purposes of codification was translated as "title 26" thus requiring no change in text.

Subsec. (c)(2). Pub. L. 101–239, § 7894(g)(4)(A), substituted "section 3713 of title 31" for "section 3466 of the Revised Statutes (31 U.S.C. 191)".

Subsec. (f). Pub. L. 101–239, § 7881(f)(10)(C), added subsec. (f).

1987—Subsec. (a). Pub. L. 100–203, § 9312(b)(2)(B)(i), substituted "to the extent such amount does not exceed 30 percent of the collective net worth of all persons described in section 1362(a) of this title" for "to the extent of an amount equal to the unpaid amount described in section 1362(b)(1)(A)(i) of this title" in two places.

Pub. L. 100–203, § 9312(b)(2)(C)(ii), inserted at end "The preceding provisions of this subsection shall be applied in a manner consistent with the provisions of section 1364(d) of this title relating to treatment of multiple controlled groups."

1986—Pub. L. 99–272, § 11016(a)(6)(B)(i), struck out "of employer" after "liability" in section catchline.

Subsec. (a). Pub. L. 99–272, § 11016(a)(6)(B)(ii), substituted "person liable" for "employer or employers liable", "neglects or refuses" for "neglect or refuse", and "such person" for "such employer or employers" and inserted "to the extent of an amount equal to the unpaid amount described in section 1362(b)(1)(A)(i) of this title" in two places.

Subsec. (c)(1). Pub. L. 99–272, § 11016(a)(6)(B)(vi), substituted par. (1) for former par. (1) which read as follows: "Except as otherwise provided under this section, the priority of the lien imposed under subsection (a) of this section shall be determined in the same manner as under section 6323 of title 26. Such section 6323 shall be applied by substituting 'lien imposed by section 4068 of the Employee Retirement Income Security Act of 1974' for 'lien imposed by section 6321'; 'corporation' for 'Secretary or his delegate'; 'employer liability lien' for 'tax lien'; 'employer' for 'taxpayer'; 'lien arising under section 4068(a) of the Employee Retirement Income Security Act of 1974' for 'assessment of the tax'; and 'payment of the loan value is made to the corporation' for 'satisfaction of a levy pursuant to section 6332(b)'; each place such terms appear."

Subsec. (d)(1), (2). Pub. L. 99–272, § 11016(a)(6)(B)(iii), (iv), substituted "liable person" for "employer" wherever appearing.

Subsec. (e). Pub. L. 99–272, § 11016(a)(6)(B)(v), (c)(14), struck out ", with the consent of the board of directors," after "corporation determines" and substituted "liable person" for "employer or employers".

1978—Subsec. (c)(2). Pub. L. 95–598 substituted "a case under title 11 or in" and "title 11" for "the case of bankruptcy or" and "the Bankruptcy Act".

EFFECTIVE DATE OF 1989 AMENDMENT

Amendment by section 7881(f)(3)(B), (10)(C), (12) of Pub. L. 101–239 effective, except as otherwise provided, as if included in the provision of the Pension Protection Act, Pub. L. 100–203, §§ 9302–9346, to which such amendment relates, see section 7882 of Pub. L. 101–239, set out as a note under section 401 of Title 26, Internal Revenue Code.

Amendment by section 7891(a)(1) of Pub. L. 101–239 effective, except as otherwise provided, as if included in the provision of the Tax Reform Act of 1986, Pub. L. 99–514, to which such amendment relates, see section 7891(f) of Pub. L. 101–239, set out as a note under section 1002 of this title.

Section 7894(g)(4)(B) of Pub. L. 101–239 provided that: "The amendment made by subparagraph (A) [amending this section] shall take effect as if originally included in section 3 of Public Law 97–258."

EFFECTIVE DATE OF 1987 AMENDMENT

Amendment by Pub. L. 100–203 applicable with respect to plan terminations under section 1341 of this title with respect to which notices of intent to terminate are provided under section 1341(a)(2) of this title after Dec. 17, 1987, and plan terminations with respect to which proceedings are instituted by the Pension Benefit Guaranty Corporation under section 1342 of this title after that date, see section 9312(d)(1) of Pub. L. 100–203, as amended, set out as a note under section 1301 of this title.

EFFECTIVE DATE OF 1986 AMENDMENT

Amendment by Pub. L. 99–272 effective Jan. 1, 1986, with certain exceptions, see section 11019 of Pub. L. 99–272, set out as a note under section 1341 of this title.

EFFECTIVE DATE OF 1978 AMENDMENT

Amendment by Pub. L. 95–598 effective Oct. 1, 1979, see section 402(a) of Pub. L. 95–598, set out as an Effective Date note preceding section 101 of Title 11, Bankruptcy.

§ 1369. Treatment of transactions to evade liability; effect of corporate reorganization

(a) Treatment of transactions to evade liability

If a principal purpose of any person in entering into any transaction is to evade liability to which such person would be subject under this subtitle and the transaction becomes effective within five years before the termination date of the termination on which such liability would be based, then such person and the members of such person's controlled group (determined as of the termination date) shall be subject to liability under this subtitle in connection with such termination as if such person were a contributing sponsor of the terminated plan as of the termination date. This subsection shall not cause any person to be liable under this subtitle in connection with such plan termination for any increases or improvements in the benefits provided under the plan which are adopted after the date on which the transaction referred to in the preceding sentence becomes effective.

(b) Effect of corporate reorganization

For purposes of this subtitle, the following rules apply in the case of certain corporate reorganizations:

(1) Change of identity, form, etc.

If a person ceases to exist by reason of a reorganization which involves a mere change in identity, form, or place of organization, however effected, a successor corporation resulting from such reorganization shall be treated as the person to whom this subtitle applies.

(2) Liquidation into parent corporation

If a person ceases to exist by reason of liquidation into a parent corporation, the parent corporation shall be treated as the person to whom this subtitle applies.

(3) Merger, consolidation, or division

If a person ceases to exist by reason of a merger, consolidation, or division, the successor corporation or corporations shall be treated as the person to whom this subtitle applies.

(Pub. L. 93–406, title IV, § 4069, as added Pub. L. 99–272, title XI, § 11013(a), Apr. 7, 1986, 100 Stat. 260.)

EFFECTIVE DATE

Section 11013(b) of Pub. L. 99–272 provided that: "Section 4069(a) of the Employee Retirement Income Security Act of 1974 (as added by subsection (a)) [subsec. (a) of this section] shall apply with respect to transactions becoming effective on or after January 1, 1986."

Section effective Jan. 1, 1986, with certain exceptions, see section 11019 of Pub. L. 99–272, set out as an Effective Date of 1986 Amendment note under section 1341 of this title.

§ 1370. Enforcement authority relating to terminations of single-employer plans

(a) In general

Any person who is with respect to a single-employer plan a fiduciary, contributing sponsor, member of a contributing sponsor's controlled group, participant, or beneficiary, and is adversely affected by an act or practice of any party (other than the corporation) in violation of any provision of section 1341, 1342, 1362, 1363, 1364, or 1369 of this title, or who is an employee organization representing such a participant or beneficiary so adversely affected for purposes of collective bargaining with respect to such plan, may bring an action—

(1) to enjoin such act or practice, or

(2) to obtain other appropriate equitable relief (A) to redress such violation or (B) to enforce such provision.

(b) Status of plan as party to action and with respect to legal process

A single-employer plan may be sued under this section as an entity. Service of summons, subpoena, or other legal process of a court upon a trustee or an administrator of a single-employer plan in such trustee's or administrator's capacity as such shall constitute service upon the plan. If a plan has not designated in the summary plan description of the plan an individual as agent for the service of legal process, service upon any contributing sponsor of the plan shall constitute such service. Any money judgment under this section against a single-employer plan shall be enforceable only against the plan as an entity and shall not be enforceable against any other person unless liability against such person is established in such person's individual capacity.

(c) Jurisdiction and venue

The district courts of the United States shall have exclusive jurisdiction of civil actions under this section. Such actions may be brought in the district where the plan is administered, where the violation took place, or where a defendant resides or may be found, and process may be served in any other district where a defendant resides or may be found. The district courts of the United States shall have jurisdiction, without regard to the amount in controversy or the citizenship of the parties, to grant the relief provided for in subsection (a) of this section in any action.

(d) Right of corporation to intervene

A copy of the complaint or notice of appeal in any action under this section shall be served upon the corporation by certified mail. The corporation shall have the right in its discretion to intervene in any action.

(e) Awards of costs and expenses

(1) General rule

In any action brought under this section, the court in its discretion may award all or a portion of the costs and expenses incurred in connection with such action, including reasonable attorney's fees, to any party who prevails or substantially prevails in such action.

(2) Exemption for plans

Notwithstanding the preceding provisions of this subsection, no plan shall be required in any action to pay any costs and expenses (including attorney's fees).

(f) Limitation on actions

(1) In general

Except as provided in paragraph (3), an action under this section may not be brought after the later of—

(A) 6 years after the date on which the cause of action arose, or

(B) 3 years after the applicable date specified in paragraph (2).

(2) Applicable date

(A) General rule

Except as provided in subparagraph (B), the applicable date specified in this paragraph is the earliest date on which the plaintiff acquired or should have acquired actual knowledge of the existence of such cause of action.

(B) Special rule for plaintiffs who are fiduciaries

In the case of a plaintiff who is a fiduciary bringing the action in the exercise of fiduciary duties, the applicable date specified in this paragraph is the date on which the plaintiff became a fiduciary with respect to the plan if such date is later than the date described in subparagraph (A).

(3) Cases of fraud or concealment

In the case of fraud or concealment, the period described in paragraph (1)(B) shall be extended to 6 years after the applicable date specified in paragraph (2).

(Pub. L. 93–406, title IV, § 4070, as added Pub. L. 99–272, title XI, § 11014(a), Apr. 7, 1986, 100 Stat. 261; amended Pub. L. 101–239, title VII, § 7881(f)(8), Dec. 19, 1989, 103 Stat. 2440.)

AMENDMENTS

1989—Subsec. (a). Pub. L. 101–239 struck out "1349," after "section 1341, 1342,".

EFFECTIVE DATE OF 1989 AMENDMENT

Amendment by Pub. L. 101–239 effective, except as otherwise provided, as if included in the provision of the Pension Protection Act, Pub. L. 100–203, §§ 9302–9346, to which such amendment relates, see section 7882 of Pub. L. 101–239, set out as a note under section 401 of Title 26, Internal Revenue Code.

EFFECTIVE DATE

Section effective Jan. 1, 1986, with certain exceptions, see section 11019 of Pub. L. 99–272, set out as an Effective Date of 1986 Amendment note under section 1341 of this title.

§ 1371. Penalty for failure to timely provide required information

The corporation may assess a penalty, payable to the corporation, against any person who fails to provide any notice or other material information required under this subtitle, subtitle A, B, or C of this subchapter, or section 1083(k)(4) of this title,,[1] or any regulations prescribed under any such subtitle or such section, within the applicable time limit specified therein. Such penalty shall not exceed $1,000 for each day for which such failure continues.

(Pub. L. 93–406, title IV, § 4071, as added Pub. L. 100–203, title IX, § 9314(c)(1), Dec. 22, 1987, 101 Stat. 1330–367; amended Pub. L. 101–239, title VII, § 7881(g)(8), (i)(3)(B), Dec. 19, 1989, 103 Stat. 2442; Pub. L. 109–280, title I, § 107(b)(5), Aug. 17, 2006, 120 Stat. 820; Pub. L. 110–458, title I, § 101(d)(1)(B), Dec. 23, 2008, 122 Stat. 5099.)

AMENDMENTS

2008—Pub. L. 110–458 substituted "or section 1083(k)(4) of this title," for "as section 1083(k)(4) or 1085b(e) of this title".

2006—Pub. L. 109–280 substituted "1083(k)(4)" for "1082(f)(4)".

1989—Pub. L. 101–239, § 7881(i)(3)(B), substituted ", subtitle A, B, or C of this subchapter, as section 1082(f)(4) or 1085b(e) of this title" for "or subtitle A, B, or C" and inserted "or such section" after "such subtitle".

Pub. L. 101–239, § 7881(g)(8), made clarifying amendment to directory language of Pub. L. 100–203, § 9314(c)(1), resulting in no change in text.

EFFECTIVE DATE OF 2008 AMENDMENT

Amendment by Pub. L. 110–458 effective as if included in the provisions of Pub. L. 109–280 to which the amendment relates, except as otherwise provided, see section 112 of Pub. L. 110–458, set out as a note under section 72 of Title 26, Internal Revenue Code.

EFFECTIVE DATE OF 2006 AMENDMENT

Amendment by Pub. L. 109–280 applicable to plan years beginning after 2007, see section 107(e) of Pub. L. 109–280, set out as a note under section 1021 of this title.

EFFECTIVE DATE OF 1989 AMENDMENT

Amendment by Pub. L. 101–239 effective, except as otherwise provided, as if included in the provision of the Pension Protection Act, Pub. L. 100–203, §§ 9302–9346, to which such amendment relates, see section 7882 of Pub. L. 101–239, set out as a note under section 401 of Title 26, Internal Revenue Code.

APPLICABILITY OF AMENDMENTS BY SUBTITLES A AND B OF TITLE I OF PUB. L. 109–280

For special rules on applicability of amendments by subtitles A (§§ 101–107) and B (§§ 111–116) of title I of Pub. L. 109–280 to certain eligible cooperative plans, PBGC settlement plans, and eligible government contractor plans, see sections 104, 105, and 106 of Pub. L. 109–280, set out as notes under section 401 of Title 26, Internal Revenue Code.

SUBTITLE E—SPECIAL PROVISIONS FOR MULTIEMPLOYER PLANS

AMENDMENTS

1980—Pub. L. 96–364, title I, § 104, Sept. 26, 1980, 94 Stat. 1217, added subtitle heading. Former subtitle E heading "Effective Date; Special Rules" was struck out. See subtitle F of this subchapter.

PART 1—EMPLOYER WITHDRAWALS

§ 1381. Withdrawal liability established; criteria and definitions

(a) If an employer withdraws from a multiemployer plan in a complete withdrawal or a partial withdrawal, then the employer is liable to the plan in the amount determined under this part to be the withdrawal liability.

(b) For purposes of subsection (a) of this section—

(1) The withdrawal liability of an employer to a plan is the amount determined under section 1391 of this title to be the allocable amount of unfunded vested benefits, adjusted—

(A) first, by any de minimis reduction applicable under section 1389 of this title,

(B) next, in the case of a partial withdrawal, in accordance with section 1386 of this title,

(C) then, to the extent necessary to reflect the limitation on annual payments under section 1399(c)(1)(B) of this title, and

(D) finally, in accordance with section 1405 of this title.

(2) The term "complete withdrawal" means a complete withdrawal described in section 1383 of this title.

(3) The term "partial withdrawal" means a partial withdrawal described in section 1385 of this title.

(Pub. L. 93–406, title IV, § 4201, as added Pub. L. 96–364, title I, § 104(2), Sept. 26, 1980, 94 Stat. 1217.)

PRIOR PROVISIONS

A prior section 1381, Pub. L. 93–406, title IV, § 4402, formerly § 4082, Sept. 2, 1974, 88 Stat. 1034; S.Res. 4, Feb. 4, 1977; Pub. L. 95–214, § 1, Dec. 19, 1977, 91 Stat. 1501; S.Res. 30, Mar. 7, 1979; Pub. L. 96–24, June 19, 1979, 93 Stat. 70; Pub. L. 96–239, § 1, Apr. 30, 1980, 94 Stat. 341; Pub. L. 96–293, § 1, June 30, 1980, 94 Stat. 610, renumbered § 4402 and amended Pub. L. 96–364, title I, § 108(a)-(c)(1), Sept. 26, 1980, 94 Stat. 1267, relating to the effective dates and special rules for this subchapter, was transferred to section 1461 of this title.

EFFECTIVE DATE

Part effective Sept. 26, 1980, see section 1461(e)(2) of this title.

ELIMINATION OF RETROACTIVE APPLICATION OF AMENDMENTS MADE BY MULTIEMPLOYER PENSION PLAN AMENDMENTS ACT OF 1980, PUB. L. 96–364

Pub. L. 98–369, div. A, title V, § 558(a), (c), (d), July 18, 1984, 98 Stat. 899, provided that:

"(a) IN GENERAL.—

"(1) LIABILITY.—Any withdrawal liability incurred by an employer pursuant to part 1 of subtitle E of title IV of the Employee Retirement Income Security Act of 1974 (29 U.S.C. 1381 et seq.) as a result of the complete or partial withdrawal of such employer from a multiemployer plan before September 26, 1980, shall be void.

"(2) REFUNDS.—Any amounts paid by an employer to a plan sponsor as a result of such withdrawal liability shall be refunded by the plan sponsor to the employer with interest (in accordance with section 401(a)(2) [26 U.S.C. 401(a)(2)]), less a reasonable amount for administrative expenses incurred by the plan sponsor (other than legal expenses incurred with respect to the plan) in calculating, assessing, and refunding such amounts.

"(c) NO INCREASE IN LIABILITY.—The amendments made by this section [amending sections 1391, 1397, 1399, 1415 and 1461 of this title and provisions set out as a note under section 1385 of this title] shall not be construed to increase the liability incurred by any employer pursuant to part 1 of subtitle E of title IV of the

[1] So in original.

Employee Retirement Income Security Act of 1974 (29 U.S.C. 1381 et seq.), as in effect immediately before the amendments made by subsection (b) [amending sections 1391, 1397, 1399, 1415, and 1461 of this title and provisions set out as a note under section 1385 of this title], as a result of the complete or partial withdrawal of such employer from a multiemployer plan prior to September 26, 1980.

"(d) SPECIAL RULE FOR CERTAIN BINDING AGREEMENTS.—In the case of an employer who, on September 26, 1980, has a binding agreement to withdraw from a multiemployer plan, subsection (a)(1) shall be applied by substituting 'December 31, 1980' for 'September 26, 1980'."

APPLICABILITY TO CERTAIN EMPLOYERS WITHDRAWN BEFORE SEPT. 26, 1980, FROM MULTIEMPLOYER PLAN COVERING EMPLOYEES IN SEAGOING INDUSTRY; EFFECTIVE DATE, COVERAGE, ETC.

Section 108(c)(4) of Pub. L. 96–364 provided that: "In the case of an employer who withdrew before the date of enactment of this Act [Sept. 26, 1980] from a multiemployer plan covering employees in the seagoing industry (as determined by the corporation), sections 4201 through 4219 of the Employee Retirement Income Security Act of 1974, as added by this Act, [section 1381 through 1399 of this title], are effective as of May 3, 1979. For the purpose of applying section 4217 [section 1397 of this title] for purposes of the preceding sentence, the date 'May 2, 1979,' shall be substituted for 'April 28, 1980,' and the date 'May 3, 1979' shall be substituted for 'April 29, 1980'. For purposes of this paragraph, terms which are used in title IV of the Employee Retirement Income Security Act of 1974 [this subchapter], or in regulations prescribed under that title, and which are used in the preceding sentence have the same meaning as when used in that Act [see Short Title note set out under sections 1001 of this title] or those regulations. For purposes of this paragraph, the term 'employer' includes only a substantial employer covering employees in the seagoing industry (as so determined) in connection with ports on the West Coast of the United States, but does not include an employer who withdrew from a plan because of a change in the collective bargaining representative."

§ 1382. Determination and collection of liability; notification of employer

When an employer withdraws from a multiemployer plan, the plan sponsor, in accordance with this part, shall—

(1) determine the amount of the employer's withdrawal liability,

(2) notify the employer of the amount of the withdrawal liability, and

(3) collect the amount of the withdrawal liability from the employer.

(Pub. L. 93–406, title IV, § 4202, as added Pub. L. 96–364, title I, § 104(2), Sept. 26, 1980, 94 Stat. 1218.)

§ 1383. Complete withdrawal

(a) Determinative factors

For purposes of this part, a complete withdrawal from a multiemployer plan occurs when an employer—

(1) permanently ceases to have an obligation to contribute under the plan, or

(2) permanently ceases all covered operations under the plan.

(b) Building and construction industry

(1) Notwithstanding subsection (a) of this section, in the case of an employer that has an obligation to contribute under a plan for work performed in the building and construction industry, a complete withdrawal occurs only as described in paragraph (2), if—

(A) substantially all the employees with respect to whom the employer has an obligation to contribute under the plan perform work in the building and construction industry, and

(B) the plan—

(i) primarily covers employees in the building and construction industry, or

(ii) is amended to provide that this subsection applies to employers described in this paragraph.

(2) A withdrawal occurs under this paragraph if—

(A) an employer ceases to have an obligation to contribute under the plan, and

(B) the employer—

(i) continues to perform work in the jurisdiction of the collective bargaining agreement of the type for which contributions were previously required, or

(ii) resumes such work within 5 years after the date on which the obligation to contribute under the plan ceases, and does not renew the obligation at the time of the resumption.

(3) In the case of a plan terminated by mass withdrawal (within the meaning of section 1341a(a)(2) of this title), paragraph (2) shall be applied by substituting "3 years" for "5 years" in subparagraph (B)(ii).

(c) Entertainment industry

(1) Notwithstanding subsection (a) of this section, in the case of an employer that has an obligation to contribute under a plan for work performed in the entertainment industry, primarily on a temporary or project-by-project basis, if the plan primarily covers employees in the entertainment industry, a complete withdrawal occurs only as described in subsection (b)(2) of this section applied by substituting "plan" for "collective bargaining agreement" in subparagraph (B)(i) thereof.

(2) For purposes of this subsection, the term "entertainment industry" means—

(A) theater, motion picture (except to the extent provided in regulations prescribed by the corporation), radio, television, sound or visual recording, music, and dance, and

(B) such other entertainment activities as the corporation may determine to be appropriate.

(3) The corporation may by regulation exclude a group or class of employers described in the preceding sentence from the application of this subsection if the corporation determines that such exclusion is necessary—

(A) to protect the interest of the plan's participants and beneficiaries, or

(B) to prevent a significant risk of loss to the corporation with respect to the plan.

(4) A plan may be amended to provide that this subsection shall not apply to a group or class of employers under the plan.

(d) Other determinative factors

(1) Notwithstanding subsection (a) of this section, in the case of an employer who—

(A) has an obligation to contribute under a plan described in paragraph (2) primarily for work described in such paragraph, and

(B) does not continue to perform work within the jurisdiction of the plan,

a complete withdrawal occurs only as described in paragraph (3).

(2) A plan is described in this paragraph if substantially all of the contributions required under the plan are made by employers primarily engaged in the long and short haul trucking industry, the household goods moving industry, or the public warehousing industry.

(3) A withdrawal occurs under this paragraph if—

(A) an employer permanently ceases to have an obligation to contribute under the plan or permanently ceases all covered operations under the plan, and

(B) either—

(i) the corporation determines that the plan has suffered substantial damage to its contribution base as a result of such cessation, or

(ii) the employer fails to furnish a bond issued by a corporate surety company that is an acceptable surety for purposes of section 1112 of this title, or an amount held in escrow by a bank or similar financial institution satisfactory to the plan, in an amount equal to 50 percent of the withdrawal liability of the employer.

(4) If, after an employer furnishes a bond or escrow to a plan under paragraph (3)(B)(ii), the corporation determines that the cessation of the employer's obligation to contribute under the plan (considered together with any cessations by other employers), or cessation of covered operations under the plan, has resulted in substantial damage to the contribution base of the plan, the employer shall be treated as having withdrawn from the plan on the date on which the obligation to contribute or covered operations ceased, and such bond or escrow shall be paid to the plan. The corporation shall not make a determination under this paragraph more than 60 months after the date on which such obligation to contribute or covered operations ceased.

(5) If the corporation determines that the employer has no further liability under the plan either—

(A) because it determines that the contribution base of the plan has not suffered substantial damage as a result of the cessation of the employer's obligation to contribute or cessation of covered operations (considered together with any cessation of contribution obligation, or of covered operations, with respect to other employers), or

(B) because it may not make a determination under paragraph (4) because of the last sentence thereof,

then the bond shall be cancelled or the escrow refunded.

(6) Nothing in this subsection shall be construed as a limitation on the amount of the withdrawal liability of any employer.

(e) Date of complete withdrawal

For purposes of this part, the date of a complete withdrawal is the date of the cessation of the obligation to contribute or the cessation of covered operations.

(f) Special liability withdrawal rules for industries other than construction and entertainment industries; procedures applicable to amend plans

(1) The corporation may prescribe regulations under which plans in industries other than the construction or entertainment industries may be amended to provide for special withdrawal liability rules similar to the rules described in subsections (b) and (c) of this section.

(2) Regulations under paragraph (1) shall permit use of special withdrawal liability rules—

(A) only in industries (or portions thereof) in which, as determined by the corporation, the characteristics that would make use of such rules appropriate are clearly shown, and

(B) only if the corporation determines, in each instance in which special withdrawal liability rules are permitted, that use of such rules will not pose a significant risk to the corporation under this subchapter.

(Pub. L. 93–406, title IV, § 4203, as added Pub. L. 96–364, title I, § 104(2), Sept. 26, 1980, 94 Stat. 1218.)

§ 1384. Sale of assets

(a) Complete or partial withdrawal not occurring as a result of sale and subsequent cessation of covered operations or cessation of obligation to contribute to covered operations; continuation of liability of seller

(1) A complete or partial withdrawal of an employer (hereinafter in this section referred to as the "seller") under this section does not occur solely because, as a result of a bona fide, arm's-length sale of assets to an unrelated party (hereinafter in this section referred to as the "purchaser"), the seller ceases covered operations or ceases to have an obligation to contribute for such operations, if—

(A) the purchaser has an obligation to contribute to the plan with respect to the operations for substantially the same number of contribution base units for which the seller had an obligation to contribute to the plan;

(B) the purchaser provides to the plan for a period of 5 plan years commencing with the first plan year beginning after the sale of assets, a bond issued by a corporate surety company that is an acceptable surety for purposes of section 1112 of this title, or an amount held in escrow by a bank or similar financial institution satisfactory to the plan, in an amount equal to the greater of—

(i) the average annual contribution required to be made by the seller with respect to the operations under the plan for the 3 plan years preceding the plan year in which the sale of the employer's assets occurs, or

(ii) the annual contribution that the seller was required to make with respect to the operations under the plan for the last plan year before the plan year in which the sale of the assets occurs,

which bond or escrow shall be paid to the plan if the purchaser withdraws from the plan, or fails to make a contribution to the plan when due, at any time during the first 5 plan years beginning after the sale; and

(C) the contract for sale provides that, if the purchaser withdraws in a complete withdrawal, or a partial withdrawal with respect to operations, during such first 5 plan years, the seller is secondarily liable for any withdrawal liability it would have had to the plan with respect to the operations (but for this section) if the liability of the purchaser with respect to the plan is not paid.

(2) If the purchaser—

(A) withdraws before the last day of the fifth plan year beginning after the sale, and

(B) fails to make any withdrawal liability payment when due,

then the seller shall pay to the plan an amount equal to the payment that would have been due from the seller but for this section.

(3)(A) If all, or substantially all, of the seller's assets are distributed, or if the seller is liquidated before the end of the 5 plan year period described in paragraph (1)(C), then the seller shall provide a bond or amount in escrow equal to the present value of the withdrawal liability the seller would have had but for this subsection.

(B) If only a portion of the seller's assets are distributed during such period, then a bond or escrow shall be required, in accordance with regulations prescribed by the corporation, in a manner consistent with subparagraph (A).

(4) The liability of the party furnishing a bond or escrow under this subsection shall be reduced, upon payment of the bond or escrow to the plan, by the amount thereof.

(b) Liability of purchaser

(1) For the purposes of this part, the liability of the purchaser shall be determined as if the purchaser had been required to contribute to the plan in the year of the sale and the 4 plan years preceding the sale the amount the seller was required to contribute for such operations for such 5 plan years.

(2) If the plan is in reorganization in the plan year in which the sale of assets occurs, the purchaser shall furnish a bond or escrow in an amount equal to 200 percent of the amount described in subsection (a)(1)(B) of this section.

(c) Variances or exemptions from continuation of liability of seller; procedures applicable

The corporation may by regulation vary the standards in subparagraphs (B) and (C) of subsection (a)(1) of this section if the variance would more effectively or equitably carry out the purposes of this subchapter. Before it promulgates such regulations, the corporation may grant individual or class variances or exemptions from the requirements of such subparagraphs if the particular case warrants it. Before granting such an individual or class variance or exemption, the corporation—

(1) shall publish notice in the Federal Register of the pendency of the variance or exemption,

(2) shall require that adequate notice be given to interested persons, and

(3) shall afford interested persons an opportunity to present their views.

(d) "Unrelated party" defined

For purposes of this section, the term "unrelated party" means a purchaser or seller who does not bear a relationship to the seller or purchaser, as the case may be, that is described in section 267(b) of title 26, or that is described in regulations prescribed by the corporation applying principles similar to the principles of such section.

(Pub. L. 93–406, title IV, § 4204, as added Pub. L. 96–364, title I, § 104(2), Sept. 26, 1980, 94 Stat. 1220; amended Pub. L. 101–239, title VII, § 7891(a)(1), Dec. 19, 1989, 103 Stat. 2445.)

AMENDMENTS

1989—Subsec. (d). Pub. L. 101–239 substituted "Internal Revenue Code of 1986" for "Internal Revenue Code of 1954", which for purposes of codification was translated as "title 26" thus requiring no change in text.

EFFECTIVE DATE OF 1989 AMENDMENT

Amendment by Pub. L. 101–239 effective, except as otherwise provided, as if included in the provision of the Tax Reform Act of 1986, Pub. L. 99–514, to which such amendment relates, see section 7891(f) of Pub. L. 101–239, set out as a note under section 1002 of this title.

§ 1385. Partial withdrawals

(a) Determinative factors

Except as otherwise provided in this section, there is a partial withdrawal by an employer from a plan on the last day of a plan year if for such plan year—

(1) there is a 70-percent contribution decline, or

(2) there is a partial cessation of the employer's contribution obligation.

(b) Criteria applicable

For purposes of subsection (a) of this section—

(1)(A) There is a 70-percent contribution decline for any plan year if during each plan year in the 3-year testing period the employer's contribution base units do not exceed 30 percent of the employer's contribution base units for the high base year.

(B) For purposes of subparagraph (A)—

(i) The term "3-year testing period" means the period consisting of the plan year and the immediately preceding 2 plan years.

(ii) The number of contribution base units for the high base year is the average number of such units for the 2 plan years for which the employer's contribution base units were the highest within the 5 plan years immediately preceding the beginning of the 3-year testing period.

(2)(A) There is a partial cessation of the employer's contribution obligation for the plan year if, during such year—

(i) the employer permanently ceases to have an obligation to contribute under one or more but fewer than all collective bargaining agreements under which the employer has been obligated to contribute under the plan but continues to perform work in the jurisdiction of the collective bargaining agreement of the type for which contributions were previously required or transfers such work to another location or to an entity or entities owned or controlled by the employer, or

(ii) an employer permanently ceases to have an obligation to contribute under the plan with respect to work performed at one or more but fewer than all of its facilities, but continues to perform work at the facility of the type for which the obligation to contribute ceased.

(B) For purposes of subparagraph (A), a cessation of obligations under a collective bargaining agreement shall not be considered to have occurred solely because, with respect to the same plan, one agreement that requires contributions to the plan has been substituted for another agreement.

(c) Retail food industry

(1) In the case of a plan in which a majority of the covered employees are employed in the retail food industry, the plan may be amended to provide that this section shall be applied with respect to such plan—

(A) by substituting "35 percent" for "70 percent" in subsections (a) and (b) of this section, and

(B) by substituting "65 percent" for "30 percent" in subsection (b) of this section.

(2) Any amendment adopted under paragraph (1) shall provide rules for the equitable reduction of withdrawal liability in any case in which the number of the plan's contribution base units, in the 2 plan years following the plan year of withdrawal of the employer, is higher than such number immediately after the withdrawal.

(3) Section 1388 of this title shall not apply to a plan which has been amended under paragraph (1).

(d) Continuation of liability of employer for partial withdrawal under amended plan

In the case of a plan described in section 404(c) of title 26, or a continuation thereof, the plan may be amended to provide rules setting forth other conditions consistent with the purposes of this chapter under which an employer has liability for partial withdrawal.

(Pub. L. 93–406, title IV, §4205, as added Pub. L. 96–364, title I, §104(2), Sept. 26, 1980, 94 Stat. 1221; amended Pub. L. 101–239, title VII, §7891(a)(1), Dec. 19, 1989, 103 Stat. 2445; Pub. L. 109–280, title II, §204(b)(1), Aug. 17, 2006, 120 Stat. 887.)

REFERENCES IN TEXT

This chapter, referred to in subsec. (d), was in the original "this Act", meaning Pub. L. 93–406, known as the Employee Retirement Income Security Act of 1974. Titles I, III, and IV of such Act are classified principally to this chapter. For complete classification of this Act to the Code, see Short Title note set out under section 1001 of this title and Tables.

AMENDMENTS

2006—Subsec. (b)(2)(A)(i). Pub. L. 109–280 inserted "or to an entity or entities owned or controlled by the employer" after "to another location".

1989—Subsec. (d). Pub. L. 101–239 substituted "Internal Revenue Code of 1986" for "Internal Revenue Code of 1954", which for purposes of codification was translated as "title 26" thus requiring no change in text.

EFFECTIVE DATE OF 2006 AMENDMENT

Pub. L. 109–280, title II, §204(b)(2), Aug. 17, 2006, 120 Stat. 887, provided that: "The amendment made by this subsection [amending this section] shall apply with respect to work transferred on or after the date of the enactment of this Act [Aug. 17, 2006]."

EFFECTIVE DATE OF 1989 AMENDMENT

Amendment by Pub. L. 101–239 effective, except as otherwise provided, as if included in the provision of the Tax Reform Act of 1986, Pub. L. 99–514, to which such amendment relates, see section 7891(f) of Pub. L. 101–239, set out as a note under section 1002 of this title.

APPLICABILITY TO CERTAIN EMPLOYERS ENGAGED IN TRADE OR BUSINESS OF SHIPPING BULK CARGOES IN GREAT LAKES MARITIME INDUSTRY

Section 108(c)(2) of Pub. L. 96–364 provided that:

"(A) For the purpose of applying section 4205 of the Employee Retirement Income Security Act of 1974 [this section] in the case of an employer described in subparagraph (B)—

"(i) 'more than 75 percent' shall be substituted for '70 percent' in subsections (a) and (b) of such section.

"(ii) '25 percent or less' shall be substituted for '30 percent' in subsection (b) of such section, and

"(iii) the number of contribution units for the high base year shall be the average annual number of such units for calendar years 1970 and 1971.

"(B) An employer is described in this subparagraph if—

"(i) the employer is engaged in the trade or business of shipping bulk cargoes in the Great Lakes Maritime Industry, and whose fleet consists of vessels the gross registered tonnage of which was at least 7,800, as stated in the American Bureau of Shipping Record, and

"(ii) whose fleet during any 5 years from the period 1970 through and including 1979 has experienced a 33 percent or more increase in the contribution units as measured from the average annual contribution units for the calendar years 1970 and 1971."

APPLICABILITY TO SPECIFIED PLAN YEAR, CESSATION OF CONTRIBUTION OBLIGATIONS, AND CONTRIBUTION BASE UNITS OF EMPLOYER

Section 108(d) of Pub. L. 96–364, as amended by Pub. L. 98–369, div. A, title V, §558(b)(2), July 18, 1984, 98 Stat. 899, provided that: "For purposes of section 4205 of the Employee Retirement Income Security Act of 1974 [this section]—

"(1) subsection (a)(1) of such section shall not apply to any plan year beginning before September 26, 1982,

"(2) subsection (a)(2) of such section shall not apply with respect to any cessation of contribution obligations occurring before September 26, 1980, and

"(3) in applying subsection (b) of such section, the employer's contribution base units for any plan year ending before September 26, 1980, shall be deemed to be equal to the employer's contribution base units for the last plan year ending before such date."

LIABILITY OF CERTAIN EMPLOYERS ANNOUNCING PUBLICLY BEFORE DECEMBER 13, 1979, TOTAL CESSATION OF COVERED OPERATIONS AT A FACILITY IN A STATE; AMOUNT, COVERAGE, DETERMINATIVE FACTORS, ETC.

Section 108(e) of Pub. L. 96–364 provided that:

"(1) In the case of a partial withdrawal under section 4205 of the Employee Retirement Income Security Act of 1974 [this section], an employer who—

"(A) before December 13, 1979, had publicly announced the total cessation of covered operations at a facility in a State (and such cessation occurred within 12 months after the announcement),

"(B) had not been obligated to make contributions to the plan on behalf of the employees at such facility for more than 8 years before the discontinuance of contributions, and

"(C) after the discontinuance of contributions does not within 1 year after the date of the partial withdrawal perform work in the same State of the type for which contributions were previously required, shall be liable under such section with respect to such partial withdrawal in an amount not greater than the amount determined under paragraph (2).

"(2) The amount determined under this paragraph is the excess (if any) of—

"(A) the present value (on the withdrawal date) of the benefits under the plan which—

"(i) were vested on the withdrawal date (or, if earlier, at the time of separation from service with the employer at the facility),

"(ii) were accrued by employees who on December 13, 1979 (or, if earlier, at the time of separation from service with the employer at the facility), were employed at the facility, and

"(iii) are attributable to service with the withdrawing employer, over

"(B)(i) the sum of—

"(I) all employer contributions to the plan on behalf of employees at the facility before the withdrawal date,

"(II) interest (to the withdrawal date) on amounts described in subclause (I), and

"(III) $100,000, reduced by

"(ii) the sum of—

"(I) the benefits paid under the plan on or before the withdrawal date with respect to former employees who separated from employment at the facility, and

"(II) interest (to the withdrawal date) on amounts described in subclause (I).

"(3) For purposes of paragraph (2)—

"(A) actuarial assumptions shall be those used in the last actuarial report completed before December 13, 1979,

"(B) the term 'withdrawal date' means the date on which the employer ceased work at the facility of the type for which contributions were previously required, and

"(C) the term 'facility' means the facility referred to in paragraph (1)."

§1386. Adjustment for partial withdrawal; determination of amount; reduction for partial withdrawal liability; procedures applicable

(a) The amount of an employer's liability for a partial withdrawal, before the application of sections 1399(c)(1) and 1405 of this title, is equal to the product of—

(1) the amount determined under section 1391 of this title, and adjusted under section 1389 of this title if appropriate, determined as if the employer had withdrawn from the plan in a complete withdrawal—

(A) on the date of the partial withdrawal, or

(B) in the case of a partial withdrawal described in section 1385(a)(1) of this title (relating to 70-percent contribution decline), on the last day of the first plan year in the 3-year testing period,

multiplied by

(2) a fraction which is 1 minus a fraction—

(A) the numerator of which is the employer's contribution base units for the plan year following the plan year in which the partial withdrawal occurs, and

(B) the denominator of which is the average of the employer's contribution base units for—

(i) except as provided in clause (ii), the 5 plan years immediately preceding the plan year in which the partial withdrawal occurs, or

(ii) in the case of a partial withdrawal described in section 1385(a)(1) of this title (relating to 70-percent contribution decline), the 5 plan years immediately preceding the beginning of the 3-year testing period.

(b)(1) In the case of an employer that has withdrawal liability for a partial withdrawal from a plan, any withdrawal liability of that employer for a partial or complete withdrawal from that plan in a subsequent plan year shall be reduced by the amount of any partial withdrawal liability (reduced by any abatement or reduction of such liability) of the employer with respect to the plan for a previous plan year.

(2) The corporation shall prescribe such regulations as may be necessary to provide for proper adjustments in the reduction provided by paragraph (1) for—

(A) changes in unfunded vested benefits arising after the close of the prior year for which partial withdrawal liability was determined,

(B) changes in contribution base units occurring after the close of the prior year for which partial withdrawal liability was determined, and

(C) any other factors for which it determines adjustment to be appropriate,

so that the liability for any complete or partial withdrawal in any subsequent year (after the application of the reduction) properly reflects the employer's share of liability with respect to the plan.

(Pub. L. 93–406, title IV, §4206, as added Pub. L. 96–364, title I, §104(2), Sept. 26, 1980, 94 Stat. 1222.)

§1387. Reduction or waiver of complete withdrawal liability; procedures and standards applicable

(a) The corporation shall provide by regulation for the reduction or waiver of liability for a complete withdrawal in the event that an employer who has withdrawn from a plan subsequently resumes covered operations under the plan or renews an obligation to contribute under the plan, to the extent that the corporation determines that reduction or waiver of withdrawal liability is consistent with the purposes of this chapter.

(b) The corporation shall prescribe by regulation a procedure and standards for the amendment of plans to provide alternative rules for the reduction or waiver of liability for a complete withdrawal in the event that an employer who has withdrawn from the plan subsequently resumes covered operations or renews an obligation to contribute under the plan. The rules may apply only to the extent that the rules are consistent with the purposes of this chapter.

(Pub. L. 93–406, title IV, §4207, as added Pub. L. 96–364, title I, §104(2), Sept. 26, 1980, 94 Stat. 1223.)

References in Text

This chapter, referred to in text, was in the original "this Act", meaning Pub. L. 93–406, known as the Employee Retirement Income Security Act of 1974. Titles I, III, and IV of such Act are classified principally to this chapter. For complete classification of this Act to the Code see Short Title note set out under section 1001 of this title and Tables.

§ 1388. Reduction of partial withdrawal liability

(a) Obligation of employer for payments for partial withdrawal for plan years beginning after the second consecutive plan year following the partial withdrawal year; criteria applicable; furnishing of bond in lieu of payment of partial withdrawal liability

(1) If, for any 2 consecutive plan years following the plan year in which an employer has partially withdrawn from a plan under section 1385(a)(1) of this title (referred to elsewhere in this section as the "partial withdrawal year"), the number of contribution base units with respect to which the employer has an obligation to contribute under the plan for each such year is not less than 90 percent of the total number of contribution base units with respect to which the employer had an obligation to contribute under the plan for the high base year (within the meaning of section 1385(b)(1)(B)(ii) of this title), then the employer shall have no obligation to make payments with respect to such partial withdrawal (other than delinquent payments) for plan years beginning after the second consecutive plan year following the partial withdrawal year.

(2)(A) For any plan year for which the number of contribution base units with respect to which an employer who has partially withdrawn under section 1385(a)(1) of this title has an obligation to contribute under the plan equals or exceeds the number of units for the highest year determined under paragraph (1) without regard to "90 percent of", the employer may furnish (in lieu of payment of the partial withdrawal liability determined under section 1386 of this title) a bond to the plan in the amount determined by the plan sponsor (not exceeding 50 percent of the annual payment otherwise required).

(B) If the plan sponsor determines under paragraph (1) that the employer has no further liability to the plan for the partial withdrawal, then the bond shall be cancelled.

(C) If the plan sponsor determines under paragraph (1) that the employer continues to have liability to the plan for the partial withdrawal, then—

(i) the bond shall be paid to the plan,

(ii) the employer shall immediately be liable for the outstanding amount of liability due with respect to the plan year for which the bond was posted, and

(iii) the employer shall continue to make the partial withdrawal liability payments as they are due.

(b) Obligation of employer for payments for partial withdrawal for plan years beginning after the second consecutive plan year; other criteria applicable

If—

(1) for any 2 consecutive plan years following a partial withdrawal under section 1385(a)(1) of this title, the number of contribution base units with respect to which the employer has an obligation to contribute for each such year exceeds 30 percent of the total number of contribution base units with respect to which the employer had an obligation to contribute for the high base year (within the meaning of section 1385(b)(1)(B)(ii) of this title,[1] and

(2) the total number of contribution base units with respect to which all employers under the plan have obligations to contribute in each of such 2 consecutive years is not less than 90 percent of the total number of contribution base units for which all employers had obligations to contribute in the partial withdrawal plan year;

then, the employer shall have no obligation to make payments with respect to such partial withdrawal (other than delinquent payments) for plan years beginning after the second such consecutive plan year.

(c) Pro rata reduction of amount of partial withdrawal liability payment of employer for plan year following partial withdrawal year

In any case in which, in any plan year following a partial withdrawal under section 1385(a)(1) of this title, the number of contribution base units with respect to which the employer has an obligation to contribute for such year equals or exceeds 110 percent (or such other percentage as the plan may provide by amendment and which is not prohibited under regulations prescribed by the corporation) of the number of contribution base units with respect to which the employer had an obligation to contribute in the partial withdrawal year, then the amount of the employer's partial withdrawal liability payment for such year shall be reduced pro rata, in accordance with regulations prescribed by the corporation.

(d) Building and construction industry; entertainment industry

(1) An employer to whom section 1383(b)[2] of this title (relating to the building and construction industry) applies is liable for a partial withdrawal only if the employer's obligation to contribute under the plan is continued for no more than an insubstantial portion of its work in the craft and area jurisdiction of the collective bargaining agreement of the type for which contributions are required.

(2) An employer to whom section 1383(c)[2] of this title (relating to the entertainment industry) applies shall have no liability for a partial withdrawal except under the conditions and to the extent prescribed by the corporation by regulation.

(e) Reduction or elimination of partial withdrawal liability under any conditions; criteria; procedures applicable

(1) The corporation may prescribe regulations providing for the reduction or elimination of partial withdrawal liability under any conditions with respect to which the corporation determines that reduction or elimination of partial withdrawal liability is consistent with the purposes of this chapter.

(2) Under such regulations, reduction of withdrawal liability shall be provided only with respect to subsequent changes in the employer's contributions for the same operations, or under the same collective bargaining agreement, that

[1] So in original. Probably should be "title),".

[2] See References in Text note below.

gave rise to the partial withdrawal, and changes in the employer's contribution base units with respect to other facilities or other collective bargaining agreements shall not be taken into account.

(3) The corporation shall prescribe by regulation a procedure by which a plan may by amendment adopt rules for the reduction or elimination of partial withdrawal liability under any other conditions, subject to the approval of the corporation based on its determination that adoption of such rules by the plan is consistent with the purposes of this chapter.

(Pub. L. 93–406, title IV, §4208, as added Pub. L. 96–364, title I, §104(2), Sept. 26, 1980, 94 Stat. 1224.)

REFERENCES IN TEXT

"Section 1383(b) of this title" and "section 1383(c) of this title", referred to in subsec. (d), were in the original "section 4202(b)" and "section 4202(c)", respectively, meaning section 4202(b) and section 4202(c) of the Employee Retirement Income Security Act of 1974 and were editorially translated as the probable intent of Congress in view of section 4202 of the Employee Retirement Income Security Act of 1974, which is classified to section 1382 of this title, not having subsection designations and the subject matter of section 4203 of the Act which is classified to section 1383 of this title.

This chapter, referred to in subsec. (e)(1), (3), was in the original "this Act", meaning Pub. L. 93–406, known as the Employee Retirement Income Security Act of 1974. Titles I, III, and IV of such Act are classified principally to this chapter. For complete classification of this Act to the Code, see Short Title note set out under section 1001 of this title and Tables.

§1389. De minimis rule

(a) Reduction of unfunded vested benefits allocable to employer withdrawn from plan

Except in the case of a plan amended under subsection (b) of this section, the amount of the unfunded vested benefits allocable under section 1391 of this title to an employer who withdraws from a plan shall be reduced by the smaller of—

(1) ¾ of 1 percent of the plan's unfunded vested obligations (determined as of the end of the plan year ending before the date of withdrawal), or

(2) $50,000,

reduced by the amount, if any, by which the unfunded vested benefits allowable to the employer, determined without regard to this subsection, exceeds $100,000.

(b) Amendment of plan for reduction of amount of unfunded vested benefits allocable to employer withdrawn from plan

A plan may be amended to provide for the reduction of the amount determined under section 1391 of this title by not more than the greater of—

(1) the amount determined under subsection (a) of this section, or

(2) the lesser of—

(A) the amount determined under subsection (a)(1) of this section, or

(B) $100,000,

reduced by the amount, if any, by which the amount determined under section 1391 of this title for the employer, determined without regard to this subsection, exceeds $150,000.

(c) Nonapplicability

This section does not apply—

(1) to an employer who withdraws in a plan year in which substantially all employers withdraw from the plan, or

(2) in any case in which substantially all employers withdraw from the plan during a period of one or more plan years pursuant to an agreement or arrangement to withdraw, to an employer who withdraws pursuant to such agreement or arrangement.

(d) Presumption of employer withdrawal from plan pursuant to agreement or arrangement applicable in action or proceeding to determine or collect withdrawal liability

In any action or proceeding to determine or collect withdrawal liability, if substantially all employers have withdrawn from a plan within a period of 3 plan years, an employer who has withdrawn from such plan during such period shall be presumed to have withdrawn from the plan pursuant to an agreement or arrangement, unless the employer proves otherwise by a preponderance of the evidence.

(Pub. L. 93–406, title IV, §4209, as added Pub. L. 96–364, title I, §104(2), Sept. 26, 1980, 94 Stat. 1225.)

§1390. Nonapplicability of withdrawal liability for certain temporary contribution obligation periods; exception

(a) An employer who withdraws from a plan in complete or partial withdrawal is not liable to the plan if the employer—

(1) first had an obligation to contribute to the plan after September 26, 1980,

(2) had an obligation to contribute to the plan for no more than the lesser of—

(A) 6 consecutive plan years preceding the date on which the employer withdraws, or

(B) the number of years required for vesting under the plan,

(3) was required to make contributions to the plan for each such plan year in an amount equal to less than 2 percent of the sum of all employer contributions made to the plan for each such year, and

(4) has never avoided withdrawal liability because of the application of this section with respect to the plan.

(b) Subsection (a) of this section shall apply to an employer with respect to a plan only if—

(1) the plan is amended to provide that subsection (a) of this section applies;

(2) the plan provides, or is amended to provide, that the reduction under section 411(a)(3)(E) of title 26 applies with respect to the employees of the employer; and

(3) the ratio of the assets of the plan for the plan year preceding the first plan year for which the employer was required to contribute to the plan to the benefit payments made during that plan year was at least 8 to 1.

(Pub. L. 93–406, title IV, §4210, as added Pub. L. 96–364, title I, §104(2), Sept. 26, 1980, 94 Stat. 1226; amended Pub. L. 101–239, title VII, §7891(a)(1), Dec. 19, 1989, 103 Stat. 2445; Pub. L. 109–280, title II, §204(c)(1), Aug. 17, 2006, 120 Stat. 887.)

AMENDMENTS

2006—Subsec. (b)(1) to (4). Pub. L. 109–280 redesignated pars. (2) to (4) as (1) to (3), respectively, and struck out former par. (1) which read as follows: "the plan is not a plan which primarily covers employees in the building and construction industry;".

1989—Subsec. (b)(3). Pub. L. 101–239 substituted "Internal Revenue Code of 1986" for "Internal Revenue Code of 1954", which for purposes of codification was translated as "title 26" thus requiring no change in text.

EFFECTIVE DATE OF 2006 AMENDMENT

Pub. L. 109–280, title II, §204(c)(3), Aug. 17, 2006, 120 Stat. 887, provided that: "The amendments made by this subsection [amending this section and section 1391 of this title] shall apply with respect to plan withdrawals occurring on or after January 1, 2007."

EFFECTIVE DATE OF 1989 AMENDMENT

Amendment by Pub. L. 101–239 effective, except as otherwise provided, as if included in the provision of the Tax Reform Act of 1986, Pub. L. 99–514, to which such amendment relates, see section 7891(f) of Pub. L. 101–239, set out as a note under section 1002 of this title.

§ 1391. Methods for computing withdrawal liability

(a) Determination of amount of unfunded vested benefits allocable to employer withdrawn from plan

The amount of the unfunded vested benefits allocable to an employer that withdraws from a plan shall be determined in accordance with subsection (b), (c), or (d) of this section.

(b) Factors determining computation of amount of unfunded vested benefits allocable to employer withdrawn from plan

(1) Except as provided in subsections (c) and (d) of this section, the amount of unfunded vested benefits allocable to an employer that withdraws is the sum of—

(A) the employer's proportional share of the unamortized amount of the change in the plan's unfunded vested benefits for plan years ending after September 25, 1980, as determined under paragraph (2),

(B) the employer's proportional share, if any, of the unamortized amount of the plan's unfunded vested benefits at the end of the plan year ending before September 26, 1980, as determined under paragraph (3); and

(C) the employer's proportional share of the unamortized amounts of the reallocated unfunded vested benefits (if any) as determined under paragraph (4).

If the sum of the amounts determined with respect to an employer under paragraphs (2), (3), and (4) is negative, the unfunded vested benefits allocable to the employer shall be zero.

(2)(A) An employer's proportional share of the unamortized amount of the change in the plan's unfunded vested benefits for plan years ending after September 25, 1980, is the sum of the employer's proportional shares of the unamortized amount of the change in unfunded vested benefits for each plan year in which the employer has an obligation to contribute under the plan ending—

(i) after such date, and

(ii) before the plan year in which the withdrawal of the employer occurs.

(B) The change in a plan's unfunded vested benefits for a plan year is the amount by which—

(i) the unfunded vested benefits at the end of the plan year; exceeds

(ii) the sum of—

(I) the unamortized amount of the unfunded vested benefits for the last plan year ending before September 26, 1980, and

(II) the sum of the unamortized amounts of the change in unfunded vested benefits for each plan year ending after September 25, 1980, and preceding the plan year for which the change is determined.

(C) The unamortized amount of the change in a plan's unfunded vested benefits with respect to a plan year is the change in unfunded vested benefits for the plan year, reduced by 5 percent of such change for each succeeding plan year.

(D) The unamortized amount of the unfunded vested benefits for the last plan year ending before September 26, 1980, is the amount of the unfunded vested benefits as of the end of that plan year reduced by 5 percent of such amount for each succeeding plan year.

(E) An employer's proportional share of the unamortized amount of a change in unfunded vested benefits is the product of—

(i) the unamortized amount of such change (as of the end of the plan year preceding the plan year in which the employer withdraws); multiplied by

(ii) a fraction—

(I) the numerator of which is the sum of the contributions required to be made under the plan by the employer for the year in which such change arose and for the 4 preceding plan years, and

(II) the denominator of which is the sum for the plan year in which such change arose and the 4 preceding plan years of all contributions made by employers who had an obligation to contribute under the plan for the plan year in which such change arose reduced by the contributions made in such years by employers who had withdrawn from the plan in the year in which the change arose.

(3) An employer's proportional share of the unamortized amount of the plan's unfunded vested benefits for the last plan year ending before September 26, 1980, is the product of—

(A) such unamortized amount; multiplied by—

(B) a fraction—

(i) the numerator of which is the sum of all contributions required to be made by the employer under the plan for the most recent 5 plan years ending before September 26, 1980, and

(ii) the denominator of which is the sum of all contributions made for the most recent 5 plan years ending before September 26, 1980, by all employers—

(I) who had an obligation to contribute under the plan for the first plan year ending on or after such date, and

(II) who had not withdrawn from the plan before such date.

(4)(A) An employer's proportional share of the unamortized amount of the reallocated unfunded vested benefits is the sum of the employer's proportional share of the unamortized amount of the reallocated unfunded vested benefits for each plan year ending before the plan year in which the employer withdrew from the plan.

(B) Except as otherwise provided in regulations prescribed by the corporation, the reallocated unfunded vested benefits for a plan year is the sum of—

(i) any amount which the plan sponsor determines in that plan year to be uncollectible for reasons arising out of cases or proceedings under title 11, or similar proceedings.[1]

(ii) any amount which the plan sponsor determines in that plan year will not be assessed as a result of the operation of section 1389, 1399(c)(1)(B), or 1405 of this title against an employer to whom a notice described in section 1399 of this title has been sent, and

(iii) any amount which the plan sponsor determines to be uncollectible or unassessable in that plan year for other reasons under standards not inconsistent with regulations prescribed by the corporation.

(C) The unamortized amount of the reallocated unfunded vested benefits with respect to a plan year is the reallocated unfunded vested benefits for the plan year, reduced by 5 percent of such reallocated unfunded vested benefits for each succeeding plan year.

(D) An employer's proportional share of the unamortized amount of the reallocated unfunded vested benefits with respect to a plan year is the product of—

(i) the unamortized amount of the reallocated unfunded vested benefits (as of the end of the plan year preceding the plan year in which the employer withdraws); multiplied by

(ii) the fraction defined in paragraph (2)(E)(ii).

(c) Amendment of multiemployer plan for determination respecting amount of unfunded vested benefits allocable to employer withdrawn from plan; factors determining computation of amount

(1) A multiemployer plan, other than a plan which primarily covers employees in the building and construction industry, may be amended to provide that the amount of unfunded vested benefits allocable to an employer that withdraws from the plan is an amount determined under paragraph (2), (3), (4), or (5) of this subsection, rather than under subsection (b) or (d) of this section. A plan described in section 1383(b)(1)(B)(i) of this title (relating to the building and construction industry) may be amended, to the extent provided in regulations prescribed by the corporation, to provide that the amount of the unfunded vested benefits allocable to an employer not described in section 1383(b)(1)(A) of this title shall be determined in a manner different from that provided in subsection (b) of this section.

(2)(A) The amount of the unfunded vested benefits allocable to any employer under this paragraph is the sum of the amounts determined under subparagraphs (B) and (C).

[1] So in original. The period probably should be a comma.

(B) The amount determined under this subparagraph is the product of—

(i) the plan's unfunded vested benefits as of the end of the last plan year ending before September 26, 1980, reduced as if those obligations were being fully amortized in level annual installments over 15 years beginning with the first plan year ending on or after such date; multiplied by

(ii) a fraction—

(I) the numerator of which is the sum of all contributions required to be made by the employer under the plan for the last 5 plan years ending before September 26, 1980, and

(II) the denominator of which is the sum of all contributions made for the last 5 plan years ending before September 26, 1980, by all employers who had an obligation to contribute under the plan for the first plan year ending after September 25, 1980, and who had not withdrawn from the plan before such date.

(C) The amount determined under this subparagraph is the product of—

(i) an amount equal to—

(I) the plan's unfunded vested benefits as of the end of the plan year preceding the plan year in which the employer withdraws, less

(II) the sum of the value as of such date of all outstanding claims for withdrawal liability which can reasonably be expected to be collected, with respect to employers withdrawing before such plan year, and that portion of the amount determined under subparagraph (B)(i) which is allocable to employers who have an obligation to contribute under the plan in the plan year preceding the plan year in which the employer withdraws and who also had an obligation to contribute under the plan for the first plan year ending after September 25, 1980; multiplied by

(ii) a fraction—

(I) the numerator of which is the total amount required to be contributed under the plan by the employer for the last 5 plan years ending before the date on which the employer withdraws, and

(II) the denominator of which is the total amount contributed under the plan by all employers for the last 5 plan years ending before the date on which the employer withdraws, increased by the amount of any employer contributions owed with respect to earlier periods which were collected in those plan years, and decreased by any amount contributed by an employer who withdrew from the plan under this part during those plan years.

(D) The corporation may by regulation permit adjustments in any denominator under this section, consistent with the purposes of this subchapter, where such adjustment would be appropriate to ease administrative burdens of plan sponsors in calculating such denominators.

(3) The amount of the unfunded vested benefits allocable to an employer under this paragraph is the product of—

(A) the plan's unfunded vested benefits as of the end of the plan year preceding the plan year in which the employer withdraws, less the value as of the end of such year of all outstanding claims for withdrawal liability which can reasonably be expected to be collected from employers withdrawing before such year; multiplied by

(B) a fraction—

(i) the numerator of which is the total amount required to be contributed by the employer under the plan for the last 5 plan years ending before the withdrawal, and

(ii) the denominator of which is the total amount contributed under the plan by all employers for the last 5 plan years ending before the withdrawal, increased by any employer contributions owed with respect to earlier periods which were collected in those plan years, and decreased by any amount contributed to the plan during those plan years by employers who withdrew from the plan under this section during those plan years.

(4)(A) The amount of the unfunded vested benefits allocable to an employer under this paragraph is equal to the sum of—

(i) the plan's unfunded vested benefits which are attributable to participants' service with the employer (determined as of the end of the plan year preceding the plan year in which the employer withdraws), and

(ii) the employer's proportional share of any unfunded vested benefits which are not attributable to service with the employer or other employers who are obligated to contribute under the plan in the plan year preceding the plan year in which the employer withdraws (determined as of the end of the plan year preceding the plan year in which the employer withdraws).

(B) The plan's unfunded vested benefits which are attributable to participants' service with the employer is the amount equal to the value of nonforfeitable benefits under the plan which are attributable to participants' service with such employer (determined under plan rules not inconsistent with regulations of the corporation) decreased by the share of plan assets determined under subparagraph (C) which is allocated to the employer as provided under subparagraph (D).

(C) The value of plan assets determined under this subparagraph is the value of plan assets allocated to nonforfeitable benefits which are attributable to service with the employers who have an obligation to contribute under the plan in the plan year preceding the plan year in which the employer withdraws, which is determined by multiplying—

(i) the value of the plan assets as of the end of the plan year preceding the plan year in which the employer withdraws, by

(ii) a fraction—

(I) the numerator of which is the value of nonforfeitable benefits which are attributable to service with such employers, and

(II) the denominator of which is the value of all nonforfeitable benefits under the plan

as of the end of the plan year.

(D) The share of plan assets, determined under subparagraph (C), which is allocated to the employer shall be determined in accordance with one of the following methods which shall be adopted by the plan by amendment:

(i) by multiplying the value of plan assets determined under subparagraph (C) by a fraction—

(I) the numerator of which is the value of the nonforfeitable benefits which are attributable to service with the employer, and

(II) the denominator of which is the value of the nonforfeitable benefits which are attributable to service with all employers who have an obligation to contribute under the plan in the plan year preceding the plan year in which the employer withdraws;

(ii) by multiplying the value of plan assets determined under subparagraph (C) by a fraction—

(I) the numerator of which is the sum of all contributions (accumulated with interest) which have been made to the plan by the employer for the plan year preceding the plan year in which the employer withdraws and all preceding plan years; and

(II) the denominator of which is the sum of all contributions (accumulated with interest) which have been made to the plan (for the plan year preceding the plan year in which the employer withdraws and all preceding plan years) by all employers who have an obligation to contribute to the plan for the plan year preceding the plan year in which the employer withdraws; or

(iii) by multiplying the value of plan assets under subparagraph (C) by a fraction—

(I) the numerator of which is the amount determined under clause (ii)(I) of this subparagraph, less the sum of benefit payments (accumulated with interest) made to participants (and their beneficiaries) for the plan years described in such clause (ii)(I) which are attributable to service with the employer; and

(II) the denominator of which is the amount determined under clause (ii)(II) of this subparagraph, reduced by the sum of benefit payments (accumulated with interest) made to participants (and their beneficiaries) for the plan years described in such clause (ii)(II) which are attributable to service with respect to the employers described in such clause (ii)(II).

(E) The amount of the plan's unfunded vested benefits for a plan year preceding the plan year in which an employer withdraws, which is not attributable to service with employers who have an obligation to contribute under the plan in the plan year preceding the plan year in which such employer withdraws, is equal to—

(i) an amount equal to—

(I) the value of all nonforfeitable benefits under the plan at the end of such plan year, reduced by

(II) the value of nonforfeitable benefits under the plan at the end of such plan year which are attributable to participants' service with employers who have an obligation to contribute under the plan for such plan year; reduced by

(ii) an amount equal to—

(I) the value of the plan assets as of the end of such plan year, reduced by

(II) the value of plan assets as of the end of such plan year as determined under subparagraph (C); reduced by

(iii) the value of all outstanding claims for withdrawal liability which can reasonably be expected to be collected with respect to employers withdrawing before the year preceding the plan year in which the employer withdraws.

(F) The employer's proportional share described in subparagraph (A)(ii) for a plan year is the amount determined under subparagraph (E) for the employer, but not in excess of an amount which bears the same ratio to the sum of the amounts determined under subparagraph (E) for all employers under the plan as the amount determined under subparagraph (C) for the employer bears to the sum of the amounts determined under subparagraph (C) for all employers under the plan.

(G) The corporation may prescribe by regulation other methods which a plan may adopt for allocating assets to determine the amount of the unfunded vested benefits attributable to service with the employer and to determine the employer's share of unfunded vested benefits not attributable to service with employers who have an obligation to contribute under the plan in the plan year in which the employer withdraws.

(5)(A) The corporation shall prescribe by regulation a procedure by which a plan may, by amendment, adopt any other alternative method for determining an employer's allocable share of unfunded vested benefits under this section, subject to the approval of the corporation based on its determination that adoption of the method by the plan would not significantly increase the risk of loss to plan participants and beneficiaries or to the corporation.

(B) The corporation may prescribe by regulation standard approaches for alternative methods, other than those set forth in the preceding paragraphs of this subsection, which a plan may adopt under subparagraph (A), for which the corporation may waive or modify the approval requirements of subparagraph (A). Any alternative method shall provide for the allocation of substantially all of a plan's unfunded vested benefits among employers who have an obligation to contribute under the plan.

(C) Unless the corporation by regulation provides otherwise, a plan may be amended to provide that a period of more than 5 but not more than 10 plan years may be used for determining the numerator and denominator of any fraction which is used under any method authorized under this section for determining an employer's allocable share of unfunded vested benefits under this section.

(D) The corporation may by regulation permit adjustments in any denominator under this section, consistent with the purposes of this subchapter, where such adjustment would be appropriate to ease administrative burdens of plan sponsors in calculating such denominators.

(E) FRESH START OPTION.—Notwithstanding paragraph (1), a plan may be amended to provide that the withdrawal liability method described in subsection (b) shall be applied by substituting the plan year which is specified in the amendment and for which the plan has no unfunded vested benefits for the plan year ending before September 26, 1980.

(d) Method of calculating allocable share of employer of unfunded vested benefits set forth in subsection (c)(3) of this section; applicability of certain statutory provisions

(1) The method of calculating an employer's allocable share of unfunded vested benefits set forth in subsection (c)(3) of this section shall be the method for calculating an employer's allocable share of unfunded vested benefits under a plan to which section 404(c) of title 26, or a continuation of such a plan, applies, unless the plan is amended to adopt another method authorized under subsection (b) or (c) of this section.

(2) Sections 1384, 1389, 1399(c)(1)(B), and 1405 of this title shall not apply with respect to the withdrawal of an employer from a plan described in paragraph (1) unless the plan is amended to provide that any of such sections apply.

(e) Reduction of liability of withdrawn employer in case of transfer of liabilities to another plan incident to withdrawal or partial withdrawal of employer

In the case of a transfer of liabilities to another plan incident to an employer's withdrawal or partial withdrawal, the withdrawn employer's liability under this part shall be reduced in an amount equal to the value, as of the end of the last plan year ending on or before the date of the withdrawal, of the transferred unfunded vested benefits.

(f) Computations applicable in case of withdrawal following merger of multiemployer plans

In the case of a withdrawal following a merger of multiemployer plans, subsection (b), (c), or (d) of this section shall be applied in accordance with regulations prescribed by the corporation; except that, if a withdrawal occurs in the first plan year beginning after a merger of multiemployer plans, the determination under this section shall be made as if each of the multiemployer plans had remained separate plans.

(Pub. L. 93–406, title IV, §4211, as added Pub. L. 96–364, title I, §104(2), Sept. 26, 1980, 94 Stat. 1226; amended Pub. L. 98–369, div. A, title V, §558(b)(1)(A), (B), July 18, 1984, 98 Stat. 899; Pub. L. 101–239, title VII, §7891(a)(1), Dec. 19, 1989, 103 Stat. 2445; Pub. L. 109–280, title II, §204(c)(2), Aug. 17, 2006, 120 Stat. 887.)

AMENDMENTS

2006—Subsec. (c)(5)(E). Pub. L. 109–280 added subpar. (E).

1989—Subsec. (d)(1). Pub. L. 101–239 substituted "Internal Revenue Code of 1986" for "Internal Revenue Code of 1954", which for purposes of codification was translated as "title 26" thus requiring no change in text.

1984—Subsec. (b). Pub. L. 98–369, §558(b)(1)(A), (B), substituted "September 25, 1980" for "April 28, 1980" in pars. (1)(A) and (2)(A), (B)(ii)(II), and "September 26, 1980" for "April 29, 1980" in pars. (1)(B) and (2)(B)(ii)(I), (D), and in par. (3) in provisions preceding subpar. (A) and in subpar. (B)(i), (ii).

Subsec. (c)(2). Pub. L. 98–369, §558(b)(1)(A), (B), substituted "September 25, 1980" for "April 28, 1980" in subpars. (B)(ii)(II) and (C)(i)(II) and "September 26, 1980" for "April 29, 1980" in subpar. (B)(i), (ii)(I), (II).

EFFECTIVE DATE OF 2006 AMENDMENT

Amendment by Pub. L. 109–280 applicable with respect to plan withdrawals occurring on or after Jan. 1, 2007, see section 204(c)(3) of Pub. L. 109–280, set out as a note under section 1390 of this title.

EFFECTIVE DATE OF 1989 AMENDMENT

Amendment by Pub. L. 101–239 effective, except as otherwise provided, as if included in the provision of the Tax Reform Act of 1986, Pub. L. 99–514, to which such amendment relates, see section 7891(f) of Pub. L. 101–239, set out as a note under section 1002 of this title.

§ 1392. Obligation to contribute

(a) "Obligation to contribute" defined

For purposes of this part, the term "obligation to contribute" means an obligation to contribute arising—

(1) under one or more collective bargaining (or related) agreements, or

(2) as a result of a duty under applicable labor-management relations law, but

does not include an obligation to pay withdrawal liability under this section or to pay delinquent contributions.

(b) Payments of withdrawal liability not considered contributions

Payments of withdrawal liability under this part shall not be considered contributions for purposes of this part.

(c) Transactions to evade or avoid liability

If a principal purpose of any transaction is to evade or avoid liability under this part, this part shall be applied (and liability shall be determined and collected) without regard to such transaction.

(Pub. L. 93–406, title IV, § 4212, as added Pub. L. 96–364, title I, § 104(2), Sept. 26, 1980, 94 Stat. 1233.)

§ 1393. Actuarial assumptions

(a) Use by plan actuary in determining unfunded vested benefits of a plan for computing withdrawal liability of employer

The corporation may prescribe by regulation actuarial assumptions which may be used by a plan actuary in determining the unfunded vested benefits of a plan for purposes of determining an employer's withdrawal liability under this part. Withdrawal liability under this part shall be determined by each plan on the basis of—

(1) actuarial assumptions and methods which, in the aggregate, are reasonable (taking into account the experience of the plan and reasonable expectations) and which, in combination, offer the actuary's best estimate of anticipated experience under the plan, or

(2) actuarial assumptions and methods set forth in the corporation's regulations for purposes of determining an employer's withdrawal liability.

(b) Factors determinative of unfunded vested benefits of plan for computing withdrawal liability of employer

In determining the unfunded vested benefits of a plan for purposes of determining an employer's withdrawal liability under this part, the plan actuary may—

(1) rely on the most recent complete actuarial valuation used for purposes of section 412 of title 26 and reasonable estimates for the interim years of the unfunded vested benefits, and

(2) in the absence of complete data, rely on the data available or on data secured by a sampling which can reasonably be expected to be representative of the status of the entire plan.

(c) Determination of amount of unfunded vested benefits

For purposes of this part, the term "unfunded vested benefits" means with respect to a plan, an amount equal to—

(A) the value of nonforfeitable benefits under the plan, less

(B) the value of the assets of the plan.

(Pub. L. 93–406, title IV, § 4213, as added Pub. L. 96–364, title I, § 104(2), Sept. 26, 1980, 94 Stat. 1233; amended Pub. L. 101–239, title VII, § 7891(a)(1), Dec. 19, 1989, 103 Stat. 2445.)

AMENDMENTS

1989—Subsec. (b)(1). Pub. L. 101–239 substituted "Internal Revenue Code of 1986" for "Internal Revenue Code of 1954", which for purposes of codification was translated as "title 26" thus requiring no change in text.

EFFECTIVE DATE OF 1989 AMENDMENT

Amendment by Pub. L. 101–239 effective, except as otherwise provided, as if included in the provision of the Tax Reform Act of 1986, Pub. L. 99–514, to which such amendment relates, see section 7891(f) of Pub. L. 101–239, set out as a note under section 1002 of this title.

§ 1394. Application of plan amendments; exception

(a) No plan rule or amendment adopted after January 31, 1981, under section 1389 or 1391(c) of this title may be applied without the employer's consent with respect to liability for a withdrawal or partial withdrawal which occurred before the date on which the rule or amendment was adopted.

(b) All plan rules and amendments authorized under this part shall operate and be applied uniformly with respect to each employer, except that special provisions may be made to take into account the creditworthiness of an employer. The plan sponsor shall give notice to all employers who have an obligation to contribute under the plan and to all employee organizations representing employees covered under the plan of any plan rules or amendments adopted pursuant to this section.

(Pub. L. 93–406, title IV, § 4214, as added Pub. L. 96–364, title I, § 104(2), Sept. 26, 1980, 94 Stat. 1234.)

§ 1395. Plan notification to corporation of potentially significant withdrawals

The corporation may, by regulation, require the plan sponsor of a multiemployer plan to provide notice to the corporation when the withdrawal from the plan by any employer has resulted, or will result, in a significant reduction in the amount of aggregate contributions under the plan made by employers.

(Pub. L. 93–406, title IV, § 4215, as added Pub. L. 96–364, title I, § 104(2), Sept. 26, 1980, 94 Stat. 1234.)

§ 1396. Special rules for plans under section 404(c) of title 26

(a) Amount of withdrawal liability; determinative factors

In the case of a plan described in subsection (b) of this section—

(1) if an employer withdraws prior to a termination described in section 1341a(a)(2) of this title, the amount of withdrawal liability to be paid in any year by such employer shall be an amount equal to the greater of—

(A) the amount determined under section 1399(c)(1)(C)(i) of this title, or

(B) the product of—

(i) the number of contribution base units for which the employer would have been required to make contributions for the prior plan year if the employer had not withdrawn, multiplied by

(ii) the contribution rate for the plan year which would be required to meet the amortization schedules contained in section 1423(d)(3)(B)(ii) of this title (determined without regard to any limitation on such rate otherwise provided by this subchapter)

except that an employer shall not be required to pay an amount in excess of the withdrawal liability computed with interest; and

(2) the withdrawal liability of an employer who withdraws after December 31, 1983, as a result of a termination described in section 1341a(a)(2) of this title which is agreed to by the labor organization that appoints the employee representative on the joint board of trustees which sponsors the plan, shall be determined under subsection (c) of this section if—

(A) as a result of prior employer withdrawals in any plan year commencing after January 1, 1980, the number of contribution base units is reduced to less than 67 percent of the average number of such units for the calendar years 1974 through 1979; and

(B) at least 50 percent of the withdrawal liability attributable to the first 33 percent decline described in subparagraph (A) has been determined by the plan sponsor to be uncollectible within the meaning of regulations of the corporation of general applicability; and

(C) the rate of employer contributions under the plan for each plan year following the first plan year beginning after September 26, 1980 and preceding the termination date equals or exceeds the rate described in section 1423(d)(3) of this title.

(b) Covered plans

A plan is described in this subsection if—

(1) it is a plan described in section 404(c) of title 26 or a continuation thereof; and

(2) participation in the plan is substantially limited to individuals who retired prior to January 1, 1976.

(c) Amount of liability of employer; "a year of signatory service" defined

(1) The amount of an employer's liability under this paragraph is the product of—

(A) the amount of the employer's withdrawal liability determined without regard to this section, and

(B) the greater of 90 percent, or a fraction—

(i) the numerator of which is an amount equal to the portion of the plan's unfunded vested benefits that is attributable to plan participants who have a total of 10 or more years of signatory service, and

(ii) the denominator of which is an amount equal to the total unfunded vested benefits of the plan.

(2) For purposes of paragraph (1), the term "a year of signatory service" means a year during any portion of which a participant was employed for an employer who was obligated to contribute in that year, or who was subsequently obligated to contribute.

(Pub. L. 93–406, title IV, § 4216, as added Pub. L. 96–364, title I, § 104(2), Sept. 26, 1980, 94 Stat. 1234.)

§ 1397. Application of part in case of certain pre-1980 withdrawals; adjustment of covered plan

(a) For the purpose of determining the amount of unfunded vested benefits allocable to an employer for a partial or complete withdrawal from a plan which occurs after September 25, 1980, and for the purpose of determining whether there has been a partial withdrawal after such date, the amount of contributions, and the number of contribution base units, of such employer properly allocable—

(1) to work performed under a collective bargaining agreement for which there was a permanent cessation of the obligation to contribute before September 26, 1980, or

(2) to work performed at a facility at which all covered operations permanently ceased before September 26, 1980, or for which there was a permanent cessation of the obligation to contribute before that date,

shall not be taken into account.

(b) A plan may, in a manner not inconsistent with regulations, which shall be prescribed by the corporation, adjust the amount of unfunded vested benefits allocable to other employers under a plan maintained by an employer described in subsection (a) of this section.

(Pub. L. 93–406, title IV, § 4217, as added Pub. L. 96–364, title I, § 104(2), Sept. 26, 1980, 94 Stat. 1235; amended Pub. L. 98–369, div. A, title V, § 558(b)(1)(A), (B), July 18, 1984, 98 Stat. 899.)

AMENDMENTS

1984—Subsec. (a). Pub. L. 98–369, § 558(b)(1)(A), (B), substituted "September 25, 1980" for "April 28, 1980" in provisions preceding par. (1) and "September 26, 1980" for "April 29, 1980" in pars. (1) and (2).

§ 1398. Withdrawal not to occur because of change in business form or suspension of contributions during labor dispute

Notwithstanding any other provision of this part, an employer shall not be considered to have withdrawn from a plan solely because—

(1) an employer ceases to exist by reason of—

(A) a change in corporate structure described in section 1369(b) of this title, or

(B) a change to an unincorporated form of business enterprise,

if the change causes no interruption in employer contributions or obligations to contribute under the plan, or

(2) an employer suspends contributions under the plan during a labor dispute involving its employees.

For purposes of this part, a successor or parent corporation or other entity resulting from any such change shall be considered the original employer.

(Pub. L. 93–406, title IV, § 4218, as added Pub. L. 96–364, title I, § 104(2), Sept. 26, 1980, 94 Stat. 1236; amended Pub. L. 99–514, title XVIII, § 1879(u)(4), as added Pub. L. 101–239, title VII, § 7862(b)(1)(C), Dec. 19, 1989, 103 Stat. 2432; Pub. L. 101–239, title VII, § 7893(f), Dec. 19, 1989, 103 Stat. 2447.)

AMENDMENTS

1989—Par. (1)(A). Pub. L. 101–239, § 7893(f), made identical amendment to that of Pub. L. 99–514, § 1879(u)(4), as added by Pub. L. 101–239, § 7862(b)(1)(C), see below.

Pub. L. 101–239, § 7862(b)(1)(C), added Pub. L. 99–514, § 1879(u)(4), see 1986 Amendment note below.

1986—Par. (1)(A). Pub. L. 99–514, § 1879(u)(4), as added by Pub. L. 101–239, § 7862(b)(1)(C), substituted "section 1369(b) of this title" for "section 1362(d) of this title".

EFFECTIVE DATE OF 1989 AMENDMENT

Amendment by section 7862(b)(1)(C) of Pub. L. 101–239 effective as if included in the provision of the Tax Reform Act of 1986, Pub. L. 99–514, to which such amendment relates, see section 7863 of Pub. L. 101–239, set out as a note under section 106 of Title 26, Internal Revenue Code.

Amendment by section 7893(f) of Pub. L. 101–239 effective as if included in the provision of the Single-Employer Pension Plan Amendments Act of 1986, Pub. L. 99–272, title XI, to which such amendment relates, see section 7893(h) of Pub. L. 101–239, set out as a note under section 1002 of this title.

PLAN AMENDMENTS NOT REQUIRED UNTIL JANUARY 1, 1989

For provisions directing that if any amendments made by subtitle A or subtitle C of title XI [§§ 1101–1147 and 1171–1177] or title XVIII [§§ 1800–1899A] of Pub. L. 99–514 require an amendment to any plan, such plan amendment shall not be required to be made before the first plan year beginning on or after Jan. 1, 1989, see section 1140 of Pub. L. 99–514, as amended, set out as a note under section 401 of Title 26, Internal Revenue Code.

§ 1399. Notice, collection, etc., of withdrawal liability

(a) Furnishing of information by employer to plan sponsor

An employer shall, within 30 days after a written request from the plan sponsor, furnish such information as the plan sponsor reasonably determines to be necessary to enable the plan sponsor to comply with the requirements of this part.

(b) Notification, demand for payment, and review upon complete or partial withdrawal by employer

(1) As soon as practicable after an employer's complete or partial withdrawal, the plan sponsor shall—

(A) notify the employer of—

(i) the amount of the liability, and

(ii) the schedule for liability payments, and

(B) demand payment in accordance with the schedule.

(2)(A) No later than 90 days after the employer receives the notice described in paragraph (1), the employer—

(i) may ask the plan sponsor to review any specific matter relating to the determination of the employer's liability and the schedule of payments,

(ii) may identify any inaccuracy in the determination of the amount of the unfunded vested benefits allocable to the employer, and

(iii) may furnish any additional relevant information to the plan sponsor.

(B) After a reasonable review of any matter raised, the plan sponsor shall notify the employer of—

(i) the plan sponsor's decision,

(ii) the basis for the decision, and

(iii) the reason for any change in the determination of the employer's liability or schedule of liability payments.

(c) Payment requirements; amount, etc.

(1)(A)(i) Except as provided in subparagraphs (B) and (D) of this paragraph and in paragraphs (4) and (5), an employer shall pay the amount determined under section 1391 of this title, adjusted if appropriate first under section 1389 of this title and then under section 1386 of this title over the period of years necessary to amortize the amount in level annual payments determined under subparagraph (C), calculated as if the first payment were made on the first day of the plan year following the plan year in which the withdrawal occurs and as if each subsequent payment were made on the first day of each subsequent plan year. Actual payment shall commence in accordance with paragraph (2).

(ii) The determination of the amortization period described in clause (i) shall be based on the assumptions used for the most recent actuarial valuation for the plan.

(B) In any case in which the amortization period described in subparagraph (A) exceeds 20 years, the employer's liability shall be limited to the first 20 annual payments determined under subparagraph (C).

(C)(i) Except as provided in subparagraph (E), the amount of each annual payment shall be the product of—

(I) the average annual number of contribution base units for the period of 3 consecutive plan years, during the period of 10 consecutive plan years ending before the plan year in which the withdrawal occurs, in which the number of contribution base units for which the employer had an obligation to contribute under the plan is the highest, and

(II) the highest contribution rate at which the employer had an obligation to contribute under the plan during the 10 plan years ending with the plan year in which the withdrawal occurs.

For purposes of the preceding sentence, a partial withdrawal described in section 1385(a)(1) of this title shall be deemed to occur on the last day of the first year of the 3-year testing period described in section 1385(b)(1)(B)(i) of this title.

(ii)(I) A plan may be amended to provide that for any plan year ending before 1986 the amount of each annual payment shall be (in lieu of the amount determined under clause (i)) the average of the required employer contributions under the plan for the period of 3 consecutive plan years (during the period of 10 consecutive plan years ending with the plan year preceding the plan year in which the withdrawal occurs) for which such required contributions were the highest.

(II) Subparagraph (B) shall not apply to any plan year to which this clause applies.

(III) This clause shall not apply in the case of any withdrawal described in subparagraph (D).

(IV) If under a plan this clause applies to any plan year but does not apply to the next plan year, this clause shall not apply to any plan year after such next plan year.

(V) For purposes of this clause, the term "required contributions" means, for any period, the amounts which the employer was obligated to contribute for such period (not taking into account any delinquent contribution for any other period).

(iii) A plan may be amended to provide that for the first plan year ending on or after September 26, 1980, the number "5" shall be substituted for the number "10" each place it appears in clause (i) or clause (ii) (whichever is appropriate). If the plan is so amended, the number "5" shall be increased by one for each succeeding plan year until the number "10" is reached.

(D) In any case in which a multiemployer plan terminates by the withdrawal of every employer from the plan, or in which substantially all the employers withdraw from a plan pursuant to an agreement or arrangement to withdraw from the plan—

(i) the liability of each such employer who has withdrawn shall be determined (or redetermined) under this paragraph without regard to subparagraph (B), and

(ii) notwithstanding any other provision of this part, the total unfunded vested benefits of the plan shall be fully allocated among all such employers in a manner not inconsistent with regulations which shall be prescribed by the corporation.

Withdrawal by an employer from a plan, during a period of 3 consecutive plan years within which substantially all the employers who have an obligation to contribute under the plan withdraw, shall be presumed to be a withdrawal pursuant to an agreement or arrangement, unless the employer proves otherwise by a preponderance of the evidence.

(E) In the case of a partial withdrawal described in section 1385(a) of this title, the amount of each annual payment shall be the product of—

(i) the amount determined under subparagraph (C) (determined without regard to this subparagraph), multiplied by

(ii) the fraction determined under section 1386(a)(2) of this title.

(2) Withdrawal liability shall be payable in accordance with the schedule set forth by the plan sponsor under subsection (b)(1) of this section beginning no later than 60 days after the date of the demand notwithstanding any request for review or appeal of determinations of the amount of such liability or of the schedule.

(3) Each annual payment determined under paragraph (1)(C) shall be payable in 4 equal installments due quarterly, or at other intervals specified by plan rules. If a payment is not made when due, interest on the payment shall accrue from the due date until the date on which the payment is made.

(4) The employer shall be entitled to prepay the outstanding amount of the unpaid annual withdrawal liability payments determined under paragraph (1)(C), plus accrued interest, if any, in whole or in part, without penalty. If the prepayment is made pursuant to a withdrawal which is later determined to be part of a withdrawal described in paragraph (1)(D), the withdrawal liability of the employer shall not be limited to the amount of the prepayment.

(5) In the event of a default, a plan sponsor may require immediate payment of the outstanding amount of an employer's withdrawal liability, plus accrued interest on the total outstanding liability from the due date of the first payment which was not timely made. For purposes of this section, the term "default" means—

(A) the failure of an employer to make, when due, any payment under this section, if the failure is not cured within 60 days after the employer receives written notification from the plan sponsor of such failure, and

(B) any other event defined in rules adopted by the plan which indicates a substantial likelihood that an employer will be unable to pay its withdrawal liability.

(6) Except as provided in paragraph (1)(A)(ii), interest under this subsection shall be charged at rates based on prevailing market rates for comparable obligations, in accordance with regulations prescribed by the corporation.

(7) A multiemployer plan may adopt rules for other terms and conditions for the satisfaction of an employer's withdrawal liability if such rules—

(A) are consistent with this chapter, and

(B) are not inconsistent with regulations of the corporation.

(8) In the case of a terminated multiemployer plan, an employer's obligation to make payments under this section ceases at the end of the plan year in which the assets of the plan (exclusive of withdrawal liability claims) are sufficient to meet all obligations of the plan, as determined by the corporation.

(d) Applicability of statutory prohibitions

The prohibitions provided in section 1106(a) of this title do not apply to any action required or permitted under this part.

(Pub. L. 93–406, title IV, § 4219, as added Pub. L. 96–364, title I, § 104(2), Sept. 26, 1980, 94 Stat. 1236; amended Pub. L. 98–369, div. A, title V, § 558(b)(1)(B), July 18, 1984, 98 Stat. 899.)

REFERENCES IN TEXT

This chapter, referred to in subsec. (c)(7)(A), was in the original "this Act", meaning Pub. L. 93–406, known as the Employee Retirement Income Security Act of 1974. Titles I, III, and IV of such Act are classified principally to this chapter. For complete classification of this Act to the Code, see Short Title note set out under section 1001 of this title and Tables.

AMENDMENTS

1984—Subsec. (c)(1)(C)(iii). Pub. L. 98–369 substituted "September 26, 1980" for "April 29, 1980".

§ 1400. Approval of amendments

(a) Amendment of covered multiemployer plan; procedures applicable

Except as provided in subsection (b) of this section, if an amendment to a multiemployer plan authorized by any preceding section of this part is adopted more than 36 months after the effective date of this section, the amendment shall be effective only if the corporation approves the amendment, or, within 90 days after the corporation receives notice and a copy of the amendment from the plan sponsor, fails to disapprove the amendment.

(b) Amendment respecting methods for computing withdrawal liability

An amendment permitted by section 1391(c)(5) of this title may be adopted only in accordance with that section.

(c) Criteria for disapproval by corporation

The corporation shall disapprove an amendment referred to in subsection (a) or (b) of this section only if the corporation determines that the amendment creates an unreasonable risk of loss to plan participants and beneficiaries or to the corporation.

(Pub. L. 93–406, title IV, § 4220, as added Pub. L. 96–364, title I, § 104(2), Sept. 26, 1980, 94 Stat. 1239.)

REFERENCES IN TEXT

For the effective date of this section, referred to in subsec. (a), see 1461(e)(2) of this title.

§ 1401. Resolution of disputes

(a) Arbitration proceedings; matters subject to arbitration, procedures applicable, etc.

(1) Any dispute between an employer and the plan sponsor of a multiemployer plan concerning a determination made under sections 1381 through 1399 of this title shall be resolved through arbitration. Either party may initiate the arbitration proceeding within a 60-day period after the earlier of—

(A) the date of notification to the employer under section 1399(b)(2)(B) of this title, or

(B) 120 days after the date of the employer's request under section 1399(b)(2)(A) of this title.

The parties may jointly initiate arbitration within the 180-day period after the date of the plan sponsor's demand under section 1399(b)(1) of this title.

(2) An arbitration proceeding under this section shall be conducted in accordance with fair and equitable procedures to be promulgated by the corporation. The plan sponsor may purchase insurance to cover potential liability of the arbitrator. If the parties have not provided for the costs of the arbitration, including arbitrator's fees, by agreement, the arbitrator shall assess such fees. The arbitrator may also award reasonable attorney's fees.

(3)(A) For purposes of any proceeding under this section, any determination made by a plan sponsor under sections 1381 through 1399 of this title and section 1405 of this title is presumed correct unless the party contesting the determination shows by a preponderance of the evidence that the determination was unreasonable or clearly erroneous.

(B) In the case of the determination of a plan's unfunded vested benefits for a plan year, the determination is presumed correct unless a party contesting the determination shows by a preponderance of evidence that—

(i) the actuarial assumptions and methods used in the determination were, in the aggregate, unreasonable (taking into account the experience of the plan and reasonable expectations), or

(ii) the plan's actuary made a significant error in applying the actuarial assumptions or methods.

(b) Alternative collection proceedings; civil action subsequent to arbitration award; conduct of arbitration proceedings

(1) If no arbitration proceeding has been initiated pursuant to subsection (a) of this section, the amounts demanded by the plan sponsor under section 1399(b)(1) of this title shall be due and owing on the schedule set forth by the plan sponsor. The plan sponsor may bring an action in a State or Federal court of competent jurisdiction for collection.

(2) Upon completion of the arbitration proceedings in favor of one of the parties, any party thereto may bring an action, no later than 30 days after the issuance of an arbitrator's award, in an appropriate United States district court in accordance with section 1451 of this title to enforce, vacate, or modify the arbitrator's award.

(3) Any arbitration proceedings under this section shall, to the extent consistent with this subchapter, be conducted in the same manner, subject to the same limitations, carried out with the same powers (including subpena power), and enforced in United States courts as an arbitration proceeding carried out under title 9.

(c) Presumption respecting finding of fact by arbitrator

In any proceeding under subsection (b) of this section, there shall be a presumption, rebuttable only by a clear preponderance of the evidence, that the findings of fact made by the arbitrator were correct.

(d) Payments by employer prior and subsequent to determination by arbitrator; adjustments; failure of employer to make payments

Payments shall be made by an employer in accordance with the determinations made under this part until the arbitrator issues a final decision with respect to the determination submitted for arbitration, with any necessary adjustments in subsequent payments for overpayments or underpayments arising out of the decision of the arbitrator with respect to the determination. If the employer fails to make timely payment in accordance with such final decision, the employer shall be treated as being delinquent in the making of a contribution required under the plan (within the meaning of section 1145 of this title).

(e) Procedures applicable to certain disputes

(1) In general

If—

(A) a plan sponsor of a plan determines that—

(i) a complete or partial withdrawal of an employer has occurred, or

(ii) an employer is liable for withdrawal liability payments with respect to the complete or partial withdrawal of an employer from the plan,

(B) such determination is based in whole or in part on a finding by the plan sponsor under section 1392(c) of this title that a principal purpose of a transaction that occurred before January 1, 1999, was to evade or avoid withdrawal liability under this subtitle, and

(C) such transaction occurred at least 5 years before the date of the complete or partial withdrawal,

then the special rules under paragraph (2) shall be used in applying subsections (a) and (d) of this section and section 1399(c) of this title to the employer.

(2) Special rules

(A) Determination

Notwithstanding subsection (a)(3) of this section—

(i) a determination by the plan sponsor under paragraph (1)(B) shall not be presumed to be correct, and

(ii) the plan sponsor shall have the burden to establish, by a preponderance of the evidence, the elements of the claim under section 1392(c) of this title that a principal purpose of the transaction was to evade or avoid withdrawal liability under this subtitle.

Nothing in this subparagraph shall affect the burden of establishing any other element of a claim for withdrawal liability under this subtitle.

(B) Procedure

Notwithstanding subsection (d) of this section and section 1399(c) of this title, if an employer contests the plan sponsor's determination under paragraph (1) through an arbitration proceeding pursuant to subsection (a) of this section, or through a claim brought in a court of competent jurisdiction, the employer shall not be obligated to make any withdrawal liability payments until a final decision in the arbitration proceeding, or in court, upholds the plan sponsor's determination.

(f) Procedures applicable to certain disputes

(1) IN GENERAL.—If—

(A) a plan sponsor of a plan determines that—

(i) a complete or partial withdrawal of an employer has occurred, or

(ii) an employer is liable for withdrawal liability payments with respect to such complete or partial withdrawal, and

(B) such determination is based in whole or in part on a finding by the plan sponsor under section 1392(c) of this title that a principal purpose of any transaction which occurred after December 31, 1998, and at least 5 years (2 years in the case of a small employer) before the date of the complete or partial withdrawal was to evade or avoid withdrawal liability under this subtitle,

then the person against which the withdrawal liability is assessed based solely on the application of section 1392(c) of this title may elect to use the special rule under paragraph (2) in applying subsection (d) of this section and section 1399(c) of this title to such person.

(2) SPECIAL RULE.—Notwithstanding subsection (d) and section 1399(c) of this title, if an electing person contests the plan sponsor's determination with respect to withdrawal liability payments under paragraph (1) through an arbitration proceeding pursuant to subsection (a), through an action brought in a court of competent jurisdiction for review of such an arbitration decision, or as otherwise permitted by law, the electing person shall not be obligated to make the withdrawal liability payments until a final decision in the arbitration proceeding, or in court, upholds the plan sponsor's determination, but only if the electing person—

(A) provides notice to the plan sponsor of its election to apply the special rule in this paragraph within 90 days after the plan sponsor notifies the electing person of its liability by reason of the application of section 1392(c) of this title; and

(B) if a final decision in the arbitration proceeding, or in court, of the withdrawal liability dispute has not been rendered within 12 months from the date of such notice, the electing person provides to the plan, effective as of the first day following the 12-month period, a bond issued by a corporate surety company that is an acceptable surety for purposes of section 1112 of this title, or an amount held in escrow by a bank or similar financial institution satisfactory to the plan, in an amount equal to the sum of the withdrawal liability payments that would otherwise be due under subsection (d) and section 1399(c) of this title for the 12-month period beginning with the first anniversary of such notice. Such bond or escrow shall remain in effect until there is a final decision in the arbitration proceeding, or in court, of the withdrawal liability dispute, at which time such bond or escrow shall be paid to the plan if such final decision upholds the plan sponsor's determination.

(3) DEFINITION OF SMALL EMPLOYER.—For purposes of this subsection—

(A) IN GENERAL.—The term "small employer" means any employer which, for the calendar year in which the transaction referred to in paragraph (1)(B) occurred and for each of the 3 preceding years, on average—

(i) employs not more than 500 employees, and

(ii) is required to make contributions to the plan for not more than 250 employees.

(B) CONTROLLED GROUP.—Any group treated as a single employer under subsection (b)(1) of section 1301 of this title, without regard to any transaction that was a basis for the plan's finding under section 1392 of this title, shall be treated as a single employer for purposes of this subparagraph.

(4) ADDITIONAL SECURITY PENDING RESOLUTION OF DISPUTE.—If a withdrawal liability dispute to which this subsection applies is not concluded by 12 months after the electing person posts the bond or escrow described in paragraph (2), the electing person shall, at the start of each succeeding 12-month period, provide an additional bond or amount held in escrow equal to the sum of the withdrawal liability payments that would otherwise be payable to the plan during that period.

(5) The liability of the party furnishing a bond or escrow under this subsection shall be reduced, upon the payment of the bond or escrow to the plan, by the amount thereof.

(Pub. L. 93–406, title IV, § 4221, as added Pub. L. 96–364, title I, § 104(2), Sept. 26, 1980, 94 Stat. 1239; amended Pub. L. 108–218, title II, § 202(a), Apr. 10, 2004, 118 Stat. 608; Pub. L. 109–280, title II, § 204(d)(1), Aug. 17, 2006, 120 Stat. 887; Pub. L. 110–458, title I, § 105(b)(2), Dec. 23, 2008, 122 Stat. 5105.)

AMENDMENTS

2008—Subsecs. (e) to (g). Pub. L. 110–458 redesignated subsecs. (f) and (g) as (e) and (f), respectively, and struck out former subsec. (e). Prior to amendment, text read as follows: "If any employer requests in writing that the plan sponsor make available to the employer general information necessary for the employer to compute its withdrawal liability with respect to the plan (other than information which is unique to that employer), the plan sponsor shall furnish the information to the employer without charge. If any employer requests in writing that the plan sponsor make an estimate of such employer's potential withdrawal liability with respect to the plan or to provide information unique to that employer, the plan sponsor may require the employer to pay the reasonable cost of making such estimate or providing such information."

2006—Subsec. (g). Pub. L. 109–280 added subsec. (g).

2004—Subsec. (f). Pub. L. 108–218 added subsec. (f).

EFFECTIVE DATE OF 2008 AMENDMENT

Amendment by Pub. L. 110–458 effective as if included in the provisions of Pub. L. 109–280 to which the amendment relates, except as otherwise provided, see section 112 of Pub. L. 110–458, set out as a note under section 72 of Title 26, Internal Revenue Code.

EFFECTIVE DATE OF 2006 AMENDMENT

Pub. L. 109–280, title II, § 204(d)(2), Aug. 17, 2006, 120 Stat. 889, provided that: "The amendments made by this subsection [amending this section] shall apply to any person that receives a notification under section 4219(b)(1) of the Employee Retirement Income Security Act of 1974 [29 U.S.C. 1399(b)(1)] on or after the date of enactment of this Act [Aug. 17, 2006] with respect to a transaction that occurred after December 31, 1998."

EFFECTIVE DATE OF 2004 AMENDMENT

Pub. L. 108–218, title II, § 202(b), Apr. 10, 2004, 118 Stat. 609, provided that: "The amendments made by this section [amending this section] shall apply to any employer that receives a notification under section 4219(b)(1) of the Employee Retirement Income Security Act of 1974 (29 U.S.C. 1399(b)(1)) after October 31, 2003."

§ 1402. Reimbursements for uncollectible withdrawal liability

(a) Required supplemental program to reimburse for payments due from employers uncollectible as a result of employer involvement in bankruptcy case or proceedings; program participation, premiums, etc.

By May 1, 1982, the corporation shall establish by regulation a supplemental program to reimburse multiemployer plans for withdrawal liability payments which are due from employers and which are determined to be uncollectible for reasons arising out of cases or proceedings involving the employers under title 11, or similar cases or proceedings. Participation in the supplemental program shall be on a voluntary basis, and a plan which elects coverage under the program shall pay premiums to the corporation in accordance with a premium schedule which shall be prescribed from time to time by the corporation. The premium schedule shall contain such rates and bases for the application of such rates as the corporation considers to be appropriate.

(b) Discretionary supplemental program to reimburse for payments due from employers uncollectible for other appropriate reasons

The corporation may provide under the program for reimbursement of amounts of withdrawal liability determined to be uncollectible for any other reasons the corporation considers appropriate.

(c) Payment of cost of program

The cost of the program (including such administrative and legal costs as the corporation considers appropriate) may be paid only out of premiums collected under such program.

(d) Terms and conditions, limitations, etc., of supplemental program

The supplemental program may be offered to eligible plans on such terms and conditions, and with such limitations with respect to the payment of reimbursements (including the exclusion of de minimis amounts of uncollectible employer liability, and the reduction or elimination of reimbursements which cannot be paid from collected premiums) and such restrictions on withdrawal from the program, as the corporation considers necessary and appropriate.

(e) Arrangements by corporation with private insurers for implementation of program; election of coverage by participating plans with private insurers

The corporation may enter into arrangements with private insurers to carry out in whole or in part the program authorized by this section and may require plans which elect coverage under the program to elect coverage by those private insurers.

(Pub. L. 93–406, title IV, § 4222, as added Pub. L. 96–364, title I, § 104(2), Sept. 26, 1980, 94 Stat. 1240.)

§1403. Withdrawal liability payment fund

(a) Establishment of or participation in fund by plan sponsors

The plan sponsors of multiemployer plans may establish or participate in a withdrawal liability payment fund.

(b) Definitions

For purposes of this section, the term "withdrawal liability payment fund", and the term "fund", mean a trust which—

(1) is established and maintained under section 501(c)(22) of title 26,

(2) maintains agreements which cover a substantial portion of the participants who are in multiemployer plans which (under the rules of the trust instrument) are eligible to participate in the fund,

(3) is funded by amounts paid by the plans which participate in the fund, and

(4) is administered by a Board of Trustees, and in the administration of the fund there is equal representation of—

(A) trustees representing employers who are obligated to contribute to the plans participating in the fund, and

(B) trustees representing employees who are participants in plans which participate in the fund.

(c) Payments to plan; amount, criteria, etc.

(1) If an employer withdraws from a plan which participates in a withdrawal liability payment fund, then, to the extent provided in the trust, the fund shall pay to that plan—

(A) the employer's unattributable liability,

(B) the employer's withdrawal liability payments which would have been due but for section 1388, 1389, 1399, or 1405 of this title,

(C) the employer's withdrawal liability payments to the extent they are uncollectible.

(2) The fund may provide for the payment of the employer's attributable liability if the fund—

(A) provides for the payment of both the attributable and the unattributable liability of the employer in a single payment, and

(B) is subrogated to all rights of the plan against the employer.

(3) For purposes of this section, the term—

(A) "attributable liability" means the excess, if any, determined under the provisions of a plan not inconsistent with regulations of the corporation, of—

(i) the value of vested benefits accrued as a result of service with the employer, over

(ii) the value of plan assets attributed to the employer, and

(B) "unattributable liability" means the excess of withdrawal liability over attributable liability.

Such terms may be further defined, and the manner in which they shall be applied may be prescribed, by the corporation by regulation.

(4)(A) The trust of a fund shall be maintained for the exclusive purpose of paying—

(i) any amount described in paragraph (1) and paragraph (2), and

(ii) reasonable and necessary administrative expenses in connection with the establishment and operation of the trust and the processing of claims against the fund.

(B) The amounts paid by a plan to a fund shall be deemed a reasonable expense of administering the plan under sections 1103(c)(1) and 1104(a)(1)(A)(ii) of this title, and the payments made by a fund to a participating plan shall be deemed services necessary for the operation of the plan within the meaning of section 1108(b)(2) of this title or within the meaning of section 4975(d)(2) of title 26.

(d) Application of payments by plan

(1) For purposes of this part—

(A) only amounts paid by the fund to a plan under subsection (c)(1)(A) of this section shall be credited to withdrawal liability otherwise payable by the employer, unless the plan otherwise provides, and

(B) any amounts paid by the fund under subsection (c) of this section to a plan shall be treated by the plan as a payment of withdrawal liability to such plan.

(2) For purposes of applying provisions relating to the funding standard accounts (and minimum contribution requirements), amounts paid from the plan to the fund shall be applied to reduce the amount treated as contributed to the plan.

(e) Subrogation of fund to rights of plan

The fund shall be subrogated to the rights of the plan against the employer that has withdrawn from the plan for amounts paid by a fund to a plan under—

(1) subsection (c)(1)(A) of this section, to the extent not credited under subsection (d)(1)(A) of this section, and

(2) subsection (c)(1)(C) of this section.

(f) Discharge of rights of fiduciary of fund; standards applicable, etc.

Notwithstanding any other provision of this chapter, a fiduciary of the fund shall discharge the fiduciary's duties with respect to the fund in accordance with the standards for fiduciaries prescribed by this chapter (to the extent not inconsistent with the purposes of this section), and in accordance with the documents and instruments governing the fund insofar as such documents and instruments are consistent with the provisions of this chapter (to the extent not inconsistent with the purposes of this section). The provisions of the preceding sentence shall supersede any and all State laws relating to fiduciaries insofar as they may now or hereafter relate to a fund to which this section applies.

(g) Prohibition on payments from fund to plan where certain labor negotiations involve employer withdrawn or partially withdrawn from plan and continuity of labor organization representing employees continues

No payments shall be made from a fund to a plan on the occasion of a withdrawal or partial withdrawal of an employer from such plan if the employees representing the withdrawn contribution base units continue, after such withdrawal, to be represented under section 159 of this title (or other applicable labor laws) in negotiations with such employer by the labor organization which represented such employees immediately preceding such withdrawal.

(h) **Purchase of insurance by employer**

Nothing in this section shall be construed to prohibit the purchase of insurance by an employer from any other person, to limit the circumstances under which such insurance would be payable, or to limit in any way the terms and conditions of such insurance.

(i) **Promulgation of regulations for establishment and maintenance of fund**

The corporation may provide by regulation rules not inconsistent with this section governing the establishment and maintenance of funds, but only to the extent necessary to carry out the purposes of this part (other than section 1402 of this title).

(Pub. L. 93–406, title IV, § 4223, as added Pub. L. 96–364, title I, § 104(2), Sept. 26, 1980, 94 Stat. 1241; amended Pub. L. 101–239, title VII, § 7891(a), Dec. 19, 1989, 103 Stat. 2445.)

REFERENCES IN TEXT

This chapter, referred to in subsec. (f), was in the original "this Act", meaning Pub. L. 93–406, known as the Employee Retirement Income Security Act of 1974. Titles I, III, and IV of such Act are classified principally to this chapter. For complete classification of this Act to the Code, see Short Title note set out under section 1001 of this title and Tables.

AMENDMENTS

1989—Subsecs. (b)(1), (c)(4)(B). Pub. L. 101–239 substituted "Internal Revenue Code of 1986" for "Internal Revenue Code of 1954", which for purposes of codification was translated as "title 26" thus requiring no change in text.

EFFECTIVE DATE OF 1989 AMENDMENT

Amendment by Pub. L. 101–239 effective, except as otherwise provided, as if included in the provision of the Tax Reform Act of 1986, Pub. L. 99–514, to which such amendment relates, see section 7891(f) of Pub. L. 101–239, set out as a note under section 1002 of this title.

§ 1404. Alternative method of withdrawal liability payments

A multiemployer plan may adopt rules providing for other terms and conditions for the satisfaction of an employer's withdrawal liability if such rules are consistent with this chapter and with such regulations as may be prescribed by the corporation.

(Pub. L. 93–406, title IV, § 4224, as added Pub. L. 96–364, title I, § 104(2), Sept. 26, 1980, 94 Stat. 1242.)

REFERENCES IN TEXT

This chapter, referred to in text, was in the original "this Act", meaning Pub. L. 93–406, known as the Employee Retirement Income Security Act of 1974. Titles I, III, and IV of such Act are classified principally to this chapter. For complete classification of this Act to the Code, see Short Title note set out under section 1001 of this title and Tables.

§ 1405. Limitation on withdrawal liability

(a) **Unfunded vested benefits allocable to employer in bona fide sale of assets of employer in arms-length transaction to unrelated party; maximum amount; determinative factors**

(1) In the case of bona fide sale of all or substantially all of the employer's assets in an arm's-length transaction to an unrelated party (within the meaning of section 1384(d) of this title), the unfunded vested benefits allocable to an employer (after the application of all sections of this part having a lower number designation than this section), other than an employer undergoing reorganization under title 11 or similar provisions of State law, shall not exceed the greater of—

(A) a portion (determined under paragraph (2)) of the liquidation or dissolution value of the employer (determined after the sale or exchange of such assets), or

(B) in the case of a plan using the attributable method of allocating withdrawal liability, the unfunded vested benefits attributable to employees of the employer.

(2) For purposes of paragraph (1), the portion shall be determined in accordance with the following table:

If the liquidation or distribution value of the employer after the sale or exchange is—	The portion is—
Not more than $5,000,000	30 percent of the amount.
More than $5,000,000, but not more than $10,000,000.	$1,500,000, plus 35 percent of the amount in excess of $5,000,000.
More than $10,000,000, but not more than $15,000,000.	$3,250,000, plus 40 percent of the amount in excess of $10,000,000.
More than $15,000,000, but not more than $17,500,000.	$5,250,000, plus 45 percent of the amount in excess of $15,000,000.
More than $17,500,000, but not more than $20,000,000.	$6,375,000, plus 50 percent of the amount in excess of $17,500,000.
More than $20,000,000, but not more than $22,500,000.	$7,625,000, plus 60 percent of the amount in excess of $20,000,000.
More than $22,500,000, but not more than $25,000,000.	$9,125,000, plus 70 percent of the amount in excess of $22,500,000.
More than $25,000,000	$10,875,000, plus 80 percent of the amount in excess of $25,000,000.

(b) **Unfunded vested benefits allocable to insolvent employer undergoing liquidation or dissolution; maximum amount; determinative factors**

In the case of an insolvent employer undergoing liquidation or dissolution, the unfunded vested benefits allocable to that employer shall not exceed an amount equal to the sum of—

(1) 50 percent of the unfunded vested benefits allocable to the employer (determined without regard to this section), and

(2) that portion of 50 percent of the unfunded vested benefits allocable to the employer (as determined under paragraph (1)) which does not exceed the liquidation or dissolution value of the employer determined—

(A) as of the commencement of liquidation or dissolution, and

(B) after reducing the liquidation or dissolution value of the employer by the amount determined under paragraph (1).

(c) Property not subject to enforcement of liability; precondition

To the extent that the withdrawal liability of an employer is attributable to his obligation to contribute to or under a plan as an individual (whether as a sole proprietor or as a member of a partnership), property which may be exempt from the estate under section 522 of title 11 or under similar provisions of law, shall not be subject to enforcement of such liability.

(d) Insolvency of employer; liquidation or dissolution value of employer

For purposes of this section—

(1) an employer is insolvent if the liabilities of the employer, including withdrawal liability under the plan (determined without regard to subsection (b) of this section), exceed the assets of the employer (determined as of the commencement of the liquidation or dissolution), and

(2) the liquidation or dissolution value of the employer shall be determined without regard to such withdrawal liability.

(e) One or more withdrawals of employer attributable to same sale, liquidation, or dissolution

In the case of one or more withdrawals of an employer attributable to the same sale, liquidation, or dissolution, under regulations prescribed by the corporation—

(1) all such withdrawals shall be treated as a single withdrawal for the purpose of applying this section, and

(2) the withdrawal liability of the employer to each plan shall be an amount which bears the same ratio to the present value of the withdrawal liability payments to all plans (after the application of the preceding provisions of this section) as the withdrawal liability of the employer to such plan (determined without regard to this section) bears to the withdrawal liability of the employer to all such plans (determined without regard to this section).

(Pub. L. 93–406, title IV, § 4225, as added Pub. L. 96–364, title I, § 104(2), Sept. 26, 1980, 94 Stat. 1243; amended Pub. L. 109–280, title II, § 204(a)(1), (2), Aug. 17, 2006, 120 Stat. 886, 887.)

AMENDMENTS

2006—Subsec. (a)(1)(B). Pub. L. 109–280, § 204(a)(2), amended subpar. (B) generally. Prior to amendment, subpar. (B) read as follows: "the unfunded vested benefits attributable to employees of the employer."

Subsec. (a)(2). Pub. L. 109–280, § 204(a)(1), added table and struck out former table which provided for a portion of: 30 percent of the amount if the liquidation or dissolution value of the employer after the sale or exchange is not more than $2,000,000; $600,000, plus 35 percent of the amount in excess of $2,000,000, if the employer's liquidation or dissolution value is more than $2,000,000, but not more than $4,000,000; $1,300,000, plus 40 percent of the amount in excess of $4,000,000, if the employer's liquidation or dissolution value is more than $4,000,000, but not more than $6,000,000; $2,100,000, plus 45 percent of the amount in excess of $6,000,000, if the employer's liquidation or dissolution value is more than $6,000,000, but not more than $7,000,000; $2,550,000, plus 50 percent of the amount in excess of $7,000,000, if the employer's liquidation or dissolution value is more than $7,000,000, but not more than $8,000,000; $3,050,000, plus 60 percent of the amount in excess of $8,000,000, if the employer's liquidation or dissolution value is more than $8,000,000, but not more than $9,000,000; $3,650,000, plus 70 percent of the amount in excess of $9,000,000, if the employer's liquidation or dissolution value is more than $9,000,000, but not more than $10,000,000; and $4,350,000, plus 80 percent of the amount in excess of $10,000,000, if the employer's liquidation or dissolution value is more than $10,000,000.

EFFECTIVE DATE OF 2006 AMENDMENT

Pub. L. 109–280, title II, § 204(a)(3), Aug. 17, 2006, 120 Stat. 887, provided that: "The amendments made by this subsection [amending this section] shall apply to sales occurring on or after January 1, 2007."

PART 2—MERGER OR TRANSFER OF PLAN ASSETS OR LIABILITIES

§ 1411. Mergers and transfers between multiemployer plans

(a) Authority of plan sponsor

Unless otherwise provided in regulations prescribed by the corporation, a plan sponsor may not cause a multiemployer plan to merge with one or more multiemployer plans, or engage in a transfer of assets and liabilities to or from another multiemployer plan, unless such merger or transfer satisfies the requirements of subsection (b) of this section.

(b) Criteria

A merger or transfer satisfies the requirements of this section if—

(1) in accordance with regulations of the corporation, the plan sponsor of a multiemployer plan notifies the corporation of a merger with or transfer of plan assets or liabilities to another multiemployer plan at least 120 days before the effective date of the merger or transfer;

(2) no participant's or beneficiary's accrued benefit will be lower immediately after the effective date of the merger or transfer than the benefit immediately before that date;

(3) the benefits of participants and beneficiaries are not reasonably expected to be subject to suspension under section 1426 of this title; and

(4) an actuarial valuation of the assets and liabilities of each of the affected plans has been performed during the plan year preceding the effective date of the merger or transfer, based upon the most recent data available as of the day before the start of that plan year, or other valuation of such assets and liabilities performed under such standards and procedures as the corporation may prescribe by regulation.

(c) Actions not deemed violation of section 1106(a) or (b)(2) of this title

The merger of multiemployer plans or the transfer of assets or liabilities between multiemployer plans, shall be deemed not to constitute a violation of the provisions of section 1106(a) of this title or section 1106(b)(2) of this title if the corporation determines that the merger or transfer otherwise satisfies the requirements of this section.

(d) Nature of plan to which liabilities are transferred

A plan to which liabilities are transferred under this section is a successor plan for purposes of section 1322a(b)(2)(B) of this title.

(Pub. L. 93–406, title IV, § 4231, as added Pub. L. 96–364, title I, § 104(2), Sept. 26, 1980, 94 Stat. 1244.)

EFFECTIVE DATE

Part effective Sept. 26, 1980, except as specifically provided, see section 1461(e) of this title.

§ 1412. Transfers between a multiemployer plan and a single-employer plan

(a) General authority

A transfer of assets or liabilities between, or a merger of, a multiemployer plan and a single-employer plan shall satisfy the requirements of this section.

(b) Accrued benefit of participant or beneficiary not lower immediately after effective date of transfer or merger

No accrued benefit of a participant or beneficiary may be lower immediately after the effective date of a transfer or merger described in subsection (a) of this section than the benefit immediately before that date.

(c) Liability of multiemployer plan to corporation where single-employer plan terminates within 60 months after effective date of transfer; amount of liability, exemption, etc.

(1) Except as provided in paragraphs (2) and (3), a multiemployer plan which transfers liabilities to a single-employer plan shall be liable to the corporation if the single-employer plan terminates within 60 months after the effective date of the transfer. The amount of liability shall be the lesser of—

(A) the amount of the plan asset insufficiency of the terminated single-employer plan, less 30 percent of the net worth of the employer who maintained the single-employer plan, determined in accordance with section 1362 or 1364 this title, or

(B) the value, on the effective date of the transfer, of the unfunded benefits transferred to the single-employer plan which are guaranteed under section 1322 of this title.

(2) A multiemployer plan shall be liable to the corporation as provided in paragraph (1) unless, within 180 days after the corporation receives an application (together with such information as the corporation may reasonably require for purposes of such application) from the multiemployer plan sponsor for a determination under this paragraph—

(A) the corporation determines that the interests of the plan participants and beneficiaries and of the corporation are adequately protected, or

(B) fails to make any determination regarding the adequacy with which such interests are protected with respect to such transfer of liabilities.

If, after the receipt of such application, the corporation requests from the plan sponsor additional information necessary for the determination, the running of the 180-day period shall be suspended from the date of such request until the receipt by the corporation of the additional information requested. The corporation may by regulation prescribe procedures and standards for the issuance of determinations under this paragraph. This paragraph shall not apply to any application submitted less than 180 days after September 26, 1980.

(3) A multiemployer plan shall not be liable to the corporation as provided in paragraph (1) in the case of a transfer from the multiemployer plan to a single-employer plan of liabilities which accrued under a single-employer plan which merged with the multiemployer plan, if, the value of liabilities transferred to the single-employer plan does not exceed the value of the liabilities for benefits which accrued before the merger, and the value of the assets transferred to the single-employer plan is substantially equal to the value of the assets which would have been in the single-employer plan if the employer had maintained and funded it as a separate plan under which no benefits accrued after the date of the merger.

(4) The corporation may make equitable arrangements with multiemployer plans which are liable under this subsection for satisfaction of their liability.

(d) Guarantee of benefits under single-employer plan

Benefits under a single-employer plan to which liabilities are transferred in accordance with this section are guaranteed under section 1322 of this title to the extent provided in that section as of the effective date of the transfer and the plan is a successor plan.

(e) Transfer of liabilities by multiemployer plan to single-employer plan

(1) Except as provided in paragraph (2), a multiemployer plan may not transfer liabilities to a single-employer plan unless the plan sponsor of the plan to which the liabilities would be transferred agrees to the transfer.

(2) In the case of a transfer described in subsection (c)(3) of this section, paragraph (1) of this subsection is satisfied by the advance agreement to the transfer by the employer who will be obligated to contribute to the single-employer plan.

(f) Additional requirements by corporation for protection of interests of plan participants, beneficiaries and corporation; approval by corporation of transfer of assets or liabilities to single-employer plan from plan in reorganization; covered transfers in connection with termination

(1) The corporation may prescribe by regulation such additional requirements with respect to the transfer of assets or liabilities as may be necessary to protect the interests of plan participants and beneficiaries and the corporation.

(2) Except as otherwise determined by the corporation, a transfer of assets or liabilities to a single-employer plan from a plan in reorganization under section 1421 of this title is not effec-

tive unless the corporation approves such transfer.

(3) No transfer to which this section applies, in connection with a termination described in section 1341a(a)(2) of this title shall be effective unless the transfer meets such requirements as may be established by the corporation to prevent an increase in the risk of loss to the corporation.

(Pub. L. 93–406, title IV, §4232, as added Pub. L. 96–364, title I, §104(2), Sept. 26, 1980, 94 Stat. 1245.)

§1413. Partition

(a) Authority of corporation

The corporation may order the partition of a multiemployer plan in accordance with this section.

(b) Authority of plan sponsor upon application to corporation for partition order; procedures applicable to corporation

A plan sponsor may apply to the corporation for an order partitioning a plan. The corporation may not order the partition of a plan except upon notice to the plan sponsor and the participants and beneficiaries whose vested benefits will be affected by the partition of the plan, and upon finding that—

(1) a substantial reduction in the amount of aggregate contributions under the plan has resulted or will result from a case or proceeding under title 11 with respect to an employer;

(2) the plan is likely to become insolvent;

(3) contributions will have to be increased significantly in reorganization to meet the minimum contribution requirement and prevent insolvency; and

(4) partition would significantly reduce the likelihood that the plan will become insolvent.

(c) Authority of corporation notwithstanding pendency of partition proceeding

The corporation may order the partition of a plan notwithstanding the pendency of a proceeding described in subsection (b)(1) of this section.

(d) Scope of partition order

The corporation's partition order shall provide for a transfer of no more than the nonforfeitable benefits directly attributable to service with the employer referred to in subsection (b)(1) of this section and an equitable share of assets.

(e) Nature of plan created by partition

The plan created by the partition is—

(1) a successor plan to which section 1322a of this title applies, and

(2) a terminated multiemployer plan to which section 1341a(d) of this title applies, with respect to which only the employer described in subsection (b)(1) of this section has withdrawal liability, and to which section 1368 of this title applies.

(f) Authority of corporation to obtain decree partitioning plan and appointing trustee for terminated portion of partitioned plan

The corporation may proceed under section 1342(c) through (h) of this title for a decree partitioning a plan and appointing a trustee for the terminated portion of a partitioned plan. The court may order the partition of a plan upon making the findings described in subsection (b)(1) through (4) of this section, and subject to the conditions set forth in subsections (c) through (e) of this section.

(Pub. L. 93–406, title IV, §4233, as added Pub. L. 96–364, title I, §104(2), Sept. 26, 1980, 94 Stat. 1246.)

§1414. Asset transfer rules

(a) Applicability and scope

A transfer of assets from a multiemployer plan to another plan shall comply with asset-transfer rules which shall be adopted by the multiemployer plan and which—

(1) do not unreasonably restrict the transfer of plan assets in connection with the transfer of plan liabilities, and

(2) operate and are applied uniformly with respect to each proposed transfer, except that the rules may provide for reasonable variations taking into account the potential financial impact of a proposed transfer on the multiemployer plan.

Plan rules authorizing asset transfers consistent with the requirements of section 1412(c)(3) of this title shall be considered to satisfy the requirements of this subsection.

(b) Exemption of de minimis transfers

The corporation shall prescribe regulations which exempt de minimis transfers of assets from the requirements of this part.

(c) Written reciprocity agreements

This part shall not apply to transfers of assets pursuant to written reciprocity agreements, except to the extent provided in regulations prescribed by the corporation.

(Pub. L. 93–406, title IV, §4234, as added Pub. L. 96–364, title I, §104(2), Sept. 26, 1980, 94 Stat. 1247.)

§1415. Transfers pursuant to change in bargaining representative

(a) Authority to transfer from old plan to new plan pursuant to employee participation in another multiemployer plan after certified change of representative

In any case in which an employer has completely or partially withdrawn from a multiemployer plan (hereafter in this section referred to as the "old plan") as a result of a certified change of collective bargaining representative occurring after September 25, 1980, if participants of the old plan who are employed by the employer will, as a result of that change, participate in another multiemployer plan (hereafter in this section referred to as the "new plan"), the old plan shall transfer assets and liabilities to the new plan in accordance with this section.

(b) Notification by employer of plan sponsor of old plan; notification by plan sponsor of old plan of employer and plan sponsor of new plan; appeal by new plan to prevent transfer; further proceedings

(1) The employer shall notify the plan sponsor of the old plan of a change in multiemployer

plan participation described in subsection (a) of this section no later than 30 days after the employer determines that the change will occur.

(2) The plan sponsor of the old plan shall—

(A) notify the employer of—

(i) the amount of the employer's withdrawal liability determined under part 1 of this subtitle with respect to the withdrawal,

(ii) the old plan's intent to transfer to the new plan the nonforfeitable benefits of the employees who are no longer working in covered service under the old plan as a result of the change of bargaining representative, and

(iii) the amount of assets and liabilities which are to be transferred to the new plan, and

(B) notify the plan sponsor of the new plan of the benefits, assets, and liabilities which will be transferred to the new plan.

(3) Within 60 days after receipt of the notice described in paragraph (2)(B), the new plan may file an appeal with the corporation to prevent the transfer. The transfer shall not be made if the corporation determines that the new plan would suffer substantial financial harm as a result of the transfer. Upon notification described in paragraph (2), if—

(A) the employer fails to object to the transfer within 60 days after receipt of the notice described in paragraph (2)(A), or

(B) the new plan either—

(i) fails to file such an appeal, or

(ii) the corporation, pursuant to such an appeal, fails to find that the new plan would suffer substantial financial harm as a result of the transfer described in the notice under paragraph (2)(B) within 180 days after the date on which the appeal is filed,

then the plan sponsor of the old plan shall transfer the appropriate amount of assets and liabilities to the new plan.

(c) Reduction of amount of withdrawal liability of employer upon transfer of appropriate amount of assets and liabilities by plan sponsor of old plan to new plan

If the plan sponsor of the old plan transfers the appropriate amount of assets and liabilities under this section to the new plan, then the amount of the employer's withdrawal liability (as determined under section 1381(b) of this title without regard to such transfer and this section) with respect to the old plan shall be reduced by the amount by which—

(1) the value of the unfunded vested benefits allocable to the employer which were transferred by the plan sponsor of the old plan to the new plan, exceeds

(2) the value of the assets transferred.

(d) Escrow payments by employer upon complete or partial withdrawal and prior to transfer

In any case in which there is a complete or partial withdrawal described in subsection (a) of this section, if—

(1) the new plan files an appeal with the corporation under subsection (b)(3) of this section, and

(2) the employer is required by section 1399 of this title to begin making payments of withdrawal liability before the earlier of—

(A) the date on which the corporation finds that the new plan would not suffer substantial financial harm as a result of the transfer, or

(B) the last day of the 180-day period beginning on the date on which the new plan files its appeal,

then the employer shall make such payments into an escrow held by a bank or similar financial institution satisfactory to the old plan. If the transfer is made, the amounts paid into the escrow shall be returned to the employer. If the transfer is not made, the amounts paid into the escrow shall be paid to the old plan and credited against the employer's withdrawal liability.

(e) Prohibition on transfer of assets to new plan by plan sponsor of old plan; exemptions

(1) Notwithstanding subsection (b) of this section, the plan sponsor shall not transfer any assets to the new plan if—

(A) the old plan is in reorganization (within the meaning of section 1421(a) of this title), or

(B) the transfer of assets would cause the old plan to go into reorganization (within the meaning of section 1421(a) of this title).

(2) In any case in which a transfer of assets from the old plan to the new plan is prohibited by paragraph (1), the plan sponsor of the old plan shall transfer—

(A) all nonforfeitable benefits described in subsection (b)(2) of this section, if the value of such benefits does not exceed the withdrawal liability of the employer with respect to such withdrawal, or

(B) such nonforfeitable benefits having a value equal to the withdrawal liability of the employer, if the value of such benefits exceeds the withdrawal liability of the employer.

(f) Agreement between plan sponsors of old plan and new plan to transfer in compliance with other statutory provisions; reduction of withdrawal liability of employer from old plan; amount of withdrawal liability of employer to new plan

(1) Notwithstanding subsections (b) and (e) of this section, the plan sponsors of the old plan and the new plan may agree to a transfer of assets and liabilities that complies with sections 1411 and 1414 of this title, rather than this section, except that the employer's liability with respect to the withdrawal from the old plan shall be reduced under subsection (c) of this section as if assets and liabilities had been transferred in accordance with this section.

(2) If the employer withdraws from the new plan within 240 months after the effective date of a transfer of assets and liabilities described in this section, the amount of the employer's withdrawal liability to the new plan shall be the greater of—

(A) the employer's withdrawal liability determined under part 1 of this subtitle with respect to the new plan, or

(B) the amount by which the employer's withdrawal liability to the old plan was reduced under subsection (c) of this section, reduced by 5 percent for each 12-month period following the effective date of the transfer and ending before the date of the withdrawal from the new plan.

(g) Definitions

For purposes of this section—

(1) "appropriate amount of assets" means the amount by which the value of the nonforfeitable benefits to be transferred exceeds the amount of the employer's withdrawal liability to the old plan (determined under part 1 of this subtitle without regard to section 1391(e) of this title), and

(2) "certified change of collective bargaining representative" means a change of collective bargaining representative certified under the Labor-Management Relations Act, 1947 [29 U.S.C. 141 et seq.], or the Railway Labor Act [45 U.S.C. 151 et seq.].

(Pub. L. 93-406, title IV, §4235, as added Pub. L. 96-364, title I, §104(2), Sept. 26, 1980, 94 Stat. 1247; amended Pub. L. 98-369, div. A, title V, §558(b)(1)(A), July 18, 1984, 98 Stat. 899.)

REFERENCES IN TEXT

The Labor-Management Relations Act, 1947, referred to in subsec. (g)(2), is act June 23, 1947, ch. 120, 61 Stat. 136, as amended, which is classified principally to chapter 7 (§141 et seq.) of this title. For complete classification of this Act to the Code, see section 141 of this title and Tables.

The Railway Labor Act, referred to in subsec. (g)(2), is act May 20, 1926, ch. 347, 44 Stat. 577, as amended, which is classified principally to chapter 8 (§151 et seq.) of Title 45, Railroads. For complete classification of this Act to the Code, see section 151 of Title 45 and Tables.

AMENDMENTS

1984—Subsec. (a). Pub. L. 98-369 substituted "September 25, 1980" for "April 28, 1980".

EFFECTIVE DATE

Section effective Sept. 26, 1980, see section 1461(e)(4) of this title.

PART 3—REORGANIZATION; MINIMUM CONTRIBUTION REQUIREMENT FOR MULTIEMPLOYER PLANS

§1421. Reorganization status

(a) Reorganization index of plan for plan year greater than zero

A multiemployer plan is in reorganization for a plan year if the plan's reorganization index for that year is greater than zero.

(b) Determination of reorganization index of plan for plan year; applicable factors, definitions, etc.

(1) A plan's reorganization index for any plan year is the excess of—

(A) the vested benefits charge for such year, over

(B) the net charge to the funding standard account for such year.

(2) For purposes of this part, the net charge to the funding standard account for any plan year is the excess (if any) of—

(A) the charges to the funding standard account for such year under section 412(b)(2)[1] of title 26, over

(B) the credits to the funding standard account under section 412(b)(3)(B)[1] of title 26.

(3) For purposes of this part, the vested benefits charge for any plan year is the amount which would be necessary to amortize the plan's unfunded vested benefits as of the end of the base plan year in equal annual installments—

(A) over 10 years, to the extent such benefits are attributable to persons in pay status, and

(B) over 25 years, to the extent such benefits are attributable to other participants.

(4)(A) The vested benefits charge for a plan year shall be based on an actuarial valuation of the plan as of the end of the base plan year, adjusted to reflect—

(i) any—

(I) decrease of 5 percent or more in the value of plan assets, or increase of 5 percent or more in the number of persons in pay status, during the period beginning on the first day of the plan year following the base plan year and ending on the adjustment date, or

(II) at the election of the plan sponsor, actuarial valuation of the plan as of the adjustment date or any later date not later than the last day of the plan year for which the determination is being made,

(ii) any change in benefits under the plan which is not otherwise taken into account under this subparagraph and which is pursuant to any amendment—

(I) adopted before the end of the plan year for which the determination is being made, and

(II) effective after the end of the base plan year and on or before the end of the plan year referred to in subclause (I), and

(iii) any other event (including an event described in subparagraph (B)(i)(I)) which, as determined in accordance with regulations prescribed by the Secretary, would substantially increase the plan's vested benefit charge.

(B)(i) In determining the vested benefits charge for a plan year following a plan year in which the plan was not in reorganization, any change in benefits which—

(I) results from the changing of a group of participants from one benefit level to another benefit level under a schedule of plan benefits as a result of changes in a collective bargaining agreement, or

(II) results from any other change in a collective bargaining agreement,

shall not be taken into account except to the extent provided in regulations prescribed by the Secretary of the Treasury.

(ii) Except as otherwise determined by the Secretary of the Treasury, in determining the vested benefits charge for any plan year following any plan year in which the plan was in reorganization, any change in benefits—

(I) described in clause (i)(I), or

(II) described in clause (i)(II) as determined under regulations prescribed by the Secretary of the Treasury,

shall, for purposes of subparagraph (A)(ii), be treated as a change in benefits pursuant to an amendment to a plan.

(5)(A) For purposes of this part, the base plan year for any plan year is—

[1] See References in Text note below.

(i) if there is a relevant collective bargaining agreement, the last plan year ending at least 6 months before the relevant effective date, or

(ii) if there is no relevant collective bargaining agreement, the last plan year ending at least 12 months before the beginning of the plan year.

(B) For purposes of this part, a relevant collective bargaining agreement is a collective bargaining agreement—

(i) which is in effect for at least 6 months during the plan year, and

(ii) which has not been in effect for more than 36 months as of the end of the plan year.

(C) For purposes of this part, the relevant effective date is the earliest of the effective dates for the relevant collective bargaining agreements.

(D) For purposes of this part, the adjustment date is the date which is—

(i) 90 days before the relevant effective date, or

(ii) if there is no relevant effective date, 90 days before the beginning of the plan year.

(6) For purposes of this part, the term "person in pay status" means—

(A) a participant or beneficiary on the last day of the base plan year who, at any time during such year, was paid an early, late, normal, or disability retirement benefit (or a death benefit related to a retirement benefit), and

(B) to the extent provided in regulations prescribed by the Secretary of the Treasury, any other person who is entitled to such a benefit under the plan.

(7) For purposes of paragraph (3)—

(A) in determining the plan's unfunded vested benefits, plan assets shall first be allocated to the vested benefits attributable to persons in pay status, and

(B) the vested benefits charge shall be determined without regard to reductions in accrued benefits under section 1425 of this title which are first effective in the plan year.

(8) For purposes of this part, any outstanding claim for withdrawal liability shall not be considered a plan asset, except as otherwise provided in regulations prescribed by the Secretary of the Treasury.

(9) For purposes of this part, the term "unfunded vested benefits" means with respect to a plan, an amount (determined in accordance with regulations prescribed by the Secretary of the Treasury) equal to—

(A) the value of nonforfeitable benefits under the plan, less

(B) the value of assets of the plan.

(c) Payment of benefits to participants

Except as provided in regulations prescribed by the corporation, while a plan is in reorganization a benefit with respect to a participant (other than a death benefit) which is attributable to employer contributions and which has a value of more than $1,750 may not be paid in a form other than an annuity which (by itself or in combination with social security, railroad retirement, or workers' compensation benefits) provides substantially level payments over the life of the participant.

(d) Terminated multiemployer plans

Any multiemployer plan which terminates under section 1341a(a)(2) of this title shall not be considered in reorganization after the last day of the plan year in which the plan is treated as having terminated.

(Pub. L. 93–406, title IV, §4241, as added Pub. L. 96–364, title I, §104(2), Sept. 26, 1980, 94 Stat. 1249; amended Pub. L. 101–239, title VII, §7891(a)(1), Dec. 19, 1989, 103 Stat. 2445.)

REFERENCES IN TEXT

Section 412, referred to in subsec. (b)(2), was amended generally by Pub. L. 109–280, title I, §111(a), Aug. 17, 2006, 120 Stat. 820, and as so amended, section 412 no longer contains a subsec. (b)(3)(B) and section 412(b)(2) no longer relates to charges to the funding standard account.

AMENDMENTS

1989—Subsec. (b)(2)(A). Pub. L. 101–239 substituted "Internal Revenue Code of 1986" for "Internal Revenue Code of 1954", which for purposes of codification was translated as "title 26" thus requiring no change in text.

EFFECTIVE DATE OF 1989 AMENDMENT

Amendment by Pub. L. 101–239 effective, except as otherwise provided, as if included in the provision of the Tax Reform Act of 1986, Pub. L. 99–514, to which such amendment relates, see section 7891(f) of Pub. L. 101–239, set out as a note under section 1002 of this title.

EFFECTIVE DATE

Part, relating to multiemployer plan reorganization, effective, with respect to each plan, on the first day of the first plan year beginning on or after the earlier of the date on which the last collective-bargaining agreement providing for employer contributions under the plan, which was in effect on Sept. 26, 1980, expires, without regard to extensions agreed to after Sept. 26, 1980, or three years after Sept. 26, 1980, see section 1461(e)(3) of this title.

§1422. Notice of reorganization and funding requirements

(a)(1) If—

(A) a multiemployer plan is in reorganization for a plan year, and

(B) section 1423 of this title would require an increase in contributions for such plan year,

the plan sponsor shall notify the persons described in paragraph (2) that the plan is in reorganization and that, if contributions to the plan are not increased, accrued benefits under the plan may be reduced or an excise tax may be imposed (or both such reduction and imposition may occur).

(2) The persons described in this paragraph are—

(A) each employer who has an obligation to contribute under the plan (within the meaning of section 1381(h)(5) of this title), and

(B) each employee organization which, for purposes of collective bargaining, represents plan participants employed by such an employer.

(3) The determination under paragraph (1)(B) shall be made without regard to the overburden credit provided by section 1424 of this title.

(b) The corporation may prescribe additional or alternative requirements for assuring, in the case of a plan with respect to which notice is required by subsection (a)(1) of this section, that the persons described in subsection (a)(2) of this section—

(1) receive appropriate notice that the plan is in reorganization,

(2) are adequately informed of the implications of reorganization status, and

(3) have reasonable access to information relevant to the plan's reorganization status.

(Pub. L. 93–406, title IV, §4242, as added Pub. L. 96–364, title I, §104(2), Sept. 26, 1980, 94 Stat. 1251.)

§1423. Minimum contribution requirement

(a) Maintenance of funding standard account; amount of accumulated funding deficiency

(1) For any plan year for which a plan is in reorganization—

(A) the plan shall continue to maintain its funding standard account while it is in reorganization, and

(B) the plan's accumulated funding deficiency under section 1084(a) of this title for such plan year shall be equal to the excess (if any) of—

(i) the sum of the minimum contribution requirement for such plan year (taking into account any overburden credit under section 1424(a) of this title) plus the plan's accumulated funding deficiency for the preceding plan year (determined under this section if the plan was in reorganization during such year or under section 1084(a) of this title if the plan was not in reorganization), over

(ii) amounts considered contributed by employers to or under the plan for the plan year (increased by any amount waived under subsection (f) of this section for the plan year).

(2) For purposes of paragraph (1), withdrawal liability payments (whether or not received) which are due with respect to withdrawals before the end of the base plan year shall be considered amounts contributed by the employer to or under the plan if, as of the adjustment date, it was reasonable for the plan sponsor to anticipate that such payments would be made during the plan year.

(b) Determination of amount; applicable factors

(1) Except as otherwise provided in this section, for purposes of this part the minimum contribution requirement for a plan year in which a plan is in reorganization is an amount equal to the excess of—

(A) the sum of—

(i) the plan's vested benefits charge for the plan year, and

(ii) the increase in normal cost for the plan year determined under the entry age normal funding method which is attributable to plan amendments adopted while the plan was in reorganization, over

(B) the amount of the overburden credit (if any) determined under section 1424 of this title for the plan year.

(2) If the plan's current contribution base for the plan year is less than the plan's valuation contribution base for the plan year, the minimum contribution requirement for such plan year shall be equal to the product of the amount determined under paragraph (1) (after any adjustment required by this part other than this paragraph) and a fraction—

(A) the numerator of which is the plan's current contribution base for the plan year, and

(B) the denominator of which is the plan's valuation contribution base for the plan year.

(3)(A) If the vested benefits charge for a plan year of a plan in reorganization is less than the plan's cash-flow amount for the plan year, the plan's minimum contribution requirement for the plan year is the amount determined under paragraph (1) (determined before the application of paragraph (2)) after substituting the term "cash-flow amount" for the term "vested benefits charge" in paragraph (1)(A).

(B) For purposes of subparagraph (A), a plan's cash-flow amount for a plan year is an amount equal to—

(i) the amount of the benefits payable under the plan for the base plan year, plus the amount of the plan's administrative expenses for the base plan year, reduced by

(ii) the value of the available plan assets for the base plan year determined under regulations prescribed by the Secretary of the Treasury,

adjusted in a manner consistent with section 1421(b)(4) of this title.

(c) Current contribution base; valuation contribution base

(1) For purposes of this part, a plan's current contribution base for a plan year is the number of contribution base units with respect to which contributions are required to be made under the plan for that plan year, determined in accordance with regulations prescribed by the Secretary of the Treasury.

(2)(A) Except as provided in subparagraph (B), for purposes of this part a plan's valuation contribution base is the number of contribution base units for which contributions were received for the base plan year—

(i) adjusted to reflect declines in the contribution base which have occurred (or could reasonably be anticipated) as of the adjustment date for the plan year referred to in paragraph (1),

(ii) adjusted upward (in accordance with regulations prescribed by the Secretary of the Treasury) for any contribution base reduction in the base plan year caused by a strike or lockout or by unusual events, such as fire, earthquake, or severe weather conditions, and

(iii) adjusted (in accordance with regulations prescribed by the Secretary of the Treasury) for reductions in the contribution base resulting from transfers of liabilities.

(B) For any plan year—

(i) in which the plan is insolvent (within the meaning of section 1426(b)(1) of this title), and

(ii) beginning with the first plan year beginning after the expiration of all relevant collective bargaining agreements which were in effect in the plan year in which the plan became insolvent,

the plan's valuation contribution base is the greater of the number of contribution base units for which contributions were received for the first or second plan year preceding the first plan year in which the plan is insolvent, adjusted as provided in clause (ii) or (iii) of subparagraph (A).

(d) Maximum amount; amount of funding standard requirement; applicability to plan amendments increasing benefits

(1) Under regulations prescribed by the Secretary of the Treasury, the minimum contribution requirement applicable to any plan for any plan year which is determined under subsection (b) of this section (without regard to subsection (b)(2) of this section) shall not exceed an amount which is equal to the sum of—

(A) the greater of—

(i) the funding standard requirement for such plan year, or

(ii) 107 percent of—

(I) if the plan was not in reorganization in the preceding plan year, the funding standard requirement for such preceding plan year, or

(II) if the plan was in reorganization in the preceding plan year, the sum of the amount determined under this subparagraph for the preceding plan year and the amount (if any) determined under subparagraph (B) for the preceding plan year, plus

(B) if for the plan year a change in benefits is first required to be considered in computing the charges under section 412(b)(2)(A) or (B)[1] of title 26, the sum of—

(i) the increase in normal cost for a plan year determined under the entry age normal funding method due to increases in benefits described in section 1421(b)(4)(A)(ii) of this title (determined without regard to section 1421(b)(4)(B)(i) of this title), and

(ii) the amount necessary to amortize in equal annual installments the increase in the value of vested benefits under the plan due to increases in benefits described in clause (i) over—

(I) 10 years, to the extent such increase in value is attributable to persons in pay status, or

(II) 25 years, to the extent such increase in value is attributable to other participants.

(2) For purposes of paragraph (1), the funding standard requirement for any plan year is an amount equal to the net charge to the funding standard account for such plan year (as defined in section 1421(b)(2) of this title).

(3)(A) In the case of a plan described in section 1396(b) of this title, if a plan amendment which increases benefits is adopted after January 1, 1980—

(i) paragraph (1) shall apply only if the plan is a plan described in subparagraph (B), and

(ii) the amount under paragraph (1) shall be determined without regard to paragraph (1)(B).

(B) A plan is described in this subparagraph if—

(i) the rate of employer contributions under the plan for the first plan year beginning on or after the date on which an amendment increasing benefits is adopted, multiplied by the valuation contribution base for that plan year, equals or exceeds the sum of—

(I) the amount that would be necessary to amortize fully, in equal annual installments, by July 1, 1986, the unfunded vested benefits attributable to plan provisions in effect on July 1, 1977 (determined as of the last day of the base plan year); and

(II) the amount that would be necessary to amortize fully, in equal annual installments, over the period described in subparagraph (C), beginning with the first day of the first plan year beginning on or after the date on which the amendment is adopted, the unfunded vested benefits (determined as of the last day of the base plan year) attributable to each plan amendment after July 1, 1977; and

(ii) the rate of employer contributions for each subsequent plan year is not less than the lesser of—

(I) the rate which when multiplied by the valuation contribution base for that subsequent plan year produces the annual amount that would be necessary to complete the amortization schedule described in clause (i), or

(II) the rate for the plan year immediately preceding such subsequent plan year, plus 5 percent of such rate.

(C) The period determined under this subparagraph is the lesser of—

(i) 12 years, or

(ii) a period equal in length to the average of the remaining expected lives of all persons receiving benefits under the plan.

(4) Paragraph (1) shall not apply with respect to a plan, other than a plan described in paragraph (3), for the period of consecutive plan years in each of which the plan is in reorganization, beginning with a plan year in which occurs the earlier of the date of the adoption or the effective date of any amendment of the plan which increases benefits with respect to service performed before the plan year in which the adoption of the amendment occurred.

(e) Adjustment of vested benefits charge

In determining the minimum contribution requirement with respect to a plan for a plan year under subsection (b) of this section, the vested benefits charge may be adjusted to reflect a plan amendment reducing benefits under section 412(c)(8)[1] of title 26.

(f) Waiver of accumulated funding deficiency

(1) The Secretary of the Treasury may waive any accumulated funding deficiency under this section in accordance with the provisions of section 1082(c) of this title.

(2) Any waiver under paragraph (1) shall not be treated as a waived funding deficiency (within the meaning of section 1082(c)(3) of this title).

[1] See References in Text note below.

(g) Statutory methods applicable for determinations

For purposes of making any determination under this part, the requirements of section 1084(c)(3) of this title shall apply.

(Pub. L. 93–406, title IV, § 4243, as added Pub. L. 96–364, title I, § 104(2), Sept. 26, 1980, 94 Stat. 1252; amended Pub. L. 101–239, title VII, § 7891(a)(1), Dec. 19, 1989, 103 Stat. 2445; Pub. L. 109–280, title I, § 107(b)(6)–(9), Aug. 17, 2006, 120 Stat. 820.)

REFERENCES IN TEXT

Section 412, referred to in subsecs. (d)(1) and (e), was amended generally by Pub. L. 109–280, title I, § 111(a), Aug. 17, 2006, 120 Stat. 820, and as so amended, no longer contains a subsec. (b)(2)(A) or (B) or (c)(8).

AMENDMENTS

2006—Subsec. (a)(1)(B). Pub. L. 109–280, § 107(b)(6), substituted "1084(a)" for "1082(a)" in introductory provisions and cl. (i).

Subsec. (f)(1). Pub. L. 109–280, § 107(b)(7), substituted "1082(c)" for "1083(a)".

Subsec. (f)(2). Pub. L. 109–280, § 107(b)(8), substituted "1082(c)(3)" for "1083(c)".

Subsec. (g). Pub. L. 109–280, § 107(b)(9), substituted "1084(c)(3)" for "1082(c)(3)".

1989—Subsecs. (d)(1)(B), (e). Pub. L. 101–239 substituted "Internal Revenue Code of 1986" for "Internal Revenue Code of 1954", which for purposes of codification was translated as "title 26" thus requiring no change in text.

EFFECTIVE DATE OF 2006 AMENDMENT

Amendment by Pub. L. 109–280 applicable to plan years beginning after 2007, see section 107(e) of Pub. L. 109–280, set out as a note under section 1021 of this title.

EFFECTIVE DATE OF 1989 AMENDMENT

Amendment by Pub. L. 101–239 effective, except as otherwise provided, as if included in the provision of the Tax Reform Act of 1986, Pub. L. 99–514, to which such amendment relates, see section 7891(f) of Pub. L. 101–239, set out as a note under section 1002 of this title.

APPLICABILITY OF AMENDMENTS BY SUBTITLES A AND B OF TITLE I OF PUB. L. 109–280

For special rules on applicability of amendments by subtitles A (§§ 101–107) and B (§§ 111–116) of title I of Pub. L. 109–280 to certain eligible cooperative plans, PBGC settlement plans, and eligible government contractor plans, see sections 104, 105, and 106 of Pub. L. 109–280, set out as notes under section 401 of Title 26, Internal Revenue Code.

§ 1424. Overburden credit against minimum contribution requirement

(a) Applicability of overburden credit to determinations

For purposes of determining the minimum contribution requirement under section 1423 of this title (before the application of section 1423(b)(2) or (d) of this title) the plan sponsor of a plan which is overburdened for the plan year shall apply an overburden credit against the plan's minimum contribution requirement for the plan year (determined without regard to section 1423(b)(2) or (d) of this title and without regard to this section).

(b) Determination of overburden status of plan

A plan is overburdened for a plan year if—

(1) the average number of pay status participants under the plan in the base plan year exceeds the average of the number of active participants in the base plan year and the 2 plan years preceding the base plan year, and

(2) the rate of employer contributions under the plan equals or exceeds the greater of—

(A) such rate for the preceding plan year, or

(B) such rate for the plan year preceding the first year in which the plan is in reorganization.

(c) Amount of overburden credit

The amount of the overburden credit for a plan year is the product of—

(1) one-half of the average guaranteed benefit paid for the base plan year, and

(2) the overburden factor for the plan year.

The amount of the overburden credit for a plan year shall not exceed the amount of the minimum contribution requirement for such year (determined without regard to this section).

(d) Amount of overburden factor

For purposes of this section, the overburden factor of a plan for the plan year is an amount equal to—

(1) the average number of pay status participants for the base plan year, reduced by

(2) the average of the number of active participants for the base plan year and for each of the 2 plan years preceding the base plan year.

(e) Definitions; determinative factors

For purposes of this section—

(1) The term "pay status participant" means, with respect to a plan, a participant receiving retirement benefits under the plan.

(2) The number of active participants for a plan year shall be the sum of—

(A) the number of active employees who are participants in the plan and on whose behalf contributions are required to be made during the plan year;

(B) the number of active employees who are not participants in the plan but who are in an employment unit covered by a collective bargaining agreement which requires the employees' employer to contribute to the plan, unless service in such employment unit was never covered under the plan or a predecessor thereof, and

(C) the total number of active employees attributed to employers who made payments to the plan for the plan year of withdrawal liability pursuant to part 1 of this subtitle, determined by dividing—

(i) the total amount of such payments, by

(ii) the amount equal to the total contributions received by the plan during the plan year divided by the average number of active employees who were participants in the plan during the plan year.

The Secretary of the Treasury shall by regulation provide alternative methods of determining active participants where (by reason of irregular employment, contributions on a unit basis, or otherwise) this paragraph does not yield a representative basis for determining the credit.

(3) The term "average number" means, with respect to pay status participants for a plan year, a number equal to one-half the sum of—

(A) the number with respect to the plan as of the beginning of the plan year, and

(B) the number with respect to the plan as of the end of the plan year.

(4) The average guaranteed benefit paid is 12 times the average monthly pension payment guaranteed under section 1322a(c)(1) of this title determined under the provisions of the plan in effect at the beginning of the first plan year in which the plan is in reorganization and without regard to section 1322a(c)(2)[1] of this title.

(5) The first year in which the plan is in reorganization is the first of a period of 1 or more consecutive plan years in which the plan has been in reorganization not taking into account any plan years the plan was in reorganization prior to any period of 3 or more consecutive plan years in which the plan was not in reorganization.

(f) Eligibility of plan for overburden credit for plan year

(1) Notwithstanding any other provision of this section, a plan is not eligible for an overburden credit for a plan year if the Secretary of the Treasury finds that the plan's current contribution base for the plan year was reduced, without a corresponding reduction in the plan's unfunded vested benefits attributable to pay status participants, as a result of a change in an agreement providing for employer contributions under the plan.

(2) For purposes of paragraph (1), a complete or partial withdrawal of an employer (within the meaning of part 1 of this subtitle) does not impair a plan's eligibility for an overburden credit, unless the Secretary of the Treasury finds that a contribution base reduction described in paragraph (1) resulted from a transfer of liabilities to another plan in connection with the withdrawal.

(g) Overburden credit where 2 or more multiemployer plans merge

Notwithstanding any other provision of this section, if 2 or more multiemployer plans merge, the amount of the overburden credit which may be applied under this section with respect to the plan resulting from the merger for any of the 3 plan years ending after the effective date of the merger shall not exceed the sum of the used overburden credit for each of the merging plans for its last plan year ending before the effective date of the merger. For purposes of the preceding sentence, the used overburden credit is that portion of the credit which does not exceed the excess of the minimum contribution requirement (determined without regard to any overburden requirement under this section) over the employer contributions required under the plan.

(Pub. L. 93–406, title IV, §4244, as added Pub. L. 96–364, title I, §104(2), Sept. 26, 1980, 94 Stat. 1255.)

REFERENCES IN TEXT

Section 1322a(c)(2) of this title, referred to in subsec. (e)(4), was repealed and former section 1322a(c)(3) was redesignated section 1322a(c)(2) by Pub. L. 106–554, §1(a)(6) [title IX, §951(a)(3)], Dec. 21, 2000, 114 Stat. 2763, 2763A–586.

[1] See References in Text note below.

§1425. Adjustments in accrued benefits

(a) Amendment of multiemployer plan in reorganization to reduce or eliminate accrued benefits attributable to employer contributions ineligible for guarantee of corporation; adjustment of vested benefits charge to reflect plan amendment

(1) Notwithstanding sections 1053 and 1054 of this title, a multiemployer plan in reorganization may be amended in accordance with this section, to reduce or eliminate accrued benefits attributable to employer contributions which, under section 1322a(b) of this title, are not eligible for the corporation's guarantee. The preceding sentence shall only apply to accrued benefits under plan amendments (or plans) adopted after March 26, 1980, or under collective bargaining agreements entered into after March 26, 1980.

(2) In determining the minimum contribution requirement with respect to a plan for a plan year under section 1423(b) of this title, the vested benefits charge may be adjusted to reflect a plan amendment reducing benefits under this section or section 412(c)(8)[1] of title 26, but only if the amendment is adopted and effective no later than 2½ months after the end of the plan year, or within such extended period as the Secretary of the Treasury may prescribe by regulation under section 412(c)(10)[1] of title 26.

(b) Reduction of accrued benefits; notice by plan sponsors to plan participants and beneficiaries

(1) Accrued benefits may not be reduced under this section unless—

(A) notice has been given, at least 6 months before the first day of the plan year in which the amendment reducing benefits is adopted, to—

(i) plan participants and beneficiaries,

(ii) each employer who has an obligation to contribute (within the meaning of section 1392(a) of this title) under the plan, and

(iii) each employee organization which, for purposes of collective bargaining, represents plan participants employed by such an employer,

that the plan is in reorganization and that, if contributions under the plan are not increased, accrued benefits under the plan will be reduced or an excise tax will be imposed on employers;

(B) in accordance with regulations prescribed by the Secretary of the Treasury—

(i) any category of accrued benefits is not reduced with respect to inactive participants to a greater extent proportionally than such category of accrued benefits is reduced with respect to active participants,

(ii) benefits attributable to employer contributions other than accrued benefits and the rate of future benefit accruals are reduced at least to an extent equal to the reduction in accrued benefits of inactive participants, and

[1] See References in Text note below.

(iii) in any case in which the accrued benefit of a participant or beneficiary is reduced by changing the benefit form or the requirements which the participant or beneficiary must satisfy to be entitled to the benefit, such reduction is not applicable to—

(I) any participant or beneficiary in pay status on the effective date of the amendment, or the beneficiary of such a participant, or

(II) any participant who has attained normal retirement age, or who is within 5 years of attaining normal retirement age, on the effective date of the amendment, or the beneficiary of any such participant; and

(C) the rate of employer contributions for the plan year in which the amendment becomes effective and for all succeeding plan years in which the plan is in reorganization equals or exceeds the greater of—

(i) the rate of employer contributions, calculated without regard to the amendment, for the plan year in which the amendment becomes effective, or

(ii) the rate of employer contributions for the plan year preceding the plan year in which the amendment becomes effective.

(2) The plan sponsors shall include in any notice required to be sent to plan participants and beneficiaries under paragraph (1) information as to the rights and remedies of plan participants and beneficiaries as well as how to contact the Department of Labor for further information and assistance where appropriate.

(c) Recoupment by plan of excess benefit payment

A plan may not recoup a benefit payment which is in excess of the amount payable under the plan because of an amendment retroactively reducing accrued benefits under this section.

(d) Amendment of plan to increase or restore accrued benefits previously reduced or rate of future benefit accruals; conditions, applicable factors, etc.

(1)(A) A plan which has been amended to reduce accrued benefits under this section may be amended to increase or restore accrued benefits, or the rate of future benefit accruals, only if the plan is amended to restore levels of previously reduced accrued benefits of inactive participants and of participants who are within 5 years of attaining normal retirement age to at least the same extent as any such increase in accrued benefits or in the rate of future benefit accruals.

(B) For purposes of this subsection, in the case of a plan which has been amended under this section to reduce accrued benefits—

(i) an increase in a benefit, or in the rate of future benefit accruals, shall be considered a benefit increase to the extent that the benefit, or the accrual rate, is thereby increased above the highest benefit level, or accrual rate, which was in effect under the terms of the plan before the effective date of the amendment reducing accrued benefits, and

(ii) an increase in a benefit, or in the rate of future benefit accruals, shall be considered a benefit restoration to the extent that the benefit, or the accrual rate, is not thereby increased above the highest benefit level, or accrual rate, which was in effect under the terms of the plan immediately before the effective date of the amendment reducing accrued benefits.

(2) If a plan is amended to partially restore previously reduced accrued benefit levels, or the rate of future benefit accruals, the benefits of inactive participants shall be restored in at least the same proportions as other accrued benefits which are restored.

(3) No benefit increase under a plan may take effect in a plan year in which an amendment reducing accrued benefits under the plan, in accordance with this section, is adopted or first becomes effective.

(4) A plan is not required to make retroactive benefit payments with respect to that portion of an accrued benefit which was reduced and subsequently restored under this section.

(e) "Inactive participant" defined

For purposes of this section, "inactive participant" means a person not in covered service under the plan who is in pay status under the plan or who has a nonforfeitable benefit under the plan.

(f) Promulgation of rules; contents, etc.

The Secretary of the Treasury may prescribe rules under which, notwithstanding any other provision of this section, accrued benefit reductions or benefit increases for different participant groups may be varied equitably to reflect variations in contribution rates and other relevant factors reflecting differences in negotiated levels of financial support for plan benefit obligations.

(Pub. L. 93–406, title IV, § 4244A, as added Pub. L. 96–364, title I, § 104(2), Sept. 26, 1980, 94 Stat. 1257; amended Pub. L. 101–239, title VII, § 7891(a)(1), Dec. 19, 1989, 103 Stat. 2445.)

REFERENCES IN TEXT

Section 412, referred to in subsec. (a)(2), was amended generally by Pub. L. 109–280, title I, § 111(a), Aug. 17, 2006, 120 Stat. 820, and as so amended, no longer contains a subsec. (c)(8) or (10).

AMENDMENTS

1989—Subsec. (a)(2). Pub. L. 101–239 substituted "Internal Revenue Code of 1986" for "Internal Revenue Code of 1954", which for purposes of codification was translated as "title 26" thus requiring no change in text.

EFFECTIVE DATE OF 1989 AMENDMENT

Amendment by Pub. L. 101–239 effective, except as otherwise provided, as if included in the provision of the Tax Reform Act of 1986, Pub. L. 99–514, to which such amendment relates, see section 7891(f) of Pub. L. 101–239, set out as a note under section 1002 of this title.

§ 1426. Insolvent plans

(a) Suspension of payments of benefits; conditions, amount, etc.

Notwithstanding sections 1053 and 1054 of this title, in any case in which benefit payments under an insolvent multiemployer plan exceed the resource benefit level, any such payments of benefits which are not basic benefits shall be suspended, in accordance with this section, to the extent necessary to reduce the sum of such payments and the payments of such basic benefits to the greater of the resource benefit level or the level of basic benefits, unless an alternative procedure is prescribed by the corporation under section 1322a(g)(5) of this title.

(b) Determination of insolvency status for plan year; definitions

For purposes of this section, for a plan year—

(1) a multiemployer plan is insolvent if the plan's available resources are not sufficient to pay benefits under the plan when due for the plan year, or if the plan is determined to be insolvent under subsection (d) of this section;

(2) "resource benefit level" means the level of monthly benefits determined under subsections (c)(1) and (3) and (d)(3) of this section to be the highest level which can be paid out of the plan's available resources;

(3) "available resources" means the plan's cash, marketable assets, contributions, withdrawal liability payments, and earnings, less reasonable administrative expenses and amounts owed for such plan year to the corporation under section 1431(b)(2) of this title; and

(4) "insolvency year" means a plan year in which a plan is insolvent.

(c) Determination by plan sponsor of plan in reorganization of resource benefit level of plan for each insolvency year; uniform application of suspension of benefits; adjustments of benefit payments

(1) The plan sponsor of a plan in reorganization shall determine in writing the plan's resource benefit level for each insolvency year, based on the plan sponsor's reasonable projection of the plan's available resources and the benefits payable under the plan.

(2) The suspension of benefit payments under this section shall, in accordance with regulations prescribed by the Secretary of the Treasury, apply in substantially uniform proportions to the benefits of all persons in pay status (within the meaning of section 1421(b)(6) of this title) under the plan, except that the Secretary of the Treasury may prescribe rules under which benefit suspensions for different participant groups may be varied equitably to reflect variations in contribution rates and other relevant factors including differences in negotiated levels of financial support for plan benefit obligations.

(3) Notwithstanding paragraph (2), if a plan sponsor determines in writing a resource benefit level for a plan year which is below the level of basic benefits, the payment of all benefits other than basic benefits must be suspended for that plan year.

(4)(A) If, by the end of an insolvency year, the plan sponsor determines in writing that the plan's available resources in that insolvency year could have supported benefit payments above the resource benefit level for that insolvency year, the plan sponsor shall distribute the excess resources to the participants and beneficiaries who received benefit payments from the plan in that insolvency year, in accordance with regulations prescribed by the Secretary of the Treasury.

(B) For purposes of this paragraph, the term "excess resources" means available resources above the amount necessary to support the resource benefit level, but no greater than the amount necessary to pay benefits for the plan year at the benefit levels under the plan.

(5) If, by the end of an insolvency year, any benefit has not been paid at the resource benefit level, amounts up to the resource benefit level which were unpaid shall be distributed to the participants and beneficiaries, in accordance with regulations prescribed by the Secretary of the Treasury, to the extent possible taking into account the plan's total available resources in that insolvency year.

(6) Except as provided in paragraph (4) or (5), a plan is not required to make retroactive benefit payments with respect to that portion of a benefit which was suspended under this section.

(d) Applicability and determinations respecting plan assets; time for determinations of resource benefit level and level of basic benefits

(1) As of the end of the first plan year in which a plan is in reorganization, and at least every 3 plan years thereafter (unless the plan is no longer in reorganization), the plan sponsor shall compare the value of plan assets (determined in accordance with section 1423(b)(3)(B)(ii) of this title) for that plan year with the total amount of benefit payments made under the plan for that plan year. Unless the plan sponsor determines that the value of plan assets exceeds 3 times the total amount of benefit payments, the plan sponsor shall determine whether the plan will be insolvent in any of the next 5 plan years. If the plan sponsor makes such a determination that the plan will be insolvent in any of the next 5 plan years, the plan sponsor shall make the comparison under this paragraph at least annually until the plan sponsor makes a determination that the plan will not be insolvent in any of the next 5 plan years.

(2) If, at any time, the plan sponsor of a plan in reorganization reasonably determines, taking into account the plan's recent and anticipated financial experience, that the plan's available resources are not sufficient to pay benefits under the plan when due for the next plan year, the plan sponsor shall make such determination available to interested parties.

(3) The plan sponsor of a plan in reorganization shall determine in writing for each insolvency year the resource benefit level and the level of basic benefits no later than 3 months before the insolvency year.

(e) Notice, etc., requirements of plan sponsor of plan in reorganization regarding insolvency and resource benefit levels

(1) If the plan sponsor of a plan in reorganization determines under subsection (d)(1) or (2) of this section that the plan may become insolvent (within the meaning of subsection (b)(1) of this section), the plan sponsor shall—

(A) notify the Secretary of the Treasury, the corporation, the parties described in section 1422(a)(2) of this title, and the plan participants and beneficiaries of that determination, and

(B) inform the parties described in section 1422(a)(2) of this title and the plan participants and beneficiaries that if insolvency occurs certain benefit payments will be suspended, but that basic benefits will continue to be paid.

(2) No later than 2 months before the first day of each insolvency year, the plan sponsor of a plan in reorganization shall notify the Secretary of the Treasury, the corporation, and the parties described in paragraph (1)(B) of the resource benefit level determined in writing for that insolvency year.

(3) In any case in which the plan sponsor anticipates that the resource benefit level for an insolvency year may not exceed the level of basic benefits, the plan sponsor shall notify the corporation.

(4) Notice required by this subsection shall be given in accordance with regulations prescribed by the corporation, except that notice to the Secretary of the Treasury shall be given in accordance with regulations prescribed by the Secretary of the Treasury.

(5) The corporation may prescribe a time other than the time prescribed by this section for the making of a determination or the filing of a notice under this section.

(f) Financial assistance from corporation; conditions and criteria applicable

(1) If the plan sponsor of an insolvent plan, for which the resource benefit level is above the level of basic benefits, anticipates that, for any month in an insolvency year, the plan will not have funds sufficient to pay basic benefits, the plan sponsor may apply for financial assistance from the corporation under section 1431 of this title.

(2) A plan sponsor who has determined a resource benefit level for an insolvency year which is below the level of basic benefits shall apply for financial assistance from the corporation under section 1431 of this title.

(Pub. L. 93–406, title IV, §4245, as added Pub. L. 96–364, title I, §104(2), Sept. 26, 1980, 94 Stat. 1259; amended Pub. L. 109–280, title II, §203(a), Aug. 17, 2006, 120 Stat. 886.)

AMENDMENTS

2006—Subsec. (d)(1). Pub. L. 109–280 substituted "5 plan years" for "3 plan years" the second place it appeared and inserted at end "If the plan sponsor makes such a determination that the plan will be insolvent in any of the next 5 plan years, the plan sponsor shall make the comparison under this paragraph at least annually until the plan sponsor makes a determination that the plan will not be insolvent in any of the next 5 plan years."

EFFECTIVE DATE OF 2006 AMENDMENT

Pub. L. 109–280, title II, §203(b), Aug. 17, 2006, 120 Stat. 886, provided that: "The amendments made by this section [amending this section] shall apply with respect to determinations made in plan years beginning after 2007."

WITHDRAWAL LIABILITY OF EMPLOYER FROM PLAN TERMINATING WHILE PLAN INSOLVENT WITHIN THIS SECTION: DETERMINATIONS, FACTORS, ETC.

Section 108(c)(3) of Pub. L. 96–364 provided that:

"(A) For the purpose of determining the withdrawal liability of an employer under title IV of the Employee Retirement Income Security Act of 1974 [this subchapter] from a plan that terminates while the plan is insolvent (within the meaning of section 4245 of such Act [this section]), the plan's unfunded vested benefits shall be reduced by an amount equal to the sum of all overburden credits that were applied in determining the plan's accumulated funding deficiency for all plan years preceding the first plan year in which the plan is insolvent, plus interest thereon.

"(B) The provisions of subparagraph (A) apply only if—

"(i) the plan would have been eligible for the overburden credit in the last plan year beginning before the date of the enactment of this Act [Sept. 26, 1980], if section 4243 of the Employee Retirement Income Security Act of 1974 [section 1423 of this title] had been in effect for that plan year, and

"(ii) the Pension Benefit Guaranty Corporation determines that the reduction of unfunded vested benefits under subparagraph (A) would not significantly increase the risk of loss to the corporation."

PART 4—FINANCIAL ASSISTANCE

§1431. Assistance by corporation

(a) Authority; procedure applicable; amount

If, upon receipt of an application for financial assistance under section 1426(f) of this title or section 1441(d) of this title, the corporation verifies that the plan is or will be insolvent and unable to pay basic benefits when due, the corporation shall provide the plan financial assistance in an amount sufficient to enable the plan to pay basic benefits under the plan.

(b) Conditions; repayment terms

(1) Financial assistance shall be provided under such conditions as the corporation determines are equitable and are appropriate to prevent unreasonable loss to the corporation with respect to the plan.

(2) A plan which has received financial assistance shall repay the amount of such assistance to the corporation on reasonable terms consistent with regulations prescribed by the corporation.

(c) Assistance pending final determination of application

Pending determination of the amount described in subsection (a) of this section, the corporation may provide financial assistance in such amounts as it considers appropriate in order to avoid undue hardship to plan participants and beneficiaries.

(Pub. L. 93–406, title IV, §4261, as added Pub. L. 96–364, title I, §104(2), Sept. 26, 1980, 94 Stat. 1261.)

EFFECTIVE DATE

Part effective Sept. 26, 1980, except as specifically provided, see section 1461(e) of this title.

PART 5—BENEFITS AFTER TERMINATION

§1441. Benefits under certain terminated plans

(a) Amendment of plan by plan sponsor to reduce benefits, and suspension of benefit payments

Notwithstanding sections 1053 and 1054 of this title, the plan sponsor of a terminated multiemployer plan to which section 1341a(d) of this title applies shall amend the plan to reduce benefits, and shall suspend benefit payments, as required by this section.

(b) Determinations respecting value of nonforfeitable benefits under terminated plan and value of assets of plan

(1) The value of nonforfeitable benefits under a terminated plan referred to in subsection (a) of this section, and the value of the plan's assets, shall be determined in writing, in accordance with regulations prescribed by the corporation, as of the end of the plan year during which section 1341a(d) of this title becomes applicable to the plan, and each plan year thereafter.

(2) For purposes of this section, plan assets include outstanding claims for withdrawal liability (within the meaning of section 1301(a)(12) of this title).

(c) Amendment of plan by plan sponsor to reduce benefits for conservation of assets; factors applicable

(1) If, according to the determination made under subsection (b) of this section, the value of nonforfeitable benefits exceeds the value of the plan's assets, the plan sponsor shall amend the plan to reduce benefits under the plan to the extent necessary to ensure that the plan's assets are sufficient, as determined and certified in accordance with regulations prescribed by the corporation, to discharge when due all of the plan's obligations with respect to nonforfeitable benefits.

(2) Any plan amendment required by this subsection shall, in accordance with regulations prescribed by the Secretary of the Treasury—

(A) reduce benefits only to the extent necessary to comply with paragraph (1);

(B) reduce accrued benefits only to the extent that those benefits are not eligible for the corporation's guarantee under section 1322a(b) of this title;

(C) comply with the rules for and limitations on benefit reductions under a plan in reorganization, as prescribed in section 1425 of this title, except to the extent that the corporation prescribes other rules and limitations in regulations under this section; and

(D) take effect no later than 6 months after the end of the plan year for which it is determined that the value of nonforfeitable benefits exceeds the value of the plan's assets.

(d) Suspension of benefit payments; determinative factors; powers and duties of plan sponsor; retroactive benefit payments

(1) In any case in which benefit payments under a plan which is insolvent under paragraph (2)(A) exceed the resource benefit level, any such payments which are not basic benefits shall be suspended, in accordance with this subsection, to the extent necessary to reduce the sum of such payments and such basic benefits to the greater of the resource benefit level or the level of basic benefits, unless an alternative procedure is prescribed by the corporation in connection with a supplemental guarantee program established under section 1322a(g)(2) of this title.

(2) For purposes of this subsection, for a plan year—

(A) a plan is insolvent if—

(i) the plan has been amended to reduce benefits to the extent permitted by subsection (c) of this section, and

(ii) the plan's available resources are not sufficient to pay benefits under the plan when due for the plan year; and

(B) "resource benefit level" and "available resources" have the meanings set forth in paragraphs (2) and (3), respectively, of section 1426(b) of this title.

(3) The plan sponsor of a plan which is insolvent (within the meaning of paragraph (2)(A)) shall have the powers and duties of the plan sponsor of a plan in reorganization which is insolvent (within the meaning of section 1426(b)(1) of this title), except that regulations governing the plan sponsor's exercise of those powers and duties under this section shall be prescribed by the corporation, and the corporation shall prescribe by regulation notice requirements which assure that plan participants and beneficiaries receive adequate notice of benefit suspensions.

(4) A plan is not required to make retroactive benefit payments with respect to that portion of a benefit which was suspended under this subsection, except that the provisions of section 1426(c)(4) and (5) of this title shall apply in the case of plans which are insolvent under paragraph (2)(A), in connection with the plan year during which such section 1341a(d) of this title first became applicable to the plan and every year thereafter, in the same manner and to the same extent as such provisions apply to insolvent plans in reorganization under section 1426 of this title, in connection with insolvency years under such section 1426 of this title.

(Pub. L. 93–406, title IV, § 4281, as added Pub. L. 96–364, title I, § 104(2), Sept. 26, 1980, 94 Stat. 1261.)

EFFECTIVE DATE

Part effective Sept. 26, 1980, except as specifically provided, see section 1461(e) of this title.

PART 6—ENFORCEMENT

§ 1451. Civil actions

(a) Persons entitled to maintain actions

(1) A plan fiduciary, employer, plan participant, or beneficiary, who is adversely affected by the act or omission of any party under this subtitle with respect to a multiemployer plan, or an employee organization which represents such a plan participant or beneficiary for purposes of collective bargaining, may bring an action for appropriate legal or equitable relief, or both.

(2) Notwithstanding paragraph (1), this section does not authorize an action against the Secretary of the Treasury, the Secretary of Labor, or the corporation.

(b) Failure of employer to make withdrawal liability payment within prescribed time

In any action under this section to compel an employer to pay withdrawal liability, any failure of the employer to make any withdrawal liability payment within the time prescribed shall be treated in the same manner as a delinquent contribution (within the meaning of section 1145 of this title).

(c) Jurisdiction of Federal and State courts

The district courts of the United States shall have exclusive jurisdiction of an action under this section without regard to the amount in controversy, except that State courts of competent jurisdiction shall have concurrent jurisdiction over an action brought by a plan fiduciary to collect withdrawal liability.

(d) Venue and service of process

An action under this section may be brought in the district where the plan is administered or where a defendant resides or does business, and process may be served in any district where a defendant resides, does business, or may be found.

(e) Costs and expenses

In any action under this section, the court may award all or a portion of the costs and expenses incurred in connection with such action, including reasonable attorney's fees, to the prevailing party.

(f) Time limitations

An action under this section may not be brought after the later of—

(1) 6 years after the date on which the cause of action arose, or

(2) 3 years after the earliest date on which the plaintiff acquired or should have acquired actual knowledge of the existence of such cause of action; except that in the case of fraud or concealment, such action may be brought not later than 6 years after the date of discovery of the existence of such cause of action.

(g) Service of complaint on corporation; intervention by corporation

A copy of the complaint in any action under this section or section 1401 of this title shall be served upon the corporation by certified mail. The corporation may intervene in any such action.

(Pub. L. 93–406, title IV, §4301, as added Pub. L. 96–364, title I, §104(2), Sept. 26, 1980, 94 Stat. 1263.)

EFFECTIVE DATE

Part effective Sept. 26, 1980, except as specifically provided, see section 1461(e) of this title.

§1452. Penalty for failure to provide notice

Any person who fails, without reasonable cause, to provide a notice required under this subtitle or any implementing regulations shall be liable to the corporation in an amount up to $100 for each day for which such failure continues. The corporation may bring a civil action against any such person in the United States District Court for the District of Columbia or in any district court of the United States within the jurisdiction of which the plan assets are located, the plan is administered, or a defendant resides or does business, and process may be served in any district where a defendant resides, does business, or may be found.

(Pub. L. 93–406, title IV, §4302, as added Pub. L. 96–364, title I, §104(2), Sept. 26, 1980, 94 Stat. 1263.)

§1453. Election of plan status

(a) Authority, time, and criteria

Within one year after September 26, 1980, a multiemployer plan may irrevocably elect, pursuant to procedures established by the corporation, that the plan shall not be treated as a multiemployer plan for any purpose under this chapter or the Internal Revenue Code of 1954, if for each of the last 3 plan years ending prior to the effective date of the Multiemployer Pension Plan Amendments Act of 1980—

(1) the plan was not a multiemployer plan because the plan was not a plan described in section 1002(37)(A)(iii) of this title and section 414(f)(1)(C) of title 26 (as such provisions were in effect on the day before September 26, 1980); and

(2) the plan had been identified as a plan that was not a multiemployer plan in substantially all its filings with the corporation, the Secretary of Labor and the Secretary of the Treasury.

(b) Requirements

An election described in subsection (a) of this section shall be effective only if—

(1) the plan is amended to provide that it shall not be treated as a multiemployer plan for all purposes under this chapter and the Internal Revenue Code of 1954, and

(2) written notice of the amendment is provided to the corporation within 60 days after the amendment is adopted.

(c) Effective date

An election described in subsection (a) of this section shall be treated as being effective as of September 26, 1980.

(Pub. L. 93–406, title IV, §4303, as added Pub. L. 96–364, title I, §108(f), Sept. 26, 1980, 94 Stat. 1270.)

REFERENCES IN TEXT

This chapter, referred to in subsecs. (a) and (b)(1), was in the original "this Act", meaning Pub. L. 93–406, known as the Employee Retirement Income Security Act of 1974. Titles I, III, and IV of such Act are classified principally to this chapter. For complete classification of this Act to the Code, see Short Title note set out under section 1001 of this title and Tables.

The Internal Revenue Code of 1954, referred to in subsecs. (a) and (b)(1), was redesignated the Internal Revenue Code of 1986 by Pub. L. 99–514, §2, Oct. 22, 1986, 100 Stat. 2095, and is classified to Title 26, Internal Revenue Code.

For the effective date of the Multiemployer Pension Plan Amendments Act of 1980, referred to in subsec. (a), see section 1461(e) of this title.

SUBTITLE F—TRANSITION RULES AND EFFECTIVE DATES

AMENDMENTS

1980—Pub. L. 96–364, title I, §104(1), Sept. 26, 1980, 94 Stat. 1217, substituted "Subtitle F—Transition Rules and Effective Dates" for "Subtitle E—Effective Date; Special Rules".

§1461. Effective date; special rules

(a) The provisions of this subchapter take effect on September 2, 1974.

(b) Notwithstanding the provisions of subsection (a) of this section, the corporation shall pay benefits guaranteed under this subchapter with respect to any plan—

(1) which is not a multiemployer plan,

(2) which terminates after June 30, 1974, and before September 2, 1974,

(3) to which section 1321 of this title would apply if that section were effective beginning on July 1, 1974, and

(4) with respect to which a notice is filed with the Secretary of Labor and received by him not later than 10 days after September 2, 1974, except that, for reasonable cause shown, such notice may be filed with the Secretary of Labor and received by him not later than October 31, 1974, stating that the plan is a plan described in paragraphs (1), (2), and (3).

The corporation shall not pay benefits guaranteed under this subchapter with respect to a plan described in the preceding sentence unless the corporation finds substantial evidence that the plan was terminated for a reasonable business purpose and not for the purpose of obtaining the payment of benefits by the corporation under this subchapter or for the purpose of avoiding the liability which might be imposed under subtitle D of this subchapter if the plan terminated on or after September 2, 1974. The provisions of subtitle D of this subchapter do not apply in the case of such a plan which terminates before September 2, 1974. For purposes of determining whether a plan is a plan described in paragraph (2), the provisions of section 1348 of this title shall not apply, but the corporation shall make the determination on the basis of the date on which benefits ceased to accrue or on any other reasonable basis consistent with the purposes of this subsection.

(c)(1) Except as provided in paragraphs (2), (3), and (4), the corporation shall not pay benefits guaranteed under this subchapter with respect to a multiemployer plan which terminates before August 1, 1980. Whenever the corporation exercises the authority granted under paragraph (2) or (3), the corporation shall notify the Committee on Education and Labor and the Committee on Ways and Means of the House of Representatives, and the Committee on Labor and Public Welfare and the Committee on Finance of the Senate.

(2) The corporation may, in its discretion, pay benefits guaranteed under this subchapter with respect to a multiemployer plan which terminates after September 2, 1974 and before August 1, 1980, if—

(A) the plan was maintained during the 60 months immediately preceding the date on which the plan terminates, and

(B) the corporation determines that the payment by the corporation of benefits guaranteed under this subchapter with respect to that plan will not jeopardize the payments the corporation anticipates it may be required to make in connection with benefits guaranteed under this subchapter with respect to multiemployer plans which terminate after July 31, 1980.

(3) Notwithstanding any provision of section 1321 or 1322 of this title which would prevent such payments, the corporation, in carrying out its authority under paragraph (2), may pay benefits guaranteed under this subchapter with respect to a multiemployer plan described in paragraph (2) in any case in which those benefits would otherwise not be payable if—

(A) the plan has been in effect for at least 5 years,

(B) the plan has been in substantial compliance with the funding requirements for a qualified plan with respect to the employees and former employees in those employment units on the basis of which the participating employers have contributed to the plan for the preceding 5 years, and

(C) the participating employers and employee organization or organizations had no reasonable recourse other than termination.

(4) If the corporation determines, under paragraph (2) or (3), that it will pay benefits guaranteed under this subchapter with respect to a multiemployer plan which terminates before August 1, 1980, the corporation—

(A) may establish requirements for the continuation of payments which commenced before January 2, 1974, with respect to retired participants under the plan,

(B) may not, notwithstanding any other provision of this subchapter, make payments with respect to any participant under such a plan who, on January 1, 1974, was receiving payment of retirement benefits, in excess of the amounts and rates payable with respect to such participant on that date,

(C) may not make any payments with respect to benefits guaranteed under this subchapter in connection with such a plan which are derived, directly or indirectly, from amounts borrowed under section 1305(c) of this title, and

(D) shall review from time to time payments made under the authority granted to it by paragraphs (2) and (3), and reduce or terminate such payments to the extent necessary to avoid jeopardizing the ability of the corporation to make payments of benefits guaranteed under this subchapter in connection with multiemployer plans which terminate after July 31, 1980, without increasing premium rates for such plans.

(d) Notwithstanding any other provision of this subchapter, guaranteed benefits payable by the corporation pursuant to its discretionary authority under this section shall continue to be paid at the level guaranteed under section 1322 of this title, without regard to any limitation on payment under subparagraph (C) or (D) of subsection (c)(4) of this section.

(e)(1) Except as provided in paragraphs (2), (3), and (4), the amendments to this chapter made by the Multiemployer Pension Plan Amendments Act of 1980 shall take effect on September 26, 1980.

(2)(A) Except as provided in this paragraph, part 1 of subtitle E of this subchapter, relating to withdrawal liability, takes effect on September 26, 1980.

(B) For purposes of determining withdrawal liability under part 1 of subtitle E of this subchapter, an employer who has withdrawn from a plan shall be considered to have withdrawn from a multiemployer plan if, at the time of the withdrawal, the plan was a multiemployer plan as defined in section 1301(a)(3) of this title as in effect at the time of the withdrawal.

(3) Sections 1421 through 1426 of this title, relating to multiemployer plan reorganization, shall take effect, with respect to each plan, on

the first day of the first plan year beginning on or after the earlier of—

(A) the date on which the last collective bargaining agreement providing for employer contributions under the plan, which was in effect on September 26, 1980, expires, without regard to extensions agreed to on or after September 26, 1980, or

(B) 3 years after September 26, 1980.

(4) Section 1415 of this title shall take effect on September 26, 1980.

(f)(1) In the event that before September 26, 1980, the corporation has determined that—

(A) an employer has withdrawn from a multiemployer plan under section 1363 of this title, and

(B) the employer is liable to the corporation under such section,

the corporation shall retain the amount of liability paid to it or furnished in the form of a bond and shall pay such liability to the plan in the event the plan terminates in accordance with section 1341a(a)(2) of this title before the earlier of September 26, 1985, or the day after the 5-year period commencing on the date of such withdrawal.

(2) In any case in which the plan is not so terminated within the period described in paragraph (1), the liability of the employer is abated and any payment held in escrow shall be refunded without interest to the employer or the employer's bond shall be cancelled.

(g)(1) In any case in which an employer or employers withdrew from a multiemployer plan before the effective date of part 1 of subtitle E of this subchapter, the corporation may—

(A) apply section 1363(d) of this title, as in effect before the amendments made by the Multiemployer Pension Plan Amendments Act of 1980, to such plan,

(B) assess liability against the withdrawn employer with respect to the resulting terminated plan,

(C) guarantee benefits under the terminated plan under section 1322 of this title, as in effect before such amendments, and

(D) if necessary, enforce such action through suit brought under section 1303 of this title.

(2) The corporation shall use the revolving fund used by the corporation with respect to basic benefits guaranteed under section 1322a of this title in guaranteeing benefits under a terminated plan described in this subsection.

(h)(1) In the case of an employer who entered into a collective bargaining agreement—

(A) which was effective on January 12, 1979, and which remained in effect through May 15, 1982, and

(B) under which contributions to a multiemployer plan were to cease on January 12, 1982,

any withdrawal liability incurred by the employer pursuant to part 1 of subtitle E of this subchapter as a result of the complete or partial withdrawal of the employer from the multiemployer plan before January 16, 1982, shall be void.

(2) In any case in which—

(A) an employer engaged in the grocery wholesaling business—

(i) had ceased all covered operations under a multiemployer plan before June 30, 1981, and had relocated its operations to a new facility in another State, and

(ii) had notified a local union representative on May 14, 1980, that the employer had tentatively decided to discontinue operations and relocate to a new facility in another State, and

(B) all State and local approvals with respect to construction of and commencement of operations at the new facility had been obtained, a contract for construction had been entered into, and construction of the new facility had begun before September 26, 1980,

any withdrawal liability incurred by the employer pursuant to part 1 of subtitle E of this subchapter as a result of the complete or partial withdrawal of the employer from the multiemployer plan before June 30, 1981, shall be void.

(i) The preceding provisions of this section shall not apply with respect to amendments made to this subchapter in provisions enacted after October 22, 1986.

(Pub. L. 93–406, title IV, §4402, formerly §4082, Sept. 2, 1974, 88 Stat. 1034; S. Res. 4, Feb. 4, 1977; Pub. L. 95–214, §1, Dec. 19, 1977, 91 Stat. 1501; S. Res. 30, Mar. 7, 1979; Pub. L. 96–24, June 19, 1979, 93 Stat. 70; Pub. L. 96–239, Apr. 30, 1980, 94 Stat. 341; Pub. L. 96–293, §1, June 30, 1980, 94 Stat. 610; renumbered and amended Pub. L. 96–364, title I, §108(a)–(c)(1), Sept. 26, 1980, 94 Stat. 1267; Pub. L. 98–369, div. A, title V, §558(b)(1)(B), (C), July 18, 1984, 98 Stat. 899; Pub. L. 99–514, title XVIII, §1852(i), Oct. 22, 1986, 100 Stat. 2869; Pub. L. 101–239, title VII, §§7862(a), 7894(h)(5)(A), Dec. 19, 1989, 103 Stat. 2431, 2451.)

REFERENCES IN TEXT

This chapter, referred to in subsec. (e)(1), was in the original "this Act", meaning Pub. L. 93–406, known as the Employee Retirement Income Security Act of 1974. Titles I, III, and IV of such Act are classified principally to this chapter. For complete classification of this Act to the Code, see Short Title note set out under section 1001 of this title and Tables.

The Multiemployer Pension Plan Amendments Act of 1980, referred to in subsecs. (e)(1) and (g)(1)(A), is Pub. L. 96–364, Sept. 26, 1980, 94 Stat. 1208. For complete classification of this Act to the Code, see Short Title of 1980 Amendment note set out under section 1001 of this title and Tables.

For the effective date of part 1 of subtitle E of this subchapter, referred to in subsec. (g)(1), see subsec. (e)(2) of this section.

CODIFICATION

Section was formerly classified to section 1381 of this title.

AMENDMENTS

1989—Subsec. (h)(1). Pub. L. 101–239, §7862(a), substituted "before January 16, 1982" for "before January 12, 1982" in concluding provisions.

Subsec. (i). Pub. L. 101–239, §7894(h)(5)(A), added subsec. (i).

1986—Subsec. (h). Pub. L. 99–514 added subsec. (h).

1984—Subsec. (e)(2)(A), (4). Pub. L. 98–369, §558(b)(1)(B), substituted "September 26, 1980" for "April 29, 1980".

Subsec. (f)(1). Pub. L. 98–369, §558(b)(1)(C), substituted "September 26, 1985" for "April 29, 1985".

1980—Subsec. (c)(1). Pub. L. 96–293, §1(1), substituted "August 1, 1980" for "July 1, 1980".

Pub. L. 96–239, § 1(1), substituted "July 1, 1980" for "May 1, 1980".

Subsec. (c)(2). Pub. L. 96–293, § 1(1), (2), substituted "August 1, 1980" for "July 1, 1980" in provisions preceding subpar. (A) and "July 31, 1980" for "June 30, 1980" in subpar. (B).

Pub. L. 96–239, § 1(1), (2), substituted "July 1, 1980" for "May 1, 1980" in provisions preceding subpar. (A) and "June 30, 1980" for "April 30, 1980" in subpar. (B).

Subsec. (c)(4). Pub. L. 96–293, § 1(1), (2), substituted "August 1, 1980" for "July 1, 1980" in provisions preceding subpar. (A) and "July 31, 1980" for "June 30, 1980" in subpar. (D).

Pub. L. 96–239, § 1(1), (2), substituted "July 1, 1980" for "May 1, 1980" in provisions preceding subpar. (A) and "June 30, 1980" for "April 30, 1980" in subpar. (D).

Subsec. (d). Pub. L. 96–364, § 108(b), added subsec. (d). Former subsec. (d), which related to report to Congressional committees respecting anticipated financial condition of program for mandatory coverage of multiemployer plans, was struck out.

Subsec. (e). Pub. L. 96–364, § 108(c)(1), added subsec. (e). Former subsec. (e), which related to annual insurance premium payable to Corporation for coverage of guaranteed basic benefits, was struck out.

Subsecs. (f), (g). Pub. L. 96–364, § 108(c)(1), added subsecs. (f) and (g).

1979—Subsec. (c)(1). Pub. L. 96–24, § 1(1), substituted "May 1, 1980" for "July 1, 1979".

Subsec. (c)(2). Pub. L. 96–24, § 1(1), (2), substituted "May 1, 1980" for "July 1, 1979" in provisions preceding subpar. (A) and "April 30, 1980" for "June 30, 1979" in subpar. (B).

Subsec. (c)(4). Pub. L. 96–24, § 1(1), (2), substituted "May 1, 1980" for "July 1, 1979" in provisions preceding subpar. (A) and "April 30, 1980" for "June 30, 1979" in subpar. (D).

1977—Subsec. (c)(1). Pub. L. 95–214, § 1(a)(1), substituted "July 1, 1979" for "January 1, 1978".

Subsec. (c)(2). Pub. L. 95–214, § 1(a)(2), substituted "July 1, 1979" for "January 1, 1978" in provisions preceding subpar. (A).

Subsec. (c)(2)(B). Pub. L. 95–214, § 1(a)(3), substituted "June 30, 1979" for "December 31, 1977".

Subsec. (c)(4). Pub. L. 95–214, § 1(a)(4), substituted "July 1, 1979" for "January 1, 1978" in provisions preceding subpar. (A).

Subsec. (c)(4)(D). Pub. L. 95–214, § 1(a)(5), substituted "June 30, 1979" for "December 31, 1977".

Subsecs. (d), (e). Pub. L. 95–214, § 1(b), added subsecs. (d) and (e).

Change of Name

Committee on Labor and Public Welfare of Senate abolished and replaced by Committee on Human Resources of Senate, effective Feb. 11, 1977. See Rule XXV of Standing Rules of Senate, as amended by Senate Resolution No. 4 (popularly cited as the "Committee System Reorganization Amendments of 1977"), approved Feb. 4, 1977. Committee on Human Resources of Senate changed to Committee on Labor and Human Resources of Senate, effective Mar. 7, 1979, by Senate Resolution No. 30, 96th Congress. See, also, Rule XXV of Standing Rules of Senate adopted Nov. 14, 1979. Committee on Labor and Human Resources of Senate changed to Committee on Health, Education, Labor, and Pensions of Senate by Senate Resolution No. 20, One Hundred Sixth Congress, Jan. 19, 1999.

Effective Date of 1989 Amendment

Amendment by section 7862(a) of Pub. L. 101–239 effective as if included in the provision of the Tax Reform Act of 1986, Pub. L. 99–514, to which such amendment relates, see section 7863 of Pub. L. 101–239, set out as a note under section 106 of Title 26, Internal Revenue Code.

Section 7894(h)(5)(B) of Pub. L. 101–239 provided that: "The amendment made by subparagraph (A) [amending this section] shall take effect as if originally included in the Reform Act [Pub. L. 99–514]."

Effective Date of 1986 Amendment

Amendment by Pub. L. 99–514 effective, except as otherwise provided, as if included in the provisions of the Tax Reform Act of 1984, Pub. L. 98–369, div. A, to which such amendment relates, see section 1881 of Pub. L. 99–514, set out as a note under section 48 of Title 26, Internal Revenue Code.

Plan Amendments Not Required Until January 1, 1989

For provisions directing that if any amendments made by subtitle A or subtitle C of title XI [§§ 1101–1147 and 1171–1177] or title XVIII [§§ 1800–1899A] of Pub. L. 99–514 require an amendment to any plan, such plan amendment shall not be required to be made before the first plan year beginning on or after Jan. 1, 1989, see section 1140 of Pub. L. 99–514, as amended, set out as a note under section 401 of Title 26, Internal Revenue Code.

Actions Taken Before Regulations Are Prescribed

Section 405 of Pub. L. 96–364 provided that:

"(a) Except as otherwise provided in the amendments made by this Act [see Short Title of 1980 Amendment note set out under section 1001 of this title] and in subsection (b), if the way in which any such amendment will apply to a particular circumstance is to be set forth in regulations, any reasonable action during the period before such regulations take effect shall be treated as complying with such regulations for such period.

"(b) Subsection (a) shall not apply to any action which violates any instruction issued, or temporary rule prescribed, by the agency having jurisdiction but only if such instruction or rule was published, or furnished to the party taking the action, before such action was taken."

CHAPTER 19—JOB TRAINING PARTNERSHIP

§§ 1501 to 1505. Repealed. Pub. L. 105–220, title I, § 199(b)(2), Aug. 7, 1998, 112 Stat. 1059

Section 1501, Pub. L. 97–300, § 2, Oct. 13, 1982, 96 Stat. 1324; Pub. L. 102–367, title I, § 101(b), Sept. 7, 1992, 106 Stat. 1022, stated purpose of this chapter.

Section 1502, Pub. L. 97–300, § 3, Oct. 13, 1982, 96 Stat. 1324; Pub. L. 100–418, title VI, § 6303, Aug. 23, 1988, 102 Stat. 1538; Pub. L. 100–628, title VII, § 714(d), Nov. 7, 1988, 102 Stat. 3256; Pub. L. 101–549, title XI, § 1101(b)(2), Nov. 15, 1990, 104 Stat. 2712; Pub. L. 102–367, title I, § 102(a), Sept. 7, 1992, 106 Stat. 1023, authorized appropriations.

Section 1503, Pub. L. 97–300, § 4, Oct. 13, 1982, 96 Stat. 1325; Pub. L. 98–524, § 4(a)(1), Oct. 19, 1984, 98 Stat. 2487; Pub. L. 99–159, title VII, § 713(b)(1), Nov. 22, 1985, 99 Stat. 907; Pub. L. 99–496, §§ 14(b)(1), 15(a), Oct. 16, 1986, 100 Stat. 1265; Pub. L. 100–77, title VII, § 740(a), July 22, 1987, 101 Stat. 531; Pub. L. 102–54, § 13(k)(2)(A), June 13, 1991, 105 Stat. 276; Pub. L. 102–235, § 3, Dec. 12, 1991, 105 Stat. 1807; Pub. L. 102–367, title I, § 103(a), (b)(1), title VII, § 702(a)(1)–(3), Sept. 7, 1992, 106 Stat. 1024, 1026, 1111, 1112; Pub. L. 103–382, title III, § 391(n)(1), Oct. 20, 1994, 108 Stat. 4023; Pub. L. 104–193, title I, § 110(n)(1), Aug. 22, 1996, 110 Stat. 2174, defined terms used in this chapter. See section 2801 of this title.

Section 1504, Pub. L. 97–300, title VI, § 604, formerly title V, § 504, Oct. 13, 1982, 96 Stat. 1399; renumbered title VI, § 604, Pub. L. 100–628, title VII, § 712(a)(1), (2), Nov. 7, 1988, 102 Stat. 3248, related to enforcement of Military Selective Service Act. See section 2939 of this title.

Section 1505, Pub. L. 97–300, title VI, § 605, formerly title V, § 505, as added Pub. L. 100–418, title VI, § 6307(a), Aug. 23, 1988, 102 Stat. 1541; renumbered title VI, § 505, Pub. L. 100–628, title VII, § 712(a)(1), Nov. 7, 1988, 102 Stat. 3248; renumbered § 605, Pub. L. 102–367, title VII, § 702(a)(20), Sept. 7, 1992, 106 Stat. 1113, related to State job bank systems.

EFFECTIVE DATE OF REPEAL

Pub. L. 105–220, title I, §199(c)(2)(B), Aug. 7, 1998, 112 Stat. 1059, provided that: "The repeal made by subsection (b)(2) [repealing this chapter and provisions set out as a note under section 801 of this title] shall take effect on July 1, 2000."

SHORT TITLE OF 1992 AMENDMENT

Pub. L. 102–367, §1, Sept. 7, 1992, 106 Stat. 1021, provided that: "This Act [enacting sections 1519, 1601 to 1606, 1630 to 1635, 1641 to 1646, 1673, 1734, 1735, 1782 to 1784b, and 1792 to 1792b of this title, amending sections 1501 to 1503, 1505, 1511, 1512, 1514 to 1518, 1531 to 1535, 1551 to 1554, 1571, 1572, 1574 to 1577, 1580, 1583, 1652, 1661, 1661c, 1661d, 1662a, 1662c, 1662e, 1671, 1672, 1693, 1696 to 1698, 1703, 1703a, 1706, 1707, 1731 to 1733, 1737, 1752 to 1754, 1772, 1773, 1781, and 1791 to 1791h of this title, section 2014 of Title 7, Agriculture, and sections 1205a and 2322 of Title 20, Education, repealing sections 1591, 1601 to 1605, 1630 to 1634, and 1734 to 1736 of this title, omitting sections 1791i and 1791j of this title, and enacting provisions set out as notes under sections 1501, 1602, and 1642 of this title] may be cited as the 'Job Training Reform Amendments of 1992'."

SHORT TITLE OF 1991 AMENDMENT

Pub. L. 102–235, §1, Dec. 12, 1991, 105 Stat. 1806, provided that: "This Act [enacting section 1737 of this title, amending sections 1503, 1514, 1531 to 1533, and 1604 of this title, and enacting provisions set out as notes under sections 1501, 1514, and 1737 of this title] may be cited as the 'Nontraditional Employment for Women Act'."

SHORT TITLE OF 1988 AMENDMENTS

Pub. L. 100–628, title VII, §711, Nov. 7, 1988, 102 Stat. 3248, provided that: "This subtitle [subtitle B (§§711–714) of title VII of Pub. L. 100–628, enacting sections 1583 and 1791 to 1791j of this title, amending sections 49, 49a, 49b, 49d, 49e to 49j, 49*l*, 49*l*–1, 1502, 1504, 1505, 1514, 1516, 1531, and 1602 of this title and section 602 of Title 42, The Public Health and Welfare, and amending provisions set out as a note under section 49 of this title] may be cited as the 'Jobs for Employable Dependent Individuals Act'."

Pub. L. 100–418, title VI, §6301, Aug. 23, 1988, 102 Stat. 1524, provided that "This title", meaning subtitle D (§§6301–6307) of title VI of Pub. L. 100–418, which enacted sections 565 and 1505 of this title, amended subchapter III of this chapter and sections 1502, 1516, 1532, and 1752 of this title, and enacted provisions set out as notes under section 1651 of this title, could be cited as the "Economic Dislocation and Worker Adjustment Assistance Act", prior to repeal by Pub. L. 103–382, title III, §391(i), Oct. 20, 1994, 108 Stat. 4023.

SHORT TITLE OF 1986 AMENDMENT

Pub. L. 99–496, §1, Oct. 16, 1986, 100 Stat. 1261, provided that: "This Act [enacting sections 1582, 1630, and 1736 of this title and amending sections 1503, 1511, 1516, 1518, 1531, 1533, 1534, 1602, 1603, 1631 to 1634, 1651, 1652, 1707, and 1733 of this title] may be cited as the 'Job Training Partnership Act Amendments of 1986'."

SHORT TITLE

Pub. L. 97–300, §1, Oct. 13, 1982, 96 Stat. 1322, which provided that Pub. L. 97–300 (enacting this chapter) could be cited as the "Job Training Partnership Act", was repealed by Pub. L. 105–220, title I, §199(b)(2), (c)(2)(B), Aug. 7, 1998, 112 Stat. 1059, effective July 1, 2000.

§1506. Transferred

CODIFICATION

Section, Pub. L. 101–649, title VIII, §801, Nov. 29, 1990, 104 Stat. 5087, which related to educational assistance and training, was transferred to section 2920 of this title.

SUBCHAPTER I—JOB TRAINING AND EMPLOYMENT ASSISTANCE SYSTEM

PART A—SERVICE DELIVERY SYSTEM

§§1511 to 1519. Repealed. Pub. L. 105–220, title I, §199(b)(2), Aug. 7, 1998, 112 Stat. 1059

Section 1511, Pub. L. 97–300, title I, §101, Oct. 13, 1982, 96 Stat. 1327; Pub. L. 99–496, §2, Oct. 16, 1986, 100 Stat. 1261; Pub. L. 102–367, title I, §111, Sept. 7, 1992, 106 Stat. 1026, related to establishment of service delivery areas.

Section 1512, Pub. L. 97–300, title I, §102, Oct. 13, 1982, 96 Stat. 1328; Pub. L. 102–367, title I, §112, Sept. 7, 1992, 106 Stat. 1026, related to private industry councils.

Section 1513, Pub. L. 97–300, title I, §103, Oct. 13, 1982, 96 Stat. 1330; Pub. L. 97–404, §1(a), Dec. 31, 1982, 96 Stat. 2026, related to functions of private industry councils.

Section 1514, Pub. L. 97–300, title I, §104, Oct. 13, 1982, 96 Stat. 1331; Pub. L. 100–628, title VII, §714(a), Nov. 7, 1988, 102 Stat. 3255; Pub. L. 102–235, §4, Dec. 12, 1991, 105 Stat. 1807; Pub. L. 102–367, title I, §113, Sept. 7, 1992, 106 Stat. 1027, related to job training plan.

Section 1515, Pub. L. 97–300, title I, §105, Oct. 13, 1982, 96 Stat. 1332; Pub. L. 102–367, title I, §114, Sept. 7, 1992, 106 Stat. 1030, related to review and approval of plan.

Section 1516, Pub. L. 97–300, title I, §106, Oct. 13, 1982, 96 Stat. 1333; Pub. L. 97–404, §1(b), Dec. 31, 1982, 96 Stat. 2026; Pub. L. 99–496, §15(b), Oct. 16, 1986, 100 Stat. 1266; Pub. L. 100–418, title VI, §6304(a), Aug. 23, 1988, 102 Stat. 1538; Pub. L. 100–628, title VII, §§713(b), 714(b), Nov. 7, 1988, 102 Stat. 3255, 3256; Pub. L. 102–367, title I, §115(a), Sept. 7, 1992, 106 Stat. 1030; Pub. L. 104–193, title I, §110(n)(2), Aug. 22, 1996, 110 Stat. 2174, related to performance standards.

Section 1517, Pub. L. 97–300, title I, §107, Oct. 13, 1982, 96 Stat. 1335; Pub. L. 102–367, title I, §116, Sept. 7, 1992, 106 Stat. 1034, related to selection of service providers.

Section 1518, Pub. L. 97–300, title I, §108, Oct. 13, 1982, 96 Stat. 1336; Pub. L. 97–404, §1(c), Dec. 31, 1982, 96 Stat. 2026; Pub. L. 99–496, §15(c), Oct. 16, 1986, 100 Stat. 1266; Pub. L. 102–367, title I, §117, Sept. 7, 1992, 106 Stat. 1035, related to limitation on certain costs.

Section 1519, Pub. L. 97–300, title I, §109, as added Pub. L. 102–367, title I, §118, Sept. 7, 1992, 106 Stat. 1036, related to recapture and reallotment of unobligated funds.

EFFECTIVE DATE OF REPEAL

Repeal effective July 1, 2000, see section 199(c)(2)(B) of Pub. L. 105–220, set out as a note under section 1501 of this title.

PART B—ADDITIONAL STATE RESPONSIBILITIES

§§1531 to 1537. Repealed. Pub. L. 105–220, title I, §199(b)(2), Aug. 7, 1998, 112 Stat. 1059

Section 1531, Pub. L. 97–300, title I, §121, Oct. 13, 1982, 96 Stat. 1337; Pub. L. 99–496, §15(d), Oct. 16, 1986, 100 Stat. 1266; Pub. L. 99–570, title XI, §11004(a), Oct. 27, 1986, 100 Stat. 3207–168; Pub. L. 100–628, title VII, §714(c), Nov. 7, 1988, 102 Stat. 3256; Pub. L. 102–54, §13(k)(2)(B), June 13, 1991, 105 Stat. 277; Pub. L. 102–235, §5, Dec. 12, 1991, 105 Stat. 1807; Pub. L. 102–367, title I, §121, title VII, §702(a)(4), Sept. 7, 1992, 106 Stat. 1037, 1112; Pub. L. 104–193, title I, §110(n)(3), Aug. 22, 1996, 110 Stat. 2174, related to Governor's coordination and special services plan.

Section 1532, Pub. L. 97–300, title I, §122, Oct. 13, 1982, 96 Stat. 1339; Pub. L. 97–404, §1(d), Dec. 31, 1982, 96 Stat. 2026; Pub. L. 98–524, §4(a)(2), Oct. 19, 1984, 98 Stat. 2487; Pub. L. 100–418, title VI, §6304(b), Aug. 23, 1988, 102 Stat. 1538; Pub. L. 102–235, §6, Dec. 12, 1991, 105 Stat. 1808; Pub. L. 102–367, title VI, §601(b)(3), title VII, §702(a)(5), Sept. 7, 1992, 106 Stat. 1103, 1112, related to State job training coordinating council.

Section 1533, Pub. L. 97–300, title I, §123, Oct. 13, 1982, 96 Stat. 1341; Pub. L. 99–496, §§3, 15(e), Oct. 16, 1986, 100 Stat. 1261, 1266; Pub. L. 101–392, §5(a)(1), Sept. 25, 1990,

104 Stat. 758; Pub. L. 102–235, § 7, Dec. 12, 1991, 105 Stat. 1808; Pub. L. 102–367, title I, § 122, Sept. 7, 1992, 106 Stat. 1038; Pub. L. 104–193, title I, § 110(n)(4), Aug. 22, 1996, 110 Stat. 2174, related to State education coordination and grants.

Section 1534, Pub. L. 97–300, title I, § 124, Oct. 13, 1982, 96 Stat. 1341; Pub. L. 99–496, § 15(f), Oct. 16, 1986, 100 Stat. 1266; Pub. L. 102–367, title I, § 123, Sept. 7, 1992, 106 Stat. 1041, related to identification of additional imposed requirements.

Section 1535, Pub. L. 97–300, title I, § 125, Oct. 13, 1982, 96 Stat. 1342; Pub. L. 97–404, § 1(e), Dec. 31, 1982, 96 Stat. 2026; Pub. L. 98–524, § 4(a)(3), Oct. 19, 1984, 98 Stat. 2487; Pub. L. 102–367, title I, § 124, title VII, § 702(a)(6), Sept. 7, 1992, 106 Stat. 1041, 1112, related to State labor market information programs.

Section 1536, Pub. L. 97–300, title I, § 126, Oct. 13, 1982, 96 Stat. 1343, related to authority of State legislature. See section 2941 of this title.

Section 1537, Pub. L. 97–300, title I, § 127, Oct. 13, 1982, 96 Stat. 1343, related to interstate agreements. See section 2941 of this title.

EFFECTIVE DATE OF REPEAL

Repeal effective July 1, 2000, see section 199(c)(2)(B) of Pub. L. 105–220, set out as a note under section 1501 of this title.

PART C—PROGRAM REQUIREMENTS FOR SERVICE DELIVERY SYSTEM

§§ 1551 to 1555. Repealed. Pub. L. 105–220, title I, § 199(b)(2), Aug. 7, 1998, 112 Stat. 1059

Section 1551, Pub. L. 97–300, title I, § 141, Oct. 13, 1982, 96 Stat. 1343; Pub. L. 97–404, § 1(f), Dec. 31, 1982, 96 Stat. 2026; Pub. L. 100–77, title VII, § 740(b), July 22, 1987, 101 Stat. 531; Pub. L. 102–367, title I, § 131, Sept. 7, 1992, 106 Stat. 1042; Pub. L. 102–484, div. D, title XLIV, § 4467(f), Oct. 23, 1992, 106 Stat. 2751; Pub. L. 103–160, div. A, title XIII, § 1336, Nov. 30, 1993, 107 Stat. 1805, related to general program requirements for service delivery system.

Section 1552, Pub. L. 97–300, title I, § 142, Oct. 13, 1982, 96 Stat. 1345; Pub. L. 97–404, § 1(g), Dec. 31, 1982, 96 Stat. 2026; Pub. L. 102–367, title I, § 132, Sept. 7, 1992, 106 Stat. 1045, related to benefits for participating individuals. See section 2931(a) of this title.

Section 1553, Pub. L. 97–300, title I, § 143, Oct. 13, 1982, 96 Stat. 1345; Pub. L. 97–404, § 1(h), Dec. 31, 1982, 96 Stat. 2026; Pub. L. 102–367, title I, § 133, Sept. 7, 1992, 106 Stat. 1045, related to labor standards. See section 2931(b) of this title.

Section 1554, Pub. L. 97–300, title I, § 144, Oct. 13, 1982, 96 Stat. 1346; Pub. L. 102–367, title I, § 134(a), Sept. 7, 1992, 106 Stat. 1045, related to grievance procedure. See section 2931(c) of this title.

Section 1555, Pub. L. 97–300, title I, § 145, Oct. 13, 1982, 96 Stat. 1347, prohibited Federal control of education.

EFFECTIVE DATE OF REPEAL

Repeal effective July 1, 2000, see section 199(c)(2)(B) of Pub. L. 105–220, set out as a note under section 1501 of this title.

PART D—FEDERAL AND FISCAL ADMINISTRATIVE PROVISIONS

§§ 1571 to 1583. Repealed. Pub. L. 105–220, title I, § 199(b)(2), Aug. 7, 1998, 112 Stat. 1059

Section 1571, Pub. L. 97–300, title I, § 161, Oct. 13, 1982, 96 Stat. 1347; Pub. L. 100–495, § 1, Oct. 17, 1988, 102 Stat. 2454; Pub. L. 102–367, title VII, § 702(a)(7), (8), Sept. 7, 1992, 106 Stat. 1112, related to program year. See section 2939(g) of this title.

Section 1572, Pub. L. 97–300, title I, § 162, Oct. 13, 1982, 96 Stat. 1347; Pub. L. 102–367, title I, § 141, Sept. 7, 1992, 106 Stat. 1046, related to prompt allocation of funds. See section 2932 of this title.

Section 1573, Pub. L. 97–300, title I, § 163, Oct. 13, 1982, 96 Stat. 1348, related to monitoring for compliance with chapter. See section 2933 of this title.

Section 1574, Pub. L. 97–300, title I, § 164, Oct. 13, 1982, 96 Stat. 1348; Pub. L. 102–367, title I, § 142, Sept. 7, 1992, 106 Stat. 1046, related to fiscal controls and sanctions. See section 2934 of this title.

Section 1575, Pub. L. 97–300, title I, § 165, Oct. 13, 1982, 96 Stat. 1350; Pub. L. 102–367, title I, § 143, Sept. 7, 1992, 106 Stat. 1048, related to reports, recordkeeping, and investigations. See section 2935 of this title.

Section 1576, Pub. L. 97–300, title I, § 166, Oct. 13, 1982, 96 Stat. 1351; Pub. L. 102–367, title I, § 134(b), Sept. 7, 1992, 106 Stat. 1046, related to administrative adjudication. See section 2936 of this title.

Section 1577, Pub. L. 97–300, title I, § 167, Oct. 13, 1982, 96 Stat. 1352; Pub. L. 102–367, title I, §§ 103(b)(2), 144, Sept. 7, 1992, 106 Stat. 1026, 1051, related to requirements for nondiscrimination. See section 2938 of this title.

Section 1578, Pub. L. 97–300, title I, § 168, Oct. 13, 1982, 96 Stat. 1353, related to judicial review. See section 2937 of this title.

Section 1579, Pub. L. 97–300, title I, § 169, Oct. 13, 1982, 96 Stat. 1353, contained administrative provisions. See section 2939 of this title.

Section 1580, Pub. L. 97–300, title I, § 170, Oct. 13, 1982, 96 Stat. 1354; Pub. L. 102–367, title I, § 145, Sept. 7, 1992, 106 Stat. 1052, related to utilization of services and facilities. See section 2939(e) of this title.

Section 1581, Pub. L. 97–300, title I, § 171, Oct. 13, 1982, 96 Stat. 1354, related to obligational authority. See section 2939(f) of this title.

Section 1582, Pub. L. 97–300, title I, § 172, as added Pub. L. 99–496, § 4, Oct. 16, 1986, 100 Stat. 1261, related to Presidential awards for outstanding private sector involvement in job training programs.

Section 1583, Pub. L. 97–300, title I, § 173, formerly § 172, as added Pub. L. 100–628, title VII, § 714(e)(1), Nov. 7, 1988, 102 Stat. 3256; renumbered § 173 and amended Pub. L. 102–367, title I, § 103(b)(3), title VII, § 702(a)(9), Sept. 7, 1992, 106 Stat. 1026, 1112, related to construction of chapter.

EFFECTIVE DATE OF REPEAL

Repeal effective July 1, 2000, see section 199(c)(2)(B) of Pub. L. 105–220, set out as a note under section 1501 of this title.

PART E—MISCELLANEOUS PROVISIONS

§ 1591. Repealed. Pub. L. 102–367, title VII, § 702(a)(10), Sept. 7, 1992, 106 Stat. 1112

Section, Pub. L. 97–300, title I, § 181, Oct. 13, 1982, 96 Stat. 1354; Pub. L. 97–404, § 1(i), Dec. 31, 1982, 96 Stat. 2026, related to transition between the Comprehensive Employment Training Act and this chapter.

EFFECTIVE DATE OF REPEAL

Repeal effective July 1, 1993, see section 701(a) of Pub. L. 102–367, formerly set out as an Effective Date of 1992 Amendment; Transition Provisions note under section 1501 of this title.

§ 1592. Repealed. Pub. L. 105–220, title I, § 199(b)(2), Aug. 7, 1998, 112 Stat. 1059

Section, Pub. L. 97–300, title I, § 183, Oct. 13, 1982, 96 Stat. 1357, related to statutory references to Comprehensive Employment and Training Act.

EFFECTIVE DATE OF REPEAL

Repeal effective July 1, 2000, see section 199(c)(2)(B) of Pub. L. 105–220, set out as a note under section 1501 of this title.

SUBCHAPTER II—TRAINING SERVICES FOR THE DISADVANTAGED

PART A—ADULT TRAINING PROGRAM

§§1601 to 1606. Repealed. Pub. L. 105–220, title I, §199(b)(2), Aug. 7, 1998, 112 Stat. 1059

Section 1601, Pub. L. 97–300, title II, §201, as added Pub. L. 102–367, title II, §201, Sept. 7, 1992, 106 Stat. 1052, stated purpose of adult training program.

A prior section 1601, Pub. L. 97–300, title II, §201, Oct. 13, 1982, 96 Stat. 1358, related to allotment of funds under adult and youth programs, prior to repeal by Pub. L. 102–367, title II, §201, title VII, §701(a), Sept. 7, 1992, 106 Stat. 1052, 1103, effective July 1, 1993.

Section 1602, Pub. L. 97–300, title II, §202, as added Pub. L. 102–367, title VII, §701(c)(1), Sept. 7, 1992, 106 Stat. 1104, related to allotment and allocation.

A prior section 1602, Pub. L. 97–300, title II, §202, Oct. 13, 1982, 96 Stat. 1359; Pub. L. 99–496, §§5(a), 6, Oct. 16, 1986, 100 Stat. 1262; Pub. L. 100–628, title VII, §713(a), Nov. 7, 1988, 102 Stat. 3255, related to allocation within States of funds under this subchapter, prior to repeal by Pub. L. 102–367, title II, §201, title VII, §701(a), Sept. 7, 1992, 106 Stat. 1052, 1103, effective July 1, 1993.

Section 1603, Pub. L. 97–300, title II, §203, as added Pub. L. 102–367, title II, §203, Sept. 7, 1992, 106 Stat. 1055; amended Pub. L. 104–193, title I, §110(n)(5), Aug. 22, 1996, 110 Stat. 2174, related to eligibility for services.

A prior section 1603, Pub. L. 97–300, title II, §203, Oct. 13, 1982, 96 Stat. 1360; Pub. L. 97–404, §2, Dec. 31, 1982, 96 Stat. 2026; Pub. L. 99–496, §7, Oct. 16, 1986, 100 Stat. 1263; Pub. L. 99–570, title XI, §11004(b), Oct. 27, 1986, 100 Stat. 3207–169, related to eligibility for training services for the disadvantaged, prior to repeal by Pub. L. 102–367, title II, §201, title VII, §701(a), Sept. 7, 1992, 106 Stat. 1052, 1103, effective July 1, 1993.

Section 1604, Pub. L. 97–300, title II, §204, as added Pub. L. 102–367, title II, §203, Sept. 7, 1992, 106 Stat. 1055; amended Pub. L. 104–193, title I, §110(n)(6), Aug. 22, 1996, 110 Stat. 2174, related to program design.

A prior section 1604, Pub. L. 97–300, title II, §204, Oct. 13, 1982, 96 Stat. 1361; Pub. L. 101–392, §5(a)(2), Sept. 25, 1990, 104 Stat. 758; Pub. L. 102–235, §8, Dec. 12, 1991, 105 Stat. 1809, related to use of funds for training services for the disadvantaged, prior to repeal by Pub. L. 102–367, title II, §201, title VII, §701(a), Sept. 7, 1992, 106 Stat. 1052, 1103, effective July 1, 1993.

Section 1605, Pub. L. 97–300, title II, §205, as added Pub. L. 102–367, title II, §203, Sept. 7, 1992, 106 Stat. 1060; amended Pub. L. 104–193, title I, §110(n)(7), Aug. 22, 1996, 110 Stat. 2174, related to linkages with other Federal programs.

A prior section 1605, Pub. L. 97–300, title II, §205, Oct. 13, 1982, 96 Stat. 1362, related to exemplary youth programs, prior to repeal by Pub. L. 102–367, title II, §201, title VII, §701(a), Sept. 7, 1992, 106 Stat. 1052, 1103, effective July 1, 1993.

Section 1606, Pub. L. 97–300, title II, §206, as added Pub. L. 102–367, title II, §203, Sept. 7, 1992, 106 Stat. 1061, related to transfer of funds.

EFFECTIVE DATE OF REPEAL

Repeal effective July 1, 2000, see section 199(c)(2)(B) of Pub. L. 105–220, set out as a note under section 1501 of this title.

PART B—SUMMER YOUTH EMPLOYMENT AND TRAINING PROGRAM

§§1630 to 1635. Repealed. Pub. L. 105–220, title I, §199(b)(2), Aug. 7, 1998, 112 Stat. 1059

Section 1630, Pub. L. 97–300, title II, §251, as added Pub. L. 102–367, title II, §204, Sept. 7, 1992, 106 Stat. 1061, stated purpose of Summer Youth Employment and Training Program.

A prior section 1630, Pub. L. 97–300, title II, §251, as added Pub. L. 99–496, §8(a)(2), Oct. 16, 1986, 100 Stat. 1263, stated purpose of summer youth employment and training programs, prior to repeal by Pub. L. 102–367, title II, §201, title VII, §701(a), Sept. 7, 1992, 106 Stat. 1052, 1103, effective July 1, 1993.

Section 1631, Pub. L. 97–300, title II, §252, as added Pub. L. 102–367, title II, §204, Sept. 7, 1992, 106 Stat. 1061, related to allotments and allocations.

A prior section 1631, Pub. L. 97–300, title II, §252, formerly §251, Oct. 13, 1982, 96 Stat. 1364; renumbered §252 and amended Pub. L. 99–496, §§5(b), 8(a)(1), Oct. 16, 1986, 100 Stat. 1262, 1263, related to allotment of funding for summer youth employment and training programs, prior to repeal by Pub. L. 102–367, title II, §201, title VII, §701(a), Sept. 7, 1992, 106 Stat. 1052, 1103, effective July 1, 1993.

Section 1632, Pub. L. 97–300, title II, §253, as added Pub. L. 102–367, title II, §204, Sept. 7, 1992, 106 Stat. 1061; amended Pub. L. 103–227, title X, §1016(a)(1)–(2)(B), Mar. 31, 1994, 108 Stat. 267; Pub. L. 104–193, title I, §110(n)(8), Aug. 22, 1996, 110 Stat. 2174, related to use of funds.

A prior section 1632, Pub. L. 97–300, title II, §253, formerly §252, Oct. 13, 1982, 96 Stat. 1364; renumbered §253 and amended Pub. L. 99–496, §8(a)(1), (b), Oct. 16, 1986, 100 Stat. 1263, related to use of funds for summer youth employment and training programs, prior to repeal by Pub. L. 102–367, title II, §201, title VII, §701(a), Sept. 7, 1992, 106 Stat. 1052, 1103, effective July 1, 1993.

Section 1633, Pub. L. 97–300, title II, §254, as added Pub. L. 102–367, title II, §204, Sept. 7, 1992, 106 Stat. 1062; amended Pub. L. 103–227, title X, §1016(a)(2)(C), Mar. 31, 1994, 108 Stat. 268; Pub. L. 106–78, title VII, §752(b)(12), Oct. 22, 1999, 113 Stat. 1169, contained limitations relating to conduct of Summer Youth Employment and Training Program.

A prior section 1633, Pub. L. 97–300, title II, §254, formerly §253, Oct. 13, 1982, 96 Stat. 1364; renumbered §254 and amended Pub. L. 99–496, §§8(a)(1), 9, Oct. 16, 1986, 100 Stat. 1263, 1264, related to limitations on summer youth employment and training programs, prior to repeal by Pub. L. 102–367, title II, §201, title VII, §701(a), Sept. 7, 1992, 106 Stat. 1052, 1103, effective July 1, 1993.

Section 1634, Pub. L. 97–300, title II, §255, as added Pub. L. 102–367, title II, §204, Sept. 7, 1992, 106 Stat. 1063, related to responsibilities for planning and administration of funds and establishment of goals.

A prior section 1634, Pub. L. 97–300, title II, §255, formerly §254, Oct. 13, 1982, 96 Stat. 1364; renumbered §255 and amended Pub. L. 99–496, §8(a)(1), (c), Oct. 16, 1986, 100 Stat. 1263, related to private industry councils and service delivery areas, prior to repeal by Pub. L. 102–367, title II, §201, title VII, §701(a), Sept. 7, 1992, 106 Stat. 1052, 1103, effective July 1, 1993.

Section 1635, Pub. L. 97–300, title II, §256, as added Pub. L. 102–367, title II, §205, Sept. 7, 1992, 106 Stat. 1063; amended Pub. L. 103–227, title X, §1016(b), Mar. 31, 1994, 108 Stat. 268, related to transfer of funds.

EFFECTIVE DATE OF REPEAL

Repeal effective July 1, 2000, see section 199(c)(2)(B) of Pub. L. 105–220, set out as a note under section 1501 of this title.

PART C—YOUTH TRAINING PROGRAM

§§1641 to 1646. Repealed. Pub. L. 105–220, title I, §199(b)(2), Aug. 7, 1998, 112 Stat. 1059

Section 1641, Pub. L. 97–300, title II, §261, as added Pub. L. 102–367, title II, §206, Sept. 7, 1992, 106 Stat. 1063, stated purpose of youth training program.

Section 1642, Pub. L. 97–300, title II, §262, as added Pub. L. 102–367, title VII, §701(f)(1), Sept. 7, 1992, 106 Stat. 1107, related to allotment and allocation.

Section 1643, Pub. L. 97–300, title II, §263, as added Pub. L. 102–367, title II, §208, Sept. 7, 1992, 106 Stat. 1066; amended Pub. L. 103–382, title III, §391(n)(2), (3), Oct. 20, 1994, 108 Stat. 4024; Pub. L. 106–78, title VII, §752(b)(12), Oct. 22, 1999, 113 Stat. 1169, related to eligibility for services.

Section 1644, Pub. L. 97–300, title II, §264, as added Pub. L. 102–367, title II, §208, Sept. 7, 1992, 106 Stat. 1068;

amended Pub. L. 104–193, title I, § 110(n)(9), Aug. 22, 1996, 110 Stat. 2174, related to program design.

Section 1645, Pub. L. 97–300, title II, § 265, as added Pub. L. 102–367, title II, § 208, Sept. 7, 1992, 106 Stat. 1071; amended Pub. L. 103–382, title III, § 391(n)(4), Oct. 20, 1994, 108 Stat. 4024; Pub. L. 104–193, title I, § 110(n)(10), Aug. 22, 1996, 110 Stat. 2174, related to linkages with other agencies and programs.

Section 1646, Pub. L. 97–300, title II, § 266, as added Pub. L. 102–367, title II, § 208, Sept. 7, 1992, 106 Stat. 1073, related to transfer of funds.

EFFECTIVE DATE OF REPEAL

Repeal effective July 1, 2000, see section 199(c)(2)(B) of Pub. L. 105–220, set out as a note under section 1501 of this title.

SUBCHAPTER III—EMPLOYMENT AND TRAINING ASSISTANCE FOR DISLOCATED WORKERS

§§ 1651 to 1653. Repealed. Pub. L. 105–220, title I, § 199(b)(2), Aug. 7, 1998, 112 Stat. 1059

Section 1651, Pub. L. 97–300, title III, § 301, as added Pub. L. 100–418, title VI, § 6302(a), Aug. 23, 1988, 102 Stat. 1524, defined terms.

A prior section 1651, Pub. L. 97–300, title III, § 301, Oct. 13, 1982, 96 Stat. 1364; Pub. L. 99–496, § 10, Oct. 16, 1986, 100 Stat. 1264, related to allocation of funds, prior to the general revision of this subchapter by Pub. L. 100–418.

Section 1652, Pub. L. 97–300, title III, § 302, as added Pub. L. 100–418, title VI, § 6302(a), Aug. 23, 1988, 102 Stat. 1525; amended Pub. L. 102–367, title I, § 102(b), title VII, § 702(a)(11), Sept. 7, 1992, 106 Stat. 1024, 1112, related to allotment.

A prior section 1652, Pub. L. 97–300, title III, § 302, Oct. 13, 1982, 96 Stat. 1365; Pub. L. 99–496, § 11, Oct. 16, 1986, 100 Stat. 1264, related to identification of dislocated workers, prior to the general revision of this subchapter by Pub. L. 100–418.

Section 1653, Pub. L. 97–300, title III, § 303, as added Pub. L. 100–418, title VI, § 6302(a), Aug. 23, 1988, 102 Stat. 1527, related to recapture and reallotment of unexpended funds.

Prior sections 1653 to 1658 were omitted in the general revision of this subchapter by Pub. L. 100–418.

Section 1653, Pub. L. 97–300, title III, § 303, Oct. 13, 1982, 96 Stat. 1366, authorized activities under provisions of former subchapter.

Section 1654, Pub. L. 97–300, title III, § 304, Oct. 13, 1982, 96 Stat. 1366, related to matching requirements for funds.

Section 1655, Pub. L. 97–300, title III, § 305, Oct. 13, 1982, 96 Stat. 1367, related to program review.

Section 1656, Pub. L. 97–300, title III, § 306, Oct. 13, 1982, 96 Stat. 1367, related to consultation with labor organizations.

Section 1657, Pub. L. 97–300, title III, § 307, Oct. 13, 1982, 96 Stat. 1367, related to limitations on availability of funds.

Section 1658, Pub. L. 97–300, title III, § 308, Oct. 13, 1982, 96 Stat. 1367; Pub. L. 97–404, § 3, Dec. 31, 1982, 96 Stat. 2026, related to State plans and coordination with other programs.

EFFECTIVE DATE OF REPEAL

Repeal effective July 1, 2000, see section 199(c)(2)(B) of Pub. L. 105–220, set out as a note under section 1501 of this title.

PART A—STATE DELIVERY OF SERVICES

§§ 1661 to 1661f. Repealed. Pub. L. 105–220, title I, § 199(b)(2), Aug. 7, 1998, 112 Stat. 1059

Section 1661, Pub. L. 97–300, title III, § 311, as added Pub. L. 100–418, title VI, § 6302(a), Aug. 23, 1988, 102 Stat. 1527; amended Pub. L. 102–367, title I, § 115(b), title VII, § 702(a)(12), Sept. 7, 1992, 106 Stat. 1034, 1112; Pub. L. 102–484, div. D, title XLIV, § 4467(a), Oct. 23, 1992, 106 Stat. 2750, related to State plans.

Section 1661a, Pub. L. 97–300, title III, § 312, as added Pub. L. 100–418, title VI, § 6302(a), Aug. 23, 1988, 102 Stat. 1529, related to substate grantees.

Section 1661b, Pub. L. 97–300, title III, § 313, as added Pub. L. 100–418, title VI, § 6302(a), Aug. 23, 1988, 102 Stat. 1531, related to substate plans.

Section 1661c, Pub. L. 97–300, title III, § 314, as added Pub. L. 100–418, title VI, § 6302(a), Aug. 23, 1988, 102 Stat. 1532; amended Pub. L. 101–392, § 5(a)(3), Sept. 25, 1990, 104 Stat. 759; Pub. L. 102–367, title III, § 301, Sept. 7, 1992, 106 Stat. 1073; Pub. L. 102–484, div. D, title XLIV, § 4467(b)–(d), Oct. 23, 1992, 106 Stat. 2750, related to use of funds and services to be provided.

Section 1661d, Pub. L. 97–300, title III, § 315, as added Pub. L. 100–418, title VI, § 6302(a), Aug. 23, 1988, 102 Stat. 1535; amended Pub. L. 102–367, title III, § 302, Sept. 7, 1992, 106 Stat. 1073, related to limitation on uses of funds.

Section 1661e, Pub. L. 97–300, title III, § 316, as added Pub. L. 100–418, title VI, § 6302(a), Aug. 23, 1988, 102 Stat. 1535, related to retraining services availability.

Section 1661f, Pub. L. 97–300, title III, § 317, as added Pub. L. 100–418, title VI, § 6302(a), Aug. 23, 1988, 102 Stat. 1536, related to functions of State job training coordinating council.

EFFECTIVE DATE OF REPEAL

Repeal effective July 1, 2000, see section 199(c)(2)(B) of Pub. L. 105–220, set out as a note under section 1501 of this title.

PART B—FEDERAL RESPONSIBILITIES

§§ 1662 to 1662e. Repealed. Pub. L. 105–220, title I, § 199(b)(2), Aug. 7, 1998, 112 Stat. 1059

Section 1662, Pub. L. 97–300, title III, § 321, as added Pub. L. 100–418, title VI, § 6302(a), Aug. 23, 1988, 102 Stat. 1536, related to Federal administration.

Section 1662a, Pub. L. 97–300, title III, § 322, as added Pub. L. 100–418, title VI, § 6302(a), Aug. 23, 1988, 102 Stat. 1536; amended Pub. L. 102–367, title I, § 115(b), Sept. 7, 1992, 106 Stat. 1034, related to Federal delivery of dislocated worker services.

Section 1662b, Pub. L. 97–300, title III, § 323, as added Pub. L. 100–418, title VI, § 6302(a), Aug. 23, 1988, 102 Stat. 1537, related to allowable activities.

Section 1662c, Pub. L. 97–300, title III, § 324, as added Pub. L. 100–418, title VI, § 6302(a), Aug. 23, 1988, 102 Stat. 1538; amended Pub. L. 102–367, title III, § 303, Sept. 7, 1992, 106 Stat. 1074, related to demonstration programs.

Section 1662d, Pub. L. 97–300, title III, § 325, as added Pub. L. 101–510, div. D, title XLII, § 4202, Nov. 5, 1990, 104 Stat. 1852; amended Pub. L. 102–484, div. D, title XLIV, § 4467(e), Oct. 23, 1992, 106 Stat. 2751; Pub. L. 103–337, div. A, title XI, §§ 1136(b), 1137(a), Oct. 5, 1994, 108 Stat. 2878, related to defense conversion adjustment program.

Section 1662d–1, Pub. L. 97–300, title III, § 325A, as added Pub. L. 102–484, div. D, title XLIV, § 4465(a), Oct. 23, 1992, 106 Stat. 2742; amended Pub. L. 103–160, div. A, title XIII, § 1339, Nov. 30, 1993, 107 Stat. 1807; Pub. L. 103–337, div. A, title XI, §§ 1136(a), 1137(b), Oct. 5, 1994, 108 Stat. 2878, 2879, related to defense diversification program.

Section 1662e, Pub. L. 97–300, title III, § 326, as added Pub. L. 101–549, title XI, § 1101(a), Nov. 15, 1990, 104 Stat. 2709; amended Pub. L. 102–367, title I, § 102(b), Sept. 7, 1992, 106 Stat. 1024, related to clean air employment transition assistance.

EFFECTIVE DATE OF REPEAL

Repeal effective July 1, 2000, see section 199(c)(2)(B) of Pub. L. 105–220, set out as a note under section 1501 of this title.

SUBCHAPTER IV—FEDERALLY ADMINISTERED PROGRAMS

PART A—EMPLOYMENT AND TRAINING PROGRAMS FOR NATIVE AMERICANS AND MIGRANT AND SEASONAL FARMWORKERS

§§ 1671 to 1673. Repealed. Pub. L. 105–220, title I, § 199(b)(2), Aug. 7, 1998, 112 Stat. 1059

Section 1671, Pub. L. 97–300, title IV, § 401, Oct. 13, 1982, 96 Stat. 1368; Pub. L. 97–404, § 4(a), Dec. 31, 1982, 96 Stat. 2026; Pub. L. 102–367, title IV, § 401(a)–(d), Sept. 7, 1992, 106 Stat. 1074–1076, related to Native American employment and training programs. See section 2911 of this title.

Section 1672, Pub. L. 97–300, title IV, § 402, Oct. 13, 1982, 96 Stat. 1369; Pub. L. 97–404, § 4(b), Dec. 31, 1982, 96 Stat. 2026; Pub. L. 102–367, title IV, § 401(e), (f), Sept. 7, 1992, 106 Stat. 1076, related to migrant and seasonal farmworker employment and training programs. See section 2912 of this title.

Section 1673, Pub. L. 97–300, title IV, § 403, as added Pub. L. 102–367, title IV, § 401(g), Sept. 7, 1992, 106 Stat. 1076, related to grant procedures. See section 2912(g) of this title.

EFFECTIVE DATE OF REPEAL

Repeal effective July 1, 2000, see section 199(c)(2)(B) of Pub. L. 105–220, set out as a note under section 1501 of this title.

PART B—JOB CORPS

§§ 1691 to 1709. Repealed. Pub. L. 105–220, title I, § 199(b)(2), Aug. 7, 1998, 112 Stat. 1059

Section 1691, Pub. L. 97–300, title IV, § 421, Oct. 13, 1982, 96 Stat. 1370, stated purpose of Job Corps program. See section 2881 of this title.

Section 1692, Pub. L. 97–300, title IV, § 422, Oct. 13, 1982, 96 Stat. 1370, established the Job Corps. See section 2883 of this title.

Section 1693, Pub. L. 97–300, title IV, § 423, Oct. 13, 1982, 96 Stat. 1370; Pub. L. 102–367, title I, § 103(b)(4), title IV, § 402(a), Sept. 7, 1992, 106 Stat. 1026, 1076, related to eligibility of individuals for the Job Corps. See section 2884 of this title.

Section 1694, Pub. L. 97–300, title IV, § 424, Oct. 13, 1982, 96 Stat. 1371, contained general provisions relating to screening and selection of applicants. See section 2885 of this title.

Section 1695, Pub. L. 97–300, title IV, § 425, Oct. 13, 1982, 96 Stat. 1372; Pub. L. 98–473, title II, § 231, Oct. 12, 1984, 98 Stat. 2031, contained special limitations relating to screening and selection of applicants. See section 2885 of this title.

Section 1696, Pub. L. 97–300, title IV, § 426, Oct. 13, 1982, 96 Stat. 1372; Pub. L. 102–367, title IV, § 402(b), Sept. 7, 1992, 106 Stat. 1076, related to enrollment and assignment. See section 2886 of this title.

Section 1697, Pub. L. 97–300, title IV, § 427, Oct. 13, 1982, 96 Stat. 1372; Pub. L. 98–524, § 4(a)(4), Oct. 19, 1984, 98 Stat. 2487; Pub. L. 102–367, title IV, § 402(c), (d), Sept. 7, 1992, 106 Stat. 1076, 1077, related to Job Corps centers. See section 2887 of this title.

Section 1698, Pub. L. 97–300, title IV, § 428, Oct. 13, 1982, 96 Stat. 1373; Pub. L. 102–367, title IV, § 402(e), Sept. 7, 1992, 106 Stat. 1077, related to program activities. See section 2888 of this title.

Section 1699, Pub. L. 97–300, title IV, § 429, Oct. 13, 1982, 96 Stat. 1374; Pub. L. 103–239, title VII, § 731, May 4, 1994, 108 Stat. 607; Pub. L. 104–193, title I, § 110(n)(11), Aug. 22, 1996, 110 Stat. 2174, related to allowances and support. See section 2890 of this title.

Section 1700, Pub. L. 97–300, title IV, § 430, Oct. 13, 1982, 96 Stat. 1375, related to standards of conduct. See section 2892 of this title.

Section 1701, Pub. L. 97–300, title IV, § 431, Oct. 13, 1982, 96 Stat. 1375, related to community participation.

Section 1702, Pub. L. 97–300, title IV, § 432, Oct. 13, 1982, 96 Stat. 1376, related to counseling and placement. See sections 2889 and 2890 of this title.

Section 1703, Pub. L. 97–300, title IV, § 433, Oct. 13, 1982, 96 Stat. 1376; Pub. L. 102–367, title VII, § 702(a)(13), Sept. 7, 1992, 106 Stat. 1112, related to experimental and developmental projects and coordination with other programs. See section 2896 of this title.

Section 1703a, Pub. L. 97–300, title IV, § 433A, as added Pub. L. 101–645, title VI, § 622, Nov. 29, 1990, 104 Stat. 4744; amended Pub. L. 102–367, title VII, § 702(a)(14), Sept. 7, 1992, 106 Stat. 1112, related to Job Corps centers for homeless families.

Section 1704, Pub. L. 97–300, title IV, § 434, Oct. 13, 1982, 96 Stat. 1378, related to advisory boards and committees. See section 2895 of this title.

Section 1705, Pub. L. 97–300, title IV, § 435, Oct. 13, 1982, 96 Stat. 1378, related to participation of the States.

Section 1706, Pub. L. 97–300, title IV, § 436, Oct. 13, 1982, 96 Stat. 1378; Pub. L. 102–367, title VII, § 702(a)(15), Sept. 7, 1992, 106 Stat. 1112, related to application of provisions of Federal law. See section 2897 of this title.

Section 1707, Pub. L. 97–300, title IV, § 437, Oct. 13, 1982, 96 Stat. 1379; Pub. L. 99–496, § 12, Oct. 16, 1986, 100 Stat. 1264; Pub. L. 102–367, title IV, § 402(f), Sept. 7, 1992, 106 Stat. 1077, contained special provisions relating to enrollment of women, documents and data, taxation, and management fees. See section 2898 of this title.

Section 1708, Pub. L. 97–300, title IV, § 438, Oct. 13, 1982, 96 Stat. 1379, contained general provisions relating to dissemination of information, collections, and expenditures. See section 2900 of this title.

Section 1709, Pub. L. 97–300, title IV, § 439, Oct. 13, 1982, 96 Stat. 1380, related to donations. See section 2898(f) of this title.

EFFECTIVE DATE OF REPEAL

Repeal effective July 1, 2000, see section 199(c)(2)(B) of Pub. L. 105–220, set out as a note under section 1501 of this title.

PART C—VETERANS' EMPLOYMENT PROGRAMS

§ 1721. Repealed. Pub. L. 105–220, title I, § 199(b)(2), Aug. 7, 1998, 112 Stat. 1059

Section, Pub. L. 97–300, title IV, § 441, Oct. 13, 1982, 96 Stat. 1380; Pub. L. 99–619, § 2(b)(3), Nov. 6, 1986, 100 Stat. 3491; Pub. L. 102–54, § 13(k)(2)(C), June 13, 1991, 105 Stat. 277; Pub. L. 103–446, title XII, § 1203(c)(2), Nov. 2, 1994, 108 Stat. 4690, authorized veterans' employment programs. See section 2913 of this title.

EFFECTIVE DATE OF REPEAL

Repeal effective July 1, 2000, see section 199(c)(2)(B) of Pub. L. 105–220, set out as a note under section 1501 of this title.

PART D—NATIONAL ACTIVITIES

§§ 1731 to 1735. Repealed. Pub. L. 105–220, title I, § 199(b)(2), Aug. 7, 1998, 112 Stat. 1059

Section 1731, Pub. L. 97–300, title IV, § 451, Oct. 13, 1982, 96 Stat. 1381; Pub. L. 102–367, title IV, § 403(a)(1), Sept. 7, 1992, 106 Stat. 1077, related to national partnership and special training programs.

Section 1732, Pub. L. 97–300, title IV, § 452, Oct. 13, 1982, 96 Stat. 1381; Pub. L. 102–367, title IV, § 403(a)(2), Sept. 7, 1992, 106 Stat. 1078, related to research, demonstration, and evaluation.

Section 1733, Pub. L. 97–300, title IV, § 453, Oct. 13, 1982, 96 Stat. 1382; Pub. L. 99–496, § 13, Oct. 16, 1986, 100 Stat. 1265; Pub. L. 102–367, title IV, § 403(a)(3), Sept. 7, 1992, 106 Stat. 1080, related to capacity building, information, dissemination, and replication activities.

Section 1734, Pub. L. 97–300, title IV, § 454, as added Pub. L. 102–367, title IV, § 403(b), Sept. 7, 1992, 106 Stat. 1084; amended Pub. L. 104–193, title I, § 110(n)(12), Aug.

22, 1996, 110 Stat. 2174, related to guidance on eligibility verification.

A prior section 1734, Pub. L. 97–300, title IV, §454, Oct. 13, 1982, 96 Stat. 1383; Pub. L. 97–404, §4(c), Dec. 31, 1982, 96 Stat. 2026, related to evaluation of effectiveness of programs, activities, and projects authorized by this chapter, prior to repeal by Pub. L. 102–367, title IV, §403(a)(4), title VII, §701(a), Sept. 7, 1992, 106 Stat. 1084, 1103, effective July 1, 1993.

Section 1735, Pub. L. 97–300, title IV, §455, as added Pub. L. 102–367, title IV, §404(a), Sept. 7, 1992, 106 Stat. 1084; amended Pub. L. 104–193, title I, §110(n)(13), Aug. 22, 1996, 110 Stat. 2174, related to uniform reporting requirements.

A prior section 1735, Pub. L. 97–300, title IV, §455, Oct. 13, 1982, 96 Stat. 1383, related to personnel training and technical assistance with respect to programs under this chapter, prior to repeal by Pub. L. 102–367, title IV, §403(a)(4), title VII, §701(a), Sept. 7, 1992, 106 Stat. 1084, 1103, effective July 1, 1993.

EFFECTIVE DATE OF REPEAL

Repeal effective July 1, 2000, see section 199(c)(2)(B) of Pub. L. 105–220, set out as a note under section 1501 of this title.

§1736. Repealed. Pub. L. 102–367, title IV, §403(a)(4), Sept. 7, 1992, 106 Stat. 1084

Section, Pub. L. 97–300, title IV, §456, as added Pub. L. 99–496, §14(a), Oct. 16, 1986, 100 Stat. 1265, related to projects designed to serve populations with multiple barriers to employment.

EFFECTIVE DATE OF REPEAL

Repeal effective July 1, 1993, see section 701(a) of Pub. L. 102–367, formerly set out as an Effective Date of 1992 Amendment; Transition Provisions note under section 1501 of this title.

§1737. Repealed. Pub. L. 105–220, title I, §199(b)(2), Aug. 7, 1998, 112 Stat. 1059

Section, Pub. L. 97–300, title IV, §456, formerly §457, as added Pub. L. 102–235, §9, Dec. 12, 1991, 105 Stat. 1809; renumbered §456 and amended Pub. L. 102–367, title IV, §403(a)(5), Sept. 7, 1992, 106 Stat. 1084, related to nontraditional employment demonstration program.

A prior section 456 of Pub. L. 97–300 was classified to section 1736 of this title, prior to repeal by Pub. L. 102–367, title IV, §403(a)(4), Sept. 7, 1992, 106 Stat. 1084.

EFFECTIVE DATE OF REPEAL

Repeal effective July 1, 2000, see section 199(c)(2)(B) of Pub. L. 105–220, set out as a note under section 1501 of this title.

PART E—LABOR MARKET INFORMATION

§§1751 to 1755. Repealed. Pub. L. 105–220, title I, §199(b)(2), Aug. 7, 1998, 112 Stat. 1059

Section 1751, Pub. L. 97–300, title IV, §461, Oct. 13, 1982, 96 Stat. 1383; Pub. L. 98–524, §4(a)(5), Oct. 19, 1984, 98 Stat. 2488, related to labor market information and availability of funds.

Section 1752, Pub. L. 97–300, title IV, §462, Oct. 13, 1982, 96 Stat. 1384; Pub. L. 100–418, title VI, §6306(a), Aug. 23, 1988, 102 Stat. 1540; Pub. L. 102–367, title IV, §405(a), title VII, §702(a)(16), Sept. 7, 1992, 106 Stat. 1085, 1112, related to cooperative labor market information program.

Section 1753, Pub. L. 97–300, title IV, §463, Oct. 13, 1982, 96 Stat. 1384; Pub. L. 97–404, §4(d), Dec. 31, 1982, 96 Stat. 2027; Pub. L. 98–524, §4(a)(6)(A), (D), Oct. 19, 1984, 98 Stat. 2488; Pub. L. 99–159, title VII, §713(b)(2), Nov. 22, 1985, 99 Stat. 907; Pub. L. 102–367, title IV, §405(b), Sept. 7, 1992, 106 Stat. 1085, related to special Federal responsibilities.

Section 1754, Pub. L. 97–300, title IV, §464, Oct. 13, 1982, 96 Stat. 1385; Pub. L. 97–404, §4(e), Dec. 31, 1982, 96 Stat. 2027; Pub. L. 98–524, §4(a)(6)(B), (C), (E), Oct. 19, 1984, 98 Stat. 2488; Pub. L. 102–367, title IV, §405(c), Sept. 7, 1992, 106 Stat. 1085, related to National Occupational Information Coordinating Committee.

Section 1755, Pub. L. 97–300, title IV, §465, Oct. 13, 1982, 96 Stat. 1386; Pub. L. 102–83, §5(c)(2), Aug. 6, 1991, 105 Stat. 406, related to job bank program.

EFFECTIVE DATE OF REPEAL

Repeal effective July 1, 2000, see section 199(c)(2)(B) of Pub. L. 105–220, set out as a note under section 1501 of this title.

PART F—NATIONAL COMMISSION FOR EMPLOYMENT POLICY

§§1771 to 1775. Repealed. Pub. L. 105–220, title I, §199(b)(2), Aug. 7, 1998, 112 Stat. 1059

Section 1771, Pub. L. 97–300, title IV, §471, Oct. 13, 1982, 96 Stat. 1387, stated purpose to establish National Commission for Employment Policy.

Section 1772, Pub. L. 97–300, title IV, §472, Oct. 13, 1982, 96 Stat. 1387; Pub. L. 98–524, §4(a)(7), Oct. 19, 1984, 98 Stat. 2488; Pub. L. 102–367, title VII, §702(a)(17), Sept. 7, 1992, 106 Stat. 1112, established National Commission for Employment Policy.

Section 1773, Pub. L. 97–300, title IV, §473, Oct. 13, 1982, 96 Stat. 1388; Pub. L. 98–524, §4(a)(8), Oct. 19, 1984, 98 Stat. 2488; Pub. L. 102–367, title VII, §702(a)(18), Sept. 7, 1992, 106 Stat. 1112, related to functions of Commission.

Section 1774, Pub. L. 97–300, title IV, §474, Oct. 13, 1982, 96 Stat. 1389, contained administrative provisions.

Section 1775, Pub. L. 97–300, title IV, §475, Oct. 13, 1982, 96 Stat. 1389, related to annual reports by Commission.

EFFECTIVE DATE OF REPEAL

Repeal effective July 1, 2000, see section 199(c)(2)(B) of Pub. L. 105–220, set out as a note under section 1501 of this title.

PART G—TRAINING TO FULFILL AFFIRMATIVE ACTION OBLIGATIONS

§1781. Repealed. Pub. L. 105–220, title I, §199(b)(2), Aug. 7, 1998, 112 Stat. 1059

Section, Pub. L. 97–300, title IV, §481, Oct. 13, 1982, 96 Stat. 1390; Pub. L. 102–367, title VII, §702(a)(19), Sept. 7, 1992, 106 Stat. 1112, related to training to fulfill affirmative action obligations.

EFFECTIVE DATE OF REPEAL

Repeal effective July 1, 2000, see section 199(c)(2)(B) of Pub. L. 105–220, set out as a note under section 1501 of this title.

PART H—YOUTH FAIR CHANCE PROGRAM

§§1782 to 1782h. Repealed. Pub. L. 105–220, title I, §199(b)(2), Aug. 7, 1998, 112 Stat. 1059

Section 1782, Pub. L. 97–300, title IV, §491, as added Pub. L. 102–367, title IV, §406, Sept. 7, 1992, 106 Stat. 1086, stated purpose of Youth Fair Chance program.

Section 1782a, Pub. L. 97–300, title IV, §492, as added Pub. L. 102–367, title IV, §406, Sept. 7, 1992, 106 Stat. 1086, authorized national program of Youth Fair Chance grants.

Section 1782b, Pub. L. 97–300, title IV, §493, as added Pub. L. 102–367, title IV, §406, Sept. 7, 1992, 106 Stat. 1087, related to applications for grants.

Section 1782c, Pub. L. 97–300, title IV, §494, as added Pub. L. 102–367, title IV, §406, Sept. 7, 1992, 106 Stat. 1089; amended Pub. L. 103–50, ch. V, §502, July 2, 1993, 107 Stat. 254, related to grant agreements.

Section 1782d, Pub. L. 97–300, title IV, § 495, as added Pub. L. 102–367, title IV, § 406, Sept. 7, 1992, 106 Stat. 1090, related to job guarantees.

Section 1782e, Pub. L. 97–300, title IV, § 496, as added Pub. L. 102–367, title IV, § 406, Sept. 7, 1992, 106 Stat. 1091, related to payments and Federal share.

Section 1782f, Pub. L. 97–300, title IV, § 497, as added Pub. L. 102–367, title IV, § 406, Sept. 7, 1992, 106 Stat. 1091, related to reporting procedures.

Section 1782g, Pub. L. 97–300, title IV, § 498, as added Pub. L. 102–367, title IV, § 406, Sept. 7, 1992, 106 Stat. 1091, related to Federal responsibilities.

Section 1782h, Pub. L. 97–300, title IV, § 498A, as added Pub. L. 102–367, title IV, § 406, Sept. 7, 1992, 106 Stat. 1092, defined "participating community", "high poverty area", and "target area".

EFFECTIVE DATE OF REPEAL

Repeal effective July 1, 2000, see section 199(c)(2)(B) of Pub. L. 105–220, set out as a note under section 1501 of this title.

PART I—MICROENTERPRISE GRANTS PROGRAM

§ 1783. Repealed. Pub. L. 105–220, title I, § 199(b)(2), Aug. 7, 1998, 112 Stat. 1059

Section, Pub. L. 97–300, title IV, § 499, as added Pub. L. 102–367, title IV, § 407, Sept. 7, 1992, 106 Stat. 1093, authorized microenterprise grants program.

EFFECTIVE DATE OF REPEAL

Repeal effective July 1, 2000, see section 199(c)(2)(B) of Pub. L. 105–220, set out as a note under section 1501 of this title.

PART J—DISASTER RELIEF EMPLOYMENT ASSISTANCE

§§ 1784 to 1784b. Repealed. Pub. L. 105–220, title I, § 199(b)(2), Aug. 7, 1998, 112 Stat. 1059

Section 1784, Pub. L. 97–300, title IV, § 499A, as added Pub. L. 102–367, title IV, § 408, Sept. 7, 1992, 106 Stat. 1094, authorized disaster relief employment assistance.

Section 1784a, Pub. L. 97–300, title IV, § 499B, as added Pub. L. 102–367, title IV, § 408, Sept. 7, 1992, 106 Stat. 1095, related to use of funds.

Section 1784b, Pub. L. 97–300, title IV, § 499C, as added Pub. L. 102–367, title IV, § 408, Sept. 7, 1992, 106 Stat. 1095, defined term "unit of general local government".

EFFECTIVE DATE OF REPEAL

Repeal effective July 1, 2000, see section 199(c)(2)(B) of Pub. L. 105–220, set out as a note under section 1501 of this title.

SUBCHAPTER V—JOBS FOR EMPLOYABLE DEPENDENT INDIVIDUALS INCENTIVE BONUS PROGRAM

§§ 1791 to 1791h. Repealed. Pub. L. 105–220, title I, § 199(b)(2), Aug. 7, 1998, 112 Stat. 1059

Section 1791, Pub. L. 97–300, title V, § 501, as added Pub. L. 100–628, title VII, § 712(a)(3), Nov. 7, 1988, 102 Stat. 3248; amended Pub. L. 102–367, title V, § 501, Sept. 7, 1992, 106 Stat. 1096; Pub. L. 104–193, title I, § 110(n)(14), Aug. 22, 1996, 110 Stat. 2174, stated purpose of jobs for employable dependent individuals incentive bonus program.

A prior section 501 of Pub. L. 97–300, which enacted sections 49e, 49f, 49*l*, and 49*l*–1 of this title, amended sections 49 to 49b, 49d, and 49g to 49j of this title, and enacted provisions set out as a note under section 49 of this title, was renumbered section 601 of Pub. L. 97–300.

Section 1791a, Pub. L. 97–300, title V, § 502, as added Pub. L. 100–628, title VII, § 712(a)(3), Nov. 7, 1988, 102 Stat. 3248; amended Pub. L. 102–367, title V, § 501, Sept. 7, 1992, 106 Stat. 1096, related to payments to States.

A prior section 502 of Pub. L. 97–300, which amended sections 632 and 633 of Title 42, The Public Health and Welfare, was renumbered section 602 of Pub. L. 97–300.

Section 1791b, Pub. L. 97–300, title V, § 503, as added Pub. L. 100–628, title VII, § 712(a)(3), Nov. 7, 1988, 102 Stat. 3249; amended Pub. L. 102–367, title V, § 501, Sept. 7, 1992, 106 Stat. 1096, related to amount of incentive bonus.

A prior section 503 of Pub. L. 97–300, which amended section 602 of Title 42, The Public Health and Welfare, was renumbered section 603 of Pub. L. 97–300.

Section 1791c, Pub. L. 97–300, title V, § 504, as added Pub. L. 100–628, title VII, § 712(a)(3), Nov. 7, 1988, 102 Stat. 3249; amended Pub. L. 102–367, title V, § 501, Sept. 7, 1992, 106 Stat. 1097, related to use of incentive bonus funds.

A prior section 504 of Pub. L. 97–300 was renumbered section 604 and was classified to section 1504 of this title prior to repeal by Pub. L. 105–220.

Section 1791d, Pub. L. 97–300, title V, § 505, as added Pub. L. 100–628, title VII, § 712(a)(3), Nov. 7, 1988, 102 Stat. 3250; amended Pub. L. 102–367, title V, § 501, Sept. 7, 1992, 106 Stat. 1097, related to notices and applications.

Another section 505 of title VI of Pub. L. 97–300, as added Pub. L. 100–418, title VI, § 6307(a), Aug. 23, 1988, 102 Stat. 1541, and amended, was renumbered section 605 of title VI of Pub. L. 97–300 by Pub. L. 102–367, title VII, § 702(a)(20), Sept. 7, 1992, 106 Stat. 1113, and was classified to section 1505 of this title, prior to repeal by Pub. L. 105–220.

Section 1791e, Pub. L. 97–300, title V, § 506, as added Pub. L. 100–628, title VII, § 712(a)(3), Nov. 7, 1988, 102 Stat. 3251; amended Pub. L. 102–367, title V, § 501, Sept. 7, 1992, 106 Stat. 1098; Pub. L. 104–193, title I, § 110(n)(15), Aug. 22, 1996, 110 Stat. 2174, related to eligibility for incentive bonuses.

Section 1791f, Pub. L. 97–300, title V, § 507, as added Pub. L. 100–628, title VII, § 712(a)(3), Nov. 7, 1988, 102 Stat. 3252; amended Pub. L. 102–367, title V, § 501, Sept. 7, 1992, 106 Stat. 1098, related to information and data collection.

Section 1791g, Pub. L. 97–300, title V, § 508, as added Pub. L. 100–628, title VII, § 712(a)(3), Nov. 7, 1988, 102 Stat. 3252; amended Pub. L. 102–367, title V, § 501, Sept. 7, 1992, 106 Stat. 1099; Pub. L. 104–193, title I, § 110(n)(16), Aug. 22, 1996, 110 Stat. 2175, related to evaluations and reports.

Section 1791h, Pub. L. 97–300, title V, § 509, as added Pub. L. 100–628, title VII, § 712(a)(3), Nov. 7, 1988, 102 Stat. 3253; amended Pub. L. 102–367, title V, § 501, Sept. 7, 1992, 106 Stat. 1099, related to implementing regulations.

EFFECTIVE DATE OF REPEAL

Repeal effective July 1, 2000, see section 199(c)(2)(B) of Pub. L. 105–220, set out as a note under section 1501 of this title.

§§ 1791i, 1791j. Omitted

CODIFICATION

Sections 1791i and 1791j of this title were omitted in the general revision of this subchapter by Pub. L. 102–367, title V, § 501, title VII, § 701(a), Sept. 7, 1992, 106 Stat. 1099, 1103, effective July 1, 1993.

Section 1791i, Pub. L. 97–300, title V, § 510, as added Pub. L. 100–628, title VII, § 712(a)(3), Nov. 7, 1988, 102 Stat. 3253, related to awards to States for start-up costs for participation in the incentive bonus program.

Section 1791j, Pub. L. 97–300, title V, § 511, as added Pub. L. 100–628, title VII, § 712(a)(3), Nov. 7, 1988, 102 Stat. 3254, related to evaluation and performance standards for the incentive bonus program.

SUBCHAPTER VI—STATE HUMAN RESOURCE INVESTMENT COUNCIL

§§ 1792 to 1792b. Repealed. Pub. L. 105–220, title I, § 199(b)(2), Aug. 7, 1998, 112 Stat. 1059

Section 1792, Pub. L. 97–300, title VII, § 701, as added Pub. L. 102–367, title VI, § 601(a), Sept. 7, 1992, 106 Stat. 1099; amended Pub. L. 104–193, title I, § 110(n)(17), Aug. 22, 1996, 110 Stat. 2175, related to establishment and functions of State human resource investment councils.

Section 1792a, Pub. L. 97–300, title VII, § 702, as added Pub. L. 102–367, title VI, § 601(a), Sept. 7, 1992, 106 Stat. 1101, related to composition of Councils.

Section 1792b, Pub. L. 97–300, title VII, § 703, as added Pub. L. 102–367, title VI, § 601(a), Sept. 7, 1992, 106 Stat. 1102, related to administration of Councils.

EFFECTIVE DATE OF REPEAL

Repeal effective July 1, 2000, see section 199(c)(2)(B) of Pub. L. 105–220, set out as a note under section 1501 of this title.

CHAPTER 20—MIGRANT AND SEASONAL AGRICULTURAL WORKER PROTECTION

§ 1801. Congressional statement of purpose

It is the purpose of this chapter to remove the restraints on commerce caused by activities detrimental to migrant and seasonal agricultural workers; to require farm labor contractors to register under this chapter; and to assure necessary protections for migrant and seasonal agricultural workers, agricultural associations, and agricultural employers.

(Pub. L. 97–470, § 2, Jan. 14, 1983, 96 Stat. 2584.)

EFFECTIVE DATE

Section 524 of Pub. L. 97–470 provided in part that: "The provisions of this Act [enacting this chapter and repealing chapter 52 (§ 2041 et seq.) of Title 7, Agriculture] shall take effect ninety days from the date of enactment [Jan. 14, 1983]."

SHORT TITLE

Section 1 of Pub. L. 97–470 provided in part that this Act [enacting this chapter and repealing chapter 52 (§ 2041 et seq.) of Title 7, Agriculture] may be cited as the "Migrant and Seasonal Agricultural Worker Protection Act".

§ 1802. Definitions

As used in this chapter—

(1) The term "agricultural association" means any nonprofit or cooperative association of farmers, growers, or ranchers, incorporated or qualified under applicable State law, which recruits, solicits, hires, employs, furnishes, or transports any migrant or seasonal agricultural worker.

(2) The term "agricultural employer" means any person who owns or operates a farm, ranch, processing establishment, cannery, gin, packing shed or nursery, or who produces or conditions seed, and who either recruits, solicits, hires, employs, furnishes, or transports any migrant or seasonal agricultural worker.

(3) The term "agricultural employment" means employment in any service or activity included within the provisions of section 3(f) of the Fair Labor Standards Act of 1938 (29 U.S.C. 203(f)), or section 3121(g) of title 26 and the handling, planting, drying, packing, packaging, processing, freezing, or grading prior to delivery for storage of any agricultural or horticultural commodity in its unmanufactured state.

(4) The term "day-haul operation" means the assembly of workers at a pick-up point waiting to be hired and employed, transportation of such workers to agricultural employment, and the return of such workers to a drop-off point on the same day.

(5) The term "employ" has the meaning given such term under section 3(g) of the Fair Labor Standards Act of 1938 (29 U.S.C. 203(g)) for the purposes of implementing the requirements of that Act [29 U.S.C. 201 et seq.].

(6) The term "farm labor contracting activity" means recruiting, soliciting, hiring, employing, furnishing, or transporting any migrant or seasonal agricultural worker.

(7) The term "farm labor contractor" means any person, other than an agricultural employer, an agricultural association, or an employee of an agricultural employer or agricultural association, who, for any money or other

valuable consideration paid or promised to be paid, performs any farm labor contracting activity.

(8)(A) Except as provided in subparagraph (B), the term "migrant agricultural worker" means an individual who is employed in agricultural employment of a seasonal or other temporary nature, and who is required to be absent overnight from his permanent place of residence.

(B) The term "migrant agricultural worker" does not include—

(i) any immediate family member of an agricultural employer or a farm labor contractor; or

(ii) any temporary nonimmigrant alien who is authorized to work in agricultural employment in the United States under sections 1101(a)(15)(H)(ii)(a) and 1184(c) of title 8.

(9) The term "person" means any individual, partnership, association, joint stock company, trust, cooperative, or corporation.

(10)(A) Except as provided in subparagraph (B), the term "seasonal agricultural worker" means an individual who is employed in agricultural employment of a seasonal or other temporary nature and is not required to be absent overnight from his permanent place of residence—

(i) when employed on a farm or ranch performing field work related to planting, cultivating, or harvesting operations; or

(ii) when employed in canning, packing, ginning, seed conditioning or related research, or processing operations, and transported, or caused to be transported, to or from the place of employment by means of a day-haul operation.

(B) The term "seasonal agricultural worker" does not include—

(i) any migrant agricultural worker;

(ii) any immediate family member of an agricultural employer or a farm labor contractor; or

(iii) any temporary nonimmigrant alien who is authorized to work in agricultural employment in the United States under sections 1101(a)(15)(H)(ii)(a) and 1184(c) of title 8.

(11) The term "Secretary" means the Secretary of Labor or the Secretary's authorized representative.

(12) The term "State" means any of the States of the United States, the District of Columbia, the Virgin Islands, the Commonwealth of Puerto Rico, and Guam.

(Pub. L. 97–470, §3, Jan. 14, 1983, 96 Stat. 2584; Pub. L. 99–514, §2, Oct. 22, 1986, 100 Stat. 2095; Pub. L. 99–603, title I, §101(b)(1)(A), Nov. 6, 1986, 100 Stat. 3372.)

REFERENCES IN TEXT

That Act, referred to in par. (5), is act June 25, 1938, ch. 676, 52 Stat. 1060, as amended, known as the Fair Labor Standards Act of 1938, which is classified generally to chapter 8 (§201 et seq.) of this title. For complete classification of this Act to the Code, see section 201 of this title and Tables.

AMENDMENTS

1986—Par. (3). Pub. L. 99–514 substituted "Internal Revenue Code of 1986" for "Internal Revenue Code of 1954", which for purposes of codification was translated as "title 26" thus requiring no change in text.

Pars. (8)(B)(ii), (10)(B)(iii). Pub. L. 99–603 substituted "1101(a)(15)(H)(ii)(a)" for "1101(a)(15)(H)(ii)".

EFFECTIVE DATE OF 1986 AMENDMENT

Section 101(b)(2) of Pub. L. 99–603, as amended by Pub. L. 100–525, §2(a)(2), Oct. 24, 1988, 102 Stat. 2610, provided that: "The amendments made by paragraph (1) [amending this section and sections 1813 and 1851 of this title and repealing section 1816 of this title] shall apply to the employment, recruitment, referral, or utilization of the services of an individual occurring on or after the first day of the seventh month beginning after the date of the enactment of this Act [Nov. 6, 1986]; except that if the provisions of section 274A of the Immigration and Nationality Act [8 U.S.C. 1324a] are terminated as of a date under [former] subsection (*l*) of such section, then such amendments shall no longer apply as of such date." [The provisions of section 1324a of Title 8, Aliens and Nationality, were not terminated under subsection (*l*) of section 1324a, and that subsection was repealed by Pub. L. 104–208.]

§ 1803. Applicability of chapter

(a) The following persons are not subject to this chapter:

(1) FAMILY BUSINESS EXEMPTION.—Any individual who engages in a farm labor contracting activity on behalf of a farm, processing establishment, seed conditioning establishment, cannery, gin, packing shed, or nursery, which is owned or operated exclusively by such individual or an immediate family member of such individual, if such activities are performed only for such operation and exclusively by such individual or an immediate family member, but without regard to whether such individual has incorporated or otherwise organized for business purposes.

(2) SMALL BUSINESS EXEMPTION.—Any person, other than a farm labor contractor, for whom the man-days exemption for agricultural labor provided under section 13(a)(6)(A) of the Fair Labor Standards Act of 1938 (29 U.S.C. 213(a)(6)(A)) is applicable.

(3) OTHER EXEMPTIONS.—(A) Any common carrier which would be a farm labor contractor solely because the carrier is engaged in the farm labor contracting activity of transporting any migrant or seasonal agricultural worker.

(B) Any labor organization, as defined in section 2(5) of the Labor Management Relations Act (29 U.S.C. 152(5)) (without regard to the exclusion of agricultural employees in that Act [29 U.S.C. 141 et seq.]) or as defined under applicable State labor relations law.

(C) Any nonprofit charitable organization or public or private nonprofit educational institution.

(D) Any person who engages in any farm labor contracting activity solely within a twenty-five mile intrastate radius of such person's permanent place of residence and for not more than thirteen weeks per year.

(E) Any custom combine, hay harvesting, or sheep shearing operation.

(F) Any custom poultry harvesting, breeding, debeaking, desexing, or health service operation provided the employees of the operation are not regularly required to be away from their permanent place of residence other than during their normal working hours.

(G)(i) Any person whose principal occupation or business is not agricultural employment, when supplying full-time students or other individuals whose principal occupation is not agricultural employment to detassel, rogue, or otherwise engage in the production of seed and to engage in related and incidental agricultural employment, unless such full-time students or other individuals are required to be away from their permanent place of residence overnight or there are individuals under eighteen years of age who are providing transportation on behalf of such person.

(ii) Any person to the extent he is supplied with students or other individuals for agricultural employment in accordance with clause (i) of this subparagraph by a person who is exempt under such clause.

(H)(i) Any person whose principal occupation or business is not agricultural employment, when supplying full-time students or other individuals whose principal occupation is not agricultural employment to string or harvest shade grown tobacco and to engage in related and incidental agricultural employment, unless there are individuals under eighteen years of age who are providing transportation on behalf of such person.

(ii) Any person to the extent he is supplied with students or other individuals for agricultural employment in accordance with clause (i) of this subparagraph by a person who is exempt under such clause.

(I) Any employee of any person described in subparagraphs (A) through (H) when performing farm labor contracting activities exclusively for such person.

(b) Subchapter I of this chapter does not apply to any agricultural employer or agricultural association or to any employee of such an employer or association.

(Pub. L. 97–470, § 4, Jan. 14, 1983, 96 Stat. 2585.)

REFERENCES IN TEXT

That Act, referred to in subsec. (a)(3)(B), is act June 23, 1947, ch. 120, 61 Stat. 136, as amended, known as the Labor Management Relations Act, 1947, which is classified principally to chapter 7 (§ 141 et seq.) of this title. For complete classification of this Act to the Code, see section 141 of this title and Tables.

SUBCHAPTER I—FARM LABOR CONTRACTORS

§ 1811. Certificate of registration required

(a) Persons engaged in any farm labor contracting activity

No person shall engage in any farm labor contracting activity, unless such person has a certificate of registration from the Secretary specifying which farm labor contracting activities such person is authorized to perform.

(b) Hire, employ, or use of any individual to perform farm labor contracting activities by farm labor contractor; liability of farm labor contractor for violations

A farm labor contractor shall not hire, employ, or use any individual to perform farm labor contracting activities unless such individual has a certificate of registration, or a certificate of registration as an employee of the farm labor contractor employer, which authorizes the activity for which such individual is hired, employed, or used. The farm labor contractor shall be held responsible for violations of this chapter or any regulation under this chapter by any employee regardless of whether the employee possesses a certificate of registration based on the contractor's certificate of registration.

(c) Possession and exhibition of certificate

Each registered farm labor contractor and registered farm labor contractor employee shall carry at all times while engaging in farm labor contracting activities a certificate of registration and, upon request, shall exhibit that certificate to all persons with whom they intend to deal as a farm labor contractor or farm labor contractor employee.

(d) Refusal or failure to produce certificate

The facilities and the services authorized by the Act of June 6, 1933 (29 U.S.C. 49 et seq.), known as the Wagner-Peyser Act, shall be denied to any farm labor contractor upon refusal or failure to produce, when asked, a certificate of registration.

(Pub. L. 97–470, title I, § 101, Jan. 14, 1983, 96 Stat. 2587.)

REFERENCES IN TEXT

The Wagner-Peyser Act, referred to in subsec. (d), is act June 6, 1933, ch. 49, 48 Stat. 113, as amended, which is classified generally to chapter 4B (§ 49 et seq.) of this title. For complete classification of this Act to the Code, see Short Title note set out under section 49 of this title and Tables.

§ 1812. Issuance of certificate of registration

The Secretary, after appropriate investigation and approval, shall issue a certificate of registration (including a certificate of registration as an employee of a farm labor contractor) to any person who has filed with the Secretary a written application containing the following:

(1) a declaration, subscribed and sworn to by the applicant, stating the applicant's permanent place of residence, the farm labor contracting activities for which the certificate is requested, and such other relevant information as the Secretary may require;

(2) a statement identifying each vehicle to be used to transport any migrant or seasonal agricultural worker and, if the vehicle is or will be owned or controlled by the applicant, documentation showing that the applicant is in compliance with the requirements of section 1841 of this title with respect to each such vehicle;

(3) a statement identifying each facility or real property to be used to house any migrant agricultural worker and, if the facility or real property is or will be owned or controlled by the applicant, documentation showing that the applicant is in compliance with section 1823 of this title with respect to each such facility or real property;

(4) a set of fingerprints of the applicant; and

(5) a declaration, subscribed and sworn to by the applicant, consenting to the designation

by a court of the Secretary as an agent available to accept service of summons in any action against the applicant, if the applicant has left the jurisdiction in which the action is commenced or otherwise has become unavailable to accept service.

(Pub. L. 97–470, title I, §102, Jan. 14, 1983, 96 Stat. 2587.)

§1813. Registration determinations

(a) Grounds for refusal to issue or renew, suspension, or revocation of certificate

In accordance with regulations, the Secretary may refuse to issue or renew, or may suspend or revoke, a certificate of registration (including a certificate of registration as an employee of a farm labor contractor) if the applicant or holder—

(1) has knowingly made any misrepresentation in the application for such certificate;

(2) is not the real party in interest in the application or certificate of registration and the real party in interest is a person who has been refused issuance or renewal of a certificate, has had a certificate suspended or revoked, or does not qualify under this section for a certificate;

(3) has failed to comply with this chapter or any regulation under this chapter;

(4) has failed—

(A) to pay any court judgment obtained by the Secretary or any other person under this chapter or any regulation under this chapter or under the Farm Labor Contractor Registration Act of 1963 [7 U.S.C. 2041 et seq.] or any regulation under such Act, or

(B) to comply with any final order issued by the Secretary as a result of a violation of this chapter or any regulation under this chapter or a violation of the Farm Labor Contractor Registration Act of 1963 or any regulation under such Act;

(5) has been convicted within the preceding five years—

(A) of any crime under State or Federal law relating to gambling, or to the sale, distribution or possession of alcoholic beverages, in connection with or incident to any farm labor contracting activities; or

(B) of any felony under State or Federal law involving robbery, bribery, extortion, embezzlement, grand larceny, burglary, arson, violation of narcotics laws, murder, rape, assault with intent to kill, assault which inflicts grievous bodily injury, prostitution, peonage, or smuggling or harboring individuals who have entered the United States illegally; or

(6) has been found to have violated paragraph (1) or (2) of section 1324a(a) of title 8.

(b) Administrative review procedures applicable

(1) The person who is refused the issuance or renewal of a certificate or whose certificate is suspended or revoked under subsection (a) of this section shall be afforded an opportunity for agency hearing, upon request made within thirty days after the date of issuance of the notice of the refusal, suspension, or revocation. In such hearing, all issues shall be determined on the record pursuant to section 554 of title 5. If no hearing is requested as herein provided, the refusal, suspension, or revocation shall constitute a final and unappealable order.

(2) If a hearing is requested, the initial agency decision shall be made by an administrative law judge, and such decision shall become the final order unless the Secretary modifies or vacates the decision. Notice of intent to modify or vacate the decision of the administrative law judge shall be issued to the parties within thirty days after the decision of the administrative law judge. A final order which takes effect under this paragraph shall be subject to review only as provided under subsection (c) of this section.

(c) Judicial review procedures applicable

Any person against whom an order has been entered after an agency hearing under this section may obtain review by the United States district court for any district in which he is located or the United States District Court for the District of Columbia by filing a notice of appeal in such court within thirty days from the date of such order, and simultaneously sending a copy of such notice by registered mail to the Secretary. The Secretary shall promptly certify and file in such court the record upon which the order was based. The findings of the Secretary shall be set aside only if found to be unsupported by substantial evidence as provided by section 706(2)(E) of title 5. Any final decision, order, or judgment of such District Court concerning such review shall be subject to appeal as provided in chapter 83 of title 28.

(Pub. L. 97–470, title I, §103, Jan. 14, 1983, 96 Stat. 2588; Pub. L. 99–603, title I, §101(b)(1)(B), Nov. 6, 1986, 100 Stat. 3372.)

REFERENCES IN TEXT

The Farm Labor Contractor Registration Act of 1963, referred to in subsec. (a)(4), is Pub. L. 88–582, Sept. 7, 1964, 78 Stat. 920, as amended, which was classified generally to chapter 52 (§2041 et seq.) of Title 7, Agriculture, and was repealed by Pub. L. 97–470, title V, §523, Jan. 14, 1983, 96 Stat. 2600. See section 1801 et seq. of this title.

AMENDMENTS

1986—Subsec. (a)(6). Pub. L. 99–603 added par. (6).

EFFECTIVE DATE OF 1986 AMENDMENT

Amendment by Pub. L. 99–603 applicable to employment, recruitment, referral, or utilization of services of an individual occurring on or after first day of seventh month beginning after Nov. 6, 1986, see section 101(b)(2) of Pub. L. 99–603, as amended, set out as a note under section 1802 of this title.

§1814. Transfer or assignment; expiration; renewal

(a) Transfer or assignment prohibited

A certificate of registration may not be transferred or assigned.

(b) Expiration; renewals

(1) Unless earlier suspended or revoked, a certificate shall expire twelve months from the date of issuance, except that (A) certificates issued under this chapter during the period beginning December 1, 1982, and ending November 30,

1983, may be issued for a period of up to twenty-four months for the purpose of an orderly transition to registration under this chapter, (B) a certificate may be temporarily extended by the filing of an application with the Secretary at least thirty days prior to its expiration date, and (C) the Secretary may renew a certificate for additional twelve-month periods or for periods in excess of twelve months but not in excess of twenty-four months.

(2) Eligibility for renewals for periods of more than twelve months shall be limited to farm labor contractors who have not been cited for a violation of this chapter, or any regulation under this chapter, or the Farm Labor Contractor Registration Act of 1963 [7 U.S.C. 2041 et seq.], or any regulation under such Act, during the preceding five years.

(Pub. L. 97–470, title I, §104, Jan. 14, 1983, 96 Stat. 2589.)

REFERENCES IN TEXT

The Farm Labor Contractor Registration Act of 1963, referred to in subsec. (b)(2), is Pub. L. 88–582, Sept. 7, 1964, 78 Stat. 920, as amended, which was classified generally to chapter 52 (§2041 et seq.) of Title 7, Agriculture, and was repealed by Pub. L. 97–470, title V, §523, Jan. 14, 1983, 96 Stat. 2600. See section 1801 et seq. of this title.

§1815. Notice of address change; amendment of certificate of registration

During the period for which the certificate of registration is in effect, each farm labor contractor shall—

(1) provide to the Secretary within thirty days a notice of each change of permanent place of residence; and

(2) apply to the Secretary to amend the certificate of registration whenever the farm labor contractor intends to—

(A) engage in another farm labor contracting activity,

(B) use, or cause to be used, another vehicle than that covered by the certificate to transport any migrant or seasonal agricultural worker, or

(C) use, or cause to be used, another real property or facility to house any migrant agricultural worker than that covered by the certificate.

(Pub. L. 97–470, title I, §105, Jan. 14, 1983, 96 Stat. 2589.)

§1816. Repealed. Pub. L. 99–603, title I, §101(b)(1)(C), Nov. 6, 1986, 100 Stat. 3372

Section, Pub. L. 97–470, title I, §106, Jan. 14, 1983, 96 Stat. 2589, prohibited employment of illegal aliens.

EFFECTIVE DATE OF REPEAL

Repeal applicable to employment, recruitment, referral, or utilization of services of an individual occurring on or after first day of seventh month beginning after Nov. 6, 1986, see section 101(b)(2) of Pub. L. 99–603, as amended, set out as an Effective Date of 1986 Amendment note under section 1802 of this title.

SUBCHAPTER II—MIGRANT AGRICULTURAL WORKER PROTECTIONS

§1821. Information and recordkeeping requirements

(a) Written disclosure requirements imposed upon recruiters

Each farm labor contractor, agricultural employer, and agricultural association which recruits any migrant agricultural worker shall ascertain and disclose in writing to each such worker who is recruited for employment the following information at the time of the worker's recruitment:

(1) the place of employment;

(2) the wage rates to be paid;

(3) the crops and kinds of activities on which the worker may be employed;

(4) the period of employment;

(5) the transportation, housing, and any other employee benefit to be provided, if any, and any costs to be charged for each of them;

(6) the existence of any strike or other concerted work stoppage, slowdown, or interruption of operations by employees at the place of employment;

(7) the existence of any arrangements with any owner or agent of any establishment in the area of employment under which the farm labor contractor, the agricultural employer, or the agricultural association is to receive a commission or any other benefit resulting from any sales by such establishment to the workers; and

(8) whether State workers' compensation insurance is provided, and, if so, the name of the State workers' compensation insurance carrier, the name of the policyholder of such insurance, the name and the telephone number of each person who must be notified of an injury or death, and the time period within which such notice must be given.

Compliance with the disclosure requirement of paragraph (8) for a migrant agricultural worker may be met if such worker is given a photocopy of any notice regarding workers' compensation insurance required by law of the State in which such worker is employed. Such worker shall be given such disclosure regarding workers' compensation at the time of recruitment or if sufficient information is unavailable at that time, at the earliest practicable time but in no event later than the commencement of work.

(b) Posting requirements imposed upon employers

Each farm labor contractor, agricultural employer, and agricultural association which employs any migrant agricultural worker shall, at the place of employment, post in a conspicuous place a poster provided by the Secretary setting forth the rights and protections afforded such workers under this chapter, including the right of a migrant agricultural worker to have, upon request, a written statement provided by the farm labor contractor, agricultural employer, or agricultural association, of the information described in subsection (a) of this section. Such employer shall provide upon request, a written statement of the information described in subsection (a) of this section.

(c) Posting or notice requirements imposed upon housing providers

Each farm labor contractor, agricultural employer, and agricultural association which provides housing for any migrant agricultural worker shall post in a conspicuous place or present to such worker a statement of the terms and conditions, if any, of occupancy of such housing.

(d) Recordkeeping and information requirements imposed upon employers

Each farm labor contractor, agricultural employer, and agricultural association which employs any migrant agricultural worker shall—

(1) with respect to each such worker, make, keep, and preserve records for three years of the following information:

(A) the basis on which wages are paid;

(B) the number of piecework units earned, if paid on a piecework basis;

(C) the number of hours worked;

(D) the total pay period earnings;

(E) the specific sums withheld and the purpose of each sum withheld; and

(F) the net pay; and

(2) provide to each such worker for each pay period, an itemized written statement of the information required by paragraph (1) of this subsection.

(e) Furnishing of records by farm labor contractor; maintenance of records by recipient

Each farm labor contractor shall provide to any other farm labor contractor, and to any agricultural employer and agricultural association to which such farm labor contractor has furnished migrant agricultural workers, copies of all records with respect to each such worker which such farm labor contractor is required to retain by subsection (d)(1) of this section. The recipient of such records shall keep them for a period of three years from the end of the period of employment.

(f) Prohibition on knowingly providing false or misleading information to workers

No farm labor contractor, agricultural employer, or agricultural association shall knowingly provide false or misleading information to any migrant agricultural worker concerning the terms, conditions, or existence of agricultural employment required to be disclosed by subsection (a), (b), (c), or (d) of this section.

(g) Form and language requirements

The information required to be disclosed by subsections (a) through (c) of this section to migrant agricultural workers shall be provided in written form. Such information shall be provided in English or, as necessary and reasonable, in Spanish or other language common to migrant agricultural workers who are not fluent or literate in English. The Department of Labor shall make forms available in English, Spanish, and other languages, as necessary, which may be used in providing workers with information required under this section.

(Pub. L. 97–470, title II, §201, Jan. 14, 1983, 96 Stat. 2590; Pub. L. 104–49, §4(a), Nov. 15, 1995, 109 Stat. 434.)

AMENDMENTS

1995—Subsec. (a). Pub. L. 104–49 added par. (8) and concluding provisions.

EFFECTIVE DATE OF 1995 AMENDMENT

Section 4(c) of Pub. L. 104–49 provided that: "The amendments made by subsections (a) and (b) [amending this section and section 1831 of this title] shall take effect upon the expiration of 90 days after the date final regulations are issued by the Secretary of Labor to implement such amendments." [Final regulations implementing Pub. L. 104–49 were signed May 13, 1996, published May 16, 1996, 61 F.R. 24858, and effective the same day.]

§1822. Wages, supplies, and other working arrangements

(a) Payment of wages

Each farm labor contractor, agricultural employer, and agricultural association which employs any migrant agricultural worker shall pay the wages owed to such worker when due.

(b) Purchase of goods or services by worker

No farm labor contractor, agricultural employer, or agricultural association shall require any migrant agricultural worker to purchase any goods or services solely from such farm labor contractor, agricultural employer, or agricultural association.

(c) Violation of terms of working arrangement

No farm labor contractor, agricultural employer, or agricultural association shall, without justification, violate the terms of any working arrangement made by that contractor, employer, or association with any migrant agricultural worker.

(Pub. L. 97–470, title II, §202, Jan. 14, 1983, 96 Stat. 2591.)

§1823. Safety and health of housing

(a) Compliance with substantive Federal and State safety and health standards

Except as provided in subsection (c) of this section, each person who owns or controls a facility or real property which is used as housing for migrant agricultural workers shall be responsible for ensuring that the facility or real property complies with substantive Federal and State safety and health standards applicable to that housing.

(b) Certification that applicable safety and health standards met; posting of certificate of occupancy; retention of certificate and availability for inspection and review; occupancy prior to inspection

(1) Except as provided in subsection (c) of this section and paragraph (2) of this subsection, no facility or real property may be occupied by any migrant agricultural worker unless either a State or local health authority or other appropriate agency has certified that the facility or property meets applicable safety and health standards. No person who owns or controls any such facility or property shall permit it to be occupied by any migrant agricultural worker unless a copy of the certification of occupancy is posted at the site. The receipt and posting of a certificate of occupancy does not relieve any

person of responsibilities under subsection (a) of this section. Each such person shall retain the original certification for three years and shall make it available for inspection and review in accordance with section 1862 of this title.

(2) Notwithstanding paragraph (1) of this subsection, if a request for the inspection of a facility or real property is made to the appropriate State or local agency at least forty-five days prior to the date on which it is occupied by migrant agricultural workers and such agency has not conducted an inspection by such date, the facility or property may be so occupied.

(c) Applicability to providers of housing on a commercial basis to the general public

This section does not apply to any person who, in the ordinary course of that person's business, regularly provides housing on a commercial basis to the general public and who provides housing to migrant agricultural workers of the same character and on the same or comparable terms and conditions as is provided to the general public.

(Pub. L. 97–470, title II, §203, Jan. 14, 1983, 96 Stat. 2591.)

SUBCHAPTER III—SEASONAL AGRICULTURAL WORKER PROTECTIONS

§ 1831. Information and recordkeeping requirements

(a) Written disclosure requirements imposed upon recruiters

(1) Each farm labor contractor, agricultural employer, and agricultural association which recruits any seasonal agricultural worker (other than day-haul workers described in section 1802(10)(A)(ii) of this title) shall ascertain and, upon request, disclose in writing the following information when an offer of employment is made to such worker:

(A) the place of employment;

(B) the wage rates to be paid;

(C) the crops and kinds of activities on which the worker may be employed;

(D) the period of employment;

(E) the transportation and any other employee benefit to be provided, if any, and any costs to be charged for each of them;

(F) the existence of any strike or other concerted work stoppage, slowdown, or interruption of operations by employees at the place of employment;

(G) the existence of any arrangements with any owner or agent of any establishment in the area of employment under which the farm labor contractor, the agricultural employer, or the agricultural association is to receive a commission or any other benefit resulting from any sales by such establishment to the workers; and

(H) whether State workers' compensation insurance is provided, and, if so, the name of the State workers' compensation insurance carrier, the name of the policyholder of such insurance, the name and the telephone number of each person who must be notified of an injury or death, and the time period within which such notice must be given.

Compliance with the disclosure requirement of subparagraph (H) may be met if such worker is given, upon request, a photocopy of any notice regarding workers' compensation insurance required by law of the State in which such worker is employed.

(2) Each farm labor contractor, agricultural employer, and agricultural association which recruits seasonal agricultural workers through use of a day-haul operation described in section 1802(10)(A)(ii) of this title shall ascertain and disclose in writing to the worker at the place of recruitment the information described in paragraph (1).

(b) Posting requirements imposed upon employers

Each farm labor contractor, agricultural employer, and agricultural association which employs any seasonal agricultural worker shall, at the place of employment, post in a conspicuous place a poster provided by the Secretary setting forth the rights and protections afforded such workers under this chapter, including the right of a seasonal agricultural worker to have, upon request, a written statement provided by the farm labor contractor, agricultural employer, or agricultural association, of the information described in subsection (a) of this section. Such employer shall provide, upon request, a written statement of the information described in subsection (a) of this section.

(c) Recordkeeping and information requirements imposed upon employers

Each farm labor contractor, agricultural employer, and agricultural association which employs any seasonal agricultural worker shall—

(1) with respect to each such worker, make, keep, and preserve records for three years of the following information:

(A) the basis on which wages are paid;

(B) the number of piecework units earned, if paid on a piecework basis;

(C) the number of hours worked;

(D) the total pay period earnings;

(E) the specific sums withheld and the purpose of each sum withheld; and

(F) the net pay; and

(2) provide to each such worker for each pay period, an itemized written statement of the information required by paragraph (1) of this subsection.

(d) Furnishing of records by farm labor contractor; maintenance of records by recipient

(1)[1] Each farm labor contractor shall provide to any other farm labor contractor and to any agricultural employer and agricultural association to which such farm labor contractor has furnished seasonal agricultural workers, copies of all records with respect to each such worker which such farm labor contractor is required to retain by subsection (c)(1) of this section. The recipient of these records shall keep them for a period of three years from the end of the period of employment.

(e) Prohibition on knowingly providing false or misleading information to workers

No farm labor contractor, agricultural employer, or agricultural association shall know-

[1] So in original. No par. (2) has been enacted.

ingly provide false or misleading information to any seasonal agricultural worker concerning the terms, conditions, or existence of agricultural employment required to be disclosed by subsection (a), (b), or (c) of this section.

(f) Form and language requirements

The information required to be disclosed by subsections (a) and (b) of this section to seasonal agricultural workers shall be provided in written form. Such information shall be provided in English or, as necessary and reasonable, in Spanish or other language common to seasonal agricultural workers who are not fluent or literate in English. The Department of Labor shall make forms available in English, Spanish, and other languages, as necessary, which may be used in providing workers with information required under this section.

(Pub. L. 97–470, title III, §301, Jan. 14, 1983, 96 Stat. 2592; Pub. L. 104–49, §4(b), Nov. 15, 1995, 109 Stat. 434.)

AMENDMENTS

1995—Subsec. (a)(1). Pub. L. 104–49 added subpar. (H) and concluding provisions.

EFFECTIVE DATE OF 1995 AMENDMENT

Amendment by Pub. L. 104–49 effective upon expiration of 90 days after the date final regulations are issued by Secretary of Labor to implement such amendment, see section 4(c) of Pub. L. 104–49, set out as a note under section 1821 of this title.

§1832. Wages, supplies, and other working arrangements

(a) Payment of wages

Each farm labor contractor, agricultural employer, and agricultural association which employs any seasonal agricultural worker shall pay the wages owed to such worker when due.

(b) Purchase of goods or services by worker

No farm labor contractor, agricultural employer, or agricultural association shall require any seasonal agricultural worker to purchase any goods or services solely from such farm labor contractor, agricultural employer, or agricultural association.

(c) Violation of terms of working arrangement

No farm labor contractor, agricultural employer, or agricultural association shall, without justification, violate the terms of any working arrangement made by that contractor, employer, or association with any seasonal agricultural worker.

(Pub. L. 97–470, title III, §302, Jan. 14, 1983, 96 Stat. 2593.)

SUBCHAPTER IV—FURTHER PROTECTIONS FOR MIGRANT AND SEASONAL AGRICULTURAL WORKERS

§1841. Motor vehicle safety

(a) Mode of transportation subject to coverage

(1) Except as provided in paragraph (2), this section applies to the transportation of any migrant or seasonal agricultural worker.

(2) This section does not apply to the transportation of any migrant or seasonal agricultural worker on a tractor, combine, harvester, picker, or other similar machinery and equipment while such worker is actually engaged in the planting, cultivating, or harvesting of any agricultural commodity or the care of livestock or poultry.

(b) Applicability of standards, licensing, and insurance requirements; promulgation of regulations for standards; criteria, etc., for regulations; amount of insurance required

(1) When using, or causing to be used, any vehicle for providing transportation to which this section applies, each agricultural employer, agricultural association, and farm labor contractor shall—

(A) ensure that such vehicle conforms to the standards prescribed by the Secretary under paragraph (2) of this subsection and other applicable Federal and State safety standards,

(B) ensure that each driver has a valid and appropriate license, as provided by State law, to operate the vehicle, and

(C) have an insurance policy or a liability bond that is in effect which insures the agricultural employer, the agricultural association, or the farm labor contractor against liability for damage to persons or property arising from the ownership, operation, or the causing to be operated, of any vehicle used to transport any migrant or seasonal agricultural worker.

(2)(A) For purposes of paragraph (1)(A), the Secretary shall prescribe such regulations as may be necessary to protect the health and safety of migrant and seasonal agricultural workers.

(B) To the extent consistent with the protection of the health and safety of migrant and seasonal agricultural workers, the Secretary shall, in promulgating regulations under subparagraph (A), consider, among other factors—

(i) the type of vehicle used,

(ii) the passenger capacity of the vehicle,

(iii) the distance which such workers will be carried in the vehicle,

(iv) the type of roads and highways on which such workers will be carried in the vehicle,

(v) the extent to which a proposed standard would cause an undue burden on agricultural employers, agricultural associations, or farm labor contractors.

(C) Standards prescribed by the Secretary under subparagraph (A) shall be in addition to, and shall not supersede or modify, any standard under part B of subtitle IV of title 49, or regulations issued thereunder, which is independently applicable to transportation to which this section applies. A violation of any such standard shall also constitute a violation under this chapter.

(D) In the event that the Secretary fails for any reason to prescribe standards under subparagraph (A) by the effective date of this chapter, the standards prescribed under section 31502 of title 49, relating to the transportation of migrant workers, shall, for purposes of paragraph (1)(A), be deemed to be the standards prescribed by the Secretary under this paragraph, and shall, as appropriate and reasonable in the circumstances, apply (i) without regard to the mileage and boundary line limitations contained in such section, and (ii) until superseded by standards actually prescribed by the Secretary in accordance with this paragraph.

(3) The level of insurance required under paragraph (1)(C) shall be determined by the Secretary considering at least the factors set forth in paragraph (2)(B) and similar farmworker transportation requirements under State law.

(c) Adjustments of insurance requirements in the event of workers' compensation coverage

If an agricultural employer, agricultural association, or farm labor contractor is the employer of any migrant or seasonal agricultural worker for purposes of a State workers' compensation law and such employer provides workers' compensation coverage for such worker in the case of bodily injury or death as provided by such State law, the following adjustments in the requirements of subsection (b)(1)(C) of this section relating to having an insurance policy or liability bond apply:

(1) No insurance policy or liability bond shall be required of the employer, if such workers are transported only under circumstances for which there is coverage under such State law.

(2) An insurance policy or liability bond shall be required of the employer for circumstances under which coverage for the transportation of such workers is not provided under such State law.

(d) Time for promulgation of regulations for standards implementing requirements; revision of standards

The Secretary shall, by regulations promulgated in accordance with section 1861 of this title not later than the effective date of this chapter, prescribe the standards required for the purposes of implementing this section. Any subsequent revision of such standards shall also be accomplished by regulation promulgated in accordance with such section.

(Pub. L. 97–470, title IV, §401, Jan. 14, 1983, 96 Stat. 2594; Pub. L. 104–49, §5(a), Nov. 15, 1995, 109 Stat. 434; Pub. L. 104–88, title III, §333, Dec. 29, 1995, 109 Stat. 953.)

References in Text

The effective date of this chapter, referred to in subsecs. (b)(2)(D) and (d), is the effective date of Pub. L. 97–470, which is ninety days from the date of enactment of Pub. L. 97–470, which was approved Jan. 14, 1983.

Codification

In subsec. (b)(2)(D), "section 31502 of title 49" substituted for "section 3102 of title 49" on authority of Pub. L. 103–272, §§1(c), (e), 6(b), July 5, 1994, 108 Stat. 745, 862, 1029, 1378. Previously, "section 3102 of title 49" substituted for "section 204(a)(3a) of the Interstate Commerce Act (49 U.S.C. 304(a)(3a))" on authority of Pub. L. 97–449, §6(b), Jan. 12, 1983, 96 Stat. 2443, the first section of which enacted subtitle I (§101 et seq.) and chapter 31 (§3101 et seq.) of subtitle II of Title 49, Transportation.

Amendments

1995—Subsec. (b)(2)(C). Pub. L. 104–88 substituted "part B of subtitle IV of title 49" for "part II of the Interstate Commerce Act, or any successor provision of subtitle IV of title 49".

Subsec. (b)(3). Pub. L. 104–49 amended par. (3) generally. Prior to amendment, par. (3) read as follows: "The level of the insurance required by paragraph (1)(C) shall be at least the amount currently required for common carriers of passengers under part II of the Interstate Commerce Act, and any successor provision of subtitle IV of title 49, and regulations prescribed thereunder."

Effective Date of 1995 Amendments

Amendment by Pub. L. 104–88 effective Jan. 1, 1996, see section 2 of Pub. L. 104–88, set out as an Effective Date note under section 701 of Title 49, Transportation.

Section 5(c) of Pub. L. 104–49 provided that: "The amendment made by subsection (a) [amending this section] takes effect upon the expiration of 180 days after the date of enactment of this Act [Nov. 15, 1995] or upon the issuance of final regulations under subsection (b) [set out below], whichever occurs first."

Regulations

Section 5(b) of Pub. L. 104–49 provided that: "Within 180 days of the date of the enactment of this Act [Nov. 15, 1995], the Secretary of Labor shall promulgate regulations establishing insurance levels under section 401(b)(3) of the Migrant and Seasonal Agricultural Worker Protection Act (29 U.S.C. 1841(b)(3)) as amended by subsection (a)." [Final regulations implementing Pub. L. 104–49 were signed May 13, 1996, published May 16, 1996, 61 F.R. 24858, and effective the same day.]

§1842. Confirmation of registration

No person shall utilize the services of any farm labor contractor to supply any migrant or seasonal agricultural worker unless the person first takes reasonable steps to determine that the farm labor contractor possesses a certificate of registration which is valid and which authorizes the activity for which the contractor is utilized. In making that determination, the person may rely upon either possession of a certificate of registration, or confirmation of such registration by the Department of Labor. The Secretary shall maintain a central public registry of all persons issued a certificate of registration.

(Pub. L. 97–470, title IV, §402, Jan. 14, 1983, 96 Stat. 2595.)

§1843. Information on employment conditions

Each farm labor contractor, without regard to any other provisions of this chapter, shall obtain at each place of employment and make available for inspection to every worker he furnishes for employment, a written statement of the conditions of such employment as described in sections 1821(b) and 1831(b) of this title.

(Pub. L. 97–470, title IV, §403, Jan. 14, 1983, 96 Stat. 2595.)

§1844. Compliance with written agreements

(a) Applicability to contracting activity or worker protection

No farm labor contractor shall violate, without justification, the terms of any written agreements made with an agricultural employer or an agricultural association pertaining to any contracting activity or worker protection under this chapter.

(b) Statutory liability

Written agreements under this section do not relieve a person of any responsibility that such person would otherwise have under this chapter.

(Pub. L. 97–470, title IV, §404, Jan. 14, 1983, 96 Stat. 2596.)

SUBCHAPTER V—GENERAL PROVISIONS

PART A—ENFORCEMENT PROVISIONS

§ 1851. Criminal sanctions

(a) Violations of chapter or regulations

Any person who willfully and knowingly violates this chapter or any regulation under this chapter shall be fined not more than $1,000 or sentenced to prison for a term not to exceed one year, or both. Upon conviction for any subsequent violation of this chapter or any regulation under this chapter, the defendant shall be fined not more than $10,000 or sentenced to prison for a term not to exceed three years, or both.

(b) Violations of section 1324a(a) of title 8

If a farm labor contractor who commits a violation of paragraph (1) or (2) of section 1324a(a) of title 8 has been refused issuance or renewal of, or has failed to obtain, a certificate of registration or is a farm labor contractor whose certificate has been suspended or revoked, the contractor shall, upon conviction, be fined not more than $10,000 or sentenced to prison for a term not to exceed three years, or both.

(Pub. L. 97–470, title V, § 501, Jan. 14, 1983, 96 Stat. 2596; Pub. L. 99–603, title I, § 101(b)(1)(D), Nov. 6, 1986, 100 Stat. 3372.)

AMENDMENTS

1986—Subsec. (b). Pub. L. 99–603 substituted "paragraph (1) or (2) of section 1324a(a) of title 8" for "section 1816 of this title".

EFFECTIVE DATE OF 1986 AMENDMENT

Amendment by Pub. L. 99–603 applicable to employment, recruitment, referral, or utilization of services of an individual occurring on or after first day of seventh month beginning after Nov. 6, 1986, see section 101(b)(2) of Pub. L. 99–603, as amended, set out as a note under section 1802 of this title.

§ 1852. Judicial enforcement

(a) Injunctive relief

The Secretary may petition any appropriate district court of the United States for temporary or permanent injunctive relief if the Secretary determines that this chapter, or any regulation under this chapter, has been violated.

(b) Control of civil litigation

Except as provided in section 518(a) of title 28, relating to litigation before the Supreme Court, the Solicitor of Labor may appear for and represent the Secretary in any civil litigation brought under this chapter, but all such litigation shall be subject to the direction and control of the Attorney General.

(Pub. L. 97–470, title V, § 502, Jan. 14, 1983, 96 Stat. 2596.)

§ 1853. Administrative sanctions

(a) Civil money penalties for violations; criteria for assessment

(1) Subject to paragraph (2), any person who commits a violation of this chapter or any regulation under this chapter, may be assessed a civil money penalty of not more than $1,000 for each violation.

(2) In determining the amount of any penalty to be assessed under paragraph (1), the Secretary shall take into account (A) the previous record of the person in terms of compliance with this chapter and with comparable requirements of the Farm Labor Contractor Registration Act of 1963 [7 U.S.C. 2041 et seq.], and with regulations promulgated under this chapter and such Act, and (B) the gravity of the violation.

(b) Administrative review

(1) The person assessed shall be afforded an opportunity for agency hearing, upon request made within thirty days after the date of issuance of the notice of assessment. In such hearing, all issues shall be determined on the record pursuant to section 554 of title 5. If no hearing is requested as herein provided, the assessment shall constitute a final and unappealable order.

(2) If a hearing is requested, the initial agency decision shall be made by an administrative law judge, and such decision shall become the final order unless the Secretary modifies or vacates the decision. Notice of intent to modify or vacate the decision of the administrative law judge shall be issued to the parties within thirty days after the decision of the administrative law judge. A final order which takes effect under this paragraph shall be subject to review only as provided under subsection (c) of this section.

(c) Judicial review

Any person against whom an order imposing a civil money penalty has been entered after an agency hearing under this section may obtain review by the United States district court for any district in which he is located or the United States District Court for the District of Columbia by filing a notice of appeal in such court within thirty days from the date of such order, and simultaneously sending a copy of such notice by registered mail to the Secretary. The Secretary shall promptly certify and file in such court the record upon which the penalty was imposed. The findings of the Secretary shall be set aside only if found to be unsupported by substantial evidence as provided by section 706(2)(E) of title 5. Any final decision, order, or judgment of such District Court concerning such review shall be subject to appeal as provided in chapter 83 of title 28.

(d) Failure to pay assessment; maintenance of action

If any person fails to pay an assessment after it has become a final and unappealable order, or after the court has entered final judgment in favor of the agency, the Secretary shall refer the matter to the Attorney General, who shall recover the amount assessed by action in the appropriate United States district court. In such action the validity and appropriateness of the final order imposing the penalty shall not be subject to review.

(e) Payment of penalties into Treasury of United States

All penalties collected under authority of this section shall be paid into the Treasury of the United States.

(Pub. L. 97–470, title V, § 503, Jan. 14, 1983, 96 Stat. 2596.)

REFERENCES IN TEXT

The Farm Labor Contractor Registration Act of 1963, referred to in subsec. (a)(2), is Pub. L. 88–582, Sept. 7, 1964, 78 Stat. 920, as amended, which was classified generally to chapter 52 (§ 2041 et seq.) of Title 7, Agriculture, and was repealed by Pub. L. 97–470, title V, § 523, Jan. 14, 1983, 96 Stat. 2600. See section 1801 et seq. of this title.

§ 1854. Private right of action

(a) Maintenance of civil action in district court by aggrieved person

Any person aggrieved by a violation of this chapter or any regulation under this chapter by a farm labor contractor, agricultural employer, agricultural association, or other person may file suit in any district court of the United States having jurisdiction of the parties, without respect to the amount in controversy and without regard to the citizenship of the parties and without regard to exhaustion of any alternative administrative remedies provided herein.

(b) Appointment of attorney and commencement of action

Upon application by a complainant and in such circumstances as the court may deem just, the court may appoint an attorney for such complainant and may authorize the commencement of the action.

(c) Award of damages or other equitable relief; amount; criteria; appeal

(1) If the court finds that the respondent has intentionally violated any provision of this chapter or any regulation under this chapter, it may award damages up to and including an amount equal to the amount of actual damages, or statutory damages of up to $500 per plaintiff per violation, or other equitable relief, except that (A) multiple infractions of a single provision of this chapter or of regulations under this chapter shall constitute only one violation for purposes of determining the amount of statutory damages due a plaintiff; and (B) if such complaint is certified as a class action, the court shall award no more than the lesser of up to $500 per plaintiff per violation, or up to $500,000 or other equitable relief.

(2) In determining the amount of damages to be awarded under paragraph (1), the court is authorized to consider whether an attempt was made to resolve the issues in dispute before the resort to litigation.

(3) Any civil action brought under this section shall be subject to appeal as provided in chapter 83 of title 28.

(d) Workers' compensation benefits; exclusive remedy

(1) Notwithstanding any other provision of this chapter, where a State workers' compensation law is applicable and coverage is provided for a migrant or seasonal agricultural worker, the workers' compensation benefits shall be the exclusive remedy for loss of such worker under this chapter in the case of bodily injury or death in accordance with such State's workers' compensation law.

(2) The exclusive remedy prescribed by paragraph (1) precludes the recovery under subsection (c) of this section of actual damages for loss from an injury or death but does not preclude recovery under subsection (c) of this section for statutory damages or equitable relief, except that such relief shall not include back or front pay or in any manner, directly or indirectly, expand or otherwise alter or affect (A) a recovery under a State workers' compensation law or (B) rights conferred under a State workers' compensation law.

(e) Expansion of statutory damages

If the court finds in an action which is brought by or for a worker under subsection (a) of this section in which a claim for actual damages is precluded because the worker's injury is covered by a State workers' compensation law as provided by subsection (d) of this section that—

(1)(A) the defendant in the action violated section 1841(b) of this title by knowingly requiring or permitting a driver to drive a vehicle for the transportation of migrant or seasonal agricultural workers while under the influence of alcohol or a controlled substance (as defined in section 802 of title 21) and the defendant had actual knowledge of the driver's condition, and

(B) such violation resulted in injury to or death of the migrant or seasonal worker by or for whom the action was brought and such injury or death arose out of and in the course of employment as determined under the State workers' compensation law,

(2)(A) the defendant violated a safety standard prescribed by the Secretary under section 1841(b) of this title which the defendant was determined in a previous judicial or administrative proceeding to have violated, and

(B) such safety violation resulted in an injury or death described in paragraph (1)(B),

(3)(A)(i) the defendant willfully disabled or removed a safety device prescribed by the Secretary under section 1841(b) of this title, or

(ii) the defendant in conscious disregard of the requirements of section 1841(b) of this title failed to provide a safety device required under such section, and

(B) such disablement, removal, or failure to provide a safety device resulted in an injury or death described in paragraph (1)(B), or

(4)(A) the defendant violated a safety standard prescribed by the Secretary under section 1841(b) of this title,

(B) such safety violation resulted in an injury or death described in paragraph (1)(B), and

(C) the defendant at the time of the violation of section 1841(b) of this title also was—

(i) an unregistered farm labor contractor in violation of section 1811(a) of this title, or

(ii) a person who utilized the services of a farm labor contractor of the type specified in clause (i) without taking reasonable steps to determine that the farm labor contractor possessed a valid certificate of registration authorizing the performance of the farm labor contracting activities which the contractor was requested or permitted to perform with the knowledge of such person,

the court shall award not more than $10,000 per plaintiff per violation with respect to whom the court made the finding described in paragraph

(1), (2), (3), or (4), except that multiple infractions of a single provision of this chapter shall constitute only one violation for purposes of determining the amount of statutory damages due to a plaintiff under this subsection and in the case of a class action, the court shall award not more than the lesser of up to $10,000 per plaintiff or up to $500,000 for all plaintiffs in such class action.

(f) Tolling of statute of limitations

If it is determined under a State workers' compensation law that the workers' compensation law is not applicable to a claim for bodily injury or death of a migrant or seasonal agricultural worker, the statute of limitations for bringing an action for actual damages for such injury or death under subsection (a) of this section shall be tolled for the period during which the claim for such injury or death under such State workers' compensation law was pending. The statute of limitations for an action for other actual damages, statutory damages, or equitable relief arising out of the same transaction or occurrence as the injury or death of the migrant or seasonal agricultural worker shall be tolled for the period during which the claim for such injury or death was pending under the State workers' compensation law.

(Pub. L. 97–470, title V, §504, Jan. 14, 1983, 96 Stat. 2597; Pub. L. 102–392, title III, §325(a), Oct. 6, 1992, 106 Stat. 1728; Pub. L. 104–49, §§1(a)(2), 2(a), 3, Nov. 15, 1995, 109 Stat. 432, 433.)

AMENDMENTS

1995—Subsec. (d). Pub. L. 104–49, §1(a)(2), amended subsec. (d) generally. Prior to amendment, subsec. (d) read as follows:

"(d)(1) Notwithstanding any other provision of this chapter, where a State workers' compensation law is applicable and coverage is provided for a migrant or seasonal agricultural worker, the workers' compensation benefits shall be the exclusive remedy for loss of such worker under this chapter in the case of bodily injury or death.

"(2) The exclusive remedy prescribed by paragraph (1) precludes the recovery under subsection (c) of this section of actual damages for loss from an injury or death but does not preclude recovery under subsection (c) of this section for statutory damages or an injunction."

Subsec. (e). Pub. L. 104–49, §2(a), added subsec. (e).

Subsec. (f). Pub. L. 104–49, §3, added subsec. (f).

1992—Subsec. (d). Pub. L. 102–392 added subsec. (d).

EFFECTIVE DATE OF 1995 AMENDMENT

Section 1(b) of Pub. L. 104–49 provided that: "The amendment made by subsection (a)(2) [amending this section] shall apply to all cases in which a final judgment has not been entered."

Section 2(b) of Pub. L. 104–49 provided that: "The amendment made by subsection (a) [amending this section] shall apply to all cases in which a final judgment has not been entered."

EFFECTIVE DATE OF 1992 AMENDMENT

Section 325(c) of Pub. L. 102–392 provided that the amendment of this section by section 325(a) of Pub. L. 102–392 would apply to actions commenced after Oct. 6, 1992, but not after the expiration of 9 months after such date, with waiver and extension provisions for certain actions, prior to repeal by Pub. L. 104–49, §1(a)(1), Nov. 15, 1995, 109 Stat. 432.

§1855. Discrimination prohibited

(a) Prohibited activities

No person shall intimidate, threaten, restrain, coerce, blacklist, discharge, or in any manner discriminate against any migrant or seasonal agricultural worker because such worker has, with just cause, filed any complaint or instituted, or caused to be instituted, any proceeding under or related to this chapter, or has testified or is about to testify in any such proceedings, or because of the exercise, with just cause, by such worker on behalf of himself or others of any right or protection afforded by this chapter.

(b) Proceedings for redress of violations

A migrant or seasonal agricultural worker who believes, with just cause, that he has been discriminated against by any person in violation of this section may, within 180 days after such violation occurs, file a complaint with the Secretary alleging such discrimination. Upon receipt of such complaint, the Secretary shall cause such investigation to be made as he deems appropriate. If upon such investigation, the Secretary determines that the provisions of this section have been violated, the Secretary shall bring an action in any appropriate United States district court against such person. In any such action the United States district courts shall have jurisdiction, for cause shown, to restrain violation of subsection (a) of this section and order all appropriate relief, including rehiring or reinstatement of the worker, with back pay, or damages.

(Pub. L. 97–470, title V, §505, Jan. 14, 1983, 96 Stat. 2598.)

§1856. Waiver of rights

Agreements by employees purporting to waive or to modify their rights under this chapter shall be void as contrary to public policy, except that a waiver or modification of rights in favor of the Secretary shall be valid for purposes of enforcement of this chapter.

(Pub. L. 97–470, title V, §506, Jan. 14, 1983, 96 Stat. 2598.)

PART B—ADMINISTRATIVE PROVISIONS

§1861. Rules and regulations

The Secretary may issue such rules and regulations as are necessary to carry out this chapter, consistent with the requirements of chapter 5 of title 5.

(Pub. L. 97–470, title V, §511, Jan. 14, 1983, 96 Stat. 2598.)

§1862. Authority to obtain information

(a) Investigation and inspection authority concerning places, records, etc.

To carry out this chapter the Secretary, either pursuant to a complaint or otherwise, shall, as may be appropriate, investigate, and in connection therewith, enter and inspect such places (including housing and vehicles) and such records (and make transcriptions thereof), question such persons and gather such information to determine compliance with this chapter, or regulations prescribed under this chapter.

(b) Attendance and testimony of witnesses, and production of evidence; subpena authority

The Secretary may issue subpenas requiring the attendance and testimony of witnesses or the production of any evidence in connection with such investigations. The Secretary may administer oaths, examine witnesses, and receive evidence. For the purpose of any hearing or investigation provided for in this chapter, the authority contained in sections 49 and 50 of title 15, relating to the attendance of witnesses and the production of books, papers, and documents, shall be available to the Secretary. The Secretary shall conduct investigations in a manner which protects the confidentiality of any complainant or other party who provides information to the Secretary in good faith.

(c) Prohibited activities

It shall be a violation of this chapter for any person to unlawfully resist, oppose, impede, intimidate, or interfere with any official of the Department of Labor assigned to perform an investigation, inspection, or law enforcement function pursuant to this chapter during the performance of such duties.

(Pub. L. 97–470, title V, §512, Jan. 14, 1983, 96 Stat. 2598.)

§ 1863. Agreements with Federal and State agencies

(a) Scope of agreements

The Secretary may enter into agreements with Federal and State agencies (1) to use their facilities and services, (2) to delegate, subject to subsection (b) of this section, to Federal and State agencies such authority, other than rulemaking, as may be useful in carrying out this chapter, and (3) to allocate or transfer funds to, or otherwise pay or reimburse, such agencies for expenses incurred pursuant to agreements under clause (1) or (2) of this section.

(b) Delegation of authority pursuant to written State plan

Any delegation to a State agency pursuant to subsection (a)(2) of this section shall be made only pursuant to a written State plan which—

(1) shall include a description of the functions to be performed, the methods of performing such functions, and the resources to be devoted to the performance of such functions; and

(2) provides assurances satisfactory to the Secretary that the State agency will comply with its description under paragraph (1) and that the State agency's performance of functions so delegated will be at least comparable to the performance of such functions by the Department of Labor.

(Pub. L. 97–470, title V, §513, Jan. 14, 1983, 96 Stat. 2599.)

PART C—MISCELLANEOUS PROVISIONS

§ 1871. State laws and regulations

This chapter is intended to supplement State law, and compliance with this chapter shall not excuse any person from compliance with appropriate State law and regulation.

(Pub. L. 97–470, title V, §521, Jan. 14, 1983, 96 Stat. 2599.)

§ 1872. Transition provision

The Secretary may deny a certificate of registration to any farm labor contractor, as defined in this chapter, who has a judgment outstanding against him under the Farm Labor Contractor Registration Act of 1963 (7 U.S.C. 2041 et seq.), or is subject to a final order of the Secretary under that Act assessing a civil money penalty which has not been paid. Any findings under the Farm Labor Contractor Registration Act of 1963 may also be applicable to determinations of willful and knowing violations under this chapter.

(Pub. L. 97–470, title V, §522, Jan. 14, 1983, 96 Stat. 2599.)

REFERENCES IN TEXT

The Farm Labor Contractor Registration Act of 1963, referred to in text, is Pub. L. 88–582, Sept. 7, 1964, 78 Stat. 920, as amended, which was classified generally to chapter 52 (§ 2041 et seq.) of Title 7, Agriculture, and was repealed by Pub. L. 97–470, title V, § 523, Jan. 14, 1983, 96 Stat. 2600. See section 1801 et seq. of this title.

CHAPTER 21—HELEN KELLER NATIONAL CENTER FOR YOUTHS AND ADULTS WHO ARE DEAF-BLIND

Sec.

§ 1901. Congressional findings

The Congress finds that—

(1) deaf-blindness is among the most severe of all forms of disabilities, and there is a great and continuing need for services and training to help individuals who are deaf-blind attain the highest possible level of development;

(2) due to the rubella epidemic of the 1960's, the rapidly increasing number of older persons many of whom are experiencing significant losses of both vision and hearing, and recent advances in medical technology that have sustained the lives of many severely disabled individuals, including individuals who are deaf-blind, who might not otherwise have survived, the need for services for individuals who are deaf-blind is even more pressing now than in the past;

(3) helping individuals who are deaf-blind to become self-sufficient, independent, and employable by providing the services and training necessary to accomplish that end will benefit the Nation, both economically and socially;

(4) the Helen Keller National Center for Youths and Adults who are Deaf-Blind is a vital national resource for meeting the needs of individuals who are deaf-blind and no State currently has the facilities or personnel to meet such needs;

(5) the Federal Government has made a substantial investment in capital, equipment, and operating funds for such Center since it was established; and

(6) it is in the national interest to continue to provide support for the Center, and it is a proper function of the Federal Government to be the primary source of such support.

(Pub. L. 98–221, title II, § 202, Feb. 22, 1984, 98 Stat. 32; Pub. L. 102–569, title IX, §§ 901, 908(a), (c)(1), Oct. 29, 1992, 106 Stat. 4482, 4485, 4486.)

PRIOR PROVISIONS

Provisions for the establishment, operation, and funding of the Helen Keller National Center for Deaf-Blind Youths and Adults, similar to those comprising this chapter, were contained in section 777c of this title prior to the repeal of that section and the enactment of this chapter by Pub. L. 98–221. Prior thereto provisions similar to those comprising this chapter and authorizing appropriations for fiscal years ending June 30, 1974, June 30, 1975, June 30, 1976, Sept. 30, 1977, and Sept. 30, 1978, for the establishment of the Helen Keller National Center for Deaf-Blind Youths and Adults were contained in former section 305 of Pub. L. 93–112, title III, Sept. 26, 1973, 87 Stat. 383, as amended by Pub. L. 93–516, title I, § 107, Dec. 7, 1974, 88 Stat. 1619; Pub. L. 93–651, title I, § 107, Nov. 21, 1974, 89 Stat. 2–4; Pub. L. 94–230, §§ 7, 11(b)(10), Mar. 15, 1976, 90 Stat. 212, 213; Pub. L. 94–288, §§ 1, 2, May 21, 1976, 90 Stat. 520, which was classified to section 775 of this title. Section 109(1) of Pub. L. 95–602 redesignated former section 305 as section 313 of Pub. L. 93–112. Section 313 of Pub. L. 93–112, as amended generally by section 116(2) of Pub. L. 95–602, was classified to section 777c of this title.

Prior similar provisions were also contained in former section 42a of this title.

AMENDMENTS

1992—Par. (1). Pub. L. 102–569, § 908(a), substituted "individuals who are deaf-blind" for "deaf-blind individuals".

Par. (2). Pub. L. 102–569, §§ 901(1), 908(a), inserted ", the rapidly increasing number of older persons many of whom are experiencing significant losses of both vision and hearing," after "1960's" and substituted "individuals who are deaf-blind" for "deaf-blind individuals" in two places.

Par. (3). Pub. L. 102–569, § 908(a), substituted "individuals who are deaf-blind" for "deaf-blind individuals".

Par. (4). Pub. L. 102–569, § 908(a), (c)(1), substituted "Youths and Adults who are Deaf-Blind" for "Deaf-Blind Youths and Adults" and "individuals who are deaf-blind" for "deaf-blind individuals".

Par. (5). Pub. L. 102–569, § 901(2), substituted "made a substantial investment" for "invested approximately $10,000,000".

SHORT TITLE

Section 201 of Pub. L. 98–221 provided that: "This title [enacting this chapter, amending section 777 of this title, and repealing section 777c of this title] may be cited as the 'Helen Keller National Center Act'."

§ 1902. Continued operation of Center

(a) Administration by Secretary of Education

The Secretary of Education shall continue to administer and support the Helen Keller National Center for Youths and Adults who are Deaf-Blind in the same manner as such Center was administered prior to February 22, 1984, to the extent such manner of administration is not inconsistent with any purpose described in subsection (b) of this section or any other requirement of this chapter.

(b) Purposes of Center

The purposes of the Center are to—

(1) provide specialized intensive services, or any other services, at the Center or anywhere else in the United States, which are necessary to encourage the maximum personal development of any individual who is deaf-blind;

(2) train family members of individuals who are deaf-blind at the Center or anywhere else in the United States, in order to assist family members in providing and obtaining appropriate services for the individual who is deaf-blind;

(3) train professionals and allied personnel at the Center or anywhere else in the United States to provide services to individuals who are deaf-blind; and

(4) conduct applied research, development programs, and demonstrations with respect to communication techniques, teaching methods, aids and devices, and delivery of services.

(Pub. L. 98–221, title II, § 203, Feb. 22, 1984, 98 Stat. 33; Pub. L. 102–569, title IX, §§ 902, 908, Oct. 29, 1992, 106 Stat. 4482, 4485.)

REFERENCES IN TEXT

This chapter, referred to in subsec. (a), was in the original "this title", meaning title II of Pub. L. 98–221, Feb. 22, 1984, 98 Stat. 32, which is classified generally to this chapter (§ 1901 et seq.). For complete classification of this title to the Code, see Short Title note set out under section 1901 of this title and Tables. For complete classification of this Act to the Code, see Short Title of 1984 Amendment note set out under section 701 of this title and Tables.

AMENDMENTS

1992—Pub. L. 102–569, § 908(c)(2), amended section catchline.

Subsec. (a). Pub. L. 102–569, §§ 902(1)–(3), 908(c)(1), redesignated subsec. (b) as (a), substituted "Youths and Adults who are Deaf-Blind" for "Deaf-Blind Youths and Adults", "prior to February 22, 1984" for "pursuant to section 313 of the Rehabilitation Act of 1973", and "subsection (b)" for "subsection (c)", and struck out former subsec. (a) which repealed section 777c of this title.

Subsecs. (b), (c). Pub. L. 102–569, §§ 902(2), (4), 908(a), (b), redesignated subsec. (c) as (b), substituted "individual who is deaf-blind" for "deaf-blind individual" in par. (1), added par. (2), redesignated former par. (2) as (3) and substituted "individuals who are deaf-blind" for "deaf-blind individuals", and redesignated former par. (3) as (4). Former subsec. (b) redesignated (a).

§ 1903. Audit; monitoring and evaluation

(a) The books and accounts of the Center shall be audited annually by an independent auditor in the manner prescribed by the Secretary and a report on each such audit shall be submitted by the auditor to the Secretary within 15 days following the completion of the audit and acceptance of the audit by the Center.

(b)(1) The Secretary shall establish procedures for monitoring, on a regular basis, the services performed and the training conducted by the Center.

(2) The Secretary shall, in addition to the regular monitoring required under paragraph (1), conduct an evaluation of the operation of the Center at the end of each fiscal year. A written report of such evaluation shall be submitted to the President, the Clerk of the House of Representatives, and the Secretary of the Senate

within one hundred and eighty days after the end of the fiscal year for which such evaluation was conducted. The first such report shall be submitted for fiscal year 1983.

(Pub. L. 98–221, title II, § 204, Feb. 22, 1984, 98 Stat. 33; Pub. L. 102–569, title IX, § 903, Oct. 29, 1992, 106 Stat. 4482.)

AMENDMENTS

1992—Subsec. (a). Pub. L. 102–569 substituted "within 15 days following the completion of the audit and acceptance of the audit by the Center" for "at such time as the Secretary shall prescribe".

TERMINATION OF REPORTING REQUIREMENTS

For termination, effective May 15, 2000, of provisions in subsec. (b)(2) of this section relating to submitting a written report to the Clerk of the House of Representatives and the Secretary of the Senate, see section 3003 of Pub. L. 104–66, as amended, set out as a note under section 1113 of Title 31, Money and Finance, and page 81 of House Document No. 103–7.

§ 1904. Authorization of appropriations

(a) There are authorized to be appropriated to carry out the provisions of this chapter such sums as may be necessary for each of the fiscal years 1999 through 2003. Such sums shall remain available until expended.

(b) Any appropriation Act containing any appropriation authorized by subsection (a) of this section shall contain a statement of the specific amount being made available to the Center.

(Pub. L. 98–221, title II, § 205, Feb. 22, 1984, 98 Stat. 33; Pub. L. 99–506, title IX, § 901, Oct. 21, 1986, 100 Stat. 1840; Pub. L. 100–630, title V, § 501, Nov. 7, 1988, 102 Stat. 3317; Pub. L. 102–52, § 9(a), June 6, 1991, 105 Stat. 263; Pub. L. 102–569, title IX, § 904, Oct. 29, 1992, 106 Stat. 4482; Pub. L. 105–220, title IV, § 412(a), Aug. 7, 1998, 112 Stat. 1241.)

AMENDMENTS

1998—Subsec. (a). Pub. L. 105–220 substituted "1999 through 2003" for "1993 through 1997".

1992—Subsec. (a). Pub. L. 102–569 substituted "1993 through 1997" for "1987 through 1992".

1991—Subsec. (a). Pub. L. 102–52 substituted "1992" for "1991".

1988—Subsec. (a). Pub. L. 100–630 substituted "1991" for "1990".

1986—Subsec. (a). Pub. L. 99–506 amended first sentence generally. Prior to amendment, first sentence read as follows: "There are authorized to be appropriated $4,000,000 for the fiscal year 1984, $4,200,000 for the fiscal year 1985, and $4,300,000 for the fiscal year 1986 to carry out the provisions of this chapter."

§ 1905. Definitions

For purposes of this chapter—

(1) the terms "Helen Keller National Center for Youths and Adults who are Deaf-Blind" and "Center" mean the Helen Keller National Center for Youths and Adults who are Deaf-Blind, and its affiliated network, operated pursuant to this chapter;

(2) the term "individual who is deaf-blind" means any individual—

(A)(i) who has a central visual acuity of 20/200 or less in the better eye with corrective lenses, or a field defect such that the peripheral diameter of visual field subtends an angular distance no greater than 20 degrees, or a progressive visual loss having a prognosis leading to one or both these conditions;

(ii) who has a chronic hearing impairment so severe that most speech cannot be understood with optimum amplification, or a progressive hearing loss having a prognosis leading to this condition; and

(iii) for whom the combination of impairments described in clauses (i) and (ii) cause extreme difficulty in attaining independence in daily life activities, achieving psychosocial adjustment, or obtaining a vocation;

(B) who despite the inability to be measured accurately for hearing and vision loss due to cognitive or behavioral constraints, or both, can be determined through functional and performance assessment to have severe hearing and visual disabilities that cause extreme difficulty in attaining independence in daily life activities, achieving psychosocial adjustment, or obtaining vocational objectives; or

(C) meets such other requirements as the Secretary may prescribe by regulation; and

(3) the term "Secretary" means the Secretary of Education.

(Pub. L. 98–221, title II, § 206, Feb. 22, 1984, 98 Stat. 34; Pub. L. 102–569, title IX, §§ 905, 908(c)(1), Oct. 29, 1992, 106 Stat. 4482, 4486.)

AMENDMENTS

1992—Par. (1). Pub. L. 102–569, §§ 905(1), 908(c)(1), substituted "Youths and Adults who are Deaf-Blind" for "Deaf-Blind Youths and Adults" in two places and struck out "section 313 of the Rehabilitation Act of 1973 and continued under" after "operated pursuant to".

Par. (2). Pub. L. 102–569, § 905(2), amended par. (2) generally, substituting present provisions for provisions defining "deaf-blind individual".

§ 1906. Construction; effect on agreements

This chapter shall not be construed as modifying or affecting any agreement between the Department of Education or any other department or agency of the United States and the Helen Keller Services for the Blind, Incorporated, or any successor to or assignee of such corporation, with respect to the Center.

(Pub. L. 98–221, title II, § 207, Feb. 22, 1984, 98 Stat. 34; Pub. L. 102–569, title IX, § 906, Oct. 29, 1992, 106 Stat. 4483.)

AMENDMENTS

1992—Pub. L. 102–569 substituted "Helen Keller Services for the Blind, Incorporated" for "Industrial Home for the Blind, Incorporated".

§ 1907. Helen Keller National Center Federal Endowment Fund

(a) Establishment

The Secretary and the Board of Directors of the Helen Keller National Center are authorized to establish the Helen Keller National Center Federal Endowment Fund (hereafter in this section referred to as the "Endowment Fund") in accordance with the provisions of this section, to promote the financial independence of the Helen Keller National Center. The Secretary and the Board may enter into such agreements as may be necessary to carry out the purposes of this section.

(b) Federal payments

(1) In general

The Secretary shall make payments to the Endowment Fund from amounts appropriated pursuant to subsection (h) of this section, consistent with the provisions of this section.

(2) Amount of payment

Subject to the availability of appropriations, the Secretary shall make payments to the Endowment Fund in amounts equal to sums contributed to the Endowment Fund from non-Federal sources (excluding transfers from other endowment funds of the Center).

(c) Investments

(1) In general

The Center, in investing the Endowment Fund corpus and income, shall exercise the judgment and care, under the prevailing circumstances, which a person of prudence, discretion, and intelligence would exercise in the management of that person's own business affairs.

(2) Limitations

(A) Federally insured investments and other investments

The Endowment Fund corpus and income shall be invested in federally insured bank savings accounts or comparable interest bearing accounts, certificates of deposit, money market funds, mutual funds, obligations of the United States, or other low-risk instruments and securities in which a regulated insurance company may invest under the laws of the State of New York.

(B) Real estate

The Endowment Fund corpus and income may not be invested in real estate.

(C) Conflict of interest

The Endowment Fund corpus or income may not be invested in instruments or securities issued by an organization in which an executive officer is a controlling shareholder, director, or owner within the meaning of Federal securities laws and other applicable laws.

(D) Encumbrances

The Center may not assign, hypothecate, encumber, or create a lien on the Endowment Fund corpus without specific written authorization of the Secretary.

(d) Withdrawals and expenditures

(1) In general

For a 20-year period following the receipt of a payment under this section, the Center shall not withdraw or expend the Federal payment or matching contribution made to the Endowment Fund corpus. On the expiration of such period, the Center may use the Endowment Fund corpus plus any of the Endowment Fund income for any purpose that benefits individuals who are deaf-blind.

(2) Operational and commercial expenses

(A) In general

The Helen Keller National Center may withdraw or expend the Endowment Fund income for any expenses necessary for the operation of the Center, including expenses of operations and maintenance, administration, academic and support personnel, construction and renovation, community and client services programs, technical assistance, and research.

(B) Limitation

The Center may not withdraw or expend the Endowment Fund income for any commercial purpose.

(3) Limitations and waiver of limitations

(A) In general

Except as provided in subparagraph (B), the Center shall not withdraw or expend more than 50 percent of the total aggregate Endowment Fund income earned prior to the time of withdrawal or expenditure.

(B) Exception

The Secretary may permit the Center to withdraw or expend more than 50 percent of its total aggregate endowment income where the Center demonstrates to the Secretary's satisfaction that such withdrawal or expenditure is necessary because of—

(i) a financial emergency, such as a pending insolvency or temporary liquidity problem;

(ii) a life-threatening situation occasioned by a natural disaster or arson; or

(iii) another unusual occurrence or exigent circumstance.

(e) Reporting requirements

(1) Financial records

The Helen Keller National Center shall keep accurate financial records relating to the operation of the Endowment Fund.

(2) Audit and report

(A) Audit

The Center shall arrange for the conduct of an annual financial and compliance audit of the Endowment Fund in the manner prescribed by the Secretary pursuant to section 1903(a) of this title.

(B) Report

The Center shall submit a copy of the report on the audit required under subparagraph (A) to the Secretary within 15 days after completion of the audit and acceptance of the audit by the Center.

(3) Annual report

Not later than 60 days after the end of each fiscal year, the Center shall provide to the Secretary an annual report on the uses of funds provided by the Federal endowment program authorized under this section. Such report shall contain such information, and be in such form as the Secretary may require.

(f) Recovery of payments

After notice and an opportunity for a hearing, the Secretary is authorized to recover any Federal payments made under this section if the Helen Keller National Center—

(1) makes a withdrawal or expenditure from the Endowment Fund corpus or income which is not consistent with the provisions of this section;

(2) fails to comply with the investment standards and limitations under this section; or

(3) fails to account properly to the Secretary concerning the investment of or expenditures from the Endowment Fund corpus or income.

(g) Definitions

For the purposes of this section:

(1) Endowment fund

The term "endowment fund" means a fund, or a tax-exempt foundation, established and maintained by the Helen Keller National Center for the purpose of generating income for the support of the Center.

(2) Endowment Fund corpus

The term "Endowment Fund corpus" means an amount equal to the Federal payments made to the Endowment Fund and amounts contributed to the Endowment Fund from non-Federal sources.

(3) Endowment Fund income

The term "Endowment Fund income" means an amount equal to the total market value of the Endowment Fund minus the Endowment Fund corpus.

(h) Authorization of appropriations

There are authorized to be appropriated to carry out this section, such sums as may be necessary for each of the fiscal years 1999 through 2003. Such sums shall remain available until expended.

(Pub. L. 98–221, title II, § 208, as added Pub. L. 102–569, title IX, § 907, Oct. 29, 1992, 106 Stat. 4483; amended Pub. L. 105–220, title IV, § 412(b), Aug. 7, 1998, 112 Stat. 1241.)

AMENDMENTS

1998—Subsec. (h). Pub. L. 105–220 substituted "1999 through 2003" for "1993 through 1997".

§ 1908. Registry

(a) In general

To assist the Center in providing services to individuals who are deaf-blind, the Center may establish and maintain registries of such individuals in each of the regional field offices of the network of the Center.

(b) Voluntary provision of information

No individual who is deaf-blind may be required to provide information to the Center for any purpose with respect to a registry established under subsection (a) of this section.

(c) Nondisclosure

The Center (including the network of the Center) may not disclose information contained in a registry established under subsection (a) of this section to any individual or organization that is not affiliated with the Center, unless the individual to whom the information relates provides specific written authorization for the Center to disclose the information.

(d) Privacy rights

The requirements of section 552a of title 5 (commonly known as the "Privacy Act of 1974") shall apply to personally identifiable information contained in the registries established by the Center under subsection (a) of this section, in the same manner and to the same extent as such requirements apply to a record of an agency.

(e) Removal of information

On the request of an individual, the Center shall remove all information relating to the individual from any registry established under subsection (a) of this section.

(Pub. L. 98–221, title II, § 209, as added Pub. L. 105–220, title IV, § 412(c), Aug. 7, 1998, 112 Stat. 1241.)

CHAPTER 22—EMPLOYEE POLYGRAPH PROTECTION

§ 2001. Definitions

As used in this chapter:

(1) Commerce

The term "commerce" has the meaning provided by section 203(b) of this title.

(2) Employer

The term "employer" includes any person acting directly or indirectly in the interest of an employer in relation to an employee or prospective employee.

(3) Lie detector

The term "lie detector" includes a polygraph, deceptograph, voice stress analyzer, psychological stress evaluator, or any other similar device (whether mechanical or electrical) that is used, or the results of which are used, for the purpose of rendering a diagnostic opinion regarding the honesty or dishonesty of an individual.

(4) Polygraph

The term "polygraph" means an instrument that—

(A) records continuously, visually, permanently, and simultaneously changes in cardiovascular, respiratory, and electrodermal patterns as minimum instrumentation standards; and

(B) is used, or the results of which are used, for the purpose of rendering a diagnostic opinion regarding the honesty or dishonesty of an individual.

(5) Secretary

The term "Secretary" means the Secretary of Labor.

(Pub. L. 100–347, §2, June 27, 1988, 102 Stat. 646.)

EFFECTIVE DATE

Section 11 of Pub. L. 100–347 provided that:

"(a) IN GENERAL.—Except as provided in subsection (b), this Act [enacting this chapter] shall become effective 6 months after the date of enactment of this Act [June 27, 1988].

"(b) REGULATIONS.—Not later than 90 days after the date of enactment of this Act, the Secretary shall issue such rules and regulations as may be necessary or appropriate to carry out this Act."

SHORT TITLE

Section 1 of Pub. L. 100–347 provided that: "This Act [enacting this chapter] may be cited as the 'Employee Polygraph Protection Act of 1988'."

§2002. Prohibitions on lie detector use

Except as provided in sections 2006 and 2007 of this title, it shall be unlawful for any employer engaged in or affecting commerce or in the production of goods for commerce—

(1) directly or indirectly, to require, request, suggest, or cause any employee or prospective employee to take or submit to any lie detector test;

(2) to use, accept, refer to, or inquire concerning the results of any lie detector test of any employee or prospective employee;

(3) to discharge, discipline, discriminate against in any manner, or deny employment or promotion to, or threaten to take any such action against—

(A) any employee or prospective employee who refuses, declines, or fails to take or submit to any lie detector test, or

(B) any employee or prospective employee on the basis of the results of any lie detector test; or

(4) to discharge, discipline, discriminate against in any manner, or deny employment or promotion to, or threaten to take any such action against, any employee or prospective employee because—

(A) such employee or prospective employee has filed any complaint or instituted or caused to be instituted any proceeding under or related to this chapter,

(B) such employee or prospective employee has testified or is about to testify in any such proceeding, or

(C) of the exercise by such employee or prospective employee, on behalf of such employee or another person, of any right afforded by this chapter.

(Pub. L. 100–347, §3, June 27, 1988, 102 Stat. 646.)

§2003. Notice of protection

The Secretary shall prepare, have printed, and distribute a notice setting forth excerpts from, or summaries of, the pertinent provisions of this chapter. Each employer shall post and maintain such notice in conspicuous places on its premises where notices to employees and applicants to employment are customarily posted.

(Pub. L. 100–347, §4, June 27, 1988, 102 Stat. 647.)

§2004. Authority of Secretary

(a) In general

The Secretary shall—

(1) issue such rules and regulations as may be necessary or appropriate to carry out this chapter;

(2) cooperate with regional, State, local, and other agencies, and cooperate with and furnish technical assistance to employers, labor organizations, and employment agencies to aid in effectuating the purposes of this chapter; and

(3) make investigations and inspections and require the keeping of records necessary or appropriate for the administration of this chapter.

(b) Subpoena authority

For the purpose of any hearing or investigation under this chapter, the Secretary shall have the authority contained in sections 49 and 50 of title 15.

(Pub. L. 100–347, §5, June 27, 1988, 102 Stat. 647.)

§2005. Enforcement provisions

(a) Civil penalties

(1) In general

Subject to paragraph (2), any employer who violates any provision of this chapter may be assessed a civil penalty of not more than $10,000.

(2) Determination of amount

In determining the amount of any penalty under paragraph (1), the Secretary shall take into account the previous record of the person in terms of compliance with this chapter and the gravity of the violation.

(3) Collection

Any civil penalty assessed under this subsection shall be collected in the same manner as is required by subsections (b) through (e) of section 1853 of this title with respect to civil penalties assessed under subsection (a) of such section.

(b) Injunctive actions by Secretary

The Secretary may bring an action under this section to restrain violations of this chapter. The Solicitor of Labor may appear for and represent the Secretary in any litigation brought under this chapter. In any action brought under this section, the district courts of the United States shall have jurisdiction, for cause shown, to issue temporary or permanent restraining orders and injunctions to require compliance with this chapter, including such legal or equitable relief incident thereto as may be appropriate, including, but not limited to, employment, reinstatement, promotion, and the payment of lost wages and benefits.

(c) Private civil actions

(1) Liability

An employer who violates this chapter shall be liable to the employee or prospective employee affected by such violation. Such employer shall be liable for such legal or equitable relief as may be appropriate, including, but not limited to, employment, reinstatement, promotion, and the payment of lost wages and benefits.

(2) Court

An action to recover the liability prescribed in paragraph (1) may be maintained against the employer in any Federal or State court of competent jurisdiction by an employee or prospective employee for or on behalf of such employee, prospective employee, and other employees or prospective employees similarly situated. No such action may be commenced more than 3 years after the date of the alleged violation.

(3) Costs

The court, in its discretion, may allow the prevailing party (other than the United States) reasonable costs, including attorney's fees.

(d) Waiver of rights prohibited

The rights and procedures provided by this chapter may not be waived by contract or otherwise, unless such waiver is part of a written settlement agreed to and signed by the parties to the pending action or complaint under this chapter.

(Pub. L. 100–347, §6, June 27, 1988, 102 Stat. 647.)

§ 2006. Exemptions

(a) No application to governmental employers

This chapter shall not apply with respect to the United States Government, any State or local government, or any political subdivision of a State or local government.

(b) National defense and security exemption

(1) National defense

Nothing in this chapter shall be construed to prohibit the administration, by the Federal Government, in the performance of any counterintelligence function, of any lie detector test to—

(A) any expert or consultant under contract to the Department of Defense or any employee of any contractor of such Department; or

(B) any expert or consultant under contract with the Department of Energy in connection with the atomic energy defense activities of such Department or any employee of any contractor of such Department in connection with such activities.

(2) Security

Nothing in this chapter shall be construed to prohibit the administration, by the Federal Government, in the performance of any intelligence or counterintelligence function, of any lie detector test to—

(A)(i) any individual employed by, assigned to, or detailed to, the National Security Agency, the Defense Intelligence Agency, the National Geospatial-Intelligence Agency, or the Central Intelligence Agency,

(ii) any expert or consultant under contract to any such agency,

(iii) any employee of a contractor to any such agency,

(iv) any individual applying for a position in any such agency, or

(v) any individual assigned to a space where sensitive cryptologic information is produced, processed, or stored for any such agency; or

(B) any expert, or consultant (or employee of such expert or consultant) under contract with any Federal Government department, agency, or program whose duties involve access to information that has been classified at the level of top secret or designated as being within a special access program under section 4.2(a) of Executive Order 12356 (or a successor Executive order).

(c) FBI contractors exemption

Nothing in this chapter shall be construed to prohibit the administration, by the Federal Government, in the performance of any counterintelligence function, of any lie detector test to an employee of a contractor of the Federal Bureau of Investigation of the Department of Justice who is engaged in the performance of any work under the contract with such Bureau.

(d) Limited exemption for ongoing investigations

Subject to sections 2007 and 2009 of this title, this chapter shall not prohibit an employer from requesting an employee to submit to a polygraph test if—

(1) the test is administered in connection with an ongoing investigation involving economic loss or injury to the employer's business, such as theft, embezzlement, misappropriation, or an act of unlawful industrial espionage or sabotage;

(2) the employee had access to the property that is the subject of the investigation;

(3) the employer has a reasonable suspicion that the employee was involved in the incident or activity under investigation; and

(4) the employer executes a statement, provided to the examinee before the test, that—

(A) sets forth with particularity the specific incident or activity being investigated and the basis for testing particular employees,

(B) is signed by a person (other than a polygraph examiner) authorized to legally bind the employer,

(C) is retained by the employer for at least 3 years, and

(D) contains at a minimum—

(i) an identification of the specific economic loss or injury to the business of the employer,

(ii) a statement indicating that the employee had access to the property that is the subject of the investigation, and

(iii) a statement describing the basis of the employer's reasonable suspicion that the employee was involved in the incident or activity under investigation.

(e) Exemption for security services

(1) In general

Subject to paragraph (2) and sections 2007 and 2009 of this title, this chapter shall not prohibit the use of polygraph tests on prospective employees by any private employer whose primary business purpose consists of providing armored car personnel, personnel engaged in the design, installation, and maintenance of security alarm systems, or other uniformed or plainclothes security personnel and whose function includes protection of—

(A) facilities, materials, or operations having a significant impact on the health or safety of any State or political subdivision thereof, or the national security of the United States, as determined under rules and regulations issued by the Secretary within 90 days after June 27, 1988, including—

(i) facilities engaged in the production, transmission, or distribution of electric or nuclear power,

(ii) public water supply facilities,

(iii) shipments or storage of radioactive or other toxic waste materials, and

(iv) public transportation, or

(B) currency, negotiable securities, precious commodities or instruments, or proprietary information.

(2) Access

The exemption provided under this subsection shall not apply if the test is administered to a prospective employee who would not be employed to protect facilities, materials, operations, or assets referred to in paragraph (1).

(f) Exemption for drug security, drug theft, or drug diversion investigations

(1) In general

Subject to paragraph (2) and sections 2007 and 2009 of this title, this chapter shall not prohibit the use of a polygraph test by any employer authorized to manufacture, distribute, or dispense a controlled substance listed in schedule I, II, III, or IV of section 812 of title 21.

(2) Access

The exemption provided under this subsection shall apply—

(A) if the test is administered to a prospective employee who would have direct access to the manufacture, storage, distribution, or sale of any such controlled substance; or

(B) in the case of a test administered to a current employee, if—

(i) the test is administered in connection with an ongoing investigation of criminal or other misconduct involving, or potentially involving, loss or injury to the manufacture, distribution, or dispensing of any such controlled substance by such employer, and

(ii) the employee had access to the person or property that is the subject of the investigation.

(Pub. L. 100–347, § 7, June 27, 1988, 102 Stat. 648; Pub. L. 103–359, title V, § 501(n), Oct. 14, 1994, 108 Stat. 3430; Pub. L. 104–201, div. A, title XI, § 1122(b)(3), Sept. 23, 1996, 110 Stat. 2687; Pub. L. 110–417, [div. A], title IX, § 931(b)(3), Oct. 14, 2008, 122 Stat. 4575.)

REFERENCES IN TEXT

Executive Order 12356, referred to in subsec. (b)(2)(B), was Ex. Ord. No. 12356, Apr. 2, 1982, 47 F.R. 14874, 15557, which was set out as a note under section 435 of Title 50, War and National Defense, prior to revocation by Ex. Ord. No. 12958, § 6.1(d), Apr. 17, 1995, 60 F.R. 19843, set out as a note under section 435 of Title 50. For provisions relating to special access programs, see section 4.4 of Ex. Ord. No. 12958.

AMENDMENTS

2008—Subsec. (b)(2)(A)(i). Pub. L. 110–417 substituted "National Geospatial-Intelligence Agency" for "National Imagery and Mapping Agency".

1996—Subsec. (b)(2)(A)(i). Pub. L. 104–201 substituted "National Imagery and Mapping Agency" for "Central Imagery Office".

1994—Subsec. (b)(2)(A)(i). Pub. L. 103–359 inserted "the Central Imagery Office," after "Defense Intelligence Agency,".

EFFECTIVE DATE OF 1996 AMENDMENT

Amendment by Pub. L. 104–201 effective Oct. 1, 1996, see section 1124 of Pub. L. 104–201, set out as a note under section 193 of Title 10, Armed Forces.

§ 2007. Restrictions on use of exemptions

(a) Test as basis for adverse employment action

(1) Under ongoing investigations exemption

Except as provided in paragraph (2), the exemption under subsection (d) of section 2006 of this title shall not apply if an employee is discharged, disciplined, denied employment or promotion, or otherwise discriminated against in any manner on the basis of the analysis of a polygraph test chart or the refusal to take a polygraph test, without additional supporting evidence. The evidence required by such subsection may serve as additional supporting evidence.

(2) Under other exemptions

In the case of an exemption described in subsection (e) or (f) of such section, the exemption shall not apply if the results of an analysis of a polygraph test chart are used, or the refusal to take a polygraph test is used, as the sole basis upon which an adverse employment action described in paragraph (1) is taken against an employee or prospective employee.

(b) Rights of examinee

The exemptions provided under subsections (d), (e), and (f) of section 2006 of this title shall not apply unless the requirements described in the following paragraphs are met:

(1) All phases

Throughout all phases of the test—

(A) the examinee shall be permitted to terminate the test at any time;

(B) the examinee is not asked questions in a manner designed to degrade, or needlessly intrude on, such examinee;

(C) the examinee is not asked any question concerning—

(i) religious beliefs or affiliations,

(ii) beliefs or opinions regarding racial matters,

(iii) political beliefs or affiliations,

(iv) any matter relating to sexual behavior; and

(v) beliefs, affiliations, opinions, or lawful activities regarding unions or labor organizations; and

(D) the examiner does not conduct the test if there is sufficient written evidence by a physician that the examinee is suffering from a medical or psychological condition or undergoing treatment that might cause abnormal responses during the actual testing phase.

(2) Pretest phase

During the pretest phase, the prospective examinee—

(A) is provided with reasonable written notice of the date, time, and location of the test, and of such examinee's right to obtain and consult with legal counsel or an employee representative before each phase of the test;

(B) is informed in writing of the nature and characteristics of the tests and of the instruments involved;

(C) is informed, in writing—

(i) whether the testing area contains a two-way mirror, a camera, or any other device through which the test can be observed,

(ii) whether any other device, including any device for recording or monitoring the test, will be used, or

(iii) that the employer or the examinee may (with mutual knowledge) make a recording of the test;

(D) is read and signs a written notice informing such examinee—

(i) that the examinee cannot be required to take the test as a condition of employment,

(ii) that any statement made during the test may constitute additional supporting evidence for the purposes of an adverse employment action described in subsection (a) of this section,

(iii) of the limitations imposed under this section,

(iv) of the legal rights and remedies available to the examinee if the polygraph test is not conducted in accordance with this chapter, and

(v) of the legal rights and remedies of the employer under this chapter (including the rights of the employer under section 2008(c)(2) of this title); and

(E) is provided an opportunity to review all questions to be asked during the test and is informed of the right to terminate the test at any time.

(3) Actual testing phase

During the actual testing phase, the examiner does not ask such examinee any question relevant during the test that was not presented in writing for review to such examinee before the test.

(4) Post-test phase

Before any adverse employment action, the employer shall—

(A) further interview the examinee on the basis of the results of the test; and

(B) provide the examinee with—

(i) a written copy of any opinion or conclusion rendered as a result of the test, and

(ii) a copy of the questions asked during the test along with the corresponding charted responses.

(5) Maximum number and minimum duration of tests

The examiner shall not conduct and complete more than five polygraph tests on a calendar day on which the test is given, and shall not conduct any such test for less than a 90-minute duration.

(c) Qualifications and requirements of examiners

The exemptions provided under subsections (d), (e), and (f) of section 2006 of this title shall not apply unless the individual who conducts the polygraph test satisfies the requirements under the following paragraphs:

(1) Qualifications

The examiner—

(A) has a valid and current license granted by licensing and regulatory authorities in the State in which the test is to be conducted, if so required by the State; and

(B) maintains a minimum of a $50,000 bond or an equivalent amount of professional liability coverage.

(2) Requirements

The examiner—

(A) renders any opinion or conclusion regarding the test—

(i) in writing and solely on the basis of an analysis of polygraph test charts,

(ii) that does not contain information other than admissions, information, case facts, and interpretation of the charts relevant to the purpose and stated objectives of the test, and

(iii) that does not include any recommendation concerning the employment of the examinee; and

(B) maintains all opinions, reports, charts, written questions, lists, and other records relating to the test for a minimum period of 3 years after administration of the test.

(Pub. L. 100–347, §8, June 27, 1988, 102 Stat. 650.)

§ 2008. Disclosure of information

(a) In general

A person, other than the examinee, may not disclose information obtained during a polygraph test, except as provided in this section.

(b) Permitted disclosures

A polygraph examiner may disclose information acquired from a polygraph test only to—

(1) the examinee or any other person specifically designated in writing by the examinee;

(2) the employer that requested the test; or

(3) any court, governmental agency, arbitrator, or mediator, in accordance with due process of law, pursuant to an order from a court of competent jurisdiction.

(c) Disclosure by employer

An employer (other than an employer described in subsection (a), (b), or (c) of section 2006 of this title) for whom a polygraph test is conducted may disclose information from the test only to—

(1) a person in accordance with subsection (b) of this section; or

(2) a governmental agency, but only insofar as the disclosed information is an admission of criminal conduct.

(Pub. L. 100–347, §9, June 27, 1988, 102 Stat. 652.)

§ 2009. Effect on other law and agreements

Except as provided in subsections (a), (b), and (c) of section 2006 of this title, this chapter shall not preempt any provision of any State or local law or of any negotiated collective bargaining agreement that prohibits lie detector tests or is more restrictive with respect to lie detector tests than any provision of this chapter.

(Pub. L. 100–347, §10, June 27, 1988, 102 Stat. 653.)

CHAPTER 23—WORKER ADJUSTMENT AND RETRAINING NOTIFICATION

§2101. Definitions; exclusions from definition of loss of employment

(a) Definitions

As used in this chapter—

(1) the term "employer" means any business enterprise that employs—

(A) 100 or more employees, excluding part-time employees; or

(B) 100 or more employees who in the aggregate work at least 4,000 hours per week (exclusive of hours of overtime);

(2) the term "plant closing" means the permanent or temporary shutdown of a single site of employment, or one or more facilities or operating units within a single site of employment, if the shutdown results in an employment loss at the single site of employment during any 30-day period for 50 or more employees excluding any part-time employees;

(3) the term "mass layoff" means a reduction in force which—

(A) is not the result of a plant closing; and

(B) results in an employment loss at the single site of employment during any 30-day period for—

(i)(I) at least 33 percent of the employees (excluding any part-time employees); and

(II) at least 50 employees (excluding any part-time employees); or

(ii) at least 500 employees (excluding any part-time employees);

(4) the term "representative" means an exclusive representative of employees within the meaning of section 159(a) or 158(f) of this title or section 152 of title 45;

(5) the term "affected employees" means employees who may reasonably be expected to experience an employment loss as a consequence of a proposed plant closing or mass layoff by their employer;

(6) subject to subsection (b) of this section, the term "employment loss" means (A) an employment termination, other than a discharge for cause, voluntary departure, or retirement, (B) a layoff exceeding 6 months, or (C) a reduction in hours of work of more than 50 percent during each month of any 6-month period;

(7) the term "unit of local government" means any general purpose political subdivision of a State which has the power to levy taxes and spend funds, as well as general corporate and police powers; and

(8) the term "part-time employee" means an employee who is employed for an average of fewer than 20 hours per week or who has been employed for fewer than 6 of the 12 months preceding the date on which notice is required.

(b) Exclusions from definition of employment loss

(1) In the case of a sale of part or all of an employer's business, the seller shall be responsible for providing notice for any plant closing or mass layoff in accordance with section 2102 of this title, up to and including the effective date of the sale. After the effective date of the sale of part or all of an employer's business, the purchaser shall be responsible for providing notice for any plant closing or mass layoff in accordance with section 2102 of this title. Notwithstanding any other provision of this chapter, any person who is an employee of the seller (other than a part-time employee) as of the effective date of the sale shall be considered an employee of the purchaser immediately after the effective date of the sale.

(2) Notwithstanding subsection (a)(6) of this section, an employee may not be considered to have experienced an employment loss if the closing or layoff is the result of the relocation or consolidation of part or all of the employer's business and, prior to the closing or layoff—

(A) the employer offers to transfer the employee to a different site of employment within a reasonable commuting distance with no more than a 6-month break in employment; or

(B) the employer offers to transfer the employee to any other site of employment regardless of distance with no more than a 6-month break in employment, and the employee accepts within 30 days of the offer or of the closing or layoff, whichever is later.

(Pub. L. 100–379, §2, Aug. 4, 1988, 102 Stat. 890.)

EFFECTIVE DATE

Section 11 of Pub. L. 100–379 provided that: "This Act [enacting this chapter] shall take effect on the date which is 6 months after the date of enactment of this Act [Aug. 4, 1988], except that the authority of the Secretary of Labor under section 8 [section 2107 of this title] is effective upon enactment."

SHORT TITLE

Section 1(a) of Pub. L. 100–379 provided that: "This Act [enacting this chapter] may be cited as the 'Worker Adjustment and Retraining Notification Act'."

§2102. Notice required before plant closings and mass layoffs

(a) Notice to employees, State dislocated worker units, and local governments

An employer shall not order a plant closing or mass layoff until the end of a 60-day period after the employer serves written notice of such an order—

(1) to each representative of the affected employees as of the time of the notice or, if there

is no such representative at that time, to each affected employee; and

(2) to the State or entity designated by the State to carry out rapid response activities under section 2864(a)(2)(A) of this title, and the chief elected official of the unit of local government within which such closing or layoff is to occur.

If there is more than one such unit, the unit of local government which the employer shall notify is the unit of local government to which the employer pays the highest taxes for the year preceding the year for which the determination is made.

(b) Reduction of notification period

(1) An employer may order the shutdown of a single site of employment before the conclusion of the 60-day period if as of the time that notice would have been required the employer was actively seeking capital or business which, if obtained, would have enabled the employer to avoid or postpone the shutdown and the employer reasonably and in good faith believed that giving the notice required would have precluded the employer from obtaining the needed capital or business.

(2)(A) An employer may order a plant closing or mass layoff before the conclusion of the 60-day period if the closing or mass layoff is caused by business circumstances that were not reasonably foreseeable as of the time that notice would have been required.

(B) No notice under this chapter shall be required if the plant closing or mass layoff is due to any form of natural disaster, such as a flood, earthquake, or the drought currently ravaging the farmlands of the United States.

(3) An employer relying on this subsection shall give as much notice as is practicable and at that time shall give a brief statement of the basis for reducing the notification period.

(c) Extension of layoff period

A layoff of more than 6 months which, at its outset, was announced to be a layoff of 6 months or less, shall be treated as an employment loss under this chapter unless—

(1) the extension beyond 6 months is caused by business circumstances (including unforeseeable changes in price or cost) not reasonably foreseeable at the time of the initial layoff; and

(2) notice is given at the time it becomes reasonably foreseeable that the extension beyond 6 months will be required.

(d) Determinations with respect to employment loss

For purposes of this section, in determining whether a plant closing or mass layoff has occurred or will occur, employment losses for 2 or more groups at a single site of employment, each of which is less than the minimum number of employees specified in section 2101(a)(2) or (3) of this title but which in the aggregate exceed that minimum number, and which occur within any 90-day period shall be considered to be a plant closing or mass layoff unless the employer demonstrates that the employment losses are the result of separate and distinct actions and causes and are not an attempt by the employer to evade the requirements of this chapter.

(Pub. L. 100–379, §3, Aug. 4, 1988, 102 Stat. 891; Pub. L. 105–277, div. A, §101(f) [title VIII, §405(d)(26), (f)(18)], Oct. 21, 1998, 112 Stat. 2681–337, 2681–424, 2681–432.)

AMENDMENTS

1998—Subsec. (a)(2). Pub. L. 105–277, §101(f) [title VIII, §405(f)(18)], struck out "the State dislocated worker unit or office (referred to in section 1661(b)(2) of this title), or" before "the State or entity".

Pub. L. 105–277, §101(f) [title VIII, §405(d)(26)], substituted "to the State dislocated worker unit or office (referred to in section 1661(b)(2) of this title), or the State or entity designated by the State to carry out rapid response activities under section 2864(a)(2)(A) of this title, and the chief" for "to the State dislocated worker unit (designated or created under title III of the Job Training Partnership Act) and the chief".

EFFECTIVE DATE OF 1998 AMENDMENT

Amendment by section 101(f) [title VIII, §405(d)(26)] of Pub. L. 105–277 effective Oct. 21, 1998, and amendment by section 101(f) [title VIII, §405(f)(18)] of Pub. L. 105–277 effective July 1, 2000, see section 101(f) [title VIII, §405(g)(1), (2)(B)] of Pub. L. 105–277, set out as a note under section 3502 of Title 5, Government Organization and Employees.

§2103. Exemptions

This chapter shall not apply to a plant closing or mass layoff if—

(1) the closing is of a temporary facility or the closing or layoff is the result of the completion of a particular project or undertaking, and the affected employees were hired with the understanding that their employment was limited to the duration of the facility or the project or undertaking; or

(2) the closing or layoff constitutes a strike or constitutes a lockout not intended to evade the requirements of this chapter. Nothing in this chapter shall require an employer to serve written notice pursuant to section 2102(a) of this title when permanently replacing a person who is deemed to be an economic striker under the National Labor Relations Act [29 U.S.C. 151 et seq.]: *Provided*, That nothing in this chapter shall be deemed to validate or invalidate any judicial or administrative ruling relating to the hiring of permanent replacements for economic strikers under the National Labor Relations Act.

(Pub. L. 100–379, §4, Aug. 4, 1988, 102 Stat. 892.)

REFERENCES IN TEXT

The National Labor Relations Act, referred to in par. (2), is act July 5, 1935, ch. 372, 49 Stat. 452, as amended, which is classified generally to subchapter II (§151 et seq.) of chapter 7 of this title. For complete classification of this Act to the Code, see section 167 of this title and Tables.

§2104. Administration and enforcement of requirements

(a) Civil actions against employers

(1) Any employer who orders a plant closing or mass layoff in violation of section 2102 of this title shall be liable to each aggrieved employee who suffers an employment loss as a result of such closing or layoff for—

(A) back pay for each day of violation at a rate of compensation not less than the higher of—

(i) the average regular rate received by such employee during the last 3 years of the employee's employment; or

(ii) the final regular rate received by such employee; and

(B) benefits under an employee benefit plan described in section 1002(3) of this title, including the cost of medical expenses incurred during the employment loss which would have been covered under an employee benefit plan if the employment loss had not occurred.

Such liability shall be calculated for the period of the violation, up to a maximum of 60 days, but in no event for more than one-half the number of days the employee was employed by the employer.

(2) The amount for which an employer is liable under paragraph (1) shall be reduced by—

(A) any wages paid by the employer to the employee for the period of the violation;

(B) any voluntary and unconditional payment by the employer to the employee that is not required by any legal obligation; and

(C) any payment by the employer to a third party or trustee (such as premiums for health benefits or payments to a defined contribution pension plan) on behalf of and attributable to the employee for the period of the violation.

In addition, any liability incurred under paragraph (1) with respect to a defined benefit pension plan may be reduced by crediting the employee with service for all purposes under such a plan for the period of the violation.

(3) Any employer who violates the provisions of section 2102 of this title with respect to a unit of local government shall be subject to a civil penalty of not more than $500 for each day of such violation, except that such penalty shall not apply if the employer pays to each aggrieved employee the amount for which the employer is liable to that employee within 3 weeks from the date the employer orders the shutdown or layoff.

(4) If an employer which has violated this chapter proves to the satisfaction of the court that the act or omission that violated this chapter was in good faith and that the employer had reasonable grounds for believing that the act or omission was not a violation of this chapter the court may, in its discretion, reduce the amount of the liability or penalty provided for in this section.

(5) A person seeking to enforce such liability, including a representative of employees or a unit of local government aggrieved under paragraph (1) or (3), may sue either for such person or for other persons similarly situated, or both, in any district court of the United States for any district in which the violation is alleged to have occurred, or in which the employer transacts business.

(6) In any such suit, the court, in its discretion, may allow the prevailing party a reasonable attorney's fee as part of the costs.

(7) For purposes of this subsection, the term,[1] "aggrieved employee" means an employee who has worked for the employer ordering the plant closing or mass layoff and who, as a result of the failure by the employer to comply with section 2102 of this title, did not receive timely notice either directly or through his or her representative as required by section 2102 of this title.

(b) Exclusivity of remedies

The remedies provided for in this section shall be the exclusive remedies for any violation of this chapter. Under this chapter, a Federal court shall not have authority to enjoin a plant closing or mass layoff.

(Pub. L. 100–379, §5, Aug. 4, 1988, 102 Stat. 893.)

§2105. Procedures in addition to other rights of employees

The rights and remedies provided to employees by this chapter are in addition to, and not in lieu of, any other contractual or statutory rights and remedies of the employees, and are not intended to alter or affect such rights and remedies, except that the period of notification required by this chapter shall run concurrently with any period of notification required by contract or by any other statute.

(Pub. L. 100–379, §6, Aug. 4, 1988, 102 Stat. 894.)

§2106. Procedures encouraged where not required

It is the sense of Congress that an employer who is not required to comply with the notice requirements of section 2102 of this title should, to the extent possible, provide notice to its employees about a proposal to close a plant or permanently reduce its workforce.

(Pub. L. 100–379, §7, Aug. 4, 1988, 102 Stat. 894.)

§2107. Authority to prescribe regulations

(a) The Secretary of Labor shall prescribe such regulations as may be necessary to carry out this chapter. Such regulations shall, at a minimum, include interpretative regulations describing the methods by which employers may provide for appropriate service of notice as required by this chapter.

(b) The mailing of notice to an employee's last known address or inclusion of notice in the employee's paycheck will be considered acceptable methods for fulfillment of the employer's obligation to give notice to each affected employee under this chapter.

(Pub. L. 100–379, §8, Aug. 4, 1988, 102 Stat. 894.)

§2108. Effect on other laws

The giving of notice pursuant to this chapter, if done in good faith compliance with this chapter, shall not constitute a violation of the National Labor Relations Act [29 U.S.C. 151 et seq.] or the Railway Labor Act [45 U.S.C. 151 et seq.].

(Pub. L. 100–379, §9, Aug. 4, 1988, 102 Stat. 894.)

References in Text

The National Labor Relations Act, referred to in text, is act July 5, 1935, ch. 372, 49 Stat. 452, as amended, which is classified generally to subchapter II (§151 et seq.) of chapter 7 of this title. For complete classification of this Act to the Code, see section 167 of this title and Tables.

The Railway Labor Act, referred to in text, is act May 20, 1926, ch. 347, 44 Stat. 577, as amended, which is

[1] So in original. The comma probably should not appear.

classified principally to chapter 8 (§ 151 et seq.) of Title 45, Railroads. For complete classification of this Act to the Code, see section 151 of Title 45 and Tables.

§ 2109. Report on employment and international competitiveness

Two years after August 4, 1988, the Comptroller General shall submit to the Committee on Small Business of both the House and Senate, the Committee on Labor and Human Resources, and the Committee on Education and Labor a report containing a detailed and objective analysis of the effect of this chapter on employers (especially small- and medium-sized businesses), the economy (international competitiveness), and employees (in terms of levels and conditions of employment). The Comptroller General shall assess both costs and benefits, including the effect on productivity, competitiveness, unemployment rates and compensation, and worker retraining and readjustment.

(Pub. L. 100–379, § 10, Aug. 4, 1988, 102 Stat. 894.)

CHANGE OF NAME

Committee on Small Business of Senate changed to Committee on Small Business and Entrepreneurship of Senate. See Senate Resolution No. 123, One Hundred Seventh Congress, June 29, 2001.

Committee on Labor and Human Resources of Senate changed to Committee on Health, Education, Labor, and Pensions of Senate by Senate Resolution No. 20, One Hundred Sixth Congress, Jan. 19, 1999.

CHAPTER 24—TECHNOLOGY RELATED ASSISTANCE FOR INDIVIDUALS WITH DISABILITIES

§§ 2201, 2202. Repealed. Pub. L. 105–394, title IV, § 401, Nov. 13, 1998, 112 Stat. 3661

Section 2201, Pub. L. 100–407, § 2, Aug. 19, 1988, 102 Stat. 1044; Pub. L. 103–218, § 3, Mar. 9, 1994, 108 Stat. 51, related to findings, purposes, and policy.

Section 2202, Pub. L. 100–407, § 3, Aug. 19, 1988, 102 Stat. 1046; Pub. L. 103–218, § 4, Mar. 9, 1994, 108 Stat. 54; Pub. L. 105–244, title I, § 102(a)(9)(B), Oct. 7, 1998, 112 Stat. 1620, related to definitions.

SHORT TITLE

Pub. L. 100–407, § 1, Aug. 19, 1988, 102 Stat. 1044, provided that Pub. L. 100–407 could be cited as the "Technology-Related Assistance for Individuals With Disabilities Act of 1988", prior to repeal by Pub. L. 105–394, title IV, § 401, Nov. 13, 1998, 112 Stat. 3661.

SUBCHAPTER I—GRANTS TO STATES

§§ 2211 to 2216. Repealed. Pub. L. 105–394, title IV, § 401, Nov. 13, 1998, 112 Stat. 3661

Section 2211, Pub. L. 100–407, title I, § 101, Aug. 19, 1988, 102 Stat. 1047; Pub. L. 103–218, title I, § 101, Mar. 9, 1994, 108 Stat. 57; Pub. L. 105–220, title IV, § 414(b)(1), Aug. 7, 1998, 112 Stat. 1242, authorized program.

Section 2212, Pub. L. 100–407, title I, § 102, Aug. 19, 1988, 102 Stat. 1052; Pub. L. 103–218, title I, § 102, Mar. 9, 1994, 108 Stat. 63; Pub. L. 105–220, title IV, § 414(b)(2), Aug. 7, 1998, 112 Stat. 1242, related to development grants.

Section 2213, Pub. L. 100–407, title I, § 103, Aug. 19, 1988, 102 Stat. 1055; Pub. L. 103–218, title I, § 103, Mar. 9, 1994, 108 Stat. 70, related to extension grants.

Section 2214, Pub. L. 100–407, title I, § 104, Aug. 19, 1988, 102 Stat. 1056; Pub. L. 103–218, title I, § 104, Mar. 9, 1994, 108 Stat. 75, related to progress criteria and reports.

Section 2215, Pub. L. 100–407, title I, § 105, Aug. 19, 1988, 102 Stat. 1057; Pub. L. 101–476, title IX, § 901(a)(2), Oct. 30, 1990, 104 Stat. 1142; Pub. L. 103–218, title I, § 105, Mar. 9, 1994, 108 Stat. 76, related to administrative provisions.

Section 2216, Pub. L. 100–407, title I, § 106, Aug. 19, 1988, 102 Stat. 1058; Pub. L. 103–218, title I, § 106, Mar. 9, 1994, 108 Stat. 82, related to authorization of appropriations.

§ 2217. Repealed. Pub. L. 103–218, title I, § 107, Mar. 9, 1994, 108 Stat. 85

Section, Pub. L. 100–407, title I, § 107, Aug. 19, 1988, 102 Stat. 1058, directed Secretary of Education to conduct national evaluation of program of grants to States authorized by this subchapter and to report to Congress on results not later than Oct. 1, 1992.

SUBCHAPTER II—PROGRAMS OF NATIONAL SIGNIFICANCE

PART A—NATIONAL CLASSIFICATION SYSTEM

§ 2231. Repealed. Pub. L. 105–394, title IV, § 401, Nov. 13, 1998, 112 Stat. 3661

Section, Pub. L. 100–407, title II, § 201, as added Pub. L. 103–218, title II, § 201, Mar. 9, 1994, 108 Stat. 85, related to classification system for assistive technology devices and assistive technology services.

A prior section 2231, Pub. L. 100–407, title II, § 201, Aug. 19, 1988, 102 Stat. 1059, directed National Council on the Handicapped to study implementation, acquisition or financing assistive technology devices and services for individuals with disabilities, prior to repeal by Pub. L. 103–218, § 201.

PART B—TRAINING AND DEMONSTRATION PROJECTS

§§ 2241 to 2246. Repealed. Pub. L. 105–394, title IV, § 401, Nov. 13, 1998, 112 Stat. 3661

Section 2241, Pub. L. 100–407, title II, § 211, as added Pub. L. 103–218, title II, § 202, Mar. 9, 1994, 108 Stat. 87, related to technology training.

A prior section 2241, Pub. L. 100–407, title II, § 211, Aug. 19, 1988, 102 Stat. 1060, related to establishment of national information and program referral network, prior to repeal by Pub. L. 103–218, § 202.

Section 2242, Pub. L. 100–407, title II, § 212, as added Pub. L. 103–218, title II, § 202, Mar. 9, 1994, 108 Stat. 89, related to technology transfer.

A prior section 2242, Pub. L. 100–407, title II, § 212, Aug. 19, 1988, 102 Stat. 1060, related to feasibility studies undertaken by Secretary of Labor concerning the national information and program referral network, prior to repeal by Pub. L. 103–218, § 202.

Section 2243, Pub. L. 100–407, title II, § 213, as added Pub. L. 103–218, title II, § 202, Mar. 9, 1994, 108 Stat. 89, related to device and equipment redistribution information systems and recycling centers.

A prior section 2243, Pub. L. 100–407, title II, § 213, Aug. 19, 1988, 102 Stat. 1060, prescribed contents of study conducted by Secretary of Labor concerning the national information and program referral network, prior to repeal by Pub. L. 103–218, § 202.

Section 2244, Pub. L. 100–407, title II, § 214, as added Pub. L. 103–218, title II, § 202, Mar. 9, 1994, 108 Stat. 90, related to business opportunities for individuals with disabilities.

A prior section 2244, Pub. L. 100–407, title II, § 214, Aug. 19, 1988, 102 Stat. 1062, prescribed timetable for study conducted by Secretary of Labor concerning the national information and program referral network, prior to repeal by Pub. L. 103–218, § 202.

Section 2245, Pub. L. 100–407, title II, § 215, as added Pub. L. 103–218, title II, § 202, Mar. 9, 1994, 108 Stat. 90, related to products of universal design.

Section 2246, Pub. L. 100–407, title II, §216, as added Pub. L. 103–218, title II, §202, Mar. 9, 1994, 108 Stat. 90, related to governing standards for activities.

PART C—AUTHORIZATION OF APPROPRIATIONS

§2251. Repealed. Pub. L. 105–394, title IV, §401, Nov. 13, 1998, 112 Stat. 3661

Section, Pub. L. 100–407, title II, §221, as added Pub. L. 103–218, title II, §202, Mar. 9, 1994, 108 Stat. 91, related to authorization of appropriations.

Prior sections 2251 to 2253 and 2261 were repealed by Pub. L. 103–218, title II, §202, Mar. 9, 1994, 108 Stat. 87.

Section 2251, Pub. L. 100–407, title II, §221, Aug. 19, 1988, 102 Stat. 1062; Pub. L. 102–569, title IX, §913(1), Oct. 29, 1992, 106 Stat. 4487, related to training programs for those in need of technologically-related assistance.

Section 2252, Pub. L. 100–407, title II, §222, Aug. 19, 1988, 102 Stat. 1063; Pub. L. 102–569, title IX, §913(2), Oct. 29, 1992, 106 Stat. 4487, related to grants or contracts for technologically-related assistance public awareness projects.

Section 2253, Pub. L. 100–407, title II, §223, Aug. 19, 1988, 102 Stat. 1063, related to establishment by Secretary of Labor of program priorities implementing technologically-related assistance.

Section 2261, Pub. L. 100–407, title II, §231, Aug. 19, 1988, 102 Stat. 1063; Pub. L. 102–569, title IX, §913(3), Oct. 29, 1992, 106 Stat. 4487, which comprised part D of this subchapter, authorized demonstration and innovation projects relating to technology-related assistance.

Section 2271, Pub. L. 100–407, title II, §241, Aug. 19, 1988, 102 Stat. 1064, which comprised part E of this subchapter, authorized appropriations to carry out this subchapter, prior to repeal by Pub. L. 103–382, title III, §366, Oct. 20, 1994, 108 Stat. 3975, effective as if included in Pub. L. 103–218.

SUBCHAPTER III—ALTERNATIVE FINANCING MECHANISMS

§§2281 to 2288. Repealed. Pub. L. 105–394, title IV, §401, Nov. 13, 1998, 112 Stat. 3661

Section 2281, Pub. L. 100–407, title III, §301, as added Pub. L. 103–218, title III, §301, Mar. 9, 1994, 108 Stat. 91, related to general authority to provide alternative financing mechanisms.

Section 2282, Pub. L. 100–407, title III, §302, as added Pub. L. 103–218, title III, §301, Mar. 9, 1994, 108 Stat. 92, related to applications and procedures.

Section 2283, Pub. L. 100–407, title III, §303, as added Pub. L. 103–218, title III, §301, Mar. 9, 1994, 108 Stat. 93, related to grant administration requirements.

Section 2284, Pub. L. 100–407, title III, §304, as added Pub. L. 103–218, title III, §301, Mar. 9, 1994, 108 Stat. 93, related to financial requirements to receive a grant under section 2281 of this title.

Section 2285, Pub. L. 100–407, title III, §305, as added Pub. L. 103–218, title III, §301, Mar. 9, 1994, 108 Stat. 94, related to amount of grants.

Section 2286, Pub. L. 100–407, title III, §306, as added Pub. L. 103–218, title III, §301, Mar. 9, 1994, 108 Stat. 94, related to information and technical assistance to States.

Section 2287, Pub. L. 100–407, title III, §307, as added Pub. L. 103–218, title III, §301, Mar. 9, 1994, 108 Stat. 95, related to annual report.

Section 2288, Pub. L. 100–407, title III, §308, as added Pub. L. 103–218, title III, §301, Mar. 9, 1994, 108 Stat. 95, related to authorization of appropriations.

CHAPTER 25—DISPLACED HOMEMAKERS SELF-SUFFICIENCY ASSISTANCE

§§2301 to 2314. Repealed. Pub. L. 105–220, title I, §199(a)(3), Aug. 7, 1998, 112 Stat. 1059

Section 2301, Pub. L. 101–554, §2, Nov. 15, 1990, 104 Stat. 2751, stated findings of Congress and purpose of chapter.

Section 2302, Pub. L. 101–554, §3, Nov. 15, 1990, 104 Stat. 2751, defined terms used in chapter.

Section 2303, Pub. L. 101–554, §4, Nov. 15, 1990, 104 Stat. 2752, authorized grant program.

Section 2304, Pub. L. 101–554, §5, Nov. 15, 1990, 104 Stat. 2753, related to application and priority for competitive grants.

Section 2305, Pub. L. 101–554, §6, Nov. 15, 1990, 104 Stat. 2753, related to use of competitive grant funds.

Section 2306, Pub. L. 101–554, §7, Nov. 15, 1990, 104 Stat. 2753, related to allocation of assistance to States.

Section 2307, Pub. L. 101–554, §8, Nov. 15, 1990, 104 Stat. 2754, related to State plans.

Section 2308, Pub. L. 101–554, §9, Nov. 15, 1990, 104 Stat. 2755, related to State administration.

Section 2309, Pub. L. 101–554, §10, Nov. 15, 1990, 104 Stat. 2755, related to use of funds.

Section 2310, Pub. L. 101–554, §11, Nov. 15, 1990, 104 Stat. 2756, related to within State allocation.

Section 2311, Pub. L. 101–554, §12, Nov. 15, 1990, 104 Stat. 2756, related to eligible service providers.

Section 2312, Pub. L. 101–554, §13, Nov. 15, 1990, 104 Stat. 2756, related to national activities.

Section 2313, Pub. L. 101–554, §14, Nov. 15, 1990, 104 Stat. 2757, contained administrative provisions.

Section 2314, Pub. L. 101–554, §15, Nov. 15, 1990, 104 Stat. 2757, authorized appropriations.

EFFECTIVE DATE OF REPEAL

Pub. L. 105–220, title I, §199(c)(1), Aug. 7, 1998, 112 Stat. 1059, provided that: "The repeals made by subsection (a) [repealing sections 2301 to 2314 of this title, section 211 of former Title 40, Appendix, Public Buildings, Property, and Works, sections 11441 to 11447, 11449, and 11450 of Title 42, The Public Health and Welfare, and sections 42101 to 42106 of Title 49, Transportation, and repealing provisions set out as notes below and under section 1255a of Title 8, Aliens and Nationality] shall take effect on the date of enactment of this Act."

Pub. L. 101–554, §1, Nov. 15, 1990, 104 Stat. 2751, provided that Pub. L. 101–554, which enacted this chapter, could be cited as the "Displaced Homemakers Self-Sufficiency Assistance Act", prior to repeal by Pub. L. 105–220, title I, §199(a)(3), Aug. 7, 1998, 112 Stat. 1059.

CHAPTER 26—NATIONAL CENTER FOR THE WORKPLACE

§§2401 to 2405. Repealed. Pub. L. 105–332, §6(b)(3), Oct. 31, 1998, 112 Stat. 3128

Section 2401, Pub. L. 102–325, title XV, §1511, July 23, 1992, 106 Stat. 831, stated purpose of chapter.

Section 2402, Pub. L. 102–325, title XV, §1512, July 23, 1992, 106 Stat. 831, authorized establishment of National Center for the Workplace.

Section 2403, Pub. L. 102–325, title XV, §1513, July 23, 1992, 106 Stat. 832, related to use of funds.

Section 2404, Pub. L. 102–325, title XV, §1514, July 23, 1992, 106 Stat. 833, related to gifts and donations.

Section 2405, Pub. L. 102–325, title XV, §1515, July 23, 1992, 106 Stat. 833, authorized appropriations.

CHAPTER 27—WOMEN IN APPRENTICESHIP AND NONTRADITIONAL OCCUPATIONS

§2501. Findings; statement of purpose

(a) Findings

The Congress finds that—

(1) American businesses now and for the remainder of the 20th century will face a dramatically different labor market than the one to which they have become accustomed;

(2) two in every three new entrants to the work force will be women, and to meet labor needs such women must work in all occupational areas including in apprenticeable occupations and nontraditional occupations;

(3) women face significant barriers to their full and effective participation in apprenticeable occupations and nontraditional occupations;

(4) the business community must be prepared to address the barriers that women have to such jobs, in order to successfully integrate them into the work force; and

(5) few resources are available to employers and unions who need assistance in recruiting, training, and retaining women in apprenticeable occupations and other nontraditional occupations.

(b) Purpose

It is the purpose of this chapter to provide technical assistance to employers and labor unions to encourage employment of women in apprenticeable occupations and nontraditional occupations. Such assistance will enable business to meet the challenge of Workforce 2000 by preparing employers to successfully recruit, train, and retain women in apprenticeable occupations and nontraditional occupations and will expand the employment and self-sufficiency options of women. This purpose will be achieved by—

(1) promoting the program to employers and labor unions to inform them of the availability of technical assistance which will assist them in preparing the workplace to employ women in apprenticeable occupations and nontraditional occupations;

(2) providing grants to community-based organizations to deliver technical assistance to employers and labor unions to prepare them to recruit, train, and employ women in apprenticeable occupations and nontraditional occupations;

(3) authorizing the Department of Labor to serve as a liaison between employers, labor, and the community-based organizations providing technical assistance, through its national office and its regional administrators; and

(4) conducting a comprehensive study to examine the barriers to the participation of women in apprenticeable occupations and nontraditional occupations and to develop recommendations for the workplace to eliminate such barriers.

(Pub. L. 102–530, §2, Oct. 27, 1992, 106 Stat. 3465.)

SHORT TITLE

Section 1 of Pub. L. 102–530 provided that: "This Act [enacting this chapter] shall be cited as the 'Women in Apprenticeship and Nontraditional Occupations Act'."

§ 2502. Outreach to employers and labor unions

(a) In general

With funds available to the Secretary of Labor to carry out the operations of the Department of Labor in fiscal year 1994 and subsequent fiscal years, the Secretary shall carry out an outreach program to inform employers of technical assistance available under section 2503(a) of this title to assist employers to prepare the workplace to employ women in apprenticeable occupations and other nontraditional occupations.

(1) Under such program the Secretary shall provide outreach to employers through, but not limited to, the private industry councils in each service delivery area.

(2) The Secretary shall provide outreach to labor unions through, but not limited to, the building trade councils, joint apprenticeable occupations councils, and individual labor unions.

(b) Priority

The Secretary shall give priority to providing outreach to employers located in areas that have nontraditional employment and training programs specifically targeted to women.

(Pub. L. 102–530, §3, Oct. 27, 1992, 106 Stat. 3466.)

§ 2503. Technical assistance

(a) In general

With funds appropriated to carry out this section, the Secretary shall make grants to community-based organizations to provide technical assistance to employers and labor unions selected under subsection (b) of this section. Such technical assistance may include—

(1) developing outreach and orientation sessions to recruit women into the employers' apprenticeable occupations and nontraditional occupations;

(2) developing preapprenticeable occupations or nontraditional skills training to prepare women for apprenticeable occupations or nontraditional occupations;

(3) providing ongoing orientations for employers, unions, and workers on creating a successful environment for women in apprenticeable occupations or nontraditional occupations;

(4) setting up support groups and facilitating networks for women in nontraditional occupations on or off the job site to improve their retention;

(5) setting up a local computerized data base referral system to maintain a current list of tradeswomen who are available for work;

(6) serving as a liaison between tradeswomen and employers and tradeswomen and labor unions to address workplace issues related to gender; and

(7) conducting exit interviews with tradeswomen to evaluate their on-the-job experience and to assess the effectiveness of the program.

(b) Selection of employer and labor unions

The Secretary shall select a total of 50 employers or labor unions to receive technical assistance provided with grants made under subsection (a) of this section.

(Pub. L. 102–530, §4, Oct. 27, 1992, 106 Stat. 3466.)

§ 2504. Competitive grants

(a) In general

Each community-based organization that desires to receive a grant to provide technical assistance under section 2503(a) of this title to employers and labor unions shall submit an application to the Secretary at such time, in such manner, and accompanied by such information as the Secretary may reasonably require.

(b) Priority

In awarding grants under section 2503(a) of this title, the Secretary shall give priority to applications from community-based organizations that—

(1) demonstrate experience preparing women to gain employment in apprenticeable occupations or other nontraditional occupations;

(2) demonstrate experience working with the business community to prepare them to place women in apprenticeable occupations or other nontraditional occupations;

(3) have tradeswomen or women in nontraditional occupations as active members of the organization, as either employed staff or board members; and

(4) have experience delivering technical assistance.

(Pub. L. 102–530, §5, Oct. 27, 1992, 106 Stat. 3467.)

§2505. Applications

To be eligible to be selected under section 2503(b) of this title to receive technical assistance provided with grants made under section 2503(a) of this title, an employer or labor union shall submit an application to the Secretary at such time, in such manner and containing or accompanied by such information as the Secretary may reasonably require. At a minimum, the application should include—

(1) a description of the need for technical assistance;

(2) a description of the types of apprenticeable occupations or nontraditional occupations in which the employer or labor union would like to train or employ women;

(3) assurances that there are or will be suitable and appropriate positions available in the apprenticeable occupations program or in the nontraditional occupations being targeted; and

(4) commitments that reasonable efforts shall be made to place qualified women in apprenticeable occupations or nontraditional occupations.

(Pub. L. 102–530, §6, Oct. 27, 1992, 106 Stat. 3467.)

§2506. Liaison role of Department of Labor

The Department of Labor shall serve as a liaison among employers, labor unions, and community-based organizations. The liaison role may include—

(1) coordination of employers, labor unions, and community-based organizations with respect to technical assistance provided under section 2503(a) of this title;

(2) conducting regular assessment meetings with representatives of employers, labor unions, and community-based organizations with respect to such technical assistance; and

(3) seeking the input of employers and labor unions with respect to strategies and recommendations for improving such technical assistance.

(Pub. L. 102–530, §7, Oct. 27, 1992, 106 Stat. 3467.)

§2507. Study of barriers to participation of women in apprenticeable occupations and nontraditional occupations

(a) Study

With funds available to the Secretary to carry out the operations of the Department of Labor in fiscal years 1994 and 1995, the Secretary shall conduct a study of the participation of women in apprenticeable occupations and nontraditional occupations. The study shall examine—

(1) the barriers to participation of women in apprenticeable occupations and nontraditional occupations;

(2) strategies for overcoming such barriers;

(3) the retention rates for women in apprenticeable occupations and nontraditional occupations;

(4) strategies for retaining women in apprenticeable occupations and nontraditional occupations;

(5) the effectiveness of the technical assistance provided by the community-based organizations; and

(6) other relevant issues affecting the participation of women in apprenticeable occupations and nontraditional occupations.

(b) Report

Not later than 2 years after October 27, 1992, the Secretary shall submit to the Congress a report containing a summary of the results of the study described in subsection (a) of this section and such recommendations as the Secretary determines to be appropriate.

(Pub. L. 102–530, §8, Oct. 27, 1992, 106 Stat. 3467.)

§2508. Definitions

For purposes of this chapter:

(1) The term "community-based organization" means a community-based organization as defined in section 4(5) of the Job Training Partnership Act (29 U.S.C. 1501(5)),[1] that has demonstrated experience administering programs that train women for apprenticeable occupations or other nontraditional occupations.

(2) The term "nontraditional occupation" means jobs in which women make up 25 percent or less of the total number of workers in that occupation.

(3) The term "Secretary" means the Secretary of Labor.

(Pub. L. 102–530, §9, Oct. 27, 1992, 106 Stat. 3468.)

REFERENCES IN TEXT

Section 4(5) of the Job Training Partnership Act (29 U.S.C. 1501(5)), referred to in par. (1), was classified to section 1503(5) of this title and was repealed by Pub. L. 105–220, title I, §199(b)(2), (c)(2)(B), Aug. 7, 1998, 112 Stat. 1059, effective July 1, 2000. Pursuant to section 2940(b) of this title, references to a provision of the Job Training Partnership Act, effective Aug. 7, 1998, are deemed to refer to that provision or the corresponding provision of the Workforce Investment Act of 1998, Pub. L. 105–220, Aug. 7, 1998, 112 Stat. 936, and effective July 1, 2000, are deemed to refer to the corresponding provision of the Workforce Investment Act of 1998. For complete classification of the Workforce Investment Act of 1998

[1] See References in Text note below.

to the Code, see Short Title note set out under section 9201 of Title 20, Education, and Tables.

§2509. Technical assistance program authorization

There is authorized to be appropriated $1,000,000 to carry out section 2503 of this title.

(Pub. L. 102–530, §10, Oct. 27, 1992, 106 Stat. 3468.)

CHAPTER 28—FAMILY AND MEDICAL LEAVE

§2601. Findings and purposes

(a) Findings

Congress finds that—

(1) the number of single-parent households and two-parent households in which the single parent or both parents work is increasing significantly;

(2) it is important for the development of children and the family unit that fathers and mothers be able to participate in early childrearing and the care of family members who have serious health conditions;

(3) the lack of employment policies to accommodate working parents can force individuals to choose between job security and parenting;

(4) there is inadequate job security for employees who have serious health conditions that prevent them from working for temporary periods;

(5) due to the nature of the roles of men and women in our society, the primary responsibility for family caretaking often falls on women, and such responsibility affects the working lives of women more than it affects the working lives of men; and

(6) employment standards that apply to one gender only have serious potential for encouraging employers to discriminate against employees and applicants for employment who are of that gender.

(b) Purposes

It is the purpose of this Act—

(1) to balance the demands of the workplace with the needs of families, to promote the stability and economic security of families, and to promote national interests in preserving family integrity;

(2) to entitle employees to take reasonable leave for medical reasons, for the birth or adoption of a child, and for the care of a child, spouse, or parent who has a serious health condition;

(3) to accomplish the purposes described in paragraphs (1) and (2) in a manner that accommodates the legitimate interests of employers;

(4) to accomplish the purposes described in paragraphs (1) and (2) in a manner that, consistent with the Equal Protection Clause of the Fourteenth Amendment, minimizes the potential for employment discrimination on the basis of sex by ensuring generally that leave is available for eligible medical reasons (including maternity-related disability) and for compelling family reasons, on a gender-neutral basis; and

(5) to promote the goal of equal employment opportunity for women and men, pursuant to such clause.

(Pub. L. 103–3, §2, Feb. 5, 1993, 107 Stat. 6.)

REFERENCES IN TEXT

This Act, referred to in subsec. (b), is Pub. L. 103–3, Feb. 5, 1993, 107 Stat. 6, known as the Family and Medical Leave Act of 1993, which enacted this chapter, sections 60m and 60n of Title 2, The Congress, and sections 6381 to 6387 of Title 5, Government Organization and Employees, amended section 2105 of Title 5, and enacted provisions set out as notes below. For complete classification of this Act to the Code, see Short Title note set out below and Tables.

EFFECTIVE DATE

Section 405 title IV of Pub. L. 103–3 provided that:

"(a) TITLE III.—Title III [enacting subchapter II of this chapter] shall take effect on the date of the enactment of this Act [Feb. 5, 1993].

"(b) OTHER TITLES.—

"(1) IN GENERAL.—Except as provided in paragraph (2), titles I, II, and V and this title [enacting subchapters I and III of this chapter, sections 60m and 60n of Title 2, The Congress, and sections 6381 to 6387 of Title 5, Government Organization and Employees, and amending section 2105 of Title 5] shall take effect 6 months after the date of the enactment of this Act.

"(2) COLLECTIVE BARGAINING AGREEMENTS.—In the case of a collective bargaining agreement in effect on the effective date prescribed by paragraph (1), title I [enacting subchapter I of this chapter] shall apply on the earlier of—

"(A) the date of the termination of such agreement; or

"(B) the date that occurs 12 months after the date of the enactment of this Act."

SHORT TITLE

Section 1(a) of Pub. L. 103–3 provided that: "This Act [enacting this chapter, sections 60m and 60n of Title 2, The Congress, and sections 6381 to 6387 of Title 5, Government Organization and Employees, amending section 2105 of Title 5, and enacting provisions set out above] may be cited as the 'Family and Medical Leave Act of 1993'."

SUBCHAPTER I—GENERAL REQUIREMENTS FOR LEAVE

§2611. Definitions

As used in this subchapter:

(1) Commerce

The terms "commerce" and "industry or activity affecting commerce" mean any activity, business, or industry in commerce or in which a labor dispute would hinder or obstruct commerce or the free flow of commerce, and include "commerce" and any "industry affecting commerce", as defined in paragraphs (1) and (3) of section 142 of this title.

(2) Eligible employee

(A) In general

The term "eligible employee" means an employee who has been employed—

(i) for at least 12 months by the employer with respect to whom leave is requested under section 2612 of this title; and

(ii) for at least 1,250 hours of service with such employer during the previous 12-month period.

(B) Exclusions

The term "eligible employee" does not include—

(i) any Federal officer or employee covered under subchapter V of chapter 63 of title 5; or

(ii) any employee of an employer who is employed at a worksite at which such employer employs less than 50 employees if the total number of employees employed by that employer within 75 miles of that worksite is less than 50.

(C) Determination

For purposes of determining whether an employee meets the hours of service requirement specified in subparagraph (A)(ii), the legal standards established under section 207 of this title shall apply.

(3) Employ; employee; State

The terms "employ", "employee", and "State" have the same meanings given such terms in subsections (c), (e), and (g) of section 203 of this title.

(4) Employer

(A) In general

The term "employer"—

(i) means any person engaged in commerce or in any industry or activity affecting commerce who employs 50 or more employees for each working day during each of 20 or more calendar workweeks in the current or preceding calendar year;

(ii) includes—

(I) any person who acts, directly or indirectly, in the interest of an employer to any of the employees of such employer; and

(II) any successor in interest of an employer;

(iii) includes any "public agency", as defined in section 203(x) of this title; and

(iv) includes the Government Accountability Office and the Library of Congress.

(B) Public agency

For purposes of subparagraph (A)(iii), a public agency shall be considered to be a person engaged in commerce or in an industry or activity affecting commerce.

(5) Employment benefits

The term "employment benefits" means all benefits provided or made available to employees by an employer, including group life insurance, health insurance, disability insurance, sick leave, annual leave, educational benefits, and pensions, regardless of whether such benefits are provided by a practice or written policy of an employer or through an "employee benefit plan", as defined in section 1002(3) of this title.

(6) Health care provider

The term "health care provider" means—

(A) a doctor of medicine or osteopathy who is authorized to practice medicine or surgery (as appropriate) by the State in which the doctor practices; or

(B) any other person determined by the Secretary to be capable of providing health care services.

(7) Parent

The term "parent" means the biological parent of an employee or an individual who stood in loco parentis to an employee when the employee was a son or daughter.

(8) Person

The term "person" has the same meaning given such term in section 203(a) of this title.

(9) Reduced leave schedule

The term "reduced leave schedule" means a leave schedule that reduces the usual number of hours per workweek, or hours per workday, of an employee.

(10) Secretary

The term "Secretary" means the Secretary of Labor.

(11) Serious health condition

The term "serious health condition" means an illness, injury, impairment, or physical or mental condition that involves—

(A) inpatient care in a hospital, hospice, or residential medical care facility; or

(B) continuing treatment by a health care provider.

(12) Son or daughter

The term "son or daughter" means a biological, adopted, or foster child, a stepchild, a legal ward, or a child of a person standing in loco parentis, who is—

(A) under 18 years of age; or

(B) 18 years of age or older and incapable of self-care because of a mental or physical disability.

(13) Spouse

The term "spouse" means a husband or wife, as the case may be.

(14) Active duty

The term "active duty" means duty under a call or order to active duty under a provision of law referred to in section 101(a)(13)(B) of title 10.

(15) Contingency operation

The term "contingency operation" has the same meaning given such term in section 101(a)(13) of title 10.

(16) Covered servicemember

The term "covered servicemember" means a member of the Armed Forces, including a member of the National Guard or Reserves, who is undergoing medical treatment, recuperation, or therapy, is otherwise in outpatient status, or is otherwise on the temporary disability retired list, for a serious injury or illness.

(17) Outpatient status

The term "outpatient status", with respect to a covered servicemember, means the status of a member of the Armed Forces assigned to—

(A) a military medical treatment facility as an outpatient; or

(B) a unit established for the purpose of providing command and control of members of the Armed Forces receiving medical care as outpatients.

(18) Next of kin

The term "next of kin", used with respect to an individual, means the nearest blood relative of that individual.

(19) Serious injury or illness

The term "serious injury or illness", in the case of a member of the Armed Forces, including a member of the National Guard or Reserves, means an injury or illness incurred by the member in line of duty on active duty in the Armed Forces that may render the member medically unfit to perform the duties of the member's office, grade, rank, or rating.

(Pub. L. 103–3, title I, § 101, Feb. 5, 1993, 107 Stat. 7; Pub. L. 104–1, title II, § 202(c)(1)(A), Jan. 23, 1995, 109 Stat. 9; Pub. L. 108–271, § 8(b), July 7, 2004, 118 Stat. 814; Pub. L. 110–181, div. A, title V, § 585(a)(1), Jan. 28, 2008, 122 Stat. 128.)

AMENDMENTS

2008—Pars. (14) to (19). Pub. L. 110–181 added pars. (14) to (19).

2004—Par. (4)(A)(iv). Pub. L. 108–271 substituted "Government Accountability Office" for "General Accounting Office".

1995—Par. (4)(A)(iv). Pub. L. 104–1 added cl. (iv).

EFFECTIVE DATE OF 1995 AMENDMENT

Amendment by Pub. L. 104–1 effective one year after transmission to Congress of the study under section 1371 of Title 2, The Congress, see section 1312(e)(2) of Title 2. The study required under section 1371 of Title 2, dated Dec. 31, 1996, was transmitted to Congress by the Board of Directors of the Office of Compliance on Dec. 30, 1996.

EFFECTIVE DATE

Subchapter effective 6 months after Feb. 5, 1993, except that, in the case of collective bargaining agreements in effect on that effective date, subchapter applicable on the earlier of (1) the date of termination of such agreement, or (2) the date that occurs 12 months after Feb. 5, 1993, see section 405(b) of Pub. L. 103–3, set out as a note under section 2601 of this title.

§ 2612. Leave requirement

(a) In general

(1) Entitlement to leave

Subject to section 2613 of this title, an eligible employee shall be entitled to a total of 12 workweeks of leave during any 12-month period for one or more of the following:

(A) Because of the birth of a son or daughter of the employee and in order to care for such son or daughter.

(B) Because of the placement of a son or daughter with the employee for adoption or foster care.

(C) In order to care for the spouse, or a son, daughter, or parent, of the employee, if such spouse, son, daughter, or parent has a serious health condition.

(D) Because of a serious health condition that makes the employee unable to perform the functions of the position of such employee.

(E) Because of any qualifying exigency (as the Secretary shall, by regulation, determine) arising out of the fact that the spouse, or a son, daughter, or parent of the employee is on active duty (or has been notified of an impending call or order to active duty) in the Armed Forces in support of a contingency operation.

(2) Expiration of entitlement

The entitlement to leave under subparagraphs (A) and (B) of paragraph (1) for a birth or placement of a son or daughter shall expire at the end of the 12-month period beginning on the date of such birth or placement.

(3) Servicemember family leave

Subject to section 2613 of this title, an eligible employee who is the spouse, son, daughter, parent, or next of kin of a covered servicemember shall be entitled to a total of 26 workweeks of leave during a 12-month period to care for the servicemember. The leave described in this paragraph shall only be available during a single 12-month period.

(4) Combined leave total

During the single 12-month period described in paragraph (3), an eligible employee shall be entitled to a combined total of 26 workweeks of leave under paragraphs (1) and (3). Nothing in this paragraph shall be construed to limit the availability of leave under paragraph (1) during any other 12-month period.

(b) Leave taken intermittently or on reduced leave schedule

(1) In general

Leave under subparagraph (A) or (B) of subsection (a)(1) shall not be taken by an employee intermittently or on a reduced leave schedule unless the employee and the employer of the employee agree otherwise. Subject to paragraph (2), subsection (e)(2), and subsection (b)(5) or (f) (as appropriate) of section 2613 of this title, leave under subparagraph (C) or (D) of subsection (a)(1) or under subsection (a)(3) may be taken intermittently or on a reduced leave schedule when medically necessary. Subject to subsection (e)(3) and section 2613(f) of this title, leave under subsection (a)(1)(E) may be taken intermittently or on a reduced leave schedule. The taking of leave intermittently or on a reduced leave schedule pursuant to this paragraph shall not result in a reduction in the total amount of leave to which the employee is entitled under subsection (a) beyond the amount of leave actually taken.

(2) Alternative position

If an employee requests intermittent leave, or leave on a reduced leave schedule, under subparagraph (C) or (D) of subsection (a)(1) or under subsection (a)(3), that is foreseeable based on planned medical treatment, the employer may require such employee to transfer temporarily to an available alternative position offered by the employer for which the employee is qualified and that—

(A) has equivalent pay and benefits; and

(B) better accommodates recurring periods of leave than the regular employment position of the employee.

(c) Unpaid leave permitted

Except as provided in subsection (d), leave granted under subsection (a) may consist of unpaid leave. Where an employee is otherwise exempt under regulations issued by the Secretary pursuant to section 213(a)(1) of this title, the compliance of an employer with this subchapter by providing unpaid leave shall not affect the exempt status of the employee under such section.

(d) Relationship to paid leave

(1) Unpaid leave

If an employer provides paid leave for fewer than 12 workweeks (or 26 workweeks in the case of leave provided under subsection (a)(3)), the additional weeks of leave necessary to attain the 12 workweeks (or 26 workweeks, as appropriate) of leave required under this subchapter may be provided without compensation.

(2) Substitution of paid leave

(A) In general

An eligible employee may elect, or an employer may require the employee, to substitute any of the accrued paid vacation leave, personal leave, or family leave of the employee for leave provided under subparagraph (A), (B), (C), or (E) of subsection (a)(1) for any part of the 12-week period of such leave under such subsection.

(B) Serious health condition

An eligible employee may elect, or an employer may require the employee, to substitute any of the accrued paid vacation leave, personal leave, or medical or sick leave of the employee for leave provided under subparagraph (C) or (D) of subsection (a)(1) for any part of the 12-week period of such leave under such subsection, except that nothing in this subchapter shall require an employer to provide paid sick leave or paid medical leave in any situation in which such employer would not normally provide any such paid leave. An eligible employee may elect, or an employer may require the employee, to substitute any of the accrued paid vacation leave, personal leave, family leave, or medical or sick leave of the employee for leave provided under subsection (a)(3) for any part of the 26-week period of such leave under such subsection, except that nothing in this subchapter requires an employer to provide paid sick leave or paid medical leave in any situation in which the employer would not normally provide any such paid leave.

(e) Foreseeable leave

(1) Requirement of notice

In any case in which the necessity for leave under subparagraph (A) or (B) of subsection (a)(1) is foreseeable based on an expected birth or placement, the employee shall provide the employer with not less than 30 days' notice, before the date the leave is to begin, of the employee's intention to take leave under such subparagraph, except that if the date of the birth or placement requires leave to begin in less than 30 days, the employee shall provide such notice as is practicable.

(2) Duties of employee

In any case in which the necessity for leave under subparagraph (C) or (D) of subsection (a)(1) or under subsection (a)(3) is foreseeable based on planned medical treatment, the employee—

(A) shall make a reasonable effort to schedule the treatment so as not to disrupt unduly the operations of the employer, subject to the approval of the health care provider of the employee or the health care provider of the son, daughter, spouse, or parent of the employee, as appropriate; and

(B) shall provide the employer with not less than 30 days' notice, before the date the leave is to begin, of the employee's intention to take leave under such subparagraph, except that if the date of the treatment requires leave to begin in less than 30 days, the employee shall provide such notice as is practicable.

(3) Notice for leave due to active duty of family member

In any case in which the necessity for leave under subsection (a)(1)(E) is foreseeable, whether because the spouse, or a son, daughter, or parent, of the employee is on active duty, or because of notification of an impending call or order to active duty in support of a contingency operation, the employee shall provide such notice to the employer as is reasonable and practicable.

(f) Spouses employed by same employer

(1) In general

In any case in which a husband and wife entitled to leave under subsection (a) are employed by the same employer, the aggregate number of workweeks of leave to which both may be entitled may be limited to 12 workweeks during any 12-month period, if such leave is taken—

(A) under subparagraph (A) or (B) of subsection (a)(1); or

(B) to care for a sick parent under subparagraph (C) of such subsection.

(2) Servicemember family leave

(A) In general

The aggregate number of workweeks of leave to which both that husband and wife may be entitled under subsection (a) may be limited to 26 workweeks during the single 12-month period described in subsection (a)(3) if the leave is—

(i) leave under subsection (a)(3); or

(ii) a combination of leave under subsection (a)(3) and leave described in paragraph (1).

(B) Both limitations applicable

If the leave taken by the husband and wife includes leave described in paragraph (1), the limitation in paragraph (1) shall apply to the leave described in paragraph (1).

(Pub. L. 103–3, title I, §102, Feb. 5, 1993, 107 Stat. 9; Pub. L. 110–181, div. A, title V, §585(a)(2), (3)(A)–(D), Jan. 28, 2008, 122 Stat. 129, 130.)

AMENDMENTS

2008—Subsec. (a)(1)(E). Pub. L. 110–181, §585(a)(2)(A), added subpar. (E).

Subsec. (a)(3), (4). Pub. L. 110–181, §585(a)(2)(B), added pars. (3) and (4).

Subsec. (b)(1). Pub. L. 110–181, §585(a)(3)(A)(i), (ii), in second sentence, substituted "subsection (b)(5) or (f) (as appropriate) of section 2613" for "section 2613(b)(5)" and inserted "or under subsection (a)(3)" after "subsection (a)(1)" and, after second sentence, inserted "Subject to subsection (e)(3) and section 2613(f) of this title, leave under subsection (a)(1)(E) may be taken intermittently or on a reduced leave schedule."

Subsec. (b)(2). Pub. L. 110–181, §585(a)(3)(A)(iii), inserted "or under subsection (a)(3)" after "subsection (a)(1)".

Subsec. (d)(1). Pub. L. 110–181, §585(a)(3)(B)(i), inserted "(or 26 workweeks in the case of leave provided under subsection (a)(3))" after "fewer than 12 workweeks" and "(or 26 workweeks, as appropriate)" after "attain the 12 workweeks".

Subsec. (d)(2)(A). Pub. L. 110–181, §585(a)(3)(B)(ii), substituted "(C), or (E)" for "or (C)".

Subsec. (d)(2)(B). Pub. L. 110–181, §585(a)(3)(B)(iii), inserted at end "An eligible employee may elect, or an employer may require the employee, to substitute any of the accrued paid vacation leave, personal leave, family leave, or medical or sick leave of the employee for leave provided under subsection (a)(3) for any part of the 26-week period of such leave under such subsection, except that nothing in this subchapter requires an employer to provide paid sick leave or paid medical leave in any situation in which the employer would not normally provide any such paid leave."

Subsec. (e)(2). Pub. L. 110–181, §585(a)(3)(C)(i), inserted "or under subsection (a)(3)" after "subsection (a)(1)" in introductory provisions.

Subsec. (e)(3). Pub. L. 110–181, §585(a)(3)(C)(ii), added par. (3).

Subsec. (f). Pub. L. 110–181, §585(a)(3)(D), designated existing provisions as par. (1) and inserted heading, redesignated former pars. (1) and (2) as subpars. (A) and (B), respectively, of par. (1), realigned margins, and added par. (2).

§2613. Certification

(a) In general

An employer may require that a request for leave under subparagraph (C) or (D) of paragraph (1) or paragraph (3) of section 2612(a) of this title be supported by a certification issued by the health care provider of the eligible employee or of the son, daughter, spouse, or parent of the employee, or of the next of kin of an individual in the case of leave taken under such paragraph (3), as appropriate. The employee shall provide, in a timely manner, a copy of such certification to the employer.

(b) Sufficient certification

Certification provided under subsection (a) of this section shall be sufficient if it states—

(1) the date on which the serious health condition commenced;

(2) the probable duration of the condition;

(3) the appropriate medical facts within the knowledge of the health care provider regarding the condition;

(4)(A) for purposes of leave under section 2612(a)(1)(C) of this title, a statement that the eligible employee is needed to care for the son, daughter, spouse, or parent and an estimate of the amount of time that such employee is needed to care for the son, daughter, spouse, or parent; and

(B) for purposes of leave under section 2612(a)(1)(D) of this title, a statement that the employee is unable to perform the functions of the position of the employee;

(5) in the case of certification for intermittent leave, or leave on a reduced leave schedule, for planned medical treatment, the dates on which such treatment is expected to be given and the duration of such treatment;

(6) in the case of certification for intermittent leave, or leave on a reduced leave schedule, under section 2612(a)(1)(D) of this title, a statement of the medical necessity for the intermittent leave or leave on a reduced leave schedule, and the expected duration of the intermittent leave or reduced leave schedule; and

(7) in the case of certification for intermittent leave, or leave on a reduced leave schedule, under section 2612(a)(1)(C) of this title, a statement that the employee's intermittent leave or leave on a reduced leave schedule is necessary for the care of the son, daughter, parent, or spouse who has a serious health condition, or will assist in their recovery, and the expected duration and schedule of the intermittent leave or reduced leave schedule.

(c) Second opinion

(1) In general

In any case in which the employer has reason to doubt the validity of the certification provided under subsection (a) of this section for leave under subparagraph (C) or (D) of section 2612(a)(1) of this title, the employer may require, at the expense of the employer, that the eligible employee obtain the opinion of a second health care provider designated or approved by the employer concerning any information certified under subsection (b) of this section for such leave.

(2) Limitation

A health care provider designated or approved under paragraph (1) shall not be employed on a regular basis by the employer.

(d) Resolution of conflicting opinions

(1) In general

In any case in which the second opinion described in subsection (c) of this section differs from the opinion in the original certification provided under subsection (a) of this section, the employer may require, at the expense of the employer, that the employee obtain the opinion of a third health care provider designated or approved jointly by the employer and the employee concerning the information certified under subsection (b) of this section.

(2) Finality

The opinion of the third health care provider concerning the information certified under subsection (b) of this section shall be considered to be final and shall be binding on the employer and the employee.

(e) Subsequent recertification

The employer may require that the eligible employee obtain subsequent recertifications on a reasonable basis.

(f) Certification related to active duty or call to active duty

An employer may require that a request for leave under section 2612(a)(1)(E) of this title be supported by a certification issued at such time and in such manner as the Secretary may by regulation prescribe. If the Secretary issues a regulation requiring such certification, the employee shall provide, in a timely manner, a copy of such certification to the employer.

(Pub. L. 103–3, title I, §103, Feb. 5, 1993, 107 Stat. 11; Pub. L. 110–181, div. A, title V, §585(a)(3)(E), Jan. 28, 2008, 122 Stat. 130.)

AMENDMENTS

2008—Subsec. (a). Pub. L. 110–181, §585(a)(3)(E)(i), substituted "paragraph (1) or paragraph (3) of section 2612(a)" for "section 2612(a)(1)" and inserted "or of the next of kin of an individual in the case of leave taken under such paragraph (3)," after "parent of the employee,".

Subsec. (f). Pub. L. 110–181, §585(a)(3)(E)(ii), added subsec. (f).

§2614. Employment and benefits protection

(a) Restoration to position

(1) In general

Except as provided in subsection (b) of this section, any eligible employee who takes leave under section 2612 of this title for the intended purpose of the leave shall be entitled, on return from such leave—

(A) to be restored by the employer to the position of employment held by the employee when the leave commenced; or

(B) to be restored to an equivalent position with equivalent employment benefits, pay, and other terms and conditions of employment.

(2) Loss of benefits

The taking of leave under section 2612 of this title shall not result in the loss of any employment benefit accrued prior to the date on which the leave commenced.

(3) Limitations

Nothing in this section shall be construed to entitle any restored employee to—

(A) the accrual of any seniority or employment benefits during any period of leave; or

(B) any right, benefit, or position of employment other than any right, benefit, or position to which the employee would have been entitled had the employee not taken the leave.

(4) Certification

As a condition of restoration under paragraph (1) for an employee who has taken leave under section 2612(a)(1)(D) of this title, the employer may have a uniformly applied practice or policy that requires each such employee to receive certification from the health care provider of the employee that the employee is able to resume work, except that nothing in this paragraph shall supersede a valid State or local law or a collective bargaining agreement that governs the return to work of such employees.

(5) Construction

Nothing in this subsection shall be construed to prohibit an employer from requiring an employee on leave under section 2612 of this title to report periodically to the employer on the status and intention of the employee to return to work.

(b) Exemption concerning certain highly compensated employees

(1) Denial of restoration

An employer may deny restoration under subsection (a) of this section to any eligible employee described in paragraph (2) if—

(A) such denial is necessary to prevent substantial and grievous economic injury to the operations of the employer;

(B) the employer notifies the employee of the intent of the employer to deny restoration on such basis at the time the employer determines that such injury would occur; and

(C) in any case in which the leave has commenced, the employee elects not to return to employment after receiving such notice.

(2) Affected employees

An eligible employee described in paragraph (1) is a salaried eligible employee who is among the highest paid 10 percent of the employees employed by the employer within 75 miles of the facility at which the employee is employed.

(c) Maintenance of health benefits

(1) Coverage

Except as provided in paragraph (2), during any period that an eligible employee takes leave under section 2612 of this title, the employer shall maintain coverage under any "group health plan" (as defined in section 5000(b)(1) of title 26) for the duration of such leave at the level and under the conditions coverage would have been provided if the employee had continued in employment continuously for the duration of such leave.

(2) Failure to return from leave

The employer may recover the premium that the employer paid for maintaining coverage for the employee under such group health plan during any period of unpaid leave under section 2612 of this title if—

(A) the employee fails to return from leave under section 2612 of this title after the period of leave to which the employee is entitled has expired; and

(B) the employee fails to return to work for a reason other than—

(i) the continuation, recurrence, or onset of a serious health condition that entitles the employee to leave under subparagraph (C) or (D) of section 2612(a)(1) of this title or under section 2612(a)(3) of this title; or

(ii) other circumstances beyond the control of the employee.

(3) Certification

(A) Issuance

An employer may require that a claim that an employee is unable to return to work because of the continuation, recurrence, or onset of the serious health condition described in paragraph (2)(B)(i) be supported by—

(i) a certification issued by the health care provider of the son, daughter, spouse, or parent of the employee, as appropriate, in the case of an employee unable to return to work because of a condition specified in section 2612(a)(1)(C) of this title;

(ii) a certification issued by the health care provider of the eligible employee, in the case of an employee unable to return to work because of a condition specified in section 2612(a)(1)(D) of this title; or

(iii) a certification issued by the health care provider of the servicemember being cared for by the employee, in the case of an employee unable to return to work because of a condition specified in section 2612(a)(3) of this title.

(B) Copy

The employee shall provide, in a timely manner, a copy of such certification to the employer.

(C) Sufficiency of certification

(i) Leave due to serious health condition of employee

The certification described in subparagraph (A)(ii) shall be sufficient if the certification states that a serious health condition prevented the employee from being able to perform the functions of the position of the employee on the date that the leave of the employee expired.

(ii) Leave due to serious health condition of family member

The certification described in subparagraph (A)(i) shall be sufficient if the certification states that the employee is needed to care for the son, daughter, spouse, or parent who has a serious health condition on the date that the leave of the employee expired.

(Pub. L. 103–3, title I, § 104, Feb. 5, 1993, 107 Stat. 12; Pub. L. 110–181, div. A, title V, § 585(a)(3)(F), Jan. 28, 2008, 122 Stat. 131.)

AMENDMENTS

2008—Subsec. (c)(2)(B)(i). Pub. L. 110–181, § 585(a)(3)(F)(i), inserted "or under section 2612(a)(3) of this title" before semicolon.

Subsec. (c)(3)(A)(iii). Pub. L. 110–181, § 585(a)(3)(F)(ii), added cl. (iii).

§ 2615. Prohibited acts

(a) Interference with rights

(1) Exercise of rights

It shall be unlawful for any employer to interfere with, restrain, or deny the exercise of or the attempt to exercise, any right provided under this subchapter.

(2) Discrimination

It shall be unlawful for any employer to discharge or in any other manner discriminate against any individual for opposing any practice made unlawful by this subchapter.

(b) Interference with proceedings or inquiries

It shall be unlawful for any person to discharge or in any other manner discriminate against any individual because such individual—

(1) has filed any charge, or has instituted or caused to be instituted any proceeding, under or related to this subchapter;

(2) has given, or is about to give, any information in connection with any inquiry or proceeding relating to any right provided under this subchapter; or

(3) has testified, or is about to testify, in any inquiry or proceeding relating to any right provided under this subchapter.

(Pub. L. 103–3, title I, § 105, Feb. 5, 1993, 107 Stat. 14.)

§ 2616. Investigative authority

(a) In general

To ensure compliance with the provisions of this subchapter, or any regulation or order issued under this subchapter, the Secretary shall have, subject to subsection (c) of this section, the investigative authority provided under section 211(a) of this title.

(b) Obligation to keep and preserve records

Any employer shall make, keep, and preserve records pertaining to compliance with this subchapter in accordance with section 211(c) of this title and in accordance with regulations issued by the Secretary.

(c) Required submissions generally limited to annual basis

The Secretary shall not under the authority of this section require any employer or any plan, fund, or program to submit to the Secretary any books or records more than once during any 12-month period, unless the Secretary has reasonable cause to believe there may exist a violation of this subchapter or any regulation or order issued pursuant to this subchapter, or is investigating a charge pursuant to section 2617(b) of this title.

(d) Subpoena powers

For the purposes of any investigation provided for in this section, the Secretary shall have the subpoena authority provided for under section 209 of this title.

(Pub. L. 103–3, title I, § 106, Feb. 5, 1993, 107 Stat. 15.)

§2617. Enforcement

(a) Civil action by employees

(1) Liability

Any employer who violates section 2615 of this title shall be liable to any eligible employee affected—

(A) for damages equal to—

(i) the amount of—

(I) any wages, salary, employment benefits, or other compensation denied or lost to such employee by reason of the violation; or

(II) in a case in which wages, salary, employment benefits, or other compensation have not been denied or lost to the employee, any actual monetary losses sustained by the employee as a direct result of the violation, such as the cost of providing care, up to a sum equal to 12 weeks (or 26 weeks, in a case involving leave under section 2612(a)(3) of this title) of wages or salary for the employee;

(ii) the interest on the amount described in clause (i) calculated at the prevailing rate; and

(iii) an additional amount as liquidated damages equal to the sum of the amount described in clause (i) and the interest described in clause (ii), except that if an employer who has violated section 2615 of this title proves to the satisfaction of the court that the act or omission which violated section 2615 of this title was in good faith and that the employer had reasonable grounds for believing that the act or omission was not a violation of section 2615 of this title, such court may, in the discretion of the court, reduce the amount of the liability to the amount and interest determined under clauses (i) and (ii), respectively; and

(B) for such equitable relief as may be appropriate, including employment, reinstatement, and promotion.

(2) Right of action

An action to recover the damages or equitable relief prescribed in paragraph (1) may be maintained against any employer (including a public agency) in any Federal or State court of competent jurisdiction by any one or more employees for and in behalf of—

(A) the employees; or

(B) the employees and other employees similarly situated.

(3) Fees and costs

The court in such an action shall, in addition to any judgment awarded to the plaintiff, allow a reasonable attorney's fee, reasonable expert witness fees, and other costs of the action to be paid by the defendant.

(4) Limitations

The right provided by paragraph (2) to bring an action by or on behalf of any employee shall terminate—

(A) on the filing of a complaint by the Secretary in an action under subsection (d) of this section in which restraint is sought of any further delay in the payment of the amount described in paragraph (1)(A) to such employee by an employer responsible under paragraph (1) for the payment; or

(B) on the filing of a complaint by the Secretary in an action under subsection (b) of this section in which a recovery is sought of the damages described in paragraph (1)(A) owing to an eligible employee by an employer liable under paragraph (1),

unless the action described in subparagraph (A) or (B) is dismissed without prejudice on motion of the Secretary.

(b) Action by Secretary

(1) Administrative action

The Secretary shall receive, investigate, and attempt to resolve complaints of violations of section 2615 of this title in the same manner that the Secretary receives, investigates, and attempts to resolve complaints of violations of sections 206 and 207 of this title.

(2) Civil action

The Secretary may bring an action in any court of competent jurisdiction to recover the damages described in subsection (a)(1)(A) of this section.

(3) Sums recovered

Any sums recovered by the Secretary pursuant to paragraph (2) shall be held in a special deposit account and shall be paid, on order of the Secretary, directly to each employee affected. Any such sums not paid to an employee because of inability to do so within a period of 3 years shall be deposited into the Treasury of the United States as miscellaneous receipts.

(c) Limitation

(1) In general

Except as provided in paragraph (2), an action may be brought under this section not later than 2 years after the date of the last event constituting the alleged violation for which the action is brought.

(2) Willful violation

In the case of such action brought for a willful violation of section 2615 of this title, such action may be brought within 3 years of the date of the last event constituting the alleged violation for which such action is brought.

(3) Commencement

In determining when an action is commenced by the Secretary under this section for the purposes of this subsection, it shall be considered to be commenced on the date when the complaint is filed.

(d) Action for injunction by Secretary

The district courts of the United States shall have jurisdiction, for cause shown, in an action brought by the Secretary—

(1) to restrain violations of section 2615 of this title, including the restraint of any withholding of payment of wages, salary, employment benefits, or other compensation, plus interest, found by the court to be due to eligible employees; or

(2) to award such other equitable relief as may be appropriate, including employment, reinstatement, and promotion.

(e) Solicitor of Labor

The Solicitor of Labor may appear for and represent the Secretary on any litigation brought under this section.

(f) Government Accountability Office and Library of Congress

In the case of the Government Accountability Office and the Library of Congress, the authority of the Secretary of Labor under this subchapter shall be exercised respectively by the Comptroller General of the United States and the Librarian of Congress.

(Pub. L. 103–3, title I, § 107, Feb. 5, 1993, 107 Stat. 15; Pub. L. 104–1, title II, § 202(c)(1)(B), Jan. 23, 1995, 109 Stat. 9; Pub. L. 108–271, § 8(b), July 7, 2004, 118 Stat. 814; Pub. L. 110–181, div. A, title V, § 585(a)(3)(G), Jan. 28, 2008, 122 Stat. 131.)

AMENDMENTS

2008—Subsec. (a)(1)(A)(i)(II). Pub. L. 110–181 inserted "(or 26 weeks, in a case involving leave under section 2612(a)(3) of this title)" after "12 weeks".

2004—Subsec. (f). Pub. L. 108–271 substituted "Government Accountability Office" for "General Accounting Office" in heading and text.

1995—Subsec. (f). Pub. L. 104–1 added subsec. (f).

EFFECTIVE DATE OF 1995 AMENDMENT

Amendment by Pub. L. 104–1 effective one year after transmission to Congress of the study under section 1371 of Title 2, The Congress, see section 1312(e)(2) of Title 2. The study required under section 1371 of Title 2, dated Dec. 31, 1996, was transmitted to Congress by the Board of Directors of the Office of Compliance on Dec. 30, 1996.

§ 2618. Special rules concerning employees of local educational agencies

(a) Application

(1) In general

Except as otherwise provided in this section, the rights (including the rights under section 2614 of this title, which shall extend throughout the period of leave of any employee under this section), remedies, and procedures under this subchapter shall apply to—

(A) any "local educational agency" (as defined in section 7801 of title 20) and an eligible employee of the agency; and

(B) any private elementary or secondary school and an eligible employee of the school.

(2) Definitions

For purposes of the application described in paragraph (1):

(A) Eligible employee

The term "eligible employee" means an eligible employee of an agency or school described in paragraph (1).

(B) Employer

The term "employer" means an agency or school described in paragraph (1).

(b) Leave does not violate certain other Federal laws

A local educational agency and a private elementary or secondary school shall not be in violation of the Individuals with Disabilities Education Act (20 U.S.C. 1400 et seq.), section 794 of this title, or title VI of the Civil Rights Act of 1964 (42 U.S.C. 2000d et seq.), solely as a result of an eligible employee of such agency or school exercising the rights of such employee under this subchapter.

(c) Intermittent leave or leave on reduced schedule for instructional employees

(1) In general

Subject to paragraph (2), in any case in which an eligible employee employed principally in an instructional capacity by any such educational agency or school requests leave under subparagraph (C) or (D) of section 2612(a)(1) of this title or under section 2612(a)(3) of this title that is foreseeable based on planned medical treatment and the employee would be on leave for greater than 20 percent of the total number of working days in the period during which the leave would extend, the agency or school may require that such employee elect either—

(A) to take leave for periods of a particular duration, not to exceed the duration of the planned medical treatment; or

(B) to transfer temporarily to an available alternative position offered by the employer for which the employee is qualified, and that—

(i) has equivalent pay and benefits; and

(ii) better accommodates recurring periods of leave than the regular employment position of the employee.

(2) Application

The elections described in subparagraphs (A) and (B) of paragraph (1) shall apply only with respect to an eligible employee who complies with section 2612(e)(2) of this title.

(d) Rules applicable to periods near conclusion of academic term

The following rules shall apply with respect to periods of leave near the conclusion of an academic term in the case of any eligible employee employed principally in an instructional capacity by any such educational agency or school:

(1) Leave more than 5 weeks prior to end of term

If the eligible employee begins leave under section 2612 of this title more than 5 weeks prior to the end of the academic term, the agency or school may require the employee to continue taking leave until the end of such term, if—

(A) the leave is of at least 3 weeks duration; and

(B) the return to employment would occur during the 3-week period before the end of such term.

(2) Leave less than 5 weeks prior to end of term

If the eligible employee begins leave under subparagraph (A), (B), or (C) of section 2612(a)(1) of this title or under section 2612(a)(3) of this title during the period that commences 5 weeks prior to the end of the academic term, the agency or school may require the employee to continue taking leave until the end of such term, if—

(A) the leave is of greater than 2 weeks duration; and

(B) the return to employment would occur during the 2-week period before the end of such term.

(3) Leave less than 3 weeks prior to end of term

If the eligible employee begins leave under subparagraph (A), (B), or (C) of section 2612(a)(1) of this title or under section 2612(a)(3) of this title during the period that commences 3 weeks prior to the end of the academic term and the duration of the leave is greater than 5 working days, the agency or school may require the employee to continue to take leave until the end of such term.

(e) Restoration to equivalent employment position

For purposes of determinations under section 2614(a)(1)(B) of this title (relating to the restoration of an eligible employee to an equivalent position), in the case of a local educational agency or a private elementary or secondary school, such determination shall be made on the basis of established school board policies and practices, private school policies and practices, and collective bargaining agreements.

(f) Reduction of amount of liability

If a local educational agency or a private elementary or secondary school that has violated this subchapter proves to the satisfaction of the court that the agency, school, or department had reasonable grounds for believing that the underlying act or omission was not a violation of this subchapter, such court may, in the discretion of the court, reduce the amount of the liability provided for under section 2617(a)(1)(A) of this title to the amount and interest determined under clauses (i) and (ii), respectively, of such section.

(Pub. L. 103–3, title I, §108, Feb. 5, 1993, 107 Stat. 17; Pub. L. 103–382, title III, §394(e), Oct. 20, 1994, 108 Stat. 4027; Pub. L. 107–110, title X, §1076(v), Jan. 8, 2002, 115 Stat. 2093; Pub. L. 110–181, div. A, title V, §585(a)(3)(H), Jan. 28, 2008, 122 Stat. 131.)

REFERENCES IN TEXT

The Individuals with Disabilities Education Act, referred to in subsec. (b), is title VI of Pub. L. 91–230, Apr. 13, 1970, 84 Stat. 175, as amended, which is classified generally to chapter 33 (§1400 et seq.) of Title 20, Education. For complete classification of this Act to the Code, see section 1400 of Title 20 and Tables.

The Civil Rights Act of 1964, referred to in subsec. (b), is Pub. L. 88–352, July 2, 1964, 78 Stat. 241, as amended. Title VI of the Act is classified generally to subchapter V (§2000d et seq.) of chapter 21 of Title 42, The Public Health and Welfare. For complete classification of this Act to the Code, see Short Title note set out under section 2000a of Title 42 and Tables.

AMENDMENTS

2008—Subsecs. (c)(1), (d)(2), (3). Pub. L. 110–181 inserted "or under section 2612(a)(3) of this title" after "section 2612(a)(1) of this title".

2002—Subsec. (a)(1)(A). Pub. L. 107–110 substituted "section 7801 of title 20" for "section 8801 of title 20".

1994—Subsec. (a)(1)(A). Pub. L. 103–382 substituted "section 8801 of title 20" for "section 2891(12) of title 20".

EFFECTIVE DATE OF 2002 AMENDMENT

Amendment by Pub. L. 107–110 effective Jan. 8, 2002, except with respect to certain noncompetitive programs and competitive programs, see section 5 of Pub. L. 107–110, set out as an Effective Date note under section 6301 of Title 20, Education.

§2619. Notice

(a) In general

Each employer shall post and keep posted, in conspicuous places on the premises of the employer where notices to employees and applicants for employment are customarily posted, a notice, to be prepared or approved by the Secretary, setting forth excerpts from, or summaries of, the pertinent provisions of this subchapter and information pertaining to the filing of a charge.

(b) Penalty

Any employer that willfully violates this section may be assessed a civil money penalty not to exceed $100 for each separate offense.

(Pub. L. 103–3, title I, §109, Feb. 5, 1993, 107 Stat. 19.)

SUBCHAPTER II—COMMISSION ON LEAVE

§2631. Establishment

There is established a commission to be known as the Commission on Leave (referred to in this subchapter as the "Commission").

(Pub. L. 103–3, title III, §301, Feb. 5, 1993, 107 Stat. 23.)

§2632. Duties

The Commission shall—

(1) conduct a comprehensive study of—

(A) existing and proposed mandatory and voluntary policies relating to family and temporary medical leave, including policies provided by employers not covered under this Act;

(B) the potential costs, benefits, and impact on productivity, job creation and business growth of such policies on employers and employees;

(C) possible differences in costs, benefits, and impact on productivity, job creation and business growth of such policies on employers based on business type and size;

(D) the impact of family and medical leave policies on the availability of employee benefits provided by employers, including employers not covered under this Act;

(E) alternate and equivalent State enforcement of subchapter I of this chapter with respect to employees described in section 2618(a) of this title;

(F) methods used by employers to reduce administrative costs of implementing family and medical leave policies;

(G) the ability of the employers to recover, under section 2614(c)(2) of this title, the premiums described in such section; and

(H) the impact on employers and employees of policies that provide temporary wage replacement during periods of family and medical leave.

(2) not later than 2 years after the date on which the Commission first meets, prepare

and submit, to the appropriate Committees of Congress, a report concerning the subjects listed in paragraph (1).

(Pub. L. 103–3, title III, §302, Feb. 5, 1993, 107 Stat. 23.)

REFERENCES IN TEXT

This Act, referred to in par. (1)(A), (D), is Pub. L. 103–3, Feb. 5, 1993, 107 Stat. 6, known as the Family and Medical Leave Act of 1993, which enacted this chapter, sections 60m and 60n of Title 2, The Congress, and sections 6381 to 6387 of Title 5, Government Organization and Employees, amended section 2105 of Title 5, and enacted provisions set out as notes under section 2601 of this title. For complete classification of this Act to the Code, see Short Title note set out under section 2601 of this title and Tables.

§2633. Membership

(a) Composition

(1) Appointments

The Commission shall be composed of 12 voting members and 4 ex officio members to be appointed not later than 60 days after February 5, 1993, as follows:

(A) Senators

One Senator shall be appointed by the Majority Leader of the Senate, and one Senator shall be appointed by the Minority Leader of the Senate.

(B) Members of House of Representatives

One Member of the House of Representatives shall be appointed by the Speaker of the House of Representatives, and one Member of the House of Representatives shall be appointed by the Minority Leader of the House of Representatives.

(C) Additional members

(i) Appointment

Two members each shall be appointed by—

(I) the Speaker of the House of Representatives;

(II) the Majority Leader of the Senate;

(III) the Minority Leader of the House of Representatives; and

(IV) the Minority Leader of the Senate.

(ii) Expertise

Such members shall be appointed by virtue of demonstrated expertise in relevant family, temporary disability, and labor management issues. Such members shall include representatives of employers, including employers from large businesses and from small businesses.

(2) Ex officio members

The Secretary of Health and Human Services, the Secretary of Labor, the Secretary of Commerce, and the Administrator of the Small Business Administration shall serve on the Commission as nonvoting ex officio members.

(b) Vacancies

Any vacancy on the Commission shall be filled in the manner in which the original appointment was made. The vacancy shall not affect the power of the remaining members to execute the duties of the Commission.

(c) Chairperson and vice chairperson

The Commission shall elect a chairperson and a vice chairperson from among the members of the Commission.

(d) Quorum

Eight members of the Commission shall constitute a quorum for all purposes, except that a lesser number may constitute a quorum for the purpose of holding hearings.

(Pub. L. 103–3, title III, §303, Feb. 5, 1993, 107 Stat. 24.)

§2634. Compensation

(a) Pay

Members of the Commission shall serve without compensation.

(b) Travel expenses

Members of the Commission shall be allowed reasonable travel expenses, including a per diem allowance, in accordance with section 5703 of title 5 when performing duties of the Commission.

(Pub. L. 103–3, title III, §304, Feb. 5, 1993, 107 Stat. 25.)

§2635. Powers

(a) Meetings

The Commission shall first meet not later than 30 days after the date on which all members are appointed, and the Commission shall meet thereafter on the call of the chairperson or a majority of the members.

(b) Hearings and sessions

The Commission may hold such hearings, sit and act at such times and places, take such testimony, and receive such evidence as the Commission considers appropriate. The Commission may administer oaths or affirmations to witnesses appearing before it.

(c) Access to information

The Commission may secure directly from any Federal agency information necessary to enable it to carry out this subchapter, if the information may be disclosed under section 552 of title 5. Subject to the previous sentence, on the request of the chairperson or vice chairperson of the Commission, the head of such agency shall furnish such information to the Commission.

(d) Use of facilities and services

Upon the request of the Commission, the head of any Federal agency may make available to the Commission any of the facilities and services of such agency.

(e) Personnel from other agencies

On the request of the Commission, the head of any Federal agency may detail any of the personnel of such agency to serve as an Executive Director of the Commission or assist the Commission in carrying out the duties of the Commission. Any detail shall not interrupt or otherwise affect the civil service status or privileges of the Federal employee.

(f) Voluntary service

Notwithstanding section 1342 of title 31, the chairperson of the Commission may accept for the Commission voluntary services provided by a member of the Commission.

(Pub. L. 103–3, title III, §305, Feb. 5, 1993, 107 Stat. 25.)

§2636. Termination

The Commission shall terminate 30 days after the date of the submission of the report of the Commission to Congress.

(Pub. L. 103–3, title III, §306, Feb. 5, 1993, 107 Stat. 25.)

SUBCHAPTER III—MISCELLANEOUS PROVISIONS

§2651. Effect on other laws

(a) Federal and State antidiscrimination laws

Nothing in this Act or any amendment made by this Act shall be construed to modify or affect any Federal or State law prohibiting discrimination on the basis of race, religion, color, national origin, sex, age, or disability.

(b) State and local laws

Nothing in this Act or any amendment made by this Act shall be construed to supersede any provision of any State or local law that provides greater family or medical leave rights than the rights established under this Act or any amendment made by this Act.

(Pub. L. 103–3, title IV, §401, Feb. 5, 1993, 107 Stat. 26.)

REFERENCES IN TEXT

This Act, referred to in text, is Pub. L. 103–3, Feb. 5, 1993, 107 Stat. 6, known as the Family and Medical Leave Act of 1993, which enacted this chapter, sections 60m and 60n of Title 2, The Congress, and sections 6381 to 6387 of Title 5, Government Organization and Employees, amended section 2105 of Title 5, and enacted provisions set out as notes under section 2601 of this title. For complete classification of this Act to the Code, see Short Title note set out under section 2601 of this title and Tables.

EFFECTIVE DATE

Subchapter effective 6 months after Feb. 5, 1993, see section 405(b)(1) of Pub. L. 103–3, set out as a note under section 2601 of this title.

§2652. Effect on existing employment benefits

(a) More protective

Nothing in this Act or any amendment made by this Act shall be construed to diminish the obligation of an employer to comply with any collective bargaining agreement or any employment benefit program or plan that provides greater family or medical leave rights to employees than the rights established under this Act or any amendment made by this Act.

(b) Less protective

The rights established for employees under this Act or any amendment made by this Act shall not be diminished by any collective bargaining agreement or any employment benefit program or plan.

(Pub. L. 103–3, title IV, §402, Feb. 5, 1993, 107 Stat. 26.)

REFERENCES IN TEXT

This Act, referred to in text, is Pub. L. 103–3, Feb. 5, 1993, 107 Stat. 6, known as the Family and Medical Leave Act of 1993, which enacted this chapter, sections 60m and 60n of Title 2, The Congress, and sections 6381 to 6387 of Title 5, Government Organization and Employees, amended section 2105 of Title 5, and enacted provisions set out as notes under section 2601 of this title. For complete classification of this Act to the Code, see Short Title note set out under section 2601 of this title and Tables.

§2653. Encouragement of more generous leave policies

Nothing in this Act or any amendment made by this Act shall be construed to discourage employers from adopting or retaining leave policies more generous than any policies that comply with the requirements under this Act or any amendment made by this Act.

(Pub. L. 103–3, title IV, §403, Feb. 5, 1993, 107 Stat. 26.)

REFERENCES IN TEXT

This Act, referred to in text, is Pub. L. 103–3, Feb. 5, 1993, 107 Stat. 6, known as the Family and Medical Leave Act of 1993, which enacted this chapter, sections 60m and 60n of Title 2, The Congress, and sections 6381 to 6387 of Title 5, Government Organization and Employees, amended section 2105 of Title 5, and enacted provisions set out as notes under section 2601 of this title. For complete classification of this Act to the Code, see Short Title note set out under section 2601 of this title and Tables.

§2654. Regulations

The Secretary of Labor shall prescribe such regulations as are necessary to carry out subchapter I of this chapter and this subchapter not later than 120 days after February 5, 1993.

(Pub. L. 103–3, title IV, §404, Feb. 5, 1993, 107 Stat. 26.)

CHAPTER 29—WORKERS TECHNOLOGY SKILL DEVELOPMENT

§2701. Findings

The Congress finds and declares the following:

(1) In an increasingly competitive world economy, the companies and nations that lead in the rapid development, commercialization, and application of new and advanced technologies, and in the high-quality, competitively priced production of goods and services, will lead in economic growth, employment, and high living standards.

(2) While the United States remains the world leader in science and invention, it has not done well in rapidly making the transition from achievement in its research laboratories to high-quality, competitively priced produc-

tion of goods and services. This lag and the unprecedented competitive challenge that the United States has faced from abroad have contributed to a drop in real wages and living standards.

(3) Companies that are successfully competitive in the rapid development, commercialization, application, and implementation of advanced technologies, and in the successful delivery of goods and services, recognize that worker participation and labor-management cooperation in the deployment, application, and implementation of advanced workplace technologies make an important contribution to high-quality, competitively priced production of goods and services and in maintaining and improving real wages for workers.

(4) The Federal Government has an important role in encouraging and augmenting private sector efforts relating to the development, application, manufacture, and deployment of new and advanced technologies. The role should be to—

(A) work with private companies, States, worker organizations, nonprofit organizations, and institutions of higher education to ensure the development, application, production, and implementation of new and advanced technologies to promote the improvement of workers' skills, wages, job security, and working conditions, and a healthy environment;

(B) encourage worker and worker organization participation in the development, commercialization, evaluation, selection, application, and implementation of new and advanced technologies in the workplace; and

(C) promote the use and integration of new and advanced technologies in the workplace that enhance workers' skills.

(5) In working with the private sector to promote the technological leadership and economic growth of the United States, the Federal Government has a responsibility to ensure that Federal technology programs help the United States to remain competitive and to maintain and improve living standards and to create and retain secure jobs in economically stable communities.

(Pub. L. 103–382, title V, §542, Oct. 20, 1994, 108 Stat. 4051.)

SHORT TITLE

Section 541 of Pub. L. 103–382 provided that: "This part [part D (§§541–547) of title V of Pub. L. 103–382, enacting this chapter] may be cited as the 'Workers Technology Skill Development Act'."

STUDY AND REPORT ON THE "DIGITAL DIVIDE"

Pub. L. 106–313, title I, §115, Oct. 17, 2000, 114 Stat. 1262, provided that:

"(a) STUDY.—The Secretary of Commerce shall conduct a review of existing public and private high-tech workforce training programs in the United States.

"(b) REPORT.—Not later than 18 months after the date of enactment of this Act [Oct. 17, 2000], the Secretary of Commerce shall submit a report to Congress setting forth the findings of the study conducted under subsection (a)."

REPORT ON OLDER WORKERS IN INFORMATION TECHNOLOGY FIELD

Pub. L. 105–277, div. C, title IV, §417, Oct. 21, 1998, 112 Stat. 2681–656, provided that:

"(a) STUDY.—The Director of the National Science Foundation shall enter into a contract with the President of the National Academy of Sciences to conduct a study, using the best available data, assessing the status of older workers in the information technology field. The study shall consider the following:

"(1) The existence and extent of age discrimination in the information technology workplace.

"(2) The extent to which there is a difference, based on age, in—

"(A) promotion and advancement;

"(B) working hours;

"(C) telecommuting;

"(D) salary; and

"(E) stock options, bonuses, and other benefits.

"(3) The relationship between rates of advancement, promotion, and compensation to experience, skill level, education, and age.

"(4) Differences in skill level on the basis of age.

"(b) REPORT.—Not later than October 1, 2000, the Director of the National Science Foundation shall submit to the Committees on the Judiciary of the United States House of Representatives and the Senate a report containing the results of the study described in subsection (a)."

REPORT ON HIGH TECHNOLOGY LABOR MARKET NEEDS

Pub. L. 105–277, div. C, title IV, §418(a), Oct. 21, 1998, 112 Stat. 2681–656, provided that:

"(1) IN GENERAL.—The Director of the National Science Foundation shall conduct a study to assess labor market needs for workers with high technology skills during the next 10 years. The study shall investigate and analyze the following:

"(A) Future training and education needs of companies in the high technology and information technology sectors and future training and education needs of United States students to ensure that students' skills at various levels are matched to the needs in such sectors.

"(B) An analysis of progress made by educators, employers, and government entities to improve the teaching and educational level of American students in the fields of math, science, computer science, and engineering since 1998.

"(C) An analysis of the number of United States workers currently or projected to work overseas in professional, technical, and managerial capacities.

"(D) The relative achievement rates of United States and foreign students in secondary schools in a variety of subjects, including math, science, computer science, English, and history.

"(E) The relative performance, by subject area, of United States and foreign students in postsecondary and graduate schools as compared to secondary schools.

"(F) The needs of the high technology sector for foreign workers with specific skills and the potential benefits and costs to United States employers, workers, consumers, postsecondary educational institutions, and the United States economy, from the entry of skilled foreign professionals in the fields of science and engineering.

"(G) The needs of the high technology sector to adapt products and services for export to particular local markets in foreign countries.

"(H) An examination of the amount and trend of moving the production or performance of products and services now occurring in the United States abroad.

"(2) REPORT.—Not later than October 1, 2000, the Director of the National Science Foundation shall submit to the Committees on the Judiciary of the United States House of Representatives and the Senate a report containing the results of the study described in paragraph (1).

"(3) INVOLVEMENT.—The study under paragraph (1) shall be conducted in a manner that ensures the participation of individuals representing a variety of points of view."

TWENTY-FIRST CENTURY WORKFORCE COMMISSION

Pub. L. 105–220, title III, subtitle C, Aug. 7, 1998, 112 Stat. 1087, as amended by Pub. L. 105–277, div. A, §101(f) [title VIII, §401(15)], Oct. 21, 1998, 112 Stat. 2681–337, 2681–412, known as the "Twenty-First Century Workforce Commission Act", established the Commission to study all matters relating to the information technology workforce in the United States, including skills necessary to enter the information technology workforce, ways to expand the number of skilled information technology workers, and the relative efficacy of programs in the United States and foreign countries to train information technology workers, and to submit a report to the President and Congress of its findings, conclusions, and recommendations for legislative and administrative actions, and provided for powers of the Commission, compensation of members, employment of staff, authorization of appropriations, and termination of the Commission 90 days after submission of its final report, which was released June 27, 2000.

§2702. Purposes

The purposes of this chapter are to—

(1) improve the ability of workers and worker organizations to recognize, develop, assess, and improve strategies for successfully integrating workers and worker organizations into the process of evaluating, selecting, and implementing advanced workplace technologies, and advanced workplace practices in a manner that creates and maintains stable well-paying jobs for workers; and

(2) assist workers and worker organizations in developing the expertise necessary for effective participation with employers in the development of strategies and programs for the successful evaluation, selection, and implementation of advanced workplace technologies and advanced workplace practices through the provision of a range of education, training, and related services.

(Pub. L. 103–382, title V, §543, Oct. 20, 1994, 108 Stat. 4052.)

§2703. Definitions

As used in this chapter:

(1) Advanced workplace practices

The term "advanced workplace practices" means innovations in work organization and performance, including high-performance workplace systems, flexible production techniques, quality programs, continuous improvement, concurrent engineering, close relationships between suppliers and customers, widely diffused decisionmaking and work teams, and effective integration of production technology, worker skills and training, and workplace organization, and such other characteristics as determined appropriate by the Secretary of Labor, in consultation with the Secretary of Commerce.

(2) Advanced workplace technologies

The term "advanced workplace technologies" includes—

(A) numerically controlled machine tools, robots, automated process control equipment, computerized flexible manufacturing systems, associated computer software, and other technology for improving the manufacturing and industrial production of goods and commercial services, which advance the state-of-the-art; or

(B) novel industrial and commercial techniques and processes not previously generally available that improve quality, productivity, and practices, including engineering design, quality assurance, concurrent engineering, continuous process production technology, inventory management, upgraded worker skills, communications with customers and suppliers, and promotion of sustainable economic growth.

(3) Department

The term "Department" means the Department of Labor.

(4) Nonprofit organization

The term "nonprofit organization" means a tax-exempt organization, as described in paragraph (3), (4), or (5) of section 501(c) of title 26.

(5) Secretary

The term "Secretary" means the Secretary of Labor.

(6) Worker organization

The term "worker organization" means a labor organization within the meaning of section 501(c)(5) of title 26.

(Pub. L. 103–382, title V, §544, Oct. 20, 1994, 108 Stat. 4053.)

§2704. Grants

(a) In general

The Secretary of Labor, after consultation with the Secretary of Commerce, shall, to the extent appropriations are available, award grants to eligible entities to carry out the purposes described in section 2702 of this title.

(b) Eligibility

To be eligible to receive a grant under this section, an entity shall—

(1) be a nonprofit organization, or a partnership consortium of such organizations;

(2) prepare and submit to the Secretary an application at such time, in such manner, and containing such information as the Secretary may require, including a description of the activities that the entity will carry out using amounts received under the grant; and

(3) agree to make available (directly or through donations from public or private entities) non-Federal contributions toward the costs of the activities to be conducted with grant funds, in an amount equal to the amount required under subsection (d) of this section.

(c) Use of amounts

An entity shall use amounts received under a grant awarded under this section to carry out the purposes described in section 2702 of this title through activities such as—

(1) the provision of technical assistance to workers, worker organizations, employers, State economic development agencies, State industrial extension programs, Advanced Technology Centers, and National Manufacturing Technology Centers to identify advanced workplace practices and strategies

that enhance the effective evaluation, selection, and implementation of advanced workplace technologies;

(2) the researching and identification of new and advanced workplace technologies, and advanced workplace practices that promote the improvement of workers' skills, wages, working conditions, and job security, that research the link between advanced workplace practices and long-term corporate performance, and which are consistent with the needs of local communities and the need for a healthy environment; and

(3) the development and dissemination of training programs and materials to be used for and by workers, worker organizations, employers, State economic development agencies, State industrial extension programs, Advanced Technology Centers, and National Manufacturing Technology Centers relating to the activities and services provided pursuant to paragraphs (1) and (2), and regarding successful practices including practices which address labor-management cooperation and the involvement of workers in the design, development, and implementation of workplace practices and technologies.

(d) Terms of grants and non-Federal shares

(1) Terms

Grants awarded under this section shall be for a term not to exceed six years.

(2) Non-Federal share

Amounts required to be contributed by an entity under subsection (b)(3) of this section shall equal—

(A) an amount equal to 15 percent of the amount provided under the grant in the first year for which the grant is awarded;

(B) an amount equal to 20 percent of the amount provided under the grant in the second year for which the grant is awarded;

(C) an amount equal to 33 percent of the amount provided under the grant in the third year for which the grant is awarded;

(D) an amount equal to 40 percent of the amount provided under the grant in the fourth year for which the grant is awarded; and

(E) an amount equal to 50 percent of the amount provided under the grant in the fifth and sixth years for which the grant is awarded.

(e) Evaluation

The Department shall develop mechanisms for evaluating the effectiveness of the use of a grant awarded under this section in carrying out the purposes under section 2702 of this title and, not later than two years after October 20, 1994, and every two years thereafter, prepare and submit a report to Congress concerning such evaluation.

(Pub. L. 103–382, title V, §545, Oct. 20, 1994, 108 Stat. 4053.)

§ 2705. Identification and dissemination of best practices

(a) In general

(1) Information

The Secretary, in cooperation and after consultation with the Secretary of Commerce, shall assist workers, worker organizations, and employers in successfully adopting advanced workplace technologies, and advanced workplace practices by identifying, collecting, and disseminating information on best workplace practices and workplace assessment tools, including—

(A) methods, techniques, and successful models of labor-management cooperation and of worker and worker organization participation in the development, evaluation, selection, and implementation of new and advanced workplace technologies, and advanced workplace practices;

(B) methods, techniques, and successful models for the design and implementation of new and advanced workplace practices;

(C) methods, techniques, and successful models for the design and implementation of advanced forms of work organization; and

(D) methods, techniques, and successful models for the assessment of worker skills and training needs relating to the effective development, evaluation, selection, and implementation of advanced workplace technologies, and advanced workplace practices.

(2) Contents

Such information on best workplace practices shall include—

(A) summaries and analyses of best practice cases;

(B) criteria for assessment of current workplace practices; and

(C) information on the best available education and training materials and services relating to the development, implementation, and operation of systems utilizing new and advanced workplace technologies, and advanced workplace practices.

(b) Distribution

The information and materials developed under this section shall be distributed through an appropriate entity designated by the Secretary of Commerce to the Regional Centers for the Transfer of Manufacturing Technology, to the Manufacturing Outreach Center, to other technology training entities, and directly to others as determined appropriate by the Secretary of Labor and the Secretary of Commerce.

(Pub. L. 103–382, title V, §546, Oct. 20, 1994, 108 Stat. 4055.)

§ 2706. Authorization of appropriations

(a) In general

There are authorized to be appropriated to carry out this chapter such sums as may be necessary for each of the fiscal years 1995 through 1997.

(b) Availability

Amounts appropriated under subsection (a) of this section shall remain available until expended.

(Pub. L. 103–382, title V, §547, Oct. 20, 1994, 108 Stat. 4055.)

CHAPTER 30—WORKFORCE INVESTMENT SYSTEMS

SUBCHAPTER I—WORKFORCE INVESTMENT DEFINITIONS

§ 2801. Definitions

In this chapter:

(1) Adult

Except in sections 2852 and 2862 of this title, the term "adult" means an individual who is age 18 or older.

(2) Adult education; adult education and literacy activities

The terms "adult education" and "adult education and literacy activities" have the meanings given the terms in section 9202 of title 20.

(3) Area vocational education school

The term "area vocational education school" has the meaning given the term "area career and technical education school" in section 2302 of title 20.

(4) Basic skills deficient

The term "basic skills deficient" means, with respect to an individual, that the individual has English reading, writing, or computing skills at or below the 8th grade level on a generally accepted standardized test or a comparable score on a criterion-referenced test.

(5) Case management

The term "case management" means the provision of a client-centered approach in the delivery of services, designed—

(A) to prepare and coordinate comprehensive employment plans, such as service strategies, for participants to ensure access to necessary workforce investment activities and supportive services, using, where feasible, computer-based technologies; and

(B) to provide job and career counseling during program participation and after job placement.

(6) Chief elected official

The term "chief elected official" means—

(A) the chief elected executive officer of a unit of general local government in a local area; and

(B) in a case in which a local area includes more than one unit of general local government, the individuals designated under the agreement described in section 2832(c)(1)(B) of this title.

(7) Community-based organization

The term "community-based organization" means a private nonprofit organization that is representative of a community or a significant segment of a community and that has demonstrated expertise and effectiveness in the field of workforce investment.

(8) Customized training

The term "customized training" means training—

(A) that is designed to meet the special requirements of an employer (including a group of employers);

(B) that is conducted with a commitment by the employer to employ an individual on successful completion of the training; and

(C) for which the employer pays for not less than 50 percent of the cost of the training.

(9) Dislocated worker

The term "dislocated worker" means an individual who—

(A)(i) has been terminated or laid off, or who has received a notice of termination or layoff, from employment;

(ii)(I) is eligible for or has exhausted entitlement to unemployment compensation; or

(II) has been employed for a duration sufficient to demonstrate, to the appropriate entity at a one-stop center referred to in section 2864(c) of this title, attachment to the workforce, but is not eligible for unemployment compensation due to insufficient earnings or having performed services for an employer that were not covered under a State unemployment compensation law; and

(iii) is unlikely to return to a previous industry or occupation;

(B)(i) has been terminated or laid off, or has received a notice of termination or layoff, from employment as a result of any permanent closure of, or any substantial layoff at, a plant, facility, or enterprise;

(ii) is employed at a facility at which the employer has made a general announcement that such facility will close within 180 days; or

(iii) for purposes of eligibility to receive services other than training services described in section 2864(d)(4) of this title, intensive services described in section 2864(d)(3) of this title, or supportive services, is employed at a facility at which the employer has made a general announcement that such facility will close;

(C) was self-employed (including employment as a farmer, a rancher, or a fisherman) but is unemployed as a result of general economic conditions in the community in which the individual resides or because of natural disasters; or

(D) is a displaced homemaker.

(10) Displaced homemaker

The term "displaced homemaker" means an individual who has been providing unpaid services to family members in the home and who—

(A) has been dependent on the income of another family member but is no longer supported by that income; and

(B) is unemployed or underemployed and is experiencing difficulty in obtaining or upgrading employment.

(11) Economic development agencies

The term "economic development agencies" includes local planning and zoning commissions or boards, community development agencies, and other local agencies and institutions responsible for regulating, promoting, or assisting in local economic development.

(12) Eligible provider

The term "eligible provider", used with respect to—

(A) training services, means a provider who is identified in accordance with section 2842(e)(3) of this title;

(B) intensive services, means a provider who is identified or awarded a contract as described in section 2864(d)(3)(B) of this title;

(C) youth activities, means a provider who is awarded a grant or contract in accordance with section 2843 of this title; or

(D) other workforce investment activities, means a public or private entity selected to be responsible for such activities, such as a one-stop operator designated or certified under section 2841(d) of this title.

(13) Eligible youth

Except as provided in subchapters III and IV of this chapter, the term "eligible youth" means an individual who—

(A) is not less than age 14 and not more than age 21;

(B) is a low-income individual; and

(C) is an individual who is one or more of the following:

(i) Deficient in basic literacy skills.

(ii) A school dropout.

(iii) Homeless, a runaway, or a foster child.

(iv) Pregnant or a parent.

(v) An offender.

(vi) An individual who requires additional assistance to complete an educational program, or to secure and hold employment.

(14) Employment and training activity

The term "employment and training activity" means an activity described in section 2864 of this title that is carried out for an adult or dislocated worker.

(15) Family

The term "family" means two or more persons related by blood, marriage, or decree of court, who are living in a single residence, and are included in one or more of the following categories:

(A) A husband, wife, and dependent children.

(B) A parent or guardian and dependent children.

(C) A husband and wife.

(16) Governor

The term "Governor" means the chief executive of a State.

(17) Individual with a disability

(A) In general

The term "individual with a disability" means an individual with any disability (as defined in section 12102 of title 42).

(B) Individuals with disabilities

The term "individuals with disabilities" means more than one individual with a disability.

(18) Labor market area

The term "labor market area" means an economically integrated geographic area within which individuals can reside and find employment within a reasonable distance or can readily change employment without changing their place of residence. Such an area shall be identified in accordance with criteria used by the Bureau of Labor Statistics of the Department of Labor in defining such areas or similar criteria established by a Governor.

(19) Literacy

The term "literacy" has the meaning given the term in section 9202 of title 20.

(20) Local area

The term "local area" means a local workforce investment area designated under section 2831 of this title.

(21) Local board

The term "local board" means a local workforce investment board established under section 2832 of this title.

(22) Local performance measure

The term "local performance measure" means a performance measure established under section 2871(c) of this title.

(23) Local educational agency

The term "local educational agency" has the meaning given the term in section 7801 of title 20.

(24) Lower living standard income level

The term "lower living standard income level" means that income level (adjusted for regional, metropolitan, urban, and rural differences and family size) determined annually by the Secretary based on the most recent lower living family budget issued by the Secretary.

(25) Low-income individual

The term "low-income individual" means an individual who—

(A) receives, or is a member of a family that receives, cash payments under a Federal, State, or local income-based public assistance program;

(B) received an income, or is a member of a family that received a total family income, for the 6-month period prior to application for the program involved (exclusive of unemployment compensation, child support payments, payments described in subparagraph (A), and old-age and survivors insurance benefits received under section 402 of title 42) that, in relation to family size, does not exceed the higher of—

(i) the poverty line, for an equivalent period; or

(ii) 70 percent of the lower living standard income level, for an equivalent period;

(C) is a member of a household that receives (or has been determined within the 6-month period prior to application for the program involved to be eligible to receive) supplemental nutrition assistance program benefits pursuant to the Food and Nutrition Act of 2008 (7 U.S.C. 2011 et seq.);

(D) qualifies as a homeless individual, as defined in subsections (a) and (c) of section 11302 of title 42;

(E) is a foster child on behalf of whom State or local government payments are made; or

(F) in cases permitted by regulations promulgated by the Secretary of Labor, is an individual with a disability whose own income meets the requirements of a program described in subparagraph (A) or of subparagraph (B), but who is a member of a family whose income does not meet such requirements.

(26) Nontraditional employment

The term "nontraditional employment" refers to occupations or fields of work for which individuals from one gender comprise less than 25 percent of the individuals employed in each such occupation or field of work.

(27) Offender

The term "offender" means any adult or juvenile—

(A) who is or has been subject to any stage of the criminal justice process, for whom services under this Act may be beneficial; or

(B) who requires assistance in overcoming artificial barriers to employment resulting from a record of arrest or conviction.

(28) Older individual

The term "older individual" means an individual age 55 or older.

(29) One-stop operator

The term "one-stop operator" means 1 or more entities designated or certified under section 2841(d) of this title.

(30) One-stop partner

The term "one-stop partner" means—

(A) an entity described in section 2841(b)(1) of this title; and

(B) an entity described in section 2841(b)(2) of this title that is participating, with the approval of the local board and chief elected official, in the operation of a one-stop delivery system.

(31) On-the-job training

The term "on-the-job training" means training by an employer that is provided to a paid participant while engaged in productive work in a job that—

(A) provides knowledge or skills essential to the full and adequate performance of the job;

(B) provides reimbursement to the employer of up to 50 percent of the wage rate of the participant, for the extraordinary costs of providing the training and additional supervision related to the training; and

(C) is limited in duration as appropriate to the occupation for which the participant is being trained, taking into account the content of the training, the prior work experience of the participant, and the service strategy of the participant, as appropriate.

(32) Outlying area

The term "outlying area" means the United States Virgin Islands, Guam, American Samoa, the Commonwealth of the Northern Mariana Islands, the Republic of the Marshall Islands, the Federated States of Micronesia, and the Republic of Palau.

(33) Out-of-school youth

The term "out-of-school youth" means—

(A) an eligible youth who is a school dropout; or

(B) an eligible youth who has received a secondary school diploma or its equivalent but is basic skills deficient, unemployed, or underemployed.

(34) Participant

The term "participant" means an individual who has been determined to be eligible to participate in and who is receiving services (except followup services authorized under this chapter) under a program authorized by this chapter. Participation shall be deemed to commence on the first day, following determination of eligibility, on which the individual began receiving subsidized employment, training, or other services provided under this chapter.

(35) Postsecondary educational institution

The term "postsecondary educational institution" means an institution of higher education, as defined in section 1002 of title 20.

(36) Poverty line

The term "poverty line" means the poverty line (as defined by the Office of Management and Budget, and revised annually in accordance with section 9902(2) of title 42) applicable to a family of the size involved.

(37) Public assistance

The term "public assistance" means Federal, State, or local government cash payments for which eligibility is determined by a needs or income test.

(38) Rapid response activity

The term "rapid response activity" means an activity provided by a State, or by an entity designated by a State, with funds provided by the State under section 2864(a)(1)(A) of this title, in the case of a permanent closure or mass layoff at a plant, facility, or enterprise, or a natural or other disaster, that results in mass job dislocation, in order to assist dislocated workers in obtaining reemployment as soon as possible, with services including—

(A) the establishment of onsite contact with employers and employee representatives—

(i) immediately after the State is notified of a current or projected permanent closure or mass layoff; or

(ii) in the case of a disaster, immediately after the State is made aware of mass job dislocation as a result of such disaster;

(B) the provision of information and access to available employment and training activities;

(C) assistance in establishing a labor-management committee, voluntarily agreed to by labor and management, with the ability to devise and implement a strategy for assessing the employment and training needs of dislocated workers and obtaining services to meet such needs;

(D) the provision of emergency assistance adapted to the particular closure, layoff, or disaster; and

(E) the provision of assistance to the local community in developing a coordinated response and in obtaining access to State economic development assistance.

(39) School dropout

The term "school dropout" means an individual who is no longer attending any school and who has not received a secondary school diploma or its recognized equivalent.

(40) Secondary school

The term "secondary school" has the meaning given the term in section 7801 of title 20.

(41) Secretary

The term "Secretary" means the Secretary of Labor, and the term means such Secretary for purposes of section 9273 of title 20.

(42) State

The term "State" means each of the several States of the United States, the District of Columbia, and the Commonwealth of Puerto Rico.

(43) State adjusted level of performance

The term "State adjusted level of performance" means a level described in clause (iii) or (v) of section 2871(b)(3)(A) of this title.

(44) State board

The term "State board" means a State workforce investment board established under section 2821 of this title.

(45) State performance measure

The term "State performance measure" means a performance measure established under section 2871(b) of this title.

(46) Supportive services

The term "supportive services" means services such as transportation, child care, dependent care, housing, and needs-related payments, that are necessary to enable an individual to participate in activities authorized under this chapter, consistent with the provisions of this chapter.

(47) Unemployed individual

The term "unemployed individual" means an individual who is without a job and who wants and is available for work. The determination of whether an individual is without a job shall be made in accordance with the criteria used by the Bureau of Labor Statistics of the Department of Labor in defining individuals as unemployed.

(48) Unit of general local government

The term "unit of general local government" means any general purpose political subdivision of a State that has the power to levy taxes and spend funds, as well as general corporate and police powers.

(49) Veteran; related definition

(A) Veteran

The term "veteran" means an individual who served in the active military, naval, or air service, and who was discharged or released from such service under conditions other than dishonorable.

(B) Recently separated veteran

The term "recently separated veteran" means any veteran who applies for participation under this chapter within 48 months after the discharge or release from active military, naval, or air service.

(50) Vocational education

The term "vocational education" has the meaning given the term "career and technical education" in section 2302 of title 20.

(51) Workforce investment activity

The term "workforce investment activity" means an employment and training activity, and a youth activity.

(52) Youth activity

The term "youth activity" means an activity described in section 2854 of this title that is carried out for eligible youth (or as described in section 2854(c)(5) of this title).

(53) Youth council

The term "youth council" means a council established under section 2832(h) of this title.

(Pub. L. 105–220, title I, §101, Aug. 7, 1998, 112 Stat. 939; Pub. L. 105–244, title I, §102(d)(1), Oct. 7, 1998, 112 Stat. 1622; Pub. L. 105–332, §3(f), Oct. 31, 1998, 112 Stat. 3126; Pub. L. 106–400, §2, Oct. 30, 2000, 114 Stat. 1675; Pub. L. 107–110, title X, §1076(w), Jan. 8, 2002, 115 Stat. 2093; Pub. L. 109–270, §2(h)(1), (2), Aug. 12, 2006, 120 Stat. 747; Pub. L. 110–234, title IV, §4002(b)(1)(B), (E), (2)(R), May 22, 2008, 122 Stat. 1096, 1097; Pub. L. 110–246, §4(a), title IV, §4002(b)(1)(B), (E), (2)(R), June 18, 2008, 122 Stat. 1664, 1857, 1858.)

REFERENCES IN TEXT

This chapter, referred to in text, was in the original "this title" meaning title I of Pub. L. 105–220, Aug. 7, 1998, 112 Stat. 939, as amended, which enacted this chapter, repealed sections 1501 to 1505, 1511 to 1583, 1592 to 1735, 1737 to 1791h, 1792 to 1792b, 2301 to 2314 of this title, section 211 of former Title 40, Appendix, Public Buildings, Property, and Works, sections 11421, 11441 to 11447, 11449, 11450, 11461 to 11466, 11471, and 11472 of Title 42, The Public Health and Welfare, and sections 42101 to 42106 of Title 49, Transportation, enacted provisions set out as notes under sections 1501, 2301, and 2940 of this title and section 11421 of Title 42, and repealed provisions set out as notes under sections 801 and 2301 of this title and section 1255a of Title 8, Aliens and Nationality. For complete classification of title I to the Code, see Tables.

The Food and Nutrition Act of 2008, referred to in par. (25)(C), is Pub. L. 88–525, Aug. 31, 1964, 78 Stat. 703, which is classified generally to chapter 51 (§2011 et seq.) of Title 7, Agriculture. For complete classification of this Act to the Code, see Short Title note set out under section 2011 of Title 7 and Tables.

This Act, referred to in par. (27)(A), is Pub. L. 105–220, Aug. 7, 1998, 112 Stat. 936, as amended, known as the Workforce Investment Act of 1998. For complete classification of this Act to the Code, see Short Title note set out under section 9201 of Title 20, Education, and Tables.

CODIFICATION

Pub. L. 110–234 and Pub. L. 110–246 made identical amendments to this section. The amendments by Pub. L. 110–234 were repealed by section 4(a) of Pub. L. 110–246.

PRIOR PROVISIONS

Provisions similar to this section were contained in section 1503 of this title prior to repeal by Pub. L. 105–220.

AMENDMENTS

2008—Par. (25)(C). Pub. L. 110–246, §4002(b)(1)(B), (E), (2)(R), substituted "supplemental nutrition assistance program benefits" for "food stamps" and "Food and Nutrition Act of 2008" for "Food Stamp Act of 1977".

2006—Par. (3). Pub. L. 109–270, §2(h)(1), substituted "given the term 'area career and technical education school'" for "given the term" and made technical amendment to reference in original act which appears in text as reference to section 2302 of title 20.

Par. (50). Pub. L. 109–270, §2(h)(2), substituted "given the term 'career and technical education' in section 2302 of title 20." for "given the term in section 2471 of title 20."

2002—Pars. (23), (40). Pub. L. 107–110 substituted "section 7801 of title 20" for "section 8801 of title 20".

2000—Par. (25)(D). Pub. L. 106–400 made technical amendment to reference in original act which appears in text as reference to section 11302 of title 42.

1998—Par. (3). Pub. L. 105–332 substituted "section 2302 of title 20" for "section 2471 of title 20".

Par. (35). Pub. L. 105–244 substituted "section 1002 of title 20" for "section 1088 of title 20".

EFFECTIVE DATE OF 2008 AMENDMENT

Amendment of this section and repeal of Pub. L. 110–234 by Pub. L. 110–246 effective May 22, 2008, the date of enactment of Pub. L. 110–234, except as otherwise provided, see section 4 of Pub. L. 110–246, set out as an Effective Date note under section 8701 of Title 7, Agriculture.

Amendment by section 4002(b)(1)(B), (E), (2)(R) of Pub. L. 110–246 effective Oct. 1, 2008, see section 4407 of Pub. L. 110–246, set out as a note under section 1161 of Title 2, The Congress.

EFFECTIVE DATE OF 2002 AMENDMENT

Amendment by Pub. L. 107–110 effective Jan. 8, 2002, except with respect to certain noncompetitive programs and competitive programs, see section 5 of Pub. L. 107–110, set out as an Effective Date note under section 6301 of Title 20, Education.

EFFECTIVE DATE OF 1998 AMENDMENT

Amendment by Pub. L. 105–244 effective Oct. 1, 1998, except as otherwise provided in Pub. L. 105–244, see section 3 of Pub. L. 105–244, set out as a note under section 1001 of Title 20, Education.

SHORT TITLE OF 2007 AMENDMENT

Pub. L. 110–140, title X, § 1001, Dec. 19, 2007, 121 Stat. 1748, provided that: "This title [amending section 2916 of this title] may be cited as the 'Green Jobs Act of 2007'."

SHORT TITLE OF 2006 AMENDMENT

Pub. L. 109–281, § 1, Sept. 22, 2006, 120 Stat. 1173, provided that: "This Act [enacting section 2918a of this title, amending section 2939 of this title, section 1701u of Title 12, Banks and Banking, section 4183 of Title 25, Indians, and section 12870 of Title 42, The Public Health and Welfare, repealing sections 12899 to 12899i of Title 42, and enacting provisions set out as notes under section 2918a of this title and section 1701u of Title 12] may be cited as the 'YouthBuild Transfer Act'."

DECLARATION OF POLICY

Pub. L. 102–367, title I, § 101(a), Sept. 7, 1992, 106 Stat. 1022, provided that: "In recognition of the training needs of low-income adults and youth, the Congress declares it to be the policy of the United States to—

"(1) provide financial assistance to States and local service delivery areas to meet the training needs of such low-income adults and youth, and to assist such individuals in obtaining unsubsidized employment;

"(2) increase the funds available for programs under title II of the Job Training Partnership Act ([former] 29 U.S.C. 1601 et seq.) by not less than 10 percent of the baseline each fiscal year to provide for growth in the percentage of eligible adults and youth served above the 5 percent of the eligible population that is currently served; and

"(3) encourage the provision of longer, more comprehensive, education, training, and employment services to the eligible population, which also requires increased funding in order to maintain current service levels."

TRANSITIONAL PROVISIONS

For provisions relating to transition from authority under the Job Training Partnership Act (29 U.S.C. 1501 et seq.) to the workforce investment systems established under this chapter, including provisions relating to regulations, expenditures, and reorganization of functions in the Department of Labor, see section 9276 of Title 20, Education.

EXECUTIVE ORDER NO. 13174

Ex. Ord. No. 13174, Oct. 27, 2000, 65 F.R. 65705, which established the Commission on Workers, Communities, and Economic Change in the New Economy, was revoked by Ex. Ord. No. 13218, § 3(b), June 20, 2001, 66 F.R. 33629, set out below.

EX. ORD. NO. 13218. 21ST CENTURY WORKFORCE INITIATIVE

Ex. Ord. No. 13218, June 20, 2001, 66 F.R. 33627, provided:

By the authority vested in me as President by the Constitution and laws of the United States of America, including the Federal Advisory Committee Act, as amended (5 U.S.C. App.), and in order to promote the study and the development of strategies to address the needs of the 21st century workforce, it is hereby ordered as follows:

SECTION 1. *Establishment of the Office of the 21st Century Workforce.* (a) The Secretary of Labor is hereby directed to establish within the Department of Labor the Office of the 21st Century Workforce. The Office shall provide a focal point for the identification and study of issues relating to the workforce of the United States and the development of strategies for effectively addressing such issues.

(b) The Office of the 21st Century Workforce shall gather and disseminate information relating to workforce issues by conducting summits, conferences, field hearings, meetings, and other appropriate forums designed to encourage the participation of organizations and individuals interested in such issues, including business and labor organizations, academicians, employers, employees, and public officials at the local, State, and Federal levels.

(c) Among the issues to be addressed by the Office of the 21st Century Workforce shall be the identification of the ways in which the Department of Labor may streamline and update the information and services made available to the workforce by the Department; eliminate duplicative or overlapping rules and regulations; and eliminate statutory and regulatory barriers to assisting the workforce in successfully adapting to the challenges of the 21st century.

SEC. 2. *Establishment of the Council on the 21st Century Workforce.*

(a) *Establishment and Composition of the Council.*

(i) There is hereby established the "President's Council on the 21st Century Workforce" (Council).

(ii) The Council shall be composed of not more than 13 members who shall be appointed by the President. The membership shall include individuals who represent the views of business and labor organizations, Federal, State, and local governments, academicians and educators, and such other associations and entities as the President determines are appropriate. In addition, the Secretary of Labor and the Director of the Office of Personnel Management shall serve as ex officio members representing the views of the Federal Government. The Secretary of Labor shall be the Chairperson of the Council.

(b) *Functions of the Council.* The Council shall provide information and advice to the President through the Secretary of Labor, the Office of the 21st Century Workforce within the Department of Labor, and other appropriate Federal officials relating to issues affecting the 21st century workforce. These activities shall include:

(i) assessing the effects of rapid technological changes, demographic trends, globalization, changes in work processes, and the need for new and enhanced skills for workers, employers, and other related sectors of society;

(ii) examining current and alternative approaches to assisting workers and employers in adjusting to and benefitting from such changes, including opportunities for workplace education, retraining, access to assistive technologies and workplace supports, and skills upgrading;

(iii) identifying impediments to the adjustment to such changes by workers and employers and recommending approaches and policies that could remove those impediments;

(iv) assisting the Office of the 21st Century Workforce in reviewing programs carried out by the Department of Labor and identifying changes to such programs that would stream line [sic] and update their effectiveness in meeting the needs of the workforce; and

(v) analyzing such additional issues relating to the workforce and making such reports as the President or the Secretary of Labor may request.

(c) *Administration of the Council.*

(i) The Council shall meet on the call of the Chairperson, at a time and place designated by the Chairperson. The Chairperson may form subcommittees or working groups within the Council to address particular matters.

(ii) The Council may from time to time prescribe such procedures and policies relating to the activities of the Council as are not inconsistent with law or with the provisions of this order.

(iii) Each member of the Council who is not an officer or employee of the Federal Government shall serve without compensation but shall be allowed travel expenses, including per diem in lieu of subsistence, as authorized by law for persons serving intermittently in Federal service (5 U.S.C. 5701–5707).

(iv) The Department of Labor shall make available appropriate funding and administrative support to assist the Council in carrying out the functions under this section, including necessary office space, equipment, supplies, staff, and services. The Secretary of Labor shall perform the functions of the President under the Federal Advisory Committee Act (5 U.S.C. App.), as amended, except that of reporting to the Congress, with respect to the Council in accordance with the guidelines and procedures established by the Administrator of General Services.

(v) The heads of executive agencies shall, to the extent permitted by law, provide the Council with such information as it may require for purposes of carrying out the functions described in this section.

(d) *Termination of the Council.* The Council shall terminate 2 years from the date of this order unless extended by the President prior to such date.

SEC. 3. *Effect on Prior Orders.*

(a) [Amended Ex. Ord. No. 13111, 5 U.S.C. 4103 note.]

(b) *Revocation of Executive Order 13174.* Executive Order 13174 of October 27, 2000, relating to the establishment of the Commission on Workers, Communities, and Economic Change in the New Economy, is revoked.

GEORGE W. BUSH.

SUBCHAPTER II—STATEWIDE AND LOCAL WORKFORCE INVESTMENT SYSTEMS

§2811. Purpose

The purpose of this subchapter is to provide workforce investment activities, through statewide and local workforce investment systems, that increase the employment, retention, and earnings of participants, and increase occupational skill attainment by participants, and, as a result, improve the quality of the workforce, reduce welfare dependency, and enhance the productivity and competitiveness of the Nation.

(Pub. L. 105–220, title I, §106, Aug. 7, 1998, 112 Stat. 945.)

PART A—STATE PROVISIONS

§2821. State workforce investment boards

(a) In general

The Governor of a State shall establish a State workforce investment board to assist in the development of the State plan described in section 2822 of this title and to carry out the other functions described in subsection (d) of this section.

(b) Membership

(1) In general

The State Board shall include—

(A) the Governor;

(B) 2 members of each chamber of the State legislature, appointed by the appropriate presiding officers of each such chamber; and

(C) representatives appointed by the Governor, who are—

(i) representatives of business in the State, who—

(I) are owners of businesses, chief executives or operating officers of businesses, and other business executives or employers with optimum policymaking or hiring authority, including members of local boards described in section 2832(b)(2)(A)(i) of this title;

(II) represent businesses with employment opportunities that reflect the employment opportunities of the State; and

(III) are appointed from among individuals nominated by State business organizations and business trade associations;

(ii) chief elected officials (representing both cities and counties, where appropriate);

(iii) representatives of labor organizations, who have been nominated by State labor federations;

(iv) representatives of individuals and organizations that have experience with respect to youth activities;

(v) representatives of individuals and organizations that have experience and expertise in the delivery of workforce investment activities, including chief executive officers of community colleges and community-based organizations within the State;

(vi)(I) the lead State agency officials with responsibility for the programs and activities that are described in section 2841(b) of this title and carried out by one-stop partners; and

(II) in any case in which no lead State agency official has responsibility for such a program, service, or activity, a representative in the State with expertise relating to such program, service, or activity; and

(vii) such other representatives and State agency officials as the Governor may designate, such as the State agency officials responsible for economic development and juvenile justice programs in the State.

(2) Authority and regional representation of board members

Members of the board that represent organizations, agencies, or other entities shall be individuals with optimum policymaking authority within the organizations, agencies, or entities. The members of the board shall represent diverse regions of the State, including urban, rural, and suburban areas.

(3) Majority

A majority of the members of the State Board shall be representatives described in paragraph (1)(C)(i).

(c) Chairperson

The Governor shall select a chairperson for the State Board from among the representatives described in subsection (b)(1)(C)(i) of this section.

(d) Functions

The State Board shall assist the Governor in—

(1) development of the State plan;

(2) development and continuous improvement of a statewide system of activities that are funded under this subchapter or carried out through a one-stop delivery system described in section 2864(c) of this title that receives funds under this subchapter (referred to in this chapter as a "statewide workforce investment system"), including—

(A) development of linkages in order to assure coordination and nonduplication among the programs and activities described in section 2841(b) of this title; and

(B) review of local plans;

(3) commenting at least once annually on the measures taken pursuant to section 2323(b)(3) of title 20;

(4) designation of local areas as required in section 2831 of this title;

(5) development of allocation formulas for the distribution of funds for adult employment and training activities and youth activities to local areas as permitted under sections 2853(b)(3)(B) and 2863(b)(3)(B) of this title;

(6) development and continuous improvement of comprehensive State performance measures, including State adjusted levels of performance, to assess the effectiveness of the workforce investment activities in the State as required under section 2871(b) of this title;

(7) preparation of the annual report to the Secretary described in section 2871(d) of this title;

(8) development of the statewide employment statistics system described in section 49*l*-2(e) of this title; and

(9) development of an application for an incentive grant under section 9273 of title 20.

(e) Alternative entity

(1) In general

For purposes of complying with subsections (a), (b), and (c) of this section, a State may use any State entity (including a State council, State workforce development board, combination of regional workforce development boards, or similar entity) that—

(A) was in existence on December 31, 1997;

(B)(i) was established pursuant to section 122 or title VII of the Job Training Partnership Act, as in effect on December 31, 1997; or

(ii) is substantially similar to the State board described in subsections (a), (b), and (c) of this section; and

(C) includes representatives of business in the State and representatives of labor organizations in the State.

(2) References

References in this Act to a State board shall be considered to include such an entity.

(f) Conflict of interest

A member of a State board may not—

(1) vote on a matter under consideration by the State board—

(A) regarding the provision of services by such member (or by an entity that such member represents); or

(B) that would provide direct financial benefit to such member or the immediate family of such member; or

(2) engage in any other activity determined by the Governor to constitute a conflict of interest as specified in the State plan.

(g) Sunshine provision

The State board shall make available to the public, on a regular basis through open meetings, information regarding the activities of the State board, including information regarding the State plan prior to submission of the plan, information regarding membership, and, on request, minutes of formal meetings of the State board.

(Pub. L. 105–220, title I, § 111, Aug. 7, 1998, 112 Stat. 945; Pub. L. 105–277, div. A, § 101(f) [title VIII, § 401(1)], Oct. 21, 1998, 112 Stat. 2681–337, 2681–411; Pub. L. 109–270, § 2(h)(3), Aug. 12, 2006, 120 Stat. 747.)

REFERENCES IN TEXT

This chapter, referred to in subsec. (d)(2), was in the original "this title" meaning title I of Pub. L. 105–220, Aug. 7, 1998, 112 Stat. 939, as amended, which enacted this chapter, repealed sections 1501 to 1505, 1511 to 1583, 1592 to 1735, 1737 to 1791h, 1792 to 1792b, 2301 to 2314 of this title, section 211 of former Title 40, Appendix, Public Buildings, Property, and Works, sections 11421, 11441 to 11447, 11449, 11450, 11461 to 11466, 11471, and 11472 of Title 42, The Public Health and Welfare, and sections 42101 to 42106 of Title 49, Transportation, enacted provisions set out as notes under sections 1501, 2301, and 2940 of this title and section 11421 of Title 42, and repealed provisions set out as notes under sections 801 and 2301 of this title and section 1255a of Title 8, Aliens and Nationality. For complete classification of title I to the Code, see Tables.

The Job Training Partnership Act, referred to in subsec. (e)(1)(B)(i), is Pub. L. 97–300, Oct. 13, 1982, 96 Stat. 1322, as amended. Section 122 and title VII of the Act were classified to section 1532 and subchapter VI (§ 1792 et seq.) of chapter 19 of this title, respectively, prior to repeal by Pub. L. 105–220, title I, § 199(b)(2), (c)(2)(B), Aug. 7, 1998, 112 Stat. 1059, effective July 1, 2000. For complete classification of this Act to the Code, see Tables.

This Act, referred to in subsec. (e)(2), is Pub. L. 105–220, Aug. 7, 1998, 112 Stat. 936, as amended, known as the Workforce Investment Act of 1998. For complete classification of this Act to the Code, see Short Title note set out under section 9201 of Title 20, Education, and Tables.

AMENDMENTS

2006—Subsec. (d)(3). Pub. L. 109–270 substituted "section 2323(b)(3) of title 20" for "section 2323(b)(14) of title 20".

1998—Subsec. (c). Pub. L. 105–277 substituted "Chairperson" for "Chairman" in heading.

§ 2822. State plan

(a) In general

For a State to be eligible to receive an allotment under section 2852 or 2862 of this title, or to receive financial assistance under the Wagner-Peyser Act (29 U.S.C. 49 et seq.), the Governor of the State shall submit to the Secretary for consideration by the Secretary, a single State plan (referred to in this chapter as the "State plan") that outlines a 5-year strategy for the statewide workforce investment system of the State and that meets the requirements of section 2821 of this title and this section.

(b) Contents

The State plan shall include—

(1) a description of the State board, including a description of the manner in which such board collaborated in the development of the State plan and a description of how the board will continue to collaborate in carrying out the functions described in section 2821(d) of this title;

(2) a description of State-imposed requirements for the statewide workforce investment system;

(3) a description of the State performance accountability system developed for the workforce investment activities to be carried out

through the statewide workforce investment system, that includes information identifying State performance measures as described in section 2871(b)(3)(A)(ii) of this title;

(4) information describing—

(A) the needs of the State with regard to current and projected employment opportunities, by occupation;

(B) the job skills necessary to obtain such employment opportunities;

(C) the skills and economic development needs of the State; and

(D) the type and availability of workforce investment activities in the State;

(5) an identification of local areas designated in the State, including a description of the process used for the designation of such areas;

(6) an identification of criteria to be used by chief elected officials for the appointment of members of local boards based on the requirements of section 2832 of this title;

(7) the detailed plans required under section 8 of the Wagner-Peyser Act (29 U.S.C. 49g);

(8)(A) a description of the procedures that will be taken by the State to assure coordination of and avoid duplication among—

(i) workforce investment activities authorized under this chapter;

(ii) other activities authorized under this chapter;

(iii) programs authorized under the Wagner-Peyser Act (29 U.S.C. 49 et seq.), title II of this Act [20 U.S.C. 9201 et seq.], title I of the Rehabilitation Act of 1973 (29 U.S.C. 720 et seq.), part A of title IV of the Social Security Act (42 U.S.C. 601 et seq.), and section 6(d)(4) of the Food and Nutrition Act of 2008 (7 U.S.C. 2015(d)(4)), activities authorized under title V of the Older Americans Act of 1965 (42 U.S.C. 3056 et seq.), and career and technical education activities at the postsecondary level authorized under the Carl D. Perkins Career and Technical Education Act of 2006 (20 U.S.C. 2301 et seq.);

(iv) work programs authorized under section 6(*o*) of the Food and Nutrition Act of 2008 (7 U.S.C. 2015(*o*));

(v) activities authorized under chapter 2 of title II of the Trade Act of 1974 (19 U.S.C. 2271 et seq.);

(vi) activities authorized under chapter 41 of title 38;

(vii) employment and training activities carried out under the Community Services Block Grant Act (42 U.S.C. 9901 et seq.);

(viii) activities authorized under the National and Community Service Act of 1990 (42 U.S.C. 12501 et seq.);

(ix) employment and training activities carried out by the Department of Housing and Urban Development; and

(x) programs authorized under State unemployment compensation laws (in accordance with applicable Federal law); and

(B) a description of the common data collection and reporting processes used for the programs and activities described in subparagraph (A);

(9) a description of the process used by the State, consistent with section 2821(g) of this title, to provide an opportunity for public comment, including comment by representatives of businesses and representatives of labor organizations, and input into development of the plan, prior to submission of the plan;

(10) information identifying how the State will use funds the State receives under this subchapter to leverage other Federal, State, local, and private resources, in order to maximize the effectiveness of such resources, and to expand the participation of business, employees, and individuals in the statewide workforce investment system;

(11) assurances that the State will provide, in accordance with section 2934 of this title for fiscal control and fund accounting procedures that may be necessary to ensure the proper disbursement of, and accounting for, funds paid to the State through the allotments made under sections 2852 and 2862 of this title;

(12)(A) a description of the methods and factors the State will use in distributing funds to local areas for youth activities and adult employment and training activities under sections 2853(b)(3)(B) and 2863(b)(3)(B) of this title, including—

(i) a description of how the individuals and entities represented on the State board were involved in determining such methods and factors of distribution; and

(ii) a description of how the State consulted with chief elected officials in local areas throughout the State in determining such distribution;

(B) assurances that the funds will be distributed equitably throughout the State, and that no local areas will suffer significant shifts in funding from year to year; and

(C) a description of the formula prescribed by the Governor pursuant to section 2863(b)(2)(B) of this title for the allocation of funds to local areas for dislocated worker employment and training activities;

(13) information specifying the actions that constitute a conflict of interest prohibited in the State for purposes of sections 2821(f) and 2832(g) of this title;

(14) with respect to the one-stop delivery systems described in section 2864(c) of this title (referred to individually in this chapter as a "one-stop delivery system"), a description of the strategy of the State for assisting local areas in development and implementation of fully operational one-stop delivery systems in the State;

(15) a description of the appeals process referred to in section 2831(a)(5) of this title;

(16) a description of the competitive process to be used by the State to award grants and contracts in the State for activities carried out under this chapter;

(17) with respect to the employment and training activities authorized in section 2864 of this title—

(A) a description of—

(i) the employment and training activities that will be carried out with the funds received by the State through the allotment made under section 2862 of this title;

(ii) how the State will provide rapid response activities to dislocated workers from funds reserved under section 2863(a)(2) of this title for such purposes, including the designation of an identifiable State rapid response dislocated worker unit to carry out statewide rapid response activities;

(iii) the procedures the local boards in the State will use to identify eligible providers of training services described in section 2864(d)(4) of this title (other than on-the-job training or customized training), as required under section 2842 of this title; and

(iv) how the State will serve the employment and training needs of dislocated workers (including displaced homemakers), low-income individuals (including recipients of public assistance), individuals training for nontraditional employment, and other individuals with multiple barriers to employment (including older individuals and individuals with disabilities); and

(B) an assurance that veterans will be afforded the employment and training activities by the State, to the extent practicable; and

(18) with respect to youth activities authorized in section 2854 of this title, information—

(A) describing the State strategy for providing comprehensive services to eligible youth, particularly those eligible youth who are recognized as having significant barriers to employment;

(B) identifying the criteria to be used by local boards in awarding grants for youth activities, including criteria that the Governor and local boards will use to identify effective and ineffective youth activities and providers of such activities;

(C) describing how the State will coordinate the youth activities carried out in the State under section 2854 of this title with the services provided by Job Corps centers in the State (where such centers exist); and

(D) describing how the State will coordinate youth activities described in subparagraph (C) with activities carried out through the youth opportunity grants under section 2914 of this title.

(c) Plan submission and approval

A State plan submitted to the Secretary under this section by a Governor shall be considered to be approved by the Secretary at the end of the 90-day period beginning on the day the Secretary receives the plan, unless the Secretary makes a written determination, during the 90-day period, that—

(1) the plan is inconsistent with the provisions of this chapter; or

(2) in the case of the portion of the plan described in section 8(a) of the Wagner-Peyser Act (29 U.S.C. 49g(a)), the portion does not satisfy the criteria for approval provided in section 8(d) of such Act.

(d) Modifications to plan

A State may submit modifications to a State plan in accordance with the requirements of this section and section 2821 of this title as necessary during the 5-year period covered by the plan.

(Pub. L. 105–220, title I, § 112, Aug. 7, 1998, 112 Stat. 948; Pub. L. 105–277, div. A, § 101(f) [title VIII, § 401(2)], Oct. 21, 1998, 112 Stat. 2681–337, 2681–411; Pub. L. 109–270, § 2(h)(4), Aug. 12, 2006, 120 Stat. 748; Pub. L. 110–234, title IV, § 4002(b)(1)(B), (2)(R), May 22, 2008, 122 Stat. 1096, 1097; Pub. L. 110–246, § 4(a), title IV, § 4002(b)(1)(B), (2)(R), June 18, 2008, 122 Stat. 1664, 1857, 1858.)

REFERENCES IN TEXT

The Wagner-Peyser Act, referred to in subsecs. (a) and (b)(8)(A)(iii), is act June 6, 1933, ch. 49, 48 Stat. 113, as amended, which is classified generally to chapter 4B (§ 49 et seq.) of this title. For complete classification of this Act to the Code, see Short Title note set out under section 49 of this title and Tables.

Title II of this Act, referred to in subsec. (b)(8)(A)(iii), is title II of Pub. L. 105–220, Aug. 7, 1998, 112 Stat. 1059, as amended, known as the Adult Education and Family Literacy Act, which is classified principally to subchapter I (§ 9201 et seq.) of chapter 73 of Title 20, Education. For complete classification of this Act to the Code, see Short Title note set out under section 9201 of Title 20 and Tables.

The Rehabilitation Act of 1973, referred to in subsec. (b)(8)(A)(iii), is Pub. L. 93–112, Sept. 26, 1973, 87 Stat. 355, as amended. Title I of the Act is classified generally to subchapter I (§ 720 et seq.) of chapter 16 of this title. For complete classification of this Act to the Code, see Short Title note set out under section 701 of this title and Tables.

The Social Security Act, referred to in subsec. (b)(8)(A)(iii), is act Aug. 14, 1935, ch. 531, 49 Stat. 620, as amended. Part A of title IV of the Act is classified generally to part A (§ 601 et seq.) of subchapter IV of chapter 7 of Title 42, The Public Health and Welfare. For complete classification of this Act to the Code, see section 1305 of Title 42 and Tables.

The Older Americans Act of 1965, referred to in subsec. (b)(8)(A)(iii), is Pub. L. 89–73, July 14, 1965, 79 Stat. 218, as amended. Title V of the Act, known as the Older American Community Service Employment Act, is classified generally to subchapter IX (§ 3056 et seq.) of chapter 35 of Title 42, The Public Health and Welfare. For complete classification of this Act to the Code, see Short Title note set out under section 3001 of Title 42 and Tables.

The Carl D. Perkins Career and Technical Education Act of 2006, referred to in subsec. (b)(8)(A)(iii), is Pub. L. 88–210, Dec. 18, 1963, 77 Stat. 403, as amended generally by Pub. L. 109–270, § 1(b), Aug. 12, 2006, 120 Stat. 683, which is classified generally to chapter 44 (§ 2301 et seq.) of Title 20, Education. For complete classification of this Act to the Code, see Short Title note set out under section 2301 of Title 20 and Tables.

The Trade Act of 1974, referred to in subsec. (b)(8)(A)(v), is Pub. L. 93–618, Jan. 3, 1975, 88 Stat. 1978, as amended. Chapter 2 of title II of the Act is classified generally to part 2 (§ 2271 et seq.) of subchapter II of chapter 12 of Title 19, Customs Duties. For complete classification of this Act to the Code, see section 2101 of Title 19 and Tables.

The Community Services Block Grant Act, referred to in subsec. (b)(8)(A)(vii), is subtitle B (§§ 671–683) of title VI of Pub. L. 97–35, Aug. 13, 1981, 95 Stat. 511, as amended, which is classified generally to chapter 106 (§ 9901 et seq.) of Title 42, The Public Health and Welfare. For complete classification of this Act to the Code, see Short Title note set out under section 9901 of Title 42 and Tables.

The National and Community Service Act of 1990, referred to in subsec. (b)(8)(A)(viii), is Pub. L. 101–610, Nov. 16, 1990, 104 Stat. 3127, as amended, which is classified principally to chapter 129 (§ 12501 et seq.) of Title 42, The Public Health and Welfare. For complete classification of this Act to the Code, see Short Title note set out under section 12501 of Title 42 and Tables.

CODIFICATION

Pub. L. 110–234 and Pub. L. 110–246 made identical amendments to this section. The amendments by Pub. L. 110–234 were repealed by section 4(a) of Pub. L. 110–246.

AMENDMENTS

2008—Subsec. (b)(8)(A)(iii), (iv). Pub. L. 110–246, §4002(b)(1)(B), (2)(R), substituted "Food and Nutrition Act of 2008" for "Food Stamp Act of 1977".

2006—Subsec. (b)(8)(A)(iii). Pub. L. 109–270 substituted "career and technical education activities at the postsecondary level" for "postsecondary vocational education activities" and "Carl D. Perkins Career and Technical Education Act of 2006" for "Carl D. Perkins Vocational and Applied Technology Education Act".

1998—Subsec. (c)(1). Pub. L. 105–277 substituted "; or" for "; and".

EFFECTIVE DATE OF 2008 AMENDMENT

Amendment of this section and repeal of Pub. L. 110–234 by Pub. L. 110–246 effective May 22, 2008, the date of enactment of Pub. L. 110–234, except as otherwise provided, see section 4 of Pub. L. 110–246, set out as an Effective Date note under section 8701 of Title 7, Agriculture.

Amendment by section 4002(b)(1)(B), (2)(R) of Pub. L. 110–246 effective Oct. 1, 2008, see section 4407 of Pub. L. 110–246, set out as a note under section 1161 of Title 2, The Congress.

PART B—LOCAL PROVISIONS

§2831. Local workforce investment areas

(a) Designation of areas

(1) In general

(A) Process

Except as provided in subsection (b) of this section, and consistent with paragraphs (2), (3), and (4), in order for a State to receive an allotment under section 2852 or 2862 of this title, the Governor of the State shall designate local workforce investment areas within the State—

(i) through consultation with the State board; and

(ii) after consultation with chief elected officials and after consideration of comments received through the public comment process as described in section 2822(b)(9) of this title.

(B) Considerations

In making the designation of local areas, the Governor shall take into consideration the following:

(i) Geographic areas served by local educational agencies and intermediate educational agencies.

(ii) Geographic areas served by postsecondary educational institutions and area vocational education schools.

(iii) The extent to which such local areas are consistent with labor market areas.

(iv) The distance that individuals will need to travel to receive services provided in such local areas.

(v) The resources of such local areas that are available to effectively administer the activities carried out under this subchapter.

(2) Automatic designation

The Governor shall approve any request for designation as a local area—

(A) from any unit of general local government with a population of 500,000 or more;

(B) of the area served by a rural concentrated employment program grant recipient of demonstrated effectiveness that served as a service delivery area or substate area under the Job Training Partnership Act, if the grant recipient has submitted the request; and

(C) of an area that served as a service delivery area under section 101(a)(4)(A)(ii) of the Job Training Partnership Act (as in effect on the day before August 7, 1998) in a State that has a population of not more than 1,100,000 and a population density greater than 900 persons per square mile.

(3) Temporary and subsequent designation

(A) Criteria

Notwithstanding paragraph (2)(A), the Governor shall approve any request, made not later than the date of submission of the initial State plan under this subchapter, for temporary designation as a local area from any unit of general local government (including a combination of such units) with a population of 200,000 or more that was a service delivery area under the Job Training Partnership Act on the day before August 7, 1998, if the Governor determines that the area—

(i) performed successfully, in each of the last 2 years prior to the request for which data are available, in the delivery of services to participants under part A of title II and title III of the Job Training Partnership Act (as in effect on such day); and

(ii) has sustained the fiscal integrity of the funds used by the area to carry out activities under such part and title.

(B) Duration and subsequent designation

A temporary designation under this paragraph shall be for a period of not more than 2 years, after which the designation shall be extended until the end of the period covered by the State plan if the Governor determines that, during the temporary designation period, the area substantially met (as defined by the State board) the local performance measures for the local area and sustained the fiscal integrity of the funds used by the area to carry out activities under this subchapter.

(C) Technical assistance

The Secretary shall provide the States with technical assistance in making the determinations required by this paragraph. The Secretary shall not issue regulations governing determinations to be made under this paragraph.

(D) Performed successfully

In this paragraph, the term "performed successfully" means that the area involved met or exceeded the performance standards for activities administered in the area that—

(i) are established by the Secretary for each year and modified by the adjustment methodology of the State (used to account for differences in economic conditions, participant characteristics, and combination of services provided from the combination assumed for purposes of the established standards of the Secretary); and

(ii)(I) if the area was designated as both a service delivery area and a substate area under the Job Training Partnership Act (as in effect on the day before August 7, 1998)—

(aa) relate to job retention and earnings, with respect to activities carried out under part A of title II of such Act (as in effect on such day); and

(bb) relate to entry into employment, with respect to activities carried out under title III of such Act (as in effect on such day);

(II) if the area was designated only as a service delivery area under such Act (as in effect on such day), relate to the standards described in subclause (I)(aa); or

(III) if the area was only designated as a substate area under such Act (as in effect on such day), relate to the standards described in subclause (I)(bb).

(E) Sustained the fiscal integrity

In this paragraph, the term "sustained the fiscal integrity", used with respect to funds used by a service delivery area or local area, means that the Secretary has not made a final determination during any of the last 3 years for which data are available, prior to the date of the designation request involved, that either the grant recipient or the administrative entity of the area misexpended the funds due to willful disregard of the requirements of the Act involved, gross negligence, or failure to observe accepted standards of administration.

(4) Designation on recommendation of State board

The Governor may approve a request from any unit of general local government (including a combination of such units) for designation (including temporary designation) as a local area if the State board determines, taking into account the factors described in clauses (i) through (v) of paragraph (1)(B), and recommends to the Governor, that such area should be so designated.

(5) Appeals

A unit of general local government (including a combination of such units) or grant recipient that requests but is not granted designation of an area as a local area under paragraph (2) or (3) may submit an appeal to the State board under an appeal process established in the State plan. If the appeal does not result in such a designation, the Secretary, after receiving a request for review from the unit or grant recipient and on determining that the unit or grant recipient was not accorded procedural rights under the appeal process established in the State plan or that the area meets the requirements of paragraph (2) or (3), as appropriate, may require that the area be designated as a local area under such paragraph.

(b) Small States

The Governor of any State that was a single State service delivery area under the Job Training Partnership Act as of July 1, 1998, may designate the State as a single State local area for the purposes of this chapter. In the case of such a designation, the Governor shall identify the State as a local area under section 2822(b)(5) of this title.

(c) Regional planning and cooperation

(1) Planning

As part of the process for developing the State plan, a State may require regional planning by local boards for a designated region in the State. The State may require the local boards for a designated region to participate in a regional planning process that results in the establishment of regional performance measures for workforce investment activities authorized under this subchapter. The State may award regional incentive grants to the designated regions that meet or exceed the regional performance measures.

(2) Information sharing

The State may require the local boards for a designated region to share, in feasible cases, employment statistics, information about employment opportunities and trends, and other types of information that would assist in improving the performance of all local areas in the designated region on local performance measures.

(3) Coordination of services

The State may require the local boards for a designated region to coordinate the provision of workforce investment activities authorized under this subchapter, including the provision of transportation and other supportive services, so that services provided through the activities may be provided across the boundaries of local areas within the designated region.

(4) Interstate regions

Two or more States that contain an interstate region that is a labor market area, economic development region, or other appropriate contiguous subarea of the States may designate the area as a designated region for purposes of this subsection, and jointly exercise the State functions described in paragraphs (1) through (3).

(5) Definitions

In this subsection:

(A) Designated region

The term "designated region" means a combination of local areas that are partly or completely in a single labor market area, economic development region, or other appropriate contiguous subarea of a State, that is designated by the State, except as provided in paragraph (4).

(B) Local board for a designated region

The term "local board for a designated region" means a local board for a local area in a designated region.

(Pub. L. 105–220, title I, § 116, Aug. 7, 1998, 112 Stat. 951; Pub. L. 105–277, div. A, § 101(f) [title

VIII, § 401(3)], Oct. 21, 1998, 112 Stat. 2681–337, 2681–411.)

REFERENCES IN TEXT

The Job Training Partnership Act, referred to in subsecs. (a)(2)(B), (C), (3) and (b), is Pub. L. 97–300, Oct. 13, 1982, 96 Stat. 1322, as amended, which was classified generally to chapter 19 (§ 1501 et seq.) of this title, prior to repeal by Pub. L. 105–220, title I, § 199(b)(2), (c)(2)(B), Aug. 7, 1998, 112 Stat. 1059. Part A of title II and title III of the Act were classified generally to part A (§ 1601 et seq.) of subchapter II and subchapter III (§ 1651 et seq.), respectively, of chapter 19 of this title, prior to repeal by Pub. L. 105–220. Section 101 of the Act was classified to section 1511 of this title, prior to repeal by Pub. L. 105–220. For complete classification of this Act to the Code, see Tables.

This chapter, referred to in subsec. (b), was in the original "this title" meaning title I of Pub. L. 105–220, Aug. 7, 1998, 112 Stat. 939, as amended, which enacted this chapter, repealed sections 1501 to 1505, 1511 to 1583, 1592 to 1735, 1737 to 1791h, 1792 to 1792b, 2301 to 2314 of this title, section 211 of former Title 40, Appendix, Public Buildings, Property, and Works, sections 11421, 11441 to 11447, 11449, 11450, 11461 to 11466, 11471, and 11472 of Title 42, The Public Health and Welfare, and sections 42101 to 42106 of Title 49, Transportation, enacted provisions set out as notes under sections 1501, 2301, and 2940 of this title and section 11421 of Title 42, and repealed provisions set out as notes under sections 801 and 2301 of this title and section 1255a of Title 8, Aliens and Nationality. For complete classification of title I to the Code, see Tables.

AMENDMENTS

1998—Subsec. (a)(3)(D)(ii)(I)(aa). Pub. L. 105–277 substituted "; and" for "; or".

§ 2832. Local workforce investment boards

(a) Establishment

There shall be established in each local area of a State, and certified by the Governor of the State, a local workforce investment board, to set policy for the portion of the statewide workforce investment system within the local area (referred to in this chapter as a "local workforce investment system").

(b) Membership

(1) State criteria

The Governor of the State, in partnership with the State board, shall establish criteria for use by chief elected officials in the local areas for appointment of members of the local boards in such local areas in accordance with the requirements of paragraph (2).

(2) Composition

Such criteria shall require, at a minimum, that the membership of each local board—

(A) shall include—

(i) representatives of business in the local area, who—

(I) are owners of businesses, chief executives or operating officers of businesses, and other business executives or employers with optimum policymaking or hiring authority;

(II) represent businesses with employment opportunities that reflect the employment opportunities of the local area; and

(III) are appointed from among individuals nominated by local business organizations and business trade associations;

(ii) representatives of local educational entities, including representatives of local educational agencies, local school boards, entities providing adult education and literacy activities, and postsecondary educational institutions (including representatives of community colleges, where such entities exist), selected from among individuals nominated by regional or local educational agencies, institutions, or organizations representing such local educational entities;

(iii) representatives of labor organizations (for a local area in which employees are represented by labor organizations), nominated by local labor federations, or (for a local area in which no employees are represented by such organizations), other representatives of employees;

(iv) representatives of community-based organizations (including organizations representing individuals with disabilities and veterans, for a local area in which such organizations are present);

(v) representatives of economic development agencies, including private sector economic development entities; and

(vi) representatives of each of the one-stop partners; and

(B) may include such other individuals or representatives of entities as the chief elected official in the local area may determine to be appropriate.

(3) Authority of board members

Members of the board that represent organizations, agencies, or other entities shall be individuals with optimum policymaking authority within the organizations, agencies, or entities.

(4) Majority

A majority of the members of the local board shall be representatives described in paragraph (2)(A)(i).

(5) Chairperson

The local board shall elect a chairperson for the local board from among the representatives described in paragraph (2)(A)(i).

(c) Appointment and certification of board

(1) Appointment of board members and assignment of responsibilities

(A) In general

The chief elected official in a local area is authorized to appoint the members of the local board for such area, in accordance with the State criteria established under subsection (b) of this section.

(B) Multiple units of local government in area

(i) In general

In a case in which a local area includes more than 1 unit of general local government, the chief elected officials of such units may execute an agreement that specifies the respective roles of the individual chief elected officials—

(I) in the appointment of the members of the local board from the individuals nominated or recommended to be such members in accordance with the criteria established under subsection (b) of this section; and

(II) in carrying out any other responsibilities assigned to such officials under this subchapter.

(ii) Lack of agreement

If, after a reasonable effort, the chief elected officials are unable to reach agreement as provided under clause (i), the Governor may appoint the members of the local board from individuals so nominated or recommended.

(C) Concentrated employment programs

In the case of a local area designated in accordance with section 2831(a)(2)(B) of this title, the governing body of the concentrated employment program involved shall act in consultation with the chief elected official in the local area to appoint members of the local board, in accordance with the State criteria established under subsection (b) of this section, and to carry out any other responsibility relating to workforce investment activities assigned to such official under this Act.

(2) Certification

(A) In general

The Governor shall, once every 2 years, certify 1 local board for each local area in the State.

(B) Criteria

Such certification shall be based on criteria established under subsection (b) of this section and, for a second or subsequent certification, the extent to which the local board has ensured that workforce investment activities carried out in the local area have enabled the local area to meet the local performance measures.

(C) Failure to achieve certification

Failure of a local board to achieve certification shall result in reappointment and certification of another local board for the local area pursuant to the process described in paragraph (1) and this paragraph.

(3) Decertification

(A) Fraud, abuse, failure to carry out functions

Notwithstanding paragraph (2), the Governor may decertify a local board, at any time after providing notice and an opportunity for comment, for—

(i) fraud or abuse; or

(ii) failure to carry out the functions specified for the local board in any of paragraphs (1) through (7) of subsection (d) of this section.

(B) Nonperformance

Notwithstanding paragraph (2), the Governor may decertify a local board if a local area fails to meet the local performance measures for such local area for 2 consecutive program years (in accordance with section 2871(h) of this title).

(C) Plan

If the Governor decertifies a local board for a local area under subparagraph (A) or (B), the Governor may require that a new local board be appointed and certified for the local area pursuant to a reorganization plan developed by the Governor, in consultation with the chief elected official in the local area, and in accordance with the criteria established under subsection (b) of this section.

(4) Single State area

Notwithstanding subsection (b) of this section and paragraphs (1) and (2), if a State described in section 2831(b) of this title indicates in the State plan that the State will be treated as a local area for purposes of the application of this chapter, the Governor may designate the State board to carry out any of the functions described in subsection (d) of this section.

(d) Functions of local board

The functions of the local board shall include the following:

(1) Local plan

Consistent with section 2833 of this title, each local board, in partnership with the chief elected official for the local area involved, shall develop and submit a local plan to the Governor.

(2) Selection of operators and providers

(A) Selection of one-stop operators

Consistent with section 2841(d) of this title, the local board, with the agreement of the chief elected official—

(i) shall designate or certify one-stop operators as described in section 2841(d)(2)(A) of this title; and

(ii) may terminate for cause the eligibility of such operators.

(B) Selection of youth providers

Consistent with section 2843 of this title, the local board shall identify eligible providers of youth activities in the local area by awarding grants or contracts on a competitive basis, based on the recommendations of the youth council.

(C) Identification of eligible providers of training services

Consistent with section 2842 of this title, the local board shall identify eligible providers of training services described in section 2864(d)(4) of this title in the local area.

(D) Identification of eligible providers of intensive services

If the one-stop operator does not provide intensive services in a local area, the local board shall identify eligible providers of intensive services described in section 2864(d)(3) of this title in the local area by awarding contracts.

(3) Budget and administration

(A) Budget

The local board shall develop a budget for the purpose of carrying out the duties of the local board under this section, subject to the approval of the chief elected official.

(B) **Administration**

(i) **Grant recipient**

(I) **In general**

The chief elected official in a local area shall serve as the local grant recipient for, and shall be liable for any misuse of, the grant funds allocated to the local area under sections 2853 and 2863 of this title, unless the chief elected official reaches an agreement with the Governor for the Governor to act as the local grant recipient and bear such liability.

(II) **Designation**

In order to assist in the administration of the grant funds, the chief elected official or the Governor, where the Governor serves as the local grant recipient for a local area, may designate an entity to serve as a local grant subrecipient for such funds or as a local fiscal agent. Such designation shall not relieve the chief elected official or the Governor of the liability for any misuse of grant funds as described in subclause (I).

(III) **Disbursal**

The local grant recipient or an entity designated under subclause (II) shall disburse such funds for workforce investment activities at the direction of the local board, pursuant to the requirements of this chapter, if the direction does not violate a provision of this Act. The local grant recipient or entity designated under subclause (II) shall disburse the funds immediately on receiving such direction from the local board.

(ii) **Staff**

The local board may employ staff.

(iii) **Grants and donations**

The local board may solicit and accept grants and donations from sources other than Federal funds made available under this Act.

(4) **Program oversight**

The local board, in partnership with the chief elected official, shall conduct oversight with respect to local programs of youth activities authorized under section 2854 of this title, local employment and training activities authorized under section 2864 of this title, and the one-stop delivery system in the local area.

(5) **Negotiation of local performance measures**

The local board, the chief elected official, and the Governor shall negotiate and reach agreement on local performance measures as described in section 2871(c) of this title.

(6) **Employment statistics system**

The local board shall assist the Governor in developing the statewide employment statistics system described in section 49*l*–2(e) of this title.

(7) **Employer linkages**

The local board shall coordinate the workforce investment activities authorized under this subchapter and carried out in the local area with economic development strategies and develop other employer linkages with such activities.

(8) **Connecting, brokering, and coaching**

The local board shall promote the participation of private sector employers in the statewide workforce investment system and ensure the effective provision, through the system, of connecting, brokering, and coaching activities, through intermediaries such as the one-stop operator in the local area or through other organizations, to assist such employers in meeting hiring needs.

(e) **Sunshine provision**

The local board shall make available to the public, on a regular basis through open meetings, information regarding the activities of the local board, including information regarding the local plan prior to submission of the plan, and regarding membership, the designation and certification of one-stop operators, and the award of grants or contracts to eligible providers of youth activities, and on request, minutes of formal meetings of the local board.

(f) **Limitations**

(1) **Training services**

(A) **In general**

Except as provided in subparagraph (B), no local board may provide training services described in section 2864(d)(4) of this title.

(B) **Waivers of training prohibition**

The Governor of the State in which a local board is located may, pursuant to a request from the local board, grant a written waiver of the prohibition set forth in subparagraph (A) (relating to the provision of training services) for a program of training services, if the local board—

(i) submits to the Governor a proposed request for the waiver that includes—

(I) satisfactory evidence that there is an insufficient number of eligible providers of such a program of training services to meet local demand in the local area;

(II) information demonstrating that the board meets the requirements for an eligible provider of training services under section 2842 of this title; and

(III) information demonstrating that the program of training services prepares participants for an occupation that is in demand in the local area;

(ii) makes the proposed request available to eligible providers of training services and other interested members of the public for a public comment period of not less than 30 days; and

(iii) includes, in the final request for the waiver, the evidence and information described in clause (i) and the comments received pursuant to clause (ii).

(C) **Duration**

A waiver granted to a local board under subparagraph (B) shall apply for a period of not to exceed 1 year. The waiver may be renewed for additional periods of not to exceed 1 year, pursuant to requests from the local board, if the board meets the requirements of subparagraph (B) in making the requests.

(D) Revocation

The Governor may revoke a waiver granted under this paragraph during the appropriate period described in subparagraph (C) if the Governor determines that the local board involved has engaged in a pattern of inappropriate referrals to training services operated by the local board.

(2) Core services; intensive services; designation or certification as one-stop operators

A local board may provide core services described in section 2864(d)(2) of this title or intensive services described in section 2864(d)(3) of this title through a one-stop delivery system described in section 2864(c) of this title or be designated or certified as a one-stop operator only with the agreement of the chief elected official and the Governor.

(3) Limitation on authority

Nothing in this Act shall be construed to provide a local board with the authority to mandate curricula for schools.

(g) Conflict of interest

A member of a local board may not—

(1) vote on a matter under consideration by the local board—

(A) regarding the provision of services by such member (or by an entity that such member represents); or

(B) that would provide direct financial benefit to such member or the immediate family of such member; or

(2) engage in any other activity determined by the Governor to constitute a conflict of interest as specified in the State plan.

(h) Youth council

(1) Establishment

There shall be established, as a subgroup within each local board, a youth council appointed by the local board, in cooperation with the chief elected official for the local area.

(2) Membership

The membership of each youth council—

(A) shall include—

(i) members of the local board described in subparagraph (A) or (B) of subsection (b)(2) of this section with special interest or expertise in youth policy;

(ii) representatives of youth service agencies, including juvenile justice and local law enforcement agencies;

(iii) representatives of local public housing authorities;

(iv) parents of eligible youth seeking assistance under this subchapter;

(v) individuals, including former participants, and representatives of organizations, that have experience relating to youth activities; and

(vi) representatives of the Job Corps, as appropriate; and

(B) may include such other individuals as the chairperson of the local board, in cooperation with the chief elected official, determines to be appropriate.

(3) Relationship to local board

Members of the youth council who are not members of the local board described in subparagraphs (A) and (B) of subsection (b)(2) of this section shall be voting members of the youth council and nonvoting members of the board.

(4) Duties

The duties of the youth council include—

(A) developing the portions of the local plan relating to eligible youth, as determined by the chairperson of the local board;

(B) subject to the approval of the local board and consistent with section 2843 of this title—

(i) recommending eligible providers of youth activities, to be awarded grants or contracts on a competitive basis by the local board to carry out the youth activities; and

(ii) conducting oversight with respect to the eligible providers of youth activities, in the local area;

(C) coordinating youth activities authorized under section 2854 of this title in the local area; and

(D) other duties determined to be appropriate by the chairperson of the local board.

(i) Alternative entity

(1) In general

For purposes of complying with subsections (a), (b), and (c) of this section, and paragraphs (1) and (2) of subsection (h) of this section, a State may use any local entity (including a local council, regional workforce development board, or similar entity) that—

(A) is established to serve the local area (or the service delivery area that most closely corresponds to the local area);

(B) is in existence on December 31, 1997;

(C)(i) is established pursuant to section 1512 of this title, as in effect on December 31, 1997; or

(ii) is substantially similar to the local board described in subsections (a), (b), and (c) of this section, and paragraphs (1) and (2) of subsection (h) of this section; and

(D) includes—

(i) representatives of business in the local area; and

(ii)(I) representatives of labor organizations (for a local area in which employees are represented by labor organizations), nominated by local labor federations; or

(II) other representatives of employees in the local area (for a local area in which no employees are represented by such organizations).

(2) References

References in this Act to a local board or a youth council shall be considered to include such an entity or a subgroup of such an entity, respectively.

(Pub. L. 105–220, title I, §117, Aug. 7, 1998, 112 Stat. 954; Pub. L. 105–277, div. A, §101(f) [title

VIII, § 401(4)], Oct. 21, 1998, 112 Stat. 2681–337, 2681–411.)

REFERENCES IN TEXT

This Act, referred to in subsecs. (c)(1)(C), (d)(3)(B)(i)(III), (iii), (f)(3), and (i)(2), is Pub. L. 105–220, Aug. 7, 1998, 112 Stat. 936, as amended, known as the Workforce Investment Act of 1998. For complete classification of this Act to the Code, see Short Title note set out under section 9201 of Title 20, Education, and Tables.

Section 1512 of this title, referred to in subsec. (i)(1)(C)(i), was repealed by Pub. L. 105–220, title I, § 199(b)(2), Aug. 7, 1998, 112 Stat. 1059, effective July 1, 2000.

AMENDMENTS

1998—Subsec. (f)(1)(D). Pub. L. 105–277, § 101(f) [title VIII, § 401(4)(A)], substituted "if the Governor" for "if the State".

Subsec. (i)(1)(D)(ii)(II). Pub. L. 105–277, § 101(f) [title VIII, § 401(4)(B)], added subcl. (II) and struck out former subcl. (II) which read as follows: "(for a local area in which no employees are represented by such organizations), other representatives of employees in the local area."

§ 2833. Local plan

(a) In general

Each local board shall develop and submit to the Governor a comprehensive 5-year local plan (referred to in this chapter as the "local plan"), in partnership with the appropriate chief elected official. The plan shall be consistent with the State plan.

(b) Contents

The local plan shall include—

(1) an identification of—

(A) the workforce investment needs of businesses, jobseekers, and workers in the local area;

(B) the current and projected employment opportunities in the local area; and

(C) the job skills necessary to obtain such employment opportunities;

(2) a description of the one-stop delivery system to be established or designated in the local area, including—

(A) a description of how the local board will ensure the continuous improvement of eligible providers of services through the system and ensure that such providers meet the employment needs of local employers and participants; and

(B) a copy of each memorandum of understanding described in section 2841(c) of this title (between the local board and each of the one-stop partners) concerning the operation of the one-stop delivery system in the local area;

(3) a description of the local levels of performance negotiated with the Governor and chief elected official pursuant to section 2871(c) of this title, to be used to measure the performance of the local area and to be used by the local board for measuring the performance of the local fiscal agent (where appropriate), eligible providers, and the one-stop delivery system, in the local area;

(4) a description and assessment of the type and availability of adult and dislocated worker employment and training activities in the local area;

(5) a description of how the local board will coordinate workforce investment activities carried out in the local area with statewide rapid response activities, as appropriate;

(6) a description and assessment of the type and availability of youth activities in the local area, including an identification of successful providers of such activities;

(7) a description of the process used by the local board, consistent with subsection (c) of this section, to provide an opportunity for public comment, including comment by representatives of businesses and comment by representatives of labor organizations, and input into the development of the local plan, prior to submission of the plan;

(8) an identification of the entity responsible for the disbursal of grant funds described in section 2832(d)(3)(B)(i)(III) of this title, as determined by the chief elected official or the Governor under section 2832(d)(3)(B)(i) of this title;

(9) a description of the competitive process to be used to award the grants and contracts in the local area for activities carried out under this subchapter; and

(10) such other information as the Governor may require.

(c) Process

Prior to the date on which the local board submits a local plan under this section, the local board shall—

(1) make available copies of a proposed local plan to the public through such means as public hearings and local news media;

(2) allow members of the local board and members of the public, including representatives of business and representatives of labor organizations, to submit comments on the proposed local plan to the local board, not later than the end of the 30-day period beginning on the date on which the proposed local plan is made available; and

(3) include with the local plan submitted to the Governor under this section any such comments that represent disagreement with the plan.

(d) Plan submission and approval

A local plan submitted to the Governor under this section shall be considered to be approved by the Governor at the end of the 90-day period beginning on the day the Governor receives the plan, unless the Governor makes a written determination during the 90-day period that—

(1) deficiencies in activities carried out under this subchapter have been identified, through audits conducted under section 2934 of this title or otherwise, and the local area has not made acceptable progress in implementing corrective measures to address the deficiencies; or

(2) the plan does not comply with this chapter.

(Pub. L. 105–220, title I, § 118, Aug. 7, 1998, 112 Stat. 961.)

PART C—WORKFORCE INVESTMENT ACTIVITIES PROVIDERS

§ 2841. Establishment of one-stop delivery systems

(a) In general

Consistent with the State plan, the local board for a local area, with the agreement of the chief elected official for the local area, shall—

(1) develop and enter into the memorandum of understanding described in subsection (c) of this section with one-stop partners;

(2) designate or certify one-stop operators under subsection (d) of this section; and

(3) conduct oversight with respect to the one-stop delivery system in the local area.

(b) One-stop partners

(1) Required partners

(A) In general

Each entity that carries out a program or activities described in subparagraph (B) shall—

(i) make available to participants, through a one-stop delivery system, the services described in section 2864(d)(2) of this title that are applicable to such program or activities; and

(ii) participate in the operation of such system consistent with the terms of the memorandum described in subsection (c) of this section, and with the requirements of the Federal law in which the program or activities are authorized.

(B) Programs and activities

The programs and activities referred to in subparagraph (A) consist of—

(i) programs authorized under this chapter;

(ii) programs authorized under the Wagner-Peyser Act (29 U.S.C. 49 et seq.);

(iii) adult education and literacy activities authorized under title II [20 U.S.C. 9201 et seq.];

(iv) programs authorized under title I of the Rehabilitation Act of 1973 (29 U.S.C. 720 et seq.) (other than part C of title I of such Act [29 U.S.C. 741] and subject to subsection (f) of this section);

(v) programs authorized under section 403(a)(5) of the Social Security Act (42 U.S.C. 603(a)(5)) (as added by section 5001 of the Balanced Budget Act of 1997);

(vi) activities authorized under title V of the Older Americans Act of 1965 (42 U.S.C. 3056 et seq.);

(vii) career and technical education activities at the postsecondary level authorized under the Carl D. Perkins Career and Technical Education Act of 2006 (20 U.S.C. 2301 et seq.);

(viii) activities authorized under chapter 2 of title II of the Trade Act of 1974 (19 U.S.C. 2271 et seq.);

(ix) activities authorized under chapter 41 of title 38;

(x) employment and training activities carried out under the Community Services Block Grant Act (42 U.S.C. 9901 et seq.);

(xi) employment and training activities carried out by the Department of Housing and Urban Development; and

(xii) programs authorized under State unemployment compensation laws (in accordance with applicable Federal law).

(2) Additional partners

(A) In general

In addition to the entities described in paragraph (1), other entities that carry out a human resource program described in subparagraph (B) may—

(i) make available to participants, through the one-stop delivery system, the services described in section 2864(d)(2) of this title that are applicable to such program; and

(ii) participate in the operation of such system consistent with the terms of the memorandum described in subsection (c) of this section, and with the requirements of the Federal law in which the program is authorized;

if the local board and chief elected official involved approve such participation.

(B) Programs

The programs referred to in subparagraph (A) may include—

(i) programs authorized under part A of title IV of the Social Security Act (42 U.S.C. 601 et seq.);

(ii) programs authorized under section 2015(d)(4) of title 7;

(iii) work programs authorized under section 2015(*o*) of title 7;

(iv) programs authorized under the National and Community Service Act of 1990 (42 U.S.C. 12501 et seq.); and

(v) other appropriate Federal, State, or local programs, including programs in the private sector.

(c) Memorandum of understanding

(1) Development

The local board, with the agreement of the chief elected official, shall develop and enter into a memorandum of understanding (between the local board and the one-stop partners), consistent with paragraph (2), concerning the operation of the one-stop delivery system in the local area.

(2) Contents

Each memorandum of understanding shall contain—

(A) provisions describing—

(i) the services to be provided through the one-stop delivery system;

(ii) how the costs of such services and the operating costs of the system will be funded;

(iii) methods for referral of individuals between the one-stop operator and the one-stop partners, for the appropriate services and activities; and

(iv) the duration of the memorandum and the procedures for amending the memorandum during the term of the memorandum; and

(B) such other provisions, consistent with the requirements of this chapter, as the parties to the agreement determine to be appropriate.

(d) One-stop operators

(1) Designation and certification

Consistent with paragraphs (2) and (3), the local board, with the agreement of the chief elected official, is authorized to designate or certify one-stop operators and to terminate for cause the eligibility of such operators.

(2) Eligibility

To be eligible to receive funds made available under this subchapter to operate a one-stop center referred to in section 2864(c) of this title, an entity (which may be a consortium of entities)—

(A) shall be designated or certified as a one-stop operator—

(i) through a competitive process; or

(ii) in accordance with an agreement reached between the local board and a consortium of entities that, at a minimum, includes 3 or more of the one-stop partners described in subsection (b)(1) of this section; and

(B) may be a public or private entity, or consortium of entities, of demonstrated effectiveness, located in the local area, which may include—

(i) a postsecondary educational institution;

(ii) an employment service agency established under the Wagner-Peyser Act (29 U.S.C. 49 et seq.), on behalf of the local office of the agency;

(iii) a private, nonprofit organization (including a community-based organization);

(iv) a private for-profit entity;

(v) a government agency; and

(vi) another interested organization or entity, which may include a local chamber of commerce or other business organization.

(3) Exception

Elementary schools and secondary schools shall not be eligible for designation or certification as one-stop operators, except that nontraditional public secondary schools and area vocational education schools shall be eligible for such designation or certification.

(e) Established one-stop delivery system

If a one-stop delivery system has been established in a local area prior to August 7, 1998, the local board, the chief elected official, and the Governor involved may agree to certify an entity carrying out activities through the system as a one-stop operator for purposes of subsection (d) of this section, consistent with the requirements of subsection (b) of this section, of the memorandum of understanding, and of section 2864(c) of this title.

(f) Application to certain vocational rehabilitation programs

(1) Limitation

Nothing in this section shall be construed to apply to part C of title I of the Rehabilitation Act of 1973 (29 U.S.C. 741).

(2) Client assistance

Nothing in this Act shall be construed to require that any entity carrying out a client assistance program authorized under section 112 of the Rehabilitation Act of 1973 (29 U.S.C. 732)—

(A) violate the requirement of section 112(c)(1)(A) of that Act that the entity be independent of any agency which provides treatment, services, or rehabilitation to individuals under that Act [29 U.S.C. 701 et seq.]; or

(B) carry out any activity not authorized under section 112 of that Act (including appropriate Federal regulations).

(Pub. L. 105–220, title I, §121, Aug. 7, 1998, 112 Stat. 963; Pub. L. 105–332, §5(a), Oct. 31, 1998, 112 Stat. 3127; Pub. L. 109–270, §2(h)(5), Aug. 12, 2006, 120 Stat. 748; Pub. L. 110–234, title IV, §4002(b)(1)(B), (2)(R), May 22, 2008, 122 Stat. 1096, 1097; Pub. L. 110–246, §4(a), title IV, §4002(b)(1)(B), (2)(R), June 18, 2008, 122 Stat. 1664, 1857, 1858.)

REFERENCES IN TEXT

This chapter, referred to in subsecs. (b)(1)(B)(i) and (c)(2)(B), was in the original "this title" meaning title I of Pub. L. 105–220, Aug. 7, 1998, 112 Stat. 939, as amended, which enacted this chapter, repealed sections 1501 to 1505, 1511 to 1583, 1592 to 1735, 1737 to 1791h, 1792 to 1792b, 2301 to 2314 of this title, section 211 of former Title 40, Appendix, Public Buildings, Property, and Works, sections 11421, 11441 to 11447, 11449, 11450, 11461 to 11466, 11471, and 11472 of Title 42, The Public Health and Welfare, and sections 42101 to 42106 of Title 49, Transportation, enacted provisions set out as notes under sections 1501, 2301, and 2940 of this title and section 11421 of Title 42, and repealed provisions set out as notes under sections 801 and 2301 of this title and section 1255a of Title 8, Aliens and Nationality. For complete classification of title I to the Code, see Tables.

The Wagner-Peyser Act, referred to in subsecs. (b)(1)(B)(ii) and (d)(2)(B)(ii), is act June 6, 1933, ch. 49, 48 Stat. 113, as amended, which is classified generally to chapter 4B (§49 et seq.) of this title. For complete classification of this Act to the Code, see Short Title note set out under section 49 of this title and Tables.

Title II, referred to in subsec. (b)(1)(B)(iii), is title II of Pub. L. 105–220, Aug. 7, 1998, 112 Stat. 1059, as amended, known as the Adult Education and Family Literacy Act, which is classified principally to subchapter I (§9201 et seq.) of chapter 73 of Title 20, Education. For complete classification of this Act to the Code, see Short Title note set out under section 9201 of Title 20 and Tables.

The Rehabilitation Act of 1973, referred to in subsecs. (b)(1)(B)(iv) and (f), is Pub. L. 93–112, Sept. 26, 1973, 87 Stat. 355, as amended, which is classified generally to chapter 16 (§701 et seq.) of this title. Title I of the Act is classified generally to subchapter I (§720 et seq.) of chapter 16 of this title. Part C of title I of the Act is classified generally to part C (§741) of subchapter I of chapter 16 of this title. For complete classification of this Act to the Code, see Short Title note set out under section 701 of this title and Tables.

The Older Americans Act of 1965, referred to in subsec. (b)(1)(B)(vi), is Pub. L. 89–73, July 14, 1965, 79 Stat. 218, as amended. Title V of the Act, known as the Older American Community Service Employment Act, is classified generally to subchapter IX (§3056 et seq.) of chapter 35 of Title 42, The Public Health and Welfare. For complete classification of this Act to the Code, see Short Title note set out under section 3001 of Title 42 and Tables.

The Carl D. Perkins Career and Technical Education Act of 2006, referred to in subsec. (b)(1)(B)(vii), is Pub.

L. 88–210, Dec. 18, 1963, 77 Stat. 403, as amended generally by Pub. L. 109–270, § 1(b), Aug. 12, 2006, 120 Stat. 683, which is classified generally to chapter 44 (§ 2301 et seq.) of Title 20, Education. For complete classification of this Act to the Code, see Short Title note set out under section 2301 of Title 20 and Tables.

The Trade Act of 1974, referred to in subsec. (b)(1)(B)(viii), is Pub. L. 93–618, Jan. 3, 1975, 88 Stat. 1978, as amended. Chapter 2 of title II of the Act is classified principally to part 2 (§ 2271 et seq.) of subchapter II of chapter 12 of Title 19, Customs Duties. For complete classification of this Act to the Code, see References in Text note set out under section 2101 of Title 19 and Tables.

The Community Services Block Grant Act, referred to in subsec. (b)(1)(B)(x), is subtitle B (§§ 671–683) of title VI of Pub. L. 97–35, Aug. 13, 1981, 95 Stat. 511, as amended, which is classified generally to chapter 106 (§ 9901 et seq.) of Title 42, The Public Health and Welfare. For complete classification of this Act to the Code, see Short Title note set out under section 9901 of Title 42 and Tables.

The Social Security Act, referred to in subsec. (b)(2)(B)(i), is act Aug. 14, 1935, ch. 531, 49 Stat. 620, as amended. Part A of title IV of the Act is classified generally to part A (§ 601 et seq.) of subchapter IV of chapter 7 of Title 42, The Public Health and Welfare. For complete classification of this Act to the Code, see section 1305 of Title 42 and Tables.

The National and Community Service Act of 1990, referred to in subsec. (b)(2)(B)(iv), is Pub. L. 101–610, Nov. 16, 1990, 104 Stat. 3127, as amended, which is classified principally to chapter 129 (§ 12501 et seq.) of Title 42, The Public Health and Welfare. For complete classification of this Act to the Code, see Short Title note set out under section 12501 of Title 42 and Tables.

This Act, referred to in subsec. (f)(2), is Pub. L. 105–220, Aug. 7, 1998, 112 Stat. 936, as amended, known as the Workforce Investment Act of 1998. For complete classification of this Act to the Code, see Short Title note set out under section 9201 of Title 20, Education, and Tables.

CODIFICATION

Pub. L. 110–234 and Pub. L. 110–246 made identical amendments to this section. The amendments by Pub. L. 110–234 were repealed by section 4(a) of Pub. L. 110–246.

AMENDMENTS

2008—Subsec. (b)(2)(B)(ii), (iii). Pub. L. 110–246, § 4002(b)(1)(B), (2)(R), made technical amendment to references in original act which appear in text as references to section 2015 of title 7.

2006—Subsec. (b)(1)(B)(vii). Pub. L. 109–270 substituted "career and technical education activities at the postsecondary level" for "postsecondary vocational education activities" and "Carl D. Perkins Career and Technical Education Act of 2006" for "Carl D. Perkins Vocational and Applied Technology Education Act".

1998—Subsec. (b)(1)(B)(iv). Pub. L. 105–332, § 5(a)(1), inserted "(other than part C of title I of such Act and subject to subsection (f) of this section)" before semicolon.

Subsec. (f). Pub. L. 105–332, § 5(a)(2), added subsec. (f).

EFFECTIVE DATE OF 2008 AMENDMENT

Amendment of this section and repeal of Pub. L. 110–234 by Pub. L. 110–246 effective May 22, 2008, the date of enactment of Pub. L. 110–234, except as otherwise provided, see section 4 of Pub. L. 110–246, set out as an Effective Date note under section 8701 of Title 7, Agriculture.

Amendment by section 4002(b)(1)(B), (2)(R) of Pub. L. 110–246 effective Oct. 1, 2008, see section 4407 of Pub. L. 110–246, set out as a note under section 1161 of Title 2, The Congress.

§ 2842. Identification of eligible providers of training services

(a) Eligibility requirements

(1) In general

Except as provided in subsection (h) of this section, to be identified as an eligible provider of training services described in section 2864(d)(4) of this title (referred to in this section as "training services") in a local area and to be eligible to receive funds made available under section 2863(b) of this title for the provision of training services, a provider of such services shall meet the requirements of this section.

(2) Providers

Subject to the provisions of this section, to be eligible to receive the funds, the provider shall be—

(A) a postsecondary educational institution that—

(i) is eligible to receive Federal funds under title IV of the Higher Education Act of 1965 (20 U.S.C. 1070 et seq. [and 42 U.S.C. 2751 et seq.]); and

(ii) provides a program that leads to an associate degree, baccalaureate degree, or certificate;

(B) an entity that carries out programs under the Act of August 16, 1937 (commonly known as the "National Apprenticeship Act" 50 Stat. 664, chapter 663; 29 U.S.C. 50 et seq.); or

(C) another public or private provider of a program of training services.

(b) Initial eligibility determination

(1) Postsecondary educational institutions and entities carrying out apprenticeship programs

To be initially eligible to receive funds as described in subsection (a) of this section to carry out a program described in subparagraph (A) or (B) of subsection (a)(2) of this section, a provider described in subparagraph (A) or (B), respectively, of subsection (a)(2) of this section shall submit an application, to the local board for the local area in which the provider desires to provide training services, at such time, in such manner, and containing such information as the local board may require.

(2) Other eligible providers

(A) Procedure

Each Governor of a State shall establish a procedure for use by local boards in the State in determining the initial eligibility of a provider described in subsection (a)(2)(C) of this section to receive funds as described in subsection (a) of this section for a program of training services, including the initial eligibility of—

(i) a postsecondary educational institution to receive such funds for a program not described in subsection (a)(2)(A) of this section; and

(ii) a provider described in subsection (a)(2)(B) of this section to receive such funds for a program not described in subsection (a)(2)(B) of this section.

(B) Recommendations

In developing such procedure, the Governor shall solicit and take into consideration the recommendations of local boards and providers of training services within the State.

(C) Opportunity to submit comments

The Governor shall provide an opportunity, during the development of the procedure, for interested members of the public, including representatives of business and labor organizations, to submit comments on such procedure.

(D) Requirements

In establishing the procedure, the Governor shall require that, to be initially eligible to receive funds as described in subsection (a) of this section for a program, a provider described in subsection (a)(2)(C) of this section—

(i) shall submit an application, to the local board for the local area in which the provider desires to provide training services, at such time and in such manner as may be required, and containing a description of the program;

(ii) if the provider provides training services through a program on the date of application, shall include in the application an appropriate portion of the performance information and program cost information described in subsection (d) of this section for the program, as specified in the procedure, and shall meet appropriate levels of performance for the program, as specified in the procedure; and

(iii) if the provider does not provide training services on such date, shall meet appropriate requirements, as specified in the procedure.

(c) Subsequent eligibility determination

(1) Procedure

Each Governor of a State shall establish a procedure for use by local boards in the State in determining the eligibility of a provider described in subsection (a)(2) of this section to continue to receive funds as described in subsection (a) of this section for a program after an initial period of eligibility under subsection (b) of this section (referred to in this section as "subsequent eligibility").

(2) Recommendations

In developing such procedure, the Governor shall solicit and take into consideration the recommendations of local boards and providers of training services within the State.

(3) Opportunity to submit comments

The Governor shall provide an opportunity, during the development of the procedure, for interested members of the public, including representatives of business and labor organizations, to submit comments on such procedure.

(4) Considerations

In developing such procedure, the Governor shall ensure that the procedure requires the local boards to take into consideration, in making the determinations of subsequent eligibility—

(A) the specific economic, geographic, and demographic factors in the local areas in which providers seeking eligibility are located; and

(B) the characteristics of the populations served by providers seeking eligibility, including the demonstrated difficulties in serving such populations, where applicable.

(5) Requirements

In establishing the procedure, the Governor shall require that, to be eligible to continue to receive funds as described in subsection (a) of this section for a program after the initial period of eligibility, a provider described in subsection (a)(2) of this section shall—

(A) submit the performance information and program cost information described in subsection (d)(1) of this section for the program and any additional information required to be submitted in accordance with subsection (d)(2) of this section for the program annually to the appropriate local board at such time and in such manner as may be required; and

(B) annually meet the performance levels described in paragraph (6) for the program, as demonstrated utilizing quarterly records described in section 2871 of this title, in a manner consistent with section 2871 of this title.

(6) Levels of performance

(A) In general

At a minimum, the procedure described in paragraph (1) shall require the provider to meet minimum acceptable levels of performance based on the performance information referred to in paragraph (5)(A).

(B) Higher levels of performance eligibility

The local board may require higher levels of performance than the levels referred to in subparagraph (A) for subsequent eligibility to receive funds as described in subsection (a) of this section.

(d) Performance and cost information

(1) Required information

For a provider of training services to be determined to be subsequently eligible under subsection (c) of this section to receive funds as described in subsection (a) of this section, such provider shall, under subsection (c) of this section, submit—

(A) verifiable program-specific performance information consisting of—

(i) program information, including—

(I) the program completion rates for all individuals participating in the applicable program conducted by the provider;

(II) the percentage of all individuals participating in the applicable program who obtain unsubsidized employment, which may also include information specifying the percentage of the individuals who obtain unsubsidized employment in an occupation related to the program conducted; and

(III) the wages at placement in employment of all individuals participating in the applicable program; and

(ii) training services information for all participants who received assistance under section 2864 of this title to participate in the applicable program, including—

(I) the percentage of participants who have completed the applicable program and who are placed in unsubsidized employment;

(II) the retention rates in unsubsidized employment of participants who have completed the applicable program, 6 months after the first day of the employment;

(III) the wages received by participants who have completed the applicable program, 6 months after the first day of the employment involved; and

(IV) where appropriate, the rates of licensure or certification, attainment of academic degrees or equivalents, or attainment of other measures of skills, of the graduates of the applicable program; and

(B) information on program costs (such as tuition and fees) for participants in the applicable program.

(2) Additional information

Subject to paragraph (3), in addition to the performance information described in paragraph (1)—

(A) the Governor may require that a provider submit, under subsection (c) of this section, such other verifiable program-specific performance information as the Governor determines to be appropriate to obtain such subsequent eligibility, which may include information relating to—

(i) retention rates in employment and the subsequent wages of all individuals who complete the applicable program;

(ii) where appropriate, the rates of licensure or certification of all individuals who complete the program; and

(iii) the percentage of individuals who complete the program who attain industry-recognized occupational skills in the subject, occupation, or industry for which training is provided through the program, where applicable; and

(B) the Governor, or the local board, may require a provider to submit, under subsection (c) of this section, other verifiable program-specific performance information to obtain such subsequent eligibility.

(3) Conditions

(A) In general

If the Governor or a local board requests additional information under paragraph (2) that imposes extraordinary costs on providers, or if providers experience extraordinary costs in the collection of information required under paragraph (1)(A)(ii), the Governor or the local board shall provide access to cost-effective methods for the collection of the information involved, or the Governor shall provide additional resources to assist providers in the collection of such information from funds made available as described in sections 2853(a) and 2863(a)(1) of this title, as appropriate.

(B) Higher education eligibility requirements

The local board and the designated State agency described in subsection (i) of this section may accept program-specific performance information consistent with the requirements for eligibility under title IV of the Higher Education Act of 1965 (20 U.S.C. 1070 et seq. [and 42 U.S.C. 2751 et seq.]) from a provider for purposes of enabling the provider to fulfill the applicable requirements of this subsection, if such information is substantially similar to the information otherwise required under this subsection.

(e) Local identification

(1) In general

The local board shall place on a list providers submitting an application under subsection (b)(1) of this section and providers determined to be initially eligible under subsection (b)(2) of this section, and retain on the list providers determined to be subsequently eligible under subsection (c) of this section, to receive funds as described in subsection (a) of this section for the provision of training services in the local area served by the local board. The list of providers shall be accompanied by any performance information and program cost information submitted under subsection (b) or (c) of this section by the provider.

(2) Submission to State agency

On placing or retaining a provider on the list, the local board shall submit, to the designated State agency described in subsection (i) of this section, the list and the performance information and program cost information referred to in paragraph (1). If the agency determines, within 30 days after the date of the submission, that the provider does not meet the performance levels described in subsection (c)(6) of this section for the program (where applicable), the agency may remove the provider from the list for the program. The agency may not remove from the list an agency submitting an application under subsection (b)(1) of this section.

(3) Identification of eligible providers

A provider who is placed or retained on the list under paragraph (1), and is not removed by the designated State agency under paragraph (2), for a program, shall be considered to be identified as an eligible provider of training services for the program.

(4) Availability

(A) State list

The designated State agency shall compile a single list of the providers identified under paragraph (3) from all local areas in the State and disseminate such list, and the performance information and program cost information described in paragraph (1), to the one-stop delivery systems within the State.

Such list and information shall be made widely available to participants in employment and training activities authorized under section 2864 of this title and others through the one-stop delivery system.

(B) Selection from State list

Individuals eligible to receive training services under section 2864(d)(4) of this title shall have the opportunity to select any of the eligible providers, from any of the local areas in the State, that are included on the list described in subparagraph (A) to provide the services, consistent with the requirements of section 2864 of this title.

(5) Acceptance of individual training accounts by other States

States may enter into agreements, on a reciprocal basis, to permit eligible providers of training services in a State to accept individual training accounts provided in another State.

(f) Enforcement

(1) Accuracy of information

If the designated State agency, after consultation with the local board involved, determines that an eligible provider or individual supplying information on behalf of the provider intentionally supplies inaccurate information under this section, the agency shall terminate the eligibility of the provider to receive funds described in subsection (a) of this section for any program for a period of time, but not less than 2 years.

(2) Noncompliance

If the designated State agency, or the local board working with the State agency, determines that an eligible provider described in subsection (a) of this section substantially violates any requirement under this Act, the agency, or the local board working with the State agency, may terminate the eligibility of such provider to receive funds described in subsection (a) of this section for the program involved or take such other action as the agency or local board determines to be appropriate.

(3) Repayment

A provider whose eligibility is terminated under paragraph (1) or (2) for a program shall be liable for repayment of all funds described in subsection (a) of this section received for the program during any period of noncompliance described in such paragraph.

(4) Construction

This subsection and subsection (g) of this section shall be construed to provide remedies and penalties that supplement, but do not supplant, other civil and criminal remedies and penalties.

(g) Appeal

The Governor shall establish procedures for providers of training services to appeal a denial of eligibility by the local board or the designated State agency under subsection (b), (c), or (e) of this section, a termination of eligibility or other action by the board or agency under subsection (f) of this section, or a denial of eligibility by a one-stop operator under subsection (h) of this section. Such procedures shall provide an opportunity for a hearing and prescribe appropriate time limits to ensure prompt resolution of the appeal.

(h) On-the-job training or customized training exception

(1) In general

Providers of on-the-job training or customized training shall not be subject to the requirements of subsections (a) through (e) of this section.

(2) Collection and dissemination of information

A one-stop operator in a local area shall collect such performance information from on-the-job training and customized training providers as the Governor may require, determine whether the providers meet such performance criteria as the Governor may require, and disseminate information identifying providers that meet the criteria as eligible providers, and the performance information, through the one-stop delivery system. Providers determined to meet the criteria shall be considered to be identified as eligible providers of training services.

(i) Administration

The Governor shall designate a State agency to make the determinations described in subsection (e)(2) of this section, take the enforcement actions described in subsection (f) of this section, and carry out other duties described in this section.

(Pub. L. 105–220, title I, §122, Aug. 7, 1998, 112 Stat. 965.)

REFERENCES IN TEXT

The Higher Education Act of 1965, referred to in subsecs. (a)(2)(A)(i) and (d)(3)(B), is Pub. L. 89–329, Nov. 8, 1965, 79 Stat. 1219, as amended. Title IV of the Act is classified generally to subchapter IV (§1070 et seq.) of chapter 28 of Title 20, Education, and part C (§2751 et seq.) of subchapter I of chapter 34 of Title 42, The Public Health and Welfare. For complete classification of this Act to the Code, see Short Title note set out under section 1001 of Title 20 and Tables.

The National Apprenticeship Act, referred to in subsec. (a)(2)(B), is act Aug. 16, 1937, ch. 663, 50 Stat. 664, as amended, which is classified generally to chapter 4C (§50 et seq.) of this title. For complete classification of this Act to the Code, see Short Title note set out under section 50 of this title and Tables.

This Act, referred to in subsec. (f)(2), is Pub. L. 105–220, Aug. 7, 1998, 112 Stat. 936, as amended, known as the Workforce Investment Act of 1998. For complete classification of this Act to the Code, see Short Title note set out under section 9201 of Title 20, Education, and Tables.

§2843. Identification of eligible providers of youth activities

From funds allocated under paragraph (2)(A) or (3) of section 2853(b) of this title to a local area, the local board for such area shall identify eligible providers of youth activities by awarding grants or contracts on a competitive basis, based on the recommendations of the youth council and on the criteria contained in the State plan, to the providers to carry out the activities, and shall conduct oversight with respect to the providers, in the local area.

(Pub. L. 105–220, title I, § 123, Aug. 7, 1998, 112 Stat. 971.)

PART D—YOUTH ACTIVITIES

§ 2851. General authorization

The Secretary shall make an allotment under section 2852(b)(1)(C) of this title to each State that meets the requirements of section 2822 of this title and a grant to each outlying area that complies with the requirements of this chapter, to assist the State or outlying area, and to enable the State or outlying area to assist local areas, for the purpose of providing workforce investment activities for eligible youth in the State or outlying area and in the local areas.

(Pub. L. 105–220, title I, § 126, Aug. 7, 1998, 112 Stat. 971.)

REFERENCES IN TEXT

This chapter, referred to in text, was in the original "this title" meaning title I of Pub. L. 105–220, Aug. 7, 1998, 112 Stat. 939, as amended, which enacted this chapter, repealed sections 1501 to 1505, 1511 to 1583, 1592 to 1735, 1737 to 1791h, 1792 to 1792b, 2301 to 2314 of this title, section 211 of former Title 40, Appendix, Public Buildings, Property, and Works, sections 11421, 11441 to 11447, 11449, 11450, 11461 to 11466, 11471, and 11472 of Title 42, The Public Health and Welfare, and sections 42101 to 42106 of Title 49, Transportation, enacted provisions set out as notes under sections 1501, 2301, and 2940 of this title and section 11421 of Title 42, and repealed provisions set out as notes under sections 801 and 2301 of this title and section 1255a of Title 8, Aliens and Nationality. For complete classification of title I to the Code, see Tables.

§ 2852. State allotments

(a) In general

The Secretary shall—

(1) for each fiscal year in which the amount appropriated under section 2872(a) of this title exceeds $1,000,000,000, reserve a portion determined under subsection (b)(1)(A) of this section of the amount appropriated under section 2872(a) of this title for use under sections 2912 (relating to migrant and seasonal farmworker programs) and 2914 (relating to youth opportunity grants) of this title; and

(2) use the remainder of the amount appropriated under section 2872(a) of this title for a fiscal year to make allotments and grants in accordance with subparagraphs (B) and (C) of subsection (b)(1) of this section and make funds available for use under section 2911 of this title (relating to Native American programs).

(b) Allotment among States

(1) Youth activities

(A) Youth opportunity grants

(i) In general

For each fiscal year in which the amount appropriated under section 2872(a) of this title exceeds $1,000,000,000, the Secretary shall reserve a portion of the amount to provide youth opportunity grants and other activities under section 2914 of this title (relating to youth opportunity grants) and provide youth activities under section 2912 of this title (relating to migrant and seasonal farmworker programs).

(ii) Portion

The portion referred to in clause (i) shall equal, for a fiscal year—

(I) except as provided in subclause (II), the difference obtained by subtracting $1,000,000,000 from the amount appropriated under section 2872(a) of this title for the fiscal year; or

(II) for any fiscal year in which the amount is $1,250,000,000 or greater, $250,000,000.

(iii) Youth activities for farmworkers

From the portion described in clause (i) for a fiscal year, the Secretary shall make available 4 percent of such portion to provide youth activities under section 2912 of this title.

(iv) Role model academy project

From the portion described in clause (i) for fiscal year 1999, the Secretary shall make available such sums as the Secretary determines to be appropriate to carry out section 2914(g) of this title.

(B) Outlying areas

(i) In general

From the amount made available under subsection (a)(2) of this section for a fiscal year, the Secretary shall reserve not more than ¼ of 1 percent of the amount appropriated under section 2872(a) of this title for the fiscal year—

(I) to provide assistance to the outlying areas to carry out youth activities and statewide workforce investment activities; and

(II) for each of fiscal years 1999, 2000, and 2001, to carry out the competition described in clause (ii), except that the funds reserved to carry out such clause for any such fiscal year shall not exceed the amount reserved for the Freely Associated States for fiscal year 1997, from amounts reserved under sections 252(a) and 262(a)(1) of the Job Training Partnership Act (as in effect on the day before August 7, 1998).

(ii) Limitation for Freely Associated States

(I) Competitive grants

The Secretary shall use funds described in clause (i)(II) to award grants to Guam, American Samoa, the Commonwealth of the Northern Mariana Islands, and the Freely Associated States to carry out youth activities and statewide workforce investment activities.

(II) Award basis

The Secretary shall award grants pursuant to subclause (I) on a competitive basis and pursuant to the recommendations of experts in the field of employment and training, working through the Pacific Region Educational Laboratory in Honolulu, Hawaii.

(III) Assistance requirements

Any Freely Associated State that desires to receive assistance under this subparagraph shall submit an application to the Secretary and shall include in the application for assistance—

(aa) information demonstrating that the Freely Associated State will meet all conditions that apply to States under this chapter;

(bb) an assurance that, notwithstanding any other provision of this chapter, the Freely Associated State will use such assistance only for the direct provision of services; and

(cc) such other information and assurances as the Secretary may require.

(IV) Termination of eligibility

Notwithstanding any other provision of law, the Freely Associated States shall not receive any assistance under this subparagraph for any program year that begins after September 30, 2001.

(V) Administrative costs

The Secretary may provide not more than 5 percent of the funds made available for grants under subclause (I) to pay the administrative costs of the Pacific Region Educational Laboratory in Honolulu, Hawaii, regarding activities assisted under this clause.

(iii) Additional requirement

The provisions of Public Law 95–134, permitting the consolidation of grants by the outlying areas, shall not apply to assistance provided to those areas, including the Freely Associated States, under this subparagraph.

(C) States

(i) In general

After determining the amounts to be reserved under subparagraph (A) (if any) and subparagraph (B), the Secretary shall—

(I) from the amount referred to in subsection (a)(2) of this section for a fiscal year, make available not more than 1.5 percent to provide youth activities under section 2911 of this title (relating to Native Americans); and

(II) allot the remainder of the amount referred to in subsection (a)(2) of this section for a fiscal year to the States pursuant to clause (ii) for youth activities and statewide workforce investment activities.

(ii) Formula

Subject to clauses (iii) and (iv), of the remainder—

(I) 33⅓ percent shall be allotted on the basis of the relative number of unemployed individuals in areas of substantial unemployment in each State, compared to the total number of unemployed individuals in areas of substantial unemployment in all States;

(II) 33⅓ percent shall be allotted on the basis of the relative excess number of unemployed individuals in each State, compared to the total excess number of unemployed individuals in all States; and

(III) 33⅓ percent shall be allotted on the basis of the relative number of disadvantaged youth in each State, compared to the total number of disadvantaged youth in all States, except as described in clause (iii).

(iii) Calculation

In determining an allotment under clause (ii)(III) for any State in which there is a local area designated under section 2831(a)(2)(B) of this title (relating to the area served by a rural concentrated employment program grant recipient), the allotment shall be based on the higher of—

(I) the number of individuals who are age 16 through 21 in families with an income below the low-income level in such area; or

(II) the number of disadvantaged youth in such area.

(iv) Minimum and maximum percentages and minimum allotments

In making allotments under this subparagraph, the Secretary shall ensure the following:

(I) Minimum percentage and allotment

Subject to subclause (IV), the Secretary shall ensure that no State shall receive an allotment for a fiscal year that is less than the greater of—

(aa) an amount based on 90 percent of the allotment percentage of the State for the preceding fiscal year; or

(bb) 100 percent of the total of the allotments of the State under sections 252 and 262 of the Job Training Partnership Act (as in effect on the day before August 7, 1998) for fiscal year 1998.

(II) Small State minimum allotment

Subject to subclauses (I), (III), and (IV), the Secretary shall ensure that no State shall receive an allotment under this subparagraph that is less than the total of—

(aa) $\frac{3}{10}$ of 1 percent of $1,000,000,000 of the remainder described in clause (i)(II) for the fiscal year; and

(bb) if the remainder described in clause (i)(II) for the fiscal year exceeds $1,000,000,000, $\frac{2}{5}$ of 1 percent of the excess.

(III) Maximum percentage

Subject to subclause (I), the Secretary shall ensure that no State shall receive an allotment percentage for a fiscal year that is more than 130 percent of the allotment percentage of the State for the preceding fiscal year.

(IV) Minimum funding

In any fiscal year in which the remainder described in clause (i)(II) does not exceed $1,000,000,000, the minimum allotments under subclauses (I) and (II) shall be calculated by the methodology for calculating the corresponding allotments under parts B and C of title II of the Job Training Partnership Act, as in effect on July 1, 1998.

(2) Definitions

For the purpose of the formula specified in paragraph (1)(C):

(A) Allotment percentage

The term "allotment percentage", used with respect to fiscal year 2000 or a subsequent fiscal year, means a percentage of the remainder described in paragraph (1)(C)(i)(II) that is received through an allotment made under paragraph (1)(C) for the fiscal year. The term, used with respect to fiscal year 1998 or 1999, means the percentage of the amounts allotted to States under sections 252(b) and 262(a) of the Job Training Partnership Act (as in effect on the day before August 7, 1998) that is received under such sections by the State involved for fiscal year 1998 or 1999.

(B) Area of substantial unemployment

The term "area of substantial unemployment" means any area that is of sufficient size and scope to sustain a program of workforce investment activities carried out under this subchapter and that has an average rate of unemployment of at least 6.5 percent for the most recent 12 months, as determined by the Secretary. For purposes of this subparagraph, determinations of areas of substantial unemployment shall be made once each fiscal year.

(C) Disadvantaged youth

Subject to paragraph (3), the term "disadvantaged youth" means an individual who is age 16 through 21 who received an income, or is a member of a family that received a total family income, that, in relation to family size, does not exceed the higher of—

(i) the poverty line; or

(ii) 70 percent of the lower living standard income level.

(D) Excess number

The term "excess number" means, used with respect to the excess number of unemployed individuals within a State, the higher of—

(i) the number that represents the number of unemployed individuals in excess of 4.5 percent of the civilian labor force in the State; or

(ii) the number that represents the number of unemployed individuals in excess of 4.5 percent of the civilian labor force in areas of substantial unemployment in such State.

(E) Low-income level

The term "low-income level" means $7,000 with respect to income in 1969, and for any later year means that amount that bears the same relationship to $7,000 as the Consumer Price Index for that year bears to the Consumer Price Index for 1969, rounded to the nearest $1,000.

(3) Special rule

For the purpose of the formula specified in paragraph (1)(C), the Secretary shall, as appropriate and to the extent practicable, exclude college students and members of the Armed Forces from the determination of the number of disadvantaged youth.

(4) Definition

In this subsection, the term "Freely Associated State" means the Republic of the Marshall Islands, the Federated States of Micronesia, and the Republic of Palau.

(c) Reallotment

(1) In general

The Secretary shall, in accordance with this subsection, reallot to eligible States amounts that are allotted under this section for youth activities and statewide workforce investment activities and that are available for reallotment.

(2) Amount

The amount available for reallotment for a program year is equal to the amount by which the unobligated balance of the State allotment under this section for such activities, at the end of the program year prior to the program year for which the determination under this paragraph is made, exceeds 20 percent of such allotment for the prior program year.

(3) Reallotment

In making reallotments to eligible States of amounts available pursuant to paragraph (2) for a program year, the Secretary shall allot to each eligible State an amount based on the relative amount allotted to such State under this section for such activities for the prior program year, as compared to the total amount allotted to all eligible States under this section for such activities for such prior program year.

(4) Eligibility

For purposes of this subsection, an eligible State means a State that has obligated at least 80 percent of the State allotment under this section for such activities for the program year prior to the program year for which the determination under paragraph (2) is made.

(5) Procedures

The Governor of each State shall prescribe uniform procedures for the obligation of funds by local areas within the State in order to avoid the requirement that funds be made available for reallotment under this subsection. The Governor shall further prescribe equitable procedures for making funds available from the State and local areas in the event that a State is required to make funds available for reallotment under this subsection.

(Pub. L. 105–220, title I, § 127, Aug. 7, 1998, 112 Stat. 971.)

REFERENCES IN TEXT

Public Law 95–134, referred to in subsec. (b)(1)(B)(iii), is Pub. L. 95–134, Oct. 15, 1977, 91 Stat. 1159, as amended. Provisions relating to consolidation of grants are contained in section 501 of Pub. L. 95–134 which is classified to section 1469a of Title 48, Territories and Insular Possessions.

The Job Training Partnership Act, referred to in subsec. (b)(1)(B)(i)(II), (C)(iv)(I)(bb), (IV), (2)(A), is Pub. L. 97–300, Oct. 13, 1982, 96 Stat. 1322, as amended, which was repealed by Pub. L. 105–220, title I, §199(b)(2), (c)(2)(B), Aug. 7, 1998, 112 Stat. 1059, effective July 1, 2000. Parts B and C of title II of the Act were classified generally to parts B (§1630 et seq.) and C (§1641 et seq.) of subchapter II of chapter 19 of this title, respectively, prior to repeal by Pub. L. 105–220. Sections 252 and 262 of the Act were classified to sections 1631 and 1642 of this title, respectively, prior to repeal by Pub. L. 105–220. For complete classification of this Act to the Code, see Tables.

§2853. Within State allocations

(a) Reservations for State activities

(1) In general

The Governor of a State shall reserve not more than 15 percent of each of the amounts allotted to the State under section 2852(b)(1)(C) of this title and paragraphs (1)(B) and (2)(B) of section 2862(b) of this title for a fiscal year for statewide workforce investment activities.

(2) Use of funds

Regardless of whether the reserved amounts were allotted under section 2852(b)(1)(C) of this title, or under paragraph (1)(B) or (2)(B) of section 2862(b) of this title, the Governor may use the reserved amounts to carry out statewide youth activities described in section 2854(b) of this title or statewide employment and training activities, for adults or for dislocated workers, described in paragraph (2)(B) or (3) of section 2864(a) of this title.

(b) Within State allocation

(1) Methods

The Governor, acting in accordance with the State plan, and after consulting with chief elected officials in the local areas, shall allocate the funds that are allotted to the State for youth activities and statewide workforce investment activities under section 2852(b)(1)(C) of this title and are not reserved under subsection (a) of this section, in accordance with paragraph (2) or (3).

(2) Formula allocation

(A) Youth activities

(i) Allocation

In allocating the funds described in paragraph (1) to local areas, a State may allocate—

(I) 33⅓ percent of the funds on the basis described in section 2852(b)(1)(C)(ii)(I) of this title;

(II) 33⅓ percent of the funds on the basis described in section 2852(b)(1)(C)(ii)(II) of this title; and

(III) 33⅓ percent of the funds on the basis described in clauses (ii)(III) and (iii) of section 2852(b)(1)(C) of this title.

(ii) Minimum percentage

Effective at the end of the second full fiscal year after the date on which a local area is designated under section 2831 of this title, the local area shall not receive an allocation percentage for a fiscal year that is less than 90 percent of the average allocation percentage of the local area for the 2 preceding fiscal years. Amounts necessary for increasing such allocations to local areas to comply with the preceding sentence shall be obtained by ratably reducing the allocations to be made to other local areas under this subparagraph.

(iii) Definition

The term "allocation percentage", used with respect to fiscal year 2000 or a subsequent fiscal year, means a percentage of the funds referred to in clause (i), received through an allocation made under this subparagraph, for the fiscal year.

(B) Application

For purposes of carrying out subparagraph (A)—

(i) references in section 2852(b) of this title to a State shall be deemed to be references to a local area;

(ii) references in section 2852(b) of this title to all States shall be deemed to be references to all local areas in the State involved; and

(iii) except as described in clause (i), references in section 2852(b)(1) of this title to the term "excess number" shall be considered to be references to the term as defined in section 2852(b)(2) of this title.

(3) Youth discretionary allocation

In lieu of making the allocation described in paragraph (2)(A), in allocating the funds described in paragraph (1) to local areas, a State may distribute—

(A) a portion equal to not less than 70 percent of the funds in accordance with paragraph (2)(A); and

(B) the remaining portion of the funds on the basis of a formula that—

(i) incorporates additional factors (other than the factors described in paragraph (2)(A)) relating to—

(I) excess youth poverty in urban, rural, and suburban local areas; and

(II) excess unemployment above the State average in urban, rural, and suburban local areas; and

(ii) was developed by the State board and approved by the Secretary as part of the State plan.

(4) Limitation

(A) In general

Of the amount allocated to a local area under this subsection and section 2863(b) of this title for a fiscal year, not more than 10 percent of the amount may be used by the local board for the administrative cost of carrying out local workforce investment activities described in subsection (d) or (e) of section 2864 of this title or in section 2854(c) of this title.

(B) Use of funds

Funds made available for administrative costs under subparagraph (A) may be used for the administrative cost of any of the local workforce investment activities described in subsection (d) or (e) of section 2864 of this title or in section 2854(c) of this title, regardless of whether the funds were allocated under this subsection or section 2863(b) of this title.

(C) Regulations

The Secretary, after consulting with the Governors, shall develop and issue regulations that define the term "administrative cost" for purposes of this chapter. Such definition shall be consistent with generally accepted accounting principles.

(c) Reallocation among local areas

(1) In general

The Governor may, in accordance with this subsection, reallocate to eligible local areas within the State amounts that are allocated under paragraph (2)(A) or (3) of subsection (b) of this section for youth activities and that are available for reallocation.

(2) Amount

The amount available for reallocation for a program year is equal to the amount by which the unobligated balance of the local area allocation under paragraph (2)(A) or (3) of subsection (b) of this section for such activities, at the end of the program year prior to the program year for which the determination under this paragraph is made exceeds 20 percent of such allocation for the prior program year.

(3) Reallocation

In making reallocations to eligible local areas of amounts available pursuant to paragraph (2) for a program year, the Governor shall allocate to each eligible local area within the State an amount based on the relative amount allocated to such local area under subsection (b)(3) of this section for such activities for the prior program year, as compared to the total amount allocated to all eligible local areas in the State under subsection (b)(3) of this section for such activities for such prior program year. For purposes of this paragraph, local areas that received allocations under subsection (b)(2)(A) of this section for the prior program year shall be treated as if the local areas received allocations under subsection (b)(3) of this section for such year.

(4) Eligibility

For purposes of this subsection, an eligible local area means a local area that has obligated at least 80 percent of the local area allocation under paragraph (2)(A) or (3) of subsection (b) of this section for such activities, for the program year prior to the program year for which the determination under paragraph (2) is made.

(Pub. L. 105–220, title I, §128, Aug. 7, 1998, 112 Stat. 976.)

§2854. Use of funds for youth activities

(a) Purposes

The purposes of this section are—

(1) to provide, to eligible youth seeking assistance in achieving academic and employment success, effective and comprehensive activities, which shall include a variety of options for improving educational and skill competencies and provide effective connections to employers;

(2) to ensure on-going mentoring opportunities for eligible youth with adults committed to providing such opportunities;

(3) to provide opportunities for training to eligible youth;

(4) to provide continued supportive services for eligible youth;

(5) to provide incentives for recognition and achievement to eligible youth; and

(6) to provide opportunities for eligible youth in activities related to leadership, development, decisionmaking, citizenship, and community service.

(b) Statewide youth activities

(1) In general

Funds reserved by a Governor for a State as described in sections 2853(a) and 2863(a)(1) of this title—

(A) shall be used to carry out the statewide youth activities described in paragraph (2); and

(B) may be used to carry out any of the statewide youth activities described in paragraph (3),

regardless of whether the funds were allotted to the State under section 2852(b)(1) of this title or under paragraph (1) or (2) of section 2862(b) of this title.

(2) Required statewide youth activities

A State shall use funds reserved as described in sections 2853(a) and 2863(a)(1) of this title (regardless of whether the funds were allotted to the State under section 2852(b)(1) of this title or paragraph (1) or (2) of section 2862(b) of this title) to carry out statewide youth activities, which shall include—

(A) disseminating a list of eligible providers of youth activities described in section 2843 of this title;

(B) carrying out activities described in clauses (ii) through (vi) of section 2864(a)(2)(B) of this title, except that references in such clauses to activities authorized under section 2864 of this title shall be considered to be references to activities authorized under this section; and

(C) providing additional assistance to local areas that have high concentrations of eligible youth to carry out the activities described in subsection (c) of this section.

(3) Allowable statewide youth activities

A State may use funds reserved as described in sections 2853(a) and 2863(a)(1) of this title (regardless of whether the funds were allotted to the State under section 2852(b)(1) of this title or paragraph (1) or (2) of section 2862(b) of this title) to carry out additional statewide youth activities, which may include—

(A) carrying out activities described in clauses (i), (ii), (iii), (iv)(II), and (vi)(II) of section 2864(a)(3)(A) of this title, except that references in such clauses to activities authorized under section 2864 of this title shall be considered to be references to activities authorized under this section; and

(B) carrying out, on a statewide basis, activities described in subsection (c) of this section.

(4) Prohibition

No funds described in this subsection or section 2864(a) of this title shall be used to develop or implement education curricula for school systems in the State.

(c) Local elements and requirements

(1) Program design

Funds allocated to a local area for eligible youth under paragraph (2)(A) or (3), as appropriate, of section 2853(b) of this title shall be used to carry out, for eligible youth, programs that—

(A) provide an objective assessment of the academic levels, skill levels, and service needs of each participant, which assessment shall include a review of basic skills, occupational skills, prior work experience, employability, interests, aptitudes (including interests and aptitudes for nontraditional jobs), supportive service needs, and developmental needs of such participant, except that a new assessment of a participant is not required if the provider carrying out such a program determines it is appropriate to use a recent assessment of the participant conducted pursuant to another education or training program;

(B) develop service strategies for each participant that shall identify an employment goal (including, in appropriate circumstances, nontraditional employment), appropriate achievement objectives, and appropriate services for the participant taking into account the assessment conducted pursuant to subparagraph (A), except that a new service strategy for a participant is not required if the provider carrying out such a program determines it is appropriate to use a recent service strategy developed for the participant under another education or training program; and

(C) provide—

(i) preparation for postsecondary educational opportunities, in appropriate cases;

(ii) strong linkages between academic and occupational learning;

(iii) preparation for unsubsidized employment opportunities, in appropriate cases; and

(iv) effective connections to intermediaries with strong links to—

(I) the job market; and

(II) local and regional employers.

(2) Program elements

The programs described in paragraph (1) shall provide elements consisting of—

(A) tutoring, study skills training, and instruction, leading to completion of secondary school, including dropout prevention strategies;

(B) alternative secondary school services, as appropriate;

(C) summer employment opportunities that are directly linked to academic and occupational learning;

(D) as appropriate, paid and unpaid work experiences, including internships and job shadowing;

(E) occupational skill training, as appropriate;

(F) leadership development opportunities, which may include community service and peer-centered activities encouraging responsibility and other positive social behaviors during non-school hours, as appropriate;

(G) supportive services;

(H) adult mentoring for the period of participation and a subsequent period, for a total of not less than 12 months;

(I) followup services for not less than 12 months after the completion of participation, as appropriate; and

(J) comprehensive guidance and counseling, which may include drug and alcohol abuse counseling and referral, as appropriate.

(3) Additional requirements

(A) Information and referrals

Each local board shall ensure that each participant or applicant who meets the minimum income criteria to be considered an eligible youth shall be provided—

(i) information on the full array of applicable or appropriate services that are available through the local board or other eligible providers or one-stop partners, including those receiving funds under this subchapter; and

(ii) referral to appropriate training and educational programs that have the capacity to serve the participant or applicant either on a sequential or concurrent basis.

(B) Applicants not meeting enrollment requirements

Each eligible provider of a program of youth activities shall ensure that an eligible applicant who does not meet the enrollment requirements of the particular program or who cannot be served shall be referred for further assessment, as necessary, and referred to appropriate programs in accordance with subparagraph (A) to meet the basic skills and training needs of the applicant.

(C) Involvement in design and implementation

The local board shall ensure that parents, participants, and other members of the community with experience relating to programs for youth are involved in the design and implementation of the programs described in paragraph (1).

(4) Priority

(A) In general

At a minimum, 30 percent of the funds described in paragraph (1) shall be used to provide youth activities to out-of-school youth.

(B) Exception

A State that receives a minimum allotment under section 2852(b)(1) of this title in accordance with section 2852(b)(1)(C)(iv)(II) of this title or under section 2862(b)(1) of this title in accordance with section 2862(b)(1)(B)(iv)(II) of this title may reduce the percentage described in subparagraph (A) for a local area in the State, if—

(i) after an analysis of the eligible youth population in the local area, the State determines that the local area will be unable to meet the percentage described in subparagraph (A) due to a low number of out-of-school youth; and

(ii)(I) the State submits to the Secretary, for the local area, a request including a proposed reduced percentage for purposes of subparagraph (A), and the summary of the eligible youth population analysis; and

(II) the request is approved by the Secretary.

(5) Exceptions

Not more than 5 percent of participants assisted under this section in each local area may be individuals who do not meet the minimum income criteria to be considered eligible youth, if such individuals are within one or more of the following categories:

(A) Individuals who are school dropouts.

(B) Individuals who are basic skills deficient.

(C) Individuals with educational attainment that is one or more grade levels below the grade level appropriate to the age of the individuals.

(D) Individuals who are pregnant or parenting.

(E) Individuals with disabilities, including learning disabilities.

(F) Individuals who are homeless or runaway youth.

(G) Individuals who are offenders.

(H) Other eligible youth who face serious barriers to employment as identified by the local board.

(6) Prohibitions

(A) Prohibition against Federal control of education

No provision of this Act shall be construed to authorize any department, agency, officer, or employee of the United States to exercise any direction, supervision, or control over the curriculum, program of instruction, administration, or personnel of any educational institution, school, or school system, or over the selection of library resources, textbooks, or other printed or published instructional materials by any educational institution, school, or school system.

(B) Nonduplication

All of the funds made available under this Act shall be used in accordance with the requirements of this Act. None of the funds made available under this Act may be used to provide funding under the School-to-Work Opportunities Act of 1994 (20 U.S.C. 6101 et seq.) or to carry out, through programs funded under this Act, activities that were funded under the School-to-Work Opportunities Act of 1994, unless the programs funded under this Act serve only those participants eligible to participate in the programs under this Act.

(C) Noninterference and nonreplacement of regular academic requirements

No funds described in paragraph (1) shall be used to provide an activity for eligible youth who are not school dropouts if participation in the activity would interfere with or replace the regular academic requirements of the youth.

(7) Linkages

In coordinating the programs authorized under this section, youth councils shall establish linkages with educational agencies responsible for services to participants as appropriate.

(8) Volunteers

The local board shall make opportunities available for individuals who have successfully participated in programs carried out under this section to volunteer assistance to participants in the form of mentoring, tutoring, and other activities.

(Pub. L. 105–220, title I, § 129, Aug. 7, 1998, 112 Stat. 978.)

REFERENCES IN TEXT

This Act, referred to in subsec. (c)(6)(A), (B), is Pub. L. 105–220, Aug. 7, 1998, 112 Stat. 936, as amended, known as the Workforce Investment Act of 1998. For complete classification of this Act to the Code, see Short Title note set out under section 9201 of Title 20, Education, and Tables.

The School-to-Work Opportunities Act of 1994, referred to in subsec. (c)(6)(B), is Pub. L. 103–239, May 4, 1994, 108 Stat. 568, as amended, which is classified principally to chapter 69 (§ 6101 et seq.) of Title 20, Education. For complete classification of this Act to the Code, see Short Title note set out under section 6101 of Title 20 and Tables.

PART E—ADULT AND DISLOCATED WORKER EMPLOYMENT AND TRAINING ACTIVITIES

§ 2861. General authorization

The Secretary shall make allotments under paragraphs (1)(B) and (2)(B) of section 2862(b) of this title to each State that meets the requirements of section 2822 of this title and a grant to each outlying area that complies with the requirements of this chapter, to assist the State or outlying area, and to enable the State or outlying area to assist local areas, for the purpose of providing workforce investment activities for adults, and dislocated workers, in the State or outlying area and in the local areas.

(Pub. L. 105–220, title I, § 131, Aug. 7, 1998, 112 Stat. 982.)

REFERENCES IN TEXT

This chapter, referred to in text, was in the original "this title" meaning title I of Pub. L. 105–220, Aug. 7, 1998, 112 Stat. 939, as amended, which enacted this chapter, repealed sections 1501 to 1505, 1511 to 1583, 1592 to 1735, 1737 to 1791h, 1792 to 1792b, 2301 to 2314 of this title, section 211 of former Title 40, Appendix, Public Buildings, Property, and Works, sections 11421, 11441 to 11447, 11449, 11450, 11461 to 11466, 11471, and 11472 of Title 42,

The Public Health and Welfare, and sections 42101 to 42106 of Title 49, Transportation, enacted provisions set out as notes under sections 1501, 2301, and 2940 of this title and section 11421 of Title 42, and repealed provisions set out as notes under sections 801 and 2301 of this title and section 1255a of Title 8, Aliens and Nationality. For complete classification of title I to the Code, see Tables.

§2862. State allotments

(a) In general

The Secretary shall—

(1) make allotments and grants from the total amount appropriated under section 2872(b) of this title for a fiscal year in accordance with subsection (b)(1) of this section; and

(2)(A) reserve 20 percent of the amount appropriated under section 2872(c) of this title for a fiscal year for use under subsection (b)(2)(A) of this section, and under sections 2915(b) (relating to dislocated worker technical assistance), 2916(d) (relating to dislocated worker projects), and 2918 (relating to national emergency grants, other than under subsection[1] (a)(4), (f), and (g)) of this title; and

(B) make allotments from 80 percent of the amount appropriated under section 2872(c) of this title for a fiscal year in accordance with subsection (b)(2)(B) of this section.

(b) Allotment among States

(1) Adult employment and training activities

(A) Reservation for outlying areas

(i) In general

From the amount made available under subsection (a)(1) of this section for a fiscal year, the Secretary shall reserve not more than 1/4 of 1 percent to provide assistance to the outlying areas.

(ii) Applicability of additional requirements

From the amount reserved under clause (i), the Secretary shall provide assistance to the outlying areas for adult employment and training activities and statewide workforce investment activities in accordance with the requirements of section 2852(b)(1)(B) of this title, except that the reference in section 2852(b)(1)(B)(i)(II) of this title to sections 252(d) and 262(a)(1) of the Job Training Partnership Act shall be deemed to be a reference to section 202(a)(1) of the Job Training Partnership Act (as in effect on the day before August 7, 1998).

(B) States

(i) In general

After determining the amount to be reserved under subparagraph (A), the Secretary shall allot the remainder of the amount referred to in subsection (a)(1) of this section for a fiscal year to the States pursuant to clause (ii) for adult employment and training activities and statewide workforce investment activities.

(ii) Formula

Subject to clauses (iii) and (iv), of the remainder—

(I) 33 1/3 percent shall be allotted on the basis of the relative number of unemployed individuals in areas of substantial unemployment in each State, compared to the total number of unemployed individuals in areas of substantial unemployment in all States;

(II) 33 1/3 percent shall be allotted on the basis of the relative excess number of unemployed individuals in each State, compared to the total excess number of unemployed individuals in all States; and

(III) 33 1/3 percent shall be allotted on the basis of the relative number of disadvantaged adults in each State, compared to the total number of disadvantaged adults in all States, except as described in clause (iii).

(iii) Calculation

In determining an allotment under clause (ii)(III) for any State in which there is a local area designated under section 2831(a)(2)(B) of this title, the allotment shall be based on the higher of—

(I) the number of adults in families with an income below the low-income level in such area; or

(II) the number of disadvantaged adults in such area.

(iv) Minimum and maximum percentages and minimum allotments

In making allotments under this subparagraph, the Secretary shall ensure the following:

(I) Minimum percentage and allotment

Subject to subclause (IV), the Secretary shall ensure that no State shall receive an allotment for a fiscal year that is less than the greater of—

(aa) an amount based on 90 percent of the allotment percentage of the State for the preceding fiscal year; or

(bb) 100 percent of the allotment of the State under section 202 of the Job Training Partnership Act (as in effect on the day before August 7, 1998) for fiscal year 1998.

(II) Small State minimum allotment

Subject to subclauses (I), (III), and (IV), the Secretary shall ensure that no State shall receive an allotment under this subparagraph that is less than the total of—

(aa) 3/10 of 1 percent of $960,000,000 of the remainder described in clause (i) for the fiscal year; and

(bb) if the remainder described in clause (i) for the fiscal year exceeds $960,000,000, 2/5 of 1 percent of the excess.

(III) Maximum percentage

Subject to subclause (I), the Secretary shall ensure that no State shall receive an allotment percentage for a fiscal year that is more than 130 percent of the allotment percentage of the State for the preceding fiscal year.

[1] So in original. Probably should be "subsections".

(IV) Minimum funding

In any fiscal year in which the remainder described in clause (i) does not exceed $960,000,000, the minimum allotments under subclauses (I) and (II) shall be calculated by the methodology for calculating the corresponding allotments under part A of title II of the Job Training Partnership Act, as in effect on July 1, 1998.

(v) Definitions

For the purpose of the formula specified in this subparagraph:

(I) Adult

The term "adult" means an individual who is not less than age 22 and not more than age 72.

(II) Allotment percentage

The term "allotment percentage", used with respect to fiscal year 2000 or a subsequent fiscal year, means a percentage of the remainder described in clause (i) that is received through an allotment made under this subparagraph for the fiscal year. The term, used with respect to fiscal year 1998 or 1999, means the percentage of the amounts allotted to States under section 202(a) of the Job Training Partnership Act (as in effect on the day before August 7, 1998) that is received under such section by the State involved for fiscal year 1998 or 1999.

(III) Area of substantial unemployment

The term "area of substantial unemployment" means any area that is of sufficient size and scope to sustain a program of workforce investment activities carried out under this subchapter and that has an average rate of unemployment of at least 6.5 percent for the most recent 12 months, as determined by the Secretary. For purposes of this subclause, determinations of areas of substantial unemployment shall be made once each fiscal year.

(IV) Disadvantaged adult

Subject to subclause (V), the term "disadvantaged adult" means an adult who received an income, or is a member of a family that received a total family income, that, in relation to family size, does not exceed the higher of—

(aa) the poverty line; or

(bb) 70 percent of the lower living standard income level.

(V) Disadvantaged adult special rule

The Secretary shall, as appropriate and to the extent practicable, exclude college students and members of the Armed Forces from the determination of the number of disadvantaged adults.

(VI) Excess number

The term "excess number" means, used with respect to the excess number of unemployed individuals within a State, the higher of—

(aa) the number that represents the number of unemployed individuals in excess of 4.5 percent of the civilian labor force in the State; or

(bb) the number that represents the number of unemployed individuals in excess of 4.5 percent of the civilian labor force in areas of substantial unemployment in such State.

(2) Dislocated worker employment and training

(A) Reservation for outlying areas

(i) In general

From the amount made available under subsection (a)(2)(A) of this section for a fiscal year, the Secretary shall reserve not more than ¼ of 1 percent of the amount appropriated under section 2872(c) of this title for the fiscal year to provide assistance to the outlying areas.

(ii) Applicability of additional requirements

From the amount reserved under clause (i), the Secretary shall provide assistance to the outlying areas for dislocated worker employment and training activities and statewide workforce investment activities in accordance with the requirements of section 2852(b)(1)(B) of this title, except that the reference in section 2852(b)(1)(B)(i)(II) of this title to sections 252(a) and 262(a)(1) of the Job Training Partnership Act shall be deemed to be a reference to section 302(e) of the Job Training Partnership Act (as in effect on the day before August 7, 1998).

(B) States

(i) In general

The Secretary shall allot the amount referred to in subsection (a)(2)(B) of this section for a fiscal year to the States pursuant to clause (ii) for dislocated worker employment and training activities and statewide workforce investment activities.

(ii) Formula

Of the amount—

(I) 33⅓ percent shall be allotted on the basis of the relative number of unemployed individuals in each State, compared to the total number of unemployed individuals in all States;

(II) 33⅓ percent shall be allotted on the basis of the relative excess number of unemployed individuals in each State, compared to the total excess number of unemployed individuals in all States; and

(III) 33⅓ percent shall be allotted on the basis of the relative number of individuals in each State who have been unemployed for 15 weeks or more, compared to the total number of individuals in all States who have been unemployed for 15 weeks or more.

(iii) Definition

In this subparagraph, the term "excess number" means, used with respect to the excess number of unemployed individuals within a State, the number that represents the number of unemployed individuals in excess of 4.5 percent of the civilian labor force in the State.

(3) Definitions

For the purpose of the formulas specified in this subsection:

(A) Freely Associated States

The term "Freely Associated States" means the Republic of the Marshall Islands, the Federated States of Micronesia, and the Republic of Palau.

(B) Low-income level

The term "low-income level" means $7,000 with respect to income in 1969, and for any later year means that amount that bears the same relationship to $7,000 as the Consumer Price Index for that year bears to the Consumer Price Index for 1969, rounded to the nearest $1,000.

(c) Reallotment

(1) In general

The Secretary shall, in accordance with this subsection, reallot to eligible States amounts that are allotted under this section for employment and training activities and statewide workforce investment activities and that are available for reallotment.

(2) Amount

The amount available for reallotment for a program year is equal to the amount by which the unobligated balance of the State allotments under this section for such activities, at the end of the program year prior to the program year for which the determination under this paragraph is made, exceeds 20 percent of such allotments for the prior program year.

(3) Reallotment

In making reallotments to eligible States of amounts available pursuant to paragraph (2) for a program year, the Secretary shall allot to each eligible State an amount based on the relative amount allotted to such State under this section for such activities for the prior program year, as compared to the total amount allotted to all eligible States under this section for such activities for such prior program year.

(4) Eligibility

For purposes of this subsection, an eligible State means a State that has obligated at least 80 percent of the State allotment under this section for such activities for the program year prior to the program year for which the determination under paragraph (2) is made.

(5) Procedures

The Governor of each State shall prescribe uniform procedures for the obligation of funds by local areas within the State in order to avoid the requirement that funds be made available for reallotment under this subsection. The Governor shall further prescribe equitable procedures for making funds available from the State and local areas in the event that a State is required to make funds available for reallotment under this subsection.

(Pub. L. 105–220, title I, §132, Aug. 7, 1998, 112 Stat. 983; Pub. L. 107–210, div. A, title II, §203(d), Aug. 6, 2002, 116 Stat. 969.)

REFERENCES IN TEXT

The Job Training Partnership Act, referred to in subsec. (b)(1)(A)(ii), (B)(iv)(I)(bb), (IV), (v)(II), (2)(A)(ii), is Pub. L. 97–300, Oct. 13, 1982, 96 Stat. 1322, as amended, which was repealed by Pub. L. 105–220, title I, §199(b)(2), (c)(2)(B), Aug. 7, 1998, 112 Stat. 1059, effective July 1, 2000. Part A of title II of the Act was classified generally to part A (§1601 et seq.) of subchapter II of chapter 19 of this title, prior to repeal by Pub. L. 105–220. Sections 202, 252, 262, and 302 of the Act were classified to sections 1602, 1631, 1642, and 1652 of this title, respectively, prior to repeal by Pub. L. 105–220. For complete classification of this Act to the Code, see Tables.

AMENDMENTS

2002—Subsec. (a)(2)(A). Pub. L. 107–210 inserted ", other than under subsection (a)(4), (f), and (g)" after "national emergency grants".

EFFECTIVE DATE OF 2002 AMENDMENT

Amendment by Pub. L. 107–210 applicable to petitions for certification filed under part 2 or 3 of subchapter II of chapter 12 of Title 19, Customs Duties, on or after the date that is 90 days after Aug. 6, 2002, except as otherwise provided, see section 151 of Pub. L. 107–210, set out as a note preceding section 2271 of Title 19.

CONSTRUCTION OF 2002 AMENDMENT

Nothing in amendment by Pub. L. 107–210, other than provisions relating to COBRA continuation coverage and reporting requirements, to be construed as creating new mandate on any party regarding health insurance coverage, see section 203(f) of Pub. L. 107–210, set out as a note under section 2918 of this title.

§2863. Within State allocations

(a) Reservations for State activities

(1) Statewide workforce investment activities

The Governor of a State shall make the reservation required under section 2853(a) of this title.

(2) Statewide rapid response activities

The Governor of the State shall reserve not more than 25 percent of the total amount allotted to the State under section 2862(b)(2)(B) of this title for a fiscal year for statewide rapid response activities described in section 2864(a)(2)(A) of this title.

(b) Within State allocation

(1) Methods

The Governor, acting in accordance with the State plan, and after consulting with chief elected officials in the local areas, shall allocate—

(A) the funds that are allotted to the State for adult employment and training activities and statewide workforce investment activities under section 2862(b)(1)(B) of this title and are not reserved under subsection (a)(1) of this section, in accordance with paragraph (2) or (3); and

(B) the funds that are allotted to the State for dislocated worker employment and training activities under section 2862(b)(2)(B) of this title and are not reserved under paragraph (1) or (2) of subsection (a) of this section, in accordance with paragraph (2).

(2) Formula allocations

(A) Adult employment and training activities

(i) Allocation

In allocating the funds described in paragraph (1)(A) to local areas, a State may allocate—

(I) 33⅓ percent of the funds on the basis described in section 2862(b)(1)(B)(ii)(I) of this title;

(II) 33⅓ percent of the funds on the basis described in section 2862(b)(1)(B)(ii)(II) of this title; and

(III) 33⅓ percent of the funds on the basis described in clauses (ii)(III) and (iii) of section 2862(b)(1)(B) of this title.

(ii) Minimum percentage

Effective at the end of the second full fiscal year after the date on which a local area is designated under section 2831 of this title, the local area shall not receive an allocation percentage for a fiscal year that is less than 90 percent of the average allocation percentage of the local area for the 2 preceding fiscal years. Amounts necessary for increasing such allocations to local areas to comply with the preceding sentence shall be obtained by ratably reducing the allocations to be made to other local areas under this subparagraph.

(iii) Definition

The term "allocation percentage", used with respect to fiscal year 2000 or a subsequent fiscal year, means a percentage of the funds referred to in clause (i), received through an allocation made under this subparagraph, for the fiscal year.

(B) Dislocated worker employment and training activities

(i) Formula

In allocating the funds described in paragraph (1)(B) to local areas, a State shall allocate the funds based on an allocation formula prescribed by the Governor of the State. Such formula may be amended by the Governor not more than once for each program year. Such formula shall utilize the most appropriate information available to the Governor to distribute amounts to address the State's worker readjustment assistance needs.

(ii) Information

The information described in clause (i) shall include insured unemployment data, unemployment concentrations, plant closing and mass layoff data, declining industries data, farmer-rancher economic hardship data, and long-term unemployment data.

(C) Application

For purposes of carrying out subparagraph (A)—

(i) references in section 2862(b) of this title to a State shall be deemed to be references to a local area;

(ii) references in section 2862(b) of this title to all States shall be deemed to be references to all local areas in the State involved; and

(iii) except as described in clause (i), references in section 2862(b)(1) of this title to the term "excess number" shall be considered to be references to the term as defined in section 2862(b)(1) of this title.

(3) Adult employment and training discretionary allocations

In lieu of making the allocation described in paragraph (2)(A), in allocating the funds described in paragraph (1)(A) to local areas, a State may distribute—

(A) a portion equal to not less than 70 percent of the funds in accordance with paragraph (2)(A); and

(B) the remaining portion of the funds on the basis of a formula that—

(i) incorporates additional factors (other than the factors described in paragraph (2)(A)) relating to—

(I) excess poverty in urban, rural, and suburban local areas; and

(II) excess unemployment above the State average in urban, rural, and suburban local areas; and

(ii) was developed by the State board and approved by the Secretary as part of the State plan.

(4) Transfer authority

A local board may transfer, if such a transfer is approved by the Governor, not more than 20 percent of the funds allocated to the local area under paragraph (2)(A) or (3), and 20 percent of the funds allocated to the local area under paragraph (2)(B), for a fiscal year between—

(A) adult employment and training activities; and

(B) dislocated worker employment and training activities.

(5) Allocation

(A) In general

The Governor of the State shall allocate the funds described in paragraph (1) to local areas under paragraphs (2) and (3) for the purpose of providing a single system of employment and training activities for adults and dislocated workers in accordance with subsections (d) and (e) of section 2864 of this title.

(B) Additional requirements

(i) Adults

Funds allocated under paragraph (2)(A) or (3) shall be used by a local area to contribute proportionately to the costs of the one-stop delivery system described in section 2864(c) of this title in the local area, and to pay for employment and training activities provided to adults in the local area, consistent with section 2864 of this title.

(ii) Dislocated workers

Funds allocated under paragraph (2)(B) shall be used by a local area to contribute proportionately to the costs of the one-stop delivery system described in section 2864(c) of this title in the local area, and to pay for employment and training activities provided to dislocated workers in the local area, consistent with section 2864 of this title.

(c) Reallocation among local areas

(1) In general

The Governor may, in accordance with this subsection, reallocate to eligible local areas within the State amounts that are allocated under paragraph (2)(A) or (3) of subsection (b) of this section for adult employment and training activities and that are available for reallocation.

(2) Amount

The amount available for reallocation for a program year is equal to the amount by which the unobligated balance of the local area allocation under paragraph (2)(A) or (3) of subsection (b) of this section for such activities, at the end of the program year prior to the program year for which the determination under this paragraph is made exceeds 20 percent of such allocation for the prior program year.

(3) Reallocation

In making reallocations to eligible local areas of amounts available pursuant to paragraph (2) for a program year, the Governor shall allocate to each eligible local area within the State an amount based on the relative amount allocated to such local area under subsection (b)(3) of this section for such activities for the prior program year, as compared to the total amount allocated to all eligible local areas in the State under subsection (b)(3) of this section for such activities for such prior program year. For purposes of this paragraph, local areas that received allocations under subsection (b)(2)(A) of this section for the prior program year shall be treated as if the local areas received allocations under subsection (b)(3) of this section for such year.

(4) Eligibility

For purposes of this subsection, an eligible local area means a local area that has obligated at least 80 percent of the local area allocation under paragraph (2)(A) or (3) of subsection (b) of this section for such activities, for the program year prior to the program year for which the determination under paragraph (2) is made.

(Pub. L. 105–220, title I, §133, Aug. 7, 1998, 112 Stat. 987.)

§2864. Use of funds for employment and training activities

(a) Statewide employment and training activities

(1) In general

Funds reserved by a Governor for a State—

(A) as described in section 2863(a)(2) of this title shall be used to carry out the statewide rapid response activities described in paragraph (2)(A); and

(B) as described in sections 2853(a) and 2863(a)(1) of this title—

(i) shall be used to carry out the statewide employment and training activities described in paragraph (2)(B); and

(ii) may be used to carry out any of the statewide employment and training activities described in paragraph (3),

regardless of whether the funds were allotted to the State under section 2852(b)(1) of this title or under paragraph (1) or (2) of section 2862(b) of this title.

(2) Required statewide employment and training activities

(A) Statewide rapid response activities

A State shall use funds reserved as described in section 2863(a)(2) of this title to carry out statewide rapid response activities, which shall include—

(i) provision of rapid response activities, carried out in local areas by the State or by an entity designated by the State, working in conjunction with the local boards and the chief elected officials in the local areas; and

(ii) provision of additional assistance to local areas that experience disasters, mass layoffs or plant closings, or other events that precipitate substantial increases in the number of unemployed individuals, carried out in local areas by the State or by an entity designated by the State, working in conjunction with the local boards and the chief elected officials in the local areas.

(B) Other required statewide employment and training activities

A State shall use funds reserved as described in sections 2853(a) and 2863(a)(1) of this title (regardless of whether the funds were allotted to the State under section 2852(b)(1) of this title or paragraph (1) or (2) of section 2862(b) of this title) to carry out other statewide employment and training activities, which shall include—

(i) disseminating the State list of eligible providers of training services, including eligible providers of nontraditional training services, information identifying eligible providers of on-the-job training and customized training, and performance information and program cost information, as described in subsections (e) and (h) of section 2842 of this title;

(ii) conducting evaluations, under section 2871(e) of this title, of activities authorized in this section, in coordination with the activities carried out under section 2917 of this title;

(iii) providing incentive grants to local areas for regional cooperation among local boards (including local boards for a designated region as described in section 2831(c) of this title), for local coordination of activities carried out under this Act, and for exemplary performance by local areas on the local performance measures;

(iv) providing technical assistance to local areas that fail to meet local performance measures;

(v) assisting in the establishment and operation of one-stop delivery systems described in subsection (c) of this section; and

(vi) operating a fiscal and management accountability information system under section 2871(f) of this title.

(3) Allowable statewide employment and training activities

(A) In general

A State may use funds reserved as described in sections 2853(a) and 2863(a)(1) of this title (regardless of whether the funds were allotted to the State under section 2852(b)(1) of this title or paragraph (1) or (2) of section 2862(b) of this title) to carry out additional statewide employment and training activities, which may include—

(i) subject to subparagraph (B), administration by the State of the activities authorized under this section;

(ii) provision of capacity building and technical assistance to local areas, one-stop operators, one-stop partners, and eligible providers, including the development and training of staff and the development of exemplary program activities;

(iii) conduct of research and demonstrations;

(iv)(I) implementation of innovative incumbent worker training programs, which may include the establishment and implementation of an employer loan program to assist in skills upgrading; and

(II) the establishment and implementation of programs targeted to empowerment zones and enterprise communities;

(v) support for the identification of eligible providers of training services as required under section 2842 of this title;

(vi)(I) implementation of innovative programs for displaced homemakers, which for purposes of this subclause may include an individual who is receiving public assistance and is within 2 years of exhausting lifetime eligibility under part A of title IV of the Social Security Act (42 U.S.C. 601 et seq.); and

(II) implementation of programs to increase the number of individuals training for and placed in nontraditional employment; and

(vii) carrying out other activities authorized in this section that the State determines to be necessary to assist local areas in carrying out activities described in subsection (d) or (e) of this section through the statewide workforce investment system.

(B) Limitation

(i) In general

Of the funds allotted to a State under sections 2852(b) and 2862(b) of this title and reserved as described in sections 2853(a) and 2863(a)(1) of this title for a fiscal year—

(I) not more than 5 percent of the amount allotted under section 2852(b)(1) of this title;

(II) not more than 5 percent of the amount allotted under section 2862(b)(1) of this title; and

(III) not more than 5 percent of the amount allotted under section 2862(b)(2) of this title,

may be used by the State for the administration of youth activities carried out under section 2854 of this title and employment and training activities carried out under this section.

(ii) Use of funds

Funds made available for administrative costs under clause (i) may be used for the administrative cost of any of the statewide youth activities or statewide employment and training activities, regardless of whether the funds were allotted to the State under section 2852(b)(1) of this title or paragraph (1) or (2) of section 2862(b) of this title.

(b) Local employment and training activities

Funds allocated to a local area for adults under paragraph (2)(A) or (3), as appropriate, of section 2863(b) of this title, and funds allocated to a local area for dislocated workers under section 2863(b)(2)(B) of this title—

(1) shall be used to carry out employment and training activities described in subsection (d) of this section for adults or dislocated workers, respectively; and

(2) may be used to carry out employment and training activities described in subsection (e) of this section for adults or dislocated workers, respectively.

(c) Establishment of one-stop delivery system

(1) In general

There shall be established in a State that receives an allotment under section 2862(b) of this title a one-stop delivery system, which—

(A) shall provide the core services described in subsection (d)(2) of this section;

(B) shall provide access to intensive services and training services as described in paragraphs (3) and (4) of subsection (d) of this section, including serving as the point of access to individual training accounts for training services to participants in accordance with subsection (d)(4)(G) of this section;

(C) shall provide access to the activities carried out under subsection (e) of this section, if any;

(D) shall provide access to programs and activities carried out by one-stop partners and described in section 2841(b) of this title; and

(E) shall provide access to the information described in section 15 of the Wagner-Peyser Act [29 U.S.C. 49*l*–2] and all job search, placement, recruitment, and other labor exchange services authorized under the Wagner-Peyser Act (29 U.S.C. 49 et seq.).

(2) One-stop delivery

At a minimum, the one-stop delivery system—

(A) shall make each of the programs, services, and activities described in paragraph (1) accessible at not less than one physical center in each local area of the State; and

(B) may also make programs, services, and activities described in paragraph (1) available—

(i) through a network of affiliated sites that can provide one or more of the programs, services, and activities to individuals; and

(ii) through a network of eligible one-stop partners—

(I) in which each partner provides one or more of the programs, services, and activities to such individuals and is accessible at an affiliated site that consists of a physical location or an electronically or technologically linked access point; and

(II) that assures individuals that information on the availability of the core services will be available regardless of where the individuals initially enter the statewide workforce investment system, including information made available through an access point described in subclause (I).

(3) Specialized centers

The centers and sites described in paragraph (2) may have a specialization in addressing special needs, such as the needs of dislocated workers.

(d) Required local employment and training activities

(1) In general

(A) Allocated funds

Funds allocated to a local area for adults under paragraph (2)(A) or (3), as appropriate, of section 2863(b) of this title, and funds allocated to the local area for dislocated workers under section 2863(b)(2)(B) of this title, shall be used—

(i) to establish a one-stop delivery system described in subsection (c) of this section;

(ii) to provide the core services described in paragraph (2) to adults and dislocated workers, respectively, through the one-stop delivery system in accordance with such paragraph;

(iii) to provide the intensive services described in paragraph (3) to adults and dislocated workers, respectively, described in such paragraph; and

(iv) to provide training services described in paragraph (4) to adults and dislocated workers, respectively, described in such paragraph.

(B) Other funds

A portion of the funds made available under Federal law authorizing the programs and activities described in section 2841(b)(1)(B) of this title, including the Wagner-Peyser Act (29 U.S.C. 49 et seq.), shall be used as described in clauses (i) and (ii) of subparagraph (A), to the extent not inconsistent with the Federal law involved.

(2) Core services

Funds described in paragraph (1)(A) shall be used to provide core services, which shall be available to individuals who are adults or dislocated workers through the one-stop delivery system and shall, at a minimum, include—

(A) determinations of whether the individuals are eligible to receive assistance under this subchapter;

(B) outreach, intake (which may include worker profiling), and orientation to the information and other services available through the one-stop delivery system;

(C) initial assessment of skill levels, aptitudes, abilities, and supportive service needs;

(D) job search and placement assistance, and where appropriate, career counseling;

(E) provision of employment statistics information, including the provision of accurate information relating to local, regional, and national labor market areas, including—

(i) job vacancy listings in such labor market areas;

(ii) information on job skills necessary to obtain the jobs described in clause (i); and

(iii) information relating to local occupations in demand and the earnings and skill requirements for such occupations; and

(F) provision of performance information and program cost information on eligible providers of training services as described in section 2842 of this title, provided by program, and eligible providers of youth activities described in section 2843 of this title, providers of adult education described in title II [20 U.S.C. 9201 et seq.], providers of career and technical education activities at the postsecondary level, and career and technical education activities available to school dropouts, under the Carl D. Perkins Career and Technical Education Act of 2006 (20 U.S.C. 2301 et seq.), and providers of vocational rehabilitation program activities described in title I of the Rehabilitation Act of 1973 (29 U.S.C. 720 et seq.);

(G) provision of information regarding how the local area is performing on the local performance measures and any additional performance information with respect to the one-stop delivery system in the local area;

(H) provision of accurate information relating to the availability of supportive services, including child care and transportation, available in the local area, and referral to such services, as appropriate;

(I) provision of information regarding filing claims for unemployment compensation;

(J) assistance in establishing eligibility for—

(i) welfare-to-work activities authorized under section 403(a)(5) of the Social Security Act [42 U.S.C. 603(a)(5)] (as added by section 5001 of the Balanced Budget Act of 1997) available in the local area; and

(ii) programs of financial aid assistance for training and education programs that are not funded under this Act and are available in the local area; and

(K) followup services, including counseling regarding the workplace, for participants in workforce investment activities authorized under this subchapter who are placed in unsubsidized employment, for not less than 12 months after the first day of the employment, as appropriate.

(3) Intensive services

(A) In general

Funds allocated to a local area for adults under paragraph (2)(A) or (3), as appropriate, of section 2863(b) of this title, and funds allocated to the local area for dislocated workers under section 2863(b)(2)(B) of this title, shall be used to provide intensive services to adults and dislocated workers, respectively—

(i)(I) who are unemployed and are unable to obtain employment through core services provided under paragraph (2); and

(II) who have been determined by a one-stop operator to be in need of more intensive services in order to obtain employment; or

(ii) who are employed, but who are determined by a one-stop operator to be in need of such intensive services in order to obtain or retain employment that allows for self-sufficiency.

(B) Delivery of services

Such intensive services shall be provided through the one-stop delivery system—

(i) directly through one-stop operators identified pursuant to section 2841(d) of this title; or

(ii) through contracts with service providers, which may include contracts with public, private for-profit, and private non-profit service providers, approved by the local board.

(C) Types of services

Such intensive services may include the following:

(i) Comprehensive and specialized assessments of the skill levels and service needs of adults and dislocated workers, which may include—

(I) diagnostic testing and use of other assessment tools; and

(II) in-depth interviewing and evaluation to identify employment barriers and appropriate employment goals.

(ii) Development of an individual employment plan, to identify the employment goals, appropriate achievement objectives, and appropriate combination of services for the participant to achieve the employment goals.

(iii) Group counseling.

(iv) Individual counseling and career planning.

(v) Case management for participants seeking training services under paragraph (4).

(vi) Short-term prevocational services, including development of learning skills, communication skills, interviewing skills, punctuality, personal maintenance skills, and professional conduct, to prepare individuals for unsubsidized employment or training.

(4) Training services

(A) In general

Funds allocated to a local area for adults under paragraph (2)(A) or (3), as appropriate, of section 2863(b) of this title, and funds allocated to a local area for dislocated workers under section 2863(b)(2)(B) of this title shall be used to provide training services to adults and dislocated workers, respectively—

(i) who have met the eligibility requirements for intensive services under paragraph (3)(A) and who are unable to obtain or retain employment through such services;

(ii) who after an interview, evaluation, or assessment, and case management, have been determined by a one-stop operator or one-stop partner, as appropriate, to be in need of training services and to have the skills and qualifications to successfully participate in the selected program of training services;

(iii) who select programs of training services that are directly linked to the employment opportunities in the local area involved or in another area in which the adults or dislocated workers receiving such services are willing to relocate;

(iv) who meet the requirements of subparagraph (B); and

(v) who are determined to be eligible in accordance with the priority system, if any, in effect under subparagraph (E).

(B) Qualification

(i) Requirement

Except as provided in clause (ii), provision of such training services shall be limited to individuals who—

(I) are unable to obtain other grant assistance for such services, including Federal Pell Grants established under title IV of the Higher Education Act of 1965 (20 U.S.C. 1070 et seq. [and 42 U.S.C. 2751 et seq.]); or

(II) require assistance beyond the assistance made available under other grant assistance programs, including Federal Pell Grants.

(ii) Reimbursements

Training services may be provided under this paragraph to an individual who otherwise meets the requirements of this paragraph while an application for a Federal Pell Grant is pending, except that if such individual is subsequently awarded a Federal Pell Grant, appropriate reimbursement shall be made to the local area from such Federal Pell Grant.

(C) Provider qualification

Training services shall be provided through providers identified in accordance with section 2842 of this title.

(D) Training services

Training services may include—

(i) occupational skills training, including training for nontraditional employment;

(ii) on-the-job training;

(iii) programs that combine workplace training with related instruction, which may include cooperative education programs;

(iv) training programs operated by the private sector;

(v) skill upgrading and retraining;

(vi) entrepreneurial training;

(vii) job readiness training;

(viii) adult education and literacy activities provided in combination with services described in any of clauses (i) through (vii); and

(ix) customized training conducted with a commitment by an employer or group of employers to employ an individual upon successful completion of the training.

(E) Priority

In the event that funds allocated to a local area for adult employment and training activities under paragraph (2)(A) or (3) of section 2863(b) of this title are limited, priority shall be given to recipients of public assistance and other low-income individuals for intensive services and training services. The appropriate local board and the Governor shall direct the one-stop operators in the local area with regard to making determinations related to such priority.

(F) Consumer choice requirements

(i) In general

Training services provided under this paragraph shall be provided in a manner that maximizes consumer choice in the selection of an eligible provider of such services.

(ii) Eligible providers

Each local board, through one-stop centers referred to in subsection (c) of this section, shall make available—

(I) the State list of eligible providers of training services required under section 2842(e) of this title, with a description of the programs through which the providers may offer the training services, and the information identifying eligible providers of on-the-job training and customized training required under section 2842(h) of this title; and

(II) the performance information and performance cost information relating to eligible providers of training services described in subsections (e) and (h) of section 2842 of this title.

(iii) Individual training accounts

An individual who seeks training services and who is eligible pursuant to subparagraph (A), may, in consultation with a case manager, select an eligible provider of training services from the list or identifying information for providers described in clause (ii)(I). Upon such selection, the one-stop operator involved shall, to the extent practicable, refer such individual to the eligible provider of training services, and arrange for payment for such services through an individual training account.

(G) Use of individual training accounts

(i) In general

Except as provided in clause (ii), training services provided under this paragraph shall be provided through the use of individual training accounts in accordance with this paragraph, and shall be provided to eligible individuals through the one-stop delivery system.

(ii) Exceptions

Training services authorized under this paragraph may be provided pursuant to a contract for services in lieu of an individual training account if the requirements of subparagraph (F) are met and if—

(I) such services are on-the-job training provided by an employer or customized training;

(II) the local board determines there are an insufficient number of eligible providers of training services in the local area involved (such as in a rural area) to accomplish the purposes of a system of individual training accounts; or

(III) the local board determines that there is a training services program of demonstrated effectiveness offered in the local area by a community-based organization or another private organization to serve special participant populations that face multiple barriers to employment.

(iii) Linkage to occupations in demand

Training services provided under this paragraph shall be directly linked to occupations that are in demand in the local area, or in another area to which an adult or dislocated worker receiving such services is willing to relocate, except that a local board may approve training services for occupations determined by the local board to be in sectors of the economy that have a high potential for sustained demand or growth in the local area.

(iv) Definition

In this subparagraph, the term "special participant population that faces multiple barriers to employment" means a population of low-income individuals that is included in one or more of the following categories:

(I) Individuals with substantial language or cultural barriers.

(II) Offenders.

(III) Homeless individuals.

(IV) Other hard-to-serve populations as defined by the Governor involved.

(e) Permissible local employment and training activities

(1) Discretionary one-stop delivery activities

Funds allocated to a local area for adults under paragraph (2)(A) or (3), as appropriate, of section 2863(b) of this title, and funds allocated to the local area for dislocated workers under section 2863(b)(2)(B) of this title, may be used to provide, through one-stop delivery described in subsection (c)(2) of this section—

(A) customized screening and referral of qualified participants in training services described in subsection (d)(4) of this section to employment; and

(B) customized employment-related services to employers on a fee-for-service basis.

(2) Supportive services

Funds allocated to a local area for adults under paragraph (2)(A) or (3), as appropriate, of section 2863(b) of this title, and funds allocated to the local area for dislocated workers under section 2863(b)(2)(B) of this title, may be used to provide supportive services to adults and dislocated workers, respectively—

(A) who are participating in programs with activities authorized in any of paragraphs (2), (3), or (4) of subsection (d) of this section; and

(B) who are unable to obtain such supportive services through other programs providing such services.

(3) Needs-related payments

(A) In general

Funds allocated to a local area for adults under paragraph (2)(A) or (3), as appropriate, of section 2863(b) of this title, and funds allocated to the local area for dislocated workers under section 2863(b)(2)(B) of this title, may be used to provide needs-related payments to adults and dislocated workers, respectively, who are unemployed and do not qualify for (or have ceased to qualify for) unemployment compensation for the purpose of enabling such individuals to participate in programs of training services under subsection (d)(4) of this section.

(B) Additional eligibility requirements

In addition to the requirements contained in subparagraph (A), a dislocated worker who has ceased to qualify for unemployment compensation may be eligible to receive needs-related payments under this paragraph only if such worker was enrolled in the training services—

(i) by the end of the 13th week after the most recent layoff that resulted in a determination of the worker's eligibility for employment and training activities for dislocated workers under this subchapter; or

(ii) if later, by the end of the 8th week after the worker is informed that a short-term layoff will exceed 6 months.

(C) Level of payments

The level of a needs-related payment made to a dislocated worker under this paragraph shall not exceed the greater of—

(i) the applicable level of unemployment compensation; or

(ii) if such worker did not qualify for unemployment compensation, an amount equal to the poverty line, for an equivalent period, which amount shall be adjusted to reflect changes in total family income.

(Pub. L. 105–220, title I, § 134, Aug. 7, 1998, 112 Stat. 990; Pub. L. 105–277, div. A, § 101(f) [title VIII, § 401(5)], Oct. 21, 1998, 112 Stat. 2681–337, 2681–411; Pub. L. 109–270, § 2(h)(6), Aug. 12, 2006, 120 Stat. 748.)

REFERENCES IN TEXT

This Act, referred to in subsecs. (a)(2)(B)(iii) and (d)(2)(J)(ii), is Pub. L. 105–220, Aug. 7, 1998, 112 Stat. 936, as amended, known as the Workforce Investment Act of 1998. For complete classification of this Act to the Code, see Short Title note set out under section 9201 of Title 20, Education, and Tables.

The Social Security Act, referred to in subsec. (a)(3)(A)(vi)(I), is act Aug. 14, 1935, ch. 531, 49 Stat. 620, as amended. Part A of title IV of the Act is classified generally to part A (§ 601 et seq.) of subchapter IV of chapter 7 of Title 42, The Public Health and Welfare. For complete classification of this Act to the Code, see section 1305 of Title 42 and Tables.

The Wagner-Peyser Act, referred to in subsecs. (c)(1)(E) and (d)(1)(B), is act June 6, 1933, ch. 49, 48 Stat. 113, as amended, which is classified generally to chapter 4B (§ 49 et seq.) of this title. For complete classification of this Act to the Code, see Short Title note set out under section 49 of this title and Tables.

Title II, referred to in subsec. (d)(2)(F), is title II of Pub. L. 105–220, Aug. 7, 1998, 112 Stat. 1059, as amended, known as the Adult Education and Family Literacy Act, which is classified principally to subchapter I (§ 9201 et seq.) of chapter 73 of Title 20, Education. For complete classification of this Act to the Code, see Short Title note set out under section 9201 of Title 20 and Tables.

The Carl D. Perkins Career and Technical Education Act of 2006, referred to in subsec. (d)(2)(F), is Pub. L. 88–210, Dec. 18, 1963, 77 Stat. 403, as amended generally by Pub. L. 109–270, § 1(b), Aug. 12, 2006, 120 Stat. 683, which is classified generally to chapter 44 (§ 2301 et seq.) of Title 20, Education. For complete classification of this Act to the Code, see Short Title note set out under section 2301 of Title 20 and Tables.

The Rehabilitation Act of 1973, referred to in subsec. (d)(2)(F), is Pub. L. 93–112, Sept. 26, 1973, 87 Stat. 355, as amended. Title I of the Act is classified generally to subchapter I (§ 720 et seq.) of chapter 16 of this title. For complete classification of this Act to the Code, see Short Title note set out under section 701 of this title and Tables.

The Higher Education Act of 1965, referred to in subsec. (d)(4)(B)(i)(I), is Pub. L. 89–329, Nov. 8, 1965, 79 Stat. 1219, as amended. Title IV of the Act is classified generally to subchapter IV (§ 1070 et seq.) of chapter 28 of Title 20, Education, and part C (§ 2751 et seq.) of subchapter I of chapter 34 of Title 42, The Public Health and Welfare. For complete classification of this Act to the Code, see Short Title note set out under section 1001 of Title 20 and Tables.

AMENDMENTS

2006—Subsec. (d)(2)(F). Pub. L. 109–270 substituted "career and technical education activities at the postsecondary level, and career and technical education activities available to school dropouts, under the Carl D. Perkins Career and Technical Education Act of 2006" for "postsecondary vocational education activities and vocational education activities available to school dropouts under the Carl D. Perkins Vocational and Applied Technology Education Act".

1998—Subsec. (d)(4)(F)(iii). Pub. L. 105–277 added cl. (iii).

PART F—GENERAL PROVISIONS

§ 2871. Performance accountability system

(a) Purpose

The purpose of this section is to establish a comprehensive performance accountability system, comprised of the activities described in this section, to assess the effectiveness of States and local areas in achieving continuous improvement of workforce investment activities funded under this subchapter, in order to optimize the return on investment of Federal funds in statewide and local workforce investment activities.

(b) State performance measures

(1) In general

For each State, the State performance measures shall consist of—

(A)(i) the core indicators of performance described in paragraph (2)(A) and the customer satisfaction indicator of performance described in paragraph (2)(B); and

(ii) additional indicators of performance (if any) identified by the State under paragraph (2)(C); and

(B) a State adjusted level of performance for each indicator described in subparagraph (A).

(2) Indicators of performance

(A) Core indicators of performance

(i) In general

The core indicators of performance for employment and training activities authorized under section 2864 of this title (except for self-service and informational activities) and (for participants who are eligible youth age 19 through 21) for youth activities authorized under section 2854 of this title shall consist of—

(I) entry into unsubsidized employment;

(II) retention in unsubsidized employment 6 months after entry into the employment;

(III) earnings received in unsubsidized employment 6 months after entry into the employment; and

(IV) attainment of a recognized credential relating to achievement of educational skills, which may include attainment of a secondary school diploma or its recognized equivalent, or occupational skills, by participants who enter unsubsidized employment, or by participants who are eligible youth age 19 through 21 who enter postsecondary education, advanced training, or unsubsidized employment.

(ii) Core indicators for eligible youth

The core indicators of performance (for participants who are eligible youth age 14 through 18) for youth activities authorized under section 2854 of this title, shall include—

(I) attainment of basic skills and, as appropriate, work readiness or occupational skills;

(II) attainment of secondary school diplomas and their recognized equivalents; and

(III) placement and retention in postsecondary education or advanced training, or placement and retention in military service, employment, or qualified apprenticeships.

(B) Customer satisfaction indicators

The customer satisfaction indicator of performance shall consist of customer satisfaction of employers and participants with services received from the workforce investment activities authorized under this subchapter. Customer satisfaction may be measured through surveys conducted after the conclusion of participation in the workforce investment activities.

(C) Additional indicators

A State may identify in the State plan additional indicators for workforce investment activities authorized under this subchapter.

(3) Levels of performance

(A) State adjusted levels of performance for core indicators and customer satisfaction indicator

(i) In general

For each State submitting a State plan, there shall be established, in accordance with this subparagraph, levels of performance for each of the core indicators of performance described in paragraph (2)(A) and the customer satisfaction indicator described in paragraph (2)(B) for workforce investment activities authorized under this subchapter. The levels of performance established under this subparagraph shall, at a minimum—

(I) be expressed in an objective, quantifiable, and measurable form; and

(II) show the progress of the State toward continuously improving in performance.

(ii) Identification in State plan

Each State shall identify, in the State plan submitted under section 2822 of this title, expected levels of performance for each of the core indicators of performance and the customer satisfaction indicator of performance, for the first 3 program years covered by the State plan.

(iii) Agreement on State adjusted levels of performance for first 3 years

In order to ensure an optimal return on the investment of Federal funds in workforce investment activities authorized under this subchapter, the Secretary and each Governor shall reach agreement on levels of performance for each of the core indicators of performance and the customer satisfaction indicator of performance, for the first 3 program years covered by the State plan, taking into account the levels identified in the State plan under clause (ii) and the factors described in clause (iv). The levels agreed to under this clause shall be considered to be the State adjusted levels of performance for the State for such years and shall be incorporated into the State plan prior to the approval of such plan.

(iv) Factors

The agreement described in clause (iii) or (v) shall take into account—

(I) the extent to which the levels involved will assist the State in attaining a high level of customer satisfaction;

(II) how the levels involved compare with the State adjusted levels of performance established for other States, taking into account factors including differences in economic conditions, the characteristics of participants when the participants entered the program, and the services to be provided; and

(III) the extent to which such levels involved promote continuous improvement in performance on the performance measures by such State and ensure optimal return on the investment of Federal funds.

(v) Agreement on State adjusted levels of performance for 4th and 5th years

Prior to the 4th program year covered by the State plan, the Secretary and each Governor shall reach agreement on levels of performance for each of the core indicators of performance and the customer satisfaction indicator of performance, for the 4th and 5th program years covered by the State plan, taking into account the factors described in clause (iv). The levels agreed to under this clause shall be considered to be the State adjusted levels of performance for the State for such years and shall be incorporated into the State plan.

(vi) Revisions

If unanticipated circumstances arise in a State resulting in a significant change in the factors described in clause (iv)(II), the Governor may request that the State adjusted levels of performance agreed to under clause (iii) or (v) be revised. The Secretary, after collaboration with the representatives described in subsection (i) of this section, shall issue objective criteria and methods for making such revisions.

(B) Levels of performance for additional indicators

The State may identify, in the State plan, State levels of performance for each of the additional indicators described in paragraph (2)(C). Such levels shall be considered to be State adjusted levels of performance for purposes of this chapter.

(c) Local performance measures

(1) In general

For each local area in a State, the local performance measures shall consist of—

(A)(i) the core indicators of performance described in subsection (b)(2)(A) of this section, and the customer satisfaction indicator of performance described in subsection (b)(2)(B) of this section, for activities described in such subsections, other than statewide workforce investment activities; and

(ii) additional indicators of performance (if any) identified by the State under subsection (b)(2)(C) of this section for activities described in such subsection, other than statewide workforce investment activities; and

(B) a local level of performance for each indicator described in subparagraph (A).

(2) Local level of performance

The local board, the chief elected official, and the Governor shall negotiate and reach agreement on the local levels of performance based on the State adjusted levels of performance established under subsection (b) of this section.

(3) Determinations

In determining such local levels of performance, the local board, the chief elected official, and the Governor shall take into account the specific economic, demographic, and other characteristics of the populations to be served in the local area.

(d) Report

(1) In general

Each State that receives an allotment under section 2852 or 2862 of this title shall annually prepare and submit to the Secretary a report on the progress of the State in achieving State performance measures, including information on the levels of performance achieved by the State with respect to the core indicators of performance and the customer satisfaction indicator. The annual report also shall include information regarding the progress of local areas in the State in achieving local performance measures, including information on the levels of performance achieved by the areas with respect to the core indicators of performance and the customer satisfaction indicator. The report also shall include information on the status of State evaluations of workforce investment activities described in subsection (e) of this section.

(2) Additional information

In preparing such report, the State shall include, at a minimum, information on participants in workforce investment activities authorized under this subchapter relating to—

(A) entry by participants who have completed training services provided under section 2864(d)(4) of this title into unsubsidized employment related to the training received;

(B) wages at entry into employment for participants in workforce investment activities who entered unsubsidized employment, including the rate of wage replacement for such participants who are dislocated workers;

(C) cost of workforce investment activities relative to the effect of the activities on the performance of participants;

(D) retention and earnings received in unsubsidized employment 12 months after entry into the employment;

(E) performance with respect to the indicators of performance specified in subsection (b)(2)(A) of this section of participants in workforce investment activities who received the training services compared with the performance of participants in workforce investment activities who received only services other than the training services (excluding participants who received only self-service and informational activities); and

(F) performance with respect to the indicators of performance specified in subsection (b)(2)(A) of this section of recipients of public assistance, out-of-school youth, veterans, individuals with disabilities, displaced homemakers, and older individuals.

(3) Information dissemination

The Secretary—

(A) shall make the information contained in such reports available to the general public through publication and other appropriate methods;

(B) shall disseminate State-by-State comparisons of the information; and

(C) shall provide the appropriate congressional committees with copies of such reports.

(e) Evaluation of State programs

(1) In general

Using funds made available under this subchapter, the State, in coordination with local boards in the State, shall conduct ongoing evaluation studies of workforce investment activities carried out in the State under this subchapter in order to promote, establish, implement, and utilize methods for continuously improving the activities in order to achieve high-level performance within, and high-level outcomes from, the statewide workforce investment system. To the maximum extent practicable, the State shall coordinate the evaluations with the evaluations provided for by the Secretary under section 2917 of this title.

(2) Design

The evaluation studies conducted under this subsection shall be designed in conjunction with the State board and local boards and shall include analysis of customer feedback and outcome and process measures in the statewide workforce investment system. The studies may include use of control groups.

(3) Results

The State shall periodically prepare and submit to the State board, and local boards in the State, reports containing the results of evaluation studies conducted under this subsection, to promote the efficiency and effectiveness of the statewide workforce investment system in improving employability for jobseekers and competitiveness for employers.

(f) Fiscal and management accountability information systems

(1) In general

Using funds made available under this subchapter, the Governor, in coordination with local boards and chief elected officials in the State, shall establish and operate a fiscal and management accountability information system based on guidelines established by the Secretary after consultation with the Governors, local elected officials, and one-stop partners. Such guidelines shall promote efficient collection and use of fiscal and management information for reporting and monitoring the use of funds made available under this subchapter and for preparing the annual report described in subsection (d) of this section.

(2) Wage records

In measuring the progress of the State on State and local performance measures, a State shall utilize quarterly wage records, consistent with State law. The Secretary shall make arrangements, consistent with State law, to ensure that the wage records of any State are available to any other State to the extent that such wage records are required by the State in carrying out the State plan of the State or completing the annual report described in subsection (d) of this section.

(3) Confidentiality

In carrying out the requirements of this Act, the State shall comply with section 1232g of title 20.

(g) Sanctions for State failure to meet State performance measures

(1) States

(A) Technical assistance

If a State fails to meet State adjusted levels of performance relating to indicators described in subparagraph (A) or (B) of subsection (b)(2) of this section for a program for any program year, the Secretary shall, upon request, provide technical assistance in accordance with section 2915 of this title, including assistance in the development of a performance improvement plan.

(B) Reduction in amount of grant

If such failure continues for a second consecutive year, or if a State fails to submit a report under subsection (d) of this section for any program year, the Secretary may reduce by not more than 5 percent, the amount of the grant that would (in the absence of this paragraph) be payable to the State under such program for the immediately succeeding program year. Such penalty shall be based on the degree of failure to meet State adjusted levels of performance.

(2) Funds resulting from reduced allotments

The Secretary shall use an amount retained, as a result of a reduction in an allotment to a State made under paragraph (1)(B), to provide incentive grants under section 9273 of title 20.

(h) Sanctions for local area failure to meet local performance measures

(1) Technical assistance

If a local area fails to meet levels of performance relating to indicators described in subparagraph (A) or (B) of subsection (b)(2) of this section for a program for any program year, the Governor, or upon request by the Governor, the Secretary, shall provide technical assistance, which may include assistance in the development of a performance improvement plan, or the development of a modified local plan.

(2) Corrective actions

(A) In general

If such failure continues for a second consecutive year, the Governor shall take corrective actions, which may include development of a reorganization plan through which the Governor may—

(i) require the appointment and certification of a new local board (consistent with the criteria established under section 2832(b) of this title);

(ii) prohibit the use of eligible providers and one-stop partners identified as achieving a poor level of performance; or

(iii) take such other actions as the Governor determines are appropriate.

(B) Appeal by local area

(i) Appeal to Governor

A local area that is subject to a reorganization plan under subparagraph (A) may, not later than 30 days after receiving notice of the reorganization plan, appeal to the Governor to rescind or revise such plan. In such case, the Governor shall make a final decision not later then 30 days after the receipt of the appeal.

(ii) Subsequent action

The local area may, not later than 30 days after receiving a decision from the Governor pursuant to clause (i), appeal such decision to the Secretary. In such case, the Secretary shall make a final decision not later than 30 days after the receipt of the appeal.

(C) Effective date

The decision made by the Governor under clause (i) of subparagraph (B) shall become effective at the time the Governor issues the decision pursuant to such clause. Such decision shall remain effective unless the Secretary rescinds or revises such plan pursuant to clause (ii) of subparagraph (B).

(i) Other measures and terminology

(1) Responsibilities

In order to ensure nationwide comparability of performance data, the Secretary, after collaboration with representatives of appropriate Federal agencies, and representatives of States and political subdivisions, business and industry, employees, eligible providers of employment and training activities, educators, and participants, with expertise regarding workforce investment policies and workforce investment activities, shall issue—

(A) definitions for information required to be reported under subsection (d)(2) of this section;

(B) terms for a menu of additional indicators of performance described in subsection (b)(2)(C) of this section to assist States in assessing their progress toward State workforce investment goals; and

(C) objective criteria and methods described in subsection (b)(3)(A)(vi) of this section for making revisions to levels of performance.

(2) Definitions for core indicators

The Secretary and the representatives described in paragraph (1) shall participate in the activities described in section 9272 of title 20 concerning the issuance of definitions for indicators of performance described in subsection (b)(2)(A) of this section.

(3) Assistance

The Secretary shall make the services of staff available to the representatives to assist the representatives in participating in the collaboration described in paragraph (1) and in the activities described in section 9272 of title 20.

(Pub. L. 105–220, title I, §136, Aug. 7, 1998, 112 Stat. 999.)

References in Text

This chapter, referred to in subsec. (b)(3)(B), was in the original "this title" meaning title I of Pub. L. 105–220, Aug. 7, 1998, 112 Stat. 939, as amended, which enacted this chapter, repealed sections 1501 to 1505, 1511 to 1583, 1592 to 1735, 1737 to 1791h, 1792 to 1792b, 2301 to 2314 of this title, section 211 of former Title 40, Appendix, Public Buildings, Property, and Works, sections 11421, 11441 to 11447, 11449, 11450, 11461 to 11466, 11471, and 11472 of Title 42, The Public Health and Welfare, and sections 42101 to 42106 of Title 49, Transportation, enacted provisions set out as notes under sections 1501, 2301, and 2940 of this title and section 11421 of Title 42, and repealed provisions set out as notes under sections 801 and 2301 of this title and section 1255a of Title 8, Aliens and Nationality. For complete classification of title I to the Code, see Tables.

This Act, referred to in subsec. (f)(3), is Pub. L. 105–220, Aug. 7, 1998, 112 Stat. 936, as amended, known as the Workforce Investment Act of 1998. For complete classification of this Act to the Code, see Short Title note set out under section 9201 of Title 20, Education, and Tables.

§ 2872. Authorization of appropriations

(a) Youth activities

There are authorized to be appropriated to carry out the activities described in section 2852(a) of this title, such sums as may be necessary for each of fiscal years 1999 through 2003.

(b) Adult employment and training activities

There are authorized to be appropriated to carry out the activities described in section 2862(a)(1) of this title, such sums as may be necessary for each of fiscal years 1999 through 2003.

(c) Dislocated worker employment and training activities

There are authorized to be appropriated to carry out the activities described in section 2862(a)(2) of this title, such sums as may be necessary for each of fiscal years 1999 through 2003.

(Pub. L. 105–220, title I, §137, Aug. 7, 1998, 112 Stat. 1006.)

SUBCHAPTER III—JOB CORPS

§ 2881. Purposes

The purposes of this subchapter are—

(1) to maintain a national Job Corps program, carried out in partnership with States and communities, to assist eligible youth who need and can benefit from an intensive program, operated in a group setting in residential and nonresidential centers, to become more responsible, employable, and productive citizens;

(2) to set forth standards and procedures for selecting individuals as enrollees in the Job Corps;

(3) to authorize the establishment of Job Corps centers in which enrollees will participate in intensive programs of activities described in this subchapter; and

(4) to prescribe various other powers, duties, and responsibilities incident to the operation and continuing development of the Job Corps.

(Pub. L. 105–220, title I, §141, Aug. 7, 1998, 112 Stat. 1006.)

PRIOR PROVISIONS

Provisions similar to this section were contained in section 1691 of this title prior to repeal by Pub. L. 105–220.

§2882. Definitions

In this subchapter:

(1) Applicable local board

The term "applicable local board" means a local board—

(A) that provides information for a Job Corps center on local employment opportunities and the job skills needed to obtain the opportunities; and

(B) that serves communities in which the graduates of the Job Corps center seek employment.

(2) Applicable one-stop center

The term "applicable one-stop center" means a one-stop customer service center that provides services, such as referral, intake, recruitment, and placement, to a Job Corps center.

(3) Enrollee

The term "enrollee" means an individual who has voluntarily applied for, been selected for, and enrolled in the Job Corps program, and remains with the program, but has not yet become a graduate.

(4) Former enrollee

The term "former enrollee" means an individual who has voluntarily applied for, been selected for, and enrolled in the Job Corps program, but left the program before completing the requirements of a vocational training program, or receiving a secondary school diploma or recognized equivalent, as a result of participation in the Job Corps program.

(5) Graduate

The term "graduate" means an individual who has voluntarily applied for, been selected for, and enrolled in the Job Corps program and has completed the requirements of a vocational training program, or received a secondary school diploma or recognized equivalent, as a result of participation in the Job Corps program.

(6) Job Corps

The term "Job Corps" means the Job Corps described in section 2883 of this title.

(7) Job Corps center

The term "Job Corps center" means a center described in section 2887 of this title.

(8) Operator

The term "operator" means an entity selected under this subchapter to operate a Job Corps center.

(9) Region

The term "region" means an area served by a regional office of the Employment and Training Administration.

(10) Service provider

The term "service provider" means an entity selected under this subchapter to provide services described in this subchapter to a Job Corps center.

(Pub. L. 105–220, title I, §142, Aug. 7, 1998, 112 Stat. 1006.)

§2883. Establishment

There shall be within the Department of Labor a "Job Corps".

(Pub. L. 105–220, title I, §143, Aug. 7, 1998, 112 Stat. 1007.)

PRIOR PROVISIONS

Provisions similar to this section were contained in section 1692 of this title prior to repeal by Pub. L. 105–220.

§2883a. Office of Job Corps

Not later than 90 days after December 30, 2005, the Secretary of Labor shall permanently establish and maintain an Office of Job Corps within the Office of the Secretary, in the Department of Labor, to carry out the functions (including duties, responsibilities, and procedures) of subtitle C of title I of the Workforce Investment Act of 1998 (29 U.S.C. 2881 et seq.). The Secretary shall appoint a senior member of the civil service to head that Office of Job Corps and carry out subtitle C. The Secretary shall transfer funds appropriated for the program carried out under that subtitle C, including the administration of such program, to the head of that Office of Job Corps. The head of that Office of Job Corps shall have contracting authority and shall receive support as necessary from the Assistant Secretary for Administration and Management with respect to contracting functions and the Assistant Secretary for Policy with respect to research and evaluation functions.

(Pub. L. 109–149, title I, §102, Dec. 30, 2005, 119 Stat. 2842.)

REFERENCES IN TEXT

The Workforce Investment Act of 1998, referred to in text, is Pub. L. 105–220, Aug. 7, 1998, 112 Stat. 936, as amended. Subtitle C of title I of the Act is classified generally to this subchapter. For complete classification of this Act to the Code, see Short Title note set out under section 9201 of Title 20, Education, and Tables.

CODIFICATION

Section was enacted as part of the Department of Labor Appropriations Act, 2006, and also as part of the Departments of Labor, Health and Human Services, and Education, and Related Agencies Appropriations Act, 2006, and not as part of title I of the Workforce Investment Act of 1998 which comprises this chapter.

§2884. Individuals eligible for the Job Corps

To be eligible to become an enrollee, an individual shall be—

(1) not less than age 16 and not more than age 21 on the date of enrollment, except that—

(A) not more than 20 percent of the individuals enrolled in the Job Corps may be not less than age 22 and not more than age 24 on the date of enrollment; and

(B) either such maximum age limitation may be waived by the Secretary, in accordance with regulations of the Secretary, in the case of an individual with a disability;

(2) a low-income individual; and

(3) an individual who is one or more of the following:

(A) Basic skills deficient.

(B) A school dropout.

(C) Homeless, a runaway, or a foster child.

(D) A parent.

(E) An individual who requires additional education, vocational training, or intensive counseling and related assistance, in order to participate successfully in regular schoolwork or to secure and hold employment.

(Pub. L. 105–220, title I, § 144, Aug. 7, 1998, 112 Stat. 1007.)

PRIOR PROVISIONS

Provisions similar to this section were contained in section 1693 of this title prior to repeal by Pub. L. 105–220.

§ 2885. Recruitment, screening, selection, and assignment of enrollees

(a) Standards and procedures

(1) In general

The Secretary shall prescribe specific standards and procedures for the recruitment, screening, and selection of eligible applicants for the Job Corps, after considering recommendations from the Governors, local boards, and other interested parties.

(2) Methods

In prescribing standards and procedures under paragraph (1), the Secretary, at a minimum, shall—

(A) prescribe procedures for informing enrollees that drug tests will be administered to the enrollees and the results received within 45 days after the enrollees enroll in the Job Corps;

(B) establish standards for recruitment of Job Corps applicants;

(C) establish standards and procedures for—

(i) determining, for each applicant, whether the educational and vocational needs of the applicant can best be met through the Job Corps program or an alternative program in the community in which the applicant resides; and

(ii) obtaining from each applicant pertinent data relating to background, needs, and interests for determining eligibility and potential assignment;

(D) where appropriate, take measures to improve the professional capability of the individuals conducting screening of the applicants; and

(E) assure that an appropriate number of enrollees are from rural areas.

(3) Implementation

To the extent practicable, the standards and procedures shall be implemented through arrangements with—

(A) applicable one-stop centers;

(B) community action agencies, business organizations, and labor organizations; and

(C) agencies and individuals that have contact with youth over substantial periods of time and are able to offer reliable information about the needs and problems of youth.

(4) Consultation

The standards and procedures shall provide for necessary consultation with individuals and organizations, including court, probation, parole, law enforcement, education, welfare, and medical authorities and advisers.

(5) Reimbursement

The Secretary is authorized to enter into contracts with and make payments to individuals and organizations for the cost of conducting recruitment, screening, and selection of eligible applicants for the Job Corps, as provided for in this section. The Secretary shall make no payment to any individual or organization solely as compensation for referring the names of applicants for the Job Corps.

(b) Special limitations on selection

(1) In general

No individual shall be selected as an enrollee unless the individual or organization implementing the standards and procedures described in subsection (a) of this section determines that—

(A) there is a reasonable expectation that the individual considered for selection can participate successfully in group situations and activities, and is not likely to engage in behavior that would prevent other enrollees from receiving the benefit of the Job Corps program or be incompatible with the maintenance of sound discipline and satisfactory relationships between the Job Corps center to which the individual might be assigned and communities surrounding the Job Corps center;

(B) the individual manifests a basic understanding of both the rules to which the individual will be subject and of the consequences of failure to observe the rules; and

(C) the individual has passed a background check conducted in accordance with procedures established by the Secretary.

(2) Individuals on probation, parole, or supervised release

An individual on probation, parole, or supervised release may be selected as an enrollee only if release from the supervision of the probation or parole official involved is satisfactory to the official and the Secretary and does not violate applicable laws (including regulations). No individual shall be denied a position in the Job Corps solely on the basis of individual contact with the criminal justice system.

(c) Assignment plan

(1) In general

Every 2 years, the Secretary shall develop and implement an assignment plan for assigning enrollees to Job Corps centers. In developing the plan, the Secretary shall, based on the analysis described in paragraph (2), establish targets, applicable to each Job Corps center, for—

(A) the maximum attainable percentage of enrollees at the Job Corps center that reside in the State in which the center is located; and

(B) the maximum attainable percentage of enrollees at the Job Corps center that reside in the region in which the center is located, and in surrounding regions.

(2) Analysis

In order to develop the plan described in paragraph (1), the Secretary shall, every 2 years, analyze, for the Job Corps center—

(A) the size of the population of individuals eligible to participate in Job[1] Corps in the State and region in which the Job Corps center is located, and in surrounding regions;

(B) the relative demand for participation in the Job Corps in the State and region, and in surrounding regions; and

(C) the capacity and utilization of the Job Corps center, including services provided through the center.

(d) Assignment of individual enrollees

(1) In general

After an individual has been selected for the Job Corps in accordance with the standards and procedures of the Secretary under subsection (a) of this section, the enrollee shall be assigned to the Job Corps center that is closest to the home of the enrollee, except that the Secretary may waive this requirement if—

(A) the enrollee chooses a vocational training program, or requires an English literacy program, that is not available at such center;

(B) the enrollee would be unduly delayed in participating in the Job Corps program because the closest center is operating at full capacity; or

(C) the parent or guardian of the enrollee requests assignment of the enrollee to another Job Corps center due to circumstances in the community of the enrollee that would impair prospects for successful participation in the Job Corps program.

(2) Enrollees who are younger than 18

An enrollee who is younger than 18 shall not be assigned to a Job Corps center other than the center closest to the home of the enrollee pursuant to paragraph (1) if the parent or guardian of the enrollee objects to the assignment.

(Pub. L. 105–220, title I, § 145, Aug. 7, 1998, 112 Stat. 1007.)

PRIOR PROVISIONS

Provisions similar to this section were contained in sections 1694 to 1696 of this title prior to repeal by Pub. L. 105–220.

§ 2886. Enrollment

(a) Relationship between enrollment and military obligations

Enrollment in the Job Corps shall not relieve any individual of obligations under the Military Selective Service Act (50 U.S.C. App. 451 et seq.).

(b) Period of enrollment

No individual may be enrolled in the Job Corps for more than 2 years, except—

(1) in a case in which completion of an advanced career training program under section 2888(c) of this title would require an individual to participate in the Job Corps for not more than one additional year; or

(2) as the Secretary may authorize in a special case.

(Pub. L. 105–220, title I, § 146, Aug. 7, 1998, 112 Stat. 1010.)

REFERENCES IN TEXT

The Military Selective Service Act, referred to in subsec. (a), is act June 24, 1948, ch. 625, 62 Stat. 604, as amended, which is classified principally to section 451 et seq. of Title 50, Appendix, War and National Defense. For complete classification of this Act to the Code, see References in Text note set out under section 451 of Title 50, Appendix, and Tables.

PRIOR PROVISIONS

Provisions similar to this section were contained in section 1696 of this title prior to repeal by Pub. L. 105–220.

§ 2887. Job Corps centers

(a) Operators and service providers

(1) Eligible entities

(A) Operators

The Secretary shall enter into an agreement with a Federal, State, or local agency, an area vocational education school or residential vocational school, or a private organization, for the operation of each Job Corps center.

(B) Providers

The Secretary may enter into an agreement with a local entity to provide activities described in this subchapter to the Job Corps center.

(2) Selection process

(A) Competitive basis

Except as provided in subsections (c) and (d) of section 253 of title 41, the Secretary shall select on a competitive basis an entity to operate a Job Corps center and entities to provide activities described in this subchapter to the Job Corps center. In developing a solicitation for an operator or service provider, the Secretary shall consult with the Governor of the State in which the center is located, the industry council for the Job Corps center (if established), and the applicable local board regarding the contents of such solicitation, including elements that will promote the consistency of the activities carried out through the center with the objectives set forth in the State plan or in a local plan.

(B) Recommendations and considerations

(i) Operators

In selecting an entity to operate a Job Corps center, the Secretary shall consider—

(I) the ability of the entity to coordinate the activities carried out through the Job Corps center with activities carried out under the appropriate State plan and local plans;

[1] So in original. Probably should be preceded by "the".

(II) the degree to which the vocational training that the entity proposes for the center reflects local employment opportunities in the local areas in which enrollees at the center intend to seek employment;

(III) the degree to which the entity is familiar with the surrounding communities, applicable one-stop centers, and the State and region in which the center is located; and

(IV) the past performance of the entity, if any, relating to operating or providing activities described in this subchapter to a Job Corps center.

(ii) Providers

In selecting a service provider for a Job Corps center, the Secretary shall consider the factors described in subclauses (I) through (IV) of clause (i), as appropriate.

(b) Character and activities

Job Corps centers may be residential or nonresidential in character, and shall be designed and operated so as to provide enrollees, in a well-supervised setting, with access to activities described in this subchapter. In any year, no more than 20 percent of the individuals enrolled in the Job Corps may be nonresidential participants in the Job Corps.

(c) Civilian Conservation Centers

(1) In general

The Job Corps centers may include Civilian Conservation Centers operated under agreements with the Secretary of Agriculture or the Secretary of the Interior, located primarily in rural areas, which shall provide, in addition to other vocational training and assistance, programs of work experience to conserve, develop, or manage public natural resources or public recreational areas or to develop community projects in the public interest.

(2) Selection process

The Secretary may select an entity to operate a Civilian Conservation Center on a competitive basis, as provided in subsection (a) of this section, if the center fails to meet such national performance standards as the Secretary shall establish.

(d) Indian tribes

(1) General authority

The Secretary may enter into agreements with Indian tribes to operate Job Corps centers for Indians.

(2) Definitions

In this subsection, the terms "Indian" and "Indian tribe", have the meanings given such terms in subsections (d) and (e), respectively, of section 450b of title 25.

(Pub. L. 105–220, title I, § 147, Aug. 7, 1998, 112 Stat. 1010.)

PRIOR PROVISIONS

Provisions similar to this section were contained in section 1697 of this title prior to repeal by Pub. L. 105–220.

§ 2888. Program activities

(a) Activities provided by Job Corps centers

(1) In general

Each Job Corps center shall provide enrollees with an intensive, well organized, and fully supervised program of education, vocational training, work experience, recreational activities, physical rehabilitation and development, and counseling. Each Job Corps center shall provide enrollees assigned to the center with access to core services described in section 2864(d)(2) of this title and the intensive services described in section 2864(d)(3) of this title.

(2) Relationship to opportunities

(A) In general

The activities provided under this subsection shall provide work-based learning throughout the enrollment of the enrollees and assist the enrollees in obtaining meaningful unsubsidized employment, participating in secondary education or postsecondary education programs, enrolling in other suitable vocational training programs, or satisfying Armed Forces requirements, on completion of their enrollment.

(B) Link to employment opportunities

The vocational training provided shall be linked to the employment opportunities in the local area in which the enrollee intends to seek employment after graduation.

(b) Education and vocational training

The Secretary may arrange for education and vocational training of enrollees through local public or private educational agencies, vocational educational institutions, or technical institutes, whenever such entities provide education and training substantially equivalent in cost and quality to that which the Secretary could provide through other means.

(c) Advanced career training programs

(1) In general

The Secretary may arrange for programs of advanced career training for selected enrollees in which the enrollees may continue to participate for a period of not to exceed 1 year in addition to the period of participation to which the enrollees would otherwise be limited. The advanced career training may be provided through the eligible providers of training services identified under section 2842 of this title.

(2) Benefits

(A) In general

During the period of participation in an advanced career training program, an enrollee shall be eligible for full Job Corps benefits, or a monthly stipend equal to the average value of the residential support, food, allowances, and other benefits provided to enrollees assigned to residential Job Corps centers.

(B) Calculation

The total amount for which an enrollee shall be eligible under subparagraph (A) shall be reduced by the amount of any scholarship or other educational grant assistance received by such enrollee for advanced career training.

(3) Demonstration

Each year, any operator seeking to enroll additional enrollees in an advanced career training program shall demonstrate that participants in such program have achieved a satisfactory rate of completion and placement in training-related jobs before the operator may carry out such additional enrollment.

(d) Continued services

The Secretary shall also provide continued services to graduates, including providing counseling regarding the workplace for 12 months after the date of graduation of the graduates. In selecting a provider for such services, the Secretary shall give priority to one-stop partners.

(e) Child care

The Secretary shall, to the extent practicable, provide child care at or near Job Corps centers, for individuals who require child care for their children in order to participate in the Job Corps.

(Pub. L. 105–220, title I, §148, Aug. 7, 1998, 112 Stat. 1011.)

PRIOR PROVISIONS

Provisions similar to this section were contained in section 1698 of this title prior to repeal by Pub. L. 105–220.

§2889. Counseling and job placement

(a) Counseling and testing

The Secretary shall arrange for counseling and testing for each enrollee at regular intervals to measure progress in the education and vocational training programs carried out through the Job Corps.

(b) Placement

The Secretary shall arrange for counseling and testing for enrollees prior to their scheduled graduations to determine their capabilities and, based on their capabilities, shall make every effort to arrange to place the enrollees in jobs in the vocations for which the enrollees are trained or to assist the enrollees in obtaining further activities described in this subchapter. In arranging for the placement of graduates in jobs, the Secretary shall utilize the one-stop delivery system to the fullest extent possible.

(c) Status and progress

The Secretary shall determine the status and progress of enrollees scheduled for graduation and make every effort to assure that their needs for further activities described in this subchapter are met.

(d) Services to former enrollees

The Secretary may provide such services as the Secretary determines to be appropriate under this subchapter to former enrollees.

(Pub. L. 105–220, title I, §149, Aug. 7, 1998, 112 Stat. 1012.)

PRIOR PROVISIONS

Provisions similar to this section were contained in section 1702 of this title prior to repeal by Pub. L. 105–220.

§2890. Support

(a) Personal allowances

The Secretary may provide enrollees assigned to Job Corps centers with such personal allowances as the Secretary may determine to be necessary or appropriate to meet the needs of the enrollees.

(b) Readjustment allowances

(1) Graduates

The Secretary shall arrange for a readjustment allowance to be paid to graduates. The Secretary shall arrange for the allowance to be paid at the one-stop center nearest to the home of the graduate who is returning home, or at the one-stop center nearest to the location where the graduate has indicated an intent to seek employment. If the Secretary uses any organization, in lieu of a one-stop center, to provide placement services under this Act, the Secretary shall arrange for that organization to pay the readjustment allowance.

(2) Former enrollees

The Secretary may provide for a readjustment allowance to be paid to former enrollees. The provision of the readjustment allowance shall be subject to the same requirements as are applicable to the provision of the readjustment allowance paid to graduates under paragraph (1).

(Pub. L. 105–220, title I, §150, Aug. 7, 1998, 112 Stat. 1013.)

REFERENCES IN TEXT

This Act, referred to in subsec. (b)(1), is Pub. L. 105–220, Aug. 7, 1998, 112 Stat. 936, as amended, known as the Workforce Investment Act of 1998. For complete classification of this Act to the Code, see Short Title note set out under section 9201 of Title 20, Education, and Tables.

PRIOR PROVISIONS

Provisions similar to this section were contained in sections 1699 and 1702 of this title prior to repeal by Pub. L. 105–220.

§2891. Operating plan

(a) In general

The provisions of the contract between the Secretary and an entity selected to operate a Job Corps center shall, at a minimum, serve as an operating plan for the Job Corps center.

(b) Additional information

The Secretary may require the operator, in order to remain eligible to operate the Job Corps center, to submit such additional information as the Secretary may require, which shall be considered part of the operating plan.

(c) Availability

The Secretary shall make the operating plan described in subsections (a) and (b) of this section, excluding any proprietary information, available to the public.

(Pub. L. 105–220, title I, §151, Aug. 7, 1998, 112 Stat. 1013.)

§ 2892. Standards of conduct

(a) Provision and enforcement

The Secretary shall provide, and directors of Job Corps centers shall stringently enforce, standards of conduct within the centers. Such standards of conduct shall include provisions forbidding the actions described in subsection (b)(2)(A) of this section.

(b) Disciplinary measures

(1) In general

To promote the proper moral and disciplinary conditions in the Job Corps, the directors of Job Corps centers shall take appropriate disciplinary measures against enrollees. If such a director determines that an enrollee has committed a violation of the standards of conduct, the director shall dismiss the enrollee from the Job Corps if the director determines that the retention of the enrollee in the Job Corps will jeopardize the enforcement of such standards or diminish the opportunities of other enrollees.

(2) Zero tolerance policy and drug testing

(A) Guidelines

The Secretary shall adopt guidelines establishing a zero tolerance policy for an act of violence, for use, sale, or possession of a controlled substance, for abuse of alcohol, or for other illegal or disruptive activity.

(B) Drug testing

The Secretary shall require drug testing of all enrollees for controlled substances in accordance with procedures prescribed by the Secretary under section 2885(a) of this title.

(C) Definitions

In this paragraph:

(i) Controlled substance

The term "controlled substance" has the meaning given the term in section 802 of title 21.

(ii) Zero tolerance policy

The term "zero tolerance policy" means a policy under which an enrollee shall be automatically dismissed from the Job Corps after a determination by the director that the enrollee has carried out an action described in subparagraph (A).

(c) Appeal

A disciplinary measure taken by a director under this section shall be subject to expeditious appeal in accordance with procedures established by the Secretary.

(Pub. L. 105–220, title I, § 152, Aug. 7, 1998, 112 Stat. 1013.)

PRIOR PROVISIONS

Provisions similar to this section were contained in section 1700 of this title prior to repeal by Pub. L. 105–220.

§ 2893. Community participation

(a) Business and Community Liaison

Each Job Corps center shall have a Business and Community Liaison (referred to in this Act as a "Liaison"), designated by the director of the center.

(b) Responsibilities

The responsibilities of the Liaison shall include—

(1) establishing and developing relationships and networks with—

(A) local and distant employers; and

(B) applicable one-stop centers and applicable local boards,

for the purpose of providing job opportunities for Job Corps graduates; and

(2) establishing and developing relationships with members of the community in which the Job Corps center is located, informing members of the community about the projects of the Job Corps center and changes in the rules, procedures, or activities of the center that may affect the community, and planning events of mutual interest to the community and the Job Corps center.

(c) New centers

The Liaison for a Job Corps center that is not yet operating shall establish and develop the relationships and networks described in subsection (b) of this section at least 3 months prior to the date on which the center accepts the first enrollee at the center.

(Pub. L. 105–220, title I, § 153, Aug. 7, 1998, 112 Stat. 1014.)

REFERENCES IN TEXT

This Act, referred to in subsec. (a), is Pub. L. 105–220, Aug. 7, 1998, 112 Stat. 936, as amended, known as the Workforce Investment Act of 1998. For complete classification of this Act to the Code, see Short Title note set out under section 9201 of Title 20, Education, and Tables.

§ 2894. Industry councils

(a) In general

Each Job Corps center shall have an industry council, appointed by the director of the center after consultation with the Liaison, in accordance with procedures established by the Secretary.

(b) Industry council composition

(1) In general

An industry council shall be comprised of—

(A) a majority of members who shall be local and distant owners of business concerns, chief executives or chief operating officers of nongovernmental employers, or other private sector employers, who—

(i) have substantial management, hiring, or policy responsibility; and

(ii) represent businesses with employment opportunities that reflect the employment opportunities of the applicable local area;

(B) representatives of labor organizations (where present) and representatives of employees; and

(C) enrollees and graduates of the Job Corps.

(2) Local board

The industry council may include members of the applicable local boards who meet the requirements described in paragraph (1).

(c) Responsibilities

The responsibilities of the industry council shall be—

(1) to work closely with all applicable local boards in order to determine, and recommend to the Secretary, appropriate vocational training for the center;

(2) to review all the relevant labor market information to—

(A) determine the employment opportunities in the local areas in which the enrollees intend to seek employment after graduation;

(B) determine the skills and education that are necessary to obtain the employment opportunities; and

(C) recommend to the Secretary the type of vocational training that should be implemented at the center to enable the enrollees to obtain the employment opportunities; and

(3) to meet at least once every 6 months to reevaluate the labor market information, and other relevant information, to determine, and recommend to the Secretary, any necessary changes in the vocational training provided at the center.

(d) New centers

The industry council for a Job Corps center that is not yet operating shall carry out the responsibilities described in subsection (c) of this section at least 3 months prior to the date on which the center accepts the first enrollee at the center.

(Pub. L. 105–220, title I, §154, Aug. 7, 1998, 112 Stat. 1015.)

§2895. Advisory committees

The Secretary may establish and use advisory committees in connection with the operation of the Job Corps program, and the operation of Job Corps centers, whenever the Secretary determines that the availability of outside advice and counsel on a regular basis would be of substantial benefit in identifying and overcoming problems, in planning program or center development, or in strengthening relationships between the Job Corps and agencies, institutions, or groups engaged in related activities.

(Pub. L. 105–220, title I, §155, Aug. 7, 1998, 112 Stat. 1015.)

PRIOR PROVISIONS

Provisions similar to this section were contained in section 1704 of this title prior to repeal by Pub. L. 105–220.

§2896. Experimental, research, and demonstration projects

The Secretary may carry out experimental, research, or demonstration projects relating to carrying out the Job Corps program and may waive any provisions of this subchapter that the Secretary finds would prevent the Secretary from carrying out the projects.

(Pub. L. 105–220, title I, §156, Aug. 7, 1998, 112 Stat. 1016.)

§2897. Application of provisions of Federal law

(a) Enrollees not considered to be Federal employees

(1) In general

Except as otherwise provided in this subsection and in section 8143(a) of title 5, enrollees shall not be considered to be Federal employees and shall not be subject to the provisions of law relating to Federal employment, including such provisions regarding hours of work, rates of compensation, leave, unemployment compensation, and Federal employee benefits.

(2) Provisions relating to taxes and social security benefits

For purposes of title 26 and title II of the Social Security Act (42 U.S.C. 401 et seq.), enrollees shall be deemed to be employees of the United States and any service performed by an individual as an enrollee shall be deemed to be performed in the employ of the United States.

(3) Provisions relating to compensation to Federal employees for work injuries

For purposes of subchapter I of chapter 81 of title 5 (relating to compensation to Federal employees for work injuries), enrollees shall be deemed to be civil employees of the Government of the United States within the meaning of the term "employee" as defined in section 8101 of title 5, and the provisions of such subchapter shall apply as specified in section 8143(a) of title 5.

(4) Federal tort claims provisions

For purposes of the Federal tort claims provisions in title 28, enrollees shall be considered to be employees of the Government.

(b) Adjustments and settlements

Whenever the Secretary finds a claim for damages to a person or property resulting from the operation of the Job Corps to be a proper charge against the United States, and the claim is not cognizable under section 2672 of title 28, the Secretary may adjust and settle the claim in an amount not exceeding $1,500.

(c) Personnel of the uniformed services

Personnel of the uniformed services who are detailed or assigned to duty in the performance of agreements made by the Secretary for the support of the Job Corps shall not be counted in computing strength under any law limiting the strength of such services or in computing the percentage authorized by law for any grade in such services.

(Pub. L. 105–220, title I, §157, Aug. 7, 1998, 112 Stat. 1016.)

REFERENCES IN TEXT

The Social Security Act, referred to in subsec. (a)(2), is act Aug. 14, 1935, ch. 531, 49 Stat. 620, as amended. Title II of the Act is classified generally to subchapter II (§401 et seq.) of chapter 7 of Title 42, The Public Health and Welfare. For complete classification of this Act to the Code, see section 1305 of Title 42 and Tables.

PRIOR PROVISIONS

Provisions similar to this section were contained in section 1706 of this title prior to repeal by Pub. L. 105–220.

§2898. Special provisions

(a) Enrollment

The Secretary shall ensure that women and men have an equal opportunity to participate in the Job Corps program, consistent with section 2885 of this title.

(b) Studies, evaluations, proposals, and data

The Secretary shall assure that all studies, evaluations, proposals, and data produced or developed with Federal funds in the course of carrying out the Job Corps program shall become the property of the United States.

(c) Transfer of property

(1) In general

Notwithstanding title II of the Federal Property and Administrative Services Act of 1949[1] and any other provision of law, the Secretary and the Secretary of Education shall receive priority by the Secretary of Defense for the direct transfer, on a nonreimbursable basis, of the property described in paragraph (2) for use in carrying out programs under this Act or under any other Act.

(2) Property

The property described in this paragraph is real and personal property under the control of the Department of Defense that is not used by such Department, including property that the Secretary of Defense determines is in excess of current and projected requirements of such Department.

(d) Gross receipts

Transactions conducted by a private for-profit or nonprofit entity that is an operator or service provider for a Job Corps center shall not be considered to be generating gross receipts. Such an operator or service provider shall not be liable, directly or indirectly, to any State or subdivision of a State (nor to any person acting on behalf of such a State or subdivision) for any gross receipts taxes, business privilege taxes measured by gross receipts, or any similar taxes imposed on, or measured by, gross receipts in connection with any payments made to or by such entity for operating or providing services to a Job Corps center. Such an operator or service provider shall not be liable to any State or subdivision of a State to collect or pay any sales, excise, use, or similar tax imposed on the sale to or use by such operator or service provider of any property, service, or other item in connection with the operation of or provision of services to a Job Corps center.

(e) Management fee

The Secretary shall provide each operator and (in an appropriate case, as determined by the Secretary) service provider with an equitable and negotiated management fee of not less than 1 percent of the amount of the funding provided under the appropriate agreement specified in section 2887 of this title.

(f) Donations

The Secretary may accept on behalf of the Job Corps or individual Job Corps centers charitable donations of cash or other assistance, including equipment and materials, if such donations are available for appropriate use for the purposes set forth in this subchapter.

(g) Sale of property

Notwithstanding any other provision of law, if the Administrator of General Services sells a Job Corps center facility, the Administrator shall transfer the proceeds from the sale to the Secretary, who shall use the proceeds to carry out the Job Corps program.

(Pub. L. 105–220, title I, §158, Aug. 7, 1998, 112 Stat. 1016.)

REFERENCES IN TEXT

The Federal Property and Administrative Services Act of 1949, referred to in subsec. (c)(1), is act June 30, 1949, ch. 288, 63 Stat. 377, as amended. Title II of the Act, which was classified principally to subchapter II (§§481, 483, 484, 485, 486, 487 to 490, 491, 492) of chapter 10 and section 758 of former Title 40, Public Buildings, Property, and Works, was repealed by Pub. L. 107–217, §6(b), Aug. 21, 2002, 116 Stat. 1304, the first section of which enacted Title 40, Public Buildings, Property, and Works. For disposition of sections of former Title 40 to revised Title 40, see Table preceding section 101 of Title 40. For complete classification of this Act to the Code, see Tables.

PRIOR PROVISIONS

Provisions similar to this section were contained in sections 1707 and 1709 of this title prior to repeal by Pub. L. 105–220.

§2899. Management information

(a) Financial management information system

(1) In general

The Secretary shall establish procedures to ensure that each operator, and each service provider, maintains a financial management information system that will provide—

(A) accurate, complete, and current disclosures of the costs of Job Corps operations; and

(B) sufficient data for the effective evaluation of activities carried out through the Job Corps program.

(2) Accounts

Each operator and service provider shall maintain funds received under this subchapter in accounts in a manner that ensures timely and accurate reporting as required by the Secretary.

(3) Fiscal responsibility

Operators shall remain fiscally responsible and control costs, regardless of whether the funds made available for Job Corps centers are incrementally increased or decreased between fiscal years.

(b) Audit

(1) Access

The Secretary, the Inspector General of the Department of Labor, the Comptroller General of the United States, and any of their duly authorized representatives, shall have access to any books, documents, papers, and records of the operators and service providers described in subsection (a) of this section that are perti-

[1] See References in Text note below.

nent to the Job Corps program, for purposes of conducting surveys, audits, and evaluations of the operators and service providers.

(2) Surveys, audits, and evaluations

The Secretary shall survey, audit, or evaluate, or arrange for the survey, audit, or evaluation of, the operators and service providers, using Federal auditors or independent public accountants. The Secretary shall conduct such surveys, audits, or evaluations not less often than once every 3 years.

(c) Information on indicators of performance

(1) Establishment

The Secretary shall, with continuity and consistency from year to year, establish indicators of performance, and expected levels of performance for Job Corps centers and the Job Corps program, relating to—

(A) the number of graduates and the rate of such graduation, analyzed by type of vocational training received through the Job Corps program and by whether the vocational training was provided by a local or national service provider;

(B) the number of graduates who entered unsubsidized employment related to the vocational training received through the Job Corps program and the number who entered unsubsidized employment not related to the vocational training received, analyzed by whether the vocational training was provided by a local or national service provider and by whether the placement in the employment was conducted by a local or national service provider;

(C) the average wage received by graduates who entered unsubsidized employment related to the vocational training received through the Job Corps program and the average wage received by graduates who entered unsubsidized employment unrelated to the vocational training received;

(D) the average wage received by graduates placed in unsubsidized employment after completion of the Job Corps program—

(i) on the first day of the employment;

(ii) 6 months after the first day of the employment; and

(iii) 12 months after the first day of the employment,

analyzed by type of vocational training received through the Job Corps program;

(E) the number of graduates who entered unsubsidized employment and were retained in the unsubsidized employment—

(i) 6 months after the first day of the employment; and

(ii) 12 months after the first day of the employment;

(F) the number of graduates who entered unsubsidized employment—

(i) for 32 hours per week or more;

(ii) for not less than 20 but less than 32 hours per week; and

(iii) for less than 20 hours per week;

(G) the number of graduates who entered postsecondary education or advanced training programs, including apprenticeship programs, as appropriate; and

(H) the number of graduates who attained job readiness and employment skills.

(2) Performance of recruiters

The Secretary shall also establish performance measures, and expected performance levels on the performance measures, for local and national recruitment service providers serving the Job Corps program. The performance measures shall relate to the number of enrollees retained in the Job Corps program for 30 days and for 60 days after initial placement in the program.

(3) Report

The Secretary shall collect, and annually submit a report to the appropriate committees of Congress containing, information on the performance of each Job Corps center, and the Job Corps program, on the core performance measures, as compared to the expected performance level for each performance measure. The report shall also contain information on the performance of the service providers described in paragraph (2) on the performance measures established under such paragraph, as compared to the expected performance levels for the performance measures.

(d) Additional information

The Secretary shall also collect, and submit in the report described in subsection (c) of this section, information on the performance of each Job Corps center, and the Job Corps program, regarding—

(1) the number of enrollees served;

(2) the average level of learning gains for graduates and former enrollees;

(3) the number of former enrollees and graduates who entered the Armed Forces;

(4) the number of former enrollees who entered postsecondary education;

(5) the number of former enrollees who entered unsubsidized employment related to the vocational training received through the Job Corps program and the number who entered unsubsidized employment not related to the vocational training received;

(6) the number of former enrollees and graduates who obtained a secondary school diploma or its recognized equivalent;

(7) the number and percentage of dropouts from the Job Corps program including the number dismissed under the zero tolerance policy described in section 2892(b) of this title; and

(8) any additional information required by the Secretary.

(e) Methods

The Secretary may collect the information described in subsections (c) and (d) of this section using methods described in section 2871(f)(2) of this title consistent with State law.

(f) Performance assessments and improvements

(1) Assessments

The Secretary shall conduct an annual assessment of the performance of each Job Corps center. Based on the assessment, the Secretary shall take measures to continuously improve the performance of the Job Corps program.

(2) Performance improvement plans

With respect to a Job Corps center that fails to meet the expected levels of performance relating to the core performance measures specified in subsection (c) of this section, the Secretary shall develop and implement a performance improvement plan. Such a plan shall require action including—

(A) providing technical assistance to the center;

(B) changing the vocational training offered at the center;

(C) changing the management staff of the center;

(D) replacing the operator of the center;

(E) reducing the capacity of the center;

(F) relocating the center; or

(G) closing the center.

(3) Additional performance improvement plans

In addition to the performance improvement plans required under paragraph (2), the Secretary may develop and implement additional performance improvement plans. Such a plan shall require improvements, including the actions described in paragraph (2), for a Job Corps center that fails to meet criteria established by the Secretary other than the expected levels of performance described in paragraph (2).

(g) Closure of Job Corps center

Prior to the closure of any Job Corps center, the Secretary shall ensure—

(1) that the proposed decision to close the center is announced in advance to the general public through publication in the Federal Register or other appropriate means;

(2) the establishment of a reasonable comment period, not to exceed 30 days, for interested individuals to submit written comments to the Secretary; and

(3) that the Member of Congress who represents the district in which such center is located is notified within a reasonable period of time in advance of any final decision to close the center.

(Pub. L. 105–220, title I, § 159, Aug. 7, 1998, 112 Stat. 1017; Pub. L. 105–277, div. A, § 101(f) [title VIII, § 401(6)], Oct. 21, 1998, 112 Stat. 2681–337, 2681–411.)

AMENDMENTS

1998—Subsec. (c)(1)(G). Pub. L. 105–277, § 101(f) [title VIII, § 401(6)(A)], substituted "postsecondary" for "post-secondary".

Subsec. (c)(3). Pub. L. 105–277, § 101(f) [title VIII, § 401(6)(B)], substituted "containing," for "containing".

Subsec. (d)(4). Pub. L. 105–277, § 101(f) [title VIII, § 401(6)(A)], substituted "postsecondary" for "post-secondary".

§ 2900. General provisions

The Secretary is authorized to—

(1) disseminate, with regard to the provisions of section 3204 of title 39, data and information in such forms as the Secretary shall determine to be appropriate, to public agencies, private organizations, and the general public;

(2) subject to section 2897(b) of this title, collect or compromise all obligations to or held by the Secretary and exercise all legal or equitable rights accruing to the Secretary in connection with the payment of obligations until such time as such obligations may be referred to the Attorney General for suit or collection; and

(3) expend funds made available for purposes of this subchapter—

(A) for printing and binding, in accordance with applicable law (including regulation); and

(B) without regard to any other law (including regulation), for rent of buildings and space in buildings and for repair, alteration, and improvement of buildings and space in buildings rented by the Secretary, except that the Secretary shall not expend funds under the authority of this subparagraph—

(i) except when necessary to obtain an item, service, or facility, that is required in the proper administration of this subchapter, and that otherwise could not be obtained, or could not be obtained in the quantity or quality needed, or at the time, in the form, or under the conditions in which the item, service, or facility is needed; and

(ii) prior to having given written notification to the Administrator of General Services (if the expenditure would affect an activity that otherwise would be under the jurisdiction of the General Services Administration) of the intention of the Secretary to make the expenditure, and the reasons and justifications for the expenditure.

(Pub. L. 105–220, title I, § 160, Aug. 7, 1998, 112 Stat. 1020.)

PRIOR PROVISIONS

Provisions similar to this section were contained in section 1708 of this title prior to repeal by Pub. L. 105–220.

§ 2901. Authorization of appropriations

There are authorized to be appropriated to carry out this subchapter such sums as may be necessary for each of the fiscal years 1999 through 2003.

(Pub. L. 105–220, title I, § 161, Aug. 7, 1998, 112 Stat. 1021.)

SUBCHAPTER IV—NATIONAL PROGRAMS

§ 2911. Native American programs

(a) Purpose

(1) In general

The purpose of this section is to support employment and training activities for Indian, Alaska Native, and Native Hawaiian individuals in order—

(A) to develop more fully the academic, occupational, and literacy skills of such individuals;

(B) to make such individuals more competitive in the workforce; and

(C) to promote the economic and social development of Indian, Alaska Native, and Native Hawaiian communities in accordance with the goals and values of such communities.

(2) Indian policy

All programs assisted under this section shall be administered in a manner consistent with the principles of the Indian Self-Determination and Education Assistance Act (25 U.S.C. 450 et seq.) and the government-to-government relationship between the Federal Government and Indian tribal governments.

(b) Definitions

As used in this section:

(1) Alaska Native

The term "Alaska Native" means a Native as such term is defined in section 1602(b) of title 43.

(2) Indian, Indian tribe, and tribal organization

The terms "Indian", "Indian tribe", and "tribal organization" have the meanings given such terms in subsections (d), (e), and (*l*), respectively, of section 4 of the Indian Self-Determination and Education Assistance Act (25 U.S.C. 450b).

(3) Native Hawaiian and Native Hawaiian organization

The terms "Native Hawaiian" and "Native Hawaiian organization" have the meanings given such terms in section 7517 of title 20.

(c) Program authorized

(1) In general

The Secretary shall, on a competitive basis, make grants to, or enter into contracts or cooperative agreements with, Indian tribes, tribal organizations, Alaska Native entities, Indian-controlled organizations serving Indians, or Native Hawaiian organizations to carry out the authorized activities described in subsection (d) of this section.

(2) Exception

The competition for grants, contracts, or cooperative agreements conducted under paragraph (1) shall be conducted every 2 years, except that if a recipient of such a grant, contract, or agreement has performed satisfactorily, the Secretary may waive the requirements for such competition on receipt from the recipient of a satisfactory 2-year program plan for the succeeding 2-year period of the grant, contract, or agreement.

(d) Authorized activities

(1) In general

Funds made available under subsection (c) of this section shall be used to carry out the activities described in paragraph (2) that—

(A) are consistent with this section; and

(B) are necessary to meet the needs of Indians or Native Hawaiians preparing to enter, reenter, or retain unsubsidized employment.

(2) Workforce investment activities and supplemental services

(A) In general

Funds made available under subsection (c) of this section shall be used for—

(i) comprehensive workforce investment activities for Indians or Native Hawaiians; or

(ii) supplemental services for Indian or Native Hawaiian youth on or near Indian reservations and in Oklahoma, Alaska, or Hawaii.

(B) Special rule

Notwithstanding any other provision of this section, individuals who were eligible to participate in programs under section 1671 of this title (as such section was in effect on the day before August 7, 1998) shall be eligible to participate in an activity assisted under this section.

(e) Program plan

In order to receive a grant or enter into a contract or cooperative agreement under this section an entity described in subsection (c) of this section shall submit to the Secretary a program plan that describes a 2-year strategy for meeting the needs of Indian, Alaska Native, or Native Hawaiian individuals, as appropriate, in the area served by such entity. Such plan shall—

(1) be consistent with the purpose of this section;

(2) identify the population to be served;

(3) identify the education and employment needs of the population to be served and the manner in which the activities to be provided will strengthen the ability of the individuals served to obtain or retain unsubsidized employment;

(4) describe the activities to be provided and the manner in which such activities are to be integrated with other appropriate activities; and

(5) describe, after the entity submitting the plan consults with the Secretary, the performance measures to be used to assess the performance of entities in carrying out the activities assisted under this section.

(f) Consolidation of funds

Each entity receiving assistance under subsection (c) of this section may consolidate such assistance with assistance received from related programs in accordance with the provisions of the Indian Employment, Training and Related Services Demonstration Act of 1992 (25 U.S.C. 3401 et seq.).

(g) Nonduplicative and nonexclusive services

Nothing in this section shall be construed—

(1) to limit the eligibility of any entity described in subsection (c) of this section to participate in any activity offered by a State or local entity under this Act; or

(2) to preclude or discourage any agreement, between any entity described in subsection (c) of this section and any State or local entity, to facilitate the provision of services by such entity or to the population served by such entity.

(h) Administrative provisions

(1) Organizational unit established

The Secretary shall designate a single organizational unit within the Department of Labor that shall have primary responsibility for the administration of the activities authorized under this section.

(2) Regulations

The Secretary shall consult with the entities described in subsection (c) of this section in—

(A) establishing regulations to carry out this section, including performance measures for entities receiving assistance under such subsection, taking into account the economic circumstances of such entities; and

(B) developing a funding distribution plan that takes into consideration previous levels of funding (prior to August 7, 1998) to such entities.

(3) Waivers

(A) In general

With respect to an entity described in subsection (c) of this section, the Secretary, notwithstanding any other provision of law, may, pursuant to a request submitted by such entity that meets the requirements established under subparagraph (B), waive any of the statutory or regulatory requirements of this chapter that are inconsistent with the specific needs of the entities described in such subsection, except that the Secretary may not waive requirements relating to wage and labor standards, worker rights, participation and protection of workers and participants, grievance procedures, and judicial review.

(B) Request and approval

An entity described in subsection (c) of this section that requests a waiver under subparagraph (A) shall submit a plan to the Secretary to improve the program of workforce investment activities carried out by the entity, which plan shall meet the requirements established by the Secretary and shall be generally consistent with the requirements of section 2939(i)(4)(B) of this title.

(4) Advisory council

(A) In general

Using funds made available to carry out this section, the Secretary shall establish a Native American Employment and Training Council to facilitate the consultation described in paragraph (2).

(B) Composition

The Council shall be composed of individuals, appointed by the Secretary, who are representatives of the entities described in subsection (c) of this section.

(C) Duties

The Council shall advise the Secretary on all aspects of the operation and administration of the programs assisted under this section, including the selection of the individual appointed as the head of the unit established under paragraph (1).

(D) Personnel matters

(i) Compensation of members

Members of the Council shall serve without compensation.

(ii) Travel expenses

The members of the Council shall be allowed travel expenses, including per diem in lieu of subsistence, at rates authorized for employees of agencies under subchapter I of chapter 57 of title 5, while away from their homes or regular places of business in the performance of services for the Council.

(iii) Administrative support

The Secretary shall provide the Council with such administrative support as may be necessary to perform the functions of the Council.

(E) Chairperson

The Council shall select a chairperson from among its members.

(F) Meetings

The Council shall meet not less than twice each year.

(G) Application

Section 14 of the Federal Advisory Committee Act (5 U.S.C. App.) shall not apply to the Council.

(5) Technical assistance

The Secretary, acting through the unit established under paragraph (1), is authorized to provide technical assistance to entities described in subsection (c) of this section that receive assistance under subsection (c) of this section to enable such entities to improve the activities authorized under this section that are provided by such entities.

(6) Agreement for certain federally recognized Indian tribes to transfer funds to the program

A federally recognized Indian tribe that administers funds provided under this section and funds provided by more than one State under other sections of this chapter may enter into an agreement with the Secretary and the Governors of the affected States to transfer the funds provided by the States to the program administered by the tribe under this section.

(i) Compliance with single audit requirements; related requirement

Grants, contracts, and cooperative agreements entered into under this section shall be subject to the requirements of chapter 75 of subtitle V of title 31 (enacted by the Single Audit Act of 1984) and charging of costs under this section shall be subject to appropriate circulars issued by the Office of Management and Budget.

(j) Assistance to American Samoans in Hawaii

(1) In general

Notwithstanding any other provision of law, the Secretary is authorized to provide assistance to American Samoans who reside in Hawaii for the co-location of federally funded and State-funded workforce investment activities.

(2) Authorization of appropriations

There are authorized to be appropriated for fiscal year 1999 such sums as may be necessary to carry out this subsection.

(Pub. L. 105–220, title I, §166, Aug. 7, 1998, 112 Stat. 1021; Pub. L. 105–277, div. A, §101(f) [title VIII, §401(7)], Oct. 21, 1998, 112 Stat. 2681–337, 2681–411; Pub. L. 107–110, title VII, §702(g), Jan. 8, 2002, 115 Stat. 1947.)

REFERENCES IN TEXT

The Indian Self-Determination and Education Assistance Act, referred to in subsec. (a)(2), is Pub. L. 93–638, Jan. 4, 1975, 88 Stat. 2203, as amended, which is classified principally to subchapter II (§450 et seq.) of chapter 14 of Title 25, Indians. For complete classification of this Act to the Code, see Short Title note set out under section 450 of Title 25 and Tables.

Section 1671 of this title, referred to in subsec. (d)(2)(B), was repealed by Pub. L. 105–220, title I, §199(b)(2), Aug. 7, 1998, 112 Stat. 1059, effective July 1, 2000.

The Indian Employment, Training and Related Services Demonstration Act of 1992, referred to in subsec. (f), is Pub. L. 102–477, Oct. 23, 1992, 106 Stat. 2302, as amended, which is classified generally to chapter 36 (§3401 et seq.) of Title 25, Indians. For complete classification of this Act to the Code, see Short Title note set out under section 3401 of Title 25 and Tables.

This Act, referred to in subsec. (g)(1), is Pub. L. 105–220, Aug. 7, 1998, 112 Stat. 936, as amended, known as the Workforce Investment Act of 1998. For complete classification of this Act to the Code, see Short Title note set out under section 9201 of Title 20, Education, and Tables.

This chapter, referred to in subsec. (h)(3)(A), (6), was in the original "this title" meaning title I of Pub. L. 105–220, Aug. 7, 1998, 112 Stat. 939, as amended, which enacted this chapter, repealed sections 1501 to 1505, 1511 to 1583, 1592 to 1735, 1737 to 1791h, 1792 to 1792b, 2301 to 2314 of this title, section 211 of former Title 40, Appendix, Public Buildings, Property, and Works, sections 11421, 11441 to 11447, 11449, 11450, 11461 to 11466, 11471, and 11472 of Title 42, The Public Health and Welfare, and sections 42101 to 42106 of Title 49, Transportation, enacted provisions set out as notes under sections 1501, 2301, and 2940 of this title and section 11421 of Title 42, and repealed provisions set out as notes under sections 801 and 2301 of this title and section 1255a of Title 8, Aliens and Nationality. For complete classification of title I to the Code, see Tables.

The Federal Advisory Committee Act, referred to in subsec. (h)(4)(G), is Pub. L. 92–463, Oct. 6, 1972, 86 Stat. 770, as amended, which is set out in the Appendix to Title 5, Government Organization and Employees.

The Single Audit Act of 1984, referred to in subsec. (i), is Pub. L. 98–502, Oct. 19, 1984, 98 Stat. 2327, which enacted chapter 75 (§7501 et seq.) of Title 31, Money and Finance, and provisions set out as notes under section 7501 of Title 31. For complete classification of this Act to the Code, see Short Title of 1984 Amendment note set out under section 7501 of Title 31 and Tables.

PRIOR PROVISIONS

Provisions similar to this section were contained in sections 1671 and 1673 of this title prior to repeal by Pub. L. 105–220.

AMENDMENTS

2002—Subsec. (b)(3). Pub. L. 107–110 substituted "section 7517 of title 20" for "paragraphs (1) and (3), respectively, of section 7912 of title 20".

1998—Subsec. (h)(3)(A). Pub. L. 105–277 substituted "subparagraph (B)" for "paragraph (2)".

EFFECTIVE DATE OF 2002 AMENDMENT

Amendment by Pub. L. 107–110 effective Jan. 8, 2002, except with respect to certain noncompetitive programs and competitive programs, see section 5 of Pub. L. 107–110, set out as an Effective Date note under section 6301 of Title 20, Education.

§2912. Migrant and seasonal farmworker programs

(a) In general

Every 2 years, the Secretary shall, on a competitive basis, make grants to, or enter into contracts with, eligible entities to carry out the activities described in subsection (d) of this section.

(b) Eligible entities

To be eligible to receive a grant or enter into a contract under this section, an entity shall have an understanding of the problems of eligible migrant and seasonal farmworkers (including dependents), a familiarity with the area to be served, and the ability to demonstrate a capacity to administer effectively a diversified program of workforce investment activities (including youth activities) and related assistance for eligible migrant and seasonal farmworkers.

(c) Program plan

(1) In general

To be eligible to receive a grant or enter into a contract under this section, an entity described in subsection (b) of this section shall submit to the Secretary a plan that describes a 2-year strategy for meeting the needs of eligible migrant and seasonal farmworkers in the area to be served by such entity.

(2) Contents

Such plan shall—

(A) identify the education and employment needs of the population to be served and the manner in which the services to be provided will strengthen the ability of the eligible migrant and seasonal farmworkers and dependents to obtain or retain unsubsidized employment or stabilize their unsubsidized employment;

(B) describe the related assistance and supportive services to be provided and the manner in which such assistance and services are to be integrated and coordinated with other appropriate services; and

(C) describe the indicators of performance to be used to assess the performance of such entity in carrying out the activities assisted under this section.

(3) Administration

Grants and contracts awarded under this section shall be centrally administered by the Department of Labor and competitively awarded by the Secretary using procedures consistent with standard Federal Government competitive procurement policies.

(4) Competition

(A) In general

The competition for grants made and contracts entered into under this section shall be conducted every 2 years.

(B) Exception

Notwithstanding subparagraph (A), if a recipient of such a grant or contract has performed satisfactorily under the terms of the grant agreement or contract, the Secretary may waive the requirement for such competition for such recipient upon receipt from the recipient of a satisfactory 2-year plan described in paragraph (1) for the succeeding 2-year grant or contract period. The Secretary may exercise the waiver authority of the preceding sentence not more than once during any 4-year period with respect to any single recipient.

(d) Authorized activities

Funds made available under this section and section 2852(b)(1)(A)(iii) of this title shall be used to carry out workforce investment activities (including youth activities) and provide related assistance for eligible migrant and seasonal farmworkers, which may include employment, training, educational assistance, literacy assistance, an English language program, worker safety training, housing, supportive services, dropout prevention activities, followup services for those individuals placed in employment, self-employment and related business enterprise development education as needed by eligible migrant and seasonal farmworkers and identified pursuant to the plan required by subsection (c) of this section, and technical assistance relating to capacity enhancement in such areas as management information technology.

(e) Consultation with Governors and local boards

In making grants and entering into contracts under this section, the Secretary shall consult with the Governors and local boards of the States in which the eligible entities will carry out the activities described in subsection (d) of this section.

(f) Regulations

The Secretary shall consult with eligible migrant and seasonal farmworkers groups and States in establishing regulations to carry out this section, including performance measures for eligible entities that take into account the economic circumstances and demographics of eligible migrant and seasonal farmworkers.

(g) Compliance with single audit requirements; related requirement

Grants and contracts entered into under this section shall be subject to the requirements of chapter 75 of subtitle V of title 31 (enacted by the Single Audit Act of 1984) and charging of costs under this section shall be subject to appropriate circulars issued by the Office of Management and Budget.

(h) Definitions

In this section:

(1) Disadvantaged

The term "disadvantaged", used with respect to a farmworker, means a farmworker whose income, for 12 consecutive months out of the 24 months prior to application for the program involved, does not exceed the higher of—

(A) the poverty line (as defined in section 334(a)(2)(B))[1] for an equivalent period; or

(B) 70 percent of the lower living standard income level, for an equivalent period.

[1] See References in Text note below.

(2) Eligible migrant and seasonal farmworkers

The term "eligible migrant and seasonal farmworkers" means individuals who are eligible migrant farmworkers or are eligible seasonal farmworkers.

(3) Eligible migrant farmworker

The term "eligible migrant farmworker" means—

(A) an eligible seasonal farmworker described in paragraph (4)(A) whose agricultural labor requires travel to a job site such that the farmworker is unable to return to a permanent place of residence within the same day; and

(B) a dependent of the farmworker described in subparagraph (A).

(4) Eligible seasonal farmworker

The term "eligible seasonal farmworker" means—

(A) a disadvantaged person who, for 12 consecutive months out of the 24 months prior to application for the program involved, has been primarily employed in agricultural labor that is characterized by chronic unemployment or underemployment; and

(B) a dependent of the person described in subparagraph (A).

(Pub. L. 105–220, title I, § 167, Aug. 7, 1998, 112 Stat. 1025; Pub. L. 105–277, div. A, § 101(f) [title VIII, § 401(8)], Oct. 21, 1998, 112 Stat. 2681–337, 2681–411.)

REFERENCES IN TEXT

The Single Audit Act of 1984, referred to in subsec. (g), is Pub. L. 98–502, Oct. 19, 1984, 98 Stat. 2327, which enacted chapter 75 (§ 7501 et seq.) of Title 31, Money and Finance, and provisions set out as notes under section 7501 of Title 31. For complete classification of this Act to the Code, see Short Title of 1984 Amendment note set out under section 7501 of Title 31 and Tables.

Section 334, referred to in subsec. (h)(1)(A), is section 334 of Pub. L. 105–220, which is set out as a note under section 2701 of this title. However, section 334 does not contain a subsec. (a)(2)(B) and does not define the term "poverty line". "Poverty line" is defined for purposes of this chapter in section 2801 of this title.

PRIOR PROVISIONS

Provisions similar to this section were contained in sections 1672 and 1673 of this title prior to repeal by Pub. L. 105–220.

AMENDMENTS

1998—Subsec. (d). Pub. L. 105–277 inserted "and section 2852(b)(1)(A)(iii) of this title" after "this section".

§ 2913. Veterans' workforce investment programs

(a) Authorization

(1) In general

The Secretary shall conduct, directly or through grants or contracts, programs to meet the needs for workforce investment activities of veterans with service-connected disabilities, veterans who have significant barriers to employment, veterans who served on active duty in the armed forces during a war or in a campaign or expedition for which a campaign badge has been authorized, and recently separated veterans.

(2) Conduct of programs

Programs supported under this section may be conducted through grants and contracts with public agencies and private nonprofit organizations, including recipients of Federal assistance under other provisions of this chapter, that the Secretary determines have an understanding of the unemployment problems of veterans described in paragraph (1), familiarity with the area to be served, and the capability to administer effectively a program of workforce investment activities for such veterans.

(3) Required activities

Programs supported under this section shall include—

(A) activities to enhance services provided to veterans by other providers of workforce investment activities funded by Federal, State, or local government;

(B) activities to provide workforce investment activities to such veterans that are not adequately provided by other public providers of workforce investment activities; and

(C) outreach and public information activities to develop and promote maximum job and job training opportunities for such veterans and to inform such veterans about employment, job training, on-the-job training and educational opportunities under this chapter, under title 38, and under other provisions of law, which activities shall be coordinated with activities provided through the one-stop centers described in section 2864(c) of this title.

(b) Administration of programs

(1) In general

The Secretary shall administer programs supported under this section through the Assistant Secretary for Veterans' Employment and Training.

(2) Additional responsibilities

In carrying out responsibilities under this section, the Assistant Secretary for Veterans' Employment and Training shall—

(A) be responsible for the awarding of grants and contracts and the distribution of funds under this section and for the establishment of appropriate fiscal controls, accountability, and program performance measures for recipients of grants and contracts under this section; and

(B) consult with the Secretary of Veterans Affairs and take steps to ensure that programs supported under this section are coordinated, to the maximum extent feasible, with related programs and activities conducted under title 38, including programs and activities conducted under chapter 63 of such title, chapters 30, 31, 32, and 34 of such title, and sections 1712A, 1720A, 3687, and 4103A of such title.

(Pub. L. 105–220, title I, §168, Aug. 7, 1998, 112 Stat. 1027; Pub. L. 109–233, title IV, §402(e)(4), June 15, 2006, 120 Stat. 411.)

PRIOR PROVISIONS

Provisions similar to this section were contained in section 1721 of this title prior to repeal by Pub. L. 105–220.

AMENDMENTS

2006—Subsec. (b)(2)(B). Pub. L. 109–233 substituted "chapter 63" for "subchapter II of chapter 77".

COORDINATION OF INFORMATION AND ASSISTANCE

Pub. L. 100–689, title IV, §402, Nov. 18, 1988, 100 Stat. 4178, as amended by Pub. L. 105–277, div. A, §101(f) [title VIII, §405(d)(24), (f)(16)], Oct. 21, 1998, 112 Stat. 2681–337, 2681–423, 2681–432, provided that:

"(a) PURPOSE.—It is the purpose of this section to ensure that veterans who are dislocated workers eligible for assistance under title I of the Workforce Investment Act of 1998 [29 U.S.C. 2801 et seq.] or are otherwise unemployed receive, to the extent feasible, assistance (including information on vocational guidance or vocational counseling, or information on both vocational guidance or vocational counseling), including information on counseling, needed by such veterans—

"(1) to apply for services and benefits for which they are eligible as veterans, dislocated workers, or unemployed persons;

"(2) to obtain resolution of questions and problems relating to such services and benefit[s]; and

"(3) to initiate any authorized administrative appeals of determinations or other actions relating to such services and benefits.

"(b) MEMORANDUM OF UNDERSTANDING.—(1) Not later than one year after the date of the enactment of this Act [Nov. 18, 1988], the Secretary of Labor and the Administrator of Veterans' Affairs shall enter into a memorandum of understanding to carry out the purpose of this section. The memorandum shall include provisions that define the relationships and responsibilities of the Veterans' Administration, the Department of Labor, and State and local agencies with respect to the provision of the following information, forms, and assistance:

"(A) Information on services and benefits referred to in subsection (d).

"(B) All application forms and related forms necessary for individuals to apply for such services and to claim such benefits.

"(C) Assistance in resolving questions and problems relating to receipt of such services and benefits.

"(D) Assistance in contacting other Federal Government offices and State offices where such services or benefits are provided or administered.

"(2) The memorandum of understanding entered into pursuant to paragraph (1) shall include a provision for the periodic evaluation, by the Secretary of Labor and the Administrator of Veterans' Affairs, of the implementation of their respective responsibilities under such memorandum.

"(c) COORDINATION OF DEPARTMENT OF LABOR ACTIVITIES.—The Assistant Secretary of Labor for Veterans' Employment and Training, in consultation with the unit or office designated or created under section 322(b) of the Job Training Partnership Act [former 29 U.S.C. 1662a(b)] or any successor to such unit or office under title I of the Workforce Investment Act of 1998 [29 U.S.C. 2801 et seq.], shall, except as the Secretary of Labor may otherwise direct, coordinate the activities of the components of the Department of Labor performing the responsibilities of the Secretary of Labor under this section.

"(d) COVERED SERVICES AND BENEFITS.—This section applies with respect to the following services and benefits:

"(1) Employment assistance under—

"(A) title I of the Workforce Investment Act of 1998 [29 U.S.C. 2801 et seq.]; and

"(B) the Veterans' Job Training Act (97 Stat. 443; 29 U.S.C. 1721 note [now set out below]).

"(2) Employment and training activities for dislocated workers under title I of the Workforce Investment Act of 1998 [29 U.S.C. 2801 et seq.].

"(3) Employment assistance and unemployment compensation under the trade adjustment assistance program provided in chapter 2 of title II of the Trade Act of 1974 (29 [19] U.S.C. 2271 et seq.) and under any other program administered by the Employment and Training Administration of the Department of Labor.

"(4) Educational assistance under—

"(A) the Adult Education Act ([former] 20 U.S.C. 1201 et seq.); and

"(B) chapters 30, 31, 32, 34, and 35 of title 38, United States Code, and chapter 106 of title 10, United States Code.

"(5) Certification of a veteran as a member of a targeted group eligible for the targeted jobs credit determined under section 51 of the Internal Revenue Code of 1986 [26 U.S.C. 51].

"(e) DEFINITION.—In this section, the term 'veteran' has the meaning given such term in section 101(2) of title 38, United States Code."

VETERANS' JOB TRAINING ACT

Pub. L. 98–77, Aug. 15, 1983, 97 Stat. 443, as amended by Pub. L. 98–160, title VII, §704, Nov. 21, 1983, 97 Stat. 1011; Pub. L. 98–543, title II, §212, Oct. 24, 1984, 98 Stat. 2744; Pub. L. 99–108, §4, Sept. 30, 1985, 99 Stat. 481; Pub. L. 99–238, title II, §201(a)(1), (b)–(e), Jan. 13, 1986, 99 Stat. 1767, 1768; Pub. L. 100–77, title IX, §901, July 22, 1987, 101 Stat. 538; Pub. L. 100–227, title II, §201, Dec. 31, 1987, 101 Stat. 1555; Pub. L. 100–323, §§11(a)(1), (2), (3)(B), (4), (b)–(f), 15(b)(2), (c)(2), May 20, 1988, 102 Stat. 567–570, 574; Pub. L. 102–40, title IV, §402(d)(2), May 7, 1991, 105 Stat. 239; Pub. L. 102–83, §5(c)(2), Aug. 6, 1991, 105 Stat. 406; Pub. L. 105–277, div. A, §101(f) [title VIII, §405(d)(25), (f)(17)], Oct. 21, 1998, 112 Stat. 2681–337, 2681–423, 2681–432, provided that:

"SHORT TITLE

"SECTION 1. This Act may be cited as the 'Veterans' Job Training Act'.

"PURPOSE

"SEC. 2. The purpose of this Act is to address the problem of severe and continuing unemployment among veterans by providing, in the form of payments to defray the costs of training, incentives to employers to hire and train certain wartime veterans who have been unemployed for long periods of time for stable and permanent positions that involve significant training.

"DEFINITIONS

"SEC. 3. For the purposes of this Act:

"(1) The term 'Administrator' means the Administrator of Veterans' Affairs.

"(2) The term 'Secretary' means the Secretary of Labor.

"(3) The terms 'veteran', 'Korean conflict', 'compensation', 'service-connected', 'State', 'active military, naval, or air service', and 'Vietnam era', have the meanings given such terms in paragraphs (2), (9), (13), (16), (20), (24), and (29), respectively, of section 101 of title 38, United States Code.

"ESTABLISHMENT OF PROGRAM

"SEC. 4. (a) The Administrator and, to the extent specifically provided by this Act, the Secretary shall carry out a program in accordance with this Act to assist eligible veterans in obtaining employment through training for employment in stable and permanent positions that involve significant training. The program shall be carried out through payments to employers who employ and train eligible veterans in such jobs in order to assist such employers in defraying the costs of necessary training.

"(b) The Secretary shall carry out the Secretary's responsibilities under this Act through the Assistant Secretary of Labor for Veterans' Employment and Training established under section 4102A of title 38, United States Code.

"ELIGIBILITY FOR PROGRAM; DURATION OF ASSISTANCE

"SEC. 5. (a)(1) To be eligible for participation in a job training program under this Act, a veteran must be a Korean conflict or Vietnam-era veteran who—

"(A) is unemployed at the time of applying for participation in a program under this Act; and

"(B) has been unemployed for at least 10 of the 15 weeks immediately preceding the date of such veteran's application for participation in a program under this Act.

"(2) For purposes of paragraph (1), the term 'Korean conflict or Vietnam-era veteran' means a veteran—

"(A) who served in the active military, naval, or air service for a period of more than one hundred and eighty days, any part of which was during the Korean conflict or the Vietnam era; or

"(B) who served in the active military, naval, or air service during the Korean conflict or the Vietnam era and—

"(i) was discharged or released therefrom for a service-connected disability; or

"(ii) is entitled to compensation (or but for the receipt of retirement pay would be entitled to compensation).

"(3) For purposes of paragraph (1), a veteran shall be considered to be unemployed during any period the veteran is without a job and wants and is available for work.

"(b)(1) A veteran who desires to participate in a program of job training under this Act shall submit to the Administrator an application for participation in such a program. Such an application—

"(A) shall include a certification by the veteran that the veteran is unemployed and meets the other criteria for eligibility prescribed by subsection (a); and

"(B) shall be in such form and contain such additional information as the Administrator may prescribe.

"(2)(A) Subject to subparagraph (B), the Administrator shall approve an application by a veteran for participation in a program of job training under this Act unless the Administrator finds that the veteran is not eligible to participate in a program of job training under this Act.

"(B) The Administrator may withhold approval of an application of a veteran under this Act if the Administrator determines that, because of limited funds available for the purpose of making payments to employers under this Act, it is necessary to limit the number of participants in programs under this Act.

"(3)(A) Subject to section 14(c), the Administrator shall certify as eligible for participation under this Act a veteran whose application is approved under this subsection and shall furnish the veteran with a certificate of that veteran's eligibility for presentation to an employer offering a program of job training under this Act. Any such certificate shall expire 90 days after it is furnished to the veteran. The date on which a certificate is furnished to a veteran under this paragraph shall be stated on the certificate.

"(B) A certificate furnished under this paragraph may, upon the veteran's application, be renewed in accordance with the terms and conditions of subparagraph (A).

"(c) The maximum period of training for which assistance may be provided on behalf of a veteran under this Act is—

"(1) fifteen months in the case of—

"(A) a veteran with a service-connected disability rated at 30 percent or more; or

"(B) a veteran with a service-connected disability rated at 10 percent or 20 percent who has been determined under section 3106 of title 38, United States Code, to have a serious employment handicap; and

"(2) nine months in the case of any other veteran.

"EMPLOYER JOB TRAINING PROGRAMS

"SEC. 6. (a)(1) Except as provided in paragraph (2), in order to be approved as a program of job training under this Act, a program of job training of an employer approved under section 7 must provide training for a period of not less than six months in an occupation in a growth industry, in an occupation requiring the use of new technological skills, or in an occupation for which demand for labor exceeds supply.

"(2) A program of job training providing training for a period of at least three but less than six months may be approved if the Administrator determines (in accordance with standards which the Administrator shall prescribe) that the purpose of this Act would be met through that program.

"(b) Subject to section 10 and the other provisions of this Act, a veteran who has been approved for participation in a program of job training under this Act and has a current certificate of eligibility for such participation may enter a program of job training that has been approved under section 7 and that is offered to the veteran by the employer.

"APPROVAL OF EMPLOYER PROGRAMS

"SEC. 7. (a)(1) An employer may be paid assistance under section 8(a) on behalf of an eligible veteran employed by such employer and participating in a program of job training offered by that employer only if the program is approved under this section and in accordance with such procedures as the Administrator may by regulation prescribe.

"(2) Except as provided in subsection (b), the Administrator shall approve a proposed program of job training of an employer unless the Administrator determines that the application does not contain a certification and other information meeting the requirements established under this Act or that withholding of approval is warranted under subsection (g).

"(b) The Administrator may not approve a program of job training—

"(1) for employment which consists of seasonal, intermittent, or temporary jobs;

"(2) for employment under which commissions are the primary source of income;

"(3) for employment which involves political or religious activities;

"(4) for employment with any department, agency, instrumentality, or branch of the Federal Government (including the United States Postal Service and the Postal Rate Commission [Postal Regulatory Commission]); or

"(5) if the training will not be carried out in a State.

"(c) An employer offering a program of job training that the employer desires to have approved for the purposes of this Act shall submit to the Administrator a written application for such approval. Such application shall be in such form as the Administrator shall prescribe.

"(d) An application under subsection (c) shall include a certification by the employer of the following:

"(1) That the employer is planning that, upon a veteran's completion of the program of job training, the employer will employ the veteran in a position for which the veteran has been trained and that the employer expects that such a position will be available on a stable and permanent basis to the veteran at the end of the training period.

"(2) That the wages and benefits to be paid to a veteran participating in the employer's program of job training will be not less than the wages and benefits normally paid to other employees participating in a comparable program of job training.

"(3) That the employment of a veteran under the program—

"(A) will not result in the displacement of currently employed workers (including partial displacement such as a reduction in the hours of nonovertime work, wages, or employment benefits); and

"(B) will not be in a job (i) while any other individual is on layoff from the same or any substantially equivalent job, or (ii) the opening for which was created as a result of the employer having terminated the employment of any regular employee or otherwise having reduced its work force with the intention of hiring a veteran in such job under this Act.

"(4) That the employer will not employ in the program of job training a veteran who is already qualified by training and experience for the job for which training is to be provided.

"(5) That the job which is the objective of the training program is one that involves significant training.

"(6) That the training content of the program is adequate, in light of the nature of the occupation for which training is to be provided and of comparable training opportunities in such occupation, to accomplish the training objective certified under clause (2) of subsection (e).

"(7) That each participating veteran will be employed full time in the program of job training.

"(8) That the training period under the proposed program is not longer than the training periods that employers in the community customarily require new employees to complete in order to become competent in the occupation or job for which training is to be provided.

"(9) That there are in the training establishment or place of employment such space, equipment, instructional material, and instructor personnel as needed to accomplish the training objective certified under clause (2) of subsection (e).

"(10) That the employer will keep records adequate to show the progress made by each veteran participating in the program and otherwise to demonstrate compliance with the requirements established under this Act.

"(11) That the employer will furnish each participating veteran, before the veteran's entry into training, with a copy of the employer's certification under this subsection and will obtain and retain the veteran's signed acknowledgment of having received such certification.

"(12) That, as applicable, the employer will provide each participating veteran with the full opportunity to participate in a personal interview pursuant to section 14(b)(1)(A) during the veteran's normal workday.

"(13) That the program meets such other criteria as the Administrator may determine are essential for the effective implementation of the program established by this Act.

"(e) A certification under subsection (d) shall include—

"(1) a statement indicating (A) the total number of hours of participation in the program of job training to be offered a veteran, (B) the length of the program of job training, and (C) the starting rate of wages to be paid to a participant in the program; and

"(2) a description of the training content of the program (including any agreement the employer has entered into with an educational institution under section 10) and of the objective of the training.

"(f)(1) Except as specified in paragraph (2), each matter required to be certified to in paragraphs (1) through (11) of subsection (d) shall be considered to be a requirement established under this Act.

"(2)(A) For the purposes of section 8(c), only matters required to be certified in paragraphs (1) through (10) of subsection (d) shall be so considered.

"(B) For the purposes of section 11, a matter required to be certified under paragraph (12) of subsection (d) shall also be so considered.

"(g) In accordance with regulations which the Administrator shall prescribe, the Administrator may withhold approval of an employer's proposed program of job training pending the outcome of an investigation under section 12 and, based on the outcome of such an investigation, may disapprove such program.

"(h) For the purposes of this section, approval of a program of apprenticeship or other on-job training for the purposes of section 3687 of title 38, United States Code, shall be considered to meet all requirements established under the provisions of this Act (other than subsections (b) and (d)(3)) for approval of a program of job training.

"PAYMENTS TO EMPLOYERS; OVERPAYMENT

"SEC. 8. (a)(1) Except as provided in paragraph (3) and subsection (b) and subject to the provisions of section

9, the Administrator shall make quarterly payments to an employer of a veteran participating in an approved program of job training under this Act. Subject to section 5(c) and paragraph (2), the amount paid to an employer on behalf of a veteran for any period of time shall be 50 percent of the product of (A) the starting hourly rate of wages paid to the veteran by the employer (without regard to overtime or premium pay), and (B) the number of hours worked by the veteran during that period.

"(2) The total amount that may be paid to an employer on behalf of a veteran participating in a program of job training under this Act is $10,000.

"(3) In order to relieve financial burdens on business enterprises with relatively few numbers of employees, the Administrator may make payments under this Act on a monthly, rather than quarterly, basis to an employer with a number of employees less than a number which shall be specified in regulations which the Administrator shall prescribe for the purposes of this paragraph.

"(b) Payment may not be made to an employer for a period of training under this Act on behalf of a veteran until the Administrator has received—

"(1) from the veteran, a certification that the veteran was employed full time by the employer in a program of job training during such period; and

"(2) from the employer, a certification—

"(A) that the veteran was employed by the employer during that period and that the veteran's performance and progress during such period were satisfactory; and

"(B) of the number of hours worked by the veteran during that period.

With respect to the first such certification by an employer with respect to a veteran, the certification shall indicate the date on which the employment of the veteran began and the starting hourly rate of wages paid to the veteran (without regard to overtime or premium pay).

"(c)(1)(A) Whenever the Administrator finds that an overpayment under this Act has been made to an employer on behalf of a veteran as a result of a certification, or information contained in an application, submitted by an employer which was false in any material respect, the amount of such overpayment shall constitute a liability of the employer to the United States.

"(B) Whenever the Administrator finds that an employer has failed in any substantial respect to comply for a period of time with a requirement established under this Act (unless the employer's failure is the result of false or incomplete information provided by the veteran), each amount paid to the employer on behalf of a veteran for that period shall be considered to be an overpayment under this Act, and the amount of such overpayment shall constitute a liability of the employer to the United States.

"(2) Whenever the Administrator finds that an overpayment under this Act has been made to an employer on behalf of a veteran as a result of a certification by the veteran, or as a result of information provided to an employer or contained in an application submitted by the veteran, which was willfully or negligently false in any material respect, the amount of such overpayment shall constitute a liability of the veteran to the United States.

"(3) Any overpayment referred to in paragraph (1) or (2) may be recovered in the same manner as any other debt due the United States. Any overpayment recovered shall be credited to funds available to make payments under this Act. If there are no such funds, any overpayment recovered shall be deposited into the Treasury.

"(4) Any overpayment referred to in paragraph (1) or (2) may be waived, in whole or in part, in accordance with the terms and conditions set forth in section 5302 of title 38, United States Code.

"ENTRY INTO PROGRAM OF JOB TRAINING

"SEC. 9. Notwithstanding any other provision of this Act, the Administrator may withhold or deny approval of a veteran's entry into an approved program of job training if the Administrator determines that funds are not available to make payments under this Act on behalf of the veteran to the employer offering that program. Before the entry of a veteran into an approved program of job training of an employer for purposes of assistance under this Act, the employer shall notify the Administrator of the employer's intention to employ that veteran. The veteran may begin such program of job training with the employer two weeks after the notice is transmitted to the Administrator unless within that time the employer has received notice from the Administrator that approval of the veteran's entry into that program of job training must be withheld or denied in accordance with this section.

"PROVISION OF TRAINING THROUGH EDUCATIONAL INSTITUTIONS

"SEC. 10. An employer may enter into an agreement with an educational institution that has been approved for the enrollment of veterans under chapter 34 of title 38, United States Code, in order that such institution may provide a program of job training (or a portion of such a program) under this Act. When such an agreement has been entered into, the application of the employer under section 7 shall so state and shall include a description of the training to be provided under the agreement.

"DISCONTINUANCE OF APPROVAL OF PARTICIPATION IN CERTAIN EMPLOYER PROGRAMS

"SEC. 11. (a) If the Administrator finds at any time that a program of job training previously approved by the Administrator for the purposes of this Act thereafter fails to meet any of the requirements established under this Act, the Administrator may immediately disapprove further participation by veterans in that program. The Administrator shall provide to the employer concerned, and to each veteran participating in the employer's program, a statement of the reasons for, and an opportunity for a hearing with respect to, such disapproval. The employer and each such veteran shall be notified of such disapproval, the reasons for such disapproval, and the opportunity for a hearing. Notification shall be by a certified or registered letter, and a return receipt shall be secured.

"(b)(1) If the Administrator determines that the rate of veterans' successful completion of an employer's programs of job training previously approved by the Administrator for the purposes of this Act is disproportionately low because of deficiencies in the quality of such programs, the Administrator shall disapprove participation in such programs on the part of veterans who had not begun such participation on the date that the employer is notified of the disapproval. In determining whether any such rate is disproportionately low because of such deficiencies, the Administrator shall take into account appropriate data, including—

"(A) the quarterly data provided by the Secretary with respect to the number of veterans who receive counseling in connection with training under this Act, are referred to employers under this Act, participate in job training under this Act, complete such training or do not complete such training, and the reasons for noncompletion; and

"(B) data compiled through the particular employer's compliance surveys.

"(2) With respect to a disapproval under paragraph (1), the Administrator shall provide to the employer concerned the kind of statement, opportunity for hearing, and notice described in subsection (a).

"(3) A disapproval under paragraph (1) shall remain in effect until such time as the Administrator determines that adequate remedial action has been taken.

"INSPECTION OF RECORDS; INVESTIGATIONS

"SEC. 12. (a) The records and accounts of employers pertaining to veterans on behalf of whom assistance has been paid under this Act, as well as other records that the Administrator determines to be necessary to ascertain compliance with the requirements established under this Act, shall be available at reasonable times for examination by authorized representatives of the Federal Government.

"(b) The Administrator may monitor employers and veterans participating in programs of job training under this Act to determine compliance with the requirements established under this Act.

"(c) The Administrator may investigate any matter the Administrator considers necessary to determine compliance with the requirements established under this Act. The investigations authorized by this subsection may include examining records (including making certified copies of records), questioning employees, and entering into any premises or onto any site where any part of a program of job training is conducted under this Act, or where any of the records of the employer offering or providing such program are kept.

"(d) The Administrator may administer functions under subsections (b) and (c) in accordance with an agreement between the Administrator and the Secretary providing for the administration of such subsections (or any portion of such subsections) by the Department of Labor. Under such an agreement, any entity of the Department of Labor specified in the agreement may administer such subsections, notwithstanding section 4(b).

"COORDINATION WITH OTHER PROGRAMS

"SEC. 13. (a)(1) Assistance may not be paid under this Act to an employer on behalf of a veteran for any period of time described in paragraph (2) and to such veteran under chapter 31, 32, 34, 35, or 36 of title 38, United States Code, for the same period of time.

"(2) A period of time referred to in paragraph (1) is the period of time beginning on the date on which the veteran enters into an approved program of job training of an employer for purposes of assistance under this Act and ending on the last date for which such assistance is payable.

"(b) Assistance may not be paid under this Act to an employer on behalf of an eligible veteran for any period if the employer receives for that period any other form of assistance on account of the training or employment of the veteran, including assistance under title I of the Workforce Investment Act of 1998 [29 U.S.C. 2801 et seq.] or a credit under section 44B of the Internal Revenue Code of 1954 (26 U.S.C. 44B) (relating to credit for employment of certain new employees).

"(c) Assistance may not be paid under this Act on behalf of a veteran who has completed a program of job training under this Act.

"COUNSELING

"SEC. 14. (a)(1) The Administrator and the Secretary may, upon request, provide employment counseling services to any veteran eligible to participate under this Act in order to assist such veteran in selecting a suitable program of job training under this Act.

"(2) The Administrator shall, after consultation with the Secretary, provide a program of job-readiness skills development and counseling services designed to assist veterans in need of such assistance in finding, applying for, and successfully participating in a suitable program of job training under this Act. As part of providing such services, the Administrator shall coordinate activities, to the extent practicable, with the readjustment counseling program described in section 1712A of title 38, United States Code. The Administrator shall advise veterans participating under this Act of the availability of such services and encourage them to request such services whenever appropriate.

"(b)(1) The Secretary shall provide for a program under which—

"(A) except as provided in paragraph (2), a disabled veteran's outreach program specialist appointed under section 4103A(a) of title 38, United States Code, is assigned as a case manager for each veteran participating in a program of job training under this Act;

"(B) the veteran has an in-person interview with the case manager not later than 60 days after entering into a program of training under this Act; and

"(C) periodic (not less frequent than monthly) contact is maintained with each such veteran for the purpose of (i) avoiding unnecessary termination of employment, (ii) referring the veteran to appropriate counseling, if necessary, (iii) facilitating the veteran's successful completion of such program, and (iv) following up with the employer and the veteran in order to determine the veteran's progress in the program and the outcome regarding the veteran's participation in and successful completion of the program.

"(2) No case manager shall be assigned pursuant to paragraph (1)(A)—

"(A) for a veteran if, on the basis of a recommendation made by a disabled veterans' outreach program specialist, the Secretary determines that there is no need for a case manager for such veteran; or

"(B) in the case of the employees of an employer, if the Secretary determines that—

"(i) the employer has an appropriate and effective employee assistance program that is available to all veterans participating in the employer's programs of job training under this Act; or

"(ii) the rate of veterans' successful completion of the employer's programs of job training under this Act, either cumulatively or during the previous program year, is 60 percent or higher.

"(3) The Secretary and the Administrator shall jointly provide, to the extent feasible—

"(A) a program of counseling or other services (to be provided pursuant to subchapter IV of chapter 3 [see chapter 63] of title 38, United States Code, and sections 1712A, 4103A, and 4104 of such title) designed to resolve difficulties that may be encountered by veterans during their training under this Act; and

"(B) a program of information services under which—

"(i) each veteran who enters into a program of job training under this Act and each employer participating under this Act is informed of the supportive services and resources available to the veteran (I) under clauses (A) and (B), (II) through Veterans' Administration counseling and career-development activities (especially, in the case of a Vietnam-era veteran, readjustment counseling services under section 1712A of such title) and under title I of the Workforce Investment Act of 1998 [29 U.S.C. 2801 et seq.], and (III) through other appropriate agencies in the community; and

"(ii) veterans and employers are encouraged to request such services whenever appropriate.

"(c) Before a veteran who voluntarily terminates from a program of job training under this Act or is involuntarily terminated from such program by the employer may be eligible to be provided with a further certificate, or renewal of certification, of eligibility for participation under this Act, such veteran must be provided by the Secretary, after consultation with the Administrator, with a case manager.

"(d) Payments made under this Act pursuant to contracts entered into for the provision of job-readiness skills development and counseling services under subsection (a)(2) may only be paid out of the same account used to make payments under section 3104(a)(7) of title 38, United States Code, and the amount paid out of such account in any fiscal year for such services shall not exceed an amount equal to 5 percent of the amount obligated to carry out this Act for such fiscal year, except that for fiscal year 1988 the amount shall not exceed 5 percent of the amount available to carry out this Act on October 1, 1987.

"INFORMATION AND OUTREACH; USE OF AGENCY RESOURCES

"SEC. 15. (a)(1) The Administrator and the Secretary shall jointly provide for an outreach and public information program—

"(A) to inform veterans about the employment and job training opportunities available under this Act, under chapters 31, 34, 36, 41, and 42 of title 38, United States Code, and under other provisions of law; and

"(B) to inform private industry and business concerns (including small business concerns), public agencies and organizations, educational institutions, trade associations, and labor unions about the job training opportunities available under, and the advantages of participating in, the program established by this Act.

"(2) The Secretary, in consultation with the Administrator, shall promote the development of employment and job training opportunities for veterans by encouraging potential employers to make programs of job training under this Act available for eligible veterans, by advising other appropriate Federal departments and agencies of the program established by this Act, and by advising employers of applicable responsibilities under chapters 41 and 42 of title 38, United States Code, with respect to veterans.

"(b) The Administrator and the Secretary shall coordinate the outreach and public information program under subsection (a)(1), and job development activities under subsection (a)(2), with job counseling, placement, job development, and other services provided for under chapters 41 and 42 of title 38, United States Code, and with other similar services offered by other public agencies and organizations.

"(c)(1) The Administrator and the Secretary shall make available in regional and local offices of the Veterans' Administration and the Department of Labor such personnel as are necessary to facilitate the effective implementation of this Act.

"(2) In carrying out the responsibilities of the Secretary under this Act, the Secretary shall make maximum use of the services of Directors and Assistant Directors for Veterans' Employment and Training, disabled veterans' outreach program specialists, and employees of local offices appointed pursuant to sections 4103, 4103A, and 4104 of title 38, United States Code. The Secretary shall also use such resources as are available under title I of the Workforce Investment Act of 1998 [29 U.S.C. 2801 et seq.]. To the extent that the Administrator withholds approval of veterans' applications under this Act pursuant to section 5(b)(2)(B), the Secretary shall take steps to assist such veterans in taking advantage of opportunities that may be available to them under title I of the Workforce Investment Act of 1998 [29 U.S.C. 2801 et seq.] or under any other program carried out with funds provided by the Secretary.

"(d) The Secretary shall request and obtain from the Administrator of the Small Business Administration a list of small business concerns and shall, on a regular basis, update such list. Such list shall be used to identify and promote possible training and employment opportunities for veterans.

"(e) The Administrator and the Secretary shall assist veterans and employers desiring to participate under this Act in making application and completing necessary certifications.

"(f) The Secretary shall, on a not less frequent than quarterly basis, collect and compile from the heads of State employment services and Directors for Veterans' Employment and Training for each State information available to such heads and Directors, and derived from programs carried out in their respective States, with respect to the numbers of veterans who receive counseling services pursuant to section 14, who are referred to employers participating under this Act, who participate in programs of job training under this Act, and who complete such programs, and the reasons for veterans' noncompletion.

"AUTHORIZATION OF APPROPRIATIONS

"SEC. 16. (a) There is authorized to be appropriated to the Veterans' Administration (1) $150,000,000 for each of fiscal years 1984 and 1985, (2) a total of $65,000,000 for fiscal years 1986, and 1987, and (3) $60,000,000 for each of the fiscal years 1988 and 1989 for the purpose of making payments to employers under this Act and for the purpose of section 18 of this Act. Amounts appropriated pursuant to this section shall remain available until September 30, 1991.

"(b) Notwithstanding any other provision of law, any funds appropriated under subsection (a) for any fiscal year which are obligated for the purpose of making payments under section 8 on behalf of a veteran (including funds so obligated which previously had been obligated for such purpose on behalf of another veteran and were thereafter deobligated) and are later deobligated shall immediately upon deobligation become available to the Administrator for obligation for such purpose. The further obligation of such funds by the Administrator for such purpose shall not be delayed, directly or indirectly, in any manner by any officer or employee in the executive branch.

"TIME PERIODS FOR APPLICATION AND INITIATION OF TRAINING

"SEC. 17. Assistance may not be paid to an employer under this Act—

"(1) on behalf of a veteran who initially applies for a program of job training under this Act after September 30, 1989; or

"(2) for any such program which begins after March 31, 1990.

"EXPANSION OF TARGETED DELIMITING DATE EXTENSION

"SEC. 18. (a) Subject to the limitation on the availability of funds set forth in subsection (b), an associate degree program which is predominantly vocational in content may be considered by the Administrator, for the purposes of section 3462(a)(3) of title 38, United States Code, to be a course with an approved vocational objective if such degree program meets the requirements established in such title for approval of such program.

"(b) Funds for the purpose of carrying out subsection (a) shall be derived only from amounts appropriated pursuant to the authorizations of appropriations in section 16. Not more than a total of $25,000,000 of amounts so appropriated for fiscal years 1984 and 1985 shall be available for that purpose.

"EFFECTIVE DATE

"SEC. 19. This Act shall take effect on October 1, 1983."

[Amendment of Pub. L. 98–77, set out above, by Pub. L. 100–323 effective on 60th day after May 20, 1988, see section 16(b)(2) of Pub. L. 100–323, set out as a note under section 3104 of Title 38, Veterans' Benefits.]

[Pub. L. 99–238, title II, §201(f), Jan. 13, 1986, 99 Stat. 1768, provided that:

["(1) Except as provided in paragraph (2), the amendments made by this section [amending Pub. L. 98–77 above] shall take effect on the date of the enactment of this Act [Jan. 13, 1986].

["(2) The amendment made by subsection (e)(2) [amending section 17(a)(1) of Pub. L. 98–77 above] shall take effect on February 1, 1986."]

COORDINATION WITH PROGRAMS UNDER OTHER LAWS

For provisions requiring coordination of programs under section 3116(b) of Title 38, Veterans' Benefits, with programs under the Veterans' Job Training Act, Pub. L. 98–77, set out above, see section 202 of Pub. L. 99–238, set out as a note under section 3116 of Title 38.

§2914. Youth opportunity grants

(a) Grants

(1) In general

Using funds made available under section 2852(b)(1)(A) of this title, the Secretary shall make grants to eligible local boards and eligible entities described in subsection (d) of this section to provide activities described in subsection (b) of this section for youth to increase the long-term employment of youth who live in empowerment zones, enterprise communities, and high poverty areas and who seek assistance.

(2) Definition

In this section, the term "youth" means an individual who is not less than age 14 and not more than age 21.

(3) Grant period

The Secretary may make a grant under this section for a 1-year period, and may renew the grant for each of the 4 succeeding years.

(4) Grant awards

In making grants under this section, the Secretary shall ensure that grants are distributed equitably among local boards and entities serving urban areas and local boards and entities serving rural areas, taking into consideration the poverty rate in such urban and rural areas, as described in subsection (c)(3)(B) of this section.

(b) Use of funds

(1) In general

A local board or entity that receives a grant under this section shall use the funds made available through the grant to provide activities that meet the requirements of section 2854 of this title, except as provided in paragraph (2), as well as youth development activities such as activities relating to leadership development, citizenship, and community service, and recreation activities.

(2) Intensive placement and followup services

In providing activities under this section, a local board or entity shall provide—

(A) intensive placement services; and

(B) followup services for not less than 24 months after the completion of participation in the other activities described in this subsection, as appropriate.

(c) Eligible local boards

To be eligible to receive a grant under this section, a local board shall serve a community that—

(1) has been designated as an empowerment zone or enterprise community under section 1391 of title 26;

(2)(A) is a State without a zone or community described in paragraph (1); and

(B) has been designated as a high poverty area by the Governor of the State; or

(3) is 1 of 2 areas in a State that—

(A) have been designated by the Governor as areas for which a local board may apply for a grant under this section; and

(B) meet the poverty rate criteria set forth in subsections (a)(4), (b), and (d) of section 1392 of title 26.

(d) Eligible entities

To be eligible to receive a grant under this section, an entity (other than a local board) shall—

(1) be a recipient of financial assistance under section 2911 of this title; and

(2) serve a community that—

(A) meets the poverty rate criteria set forth in subsections (a)(4), (b), and (d) of section 1392 of title 26; and

(B) is located on an Indian reservation or serves Oklahoma Indians or Alaska Natives.

(e) Application

To be eligible to receive a grant under this section, a local board or entity shall submit an application to the Secretary at such time, in such manner, and containing such information as the Secretary may require, including—

(1) a description of the activities that the local board or entity will provide under this section to youth in the community described in subsection (c) of this section;

(2) a description of the performance measures negotiated under subsection (f) of this section, and the manner in which the local boards or entities will carry out the activities to meet the performance measures;

(3) a description of the manner in which the activities will be linked to activities described in section 2854 of this title; and

(4) a description of the community support, including financial support through leveraging additional public and private resources, for the activities.

(f) Performance measures

(1) In general

The Secretary shall negotiate and reach agreement with the local board or entity on performance measures for the indicators of performance referred to in subparagraphs (A) and (B) of section 2871(b)(2) of this title that will be used to evaluate the performance of the local board or entity in carrying out the activities described in subsection (b) of this section. Each local performance measure shall consist of such a[1] indicator of performance, and a performance level referred to in paragraph (2).

(2) Performance levels

The Secretary shall negotiate and reach agreement with the local board or entity regarding the levels of performance expected to be achieved by the local board or entity on the indicators of performance.

(g) Role model academy project

(1) In general

Using the funds made available pursuant to section 2852(b)(1)(A)(iv) of this title for fiscal year 1999, the Secretary shall provide assistance to an entity to carry out a project establishing a role model academy for out-of-school youth.

(2) Residential center

The entity shall use the assistance to establish an academy that consists of a residential center located on the site of a military installation closed or realigned pursuant to a law providing for closures and realignments of such installations.

(3) Services

The academy established pursuant to this subsection shall provide services that—

[1] So in original. Probably should be "an".

(A) utilize a military style model that emphasizes leadership skills and discipline, or another model of demonstrated effectiveness; and

(B) include vocational training, secondary school course work leading to a secondary school diploma or recognized equivalent, and the use of mentors who serve as role models and who provide academic training and career counseling to the youth.

(Pub. L. 105–220, title I, § 169, Aug. 7, 1998, 112 Stat. 1028; Pub. L. 106–113, div. B, § 1000(a)(4) [title V, § 518], Nov. 29, 1999, 113 Stat. 1535, 1501A–276.)

AMENDMENTS

1999—Subsec. (d)(2)(B). Pub. L. 106–113 substituted "or Alaska Natives." for "or Alaska Native villages or Native groups (as such terms are defined in section 1602 of title 43)."

§ 2915. Technical assistance

(a) General technical assistance

(1) In general

The Secretary shall provide, coordinate, and support the development of, appropriate training, technical assistance, staff development, and other activities, including assistance in replicating programs of demonstrated effectiveness, to States and localities, and, in particular, to assist States in making transitions from carrying out activities under the provisions of law repealed under section 199[1] to carrying out activities under this chapter.

(2) Form of assistance

In carrying out paragraph (1) on behalf of a State, or recipient of financial assistance under any of sections 2911 through 2914 of this title, the Secretary, after consultation with the State or grant recipient, may award grants and enter into contracts and cooperative agreements.

(3) Limitation

Grants or contracts awarded under paragraph (1) to entities other than States or local units of government that are for amounts in excess of $100,000 shall only be awarded on a competitive basis.

(b) Dislocated worker technical assistance

(1) Authority

Of the amounts available pursuant to section 2862(a)(2) of this title, the Secretary shall reserve not more than 5 percent of such amounts to provide technical assistance to States that do not meet the State performance measures described in section 2871 of this title with respect to employment and training activities for dislocated workers. Using such reserved funds, the Secretary may provide such assistance to other States, local areas, and other entities involved in providing assistance to dislocated workers, to promote the continuous improvement of assistance provided to dislocated workers, under this chapter.

[1] See References in Text note below.

(2) Training

Amounts reserved under this subsection may be used to provide for the training of staff, including specialists, who provide rapid response services. Such training shall include instruction in proven methods of promoting, establishing, and assisting labor-management committees. Such projects shall be administered through the dislocated worker office described in section 2918(b) of this title.

(Pub. L. 105–220, title I, § 170, Aug. 7, 1998, 112 Stat. 1030; Pub. L. 105–277, div. A, § 101(f) [title VIII, § 401(9), (10)], Oct. 21, 1998, 112 Stat. 2681–337, 2681–411.)

REFERENCES IN TEXT

Section 199, referred to in subsec. (a)(1), is section 199 of Pub. L. 105–220, title I, Aug. 7, 1998, 112 Stat. 1058. Section 199 repealed sections 1501 to 1505, 1511 to 1583, 1592 to 1735, 1737, 1751 to 1791h, 1792 to 1792b, and 2301 to 2314 of this title, section 211 of former Title 40, Appendix, Public Buildings, Property, and Works, sections 11421, 11441 to 11447, 11449, 11450, 11461 to 11466, 11471, and 11472 of Title 42, The Public Health and Welfare, sections 42101 to 42106 of Title 49, Transportation, and provisions set out as notes under sections 801, 1501, and 2301 of this title and section 1255a of Title 8, Aliens and Nationality. For complete classification of this section to the Code, see Tables.

AMENDMENTS

1998—Subsec. (a)(1). Pub. L. 105–277, § 101(f) [title VIII, § 401(9)], substituted "carrying out activities under this chapter" for "carry out activities under this chapter".

Subsec. (b)(2). Pub. L. 105–277, § 101(f) [title VIII, § 401(10)], substituted "section 2918(b)" for "section 2919(b)".

§ 2916. Demonstration, pilot, multiservice, research, and multistate projects

(a) Strategic plan

(1) In general

After consultation with States, localities, and other interested parties, the Secretary shall, every 2 years, publish in the Federal Register, a plan that describes the demonstration and pilot (including dislocated worker demonstration and pilot), multiservice, research, and multistate project priorities of the Department of Labor concerning employment and training for the 5-year period following the submission of the plan. Copies of the plan shall be transmitted to the appropriate committees of Congress.

(2) Factors

The plan published under paragraph (1) shall contain strategies to address national employment and training problems and take into account factors such as—

(A) the availability of existing research (as of the date of the publication);

(B) the need to ensure results that have interstate validity;

(C) the benefits of economies of scale and the efficiency of proposed projects; and

(D) the likelihood that the results of the projects will be useful to policymakers and stakeholders in addressing employment and training problems.

(b) Demonstration and pilot projects

(1) In general

Under a plan published under subsection (a) of this section, the Secretary shall, through grants or contracts, carry out demonstration and pilot projects for the purpose of developing and implementing techniques and approaches, and demonstrating the effectiveness of specialized methods, in addressing employment and training needs. Such projects shall include the provision of direct services to individuals to enhance employment opportunities and an evaluation component and may include—

(A) the establishment of advanced manufacturing technology skill centers developed through local partnerships of industry, labor, education, community-based organizations, and economic development organizations to meet unmet, high-tech skill needs of local communities;

(B) projects that provide training to upgrade the skills of employed workers who reside and are employed in enterprise communities or empowerment zones;

(C) programs conducted jointly with the Department of Defense to develop training programs utilizing computer-based and other innovative learning technologies;

(D) projects that promote the use of distance learning, enabling students to take courses through the use of media technology such as videos, teleconferencing computers, and the Internet;

(E) projects that assist in providing comprehensive services to increase the employment rates of out-of-school youth residing in targeted high poverty areas within empowerment zones and enterprise communities;

(F) the establishment of partnerships with national organizations with special expertise in developing, organizing, and administering employment and training services, for individuals with disabilities, at the national, State, and local levels;

(G) projects to assist public housing authorities that provide, to public housing residents, job training programs that demonstrate success in upgrading the job skills and promoting employment of the residents; and

(H) projects that assist local areas to develop and implement local self-sufficiency standards to evaluate the degree to which participants in programs under this chapter are achieving self-sufficiency.

(2) Limitations

(A) Competitive awards

Grants or contracts awarded for carrying out demonstration and pilot projects under this subsection shall be awarded in accordance with generally applicable Federal requirements.

(B) Eligible entities

Grants or contracts may be awarded under this subsection only to—

(i) entities with recognized expertise in—

(I) conducting national demonstration projects;

(II) utilizing state-of-the-art demonstration methods; or

(III) conducting evaluations of workforce investment projects; or

(ii) State and local entities with expertise in operating or overseeing workforce investment programs.

(C) Time limits

The Secretary shall establish appropriate time limits for carrying out demonstration and pilot projects under this subsection.

(c) Multiservice projects, research projects, and multistate projects

(1) Multiservice projects

Under a plan published under subsection (a) of this section, the Secretary shall, through grants or contracts, carry out multiservice projects—

(A) that will test an array of approaches to the provision of employment and training services to a variety of targeted populations;

(B) in which the entity carrying out the project, in conjunction with employers, organized labor, and other groups such as the disability community, will design, develop, and test various training approaches in order to determine effective practices; and

(C) that will assist in the development and replication of effective service delivery strategies for targeted populations for the national employment and training system as a whole.

(2) Research projects

(A) In general

Under a plan published under subsection (a) of this section, the Secretary shall, through grants or contracts, carry out research projects that will contribute to the solution of employment and training problems in the United States.

(B) Formula improvement study and report

(i) Study

The Secretary shall conduct a 2-year study concerning improvements in the formulas described in section 2862(b)(1)(B) of this title and paragraphs (2)(A) and (3) of section 2863(b) of this title (regarding distributing funds under subchapter II of this chapter to States and local areas for adult employment and training activities). In conducting the study, the Secretary shall examine means of improving the formulas by—

(I) developing formulas based on statistically reliable data;

(II) developing formulas that are consistent with the goals and objectives of this chapter; and

(III) developing formulas based on organizational and financial stability of State boards and local boards.

(ii) Report

The Secretary shall prepare and submit to Congress a report containing the results of the study, including recommendations for improved formulas.

(3) Multistate projects

(A) In general

(i) Authority

Under a plan published under subsection (a) of this section, the Secretary may, through grants or contracts, carry out multistate projects that require demonstrated expertise that is available at the national level to effectively disseminate best practices and models for implementing employment and training services, address the specialized employment and training needs of particular service populations, or address industry-wide skill shortages.

(ii) Design of grants

Grants or contracts awarded under this subsection shall be designed to obtain information relating to the provision of services under different economic conditions or to various demographic groups in order to provide guidance at the national and State levels about how best to administer specific employment and training services.

(4) Limitations

(A) Competitive awards

Grants or contracts awarded for carrying out projects under this subsection in amounts that exceed $100,000 shall be awarded only on a competitive basis, except that a noncompetitive award may be made in the case of a project that is funded jointly with other public or private sector entities that provide a substantial portion of assistance under the grant or contract for the project.

(B) Time limits

A grant or contract shall not be awarded under this subsection to the same organization for more than 3 consecutive years unless such grant or contract is competitively reevaluated within such period.

(C) Peer review

(i) In general

The Secretary shall utilize a peer review process—

(I) to review and evaluate all applications for grants in amounts that exceed $500,000 that are submitted under this section; and

(II) to review and designate exemplary and promising programs under this section.

(ii) Availability of funds

The Secretary is authorized to use funds provided under this section to carry out peer review activities under this subparagraph.

(D) Priority

In awarding grants or contracts under this subsection, priority shall be provided to entities with nationally recognized expertise in the methods, techniques, and knowledge of workforce investment activities and shall include appropriate time limits, established by the Secretary, for the duration of such projects.

(d) Dislocated worker projects

Of the amount made available pursuant to section 2862(a)(2)(A) of this title for any program year, the Secretary shall use not more than 10 percent of such amount to carry out demonstration and pilot projects, multiservice projects, and multistate projects, relating to the employment and training needs of dislocated workers. Of the requirements of this section, such projects shall be subject only to the provisions relating to review and evaluation of applications under subsection (c)(4)(C) of this section. Such projects may include demonstration and pilot projects relating to promoting self-employment, promoting job creation, averting dislocations, assisting dislocated farmers, assisting dislocated fishermen, and promoting public works. Such projects shall be administered through the dislocated worker office described in section 2918(b) of this title.

(e) Energy efficiency and renewable energy worker training program

(1) Grant program

(A) In general

Not later than 6 months after December 19, 2007, the Secretary, in consultation with the Secretary of Energy, shall establish an energy efficiency and renewable energy worker training program under which the Secretary shall carry out the activities described in paragraph (2) to achieve the purposes of this subsection.

(B) Eligibility

For purposes of providing assistance and services under the program established under this subsection—

(i) target populations of eligible individuals to be given priority for training and other services shall include—

(I) workers impacted by national energy and environmental policy;

(II) individuals in need of updated training related to the energy efficiency and renewable energy industries;

(III) veterans, or past and present members of reserve components of the Armed Forces;

(IV) unemployed individuals;

(V) individuals, including at-risk youth, seeking employment pathways out of poverty and into economic self-sufficiency; and

(VI) formerly incarcerated, adjudicated, nonviolent offenders; and

(ii) energy efficiency and renewable energy industries eligible to participate in a program under this subsection include—

(I) the energy-efficient building, construction, and retrofits industries;

(II) the renewable electric power industry;

(III) the energy efficient and advanced drive train vehicle industry;

(IV) the biofuels industry;

(V) the deconstruction and materials use industries;

(VI) the energy efficiency assessment industry serving the residential, commercial, or industrial sectors; and

(VII) manufacturers that produce sustainable products using environmentally sustainable processes and materials.

(2) Activities

(A) National research program

Under the program established under paragraph (1), the Secretary, acting through the Bureau of Labor Statistics, where appropriate, shall collect and analyze labor market data to track workforce trends resulting from energy-related initiatives carried out under this subsection. Activities carried out under this paragraph shall include—

(i) tracking and documentation of academic and occupational competencies as well as future skill needs with respect to renewable energy and energy efficiency technology;

(ii) tracking and documentation of occupational information and workforce training data with respect to renewable energy and energy efficiency technology;

(iii) collaborating with State agencies, workforce investments boards, industry, organized labor, and community and nonprofit organizations to disseminate information on successful innovations for labor market services and worker training with respect to renewable energy and energy efficiency technology;

(iv) serving as a clearinghouse for best practices in workforce development, job placement, and collaborative training partnerships;

(v) encouraging the establishment of workforce training initiatives with respect to renewable energy and energy efficiency technologies;

(vi) linking research and development in renewable energy and energy efficiency technology with the development of standards and curricula for current and future jobs;

(vii) assessing new employment and work practices including career ladder and upgrade training as well as high performance work systems; and

(viii) providing technical assistance and capacity building to national and State energy partnerships, including industry and labor representatives.

(B) National Energy Training Partnership Grants

(i) In general

Under the program established under paragraph (1), the Secretary shall award National Energy Training Partnerships Grants on a competitive basis to eligible entities to enable such entities to carry out training that leads to economic self-sufficiency and to develop an energy efficiency and renewable energy industries workforce. Grants shall be awarded under this subparagraph so as to ensure geographic diversity with at least 2 grants awarded to entities located in each of the 4 Petroleum Administration for Defense Districts with no subdistricts, and at least 1 grant awarded to an entity located in each of the subdistricts of the Petroleum Administration for Defense District with subdistricts.

(ii) Eligibility

To be eligible to receive a grant under clause (i), an entity shall be a nonprofit partnership that—

(I) includes the equal participation of industry, including public or private employers, and labor organizations, including joint labor-management training programs, and may include workforce investment boards, community-based organizations, qualified service and conservation corps, educational institutions, small businesses, cooperatives, State and local veterans agencies, and veterans service organizations; and

(II) demonstrates—

(aa) experience in implementing and operating worker skills training and education programs;

(bb) the ability to identify and involve in training programs carried out under this grant, target populations of individuals who would benefit from training and be actively involved in activities related to energy efficiency and renewable energy industries; and

(cc) the ability to help individuals achieve economic self-sufficiency.

(iii) Priority

Priority shall be given to partnerships which leverage additional public and private resources to fund training programs, including cash or in-kind matches from participating employers.

(C) State labor market research, information, and labor exchange research program

(i) In general

Under the program established under paragraph (1), the Secretary shall award competitive grants to States to enable such States to administer labor market and labor exchange information programs that include the implementation of the activities described in clause (ii), in coordination with the one-stop delivery system.

(ii) Activities

A State shall use amounts awarded under a grant under this subparagraph to provide funding to the State agency that administers the Wagner-Peyser Act [29 U.S.C. 49 et seq.] and State unemployment compensation programs to carry out the following activities using State agency merit staff:

(I) The identification of job openings in the renewable energy and energy efficiency sector.

(II) The administration of skill and aptitude testing and assessment for workers.

(III) The counseling, case management, and referral of qualified job seekers to openings and training programs, including energy efficiency and renewable energy training programs.

(D) State energy training partnership program

(i) In general

Under the program established under paragraph (1), the Secretary shall award competitive grants to States to enable such States to administer renewable energy and energy efficiency workforce development programs that include the implementation of the activities described in clause (ii).

(ii) Partnerships

A State shall use amounts awarded under a grant under this subparagraph to award competitive grants to eligible State Energy Sector Partnerships to enable such Partnerships to coordinate with existing apprenticeship and labor management training programs and implement training programs that lead to the economic self-sufficiency of trainees.

(iii) Eligibility

To be eligible to receive a grant under this subparagraph, a State Energy Sector Partnership shall—

(I) consist of nonprofit organizations that include equal participation from industry, including public or private nonprofit employers, and labor organizations, including joint labor-management training programs, and may include representatives from local governments, the workforce investment system, including one-stop career centers, community based organizations, qualified service and conservation corps, community colleges, and other post-secondary institutions, small businesses, cooperatives, State and local veterans agencies, and veterans service organizations;

(II) demonstrate experience in implementing and operating worker skills training and education programs; and

(III) demonstrate the ability to identify and involve in training programs, target populations of workers who would benefit from training and be actively involved in activities related to energy efficiency and renewable energy industries.

(iv) Priority

In awarding grants under this subparagraph, the Secretary shall give priority to States that demonstrate that activities under the grant—

(I) meet national energy policies associated with energy efficiency, renewable energy, and the reduction of emissions of greenhouse gases;

(II) meet State energy policies associated with energy efficiency, renewable energy, and the reduction of emissions of greenhouse gases; and

(III) leverage additional public and private resources to fund training programs, including cash or in-kind matches from participating employers.

(v) Coordination

A grantee under this subparagraph shall coordinate activities carried out under the grant with existing other appropriate training programs, including apprenticeship and labor management training programs, including such activities referenced in paragraph (3)(A), and implement training programs that lead to the economic self-sufficiency of trainees.

(E) Pathways Out of Poverty Demonstration Program

(i) In general

Under the program established under paragraph (1), the Secretary shall award competitive grants of sufficient size to eligible entities to enable such entities to carry out training that leads to economic self-sufficiency. The Secretary shall give priority to entities that serve individuals in families with income of less than 200 percent of the sufficiency standard for the local areas where the training is conducted that specifies, as defined by the State, or where such standard is not established, the income needs of families, by family size, the number and ages of children in the family, and sub-State geographical considerations. Grants shall be awarded to ensure geographic diversity.

(ii) Eligible entities

To be eligible to receive a grant an entity shall be a partnership that—

(I) includes community-based nonprofit organizations, educational institutions with expertise in serving low-income adults or youth, public or private employers from the industry sectors described in paragraph (1)(B)(ii), and labor organizations representing workers in such industry sectors;

(II) demonstrates a record of successful experience in implementing and operating worker skills training and education programs;

(III) coordinates activities, where appropriate, with the workforce investment system; and

(IV) demonstrates the ability to recruit individuals for training and to support such individuals to successful completion in training programs carried out under this grant, targeting populations of workers who are or will be engaged in activities related to energy efficiency and renewable energy industries.

(iii) Priorities

In awarding grants under this paragraph, the Secretary shall give priority to applicants that—

(I) target programs to benefit low-income workers, unemployed youth and adults, high school dropouts, or other underserved sectors of the workforce within areas of high poverty;

(II) ensure that supportive services are integrated with education and training, and delivered by organizations with direct access to and experience with targeted populations;

(III) leverage additional public and private resources to fund training programs, including cash or in-kind matches from participating employers;

(IV) involve employers and labor organizations in the determination of relevant skills and competencies and ensure that the certificates or credentials that result from the training are employer-recognized;

(V) deliver courses at alternative times (such as evening and weekend programs) and locations most convenient and accessible to participants and link adult remedial education with occupational skills training; and

(VI) demonstrate substantial experience in administering local, municipal, State, Federal, foundation, or private entity grants.

(iv) Data collection

Grantees shall collect and report the following information:

(I) The number of participants.

(II) The demographic characteristics of participants, including race, gender, age, parenting status, participation in other Federal programs, education and literacy level at entry, significant barriers to employment (such as limited English proficiency, criminal record, addiction or mental health problem requiring treatment, or mental disability).

(III) The services received by participants, including training, education, and supportive services.

(IV) The amount of program spending per participant.

(V) Program completion rates.

(VI) Factors determined as significantly interfering with program participation or completion.

(VII) The rate of job placement and the rate of employment retention after 1 year.

(VIII) The average wage at placement, including any benefits, and the rate of average wage increase after 1 year.

(IX) Any post-employment supportive services provided.

The Secretary shall assist grantees in the collection of data under this clause by making available, where practicable, low-cost means of tracking the labor market outcomes of participants, and by providing standardized reporting forms, where appropriate.

(3) Activities

(A) In general

Activities to be carried out under a program authorized by subparagraph (B), (D), or (E) of paragraph (2) shall be coordinated with existing systems or providers, as appropriate. Such activities may include—

(i) occupational skills training, including curriculum development, on-the-job training, and classroom training;

(ii) safety and health training;

(iii) the provision of basic skills, literacy, GED, English as a second language, and job readiness training;

(iv) individual referral and tuition assistance for a community college training program, or any training program leading to an industry-recognized certificate;

(v) internship programs in fields related to energy efficiency and renewable energy;

(vi) customized training in conjunction with an existing registered apprenticeship program or labor-management partnership;

(vii) incumbent worker and career ladder training and skill upgrading and retraining;

(viii) the implementation of transitional jobs strategies; and

(ix) the provision of supportive services.

(B) Outreach activities

In addition to the activities authorized under subparagraph (A), activities authorized for programs under subparagraph (E) of paragraph (2) may include the provision of outreach, recruitment, career guidance, and case management services.

(4) Worker protections and nondiscrimination requirements

(A) Application of WIA

The provisions of sections 2931 and 2938 of this title shall apply to all programs carried out with assistance under this subsection.

(B) Consultation with labor organizations

If a labor organization represents a substantial number of workers who are engaged in similar work or training in an area that is the same as the area that is proposed to be funded under this Act, the labor organization shall be provided an opportunity to be consulted and to submit comments in regard to such a proposal.

(5) Performance measures

(A) In general

The Secretary shall negotiate and reach agreement with the eligible entities that receive grants and assistance under this section on performance measures for the indicators of performance referred to in subparagraphs (A) and (B) of section 2871(b)(2) of this title that will be used to evaluate the performance of the eligible entity in carrying out the activities described in subsection (e)(2). Each performance measure shall consist of such an indicator of performance, and a performance level referred to in subparagraph (B).

(B) Performance levels

The Secretary shall negotiate and reach agreement with the eligible entity regarding the levels of performance expected to be achieved by the eligible entity on the indicators of performance.

(6) Report

(A) Status report

Not later than 18 months after December 19, 2007, the Secretary shall transmit a report to the Senate Committee on Energy and Natural Resources, the Senate Committee on Health, Education, Labor, and Pensions, the House Committee on Education and Labor, and the House Committee on Energy and Commerce on the training program established by this subsection. The report shall include a description of the entities receiving funding and the activities carried out by such entities.

(B) Evaluation

Not later than 3 years after December 19, 2007, the Secretary shall transmit to the Senate Committee on Energy and Natural Resources, the Senate Committee on Health, Education, Labor, and Pensions, the House Committee on Education and Labor, and the House Committee on Energy and Commerce an assessment of such program and an evaluation of the activities carried out by entities receiving funding from such program.

(7) Definition

As used in this subsection, the term "renewable energy" has the meaning given such term in section 15852(b)(2) of title 42.

(8) Authorization of appropriations

There is authorized to be appropriated to carry out this subsection, $125,000,000 for each fiscal year, of which—

(A) not to exceed 20 percent of the amount appropriated in each such fiscal year shall be made available for, and shall be equally divided between, national labor market research and information under paragraph (2)(A) and State labor market information and labor exchange research under paragraph (2)(C), and not more than 2 percent of such amount shall be for the evaluation and report required under paragraph (4);[1]

(B) 20 percent shall be dedicated to Pathways Out of Poverty Demonstration Programs under paragraph (2)(E); and

(C) the remainder shall be divided equally between National Energy Partnership Training Grants under paragraph (2)(B) and State energy training partnership grants under paragraph (2)(D).

(Pub. L. 105–220, title I, § 171, Aug. 7, 1998, 112 Stat. 1031; Pub. L. 105–277, div. A, § 101(f) [title VIII, § 401(11)], Oct. 21, 1998, 112 Stat. 2681–337, 2681–411; Pub. L. 110–140, title X, § 1002, Dec. 19, 2007, 121 Stat. 1748.)

REFERENCES IN TEXT

The Wagner-Peyser Act, referred to in subsec. (e)(2)(C)(ii), is act June 6, 1933, ch. 49, 48 Stat. 113, which is classified generally to chapter 4B (§ 49 et seq.) of this title. For complete classification of this Act to the Code, see Short Title note set out under section 49 of this title and Tables.

This Act, referred to in subsec. (e)(4)(B), is Pub. L. 105–220, Aug. 7, 1998, 112 Stat. 936, known as the Workforce Investment Act of 1998. For complete classification of this Act to the Code, see Short Title note set out under section 9201 of Title 20, Education, and Tables.

AMENDMENTS

2007—Subsec. (e). Pub. L. 110–140 added subsec. (e).

1998—Subsec. (b)(2)(A). Pub. L. 105–277, which directed the amendment of subsec. (b)(2) of this section by substituting "in accordance with generally applicable Federal requirements." for "'only on a competitive' and all that follows through the period", was executed to subsec. (b)(2)(A) by making the substitution for "only on a competitive basis, except that a noncompetitive award may be made in the case of a project that is funded jointly with other public or private sector entities that provide a portion of the funding for the project.", to reflect the probable intent of Congress.

EFFECTIVE DATE OF 2007 AMENDMENT

Amendment by Pub. L. 110–140 effective on the date that is 1 day after Dec. 19, 2007, see section 1601 of Pub. L. 110–140, set out as an Effective Date note under section 1824 of Title 2, The Congress.

DEMONSTRATION PROGRAMS AND PROJECTS TO PROVIDE TECHNICAL SKILLS TRAINING FOR WORKERS

Pub. L. 105–277, div. C, title IV, § 414(c), Oct. 21, 1998, 112 Stat. 2681–653, as amended, formerly set out as a note under this section, was transferred and is classified to section 2916a of this title.

§ 2916a. Job training grants

(1) In general

The Secretary of Labor shall use funds available under section 1356(s)(2) of title 8 to award grants to eligible entities to provide job training and related activities for workers to assist them in obtaining or upgrading employment in industries and economic sectors identified pursuant to paragraph (4) that are projected to experience significant growth and ensure that job training and related activities funded by such grants are coordinated with the public workforce investment system.

(2) Use of funds

(A) Training provided

Funds under this section may be used to provide job training services and related activities that are designed to assist workers (including unemployed and employed workers) in gaining the skills and competencies needed to obtain or upgrade career ladder employment positions in the industries and economic sectors identified pursuant to paragraph (4).

(B) Enhanced training programs and information

In order to facilitate the provision of job training services described in subparagraph (A), funds under this section may be used to assist in the development and implementation of model activities such as developing appropriate curricula to build core competencies and train workers, identifying and disseminating career and skill information, and increasing the integration of community and technical college activities with activities of businesses and the public workforce investment system to meet the training needs for the industries and economic sectors identified pursuant to paragraph (4).

(3) Eligible entities

Grants under this section may be awarded to partnerships of private and public sector entities, which may include—

(A) businesses or business-related nonprofit organizations, such as trade associations;

---

[1] So in original. Probably should be paragraph "(6)".

(B) education and training providers, including community colleges and other community-based organizations; and

(C) entities involved in administering the workforce investment system established under title I of the Workforce Investment Act of 1998 [29 U.S.C. 2801 et seq.], and economic development agencies.

(4) High growth industries and economic sectors

For purposes of this section, the Secretary of Labor, in consultation with State workforce investment boards, shall identify industries and economic sectors that are projected to experience significant growth, taking into account appropriate factors, such as the industries and sectors that—

(A) are projected to add substantial numbers of new jobs to the economy;

(B) are being transformed by technology and innovation requiring new skill sets for workers;

(C) are new and emerging businesses that are projected to grow; or

(D) have a significant impact on the economy overall or on the growth of other industries and economic sectors.

(5) Equitable distribution

In awarding grants under this section, the Secretary of Labor shall ensure an equitable distribution of such grants across geographically diverse areas.

(6) Leveraging of resources and authority to require match

(A) Leveraging of resources

In awarding grants under this section, the Secretary of Labor shall take into account, in addition to other factors the Secretary determines are appropriate—

(i) the extent to which resources other than the funds provided under this section will be made available by the eligible entities applying for grants to support the activities carried out under this section; and

(ii) the ability of such entities to continue to carry out and expand such activities after the expiration of the grants.

(B) Authority to require match

The Secretary of Labor may require the provision of specified levels of a matching share of cash or noncash resources from resources other than the funds provided under this section for projects funded under this section.

(7) Performance accountability

The Secretary of Labor shall require grantees to report on the employment outcomes obtained by workers receiving training under this section using indicators of performance that are consistent with other indicators used for employment and training programs administered by the Secretary, such as entry into employment, retention in employment, and increases in earnings. The Secretary of Labor may also require grantees to participate in evaluations of projects carried out under this section.

(Pub. L. 105–277, div. C, title IV, § 414(c), Oct. 21, 1998, 112 Stat. 2681–653; Pub. L. 106–313, title I, § 111, Oct. 17, 2000, 114 Stat. 1257; Pub. L. 108–447, div. J, title IV, § 428, Dec. 8, 2004, 118 Stat. 3358.)

REFERENCES IN TEXT

The Workforce Investment Act of 1998, referred to in par. (3)(C), is Pub. L. 105–220, Aug. 7, 1998, 112 Stat. 936, as amended. Title I of the Act is classified principally to this chapter. For complete classification of this Act to the Code, see Short Title note set out under section 9201 of Title 20, Education, and Tables.

CODIFICATION

Section was formerly set out as a note under section 2916 of this title.

Section was enacted as part of the American Competitiveness and Workforce Improvement Act of 1998 and also as part of the Omnibus Consolidated and Emergency Supplemental Appropriations Act, 1999, and not as part of title I of the Workforce Investment Act of 1998 which comprises this chapter.

AMENDMENTS

2004—Pub. L. 108–447 amended section catchline and text generally, substituting provisions relating to job training grants for provisions relating to demonstration programs and projects to provide technical skills training for workers.

2000—Pub. L. 106–313 amended section catchline and text generally. Prior to amendment, text read as follows:

"(1) IN GENERAL.—In establishing demonstration programs under section 1732(c) of this title, as in effect on October 21, 1998, or demonstration programs or projects under section 2916(b) of this title, the Secretary of Labor shall use funds available under section 1356(s)(2) of title 8 to establish demonstration programs or projects to provide technical skills training for workers, including both employed and unemployed workers.

"(2) GRANTS.—The Secretary of Labor shall award grants to carry out the programs and projects described in paragraph (1) to—

"(A)(i) private industry councils established under section 1512 of this title, as in effect on October 21, 1998; or

"(ii) local boards that will carry out such programs or projects through one-stop delivery systems established under section 2841 of this title; or

"(B) regional consortia of councils or local boards described in subparagraph (A)."

EFFECTIVE DATE OF 2004 AMENDMENT

Amendment by Pub. L. 108–447 effective 90 days after Dec. 8, 2004, see section 430(a) of Pub. L. 108–447, set out as a note under section 1182 of Title 8, Aliens and Nationality.

§ 2917. Evaluations

(a) Programs and activities carried out under this chapter

For the purpose of improving the management and effectiveness of programs and activities carried out under this chapter, the Secretary shall provide for the continuing evaluation of the programs and activities, including those programs and activities carried out under section 2916 of this title. Such evaluations shall address—

(1) the general effectiveness of such programs and activities in relation to their cost, including the extent to which the programs and activities—

(A) improve the employment competencies of participants in comparison to comparably-situated individuals who did not participate in such programs and activities; and

(B) to the extent feasible, increase the level of total employment over the level that would have existed in the absence of such programs and activities;

(2) the effectiveness of the performance measures relating to such programs and activities;

(3) the effectiveness of the structure and mechanisms for delivery of services through such programs and activities;

(4) the impact of the programs and activities on the community and participants involved;

(5) the impact of such programs and activities on related programs and activities;

(6) the extent to which such programs and activities meet the needs of various demographic groups; and

(7) such other factors as may be appropriate.

(b) Other programs and activities

The Secretary may conduct evaluations of other federally funded employment-related programs and activities under other provisions of law.

(c) Techniques

Evaluations conducted under this section shall utilize appropriate methodology and research designs, including the use of control groups chosen by scientific random assignment methodologies. The Secretary shall conduct as least 1 multisite control group evaluation under this section by the end of fiscal year 2005.

(d) Reports

The entity carrying out an evaluation described in subsection (a) or (b) of this section shall prepare and submit to the Secretary a draft report and a final report containing the results of the evaluation.

(e) Reports to Congress

Not later than 30 days after the completion of such a draft report, the Secretary shall transmit the draft report to the Committee on Education and the Workforce of the House of Representatives and the Committee on Labor and Human Resources of the Senate. Not later than 60 days after the completion of such a final report, the Secretary shall transmit the final report to such committees of the Congress.

(f) Coordination

The Secretary shall ensure the coordination of evaluations carried out by States pursuant to section 2871(e) of this title with the evaluations carried out under this section.

(Pub. L. 105–220, title I, §172, Aug. 7, 1998, 112 Stat. 1034.)

CHANGE OF NAME

Committee on Education and the Workforce of House of Representatives changed to Committee on Education and Labor of House of Representatives by House Resolution No. 6, One Hundred Tenth Congress, Jan. 5, 2007. Committee on Labor and Human Resources of Senate changed to Committee on Health, Education, Labor, and Pensions of Senate by Senate Resolution No. 20, One Hundred Sixth Congress, Jan. 19, 1999.

§ 2918. National emergency grants

(a) In general

The Secretary is authorized to award national emergency grants in a timely manner—

(1) to an entity described in subsection (c) of this section to provide employment and training assistance to workers affected by major economic dislocations, such as plant closures, mass layoffs, or closures and realignments of military installations;

(2) to provide assistance to the Governor of any State within the boundaries of which is an area that has suffered an emergency or a major disaster as defined in paragraphs (1) and (2), respectively, of section 5122 of title 42 (referred to in this section as the "disaster area") to provide disaster relief employment in the area;

(3) to provide additional assistance to a State or local board for eligible dislocated workers in a case in which the State or local board has expended the funds provided under this section to carry out activities described in paragraphs (1) and (2) and can demonstrate the need for additional funds to provide appropriate services for such workers, in accordance with requirements prescribed by the Secretary; and

(4) from funds appropriated under section 2919(c) of this title—

(A) to a State or entity (as defined in subsection (c)(1)(B) of this section) to carry out subsection (f) of this section, including providing assistance to eligible individuals; and

(B) to a State or entity (as so defined) to carry out subsection (g) of this section, including providing assistance to eligible individuals.

(b) Administration

The Secretary shall designate a dislocated worker office to coordinate the functions of the Secretary under this chapter relating to employment and training activities for dislocated workers, including activities carried out under the national emergency grants.

(c) Employment and training assistance requirements

(1) Grant recipient eligibility

(A) Application

To be eligible to receive a grant under subsection (a)(1) of this section, an entity shall submit an application to the Secretary at such time, in such manner, and containing such information as the Secretary may require.

(B) Eligible entity

In this paragraph, the term "entity" means a State, a local board, an entity described in section 2911(c) of this title, entities determined to be eligible by the Governor of the State involved, and other entities that demonstrate to the Secretary the capability to effectively respond to the circumstances relating to particular dislocations.

(2) Participant eligibility

(A) In general

In order to be eligible to receive employment and training assistance under a national emergency grant awarded pursuant to subsection (a)(1) of this section, an individual shall be—

(i) a dislocated worker;

(ii) a civilian employee of the Department of Defense or the Department of Energy employed at a military installation that is being closed, or that will undergo realignment, within the next 24 months after the date of the determination of eligibility;

(iii) an individual who is employed in a nonmanagerial position with a Department of Defense contractor, who is determined by the Secretary of Defense to be at-risk of termination from employment as a result of reductions in defense expenditures, and whose employer is converting operations from defense to nondefense applications in order to prevent worker layoffs; or

(iv) a member of the Armed Forces who—

(I) was on active duty or full-time National Guard duty;

(II)(aa) is involuntarily separated (as defined in section 1141 of title 10) from active duty or full-time National Guard duty; or

(bb) is separated from active duty or full-time National Guard duty pursuant to a special separation benefits program under section 1174a of title 10 or the voluntary separation incentive program under section 1175 of that title;

(III) is not entitled to retired or retained pay incident to the separation described in subclause (II); and

(IV) applies for such employment and training assistance before the end of the 180-day period beginning on the date of that separation.

(B) Retraining assistance

The individuals described in subparagraph (A)(iii) shall be eligible for retraining assistance to upgrade skills by obtaining marketable skills needed to support the conversion described in subparagraph (A)(iii).

(C) Additional requirements

The Secretary shall establish and publish additional requirements related to eligibility for employment and training assistance under the national emergency grants to ensure effective use of the funds available for this purpose.

(D) Definitions

In this paragraph, the terms "military institution"[1] and "realignment" have the meanings given the terms in section 2910 of the Defense Base Closure and Realignment Act of 1990 (Public Law 101–510; 10 U.S.C. 2687 note).

(d) Disaster relief employment assistance requirements

(1) In general

Funds made available under subsection (a)(2) of this section—

(A) shall be used to provide disaster relief employment on projects that provide food, clothing, shelter, and other humanitarian assistance for disaster victims, and projects regarding demolition, cleaning, repair, renovation, and reconstruction of damaged and destroyed structures, facilities, and lands located within the disaster area;

(B) may be expended through public and private agencies and organizations engaged in such projects; and

(C) may be expended to provide employment and training activities.

(2) Eligibility

An individual shall be eligible to be offered disaster relief employment under subsection (a)(2) of this section if such individual is a dislocated worker, is a long-term unemployed individual, or is temporarily or permanently laid off as a consequence of the disaster.

(3) Limitations on disaster relief employment

No individual shall be employed under subsection (a)(2) of this section for more than 6 months for work related to recovery from a single natural disaster.

(e) Additional assistance

(1) In general

From the amount appropriated and made available to carry out this section for any program year, the Secretary shall use not more than $15,000,000 to make grants to not more than 8 States to provide employment and training activities under section 2864 of this title, in accordance with subchapter II of this chapter.

(2) Eligible States

The Secretary shall make a grant under paragraph (1) to a State for a program year if—

(A)(i) the amount of the allotment that would be made to the State for the program year under the formula specified in section 1602(a) of this title, as in effect on July 1, 1998; is greater than

(ii) the amount of the allotment that would be made to the State for the program year under the formula specified in section 2862(b)(1)(B) of this title; and

(B) the State is 1 of the 8 States with the greatest quotient obtained by dividing—

(i) the amount described in subparagraph (A)(i); by

(ii) the amount described in subparagraph (A)(ii).

(3) Amount of grants

Subject to paragraph (1), the amount of the grant made under paragraph (1) to a State for a program year shall be based on the difference between—

(A) the amount of the allotment that would be made to the State for the program year under the formula specified in section 1602(a) of this title, as in effect on July 1, 1998; and

(B) the amount of the allotment that would be made to the State for the program year under the formula specified in section 2862(b)(1)(B) of this title.

(4) Allocation of funds

A State that receives a grant under paragraph (1) for a program year—

[1] So in original. Probably should be "'military installation'".

(A) shall allocate funds made available through the grant on the basis of the formula used by the State to allocate funds within the State for that program year under—

(i) paragraph (2)(A) or (3) of section 2863(b) of this title; or

(ii) paragraph (2)(B) of section 2863(b) of this title; and

(B) shall use the funds in the same manner as the State uses other funds allocated under the appropriate paragraph of section 2863(b) of this title.

(f) Health insurance coverage assistance for eligible individuals

(1) In general

Funds made available to a State or entity under paragraph (4)(A) of subsection (a) of this section may be used by the State or entity for the following:

(A) Health insurance coverage

To assist an eligible individual and such individual's qualifying family members in enrolling in qualified health insurance.

(B) Administrative and start-up expenses

To pay the administrative expenses related to the enrollment of eligible individuals and such individuals' qualifying family members in qualified health insurance, including—

(i) eligibility verification activities;

(ii) the notification of eligible individuals of available qualified health insurance options;

(iii) processing qualified health insurance costs credit eligibility certificates provided for under section 7527 of title 26;

(iv) providing assistance to eligible individuals in enrolling in qualified health insurance;

(v) the development or installation of necessary data management systems; and

(vi) any other expenses determined appropriate by the Secretary, including start-up costs and on going administrative expenses to carry out clauses (iv) through (ix) of paragraph (2)(A).

(2) Qualified health insurance

For purposes of this subsection and subsection (g) of this section—

(A) In general

The term "qualified health insurance" means any of the following:

(i) Coverage under a COBRA continuation provision (as defined in section 1191b(d)(1) of this title).

(ii) State-based continuation coverage provided by the State under a State law that requires such coverage.

(iii) Coverage offered through a qualified State high risk pool (as defined in section 300gg–44(c)(2) of title 42).

(iv) Coverage under a health insurance program offered for State employees.

(v) Coverage under a State-based health insurance program that is comparable to the health insurance program offered for State employees.

(vi) Coverage through an arrangement entered into by a State and—

(I) a group health plan (including such a plan which is a multiemployer plan as defined in section 1002(37) of this title),

(II) an issuer of health insurance coverage,

(III) an administrator, or

(IV) an employer.

(vii) Coverage offered through a State arrangement with a private sector health care coverage purchasing pool.

(viii) Coverage under a State-operated health plan that does not receive any Federal financial participation.

(ix) Coverage under a group health plan that is available through the employment of the eligible individual's spouse.

(x) In the case of any eligible individual and such individual's qualifying family members, coverage under individual health insurance if the eligible individual was covered under individual health insurance during the entire 30-day period that ends on the date that such individual became separated from the employment which qualified such individual for—

(I) in the case of an eligible TAA recipient, the allowance described in section 35(c)(2) of title 26,

(II) in the case of an eligible alternative TAA recipient, the benefit described in section 35(c)(3)(B) of such title, or

(III) in the case of any eligible PBGC pension recipient, the benefit described in section 35(c)(4)(B) of such title.

For purposes of this clause, the term "individual health insurance" means any insurance which constitutes medical care offered to individuals other than in connection with a group health plan and does not include Federal- or State-based health insurance coverage.

(B) Requirements for State-based coverage

(i) In general

The term "qualified health insurance" does not include any coverage described in clauses (ii) through (viii) of subparagraph (A) unless the State involved has elected to have such coverage treated as qualified health insurance under this paragraph and such coverage meets the following requirements:

(I) Guaranteed issue

Each qualifying individual is guaranteed enrollment if the individual pays the premium for enrollment or provides a qualified health insurance costs credit eligibility certificate described in section 7527 of title 26 and pays the remainder of such premium.

(II) No imposition of preexisting condition exclusion

No pre-existing condition limitations are imposed with respect to any qualifying individual.

(III) Nondiscriminatory premium

The total premium (as determined without regard to any subsidies) with respect to a qualifying individual may not be greater than the total premium (as so determined) for a similarly situated individual who is not a qualifying individual.

(IV) Same benefits

Benefits under the coverage are the same as (or substantially similar to) the benefits provided to similarly situated individuals who are not qualifying individuals.

(ii) Qualifying individual

For purposes of this subparagraph, the term "qualifying individual" means—

(I) an eligible individual for whom, as of the date on which the individual seeks to enroll in clauses (ii) through (viii) of subparagraph (A), the aggregate of the periods of creditable coverage (as defined in section 9801(c) of title 26) is 3 months or longer and who, with respect to any month, meets the requirements of clauses (iii) and (iv) of section 35(b)(1)(A) of such title; and

(II) the qualifying family members of such eligible individual.

(C) Exception

The term "qualified health insurance" shall not include—

(i) a flexible spending or similar arrangement, and

(ii) any insurance if substantially all of its coverage is of excepted benefits described in section 1191b(c) of this title.

(3) Availability of funds

(A) Expedited procedures

With respect to applications submitted by States or entities for grants under this subsection, the Secretary shall—

(i) not later than 15 days after the date on which the Secretary receives a completed application from a State or entity, notify the State or entity of the determination of the Secretary with respect to the approval or disapproval of such application;

(ii) in the case of an application of a State or other entity that is disapproved by the Secretary, provide technical assistance, at the request of the State or entity, in a timely manner to enable the State or entity to submit an approved application; and

(iii) develop procedures to expedite the provision of funds to States and entities with approved applications.

(B) Availability and distribution of funds

The Secretary shall ensure that funds made available under section 2919(c)(1)(A) of this title to carry out subsection (a)(4)(A) of this section are available to States and entities throughout the period described in section 2919(c)(2)(A) of this title.

(4) Eligible individual defined

For purposes of this subsection and subsection (g) of this section, the term "eligible individual" means—

(A) an eligible TAA recipient (as defined in section 35(c)(2) of title 26),

(B) an eligible alternative TAA recipient (as defined in section 35(c)(3) of title 26), and

(C) an eligible PBGC pension recipient (as defined in section 35(c)(4) of title 26),

who, as of the first day of the month, does not have other specified coverage and is not imprisoned under Federal, State, or local authority.

(5) Qualifying family member defined

For purposes of this subsection and subsection (g) of this section—

(A) In general

The term "qualifying family member" means—

(i) the eligible individual's spouse, and

(ii) any dependent of the eligible individual with respect to whom the individual is entitled to a deduction under section 151(c) of title 26.

Such term does not include any individual who has other specified coverage.

(B) Special dependency test in case of divorced parents, etc.

If paragraph (2) or (4) of section 152(e) of such title applies to any child with respect to any calendar year, in the case of any taxable year beginning in such calendar year, such child shall be treated as described in subparagraph (A)(ii) with respect to the custodial parent (within the meaning of section 152(e)(1) of such title) and not with respect to the noncustodial parent.

(6) State

For purposes of this subsection and subsection (g) of this section, the term "State" includes an entity as defined in subsection (c)(1)(B) of this section.

(7) Other specified coverage

For purposes of this subsection, an individual has other specified coverage for any month if, as of the first day of such month—

(A) Subsidized coverage

(i) In general

Such individual is covered under any insurance which constitutes medical care (except insurance substantially all of the coverage of which is of excepted benefits described in section 9832(c) of title 26) under any health plan maintained by any employer (or former employer) of the taxpayer or the taxpayer's spouse and at least 50 percent of the cost of such coverage (determined under section 4980B of such title) is paid or incurred by the employer.

(ii) Eligible alternative TAA recipients

In the case of an eligible alternative TAA recipient (as defined in section 35(c)(3) of title 26), such individual is either—

(I) eligible for coverage under any qualified health insurance (other than insurance described in clause (i), (ii), or (vi) of paragraph (2)(A)) under which at least 50 percent of the cost of coverage (determined under section 4980B(f)(4) of such title) is paid or incurred by an employer (or former employer) of the taxpayer or the taxpayer's spouse, or

(II) covered under any such qualified health insurance under which any portion of the cost of coverage (as so determined) is paid or incurred by an employer (or former employer) of the taxpayer or the taxpayer's spouse.

(iii) Treatment of cafeteria plans

For purposes of clauses (i) and (ii), the cost of coverage shall be treated as paid or incurred by an employer to the extent the coverage is in lieu of a right to receive cash or other qualified benefits under a cafeteria plan (as defined in section 125(d) of title 26).

(B) Coverage under Medicare, Medicaid, or SCHIP

Such individual—

(i) is entitled to benefits under part A of title XVIII of the Social Security Act [42 U.S.C. 1395c et seq.] or is enrolled under part B of such title [42 U.S.C. 1395j et seq.], or

(ii) is enrolled in the program under title XIX [42 U.S.C. 1396 et seq.] or XXI [42 U.S.C. 1397aa et seq.] of such Act (other than under section 1928 of such Act [42 U.S.C. 1396s]).

(C) Certain other coverage

Such individual—

(i) is enrolled in a health benefits plan under chapter 89 of title 5, or

(ii) is entitled to receive benefits under chapter 55 of title 10.

(g) Interim health insurance coverage and other assistance

(1) In general

Funds made available to a State or entity under paragraph (4)(B) of subsection (a) of this section may be used by the State or entity to provide assistance and support services to eligible individuals, including health care coverage to the extent provided under subsection (f)(1)(A) of this section, transportation, child care, dependent care, and income assistance.

(2) Income support

With respect to any income assistance provided to an eligible individual with such funds, such assistance shall supplement and not supplant other income support or assistance provided under chapter 2 of title II of the Trade Act of 1974 (19 U.S.C. 2271 et seq.) (as in effect on the day before the effective date of the Trade Act of 2002) or the unemployment compensation laws of the State where the eligible individual resides.

(3) Health insurance coverage

With respect to any assistance provided to an eligible individual with such funds in enrolling in qualified health insurance, the following rules shall apply:

(A) The State or entity may provide assistance in obtaining such coverage to the eligible individual and to such individual's qualifying family members.

(B) Such assistance shall supplement and may not supplant any other State or local funds used to provide health care coverage and may not be included in determining the amount of non-Federal contributions required under any program.

(4) Availability of funds

(A) Expedited procedures

With respect to applications submitted by States or entities for grants under this subsection, the Secretary shall—

(i) not later than 15 days after the date on which the Secretary receives a completed application from a State or entity, notify the State or entity of the determination of the Secretary with respect to the approval or disapproval of such application;

(ii) in the case of an application of a State or entity that is disapproved by the Secretary, provide technical assistance, at the request of the State or entity, in a timely manner to enable the State or entity to submit an approved application; and

(iii) develop procedures to expedite the provision of funds to States and entities with approved applications.

(B) Availability and distribution of funds

The Secretary shall ensure that funds made available under section 2919(c)(1)(B) of this title to carry out subsection (a)(4)(B) of this section are available to States and entities throughout the period described in section 2919(c)(2)(B) of this title.

(5) Inclusion of certain individuals as eligible individuals

For purposes of this subsection, the term "eligible individual" includes an individual who is a member of a group of workers certified after April 1, 2002, under chapter 2 of title II of the Trade Act of 1974 [19 U.S.C. 2271 et seq.] (as in effect on the day before the effective date of the Trade Act of 2002) and is participating in the trade adjustment allowance program under such chapter (as so in effect) or who would be determined to be participating in such program under such chapter (as so in effect) if such chapter were applied without regard to section 231(a)(3)(B) of the Trade Act of 1974 [19 U.S.C. 2291(a)(3)(B)] (as so in effect).

(Pub. L. 105–220, title I, §173, Aug. 7, 1998, 112 Stat. 1035; Pub. L. 105–277, div. A, §101(f) [title VIII, §401(12)], Oct. 21, 1998, 112 Stat. 2681–337, 2681–411, 2681–435; Pub. L. 107–210, div. A, title II, §203(a), (b), Aug. 6, 2002, 116 Stat. 963.)

REFERENCES IN TEXT

Section 1602 of this title, referred to in subsec. (e)(2)(A)(i), (3)(A), was repealed by Pub. L. 105–220, title I, §199(b)(2), Aug. 7, 1998, 112 Stat. 1059, effective July 1, 2000.

The Social Security Act, referred to in subsec. (f)(7)(B), is act Aug. 14, 1935, ch. 531, 49 Stat. 620, as amended. Parts A and B of title XVIII of the Act are classified generally to parts A (§1395c et seq.) and B (§1395j et seq.), respectively, of subchapter XVIII of chapter 7 of Title 42, The Public Health and Welfare.

Titles XIX and XXI of the Act are classified generally to subchapters XIX (§ 1396 et seq.) and XXI (§ 1397aa et seq.), respectively, of chapter 7 of Title 42. For complete classification of this Act to the Code, see section 1305 of Title 42 and Tables.

Chapter 2 of title II of the Trade Act of 1974 (19 U.S.C. 2271 et seq.) (as in effect on the day before the effective date of the Trade Act of 2002), referred to in subsec. (g)(2), (5), is chapter 2 of title II of Pub. L. 93–618, Jan. 3, 1975, 88 Stat. 1978, as amended, as in effect on the day before the effective date of Pub. L. 107–210. Chapter 2 of title II of Pub. L. 93–618 is classified generally to part 2 (§ 2271 et seq.) of subchapter II of chapter 12 of Title 19, Customs Duties. For effective date provisions applicable to certain amendments by Pub. L. 107–210 to chapter 2 of title II of Pub. L. 93–618, see Effective Date of 2002 Amendment note set out preceding section 2271 of Title 19. For complete classification of Pub. L. 93–618 to the Code, see section 2101 of Title 19 and Tables.

AMENDMENTS

2002—Subsec. (a)(4). Pub. L. 107–210, § 203(a), added par. (4).

Subsecs. (f), (g). Pub. L. 107–210, § 203(b), added subsecs. (f) and (g).

1998—Subsec. (a)(2). Pub. L. 105–277, § 101(f) [title VIII, § 401(12)], made technical amendment to reference in original act which appears in text as reference to section 5122 of title 42.

Subsec. (e). Pub. L. 105–277, § 101(f) [title VIII], added subsec. (e).

EFFECTIVE DATE OF 2002 AMENDMENT

Amendment by Pub. L. 107–210 applicable to petitions for certification filed under part 2 or 3 of subchapter II of chapter 12 of Title 19, Customs Duties, on or after the date that is 90 days after Aug. 6, 2002, except as otherwise provided, see section 151 of Pub. L. 107–210, set out as a note preceding section 2271 of Title 19.

CONSTRUCTION OF 2002 AMENDMENT

Pub. L. 107–210, div. A, title II, § 203(f), Aug. 6, 2002, 116 Stat. 972, provided that: "Nothing in this title [enacting sections 35, 6050T, and 7527 of Title 26, Internal Revenue Code, and section 300gg–45 of Title 42, The Public Health and Welfare, amending this section, sections 1165, 2862, and 2919 of this title, sections 4980B, 6103, 6724, and 7213A of Title 26, section 1324 of Title 31, Money and Finance, and section 300bb–5 of Title 42, renumbering section 35 of Title 26 as section 36 of Title 26, and enacting provisions set out as notes under sections 35 and 6050T of Title 26] (or the amendments made by this title), other than provisions relating to COBRA continuation coverage and reporting requirements, shall be construed as creating any new mandate on any party regarding health insurance coverage."

§ 2918a. YouthBuild program

(a) Statement of purpose

The purposes of this section are—

(1) to enable disadvantaged youth to obtain the education and employment skills necessary to achieve economic self-sufficiency in occupations in demand and postsecondary education and training opportunities;

(2) to provide disadvantaged youth with opportunities for meaningful work and service to their communities;

(3) to foster the development of employment and leadership skills and commitment to community development among youth in low-income communities; and

(4) to expand the supply of permanent affordable housing for homeless individuals and low-income families by utilizing the energies and talents of disadvantaged youth.

(b) Definitions

In this section:

(1) Adjusted income

The term "adjusted income" has the meaning given the term in section 1437a(b) of title 42.

(2) Applicant

The term "applicant" means an eligible entity that has submitted an application under subsection (c).

(3) Eligible entity

The term "eligible entity" means a public or private nonprofit agency or organization (including a consortium of such agencies or organizations), including—

(A) a community-based organization;

(B) a faith-based organization;

(C) an entity carrying out activities under this chapter, such as a local board;

(D) a community action agency;

(E) a State or local housing development agency;

(F) an Indian tribe or other agency primarily serving Indians;

(G) a community development corporation;

(H) a State or local youth service or conservation corps; and

(I) any other entity eligible to provide education or employment training under a Federal program (other than the program carried out under this section).

(4) Homeless individual

The term "homeless individual" has the meaning given the term in section 11302 of title 42.

(5) Housing development agency

The term "housing development agency" means any agency of a State or local government, or any private nonprofit organization, that is engaged in providing housing for homeless individuals or low-income families.

(6) Income

The term "income" has the meaning given the term in section 1437a(b) of title 42.

(7) Indian; Indian tribe

The terms "Indian" and "Indian tribe" have the meanings given such terms in section 450b of title 25.

(8) Individual of limited English proficiency

The term "individual of limited English proficiency" means an eligible participant under this section who meets the criteria set forth in section 9202(10) of title 20.

(9) Low-income family

The term "low-income family" means a family described in section 1437a(b)(2) of title 42.

(10) Qualified national nonprofit agency

The term "qualified national nonprofit agency" means a nonprofit agency that—

(A) has significant national experience providing services consisting of training, information, technical assistance, and data management to YouthBuild programs or similar projects; and

(B) has the capacity to provide those services.

(11) Registered apprenticeship program

The term "registered apprenticeship program" means an apprenticeship program—

(A) registered under the Act of August 16, 1937 (commonly known as the "National Apprenticeship Act"; 50 Stat. 664, chapter 663; 20[1] U.S.C. 50 et seq.); and

(B) that meets such other criteria as may be established by the Secretary under this section.

(12) Transitional housing

The term "transitional housing" means housing provided for the purpose of facilitating the movement of homeless individuals to independent living within a reasonable amount of time. The term includes housing primarily designed to serve deinstitutionalized homeless individuals and other homeless individuals who are individuals with disabilities or members of families with children.

(13) YouthBuild program

The term "YouthBuild program" means any program that receives assistance under this section and provides disadvantaged youth with opportunities for employment, education, leadership development, and training through the rehabilitation or construction of housing for homeless individuals and low-income families, and of public facilities.

(c) YouthBuild grants

(1) Amounts of grants

The Secretary is authorized to make grants to applicants for the purpose of carrying out YouthBuild programs approved under this section.

(2) Eligible activities

An entity that receives a grant under this subsection shall use the funds made available through the grant to carry out a YouthBuild program, which may include the following activities:

(A) Education and workforce investment activities including—

(i) work experience and skills training (coordinated, to the maximum extent feasible, with preapprenticeship and registered apprenticeship programs) in the rehabilitation and construction activities described in subparagraphs (B) and (C);

(ii) occupational skills training;

(iii) other paid and unpaid work experiences, including internships and job shadowing;

(iv) services and activities designed to meet the educational needs of participants, including—

(I) basic skills instruction and remedial education;

(II) language instruction educational programs for individuals with limited English proficiency;

(III) secondary education services and activities, including tutoring, study skills training, and dropout prevention activities, designed to lead to the attainment of a secondary school diploma, General Education Development (GED) credential, or other State-recognized equivalent (including recognized alternative standards for individuals with disabilities);

(IV) counseling and assistance in obtaining postsecondary education and required financial aid; and

(V) alternative secondary school services;

(v) counseling services and related activities, such as comprehensive guidance and counseling on drug and alcohol abuse and referral;

(vi) activities designed to develop employment and leadership skills, which may include community service and peer-centered activities encouraging responsibility and other positive social behaviors, and activities related to youth policy committees that participate in decision-making related to the program;

(vii) supportive services and provision of need-based stipends necessary to enable individuals to participate in the program and supportive services to assist individuals, for a period not to exceed 12 months after the completion of training, in obtaining or retaining employment, or applying for and transitioning to postsecondary education; and

(viii) job search and assistance.

(B) Supervision and training for participants in the rehabilitation or construction of housing, including residential housing for homeless individuals or low-income families, or transitional housing for homeless individuals.

(C) Supervision and training for participants in the rehabilitation or construction of community and other public facilities, except that not more than 10 percent of funds appropriated to carry out this section may be used for such supervision and training.

(D) Payment of administrative costs of the applicant, except that not more than 15 percent of the amount of assistance provided under this subsection to the grant recipient may be used for such costs.

(E) Adult mentoring.

(F) Provision of wages, stipends, or benefits to participants in the program.

(G) Ongoing training and technical assistance that are related to developing and carrying out the program.

(H) Follow-up services.

(3) Application

(A) Form and procedure

To be qualified to receive a grant under this subsection, an eligible entity shall submit an application at such time, in such manner, and containing such information as the Secretary may require.

(B) Minimum requirements

The Secretary shall require that the application contain, at a minimum—

[1] So in original. Probably should be "29".

(i) labor market information for the labor market area where the proposed program will be implemented, including both current data (as of the date of submission of the application) and projections on career opportunities in growing industries;

(ii) a request for the grant, specifying the amount of the grant requested and its proposed uses;

(iii) a description of the applicant and a statement of its qualifications, including a description of the applicant's relationship with local boards, one-stop operators, local unions, entities carrying out registered apprenticeship programs, other community groups, and employers, and the applicant's past experience, if any, with rehabilitation or construction of housing or public facilities, and with youth education and employment training programs;

(iv) a description of the proposed site for the proposed program;

(v) a description of the educational and job training activities, work opportunities, postsecondary education and training opportunities, and other services that will be provided to participants, and how those activities, opportunities, and services will prepare youth for employment in occupations in demand in the labor market area described in clause (i);

(vi) a description of the proposed rehabilitation or construction activities to be undertaken under the grant and the anticipated schedule for carrying out such activities;

(vii) a description of the manner in which eligible youth will be recruited and selected as participants, including a description of arrangements that will be made with local boards, one-stop operators, community- and faith-based organizations, State educational agencies or local educational agencies (including agencies of Indian tribes), public assistance agencies, the courts of jurisdiction, agencies operating shelters for homeless individuals and other agencies that serve youth who are homeless individuals, foster care agencies, and other appropriate public and private agencies;

(viii) a description of the special outreach efforts that will be undertaken to recruit eligible young women (including young women with dependent children) as participants;

(ix) a description of the specific role of employers in the proposed program, such as their role in developing the proposed program and assisting in service provision and in placement activities;

(x) a description of how the proposed program will be coordinated with other Federal, State, and local activities and activities conducted by Indian tribes, such as local workforce investment activities, vocational education programs, adult and language instruction educational programs, activities conducted by public schools, activities,[2] conducted by community colleges, national service programs, and other job training provided with funds available under this chapter;

(xi) assurances that there will be a sufficient number of adequately trained supervisory personnel in the proposed program;

(xii) a description of results to be achieved with respect to common indicators of performance for youth and lifelong learning, as identified by the Secretary;

(xiii) a description of the applicant's relationship with local building trade unions regarding their involvement in training to be provided through the proposed program, the relationship of the proposed program to established registered apprenticeship programs and employers, and the ability of the applicant to grant industry-recognized skill certification through the program;

(xiv) a description of activities that will be undertaken to develop the leadership skills of participants;

(xv) a detailed budget and a description of the system of fiscal controls, and auditing and accountability procedures, that will be used to ensure fiscal soundness for the proposed program;

(xvi) a description of the commitments for any additional resources (in addition to the funds made available through the grant) to be made available to the proposed program from—

(I) the applicant;

(II) recipients of other Federal, State or local housing and community development assistance who will sponsor any part of the rehabilitation, construction, operation and maintenance, or other housing and community development activities undertaken as part of the proposed program; or

(III) entities carrying out other Federal, State, or local activities or activities conducted by Indian tribes, including vocational education programs, adult and language instruction educational programs, and job training provided with funds available under this chapter;

(xvii) information identifying, and a description of, the financing proposed for any—

(I) rehabilitation of the property involved;

(II) acquisition of the property; or

(III) construction of the property;

(xviii) information identifying, and a description of, the entity that will operate and manage the property;

(xix) information identifying, and a description of, the data collection systems to be used;

(xx) a certification, by a public official responsible for the housing strategy for the State or unit of general local government within which the proposed program is located, that the proposed program is consistent with the housing strategy; and

(xxi) a certification that the applicant will comply with the requirements of the

[2] So in original. The comma probably should not appear.

Fair Housing Act (42 U.S.C. 3601 et seq.) and will affirmatively further fair housing.

(4) Selection criteria

For an applicant to be eligible to receive a grant under this subsection, the applicant and the applicant's proposed program shall meet such selection criteria as the Secretary shall establish under this section, which shall include criteria relating to—

(A) the qualifications or potential capabilities of an applicant;

(B) an applicant's potential for developing a successful YouthBuild program;

(C) the need for an applicant's proposed program, as determined by the degree of economic distress of the community from which participants would be recruited (measured by indicators such as poverty, youth unemployment, and the number of individuals who have dropped out of secondary school) and of the community in which the housing and public facilities proposed to be rehabilitated or constructed is located (measured by indicators such as incidence of homelessness, shortage of affordable housing, and poverty);

(D) the commitment of an applicant to providing skills training, leadership development, and education to participants;

(E) the focus of a proposed program on preparing youth for occupations in demand or postsecondary education and training opportunities;

(F) the extent of an applicant's coordination of activities to be carried out through the proposed program with local boards, one-stop operators, and one-stop partners participating in the operation of the one-stop delivery system involved, or the extent of the applicant's good faith efforts in achieving such coordination;

(G) the extent of the applicant's coordination of activities with public education, criminal justice, housing and community development, national service, or postsecondary education or other systems that relate to the goals of the proposed program;

(H) the extent of an applicant's coordination of activities with employers in the local area involved;

(I) the extent to which a proposed program provides for inclusion of tenants who were previously homeless individuals in the rental housing provided through the program;

(J) the commitment of additional resources (in addition to the funds made available through the grant) to a proposed program by—

(i) an applicant;

(ii) recipients of other Federal, State, or local housing and community development assistance who will sponsor any part of the rehabilitation, construction, operation and maintenance, or other housing and community development activities undertaken as part of the proposed program; or

(iii) entities carrying out other Federal, State, or local activities or activities conducted by Indian tribes, including vocational education programs, adult and language instruction educational programs, and job training provided with funds available under this chapter;

(K) the applicant's potential to serve different regions, including rural areas and States that have not previously received grants for YouthBuild programs; and

(L) such other factors as the Secretary determines to be appropriate for purposes of carrying out the proposed program in an effective and efficient manner.

(5) Approval

To the extent practicable, the Secretary shall notify each applicant, not later than 5 months after the date of receipt of the application by the Secretary, whether the application is approved or not approved.

(d) Use of housing units

Residential housing units rehabilitated or constructed using funds made available under subsection (c) shall be available solely—

(1) for rental by, or sale to, homeless individuals or low-income families; or

(2) for use as transitional or permanent housing, for the purpose of assisting in the movement of homeless individuals to independent living.

(e) Additional program requirements

(1) Eligible participants

(A) In general

Except as provided in subparagraph (B), an individual may participate in a YouthBuild program only if such individual is—

(i) not less than age 16 and not more than age 24, on the date of enrollment;

(ii) a member of a low-income family, a youth in foster care (including youth aging out of foster care), a youth offender, a youth who is an individual with a disability, a child of incarcerated parents, or a migrant youth; and

(iii) a school dropout.

(B) Exception for individuals not meeting income or educational need requirements

Not more than 25 percent of the participants in such program may be individuals who do not meet the requirements of clause (ii) or (iii) of subparagraph (A), but who—

(i) are basic skills deficient, despite attainment of a secondary school diploma, General Education Development (GED) credential, or other State-recognized equivalent (including recognized alternative standards for individuals with disabilities); or

(ii) have been referred by a local secondary school for participation in a YouthBuild program leading to the attainment of a secondary school diploma.

(2) Participation limitation

An eligible individual selected for participation in a YouthBuild program shall be offered full-time participation in the program for a period of not less than 6 months and not more than 24 months.

(3) Minimum time devoted to educational services and activities

A YouthBuild program receiving assistance under subsection (c) shall be structured so that participants in the program are offered—

(A) education and related services and activities designed to meet educational needs, such as those specified in clauses (iv) through (vii) of subsection (c)(2)(A), during at least 50 percent of the time during which the participants participate in the program; and

(B) work and skill development activities such as those specified in clauses (i), (ii), (iii), and (viii) of subsection (c)(2)(A), during at least 40 percent of the time during which the participants participate in the program.

(4) Authority restriction

No provision of this section may be construed to authorize any agency, officer, or employee of the United States to exercise any direction, supervision, or control over the curriculum, program of instruction, administration, or personnel of any educational institution (including a school) or school system, or over the selection of library resources, textbooks, or other printed or published instructional materials by any educational institution or school system.

(5) State and local standards

All educational programs and activities supported with funds provided under subsection (c) shall be consistent with applicable State and local educational standards. Standards and procedures for the programs and activities that relate to awarding academic credit for and certifying educational attainment in such programs and activities shall be consistent with applicable State and local educational standards.

(f) Management and technical assistance

(1) Secretary assistance

The Secretary may enter into contracts with 1 or more entities to provide assistance to the Secretary in the management, supervision, and coordination of the program carried out under this section.

(2) Technical assistance

(A) Contracts and grants

The Secretary shall enter into contracts with or make grants to 1 or more qualified national nonprofit agencies, in order to provide training, information, technical assistance, and data management to recipients of grants under subsection (c).

(B) Reservation of funds

Of the amounts available under subsection (h) to carry out this section for a fiscal year, the Secretary shall reserve 5 percent to carry out subparagraph (A).

(3) Capacity building grants

(A) In general

In each fiscal year, the Secretary may use not more than 3 percent of the amounts available under subsection (h) to award grants to 1 or more qualified national nonprofit agencies to pay for the Federal share of the cost of capacity building activities.

(B) Federal share

The Federal share of the cost described in subparagraph (A) shall be 25 percent. The non-Federal share shall be provided from private sources.

(g) Subgrants and contracts

Each recipient of a grant under subsection (c) to carry out a YouthBuild program shall provide the services and activities described in this section directly or through subgrants, contracts, or other arrangements with local educational agencies, postsecondary educational institutions, State or local housing development agencies, other public agencies, including agencies of Indian tribes, or private organizations.

(h) Authorization of appropriations

(1) In general

There are authorized to be appropriated for each of fiscal years 2007 through 2012 such sums as may be necessary to carry out this section.

(2) Fiscal year

Notwithstanding section 2939(g) of this title, appropriations for any fiscal year for programs and activities carried out under this section shall be available for obligation only on the basis of a fiscal year.

(Pub. L. 105–220, title I, §173A, as added Pub. L. 109–281, §2(a), Sept. 22, 2006, 120 Stat. 1173.)

REFERENCES IN TEXT

This chapter, referred to in subsecs. (b)(3)(C) and (c)(3)(B)(x), (xvi)(III), (4)(J)(iii), was in the original "this title" meaning title I of Pub. L. 105–220, Aug. 7, 1998, 112 Stat. 939, which enacted this chapter, repealed sections 1501 to 1505, 1511 to 1583, 1592 to 1735, 1737 to 1791h, 1792 to 1792b, 2301 to 2314 of this title, section 211 of former Title 40, Appendix, Public Buildings, Property, and Works, sections 11421, 11441 to 11447, 11449, 11450, 11461 to 11466, 11471, and 11472 of Title 42, The Public Health and Welfare, and sections 42101 to 42106 of Title 49, Transportation, enacted provisions set out as notes under sections 1501, 2301, and 2940 of this title and section 11421 of Title 42, and repealed provisions set out as notes under sections 801 and 2301 of this title and section 1255a of Title 8, Aliens and Nationality. For complete classification of title I to the Code, see Tables.

Act of August 16, 1937, commonly known as the National Apprenticeship Act, referred to in subsec. (b)(11)(A), is act Aug. 16, 1937, ch. 663, 50 Stat. 664, which is classified generally to chapter 4C (§50 et seq.) of this title. For complete classification of this Act to the Code, see Short Title note set out under section 50 of this title and Tables.

The Fair Housing Act, referred to in subsec. (c)(3)(B)(xxi), is title VIII of Pub. L. 90–284, Apr. 11, 1968, 82 Stat. 81, which is classified principally to subchapter I (§3601 et seq.) of chapter 45 of Title 42, The Public Health and Welfare. For complete classification of this Act to the Code, see Short Title note set out under section 3601 of Title 42 and Tables.

EFFECTIVE DATE

Section effective Sept. 22, 2006, see section 2(f) of Pub. L. 109–281, set out as an Effective Date of 2006 Amendment note under section 1701u of Title 12, Banks and Banking.

TRANSFER OF FUNCTIONS AND SAVINGS PROVISIONS

Pub. L. 109–281, §3, Sept. 22, 2006, 120 Stat. 1182, provided that:

"(a) DEFINITIONS.—For purposes of this section, unless otherwise provided or indicated by the context—

"(1) the term 'Federal agency' has the meaning given to the term 'agency' by section 551(1) of title 5, United States Code;

"(2) the term 'function' means any duty, obligation, power, authority, responsibility, right, privilege, activity, or program; and

"(3) the term 'office' includes any office, administration, agency, institute, unit, organizational entity, or component thereof.

"(b) TRANSFER OF FUNCTIONS.—There are transferred to the Department of Labor all functions which the Secretary of Housing and Urban Development exercised before the effective date of this section (including all related functions of any officer or employee of the Department of Housing and Urban Development) relating to subtitle D of title IV of the Cranston-Gonzalez National Affordable Housing Act (42 U.S.C. 12899 et seq.).

"(c) DETERMINATIONS OF CERTAIN FUNCTIONS BY THE OFFICE OF MANAGEMENT AND BUDGET.—If necessary, the Office of Management and Budget shall make any determination of the functions that are transferred under subsection (b).

"(d) PERSONNEL PROVISIONS.—

"(1) APPOINTMENTS.—The Secretary of Labor may appoint and fix the compensation of such officers and employees, including investigators, attorneys, and administrative law judges, as may be necessary to carry out the respective functions transferred under this section. Except as otherwise provided by law, such officers and employees shall be appointed in accordance with the civil service laws and their compensation fixed in accordance with title 5, United States Code.

"(2) EXPERTS AND CONSULTANTS.—The Secretary of Labor may obtain the services of experts and consultants in accordance with section 3109 of title 5, United States Code, and compensate such experts and consultants for each day (including traveltime) at rates not in excess of the rate of pay for level IV of the Executive Schedule under section 5315 of such title. The Secretary of Labor may pay experts and consultants who are serving away from their homes or regular place of business travel expenses and per diem in lieu of subsistence at rates authorized by sections 5702 and 5703 of such title for persons in Government service employed intermittently.

"(e) DELEGATION AND ASSIGNMENT.—Except where otherwise expressly prohibited by law or otherwise provided by this section, the Secretary of Labor may delegate any of the functions transferred to the Secretary of Labor by this section and any function transferred or granted to the Secretary of Labor after the effective date of this section to such officers and employees of the Department of Labor as the Secretary of Labor may designate, and may authorize successive redelegations of such functions as may be necessary or appropriate. No delegation of functions by the Secretary of Labor under this subsection or under any other provision of this section shall relieve the Secretary of Labor of responsibility for the administration of such functions.

"(f) REORGANIZATION.—The Secretary of Labor is authorized to allocate or reallocate any function transferred under subsection (b) among the officers of the Department of Labor, and to establish, consolidate, alter, or discontinue such organizational entities in the Department of Labor as may be necessary or appropriate.

"(g) RULES.—The Secretary of Labor is authorized to prescribe, in accordance with the provisions of chapters 5 and 6 of title 5, United States Code, such rules and regulations as the Secretary of Labor determines necessary or appropriate to administer and manage the functions of the Department of Labor.

"(h) TRANSFER AND ALLOCATIONS OF APPROPRIATIONS.—Except as otherwise provided in this section, the assets, liabilities, grants, contracts, property, records, and unexpended balances of appropriations, authorizations, allocations, and other funds used, held, arising from, available to, or to be made available in connection with the functions transferred by this section, subject to section 1531 of title 31, United States Code, shall be transferred to the Department of Labor. Unexpended funds transferred pursuant to this subsection shall be used only for the purposes for which the funds were originally authorized and appropriated.

"(i) TRANSFERS.—The Director of the Office of Management and Budget, at such time or times as the Director shall provide, is authorized to make such determinations as may be necessary with regard to the functions transferred by this section, and to make such dispositions of assets, liabilities, grants, contracts, property, records, and unexpended balances of appropriations, authorizations, allocations, and other funds used, held, arising from, available to, or to be made available in connection with such functions, subject to section 1531 of title 31, United States Code, as may be necessary to carry out the provisions of this section. The Director of the Office of Management and Budget shall provide for the termination of the affairs of all entities terminated by this section and for such further measures and dispositions as may be necessary to effectuate the purposes of this section.

"(j) SAVINGS PROVISIONS.—

"(1) CONTINUING EFFECT OF LEGAL DOCUMENTS.—All orders, determinations, rules, regulations, permits, agreements, grants, contracts, certificates, licenses, registrations, privileges, and other administrative actions—

"(A) which have been issued, made, granted, or allowed to become effective by the President, any Federal agency or official thereof, or by a court of competent jurisdiction, in the performance of functions which are transferred under this section; and

"(B) which are in effect at the time this section takes effect, or were final before the effective date of this section and are to become effective on or after the effective date of this section,

shall continue in effect according to their terms until modified, terminated, superseded, set aside, or revoked in accordance with law by the President, the Secretary of Labor or other authorized official, a court of competent jurisdiction, or by operation of law.

"(2) PROCEEDINGS NOT AFFECTED.—The provisions of this section shall not affect any proceedings, including notices of proposed rulemaking, or any application for any license, permit, certificate, or financial assistance pending before the Department of Housing and Urban Development at the time this section takes effect, with respect to functions transferred by this section but such proceedings and applications shall be continued. Orders shall be issued in such proceedings, appeals shall be taken therefrom, and payments shall be made pursuant to such orders, as if this section had not been enacted, and orders issued in any such proceedings shall continue in effect until modified, terminated, superseded, or revoked by a duly authorized official, by a court of competent jurisdiction, or by operation of law. Nothing in this paragraph shall be deemed to prohibit the discontinuance or modification of any such proceeding under the same terms and conditions and to the same extent that such proceeding could have been discontinued or modified if this section had not been enacted.

"(3) SUITS NOT AFFECTED.—The provisions of this section shall not affect suits commenced before the effective date of this section, and in all such suits, proceedings shall be had, appeals taken, and judgments rendered in the same manner and with the same effect as if this section had not been enacted.

"(4) NONABATEMENT OF ACTIONS.—No suit, action, or other proceeding commenced by or against the Department of Housing and Urban Development, or by or against any individual in the official capacity of such individual as an officer of the Department of Housing and Urban Development, shall abate by reason of the enactment of this section.

"(5) ADMINISTRATIVE ACTIONS RELATING TO PROMULGATION OF REGULATIONS.—Any administrative action relating to the preparation or promulgation of a regulation by the Department of Housing and Urban Development relating to a function transferred under this section may be continued by the Department of Labor with the same effect as if this section had not been enacted.

"(k) SEPARABILITY.—If a provision of this section or its application to any person or circumstance is held invalid, neither the remainder of this section nor the application of the provision to other persons or circumstances shall be affected.

"(*l*) TRANSITION.—The Secretary of Labor is authorized to utilize—

"(1) the services of such officers, employees, and other personnel of the Department of Housing and Urban Development with respect to functions transferred to the Department of Labor by this section; and

"(2) funds appropriated to such functions for such period of time,

as may reasonably be needed to facilitate the orderly implementation of this section.

"(m) ACCOMPLISHING ORDERLY TRANSFER.—Consistent with the requirements of this section, the Secretary of Labor and the Secretary of Housing and Urban Development shall take such actions as the Secretaries determine are appropriate to accomplish the orderly transfer of functions as described in subsection (b).

"(n) ADMINISTRATION OF PRIOR GRANTS.—Notwithstanding any other provision of this Act [See Short Title of 2006 Amendment note set out under section 2801 of this title], grants awarded under subtitle D of title IV of the Cranston-Gonzalez National Affordable Housing Act (42 U.S.C. 12899 et seq.) with funds appropriated for fiscal year 2006 or a preceding fiscal year shall be subject to the continuing authority of the Secretary of Housing and Urban Development under the provisions of such subtitle, as in effect on the day before the date of enactment of this Act [Sept. 22, 2006], until the authority to expend applicable funds for the grants, as specified by the Secretary of Housing and Urban Development, has expired and the Secretary has completed the administrative responsibilities associated with the grants.

"(*o*) REFERENCES.—A reference in any other Federal law, Executive order, rule, regulation, or delegation of authority, or any document of or relating to—

"(1) the Secretary of Housing and Urban Development with regard to functions transferred under subsection (b), shall be deemed to refer to the Secretary of Labor; and

"(2) the Department of Housing and Urban Development with regard to functions transferred under subsection (b), shall be deemed to refer to the Department of Labor.

"(p) EFFECTIVE DATE.—This section takes effect on the earlier of—

"(1) the date of enactment of this Act [Sept. 22, 2006]; and

"(2) September 30, 2006."

§2919. Authorization of appropriations

(a) Native American programs; migrant and seasonal farmworker programs; veterans' workforce investment programs

(1) In general

Subject to paragraph (2), there are authorized to be appropriated to carry out sections 2911 through 2913 of this title such sums as may be necessary for each of the fiscal years 1999 through 2003.

(2) Reservations

Of the amount appropriated pursuant to the authorization of appropriations under paragraph (1) for a fiscal year, the Secretary shall—

(A) reserve not less than $55,000,000 for carrying out section 2911 of this title;

(B) reserve not less than $70,000,000 for carrying out section 2912 of this title; and

(C) reserve not less than $7,300,000 for carrying out section 2913 of this title.

(b) Technical assistance; demonstration and pilot projects; evaluations; incentive grants

(1) In general

Subject to paragraph (2), there are authorized to be appropriated to carry out sections 2915 through 2917 of this title and section 9273 of title 20 such sums as may be necessary for each of the fiscal years 1999 through 2003.

(2) Reservations

Of the amount appropriated pursuant to the authorization of appropriations under paragraph (1) for a fiscal year, the Secretary shall—

(A)(i) for fiscal year 1999, reserve up to 40 percent for carrying out section 2915 of this title (other than subsection (b) of such section);

(ii) for fiscal year 2000, reserve up to 25 percent for carrying out section 2915 of this title (other than subsection (b) of such section); and

(iii) for each of the fiscal years 2001 through 2003, reserve up to 20 percent for carrying out section 2915 of this title (other than subsection (b) of such section);

(B)(i) for fiscal year 1999, reserve not less than 50 percent for carrying out section 2916 of this title; and

(ii) for each of the fiscal years 2000 through 2003, reserve not less than 45 percent for carrying out section 2916 of this title;

(C)(i) for fiscal year 1999, reserve not less than 10 percent for carrying out section 2917 of this title; and

(ii) for each of the fiscal years 2000 through 2003, reserve not less than 10 percent for carrying out section 2917 of this title; and

(D)(i) for fiscal year 1999, reserve no funds for carrying out section 9273 of title 20;

(ii) for fiscal year 2000, reserve up to 20 percent for carrying out section 9273 of title 20; and

(iii) for each of the fiscal years 2001 through 2003, reserve up to 25 percent for carrying out section 9273 of title 20.

(c) Assistance for eligible workers

(1) Authorization and appropriation for fiscal year 2002

There are authorized to be appropriated and appropriated—

(A) to carry out subsection (a)(4)(A) of section 2918 of this title, $10,000,000 for fiscal year 2002; and

(B) to carry out subsection (a)(4)(B) of section 2918 of this title, $50,000,000 for fiscal year 2002.

(2) Authorization of appropriations for subsequent fiscal years

There are authorized to be appropriated—

(A) to carry out subsection (a)(4)(A) of section 2918 of this title, $60,000,000 for each of fiscal years 2003 through 2007; and

(B) to carry out subsection (a)(4)(B) of section 2918 of this title—

(i) $100,000,000 for fiscal year 2003; and

(ii) $50,000,000 for fiscal year 2004.

(3) Availability of funds

Funds appropriated pursuant to—

(A) paragraphs (1)(A) and (2)(A) for each fiscal year shall, notwithstanding section 2939(g) of this title, remain available for obligation during the pendency of any outstanding claim under the Trade Act of 1974 [19 U.S.C. 2101 et seq.], as amended by the Trade Act of 2002; and

(B) paragraph[1] (1)(B) and (2)(B), for each fiscal year shall, notwithstanding section 2939(g) of this title, remain available during the period that begins on August 6, 2002, and ends on September 30, 2004.

(Pub. L. 105–220, title I, §174, Aug. 7, 1998, 112 Stat. 1037; Pub. L. 107–210, div. A, title II, §203(c), Aug. 6, 2002, 116 Stat. 969.)

REFERENCES IN TEXT

The Trade Act of 1974, as amended by the Trade Act of 2002, referred to in subsec. (c)(3)(A), is Pub. L. 93–618, Jan. 3, 1975, 88 Stat. 1978, as amended by Pub. L. 107–210, which is classified principally to chapter 12 (§2101 et seq.) of Title 19, Customs Duties. For complete classification of this Act to the Code, see References in Text note set out under section 2101 of Title 19 and Tables.

AMENDMENTS

2002—Subsec. (c). Pub. L. 107–210 added subsec. (c).

EFFECTIVE DATE OF 2002 AMENDMENT

Amendment by Pub. L. 107–210 applicable to petitions for certification filed under part 2 or 3 of subchapter II of chapter 12 of Title 19, Customs Duties, on or after the date that is 90 days after Aug. 6, 2002, except as otherwise provided, see section 151 of Pub. L. 107–210, set out as a note preceding section 2271 of Title 19.

CONSTRUCTION OF 2002 AMENDMENT

Nothing in amendment by Pub. L. 107–210, other than provisions relating to COBRA continuation coverage and reporting requirements, to be construed as creating new mandate on any party regarding health insurance coverage, see section 203(f) of Pub. L. 107–210, set out as a note under section 2918 of this title.

§ 2920. Educational assistance and training

(a) Use of fund

The Secretary of Labor shall provide for grants to States to provide educational assistance and training for United States workers. The Secretary shall consult with the Secretary of Education in making grants under this section.

(b) Allocation of funds

Within the purposes described in subsection (a) of this section, funds in the account used under this section shall be allocated among the States based on a formula, established jointly by the Secretaries of Labor and Education, that takes into consideration—

(1) the location of foreign workers admitted into the United States,

(2) the location of individuals in the United States requiring and desiring the educational assistance and training for which the funds can be applied, and

(3) the location of unemployed and underemployed United States workers.

(c) Disbursement to States

(1) Within the purposes and allocations established under this section, disbursements shall be made to the States, in accordance with grant applications submitted to and approved jointly by the Secretaries of Labor and Education, to be applied in a manner consistent with the guidelines established by such Secretaries in consultation with the States. In applying such grants, the States shall consider providing funding to joint labor-management trust funds and other such non-profit organizations which have demonstrated capability and experience in directly training and educating workers.

(2) Not more than 5 percent of the funds disbursed to any State under this section may be used for administrative expenses.

(d) Limitation on Federal overhead

The Secretaries shall provide that not more than 2 percent of the amount of funds disbursed to States under this section may be used by the Federal Government in the administration of this section.

(e) Annual report

The Secretary of Labor shall report annually to the Congress on the grants to States provided under this section.

(f) "State" defined

In this section, the term "State" has the meaning given such term in section 1101(a)(36) of title 8.

(Pub. L. 101–649, title VIII, §801, Nov. 29, 1990, 104 Stat. 5087.)

CODIFICATION

Section was enacted as part of the Immigration Act of 1990, and not as part of title I of the Workforce Investment Act of 1998 which comprises this chapter.

Section was formerly classified to section 1506 of this title.

SUBCHAPTER V—ADMINISTRATION

§ 2931. Requirements and restrictions

(a) Benefits

(1) Wages

(A) In general

Individuals in on-the-job training or individuals employed in activities under this chapter shall be compensated at the same rates, including periodic increases, as trainees or employees who are similarly situated in similar occupations by the same employer and who have similar training, experience, and skills, and such rates shall be in accordance with applicable law, but in no event less than the higher of the rate specified in section 206(a)(1) of this title or the applicable State or local minimum wage law.

(B) Rule of construction

The reference in subparagraph (A) to section 206(a)(1) of this title—

[1] So in original. Probably should be "paragraphs".

(i) shall be deemed to be a reference to section 206(a)(3)[1] of this title for individuals in American Samoa; and

(ii) shall not be applicable for individuals in other territorial jurisdictions in which section 206 of this title does not apply.

(2) Treatment of allowances, earnings, and payments

Allowances, earnings, and payments to individuals participating in programs under this chapter shall not be considered as income for the purposes of determining eligibility for and the amount of income transfer and in-kind aid furnished under any Federal or federally assisted program based on need, other than as provided under the Social Security Act (42 U.S.C. 301 et seq.).

(b) Labor standards

(1) Limitations on activities that impact wages of employees

No funds provided under this chapter shall be used to pay the wages of incumbent employees during their participation in economic development activities provided through a statewide workforce investment system.

(2) Displacement

(A) Prohibition

A participant in a program or activity authorized under this chapter (referred to in this section as a "specified activity") shall not displace (including a partial displacement, such as a reduction in the hours of nonovertime work, wages, or employment benefits) any currently employed employee (as of the date of the participation).

(B) Prohibition on impairment of contracts

A specified activity shall not impair an existing contract for services or collective bargaining agreement, and no such activity that would be inconsistent with the terms of a collective bargaining agreement shall be undertaken without the written concurrence of the labor organization and employer concerned.

(3) Other prohibitions

A participant in a specified activity shall not be employed in a job if—

(A) any other individual is on layoff from the same or any substantially equivalent job;

(B) the employer has terminated the employment of any regular employee or otherwise reduced the workforce of the employer with the intention of filling the vacancy so created with the participant; or

(C) the job is created in a promotional line that will infringe in any way upon the promotional opportunities of currently employed individuals (as of the date of the participation).

(4) Health and safety

Health and safety standards established under Federal and State law otherwise applicable to working conditions of employees shall be equally applicable to working conditions of participants engaged in specified activities. To the extent that a State workers' compensation law applies, workers' compensation shall be provided to participants on the same basis as the compensation is provided to other individuals in the State in similar employment.

(5) Employment conditions

Individuals in on-the-job training or individuals employed in programs and activities under this chapter, shall be provided benefits and working conditions at the same level and to the same extent as other trainees or employees working a similar length of time and doing the same type of work.

(6) Opportunity to submit comments

Interested members of the public, including representatives of businesses and of labor organizations, shall be provided an opportunity to submit comments to the Secretary with respect to programs and activities proposed to be funded under subchapter II of this chapter.

(7) No impact on union organizing

Each recipient of funds under this chapter shall provide to the Secretary assurances that none of such funds will be used to assist, promote, or deter union organizing.

(c) Grievance procedure

(1) In general

Each State and local area receiving an allotment under this chapter shall establish and maintain a procedure for grievances or complaints alleging violations of the requirements of this chapter from participants and other interested or affected parties. Such procedure shall include an opportunity for a hearing and be completed within 60 days after the filing of the grievance or complaint.

(2) Investigation

(A) In general

The Secretary shall investigate an allegation of a violation described in paragraph (1) if—

(i) a decision relating to such violation has not been reached within 60 days after the date of the filing of the grievance or complaint and either party appeals to the Secretary; or

(ii) a decision relating to such violation has been reached within such 60 days and the party to which such decision is adverse appeals such decision to the Secretary.

(B) Additional requirement

The Secretary shall make a final determination relating to an appeal made under subparagraph (A) no later than 120 days after receiving such appeal.

(3) Remedies

Remedies that may be imposed under this section for a violation of any requirement of this chapter shall be limited—

(A) to suspension or termination of payments under this chapter;

(B) to prohibition of placement of a participant with an employer that has violated any requirement under this chapter;

[1] See References in Text note below.

(C) where applicable, to reinstatement of an employee, payment of lost wages and benefits, and reestablishment of other relevant terms, conditions, and privileges of employment; and

(D) where appropriate, to other equitable relief.

(4) Rule of construction

Nothing in paragraph (3) shall be construed to prohibit a grievant or complainant from pursuing a remedy authorized under another Federal, State, or local law for a violation of this chapter.

(d) Relocation

(1) Prohibition on use of funds to encourage or induce relocation

No funds provided under this chapter shall be used, or proposed for use, to encourage or induce the relocation of a business or part of a business if such relocation would result in a loss of employment for any employee of such business at the original location and such original location is within the United States.

(2) Prohibition on use of funds for customized or skill training and related activities after relocation

No funds provided under this chapter for an employment and training activity shall be used for customized or skill training, on-the-job training, or company-specific assessments of job applicants or employees, for any business or part of a business that has relocated, until the date that is 120 days after the date on which such business commences operations at the new location, if the relocation of such business or part of a business results in a loss of employment for any employee of such business at the original location and such original location is within the United States.

(3) Repayment

If the Secretary determines that a violation of paragraph (1) or (2) has occurred, the Secretary shall require the State that has violated such paragraph to repay to the United States an amount equal to the amount expended in violation of such paragraph.

(e) Limitation on use of funds

No funds available under this chapter shall be used for employment generating activities, economic development activities, investment in revolving loan funds, capitalization of businesses, investment in contract bidding resource centers, and similar activities that are not directly related to training for eligible individuals under this chapter. No funds available under subchapter II of this chapter shall be used for foreign travel.

(f) Testing and sanctioning for use of controlled substances

(1) In general

Notwithstanding any other provision of law, a State shall not be prohibited by the Federal Government from—

(A) testing participants in programs under subchapter II of this chapter for the use of controlled substances; and

(B) sanctioning such participants who test positive for the use of such controlled substances.

(2) Additional requirements

(A) Period of sanction

In sanctioning participants in programs under subchapter II of this chapter who test positive for the use of controlled substances—

(i) with respect to the first occurrence for which a participant tests positive, a State may exclude the participant from the program for a period not to exceed 6 months; and

(ii) with respect to the second occurrence and each subsequent occurrence for which a participant tests positive, a State may exclude the participant from the program for a period not to exceed 2 years.

(B) Appeal

The testing of participants and the imposition of sanctions under this subsection shall be subject to expeditious appeal in accordance with due process procedures established by the State.

(C) Privacy

A State shall establish procedures for testing participants for the use of controlled substances that ensure a maximum degree of privacy for the participants.

(4)[2] Funding requirement

In testing and sanctioning of participants for the use of controlled substances in accordance with this subsection, the only Federal funds that a State may use are the amounts made available for the administration of statewide workforce investment activities under section 2864(a)(3)(B) of this title.

(Pub. L. 105–220, title I, §181, Aug. 7, 1998, 112 Stat. 1038.)

REFERENCES IN TEXT

This chapter, referred to in text, was in the original "this title" meaning title I of Pub. L. 105–220, Aug. 7, 1998, 112 Stat. 939, as amended, which enacted this chapter, repealed sections 1501 to 1505, 1511 to 1583, 1592 to 1735, 1737 to 1791h, 1792 to 1792b, 2301 to 2314 of this title, section 211 of former Title 40, Appendix, Public Buildings, Property, and Works, sections 11421, 11441 to 11447, 11449, 11450, 11461 to 11466, 11471, and 11472 of Title 42, The Public Health and Welfare, and sections 42101 to 42106 of Title 49, Transportation, enacted provisions set out as notes under sections 1501, 2301, and 2940 of this title and section 11421 of Title 42, and repealed provisions set out as notes under sections 801 and 2301 of this title and section 1255a of Title 8, Aliens and Nationality. For complete classification of title I to the Code, see Tables.

Section 206(a)(3) of this title, referred to in subsec. (a)(1)(B)(i), was repealed and section 206(a)(4) of this title was redesignated section 206(a)(3) by Pub. L. 110–28, title VIII, §8103(c)(1)(B), May 25, 2007, 121 Stat. 189.

The Social Security Act, referred to in subsec. (a)(2), is act Aug. 14, 1935, ch. 531, 49 Stat. 620, as amended, which is classified generally to chapter 7 (§301 et seq.) of Title 42, The Public Health and Welfare. For complete classification of this Act to the Code, see section 1305 of Title 42 and Tables.

[2] So in original. No par. (3) has been enacted.

PRIOR PROVISIONS

Provisions similar to this section were contained in sections 1551 to 1554 of this title prior to repeal by Pub. L. 105–220.

§2932. Prompt allocation of funds

(a) Allotments based on latest available data

All allotments to States and grants to outlying areas under this chapter shall be based on the latest available data and estimates satisfactory to the Secretary. All data relating to disadvantaged adults and disadvantaged youth shall be based on the most recent satisfactory data from the Bureau of the Census.

(b) Publication in Federal Register relating to formula funds

Whenever the Secretary allots funds required to be allotted under this chapter, the Secretary shall publish in a timely fashion in the Federal Register the proposed amount to be distributed to each recipient of the funds.

(c) Requirement for funds distributed by formula

All funds required to be allotted under section 2852 or 2862 of this title shall be allotted within 45 days after the date of enactment of the Act appropriating the funds, except that, if such funds are appropriated in advance as authorized by section 2939(g) of this title, such funds shall be allotted or allocated not later than the March 31 preceding the program year for which such funds are to be available for obligation.

(d) Publication in Federal Register relating to discretionary funds

Whenever the Secretary utilizes a formula to allot or allocate funds made available for distribution at the Secretary's discretion under this chapter, the Secretary shall, not later than 30 days prior to such allotment or allocation, publish such formula in the Federal Register for comments along with the rationale for the formula and the proposed amounts to be distributed to each State and local area. After consideration of any comments received, the Secretary shall publish final allotments and allocations in the Federal Register.

(e) Availability of funds

Funds shall be made available under sections 2853 and 2863 of this title for a local area not later than 30 days after the date the funds are made available to the Governor involved, under section 2852 or 2862 of this title (as the case may be), or 7 days after the date the local plan for the area is approved, whichever is later.

(Pub. L. 105–220, title I, §182, Aug. 7, 1998, 112 Stat. 1041.)

PRIOR PROVISIONS

Provisions similar to this section were contained in section 1572 of this title prior to repeal by Pub. L. 105–220.

§2933. Monitoring

(a) In general

The Secretary is authorized to monitor all recipients of financial assistance under this chapter to determine whether the recipients are complying with the provisions of this chapter, including the regulations issued under this chapter.

(b) Investigations

The Secretary may investigate any matter the Secretary determines to be necessary to determine the compliance of the recipients with this chapter, including the regulations issued under this chapter. The investigations authorized by this subsection may include examining records (including making certified copies of the records), questioning employees, and entering any premises or onto any site in which any part of a program or activity of such a recipient is conducted or in which any of the records of the recipient are kept.

(c) Additional requirement

For the purpose of any investigation or hearing conducted under this chapter by the Secretary, the provisions of section 49 of title 15 (relating to the attendance of witnesses and the production of documents) apply to the Secretary, in the same manner and to the same extent as the provisions apply to the Federal Trade Commission.

(Pub. L. 105–220, title I, §183, Aug. 7, 1998, 112 Stat. 1042.)

PRIOR PROVISIONS

Provisions similar to this section were contained in section 1573 of this title prior to repeal by Pub. L. 105–220.

§2934. Fiscal controls; sanctions

(a) Establishment of fiscal controls by States

(1) In general

Each State shall establish such fiscal control and fund accounting procedures as may be necessary to assure the proper disbursal of, and accounting for, Federal funds allocated to local areas under subchapter II of this chapter. Such procedures shall ensure that all financial transactions carried out under subchapter II of this chapter are conducted and records maintained in accordance with generally accepted accounting principles applicable in each State.

(2) Cost principles

(A) In general

Each State (including the Governor of the State), local area (including the chief elected official for the area), and provider receiving funds under this chapter shall comply with the applicable uniform cost principles included in the appropriate circulars of the Office of Management and Budget for the type of entity receiving the funds.

(B) Exception

The funds made available to a State for administration of statewide workforce investment activities in accordance with section 2864(a)(3)(B) of this title shall be allocable to the overall administration of workforce investment activities, but need not be specifically allocable to—

(i) the administration of adult employment and training activities;

(ii) the administration of dislocated worker employment and training activities; or

(iii) the administration of youth activities.

(3) Uniform administrative requirements

(A) In general

Each State (including the Governor of the State), local area (including the chief elected official for the area), and provider receiving funds under this chapter shall comply with the appropriate uniform administrative requirements for grants and agreements applicable for the type of entity receiving the funds, as promulgated in circulars or rules of the Office of Management and Budget.

(B) Additional requirement

Procurement transactions under this chapter between local boards and units of State or local governments shall be conducted only on a cost-reimbursable basis.

(4) Monitoring

Each Governor of a State shall conduct on an annual basis onsite monitoring of each local area within the State to ensure compliance with the uniform administrative requirements referred to in paragraph (3).

(5) Action by Governor

If the Governor determines that a local area is not in compliance with the uniform administrative requirements referred to in paragraph (3), the Governor shall—

(A) require corrective action to secure prompt compliance; and

(B) impose the sanctions provided under subsection (b) of this section in the event of failure to take the required corrective action.

(6) Certification

The Governor shall, every 2 years, certify to the Secretary that—

(A) the State has implemented the uniform administrative requirements referred to in paragraph (3);

(B) the State has monitored local areas to ensure compliance with the uniform administrative requirements as required under paragraph (4); and

(C) the State has taken appropriate action to secure compliance pursuant to paragraph (5).

(7) Action by the Secretary

If the Secretary determines that the Governor has not fulfilled the requirements of this subsection, the Secretary shall—

(A) require corrective action to secure prompt compliance; and

(B) impose the sanctions provided under subsection (e) of this section in the event of failure of the Governor to take the required appropriate action to secure compliance.

(b) Substantial violation

(1) Action by Governor

If, as a result of financial and compliance audits or otherwise, the Governor determines that there is a substantial violation of a specific provision of this chapter, and corrective action has not been taken, the Governor shall—

(A) issue a notice of intent to revoke approval of all or part of the local plan affected; or

(B) impose a reorganization plan, which may include—

(i) decertifying the local board involved;

(ii) prohibiting the use of eligible providers;

(iii) selecting an alternative entity to administer the program for the local area involved;

(iv) merging the local area into one or more other local areas; or

(v) making other such changes as the Secretary or Governor determines necessary to secure compliance.

(2) Appeal

(A) In general

The actions taken by the Governor pursuant to subparagraphs (A) and (B) of paragraph (1) may be appealed to the Secretary and shall not become effective until—

(i) the time for appeal has expired; or

(ii) the Secretary has issued a decision.

(B) Additional requirement

The Secretary shall make a final decision under subparagraph (A) not later than 45 days after the receipt of the appeal.

(3) Action by the Secretary

If the Governor fails to promptly take the actions required under paragraph (1), the Secretary shall take such actions.

(c) Repayment of certain amounts to the United States

(1) In general

Every recipient of funds under this chapter shall repay to the United States amounts found not to have been expended in accordance with this chapter.

(2) Offset of repayment

If the Secretary determines that a State has expended funds made available under this chapter in a manner contrary to the requirements of this chapter, the Secretary may offset repayment of such expenditures against any other amount to which the State is or may be entitled, except as provided under subsection (d)(1) of this section.

(3) Repayment from deduction by State

If the Secretary requires a State to repay funds as a result of a determination that a local area of the State has expended funds contrary to the requirements of this chapter, the Governor of the State may use an amount deducted under paragraph (4) to repay the funds, except as provided under subsection (e)(1)[1] of this section.

(4) Deduction by State

The Governor may deduct an amount equal to the misexpenditure described in paragraph (3) from subsequent program year allocations to the local area from funds reserved for the administrative costs of the local programs involved, as appropriate.

---

[1] So in original. Probably should be subsection "(d)(1)".

(5) Limitations

A deduction made by a State as described in paragraph (4) shall not be made until such time as the Governor has taken appropriate corrective action to ensure full compliance within such local area with regard to appropriate expenditures of funds under this chapter.

(d) Repayment of amounts

(1) In general

Each recipient of funds under this chapter shall be liable to repay the amounts described in subsection (c)(1) of this section, from funds other than funds received under this chapter, upon a determination by the Secretary that the misexpenditure of funds was due to willful disregard of the requirements of this chapter, gross negligence, failure to observe accepted standards of administration, or a pattern of misexpenditure as described in paragraphs (2) and (3) of subsection (c) of this section. No such determination shall be made under this subsection or subsection (c) of this section until notice and opportunity for a fair hearing has been given to the recipient.

(2) Factors in imposing sanctions

In determining whether to impose any sanction authorized by this section against a recipient for violations by a subgrantee or contractor of such recipient under this chapter (including the regulations issued under this chapter), the Secretary shall first determine whether such recipient has adequately demonstrated that the recipient has—

(A) established and adhered to an appropriate system for the award and monitoring of grants and contracts with subgrantees and contractors that contains acceptable standards for ensuring accountability;

(B) entered into a written grant agreement or contract with such subgrantee or contractor that established clear goals and obligations in unambiguous terms;

(C) acted with due diligence to monitor the implementation of the grant agreement or contract, including the carrying out of the appropriate monitoring activities (including audits) at reasonable intervals; and

(D) taken prompt and appropriate corrective action upon becoming aware of any evidence of a violation of this chapter, including regulations issued under this chapter, by such subgrantee or contractor.

(3) Waiver

If the Secretary determines that the recipient has demonstrated substantial compliance with the requirements of paragraph (2), the Secretary may waive the imposition of sanctions authorized by this section upon such recipient. The Secretary is authorized to impose any sanction consistent with the provisions of this chapter and any applicable Federal or State law directly against any subgrantee or contractor for violation of this chapter, including regulations issued under this chapter.

(e) Immediate termination or suspension of assistance in emergency situations

In emergency situations, if the Secretary determines it is necessary to protect the integrity of the funds or ensure the proper operation of the program or activity involved, the Secretary may immediately terminate or suspend financial assistance, in whole or in part, to the recipient if the recipient is given prompt notice and the opportunity for a subsequent hearing within 30 days after such termination or suspension. The Secretary shall not delegate any of the functions or authority specified in this subsection, other than to an officer whose appointment is required to be made by and with the advice and consent of the Senate.

(f) Discrimination against participants

If the Secretary determines that any recipient under this chapter has discharged or in any other manner discriminated against a participant or against any individual in connection with the administration of the program involved, or against any individual because such individual has filed any complaint or instituted or caused to be instituted any proceeding under or related to this chapter, or has testified or is about to testify in any such proceeding or investigation under or related to this chapter, or otherwise unlawfully denied to any individual a benefit to which that individual is entitled under the provisions of this chapter or the Secretary's regulations, the Secretary shall, within 30 days, take such action or order such corrective measures, as necessary, with respect to the recipient or the aggrieved individual, or both.

(g) Remedies

The remedies described in this section shall not be construed to be the exclusive remedies available for violations described in this section.

(Pub. L. 105–220, title I, §184, Aug. 7, 1998, 112 Stat. 1042.)

PRIOR PROVISIONS

Provisions similar to this section were contained in section 1574 of this title prior to repeal by Pub. L. 105–220.

§2935. Reports; recordkeeping; investigations

(a) Reports

(1) In general

Recipients of funds under this chapter shall keep records that are sufficient to permit the preparation of reports required by this chapter and to permit the tracing of funds to a level of expenditure adequate to ensure that the funds have not been spent unlawfully.

(2) Submission to the Secretary

Every such recipient shall maintain such records and submit such reports, in such form and containing such information, as the Secretary may require regarding the performance of programs and activities carried out under this chapter. Such records and reports shall be submitted to the Secretary but shall not be required to be submitted more than once each quarter unless specifically requested by Congress or a committee of Congress, in which case an estimate may be provided.

(3) Maintenance of standardized records

In order to allow for the preparation of the reports required under subsection (c) of this section, such recipients shall maintain standardized records for all individual participants and provide to the Secretary a sufficient number of such records to provide for an adequate analysis of the records.

(4) Availability to the public

(A) In general

Except as provided in subparagraph (B), records maintained by such recipients pursuant to this subsection shall be made available to the public upon request.

(B) Exception

Subparagraph (A) shall not apply to—

(i) information, the disclosure of which would constitute a clearly unwarranted invasion of personal privacy; and

(ii) trade secrets, or commercial or financial information, that is obtained from a person and privileged or confidential.

(C) Fees to recover costs

Such recipients may charge fees sufficient to recover costs applicable to the processing of requests for records under subparagraph (A).

(b) Investigations of use of funds

(1) In general

(A) Secretary

In order to evaluate compliance with the provisions of this chapter, the Secretary shall conduct, in several States, in each fiscal year, investigations of the use of funds received by recipients under this chapter.

(B) Comptroller General of the United States

In order to ensure compliance with the provisions of this chapter, the Comptroller General of the United States may conduct investigations of the use of funds received under this chapter by any recipient.

(2) Prohibition

In conducting any investigation under this chapter, the Secretary or the Comptroller General of the United States may not request the compilation of any information that the recipient is not otherwise required to compile and that is not readily available to such recipient.

(3) Audits

(A) In general

In carrying out any audit under this chapter (other than any initial audit survey or any audit investigating possible criminal or fraudulent conduct), either directly or through grant or contract, the Secretary, the Inspector General of the Department of Labor, or the Comptroller General of the United States shall furnish to the State, recipient, or other entity to be audited, advance notification of the overall objectives and purposes of the audit, and any extensive recordkeeping or data requirements to be met, not later than 14 days (or as soon as practicable), prior to the commencement of the audit.

(B) Notification requirement

If the scope, objectives, or purposes of the audit change substantially during the course of the audit, the entity being audited shall be notified of the change as soon as practicable.

(C) Additional requirement

The reports on the results of such audits shall cite the law, regulation, policy, or other criteria applicable to any finding contained in the reports.

(D) Rule of construction

Nothing contained in this chapter shall be construed so as to be inconsistent with the Inspector General Act of 1978 (5 U.S.C. App.) or government auditing standards issued by the Comptroller General of the United States.

(c) Accessibility of reports

Each State, each local board, and each recipient (other than a subrecipient, subgrantee, or contractor of a recipient) receiving funds under this chapter—

(1) shall make readily accessible such reports concerning its operations and expenditures as shall be prescribed by the Secretary;

(2) shall prescribe and maintain comparable management information systems, in accordance with guidelines that shall be prescribed by the Secretary, designed to facilitate the uniform compilation, cross tabulation, and analysis of programmatic, participant, and financial data, on statewide, local area, and other appropriate bases, necessary for reporting, monitoring, and evaluating purposes, including data necessary to comply with section 2938 of this title; and

(3) shall monitor the performance of providers in complying with the terms of grants, contracts, or other agreements made pursuant to this chapter.

(d) Information to be included in reports

(1) In general

The reports required in subsection (c) of this section shall include information regarding programs and activities carried out under this chapter pertaining to—

(A) the relevant demographic characteristics (including race, ethnicity, sex, and age) and other related information regarding participants;

(B) the programs and activities in which participants are enrolled, and the length of time that participants are engaged in such programs and activities;

(C) outcomes of the programs and activities for participants, including the occupations of participants, and placement for participants in nontraditional employment;

(D) specified costs of the programs and activities; and

(E) information necessary to prepare reports to comply with section 2938 of this title.

(2) Additional requirement

The Secretary shall ensure that all elements of the information required for the reports described in paragraph (1) are defined and reported uniformly.

(e) Quarterly financial reports

(1) In general

Each local board in the State shall submit quarterly financial reports to the Governor with respect to programs and activities carried out under this chapter. Such reports shall include information identifying all program and activity costs by cost category in accordance with generally accepted accounting principles and by year of the appropriation involved.

(2) Additional requirement

Each State shall submit to the Secretary, on a quarterly basis, a summary of the reports submitted to the Governor pursuant to paragraph (1).

(f) Maintenance of additional records

Each State and local board shall maintain records with respect to programs and activities carried out under this chapter that identify—

(1) any income or profits earned, including such income or profits earned by subrecipients; and

(2) any costs incurred (such as stand-in costs) that are otherwise allowable except for funding limitations.

(g) Cost categories

In requiring entities to maintain records of costs by category under this chapter, the Secretary shall require only that the costs be categorized as administrative or programmatic costs.

(Pub. L. 105–220, title I, §185, Aug. 7, 1998, 112 Stat. 1046.)

REFERENCES IN TEXT

The Inspector General Act of 1978, referred to in subsec. (b)(3)(D), is Pub. L. 95–452, Oct. 12, 1978, 92 Stat. 1101, as amended, which is set out in the Appendix to Title 5, Government Organization and Employees.

PRIOR PROVISIONS

Provisions similar to this section were contained in section 1575 of this title prior to repeal by Pub. L. 105–220.

§2936. Administrative adjudication

(a) In general

Whenever any applicant for financial assistance under this chapter is dissatisfied because the Secretary has made a determination not to award financial assistance in whole or in part to such applicant, the applicant may request a hearing before an administrative law judge of the Department of Labor. A similar hearing may also be requested by any recipient for whom a corrective action has been required or a sanction has been imposed by the Secretary under section 2934 of this title.

(b) Appeal

The decision of the administrative law judge shall constitute final action by the Secretary unless, within 20 days after receipt of the decision of the administrative law judge, a party dissatisfied with the decision or any part of the decision has filed exceptions with the Secretary specifically identifying the procedure, fact, law, or policy to which exception is taken. Any exception not specifically urged shall be deemed to have been waived. After the 20-day period the decision of the administrative law judge shall become the final decision of the Secretary unless the Secretary, within 30 days after such filing, has notified the parties that the case involved has been accepted for review.

(c) Time limit

Any case accepted for review by the Secretary under subsection (b) of this section shall be decided within 180 days after such acceptance. If the case is not decided within the 180-day period, the decision of the administrative law judge shall become the final decision of the Secretary at the end of the 180-day period.

(d) Additional requirement

The provisions of section 2937 of this title shall apply to any final action of the Secretary under this section.

(Pub. L. 105–220, title I, §186, Aug. 7, 1998, 112 Stat. 1048.)

PRIOR PROVISIONS

Provisions similar to this section were contained in section 1576 of this title prior to repeal by Pub. L. 105–220.

§2937. Judicial review

(a) Review

(1) Petition

With respect to any final order by the Secretary under section 2936 of this title by which the Secretary awards, declines to award, or only conditionally awards, financial assistance under his[1] chapter, or any final order of the Secretary under section 2936 of this title with respect to a corrective action or sanction imposed under section 2934 of this title, any party to a proceeding which resulted in such final order may obtain review of such final order in the United States Court of Appeals having jurisdiction over the applicant or recipient of funds involved, by filing a review petition within 30 days after the date of issuance of such final order.

(2) Action on petition

The clerk of the court shall transmit a copy of the review petition to the Secretary who shall file the record on which the final order was entered as provided in section 2112 of title 28. The filing of a review petition shall not stay the order of the Secretary, unless the court orders a stay. Petitions filed under this subsection shall be heard expeditiously, if possible within 10 days after the date of filing of a reply to the petition.

(3) Standard and scope of review

No objection to the order of the Secretary shall be considered by the court unless the objection was specifically urged, in a timely manner, before the Secretary. The review shall be limited to questions of law and the findings of fact of the Secretary shall be conclusive if supported by substantial evidence.

[1] So in original. Probably should be "this".

(b) Judgment

The court shall have jurisdiction to make and enter a decree affirming, modifying, or setting aside the order of the Secretary in whole or in part. The judgment of the court regarding the order shall be final, subject to certiorari review by the Supreme Court as provided in section 1254(1) of title 28.

(Pub. L. 105–220, title I, §187, Aug. 7, 1998, 112 Stat. 1049.)

PRIOR PROVISIONS

Provisions similar to this section were contained in section 1578 of this title prior to repeal by Pub. L. 105–220.

§ 2938. Nondiscrimination

(a) In general

(1) Federal financial assistance

For the purpose of applying the prohibitions against discrimination on the basis of age under the Age Discrimination Act of 1975 (42 U.S.C. 6101 et seq.), on the basis of disability under section 504 of the Rehabilitation Act of 1973 (29 U.S.C. 794), on the basis of sex under title IX of the Education Amendments of 1972 (20 U.S.C. 1681 et seq.), or on the basis of race, color, or national origin under title VI of the Civil Rights Act of 1964 (42 U.S.C. 2000d et seq.), programs and activities funded or otherwise financially assisted in whole or in part under this Act are considered to be programs and activities receiving Federal financial assistance.

(2) Prohibition of discrimination regarding participation, benefits, and employment

No individual shall be excluded from participation in, denied the benefits of, subjected to discrimination under, or denied employment in the administration of or in connection with, any such program or activity because of race, color, religion, sex (except as otherwise permitted under title IX of the Education Amendments of 1972 [20 U.S.C. 1681 et seq.]), national origin, age, disability, or political affiliation or belief.

(3) Prohibition on assistance for facilities for sectarian instruction or religious worship

Participants shall not be employed under this chapter to carry out the construction, operation, or maintenance of any part of any facility that is used or to be used for sectarian instruction or as a place for religious worship (except with respect to the maintenance of a facility that is not primarily or inherently devoted to sectarian instruction or religious worship, in a case in which the organization operating the facility is part of a program or activity providing services to participants).

(4) Prohibition on discrimination on basis of participant status

No person may discriminate against an individual who is a participant in a program or activity that receives funds under this chapter, with respect to the terms and conditions affecting, or rights provided to, the individual, solely because of the status of the individual as a participant.

(5) Prohibition on discrimination against certain noncitizens

Participation in programs and activities or receiving funds under this chapter shall be available to citizens and nationals of the United States, lawfully admitted permanent resident aliens, refugees, asylees, and parolees, and other immigrants authorized by the Attorney General to work in the United States.

(b) Action of Secretary

Whenever the Secretary finds that a State or other recipient of funds under this chapter has failed to comply with a provision of law referred to in subsection (a)(1) of this section, or with paragraph (2), (3), (4), or (5) of subsection (a) of this section, including an applicable regulation prescribed to carry out such provision or paragraph, the Secretary shall notify such State or recipient and shall request that the State or recipient comply. If within a reasonable period of time, not to exceed 60 days, the State or recipient fails or refuses to comply, the Secretary may—

(1) refer the matter to the Attorney General with a recommendation that an appropriate civil action be instituted; or

(2) take such other action as may be provided by law.

(c) Action of Attorney General

When a matter is referred to the Attorney General pursuant to subsection (b)(1) of this section, or whenever the Attorney General has reason to believe that a State or other recipient of funds under this chapter is engaged in a pattern or practice of discrimination in violation of a provision of law referred to in subsection (a)(1) of this section or in violation of paragraph (2), (3), (4), or (5) of subsection (a) of this section, the Attorney General may bring a civil action in any appropriate district court of the United States for such relief as may be appropriate, including injunctive relief.

(d) Job Corps

For the purposes of this section, Job Corps members shall be considered as the ultimate beneficiaries of Federal financial assistance.

(e) Regulations

The Secretary shall issue regulations necessary to implement this section not later than one year after August 7, 1998. Such regulations shall adopt standards for determining discrimination and procedures for enforcement that are consistent with the Acts referred to in a[1] subsection (a)(1) of this section, as well as procedures to ensure that complaints filed under this section and such Acts are processed in a manner that avoids duplication of effort.

(Pub. L. 105–220, title I, §188, Aug. 7, 1998, 112 Stat. 1049.)

REFERENCES IN TEXT

The Age Discrimination Act of 1975, referred to in subsec. (a)(1), is title III of Pub. L. 94–135, Nov. 28, 1975, 89 Stat. 728, as amended, which is classified generally to chapter 76 (§6101 et seq.) of Title 42, The Public Health and Welfare. For complete classification of this

[1] So in original.

Act to the Code, see Short Title note set out under section 6101 of Title 42 and Tables.

The Education Amendments of 1972, referred to in subsec. (a)(1), (2), is Pub. L. 92–318, June 23, 1972, 86 Stat. 235, as amended. Title IX of the Act, known as the Patsy Takemoto Mink Equal Opportunity in Education Act, is classified principally to chapter 38 (§1681 et seq.) of Title 20, Education. For complete classification of title IX to the Code, see Short Title note set out under section 1681 of Title 20 and Tables.

The Civil Rights Act of 1964, referred to in subsec. (a)(1), is Pub. L. 88–352, July 2, 1964, 78 Stat. 241, as amended. Title VI of the Act is classified generally to subchapter V (§2000d et seq.) of chapter 21 of Title 42, The Public Health and Welfare. For complete classification of this Act to the Code, see Short Title note set out under section 2000a of Title 42 and Tables.

This Act, referred to in subsec. (a)(1), is Pub. L. 105–220, Aug. 7, 1998, 112 Stat. 936, as amended, known as the Workforce Investment Act of 1998. For complete classification of this Act to the Code, see Short Title note set out under section 9201 of Title 20, Education, and Tables.

PRIOR PROVISIONS

Provisions similar to this section were contained in section 1577 of this title prior to repeal by Pub. L. 105–220.

ABOLITION OF IMMIGRATION AND NATURALIZATION SERVICE AND TRANSFER OF FUNCTIONS

For abolition of Immigration and Naturalization Service, transfer of functions, and treatment of related references, see note set out under section 1551 of Title 8, Aliens and Nationality.

§2939. Administrative provisions

(a) In general

The Secretary may, in accordance with chapter 5 of title 5, prescribe rules and regulations to carry out this chapter only to the extent necessary to administer and ensure compliance with the requirements of this chapter. Such rules and regulations may include provisions making adjustments authorized by section 6504 of title 31. All such rules and regulations shall be published in the Federal Register at least 30 days prior to their effective dates. Copies of each such rule or regulation shall be transmitted to the appropriate committees of Congress on the date of such publication and shall contain, with respect to each material provision of such rule or regulation, a citation to the particular substantive section of law that is the basis for the provision.

(b) Acquisition of certain property and services

The Secretary is authorized, in carrying out this chapter, to accept, purchase, or lease in the name of the Department of Labor, and employ or dispose of in furtherance of the purposes of this chapter, any money or property, real, personal, or mixed, tangible or intangible, received by gift, devise, bequest, or otherwise, and to accept voluntary and uncompensated services notwithstanding the provisions of section 1342 of title 31.

(c) Authority to enter into certain agreements and to make certain expenditures

The Secretary may make such grants, enter into such contracts or agreements, establish such procedures, and make such payments, in installments and in advance or by way of reimbursement, or otherwise allocate or expend such funds under this chapter, as may be necessary to carry out this chapter, including making expenditures for construction, repairs, and capital improvements, and including making necessary adjustments in payments on account of overpayments or underpayments.

(d) Annual report

The Secretary shall prepare and submit to Congress an annual report regarding the programs and activities carried out under this chapter. The Secretary shall include in such report—

(1) a summary of the achievements, failures, and problems of the programs and activities in meeting the objectives of this chapter;

(2) a summary of major findings from research, evaluations, pilot projects, and experiments conducted under this chapter in the fiscal year prior to the submission of the report;

(3) recommendations for modifications in the programs and activities based on analysis of such findings; and

(4) such other recommendations for legislative or administrative action as the Secretary determines to be appropriate.

(e) Utilization of services and facilities

The Secretary is authorized, in carrying out this chapter, under the same procedures as are applicable under subsection (c) of this section or to the extent permitted by law other than this chapter, to accept and use the services and facilities of departments, agencies, and establishments of the United States. The Secretary is also authorized, in carrying out this chapter, to accept and use the services and facilities of the agencies of any State or political subdivision of a State, with the consent of the State or political subdivision.

(f) Obligational authority

Notwithstanding any other provision of this chapter, the Secretary shall have no authority to enter into contracts, grant agreements, or other financial assistance agreements under this chapter except to such extent and in such amounts as are provided in advance in appropriations Acts.

(g) Program year

(1) In general

(A) Program year

Except as provided in subparagraph (B) and section 2918a of this title, appropriations for any fiscal year for programs and activities carried out under this chapter shall be available for obligation only on the basis of a program year. The program year shall begin on July 1 in the fiscal year for which the appropriation is made.

(B) Youth activities

The Secretary may make available for obligation, beginning April 1 of any fiscal year, funds appropriated for such fiscal year to carry out youth activities under subchapter II of this chapter.

(2) Availability

Funds obligated for any program year for a program or activity carried out under this chapter may be expended by each State receiving such funds during that program year and the 2 succeeding program years. Funds obligated for any program year for a program or activity carried out under section 2916 or 2917 of this title shall remain available until expended. Funds received by local areas from States under this chapter during a program year may be expended during that program year and the succeeding program year. No amount of the funds described in this paragraph shall be deobligated on account of a rate of expenditure that is consistent with a State plan, an operating plan described in section 2891 of this title, or a plan, grant agreement, contract, application, or other agreement described in subchapter IV of this chapter, as appropriate.

(h) Enforcement of Military Selective Service Act

The Secretary shall ensure that each individual participating in any program or activity established under this chapter, or receiving any assistance or benefit under this chapter, has not violated section 3 of the Military Selective Service Act (50 U.S.C. App. 453) by not presenting and submitting to registration as required pursuant to such section. The Director of the Selective Service System shall cooperate with the Secretary to enable the Secretary to carry out this subsection.

(i) Waivers and special rules

(1) Existing waivers

With respect to a State that has been granted a waiver under the provisions relating to training and employment services of the Department of Labor in title I of the Departments of Labor, Health and Human Services, and Education, and Related Agencies Appropriations Act, 1998 (Public Law 105–78; 111 Stat. 1467), the authority provided under such waiver shall continue in effect and apply, and include a waiver of the related provisions of subchapter II of this chapter and this subchapter, for the duration of the initial waiver.

(2) Special rule regarding designated areas

A State that has enacted, not later than December 31, 1997, a State law providing for the designation of service delivery areas for the delivery of workforce investment activities, may use such areas as local areas under this chapter, notwithstanding section 2831 of this title.

(3) Special rule regarding sanctions

A State that enacts, not later than December 31, 1997, a State law providing for the sanctioning of such service delivery areas for failure to meet performance measures for workforce investment activities, may use the State law to sanction local areas for failure to meet State performance measures under this chapter.

(4) General waivers of statutory or regulatory requirements

(A) General authority

Notwithstanding any other provision of law, the Secretary may waive for a State, or a local area in a State, pursuant to a request submitted by the Governor of the State (in consultation with appropriate local elected officials) that meets the requirements of subparagraph (B)—

(i) any of the statutory or regulatory requirements of subchapter II of this chapter or this subchapter (except for requirements relating to wage and labor standards, including nondisplacement protections, worker rights, participation and protection of workers and participants, grievance procedures and judicial review, nondiscrimination, allocation of funds to local areas, eligibility of providers or participants, the establishment and functions of local areas and local boards, and procedures for review and approval of plans); and

(ii) any of the statutory or regulatory requirements of sections 49g through 49i of this title (excluding requirements relating to the provision of services to unemployment insurance claimants and veterans, and requirements relating to universal access to basic labor exchange services without cost to jobseekers).

(B) Requests

A Governor requesting a waiver under subparagraph (A) shall submit a plan to the Secretary to improve the statewide workforce investment system that—

(i) identifies the statutory or regulatory requirements that are requested to be waived and the goals that the State or local area in the State, as appropriate, intends to achieve as a result of the waiver;

(ii) describes the actions that the State or local area, as appropriate, has undertaken to remove State or local statutory or regulatory barriers;

(iii) describes the goals of the waiver and the expected programmatic outcomes if the request is granted;

(iv) describes the individuals impacted by the waiver; and

(v) describes the process used to monitor the progress in implementing such a waiver, and the process by which notice and an opportunity to comment on such request has been provided to the local board.

(C) Conditions

Not later than 90 days after the date of the original submission of a request for a waiver under subparagraph (A), the Secretary shall provide a waiver under this paragraph if and only to the extent that—

(i) the Secretary determines that the requirements requested to be waived impede the ability of the State or local area, as appropriate, to implement the plan described in subparagraph (B); and

(ii) the State has executed a memorandum of understanding with the Secretary requiring such State to meet, or ensure that the local area meets, agreed-upon outcomes and to implement other appropriate measures to ensure accountability.

(Pub. L. 105–220, title I, § 189, Aug. 7, 1998, 112 Stat. 1051; Pub. L. 105–277, div. A, § 101(f) [title

VIII, §401(13)], Oct. 21, 1998, 112 Stat. 2681-337, 2681-411; Pub. L. 109-281, §2(c), Sept. 22, 2006, 120 Stat. 1181.)

REFERENCES IN TEXT

Title I of the Departments of Labor, Health and Human Services, and Education, and related Agencies Appropriations Act, 1998, referred to in subsec. (i)(1), is title I of Pub. L. 105-78, Nov. 13, 1997, 111 Stat. 1467.

CODIFICATION

In subsec. (a), "section 6504 of title 31" substituted for "section 204 of the Intergovernmental Cooperation Act of 1968" on authority of Pub. L. 97-258, §4(b), Sept. 13, 1982, 96 Stat. 1067, the first section of which enacted Title 31, Money and Finance.

PRIOR PROVISIONS

Provisions similar to this section were contained in sections 1504, 1571, and 1579 to 1581 of this title prior to repeal by Pub. L. 105-220.

AMENDMENTS

2006—Subsec. (g)(1)(A). Pub. L. 109-281 inserted "and section 2918a of this title" after "Except as provided in subparagraph (B)".

1998—Subsec. (i)(1). Pub. L. 105-277 substituted "1998 (Public Law 105-78; 111 Stat. 1467)" for "1997 (Public Law 104-208; 110 Stat. 3009-234)". The substitution was made to reflect the probable intent of Congress, in the absence of closing quotation marks designating the provisions to be inserted.

EFFECTIVE DATE OF 2006 AMENDMENT

Amendment by Pub. L. 109-281 effective Sept. 22, 2006, see section 2(f) of Pub. L. 109-281, set out as a note under section 1701u of Title 12, Banks and Banking.

§2940. References

(a) References to Comprehensive Employment and Training Act

Except as otherwise specified, a reference in a Federal law (other than a reference in a provision amended by the Reading Excellence Act) to a provision of the Comprehensive Employment and Training Act—

(1) effective on August 7, 1998, shall be deemed to refer to the corresponding provision of the Job Training Partnership Act or of the Workforce Investment Act of 1998; and

(2) effective on July 1, 2000, shall be deemed to refer to the corresponding provision of the Workforce Investment Act of 1998.

(b) References to Job Training Partnership Act

Except as otherwise specified, a reference in a Federal law (other than a reference in this Act or a reference in a provision amended by the Reading Excellence Act) to a provision of the Job Training Partnership Act—

(1) effective on August 7, 1998, shall be deemed to refer to that provision or the corresponding provision of the Workforce Investment Act of 1998; and

(2) effective on July 1, 2000, shall be deemed to refer to the corresponding provision of the Workforce Investment Act of 1998.

(Pub. L. 105-220, title I, §190, Aug. 7, 1998, 112 Stat. 1054; Pub. L. 105-277, div. A, §101(f) [title VIII, §405(h)(1)], Oct. 21, 1998, 112 Stat. 2681-337, 2681-435.)

REFERENCES IN TEXT

The Comprehensive Employment and Training Act, referred to in subsec. (a), is Pub. L. 93-203, Dec. 28, 1973, 87 Stat. 839, as amended, which was classified generally to chapter 17 (§801 et seq.) of this title, and was repealed by section 184(a)(1) of the Job Training Partnership Act, Pub. L. 97-300, title I, Oct. 13, 1982, 96 Stat. 1357.

The Reading Excellence Act, referred to in text, is section 101(f) [title VIII] of Pub. L. 105-277, div. A, Oct. 21, 1998, 112 Stat. 2681-337, 2681-391. The provisions of title VIII of section 101(f) appear at 112 Stat. 2681-391 to 2681-435. For complete classification of this Act to the Code, see Tables.

The Job Training Partnership Act, referred to in subsecs. (a)(1) and (b), is Pub. L. 97-300, Oct. 13, 1982, 96 Stat. 1322, as amended, which was classified generally to chapter 19 (§1501 et seq.) of this title, prior to repeal by Pub. L. 105-220, title I, §199(b)(2), (c)(2)(B), Aug. 7, 1998, 112 Stat. 1059. For complete classification of this Act to the Code, see Tables.

The Workforce Investment Act of 1998, referred to in text, is Pub. L. 105-220, Aug. 7, 1998, 112 Stat. 936, as amended. For complete classification of this Act to the Code, see Short Title note set out under section 9201 of Title 20, Education, and Tables.

This Act, referred to in subsec. (b), is the Workforce Investment Act of 1998. See note above.

AMENDMENTS

1998—Pub. L. 105-277 amended section catchline and text generally. Prior to amendment, text read as follows: "Effective on August 7, 1998, all references in any other provision of law (other than section 665 of title 18) to the Comprehensive Employment and Training Act, or to the Job Training Partnership Act, as the case may be, shall be deemed to refer to the 'Workforce Investment Act of 1998.'"

EFFECTIVE DATE OF 1998 AMENDMENT

Pub. L. 105-277, div. A, §101(f) [title VIII, §405(h)(2)], Oct. 21, 1998, 112 Stat. 2681-337, 2681-435, provided that: "The amendment made by paragraph (1) [amending this section] shall take effect as if included in the Workforce Investment Act of 1998 [Pub. L. 105-220]."

PREPARATION OF LEGISLATION TO MAKE TECHNICAL AND CONFORMING AMENDMENTS

Pub. L. 105-220, title I, §199A, Aug. 7, 1998, 112 Stat. 1059, as amended by Pub. L. 105-277, div. A, §101(f) [title VIII, §405(h)(3)], Oct. 21, 1998, 112 Stat. 2681-337, 2681-435, provided that:

"(a) PREPARATION.—After consultation with the appropriate committees of Congress and the Director of the Office of Management and Budget, the Secretary shall prepare recommended legislation containing technical and conforming amendments to reflect the changes made by this subtitle [subtitle F (§§199, 199A) of title I of Pub. L. 105-220, repealing sections 1501 to 1505, 1511 to 1583, 1592 to 1735, 1737, 1751 to 1791h, 1792 to 1792b, and 2301 to 2314 of this title, section 211 of former Title 40, Appendix, Public Buildings, Property, and Works, sections 11421, 11441 to 11447, 11449, 11450, 11461 to 11466, 11471, and 11472 of Title 42, The Public Health and Welfare, and sections 42101 to 42106 of Title 49, Transportation, enacting provisions set out as notes under sections 1501 and 2301 of this title and section 11421 of Title 42, and repealing provisions set out as notes under sections 1501 and 2301 of this title and section 1255a of Title 8, Aliens and Nationality].

"(b) SUBMISSION TO CONGRESS.—Not later than 6 months after the date of enactment of this Act [Aug. 7, 1998], the Secretary shall submit to Congress the recommended legislation referred to under subsection (a)."

§2941. State legislative authority

(a) Authority of State legislature

Nothing in this chapter shall be interpreted to preclude the enactment of State legislation providing for the implementation, consistent with the provisions of this chapter, of the activities assisted under this chapter. Any funds received by a State under this chapter shall be subject to appropriation by the State legislature, consistent with the terms and conditions required under this chapter.

(b) Interstate compacts and cooperative agreements

In the event that compliance with provisions of this chapter would be enhanced by compacts and cooperative agreements between States, the consent of Congress is given to States to enter into such compacts and agreements to facilitate such compliance, subject to the approval of the Secretary.

(Pub. L. 105–220, title I, § 191, Aug. 7, 1998, 112 Stat. 1054.)

PRIOR PROVISIONS

Provisions similar to this section were contained in sections 1536 and 1537 of this title prior to repeal by Pub. L. 105–220.

§ 2942. Workforce flexibility plans

(a) Plans

A State may submit to the Secretary, and the Secretary may approve, a workforce flexibility plan under which the State is authorized to waive, in accordance with the plan—

(1) any of the statutory or regulatory requirements applicable under this chapter to local areas, pursuant to applications for such waivers from the local areas, except for requirements relating to the basic purposes of this chapter, wage and labor standards, grievance procedures and judicial review, nondiscrimination, eligibility of participants, allocation of funds to local areas, establishment and functions of local areas and local boards, review and approval of local plans, and worker rights, participation, and protection;

(2) any of the statutory or regulatory requirements applicable under sections 49g through 49i of this title to the State, except for requirements relating to the provision of services to unemployment insurance claimants and veterans, and to universal access to basic labor exchange services without cost to jobseekers; and

(3) any of the statutory or regulatory requirements applicable under the Older Americans Act of 1965 (42 U.S.C. 3001 et seq.) to State agencies on aging with respect to activities carried out using funds allotted under section 506(a)(3)[1] of such Act (42 U.S.C. 3056d(a)(3)), except for requirements relating to the basic purposes of such Act, wage and labor standards, eligibility of participants in the activities, and standards for agreements.

(b) Content of plans

A workforce flexibility plan implemented by a State under subsection (a) of this section shall include descriptions of—

(1)(A) the process by which local areas in the State may submit and obtain approval by the State of applications for waivers of requirements applicable under this chapter; and

(B) the requirements described in subparagraph (A) that are likely to be waived by the State under the plan;

(2) the requirements applicable under sections 49g through 49i of this title that are proposed to be waived, if any;

(3) the requirements applicable under the Older Americans Act of 1965 [42 U.S.C. 3001 et seq.] that are proposed to be waived, if any;

(4) the outcomes to be achieved by the waivers described in paragraphs (1) through (3); and

(5) other measures to be taken to ensure appropriate accountability for Federal funds in connection with the waivers.

(c) Periods

The Secretary may approve a workforce flexibility plan for a period of not more than 5 years.

(d) Opportunity for public comments

Prior to submitting a workforce flexibility plan to the Secretary for approval, the State shall provide to all interested parties and to the general public adequate notice and a reasonable opportunity for comment on the waiver requests proposed to be implemented pursuant to such plan.

(Pub. L. 105–220, title I, § 192, Aug. 7, 1998, 112 Stat. 1054; Pub. L. 105–277, div. A, § 101(f) [title VIII, § 401(14)], Oct. 21, 1998, 112 Stat. 2681–337, 2681–411.)

REFERENCES IN TEXT

The Older Americans Act of 1965, referred to in subsecs. (a)(3) and (b)(3), is Pub. L. 89–73, July 14, 1965, 79 Stat. 218, as amended, which is classified generally to chapter 35 (§ 3001 et seq.) of Title 42, The Public Health and Welfare. Section 506 of the Act, which is classified to section 3056d of Title 42, was amended generally by Pub. L. 109–365, title V, § 501, Oct. 17, 2006, 120 Stat 2563, and provisions formerly appearing in subsec. (a)(3) of that section are now contained in subsec. (e). For complete classification of this Act to the Code, see Short Title note set out under section 3001 of Title 42 and Tables.

AMENDMENTS

1998—Subsec. (a)(2). Pub. L. 105–277 struck out comma before "to the State, except".

Subsec. (a)(3). Pub. L. 105–277 substituted ") to" for "), to".

WORKFORCE FLEXIBILITY PARTNERSHIP DEMONSTRATION PROGRAM

Pub. L. 105–78, title I, Nov. 13, 1997, 111 Stat. 1469, provided in part: "That the Secretary of Labor shall establish a workforce flexibility (work-flex) partnership demonstration program under which the Secretary shall authorize not more than six States, of which at least three States shall each have populations not in excess of 3,500,000, with a preference given to those States that have been designated Ed-Flex Partnership States under section 311(e) of Public Law 103–227 [20 U.S.C. 5891(e)], to waive any statutory or regulatory requirement applicable to service delivery areas or substate areas within the State under titles I–III of the Job Training Partnership Act [former 29 U.S.C. 1511 et seq., 1601 et seq., 1651 et seq.] (except for requirements relating to wage and labor standards, grievance procedures and judicial review, nondiscrimination, allotment of funds, and eligibility), and any of the statutory or regulatory requirements of sections 8–10 of the Wagner-Peyser Act [29 U.S.C. 49g–49i] (except for requirements relating to the provision of services to unemployment insurance claimants and veterans, and to

[1] See References in Text note below.

universal access to basic labor exchange services without cost to job seekers), for a duration not to exceed the waiver period authorized under section 311(e) of Public Law 103–227, pursuant to a plan submitted by such States and approved by the Secretary for the provision of workforce employment and training activities in the States, which includes a description of the process by which service delivery areas and substate areas may apply for and have waivers approved by the State, the requirements of the Wagner-Peyser Act [29 U.S.C. 49 et seq.] to be waived, the outcomes to be achieved and other measures to be taken to ensure appropriate accountability for Federal funds."

[References to a provision of the Job Training Partnership Act, effective Aug. 7, 1998, are deemed to refer to that provision or the corresponding provision of the Workforce Investment Act of 1998, Pub. L. 105–220, Aug. 7, 1998, 112 Stat. 936, and effective July 1, 2000, are deemed to refer to the corresponding provision of the Workforce Investment Act of 1998, see section 2940(b) of this title. For complete classification of the Workforce Investment Act of 1998 to the Code, see Short Title note set out under section 9201 of Title 20, Education, and Tables.]

Similar provisions were contained in the following prior appropriations act:

Pub. L. 104–208, div. A, title I, § 101(e) [title I], Sept. 30, 1996, 110 Stat. 3009–233, 3009–234.

§ 2943. Transfer of Federal equity in State employment security real property to the States

(a) Transfer of Federal equity

Notwithstanding any other provision of law, any Federal equity acquired in real property through grants to States awarded under title III of the Social Security Act (42 U.S.C. 501 et seq.) or under the Wagner-Peyser Act (29 U.S.C. 49 et seq.) is transferred to the States that used the grants for the acquisition of such equity. The portion of any real property that is attributable to the Federal equity transferred under this section shall be used to carry out activities authorized under this Act, the Wagner-Peyser Act (29 U.S.C. 49 et seq.), or title III of the Social Security Act (42 U.S.C. 501 et seq.). Any disposition of such real property shall be carried out in accordance with the procedures prescribed by the Secretary and the portion of the proceeds from the disposition of such real property that is attributable to the Federal equity transferred under this section shall be used to carry out activities authorized under this Act, the Wagner-Peyser Act, or title III of the Social Security Act.

(b) Limitation on use

A State shall not use funds awarded under this Act, the Wagner-Peyser Act [29 U.S.C. 49 et seq.], or title III of the Social Security Act [42 U.S.C. 501 et seq.] to amortize the costs of real property that is purchased by any State on or after February 15, 2007.

(Pub. L. 105–220, title I, § 193, Aug. 7, 1998, 112 Stat. 1055; Pub. L. 109–289, div. B, title II, § 20610, as added Pub. L. 110–5, § 2, Feb. 15, 2007, 121 Stat. 30.)

References in Text

The Social Security Act, referred to in text, is act Aug. 14, 1935, ch. 531, 49 Stat. 620. Title III of the Act is classified generally to subchapter III (§ 501 et seq.) of chapter 7 of Title 42, The Public Health and Welfare. For complete classification of this Act to the Code, see section 1305 of Title 42 and Tables.

The Wagner-Peyser Act, referred to in text, is act June 6, 1933, ch. 49, 48 Stat. 113, which is classified generally to chapter 4B (§ 49 et seq.) of this title. For complete classification of this Act to the Code, see Short Title note set out under section 49 of this title and Tables.

This Act, referred to in text, is Pub. L. 105–220, Aug. 7, 1998, 112 Stat. 936, known as the Workforce Investment Act of 1998. For complete classification of this Act to the Code, see Short Title note set out under section 9201 of Title 20, Education, and Tables.

Amendments

2007—Pub. L. 110–5 added Pub. L. 109–289, § 20610. See 2006 Amendment note below.

2006—Pub. L. 109–289, § 20610, as added by Pub. L. 110–5, amended section catchline and text generally. Prior to amendment, text related to use of State real property for a one-stop service delivery system.

§ 2944. Continuation of State activities and policies

(a) In general

Notwithstanding any other provision of this chapter, the Secretary may not deny approval of a State plan for a covered State, or an application of a covered State for financial assistance, under this chapter or find a covered State (including a State board or Governor), or a local area (including a local board or chief elected official) in a covered State, in violation of a provision of this chapter, on the basis that—

(1)(A) the State proposes to allocate or disburse, allocates, or disburses, within the State, funds made available to the State under section 2852 or 2862 of this title in accordance with the allocation formula for the type of activities involved, or in accordance with a disbursal procedure or process, used by the State under prior consistent State laws; or

(B) a local board in the State proposes to disburse, or disburses, within the local area, funds made available to a State under section 2852 or 2862 of this title in accordance with a disbursal procedure or process used by a private industry council under prior consistent State law;

(2) the State proposes to carry out or carries out a State procedure through which local areas use, as fiscal agents for funds made available to the State under section 2852 or 2862 of this title and allocated within the State, fiscal agents selected in accordance with a process established under prior consistent State laws;

(3) the State proposes to carry out or carries out a State procedure through which the local board in the State (or the local boards, the chief elected officials in the State, and the Governor) designate or select the one-stop partners and one-stop operators of the statewide system in the State under prior consistent State laws, in lieu of making the designation, or certification described in section 2841 of this title (regardless of the date the one-stop delivery systems involved have been established);

(4) the State proposes to carry out or carries out a State procedure through which the persons responsible for selecting eligible providers for purposes of subchapter II of this chapter are permitted to determine that a provider

shall not be selected to provide both intake services under section 2864(d)(2) of this title and training services under section 2864(d)(4) of this title, under prior consistent State laws;

(5) the State proposes to designate or designates a State board, or proposes to assign or assigns functions and roles of the State board (including determining the time periods for development and submission of a State plan required under section 2822 of this title), for purposes of subchapter II of this chapter in accordance with prior consistent State laws; or

(6) a local board in the State proposes to use or carry out, uses, or carries out a local plan (including assigning functions and roles of the local board) for purposes of subchapter II of this chapter in accordance with the authorities and requirements applicable to local plans and private industry councils under prior consistent State laws.

(b) Definition

In this section:

(1) Covered State

The term "covered State" means a State that enacted State laws described in paragraph (2).

(2) Prior consistent State laws

The term "prior consistent State laws" means State laws, not inconsistent with the Job Training Partnership Act or any other applicable Federal law, that took effect on September 1, 1993, September 1, 1995, and September 1, 1997.

(Pub. L. 105–220, title I, § 194, Aug. 7, 1998, 112 Stat. 1056.)

REFERENCES IN TEXT

The Job Training Partnership Act, referred to in subsec. (b)(2), is Pub. L. 97–300, Oct. 13, 1982, 96 Stat. 1322, as amended, which was classified generally to chapter 19 (§ 1501 et seq.) of this title, prior to repeal by Pub. L. 105–220, title I, § 199(b)(2), (c)(2)(B), Aug. 7, 1998, 112 Stat. 1059, effective July 1, 2000.

§ 2945. General program requirements

Except as otherwise provided in this chapter, the following conditions are applicable to all programs under this chapter:

(1) Each program under this chapter shall provide employment and training opportunities to those who can benefit from, and who are most in need of, such opportunities. In addition, efforts shall be made to develop programs which contribute to occupational development, upward mobility, development of new careers, and opportunities for nontraditional employment.

(2) Funds provided under this chapter shall only be used for activities that are in addition to those that would otherwise be available in the local area in the absence of such funds.

(3)(A) Any local area may enter into an agreement with another local area (including a local area that is a city or county within the same labor market) to pay or share the cost of educating, training, or placing individuals participating in programs assisted under this chapter, including the provision of supportive services.

(B) Such agreement shall be approved by each local board providing guidance to the local area and shall be described in the local plan under section 2833 of this title.

(4) On-the-job training contracts under this chapter shall not be entered into with employers who have received payments under previous contracts and have exhibited a pattern of failing to provide on-the-job training participants with continued long-term employment as regular employees with wages and employment benefits (including health benefits) and working conditions at the same level and to the same extent as other employees working a similar length of time and doing the same type of work.

(5) No person or organization may charge an individual a fee for the placement or referral of the individual in or to a workforce investment activity under this chapter.

(6) The Secretary shall not provide financial assistance for any program under this chapter that involves political activities.

(7)(A) Income under any program administered by a public or private nonprofit entity may be retained by such entity only if such income is used to continue to carry out the program.

(B) Income subject to the requirements of subparagraph (A) shall include—

(i) receipts from goods or services (including conferences) provided as a result of activities funded under this chapter;

(ii) funds provided to a service provider under this chapter that are in excess of the costs associated with the services provided; and

(iii) interest income earned on funds received under this chapter.

(C) For purposes of this paragraph, each entity receiving financial assistance under this chapter shall maintain records sufficient to determine the amount of such income received and the purposes for which such income is expended.

(8)(A) The Secretary shall notify the Governor and the appropriate local board and chief elected official of, and consult with the Governor and such board and official concerning, any activity to be funded by the Secretary under this chapter within the corresponding State or local area.

(B) The Governor shall notify the appropriate local board and chief elected official of, and consult with such board and official concerning, any activity to be funded by the Governor under this chapter within the corresponding local area.

(9)(A) All education programs for youth supported with funds provided under part D of subchapter II of this chapter shall be consistent with applicable State and local educational standards.

(B) Standards and procedures with respect to awarding academic credit and certifying educational attainment in programs conducted under such part shall be consistent with the requirements of applicable State and local law, including regulation.

(10) No funds available under this chapter may be used for public service employment ex-

cept as specifically authorized under this chapter.

(11) The Federal requirements governing the chapter, use, and disposition of real property, equipment, and supplies purchased with funds provided under this chapter shall be the Federal requirements generally applicable to Federal grants to States and local governments.

(12) Nothing in this chapter shall be construed to provide an individual with an entitlement to a service under this chapter.

(13) Services, facilities, or equipment funded under this chapter may be used, as appropriate, on a fee-for-service basis, by employers in a local area in order to provide employment and training activities to incumbent workers—

(A) when such services, facilities, or equipment are not in use for the provision of services for eligible participants under this chapter;

(B) if such use for incumbent workers would not have an adverse affect[1] on the provision of services to eligible participants under this chapter; and

(C) if the income derived from such fees is used to carry out the programs authorized under this chapter.

(Pub. L. 105–220, title I, §195, Aug. 7, 1998, 112 Stat. 1057.)

CHAPTER 31—ASSISTIVE TECHNOLOGY FOR INDIVIDUALS WITH DISABILITIES

Sec.

§3001. Findings and purposes

(a) Findings

Congress finds the following:

(1) Over 54,000,000 individuals in the United States have disabilities, with almost half experiencing severe disabilities that affect their ability to see, hear, communicate, reason, walk, or perform other basic life functions.

(2) Disability is a natural part of the human experience and in no way diminishes the right of individuals to—

(A) live independently;

(B) enjoy self-determination and make choices;

(C) benefit from an education;

(D) pursue meaningful careers; and

(E) enjoy full inclusion and integration in the economic, political, social, cultural, and educational mainstream of society in the United States.

(3) Technology is one of the primary engines for economic activity, education, and innovation in the Nation, and throughout the world. The commitment of the United States to the development and utilization of technology is one of the main factors underlying the strength and vibrancy of the economy of the United States.

(4) As technology has come to play an increasingly important role in the lives of all persons in the United States, in the conduct of business, in the functioning of government, in the fostering of communication, in the conduct of commerce, and in the provision of education, its impact upon the lives of individuals with disabilities in the United States has been comparable to its impact upon the remainder of the citizens of the United States. Any development in mainstream technology will have profound implications for individuals with disabilities in the United States.

(5) Substantial progress has been made in the development of assistive technology devices, including adaptations to existing devices that facilitate activities of daily living that significantly benefit individuals with disabilities of all ages. These devices, including adaptations, increase involvement in, and reduce expenditures associated with, programs and activities that facilitate communication, ensure independent functioning, enable early childhood development, support educational achievement, provide and enhance employment options, and enable full participation in community living for individuals with disabilities. Access to such devices can also reduce expenditures associated with early childhood intervention, education, rehabilitation and training, health care, employment, residential living, independent living, recreation opportunities, and other aspects of daily living.

(6) Over the last 15 years, the Federal Government has invested in the development of comprehensive statewide programs of technology-related assistance, which have proven effective in assisting individuals with disabilities in accessing assistive technology devices and assistive technology services. This partnership between the Federal Government and the States provided an important service to individuals with disabilities by strengthening the capacity of each State to assist individuals with disabilities of all ages meet their assistive technology needs.

(7) Despite the success of the Federal-State partnership in providing access to assistive technology devices and assistive technology services, there is a continued need to provide information about the availability of assistive technology, advances in improving accessibility and functionality of assistive technology, and appropriate methods to secure and utilize assistive technology in order to maximize the independence and participation of individuals with disabilities in society.

(8) The combination of significant recent changes in Federal policy (including changes to section 794d of this title, accessibility provisions of the Help America Vote Act of 2002 (42 U.S.C. 15301 et seq.), and the amendments made to the Elementary and Secondary Education Act of 1965 (20 U.S.C. 6301 et seq.) by the No Child Left Behind Act of 2001) and the rapid and unending evolution of technology require a Federal-State investment in State assistive

[1] So in original. Probably should be "effect".

technology systems to continue to ensure that individuals with disabilities reap the benefits of the technological revolution and participate fully in life in their communities.

(b) Purposes

The purposes of this chapter are—

(1) to support State efforts to improve the provision of assistive technology to individuals with disabilities through comprehensive statewide programs of technology-related assistance, for individuals with disabilities of all ages, that are designed to—

(A) increase the availability of, funding for, access to, provision of, and training about assistive technology devices and assistive technology services;

(B) increase the ability of individuals with disabilities of all ages to secure and maintain possession of assistive technology devices as such individuals make the transition between services offered by educational or human service agencies or between settings of daily living (for example, between home and work);

(C) increase the capacity of public agencies and private entities to provide and pay for assistive technology devices and assistive technology services on a statewide basis for individuals with disabilities of all ages;

(D) increase the involvement of individuals with disabilities and, if appropriate, their family members, guardians, advocates, and authorized representatives, in decisions related to the provision of assistive technology devices and assistive technology services;

(E) increase and promote coordination among State agencies, between State and local agencies, among local agencies, and between State and local agencies and private entities (such as managed care providers), that are involved or are eligible to be involved in carrying out activities under this chapter;

(F) increase the awareness and facilitate the change of laws, regulations, policies, practices, procedures, and organizational structures, that facilitate the availability or provision of assistive technology devices and assistive technology services; and

(G) increase awareness and knowledge of the benefits of assistive technology devices and assistive technology services among targeted individuals and entities and the general population; and

(2) to provide States with financial assistance that supports programs designed to maximize the ability of individuals with disabilities and their family members, guardians, advocates, and authorized representatives to obtain assistive technology devices and assistive technology services.

(Pub. L. 105–394, §2, Nov. 13, 1998, 112 Stat. 3628; Pub. L. 108–364, §2, Oct. 25, 2004, 118 Stat. 1707.)

REFERENCES IN TEXT

The Help America Vote Act of 2002, referred to in subsec. (a)(8), is Pub. L. 107–252, Oct. 29, 2002, 116 Stat. 1666, which is classified principally to chapter 146 (§15301 et seq.) of Title 42, The Public Health and Welfare. For complete classification of this Act to the Code, see Short Title note set out under section 15301 of Title 42 and Tables.

The Elementary and Secondary Education Act of 1965, referred to in subsec. (a)(8), is Pub. L. 89–10, Apr. 11, 1965, 79 Stat. 27, as amended, which is classified generally to chapter 70 (§6301 et seq.) of Title 20, Education. For complete classification of this Act to the Code, see Short Title note set out under section 6301 of Title 20 and Tables.

The No Child Left Behind Act of 2001, referred to in subsec. (a)(8), is Pub. L. 107–110, Jan. 8, 2002, 115 Stat. 1425, as amended. For complete classification of this Act to the Code, see Short Title of 2002 Amendment note set out under section 6301 of Title 20, Education, and Tables.

AMENDMENTS

2004—Pub. L. 108–364 amended section catchline and text generally. Prior to amendment, text consisted of subsecs. (a) and (b) relating to findings and purposes.

SHORT TITLE OF 2004 AMENDMENT

Pub. L. 108–364, §1, Oct. 25, 2004, 118 Stat. 1707, provided that: "This Act [enacting sections 3003 to 3007 of this title, amending this section, sections 763, 781, 792, and 3002 of this title, and sections 15024, 15025, 15043, and 15064 of Title 42, The Public Health and Welfare, omitting sections 3011 to 3015, 3031 to 3037, and 3051 to 3058 of this title, and amending provisions set out as a note under this section] may be cited as the 'Assistive Technology Act of 2004'."

SHORT TITLE

Pub. L. 105–394, §1(a), Nov. 13, 1998, 112 Stat. 3627, as amended by Pub. L. 108–364, §2, Oct. 25, 2004, 118 Stat. 1707, provided that: "This Act [enacting this chapter] may be cited as the 'Assistive Technology Act of 1998'."

§3002. Definitions

In this chapter:

(1) Adult service program

The term "adult service program" means a program that provides services to, or is otherwise substantially involved with the major life functions of, individuals with disabilities. Such term includes—

(A) a program providing residential, supportive, or employment services, or employment-related services, to individuals with disabilities;

(B) a program carried out by a center for independent living, such as a center described in part C of title VII of the Rehabilitation Act of 1973 (29 U.S.C. 796f et seq.);

(C) a program carried out by an employment support agency connected to adult vocational rehabilitation, such as a one-stop partner, as defined in section 2801 of this title; and

(D) a program carried out by another organization or vender licensed or registered by the designated State agency, as defined in section 7 of the Rehabilitation Act of 1973 (29 U.S.C. 705).

(2) American Indian consortium

The term "American Indian consortium" means an entity that is an American Indian Consortium (as defined in section 102 of Developmental Disabilities Assistance and Bill of Rights Act of 2000 (42 U.S.C. 15002)), and that is established to provide protection and advocacy services for purposes of receiving funding under subtitle C of title I of such Act (42 U.S.C. 15041 et seq.).

(3) Assistive technology

The term "assistive technology" means technology designed to be utilized in an assistive technology device or assistive technology service.

(4) Assistive technology device

The term "assistive technology device" means any item, piece of equipment, or product system, whether acquired commercially, modified, or customized, that is used to increase, maintain, or improve functional capabilities of individuals with disabilities.

(5) Assistive technology service

The term "assistive technology service" means any service that directly assists an individual with a disability in the selection, acquisition, or use of an assistive technology device. Such term includes—

(A) the evaluation of the assistive technology needs of an individual with a disability, including a functional evaluation of the impact of the provision of appropriate assistive technology and appropriate services to the individual in the customary environment of the individual;

(B) a service consisting of purchasing, leasing, or otherwise providing for the acquisition of assistive technology devices by individuals with disabilities;

(C) a service consisting of selecting, designing, fitting, customizing, adapting, applying, maintaining, repairing, replacing, or donating assistive technology devices;

(D) coordination and use of necessary therapies, interventions, or services with assistive technology devices, such as therapies, interventions, or services associated with education and rehabilitation plans and programs;

(E) training or technical assistance for an individual with a disability or, where appropriate, the family members, guardians, advocates, or authorized representatives of such an individual;

(F) training or technical assistance for professionals (including individuals providing education and rehabilitation services and entities that manufacture or sell assistive technology devices), employers, providers of employment and training services, or other individuals who provide services to, employ, or are otherwise substantially involved in the major life functions of individuals with disabilities; and

(G) a service consisting of expanding the availability of access to technology, including electronic and information technology, to individuals with disabilities.

(6) Capacity building and advocacy activities

The term "capacity building and advocacy activities" means efforts that—

(A) result in laws, regulations, policies, practices, procedures, or organizational structures that promote consumer-responsive programs or entities; and

(B) facilitate and increase access to, provision of, and funding for, assistive technology devices and assistive technology services, in order to empower individuals with disabilities to achieve greater independence, productivity, and integration and inclusion within the community and the workforce.

(7) Comprehensive statewide program of technology-related assistance

The term "comprehensive statewide program of technology-related assistance" means a consumer-responsive program of technology-related assistance for individuals with disabilities, implemented by a State, and equally available to all individuals with disabilities residing in the State, regardless of their type of disability, age, income level, or location of residence in the State, or the type of assistive technology device or assistive technology service required.

(8) Consumer-responsive

The term "consumer-responsive"—

(A) with regard to policies, means that the policies are consistent with the principles of—

(i) respect for individual dignity, personal responsibility, self-determination, and pursuit of meaningful careers, based on informed choice, of individuals with disabilities;

(ii) respect for the privacy, rights, and equal access (including the use of accessible formats) of such individuals;

(iii) inclusion, integration, and full participation of such individuals in society;

(iv) support for the involvement in decisions of a family member, a guardian, an advocate, or an authorized representative, if an individual with a disability requests, desires, or needs such involvement; and

(v) support for individual and systems advocacy and community involvement; and

(B) with respect to an entity, program, or activity, means that the entity, program, or activity—

(i) is easily accessible to, and usable by, individuals with disabilities and, when appropriate, their family members, guardians, advocates, or authorized representatives;

(ii) responds to the needs of individuals with disabilities in a timely and appropriate manner; and

(iii) facilitates the full and meaningful participation of individuals with disabilities (including individuals from underrepresented populations and rural populations) and their family members, guardians, advocates, and authorized representatives, in—

(I) decisions relating to the provision of assistive technology devices and assistive technology services to such individuals; and

(II) decisions related to the maintenance, improvement, and evaluation of the comprehensive statewide program of technology-related assistance, including decisions that affect capacity building and advocacy activities.

(9) Disability

The term "disability" means a condition of an individual that is considered to be a disability or handicap for the purposes of any Federal law other than this chapter or for the purposes of the law of the State in which the individual resides.

(10) Individual with a disability; individuals with disabilities

(A) Individual with a disability

The term "individual with a disability" means any individual of any age, race, or ethnicity—

(i) who has a disability; and

(ii) who is or would be enabled by an assistive technology device or an assistive technology service to minimize deterioration in functioning, to maintain a level of functioning, or to achieve a greater level of functioning in any major life activity.

(B) Individuals with disabilities

The term "individuals with disabilities" means more than 1 individual with a disability.

(11) Institution of higher education

The term "institution of higher education" has the meaning given such term in section 1001(a) of title 20, and includes a community college receiving funding under the Tribally Controlled Colleges and Universities Assistance Act of 1978 (25 U.S.C. 1801 et seq.).

(12) Protection and advocacy services

The term "protection and advocacy services" means services that—

(A) are described in subtitle C of title I of the Developmental Disabilities Assistance and Bill of Rights Act of 2000 (42 U.S.C. 15041 et seq.), the Protection and Advocacy for Individuals with Mental Illness Act (42 U.S.C. 10801 et seq.), or section 509 of the Rehabilitation Act of 1973 (29 U.S.C. 794e); and

(B) assist individuals with disabilities with respect to assistive technology devices and assistive technology services.

(13) Secretary

The term "Secretary" means the Secretary of Education.

(14) State

(A) In general

Except as provided in subparagraph (B), the term "State" means each of the 50 States of the United States, the District of Columbia, the Commonwealth of Puerto Rico, the United States Virgin Islands, Guam, American Samoa, and the Commonwealth of the Northern Mariana Islands.

(B) Outlying areas

In section 3003(b) of this title:

(i) Outlying area

The term "outlying area" means the United States Virgin Islands, Guam, American Samoa, and the Commonwealth of the Northern Mariana Islands.

(ii) State

The term "State" does not include the United States Virgin Islands, Guam, American Samoa, and the Commonwealth of the Northern Mariana Islands.

(15) State assistive technology program

The term "State assistive technology program" means a program authorized under section 3003 of this title.

(16) Targeted individuals and entities

The term "targeted individuals and entities" means—

(A) individuals with disabilities of all ages and their family members, guardians, advocates, and authorized representatives;

(B) underrepresented populations, including the aging workforce;

(C) individuals who work for public or private entities (including centers for independent living described in part C of title VII of the Rehabilitation Act of 1973 (29 U.S.C. 796f et seq.), insurers, or managed care providers) that have contact, or provide services to, with individuals with disabilities;

(D) educators at all levels (including providers of early intervention services, elementary schools, secondary schools, community colleges, and vocational and other institutions of higher education) and related services personnel;

(E) technology experts (including web designers and procurement officials);

(F) health, allied health, and rehabilitation professionals and hospital employees (including discharge planners);

(G) employers, especially small business employers, and providers of employment and training services;

(H) entities that manufacture or sell assistive technology devices;

(I) entities that carry out community programs designed to develop essential community services in rural and urban areas; and

(J) other appropriate individuals and entities, as determined for a State by the State.

(17) Technology-related assistance

The term "technology-related assistance" means assistance provided through capacity building and advocacy activities that accomplish the purposes described in section 3001(b) of this title.

(18) Underrepresented population

The term "underrepresented population" means a population that is typically underrepresented in service provision, and includes populations such as persons who have low-incidence disabilities, persons who are minorities, poor persons, persons with limited English proficiency, older individuals, or persons from rural areas.

(19) Universal design

The term "universal design" means a concept or philosophy for designing and delivering products and services that are usable by people with the widest possible range of functional capabilities, which include products and services that are directly accessible (without requiring assistive technologies) and products and services that are interoperable with assistive technologies.

(Pub. L. 105–394, §3, Nov. 13, 1998, 112 Stat. 3631; Pub. L. 106–402, title IV, §401(b)(4)(A), Oct. 30,

2000, 114 Stat. 1738; Pub. L. 108–364, §2, Oct. 25, 2004, 118 Stat. 1709; Pub. L. 110–315, title IX, §941(k)(2)(K), Aug. 14, 2008, 122 Stat. 3467.)

REFERENCES IN TEXT

The Rehabilitation Act of 1973, referred to in pars. (1)(B) and (16)(C), is Pub. L. 93–112, Sept. 26, 1973, 87 Stat. 355. Part C of title VII of the Act is classified generally to subpart 3 (§796f et seq.) of part A of subchapter VII of chapter 16 of this title. For complete classification of this Act to the Code, see Short Title note set out under section 701 of this title and Tables.

The Developmental Disabilities Assistance and Bill of Rights Act of 2000, referred to in pars. (2) and (12)(A), is Pub. L. 106–402, Oct. 30, 2000, 114 Stat. 1677. Subtitle C of title I of the Act is classified generally to part C (§15041 et seq.) of subchapter I of chapter 144 of Title 42, The Public Health and Welfare. For complete classification of this Act to the Code, see Short Title note set out under section 15001 of Title 42 and Tables.

The Tribally Controlled Colleges and Universities Assistance Act of 1978, referred to in par. (11), is Pub. L. 95–471, Oct. 17, 1978, 92 Stat. 1325, which is classified principally to chapter 20 (§1801 et seq.) of Title 25, Indians. For complete classification of this Act to the Code, see Short Title note set out under section 1801 of Title 25 and Tables.

The Protection and Advocacy for Individuals with Mental Illness Act, referred to in par. (12)(A), is Pub. L. 99–319, May 23, 1986, 100 Stat. 478, which is classified generally to chapter 114 (§10801 et seq.) of Title 42, The Public Health and Welfare. For complete classification of this Act to the Code, see Short Title note set out under section 10801 of Title 42 and Tables.

AMENDMENTS

2008—Par. (11). Pub. L. 110–315 substituted "the Tribally Controlled Colleges and Universities Assistance Act of 1978" for "the Tribally Controlled College or University Assistance Act of 1978".

2004—Pub. L. 108–364 amended section catchline and text generally. Prior to amendment, text consisted of subsecs. (a) and (b) relating to definitions and references.

2000—Subsec. (a)(11)(A). Pub. L. 106–402 substituted "subtitle C of the Developmental Disabilities Assistance and Bill of Rights Act of 2000" for "part C of the Developmental Disabilities Assistance and Bill of Rights Act (42 U.S.C. 6041 et seq.)".

§3003. State grants for assistive technology

(a) Grants to States

The Secretary shall award grants under subsection (b) to States to maintain comprehensive statewide programs of technology-related assistance to support programs that are designed to maximize the ability of individuals with disabilities across the human lifespan and across the wide array of disabilities, and their family members, guardians, advocates, and authorized representatives, to obtain assistive technology, and that are designed to increase access to assistive technology.

(b) Amount of financial assistance

(1) In general

From funds made available to carry out this section, the Secretary shall award a grant to each eligible State and eligible outlying area from an allotment determined in accordance with paragraph (2).

(2) Calculation of State grants

(A) Base year

Except as provided in subparagraphs (B) and (C), the Secretary shall allot to each State and outlying area for a fiscal year an amount that is not less than the amount the State or outlying area received under the grants provided under section 3011 of this title (as in effect on the day before October 25, 2004) for fiscal year 2004.

(B) Ratable reduction

(i) In general

If funds made available to carry out this section for any fiscal year are insufficient to make the allotments required for each State and outlying area under subparagraph (A) for such fiscal year, the Secretary shall ratably reduce the allotments for such fiscal year.

(ii) Additional funds

If, after the Secretary makes the reductions described in clause (i), additional funds become available to carry out this section for the fiscal year, the Secretary shall ratably increase the allotments, until the Secretary has allotted the entire base year amount.

(C) Higher appropriation years

Except as provided in subparagraph (D), for a fiscal year for which the amount of funds made available to carry out this section is greater than the base year amount, the Secretary shall—

(i) make the allotments described in subparagraph (A);

(ii) from a portion of the remainder of the funds after the Secretary makes the allotments described in clause (i), the Secretary shall—

(I) from 50 percent of the portion, allot to each State or outlying area an equal amount; and

(II) from 50 percent of the portion, allot to each State or outlying area an amount that bears the same relationship to such 50 percent as the population of the State or outlying area bears to the population of all States and outlying areas,

until each State has received an allotment of not less than $410,000 and each outlying area has received an allotment of $125,000 under clause (i) and this clause;

(iii) from the remainder of the funds after the Secretary makes the allotments described in clause (ii), the Secretary shall—

(I) from 80 percent of the remainder allot to each State an amount that bears the same relationship to such 80 percent as the population of the State bears to the population of all States; and

(II) from 20 percent of the remainder, allot to each State an equal amount.

(D) Special rule for fiscal year 2005

Notwithstanding subparagraph (C), if the amount of funds made available to carry out this section for fiscal year 2005 is greater than the base year amount, the Secretary may award grants on a competitive basis for periods of 1 year to States or outlying areas in accordance with the requirements of subchapter III of this chapter[1] (as in effect on the day before October 25, 2004) to develop, support, expand, or administer an alternative financing program.

(E) Base year amount

In this paragraph, the term "base year amount" means the total amount received by all States and outlying areas under the grants described in subparagraph (A) for fiscal year 2004.

(c) Lead agency, implementing entity, and advisory council

(1) Lead agency and implementing entity

(A) Lead agency

(i) In general

The Governor of a State shall designate a public agency as a lead agency—

(I) to control and administer the funds made available through the grant awarded to the State under this section; and

(II) to submit the application described in subsection (d) on behalf of the State, to ensure conformance with Federal and State accounting requirements.

(ii) Duties

The duties of the lead agency shall include—

(I) preparing the application described in subsection (d) and carrying out State activities described in that application, including making programmatic and resource allocation decisions necessary to implement the comprehensive statewide program of technology-related assistance;

(II) coordinating the activities of the comprehensive statewide program of technology-related assistance among public and private entities, including coordinating efforts related to entering into interagency agreements, and maintaining and evaluating the program; and

(III) coordinating efforts related to the active, timely, and meaningful participation by individuals with disabilities and their family members, guardians, advocates, or authorized representatives, and other appropriate individuals, with respect to activities carried out through the grant.

(B) Implementing entity

The Governor may designate an agency, office, or other entity to carry out State activities under this section (referred to in this section as the "implementing entity"), if such implementing entity is different from the lead agency. The implementing agency shall carry out responsibilities under this chapter through a subcontract or another administrative agreement with the lead agency.

(C) Change in agency or entity

(i) In general

On obtaining the approval of the Secretary, the Governor may redesignate the lead agency, or the implementing entity, if the Governor shows to the Secretary good cause why the entity designated as the lead agency, or the implementing entity, respectively, should not serve as that agency or entity, respectively. The Governor shall make the showing in the application described in subsection (d).

(ii) Construction

Nothing in this paragraph shall be construed to require the Governor of a State to change the lead agency or implementing entity of the State to an agency other than the lead agency or implementing entity of such State as of October 25, 2004.

(2) Advisory council

(A) In general

There shall be established an advisory council to provide consumer-responsive, consumer-driven advice to the State for, planning of, implementation of, and evaluation of the activities carried out through the grant, including setting the measurable goals described in subsection (d)(3).

(B) Composition and representation

(i) Composition

The advisory council shall be composed of—

(I) individuals with disabilities that use assistive technology or the family members or guardians of the individuals;

(II) a representative of the designated State agency, as defined in section 7 of the Rehabilitation Act of 1973 (29 U.S.C. 705) and the State agency for individuals who are blind (within the meaning of section 101 of that Act (29 U.S.C. 721)), if such agency is separate;

(III) a representative of a State center for independent living described in part C of title VII of the Rehabilitation Act of 1973 (29 U.S.C. 796f et seq.);

(IV) a representative of the State workforce investment board established under section 111 of the Workforce Investment Act of 1998 (29 U.S.C. 2821);

(V) a representative of the State educational agency, as defined in section 7801 of title 20; and

(VI) representatives of other State agencies, public agencies, or private organizations, as determined by the State.

(ii) Majority

(I) In general

A majority, not less than 51 percent, of the members of the advisory council, shall be members appointed under clause (i)(I).

(II) Representatives of agencies

Members appointed under subclauses (II) through (VI) of clause (i) shall not count toward the majority membership requirement established in subclause (I).

(iii) Representation

The advisory council shall be geographically representative of the State and re-

[1] See References in Text note below.

flect the diversity of the State with respect to race, ethnicity, types of disabilities across the age span, and users of types of services that an individual with a disability may receive.

(C) Expenses

The members of the advisory council shall receive no compensation for their service on the advisory council, but shall be reimbursed for reasonable and necessary expenses actually incurred in the performance of official duties for the advisory council.

(D) Period

The members of the State advisory council shall be appointed not later than 120 days after October 25, 2004.

(E) Impact on existing statutes, rules, or policies

Nothing in this paragraph shall be construed to affect State statutes, rules, or official policies relating to advisory bodies for State assistive technology programs or require changes to governing bodies of incorporated agencies who carry out State assistive technology programs.

(d) Application

(1) In general

Any State that desires to receive a grant under this section shall submit an application to the Secretary, at such time, in such manner, and containing such information as the Secretary may require.

(2) Lead agency and implementing entity

The application shall contain information identifying and describing the lead agency referred to in subsection (c)(1)(A). The application shall contain information identifying and describing the implementing entity referred to in subsection (c)(1)(B), if the Governor of the State designates such an entity.

(3) Measurable goals

The application shall include—

(A) measurable goals, and a timeline for meeting the goals, that the State has set for addressing the assistive technology needs of individuals with disabilities in the State related to—

(i) education, including goals involving the provision of assistive technology to individuals with disabilities who receive services under the Individuals with Disabilities Education Act (20 U.S.C. 1400 et seq.);

(ii) employment, including goals involving the State vocational rehabilitation program carried out under title I of the Rehabilitation Act of 1973 (29 U.S.C. 720 et seq.);

(iii) telecommunication and information technology; and

(iv) community living; and

(B) information describing how the State will quantifiably measure the goals to determine whether the goals have been achieved.

(4) Involvement of public and private entities

The application shall describe how various public and private entities were involved in the development of the application and will be involved in the implementation of the activities to be carried out through the grant, including—

(A) in cases determined to be appropriate by the State, a description of the nature and extent of resources that will be committed by public and private collaborators to assist in accomplishing identified goals; and

(B) a description of the mechanisms established to ensure coordination of activities and collaboration between the implementing entity, if any, and the State.

(5) Implementation

The application shall include a description of—

(A) how the State will implement each of the required activities described in subsection (e), except as provided in subsection (e)(6)(A); and

(B) how the State will allocate and utilize grant funds to implement the activities, including describing proposed budget allocations and planned procedures for tracking expenditures for activities described in paragraphs (2) and (3) of subsection (e).

(6) Assurances

The application shall include assurances that—

(A) the State will annually collect data related to the required activities implemented by the State under this section in order to prepare the progress reports required under subsection (f);

(B) funds received through the grant—

(i) will be expended in accordance with this section; and

(ii) will be used to supplement, and not supplant, funds available from other sources for technology-related assistance, including the provision of assistive technology devices and assistive technology services;

(C) the lead agency will control and administer the funds received through the grant;

(D) the State will adopt such fiscal control and accounting procedures as may be necessary to ensure proper disbursement of and accounting for the funds received through the grant;

(E) the physical facility of the lead agency and implementing entity, if any, meets the requirements of the Americans with Disabilities Act of 1990 (42 U.S.C. 12101 et seq.) regarding accessibility for individuals with disabilities;

(F) a public agency or an individual with a disability holds title to any property purchased with funds received under the grant and administers that property;

(G) activities carried out in the State that are authorized under this chapter, and supported by Federal funds received under this chapter, will comply with the standards established by the Architectural and Transportation Barriers Compliance Board under section 508 of the Rehabilitation Act of 1973 (20[2] U.S.C. 794d); and

[2] So in original. Probably should be "(29".

(H) the State will—

(i) prepare reports to the Secretary in such form and containing such information as the Secretary may require to carry out the Secretary's functions under this chapter; and

(ii) keep such records and allow access to such records as the Secretary may require to ensure the correctness and verification of information provided to the Secretary under this subparagraph.

(7) State support

The application shall include a description of the activities described in paragraphs (2) and (3) of subsection (e) that the State will support with State funds.

(e) Use of funds

(1) In general

(A) Required activities

Except as provided in subparagraph (B) and paragraph (6), any State that receives a grant under this section shall use a portion of the funds made available through the grant to carry out activities described in paragraphs (2) and (3).

(B) State or non-Federal financial support

A State shall not be required to use a portion of the funds made available through the grant to carry out the category of activities described in subparagraph (A), (B), (C), or (D) of paragraph (2) if, in that State—

(i) financial support is provided from State or other non-Federal resources or entities for that category of activities; and

(ii) the amount of the financial support is comparable to, or greater than, the amount of the portion of the funds made available through the grant that the State would have expended for that category of activities, in the absence of this subparagraph.

(2) State-level activities

(A) State financing activities

The State shall support State financing activities to increase access to, and funding for, assistive technology devices and assistive technology services (which shall not include direct payment for such a device or service for an individual with a disability but may include support and administration of a program to provide such payment), including development of systems to provide and pay for such devices and services, for targeted individuals and entities described in section 3002(16)(A) of this title, including—

(i) support for the development of systems for the purchase, lease, or other acquisition of, or payment for, assistive technology devices and assistive technology services; or

(ii) support for the development of State-financed or privately financed alternative financing systems of subsidies (which may include conducting an initial 1-year feasibility study of, improving, administering, operating, providing capital for, or collaborating with an entity with respect to, such a system) for the provision of assistive technology devices, such as—

(I) a low-interest loan fund;

(II) an interest buy-down program;

(III) a revolving loan fund;

(IV) a loan guarantee or insurance program;

(V) a program providing for the purchase, lease, or other acquisition of assistive technology devices or assistive technology services; or

(VI) another mechanism that is approved by the Secretary.

(B) Device reutilization programs

The State shall directly, or in collaboration with public or private entities, carry out assistive technology device reutilization programs that provide for the exchange, repair, recycling, or other reutilization of assistive technology devices, which may include redistribution through device sales, loans, rentals, or donations.

(C) Device loan programs

The State shall directly, or in collaboration with public or private entities, carry out device loan programs that provide short-term loans of assistive technology devices to individuals, employers, public agencies, or others seeking to meet the needs of targeted individuals and entities, including others seeking to comply with the Individuals with Disabilities Education Act (20 U.S.C. 1400 et seq.), the Americans with Disabilities Act of 1990 (42 U.S.C. 12101 et seq.), and section 504 of the Rehabilitation Act of 1973 (29 U.S.C. 794).

(D) Device demonstrations

(i) In general

The State shall directly, or in collaboration with public and private entities, such as one-stop partners, as defined in section 101 of the Workforce Investment Act of 1998 (29 U.S.C. 2801), demonstrate a variety of assistive technology devices and assistive technology services (including assisting individuals in making informed choices regarding, and providing experiences with, the devices and services), using personnel who are familiar with such devices and services and their applications.

(ii) Comprehensive information

The State shall directly, or through referrals, provide to individuals, to the extent practicable, comprehensive information about State and local assistive technology venders, providers, and repair services.

(3) State leadership activities

(A) In general

A State that receives a grant under this section shall use a portion of not more than 40 percent of the funds made available through the grant to carry out the activities described in subparagraph (B). From that portion, the State shall use at least 5 percent of the portion for activities described in subparagraph (B)(i)(III).

(B) Required activities

(i) Training and technical assistance

(I) In general

The State shall directly, or provide support to public or private entities with demonstrated expertise in collaborating with public or private agencies that serve individuals with disabilities, to develop and disseminate training materials, conduct training, and provide technical assistance, for individuals from local settings statewide, including representatives of State and local educational agencies, other State and local agencies, early intervention programs, adult service programs, hospitals and other health care facilities, institutions of higher education, and businesses.

(II) Authorized activities

In carrying out activities under subclause (I), the State shall carry out activities that enhance the knowledge, skills, and competencies of individuals from local settings described in subclause (I), which may include—

(aa) general awareness training on the benefits of assistive technology and the Federal, State, and private funding sources available to assist targeted individuals and entities in acquiring assistive technology;

(bb) skills-development training in assessing the need for assistive technology devices and assistive technology services;

(cc) training to ensure the appropriate application and use of assistive technology devices, assistive technology services, and accessible technology for e-government functions;

(dd) training in the importance of multiple approaches to assessment and implementation necessary to meet the individualized needs of individuals with disabilities; and

(ee) technical training on integrating assistive technology into the development and implementation of service plans, including any education, health, discharge, Olmstead, employment, or other plan required under Federal or State law.

(III) Transition assistance to individuals with disabilities

The State shall directly, or provide support to public or private entities to, develop and disseminate training materials, conduct training, facilitate access to assistive technology, and provide technical assistance, to assist—

(aa) students with disabilities, within the meaning of the Individuals with Disabilities Education Act (20 U.S.C. 1400 et seq.), that receive transition services; and

(bb) adults who are individuals with disabilities maintaining or transitioning to community living.

(ii) Public-awareness activities

(I) In general

The State shall conduct public-awareness activities designed to provide information to targeted individuals and entities relating to the availability, benefits, appropriateness, and costs of assistive technology devices and assistive technology services, including—

(aa) the development of procedures for providing direct communication between providers of assistive technology and targeted individuals and entities, which may include partnerships with entities in the statewide and local workforce investment systems established under the Workforce Investment Act of 1998 (29 U.S.C. 2801 et seq.), State vocational rehabilitation centers, public and private employers, or elementary and secondary public schools;

(bb) the development and dissemination, to targeted individuals and entities, of information about State efforts related to assistive technology; and

(cc) the distribution of materials to appropriate public and private agencies that provide social, medical, educational, employment, and transportation services to individuals with disabilities.

(II) Collaboration

The State shall collaborate with entities that receive awards under paragraphs (1) and (3) of section 3005(b) of this title to carry out public-awareness activities focusing on infants, toddlers, children, transition-age youth, employment-age adults, seniors, and employers.

(III) Statewide information and referral system

(aa) In general

The State shall directly, or in collaboration with public or private (such as nonprofit) entities, provide for the continuation and enhancement of a statewide information and referral system designed to meet the needs of targeted individuals and entities.

(bb) Content

The system shall deliver information on assistive technology devices, assistive technology services (with specific data regarding provider availability within the State), and the availability of resources, including funding through public and private sources, to obtain assistive technology devices and assistive technology services. The system shall also deliver information on the benefits of assistive technology devices and assistive technology services with respect to enhancing the capacity of individuals with disabilities of all ages to perform activities of daily living.

(iii) Coordination and collaboration

The State shall coordinate activities described in paragraph (2) and this paragraph, among public and private entities that are responsible for policies, procedures, or funding for the provision of assistive technology devices and assistive technology services to individuals with disabilities, service providers, and others to improve access to assistive technology devices and assistive technology services for individuals with disabilities of all ages in the State.

(4) Indirect costs

Not more than 10 percent of the funds made available through a grant to a State under this section may be used for indirect costs.

(5) Prohibition

Funds made available through a grant to a State under this section shall not be used for direct payment for an assistive technology device for an individual with a disability.

(6) State flexibility

(A) In general

Notwithstanding paragraph (1)(A) and subject to subparagraph (B), a State may use funds that the State receives under a grant awarded under this section to carry out any 2 or more of the activities described in paragraph (2).

(B) Special rule

Notwithstanding paragraph (3)(A), any State that exercises its authority under subparagraph (A)—

(i) shall carry out each of the required activities described in paragraph (3)(B); and

(ii) shall use not more than 30 percent of the funds made available through the grant to carry out the activities described in paragraph (3)(B).

(f) Annual progress reports

(1) Data collection

States shall participate in data collection as required by law, including data collection required for preparation of the reports described in paragraph (2).

(2) Reports

(A) In general

Each State shall prepare and submit to the Secretary an annual progress report on the activities funded under this chapter, at such time, and in such manner, as the Secretary may require.

(B) Contents

The report shall include data collected pursuant to this section. The report shall document, with respect to activities carried out under this section in the State—

(i) the type of State financing activities described in subsection (e)(2)(A) used by the State;

(ii) the amount and type of assistance given to consumers of the State financing activities described in subsection (e)(2)(A) (who shall be classified by type of assistive technology device or assistive technology service financed through the State financing activities, and geographic distribution within the State), including—

(I) the number of applications for assistance received;

(II) the number of applications approved and rejected;

(III) the default rate for the financing activities;

(IV) the range and average interest rate for the financing activities;

(V) the range and average income of approved applicants for the financing activities; and

(VI) the types and dollar amounts of assistive technology financed;

(iii) the number, type, and length of time of loans of assistive technology devices provided to individuals with disabilities, employers, public agencies, or public accommodations through the device loan program described in subsection (e)(2)(C), and an analysis of the individuals with disabilities who have benefited from the device loan program;

(iv) the number, type, estimated value, and scope of assistive technology devices exchanged, repaired, recycled, or reutilized (including redistributed through device sales, loans, rentals, or donations) through the device reutilization program described in subsection (e)(2)(B), and an analysis of the individuals with disabilities that have benefited from the device reutilization program;

(v) the number and type of device demonstrations and referrals provided under subsection (e)(2)(D), and an analysis of individuals with disabilities who have benefited from the demonstrations and referrals;

(vi)(I) the number and general characteristics of individuals who participated in training under subsection (e)(3)(B)(i) (such as individuals with disabilities, parents, educators, employers, providers of employment services, health care workers, counselors, other service providers, or vendors) and the topics of such training; and

(II) to the extent practicable, the geographic distribution of individuals who participated in the training;

(vii) the frequency of provision and nature of technical assistance provided to State and local agencies and other entities;

(viii) the number of individuals assisted through the public-awareness activities and statewide information and referral system described in subsection (e)(3)(B)(ii);

(ix) the outcomes of any improvement initiatives carried out by the State as a result of activities funded under this section, including a description of any written policies, practices, and procedures that the State has developed and implemented regarding access to, provision of, and funding for, assistive technology devices, and assistive technology services, in the contexts of education, health care, employment, community living, and information technology and telecommunications, including e-government;

(x) the source of leveraged funding or other contributed resources, including resources provided through subcontracts or other collaborative resource-sharing agreements, from and with public and private entities to carry out State activities described in subsection (e)(3)(B)(iii), the number of individuals served with the contributed resources for which information is not reported under clauses (i) through (ix) or clause (xi) or (xii), and other outcomes accomplished as a result of such activities carried out with the contributed resources; and

(xi) the level of customer satisfaction with the services provided.

(Pub. L. 105–394, §4, as added Pub. L. 108–364, §2, Oct. 25, 2004, 118 Stat. 1714.)

REFERENCES IN TEXT

Section 3011 of this title, referred to in subsec. (b)(2)(A), was omitted in the general amendment of this chapter by Pub. L. 108–364, §2, Oct. 25, 2004, 118 Stat. 1707.

Subchapter III of this chapter, referred to in subsec. (b)(2)(D), which consisted of sections 3051 to 3058 of this title, was omitted in the general amendment of this chapter by Pub. L. 108–364, §2, Oct. 25, 2004, 118 Stat. 1707.

The Rehabilitation Act of 1973, referred to in subsecs. (c)(2)(B)(i)(III) and (d)(3)(A)(ii), is Pub. L. 93–112, Sept. 26, 1973, 87 Stat. 355, as amended. Title I of the Act is classified generally to subchapter I (§720 et seq.) of chapter 16 of this title. Part C of title VII of the Act is classified generally to subpart 3 (§796f et seq.) of part A of subchapter VII of chapter 16 of this title. For complete classification of this Act to the Code, see Short Title note set out under section 701 of this title and Tables.

The Individuals with Disabilities Education Act, referred to in subsecs. (d)(3)(A)(i) and (e)(2)(C), (3)(B)(i)(III)(aa), is title VI of Pub. L. 91–230, Apr. 13, 1970, 84 Stat. 175, as amended, which is classified generally to chapter 33 (§1400 et seq.) of Title 20, Education. For complete classification of this Act to the Code, see section 1400 of Title 20 and Tables.

The Americans with Disabilities Act of 1990, referred to in subsecs. (d)(6)(E) and (e)(2)(C), is Pub. L. 101–336, July 26, 1990, 104 Stat. 327, as amended, which is classified principally to chapter 126 (§12101 et seq.) of Title 42, The Public Health and Welfare. For complete classification of this Act to the Code, see Short Title note set out under section 12101 of Title 42 and Tables.

The Workforce Investment Act of 1998, referred to in subsec. (e)(3)(B)(ii)(I)(aa), is Pub. L. 105–220, Aug. 7, 1998, 112 Stat. 936, as amended. For complete classification of this Act to the Code, see Short Title note set out under section 9201 of Title 20, Education, and Tables.

§3004. State grants for protection and advocacy services related to assistive technology

(a) Grants

(1) In general

The Secretary shall make grants under subsection (b) to protection and advocacy systems in each State for the purpose of enabling such systems to assist in the acquisition, utilization, or maintenance of assistive technology devices or assistive technology services for individuals with disabilities.

(2) General authorities

In providing such assistance, protection and advocacy systems shall have the same general authorities as the systems are afforded under subtitle C of title I of the Developmental Disabilities Assistance and Bill of Rights Act of 2000 (42 U.S.C. 15041 et seq.), as determined by the Secretary.

(b) Grants

(1) Reservation

For each fiscal year, the Secretary shall reserve such sums as may be necessary to carry out paragraph (4).

(2) Population basis

From the funds appropriated under section 3007(b) of this title for a fiscal year and remaining after the reservation required by paragraph (1) has been made, the Secretary shall make a grant to a protection and advocacy system within each State in an amount bearing the same ratio to the remaining funds as the population of the State bears to the population of all States.

(3) Minimums

Subject to the availability of appropriations, the amount of a grant to a protection and advocacy system under paragraph (2) for a fiscal year shall—

(A) in the case of a protection and advocacy system located in American Samoa, Guam, the United States Virgin Islands, or the Commonwealth of the Northern Mariana Islands, not be less than $30,000; and

(B) in the case of a protection and advocacy system located in a State not described in subparagraph (A), not be less than $50,000.

(4) Payment to the system serving the American Indian Consortium

(A) In general

The Secretary shall make grants to the protection and advocacy system serving the American Indian Consortium to provide services in accordance with this section.

(B) Amount of grants

The amount of such grants shall be the same as the amount provided under paragraph (3)(A).

(c) Direct payment

Notwithstanding any other provision of law, the Secretary shall pay directly to any protection and advocacy system that complies with this section, the total amount of the grant made for such system under this section, unless the system provides otherwise for payment of the grant amount.

(d) Certain States

(1) Grant to lead agency

Notwithstanding any other provision of this section, with respect to a State that, on November 12, 1998, was described in section 2212(f)(1)[1] of this title, the Secretary shall pay the amount of the grant described in subsection (a), and made under subsection (b), to the lead agency designated under section 3003(c)(1) of this title for the State.

(2) Distribution of funds

A lead agency to which a grant amount is paid under paragraph (1) shall determine the

[1] See References in Text note below.

manner in which funds made available through the grant will be allocated among the entities that were providing protection and advocacy services in that State on the date described in such paragraph, and shall distribute funds to such entities. In distributing such funds, the lead agency shall not establish any additional eligibility or procedural requirements for an entity in the State that supports protection and advocacy services through a protection and advocacy system. Such an entity shall comply with the same requirements (including reporting and enforcement requirements) as any other entity that receives funding under this section.

(3) Application of provisions

Except as provided in this subsection, the provisions of this section shall apply to the grant in the same manner, and to the same extent, as the provisions apply to a grant to a system.

(e) Carryover

Any amount paid to an eligible system for a fiscal year under this section that remains unobligated at the end of such fiscal year shall remain available to such system for obligation during the subsequent fiscal year. Program income generated from such amount shall remain available for 2 additional fiscal years after the year in which such amount was paid to an eligible system and may only be used to improve the awareness of individuals with disabilities about the accessibility of assistive technology and assist such individuals in the acquisition, utilization, or maintenance of assistive technology devices or assistive technology services.

(f) Report to Secretary

An entity that receives a grant under this section shall annually prepare and submit to the Secretary a report that contains such information as the Secretary may require, including documentation of the progress of the entity in—

(1) conducting consumer-responsive activities, including activities that will lead to increased access, for individuals with disabilities, to funding for assistive technology devices and assistive technology services;

(2) engaging in informal advocacy to assist in securing assistive technology devices and assistive technology services for individuals with disabilities;

(3) engaging in formal representation for individuals with disabilities to secure systems change, and in advocacy activities to secure assistive technology devices and assistive technology services for individuals with disabilities;

(4) developing and implementing strategies to enhance the long-term abilities of individuals with disabilities and their family members, guardians, advocates, and authorized representatives to advocate the provision of assistive technology devices and assistive technology services to which the individuals with disabilities are entitled under law other than this chapter;

(5) coordinating activities with protection and advocacy services funded through sources other than this chapter, and coordinating activities with the capacity building and advocacy activities carried out by the lead agency; and

(6) effectively allocating funds made available under this section to improve the awareness of individuals with disabilities about the accessibility of assistive technology and assist such individuals in the acquisition, utilization, or maintenance of assistive technology devices or assistive technology services.

(g) Reports and updates to State agencies

An entity that receives a grant under this section shall prepare and submit to the lead agency of the State designated under section 3003(c)(1) of this title the report described in subsection (f) and quarterly updates concerning the activities described in subsection (f).

(h) Coordination

On making a grant under this section to an entity in a State, the Secretary shall solicit and consider the opinions of the lead agency of the State with respect to efforts at coordination of activities, collaboration, and promoting outcomes between the lead agency and the entity that receives the grant under this section.

(Pub. L. 105–394, §5, as added Pub. L. 108–364, §2, Oct. 25, 2004, 118 Stat. 1725.)

REFERENCES IN TEXT

The Developmental Disabilities Assistance and Bill of Rights Act of 2000, referred to in subsec. (a)(2), is Pub. L. 106–402, Oct. 30, 2000, 114 Stat. 1677, as amended. Subtitle C of title I of the Act is classified generally to part C (§15041 et seq.) of subchapter I of chapter 144 of Title 42, The Public Health and Welfare. For complete classification of this Act to the Code, see Short Title note set out under section 15001 of Title 42 and Tables.

Section 2212 of this title, referred to in subsec. (d)(1), was repealed by Pub. L. 105–394, title IV, §401, Nov. 13, 1998, 112 Stat. 3661.

§3005. National activities

(a) In general

In order to support activities designed to improve the administration of this chapter, the Secretary, under subsection (b)—

(1) may award, on a competitive basis, grants, contracts, and cooperative agreements to entities to support activities described in paragraphs (1) and (2) of subsection (b); and

(2) shall award, on a competitive basis, grants, contracts, and cooperative agreements to entities to support activities described in paragraphs (3), (4), and (5) of subsection (b).

(b) Authorized activities

(1) National public-awareness toolkit

(A) National public-awareness toolkit

The Secretary may award a 1-time grant, contract, or cooperative agreement to an eligible entity to support a training and technical assistance program that—

(i) expands public-awareness efforts to reach targeted individuals and entities;

(ii) contains appropriate accessible multimedia materials to reach targeted individuals and entities, for dissemination to State assistive technology programs; and

(iii) in coordination with State assistive technology programs, provides meaningful and up-to-date information to targeted individuals and entities about the availability of assistive technology devices and assistive technology services.

(B) Eligible entity

To be eligible to receive the grant, contract, or cooperative agreement, an entity shall develop a partnership that—

(i) shall consist of—

(I) a lead agency or implementing entity for a State assistive technology program or an organization or association that represents implementing entities for State assistive technology programs;

(II) a private or public entity from the media industry;

(III) a private entity from the assistive technology industry; and

(IV) a private employer or an organization or association that represents private employers;

(ii) may include other entities determined by the Secretary to be necessary; and

(iii) may include other entities determined by the applicant to be appropriate.

(2) Research and development

(A) In general

The Secretary may award grants, contracts, or cooperative agreements to eligible entities to carry out research and development of assistive technology that consists of—

(i) developing standards for reliability and accessibility of assistive technology, and standards for interoperability (including open standards) of assistive technology with information technology, telecommunications products, and other assistive technology; or

(ii) developing assistive technology that benefits individuals with disabilities or developing technologies or practices that result in the adaptation, maintenance, servicing, or improvement of assistive technology devices.

(B) Eligible entities

Entities eligible to receive a grant, contract, or cooperative agreement under this paragraph shall include—

(i) providers of assistive technology services and assistive technology devices;

(ii) institutions of higher education, including University Centers for Excellence in Developmental Disabilities Education, Research, and Service authorized under subtitle D of title I of the Developmental Disabilities Assistance and Bill of Rights Act of 2000 (42 U.S.C. 15061 et seq.), or such institutions offering rehabilitation engineering programs, computer science programs, or information technology programs;

(iii) manufacturers of assistive technology devices; and

(iv) professionals, individuals, organizations, and agencies providing services or employment to individuals with disabilities.

(C) Collaboration

An entity that receives a grant, contract, or cooperative agreement under this paragraph shall, in developing and implementing the project carried out through the grant, contract, or cooperative agreement coordinate activities with the lead agency for the State assistive technology program (or a national organization that represents such programs) and the State advisory council described in section 3003(c)(2) of this title (or a national organization that represents such councils).

(3) State training and technical assistance

(A) Training and technical assistance efforts

The Secretary shall award a grant, contract, or cooperative agreement to an entity to support a training and technical assistance program that—

(i) addresses State-specific information requests concerning assistive technology from entities funded under this chapter and public entities not funded under this chapter, including—

(I) requests for information on effective approaches to Federal-State coordination of programs for individuals with disabilities, related to improving funding for or access to assistive technology devices and assistive technology services for individuals with disabilities of all ages;

(II) requests for state-of-the-art, or model, Federal, State, and local laws, regulations, policies, practices, procedures, and organizational structures, that facilitate, and overcome barriers to, funding for, and access to, assistive technology devices and assistive technology services;

(III) requests for information on effective approaches to developing, implementing, evaluating, and sustaining activities described in sections 3003 and 3004 of this title and related to improving funding for or access to assistive technology devices and assistive technology services for individuals with disabilities of all ages, and requests for assistance in developing corrective action plans;

(IV) requests for examples of policies, practices, procedures, regulations, or judicial decisions that have enhanced or may enhance access to funding for assistive technology devices and assistive technology services for individuals with disabilities;

(V) requests for information on effective approaches to the development of consumer-controlled systems that increase access to, funding for, and awareness of, assistive technology devices and assistive technology services; and

(VI) other requests for training and technical assistance from entities funded under this chapter and public and private entities not funded under this chapter;

(ii) assists targeted individuals and entities by disseminating information about—

(I) Federal, State, and local laws, regulations, policies, practices, procedures, and organizational structures, that facilitate, and overcome barriers to, funding for, and access to, assistive technology devices and assistive technology services, to promote fuller independence, productivity, and inclusion in society for individuals with disabilities of all ages; and

(II) technical assistance activities undertaken under clause (i);

(iii) provides State-specific, regional, and national training and technical assistance concerning assistive technology to entities funded under this chapter, other entities funded under this chapter, and public and private entities not funded under this chapter, including—

(I) annually providing a forum for exchanging information concerning, and promoting program and policy improvements in, required activities of the State assistive technology programs;

(II) facilitating onsite and electronic information sharing using state-of-the-art Internet technologies such as real-time online discussions, multipoint video conferencing, and web-based audio/video broadcasts, on emerging topics that affect State assistive technology programs;

(III) convening experts from State assistive technology programs to discuss and make recommendations with regard to national emerging issues of importance to individuals with assistive technology needs;

(IV) sharing best practice and evidence-based practices among State assistive technology programs;

(V) maintaining an accessible website that includes a link to State assistive technology programs, appropriate Federal departments and agencies, and private associations and developing a national toll-free number that links callers from a State with the State assistive technology program in their State;

(VI) developing or utilizing existing (as of the date of the award involved) model cooperative volume-purchasing mechanisms designed to reduce the financial costs of purchasing assistive technology for required and discretionary activities identified in section 3003 of this title, and reducing duplication of activities among State assistive technology programs; and

(VII) providing access to experts in the areas of banking, microlending, and finance, for entities funded under this chapter, through site visits, teleconferences, and other means, to ensure access to information for entities that are carrying out new programs or programs that are not making progress in achieving the objectives of the programs; and

(iv) includes such other activities as the Secretary may require.

(B) Eligible entities

To be eligible to receive a grant, contract, or cooperative agreement under this paragraph, an entity shall have (directly or through grant or contract)—

(i) experience and expertise in administering programs, including developing, implementing, and administering the required and discretionary activities described in sections 3003 and 3004 of this title, and providing technical assistance; and

(ii) documented experience in and knowledge about banking, finance, and microlending.

(C) Collaboration

In developing and providing training and technical assistance under this paragraph, including activities identified as priorities, a recipient of a grant, contract, or cooperative agreement under this paragraph shall collaborate with other organizations, in particular—

(i) organizations representing individuals with disabilities;

(ii) national organizations representing State assistive technology programs;

(iii) organizations representing State officials and agencies engaged in the delivery of assistive technology;

(iv) the data-collection and reporting providers described in paragraph (5); and

(v) other providers of national programs or programs of national significance funded under this chapter.

(4) National information Internet system

(A) In general

The Secretary shall award a grant, contract, or cooperative agreement to an entity to renovate, update, and maintain the National Public Internet Site established under this chapter (as in effect on the day before October 25, 2004).

(B) Features of Internet site

The National Public Internet Site shall contain the following features:

(i) Availability of information at any time

The site shall be designed so that any member of the public may obtain information posted on the site at any time.

(ii) Innovative automated intelligent agent

The site shall be constructed with an innovative automated intelligent agent that is a diagnostic tool for assisting users in problem definition and the selection of appropriate assistive technology devices and assistive technology services resources.

(iii) Resources

(I) Library on assistive technology

The site shall include access to a comprehensive working library on assistive technology for all environments, including home, workplace, transportation, and other environments.

(II) Information on accommodating individuals with disabilities

The site shall include access to evidence-based research and best practices concerning how assistive technology can be used to accommodate individuals with disabilities in the areas of education, employment, health care, community living, and telecommunications and information technology.

(III) Resources for a number of disabilities

The site shall include resources relating to the largest possible number of disabilities, including resources relating to low-level reading skills.

(iv) Links to private-sector resources and information

To the extent feasible, the site shall be linked to relevant private-sector resources and information, under agreements developed between the recipient of the grant, contract, or cooperative agreement and cooperating private-sector entities.

(v) Links to public-sector resources and information

To the extent feasible, the site shall be linked to relevant public-sector resources and information, such as the Internet sites of the Office of Special Education and Rehabilitation Services of the Department of Education, the Office of Disability Employment Policy of the Department of Labor, the Small Business Administration, the Architectural and Transportation Barriers Compliance Board, the National Institute of Standards and Technology, the Jobs Accommodation Network funded by the Office of Disability Employment Policy of the Department of Labor, and other relevant sites.

(vi) Minimum library components

At a minimum, the site shall maintain updated information on—

(I) State assistive technology program demonstration sites where individuals may try out assistive technology devices;

(II) State assistive technology program device loan program sites where individuals may borrow assistive technology devices;

(III) State assistive technology program device reutilization program sites;

(IV) alternative financing programs or State financing systems operated through, or independently of, State assistive technology programs, and other sources of funding for assistive technology devices; and

(V) various programs, including programs with tax credits, available to employers for hiring or accommodating employees who are individuals with disabilities.

(C) Eligible entity

To be eligible to receive a grant, contract, or cooperative agreement under this paragraph, an entity shall be a nonprofit organization, for-profit organization, or institution of higher education, that—

(i) emphasizes research and engineering;

(ii) has a multidisciplinary research center; and

(iii) has demonstrated expertise in—

(I) working with assistive technology and intelligent agent interactive information dissemination systems;

(II) managing libraries of assistive technology and disability-related resources;

(III) delivering to individuals with disabilities education, information, and referral services, including technology-based curriculum-development services for adults with low-level reading skills;

(IV) developing cooperative partnerships with the private sector, particularly with private-sector computer software, hardware, and Internet services entities; and

(V) developing and designing advanced Internet sites.

(5) Data-collection and reporting assistance

(A) In general

The Secretary shall award grants, contracts, and cooperative agreements to entities to assist the entities in carrying out State assistive technology programs in developing and implementing effective data-collection and reporting systems that—

(i) focus on quantitative and qualitative data elements;

(ii) measure the outcomes of the required activities described in section 3003 of this title that are implemented by the States and the progress of the States toward achieving the measurable goals described in section 3003(d)(3) of this title;

(iii) provide States with the necessary information required under this chapter or by the Secretary for reports described in section 3003(f)(2) of this title; and

(iv) help measure the accrued benefits of the activities to individuals who need assistive technology.

(B) Eligible entities

To be eligible to receive a grant, contract, or cooperative agreement under this paragraph, an entity shall have personnel with—

(i) documented experience and expertise in administering State assistive technology programs;

(ii) experience in collecting and analyzing data associated with implementing required and discretionary activities;

(iii) expertise necessary to identify additional data elements needed to provide comprehensive reporting of State activities and outcomes; and

(iv) experience in utilizing data to provide annual reports to State policymakers.

(c) Application

To be eligible to receive a grant, contract, or cooperative agreement under this section, an entity shall submit an application to the Secretary at such time, in such manner, and containing such information as the Secretary may require.

(d) Input

With respect to the activities described in subsection (b) to be funded under this section, including the national and regionally based training and technical assistance efforts carried out through the activities, in designing the activities the Secretary shall consider, and in providing the activities providers shall include, input of the directors of comprehensive statewide programs of technology-related assistance, directors of alternative financing programs, and other individuals the Secretary determines to be appropriate, especially—

(1) individuals with disabilities who use assistive technology and understand the barriers to the acquisition of such technology and assistive technology services;

(2) family members, guardians, advocates, and authorized representatives of such individuals;

(3) individuals employed by protection and advocacy systems funded under section 3004 of this title;

(4) relevant employees from Federal departments and agencies, other than the Department of Education;

(5) representatives of businesses; and

(6) venders and public and private researchers and developers.

(Pub. L. 105–394, §6, as added Pub. L. 108–364, §2, Oct. 25, 2004, 118 Stat. 1727; amended Pub. L. 110–69, title III, §3002(c)(7), Aug. 9, 2007, 121 Stat. 587.)

REFERENCES IN TEXT

The Developmental Disabilities Assistance and Bill of Rights Act of 2000, referred to in subsec. (b)(2)(B)(ii), is Pub. L. 106–402, Oct. 30, 2000, 114 Stat. 1677, as amended. Subtitle D of title I of the Act is classified generally to part D (§15061 et seq.) of subchapter I of chapter 144 of Title 42, The Public Health and Welfare. For complete classification of this Act to the Code, see Short Title note set out under section 15001 of Title 42 and Tables.

AMENDMENTS

2007—Subsec. (b)(4)(B)(v). Pub. L. 110–69 substituted "the National Institute of Standards and Technology," for "the Technology Administration of the Department of Commerce,".

§3006. Administrative provisions

(a) General administration

(1) In general

Notwithstanding any other provision of law, the Assistant Secretary for Special Education and Rehabilitative Services of the Department of Education, acting through the Rehabilitation Services Administration, shall be responsible for the administration of this chapter.

(2) Collaboration

The Assistant Secretary for Special Education and Rehabilitative Services shall consult with the Office of Special Education Programs, the Rehabilitation Services Administration, and the National Institute on Disability and Rehabilitation Research in the Office of Special Education and Rehabilitative Services, and appropriate Federal entities in the administration of this chapter.

(3) Administration

In administering this chapter, the Rehabilitation Services Administration shall ensure that programs funded under this chapter will address the needs of individuals with disabilities of all ages, whether the individuals will use the assistive technology to obtain or maintain employment, to obtain education, or for other reasons.

(4) Orderly transition

(A) In general

The Secretary shall take such steps as the Secretary determines to be appropriate to provide for the orderly transition to, and implementation of, programs authorized by this chapter, from programs authorized by this chapter, as in effect on the day before October 25, 2004.

(B) Cessation of effectiveness

Subparagraph (A) ceases to be effective on the date that is 6 months after October 25, 2004.

(b) Review of participating entities

(1) In general

The Secretary shall assess the extent to which entities that receive grants under this chapter are complying with the applicable requirements of this chapter and achieving measurable goals that are consistent with the requirements of the grant programs under which the entities received the grants.

(2) Provision of information

To assist the Secretary in carrying out the responsibilities of the Secretary under this section, the Secretary may require States to provide relevant information, including the information required under subsection (d).

(c) Corrective action and sanctions

(1) Corrective action

If the Secretary determines that an entity that receives a grant under this chapter fails to substantially comply with the applicable requirements of this chapter, or to make substantial progress toward achieving the measurable goals described in subsection (b)(1) with respect to the grant program, the Secretary shall assist the entity, through technical assistance funded under section 3005 of this title or other means, within 90 days after such determination, to develop a corrective action plan.

(2) Sanctions

If the entity fails to develop and comply with a corrective action plan described in paragraph (1) during a fiscal year, the entity shall be subject to 1 of the following corrective actions selected by the Secretary:

(A) Partial or complete termination of funding under the grant program, until the entity develops and complies with such a plan.

(B) Ineligibility to participate in the grant program in the following year.

(C) Reduction in the amount of funding that may be used for indirect costs under section 3003 of this title for the following year.

(D) Required redesignation of the lead agency designated under section 3003(c)(1) of this title or an entity responsible for administering the grant program.

(3) **Appeals procedures**

The Secretary shall establish appeals procedures for entities that are determined to be in noncompliance with the applicable requirements of this chapter, or have not made substantial progress toward achieving the measurable goals described in subsection (b)(1).

(4) **Secretarial action**

As part of the annual report required under subsection (d), the Secretary shall describe each such action taken under paragraph (1) or (2) and the outcomes of each such action.

(5) **Public notification**

The Secretary shall notify the public, by posting on the Internet website of the Department of Education, of each action taken by the Secretary under paragraph (1) or (2). As a part of such notification, the Secretary shall describe each such action taken under paragraph (1) or (2) and the outcomes of each such action.

(d) **Annual report to Congress**

(1) **In general**

Not later than December 31 of each year, the Secretary shall prepare, and submit to the President and to the Committee on Education and the Workforce of the House of Representatives and the Committee on Health, Education, Labor, and Pensions of the Senate, a report on the activities funded under this chapter to improve the access of individuals with disabilities to assistive technology devices and assistive technology services.

(2) **Contents**

Such report shall include—

(A) a compilation and summary of the information provided by the States in annual progress reports submitted under section 3003(f) of this title; and

(B) a summary of the State applications described in section 3003(d) of this title and an analysis of the progress of the States in meeting the measurable goals established in State applications under section 3003(d)(3) of this title.

(e) **Construction**

Nothing in this section shall be construed to affect the enforcement authority of the Secretary, another Federal officer, or a court under part D of the General Education Provisions Act (20 U.S.C. 1234 et seq.) or other applicable law.

(f) **Effect on other assistance**

This chapter may not be construed as authorizing a Federal or State agency to reduce medical or other assistance available, or to alter eligibility for a benefit or service, under any other Federal law.

(g) **Rule**

This chapter (as in effect on the day before October 25, 2004) shall apply to funds appropriated under this chapter for fiscal year 2004.

(Pub. L. 105–394, §7, as added Pub. L. 108–364, §2, Oct. 25, 2004, 118 Stat. 1734.)

REFERENCES IN TEXT

The General Education Provisions Act, referred to in subsec. (e), is title IV of Pub. L. 90–247, Jan. 2, 1968, 81 Stat. 814, as amended. Part D of the Act is classified generally to subchapter IV (§1234 et seq.) of chapter 31 of Title 20, Education. For complete classification of this Act to the Code, see section 1221 of Title 20 and Tables.

CHANGE OF NAME

Committee on Education and the Workforce of House of Representatives changed to Committee on Education and Labor of House of Representatives by House Resolution No. 6, One Hundred Tenth Congress, Jan. 5, 2007.

§ 3007. Authorization of appropriations

(a) **State grants for assistive technology and national activities**

(1) **In general**

There are authorized to be appropriated to carry out sections 3003 and 3005 of this title such sums as may be necessary for each of fiscal years 2005 through 2010.

(2) **Reservation**

(A) **Definition**

In this paragraph, the term "higher appropriation year" means a fiscal year for which the amount appropriated under paragraph (1) and made available to carry out section 3003 of this title is at least $665,000 greater than the amount that—

(i) was appropriated under section 3015 of this title (as in effect on October 1, 2003) for fiscal year 2004; and

(ii) was not reserved for grants under section 3012 or 3014 of this title (as in effect on such date) for fiscal year 2004.

(B) **Amount reserved for national activities**

Of the amount appropriated under paragraph (1) for a fiscal year—

(i) not more than $1,235,000 may be reserved to carry out section 3005 of this title, except as provided in clause (ii); and

(ii) for a higher appropriation year—

(I) not more than $1,900,000 may be reserved to carry out section 3005 of this title; and

(II) of the amount so reserved, the portion exceeding $1,235,000 shall be used to carry out paragraphs (1) and (2) of section 3005(b) of this title.

(b) **State grants for protection and advocacy services related to assistive technology**

There are authorized to be appropriated to carry out section 3004 of this title $4,419,000 for fiscal year 2005 and such sums as may be necessary for each of fiscal years 2006 through 2010.

(Pub. L. 105–394, §8, as added Pub. L. 108–364, §2, Oct. 25, 2004, 118 Stat. 1736.)

REFERENCES IN TEXT

Sections 3012, 3014, and 3015 of this title, referred to in subsec. (a)(2)(A), were omitted in the general amendment of this chapter by Pub. L. 108–364, §2, Oct. 25, 2004, 118 Stat. 1707.

§§ 3011 to 3015. Omitted

Sections, comprising subchapter I of this chapter "State Grant Programs", were omitted in the general amendment of this chapter by Pub. L. 108–364, §2, Oct. 25, 2004, 118 Stat. 1707.

Section 3011, Pub. L. 105–394, title I, §101, Nov. 13, 1998, 112 Stat. 3635, provided for continuity grants for

States that received funding for a limited period for technology-related assistance.

Section 3012, Pub. L. 105–394, title I, §102, Nov. 13, 1998, 112 Stat. 3644; Pub. L. 106–402, title IV, §401(b)(4)(B), Oct. 30, 2000, 114 Stat. 1738, provided for State grants for protection and advocacy related to assistive technology.

Section 3013, Pub. L. 105–394, title I, §103, Nov. 13, 1998, 112 Stat. 3646, related to administrative provisions.

Section 3014, Pub. L. 105–394, title I, §104, Nov. 13, 1998, 112 Stat. 3648, related to a technical assistance program.

Section 3015, Pub. L. 105–394, title I, §105, Nov. 13, 1998, 112 Stat. 3651, authorized appropriations.

§§ 3031 to 3037. Omitted

Sections, comprising subchapter II of this chapter, "National Activities", were omitted in the general amendment of this chapter by Pub. L. 108–364, §2, Oct. 25, 2004, 118 Stat. 1707.

Section 3031, Pub. L. 105–394, title II, §211, Nov. 13, 1998, 112 Stat. 3654, related to small business incentives.

Section 3032, Pub. L. 105–394, title II, §212, Nov. 13, 1998, 112 Stat. 3654, related to technology transfer and universal design.

Section 3033, Pub. L. 105–394, title II, §213, Nov. 13, 1998, 112 Stat. 3655, related to universal design in products and the built environment.

Section 3034, Pub. L. 105–394, title II, §214, Nov. 13, 1998, 112 Stat. 3655, related to assistive technology outreach programs.

Section 3035, Pub. L. 105–394, title II, §215, Nov. 13, 1998, 112 Stat. 3656, related to training pertaining to rehabilitation engineers and technicians.

Section 3036, Pub. L. 105–394, title II, §216, Nov. 13, 1998, 112 Stat. 3656, related to the President's Committee on Employment of People With Disabilities.

Section 3037, Pub. L. 105–394, title II, §217, Nov. 13, 1998, 112 Stat. 3657, authorized appropriations.

§§ 3051 to 3058. Omitted

Sections, comprising subchapter III of this chapter, "Alternative Financing Mechanisms", were omitted in the general amendment of this chapter by Pub. L. 108–364, §2, Oct. 25, 2004, 118 Stat. 1707.

Section 3051, Pub. L. 105–394, title III, §301, Nov. 13, 1998, 112 Stat. 3657, related to the general authority of the Secretary.

Section 3052, Pub. L. 105–394, title III, §302, Nov. 13, 1998, 112 Stat. 3657, related to the amount of grants.

Section 3053, Pub. L. 105–394, title III, §303, Nov. 13, 1998, 112 Stat. 3658, related to grant applications and procedures.

Section 3054, Pub. L. 105–394, title III, §304, Nov. 13, 1998, 112 Stat. 3659, related to contracts with community-based organizations.

Section 3055, Pub. L. 105–394, title III, §305, Nov. 13, 1998, 112 Stat. 3660, related to grant administration requirements.

Section 3056, Pub. L. 105–394, title III, §306, Nov. 13, 1998, 112 Stat. 3660, related to grant information and technical assistance.

Section 3057, Pub. L. 105–394, title III, §307, Nov. 13, 1998, 112 Stat. 3660, related to annual reports.

Section 3058, Pub. L. 105–394, title III, §308, Nov. 13, 1998, 112 Stat. 3661, authorized appropriations.

Made in United States
North Haven, CT
04 November 2026

21764771R00417